20° 40° 60° 80° 100° 120° 140° 160°

OCEAN

60°

NAY

SWEDEN
FINLAND
K
ESTONIA
LATVIA
LITHUANIA
BELARUS
CZECH REPUBLIC
SLOVAK REPUBLIC
SLOVENIA
HUNGARY
CROATIA
POLAND
GERMANY
AUS.
ROMANIA
UKRAINE
MOLDOVA

RUSSIAN FEDERATION

ITALY
ALBANIA
BOSNIA-HERZEGOVINA
SERBIA
BULGARIA
MACEDONIA
GEORGIA
GREECE
TURKEY
ARMENIA
MALTA
CYPRUS
TUNISIA
LEBANON
SYRIA
ISRAEL
IRAQ
JORDAN
EGYPT
BAHRAIN
LIBYA

KAZAKHSTAN

UZBEKISTAN
TURKMENISTAN

KYRGYZSTAN
TAJIKISTAN

MONGOLIA

NORTH
KOREA
SOUTH
KOREA

JAPAN

60°

40°

AZERBAIJAN
IRAN
KUWAIT
QATAR
AFGHANISTAN

PEOPLE'S REPUBLIC OF CHINA

NEPAL
BHUTAN
PAKISTAN

SAUDI
ARABIA
UNITED
ARAB
EMIRATES
OMAN
YEMEN

INDIA

MYANMAR (BURMA)

PACIFIC

OCEAN Tropic of Cancer

TAIWAN

20°

NIGER
CHAD
SUDAN
ERITREA

DJIBOUTI

BANGLADESH
THAILAND

LAOS

VIETNAM

PHILIPPINES

MARSHALL
ISLANDS

GERIA
CAMEROON
UGANDA
ETHIOPIA
SOMALIA

SRI LANKA
MALDIVES

CAMBODIA
BRUNEI
MALAYSIA

MICRONESIA
Equator

KIRIBATI 0°

RWANDA
BURUNDI
Democratic
Republic
of Congo
KENYA

SINGAPORE

NAURU

SOLOMON
ISLANDS

PAPUA
NEW GUINEA

TANZANIA

SEYCHELLES

INDONESIA

TUVALU

ANGOLA
MALAWI
COMOROS
MOZAMBIQUE

INDIAN
OCEAN

EAST TIMOR

VANUATU

FIJI

20°

ZAMBIA
MADAGASCAR
MAURITIUS

Tropic of Capricorn

AUSTRALIA

NEW CALEDONIA
(FRANCE)

NAMIBIA
BOTSWANA

ZIMBABWE
SWAZILAND

40°

SOUTH
AFRICA
LESOTHO

NEW ZEALAND

60°

Antarctic Circle

0   1,000   2,000 Miles

80°

0   1,000 2,000 3,000 Kilometers

COMBINED VOLUME

EIGHTH EDITION

THE HERITAGE OF
World Civilizations

ALBERT M. CRAIG ◆ Harvard University

WILLIAM A. GRAHAM ◆ Harvard University

DONALD KAGAN ◆ Yale University

STEVEN OZMENT ◆ Harvard University

FRANK M. TURNER ◆ Yale University

PEARSON
Prentice
Hall

Upper Saddle River, NJ 07458

Executive Editor: Charles Cavaliere
Editorial Assistants: Lauren Aylward, Maureen Diana
Director of Marketing: Brandy Dawson
Senior Marketing Manager: Kate Mitchell
Marketing Assistant: Jennifer Lang
Director, Media and Assessment: Shannon Gattens
Media Project Manager: Brian Hyland
Senior Managing Editor: Mary Carnis
Production Project Manager: Kathy Sleys
Operations Supervisor: Mary Ann Gloriande
Senior Art Director: Maria Lange
Art Directors: Anne Nieglos, Suzanne Duda
Interior/Cover Design: Karen Quigley
Design Support: Michael Frubheis
Cover Illustration/Photo: © Yann Arthus-Bertrand / Altitude
AV Project Manager: Mirella Signoretto
Manager, Rights and Permissions: Zina Arabia
Manager, Visual Research: Beth Brenzel
Photo Researcher: Teri Stratford
Image Permission Coordinator: Michelina Viscusi
Composition/Full-Service Project Management: Frank Weihenig, Preparé, Inc.
Printer/Binder: R. R. Donnelley & Sons, Inc.

Credits and acknowledgments borrowed from other sources and reproduced, with permission, in this textbook appear on appropriate page within text (or on page C-1).

Pearson Education Ltd.
Pearson Education Singapore, Pte. Ltd.
Pearson Education, Canada, Ltd.
Pearson Education–Japan

Pearson Education Australia PTY, Ltd.
Pearson Education North Asia Ltd.
Pearson Educación de Mexico, S.A. de C.V.
Pearson Education Malaysia, Pte. Ltd.

10 9 8 7 6 5 4 3 2 1
ISBN 13: 978-0-13-601387-7
ISBN 10:   0-13-601387-2

Brief Contents

Contents

Part 1 HUMAN ORIGINS AND EARLY CIVILIZATIONS TO 500 B.C.E. ◆ 3

Part 2   EMPIRES AND CULTURES OF THE ANCIENT WORLD, 1000 B.C.E. TO 500 C.E. ◆ 85

Part 3   CONSOLIDATION AND INTERACTION OF WORLD CIVILIZATIONS, 500 C.E. TO 1500 C.E. ◆ 243

Part 5   ENLIGHTENMENT AND REVOLUTION IN THE ATLANTIC WORLD, 1700–1850 ◆ 673

CHAPTER 24   POLITICAL CONSOLIDATION IN NINETEENTH-CENTURY EUROPE AND NORTH AMERICA,   742

Global Perspective: European and North American Political Consolidation   744

Part 6   INTO THE MODERN WORLD, 1815–1949 ◆ 777

CHAPTER 25   NORTHERN TRANSATLANTIC ECONOMY AND SOCIETY, 1815–1914   778

Global Perspective: The Building of Northern Transatlantic Supremacy   780

CHAPTER 26 LATIN AMERICA FROM INDEPENDENCE TO THE 1940s 816

CHAPTER 27 INDIA, THE ISLAMIC HEARTLANDS, AND AFRICA, 1800–1945 844

Part 7   GLOBAL CONFLICT AND CHANGE, 1900–PRESENT ◆ 919

Documents

Maps

Preface

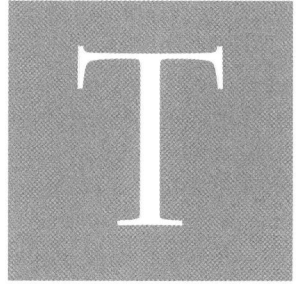

The response of the United States to the events of September 11, 2001, including the war in Iraq and Afghanistan, have brought upon the world a new awareness of human history in a global context. Prior to the attacks on New York and Washington and the subsequent U.S. intervention in the Middle East, readers in North America generally understood world history and globalism as academic concepts. They now understand them as realities shaping their daily lives and experience. The immediate pressures of the present and of the foreseeable future draw us to seek a more certain and extensive understanding of the past.

The idea of globalization is now a pressing reality on the lives of nations, affecting the domestic security of their citizens, the deployment of armed forces, their standard of living, and, increasingly, the environment. We have certainly entered a new era in which no active citizen or educated person can escape the necessity of understanding the past in global terms. Both the historical experience and the moral, political, and religious values of the different world civilizations now demand our attention and our understanding. It is our hope that in these new, challenging times *The Heritage of World Civilizations* will provide one path to such knowledge.

The Roots of Globalization

Globalization—that is, the increasing interaction and interdependency of the various regions of the world—has resulted from two major historical developments: the closing of the European era of world history and the rise of technology.

From approximately 1500 C.E. to the middle of the twentieth century, Europeans gradually came to dominate the world through colonization (most particularly in North and South America), state-building, economic productivity, and military power. That era of European dominance ended during the third quarter of the twentieth century after Europe had brought unprecedented destruction on itself during World War II and as the nations of Asia, the Near East, and Africa achieved new positions on the world scene. Their new political independence, their control over strategic natural resources, and the expansion of their economies (especially those of the nations of the Pacific rim of Asia), and in some cases their access to nuclear weapons have changed the shape of world affairs.

Further changing the world political and social situation has been a growing discrepancy in the economic development of different regions that is often portrayed as a problem between the northern and southern hemispheres. Beyond the emergence of this economic disparity has been the remarkable advance of radical political Islamism during the past forty years. In the midst of all these developments, as a result of the political collapse of the former Soviet Union, the United States has emerged as the single major world power, though its position is increasingly being challenged by China, whose increasing economic might now rivals that of the United States and whose military has embarked on a rapid buildup of its forces.

The second historical development that continues to fuel the pace of globalization is the advance of technology, associated most importantly with transportation, military weapons, and electronic communication. The advances in transportation over the past two centuries including ships, railways, and airplanes have made more parts of the world and its resources accessible to more people in ever shorter spans of time. Over the past century and a half, military weapons of increasingly destructive power enabled Europeans and then later the United States to dominate other regions of the globe. Now, the spread of these weapons means that any nation with sophisticated military technology can threaten other nations, no matter how far away. Furthermore, technologies that originated in the West from the early twentieth century to the present have been turned against the West. More recently, the electronic revolution associated with computer technology and most particularly the Internet has sparked unprecedented speed and complexity in global communications. It is astonishing to recall that personal computers have been generally available for less than twenty-five years and the rapid personal communication associated with them has existed for less than fifteen years.

Why not, then, focus only on new factors in the modern world, such as the impact of technology and the end of the European era? To do so would ignore the very deep roots that these developments have in the past. More important, the events of recent years demonstrate, as the authors of this book have long contended, that the major religious traditions continue to shape and drive the modern world as well as the world of the past. The religious traditions link today's civilizations to their most ancient roots. We believe this emphasis on the great religious traditions recognizes not only a factor that has shaped the past, but one that is profoundly and dynamically alive in our world today.

Strengths of the Text

Balanced and Flexible Presentation   In this edition, as in past editions, we have sought to present world history fairly, accurately, and in a way that does justice to its great variety. History has many facets, no one of which can account for the others. Any attempt to tell the story of civilization from a single perspective, no matter how timely, is bound to neglect or suppress some important part of that story.

Historians have recently brought a vast array of new tools and concepts to bear on the study of history. Our coverage introduces students to various aspects of social and intellectual history as well as to the more traditional political, diplomatic, and military coverage. We firmly believe that only through an appreciation of all pathways to understanding of the past can the real heritage of world civilizations be claimed.

The Heritage of World Civilizations, Eighth Edition is designed to accommodate a variety of approaches to a course in world history, allowing teachers to stress what is most important to them. Some teachers will ask students to read all the chapters. Others will select among them to reinforce assigned readings and lectures.

Clarity and Accessibility   Good narrative history requires clear, vigorous prose. Our goal has been to make our presentation fully accessible to students without compromising on vocabulary or conceptual level. We hope this effort will benefit both teachers and students.

Current Scholarship   As in previous editions, changes in this edition reflect our determination to incorporate the most recent developments in historical scholarship and the expanding concerns of professional historians. To better highlight the dynamic processes of world history, significant new and expanded coverage of prehistory, Africa, East Asia, Southeast Asia, the Atlantic World, and the Middle East has been added to the Eighth Edition.

Content and Organization   The many changes in content and organization in this edition of *The Heritage of World Civilizations* reflect our ongoing effort to present a truly global survey of world civilizations that at the same time gives a rich picture of the history of individual regions:

◆ **Global Approach.** The Eighth Edition continues to explicitly highlight the connections and parallels in global history among regions of the world. Each chapter begins with a "Global Perspective" essay that succinctly places in a wider, global framework the regions and topics that are to be discussed with an emphasis on the connections, parallels, and comparisons between and among different cultures. In addition, each of the seven parts opens with a two-page global map that visually depicts the key themes in the chapters that follow.

◆ **Expanded Map Program.** As in previous editions, great attention has been paid to extending and refining the map program for *The Heritage of World Civilizations*. The Eighth Edition includes twenty-four new maps that graphically illustrate key developments in global history. In addition, when appropriate, existing maps in the text have been redesigned and modified for greater visual appeal and accuracy. Many maps are now accompanied by a global locator that helps students situate the main map in a wider geographical setting.

Maps new to the Eighth Edition:

Early Human Migrations
Mohenjo-Daro
Centers of Greek Philosophy
Early Korean States
Vietnam and Neighboring Southeast Asia
Great Zimbabwe
The Russian Empire, ca. 1500
European Explorations of the Americas, ca. 1550
Origins of African Slaves Sent to the Americas
Korea During the Choson Era
India under the Mughals
Subscriptions to the *Encyclopedia*
The Haitian Revolution
The Languages of Europe, ca. 1850
British India, 1820 and 1856
West Asia, Central Asia, and the Mediterranean, ca. 1850.
Nineteenth-Century Reform Movements in Africa and Arabia
The Long March
The Colonial Economy of Africa, 1880–1914
The American Domain, ca. 1900
The Growth of European Union
Displaced Peoples in Europe after World War II
Distribution of HIV in Africa

A listing of all the maps in the text can be found on pp. xxiii-xxiv.

◆ **Improved Organization and New Scholarship.** Though the number of chapters remains unchanged in the Eighth Edition, the organization of several chapters has been revised to improve narrative flow and highlight important topics more clearly. Chapter 5, on the early history of Africa, now includes extensive discussion of the sources and tools used by anthropologists and historians in their work. Chapter 9, formerly devoted to the early history of Japan, now takes a wider perspective in examining early state formation and cultural developments in Korea and Vietnam as well. Chapter 10 now includes discussion of Nestorian Christianity. The coverage of African history from 1000 to 1700 has been moved to Chapter 14 to more fully integrate the discussion of crucial African developments in this period with developments in Europe and the Americas during this time. Chapter 18, on the formation of an Atlantic World in the sixteenth–eighteenth centuries, now includes extensive treatment of the Columbian exchange and the most recent data on the slave trade. Chapter 27, on India, the Islamic world, and Africa in the nineteenth and early twentieth centuries, has been extensively revised to sharpen the perspective of native peoples on the experience of imperialism. Chapter 32's discussion of the West since World War II now presents coverage of climate change and the tensions this has caused between the United States and Europe. Chapter 34, the final chapter, has been extensively revised to highlight important recent events in Africa, Latin America, South Asia, and the Middle East.

◆ **New Design and Photo Program.** The entire text has been set in a crisp and engaging new design. Each of the 34 chapters includes photos never before included in previous editions of the text. Seven new graphs and tables have also been added to the text to help students visualize important data.

Pedagogical Features

This edition retains many of the pedagogical features of previous editions, while providing increased assessment opportunities.

◆ **NEW** Interpreting the Past feature, found at the end of each chapter, presents students with sources from both the text and on MyHistoryLab/Primary Source, that shed light on a significant problem in world history. Problems include the nature of kingship in early societies, Islam's encounter with the "other," perspectives on the Atlantic slave trade, Japan's relations with the outside world during the Tokugawa shogunate, and feminism and civil rights after World War II. Students are asked to consider how the sources relate to each other and how they shed light on the problems historians face in interpreting the past.

◆ **Two-page Global Maps** open each of the seven parts of the book. These provide a visual and geographical overview of the key themes presented in the chapters that follow. Introduction and questions help students make connections across time and space.

◆ **Global Perspective Essays** introduce the key problems of each chapter and place them in a global and historical context. Focus Questions prompt students to consider the causes, connections, and consequences of the topics they will encounter in the main narrative.

◆ **Religions of the World** essays examine the historical impact of each of the world's great religious traditions: Judaism, Christianity, Islam, Buddhism, and Hinduism.

◆ **Chapter Outlines** open each chapter and help students easily access important topics for study and review.

◆ **Overview Tables** summarize key concepts and reinforce material presented in the main narrative.

◆ **Chronologies** within each chapter help students situate key events in time.

◆ **Documents**, including selections from sacred books, poems, philosophical tracts, political manifestos, letters, and travel accounts, expose students to the raw material of history, providing an intimate contact with peoples of the past. Questions accompanying the source documents direct students toward important, thought-provoking issues and help them relate the documents to the main narrative.

◆ **Key Terms** are boldfaced in the text, listed (with page reference) at the end of each chapter (along with phonetic spellings when appropriate), and are defined in the book's glossary.

◆ **Interactive Maps**, usually one per chapter, prompt students to explore the relationship between geography and history in a dynamic fashion.

◆ **Chapter Summaries** conclude each chapter, organized by subtopic, and recap important points.

◆ **Chapter Review Questions** help students interpret the broad themes of each chapter. These questions can be used for class discussion and essay topics.

A Note on Dates and Transliteration

We have used B.C.E. (before the common era) and C.E. (common era) instead of B.C. (before Christ) and A.D. (anno domini, the year of our Lord) to designate dates.

Until recently, most scholarship on China used the Wade-Giles system of romanization for Chinese names and terms. China, today, however, uses another system known as pinyin. Virtually all Western newspapers have adopted it. In order that students may move easily from the present text to the existing body of advanced scholarship on Chinese history, we now use the pinyin system throughout the text.

Also, we have followed the currently accepted English transliterations of Arabic words. For example, today Koran is being replaced by the more accurate Qur'an; similarly Muhammad is preferable to Mohammed and Muslim to Moslem. We have not tried to distinguish the letters 'ayn and *hamza*; both are rendered by a simple apostrophe (') as in Shi'ite. With regard to Sanskritic transliteration, we have not distinguished linguals and dentals, and both palatal and lingual *s* are rendered *sh*, as in Shiva and Upanishad.

Support Materials

The Heritage of World Civilizations, Eighth Edition, comes with an extensive package of support materials for teachers and students.

For Instructors

- **The Instructor's Manual/Test-Item File** includes chapter outlines, overviews, key concepts, discussion questions, suggestions for useful audiovisual resources, and approximately 1,500 test items (essay, multiple choice, true/false, and matching).
- **Test Manager** is a computerized test management program for Windows and Macintosh environments. The program allows instructors to select items from the test-item file to create tests. It also allows for online testing.
- **The Instructor's Resource Center** (*www.prenhall.com*) Text-specific materials, such as the instructor's manual, the test-item file, map files, and PowerPoint™ presentations, are available for downloading by adopters.
- **myhistorylab** *http://www.myhistorylab.com* With the best of Prentice Hall's multimedia solutions in one easy-to-use place, MyHistoryLab for *The Heritage of World Civilizations* offers students and instructors a state-of-the-art, interactive solution for world history. Organized by the main subtopics of *The World*, and delivered within a course-management platform, MyHistoryLab supplements and enriches the classroom experience and can form the basis for an online course.

For the Student

- Extensively revised and updated, the **Primary Source: Documents in Global History DVD** is both an immense collection of textual and visual documents in world history and an indispensable tool for working with sources. Extensively developed with the guidance of historians and teachers, the revised and updated DVD version includes over 800 sources in world history—from cave art to satellite images of the Earth from space. More sources from Africa, Latin America, and Southeast Asia have been added to this revised and updated DVD version. All sources are accompanied by headnotes, focus questions, and are searchable by topic, region, or time period.
- **World History Study Site** (*www.prenhall.com*) This course-based, open-access online companion provides a wealth of resources for both students and professors, including test questions, flash cards, links for further research, and Web-based assignments.

vango notes **Hear it. Get it.** Study on the go with **VangoNotes**. VangoNotes is a digital audio study guide that can be downloaded to a mp3 player. Students can study wherever they are or whatever they are doing by listening to the following for each chapter of the *Heritage of World Civilizations*:

- **Big Ideas**: Your "need to know" for each chapter
- **Practice Test**: A gut check for the Big Ideas—tells students what they need to keep studying
- **Rapid Review**: A quick drill session

VangoNotes are **flexible**; students can download all the material directly to their mp3 players, or only the chapters they need. *http://www.vangonotes.com*

- **Study Guide, Volumes I and II** includes practice tests, essay questions, and map exercises
- Titles from the renowned **Penguin Classics** series can be bundled with *The Heritage of World Civilizations* for a nominal charge. Please contact your Pearson Arts and Sciences sales representative for details.
- **The Prentice Hall Atlas of World History, Second Edition** includes over 100 full-color maps in world history, drawn by Dorling Kindersley, one of the world's most respected cartographic publishers. Copies of the Atlas can be bundled with *The World* for a nominal charge. Contact your Pearson Arts and Sciences sales representative for details.

Pearson Prentice Hall is pleased to serve as a sponsor of the The World History Association Teaching Prize and The

World History Association and Phi Alpha Theta Student Paper Prize (undergraduate and graduate divisions). Both of these prizes are awarded annually. For more information, contact thewha@hawaii.edu

Acknowledgments

We are grateful to the many scholars and teachers whose thoughtful and often detailed comments helped shape this as well as previous editions of *The Heritage of World Civilizations*. The advice and guidance provided by Katie Janssen on the coverage of African history and Thomas M. Ricks on the coverage of Islam and the Middle East is especially appreciated. We also thank Frank Karpiel and Jonathan Perry, who helped compose the new "Interpreting the Past" sections.

Reviewers of the Seventh Edition

W. Nathan Alexander, *Troy University*

Douglas Chambers, *University of Southern Mississippi*

Barry Hankins, *Baylor University*

Don Knox, *Wayland Baptist University*

Garth Montgomery, *Radford University*

George S. Pabis, *Georgia Perimeter College*

Anthony R. Santoro, *Christopher Newport University*

Linda B. Scherr, *Mercer County Community College*

Deborah Vess, *Georgia College and State University*

Gilmar Visoni, *Queensborough Community College*

Reviewers of Previous Editions

Wayne Ackerson, *Salisbury State University*

Jack Martin Balcer, *Ohio State University*

Charmarie J. Blaisdell, *Northeastern University*

Deborah Buffton, *University of Wisconsin at La Crosse*

Loretta Burns, *Mankato State University*

Gayle K. Brunelle, *California State University, Fullerton*

Chun-shu Chang, *University of Michigan, Ann Arbor*

Mark Chavalas, *University of Wisconsin at La Crosse*

Anthony Cheeseboro, *Southern Illinois University at Edwardsville*

William J. Courteney, *University of Wisconsin*

Samuel Willard Crompton, *Holyoke Community College*

James B. Crowley, *Yale University*

Bruce Cummings, *The University of Chicago*

Stephen F. Dale, *Ohio State University, Columbus*

Clarence B. Davis, *Marian College*

Raymond Van Dam, *University of Michigan, Ann Arbor*

Bill Donovan, *Loyola University of Maryland*

Wayne Farris, *University of Tennessee*

Anita Fisher, *Clark College*

Suzanne Gay, *Oberlin College*

Katrina A. Glass, *United States Military Academy*

Robert Gerlich, *Loyola University*

Samuel Robert Goldberger, *Capital Community-Technical College*

Andrew Gow, *University of Alberta*

Katheryn L. Green, *University of Wisconsin, Madison*

David Griffiths, *University of North Carolina, Chapel Hill*

Louis Haas, *Duquesne University*

Joseph T. Hapak, *Moraine Valley Community College*

Hue-Tam Ho Tai, *Harvard University*

David Kieft, *University of Minnesota*

Frederick Krome, *Northern Kentucky University*

Lisa M. Lane, *Mira Costa College*

Richard Law, *Washington State University*

David Lelyveld, *Columbia University*

Jan Lewis, *Rutgers University, Newark*

James C. Livingston, *College of William and Mary*

Richard L. Moore Jr. , *St. Augustine's College*

Beth Nachison, *Southern Connecticut State University*

Robin S. Oggins, *Binghamton University*

Louis A. Perez Jr. , *University of South Florida*

Jonathan Perry, *University of South Florida*

Cora Ann Presley, *Tulane University*

Norman Raiford, *Greenville Technical College*

Norman Ravitch, *University of California, Riverside*

Thomas M. Ricks, *University of Pennsylvania*

Philip F. Riley, *James Madison University*

Thomas Robisheaux, *Duke University*

William S. Rodner, *Tidewater Community College*

David Ruffley, *United States Air Force Academy*

Dankwart A. Rustow, *The City University of New York*

James J. Sack, *University of Illinois at Chicago*

William Schell, *Murray State University*

Marvin Slind, *Washington State University*

Daniel Scavone, *University of Southern Indiana*

Roger Schlesinger, *Washington State University*

Charles C. Stewart, *University of Illinois*

Nancy L. Stockdale, *University of Central Florida*

Carson Tavenner, *United States Air Force Academy*

Truong-bu Lam, *University of Hawaii*

Harry L. Watson, *Loyola College of Maryland*

William B. Whisenhunt, *College of DuPage*

Paul Varley, *Columbia University*

Finally, we would like to thank the dedicated people who helped produce this revision: our editor, Charles Cavaliere; Karen Quigley and Anne Nieglos who created the handsome new design for this edition; Kathleen Sleys, our project manager; Mary Ann Gloriande, our senior operations supervisor, and Frank Weihenig, our production editor.

A.M.C
W.A.G
D.K
S.O
F.M.T

About the Authors

Albert M. Craig is the Harvard-Yenching Research Professor of History Emeritus at Harvard University, where he has taught since 1959. A graduate of Northwestern University, he received his Ph.D. at Harvard University. He has studied at Strasbourg University and at Kyoto, Keio, and Tokyo universities in Japan. He is the author of *Choshu in the Meiji Restoration* (1961), *The Heritage of Chinese Civilization* (2001), and, with others, of *East Asia, Tradition and Transformation* (1989). He is the editor of *Japan, A Comparative View* (1973) and co-editor of *Personality in Japanese History* (1970). At present he is engaged in research on the thought of Fukuzawa Yukichi. For eleven years (1976–1987) he was the director of the Harvard-Yenching Institute. He has also been a visiting professor at Kyoto and Tokyo universities. He has received Guggenheim, Fulbright, and Japan Foundation Fellowships. In 1988 he was awarded the Order of the Rising Sun by the Japanese government.

William A. Graham is Albertson Professor of Middle Eastern Studies in the Faculty of Arts and Sciences and O'Brian Professor of Divinity and Dean in the Faculty of Divinity at Harvard University, where he has taught for thirty-four years. He has directed the Center for Middle Eastern Studies and chaired the Department of Near Eastern Languages and Civilizations, the Committee on the Study of Religion, and the Core Curriculum Committee on Foreign Cultures. He received his BA in Comparative Literature from University of North Carolina, Chapel Hill, an A.M. and Ph.D. in History of Religion from Harvard, and studied also in Göttingen, Tübingen, Lebanon, and London. He is former chair of the Council on Graduate Studies in Religion (U.S. and Canada). In 2000 he received the quinquennial Award for Excellence in Research in Islamic History and Culture from the Research Centre for Islamic History, Art and Culture (IRCICA) of the Organisation of the Islamic Conference. He has held John Simon Guggenheim and Alexander von Humboldt research fellowships and is a fellow of the American Academy of Arts and Sciences. Among his publications are *Beyond the Written Word: Oral Aspects of Scripture in the History of Religion* (1987); *Divine Word and Prophetic Word in Early Islam* (1977—ACLS History of Religions Prize, 1978); and *Three Faiths, One God* (co-authored, 2003).

Donald Kagan is Sterling Professor of History and Classics at Yale University, where he has taught since 1969. He received the A.B. degree in history from Brooklyn College, the M.A. in classics from Brown University, and the Ph.D. in history from Ohio State University. During 1958–1959 he studied at the American School of Classical Studies as a Fulbright Scholar. He has received three awards for undergraduate teaching at Cornell and Yale. He is the author of a history of Greek political thought, *The Great Dialogue* (1965); a four-volume history of the Peloponnesian war, *The Origins of the Peloponnesian War* (1969); *The Archidamian War* (1974); *The Peace of Nicias and the Sicilian Expedition* (1981); *The Fall of the Athenian Empire* (1987); a biography of Pericles, *Pericles of Athens and the Birth of Democracy* (1991); *On the Origins of War* (1995), and *The Peloponnesian War* (2003). He is coauthor, with Frederick W. Kagan of *While America Sleeps* (2000). With Brian Tierney and L. Pearce Williams, he is the editor of *Great Issues in Western Civilization*, a collection of readings. He was awarded the National Humanities Medal for 2002.

Steven Ozment is McLean Professor of Ancient and Modern History at Harvard University. He has taught Western Civilization at Yale, Stanford, and Harvard. He is the author of nine books. *The Age of Reform, 1250–1550* (1980), won the Schaff Prize, and was nominated for the 1981 National Book Award. Five of his books have been selections of the History Book Club: *Magdalena and Balthasar: An Intimate Portrait of Life in Sixteenth Century Europe* (1986), *Three Behaim Boys: Growing Up in Early Modern Germany* (1990), *Protestants: The Birth of A Revolution* (1992), *The Burgermeister's Daughter: Scandal in a Sixteenth Century German Town* (1996), and *Flesh and Spirit: Private Life in Early Modern Germany* (1999). His most recent book is *Ancestors: The Loving Family of Old Europe* (2001). *A Mighty Fortress: A New History of the German People*, was published in January 2004.

Frank M. Turner is John Hay Whitney Professor of History at Yale University and Director of the Beinecke Rare Book and Manuscript Library at Yale University, where he served as University Provost from 1988 to 1992. He received his B.A. degree from the College of William and Mary and his Ph.D. from Yale. He has received the Yale College Award for Distinguished Undergraduate Teaching. He has directed a National Endowment for the Humanities Summer Institute. His scholarly research has received the support of fellowships from the National Endowment for the Humanities, the Guggenheim Foundation, and the Woodrow Wilson Center. He is the author of *Between Science and Religion: The Reaction to Scientific Naturalism in Late Victorian England* (1974), *The Greek Heritage in Victorian Britain* (1981), which received the British Council Prize of the Conference on British Studies and the Yale Press Governors Award, *Contesting Cultural Authority: Essays in Victorian Intellectual Life* (1993), and *John Henry Newman: The Challenge to Evangelical Religion* (2002). He has also contributed numerous articles to journals and has served on the editorial advisory boards of *The Journal of Modern History*, *Isis*, and *Victorian Studies*. He edited *The Idea of a University*, by John Henry Newman (1996), *Reflections on the Revolution in France by Edmund Burke* (2003), and *Apologia Pro Vita Sua and Six Sermons* by John Henry Newman (2008). He served as a Trustee of Connecticut College from 1996–2006. In 2003, Professor Turner was appointed Director of the Beinecke Rare Book and Manuscript Library at Yale University.

THE HERITAGE OF

World Civilizations

*H*omo sapiens—modern humans—first appeared about one hundred thousand years ago. Since then the pace of human control over the environment has constantly accelerated. It took humans tens of thousands of years to domesticate animals and to master the rudiments of agriculture. It took humans another seven thousand years to nine thousand years to develop cities, systems of writing, and bronze and iron. Several hundred years later the great religious and philosophical revolutions of the ancient world occurred, followed by the empires of China, Iran, and Rome.

NORTH
AMERICA

Temple of the Sun, Palenque, southern Mexico, 300–600 C.E.
Temples such as this Mayan pyramid formed the cultural centers of many early civilizations. *(See pages 41–43).*

Egyptian peasants plowing with oxen, 1400 B.C.E.
Agriculture transformed the societies of the ancient world.
(See pages 18–24).

SOUTH
AMERICA

1

HUMAN ORIGINS AND EARLY CIVILIZATIONS TO 500 B.C.E.

Cave Art showing bison, rhinoceroses, and horses, from Chauvet, southern France, circa 25,000 B.C.E— 30,000 B.C.E *(See pages 6–8).*

Laozi, the founder of Daoism. *(See pages 54–55).*

ASIA

EUROPE

Ziggurat from Ur, in modern Iraq (ca. 2100 – 2050 B.C.E.). Monumental religious architecture is characteristic of many early civilizations. *(See pages 12–24).*

AFRICA

AUSTRALIA

Carved stone. Discovered in 2001, this 75,000-year-old ochre slab from South Africa is carved with lines and markings. It may be the world's oldest calendar. *(See pages 6–8).*

Making Connections

1

What is the relationship between the development of agriculture and the rise of cities?

2

What is the evidence for contact and exchange between early civilizations?

1

The Birth of Civilization

SCIENTISTS ESTIMATE THAT THE EARTH MAY BE AS many as six billion years old and that the first humanlike creatures appeared in Africa perhaps 3 to 5 million years ago. Some 1 to 2 million years ago, erect and tool-using early humans spread over much of Africa, Europe, and Asia (see Map 1–1). Our own species, *Homo sapiens*, probably emerged some 200,000 years ago, and the earliest remains of fully modern humans date to about 100,000 years ago.

The earliest humans lived by hunting, fishing, and collecting wild plants. Only some 10,000 years ago did they learn to cultivate plants, herd animals, and make airtight pottery for storage. These discoveries transformed them from gatherers to producers and allowed them to grow in number and to lead a settled life. Beginning about 5,000 years ago a far more complex way of life began to appear in some parts of the world. In these places humans learned how to increase harvests through irrigation and other methods, making possible much larger populations. They came together in towns, cities, and other centers, where they erected

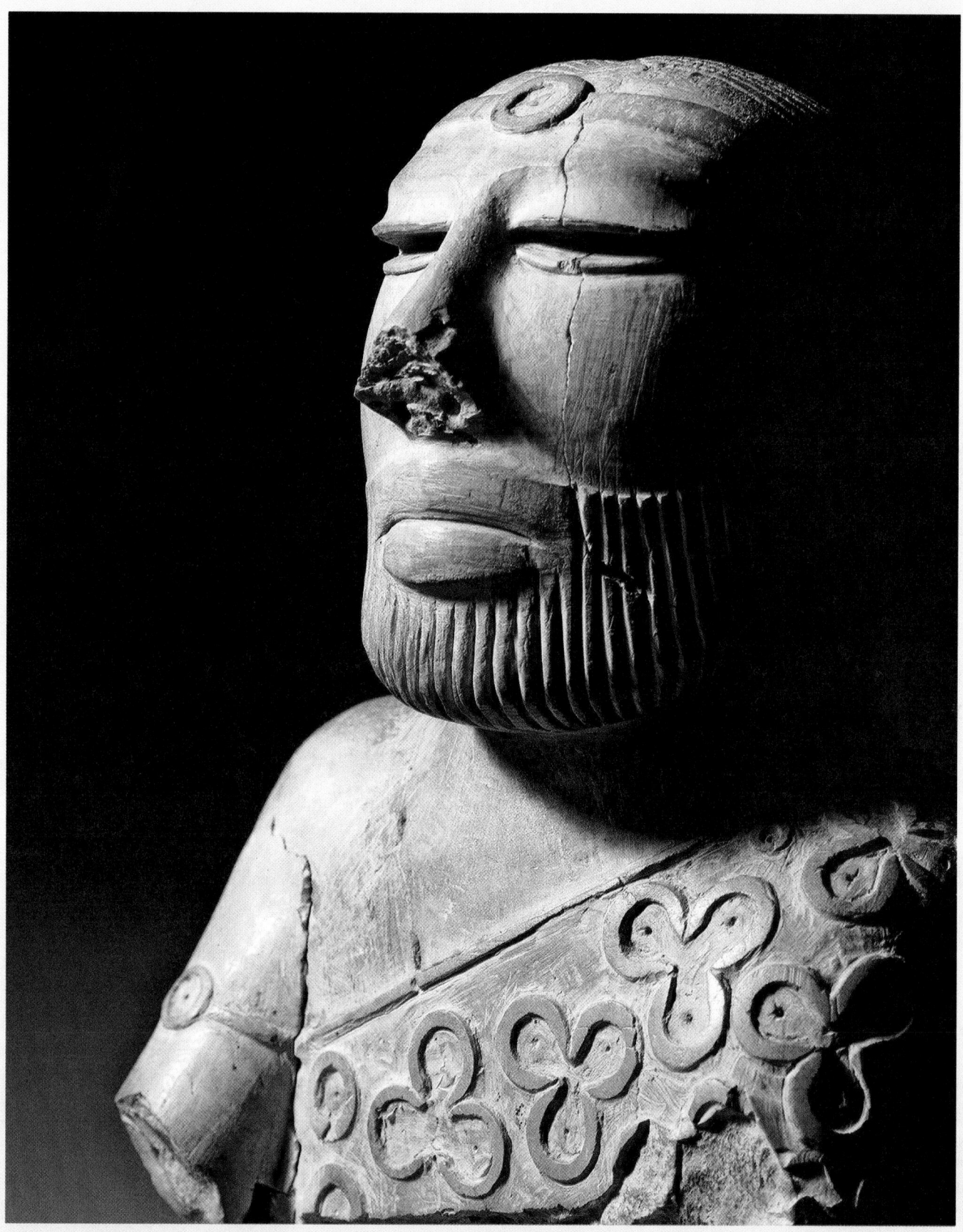

A carved or etched limestone statue, from about 2500 B.C.E., believed by scholars to be a king or a priest from Mohenjo-Daro in the Indus valley in present-day Pakistan.

Civilizations

The World

The way of life of prehistoric cave dwellers differed immensely from that of today's civilized world. Yet the few millennia in which we have been civilized are but a tiny fraction of the long span of human existence. Especially during the recent millennia, changes in our culture/way of life have far outpaced changes in our bodies. We retain the emotional makeup and motor reflexes of prehistoric men and women while living highly organized and often sedentary lives.

We might best view the early civilizations by asking how they fit into the sweep of history. One notable feature of human history is the acceleration in the pace of change. From the time that modern humans first appeared 100,000 years ago until 7000 B.C.E., few changes occurred. Humans migrated from Africa to other parts of the world and adapted to new climes. All lived by hunting, fishing, and gathering. The chief advance in technology during this longest span of human existence was from rough to smooth stone weapons and tools.

Then, from about 7000 B.C.E., innovations began. Humans learned to till the soil, domesticate animals, and make pots for the storage of food. A few millennia later, bronze was discovered and the so-called river valley civilizations formed along the Nile, the Tigris-Euphrates, the Indus, and the Yellow River. Cities rose. Writing was invented. Societies divided into classes or castes: most members engaged in farming, a few traded, and others assumed military, priestly, or governmental roles. As these civilizations expanded, they became richer, more populous, and more powerful.

The last millennium B.C.E. witnessed two major developments. One was the emergence, during 600–300 B.C.E., of the religious and philosophical revolutions that would indelibly mark their respective civilizations: monotheistic Judaism from which would later develop the world religions of Christianity and Islam; Hinduism and Buddhism in southern Asia; the philosophies of Greece and China. The second development was the rise of the iron-age empires—the Roman, the Mauryan along the Ganges, the Han in China—during the centuries straddling the end of the millennium.

impressive structures and where industry and commerce flourished. They developed writing, enabling them to keep inventories of food and other resources. Specialized occupations emerged, complex religions took form, and social divisions increased. These changes marked the birth of civilization. ■

Early Humans and Their Culture

Humans, unlike other animals, are cultural beings. **Culture** is the sum total of the ways of living built up by a group and passed on from one generation to another. Culture includes behavior such as courtship or child-rearing practices; material things such as tools, clothing, and shelter; and ideas, institutions, and beliefs. Language, apparently a uniquely

human trait, lies behind our ability to create ideas and institutions and to transmit culture from one generation to another. Our flexible and dexterous hands enable us to hold and make tools and so to create the material artifacts of culture. Because culture is learned and not inherited, it permits rapid adaptation to changing conditions, making possible the spread of humanity to almost all the lands of the globe.

The Paleolithic Age

Anthropologists designate early human cultures by their tools. The earliest period—the **Paleolithic Age** (from the Greek, "old stone")—dates from the earliest use of stone tools some 1 million years ago to about 10,000 B.C.E. During this immensely long period, people were hunters, fishers, and gatherers, but not producers, of food. They learned to make and use increasingly sophisticated tools of stone

After the fall of these early empires, swift changes occurred. For a millennium, Europe and Byzantium fell behind, while China and the Middle East led in technology and the arts of government. But by 1500 Europe had caught up, and after 1700, it led. India had invented Arabic numerals, and Arab thinkers inspired the Renaissance, but it was Europe that produced Copernicus and Newton.

The nineteenth century saw the invention of the steam engine, the steamship, the locomotive, the telegraph and telephone, and the automobile. After that came electric lights, the radio, and, in the century that followed, the airplane.

In the twentieth century, invention and scientific discovery became institutionalized in university, corporate, and government laboratories. Ever larger amounts of resources were committed to research. By the beginning of the twenty-first century man had walked on the moon, deciphered the human genome, and unlocked the power of the atom. Today, as discoveries occur ever more rapidly, we cannot imagine the science of a hundred years into the future.

If this process of accelerating change had its origins in 7000 B.C.E., what was the original impetus? Does the logic of nature dictate that once agriculture develops, cities will rise in alluvial valleys favorable to cultivation? Was it inevitable that the firing of clay to produce pots would produce metals from metallic oxides and lead to the discovery of smelting? Did the formation of aristocratic and priestly classes automatically lead to record keeping and writing? If so, it is not at all surprising that parallel and independent developments should have occurred in regions as widely separated as China and the Middle East.

Or was the almost simultaneous rise of the ancient Eurasian civilizations the result of **diffusion**? Did migrating peoples carry seeds, new tools, and metals over long distances? The available evidence provides no definitive answer. Understanding the origins of the early civilizations and the lives of the men and women who lived in them from what is left of their material culture is like reconstructing a dinosaur from a broken tooth and a fragment of jawbone.

Focus Questions

◆ What were the processes behind the creation of early civilizations?

◆ What are the similarities and differences among the world's earliest civilizations?

◆ Why has the pace of change accelerated with time?

and perishable materials like wood; they learned to make and control fire; and they acquired language and the ability to use it to pass on what they had learned.

These early humans, dependent on nature for food and vulnerable to wild beasts and natural disasters, may have developed responses to the world rooted in fear of the unknown—of the uncertainties of human life or the overpowering forces of nature. Religious and magical beliefs and practices may have emerged in an effort to propitiate or coerce the superhuman forces thought to animate or direct the natural world. Evidence of religious faith and practice, as well as of magic, goes as far back as archaeology can take us. Fear or awe, exultation, gratitude, and empathy with the natural world must all have figured in the cave art and in the ritual practices, such as burial, that we find evidenced at Paleolithic sites around the globe. The sense that there is more to the world than meets the eye—in other words, the religious response to the world—seems to be as old as humankind.

During the Paleolithic Age, most likely relatively near its close, humans, probably pursuing game, crossed from Asia through the region of the Bering Sea, which was then dry land, into the American continent (see Map 1–1). This migration would ultimately separate their descendants from other human groups for many thousands of years. In their isolation, however, the inhabitants of the Americas experienced cultural changes parallel to those of Eurasia and Africa.

The style of life and the level of technology of the Paleolithic period could support only a sparsely settled society. If hunters were too numerous, game would not suffice. In Paleolithic times people were subject to the same natural and ecological constraints that today mantain a balance between wolves and deer in Alaska.

SOURCE Hominid tools

The spread of modern humans

→ possible colonization route
◆ major site 50,000–12,000 BCE
▨ extent of ice sheet 18,000 BCE
▨ extent of ice sheet 10,000 BCE
········ coastline 18,000 BCE
------ ancient river
▨ ancient lake

Map 1–1. Early Human Migrations.

Paleolithic society was probably characterized by a division of labor by sex. Men most likely hunted, fished, and fought other families, clans, and tribes. Women, less mobile because of childbearing, most likely gathered nuts, berries, and wild grains, wove baskets, and made clothing. Women gathering food probably discovered how to plant and care for seeds, knowledge that eventually led to agriculture and the Neolithic revolution.

The Neolithic Age

Only a few Paleolithic societies made the initial shift from hunting and gathering to agriculture. Anthropologists and archaeologists disagree as to why, but however it happened, some 10,000 years ago parts of what we now call the Near East began to change from a nomadic hunter-gatherer culture to a more settled agricultural one.

Last dwarf mammoths
become extinct c.3000 BCE

Wrangel
Island

Settled by c.45,000 BCE

Volga

◇ Sunghir

Ob'

S i b e r i a

Yenisey

Lena

Pushkari

◇ Kostienki

◇ Mezhirich

dmostí
ní
tonice

Black Sea
Lake

Caspian Sea

Aral
Sea

Lake
Konya

◇ Mal'ta

A S I A

G o b i

Amur

Yellow River

◇ Zhoukoudian

Japan

Honshu

◇ Hoshino

Yangtze

◇ Fukui

Earliest settlers
c.40,000 BCE

Ili

◇ Shanidar

Tigris

Euphrates

H i m a l a y a s

◇ Yuanmou

First evidence of
human burials

Haua
Fleah

◇ Nazlet Khatir

Indus

Ganges

Nile

A r a b i a n
P e n i n s u l a

◇ Bhimbetka

I n d i a

◇ Patne

Maba

East Asia:
Earliest evidence for
hominid colonization
dates to c.1.7 million
years ago

Philippine
Islands

First settled
c.60,000 BCE

P
A
C
I
F
I
C

O
C
E
A
N

Mekong

RICA

Lake
Galla

Congo

Lake
Victoria

I N D I A N

O C E A N

◇ Tabon Cave

Sunda

◇ Niah Cave

Borneo

◇ Pamwak

Olduvai Gorge:
Site of first discoveries of
Australopithecus boisei and
Homo habilis, dating from
c.2.5 million years ago

New
Guinea

◇ Nombe

Solomon
Islands

◇ Olduvai Gorge

◇ Kisese

Great Rift Valley

Sumatra

Java

Earliest evidence
of use of boats

◇ Kosipe

Sahul

Migration of early
modern humans begins
c.150,000 years ago

Australia:
Fully modern humans colonize Aus
from Southeast Asia, from c.60,000
ago; they utilize land bridges creat
lowered sea levels during last Ice A

Zimbe

Lake
akgadikgadi

Southern Africa:
From c.120,000 years ago,
early hominids colonize
more marginal areas
of Africa

Madagascar

Lake
Car pentaria

◇ Koolan

◇ Cuckadoo

◇ Lion Cave

◇ Border Cave

Kalahari
Desert

rican
rt

◇ Puritjarra

◇ Kenniff Cave

Orange River

as
ver
uth

A u s t r a l i a

◇ Koonalda Cave

Darling

◇ Arumvale

◇ Panaramitee

◇ Lake Mungo

Earliest evidence of
human cremation
c.26,000 BCE

Lake
Napait

◇ Kow Swamp

◇ Keilor

New Zealand

Tasmania

◇ Beginner's Luck Cave

◇ Bone Cave

Because the shift to agriculture coincided with advances in stone tool technology—the development of greater precision, for example, in chipping and grinding—this period is called the Neolithic Age (from the Greek, "new stone"). Productive animals, such as sheep and goats, and food crops, such as wheat and barley, were first domesticated in the mountain foothills where they already lived or grew in the wild. Once they had domesticated these plants and animals, people could move to areas where these plants

and animals did not occur naturally, such as the river valleys of the region. The invention of pottery during the Neolithic Age enabled people to store surplus foods and liquids and to transport them, as well as to cook agricultural products that were difficult to eat or digest raw. They made cloth from flax and wool. Crops required constant care from planting to harvest, so Neolithic farmers built permanent dwellings. The earliest of these tended to be circular huts, large enough to house only one or two people

Wondjina. An image depicting cloud and rain spirits from Chamberlain Gorge in western Australia, painted perhaps 12,000 years ago.

suggesting that most Neolithic villagers had about the same level of wealth and social status. A few items, such as stones and shells, were traded long distance, but Neolithic villages tended to be self-sufficient.

Two larger Neolithic settlements do not fit this village pattern. One was found at Çatal Hüyük, in a fertile agricultural region about 150 miles south of Ankara, the capital of present-day Turkey. This was a large town covering over fifteen acres, with a population probably well over six thousand people. The houses were clustered so closely that they had no doors but were entered by ladders from the roofs. Many were decorated inside with sculptures of animal heads and horns, as well as paintings that were apparently redone regularly. Some appear to depict ritual or festive occasions involving men and women. One is the world's oldest landscape picture, showing a nearby volcano exploding. The agriculture, arts, and crafts of this town were astonishingly diversified and at a much higher level of attainment than in other, smaller settlements of the period. The site of Jericho, an oasis around a spring near the Dead Sea, was occupied as early as 12,000 B.C.E. Around 8000 B.C.E. a town of eight to ten acres grew up, surrounded by a massive stone wall with at least one tower against the inner face. Although this wall may have been for defense, scholars dispute its use because no other Neolithic settlement has been found with fortifications. The inhabitants of Neolithic Jericho had a mixed agricultural, herding, and hunting economy and may have traded salt. They had no pottery but plastered the skulls of their dead to make realistic memorial portraits of them. These two sites show that the economy and the settlement patterns of the Neolithic period may be more complicated than many scholars have thought.

and clustered in groups around a central storage place. Later people built square and rectangular family-sized houses with individual storage places and enclosures to house livestock. Houses in a Neolithic village were normally all the same size and were built on the same plan,

Throughout the Paleolithic Age, the human population had been small and relatively stable. The shift from food gathering to food production may not have been associated with an immediate change in population, but over time in the regions where agriculture and animal husbandry appeared, the number of human beings grew at an unprecedented rate. One reason for this is that farmers usually had larger families than hunters. Their children began to work and matured at a younger age than the children of hunters. When animals and plants were domesticated and brought to the river valleys, the relationship between human beings and nature was changed forever. People had learned to control nature, a vital prerequisite for the emergence of civilization. But farmers had to work harder and longer than hunters did, and they had to stay

Çatal Hüyük. The diagram reconstructs part of Çatal Hüyük on the basis of archaeological findings. *Reprinted by permission of the Catalhoyuk Research Project.*

in one place. Herders, on the other hand, often moved from place to place in search of pasture and water, returning to their villages in the spring. Some scholars refer to the dramatic changes in subsistence, settlement, technology, and population of this time as the **Neolithic Revolution**. The earliest Neolithic societies appeared in the Middle East about 8000 B.C.E., in China about 4000 B.C.E., and in India about 3600 B.C.E. Neolithic agriculture was based on wheat and barley in the Middle East, on millet and rice in China, and on corn in Mesoamerica, several millennia later.

The Bronze Age and the Birth of Civilization

Neolithic agricultural villages and herding cultures gradually replaced Paleolithic culture in much of the world. Then another major shift occurred, first in the plains along the Tigris and Euphrates Rivers in the region the Greeks and Romans called **Mesopotamia** (modern Iraq), later in the valley of the Nile River in Egypt, and somewhat later in India and the Yellow River basin in China. This shift was initially associated with the growth of towns alongside villages, creating a hierarchy of larger and smaller settlements in the same region. Some towns then grew into much larger urban centers and often drew populations into them, so that

nearby villages and towns declined. The urban centers, or cities, usually had monumental buildings, such as temples and fortifications. These were vastly larger than individual houses and could be built only by the sustained effort of hundreds and even thousands of people over many years. Elaborate representational artwork appeared, sometimes made of rare and imported materials. New technologies, such as smelting and the manufacture of metal tools and weapons, were characteristic of urban life. Commodities like pottery and textiles that had been made in individual houses in villages were mass produced in cities, which also were characterized by social stratification—that is, different classes of people based on factors such as control of resources, family, religious or political authority, and personal wealth. The earliest writing is also associated with the growth of cities. Writing, like representational art, was a powerful means of communicating over space and time and was probably invented to deal with urban problems of management and record keeping. These attributes—urbanism; technological, industrial, and social change; long-distance trade; and new methods of symbolic communication—are defining characteristics of the form of human culture called **civilization**. At about the time the earliest civilizations were emerging, someone discovered how to combine tin and copper to make a stronger and more useful material—bronze. Archaeologists coined the term **Bronze Age** to refer to the period 3100–1200 B.C.E. in the Near East and eastern Mediterranean.

Early Civilizations in the Middle East to About 1000 B.C.E.

By 4000 B.C.E., people had settled in large numbers in the river-watered lowlands of Mesopotamia and Egypt. By about 3000 B.C.E., when the invention of writing gave birth to history, urban life and the organization of society into centralized states were well established in the valleys of the Tigris and Euphrates Rivers in Mesopotamia and the Nile River in Egypt.

Much of the urban population consists of people who do not grow their own food, so urban life is possible only where farmers and stockbreeders can be made to produce a substantial surplus beyond their own needs. Also, some process has to be in place so that this surplus can be collected and redeployed to sustain city dwellers. Moreover, efficient farming of plains alongside rivers requires intelligent management of water resources for irrigation. In Mesopotamia, irrigation was essential, because in the south (Babylonia), rainfall was insufficient to sustain crops. Furthermore, the rivers, fed by melting snows in Armenia, rose to flood the fields in the spring, about the time for harvest, when water was not needed. When water was needed for the autumn planting, less was available. This meant that people had to build dikes to keep the rivers from flooding the fields in the spring and had to devise means to store water for use in the autumn. The Mesopotamians became skilled at that activity early on. In Egypt, on the other hand, the Nile River flooded at the right moment for cultivation, so irrigation was simply a matter of directing the water to the fields. In Mesopotamia, villages, towns, and cities tended to be strung along natural watercourses and, eventually, man-made canal systems. Thus, control of water could be important in warfare; an enemy could cut off water upstream of a city to force it to submit. Because the Mesopotamian plain was flat, branches of the rivers often changed their courses, and people would have to abandon their cities and move to new locations. Archaeologists once believed that urban life and centralized government arose in response to the need to regulate irrigation. This theory supposed that only a strong central authority could construct and maintain the necessary waterworks. More recently, archaeologists have shown that large-scale irrigation appeared only long after urban civilization had already developed, so major waterworks were a consequence of urbanism, not a cause of it.

Mesopotamian Civilization

The first civilization appears to have arisen in Mesopotamia. The region is divided into two ecological zones, roughly north and south of modern Baghdad. In the south (Babylonia), as noted, irrigation is vital; in the north (Assyria), agriculture is possible with rainfall and wells. The south has high yields from irrigated lands, while the north has lower yields, but much more land under cultivation, so it can produce more than the south. The oldest Mesopotamian cities seem to have been founded by a people called the Sumerians during the fourth millennium B.C.E. in the land of Sumer, which is the southern half of Babylonia. By 3000 B.C.E., the Sumerian city of Uruk was the largest city in the world (see Map 1–2). Colonies of people from Uruk built cities and outposts in northern Syria and southern Anatolia. One of these, at Habubah Kabirah on the Euphrates River in Syria, was built on a regular plain on virgin ground, with strong defensive walls, but was abandoned after a few generations and never inhabited again. No one knows how the Sumerians were able to establish colonies so far from their homeland or even what their purpose was. They may have been trading centers.

From about 2800 to 2370 B.C.E., in what is called the Early Dynastic period, several Sumerian city-states existed in southern Mesopotamia, arranged in north–south lines along the major watercourses. Among these cities were Uruk, Ur, Nippur, Shuruppak, and Lagash. Some of the city-states formed leagues among themselves that apparently had both political and religious significance. Quarrels over water and agricultural land led to incessant warfare, and in time, stronger towns and leagues conquered weaker ones and expanded to form kingdoms ruling several city-states.

Unlike the Sumerians, the people who occupied northern Mesopotamia and Syria spoke mostly Semitic languages (that is, languages in the same family as Arabic and Hebrew). The Sumerian language is not related to any language known today. Many of these Semitic peoples absorbed aspects of Sumerian culture, especially writing. At the western end of this broad territory, at Ebla in northern Syria, scribes kept records using Sumerian writing and studied Sumerian word lists. In northern Babylonia, the Mesopotamians believed that the large city of Kish had history's first kings. In the far east of this territory, not far from modern Baghdad, a people known as the Akkadians established their own kingdom at a capital city called Akkade, under their first king, Sargon, who had been a servant of the king of Kish.

The Akkadians conquered all the Sumerian city-states and invaded southwestern Iran and northern Syria. This was history's first empire, having a heartland, provinces, and an absolute ruler. It included numerous peoples, cities, lan-

Map 1–2.   The Ancient Near East. Two river valley civilizations thrived in the Ancient Near East: Egypt, which was united into a single state, and Mesopotamia, which was long divided into a number of city-states.

guages, and cultures, as well as different ecological zones, under one rule. Sargon's name became legendary as the first great conqueror of history. His grandson, Naram-Sin, ruled from the Persian Gulf to the Mediterranean Sea, with a standardized administration, vast wealth and power, and a grand style that to later Mesopotamians was a high point of their history. Naram-Sin even declared himself a god and had temples built to himself, something no Sumerian ruler had ever done. External attack and internal weakness destroyed the Akkadian Empire, but several smaller states flourished independently, notably Lagash in Sumer, under its ruler Gudea.

About 2125 B.C.E. the Sumerian city of Ur rose to dominance, and the rulers of the Third Dynasty of Ur established an empire built on the foundation of the Akkadian Empire, but far smaller. In this period, Sumerian culture and literature flourished. Epic poems were composed, glorifying the deeds of the ancestors of the kings of Ur. A highly centralized administration kept detailed records of agriculture, animal husbandry, commerce, and other mat-

ters. Over a hundred thousand of these documents have been found in the ruins of Sumerian cities. After little more

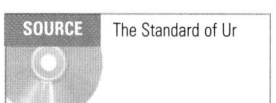

SOURCE   The Standard of Ur

than a century of prominence, the kingdom of Ur disintegrated in the face of famine and invasion. From the east, the Elamites attacked the city of Ur and captured the king. From the north and west, a Semitic-speaking people, the Amorites, invaded Mesopotamia in large numbers, settling around the Sumerian cities and eventually founding their own dynasties in some of them, such as at Uruk, Babylon, Isin, and Larsa.

The fall of the Third Dynasty of Ur ended Sumerian rule, and the Sumerians gradually disappeared as an identifiable group. The Sumerian language survived only in writing as the learned language of Babylonia taught in schools and used by priests and scholars. So great was the respect for Sumerian that seventeen centuries after the fall of Ur, when Alexander the Great arrived in Babylon, Sumerian was still used there as a scholarly and religious language.

For some time after the fall of Ur, there was relative peace in Babylonia under the Amorite kings of Isin, who used Sumerian at their court and considered themselves the successors of the kings of Ur. Eventually, another Amorite dynasty at the city of Larsa contested control of Babylonia, and a period of warfare began, mostly centering around attacks on strategic points on waterways. A powerful new dynasty at Babylon defeated Isin, Larsa, and other rivals and dominated Mesopotamia for nearly three hundred years. Its high point was the reign of its most famous king, Hammurabi (r. ca. 1792–1750 B.C.E.), best known today for the collection of laws that bears his name. (See Document, "The Code of Hammurabi.") Hammurabi destroyed the great city of Mari on the Euphrates and created a kingdom embracing most of Mesopotamia.

Writing and Mathematics   Government, business, and scholarship required an effective writing system. The Sumerians invented the writing system now known as **cuneiform** (from the Latin *cuneus*, "wedge") because of the wedge-shaped marks they made by writing on clay tablets with a cut-reed stylus. At first the writing system was sketchy, giving only a few elements of a sentence to help a reader remember something that he probably already knew. Later, people thought to write whole sentences in the order in which they were to be spoken, so writing could communicate new information to a reader. The Sumerian writing system used several thousand characters, some of which stood for words and some for sounds. Some characters stood for many different sounds or words, and some sounds could be written using a choice of many different characters. The result was a writing system that was difficult to learn. Sumerian students were fond of complaining about their unfair teachers, the difficulty of their schoolwork, and their too-short vacations. Sumerian and Babylonian schools em-

SOURCE | Sumerian Cuneiform Tablet

phasized language and literature, accounting, legal practice, and mathematics, especially geometry, along with memorization of much abstract knowledge that had no relevance to everyday life. The ability to read and write was restricted to an elite who could afford to go to school. Success in school and factors such as good family connections meant that a literate Sumerian could find employment as a clerk, surveyor, teacher, diplomat, or administrator.

The Sumerians also began the development of mathematics. The earliest Sumerian records suggest that before 3000 B.C.E. people had not yet conceptualized the idea of numbers independently of counting specific things. Therefore, the earliest writing used different numerals for counting different things, and the numerals had no independent value. (For example, the same sign could be 10 or 18, depending on what was counted.) Once an independent concept of number was established, mathematics developed rapidly. The Sumerian system was based on the number 60 (sexagesimal), rather than the number 10 (decimal), the system in general use today. Sumerian counting survives in the modern 60-minute hour and the circle of 360 degrees. By the time of Hammurabi, the Mesopotamians were expert in many types of mathematics, including mathematical astronomy. The calendar the Mesopotamians used had twelve lunar months of thirty days each. To keep it in accordance with the solar year and the seasons, the Mesopotamians occasionally introduced a thirteenth month.

Religion   The Sumerians and their successors worshiped many gods and goddesses. They visualized these in human form, with human needs and weaknesses. Most of the gods were identified with some natural phenomenon such as the sky, fresh water, or storms. They differed from humans in their greater power, sublime position in the universe, and immortality. The Mesopotamians believed that the human race was created to serve the gods

Akkadian Victory Stele. The victory stele of Naram-Sin, King of Akkad, over the mountain-dwelling Lullubi, Mesopotamian, Akkadian period, ca. 2230 B.C.E. (pink sandstone). The king, wearing the horned helmet denoting divine power, strides forward at the head of his army. This is one of the finest sculptures to survive from the Akkadian period. *Louvre, Paris, France. The Bridgeman Art Library International Ltd.*

The Code of Hammurabi

Document

The Code of Hammurabi (r. 1792–1750 B.C.E.) was only one of many law codes that Mesopotamian societies produced, probably because in this culture rulers were not considered divine. As a result, civil law codes, separate from religious regulations, were necessary to govern human behavior. From a modern perspective, Mesopotamian law codes such as that of Hammurabi seem unjust, in that they prescribed different rights, responsibilities, and punishments, depending on gender, class, and whether a person was enslaved or free. But they represent an enormous advance in legal thought because they codified and standardized laws and punishments, which made the legal process less dependent on the whims or favoritism of rulers or judges. They also offer invaluable evidence to historians about the social structures and culture of the society that produced them.

◆ What do the passages suggest about the way Mesopotamians viewed the role of marriage in society, and the role of women in marriage? If you formed your judgment about the roles women played in Babylonian society from passages 129, 137, and 138 alone, you might assume that women primarily reared children and were confined to the home. What do the other passages here reveal about other roles that women played in this culture? What does this difference suggest about the importance of evidence and the accidents of its survival in understanding the lives of women in history?

109. If rebels meet in the house of a wineseller and she does not seize them and take them to the palace, that wineseller shall be slain.

110. If a priestess who has not remained in the temple, shall open a wine-shop, or enter a wine-shop for a drink, that woman shall be burned.

117. If a man has contracted a debt, and has given his wife, his son, his daughter for silver or for labor, three years shall they serve in the house of their purchaser or bondsmaster; in the fourth year they shall regain their original condition.

129. If the wife of a man is found lying with another male, they shall be bound and thrown into the water. If the husband lets his wife live, then the king shall let his servant live . . .

137. If a man had decided to divorce . . . a wife who has presented him with children, then he shall give back to that woman her dowry, and he shall give her the use of field, garden, and property, and she shall bring up her children. After she has brought up her children, she shall take a son's portion of all that is given to her children, and she marry the husband of her heart.

138. If a man divorces his spouse who has not borne him children, he shall give to her all the silver of the bride-price, and restore to her the dowry which she brought from the house of her father, and so he shall divorce her.

Source: *The Human Record*, vol. I, Alfred J. Andrea, James H. Overfield, eds., pp. 14–15. Their source is Chilperic Edwards, *The Hammurabi Code* (1904), pp. 23–80.

and to relieve the gods of the necessity of providing for themselves. The gods were considered universal, but also as residing in specific places, usually one important god or goddess in each city. Mesopotamian temples were run like great households where the gods were fed lavish meals, entertained with music, and honored with devotion and ritual. There were gardens for their pleasure and bedrooms to retire to at night. The images of the gods were dressed and adorned with the finest materials. Theologians organized the gods into families and generations. Human social institutions, such as kingship, or crafts, such as carpentry, were associated with specific gods, so the boundaries between human and divine society were not always clearly drawn. Since the great gods were visualized like human rulers, remote from the common people and their concerns, the Mesopotamians imagined another, more personal intercessor god who was supposed to look after a person, rather like a guardian spirit. The public festivals of the gods were important holidays, with parades, ceremonies, and special foods. People wore their best clothes and celebrated their city and its gods. The Mesopotamians were religiously tolerant and readily accepted the possibility that different people might have different gods.

The Mesopotamians had a vague and gloomy picture of the afterworld. The winged spirits of the dead were recognizable as individuals. They were confined to a dusty, dark netherworld, doomed to perpetual hunger and thirst unless someone offered them food and drink. Some spirits escaped to haunt human beings. There was no preferential treatment in the afterlife for those who had led religious or virtuous lives—everyone was in equal misery. Mesopotamian families often had a ceremony to remember and honor their dead. People were usually buried together with goods such as pottery and ornaments. In the Early Dynastic period, certain kings were buried with a large retinue of attendants, including soldiers and musicians, who apparently took poison during the funeral ceremony and were buried where they fell. But this practice soon disappeared. Children were sometimes buried under the floors of houses. Some families used burial vaults, others large cemeteries. No tombstones or inscriptions identified the deceased. Mesopotamian religion focused on problems of this world and how to lead a good life before dying.

The Mesopotamian peoples who came after the Sumerians believed that the gods revealed a person's destiny to those who could understand the omens, or indications of what was going to happen. The Babylonians therefore developed an elaborate science of divination based on chance observations, such as a cat walking in the street, and on ritual procedures, such as asking a question of the gods and then slaughtering a sheep to examine its liver and entrails for certain marks and features. Some omens, such as monstrous births or eclipses, were thought to apply to the government, while others, such as birds flying over a person's house, were thought to apply to the individual. Thousands of omens, including both the observation and the outcome thereof, were compiled into huge encyclopedias that scholars could consult. Divination was often done before making major decisions and to discover the causes of illness, unhappiness, and failure. The hope was to avert unfavorable future events by discovering them in time and carrying out rituals or avoiding certain actions. Diviners were paid professionals, not priests. Witchcraft was also widely feared and blamed for illnesses and harm

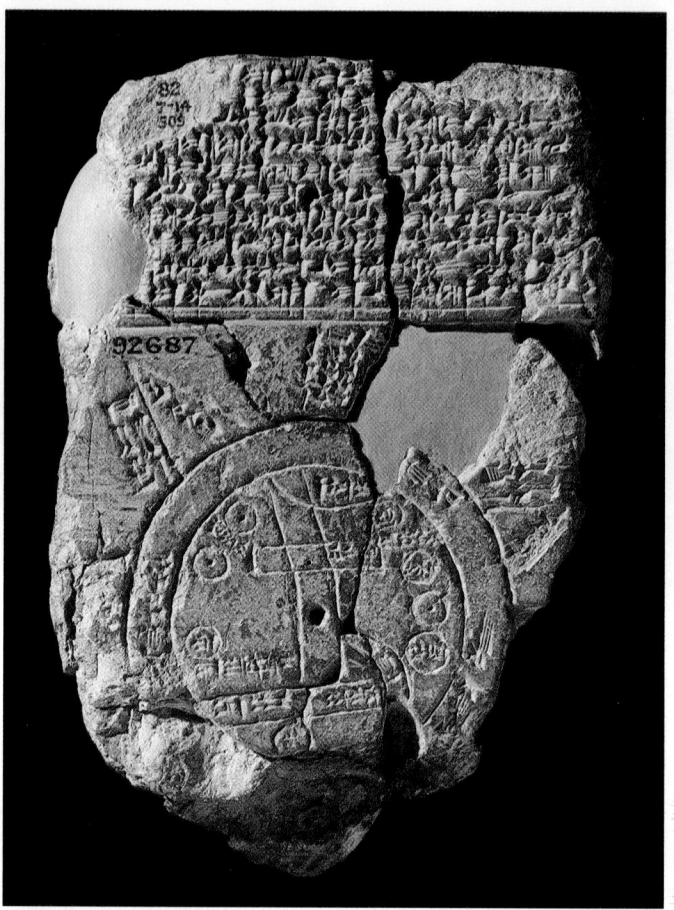

Babylonian World Map. This clay tablet from the Neo-Babylonian period (612–539 B.C.E.) shows a map of the world as seen by the Babylonians. The "Salt Sea" is shown as a circle. An arc inside it is labeled "Mountains." Below it is a rectangular box marked "Babylon," and to the right of the box is a small circle marked "Assyria." *Courtesy of the Trustees of the British Museum. © The British Museum.*

to people. There were many rituals against witchcraft, such as making a figurine of a witch and burning it, thereby burning up the witchcraft.

Religion played a large part in the literature and art of Mesopotamia. Epic poems told of the deeds of the gods, such as how the world was created and organized, of a great flood the gods sent to wipe out the human race, and of the hero-king Gilgamesh, who tried to escape death by going on a fantastic journey to find the sole survivor of the great flood. (See Document, "The Babylonian Story of the Flood.") The presence of many literary and artistic works that were not religious in character suggests that religion did not dominate all aspects of the Mesopotamians' lives. Religious architecture took the form of great temple complexes in the major cities. The most imposing religious structure was the *ziggurat*, a tower in stages, sometimes with a small chamber on top. The terraces may have been planted with trees to resemble a mountain. Poetry about ziggurats often compares them to mountains, with their peaks in the sky and their roots in the netherworld, linking heaven to earth, but their precise purpose is not known. Eroded remains of many of these monumental structures still dot the Iraqi landscape. Through the Bible, they have entered Western tradition as the Tower of Babel.

Society Hundreds of thousands of cuneiform texts from the early third millennium B.C.E. until the third century B.C.E. reveal a full and detailed picture of how peoples in ancient Mesopotamia conducted their lives and of the social conditions in which they lived. From the time of Hammurabi, for example, there are many royal letters to and from the various rulers of the age, letters from the king to his subordinates, administrative records from many different cities, and numerous letters and documents belonging to private families.

Categorizing the laws of Hammurabi according to the aspects of life with which they deal reveals much about Babylonian life in his time. The third largest category of laws deals with commerce, relating to such issues as contracts, debts, rates of interest, security, and default. Business documents of Hammurabi's time show how people invested their money in land, moneylending, government contracts, and international trade. Some of these laws regulate professionals, such as builders, judges, and surgeons. The second largest category of laws deals with land tenure, especially land given by the king to soldiers and marines in return for their service. The letters of Hammurabi that deal with land tenure show that he was concerned to uphold individual rights of landholders against powerful officials who tried to take their land from them. The largest category of laws relates to the family and its maintenance and protection, including marriage, inheritance, and adoption.

Parents usually arranged marriages, and betrothal was followed by the signing of a marriage contract. The bride usually left her own family to join her husband's. The husband-to-be could make a bridal payment, and the father of the bride-to-be provided a dowry for his daughter in money,

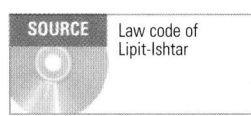
SOURCE Law code of Lipit-Ishtar

land, or objects. A marriage started out monogamous, but a husband whose wife was childless or sickly could take a second wife. Sometimes husbands also sired children from domestic slave women. Women could own their own property and do business on their own. Women divorced by their husbands without good cause could get back their dowry. A woman seeking divorce could also recover her dowry if her husband could not convict her of wrongdoing. A married woman's place was thought to be in the home, but hundreds of letters between wives and husbands show them as equal partners in the ventures of life. Single women who were not part of families could establish a business on their own, often as tavern owners or moneylenders, or could be associated with temples, sometimes working as midwives and wet nurses, or taking care of orphaned children.

Slavery: Chattel Slaves and Debt Slaves There were two main types of slavery in Mesopotamia: chattel and debt slavery. Chattel slaves were bought like any other piece of property and had no legal rights. They had to wear their hair in a certain way and were sometimes branded or tattooed on their hands. They were often non-Mesopotamians bought from slave merchants. Prisoners of war could also be enslaved. Chattel slaves were expensive luxuries during most of Mesopotamian history. They were used in domestic service rather than in production, such as field work. A wealthy household might have five or six slaves, male and female.

Debt slavery was more common than chattel slavery. Rates of interest were high, as much as 33⅓ percent, so people often defaulted on loans. One reason the interest rates were so high was that the government periodically canceled certain types of debts, debt slavery, and obligations, so lenders ran the risk of losing their money. If debtors had pledged themselves or members of their families as surety for a loan, they became the slave of the creditor; their labor went to pay the interest on the loan. Debt slaves could not be sold but could redeem their freedom by paying off the loan. True chattel slavery did not become common until the Neo-Babylonian period (612–539 B.C.E.).

Although laws against fugitive slaves or slaves who denied their masters were harsh—the Code of Hammurabi permits the death penalty for anyone who sheltered or helped a runaway slave to escape—Mesopotamian slavery appears enlightened compared with other slave systems in history. Slaves were generally of the same people as their masters. They had been enslaved because of misfortune from which their masters were not immune, and they generally labored alongside them. Slaves could engage in business and, with certain restrictions, hold property. They could marry free men or women, and the resulting children would normally be free. A slave who acquired the means could buy his or her freedom. Children of a slave by a master might be allowed to share his property after his death. Notwithstanding these policies, slaves were property, subject to an owner's will and had little legal protection.

The Babylonian Story of the Flood

Document

The passage that follows is part of the Babylonian *Epic of Gilgamesh*. It did not form a part of the original epic but was added at some point from an earlier independent Babylonian *Story of the Flood*. Gilgamesh was a legendary king who became terrified of death when his best friend and companion died. He resolved to locate Utanapishtim, who, with his wife, was the only survivor of the great flood, in order to ask him how he, too, could escape death. After many adventures, Gilgamesh crossed the distant ocean and the "waters of death" to ask Utanapishtim the secret of eternal life. In response, Utanapishtim narrated the story of the great flood. Note the similarities and the differences between this and the biblical story of Noah.

◆ How is this tale similar to the story of Noah in the Book of Genesis in the Hebrew Bible? How is it different?

Six days and seven nights
The wind continued, the deluge and windstorm levelled
    the land.
When the seventh day arrived,
The windstorm and deluge left off their battle,
Which had struggled, like a woman in labor.
The sea grew calm, the tempest stilled, the deluge
    ceased,
I looked at the weather, stillness reigned,
And the whole human race had turned into clay.
The landscape was flat as a rooftop.
I opened the hatch, sunlight fell upon my face.
Falling to my knees, I sat down weeping,
Tears running down my face.
I looked at the edges of the world, the borders of the sea,
At twelve times sixty double leagues the periphery
    emerged.
The boat had come to rest on Mount Nimush,
Mount Nimush held the boat fast, not letting it move.
One day, a second day Mount Nimush held the boat fast,
    not letting it move.
A third day, a fourth day Mount Nimush held the boat
    fast, not letting it move.
A fifth day, a sixth day Mount Nimush held the boat fast,
    not letting it move.
When the seventh day arrived,
I brought out a dove and set it free.
The dove went off and returned,

No landing place came to its view, so it turned back.
I brought out a swallow and set it free,
The swallow went off and returned,
No landing space came to its view, so it turned back.
I brought out a raven and set it free.
The raven went off and saw the ebbing of the waters.
It ate, preened, left droppings, did not turn back.
I released all to the four directions,
I brought out an offering and offered it to the four
    directions.
I set up an incense burner on the summit of the
    mountain,
I arranged seven and seven cult vessels,
I heaped reeds, cedar, and myrtle in their bowls.
The gods smelled the savor,
The gods smelled the sweet savor,
The gods crowded round the sacrificer like flies.
As soon as the Belet-ili arrived,
She held up the great fly-ornaments that Anu had made
    in his ardor:
'O ye gods, as surely as I shall not forget these lapis
    pendants on my neck,
'I shall be mindful of these days and not forget, not ever!

"The Babylonian Story of the Flood" from Babylonian *Epic of Gilgamesh*, trans. by Benjamin R. Foster, from *The Epic of Gilgamesh* © 2001 W. W. Norton & Co. Used by permission of W. W. Norton Company, Inc.

Egyptian Civilization

As Mesopotamian civilization arose in the valley of the Tigris and Euphrates, another great civilization emerged in Egypt, centered on the Nile River. From its sources in Lake Victoria and the Ethiopian highlands, the Nile flows north some four thousand miles to the Mediterranean. Ancient Egypt included the 750-mile stretch of smooth, navigable river from Aswan to the sea. South of Aswan the river's course is interrupted by several cataracts—rocky areas of rapids and whirlpools.

The Egyptians recognized two sets of geographical divisions in their country. Upper (southern) Egypt consisted of the narrow valley of the Nile. Lower (northern) Egypt referred to the broad triangular area, named by the Greeks after their letter *delta*, formed by the Nile as it branches out to empty into the Mediterranean. They also made a distinction between what they termed the "black land," the dark fertile fields along the Nile, and the "red land," the desert cliffs and plateaus bordering the valley.

The Nile alone made agriculture possible in Egypt's desert environment. Each year the rains of central Africa caused the river to rise over its floodplain, cresting in September and October. In places the plain extends several miles on either side; elsewhere the cliffs slope down to the water's edge. When the floodwaters receded, they left a rich layer of organically fertile silt. The construction and maintenance of canals, dams, and irrigation ditches to control the river's water, together with careful planning and organization of planting and harvesting, produced agricultural prosperity unmatched in the ancient world.

The Nile served as the major highway connecting Upper and Lower Egypt (see Map 1–3). There was also a network of desert roads running north and south, as well as routes across the eastern desert to the Sinai and the Red Sea. Other tracks led to oases in the western desert. Thanks to geography and climate, Egypt was more isolated and enjoyed far more security than Mesopotamia. This security, along with the predictable flood calendar, gave Egyptian civilization a more optimistic outlook than the civilizations of the Tigris and Euphrates, which were more prone to storms, flash floods, and invasions.

The three thousand year span of ancient Egyptian history is traditionally divided into thirty-one royal dynasties, from the first, said to have been founded by Menes, the king who orig-

Making Bread. A hallmark of the early river civilizations was the development of techniques to increase harvests. This statue from the Old Kingdom in Egypt (ca. 2700–2200 B.C.E.) shows a woman grinding wheat for bread. *Kenneth Garrettings/National Geographic Society.*

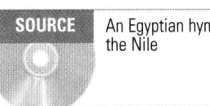
SOURCE An Egyptian hymn to the Nile

inally united Upper and Lower Egypt, to the last, conquered by Alexander the Great in 332 B.C.E. (as we shall see in Chapter 3). Ptolemy, one of Alexander's generals, founded the Ptolemaic Dynasty, whose last ruler was Cleopatra. In 30 B.C.E. the Romans defeated Egypt, effectively ending the independent existence of a civilization that had lasted three millennia.

The unification of Upper and Lower Egypt was vital, for it meant that the entire river valley could benefit from an unimpeded distribution of resources. Three times in its history, Egypt experienced a century or more of political and social disintegration, known as Intermediate periods. During these eras, rival dynasties often set up separate power bases in Upper and Lower Egypt until a strong leader reunified the land.

The Old Kingdom (2700–2200 B.C.E.) The Old Kingdom represents the culmination of the cultural and historical developments of the Early Dynastic period. For over four hundred

Chronology

Key Events and People in Mesopotamian History

ca. 3500 B.C.E.	Development of Sumerian cities, especially Uruk
ca. 2800–2370 B.C.E.	Early Dynastic period of Sumerian city-states
ca. 2370 B.C.E.	Sargon establishes Akkadian Dynasty and Empire
ca. 2125–2027 B.C.E.	Third Dynasty of Ur
ca. 2000–1800 B.C.E.	Establishment of Amorites in Mesopotamia
ca. 1792–1750 B.C.E.	Reign of Hammurabi
ca. 1550 B.C.E.	Establishment of Kassite Dynasty at Babylon

Pyramids at Giza. The three largest pyramids of Egypt, located at Giza, near Cairo, are the colossal tombs of pharaohs of the Fourth Dynasty (ca. 2640–2510 B.C.E.): Khufu (right), Chafre (center), and Menkaure (left). The small pyramids and tombs at their bases were those of the pharaohs' queens and officials. *Pictor/Uniphoto Picture Agency.*

years, Egypt enjoyed internal stability and great prosperity. During this period, the **pharaoh** was a king who was also a god (the term comes from the Egyptian for "great house," much as we use "White House" to refer to the president). From his capital at Memphis, the god-king administered Egypt according to set principles—prime among them was *maat*, an ideal of order, justice, and truth. In return for the king's building and maintaining temples, the gods preserved the equilibrium of the state and ensured the king's continuing power, which was absolute. Because the king was obligated to act infallibly in a benign and beneficent manner, the welfare of the people of Egypt was automatically guaranteed and safeguarded.

Nothing better illustrates the nature of Old Kingdom royal power than the pyramids built as pharaonic tombs. Beginning in the Early Dynastic period, kings constructed increasingly elaborate burial complexes in Upper Egypt. Djoser, a Third Dynasty king, was the first to erect a monumental six-step pyramid of hard stone. Subsequent pharaohs built other stepped pyramids until Snefru, the founder of the Fourth Dynasty, converted a stepped pyramid to a true pyramid over the course of putting up three monuments.

Djoser's son Khufu (Cheops in the Greek version of his name) chose the desert plateau of Giza, south of Memphis, as the site for the largest pyramid ever constructed. Its dimensions are prodigious: 481 feet high, 756 feet long on each side, and its base covering 13.1 acres. The pyramid is made of 2.3 million stone blocks averaging 2.5 tons each. It is also a geometrical wonder, deviating from absolutely level and square only by the most minute measurements using the latest modern devices. Khufu's successors, Khafre (Chephren) and Menkaure (Mycerinus), built equally perfect pyramids at Giza, and together the three constitute one of the most extraordinary achievements in human history. Khafre also built the huge composite creature, part lion and part human, which the Greeks named the Sphinx. Recent research has shown that the Sphinx played a crucial role in the solar cult aspects of the pyramid complex.

The pyramids are remarkable not only for the great technical skill they demonstrate, but also for the concentration of resources they represent. They are evidence that the pharaohs controlled vast wealth and had the power to focus and organize enormous human effort over the years it took to build each pyramid. They also provide a visible indication of the nature of the Egyptian state: The pyramids, like the pharaohs, tower above the land, while the low tombs at their base, like the officials buried there, seem to huddle in relative unimportance.

Originally, the pyramids and their associated cult buildings contained statuary, offerings, and all that the pharaoh needed for the afterlife. Despite great precautions and ingenious concealment methods, tomb robbers took nearly everything, leaving little for modern archaeologists to recover. Several full-size wooden boats have been found, however, still in their own graves at the base of the pyramids, ready for the pharaoh's journeys in the next world. Recent excavations have uncovered remains of the large town built to house the thousands of pyramid builders, including the farmers who worked at Giza during the annual flooding of their fields.

Numerous officials, both members of the royal family and nonroyal men of ability, aided the god-kings. The highest office was the *vizier* (a modern term from Arabic). Central offices dealing with granaries, surveys, assessments, taxes, and salaries administered the land. Water management was local rather than on a national level. Upper and Lower Egypt were divided into *nomes*, or districts, each governed by a *nomarch*, or governor, and his local officials. The kings could also appoint royal officials to oversee groups of nomes or to supervise pharaonic landholdings throughout Egypt.

The First Intermediate Period and Middle Kingdom (2200–1630 B.C.E.)

Toward the end of the Old Kingdom, for a combination of political and economic reasons, absolute pharaonic power waned as the nomarchs and other officials became more independent and influential. About 2200 B.C.E. the Old Kingdom collapsed and gave way to the decentralization and disorder of the First Intermediate period, which lasted until about 2025 B.C.E. Eventually, the kings of Dynasty 11, based in Thebes in Upper Egypt, defeated the rival Dynasty 10, based in a city south of Giza.

Amunemhet I, the founder of Dynasty 12 and the Middle Kingdom, probably began his career as a successful vizier under an Eleventh Dynasty king. After reuniting Upper and Lower Egypt, he turned his attention to making three important and long-lasting administrative changes. First, he moved his royal residence from Thebes to a brand-new town, just south of the old capital at Memphis, signaling a fresh start rooted in past glories. Second, he reorganized the nome structure by more clearly defining the nomarchs' duties to the state, granting them some local autonomy within the royal structure. Third, he established a co-regency system to smooth transitions from one reign to another.

Amunemhet I and the other Middle Kingdom pharaohs sought to evoke the past by building pyramid complexes like those of the later Old Kingdom rulers. Yet the events of the First Intermediate period had irrevocably changed the nature of Egyptian kingship. Gone was the absolute, distant god-king; the king was now more directly concerned with his people. In art, instead of the supremely confident faces of the Old Kingdom pharaohs, the Middle Kingdom rulers seem thoughtful, careworn, and brooding.

Egypt's relations with its neighbors became more aggressive during the Middle Kingdom. To the south, royal fortresses were built to control Nubia and the growing trade in African resources. To the north and east, Syria and Palestine increasingly came under Egyptian influence, even as fortifications sought to prevent settlers from the Levant from moving into the Delta.

The Second Intermediate Period and the New Kingdom (1630–1075 B.C.E.)

For some unknown reason, during Dynasty 13, the kingship changed hands rapidly and the western Delta established itself as an independent Dynasty 14, ushering in the Second Intermediate period. The eastern Delta, with its expanding Asiatic populations, came under the control of the Hyksos (Dynasty 15) and minor Asiatic kings (Dynasty 16). Meanwhile, the Dynasty 13 kings left their northern capital and regrouped in Thebes (Dynasty 17).

Though much later sources describe the Hyksos ("chief of foreign lands" in Egyptian) as ruthless invaders from parts unknown, they were almost certainly Amorites from the Levant, part of the gradual infiltration of the Delta during the Middle Kingdom. Ongoing excavations at the Hyksos capital of Avaris in the eastern Delta have revealed architecture, pottery, and other goods consistent with that cultural background. After nearly a century of rule, the Hyksos were expelled, a process begun by Kamose, the last king of Dynasty 17, and completed by his brother Ahmose, the first king of the Eighteenth Dynasty and the founder of the New Kingdom.

During the Eighteenth Dynasty, Egypt pursued foreign expansion with renewed vigor. Military expeditions reached as far north as the Euphrates in Syria, with frequent campaigns in the Levant. To the south, major Egyptian temples were built in the Sudan, almost thirteen hundred miles from Memphis. Egypt's economic and political power was at its height.

Egypt's position was reflected in the unprecedented luxury and cosmopolitanism of the royal court and in the

Chronology

Major Periods in Ancient Egyptian History (Dynasties in Roman Numerals)

3100–2700 B.C.E.	Early Dynastic period (I–II)
2700–2200 B.C.E.	Old Kingdom (III–VI)
2200–2025 B.C.E.	First Intermediate period (VII–XI)
2025–1630 B.C.E.	Middle Kingdom (XII–XIII)
1630–1550 B.C.E.	Second Intermediate period (XIV–XVII)
1550–1075 B.C.E.	New Kingdom (XVIII–XX)

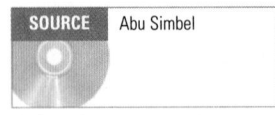

SOURCE Abu Simbel

ambitious palace and temple projects undertaken throughout the country. Perhaps to foil tomb robbers, the Eighteenth Dynasty pharaohs were the first to cut their tombs deep into the rock cliffs of a desolate valley in Thebes, known today as the Valley of the Kings. To date, only one intact royal tomb has been discovered there, that of the young Eighteenth Dynasty king Tutankhamun, and even it had been disturbed shortly after his death. The thousands of goods buried with him, many of them marvels of craftsmanship, give a glimpse of Egypt's material wealth during this period.

Following the premature death of Tutankhamun in 1323 B.C.E., a military commander named Horemheb assumed the kingship, which passed in turn to his own army commander, Ramses I. The Ramessides of Dynasty 19 undertook numerous monumental projects, among them Ramses II's rock-cut temples at Abu Simbel, south of the First Cataract, which had to be moved to a higher location when the Aswan High Dam was built in the 1960s. There and elsewhere, Ramses II left textual and pictorial accounts of his battle in 1285 B.C.E. against the Hittites at Kadesh on the Orontes in Syria. Sixteen years later, the Egyptians and Hittites signed a formal peace treaty, forging an alliance against an increasingly volatile political situation in the Middle East and the eastern Mediterranean during the thirteenth century B.C.E.

Merneptah, one of the hundred offspring of Ramses II, held off a hostile Libyan attack, as well as incursions by the Sea Peoples, a loose coalition of Mediterranean raiders who seem to have provoked and taken advantage of unsettled conditions. One of Merneptah's inscriptions commemorating his military triumphs contains the first known mention of Israel.

Despite Merneptah's efforts, by the end of the Twentieth Dynasty, Egypt's period of imperial glory had passed. The next thousand years witnessed a Third Intermediate period, a Saite renaissance, Persian domination, conquest by Alexander the Great, the Ptolemaic period, and finally, defeat at the hands of the Roman emperor Octavian in 30 B.C.E.

Language and Literature

Writing first appears in Egypt about 3000 B.C.E. While the impetus for the first Egyptian writing probably came from Mesopotamia, the Egyptians may have invented it on their own. The writing system, dubbed **hieroglyphs** ("sacred carvings") by the Greeks, was highly sophisticated, involving hundreds of picture signs that remained relatively constant in the way they were rendered for over three thousand years. Many of them formed a syllabary of one, two, or three consonantal sounds, while some conveyed a word's meaning or category, either independently or added to the end of the word. Texts were usually written horizontally from right to left but could be written from left to right, as well as vertically from top to bottom in both horizontal directions. A cursive version of hieroglyphs was used for business documents and literary texts, which were penned rapidly in black and red ink. The Egyptian language, part of the Afro-Asiatic (or Hamito-Semitic) family, evolved through several stages—Old, Middle, and Late Egyptian, Demotic, and Coptic—thus giving it a history of continuous recorded use well into the Medieval period.

Egyptian literature includes narratives, myths, books of instruction in wisdom, letters, religious texts, and poetry, written on papyri, limestone flakes, and potsherds. (See Document, "Love Poems from the New Kingdom.") Unfortunately, only a small fraction of this enormous literature has survived, and many texts are incomplete. Though they surely existed, we have no epics or dramas from ancient Egypt. Such nonliterary documents as lists of kings, autobiographies in tombs, wine jar labels, judicial records, astronomical observations, and medical and other scientific texts are invaluable for our understanding of Egyptian history and civilization.

Religion: Gods and Temples Egyptian religion encompasses a multitude of concepts that often seem mutually contradictory to us. Three separate explanations for the origin of the universe were formulated, each based in the philosophical traditions of a venerable Egyptian city. The cosmogony of Heliopolis, north of Memphis, held that the creator–sun god Atum (also identified as Re) emerged from the darkness of a vast sea to stand upon a primeval mound, containing within himself the life force of the gods he was to create. At Memphis, it was the god Ptah who created the other gods by uttering their names. Further south, at Hermopolis, eight

Seated Egyptian Scribe. One of the hallmarks of the early river valley civilizations was the development of writing. Ancient Egyptian scribes had to undergo rigorous training but were rewarded with a position of respect and privilege. This statue from the Fifth Dynasty (ca. 2510–2460 B.C.E.) is of painted limestone and measures 21 inches (53 cm) in height. *Musée du Louvre, Paris, © Giraudon/Art Resource, N.Y.*

male and female entities within a primordial slime suddenly exploded, and the energy that resulted created the sun and Atum, from which the rest came.

The Egyptian gods, or pantheon, defy neat categorization, in part because of the common tendency to combine the character and function of one or more gods. Amun, one of the eight entities in the Hermopolitan cosmogony, provides a good example. Thebes, Amun's cult center, rose to prominence in the Middle Kingdom. In the New Kingdom, Amun was elevated above his seven cohorts and took on aspects of the sun god Re to become Amun-Re.

Not surprisingly in a nearly rainless land, solar cults and mythologies were highly developed. Much thought was devoted to conceptualizing what happened as the sun god made his perilous way through the underworld in the night hours between sunset and sunrise. Three long texts trace Re's journey as he vanquishes immense snakes and other foes.

The Eighteenth Dynasty was one of several periods during which solar cults were in ascendancy. Early in his reign, Amunhotep IV promoted a single, previously minor aspect of the sun, the Aten ("disc") above Re himself and the rest of the gods. He declared that the Aten was the creator god who brought life to mankind and all living beings, with himself and his queen Nefertiti the sole mediators between the Aten and the people. For religious and political reasons still imperfectly understood, he went further, changing his name to Akhenaten ("the effective spirit of the Aten"), building a new capital called Akhetaten ("the horizon of the Aten") near Amarna north of Thebes and chiseling out the name of Amun from inscriptions everywhere. Shortly after his death, Amarna was abandoned and partially razed. A large diplomatic archive of tablets written in Akkadian was left at the site, which give us a vivid, if one-sided, picture of the political correspondence of the day. During the reigns of Akhenaten's successors, Tutankhamun (born Tutankhaten) and Horemheb, Amun was restored to his former position, and Akhenaten's monuments were defaced and even demolished.

In representations, Egyptian gods have human bodies, possess human or animal heads, and wear crowns, celestial discs, or thorns. The lone exception is the Aten, made nearly abstract by Akhenaten, who altered its image to a plain disc with solar rays ending in small hands holding the hieroglyphic sign for life to the nostrils of Akhenaten and Nefertiti. The gods were thought to reside in their cult centers, where, from the New Kingdom on, increasingly ostentatious temples were built and staffed by full-time priests. At Thebes, for instance, for over two thousand years successive kings enlarged the great Karnak temple complex dedicated to Amun. Though the ordinary person could not enter a temple precinct, great

Love Poems from the New Kingdom

Document

Numerous love poems from ancient Egypt reveal the Egyptians' love of life through their frank sensuality.

◆ How does the girl in the first poem propose to escape the supervision of her parents? What ails the young man in the second poem?

SHE: Love, how I'd love to slip down to the pond, bathe with you close by on the bank.
Just for you I'd wear my new Memphis swimsuit, made of sheer linen, fit for a queen—Come see how it looks in the water!
Couldn't I coax you to wade in with me? Let the cool creep slowly around us?
Then I'd dive deep down and come up for you dripping,
Let you fill your eyes with the little red fish that I'd catch.
And I'd say, standing there tall in the shallows:
Look at my fish, love, how it lies in my hand,
How my fingers caress it, slip down its sides . . .
But then I'd say softer, eyes bright with your seeing:

A gift, love. No words.
Come closer and look, it's all me.

HE: I think I'll go home and lie very still, feigning terminal illness.
Then the neighbors will all troop over to stare, my love, perhaps, among them.
How she'll smile while the specialists snarl in their teeth!—she perfectly well knows what ails me.

From *Love Songs of the New Kingdom*, trans. from the Ancient Egyptian by John L. Foster, copyright © 1969, 1970, 1971, 1972, 1973, and 1974 by John L. Foster, pp. 20 and 72. By permission of the University of Texas Press.

Scene from the *Book of the Dead*. The Egyptians believed in the possibility of life after death through the god Osiris. Before the person could be presented to Osiris, forty-two assessor-gods tested aspects of the person's life. In this scene from a papyrus manuscript of the *Book of the Dead*, the deceased and his wife (on the left) watch the scales of justice weighing his heart (on the left side of the scales) against the feather of truth. The jackal-headed god Anubis also watches the scales, while the ibis-headed god Thoth keeps the record. *British Museum, London/The Bridgeman Art Library International Ltd.*

festivals took place for all to see. During Amun's major festival of Opet, the statue of the god traveled in a divine boat along the Nile, whose banks were thronged with spectators.

Worship and the Afterlife   Most Egyptians worshiped at small local shrines. They left offerings to the chosen gods, as well as votive inscriptions with simple prayers. Private houses often had niches containing busts for ancestor worship and statues of household deities. The Egyptians strongly believed in the power of magic, dreams, and oracles, and they possessed a wide variety of amulets to ward off evil.

The Egyptians thought that the afterlife was full of dangers, which could be overcome by magical means, among them the spells in the *Book of the Dead*. The goals were to join and be identified with the gods, especially Osiris, or to sail in the "boat of millions." Originally only the king could hope to enjoy immortality with the gods, but gradually this became available to all. Since the Egyptians believed that the preservation of the body was essential for continued existence in the afterlife, early on they developed mummification, a process that by the New Kingdom took seventy days. How lavishly tombs were prepared and decorated varied over the course of Egyptian history and in accordance with the wealth of a family. A high-ranking Dynasty 18 official, for example, typically had a Theban rock-cut tomb of several rooms embellished with scenes from daily life and funerary texts, as well as provisions and equipment for the afterlife, statuettes of workers, and a place for descendants to leave offerings.

Women in Egyptian Society   It is difficult to assess the position of women in Egyptian society, because our pictorial and textual evidence comes almost entirely from male sources. Women's prime roles were connected with the management of the household. They could not hold office, go to scribal schools, or become artisans. Nevertheless, women could own and control property, sue for divorce, and, at least in theory, enjoy equal legal protection.

Royal women often wielded considerable influence, particularly in the Eighteenth Dynasty. The most remarkable was Hatshepsut, daughter of Thutmosis I and widow of Thutmosis II, who ruled as pharaoh for nearly twenty years. Many Egyptian queens held the title "god's wife of Amun," a power base of great importance.

In art, royal and nonroyal women are conventionally shown smaller than their husbands or sons, yet it is probably of greater significance that they are so frequently depicted in such a wide variety of contexts. Much care was lavished on details of their gestures, clothing, and hairstyles. With their husbands, they attend banquets, boat in the papyrus marshes, make and receive offerings, and supervise the myriad affairs of daily life.

Slaves   Slaves did not become numerous in Egypt until the growth of Egyptian imperial power in the Middle Kingdom (2052–1786 B.C.E.). During that period, black Africans from Nubia to the south and Asians from the east were captured in war and brought back to Egypt as slaves. The great period of Egyptian imperial expansion, the New Kingdom (1550–1075 B.C.E.), vastly increased the number of slaves and captives in Egypt. Sometimes an entire people were enslaved, as the Hebrews were, according to the Bible.

Slaves in Egypt performed many tasks. They labored in the fields with the peasants, in the shops of artisans, and as domestic servants. Others worked as policemen and soldiers. Many slaves labored to erect the great temples, obelisks, and other huge monuments of Egypt's imperial age. As in Mesopotamia, slaves were branded for identification and to help prevent their escape. Egyptian slaves could be freed, although manumission seems to have been rare. Nonetheless, former slaves were not set apart and could expect to be assimilated into the mass of the population.

Map Exploration

To explore this map further, go to http://www.prenhall.com/craig_maps

Map 1–3. The Near East and Greece, ca. 1400 B.C.E. About 1400 B.C.E., the Near East was divided among four empires. Egypt extended south to Nubia and north through Palestine and Phoenicia. Kassites ruled in Mesopotamia, Hittites in Asia Minor, and the Mitannians in Assyrian lands. In the Aegean, the Mycenaean kingdoms were at their height.

Ancient Near Eastern Empires

In the time of the Eighteenth Dynasty in Egypt, new groups of peoples had established themselves in the Near East: the Kassites in Babylonia, the Hittites in Asia Minor, and the Mitannians in northern Syria and Mesopotamia (see Map 1–3). The Kassites and Mitannians were warrior peoples who ruled as a minority over more civilized folk and absorbed their culture. The Hittites established a kingdom of their own and forged an empire that lasted some two hundred years.

The Hittites

The Hittites were an Indo-European people, speaking a language related to Greek and Sanskrit. By about 1500 B.C.E., they established a strong, centralized government with a capital at Hattusas (near Ankara, the capital of modern Turkey). Between 1400 and 1200 B.C.E., they emerged as a leading military power in the Middle East and contested Egypt's ambitions to control Palestine and Syria. This struggle culminated in a great battle between the Egyptian and Hittite

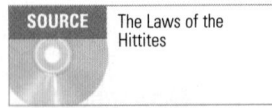 **SOURCE** The Laws of the Hittites

armies at Kadesh in northern Syria (1285 B.C.E.) and ended as a standoff. The Hittites also broke the power of the Mitannian state in northern Syria. The Hittites adopted Mesopotamian writing and many aspects of Mesopotamian culture, especially through the Hurrian peoples of northern Syria and southern Anatolia. Their extensive historical records are the first to mention the Greeks, whom the Hittites called Ahhiyawa (the Achaeans of Homer). By 1200 B.C.E., the Hittite Kingdom disappeared, swept away in the general invasions and collapse of the Middle Eastern nation-states at that time. Successors to the empire, called the Neo-Hittite states, flourished in southern Asia Minor and northern Syria until the Assyrians destroyed them in the first millennium B.C.E.

The government of the Hittites was different from that of Mesopotamia in that Hittite kings did not claim to be divine or even to be the chosen representatives of the gods. In the early period, a council of nobles limited the king's power, and the assembled army had to ratify his succession to the throne.

The Discovery of Iron An important technological change took place in northern Anatolia, somewhat earlier than the creation of the Hittite Kingdom, but perhaps within its region. This was the discovery of how to smelt iron and the decision to use it rather than copper or bronze to manufacture weapons and tools. Archaeologists refer to the period after 1100 B.C.E. as the Iron Age.

The Kassites

The Kassites were a people of unknown origin who spoke their own Kassite language and who established at Babylon a dynasty that ruled for nearly five hundred years. The Kassites were organized into large tribal families and carved out great domains for themselves in Babylonia. They promoted Babylonian

Assyrian Palace Relief. This eighth-century B.C.E. relief of a hero gripping a lion formed part of the decoration of an Assyrian palace. The immense size of the figure and his powerful limbs and muscles may well have suggested the might of the Assyrian king. *Giraudon/Art Resource, N.Y.*

culture, and many of the most important works of Babylonian literature were written during their rule. Under the Kassites, Babylonia became one of the great nation-states of the late Bronze Age, along with Mitanni on the upper Euphrates, Assyria, Egypt, and the empire of the Hittites in Anatolia. The kings of these states frequently wrote to each other and exchanged lavish gifts. They supported a military aristocracy based on horses and chariots, the prestige weaponry of the age. Though equally matched in power, the kings of this time conspired against each other, with Egypt and the Hittites hoping to control Syria and Palestine, and Babylonia and Assyria testing each other's borders. Their wars were often inconclusive.

The Mitannians

The Mitannians belonged to a large group of people called the Hurrians, some of whom had been living in Mesopotamia and Syria in the time of the kings of Akkad and Ur. Their language is imperfectly understood, and the location of their capital city, Washukanni, is uncertain. The Hurrians were important mediators of Mesopotamian culture to Syria and Anatolia. They developed the art of chariot warfare and horse training to a high degree and created a large state that reached from the Euphrates to the foothills of Iran. The Hittites destroyed their kingdom, and the Assyrian empire eventually incorporated what was left of it.

The Assyrians

The Assyrians were originally a people living in Assur, a city in northern Mesopotamia on the Tigris River. They spoke a Semitic language closely related to Babylonian. They had a proud, independent culture heavily influenced by Babylonia. Assur had been an early center for trade but emerged as a political power during the fourteenth century B.C.E., after the decline of Mitanni. The first Assyrian Empire spread north and west against the neo-Hittite states but was brought to an end in the general collapse of Near Eastern states at the end of the second millennium. A people called the Arameans, a Semitic nomadic

An Assyrian Woman Writes to Her Husband, ca. 1800 B.C.E.

Document

The wives of early Assyrian businessmen were often active in their husbands' business affairs. They made extra money for themselves by having slave girls weave textiles that the husbands then sold on business trips. Their letters are among the largest groups of women's records from the ancient world. The woman writing this letter, Taram-Kubi, complains of her husband's selfishness and points out all the matters she has worked on during his absence on business.

◆ What functions did this woman perform on behalf of the family? How do you judge her real power in regard to her husband? On what evidence do you base that judgment? What does this document reveal about the place of women in Assyrian society?

You wrote to me saying, "You'll need to safeguard the bracelets and rings which are there so they'll be available [to buy] food." In fact you sent [the man] Ilum-bani a half pound of gold! Which are the bracelets you left me? When you left, you didn't leave me an ounce of silver, you picked the house clean and took away everything! After you left, there was a severe famine in the city. Not so much as a quart of grain did you leave me, I always had to buy grain for our food. Besides that, I paid the assessment for the divine icon(?); in fact, I paid for my part in full. Besides that,

I paid over to the Town Hall the grain owed [the man] Atata. What is the extravagance you keep writing to me about? There is nothing for us to eat—we're the ones being extravagant? I picked up whatever I had to hand and sent it to you—today I'm living in an empty house. It's high time you sent me the money realized on my weavings, in silver, from what you have to hand, so I can buy ten quarts of grain!

Trans. by Benjamin R. Foster, 1999.

---

and agricultural people originally from northern Syria who spoke a language called Aramaic, invaded Assyria. Aramaic is still used in parts of the Near East and is one of the languages of medieval Jewish and Middle Eastern Christian culture.

The Second Assyrian Empire

After 1000 B.C.E., the Assyrians began a second period of expansion, and by 665 B.C.E. they controlled all of Mesopotamia, much of southern Asia Minor, Syria, Palestine, and Egypt to its southern frontier. They succeeded thanks to a large, well-disciplined army and a society that valued military skills. Some Assyrian kings boasted of their atrocities, so that their names inspired terror throughout the Near East. They constructed magnificent palaces at Nineveh and Nimrud (near modern Mosul, Iraq), surrounded by parks and gardens. The walls of the reception rooms and hallways were decorated with stone reliefs and inscriptions proclaiming the power and conquests of the king. (See Document, "An Assyrian Woman Writes to Her Husband, ca. 1800 B.C.E.")

The Assyrians organized their empire into provinces with governors, military garrisons, and administration for taxation, communications, and intelligence. Important officers were assigned large areas of land throughout the empire, and agricultural colonies were set up in key regions to store up supplies for military actions beyond the frontiers. Vassal kings had to send tribute and delegations to the Assyrian capital every year. Tens of thousands of people were forcibly displaced from their homes and resettled in other areas of the empire, partly to populate sparsely inhabited regions, partly to diminish resistance to Assyrian rule. Among those resettled were the people of the kingdom of Israel, which the Assyrians invaded and destroyed.

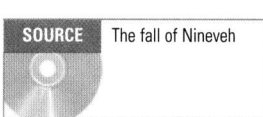 SOURCE The fall of Nineveh

The empire became too large to govern efficiently. The last years of Assyria are obscure, but civil war apparently divided the country. The Medes, a powerful people from western and central Iran, had been expanding across the Iranian plateau. They were feared for their cavalry and archers, against which traditional Middle Eastern armies were ineffective. The Medes attacked Assyria and were joined by the Babylonians, who had always been restive under Assyrian rule, under the leadership of a general named Nebuchadnezzar. In 612 B.C.E., they so thoroughly destroyed the Assyrian cities, including Nineveh, that Assyria never recovered. The ruins of the great Assyrian palaces lay untouched until archaeologists began to explore them in the nineteenth century.

The Neo-Babylonians

The Medes did not follow up on their conquests, so Nebuchadnezzar took over much of the Assyrian Empire. Under him and his successors, Babylon grew into one of the greatest cities of the world. The Greek traveler Herodotus described its wonders, including its great temples, fortification walls, boulevards, parks, and palaces, to a Greek readership that had never seen the like. Babylon prospered as a center of world trade, linking Egypt, India, Iran, and Syria-Palestine by land and sea routes. For centuries, an astronomical center at Babylon kept detailed records of observations that were the longest running chronicle of the ancient world. Nebuchadnezzar's dynasty did not last long, and the government passed to various men in rapid succession. The last independent king of Babylon set up a second capital in the Arabian desert and tried to force the Babylonians to honor the moon god above all other gods. He allowed dishonest or incompetent speculators to lease huge areas of temple land for their personal profit. These policies proved unpopular—some said that the king was insane—and many Babylonians may have welcomed the Persian conquest that came in 539 B.C.E. After that, Babylonia began another, even more prosperous phase of its history as one of the most important provinces of another great Eastern empire, that of the Persians. We shall return to the Persians in Chapter 4.

Chronology

Key Events in the History of Ancient Near Eastern Empires

ca. 1400–1200 B.C.E.	Hittite Empire
ca. 1100 B.C.E.	Rise of Assyrian power
732–722 B.C.E.	Assyrian conquest of Syria-Palestine
671 B.C.E.	Assyrian conquest of Egypt
612 B.C.E.	Destruction of Assyrian capital at Nineveh
612–539 B.C.E.	Neo-Babylonian (Chaldean) Empire

Early Indian Civilization

To the east of Mesopotamia, beyond the Iranian plateau and the mountains of Baluchistan, the Asian continent bends sharply southward below the Himalayan mountain barrier to form the Indian subcontinent (see Map 1–4). Several sizable rivers flow west and south out of the Himalayas in Kashmir and the Punjab (*Panjab,* "five rivers"), merging into the single stream of the Indus River in Sind before emptying into the Indian Ocean. The headwaters of south Asia's other great river system—the Ganges and its tributaries—are also in the Himalayas but flow south and east to the Bay of Bengal on the opposite side of the subcontinent.

The earliest evidence of a settled, neolithic way of life on the subcontinent comes from the foothills of Sind and Baluchistan and dates to about 5500 B.C.E. with evidence of barley and wheat cultivation, baked brick dwellings, and, later, domestication of animals such as goats, sheep, and cows, and, after about 4000 B.C.E., metalworking. The subcontinent's earliest literate, urban civilization arose in the valley of the Indus River sometime after 2600 B.C.E. and by about 2300 B.C.E. was trading with Mesopotamia. Known as the Indus Valley culture (or the **Harappan** civilization, after the archaeological site at which it was first recognized), it lasted only a few centuries and left many unanswered questions about its history and culture. The region's second identifiable civilization was of a different character. Dating to about 1500 B.C.E., it is known as the Vedic Aryan civilization—after the nomadic Indo-European immigrant people, or **Aryans**, who founded it, and their holy texts, or **Vedas**. This civilization endured for nearly a thousand years without cities or writing, but its religious and social traditions commingled with older traditions in the subcontinent—notably that of the Indus culture—to form the Indian civilization as it has developed in the past 2,500 years.

The Indus Civilization

Archaeologists discovered the existence of the Indus culture at the site of Harappa in the 1920s. Since then, some seventy cities, the largest being Harappa and Mohenjo-Daro, have been identified over a vast area from the Himalayan foothills west and south on the coasts of the Arabian Sea. This urban civilization had bronze tools, writing, covered drainage systems, and a diversified social and economic organization. Because it disappeared before 1500 B.C.E. and its writing is still undeciphered, it remains the least understood of the early river valley civilizations. Archaeological evidence and inferences from later Indian life, however, allow us to reconstruct something of its highly developed and once thriving culture.

Map 1–4. Indus and Vedic Aryan Cultures. Indus culture likely influenced the Vedic Aryans, although the influence cannot be proved. Some scholars surmise, for example, that the fortified Aryan city of Hariyupiya, mentioned in later texts, may have been the same site as the older Indus city of Harappa.

General Character The Indus culture covered an area many times larger than either Middle Kingdom Egypt or Third Dynasty Ur, yet the archaeological finds show it to have been remarkably homogeneous. City layouts, building construction, weights and measures, seal inscriptions, patterned pottery and figurines, and even the burnt brick used for buildings and flood walls are unusually uniform in all Indus towns, suggesting an integrated economic system and good internal communications.

Indus culture was also remarkably constant over time. Because the main cities and towns lay in river lowlands subject to flooding, they were rebuilt often, with each reconstruction closely following the previous pattern. Similarly, the Indus script, known from more than two thousand stamp seals and apparently using both pictographic and phonetic symbols, shows no evidence of change over time. This evidence of stability, regularity, and traditionalism has led scholars to speculate that a centralized government, perhaps a conservative (priestly) theocracy rather than a more unstable royal dynasty and court, controlled this far-flung society.

Cities Harappa and Mohenjo-Daro both apparently had populations of more than thirty-five thousand and were meticulously designed on a similar plan. To the west of each

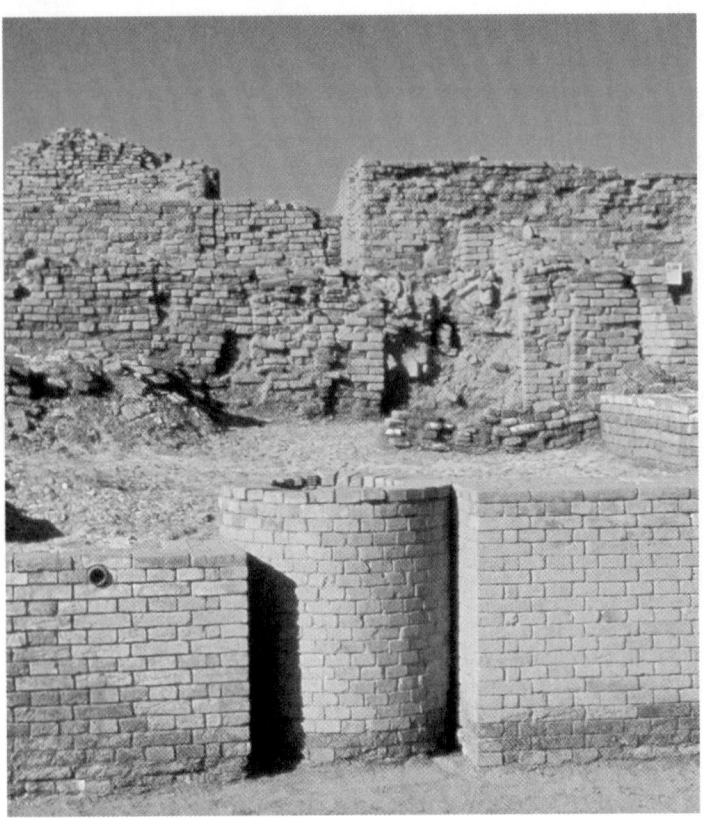

Ancient Mohenjo-Daro. Like most cities of the Indus Valley civilization, Mohenjo-Daro was built principally of mud brick. The structures are laid on straight lines; streets cross each other at right angles. The impression is one of order, prosperity, and civic discipline. *Borromeo/Art Resource, N.Y.*

stood a large, walled citadel on a raised rectangular platform about eight hundred by fourteen hundred feet in size. East of this the town proper was laid out on a north–south, east–west grid of main avenues, some as wide as thirty feet. The citadel apparently contained the main public buildings. A large bath with a brick-lined pool, a subterranean furnace, and columned porticoes have been excavated at Mohenjo-Daro. Both Harappa and Mohenjo-Daro had buildings tentatively identified as temples.

The periphery of each city had a cemetery and a large granary for food storage. The town "blocks" formed by the main avenues were crisscrossed by small, less rigidly planned lanes, off which opened private houses, sometimes of more than one story. The typical house was built around a central courtyard and presented only blank walls to the lanes or streets outside, an arrangement still common in many Near Eastern and south Asian cities.

Perhaps the most striking feature of these cities was a complex system of covered drains and sewers. Private houses were serviced by wells, bathrooms, and latrines, and the great bath at Mohenjo-Daro was filled from its own large well. The drainage system that served these facilities was an

engineering feat unrivaled until the time of the Romans, nearly two thousand years later (see Map 1–5).

Economic Life The economy of the Indus state or states was based on agriculture. Wheat and barley were the main crops; rice, peas, lentils, sesame, dates, and cotton were also important. Cattle, dogs, cats, goats, sheep, and fowl were raised, and elephants and water buffalo were likely used as beasts of burden. The Indus Valley people wove cloth from cotton, made metal tools, and used the potter's wheel.

Evidence points to trade between the Indus culture and Mesopotamia. Indus stone stamp seals have been found in Mesopotamia, and Akkadian texts mention a "Melukka" region, perhaps the Indus basin, as a source of ivory, precious stones, and other wares. The island of Bahrain in the Persian Gulf may have been a staging point for Indus-Mesopotamian sea trade. Metals and semiprecious stones were apparently imported into the Indus region from present-day Iran and Afghanistan, as well as from central Asia, from farther south on the Indian peninsula, and perhaps from Arabia. Similarities in artistic styles suggest that trade contacts resulted in cultural borrowings.

Material Culture Among the most striking accomplishments of the Indus culture are fine bronze and stone sculptures. Other evidence of the skill of Indus artisans includes copper and bronze tools and vessels, black-on-red painted pottery, dressed stonework, stone and terra-cotta figurines and toys, silver vessels and ornaments, gold jewelry, and dyed woven fabric. Indus stamp seals, which provide the only examples of the still undeciphered Indus script, also bear representations of animals, humans, and what are thought to be divine or semidivine beings. Similar figures are also found on paint-

Map 1–5. Mohenjo-Daro

ed pottery and engraved copper tablets. Compared with the art of Egypt or Mesopotamia, this art seems limited, however. Except for some decorative brickwork, no monumental friezes, mosaics, or sculpture have been found.

Religion The Indus remains reveal somewhat more regarding the religious realm. The elaborate bath facilities suggest that ritual bathing and water purification rites were important, as they still are in India today. The stone images from the so-called temples of Mohenjo-Daro and the more common terra-cotta figurines from other sites also suggest links to later Indian religious practices and symbols. The many images of male animals such as the humped bull might be symbols of power and fertility or might indicate animal worship. A recurring image of a male figure with leafy headdress and horns, often seated in a posture associated later in India with yogic meditation, has been likened to the Vedic Aryan "Lord of All Creatures." He has features in common with the Hindu god Shiva, especially where he is depicted with three faces and an erect phallus. Also found in Indus artifacts are the pipal tree and the left-handed swastika, both symbols later important to Hindus.

Terra-cotta figurines of females, often pregnant or carrying a child, are similar to female images in several prehistoric cultures. As possible precursors of Shiva's consort (known as Devi, Durga, and by other names), they too may represent an element of pre-Aryan religion that reemerged later to figure in "Hindu" culture. Yet other aspects of Indus religion—burial customs, for example—are not clearly related to later Indian practices. They remind us, however, that the Indus peoples, like all others, had their own ways of coming to terms with the mysteries of birth, life, and death.

The Passing of Indus Civilization

Sometime in the period from about 1800 to 1700 B.C.E., Indus civilization disappeared. It is not clear whether its demise was related to the warlike Aryan invaders who may first have appeared in the upper Indus about 1800 B.C.E. and later used their horse-drawn chariots to subdue indigenous peoples and move across the north Indian plains. Some scholars think it was destroyed by abnormal flooding (perhaps from careless damming of the Indus), changes in the course of the Indus, collapse of military power, or a long period of dessication even before the Aryans ar-

Indus Stamp Seal. Note the familiar humped bull of India on this stone stamp seal. © Scala/Art Resource, N.Y.

rived. Regardless of cause, the Indus culture disappeared by about 1700 B.C.E. and remains too shadowy for us to measure its proper influence. Nonetheless, these predecessors of the Aryans likely made significant contributions to later life in the subcontinent in ways that we have yet to discover.

The Vedic Aryan Civilization

We know more about the Aryan culture that effectively "refounded" Indian civilization around 1500 B.C.E. Yet unlike

SOURCE Selections from the *Rig Veda*

Indus civilization, it was not urban and left neither city ruins nor substantial artifacts beyond tools, weapons, and pottery. Virtually our only source of knowledge about ancient Aryan life are the words of the Vedas, the Aryan sacred texts—hence we know the culture as "Vedic." Although the latest Vedic texts date from perhaps 500 B.C.E., the earliest may go back to 1700 B.C.E. Transmitted orally through the centuries, the Vedas were not written down until writing was reintroduced to India sometime after 700 B.C.E. (Indeed, until recently, writing down the Vedas at all was shunned in favor of memorization and recitation among the Brahmans.) The Vedas are ritual, priestly, and speculative, not historical works. They reveal little about events but do offer insight into the religion, society, values, and thought of early Aryan India.

Veda, which means "knowledge," is the collective term for the texts still recognized today by most Indians as the holiest sources of their tradition. For Hindus, Veda is the eternal wisdom of primordial seers preserved for thousands of years in an unbroken oral tradition. The Vedas are the four major compilations of Vedic ritual, explanatory, and speculative texts. The collection of 1,028 religious hymns known as the *Rig-Veda* represents the oldest materials of the Vedas. The latest of these hymns date from about 1000 B.C.E., the oldest from perhaps 1700–1200 B.C.E., when the Aryans spread across the northern plains to the upper reaches of the Ganges.

Aryan is a different kind of term. The second-millennium invaders of northern India called themselves *Aryas* as opposed to the peoples whom they conquered. Vedic Sanskrit, the language of the invaders, gave this word to later Sanskrit as a term for "noble" or "free-born" (*arya*). The word is found also in old Iranian, or Persian, texts, and even the term

Iran is derived from the Old Persian equivalent of *arya*. It was apparently the original name of peoples who migrated out of the steppeland between Eastern Europe and Central Asia into Europe, Greece, Anatolia, the Iranian plateau, and India during the second and first millennia B.C.E. Those who came to India are thus more precisely designated Indo-Aryans, or Vedic Aryans.

In the nineteenth century, *Aryan* was the term applied to the widespread language group known more commonly today as **Indo-European**. To this widely distributed family belong Greek, Latin, the Romance and Germanic languages, the Slavic tongues, and the Indo-Iranian languages, including Persian and Sanskrit and their derivatives. The Nazis perversely misused "Aryan" to refer to a white "master race." Today most scholars use *Aryan* only to identify the Indo-European speakers who invaded India and the Iranian plateau in the second millennium B.C.E. and the Indo-Iranian languages.

"Aryanizing" of North India   The Vedic Aryans were semi-nomadic warriors who reached India in small tribal groups through the mountain passes of the Hindu Kush. They were horsemen and cattle herders rather than farmers and city builders. They left their mark not in material culture, but in the changes that their conquests brought to the regions they overran: a new language, social organization, techniques of warfare, and religious forms and ideas.

The early Aryans penetrated first into the Punjab and the Indus Valley around 1800–1500 B.C.E., presumably in search of grazing lands for their livestock. Their horses, chariots, and copper-bronze weapons likely gave them military superiority over the Indus peoples or their successors. Rig-Vedic hymns echo these early conflicts. The god Indra, for example, is hailed as the warrior who smashes the fortifications of enemies (Indus citadels?) and slays the great serpent who had blocked the rivers (referring to the destruction of the dams that controlled the Indus waters?). The references to human rather than divine warriors in some later Rig-Vedic hymns may reflect actual historical events. One late hymn praises the king of the *Bharatas*, giving us the Indian name for modern India, *Bharat*, "land of the Bharatas."

During the Rig-Vedic age (ca. 1700–1000 B.C.E.), the newcomers settled in the Punjab and beyond, where they took up agriculture and stockbreeding. How far they penetrated before 1000 B.C.E. is not clear, but their main locus remained the Punjab and the plains west of the Yamuna River. Then, between about 1000 and 500 B.C.E., the *Late Vedic Age*, these Aryan Indians spread across the plain between the Yamuna and the Ganges and eastward. They cleared (probably by burning) the heavy forests that covered this region and then settled there. They also moved farther northeast to the Himalayan foothills and southeast along the Ganges, in what

was to be the cradle of subsequent Indian civilization. During this age the importance of the Punjab receded.

The late Vedic period is also called the Brahmanic Age because it was dominated by the priestly religion of the Brahman class, as evidenced in commentaries called the *Brahmanas* (ca. 1000–800 or 600 B.C.E.). It is also sometimes called the Epic Age because it provided the setting for India's two classical epics, the **Mahabharata** and the **Ramayana**. Both were composed much later, probably between 400 B.C.E. and 200 C.E., but contain older material and refer to older events. The *Mahabharata*, the world's longest epic poem, centers on the rivalry of two Aryan clans in the region northwest of modern Delhi, perhaps around 900 B.C.E. The *Ramayana* tells of the legendary, dramatic adventures of King Rama. Both epics reflect the complex cultural and social mixing of Aryan and other earlier subcontinent peoples.

By about 200 C.E., this mixing produced a distinctive new "Indian" civilization over most of the subcontinent. Its basis was clearly Aryan, but its language, society, and religion incorporated many non-Aryan elements. Harappan culture vanished, but both it and other regional cultures contributed to the formation of Indian culture as we know it.

Vedic Aryan Society   Aryan society was apparently patrilineal—with succession and inheritance in the male line—and its gods were likewise predominantly male. Marriage appears to have been monogamous, and widows could remarry. Related families formed larger kin groups. The largest social grouping was the tribe, ruled by a chieftain or **raja** ("king" in Sanskrit), who shared power with a tribal council. In early Vedic days the ruler was chosen for his prowess; his chief responsibility was to lead in battle, and he had no priestly function or sacred authority. A chief priest looked after the sacrifices on which religious life centered. By the Brahmanic age the king, with the help of priests, had assumed the role of judge in legal matters and become a hereditary ruler claiming divine qualities. The power of the priestly class had also increased.

Although there were probably subgroups of warriors and priests, Aryan society seems originally to have had only two basic divisions: noble and common. The Dasas—the darker, conquered peoples—came to form a third group (together with those who intermarried with them) of the socially excluded. Over time, a more rigid scheme of four social classes (excluding the non-Aryan Dasas) evolved. By the late Rig-Vedic period, religious theory explicitly sanctioned these four divisions, or *varnas*—the priestly (*Brahman*), the warrior/noble (*Kshatriya*), the peasant/tradesman (*Vaishya*), and the servant (*Shudra*). Only the members of the three upper classes participated fully in social, political, and religious life. This scheme underlies the rigid caste system that later became fundamental to Indian society.

Material Culture The early, seminomadic Aryans lived simply in wood-and-thatch or, later, mud-walled dwellings. They measured wealth in cattle and were accomplished at carpentry and bronze working (iron probably was not known in India before 1000 B.C.E.). They used gold for ornamentation and produced woolen textiles. They also cultivated some crops, especially grains, and were familiar with intoxicating drinks, including soma, used in religious rites, and a kind of mead.

References to singing, dancing, and musical instruments suggest that music was a favored pastime in the Vedic period. Gambling, especially dicing, appears to have been popular. One of the few secular pieces among the Vedic hymns is a "Gambler's Lament," which closes with a plea to the dice: "Take pity on us. Do not bewitch us with your fierce magic. Let no one be trapped by the brown dice!"

The Brahmanic Age left few material remains. Urban culture remained undeveloped, although mud-brick towns appeared as new lands were cleared for cultivation. Established kingdoms with fixed capitals now existed. Trade grew, especially along the Ganges, although there is no evidence of a coinage system. Later texts mention specialized artisans, including goldsmiths, basket makers, weavers, potters, and entertainers. Writing had been reintroduced to India around 700 B.C.E., perhaps from Mesopotamia along with traded goods.

Religion Vedic India's main identifiable contributions to later history were religious. The Vedas reflect the broad development of Vedic Brahmanic religion in the millennium after the coming of the first Aryans. They tell us primarily about the public cult and domestic rituals of the Aryan upper classes. Among the rest of the population, non-Aryan practices and ideas likely continued to flourish. Apparently non-Aryan elements are visible occasionally even in the Vedic texts themselves, especially later ones. The Upanishads (after ca. 800 B.C.E.) thus refers to fertility and female deities, ritual pollution and ablutions, and the transmigration of the soul after death.

The central Vedic cult—controlled by priests serving a military aristocracy—remained dominant until the middle of the first millennium B.C.E. By that time other, perhaps older, religious forms were evidently asserting themselves among the populace. The increasing ritual formalism of Brahmanic religion provoked challenges both in popular practice and in religious thought that culminated in Buddhist, Jain, and Hindu traditions of piety and practice (see Chapter 2).

The earliest Indo-Aryans seem to have worshiped numerous gods, most of whom embodied or were associated with powers of nature. The Rig-Vedic hymns are addressed to anthropomorphic deities linked to natural phenomena such as the sky, the clouds, and the sun. These gods are comparable to those of ancient Greece (see Chapter 3) and are apparently distantly related to them through the Indo-European heritage the Greeks and Aryans shared. The name of the Aryan father-god Dyaus, for example, is linguistically related to the Greek Zeus. In Vedic India, however, unlike Greece, the father-god had become less important than his children, especially Indra, god of war and the storm, who led his heavenly warriors across the sky to slay dragons or other enemies with his thunderbolt. (See Document, "Hymn to Indra.")

Also of major importance was Varuna, who may have had connections with the later Iranian god Ahura Mazda (see Chapter 4) and the Greek god of the heavens, Uranos. Varuna was more remote from human affairs than Indra. Depicted as a regal figure seated on his heavenly throne, he guarded the cosmic order, *Rta*, which was both the law of nature and the universal moral law or truth. As the god who commanded awe and demanded righteous behavior, Varuna had characteristics of a supreme, omnipresent divinity.

Another prominent Vedic god was Agni, the god of fire (his name, which is the Sanskrit word for fire, is related to Latin *ignis*, "fire," and thus to English *ignite*). He mediated between heaven and earth through the fire sacrifice, and was thus the god of sacrifice and the priests. He was also

Chronology

Ancient India

ca. 2250–1750 (2500–1500?) B.C.E.	Indus (Harappan) civilization (written script still undeciphered)
ca. 1800–1500 B.C.E.	Aryan peoples invade northwestern India
ca. 1500–1000 B.C.E.	Rig-Vedic period: composition of Rig-Vedic hymns; Punjab as center of Indo-Aryan civilization
ca. 1000–500 B.C.E.	Late Vedic period: Doab as center of Indo-Aryan civilization
ca. 1000–800/600 B.C.E.	Composition of Brahmanas and other Vedic texts
ca. 800–500 B.C.E.	Composition of major Upanishads
ca. 700–500 B.C.E.	Probable reintroduction of writing
ca. 400 B.C.E.–200 C.E.	Composition of great epics, the *Mahabharata* and *Ramayana*

Hymn to Indra

Document

This hymn celebrates the greatest deed ascribed to Indra, the slaying of the dragon Vritra to release the waters needed by people and livestock (which is also heralded at one point in the hymn as the act of creation itself). These waters are apparently those of the dammed-up rivers, but possibly also the rains as well. This victory also symbolizes the victory of the Aryans over the dark-skinned Dasas. Note the sexual as well as water imagery. The *kadrukas* may be the bowls used for soma in the sacrifice. The *vajra* is Indra's thunderbolt; the name *Dasa* for the lord of the waters is also that used for the peoples defeated by the Aryans and for all enemies of Indra, of whom the *Pani* tribe is one.

◆ **What are the main kinds of imagery used for Indra and his actions in the hymn? What divine acts does the hymn ascribe to Indra?**

Indra's heroic deeds, indeed, will I proclaim, the first ones which the wielder of the vajra accomplished. He killed the dragon, released the waters, and split open the sides of the mountains.

He killed the dragon lying spread out on the mountain; for him Tvashtar fashioned the roaring vajra. Like bellowing cows, the waters, gliding, have gone down straightway to the ocean.

Showing off his virile power he chose soma; from the three kadrukas he drank of the extracted soma. The bounteous god took up the missile, the vajra; he killed the firstborn among the dragons.

When you, O Indra, killed the first-born among the dragons and further overpowered the wily tricks (maya) of the tricksters, bringing forth, at that very moment, the sun, the heaven and the dawn—since then, indeed, have you not come across another enemy. Indra killed Vritra, the greater enemy, the shoulderless one, with his mighty and fatal weapon, the vajra. Like branches of a tree lopped off with an axe, the dragon lies prostrate upon the earth. . . .

Over him, who lay in that manner like a shattered reed flowed the waters for the sake of man. At the feet of the very waters, which Vritra had [once] enclosed with his might, the dragon [now] lay [prostrate]. . . .

With the Dasa as their lord and with the dragon as their warder, the waters remained imprisoned, like cows held by the Pani. Having killed Vritra, [Indra] threw open the cleft of waters which had been closed.

You became the hair of a horse's tail, O Indra, when he [Vritra] struck at your sharp-pointed vajra—the one god [eka deva] though you were. You won the cows, O brave one, you won soma; you released the seven rivers, so that they should flow. . . .

Indra, who wields the vajra in his hand, is the lord of what moves and what remains rested, of what is peaceful and what is horned. He alone rules over the tribes as their king; he encloses them as does a rim the spokes.

—*Rig-Veda 1.32*

god of the hearth, and thus of the home. Like flame itself, he was a mysterious deity.

Other Vedic gods include Soma, the god of the hallucinogenic soma plant and the drink made from it; Ushas, goddess of dawn (one of few female deities); Yama, god of the dead; Rudra, the archer and storm god; Vishnu, a solar deity; and the sun god, Surya. The Vedic hymns praise each god they address as possessing almost all powers, including those associated with other gods.

Ritual sacrifice was the central focus of Vedic religion, its goal apparently to invoke the presence of the gods to

whom an offering was made rather than to expiate sins or express thanksgiving. Drinking soma juice was part of the ritual. A recurring theme of the Vedic hymns that accompanied the rituals is the desire for prosperity, health, and victory. Fire sacrifices were particularly important.

The late Vedic texts emphasize magical and cosmic aspects of ritual and sacrifice. Indeed, some of the *Brahmanas* maintain that only exacting performance of the sacrifice can maintain the world order.

The word *Brahman*, originally used to designate the ritual utterance or word of power, came to refer also to the

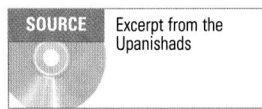
SOURCE Excerpt from the Upanishads

generalized divine power present in the sacrifice. In the **Upanishads**, some of the latest Vedic texts and the ones most concerned with speculation about the universe, *Brahman* was extended to refer to the Absolute, the transcendent principle of reality. As the guardian of ritual and the master of the sacred word, the priest was known throughout the Vedic Aryan period by a related word, *Brahmana*, for which the English is *Brahman*. Echoes of these associations were to lend force in later Hindu tradition to the special status of the Brahman caste groups as the highest social class (see Chapter 4).

Early Chinese Civilization

Neolithic Origins in the Yellow River Valley

Agriculture began in China about 4000 B.C.E. in the basin of the southern bend of the Yellow River. This is the northernmost of east Asia's four great river systems. The others are the Yangtze in central China, the West River in southern China, and the Red River in what is today northern Vietnam (see Map 1–6). All drain eastward into the Pacific Ocean. In recent millennia, the Yellow River has flowed through a deforested plain, cold in winter and subject to periodic droughts. But in 4000 B.C.E., its climate was warmer, with

Map 1–6. Bronze Age China During the Shang Dynasty, 1766–1050 B.C.E. Anyang was a late Shang dynasty capital. Sian and Luoyang were the capitals of the Western and Eastern Zhou.

forested highlands in the west and swampy marshes to the east. The bamboo rat that today can be found only in semitropical Southeast Asia lived along the Yellow River.

The chief crop of China's agricultural revolution was millet. A second agricultural development focusing on rice may have occurred on the Huai River between the Yellow River and the Yangtze near the coast. In time, wheat entered China from the west. The early Chinese cleared land and burned its cover to plant millet and cabbage and, later, rice and soybeans. When the soil became exhausted, fields were abandoned, and sometimes early villages were abandoned, too. Tools were of stone: axes, hoes, spades, and sickle-shaped knives. The early Chinese domesticated pigs, sheep, cattle, dogs, and chickens. Game was also plentiful, and hunting continued to be important to the village economy. In excavated village garbage heaps of ancient China are found the bones of deer, wild cattle, antelopes, rhinoceros, hares, and marmots. Grain was stored in pottery painted in bold, geometric designs of red and black. This pottery gave way to a harder, thin black pottery, made on a potter's wheel, whose use spread west along the Yellow River and south to the Yangtze. The tripodal shapes of Neolithic pots prefigure later Chinese bronzes.

The earliest cultivators lived in wattle-and-daub pit dwellings with wooden support posts and sunken, plastered floors. Their villages were located in isolated clearings along slopes of river valleys. Archaeological finds of weapons and remains of earthen walls suggest tribal warfare between villages. Little is known of the religion of these people, although some evidence indicates the worship of ancestral spirits. They practiced divination by applying heat to a hole drilled in the shoulder bone of a steer or the undershell of a tortoise and then interpreting the resulting cracks in the bone. They buried their dead in cemeteries with jars of food. Tribal leaders wore rings and beads of jade.

Early Bronze Age: The Shang

The traditional history of China tells of three ancient dynasties: Xia (2205–1766 B.C.E.), Shang (1766–1050 B.C.E.), and Zhou (1050–256 B.C.E.). Until early in this century, historians thought the first two were legendary. Then, in the 1920s, archaeological excavations at "the wastes of Yin" near present-day Anyang uncovered the ruins of a walled city that had been a late Shang capital (see Map 1–6). Other Shang cities have been discovered more recently. The ruins contained the archives of the department of divination of the Shang court, with thousands on thousands of "oracle bones" incised with archaic Chinese writing. The names of kings on the bones fit almost perfectly those of the traditional historical record. This evidence that the Shang actually existed

has led historians to suggest that the Xia may also have been an actual dynasty. Perhaps the Xia was a late Neolithic black-pottery kingdom; perhaps it already had bronze and was responsible for the earliest, still missing stage of Chinese writing.

The characteristic political institution of Bronze Age China was the city-state. The largest was the Shang capital, which, frequently moved, lacked the monumental architecture of Egypt or Mesopotamia. The walled city contained public buildings, altars, and the residences of the aristocracy; it was surrounded by a sea of Neolithic tribal villages. By late Shang times, several such cities were spotted across the north China plain. The Shang kings possessed political, economic, social, and religious authority. When they died, they were sometimes succeeded by younger brothers and sometimes by sons. The rulers of other city-states acknowledged their authority.

The military aristocracy went to war in chariots, supported by levies of foot soldiers. Their weapons were spears and powerful compound bows. Accounts tell of armies of three or four thousand troops and of a battle involving thirteen thousand. The Shang fought against barbarian tribes and, occasionally, against other city-states in rebellion against Shang rule. Captured prisoners were enslaved.

The three most notable features of Shang China were writing, bronzes, and the appearance of social classes. (See "Chinese Writing.") Scribes at the Shang court kept records on strips of bamboo, but these have not survived. What have survived are inscriptions on bronze artifacts and the oracle bones. Some bones contain the question put to the oracle, the answer, and the outcome of the matter. Representative questions were: Which ancestor is causing the king's earache? If the king goes hunting at Ch'i, will there be a disaster? Will the king's child be a son? If the king sends his army to attack an enemy, will the deity help him? Was a sacrifice acceptable to ancestral deities?

What we know of Shang religion is based on the bones. The Shang believed in a supreme "Deity Above," who had authority over the human world. Also serving at the court of

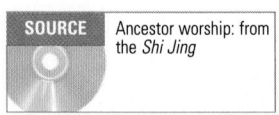
SOURCE Ancestor worship: from the *Shi Jing*

the Deity Above were lesser natural deities—the sun, moon, earth, rain, wind, and the six clouds. Even the Shang king sacrificed not to the Deity Above but to his ancestors, who interceded with the Deity Above on the king's behalf. Kings, while alive at least, were not considered divine but were the high priests of the state.

In Shang times, as later, religion in China was closely associated with cosmology. The Shang people observed the movements of the planets and stars and reported eclipses. Celestial happenings were seen as omens from the gods. The chief cosmologists also recorded events at the court. The Shang calendar had a month of 30 days and a year of 360 days. Adjustments were made periodically by adding an extra month. The calendar was used by the king to tell his people when to sow and when to reap.

Bronze appeared in China about 2000 B.C.E., a thousand years later than in Mesopotamia and five hundred years later than in India. The Shang likely developed bronze technology independently, however, because Shang methods of casting were more advanced than those of Mesopotamia, and because the designs on its bronzes emerged directly from those of the preceding black-pottery culture. Bronze was used for weapons, armor, and chariot fittings, and for a variety of ceremonial vessels of amazing fineness and beauty.

Among the Shang, as with other early river valley civilizations, the increasing control of nature through agriculture and metallurgy was accompanied by the emergence of a rigidly stratified society in which the many were compelled to serve the few. A monopoly of bronze weapons enabled aristocrats to exploit other groups. A hierarchy of class defined life in the Chinese city-state. The king and the officials of his court lived within the walled city. Their houses were spacious, built above the ground with roofs supported by rows of wooden pillars, resting on foundation stones. Their lifestyle was opulent for ancient times. They wore fine clothes, feasted at banquets, and drank wine from bronze vessels. In contrast, a far larger population of agricultural workers lived outside the city in cramped pit dwellings. Their life was meager and hard. Archaeological excavations of their underground hovels have uncovered only clay pots.

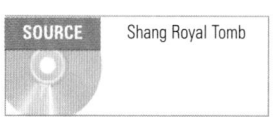
SOURCE Shang Royal Tomb

Nowhere was the gulf between the royal lineage and the baseborn more apparent than it was in the Shang institution of human sacrifice. One Shang tomb thirty-nine feet long, twenty-six feet wide, and twenty-six feet deep contained the decapitated bodies of humans, horses, and dogs, as well as ornaments of bone, stone, and jade. When a king died, hundreds of slaves or prisoners of war, sometimes together with those who had served the king during his lifetime, might be buried with him. Sacrifices also were made when a palace or an altar was built.

Oracle Bone. Inscribed oracle bone from the Shang Dynasty city of Anyang.

Late Bronze Age: The Western Zhou

To the west of the area of Shang rule, in the valley of the Wei River, a tributary of the Yellow River, lived the Zhou people. Culturally closer to the Neolithic black-pottery people, they were less civilized and more warlike than the Shang. References to the Zhou in the Shang oracle bones indicate that the Shang had relations with them—sometimes friendly, sometimes hostile. According to the traditional historical record, the last Shang kings were weak, cruel, and tyrannical. By 1050 B.C.E., they had been debilitated by campaigns against nomads in the north and rebellious tribes in the east. Taking advantage of this opportunity, the Zhou made alliances with disaffected city-states and swept in, conquering the Shang.

In most respects, the Zhou continued the Shang pattern of life and rule. The agrarian-based city-state continued to be the basic unit of society, and it is estimated that there were about two hundred of them in the eighth century B.C.E. The Zhou social hierarchy was not unlike that of the Shang, with kings and lords at the top, officials and warriors below them, and peasants and slaves at the bottom. Slaves served primarily as domestic servants. The Zhou assimilated Shang culture, continuing without interruption the development of China's ideographic writing. The Zhou also maintained the practice of casting bronze ceremonial vessels, but their vessels lack the fineness that set the Shang above the rest of the Bronze Age world.

The Zhou kept their capital in the west but set up a secondary capital at Luoyang, along the southern bend of the Yellow River (see Map 1–6). They appointed their kinsmen or other aristocratic allies to rule in other city-states. Blood or lineage ties were essential to the Zhou pattern of rule. The Zhou king was the head of the senior branch of the family. He performed the sacrifices to the Deity Above for the entire family. The rankings of the lords of other princely states reflected their degree of closeness to the senior line of Zhou kings.

One difference between the Shang and the Zhou was in the nature of the political legitimacy each claimed. The Shang kings, descended from shamanistic (priestly) rulers,

Chinese Writing

The Chinese system of writing dates back at least to the Shang dynasty (1766–1050 B.C.E.), when animal bones and tortoise shells (the so-called oracle bones) were incised for the purpose of divination. About half of the three thousand characters used in Shang times have been deciphered. They evolved over the centuries into the fifty thousand characters found in the largest dictionaries. But even today only about three or four thousand are in common use. A scholar may know twice that number.

Characters developed from little pictures. Note the progressive stylization. By 200 B.C.E., the writing had become standardized and close to the modern form of the printed character.

	Shang (1400 B.C.E.)	Zhou (600 B.C.E.)	Seal Script (200 B.C.E.)	Modern
Sun				
Moon				
Tree				
Bird				
Mouth				
Horse				

Other characters combined two pictures to express an idea. The following examples use modern characters:

Sun	日	+ moon	月	= bright	明	
Mouth	口	+ bird	鳥	= to chirp	鳴	
Woman	女	+ child	子	= good	好	
Tree	木	+ sun	日	= east	東	

It was a matter of convention that the sun behind a tree meant the rising sun in the east and not the setting sun in the west.

Characters were formed several other ways. In one, a sound element was combined with a meaning element. Chinese has many homonyms, or words with the same sound. The character, for example, is read *tai* and means "elevation" or "to raise up." But in spoken Chinese, there are other words with the same sound that mean "moss," "trample," "a nag," and "idle." Thus,

Tai	台	+ grass	艹	= moss	苔	
Tai	台	+ foot	足	= trample	跆	
Tai	台	+ horse	馬	= a nag	駘	
Tai	台	+ heart	心	= idle	怠	

In each case the sound comes from the 台, and the meaning from the other element. Note that the 台 may be at the bottom, the top, or the right. This positioning, too, is a matter of convention.

Tables by A. Craig; calligraphy by Teruko Craig.

had a built-in religious authority and needed no theory to justify their rule. But the Zhou, having conquered the Shang, needed a rationale for why they, and not the Shang, were now the rightful rulers. Their argument was that Heaven (the name for the supreme being that gradually replaced the Deity Above during the early Zhou), appalled by the wickedness of the last Shang king, had withdrawn its mandate to rule from the Shang, awarding it instead to the Zhou. This concept of the **Mandate of Heaven** was subsequently invoked by every dynasty in China down to the twenty-first century. The ideograph for Heaven is related to that for man, and the concept initially had human, or anthropomorphic, attributes. In the later Zhou, however, although it continued to be viewed as having a moral will, Heaven became less anthropomorphic and more of an abstract metaphysical force.

Iron Age: The Eastern Zhou

In 771 B.C.E. the Wei Valley capital of the Western Zhou was overrun by barbarians. The explanation of the event in Chinese tradition calls to mind the story of "the boy who cried wolf." The last Western Zhou king was so infatuated with a favorite concubine that he repeatedly lit bonfires signaling a barbarian attack. His concubine would clap her hands in delight at the sight of the army assembled in martial splendor. But the army tired of the charade, and when invaders actually came, the king's beacons were ignored. The king was killed and the Zhou capital sacked. The heir to the throne, with some members of the court, escaped to the secondary capital at Luoyang, two hundred miles to the east and just south of the bend in the Yellow River, beginning the Eastern Zhou period.

The first phase of the Eastern Zhou, sometimes called the Spring and Autumn period after a classic history by that name, lasted until 481 B.C.E. After their flight to Luoyang, the Zhou kings were never able to reestablish their old authority. By the early seventh century B.C.E., Luoyang's political power was nominal, although it remained a center of culture and ritual observances. (See Document, "Human Sacrifice in Early China.") Kinship and religious ties to the Zhou house had worn thin, and it no longer had the military strength to reim-

Bronze Vessel from the Shang Dynasty.
The little elephant on top forms the handle of the lid. Wine was poured through the spout formed by the big elephant's trunk.
The Freer Gallery of Art, Smithsonian Institution, Washington, D.C.

pose its rule. During the seventh and sixth centuries B.C.E. the political configuration was an equilibrium of many small principalities on the north-central plain surrounded by larger, wholly autonomous territorial states along the borders of the plain (see Map 1–7). The larger states consolidated the areas within their borders, absorbed tribal peoples, and expanded, conquering states on their periphery.

To defend themselves against the more aggressive territorial states, and in the absence of effective Zhou authority, smaller states entered defensive alliances. The earliest alliance, of 681 B.C.E., was directed against the half-barbarian state of Chu, which straddled the Yangzi in the south. Princes and lords of smaller states elected as their *hegemon* (or military overlord) the lord of a northern territorial state and pledged him their support. At the formal ceremony that established the alliance, a bull was sacrificed. The hegemon and other lords smeared its blood on their mouths and swore oaths to the gods to uphold the alliance. That the oaths were not always upheld can be surmised from the Chinese expression, "to break an oath while the blood is still wet on one's lips."

During the next two centuries, alliances shifted and hegemons changed. At best, alliances only slowed down the pace of military aggrandizement.

The second phase of the Eastern Zhou is known as the Warring States period after a chronicle of the same name treating the years from 401 to 256 B.C.E. By the fifth century B.C.E., all defensive alliances had collapsed. Strong states swallowed their weaker neighbors. The border states grew in size and power. Interstate stability disappeared. By the fourth century B.C.E., only eight or nine great territorial states remained as contenders. The only question was which one would defeat the others and go on to unify China.

Three basic changes in Chinese society contributed to the rise of large territorial states. One was the expansion of population and agricultural lands. The walled cities of the Shang and Western Zhou had been like oases in the wilds, bounded by

Map 1–7. Early Iron Age Territorial States in China During the Sixth Century B.C.E. After the fall of the Western Zhou in China in 771 B.C.E., large territorial states formed that became increasingly independent of the later Zhou kings.

Human Sacrifice in Early China

By the seventh century B.C.E. human sacrifice was less frequent in China but still happened. This poem was composed when Duke Mu of the state of Qin died in 631 B.C.E. (For want of better terms, Chinese titles are usually translated into roughly equivalent titles among the English nobility.) Were human feelings different, as Professor K. C. Chang has asked, a thousand years earlier during the Shang? The poem suggests that despite religious belief and the honor accorded the victims, they may not have gone gladly to the grave. Note the identification of Heaven with "that blue one," the sky.

◆ We believe today that it is honorable to die in war for one's nation. How is that different from dying to serve one's lord in the afterlife?

"Kio" sings the oriole
As it lights on the thorn-bush.
Who went with Duke Mu to the grave?
Yen-hsi of the clan Tsu-chu.
Now this Yen-hsi
Was the pick of all our men;
But as he drew near the tomb-hole
His limbs shook with dread.
That blue one, Heaven,
Takes all our good men.
Could we but ransom him
There are a hundred would give their lives.
"Kio" sings the oriole
As it lights on the mulberry-tree.

Who went with Duke Mu to the grave?
Chung-hang of the clan Tsu-chu.
Now this Chung-hang
Was the sturdiest of all our men;
But as he drew near the tomb-hole
His limbs shook with dread.
That blue one, Heaven,
Takes all our good men.
Could we but ransom him
There are a hundred would give their lives.

From *The Book of Songs*, trans. by Arthur Waley (New York: Grove Press, 1960), p. 311.

---

plains, marshes, and forests. Game was plentiful; thus, hunting, along with sheep and cattle breeding, supplemented agriculture. But in the Eastern Zhou, as population grew, wilds began to disappear, the economy became almost entirely agricultural, and hunting became an aristocratic pastime. Friction arose over boundaries as states began to abut. These changes accelerated in the late sixth century B.C.E. after the start of the Iron Age. With iron tools, farmers cleared new lands and plowed deeper, raising yields and increasing agricultural surpluses. Irrigation and drainage canals became important for the first time. Serfs gave way to independent farmers, who bought and sold land. By the third century B.C.E., China had about 20 million people, making it the most populous country in the world, a distinction it has never lost.

A second development was the rise of commerce. Roads built for war were used by merchants. Goods were transported by horses, oxcarts, riverboats, and the camel, which entered China in the third century B.C.E. The products of one region were traded for those of another. Copper coins joined bolts of silk and precious metals as media of exchange. Rich merchants rivaled in lifestyle the landowning lower nobility. New outer walls were added to cities to provide for expanded merchant quarters. Bronze bells and mirrors, clay figurines, lacquer boxes, and musical instruments found in late Zhou tombs give ample evidence that the material and artistic culture of China leaped ahead during this period, despite its endemic wars.

A third change that doomed the city-state was the rise of a new kind of army. The war chariots of the old aristocracy, practical only on level terrain, gave way to cavalry armed with crossbows. Most of the fighting was done by conscript foot soldiers. Armies of the territorial states numbered in the hundreds of thousands. The old nobility gave way to professional commanders. The old aristocratic etiquette, which governed behavior even in battle, gave way to military tactics that were bloody and ruthless. Prisoners were often massacred.

Change also affected government. Lords of the new territorial states began to style themselves as kings, taking the title that previously only Zhou royalty had enjoyed. At some courts, the hereditary nobility began to

Chronology

Early China

4000 B.C.E.	Neolithic agricultural villages
1766 B.C.E.	Bronze Age city-states, aristocratic charioteers, pictographic writing
771 B.C.E.	Iron Age territorial states
500 B.C.E.	Age of philosophers
221 B.C.E.	China is unified

decline, supplanted by ministers appointed for their knowledge of statecraft. To survive, new states had to transform their agricultural and commercial wealth into military strength. To collect taxes, conscript soldiers, and administer the affairs of state required records and literate officials. Academies were established to fill the need. Beneath the ministers, a literate bureaucracy developed. Its members were referred to as *shi*, a term that had once meant "warrior" but gradually came to mean "scholar-bureaucrat." The *shi* were of mixed social origins, including petty nobility, literate members of the old warrior class, landlords, merchants, and rising commoners. From this class, as we will see in Chapter 2, came the philosophers who created the "one hundred schools" and transformed the culture of China.

The Rise of Civilization in the Americas

During the last ice age the Bering region between Siberia and Alaska was dry land. Sometime before twelve thousand years ago, and perhaps as early as thirty thousand years ago, humans crossed this land bridge, probably in several migrations. Over many centuries these Asian immigrants moved south and east until they eventually crossed the more than eleven thousand miles to the tip of South America and the more than four thousand miles to the eastern regions of North America. In light of the vast distances and imposing geographic barriers involved, these ancient migrations must have been as heroic as any in human history. From them a wide variety of original American cultures and many hundreds of languages arose.

The earliest immigrants to the Americas, like all other Paleolithic peoples, lived by hunting, fishing, and gathering. At the time of the initial migrations, herds of

large game animals such as mammoths were plentiful. By the end of the Ice Age, however, mammoths and many other forms of game had become extinct in the Americas. Compared to Africa and Eurasia, many parts of North and South America were poor in animal resources and the rich source of protein they provide. Neither horses nor cattle populated the American continents. Where fishing or small game were not sufficiently plentiful, people had to rely on protein from vegetable sources. One result was the remarkable manner in which the original Americans participated in the Neolithic revolution. American production of plants providing protein far outpaced that of European agriculture. In this regard one of the most important early developments was the cultivation of maize (corn). Wherever maize could be extensively grown, a major ingredient in the food supply was secured. The cultivation of maize appears to have been in place in Mexico by approximately 4000 B.C.E. and to have developed farther south somewhat later. Other important foods were potatoes (developed in the Andes), manioc, squash, beans, peppers, and tomatoes. Many of these foods entered the diet of Europeans, Asians, and other peoples after the European conquest of the Americas in the sixteenth century C.E.

Eventually four areas of relatively dense settlement emerged in the Americas. One of these, in the Pacific Northwest in the area around Puget Sound, depended on the region's extraordinary abundance of fish rather than on agriculture; this area did not develop urbanized states. Another was the Mississippi Valley, where, based on maize agriculture, the inhabitants developed a high level of social and political integration that had collapsed several centuries before European contact. The other two, Mesoamerica and the Andean region of South America, saw the emergence of strong, long-lasting states. In other regions with maize agriculture and settled village life—notably the North American

Chronology

Early Civilizations of Mesoamerica

1500–400 B.C.E.	The Olmecs
200–750 C.E.	The Classic period in central Mexico. Dominance of Teotihuacán in the Valley of Mexico and Monte Alban in the Valley of Oaxaca
150–900 C.E.	The Classic period of Mayan civilization in the Yucatán and Guatemala

Map 1–8. Civilization in Mesoamerica and the Andes. Both Mesoamerica and the Andean region of South America saw the development of a series of civilizations beginning between 1500 and 1000 B.C.E.

Southwest—food supplies might have been too insecure to support the development of states.

Chapter 14 examines Mesoamerican and Andean civilization in detail. Here we give only a brief overview of their development. **Mesoamerica**, which extends from the central part of modern Mexico into Central America, is a region of great geographical diversity, ranging from tropical rain forest to semiarid mountains (see Map 1–8). Archaeologists traditionally divide its preconquest history into three broad periods: Pre-Classic or Formative (2000 B.C.E.–150 C.E.), Classic (150–900 C.E.), and Post-Classic (900–1521). The earliest Mesoamerican civilization, that of the Olmecs, arose during the Pre-Classic on the Gulf Coast beginning approximately 1500 B.C.E. The Olmec centers at San Lorenzo (c. 1200–c. 900 B.C.E.) and La Venta (c. 900–c. 400 B.C.E.) exhibit many of the characteristics of later Mesoamerican cities, including the symmetrical arrangement of large platforms, plazas, and other monumental structures along a central axis and possibly courts for the ritual ball game played throughout

Mesoamerica at the time of the Spanish conquest. Writing developed in Mesoamerica during the Late Formative period. As we will see in Chapter 14, succeeding civilizations—including the Classic period civilization of Teotihuacán, the Post-Classic civilizations of the Toltecs and Aztecs, and the Classic and Post-Classic civilization of the Mayas—created large cities, developed sophisticated calendar systems, and were organized in complex social and political structures.

The Andean region is one of dramatic contrasts. Along its western edge, the narrow coastal plain is one of the driest deserts in the world. The Andes rise abruptly from the coastal plain and then descend gradually into the Amazon basin to the east. Agriculture is possible on the coast only in the valleys of the many rivers that flow from the Andes into the Pacific. The earliest monumental architecture in the Andean region, built on the coast at the site of Aspero by people who depended on a combination of agriculture and the Pacific's rich marine resources, dates to about 2750 B.C.E., contemporary with the Great Pyramids of Egypt's Old Kingdom.

From 800 to 200 B.C.E. a civilization associated with the site of Chavín de Huantar in the highlands of Peru exerted great influence in the Andes. Artifacts in the distinctive Chavín style can be found over a large area dating to this period, which archaeologists call the Early Horizon. In many areas, this was a time of technical innovation, including pottery, textiles, and metallurgy. Whether the spread of the Chavín style represents actual political integration or the influence of a strong religious center is not known. The period following the decline of Chavín, which archaeologists call the Early Intermediate period, saw the development of distinctive cultures in several regions. Notable among these are the Moche culture on the northern coast of Peru and the Nazca culture on the southern coast. A second period of transregional integration—called the Middle Horizon—occurred around 600 C.E., this time probably associated with empires centered on the highland sites of Huari and Tiahuanaco. The succeeding Late Intermediate period was dominated on the northern coast of Peru by the Chimu successors of the Moche state. This period ended with the founding of the vast, tightly controlled empire of the Incas in the fourteenth and fifteenth centuries C.E.

Olmec Head. This colossal Olmec head, now in the Museo Nacional de Antropologia in Mexico City, was excavated at San Lorenzo. Carved of basalt, it may be a portrait of an Olmec ruler. Olmec civilization thrived between 1500 and 800 B.C.E.

in the Tigris and Euphrates valleys in Mesopotamia, then along the Nile River in Egypt, and somewhat later in the Indus valley in India and the Yellow River basin in China. Each of these early civilizations developed urban centers, monumental architecture, a hierarchical society, and a system of writing. The period is known as the Bronze Age because it coincided with the discovery of the technique for making bronze tools and weapons.

Summary

The Emergence of Civilization. Beginning in 10,000 B.C.E. human beings shifted from a hunter-gather way of life to one marked by settled agriculture and the domestication of animals—a shift known as the "Neolithic Revolution." Between 4000 and 3000 B.C.E., civilization began to appear

Chronology

Early Civilization of the Andes

ca. 2750 B.C.E.?	Monumental architecture at Aspero
800–200 B.C.E.?	Chavín (Early Horizon)
200 B.C.E.–600 C.E.	Early Intermediate period (Moche on the northern coast of Peru, Nazca on the southern coast)

Mesopotamia. The Sumerians founded the oldest Mesopotamian cities around 3000 B.C.E. Beginning around 2370 B.C.E., the Sumerian city-states were conquered and absorbed in turn by the Akkadian, Babylonian, and Assyrian Empires. The Sumerians passed much of their civilization down to their successors: a system of writing on clay tablets called *cuneiform*, the worship of gods based on natural forces, semidivine kings, and a highly developed bureaucracy.

Egypt. Watered by the Nile River and protected by deserts and the sea, Egyptian civilization was more secure and peaceful than that of Mesopotamia. Egypt became a unified kingdom around 2700 B.C.E. Religion dominated Egyptian life. The kings, or pharaohs, were considered gods on whom the lives and prosperity of their people depended. Egyptian history is divided into three main periods: Old Kingdom (2700–2200 B.C.E.), Middle Kingdom (2052–1786 B.C.E.), and New Kingdom (1575–1087 B.C.E.). Under the New Kingdom, Egypt contended for mastery of the Near East with the Hittite Empire.

Indus Civilization. By 2300 B.C.E. at least 70 Indus cities, the largest being Harappa and Mohenjo-Daro, had developed a sophisticated urban culture. Between 1800 and 1700 B.C.E., Indus civilization disappeared for unknown reasons. In its place, Indo-European (or Aryan) invaders established the "Vedic" culture, named after the ritual writings known as the Vedas. In turn, Vedic culture evolved into a "new" Indian civilization that spread over the whole subcontinent.

China. The Shang Dynasty (1766–1050 B.C.E.) founded the earliest known Bronze Age civilization in China. The Shang and their successors, the Zhou (1050–256 B.C.E.), ruled as warrior aristocrats from city-states that fought outsiders and each other. By the fourth century B.C.E., as population and commerce expanded, rulers needed bigger armies to defend their states and trained bureaucrats to administer them. The result was the consolidation of many petty states into a few large territorial units.

The Americas. The first civilizations in the Americas arose in places that produced an agricultural surplus. In Mesoamerica (central Mexico and Central America) this was based on the cultivation of maize (corn). In the Andes valleys, it was based on a combination of agriculture and the rich marine resources of the Pacific. The Olmecs (1500–400 B.C.E.) established the first civilization in Mesoamerica, whereas the first monumental architecture appeared in the Andes region around 2750 B.C.E.

Review Questions

1. How was life during the Paleolithic Age different from that in the Neolithic Age? What advances in agriculture and human development had taken place by the end of the Neolithic era? Is it valid to speak of a "Neolithic Revolution"?

2. What defines civilization? What are the similarities and differences among the world's earliest civilizations?

3. What general conclusions can you draw about the differences in the political and intellectual outlooks of the civilizations of Egypt and Mesopotamia? Compare especially Egyptian and Mesopotamian religious views. In what ways did the regional geography influence the religious outlooks of these two civilizations?

4. Why were the Assyrians so successful in establishing their Near Eastern Empire? How did their empire differ from that of the Hittites or Egyptians? In what ways did this empire benefit the civilized Middle East? Why did the Assyrian Empire ultimately fail to survive?

5. How does the early history of Indian civilization differ from that of the river valley civilizations of China, Mesopotamia, and Egypt? What does the evidence suggest were the social, economic, and political differences between the Indus civilization and the Vedic Aryan civilization?

INTERPRETING THE PAST

The King in Early World Civilizations

In his 1817 poem "Ozymandias," Percy Bysshe Shelley envisioned a traveler stumbling across a ruined pedestal in a trackless desert that read, "My name is Ozymandias, King of Kings: Look on my works, ye mighty, and despair!" While Shelley suggested that fame is temporary, an important feature of the earliest world civilizations is the centrality of their kings, many of whom were clearly as proud and self-important as the fictional "Ozymandias." In fact, one could argue that powerful monarchs facilitated the organization and discipline that made these civilizations possible.

Sources from Chapter One

Drawing on the visual and literary evidence available in this chapter, analyze the way in which ancient rulers were depicted. Consider, for example, the images of kings in the Victory Stele of the Akkadian king Naram-Sin (p. 14), the Assyrian palace relief of a king clutching a lion (p. 26), and the sculpted face of an Olmec ruler in Mexico (p. 43).

Sources from the Primary Source DVD / MyHistoryLab

 Read the excerpts from the *Amarna Letters* and the letter from the pharaoh to Harkhuf the explorer (Egypt), Liu the Duke, and Tan-Fu the

6. What were the stages of early Chinese history? What led each to evolve toward the next?

7. From the appearance of civilization in the Americas, what can you conclude about the factors that give rise to it?

Key Terms

Aryans (AIR-ee-uhns) (p. 28)

Bronze Age (p. 12)

civilization (p. 11)

culture (p. 6)

cuneiform (koo-NAY-form) (p. 14)

diffusion (p. 7)

Harappan (p. 28)

hieroglyphs (p. 22)

Indo-European (p. 32)

Mahabharata and *Ramayana* (p. 32)

Mandate of Heaven (p. 38)

Mesoamerica (p. 42)

Mesopotamia (p. 11)

Neolithic Revolution (p. 11)

Paleolithic Age (p. 6)

pharaoh (p. 20)

raja (rah-JAH) (p. 32)

Upanishads (oo-PAHN-ee-shahdz) (p. 35)

Vedas (vay-DAHZ) (p. 28)

Note: To learn more about the topics in this chapter, please turn to the Suggested Readings at the end of the book. For additional sources related to this chapter please see the Primary Source DVD at the back of this text or MyHistoryLab.

Duke from the *Shi Jing* (China). Examine as well the photographs of the Standard of Ur (Sumer) and the temple of Abu Simbel (Egypt).

Questions

How do these rulers appear, and why?

How is a king's power described and reinforced in these documents?

How did these kings, armed with visual and literary supports to their power, impose their will on their officials and the people at large?

Four Great Revolutions in Thought and Religion

- ◆ Comparing the Four Great Revolutions
- ◆ Philosophy in China
- ◆ Religion in India
- ◆ The Religion of the Israelites
- ◆ Greek Philosophy

LL HUMAN CULTURES DEVELOP RELIGIOUS or philosophical systems. Some scientists have even debated whether humans are somehow "hard-wired" biologically to tend toward religious beliefs. Regardless of the outcome of that debate, clearly religion and philosophy meet profound human psychological needs. They offer people explanations of where they and their societies came from, why they exist, and what the future holds for them, in this life and beyond. ■

Comparing the Four Great Revolutions

The most straightforward case is that of China. Both geographically and culturally, its philosophical breakthrough grew directly out of the earlier river valley civilization. No such continuity existed elsewhere in the world. The natural barriers of the Central Asian steppes, mountain ranges, and deserts allowed China to develop its own unique culture relatively undisturbed and uninfluenced by outside forces.

The sharpest contrast with China is the Indian subcontinent, which lacked geographic and cultural continuity. By the middle of the second millennium B.C.E., the Indus

The Way. Detail from a twelfth-century Daoist scroll, showing the feats of the "Eight Immortals," the most famous characters in Daoist folklore. The landscape evokes the ineffability and mystery of Dao, or "the way."

Philosophy and Religion

Greece

Near East

India China

Between 800 and 300 B.C.E, four philosophical or religious revolutions shaped the subsequent history of the world. The names of many involved in these revolutions are world-famous—Socrates, Plato, Aristotle, the Buddha, Isaiah, and Confucius. All the revolutions occurred in or near the four heartland areas in which the river valley civilizations (described in Chapter 1) had appeared fifteen hundred or more years earlier. The transition from the early river valley civilizations to the intellectual and spiritual breakthroughs of the middle of the first millennium B.C.E. is schematized in Figure 2–1.

Before considering each of the original breakthroughs that occurred between 800 and 300 B.C.E., we might ask whether they have anything in common. Five points are worth noting.

1. All the philosophical or religious revolutions occurred in or near the original river valley civilizations. These areas contained the most advanced cultures of the ancient world. They had sophisticated agriculture, cities with many literate inhabitants, and specialized trades and professions. In short, they had the material preconditions for breakthroughs in religion and thought.

2. Each of the revolutions in thought and ethos was born of a crisis in the ancient world. The appearance of iron meant better tools and weapons and, by extension, greater riches and more powerful armies. Old societies began to change and then to disintegrate. Old aristocratic and priestly codes of behavior broke down, producing a demand for more universalized rules of behavior, in other words, for ethics. The very relation of humans to nature or to the universe seemed to be changing. This predicament led to new visions of social and political order. The similarity between the Jewish Messiah, the Chinese sage-king, and Plato's philosopher-king is more than accidental. Each was a response to a crisis in a society of the

civilization had collapsed. It was replaced by the culture of the Indo-Aryan warriors who swept in from the northwest. Absorbing many particulars from the earlier tradition, they built a new civilization on the plains farther east along the mighty Ganges River. The great tradition of Indian thought and religion emerged after 600 B.C.E. from this Ganges civilization.

In southwest Asia and along the shores of the Mediterranean, the transition was more complex than that in either China or India. No direct line of development can be traced from the Nile civilization of ancient Egypt or the civilization of the Tigris-Euphrates river valley to Greek philosophy or to Judaic monotheism. Rather, the ancient river valley civilizations evolved into a complex amalgam that we call ancient

Near Eastern civilization. This cosmopolitan culture included diverse older religious, mythical, and cosmological traditions, as well as newer mystery cults. The Greeks and the ancient Hebrews were two among many outside peoples who invaded this region, settled down, and both absorbed and contributed to the composite civilization.

Judaic monotheism and Greek philosophy—representing different outgrowths of this amalgam—were each important in their own right. They have continued as vital elements in Western and Near Eastern civilizations. But their greatest influence occurred centuries later when they helped shape first Christianity and then Islam. The major cultural zones in world history since the mid–first millennium C.E. are the Chinese, the Indian, the Western Christian, and the Islamic. But ancient world. Each would reconnect ethics to history and restore order to a troubled society.

3. The number of philosophical and religious revolutions can be counted on the fingers of one hand. The reason is not that humans' creativity dried up after 300 B.C.E., but that subsequent breakthroughs and advances tended to occur within the original traditions, which, absorbing new energies, continued to evolve.

4. After the first- and second-stage transformations, much of the cultural history of the world involves the spread of cultures derived from these original heartlands to ever-wider spheres. Christianity spread to northern and eastern Europe, the Americas, and parts of Asia and Africa; Buddhism to central, southeastern, and eastern Asia; Confucianism to Korea, Vietnam, and Japan; and Islam to Africa, southeastern Europe, and southern, central, and southeastern Asia. Sometimes the spread was the result of movements of people; other areas were like dry grasslands needing only the spark of the new ideas to be ignited. Typically, the process spread out over centuries.

5. Once a cultural pattern was set, it usually endured. Each major culture was resistant to the others and was only rarely displaced. Even in modern times, although the culture of modern science, and the learning associated with it, has penetrated every cultural zone, it has reshaped—and is reshaping, not displacing—the major cultures. Only Confucianism, the most secular of the traditional cultures, crumbled at the touch of science, and even its ethos remains a potent force in east Asian societies. These major cultures endured because they were not only responses to particular crises, but also attempts to answer universal questions concerning the human condition: What are human beings? What is our relation to the universe? How should we relate to others?

Focus Questions

◆ Why do you think so many revolutionary philosophical and religious ideas emerged at about the same time in many different regions? Do these ideas share any fundamental concerns?

◆ Why is this period in Eurasian history sometimes referred to as the "axial age"?

the latter two were formed much later than the Chinese and the Indian. They represent a second-stage formation of which the first stage comprised the Judaic and the Greek (see Figure 2–1).

Philosophy in China

The beauty of ancient Shang bronzes is breathtaking, but they also have an archaic strangeness. Like Olmec stone sculpture of prehistoric America, they are products of a culture so far removed from our own as to be almost incomprehensible. By contrast, the humanism of the Confucian writings and the poetry of the Eastern Zhou (771–256 B.C.E.) speak to us directly. However much the philosophies of these centuries grew out of the earlier matrix of archaic culture, they mark a break with it and the beginning of what we think of today as the Chinese tradition.

The background of the philosophical revolution in China was the disintegration of the old Zhou society (see Chapter 1 for details). New territorial states replaced the many Zhou city-states. Ruthless, upstart, peasant armies, augmented by an Early Iron Age cavalry armed with crossbows, began to replace the old nobility, who had gone to war in chariots. A rising merchant class disrupted the formerly stable agricultural economy. As the old etiquette crumbled and old rituals lost their force, a search began for new principles by which to recreate a peaceful society and new rules by which to live.

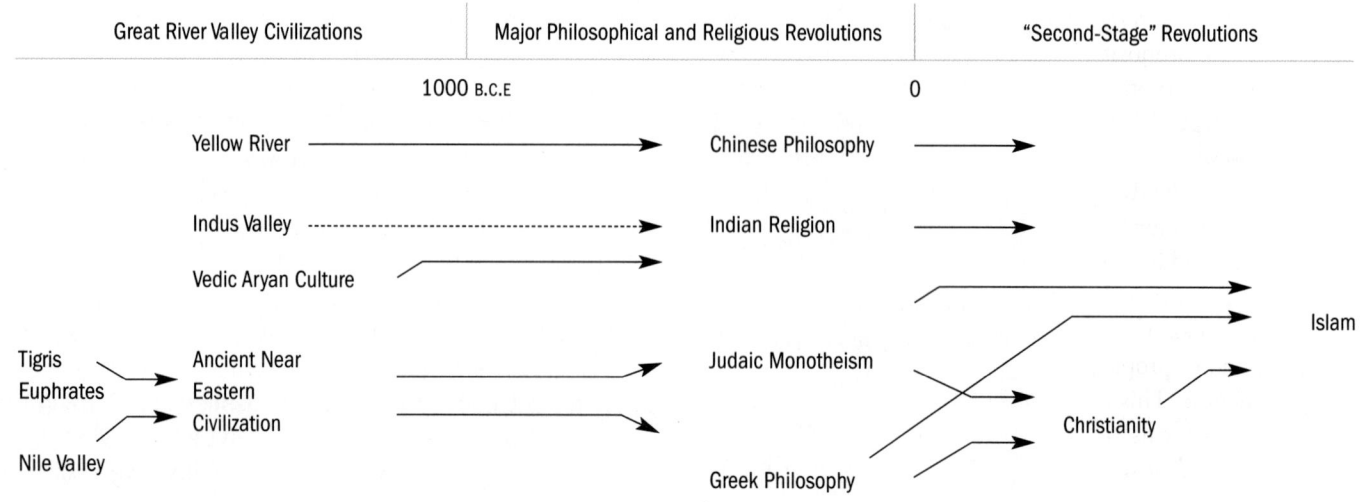

| Great River Valley Civilizations | Major Philosophical and Religious Revolutions | "Second-Stage" Revolutions |

Figure 2–1. "First-Stage" and "Second-Stage" Revolutions.

Of the four great revolutions in thought of the first millennium B.C.E., the Chinese was more akin, perhaps, to the Greek than to the Indian religious transformations or to Judaic monotheism. Just as Greece had a gamut of philosophies, so in China there were the "one hundred schools." (When Mao Zedong said in 1956, "Let the one hundred flowers bloom"—encouraging a momentary easing of intellectual repression—he was referring to the creative era of Zhou philosophy.) Whereas Greek thought was speculative and more concerned with the world of nature, Chinese thought was sociopolitical and more practical. Even the Daoist sages, who were inherently apolitical, found it necessary to offer a political philosophy. Chinese thought also had far greater staying power than Greek thought, which only a few centuries after the glory of Athens was submerged by Christianity. It became the handmaiden of theology and did not reemerge as an independent force until the Renaissance. In contrast, Chinese philosophy, although challenged by Buddhism, remained dominant until the early twentieth century. How were these early philosophies able to maintain such a grip on China when the cultures of every other part of the world fell under the sway of religions?

Part of the answer is that most Chinese philosophy had a religious dimension. But it was another kind of religion, with assumptions different from those derived from Judaic roots. In the Christian or Islamic worldview, there is a God who, however concerned with humankind, is not of this world. This worldview leads to dualism, the distinction between an otherworld, which is supernatural, and this world, which is natural.

In the Chinese worldview, the two spheres are not separate: The cosmos is single, continuous, and nondualistic. It includes heaven, earth, and man. Heaven is above. Earth is below. Man, ideally guided by a wise and virtuous ruler, stands in between and regulates or harmonizes the cosmological forces of heaven and earth by the power of his virtue and by performing the sacrifices. The forms that this cosmology took under the last Manchu Dynasty (1644–1912) can be seen today in the city of Beijing: The Temple of Heaven is in the south; the Temple of Earth is in the northeast; and the Imperial Palace is—symbolically, at least—in between. To say that the emperor's sacrifices at the Temple of Heaven were secular (and, therefore, not religious) or religious (and not secular) misses the point. It projects our own dualistic assumptions onto China. Similarly, when we speak of the Daoist sage becoming one with nature, it is not the nature of a twenty-first-century natural scientist; it is a nature that contains metaphysical and cosmological forces that our worldview might label as religious.

Most of the one hundred schools—if, in fact, there were that many—are unknown today. Many works disappeared in the book burning of the Qin Dynasty (256–221 B.C.E.). But apart from the three major schools of Confucianism, Daoism, and Legalism, texts of enough other schools have survived to convey a sense of the range and vitality of Zhou thought:

1. *Rhetoricians.* This school taught the arts of persuasion to be used in diplomatic negotiations. Its principal work instructed the rulers of territorial states by using historical anecdote. A practical work, it was popular for its humor and lively style.

2. *Logicians.* This school taught logic and relativity. For example, one proposition was "The south has no limit and has a limit." Another was "A white horse is not a horse": The concept of *horse* is not the same as the concept of *white horse.*

3. *Strategists.* *The Art of War* by Sunzi became the classic of military science in China and is studied today by guerrillas and in military academies around the world. It praises the general who wins victories without battles but also talks of organizing states for war, of supply, of spies, and of propaganda.

4. *Cosmologists.* This school described the functions of the cosmos in terms of *yin* and *yang,* the complementary negative and positive forces of nature, and in terms of the five elements (metal, wood, earth, fire, and water). Its ideas were later absorbed by other schools.

5. *Mohists.* Mozi (470–391 B.C.E.) was an early critic of Confucius. His goals were peace, wealth, and the increase of population. He taught an ethic of universal love—to overcome a selfish human nature. He preached discipline and austerity and was critical of whatever lacked utility, including music and the other arts, elaborate funerals, wasteful rites, and, above all, war. To achieve his goals, Mozi argued for a strong state: Subjects must obey their rulers, who in turn must obey Heaven. Heaven would punish evil and reward good. To promote peace, Mozi organized his followers into military units to aid states that were attacked.

Confucianism

Confucius was born in 551 B.C.E. in a minor state in northeastern China. He probably belonged to the lower nobility or the knightly class, because he received an education in

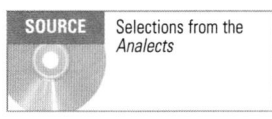
SOURCE Selections from the *Analects*

writing, music, and rituals. His father died when Confucius was young, so he may have known privation. He made his living by teaching. He traveled with his disciples from state to state, seeking a ruler who would put his ideas into practice. Although he may once have held a minor position, his ideas were rejected as impractical. He died in 479 B.C.E., honored as a teacher and scholar but having failed to find a ruler to advise. The name *Confucius* is the Latinized form of *Kong Fuzi,* or *Master Kong,* as he is known in China.

We know of Confucius only through the *Analects,* his sayings collected by his disciples, or perhaps by their disciples. They are mostly in the form of "The Master said," followed by his words. (See Document, "Confucius Defines the Gentleman.") The picture that emerges is of a man of mod-

eration, propriety, optimism, good sense, and wisdom. In an age of cruelty and superstition, he was humane, rational, and upright, demanding much of others and more of himself. Asked about death, he replied, "You do not understand even life. How can you understand death?"[1] Asked about how to serve the spirits and the gods, in which he did not disbelieve, he answered, "You are not able even to serve man. How can you serve the spirits?"

Confucius described himself as a transmitter and a conservator of tradition, not an innovator. He idealized the early Shang and Zhou kings as paragons of virtue and particularly saw early Zhou society as a golden age. He sought the secrets of this golden age in its writings. Some of these writings, along with later texts, became the Confucian classics, which through most of Chinese history had an authority not unlike Scripture in the West. Five of the thirteen classics were the following:

1. *The Book of Changes* (also known as the *Classic of Divination*). A handbook for diviners, this book was later seen as containing metaphysical truths about the universe.

2. *The Book of History.* This book contains documents and speeches from the early Zhou, some authentic. Chinese tradition holds that it was edited by Confucius. It was interpreted as the record of sage-kings.

3. *The Book of Poetry.* This book contains some three hundred poems from the early Zhou. Representing a sophisticated literary tradition, it includes love songs as well as poems of friendship, ritual, and politics. Many were given political and moral interpretations in later times.

4. *The Book of Rites.* This book includes both rituals and rules of etiquette. Rites were important to Confucians, both as a support for proper behavior and because they were seen as corresponding to the forces of nature.

5. *The Spring and Autumn Annals.* A brief record of the major occurrences from 722 to 481 B.C.E. in the state where Confucius was born, this book, according to Chinese tradition, was edited by Confucius and reflected his moral judgments on past historical figures.

Basing his teachings on these writings, Confucius proposed to resolve the turmoil of his own age by a return to the good old ways of the early Zhou. When asked about government, he said, "Let the ruler be a ruler, the subject a subject, the father a father, the son a son." (The five Confucian relationships were ruler–subject, father–son, husband–wife,

---

[1] This quotation and all quotations from Confucius in this passage are from Confucius, *The Analects,* trans. by D. C. Lau (Penguin Books, 1979).

Confucius, depicted wearing the robes of a scholar of a later age.
Collection of the National Palace Museum, Taipei, Taiwan.

older brother–younger brother, and friend–friend.) If everyone fulfilled the duties of his or her status, then harmony would prevail. Confucius understood the fundamental truth that the well-being of a society depends on the morality of its members. His vision was of an unbroken social harmony extending from the individual family member to the monarch.

But a return to the early Zhou was impossible. China was undergoing a dynamic transition from hundreds of small city-states to a few large territorial states. Specialized classes were appearing. Old rituals no longer worked. It was thus

not enough to stress basic human relationships. The genius of Confucius was to transform the old aristocratic code into a new ethic that any educated Chinese could practice. His reinterpretation of the early Zhou tradition can be seen in the concept of the junzi. This term literally meant "the son of the ruler" (or the aristocrat). Confucius redefined it to mean one of noble behavior, a person with the inner virtues of humanity, integrity, righteousness, altruism, and loyalty, and an outward demeanor and propriety to match.

This redefinition was not unlike the change in the meaning of *gentleman* in England, from "one who is gentle-born" to "one who is gentle-behaved." But whereas *gentleman* remained a fairly superficial category in the West, in China *junzi* went deeper. Confucius saw ethics as grounded in nature. The true gentleman was in touch with his own basic nature, which in turn was a part of the cosmic order. Confucius expressed this saying: "Heaven is the author of the virtue that is in me." Confucius's description of his own passage through life goes far beyond good manners: "At fifteen I set my heart on learning; at thirty I took my stand; at forty I came to be free from doubts; at fifty I understood the Decree of Heaven; at sixty my ear was attuned; at seventy I followed my heart's desire without overstepping the line."

Confucius often contrasted the gentleman with the small or common person. The gentleman, educated in the classics and cultivating the Way, understands moral action. The common people, in contrast, "can be made to follow a path but not to understand it." Good government for Confucius depended on the appointment to office of good men, who would serve as examples for the multitude: "Just desire the good yourself and the common people will be good. The virtue of the gentleman is like wind; the virtue of the small man is like grass. Let the wind blow over the grass and it is sure to bend." Beyond the gentleman was the sage-king, who possessed an almost mystical virtue and power. For Confucius, the early Zhou kings were clearly sages. But he wrote, "I have no hopes of meeting a sage. I would be content if I met someone who is a gentleman."

Confucianism was not adopted as the official philosophy of China until the second century B.C.E., during the Han Dynasty (202 B.C.E.–9 C.E., see Chapter 7). But two other important Confucian philosophers had appeared in the meantime. Mencius (370–290 B.C.E.) represents the idealistic extension of Confucius's thought. His interpretation was accepted during most of history. He is famous for his argument that humans tend toward the good just as water runs downward. The role of education, therefore, is to uncover and cultivate that innate goodness. Moreover, just as humans tend toward the good, so does Heaven possess a moral will. The will of Heaven is that a government should see to the education and well-

Confucius Defines the Gentleman

For more than two thousand years in China, the cultural ideal was the gentleman, who combined knowledge of the ancient sages with an inner morality and outer propriety.

◆ How does the injunction "to repay an injury with straightness" compare to the Christian injunction to turn the other cheek? Which do you think is more appropriate?

The Master said, "I never enlighten anyone who has not been driven to distraction by trying to understand a difficulty or who has not got into a frenzy trying to put his ideas into words.

"When I have pointed out one corner of a square to anyone and he does not come back with the other three, I will not point it out to him a second time."

The Master said, "Yu, shall I tell you what it is to know? To say you know when you know, and to say you do not when you do not, that is knowledge."

The Master said, "Is it not a pleasure, having learned something, to try it out at due intervals? Is it not a joy to have friends come from afar? Is it not gentlemanly not to take offence when others fail to appreciate your abilities?"

Someone said, "Repay an injury with a good turn. What do you think of this saying?" The Master said, "What, then, do you repay a good turn with? You repay an injury with straightness, but you repay a good turn with a good turn."

Lin Fang asked about the basis of the rites. The Master said, "A noble question indeed! With the rites, it is better to err on the side of frugality than on the side of extravagance; in mourning, it is better to err on the side of grief than on the side of formality."

The Master said, "I suppose I should give up hope. I have yet to meet the man who is as fond of virtue as he is of beauty in women."

The Master said, "The gentleman agrees with others without being an echo. The small man echoes without being in agreement."

The Master said, "The gentleman is at ease without being arrogant; the small man is arrogant without being at ease."

The Master said, "There is no point in seeking the views of a gentleman who, though he sets his heart on the Way, is ashamed of poor food and poor clothes."

Confucius, *The Analects*, trans. by D. C. Lau (New York: Penguin Classics, 1979), © D. C. Lau, 1979.

---

being of its people. The rebellion of people against a government is the primary evidence that Heaven has withdrawn its mandate. At times in Chinese history, only lip service was paid to a concern for the people. In fact, rebellions occurred more often against weak governments than against harsh ones. But the idea that government ought to care for the people became a permanent part of the Confucian tradition.

The other influential Confucian philosopher was Xunzi (300–237 B.C.E.), who represents a tough-minded extension of Confucius's thought. Xunzi felt Heaven was amoral, indifferent to whether China was ruled by a tyrant or a sage. He believed human nature was bad or at least that desires and emotions, if unchecked and unrefined, led to social conflict. So he emphasized etiquette and education as restraints on an unruly human nature, and good institutions, including punishments and rewards, as a means for shaping behavior. These ideas influenced the thinkers of the Legalist school.

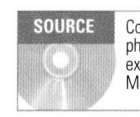
SOURCE Confucian political philosophy: an excerpt from Mencius.

Chronology

China

551–479 B.C.E.	Confucius
370–290 B.C.E.	Mencius
Fourth century B.C.E.	Laozi
221 B.C.E.	Qin unifies China

Daoism

It is often said that the Chinese have been Confucian while in office and Daoist in their private lives. **Daoism** offered a refuge from the burden of social responsibilities. The classics of the school are the *Laozi*, dating from the fourth century B.C.E., and the *Zhuangzi*, dating from about a century later.

The central concept of Daoism is the *Dao*, or Way. It is mysterious, ineffable, and cannot be named. It is the creator of the universe, the sustainer of the universe, and the process or flux of the universe. The *Dao* functions on a cosmic, not a human, scale. As the *Laozi* put it, "Heaven and Earth are ruthless, and treat the myriad creatures as straw dogs; the sage (in accord with the *Dao*) is ruthless, and treats the people as straw dogs."[2]

What does it mean to be a sage? How does a human join the rhythms of nature? The answer given by the *Laozi* is by regaining or returning to an original simplicity. Various similes describe this state: "to return to the infinite," "to return to being a babe," or "to return to being the uncarved block." To attain this state, one must "learn to be without learning." Knowledge is bad because it creates distinctions, and because it leads to the succession of ideas and images that interfere with participation in the *Dao*. One must also learn to be without desires beyond the immediate and simple needs of nature: "The nameless uncarved block is but freedom from desire."

If the sage treats the people as straw dogs, it would appear that he is beyond good and evil. But elsewhere in the *Laozi*, the sage is described as one who "excels in saving people." If not a contradiction, this is at least a paradox. The resolution is that the sage is clearly beyond morality but is not immoral or even amoral. On the contrary, by being in harmony with the *Dao*, the sage is impeccably moral—as one who clings to the forms of morality or makes morality a goal could never be. So in the *Laozi* it is written, "Exterminate benevolence, discard rectitude, and the people will again be filial; exterminate ingenuity, discard profit, and there will be no more thieves and bandits." In this formulation we also see the basis for the political philosophy of Daoism, which can be summed up as "not doing" (*wuwei*). This means something between "doing nothing" and "being, but not acting." In this concept, there is some overlap with Confucianism. The Confucian sage-king exerts a moral force by dint of his inter-

Laozi, the founder of Daoism, as imagined by a later artist. *Courtesy of the Freer Gallery of Art, Smithsonian Institution, Washington, D.C. (72.1).*

nal accord with nature. A perfect Confucian sage could rule without doing. Confucius said, "If there was a ruler who achieved order without taking any action, it was, perhaps, Shun [the sage-emperor]. There was nothing for him to do but to hold himself in a respectful posture and to face due south." In Daoism, all true sages had this Shun-like power to rule without action: "The Way never acts yet nothing is left undone. Should lords and princes be able to hold fast to it, the myriad creatures will be transformed of their own accord." Or, says the *Laozi*, "I am free from desire and the people of themselves become simple like the uncarved block." The sage acts without acting, and "when his task is accomplished and his work is done, the people will say, 'It happened to us naturally.'" (See Document, "Daoism.")

Along with the basic Daoist prescription of becoming one with the *Dao* are two other assumptions or principles. One is that any action pushed to an extreme will initiate a countervailing reaction in the direction of the opposite extreme. The other is that too much government, even good government, can become oppressive by its very weight. As the *Laozi* put it, "The people are hungry; it is because those in authority eat up too much in taxes that the peo-

---

[2] All quotations from the Laozi are from *Tao Te Ching,* trans. by D. C. Lau (Penguin Books, 1963).

Daoism

Can inner, transformative, religious experience take people beyond everyday worldly concerns and imbue them with moral charisma or moral authority? What other religions might call "supernatural," Daoism sees as truly natural.

◆ How does the Way in Daoism compare with Confucius's use of the same term?

LAOZI TELLS OF THE WAY OF THE SAGE

> The way that can be spoken of
> Is not the constant way;
> The name that can be named
> Is not the constant name.
> The nameless was the beginning of heaven and earth;
> The named was the mother of the myriad creatures.
> The spirit of the valley never dies
> This is called the mysterious female.
> The gateway of the mysterious female
> Is called the root of heaven and earth.
> Dimly visible, it seems as if it were there,
> Yet use will never drain it.
> There is a thing confusedly formed,
> Born before heaven and earth.
> Silent and void
> It stands alone and does not change,
> Goes round and does not weary.
> It is capable of being the mother of the world.
> I know not its name
> So I style it "the way."

When the way prevails in the empire, fleetfooted horses are relegated to ploughing the fields; when the way does not prevail in the empire, war-horses breed on the border.

> One who knows does not speak; one who speaks does not know.
> Therefore the sage puts his person last and it comes first,
> Treats it as extraneous to himself and it is preserved.

Is it not because he is without thought of self that he is able to accomplish his private ends?

ZHUANGZI COMPARES GOVERNMENTAL OFFICE TO A DEAD RAT

When Hui Tzu was prime minister of Liang, Zhuangzi set off to visit him. Someone said to Xunzi, "Zhuangzi is coming because he wants to replace you as prime minister!" With this Xunzi was filled with alarm and searched all over the state for three days and three nights trying to find Zhuangzi. Zhuangzi then came to see him and said, "In the south there is a bird called the Yuan-ch'u—I wonder if you've ever heard of it? The Yuan-ch'u rises up from the South Sea and flies to the North Sea, and it will rest on nothing but the Wu-t'ung tree, eat nothing but the fruit of the Lien, and drink only from springs of sweet water. Once there was an owl who had gotten hold of a half-rotten old rat, and as the Yuan-ch'u passed by, it raised its head, looked up at the Yuan-ch'u, and said, 'Shoo!' Now that you have this Liang state of yours, are you trying to shoo me?"

ple are hungry. The people are difficult to govern; it is because those in authority are too fond of action that the people are difficult to govern." Elsewhere, the same idea was expressed in even homelier terms: "Govern a large state as you would cook small fish," that is, without too much stirring.

Legalism

A third great current in classical Chinese thought, and by far the most influential in its own age, was **Legalism**. Like the philosophers of other schools, the Legalists were concerned with ending the wars that plagued China. True peace, they believed, required a united country and a strong state. They favored conscription and considered war a means of extending state power.

The Legalists did not seek a model in the distant past. In ancient times, said one, there were fewer people and more food, so it was easier to rule; different conditions require new principles of government. Nor did the Legalists model their state on a heavenly order of values. Human nature is selfish, argued both of the leading Legalists, Han Feizi (d. 233 B.C.E.) and Li Si (d. 208 B.C.E.). It is human to like rewards or pleasure and to dislike punishments or pain. If laws are severe and impartial, if what strengthens the state is rewarded and what weakens the state is punished, then a strong state and a good society will ensue. (See Document, "Legalism.")

Laws, therefore, should contain incentives for loyalty and bravery in battle, and for obedience, diligence, and frugality in everyday life. The Legalists despised merchants as parasites and approved of productive farmers. They particularly despised purveyors of doctrines different from their own and were critical of rulers who honored philosophers while ignoring their philosophies.

Legalism was the philosophy of the state of Qin, which destroyed the Zhou in 256 B.C.E. and unified China in 221 B.C.E. Because Qin laws were cruel and severe, and because Legalism put human laws above an ethic modeled on Heaven, later generations of Chinese have denounced its doctrines. They saw it, not without justification, as a philosophy that consumed its founders: Han Feizi became an official of the Qin state but was eventually poisoned in a prison cell by Li Si, who was jealous of his growing influence. Li Si, although he became prime minister of Qin, was killed in 208 B.C.E. in a political struggle with a court eunuch. Yet for all the abuse heaped on Legalist doctrines, its legacy of administrative and criminal laws became a vital part of subsequent dynastic China. Even Confucian statesmen could not do without them.

Religion in India

By 400 B.C.E., new social and religious forms took shape on the Indian subcontinent that drew both on the older traditions of the Aryan noble and priestly elites, and on non-Aryan ideas and practices. This tradition took its classical "Indian" shape in the early first millennium C.E. When its fundamental institutions and ideas came to prevail virtually throughout the subcontinent. Despite staggering internal diversity and divisions, and long periods of foreign rule, this Indian culture has survived for over two thousand years as a

coherent tradition of cultural heritage, social organization, and religious worldview.

"Hindu" and "Indian"

Indian culture and tradition include more than the word **Hindu** commonly implies today. Earlier, *Hindu* simply meant "Indian." Taken from the Indo-Iranian name for the Indus, it was the term outsiders, like the Persians and the Greeks, used for the people or land of the subcontinent. Later, first invading Muslims, then Europeans, used Hindu to characterize the most prominent religious and social institutions of India as a whole. Heading the list of such "Hindu" institutions were the concept of transmigration, the sacredness of the Vedas and the cow, worship of Shiva and Vishnu, and caste distinctions. Most Indians in the past twenty-five hundred years have accepted these institutions, but Indian Buddhists, Jains, Muslims, Sikhs, and Christians have rejected some or all of them.

Hindu is not a term for any single or uniform religious community. "Hindu" religion and culture lumps together an immense diversity of social, racial, linguistic, and religious groups.

Indian, on the other hand, commonly refers today to all native inhabitants of the subcontinent, whatever their beliefs. In this book we shall generally use the term *Indian* in this inclusive sense when referring to the subcontinent or its peoples. However, for the period before the arrival of Muslim culture (ca. 1000 C.E.), we will use *Indian* also to refer to the distinctively Indian tradition of thought and culture that began around the middle of the first millennium B.C.E. and achieved its classical formulation in the Hindu society and religion of the first millennium C.E.

Historical Background

We saw in Chapter 1 how, in the late Vedic or Brahmanic period, a priest-centered cult dominated the upper classes of Aryanized northern Indian society. By the sixth century B.C.E., this had become an elite, esoteric cult to which most people had little or no access. Elaborate animal sacrifices on behalf of Aryan rulers were an economic burden on the peasants, whose livestock provided the victims. Such sacrifices were also largely irrelevant to the religious concerns of both peasants and town dwellers. New, ascetic tendencies questioned the basic values and practices of the older Aryan religion. During the seventh and sixth centuries B.C.E., skepticism in religious matters accompanied social and political upheavals.

Legalism

Document

According to Legalism, the state can only regulate behavior, it cannot affect the inner dimensions of human life. Rewards and punishments, furthermore, are far more efficient in controlling behavior than moral appeals.

◆ Do the tenets of Legalism have any modern parallels? What do you think of Legalism as a philosophy of government? As an approach to the problem of crime? How does Legalism compare with other approaches to law, leadership, and government?

HAN FEIZI ARGUES FOR THE EFFICACY OF PUNISHMENTS

Now take a young fellow who is a bad character. His parents may get angry at him, but he never makes any change. The villagers may reprove him, but he is not moved. His teachers and elders may admonish him, but he never reforms. The love of his parents, the efforts of the villagers, and the wisdom of his teachers and elders—all the three excellent disciplines are applied to him, and yet not even a hair on his shins is altered. It is only after the district magistrate sends out his soldiers and in the name of the law searches for wicked individuals that the young man becomes afraid and changes his ways and alters his deeds. So while the love of parents is not sufficient to discipline the children, the severe penalties of the district magistrate are. This is because men became naturally spoiled by love, but are submissive to authority. . . .

That being so, rewards should be rich and certain so that the people will be attracted by them; punishments should be severe and definite so that the people will fear them; and laws should be uniform and steadfast so that the people will be familiar with them. Consequently, the sovereign should show no wavering in bestowing rewards and grant no pardon in administering punishments, and he should add honor to rewards and disgrace to punishments—when this is done, then both the worthy and the unworthy will want to exert themselves. . . .

HAN FEIZI ATTACKS CONFUCIANISM

There was once a man of Sung who tilled his field. In the midst of his field stood the stump of a tree, and one day a hare, running at full speed, bumped into the stump, broke its neck, and died. Thereupon the man left his plow and kept watch at the stump, hoping that he would get another hare. But he never caught another hare, and was only ridiculed by the people of Sung. Now those who try to rule the people of the present age with the conduct of government of the early kings are all doing exactly the same thing as that fellow who kept watch by the stump. . . .

Those who are ignorant about government insistently say: "Win the hearts of the people." If order could be procured by winning the hearts of the people, then even the wise ministers Yi Yin and Kuan Chung would be of no use. For all that the ruler would need to do would be just to listen to the people. Actually, the intelligence of the people is not to be relied upon any more than the mind of a baby. If the baby does not have his head shaved, his sores will recur; if he does not have his boil cut open, his illness will go from bad to worse. However, in order to shave his head or open the boil someone has to hold the baby while the affectionate mother is performing the work, and yet he keeps crying and yelling incessantly. The baby does not understand that suffering a small pain is the way to obtain a great benefit.

Now, the sovereign urges the tillage of land and the cultivation of pastures for the purpose of increasing production for the people, but they think the sovereign is cruel. The sovereign regulates penalties and increases punishments for the purpose of repressing the wicked, but the people think the sovereign is severe. Again he levies taxes in cash and in grain to fill up the granaries and treasuries in order to relieve famine and provide for the army, but they think the sovereign is greedy. Finally, he insists upon universal military training without personal favoritism, and urges his forces to fight hard in order to take the enemy captive, but the people think the sovereign is violent. These four measures are methods for attaining order and maintaining peace, but the people are too ignorant to appreciate them.

The latest Vedic texts themselves reflected a reaction against excessive emphasis on the power of sacrifice and ritual, accumulation of worldly wealth and power, and hope for an afterlife in a paradise. The treatises of the **Brahmanas** (ca. 1000–800 B.C.E.) dealt with the ritual application of the old Vedic texts, the explanation of Vedic rites and mythology, and the theory of the sacrifice. Early on they focused on controlling the sacred power (*Brahman*) of the sacrificial ritual, but they gradually stressed acquiring this power through knowledge instead of ritual.

This tendency became central in the Upanishads (ca. 800–500 B.C.E.). The Upanishadic sages and the early Jains and Buddhists (fifth century B.C.E.) shared certain revolutionary ideas and concerns. Their thinking and piety influenced not only all later Indian intellectual thought but also, through the spread of the Buddhist tradition, much of the intellectual and religious life of east and southeast Asia as well. Thus, the middle centuries of the first millennium B.C.E. in India began a religious and philosophical revolution that ranks alongside those of Chinese philosophy and religion, Judaic monotheism, and Greek philosophy as a turning point in the history of civilization.

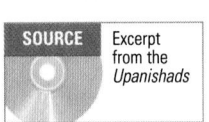
SOURCE Excerpt from the *Upanishads*

The Upanishadic Worldview

In the Upanishads two new emphases emerge: knowledge over ritual and immortality in terms of escape from existence itself. These were already evident in two sentences from the prayer of an early Upanishadic thinker who said, "From the unreal lead me to the Real. . . . From death lead me to immortality." The first sentence points to the Upanishadic focus on speculation about the nature of things, the quest for ultimate truth. Here knowledge, not the sacred word or act, has become the ultimate source of power. The second sentence reflects a new concern with life after death. The old Vedic ideal of living a full and upright life so as to attain an afterlife among the gods no longer appears adequate. Immortality is now interpreted in terms of escape from mundane existence in any form. These two Upanishadic emphases gave birth to ideas that were to change the shape of Indian thought forever. They also provide the key to its basic worldview.

The Nature of Reality   The quest for knowledge by the Upanishadic sages focused on the nature of the individual self (*atman*) and its relation to ultimate reality (*Brahman*). The gods are now merely part of the total scheme of things, subject to the laws of existence, and not to be put on the same plane with the transcendent Absolute. Prayer and sacrifice to particular gods for their help continue; but the higher goal is realization of *Brahman* through mental action alone, not ritual performance.

The culmination of Upanishadic speculation is the recognition that the way to the Absolute is through the self. Through contemplation, ***atman-Brahman*** is recognized not as a deity, but as the principle of reality itself: the unborn, unmade, unitary, unchanging infinite. Of this reality, all that can be said is that it is "neither this nor that," because the ultimate cannot be conceptualized or described in finite terms. Beneath the impermanence of ordinary reality is the changeless *Brahman*, to which every being's immortal self belongs and of which it partakes. The difficulty is recognizing this self, and with it the Absolute, while one is enmeshed in mortal existence. (See Document, "Discussions of Brahman and Atman from the *Upanishads*.")

A second, related focus of Upanishadic inquiry was the nature of "normal" existence. The realm of life is seen to be ultimately impermanent, ever changing. What seem to be "solid" things—the physical world, our bodies and personalities, worldly success—are revealed in the *Upanishads* as insubstantial and, impermanent. Even happiness is transient. Existence is neither satisfying nor lasting. Only *Brahman* is eternal, unchanging. This perception already shows a marked tendency toward the Buddhist emphasis on impermanence and suffering as the fundamental facts of existence.

Life After Death   The new understanding of immortality that emerges in the Upanishads is related to these basic perceptions about the self, the Absolute, and the world of existence. The Upanishadic sages conceived of existence as a ceaseless cycle, a never-ending alternation between life and death. This idea became the basic assumption of all Indian thought and religious life.

The idea of the endless cycle of existence, or ***samsara***, is only superficially similar to our idea of "transmigration" of souls. For Indians, it is the key to understanding reality. Furthermore, it is not a liberating, but a burdensome reality: the terrifying prospect of endless "redeath" as the normal lot of all beings in this world, whether animals, plants, humans, or gods. This is the fundamental problem for all later Indian thought.

Karma   The key to resolving the dilemma of *samsara* lies in the concept of ***karma***, which in Sanskrit literally means "work" or "action." At base, it is the concept that every action has its inevitable effects, sooner or later; as long as there is action of mind or body, there is continued effect and hence continued existence. Good deeds bring good results, perhaps even rebirth in a heaven or as a god, and evil ones bring

Discussions of Brahman and Atman from the Upanishads

Document

Much of the *Upanishads* is couched in the form of teacher-student dialogue. The following two selections are responses of teachers to the questions of their disciples.

◆ Does either of these passages provide a guide to salvation? If so, why, and what is the suggested path to salvation? In what sense and degree are the passages concerned with ignorance and enlightenment?

A REPORT OF THE SAGE SANDILYA'S STATEMENT ABOUT THE IDENTITY OF ATMAN AND BRAHMAN

Verily, this whole world is Brahman. Tranquil, let one worship it as that from which he came forth, as that into which he will be dissolved, as that in which he breathes. Now, verily, a person consists of purpose. According to the purpose which a person has in this world, thus does he become on departing hence. So let him form for himself a purpose. He who consists of mind, whose body is life, whose form is light, whose conception is truth, whose soul [*atman*] is space, containing all odors, containing all tastes, encompassing this whole world, the unspeaking, the unconcerned—this Soul of mine within the heart is smaller than a grain of rice, or a barley-corn, or a mustard-seed, or a grain of millet; or the kernel of a grain of millet; this Soul of mine within the heart is greater than the earth, greater than the atmosphere, greater than the sky, greater than these worlds. Containing all works, containing all desires, containing all odors, containing all tastes, encompassing this whole world, the unspeaking, the unconcerned—this Soul of mine within the heart, this is Brahman. Into him I shall enter on departing hence. If one would believe this, he would have no more doubt."— Thus used Sandilya to say. . . .

—*Chandogya Upanishad 3.14*

THE YOUNG BRAHMAN, SHVETAKETU, IS INSTRUCTED IN THE IDENTITY OF ATMAN AND BRAHMAN BY HIS FATHER

"These rivers, my dear, flow, the eastern toward the east, the western toward the west. They go just from the ocean to the ocean. They become the ocean itself. As there they know not 'I am this one,' 'I am that one'—even so, indeed, my dear, all creatures here, though they have come forth from Being, know not 'We have come forth from Being.' Whatever they are in this world, whether tiger, or lion, or wolf, or boar, or worm, or fly, or gnat, or mosquito, that they become. That which is the finest essence—this whole world has that as its soul. That is Reality. That is *Atman*. That art thou, Shvetaketu."

—*Chandogya Upanishad 6.10*

Selections taken with minor changes from *The Thirteen Principal Upanishads*, 2nd ed., Robert Ernest Hume, trans. Copyright © 1931, Oxford University Press, pp. 209–210, 246–247. Reprinted by permission of Oxford University Press, New Delhi.

evil consequences, whether in this life or by rebirth in the next, whether in the everyday world or in the lower worlds of hell. Because of the fundamental impermanence of everything in existence (heavens and hells included), good as well as evil is temporary. The flux of existence knows only movement, change, endless cause and effect far transcending a mere human life-span, or even a mere world eon.

Solutions The Indian tradition developed two kinds of solutions to the problem of *samsara*. The first involves a strategy of maximizing good actions and minimizing bad actions to achieve the best possible rebirth in one's next round of existence. The second, and more radical, solution seeks "liberation" (*moksha*) from existence: escaping all karmic effects by escaping action itself.

The first strategy has been followed by the great masses of Hindus, Buddhists, and Jains over the centuries. It has been characterized by Franklin Edgerton as the "ordinary norm," as opposed to the "extraordinary norm," the path of only the select elite, the greatest seekers of Upanishadic truth, Jain asceticism, or the Buddhist Middle Path. Essentially, the ordinary norm aims at living according to a code of social and moral responsibility. The most significant such codes in Indian history are those of the masses of Hindus, Buddhists, and Jains over the centuries. On the other hand, the seekers of the extraordinary norm usually follow an ascetic discipline aimed at transcending action, at withdrawal from the karmic cycle altogether and consequent release (*moksha*) from cause and effect, good and evil, birth and rebirth. These two characteristic Indian responses to the problem posed by *samsara* underlie the fundamental forms of Indian thought and piety that took shape in the mid- to late first millennium B.C.E.

Social Responsibility: Dharma *as Ideal*

The "ordinary norm" of life in the various traditions of Indian religiousness can be summarized as life lived according to **dharma**. Although *dharma* has many meanings, its most common is similar to that of the Vedic Aryan concept of *Rta* (see Chapter 1). In this sense, it means "the right (order of things)," "moral law," "right conduct," or even "duty." It includes the cosmic order (compare the Chinese *Dao*) as well as the right conduct of political, commercial, social, and religious affairs and individual moral responsibility. For most people—those we might call the laity, as distinguished from monks and ascetics—life according to *dharma* is the life of moral action that will lead to a better birth in the next round of existence.

Life according to *dharma* has several implications. First, it accepts action in the world of *samsara* as necessary and legitimate. Second, it demands acceptance of the responsibilities appropriate to one's sex, class and caste group, stage in life, and other life circumstances. Third, it allows for legitimate self-interest: One's duty is to do things that acquire merit for one's eternal *atman* and to avoid those that bring evil consequences. Fourth, rebirth in heaven, in paradise, is the highest goal attainable through the life of *dharma*. However (fifth), all achievement in the world of *dharma* (which is also the world of *samsara*), even the attainment of heaven, is ultimately subject to change. (See Document, "The 'Turning of the Wheel of the Dharma': Basic Teachings of the Buddha.")

Ascetic Discipline: Moksha *as Ideal*

For those who abandon the world of ordinary life to gain freedom from *samsara*, the implications for living are in direct contrast to those of the ordinary norm. First, any action, good or bad, is at least counterproductive, for action produces only more action, more *karma*, more rebirth. Second, nonaction is achieved only by withdrawal from "normal" existence. The person seeking release from *samsara* has to move beyond the usual responsibilities of family and society. Most often, this involves becoming a "renouncer" (*sannyasi*)—whether a Hindu hermit, yogi, or wanderer, or a Jain or Buddhist monk. Third, this renunciation of the world and its goals demands selflessness, absence of ego. One must give up the desires and attachments that the self normally needs to function in the world. Fourth, the highest goal is not rebirth in heaven, but liberation (*moksha*) from all rebirth and redeath. Finally, this *moksha* is permanent. Its realization means no more becoming, no more suffering in the realm of *samsara*. Permanence, eternity, transcendence, and freedom from suffering are its attributes.

Seekers of the Extraordinary Norm   The ideas that led individuals to seek the extraordinary norm were first fully elaborated in the Upanishads. These ideas appealed to an increasing number of persons who abandoned both the ritualistic religious practices and the society of class distinctions and material concerns around them. Many of these seekers were of warrior-noble (*Kshatriya*), not Brahmanic, birth. They took up the wandering or hermitic existence of the ascetic, seeking spiritual powers in yogic meditation and self-denial or even self-torture. Such seekers wanted to transcend bodily existence to realize the Absolute.

In the sixth century B.C.E., teachers of new ideas appeared, especially in the lower Ganges basin, in the area of Magadha (modern Bihar). Most of them rejected traditional religious practices as well as the authority of the Vedas in favor of ascetic discipline as the true spiritual path. The ideas and practices of two of these teachers became the foundations of new and lasting traditions of piety and faith, those of the Jains and the Buddhists.

Mahavira and the Jain Tradition

The **Jains** are an Indian community that traces its tradition to Vardhamana, known as Mahavira ("the great hero"), who is traditionally believed to have lived from about 540 to 468 B.C.E. The Jains consider Mahavira as the final *Jina* ("victor" over *samsara*) or *Tirthankara* ("ford maker," one who finds a way across the waters of existence), in a line of twenty-four great teachers who have appeared in the latter, degenerative half of the present-world time cycle. The Jains (or *Jainas*, "adherents of the *Jina*") see in Mahavira not a god, but a human teacher who found and taught the way to extricate the self, or soul, from the bonds of the material world and its karmic accretions.

In the Jain view, there is no beginning or end to phenomenal existence, only innumerable, ceaseless cycles of generation and degeneration. The universe is alive from end to end with an infinite number of souls, all immortal, omniscient, and pure in their essence.

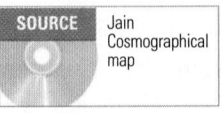
SOURCE   Jain Cosmographical map

Chronology

India

ca. 800–500 B.C.E.	The Upanishads
540–ca. 468 B.C.E.	Mahavira, the Jina/Vardamana
ca. 566–ca. 486 B.C.E.	Siddhartha Gautama, the Buddha

But all are trapped in *samsara*, whether as animals, gods, humans, plants, or even inanimate stones or fire. *Karma* here takes on a quasi-material form: Any thought, word, or deed attracts karmic matter that clings to and encumbers the soul. The greatest amounts come from evil acts, especially those done out of hate, greed, or cruelty to any other being.

Mahavira's path to release focused on eliminating evil thoughts and acts, especially those harmful to others. His radical ascetic practice aimed at destroying karmic defilements and, ultimately, all actions leading to further karmic bondage. At the age of thirty, Mahavira began practicing the radical self-denial of a wandering ascetic, eventually even giving up clothing altogether. After twelve years of self-deprivation and yogic meditation, he attained enlightenment. Then, for some thirty years, he went about teaching his discipline to others. At the age of seventy-two he chose to fast to death to burn out the last karmic residues, an action that some of the most advanced Jain ascetics have emulated down to the present day.

It would, however, be wrong to think of the Jain tradition in terms only of the extreme ascetic practices of some Jain mendicants. Jain monks are bound basically by the five great vows they share with other monastic traditions like the Buddhist and the Christian: not to kill, steal, lie, engage in sexual activity, or own anything.

Most Jains are not monks. Today there is a thriving lay community of perhaps 3 million Jains, most in western India (Gujarat and Rajasthan). Laypersons have close ties to the monks and nuns, whom they support with gifts and food. Many Jain laypersons spend periods of their lives in retreat with monks or nuns. They are vegetarians and regard *ahimsa* ("noninjury") to any being as paramount. Compassion is the great virtue for them, as for Buddhists. The merit of serving the extraordinary-norm seekers who adopt the mendicant life and of living a life according to the high standards of the community provides a goal even for those who as laypersons are following the ordinary norm.

The Buddha's Middle Path

It can be argued that India's greatest contribution to world civilization was the Buddhist tradition, which ultimately faded out in India. Yet there it was born, developed its basic contours, and left its mark on Hindu and Jain religion and culture. Like the two other great universalist traditions, Christianity and Islam, it traces its origins to a single figure who for centuries has loomed larger than life for the faithful.

This figure is Siddhartha Gautama, known as the "sage of the Shakya tribe (Shakyamuni)" and, above all, as the Buddha, or "Enlightened/Awakened One." A contemporary of Mahavira, Gautama was also born (ca. 566 B.C.E.) of a *Kshatriya* family in comfortable—if not, as legend has it, royal—circumstances. His people lived near the modern Nepalese border in the Himalayan foothills. The traditional story of how Gautama came to teach the Middle Path to liberation from *samsara* begins with his sheltered life of ease as a young married prince.

At the age of twenty-nine, Gautama first perceived the reality of aging, sickness, and death as the human lot. Revolted at his previous delight in sensual pleasures and even his wife and child, he abandoned his home and family to

Jain Nuns, Northern India.

Fasting Buddha. Before Gautama arrived at the "Middle Path," he practiced severe austerities for six years. This fourth-to second-century B.C.E. statue of a fasting Buddha from Gandhara (in present-day Pakistan) reflects the Greek influence on early Buddhist sculpture. *Borromeo, EPA/Art Resource, N.Y.*

Noble Truths: (1) all life is *dukkha*, or suffering; (2) the source of suffering is desiring; (3) the cessation of desiring is the way to end suffering; and (4) the path to this end is eightfold: Right Understanding, Right Thought, Right Speech, Right Action, Right Livelihood, Right Effort, Right Mindfulness, and Right Concentration. The key idea of the Buddha's teaching, or *dharma*, is that everything in the world of existence is causally linked. The essential fact of existence is *dukkha*: For no pleasure—however great—is permanent (here we see the Buddhist variation on the central Indian theme of *samsara*).

Thus, Buddhist discipline focuses on the moral Eightfold Path, and the cardinal virtue of compassion for all beings, as the way to eliminate the selfish desiring that is the root of *samsara* and its unavoidable suffering. The Buddha himself had attained this goal; when he died (ca. 486 B.C.E.) after a life of teaching others how to master desiring, he passed from the round of existence forever. In Buddhist terminology, he attained nirvana, the extinguishing of karmic bondage. This attainment became the starting point for the growth and eventual spread of the Buddhist *dharma*, which was to assume new and diverse forms in its long history.

The Buddhist movement, like the Jain, included not only those who were willing to renounce marriage and normal occupations to become part of the Buddha's communities of monks or nuns, but also laypersons who would strive to live by the high moral standards of the tradition and support those who became mendicants in attaining full release. Buddhist tradition, again like that of the Jains, encompassed from the outset seekers of both the extraordinary and the ordinary norms in their present lives. This dual community has remained characteristic of all forms of Buddhism wherever it is practiced. Later we shall see how varied these forms have been historically. But however much the essentially a-theistic, a-ritualistic, and pragmatic tradition was later modified and expanded (so that popular Buddhism would cultivate even theistic devotion to a divinized Buddha and other enlightened beings), the fundamental vision persisted of a humanly attainable wisdom that leads to compassion and release.

The varying visions of Upanishadic, Jain, and Buddhist thought proved durable, albeit in different ways and degrees in India itself, as we have noted. The later emergence of "Hindu" tradition drew on all three of these revolutionary strands in Indian thought and integrated parts of their fundamental ideas about the universe, human life, morality, and society into the cultic and mythic strands of both Brahmanic and popular Indian practice.

seek an answer to the dilemma of the endless cycle of mortal existence. After this Great Renunciation, he studied first with renowned teachers and then took up extreme ascetic disciplines of penance and self-mortification. Still unsatisfied, Gautama turned finally to intense yogic meditation under a pipal tree in the place near Varanasi (Banaras) known as Gaya. In one historic night, he moved through different levels of trance, during which he realized all of his past lives, the reality of the cycle of existence of all beings, and how to stop the karmic outflows that fuel suffering. Thus he became the Buddha; that is, he achieved full enlightenment—the omniscient consciousness of reality as it truly is. Having realized the truth of suffering existence, he pledged himself to achieving release for all beings.

From the time of the experience under the Bodh tree, or "Enlightenment Tree," Gautama devoted the last of his earthly lives before his final release to teaching others his Middle Path between asceticism and indulgence. This path has been the core of Buddhist faith and practice ever since. It begins with realizing the Four

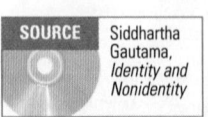

SOURCE   Siddhartha Gautama, Identity and Nonidentity

The "Turning of the Wheel of the Dharma": Basic Teachings of the Buddha

Document

Following are selections from the sermon said to have been the first preached by the Buddha. It was directed at five former companions with whom he had practiced extreme austerities. When he abandoned asceticism to meditate under the Bodh tree, they had become disillusioned and left him. This sermon is said to have made them the first to follow him. Because it set in motion the Buddha's teaching, or *Dharma*, on earth, it is usually described as "setting in motion the wheel of Dharma." The text is from the *Dhammacakkappavattanasutta*.

◆ What extremes does the Middle Path try to avoid? What emotion drives the chain of suffering? How does the "knowledge" that brings salvation compare to the knowledge sought in the Hindu tradition?

Thus have I heard. The Blessed One was once living in the Deer Park at Isipatana (the Resort of Seers) near Baranasi (Benares). There he addressed the group of five *bhikkhus*.

"Bhikkhus, these two extremes ought not to be practiced by one who has gone forth from the household life. What are the two? There is devotion to the indulgence of sense-pleasures, which is low, common, the way of ordinary people, unworthy and unprofitable; and there is devotion to self-mortification, which is painful, unworthy and unprofitable.

"Avoiding both these extremes, the Tathagata has realized the Middle Path: it gives vision, it gives knowledge, and it leads to calm, to insight, to enlightenment, to Nibbana. And what is that Middle Path? It is simply the Noble Eightfold Path, namely, right view, right thought, right speech, right action, right livelihood, right effort, right mindfulness, right concentration. This is the Middle Path realized by the Tathagata, which gives vision, which gives knowledge, and which leads to calm, to insight, to enlightenment, to Nibbana. . . .

"The Noble Truth of suffering (*Dukkha*) is this: Birth is suffering; aging is suffering; sickness is suffering; death is suffering; sorrow and lamentation, pain, grief and despair are suffering; association with the unpleasant is suffering; dissociation from the pleasant is suffering; not to get what one wants is suffering—in brief, the five aggregates of attachment are suffering.

"The Noble Truth of the origin of suffering is this: It is this thirst (craving) which produces re-existence and re-becoming, bound up with passionate greed. It finds fresh delight now here and now there, namely, thirst for nonexistence (self-annihilation).

"The Noble Truth of the Cessation of suffering is this: It is the complete cessation of that very thirst, giving it up, renouncing it, emancipating oneself from it, detaching oneself from it.

"The Noble Truth of the Path leading to the Cessation of suffering is this: It is simply the Noble Eightfold Path. . . .

"'This is the Noble Truth of Suffering (*Dukkha*)': such was the vision, the knowledge, the wisdom, the science, the light, that arose in me with regard to things not heard before. 'This suffering, as a noble truth, should be fully understood.'

"'This is the Noble Truth of the Cessation of suffering': such was the vision, 'This Cessation of suffering, as a noble truth, should be realized.'

"'This is the Noble Truth of the Path leading to the Cessation of suffering': such was the vision, 'This Path leading to the Cessation of suffering, as a noble truth, has been followed (cultivated).'

"As long as my vision of true knowledge was not fully clear regarding the Four Noble Truths, I did not claim to have realized the perfect Enlightenment that is supreme in the world with its gods, in this world with its recluses and brahmanas, with its princes and men. But when my vision of true knowledge was fully clear regarding the Four Noble Truths, then I claimed to have realized the perfect Enlightenment that is supreme in the world with its gods, in this world with its recluses and brahmanas, with its princes and men. And a vision of true knowledge arose in me thus: My heart's deliverance is unassailable. This is the last birth. Now there is no more re-becoming (rebirth)."

This the Blessed One said. The group of five bhikkhus was glad, and they rejoiced at his words.

—*Samyutta-nikaya, LVI, II*

From *What the Buddha Taught* by Walpola Rahula. Copyright © 1974 by W. Rahula, pp. 92–94. Used by permission of Grove Atlantic Inc.

The Religion of the Israelites

The ancient Near East was a **polytheistic** world; its people worshiped many gods. They worshiped local or regional gods and goddesses. Some of these deities were associated with natural phenomena such as mountains or animals, the sky or the earth. For example, Shamash in Mesopotamia and Re in Egypt were both sun gods. Others were tribal or local deities, such as Marduk in Babylonia or Atum, the patron god of the Egyptian city of On (Heliopolis). Still others represented elemental powers of this world or the next, as with Baal, the fertility god of the Canaanites, and Ishtar, whom the Assyrians worshiped as goddess of love and of war. Furthermore, from our perspective, the gods were represented largely as capricious, amoral beings who were no more affected by the actions of humans than were the natural forces that some of them represented.

If the gods were many and diverse, so too were the religious traditions of the ancient Near Eastern world. Even the major traditions of religious thought in Egypt and Mesopotamia did not offer comprehensive interpretations of human life that linked history and human destiny to a transcendent or eternal realm of meaning beyond this world—or at least no one interpretation was able to predominate in this pluralistic, religiously fragmented region.

Out of this polytheistic and pluralistic world came the great tradition of monotheistic faith represented historically in the Jewish, Christian, and Islamic communities. This tradition traces its origin not to any of the great imperial cultures of the ancient world, but to the small nation of the Israelites, or Hebrews. Although they were people from a tiny tribe, people whose external fortunes were at the mercy of the ebb and flow of the great dynasties and empires of the second and first millennia B.C.E., their impact on world civilization was far greater than that of their giant neighbors. For all the glories of the major civilizations of the Fertile Crescent and Nile valley, it was the Israelites, not the Babylonians or Egyptians, who generated a tradition that significantly affected later history. This tradition was ethical monotheism.

Monotheism, faith in a single, all-powerful God as the sole Creator, Sustainer, and Ruler of the universe, may be older than the Hebrews, but its first clear historical manifestation was with them. It was among the Hebrew tribes that emphasis on the moral demands and responsibilities that the one God placed on individual and community was first definitively linked to human history itself, and that history to a divine plan. This historically based ethical and monotheistic tradition culminated in the Jewish, Christian, and Islamic religions, but its direction was set among the ancient Hebrews.

The path from the appearance of the Hebrews as a nomadic people in the northern Arabian Peninsula, sometime after 2000 B.C.E., to the full flowering of Judaic monotheism in the mid–first millennium B.C.E. was a long one. Before we turn to the monotheistic revolution itself, we need to look briefly at this history.

From Hebrew Nomads to the Israelite Nation

The history of the Hebrews, later known as Israelites, must be pieced together from various sources. The records of their ancient Near Eastern neighbors mention the Hebrews only rarely, so historians must rely on their own accounts as compiled in the Hebrew Bible (the Old Testament in Christian terminology). It was not intended as a history in the contemporary sense; rather, it is a complicated collection of historical narrative, wisdom literature, poetry, law, and religious witness. Scholars once tended to discard the Bible as a source for historians, but the trend today is to take it seriously while using it cautiously and critically. Although its earliest writings go back at most to the ninth century B.C.E. (it was fixed in its present form only in the second century C.E.), it contains much older oral materials that allow us at least some glimpses of the earliest history of the Hebrew people.

We need not reject the core reality of the tradition that the Hebrew Abraham came from Ur in southern Mesopotamia and wandered west with his Hebrew clan to tend his flocks in the land later known as Palestine. Such a movement would be in accord with what we know of a general westward migration of seminomadic tribes from Mesopotamia after about 1950 B.C.E. Any precise dating of the arrival of the Hebrews in Palestine is impossible, but it was likely between 1900 and 1600 B.C.E.

It is with Moses, at about the beginning of the thirteenth century B.C.E., that the Hebrews tread clearly upon the stage of history. Some of Abraham's people had settled in the Palestinian region, but others apparently wandered farther, into Egypt, perhaps with the Hyksos invaders (see Chapter 1). By about 1400 B.C.E., as the biblical narrative tells it, they had become a settled but subjected, even enslaved, people there. Under Moses, some of the Egyptian Israelites fled Egypt to find a new homeland to the east, from which Abraham's descendants had come. They may then have wandered in the Sinai Desert and elsewhere for several decades before reaching Canaan, the province of Palestine that is described in the Bible as their promised homeland. The Bible presents this experience as the key event in Israel's history: the forging of the covenant, or

God the Sole Creator, as painted by the British poet and artist William Blake (1757–1827).

mutual pact, between God, or Yahweh, and his people. We interpret this Exodus as the time when the Israelites emerged as a nation, a people with a sense of community and common faith.

By about 1200 B.C.E., they had displaced the Canaanite inhabitants of ancient Palestine. After perhaps two centuries of consolidation as a loose federation of tribes, the now settled nation reached its peak as a kingdom under David (r. ca. 1000–961 B.C.E.) and Solomon (r. ca. 961–922 B.C.E.). But in the ninth century B.C.E., the kingdom split into two parts: Israel in the north and Judah, with its capital at Jerusalem, in the south (see map 2–1).

The rise of great empires around them brought disaster to the Israelites. The Northern Kingdom fell to the Assyrians in 722 B.C.E.; its people were scattered and, according to tradition, lost forever—the so-called ten lost tribes. Only the kingdom of Judah, with its seat at Jerusalem, remained, and

after that we may call the Israelites Jews. In 586 B.C.E., Judah was defeated by the Neo-Babylonian king Nebuchadnezzar II (d. 562 B.C.E.). He destroyed the Jewish cult center, the great Temple built by Solomon, and carried off the cream of the Jewish nation as exiles to be resettled in Babylon. There, in the "Babylonian captivity" of the Exile, without a temple, the Jews clung to their traditions and faith. After the new Persian dynasty of the Achaemenids defeated the Babylonians in 539 B.C.E., the Jews were allowed to return and resettle in their homeland. Many, but not all, of the exiles did return, and by about 516 B.C.E., they erected a second temple in a restored Jerusalem.

The new Judaic state continued for centuries to be dominated by foreign peoples but was able to maintain its religious and national identity and occasionally to assert itself. However, it was again destroyed and its people dispersed after the Romans' destruction of Jerusalem, in 70 C.E. and again in 132 C.E. By this era, however, the Jews had developed a religious worldview that would long outlive any Judaic national state.

The Monotheistic Revolution

The fate of this small nation would be of little interest were it not for its unique religious achievement. It developed a tradition of faith that amounted to a revolution in ways of thinking about the human condition, the meaning of life and history, and the nature of the Divine. It was not the overt history of the Judaic state down to its catastrophic end in 132 C.E. that was to have lasting historical importance, but what the Jews made of that history—how they interpreted it and built upon it a lasting Jewish culture and identity. The revolutionary character of this interpretation lay in its uniquely moralistic understanding of human life and history and the uncompromising monotheism on which it was based.

At the root of this monotheistic tradition stands the figure of Abraham. Not only Jews but also Christians and Muslims look to him as the symbolic founder of their monotheistic faith. The Hebrews in Abraham's time were probably much like other primitive tribal peoples in their religious attitudes. For them, the world must have been alive with supernatural powers: ancestral spirits, personifications of the forces of nature, and deities of local places. Abraham probably conceived of his Lord simply as his chosen deity among the many divinities who might be worshiped. Yet for the strength of his faith in his God, the biblical account recognizes him as the "Father of the Faithful," the first of the Hebrew patriarchs to make a **covenant** with the God who would become unique and supreme. In this, Abraham

Map Exploration

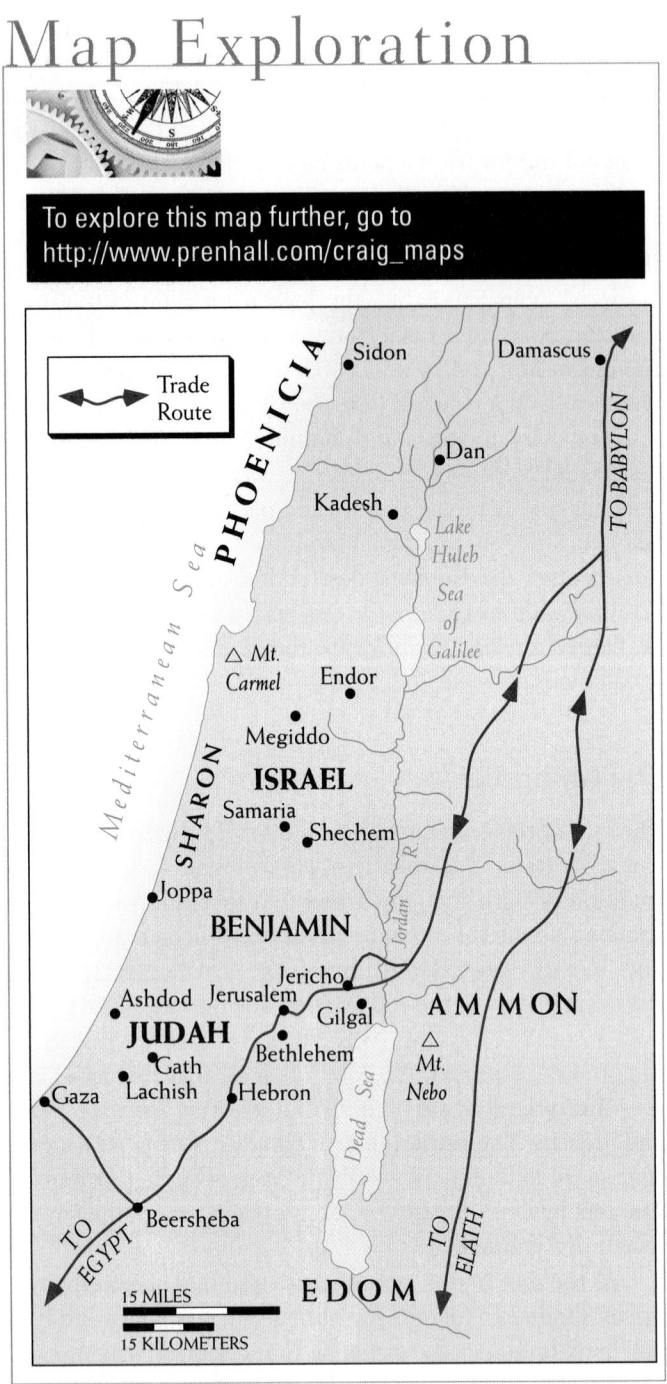

To explore this map further, go to
http://www.prenhall.com/craig_maps

Map 2–1. Ancient Palestine. The Hebrews established a unified kingdom under Kings David and Solomon in the 10th century B.C.E. After Solomon, the kingdom was divided into Israel in the north and Judah, with its capital, Jerusalem, in the south. North of Israel were the great commercial cities of Phoenicia.

promised to serve only him, and his God promised to bless his descendants and guide them as his special people.

After Abraham, the next major step came with Moses. As with Abraham's faith, it is difficult to say how much the Mo-

saic covenant at Sinai actually marked the achievement of an exclusively monotheistic faith. A notion of the supremacy of Yahweh is reflected in the biblical emphasis on the Israelites' rejection of all other gods after Sinai—and on their subsequent victory, through Yahweh's might, over the Canaanites. Certainly, the covenant event was decisive in uniting the Israelites as a people with a special relationship to God. At Sinai, they received both God's holy Law (the Torah) and his promise of protection and guidance as long as they kept the Law. This was the pivotal moment in the monotheistic revolution that came to full fruition only several hundred years later. But from the later perspective of the biblical redactors at least, from Sinai forward the Israelites saw themselves as God's chosen people among the nations and their history as the history of the mighty acts of the one God.

The monotheistic revolution might thus be said to have begun with Abraham or Moses. Historically, we can trace it primarily from the bipartite division of the Israelite kingdom in 922 B.C.E. After this, men and women known as the *prophets* arose. These inspired messengers of God were sent to call their people back from worship of false gods to faith in the one true God, and from immorality to obedience to God's commandments.

The important point in the colorful history of the great and lesser prophets is that their activity was closely linked to

SOURCE The Book of Job

the saga of Israelite national success, exile, and return in the mid–first millennium B.C.E. In the biblical interpretation of these events, we can see the progressive consolidation of Judaic religion. This consolidation, even amidst the political demise of the Israelite kingdom, was largely the work of the prophets. Their concern with purifying Jewish faith, and with morality, focused in particular on two ideas that proved central to Judaic monotheism.

The first seminal idea for the Jews was the significance of history in the divine plan. Calling on the Jews' awareness of the Sinai covenant, the prophets saw in Israel's past and present troubles God's punishment for failing in their covenant duties. Their prophecies of coming disaster from their enemies were based on the conviction that unless Israel changed its ways, more punishment would follow. But they were not only prophets of doom. When the predicted disasters arrived, their vision extended to seeing Israel as the "suffering servant" among the nations, the people who, by their trials, would purify other nations and bring them ultimately to God. Here the nationalistic, particularistic focus of previous Israelite religion gave way to a more complete, universalist monotheism: Yahweh was now God of all, even the Babylonians or Assyrians.

Exile of the Israelites. In 722 B.C.E. the northern part of Jewish Palestine, the kingdom of Israel, was conquered by the Assyrians. Its people were driven from their homeland and exiled all over the vast Assyrian Empire. This wall carving in low relief comes from the palace of the Assyrian king Sennacherib at Nineveh. It shows the Jews with their cattle and baggage going into exile. *Erich Lessing/Art Resource, N.Y.*

The second central idea emphasized the nature of Yahweh. The prophets saw in him the transcendent ideal of justice and goodness. From this view followed naturally the demand for justice and goodness, individually and collectively, among his worshipers. God was a righteous God who expected righteousness from human beings. (See Document, "God's Purpose with Israel.") No longer could he be only the object of a sacrificial cult: he was a moral God who demanded goodness, not blood offerings or empty prayers. A corollary of God's goodness was his love for his people, as the prophet Hosea (late eighth century B.C.E.) emphasized. However much he might have to punish them for their sins, God would finally lead them back to his favor.

The crux of the breakthrough to ethical monotheism lay in linking the Lord of the Universe to history and morality. The Almighty Creator was seen as actively concerned with the actions and fates of his human creatures as exemplified in Israel. This concern was reflected in God's involvement in history, which thus took on transcendent meaning. God had created humankind for an ultimately good purpose; they were called to be just and good like their Creator, for they were involved in the fulfillment of his divine purpose. This fulfillment would come in the restoration of Israel as a people purified of their sins: "I will put my law within them, and I will write it upon their hearts; and I will be their God, and they shall be my people" (Jeremiah 31:33).

Even after the exile, however, the realization of the prophesied days of peace and blessedness under God's rule clearly still had not come. Jews were scattered from Egypt to Babylonia, and their homeland was controlled by foreign powers. This context brought forth the late prophetic concept that history's culmination would come in a future Messianic age. Faith and morality were tied to human destiny, even without the still later Jewish idea that a Day of Judgment would cap the golden age of the **Messiah**, the redeemer who Jews believed would establish the kingdom of God on earth. The significance of these ideas, some of which might have come from the Jews' encounter with Zoroastrian traditions during the exile, did not stop with Judaic religion. They played a key role in similar Christian and Muslim ideas of a Messianic deliverer, resurrection of the body, and a life after death.

Alongside the prophets, the other key element in the monotheistic revolution of the Jews was the Law itself. The Law is embodied in the five books of the Torah (the Pentateuch, or "five books": Genesis, Exodus, Leviticus, Numbers, and Deuteronomy). The central place of the Law in Jewish life was reestablished, after a period of decline, by King Josiah of Judah (ca. 649–609 B.C.E.) shortly before the fall of Jerusalem and the exile. Its presence and importance in Judaic faith enabled the Jews in exile to survive the loss of the Temple and its priestly cult, thereby fixing the Torah

The Fall. The German artist Albrecht Dürer (1471–1528) engraved this image of the biblical first humans whose creation and fall are recounted in Genesis. God's covenant with humankind is central to his divine plan. However much he might punish people for their sins, God would finally lead them back to his favor.

The evolution of Judaic monotheistic faith was the beginning of one of the major traditions of world religion. For the first time, a nation defined itself not primarily by dynastic, linguistic, or geographic considerations, but by shared religious faith and practice. This was something new in human history. It was later to have still greater effects when not only Judaic but also Christian and Muslim traditions would change the face of much of the world.

Greek Philosophy

Greek thought offered different approaches and answers to many of the same concerns as those of the original monotheists. Calling attention to some of those differences will help to identify the distinctive outlook of the Greeks and of the later cultures of Western civilization that have drawn heavily on it.

Greek ideas had much in common with those of earlier peoples. The Greek gods had most of the characteristics of the Mesopotamian deities; magic and incantations played a part in Greek lives; and their law was usually connected with divinity. Many, if not most, Greeks in the ancient world must have lived with notions similar to those held by other peoples. But surprisingly, some Greeks developed ideas that were strikingly different and,

even over Jerusalem as the ultimate earthly focus of faith in God. Its centrality for the Judaic nation was reaffirmed after the reestablishment of the Temple by the prophets Ezra and Nehemiah in the fifth century B.C.E.

In the second century B.C.E., the enduring role of the Torah was ensured by its physical compilation, together with the books of the prophets and other writings, into the Holy Scriptures, or Bible (from the Greek *bibloi*, "books"). The Torah has not only the Law itself, but also the record of the Jews' journey to the recognition of God's law for his people. A holy, authoritative, divinely revealed scripture as an element of Judaic monotheism had revolutionary consequences, not only for Jews, but also for Christians and Muslims. It put the seal on the monotheistic revolution that had made the sovereignty and righteousness of God the focal points of faith.

Chronology

The Israelites

ca. 1000–961 B.C.E.	Reign of King David
ca. 961–922 B.C.E.	Reign of King Solomon
722 B.C.E.	Assyrian conquest of Israel (Northern Kingdom)
586 B.C.E.	Destruction of Jerusalem; fall of Judah (Southern Kingdom); Babylonian captivity
539 B.C.E.	Restoration of Temple; return of exiles

God's Purpose with Israel

Document

According to Jewish tradition, the Ten Commandments that Moses received from God for the Israelites are given in two different places in the Torah, with slightly different wording in each. The Exodus passage is one of these; the other is in Deuteronomy 5, the chapter immediately followed by the second passage cited here, Deuteronomy 6:1–9. This latter passage contains the fundamental statement of Judaic faith (verses 4–5), known as the *Shema* ("Hear," the word that begins this divine command).

◆ How do these passages exemplify the moral consciousness and utter faith in God that Jewish monotheism is built upon?

And God spoke all these words, saying,

"I am the Lord your God, who brought you out of the land of Egypt, out of the house of bondage.

"You shall have no other gods before me.

"You shall not make for yourself a graven image, or any likeness of anything that is in heaven above, or that is in the earth beneath, or that is in the water under the earth; you shall not bow down to them or serve them; for I the Lord your God am a jealous God, visiting the iniquity of the fathers upon the children to the third and the fourth generation of those who hate me, but showing steadfast love to thousands of those who love me and keep my commandments.

"You shall not take the name of the Lord your God in vain; for the Lord will not hold him guiltless who takes his name in vain.

"Remember the sabbath day, to keep it holy. Six days you shall labor, and do all your work; but the seventh day is a sabbath to the Lord your God; in it you shall not do any work, you, or your son, or your daughter, your manservant, or your maidservant, or your cattle, or the sojourner who is within your gates; for in six days the Lord made heaven and earth, the sea, and all that is in them and rested the seventh day; therefore the Lord blessed the sabbath day and hallowed it.

"Honor your father and your mother, that your days may be long in the land which the Lord your God gives you.

"You shall not kill.

"You shall not commit adultery.

"You shall not steal.

"You shall not bear false witness against your neighbor.

"You shall not covet your neighbor's house; you shall not covet your neighbor's wife, or his manservant, or his maidservant, or his ox, or his ass, or anything that is your neighbor's."

—*Exodus 20:1–17*

"Now this is the commandment, the statutes and the ordinances which the Lord your God commanded me to teach you, that you may do them in the land to which you are going over, to possess it; that you may fear the Lord your God, you and your son and your son's son, by keeping all his statutes and his commandments, which I command you, all the days of your life; and that your days may be prolonged. Hear therefore, O Israel, and be careful to do them; that it may go well with you, and that you may multiply greatly, as the Lord, the God of your fathers, has promised you, in a land flowing with milk and honey.

"Hear, O Israel: The Lord our God is one Lord, and you shall love the Lord your God with all your heart, and with all your soul, and with all your might. And these words which I command you this day shall be upon your heart; and you shall teach them diligently to your children, and shall talk of them when you sit in your house, and when you walk by the way, and when you lie down, and when you rise. And you shall bind them as a sign upon your hand, and they shall be as frontlets between your eyes. And you shall write them on the doorposts of your house and on your gates.

—*Deuteronomy 6:1–9*

Four Great Systems of Thought and Religion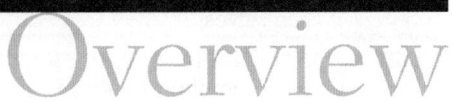

Between 800 B.C.E. and 300 B.C.E., four philosophical or religious revolutions occurred that shaped the subsequent history of the world. These revolutions, which were attempts to answer universal questions about the human condition, established cultural patterns that have endured to the present day.

CHINESE PHILOSOPHY

Three principal schools: Confucianism, Daoism, Legalism. Each school was concerned with social and political issues, how individuals interact with each other and the state, and the question of how to lead an ethical life that was in harmony with nature and the cosmos.

INDIAN RELIGION

Hinduism, Jains, Buddhism. Indian religion saw existence as an endless cycle of birth and rebirth (*samsara*). *Karma*, the concept that every action has good or evil effects, was the key to resolving the dilemma of *samsara*. Good actions could result in a person's being reborn in a higher state, even as a god. Complete withdrawal from the world could lead to escape from *samsara* into nonexistence.

HEBREW MONOTHEISM

The Hebrews, or Israelites, were the first people in history to base their identity as a nation in faith in a single, all-powerful God who made ethical demands and placed responsibilities on them as individuals and as a community. History, itself, was the unfolding of a divine plan for human beings. Through the Christian and Muslim traditions, Hebrew monotheism would profoundly influence much of the world.

GREEK PHILOSOPHY

Beginning in the sixth century B.C.E., Greek thinkers were the first to try to explain the natural world without reference to supernatural powers. Later Greek thinkers used rational analysis to investigate ethical, political, and social problems: how human beings should govern themselves, live in society, and act toward each other. The Greek tradition of rational inquiry lies at the root of all subsequent Western science and philosophy.

---

in so doing, set a part of humankind on an entirely new path. As early as the sixth century B.C.E., Greeks living in the Ionian cities of Asia Minor raised questions and suggested answers about nature that produced an intellectual revolution. In speculating about the nature of the world and its origin, they made guesses that were completely naturalistic and included no reference to supernatural powers. One historian of Greek thought, discussing the views of Thales (624–545 B.C.E.), the first Greek philosopher, put the case particularly well:

In one of the Babylonian legends it says: "All the lands were sea. Marduk bound a rush mat upon the face of the waters, he made dirt and piled it beside the rush mat." What Thales did was to leave Marduk out. He, too, said

that everything was once water. But he thought that earth and everything else had been formed out of water by a natural process, like the silting up of the Delta of the Nile. It is an admirable beginning, the whole point of which is that it gathers together into a coherent picture a number of observed facts without letting Marduk in.[3]

By putting the question of the world's origin in a naturalistic form, Thales may have initiated the unreservedly rational investigation of the universe, and in so doing, initiated both Western philosophy and Western science.

---

[3] Benjamin Farrington, *Greek Science* (London: Penguin Books, 1953), p. 37.

The same relentlessly rational approach was applied even to the gods themselves. In the same century as Thales, Xenophanes of Colophon expressed the opinion that humans think of the gods as resembling themselves, that like themselves they were born, that they wear clothes like theirs, and that they have voices and bodies like theirs. If oxen, horses, and lions had hands and could paint like humans, Xenophanes argued, they would paint gods in their own image; the oxen would draw gods like oxen and the horses like horses. Thus Africans believed in flat-nosed, black-faced gods, and the Thracians in gods with blue eyes and red hair.[4] In the fifth century B.C.E. Protagoras of Abdera (ca. 490–420 B.C.E.) went so far in the direction of agnosticism as to say, "About the gods I can have no knowledge either that they are or that they are not or what is their nature."[5]

This rationalistic, skeptical way of thinking carried over into practical matters as well. The school of medicine led by Hippocrates of Cos (ca. 400 B.C.E.) attempted to understand, diagnose, and cure disease without recourse to supernatural forces or beings. One of the Hippocratics wrote of the mysterious disease epilepsy:

It seems to me that the disease is no more divine than any other. It has a natural cause, just as other diseases have. Men think it divine merely because they do not understand it. But if they called everything divine which they do not understand, why, there would be no end of divine things.[6]

By the fifth century B.C.E., it was possible for the historian Thucydides (ca. 460–400 B.C.E.) to analyze and explain the behavior of humans in society completely in terms of human nature and chance, leaving no place for the gods or supernatural forces.

The relative unimportance of divine or supernatural forces also characterized Greek views of law and justice. Most Greeks, of course, liked to think that law came ultimately from the gods. In practice, however, and especially in the democratic states, they understood that laws were made by humans and should be obeyed because they represented the expressed consent of the citizens. Law, according to the fourth-century B.C.E. statesman Demosthenes (384–322 B.C.E.), was "a general covenant of the whole State, in accordance with which all men in that State ought to regulate their lives."[7]

These ideas, so different from any that came before the Greeks, open the discussion of most of the issues that appear in the long history of civilization and that remain major concerns in the modern world: What is the nature of the universe and how can it be controlled? Are there divine powers, and if so, what is humanity's relationship to them? Are law and justice human, divine, or both? What is the place in human society of freedom, obedience, and reverence? The Greeks confronted and intensified these and many other problems.

Reason and the Scientific Spirit

The rational spirit characteristic of Greek culture blossomed in the sixth century B.C.E. into the intellectual examination of the physical world and the place of humankind in it that we call philosophy. It is not surprising that the first steps along this path were taken in Ionia on the coast of Asia Minor, which was on the fringe of the Greek world and therefore in touch with foreign ideas and the learning of the East (see Map 2–2). The Ionians were among the first to recognize that the Greek account of how the world was created and maintained and of the place of humans in it was not universally accepted. Perhaps this realization helped spark the first attempts at disciplined philosophical inquiry.

We have already met Thales of Miletus. He believed that the earth floated on water and that water was the primary substance. This idea was not new; what was new was the absence of any magical or mythical elements in the explanation. Thales observed, as any person can, that water has many forms: liquid, solid, and gaseous. He saw that it could "create" land by alluvial deposit and that it was necessary for all life. These observations he organized by reason into a single explanation that accounted for many phenomena without any need for the supernatural. The first philosopher thus set the tone for future investigations. Greek philosophers assumed that the world was knowable, rational, and simple.

The search for fundamental rational explanations of phenomena was carried forward by another Milesian, Anaximander (ca. 611–546 B.C.E.). He imagined that the basic element was something undefined, "unlimited." The world emerged from this basic element as the result of an interaction of opposite forces—wet and dry, hot and cold. Anaximander pictured the universe in eternal motion, with all sensible things emerging from the "unlimited," then decaying and returning to it. He also argued that human beings originated in water and had evolved to the present state through several stages, including that of a fish.

Anaximenes, another Milesian who flourished about 546 B.C.E., believed air was primary. It took different forms as a result of the purely physical processes of rarefaction and condensation.

Heraclitus of Ephesus, who lived near the end of the sixth century B.C.E., carried the dialogue further. His famous saying, "All is motion," raised important problems. If all is

---

[4] Frankfort et al., *Before Philosophy* (1949), pp. 14–16.
[5] Hermann Diels, *Fragmente der Vorsokratiker*, 5th ed., ed. by Walther Kranz (Berlin: Weidmann, 1934–1938), Frg. 4.
[6] Ibid., Frgs. 14–16.
[7] *Against Aristogeiton*, p. 16.

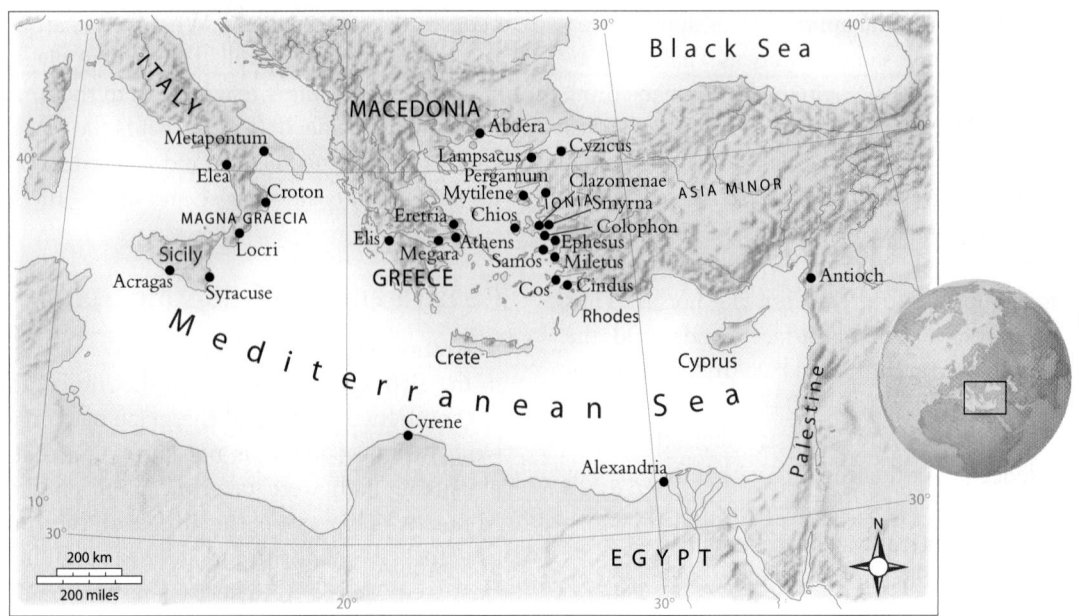

Map 2–2.   Centers of Greek Philosophy

constantly in motion, nothing ever really exists. Yet Heraclitus believed that the world order was governed by a guiding principle, the *Logos*, and that though phenomena changed, the *Logos* did not. *Logos* has several meanings, among them "word," "language," "speech," and "reason." So when Heraclitus said that the physical world was governed by *Logos*, he implied that it could be explained by reason. Speculations about the physical world, what we would call natural science, thus soon led the way toward even more difficult philosophical speculations about language, about the manner of human thought, and about knowledge itself.

In opposition to Heraclitus, the fifth-century B.C.E. philosopher Parmenides of Elea and his pupil Zeno argued that change was only an illusion of the senses. Reason and reflection showed that reality was fixed and unchanging because it seemed evident that nothing could be created out of nothingness. Such fundamental speculations were carried forward by Empedocles of Acragas (fl. ca. 450 B.C.E.), who spoke of four basic elements: fire, water, earth, and air. Like Parmenides, he thought that reality was permanent but not immobile, for the four elements were moved by two primary forces, Love and Strife, or, as we might be inclined to say, attraction and repulsion.

This theory was clearly a step on the road to the atomic theory of Leucippus of Miletus (fl. fifth century B.C.E.) and Democritus of Abdera (ca. 460–370 B.C.E.). They believed that the world consisted of innumerable tiny, solid particles (atoms) that could not be divided or modified and that moved about in the void. The size of the atoms and the arrangement in which they were joined with others produced the secondary qualities that the senses could per-

ceive, such as color and shape. These qualities—unlike the atoms themselves, which were natural—were merely conventional. Anaxagoras of Clazomenae (ca. 500–428 B.C.E.) had previously spoken of tiny fundamental particles called *seeds* that were put together on a rational basis by a force called *nous*, or "mind." Thus, Anaxagoras suggested a distinction between matter and mind. But the **atomists** regarded "soul," or "mind," as material and believed that everything was guided by purely physical laws. In the arguments of Anaxagoras and the atomists, we have the beginning of the philosophical debate between materialism and idealism that has continued through the ages. (See Document, "The Atomists' Account of the Origin of the World Order.")

These discussions interested few; indeed, most Greeks were suspicious of such speculations. A far more influential debate was begun by a group of professional teachers who emerged in the mid–fifth century B.C.E. Called **Sophists**, they traveled about and received pay for teaching practical techniques of persuasion, such as rhetoric, which were highly valued in democracies like Athens. Some claimed to teach wisdom and even virtue. (See Document, "The Sophists: From Rational Inquiry to Skepticism.") They did not speculate about the physical universe but applied reasoned analysis to human beliefs and institutions. This human focus was characteristic of fifth-century B.C.E. thought, as was the central problem that the Sophists considered: They discovered the tension and even the contradiction between nature and custom, or law. The more traditional among them argued that law itself was in accord with nature, and this view fortified the traditional beliefs about the **polis**, the Greek city-state (see Chapter 3).

The Atomists' Account of the Origin of the World Order

Document

Leucippus and Democritus were Greek thinkers of the fifth century B.C.E. who originated the theory that the world is entirely material, made up of atoms and the void, moving through space without external guidance. As these selections show, they provided a fundamental explanation of things that was purely natural, without divine or mythical intervention. Their view was passed on and later influenced such Renaissance scientists as Galileo.

◆ Compare the atomists' explanation of the origins of the world with that presented in the box entitled "Hymn to Indra" in Chapter 1. How do these explanations of the nature of things and how they got that way differ from those offered by different civilizations and by the Greeks before the sixth century B.C.E.? What are the consequences and significance of this new way of looking at the universe?

1. The world-orders arise in this way. Many bodies of all sorts of shapes "split off" from the infinite into a great void where, being gathered together, they give rise to a single vortex, in which, colliding and circling in all sorts of ways, they begin to separate apart, like to like. Being unable to circle in equilibrium any longer because of their congestion, the light bodies go off into the outer void like chaff, while the rest "remain together" and, becoming entangled, unite their motions and produce first a spherical structure. This stands apart like a "membrane," containing in itself all sorts of bodies; and, because of the resistance of the middle, as these revolve the surrounding membrane becomes thin as contiguous bodies continually flow together because of contact with the vortex. And in this way the earth arose, the bodies which were carried to the middle remaining together. Again, the surrounding membrane increases because of the acquisition of bodies from without; and as it moves with the vortex, whatever it touches it adds to itself. Certain of these, becoming entangled, form a structure at first very watery and muddy; but afterward they dry out, being carried about with the rotation of the whole, and ignite to form the substance of the heavenly bodies.

2. Certainly the atoms did not arrange themselves in order by design or intelligence, nor did they propound what movements each should make. But rather myriad atoms, swept along through infinite time or myriad paths by blows and their own weight, have come together in every possible way and tried out every combination that they could possibly create. So it happens that, after roaming the world for aeons of time in making trial of every combination and movement, at length they come together—those atoms whose sudden coincidence often becomes the origin of mighty things: of earth and sea and sky and the species of living things.

The first selection is from Diogenes Laertius 9.31; the second is from Lucretius, *De Rerum Naturae* 5.419–431. Both selections from John Mansley Robinson, *An Introduction to Early Greek Philosophy.* Copyright © 1968 by John Mansley Robinson. Used with permission of the author.

Others argued that laws were merely conventional and not in accord with nature. The law was not of divine origin but merely the result of an agreement among people. It could not pretend to be a positive moral force but merely had the negative function of preventing people from harming each other. The most extreme Sophists argued that law was contrary to nature, a trick whereby the weak controlled the strong. Critias (ca. 460–403 B.C.E.) went so far as to say that the gods themselves had been invented by some clever man to deter people from doing what they wished. Such ideas attacked the theoretical foundations of the *polis* and helped provoke the philosophical responses of Plato and Aristotle in the next century.

Political and Moral Philosophy

Like thinkers in other parts of the world around the middle of the first millennium B.C.E., some Greeks were vitally concerned with the formulation of moral principles for the governance of the state and the regulation of individual life, as well as with more abstract problems of the nature of existence and transcendence. Nowhere is the Greek concern with ethical, political, and religious issues clearer than in the philosophical tradition that began with Socrates in the latter half of the fifth century B.C.E. That tradition continued with Socrates' pupil Plato and with Plato's pupil Aristotle. Aristotle also had great interest in and made great contributions to the scientific understanding of the physical world, but he is perhaps more important for his impact on later Western and Islamic metaphysics.

The three philosophical giants of Hellenic political and moral philosophy were Socrates, Plato, and Aristotle. The starting point for all three was the social and political reality of the Greek city-state, or *polis*. The greatest crisis for the *polis* was the Great Peloponnesian War (435–404 B.C.E.), which is discussed in Chapter 3. Probably the most complicated response to this crisis may be found in the life and teachings of Socrates (469–399 B.C.E.). Because he wrote nothing, our knowledge of him comes chiefly from his disciples Plato and Xenophon (ca. 435–354 B.C.E.) and from later tradition. Although as a young man Socrates was interested in speculations about the physical world, he later turned to the investigation of ethics and morality. As the Roman writer and statesman Cicero (106–43 B.C.E.) put it, he brought philosophy down from the heavens.

Socrates was committed to the search for truth and for the knowledge about human affairs that he believed reason could reveal. His method was to go among men, particularly those reputed to know something, like craftsmen, poets, and politicians, to question and cross-examine them. The result was always the same: Those he questioned might have technical information and skills but seldom had any knowledge of the fundamental principles of human behavior. It is understandable that Athenians so exposed should become angry with their examiner, and it is not surprising that they thought Socrates was undermining the beliefs and values of the *polis*. Socrates' unconcealed contempt for democracy, which seemingly relied on ignorant amateurs to make important political decisions without any certain knowledge, created further hostility. Moreover, his insistence on the primacy of his own individualism and his determination to pursue philosophy even against the wishes of his fellow citizens reinforced this hostility and the prejudice that went with it.

Unlike the Sophists, Socrates did not accept pay for his teaching; he professed ignorance and denied that he taught at all. His individualism, moreover, was unlike the worldly hedonism of some of the Sophists. It was not wealth or pleasure or power that he urged people to seek, but "the greatest improvement of the soul." He differed also from the more radical Sophists in denying that the *polis* and its laws were merely conventional. He thought, on the contrary, that

they had a legitimate claim on the citizen, and he proved it in the most convincing fashion. In 399 B.C.E., he was condemned to death by an Athenian jury on the charges of bringing new gods into the city and of corrupting its youth. His dialectical inquiries had angered many important people, and his criticism of democracy must have been viewed with suspicion. He was given a chance to escape, but in Plato's *Crito* we are told of his refusal to do so because of his veneration of the laws.

Socrates' career set the stage for later responses to the travail of the *polis*; he recognized its difficulties and criticized its shortcomings. Although he turned away from an active political life, he did not abandon the idea of the *polis*. He fought as a soldier in its defense, obeyed its laws, and sought to use reason to put its values on a sound foundation.

The Cynics   One branch of Socratic thought—the concern with personal morality and one's own soul, the disdain for worldly pleasure and wealth, and the withdrawal from political life—was developed and then distorted almost beyond recognition by the Cynic school. Antisthenes (ca. 455–360 B.C.E.), a follower of Socrates, is said to have been its founder, but its most famous exemplar was Diogenes of Sinope (ca. 400–325 B.C.E.). Socrates disparaged wealth and worldly comfort, so Diogenes wore rags and lived in a tub. He performed shameful acts in public and made his living by begging to show his rejection of convention. He believed that happiness lay in satisfying natural needs in the simplest and most direct way. Because actions to this end, being natural, could not be indecent, they could and should be done publicly.

Socrates questioned the theoretical basis for popular religious beliefs; the Cynics ridiculed all religious observances. As Plato said, Diogenes was Socrates gone mad. Beyond that, the way of the Cynics contradicted important Socratic beliefs. Socrates believed that virtue was not a matter of birth but of knowledge, and that people did wrong only through ignorance of what is virtuous. The Cynics, on the contrary, believed that virtue was an affair of deeds and did not need a store of words and learning. Wisdom and happiness came from pursuing the proper style of life, not from philosophy. The Cynics moved even further from Socrates by abandoning the concept of the *polis* entirely. When Diogenes was asked about his citizenship, he answered that he was *kosmopolites*, a citizen of the world. The Cynics plainly had turned away from the past, and their views anticipated those of the Hellenistic Age (see Chapter 3).

Plato   Plato (429–347 B.C.E.) was the most important of Socrates' associates and is a perfect example of the pupil who becomes greater than his master. He was the first systematic philosopher and therefore the first to place political ideas in

"The Death of Socrates" by Jacques-Louis David (1748–1825), the leading Neoclassical painter of his day. David used themes from the supposedly morally austere and virtuous world of ancient Greece to comment on the decadence and corruption of contemporary France.

their full philosophical context. He was also a writer of genius, leaving us twenty-six philosophical discussions. (See Document, "Plato on the Role of Women in His Utopian Republic.") Almost all are in the form of dialogues, which dramatize the examination of difficult and complicated philosophical problems and make them somewhat entertaining.

Born of a noble Athenian family, Plato looked forward to an active political career until he was discouraged by the excesses of Athenian politics and the execution of Socrates. Twice he went to Sicily in the hope of producing a model state at Syracuse under that city's rulers, but without success. In 386 B.C.E., Plato founded the Academy, a center of philosophical investigation and a school for training statesmen and citizens that had a powerful impact on Greek thought and endured until it was closed in the sixth century C.E.

Like Socrates, Plato firmly believed in the *polis* and its values. Its virtues were order, harmony, and justice, and one of its main objects was to produce good people. Like his master, and unlike the radical Sophists, Plato thought that

the *polis* was in accord with nature. He accepted Socrates' doctrine of the identity of virtue and knowledge and made it plain what that knowledge was: *episteme*, science, a body of true and unchanging wisdom open to only a few philosophers whose training, character, and intellect allowed them to see reality. Only such people were qualified to rule; they themselves would prefer the life of pure contemplation but would accept their responsibility and take their turn as philosopher-kings. The training of such men required a specialization of function and a subordination of the individual to the community. This specialization would lead to Plato's definition of justice: that each man should do only that one thing to which his nature was best suited.

Plato understood that the *polis* of his day suffered from terrible internal stress, class struggle, and factional divisions. His solution, however, was not that of some Greeks—that is, conquest and resulting economic prosperity. For Plato the answer was in moral and political reform. The way to harmony was to destroy the causes of strife: private

The Sophists: From Rational Inquiry to Skepticism

Document

The rational spirit inherent in Greek thought was carried to remarkable and dangerous extremes by the Sophists in the fifth century B.C.E. As these three selections suggest, they questioned even the nature, the existence, and the origin of the gods, subjecting these matters to rational analysis.

◆ What was new in the thinking of the Sophists? How was it similar to the thought of the atomists (Democritus and Leucippus)? How was it different? In what ways were Sophist ideas threatening to the Greek way of life?

1. Concerning the gods, I do not know whether they exist or not. For many are the obstacles to knowledge: the obscurity of the subject and the brevity of human life.

2. Prodicus says that the ancients worshiped as gods the sun, the moon, rivers, springs, and all things useful to human life, simply because of their usefulness—just as the Egyptians deify the Nile. For this reason bread is worshiped as Demeter, wine as Dionysus, water as Poseidon, fire as Hephaestus, and so on for each of the things that are useful to men.

3. There was a time when the life of man was disorderly and bestial and subject to brute force; when there was no reward for the good and no punishment for the bad. At that time, I think, men enacted laws in order that justice might be absolute ruler and have arrogance as its slave; and if anyone did wrong he was punished. Then, when the laws prohibited them from doing deeds of violence, they began to do them secretly. Then, I think, some shrewd and wise man invented fear of the gods for mortals, so that there might be some deterrent to the wicked even if they did or said or thought something in secret. Therefore he introduced the divine, saying that there is a god, flourishing with immortal life, hearing and seeing with his mind, thinking of all things and watching over

them and having a divine nature; who will hear everything that is said among mortals and will be able to see all that is done. And if you plan any evil in secret it will not escape the notice of the gods, for they are of surpassing intelligence. In speaking thus he introduced the prettiest of teachings, concealing the truth under a false account. And in order that he might better strike fear into the hearts of men he told them that the gods dwell in that place which he knew to be a source of fears to mortals—and of benefits too—namely, the upper periphery where they saw lightnings and heard the dreaded rumblings of thunder and saw the starry body of the heaven, the beauteous embroidery of that wise craftsman Time, where the bright glowing mass of the sun moves and whence dark rains descend to earth. With such fears did he surround men, and by means of them he established the deity securely in a place befitting his dignity, and quenched lawlessness. Thus, I think, did some man first persuade mortals to believe in a race of gods.

The first selection is from Diogenes Laertius 9.51; the next two are from Sextus Empiricus, *Against the Schoolmasters* 9.18, 9.54. From John Mansley Robinson, *An Introduction to Early Greek Philosophy.* Copyright © 1968 by John Mansley Robinson. Used with permission of the author.

---

property, the family—anything, in short, that stood between the individual citizen and devotion to the *polis.*

The concern for the redemption of the *polis* was at the heart of Plato's system of philosophy. He began by asking the traditional questions: What is a good man, and how is he made? The goodness of a human being was a theme that belonged to moral philosophy, and when it became a function of the state, the question became part of political philosophy. Because goodness depended on knowledge of the good, it required a theory of knowledge and an investigation of what the knowledge was that was required for goodness. The answer

must be metaphysical and so required a full examination of metaphysics. Even when the philosopher knew the good, however, the question remained of how the state could bring

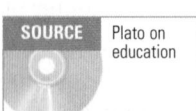 SOURCE Plato on education

its citizens to the necessary comprehension of that knowledge. The answer required a theory of education. Even purely logical and metaphysical questions, therefore, were subordinate to the overriding political questions. Plato's need to find a satisfactory foundation for the beleaguered *polis* thus contributed to the birth of systematic philosophy.

Aristotle Aristotle (384–322 B.C.E.) was a pupil of Plato and owed much to the thought of his master, but his different experience and cast of mind led him in new directions. He was born in northern Greece, the son of the court doctor of neighboring Macedon. As a young man, he came to study at the Academy, where he stayed until Plato's death. Then he joined a Platonic colony at Assos in Asia Minor, and from there, he moved to Mytilene. In both places, he carried on research in marine biology, and biological interests played a large part in all his thoughts. In 342 B.C.E., Philip, the king of Macedon, appointed him tutor to his son, the young Alexander (see Chapter 3). In 336 he returned to Athens, where he founded his own school, the Lyceum (or the Peripatos, as it was also called, based on the covered walk within it). In later years, its members were called Peripatetics. On the death of Alexander in 323 B.C.E., the Athenians rebelled against Macedonian rule, and Aristotle found it wise to leave Athens. He died the following year.

The Lyceum was different from the Academy. Its members took little interest in mathematics and were concerned with gathering, ordering, and analyzing all human knowledge. Aristotle wrote dialogues on the Platonic model, but none have survived. He and his students also prepared many collections of information to serve as the basis for scientific works, but of them only one remains, the *Constitution of the Athenians*, one of 158 constitutional treatises. Almost all we possess of his work is in the form of philosophical and scientific studies, whose loose organization and style suggest that they were lecture notes. The range of treated subjects is astonishing, including logic, physics, astronomy, biology, ethics, rhetoric, literary criticism, and politics.

In each field, the method was the same. Aristotle began with observation of the empirical evidence, which in some cases was physical and in others was common opinion. To this body of information he applied reason and discovered inconsistencies or difficulties. To deal with these, he introduced metaphysical principles to explain the problems or to reconcile the inconsistencies. His view on all subjects, like Plato's, was teleological; that is, he recognized purposes apart from and greater than the will of the individual human being. Plato's purposes, however, were contained in the Ideas, or Forms—transcendental concepts outside the experience of most people. For Aristotle, the purposes of most things were easily inferred by observing their behavior in the world.

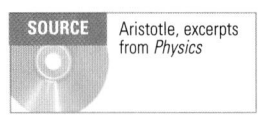

SOURCE
Aristotle, excerpts from *Physics*

Aristotle's most striking characteristics are his moderation and common sense. His epistemology finds room for both reason and experience; his metaphysics gives meaning and reality to both mind and body; his ethics aims at the good life, which is the contemplative life, but recognizes the necessity for moderate wealth, comfort, and pleasure.

All these qualities are evident in Aristotle's political thought. Like Plato, he opposed the Sophists' assertion that the *polis* was contrary to nature and the result of mere convention. His response was to apply to politics the teleology that he saw in all nature. In his view, matter existed to achieve an end, and it developed until it achieved its form, which was its end. There was constant development from matter to form, from potential to actual. Therefore, human primitive instincts could be seen as the matter out of which the human's potential as a political being could be realized. The *polis* made individuals self-sufficient and allowed the full realization of their potentiality. It was therefore natural. It was also the highest point in the evolution of the social institutions that serve the human need to continue the species: marriage, household, village, and finally, *polis*. For Aristotle, the purpose of the *polis* was neither economic nor military, but moral: "The end of the state is the good life," the life lived "for the sake of noble actions," a life of virtue and morality.[8]

Characteristically, Aristotle was less interested in the best state—the utopia that required philosophers to rule it—than in the best state practically possible, one that would combine justice with stability. The constitution for that state he called *politeia*, not the best constitution, but the next best, the one most suited to and most possible for most states. Its quality was moderation, and it naturally gave power to neither the rich nor the poor but to the middle class, which also had to be the most numerous. The middle class possessed many virtues: Because of its moderate wealth, it was free of the arrogance of the rich and the malice of the poor. For this reason, it was the most stable class. The stability of the constitution also came from being a mixed constitution, blending in some way the laws of democracy and those of oligarchy. Aristotle's scheme was unique because of its realism and the breadth of its vision.

All the political thinkers of the fourth century B.C.E. recognized that the *polis* was in danger and hoped to save it. All recognized the economic and social troubles that threatened it. Isocrates (436–338 B.C.E.), a contemporary of Plato and Aristotle, urged a program of imperial conquest as a cure for poverty and revolution. Plato saw the folly of solving a political and moral problem by purely economic means and resorted to the creation of utopias. Aristotle combined the practical analysis of political and economic realities with the moral and political purposes of the traditional defenders of the *polis*. The result was a passionate

---

[8] Aristotle, *Politics*, 1280b, 1281a.

Plato on the Role of Women in His Utopian Republic

The Greek invention of reasoned intellectual analysis of all things led the philosopher Plato to consider the problem of justice, which is the subject of his most famous dialogue, *The Republic*. This inquiry leads him to sketch out a utopian state in which justice may be found and where the most radical arrangements may be necessary. These include the equality of the sexes and the destruction of the family in favor of the practice of men having wives and children in common. In the following excerpts he argues for the fundamental equality of men and women and that women are no less appropriate than men as Guardians, leaders of the state.

◆ What are Plato's reasons for treating men and women the same? What objections could be raised to that practice? Would that policy, even if appropriate in Plato's utopia, also be suitable to conditions in the real world of classical Athens? In the world of today?

"If, then, we use the women for the same things as the men, they must also be taught the same things."

"Yes."

"Now music and gymnastics were given to the men."

"Yes."

"Then these two arts, and what has to do with war, must be assigned to the women also, and they must be used in the same ways."

"On the basis of what you say," he said, "it's likely."

"Perhaps," I said, "compared to what is habitual, many of the things now being said would look ridiculous if they were to be done as is said."

"Indeed they would," he said.

"Well," I said, "since we've started to speak, we mustn't be afraid of all the jokes—of whatever kind—the wits might make if such a change took place in gymnastic, in music and, not the least, in the bearing of arms and the riding of horses."

"Then," I said, "if either the class of men or that of women shows its superiority in some art or other practice then we'll say that that art must be assigned to it. But if they look as though they differ in this alone, that the female bears and the male mounts, we'll assert that it has not thereby yet been proved that a woman differs from a man with respect to what we're talking about; rather, we'll still suppose that our Guardians and their women must practice the same things."

"And rightly," he said.

"Therefore, my friend, there is no practice of a city's governors which belongs to woman because she's woman, or to man because he's man; but the natures are scattered alike among both animals; and woman participates according to nature in all practices, and man in all, but in all of them woman is weaker than man."

"Certainly."

"So, shall we assign all of them to men and none to women?"

"How could we?"

"For I suppose there is, as we shall assert, one woman apt at medicine and another not, one woman apt at music and another unmusical by nature."

"Of course."

"And isn't there then also one apt at gymnastic and at war, and another unwarlike and no lover of gymnastic?"

"I suppose so."

"And what about this? Is there a lover of wisdom and a hater of wisdom? And one who is spirited and another without spirit?"

"Yes, there are these too."

"There is, therefore, one woman fit for guarding and another not, or wasn't it a nature of this sort we also selected for the men fit for guarding?"

"Certainly, that was it."

From *The Republic of Plato*, 2nd ed., trans. by Allan Bloom. Copyright © 1968 by Allan Bloom. Preface to paperback edition, © 1991 by Allan Bloom. pp. 130–134. Reprinted by permission of Basic Books, a member of Perseus Books, L.L.C.

confidence in the virtues of moderation and of the middle class, and the proposal of a constitution that would give it power. It is ironic that the ablest defense of the *polis* came soon before its demise.

The concern with an understanding of nature in a purely rational, scientific way remained strong through the fifth century B.C.E., culminating in the work of the formulators of the atomic theory, Democritus and Leucip-

Chronology

Major Greek Philosophers

469–399 B.C.E.	Socrates
429–347 B.C.E.	Plato
384–322 B.C.E.	Aristotle

pus, and in that of the medical school founded by Hippocrates of Cos. In the mid–fifth century B.C.E., however, men like the Sophists and Socrates turned their attention to humankind and to ethical, political, and religious questions. This latter tradition of inquiry led, by way of Plato, Aristotle (in his metaphysical thought), and the Stoics, to Christianity; it had, as well, a substantial impact on Judaic and Islamic thought. The former tradition of thought, following a line from the natural philosophers, the Sophists, Aristotle (in his scientific thought), and the Epicureans, had to wait until the Renaissance in Western Europe to exert an influence. Since the eighteenth century, this line of Greek thought has been the more influential force in Western civilization. It may not be too much to say that since the Enlightenment of that century, the Western world has been engaged in a debate between the two strands of the Greek intellectual tradition. As Western influence has spread over the world in recent times, that debate has become of universal importance, for other societies have not separated the religious and philosophical from the scientific and physical realms as radically as has the modern West.

Summary

The Four Great Philosophical and Religious Revolutions. Between 800 and 300 B.C.E., four philosophical and religious revolutions arose that were to shape the subsequent history of the world. These were Chinese philosophy, Indian religion, Hebrew monotheism, and Greek philosophy.

Chinese Philosophy. Traditional Chinese philosophical thought, which took shape with the teachings of Confucius in the sixth century B.C.E., remained dominant in China until the early twentieth century. It was concerned with social and political issues and sought to teach human beings how to live harmoniously and ethically under Heaven by prescribing the correct relationships between ruler and sub-

ject, father and son, older and younger brother, husband and wife, and friend and friend. Confucianism became the official philosophy of China in the second century B.C.E. Other Chinese philosophies were Daoism, a mystical way of thought that offered a refuge from social responsibilities, and Legalism, which taught that a good society requires a strong state that enforces the law and punishes wrongdoers.

Indian Religion. Hinduism, the dominant Indian religious tradition, took shape by 400 B.C.E. In Indian religion, existence was an endless alteration between life and death (*samsara*). The escape from this dilemma lay in the concept of *karma*, the idea that good actions (*dharma*) could lead to rebirth as a higher being, even a god, or to escape the cycle entirely and cease to exist entirely (*moksha*).

Another Indian religious tradition, the Jains, sought to liberate the soul from the bonds of the material world by eliminating evil acts. Although there are few Indian Buddhists today, Buddhism traces its origins to the teachings of an Indian, Siddhartha Gautama (b. ca. 566 B.C.E.). Buddhism holds that escape from *samsara* lies in following a moral path of right understanding and actions and in having compassion for all beings.

Hebrew Monotheism. Monotheism is the faith in a single, all-powerful God as the sole creator, sustainer, and ruler of the universe. The Hebrews were the first people to emphasize the moral demands that the one God, Yahweh, placed on individual and community and to see history as the unfolding of a divine plan. The Hebrews, or Jews, were the first people in history to be defined by shared religious faith and practice. Through the Christian and Muslim traditions, Judaic monotheism would change the face of much of the world.

Greek Philosophy. The Greeks were the first to initiate the unreservedly rational investigation of the universe. They thus became the forerunners of Western philosophy and science. In the sixth and fifth centuries B.C.E., Greek thinkers, such as Thales of Miletus and Heraclitus, sought to explain natural phenomena without recourse to divine intervention. In the later fifth century and the fourth century B.C.E., philosophers, such as Socrates, Plato, and Aristotle, applied the same rational, inquisitive approach to the study of moral and political issues in the life of the Greek city state, or *polis*.

Review Questions

1. Is your outlook on life closer to Confucianism, Daoism, or Legalism? What specifically makes you favor one over the others?

2. Which fundamental assumptions about the world, the individual, and reality do the Jain, Hindu, and Buddhist traditions share? How do these assumptions compare with those that underlie Chinese philosophy, Jewish religious thought, and Greek philosophy?

3. How did the monotheism of the Hebrews differ from that of Egypt's Akhenaten (Chapter 1)? To what extent did their faith bind the Jews politically? Why was the concept of monotheism so radical for Near Eastern civilization?

4. In what ways did the ideas of the Greeks differ from those of other ancient peoples? How do Aristotle's political and ethical ideas compare with those of Confucius? What were Socrates' contributions to the development of philosophy?

Key Terms

atman-Brahman (p. 58)

atomists (p. 72)

Brahmanas (p. 58)

covenant (p. 65)

Daoism (daow-ihzm) (p. 54)

dharma (p. 60)

Hindu (p. 56)

Jains (p. 60)

karma (p. 58)

INTERPRETING THE PAST

Socrates in Asia: The Quest for Enlightenment in World Religions

Sources from My History Lab / Primary Source DVD

1) The Book of Job and Jewish Literature
2) Vardhamana Mahavira on Jainism
3) Siddhartha Gautama on Identity
4) Confucius, selections from the *Analects*
5) Plato, *The Republic*, excerpts

Throughout his life in Athens, Socrates (469–399 B.C.E.) pestered and needled his fellow citizens with questions like, 'What is the good life?', initiating a series of "Socratic dialogues", during which he would con-

tinue to bombard an unfortunate person with questions until the latter gave up in frustration. Taking pride in being Athens' "gadfly," Socrates was amazed that a democratic jury wished him to die, officially for "corrupting the youth" and "disrespecting the state's gods". While he protested in court that the proper punishment for his crime was to be treated to a dinner every night at state expense, he dutifully drank his hemlock.

But what if Socrates had chosen to go into exile, rather than drinking the poison (which might actually have been the intent and hope of Athens' leaders), and then began a tour of Asia in order to find enlightenment? His hosts, though at first appalled by this elderly, unattractive, and rather unwashed man asking his usual questions, might graciously have shared with him what they believed the good life to be.

For this assignment, determine what Socrates might have been told by Confucian philosophers; the adherents of Buddhism, Vardhamana Mahavira on Jainism, and the worshipers of the Hebrews' God, about how an enlightened person should live.

Legalism (p. 55)

Messiah (p. 67)

monotheism (p. 64)

polis (POH-lihs) (p. 72)

polytheistic (p. 64)

samsara (p. 58)

Sophists (p. 72)

Note: To learn more about the topics in this chapter, please turn to the Suggested Readings at the end of the book. For additional sources related to this chapter please see the Primary Source DVD at the back of this text or MyHistoryLab.

However, Socrates had come to his own understanding of the good life under the influence of Greek philosophy, as represented in the document from *The Republic* listed above. Describe what the Greeks' approach to philosophy seems to have been.

Questions

Socrates was a keen listener (when he wasn't interrupting with more questions)—would he have heard anything similar in what each group said? What, specifically?

Would anything that he heard on his extensive travels have sounded familiar? If so, what?

How does Greek philosophy compare with the Hebrews? With Confucius? With the Buddha and Vardhamana Mahavira?

Monotheism, the belief in a unique God who is the Creator of the universe and its all-powerful Ruler, first became a central and lasting element in religion among the Hebrews, later called Israelites and also Jews. Their religion, more than the many forms of polytheistic worship that characterized the ancient world, demanded moral rectitude and placed ethical responsibilities both on individuals and on the community as a whole. Their God had a divine plan for human history, which was linked to the behavior of his chosen people. This vision of the exclusive worship of the true God, obedience to the laws governing the community that derive from him, and a strong ethical responsibility was connected to humanity's historical experience in this world. Ultimately it gave rise to three great religions: Judaism, Christianity, and Islam.

At the beginning of this tradition stands Abraham, whom all three religions recognize as the founder. According to the Torah (the first five books of the Hebrew Bible; the Christian Old Testament), Abraham entered into a covenant with God in which he promised to worship only this God, who in turn promised to make Abraham's descendants his own chosen people—chosen to worship him, to obey his Laws, and to undertake a special set of moral responsibilities. God renewed the covenant with Moses at Mount Sinai when he freed the Israelites from Egyptian bondage. He promised them the land of Canaan (later called Palestine and part of which is now the state of Israel) and gave them the Law (the Torah), including the Ten Commandments, by which they were to guide their lives. As long as they lived by his Law, God would give them his guidance and protection.

In time the Israelites formed themselves into a kingdom that remained unified from about 1000 to 922 B.C.E. In the period after its division, prophets emerged. Thought to be inspired by God, they chastised the Israelites for their lapses

"In the Beginning." The Hebrew word *Beresheet*, which means "in the beginning," opens the Book of Genesis. The Jews are people of the Book, and foremost among their sacred writings is the Hebrew Bible.

into idolatry and immorality. Even as the kingdom was disintegrating and the Israelites falling under the control of alien empires, the prophets preached social reform and a return to God's laws. The prophets saw Israel's misfortune as punishment for failing to keep the covenant and predicted disaster if the Israelites did not change their ways. When disasters came—the Jewish kingdoms captured, the people enslaved and exiled—the prophets interpreted Israel's status as a chosen people to mean that their sufferings would make them "a light unto the nations," leading other nations to the true worship of one God.

The prophets also preached that God was righteous and demanded righteousness from his people. But he was also a God of justice; although he might need to punish his people for their sins, he would one day reward them with divine favor. Traditional Jewish belief expects that the Messiah, or Anointed One, will someday come and establish God's kingdom on earth. He will introduce an age of universal brotherhood in which all nations will acknowledge the one true God.

The Jews are people of the Book, and foremost among their sacred writings is the Hebrew Bible, consisting of the Five Books of Moses (the Torah), the books of the prophets, and other writings. The Torah is the source of Jewish Law. Over the centuries new experiences required new interpretation of the Law, which was accomplished by the oral Law, no less sacred than the written Law. Compilations of interpretation and commentary by rabbis (wise and learned teachers) were brought together to form the Talmud.

The destruction of their temple in Jerusalem by the Romans in 70 C.E. hastened the scattering of the Jews throughout the empire. Thereafter almost all Jews lived in the Diaspora (dispersion), without a homeland, a political community, or a national or religious center. In the fifth and sixth centuries the decline of the Sassanid Empire in Iran and the collapse of the Western Roman Empire undermined the institutions in which the Jews had found a stable way of life. In the seventh and eighth centuries the missionary zeal of the Christian church also brought hard times for the Jews in Western Europe and in the Byzantine East. In the West, their condition improved in the ninth century under Charlemagne and his successors.

Under Islam, Jews, like Christians, were tolerated as people of the Book. Jewish settlements flourished throughout the Islamic world. After the Islamic conquest of Spain in 711, the Jews there enjoyed an almost three-hundred-year-long golden age. During this period of extraordinary intellectual and cultural accomplishment, Jews practiced their religion openly and flourished economically.

The beginning of the Crusades in the eleventh century brought renewed persecution of the Jews in both the Christian and Islamic worlds. In the wake of the Christian reconquest of Spain, Jews were persecuted, killed, forced to convert, and finally expelled in 1492.

By the Middle Ages, Jews had divided into two distinct branches: those who lived in Christian Europe, called *Ashkenazim*, and those in the Muslim world, particularly Spain, called *Sephardim*. The Sephardim, with greater opportunities, developed a more secular life. Their language, Ladino, combined Hebrew and Spanish elements. The Ashkenazim, scattered in tiny communities, were forced to turn inward. Centered in German lands, they developed Yiddish, a combination of Hebrew and German. In time Yiddish became the language of most Jews in northern Europe, although the Torah was always read and studied in Hebrew.

Two of the dominant influences on modern Judaism have been Zionism—the effort to found a Jewish nation—and the death of some 6 million Jews in the Holocaust of World War II. Bolstered by the determination of Jews never again to find themselves victimized by the forces of anti-Semitism, the Zionist movement culminated in the founding of the state of Israel in 1948.

The adherents of Judaism are divided into several groups—Reform, Reconstruction, Conservative, and Orthodox—each holding significantly different views about the place of tradition and the traditional law in the modern world. All, however, would give assent to the saying of Hillel, the great Talmudic teacher of the first century B.C.E.: "What is distasteful to you do not to your fellow man. This is the Law, all the rest is commentary. Now go and study."

◆ **In what ways did Judaism differ from the polytheistic religions?**

◆ **What elements of the religion helped it persist through the ages?**

Persecution of the Jews. This 1900 painting, *After the Pogrom*, by the Polish painter Maurycy Minkowski, shows a group of women and children in the aftermath of a pogrom, an organized persecution of Jews that were once common in eastern Europe and Russia. Pogroms often became massacres. Encouraged by the Russian government, pogroms were particularly brutal in the late 19th and early 20th centuries. *Gift of Mr. and Mrs. Lester Klein/Jewish Museum/Art Resource, N.Y.*

The last five hundred years before the beginning of the common era and the two centuries that followed saw the appearance in Eurasia of great empires in Iran, India, and China, and of the Roman Empire in the Mediterranean. The growth of trade also facilitated cultural exchange in Africa. Although each arose in response to local conditions, they shared common features: centralized monarchies, large armies, well-organized bureaucracies, efficient taxation, and organized religions.

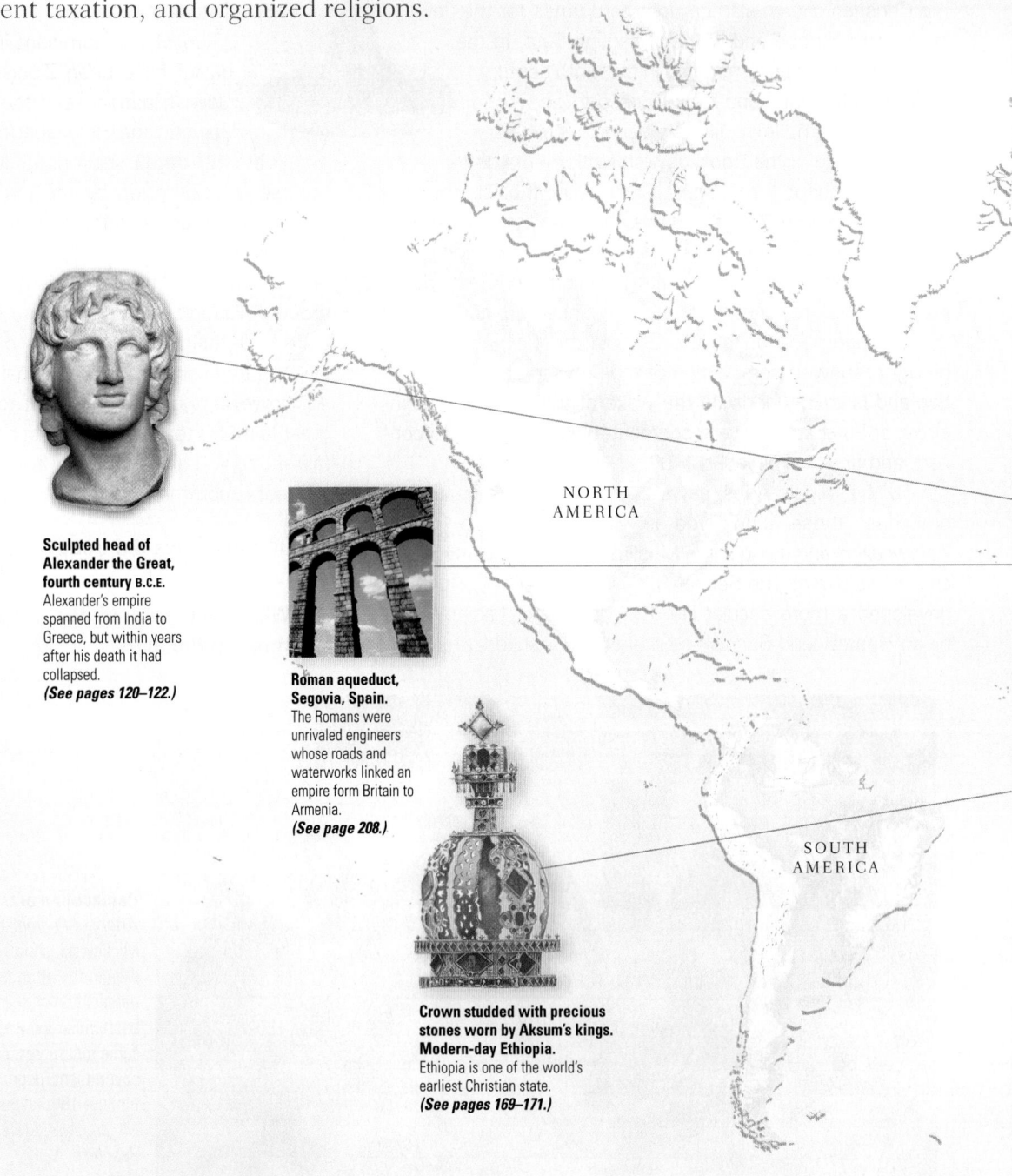

Sculpted head of Alexander the Great, fourth century B.C.E.
Alexander's empire spanned from India to Greece, but within years after his death it had collapsed.
(See pages 120–122.)

Roman aqueduct, Segovia, Spain.
The Romans were unrivaled engineers whose roads and waterworks linked an empire form Britain to Armenia.
(See page 208.)

Crown studded with precious stones worn by Aksum's kings. Modern-day Ethiopia.
Ethiopia is one of the world's earliest Christian state.
(See pages 169–171.)

NORTH
AMERICA

SOUTH
AMERICA

Pectoral, from the tomb of a Scythian at Ordzhonikidze, Caucasus Mountains, fourth century B.C.E.
Nomadic people such as the Scythians dominated the Eurasian steppes and challenged sedentary societies.
(See pages 148–150)

Seated Buddha, showing Greek influence.
Successors to Alexander the Great founded the Kingdom of Gandhara (present-day western Pakistan).
(See pages 147–148.)

Painted banner from the tomb of an aristocratic lady, Hunan Province, China, Han dynasty, ca. 160 B.C.E.
Although women rarely ruled in the ancient world, they could be conducts of power and authority, and their clothing and jewelry also became symbols of their husbands' wealth and influence.
(See pages 228–334).

ASIA

EUROPE

AFRICA

AUSTRALIA

Daric, a gold coin first minted under Darius I of Persia, fourth century B.C.E.
The Achaemenid empire of Persia commanded a central position along Eurasian trade routes.
(See pages 132–139).

Making Connections

1

What role did trade play in the foundation of early empires in Eurasia?

2

How did cultural exchange influence states and societies in the ancient world?

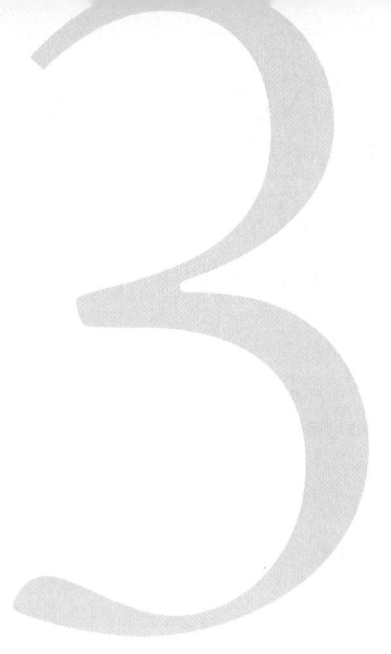

Greek and Hellenistic Civilization

- ◆ The Bronze Age on Crete and on the Mainland to ca. 1150 B.C.E.
- ◆ Greek "Middle Age" to ca. 750 B.C.E.
- ◆ The *Polis*
- ◆ Expansion of the Greek World
- ◆ Life in Archaic Greece
- ◆ Major City-States
- ◆ The Persian Wars
- ◆ Classical Greece
- ◆ Emergence of the Hellenistic World
- ◆ Hellenistic Culture

BOUT 2000 B.C.E., GREEK–SPEAKING PEOPLES SETTLED the lands surrounding the Aegean Sea at the eastern end of the Mediterranean, where they came in touch with the more advanced and earlier civilizations of the Near East, including the rich cultures of Egypt, Asia Minor, the Syria-Palestine region, and Mesopotamia. Adapting from these predecessors, the Greeks forged their own way of life, forming a set of ideas, values, and institutions that would spread far beyond their homeland. The foundation of this way of life was the independent city-state, or *polis* (plural *poleis*). In the eighth century B.C.E. the Greeks began to expand beyond the Aegean, establishing *poleis* on the shores of the Mediterranean Sea and, pushing on through the Dardanelles, placing many settlements on the coasts of the Black Sea in southern Russia and as far east as the approaches to the Caucasus Mountains. The center of Greek life, however, remained the Aegean Sea and the lands in and around it.

Early in the fifth century B.C.E., the great Persian Empire (see Chapter 4) threatened to extinguish

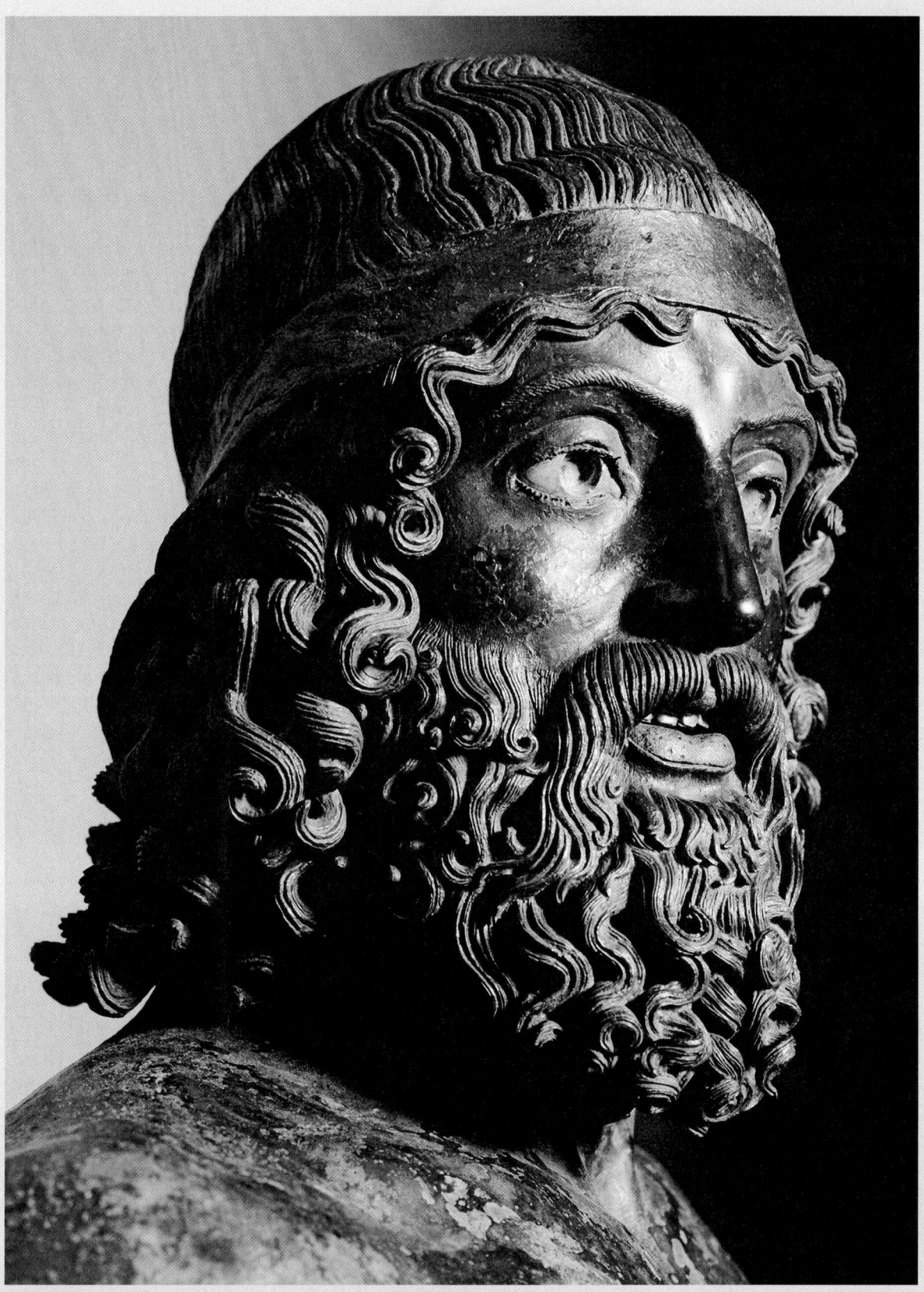

Bronze Statue. In 1972 this striking bronze statue was found off the coast of Riace, southern Italy. Possibly a votive statue from the sanctuary of Delphi in Greece, it may have been the work of the sculptor Phidias (ca. 490–430 B.C.E).

The Achievement of Greek and Hellenistic Civilization

Greece

Hellenic civilization lies at the root of Western civilization, and it has powerfully influenced the modern world. It emerged from the collapse of the Bronze Age Mycenaean civilization. However, it had little in common with Mycenaean civilization and the Bronze Age civilization of Crete or with other early civilizations—in Mesopotamia, Palestine-Syria, China, India, and elsewhere. These civilizations were characterized by strong, centralized monarchical governments ruling through tightly organized, large bureaucracies; hierarchical social systems; professional standing armies; and a regular system of taxation to support it all. To varying degrees, they all tended to cultural stability and uniformity. Hellenic civilization departed sharply from this pattern of development.

The crucial unit of the Greek way of life—forged in poverty and isolation following the Mycenaean collapse—was the *polis*, the Hellenic city-state. There were hundreds of *poleis*, ranging in size from a few thousand inhabitants to hundreds of thousands. Each evoked a kind of loyalty and attachment in its citizens that made it unthinkable for them to allow it to be part of a larger political unit. The result was a dynamic, many-faceted, competitive, sometimes chaotic society in which rivalry for excellence and victory had the highest value. This competitiveness led to almost constant warfare, but it also inspired the Greeks' extraordinary achievements in literature and art.

The Classical Age, which followed in the wake of the Greeks' heroic defense of their homeland against the armies of the powerful Persian Empire in the early sixth century B.C.E., was a period of unparalleled achievement. While the rest of the world's civilizations remained monarchical, hierarchical, command societies, Athens, the seat of an Aegean empire, developed democratic government to an extent not seen again until modern times. Athenian citizenship—although limited to adult males of native parentage—granted

Greek independence. The Greeks, however, led by the city-states of Sparta and Athens, won a remarkable victory over the Persians, securing for themselves a period of freedom and autonomy during which they realized their greatest political and cultural achievements. In Athens, especially, the victory produced a great sense of confidence and ambition. Sparta withdrew from active leadership against the Persians, leaving the Delian League—an alliance of Greek cities led by Athens—to fill the vacuum. The Delian League soon turned into the Athenian Empire.

At the same time that it tightened its hold over the Greek cities in and around the Aegean Sea, Athens developed an extraordinarily democratic constitution at home. Fears and jealousies of this new kind of state and empire created a split in the Greek world that led to a series of major wars.

These wars impoverished Greece and left it vulnerable to conquest. In 338 B.C.E. Philip of Macedon conquered the Greek states, ending the age of the *polis*. The conquests of Philip's son, Alexander, however, spread Greek culture far from its homeland, to Egypt and into Asia. Preserved and adapted by the Romans, Greek culture powerfully influenced the society of Western Europe in the Middle Ages and dominated the Byzantine Empire in the same period.

full and active participation in every decision of the state without regard to wealth or class.

Despite the unique aspects of its culture, however, Greece was also deeply influenced by its neighbors, especially in its earliest stages. The influences of Egyptian art, for example, on early Greek sculpture are evident in the style and stance of statues, jewelry, and figurines. The Greeks adopted the Phoenician alphabet as the basis for their own. These influences are not surprising, as the Minoans and Mycenaeans, whose legacies were of great importance to the evolution of classical Greek culture, were deeply enmeshed in Mediterranean trade. Seafaring and trade were equally fundamental to archaic and classical Greek society. Nonetheless, as in the case of political development and the unique *polis*-centered way of life, the Greeks adapted and made uniquely their own the artistic styles, alphabet, and intellectual ideas they borrowed from their neighbors.

Even more significant, however, was the influence of Greek culture in world history. The culture of democratic yet imperial Athens gave rise to the greatest artistic, literary, and philosophical achievements of the Greek classical period, achievements that became integral to Roman culture and, via the Greco-Roman cultural synthesis, a pillar of European civilization. The conquests of Alexander and the Hellenistic states that followed in their wake spread Greek culture over a remarkably wide area and made a significant and lasting impression on the conquered societies and their neighbors. The Seleucid dynasty ruled some parts of the Persian Empire for almost two centuries. As we will see in Chapter 4, a group of Greeks who broke away from the Seleucids carried Hellenistic culture even farther east, to the Indus valley in northwest India, creating the Indo-Greek Bactrian society. In art, Hellenistic influence reached even as far away as China. In the West, of course, the legacy of Hellenism was more substantial and enduring, powerfully shaping the culture of the Roman Empire that ultimately dominated the entire Mediterranean world.

Focus Questions

◆ Why are the achievements of Greek culture so fundamental to the development of Western civilization?

◆ In what ways was Greece influenced by neighboring civilizations? Which civilizations had the most influence on Greek culture, and why?

◆ How did the Hellenistic era differ from the Hellenic? What made Hellenistic culture more cosmopolitan than Hellenic culture?

The civilization emerging from the Greek and Roman experience spread across Europe and in time crossed the Atlantic to the Western Hemisphere. ■

The Bronze Age on Crete and on the Mainland to ca. 1150 B.C.E.

One source of Greek civilization was the culture of the large island of Crete in the Mediterranean. With Greece to the north, Egypt to the south, and Asia to the east, Crete was a cultural bridge between the older civilizations and the new one of the Greeks.

The Minoans

In the third and second millennia B.C.E., a Bronze Age civilization arose on Crete that powerfully influenced the islands of the Aegean and the mainland of Greece (see Map 3–1). This civilization is called **Minoan**, after Minos, the legendary king of Crete. Scholars have divided Minoan history into three major periods—Early, Middle, and Late Minoan—with some subdivisions. Dates for Bronze Age settlements on the Greek mainland, for which the term *Helladic* is used, are derived from the same chronological scheme.

The civilization of the Middle and Late Minoan periods in eastern and central Crete centered on several great palaces, including those at Phaestus, Haghia Triada, and,

Map 3–1. The Aegean Area in the Bronze Age. The Bronze Age in the Aegean area lasted from ca. 1900 to ca. 1100 B.C.E. Its culture on Crete is called Minoan and was at its height about 1900–1400 B.C.E. Bronze Age Helladic culture on the mainland flourished from ca. 1600 to 1200 B.C.E.

most important, Cnossus. The distinctive and striking art and architecture of these palaces reflect the influence of Syria, Asia Minor, and Egypt but have a uniquely Cretan style and quality. Minoan cities lacked strong defensive walls, suggesting that they were not built for defense.

Along with palaces, paintings, pottery, jewelry, and other valuable objects, excavations at Minoan sites have revealed clay writing tablets like those found in Mesopotamia. Tablets found at the royal palace at Cnossus, accidentally preserved when a great fire that destroyed the palace hardened them, have three distinct kinds of writing on them. One has proved to be an early form of Greek. The contents

of the tablets, primarily inventories, reveal an organization centered on the palace and ruled by a king who was supported by an extensive bureaucracy that kept remarkably detailed records. This sort of organization is typical of early civilizations in the Near East but, as we shall see, is nothing like that of the Greeks after the Bronze Age. Yet some of the inventories were written in a form of Greek. Why should Minoans, who were not Greek, write in a language not their own? This question raises the larger one of what the relationship was between Crete and the Greek mainland during the Bronze Age, leading us to an examination of mainland, or Helladic, culture.

A Minoan Fresco. Acrobats leaping over a charging bull, from the east wing of the Minoan-period palace at Cnossus on the island of Crete. It is not known whether such acrobatic displays were for entertainment or were part of some religious ritual. *Scala/Art Resource, N.Y.*

The Mycenaeans

In the third millennium B.C.E., most of the Greek mainland, including many of the sites of later Greek cities, was settled by people who used metal, built some impressive houses, and traded with Crete and the islands of the Aegean. The names they gave to places—names that were sometimes preserved by later invaders—make it clear that they were not Greeks and that they spoke a language that was not Indo-European (the language family to which Greek belongs).

Not long after 2000 B.C.E., many of the Early Helladic sites were destroyed by fire, some were abandoned, and still others appear to have yielded peacefully to an invading people. These signs of invasion, which mark the beginning of the Middle Helladic period, probably signal the arrival of the Greeks.

The shaft graves cut into the rock at the royal palace-fortress of Mycenae show that by the Late Helladic the conquerors had prospered and sometimes became very rich. At Mycenae the richest finds come from the period after 1600 B.C.E. The city's wealth and power reached their peak during this time, and the culture of the whole mainland during the Late Helladic period goes by the name **Mycenaean**. Greek invaders also established themselves in a still flourishing Crete, and there is good reason to believe that at the height of Mycenaean power (1400–1200 B.C.E.) Crete was part of the Mycenaean world.

Excavations at Mycenae, Pylos, and other Mycenaean sites reveal a culture influenced by, but very different from, Minoan culture. Mycenae and Pylos, like Cnossus, were built some distance from the sea. Defense against attack, however, was plainly foremost in the minds of the founders of the Mycenaean cities. Both were built on hills in positions commanding the neighboring territory. The Mycenaean people were warriors, as their art, architecture, and weapons reveal. All available evidence suggests that they were led by strong kings who, with their retainers, lived in palaces protected by defensive walls while most of the population lived outside the walls. Like the palaces of Crete, Mycenaean palaces were adorned with murals, but instead of the peaceful scenery and games depicted on the Cretan murals, the Mycenaean murals depicted scenes of war and boar hunting.

About 1500 B.C.E. *tholos* tombs—large, beehivelike chambers cut into hillsides—replaced the earlier, already impressive, shaft graves. The *tholos* tombs, built of enormous, well-cut, fitted stones, were approached through an unroofed passage cut horizontally into the side of the hill. The lintel block alone of one of these tombs weighs over a hundred tons. Only a strong king whose wealth was great, whose power was unquestioned, and who commanded the labor of many could undertake such a project. His wealth probably came from plundering raids, piracy, and trade. Some of this trade went westward to Italy and Sicily, but most of it was with the islands of the Aegean, the coastal towns of Asia Minor, and the cities of Syria, Egypt, and Crete. The Mycenaeans exchanged pottery, olive oil, and animal hides for jewels and other luxuries.

Further evidence that the Mycenaean world was made up of a number of independent, powerful, and well-organized monarchies comes from the many clay tablets with Mycenaean writing found throughout the mainland, and in particular from a large collection of tablets found at Pylos. These reveal a society similar to that of Cnossus on Crete. A king whose title was *wanax* held a royal domain, appointed officials, commanded servants, and kept a close record of what he owned and what was owed to him.

The Fall of Mycenaean Power At the height of their power (1400–1200 B.C.E.), the Mycenaeans were prosperous and active. They enlarged their cities, expanded their trade, and even established commercial colonies in the east. They are mentioned in the archives of the Hittite kings of Asia Minor. They are named as marauders of the Nile Delta in Egyptian records. Sometime about 1250 B.C.E. they probably sacked Troy, on the coast of northwestern Asia Minor, giving rise to the epic poems of Homer, the ***Iliad*** and the ***Odyssey***

(see Map 3–1). Around the year 1200 B.C.E., however, the Mycenaean world showed signs of great trouble; by 1100 B.C.E. it was gone: Its palaces were destroyed; many of its cities abandoned; and its art, its pattern of life, its system of writing buried and forgotten.

The reasons for the collapse of Mycenaean civilization are not known for certain. Greek legends attribute it to a new wave of Greek invaders, the Dorians, into the Greek mainland from the north. The legends identify the Dorians as a rude people who spoke a Greek dialect different from that of the Mycenaean peoples. The legend of "The Return of the Heraclidae," for example, recounts how the Dorians joined one of the Greek tribes, the Heraclidae, in an attack on the southern Greek peninsula of Peloponnesus, which was repulsed. A hundred years later they returned and gained full control.

Greek "Middle Age" to ca. 750 B.C.E.

The immediate effects of the Mycenaean collapse were disastrous. Palaces were destroyed, the kings and bureaucrats who managed them were swept away, and the wealth and organization that had supported artists and merchants evaporated. Greece entered a dark "middle age" about which little is known. Many villages were abandoned and never resettled. Some of their inhabitants probably turned to a nomadic life, and many undoubtedly perished.

Another result of the turmoil surrounding the Mycenaean collapse was the spread of the Greek people eastward from the mainland to the Aegean islands and the coast of Asia Minor. The Dorians, after occupying most of the Peloponnesus, swept across the Aegean to occupy the southern islands and the southern part of the Anatolian coast. Another group, known as the Ionians, spread from Attica and Euboea to the Cyclades and the central Anatolian coast, which came to be called Ionia.

These migrations made the Aegean a Greek lake. Trade with the old civilizations of the Near East, however, was virtually ended by the fall of the advanced Minoan and Mycenaean civilizations; nor was there much internal trade among the different parts of Greece. The Greeks were forced to turn inward, and each community was left largely to its own devices. The Near East was also in disarray at this time, and no great power arose to impose its ways and its will on the helpless people who lived about the Aegean. The Greeks were allowed time to recover from their disaster and to create their unique style of life.

Age of Homer

For a picture of society in these dark ages, the best source is Homer. His epic poems the *Iliad* and the *Odyssey* emerged from a tradition of oral poetry whose roots extend into the Mycenaean Age. Through the centuries bards had sung tales of the heroes who had fought at Troy, using verse arranged in rhythmic formulas to aid the memory. In this way some very old material was preserved into the eighth century B.C.E., when the poems attributed to Homer were finally written down.

Although the poems tell of the deeds of Mycenaean heroes, the world they describe seems to be that of the tenth and ninth centuries B.C.E. rather than the earlier Mycenaean. Homer's heroes are not buried in *tholos* tombs but are cremated; they worship gods in temples, whereas the Mycenaeans had no temples; and although they

The Trojan Horse, Depicted on a Seventh-Century B.C.E. Greek Vase. According to legend, the Greeks finally defeated Troy by pretending to abandon their siege of the city, leaving behind a giant wooden horse. Soldiers hidden in the horse opened the gates of the city to their compatriots after the Trojans had brought it within their walls. Note the wheels on the horse and the Greek soldiers who are hiding inside it holding weapons and armor. *Deutsches Archäologisches Institut, Athens: Mycon 70.*

have chariots, like the Mycenaeans, they do not know their proper use in warfare.

Government In the Homeric poems the power of the kings is much less than that of the Mycenaean rulers. Homeric kings were limited in their ability to make important decisions by the need to consult a council of nobles. The nobles felt free to discuss matters in vigorous language and in opposition to the king's wishes. In the *Iliad*, Achilles does not hesitate to address Agamemnon, the "most kingly" commander of the Trojan expedition, in these words: "you with a dog's face and a deer's heart." Such language may have been impolite, but it was not treasonous. The king could ignore the council's advice, but it was risky for him to do so.

The right to speak in council was limited to noblemen, but the common people could not be ignored. If a king planned a war or a major change of policy during a campaign, he would not fail to call the common soldiers to an assembly; they could listen and express their feelings by acclamation, though they could not take part in the debate. Homer shows that even in these early times the Greeks, unlike their predecessors and contemporaries, practiced some forms of limited constitutional government.

Society Despite the accommodation for noblemen and commoners, Homeric society was sharply divided into classes, the most important division being the one between nobles and everyone else. We do not know the origin of this distinction, but we cannot doubt that at this time Greek society was aristocratic. Birth determined noble status, and wealth usually accompanied it. Below the nobles were two other classes: *thetes* and slaves. *Thetes* worked the land, but we do not know whether they owned outright the land they worked (and so were free to sell it) or worked a hereditary plot that belonged to their clan (and was therefore not theirs to dispose of as they chose).

Those *thetes* who were landless laborers endured the worst condition in Homeric society. Slaves, at least, were attached to family households and so were protected and fed. In a world where membership in a settled group gave the only security, free laborers were desperately vulnerable. Slaves were few in number and were mostly women who served as maids and concubines. Some male slaves worked

as shepherds. Few, if any, worked in agriculture, which depended chiefly on free labor throughout Greek history.

Homeric Values The Homeric poems reflect an aristocratic code of values that powerfully influenced all future Greek thought. Homer was the schoolbook of the Greeks. They memorized his texts, settled diplomatic disputes by citing passages in them, and emulated the behavior and cherished the values they found in them. Those values were physical prowess; courage; and fierce protection of one's family, friends, and property, and above all, one's personal honor and reputation. Speed of foot, strength, and, most of all, excellence at fighting make a man great, and all these attributes serve to promote personal honor. The great hero of the *Iliad*, Achilles, refuses to fight in battle, allowing his fellow Greeks to be slain and almost defeated, because Agamemnon has wounded his honor by taking away his battle prize. He returns to the army not out of a sense of duty but to avenge the death of his dear friend Patroclus. Odysseus, the hero of the *Odyssey*, returning home after his wanderings, ruthlessly kills the many suitors who had, in his long absence, sought to marry his wife, Penelope; they had dishonored him by consuming his wealth, wooing Penelope, and scorning his son.

The highest virtue in Homeric society was *arete*—manliness, courage in the most general sense, and the excellence proper to a hero. This quality was best revealed in a contest, or *agon*. Homeric battles are not primarily group combats, but a series of individual contests between great champions. One of the prime forms of entertainment is the athletic contest, and the funeral of Patroclus is celebrated by such a contest.

Attic Wine Cup. Painted ca. 490 B.C.E., this cup depicts a scene from Homer's *Iliad*: Priam, King of Troy, begs the Greek hero Achilles to return the body of the old man's son, Hector, the great Trojan warrior. *Vase Painting. Classical Greek 5th B.C.E. Brygos Painter. Troyan King Priamus begs Achilles to give him the body of Hector, his slain son; Hector's body lies under Achilles' bed. Red-figured Attic skyphos from Caere, around 490 B.C.E. H: 25 cm. Inv. IV 3710. Kunsthistorisches Museum, Vienna, Austria. Erich Lessing/Art Resouce, N.Y.*

Husband and Wife in Homer's Troy   Document

Homer's poems provide a picture of early Greek ideas and institutions. In the *Iliad*, the poet tells of the return from battle of the Trojan hero Hector. He is greeted by his loving, "warm, generous wife," Andromache, who is carrying their baby son. Hector reaches for the boy, who is frightened to tears by the plume on his father's helmet. The father removes the helmet and prays that his son will grow up to be called "a better man than his father . . . a joy to his mother's heart." The rest of the scene reveals the character of their marriage and the division of responsibility between men and women in their world.

◆ How does Homer depict the feelings of husband and wife toward one another? What are the tasks of the aristocratic woman revealed in this passage? What can be learned about the attitude towards death and duty?

So Hector prayed and placed his son in the arms of his loving wife. Andromache pressed the child to her scented breast, smiling through her tears. Her husband noticed, and filled with pity now, Hector stroked her gently, trying to reassure her, repeating her name: "Andromache, dear one; why so desperate? Why so much grief for me? No man will hurl me down to Death, against my fate. And fate? No one alive has ever escaped it, neither brave man nor coward, I tell you—it's born with us the day that we are born. So please go home and tend to your own tasks, the distaff and the loom, and keep the women working hard as well. As for the fighting, men will see to that, all who were born in Troy but I most of all."

Hector aflash in arms took up his horsehair-crested helmet once again. And his loving wife went home, turning, glancing back again and again and weeping live warm tears. She quickly reached the sturdy house of Hector, man-killing Hector, and found her women gathered there inside and stirred them all to a high pitch of mourning. So in his house they raised the dirges for the dead, for Hector still alive, his people were so convinced that never again would he come home from battle, never escape the Argives' rage and bloody hands.

The central ethical idea in Homer can be found in the instructions that the father of Achilles gives to his son when he sends him off to fight at Troy: "Always be the best and distinguished above others." The father of another Homeric hero has given his son exactly the same orders and has added to them the injunction: "Do not bring shame on the family of your fathers who were by far the best in Ephyre and in wide Lycia." Here in a nutshell are the chief values of the aristocrats of Homer's world: to vie for individual supremacy in *arete* and to defend and increase the honor of the family. These would remain prominent aristocratic values long after Homeric society was only a memory. (See Document, "Husband and Wife in Homer's Troy.")

The *Polis*

The characteristic Greek institution was the *polis*. The common translation of that word as "city-state" is misleading, for it says both too much and too little. All Greek *poleis* began as little more than agricultural villages or towns, and many stayed that way, so the word *city* is inappropriate. All of them were states, in the sense of being independent political units, but they were much more than that. The *polis* was thought of as a community of relatives; all its citizens, who were theoretically descended from a common ancestor, belonged to subgroups such as fighting brotherhoods (*phratries*), clans, and tribes. They worshiped the gods in common ceremonies.

Aristotle (see Chapter 2) argued that the *polis* was a natural growth and that the human being is by nature "an animal who lives in a *polis*." Humans alone have the power of speech and from it derive the ability to distinguish good from bad and right from wrong, "and the sharing of these things is what makes a household and a *polis*." Therefore, humans who are incapable of sharing these things or who are so self-sufficient that they have no need of them are not humans at all, but either wild beasts or gods. Without law and justice humans are the worst and most dangerous of the animals. With them they can be the best, and justice exists only in the *polis*. These high claims were made in the fourth century B.C.E., hundreds of years after the *polis* came into existence, but they accurately reflect an attitude that was present from the first.

Development of the *Polis*

Originally the word *polis* referred only to a citadel, an elevated, defensible rock to which the farmers of the neighboring area could retreat in case of attack. The **Acropolis** in Athens and the hill called Acrocorinth in Corinth are examples. For some time such high places and the adjacent farms made up the *polis*. The towns grew gradually and without planning, as their narrow, winding, and disorderly streets show. For centuries they had no walls. Unlike the city-states of the Near East, they were not placed for commercial convenience on rivers or the sea. Nor did they grow up around a temple to serve the needs of priests and to benefit from the needs of worshipers. The availability of farmland and of a natural fortress determined their location. They were placed either well inland or far enough away from the sea to avoid piratical raids. Only later and gradually did the **agora**—a marketplace and civic center—appear within the *polis*. The *agora* was to become the heart of the Greeks' remarkable social life, distinguished by conversation and argument carried on in the open air.

Some *poleis* probably came into existence early in the eighth century B.C.E. The institution was certainly common by the middle of that century, for all the colonies that were established by the Greeks in the years after 750 B.C.E. took the form of the *polis*. Once the new institution had been fully established, true monarchy disappeared. In some places kings survived, but they were almost always only ceremonial figures without power. The original form of the *polis* was an aristocratic republic dominated by the nobility through its council of nobles and its monopoly of the magistracies.

The Hoplite Phalanx

Crucial to the development of the *polis* was a new military strategy. In earlier times the brunt of fighting had been carried on by small troops of cavalry and individual "champions" who first threw their spears and then came to close quarters with swords. Toward the end of the eighth century B.C.E., however, the **hoplite phalanx** came into being and remained the basis of Greek warfare thereafter.

The hoplite was a heavily armed infantryman who fought with a spear and a large shield. These soldiers were arrayed in close order, usually at least eight ranks

deep, to form a phalanx. As long as the hoplites fought bravely and held their ground, there would be few casualties and no defeat, but if they gave way, the result was usually a rout. All depended on the discipline, strength, and courage of the individual soldier. At its best, the phalanx could withstand cavalry charges and defeat infantries not as well protected or disciplined. Until defeated by the Roman legion, it was the dominant military force in the eastern Mediterranean.

The usual hoplite battle in Greece was between the armies of two *poleis* quarreling over a piece of land. One army invaded the territory of the other when its crops were almost ready for harvest. The defending army had no choice but to protect the fields. If the defenders were beaten, the fields were captured or destroyed and the people of the *polis* might starve. This style of fighting produced a single decisive battle that reduced the time lost in fighting other kinds of warfare; it spared the houses, livestock, and other capital of the farmer-soldiers who made up the phalanx, and it minimized casualties. It perfectly suited the farmer-soldier-citizen who was the backbone of the *polis* and, by keeping wars short and limiting their destructiveness and expense, it helped the *polis* prosper.

The phalanx and the *polis* arose together, and both heralded the decline of kings. The immediate beneficiaries of the royal decline were aristocrats, but because the phalanx, and with it the *polis*, depended on farmers working small holdings as well as aristocrats, the wishes of the small farmers could not for long be wholly ignored. The rise of the hoplite phalanx created a bond between aristocrats and family farmers who fought in it side by side, and this bond helps explain why class conflicts were muted for some time in Greece. It also guaranteed, however, that the aristocrats, who dominated the *poleis* at first, would not always be unchallenged.

Expansion of the Greek World

From the middle of the eighth century B.C.E. until well into the sixth, the Greeks vastly expanded the territory they controlled, their wealth, and their contacts with other peoples. A burst of colonizing activity placed *poleis* from Spain to the Black Sea. A century earlier a few Greeks had established trading posts in Syria. There they had learned new techniques in art and crafts and much more from the older civilizations of the Near East. About 750 B.C.E. they borrowed a writing system from one of the Semitic scripts and added vowels to create the first true alphabet. The new Greek alphabet was easier to learn than any earlier writing system and made possible a widely literate society.

To explore this map further, go to http://www.prenhall.com/craig_maps

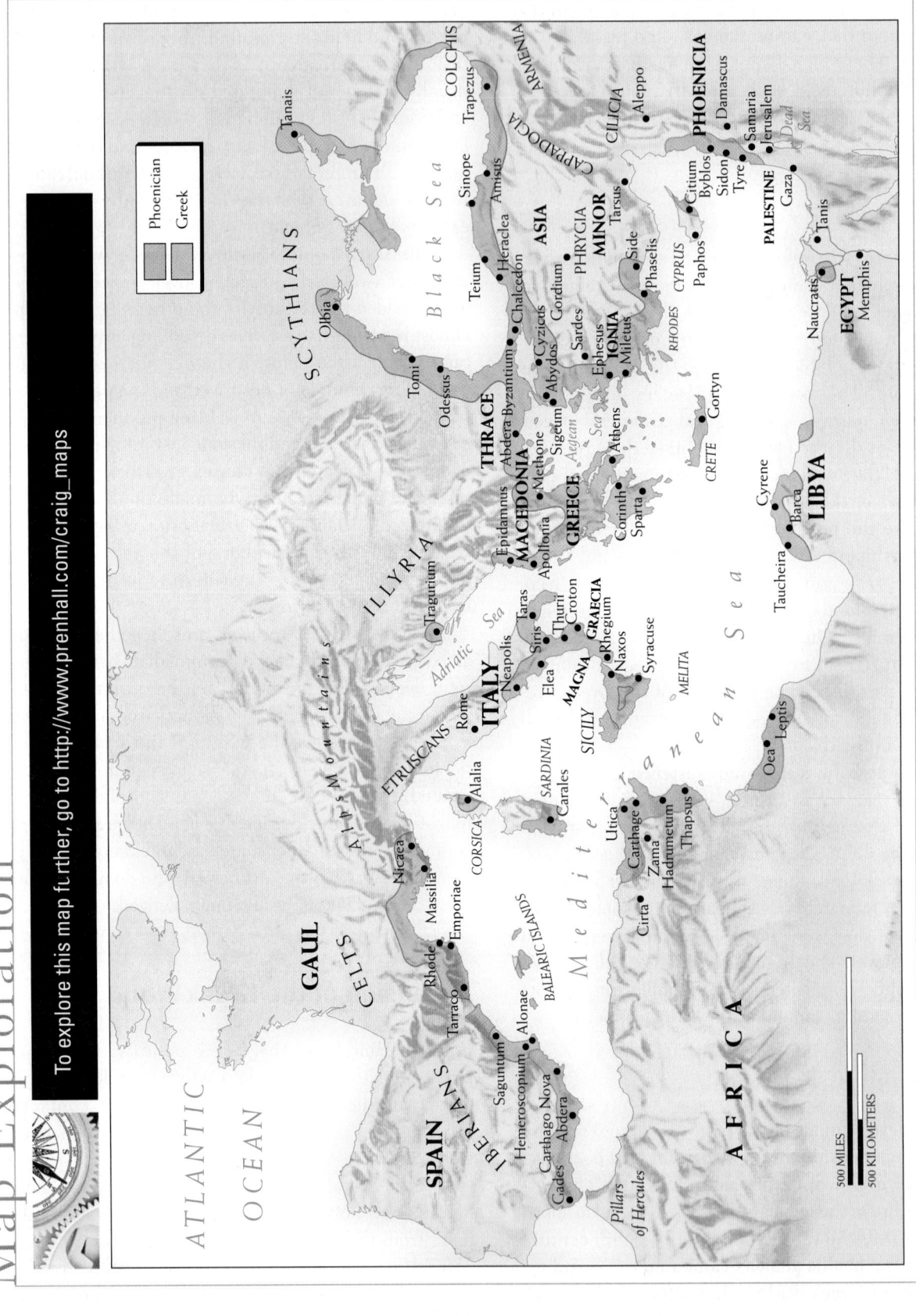

Map 3–2. Phoenician and Greek Colonization. Most of the coastline of the Mediterranean and Black Seas was populated by Greek or Phoenician colonies. The Phoenicians were a commercial people who planted their colonies in North Africa, Spain, Sicily, and Sardinia, chiefly in the ninth century B.C.E. The height of Greek colonization came later, between ca. 750 and 550 B.C.E.

Greek Colonies

Syria and its neighboring territory were too strong to penetrate, so the Greeks settled the sparsely populated southern coast of Macedonia and the Chalcidian peninsula (see Map 3–2). Southern Italy and eastern Sicily were even more inviting areas. Before long, there were so many Greek colonies in Italy and Sicily that the Romans called the whole region **Magna Graecia** ("Great Greece"). The Greeks also put colonies in Spain and southern France. In the seventh century B.C.E. Greek colonists settled the coasts of the northeastern Mediterranean, the Black Sea, and the straits connecting them. At about the same time they established settlements on the eastern part of the north African coast. The Greeks now had outposts throughout the Mediterranean world. Most colonies, although independent, were friendly with their mother cities. Each might ask the other for aid in time of trouble and expect to receive a friendly hearing, although neither was obliged to help.

Colonization had a powerful influence on Greek life. By relieving the pressure and land hunger of a growing population, it provided a safety valve that allowed the *poleis* to escape civil wars. By confronting them with the differences between themselves and the new peoples they met, colonization gave the Greeks a sense of cultural identity and fostered a **Panhellenic** ("all-Greek") spirit that led to the establishment of a number of common religious festivals. The most important of these were at Olympia, Delphi, Corinth, and Nemea.

Colonization also encouraged trade and industry. The influx of new wealth from abroad and the increased demand for goods from the homeland stimulated a more intensive use of the land and an emphasis on crops for export, chiefly the olive and the wine grape. The manufacture of pottery, tools, weapons, and fine metalwork as well as perfumed oil, the soap of the ancient Mediterranean world, was likewise encouraged. New opportunities allowed some men, sometimes outside the nobility, to become wealthy and important. These newly enriched became a troublesome element in the aristocratic *poleis*, for, although increasingly important in the life of their states, they were barred from political power, religious privileges, and social acceptance by the ruling aristocrats. These conditions soon created a crisis in many states.

The Tyrants (CA. 700–500 B.C.E.)

In some cities, perhaps only a small percentage of the more than one thousand Greek *poleis*, the crisis produced by new economic and social conditions led to or intensified factional divisions within the ruling aristocracy. In the years between 700 and 500 B.C.E., the result was often the establishment of a tyranny.

The Rise of Tyranny A tyrant was a monarch who had gained power in an unorthodox but not necessarily wicked way and who exercised a strong one-man rule that might well be beneficent and popular.

The founding tyrant was usually a member of the ruling aristocracy who either had a personal grievance or led an unsuccessful faction. He often rose to power because of his military ability and support from the hoplites. He generally had the support of the politically powerless newly wealthy and the poor farmers. When he took power he often expelled many of his aristocratic opponents and divided at least some of their land among his supporters. He pleased his commercial and industrial supporters by destroying the privileges of the old aristocracy and by fostering trade and colonization.

The tyrants presided over a period of population growth that saw an increase especially in the number of city dwellers. They responded with a program of public works that included the improvement of drainage systems, care for the water supply, the construction and organization of marketplaces, the building and strengthening of city walls, and the erection of temples. They introduced new local festivals and elaborated the old ones. They were active in the patronage of the arts, supporting poets and artisans with gratifying results. All this activity contributed to the tyrant's popularity, to the prosperity of his city, and to his self-esteem.

In most cases the tyrant's rule was secured by a personal bodyguard and mercenary soldiers. An armed citizenry,

Chronology

Rise of Greece

ca. 2900–1150 B.C.E.	Minoan period
ca. 1900 B.C.E.	Probable date of the arrival of the Greeks on the mainland
ca. 1600–1150 B.C.E.	Mycenaean period
ca. 1250 B.C.E.	Sack of Troy (?)
ca. 1200–1150 B.C.E.	Destruction of Mycenaean centers in Greece
ca. 1100–750 B.C.E.	Dark ages
ca. 750–500 B.C.E.	Major period of Greek colonization
ca. 725 B.C.E.	Probable date of Homer
ca. 700 B.C.E.	Probable date of Hesiod
ca. 700–500 B.C.E.	Major period of Greek tyranny

necessary for an aggressive foreign policy, would have been dangerous, so the tyrants usually pursued a program of peaceful alliances with other tyrants abroad and avoided war.

The End of the Tyrants By the end of the sixth century B.C.E. tyranny had disappeared from the Greek states and did not return in the same form or for the same reasons. The last tyrants were universally hated for their cruelty and repressiveness. They left bitter memories in their own states and became objects of fear and hatred everywhere.

Besides the outrages committed by individual tyrants, there was something about the very concept of tyranny that was inimical to the idea of the *polis*. The notion of the *polis* as a community to which every member must be responsible, the connection of justice with that community, and the natural aristocratic hatred of monarchy all made tyranny seem alien and offensive. The rule of a tyrant, however beneficent, was arbitrary and unpredictable. Tyranny came into being in defiance of tradition and law, and the tyrant governed without either. He was not answerable in any way to his fellow citizens.

From a longer perspective, however, the tyrants made important contributions to the development of Greek civilization. They encouraged economic changes that helped secure the future prosperity of Greece. They increased communication with the rest of the Mediterranean world and cultivated the crafts and technology, as well as the arts and literature. Most important of all, they broke the grip of the aristocracy and put the productive powers of the most active and talented of its citizens fully at the service of the *polis*.

Life in Archaic Greece

Society

As the dark ages came to an end, the features that would distinguish Greek society thereafter took shape. The role of the artisan and the merchant grew more important as contact with the non-Greek world became easier, but the great majority of people continued to make their living from the land. Wealthy aristocrats with large estates, powerful households, families, and clans, however, led very different lives from those of the poorer peasants and the independent farmers who had smaller and less fertile fields.

Farmers Ordinary country people rarely leave a record of their thoughts or activities, and we have no such record from ancient Greece. The poet Hesiod (ca. 700 B.C.E.), however, was certainly no aristocrat. He presented himself as a small farmer, and his *Works and Days* gives some idea of the life of such a farmer. (See Document, "Hesiod's Farmer's Almanac.") The crops included grain, chiefly barley but also wheat; grapes for the making of wine; olives for food, but

mainly for oil, used for cooking, lighting, and washing; green vegetables, especially beans; and some fruit. Sheep and goats provided milk and cheese. The Homeric heroes had great herds of cattle and ate lots of meat, but by Hesiod's time land fertile enough to provide fodder for cattle was needed to grow grain. He and small farmers like him tasted meat chiefly from sacrificial animals at festivals.

These farmers worked hard to make a living. Although Hesiod had the help of oxen and mules and one or two hired helpers for occasional labor, his life was one of continual toil. The hardest work came in October, at the start of the rainy season, the time for the first plowing. The plow was light and easily broken, and the work of forcing the iron tip into the earth was backbreaking, even with the help of a team of oxen. For the less fortunate farmer, the cry of the crane that announced the time of year to plow "bites the heart of the man without oxen." Autumn and winter were the time for cutting wood, building wagons, and making tools. Late winter was the time to tend to the vines, May the time to harvest the grain, July to winnow and store it. Only at the height of summer's heat did Hesiod allow for rest, but when September came it was time to harvest the grapes. No sooner was that task done than the cycle started again. The work went on under the burning sun and in the freezing cold.

Hesiod wrote nothing of pleasure or entertainment, but less austere farmers than he gathered at the blacksmith's shop for warmth and companionship in winter, and even he must have taken part in religious rites and festivals that were accompanied by some kind of entertainment. Nonetheless, the lives of ordinary farmers were certainly hard and their pleasures few.

Aristocrats Most aristocrats were rich enough to employ many hired laborers, sometimes sharecroppers and sometimes even slaves, to work their extensive lands and were therefore able to enjoy leisure for other activities. The center of aristocratic social life was the drinking party, or *symposion*. This activity was not a mere drinking bout meant to remove inhibitions and produce oblivion. The Greeks, in fact, almost always mixed their wine with water, and one of the goals of the participants was to drink as much as the others without becoming drunk.

The *symposion* was a carefully organized occasion, with a "king" chosen to set the order of events and to determine that night's mixture of wine and water. Only men took part, and they ate and drank as they reclined on couches along the walls of the room. The sessions began with prayers and libations to the gods. Usually there were games, such as dice or *kottabos*, in which wine was flicked from the cups at different targets. Sometimes dancing girls or flute girls offered entertainment. Frequently the participants provided their own amusements with songs, poetry, or even philosophical disputes. Characteristically, these took the form of contests, with some kind of prize for the winner, for aristocratic values continued to emphasize competition and the need to excel, whatever the arena.

This aspect of aristocratic life appears in the athletic contests that became widespread early in the sixth century B.C.E. The games included running events; the long jump; the discus and javelin throws; the *pentathlon*, which included all of these; box-

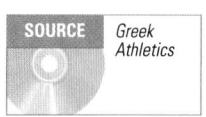 SOURCE *Greek Athletics*

ing; wrestling; and the chariot race. Only the rich could afford to raise, train, and race horses, so the chariot race was a special preserve of aristocracy. Wrestling was also especially favored by the nobility, and the *palaestra* where they practiced became an important social center for the aristocracy. The contrast between the hard, drab life of the peasants and the leisured and lively one of the aristocrats could hardly be greater.

Religion

Like most ancient peoples, the Greeks were polytheists, and religion played an important part in their lives. A great part of Greek art and literature was closely connected with religion, as was the life of the *polis* in general.

The Greek pantheon consisted of the twelve gods who lived on Mount Olympus. These were

- Zeus, the father of the gods
- Hera, his wife
- Zeus's siblings:
  Poseidon, his brother, god of the seas and earthquakes
  Hestia, his sister, goddess of the hearth
  Demeter, his sister, goddess of agriculture and marriage
- Zeus's children:
  Aphrodite, goddess of love and beauty
  Apollo, god of the sun, music, poetry, and prophecy
  Ares, god of war
  Artemis, goddess of the moon and the hunt
  Athena, goddess of wisdom and the arts
  Hephaestus, god of fire and metallurgy
- Hermes, messenger of the gods, connected with commerce and cunning

Attic Jar. From late in the sixth century B.C.E. this jar shows how olives, one of Athens's most important crops, were harvested. *Courtesy of the Trustees of the British Museum.*

The gods were seen as behaving very much as mortal humans behaved, with all the human foibles, except that they were superhuman in these as well as in their strength and immortality. On the other hand, Zeus, at least, was seen as a source of human justice, and even the Olympians were understood to be subordinate to the Fates. Each *polis* had one of the Olympians as its guardian deity and worshiped that god in its own special way, but all the gods were Panhellenic. In the eighth and seventh centuries B.C.E. common shrines were established at Olympia and at Nemea for the worship of Zeus, at Delphi for Apollo, and at the Isthmus of Corinth for Poseidon. Each held athletic contests in honor of its deity, to which all Greeks were invited and for which a sacred truce was declared.

The worship of these deities did not involve great emotion. Worshipers offered a god prayer, libations, and gifts in hopes of protection and favors. Greek religion offered no hope of immortality for the average human and little moral teaching. Most Greeks seem to have held to the common-sense notion that justice lay in paying one's debts. They thought that civic virtue consisted of worshiping the state deities in the traditional way, performing required public services, and fighting in defense of the state. To them, private morality meant to do good to one's friends and harm to one's enemies.

In the sixth century B.C.E., the influence of the cult of Apollo at Delphi and of his oracle there became very great. The oracle was the most important of several that helped satisfy human craving for a clue to the future. The priests of Apollo preached moderation; their advice was exemplified in the two famous sayings identified with Apollo: "Know thyself" and "Nothing in excess." Humans need self-control (*sophrosyne*). Its opposite is arrogance (*hubris*), which is brought on by excessive wealth or good fortune. *Hubris* leads to moral blindness and finally to divine vengeance. This theme of moderation and the dire consequences of its absence was central to Greek popular morality and appears frequently in Greek literature.

The somewhat cold religion of the Olympian gods and of the cult of Apollo did little to assuage human fears, hopes,

Hesiod's Farmer's Almanac

Document

Hesiod was a farmer and poet who lived in a village in Greece about 700 B.C.E. His poem *Works and Days* contains wisdom on several subjects, but its final section amounts to a farmer's almanac, taking readers through the year and advising them on just when each activity is demanded. Hesiod painted a picture of a very hard life for Greek farmers. In the following passage he talks about one of the few times when the farmer is free from toil, during the hottest part of summer.

◆ What might be Hesiod's purposes in writing this poem? What can be learned from this passage about the character of Greek farming? How did it differ from other modes of agriculture? What are the major virtues Hesiod associates with farming? How do they compare with the virtues celebrated by Homer?

But when House-on-Back, the snail, crawls from the
  ground up
the plants, escaping the Pleiades, it's no longer time for
  vine-digging;
time rather to put an edge to your sickles, and rout out
  your helpers.
Keep away from sitting in the shade or lying in bed till the
  sun's up
in the time of the harvest, when the sunshine scorches
  your skin dry.
This is the season to push work and bring home your
  harvest;
get up with the first light so you'll have enough to
  live on.
Dawn takes away from work a third part of the work's
  measure.
Dawn sets a man well along on his journey, in his work
  also,
Dawn, who when she shows, has numerous people
  going their ways; Dawn who puts the yoke upon many
  oxen.
But when the artichoke is in flower, and the clamorous
  cricket
sitting in his tree lets go his vociferous singing, that
  issues
from the beating of his wings, in the exhausting season
  of summer,

then is when goats are at their fattest, when the wine
  tastes best,
women are most lascivious, but the men's strength fails
  them
most, for the star Seirios shrivels them, knees and heads
  alike,
and the skin is all dried out in the heat; then, at that
  season,
one might have the shadow under the rock, and the wine
  of Biblis,
a curd cake, and all the milk that the goats can give you,
the meat of a heifer, bred in the woods, who has never
  borne a calf,
and of baby kids also. Then, too, one can sit in the shadow
and drink the bright-shining wine, his heart satiated with
  eating
and face turned in the direction where Zephyros blows
  briskly,
make three libations of water from a spring that keeps
  running forever
and has no mud in it; and pour wine for the fourth
  libation.

_____

Hesiod, *Works and Days*, trans. by Richmond Lattimore. Copyright © 1959, University of Michigan Press, Ann Arbor, MI, pp. 87, 89. Reprinted by permission.

and passions. For these needs, the Greeks turned to other deities and rites. Of them, the most popular was Dionysus, a god of nature and fertility, of the grapevine and drunkenness and sexual abandon. In some of his rites the god was followed by maenads, female devotees who cavorted by night, ate raw flesh, and were reputed to tear to pieces any creature they came across.

Poetry

The great changes sweeping through the Greek world were also reflected in the poetry of the sixth century B.C.E. The lyric style, whether sung by a chorus or one singer, predominated. Sappho of Lesbos, Anacreon of Teos, and Simonides of Cous composed personal poetry, often speaking of the pleasure and agony of love. Alcaeus of Mytilene, an aristocrat driven from his city by a tyrant, wrote bitter invective.

Perhaps the most interesting poet of the century from a political point of view was Theognis of Megara. An aristocrat who lived through a tyranny, an unusually chaotic and violent democracy, and an oligarchy that restored order but ended the rule of the old aristocracy, Theognis was the spokesman for the old, defeated aristocracy of birth. He divided everyone into two classes, the noble and the base; the former were good, the latter bad. Those nobly born must associate only with others like themselves if they were to preserve their virtue; if they mingled with the base, they became base. Those born base, on the other hand, could never become noble. Only nobles could aspire to virtue, and only nobles possessed the critical moral and intellectual qualities: respect (or honor) and judgment. These qualities could not be taught; they were innate. Even so, nobles had to guard themselves against corruption by wealth or by mingling with the base. Intermarriage between the noble and the base was especially condemned. These were the ideas of the unreconstructed nobility, whose power had been destroyed or reduced in most Greek states by this time. They remained alive in aristocratic hearts throughout the next century and greatly influenced later thinkers, including Plato.

Major City-States

Generalization about the *polis* becomes difficult not long after its appearance, for although the states had much in common, some of them developed in unique ways. Sparta and Athens, which became the two most powerful Greek states, had especially unusual histories.

Sparta

Sparta (see Map 3–3) began to assume its special character about 725 B.C.E., when population pressure and land hunger led the Spartans to conquer their western neighbor Messenia in the First Messenian War. The Spartans now had as

The God Dionysus Dances with Two Female Followers. The vase was painted in the sixth century B.C.E. *Bibliothèque Nationale de France, Paris The Parthenon.*

much land as they would ever need, and because they reduced the Messenians to **Helots**, or serfs, they no longer had to work this land themselves. When the Helots—assisted by Argos and some other Peloponnesian cities—rebelled in the Second Messenian War in about 650 B.C.E., the Spartans faced a turning point. The long and bitter war, which at one point threatened their city's existence, made it clear to the Spartans that they could not expect to keep down the Helots, who outnumbered them perhaps ten to one, and maintain the free-and-easy habits typical of most Greeks. They thus chose to introduce fundamental reforms that turned their city forever after into a military academy and camp.

Society The new system, which emerged late in the sixth century B.C.E., exerted control over each Spartan from birth, when officials of the state decided which infants, male and female, were physically fit to survive. At age seven, the Spartan boy was taken from his mother and turned over to young instructors who trained him in athletics and the military arts and taught him to endure privation, to bear physical pain, and to live off the country, by theft if necessary. The Spartan youth was enrolled in the army at twenty and lived in barracks with his companions until he was thirty. He could marry but could visit his wife only infrequently and by stealth. At thirty he became a full citizen, an "equal," and was allowed to live in his own house with his wife, although he took his meals at a public mess in the company of fifteen comrades. His food, a simple diet without much meat or wine, was provided by his own plot of land, which was worked by Helots. Only when he reached sixty could the Spartan retire from military service to his home and family.

Spartan girls did not receive military training, but they were given gymnastic training and were permitted greater freedom than among other Greeks. Like boys, they too were

Map 3–3.   The Peloponnesus. Sparta's region, Laconia, was in the Peloponnesus. Nearby states were members of the Peloponnesian League under Sparta's leadership.

indoctrinated with the idea of service to Sparta. The entire system was designed to change the natural feelings of devotion to family into a more powerful commitment to the *polis*. Privacy, luxury, and even comfort were sacrificed to the purpose of producing soldiers whose physical prowess, training, and discipline made them the best in the world. Nothing that might turn the mind away from duty was permitted. The very use of coins was forbidden for its potential to corrupt. Neither family nor money was allowed to interfere with the only ambition permitted to a Spartan male: to win glory and respect by bravery in war.

Government   In a mixture of monarchy, oligarchy, and democracy, Sparta was governed by two kings, a council of elders, and an assembly. The power of the kings was limited by law and by the rivalry that usually prevailed between them. The council of elders—twenty-eight men over sixty who were elected for life—had important judicial functions,

sitting as a court in cases involving the kings. It was also consulted before any proposal was put before the assembly. In a traditional society like Sparta's, it must have had considerable influence. The assembly, which consisted of all males over thirty, was theoretically the final authority. In practice, however, it served only to ratify the decisions of magistrates, elders, and kings, or to decide between the positions of these leading figures.

Sparta also had another, unique, governmental institution, the board of ephors. This consisted of five men elected annually by the assembly. Apparently originally intended to check the power of the kings, the ephors gradually acquired other important functions. They controlled foreign policy, oversaw the generalship of the kings on campaign, presided at the assembly, and guarded against rebellion by the Helots.

Suppression of the Helots required all the effort and energy the Spartans had. They could not expand their borders, but at the same time they could not allow unruly independent neighbors to sow unrest among the Helots. Thus when the Spartans defeated Tegea, their northern neighbor, they imposed an unusual peace, allowing the Tegeans to keep their land and their freedom in exchange for following Sparta's lead in foreign affairs and supplying Sparta with a fixed number of troops on demand. As Sparta imposed this model on other neighbors, it emerged as the leader of an alliance— known to scholars today as the Peloponnesian League—that included every Peloponnesian state except Argos. This alliance provided the Spartans with the security they needed, and made Sparta the most powerful *polis* in Greece. Thanks to Sparta and the league, by 500 B.C.E. the Greeks had a force capable of facing mighty threats from abroad.

Athens

In the seventh century B.C.E. Athens and the region of Attica (see Map 3–4) constituted a typical aristocratic *polis*. Aristocrats held the most and best land and dominated religious and political life. There was no written law. The state was governed by the **Areopagus**, a council of nobles deriving its name from the hill where it held its sessions. Annually the council elected nine magistrates, called *archons*, who joined the Areopagus after their year in office. The Areopagus, however, not the archons, was the true master of the state. A broad-based citizens' assembly, which had little power, represented the four tribes into which Attica's inhabitants were traditionally divided.

Pressure for Change In the seventh century B.C.E., quarrels within the nobility and the beginnings of an agrarian crisis dis-

Spartan Warrior. A bronze statuette from Corinth showing a warrior holding a Boeotian Shield ca. 500 B.C.E.

turbed the peaceful life of Athens. Many Athenians made their living from family farms, apparently planting wheat, the staple crop, year after year without rotating fields or using enough fertilizer. A shift to more intensive agricultural techniques and the cultivation of trees and vines, which required capital, forced some of the less successful farmers to borrow from wealthy neighbors. As their troubles grew, debtors pledged their wives, their children, and themselves as surety for new loans. Inevitably, many defaulted and were enslaved. Some were even sold abroad. Revolutionary pressures grew among the poor, who began to demand the abolition of debt and a redistribution of the land.

Reforms of Solon In 594 B.C.E., as tradition has it, the Athenians elected Solon (ca. 639–559 B.C.E.) as the only archon, with extraordinary powers to legislate and revise Athens's governing institutions. In a program called the "shaking off of burdens," Solon immediately canceled current debts and forbade future loans secured by the person of the borrower. He helped bring back many Athenians enslaved abroad and freed those in Athens enslaved for debt. Solon did not redistribute land and failed in the short run to end Athens's economic crisis. Some of his actions, however, were profoundly successful in the long run. He encouraged commerce and turned Athens in the direction that would lead it to great prosperity in the fifth century. He forbade the export of wheat, initially making wheat more available in Attica, but he also encouraged the export of olive oil and wine. As a result, by the fifth century B.C.E. much Athenian land was diverted from grain production to the cultivation of olive

Map 3–4. **Attica and Vicinity.** Citizens of all towns in Attica were also citizens of Athens.

trees and vines as cash crops, making Athens dependent on imported wheat. Solon also encouraged industry by offering citizenship to foreign artisans, stimulating the development of outstanding pottery in Attica in the sixth century.

Solon also significantly changed the way Athens was governed. He expanded citizenship—previously limited to adult males whose fathers were citizens—to include immigrant artisans and merchants, and divided the citizenry into four classes on the basis of wealth. Only men of the wealthiest two classes could be archons and sit on the Areopagus. Men of the third class could serve as hoplites and on a council of four hundred chosen by the assembly of all male citizens. The fourth class, the *thetes*, voted in the assembly and also sat on a new court of appeals that would hear almost all cases in Athens by the fifth century B.C.E.

Pisistratus the Tyrant Despite Solon's reforms, Athens succumbed to factional strife that ended when the leader of one faction, Pisistratus (605?–527 B.C.E.), a nobleman and mili-

tary hero, seized power firmly in 546 B.C.E. with the help of mercenary soldiers and made himself the city's first tyrant.

Pisistratus sought to increase the power of the central government at the expense of the nobles. To undermine their authority in the countryside, he sent out circuit judges to hear local cases. To fix attention on the capital, he engaged in great programs of public works, urban improvement, and religious piety. He built temples, expanded and improved religious centers, introduced new religious festivals, and increased the public appeal of traditional festivals. His reconstruction of Athens's agora (marketplace) helped transform it into the center of public life. To add cultural luster to his court he supported poets and artists. Throughout his rule, Pisistratus made no formal change in the institutions of government. Assembly, councils, and courts met; magistrates and councils were elected; Pisistratus merely saw to it that his supporters filled key offices. The intended effect was to blunt the sharp edge of tyranny with the appearance of constitutional government, and it worked. The rule of Pisistratus was remembered as popular and mild. The unintended effect was to give the Athenians more experience in the procedures of self-government and a growing taste for it.

Invasion by Sparta Pisistratus was succeeded by his oldest son, Hippias (r. 527–510 B.C.E.), whose rule became increasingly nervous, suspicious, and harsh after his brother Hipparchus was murdered in 514 B.C.E. Hippias was deposed and driven into exile in 510 B.C.E. when Sparta invaded Athens with the cooperation of a noble family that Hippias had exiled. The tyranny was over.

After the withdrawal of the Spartan army, some factions in the Athenian aristocracy, led by Isagoras, tried to restore the aristocracy to the position of dominance it held before Solon. Isagoras purged the citizen lists, removing those who had been enfranchised by Solon or Pisistratus and any others thought to have a doubtful claim. Isagoras, however, faced competitors, chief among them Clisthenes, of a rival aristocratic clan. In a challenge to Isagoras, Clisthenes took an unprecedented action—he turned to the people for political support and won it with a program of great popular appeal. In response, Isagoras called in the Spartans again, who expelled Clisthenes and many of his supporters. But the fire of Athenian political consciousness, ignited by Solon and kept alive under Pisistratus, had been fanned into flames by the popular appeal of Clisthenes. The people refused to tolerate an aristocratic restoration and drove out the Spartans and Isagoras with them. Clisthenes and his allies returned, ready to put their program into effect.

Clisthenes, the Founder of Democracy A central aim of Clisthenes' reforms was to diminish the influence of traditional localities and regions in Athenian life, for they were an important source of power for the nobility and of factions in the state. Clisthenes immediately enrolled the disenfranchised who had supported him in the struggle with Isagoras. He also replaced Attica's traditional four tribes with ten new tribes organized to guarantee that no region would dominate any of them. Because members of a tribe had common religious activities and fought together in regimental units, the new organization increased devotion to the _polis_, weakening regional loyalties.

Clisthenes replaced Solon's council of four hundred with a new council of five hundred, but he vested final authority in all things in the assembly of all adult male Athenian citizens. Debate in the assembly was free and open; any Athenian could submit legislation, offer amendments, or argue the merits of any question. Although Clisthenes did not alter Solon's property qualifications for officeholders, his enlargement of the citizen rolls, his diminution of the power of the aristocrats, and his elevation of the role of the assembly with its effective and

manageable council all give him a firm claim to the title of father of Athenian democracy.

Solon, Pisistratus, and Clisthenes put Athens well on the way to prosperity and democracy by the beginning of the fifth century B.C.E. It was much more centralized and united than it had been and was ready to take its place among the major states that would lead the defense of Greece against the dangers that lay ahead.

The Persian Wars

The Greeks' period of fortunate isolation and freedom ended in the sixth century B.C.E., when the Greek cities on the coast of Asia Minor came under the control first of King Croesus of Lydia (r. ca. 560–546 B.C.E.), and then in 546 B.C.E. of the powerful Persian Empire (see Chapter 4).

Ionian Rebellion

Initially the cities of Ionia (those on the central part of the west coast of Asia Minor and nearby islands) prospered under Persian rule and remained obedient. The private troubles of Aristagoras, the ambitious tyrant of Miletus, however, ended this calm and set in motion events that would threaten the independence of all the Greeks. Aristagoras had urged a Persian expedition against the island of Naxos; when it failed, he feared the consequences and organized a rebellion in Ionia in 499 B.C.E. To gain support, he overthrew the tyrannies the

Chronology

Key Events in the Early History of Sparta and Athens

ca. 725–710 B.C.E.	First Messenian War
ca. 650–625 B.C.E.	Second Messenian War
ca. 600–590 B.C.E.	Solon initiates reforms at Athens
ca. 560–550 B.C.E.	Sparta defeats Tegea: beginning of Peloponnesian League
546–527 B.C.E.	Pisistratus reigns as tyrant at Athens (main period)
510 B.C.E.	Hippias, son of Pisistratus, deposed as tyrant of Athens
ca. 508–501 B.C.E.	Clisthenes institutes reforms at Athens

Persians had installed and proclaimed democratic constitutions. Next he turned for help to the mainland Greeks, first petitioning Sparta, which refused him, and then Athens. The Athenians, who were related to the Ionians and had close ties of religion and tradition with them, agreed to send a fleet of twenty ships to help the rebels. This expedition was strengthened by five ships from Eretria in Euboea.

In 498 B.C.E., the Athenians and their allies made a swift march and a surprise attack on Sardis, the old capital of Lydia and now the seat of the Persian governor, and burned it. The revolt spread throughout the Greek cities of Asia Minor outside Ionia, but the Athenians withdrew and the Persians gradually reimposed their will. In 495 B.C.E. they defeated the Ionian fleet at Lade, and in the next year they wiped out Miletus, killing many of the city's men, transporting others to the Persian Gulf, and enslaving its women and children. The Ionian rebellion was over.

The War in Greece

In 490 B.C.E. the Persian king Darius (r. 521–486 B.C.E.) sent an expedition to punish Athens, to restore Hippias, and to gain control of the Aegean Sea. Miltiades (d. 489 B.C.E.), an Athenian who had fled from Persian service, led the city's army to a confrontation with the invaders at Marathon. A Persian victory at Marathon would have destroyed Athenian freedom and led to the conquest of all the mainland Greeks. The greatest achievements of Greek culture, most of which lay in the future, would never have occurred. But the Athenians won a decisive victory, instilling them with a sense of confidence and pride in their *polis*, their unique form of government, and themselves.

The Great Invasion   For the Persians, Marathon was only a small and temporary defeat. In 481 B.C.E. Darius's successor, Xerxes (r. 486–465 B.C.E.), gathered an army of at least 150,000 men and a navy of more than 600 ships for the conquest of Greece. In Athens, Themistocles (ca. 525–462 B.C.E.), who favored making Athens into a naval power, had become the leading politician. During his archonship in 493 B.C.E., Athens had already taken the first step in that direction by building a fortified port at Piraeus. A decade later the Athenians came upon a rich vein of silver in the state mines, and Themistocles persuaded them to use the profits to increase their

fleet. By 480 B.C.E. Athens had more than 200 ships, the backbone of a navy that was to defeat the Persians.

Of the hundreds of Greek states, only thirty-one—led by Sparta, Athens, Corinth, and Aegina—were willing to fight as the Persian army gathered south of the Hellespont. In the spring of 480 B.C.E. Xerxes launched his invasion. The Persian strategy was to march into Greece, destroy Athens, defeat the Greek army, and add the Greeks to the number of Persian subjects. The huge Persian army needed to keep in touch with the fleet for supplies. If the Greeks could defeat the Persian navy, the army could not remain in Greece long. Themistocles knew that the Aegean was subject to sudden devastating storms. His strategy was to delay the Persian army and then to bring on the kind of naval battle he might hope to win.

The Greeks chose Sparta to lead them and first confronted the Persians at Thermopylae on land and off Artemisium at sea. The opening between the mountains and the sea at Thermopylae is so narrow that it might be held by a smaller army against a much larger one. Severe storms wrecked many Persian ships while the Greek fleet waited safely in a protected harbor. Then Xerxes attacked Thermopylae, and for two days the Greeks butchered his best troops without serious loss to themselves. On the third day, however, a traitor showed the Persians a mountain trail that permitted them to come on the Greeks from behind. Many allies escaped, but Sparta's King Leonidas and the three hundred Spartans with him all died fighting. Although the naval battle at Artemisium was indecisive, the defeat at Thermopylae forced the Greek navy to withdraw. The Persian army then moved into Attica and burned Athens.

The fate of Greece was decided in a sea battle in the narrow straits to the east of the island of Salamis to which the

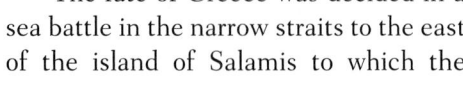

A Greek hoplite attacks a Persian soldier. The contrast between the Greek's metal body armor, large shield, and long spear and the Persian's cloth and leather garments indicates one reason the Greeks won. *Greek. Vase, Red-figured. Attic. ca. 480–470 B.C.E. Neck amphora, Nolan type. SIDE 1: "Greek warrior attacking a Persian." Said to be from Rhodes. Terracotta. H. 13-11/16 in. The Metropolitan Museum of Art, Rogers Fund, 1906 (Acc. # 06.1021.117) Photograph © The Metropolitan Museum of Art.*

Map 3–5. **Classical Greece.** Greece in the Classical period (ca. 480–338 B.C.E.) centered on the Aegean Sea. Although there were important Greek settlements in Italy, Sicily, and all around the Black Sea, the area shown in this general reference map embraced the vast majority of Greek states.

Greek fleet withdrew after the battle of Artemisium. There the Greeks destroyed more than half the Persian fleet, forcing the rest to retreat to Asia with a good part of the Persian army.

The danger, however, was not over yet. The Persian general Mardonius spent the winter in central Greece, and in the spring he unsuccessfully tried to win the Athenians away from the Greek League. The Spartan regent, Pausanias (d. ca. 470 B.C.E.), then led the largest Greek army yet assembled to confront Mardonius in Boeotia. At Plataea, in the summer of 479 B.C.E., Mardonius died in battle, and his army fled toward home. Meanwhile, the Ionian Greeks urged King Leotychidas, the Spartan commander of the fleet, to fight the Persian fleet at Samos. At Mycale, on the nearby coast, Leotychidas destroyed the Persian camp and its fleet offshore. The Persians fled the Aegean and Ionia. For the moment, at least, the Persian threat was gone.

Classical Greece

The repulse of the Persians marks the beginning of the classical period in Greece, 150 years of intense cultural achievement that has rarely if ever been matched anywhere since (see Map 3–5). The classical period was also a time of destructive conflicts among the *poleis* that in the end left them weakened and vulnerable.

The Delian League

Within two years of the Persian retreat, Greek unity, strained even during the life-and-death struggle with Persia, gave way to division. Two spheres of influence emerged—one dominated by Sparta, the other by Athens. The reasons for the split lay in the Ionian Greeks' ongoing need for protection against the Persians and the desire of many Greeks for revenge and reparations. Sparta was ill suited to lead the Greeks under these conditions, which required a long-term commitment and continual naval action. It fell to Athens, the leading naval power in Greece, to lead the effort to drive the Persians from the Aegean and the Hellespont.

In the winter of 478–477 B.C.E. the islanders, the Greeks from the coast of Asia Minor, and some from other Greek cities on the Aegean met with the Athenians on the sacred island of Delos. Swearing themselves to a permanent alliance, they vowed to free Greeks under Persian rule, to protect all against a Persian return, and to obtain compensation from the Persians by attacking their lands and taking booty. Athens was the clearly designated leader. Known as the **Delian League**, the alliance was remarkably successful, driving the Persians from Europe and the Hellespont and clearing the Aegean of pirates. A great Greek victory at the Eurymedon River in Asia Minor in 467 B.C.E. routed the Persians and added several cities to the league. Believing it necessary for their common safety, the members forced some states into the league and prevented others from leaving.

Leading Athens and the Delian League in this succession of victories was the statesman and soldier Cimon (d. 449 B.C.E.). Themistocles, the architect of the Greek victory in 480 B.C.E., was ostracized and driven from power soon after the Persian War by a coalition of his enemies, ironically ending his days at the court of the Persian king. Cimon dominated Athenian politics for almost two decades, pursuing a policy of aggressive attacks on Persia and friendly relations with Sparta. In domestic affairs, Cimon was conservative. He accepted the democratic constitution of Clisthenes, which appears to have become somewhat more limited when the aristocratic Areopagus usurped many powers from the council of five hundred, the assembly, and the popular courts after the Persian War.

The First Peloponnesian War

The Fall of Cimon   In 465 B.C.E., the island of Thasos rebelled against the league. Cimon's suppression of this rebellion after a siege of more than two years marked the first time Athenian interests alone determined league policy and was thus a significant step in the evolution of the league into an Athenian empire. Despite his success, Cimon faced a challenge at home from a faction led by Ephialtes (d. 462 B.C.E.), whose chief supporter was Pericles (ca. 495–429 B.C.E.), a member of a distinguished Athenian family. This faction wanted to reduce the power of the conservative Areopagus and increase the power of ordinary people in Athens and abroad to break with Sparta and contest its claim to leadership.

When the Thasians began their rebellion they asked Sparta to invade Athens, and the Spartans agreed. However, an earthquake, accompanied by a rebellion of the Helots that threatened the survival of Sparta, prevented the invasion. The Spartans asked for help from their allies, including the Athenians, and Cimon persuaded the Athenians, over the objections of Ephialtes, to send it. The results were disastrous for Cimon. While he was in the Peloponnesus helping the Spartans, Ephialtes stripped the Areopagus of almost all its power. Meanwhile, the Spartans, fearing "the boldness and revolutionary spirit of the Athenians," ultimately sent them home. In 461 B.C.E. Cimon was exiled, and Athens made an alliance with Argos, Sparta's traditional enemy. Almost overnight, Cimon's domestic and foreign policies had been overturned.

Outbreak of War   The policies of the confident and ambitious new regime at Athens helped bring on a conflict with Sparta known as the First **Peloponnesian War**. The war began after Megara, getting the worst of a border dispute with Corinth, withdrew from the Spartan-led Peloponnesian League and allied itself with Athens. Megara barred the way

Chronology

Greek Wars Against Persia

ca. 560–546 B.C.E.	Greek cities of Asia Minor conquered by Croesus of Lydia
546 B.C.E.	Cyrus of Persia conquers Lydia and gains control of Greek cities
499–494 B.C.E.	Greek cities rebel (Ionian rebellion)
490 B.C.E.	Battle of Marathon
480–479 B.C.E.	Xerxes' invasion of Greece
480 B.C.E.	Battles of Thermopylae, Artemisium, and Salamis
479 B.C.E.	Battles of Plataea and Mycale

from the Peloponnesus to Athens, giving Athens a strategic advantage. The Athenians made great gains during the war's early years, conquering Aegina and gaining control of Boeotia. They appeared supreme and invulnerable, controlling neighboring states and dominating the sea.

The tide turned in 454 B.C.E. The Athenian fleet, dispatched to help an Egyptian rebellion against Persia, suffered a disastrous defeat. Rebellions broke out within the Delian League, forcing Athens to make a truce in Greece to subdue its allies in the Aegean. In 449 B.C.E. Athens ended the war against Persia. In 446 B.C.E. the war on the Greek mainland broke out again. Rebellions in Boeotia and Megara opened Athens to a Spartan invasion. Rather than fight, Pericles, the commander of the Athenian army, agreed to a peace of thirty years, abandoning all Athenian possessions on the mainland in return for Spartan recognition of Athenian control of the Aegean. Greece was now divided into two blocs: Sparta and its alliance on the mainland, and Athens and what had become the Athenian Empire in the Aegean.

The Athenian Empire

After the Egyptian disaster, the Athenians moved the Delian League's treasury to Athens and began to keep one sixtieth of the league's annual revenues for themselves. Athens was clearly becoming the master and its allies mere subjects (see Map 3–6). By 445 B.C.E. only Chios, Lesbos, and Samos were autonomous and provided ships. All the other states paid tribute.

The change from alliance to empire resulted largely from the pressure of war and rebellion and the unwillingness of the allies to see to their own defenses. Within the subject states, many democratic politicians and people in the lower classes supported the empire, but it nevertheless came to be seen more and more as a tyranny. For the Athenians, however, the empire recognized by the Thirty Years' Peace of 445 B.C.E. had become the key to prosperity and security, and they were determined to defend it at any cost.

Athenian Democracy

Even as the Athenians were tightening their control over their empire, they were expanding democracy at home. Under the leadership of Pericles they evolved the freest government the world had yet seen. The hoplite class was made eligible for the archonship; in theory, no adult male was thereafter barred from that office on the basis of property class. Pericles proposed a law introducing pay for jury service, opening that important duty to the poor. Circuit judges were reintroduced, making swift impartial justice available even to the poorest residents in the countryside.

The benefits of this legislation were limited to citizens, and citizenship was sharply restricted. Pericles himself introduced a bill limiting it to those who had two citizen parents. In Greek terms this was quite natural. Democracy was the privilege of citizenship, making citizenship a valuable commodity. Limiting it would have increased its value and must have won a large majority. Participation in government in all the Greek states was also denied to slaves, resident aliens, and women.

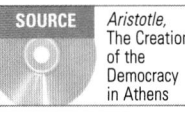

SOURCE *Aristotle, The Creation of the Democracy in Athens*

Among citizens, however, the extent of the democracy was remarkable. Every decision of the state had to be approved by the popular assembly—a collection of the people, not their representatives. Every judicial decision was subject to appeal to a popular court of not fewer than fifty-one citizens, chosen from an annual panel of jurors representative of the Athenian male population. Most officials were selected by lot, without regard to class. The main elected officials, such as the generals and the imperial treasurers, were generally nobles and almost always rich men, but the people were free to choose others. All public officials were subject to scrutiny before taking office, could be called to account and removed from office during their tenure, and were held to a compulsory examination and accounting at the end of their terms. There was no standing army; no police force, open or secret; and no way to coerce the people.

Pericles was elected to the generalship (a military office with important political influence) fifteen years in a row and thirty times in all—not because he was a dictator but because he was a persuasive speaker, a skillful politician, a respected general, an acknowledged patriot, and patently incorruptible. When he lost the people's confidence, they did not hesitate to depose him from office. In 443 B.C.E., however, he stood at the height of his power. The defeat of the Athenian fleet in the Egyptian campaign and the failure of Athens's continental campaigns persuaded him to favor a conservative policy, seeking to retain the empire in the Aegean and live at peace with the Spartans. It was in this direction that he led Athens's imperial democracy in the years after the First Peloponnesian War.

Women of Athens

Greek society, like most other societies all over the world throughout history, was dominated by men. This was true of the democratic Athens in the great days of Pericles in the fifth century B.C.E. no less than of other Greek cities. The actual position of women in classical Athens, however, has been the subject of much controversy.

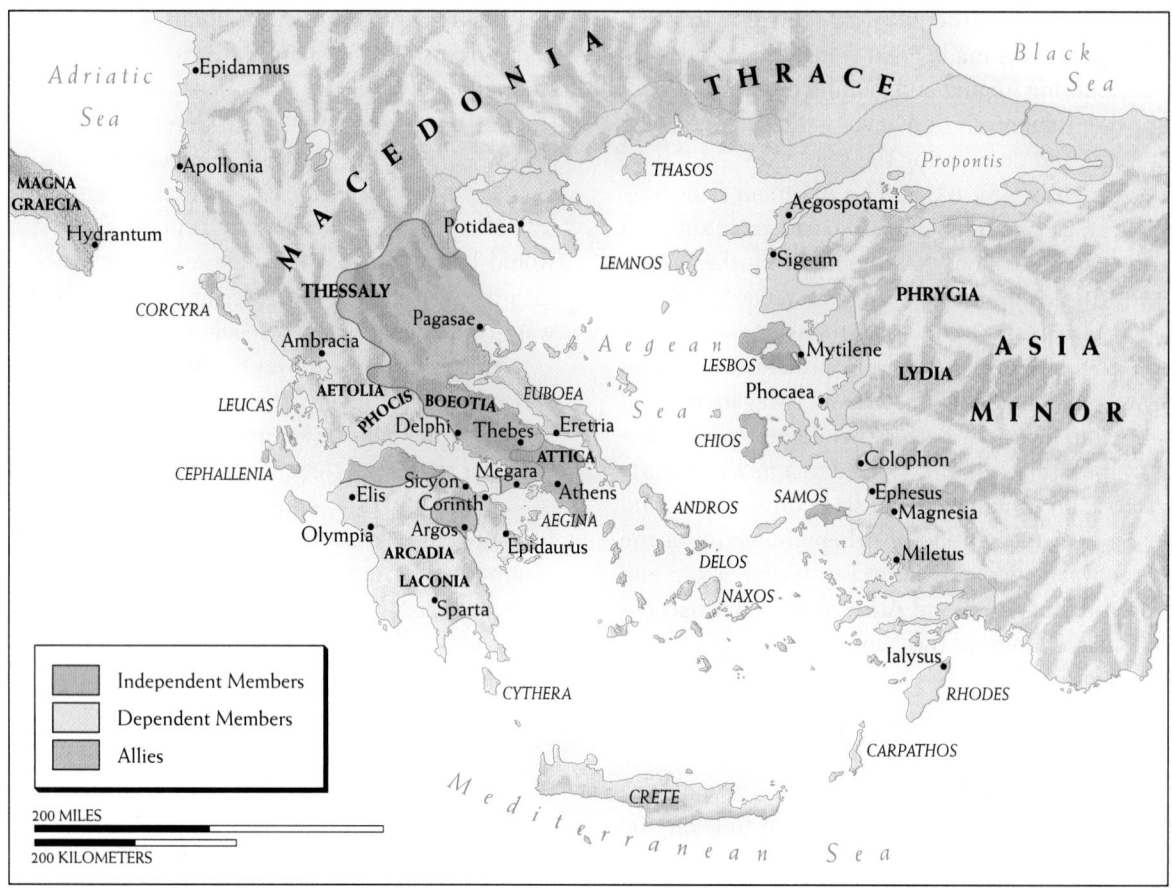

Map 3–6.   The Athenian Empire ca. 450 B.C.E. The empire at its fullest extent. We see Athens and the independent states that provided manned ships for the imperial fleet but paid no tribute, the dependent states that paid tribute, and the states allied to but not actually in the empire.

Subjection The bulk of the evidence, coming from the law, from philosophical and moral writings, and from information about the conditions of daily life and the organization of society, shows that Athenian women were excluded from most aspects of public life. Unlike Athenian men, they could not vote, take part in political assemblies, hold public office, or take any direct part at all in politics.

In private life, women were always under the control of a male guardian—a father, husband, or other appropriate male relative. Women married young, usually between the ages of twelve and eighteen; typically, their husbands were over thirty, making the relationship of a woman to her spouse similar to that of a daughter to her father. Marriages were arranged; the woman normally had no choice of husband, and her dowry was controlled by a male relative. Divorce was difficult for a woman to obtain, for she needed the approval of a male relative who had to be willing to serve as her guardian after the dissolution of the marriage. In case of divorce, the dowry returned with the woman but was controlled by her father or the appropriate male relative.

The main function and responsibility of a respectable Athenian woman of a citizen family was to produce male heirs for the household (*oikos*) of her husband. If, however, her father's *oikos* lacked a male heir, the daughter became an *epikleros,* the "heiress" to the family property. In that case she was required by law to marry a relative on her father's side in order to produce the desired male offspring. In the Athenian way of thinking, women were "lent" by one household to another for bearing and raising a male heir to continue the existence of the *oikos.*

Because the pure and legitimate lineage of the offspring was important, women were carefully segregated from men outside the family and were confined to the women's quarters in the house. Men might seek sexual gratification outside the house with prostitutes of high or low style, frequently recruited from abroad. Respectable women stayed home to raise the children, cook, weave cloth, and oversee the management of the household. The only public function of women—an important one—was in the various rituals and festivals of the state religion. Apart from these activities, Athenian women were expected to remain at home out of sight, quiet and unno-

Chronology

Key Events in Athenian History Between the Persian War and the Great Peloponnesian War

478–477 B.C.E.	Delian League founded
ca. 474–462 B.C.E.	Cimon leading politician
467 B.C.E.	Victory over Persians at Eurymedon River
465–463 B.C.E.	Rebellion of Thasos
462 B.C.E.	Ephialtes murdered; Pericles rises to leadership
461 B.C.E.	Cimon ostracized
461 B.C.E.	Reform of Areopagus
ca. 460 B.C.E.	First Peloponnesian War begins
454 B.C.E.	Athens defeated in Egypt; crisis in the Delian League
449 B.C.E.	Peace with Persia
445 B.C.E.	Thirty Years' Peace ends First Peloponnesian War

ticed. Pericles told the widows and mothers of the Athenian men who died in the first year of the Peloponnesian War only this: "Your great glory is not to fall short of your natural character, and the greatest glory of women is to be least talked about by men, whether for good or bad."

Power Evidence from mythology, from pictorial art, and from the tragedies and comedies by the great Athenian dramatists portrays women in a different light. These often show women as central characters and powerful figures in both the public and the private spheres, suggesting that the role played by Athenian women may have been more complex than their legal status suggests. For example, in Aeschylus's tragedy *Agamemnon*, Clytemnestra arranges the murder of her royal husband and establishes the tyranny of her lover, whom she dominates.

As a famous speech in Euripides' tragedy *Medea* makes clear, we are left with an apparent contradiction. In this speech, Medea paints a bleak picture of the subjugation of women as dictated by their legal status (See Document, "Medea Bemoans the Condition of Women"). Yet Medea, as depicted by Euripides, is herself a powerful

and terrifying figure who negotiates with kings. She is the central figure in a tragedy bearing her name, produced at state expense before most of the Athenian population, and written by one of Athens' greatest poets and dramatists. She is a cause of terror to the audience and, at the same time, an object of their pity and sympathy as a victim of injustice. She is certainly not "least talked about by men, whether for good or bad."

The Great Peloponnesian War

The Thirty Years' Peace of 445 B.C.E. endured little more than ten years. About 435 B.C.E. a dispute flared in a remote and unimportant part of the Greek world that ensnared Athens and Sparta, plunging them back into conflict. This new war was long and disastrous, shaking the foundations of Greek civilization.

The Spartan strategy was traditional: to invade the enemy's country and threaten the crops, forcing the enemy to defend them in a hoplite battle. Such a battle the Spartans were sure to win, because they had the better army and they and their allies outnumbered the Athenians at least two to one. Any ordinary *polis* would have yielded or fought and lost, but Athens had an enormous navy, annual income from its empire, a vast reserve fund, and long walls that connected the fortified city with the fortified port of Piraeus.

The Athenian strategy was to allow the devastation of their own land to prove that Spartan invasions could not hurt Athens. At the same time, the Athenians launched seaborne raids on the Peloponnesian coast to show that Sparta's allies could be hurt. Pericles expected that within a year or two, three at most, the Peloponnesians would become discouraged and make peace. A conflict of longer than four or five years would strain Athenian resources.

The Athenian plan required restraint and the leadership that only Pericles could provide, but Pericles died in 429 B.C.E. Ten years of war ended in stalemate. In 421 B.C.E. Athens and Sparta agreed to the Peace of Nicias, which was supposed to last for fifty years but proved far more tenuous. Neither side carried out all the commitments of the peace, and several of Sparta's allies refused to ratify it.

In 415 B.C.E. Alcibiades (ca. 450–404 B.C.E.), a young and ambitious leader, persuaded the Athenians to attack

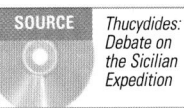
SOURCE *Thucydides: Debate on the Sicilian Expedition*

Sicily to bring it under their control. In 413 B.C.E., the entire expedition was destroyed. The Athenians lost some 200 ships, about 4,500 of their own men, and almost ten times as many allies. It was a disaster that shook Athenian prestige, reduced the power of Athens,

Medea Bemoans the Condition of Women

Document

In 431 B.C.E Euripides (ca. 485–406 B.C.E) presented his play *Medea* at the Festival of Dionysus in Athens. The heroine is a foreign woman who has unusual powers. Her description of the condition of women in the speech that follows, however, appears to be an accurate representation of the condition of women in fifth-century B.C.E. Athens.

◆ Apart form participation in politics, how did the lives of men and women differ in ancient Athens? How well or badly did that aspect of Athenian society suit the needs of the Athenian people and the state in the Classical Age? Since men had a dominant position in the state, and the state managed and financed the presentation of tragedies, how do you explain the sympathetic account of the condition of women Euripides puts into the mouth of Medea?

Of all things which are living can form a judgement
We women are the most unfortunate creatures.
First, with an excess of wealth it is required
For us to buy a husband and take for our bodies
A master; for not to take one is even worse.
And now the question is serious whether we take
A good or bad one, can say no to her marriage
She arrives among new modes of behavior and manners,
And needs prophetic power, unless she has learned
  at home,
How best to manage him who shares the bed with her.
And if we work out all this well and carefully,
And the husband lives with us and lightly bears his yoke,

Then life is enviable. If not I'd rather die.
A man, when he's tired of the company in his home,
Goes out of the house and puts an end to his boredom
And turns to a friend or companion of his own age.
But we are forced to keep our eyes on one alone.
What they say of us is that we have a peaceful time
Living at home, while they do the fighting in war.
How wrong they are! I would very much rather stand
Three times in the front of battle than bear one child.

From Euripides, *Medea in Four Tragedies*, trans. by Rex Warner, copyright © 1955, The Bodley Head.

---

provoked rebellions, and brought Persia into the war on Sparta's side.

Remarkably, the Athenians were able to continue fighting in spite of the disaster. They survived a brief oligarchic coup in 411 B.C.E. and won several important victories at sea as the war shifted to the Aegean. As their allies rebelled, however, and were sustained by fleets paid for by Persia, the Athenians saw their financial resources shrink and finally disappear. When their fleet was caught napping and was destroyed at Aegospotami in 405 B.C.E., they could not build another. The Spartans, under Lysander (d. 395 B.C.E.), a clever and ambitious general who was responsible for obtaining Persian support, cut off the food supply to Athens, starving the city into submission. In 404 B.C.E. Athens surrendered unconditionally. Its walls were dismantled, its empire was gone, and it was forbidden from rebuilding its fleet. The Great Peloponnesian War was over (See Document, "Lysistrata Ends the War.")

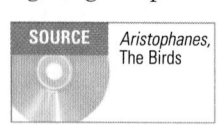

SOURCE   Aristophanes, The Birds

Struggle for Greek Leadership

The Hegemony of Sparta   The collapse of the Athenian Empire created a vacuum of power in the Aegean and opened the way for Spartan leadership, or hegemony. Fulfilling the contract that had brought them the funds to win the war, the Spartans handed the Greek cities of Asia Minor back to Persia. Under the leadership of Lysander, the Spartans stepped into the imperial role Athens had lost. Making a mockery of the Spartan promise to free the Greeks, Lysander installed a board of ten local oligarchs loyal to him and supported by a Spartan garrison in most of the cities along the European coast and the islands of the Aegean. These tributaries brought Sparta almost as much revenue as the Athenians had collected.

Limited manpower, the Helot problem, and traditional conservatism all made Sparta less than an ideal state to rule a maritime empire. Some of Sparta's allies, especially Thebes and Corinth, were alienated by Sparta's increasingly arrogant policies. In 404 B.C.E. Lysander

Greek Warship. A replica of a *trireme*, the warship that dominated naval warfare in the Mediterranean in the fourth and fifth centuries B.C.E.

installed an oligarchic government in Athens whose outrageous behavior earned it the title "Thirty Tyrants." Democratic exiles took refuge in Thebes and Corinth and created an army to challenge the oligarchy. Sparta's conservative king, Pausanias, replaced Lysander, arranging a peaceful settlement and ultimately the restoration of democracy. Thereafter, Athenian foreign policy remained under Spartan control, but otherwise Athens was free.

In 405 B.C.E. Greek mercenaries recruited with Spartan help intervened in Persia on behalf of Cyrus the Younger, who was contesting the accession to the Persian throne of his brother Artaxerxes II (r. 404–358 B.C.E.). The Greeks marched inland to Mesopotamia, defeating the Persians at Cunaxa (see Map 3–7) in 401 B.C.E. Cyrus was killed, however, and the Greeks marched back to the Black Sea and safety. Their success revealed the potential weakness of the Persian Empire.

The Greeks of Asia Minor had supported Cyrus and were now afraid of Artaxerxes' revenge. The Spartans accepted their request for aid and sent an army into Asia,

attracted by the prospect of prestige, power, and money. In 396 B.C.E. the command of this army was given to Sparta's new king, Agesilaus (444–360 B.C.E.), whose aggressive policy was to dominate Sparta until his death.

The Persians responded to Agesilaus's plundering army by seeking assistance among Greek states disaffected with Spartan domination, offering them money and other support. Thebes forged an alliance with Argos, Corinth, and Athens and engaged Sparta in the Corinthian War (395–387 B.C.E.), ending Sparta's Asian adventure. In 394 B.C.E. the Persian fleet destroyed Sparta's maritime empire. Athens, meanwhile, had rebuilt its walls, resurrected its navy, and recovered some of its lost empire. The Persians, who dictated the terms of the peace that ended the Corinthian War to the exhausted Greeks, were alarmed by this Athenian recovery and turned the management of Greece over to Sparta.

Sparta's actions grew increasingly arrogant and lawless. Agesilaus broke up all alliances except the Peloponnesian League and put friends in power in several Greek cities. In 382 B.C.E. Sparta seized Thebes during peacetime without

Lysistrata Ends the War

Aristophanes, the greatest of the Athenian comic poets, presented the play *Lysistrata* in 411 B.C.E. two decades into the Great Peloponnesian War. The central idea of the plot is that the women of Athens, led by Lysistrata, tired of the privations imposed by the war, decide to take matters into their own hands and bring the war to an end. The device they employ is to get the women on both sides to deny their marital favors to their husbands, a kind of sexual strike that quickly achieves its purpose. Before the following passage, Lysistrata has set the terms the Spartans must accept. Next she turns to the Athenians. The play is a masterful example of Athenian Old Comedy, which was almost always full of contemporary and historical political satirical references and sexual and erotic puns and jokes. The references to "Peace" in the stage directions are to an actor playing to goddess Peace.

◆ To what historic event does the passage concerning "the Tyrant's days" refer? To what does the "Promontory of Pylos" refer? What was the real role of women in Athenian political life, and what does the play tell us about it? What is the relationship between humor and reality in this play?

LYSISTRATA
(Turning to the Athenians)

Men of Athens, do you think I'll let you off?
    Have you forgotten the Tyrant's days, when you wore
    the smock of slavery, when the Spartans turned to the
    spear, cut down the pride of Thessaly, despatched
    the friends of tyranny, and dispossessed your op-
    pressors?
    Recall:
    On that great day, your only allies were Spartans;
    your liberty came at their hands, which stripped away
    your servile garb and clothed you again in Freedom!

SPARTAN
(Indicating Lysistrata)

Hain't never seed no higher type of woman.

KINESIAS
(Indicating Peace)

Never saw one I wanted so much to top.

LYSISTRATA
(Oblivious to the byplay, addressing both groups)

With such a history of mutual benefits conferred
    and received, why are you fighting? Stop this
    wickedness!
    Come to terms with each other! What prevents you?

SPARTAN
We'd a heap sight druther make Peace, if we was
indemnified with a plumb strategic location.
    (Pointing at Peace's rear)
    We'll take thet butte.

LYSISTRATA
Butte?

SPARTAN
The Promontory of Pylos—Sparta's Back Door.
    We've missed it fer a turrible spell.
(Reaching)
    Hev to keep our hand in.

KINESIAS
(Pushing him away)

The price is too high—you'll never take that!

LYSISTRATA
Oh, let them have it.

KINESIAS
What room will we have left for maneuvers?

LYSISTRATA
Demand another spot in exchange.

KINESIAS
(Surveying Peace like a map as he addresses the Spartan)

Then you hand over to us—uh, let me see—let's try
Thessaly—
(Indicating the relevant portions of Peace)

First of all, Easy Mountain. . .
then the Maniac Gulf behind it. . .
and down to Megara for the legs. . .

SPARTAN
You cain't take all of thet! Yore plumb
out of yore mind!

LYSISTRATA
(To Kinesias)

Don't argue. Let the legs go.
> *(Kinesias nods. A pause, general smiles of agreement)*

KINESIAS
(Doffing his cloak)

I feel an urgent desire to plow a few furrows.

SPARTAN
(Doffing his cloak)

Hit's time to work a few loads of fertilizer in.

LYSISTRATA

Conclude the treaty and the simple life is yours.
> If such is your decision, convene your councils,
> and then deliberate the matter with your allies.

KINESIAS

Deliberate? Allies?
> We're over-extended already!
> Wouldn't every ally approve of our position—
> Union Now?

SPARTAN

I know I kin speak for ourn.

KINESIAS

And I for ours.
> They're just a bunch of gigolos.

LYSISTRATA

I heartily approve.
> Now first attend to your purification,
> then we, the women, will welcome you to the Citadel
> and treat you to all the delights of a home-cooked banquet.
> Then you'll exchange your oaths and pledge your faith,
> and every man of you will take his wife
> and depart for home.

Aristophanes, *Lysistrata*, trans. by Douglass Parker in *Four Comedies by Aristophanes,* ed. by W. Arrowsmith (Ann Arbor: University of Michigan Press, 1969), pp. 79–81. Reprinted by permission of the University of Michigan Press.

---

warning or pretext. In 379 B.C.E. a Spartan army made a similar attempt on Athens. That action persuaded the Athenians to join with Thebes, which had rebelled from Sparta a few months earlier. In 371 B.C.E. the Thebans defeated the Spartans at Leuctra (see Map 3–5). They then encouraged the Arcadian cities of the central Peloponnesus to form a federal league and freed the Helots, helping them found a city of their own. Sparta's population had been shrinking so that it could field an army of fewer than two thousand men at Leuctra. Now, hemmed in by hostile neighbors, deprived of much of its farmland and of the slaves who had worked it, Sparta ceased to be a first-rank power. Its aggressive policies had led to ruin.

Theban Hegemony Thebes' power after its victory lay in its democratic constitution, its control over Boeotia, and the two outstanding and popular generals—Pelopidas (d. 364 B.C.E.) and Epaminondas (d. 362 B.C.E.)—who led its forces at Leuctra. Under their leadership Thebes gained dominance over the Corinthian gulf and all Greece north of Athens, challenging the reborn Athenian Empire in the Aegean. This success provoked resistance, however, and by 362 B.C.E. Thebes faced a Peloponnesian coalition as well as Athens. Epaminondas, who was once again leading a Boeotian army into the Peloponnesus, confronted this coalition at Mantinea. His army was victorious, but Epaminondas was killed, ending Theban dominance.

Chronology

The Great Peloponnesian War

435 B.C.E.	Civil war at Epidamnus
432 B.C.E.	Sparta declares war on Athens
431 B.C.E.	Peloponnesian invasion of Athens
421 B.C.E.	Peace of Nicias
415–413 B.C.E.	Athenian invasion of Sicily
405 B.C.E.	Battle of Aegospotami
404 B.C.E.	Athens surrenders

The Second Athenian Empire In 378 B.C.E. Athens organized a second confederation aimed at resisting Spartan aggression in the Aegean. Its constitution was careful to avoid the abuses of the Delian League, but the Athenians soon began to repeat them anyway. This time, however, they lacked the power to suppress resistance. When the collapse of Sparta and Thebes and the restraint of Persia removed any reason for voluntary membership, Athens's allies revolted. By

Greek Civilization

Overview

Historians divide ancient Greek civilization into periods marked by different forms of social and political organizations and by significant cultural achievements.

Minoan Based on the island of Crete, ca. 2900–1150 B.C.E., sea-based power, probably ruled by kings. Palace architecture, vivid frescoes.

Mycenaean Mainland Greece, ca. 1600–1150 B.C.E., city-states ruled by powerful kings assisted by an elaborate bureaucracy. Monumental architecture, gold-and bronzework.

Archaic Colonization from Greece to Asia Minor, southern Italy, and the coasts of the Black Sea, 700–500 B.C.E. Characteristic form of government was the *polis*, a city-state dominated by land-holding aristocrats or ruled by tyrants. Lyric poetry, natural philosophy.

Classical Golden age of Athenian civilization, fifth century B.C.E. Athens and other *poleis* became much more democratic. Drama, sculpture in marble and bronze, architecture (the Acropolis), philosophy, history.

Hellenistic Conquests of Alexander the Great (356–323 B.C.E.) spread Greek culture to Egypt and as far east as the Indus Valley. Decline of the *polis*. Domination of the Greek world by large monarchical states. Stoic and Epicurean philosophy, realistic sculputre, advances in mathematics and science.

---

355 B.C.E. Athens had to abandon most of the empire. After two centuries of almost continual warfare, the Greeks returned to the chaotic disorganization that characterized the time before the founding of the Peloponnesian League.

Culture of Classical Greece The term *classical* often suggests calm and serenity, but ironically the word that best describes the common element in Greek life, thought, art, and literature during the Classical period is tension. Among the great achievements of this era were the philosophical works of Socrates (469–399 B.C.E.), Plato (427–347 B.C.E.), and Aristotle (384–322 B.C.E.) (see Chapter 2). The arts of the time were animated by the same concern with the nature, capacities, limits, and place in the universe of human beings that animated those works.

Fifth Century B.C.E.

Two sources of tension contributed to the artistic outpouring of fifth-century B.C.E. Greece. One arose from the conflict between the Greeks' pride in their accomplishments and their concern that overreaching would bring retribution. The victory over the Persians brought a sense of exultation in the

capacity of humans to accomplish great things, and a sense of confidence in the divine justice that had subdued the arrogant pride of Xerxes. But the Greeks recognized that the fate that had met Xerxes awaited all those who reached too far, creating a sense of unease. The second source of tension was the conflict between the soaring hopes and achievements of individuals and the claims and limits put on them by their fellow citizens in the *polis*. These tensions were felt throughout Greece. They had the most spectacular consequences, however, in Athens in its golden age, the time between the Persian and the Peloponnesian Wars.

Attic Tragedy These concerns are best reflected in Attic (Athenian) tragedy, which emerged as a major form of Greek poetry in the fifth century B.C.E. The tragedies were selected in a contest and presented as part of public religious observations in honor of the god Dionysus.

Poets who wished to compete submitted their works to the archon. Each offered three tragedies, which might or might not have a common subject, and a satyr play (a comic choral dialogue with Dionysus) to close. Each of the three best competitors was awarded three actors and a chorus. The actors were paid by the state, and the chorus was

The Acropolis. It was both the religious and civic center of Athens. In its final form it is the work of Pericles and his successors in the late fifth century B.C.E. This photograph shows the Parthenon and, to its left, the Erechtheum. *Meredith Pillon, Greek National Tourism Organization.*

provided by a wealthy citizen selected by the state to perform this service as *chorego*. Most of the tragedies were performed in the theater of Dionysus on the south side of the Acropolis, where as many as thirty thousand Athenians could attend. Prizes and honors were awarded to the author, the actor, and the *choregos* voted best by a jury of Athenians chosen by lot.

Attic tragedy served as a forum for poets to raise vital issues. Until late in the century the tragedies, drawing mostly on mythological subjects, dealt solemnly with difficult questions of religion, politics, ethics, or morality. The plays of the dramatists Aeschylus (525–456 B.C.E.) and Sophocles (ca. 496–406 B.C.E.) follow this pattern. The plays of Euripides (ca. 480–406 B.C.E.) are less solemn and more concerned with individual psychology.

Old Comedy Comedy was introduced into the Dionysian festival early in the fifth century B.C.E. The great master of the genre called Old Comedy, Aristophanes (ca. 450–385 B.C.E.), the only one from whom we have complete plays, wrote political comedies filled with scathing invective and satire against such contemporary figures as Pericles, Socrates, and Euripides.

Architecture and Sculpture The great architectural achievements of Periclean Athens, like Athenian tragedy, reflect the tension generated by the union of individual genius with religious and civic responsibility. Beginning in 448 B.C.E. and

continuing to the outbreak of the Great Peloponnesian War, Pericles undertook a great building program on the Acropolis with funds from the income of the empire. The new buildings included temples to honor the city's gods and a fitting gateway to the temples. They visually projected Athenian greatness, emphasizing the city's intellectual and artistic achievements rather than its military power and providing tangible proof of Pericles' claim that Athens was "the school of Hellas,"[1] the intellectual center of all Greece.

History The first prose history ever written was an account of the Persian War by Herodotus (484?–425? B.C.E.). "The father of history," as he has deservedly been called, was born shortly before the outbreak of the war. His account goes far beyond all previous chronicles, genealogies, and geographical studies, and it attempts to explain human actions and to draw instruction from them.

Herodotus accepted the evidence of legends and oracles, although not uncritically, and often explained human events in terms of divine intervention. Yet his *History,* typical of its time, also celebrates the crucial influence of human intelligence on events, as exemplified by Miltiades at Marathon and Themistocles at Salamis. Herodotus also recognized the importance of institutions, pointing with pride to the way the Greek *polis* inspired discipline and a

---

[1] Diogenes Laertius, *Lives of Eminent Philosophers (Zeno)* (Cambridge, MA: Harvard University Press, 1931–1938).

Chronology

Spartan and Theban Hegemonies

404–403 B.C.E.	Thirty Tyrants rule at Athens
401 B.C.E.	Expedition of Cyrus, rebellious prince of Persia; Battle of Cunaxa
400–387 B.C.E.	Spartan War against Persia
398–360 B.C.E.	Reign of Agesilaus at Sparta
395–387 B.C.E.	Corinthian War
382 B.C.E.	Sparta seizes Thebes
378 B.C.E.	Second Athenian Confederation founded
371 B.C.E.	Thebans defeat Sparta at Leuctra; end of Spartan hegemony
362 B.C.E.	Battle of Mantinea; end of Theban hegemony

voluntary obedience to the law in its citizen soldiers, in contrast to the fear of punishment that motivated the Persians.

Thucydides, the historian of the Peloponnesian War, was born about 460 B.C.E. and died about 400 B.C.E., a few years after the end of the Great Peloponnesian War. His work, which was influenced by the secular, human-centered, skeptical rationalism of the Sophists (see Chapter 2), also reflects the scientific approach to medicine pioneered by his contemporary, Hippocrates of Cos (ca. 460–ca. 370 B.C.E.). The Hippocratic approach to the understanding, diagnosis, and treatment of disease combined careful observation with reason. Thucydides similarly took great pains to achieve factual accuracy and tried to use his evidence to discover meaningful patterns of human behavior. He believed that human nature was essentially unchanging, so that a wise person equipped with an understanding of history might accurately foresee events and help guide them. He believed, however, that only a few were equipped to understand history and to put its lessons to good use, and that even the wisest could be foiled by the intervention of chance in human affairs. Thucydides focused on politics, and in that area his assumptions about human nature do not seem unwarranted.

Fourth Century B.C.E

Historians often call the Great Peloponnesian War the crisis of the *polis* and the fourth century B.C.E. the period of its

decline. But the Greeks of the fourth century B.C.E. did not know that their traditional way of life was on the verge of destruction. Some looked to the past for ways to shore up the weakened structure of the *polis*; others tended toward despair and looked for new solutions; and still others averted their gaze from the public arena altogether. All of these responses are apparent in the literature, philosophy, and art of the period.

Drama   The tendency of some to turn away from the life of the *polis* and inward to everyday life, the family, and the self is apparent in the poetry of the fourth century B.C.E. A new genre, called Middle Comedy, replaced the political subjects and personal invective of the Old Comedy with comic-realistic depictions of daily life, plots of intrigue, and mild domestic satire. Significantly, the role of the chorus, which in some ways represented the *polis*, was much diminished. These trends continued, resulting in New Comedy, whose leading exponent, Menander (342–291 B.C.E.), completely abandoned mythological subjects in favor of domestic tragicomedy. Menander's gentle satire of the foibles of ordinary people and his tales of lovers temporarily thwarted before a happy ending would be familiar to viewers of modern situation comedies.

Tragedy faded as a robust and original form in the fourth century B.C.E., but the great tragedies of the previous century were commonly revived. The plays of Euripides, which rarely won first prize when originally produced, became increasingly popular in the fourth century and after. Euripides was less interested in cosmic confrontations of conflicting principles than in the psychology and behavior of individual human beings. Some of his late plays, in fact, are less like the tragedies of Aeschylus and Sophocles than forerunners of later forms such as the New Comedy. Plays like *Helena*, *Andromeda*, and *Iphigenia in Tauris* are more like fairy tales, tales of adventure, or love stories than tragedies.

Sculpture   Fourth-century sculpture reflects the same movement away from the grand, the ideal, and the general and toward the ordinary, the real, and the individual.

Emergence of the Hellenistic World

The term *Hellenistic* was coined in the nineteenth century to describe a period of three centuries during which Greek culture spread from its homeland to Egypt and far into Asia. The result was a new civilization that combined Greek and Asian elements. The Hellenistic world was larger than the world of classical Greece, and its major political units were much larger than the *poleis*, although these endured in modified forms. Hellenistic civilization had its roots in the rise to power of a dynasty in Macedonia whose armies conquered Greece and the Persian Empire in the space of two generations.

Macedonian Conquest

The kingdom of Macedon, north of Thessaly, had long served unknowingly as a buffer between the Greek states to the south and barbarian tribes farther to the north. The Macedonians were of the same stock as the Greeks and spoke a Greek dialect, and Macedonian nobles, at least, thought of themselves as Greeks. Macedon's kings, who claimed descent from Heracles and the royal house of Argos, sought to bring Greek culture into their court. By Greek standards, however, Macedon, although allowed to participate in the Olympic games, was backward and semibarbaric. It had no *poleis* and was ruled loosely by a king in a rather Homeric fashion. The king was chosen partly on the basis of descent, but gained legitimacy only with the acclamation of the army gathered in assembly. Quarrels between pretenders to the throne and even murder to secure it were not uncommon. A council of nobles checked the royal power and could reject a weak or incompetent king. Plagued by constant war with the barbarians, internal strife, loose organization, and lack of money, Macedon played no great part in Greek affairs up to the fourth century B.C.E. Once unified under a strong king, however, it was destined to play a great part in Greek affairs.

Philip of Macedon That strong king was Philip II (r. 359–336 B.C.E.), who, while still under thirty, took advantage of his appointment as regent to overthrow his infant nephew and make himself king. Like many of his predecessors, he admired Greek culture. Between 367 and 364 B.C.E. he had been a hostage in Thebes, where he learned about Greek politics and warfare from Epaminondas. His natural talents for war and diplomacy and his boundless ambition made him the ablest king in Macedonian history. After first securing his hold on the throne and pacifying the tribes on his frontiers, he began to undermine Athenian control of the northern Aegean. Gaining control of a lucrative gold and silver mining region, he began to found new cities, to bribe foreign politicians, and to reorganize his army into the finest fighting force in the world.

Invasion of Greece So armed, Philip turned south toward central Greece, threatening the vital interest of Athens. Although it still had a formidable fleet of three hundred ships, the Athens of 350 B.C.E. was not the Athens of Pericles. It had neither imperial revenue nor allies to share the burden of war, and its population was smaller than it had been in the fifth century B.C.E. The Athenians, therefore, were reluctant to go on expeditions themselves or even to send out mercenary armies under Athenian generals, for mercenaries had to be paid from Athenian coffers.

The leading critic of this cautious policy was Demosthenes (384–322 B.C.E.), one of the greatest orators in Greek history. Convinced that Philip was a dangerous enemy, Demosthenes spent most of his career urging the Athenians to resist him. Demosthenes was right. Beginning in 349 B.C.E. Philip attacked several cities in northern and central Greece, firmly establishing Macedonian power in those regions. The king of "barbarian" Macedon was elected president of the Pythian games at Delphi, and the Athenians were forced to concur in the election.

The years between 346 and 340 B.C.E. were spent in diplomatic maneuvering, each side trying to win strategically useful allies. In 340 B.C.E. Philip besieged Perinthus and Byzantium (see Map 3–5), the lifeline of Athenian commerce, and declared war. The Athenian fleet saved both cities, so in the following year Philip marched into Greece. Demosthenes rallied the Athenians and won Thebes over to the Athenian side. In 338 B.C.E., however, Philip defeated the allied forces at Chaeronea in Boeotia. The decisive blow in this great battle was a cavalry charge led by Philip's eighteen-year-old son, Alexander.

Macedonian Government of Greece Macedonian rule was not as harsh as many had feared, although in some cities Philip's supporters took power and killed or exiled their enemies. Demosthenes remained free to engage in politics. Athens was spared from attack on the condition that it give up what was left of its empire and follow the lead of Macedon. The rest of Greece was arranged in such a way as to remove all dangers to Philip's rule. To guarantee his security, Philip placed garrisons at Thebes, Chalcis, and Corinth.

In 338 B.C.E. Philip organized the Greek states into the Federal League of Corinth. The league's constitution provided its constituent states autonomy and freedom from tribute and garrisons, and called for the suppression of piracy and civil war. League delegates would make foreign policy, in theory without consulting their home governments or Philip. All this was a façade; not only was Philip of Macedon president of the league, he was also its ruler. The defeat at Chaeronea ended Greek freedom and autonomy. Although it maintained its form and internal life for some time, the *polis* had lost control of its own affairs and the special conditions that had made it unique.

Philip's choice of Corinth as the seat of his new confederacy was deliberate. It was at Corinth that the Greeks had gathered to resist a Persian invasion almost 150 years earlier, and it was there in 337 B.C.E. that Philip announced his intention to invade Persia as leader of the new league. In the spring of 336 B.C.E., however, as he prepared to begin the campaign, Philip was assassinated.

In 1977 excavations of a mound at the Macedonian village of Vergina revealed structures with extraordinarily rich associated artifacts that many scholars believe to be the royal tomb of Philip II. Philip certainly deserved so distinguished a resting place. He found Macedon a disunited kingdom of semibarbarians, despised and exploited by the Greeks. He left it a united kingdom, master and leader of the Greeks, rich, powerful, and ready to undertake the invasion of Asia.

Alexander the Great and His Successors

Philip's first son, Alexander III (356–323 B.C.E.), later called Alexander the Great, succeeded his father at the age of twenty. Along with his throne, the young king inherited his father's daring plans for the conquest of Persia.

The Conquest of Persia The usurper Cyrus and his Greek mercenaries had shown the vast and wealthy Persian Empire to be vulnerable when they penetrated deep into its interior early in the fourth century B.C.E. In 334 B.C.E. Alexander crossed the Hellespont into Asia. His army consisted of about thirty thousand infantry and five thousand cavalry; he had no navy and little money. Consequently he sought quick and decisive battles to gain money and supplies from the conquered territory. To neutralize the Persian navy he moved along the coast, depriving it of ports.

Alexander met the Persian forces of Asia Minor at the Granicus River (see Map 3–7), where he won a smashing victory in characteristic style: He led a cavalry charge across the river into the teeth of the enemy on the opposite bank, almost losing his life in the process and winning the devotion of his soldiers. The coast of Asia Minor now open, Alexander captured the coastal cities, denying them to the Persian fleet.

In 333 B.C.E. Alexander marched inland to Syria, meeting the main Persian army under King Darius III (r. 336–330 B.C.E.) at Issus. Alexander himself led the cavalry charge that broke the Persian line and sent Darius fleeing to the east. He continued along the coast and captured previously impregnable Tyre after a long and ingenious siege, putting an end to the threat of the Persian navy. He took Egypt with little trouble and was greeted as liberator, pharaoh, and son of the Egyptian god Re. While Alexander was at Tyre, Darius offered him his daughter and his entire empire west of the Euphrates River in exchange for an alliance and an end to the invasion. But Alexander wanted the whole empire and probably whatever lay beyond that.

In the spring of 331 B.C.E. Alexander marched into Mesopotamia. At Gaugamela, near the ancient Assyrian city of Nineveh, he met Darius, ready for a last stand. Once again, Alexander's tactical genius and personal leadership carried the day. The Persians were broken and Darius fled once more. Alexander entered Babylon, again hailed as liberator and king. In January of 330 B.C.E. he came to Persepolis, the Persian capital, which held splendid palaces and the royal treasury. This bonanza ended his financial troubles and put a vast sum of money into circulation, with economic consequences that lasted for centuries. After a stay of several months, Alexander burned Persepolis to dramatize the destruction of the native Persian dynasty and the completion of Hellenic revenge for the earlier Persian invasion of Greece.

Setting off after Darius, Alexander found him, dead, just south of the Caspian Sea. He had been murdered and replaced by his relative Bessus, with the support of the Persian nobility. Alexander soon captured Bessus. This pursuit, and his own great curiosity and desire to see the most distant places, took him to the frontier of India.

Near Samarkand, in the land of the Scythians, he founded the city of Alexandria Eschate ("Furthest Alexandria"), one of the many cities bearing his name that he founded as he traveled. As a part of his grand scheme of amalgamation and conquest, he married the Bactrian princess Roxane and enrolled thirty thousand young Bactrians to be trained for his army.

In 327 B.C.E. Alexander took his army through the Khyber Pass to conquer the lands around the Indus River (modern Pakistan). Reducing the region's king, Porus, to vassalage, he pushed on in the hope of reaching the river called Ocean that the Greeks believed encircled the world. Finally his weary men refused to go on. By the spring of 324 B.C.E. the army was back at the Persian Gulf, celebrating Macedonian style with a wild spree of drinking.

Death of Alexander

Alexander was filled with plans for the future: for the consolidation and organization of his empire; for geographic exploration; for new cities, roads, and harbors; perhaps even for further conquests in the West. There is even some evidence that he asked to be deified and worshiped as a god, although we cannot be sure if he really did so or what he had in mind if he did. In June of 323 B.C.E. he was overcome by a fever and died in Babylon at the age of thirty-three. His memory has never faded, and he soon became the subject of myth, legend, and romance. Some have seen in him a man of vision who transcended Greek and Macedonian ethnocentrism and sought to forge human solidarity in a great world state. Others have seen him as a calculating despot, given to drunken brawls, brutality, and murder. The truth is probably in between. Alexander was one of the greatest generals the world has seen; he never lost a battle or failed in a

Alexander and Darius. King Darius III looks back in distress as Alexander advances against his vanguard during the battle of Issus, as depicted in a Roman mosaic from the first century B.C.E.

Chronology

Rise of Macedon

359–336 B.C.E.	Reign of Philip II
338 B.C.E.	Battle of Chaeronea; Philip conquers Greece; founding of League of Corinth
336–323 B.C.E.	Reign of Alexander III, the Great
334 B.C.E.	Alexander invades Asia
333 B.C.E.	Battle of Issus
331 B.C.E.	Battle of Gaugamela
330 B.C.E.	Fall of Persepolis
327 B.C.E.	Alexander reaches Indus valley
323 B.C.E.	Death of Alexander

siege, and with a modest army, he conquered a vast empire. He had rare organizational talents, and his plan for creating a multinational empire was the only intelligent way to consolidate his conquests. He established many new cities—seventy, according to tradition—mostly along trade routes. These cities promoted commerce and prosperity and introduced Hellenic civilization into new areas. It is hard to know if even Alexander could have held together the vast new empire he had created, but his death proved that only he had a chance to succeed.

Alexander's Successors

Alexander's sudden death left his enormous empire with no clear, strong heir. His able and loyal Macedonian generals, at first hoping to preserve the empire for the Macedonian royal house, appointed themselves governors of the various provinces of the empire. The conflicting ambitions of these strong-willed men, however, soon led to prolonged warfare among them in which three of the generals were killed and all of the direct members of

Map 3–7. Alexander's Campaigns. The route taken by Alexander the Great in his conquest of the Persian Empire, 334–323 B.C.E. Starting from the Macedonian capital at Pella, he reached the Indus valley before being turned back by his own restive troops. He died of fever in Mesopotamia.

the Macedonian royal house were either executed or murdered. The murder of Roxane and her son in 310 B.C.E. left the empire with no focus, and in 306 and 305 B.C.E. the surviving governors proclaimed themselves kings of their various holdings. Three of these generals founded dynasties of significance in the spread of Hellenistic culture:

◆ Ptolemy I, 367?–283 B.C.E.; founder of the Thirty-first Dynasty in Egypt, the Ptolemies, of whom Cleopatra, who died in 30 B.C.E., was the last

◆ Seleucus I, 358?–280 B.C.E.; founder of the Seleucid Dynasty in Mesopotamia

◆ Antigonus I, 382–301 B.C.E.; founder of the Antigonid Dynasty in Asia Minor and Macedon

For the first seventy-five years or so after the death of Alexander, the world ruled by his successors enjoyed considerable prosperity. The vast sums of money he and they had put into circulation greatly increased economic activity. Opportunities for service and profit in the East attracted many Greeks and relieved their native cities of some of the pressure of the poor. The opening of vast new territories to Greek trade, the increased demand for Greek products, and the new availability of things Greeks wanted, as well as the conscious policies of the Hellenistic kings, all helped stimulate commerce. The new prosperity, however, was not evenly distributed. The urban Greeks, the Macedonians, and the Hellenized natives who made up the upper and middle classes lived lives of comfort and even luxury, but native peasants did not.

Prosperity initially tempered these distinctions. After a while, however, war, inflation, and a gradual lessening of the positive effects of the introduction of Persian wealth led to economic crisis. The kings bore down heavily on the middle classes, who were skilled in avoiding their responsibilities. The pressure on peasants and city laborers also increased, and they responded by slowing work and even by striking. In Greece, economic pressures brought clashes between rich and poor, demands for the abolition of debt and the redistribution of land, and, on occasion, civil war.

Ongoing warfare and these internal divisions made the Hellenistic kingdoms vulnerable to outside attack, and by the middle of the second century B.C.E. the expanding empire of Rome had absorbed all except Egypt. The two centuries of Hellenistic rule had great and lasting importance, however. They saw the entire eastern Mediterranean coast, Greece, Egypt, Mesopotamia, and the old Persian Empire formed into a single political, economic, and cultural unit.

Hellenistic Culture

Alexander's conquests and the establishment of the successor kingdoms, by ending the central role of the *polis* in Greek life and thought, marked a significant turning point in Greek literature, philosophy, religion, and art.

Deprived of control of their foreign affairs, their important internal arrangements determined by a foreign monarch, the postclassical cities lost the kind of political freedom that was basic to the old outlook. They were cities, perhaps—in a sense, even city-states—but not *poleis*. As time passed they lost their sovereignty, becoming municipalities within military empires. For the most part, the Greeks after Alexander turned inward, away from politics, to address their hopes and fears. The confident, sometimes arrogant, humanism of the fifth century B.C.E. gave way to a kind of resignation to fate, a recognition of helplessness before forces too great for humans to manage.

Philosophy These developments are noticeable in the changes that overtook the established schools of philosophy as well as in the emergence of two new and influential groups of philosophers, the Epicureans and the Stoics.

Plato's Academy and Aristotle's Lyceum (see Chapter 2) continued to operate, reinforcing Athens's position as the center of philosophical studies. The Lyceum turned gradually away from Aristotle's universal investigations, even from his scientific interests, to become a center chiefly of literary and historical studies. The Academy turned even further from its founder's tradition, adopting the philosophical approach known as skepticism, established by Pyrrho of Elis (ca. 365–275 B.C.E.). The Skeptics thought that nothing could be known and so consoled themselves and their followers by suggesting that nothing mattered. It was easy for them, therefore, to accept conventional morality and the world as it was. The Cynics continued to denounce convention and to advocate a crude life in accordance with nature, which some of them practiced publicly, to the shock and outrage of respectable citizens. Neither of these views had much appeal to the middle-class city dweller of the third century B.C.E., who sought some basis for choosing a way of life now that the *polis* no longer provided one ready-made.

Epicureans Epicurus of Athens (342–271 B.C.E.), who founded a school in that city in 306 B.C.E., formulated a philosophy in keeping with the new mood. The goal of this philosophy was not knowledge but happiness, which Epicurus believed could be achieved through a life based on reason.

Accepting the description of the physical universe proposed by the atomists Democritus and Leucippus (see Chapter 2), the **Epicureans** took sense perception to be the

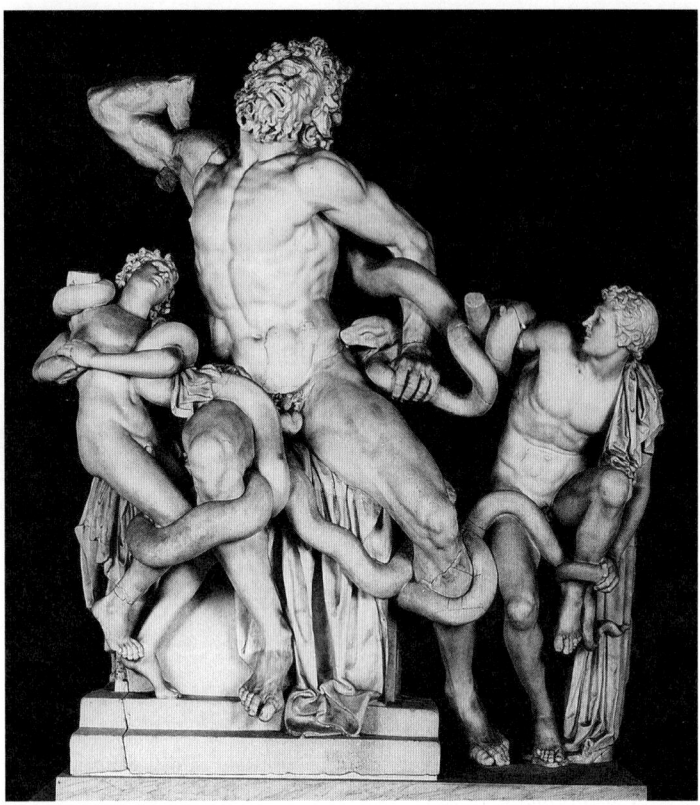

One of the Masterpieces of Hellenistic Sculpture, the _Laocoön_. This is a Roman copy. According to legend, Laocoön was a priest who warned the Trojans not to take the Greeks' wooden horse within their city. This sculpture depicts his punishment. Great serpents sent by the goddess Athena, who was on the side of the Greeks, devoured Laocoön and his sons before the horrified people of Troy. _Direzione Generale Musei Vaticani_

basis of all human knowledge. According to Epicurus, atoms were continually falling through the void and giving off images in direct contact with the senses. These falling atoms could swerve in an arbitrary, unpredictable way to produce the combinations seen in the world. When a person died, the atoms that composed the body dispersed so that the person had no further existence or perception and therefore nothing to fear after death. The gods, according to Epicurus, took no interest in human affairs. This belief amounted to a practical atheism, and the Epicureans were often thought to be atheists.

The purpose of Epicurean physics was to liberate people from the fear of death, the gods, and the supernatural. Epicurean ethics were hedonistic, identifying happiness with pleasure. But _pleasure_ for Epicurus was chiefly negative: the absence of pain and trouble. The goal of the Epicureans was _ataraxia_, the condition of being undisturbed, without trouble, pain, or responsibility. To achieve it, one should ideally have sufficient means to withdraw from worldly affairs; Epicurus even advised against marriage and children. He preached a life of genteel, restrained selfishness, which might appeal to intellectuals of means but was not calculated to be widely attractive.

Stoics The Stoic school, established by Zeno of Citium (335–263 B.C.E.) soon after Epicurus began teaching, took

its name from the Stoa Poikile, or Painted Portico, in the Athenian Agora, where Zeno and his disciples met.

Like the Epicureans, the **Stoics** sought the happiness of the individual; but unlike Epicurean philosophy, Stoic philosophy was almost indistinguishable from religion. The Stoics believed that god and nature are the same and that humans must live in harmony within themselves and with nature. The guiding principle in nature is divine reason (**_logos_**), or fire. Every human has a spark of this divinity, and after death it returns to the eternal Divine Spirit. From time to time the world is destroyed by fire, from the ashes of which a new world arises.

Human happiness, according to the Stoics, lies in the virtuous life, lived in accordance with natural law, in which "all actions promote the harmony of the spirit dwelling in the individual man with the will of him who orders the universe."

Only the wise—who know what is good, what is evil, and what is "indifferent"—can live such a life. Good and evil are dispositions of the mind or soul. Thus prudence, justice, courage, and temperance are good, whereas folly, injustice, and cowardice are evil. Life, health, pleasure, beauty, strength, wealth, and so on are neutral—morally "indifferent." The source of misery is passion, a disease of the soul and an irrational mental contraction that arises from morally indifferent things. The goal of the wise is _apatheia_, or freedom from passion.

The Stoics viewed the world as a single large _polis_ and all people as children of god. Although they did not forbid political activity, and many Stoics were politically active, they believed the usual subjects of political argument to be indifferent. With their striving for inner harmony and a life lived in accordance with the Divine Will, their fatalistic attitude, and their goal a form of apathy, the Stoics fit the post-Alexandrian world well. The spread of Stoicism eased the creation of a new political system that relied on the docile submission, not the active participation, of the governed.

Literature

The literary center of the Hellenistic world in the third and second centuries B.C.E. was Alexandria, Egypt. There, Egypt's Hellenistic rulers, the Ptolemies, had founded the

A Page from *On Floating Bodies.* Archimedes' work was covered by a 10th-century manuscript, but ultraviolet radiation reveals the original text and drawings underneath. ©*2004 Christie's Images, Inc.*

museum—a great research institute where royal funds supported scientists and scholars—and a library with almost half a million books. The library housed much of the great body of past Greek literature, most of which has since been lost. Alexandrian scholars had what they judged to be the best works copied, editing and criticizing them from the point of view of language, form, and content, and writing biographies of the authors. It is to this work that we owe the preservation of most of what remains to us of ancient literature.

The scholarly atmosphere of Alexandria stimulated the study of history and its ancillary discipline, chronology. Eratosthenes (ca. 275–195 B.C.E.) developed a chronology of important events since the Trojan War, and others undertook similar tasks. Contemporaries of Alexander, such as Ptolemy I (d. 284 B.C.E.), Aristobulus, and Nearchus, wrote apparently sober, factual accounts of his career. The fragments we have of the work of most Hellenistic historians suggest that they emphasized sensational and biographical detail over the rigorous, impersonal analysis characteristic of Thucydides.

Architecture and Sculpture

The Hellenistic monarchies greatly increased the opportunities open to architects and sculptors. Money was plentiful, rulers sought outlets for conspicuous display, new cities needed to be built and beautified, and the well-to-do created an increasing demand for objects of art. New cities were usually laid out on the grid plan introduced in the fifth century B.C.E. by Hippodamus of Miletus. Temples were built on the classical model, and the covered portico, or *stoa*, became a very popular addition to Hellenistic agoras.

Reflecting the cosmopolitan nature of the Hellenistic world, leading sculptors accepted commissions wherever they were attractive. The result was a certain uniformity, although Alexandria, Rhodes, and the kingdom of Pergamum in Asia Minor developed distinctive styles. In general, Hellenistic sculpture continued the trend that emerged in the fourth century B.C.E. toward the sentimental, emotional, and realistic and away from the balanced tension and idealism of the fifth century B.C.E. The characteristics of Hellenistic sculpture are readily apparent in the *Laocoön*, carved at Rhodes in the second century B.C.E.

Mathematics and Science

Among the most spectacular intellectual accomplishments of the Hellenistic Age were those in mathematics and science. Indeed, Alexandrian scholars were responsible for most of the scientific knowledge available to the West until the scientific revolution of the sixteenth and seventeenth centuries C.E. (See Document, "Plutarch Cites Archimedes and Hellenistic Science.")

Euclid's *Elements* (written early in the third century B.C.E.) is still the foundation for courses in plane and solid geometry. Archimedes of Syracuse (ca. 287–212 B.C.E.), who also made advances in geometry, established the theory of the lever in mechanics and invented hydrostatics.

Advances in mathematics, when applied to Babylonian astronomical tables available to Hellenistic scholars, spurred great progress in astronomy. As early as the fourth century Heraclides of Pontus (ca. 390–310 B.C.E.) had

Plutarch Cites Archimedes and Hellenistic Science

Document

Archimedes (ca. 287–212 B.C.E. was one of the great mathematicians and physicists of antiquity. He was a native of Syracuse in Sicily and a friend of its king. Plutarch discusses him in the following selection and reveals much about the ancient attitude toward applied science.

◆ What does this account reveal about the Greek attitude toward the mechanical arts? Why would Archimedes consider intellectual speculation to be superior to practical knowledge? Do you think Plutarch shared this view?

Archimedes, however, in writing to King Hiero, whose friend and near relation he was, had stated that given the force, any given weight might be moved, and even boasted, we are told, relying on the strength of demonstration, that if there were another earth, by going into it he could remove this. Hiero being struck with amazement at this, and entreating him to make good this problem by actual experiment, and show some great weight moved by a small engine, he fixed accordingly upon a ship of burden out of the king's arsenal, which could not be drawn out of the dock without great labour and many men; and, loading her with many passengers and a full freight, sitting himself the while far off, with no great endeavour, but only holding the head of the pulley in his hand and drawing the cords by degrees [he

lifted the ship]. (Yet Archimedes possessed so high a spirit, so profound a soul, and such treasures of scientific knowledge, that though these inventions had now obtained him the renown of more than human sagacity, he yet would not deign to leave behind him any commentary or writing on such subjects; but, repudiating as sordid and ignoble the whole trade of engineering, and every sort of art that lends itself to mere use and profit, he placed his whole affection and ambition in those purer speculations where there can be no reference to the vulgar needs of life. . . .

From Plutarch, "Marcellus," in *Lives of the Noble Grecians and Romans*, trans. by John Dryden, rev. by A. H. Clough (New York: Random House, n.d.), pp. 376–378.

argued that Mercury and Venus circulate around the sun and not the Earth. He appears to have made other suggestions leading in the direction of a **heliocentric theory** of the universe. It was Aristarchus of Samos (ca. 310–230 B.C.E.), however, who asserted that the sun, along with the other fixed stars, did not move and that the Earth revolved around the sun in a circular orbit and rotated on its axis while doing so. The heliocentric theory, however, did not take hold. It ran contrary not only to the traditional view codified by Aristotle, but also to what seemed to be common sense. And, of course, planetary orbits are not circular. Hipparchus of Nicaea (b. ca. 190 B.C.E.) constructed an ingenious and complicated geocentric model of the universe that did a good job of accounting for the movements of the sun, the moon, and the planets. Ptolemy of Alexandria (second century C.E.) adopted Hipparchus's system with a few improvements, and it remained dominant until the work of Copernicus, in the sixteenth century C.E.

Hellenistic scientists made progress in mapping the Earth as well as the sky. Eratosthenes of Cyrene (ca. 275–195 B.C.E.) accurately calculated the circumference of the Earth and

wrote a treatise on geography based on mathematical and physical reasoning and the reports of travelers. Eratosthenes' map (see Map 3–8) was in many ways more accurate than a later one, created by Ptolemy, which became standard during the Middle Ages.

Summary

Early Greece. Greek civilization is divided into several periods. In the Minoan and Mycenaean ages, the Greek states were ruled by powerful kings supported by elaborate bureaucracies. Invaders from the north destroyed Mycenaean civilization around 1150 B.C.E. By 750 B.C.E., during the Archaic period, Greek society took its characteristic form: the *polis* (plural *poleis*), a self-governing city-state. The most important *poleis* were Athens and Sparta. At first governed by land-owning aristocrats, then by tyrants, many *poleis* evolved more democratic forms of government by 500 B.C.E. In an effort to avoid the pressures of overpopulation and land hunger, the Greeks

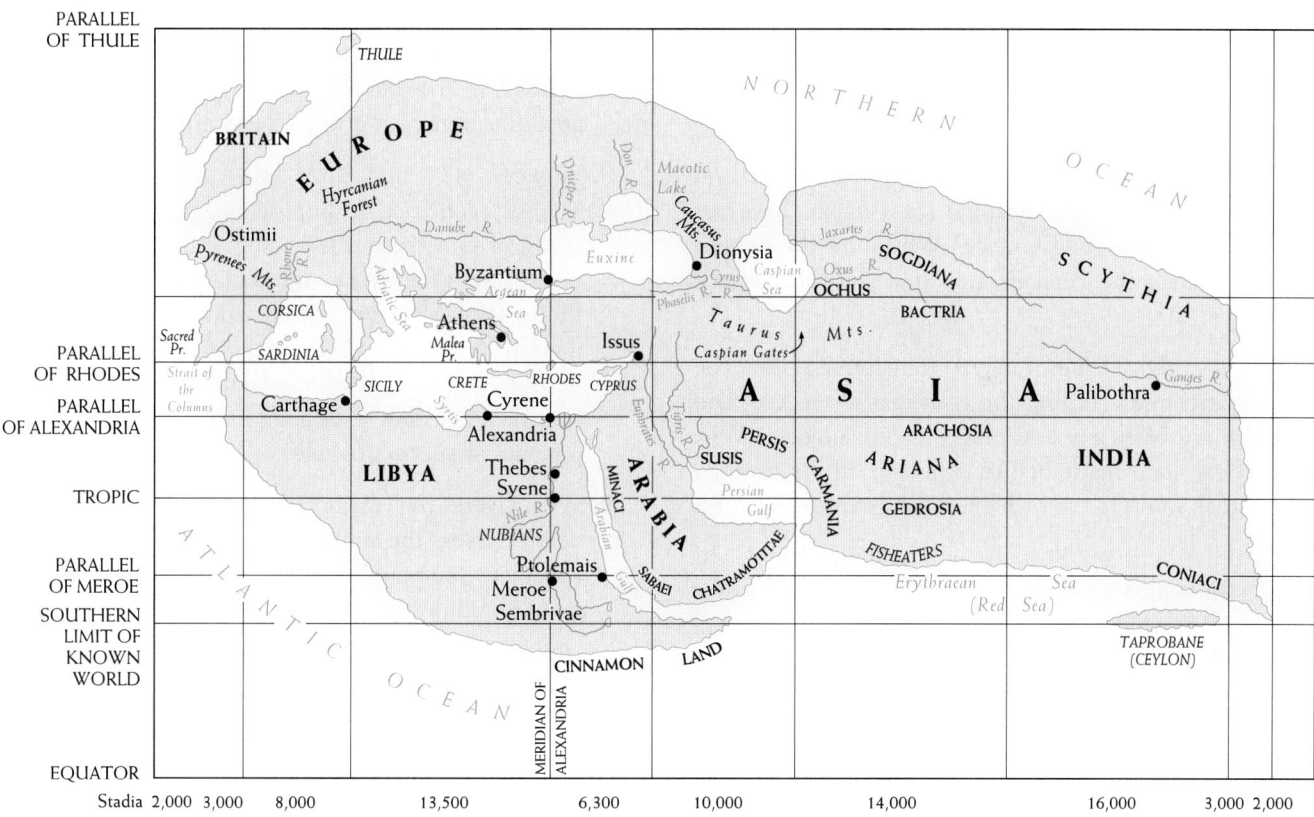

Map 3–8. The World According to Eratosthenes. Eratosthenes of Alexandria (ca. 275–195 B.C.E.) was a Hellenistic geographer. His map, reconstructed here, was remarkably accurate for its time. The world was divided by lines of "latitude" and "longitude," thus anticipating our global divisions.

established colonies around the shores of the Mediterranean and Black Seas.

Classical Greece. After defeating two Persian attempts to conquer them in the early fifth century B.C.E., the Greeks entered their Golden Age. The greatest achievements in art, literature, and philosophy of Classical Greece took place in Athens, where the government was the most democratic seen until modern times. Among the accomplishments of Greek artists, writers, and thinkers were naturalistic sculpture, tragedy and comedy, secular history, and systematic logic, all of which still influence Western art and thought.

Hellenistic Greece. The *polis* went into political and cultural decline after Sparta defeated Athens in the Great Peloponnesian War (435–404 B.C.E.). Macedon under Philip II (r. 359–336 B.C.E.) and Alexander the Great (r. 336–323 B.C.E.) came to dominate first Greece and then all the Near East from Asia Minor to northern India. Alexander's conquest of the Persian Empire spread Greek culture over a wide area and ushered in the Hellenistic era. Hellenistic Greek culture, which was fostered by the kingdoms

that succeeded Alexander's empire, was more accessible to outsiders than that of Classical Greece. Hellenistic scholars made Greek literature and science available to many different peoples who adopted it as their own. The Romans were particularly impressed. They spread Hellenistic culture across the Mediterranean world and transmitted it to later generations in the West.

Review Questions

1. Describe the Minoan civilization of Crete. How did the later Bronze Age Mycenaean civilization differ from the Minoan civilization in political organization, art motifs, and military posture? How valuable are the Homeric epics as sources of early Greek history?

2. Define the concept of *polis*. What role did geography play in its development, and why did the Greeks consider it a unique and valuable institution?

3. Compare the fundamental political, social, and economic institutions of Athens and Sparta about

500 B.C.E. Why did Sparta develop its unique form of government? What were the main stages in the transformation of Athens from an aristocratic state to a democracy between 600 and 500 B.C.E.?

4. Why did the Greeks and Persians go to war in 490 and 480 B.C.E.? What benefit could the Persians have derived from conquering Greece? Why were the Greeks able to defeat the Persians, and how did they benefit from the victory?

5. How was the Delian League transformed into the Athenian Empire during the fifth century B.C.E.? Did the empire offer any advantages to its subjects? Why was there such resistance to Athenian efforts to unify the Greek world in the fifth and fourth centuries B.C.E.?

6. Why did Athens and Sparta come to blows in the Great Peloponnesian War? What was each side's strategy for victory? Why did Sparta win the war?

7. Using examples from art, literature, and philosophy, explain the tension that characterized Greek life and thought in the classical period. How does Hellenistic art differ from that of the Classical period?

8. Between 431 and 362 B.C.E. Athens, Sparta, and Thebes each tried to impose hegemony over the city-states of Greece, but none succeeded except for short periods of time. Why did each state fail? How was Philip II of Macedon able to conquer Greece? Where does more of the credit for Philip's success lie: in Macedon's strength, or in the weakness of the Greek city-states? What does your analysis reveal about the components of successful rule?

9. What were the major consequences of Alexander's death? Assess the achievements of Alexander. Was he a conscious promoter of Greek civilization, or just an egomaniac drunk with a lust for conquest?

INTERPRETING THE PAST

The Greeks and "Homeric Values"

Text Source from MyHistoryLab / PrimarySource DVD

1. Homer: Debate Among the Greeks at Troy

Text Source from Chapter 3

1. Husband and Wife in Homer's Troy (p. 94)

Visual Sources from Chapter 3

1. The Trojan Horse (p. 92)
2. Attic Wine Cup (p. 93)
3. The Laocoön (p. 124)

PRENTICE HALL
myhistorylab
Where it's a good time to connect to the past!

When he landed in the northwestern corner of Asia Minor (modern Turkey) and began his invasion of the Persian Empire in 334 B.C.E, Alexander the Great made a pilgrimage to the site of ancient Troy, where his ancestors had, by tradition, fought in the very distant past. There, as his biographer Plutarch tells the story, "At the tomb of Achilles, who was his ancestor on his mother's side, Alexander anointed the gravestone with oil and then ran around it naked with his companions, according to the ancient custom."

Some accounts add that Alexander also lamented that he did not have a Homer of his own to record his great deeds, as Achilles did. Thus, this incident, complete with the naked revel, reveals the tremendous respect in which the Greeks, at all periods in their history, held the Homeric epics, the *Iliad* and the *Odyssey*, and the larger story of the Trojan War.

Notice how often in this chapter the Greeks' artistic legacy reflects this veneration. A series of treasures, from the Archaic vase paintings of the famous Trojan Horse and of Priam begging Achilles for the body of his son Hector, to the Hellenistic sculpture group of Laocoön and his sons being strangled by a sea monster, reflect the long-term popularity of images from this mythological war.

Key Terms

Acropolis (p. 95)

agora (p. 95)

Areopagus (p.103)

Delian League (p. 108)

Epicureans (p. 123)

heliocentric theory (p. 126)

Helots (HEH-lohtz) (p. 101)

hoplite phalanx (p. 95)

The *Iliad* and the *Odyssey* (p. 91)

logos (p. 124)

Magna Graecia (p. 97)

Minoan (p. 89)

Mycenaean (p. 91)

Panhellenic (p. 97)

Peloponnesian War (p. 108)

Stoics (p. 124)

symposion (p. 98)

Note: To learn more about the topics in this chapter, please turn to the Suggested Readings at the end of the book. For additional sources related to this chapter please see the Primary Source DVD at the back of this text or MyHistoryLab.

However, one should note that all of these images depict the sufferings of the *losers* in the war, that is, the Trojans whom the Greeks fought. Compare the images mentioned above with the document in which Hector comforts his wife, Andromache. This segment, also drawn from the *Iliad*, might make us feel sympathy for the "enemies" in this war. Another segment of the *Iliad* (the Thersites episode) might also make us less sympathetic to the Greek cause, or at least to its leaders.

Questions

Why might Greek artists have chosen to focus on images of the losers in this central story in their culture?

Do these stories demonstrate that the Greeks (or at least some of them) were able to sympathize with the fates of others? If so, what might this suggest about Greek culture?

Are we supposed to sympathize with Thersites? Is his protest against the war at all justified?

4

Iran, India, and Inner Asia to 200 C.E.

IRANIAN LANDS

◆ Ancient History

◆ The First Persian Empire in the Iranian Plateau (550–330 B.C.E.)

INDIA AND SOUTH ASIA

◆ The First Indian Empire (321–185 B.C.E.)

◆ The Consolidation of Indian Civilization (ca. 200 B.C.E.–300 C.E.)

INNER ASIA

◆ The Seleucids

◆ The Indo-Greeks

◆ Steppe Peoples

FROM THE MEDITERRANEAN TO CHINA, IN THE PERIOD from about 600 B.C.E. to 200 C.E., centralized empires flourished on an unprecedented scale—a development in which Iran and India preceded both China and the Roman West. Well before the Qin unification (221–207 B.C.E.) or the Han dynasty (202 B.C.E.–9 C.E.) in China, and long before *imperium* replaced the republic in Rome, imperial states developed in Iran. First the Elamites, in the third and the second millennia B.C.E., built regional empires centered on their homeland of

Susa (modern Khuzistan) in lowland southwestern Iran. Then the Achaemenids (ca. 539–330 B.C.E.), an Aryan dynasty from southwestern Iran, created the greatest empire yet seen, based in Babylonia and Iran. Two centuries later the Mauryans, a northeast Indian dynasty centered in the Ganges basin, founded the first great Indian empire (ca. 321–185 B.C.E.). Both of these empires, like their later Chinese and Roman counterparts, built sophisticated bureaucracies, professional armies, and strong communication systems. They also facilitated or contributed to new cultural, political, and religious developments in their domains. ■

Persepolis. Wall relief showing Babylonians bringing amphorae and a cow (upper level) and Phoenicians bringing bracelets, cups, and a war chariot pulled by two horses (lower level) to the King of Kings, Darius I (550–486 B.C.E.) king of Persia and founder of Achaemenid dynasty. From the east side of the Apadana, Persepolis, Iran.

The Indo-Iranian Worlds in Antiquity

Iran and South Asia

By the second century C.E., the Indo-Iranian worlds had developed imperial governments with power and influence far surpassing those of any before them. In and of themselves, not all of the empires were necessarily equated with what we call "civilizations"—that is, societies characterized by cities, literate culture, technological sophistication, specialized division of labor, and complex social and political structures. Yet they mark the security, military power, and wealth that are necessary for civilization. This was clearly the case in the empires of the Achaemenids and Mauryans, which are discussed in this chapter. Developments in these empires paralleled those in other regions with which the Indo-Iranian world was in contact via trade. Centralized governments like those of the Achaemenids and Mauryans were able to build the infrastructures and secure the peace necessary for contacts among civilizations. For example, the Mauryans constructed an excellent road system that subsequently became the route for Buddhism's diffusion to East and Central Asia at the same time that it was declining in India. The Achaemenids extended long-distance overland routes, developed new relations with the Eastern Mediterranean via the Indian Ocean, and resurrected the Sumerian provincial system of central and southern Mesopotamia.

In Asia this was also an era in which influential, lasting religious traditions came of age. Some spread to and took root in cultures far from their regions of origin—the Christian,

Three characteristics mark this period. First, the era saw sustained contact among the major centers of culture from the Mediterranean to China. Large-scale empires created new markets for diverse goods, both material and human (such as slaves, soldiers, and artisans); more secure trade routes; new impetus for both diplomacy and conquest; and a wider interest in the world.

Alexander the Great's conquest (334–323 B.C.E.) of the Persian Empire and the regions eastward to North India provided the impetus for the era's second characteristic—dramatic increased contact among diverse cultures, races, and religious traditions. Although Alexander's empire was ephemeral, his conquests ended the Achaemenid dynasty and allowed the rising Mauryan power to extend across North India. The Hellenes and steppe peoples of northeastern Iran and Central (Inner) Asia, who ruled first post-Alexandrine Iran and then post-Mauryan India down to the third century C.E., inherited a much wider world than those of their original homelands.

A third characteristic of this period was the rise of major religious traditions that would influence history from Africa to China. The evolution of Judaism in the Second Temple (rebuilt 520–515 B.C.E.) and early Diaspora (second century C.E.) periods, and the rise and spread of Christianity and diverse Hellenistic cults affected the history of the eastern Mediterranean and western Asia (see Chapters 2, 3, and 6). This period also saw in China the rise of Han Confucianism and classical Daoist thought (see Chapters 2 and 7); in Iranian lands the growth of the Zoroastrian tradition; in India, the emergence of an identifiable Hindu tradition and growth of the Buddhist movement; and in East Asia generally, the spread of Buddhist traditions, especially into Southeast Asia and China.

IRANIAN LANDS

"Iran" designates the vast expanse of southwest Asia bounded by the Caspian Sea and Jaxartes (Syr Darya) River to the north and northeast, the Indus valley to the southeast, the Arabian Sea and Gulf to the south, the Tigris-Euphrates basin to the west, and Armenia and the Caucasus to the

Buddhist, Confucian as well as Judaic and Hindu traditions, for example. Others, such as Zoroastrianism, never attracted a wide following in many areas outside of their homelands. Nonetheless, Zoroastrianism was a religion especially attractive to merchants, who carried it throughout Central Asia in their travels along the old Silk Road. It won some converts among other merchants from elsewhere in Asia and, more importantly, it influenced in subtle ways other religions developing in Asia and the Middle East, including Christianity, Islam and Buddhism.

In this period, another important development for the history of civilizations was an increase in cross-cultural contact, epitomized by the Hellenizing conquests of Alexander the Great. The network of roads that spanned Inner Asia made this region a cradle of syncretism in which travelers from east and west met and exchanged ideas as well as trade goods.

The Central Asian periphery of Iran and India especially provided the great meeting ground of languages, customs, ideas, arts, and religious practices among settled peoples, inhabitants of the steppe. In later centuries, Iranian and Indian cultures continued to develop distinctive, largely independent forms, and Central Asia remained a fragmented but fertile cultural melting pot. Yet developments in antiquity set in motion cross-cultural exchanges that continued apace in later centuries. In this period Romans, Iranians, and Indians (less so the Chinese) experienced increased contact with other cultures and increased influence from abroad. These contacts and influences were manifested in new, governmental structures, technological innovations, specialized skills and arts, and religious ideas.

Focus Questions

◆ In what ways did the imperial rule that developed in Iran and India during this period contribute to civilizations in and beyond these regions?

◆ Why did this period see a significant increase in cross-cultural contacts? How were these contacts manifested? Who participated in these increased contacts?

northwest (see Map 4–1). The heart of this region is the vast Iranian plateau, bounded on all sides by mountain ranges, notably the Hindu Kush, the Sulaiman chain, the Zagros, and the Elburz. In its central reaches, the plateau contains two large, uninhabitable salt deserts whose desolation is a barrier to travel even more formidable than most of the great mountain ranges.

Early (and later) peoples in the lands of Iran clustered wherever rainfall or ground water was plentiful and communication easiest. The key areas were the slopes and lowlands between the Zagros, Persis, Media, Hyrcania, and Parthia. The great Asian trade routes put Iran at the heart of east-west interchange (see Map 4–3).

Ancient History

The Elamites

The Elamites, a non-Semitic-speaking people, built a flourishing civilization in the southwestern lowlands and adjacent highlands of Susa (Elam, later Ahwaz or Khuzistan) and the neighboring regions between the Zagros and the Gulf. Even though we have tablets, monumental inscriptions, and brick imprints from Elamite remains, scholars have not determined to which language group Elamite belongs. It did, however, long outlive the Elamite state, since it was still recognized as one of three official languages in the Persian Empire of the Achaemenids. The Elamites were repeatedly at war with the great Mesopotamian dynasties of the Sumerians, Babylonians, and Assyrians from around 2700 B.C.E. until the end of the second millennium B.C.E. Their apogee came in the so-called "middle Elamite" period in the twelfth century B.C.E. While we know of Elamite attempts to contest the Assyrian power of the latter seventh and early sixth centuries, Assyrian armies set upon the Neo-Elamite rulers of the day from 692 until their complete destruction by Asshurbanipal's troops in 639 B.C.E., when their cities were ransacked and even their soil sown with salt.

The Iranian Peoples

The forefathers of the Iranian dynasts who would eventually build cities and palaces again at Susa as well in the Assyrian heartlands were Aryans. The oldest texts in ancient Persian dialects show that Aryan peoples settled on the Iranian plateau around 1100 B.C.E. Like their Vedic or Indo-Aryan relations in North India, these peoples were pastoralists—horse breeders—from the Eurasian or Central Asian steppes. The most prominent of these ancient Iranians were the Medes and the Persians. By the eighth century B.C.E., they had spread around the deserts of the plateau to settle and control its western and southwestern reaches, to which they gave their names, Media and Persis (Pars, and later Fars).

The Medes developed a tribal confederacy in western Iran, and were the predecessors of today's Kurdish peoples on both western and eastern slopes of the western Iranian Zagros mountains. By 612 B.C.E., they and the Neo-Babylonians had defeated the mighty Assyrians and broken their hold on the Fertile Crescent. The rise of Persian power under the Achaemenid clan from the seventh century B.C.E. led to the end of Median supremacy on the Iranian plateau by the time of the Achaemenid ruler Cyrus the Great around 550 B.C.E. Many of the institutions that developed in the ensuing empire were apparently based on Median practices, which the Medes in turn had often drawn from Babylonian and Assyrian models. Part of the genius of the Achaemenids' unparalleled imperial success lay in their ability to use existing institutions to build their own state and administer far-flung dominions well.

Ancient Iranian Religion

We know more about religious traditions of ancient Iran than about other aspects of its culture because our only pre-Achaemenid texts are religious. They suggest that old Iranian culture and religion were similar to those of the Vedic Aryans. The importance of water, fire, sacrifice, and the cow, as well as the names and traits of major divine beings and religious concepts, all have counterparts in Vedic texts. The emphasis was on moral order, or the "Right"—that is, *asha* or *arta* (equivalent to the Vedic *RTA*; see Chapter 1). The supreme heavenly deity was Ahura (the equivalent of the Vedic Varuna) Mazda, the "Wise Lord." However, ancient Iranian religion in the early second millennium was far from monolithic. Regional cultural variations were substantial.

Zoroaster and the Zoroastrian Tradition

The first person who stands out in Iranian history was not Cyrus, the famous founder of the Achaemenid Empire, but the great prophet-reformer of Iranian religion, Zarathustra, commonly known in the West by the Greek version of his name, Zoroaster. Until recently, the consensus was that Zoroaster lived in northeastern Iran from 628 to 551 B.C.E., but today most scholars accept a revised dating for him of no later than 1000 B.C.E. Whatever his dates, it is clear from his hymns that, not unlike the Hebrew prophets, the Buddha, and Confucius, Zoroaster presented a message of moral reform in an age of materialism, political opportunism, and ethical indifference. (See Document, "A Hymn of Zoroaster About the Two Spirits of Good and Evil.") While he is said to have gained the protection of an eastern Iranian tribal leader, his preaching probably did not become an official "state" creed during his lifetime.

Zoroaster was evidently trained as a priest in the old Iranian tradition, but his hymns, or *Gathas*, reflect his new religious vision. In these hymns we glimpse the values of a peasant-pastoralist society that was growing up alongside early urban trade centers in northeastern Iran. These values—for example, the sacralization of the cow and ox or honest dealings in trade—contrasted with those of the nomadic warrior peoples of the steppes. Zoroaster's personal experience of Ahura Mazda as the supreme deity led him to reinterpret the old sacrificial fire as Ahura's symbol. He called on people to abandon worship of all lesser deities, or *daevas*, whom he identified as demons, not gods. He exhorted his people to turn from the "Lie" (*druj*) to the "Truth" (*asha*). He warned of a "final reckoning," when the good would be rewarded with "future glory" but the wicked with "long-lasting darkness, ill food, and wailing."

By the mid–fourth century B.C.E., the Zoroastrian reform had spread into western as well as eastern Iran. The quasi-monotheistic worship of Ahura Mazda, the Wise Lord, was rapidly accommodated to the veneration of older Iranian gods by the interpretation of these deities as secondary gods or even manifestations of the Wise Lord himself. The old Iranian priestly clan of the **Magi** may have integrated Zoroastrian ideas and texts into their older, polytheistic tradition, thus becoming architects of a reformed tradition. Certainly the name "magi" was later used for the priests of the tradition that we call "Zoroastrian."

Zoroastrianism probably influenced not only Jewish, Christian, and Muslim ideas of angels, devils, the messiah, the last judgment, and afterlife, but also Buddhist concepts as well. Zoroastrianism was wiped out as a major force in Iran by the spread of Islam in the seventh and eighth centuries C.E. and later. However, its tradition continues in the faith and practice of the Parsis, a community today of perhaps 100,000 people, most of whom live in western India.

A Hymn of Zoroaster About the Two Spirits of Good and Evil

Document

The focus of Zoroaster's reform was the supremacy of Ahura Mazda (the "Wise Lord") over all the deities of the Iranian peoples' pantheon. He is pictured in the hymns, or Gathas, as the greatest of the ahuras, the divinities associated with the good. The world is seen in terms of a moral dualism of good and evil, which is represented on the divine plane in the twin spirits created by Ahura Mazda, both of whom are given the freedom to choose the Truth or the Lie. The "Very Holy [Spirit]" chose Truth ("Righteousness"), and the "Evil [spirit]" (Angra Mainyu, or Ahriman), chose the evil of "the Lie." Similarly, humans can choose the side with which they will ally themselves—the good spirit and the *ahuras*, or the evil spirit and the *daevas* ("the false gods"). This selection is from a gatha in Yasna ("Worship"), section 45 of the main Zoroastrian holy book, the Avesta.

◆ **What lesson or values does this passage teach? Is there a conflict between the seeming omnipotence ascribed to Ahura Mazda and the existence of Ahriman, the Evil Spirit? How does the sharp choice offered here compare to the Buddha's Middle Path (see "The 'Turning of the Wheel of the *Dharma*': Basic Teachings of the Buddha," in Chapter 2)?**

(1) Then shall I speak, now give ear and hearken, both you who seek from near and you from far . . . (2) Then shall I speak of the two primal Spirits of existence, of whom the Very Holy thus spoke to the Evil One: 'Neither our thoughts nor teachings nor wills, neither our choices nor words nor acts, not our inner selves nor our souls agree.' (3) Then shall I speak of the foremost (doctrine) of this existence, which Mazda the Lord, He with knowledge, declared to me. Those of you who do not act upon this manthra, even as I shall think and speak it, for them there shall be woe at the end of life. (4) Then shall I speak of the best things of this existence. I know Mazda who created it in accord with truth to be the Father of active Good Purpose. And his daughter is Devotion of good action. The all-seeing Lord is not to be deceived. (5) Then shall I speak of what the Most Holy One told me, the word to be listened to as best for men. Those who shall give for me hearkening and heed to Him, shall attain wholeness and immortality. Mazda is Lord through acts of the Good Spirit . . .

(8) Him shall I seek to turn to us by praises of reverence, for truly I have now seen with my eyes (the House) of Good Purpose, and of good act and deed, having known through Truth Him who is Lord Mazda. Then let us lay up supplications to Him in the House of Song. (9) Him shall I seek to requite for us with good purpose, Him who left to our will (the choice between) holy and unholy. May Lord Mazda by His power make us active for prospering our cattle and men, through the fair affinity of good purpose with truth. (10) Him shall I seek to glorify for us with sacrifices of devotion, Him who is known in the soul as Lord Mazda; for He has promised by His truth and good purpose that there shall be wholeness and immortality within His kingdom (khshathra), strength and perpetuity within His house.

From Mary Boyce, ed. and trans., *Textual Sources for the Study of Zoroastrianism* (Manchester, Eng.: Manchester University Press, 1984), p. 36.

The First Persian Empire in the Iranian Plateau (550–330 B.C.E.)

The Achaemenids

In October 1971 C.E., the Iranian monarch Muhammad Reza Shah (r. 1941–1979) hosted a lavish pageant amid the ruins of the ancient Persian capital of Persepolis to commemorate the 2,500-year anniversary of the beginning, under Cyrus the Great, of "the imperial glory of Iran." The shah felt his modern

secularist regime had re-created this traditional Iranian glory since the 1900s. Although the Iranian revolution of 1978 ended his heavy-handed dictatorship aimed at forging a centralized monarchy-dominated state, modern Iran does have a dual heritage: that of the rich Iranian Islamic culture and that of the far older, Indo-Iranian, Zoroastrian, and imperial culture of pre-Islamic Iran. The latter began with the Persian dynasty of the Achaemenids.

Achaemenid regional power in southwestern Iran (Persis) went back at least to Cyrus I (d. 600 B.C.E.), but the rise

Zoroastrian Priests hold hands around a devotional flame during a religious New Year's celebration in London in 1999.

of Iran as a major civilization and empire is usually dated from the reign of his famous grandson, Cyrus the Great (559–530 B.C.E.). The empire Cyrus the Great founded was anticipated in many ways by the loosely controlled empire of his predecessors, the Medes, in Anatolia (Asia Minor) and western Iran (and the Elamites to the southwest, in and beyond the Zagros). Cyrus defeated the last Median king about 550 B.C.E. He then subdued northern Assyria, Cilicia, and the kingdom of Lydia, near the Aegean coast of Asia Minor. Next, Cyrus swiftly defeated the last Babylonian king in Mesopotamia.

This event, in 539 B.C.E., symbolizes the beginning of the Achaemenid Empire, for it joined Mesopotamia and the Iranian plateau for the first time under one rule—a unity that would last for centuries (see Map 4–1). One of its results was the end of the Babylonian Exile of the Jews, for Cyrus allowed the Jews to return to their Holy Land and rebuild their temple in Jerusalem (see Chapter 2). Cyrus subsequently extended Achaemenid rule in the east before he was killed fighting steppe tribes there. His most notable legacy to his heirs was not only his ability to conquer, but also his readiness to rule through local elites and institutions rather than impose new political superstructures.

Early in his career, Cyrus had moved his capital from Susa to the old Median capital of Ecbatana (later Hamadan). He and his successors, in what was really a tribal confederation, adopted Median administrative practice, and many Medes served the new state. Thus the Bible and other sources refer to the Achaemenid rulers as the "Medes and Persians." What the Medes had set in motion, Cyrus and his heirs consolidated and expanded, so that the new Persian Empire became the most extensive the world had ever seen.

Cyrus's successor, Cambyses (r. 529–522 B.C.E.) added Egypt to the Achaemenid dominions. His brief reign was followed by a succession struggle and civil war from Babylonia to the Hindu Kush. The winner, Darius I (r. 521–486 B.C.E.), enjoyed a prosperous reign in which the Achaemenid Empire reached its greatest extent—from Egypt northeast to southern Russia and Sogdiana (Transoxiana) and east to the Indus valley. Susa and Persepolis were Darius's principal capitals. (See Document, "Inscription of Darius I: Building the Royal Palace at Susa.")

The next five rulers (486–359 B.C.E.) fared less well, and after 478 B.C.E., the Persians found themselves militarily inferior to the Greeks. Although

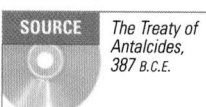

SOURCE *The Treaty of Antalcides, 387 B.C.E.*

they kept the divided Greeks at bay by clever diplomacy, Greek cultural influence grew in Asia Minor. Egyptian rebellions, succession struggles, conflict with Scythian steppe tribes, and poor leadership now plagued Achaemenid rule. Much might have been recouped by the able, energetic Artaxerxes III (r. 359–338 B.C.E.), but he was poisoned in a palace coup just as Philip of Macedon was unifying the Greeks. Philip's son Alexander was to end Achaemenid rule.

The Achaemenid State

Perhaps the greatest achievement of the Achaemenids was the relative stability of their rule. To justify their sovereignty—and the title of **Shahanshah**, "king of kings"—they claimed that Ahura Mazda had entrusted them with universal sovereignty. An inscription of Darius reads: ". . . I am king by the will of **Ahura Mazda**."[1] Other inscriptions reflect the sense—underscored by court ceremony and impressive architecture—that a ruler earned Ahura Mazda's trust through justice and uprightness. The ruler acted as

---

[1] William W. Malandra, trans., *An Introduction to Ancient Iranian Religion* (Minneapolis: University of Minnesota Press, 1983), p. 50.

Map Exploration

To explore this map further, go to http://www.prenhall.com/craig_maps

Map 4–1. The Achaemenid Persian Empire. The empire created by Cyrus had reached its fullest extent under Darius when Persia attacked Greece in 490 B.C.E. It extended from the subcontinent of India to the Aegean Sea, and even into Europe, encompassing the lands formerly ruled by Egyptians, Hittites, Babylonians, and Assyrians.

priest and sacrificer in the court rituals; a special royal fire that burned throughout his reign symbolized his role as cosmic ruler. The talents and success of the early Achaemenids strengthened their claim to divinely sanctioned royal status.

The Achaemenids, however, were tolerant of other cultural and religious traditions in ways earlier empires had not been. In part, the sheer size of their realms demanded it, but the contrast to later Roman imperial practice is striking. Even Darius's emphasis on Zoroastrian ritual and theology did not bring forced conformity or conversion to the "state cult," as his lenient treatment of the Jews shows (see Chapter 2).

The Achaemenids built a powerful army, but much of their success lay in their administrative abilities and willingness to borrow from predecessors like the Medes or Babylonians. Most of their leaders were adept at conciliation

and worked to establish what has been termed a *pax Achaemenica*.[2] They were able to maintain continuity as their state evolved from a tribal confederation into a sophisticated monarchy. The state of Cyrus, with its largely Iranian troops and tribute system of revenue, was replaced by a monarchy supported by a noble class, professional armies (led by loyal Persian elite troops), an administrative system of provinces ruled by governors called **satraps**, and fixed-yield levies of revenue.

The excellence of Achaemenid administration can also be seen in their communication and propaganda systems. Couriers linked imperial outposts with the heartlands over

---

[2] Richard N. Frye, *The Heritage of Persia* (New York: New American Library, 1966), p. 110.

Persepolis. The ruins of the famous royal complex at Persepolis, begun ca. 518 B.C.E. The foundation of the treasury is in the foreground; part of the recently restored women's quarters is visible on the left; and the tall pillars of the main audience hall stand in the rear. *Giraudon/Art Resource, N.Y.*

the borders of former states incorporated into the empire. Although *satraps* were powerful princes in their own right, the power of the "king of kings" held together the diverse provinces and tribute-paying states.

The Achaemenid Economy

Economic life from Greece to India received a substantial boost from Achaemenid success. Although Croesus had introduced a true coin-based monetary system in Lydia (sixth century B.C.E.), the Achaemenids greatly expanded on this system. Coinage was used to pay part of the workers' wages in the construction of Persepolis and displaced in-kind payment altogether under Darius. Coinage stimulated banking operations, which had declined since the heyday of Mesopotamian rule in the previous millennium. Private banking houses arose: Deposits were taken; loans made; checks accepted; leases sold; monopolies secured; and capital invested in property, shipping, canals, and commodities. The Achaemenids taxed diverse sources of income—estates, livestock, mines, trade, and production. They regulated wages and established money-goods equivalences (thus a sheep might be set at three shekels).

Agriculture remained the basic industry and normal occupation of free men. Serfs and slaves, both chattel and domestic, formed most of the labor force. Work animals were bred, bees colonized, and grapes, wheat, barley, and olives cultivated widely. Where water was scarce, the government dug irrigation canals. Rulers such as Darius mandated the transfer of fruit trees and other plants to different parts of the empire; thus from the east pistachio cultivation came to Aleppo, rice to Mesopotamia, and sesame to Egypt.

Fishing, timbering, and mining were key elements in the economy. Some industries, such as those for producing clothing, shoes, and furniture, developed alongside

well-kept highways, which also facilitated rapid troop deployment. Herodotus called the greatest of these highways, from Sardis to Susa, "the King's Road" (See Map 4–1). A network of observers and royal inspectors kept the court abreast of activities outside the capital. An efficient chancery with large archives and numerous scribes served administrative needs. The Achaemenid bureaucracy's adoption of Aramaic, which had become the common language of the Near East under the Assyrians, helped link East and West. Royal proclamations were rapidly and widely distributed, often in several languages. Achaemenid inscriptions reflect a strong emphasis on universal justice through the rule of law.

Strategic capitals in western Iran, such as Ekbatana and Susa, were important to central imperial control. The Achaemenids never had a single fixed capital; they moved the court as needed from one to another of their palaces, whether in Babylon or the Iranian highlands. The *satrapy* divisions usually reflected

Daric. A gold coin first minted under Darius I of Persia, fourth century B.C.E.

Inscription of Darius I: Building the Royal Palace at Susa

The Achaemenids, like other ancient rulers before them, used public inscriptions to underscore their accomplishments. These portions of an inscription of Darius were unearthed from the remains of Susa, the first of the two great palace-residences that he built (the second was Persepolis). They tell of his building accomplishments there and show also the extent of Achamenid power and dominion in its heyday.

◆ Why did Darius build the palace? For what does he want to be remembered? From how large an area did Darius draw the materials for his palace? What political purpose might he have had for using builders and artisans from the diverse nations and peoples that made up his empire?

. . . This is the palace which I built at Susa. From afar its ornamentation was brought. Downward the earth was dug, until I reached rock in the earth. When the excavation has been made, then rubble was packed down. . . . On that rubble the palace was constructed. And that the earth was dug downward, and that the rubble was packed down, and that the sun dried brick was moulded, the Babylonian people, it did [these tasks]. The cedar timber, this—a mountain by name Lebanon—from there was brought; the Assyrian people . . . brought it to Babylon; from Babylon the Carians and the Ionians brought it to Susa. The yak timber was brought from Gandara and from Carmania. The gold was brought from Sardis and from Bactria, which here was wrought. The precious stone lapis-lazuli and carnelian which was wrought here, this was brought from Sogdiana. The precious stone turquoise, this was brought from Chorasmia, which was wrought here. The silver and the ebony were brought from Egypt. The ornamentation with which

the wall was adorned, that from Ionia was brought. The ivory which was wrought here, was brought from Ethiopia and from Sind and from Arachosia. The stone columns which were here wrought—a village by name Abiradus, in Elam—from there were brought. The stone cutters who wrought stone, these were Ionians and Sardians. The goldsmiths who wrought the gold, these were Medes and Egyptians. The men who wrought the wood, these were Sardians and Egyptians. The men who wrought the baked brick, these were Babylonians. The men who adorned the wall, these were Medes and Egyptians. Sayeth Darius the king: At Susa a very excellent [work] was [brought to completion]. Me may Ahura Mazda protect, and Hystapes, my father, and my country.

Reprinted from R.G. Kent, *Old Persian Grammar, Texts, Lexicon.* © 1950. Reprinted by permission of the American Oriental Society, The University of Michigan, Ann Arbor, MI.

the older luxury crafts for the wealthy. The unprecedented volume of trade in Achaemenid times included large quantities of everyday household products that were now widely exchanged where earlier only luxury goods had been traded over long distances. Goods from India crossed paths with those of the Rhine valley; it was a prosperous era, marked by expanding markets—into southern Europe especially—and increased foreign travel, exploration, and investment (see Map 4–3).

The empire's overall stability for over two centuries testifies to the quality of the *pax Achaemenica*. This stable environment laid the cosmopolitan basis for the coming Hellenic influences in parts of western Asia in the wake of Alexander's conquests.

INDIA AND SOUTH ASIA

Large-scale imperial expansion came much later to the South Asian, or Indian, subcontinent than to the Iranian plateau. A cultural and religious heritage going back to the Aryan invaders of North India left its mark on the subsequent history of the vast and diverse subcontinent, despite the many languages and regional traditions that have persisted there. Only rarely, however, has the subcontinent seen political unity among even a bare majority of its inhabitants. Today's division into India, Pakistan, and Bangladesh is just the most recent. Only four times has much of the whole come under one rule: in the Mauryan,

Iranian and Indian Empires

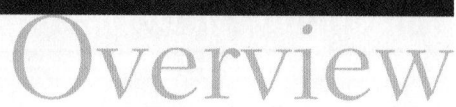

From 600 B.C.E. to 200 C.E. a series of centralized empires arose on the Iranian plateau and in India. These states built sophisticated bureaucracies, professional armies, and effective communication systems. They also contributed to new cultural, religious, and social developments.

ACHAEMENID EMPIRE, 539–330 B.C.E.

Founded by Cyrus the Great (r. 559–530 B.C.E.), it was based in the Iranian plateau and ran from Egypt to northern India. Provided a tolerant, stable, and prosperous cosmopolitan environment that paved the way for the initiation of Hellenic influences in western Asia under Alexander the Great and his successors.

MAURYAN EMPIRE, 321–185 B.C.E.

The first Indian empire, it stretched from northern India to the Deccan. Its greatest ruler was Ashoka (r. ca. 272–232 B.C.E.), who converted to Buddhism. The Mauryans helped spread Buddhism, developed strong administrative and communications systems that helped give India a sense of unity, established contact with both East and West, and fostered the growth of cities and the flourishing of art and literature.

SELEUCID EMPIRE, 312–125 B.C.E.

A successor state to Alexander's Empire. The Seleucids controlled much of the Near East from the Mediterranean to northern India for much of this period. By fusing aspects of Hellenic culture with Persian culture and politics, the Seleucids did much to preserve Hellenic culture throughout parts of western Asia.

Gupta, Mughal, and British imperial epochs. We look now at the first of these.

The First Indian Empire (321–185 B.C.E.)

Alexander the Great conquered the Achaemenids' northwest Indian provinces of Gandhara and the Indus valley in 327 B.C.E. The conquest had little or no impact on the Indian subcontinent except in Gandhara, where his passage opened the way for the increased Greek and Indian cultural interpenetration that developed under the Mauryan emperors of India. Only with the Mauryans was much of North India incorporated into the first true Indian empire.

Political Background

The basis for empire in North India was the rise of regional states and commercial towns between the seventh and fourth centuries B.C.E. The most powerful of these were the monarchies of the Ganges plains. North and northwest of the plains, in the Himalayan foothills and in the Punjab and beyond, tribal republics were more common. The Buddha and Mahavira came from two of these republics (see Chapter 2), although both spent much of their lives in the two most powerful Gangetic monarchies, Kosala and Magadha. In their lifetimes, Magadha emerged as the strongest Indian state under King Bimbisara (d. 493 B.C.E.).

Bimbisara was, as far as we know, the first king to build (possibly on the Achaemenid model) a centralized state strong enough for imperial expansion. He emphasized good roads, able administrators, and fair agricultural taxes. His son annexed Kosala, giving Magadha control of the Ganges trade. Consequently, Magadha remained preeminent in the Ganges basin, even under less competent successors. A new dynasty, the Nandas, replaced the last of these on the Magadhan throne in the mid–fourth century B.C.E., but the rise of the Mauryan clan soon dashed their imperial hopes.

Chronology

Iran to the Third Century C.E.

ca. 2000–1000 B.C.E.	Indo-Iranian (Aryan) tribes move south into the Punjab of India and the Iranian plateau
ca. 628–551 B.C.E. (or before 1000 B.C.E.?)	Traditional dating of the life of Zoroaster, probably in eastern/northeastern Iran (perhaps originally in Herat?)
559–530 B.C.E.	Reign of Cyrus the Great, Persian Achaemenid ruler
539–330 B.C.E.	Achaemenid Empire
331–330 B.C.E.	Alexander the Macedonian (d. 323 B.C.E.) conquers Achaemenid Empire
312–ca. 125 B.C.E.	Seleucids rule part of Achaemenid realm
ca. 248 B.C.E.–224 C.E.	Parthian Empire of the Arsacids in Iran, Babylonia

The Mauryans

Chandragupta Maurya (r. ca. 321–297 B.C.E.), an adventurer who seized Magadha and the Ganges basin in about 324 B.C.E., established the first true Indian empire and made Pataliputra (modern Patna) his capital (see Map 4–2). He next marched westward into the vacuum created by Alexander's departure (326 B.C.E.) and brought the Indus region and much of west-central India under his control. A treaty with the invading Seleucus (ca. 358–280 B.C.E.), Alexander's successor in Bactria, added Gandhara and Arachosia to his empire. The Greek sources say the treaty (303 B.C.E.) included a marriage alliance, possibly of a Seleucid woman to Chandragupta. Whether or not such a marriage occurred, there was much Seleucid–Mauryan contact thereafter.

Chandragupta's fame as the first Indian empire builder is rivaled by that of his Brahman minister, Kautilya. Known as the "Indian Machiavelli," Kautilya may have been the actual architect of Mauryan rule. However, he probably did not write the most famous Indian treatise on the art of government, the *Arthashastra*, even though it is ascribed to him.

Chandragupta's son and successor, Bindusara (r. ca. 297–272 B.C.E.), conquered the Deccan, the great plateau that covers central India and divides the far south (Tamilnad) from North India. Like his father, he had substantial contact with the Seleucid Greeks, including Antiochus I (r. 297–261 B.C.E.) of Syria, from whom he is said to have requested wine, figs, and a court philosopher.

Ashoka The third and greatest Mauryan, Ashoka (r. ca. 272–232 B.C.E.), left us numerous rock inscriptions—the first significant Indian written sources after the (still undeciphered) Indus seals. From Ashoka's edicts, we can piece together much of his reign and glimpse his character. In his first years as king, he conquered Kalinga, the last independent kingdom in North India and the Deccan. He thus extended Mauryan control over the whole subcontinent except the far south.

Apparently revolted by the bloody Kalinga war, Ashoka underwent a religious conversion. Thereafter he pursued the Buddhist Middle Path as his ideal in both personal and state relations. Accordingly, he forsook hunting and meat eating and championed nonviolence (*ahimsa*). He did not abandon all warfare, but he did eschew aggression in favor of "conquest by righteousness" (*dharma*). He sought by moral example to win over others to humanitarian values. In the words of one edict, he looked on his subjects as his "children." His edicts show that he pursued the laity's norm of the Buddhist *dharma*, striving to attain heaven by the merit of good actions. While stressing tolerance for all traditions, he sent envoys abroad to spread the Buddhist teaching. Among his efforts to raise standards of morality in his realm was the appointment of "*dharma* officials" to investigate public welfare and foster just government. (See Document, "The Edicts of Ashoka.")

Ashoka evidently did ease some burdens imposed on the populace by earlier governments, and he instituted many beneficial public works. However, by the end of his reign, the empire's size hampered effective administration, and under his successors, Mauryan rule disintegrated. Neither Ashoka's Buddhism nor his rejection of aggression was the cause of decline; more likely factors were economic strains and increased bureaucratic corruption, as well as his heirs' inability to claim the personal allegiances he had maintained. After his death local dynasties seized power in many areas.

Ashoka provided the model of the ideal king for later Hindu and Buddhist thought—the *chakravartin*, or universal monarch who rules with righteousness, justice, and wisdom. He is a symbol of enlightened rule with few if any equals in the history of East or West.

The Mauryan State Mauryan bureaucracy was marked by centralization, standardization, and efficiency in long-distance

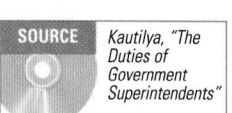

Map 4–2. Southwest Asia and India ca. 250 B.C.E. This map shows not only the major cities and regions of the Iranian lands and the Indian subcontinent, but also the neighboring eastern Mediterranean world. Although the Mediterranean was closely tied to the Iranian plateau from Achaemenid times onward, its contacts with India in the wake of the conquests of Alexander the Great were many and varied.

communications; civil and military organization; tax collection; and information gathering (by a secret service). The fundamental unit of government, as before and ever after, was the village, with its headman and council. Groups of villages formed districts within the larger provincial unit. Governors sent from the capital controlled most provinces although some local rulers were confirmed in these positions also, much as under the Achaemenids (who were probably a model for Mauryan imperialism).

SOURCE Kautilya, "The Duties of Government Superintendents"

The administration of the empire depended primarily on the king himself, who had an advisory council to assist him. Still, it was the king who commanded full allegiance of all subjects. Each of the three great Mauryan kings was associated with one of the "new" religious movements of the age: Chandragupta with the Jains (see Chapter 2), his son

with the ascetic Ajivikas, and Ashoka with the Buddhists. Such links must have strengthened Mauryan claims to righteous leadership. The reputed ceremonialism of the Mauryan court probably also enhanced royal authority.

Revenues in the Mauryan empire came primarily from taxing the produce of the land, which was regarded as the king's property. Urban trade and production were also taxed heavily. The Mauryan economic system also involved **slavery**, although most of it was domestic labor, often a kind of temporary indentured service.

The Mauryan Legacy An imperial ideal, a strengthened Buddhist movement, and strong central administration were among the Mauryans' gifts to Indian sub-continental culture. They also left behind new cosmopolitan traditions of external relations and internal communication that encouraged cultural development and discouraged provincialism. Their many contacts with the West reflect their international perspective, as do the Ashokan edicts, which were executed in various languages and scripts. The edicts suggest that writing and reading must have been common by this time (perhaps because of Buddhist monastic schooling?). The Mauryans' excellent road system facilitated unprecedented internal and external contacts, above all west to Herat and northwest to Bactria. These roads would later be the routes for Buddhism's spread to Central Asia and China, as well as corridors for successive invaders of the subcontinent moving in the opposite direction.

This era also saw the flourishing of cities across the empire: Pataliputra, Varanasi (Banaras), Ayodhya, Prayag (modern Allahabad), Ujjain, Taxila, and Qandahar. They were centers for arts, crafts, industry, literature, and education. The architecture of the Mauryan capital, Pataliputra, has not survived because of its wood-and-brick construction. But Greek travelers such as Megasthenes (who was active around 300 B.C.E.) reported that its glories surpassed those of the Achaemenid palaces. Certainly the stone buildings and sculpture of the Ashokan period reflect sophisticated aesthetics and technique, as well as strong Persian and Greek influence.

The Consolidation of Indian Civilization (ca. 200 B.C.E.–300 C.E.)

In the post-Mauryan period, the history of North India was dominated by the influx of various foreign peoples whom we shall consider shortly. In the rest of the subcontinent, indigenous Indian dynasties held sway, often controlling regional empires that became centers for developing Indian cultural styles. In this period a general pattern of regional and local political autonomy arose that would be

The Lion Capital of Sarnath. This famous Ashokan column capital was taken by India as its state seal after independence in 1947. It reflects both Persian and Greek influences. Originally the capital stood atop a mighty pillar some 50 feet high; the lions supported a huge stone chakra, the Buddhist "Wheel of the *Dharma*," the symbol of universal law. *Bridgeman-Giraudon/Art Resource, N.Y.*

broken only by the empire built much later by the Guptas (320 C.E.–ca. 550; see Chapter 10). However, religiously and culturally, the centuries between the Mauryans and the Guptas still saw the consolidation of transregional patterns and styles that helped shape permanently Indian and, through the diffusion of Buddhism, Asian civilization.

The Economic Base

Although agriculture remained the basis of the post-Mauryan economy, India's merchant classes prospered, as their patronage of Buddhist and Jain buildings shows. The fine Mauryan road system facilitated trade throughout India. India became a center of world trade, largely because of Chinese and Roman demand for Indian luxury goods—jewels, semiprecious stones, sandalwood, teak, spices, cotton and silk textiles, exotic animals, and slaves (see Map 4–3). Considerable wealth flowed in, as evidenced by archaeological finds of Roman gold coin hoards and remains of Roman trading communities in the Tamil south. Within India, guild organizations flourished and provided technical education in skilled crafts. Kings as well as the merchant classes invested in guilds. Coin minting increased after Mauryan times, and banking flourished.[3]

_____
[3] Romila Thapar, *A History of India*, vol. 1 (Harmondsworth, Eng.: Penguin Books, 1966), pp. 105–118.

The Edicts of Ashoka

Document

In the first of the two following excerpts from Ashokan edicts, the monarch explains his change of heart and conversion to nonviolence after the Kalinga war and states his determination to follow *dharma*. "The Beloved of the Gods" was the common royal epithet Ashoka used for himself. The second excerpt is from the end of Ashoka's reign and speaks of his efforts to better his and other people's lives by rule according to the dictates of *dharma*.

◆ What does Ashoka suggest is the role of the monarch? What is his concept of "conquest"? What does he think of those of other faiths and what does he want for them? What reforms does Ashoka propose, and why? Can you reconcile his expressed abhorrence of killing with his words to the forest tribes? How do these edicts compare to other approaches to law, leadership, and government?

FROM THE THIRTEENTH ROCK EDICT

When the king, Beloved of the Gods and of Gracious Mien, had been consecrated eight years Kalinga was conquered, 150,000 people were deported, 100,000 were killed, and many times that number died. But after the conquest of Kalinga, the Beloved of the Gods began to follow Righteousness [*dharma*], to love Righteousness, and to give instruction in Righteousness. Now the Beloved of the Gods regrets the conquest of Kalinga, for when an independent country is conquered people are killed, they die, or are deported, and that the Beloved of the Gods finds very painful and grievous. . . . The Beloved of the Gods will forgive as far as he can, and he even conciliates the forest tribes of his dominions; but he warns them that there is power even in the remorse of the Beloved of the Gods, and he tells them to reform, lest they be killed.

For all beings the Beloved of the Gods desires security, self-control, calm of mind, and gentleness. The Beloved of the Gods considers that the greatest victory is the victory of Righteousness; and this he has won here [in India] and even five hundred leagues beyond his frontiers in the realm of the Greek king Antiochus, and beyond Antiochus among the four kings Ptolemy, Antigonus, Magas, and Alexander. Even where the envoys of the Beloved of the Gods have not been sent men hear of the way in which he follows and teaches Righteousness, and they too follow it and will follow it. Thus he achieves a universal conquest, and conquest always gives a feeling of pleasure; yet it is but a slight pleasure, for the Beloved of the Gods only looks on that which concerns the next life as of great importance. . . .

FROM THE SEVENTH PILLAR EDICT

In the past kings sought to make the people progress in Righteousness, but they did not progress. . . . And I asked myself how I might uplift them through progress in Righteousness. . . . Thus I decided to have them instructed in Righteousness, and to issue ordinances of Righteousness, so that by hearing them the people might conform, advance in the progress of Righteousness, and themselves make great progress. . . . For that purpose many officials are employed among the people to instruct them in Righteousness and to explain it to them. . . .

Moreover I have had banyan trees planted on the roads to give shade to man and beast; I have planted mango groves, and I have had ponds dug and shelters erected along the roads at every eight kos. Everywhere I have had wells dug for the benefit of man and beast. But this benefit is but small, for in many ways the kings of olden time have worked for the welfare of the world; but what I have done has been done that men may conform to Righteousness. . . .

I have enforced the law against killing certain animals and many others, but the greatest progress of Righteousness among men comes from exhortation in favor of noninjury to life and abstention from killing living beings.

I have done this that it may endure as long as the moon and sun, and that my sons and my great-grandsons may support it; for by supporting it they will gain both this world and the next.

From *Sources of Indian Tradition*, by William Theodore de Bary. Copyright © 1988 by Columbia University Press. Reprinted with permission of the publisher.

Map 4–3. Eurasian Trade Routes ca. 100 C.E. An extensive network of overland and sea routes connected Eurasia from the Mediterranean Sea to the China mainland. The central position of the Iranian plateau, Inner Asia, and the subcontinent of India in this vast trading zone provided them with great wealth and influence, although North and East Africa and Southeast Asia formed important links as well.

High Culture

In the arts, the great achievements of the post-Mauryan era were primarily Buddhist in inspiration. Northwestern India saw the rise of the Gandharan school of Buddhist art, named after the province that covered today's Pakistani Punjab and eastern Afghanistan. In Gandharan sculpture, Hellenistic naturalism of form joined with the more recent Indian tradition of Buddha images to produce sculptural figures with flowing draped garments through which the muscular lines of the human body are discernible. In central India as early as the first century B.C.E., artists were producing stone-relief sculpture with the naturalistic, yet flowing, plastic human and animal forms that would become earmarks of the "classical" style of Indian art. The finest surviving examples are at the great Buddhist *stupas* (shrines) of Bharhut and Sanchi.

Language and literature during this period rested on the sophisticated Sanskrit grammar of Panini (ca. 300 B.C.E.?), which remains standard even today. Two masterpieces of Sanskrit culture, the epics of the *Mahabharata* and the *Ramayana*, probably took shape by 200 C.E. The first is a

composite work concerned largely with the nature of *dharma* (the moral and cosmic Law, see Chapter 2). Included in its earlier, narrative portions are systematic treatments of *dharma*, such as the Bhagavad Gita, or "Song of the Blessed Lord," the most influential of all Indian religious texts. Evidence of the rise of devotional cults is seen in the importance of Krishna in the *Mahabharata* (especially in the Gita) and Rama in the *Ramayana*. Both are major incarnations, or *avataras*, of the god Vishnu.

Religion and Society

The post-Mauryan period saw Buddhist monasticism and lay devotionalism thrive across the subcontinent. However, the Brahmans continued to dominate Vedic learning and ritual. It was also an era of diffusion of popular devotional cults of particular gods, above all Shiva and Vishnu. These traditions were to be the mainstays of all later "Hindu" religious life. The parallel development in Buddhist tradition was the rise, along with Mahayana thought (see Chapter 10), of a cult of the person of the Buddha. It focused on pilgrim-

The Great Stupa at Sanchi. This is an oustanding example of early Buddhist relic mounds. The mound, seated on an Ashokan foundation, was added to over the centuries. Magnificent carvings adorn its stone railing and gateways, one of which is shown in the left foreground. Sanchi is located in north-central India. *Dale Williams*

ages to sites where his relics were deposited or to places associated with his life. Toward the end of this age, Buddhism in its Mahayana form began to spread from India over the trade routes to Central Asia and eventually to China and Japan.

Hindu Tradition What we now call Hinduism emerged in this era. The major developments shaping a Hindu tradition were (1) the consolidation of the caste system, Brahman ascendancy, and the "high" culture of Sanskrit learning; (2) the increasing dominance of theistic devotionalism (especially the cults of Vishnu and Shiva); and (3) the intellectual reconciliation of these developments with the older ascetic and speculative traditions deriving from the Upanishadic age. These social and religious developments would continue and solidify in the Gupta era and beyond.

Buddhist Tradition Indian Buddhist monastic communities prospered under mercantile and royal patronage, especially in or near urban centers—a trait they shared with the Jains. Merchants found both traditions attractive and strongly supported Jain and Buddhist monasteries, presumably for the merit to be gained.

Chronology

India from the Sixth Century B.C.E. to the End of Mauryan Rule

ca. 600–400 B.C.E.	Late Upanishadic age: local/regional kingdoms and tribal republics along the Ganges and in Himalayan foothills, the Punjab, and northwestern India
ca. 550–324 B.C.E.	Regional empire of Maghadan kings
ca. 540–ca. 468 B.C.E.	Vardhamana Mahavira, Jain founder
ca. 537–ca. 486 B.C.E.	Siddhartha Gautama, the Buddha
330–325 B.C.E.	Alexander campaigns in Indus valley, Soghdiana, Bactria, and Punjab
324–ca. 185 B.C.E.	Mauryan Empire controls most of northern India and the Deccan
ca. 272–232 B.C.E.	Reign of the Mauryan emperor Ashoka

Buddhist lay devotion figured prominently in Indian religious life, especially in the Ganges basin. It was, however, a different tradition from the Buddhism of the theological texts, which focuses on the quest for *nirvana* and the "extraordinary norm" (see Chapter 2). The Buddha and Buddhist saints were naturally identified with popular Indian deities, and Buddhist worship easily assimilated to common Indian patterns of theistic piety. Thus popular Buddhist practice was indistinguishable from countless other devotional cults that began to dominate the Indian scene. One reason that Buddhist tradition remained only one among many Indian religious paths was its absorption into the religious variety that then and now typifies the Hindu religious scene.

INNER ASIA

The Seleucids

We have seen that Alexander's successors in Achaemenid lands, the Greek general Seleucus and his heirs, soon lost Arachosia and Gandhara to the Mauryans. They did, however, rule most of the former Achaemenid realm from about 312 to 246 B.C.E. and lesser portions until about 125 B.C.E. Alexander's policies of Hellenic-Persian fusion—the appointment of Iranians and Greeks as *satraps*, as well as large-scale Greek and Persian intermarriage—helped make viable the Seleucid rule of many eastern areas. The new "cities"—more accurately, military colonies—that Alexander left behind were bases for Seleucid control. As a foreign minority, the Seleucids had to maintain control with mercenary troops. However, the leaders of their own troops and *satrapies* gradually whittled away at Seleucid rule. Always at war, neither Seleucus (r. 311–281 B.C.E.; see Chapter 3) nor the greatest of his successors, Antiochus the Great (r. 223–187 B.C.E.), ever equaled the scale of Achaemenid rule.

In the end, Alexander's policy of linking Hellenes with Iranians in political power, marriage, and culture bore fruit more lasting than empire. The Seleucid emphasis on building Greek-style cities stimulated the Hellenization process. During the second century B.C.E., Hellenistic culture and law became new ideals among the Seleucid elites. The Seleucids welcomed into the ruling classes those non-Hellenes willing to become Hellenized. Aramaic, although declining in eastern Iran, remained the common tongue from Syria to the Hindu Kush. Greek culture penetrated but did not displace local sociocultural forms.

Zoroastrian religious tradition declined with the loss of its imperial-cult status. The many syncretic cults of the Mediterranean Hellenistic world made inroads even in the East in Seleucid and Parthian times. The later Parthians probably laid the groundwork for the subsequent revival of Zoroastrian tradition. Mystery and savior cults were becoming more popular in East and West. The new Hellenistic urban centers may have provided an environment in which the individual was less rooted in established traditions of culture and religious life. This enhanced the attractiveness of the focus on individual salvation common to many lesser Hellenistic cults and to emerging traditions like the Christian, Mahayana Buddhist, Manichaean, and Hindu devotionalist that came to dominate Eurasia over the next few centuries.

The Indo-Greeks

The farthest reach of Hellenization in the East came with the **Indo-Greeks** of Bactria.[4] About 246 B.C.E., Bactria's Greek satrap broke away from the Seleucids. His successor, Euthydemus (r. ca. 235–ca. 200 B.C.E.), extended his sway north and southwest and withstood a Seleucid attempt at reconquest by Antiochus the Great in 208 B.C.E. His son Demetrius exploited the growing Mauryan weakness and by 175 B.C.E. had crossed the Hindu Kush to conquer Arachosia. He then moved up the Indus valley to take Gandhara. Demetrius made Taxila his capital and controlled other parts of northern India. Most of the Indo-Greeks were Indian in language, culture, and religion, as their coins and inscriptions show.

Before their demise at the hands of invading steppe peoples (ca. 130–100 B.C.E.), these Indo-Greeks left their mark on civilization in all the areas around their Bactrian center. Bactria was a major source of the later Graeco-Buddhist art of Gandhara, one of history's remarkable examples of cross-cultural influence. The Indo-Greeks also probably helped spread Buddhism from India to Central Asia. The most famous of the Bactrian rulers, Menander, or Milinda (r. ca. 155–130 B.C.E.?), successor to Demetrius, is depicted as a Buddhist convert in a later Buddhist text, *The Questions of King Milinda*.

---

[4] In *The Indo-Greeks* (Oxford: Oxford University Press, 1957), A. K. Narian argues for "Indo-Greeks" as the appropriate term for these kings, who are usually called "Graeco-Bactrians" or "Euthydemids."

Steppe Peoples

In considering the Parthian Arsacid dynasty, which succeeded the Seleucids in Iran, and the steppe dynasties that followed the Indo-Greeks in Bactria and North India, separation of Iranian from Indian history is misleading. The history of North India and the Iranian plateau was dominated from about 250 B.C.E. to 300 C.E. by incursions of Iranian tribal peoples originally from the Central Asian steppes. These were neither the first nor the last such invasions from the steppe. Although commonly ignored, these pastoral **steppes peoples** have been a major force in Eurasian history.

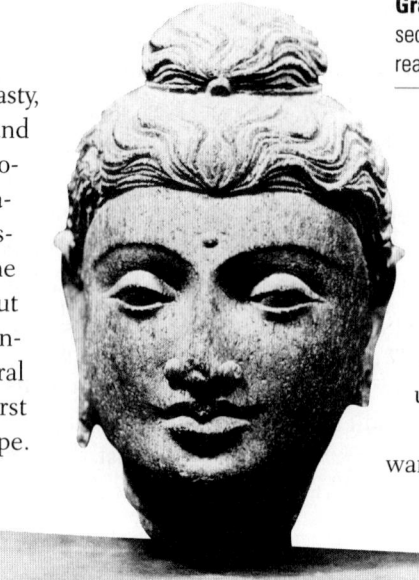

Graeco-Buddhist Art. A sculpted head of the Buddha, second century B.C.E. Hellenistic influences are evident in the realistic modeling and sculptural plasticity.

Parthians

The Parni, said to be related to the Scythians, were probably the major group of Iranian steppe peoples who first settled the area south of the Aral Sea and Oxus. In late Achaemenid times, they moved south into Parthia and eventually adopted its dialect. Thenceforward we can call them Parthians. The independent control of Parthia by the dynastic family of the Arsacids dates from about 247 B.C.E. Shortly thereafter, the Parthians began to extend their dominion onto the Iranian plateau. Under Mithradates I (ca. 171–138 B.C.E.) they emerged as a new Eurasian imperial force, the true Achaemenid successors.

Facing weak Seleucid and Indo-Greek opposition, Mithradates by about 140 B.C.E., secured a sizable empire that stretched across the Iranian plateau from Mesopotamia to Arachosia. Its center was Mithradates' new winter capital of Ctesiphon, on the Tigris. The Parthians' imperial borders varied, but from their victory over the Romans at Carrhae in 53 B.C.E. (see Chapter 6) until their fall in 233 C.E., they were the major Eurasian power alongside Rome. Eventually the constant Roman wars of their last century and the pressure of the Kushan Empire in the east weakened them sufficiently for a new Persian dynasty to replace them.

It is not easy to measure Parthian rule in Iranian lands, despite its duration and successes, because of the scarcity and bias of available sources. For much of their long reign, the Parthians were under pressure on all fronts—in Armenia, in Mesopotamia, and along their Indian and Central Asian frontiers. Yet during their rule, trade in and around their domains apparently increased, especially north over the Caucasus, on the "Silk Road" to China, and along the Indian Ocean coast (the ancient Arabs' "monsoon route," used for the spice trade with the Indies).

Culturally, the Parthians were oriented toward the Hellenistic world of their Seleucid predecessors until the mid–first century C.E., after which they seem to have experienced a kind of Iranian revival. They replaced Greek on their coins with Parthian and Aramaic, and their cities reverted to their older Iranian names. Their formerly Hellenic tastes in art turned to Iranian motifs like the hunt, the battle, and the feast. In late Parthian times, the Iranian national epic took its lasting shape. Similarly, the Magi preserved the worship of Ahura Mazda despite the success of other eastern and western cults and the common assimilation of Greek gods to Iranian ones. Still, the Parthians seem to have tolerated religious plurality. In their era, a huge variety of religious cults and cultural traditions rubbed shoulders with one another and vied for supremacy in different regions.

Sakas and Kushans

The successors of the Indo-Greeks were steppe peoples even closer to their nomadic past than the Parthians. These peoples played a major political and cultural role in Asia for centuries, especially in the Indo-Iranian region. They reflect the cosmopolitan nature of the world of Central Asia, eastern Iran, and northwestern India at this time.

Beginning about 130 B.C.E., Scythian (Saka) tribes from beyond the Jaxartes (Syr Darya) overran northeastern Iran, taking Sogdiana's Hellenic cities and then Bactria. Thus ended the Indo-Greek heyday, although the last Greek petty ruler lasted in the upper Indus valley until about 50 B.C.E. One group of Sakas extended their domain from Bactria into North India, as far as Mathura. Another went southwest into Herat and Sistan, where they encroached on the Parthians. In northwestern India the Sakas were defeated by invading Iranians known as the

Parthian Warrior. The Parthians were superb fighters and were particularly noted for the "Parthian shot," firing arrows backward while mounted on a galloping horse. It is not difficult to imagine the fear that must have gripped sedentary peoples upon the sight of such swift and mobile cavalry men. *Werner Forman Archive.*

Pahlavas, who went on to rule in northwestern India in the first century C.E.,[5] though Saka dynasties continued to rule in parts of northwestern and western India through the fourth century C.E.

The Sakas had been displaced earlier in Sogdiana by another steppe people, known from Chinese sources as the Yüeh Chih. The building of the Great Wall (ca. 215 B.C.E.) or drought in the steppes may have driven them from western China. These peoples, led by the Kushan tribe, drove the Sakas out of Bactria in the mid–first century B.C.E. About 100 years later, they swept over the mountains into northwestern India. Here they ended Pahlava rule and founded a long-lived Indian Kushan dynasty that controlled a relatively stable empire from the upper Oxus regions through Bactria, Gandhara, Arachosia, the Punjab, and over the Ganges plains as far as Varanasi (Banaras).

The Kushan kingdom of India was—along with Rome, China, and the weakened Parthian Empire of Iran—one of four major centers of civilization in Eurasia around 100 C.E. Its greatest ruler, Kanishka, reigned around either 100 or possibly 150 C.E. He was the greatest patron of Buddhism

---

[5] Tradition gives one of their rulers, Gondophares, the role of host to Saint Thomas, who is said to have brought Christianity to India. But because Gondophares probably ruled in the early to mid–first century C.E., it may be a confused report. Even if traditions of Thomas's mission to India are correct, some connect him instead with southern India.

Chronology

Indo-Greek, Iranian, Indian, and Steppe Dynasties after Alexander

312–ca. 125 B.C.E.	Seleucid rule in part of the old Achaemenid realm
ca. 248 B.C.E.–224 C.E.	Parthian empire of the Arsacids in Iran, Babylonia
246–ca. 50 B.C.E.	Indo-Greek ("Graeco-Bactrian," "Euthydemid") rulers of region from modern Afghanistan to Oxus
ca. 171–138 B.C.E.	Reign of Arsacid king Mithradates I
ca. 140 B.C.E.–ca. 100 C.E.	Movements west and south of Yüeh Chih (including Kushans) and Sythians (Sakas) into Sogdiana, then Bactria, then northwestern India
ca. 50 C.E.–ca. 250 C.E.	Height of Kushan power in Oxus to Ganges region
ca. 105 C.E.	Accession of King Kanishka to Kushan throne in Taxila (ruled about 28 years)

since Ashoka. In its heyday (the first to third centuries C.E.), Kushan power in Central Asia facilitated the missionary activity that carried Buddhism across the steppes into China. A lasting Kushan contribution was the school of Graeco-Buddhist art fostered in Gandhara by Kanishka and his successors and supported by a later Kushan dynasty for another five hundred years.

Summary

Indo-Iranian Empires. Between 600 B.C.E. and 200 C.E. imperial governments arose in the Indo-Iranian worlds whose power and influence surpassed that of any before them. The Persian Achaemenid Empire based in Iran, the Mauryan Empire in India, and the Hellenic empire of the Seleucids provided the security and wealth that permitted trade and culture to flourish from the Mediterranean to India. The Achaemenid Empire established two centuries of tolerant, stable, prosperous rule from Egypt to the borders of India. The Mauryans created the first true-empire of India, while Seleucid rule fostered Greek culture in Western Asia.

Cross-Cultural Contacts. In Asia these empires enabled widely influential, lasting religious traditions to come of age and spread—Zoroastrianism, Buddhism, Hinduism. The empires also fostered increased cross-cultural contact, especially in Central Asia where Greek, Iranian, Indian, and steppe languages, ideas, arts, customs, and religious practices intermingled. These contacts and influences were manifested in new peoples, structures of government, technological innovations, specialized skills and arts, and ethical and religious ideas.

Review Questions

1. Why was the Achaemenid Empire successful for so long? What was the political basis for Achaemenid power?

2. How was the Mauryan Empire created? What role did Greeks play in its creation? How did Ashoka develop Mauryan power and prestige?

INTERPRETING THE PAST

"Cross-Cultural Connections in Inner Asia"

Text Source from MyHistoryLab / PrimarySource DVD

1. Excerpts from The Questions of King Milinda

Text Source from Chapter 4

1. Excerpts from The Edicts of Ashoka (p. 144)

PRENTICE HALL
myhistorylab
Where it's a good time to connect to the past!

Visual Sources from Chapter 4

1. Lion Capital of Sarnath (p. 143)
2. Buddha Statue (p. 148)

Ours is not the only, and certainly not the first, era of "multicultural" interaction across geographic space. One of the best examples of cross-cultural connections in historical times can be found in the eastern Mediterranean and in West and South Asia between 400 BCE and 200 CE. Cultural concepts were transmitted across borders, as various peoples traded and came into contact with each other, and these influences can be seen in the arts, literature, historical writing, and even religious texts from this period.

Examine closely both the visual images and the explanatory captions incorporated into this chapter, seeking instances of

3. How did the role of religion in the Achaemenid Empire compare to its role in the Mauryan Empire? What influences did Zoroaster and Zoroastrian beliefs have on Achaemenid Persia?

4. Compare the Achaemenid and Mauryan Empires. What was their respective historical importance? How did each affect the world beyond its borders? How does each compare to the empires of Rome and China in the same centuries?

5. Compare the major features of the Hindu and Buddhist traditions. Why do you think Buddhism spread to Southeast and East Asia whereas Hinduism did not?

6. How did the Kushans, Sakas, and other inner Asian groups play important roles in world history?

Indo-Greeks (p. 147)

Magi (MEY-jeye) (p. 134)

satraps (sah-TRAPZ) (p. 137)

Shahanshah (p. 136)

slavery (p. 142)

steppe peoples (p. 148)

Zoroastrianism (p. 134)

Note: To learn more about the topics in this chapter, please turn to the Suggested Readings at the end of the book. For additional sources related to this chapter please see the Primary Source DVD at the back of this text or MyHistoryLab.

Key Terms

Ahura Mazda (ah-HOO-rah MAHZ-dah) (p. 136)

cross-cultural influence, in terms of artistic style and/or subject matter. Also pay close attention to the text references to Greeks in the Ashoka Edict and in the conversion account of King Milinda (Menander).

Questions

How many examples of cross-cultural influences and collaboration can you find here?

Were such interactions always favorable and respectful? What striking differences are also noticeable among the Greek, Persian, and Indian cultures?

Did these cultures always understand each other? If not, why not?

Religions of the World

The term *Hinduism* is our modern word for the whole of the diverse religious traditions of India. Until the word was coined in the nineteenth century, it (like *Buddhism*) was not even a concept in the West, let alone in India. In contemporary usage, it has become a catchall term for all the Indian religious communities that look upon the texts of the Vedas (see Chapter 1) as eternal, perfect truth.

The historical beginnings of the varied Hindu traditions can be traced to the ancient Aryan migrations into southern Asia in the second millennium B.C.E. During this era the Vedic hymns were composed. They describe a pantheon of gods not unlike that among the Greeks, the Romans, the Iranians, and other Indo-European peoples. Centered on a sacrificial cult of these gods, Vedic religion increasingly became the preserve of the Brahman priestly class of early Indian society. The Brahmans gradually elaborated a cult characterized by sacrificial rituals, purificatory rules, and fixed distinctions of birth on which India's later caste system was based. These developments are mirrored in the later Vedic, or Brahmanical, texts (ca. 1000–500 B.C.E.) that provide commentary on and instructions for ritual use of the Vedic hymns.

After about 700 B.C.E. new developments emerged. North India produced a series of religious reformers, some of whom broke with Vedic tradition and championed knowledge and ascetic discipline over purity and ritual action. Of these, the most famous were Siddhartha Gautama (the Buddha, b. ca. 563 B.C.E.) and Mahavira Vardhamana (founder of the Jain tradition, b. ca. 550 B.C.E.). Other religious leaders reinterpreted the older sacrifice as an inner activity and deepened its spiritual dimensions. Their thinking is represented especially in the Upanishads, which many Hindus consider the most sublime philosophical texts in the Indian tradition.

Developed so long ago, such notions have been part of the complex vision of existence that lies behind the myriad forms of religious life known to us as Hinduism. In this vision the immortal part of each human being, the *atman*, is enmeshed in existence, but not ultimately of it. The nature of existence is *samsara*, a ceaseless round of cause and effect determined by the inescapable consequences of *karma*, or "action." The doctrine of *karma* is a moral as well as physical economy in which every act has unavoidable results; so long as mental or physical action occurs, life and change go on repeatedly. Birth determines one's place and duties in the traditional Indian caste system. Caste is the most visible and concrete reminder of the pervasiveness of the Hindu concept of absolute causality that keeps us enmeshed in existence. The final goal is to transcend this cycle, or *samsara*, in which

we are all caught. The only way out of this otherwise endless becoming and rebirth is *moksha*, which may be gained through knowledge, action, or devotion.

On the popular level, the period after about 500 B.C.E. is most notable in Indian religious life for two developments. Both took place alongside the ever deeper entrenchment in society of caste distinctions and a supporting ethic of obligations and privileges. The first was the elaboration of ascetic traditions of inner quest and self-realization, such as that of yoga. The second was the rise of devotional worship of specific gods and goddesses who were seen by their worshipers as identical with the Ultimate—in other words, as supreme deities for those who served them. The latter development was of particular importance for popular religion in India. Evident in the famous and beloved Hindu devotional text, the Bhagavad Gita, it reached its highest level after 500 B.C.E. in the myriad movements of fervent, loving devotionalism, or *bhakti*, many of which remain important today. A striking aspect of Hindu piety

This exquisitely crafted bronze figure of Shiva dating from the 11th century C.E. depicts him as Lord of the Dance. He is surrounded by a circle of fire, which symbolizes both death and rebirth. *The Cleveland Museum of Art, 2002, Purchase from the J.H. Wade Fund 1930.331.*

has been its willingness to accommodate the focus on one "chosen deity" who is worshiped as supreme to a worldview that holds that the Divine can and does take many forms. Thus most Hindus worship one deity, but they do so in the awareness that faith in other deities can also lead one to the Ultimate.

The period between about 500 B.C.E. and 1000 C.E. saw the rise to special prominence of two gods, Vishnu and Shiva, as the primary forms in which the Supreme Lord was worshiped. Along with the mother-goddess figure, who takes various names and forms (Kali and Durga, for example), Vishnu and Shiva have remained the most important manifestations of the Divine in India. Their followers are known as Vaishnavas and

Shaivas, respectively. A few recurring phenomena and ideas can suggest something of Indian religiousness in practice.

Hindu practice is characterized especially by temple worship (*puja*), in which worshipers bring offerings of flowers, food, and the like. They especially seek out temple images for the blessing that the sight of these images brings. Another important part of Hindu devotionalism is the recitation of sacred texts, many of which are vernacular hymns of praise to a particular deity. *Mantras*, or special recitative texts from the Vedas, are thought to have extraordinary power and are used by many Hindus in their original Sanskrit form. Pilgrimage to sacred sites, especially rivers, mountains, and famous shrines, is a prominent part of Hindu religious life. India's landscape is filled with sacred sites and sacred pilgrim routes, both local and national in reputation. A prominent feature of Hindu life is preoccupation with purity and pollution, most evident in the food taboos associated with caste groupings.

The ascetic tendency in India is also highly developed. Although only a tiny minority of Indians take up a life of full renunciation, they are influential. Ascetic worshipers do not settle in one place, acquire possessions, or perform regular worship. Rather, they wander about in search of teachers and devote themselves to meditation and self-realization. Even though most Hindus have families and work at their salvation through *puja* and moral living, the ascetic ideal has an important place in the overall Indian worldview. It stands as a constant reminder of the deeper reality beyond the everyday world and any individual, life.

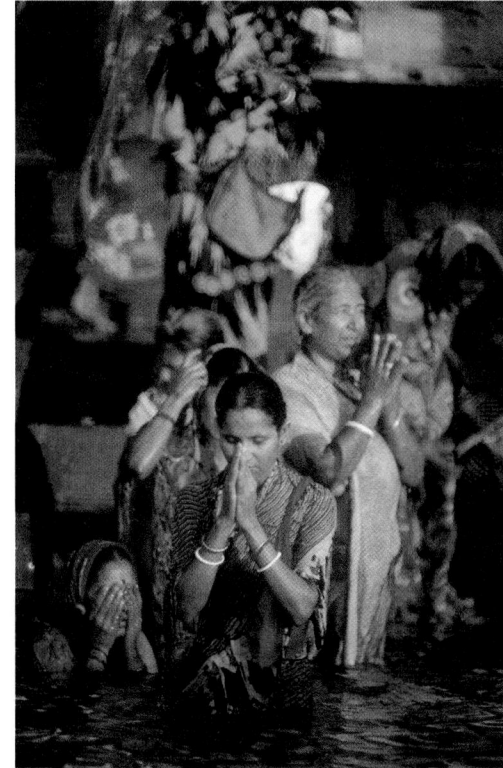

Purification rituals in the waters of the holy Ganges.
Purification rituals are part of the obligatory daily rituals of all "twice-born" Hindus. The morning rituals performed by the women here in the Ganges include greeting the sun with recitation and prayer and purification by bathing. *Ian Berry/Magnum Photos, Inc.*

◆ **Compared to other faiths that have expanded globally, such as Christianity and Islam, why has Hinduism been largely confined to India?**

◆ **How has Hinduism accomodated and absorbed different beliefs and value systems?**

Africa: Early History to 1000 C.E.

- ◆ Issues of Interpretation, Sources, and Disciplines
- ◆ Physical Description of the Continent
- ◆ African Peoples
- ◆ The Sahara and the Sudan to the Beginning of the Common Era
- ◆ Nilotic Africa and the Ethiopian Highlands
- ◆ The Western and Central Sudan
- ◆ Central, Southern, and East Africa

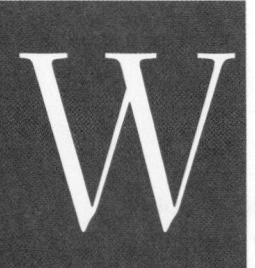

E NOW SHIFT OUR FOCUS FROM THE AN-CIENT societies that emerged north and east of the Mediterranean—the Persian, Greek, and Hellenistic worlds—to the world's second-largest continent, Africa, beginning with the earliest archaeological record. Africa forms the southern frontier of the Mediterranean world and connects to Asia through the Arabian Peninsula and the Indian Ocean. The human species originated in Africa. In the ancient world, pharaonic Egypt, the Kushite kingdoms of Napata and Meroe, and the Ethiopian state of Aksum were all major political-military powers with highly complex cultures in regular interchange with other civilizations, from Rome to India and beyond. The Bantu expansion is one of the epic migration stories of human history. The myriad ways Africans have adapted to various challenging environments provide researchers invaluable information about human societies. Finally, the difficulties of writing African history have encouraged scholars to reach beyond traditional disciplinary boundaries, thereby introducing valuable new perspectives and tools to the repertoire of all historians. ■

Rock Art from Tassili n'Ajjer National Park in Algeria, a UNESCO World Heritage Site. This painting might represent women gathering grain. It is one of a large group of works that were created between approximately 8000 B.C.E. and the early part of the common era. Although now part of the Sahara Desert, at the time this area was much wetter and supported populations of large animals (other paintings show giraffes, elephants, and other animals) and humans. *Henri Lhote Collection. Musée de l'Homme, Paris, France/© Erich Lessing/Art Resource, N.Y.*

"Traditional" Peoples and Non-Traditional Histories

Africa

People in early African societies, like people everywhere, had definite ideas about what was important in their past. They had histories. What most of them did not have was writing, and academic historians have built their craft around the interpretation of written records. African histories were generally transmitted in performances: in songs, poems, dances, rituals, and other activities that symbolically reenacted events from the past. Before the twentieth century, such performances and the artifacts they left behind (masks and costumes, rock paintings, landscapes reconfigured to accommodate ceremonies, and more) were considered beyond the purview of historians. Growing discontent with history's traditional privileging of the affairs and interests of society's elites—the emphasis on ruling dynasties, wars, exploration and invention, at the expense of describing the lives of ordinary people—eventually led historians to experiment with using different types of source material, and to subject traditional documentary sources to new types of analysis.

Historians of Africa arguably have to work harder than specialists in other regions to gather the information they need, but they also have more opportunities than most academics to collaborate with scholars in other disciplines. They often call themselves "Africanists" or "African Studies" scholars, to reflect their necessary expertise in fields such as paleontology, archeology, anthropology, linguistics, demography, and oral literature. In this they are similar to Classicists (scholars of Ancient Greece and Rome, whose training might incorporate history, ancient languages, archaeology, art history, and other fields), Women's Studies scholars (academics who examine the roles of women across cultures, and whose areas of expertise might include history, anthropology, sociology, literature, and other disciplines), and Environmental Historians (scholars who highlight the role of nature in historical narratives, and whose backgrounds might include advanced study in history, climatology, geography, biology, and other areas of knowledge), among other cross-disciplinary researchers.

Formal, university-based research in African history is still an amazingly recent phenomenon. In the academic year

Issues of Interpretation, Sources, and Disciplines

The Question of "Civilization"

In Chapter 1 we defined "civilization" in terms of a cluster of attributes—among them writing, urban life, and metallurgy—that relate to social complexity and technological development. In that sense the term identifies some common characteristics of the ancient states that emerged in the Nile valley, Mesopotamia, the Indus and Ganges valleys, and China, and also of the larger, more complex societies developed since those ancient states. However, in a broader sense, the term *civilization* is associated with the sophistication of

a people's intellectual, cultural, and artistic traditions. Too often we assume that societies that lack writing, cities, or a state bureaucracy are therefore "uncivilized." Once we move outside the Nile valley and the Ethiopian highlands, most African societies down to recent times—indeed, most societies anywhere for most of history—may not have been civilizations in the narrow sense, but they were civilized in the broader sense. African history reveals important states with writing, cities, and technology. There were, as well, many societies that were not organized as bureaucratic states with literate, urban populations, but that relied on rich, varied traditions to maintain their identities while adapting to changing circumstances and shaping their own histories.

1958–59, of the 1,735 graduate students in history in the United States, precisely one was concentrating on African history.[1] Within the past century, Africans were widely considered by intellectuals in Europe and the United States (not coincidentally, the same parts of the world where governments held colonies and legislated race-based discrimination) to be "primitive" peoples whose lives were governed by the traditions of their ancestors, largely untouched by historical processes. Events of the twentieth century—most visibly the wave of decolonization that swept Africa after the middle of the century—demonstrated that Africans had a role in world history. The development of universities in Africa and the internationalization of academia in Europe and the United States have created a small cadre of Africanists. These scholars have done important work, some of which has influenced historical studies in other parts of the world, but many basic questions in African history remain unanswered. For example, fifty years ago textbooks comparable to this one insisted that "civilization" required not only population density, political organization, and writing, but also the plow. In the intervening decades, researchers in Africa and elsewhere have proven

that in many places, plows quickly destroy the soil; the fact that some peoples prefer hoes to plows is not an example of technological backwardness, but intelligent adaptation to local conditions. As a result, this textbook and others now consider metallurgy, but not the use of plows, a hallmark of civilization. Some historians—including Africanists, and also many who specialize in women, European peasants, and other groups whose members were generally illiterate—now question whether writing is really a necessary attribute of civilization.

[1] Steven Feierman, "African Histories and the Dissolution of World History," in Bates et al., eds., *Africa and the Disciplines* (Chicago: University of Chicago Press, 1993), p. 168.

Focus Questions

◆ What are the advantages and disadvantages of emphasizing written texts as primary sources for history?

◆ Think about the histories of other regions you have already studied. Have you been aware of historians using sources other than documents in writing these histories? If so, what kinds of sources have you noticed historians using?

◆ For histories of what other regions, peoples, or topics (e.g., history of science, art history, history of religion) could scholars make good use of nonwritten sources?

Source Issues

African history has flourished in recent decades, but there is still much we do not know. Written documents, the type of evidence most historians are most comfortable using, are few and far between in ancient Africa. This shortage is especially acute for the small, local societies without writing, centralized governmental bureaucracies, or large urban centers that characterize much of sub-Saharan African history.

Stateless societies leave few historical records. Local oral traditions provide one valuable source of information (see Document, "Origins of the Gikuyu"). But even combined with reports by outside observers, oral traditions can give us access only to relatively recent history—generally no more than a few centuries.

Another source for the history of Africa's states and its stateless societies is archaeological research. The tropical climate that prevails in much of sub-Saharan Africa unfortunately destroys many types of artifacts that survive in drier regions. Nonetheless, archaeological scholarship has brought to light many formerly unknown cultures. Some of this work indicates that ancient Africa may have had large and advanced societies and states that are still unknown. The Nok and Zimbabwean cultures, for example, left impressive but hard-to-decipher remains.

A third important source consists of the reports of outside observers. It is only after about 950 C.E., however, that we get—from Islamic historians, geographers, and travelers, and still later, Europeans—much depth in descriptions of

Origins of the Gikuyu

Document

This version of the creation story of the Gikuyu in Kenya was published by Jomo Kenyatta in 1938. Kenyatta was a Gikuyu (nowadays more frequently written as "Kikuyu") who studied in London under one of the foremost anthropologists of the day, Bronislaw Malinowski. Kenyatta was a leader in political organizations opposed to British colonial rule in Kenya. When Kenya became independent in 1963, Kenyatta was the first prime minister, and he led the country until his death in 1978.

◆ Does anything in the style or content of this written document suggest that it is based on an oral tradition?

◆ In what ways might authoring this text have elevated Kenyatta's stature within Kenya? Can you imagine any potential negative consequences for Kenyatta's authorship of this text?

◆ Do you notice similarities to other creation stories?

. . . According to the tribal legend, we are told that in the beginning of things, when mankind started to populate earth, the man Gikuyu, the founder of the tribe, was called by the Mogai (the Divider of the Universe), and was given as his share the land with ravines, the rivers, the forests, the game, and all the gifts that the Lord of Nature (Mogai) bestowed on mankind. At the same time Mogai made a big mountain which he called Kere-Nyage (Mount Kenya). . . . He then took the man Gikuyu to the top of the mountain of mystery, and . . . pointed out to the Gikuyu a spot full of fig trees (*mikoyo*), right in the centre of the country. [T]he Mogai . . . commanded him to descend and establish his homestead on the selected place. . . .

Gikuyu did as was commanded by the Mogai, and when he reached the spot, he found that the Mogai had provided him with a beautiful wife whom Gikuyu named Moombi (creator or moulder). Both lived happily, and had nine daughters and no sons.

Gikuyu was very disturbed at not having a male heir. In his despair he called upon the Mogai, [who] told Gikuyu not to be perturbed. . . . He then commanded him, saying, "Go and take one lamb and one kid from your flock. Kill them under the big fig tree (*mokoyo*) [then] burn the meat as a sacrifice to me, your benefactor. When you have done this, take home your wife and daughters. After that go back to the sacred tree, and there you will find nine handsome young men who are willing to marry your daughters under any condition that will please you and your family."

Gikuyu did as he was directed. . . . [W]hen Gikuyu returned to the sacred tree, there he found the promised nine young men who greeted him warmly. . . . [H]e took the nine youths to his homestead and introduced them to his family.

The strangers were entertained and hospitably treated according to the social custom. A ram was killed and a millet gruel prepared for their food. While this was being made ready, the youths were taken to a stream nearby to wash their tired limbs. After this, they had their meal, and conversed merrily with the family and then went to bed.

Early the next morning Gikuyu rose and woke the young men to have their morning meal with him. When they finished eating, the question of marriage was discussed. Gikuyu told the young men that if they wished to marry his daughters he could give his consent only if they agreed to live in his homestead under a matriarchal system.

The young men agreed to this condition, for they could not resist the beauty of the Gikuyu daughters, nor the kindness which the family had showed them. . . . [A]fter a short time all of them were married, and soon established their own family sets. . . . Thus the nine principal Gikuyu *meherega* clans were founded.

From *Facing Mountain Kenya*, by Jomo Kenyatta, copyright Published by Vintage Books, a division of Random House, Inc. Used by permisson of Alfred A. Knopf, a division of Random House, Inc.

life and peoples in the vast reaches of Africa beyond Egypt, Ethiopia, and North Africa. Before this, only a few brief Greek and Roman accounts are available. These outside records are of mixed value. Greek and Roman observers and, later, Islamic and European writers brought strong biases to their assessments of Africa and Africans; their commentaries did much to form the stereotypes with which many still view this vast, diverse continent.

Anthropologists in the Field. Anthropologists are trained to recognize the potential benefits and risks of interacting with the people they study.

Because relatively little is known about small African communities that left no written documents, monuments, or other decipherable artifacts, surveys therefore tend to focus on the larger societies, with known rulers, armies, and towns or cities, which left their own records or were documented by outsiders. We shall try nonetheless to discuss both larger societies and states, for which we have more adequate evidence, and areas that have left us fewer sources.

History and Disciplinary Boundaries

History as we know it came of age in tandem with the European nation-states. As the structure of the modern university coalesced—with knowledge categorized into disciplines, and scholars categorized into academic departments—Europe's global dominance in technology and economic power was so great that it seemed reasonable to imagine that Europeans had advanced to a higher level than peoples in other parts of the

world. Indeed, around the time of the nineteenth-century European "Scramble for Africa" (see Chapter 27), racism combined with colonial self-interest and other factors to enable many Western intellectuals to assume that Africans (and other "primitive" peoples around the world) lived outside of historical time: their lives were the same as their ancestors' lives, no matter how many generations into the past one looked. Such people had no history. According to European nationalism, one of the criteria for nationhood was that a people have a shared history (see Chapter 24). Conveniently, then, Africans and other people who lacked history were incapable of forming their own nations.

There were interesting features of these peoples' lives, however, and academics who wanted to study them. Thus was born the discipline of anthropology. Anthropology has changed considerably over the past century, but in the nineteenth and early twentieth centuries it was meant to give formal structure to observations of the "Other," of people whose lives were utterly different from—and fundamentally unconnected to—those of contemporary Westerners.[2]

Anthropologists developed techniques for analyzing cultures based on people's everyday lives, their material culture, their myths, rituals and beliefs, and other types of sources. As historians have moved beyond colonial-era paradigms, they have found it useful to collaborate with anthropologists and scholars trained in other disciplines in their attempts to understand the African past.

Physical Description of the Continent

Africa is three and a half times the size of the continental United States and second only to Asia in total area (see Map 5–1). Because its average elevation is 660 meters, Africa has few natural harbors and islands. Steep escarpments surmount most of its narrow coasts. This has made communication with its interior difficult. Of Africa's major rivers (the Niger, Congo, Nile, Zambezi, and Orange), only the Nile has a relatively long navigable reach below its **cataracts** in upper Egypt. The vast size and sharp physical variations, from high mountains to swamplands, tropical forests, and deserts, have channeled long-distance communication and movement along certain corridors (such as the Rift Valley of East Africa, the coastal reaches of East or North Africa, the Niger or Zambezi River valley, or the Sahelian savanna lands bordering the great equatorial forest).

The special character of various regions is largely the result of Africa's position astride the equator. As a whole, its

---

[2] See Sally Falk Moore, "Changing Perspectives on a Changing Africa: The Work of Anthropology," in R. Bates et al., *Africa and the Disciplines* (1993).

Sources and Tools Typically Utilized by Historians and Anthropologists

Overview

HISTORIANS

Narrative Writing	Books, letters, diaries, newspapers and magazines
Government, Institutional, and Personal Records	Census data, tax rolls, patent applications, baptism records, business contracts, wills and other legal documents
Other Documents	Maps, portraits and other paintings, photographs
Material Culture	Local building styles, modes of transportation, technological innovation
Environmental Factors	Plagues, famines, extreme weather events (e.g. floods), natural products suitable for long-distance trade (e.g. precious metals, spices)

ANTHROPOLOGISTS

Oral Sources	Stories, myths, interviews
Performances	Songs, poems, dances, rituals and ceremonies (e.g. initiation rites, observances of births and deaths)
Other Sources	"Participant-Observation," in which the anthropologist enters into events that are later described and analyzed.
Material Culture	Everyday objects (particularly those involved in food production and consumption), shelter, artifacts associated with the practice of medicine or religion, trade goods
Environmental Factors	Population levels of humans and animals, indigenous plants, disease (in relation to humans, animals, and plant species), climate, water

climate is unusually hot. To a rough approximation, climate bands north and south of the equator on the African continent mirror each other. Over the equator, dense rain forests dominate a west–east band of tropical woodland territory from the southern coasts of West Africa across the Congo basin nearly to the Kenyan highlands. (Despite the size of this band, however, it is important to remember that tropical rain forests cover only about 5 percent of the continent.) North and south of this band (and in the Kenyan highlands), the lush rain forests give way to the **savanna**—open woodlands and grassy plains. This in turn passes into steppe and semidesert, and finally into true desert as one moves farther from the equator. In the north, the semidesert is known as the **Sahel.** The adjoining **Sahara** ("the Desert"; Arabic *al-Sahrá*) is the world's largest desert and has historically hindered contact between the Mediterranean world and sub-Saharan Africa. In southwestern Africa the desert of the **Kalahari** partially cuts off the southern plateau and coastal regions from central Africa.

Other natural factors are important to Africa's history. The soils of Africa are typically tropical in character, which means they lack much humus, or vegetable mold, and are easily leached of minerals and nutrients. Thus they are rapidly exhausted and not highly productive for long. Water is also scarce in most of Africa. Crop pests and insects such as the tsetse fly, mosquito, and locust have also hampered farming and pastoralism in Africa; the tsetse fly specifically has blocked the spread of cattle and horses to the forest regions. Still, abundant animal life has made hunting and fishing important means of survival from early times down to the present in most regions of Africa.

Africa has great mineral wealth. Salt, iron, copper, and gold have been major trade goods from early times.

Finally, we should note that Africa is often discussed in terms of several major regions: *North Africa*—all the Mediterranean coastal regions from modern Morocco through modern Libya and the northern Sahara, including the Sahel that marks the transition from mountains to true desert; **Nilotic Africa** (i.e., the lands of the Nile), roughly the area of the modern states of Egypt and Sudan; the **Sudan**, the broad belt of Sahel and savanna below the Sahara, stretching from the Atlantic east across the entire continent; *West Africa*,

Map 5–1. Africa: Physical Features and Early Sites. This map shows the major physical features of the continent and Iron Age sites of the western and central Sudan.

including the woodland coastal regions from Cape Verde to Cameroon and the desert, Sahel, and savanna of the western Sudan as far east as the Lake Chad basin; *East Africa*, from the Ethiopian highlands (a high, fertile plateau cut off by steppe, Sahel, and desert to its north and south) south over modern Kenya and Tanzania, an area split north to south by the Great Rift Valley; *central Africa*, the region north of the Kalahari, from the Chad basin across the Congo basin and southeast to Lake Tanganyika and south to the Zambezi (or, sometimes, the Limpopo) River; and *southern Africa*, from the Kalahari Desert and Zambezi (or Limpopo) south to the Cape of Good Hope.

African Peoples

Africa and Early Human Culture

Paleontological research indicates that our hominid ancestors evolved in the Great Rift Valley region of highland East Africa at least 1.5 to 1.8 million years ago. It was probably also here that, sometime before 100,000 B.C.E., modern humans—the species *Homo sapiens* (*sapiens*)—appeared and moved out to populate the world. In this sense, we are all African by descent.

The once popular view of sub-Saharan Africa as a vast region isolated from outside contact until its "discovery" by Europeans distorts reality. African goods circulated for centuries through Indian Ocean as well as Mediterranean trade. Archaeological research is documenting the existence and substantial internal movements of peoples—and hence languages, cultures, and technologies—both north–south and east–west within the continent in ancient times. Commercial links between Africa and the outside date to earliest classical antiquity. The geography of Nilotic Egypt allowed it to serve as a bridge between the rest of Africa and the Mediterranean and the Near East. Well before the common era, the peoples of the upper Nile, the Ethiopian highlands, and the coastal areas of East Africa below the Horn maintained contacts with Egypt, south Arabia, and probably India and Indonesia, via the Indian Ocean. Like Egypt, the North African coast engaged in Mediterranean trade throughout antiquity. Africa's Mediterranean littoral in particular was a place where Berber speakers mixed with other Mediterraneans such as the Phoenicians. Here the powerful Carthaginian Punic state arose in the mid–first millennium, only to fall prey to Rome (see Chapter 6).

Diffusion of Languages and Peoples

Cultural and linguistic diffusion shows that, despite the continent's natural barriers, Africans have moved extensively around the continent. Language is a particularly interesting phenomenon in Africa. Between 1,000 and 3,000 languages can be found there, depending on how one distinguishes languages from dialects. As a whole, they can be roughly divided into four major indigenous language families (the Afro-Asiatic, the Nilo-Saharan, the Niger-Kongo, and the Khoisan), plus two later arrivals (the **Austronesian** language spoken on Madagascar, and the Indo-European family from Western Europe).

The **Afro-Asiatic** language family originated near the Red Sea. It is represented in the Semitic languages (which include Arabic, Hebrew, Aramaic, and Syriac) of southwestern Asia, as well as the ancient Egyptian, Berber, Chadic, Kushitic, and Omotic languages, all of which belong basically to North and northeastern Africa. The **Nilo-Saharan** family is spread over an area generally southwest of the Afro-Asiatic group, from the upper Nile across the central Sahara into the Rift highlands of Morocco. **Niger-Kongo** languages are found to the west and south of the Nilo-Saharan group, originally from the savanna and woodlands west of the Niger bend south and southeast to central and southern Africa. Finally, **Khoisan** is a collection of loosely related languages found today in southern Africa.[3]

An Anthropologist in the Lab. Anthropologist Emma Mbua stands beside a reconstructed skeleton of *Homo erectus.*

---

[3] For the discussion of language here and later in the chapter, we rely on the summary and analysis of R. Oliver, *The African Experience* (1991), pp. 38–50, and of E. Gilbert and J. Reynolds, *Africa in World History* (2004), especially chapter 4.

Based on linguistic and archaeological investigations, Roland Oliver has attempted a plausible reconstruction of the diffusion of these language groups. He links the development of language families with a population growth that brought larger communities and extended movements of peoples. According to his interpretation, after about 8000 B.C.E., Afro-Asiatic languages from the Jordan and Nile valleys had spread to Arabia and across North Africa. Two southward extensions of these languages, from North Africa across the Sahara to the Chad basin, and from Egypt into the Ethiopian highlands and the Horn, likely occurred after 4000 B.C.E., possibly through the movement of sheep and cattle herders.

The Nilo-Saharan languages may have originated among fishing and cereal-growing societies in the Nubian region of the Nile and spread before about 5000 B.C.E. west into the Sahara. They were later largely displaced there by the southward extension of Afro-Asiatic languages into the Sahara with their pastoralist carriers. Isolated Nilo-Saharan tongues such as Zaghawa in the Tibesti, or Songhay above the Niger River, survived this influx. Nilo-Saharan languages must also have spread southeast with fisherman-farmers as far as the lakes region of the Great Rift Valley, where they were later partially displaced by Kushitic-speaking pastoralists or farmers.

The Niger-Kongo family had its homeland in the woodland savanna and equatorial forests of West and central Africa, perhaps near the Niger and Senegal headwaters west of the great bend of the Niger. Spoken by fisherfolk who may also have turned to farming, this group spread to the Atlantic coast from the Senegal River to the Cameroon mountains. Its largest subgroup, the **Bantu** speakers, later spread southward into the equatorial forestlands (largely as agriculturalists) and around the rain forests of central Africa (as herders and farmers) until they entered the eastern and southern savannas (see Map 5–2).

The fourth language family, nowadays called Khoisan, apparently covered most of the southern half of the African continent by late Neolithic times but was largely displaced by the migration of Niger-Kongo Bantu speakers. The varied peoples who were the ancestors of today's Khoisan speakers were likely still primarily hunter-gatherers at this time. Eventually, most of these peoples adopted the languages of the immigrant Bantu-speaking agriculturalists and pastoralists, making Bantu tongues the most widely dispersed African languages and confining the diverse Khoisan tongues to smaller areas than they had once covered.

The development of the complex language map of present-day Africa can thus be seen in terms of ancient developments in food production and movement of peoples and ways of life within the continent. We shall return to several of these developments later in this chapter.

"Race" and Physiological Variation

As recently as the late twentieth century, some interpreters attempted to link changes in African food production, development of local settled cultures, and even larger patterns of civilization to the apparent differences in appearance of African populations. The paleontological record consists of bones; we do not know the shade (or, more likely, shades) of early humans' skins. What little documentation exists suggests that, in recent centuries, lighter-skinned, Caucasoid African peoples have predominated in the Sahara, North Africa, and Egypt, whereas darker-skinned, Negroid peoples have been

San Hunters, Southern Africa. There are many groups in Africa with different typical physiologies, skin pigmentation, and lifeways. As with all humans, however, there are more genetic differences between individuals than between groups.

Map Exploration

To explore this map further, go to http://www.prenhall.com/craig_maps

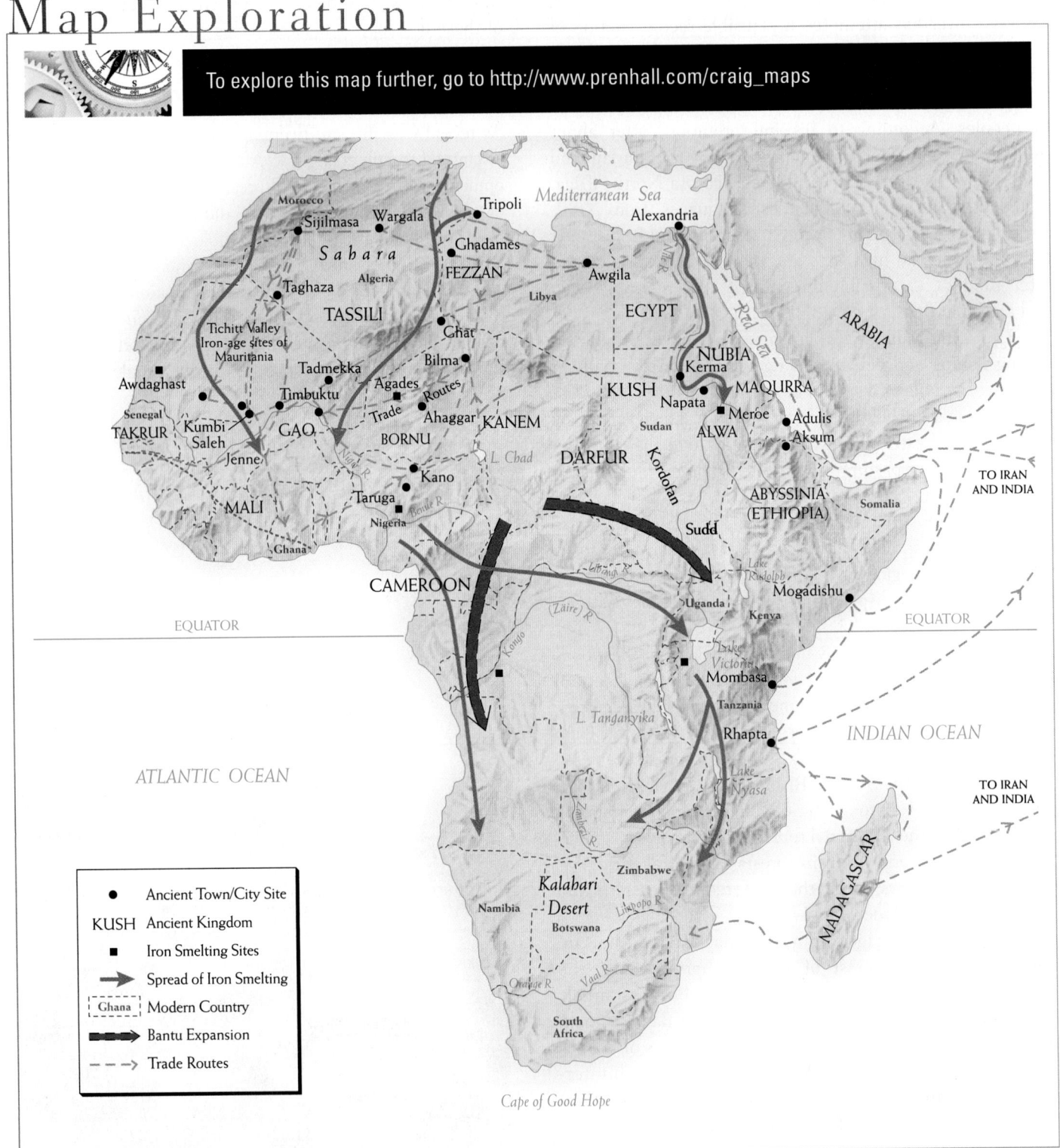

Map 5–2. **Ancient African Kingdoms and Empires.**

the majority in the rest of Africa. There are smaller numbers of other peoples, sometimes described as yellowish-brown, in southern Africa, most of whom live in herding or hunter-gatherer groups. These peoples are known as the Khoikhoi and

San or today, collectively, the Khoisan; their greatest numbers are in the Kalahari and adjacent areas of southern Africa.

Some theories have attempted to relate color or racial differences to the development and spread of everything from language, agriculture, or cattle herding to ironworking or state building in Africa. None of these theories is tenable, however, because race itself is such a problematic concept both in the historical record and in the scientific practice of biology. In the 1990s, there was a running dispute about whether ancient Egyptians were more "black" or "white," an argument in which skin pigmentation was meant to signal many other attributes. (If they were black, ancient Egyptians were assumed to be somehow more African than they already were simply by virtue of living on the African continent, whereas white Egyptians would somehow have shown greater affinity for the Mediterranean world.) In reality, ancient Egypt was a multi-ethnic society, and ancient Egyptians seem to have lived among people of many hues.

The Greeks called all the black peoples they were aware of in Africa *Ethiopians*, "those with burnt skins." The Arabs termed all of Africa south of the Sahara and Egypt *Bilad al-Sudan*, "the Land of the Blacks," and from this we get the term *Sudan*. Although ancient writers observed variations in skin tone, it is important to avoid assuming that they meant anything in particular by their observations. As with all historical records, these documents need to be read with attention to the authors' contexts and intentions.

Meanwhile, although skin color and other physiological characteristics are partially determined by genes, current research has found no genetic basis for the racial categories that humans have invented. There are more genetic differences between individuals than between groups.[4]

The Sahara and the Sudan to the Beginning of the Common Era

Early Saharan Cultures

Since the second millennium B.C.E., the vast arid wilderness of the Sahara has separated the North African and Egyptian worlds from the Sudan and West and central Africa. What is hard for us to imagine, however, is that until about 2500 B.C.E. the Sahara was arable land with lakes and rivers, trees, grasses, and a reasonable climate. During the so-called Wet Holocene period in Africa, from ca. 7500–2500 B.C.E., especially the southern half of the Sahara was positively well watered. The increased animal, fowl, reptile, and fish populations in these periods would have allowed riparian (river- and lakeside) communities of considerable size to live with ease off the land, and excavations near Khartoum in the Sudan support this likelihood.

Then, from about 2500 B.C.E., climatic changes caused the Sahara to undergo a relatively rapid dessication, and the riparian communities of this vast territory disappeared.[5]

By 1000 B.C.E., the dessication process progressed enough to make the Sahara an immense east–west expanse of largely uninhabitable desert separating most of Africa from the Mediterranean coastal rim and the Near Eastern centers of early civilization. Even then, however, regular contacts in ancient times between sub-Saharan Africa and the Mediterranean continued. Various north–south routes across the western and central Sahara were traversed by horses and carts or chariots and, most important, by migrating peoples long before the coming of the camel.

Neolithic Sudanic Cultures

From the first millennium B.C.E., preliterate but complex agricultural communities of Neolithic and Early Iron Age culture dotted the central and western reaches of the great belt of the sub-Saharan Sudan. These peoples may have once been spread farther north, in the then-arable Saharan lands they would have shared with ancestors of the Berber-speaking peoples of contemporary west-Saharan and North Africa.

This hypothesis has been bolstered by the excavation of town cultures from the mid–fifth millennium B.C.E. in Mali and Mauritania. In inland Mauritania, remains of an ancient but later agricultural civilization with as many as 200 towns have also been found. These reflect the transition from a hunting and fishing to a herding and rudimentary agricultural society. The progressive dessication of the second millennium B.C.E. may have forced these peoples farther south. Pottery found in the first-millennium settlements in places such as Jenne (in Mali) are clearly "offshoots of a Saharan pottery tradition."[6] These migrants carried with them both languages and techniques of settled agriculture, especially those based on cereal grains, as well as techniques of animal husbandry, because they kept to the savanna lands below the desert and Sahel. They also domesticated new crops using their old techniques. Assisted ultimately by knowledge of ironworking, they effected an agricultural revolution. This meant considerable population growth in the more fertile Sudanic regions, especially near the Niger and Senegal rivers and Lake Chad. (A similar spread of agricultural techniques and cattle- and sheep-raising seems to have occurred down the Rift Valley of the East African highlands.) This agricultural revolution, completed during the first millennium B.C.E., enabled new cultural centers in the sub-Saharan regions to develop.

---

[4] See Gilbert and Reynolds, chapters 1–3.

[5] Oliver, *The African Experience*, pp. 31–37.

[6] S. J. and R. J. McIntosh, *Prehistoric Investigations at Jenne, Mali* (Oxford, England: B.A.R., 1980), p. 436.

Whatever their earlier history, we know that in the first millennium B.C.E. the Sudanic peoples developed and refined techniques of settled agriculture. They must have carried these together with their languages eastward through the savannas and southward, largely along the rivers, into the tropical rain forests of central and West Africa. The result changed the face of sub-Saharan Africa, where before small groups of hunter-gatherers had predominated. With the advent of iron smelting, these settled peoples were able to develop larger and more complex societies than their predecessors.

The Early Iron Age and the Nok Culture

Features of the oldest iron-smelting furnaces commom to widely scattered sites across Africa from the seventh century B.C.E. to the fourth century C.E. suggest that smelting was both introduced to Africa from the Near East, via Egypt, and independently invented within the continent, probably in the Great Lakes region. Thence it likely spread southward into western, central, and eastern parts of the continent. The western route lay between copper- and iron-rich southern Mauritania and both the great bend of the Niger River and the middle Senegal River farther west. The central route, to which we shall return, was from the Saharan mountains into northern Nigeria. In the east, there may have been more than one route of diffusion, whether from Nubia through the highlands between the Chad basin and the Nile to the Congo basin and then the lakelands of the East African Rift, or parallel to the East African coast from the Ethiopian highlands and Nubia south to the Zambezi and Limpopo. [7]

Some of the most significant Iron Age sites have been found in what is today northeastern Nigeria, on the Jos plateau. Here archaeological digs have yielded evidence of an Iron Age people labeled the **Nok** culture (see Map 5–1). Excavations at Nok sites have yielded stone tools, iron implements, and sophisticated terra-cotta sculptures dating from about 900 B.C.E. to 200 C.E. Scholars date the introduction of iron smelting to about the sixth century B.C.E. The Nok people cleared substantial woodlands from the plateau, and combined agriculture with cattle herding.

The Nok people had the earliest Iron Age culture of West Africa. That they likely acquired this art before 500 B.C.E. by way of the Aïr Mountains to the north is further evidence of early contact among African cultures. Nok culture also produced extraordinary sculptural art, most vividly evident in magnificent burial or ritual masks. The apparent continuities of Nok sculptural traditions with those of other, later West African cultures to the south suggest that this culture influ-

A Terra-Cotta Head. This is from the Iron Age Nok culture, which occupied what is today northeastern Nigeria from about 900 B.C.E. to about 200 C.E. © Werner Forman Archive/Art Resource, N.Y./Jos Museum, Nigeria.

enced later West and central African life. These continuities suggest that ancient communities laid a basis on which later, better-known Sudanic civilizations may have built.

Nilotic Africa and the Ethiopian Highlands

The Kingdom of Kush

If we move east across the Sudan to the upper Nile basin, just above the first cataract, we come to the lower Nubian land of **Kush** (see Map 5–2). There an Egyptianized segment of Nilo-Saharan-speaking Nubians built the earliest-known literate and politically unified civilization in Africa after Pharaonic Egypt. As early as the fourth millennium B.C.E., the Old Kingdom pharaohs had subjugated and colonized Nubia. In the early second millennium B.C.E., however, an independent kingdom arose in Kush in the broad floodplain just above the third cataract of the Nile. As early as 2000 B.C.E., its capital, Kerma, had been a major trading outpost for Middle Kingdom Egypt from which (and from neighboring settlements) a stream of building materials, ivory, slaves, mercenaries, and gold flowed north down the Nile.

The early Kushite kingdom reached its zenith between the Middle and New Kingdoms of Egypt, or about 1700–1500 B.C.E. Kush appears to have been a wealthy and prosperous kingdom. Finds in the royal palace fortress ruins and tombs suggest that these Nubian kings may have taken the gold mines of lower Nubia from the weakened Egyptian

---

[7] Oliver, pp. 64–76, and Gilbert and Reynolds, chapter 4.

state in the Intermediate period. After the Hyksos invasions, with Egypt's recovery (from about 1500 B.C.E.) under the New Kingdom rulers, Kush came once more under Egyptian colonial rule and hence stronger Egyptian cultural influence. Then, sometime after 1000 B.C.E., as the New Kingdom floundered, a new Kushite state reasserted itself and by about 900 B.C.E. conquered lower as well as upper Nubia, regaining independence and the wealth from the Nubian gold mines.

The Napatan Empire

This new Kushite empire, centered first at Napata, just below the fourth Nile cataract, and then farther up the Nile at **Meroe**, was strong and lasting. It survived from the tenth century B.C.E. until the fourth century C.E., when the Ethiopian Aksumites replaced Kush as the dominant power in northeastern Africa.

Napata became the center of a new Nubian state and culture that flourished from the tenth to the seventh century B.C.E. as the successor power to pharaonic Egypt. The royal line that ruled at Napata saw themselves as Egyptian. They practiced the pharaonic custom of marrying their own sisters, a practice known to many kingship institutions around the world. They buried their royalty embalmed in pyramids in traditional Egyptian style. They used Egyptian protocol and titles. In the eighth century B.C.E., they conquered Egypt and ruled it for about a century as the Twenty-fifth pharaonic dynasty. This Kushite dynasty was driven out of Egypt proper by Assyria sometime around 650 B.C.E.

The Meroitic Empire

Forced back above the lower cataracts of the Nile by the Assyrians and kept there by the Persians, the Napatan kingdom became increasingly isolated from Egypt and the Mediterranean and developed in its own distinctive ways. When an Egyptian army sacked Napata in 591 B.C.E., the capital was relocated farther south in the prosperous city of Meroe, bringing the seat of rule closer to the geographic center of the Kushite domains. By this time the Kushite kings had extended their sway westward into Kordofan, south above the confluence of the Blue and the White Nile, and southeast to the edges of the Abyssinian plateau. Meroe now became the kingdom's densely populated political and cultural capital. In the sixth century B.C.E. it was the center of a flourishing iron industry, from which iron smelting may have spread south and west. The Meroitic state was built on a staggeringly wide network of internal African as well as intercontinental trade (see Document, "Herodotus on Carthaginian Trade and the City of Meroe"). The empire lasted until it was defeated and divided in the fourth century C.E. by Nuba peoples from west of the upper Nile. The rival trading state of **Aksum** on the Abyssinian plateau then became the dominant regional power.

Culture and Economy The heyday of Meroitic culture was from the mid–third century B.C.E. to the first century C.E. The kingdom was "middleman" for varied African goods in

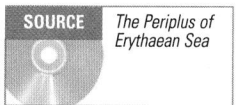

SOURCE *The Periplus of Erythaean Sea*

demand in the Mediterranean and Near East: animal skins, ebony and ivory, gold, oils and perfumes, and slaves. The Kushites traded with the Hellenistic-Roman world, southern Arabia, and India. They shipped quality iron to Aksum and the Red Sea, and the Kushite lands between the Nile and the Red Sea were a major source of gold for Egypt and the Mediterranean world. Cattle breeding and other animal husbandry and agriculture were their economic mainstays. Cotton cultivation in Kush

Ruins of the Great Amon Temple. At Gebel (Mount) Barkal at the site of Napata, near Karima, Sudan, the Napatan kings were said to have been selected here by an oracle of the Egyptian god Amon, who was believed to reside inside the mountain. *Timothy Kendall.*

Meroe. A view of the ruins.
Superstock, Inc.

preceded that of Egypt, and cotton may have been an early export of the kingdom.

This was an era of prosperity. Many monuments were built, including royal pyramids and the storied palace and walls of the capital. Fine pottery and jewelry were produced. Meroitic culture is especially renowned for its two kinds of pottery. The first, turned on wheels, was the product of an all-male industry attuned apparently to market demands; the second, made exclusively by hand by women, was largely for domestic use. This latter pottery seems to have come from an older tradition of African pottery craft found well outside the region of Kush—an indication of ancient traditions shared in varied regions of Africa and of the antiquity of African internal trade.

Rule and Administration   The political system of the Meroitic Empire, like the pharaonic, endured for centuries. There were several features that distinguished it from its Egyptian models. The king seems to have ruled strictly by customary law, presumably as interpreted by whatever clerics served the state's needs. According to Greek accounts, firm taboos limited his actions; kings who violated those taboos could be forced to commit suicide. There was also a royal election system. The priests presented several candidates for king, from among whom the god would choose the new sacred king (how, we are not told). The priests apparently considered

the king a living god, an idea found in both ancient Egypt and many other African societies.

A Kushite inscription tells us that King Aspalta (r. 593–568 B.C.E.) was elected to succeed his brother by twenty-four high officials and military leaders. Thus royal succession was within the royal family but not from father to son. Other inscriptions tell us that the succession was often through the maternal rather than the paternal line (matrilineal succession was widespread in ancient Africa). The role of the queen mother in the election appears to have been crucial—another parallel, if not a direct link, to African practices elsewhere. Indeed, the queen mother seems to have adopted formally her son's wife upon his succession. By the second century B.C.E. a woman had become sole monarch, initiating a long line of queens, or "Candaces" (*Kandake*, from the Meroitic word for "queen mother").

We know little of Meroitic administration. The empire seems to have been under the autocratic rule of the monarch, perhaps on the Egyptian model, who presided over a central administration run by numerous high officials: chiefs of the treasury, seal bearers, granary chiefs, army commanders, and chiefs of scribes and

SOURCE   Selection from Aspalta as King of Kush

Meroitic Culture. The people of Meroe produced many examples of fine pottery. This fired clay jar is decorated with giraffes and serpents. *University of Pennsylvania Museum of Archaeology and Anthropology.*

archives. The provinces were delegated to princes who must have enjoyed considerable autonomy, given the slow communications over the vast and difficult terrain of the upper Nile and eastern Sudanic region.

Society and Religion Because of the limited sources for Kushite history, we have to speculate about the social structure outside the palace circle—the ruling class of monarch and relatives, priests, courtiers and provincial nobility. We do find mention of slaves, both female domestics and male laborers drawn largely from prisoners of war. Cattle breeders, farmers, traders, artisans, and minor government functionaries probably formed an intermediate class or classes between the slaves and the rulers.

We have no direct records of Kushite religious practices, but they clearly followed Egyptian traditions for centuries. To judge from the great temples dedicated to him, Amon was the highest god for the earlier kings, and his priests were influential. By the third century B.C.E., however, gods unknown to Egypt became prominent. Most notable was Apedemak, a warrior god with a lion's head. The many lion temples associated with him (forty-six have been identified) reflect his importance. Such gods likely represented local deities who gradually took their places alongside the highest Egyptian gods.

The Aksumite Empire

A highland people who had developed their own commercially powerful trading state to the south of Kush finished off the weakened Kushite empire, apparently about 330 C.E. This was the newly Christianized state of Aksum, which centered in the northern Ethiopian, or Abyssinian, highlands where the Blue Nile rises. With the ascendancy of Aksum, our sources lapse into relative silence concerning the Nubian regions of the Nile. Not until the rise of new Christian Nubian states in the mid–sixth century can we again find clear evidence of the inheritors of the land of Kush.

The peoples of Aksum were the product of a linguistic and cultural mixing of African Kushitic speakers with Semitic speakers from Yemenite southern Arabia. This mixing occurred after southern Arabians infiltrated and settled on the Ethiopian plateau around 500 B.C.E., giving Aksum, and later Ethiopia, Semitic speech and script closely related to South Arabian. Greek and Roman sources tell of an Aksumite kingdom from at least the first century C.E. By this time the kingdom, through its chief port of Adulis, had already become the major ivory and elephant market of northeastern Africa. Adulis had been important in Ptolemaic times, when it was captured by Egypt and used as a conduit for Egyptian influence in the highlands. After Egypt fell to the

Romans, Aksum and its major port became an important cosmopolitan commercial center.

In the first two centuries C.E., their Red Sea location gave the Aksumites a strategic seat astride the important Indian Ocean trade routes that linked India and the East Indies, Iran, Arabia, and the East African coast with the Roman Mediterranean. Aksum also controlled trade between the African interior and the extra-African world, from Rome to Southeast Asia—notably exports of frankincense, ivory, and spices, but also of elephants, ebony, obsidian, slaves, gold, and other inland products.

A Giant Stela at Aksum. Dating probably from the first century C.E., this giant carved monolith is the only one remaining of seven giant stelae—the tallest of which reached a height of 33 meters—that once stood in Aksum amidst numerous smaller monoliths. Although the exact purpose of the stelae is not known, the generally accepted explanation is that they were commemorative funerary monuments. Erecting them required engineering of great sophistication. © *Werner Former Archive/Art Resource, N.Y.*

Herodotus on Carthaginian Trade and the City of Meroe

Document

Herodotus reports (in about 430 B.C.E. in the first passage below) on what he has heard of the trading practices along the western or northwestern (Atlantic) coast of Africa ("Libya") as gleaned from the Carthaginian traders who passed beyond the Strait of Gibraltar ("Pillars of Hercules"). In the second passage he describes what he knows of the country, known to him as the land of the Ethiopians, above Elephantine (Aswan) on the Nile.

◆ What can we infer from the two passages about trade and interregional contacts in Africa in the fifth century B.C.E.?

The Carthaginians also tell us that they trade with a race of men who live in a part of Libya beyond the Pillars of Hercules. On reaching this country, they unload their goods, arrange them tidily along the beach, and then, returning to their boats, raise a smoke. Seeing the smoke, the natives come down to the beach, place on the ground a certain quantity of gold in exchange for the goods, and go off again to a distance. The Carthaginians then come ashore and take a look at the gold; and if they think it represents a fair price for their wares, they collect it and go away; if, on the other hand, it seems too little, they go back aboard and wait, and the natives come and add to the gold until they are satisfied. There is perfect honesty on both sides; the Carthaginians never touch the gold until it equals in value what they have offered for sale, and the natives never touch the goods until the gold has been taken.

. . . .

I went as far as Elephantine to see what I could with my own eyes, but for the country still further south I had to be content with what I was told in answer to my questions. The most I could learn was that beyond Elephantine the country rises steeply; and in that part of the river boats have to be hauled along by the ropes—one rope on each side—much as one drags an ox. If the rope parts, the boat is gone in a moment, carried away by the force of the stream. These conditions last over a four days' journey, the river all the time winding greatly, like the Maeander, and the distance to be covered amounting to twelve *schoeni*. After this one reaches a level plain, where the river is divided by an island named Tachompso.

South of Elephantine the country is inhabited by Ethiopians who also possess half of Tachompso, the other half being occupied by Egyptians. Beyond the island is a great lake, and round its shores live nomadic tribes of Ethiopians. After crossing the lake one comes again to the stream of the Nile, which flows into it. At this point one must land and travel along the bank of the river for forty days, because sharp rocks, some showing above the water and many just awash, make the river impracticable for boats. After the forty days' journey on land one takes another boat and in twelve days reaches a big city named Meroe, said to be the capital city of the Ethiopians. The inhabitants worship Zeus and Dionysus alone of the Gods, holding them in great honor. There is an oracle of Zeus there, and they make war according to its pronouncements, taking from it both the occasion and the object of their various expeditions.

From the translation of *The Histories of Herodotus*, by Aubrey de Selincourt, rev. by A. R. Burn (New York: Penguin Classics, 1954, revised 1972). Copyright © The estate of Aubrey de Selincourt, 1954, © A. R. Burn, 1972.

By the third century C.E., Aksum was one of the most impressive states of its age. A work attributed to the prophet Mani, ca. 216–277 C.E., describes Aksum as one of the four greatest empires in the world. The Aksumites often held tributary territories across the Red Sea in southern Arabia. They also controlled northern Ethiopia and conquered Meroitic Kush. Thus they dominated some of the most fertile cultivated regions of the ancient world: their own plateau, the rich Yemenite highlands of southern Arabia, and much of the eastern Sudan across the upper Nile as far as the Sahara.

A king of kings in Aksum ruled this empire through tribute-paying vassal kings in the other subject states. By the sixth century the Aksumite king was even appointing southern Arabian kings himself. Aksum's coinage in gold, silver, and copper (it was the first tropical African state to mint these) coins symbolized both its political and economic power. The Aksumites enjoyed a long-lived economic prosperity. Goods of the Roman-Byzantine world and India and Sri Lanka, as well as of neighboring Meroe, flowed into Aksum. Vast herds and good agricultural produce also bolstered Aksumite prosperity.

Chronology

Early African Civilizations

ca. 7500–2500 B.C.E.	"Wet Holocene" period
ca. 2500 B.C.E.	Rapid dessication of Saharan region begins
ca. 2000–1000 B.C.E.	Increasing Egyptian influence in Nubia
ca. 1000–900 B.C.E.	Kushite kingdom with capital at Napata becomes independent of Egypt
751–663 B.C.E.	Kushite kings Piankhi and Taharqa rule all Egypt
ca. 600–500 B.C.E.	Meroe becomes new Kushite capital
ca. 500 B.C.E.–330 C.E.	Meroitic kingdom of Kush (height of Meroitic Kushite power ca. 250 B.C.E.–50 C.E.)
ca. 500 B.C.E.–500 C.E.?	Nok culture flourishes on Jos plateau in western Sudan (modern central Nigeria)
First century C.E.	Rise of Aksum as trading power on Ethiopian (Abyssinian) plateau
ca. 330 C.E.	Aksumite conquest of Kush

In religion, the pre-Christian paganism of Aksum resembled the pre-Islamic paganism of southern Arabia, with various gods and goddesses closely tied to natural phenomena such as the sun, moon, and stars and worshiped with animal sacrifices. Jewish, Meroitic, and even Buddhist minorities lived in the major cities of Aksum—an index of the cosmopolitanism of the society and its involvement with the larger worlds beyond the Red Sea.

In an inscription of the powerful fourth-century ruler King Ezana, we read of his conversion to Christianity, which led to the Christianizing of the kingdom as a whole. The conversion of Ezana and his realm was the work of Frumentius, a Syrian bishop of Aksum who served as secretary and treasurer to the king. Subsequently, under Alexandrian influence, the Ethiopian church became **Monophysite** (that is, it adhered to the dogma of the single, unitary nature of Christ). Yet this did not end Aksumite trade with Byzantium, however much Constantinople persecuted Monophysites at home. In the

fifth century C.E., the native Semitic language, Ge'ez, began to replace Greek in the liturgy, which proved a major step in the unique development of the Ethiopic or Abyssinian Christian church over the succeeding centuries.

Isolation of Christian Ethiopia

Aksumite trade continued to thrive through the sixth century, despite the decay of Rome. Strong enough at times to extend to the Yemen, Aksumite power was eclipsed in the end by Arab Islamic power. Nevertheless, the Aksumite state continued to exist. Having sheltered a refugee group of Muhammad's earliest Meccan converts, the Aksumites enjoyed relatively cordial relations with the new Islamic domains across the Red Sea and to the north in Egypt. But Aksum became increasingly isolated. Its center of gravity shifted south from the coast to the more rugged parts of the plateau. Here a Monophysite Christian, Ge'ez-speaking culture emerged in the region of modern Ethiopia and lasted in relative isolation until modern times, surrounded largely by Muslim peoples and states.

Ethiopia's northern neighbors, the Christian states of Maqurra and Alwa, also survived for centuries in the former Meroitic lands of the Nilotic Sudan under treaty relations with Muslim Egypt. However, incursions of the Muslim Mamluk rulers of Egypt in the fourteenth and fifteenth centuries and Arab migration from about 1300 led ultimately to the Islamization of the whole Nubian region. This left Ethiopia the sole predominantly Christian state in Africa.

The Western and Central Sudan

Agriculture, Trade, and the Rise of Urban Centers

Earlier we noted the presumed movements of Neolithic peoples southward from the Saharan regions into the western and central Sudan and ultimately into the equatorial forests. The rain forests were inhospitable to cows and horses, largely because of the animals' inability to survive the sleeping sickness (**trypanosomiasis**) carried by the tsetse fly. But the agriculturalists who brought their cereal grains and stone tools south found particularly good conditions in the savanna just north of the West African forests. By the first or second century C.E., settled agriculture, augmented by iron tools, had become the way of life of most inhabitants of the western Sudan; it had even progressed in the forest regions farther south. The savanna areas seem to have experienced a population explosion in the first few centuries C.E., especially around the Senegal River, the great northern bend in

A Camel Caravan Crossing the Sahara. The use of the camel as a beast of burden from the first century C.E. onward greatly increased trans-Saharan trade. © Michael S. Lewis/Corbis.

the Niger River, and Lake Chad. Villages, and chiefdoms of several villages, were the largest political units. As time went on, their growth provided the basis (and need) for larger towns and political units in the western Sudan to develop.

Trade also promoted or at least accompanied the eventual rise of larger political entities in the western and central Sudan. Regional and interregional trade networks in the western and central Sudan date to ancient times; as we saw earlier, contacts between the Sudanic regions and the Mediterranean were maintained throughout the first millennium B.C.E. over trans-Saharan trading routes. Extensive east–west trade connected the western Sahel to Egypt and the Nilotic Sudan. From the western Sahel this trade connected to Saharan routes and sites to the north (see Map 5–3).

By the latter first millennium B.C.E., urban settlements—such as Gao, Kumbi (or Kumbi Saleh), and Jenne—emerged in the western Sahel. Excavations at Jenne, in the upper Niger (the so-called Inland Delta) indicate that it dates from 250 B.C.E. and had a population of more than 10,000 by the late first millennium C.E.[8]

We have already noted even earlier evidence of urbanism farther west and north, in the southern Mauritanian desert. In addition, to the east, south of Lake Chad, 600 densely populated towns of the Sao, a Chadic-speaking people, can be dated to the early first millennium C.E.

---

[8] S. J. and R. J. McIntosh, pp. 41–59, 434–461; and R. Oliver, p. 90. The ensuing discussion of West African urban settlement is also taken primarily from Oliver's excellent summary of current knowledge about this subject, ibid., pp. 90–101.

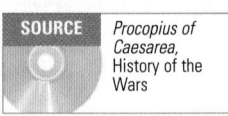

SOURCE *Procopius of Caesarea, History of the Wars*

All of these early urbanized areas combined farming with fishing and hunting, and all developed in oasis or river regions rich enough to support dense populations and trade. The existence of relatively autonomous settlements made possible loose confederations or even imperial networks as time went on (and much earlier than scholars used to think).

The introduction of the domesticated camel (the one-humped Arabian camel, or dromedary) from the east around the beginning of the Common Era increased trans-Saharan trade. By the early centuries C.E. the West African settled communities had developed important trading centers on their northern peripheries, in the Sahel near the edge of the true desert. The salt of the desert, so badly needed in the settled savanna, and the gold of West Africa, coveted in the north, were the prime trade commodities. However, many other items were also traded, including cola nuts, slaves, dates, and gum from West Africa, and horses, cattle, millet, leather, cloth, and weapons from the north.

Towns such as Awdaghast, Walata, Timbuktu, Gao, Tadmekka, and Agades were the most famous southern terminals for this trade. These centers allowed the largely Berber middlemen who plied the desert routes to cross the perilous Sahara via oasis stations en route to the North

Chronology

Nilotic Africa and the Ethiopian Highlands

ca. 500 B.C.E.	Yemenites (southern Arabians) enter and settle on the Ethiopian plateau
30 B.C.E.	Egypt becomes part of Roman Empire of Octavian
ca. 1–100 C.E.	Earliest mention (in Latin and Greek writers) of the kingdom of Aksum on Ethiopian plateau
ca. 330 C.E.	Fall of Kushite Empire to Elzana of Aksum
ca. 200–400 C.E.	Heyday of Aksumite Ethiopia
ca. 500–600 C.E.	Christianizing of the major Nubian states of Maqurra and Alwa
652 C.E.	Maqurra and Alwa make peace with Arab Muslim armies from Egypt

Map 5–3. Africa: Early Trade Routes and Early States of the Western and Central Sudan. This map shows some of the major routes of north–south trans-Saharan caravan trade and their links with Egypt and with Sudanic and forest regions of West Africa.

African coasts or even Egypt. Some of the main routes ran as follows: (1) from Awdaghast, Walata, and Timbuktu to the major desert salt-producing center of Taghaza and thence to Morocco; (2) from Timbuktu or Gao over the desert direct to Morocco; and (3) from Tadmekka and Agades to the desert market town of Ghat in the north-central Sahara and on to the coasts of Libyan North Africa. Other lines went north from the region of Lake Chad; one route stretched as far east as Egypt itself. This was not an easy means of transporting goods; a typical crossing could take two to three months.

Formation of Sudanic Kingdoms in the First Millennium

The growth of settled agricultural populations and the expansion of trade coincided with the rise of sizable states in the western and central Sudan, significantly in the Sahel

The Ruins of Kumbi Saleh belie its former glory, when it housed between 15,000–20,000 people.

and savanna border region near the great water sources below the Sahara. The most important states were located in Takrur on the Senegal River, from perhaps the fifth century, if not earlier; Ghana, between the northern bends of the Senegal and the Niger, from the fifth or sixth century; Gao, on the Niger southeast of the great bend, from before the eighth century; and Kanem, northeast of Lake Chad, from the eighth or ninth century. Although the origins and even the full extent of the major states in these areas are obscure, each represents only the first of a series of large political entities in its region. All continued to figure prominently in subsequent West African history (see Chapter 17).

The states developed by the Fulbe people of Takrur and the Soninke people of Ghana depended on their ability to draw gold for the Saharan trade with Morocco from the savanna region west of the upper Senegal. Of all the sub-Saharan kingdoms of the late first millennium, Ghana was the most famous outside of the region, largely because of its control of the gold trade. Its people built a large regional empire centered at its capital, Kumbi Saleh. Inheriting his throne by

matrilineal descent, the ruler was treated as a semidivine personage whose interaction with his subjects was mediated by a hierarchy of government ministers. An eleventh-century Arabic chronicle describes him as commanding a sizable army, including horsemen and archers, and being buried with his retainers under a dome of earth and wood. In contrast to the Soninke of Ghana, the Songhai rulers of Gao had no gold trade until the fourteenth century. Gao was oriented in its forest trade towards the lower Niger basin and in its Saharan trade toward eastern Algeria.

All of these states were based on agriculture and settled populations. By contrast, the power of Kanem, on the northwestern side of Lake Chad, originated in the borderlands of the central Sudan and southern Sahara with a nomadic federation of tribal peoples that persisted long enough for the separate tribes to merge and form a single people, the Kanuri. They then moved south to take over the sedentary societies of Kanem proper, just east of Lake Chad, and later, Bornu, west of Lake Chad. By the thirteenth century the Kanuri had themselves become sedentary. Their kingdom

Chronology

The Western and Central Sudan: Probable Dates for Founding of Regional Kingdoms

ca. 400 C.E.	Takrur (Senegal River valley) or earlier
400–600 C.E.	Ghana (in Sahel between great northern bends of the Senegal and Niger Rivers)
ca. 700–800 C.E.	Gao (on the Niger River or before southeast of great bend)
ca. 700–900 C.E.	Kanem (northeast of Lake Chad)

controlled the southern terminus of perhaps the best trans-Saharan route—that running north via good watering stations to the oasis region of Fezzan in modern central Libya and thence to the Mediterranean. We shall return to Kanem and the western Sudanic states and their later development in Chapter 15.

Central, Southern, and East Africa

The African subcontinent is that part of central, southern, and East Africa that lies south of a line from roughly the Niger Delta and Cameroon across to southern Somalia on the east coast. The few sources make it difficult to reconstruct a detailed history of this region before 1000 C.E.

Bantu Expansion and Diffusion

In the southern subcontinent, most people speak one of more than 400 languages that belong to a single language group known as **Bantu,** a subgroup of the Niger-Congo language family. All Bantu languages are as closely related as are the Germanic or Romance tongues of Europe. The proto-Bantu language probably arose south of the Benue River, in eastern Nigeria and modern Cameroon. Thence, during the latter centuries B.C.E. and the first century C.E., migrations of Bantu-speaking peoples must have carried their languages in two basic directions: (1) south into the lower Congo basin and ultimately to the southern edge of the equatorial forest in present-day northern Katanga; and (2) east around the equatorial forests into the lakes of highland East Africa (see Map 5–3).

In all these regions, Bantu tongues developed and multiplied in contact with other languages. Likewise, Bantu speakers intermixed and adapted in diverse ways. Further migrations, some in the early centuries C.E. and others perhaps as late as the eleventh century, dispersed Bantu peoples even more widely, into south-central Africa, coastal East Africa, and southern Africa. This dispersion led to the early civilization of "Great Zimbabwe" and Mapungubwe in the upper Limpopo region (treated in Chapter 17).

How the Bantu peoples managed to impose their languages on the earlier cultures of these regions remains unexplained. The proto-Bantu had apparently been fishermen and hunters who also cultivated yams, date palms, and cereals. They raised goats and possibly sheep and cattle, but they did not bring cattle with them in their migrations. Most of the migrating Bantus seem to have been mainly cereal farmers whose basic political and social unit was the village. Perhaps they had unusually strong social cohesion, which allowed them to absorb other peoples; they were apparently not military conquerors. Possibly they simply had sufficient numbers to become dominant, or they may have brought diseases with them against which the aboriginals of the forests and southern savanna had no immunities.

Bantu cultures became in time so fully interwoven with those of the peoples among whom they settled that these questions may never be answered. Bantu-Arab mixing on the eastern coasts produced the Swahili culture (see Chapter 15).

The Khoisan and Twa Peoples

In southern Africa, as already noted, we find alongside the Bantu-speaking majority a minority who speak "Khoisan." The main two peoples that constitute the Khoisan speakers are the San and the Khoikhoi. (Westerners used to refer to these groups as "Bushmen" and "Hottentots," but these names are now considered offensive.) At one time, observers believed that the Khoikhoi and the San could be distinguished from each other largely by their livelihood.[9] The Khoikhoi were labeled as herdsmen and the San as hunter-gatherers, but more recent research has challenged this. Both groups were also long seen as surviving representatives of a "primitive" stage of cultural evolution, but anthropologists and historians now reject the very notion of cultural evolution. Scholars today

---

[9] On distinctions between San and Khoikhoi, see Richard Elphick, *Kraal and Castle: Khoikhoi and the Founding of White South Africa* (New Haven: Yale University Press, 1977), pp. xxi–xxii, 3–42; on the "construction" of their respective identities and for a summary of research on their antiquity and history, see E. N. Wilmsen, *Land Filled with Flies* (Chicago: University of Chicago Press, 1989). Note also that the once widely held notion that the Bantu and the Khoikhoi arrived in southern Africa at about the same time as the first European settlers was a fabrication to justify apartheid (see Chapter 34).

Cave Painting from Namibia from at least 15,000 B.C.E., depicting rhinoceroses, giraffes, antelope, and zebra.

recognize that much of the common wisdom about these peoples results from colonialist and postcolonial prejudice, the same prejudice that accounts for the Khoisan's low social and economic status in contemporary Africa.

The San are likely the descendants of the Neolithic and Early Iron Age peoples who created the striking prehistoric rock paintings of southern Africa. They have developed linguistically and culturally diverse subgroups across southern Africa. Today they survive most prominently in the Kalahari region. The more homogeneous Khoikhoi were generally sheep- and cattle-herding pastoralists scattered across the south, yet speaking closely related Khoisan tongues. Their ancestors probably originated in northern Botswana. They were hunters who relatively late—likely between 700 and 1000 C.E.—adopted animal herding from their Bantu-speaking southern African neighbors. Thus they became primarily pastoralists and soon expanded as far south as the Cape of Good Hope. Here they flourished as pastoralist clans, until their tragic encounter with the invading Dutch colonists in the mid–seventeenth century, which resulted in their demise as a distinct people.

Sandwe, a Khoisan language, is spoken by foraging groups in Tanzania, and small foraging groups in Kenya speak similar languages. Members of these groups are probably, like the Khoikhoi and San peoples in southern Africa,

remnants of groups that inhabited East Africa prior to the arrival of the Bantu.

Interestingly, in the central African rain forests, the Twa people (commonly referred to in the West as "Pygmies") speak Bantu languages, but show other links to the Khoisan. They too are probably descendants of a population that preceded the Bantu migration.

East Africa

The history of East Africa along the coast before Islam differed from that of the inland highlands. Long-distance travel was easy and common along the seashore but less so inland. The coast had been in maritime contact with India, Arabia, and the Mediterranean via the Indian Ocean and Red Sea trade routes from at least the second century B.C.E. By contrast, we know little about the long-distance contacts of inland regions with the coastal areas until after 1000 C.E. Nonetheless, both regional inland and coastal trade must also be ancient. Both coastal and overseas trade remained important and interdependent over the centuries, because the Indian Ocean trade depended on the monsoon winds and could use only the northernmost coastal trading harbors of East Africa for round-trip voyages in the same year. The monsoon winds blow from the northeast from December to

Chronology

Movement and Contact of Peoples in Central, Southern, and East Africa

ca. 1300–1000 B.C.E.	Kushitic-speaking peoples migrate from Ethiopian plateau south along Rift Valley
ca. 400 B.C.E.–400 C.E.	Probable era of major Bantu migrations into central, East, and southeastern Africa
200–100 B.C.E.	East African coast becomes involved in Indian Ocean trade
ca. 100 B.C.E.	Probable time of first Indonesian immigration to East African coast
ca. 100–1500 C.E.	Nilotic-speaking peoples spread over upper Nile valley; Nilotic peoples spread over Rift Valley region

March and thus can carry sailing ships south from Iran, Arabia, and India only during those months; they blow from the southwest from April to August, so ships can sail from Africa northeast during those months. Local coastal shipping thus had to haul cargoes from south of Zanzibar and then transfer them to other ships for the annual round-trip voyages to Arabia and beyond.

Long-distance trade came into its own in Islamic times—about the ninth century—as an Arab monopoly. However, long before the coming of Islam, trade was apparently largely in the hands of Arabs, many of whom had settled in the East African coastal towns and in Iran and India to handle this international commerce. We can document Graeco-Roman contact with these East African centers of Red Sea and Indian Ocean trade from as early as the first century C.E. Most of the coastal trading towns apparently were independent, although Rhapta, the one town mentioned in the earliest Greek source, *The Periplus* (ca. 89 C.E.), was a dependency of a southern Arabian state.

The overseas trade was, however, evidently even more international than the earliest sources indicate. Today, Malagasy, the Austronesian language of Madagascar, points

The Great Mosque at Kilwa, ca. 1100 C.E. The Swahili city of Kilwa, on the coast of present-day Tanzania, was likely founded by Muslim traders with strong links to the Indian Ocean world. The insides of its domes were lined with Chinese porcelain. Now in ruins, this large congregational mosque was probably in its day the largest fully enclosed structure in sub-Saharan Africa.

A Tenth-Century Arab Description of the East African Coast

Document

This selection is from the famous Baghdadi scholar al-Mas'udi, who died in Cairo about 956 C.E. It treats the country of the Zanj, by which he means the coastal region of East Africa from the Horn down to Mozambique, a region that he himself visited on a voyage from Oman.

◆ In what ways does this Muslim observer seem to be critical, and in what ways laudatory, of the East Africans?

The sea of the Zanj reaches down to the country of Sofala and of the Wak-Wak which produces gold in abundance and other marvels; its climate is warm and its soil fertile. It is there that the Zanj built their capital; then they elected a king whom they called *Waklimi* . . . .

The *Waklimi* has under him all the other Zanj kings, and commands three hundred thousand men. The Zanj use the ox as a beast of burden, for their country has no horses or mules or camels and they do not even know these animals. Snow and hail are unknown to them as to all the Abyssinians. Some of their tribes have sharpened teeth and are cannibals. The territory of the Zanj begins at the canal which flows from the Upper Nile and goes down as far as the country of Sofala and the Wak-Wak. Their settlements extend over an area of about seven hundred parasangs in length and in breadth; this country is divided by valleys, mountains and stony deserts; it abounds in wild elephants but there is not so much as a single tame elephant . . . .

Although constantly employed in hunting elephants and gathering ivory, the Zanj make no use of ivory for their own domestic purposes. They wear iron instead of gold and silver . . . .

. . . *Waklimi* . . . means supreme lord; they give this title to their sovereign because he has been chosen to govern them with equity. But once he becomes tyrannical and departs from the rules of justice, they cause him to die and exclude his posterity from succession to the throne, for they claim that in thus conducting himself he ceases to be the son of the Master, that is to say of the king of heaven and earth. They call God by the name of Maklandjalu, which means supreme Master. . . .

The Zanj speak elegantly, and they have orators in their own language . . . These peoples have no code of religion; their kings follow custom, and conform in their government to a few political rules. . . . Each worships what he pleases, a plant, an animal, a mineral.

They possess a great number of islands where the coconut grows, a fruit that is eaten by all the peoples of the Zanj. One of these islands, placed one or two days' journey from the coast, has a Muslim population who provide the royal family. . . .

Translated from the French version of de Meynard and de Courteille (1864) by Basil Davidson, *The African Past* (New York: Grosset and Dunlap, 1967), pp. 108–109.

to the antiquity of contact with the East Indies. Even before the beginning of our era, bananas, coconut palms, and other crops indigenous to Southeast Asia had spread across Africa as staple foods. Further, as a result of the early regular commercial ties to distant lands of Asia, extra-African ethnic and cultural mixing has long been the rule for the East African coast; even today, its linguistic and cultural traditions are rich and varied (see Chapter 15). (See Document, "A Tenth-Century Arab Description of the East African Coast.")

East Africa also imported such items as Persian Gulf pottery, Chinese porcelain, and cotton cloth. The major African export good around which the east-coast trade revolved was ivory, which was in perennial demand from

Greece to India and even China. The slave trade was another major business. Slaves were procured, often inland, in East Africa and exported to the Arab and Persian world, as well as to India or China. Gold became important in external trade only in Islamic times, from about the tenth century onward, as we shall see in Chapter 15. Wood and cereals must also have been shipped abroad.

The history of inland East Africa south of Ethiopia is much more difficult to trace than that of the coast, again because of the absence of written sources. However, linguistic clues and other evidence indicate some key developments in the eastern highlands. These regions had seen an early diffusion of peoples from the north, and over the centuries small groups continued to move into new areas. Of the early

Manyatta. Aerial view of a contemporary Maasai settlement, or *manyatta*, in Kenya.

migrants from the north, first came peoples speaking Kushitic languages of the Afro-Asiatic family, likely cattle herders and grain cultivators. Perhaps as early as 2000 B.C.E., they pushed from their homeland on the Ethiopian plateau south down the Rift Valley as far as the southern end of Lake Tanganyika. They apparently displaced Neolithic hunter-gatherers who may have been related to the Khoisan minorities of modern East and southern Africa. Although Kushitic languages are spoken from east of Lake Rudolph northward in abundance, farther south only isolated remnants of Kushitic speakers remain today, largely in the Rift Valley in Tanzania.

Later, Nilotic-Saharan speakers moved from the southwestern side of the Ethiopian plateau west over the upper Nile valley by about 1000 C.E. Then they pushed east and south, following older Kushite paths, to spread over the Rift Valley area by the fifteenth century and subsequently much of the East African highlands of modern-day Uganda, Kenya, and Tanzania, where they supplanted their Kushite prede-cessors. Two of these Nilotic peoples were the Luo and the Maasai. The Luo spread over a 900-mile-long swath of modern Uganda and parts of southern Sudan and western Kenya, absorbing new cultural elements and adapting to new situations wherever they went. The Maasai, on the other hand, were and still are cattle pastoralists proud of their separate language, way of life, and cultural traditions. These features have distinguished them from the farming or hunting peoples whose settlements abutted their pasturages at the top of the southern Rift Valley in modern Kenya and Tanzania. Here the Maasai have concentrated and remained.

These migrations and those of the Bantu peoples, who entered the eastern highlands over many centuries, have made the highlands a melting pot of Kushitic, Nilotic, Bantu, and Khoisan groups. Their characteristics are visible in today's populations, possessing an immense diversity of languages and cultures. Here as well as anywhere we can see the radical diversity of peoples and cultures of the entire African continent mirrored in a single region.

Summary

History and Sources. Historians are challenged in their study of Africa by the paucity of written sources, and by the European prejudices that have traditionally devalued African contributions to world culture. Africanists use cross-disciplinary methods and innovative scholarship to understand Africa's past.

Geography and Migrations. The human species, *Homo sapiens* (*sapiens*) probably originated in Africa. In general, however, Africa's geography and climate tended to limit Africans' contact with peoples outside the continent. Within Africa itself, archaeology reveals that there were extensive migrations of peoples across the continent from the earliest days of African history, with widespread cross-cultural influences.

Contact with Other Cultures. In three parts of Africa, there was considerable contact with non-African civilizations. In the Nile River valley, Egypt had extensive interaction with the Nubian peoples to its south. Nubian kingdoms—Kush, Napata, Meroe, and Aksum (Ethiopia)—adopted many features of Egyptian civilization and sometimes dominated Egypt itself. Aksum adopted Christianity in the fourth century C.E.

On the coast of East Africa, trade across the Red Sea and the Indian Ocean with Arabia and east Asia fostered a distinct and sophisticated culture. Extensive trade across the Sahara between North Africa and the western and central Sudan enabled products and ideas from the Mediterranean to reach the African interior in exchange for African products, such as gold, ivory, and salt.

Review Questions

1. Why have historians generally paid more attention to pharaonic Egypt than to the societies of sub-Saharan Africa?

2. Summarize the argument for including writing among the necessary attributes of a "civilization"; summarize the argument against the writing requirement. Which argument do you find more compelling?

INTERPRETING THE PAST

Trade and Kingship in Ancient Africa

Several sources for this chapter highlight the continuous cultural and economic interactions between Africa and surrounding regions in this period. Two predominant themes emerge: first, the central importance of kingship along with the accompanying symbols of authority, and second, the evidence of wide-ranging, interconnected trading networks. In the following exercise, use the source documents and visual sources to address questions relating to cross-cultural interaction.

Text Sources from the Primary Source DVD/ MyHistoryLab for Chapter Five

 The primary sources for this chapter vary widely in perspective and time period.

Aspalta as King of Kush, dates from 600 B.C.E., *Periplus* dates from the first century C.E., and *History of the Wars* dates from 550 C.E. *Aspalta* focuses on the election of the King of Kush, in Nubia (today northern Sudan) by a group of military and religious leaders. *Periplus* offers a detailed guide to the East African coast south of Egypt's border, its natural resources, potential for trade, and inhabitants. Finally, Procopius' *History of Wars* details the struggle between the rulers of Mauretania in North Africa, the late Roman Empire, centered in Constantinople (Byzantium), and the Vandals, a barbarian tribe.

The *Aspalta* and Procopius sources show African kingdoms in conflict with neighboring regions—Egypt and Rome. In the *Aspalta*, Egyptian priesthood, religious symbolism, and the deity Amun are invoked during the selection of the leader of the Nubian kingdom of Kush. Since Kush had engaged in an ongoing series of wars with Egypt for centuries, and had occupied the larger country, the degree of influence is perhaps not surprising. The Procopius excerpt illustrates the

3. Discuss the strengths and weaknesses of the various sources and tools available to scholars of early African history.

4. What does the diffusion of peoples and languages in Africa tell us about early African history?

5. How does the political system of the Meroitic Empire compare to that of Egypt?

6. How did Aksum become a Christian state?

7. What were the most important goods for African internal trade? Which products were traded abroad? What can we learn from these trade patterns?

8. What was the role of geography in early African history? What about the specific case of Ghana? Of North Africa? Of the East African littoral? Of southern Africa?

9. Is the role of geography different in Africa than in the Near East or other regions you have studied? Explain.

10. What information presented in this chapter was most surprising to you, and why?

fierce resistance of the Mauretanii (the origin of "Moors") to Roman / Byzantine occupation, the disunion of the Moors, and the continuing threat of barbarian invasions from Vandals and later the Visigoths

Visual Sources from Chapter 5

Pyramids at Meroe (p. 168), *Giant Stela at Aksum* (p. 169),

Questions

After reading the primary sources and examining the images, note the specific details of cross-cultural influences, and of their use.

What are these influences?

For what purpose are they invoked? Who is using them?

How do these sources highlight cultural continuities in African history?

Key Terms

Afro-Asiatic (p. 162)

Aksum (AHK-suhm) (p. 167)

Austronesian (p. 162)

Bantu (BAN-tu) (pp. 163/175)

cataract (p. 159)

Kalahari (p. 160)

Khoisan (KOI-sahn) (p. 162)

Kush (koosh) (p. 166)

Meroe (MEH-roh-ee) (p. 167)

Monophysite (moh-NOH-fiss-it) (p. 171)

Niger-Kongo (p. 162)

Nilo-Saharan (p. 162)

Nilotic Africa (p. 160)

Nok (p. 166)

Sahara (p. 160)

Sahel (p. 160)

savanna (p. 160)

Sudan (p. 160)

trypanosomiasis (p. 171)

Note: To learn more about the topics in this chapter, please turn to the Suggested Readings at the end of the book. For additional sources related to this chapter please see the Primary Source DVD at the back of this text or MyHistoryLab.

Republican and Imperial Rome

THE ANCIENT ROMANS WERE RESPONSIBLE FOR one of the most remarkable achievements in history. From their city in central Italy, which began as a small village, they conquered all of Italy, then the entire Mediterranean coastline, and finally most of the Near East and much of continental Europe. Their unifying government brought centuries of peace and prosperity to this vast region, which has never been unified again, and has only rarely since enjoyed prolonged peace and stability.

When it began its expansion, Rome had a non-monarchical, republican government. Few non-monarchical governments have lasted for more than a relatively short time, and the Roman Republic, which endured for almost five hundred years and came to control a vast empire, has no parallel. The eventual fall of the republic and the imposition of an imperial monarchy under Augustus, Rome's first emperor, ended this unusual chapter in history. The transition was difficult. Romans continued to think in republican terms for generations, and many longed for the republic's restoration. Augustus skillfully

Lady Playing the Cithara. This wall painting from the first century B.C.E. comes from the villa of Publius Fannius Synistor at Pompeii and shows a woman playing a cithara, a type of lyre. Behind her a child, presumably her daughter, provides support. *Roman. Paintings. Pompeian, Boscoreale. 1st Century B.C. "Lady playing the cithara." Wall painting from the east wall of large room in the villa of Publius Fannius Synistor. Fresco on lime plaster. H. 6 ft. ½ in. (187 × 187 cm.) The Metropolitan Museum of Art, Rogers Fund, 1903 (03.14.5) Photograph © 1986 The Metropolitan Museum of Art.*

Republican and Imperial Rome

Rome

Despite the nearly continuous warfare that marked Roman history, including a long-lasting rivalry with the Sassanid Empire, it was primarily through trade that Romans came into contact with peoples beyond the borders of their empire. Strong, centralized empires in the West (Rome), in China (Han), and in India (Mauryan) were able to provide law and order to their citizens, protection to travelers, and an infrastructure that included decent roads and coinage. Likewise, merchants and missionaries found it possible to transport themselves and their goods in greater safety than ever before throughout much of Eurasia. As a result, a tenuous but continuous network of routes by land (the first Silk Road) and sea (the Arabian "monsoon route" across the Indian Ocean) linked the Roman world to China and allowed a thin but continuous stream of people, cargo, and ideas to cross Asia from east to west and from north to south. As yet the fruits of this exchange were small compared to the significance of the later, medieval Silk Road with Central Asia, whose merchants and towns were the vital intermediaries of trade and benefited the most. However, there is no doubt that Roman objects and with them some knowledge of Rome, reached China and India, and vice versa.

Nonetheless, most Romans focused their energies on internal Roman territory, which expanded considerably during the late republic and the early empire to include much of the former Hellenistic kingdoms. This is not surprising given that, despite the expansion of trade in this period, agriculture was still the primary occupation and source of income of most people in the empire. But Rome was a multicultural empire, maintained the appearance of republican institutions, helping to mask the monarchical reality. The passage of time made such deception less necessary. Hard times and chaos in the third century C.E. revealed the military foundation of the emperors' increasingly autocratic rule. Beginning in the first century C.E. emperors were declared divine after death; by the second century they were worshiped as gods while alive, like the rulers of ancient Egypt and other early empires.

Rome's legacy was not just of military prowess and superb political organization. The Romans adopted and transformed the intellectual and cultural achievements of the Greeks, creating the Graeco-Roman tradition in literature, philosophy, and art. This tradition formed the core of learning during the Middle Ages and inspired the new intellectual paths taken during the Renaissance. It remains the heart of Western civilization. ■

Prehistoric Italy

About 1000 B.C.E. bands of warlike peoples speaking a set of closely related languages we call Italic began to infiltrate Italy. By 800 B.C.E. they had occupied the highland pastures of the Apennines and soon challenged the earlier settlers for control of the tempting western plains. The Romans would emerge from among the descendants of these tough mountain people. Others who shaped the future of Italy included the Etruscans, the Greeks who colonized Sicily and southern Italy, and the Celts, who established themselves in the north around 400 B.C.E.

The Etruscans

Etruscan civilization, which was to have a powerful influence on the Romans, arose about 800 B.C.E. (see Map 6–1). The Etruscans lived in self-governing, fortified city-states. They encompassing territory and cultures in Africa and the Middle East, as well as northern and central Europe. Rome profited enormously from the territories it conquered in terms of material wealth, including foodstuffs, as Egypt quickly became the "breadbasket" of the empire. It also realized cultural benefits, especially that blending of Greek and Asian culture that characterized the Hellenistic world. But the infusion of new ideas caused tension among Romans, as many conservative Romans objected to what they viewed as corrupting Asian influences from even the much admired, and copied, Greeks, which threatened to undermine traditional Roman values and strengths.

The conquest of a vast empire had moved the Romans away from their unusual historical traditions towards the more familiar path of empire trodden by rulers in Egypt, Mesopotamia, China, India, and Iran. It is especially instructive to look at Rome from the perspective of historians who discern a "dynastic cycle" in China (see Chapter 7). The development of the Roman Empire, although by no means the same as the Chinese, fits the same pattern fairly well. Like the Former Han dynasty in China, the Roman Empire in the West fell, leaving in its wake disunity, insecurity, disorder, and poverty. Like other similar empires in the ancient world, it had been unable to sustain its "immoderate greatness."

Focus Questions

◆ Why might we describe the Roman Empire as "multicultural"? What cultures most influenced Roman culture, and why?

◆ What was it about the period from the second century B.C.E. through the third century C.E. that allowed the opening of new routes by land and sea linking Europe to Central Asia, India, and China?

◆ Why did the Roman Empire decline in the West? Which of the problems that Rome faced were internal, and which were external? How were the two connected?

constituted a military ruling class, dominating the native people they had dispossessed and exploiting them to work their lands and fight in their infantry. The Etruscan states were first ruled by kings and later by an agrarian aristocracy that governed through a council and annually elected magistrates. This aristocracy accumulated considerable wealth through agriculture, industry, piracy, and commerce with the Carthaginians of North Africa and the Greeks.

In the seventh and sixth centuries B.C.E. the Etruscans conquered Latium (which included Rome) and Campania, where they became neighbors of the Greeks of Naples. But after 500 B.C.E. Etruscan power rapidly declined. The Celts drove them from the Po valley about 400 B.C.E., and soon thereafter they lost control of their Etrurian heartland to an expanding Rome.

Royal Rome

In the sixth century B.C.E. the town of Rome in Latium came under Etruscan control. Although it had been of little

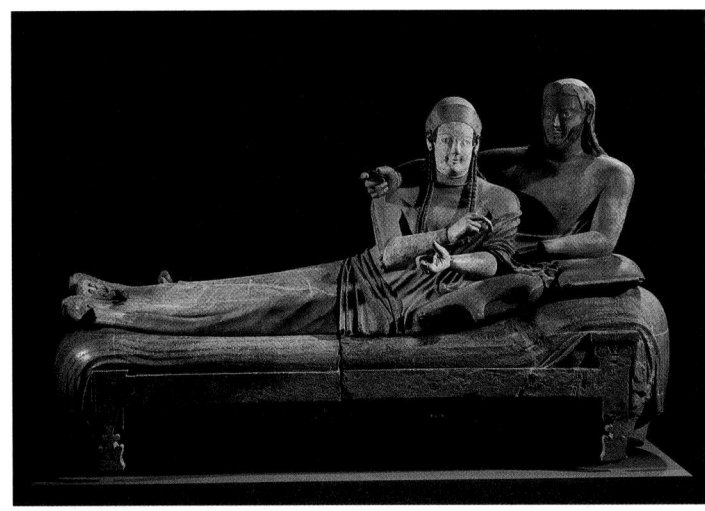

Sarcophagus of an Etruscan Couple. Much of what we know of the Etruscans comes from their funerary art. This sculpture of an Etruscan couple is part of a sarcophagus. © Erich Lessing/ Art Resource, N.Y.

Map 6–1. Ancient Italy. This map of ancient Italy and its neighbors before the expansion of Rome shows the major cities and towns as well as a number of geographical regions and the locations of some of the Italic and non-Italic peoples.

importance, it was a natural center for communication and trade. Led by Etruscan kings, the Roman army conquered most of Latium. Rome's effective political and social organization, which gave extraordinary power to its rulers, made this success possible.

Government

Roman kings had the awesome power of **imperium,** the right to issue commands and to enforce them by fines, arrests, and physical punishment, including execution. Although it

tended to remain in families, kingship was elective. The Roman Senate approved the candidate for the office, and the Roman people, voting in assembly, formally granted the *imperium.* This procedure—the granting of great power to executive officers contingent on the approval of the Senate and ultimately the people—would remain a basic characteristic of Roman government.

The king was the commander of the army, the chief priest, and the supreme judge. He conducted foreign affairs, commanded the army, and disciplined his troops, all by virtue of his *imperium.* In practice the royal power was much more limited.

The Senate, the second branch of the early Roman government, ostensibly had neither executive nor legislative power; it met only when summoned by the king and then only to advise him. In reality its authority was great, for the senators, like the king, served for life. The Senate, therefore, had continuity and experience, and it was composed of the most powerful men in the state. It could not be ignored.

The third branch of government, the curiate assembly, was made up of all citizens and divided into thirty groups. The assembly also met only when summoned by the king. Usually, the assembly was called to listen and approve. Voting was not by head but by group; a majority within each group determined its vote, and the decisions were made by majority vote of the groups. Group voting would be typical of all future forms of Roman assembly.

Family

The center of Roman life was the family. At its head stood the father, whose power and authority resembled those of the king within the state. Over his children he held broad powers analogous to *imperium;* he could sell his children into slavery, and might even kill them. Over his wife he had less power; he could not sell or kill her. In practice his power to dispose of his children was limited by other family members, by public opinion, and, most of all, by tradition. A wife could be divorced only for serious offenses, and only after she had been convicted by a court made up of her male blood relatives. The Roman woman had a respected position and the main responsibility for managing the household. The father was the chief priest of the family, leading it in daily prayers to the dead that reflected the ancestor worship central to the Roman family and state.

Clientage

Clientage was one of Rome's most important institutions. The client was "an inferior entrusted, by custom or by himself, to the protection of a stranger more powerful than he, and rendering certain services and observances in return for this protection."[1] The client was said to be in the *fides,* or trust, of his patron, giving the relationship a moral dimension. The patron provided his client with physical and legal protection and economic support. In return the client would fight for his patron, work his land, and support him politically. These mutual obligations were enforced by public opinion and tradition. When early custom was codified in the mid–fifth century B.C.E., one of the twelve tablets of laws announced: "Let the patron who has defrauded his client be accursed."[2]

In early Rome, patrons were rich and powerful, whereas clients were poor and weak, but in time, rich and powerful members of the upper classes increasingly became clients of even more powerful men. Because the client-patron relationship was hereditary and was sanctioned by religion and custom, it played an important part in the life of the Roman Republic.

Patricians and Plebeians

In the royal period Roman society was divided into two classes based on birth. The wealthy **patrician** upper class held a monopoly of power and influence. Its members alone could conduct state religious ceremonies, sit in the Senate, or hold office. They formed a closed caste by forbidding marriage outside their own group.

The **plebeian** lower class must have consisted originally of poor, dependent small farmers, laborers, and artisans, the clients of the nobility. As Rome grew, nonpatrician families acquired wealth. From early times, therefore, there were rich plebeians and patrician families that fell into poverty from incompetence or bad luck. The line between the classes and the monopoly of privileges nevertheless remained firm.

The Republic

According to Roman tradition, the outrageous behavior of the last kings provoked the noble families to revolt in 509 B.C.E., leading to the creation of the republic.

Constitution

The Roman constitution was an unwritten accumulation of laws and customs.

---

[1] E. Badian, *Foreign Clientelae (264–70 B.C.E.)* (Oxford: Oxford University Press, 1958), p. 1.
[2] *Roman Civilization: Selected Readings*, Vol. 1, ed. by Naphtali Lewis and Meyer Reinhold (New York: Columbia University Press, 1963).

Consuls The Romans were never willing to deprive their chief magistrates of the great powers their kings had exercised. They elected two patricians to the office of consul and endowed them with *imperium.* Assisting the consuls were financial officials called *quaestors.* Like the kings, the consuls led the army, had religious duties, and served as judges. Consular power, however, was limited legally, institutionally, and by custom.

The power of the consulship was granted for a year only. Each consul could overrule the other, and they shared their religious powers with others. Even the *imperium* was limited. Although the consuls had full powers of life and death while leading an army, within the sacred boundary of the city of Rome, citizens could appeal to the popular assembly all cases involving capital punishment. Besides, after their year in office, the consuls would spend the rest of their lives as members of the Senate, so only a reckless consul would ignore its advice.

The many checks on consular action tended to prevent initiative, swift action, and change, but this was just what a conservative, traditional, aristocratic republic wanted. Only in military matters did these limitations create problems. In serious crises, the consuls could, with the advice of the Senate, appoint a dictator, who would have *imperium* not subject to appeal both inside and outside the city for six months. These devices sufficed in the early republic, when Rome's battles were near home, but longer wars and more sophisticated opponents required significant changes.

In 325 B.C.E. the Romans created the office of proconsul, which permitted a consul in the field to retain command during a long campaign. Another new office, that of praetor, was primarily judicial, but praetors also had *imperium* and served as generals. They too could have their one-year term of office extended for long campaigns. Eventually there were eight praetors.

After the middle of the fifth century B.C.E. the job of identifying citizens and classifying them according to age and property was delegated to a new office, that of **censor**. The Senate elected two censors every five years. They conducted a census and drew up the citizen rolls. Because the classification fixed taxation and status, the censors had to be men of reputation, former consuls. They soon acquired additional powers and by the fourth century B.C.E. had the authority to exclude senators from the Senate on moral as well as financial grounds. As the prestige of the office grew, it came to be considered the ultimate prize of a political career.

Senate and Assembly The end of the monarchy increased the power of the Senate. Composed of leading patricians, often clan leaders and patrons with many clients, it became the only ongoing deliberative body in the Roman state and soon controlled finances and foreign policy.

Lictors. Pictured here, lictors attended the chief Roman magistrates when they appeared in public. The ax carried by one of the lictors and the bound bundle of staffs carried by the others symbolize both the power of Roman magistrates to inflict corporal punishment on Roman citizens and the limits on that power. The bound staffs symbolize the right of citizens within the city of Rome not to be punished without a trial. The ax symbolizes the power of the magistrates, as commanders of the army, to put anyone to death without a trial outside the city walls. *Alinari/Art Resource, N.Y.*

The *centuriate assemble,* the early republic's most important popular assembly, was, in a sense, the Roman army acting in a political capacity. Its basic unit was the century, theoretically one hundred fighting men who fought with the same kind of equipment. Because each man equipped himself, this organization divided the assembly into classes according to wealth.

Struggle of the Orders   Patricians monopolized power in the early republic. Plebeians were barred from all political and religious offices. In response, the plebeians launched the "struggle of the orders," a fight for political, legal, and social equality that lasted two hundred years.

Plebeians made up much of the Roman army, giving them great political leverage. They formed the plebeian tribal assembly and elected **tribunes,** officials with the power to protect plebeians from abuse by patrician magistrates. In effect, a tribune could veto any action of a magistrate or any bill in a Roman assembly or the Senate.

In 450 B.C.E. the Twelve Tables were published, the first attempt to codify Rome's harsh customs. In 445 B.C.E.

plebeians won the right to marry patricians. It was not until 367 B.C.E. that one of the consuls was allowed to be of plebeian rank. Gradually other offices, including the dictatorship and the censorship, opened to them. In 300 B.C.E. they were admitted to the most important priesthoods. In 287 B.C.E. the plebeians secured the passage of a law making the decisions of the plebeian assembly binding on all Romans without the approval of the Senate.

The victory of the plebeians allowed wealthy plebeian families to enter politics and share the privileges of the patrician aristocracy. The *nobiles*—a relatively small group of wealthy and powerful families, both patrician and plebeian— dominated the increasingly powerful Senate and controlled the highest offices of the state.

The end of the struggle of the orders brought domestic peace under a republican constitution dominated by a capable, if narrow, senatorial aristocracy. Most Romans accepted this leadership, which secured them a growing empire and many benefits.

Conquest of Italy

Initial Expansion and Gallic Invasion   By the beginning of the fourth century B.C.E. the Romans were the chief power in central Italy, but in 387 B.C.E. the Gauls, marching south from the Po valley, captured, looted, and burned Rome. Rome appeared finished, but by about 350 B.C.E. it had reclaimed the leadership of central Italy.

In 340 B.C.E. the city's Latin neighbors, the Latin League, sought to curtail Rome's expansion. In 338 B.C.E. the Romans defeated the league and dissolved it. The terms they imposed provided a model for the way they were to treat opponents as they incorporated the rest of Italy.

Roman Policy Towards the Conquered   The Romans did not destroy any of the Latin cities, nor did they treat them all alike. To some near Rome they granted full citizenship. To others farther away they granted municipal status, which included the right to local self-government and the right to trade and intermarry with Romans, but not to take part in Roman politics unless they moved to Rome and applied for citizenship. These states followed Rome's foreign policy and supplied soldiers for Rome's legions. Still other states became allies of Rome on the basis of treaties that differed from city to city. All the allies supplied troops to fight in auxiliary battalions under Roman officers, but they did not pay taxes to Rome.

The Romans established permanent colonies of veteran soldiers in conquered lands. The colonists remained Roman citizens and deterred rebellion. A network of durable roads—some still in use—connected the colonies to Rome, permitting troops to be moved swiftly to any trouble spot.

Map 6–2. The Western Mediterranean Area During the Rise of Rome. This map covers the theater of the conflict between the growing Roman dominions and those of Carthage in the third century B.C.E. The Carthaginian Empire stretched westward from Carthage along the North African coast and into southern Spain.

Rome divided its enemies and extended its influence through military force and diplomatic skill. Rebels were punished harshly and swiftly. But Rome was also generous to those who submitted. The status of a newly conquered city was not permanent. Loyal allies could improve their prospects, even gaining full Roman citizenship. This policy gave allies a stake in Rome's future and a sense of being colleagues rather than subjects. As a result, most remained loyal even when put to the severest test.

Rome and Carthage

Late in the ninth century B.C.E. the Phoenician city of Tyre had planted a colony on the North African coast, calling it the New City, or Carthage (see Map 6–2). In the sixth century B.C.E. Carthage became independent and free to take advantage of its defensible position, excellent harbor, and rich countryside. The Carthaginians expanded along the coast of North Africa west beyond the Straits of Gibraltar and east into Libya. They also gained control of southern Spain, Sardinia, Corsica, Malta, the Balearic Islands, and western Sicily. The people of these territories became Carthaginian subjects, paying tribute and serving in the Carthaginian military. Carthage claimed an absolute monopoly on trade in the western Mediterranean.

First Punic War (264–241 B.C.E.) Sicily was strategically important to both Carthage and Rome. It was there, in 264 B.C.E., that the two expanding powers first came to blows. Because the Romans called the Carthaginians Poeni or Puni (meaning "Phoenician"), the conflicts between them are called the **Punic Wars.**

Neither side made any progress against the other until the Romans built a fleet to blockade the Carthaginian ports at the western end of Sicily. Carthage capitulated in 241 B.C.E., giving up Sicily and the islands between Italy and Sicily and agreeing to pay a war indemnity, to keep its ships out of Italian waters, and not to recruit mercenaries in Italy. Neither side was to attack the allies of the other.

The terms of the peace were fair, but Rome broke them almost immediately, setting the stage for more conflict. In 238 B.C.E., while Carthage struggled to put down a revolt of unpaid mercenaries, Rome seized Sardinia and Corsica and demanded an additional indemnity. This cynical action provoked the Carthaginians without preventing them from recovering their strength to seek vengeance in the future.

A Roman Warship. Rome became a naval power late in its history, in the course of the First Punic War. Roman sailors initially lacked the skill and experience in sea warfare of their Carthaginian opponents, who could maneuver their oared ships to ram the enemy. To compensate for this disadvantage, the Romans sought to make a sea battle more like an encounter on land by devising ways to grapple enemy ships and board them with armed troops. In time they also mastered the skillful use of the ram. This picture shows a Roman ship, propelled by oars, with both ram and soldiers, ready for either kind of fight. *Direzione Generale Musei Vaticani.*

Second Punic War (218–202 B.C.E.) After 241 B.C.E., Carthage recovered strength by building a rich empire in Spain while Rome looked on with concern. In 221 B.C.E. Hannibal (247–182 B.C.E.) took command of Carthaginian forces in Spain. A few years earlier Rome had received an offer from the Spanish town of Saguntum to become the friends of Rome. The Romans accepted, thereby taking on the responsibilities of friendship with a foreign state. At first Hannibal was careful to respect Saguntum, but the Saguntines, confident of Rome's protection, began to interfere with Spanish tribes allied with Hannibal. The Romans warned Hannibal to let Saguntum alone, but he ignored Rome's warning, besieged Saguntum, and captured it.

Chronology

The Punic Wars

264–241 B.C.E.	First Punic War
238 B.C.E.	Rome seizes Sardinia and Corsica
221 B.C.E.	Hannibal takes command of Punic army in Spain
218–202 B.C.E.	Second Punic War
216 B.C.E.	Battle of Cannae
202 B.C.E.	Battle of Zama
149–146 B.C.E.	Third Punic War
146 B.C.E.	Destruction of Carthage

Rome declared war in 218 B.C.E. Starting in Spain, Hannibal launched a swift and daring invasion of Italy. By September of 218 B.C.E. he was across the Alps. His army was weary, bedraggled, and greatly reduced, but he was in Italy. Hannibal defeated the Romans in three consecutive battles, but his chances of prevailing would depend ultimately on Rome's ability to retain the loyalty of its allies.

In 216 B.C.E., at Cannae in Apulia, Hannibal destroyed a Roman army of some 80,000 men. It was the worst defeat in Roman history; Rome's prestige was shattered, and many of its allies went over to Hannibal. In 215 B.C.E. Philip V (r. 221–179 B.C.E.), king of Macedon, made an alliance with Hannibal and launched a war to recover his influence on the Adriatic. For more than a decade no Roman army would dare face Hannibal in the open field, and he was free to roam over all Italy and do as he pleased.

But crucial allies remained loyal to Rome, preventing Hannibal's victory. He had neither the numbers nor the supplies to besiege Rome or the cities of its major allies, nor did he have the equipment to take them by assault. The Romans appointed Publius Cornelius Scipio (237–183 B.C.E.), later called Scipio Africanus, to the command in Spain with proconsular *imperium*. He was a general almost as talented as Hannibal. Within a few years Scipio had conquered all Spain and had deprived Hannibal of hope of help from that region.

In 204 B.C.E. Scipio landed in Africa and forced the Carthaginians to accept a peace whose main clause was the withdrawal of Hannibal and his army from Italy. Hannibal had won every battle but lost the war. His return inspired Carthage to risk all in battle. In 202 B.C.E. Scipio and Hannibal faced each other at Zama. Rome won and the new peace terms reduced Carthage to the status of a dependent ally of Rome.

Carthage was no longer a great power. Rome ruled the seas and the entire Mediterranean coast from Italy westward.

The New Imperial System The Roman conquest of overseas territory presented a new problem. Instead of following the policy they had pursued in Italy, the Romans made Sicily, Sardinia, and Corsica provinces. It became common to extend the term of the governors of these provinces beyond a year. The governors were unchecked by colleagues and exercised full *imperium*. New magistracies, in effect, were thus created free of the limits put on the power of officials in Rome. The new populations were subjects who paid tribute instead of serving in the army. The old practice of extending citizenship, and with it loyalty to Rome, stopped at the borders of Italy. Rome collected the new taxes by "farming them out" at auction to the highest bidder. The tax collectors became powerful and wealthy by squeezing the provincials hard. These innovations were the basis for Rome's imperial organization; in time they so strained the constitution and traditions of Rome that the existence of the republic was threatened.

The Republic's Conquest of the Hellenistic World

The East By the middle of the third century B.C.E. the eastern Mediterranean had reached a stable balance of power. That equilibrium was threatened by two aggressive monarchs, Philip V of Macedon and the Seleucid Antiochus III (223–187 B.C.E.). Philip and Antiochus moved swiftly, the latter against Syria and Palestine, the former against Greek cities.

The threat that a more powerful Macedon might pose to Rome's friends, and perhaps even to Italy, persuaded the Romans to intervene. In 200 B.C.E. the Romans ordered Philip not to attack any Greek city and to pay reparations to the kingdom of Pergamum in Asia Minor. Philip refused. Two years later the Romans demanded that Philip withdraw from Greece entirely. In 197 B.C.E., with Greek support, they defeated Philip in Thessaly. The Greek cities taken from Philip were made autonomous and the freedom of the Greeks was proclaimed.

Soon after, the Romans came into conflict with Antiochus. On the pretext of freeing the Greeks from Roman domination, he landed an army on the Greek mainland. The Romans quickly drove him from Greece, and in 189 B.C.E. they crushed his army at Magnesia in Asia Minor. The peace of Apamia in the next year deprived Antiochus of his elephants and his navy and imposed a huge indemnity on him. Once again the Romans took no territory for themselves and left Greek cities in Asia free. They continued to regard

Greece, and now Asia Minor, as a kind of protectorate in which they could intervene as they chose.

In 179 B.C.E. Perseus (r. 179–168 B.C.E.) succeeded Philip V as king of Macedon. He tried to gain popularity in Greece by favoring the democratic and revolutionary forces in the cities. The Romans, troubled by this threat to stability, defeated him in 168 B.C.E. and divided Macedon into four separate republics whose citizens were forbidden to intermarry or even to do business across the new national boundaries.

The new policy reflected the stern and businesslike approach favored by the conservative censor Cato (234–149 B.C.E.). The new harshness was applied to allies and bystanders as well as to defeated opponents. Leaders of anti-Roman factions in the Greek cities were punished severely. In 146 B.C.E., for instance, the ancient and wealthy commercial city of Corinth was completely destroyed.

The public treasury benefited to such a degree from these wars that the direct property tax on Roman citizens was abolished. Part of the booty went to the victorious generals and part to their soldiers. New motives were thereby introduced into Roman foreign policy, or, perhaps, old motives were given new prominence. Foreign campaigns could bring profit to the state, rewards to the army, and wealth, fame, honor, and political power to the general.

The West Harsh as the Romans had become towards the Greeks, they treated the Spaniards, whom they considered barbarians, even worse. The Romans committed dreadful atrocities; they lied, cheated, and broke treaties in their effort to exploit and pacify the natives, who fought back

Chronology

Roman Overseas Engagements

215–205 B.C.E.	First Macedonian War
200–197 B.C.E.	Second Macedonian War
196 B.C.E.	Proclamation of Greek freedom
189 B.C.E.	Battle of Magnesia; Antiochus defeated in Asia Minor
172–168 B.C.E.	Third Macedonian War
168 B.C.E.	Battle of Pydna
154–133 B.C.E.	Roman wars in Spain
134 B.C.E.	Numantia taken

fiercely in guerrilla style. From 154 to 133 B.C.E. the fighting waxed, and it became hard to recruit Roman soldiers for the increasingly ugly war. At last, in 134 B.C.E., Scipio Aemilianus (185–129 B.C.E.) took the key city of Numantia by siege and put an end to the war in Spain.

Roman treatment of Carthage was no better. Although Carthage posed no threat, some Romans refused to abandon their hatred and fear of the traditional enemy. Cato is said to have ended all his speeches in the Senate with the same sentence, *"Ceterum censeo delendam esse Carthaginem"* ("Besides, I think that Carthage must be destroyed"). At last the Romans took advantage of a technical breach of the peace to destroy Carthage. In 146 B.C.E. Scipio Aemilianus took the city, plowed up its land, and put salt in the furrows as a symbol of the permanent abandonment of the site. The Romans incorporated Carthage as the province of Africa.

Civilization in the Early Roman Republic: Greek Influence

Among the most important changes wrought by Roman expansion overseas were those in the Roman style of life and thought brought about by close and continued association with the Greeks of the Hellenistic world. Attitudes towards the Greeks themselves ranged from admiration for their culture and history to contempt for their constant squabbling, their commercial practices, and their weakness. Such Roman aristocrats as the Scipios surrounded themselves with Greek intellectuals, like the historian Polybius (ca. 203–ca. 123 B.C.E.) and the philosopher Panaetius (ca. 185–ca. 110 B.C.E.). Conservatives, such as Cato, might speak contemptuously of the Greeks as "Greeklings" (Graeculi), but even he learned Greek and absorbed Greek culture.

Religion

Roman religion was influenced by the Greeks almost from the beginning; the Romans identified their own gods with Greek equivalents and incorporated Greek mythology into their own. For the most part, however, Roman religious practice remained simple and Italian, until the third century B.C.E. brought important new influences from the east. In 205 B.C.E. the Senate approved the public worship of Cybele, the Great Mother goddess from Asia Minor. Hers was a fertility cult accompanied by ecstatic, frenzied, and sensual rites that so shocked and outraged conservative Romans that they soon banned the cult to Romans. Similarly, the Senate banned the worship of Dionysus, or Bacchus, in 186 B.C.E. In the second century B.C.E. interest in Babylonian astrology also grew, and

the Senate's attempt in 139 B.C.E. to expel the "Chaldaeans," as the astrologers were called, did not prevent the continued influence of their superstition.

Education

Education was entirely the responsibility of the Roman family, the fathers teaching their own sons at home. It is not clear whether girls received any education in early Rome, although they certainly did later on. The boys learned to read, write, and calculate, as well as how to farm. They memorized the Twelve Tables, Rome's earliest code of law; learned how to perform religious rites; heard stories of the great deeds of early Roman history, particularly those of their ancestors; and engaged in the physical training appropriate for potential soldiers. This course of study was practical, vocational, and moral. It aimed at making the boys moral, pious, patriotic, law-abiding, and respectful of tradition.

Contact with the Greeks of southern Italy produced momentous changes. Greek teachers came to Rome and introduced the study of language, literature, and philosophy, as well as the idea of a liberal education, or what the Romans called **humanitas,** the root of our concept of the humanities. This education emphasized broad intellectual training, critical thinking, an interest in ideas, and the development of a well-rounded person.

The first need was to learn Greek, for Rome did not yet have a literature of its own. Schools were established in which the teacher, called a *grammaticus*, taught his students the Greek language and its literature, particularly the works of Homer. Thereafter, educated Romans were expected to be bilingual. Roman boys of the upper classes then studied rhetoric—the art of speaking and writing well—with Greeks who were expert in it. The Greeks considered rhetoric less important than philosophy. But the more practical Romans took to it avidly, for it was of great use in legal disputes and was becoming ever more valuable in political life.

Some Romans, however, felt that the new learning would weaken Roman moral fiber. They were able to pass laws expelling philosophers and teachers of rhetoric. But these reactionary attempts failed. The new education suited the needs of the Romans of the second century B.C.E., who found themselves changing from a rural to an urban society and who were being thrust into the sophisticated world of the Hellenistic Greeks.

By the last century of the Roman republic the new Hellenized education had become dominant. Latin literature had come into being along with Latin translations of Greek poets, which formed part of the course of study. The Greek language and literature were still central to the curriculum. Many schools were established, and the number of educated

A Master Among His Students. This carved relief from the second century C.E. shows a schoolmaster and his pupils. The one at the right is arriving late. *Rheinisches Landesmuseum, Triern, Germany/Alinari/ Art Resource, N.Y.*

people grew, extending beyond the senatorial class and outside Rome to the cities of Italy.

Girls of the upper classes were educated similarly to boys, at least through the earlier stages. They were probably taught by tutors at home rather than going to school. Young women did not study with philosophers and rhetoricians, for they were usually married by the age when the men were pursuing their higher education. Still, some women found ways to continue their education. Some became prose writers or poets. By the first century C.E. there were apparently enough learned women to provoke the complaints of a crotchety and conservative satirist:

> *Still more exasperating is the woman who begs as soon as she sits down to dinner, to discourse on poets and poetry, comparing Virgil with Homer; professors, critics, lawyers, auctioneers—even another woman—can't get a word in. She rattles on at such a rate that you'd think that all the pots and pans in the kitchen were crashing to the floor or that every bell in town was clanging. All by herself she makes as much noise as some primitive tribe chasing away an eclipse. She should learn the philosopher's lesson: "moderation is necessary even for intellectuals." And, if she still wants to appear educated and eloquent, let her dress as a man, sacrifice to men's gods and bathe in the men's baths. Wives shouldn't try to be public speakers; they shouldn't use rhetorical devices; they shouldn't read all the classics—there should be some things women don't understand. I myself cannot understand a woman who can quote the rules of grammar and never make a mistake and cites obscure, long-forgotten poets—as if men cared about such things. If she has to correct somebody let her correct her girl friends and leave her husband alone.[3]*

A rich and ambitious Roman could support a Greek philosopher in his own home, so that his son could acquire through conversation the learning and polished thought

necessary for the fully cultured gentleman. Some, like the great orator Cicero (106–43 B.C.E.), traveled to Greece to study with great teachers of rhetoric and philosophy. This style of education broadened the Romans' understanding and made them a part of the older and wider culture of the Hellenistic world, a world they had come to dominate and needed to understand.

Roman Imperialism

Rome's expansion in Italy and overseas was accomplished without a grand general plan. The new territories were acquired as a result of wars that the Romans believed were either defensive or preventive. Their foreign policy was aimed at providing security for Rome on Rome's terms, but these terms were often unacceptable to other nations and led to continued conflict. Whether intended or not, Rome's expansion brought the Romans an empire, and with it, power, wealth, and responsibilities (see Map 6–3).

Aftermath of Conquest

War and expansion changed the economic, social, and political life of Italy. Before the Punic Wars most Italians owned their own farms, which provided most of the family's needs. The Second Punic War did terrible damage to Italian farmland. Many veterans found it impossible or unprofitable to go back to their farms. Some moved to Rome to work as occasional laborers, but most stayed in the country as tenant farmers or hired hands. No

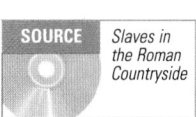 SOURCE *Slaves in the Roman Countryside*

longer landowners, they were also no longer eligible for the army. Often the land they abandoned was acquired by the wealthy who converted these farms, later called **latifundia**, into large plantations for growing cash crops—grain, olives, and grapes for wine—or into cattle ranches.

The upper classes had plenty of capital to stock and operate these estates as a result of profits from the war and from exploiting the provinces. Land was cheap, and slaves conquered in war provided cheap labor. By fair means and foul, large landholders obtained sizable quantities of public

[3] Juvenal. *Satires* 6.434–456. trans. by Roger Killian, Richard Lynch, Robert J. Rowland, and John Sims. cited by Sarah B. Pomeroy in *Goddesses, Whores, Wives, and Slaves* (New York: Schocken, 1975), p. 172.

Map Exploration

To explore this map further, go to http://www.prenhall.com/craig_maps

Territorial Extent of the Republic, 44 B.C.E.

Map 6–3. Roman Dominions of the Late Republic. This map shows the extent of the territory controlled by Rome at the time of Caesar's death in 44 B.C.E.

land and forced small farmers off it. These changes separated the people of Rome and Italy more sharply into rich and poor, landed and landless, privileged and deprived. The result was political, social, and ultimately constitutional conflict that threatened the republic.

The Gracchi

By the middle of the second century B.C.E. the problems caused by Rome's rapid expansion troubled perceptive Roman nobles. The fall in status of the peasant farmers made it harder to recruit soldiers and came to present a political threat as well. The patron's traditional control over his clients was weakened by their flight from their land. Even those former landowners who worked on the land of their patrons as tenants or hired hands were less reliable. The introduction of the secret ballot in the 130s B.C.E. made them even more independent.

Tiberius Gracchus (168–133 B.C.E.) tried to solve these problems. He became tribune in 133 B.C.E. on a program of land reform. The program aroused great hostility. When Tiberius put it before the tribal assembly, another tribune interposed his veto. Unwilling to give up, Tiberius put his bill before the tribal assembly again. Again it was vetoed, so Tiberius, strongly supported by the people, had the offending tribune removed from office, thereby violating the constitution.

Tiberius then proposed a second bill, harsher than the first and more appealing to the people, for he had despaired of conciliating the Senate. There could be no compromise: Either Tiberius or the Roman constitution must go under.

Tiberius understood the danger he would face if he stepped down from the tribunate, so he announced his candidacy for a second successive term, another blow at tradition.

At the elections a riot broke out, and a mob of senators and their clients killed Tiberius and some 300 of his followers and threw their bodies into the Tiber River. The Senate had put down the threat to its rule, but at the price of the first internal bloodshed in Roman political history.

The tribunate of Tiberius Gracchus permanently changed Roman politics. Heretofore, politics had generally involved struggles for honor and reputation between great families or coalitions of such families. Fundamental issues were rarely at stake. The revolutionary proposals of Tiberius, however, and the senatorial resort to bloodshed created a new situation.

From then on Romans could pursue a political career that was not based solely on influence within the aristocracy; pressure from the people might be an effective substitute. In the last century of the republic such politicians were called **populares**, whereas those who supported the traditional role of the Senate were called *optimates* ("the best men").

The tribunate of Gaius Gracchus (ca. 159–121 B.C.E.), brother of Tiberius, was much more dangerous to the Senate than that of Tiberius because all the tribunes of 123 B.C.E. were Gaius's supporters. There could be no veto, and tribunes could now be reelected. Gaius appealed to a variety of groups. He proposed to establish new colonies for landless veterans: two in Italy and one on the old site of Carthage. Among other popular acts, he put through a law stabilizing the price of grain in Rome.

Gaius also appealed to the equestrian order in his struggle against the Senate. The **equestrians** were rich men who could qualify to serve in the Roman cavalry, the most expensive form of military service. Many supplied goods and services to the Roman state and collected its taxes in the provinces. These wealthy men usually had the same outlook as the Senate; generally they used their profits to purchase land and to try to reach senatorial rank themselves. Still, they had a special interest in Roman expansion and in the exploitation of the provinces. When Pergamum became the Roman province of Asia in 129 B.C.E. Gaius gave them the right to collect taxes there.

Gaius easily won reelection as tribune for 122 B.C.E. He aimed at giving citizenship to the Italians, both to resolve their dissatisfaction and to add them to his political coalition. But the common people did not want to share the advantages of Roman citizenship, and the Senate seized on this proposal to drive a wedge between Gaius and his supporters.

The Romans did not reelect Gaius in 121 B.C.E., and a hostile consul provoked an incident that led to violence. The Senate established martial law. Gaius was hunted down and killed, and some 3,000 of his followers were put to death without trial.

Marius and Sulla

Before long the senatorial oligarchy faced more serious dangers arising from troubles abroad. Jugurtha (d. 104 B.C.E.) became king of Numidia, a client kingdom of Rome near Carthage, and his massacre of Roman and Italian businessmen in Numidia gained Roman attention. Pressure from the equestrians and the people forced the declaration of what became known as the Jugurthine War in 111 B.C.E.

The war dragged on until the people elected Gaius Marius (157–86 B.C.E.) to the consulship for 107 B.C.E., and the assembly, usurping the role of the Senate, assigned him to the province of Numidia. Marius was a *novus homo,* a "new man"—that is, the first in the history of his family to reach the consulship. He was outside the closed circle of the old Roman aristocracy and a political maverick.

Marius quickly defeated Jugurtha, but Jugurtha escaped and guerrilla warfare continued. Finally, Marius's subordinate, Lucius Cornelius Sulla (138–78 B.C.E.), trapped Jugurtha and brought the war to an end. Marius celebrated the victory, but Sulla, an ambitious but impoverished descendant of an old Roman family, resented being cheated of the credit. The seeds were planted for a personal rivalry that would last until Marius's death. (See Document, "Sallust on Factions and the Decline of the Republic.")

While the Romans were fighting Jugurtha, a far greater danger from barbarians threatened Rome from the north. To meet the danger, the Romans elected Marius to his second consulship when these tribes threatened again. He served five consecutive terms from 104 B.C.E. until 100 B.C.E.

Marius made important changes in the army. He began using volunteers, mostly the dispossessed farmers and rural proletarians whose problems had not been solved by the Gracchi. They enlisted for a long term of service and looked on the army as an opportunity and a career. They became semiprofessional clients of their general and sought guaranteed food, clothing, shelter, and booty from victories. They came to expect land as a form of mustering-out pay or veteran's bonus when they retired. Volunteers were most likely to join a man who was a capable soldier and influential enough to obtain what they wanted. They looked to him rather than to the state for their rewards. He on the other hand, had to obtain grants from the Senate if he was to maintain his power and reputation.

Marius's innovation created both the opportunity and the necessity for military leaders to gain enough power to challenge civilian authority. The promise of rewards won these leaders the personal loyalty of their troops that allowed them to frighten the Senate into granting their demands.

Sallust on Factions and the Decline of the Republic

Document

Sallust (86–35 B.C.E.) was a supporter of Julius Caesar and of the political faction called *populares*, translated here as "the democratic party," opponents of the *optimates*, translated here as "the nobility." In this selection from his monograph on the Jugurthine War, Sallust tries to explain Rome's troubles in the period after the destruction of Carthage in 146 B.C.E.

◆ Why did Sallust think the destruction of Carthage marked the beginning of the decline of the Roman Republic? Does his account of events seem fair and dispassionate? How would a member of "the nobility" have evaluated the same events? Is the existence of factions or "parties" inevitably harmful to a republic?

The division of the Roman state into warring factions, with all its attendant vices, had originated some years before, as a result of peace and of that material prosperity which men regard as the greatest blessing. Down to the destruction of Carthage, the people and Senate shared the government peaceably and with due restraint, and the citizens did not compete for glory or power; fear of its enemies preserved the good morals of the state. But when the people were relieved of this fear, the favourite vices of prosperity—licence and pride—appeared as a natural consequence. Thus the peace and quiet which they had longed for in time of adversity proved, when they obtained it, to be even more grievous and bitter than the adversity. For the nobles started to use their position, and the people their liberty, to gratify their selfish passions, every man snatching and seizing what he could for himself. So the whole community was split into parties, and the Republic, which hitherto had been the common interest of all, was torn asunder. The nobility had the advantage of being a close-knit body, whereas the democratic party was weakened by its loose organization,

its supporters being dispersed among a huge multitude. One small group of oligarchs had everything in its control alike in peace and war—the treasury, the provinces, public offices, all distinctions and triumphs. The people were burdened with military services and poverty, while the spoils of war were snatched by the generals and shared with a handful of friends. Meantime, the soldiers' parents or young children, if they happened to have a powerful neighbour, might well be driven from their homes. Thus the possession of power gave unlimited scope to ruthless greed, which violated and plundered everything, respecting nothing and holding nothing sacred, till finally it brought about its own downfall. For the day came when noblemen rose to power who preferred true glory to unjust dominion: then the state was shaken to its foundations by civil strife, as by an earthquake.

The Jugurthine War: The Conspiracy of Cataline by Sallust, translated by S.A. Hanford. Penguin Classics. Copyright © 1963 The Estate of S.A. Hanford. Reproduced by permission of Penguin Books Ltd.

War Against the Italian Allies (90–88 B.C.E.)

For a decade Rome ignored Italian discontent. In frustration, the Italians revolted and established a separate confederation with its own capital and its own coinage.

Employing the traditional device of divide and conquer, the Romans immediately offered citizenship to those cities that remained loyal and soon made the same offer to the rebels if they laid down their arms. By 88 B.C.E. the war against the allies was over. All the Italians became Roman citizens with the protections that citizenship offered, but they retained local self-government and a dedication to their own municipalities that made Italy flourish. The passage of

time blurred the distinction between Romans and Italians and forged them into a single nation.

Sulla's Dictatorship

Sulla had performed well during the war against the allies, and he was elected consul for 88 B.C.E. A champion of senatorial control, he won a civil war against Marius and his friends. He now held all power and had himself appointed dictator to reconstitute the state. He had enough power to make himself the permanent ruler of Rome. Yet he was traditional enough to want to restore senatorial government, reformed to prevent the misfortunes of the past.

Sulla retired to a life of ease and luxury in 79 B.C.E. He could not, however, undo the effect of his own example: a general using the loyalty of his own troops to take power and massacre his opponents, as well as innocent people. These actions proved to be far more significant than his constitutional arrangements.

The Fall of the Republic

Pompey, Crassus, and Caesar

Within a year of Sulla's death, his constitution came under assault. Marcus Licinius Crassus (115–53 B.C.E.) and Cnaeus Pompey (106–48 B.C.E.) were ambitious men whom the Senate feared. Both demanded special honors and election to the consulship for the year 70 B.C.E. They both won election and repealed most of Sulla's constitution. This led to further attacks on senatorial control and to collaboration between ambitious generals and demagogic tribunes.

In 67 B.C.E. a special law gave Pompey *imperium* for three years over the entire Mediterranean and fifty miles in from the coast. He also was given the power to raise great quantities of troops and money to rid the area of pirates. His power was then extended to fight a war that had broken out in Asia Minor. When he returned to Rome in 62 B.C.E. he had more power, prestige, and popular support than any Roman in history. The Senate and his personal enemies feared that he might emulate Sulla and establish his own rule.

Crassus had the most reason to fear Pompey's return. Although rich and influential, he did not have the confidence of the Senate, a firm political base of his own, or the kind of military glory needed to rival Pompey. During the 60s B.C.E., therefore, he allied himself with various popular leaders. The ablest of these men was Gaius Julius Caesar (100–44 B.C.E.), a descendant of an old but politically obscure patrician family.

First Triumvirate

To general surprise, Pompey disbanded his army, celebrated a great triumph, and returned to private life. He had achieved amazing things for Rome and simply wanted the Senate to approve his excellent arrangements in the east and to give land to his veterans. But the jealous and fearful Senate refused. Pompey was thus driven to an alliance with his natural enemies, Crassus and Caesar. So was born the First Triumvirate, an informal agreement among three Roman

Bust of Julius Caesar

politicians, each seeking his private goals, that further undermined the future of the republic.

Dictatorship of Julius Caesar

Caesar was rewarded with election to the consulship for 59 B.C.E. The Triumvirate's program was quickly enacted, and Caesar got the extraordinary command that would give him a chance to earn the glory and power with which to rival Pompey: the governorship of Illyricum and Gaul for five years.

Caesar was now free in Gaul to seek the military success he craved. By the time he was ready to return, after conquering the province and consolidating his gains, the Triumvirate had dissolved and a crisis was at hand. At Carrhae in 53 B.C.E. Crassus died trying to conquer the Parthians. Pompey joined the Senate in opposing Caesar.

Early in January of 49 B.C.E. the more extreme faction in the Senate ordered Pompey to defend the state and Caesar to lay down his command. For Caesar this meant exile or death, so he ordered his legions to cross the Rubicon River, the boundary of his province. This action was the first act of a civil war that ended in 45 B.C.E., when Caesar defeated the last of the enemy forces under Pompey's sons at Munda in Spain. As dictator Caesar, in Shakespeare's words, bestrode "the narrow world like a Colossus."

Caesar's innovations generally sought to make rational and orderly what was traditional and chaotic. His reforms also tended to elevate Italians and even provincials at the expense of the old Roman families, most of whom were his political enemies.

Caesar made few changes in the government of Rome, but his monopoly of military power made the whole structure a sham. He treated the Senate as his creature, sometimes with disdain. His enemies were quick to accuse him of aiming at monarchy and conspired against him. On March 15, 44 B.C.E., Caesar was stabbed to death in the Senate. The assassins regarded themselves as heroic "tyrannicides" and had no clear plan of action. No doubt they simply expected the republic to be restored in the old way, but things had gone too far for that. Instead thirteen years more of civil war ensued, at the end of which the republic received its final burial.

Second Triumvirate and the Emergence of Octavian

Caesar's heir was his grandnephew, Octavian (63 B.C.E.–14 C.E.), a youth of eighteen. He joined Marcus Antonius (Mark Antony, ca. 83–30 B.C.E.) and Lepidus (d. 13 B.C.E.), two of Caesar's officers, in the Second Triumvirate to fight the assassins. The new triumvirs defeated the enemy at Philippi in 42 B.C.E., but they soon quarreled among themselves. Octavian gained control of the western part of the empire. Antonius, together with Cleopatra (r. 51–30 B.C.E.), queen of Egypt, ruled the east. In 31 B.C.E. the forces of Octavian crushed the fleet and army of Antony and Cleopatra at Actium, resolving the conflict.

The civil wars were over, and at the age of thirty-two Octavian was absolute master of the Mediterranean world. His power was enormous, but so was the task before him. He had to restore peace, prosperity, and confidence, all of which required a constitution that would reflect the new realities without offending unduly the traditional republican prejudices that still had so firm a grip on Rome and Italy.

Chronology

The Fall of the Roman Republic

133 B.C.E.	Tribunate of Tiberius Gracchus
123–122 B.C.E.	Tribunate of Gaius Gracchus
111–105 B.C.E.	Jugurthine War
104–100 B.C.E.	Consecutive consulships of Marius
90–88 B.C.E.	War against the Italian allies
70 B.C.E.	Consulship of Crassus and Pompey
60 B.C.E.	Formation of First Triumvirate
58–50 B.C.E.	Caesar in Gaul
53 B.C.E.	Crassus killed in Battle of Carrhae
49 B.C.E.	Caesar crosses Rubicon; civil war begins
46–44 B.C.E.	Caesar's dictatorship
45 B.C.E.	End of civil war
43 B.C.E.	Formation of Second Triumvirate
42 B.C.E.	Battle of Philippi
31 B.C.E.	Octavian defeats Antony at Actium

The Augustan Principate

If the problems facing Octavian after the Battle of Actium were great, so too were his resources for addressing them. He was the master of a vast military force, the only one in the Roman world, and he had loyal and capable assistants. Yet the memory of Julius Caesar's fate was still clear in Octavian's mind; it was dangerous to flaunt unprecedented powers and to disregard all republican traditions.

Octavian's constitutional solution proved to be successful and lasting, subtle and effective. Behind the republican trappings and the apparent sharing of authority with the Senate, the government of Octavian, like that of his successors, was a monarchy. All real power—both civil and

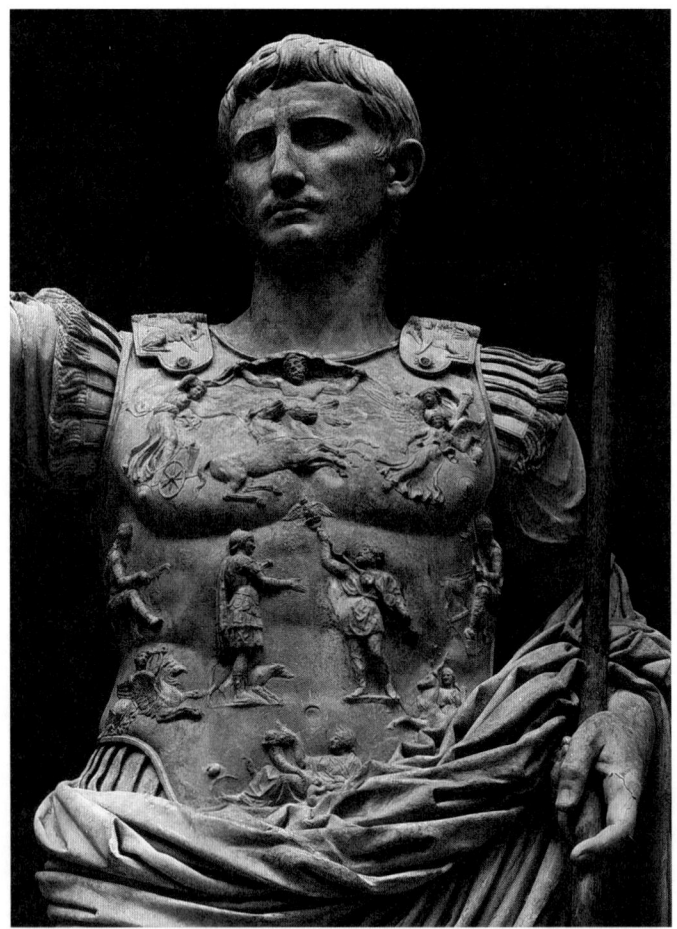

Emperor Augustus (r. 27 B.C.E.–14 C.E.). This statue, now in the Vatican, stood in the villa of Augustus's wife Livia. The figures on the elaborate breastplate are all of symbolic significance. At the top, for example, Dawn in her chariot brings in a new day under the protective mantle of the sky god; in the center, Tiberius, Augustus' successor, accepts the return of captured Roman army standards from a barbarian prince; and at the bottom, Mother Earth offers a horn of plenty. *Charitable Foundation, Gemeinnutzige Stiftung Leonard von Matt.*

military—lay with the ruler, whether he was called by the unofficial title of "first citizen" (*princeps*) like Octavian, who was the founder of the regime, or "emperor" (**imperator**) like those who followed.

On January 13, 27 B.C.E., he put forward a new plan in dramatic style, coming before the Senate to give up all his powers and provinces. In what was surely a rehearsed response, the Senate begged him to reconsider, and at last he agreed to accept the provinces of Spain, Gaul, and Syria with proconsular power for military command and to retain the consulship in Rome. The Senate would govern the other provinces as before. Because his provinces contained twenty of the twenty-six legions, his true power was undiminished, but the Senate responded with almost hysterical gratitude, voting him many honors. Among them was the semireligious title "**Augustus,**" which connoted veneration, majesty, and holiness. Historians thus speak of Rome's first emperor as Augustus and of his regime as the Principate. This would have pleased him, for it helps conceal the novel, unrepublican nature of the regime and the naked power on which it rested.

Administration

Augustus made important changes in the government of Rome, Italy, and the provinces, intending to reduce inefficiency and corruption, eliminate the threat to peace and order by ambitious individuals, and reduce the distinction between Romans and Italians, senators and equestrians. Augustus controlled the elections and saw to it that promising young men, whatever their origin, served the state as administrators and provincial governors. Thus, many equestrians and Italians who had no connection with the Roman aristocracy entered the Senate, which Augustus was always careful to treat with respect and honor.

The Augustan period was one of great prosperity, based on the wealth that Augustus had brought in by the conquest of Egypt, on the great increase in commerce and industry made possible by general peace and a vast program of public works, and on a revival of successful small farming by Augustus' resettled veterans.

The union of political and military power in the hands of the *princeps* enabled him to install rational, efficient, and stable government in the provinces for the first time.

The Army and Defense

Under Augustus, members of the armed forces became true professionals. Enlistment, chiefly by Italians, was for twenty years, but the pay was relatively good, and there were occasional bonuses and the promise of a pension on retirement in the form of money or land. Together with the auxiliaries from the provinces, these forces formed a frontier army of about 300,000 men. This was barely enough to hold the line. The Roman army permanently based in the provinces brought Roman culture to the natives. The soldiers spread their language and customs, often marrying local women and settling down there. They attracted merchants, who often became the nuclei of new towns and cities that became centers of Roman civilization. As time passed, the provincials on the frontiers became Roman citizens and helped strengthen Rome's defenses against the barbarians outside.

Religion and Morality

A century of political strife and civil war had undermined the foundations of traditional Roman society. Augustus undertook to preserve and restore the traditional values of the

Tombstone of a Roman Soldier, from Cologne, Germany, ca 100 C.E. The soldier, Marcus Valerius Celerinus, a veteran of the Tenth Legion, reclines while his wife sits in a subordinate position. A slave stands near his side, ready to serve him food and drink.

family and religion in Rome and Italy. He curbed adultery and divorce and encouraged early marriage and the procreation of legitimate children.

Augustus also worked to restore the dignity of formal Roman religion, building many temples, reviving old cults, and reorganizing and invigorating the priestly colleges; he also banned the worship of newly introduced foreign gods. During his lifetime he did not accept divine honors, although he was deified after his death; as with Julius Caesar, a state cult was dedicated to his worship.

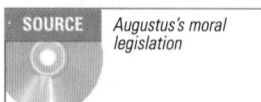

SOURCE *Augustus's moral legislation*

Civilization of the Ciceronian and Augustan Ages

The high point of Roman culture came in the last century of the republic and during the Principate of Augustus. While Greek rhetoric, philosophy, and literature served as the models for Roman writers and artists, the art and writing of both periods show uniquely Roman qualities in spirit and sometimes in form.

The Late Republic

Cicero (106–43 B.C.E.) The towering literary figure of the late republic was Cicero. He is most famous for his orations delivered in the law courts and the Senate. Together with many of his private letters, the speeches give us a clearer and fuller insight into his mind than the works of any other figure in antiquity. We see the political life of his period largely through his eyes. He also wrote treatises on rhetoric, ethics, and politics that put Greek philosophical ideas into Latin terminology and also changed them to suit Roman conditions and values.

Cicero believed in a world governed by divine and natural law that human reason could perceive and human institutions reflect. He looked to law, custom, and tradition to produce both stability and liberty. His literary style, as well as his values and ideas, was an important legacy for the Middle Ages and, reinterpreted, for the Renaissance.

Law The period from the Gracchi to the fall of the Republic was important in the development of Roman law. Before that time Roman law was essentially national and had developed chiefly by means of juridical decisions, case by case, but contact with foreign peoples and the influence of Greek ideas forced a change. From the last century of the republic on, the edicts of the *praetors,* which interpreted and even changed and added to existing law, had increasing importance in developing the Roman legal code. Quite early the edicts of the magistrates who dealt with foreigners developed the idea of the *jus gentium,* or "law of peoples," as opposed to that arising strictly from the experience of the Romans. In the first century B.C.E. the influence of Greek thought made the idea of *jus gentium* identical to that of the *jus naturale,* or "natural law," taught by the Stoics. It was this view of a world ruled by divine reason that Cicero enshrined in his treatise on the laws, *De Legibus.*

Poetry This was also the period of two of Rome's greatest poets, Lucretius and Catullus, each representing a different aspect of Rome's poetic tradition. The Hellenistic poets and literary theorists saw two functions for the poet, as entertainer and as teacher. They thought the best poet combined both roles, and the Romans adopted the same view. Lucretius (ca. 99–55 B.C.E.) pursued this path in his epic poem *De Rerum Natura* (On the Nature of Things). In it, he set forth the scientific and philosophical ideas of Epicurus and Democritus with the zeal of a missionary trying to save society from fear and superstition. He knew that his doctrine might be bitter medicine to the reader: "That is why I have tried to administer it to you in the dulcet strains of poesy, coated with the sweet honey of the Muses."[4]

Catullus (ca. 84–54 B.C.E.) was thoroughly different. His poems were personal, even autobiographical. He wrote of the joys and pains of love, he hurled invective at important contemporaries like Julius Caesar, and he amused himself in witty poetic exchanges. He offered no moral lessons and was not interested in Rome's glorious history and in contemporary politics. In a sense, he is an example of the proud, independent, pleasure-seeking nobleman who characterized part of the aristocracy at the end of the republic.

The Age of Augustus

The spirit of the Augustan Age, the golden age of Roman literature, reflected the new conditions of society (see Document, "An Ideal Roman Woman").

The old aristocratic order, with its system of independent nobles following their own particular interests, was gone. So was the world of poets of the lower orders, receiving patronage from individual aristocrats. Augustus replaced the complexity of republican patronage with a simple scheme in which all patronage flowed from the princeps, usually through his chief cultural adviser, Maecenas (d. 8 B.C.E.).

Two of the major poets of this time, Virgil and Horace, had lost their property during the civil wars. The patronage of the *princeps* allowed them the leisure and the security to write poetry and also made them dependent on him and

---

[4] Lucretius. *De Rerum Natura*, lines 931 ff. (New York: Oxford University Press, 1922).

An Ideal Roman Woman

Document

Just after the fall of the Roman republic, late in the first century B.C.E. the poet Propertius wrote an elegy in honor of a woman of the Roman nobility, Cornelia, the stepdaughter of Augustus, the ruler of the newly established Principate. She was married to the aristocrat Paullus and was the mother of three children. Propertius presents her as defending herself before the last judgment of Hades, king of the underworld. Her words were written by a man, but they seem to be an accurate representation of the values of the upper classes of Rome of both sexes.

◆ In what achievements, associations, and qualities did she take pride? What might a person of our time find absent? What limits are implied by what is missing?

I was born to this, and when the wreath of marriage
Caught up my hair, and I was a woman grown, it was
*   your bed, my Paullus, that I came to and now have left.*
*   The carving on the stone says she wed but once. O*
*   fathers long respected victors in Africa, be my defense*
*   . . .*
I asked no favours when Paullus was made censor: no
*   evil found its way within our walls.*
I do not think I have disgraced my fathers:
I set a decent pattern in these halls.
Days had a quiet rhythm: no scandal touched us from the
*   wedding torch to the torch beside my bier.*
A certain integrity is proof of breeding: the love of virtue
*   should not be born of fear.*
Whatever the judge, whatever the lot fate gives me, no
*   woman needs to blush who sits at my side . . .*

For my children I wore the mother's robe of honor;
It was no empty house I left behind.
Lepidus, Paullus, still you bring me comfort; you closed
*   my eyes when death had made me blind.*
Twice in the curule chair I have seen my brother; they
*   cheered him as a consul the day before I died.*
And you, my daughter, think of your censor-father, choose
*   one husband and live content at his side.*
Our clan will rest on the children that you give it. Secure
*   in their promise I board the boat and rejoice. Mine is*
*   the final triumph of any woman, that her spirit earns*
*   the praise of a living voice.*

Properitius, translated by Consantce Carrier, *The Poems of Properitus,* Indiana University Press © 1963. Reprinted with permission.

---

limited their freedom of expression. They wrote on subjects that were useful for his policies and that glorified him and his family, but they were not mere propagandists. For the most part, they were persuaded of the virtues of Augustus and his reign and sincerely sang its praises. Because they were poets of genius, they were also able to maintain some independence in their work.

Virgil   Virgil (70–19 B.C.E.) was the most important of the Augustan poets. His greatest work is the *Aeneid,* a long national epic that placed the history of Rome in the great tradition of the Greeks and the Trojan War. Its hero, the Trojan Aeneas, personifies the ideal Roman qualities of duty, responsibility, serious purpose, and patriotism. As the Romans' equivalent to Homer, Virgil glorified not the personal honor and excellence of the Greek epic heroes, but the civic greatness represented by Augustus and the peace and prosperity that he and the Julian family had given to imperial Rome.

Horace   Horace (65–8 B.C.E.) was won over to the Augustan cause by the patronage of Maecenas and by the attractions of the Augustan reforms. His great skills as a lyric poet are best revealed in his *Odes,* which are ingenious in their adaptation of Greek meters to the requirements of Latin verse. Two of the odes are directly in praise of Augustus, and many of them glorify the new Augustan order, the imperial family, and the empire.

SOURCE   Horace, "Dulce et Decorum est Pro Patria"

Ovid   The darker side of Augustan influence on the arts is revealed by the career of Ovid (43 B.C.E.–18 C.E.). He wrote light and entertaining love elegies that reveal the sophistication and the loose sexual code of a notorious sector of the Roman aristocracy. Their values and way of life were contrary to the seriousness and family-centered life that Augustus was trying to foster. Ovid's *Ars Amatoria,* a poetic textbook on the art of seduction, angered Augustus and was partly responsible for the poet's exile in 8 C.E. His most popular work is

Metamorphoses, a kind of mythological epic that turns Greek myths into charming stories in a graceful and lively style. Ovid's fate was an effective warning to later poets.

History The most important and influential prose writer of the time was Livy (59 B.C.E.–17 C.E.). His *History of Rome* treated the period from the legendary origins of Rome until 9 B.C.E. Only one-fourth of his work survives; of the rest we have only pitifully brief summaries. He based his history on

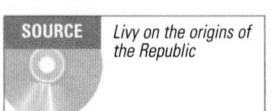
SOURCE *Livy on the origins of the Republic*

earlier accounts, and made no effort at original research. His great achievement was to tell the story of Rome in a continuous and impressive narrative. Its purpose was moral—setting up historical models as examples of good and bad behavior—and, above all, patriotic. He glorified Rome's greatness and connected it with Rome's past, just as Augustus tried to do.

Architecture and Sculpture Augustus was the great patron of the visual arts, as he was of literature. He embarked on a building program that beautified Rome, glorified his reign, and contributed to the general prosperity and his own popularity. Most of the building was influenced by the Greek classical style, which aimed at serenity and the ideal type. The greatest monument of the age is the Altar of Peace (*Ara Pacis*), dedicated in 9 B.C.E. Its walls show a procession in which Augustus and his family appear to move forward, followed by the magistrates, the Senate, and the people of Rome. There is no better symbol of the new order.

A Panel from the Ara Pacis (Altar of Peace). The altar was dedicated in 9 B.C.E. It was part of a propaganda campaign—involving poetry, architecture, myth, and history—that Augustus undertook to promote himself as the savior of Rome and the restorer of peace. This panel shows the goddess Earth and her children with cattle, sheep, and other symbols of agricultural wealth.
Saturnia, Tellus, Goddess of Earth, Air and Water. Panel from the Ara Pacis. 13–9 B.C.E. Museum of the Ara Pacis, Rome. Nimatallah/Art Resource, N.Y.

Peace and Prosperity: Imperial Rome (14–180 C.E.)

Augustus tried to cloak the monarchical nature of his government, but his successors soon abandoned all pretense. The rulers came to be called *imperator*—from which comes our word *emperor*—as well as *Caesar.* The latter title signified connection with the imperial house, and the former indicated the military power on which their authority was based. Because Augustus was ostensibly only the "first citizen" of a restored republic and his powers were theoretically voted him by the Senate and the people, he could not legally name his successor. In fact, he plainly designated his heirs by favors lavished on them and by giving them a share in the imperial power and responsibility (see Map 6–4).

Tiberius (r. 14–37 C.E.), his immediate successor, was at first embarrassed by the ambiguity of his new role, but soon the monarchical and hereditary nature of the regime became patent. Gaius (Caligula, r. 37–41 C.E.), Claudius (r. 41–54 C.E.), and Nero (r. 54–68 C.E.) were all descended from Augustus's family. The year 69, however, saw four different emperors assume power in quick succession as different Roman armies took turns placing their commanders on the throne.

Vespasian (r. 69–79 C.E.) emerged victorious from the chaos, and his sons, Titus (r. 79–81 C.E.) and Domitian (r. 81–96 C.E.), carried forward his line, the Flavian dynasty. Vespasian was the first emperor who did not come from the old Roman nobility.

The Flavian dynasty ended with the assassination of Domitian. Because Domitian had no close relative who had been designated as successor, the Senate put Nerva (r. 96–98 C.E.) on the throne to avoid chaos. He was the first of the five "good emperors," who included Trajan (r. 98–117 C.E.), Hadrian (r. 117–138 C.E.), Antoninus Pius (r. 138–161 C.E.), and Marcus Aurelius (r. 161–180 C.E.). Until Marcus Aurelius, none of these emperors had sons, so they each followed the example set by Nerva of adopting an able senator and establishing him as successor. The result was almost a century of peaceful succession and competent rule, which ended when Marcus Aurelius allowed his incompetent son, Commodus (r. 180–192 C.E.), to succeed him, with unfortunate results.

There was, of course, opposition to imperial rule. Plots and the suspicion of plots led to repression, the use of spies and paid informers, book burning, and executions. The opposition consisted chiefly of senators who looked back to republican liberty for their class. Plots and repression were most common under Nero and Domitian. From Nerva to Marcus Aurelius, however, the emperors, without yielding

Map 6–4. Provinces of the Roman Empire to 117 C.E. The growth of the empire to its greatest extent is shown in three states—at the death of Augustus in 14 B.C.E., at the death of Nerva in 98 C.E., and at the death of Trajan in 117 C.E. The division into provinces is also indicated. The inset outlines the main roads that tied the far-flung empire.

Inset map: **MAJOR ROADS OF THE ROMAN EMPIRE** — Rome, Mediterranean Sea; 500 MILES, 500 KILOMETERS

Legend:
- 14 C.E. — Death of Augustus
- 14–98 C.E. — Acquisitions, Augustus to Trajan
- 98–117 C.E. — Acquisitions During the Reign of Trajan

500 MILES, 500 KILOMETERS

Chronology

Rulers of the Early Empire

27 B.C.E.–14 C.E.	Augustus

The Julio-Claudian Dynasty

14–37 C.E.	Tiberius
37–41 C.E.	Gaius (Caligula)
41–54 C.E.	Claudius
54–68 C.E.	Nero
69 C.E.	Year of the four emperors

The Flavian Dynasty

69–79 C.E.	Vespasian
79–81 C.E.	Titus
81–96 C.E.	Domitian

The "Good Emperors"

96–98 C.E.	Nerva
98–117 C.E.	Trajan
117–138 C.E.	Hadrian
138–161 C.E.	Antoninus Pius
161–180 C.E.	Marcus Aurelius

any power, enlisted the cooperation of the upper class by courteous and modest deportment.

Administration of the Empire

From an administrative and cultural standpoint, the empire was a collection of cities and towns. Roman policy during the Principate was to raise urban centers to the status of Roman municipalities with the rights and privileges attached to them. The Romans enlisted the upper classes of the provinces in their own government, spread Roman law and culture, and won the loyalty of the influential people.

Unlike most conquered peoples the Jews found accommodation to Roman rule difficult. Their first rebellion was crushed by Vespasian's son, the future emperor Titus, in 70 C.E. At that time the Temple in Jerusalem was destroyed. A second revolt was put down in 117 C.E. Finally, when Hadrian ordered a Roman colony placed on the site of Jerusalem, Simon, who was called Bar Kochba, or "Son of the Star," led a last uprising from 132 to 135 that was brutally suppressed.

As the bureaucracy became more efficient, so did the number and scope of its functions and therefore its size. The importance and autonomy of the municipalities shrank as the central administration took a greater part in local affairs. The price paid for the increased efficiency offered by centralized control was the loss of the vitality of the cities throughout the empire.

Augustus's successors accepted his conservative and defensive foreign policy. Trajan was the first emperor to take the offensive in a sustained way. Between 101 and 106 c.e. he established the new province of Dacia between the Danube and the Carpathian Mountains. He was tempted, no doubt, by its important gold mines, but he was probably also pursuing a new general strategy: to defend the empire more aggressively by driving wedges into enemy territory. The same strategy dictated the invasion of the Parthian Empire in the east (113–117 c.e.). Trajan's early success there was astonishing, but his lines were overextended. Rebellions

Relief from the Arch of Titus. Spoils from the Temple in Jerusalem were carried in triumphal procession by Roman troops. This relief from Titus's Arch of Victory in the Roman Forum celebrates his capture of Jerusalem in 70 C.E. after a two-year siege. The Jews found it difficult to reconcile their religion with Roman rule and frequently rebelled. *Scala/Art Resource, N.Y.*

Daily Life in a Roman Provincial Town: Graffiti from Pompeii

Document

On the walls of the houses of Pompeii, buried and preserved by the eruption of Mount Vesuvius in 79 C.E., are many scribblings that give us an idea of what the life of ordinary people was like.

◆ How do these graffiti differ from those one sees in a modern American city? What do they reveal about the similarities and differences between the ordinary people of ancient Rome and the people of today? How would you account for the differences?

I

Twenty pairs of gladiators of Decimus Lucretius Satrius Valens, lifetime flamen of Nero son of Caesar Augustus, and ten pairs of gladiators of Decimus Lucretius Valens, his son, will fight at Pompeii on April 8, 9, 10, 11, 12. There will be a full card of wild beast combats, and awnings [for the spectators]. Aemilius Celer [painted this sign], all alone in the moonlight.

II

Market days: Saturday in Pompeii, Sunday in Nuceria, Monday in Atella, Tuesday in Nola, Wednesday in Cumae, Thursday in Puteoli, Friday in Rome.

III

Pleasure says: "You can get a drink here for an as [a few cents], a better drink for two, Falernian for four."

IV

A copper pot is missing from this shop. 65 sesterces reward if anybody brings it back, 20 sesterces if he reveals the thief so we can get our property back.

V

The weaver Successus loves the innkeeper's slave girl, Iris by name. She doesn't care for him, but he begs her to take pity on him. Written by his rival. So long.

[Answer by the rival:] Just because you're bursting with envy, don't pick on a handsomer man, a lady-killer and a gallant.

[Answer by the first writer:] There's nothing more to say or write. You love Iris, who doesn't care for you.

VI

Take your lewd looks and flirting eyes off another man's wife, and show some decency on your face!

VII

Anybody in love, come here. I want to break Venus' ribs with a club and cripple the goddess' loins. If she can pierce my tender breast, why can't I break her head with a club?

VIII

I write at Love's dictation and Cupid's instruction; But damn it! I don't want to be a god without you.

IX

[A prostitute's sign:] I am yours for 2 asses cash.

From Roman Civilization, *Naphtali Lewis and Meyer Reinhold*, Copyright © 1955 Columbia University Press. Reprinted with permission of the Columbia University Press.

---

sprang up, and the campaign crumbled. Trajan was forced to retreat and died before returning to Rome.

Hadrian kept Dacia but abandoned Trajan's eastern conquests. Under Hadrian the Roman defense became rigid, and initiative passed to the barbarians. Marcus Aurelius spent most of his reign resisting dangerous attacks in the east and on the Danube frontier, and these attacks put enormous pressure on the empire's resources.

Culture of the Early Empire

Literature In Latin literature, the years between the death of Augustus and the time of Marcus Aurelius are known as the Silver Age; as the name implies, work of high quality—al-

though probably inferior to that of the Augustan era—was produced. The writers of the Silver Age were gloomy, negative, and pessimistic. Criticism and satire lurk everywhere in

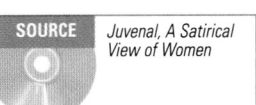
SOURCE Juvenal, A Satirical View of Women

their work. Some of the most important writers of the silver age in the first century C.E. reflected the Stoic opposition's hostility to the

growing power and personal excesses of the emperors.

The writers of the second century C.E. appear to have turned away from contemporary affairs and even recent history. Historical writing was about remote periods, so there was less danger of irritating imperial sensibilities. Scholarship was encouraged, but we hear little of poetry, especially about any dealing with dangerous subjects.

Pompeiian Woman. The Roman provincial city of Pompeii, near the Bay of Naples, was buried by an eruption of Mount Vesuvius in 79 C.E. As a result, the town, together with its private houses and their contents, was remarkably well preserved until recovery in the eighteenth century. Among the discoveries were a number of works of art, including pictorial mosaics and paintings. This depiction of a young woman, on a round panel from a house in Pompeii, is part of a larger painting that includes her husband holding a volume of Plato's writings. The woman is holding a stylus and a booklet of wax tablets and is evidently in the process of writing. Her gold earrings and hair net show that she is a fashionable person of some means. Late first century C.E. Diameter 14⅜ inches. *Sappho, idealized portrait of a girl posing as a poetess. Fresco from Pompeii, Insula occidentale. Museo Archeologico Nazionale, Naples, Italy, © Erich Lessing/Art Resource, N.Y.*

During the third century C.E. romances written in Greek became popular as an escape from contemporary realities.

Architecture   The prosperity and relative stability of the first two centuries of imperial Rome allowed the full development of Roman architecture. To the fundamental styles of buildings developed by the Greeks, the Romans added little; the great public bath and a new, free-standing amphitheater were their main innovations.

The main contribution of the Romans lay in the size of the structures they could build and in the advances in engineering that made these large structures possible. To the basic post-and-lintel construction used by the Greeks, the Romans added the semicircular arch, borrowed from the Etruscans. They also made good use of concrete, a building material first used by the Hellenistic Greeks and fully developed by the Romans. The arch combined with the post and lintel produced the great Colosseum built by the Flavian emperors. When used internally in the form of vaults and domes, the arch permitted great buildings like the baths.

One of Rome's most famous buildings, the Pantheon, begun by Augustus's friend Agrippa (63–12 B.C.E.) and rebuilt by Hadrian, combines all these elements. Its portico of Corinthian columns is of Greek origin, but its rotunda of brick-faced concrete with its domed ceiling and relieving arches is thoroughly Roman. The new engineering also made possible the construction of more mundane but more useful structures like bridges and aqueducts.

Society   Seen from the harsh perspective of human history, the first two centuries of the Roman Empire deserve their reputation as a golden age, but by the second century C.E. troubles had arisen—troubles that foreshadowed the difficult times ahead. The literary efforts of the time reveal a flight from the present and from reality and the public realm to the past, to romance, and to private pursuits. (See Document, "Daily Life in a Roman Provincial Town: Graffiti from Pompeii.") Some of the same aspects may be seen in the more prosaic world of everyday life, especially in the decline of vitality in local government.

In the first century C.E. the upper classes vied for election to municipal office and for the honor of serving their communities. By the second century much of their zeal had disappeared, and the emperors had to correct abuses in local affairs and even force unwilling members of the ruling classes to accept public office. The reluctance to serve was caused largely by the imperial practice of holding magistrates and councilmen personally and collectively responsible for revenues that were due. Some magistrates even fled to avoid their office, a practice that eventually became widespread.

All of these difficulties reflected more basic problems. The prosperity brought by the end of civil war and the influx of wealth from the east, especially Egypt, could not sustain itself beyond the first half of the second century C.E. For reasons that remain mysterious the population also seems to have declined. The cost of government kept rising as the emperors were required to maintain an expensive standing army, to keep the people in Rome happy with "bread and circuses," to pay for an increasingly large bureaucracy, and to defend the frontiers against dangerous and determined enemies.

The ever-increasing need for money compelled the emperors to raise taxes, to press hard on their subjects, and to cause inflation by debasing the coinage. These elements were to bring on the desperate crises that ultimately destroyed the empire.

A Roman Apartment House. This is a reconstruction of a typical Roman apartment house found at Ostia, Rome's port. The ground floor contained shops, and the stories above it held many apartments. *Gismondi (20th CE). Museo della Civiltá Romana, Rome, Italy/© Scala/Art Resource, N.Y.*

Life in Imperial Rome: The Apartment House

The civilization of the Roman Empire depended on the vitality of its cities. While the typical city had about 20,000 inhabitants, Rome had more than 500,000, and some scholars think it may have had more than a million. Newcomers found Rome overwhelming and were either thrilled or horrified by its size, bustle, and noise.

The mass of its inhabitants were squeezed into increasingly tall multiple dwellings. Most Romans during the imperial period lived in apartment buildings called *insulae* ("islands") that rose to five or six stories and sometimes even more. The apartments were cramped and uncomfortable, hot in summer, cold in winter, and stuffy and smoky when the stoves were lit. These buildings were also dangerous. They were lightly built of concrete and brick, far too high for their foundations, and so they often collapsed. Even more serious was the threat of fire. The floors were supported by wooden beams, and the rooms were lit by torches, candles, and oil lamps and heated by braziers. Fires broke out easily but, without running water, were not easily put out; once started, they usually led to disaster.

When we compare these apartments to the attractive public places in the city, we can easily understand why the people of Rome spent most of their time outdoors.

The Rise of Christianity

The story of how Christianity emerged, spread, survived, and ultimately conquered the Roman Empire is one of the most remarkable in history. Its origin among poor people from an unimportant and remote province of the empire gave little promise of what was to come. Christianity faced the hostility of the established religious institutions of its native Judaea and had to compete not only against the official cults of Rome and the highly sophisticated philosophies of the educated classes, but also against **"mystery religions"** like the cults of Mithra, Isis, and Osiris. The Christians also faced the opposition of the imperial government and suffered formal persecution, yet Christianity finally became the official religion of the empire.

Jesus of Nazareth

An attempt to understand this amazing outcome must begin with a discussion of Jesus of Nazareth. The most important evidence of his life and teachings is in the Gospel accounts. Their authors believed that Jesus was the Son of God and that he came into the world to redeem humanity and to bring immortality to those who believed in him and followed his way; to the Gospel writers, Jesus' resurrection was striking proof of his teachings. The Gospels also regard Jesus as a figure in history, and they recount events in his life as well as his sayings.

There is no reason to doubt that Jesus was born in the province of Judaea in the time of Augustus and that he was a most effective teacher in the tradition of the Jewish prophets. This tradition promised the coming of a Messiah (in Greek, *christos*—so *Jesus Christ* means "Jesus the Messiah"), the Redeemer who would make Israel triumph over its enemies and establish the Kingdom of God on earth. In fact, Jesus seems to have insisted that the Messiah would not establish an earthly kingdom but, at the Day of Judgment, would bring an end to the world as human beings knew it. On that day God would reward the righteous and condemn the wicked. Until that day, which his followers believed would come soon, Jesus taught the faithful to abandon sin and worldly concerns; to follow the moral code described in the Sermon on the Mount, which preached love, charity, and humility; and to believe in him and his divine mission.

Jesus won a considerable following, especially among the poor. This success caused great suspicion among the upper classes and provoked the hostility of the religious establishment in Jerusalem. They convinced the Roman governor that Jesus and his followers might be dangerous revolutionaries. He was put to death in Jerusalem by the cruel and degrading device of crucifixion, probably in 30 C.E. His followers believed that he was resurrected on the third day after his death, and that belief became a critical element in their religion. (See Document, "Mark Describes the Resurrection of Jesus.")

Although the new belief spread quickly to the Jewish communities of Syria and Asia Minor, without the conversion and career of Saint Paul it might have had only a short life as a despised Jewish heresy.

Paul of Tarsus

Paul (?5–67 C.E.) was born Saul, a citizen of the city of Tarsus in Asia Minor. Even though he was trained in Hellenistic culture and was a Roman citizen, he was a zealous member of the Jewish sect known as the **Pharisees,** who were the strictest adherents of the Jewish law. He took a vigorous part in the persecution of the early Christians until his own conversion outside Damascus in about 35 C.E. The great problem facing the early Christians was their relationship to Judaism. If the new faith was a version of Judaism, then it must adhere to the Jewish law and seek converts only among Jews. James, called the brother of Jesus, held that view, whereas Hellenist Jews tended to see Christianity as a new and universal religion.

Paul, converted and with his new name, supported the position of the Hellenists and soon won many converts among the Gentiles. Paul believed it important that the followers of Jesus be evangelists ("messengers"), to spread the gospel ("good news") of God's gracious gift. He taught that Jesus would soon return for the Day of Judgment, and that all should believe in him and accept his way. Faith in Jesus as the Christ was necessary but not sufficient for salvation, nor could good deeds alone achieve it. That final blessing of salvation was a gift of God's grace.

Organization

The new religion spread throughout the Roman Empire and even beyond its borders. It had its greatest success in the cities and among the poor and uneducated. The rites of the early communities appear to have been simple and few. Baptism by water removed original sin and permitted participation in the community and its activities. The central ritual was a common

Christ's Arrest. This Early Christian art shows Christ arrested by soldiers on the night before his crucifixion. Note that Christ is portrayed clean-shaven and dressed in the toga of a Roman aristocrat. *Hirmer Fotoarchiv, Munich.*

Mark Describes the Resurrection of Jesus

Belief that Jesus rose from the dead after his crucifixion (about 30 C.E.) was and is central to traditional Christian doctrine. The record of the resurrection in the Gospel of Mark, written a generation later (toward 70 C.E.), is the earliest we have. The significance to most Christian groups revolves about the assurance given them that death and the grave are not final and that, instead, salvation for a future life is possible. The appeal of these views was to be nearly universal in the West during the Middle Ages. The church was commonly thought to be the means of implementing the promise of salvation; hence the enormous importance of the church's sacramental system, its rules, and its clergy.

◆ Why are the stories of miracles such as the one described here important for the growth of Christianity? What is special and important about this miracle? Why is it important in the story that days passed between the death of Jesus and the opening of the tomb? Why might the early Christians believe this story? Why was belief in the resurrection important for Christianity in the centuries immediately after the life of Jesus? Is it still important today?

And when evening had come, since it was the day of Preparation, that is, the day before the sabbath, Joseph of Arimathea, a respected member of the council, who was also himself looking for the kingdom of God, took courage and went to Pilate, and asked for the body of Jesus. And Pilate wondered if he were already dead; and summoning the centurion, he asked him whether he was already dead. And when he learned from the centurion that he was dead, he granted the body to Joseph. And he bought a linen shroud, and taking him down, wrapped him in the linen shroud, and laid him in a tomb which had been hewn out of the rock; and he rolled a stone against the door of the tomb. Mary Magdalene and Mary the mother of Jesus saw where he was laid.

And when the sabbath was past, Mary Magdalene, and Mary the mother of James, and Salome, bought spices, so that they might go and anoint him. And very early on the first day of the week they went to the tomb when the sun had risen. And they were saying to one another, "Who will roll away the stone for us from the door of the tomb?" And looking up, they saw that the stone was rolled back; for it was very large. And entering the tomb, they saw a young man sitting on the right side, dressed in a white robe; and they were amazed. And he said to them, "Do not be amazed; you seek Jesus of Nazareth, who was crucified. He has risen, he is not here, see the place where they laid him. But go, tell his disciples and Peter that he is going before you to Galilee; there you will see him, as he told you." And they went out and fled from the tomb; for trembling and astonishment had come upon them; and they said nothing to any one, for they were afraid.

From the Gospel of Mark 15:42–47, 16:1–8, Revised Standard Version of the Bible (New York: Thomas Nelson and Sons, 1946, 1952).

---

meal called the **agape** ("love feast"), followed by the ceremony of the **Eucharist** ("thanksgiving"), a celebration of the Lord's Supper in which unleavened bread was eaten and unfermented wine drunk. There were also prayers, hymns, and readings from the Gospels.

At first the churches had little formal organization. Soon, it appears, affairs were placed in the hands of boards of *presbyters* ("elders") and *deacons* ("those who serve"). By the second century C.E., as their numbers grew, the Christians of each city tended to accept the authority and leadership of bishops (*episkopoi*, or "overseers"), who were elected by the congregation. As time passed, bishops extended their authority over the Christian communities in outlying towns and the countryside. The power and almost monarchical authority of the bishops were soon enhanced by the doctrine of Apostolic Succession, which asserted that the powers Jesus had given his original disciples were passed on from bishop to bishop by the rite of ordination.

The bishops kept in touch with one another, maintained communications between different Christian communities, and prevented doctrinal and sectarian splintering, which would have destroyed Christian unity. They kept internal discipline and dealt with the civil authorities. In time they began coming together in councils to settle difficult questions, to establish orthodox opinion, and even to expel as heretics those who would not accept it. Christianity could probably not have survived without such strong internal organization and government.

Persecution of Christians

The new faith soon incurred the distrust of the pagan world and of the imperial government. The Christians' refusal to worship the emperor was considered treason. The privacy and secrecy of Christian life and worship ran counter to a traditional Roman dislike of any private association, especially any of a religious nature, and the Christians thus earned the reputation of being "haters of humanity." By the end of the first

Christian Martyr. Thrown to the lions in 275 C.E. by the Romans for refusing to recant his Christian beliefs, St. Mamai is an important martyr in the iconography of Georgia, a Caucasian kingdom that embraced Christianity early in the fourth century. This gilded silver medallion, made in Georgia in the eleventh century, depicts the saint astride a lion while he bears a cross in one hand, symbolizing his triumphant victory over death and ignorance. *The Tondo of St. Mamai, from the city of Gelati, 11th c. A.D. Courtesy of the Keke-lidze Institute of Manuscripts, Tbilisi, Georgia.*

century "the name alone"—that is, simple membership in the Christian community—was a crime.

Most persecutions during this period, however, were instituted not by the government but by mobs. But even this adversity had its benefits. It weeded out the weaklings among the Christians, brought greater unity to those who remained faithful, and provided martyrs who inspired still greater devotion and dedication.

Emergence of Catholicism

Most Christians held to what even then were traditional, simple, conservative beliefs. This body of majority opinion and the church that enshrined it came to be called **Catholic,** which means "universal." Its doctrines were deemed **orthodox;** those holding contrary opinions were **heretics.**

The need to combat heretics, however, compelled the orthodox to formulate their own views more clearly and firmly. By the end of the second century an Orthodox canon had been shaped that included the Old Testament, the Gospels, and the Epistles of Paul, among other writings. The process was not completed for at least two more centuries, but a vitally important start had been made. The Orthodox declared the church itself to be the depository of Christian teaching and the bishops to be its receivers. They also drew up creeds, brief statements of faith to which true Christians should adhere. In the first century all that was required of one to be a Christian was to be baptized, to partake of the Eucharist, and to call Jesus the Lord. By the end of the second century an Orthodox Christian—that is, a member of the Catholic Church—had to accept its creed, its canon of holy writings, and the authority of the bishops. The loose structure of the apostolic church had given way to an organized body with recognized leaders able to define its faith and to exclude those who did not accept it.

Rome as a Center of the Early Church

During this same period the church in the city of Rome came to have special prominence. Besides having the largest single congregation of Christians, Rome also benefited from the tradition that both Jesus' apostles Peter and Paul were martyred there. Peter, moreover, was thought to be the first bishop of Rome, and the Gospel of Matthew (16:18) reported Jesus' statement to Peter: "Thou art Peter [in Greek, *Petros*] and upon this rock [in Greek, *petra*] I will build my church." As a result, later bishops of Rome were to claim supremacy in the Catholic Church.

The Crisis of the Third Century

The pressure on Rome's frontiers reached massive proportions in the third century C.E. In the east, by 224 C.E. a new Iranian dynasty, the Sassanids, reinvigorated Persia (see Chapter 10). They soon recovered Mesopotamia and raided deep into Roman territory.

Barbarian Invasions

On the western and northern frontiers the threat came from German tribes. The most aggressive in the third century C.E. were the Goths. In the 220s and 230s they began to put pressure on the Danube frontier, and by about 250 C.E. they overran the Balkan provinces. The need to meet these threats made the Romans weaken their western frontiers, and other Germanic peoples broke through there. There was a considerable danger that Rome would be unable to meet this challenge.

Septimius Severus (r. 193–211 C.E.) and his successors transformed the character of the Roman army. Septimius was a military usurper who owed everything to the support of his soldiers. He was prepared to make Rome into an undisguised military monarchy. Septimius drew recruits for the army increasingly from peasants of the less civilized provinces, and the result was a barbarization of Rome's military forces.

Economic Difficulties

Inflation had forced Commodus (r. 180–192 C.E.) to raise the soldiers' pay, but the Severan emperors had to double it to keep up with prices, which increased the imperial budget by as much as 25 percent. The emperors invented new taxes, debased the coinage, and even sold the palace furniture to raise money. Even then it was hard to recruit troops, and the new style of military life introduced by Septimius—with its laxer discipline, more pleasant duties, and greater opportunity for advancement, not only in the army but also in Roman society—was needed to attract men into the army. The policy proved effective for a short time but could not prevent the chaos of the late third century.

The same forces that caused problems for the army hurt society at large. The shortage of workers reduced agricultural production. As external threats distracted the emperors, they were less able to preserve domestic peace. Piracy, brigandage, and the neglect of roads and harbors hampered trade. So, too, did the debasement of the coinage and the resulting inflation. Imperial exactions and confiscations of the property of the rich removed badly needed capital from productive use.

The government now had to demand services that had once been gladly volunteered. Because the empire lived on a hand-to-mouth basis, with no significant reserve fund and no system of credit financing, the emperors had to compel the people to provide food, supplies, money, and labor. The upper classes in the cities were made to serve as administrators without pay and to meet deficits in revenue out of their own pockets. There were provincial rebellions, and peasants and even town administrators fled to escape their burdens. These difficulties weakened Rome's economic strength when it was most needed.

The Social Order

The new conditions caused important changes in the social order. The Senate and the traditional ruling class were decimated by direct attacks from hostile emperors and by economic losses. Their ranks were filled by military men. The whole state began to take on an increasingly military appearance. Distinctions among the classes by dress had been traditional since the republic, but in the third and fourth centuries C.E. people's everyday clothing became a kind of uniform that precisely revealed their status. Titles were assigned to ranks in society as to ranks in the army. The most important distinction was the one formally established by Septimius Severus, which drew a sharp line between the *honestiores* (senators, equestrians, the municipal aristocracy, and the soldiers) and the lower classes, or *humiliores*. Septimius gave the *honestiores* a privileged position before the law. They were given lighter punishments, could not be tortured, and alone had the right of appeal to the emperor.

It became more difficult to move from the lower order to the higher, another example of the growing rigidity of the late Roman Empire. Farmers were tied to their lands, artisans to their crafts, soldiers to the army, merchants and shipowners to the needs of the state, and citizens of the municipal upper class to the collection and payment of increasingly burdensome taxes. Freedom and private initiative yielded to the needs of the state and its ever-expanding control of its citizens.

Civil Disorder

By the mid–third century the empire seemed on the point of collapse, but two able soldiers, Claudius II Gothicus (r. 268–270 C.E.) and Aurelian (r. 270–275 C.E.), drove back the barbarians and stamped out disorder. The emperors who followed Aurelian on the throne were good fighters and changed Rome's system of defense. They built walls around Rome and other cities to resist barbarian attack. They drew back their best troops from the frontiers, relying chiefly on a newly organized heavy cavalry and a mobile army near the emperor's own residence. Hereafter, the army was composed largely of Germanic mercenaries whose officers gave personal loyalty to the emperor rather than to the empire. These officers became a foreign, hereditary caste of aristocrats that increasingly supplied high administrators and even emperors. In effect, the Roman people hired an army of mercenaries, only technically Roman, to protect them.

The Late Empire

The Fourth Century and Imperial Reorganization

The period from Diocletian (r. 284–305 C.E.) to Constantine (r. 306–337 C.E.) was one of reconstruction and reorganization.

Diocletian

The emperor Diocletian was a man of undistinguished birth who rose to the throne through the army. He knew that he was not a great general and that the job of defending and governing the entire empire was too great for one man. He therefore decreed the introduction of the **tetrarchy,** the rule of the empire by four men with power divided on a territorial basis (see Map 6–5). This system seemed to promise orderly, peaceful transitions instead of assassinations, chaos, and civil war.

Constantine

In 305 Diocletian retired and compelled his co-emperor to do the same. But his plan for a smooth succession failed completely. In 310 there were five competing emperors. Out of this chaos Constantine produced order. In 324 he defeated his last opponent and made himself sole emperor, uniting the empire once again; he reigned until 337.

The emperor had now become a remote figure surrounded by carefully chosen high officials. He lived in a great palace and was almost unapproachable. Those admitted to his presence had to prostrate themselves before him and kiss the hem of his robe, which was purple and had golden threads going through it. The emperor was addressed as *dominus* ("lord"), and his right to rule was not derived from the Roman people but from God. This remoteness and ceremony enhanced the dignity of the emperor and safeguarded him against assassination.

Constantine erected the new city of Constantinople on the site of ancient Byzantium on the Bosporus, which leads to both the Aegean and the Black Seas, and made it the new capital of the empire. Its strategic location was excellent for protecting the eastern and Danubian frontiers, and, surrounded on three sides by water, it was easily defended.

Administration and Finance   The autocratic rule of the emperors was carried out by a civilian bureaucracy, which was carefully separated from the military service to reduce the chances of rebellion. The entire system was supervised by a network of spies and secret police, without whom the increasingly rigid authoritarian organization could not be trusted to perform. Despite these efforts, the system was corrupt and inefficient.

The cost of maintaining a 400,000-man army as well as the vast civilian bureaucracy, the expensive imperial court, and the imperial taste for splendid buildings strained an already weak economy. Diocletian's attempts to establish a uniform and reliable currency merely increased inflation. To deal with it he resorted to price control with his Edict of Maximum Prices in 301. For each product and each kind of labor a maximum price was set, and violations were punishable by death. The edict failed, despite its harsh provisions.

Peasants unable to pay their taxes and officials unable to collect them tried to escape, and Diocletian resorted to stern regimentation to keep all in their places and at the service of the government. The terror of the third century had turned many peasants into tenant farmers who fled for protection to the country estates of powerful landowners. They were tied to the land, as were their descendants, as the caste system hardened.

Division of the Empire   The peace and unity established by Constantine did not last. His death was followed by a struggle for succession that was won by Constantius II (r. 337–361 C.E.). His death left the empire to his young cousin Julian (r. 361–363 C.E.), called by the Christians "the Apostate" as a result of his attempt to restore paganism. Julian was killed in a campaign against the Persians. His death ended the pagan revival.

The Germans in the West attacked along the Rhine, but even greater trouble was brewing along the Danube (see Map 6–6) where the Visigoths had been driven from their home in the Ukraine by the fierce Huns, a nomadic people from Central Asia. The Emperor Valentinian (r. 364–375) saw that he could not defend the empire alone and appointed his brother Valens (r. 364–378) as co-ruler. Valentinian made his own headquarters at Milan and spent the rest of his life fighting barbarians in the West. Valens was given control of the East. The empire was once again divided in two. The two emperors maintained their own courts, and the two halves of the empire became increasingly separate and different. Latin was the language of the West and Greek of the East.

Map 6–5. Divisions of the Roman Empire under Diocletian. Diocletian divided the sprawling empire into four prefectures for more effective government and defense. The inset map shows their boundaries and the large map gives some details of regions and provinces. The major division between East and West was along the line running from north to south between Pannonia and Moesia.

In 376 the hard-pressed Visigoths received permission to enter the empire to escape the Huns. When the Goths began to plunder the Balkan provinces, Valens attacked them and died, along with most of his army, at Adrianople in Thrace in 378. Theodosius (r. 379–395), an able and experienced general, was named co-ruler in the East. He tried to unify the empire again, but his death in 395 left it divided and weak.

Thereafter, the two parts of the empire went their separate and different ways. The West became increasingly rural as barbarian invasions grew. The villa, a fortified country estate, became the basic unit of life. There, *coloni* (tenant farmers) gave their services to the local magnate in return for economic assistance and protection from both barbarians and imperial officials. Many cities shrank to tiny walled fortresses ruled by military commanders and bishops. The upper classes moved to the country and asserted ever greater independence of imperial authority. The failure of

the central authority to maintain the roads and the constant danger from robber bands sharply curtailed trade and communications, forcing greater self-reliance and a more primitive style of life. By the fifth century the West was increasingly made up of isolated units of rural aristocrats and their dependent laborers. The only unifying institution was the Christian church. The pattern for the early Middle Ages in the West was already formed.

The East was different. Constantinople became the center of a vital and flourishing culture that we call *Byzantine* and that lasted until the fifteenth century. Due to its defensible location, the skill of its emperors, and the firmness and strength of its base in Asia Minor, it was able to deflect and repulse barbarian attacks. A strong navy allowed commerce to flourish in the eastern Mediterranean and, in good times, far beyond it. Cities continued to prosper, and the emperors controlled the nobility. Byzantine civilization was a unique combination of classical culture, the

Map 6–6. The Empire's Neighbors. In the fourth century the Roman Empire was nearly surrounded by ever-more threatening neighbors. The map shows where these so-called barbarians lived and the invasion routes many of them took in the fourth and fifth centuries.

Christian religion, Roman law, and Eastern artistic influences. While the West was being overrun by barbarians, the Roman Empire, in altered form, persisted in the East. While Rome shrank to an insignificant ecclesiastical town, Constantinople flourished as the seat of empire, the "New Rome," and the Byzantines called themselves "Romans." When we contemplate the decline and fall of the Roman Empire in the fourth and fifth centuries, we are speaking only of the West. A form of classical culture persisted in the Byzantine East for another thousand years.

Triumph of Christianity

Religious Currents in the Empire   In the troubled fourth and fifth centuries people sought powerful, personal deities who would bring them safety and prosperity in this world and immortality in the next. Paganism was open and tolerant, and it was by no means unusual for people to worship new deities alongside the old and even to intertwine elements of several gods to form a new amalgam by the device called **syncretism.**

Christianity's success owed something to the same causes of the popularity of other cults, which are often spoken of as its rivals. None of them, however, attained Christianity's universality, and none appears to have given the early Christians and their leaders as much competition as the ancient philosophies or the state religion (see Map 6–7).

Imperial Persecution   By the third century Christianity had taken firm hold in the Eastern provinces and Italy. As times became bad and the Christians became more numerous and visible, popular opinion blamed disasters, natural and military, on the Christians. About 250 the emperor Decius (r. 249–251) required that all citizens worship the state gods publicly. True Christians could not obey, and Decius instituted a major persecution. Valerian (r. 253–260) resumed the persecutions, partly to confiscate the wealth of rich Christians. His successors, however, let persecution lapse until the end of the century.

In 303 Diocletian launched the most serious persecution inflicted on the Christians in the Roman Empire. Because the martyrs often aroused pity and sympathy, and

Map Exploration

To explore this map further, go to http://www.prenhall.com/craig_maps

Christian Areas, 200

(A) 200

Christian Areas, 200

Expansion, 200 – 400

(B) 200 – 400

Christian Areas, 400

Expansion, 400 – 600

(C) 400 – 600

Map 6–7. The Spread of Christianity. Christianity grew swiftly in the third, fourth, fifth, and sixth centuries—especially after the conversion of the emperors in the fourth century. By 600, on the eve of the birth of the new religion of Islam, Christianity was dominant throughout the Mediterranean world and most of Western Europe.

Nag Hammadi Manuscripts. Found in Upper Egypt in 1945, these documents had been buried about 400 C.E. by members of the Gnostic community of Christians. They contain copies and translations of early Christian texts condemned as heretical by the Church. *Institute for Antiquity and Christianity, Claremont, California.*

because large ancient states were unable to carry out a program of terror with the thoroughness of modern totalitarian governments, the Christians and their church survived to enjoy what they must have considered a miraculous change of fortune. In 311 Galerius (r. 305–311), who had been one of the most vigorous persecutors, was influenced, perhaps by his Christian wife, to issue an edict of toleration permitting Christian worship.

The victory of Constantine and his emergence as sole ruler of the empire transformed Christianity from a precariously tolerated sect to the religion favored by the emperor. In 394 Theodosius forbade the celebration of pagan cults and abolished the pagan religious calendar. At his death Christianity was the official religion of the Roman Empire.

The favored position of the church attracted opportunistic converts and diluted the moral excellence and spiritual fervor of its adherents. The relationship between church and state presented the possibility that religion would become subordinate to the state, as it had traditionally been. In the East, that largely happened. In the West, the weakness of the emperors permitted church leaders to exercise remarkable independence. In 390 Ambrose (ca. 339–397), bishop of Milan, excommunicated Emperor Theodosius, and the emperor did humble penance. This act provided an important precedent for future assertions of the church's autonomy and authority, but it did not stop secular interference and influence in the church by any means.

Arianism and the Council of Nicaea Internal divisions within the church proved to be even more troubling as new

heresies emerged. The most important and the most threatening was **Arianism,** founded by a priest named Arius of Alexandria (ca. 280–336) in the fourth century. Arius's view that Jesus was not co-equal and co-eternal with God the Father did away with the mysterious concept of the Trinity, the difficult doctrine that holds that God is three persons (the Father, the Son, and the Holy Spirit) but also one in substance and essence.

Athanasius (ca. 293–373), later bishop of Alexandria, saw the Arian view as an impediment to salvation. Only if Jesus were both fully human and fully God could the transformation of humanity to divinity have taken place in him and be transmitted by him to his disciples. "Christ was made man," he said, "that we might be made divine."

To deal with the growing controversy, Constantine called a council of Christian bishops at Nicaea, not far from Constantinople, in 325. For the emperor, the question was essentially political, but for the disputants, salvation was at stake. At the Council of Nicaea the view expounded by Athanasius won out, became orthodox, and was embodied in the **Nicene Creed.** The Christian emperors hoped to unify their increasingly decentralized realms by imposing a single religion, and it did prove to be a unifying force, but it also introduced new divisions where none had previously existed.

Chronology

The Triumph of Christianity

ca. 4 B.C.E.	Jesus of Nazareth born
ca. 30 C.E.	Crucifixion of Jesus
64 C.E.	Fire at Rome: persecution by Nero
ca. 70–100 C.E.	Gospels written
ca. 250–260 C.E.	Major persecutions by Decius and Valerian
303 C.E.	Persecution by Diocletian
311 C.E.	Galerius issues Edict of Toleration
312 C.E.	Battle of Milvian Bridge; conversion of Constantine to Christianity
325 C.E.	Council of Nicaea
ca. 330 C.E.	Georgia and Armenia become first Christian kingdoms
395 C.E.	Christianity becomes official religion of Roman Empire

Arts and Letters in the Late Empire

The art and literature of the late empire reflect both the confluence of pagan and Christian ideas and traditions and the conflict between them. Much of the literature is polemical, and much of the art is propaganda.

The empire was saved from the chaos of the third century by a military revolution based on and led by provincials of lower-class origins. They brought with them the fresh winds of cultural change, which blew out not only the dust of classical culture but much of its substance as well. Yet the new ruling class thought of itself as effecting a great restoration rather than a revolution and sought to restore classical culture and absorb it. The confusion and uncertainty of the times were tempered in part, of course, by the comfort of Christianity, but the new aristocracy sought order and stability—ethical, literary, and artistic—in the classical tradition as well.

Preservation of Classical Culture

One of the main needs and accomplishments of this period was to preserve classical culture and make it available and useful to the new elite. The great classical authors were reproduced in many copies, and their works were transferred from perishable and inconvenient papyrus rolls to sturdier codices, bound volumes that were as easy to use as modern books. Scholars also digested long works like Livy's *History of Rome* into shorter versions and wrote learned commentaries and compiled grammars. Original works by pagan writers of the late empire were neither numerous nor especially distinguished.

Christian Writers

Of Christian writings, on the other hand, the late empire saw a great outpouring: Christian apologetics in poetry and prose, as well as sermons, hymns, and biblical commentaries. Christianity could also boast important scholars. Jerome (348–420), thoroughly trained in classical Latin literature and rhetoric, produced a revised version of the Bible in Latin, commonly called the Vulgate, which became the Bible used by the Catholic Church.

Probably the most important Eastern scholar was Eusebius of Caesarea (ca. 260–340). His most important contribution was his *Ecclesiastical History,* an attempt to set forth the Christian view of history. He saw history as the working out of God's will. All of history, therefore, had a purpose and a direction, and Constantine's victory and the subsequent unity of empire and church were its culmination.

The closeness and complexity of the relationship between classical pagan culture and the Christianity of the late empire 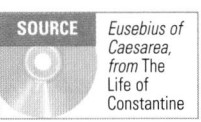 are nowhere better displayed than in the career and writings of Augustine (354–430), bishop of Hippo in North Africa. He was born at Carthage and was trained as a teacher of rhetoric. He passed through a number of intellectual way stations before his conversion to Christianity. His skill in pagan rhetoric and philosophy made him peerless among his contemporaries as a defender of Christianity and a theologian. His greatest works are his *Confessions,* an autobiography describing the road to his conversion, and *The City of God.* The latter was a response to the pagan charge that Rome's sack by the Goths in 410 was caused by the abandonment of the old gods and the advent of Christianity. The optimistic view held by some Christians that God's will worked its way in history and was easily comprehensible needed further support in the face of this disaster.

Augustine sought to separate the fate of Christianity from that of the Roman Empire. He contrasted the secular world—the city of man—with the spiritual—the City of God. Augustine argued that history was moving forward, in the spiritual sense, to the Day of Judgment, but that there was no reason to expect improvement before then in the secular sphere. The fall of Rome was neither surprising nor important, for all states were part of the city of man and therefore corrupt and mortal. Only the City of God was immortal, and it was untouched by earthly calamities.

Augustine believed that faith is essential and primary but not a substitute for reason. Instead, faith is the starting 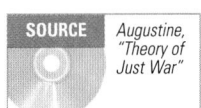 point for the liberation of human reason, the means by which people can understand what is revealed by faith.

His writings constantly reveal the presence of both Christian faith and pagan reason and the tension between them, a legacy he left to the Middle Ages.

The Problem of the Decline and Fall of the Empire in the West

Whether important to Augustine or not, the massive barbarian invasions of the fifth century ended effective imperial government in the West. For centuries people have speculated about why the ancient world collapsed. Soil exhaustion, plague, climatic change, and even poisoning from lead water pipes have been suggested as reasons for Rome's decline in population, vigor, and the capacity to defend itself. Some blame slavery and the failure to make advances in science and technology; others blame excessive government interference in the economic life; others, the destruction of the urban middle class.

The Fall of the Roman Empire in the West   Overview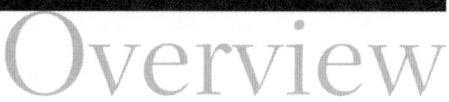

For centuries historians and social scientists have speculated why the ancient world collapsed. By contrast, the great English historian Edward Gibbon (1737–1794) wrote in his classic work *The Decline and Fall of the Roman Empire* that we should really ask not why Rome fell but why so vast an empire survived for so long. The following are some of the causes and explanations scholars have proposed for the fall of Rome. They range from the plausible to the ridiculous.

CAUSE	EXPLANATION
Climate change	A gradual drying and cooling climate destroyed the productivity of ancient agriculture on which the empire depended.
Soil exhaustion	Depleted soil around the Mediterranean no longer produced enough food to feed the population, which weakened and declined.
Lead poisoning	The use of lead pipes for drinking and cooking water led to widespread lead poisoning and sterility, especially among the upper classes who had most access to running water.
Racial pollution	Eastern immigrants to Rome—Syrians, Greeks, and Jews—sapped the vitality of the Romans and destroyed their ability to rule and defend themselves.
Slavery	The prevalence of slavery made the Romans lazy and undercut free labor.
Intellectual stagnation	The failure to make advances in science and technology—to achieve a scientific revolution—led the empire to an intellectual and economic dead end.
Social disorder	The destruction of the middle class through civil war, invasion, and over taxation wiped out the most productive and culturally aware part of the Roman population. Third-century emperors encouraged the rural poor to plunder the middle and upper classes.
Excessive government	Government exactions and regulations destroyed the operation of a market economy, which was the basis for prosperity.
Christianity	The adoption of Christianity as the official religion of the empire in the fourth century weakened the Roman state, diverted scarce resources to building and staffing churches and monasteries, and led large segments of the population to embrace pacifism.
Immorality	Gluttony, sloth, and sexual depravity replaced the old Roman virtues that had enabled Rome to conquer its empire.

Perhaps a more simple and obvious explanation can be found. The growth of so mighty an empire as Rome's was by no means inevitable. Rome's greatness had come from conquests that provided the Romans with the means to expand still further, until there were not enough Romans to conquer and govern any more peoples and territory. When pressure from outsiders grew, the Romans lacked the resources to advance and defeat the enemy as in the past. Still, the tenacity and success of their resistance were remarkable. Without new conquests to provide the immense wealth needed to defend and maintain internal prosperity, the Romans finally yielded to unprecedented onslaughts by fierce and numerous attackers.

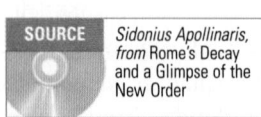
SOURCE   *Sidonius Apollinaris, from* Rome's Decay and a Glimpse of the New Order

To blame the ancients and slavery for the failure to produce an industrial and economic revolution like that of the later Western world, one capable of producing wealth without taking it from another, is to stand the problem on its head. No one yet has a satisfactory explanation for those revolutions, so it is improper to blame any institution or society for not achieving what has been achieved only once in human history, in what are still mysterious circumstances.

We may do well to think of the decline of Rome as the historian Edward Gibbon did:

The decline of Rome was the natural and inevitable effect of immoderate greatness. Prosperity ripened the principle of decay; the cause of the destruction multiplied with the extent of conquest; and, as soon as time or accident had removed the artificial supports, the stupendous fabric yielded to the pressure of its own weight. The story of the ruin is simple and obvious; and instead of inquiring why the Roman Empire was destroyed, we should rather be surprised that it had subsisted so long.[5]

This explanation allows us to see the Roman Empire as one among several great empires around the world that had similar experiences.

Summary

Republican Rome. Rome began as a small settlement in Latium in central Italy ruled by Etruscan kings; Rome became a republic in 509 B.C.E. The Roman constitution divided power between elected magistrates, the chief of whom were two consuls; an appointed Senate, whose members served for life; and popular assemblies. During the third century B.C.E., the aristocratic patricians were forced to share power with the common people, the plebians. The institution of clientage by which clients pledged their loyalty to powerful patrons in return for legal and political protection was an important part of Roman political life.

Roman Expansion. By the early fourth century, Rome had expanded to control all of Italy through a policy of conquest, alliances, colonies of Roman veterans, and generosity to foes who submitted. Between 264 and 146 B.C.E., Rome fought three wars with Carthage for control of the western Mediterranean. These Punic Wars ended with the destruction of Carthage, but led to resolve social and political disorder in Italy. Many small farmers lost their land, and efforts by the Gracchi brothers to resolve the problems ended in their murders.

In the third century B.C.E., Rome turned to the east and defeated the Hellenistic monarchies that had succeeded Alexander's empire. Macedon and Greece fell under Roman rule. This led to the adoption of Greek culture by the Roman aristocracy and the rapid Hellenization of Roman culture. By the first century B.C.E., Rome controlled most of the Mediterranean world.

The Empire and Rise of Christianity. The Roman Republic was destroyed by social unrest and rivalry among ambitious generals and politicians, the most successful of whom was Julius Caesar. After a civil war that followed Caesar's assassination in 44 B.C.E., his nephew Octavian emerged as the most powerful man in Rome. Under the title of Augustus, he set up a system that preserved the façade of republican institutions but was in fact a monarchy.

The Roman Empire stretched from Scotland to Iraq. Rome fostered the growth of cities, developed the rule of law, built a vast network of roads and other public works, and established two centuries of peace and stability. Christianity, which arose in the Roman province of Judaea in the first century C.E., spread throughout the empire despite occasional persecutions by the Roman state, which itself became Christian in the late fourth century.

Decline and Fall. In the third century C.E., the Roman peace collapsed under the pressure of invasions by barbarians in the West and the Sassanids in the East. Rival generals murdered emperors and usurped the throne. The economy declined. The state exacted more and more taxes and resources from its citizens. The emperors Diocletian and Constantine managed to halt the decline, but in the fifth century C.E. Roman authority in the West collapsed. In the East, however, a Christian Roman empire based in the city of Constantinople survived and evolved into the Byzantine empire that did much to preserve the Greek and Roman heritage for another 1,000 years.

Review Questions

1. How did the institutions of family and clientage and the establishment of patrician and plebeian classes contribute to the stability of the early Roman Republic? How important was education to the success of the republic?

2. Discuss Rome's expansion to 265 B.C.E. How was Rome able to conquer and control Italy? In their relations with Greece and Asia Minor in the second century B.C.E., were the Romans looking for security? Wealth? Power? Fame?

---

[5] Edward Gibbon, *Decline and Fall of the Roman Empire*, ed. by J. B. Bury, 2nd ed., Vol. 4 (London: J. Murray, 1909), pp. 173–174.

3. Explain the clash between the Romans and the Carthaginians in the First and Second Punic Wars. Could the wars have been avoided? How did Rome benefit from its victory over Carthage? What problems were created by this victory?

4. What were the problems that plagued the Roman Republic in the last century? What caused these problems and how did the Romans try to solve them? To what extent was the republic destroyed by ambitious generals who loved power more than Rome itself?

5. Discuss the Augustan constitution and government. What solutions did Augustus provide for the problems that had plagued the Roman Republic? Why was the Roman population willing to accept Augustus as head of the state?

6. Despite unpromising beginnings, Christianity was enormously popular by the fourth century C.E. Why were Christians persecuted by Roman authorities? What were the more important reasons for Christianity's success?

7. Consider three theories that scholars have advanced to explain the decline and fall of the Roman Empire. What are the difficulties involved in explaining the fall? What explanation would you give?

Key Terms

agape (ah-gah-PAY) (p. 209)

Arianism (p. 216)

Augustus (p. 199)

Catholic (p. 210)

censor (p. 187)

equestrians (p. 195)

Eucharist (p. 209)

heretics (p. 210)

humanitas (p. 192)

INTERPRETING THE PAST

Imperialism and its Discontents: Rome Confronts Outsiders

Text Sources from MyHistoryLab / PrimarySource DVD

1. Pliny the Elder, *Natural History*
2. Jordanes, *Deeds of the Goths*
3. Sidonius Apollinaris, *Rome's Decay*

Visual Source from MyHistoryLab / PrimarySource DVD

1. Roman Aqueduct

Visual Sources from Chapter 6

1. Map 6.2 The Western Mediterranean During the Rise of Rome (p. 189)
2. Map 6.3 Roman Dominions of the Late Republic (p. 194)

PRENTICE HALL
myhistorylab
Where it's a good time to connect to the past!

3. 'Relief from Arch of Titus' (p. 204)

For roughly five centuries the Roman Empire was the dominant superpower in the Western world, providing stability and order, while also enforcing its will with brutal measures. The Romans themselves preferred to think that they had expanded only because they were defending themselves against the aggressions of others, and they treasured the (probably mythical) notion that their ancestors were better and morally superior people, a concept they enshrined in the Latin term "*mos maiorum*" ("the behavior of the ancestors").

Although they venerated the simple and rustic ways of their predecessors, the Romans found themselves rulers of a vast empire, and the process of conquering that empire put enormous strains on their domestic politics and moral sensibilities. Comment on the rapid expansion of the empire by examining the maps in this chapter and on the benefits the Romans reaped as a result of their world domination. Also note the way the Romans celebrated their victories over their enemies, as depicted in artworks illustrating their military success.

Nevertheless, one of the consequences of Rome's mastery of the Mediterranean was its series of encounters with other *imperator* (p. 199)

imperium (p. 186)

latifundia (lah-tee-foon-dee-ah) (p. 193)

"mystery religions" (p. 207)

Nicene Creed (p. 216)

orthodox (p. 210)

patrician (p. 187)

Pharisees (p. 208)

plebeian (p. 187)

populares (p. 195)

Punic Wars (p. 189)

syncretism (p. 214)

tetrarchy (p. 212)

tribunes (p. 188)

Note: To learn more about the topics in this chapter, please turn to the Suggested Readings at the end of the book. For additional sources related to this chapter please see the Primary Source DVD at the back of this text or MyHistoryLab.

peoples and ways of thought, which the Romans often found difficult to understand. Evaluate the documents in which the Romans seemed to grapple with foreign ethnicities and ways of thought.

Questions

In what directions, and for what purposes, did the Romans expand their empire?

Did the Romans have reason to be proud of their accomplishments?

What physical examples demonstrated Roman power in the world?

How did the Romans try to make sense of "barbarians" such as the Goths and the Burgundians?

7

China's First Empire, 221 B.C.E.–589 C.E.

- ◆ Qin Unification of China
- ◆ Former Han Dynasty (206 B.C.E.–8 C.E.)
- ◆ Later Han (25–220 C.E.) and Its Aftermath
- ◆ Han Thought and Religion

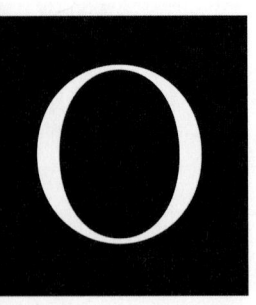

ONE HALLMARK OF CHINESE HISTORY IS ITS striking continuity of culture, language, and geography. The Shang and Zhou dynasties were centered in north China along the Yellow River or its tributary, the Wei. The capitals of China's first empire were in exactly the same areas, and north China would remain China's political center through history to the present. If Western civilization had experienced similar continuity, it would have progressed from Thebes in the valley of the Nile to Athens on the Nile; Rome on the Nile; and then, in time, to Paris, London, and Berlin on the Nile; and each of these centers of civilization would have spoken Egyptian and written in Egyptian hieroglyphics.

The many continuities in its history did not mean, however, that China was unchanging. One key turning point came in the third century B.C.E., when the old, quasi-feudal, multistate Zhou system gave way to a centralized bureaucratic government. The new centralized state built an empire stretching from the steppe in the north to Vietnam in the south.

The history of the first empire is composed of three segments: the Qin dynasty, the Former Han dynasty, and the Later Han dynasty. The English

Wudi, who reigned as Han emperor from 141–87 B.C.E, kneels before two statues of the Buddha. This scene is from the Dunhuang monastery, which was founded during Wudi's reign.

China's First Empire

China

Were there world-historical forces that produced at roughly the same time great empires in China, India, and the Mediterranean? Certainly these empires had similar features. All three came after revolutions in thought. The Han built on Zhou thought (it would be hard to imagine the Han bureaucratic state without Legalism and Confucianism), just as Rome used Greek thought, and the Mauryan Empire, Buddhist thought. In each case, the conception of universal political authority sustaining the empire derived from earlier philosophies. All three were Iron Age empires, joining their respective technologies with new organizational techniques to create superb military forces. All three had to weld together diverse regions into a single polity. All three created legacies that continued long after the empire had disappeared.

The differences between the empires are also instructive. Consider China and Rome. In China the pervasive culture—the only higher culture in the area—was Chinese, even before the first empire arose. This culture had been slowly spreading for centuries and in places outran the polity. Even the Ch'u people south of the Yangzi, while viewed as "semibarbarian" by northern Chinese, had only a variation of the same common culture. Thus cultural unity had paved the way for political unity. In contrast, the polyglot empire of Rome encompassed quite different peoples, including older civilizations. The genius of Rome, in fact, was to fashion a government and a set of laws that could contain and reconcile its diverse cultures.

Geographically, however, Rome had an easier time of it, for the Mediterranean offered direct access to most parts of the empire and was a thoroughfare for commerce. In contrast, China was largely landlocked. It was composed of several regional economic units, each of which, located in a

word *China* is derived from the name of the first dynasty. The Qin overthrew the previous Zhou dynasty in 256 B.C.E. and went on to unify China in 221 B.C.E. In reshaping China, the Qin developed such momentum that it became overextended and collapsed a single generation after the unification. The succeeding Han dynasties each lasted about 200 years, the Early Han from 206 B.C.E. to 8 C.E., the Later Han (founded by a descendant of the Former Han rulers) from 25 to 220 C.E. Historians usually treat each of the Han dynasties as a separate period of rule, although they were almost back to back and shared many institutions and cultural traits. So deep was the impression left by these two dynasties on the Chinese that even today they call themselves the "Han people"—in contrast to Mongols, Manchus, Tibetans, and other minorities—and they call their ideographs "Han writing." ∎

Qin Unification of China

Of the territorial states of the Late Zhou era, none was more innovative and ruthless than Qin. Its location on the Wei River in northwest China—the same area from which the Zhou had launched their expansion a millennium earlier—gave it strategic advantages: It controlled the passes leading out onto the Yellow River plain and so was easy to defend and was a secure base from which to attack other states. From the late fourth century B.C.E., the Qin conquered a part of Sichuan and thus controlled two of the most fertile regions of ancient China. It welcomed Legalist administrators, who developed policies for enriching the country and strengthening its military. Despite its harsh laws, farmers moved to Qin from other areas, attracted by the order and stability of its society. Its armies had been forged by centuries of warfare against the nomadic raiders whose lands half encircled it. To counter these raiders, its armies adopted nomadic skills, developing cavalry in the fourth segment of a river basin separated from the others by natural barriers, looked inward. It was the genius of Chinese administration to overcome physical and spatial barriers and integrate the country politically.

A second difference was that government in Han China was more orderly, more complex, and more competent than that of Rome. For example, civil officials controlled the Chinese military almost until the end, whereas in later Roman times, emperor after emperor was set on the throne by the army or the Praetorian Guard. The Roman Empire was not a Chinese-type, single-family dynasty.

A third difference was in the military dynamics of the two empires. Roman power was built over centuries. Its history is the story of one state growing in power by steady increments, imposing its will on others, and gradually piecing together an empire. Not until the early centuries C.E. was the whole empire in place. China, in contrast, remained a multistate system right up to 232 B.C.E. and then, in a sudden surge, was unified by one state in eleven years. The greater dynamism of China during the first empire can be explained, perhaps, by the greater military challenge it faced across its northern border: an immense Hunnish (or Xiongnu) nomadic empire. Because the threat was more serious than that any European barbarian enemy posed to Rome, the Chinese response was correspondingly massive. (Some historians say that Chinese expansion to the north and northwest drove the Huns westward, displacing Germanic tribes that flooded into Europe and pressed against Roman frontiers.)

◆ What challenges did the Roman, Han, and Mauryan Empires face in conquering and integrating new territories? How did they meet these challenges?

◆ Compare and contrast the Roman and Han Empires. What qualities did they have in common? How did they differ?

◆ What is the significance of the Silk Road as a conduit of trade, culture, and war?

century. Other states regarded the Qin as tough, crude, and brutal but recognized its formidable strengths.

In 246 B.C.E. the man who would unify China succeeded to the Qin throne at the age of thirteen. He grew to be vigorous, ambitious, intelligent, and decisive. He is famous as a Legalist autocrat, but he was also well liked by his ministers, whose advice he usually followed. (See Chapter 2 for a description of Legalism.) In 232 B.C.E., at the age of twenty-seven, he began the campaigns that destroyed the six remaining territorial states. On completing his conquests in 221 B.C.E., and to raise himself above the kings of the former territorial states, he adopted the glorious title that we translate as "emperor"—a combination of ideographs hitherto used only for gods or mythic heroes. Then, aided by officials of great talent, this First Qin Emperor set about applying to all of China the reforms that had been tried and found effective in his own realm. His accomplishments in the eleven years before his death, in 210 B.C.E., were stupendous.

Having conquered the civilized world of north China and the Yangzi River basin, the First Emperor sent his armies to conquer new lands. They reached the northern edge of the Red River basin in what is now Vietnam. They occupied China's southeastern coast and the area about the present-day city of Guangzhou (see Map 7–1). In the north and the northwest, the emperor's armies fought against the Xiongnu, Altaic-speaking Hunnish nomads. During the previous age, northern border states had built long walls to protect settled lands from incursions by horse-riding raiders. The Qin emperor had them joined into a single Great Wall that extended 1,400 miles from the Pacific Ocean into Central Asia. (By comparison, Hadrian's Wall in England was 73 miles long.) Construction of the Great Wall cost the lives of vast numbers of conscripted laborers—by some accounts, 100,000; by others, as many as 1 million.

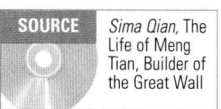
SOURCE Sima Qian, The Life of Meng Tian, Builder of the Great Wall

The most significant reform, carried out by the Legalist minister Li Si, extended the Qin system of bureaucratic

Map 7–1. The Unification of China by the Qin State. Between 232 and 221 B.C.E. the Qin state expanded and unified China.

government to the entire empire. Li Si divided China into forty prefectures, which were further subdivided into counties. The county heads were responsible to prefects, who, in turn, were responsible to the central government. Officials were chosen by ability. Bureaucratic administration was impersonal, based on laws to which all were subject. No one, for example, escaped taxation. This kind of bureaucratic centralism broke sharply with the old Zhou pattern of establishing dependent principalities for members of a ruler's family. Furthermore, to ensure the smooth functioning of local government offices, former aristocrats of the territorial states were removed from their lands and resettled in the capital, near present-day Xian. They were housed in mansions on one side of the river, from which they could gaze across at the enormous palace of the First Emperor.

Other reforms further unified the First Emperor's vast domain. Roads were built radiating out from the capital city. The emperor decreed a system of uniform weights and measures. He unified the Chinese writing system, establishing standard ideographs to replace the great variety that had hitherto prevailed. He established uniform axle lengths for carts. Even ideas did not escape the drive toward uniformity. Following the precepts of Legalism, the emperor and his advisers launched a campaign for which they have subsequently been denounced throughout Chinese history. They collected and burned the books of Confucianism and other schools, and were said to have buried alive several hundred scholars opposed to the Legalist philosophy. Only useful books on agriculture, medicine, or Legalist teachings were spared.

But the Qin had changed too much too quickly. To pay for the roads, canals, and the Great Wall, burdensome taxes were levied on the people. Commoners hated conscription and labor service, and nobles resented their loss of status. Merchants were exploited; scholars, except for Legalists, were oppressed. A Chinese historian wrote afterward: "The condemned were an innumerable multitude; those who had been tortured and mutilated formed a long procession on the roads. From the princes and ministers down to the humblest people everyone was terrified and in fear of their lives."[1] After the First Emperor died, in 210 B.C.E., intrigues broke out at court and rebellions arose in the land. At the end, the short-lived dynasty was destroyed by the domino effect of its own legal codes. When the generals sent to quell a rebellion were defeated, they joined the rebellion rather than returning to the capital and incurring the severe punishment decreed for failure. The Qin collapsed in 206 B.C.E.

In 1974 a farmer near Xian discovered the army of 8,000 life-size terra-cotta horses and soldiers that guarded the tomb of the First Emperor. The historical record tells us that in the tomb itself, under a mountain of earth, are a replica of his capital; a relief model of the Chinese world with quicksilver rivers; other warriors with chariots of bronze; and the remains of horses, noblemen, and criminals sacrificed to accompany in death the emperor whose dynasty was to have lasted for 10,000 generations.

Former Han Dynasty (206 B.C.E.–8 C.E.)

The Dynastic Cycle

Confucian historians have seen a pattern in every dynasty of long duration. They call it the **dynastic cycle**. The stages of the cycle are interpreted in terms of the "Mandate of Heaven." The cycle begins with internal wars that eventually lead to the military unification of China. Unification is proof that heaven has given the unifier the mandate to rule. Strong and vigorous, the first ruler, in the process of consolidating his political power, restores peace and order to China. Economic growth follows, almost automatically. The peak of the cycle is marked by public works, further energetic reforms, and aggressive military expansion. During this phase, China appears invincible.

---

[1] C. P. Fitzgerald, *China, A Short Cultural History* (New York: Praeger, 1935), p. 147.

The Great Wall of China. It was originally built during the Qin dynasty (256–206 B.C.E.), but what we see today is the wall as it was completely rebuilt during the Ming dynasty (1368–1644 C.E.). *Paolo Koch/Photo Researchers, Inc.*

But then the cycle turns downward. The costs of expansion, coupled with increasing opulence at the court, place a heavy burden on tax revenues just as they are beginning to decline. The vigor of the monarchs wanes. Intrigues develop at court. Central controls loosen, and provincial governors and military commanders gain autonomy. Finally, public works fall into disrepair, floods and pestilence occur, rebellions break out, and the dynasty collapses. For Confucian historians, the last emperors in a cycle are not only politically weak but morally culpable.

Early Years of the Former Han Dynasty

The first sixty years of the Han may be thought of as the early phase of its dynastic cycle. After the collapse of the Qin, one rebel general gained control of the Wei basin and went on to unify China. He became the first emperor of the Han dynasty and is known by his posthumous title of Gaozu (r. 206–195 B.C.E.). He rose from plebeian origins to become emperor, which would happen only once again in Chinese history. Gaozu built his capital at Chang'an, not far from the capitals of the previous dynasties. It took the emperor and his immediate successors many years to consolidate their power because they consciously avoided actions that would remind the populace of the hated Qin despotism. They made punishments less severe and reduced taxes. Good government prevailed, the economy rebounded, granaries were filled, and the government accumulated vast cash reserves. Later historians often singled out the early Han rulers as model sage-emperors.

Han Wudi

The second phase of the dynastic cycle began with the rule of Wudi (the "martial emperor"), who came to the throne in 141 B.C.E. at the age of sixteen and remained there for fifty-four years (141–87 B.C.E.). Wudi was daring, vigorous, and intelligent but also superstitious, suspicious, and vengeful. He wielded tremendous personal authority.

Building on the prosperity achieved by his predecessors, Wudi initiated new economic policies. He had a canal built from the Yellow River to the capital in northwest China, linking the two major economic regions of north China. He established "ever-level granaries" throughout the country so that the surplus from bumper crops could be bought and then resold in time of scarcity. To increase revenues, he levied taxes on merchants, debased the currency, and sold some offices. Wudi also moved against merchants who had built fortunes in untaxed commodities by reestablishing government monopolies—a practice of the Qin—on copper coins, salt, iron, and liquor. For fear of Wudi, no one spoke out against the monopolies, but a few years after his death, a famous debate was held at the court.

Known after the title of the chronicle as the "Salt and Iron Debate," it was frequently cited thereafter in China, and in Japan and Korea as well. On one side, quasi-Legalist officials argued that the state should enjoy the profits from the sale of salt and iron. On the other side, Confucians argued that these resources should be left in private hands, for the moral purity of officials would be sullied by dealings with merchants. The Confucian scholars who compiled the chronicle made

Terra-Cotta Soldiers of the Qin Army. Over 7,000 life-size terra-cotta soldiers were found in the tomb of the first emperor of the Qin dynasty (256–206 B.C.E.). *Adam Crowley/Getty Images, Inc./PhotoDisc, Inc.*

themselves the winner in the debate; but state monopolies became a regular part of Chinese government finance.

Wudi also aggressively expanded Chinese borders—a policy that would characterize every strong dynasty. His armies swept south into what is today northern Vietnam and northeast across Manchuria to establish a military outpost in northern Korea that would last until 313 C.E.

The Xiongnu

The principal threat to the Han was from the Xiongnu, a nomadic **pastoral people** who lived to the north. Their mounted archers could raid China and flee before an army could be sent against them. To combat them, Wudi employed the entire repertoire of policies that would become standard thereafter. When possible he "used the barbarian to control the barbarian," making allies of border nomads against more distant tribes. Allies were permitted to trade with Chinese merchants; they were awarded titles and honors; and their kings were sent Chinese princesses as brides. Poems capture the pathos of their lives on grassy steppes far from China. (See Document, "Chinese Women Among the Nomads.") When trade and titles did not work, he used force. Between 129 and 119 B.C.E. he sent several armies of more than 100,000 troops into the steppe, destroying Xiongnu power south of the Gobi Desert in southern Mongolia. To establish a strategic line of defense aimed at the heart of the Xiongnu empire further to the west, Wudi then sent 700,000 Chinese colonists to the arid Kansu panhandle and extended the Great Wall to the Yumen (Jade Gate) outpost at the eastern end of the Tarim basin. From this outpost, Chinese influence was extended over the rim oases of Central Asia, establishing the **Silk Road** that linked Chang'an with Rome (see Map 7–2).

SOURCE   *Zhang Qian, "Descriptions of the Western Regions"*

Map Exploration

To explore this map further, go to http://www.prenhall.com/craig_maps

Map 7–2. The Han Empire 206 B.C.E.–220 C.E. At the peak of Han expansion, Han armies advanced far out into the steppe north of the Great Wall and west into Central Asia. The Silk Road to Rome passed through the Tarim Basin to the Kushan Empire, and on to western Asia and the Middle East.

Government During the Former Han

To demonstrate how different they were from the Qin, early Han emperors set up some Zhou-like principalities, small, semiautonomous states with independent lords. But this was a token gesture. The principalities were closely superintended and then curtailed after several generations. Basically, despite its repudiation of the Qin and all its works, the Han continued the Qin form of centralized bureaucratic administration. Officials were organized by grades and were paid salaries in grain, plus cash or silk. They were recruited by sponsorship or recommendation: Provincial officials had the duty of recommending promising candidates. A school established at Chang'an was said to have 30,000 students by the Later Han. Bureaucracy grew until, by the first century B.C.E., there were more than 130,000 officials—perhaps not too many for a population that, by that time, had reached 60 million.

During the Han dynasty, this "Legalist" structure of government became partially Confucianized. It did not happen overnight. The first Han emperor despised Confucians as bookish pedants—he once urinated in the hat of a scholar. But Confucian ideas proved useful. The mandate of heaven provided an ethical justification for dynastic rule. A respect for old records and the written word fit in well with the vast bookkeeping the empire entailed. Gradually the Confucian classics were accepted as the standard for education. Confucianism was seen as shaping moral men who would be upright officials, even in the absence of external constraints. For Confucius had taught the transformation of self through ethical cultivation and had presented a vision of benevolent government by men who were virtuous as well as talented. No one attempted to replace laws with a code of etiquette, but increasingly laws were interpreted and applied by men with a Confucian education.

The court during the Han dynasty exhibited features that would appear in later dynasties as well. All authority centered on the emperor, the all-powerful "son of heaven." The will of a strong adult emperor was paramount. When the emperor was weak, however, or ascended to the throne when still a child, others competed to rule in his name. Four contenders for this surrogate role appeared and reappeared through Chinese history: court officials, the empress dowager, court eunuchs, and military commanders.

Court officials were selected for their ability to govern: They staffed the apparatus of government and advised the emperor directly. Apart from the emperor himself, they were usually the most powerful men in China, yet their position was often precarious. Few officials escaped being removed from office or banished once or twice during their careers. Of the seven prime ministers who served Wudi, five were executed by his order.

Of the emperor's many wives, the empress dowager was the one whose child had been named as the heir to the throne. Her influence sometimes continued even after her child became an adult emperor. But she was most powerful as a regent for a child emperor. On Gaozu's death in 195 B.C.E., for example, the Empress Lu became the regent for her child, the new emperor. Aided by her relatives, she seized control of the court and murdered a rival, and when her son was about to come of age, she had him killed and a younger son made the heir to continue her rule as regent. When she died in 180 B.C.E., loyal adherents of the imperial family who had opposed her rule massacred her relatives.

Court eunuchs came mostly from families of low social status. They were brought to the court as boys, castrated, and assigned to work as servants in the emperor's harem. They were thus in contact with the future emperor from the day he was born, became his childhood confidants, and often continued to advise him after he had gained the throne. Emperors found eunuchs useful as

Tomb Figure of Standing Attendant. This statue is from the Former Han dynasty, second century B.C.E. *The Asia Society, N. Y.: Mr. and Mrs. John D. Rockefeller 3rd Collection.*

counterweights to officials. But to the scholars who wrote China's history, the eunuchs were greedy half-men, given to evil intrigues.

Military leaders, whether generals or rebels, were the usual founders of dynasties. In the later phase of most dynasties, regional military commanders often became semi-independent rulers. A few even usurped the throne. Yet they were less powerful at the Chinese court than they were, for example, in imperial Rome, partly because the military constituted a separate category, lower in prestige than the better-educated civil officials. It was also partly because the court took great pains to prevent its generals from establishing a base of personal power. Appointments to command a Han army were given only for specific campaigns, and commanders were appointed in pairs so that each would check the other.

Another characteristic of government during the Han and subsequent dynasties was that its functions were limited. It collected taxes, maintained military forces, administered laws, supported the imperial household, and carried out public works that were beyond the powers of local jurisdictions. But government in a district that remained orderly and paid its taxes was left largely in the hands of local notables and large landowners. This pattern was not, to be sure, unique to China. Most premodern governments, even those that were bureaucratic, floated on top of their local societies and only rarely reached down and interfered in the everyday lives of their subjects.

The Silk Road

Roman ladies loved, and Roman moralists inveighed against, diaphanous gowns of Chinese silk. Wealthy Chinese coveted Roman glass and gold. Yet no camel train traveled from Chang'an all the way to Rome. Precious cargoes, moving more easily than persons, were passed across empires, like batons in relay races, from one network of merchants to another.

Chinese Women Among the Nomads

Document

The first of these selections is the lament of Xijun, a Chinese lady sent by Wudi in about 105 B.C.E. to be the wife of a nomad king of the Wusun people of Central Asia. Once there, she found her husband to be old and decrepit. He saw her only once or twice a year, when they drank a cup of wine together. They could not converse, as they had no language in common. The second selection, written centuries later, is by the Tang poet Du Fu, who visited the village of another woman sent to be the wife of a nomad king.

◆ What does the fate of the women in these poems suggest about the foreign policy of the rulers of ancient China?

1.

My people have married me
In a far corner of Earth;
Sent me away to a strange land,
To the king of the Wu-sun.
A tent is my house,
Of felt are my walls;
Raw flesh my food
With mare's milk to drink.
Always thinking of my own country,
My heart sad within.
Would I were a yellow stork
And could fly to my old home!

2.

Ten thousand ranges and valleys approach the Ching Gate
And the village in which the Lady of Light was born and bred.
She went out from the purple palace into the desert-land;
She has now become a green grave in the yellow dusk.
Her face!—Can you picture a wind of the spring?
Her spirit by moonlight returns with a tinkling
Telling her eternal sorrow.

[1] From *Chinese Poems* by Arthur Waley. Copyright © 1946 by George Allen and Unwin Ltd., an imprint of HarperCollins Publishers Ltd. Reprinted by permission of the Arthur Waley Estate.

[2] From *The Jade Mountain* translated by Witter Bynner, Copyright 1929 and renewed 1957 by Alfred A. Knopf, a division of Random House, Inc. Used by permission of Alfred A. Knopf, a division of Random House, Inc.

During the Han and later dynasties, the route began with a network of Chinese or Central Asian traders that stretched from the Chinese capital to Lanzhou in northeastern China, through the Gansu corridor to Yumen or later Dunhuang. It then crossed the inhospitable Tarim Basin, intermittently under Chinese military control, from oasis to oasis, to Kashi (Kashgar). From Kashi, the route continued in a northerly sweep to Tashkent, Samarkand, and Bukhara or in a southerly sweep to Teheran, Bagdad, and Damascus, and finally on to the Mediterranean ports of Tyre, Antioch, and Byzantium (Constantinople)—which traded with Rome. (See Map 7–2 and Map 4–3.) Of the goods that departed Chang'an, only a minute portion reached Rome, which was not a destination as much as the center of the westernmost trade net. Of goods consigned to Roman commerce, only the thinnest trickle reached China.

The Silk Road, and the alternate, more distant, and equally perilous oceanic route, points up China's isolation from other high centers of civilization. The "trip" took more than half a year; the distance was measured in thousands of miles; camel caravans at times traveled as little as fifteen miles a day. The route was hazardous, the climate extreme. Crossing deserts and mountain passes, travelers experienced cold, hunger, sandstorms, and bandits.

Most Chinese foreign trade was with their immediate steppe neighbors. The Chinese exported silk, lacquer, metal work, and later jewels, musk, and rhubarb (as a digestive for nomadic stomachs). They imported horses for their army, cattle, sheep, donkeys, and jade from Khotan and also woolens, medicines, indigo, and the occasional exotic animal. Only the most precious goods made their way to distant empires. Silk—light, compact, and valuable—was ideal. The Romans and Chinese had only the vaguest idea of where the other was located and knew nothing of the other's civilization. Romans thought silk came from a plant.

Exotic goods hawked in distant bazaars lend an aura of romance to the "Silk Road," but its true significance was as a transmission belt. In an early age China may have borrowed the chariot, compound bow, wheat, domesticated horses, and the stirrup from western Asia. Even the idea of mold-casting bronze may have come from beyond China's frontiers. Chinese technologies of paper making, iron casting, water-powered mills, and shoulder collars for draft animals, and then the compass and gunpowder, spread slowly from China to the West, sometimes over centuries. Seeds of trees and plants went in both directions, as did germs. During the late Han (in the second century C.E.), the Roman Empire lost a quarter of its population to an epidemic that, some say, appeared in China forty years later with equally dire results. During the fourteenth century, bubonic plague may have spread through the Mongol empire from southwestern China to central Asia to the Middle East, and then on to Europe as the Black Death. Missionary religions traveled the Silk Road east: Buddhism toward the end of the Han dynasty and Islam centuries later.

Decline and Usurpation

During the last decade of Wudi's rule in the early first century b.c.e., military expenses ran ahead of revenues. His successor cut back on military costs, eased economic controls, and reduced taxes. But over the next several generations, large landowners began to use their growing influence in provincial politics to avoid paying taxes. State revenues declined. The tax burden on smaller landowners and free peasants grew heavier. In 22 b.c.e., rebellions broke out in several parts of the empire. At the court, too, a decline set in. There was a succession of weak emperors. Intrigues, nepotism, and factional struggles grew apace. Even officials began to sense that the dynasty no longer had the approval of heaven. The dynastic cycle approached its end.

Chinese Galloping Horse. China traded with steppe merchants to obtain the horses needed to equip its armies against steppe warriors. Especially desired by the Chinese court were the fable "blood sweating" horses of far-off Ferghana (present-day Tajikistan). *The New York Public Library for the Performing Arts/Art Resource.*

Many at the court urged Wang Mang, the regent for the infant emperor and the nephew of an empress, to become the emperor and begin a new dynasty. Wang Mang refused several times—to demonstrate his lack of eagerness—and then accepted in 8 C.E. He drew up a program of sweeping reforms based on ancient texts. He was a Confucian yet relied on new institutional arrangements rather than moral reform to improve society. He revived ancient titles, expanded state monopolies, abolished private slavery (about 1 percent of the population), made loans to poor peasants, and then moved to confiscate large private estates.

These reforms alienated many. Merchants disliked the monopolies. Large landowners resisted the expropriation of their lands. Nature also conspired to bring down Wang Mang: The Yellow River overflowed its banks and changed its course, destroying the northern Chinese irrigation system. Several years of poor harvests produced famines. The Xiongnu overran China's northern borders. In 18 C.E., a secret peasant society rose in rebellion. In 23 C.E., rebels attacked Chang'an, and Wang Mang was killed and eaten by rebel troops. He had tried to found a new dynasty from within a decrepit court without an independent military base. The attempt was futile. Internal wars continued in China for two more years until a large landowner, who had become the leader of a rebel army, emerged triumphant in 25 C.E. Because he was from a branch of the imperial family, his new dynasty was viewed as a restoration of the Han.

Chronology

The Dynastic History of China's First Empire

256–206 B.C.E.	Qin dynasty
206 B.C.E.–8 C.E.	Former Han dynasty
25–220 C.E.	Later Han dynasty

Later Han (25–220 C.E.) and Its Aftermath

First Century

The founder of the Later Han moved his capital east to Luoyang. Under the first emperor and his two successors, there was a return to strong central government and a laissez-faire economy. Agriculture and population recovered. By the end of the first century C.E., China was as prosperous as it had been during the good years of the Former Han. The shift from pacification and recuperation to military expansion came earlier than it had during the previous dynasty. During the reign of the first emperor, south China and Vietnam were retaken. Dissension among the Xiongnu enabled the Chinese to secure an alliance with some of the southern tribes in 50 C.E., and in 89 C.E. Chinese armies crossed the Gobi Desert and defeated the northern Xiongnu. This defeat sparked the migrations, some historians say, that brought those nomadic warriors to the southern Russian steppes and then, in the fifth century C.E., to Europe, where they were known as the Huns of Attila. In 97 C.E. a Chinese general led an army to the shores of the Caspian Sea. The Chinese expansion in inner Asia, coupled with more lenient government policies towards merchants, facilitated the camel caravans that carried Chinese silk across the Tarim basin and, ultimately, to merchants in Iran, Palestine, and Rome. (See Document, "Ban Zhao's *Admonitions for Women*.")

Decline During the Second Century

Until 88 C.E. the emperors of the Later Han were vigorous; afterward they were ineffectual and short-lived. Empresses plotted to advance the fortunes of their families. Emperors turned for help to palace eunuchs, whose power at times surpassed that of officials. In 159 C.E. a conspiracy of eunuchs in the service of an emperor slaughtered the family of a scheming empress dowager and ruled at the court. When officials and students protested against the eunuch dictatorship, over 100 were killed and over 1,000 were tortured or imprisoned. In another incident in 190 C.E., a general deposed one emperor, installed another, killed the empress dowager, and massacred most of the eunuchs at the court.

In the countryside, large landowners who had been powerful from the start of the dynasty grew more so. They harbored private armies. Farmers on the estates of the mighty were reduced to serfs. The landowners used their influence to avoid taxes. Great numbers of free farmers fled south for the same purpose. The remaining freeholders paid ever-heavier taxes and labor services. Many peasants turned to neo-Daoist religious movements that provided the ideology and organization to channel their discontent into action. In 184 C.E. rebellions organized by members of the religious movements broke out against the government. Han generals suppressed the re-

bellions but stayed on to rule in the provinces they had pacified. In 220 C.E. they deposed the last Han emperor.

Aftermath of Empire

For more than three and a half centuries after the fall of the Han, China was disunited. For several generations it was divided into three kingdoms, whose heroic warriors and scheming statesmen were made famous by wandering storytellers. These figures later peopled the *Tale of the Three Kingdoms*, a great romantic epic of Chinese literature.

Chinese history during the post-Han centuries had two characteristics. The first was the dominant role played by the great aristocratic landowning families. With vast estates, huge numbers of serfs, fortified manor houses, and private armies, they were beyond the control of most governments. Because they took over many of the functions of local government, some historians describe post-Han China as having

A Green Glazed Pottery Model of a Later Han Dynasty Watchtower (87.6 × 35.6 × 38.1 cm). Note the resemblance to later Chinese Buddhist pagodas. *The Nelson-Atkins Museum of Art, Kansas City, Missouri (Purchase: Nelson Trust) © The Nelson Gallery Foundation, The Nelson-Atkins Museum of Art.*

Ban Zhao's *Admonitions for Women*

Document

Ban Zhao (45–116) was the sister of the famous historian Ban Gu. Her guide to morality, *Admonitions for Women*, was widely used during the Han dynasty. Humility is one of the seven womanly virtues about which she wrote; the others are resignation, subservience, self-abasement, obedience, cleanliness, and industry.

◆ Given the range of female personalities in Chinese society, what are some of the likely responses to this sort of moral education? Are self-control and self-discipline more likely to be associated with weakness or with strength of character?

HUMILITY

In ancient times, on the third day after a girl was born, people placed her at the base of the bed, gave her a pot shard to play with, and made a sacrifice to announce her birth. She was put below the bed to show that she was lowly and weak and should concentrate on humbling herself before others. Playing with a shard showed that she should get accustomed to hard work and concentrate on being diligent. Announcing her birth to the ancestors showed that she should focus on continuing the sacrifices. These three customs convey the unchanging path for women and the ritual traditions.

Humility means yielding and acting respectful, putting others first and oneself last, never mentioning one's own good deeds or denying one's own faults, enduring insults and bearing with mistreatment, all with due trepidation. In-dustriousness means going to bed late, getting up early, never shirking work morning or night, never refusing to take on domestic work, and completing everything that needs to be done neatly and carefully. Continuing the sacrifices means serving one's husband-master with appropriate demeanor, keeping oneself clean and pure, never joking or laughing, and preparing pure wine and food to offer to the ancestors.

There has never been a woman who had these three traits and yet ruined her reputation or fell into disgrace. If a woman loses these three traits, she will have no name to preserve and will not be able to avoid shame.

reverted to the quasi feudalism of the Zhou. The second characteristic of these centuries was that northern and southern China developed in different ways.

In the south, there followed a succession of ever-weaker dynasties with capitals at Nanjing. Although these six southern states were called dynasties—and the entire period of Chinese history from 220 B.C.E. to 589 C.E. is called the Six Dynasties era after them—they were in fact short-lived kingdoms plagued by intrigues, usurpations, and coups d'état; frequently at war with northern states; and in constant fear of their own generals. The main developments in the south were (1) continuing economic growth and the emergence of Nanjing as a thriving center of commerce; (2) the ongoing absorption of tribal peoples into Chinese society and culture; (3) large-scale immigrations of Chinese fleeing the north; and (4) the spread of Buddhism and its penetration to the heart of Chinese culture.

In the north, state formation depended on the interaction of nomads and Chinese. During the Han dynasty, Chinese invasions of the steppe had led to the incorporation of semi-Sinicized Xiongnu as the northernmost tier of the Chi-nese defense system—just as Germanic tribes had acted as the teeth and claws of the late Roman Empire. But as the Chinese state weakened, the highly mobile nomads broke loose, joined with other tribes, and began to invade China. The short-lived states that they formed are usually referred to as the "Sixteen Kingdoms." One kingdom was founded by invaders of Tibetan stock. Most spoke Altaic languages: the Xi-anbi (proto-Mongols), the Tuoba (proto-Turks), and the Ruan Ruan (who would later appear in eastern Europe as the Avars). But differences of language and stock were less important than these tribes' similarities:

1. All began as steppe nomads with a way of life different from that of agricultural China.
2. After forming states, all became at least partially Sinicized. Chinese from great families, which had preserved Han traditions, served as their tutors and administrators.
3. All were involved in wars—among themselves, against southern dynasties, or against conservative steppe tribes that resisted Sinicization.

4. Buddhism was as powerful in the north as in the south. As a universal religion, it acted as a bridge between "barbarians" and Chinese—just as Christianity was a unifying force in post-Roman Europe. The barbarian rulers of the north were especially attracted to its magical side. Usually Buddhism was made the state religion. Of the northern states, the most durable was the Northern Wei (386–534 C.E.), famed for its Buddhist sculpture.

Han Thought and Religion

Poems describe the splendor of Chang'an and Luoyang: broad boulevards, tiled gateways, open courtyards, watchtowers, and imposing walls. Most splendid of all were the palaces of emperors, with their audience halls, vast chambers, harem quarters, and parks containing artificial lakes and rare animals and birds. But today little remains of the grandeur of the Han. Whereas Roman ruins abound in Italy and circle the Mediterranean, in China nothing remains above ground. Only the items buried in tombs—pottery, bronzes, musical instruments, gold and silver jewelry, lacquerware, and clay figurines—give a glimpse of the rich material culture of the Han period. And only paintings on the walls of tombs tell us of its art.

But a wealth of written records conveys the sophistication and depth of Han culture. Perhaps the two most important areas were philosophy and history.

Han Confucianism

A major accomplishment of the early Han was the recovery of texts that had been lost during the Qin persecution of scholars. Some were retrieved from the walls of houses where they had been hidden; others were reproduced from memory by scholars. Debate arose regarding the relative authenticity of the old and new texts—a controversy that has continued until modern times. In 51 B.C.E. and again in 79 C.E. councils were held to determine the true meaning of the Confucian classics. In 175 C.E. an approved, official version of the texts was inscribed on stone tablets.

In about 100 C.E. the first dictionary was compiled. Containing about 9,000 characters, it helped promote a uniform system of writing. In Han times, as today, Chinese from the north could not converse with Chinese from the southeastern coast, but a common written language bridged differences of pronunciation, contributing to Chinese unity.

It was also in Han times that scholars began writing commentaries on the classics, a major scholarly activity throughout Chinese history. Scholars learned the classics by heart and used classical allusions in their writing.

Han philosophers also extended Zhou Confucianism by adding to it the teachings of cosmological naturalism. Zhou Confucianists had assumed that the moral force of a virtuous emperor would not only order society but also harmonize nature. Han Confucianists explained why. Dong Zhongshu (ca. 179–104 B.C.E.), for example, held that all nature was a single, interrelated system. Just as summer always follows spring, so does one color, one virtue, one planet, one element, one number, and one officer of the court always take precedence over another. All reflect the systematic workings of yang and yin and the five elements. And just as one dresses appropriately to the season, so was it important for the emperor to choose policies appropriate to the sequences inherent in nature. If he was moral, if he acted in accord with Heaven's natural system, then all would go well. But if he acted inappropriately, then Heaven would send a portent as a warning—a blue dog, a rat holding its tail in its mouth, an eclipse, or a comet. If the portent was not heeded, wonders and then misfortunes would follow. It was the Confucian scholars, of course, who claimed to understand nature's messages and advised the emperor.

Han Dynasty Tomb Painting. Court figures painted on ceramic tile in a Han dynasty tomb (Gray earthenware; hollow tiles painted in ink and colors on a whitewashed ground 73.8 × 204.7 cm). *"Lintel & Pediment of a Tomb." China, Western Han dynasty, 1st century B.C.E. Gray earthenware; hollow tiles painted in ink & colors on a whitewashed ground. 73.8 × 204.7 cm. Denman Waldo Ross Collection, & Gift of C. T. Loo. Courtesy Museum of Fine Arts, Boston.*

It is easy to criticize Han philosophy as a pseudoscientific or mechanistic view of nature, but it represented a new effort by the Chinese to encompass and comprehend the interrelationships of the natural world. This effort led to inventions like the seismograph and to advances in astronomy, music, and medicine. It was also during the Han that the Chinese invented paper, the wheelbarrow, the stern-post rudder, and the compass (known as the "south-pointing chariot").

History

The Chinese were the greatest historians of the premodern world. They wrote more history than anyone else, and what they wrote was usually more accurate. Apart from the *Spring and Autumn Annals* and the scholarship of Confucius himself, history writing in China began during the Han dynasty. Why the Chinese were so history-minded has been variously explained: Because the Chinese tradition is this-worldly; be-

A Chinese Seismograph. The suspended weight swings in the direction of the earthquake. This moves a lever and a dragon drops a ball into the mouth of one of the four waiting ceramic frogs. *National Archives and Records Administration.*

cause Confucianists were scholarly and their veneration for the classics carried over to the written word; because history was seen as a lesson book (the Chinese called it a mirror) for statesmen, and thus a necessity for the literate men who operated the centralized Chinese state.

The practice of using actual documents and firsthand accounts of events began with Sima Qian (d. 85 B.C.E.), who set out to write a history of the known world from the most ancient times down to the age of the emperor Wudi. His *Historical Records* consisted of 130 substantial chapters (with a total of over 700,000 characters) divided into "Basic Annals"; "Chronological Tables"; "Treatises" on rites, music, astronomy, the calendar, and so on; "Hereditary Houses"; and seventy chapters of "Biographies," including descriptions of foreign peoples. (See Document, "Sima Qian on the Wealthy.") A second great work, *The Book of the Han*, was written by Ban Gu (d. 92 C.E.). It applied the analytical schema of Sima Qian to a single dynasty, the Former Han, and established the pattern by which each dynasty wrote the history of its predecessor.

Neo-Daoism

As the Han dynasty waned, the effort to realize the Confucian ethic in the sociopolitical order became increasingly difficult. Some scholars abandoned Confucianism altogether in favor of **Neo-Daoism**, or "mysterious learning," as it was sometimes called. A few wrote commentaries on the classical Daoist texts that had been handed down from the Zhou. The *Zhuangzi* was especially popular. Other scholars, defining the natural as the pleasurable, withdrew from society to engage in witty "pure conversations." They discussed poetry and philosophy, played the lute, and drank wine. The most famous were the Seven Sages of the Bamboo Grove of the third century C.E.. One sage was always accompanied by a servant carrying a jug of wine and a spade—the one for his pleasure, the other to dig his grave should he die. Another wore no clothes at home. When criticized, he replied that the cosmos was his home, and his house his clothes. "Why are you in my pants?" he asked a discomfited visitor. Still another took a boat to visit a friend on a snowy night, but on arriving at his friend's door, turned around and went home. When pressed for an explanation, he said that it had been his pleasure to go, and that when the impulse died, it was his pleasure to return. This story reveals a scorn for convention coupled with an admiration for an inner spontaneity, however eccentric.

Another concern of what is called Neo-Daoism was immortality. Some sought it in dietary restrictions and yoga-like meditation, some in sexual abstinence or orgies. Others, seeking elixirs to prolong life, dabbled in alchemy, and although no magical elixir was ever found, the schools

Sima Qian on the Wealthy

More than half of the chapters in Sima Qian's *Historical Records* (early first century B.C.E.) were biographies of extraordinary men and women. He wrote of scholars, wandering knights, diviners, harsh officials and reasonable officials, wits and humorists, doctors, and moneymakers. The following is his description of the vibrant economic life of Han cities and his judgments regarding the wealthy.

◆ What economic "principles" can you derive from this passage? Can you detect an echo of Sima Qian's perspectives in present-day debates on economic policy?

Anyone who in the market towns or great cities manages in the course of a year to sell the following items: a thousand brewings of liquor; a thousand jars of pickles and sauces; a thousand jars of sirups; a thousand slaughtered cattle, sheep, and swine; a thousand chung of grain; a thousand cartloads or a thousand boat-lengths of firewood and stubble for fuel; a thousand logs of timber; ten thousand bamboo poles; a hundred horse carriages; a thousand two-wheeled ox carts; a thousand lacquered wooden vessels; brass utensils weighing thirty thousand catties; a thousand piculs of plain wooden vessels, iron vessels, or gardenia and madder dyes; two hundred horses; five hundred cattle; two thousand sheep or swine; a hundred male or female slaves; a thousand catties of tendons, horns, or cinnabar; thirty thousand catties of silken fabric, raw silk, or other fine fabrics; a thousand rolls of embroidered or patterned silk; a thousand piculs of fabrics made of vegetable fiber or raw or tanned hides; a thousand pecks of lacquer; a thousand jars of leaven or salted bean relish; a thousand catties of globe-fish or mullet; a thousand piculs of dried fish; thirty thousand catties of salted fish; three thousand piculs of jujubes or chestnuts; a thousand skins of fox or sable; a thousand piculs of lamb or sheep skins; a thousand felt mats; or a thousand chung of fruits or vegetables—such a man may live as well as the master of an estate of a thousand chariots. The same applies for anyone who has a thousand strings of cash [i.e., a million in cash] to lend out on interest. Such loans are made through a moneylender, but a greedy merchant who is too anxious for a quick return will only manage to revolve his working capital three times while a less avaricious merchant has revolved his five times. These are the principal ways of making money. There are various other occupations which bring in less than twenty percent profit, but they are not what I would call sources of wealth.

Thrift and hard work are without doubt the proper way to gain a livelihood. And yet it will be found that rich men have invariably employed some unusual scheme or method to get to the top. Plowing the fields is a rather crude way to make a living, and yet Ch'in Yang did so well at it that he became the richest man in his province. Robbing graves is a criminal offense, but T'ien Shu got his start by doing it. Gambling is a wicked pastime, but Huan Fa used it to acquire a fortune. Most fine young men would despise the thought of traveling around peddling goods, yet Yung Lo-ch'eng got rich that way. Many people would consider trading in fats a disgraceful line of business, but Yung Po made a thousand catties of gold at it. Vending sirups is a petty occupation, but the Chang family acquired ten million cash that way. It takes little skill to sharpen knives, but because the Chih family didn't mind doing it, they could eat the best of everything. Dealing in dried sheep stomachs seems like an insignificant enough trade, but thanks to it the Cho family went around with a mounted retinue. The calling of a horse doctor is a rather ignominious profession, but it enabled Chang Li to own a house so large that he had to strike a bell to summon the servants. All of these men got where they did because of their devotion and singleness of purpose.

From this we may see that there is no fixed road to wealth, and money has no permanent master. It finds its way to the man of ability like the spokes of a wheel converging upon the hub, and from the hands of the worthless it falls like shattered tiles. A family with a thousand catties of gold may stand side by side with the lord of a city; the man with a hundred million cash may enjoy the pleasures of a king. Rich men such as these deserve to be called the "untitled nobility," do they not?

Map 7–3. The Spread of Buddhism and Chinese States in 500 C.E. Buddhism originated in a Himalayan state in northwest India. It spread in one wave south to India and on to Southeast Asia as far as Java. But it also spread into northwest India, Afghanistan, Central Asia, and then to China, Korea, and Japan.

of alchemy to which the search gave rise are credited with the discovery of medicines, dyes, glazes, and gunpowder.

Meanwhile, among the common people, there arose popular religious cults that, because they included the Daoist classics among their sacred texts, are also called Neo-Daoist. Like most folk religions, they contained an amalgam of beliefs, practices, and superstitions. They had a pantheon of gods and immortals and taught that the good or evil done in this life would be rewarded or punished in the innumerable heavens or hells of an afterlife. These cults had priests, shamans who practiced faith healing, seers, and sorceresses. For a time, they also had hierarchical church organizations, but these were smashed at the end of the second century C.E. Local Daoist temples and monasteries, however, continued until modern times. With many Buddhist accretions, they furnished the religious beliefs of the bulk of the Chinese population. Even in recent decades, these sects flourished in Taiwan and Chinese communities in Southeast Asia. They were suppressed in China in the Maoist era but revived during the 1990s.

Buddhism

Central Asian missionaries, following the trade routes East, brought Buddhism to China in the first century C.E. It was at first viewed as a new Daoist sect, which is not surprising because early translators used Daoist terms to render Buddhist concepts. **Nirvana**, for example, was translated as "not doing" (*wuwei*). In the second century C.E., confusion about the two religions led to the very Chinese view that Laozi had gone to India, where the Buddha had become his disciple, and that Buddhism was the Indian form of Daoism.

Then, as the Han sociopolitical order collapsed in the third century C.E., Buddhism spread rapidly. We are reminded of the spread of Christianity at the end of the Roman Empire. Although an alien religion in China, Buddhism had some advantages over Daoism:

1. It was a doctrine of personal salvation, offering several routes to that goal.
2. It upheld high standards of personal ethics.
3. It had systematic philosophies, and during its early centuries in China, it continued to receive inspiration from India.
4. It drew on the Indian tradition of meditative practices and psychologies, which were the most sophisticated in the world.

By the fifth century C.E. Buddhism had spread over all of China (see Map 7–3). Occasionally it was persecuted by

The Peach Blossom Spring

The poet Tao Qian wrote in 380 C.E. of a lost village without taxes and untouched by the barbarian invasions and wars of the post-Han era. The simplicity and naturalness of his utopian vision were in accord, perhaps, with certain strains of Neo-Daoist thought. It struck a chord in the hearts of Chinese, and then Koreans and Japanese, inspiring a spate of paintings, poetry, and essays.

◆ Utopias are often based on religion, but this one is not. What does this suggest regarding the Chinese view of human nature?

During the T'ai-yuan period of the Ch'in [Qin] dynasty a fisherman of Wuling once rowed upstream, unmindful of the distance he had gone, when he suddenly came to a grove of peach trees in bloom. For several hundred paces on both banks of the stream there was no other kind of tree. The wild flowers growing under them were fresh and lovely, and fallen petals covered the ground—it made a great impression on the fisherman. He went on for a way with the idea of finding out how far the grove extended. It came to an end at the foot of a mountain whence issued the spring that supplied the stream. There was a small opening in the mountain and it seemed as though light was coming through it. The fisherman left his boat and entered the cave, which at first was extremely narrow, barely admitting his body; after a few dozen steps it suddenly opened out onto a broad and level plain where well-built houses were surrounded by rich fields and pretty ponds. Mulberry, bamboo and other trees and plants grew there, and criss-cross paths skirted the fields. The sounds of cocks crowing and dogs barking could be heard from one courtyard to the next. Men and women were coming and going about their work in the fields. The clothes they wore were like those of ordinary people. Old men and boys were carefree and happy.

When they caught sight of the fisherman, they asked in surprise how he had got there. The fisherman told the whole story, and was invited to go to their house, where he was served wine while they killed a chicken for a feast. When the other villagers heard about the fisherman's arrival they all came to pay him a visit. They told him that their ancestors had fled the disorders of Ch'in [Qin] times and, having taken refuge here with wives and children and neighbors, had never ventured out again; consequently they had lost all contact with the outside world. They asked what the present ruling dynasty was, for they had never heard of the Han, let alone the Wei and the Ch'in [Jin]. They sighed unhappily as the fisherman enumerated the dynasties one by one and recounted the vicissitudes of each. The visitors all asked him to come to their houses in turn, and at every house he had wine and food. He stayed several days. As he was about to go away, the people said, "There's no need to mention our existence to outsiders." After the fisherman had gone out and recovered his boat, he carefully marked the route. On reaching the city, he reported what he had found to the magistrate, who at once sent a man to follow him back to the place. They proceeded according to the marks he had made, but went astray and were unable to find the cave again.

From *The Poetry of Ta'o Ch'ien*, by J. R. Hightower, pp. 254–255. Copyright © 1970 Clarendon Press. Reprinted by permission of Oxford University Press.

Daoist emperors—in the north between 446 and 452 C.E., and again between 574 and 578 C.E. But most courts supported Buddhism. The "Bodhisattva Emperor" Wu of the southern Liang dynasty three times gave himself to a monastery and had to be ransomed back by his disgusted courtiers. Temples and monasteries abounded in both the north and the south. There were communities of women as well as of men. Chinese artists produced Buddhist painting and sculpture of surpassing beauty, and thousands of monk-scholars labored to translate sutras and philosophical treatises. Chinese monks went on pilgrimages to India.

The record left by Fa Xian, who traveled to India overland and back by sea between 399 and 413 C.E., became a prime source of Indian history. The Tang monk Xuanzang went to India from 629 until 645. Several centuries later, his pilgrimage was novelized as *Journey to the West*. The novel joins faith, magic, and adventure.

A comparison of Indian and Chinese Buddhism highlights some distinctive features of its spread. Buddhism in India had begun as a reform movement. Forget speculative philosophies and elaborate metaphysics, taught the Buddha, and concentrate on simple truths: Life is suffering, the cause

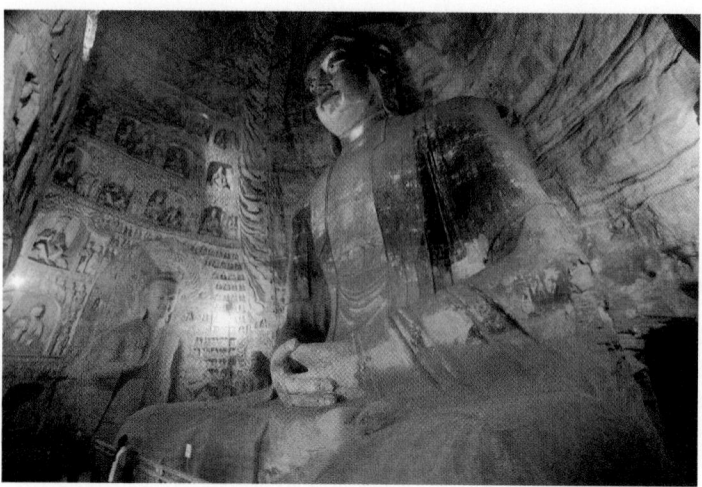

Buddha. A giant statue of the Buddha dwarfs visitors to the Yungang Grotto, in Datong, China. Note the little Buddhas in the walls of the grotto. *China Tourism Press/Chan, Yatmin/Getty Images, Inc.*

of suffering is desire, death does not stop the endless cycle of birth and rebirth; only the attainment of *nirvana* releases one from the "wheel of *karma*." Thus, in this most otherworldly of the world's religions, all of the cosmic drama of salvation was compressed into the single figure of the Buddha meditating under the Bodhi tree. Over the centuries, however, Indian Buddhism developed contending philosophies and conflicting sects and, having become virtually indistinguishable from Hinduism, was largely reabsorbed after 1000 C.E.

In China, there were a number of sects with different doctrinal positions, but the Chinese genius was more syncretic. It took in the sutras and meditative practices of early Buddhism. It took in the Mahayana philosophies that depicted a succession of Buddhas, cosmic and historical, past and future, all embodying a single ultimate reality. It also took in the sutras and practices of Buddhist devotional sects. Finally, in the Tiantai sect, the Chinese joined together these various elements as different levels of a single

INTERPRETING THE PAST

The Emperor's Dilemma

You are the emperor of China, one of the successors to the First Emperor of the Qin dynasty, who united the kingdom and carried out a systematic series of reforms and innovations. Many of these bureaucratic innovations and reforms were successful even as they were despised (universal taxation, seizure of private lands of aristocrats, conscription of peasants to build the Great Wall). A substantial amount of discontent exists among certain groups within your kingdom. However, you also possess economic and military power, bestowed on you by your effective, if brutal, predecessor. You therefore have vital decisions to make in order to ensure domestic tranquility, maintain economic prosperity, and develop effective responses to the warlike tribes and nations on the empire's vast land frontiers (see Map 7–2). Most importantly, you have to maintain the confidence of your ministers, the military, and your subjects so that you are not overthrown and/or murdered by rivals.

Text Sources from the Primary Source DVD / MyHistoryLab for Chapter 7

You have sent a series of ambassadors and emissaries to regions beyond China's frontier in the north, south, and west. (See Document, Zhang Quian "Descriptions of Western Regions," and Document "Chinese Descriptions of the Tibetans") You also are able to obtain dispatches from religious figures seeking information about a popular new religion arising to the south. (See Document, Faxien, "Record of Buddhist Countries").

Text Source from Chapter 7

Your assets—the kingdom's military power and economic wealth (See Chapter 7 Document, "Sima Qian on the Wealthy, p. 237")—allow you to commit a not unlimited amount of resources to achieve several goals. Using the information at your disposal, evaluate each option listed below:

The Options:

A. Infrastructure: Should you commit significant resources to extend the Great Wall by increasing its height and length? Should you approve the building of roads and bridges to the truth. Thus the monastic routine of a Tiantai monk would include reading sutras, sitting in meditation, and also practicing devotional exercises.

Socially, too, Buddhism adapted to China. Ancestor worship demanded heirs to perform the sacrifices. Without progeny, ancestors might become "hungry ghosts." Hence, the first son would be expected to marry and have children, whereas the second son, if he were so inclined, might become a monk. The practice also arose of holding Buddhist masses for dead ancestors. Still another difference between China and India was the more extensive regulation of Buddhism by the state in China. Just as Buddhism was not to threaten the integrity of the family, so Buddhism was not to reduce the taxes paid on land. As a result, limits were placed on the number of monasteries, nunneries, and monastic lands, and the state had to give its permission before men or women abandoned the world to enter a religious establishment. The regulations, to be sure, were not always enforced.

country's frontiers and beyond? Money will have to be allocated from the budget. Mass conscription of laborers will be required. Conscription is not a popular policy, especially if the conscriptions are lengthy or the conditions of labor are onerous. Evaluate the benefits and drawbacks of expanding the infrastructure.

B. Trade and Diplomacy: Should you open your frontiers and cities to international trade? Should you send ambassadors to all of the neighboring kingdoms in order to develop trade agreements and guarantees of safe passage for merchants and travelers? Evaluate the benefits and drawbacks of such a policy.

C. Military Conquest: Should you embark on a campaign against hostile tribes or kingdoms on your frontiers? Substantial resources would have to be allocated in the form of military force as well as funds to arm and supply them for a sustained campaign. Evaluate the benefits and drawbacks of going to war against those who might interfere with China's trade or threaten frontier settlements and stifle the kingdom's growth.

Consider the likelihood of success versus resources required for each option. Summarize your findings and integrate them into a coherent imperial policy.

Summary

Unification of China. The state of Qin unified China in 21 B.C.E. To the north it built the Great Wall to prevent incursions by the nomadic Xiongnu peoples. It ruled through a centralized bureaucracy, in line with its Legalist philosophy. But the pace of its reform was so frenetic and its legal punishments were so harsh that it alienated its people. The Qin collapsed after the death of the First Emperor.

The Two Han. The Former Han and Later Han, back-to-back dynasties, ruled China for more than four centuries (206 B.C.E.–220 C.E.). Under emperors, a pattern of centralized rule by officials educated in the Confucian classics was established. During long periods of peace and good government, literature, art, and history-writing flourished. Buddism entered China in the first century. Ever since this period, the core Chinese population has referred to itself as the "Han people."

Review Questions

1. How did Legalism help the Qin unify China? What other factors played a part? What were the main features of Qin administration? Why did the Qin collapse?

2. What was the "dynastic cycle"? In what sense was it a Confucian moral rationalization? Was a cycle of administrative and military decline especially true of Chinese government, or can we see the same pattern elsewhere?

3. Who were the players who sought power at the Han court? Did the means they used reflect the difference in their positions?

4. Did Buddhism "triumph" in China in the same sense in which Christianity triumphed in the Roman world? Compare China to the Roman Empire. What problems did both empires face and how did they try to resolve them?

Key Terms

dynastic cycle (p. 226)

Neo-Daoism (p. 236)

Nirvana (p. 238)

pastoral people (p. 228)

Silk Road (p. 228)

Note: To learn more about the topics in this chapter, please turn to the Suggested Readings at the end of the book. For additional sources related to this chapter please see the Primary Source DVD at the back of this text or MyHistoryLab.

Between 500 and 1500, the major civilizations of the world shaped themselves politically and culturally in new and lasting ways. The spread of world religions—Buddhism, Christianity, and Islam—supported the political power of new states and empires.

Woodcut of a medieval city. *This scene illustrates the close relationship between church and state in medieval Europe. The walls of the city enclose both the spires of churches and the ruler's palace in the center.* **(See pages 372–375.)**

Pre-Columbian Aztec sun stone. *Pre-Columbian American cultures also associated a ruler's sovereignty with the divine. Among the Aztecs, priests and rulers possessed access to the specialized knowledge of the calendar, which symbolized the relationship between the gods and mankind.* **(See pages 416–422.)**

NORTH AMERICA

Sultan Hasan Madrasa, Cairo, Egypt, 1356–1363. *Although the Islamic state generally preserved separate secular and religious institutions, rulers' patronage was crucial for the diffusion of Islam.* **(See pages 385–386.)**

SOUTH AMERICA

Great Mosque, Kilwa, on the Swahili coast reflects the strong Indian Ocean connections of East Africa. **(See pages 448–451.)**

CONSOLIDATION AND INTERACTION OF WORLD CIVILIZATIONS, 500 C.E. to 1500 C.E.

A Sasanian King, probably Bahram V, who probably ruled Iran from 421 to 439 C.E. Under the Sasanians, Zoroastriarism flourished.
(See pages 313–318).

Angkor Wat, in present-day Cambodia. Built in the twelfth century, it combines Hindu and Buddhist cosmological elements.
(See pages 279–282.)

ASIA

Great Wild Goose Pagoda at Ci'en Temple, Xi'an, China, Tang Dynasty, 645. *During the Tang Dynasty, Buddhism reached its greatest development, although under the patronage of the later Tang emperors a conservative reaction reasserted Confucian influence at the expense of Buddhism.* *(See pages 247–256.)*

Jōdō "Amida Buddha," Japan, Heian Period, ca. 1053. *In Heian Japan, nobles and samurai asserted their power at the expense of emperors; their patronage was crucial in the creation of Buddhist works of art such as the Amida Buddha pictured here.* *(See pages 287–297.)*

EUROPE

AFRICA

Devout Muslims circle the Ka'aba, in Mecca. Pious Muslims are obliged to make a pilgrimage to Mecca at least once in their lifetime.
(See pages 330–334.)

AUSTRALIA

Making Connections

1

How did the spread of world religions create larger, global communities?

2

Why were political leaders during this time so eager to ground their right to rule in religious terms?

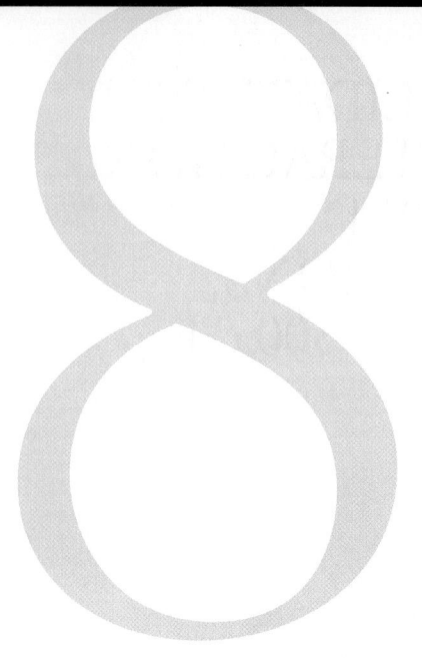

Imperial China, 589–1368

- ◆ Reestablishment of Empire: Sui (589–618) and Tang (618–907) Dynasties
- ◆ Transition to Late Imperial China: The Song Dynasty (960–1279)
- ◆ China in the Mongol World Empire: The Yuan Dynasty (1279–1368)

I F CHINESE DYNASTIES FROM THE LATE SIXTH TO THE mid–fourteenth centuries were given numbers like those of ancient Egypt, the Sui and Tang dynasties would be called the Second Empire; the Song, the Third; and the Yuan, the Fourth. Numbers would not convey the distinct personalities of these dynasties, however. The Tang (618–907) is everyone's favorite dynasty: open, cosmopolitan, expansionist, exuberant, and creative. It was the example of Tang China that decisively influenced the formation of states and high cultures in Japan, Korea, and Vietnam. Poetry during the Tang attained a peak that has not been equaled since. The Song (960–1279) rivaled the Tang in the arts; it was China's great age of painting and the most significant period for philosophy since the Zhou, when Chinese philosophy began. Although not militarily strong, the Song dynasty also witnessed an important commercial revolution. The Yuan (1279–1368) was a short-lived dynasty of rule by Mongols during which China became the most important unit in the largest empire the world has yet seen. ■

"Lady Wenji's Return to China: Wenji Arriving Home." Southern Song dynasty. Circa 1150 C.E. Lady Wenji, who lived in the second century CE, was the daughter of a high-ranking official who was abducted the nomadic Xiongnu. She eventually married and bore two sons. After twelve years in captivity she was ransomed and returned to China, leaving her children behind. Wenji's ordeal became the subject of numerous poems and paintings, such as the one shown here.

Imperial China

China

Rough parallels between China and Europe persisted until the sixth century C.E. Both saw the rise and fall of great empires. At first glance, the three and a half centuries that followed the Han dynasty appear remarkably similar to the comparable period after the collapse of the Roman Empire: Central authority broke down, private armies arose, and aristocratic estates were established. Barbarian tribes once allied to the empires invaded and pillaged large areas. Otherworldly religions entered to challenge earlier official worldviews. In China, Neo-Daoism and then Buddhism challenged Confucianism, just as Christianity challenged Roman conceptions of the sociopolitical order.

But from the late sixth century C.E., a fundamental divergence occurred. Europe tailed off into centuries of feudal disunity and backwardness. A ghost of empire lingered in the European memory. But the reality, even after centuries had passed, was that tiny areas like France (one seventeenth the size of China), Italy (one thirty-second), or Germany (one twenty-seventh) found it difficult to establish an internal unity, much less re-create a pan-European or pan-Mediterranean empire. In contrast, China, which is about the size of Europe and geographically no more natural a political unit, put a unified empire back together again, attaining new wealth, power, culture, and unified rule that has continued until the present. What explains the difference?

One reason the empire was reconstituted in China was that the victory of Buddhism in China was less complete than that of Christianity in Europe. Confucianism, and its conception of a unified empire, survived within the aristocratic families and at the courts of the Six Dynasties. It is difficult even to think of Confucianism apart from the idea of a universal ruler, aided by men of virtue and ability, ruling "all under Heaven" according to Heaven's Mandate. In contrast, the Roman concept of political order was not maintained as an independent doctrine. Moreover, empire was not a vital element in Christian thought—except perhaps in Byzantium, where the empire lasted longer than it did in Western Europe. The notion of a "Christian king" did appear

Reestablishment of Empire: Sui (589–618) and Tang (618–907) Dynasties

In the period corresponding to the European early Middle Ages, the most notable feature of Chinese history was the reunification of China, the re-creation of a centralized bureaucratic empire consciously modeled on the earlier Han dynasty (206 B.C.E.–220 C.E.). Reunification, as usual, began in the north. The first steps were taken by the Northern Wei (386–534), the most enduring of the northern Sino-Turkic states. It moved its court south to Luoyang, made Chinese the language of the court, and adopted Chinese dress and surnames. It also used the leverage of its nomadic cavalry to impose a new land tax, mobilizing resources for state use. The Northern Wei was followed by several short-lived kingdoms. Because the emperors, officials, and military commanders of these kingdoms came from the same

aristocratic stratum, the social distance between them was small, and the throne was often usurped.

The Sui Dynasty

The general of mixed Chinese-Turkic ancestry, Sui Wendi (d. 605), who came to power in 581 and began the Sui dynasty (589–618), was no exception to this rule. But he displayed great talent, unified the north, restored the tax base, reestablished a centralized bureaucratic government, and went on to conquer southern China and unify the country. During his reign, all went well. Huge palaces arose in his Wei valley capital. The Great Wall was rebuilt. The Grand Canal was constructed, linking the Yellow and Yangzi Rivers. This canal enabled the northern conquerors to tap the wealth of central and southern China. Peace was maintained with the Turkic tribes along China's northern borders. Eastern Turkic khans (chiefs) were sent Chinese princesses as brides.

in the West, but basically, the kingdom sought by Jesus was not of this world.

A second consideration was China's greater cultural homogeneity. It had a common written language that was fairly close to all varieties of spoken Chinese. Minority peoples and even barbarian conquerors—apart from the Mongols—were rapidly Sinicized. In contrast, after Rome the Mediterranean fell apart into its component cultures. Latin became the universal language of the Western church, but for most Christians it was a foreign language, a part of the mystery of the Mass, and even in Italy it became an artificial language, separate from the living tongue. European languages and cultures were divisive forces.

A third and perhaps critical factor was China's population density, at least fifteen times greater than that of France, Europe's most populous state. Population density explains why the Chinese could absorb barbarian conquerors so much more quickly than could Europe. More cultivators provided a larger agricultural surplus to the northern kingdoms than that enjoyed by comparable kingdoms in Europe. Greater numbers of people also meant better communications and a better base for commerce. To be sure, the centuries that followed the Han saw a decline in commerce and cities. In some areas barter or the use of silk as currency replaced money, but the economic level remained higher than in early medieval Europe. Several of the factors that explain the Sui-Tang regeneration of a unified empire apply equally well or better to the Song and subsequent dynasties. Comparisons across continents are difficult, but it seems likely that Tang and Song China had longer stretches of good government than any other part of the contemporary world. Not until the nineteenth century did comparable bureaucracies of talent and virtue appear in the West.

Focus Questions

◆ In what ways did China and Europe parallel each other in their development until the sixth century C.E.? How did they diverge after that?

◆ Why did China witness the reunification of empire after the fall of the Han dynasty, whereas after the fall of Rome, Europe was never again united in a single empire?

◆ Why did Tang and Song China enjoy longer stretches of good government than anywhere else in the contemporary world during the same period?

The early years of the second Sui emperor were also constructive, but then Chinese attempts to meddle in steppe politics led to hostilities and wars. The hardships and casualties in campaigns against Korea and along China's northern border produced rising discontent. Natural disasters occurred. The court became bankrupt and demoralized. Rebellions broke out, and once again, there was a free-for-all among the armies of aristocratic military commanders. The winner, and the founder of the Tang dynasty, was a relative of the Sui empress and a Sino-Turkic aristocrat of the same social background as those who had ruled before him.

Chinese historians often compare the short-lived Sui dynasty with that of the Qin (256–206 B.C.E.). Each brought all of China under a single government after centuries of disunity. Each did too much, fell, and was replaced by a long-lasting dynasty. The Tang built on the foundations that had been laid by the Sui, just as the Han had built on those of the Qin.

The Tang Dynasty

The first Tang emperor took over the Sui capital, renamed it Chang'an, and made it his own. Within a decade or so the new dynasty had extended its authority over all of China; tax revenues were adequate for government needs; and Chinese armies had begun the campaigns that would push Chinese borders out further than ever (see Map 8–1). Confucian scholars were employed at the court, Buddhist temples and monasteries flourished, and peace and order prevailed in the land. The years from 624 to 755 were the good years of the dynasty.

Government The first Tang emperor had been a provincial governor before he became a rebel general. Many of those whom he appointed to posts in his new administration were former Sui officials who had served with him. In building the new administration, he and his successors had to reconcile two conflicting sets of interests. On the one hand, the emperor wanted a bureaucratic government in which authority was centralized in his own person. On the other

Tang Government Organization

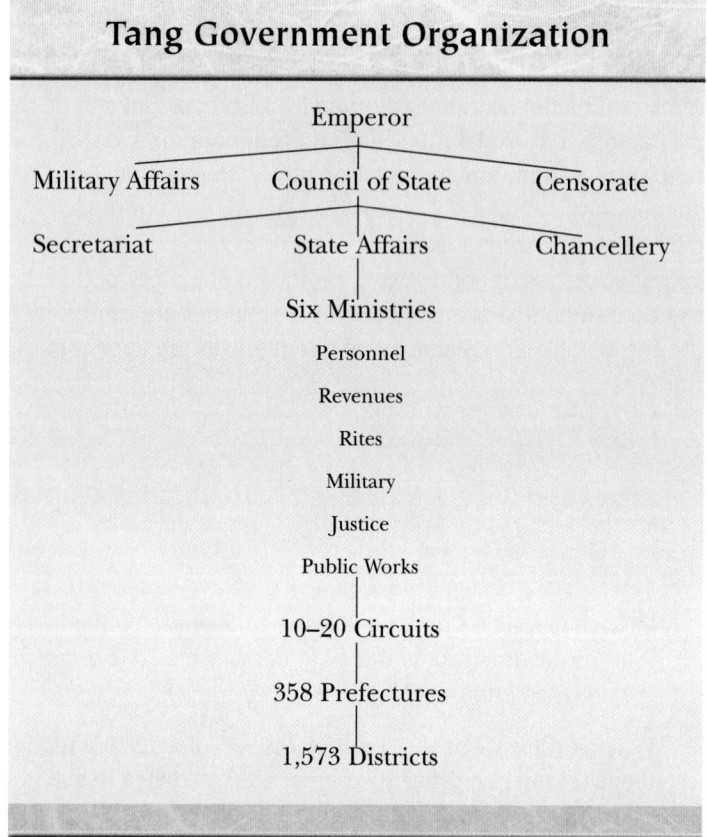

Figure 8-1.   Tang Government Organization.

hand, he had to make concessions to the aristocrats—the dominant elements in Chinese society in the Late Han—who staffed his government and continued to dominate early Tang society.

The degree to which political authority was centralized was apparent in the formal organization of the bureaucracy. At the highest level were three organs: Military Affairs, the **Censorate**, and the Council of State (see Figure 8–1). Military Affairs supervised the Tang armies, with the emperor, in effect, the commander-in-chief. The Censorate had watchdog functions: It reported instances of misgovernment directly to the emperor and could also remonstrate with the emperor when it considered his behavior improper. The Council of State was the most important body. It met daily with the emperor and was made up of the heads of the Secretariat, which drafted policies; the Chancellery, which reviewed them; and State Affairs, which carried them out. Beneath State Affairs were the Six Ministries, which continued as the core of the central government down to the twentieth century; beneath them were the several levels of local administration.

Concessions to the interests of the aristocratic families were embodied in the tax system. All land was declared to be

the property of the emperor and was then redistributed to able-bodied cultivators, who paid taxes in labor and grain. Because all able-bodied adult males received an equal allotment of land (women got less), the land-tax system was called the "equal field system." But the system was not egalitarian. Aristocrats enjoyed special exemptions and grants of "rank" and "office" lands that, in effect, confirmed their estate holdings.

Aristocrats were also favored in the recruiting of officials. Most officials either were recommended for posts or received posts because their fathers had been high officials. They were drawn almost exclusively from the aristocracy. Only a tiny percentage were recruited by examinations. Those who passed the examinations had the highest prestige and were more likely to have brilliant careers. But as only well-to-do families could afford the years of study needed to master the Confucian classics and pass the rigorous examinations, even the examination bureaucrats were usually the able among the noble. Entrance to government schools at Chang'an and the secondary capital at Luoyang was restricted to the sons of nobles and officials.

The Empress Wu   Women of the inner court continued to play a role in government. For example, Wu Zhao (626– ca. 706), a young concubine of the strong second emperor, had so entranced his weak heir by her charms that when he succeeded to the throne, she was recalled from the nunnery to which all the former wives of deceased emperors were routinely consigned and installed at the court. She poisoned or otherwise removed her rivals and became his empress. She also had murdered or exiled the statesmen who opposed her. When the emperor suffered a stroke in 660, she completely dominated the court. After his death in 683 she ruled for seven years as regent and then, deposing her son, became emperor herself, the only woman in Chinese history to hold the title. She moved the court to Luoyang in her native area and proclaimed a new dynasty. A fervent Buddhist with an interest in magic, she saw herself as the incarnation of the messianic Buddha Maitreya and built temples throughout the land. She patronized the White Horse Monastery, appointing one of her favorites as its abbot. Her sexual appetites were said to have been prodigious. She ruled China until 705, when at the age of eighty she was deposed.

After Empress Wu, no woman would ever become emperor again; yet her machinations did not seriously weaken the court. So highly centralized was power during these early years of the dynasty that the ill effects of her intrigues could be absorbed without provinces breaking away or military commanders becoming autonomous. In fact, her struggle for power may have strengthened the central gov-

Map Exploration

To explore this map further, go to http://www.prenhall.com/craig_maps

Map 8–1. The Tang Empire at Its Peak During the Eighth Century. The Tang expansion into Central Asia reopened trade routes to the Middle East and Europe. Students from Bohai, Silla (Korea), and Japan studied in the Tang capital of Chang'an and then returned, carrying with them Tang books and technology.

ernment, for, to overcome the old northwestern Chinese aristocrats, she turned not to members of her family but to the products of the examination system and to a group known as the Scholars of the North Gate. This policy broadened the base of government by bringing in aristocrats from other regions of China. The dynamism of a young dynasty may also explain why her rule coincided with the maximal geographical expansion of Tang military power.

The Chang'an of Emperor Xuan Zong Only a few years after Empress Wu was deposed—years filled with tawdry intrigues—Xuan Zong came to the throne. In reaction to Empress Wu, he appointed government commissions headed by distinguished aristocrats to reform government finances. Examination bureaucrats lost ground during his reign. The Grand Canal was repaired and extended. A new census extended the tax rolls. Wealth and prosperity returned to the court. His reign (713–756) was also culturally brilliant. Years later, while in exile, the great poet Li Bo (701–762) wrote a verse in which memories of youthful exhilaration merged with the glory of the capital of Xuan Zong:

Long ago, among the flowers and willows,
We sat drinking together at Chang'an.
The Five Barons and Seven Grandees were of our company,
But when some wild stroke was afoot
It was we who led it, yet boisterous though we were
In the arts and graces of life we could hold our own
With any dandy in the town—
In the days when there was youth in your cheeks
And I was still not old.
We galloped to the brothels, cracking our gilded whips,

We sent in our writings to the palace of the Unicorn,
Girls sang to us and danced hour by hour on tortoise-shell
    mats.
We thought, you and I, that it would be always like this.
How should we know the grasses would stir and dust rise
    on the wind?
Suddenly foreign horsemen were at the Hsien-ku Pass
Just when the blossom at the palace of Ch'in was opening
    on the sunny boughs.[1]

Chang'an was an imperial city, an administrative center that lived on taxes (see Map 8–2). It was designed to exhibit the power of the emperor and the majesty of his court. At the far north of the city, the palace faced south. The placement was traditional: Confucius, speaking of Shun, said he had only "to hold himself in a respectful posture and to face due south." In front of the palace was a complex of government offices from which an imposing five-hundred-foot-wide avenue led to the main southern gate. The city was laid out on a north–south, east–west grid, which one Tang poet compared to a chessboard. Each block of the city was administered as a ward with interior streets and gates that were locked at night. Enclosed by great walls, the city covered thirty square miles. Its population was over 1 million: half within the walls, the other half in suburbs—the largest city in the world. (The population of China in the year 750 was about 50 million—about 4 percent of the country's present-day population.) Chang'an was also a trade center from which caravans set out across Central Asia. Merchants from India, Persia, Syria, and Arabia hawked the wares of the Near East and all of Asia in its two government-controlled markets.

The Tang Empire A Chinese dynasty is like an accordion, first expanding into the territories of its barbarian neighbors and then contracting back to its original, densely populated core area. The principal threats to the Tang state were from Tibetans in the west, Turks in the northwest and north, and Khitan Mongols in Manchuria.

To protect its border, the Tang employed a four-tier policy. When nothing else would work, the Tang sent armies. But armies were expensive, and using them against nomads was like sweeping back the waves with a broom. A victory might dissolve a tribal confederation, but a decade or two later it would reappear under a new leader. For example, in 630 Tang armies defeated the eastern Turks; in 648 they took the Tarim Basin, opening trade routes to western Asia for almost a century; and in 657 they defeated the western Turks and extended Chinese influence across the Pamir

---

[1] Arthur Waley, *The Poetry and Career of Li Po.* © 1950, George Allen & Unwin Ltd, an imprint of HarperCollins Publishers, Ltd.

Chang'an

- Imperial building
- government building
- upper class district
- middle class district
- working class district

Great South Gate   2 km / 2 miles

Map 8–2. Chang'an. The great city of Chang'an had been a Chinese capital since the Han period. By the eighth century there were around a half-million people within the city walls, with the same number close by outside, making it the largest city in the world at the time. The rigorous grid structure accommodated a variety of districts, each with its own function.

Mountains to petty states near Samarkand. By 698, however, the Turks were back invading northeastern China, and between 711 and 736 they were in control of the steppe from the Oxus River to China's northern frontier.

Chinese efforts against Tibet were much the same. From 670 Tibet expanded and threatened China. In 679 it was defeated. In 714 it rose again; wars were fought from 727 to 729; and a settlement was reached in 730. But wars broke out anew. In 752 Tibet entered an alliance with the state of Nan Chao in Yunnan. In 763 Tibetan forces captured and looted Chang'an. They were driven out, but the point is that even during the good years of the Tang, no final victory was possible.

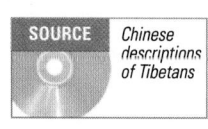

SOURCE *Chinese descriptions of Tibetans*

The human costs of sending armies far afield was detailed in a poem by Li Bo:

Last year we were fighting at the source of the Sang-kan;
This year we are fighting on the Onion River road.
We have washed our swords in the surf of Parthian seas;
We have pastured our horses among the snows of the
    T'ien Shan,
The King's armies have grown grey and old
Fighting ten thousand leagues away from home.
The Huns have no trade but battle and carnage;

They have no fields or ploughlands,
But only wastes where white bones lie among yellow sands.
Where the House of Ch'in built the great wall that was to
*   keep away the Tartars.*
There, in its turn, the House of Han lit beacons of war.
The beacons are always alight, fighting and marching
*   never stop.*
Men die in the field, slashing sword to sword;
The horses of the conquered neigh piteously to Heaven.
Crows and hawks peck for human guts,
Carry them in their beaks and hang them on the branches
*   of withered trees.*
Captains and soldiers are smeared on the bushes and grass;
The general schemed in vain.
Know therefore that the sword is a cursed thing
Which the wise man uses only if he must.[2]

The second tier of Chinese defenses was to use nomads against other nomads. The critical development for the Tang was the rise to power of the Uighur Turks. From 744 to 840, the Uighurs controlled Central Asia and were staunch allies of the Tang. Without their support, the Tang dynasty would have ended sooner.

A third tier was the defense along China's borders, including the Great Wall. At mid-dynasty, whole frontier provinces in the north and the northwest were put under military commanders, who in time came to control the provinces' civil governments as well. The bulk of the Tang military was in such frontier commands. At times their autonomy and potential as rebels were as much a threat to the Tang court as to the nomadic enemy.

Diplomacy is cheaper than war. The fourth line of defense was to bring the potential enemy into the empire as a tributary. The Tang defined the position of "tributary" with great elasticity. It included principalities truly dependent on China; Central Asian states conquered by China; enemy states, such as Tibet or the Thai state of Nan Chao in Yunnan, when they were not actually at war with China; the Korean state of Silla, which had unified the peninsula with Tang aid but had then fought Tang armies to a standstill when they attempted to impose Chinese hegemony; and wholly independent states, such as Japan. All sent embassies bearing gifts to the Tang court, which housed and fed them and sent back costly gifts in return.

For some countries these embassies had a special significance. As the only "developed nation" in eastern Asia, China was a model for countries still in the throes of statehood. An embassy gained access to the entire range of

SOURCE *Treaty between China and Tibet, 821 C.E.*

Tang culture and technology: its philosophy and writing; governmental and land systems; Buddhism; and the arts, architecture, and medicine. In 640 there were 8,000 Koreans, mostly students, in Chang'an. Never again would China exert such an influence, for never again would its neighbors be at that formative stage of development.

Rebellion and Decline From the mid–eighth century, signs of decline began to appear. China's frontiers started to contract. Tribes in Manchuria became unruly. Tibetans threatened China's western border. In 751 an overextended Tang army led by a Korean general was defeated by Arabs near Samarkand in western Asia, shutting down China's caravan trade with the West for more than five centuries. Furthermore, in 755 a Sogdian general, An Lushan, who commanded three Chinese provinces on the northeastern frontier, led his 160,000 troops in a rebellion that swept across northern China, capturing Luoyang and then Chang'an. The emperor fled to Sichuan.

The event contained an element of romance. Ten years earlier the emperor Xuan Zong had taken a young woman, Yang Guifei, from the harem of his son (he gave his son another beauty in exchange). So infatuated was he that he neglected not only the other "three thousand beauties of his inner chambers," but the business of government as well. For a while his neglect did not matter because he had an able chief minister, but when the minister died Xuan Zong appointed his concubine's second cousin to the post, initiating a chain of events that resulted in rebellion. En route to Sichuan, his soldiers, blaming Yang Guifei for their plight, strangled her. The event was later immortalized in a poem that described her "snow-white skin," "flowery face," and "moth eyebrows," as well as the "eternal sorrow" of the emperor, who, in fact, was seventy-two at the time.

Chronology

Imperial China

589–618	Sui dynasty
618–907	Tang dynasty
960–1279	Song dynasty
1279–1368	Yuan (Mongol) dynasty

[2] Waley, pp. 34–35.

Chinese Policy Towards Barbarians   Overview

For much of the history of the Chinese Empire, nomadic peoples from the west and north, whom the Chinese considered to be barbarians, posed a recurrent threat. The imperial Chinese government adopted a variety of strategies for dealing with this threat.

Armies	When nothing else worked, the Chinese went on the offensive and sent armies against the nomads. But armies were expensive, and victories over nomads were transitory. Within a few years the tribes would regroup and menace China anew.
Nomads against nomads	A second strategy was to obtain allies from the nomads along China's borders and use them against more distant nomads. To win over neighboring tribes, a variety of bribes was employed.
Border defense	In the north, an inner line of defense was the Great Wall. Also, late in dynasties, northern provinces were often placed under military governors.
Diplomacy	China sought to neutralize its neighbors by loosely attaching them to its empire. Nomadic tribes, Central Asian states, and Korea became "tributaries" of the emperor. Their rulers sent embassies bearing gifts ("tribute") to the imperial court, which fed and housed them, and sent them home with even costlier gifts and reports of China's power, wealth, splendor, and cultural achievements.

After a decade of wars and much devastation, a new emperor restored the dynasty with the help of the Uighur Turks, who looted Chang'an as part of their reward. The recovery and the century of relative peace and prosperity that followed

Relief of Tang Emperor's Horse. A bearded "barbarian" groom tends the charger of the second Tang emperor (r. 626–649). This stone relief was found on the emperor's tomb. Note the stirrup, a Chinese invention of the fourth century C.E. *A Relief of Emperor T'ai T'sung's Horse, "Autumn Dew." University of Pennsylvania Museum, Philadelphia (NEG.# S8-62840).*

illustrate the resilience of Tang institutions. China was smaller, but military governors maintained the diminished frontiers. Provincial governors were more autonomous, but taxes were still sent to the capital. Occasional rebellions were suppressed by imperial armies, sometimes led by eunuchs. Most of the emperors were weak, but three strong emperors appeared and reforms were carried out. Edwin O. Reischauer, after translating the diary of a Japanese monk who studied in China during the early ninth century, commented that the "picture of government in operation" that emerges "is amazing for the ninth century, even in China":

> *The remarkable degree of centralized control still existing, the meticulous attention to written instructions from higher authorities, and the tremendous amount of paper work involved in even the smallest matters of administration are all the more striking just because this was a period of dynastic decline.*[3]

Of the reforms of this era, none was more important than that of the land system. The official census, on which land allotments and taxes were based, showed a drop in population from 53 million before the An Lushan rebellion to 17 million

---

[3] E. O. Reischauer, *Ennin's Travels in T'ang China* (New York: Ronald Press, 1955), p. 7.

afterward. Unable to put people back on the registers, the government replaced the equal field system with a tax collected twice a year. The new system, begun in 780, lasted until the sixteenth century. Under it, a fixed quota of taxes was levied on each province. After the rebellion, government revenues from salt and iron surpassed those from land.

During the second half of the ninth century the government weakened further. Most provinces were autonomous, often under military commanders, and resisted central control. Wars were fought with the state of Nan Chao in the southwest. Bandits appeared. Droughts led to peasant uprisings. By the 880s warlords had carved all of China into independent kingdoms, and in 907 the Tang dynasty fell. But within half a century a new dynasty arose. The fall of the Tang did not lead to the centuries of division that had followed the Han. Something had changed within China.

Tang Culture The creativity of the Tang period arose from the juxtaposition and interaction of cosmopolitan, medieval Buddhist, and secular elements. The rise of each of these cultural spheres was rooted in the wealth and the social order of the re-created empire.

Tang culture was cosmopolitan not just because of its broad contacts with other cultures and peoples but also because of its openness to them. Buddhist pilgrims to India and a flow of Indian art and philosophies to China were a part of it. The voluptuousness of Indian painting and sculpture, for example, helped shape the Tang representation of the *bodhisattva*. Commercial contacts were widespread. Foreign goods were vended in Chang'an marketplaces. Communities of central and western Asians were established in the capital, and Arab and Persian quarters grew up in the seaports of southeastern China. Merchants brought their religions with them. Nestorian Christianity, Zoroastrianism, Manichaeism, Judaism, and Islam entered China at this time. Most would be swept away in the persecutions of the ninth century, but Islam and small pockets of Judaism survived until the twentieth century.

Central Asian music and musical instruments became so popular they almost displaced the native tradition. Tang ladies adopted foreign hairstyles. Dramas and acrobatic performances by western Asians could be seen in the streets of the capital. Even among the pottery figurines customarily placed in tombs there were representations of western Asian

Tang Figurine. During the Tang dynasty (618–907), well-to-do families placed glazed pottery figurines in the tombs of their dead. Perhaps they were intended to accompany and amuse the dead in the afterlife. Note the fancy chignon hairstyle of this female flutist, one figure in a musical ensemble. Today these figurines are sought by collectors around the world. *Werner Forman/Art Resource, N.Y.*

traders and Central Asian grooms, along with those of horses, camels, and court ladies that today may be seen in museums around the world. In Tang poetry, too, what was foreign was not shunned but judged on its own merits or even presented as exotically attractive. Of a gallant of Chang'an, Li Bo wrote:

> *A young man of Five Barrows suburb east*
> *of the Golden Market,*
> > *Silver saddle and white horse*
> > *cross through wind of spring.*
> > *When fallen flowers are tram-*
> > *pled all under, where is it*
> *he will roam?*
> > *With a laugh he enters the tav-*
> ern *of a lovely Turkish wench.*[4]

Later in the dynasty, another poet, Li He, wrote of service on the frontier:

> *A Tartar horn tugs at the north wind,*
> *Thistle Gate shines whiter than the stream.*
> *The sky swallows the road to Kokonor.*
> *On the Great Wall, a thousand miles of moonlight.*[5]

The Tang dynasty, although slightly less an age of faith than the preceding Six Dynasties, was nonetheless the golden age of Buddhism in China. Patronized by emperors and aristocrats, the Buddhist establishment acquired vast landholdings and great wealth. Temples and monasteries were constructed throughout China. To gain even an inkling of the beauty and sophistication of the temple architecture, the wooden sculpture, or the paintings on the temple walls, one must see Hōryūji or the ancient temples of Nara in Japan, for little of note has survived in China.

---

[4] S. Owen, *The Great Age of Chinese Poetry: The High T'ang.* © 1980, (New Haven: Yale University Press), p. 130. Reprinted by permission.
[5] A. C. Graham, *Poems of the Late T'ang,* trans. by A. C. Graham (Penguin Classics, 1965). Copyright © 1965, A. C. Graham.

Caravaneer on a Camel. The animal's shaggy mane indicates that it is a Bactrian camel from Central Asia. *Réunion des Musées Nationaux/Art Resource, N.Y.*

The single exception is the Caves of the Thousand Buddhas at Dunhuang in China's far northwest, which were sealed during the eleventh century for protection from Tibetan raiders and not rediscovered until the twentieth century. They were found to contain stone sculptures, Buddhist frescoes, and thousands of manuscripts in Chinese and Central Asian languages.

Only during the Tang did China have a "church" establishment that was at all comparable to that of medieval Europe, and even then it was subservient to the far stronger Tang state. Buddhist wealth and learning brought with them secular functions. Temples served as schools, inns, or even bathhouses. They lent money. Priests performed funerals and dispensed medicines. Occasionally the state moved to recapture the revenues monopolized by temples. The severest persecution, which marked a turn in the fortunes of Buddhism in China, occurred from 841 to 845, when an ardent Daoist emperor confiscated millions of acres of tax-exempt lands, put back on the tax registers 260,000 monks and nuns, and destroyed 4,600 monasteries and 40,000 shrines.

During the early Tang, the principal Buddhist sect was the Tiantai, but after the mid–ninth-century suppression, other sects came to the fore:

1. One devotional sect focused on Maitreya, a Buddha of the future, who will appear and create a paradise on earth. Maitreya was a cosmic messiah, not a human figure. The messianic teachings of the sect often furnished the ideology for popular uprisings and rebellions like the White Lotus, which claimed that it was renewing the world in anticipation of Maitreya's coming.

2. Another devotional or faith sect worshiped the **Amitabha Buddha**, the Lord of the Western Paradise or Pure Land. This sect taught that in the early centuries after the death of the historical Buddha, his teachings had been transmitted properly and people could obtain enlightenment by their own efforts, but that at present the Buddha's teachings had become so distorted that only by reliance on Amitabha could humans obtain salvation. All who called on Amitabha with a pure heart and perfect faith would be saved. Developing a congregational form of worship, this sect became the largest in China and deeply influenced Chinese popular religion.

3. A third sect, and the most influential among the Chinese elites, was known in China, where it began, as Chan and is better known in the West by its Japanese name, **Zen**. Zen had no cosmic Buddhas. It taught that the historical Buddha was only a man and exhorted each person to attain enlightenment by his or her own efforts. Although its monks were often the most learned in China, Zen was anti-intellectual in its emphasis on direct intuition into one's own Buddha-nature. Enlightenment was to be obtained by a regimen of physical labor and meditation. To jolt the monk into enlightenment—after he had been readied by long hours of meditation—some Zen sects used little problems not answerable by normal ratiocination: "What was your face before you were conceived?" "If all things return to the One, what does the One return to?" "From the top of a hundred-foot pole, how do you step forward?" The psychological state of the adept attempting to deal with these problems is compared to that of "a rat pursued into a blocked pipe" or "a mosquito biting an iron ball." The discipline of meditation, combined with a Zen view of nature, profoundly influenced the arts in China and subsequently in Korea and Japan as well.

A third characteristic of Tang culture was the reappearance of secular scholarship and letters. The reestablishment of centralized bureaucratic government stimulated the tradition of learning that had been partially interrupted after the fall of the Han dynasty in the third century C.E. A scholarly

A Painting from Dunhuaug Monastery showing the bodhisattva Guanyin being worshiped by the painting's donor and his family.

bureaucratic complex emerged. Most men of letters were also officials, and most high-ranking officials painted or wrote poems. An anthology of Tang poetry compiled during the Ming period (1368–1644) contained 48,900 poems by almost 2,300 authors. This secular stream of Tang culture was not ideologically anti-Buddhist. Officials were often privately sympathetic to Buddhism, but as men involved themselves in the affairs of government, their values became increasingly this-worldly.

Court historians of the Tang revived the Han practice of writing an official history of the previous dynasty. For the first time scholars wrote comprehensive institutional histories and regional and local gazetteers. They compiled dictionaries and wrote commentaries on the Confucian classics. Other scholars wrote ghost stories or tales of adventure, using the literary language. (Buddhist sermons, in contrast, were often written in the vernacular.) More paintings were Buddhist than secular, but Chinese landscape painting had its origins during the Tang. Nowhere, however, was the growth of a sec-

ular culture more evident than in poetry, the greatest achievement of Tang letters.

Whether Li Bo (701–762) can be called wholly secular is questionable. He might better be called Daoist. But he clearly was not Buddhist. Born in Sichuan, he was exceptional among Tang poets in never having sat for the civil service examinations, although he briefly held an official post at Chang'an, given in recognition of his poetry. Large and muscular, he was a swordsman and a carouser. Of the 20,000 poems he is said to have composed, 1,800 have survived, and a fair number have titles like "Bring on the Wine" or "Drinking Alone in the Moonlight." According to legend, he drowned while drunkenly attempting to embrace the reflection of the moon in a lake. His poetry is clear, powerful, passionate, and always sensitive to beauty. (See Document, "A Poem by Li Bo.") It also contains a sense of fantasy, as when he climbed a mountain and saw a star-goddess, "stepping in emptiness, pacing pure ether, her rainbow robes trailed broad sashes." Li Bo, nearer to heaven than to earth, looked down below where

> Far and wide Tartar troops were speeding,
> And flowing blood mired the wild grasses
> Where wolves and jackals all wore officials' caps.[6]

According to Li Bo, life is brief and the universe is large, but this view did not lead him to renounce the world. His Daoism was not of the quietistic strain close to Buddhism. Rather, he exulted, identifying with the primal flux of yin and yang:

> I'll wrap this Mighty Mudball of a world all up in a bag
> And be wild and free like Chaos itself![7]

Du Fu (712–770), an equally famous Tang poet, was from a literary family. He failed the metropolitan examination at the age of twenty-three and spent years in wandering and poverty. At thirty-nine he received an official appointment after presenting his poetry to the court. Four years later he was appointed to a military post. He fell into rebel hands during the An Lushan rebellion, escaped, and was reappointed to a civil post. But he was then dismissed and suffered further hardships. His poetry is less lyrical and more allusive than Li Bo's. It also reflects more compassion for human suffering: for the mother whose sons have been conscripted and sent to war; for brothers scattered by war; for his own family, to whom he returned after having been given up for dead. Like Li Bo, he felt that humans are short-lived and that nature endures. Visiting the ruins of the palace of the second Tang emperor, he saw "Grey rats scuttling over ancient tiles" and "in its shadowed chambers ghost

[6] Owen, p. 134.
[7] Owen, p. 125.

A Poem by Li Bo

Document

The great Tang poet Li Bo reputedly wrote 20,000 poems, of which 1,800 have survived.

◆ It has been said that concreteness of imagery is the genius of Chinese poetry. How does this poem support that contention?

THE RIVER MERCHANT'S WIFE: A LETTER

While my hair was still cut straight across my forehead
I played about the front gate, pulling flowers.
You came by on bamboo stilts, playing horse,
You walked about my seat, playing with blue plums.
And we went on living in the village of Chokan:
Two small people, without dislike or suspicion.
At fourteen I married My Lord you.
I never laughed, being bashful.
Lowering my head, I looked at the wall.
Called to, a thousand times, I never looked back.
At fifteen I stopped scowling,
I desired my dust to be mingled with yours
Forever and forever and forever.
Why should I climb the look out?
At sixteen you departed,
You went into far Ku-to-yen, by the river of swirling
* eddies,*
And you have been gone five months.

The monkeys make sorrowful noise overhead.
You dragged your feet when you went out.
By the gate now, the moss is grown, the different
* mosses,*
Too deep to clear them away!
The leaves fall early this autumn, in wind.
The paired butterflies are already yellow with August
Over the grass in the West garden;
They hurt me. I grow older.
If you are coming down through the narrows
* of the river Kiang,*
Please let me know beforehand,
And I will come out to meet you,
As far as Cho-fu-Sa.

"The River Merchant's Wife: A Letter" by Ezra Pound, from *Personae*. Copyright © 1926 by Ezra Pound. Reprinted by permission of New Directions Publishing Corp.

---

fires green." "Its lovely ladies are the brown soil" and only "tomb horses of stone remain." But his response to this sad scene was to

Sing wildly, let the tears cover your open hands.
Then go ever onward and on the road of your travels,
Meet none who prolong their fated years.[8]

His response was unlike that of Li Bo. It was close to Stoicism but equally un-Buddhist.

Transition to Late Imperial China: The Song Dynasty (960–1279)

Most traditional Chinese history was written in terms of the dynastic cycle, and for good reason: The pattern of rise and fall, of expansion and contraction, within each dynasty can-

---

[8] Owen, pp. 223–224.

not be denied. Certainly the Song can be viewed from this perspective. It reunified China in 960, establishing its capital at Kaifeng on the Yellow River (see Map 8–3). Mobilizing its resources effectively, it ruled for 170 years; this period is called the Northern Song. Then it weakened. In 1127 it lost the north but for another 150 years continued to rule the south from a new capital at Hangzhou in east–central China. The Southern Song fell before the Mongol onslaught in 1279.

But there is more to Chinese history than the inner logic of the dynastic cycle. Longer term changes that cut across dynastic lines were ultimately more important. One such set of changes began during the late Tang period and continued on into the Song period, affecting its economy, society, state, and culture. Taken together, these changes help to explain why China after the Tang did not relapse into centuries of disunity as it had after the Han, and why China would never again experience more than brief intervals of disunity. In this section we will skip over emperors

The Tang Poet Li Bo. As imagined by the great Song artist Liang Kai.
Tokyo National Museum/DNP Archives.Com Co., Ltd.

and empresses, eunuchs and generals, and focus instead on more fundamental transformations.

Agricultural Revolution of the Song: From Serfs to Free Farmers

Landed aristocrats had dominated local society in China during the Sui and Tang periods. The tillers of their lands were little more than serfs. Labor service was the heaviest tax, and whether performed on the office or rank lands of aristocrats or on other government lands, it created conditions of social subordination.

The aristocracy weakened, however, under the Tang and after its fall. Estates were divided among male children at each change of generation. Drawn to the capital,

the aristocracy became less a landed, and more a metropolitan, elite. After the fall of the Tang, the aristocratic estates were often seized by warlords. As the aristocracy declined, the claims of those who worked the soil grew stronger, aided by changes in the land and tax systems. With the collapse of the equal field system (described earlier), farmers could buy and sell land. The ownership of land as private property gave the cultivators greater independence. They could now move about as they pleased. Taxes paid in grain gave way during the Song to taxes in money. The commutation of the labor tax to a money tax gave the farmers more control over their own time. Conscription, the cruelest and heaviest labor tax of all, disappeared as the conscript armies of the early and middle Tang gave way to professional armies.

Changes in technology also benefited the cultivator. New strains of an early-ripening rice permitted double cropping. In the Yangzi region, extensive water-control projects were carried out, and more fertilizers were used. New commercial crops were developed. Tea, which had been introduced during the Six Dynasties as a medicine and had been drunk by monks during the Tang, became widely cultivated; cotton also became a common crop. Because taxes paid in money tended to become fixed, much of the increased productivity accrued to the cultivator. Of course, not all benefited equally; there were landlords and landless tenants as well as independent small farmers.

The disappearance of the aristocrats also increased the authority of the district magistrate, who no longer had to contend with their interference in local affairs. The Song magistrate became the sole representative of imperial authority in local society. But there were too many villages in his district for him to be involved regularly in their internal governance. As long as taxes were paid and order maintained, affairs were left in the hands of the village elites, so the Song farmer enjoyed not only a rising income and more freedom, but also substantial self-government.

One other development that began during the Song—and became vastly more important later—was the appearance of a scholar-gentry class. The typical gentry family contained at least one member who had passed the provincial civil service examination and lived in a district seat or market town. Socially and culturally, these gentry were closer to magistrates than to villagers. But they usually owned land in the villages and thus shared some interests with the local landholders. Although much less powerful than the former aristocrats, they took a hand in local affairs and at times functioned as a buffer between the village and the magistrate's office.

Commercial Revolution of the Song

Stimulated by changes in the countryside, and contributing to them as well, were demographic shifts, innovative technologies, the growth of cities, the spread of money, and rising trade. These developments varied by region, but overall the Song economy reached new prosperity.

Emergence of the Yangzi Basin   Until late in the Tang, the north had been China's most populous and productive region. But from the late ninth century the center of gravity of China's population, agricultural production, and culture shifted to the lower and eastern Yangzi region. Between 800 and 1100 the population of the region tripled as China's total population increased to about 100 million. Its rice paddies yielded more per acre than the wheat or millet fields of the north, making rice the tax base of the empire. Its wealth led to the establishment of so many schools that the government set regional quotas for the examination system to prevent the Yangzi region from dominating all of China. The Northern Song capital itself was kept in the north for strategic reasons, but it was situated at Kaifeng, further east than Luoyang, at the point where the Grand Canal, which carried tax rice from the south, joined the Yellow River.

New Technology   During the Northern Song a coal and iron-smelting industry developed in north China that provided China with better tools and weapons. Using coke and bellows to heat furnaces to the temperatures required for carbonized steel, it was the most advanced in the world.

Printing began in China with the use of carved seals. The earliest woodblock texts, mostly on Buddhist subjects, appeared in the seventh century. By the tenth century a complete edition of the classics had been published, and by the mid-Song books printed with movable type were fairly common.

Other advances during the Song were the abacus, the use of gunpowder in grenades and projectiles, and improvements in textiles and porcelains.

Rise of a Money Economy   Exchange during the Tang had been based on silk. Coins had been issued, but their circulation was limited. During the Northern Song large amounts of copper cash were coined, but the demand rose more rapidly than the supply. Coins were made with holes in the center, and 1,000 on a string constituted the usual unit for large transactions. Beginning in the Southern Song, silver was minted to complement copper cash, ten times as much silver in the late twelfth century as in the early eleventh century. Letters of credit were used by merchants, and various kinds of paper money were also issued. The penetration of money

Map 8–3. The Northern Song and Liao Empires (Top) and the Southern Song and Jin Empires (Bottom). During the Northern Song, the Mongol Liao dynasty ruled only the extreme northern edge of China. During the Southern Song, in contrast, the Manchurian Jin dynasty ruled half of China.

Irrigation Methods on a Farm in the Yangzi Valley. A farmer and his wife use their legs and feet to work the square-pallet chain pump, a boy drives a water buffalo to turn a water-pumping device, and another boy fishes. © *Photograph by Wan-go Weng/Collection of H. C. Weng.*

into the village economy was such that by 1065 tax receipts paid in money had risen to 38 million strings of cash—in comparison with a mere 2 million in mid-Tang.

Trade The growth of trade spurred the demand for money. One may distinguish among trade within economic regions, trade between regions, and foreign trade. During the Tang most cities had been administrative, supported by taxes from the countryside. Official salaries and government expenditures created a demand for services and commercial products, making the cities into islands of commerce in a noncommercial hinterland. In most of China's seven or eight economic regions this pattern continued during the Song, but in the capital, and especially in the economically advanced regions along the Yangzi, cities became the hubs of regional commercial networks, with district seats or market towns serving as secondary centers for the local markets beneath them.

As this transition occurred, cities with more than 100,000 households almost quadrupled in number. The Northern Song capital at Kaifeng is recorded as having had 260,000 households—probably more than 1 million inhabitants—and the Southern Song capital at Hangzhou had 391,000 households. Compare these capitals to those of backward Europe: London during the Northern Song had a

population of about 18,000; Rome during the Southern Song had 35,000; and Paris even a century later had fewer than 60,000.

Furthermore, these Song capitals, unlike Chang'an with its walled wards that closed at night, were open within and spread beyond their outer walls. As in present-day Chinese cities, their main avenues were lined with shops. Merchant guilds replaced government officials as the managers of marketplaces. Growing wealth also led to a taste for luxury and an increasingly secular lifestyle. Restaurants, theaters, wine shops, and brothels abounded. Entertainment quarters with fortunetellers, jugglers, chess masters, acrobats, and puppeteers sprang up. Such activity had been present in Chang'an, but the numbers increased, and now they catered to traders and rich merchants as well as to officials.

Trade between regions during the Song was limited mainly to luxury goods like silk, lacquerware, medicinal herbs, and porcelains. Only where transport was cheap—along rivers, canals, or the coast—was interregional trade in bulk commodities economical, and even then it was usually carried on only to make up for specific shortages.

Foreign trade also reached new heights during the Song. In the north, Chinese traders bought horses from Tibetan, Turkic, and Mongol border states and sold silks and tea. Along the coast, Chinese merchants took over the port trade that during the Tang had been in the hands of Korean, Arab, and Persian merchants. The new hegemony of Chinese merchants was based on improved ships using both sail and oars and equipped with watertight compartments and better rudders. Chinese captains, navigating with the aid of the compass, came to dominate the sea routes from Japan in the north to Sumatra in the south. The content of the overseas trade reflected China's advanced economy: It imported raw materials and exported finished goods. Porcelains were sent to Southeast Asia and then were carried by Arab ships to medieval trading centers on the Persian Gulf and down the coast of East Africa as far south as Zanzibar.

Government: From Aristocracy to Autocracy

The millennium of late imperial China after the Tang is often spoken of as the age of autocracy or as China's age of absolute monarchy. Earlier emperors, as we have noted, were often personally powerful, but beginning with the Song, changes occurred that made it easier for emperors to be autocrats.

One change was that Song emperors had direct personal control over more offices than their Tang predecessors. For example, the Board of Academicians, an advisory office, presented the emperor with policy options separate

"Chaste Woman" Shi

Document

Hong Mai (1123–1202 C.E.) was a collector of stories—fantastic, folkloric, and factual. Unlike the usual Confucian homilies on the proper virtues of women, his stories, and those told by other Song storytellers, contained broader perspectives. They reflected the actual diversity of Chinese society. In this story the Chinese belief in ghosts enables the wronged Ning to have a hand in the villain's downfall.

◆ Is the moral of this tale simply that justice ultimately prevails? Can a more complex interpretation be made? What does it say about the dynamics of Song society?

Ning Six of South Meadow village, in the southern suburbs of Jianchang, was a simple-minded man who concentrated on his farming. His younger brother's wife, Miss Shi, was a little sleeker than her peers. She was also ruthless and licentious, and had an adulterous affair with a youth who lived there. Whenever Ning looked askance at her she would scold him and there was not much he could do.

Once Miss Shi took a chicken, wanting to cook it. When Ning learned of it, he went into her room, demanded that she give it to him, then left with it. Miss Shi quickly cut her arm with a knife, then went to the neighbors screaming, "Because my husband is not home, brother-in-law offered me a chicken and tried to force me to have sex with him. I resisted, threatening to kill myself with the knife I was holding, and so just managed to escape."

Ning at that time had no wife, so the neighbors thought she might be telling the truth. They took them to the village headman, then the county jail. The clerks at the jail reviewed the evidence and demanded 10,000 cash to set things right. Ning was poor and stingy, and moreover, knew himself to be in the right, so stubbornly refused. The clerks sent up the dossier to the prefect Dai Qi. Dai was unable to examine it but noted that it involved an ordinary village wife who was able to protect her virtue and her body and not be violated. The administrative supervisor, Zhao Shiqing, concurred with Qi, and they sent up the case making Ning look guilty. Ning received the death penalty and Miss Shi was granted 100,000 cash, regular visits from the local officials, and a banner honoring her for her chastity. From this, she acquired a reputation as a chaste wife. The local people all realized Ning had been wronged and resented how overboard she had gone.

In the end Miss Shi had an affair with a monk at the nearby Lintian temple. Charges were brought and she received a beating and soon became ill. She saw Ning as a vengeful demon and then died. The date was the sixth month of 1177.

from those presented by the Secretariat-Chancellery. The emperor could thus use the one against the other and prevent bureaucrats in the Secretariat-Chancellery from dominating the government.

A second change was that the central government was better funded than it had been previously. Revenues in 1100 were three times the peak revenues of the Tang, partly because of the growth of population and agricultural wealth, and partly because of the establishment of government monopolies on salt, wine, and tea and various duties, fees, and taxes levied on domestic and foreign trade. During the Northern Song these commercial revenues rivaled the land tax; during the Southern Song they surpassed it. Confucian officials would continue to stress the primacy of land, but throughout late imperial China, commerce became a vital source of revenues.

A third change that strengthened the emperors was the disappearance of the aristocracy. During the Tang the emperor had come from the same Sino-Turkic aristocracy of northwestern China as most of his principal ministers, and he was essentially the organ of a state that ruled on behalf of this aristocracy. Aristocrats monopolized the high posts of government. They married among themselves and with the imperial family. They called the emperor the Son of Heaven, but they knew he was one of them. During the Song, in contrast, government officials were commoners, mostly products of the examination system. They were separated from the emperor by an enormous social gulf and saw him as a person apart.

The Song examination system was larger than that of the Tang, though smaller than under later dynasties. Whereas only 10 percent of officials had been recruited by examination during the Tang, the Song figure rose to over 50 percent and included the most important officials. The first examination was given at regional centers. The applicant took the examination in a walled cubicle under close supervision. To ensure impartiality, his answers were recopied by clerks and his name was replaced by a number before his examination was sent to the officials who would grade it. Of those who sat for the examination, only a tiny percentage passed. The second hurdle was the metropolitan examination at the national capital, where the precautions were equally elaborate. Only one in five, or about two hundred a year, passed. The average successful applicant was in his mid-thirties. The final hurdle was the palace examination, which rejected a few and assigned a ranking to the others.

To pass the examinations, the candidate had to memorize the Confucian classics, interpret selected passages, write in the literary style, compose poems on themes given by the examiners, and propose solutions to contemporary problems in terms of Confucian philosophy. The quality of the officials produced by the Song system was impressive. A parallel might be drawn with nineteenth-century Britain, where students in the classics at Oxford and Cambridge went on to become generalist bureaucrats. The Chinese examination system that flourished during the Song continued, with some interruptions, into the twentieth century. The continuity of Chinese government during this millennium rested on the examination elite, with its common culture and values.

The social base for this examination meritocracy was triangular, consisting of land, education, and office. Landed wealth paid the costs of education. A poor peasant or city dweller could not afford the years of study needed to pass the examinations. Without passing the examinations, an official position was out of reach. And without office, family wealth could not be preserved. The Chinese pattern of inheritance, as noted earlier, led to the division of property at each change of generation. Some families passed the civil service examinations for several generations running. More often, the sons of well-to-do officials did not study as hard as those with bare means. The adage "shirt sleeves to shirt sleeves in three generations" is not inappropriate to the Song and later dynasties. As China had an extended-family or clan

An Elegant Song Dynasty Wine Pot with green celadon glaze (24.8 cm high). *Ewer with carved flower sprays. Porcelain with molded and carved low-relief decoration in grayish-green glaze. Northern Song Dynasty (960–1000) .H. 9 5/8 in × W. 5 1/4 in × D. 7 3/4 in, H. 24.5 cm × W. 13.4 cm × D. 19.7 cm. China; Shaanxi province. © Gift of The Asian Art Museum Foundation.*

system, a wealthy official often provided education for the bright children of poor relations.

How the merchants related to this system is less clear. They had wealth but were despised by scholar-officials as grubby profit seekers and were barred from taking the examinations. Some merchants avoided the system altogether—a thorough education in the Confucian classics did little to fit a merchant's son for a career in commerce. Others bought land for status and security, and their sons or grandsons became eligible to take the exams. Similarly, a small peasant might build up his holdings, become a landlord, and educate a son or grandson. The system was steeply hierarchical, but it was not closed nor did it produce a new, self-perpetuating aristocracy.

Song Culture

As society and government changed during the Tang–Song transition, so too did culture. Song culture retained some of the energy of the Tang while becoming more intensely and perhaps more narrowly Chinese. The preconditions for the rich Song culture were a rising economy, an increase in the number of schools and higher literacy, and the spread of printing. Song culture was less aristocratic, less cosmopolitan, and more closely associated with the officials and the scholar-gentry, who were both its practitioners and its patrons. It also was less Buddhist than the Tang had been. Only the Zen (Chan) sect kept its vitality, and many Confucians were outspokenly anti-Buddhist and anti-Daoist. In sum, the secular culture of officials that had been a sidestream in the Tang broadened and became the mainstream during the Song.

Chinese consider the Song dynasty as the peak of their traditional culture. It was, for example, China's greatest age of pottery and porcelains. High-firing techniques were developed, and kilns were established in every area. There was a rich variety of beautiful glazes. The shapes were restrained and harmonious. Song pottery, like nothing produced in the world before it, made ceramics a major art form in East Asia. It was also an age of great historians. Sima Guang (1019–1086) wrote *A Comprehensive Mirror for Aid in Government*, which treated not a single dynasty but all Chinese history. His work was more sophisticated than previous histories in that it included a discussion of documentary sources and an explanation of why he chose to rely on one source rather than another. The greatest achievements of the Song, however, were in philosophy, poetry, and painting. (See Document, "'Chaste Woman' Shi.")

Philosophy　The Song was second only to the Zhou as a creative age in philosophy. A series of original thinkers culminated in the towering figure of Zhu Xi (1130–1200). Zhu Xi studied Daoism and Buddhism in his youth, along with Confucianism. A brilliant student, he passed the metropolitan examination at the age of eighteen. During his thirties he focused his attention on Confucianism, deepening and making more systematic its social and political ethics by joining to it certain Buddhist and native metaphysical elements. As a consequence, the new Confucianism became a viable alternative to Buddhism for Chinese intellectuals. Zhu Xi became famous as a teacher at the White Deer Grotto Academy, and his writings were widely distributed. Before the end of the Song, his Confucianism had become the standard interpretation used in the civil service examinations, and it remained so until the twentieth century.

If we search for comparable figures in other traditions, we might pick Saint Thomas Aquinas (1224–1274) of medieval Europe or the Islamic theologian al-Ghazali (1058–1111), each of whom produced a new synthesis or worldview that lasted for centuries (see Chapters 16 and 13, respectively). Aquinas combined Aristotle and Latin theology just as Zhu Xi combined Confucian philosophy and metaphysical notions from other sources. Because Zhu Xi used terms such as the "great ultimate" and because he emphasized a Zen-like meditation called "quiet sitting," some contemporary critics said his Neo-Confucian philosophy was a Buddhist wolf in the clothing of a Confucian sheep. This was unfair. Whereas Aquinas would make philosophy serve religion, Zhu Xi made religion or metaphysics serve philosophy. In his hands, the great ultimate (also known as "principle" or *li*) lost its otherworldly character and became a constituent of all things in the universe. Perhaps the Zhu Xi philosophy may be characterized as innerworldly.

Later critics often argued that Zhu Xi's teachings encouraged metaphysical speculation at the expense of practical ethics. Zhu Xi's followers replied that, on the contrary, his teachings gave practical ethics a systematic underpinning and positively contributed to individual moral responsibility. What was discovered within by Neo-Confucian quiet sitting

Song Dynasty Philosopher Zhu Xi (1130–1200). His Neo-Confucian ideas remained central down to the twentieth century. *Collection of the National Palace Museum, Taiwan, R.O.C.*

was just those positive ethical truths enunciated by Confucius over 1,000 years earlier. The new metaphysics did not change the Confucian social philosophy.

Zhu Xi himself advocated the selection of scholar-officials through schools, rather than by examinations. It is ironic that his teachings became a new orthodoxy that was maintained by the channelizing effect of the civil service examinations. Historians argue, probably correctly, that Zhu Xi's teachings were one source of stability in late imperial China. Like the examination system, the imperial institution, the scholar-gentry class, and the land system, his interpretation of Confucianism contributed to continuity and impeded change. Some historians go further and say that the emergence of the Zhu Xi orthodoxy stifled intellectual creativity during later dynasties, which probably is an overstatement. There were always contending schools.

Poetry　Song poets were in awe of those of the Tang, yet Song poets were also among China's best. A Japanese authority on Chinese literature wrote:

Tang poetry could be likened to wine, and Song poetry to tea. Wine has great power to stimulate, but one cannot drink it constantly. Tea is less stimulating, bringing to the drinker a quieter pleasure, but one which can be enjoyed more continuously.[9]

The most famous poet of the Northern Song was Su Dungpo (1037–1101), a man who participated in the full range of the culture of his age: He was a painter and a calligrapher, particularly knowledgeable about inks; he practiced Zen and wrote commentaries on the Confucian classics; he superintended engineering projects; and he was a connoisseur of cooking and wine. His life was shaped by politics. He was a conservative, believing in a limited role for government and social control through morality. (The other faction in the Song bureaucracy was the reformers, who stressed law and an expanded governmental role.)

Passing the metropolitan examination, Su rose through a succession of posts to become the governor of a province—a position of immense power. While considering death sentences, which could not be carried over into the new year, he wrote:

New Year's Eve—you'd think I could go home early
But official business keeps me.
I hold the brush and face them with tears:
Pitiful convicts in chains,
Little men who tried to fill their bellies,
Fell into the law's net, don't understand disgrace.
And I? In love with a meager stipend
I hold on to my job and miss the chance to retire.
Do not ask who is foolish or wise;
All of us alike scheme for a meal.
The ancients would have freed them a while at New
*   Year's—Would*
I dare do likewise? I am silent with shame.[10]

Eight years later, when the reformers came to power, Su himself was arrested and spent 100 days in prison, awaiting execution on a charge of slandering the emperor. Instead, he was released and exiled. He wrote, "Out the gate, I do a dance, wind blows in my face; our galloping horses race along as magpies cheer."[11] Arriving at his place of exile, he reflected:

Between heaven and earth I live,
One ant on a giant grindstone,
Trying in my petty way to walk to the right
While the turning of the mill wheel takes me
*   endlessly left.*

Though I go the way of benevolence and duty,
I can't escape from hunger and cold.[12]

But exile was soon turned to art. He farmed a plot of land at the "eastern slope" from which he took his literary name, Dungpo. Of his work there, he wrote:

A good farmer hates to wear out the land;
I'm lucky this plot was ten years fallow.
It's too soon to count on mulberries;
My best bet is a crop of wheat.
I planted seed and within the month
Dirt on the rows was showing green.
An old farmer warned me,
Don't let seedlings shoot up too fast!
If you want plenty of dumpling flour
Turn a cow or sheep in here to graze.
Good advice—I bowed my thanks;
I won't forget you when my belly's full.[13]

After 1086 the conservatives regained control of the government, and Su resumed his official career. In 1094 another shift occurred, and Su was again exiled to the distant southern island of Hainan. After still another shift, Su was on his way back to the capital when he died, in 1101. (See Document, "Su Dungpo Imagined on a Wet Day, Wearing a Rain Hat and Clogs.")

Painting In the West, penmanship and painting are quite separate, one merely a skill and the other esteemed as an art. In China, calligraphy and painting were equally appreciated and were seen as related. A scholar spent his life with brush in hand. The same qualities of line, balance, and strength needed for calligraphy carried over to painting. Chinese calligraphy is immensely pleasing even to the untutored Western eye, and it is not difficult to distinguish between the elegant strokes of Huineng, the last emperor of the Northern Song, and the powerful brushwork of the Zen monk Zhang Jizhi.

Song painting was varied—of birds or flowers; of fish or insects; of horses, monkeys, or water buffalo; of scholars, emperors, Buddhas, or Daoist immortals. But its crowning achievement was landscapes. Song landscapes are different from those of the West. Each stroke of the brush on silk or paper was final. Mistakes could not be covered up. Each element of a painting was presented in its most pleasing aspect; the painting was not constrained by single-point perspective. Paintings had no single source of illumination with light and shadow but contained an overall diffusion of light. Space was

---

[9] Kojiro Yoshikawa, *An Introduction to Sung Poetry*, trans. by Burton Watson (Cambridge: Harvard University Press, Harvard-Yenching Institute Monograph Series, 1967), p. 37.

[10] Yoshikawa, p. 119.

[11] Yoshikawa, p. 117.

[12] Yoshikawa, p. 105.

[13] Yoshikawa, pp. 119–120.

Su Dungpo Imagined on a Wet Day, Wearing a Rain Hat and Clogs

Document

After Su's death, a disciple wrote these lines.

◆ How does the sentiment in this poem relate to the Confucian humanism encountered in the document in Chapter 2?

When with tall hat and firm baton he stood in council,
The crowds were awed at the dignity of the statesman
in him.
But when in cloth cap he strolled with cane and sandals,
He greeted little children with gentle smiles.

From *An Introduction to Sung Poetry*, by Kojiro Yoshikawa, trans. by Burton Watson (Cambridge, MA: Harvard University Press, 1967). Copyright © 1967 by the Harvard-Yenching Institute, Monograph Series, poem, p. 122, illustration located on unnumbered page opposite p. 65. Reprinted by permission of Harvard-Yenching Institute.

an integral part of the painting. A typical painting might have craggy rocks or twisted pine trees in the foreground, then mist or clouds or rain to create distance, and in the background the outlines of mountains or cliffs fading into space. If the painting contained human figures at all, they were small in a natural universe that was very large. Chinese painting thus reflected the same worldview as Chinese philosophy or poetry. The painter sought to grasp the inner reality of the scene and not be bound up in surface details.

In paintings by monks or masters of the Zen school, the presentation of an intuitive vision of an inner reality became even more pronounced. Paintings of Bodhidharma, the legendary founder of the Zen sect, are often dominated by a single powerful downstroke of the brush, defining the edge of his robe. Paintings of patriarchs tearing up sutras or sweeping dust with a broom from the mirror of the mind are almost as calligraphic as paintings of bamboo. A Yuan dynasty painting in the style of Shi Ke shows the figure of a monk or sage who is dozing or meditating. A Zen "broken ink" landscape might contain rocks, water, mountains, and clouds, each represented by a few explosive strokes of the brush.

China in the Mongol World Empire: The Yuan Dynasty (1279–1368)

The Mongols created the greatest empire in the history of the world. It extended from the Caspian Sea to the Pacific

An ink on silk handscroll, Southern Song Dynasty. The vast expanse of nature is hardly affected by the human presence.

Ocean; from Russia, Siberia, and Korea in the north to Persia and Burma in the south. Invasion fleets were even sent to Java and Japan, although without success. Mongol rule in China is one chapter of this larger story.

Rise of the Mongol Empire

The Mongols, a nomadic people, lived to the north of China on grasslands where they raised horses and herded sheep. They lived in felt tents called yurts—they sometimes called themselves "the people of the felt tents." Women performed much of the work and were freer and more easygoing than women in China. Families belonged to clans and related clans to tribes. Tribes would gather during the annual migration from the summer plains to winter pasturage. Chiefs were elected, most often from noble lineages, for their courage, military prowess, judgment, and leadership. Like Manchu or Turkic, the Mongol language was Altaic.

The Mongols believed in nature deities and in the sky god above all others. Sky blue was their sacred color. They communicated with their gods through religious specialists called *shamans*. Politically divided, they traded and warred among themselves and with settled peoples on the borders of their vast grassland domains.

The founder of the Mongol Empire, Temujin, was born in 1167, the son of a tribal chief. While Temujin was still a child, his father was poisoned. He fled and after wandering for some years, returned to the tribe, avenged his father, and in time became chief himself. Through his shrewd policy of alliances and remarkable survival qualities, by the time he was forty, he had united all Mongol tribes and had been elected their great khan, or ruler. It is by the title *Genghis* (also spelled *Jenghiz* or *Chinggis*) *Khan* that he is known to history. Genghis possessed an extraordinary charisma, and his sons and grandsons also became wise and talented

leaders. Why the Mongol tribes, almost untouched by the higher civilizations of the world, should have produced such leaders at this point in history is difficult to explain.

A second conundrum is how the Mongols, who numbered only about 1.5 million, created the army that conquered vastly denser populations. Part of the answer is institutional. Genghis organized his armies into "myriads" of 10,000 troops, with decimal subdivisions of 1,000, 100, and 10. Elaborate signals were devised so that in battle, even large units could be manipulated like the fingers of a hand. Mongol tactics were superb: Units would retreat, turn, flank, and destroy their enemies. The historical record makes amply clear that Genghis's nomadic cavalry had a paralytic effect on the peoples they encountered. The Mongols were peerless horsemen, and their most dreaded weapon was the compound bow, short enough to be used from the saddle yet more powerful than the English longbow.

They were astonishingly mobile. Each man carried his own supplies. Trailing remounts, they covered vast distances quickly. In 1241, for example, a Mongol army had reached Hungary, Poland, and the shore of the Adriatic and was poised for a further advance into Western Europe. But when word arrived of the death of the great khan, the army turned and galloped back to Mongolia to help choose his successor.

When this army encountered walled cities, it learned the use of siege weapons from the enemies it had conquered. Chinese engineers were used in campaigns in Persia. The Mongols also used terror as a weapon. Inhabitants of cities that refused to surrender in the Near East and China were put to the sword. Large areas in north China and Sichuan were devastated and depopulated. Descriptions of the Mongols by those whom they conquered dwell on their physical toughness and pitiless cruelty.

But the Mongols had strengths that went beyond the strictly military. Genghis opened his armies to recruits from

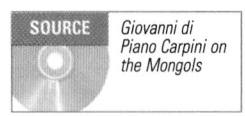

SOURCE *Giovanni di Piano Carpini on the Mongols*

the Uighur Turks, the Manchus, and other nomadic peoples. As long as they complied with the military discipline demanded of his forces, they could participate in his triumphs. In 1206 Genghis promulgated laws designed to prevent the normal wrangling and warring between tribes that would undermine his empire. Genghis also obtained thousands of pledges of personal loyalty from his followers, and he appointed these "vassals" to command his armies and staff his government. This policy gave his forces an inner coherence that countered the divisive effect of tribal loyalties.

The Mongol conquests were all the more impressive in that, unlike the earlier Arab expansion, they lacked the unifying force of religious zeal. To be sure, at an assembly of chiefs in 1206, an influential shaman revealed that it was the sky god's will that Genghis conquer the world. Yet other unabashedly frank words attributed to Genghis may reveal a truer image of what lay behind the Mongol drive to conquest: "Man's highest joy is in victory: to conquer one's enemies, to pursue them, to deprive them of their possessions, to make their beloved weep, to ride on their horses, and to embrace their wives and daughters."[14]

Genghis divided his far-flung empire among his four sons. Trade and communications were maintained between the parts, but over several generations, each of the four khanates became independent. The khanate of Chagatai was in Central Asia and remained purely nomadic. A second khanate of the Golden Horde ruled Russia from the lower Volga. The third was in Persia, and the fourth, led by those who succeeded Genghis as great khans, centered first in Mongolia and then in China (see Map 8–4).

Mongol Rule in China

The standard theory used in explaining Chinese history is the dynastic cycle. A second theory explains Chinese history in terms of the interaction between the settled peoples of China and nomads of the steppe. When strong states emerged in China, their wealth and population enabled them to expand militarily onto the steppe. But when China was weak, as was more often the case, the steppe peoples overran China. To review briefly:

Kublai Khan. Wearing ermine coat, the Mongol emperor sits on a horse amongst Mongol warriors at the hunt. At his side is his consort, Chabi. *National Palace Museum, Taiwan, R.O.C.*

1. During the Han dynasty (206 B.C.E.–220 C.E.), the most pressing problem in foreign relations was the Xiongnu Empire to the north.

2. During the centuries that followed the Han, various nomadic peoples invaded and ruled northern China.

3. The energy and institutions of these Sino-Turkic rulers of the northern dynasties shaped China's reunification during the Sui (589–618) and Tang (618–907) dynasties. The Uighur Turks also played a major role in Tang defense policy.

4. Northern border states became even more important during the Song. The Northern Song (960–1126) bought peace with payments of gold and silver to the Liao. The Southern Song (1126–1279), for all its cultural brilliance, was little more than a tributary state of the Jin dynasty, which had expanded into northern China.

From the start of the Mongol pursuit of world hegemony, the riches of China were a target, but Genghis proceeded cautiously, determined to leave no enemy at his back. He first disposed of the Tibetan state to the northwest of China and then the Manchu state of Jin that ruled north China. Mongol forces took Beijing in 1227, the year Genghis died. They went on to take Luoyang and the southern reaches of the Yellow River in 1234, and all of north China by 1241. During this time, the Mongols were interested mainly in loot. Only later did Chinese

---

[14] J. K. Fairbank, E. O. Reischauer, and A. M. Craig, *East Asia, Tradition and Transformation* (Boston: Houghton Mifflin, 1973), p. 164.

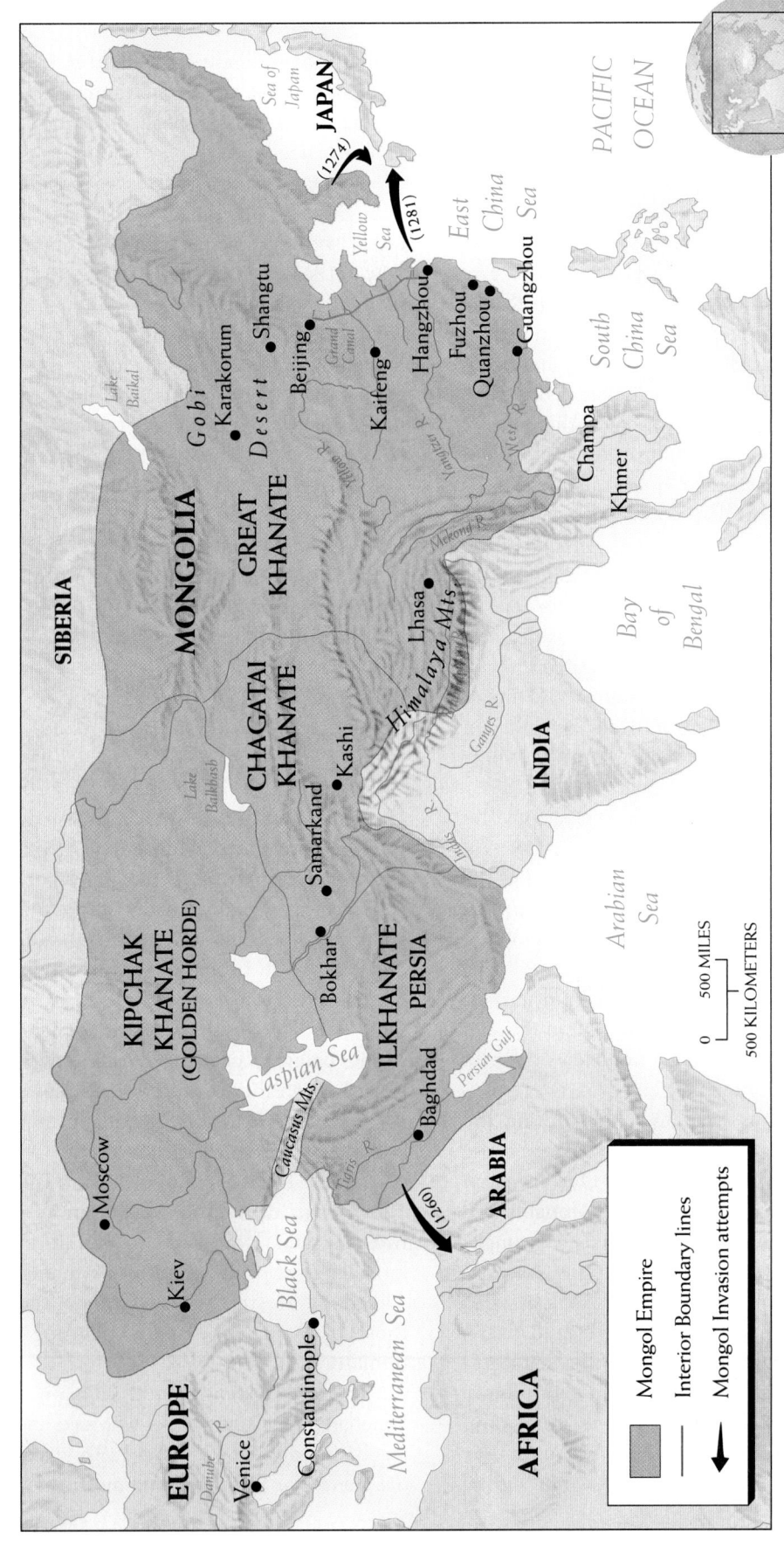

Map 8–4. The Mongol Empire in the Late thirteenth Century. Note the four khanates: the Golden Horde in Persia, Chagatai in Central Asia, and the Great Khanate extending from Mongolia to southern China.

advisers persuade them that more wealth could be obtained by taxation.

Kublai, a grandson of Genghis, was chosen as the great khan in 1260. In 1264 he moved his capital from Karakorum in Mongolia to Beijing. It was only in 1271 that he adopted a Chinese dynastic name, the Yuan, and, as a Chinese ruler, went to war with the Southern Song. Once the decision was made, the Mongols swept across southern China. The last Song stronghold fell in 1279.

Kublai Khan's rule in Beijing reflected the mixture of cultural elements in Mongol China. From Beijing, Kublai could rule as a Chinese emperor, which would not have been possible in Karakorum. He adopted the Chinese custom of hereditary succession. He rebuilt Beijing as a walled city in the Chinese style. But Beijing was far to the north of any previous Chinese capital, away from centers of wealth and population; to provision it, the Grand Canal had to be extended. From Beijing, Kublai could look out onto Manchuria and Mongolia and maintain ties with the other khanates. The city proper was for the Mongols. It was known to the West as Cambulac, "the city (baliq) of the khan." Chinese were segregated in an adjoining walled city. The palace of the khan was designed by an Arab architect; its rooms were Central Asian in style. Kublai also maintained a summer palace at Shangdu (the "Xanadu" of Samuel Taylor Coleridge's poem) in Inner Mongolia, where he could hawk and ride and hunt in Mongol style.

Early Mongol rule in northern China was rapacious and exploitative, but it later shifted towards Chinese forms of government and taxation, especially in the south and at the local level. Because it was a foreign military occupation, civil administration was highly centralized. Under the emperor was a Central Secretariat, and beneath it were ten "Moving Secretariats," which became the provinces of later dynasties. These highly centralized institutions and the arbitrary style of Mongol decision-making accelerated the trend towards absolutism that had started during the previous dynasty.

About 400,000 Mongols lived in China during the Yuan period. For such a tiny minority to control the Chinese majority, it had to stay separate. One measure was to make military service a monopoly of Mongols and their nomadic allies. Garrisons were established throughout China, with a strategic reserve on the steppe. Military officers were always regarded as more important than civil officials. A second measure was to use ethnic classifications in appointing civil officials. The highest category was the Mongols, who held the top civil and military posts. The second category included Persians, Turks, and other non-Chinese, who were given high civil posts. The third category was the northern Chinese, including

Manchus and other border peoples, and the fourth was the southern Chinese. Even when the examination system was sporadically revived after 1315, the Mongols and their allies took an easier examination; their quota was as large as that for Chinese, and they were appointed to higher offices.

The net result was an uneasy symbiosis. Chinese officials directly governed the Chinese populace, collecting taxes, settling disputes, and maintaining the local order. Few of these officials ever learned to speak Mongolian, yet without their positive cooperation, Mongol rule in China would have been impossible. The Mongols, concentrated in Beijing, large cities, and in garrisons, spoke Mongolian among themselves and usually did not bother to learn Chinese. A few exceptions wrote poetry in Chinese and painted in the Chinese style. Communication was through interpreters. When a Chinese district magistrate sent a query to the court, the ruling was made in Mongolian. (The Mongols had borrowed the alphabet of the Uighurs to transcribe their tongue.) A word-for-word translation in Chinese was written below the Mongolian and passed back down to the magistrate. As the two languages are syntactically very different, the resulting Chinese was grotesque.

Foreign Contacts and Chinese Culture

Diplomacy and trade within the greater Mongol Empire brought China into contact with other higher civilizations for the first time since the Tang period. Persia and the Arab world were especially important. Merchants, missionaries, and diplomats voyaged from the Persian Gulf and across the Indian Ocean to seaports in southeastern China. The Arab communities in Guangzhou and other ports were larger than they had been during the Song. Camel caravans carrying silks and ceramics left Beijing to pass through the Central Asian oases and on to Baghdad. Although the Mongols did not favor Chinese merchants and most trade was in other hands, Chinese trade also expanded. Chinese communities became established in Tabriz, the center of trading in western Asia, and in Moscow and Novgorod. It was during this period that knowledge of printing, gunpowder, and Chinese medicine spread to western Asia. Chinese ceramics influenced those of Persia as Chinese painting influenced Persian miniatures.

In Europe, knowledge of China was transmitted by the Venetian trader Marco Polo, who said he had served Kublai as an official between 1275 and 1292. His book, A *Description of the World*, was translated into most European languages. (See

Marco Polo Describes the City of Hangzhou

Document

Marco Polo was a Venetian. In 1300 Venice had a population of more than 100,000 and was the wealthiest Mediterranean city-state. But Polo was nonetheless unprepared for what he saw in China. Commenting on Hangzhou, China's capital during the Southern Song, he first noted its size (ten or twelve times larger than Venice), then its many canals and bridges, its streets "paved with stones and bricks," and its location between "a lake of fresh and very clear water" and "a river of great magnitude." He spoke of "the prodigious concourse of people" frequenting its ten great marketplaces and of its "capacious warehouses built of stone for the accommodation of merchants who arrive from India and other parts." He then described the life of its people.

◆ Europeans who read Marco Polo's account of China thought it was too good to be true. Would you agree?

Each of the ten market-squares is surrounded with high dwelling-houses, in the lower part of which are shops, where every kind of manufacture is carried on, and every article of trade is sold; such, amongst others, as spices, drugs, trinkets, and pearls. In certain shops nothing is vended but the wine of the country, which they are continually brewing, and serve out fresh to their customers at a moderate price. The streets connected with the market-squares are numerous, and in some of them are many cold baths, attended by servants of both sexes, to perform the offices of ablution for the men and women who frequent them, and who from their childhood have been accustomed at all times to wash in cold water, which they reckon highly conducive to health. At these bathing places, however, they have apartments provided with warm water, for the use of strangers, who from not being habituated to it, cannot bear the shock of the cold. All are in the daily practice of washing their persons, and especially before their meals.

In other streets are the habitations of the courtesans, who are here in such numbers as I dare not venture to report; and not only near the squares, which is the situation usually appropriated for their residence, but in every part of the city they are to be found, adorned with much finery, highly perfumed, occupying well-furnished houses, and attended by many female domestics. These women are accomplished, and are perfect in the arts of blandishment and dalliance, which they accompany with expressions adapted to every description of person, insomuch that strangers who have once become so enchanted by their meretricious arts, that they can never divest themselves of the impression. Thus intoxicated with sensual pleasures, when they return to their homes they report that they have been in Kin-sai [Hangzhou], or the celestial city, and pant for the time when they may be enabled to revisit paradise.

The inhabitants of the city are idolaters, and they use paper money as currency. The men as well as the women have fair complexions, and are handsome. The greater part of them are always clothed in silk, in consequence of the vast quantity of that material produced in the territory of Kin-sai, exclusively of what the merchants import from other provinces. Amongst the handicraft trades exercised in the place, there are twelve considered to be superior to the rest, as being more generally useful; for each of which there are a thousand workshops, and each shop furnishes employment for ten, fifteen, or twenty workmen, and in a few instances as many as forty; under their respective masters. The natural disposition of the native inhabitants of Kin-sai is pacific, and by the example of their former kings, who were themselves unwarlike, they have been accustomed to habits of tranquility. The management of arms is unknown to them, nor do they keep any in their houses. Contentious broils are never heard among them. They conduct their mercantile and manufacturing concerns with perfect candour and probity. They are friendly towards each other, and persons who inhabit the same street, both men and women, from the mere circumstance of neighbourhood, appear like one family. In their domestic manners they are free from jealousy or suspicion of their wives, to whom great respect is shown, and any man would be accounted infamous who should presume to use indecent expressions to a married woman. To strangers also, who visit their city in the way of commerce, they give proofs of cordiality, inviting them freely to their houses, showing them hospitable attention, and furnishing them with the best advice and assistance in their mercantile transactions. On the other hand, they dislike the sight of soldiery, not excepting the guards of the grand khan, as they preserve the recollection that by them they were deprived of the government of their native kings and rulers.

Excerpt from *The Travels of Marco Polo*, 1908, from Everyman's Library. Reprinted by permission of David Campbell Publishers, London, pp. 290–301.

The Journey of Marco Polo. Marco Polo and companions en route to China on the Silk Road.
Getty Images, Inc/Hulton Archive Photos.

Document, "Marco Polo Describes the City of Hangzhou.") Many readers doubted that a land of such wealth and culture could exist so far from Europe, but the book excited an interest in geography. When Christophe Columbus set sail in 1492, his goal was to reach Polo's Zipangu (Japan).

The greatest of all Muslim travelers, the Moroccan Ibn Battuta (1304–c. 1370) traveled throughout much of the Mongol world in the fourteenth century. His observations are a rich source of information about the societies he visited. Ever curious, he had a sharp eye for detail: "The Chinese infidels eat the flesh of swine and dogs, and sell it in their markets. They are wealthy folk and well-to-do, but they make no display either in their food or their clothes."

Other cultural contacts were fostered by the Mongol toleration or encouragement of religion. Nestorian Christianity, spreading from Persia to Central Asia, reentered China during the Mongol era. Churches were built in main cities. The mother of Kublai Khan was a Nestorian Christ-

ian. Also, several papal missions were sent from Rome to the Mongol court. An archbishopric was established in Beijing; a church was built, sermons were preached in Turkish or Mongolian, and choirboys sang hymns. Kublai sent Marco Polo's father and uncle with a letter to the pope asking for 100 intelligent men acquainted with the seven arts.

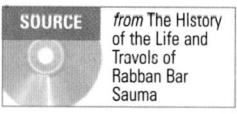
SOURCE *from* The History of the Life and Travels of Rabban Bar Sauma

Tibetan Buddhism with its magical doctrines and elaborate rites was the religion most favored by the Mongols, but Chinese Buddhism also flourished. Priests and monks of all religions were given tax exemptions. It is estimated that half a million Chinese became Buddhist monks during the Mongol century. The foreign religion that made the greatest gains was Islam, which became permanently established in Central Asia and western China. Mosques were built in the Islamic areas, in Beijing, and in southeastern port cities. Even Confucianism was regarded as a religion by the Mongols, and its teachers were exempted from taxes. But as the scholar-gentry rarely obtained important offices, they saw the Mongol era as a time of hardship.

Despite these wide contacts with other peoples and religions, the high culture of China appears to have been influenced almost not at all—partly because China had little to learn from other areas, and partly because the centers of Chinese culture were in the south, the last area to be conquered and the area least affected by Mongol rule. Also, in reaction to the Mongol conquest, Chinese culture became conservative and turned in on itself. Scholars wrote poetry in the style of the Song. New schools of painting developed, but the developments were from within the Chinese tradition, and the greatest Yuan paintings continued the style of the Song. Yuan historians wrote the official history of the dynasties that preceded it. The head of the court bureau of historiography was a Mongol, but the histories produced by his Chinese staff were in the traditional mold. As the dynasty waned, unemployed scholars wrote essays expressing loyalty toward the Song and satirizing the Mongols. Their writings were not censored: The Mongols either could not read them, did not read them, or did not care.

The major contribution to Chinese arts during the Yuan was by dramatists, who combined poetic arias with vaudeville theater to produce a new operatic drama. Performed by traveling troupes, the operas used few stage props. They relied for effect on makeup, costumes, pantomime, and stylized gestures. The women's roles were usually played by men. Except for the arias—the highlights of the performance—the dramas used vernacular Chinese, appealing to a popular audience. The unemployed scholars who wrote the scripts drew on the entire repertoire of the Song storyteller. Among the stock figures in the operas were a Robin Hood–like bandit; a famous detective-judge; the Tang monk who traveled to India; warriors and statesmen of the Three Kingdoms; and romantic heroes, villains, and ghosts. Justice always triumphed, and the dramas usually ended happily. In several famous plays the hero gets the girl, despite objections by her parents and seemingly insurmountable obstacles, by passing the civil service examinations in first place. As the examinations were not in effect during most of the Yuan, this resolution of the hero's predicament is one that looked back to the Song pattern of government. Yuan drama continued almost unchanged in later dynasties, and during the nineteenth century it merged with a form of southern Chinese theater to become today's Beijing Opera.

Last Years of the Yuan

Despite the Mongol military domination of China and the highly centralized institutions of the Mongol court, the Yuan was the shortest of China's major dynasties. Little more than a century elapsed between Kublai's move to Beijing in 1264 and the dynasty's collapse in 1368. The rule of Kublai and his successor had been effective, but thereafter a decline set in. By then, the Mongol Empire as a whole no longer lent strength to its parts. The khanates became separated by religion and culture as well as by distance. Even tribesmen in Mongolia rebelled now and then against the great khans in Beijing, who, in their eyes, had become too Chinese. The court at Beijing, too, had never really gained legitimacy. Some Chinese officials served it loyally to the end, but most Chinese saw the government as carpetbaggers and Mongol rule as a military occupation. When succession disputes, bureaucratic factionalism, and pitched battles between Mongol generals broke out, Chinese showed little inclination to rally in support of the dynasty.

Problems also arose in the countryside. Taxes were heavy, and some local officials were corrupt. The government issued excessive paper money and then refused to accept it in payment for taxes. The Yellow River changed its course, flooding the canals that carried grain to the capital. At great cost and suffering, a labor force of 150,000 workers and 20,000 soldiers rerouted the river to the south of the Shandung Peninsula. Further natural disasters during the 1350s led to popular uprisings. The White Lotus sect preached the coming of Maitreya. Regional military commanders, suppressing the rebellions, became independent of central control. Warlords arose. The warlord who ruled Sichuan was infamous for his cruelty. Important economic regions were devastated and in part depopulated by rebellions. At the end, a rebel army threatened Beijing, and the last Mongol emperor and his court fled on horses to Shangdu. When that city fell, they fled still deeper into the plains of Mongolia.

Summary

Sui and Tang Dynasties. The Sui and Tang dynasties (589–907) reunited China's empire. Under the Tang, China expanded into Central Asia, taking control of much of the lucrative Silk Road along which trade moved to the West. Chang'an, the Tang capital, became the largest city in the world. Tang culture was rich and cosmopolitan, much influenced by its contacts with other cultures and immensely influential on the cultures of Japan, Korea, and Vietnam. The Tang dynasty was also the golden age of Buddhism in China, and a variety of Buddhist sects flourished.

Song Dynasty. Under the Song dynasty (960–1279), China experienced an agricultural revolution in which large aristocratic estates worked by serfs gave way to small land holdings owned by free farmers. Advances in technology led to the invention of printing and the development of a coal and iron-smelting industry. The growth of a money economy encouraged the expansion of trade, both within China and with foreign countries. Song culture was particularly rich in philosophy, poetry, and painting.

The Mongols. After their unification by Genghis Khan (1167–1227), the Mongols created the greatest empire in history. The highly mobile Mongol cavalry overwhelmed Chinese armies. By 1279 the Mongols ruled all of China. But Mongol rule in China was short-lived and enjoyed only shallow Chinese support. Mongol rule in China ended in 1368.

Review Questions

1. Why could China re-create its empire—just 400 years after the fall of the Han—but Rome could not? Are there similarities between the Qin-Han transition and that of the Sui-Tang? Between Han and Tang expansion and contraction?

2. How did the Chinese economy change from the Tang to the Northern Song to the Southern Song? How did the polity change? How did China's relationships to surrounding states change?

3. What do Chinese poetry and art tell us about Chinese society? About women? What position did poets occupy in Chinese society?

4. What drove the Mongols to conquer most of the known world? How could their military accomplish the task? Once they conquered China, how did they rule it? What was the Chinese response to Mongol rule?

INTERPRETING THE PAST

Travelers' Accounts

The following travelers' accounts of China, southern Russia, and surrounding regions offer the reader varied perspectives into twelfth- and thirteenth-century society and culture in Asia. Analyze several of these documents in order to understand *why* they were written and *who* the potential readers/audience were.

Text Sources from the Primary Source DVD / MyHistoryLab

Lu You, *Excerpt of a Diary of a Journey to Sichuan*

Marco Polo, excerpt from *Travels*

 Excerpt from *History of Life and Travels of Rabban Bar Sauma*

Excerpt from *William of Rubruck's Account of the Mongols*

Text Source from Chapter 8

Marco Polo Describes the City of Hangzhou, p. 269.

Questions

First determine the primary themes/subjects of each account. Choose several examples of details in each account that provide clues to the writer's interest and attitudes towards these subjects.

Several of the accounts (those authored by Lu You and Marco Polo, for example) focus on journeys without obvious, specific assignments. How do these descriptions of people, places, and events differ in focus from those of modern travelers or tourists? Are there any similarities?

The other documents referred to here (those authored by Rabban Bar Sauma, William of Rubruck) are concerned with journeys with specific purposes (trade and diplomacy), sponsored by rulers. What kinds of differences

KeyTerms

Amitabha Buddha (p. 254)

Censorate (p. 248)

Zen (p. 254)

Note: To learn more about the topics in this chapter, please turn to the Suggested Readings at the end of the book. For additional sources related to this chapter please see the Primary Source DVD at the back of this text or MyHistoryLab.

Questions (continued)

are there between these accounts and the reports of contemporary government officials on international trade and diplomatic missions?

Are they any differences in themes, topics, and experiences between the Western travel-writers represented here (Marco Polo, William of Rubruck) and the Asian writers (Rabban Bar Sauma, Lu You)?

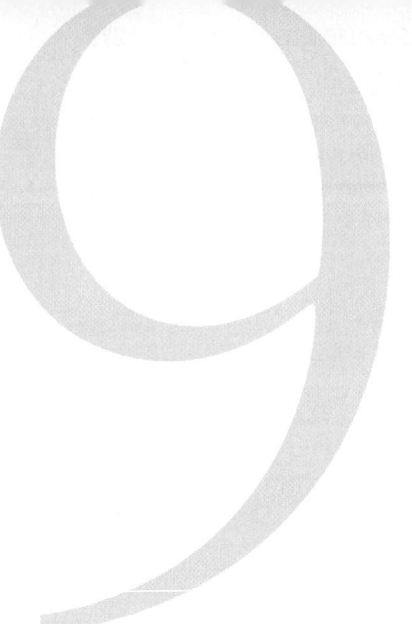

The Emergence of East Asia: Japan, Korea, and Vietnam

IETNAM, KOREA, AND JAPAN WERE AN UNLIKELY TRIO. Vietnam had jungles and elephants and was hot. Korea was a northern land with a post-tribal society and an Altaic language related to Manchurian, Mongolian, and Turkic. Japan was an island country, out in the sea to the east of the Asian mainland. In terms of spatial perception, travel from Japan to America or Europe today is safe and takes half a day; in the seventh century, travel to China was risky and took weeks.

Yet each of these three countries (along with Bohai, to the north of Korea, a country which later disappeared) took in the civilization of Tang dynasty China and made it their own. To say this, of course, means that they used it in response to their particular needs and took in what they were able to assimilate.

Are we to emphasize their similarities or differences? Certainly the way they went about the task was different. In Vietnam it was done through Chinese rule, which the Vietnamese were unable to forestall. In Korea, the rulers gained power with the help of Tang armies, which they then ousted from the peninsula. Ousting the Chinese

Early Korean Woodblock Printing. The carving of the woodblocks of the Korean *Tripitaka* (Buddhist canon) began in the early eleventh century and was completed in 1087. The original woodblocks were destroyed during the thirteenth-century Mongol invasions. The *Tripitaka Koreana* that remains today is a later edition completed in 1251 and consists of 81,200 woodblocks. It is considered to be the finest, in terms of accuracy and calligraphic beauty, among the twenty-some versions of the *Tripitaka*. *"P'alman taejanggyon" (Tripitaka Koreana). Korea, 1251. Asian Division*

East Asia

Korea

Vietnam Japan

Heartland civilizations were few in number. Most of the world became civilized as the culture and technologies of the heartlands spread into adjacent areas. In East Asia the heartland civilization of China spread to Korea, Japan, and Vietnam (and much later to Taiwan), just as Mediterranean culture spread through a barbarian Europe.

When we speak of East Asia, we refer more to culture than to geography. We stress what Japan, Korea, and Vietnam had in common. They mastered Buddhist and Confucian teachings and with them Chinese conceptions of the universe, state, and human relationships. They took in Chinese arts and technologies: painting, music, ceramics, criminal and civil law, medicine, and architecture. They learned to write using Chinese ideographs. Since their languages belonged to non-Chinese language families, it was as difficult for them to write using Chinese ideographs as it would be for us to write English using Egyptian hieroglyphics.

In the seventh century, when "East Asia" began, these countries were not blank slates on which Chinese culture could be simply inscribed. Each already had in place preconditions for the acceptance of a more advanced civilization: bronze and iron technologies, the practice of agriculture, settled village communities, and archaic states. The appeal of Chinese civilization was irresistible, but specific needs and interests conditioned its adoption. In Japan, for example, the archaic Yamato court strengthened its control over outlying regions by using Chinese political institutions and tax systems.

Japan, Korea, and Vietnam may be compared, almost as a controlled laboratory experiment, with a second half-circle of countries or regions made up of Manchuria, Mongolia, Central Asia, and Tibet. In the second half-circle, the climate was harsher, agriculture was more rudimentary, and the lifestyle was mostly nomadic and pastoral. Despite their troops, paradoxically, set the stage for their borrowing of its culture. Japan, much more distant and protected by an ocean moat, had the luxury of taking what it wanted, but it turned out that it wanted almost everything. Or so it seemed at the time. In the last analysis, the common core of what the three countries took may be more important than the way they went about it. ■

Korea

Geography has shaped Korean history. A range of mountains along its northern rim divides the Korean peninsula from Manchuria, making it a distinct geographical unit. Mountains continue south through the eastern third of Korea, while in the west and south are coastal plains and broad river valleys. The combination of mountains, rice paddies, and sea make Korea a beautiful land. The traditional name for Korea may be translated as the "land of the morning calm." Two further geographical factors vitally affected Korean history. One was that the northwestern corner of Korea was only 300 miles from the northeastern corner of historical China: close enough for Korea to be vulnerable to invasions by its powerful neighbor but far enough away so that most of the time China found it easier to treat Korea as a tributary than to control it directly. The other factor was that the southern rim of Korea was just one hundred miles from the southern Japanese island of Kyushu across the Tsushima Straits (see Map 9–1).

During its old and new stone ages, Korea was peopled by tribes migrating south from northeast Asia—from Siberia, Mongolia, and Inner Asia. They probably spoke an Altaic tongue—distantly related to Japanese and to Manchurian, Mongolian, and Turkic. They settled in Korea, though small numbers continued on to Japan after 300 B.C.E. They subsisted by hunting, gathering, and fishing, and, like other early peoples of northeast Asia, made comb-patterned pottery and lived in pit dwellings.

The Korean Bronze Age began in 1300, agriculture in 1000, and the Iron Age in 400–300 B.C.E. Most of the population lived in small villages along the coasts or rivers and only gradually spread inland. Agriculture made possible permanent settlements. Their religion was animism, the worship of the sun, moon, sea, and other forces of nature, and they communicated with the spirits of the dead through shamans. Important leaders were buried in megalithic tomb mounds.

proximity to China and their frequent contacts with it, these countries were unable or unwilling to take in its more advanced civilization. In effect, on the steppe to the north and west, the Chinese seed fell upon stony places or was scorched and withered away. But in the agricultural lands of Korea, Japan, and Vietnam it fell onto good ground and brought forth fruit.

The comparison can be extended. It seems paradoxical that Japan, Korea, and Vietnam, which took in Chinese civilization and made it their own, became independent nations in recent times, whereas Tibet, central Asia, part of Mongolia, and Manchuria, which refused Chinese civilization, were conquered and absorbed by China. (The case of Manchuria is complicated.) The explanation is partly a question of development: the regions to the west and north were less able to resist Chinese imperialism. It was partly a matter of political and cultural identity. Just as in modern times westernizing nations feel an ambivalence or even antipathy toward the "modern heartland civilization" of the West, so did Japan, Korea, and Vietnam have complex feelings toward China.

Of the three societies treated in this chapter, Korea and Vietnam were closer to China for longer periods of time, and had, as a result, a stronger Chinese imprint. Japan, which was larger, more populous, and more distant, emerged as the most distinctive variant within East Asia. To understand these countries, however, we must turn from generalizations to their historical particulars.

Focus Questions

◆ Why did Korea, Vietnam, and Japan follow a distinctive trajectory in their relationship with China compared to other regions of east and central Asia?

◆ How do the histories of Korea, Vietnam, and Japan illustrate the relationship between a "heartland civilization" and adjacent areas?

Chinese Commanderies 108 B.C.E.–313 C.E., and Korean States 313–668 C.E.

Koreans were still ruled by tribal chiefdoms, or tribal confederations, in 108 B.C.E. when the Han emperor Wudi sent an army into north Korea to menace the flank of the Xiongnu empire that spread across the steppe to the north of China. Wudi established four commanderies, with troops and forts to rule over the local village society. The most important, Lolang, was located near Pyongyang, the present-day capital of North Korea. Playing off one tribal leader against another, the Chinese maintained a partial hegemony over the peninsula for four centuries until 313 C.E., almost a century after the fall of the Han dynasty.

As the commanderies disappeared, three archaic states emerged from earlier tribal confederations: Silla in the east, Paekche in the west, and Koguryo stretching into Manchuria in the north. Their history is complex for they had varying relations with China and Japan, and often fought among themselves. Despite ups and downs, their populations increased and their aristocratic governments increased their sway over local villages. The power of their kings is reflected in the size and number of their royal tomb mounds. Chinese culture entered only as a small trickle from the northwest or by sea. Buddhism entered, too, but the indigenous animism predominated at the village level.

Silla 668–918 Of the three Korean states, Silla, the westernmost, grew stronger, and with the help of Tang (Chinese) armies, defeated the other two in 660 and 668 and unified Korea. The Chinese intended to stay and rule, but Silla forces soon drove them from Korea. After an interval, relations were reestablished: China recognized Silla as an autonomous tribute state, and Silla, for its part, sent annual missions to the Chinese court carrying tribute or gifts. Thereafter, Korea's northern flank was protected from steppe nomads by Chinese armies.

The period of Silla rule may be likened to eighth-century Nara Japan. On the one hand, borrowing from China began in earnest. The capital at Kyongju was laid out, like Chang'an, on a checkerboard pattern. Korea adopted Chinese writing, established some government offices on the Chinese model, set up a Confucian national academy to train officials, sent annual embassies to the Tang court, and

Map 9–1.   Early Korean States.

sent thousands of students to study in the Tang capital. It also embraced a range of Chinese arts, philosophies, and technologies. Buddhism was patronized by the Silla king and nobility and began to spread into the countryside. On the other hand, within the Silla government, aristocratic birth mattered more than scholarship, and most official posts were held by the well-born even after the establishment of an examination system in 788. In village Korea, the worship of nature deities continued, despite the formal introduction of Buddhism.

Silla underwent a normal end-of-dynasty decline. The waning of the Tang dynasty in China left Korea open to attacks from the northwest. There were coups at the court and rebellions in outlying regions. Rebel kingdoms fought among themselves until, in 918, a warlord general founded a new dynasty, the Koryo. The English word "Korea" is derived from this dynastic name.

Koryo 918–1392 The West knows the Koryo era for its celadon vases, which rivaled those of China, but it was creative in other ways as well. The earliest surviving history of

Korea was compiled in 1145; new genres of poetry and literature appeared; printing using moveable metallic type was invented during the thirteenth century. The Koryo was also Korea's Buddhist age: temples, monasteries, and nunneries were built throughout the land, and sculpture and art flourished. During the thirteenth century, Buddhist scholars produced in classical Chinese a printed edition of the *Tripitaka*, a huge compendium of *sutras* and other sacred writings. Confucianism was also supported by the court and taught both in state schools and private academies.

In comparison to Silla, Koryo was more "Chinese" in most respects. Government offices resembled those of China and Chinese-type laws were established. But even then, governing remained a monopoly of the aristocracy, and administrative centralization was incomplete: of the three hundred district magistrates, only one-third were officials sent out from the capital; the rest were appointed from among local nobles or dignitaries. Apart from aristocrats, Koryo society was made up of commoners (the "good people") and slaves. Commoners were burdened by heavy

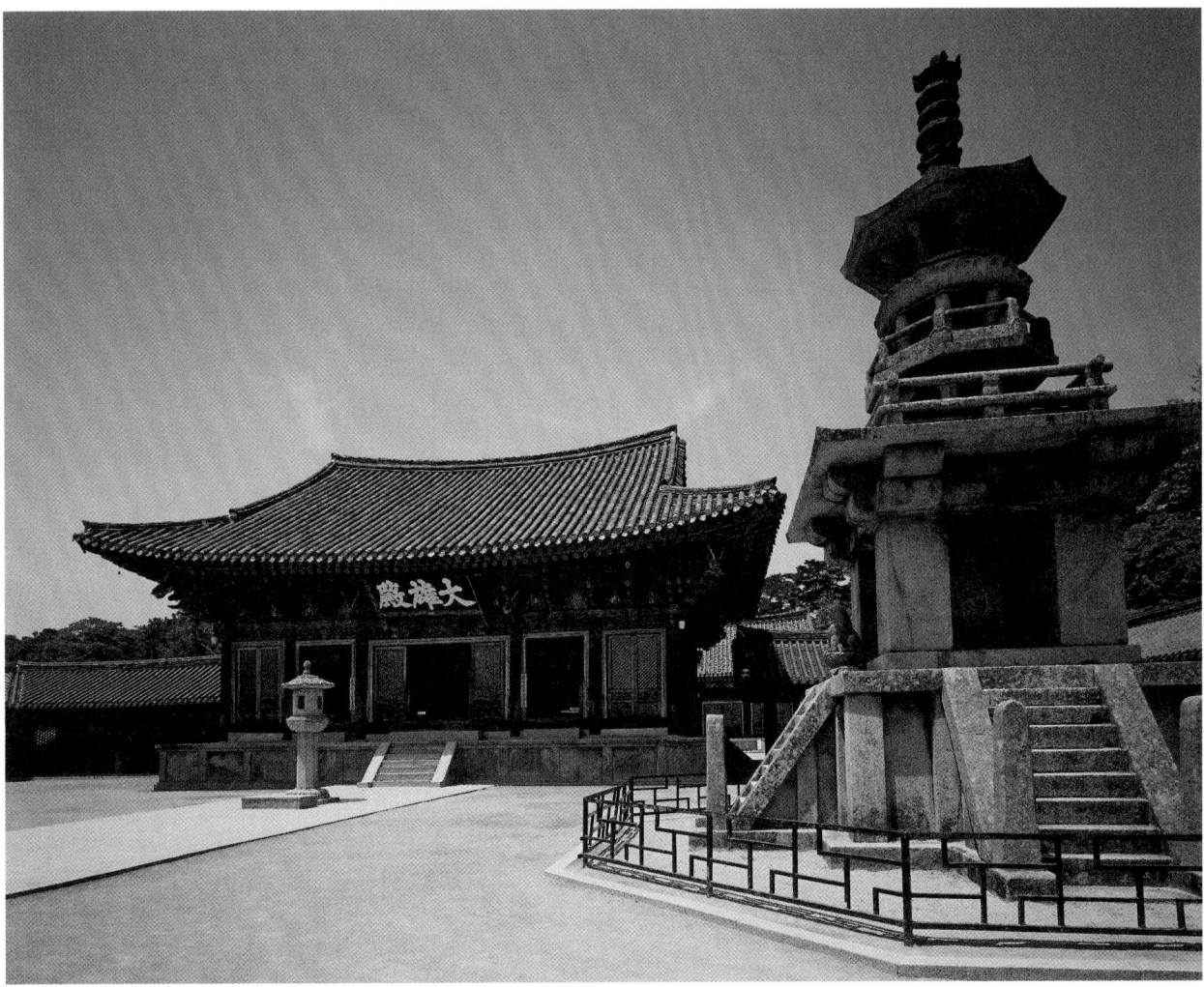

Pulguksa temple, built in 751 (and recently restored) near the ancient Silla capital of Kyongju. At right is a stupa containing a *sutra*, or relic of the Buddha.

taxes of rice, labor, and military service. Hereditary slaves were almost one-third of the entire population—more than anywhere else in East Asia.

Despite its cultural brilliance, the weaknesses of Koryo were many. For one thing, the Koryo economy was undeveloped: Trade was by barter, and money did not circulate. Chinese missions commented on the extravagance of officials in the capital and the squalor of commoners and slaves in Korea's villages. For another, aristocrats amassed estates and built private armies. By the late twelfth century, military officials had replaced civil officials at the court, and power passed into the hands of the capital guards–who have been compared to the Praetorian Guards of the late Roman Empire. Still another problem is that frequent incursions from across Korea's northern border weakened the state. The Koryo court survived as long as it did by becoming in succession the tributary of the Song, Liao, Chin, and Mongol dynasties of China. The cost of wars with the Mongols was particularly high; the demands placed on Korea by the

Mongol invasions of Japan in 1274 and 1281, which were launched from Korean ports, further weakened the court.

Vietnam

Vietnam in Southeast Asia

Four movements shaped the historical civilizations of Southeast Asia. Vietnam was touched by each and by a fifth, as well. The first was the movement of peoples and languages from north to south. Ranges of mountains rising in Tibet and South China extend southward, dividing Southeast Asia into river valleys. The Mon and Burmese peoples had moved from the southeast slopes of the Tibetan plateau into the Upper Irrawaddy by 500 B.C.E. and continued south along the Irrawaddy and Salween Rivers, founding the kingdom of Pagan in 847 C.E. Thai tribes moved south from China down the valley of the Chao Phraya River somewhat later, founding the kingdoms of

Sukhothai (1238–1419) and Ayutthaya (1350–1767). Even today Thai-speaking peoples are still to be found in several southern China provinces. The origins of the Vietnamese are less clear, but they, too, first inhabited the north and moved into present-day central and southern Vietnam only in recent historical times.

A second movement was the Indianization of Southeast Asia. Between the first and fifteenth centuries Indian traders and missionaries crossed the Bay of Bengal and established outposts throughout Southeast Asia. As Hinduism and Buddhism spread through the region, Indian-type states with god-kings were established, and Indian scripts, legal codes, literature, drama, art, and music were adopted by the indigenous peoples. Today, Burma, Thailand, and Cambodia retain an Indian-type Buddhism; on the walls of Bangkok temples are painted scenes from the great Hindu epic, the *Mahabharata*. This early wave of Buddhism reached Vietnam, but was later supplanted by Chinese Buddhism. Vietnam, too, first received Buddhism as part of this early Indian wave, though it was later supplanted by the Chinese form of that religion.

A third movement of considerable dynamism was of Arab and Indian traders who sailed across the Indian Ocean to dominate trade with the Spice Islands (the Moluccas of present-day Indonesia) between the thirteenth and fifteenth centuries. Settling on the coasts and islands of Southeast Asia, they married into local ruling families and spread the teachings of Islam. Local rulers who converted became sultans. Today Malaysia and Indonesia are predominantly Muslim. The majestic Buddhist temple at Borobudur in central Java is a monument of an earlier age, submerged today in a sea of Islamic practice. Only the Hindu island of Bali to the east of Java retains the Indian religion that once covered the entire Indonesian archipelago. The Cham state (located in what today is central Vietnam) also became Muslim. Islam did not directly affect Vietnam, though Arab and Indian traders en route to China would visit Vietnamese coastal harbors or travel up the Red River to Hanoi.

A fourth movement, much later, was the Chinese **diaspora**. The emigration of Chinese throughout the world but especially to Southeast Asia began as a trickle and gathered momentum after 1842, after the post–Opium War treaties. Most Chinese went, initially, as indentured labor to work on plantations. But in time many moved to cities and opened shops. The mercantile ethos of the Chinese was more advanced than that of peoples to the south. Even today the casual visitor to Bangkok sees shopkeepers sitting in front of their shops reading Chinese newspapers. Their children became educated; some entered banking or law. In most of Southeast Asia the urban economies were largely developed and controlled by Chinese. This created resentments and, occasionally, anti-Chinese riots. To appease the powers that be, Chinese companies routinely appointed non-Chinese politicians or generals to their boards of directors. Assimilation occurred, but at a generational pace. The greatest concentrations of Chinese, apart from Singapore (three quarters of the population), were in Malaysia, Indonesia, and Thailand. But many of the "boat people" who fled Vietnam after the Vietnam War were Chinese Vietnamese.

A fifth movement or event, which affected only Vietnam and made it a part of East Asia, was conquest by China.

Vietnamese Origins

The story of a second perspective on Vietnam might begin with its present-day geography. Vietnam has been likened to two baskets on a carrying pole. One basket is the Red River basin, centering on Hanoi in the north, the other the delta of the Mekong River centering on Saigon (today Ho Chi Minh City) in the south. The carrying pole is the narrow mountainous strip of central Vietnam, with little river valleys opening to the South China Sea (see Map 9–2).

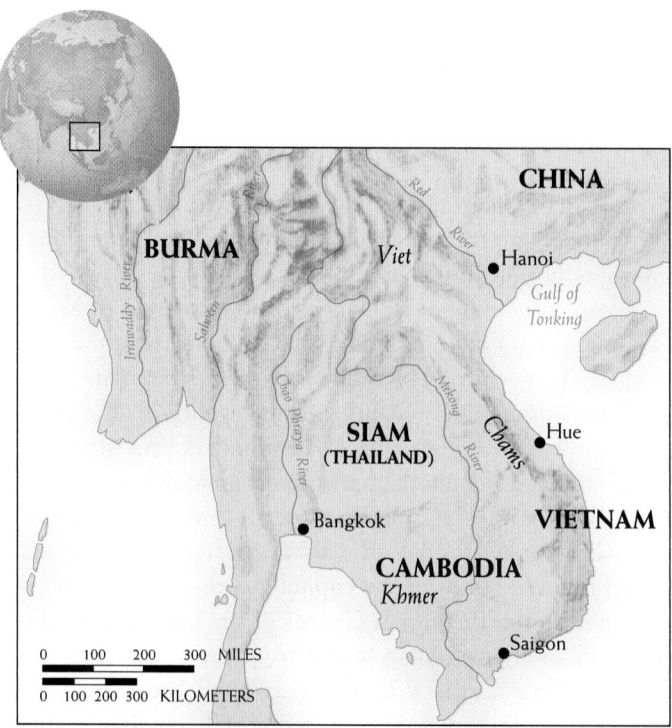

Map 9–2.   Vietnam and neighboring Southeast Asia.

Languages of East Asia

The two main language families in present-day East Asia are the Sinitic and the Ural-Altaic. They are as different from each other as they are from European tongues. The Sinitic languages are Chinese, Vietnamese, Thai, Burmese, and Tibetan. Within Chinese are several mutually unintelligible dialects.

Standard Chinese, based on the Beijing dialect, is further from Cantonese than Spanish is from French. Ural-Altaic languages are spoken to the east, north, and west of China. They include Japanese, Korean, Manchurian, Mongolian, the Turkic languages, and, in Europe, Finnish and Hungarian.

Until the late fifteenth century, the Vietnamese people inhabited only the north, that is to say, the basin of the Red River, which flows from west to east and empties into the Gulf of Tongking. The Chams, a wholly different people, closer to Indonesians than to Vietnamese, occupied central Vietnam and part of the southeastern coast. A sea-faring people who engaged in trade and piracy, the Chams became Hindu-Buddhist and later Muslim. They were united in the kingdom of Champa and waged intermittent wars against the Vietnamese to their north. A third people, the Khmers or Cambodians, inhabited the Mekong River delta, the area that is today south Vietnam. They were a part of the Hindu-Buddhist Cambodian (Khmer) empire that had its capital at Angkor in present-day Cambodia.

The early history of the Vietnamese in the Red River valley is known only through archaeology. Agriculture began early; slash and burn techniques were practiced in the highlands and crude paddy fields in the lowlands. Bronze entered, probably from China, during the first millennium B.C.E., and iron during the first or second century B.C.E. Pots made on potting wheels and bronze arrowheads and fishhooks are found in excavations, but plows were still tipped with stone. The people lived in villages under tribal leaders and worshiped the spirits of nature; men tattooed their bodies.

A Millennium of Chinese Rule: 111 B.C.E.–939 C.E.

The political history of the Vietnamese began in 208 B.C.E. when a renegade Han dynasty general formed the state of Nan Yueh. Its capital was near the present-day Chinese city of Guangzhou (Canton). It ruled over peoples in both southeastern China and the Red River basin. The Chinese ideograph for Yueh is read *Viet* in Vietnamese. The name Vietnam, literally, "Viet to the south," is derived from the name of this early state. Nan Yueh lasted for about a century until 111 B.C.E., when the armies of Han Wudi conquered it and brought it under Chinese control. After that, the Red River basin was ruled by China for more than one thousand years.

For the first seven centuries, Vietnam was governed by a Chinese military commandery—like those established in Korea and other border regions to rule over non-Chinese "barbarian" populations. The administrative center was initially a fort with a Chinese governor and Chinese troops. The governor ruled indirectly through local Vietnamese chiefs or magnates. Refugees fleeing China after the fall of the Former Han dynasty were appointed as officials in Vietnam.

In a famous incident of 39 C.E., the Trung sisters led a revolt against Chinese rule—the husband of one had been executed by the Chinese. The sisters later were made into national heroes. As a fifteenth-century Vietnamese poet put it:

All the male heroes bowed their heads in submission;
Only the two sisters proudly stood up to avenge the country.

Bronze drum engraved with intricate geometric designs from circa 800 B.C.E. Vietnam. An artifact of the early Bronze age, it was made for ceremonial purposes. Whether early Vietnamese bronze technology was indigenous or whether it came from China is an open question.

But in that age there was little sense of "country," and the only consequence of the revolt was a further strengthening of Chinese controls.

Vietnamese society changed during the centuries of Chinese rule. Early Vietnam had a matrilineal tribal society, practiced slash-and-burn agriculture, and often moved their settlements when their lands became exhausted. New agricultural techniques and metal plows, introduced from China, made possible permanent settlements and denser populations. Tribal organization gave way to village society, and matrilineal to patrilineal descent—though women continued to enjoy a higher status than in China. Buddhism entered, replacing or mingling with earlier animistic beliefs. Chinese officials sometimes married Vietnamese women, and a Sino-Vietnamese social elite arose in the capital. The influence of Chinese higher culture was initially confined to this elite.

During the Tang dynasty (618–907), Vietnam was still treated as a border region, but Chinese administration became stronger. Elements of Chinese law and, possibly, the Chinese land and tax system were introduced at this time. Also, the Red River basin was divided into provinces, which the Chinese referred to collectively as **Annam**, the "pacified south." When the French came to Vietnam in the nineteenth century, they picked up the term and called the north Vietnamese *Annamese*.

Since it was during the Tang that Japan and Korea also took in Chinese learning, one can ask whether Vietnam was a parallel case. In some regards it was. In all three societies Buddhism entered, flourished in the capitals, and gradually percolated into local areas, where it absorbed elements from earlier indigenous religions. In all three, other aspects of China's higher culture affected mainly the elites of the society, while an older way of life continued in villages with only small changes. But where Japanese and Korean rulers reached out for Chinese learning and technology and used it for their own ends, the Vietnamese had it thrust upon them. In the ninth century the Japanese devised a phonetic syllabary for the transcription of their language, and by the year 1000 were writing works such as *The Tale of Genji*—reflecting a new culture in which native and Chinese elements were fused. In Vietnam, where both the rulers and the written language were Chinese, no such transformation occurred.

Ten major revolts occurred during the thousand years of Chinese rule—not an unusual number for a Chinese border region with a non-Chinese population. The last revolt, which took place in 939, when China was weak, led to the establishment of an independent Vietnamese government. Vietnam never again became a part of China.

A Small Independent Country

The history of independent Vietnam is conventionally broken into dynastic blocs named after the ruling family. The first two dynasties were the Ly (1009–1225) and the Tran (1225–1400). Vietnamese dynasties, however, were not the strong, centralized, bureaucratic states found in China. From the beginnings of the dynasties, there were tensions between the center and periphery. At the center were the social elites who ruled the population of the Red River delta. At the periphery were magnates—powerful local figures who controlled upland peoples. Of these peripheral areas, the province of Thanh Hoa, one hundred miles south of the Hanoi capital, was of particular importance with magnates who were usually autonomous and often opposed the dynasty. Both center and periphery maintained military forces and sometimes engaged in wars. Often, several independent states coexisted during the timespan of a single "dynasty."

Chinese invasions also affected Vietnamese history. Most Chinese dynasties, as they expanded, attempted to reconquer the "south" that had once been ruled by China. Such invasions were successfully repelled, though Ming armies occupied Vietnam for twenty years beginning in 1407. But rather than defying China altogether, Vietnamese rulers found it easier to accommodate: Every Vietnamese dynasty became a "tributary" of China and sent missions that professed the Vietnamese ruler's submission to the Chinese emperor. In official communications with the Chinese "emperor," the Vietnamese rulers styled themselves as "kings," indicating their subordinate status.

Such submission, however, was purely formal. Within Vietnam, Vietnamese rulers styled themselves as "emperors" and claimed that their mandate to rule came directly from Heaven, separate but equal to the mandate received by the Chinese emperor. They also denied the universality of the Chinese imperium by referring to China not as the Middle Kingdom but as the Northern Court—their own government being the Southern Court. In 1076, a Vietnamese general fighting Chinese troops wrote the following poem:

> *The Southern emperor rules the Southern land*
> *Our destiny is writ in Heaven's Book*
> *How dare you bandits trespass on our soil*
> *You shall meet your undoing at our hands.*

We must note that the poem was in Chinese, Vietnam's only written language, and couched in the terminology of Chinese political thought.

Japan

Japanese history has three main turning points, each marked by a major influx of an outside culture and each followed by a massive restructuring of Japanese institutions. The first turning point was in the third century B.C.E., when an Old Stone Age Japan became an agricultural, metalworking society, similar to those on the Korean peninsula or in northeastern Asia. This era lasted until 600 C.E. The second turning point came during the seventh and eighth centuries, when whole complexes of Chinese culture entered Japan directly. Absorbing these, archaic Japan made the leap to a higher historical civilization associated with the writing system, technologies, and philosophies of China, and with Chinese forms of Buddhism. Japan would remain a vital part of this civilization until the third turning point, in the nineteenth century, when it encountered the West.

Japanese Origins and the Yayoi Revolution

Japanese hotly debate their origins. New archaeological finds are front-page news. Bookstores have rows of books, often popular works, asking, Who are we and where did we come from? During the ice ages, Japan was connected by land bridges to Asia. Woolly mammoths entered the northern island of Hokkaido, and elephants, saber-toothed tigers, giant elk, and other continental fauna entered the lower islands. Did humans enter as well? Because Japan's acidic volcanic soil eats up bones, there are no early skeletal remains. The earliest evidence of human habitation is that of finely shaped stone tools dating from about 30,000 B.C.E. Then, from about 10,000 B.C.E., there exists pottery, the oldest in the world, and from about 8000 B.C.E., Jōmon or "cord-pattern" pottery.

Archaeologists are baffled by the appearance of pottery in an Old Stone Age hunting gathering, and fishing society, when in all other early societies it developed along with agriculture as an aspect of New Stone Age culture.

After 8,000 years of Jōmon culture, a second phase of Japanese prehistory began about 300 B.C.E. It is called the Yayoi culture, after the area in Tokyo where its distinctive hard, pale orange pottery was first unearthed. There is no greater break in the entire Japanese record than between the Jōmon and the Yayoi. For at the beginning of the third century B.C.E. the agricultural revolution, the bronze revolution, and the iron revolution—which in the Near East, India, and China had been separated by thousands of years, and each of which singly had wrought profound transformations—burst into Japan simultaneously.

The new technologies were brought to Japan by peoples moving across the Tsushima Straits from the Korean peninsula. It is uncertain whether these immigrants came as a trickle and were absorbed—the predominant view in Japan—or whether they came in sufficient numbers to push back the indigenous Jōmon people. Physical anthropologists say that skulls from early Yayoi sites differ from those of the Jōmon.

The early Yayoi migrants, using the same seacraft by which they had crossed from Korea, spread along the coasts of northern Kyushu and western Honshu. Yayoi culture rapidly replaced that of the Jōmon as far east in Japan as the present-day city of Nagoya. After that, the Yayoi culture diffused overland into eastern Japan more slowly and with greater difficulty. Conditions were less favorable for agriculture, and a mixed agricultural-hunting economy lasted longer.

The early Yayoi "frontier settlements" were located next to their fields. Their agriculture was primitive. By the first century C.E., the Yayoi population had so expanded that wars were fought for the best land. Excavations have found extensive stone-axe industries and skulls pierced by bronze and iron arrowheads. An early Chinese chronicle describes Japan as made up of "more than one hundred countries" with wars and conflicts raging on all sides. During these wars, villages

Jōmon figurine. Along with the cord-patterned pots, the hunting and gathering Jōmon people produced mysterious figurines. Is this a female deity? Why are the eyes slitted like snow goggles? Earthenware with traces of pigment (Kamegaoka type); 24.8 cm high.
Asia Society, N.Y.: Mr. and Mrs. John D. Rockefeller 3rd Collection.

were relocated to defensible positions on low hills away from the fields. From these wars emerged a more peaceful order of regional tribal confederations and a ruling class of aristocratic warriors. Late Yayoi excavations once again reveal villages alongside fields and far fewer stone axes.

During the third century C.E. a temporary hegemony was achieved over a number of such regional tribal confederations by a queen named Pimiko. In the Chinese chronicle Pimiko is described as a shaman who "occupied herself with magic and sorcery, bewitching the people." She was mature but unmarried. "After she became the ruler, there were few who saw her. She had one thousand women as attendants but only one man. He served her food and drink and acted as a medium of communication. She resided in a palace surrounded by towers and stockades with armed guards in a state of constant vigilance."[1]

After Pimiko, references to Japan disappeared from the Chinese dynastic histories for a century and a half.

Tomb Culture, the Yamato State, and Korea

Emerging directly from Yayoi culture was an era, (300–600 C.E.), characterized by giant tomb mounds. Even today these dot the landscape of the Yamato plain near present-day Osaka. The early tombs—patterned on those in Korea—were circular mounds of earth built atop megalithic burial chambers. Later tombs were sometimes keyhole shaped. The tombs were surrounded by moats and adorned with clay cylinders and statues of warriors, scribes, musicians, houses, boats, and the like. Early tombs, like the Yayoi graves that preceded them, contained mirrors, jewels, and other ceremonial objects. From the fifth century C.E. these objects were replaced by armor, swords, spears, and military trappings, reflecting a new wave of continental influences. The flow of people and culture from the Korean peninsula into Japan that began with Yayoi was continuous into historical times.

Japan reappeared in the Chinese chronicles in the fifth century C.E. This period was also covered in the earliest

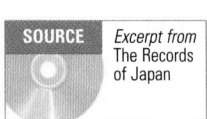

SOURCE *Excerpt from The Records of Japan*

Japanese accounts of their own history, the *Records of Ancient Matters [Kojiki]* and the *Records of Japan [Nihongi]*, compiled in 712 and 720. These records dovetail with the evidence of the tombs. The picture that emerges is of regional aristocracies under the loose hegemony of the Yamato "great kings." Historians use the geographic label "Yamato" because the courts of the great kings were located on the Yamato plain, the richest agricul-

Japanese Tomb Painting. In 1972, Japanese archaeologists found this painting on the interior wall of a megalithic burial chamber at Takamatsuzuka in Nara Prefecture. The most sophisticated tomb painting found in Japan, it dates to the 300–680 era and resembles paintings found in Korean and Chinese tombs. *Art Resource/Bildarchiv Preussischer Kulturbesitz.*

tural region of ancient Japan. The Yamato rulers also held lands and granaries throughout Japan. The tomb of the great king Nintoku is 486 meters long and 36 meters high, with twice the volume of the Great Pyramid of Egypt. By the fifth century C.E. the great kings possessed sufficient authority to commandeer laborers for such a project.

Chronology

Early Japanese History

8000–300 B.C.E.	Jōmon culture
Early Continental Influences	
300 B.C.E.–300 C.E.	Yayoi culture
300–680 C.E.	Tomb culture and the Yamato state
680–850 C.E.	Chinese Tang pattern in Nara and Early Heian Japan

---

[1] L. C. Goodrich, ed., and R. Tsunoda, trans., *Japan in the Chinese Dynastic Histories* (South Pasadena, CA: Perkins Asiatic Monographs, 1951), p. 13.

The great kings awarded Korean-type titles to court and regional aristocrats, titles that implied a national hierarchy centering on the Yamato court. That regional rulers had the same kind of political authority over their populations can be seen in the spread of tomb mounds throughout Japan.

The basic social unit of Yamato aristocratic society was the extended family (*uji*), closer in size to a Scottish clan than to a modern household. Attached to these aristocratic families were groups of specialist workers called *be*. This word was of Korean origin and was originally used to designate potters, scribes, or others with special skills who had emigrated from Korea. It was then extended to include similar groups of indigenous workers and groups of peasants. Yamato society had a small class of slaves, possibly captured in wars. Many peasants were neither slaves nor members of aristocratic clans or specialized workers' groups.

What little is known of Yamato politics suggests that the court was the scene of incessant struggles for power between aristocratic families. There were also continuing efforts by the court to control outlying regions. Although marriage alliances were established and titles awarded, rebellions were not infrequent during the fifth and sixth centuries. Finally, there were constant wars with "barbarian tribes" in southern Kyushu and eastern Honshu on the frontiers of "civilized" Japan.

During the era of the Yamato court, a three-cornered military balance had emerged on the Korean peninsula between the states of Paekche in the southwest, Silla in the east, and Koguryo in the north (see Map 9–3). Japan was an ally of Paekche and maintained extensive trade and military relations with the weak southern federation known as the Kaya States.

Map 9–3.   Yamato Japan and Korea (ca. 500 C.E.)   Paekche was Japan's ally on the Korean peninsula. Silla, Japan's enemy, was the state that would eventually unify Korea. (Note: Nara was founded in 710; Heian in 794.)

The Paekche connection enabled the Yamato court to expand its power within Japan. Imports of iron weapons and tools gave it military strength. The migration to Japan of Korean potters, weavers, scribes, metalworkers, and other artisans increased its wealth and influence. The great cultural significance of the immigrants from Korea can be gauged by the fact that many became established as noble families. Paekche also served as a conduit for the first elements of Chinese culture to enter Japan. Chinese writing was adopted for the transcription of Japanese names during the fifth or sixth century. Confucianism entered in 513, when Paekche sent a "scholar of the Five Classics." Buddhism arrived in 538 when a Paekche king sent a Buddha image, sutras, and possibly a priest.

Eventually the political balance on the peninsula shifted. In 532 Paekche turned against Japan and joined Silla in attacking and then gobbling up the Kaya States. In 660 Silla, always hostile to Japan, defeated Paekche and unified the peninsula. But the rupture of ties with Korea was less of a loss than it would have been earlier, for by this time Japan had established direct relations with China.

Religion in Early Japan

The indigenous religion of the Yamato Japanese was an animistic worship of the forces of nature, later given the name of **Shintō**, or "the way of the gods," to distinguish it from Buddhism. Shintō probably entered Japan from the continent as part of Yayoi culture. The underlying forces of nature might be embodied in a waterfall, a twisted tree, a strangely shaped boulder, a mountain, or in a great leader who would be worshiped as a deity after his death. Mount Fuji was holy not as the abode of a god but because the mountain itself was an upwelling of a vital natural force. Even today in Japan, a gnarled tree trunk may be girdled with a straw rope and set aside as an object of veneration. The more potent forces of nature such as the sea, the sun, the moon, the wind, and thunder and lightning became personified as deities. The sensitivity to nature and natural beauty that pervades Japanese art and poetry owes much to Shintō. (See Document, "Darkness and the Cave of High Heaven.")

Throughout Japan's premodern history most villages had shamans, religious specialists who, by entering a trance, could directly contact the inner forces of nature and gain the power to foretell the future or heal sickness. The queen Pimiko was such a shaman. The sorceress is also a stock figure in tales of ancient or medieval Japan. More often than not, women, receiving the command of a god, have founded the "new" religions in this tradition, even into the nineteenth and twentieth centuries.

A second aspect of early Shintō was its connection with the state and the ruling post-tribal aristocracy. Each clan, or extended family, had its own myth centering on a nature deity (*kami*) that it claimed as its original ancestor. The clan genealogy in which the line of descent was traced was a patent of nobility and a title to political authority. The head of a clan, who was also its chief priest, made sacrifices to its deity. When Japan was unified by the Yamato court, the myths of several clans were joined into a composite national myth. The deity of the Yamato great kings was the sun goddess, so she became the chief deity, while other gods assumed lesser positions appropriate to the status of their clan. Had another clan won the struggle, its deity would have become paramount—perhaps a thunder god as in ancient Greece.

The *Records of Ancient Matters* and *Records of Japan* tell of the creation of Japan, of the deeds and misdeeds of gods 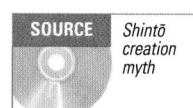 on the "plain of high heaven," and of their occasional adventures on earth or in the underworld. In mid-volume, the stories of the gods, interspersed with the genealogies of noble families, give way to stories of early emperors and early Japanese history. The Japanese emperors, today the oldest royal family in the world, were viewed as the lineal descendants of the sun goddess and as "living gods." The Great Shrine of the sun goddess at Ise has always been the most important in Japan.

The Itsukashima Shrine. On the little island of Miyajima not far from Hiroshima is the lovely Itsukashima shrine dedicated to the daughters of the Shintō god of the moon and oceans. Its outer gate (*torii*) is constructed of camphor logs to resist the salt water. Originally built in the late 6th century, it was rebuilt in the 16th.

Darkness and the Cave of High Heaven

Document

The younger brother of the sun goddess was a mischief-maker. Eventually the gods drove him out of heaven. On one occasion, he knocked a hole in the roof of a weaving hall and dropped in a dappled pony that he had skinned alive. One weaving maiden was so startled that she struck her genitals with the shuttle she was using and died.

◆ **What does this myth suggest regarding the social relations of the Shintō gods? Entering a cave and then reemerging signifies death and rebirth in the religions of many peoples. Compare this passage to "Mark Describes the Resurrection of Jesus" in Chapter 6.**

The Sun Goddess, terrified at the sight, opened the door of the heavenly rock cave, and hid herself inside. Then the Plain of High Heaven was shrouded in darkness, as was the Central Land of the Reed Plains [Japan]. An endless night prevailed. The cries of the myriad gods were like the buzzing of summer flies, and myriad calamities arose.

The eight hundred myriad gods assembled in the bed of the Quiet River of Heaven. They asked one god to think of a plan. They assembled the long-singing birds of eternal night and made them sing. They took hard rocks from the bed of the river and iron from the Heavenly Metal Mountain and called in a smith to make a mirror. They asked the Jewel Ancestor God to make a string of 500 curved jewels eight feet long. They asked other gods to remove the shoulder blade of a male deer, to obtain cherry wood from Mount Kagu, and to perform a divination. They uprooted a sacred tree, attached the string of curved jewels to its upper branches, hung the large mirror from its middle branches, and suspended offerings of white and blue cloth from its lower branches.

One god held these objects as grand offerings and another intoned sacred words. The Heavenly Hand-Strong-Male God stood hidden beside the door. A goddess bound up her sleeves with clubmoss from Mount Kagu, made a herb band from the spindle-tree, and bound together leaves of bamboograss to hold in her hands. Then she placed a wooden box face down before the rock cave, stamped on it until it resounded, and, as if possessed, she exposed her breasts and pushed her skirt-band down to her genitals. The Plain of High Heaven shook as the myriad gods broke into laughter.

The Sun Goddess, thinking this strange, opened slightly the rock-cave door and said from within: "Since I have hidden myself, I thought that the Plain of Heaven and the Central Land of the Reed Plains would all be in darkness. Why is it that the goddess makes merry and the myriad gods all laugh?"

The goddess replied: "We rejoice and are glad because there is here a god greater than you." While she spoke two other gods brought out the mirror and held it up before the Sun Goddess.

The Sun Goddess, thinking this stranger and stranger, came out the door and peered into the mirror. Then the heavenly Hand-Strong-Male God seized her hand and pulled her out. Another god drew a rope behind her and said: "You may not go back further than this."

So when the Sun Goddess had come forth, the Plain of High Heaven and the Central Land of the Reed Plains once again naturally shone in brightness.

From the *Records of Ancient Matters (Kojiki)*, trans. by Albert Craig, with appreciation to Basil Hall Chamberlain and Donald L. Phillippi.

Nara and Heian Japan

The second major turning point in Japanese history was its adoption of the higher civilization of China. This is a prime example of the worldwide process (described in Chapter 2) by which the heartland civilizations spread into outlying areas. In Japan the process occurred between the seventh and twelfth centuries and can best be understood in terms of three stages. During the seventh century the Japanese studied China; during the eighth, they implanted Chinese institutions in Japan; after that, they adapted the institutions to meet Japanese needs. By the eleventh century the creative reworking of Chinese elements had led to distinctive Japanese forms, unlike those of China but equally unlike those of the earlier Yamato court.

Court Government

The official embassies to the Tang court that began in 607 C.E. included traders, students, and Buddhist monks as well as representatives of the Yamato great kings. Like Third World students who study abroad today, Japanese who studied in China played key roles in their own government when they returned home. They brought back with them a quickening flow of technology, art, Buddhism, and knowledge of Tang legal and governmental systems. But for Yamato Japanese, the difficulties of mastering Chinese and China's philosophical culture were enormous. Actual institutional changes using the Tang model began only in the 680s with the Emperor Temmu and his successor, the Empress Jitō (r. 686–697).

Temmu's life illustrates the interplay between Japanese power politics and the adoption of Chinese institutions. He came to the throne by leading an alliance of eastern clans in rebellion against the previous great king, his nephew. The *Records of Japan* describes Temmu as "walking like a tiger through the eastern lands." He then used Chinese systems to consolidate his power. He rewarded his supporters with new court ranks and with positions in a new court government, both patterned after the Tang example. He extended the authority of the court and increased its revenues by a survey of agricultural lands and a census of their population. He promulgated a Chinese-type law code that greatly augmented the powers of the ruler. He styled himself as the "heavenly emperor," or **tennō**, which thereafter replaced the earlier title of "great king." In short, although Temmu must have admired immensely things Chinese, much of the borrowing was dictated by specific, immediate, and practical goals.

Until the eighth century the capital was usually moved each time an emperor died. Then, in 710 a new capital, intended to be permanent, was established at Nara. It was laid out on a checkerboard grid like the Chinese capital at Chang'an. But then it was moved again in 784—some say to escape the meddling in politics of powerful Buddhist temples. A final move occurred in 794 to Heian (later Kyoto) on the plain north of Nara. This site remained the capital until the move to Tokyo in 1869. Even today, Kyoto's regular geometry reflects Chinese city planning.

The superimposition of a Chinese-type capital on a still backward Japan produced as stark a contrast as any in history. In the villages, peasants—who worshiped the forces in mountains and trees—lived in pit dwellings and either planted in crude paddy fields or used slash-and-burn techniques of dryland farming. In the capital stood pillared palaces in which dwelt the emperor and nobles, descended from the gods on high. They drank wine, wore silk, and enjoyed the paintings,

Prince Shōtoku (574–622). A commanding figure at the pre-Nara Yamato court, Prince Shōtoku (shown here with two of his sons) promoted Buddism and began regular embassies to China. "This world is a lie," he wrote, reflecting the Buddhist belief in an ultimate reality beyond.

perfumes, and pottery of the Tang. Clustered about the capital were Buddhist temples, more numerous than in Nara, with soaring pagodas and sweeping tile roofs. With what awe must a peasant have viewed the city and its inhabitants!

Governments at the Nara and Heian courts were headed by emperors, who were at the same time Confucian rulers with the majesty accorded by Chinese law and Shintō rulers descended from the sun goddess. Protected by an aura of the sacred, their lineage was never usurped. It remained in place throughout the rest of Japanese history, though several emperors were killed and replaced by other family members.

Beneath the emperor, the same modified Chinese pattern prevailed. At the top was a Council of State, a powerful office from which leading clans sometimes manipulated the authority of an emperor who reigned but did not rule. Beneath the council were eight ministries—two more than in

China. One of the extra ministries was a Secretariat and the other the Imperial Household Ministry. Size affected function. China had a population of 60 million; Nara Japan had 4 or 5 million. Since there were fewer people to govern in Japan and no external enemies, more of the business of court government was with the court itself. Of the 6,000 persons in the central ministries, more than 4,000 were concerned in one way or another with the care of the imperial house. The Imperial Household Ministry, for example, had an official staff of 1,296, whereas the Treasury had 305 and Military Affairs only 198.

Local government was handled by sixty-odd provinces, which were further subdivided into districts and villages. In pre-Nara times, these outlying areas had been governed in Yamato fashion by regional clans, but under the new system, provincial governors were sent out from the capital—leaving local aristocrats to occupy the lesser position of district magistrate. This substantially increased the power of the court.

In other respects, Japanese court government was unlike that of China. There were no eunuchs. There was little tension between the emperor and the bureaucracy—the main struggles were between clans. The Tang movement from aristocracy towards meritocracy was also absent in Japan. Apart from clerks and monastics, only aristocrats were educated, and only they were appointed to important official posts. Family counted for more than grades. A feeble attempt to establish an examination elite on the Chinese model failed completely.

Even during the Nara period the elaborate apparatus of Chinese government was too much. In the words of a Chinese proverb, it was like using an axe to carve a chicken. In the early Heian period the actual functions of government were taken over by three new offices outside the Chinese system:

1. **Audit officers**. A newly appointed provincial governor had to report on the accounts of his predecessor. Agreement was rare, so from the end of the Nara period audit officers were sent to examine the books. By early Heian times these auditors had come to superintend the collection of taxes and most other capital-province relationships. They tried to halt the erosion of tax revenues. But as the quota and estate systems developed, this office had less and less to do.

2. **Bureau of archivists**. This bureau was established in 810 to record and preserve imperial decrees. Eventually it took over the executive function at the Heian court, drafting imperial decrees and attending to all aspects of the emperor's life.

3. **Police commissioners**. Established in the second decade of the ninth century to enforce laws and prosecute criminals, the commissioners eventually became responsible for all law and order in the capital. They ab-

sorbed military functions as well as those of the Ministry of Justice and the Bureau of Impeachment.

Over the course of the Heian period, control of the court also shifted, though the emperor, with the power of appointments, remained the key figure.

1. Until the mid–ninth century, some emperors actually ruled or, more often, shared power with nobles of other leading clans.

2. From 856 the northern branch of the Fujiwara clan became preeminent, and from 986 to 1086 its stranglehold on the court was absolute. The private offices of the Fujiwara house were as powerful as those of the central government, and the Fujiwara family monopolized all key government posts. They controlled the court by marrying their daughters to the emperor, forcing the emperor to retire after a son was born, and then ruling as regents in place of the new infant emperor. At times they even ruled as regents for adult emperors. Fujiwara Michinaga's words were no empty boast when he said, "As for this world, I think it is mine, nor is there a flaw in the full moon." (See Document, "Aristocratic Taste at the Fujiwara Court: Sei Shōnagon Records Her Likes and Dislikes.")

3. Fujiwara rule gave way, during the second half of the eleventh century, to rule by retired emperors. The imperial family and lesser noble houses had long resented Fujiwara domination. Disputes within the Fujiwara house itself enabled Emperor Shirakawa to regain control of the government. He reigned from 1072 to 1086 and then, abdicating at the age of thirty-three, ruled for forty-three years as retired emperor. After his death another retired emperor continued in the same pattern until 1156. Shirakawa set up offices in his quarters not unlike the private offices of the Fujiwara family. He appointed talented non-Fujiwara nobles to government posts and sought to reduce the number of tax-free estates by confiscating those of the Fujiwara. He failed in this and instead garnered huge estates for the imperial family. He also developed strong ties to regional military leaders and great temples. His sense of his own power was reflected in his words—more a boast than a lament: "The only things that do not submit to my will are the waters of the Kamo River, the roll of the dice, and the mountain-monks [of the Tendai temple on Mount Hiei to the northeast of Kyoto]." But Shirakawa's powers were exercised in a capital city that was increasingly isolated from the changes in outlying regions, and even the city itself was plagued by fires, banditry, and a sense of impending catastrophe.

Land and Taxes

The last embassy to China was in 839. By that time the frenetic borrowing of Chinese culture had slowed. The Japanese had taken in all they needed—or, perhaps, all they could handle—and were sufficiently self-confident to use Chinese ideas in innovative and flexible ways. The 350 years that followed until the end of the twelfth century were a time of assimilation and evolutionary change. Nowhere was this more evident than in the tax system.

In Nara and early Heian Japan, the economy was agricultural. The problem was to find labor to work the extensive landholdings of the government, imperial family, nobles, and temples. The solution—using the inappropriately named equal field system of China—was to distribute land to all able-bodied persons and collect from them three taxes: a light tax of grain, a light tax of cloth or other local products, and a heavy tax of labor service. But to tax persons meant knowing how many there were and where they were, and this necessitated elaborate population and land registers. Even in China, despite its sophisticated bureaucracy, the system broke down. In Japan, the marvel is that it could be carried out at all. Old registers and recent aerial photographs suggest that for a time it was, at least in western Japan. Its implementation speaks of the immense energy and ability of the early Japanese, who so quickly absorbed Chinese administrative techniques.

Whenever changes in a society are legislated or imposed from above, the results tend to be uniform. But when changes occur willy-nilly within a society, the results are usually messy and difficult to comprehend. The evolution of taxation in Heian Japan was of the second type.

One big change was from the equal field system to one of tax quotas payable in grain. Unable to maintain the elaborate records needed for the equal field system, court officials simply gave each governor a quota of taxes to collect from his province, and each governor, in turn, gave quotas to the district magistrates. Governors and magistrates, when they could, collected more than their quotas and pocketed the difference for themselves. By this means court nobles appointed as governors restored their family fortunes, while district magistrates, and the local notables and military families associated with them, transformed themselves into a new local ruling class.

A second change affecting about half the land in late Heian Japan was the conversion of tax-paying lands to tax-free estates. Court nobles and powerful temples did not like to pay taxes, so they used their influence at court to obtain immunities—exemptions from taxation for their lands. From the ninth century small landholders often commended their land to such nobles, figuring they would be better off as serfs

Chronology

Who Was in Charge at the Nara and Heian Courts?

710–856	Emperors or combinations of nobles
856–1086	Fujiwara nobles
1086–1160	Retired emperors
1160–1180	Military house of Taira

on tax-free estates than as free farmers subject to taxation. The pattern of such commendations was random, resulting in estates composed of scattered parcels of land, unlike the unified estates of Europe. The noble owners of estates appointed stewards from among local notables to manage the land. The stewards took a small slice of the cultivators' surplus for themselves, and forwarded the rest to the noble or priestly owner in Kyoto. Since the stewards were from the same stratum of local society as the district magistrates, they shared an interest in upholding the local order.

Rise of the Samurai

During the Nara period, Japan experimented with a Chinese military system based on conscription. One-third of all able-bodied men between the ages of twenty-one and sixty were taken. Conscript armies, however, proved inefficient, so in 792 the court abolished conscription and began a new system relying on local mounted warriors. Some were stationed in the capital and some in the provinces. They were official troops whose taxes were remitted in exchange for military service. The Japanese verb "to serve" is *samurau*, so those who served became **samurai**—the noun form of the verb. Then, in the mid–Heian period, the officially recruited local warriors were replaced by nonofficial private bands of local warriors. They constituted the military of Japan for the next half millennium or so, until the foot-soldier revolution of the fifteenth and sixteenth centuries.

Being a samurai was expensive. Horses, armor, and weapons were costly, and their use required long training. The primary weapon was the bow and arrow, used from the saddle. Most samurai were from well-to-do local families—district magistrates, notables, or the military families associated with them. Their initial function was to preserve local order and, possibly, to help with tax collection. But from early on they contributed at times to disorder. From the second half of the ninth century there are accounts of district

In the Heiji War of 1159–1160, regional samurai bands became involved in Kyoto court politics. This is a scroll painting of the burning of the Sanjō Palace. Handscroll; ink and colors on paper. © *Courtesy of Museum of Fine Arts, Boston.*

magistrates leading local forces against provincial governors, doubtless in connection with tax disputes.

From the early tenth century regional military coalitions or confederations began to form. They first broke into history in 935–940, when a regional military leader, a descendant of an emperor, became involved in a tax dispute. He captured several provinces, called himself the new emperor, and appointed a government of civil and military officials. The Kyoto court responded by recruiting another military band as its champion. The rebellion was quelled and the rebel leader died in battle. That the Kyoto court could summon a military band points up the connections that enabled it to manipulate local military leaders and maintain its political control of Japan.

Other regional wars followed. Many were fought in eastern Japan—the "wild east" of those days. The east was more militarized because it was the headquarters for the periodic campaigns against the tribal peoples to the north. By the middle of the twelfth century there were regional military bands in every part of Japan.

In 1156 the rising countryside military forces intruded at the Heian court. The death of the ruling retired emperor precipitated a struggle for power between another retired emperor and the reigning emperor. Each called on a Fujiwara and a local military force for backing. The force led by Taira Kiyomori defeated the one led by a Minamoto, though it was challenged again in the Heiji War of 1159–1160. Taira Kiyomori had come to Kyoto to uphold an emperor, but finding himself in charge, he stayed to rule. His pattern of rule was not unlike that of the earlier Fujiwara: He married his daughter to the new emperor and, when a son was born, he forced the emperor to retire and ruled as the maternal grandfather. Otherwise, there were few changes: Court nobles kept their Chinese court offices. The reigning emperor, who had been supported by Kiyomori, retired and exercised control over the offices of the retired emperor and the estates of the imperial family. The head of the Fujiwara family kept the now meaningless post of regent. In short, the Taira ruled as a new stratum atop the many power centers of the old court.

Aristocratic Culture and Buddhism

If the parts of a culture could be put on a scale and weighed like sugar or flour, we would conclude that the culture of Nara and early Heian Japan was overwhelmingly one of Shintō religious practices and village folkways, an extension of the culture of the late Yamato period. The tiny aristocracy, about one-tenth of 1 percent of Japan's population, was encapsulated in the routines of court life, as were Buddhist monks in the rounds of their monastic life. Most of the court culture had only recently been imported from China. There had not been time for commoners to ape their betters or for the powerful force of indigenous culture to reshape that of the elite.

The resulting cultural gap helps to explain why the aristocrats, insofar as we can tell from literature, found commoners to be odd, incomprehensible, and, indeed, hardly human. The writings of courtiers reflect little sympathy for the suffering and hardships of the people—except in Chinese-style poetry, where such feelings were expected. When the fictional Prince Genji stoops in the novel *The Tale of Genji* to an affair with an impoverished woman, she is inevitably a princess. Sei Shōnagon, who wrote the *Pillow Book*, was not atypical as a writer: She was offended by the vulgarity of mendicant nuns; laughed at an illiterate old man whose house had burned down; and found lacking in charm the eating habits of carpenters, who wolfed down their food a bowl at a time.

Heian high culture resembled a hothouse plant. It was protected by the political influence of the court. It was nourished by the flow of tax revenues and income from estates. Under these conditions, the aristocrats of the never-never land of Prince Genji indulged in a unique way of life and created canons of elegance and taste that are striking even today. The speed with which Tang culture was assimilated and reworked was amazing. A few centuries after Mediterranean culture had been introduced into northwestern Europe, there appeared nothing even remotely comparable to *The Tale of Genji* or the *Pillow Book*.

Chinese Tradition in Japan

Education at the Nara and Heian courts was largely a matter of reading Chinese books and acquiring the skills needed to compose poetry and prose in Chinese. These were daunting tasks, not only because there was no prior tradition of scholarship in Japan but also because the two languages were so dissimilar. To master written Chinese and use it for everyday written communications was as great a challenge to the Nara Japanese as it would have been to any European of the same century, but the chal-

lenge was met. From the Nara period until the nineteenth century, most philosophical and legal writings, as well as most of the histories, essays, and religious texts in Japan, were written in Chinese. From a Chinese perspective the writings may leave something to be desired. It would be astonishing if this were not the case, for the soul of language is the music of the spoken tongue. But the Japanese writers were competent, and the feelings they expressed were authentic—when not copybook exercises in the style of a Chinese master. In 883, when Sugawara Michizane wrote a poem on the death of his son, he naturally wrote it in Chinese. The poem began

Since Amaro died I cannot sleep at night;
if I do, I meet him in dreams and tears come coursing
  down.
Last summer he was over three feet tall;
this year he would have been seven years old.
He was diligent and wanted to know how to be a good son,
read his books and recited by heart the "Poem on the
  Capital."

The capital was Chang'an; the poem was one "used in Japan as a text for little boys learning to read Chinese."[2]

Japanese writings in Chinese and original Chinese works, too, shaped the Japanese cultural tradition. The late Tang poet Bo Zhuyi was widely read and appreciated, as were Du Fu and Li Bo. Despite the many differences between the two societies, Chinese history became the mirror in which Japan saw itself, its heroes and villains became the stock figures of the Japanese historical consciousness. Buddhist stories and the books of Confucianism were also consulted over the centuries for their wisdom and philosophy. The parallel might be the acceptance of such "foreign books" as the Bible and works of Plato and Aristotle in medieval and Renaissance England.

Birth of Japanese Literature

Stimulated by Chinese models, the Japanese began to compose poetry in their native tongue. The first major anthology was the *Collection of Ten Thousand Leaves* (*Man'yōshū*), compiled about 760. It contained 4,516 poems. The sentiments in the poems are fresh, sometimes simple and straightforward, but often sophisticated. They reveal a deep sensitivity to nature and strong human relationships

---

[2] From *The Country of Eight Islands*, by Hiroaki Sato and Burton Watson. Copyright © 1981 by Hiroaki Sato and Burton Watson. Used by permission of Doubleday, a division of Random House, Inc.

Aristocratic Taste at the Fujiwara Court: Sei Shōnagon Records Her Likes and Dislikes

Document

Here are some passages from the *Pillow Book* of Sei Shōnagon, one of the masterpieces of Heian Japan.

◆ In what sense can a literary work such as this also be considered a historical document? What kind of information does it provide about court life?

ELEGANT THINGS

A white coat worn over a violet waistcoat.
Duck eggs.
Shaved ice mixed with liana syrup and put in a new silver bowl.
A rosary of rock crystal.
Snow on wistaria or plum blossoms.
A pretty child eating strawberries.

FEATURES THAT I PARTICULARLY LIKE

Someone has torn up a letter and thrown it away. Picking up the pieces, one finds that many of them can be fitted together.

A person in whose company one feels awkward asks one to supply the opening or closing line of a poem. If one happens to recall it, one is very pleased. Yet often on such occasions one completely forgets something that one would normally know.

Entering the Empress's room and finding that ladies-in-waiting are crowded round her in a tight group, I go next to a pillar which is some distance from where she is sitting. What a delight it is when Her Majesty summons me to her side so that all the others have to make way!

HATEFUL THINGS

A lover who is leaving at dawn announces that he has to find his fan and his paper. "I know I put them somewhere last night," he says. Since it is pitch dark, he gropes about the room, bumping into the furniture and muttering, "Strange! Where on earth can they be?" Finally he discovers the objects. He thrusts the paper into the breast of his robe with a great rustling sound; then he snaps open his fan and busily fans away with it. Only now is he ready to take his leave. What charmless behavior! "Hateful" is an understatement.

A good lover will behave as elegantly at dawn as at any other time. He drags himself out of bed with a look of dismay on his face. The lady urges him on: "Come, my friend, it's getting light. You don't want anyone to find you here." He gives a deep sigh, as if to say that the night has not been nearly long enough and that it is agony to leave. Once up, he does not instantly pull on his trousers. Instead he comes close to the lady and whispers whatever was left unsaid during the night. Even when he is dressed, he still lingers, vaguely pretending to be fastening his sash.

Presently he raises the lattice, and the two lovers stand together by the side door while he tells her how he dreads the coming day, which will keep them apart; then he slips away. The lady watches him go, and this moment of parting will remain among her most charming memories.

IN SPRING IT IS THE DAWN

In spring it is the dawn that is most beautiful. As the light creeps over the hills, their outlines are dyed a faint red and wisps of purplish cloud trail over them.

In summer the nights. Not only when the moon shines, but on dark nights too, as the fireflies flit to and fro, and even when it rains, how beautiful it is!

In autumn the evenings, when the glittering sun sinks close to the edge of the hills and the crows fly back to their nests in threes and fours and twos; more charming still is a file of wild geese, like specks in the distant sky. When the sun has set, one's heart is moved by the sound of the wind and the hum of the insects.

In winter the early mornings. It is beautiful indeed when snow has fallen during the night, but splendid too when the ground is white with frost; or even when there is no snow or frost, but it is simply very cold and the attendants hurry from room to room stirring up the fires and bringing charcoal, how well this fits the season's mood! But as noon approaches and the cold wears off, no one bothers to keep the braziers alight, and soon nothing remains but piles of white ashes.

THINGS THAT HAVE LOST THEIR POWER

A large tree that has been blown down in a gale and lies on its side with its roots in the air.

The retreating figure of a sumo wrestler who has been defeated in a match.

A woman, who is angry with her husband about some trifling matter, leaves home and goes somewhere to hide. She is certain that he will rush about looking for her; but he does nothing of the kind and shows the most infuriating indifference. Since she cannot stay away for ever, she swallows her pride and returns.

An Album Leaf from the Ishiyama-gire. A part of a collection from the works of 36 poets compiled in the early twelfth century. The poem is by Ki no Tsurayuki (868?–945?), who in the preface to another anthology wrote: "The poetry of Japan has its roots in the human heart and flourishes in the countless leaves of words. . . . Hearing the warbler sing among the blossoms and the frog in his fresh waters—is there any living being not given to song? It is poetry which, without exertion, moves heaven and earth, stirs the feelings of gods and spirits invisible to the eye, softens the relations between men and women, calms the hearts of fierce warriors." The calligraphy is by Fujiwara no Sadanobu (1088–1154). The poem is written on layered rice paper with gold and silver and foliage designs. Even to the untutored eye, the effect is elegant. *Courtesy of The Freer Gallery of Art, Smithsonian Institution, Washington, D.C.*

script that had developed during the ninth century. A second major anthology was the *Collection of Ancient and Modern Times*, compiled in 905. It was written entirely in *kana*.

The invention of *kana* opened the gate to the most brilliant developments of the Heian period. Most of the new works and certainly the greatest were by women, as most men were busy writing Chinese. One genre of writing was the diary or travel diary. An outstanding example was the *Izumi Shikibu Diary*, in which Izumi Shikibu reveals her tempestuous loves through a record of poetic exchanges.

The greatest works of the period were by Sei Shōnagon and Murasaki Shikibu. Both were daughters of provincial officials serving at the Heian court. The *Pillow Book* of Sei Shōnagon contains sharp, satirical, amusing essays and literary jottings that reveal the demanding aristocratic taste of the early-eleventh-century Heian court, at which, as Sir George Sansom put it, "religion became an art and art a religion."[3]

The Tale of Genji, written by Murasaki Shikibu about 1010, was the world's first novel. Emerging out of a short tradition of lesser works in which prose was a setting for poetry, *Genji* is a work of sensitivity, originality, and acute psychological delineation of character, for which there was no Chinese model. It tells of the life, loves, and sorrows of Prince Genji, the son of an imperial concubine, and, after his death, of his son Kaoru. The novel spans three quarters of a century and is quasi-historical in nature, although the court society it describes is more emperor-centered than was the Fujiwara age in which Murasaki lived. The book may be seen as having had a "definite and serious purpose." In one passage Genji twits a court lady whom he finds reading an extravagant romance. She is "hardly able to lift her eyes from the book in front of her." But then Genji relents and says,

> I think far better of this art than I have led you to suppose. Even its practical value is immense. Without it what should we know of how people lived in the past, from the Age of the Gods down to the present day? For history books such as the Chronicles of Japan *show us only one small corner of life; whereas these diaries and romances, which I see piled around you, contain, I am sure, the most minute information about all sorts of people's private affairs.*[4]

between husband and wife, parents and children. They also display a love for the land of Japan and links to a Shintō past.

An early obstacle to the development of Japanese poetry was the difficulty of transcribing Japanese sounds. In the *Ten Thousand Leaves*, Chinese characters were used as phonetic symbols, but there was no standardization, and the transcription soon became unintelligible. In 951, when an empress wished to read it, a committee of poets deciphered the work and put it into *kana*, the new syllabic

---

[3] G. Sansom, *Japan, A Short Cultural History* (New York: Appleton-Century-Crofts, 1962), p. 239.

[4] R. Tsunoda, W. T. deBary, and D. Keene, eds., *Sources of the Japanese Tradition* (New York: Columbia University Press, 1958), p. 181.

Development of Japanese Writing

Overview

No two languages could be more different than Chinese and Japanese. Chinese is monosyllabic, uninflected, and tonal. Japanese is polysyllabic, highly inflected, and atonal. To adopt Chinese writing for use in Japanese was thus no easy task. What the Japanese did at first—when they were not simply learning to write in Chinese—was to use certain Chinese ideographs as a phonetic script. For example, in the *Man'yōshû*, the eighth-century poetic anthology, *shira-nami* (white wave) was written with 之 for shi, 良 for ra, 奈 for na, and 美 for mi. Over several centuries, these phonetic ideographs evolved into a unique Japanese phonetic script:

ORIGINAL CHINESE IDEOGRAPH	SIMPLIFIED IDEOGRAPH	PHONETIC SCRIPT (KANA)
之	之	し
良	良	ら
奈	奈	な
美	美	み

It is apparent in the above examples how the original ideograph was first simplified according to the rules of calligraphy and was then further simplified into a phonetic script known as *kana*. In modern Japanese, Chinese ideographs are used for nouns, verb stems, and adjectives, and the phonetic script is used for inflections and particles.

学生 は 図書館 へ 行きました Student/as for/library/to/went. (The student went to the library.)

In the above sentence, the Chinese ideographs are the forms with many strokes, and the phonetic script is shown in the simpler, cursive form.

Nara and Heian Buddhism

Buddhism came to Japan from China. The Six Sects of the Nara period each represented a separate doctrinal position within Mahayana Buddhism. Their monks trained as religious specialists in monastic communities set apart from the larger society. They studied, read sutras, copied texts, meditated, and participated in rituals. The typical monastery was a self-contained community with a Golden Hall for worship, a pagoda that housed a relic or sutra, a belfry that rang the hours of the monastic regimen, a lecture hall, a refectory, and dormitories with monks' cells.

As in China, monasteries and temples were involved with the state. In 741 the court established temples in every province to protect the state by reading sutras. Tax revenues were assigned for their support. Monks prayed for the health of the emperor and for rain in time of drought. The Temple of the Healing Buddha (Yakushiji) was built by an emperor when his consort fell ill. In China, to protect tax revenues and the family, laws limited the number of monks and nuns. In Nara Japan, where Buddhism spread only slowly outside the capital area, the same laws took on a prescriptive force: The figure that had been a limit in China became a goal in Japan. Thus the involvement of the state was patterned on that of China, but its role was more supportive.

Japan was also less culturally developed than China. Japanese came to Buddhism not from the philosophical perspectives of Confucianism or Daoism, but from the magic and mystery of Shintō. Its appeal, consequently, lay in its colorful and elaborate rituals, the beauty of its art, and the gods, demons, and angels of the Mahayana pantheon. The mastery of the philosophy took longer.

Another difference was in cultural identity. China's national self-consciousness had formed centuries earlier. Buddhism entered as a foreign cultural compound—China's only important borrowing from abroad prior to the nineteenth

The Hōryūji Temple. Built by Prince Shōtoku in 607, it contains the oldest wooden buildings in the world. They are the best surviving examples of contemporary Chinese Buddhist architecture.

century. Though Buddhism became Sinicized and accepted, its Indian origins were understood, and the sense of it as somehow "alien" contributed to its occasional persecutions during the ninth century. In contrast, Japan's national self-awareness took shape during the Nara and early Heian periods just as the entire complex of Tang civilization—including Buddhism—entered. Buddhism was no more foreign to the Japanese than all the rest of their high culture. Consequently, there was no particular bias against it, no persecutions, and it retained its vitality longer. Not until the seventeenth or eighteenth century did a few Japanese scholars become so Confucian as to be anti-Buddhist.

During the Heian era the two great new Buddhist sects were Tendai and Shingon. The monk Saichō (767–822) had founded a temple on Mount Hiei to the northwest of Kyoto in 785, nine years before the Heian period began. He went to China as a student monk in 804 and returned the following year with the teachings of the Tendai sect (*Tiantai* in

Chinese). He preached in Japan the doctrine that salvation was not solely for monastic specialists, but also for all persons who led lives of contemplation and moral purity. He instituted strict rules and a twelve-year training curriculum for novice monks at his mountain monastery. Over the next few centuries the sect grew until thousands of temples had been built on Mount Hiei. It remained a center of Japanese Buddhism until it was destroyed in the wars of the sixteenth century. Many later Japanese sects emerged from within the Tendai fold, stressing one or another doctrine of its syncretic teachings.

The Shingon sect was begun by Kûkai (774–835), who, as a youth, studied Confucianism, Taoism, and Buddhism at the court university. Deciding that Buddhism was superior, he became a monk at the age of eighteen, and in 804 he went to China with Saichō. He returned two years later bearing the Shingon doctrines and founded a monastery on Mount Kōya to the south of the Nara plain and far from the new capital. Kûkai was an extraordinary figure: a bridge builder, poet, artist, and one of three great calligraphers of the period. He is sometimes credited with inventing the *kana* syllabary and with introducing tea into Japan. Shingon doctrines center on an eternal and cosmic Buddha, of whom all other Buddhas are manifestations. *Shingon* means "true word" or "mantra," a verbal formula with mystical powers. It is sometimes called esoteric Buddhism because it had secret teachings that were passed from master to disciple. In China, Shingon died out as a sect in the persecutions of the mid–ninth century, but it was tremendously successful in Japan. Its doctrines even spread to the Tendai center on Mount Hiei. Part of the appeal was its air of mystery and its complex rituals involving signs, the manipulation of religious objects, and mandalas—maps of the cosmic Buddhist universe.

During the later Heian period, Buddhism began to be assimilated. At the village level, the folk religion of Shintō took in Buddhist elements. In the high culture of the capital, Shintō was almost entirely absorbed by Buddhism. Shintō deities came to be seen as the local manifestations of universal Buddhas. The "Great Sun Buddha" of the Shingon sect, for example, was easily identified with the sun goddess. Often, great Buddhist temples had smaller Shintō shrines on their grounds. The Buddha watched over Japan and the cosmos; the shrine deity guarded the temple itself. Not until the mid–nineteenth century was Shintō disentangled from Buddhism, and then for political ends.

Japan's Early Feudal Age

The late twelfth century marked another turning point in Japanese history. It began the shift towards rule by military houses. It saw the formation of the **bakufu** (tent government), a completely non-Chinese type of government. It saw the emergence of the **shōgun** as the *de facto* ruler of Japan—although in theory he remained a military official of the emperor. It initiated new cultural forms and changes in family and social organization.

The Kamakura Era

Taira Kiyomori's seizure of Kyoto in 1160 fell far short of being a national military hegemony, for other bands still flourished

Minamoto Yoritomo. Founder of the Kamakura Shogunate. He is depicted here in court robes as a statesman and official though he was, above all, a warrior-general.

elsewhere in Japan. After Kiyomori's victory, the Taira embraced the elegant lifestyle of the Kyoto court while ties to their base area along the Inland Sea weakened. They assumed that their tutelage over the court would be as enduring as had been that of the Fujiwara. In the meantime, the Minamoto were rebuilding their strength in eastern Japan. In 1180 Minamoto Yoritomo (1147–1199) responded to a call to arms by a disaffected prince, seized control of eastern Japan (the rich Kantō plain), and began the war that ended in 1185 with the downfall of the Taira.

Yoritomo's victory was national, for his armies had ranged over most of Japan. Afterwards, warriors from every area vied to become his vassals. Wary of the blandishments of Kyoto that had weakened the Taira, Yoritomo set up his headquarters at Kamakura, thirty miles south of present-day Tokyo, at the edge of his base of power in eastern Japan (see Map 9–4). He called his government the *bakufu* in contrast to the civil government in Kyoto. The offices he established were few and practical, and staffed by his vassals: one to deal with his samurai retainers, one to administer and execute his policies, and one to hear legal suits. The decisions of these offices, built up into a body of customary law, were codified in 1232 as the Jōei Code. Yoritomo also appointed military governors in each province and military stewards on the former estates of the Taira and others who had fought against him. These appointments carried the right to some income from the land. The remainder of the income, as earlier, went to Kyoto as taxes or as revenues to the owners of the estates.

When Yoritomo died in 1199, his widow and her Hōjō kinsmen moved to usurp the power of the Minamoto house. The widow, having taken holy orders after her husband's death, was known as the Nun Shōgun. One of her sons was pushed aside. The other became shōgun but was murdered in 1219. After that, the Hōjō ruled as regents for a puppet shōgun, just as the Fujiwara had been regents for figurehead emperors. The Kyoto court, trying to use the Hōjō usurpation, led an armed uprising against Kamakura in 1221, but it was quickly suppressed. New military stewards were then placed on the lands of those who had joined in the uprising.

Map Exploration

To explore this map further, go to http://www.prenhall.com/craig_maps

Map 9–4. Medieval Japan and the Mongol Invasions. The *bakufu* at Kamakura and the court at Kyoto were the two centers of power during the Kamakura period, 1185–1333. After 1336 the Ashikaga *bakufu* was established in Kyoto, absorbing the powers of the court.

Any society based on personal bonds faces the problem of how to transfer loyalty from one generation to another. That the Kamakura vassals fought for the Hōjō in 1221, despite the Hōjō usurpation of Minamoto rule, suggests that their loyalty had become institutional. They were loyal to the *bakufu*, which guaranteed their income from land. Their personal loyalty to the Minamoto had ended with the death of Yoritomo.

The Mongols   In 1266 Kublai Khan (see Chapter 8) sent envoys demanding that Japan submit to his rule. He had subjugated Korea in 1258, and his army looked outward

Japanese Scroll Painting. Mongol invaders battling with an intrepid samurai horseman. Note the bomb bursting in air at the upper right of this late 13th century Japanese scroll painting. © *Museum of Imperial Collections—Sanno-maru Shozo Kan. Courtesy of the International Society for Educational Information, Inc.*

across the Tsushima Straits. The Kyoto court was terrified, but the Hōjō at Kamakura refused to submit. The first Mongol invasion fleet arrived in 1274 with 30,000 troops but withdrew after initial victories. The Mongols again sent envoys; this time, they were beheaded. A second invasion of 140,000 troops, an amphibious force on a scale unprecedented in world history, arrived in 1281, two years after Kublai had completed his conquest of southern China. With gunpowder bombs and phalanxes of archers protected by a forward wall of soldiers carrying overlapping shields, the Mongol forces were formidable.

The Japanese tactics of fierce individual combat were not appropriate to their foe. But a wall of stone had been erected along the curved shoreline of Hakata Bay in northwestern Kyushu, and the Mongols were held off for two months until again **kamikaze**, or "divine winds," sank a portion of their fleet and forced the rest to withdraw. Preparations for a third expedition ended with Kublai's death in 1294.

The burden of repelling the Mongols fell on Kamakura's vassals in Kyushu. Non-Kamakura warriors of Kyushu were also mobilized to fight under the command of military governors. But as no land was taken, unlike in 1221, there were few rewards for those who had fought, and dissatisfaction was rife. Even temples and shrines demanded rewards, claiming that their prayers had brought about the divine winds.

The Question of Feudalism

Scholars often contend that Yoritomo's rule marks the start of feudalism in Japan. Feudalism may be defined in terms of three criteria: lord-vassal relationships, fiefs given in return for military service, and a warrior ethic. Do these apply to Kamakura Japan?

Certainly, the mounted warriors who made up the armies of Yoritomo were predominantly his vassals, not his kin. The Minamoto and Taira houses had originally been extended families, much like the Fujiwara or the earlier Yamato nobility. Yoritomo's brothers were among his generals. But after he came to power, he favored his vassals over his kin, and lateral blood ties gave way to vertical and political lord-vassal bonds. As for fiefs, the answer is ambiguous. Kamakura vassals received rights to income from land in exchange for military service, but the income was usually a slice of the surplus from the estates of Kyoto nonmilitary aristocrats. Fiefs, as such, did not appear until the late fifteenth century.

There is no ambiguity, however, regarding the warrior ethic, which had been developing among regional military bands for several centuries before 1185. The samurai prized martial qualities such as bravery, cunning, physical strength, and endurance. They gave their swords names. Their sports were hunting, hawking, and archery—loosing their arrows at the target while riding at full tilt. If military tales of the period are to be believed, their combat was often individual, and before engaging in battle warriors would call out their pedigrees. That is to say, warriors thought of themselves as a military aristocracy that practiced the "way of the bow and arrow," the "way of the bow and horse," the "way of the warriors," and so on. In the Buddhism-tinged *Tale of Heike*, a military romance recounting the struggle between the Taira and the Minamoto, a Taira general asks a vassal from eastern Japan,

Chronology

Government by Military Houses

1160–1180	Taira rule in Kyoto
1185–1333	Kamakura bakufu
1185	Founded by Minamoto Yoritomo
1219	Usurped by Hōjō
1221	Armed uprising by Kyoto court
1232	Formation of Jōei Code
1274 and 1281	Invasion by Mongols
1336–1467	Ashikaga bakufu
1392	End of Southern Court
1467	Start of Warring States period

"Sanemori, in the eight eastern provinces are there many men who are as mighty archers as you are?"

"Do you then consider me a mighty archer?" asked Sanemori with a scornful smile. "I can only draw an arrow thirteen handbreadths long. In the eastern provinces there are any number of warriors who can do so. There is one famed archer who never draws a shaft less than fifteen handbreadths long. So mighty is his bow that four or five ordinary men must pull together to bend it. When he shoots, his arrow can easily pierce two or three suits of armor at once. Even a warrior from a small estate has at least five hundred soldiers. They are bold horsemen who never fall, nor do they let their horses stumble on the roughest road. When they fight, they do not care if even their parents or children are killed; they ride on over their bodies and continue the battle.

"The warriors of the western province are quite different. If their parents are killed, they retire from the battle and perform Buddhist rites to console the souls of the dead. Only after the mourning is over will they fight again. If their children are slain, their grief is so deep that they cease fighting altogether. When their rations have given out, they plant rice in the fields and go out to fight only after reaping it. They dislike the heat of summer. They grumble at the severe cold of winter. This is not the way of the soldiers of the eastern provinces."[5]

[5] H. Kitagawa and B. Tsuchida, trans., *The Tale of Heike* (Tokyo: Tokyo University Press, 1975), p. 330.

Japanese Sword. From medieval times, Japanese artisans have made the world's finest swords. They became a staple export to China. Worn only by samurai, they were also an emblem of class status, distinguishing the warriors from commoners. *Philip Gatward © Dorling Kindersley.*

The Taira soldiers, according to the story, "heard his words and trembled."

The Kamakura military band thus pretty well fits our definition of feudalism. Nonetheless, qualifications are in order, as warrior bands were only a part of the whole society. One important qualification is that Kamakura Japan still had two political centers. The *bakufu* had military authority, but the Kyoto court continued the late Heian pattern of civil rule. It appointed civil governors, received tax revenues, and controlled the region about Kyoto. Noble families, retired emperors, and great Buddhist temples—in control of vast estates—also contributed to Kyoto's ongoing power. The court also remained the fount of rank and honors. After his victory in 1185, Yoritomo asked the emperor for the title of "barbarian-quelling generalissimo" (*Sei i tai shōgun*, conventionally shortened to *shōgun*). He was refused, and only after the retired emperor died in 1192 did Yoritomo get the title to match his power. Even then, the award of the title was justified because Yoritomo was a Minamoto offshoot of the imperial line.

The small size of Yoritomo's vassal band is an even more telling argument against viewing Japan as fully feudal at this time. Numbering perhaps 2,000 before 1221 and 3,000 thereafter, most of the band was concentrated in eastern Japan. But if as many as half were distributed about the rest of the country as military governors and stewards, there would have been only 100 in a region the size of Massachusetts—because Japan in 1180 was about fifteen times larger than that state. Given the difficulties of transportation and communications, how could so few have controlled such a large area? The answer is that they did not have to.

The local social order of the late Heian era continued into the Kamakura period. The Kyoto court, great temples, governors, district magistrates, and local notables—including many warriors who were not members of Yoritomo's band—functioned more or less as they had earlier. To influence the local scene, the newly appointed Kamakura vassals had to win the cooperation of the existing local power holders. In short, even if the Kamakura vassals themselves could be called feudal, they were only a thin skim on the surface of a society constructed according to older principles.

The Ashikaga Era

At times, formal political institutions seem rocklike in their stability, and history unfolds within the framework they provide. Then, almost as if a kaleidoscope had been shaken, the old institutions collapse and are swept away. In their place appear new institutions and new patterns of personal relations that, often enough, had begun to take shape within the confines of the old. It is not easy to explain the timing of such upheavals, but they are easy to recognize. One occurred in Japan between 1331 and 1336.

Various tensions had developed within late Kamakura society. The patrimony of a warrior was divided among his children. Over several generations vassals became poorer, often falling into debt. High-ranking vassals of Kamakura were dissatisfied with the Hōjō monopolization of key *bakufu* posts. In the meantime, the ties of vassals to Kamakura were weakening, while the ties to other warriors within their region were growing stronger. New regional bands were ready to emerge. The precipitating event was a revolt in 1331 by an emperor who thought emperors should actually rule. Kamakura sent Ashikaga Takauji (1305–1358), the head of a branch family of the Minamoto line, to put down the revolt. Instead he joined it, giving a clear signal to other regional lords, who threw off Kamakura's control and destroyed the Hōjō -controlled *bakufu*.

What emerged from the dust and confusion of the period from 1331 to 1336 was a new *bakufu* in Kyoto and a variety of semiautonomous regional states in the rest of Japan. Each regional state was governed by a lord, now called a **daimyo**, and a warrior band about the size of the band that had brought Yorimoto to power a century and a half earlier. The *bakufu* offices established by Ashikaga Takauji were simple and functional: a samurai office for police and military matters; an administrative office for financial matters; a documents office for land records; and a judicial board to settle disputes. They were staffed by Takauji's vassals, the most trusted vassals holding the highest posts and often concurrent appointments as military governors in the provinces surrounding Kyoto. The *bakufu* also appointed vassals to watch over its interests in the far north, in eastern Japan, and in Kyushu.

The pattern of rule in the outlying regions was diverse. Some lords held several provinces, some only one. Some had integrated most of the warriors in their areas into their bands. Others had several unassimilated military bands within their territories, forcing them to rely more on the authority of Kyoto. Formally, all regional lords or *daimyo* were the vassals of the shōgun. But the relationship was often nominal. Some regional lords lived on their lands; some lived in Kyoto.

The relationship between the *bakufu* and regional lords fluctuated from 1336 to 1467. At times, able lords made their regions into virtually independent states. At other times, the Kyoto *bakufu* became stronger. The third shōgun, for example, tightened his grip on the Kyoto court. He even relinquished the military post of shōgun—giving it to his son in 1394—in order to take the highest civil post of grand minister of state. He improved relations with the great Buddhist temples and Shintō shrines and established ties with Ming China. Most significant were his military campaigns, which dented the autonomy of regional lords outside of the inner Kyoto circle.

But even the third shōgun had to rely on his *daimyo* and their armies. To strengthen them for campaigns, he gave them the authority to levy taxes; unify in their own hands all judicial, administrative, and military matters in their regions; and take on unaffiliated warriors as their direct vassals. But in doing so, he left problems for his successors. As ties of personal loyalty wore thin, new local warrior bands began to form in the interstices of the Ashikaga regional states.

Women in Warrior Society

The Nun Shōgun was one of a long line of important women in Japan. Although historians no longer speak of an early matriarchal age, there is no denying that the central figure of Japanese mythology was the sun goddess, who ruled the Plain of High Heaven. In the late Yayoi age, the shaman ruler Pimiko was probably not an exceptional figure. She was followed by empresses during the Yamato and Nara courts, and they in turn by great women writers in the Heian period. Under the Kamakura *bakufu*, there was only one Nun Shōgun, but daughters as well as sons of warrior families often trained in archery and other military arts. Women also occasionally inherited the position of military steward. As long as society was stable, women fared relatively well. But as fighting became more common in the fourteenth century, their position began to decline, and as warfare became endemic in the fifteenth, their status plummeted. The warrior's fief—his reward for serving his lord in battle and the lord's surety for his continuing service—had become all-important. To protect it, multigeniture, in which daughters as well as sons inherited property, gave way to unigeniture, inheritance by the most able son.

Agriculture, Commerce, and Medieval Guilds

Population figures for medieval Japan are rough estimates at best, but recent scholarship suggests 6 million for the year 1200 and 15 million for 1600. Much of the increase occurred during the late Kamakura and Ashikaga periods, when the country was fairly peaceful. The increase was brought about by land reclamation and improvements in agricultural technology. Iron-edged tools became available to all. New strains of rice were developed. Irrigation and diking improved. Double cropping began with vegetables planted during the fall and winter in dry fields, which were flooded and planted with rice during the spring and summer.

In the Nara and early Heian periods, the economy was almost exclusively agricultural. Japan had no money, no commerce, and no cities—apart from Nara, which developed into a temple town living on assigned revenues, and Kyoto, where taxes were consumed. Following the example of China, the government had established a mint, but little money actually circulated. Taxes were paid in labor or grain. Commerce consisted of barter transactions, with silk or grain as the medium of exchange. Artisans produced for the noble households or temples to which they were attached. Peasants were economically self-sufficient.

From the late Heian period, partly as a side effect of fixed tax quotas, more of the growing agricultural surplus stayed in local hands, though not in the hands of the cultivators. This trend accelerated during the Kamakura and Ashikaga periods, as warriors took ever larger slices of the income of estates. As this occurred, artisans detached themselves from noble households and began to produce for a wider market. Military equipment was an early staple of commerce, but gradually *sake*, lumber, paper, vegetable oils, salt, and products of the sea also became commercialized. A demand for copper coins appeared, and since they were no longer minted in Japan, huge quantities were imported from China.

During the Kamakura period, independent merchants appeared to handle the products of artisans. Some trade networks spread over all Japan. More often, artisan and merchant guilds, not unlike those of medieval Europe, paid a fee to obtain monopoly rights in a given area. Kyoto guilds paid fees to powerful nobles or temples, and later to the Ashikaga *bakufu*. In outlying areas guild privileges were obtained from the regional lords. From the Kamakura period onward, markets were held periodically in many parts of Japan, by a river or at a crossroads. Some place-names in Japan today reveal such an origin. Yokkaichi, today an industrial city, means "fourth-day market." It began as a place where markets were held on the fourth, fourteenth, and twenty-fourth days of each month. From the fifteenth century such markets were held with increasing frequency until, eventually, permanent towns were established.

Buddhism and Medieval Culture

The Nara and Heian periods are often referred to as Japan's classical age. The period that followed—say, from 1200 to 1600—is often called medieval. It was medieval in the root sense of the word in that it lay between the other two major spans of premodern Japanese history. It also shared some characteristics that we label medieval in Europe and China. However, there is one important difference. Medieval Japanese culture was a direct outgrowth of the classical age; one can even say that during the early Kamakura there was an overlap. In contrast, Europe was torn by barbarian invasions, and a millennium separated the classical culture of Rome from high medieval culture. Even to have a Charlemagne, Europe had to wait for almost half a millennium. In China, too, the era of political disunity and barbarian invasions lasted 400 years, and it was during these years that its medieval Buddhist culture blossomed.

The results of the historical continuity in Japan are visible in every branch of its culture. The earlier poetic tradition continued with great vigor. In 1205 the compilation of the *New Collection from Ancient and Modern Times* (*Shinkokinshû*) was ordered by the same emperor who began the 1221 rebellion against Kamakura. The flat *Yamato-e* style of painting that had reached a peak in the *Genji Scrolls* continued into the medieval era with scrolls on historical and religious themes or fairy-tale adventures. Artisanal production continued without a break. The same techniques of lacquerwork with inlaid mother-of-pearl that had been employed, say, to make a cosmetic box for a Heian court lady were now applied to produce saddles for Kamakura warriors. In short, just as Heian estates continued into the Kamakura era, and just as the authority of the court continued, so did Heian culture extend into medieval Japan.

Nonetheless, medieval Japanese culture had some distinctly new characteristics. First, as the leadership of society shifted from court aristocrats to military aristocrats, new forms of literature appeared. The medieval military tales were as different from *The Tale of Genji* as the armor of the mounted warrior was from the no less colorful silken robes of the court nobility. Second, a new wave of culture entered from China. If the Nara and Heian had been shaped by Tang culture, medieval Japan—although not its institutions—was shaped by Song culture. The link is immediately apparent in the ink paintings of medieval Japan. Third, and most important, the medieval centuries were Japan's age of Buddhist faith. A religious revolution occurred during the Kamakura period and deepened during the Ashikaga.

Japanese Pietism: Pure Land and Nichiren Buddhism

Among the doctrines of the Heian Tendai sect was the belief that the true teachings of the historical Buddha had been lost and that salvation could be had only by calling on the name of Amida, the Buddha who ruled over the Western Paradise, or **Pure Land**. During the tenth and eleventh centuries, itinerant preachers began to spread Pure Land doctrines and practices beyond the narrow circles of Kyoto. Kūya (903–972), the "saint of the marketplace," for example, preached not only in Kyoto and throughout the provinces, but also even to the aboriginal Ainu in northernmost Japan.

The doctrine that the world had fallen on evil times and that only faith would suffice was given credence by earthquakes, epidemics, fires, and banditry in the capital, as well as wars throughout the land. The deepening Buddhist coloration of the age can be read in the opening lines of the thirteenth-century *Tale of Heiki*, written just two centuries after *The Tale of Genji* and the *Pillow Book*:

> *The sound of the bell of Jetavana echoes the impermanence of all things. The hue of the flowers of the teak-tree declares that they who flourish must be brought low. Yea, the proud ones are but for a moment, like an evening dream in springtime. The mighty are destroyed at the last, they are but as the dust before the wind.*[6]

Two early Kamakura figures stand out as religious geniuses who experienced the truth of Pure Land Buddhism within themselves. Hōnen (1133–1212) was perhaps the first to say that the invocation of the name of Amida alone was enough for salvation and that only faith, not works or rituals, counted. These claims brought Hōnen into conflict with the older Buddhist establishment and marked the emergence of Pure Land as a separate sect. After Hōnen came Shinran (1173–1262), who taught that even a single invocation in praise of Amida, if done with perfect faith, was sufficient for salvation. But perfect faith was a gift from Amida and could not be obtained by human effort. Shinran

Kūya Invoking Buddha.   The mid-Heian monk Kūya (903–972) preached Pure Land doctrines in Kyoto and throughout Japan. Little Buddhas emerge from his mouth. *PPS/Pacific Press Service.*

taught that pride was an obstacle to purity of heart. One of his most famous sayings is "If even a good man can be reborn in the Pure Land, how much more so a wicked man."[7] Shinran is saying that the wicked man is less inclined to assume that he is the source of his own salvation and therefore more apt to place his complete trust in Amida.

Shinran's emphasis on faith alone led him to break with many of the practices of earlier Buddhism. He ate meat, he married a nun—thereafter the Pure Land sect had a married clergy—and he taught that all occupations were equally "heavenly" if performed with a pure heart. Exiled from Kyoto, he traveled about Japan establishing "True Pure Land" congregations. (When the Jesuits arrived in Japan in the sixteenth century, they called this sect "the devil's Christianity.")

As a result of a line of distinguished teachers after Shinran, its doctrinal simplicity, and its reliance on piety, Pure Land Buddhism became the dominant form of Buddhism in Japan and remains so today. It was also the only sect in medieval Japan—apart from the Tendai sect on Mount Hiei—to develop political and military power. As a religion of faith, it developed a strong church as a protection for the saved while they were still in this world. As peasants became militarized during the fifteenth century, some Pure Land village congregations created self-defense forces. At times they rebelled against feudal lords. In one instance, Pure Land armies ruled the province of Kaga for over a century. These congregations were smashed during the late sixteenth century, and the sect depoliticized.

A second devotional sect was founded by Nichiren (1222–1282), who believed that the Lotus Sutra perfectly embodied the teachings of the Buddha. He instructed his adherents to chant, over and over, "Praise to the Lotus Sutra of the Wondrous Law," usually to the accompaniment of

---

[6] A. L. Sadler, trans., *The Tenfoot Square Hut and Tales of the Heike* (Rutland, VT, and Tokyo: Charles E. Tuttle, 1972), p. 22.

[7] Tsunoda, deBary, and Keene, p. 217.

rapid drumbeats. Like the repetition of "Praise to the Amida Buddha" in the Pure Land sect or comparable verbal formulas in other religions around the world, the chanting optimally induced a state of religious rapture. The goal of an internal spiritual transformation was common to both the devotional and the meditative sects of Buddhism. Nichiren was remarkable for a Buddhist in being both intolerant and nationalistic. He blamed the ills of his age on rival sects and asserted that only his sect could protect Japan. He predicted the Mongol invasions, and his sect claimed credit for the "divine winds" that sank the Mongol fleets. Even his adopted Buddhist name, the Sun Lotus, combined the character for the rising sun of Japan with that of the flower that had become the symbol of Buddhism.

Zen Buddhism

Meditation had long been a part of Japanese monastic practice. Zen teachings and meditation techniques were introduced by monks returning from study in Song China. Eisai (1141–1215) brought back the teachings of the Rinzai sect in 1191 and Dōgen (1200–1253) the Sōtō teachings in 1227. Eisai's sect was patronized by the Hōjō rulers in Kamakura and the Ashikaga in Kyoto. Dōgen established his sect on Japan's western coast, far from centers of political power.

Zen was a religion of paradox. Its monks were learned, yet it stressed a return to ignorance, to the uncluttered "original mind," attained in a flash of intuitive understanding. Zen was punctiliously traditional, the most Chinese of Japanese medieval sects. The authority of the Zen master over his pupil-monks was absolute. Yet Zen was also iconoclastic. Its sages were depicted in paintings as tearing up sutras to make the point that it is religious experience and not words that count. Within a rigidly structured monastic regimen, a vital give-and-take occurred as monks tested their understanding, gained through long hours of meditation, in encounters with their master. Buddhism stressed compassion for all sentient beings, yet in Japan the Zen sect included many samurai whose duty it was to kill the enemies of their lord. Some military leaders encouraged the practice of Zen among their retainers in the hope of reinforcing such a sense of duty; a handful of Hōjō, and Ashikaga rulers even went so far as to practice Zen themselves.

Zen influenced the arts of medieval Japan. (See Document, "The Arts and Zen Buddhism.") The most beautiful gardens were in Zen temples, many designed by Zen masters. The most famous, at Ryōanji, consists of fifteen rocks set in white sand. Others only slightly less austere contain moss, shrubs, trees, ponds, and streams. With these elements and within a small compass, rocks become cliffs, raked sand becomes rivers or the sea, and a little world of nature emerges.

If a garden may be said to possess philosophic stillness, the Zen gardens of Daitokuji and other Kyoto temples have it.

Zen monks, such as Josetsu, Shūbun (ca. 1415), and Sesshū (1420–1506), number among the masters of ink painting in East Asia. One painting by Josetsu shows a man trying to catch a catfish with a gourd. Like the sound of one hand clapping, the impossibility of catching a catfish with a gourd presents as art the kind of logical conundrum used to expound Zen teachings. Sesshū painted in both the broken-ink style, in which splashlike brushstrokes represent an entire mountain landscape, and a more usual calligraphic style. Because the artist's creativity itself was seen as grounded in his experience of meditation, a painting of a waterfall or a crow on a leafless branch in late fall was viewed as no less religious than a painting of the mythic Zen founder Bodhidharma.

Nō Plays

Another vital product of Ashikaga culture is the Nō play, a kind of mystery drama without parallels elsewhere in East Asia. The form has survived to the present day as the world's oldest living dramatic tradition. The play is performed on an almost square, bare wooden stage (usually outdoors) by male actors wearing robes of great beauty and carved, painted masks of enigmatic expressions. Many such masks and robes number among Japan's national treasures. The text is chanted by actors and a chorus to the accompaniment of flute and drums. The language is poetic. The action is slow and highly stylized: Circling about the stage can represent a journey, and a vertical motion of the hand, the reading of a letter. At a critical juncture in most plays, the protagonist is possessed by the spirit of another and performs a dance. (Spirit possession was commonplace in Japanese folk religion and also occurred in *The Tale of Genji*.) Several plays are shown in a single performance; comic skits called "Crazy Words" are usually interspersed between them to break the tension.

Nō plays reveal a medley of themes present in medieval culture. Some pivot on incidents in the struggle between the Taira and the Minamoto. Some are religious: A cormorant fisher is saved from the king of hell for having given lodging to a priest. Some dramatize incidents from *The Tale of Genji* or the Heian court: The famous Heian beauty and poet Ono no Komachi is possessed by the spirit of a lover she has spurned; their conflict is left to be resolved in a Buddhist afterlife. Buddhist ideas of impermanence, of this world as a place of suffering, and of the need to relinquish worldly attachments are found in many plays. Some plays are close to fairy tales: A fisherman takes the feather robe of an angel, but when she begins to sicken and grow wan, he returns the robe and she dances for him a dance that is performed only

The Arts and Zen Buddhism

Zen Buddhism in Japan developed a theory of art that influenced every department of high medieval culture. Put simply, the theory is that intuitive action is better than conscious, purposive action. The best painter is one so skilled that he no longer needs to think of technique but paints as a natural act. Substitute a sword for a brush, and the same theory applies: A warrior who has to stop to consider his next move is at a disadvantage in battle. To this concern with direct, intuitive action is added the Zen distinction between the deluded mind and the "original mind." The latter is also referred to as the "no mind," or the mind in the enlightened state. The highest intuitive action proceeds from such a state of being. This theory was applied, in time, to the performance of the actor, the skill of the potter, archery, flower arrangement, and the tea ceremony. Compare the following two passages, one by Zeami (1363–1443), the author of many Nō plays, and the other by Takuan Sōhō (1573–1645), a famous Zen master of the early Tokugawa era (see Chapter 19).

◆ **Could the same theory be applied to baseball or any other sport? If so, what effect would this have on how they are played?**

1. Sometimes spectators of the Nō say, "The moments of 'no-action' are the most enjoyable." This is an art which the actor keeps secret. Dancing and singing, movements and the different types of miming are all acts performed by the body. Moments of "no-action" occur in between. When we examine why such moments without actions are enjoyable, we find that it is due to the underlying spiritual strength of the actor which unremittingly holds the attention. He does not relax the tension when the dancing or singing come to an end or at intervals between the dialogue and the different types of miming, but maintains an unwavering inner strength. This feeling of inner strength will faintly reveal itself and bring enjoyment. However, it is undesirable for the actor to permit this inner strength to become obvious to the audience. If it is obvious, it becomes an act, and is no longer "no-action." The actions before and after an interval of "no-action" must be linked by entering the state of mindlessness in which one conceals even from oneself one's intent. This, then, is the fac-ulty of moving audiences, by linking all the artistic powers with one mind.

2. Where should a swordsman fix his mind? If he puts his mind on the physical movement of his opponent, it will be seized by the movement; if he places it on the sword of his opponent, it will be arrested by the sword; if he focuses his mind on the thought of striking his opponent, it will be carried away by the very thought; if the mind stays on his own sword, it will be captured by his sword; if he centers it on the thought of not being killed by his opponent, his mind will be overtaken by this very thought; if he keeps his mind firmly on his own or on his opponent's posture, likewise, it will be blocked by them. Thus the mind should not be fixed anywhere.

1. From *Sources of Japanese Tradition*, trans. by William Theodore de Bary. Copyright © 1958 by Columbia University. Reprinted with permission of the publisher.

2. From *The Buddhist Tradition*, by William Theodore de Bary. Copyright © 1969 by William Theodore de Bary. Reprinted by permission of Random House Inc.

in heaven. Some plays are based on stories from China: A traveler dreams an entire lifetime on a magical pillow while waiting for a bowl of millet to cook. Another play reflects the constant Japanese ambivalence towards Chinese culture: Po Chûi, the Tang poet most esteemed in Japan, rows a boat over the seas and comes to the shores of Japan, where he is met by fishermen who turn him back in the name of Japanese poetry. One fisherman speaks:

You in China make your poems and odes out of the Scriptures of India; and we have made our "uta" out of the poems and odes of China. Since then our poetry is a blend of three lands, we have named it Yamato, the great blend, and all our songs "Yamato uta."[8]

[8] A. Waley, trans., *The Nō Plays of Japan* (New York: Grove Press, 1957), p. 252.

At the end, the fisherman is transformed into the Shintō god of Japanese poetry and performs the "Sea Green Dance."

Summary

Korea and Vietnam. The peninsula that would become Korea was conquered by China in 108 B.C.E. and ruled by it for 450 years. What is today north Vietnam was conquered by China in 111 B.C.E. and ruled by it for more than a millennium. Thereafter, both countries established their own independence and cultural identity, even while adopting institutions and ideas from China.

Yamato Japan. Early Japanese history has two main turning points. The first occurred in the third century B.C.E. when an Old Stone Age Japan became an agricultural, metalworking society. The new technologies came to Japan from Korea. By the fifth century C.E., the Yamato court ruled most of Japan. It was heavily influenced by Korea until the seventh century when, in the second main turning point of

their history, the Japanese began to adopt and adapt many features of Chinese culture, including Buddhism and Chinese writing, literature, and political institutions.

Nara and Heian Japan. In this period, Japan was ruled by a civil aristocracy under the emperor. An enormous gulf existed between aristocrats and commoners. Japanese government was heavily influenced by the Chinese imperial system. Japanese culture, however, was increasingly self-confident and was aristocratic in its tastes and forms of expression. Noblewomen wrote many of the great works of Japanese literature during this age. Buddhism became increasingly assimilated.

The Early Feudal Age. In the eighth century mounted warriors called *samurai* began to dominate local society. By the late 1100s, power passed from the civil bureaucracy to military aristocrats. A series of *shōguns*, military officials, ruled in the emperor's name. The *shōguns'* power was based on their ability to command the loyalty of military vassals. Minamoto Yoritomo's seizure of power in 1185 marked the beginning of Japan's feudal age. He established the *bakufu*, or "tent government," in Kamakura. Some form of *bakufu*

INTERPRETING THE PAST

Class, Gender, and Love in Medieval Japan

The following three text sources and two images describe the creation of a strong central government in Japan, the development of a ruling system revolving around a sacrosanct emperor, and the life of the nobility at the imperial court. Your assignment is to analyze these primary source documents in order to describe the treatment of the different classes in Japanese society, the role of women, and the influence of Chinese culture on Japan.

Text Sources from the Primary Source DVD / MyHistoryLab for Chapter 9

Excerpts from the *Taika Reform Edicts*

Selections from *The Tale of Genji*

Aristocratic Taste at the Fujiwara Court: Sei Shonagon

Questions

In examining the *Taika Reform Edicts* primary source, address the following questions: What justifications are given for the centralization of power and the absolute domination of government by the imperial court? How detailed are the specific regulations, and what methods are used to ensure compliance by provincial authorities and the general population? How do these reforms address different social classes?

How is Chinese culture invoked in each of the three text documents? What topics and themes is Chinese culture associated with? (For example, see reference to the Chinese "Book of Changes"—I Ching—on the second page of the *Taika Reform Edicts* excerpt).

Both *The Tale of Genji* and the *Aristocratic Taste at the Fujiwara Court: Sei Shōnagon* excerpts offer detailed descriptions of the behavior and values of the Japanese nobility and would endure in Japan until the mid-nineteenth century. In 1274 and 1281, the Japanese, with the help of storms that destroyed the Mongol fleet, managed to defeat Mongol invaders sent by Kublai Khan. In 1336, Ashitaga Takauji moved his *bakufu* to Kyoto.

Review Questions

1. Was Korea's pattern of development more like that of Japan (the Yayoi baseline, tomb mounds, animism, and aristocracy)? Or was it closer to that of Vietnam? Is geography fate?

2. In what sense was Japanese society during the Yayoi period defined by its eastern frontier? What changes in its early frontier society led to the building of tombs and the emergence of the Yamato great kings?

3. Discuss Japan's cultural ties with China during the Nara and Heian periods. How did Chinese culture affect Japanese government and religion? How did the Japanese change what they borrowed? Was the relation

of Japanese culture to China like that of American culture to England?

4. Trace the rise in Japan of a society dominated by military lords and their vassals. Do the late Heian, Kamakura, and Ashikaga represent successive stages in the development of Japanese "feudalism"?

5. Contrast Heian court culture with the "feudal" culture of the Kamakura and Ashikaga eras. Contrast Heian Buddhism with the Kamakura Pure Land and Zen sects.

Key Terms

Annam (p. 282)

bakufu (ba-ku-fu) (p. 297)

daimyo (dye-myoh) (p. 301)

kamikaze (p. 299)

Pure Land (p. 303)

samurai (p. 290)

Shintō (p. 286)

shōgun (p. 297)

tennō (ten-noh) (p. 288)

Note: To learn more about the topics in this chapter, please turn to the Suggested Readings at the end of the book. For additional sources related to this chapter please see the Primary Source DVD at the back of this text or MyHistoryLab.

Questions (continued)

court ladies" who surrounded them in the Nara and Heian eras. What roles are women and men expected to play in this aristocratic milieu? In what way is a unique Japanese culture arising in this rarified imperial setting?

The *Taika Reform Edicts* excerpt dates from the earliest period of the consolidation of imperial rule in Japan, seeking to thoroughly reform and restructure the society. What do the description of court life in *Genji* and *Sei Shōnagon* three centuries later tell us about the spirit of reform and the imperial court?

Religions of the World

Hinduism, Buddhism, and Jainism all arose out of the spiritual ferment of Vedic India after 700 B.C.E. Buddhism shares a kinship with these other religions much as Judaism, Christianity, and Islam have a relationship.

The founder of Buddhism, Siddhartha Gautama, was born about 563 B.C.E., a prince in a petty kingdom near what is now the border of India and Nepal. He was reared amid luxury and comforts, married at sixteen, and had a child. According to legend, at age twenty-nine he saw a decrepit old man, sick and suffering, and a corpse. He suddenly realized that all humans would suffer the same fate. Gautama renounced his wealth and family and entered the life of a wandering ascetic. He visited famous teachers, for almost six years practiced extremes of ascetic self-deprivation, and finally discovered the Middle Path between self-indulgence and self-mortification. At the age of thirty-five he attained *nirvana*, becoming the *Buddha*, or the Enlightened One. The rest of his eighty years the Buddha spent teaching others the truths he had learned.

Basic to the Buddha's understanding of the human condition were the "Four Noble Truths": (1) All life is suffering—an endless chain of births and rebirths (*karma*); (2) the cause

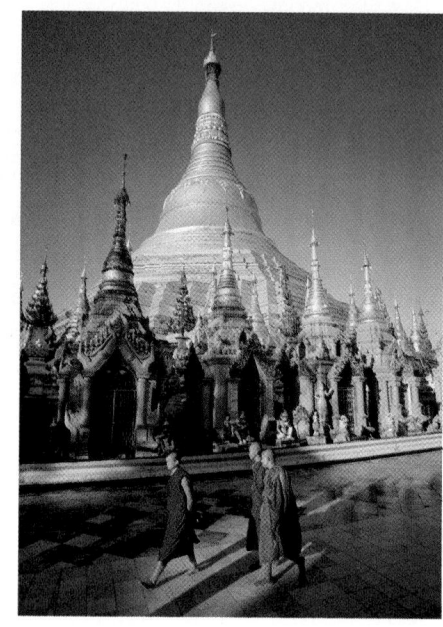

Teenage Buddist monks walk past the ornate facade and towering stupa of Shwedagon Pagoda in Yangon, Myanmar (Burma).

Two Seated Buddhas. This fifth to sixth-century C.E. painting adorns a wall of a cave in Ajanta, India. *Borromeo/Art Resource, N.Y.*

of the suffering is desire—it is desire that binds humans to the wheel of *karma*; (3) escape from suffering and endless rebirths can come only by the cessation of desire and the attainment of *nirvana*; (4) the path to *nirvana* is eightfold, requiring right views, thought, speech, actions, living, efforts, mindfulness, and meditation. Buddhists say that *nirvana* cannot be described: It is the ground of all existence, ineffable, and beyond time and space—an ultimate reality that may be experienced but not grasped intellectually.

The Buddha was a religious teacher, not a social reformer, yet his religious understanding led to ethical conclusions. He condemned the caste system that flourished in the India of his day. He denounced war, slavery, and the taking of life. He opposed appeals to miracles. He did not demand a blind faith in his doctrines: He told his followers to accept his teachings only after they had tested them against their own experience. He taught that poverty was a cause of immorality and that it was futile to attempt to suppress crime with punishments. He identified with all humanity, saying, "He who attends on the sick attends on me."

Because the goal of Buddhism is for all humans to become buddhas, some have called Buddhism the most contemplative and otherworldly of the great world religions. For the spiritually unprepared, and even for the historical Buddha, the way was not easy, and one lifetime was not enough.

Monks and nuns might practice the Eightfold Path, meditate for months and years, and experience an inner spiritual awakening, but only a few would gain enlightenment, the release from karmic causation. Most could only hope for a rebirth in a higher spiritual state—to begin again closer to the goal.

For laypeople the emphasis of Buddhism was on ethical living in human society as a preparation for a more dedicated religious quest in a future life.

Buddhism spread rapidly along the Ganges River and through northern India. In the time of King Ashoka (272–232 B.C.E.) of the Mauryas, it spread to southern India, Ceylon, and beyond. This was its great missionary age. As it spread throughout India its influence on religious practice at the village level was enormous, and its meditative techniques helped reshape Hindu yogic exercises. Eventually, however, Buddhism in India was re-Hinduized. It developed competing schools of metaphysics, a pantheon of gods and cosmic Buddhas, and devotional sects focusing on one or another of these cosmic figures. Its original character as a reform movement of Hinduism was lost, and between 500 and 1500 C.E. it was largely reabsorbed into Hinduism.

Beyond India, two major currents of Buddhism spread over Asia. One, known as the "Way of the Elders" (*Theravada*), swept through continental Southeast Asia and the islands that are today Indonesia. The Theravada teaching was close to early Indian Buddhism and, as it spread, it carried with it other strands of Indian culture as well.

Buddhism remains the predominant religion of Burma, Thailand, Cambodia, and Laos, although it must contend with more recent secular ideologies. In Thailand it remains the state religion: Thai kings rule as Buddhist monarchs; Thai boys spend short periods as Buddhist monks; and Thai temples (*wats*) continue as one center of village life. Before the spread of Islam, Buddhism also once flourished in Malaya, Sumatra, and Java.

The second major current, known as the "Greater Vehicle" (*Mahayana*), spread through northwest India to Afghanistan and Central Asia, and then to China, Tibet and Mongolia, Vietnam, Korea, and Japan. In each region the pattern that unfolded was different. In what is today Pakistan, Afghanistan, and Central Asia, Buddhism was overtaken and replaced by Islam. Mahayana doctrines entered Tibet during the sixth century C.E. and became firmly established several centuries later.

Today Tibetan Buddhism is the predominant religion of Tibet, Nepal, Sikkim, Bhutan, and Mongolia (although there it is severely curtailed by Chinese authorities). In China, and then spreading from China to Korea, Vietnam, and Japan, Ma-

Tibetan Buddhist nuns. They belong to a Tibetan sect of the Mahayana (Greater Vehicle) Buddhism that swept north to Central Asia and Tibet, and then east to China, Korea, and Japan. Behind them, prayer flags blow in the wind. *Patrick Feld/Eye Ubiquitous/Corbis.*

hayana Buddhism saw its fullest development. One key doctrine in this current was the ideal of the *bodhisattva*, a being who had gone all the way to *nirvana*, but held back in order to help others attain salvation.

Another Mahayana doctrine, that of the Chan (in China) or Zen (in Japan) sect, stressed meditation and perhaps was closer to the teachings of the historical Buddha.

In China, the Tang dynasty (618–907) was the great Buddhist age, a time of unparalleled creativity in religious art, sculpture, and music. After that, although Buddhism continued to flourish at the village level, the governing scholar-gentry class shifted to the more worldly doctrines of Neo-Confucianism. In Vietnam, Korea, and Japan, the overall process replicated that of China, but the shift occurred later and with many local variations.

During modern times Buddhism—like all structures of faith—has struggled, with the secular doctrines of the scientific, and industrial, and communist revolutions exerting a powerful influence in the nineteenth and twentieth centuries. The future is unclear, but undoubtedly Buddhism will be powerfully affected by the ongoing transformations of Asian societies.

◆ **In what way is Buddhism's relation to Hinduism parallel to Christianity's relation to Judaism?**

◆ **How do the teachings of the Buddha compare with Christian doctrine?**

10

Iran and South Asia, 200 C.E.–1000 C.E.

IRANIAN LANDS

◆ The Parthians

◆ The Sasanid Empire (224–651 C.E.)

THE INDIAN SUBCONTINENT

◆ Golden Age of the Guptas

◆ The Development of "Classical" Indian Civilization (ca. 300–1000 C.E.)

I N THIS CHAPTER WE LOOK AT WEST AND SOUTH ASIA before the spread of Islam. In Iranian lands, the Sasanids, a dynasty of Persian, Zoroastrian, imperial rulers, reigned from the breakdown of Parthian rule in the early third century C.E. to the coming of Islam in the seventh. A small ruling nobility dominated their highly centralized social and political system. During this time, the Silk Road, which connected China and the Middle East through Central Asia, developed into a thriving system of exchange between different cultures. Along with commerical merchandise and agricultural products, people exchanged ideas and influenced each other's culture, yet this was not merely a time of peace and prosperity. The Sasanid Empire was in constant competition with the Byzantine Empire, as the Achaemenid had been with the Delos Confederation. This competition finally exhausted both Sasanid and Byzantine resources. Both empires were, in time, weakened and defeated in turn by the Arab armies under the banner of Islam in the mid–seventh century.

The Buddhist temple of Borobodur, with tiers of stupas looking out over the island of Java. Built out of a half million blocks of stone, it represents a schema of the Buddhist cosmos. Construction began late in the eighth century; the temple was intended originally to be a Hindu sanctuary.

Pre-Islamic Iran and South Asia

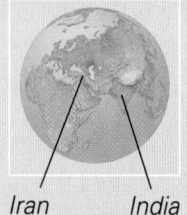

Iran   *India*

From Iran and India European perspective, the center of the world in the early centuries of the common era was the Roman-Byzantine world of late antiquity in the Mediterranean basin. However, in global perspective the loci of major political power, cultural creativity, and religious vitality throughout most of the early centuries C.E. also included Iranian lands, the Indian Ocean, India, and China.

Even in the Roman "West," by the third century C.E. "Roman" civilization remained a vital, living cultural force primarily in regions east and south of Rome itself, whereas in northwestern Europe Roman civilization endured more as a legacy still coexisting uneasily with the cultural traditions of the Germanic invaders. Roman imperial strength rapidly shifted east to Byzantium, where the influence of Africa and West Asia were prominent both politically and culturally; Alexandria, at the mouth of the Nile river, was the center of Hellenism for centuries; and the major Christian doctrinal councils were held in Asia. The perspective changes further when we consider other regions and cultures—the Sasanid imperial culture of Iran and its Zoroastrian revival, the Manichaean movement which spread throughout Central Asia to China, the completion of the *Mahabharata* and *Ramayana* epics, Gupta art and literature, Indian religious thought, and the diffusion of Mahayana Buddhism across Central Asia to China and thence to Japan.

Thus notions of a "rise of Europe" from classical antiquity to modern times do not hold, especially for the first millennium C.E., when we consider the continued expansion of lands, luxuries, and trade under the Persian and Byzantine kings, and the coming of Islam. To any impartial observer, the European world in these centuries did not hold much promise as a future global center of political or cultural life. Instead, progress and culture seemed best embodied either in Sasanid and Gupta culture in west and south Asia, in China under the Han, Sui, and Tang dynasties, and in Japan in Nara and Heian times.

In India the imperial Gupta kings presided over a cultural flowering of unprecedented magnificence until new incursions of steppe peoples from about 500 C.E.. led to political fragmentation. Nevertheless, regional empires lasted until the thirteenth century, when Islamic power under the Delhi sultans began to forge new patterns of power and culture north and south.

The coming of Islamic civilization—and its Arab and Persian sciences, and global networks—with Muslim conquerors or, more often, with Muslim traders and religious brotherhoods—took place at different times across western, southern, central, and southeast Asia. The process—sometimes peaceful and sometimes not—had differing consequences in Iran and India.

In the Iranian lands, Islamic institutions were prominent in government and public life from the early years of the Arab conquests in the mid–seventh century, although the populace in the regions of the traditional Iranian cultural sphere did not convert to Islam until much later.

In India, Arab armies penetrated the Indus region as early as 711, and Muslim rulers of Central Asian heritage controlled the Panjab from around 1000. The establishment of the military-slave-dominated Delhi Sultanate in 1205 marked the entrenchment of Islamic ruling dynasties in the Indian heartlands in the same way that the military-slave dynasty of the Mamluks ruled Egypt in the same era. Similarly, Sufi brotherhoods made significant converts in India from about the thirteenth century onward. Even earlier, in trading communities on the coasts of Gujarat and South India, Muslim settlers and converts had already provided the nuclei of smaller, often scattered Muslim communities that grew up within the larger Hindu society. ■

A revised perspective thus identifies important centers of cultural, religious, economic, and political traditions around the globe—in West, South, and East Asia, in the East Mediterranean empire of Byzantium, and in Aksumite Ethiopia. Societies in each of these regions, themselves the products of syncretistic blending of indigenous and imported cultural traditions, possessed sufficient dynamism to influence the development of neighboring peoples and in some cases exported their religions and cultures over great distances. Merchants and missionaries alike braved the hazards of travel by land and sea, carrying ideas as well as trade goods to remote regions. Wares and religions passed from hand to hand, and from mouth to mouth, on the journey from Byzantium to China, and from Africa and West Asia to India and beyond, as the centers of civilization in Africa and Asia waxed powerful. Hindu tradition and Indian culture were undergoing important internal developments, while Buddhism was finding new and rich fields for conversion in Central Asia, China, Japan, and Southeast Asia. Zoroastrian Persia appeared well on its way into a second millennium of imperial splendor under the Sasanids.

Yet with the imminent rise of the last monotheistic world religion, Islam, Iranian lands soon faced far-reaching changes—changes that would later overtake much of North and East Africa, India, and South and Southeast Asia. In the time of Chosroes Anoshirvan in the sixth century C.E.., who could have suspected that within a few hundred years Persian culture would eventually be recast in Islamic forms?

Focus Questions

◆ Why is a European perspective unhelpful for understanding the world in the first millennium C.E.? How does a global perspective offer a better understanding of the development of civilizations in this era?

◆ In what ways can the Sasanids and Guptas be considered high points for Persian and Indian civilizations?

IRANIAN LANDS

The Parthians

Parthian Arsacid rule (ca. 247 B.C.E.–223 C.E.) began in the eastern Iranian province of Parthia in Seleucid times and eventually dominated the Iranian heartlands of the Achaemenids (see Chapter 4). The Parthians even managed by 129 B.C.E. to extinguish Seleucid power east of the Euphrates. They also continued the Iranian imperial and cultural traditions of the Achaemenids. The relative Parthian tolerance of religious diversity was paralleled by the growth of regionalism in political and cultural affairs. A growing nobility built strong local power bases and became the backbone of Parthian military power. Aramaic, the common language of the empire, gradually lost ground to regional Iranian tongues after the second century B.C.E., although Greek was widely spoken.

Despite their general religious tolerance, the Parthians upheld such Zoroastrian traditions as maintenance of a royal sacred fire at a shrine in their Parthian homeland and included priestly advisers on the emperor's council. The last century or so of their rule saw increased emphasis on Iranian as opposed to foreign traditions in religious and cultural affairs, perhaps in reaction to the almost constant warfare with the Romans on their west flank and the Indo-Greek Kushan threat from Bactria to the east. By this time Christianity and Buddhism were making sufficient converts in border areas to threaten Zoroastrian tradition. These threats may have stimulated Parthian attempts to collect the largely oral Zoroastrian textual heritage. In such ways, Parthian rule laid the groundwork for the nationalistic emphases of subsequent centuries.

The Sasanid Empire (224–651 C.E.)

The Sasanids were a Persian dynasty and claimed to be the rightful Achaemenid heirs. They championed Iranian

Accolades to Shapur I

Document

This document is an inscription at a Hajiabad, Iran, cave honoring Shapur I in the western Zagros mountains. The inscription, like so many during the Sasanid reign that narrate a commemoration of a battle, or ceremonial greeting of captives, is, in this case, the designation of Shapur's future resting place or mausoleum.

◆ Are the accolades to Shapur similar to titles given to other rulers or kings of the ancient period of world history? What is the significance of mentioning Shapur's religion as "the Mazda worshiper"? While the narrative is a little wooden in its translation, can you think of ways that the shooting of the arrow has both practical and sacred meaning to the Sasanian people and their ruler?

"This is the edict of me, the Mazda worshiper, Shahpuhr, placed among the gods, King of kings of Persia and non-Persia, of celestial descent from God, son of Mazda-worshiper Artakhshatr, placed among the gods, King of kings of Persia, of celestial descent from God, grandson of Papak, placed among the gods, the King.

And when we shot this arrow, the one we shot it in the presence of the Satraps, the Princes, the Great one and the Nobles; we set the foot on this stone [in this place] and shot out the arrow at one of these targets; where the arrow was shot, however, there was no bird at hand, where, if the targets had been rightly set up, the arrow would have been found outwardly visible [above ground].

Then we ordered a target specially set apart for His Majesty to be erected in this place. The Celestial hand [of His Majesty] wrote this: 'Let no one set foot on this stone or shoot an arrow at this target'. Then I shot the arrow destined for the Royal use at these targets.

This hath the hand [of the King] written."

Edward G. Browne, *The Literary History of Persia*, Vol I: The Earliest Times to Firdawsi, Copyright © 1969 Cambridge University Press.

---

legitimacy and tried to brand the Parthians as outside invaders from the northeast who followed Hellenic and other foreign ways. The first Sasanid king, Ardashir (r. 224–ca. 239 C.E.), was a Persian warrior noble from a priestly family. The Sasanid name came from his grandfather, Sasan. Ardashir and his son, Shapur I (r. ca. 239–272), built a strong internal administration in Persia (Pars, later Fars), extended their sway to Ctesiphon (formerly Babylon), and took Bactria from the Kushans. Under Shapur's long rule, the Persian empire grew in the east, beyond the Caucasus to the north, and to the west in Syria, Armenia, and parts of Anatolia. Shapur defeated three Roman emperors, even capturing one of them, Valerian (r. 253–260). Thus he could justifiably claim to be a restorer of Iranian glory and a "king of kings," or *shahanshah* (See Document, "Accolades to Shapur I".) He also centralized and rationalized taxation, the civil ministries, and the military, although neither he nor his successors could fully contain the growing power of the nobility.

With the shift of the Roman Empire east to Byzantium in the early fourth century C.E., the stage of imperial conflict in West Asia was set for the next 350 years: between the Byzantines based in Constantinople on the Bosphorus and the Sasanids based in Ctesiphon on the Tigris. These two imperial centers were home to the two mightiest thrones of Eurasia until the coming of the Arabs. Each side won victories over the other and championed a different religious orthodoxy, but neither could ever completely conquer the other. In the sixth century each produced its greatest emperor: the Byzantine Justinian (r. 527–565) and the Sasanid Chosroes Anosharvan ("Chosroes of the Immortal Soul," r. 531–579). Yet, less than a century after their deaths, the new Arab power to the south reduced one empire dramatically and destroyed the other. Byzantium survived with the loss of most of its territory for another 800 years, but the Sasanid imperial order was swept away entirely in 651. Memory of the Sasanids did not, however, die. Chosroes, for example, became a legendary model of greatness for Persians and a symbol of imperial splendor among the Arabs. The Pahlavi monarchy in twentieth-century Iran attempted to use the historical memory of the Sasanids to legitimize its rule and to convince modern-day

Sasanid victory. Cliff-cut tombs at Nagsh-i Rustam, Iran. Stone relief depicts Philip the Arab in Roman dress kneeling before the third-century Persian King Shapur I on horseback wearing royal armor and crown, who grasps with his right hand the uplifted arms of the Byzantine Emperor Valerian. Located at the tombs of the Achaemenids, in Istakhr, Iran.

Iranians of the need to continue "2,500 years of imperial rule." The attempt was without success as the Shah of Iran was overthown ten years after that 1969 proclamation.

Society and Economy

Sasanid society was largely like that of earlier times. The extended family was the basic social unit. Zoroastrian orthodoxy recognized four classes: priests, warriors, scribes, and peasants. However, a great divide separated the royal house, the priesthood, and the warrior nobility from the common people (artisans, traders, and the rural peasantry).

The basis of the economy remained agriculture, but land became increasingly concentrated in the hands of an ever-richer minority of the royalty, nobility, and Zoroastrian priesthood. As in Roman domains, the growth of great estates was responsible for a growing imbalance between the rich few and the impoverished many, including the ever-expanding slave and captured labor force. Many small farmers were reduced to serfdom or abject poverty. The burden of land taxation, like that of conscript labor and army duty, hit hardest those least able to afford it. This produced a popular reaction, as shown by the Mazdakite movement, discussed below.

The Sasanids also closely oversaw and heavily taxed the lucrative caravan and sea trade in their territory (see Map 10–1). Silk and glass production increased under government monopoly, and the state also controlled mining. The empire's many urban centers and its foreign trade relied on a money system. It was from Jewish bankers in Babylonia

and their Persian counterparts that Europe—and in other diaspora Persian, Arab, and Armenian communities in the rest of the world—got the use of bills of exchange (the term *check* comes from a Pahlavi word).[1]

Sasanid aristocratic culture drew on diverse traditions, from Roman, Hellenic, Mesopotamian, and Bactrian-Indian to Achaemenid and other native Iranian ones. Its heyday was the reign of Chosroes. Indian influences—not only religious, as in the case of Buddhist ideas, but also artistic and scientific—were especially strong. Indian medicine and mathematics were notably in demand and transmitted west by way of the Persian Gulf and Indian Ocean maritime routes. Hellenistic culture was also revived in the academy at Jundishapur in the southwest Persian province of Khuzistan, where Nestorian Christian scholars fleeing Byzantine persecution of their doctrines on Christ's nature brought many Greco-Roman philosophical, scientific, and literary texts with them. Justinian's closing of the Greek academies in the Mediterranean only accelerated the scholarly and textual migration to Persia and to Muharraq in the Persian Gulf.

Religion

Zoroastrian Revival The Sasanids institutionalized Zoroastrian ritual and theology as state orthodoxy. Although they were continuing the Arsacid patronage of Zoroastrian worship, the Sasanids claimed to be restoring the true faith after centuries of neglect. The initial architect of this propaganda and the Zoroastrian revival was the first chief priest (*mobad*) of the empire, Tosar (or Tansar). Under Ardashir I, Tosar instituted a state institution and began to compile an authoritative, written scriptural canon known as the *Avesta*; these texts include the hymns and sayings of Zarathushtra (see Chapter 4). He may also have instituted a calendar reform and replaced all images in the temples with the sacred altar fires of Zoroastrian tradition, which burned as a symbol of the holiness of Ahura Mazda.

The most influential figure in Sasanid religious history was Tosar's successor, Kartir (or Kirdir), who served as chief priest to Shapur I and three successors (ca. 239–293). Although his zealotry was initially restrained by the religiously tolerant Shapur, Kirdir gained greater power and influence after Shapur's death. He seems to have tried to convert not only pagans, but also Christians, Buddhists, and others. His chief opponents were the Manichaeans, whom he considered Zoroastrian heretics, much as Christian groups, such as the Nestorians, saw them as Christian heretics.

[1] R. Girshman, *Iran* (Harmondsworth, U.K.: Penguin Books, 1954), pp. 341–346. "Pahlavi" is the name of the Middle Persian language that gradually replaced Aramaic as the Iranian common tongue in Sasanid times.

A Report of Mani's Words About His Mission

Document

The following excerpt is from *The Cologne Mani Codex*, a Greek biographical work on Mani's early life that has only recently been discovered. The tiny parchment "pocketbook" on which it was written dates from around 400 C.E., within 150 years of Mani's death. In it, the Manichaean author cites one of Mani's "gospels."

◆ **What does Mani's proclamation suggest he shared with other West Asian and eastern Mediterranean traditions? What rank and role does he claim for himself? What seems to be his idea of scripture?**

He wrote [thus again and] said in the Gospel of his most holy hope: "I, Mani, an apostle of Jesus Christ through the will of God, the Father of Truth, from whom I also was born, who lives and abides forever, existing before all and also abiding after all. All things which are and will be subsist through his power. For from this very one I was begotten; and I am from his will. From him all that is true was revealed to me; and I am from [his] truth. [The truth of ages which he revealed] I have seen, and [that] truth I have disclosed to my fellow travelers; peace I have announced to the children of peace, hope I have proclaimed to the immortal race. The Elect I have chosen and a path to the height I have shown to those who ascend according to this truth. Hope I have proclaimed and this revelation I have revealed. This immortal Gospel I have written, including in it these eminent mysteries, and disclosing in it the greatest works, the greatest and most august forms of the most eminently powerful works. These things which he [revealed], I have shown [to those who live from] the truest vision, which I have beheld, and the most glorious revelation revealed to me."

From *The Cologne Mani Codex*, trans. from the Greek by Ron Cameron and A. J. Dewey. Copyright © 1979, Scholars Press, p. 53. Reprinted by permission.

Manichaeism Mani (216–277 C.E.) was born of a noble Parthian family but raised in Babylonia. A cosmopolitan who spoke Aramaic, Persian, and Greek and traveled to India, Mani preached a message both similar to and sharply divergent from its Zoroastrian, Judaic, and Christian forerunners (see Document, "A Report of Mani's Words About His Mission.") **Manichaeism** centered on a radically dualistic and moralistic view of reality in which good and evil, spirit and matter, always warred. These ideas are now commonplace in the major monotheistic religions. He sought to convert others to his views, which he presented as the culmination and restoration of the original unity of Zoroastrian, Christian, and Buddhist teachings. Mani may have been the first person in history to consciously "found" a new religious tradition or to seek to create a "scripture" for his followers. He called his new system "Justice," although outsiders called it *Manichaeism*. The popularity of Mani's movement probably contributed to Kirdir's and later attempts to establish a Zoroastrian "orthodoxy" and scriptural canon.[2]

---
[2] W. C. Smith, *The Meaning and End of Religion* (New York: Harper & Row, 1962), pp. 92–98.

Chronology

Sasanid Iran

216–277	Mani
223–224 C.E.	Ardashir (r. 224–ca. 239) defeats the last Arsacid ruler, becomes *shahanshah* of Iran
ca. 225–ca. 239	Tosar chief priest (*mobad*) of realm
239–272	Reign of Shapur I; expansion of the empire east and west
ca. 239–293	Kirdir chief priest (*mobad*) of the realm
ca. 307–379	Reign of Shapur II
488–531	Reign of Kavad I; height of Mazdakite movement
528	Mazdak and many of his followers massacred
531–579	Reign of Chosroes Anosharvan at Ctesiphon
651	Death of last Sasanid; Arabs conquer Persian Empire

Manichaean Priests. This leaf from a Manichaean book (ca. eighth–ninth century c.e.) shows priests in white robes and tall hats kneeling in front of low desks. Each has a sheet of white paper, and some hold pens. Works such as this are an important source for our knowledge of Manichaean communities. *A leaf from a Manchurian book, Roko, Templek (MIK III 6368), 8th–9th century, a manuscript painting 17.2 × 11.2 cm. Museum für Indische Kunst, Staatliche Museen Preussischer Kulturbesitz, Berlin.*

Kirdir eventually had Mani executed as a heretic in 277, but Mani's movement had great consequences. It spread westward to challenge the Christian church (Saint Augustine was once a Manichaean) and eastward along the Silk Road to Central Asia and China. Its ideas figured even centuries later in both Christian and Islamic heresies. Its adherents probably carried the Western planetary calendar to China, where in some areas it was used for centuries.

Zoroastrian Orthodoxy Kirdir had firmly grounded Zoroastrian orthodoxy despite the persistence of challenges to it, such as that of Mani. This orthodoxy became the backbone of Sasanid culture. Soon the Sasanids' spoken Persian, *Pahlavi*, became the official imperial language. Eventually the Zoroastrian sacred texts were set down in Pahlavi. Throughout Sasanid times, the priesthood increased its power as the jurists and legal interpreters, as well as the liturgists and scholars, of the land. With increasing endowments of new fire temples, the church establishment also eventually controlled much of Iran's wealth.

Nestorian Christianity Nestorius (c. 386–c. 451), the Patriarch of Constantinople, had taught that the human and divine natures of Jesus Christ were distinct and separate, not unified in one person as believed by Rome and Constantinople. He preached that the Virgin Mary's title of "Mother of God" (*Theotokos*) was not appropriate, for she need only be called the "Mother of Christ" (*Christotokos*) instead. Nestorius was condemned as a heretic at the Council of Ephesus in 431, and the Sasanid kings, who were at war with the Byzantines, saw an opportunity and supported the Nestorian Christians and the Nestorian schism, opened schools to the Nestorian scholars, and allowed the Nestorian Assyrian Christians to flourish in Persia. Indeed, the Nestorian Church produced many missionaries who traveled and preached throughout Persia and Central and East Asia in the seventh and eighth centuries, reaching China in 635. Its relics can still be seen in Chinese cities, such as Xi'an.

Nestorian Christianity in China. The spread of Christianity along the Silk Road perfectly illustrates the close connection between missionary activity and trading routes in late antiquity. Although the Nestorians had little impact on Christian communities in the Mediterranean and Europe, their faith extended east along the Silk Road. The stele depicted here, built in 781 c.e.. commemorates the introduction of Nestorian Christianity to China. *Musée des Arts Asiatiques—Guimet, Paris, France. Réunion des Musées Nationaux/Art Resource. N.Y.*

Later Sasanid Developments

Despite the high Zoroastrian moral intent of many of their rulers, the Sasanid ideal of justice did not include equal distribution of the empire's bounty. The radical inequalities between the aristocracy and the masses erupted at least once in conflict with the Mazdakite movement at the end of the fifth century. Its leader, Mazdak, preached asceticism, pessimism about the evil state of the material world, the virtues of vegetarianism, tolerance, and brotherly love—all ideas apparently drawn ultimately from Manichaeism—and the need for a more equal distribution of society's goods. This appealed to the oppressed classes, although even one Sasanid ruler, Kavad I (r. 488–531), was sympathetic for a time to Mazdak's ideas of social justice. However, in 528 Kavad's third son, the later Chosroes Anosharvan, massacred Mazdak and his most important followers. Although this finished the Mazdakites, the name was still used later, in Islamic times, for various Iranian popular revolts.

THE INDIAN SUBCONTINENT

Golden Age of the Guptas

Indians have always considered the Gupta era a high point of their early civilizations. Historians have seen in it the source of "classical" norms for Hindu religion and Indian culture—the symbolic equivalent of Periclean Athens, Augustan Rome, Sasanid Persia, or Han China. The Guptas ruled when the various facets of Indian life took on the recognizable patterns of a single, if still highly diverse civilization that extended its influence over the whole subcontinent. A major factor in this development was the relative peace and stability that marked most of the Guptas' reign. (See Document, "A Chinese Traveler's Report on the Gupta Realm.")

Gupta Rule

The first Gupta king was Chandragupta (r. 320–ca. 330 C.E.). He ruled first in Magadha and then became prominent in the whole Ganges basin after he married Princess Kumaradevi, daughter of a powerful tribal leader north of the Ganges. Although their reign inaugurated Gupta power, it was their son, Samudragupta (r. ca. 330–375), and especially their grandson, Chandragupta II (r. ca. 375–415), who turned kingdom into empire and presided over the Gupta "golden age."

Chronology

India from the Gupta Age to ca. 1000 C.E.

320 C.E.–ca. 467	Gupta period
320–330	Reign of Chandragupta, first Gupta king
376–454	Reigns of Chandragupta II and Kumaragupta: Kalidasa flourishes; heyday of Gupta culture
399–414	Chinese Buddhist monk Faxien travels in India
ca. 440	Beginning of Hun invasions from Central Asia
550–ca. 1000	Regional Indian kingdoms in north and south; major Puranas composed; age of first great Vaishnava and Shaivite devotional poets in southern India
616–657	Reign of Harsha; revival of Gupta splendor and power
820	Death of Shankara, Vedantin philosopher-theologian

The Gupta realm extended from the Panjab and Kashmir south to the Narbada River in the western Deccan and east to modern Assam (see Map 10–1), and their sphere of influence included some of the Kushan and Saka kingdoms of the northwest and much of the eastern coast of India and possibly Ceylon (Sri Lanka). Unlike the Mauryans, the Guptas usually accepted a defeated ruler as a vassal prince rather than rule his kingdom directly. Seated at the old Mauryan capital, Pataliputra, Gupta splendor and power had no rival. Under Chandragupta II, India was arguably the most civilized and peaceful country in the world.

Two further Gupta kings sustained this prosperity for another half century, despite invasions by a new wave of steppe nomads, the Huns, after about 440. By about 500 the Huns had overrun western India, and the Gupta Empire collapsed

Gupta Sculpture. Fifth-century C.E. statue of Lokanatha from Sarnath, which, despite damage, shows the fine sculptural work of the important school of Gupta artists at Sarnath and the influence on them of both Graeco-Roman antecedents and native Indian traditions and conventions. *Scala/Art Resource, N.Y.*

Map Exploration

To explore this map further, go to http://www.prenhall.com/craig_maps

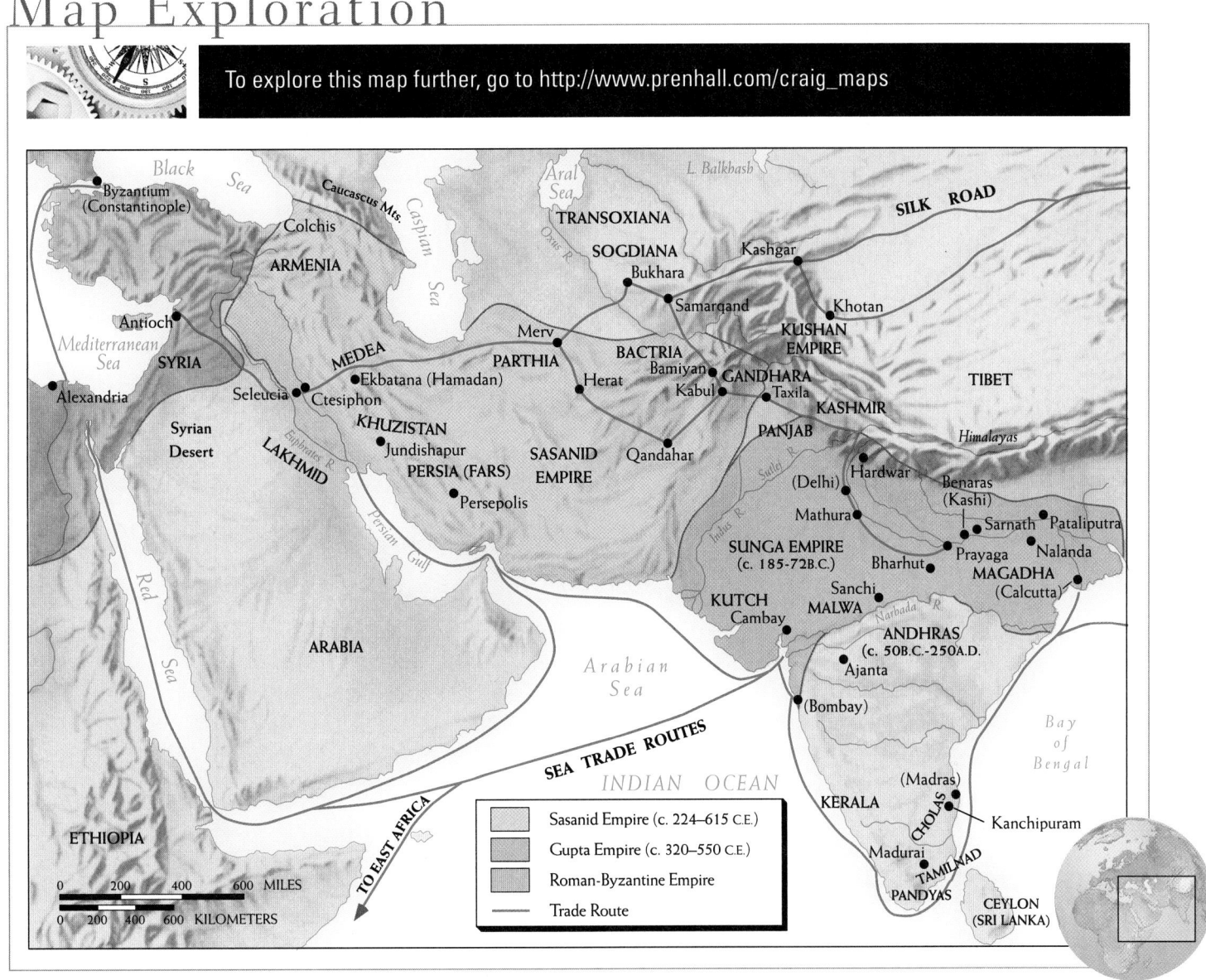

Map 10–1. International Trade Routes in Gupta and Sasanid Times. This map shows the Gupta and Sasanid Empires and the trade routes that linked them to each other and to other areas of the world.

about 550. Harsha, a descendant of the Guptas through his grandmother, did revive a semblance of former Gupta splendor between 616 and 657. His loosely held dominions again spanned North India, but when he died without heirs the empire broke up again.

The succeeding centuries before the arrival of Muslim invaders about 1000 C.E. saw several dynasties in North India share power, but no unified rule of any duration. Outside the north, several long-lived dynasties built regional empires in the western Deccan and Tamilnad (the extreme south) after Gupta times, and the main centers of Indian civilization shifted to those areas.

Gupta Culture

Indian culture experienced little new outside influence from the Gupta era until Islamic times. India's chief contacts were now with Southeast Asia and China, and most of the cultural transmission was from India eastward, not vice versa (see Map 10–2).

The claim of the Gupta era to being India's golden age of culture could be sustained solely by its magnificent architecture and sculpture, the wall paintings of the Ajanta caves, and Kalidasa's matchless drama and verse. The "Shakespeare" of Sanskrit letters, Kalidasa flourished in the time of Chandragupta II and his successor.

Map 10–2. Indian Influence in Southeast Asia, ca. 650 C.E. By the middle of the 7th century C.E., Indian traditions, art, and music exerted a pervasive influence throughout Southeast Asia, even though the number of Indians who traded and migrated there was not great.

We can see the depth of Gupta culture in the strong emphasis on education, whether in Jain and Buddhist monasteries or in Brahmanical schools. In addition to religious texts, typical subjects included rhetoric, prose and poetic composition, grammar, logic, medicine, and metaphysics. Using an older Indian number system that the Arabs transmitted to Europe as "Arabic numerals," Gupta scholars cultivated mathematics especially.

In sculpture, the monastic complex at Sarnath was a great center of activity. The superb technique and expressive serenity of Gupta style grew out of native Mathura, influenced by the Indo-Greek and Persian schools. Hindu, Jain, and Buddhist works all shared the same style and conventions. Even in handwork and luxury crafts, Gupta products achieved new levels of quality and were in great demand abroad: silks, muslin, linen, ivory and other carvings, bronze metalwork, gold and silver work, and cut stones, among others. In architecture, Gupta splendor is less evident, except in the culmination of cave-shrine (Chaitya-hall) development at Ajanta and in the earliest surviving free-standing temples in India. The Hindu temple underwent its important development in post-Gupta times, beginning in the eighth century.

A Chinese Traveler's Report on the Gupta Realm

Document

Faxien, a Chinese Buddhist monk, was the first of several Chinese known for traveling to India to study and bring back Buddhist scriptures from the intellectual centers of Buddhist thought there. He wrote an account of his travels, first through Central Asia, then all over India, then through Ceylon and Indonesia and again to China (399–414 C.E.).

◆ What things about India seem to most surprise Faxian? Is his image of Indian rule a positive one? What do his remarks say about the prestige of the Buddhist tradition and its monks in the Indian state? What does he tell us about Indian society?

On the sides of the river, both right and left, are twenty san ghârâmas [monasteries], with perhaps 3000 priests. The law of the Buddha is progressing and flourishing. Beyond the deserts are the countries of Western India. The kings of these countries are all firm believers in the law of Buddha. They remove their caps of state when they make offerings to the priests. The members of the royal household and the chief ministers personally direct the food-giving; when the distribution of food is over, they spread a carpet on the ground opposite the chief seat (the president's seat) and sit down before it. They dare not sit on couches in the presence of the priests. The rules relating to the almsgiving of kings have been handed down from the time of Buddha till now. Southward from this is the so-called middle-country (Mâdhyade′sa). The climate of this country is warm and equable, without frost or snow. The people are very well off, without poll tax or official restrictions. Only those who till the royal lands return a portion of profit of the land. If they desire to go, they go; if they like to stop, they stop. The kings govern without corporal punishment; criminals are fined, according to circumstances, lightly or heavily. Even in cases of repeated rebellion they only cut off the right hand. The king's personal attendants, who guard him on the right and left, have fixed salaries. Throughout the country the people kill no living thing nor drink wine, nor do they eat garlic or onions, with the exception of Chandâlas [outcasts] only.

The Chandâlas are named "evil men" and dwell apart from others; if they enter a town or market, they sound a piece of wood in order to separate themselves; then men, knowing who they are, avoid coming in contact with them. In this country they do not keep swine nor fowls, and do not deal in cattle; they have no shambles or wine-shops in their market places. In selling they use cowrie shells. The Chandâlas only hunt and sell flesh. Down from the time of Buddha's Nirvâna, the kings of these countries, the chief men and householders, have raised vihâras [monasteries] for the priests, and provided for their support by bestowing on them fields, houses, and gardens, with men and oxen. Engraved title-deeds were prepared and handed down from one reign to another; no one has ventured to withdraw them, so that till now there has been no interruption. All the resident priests having chambers (in these vihâras) have their beds, mats, food, drink, and clothes provided without stint; in all places this is the case. The priests ever engage themselves in doing meritorious works for the purpose of religious advancement (karma—building up their religious character), or in reciting the scriptures, or in meditation.

From "Buddhist Country Records," in Si-Yu-Ki, *Buddhist Records of the Western World*, trans. by Samuel Beal (London, 1884; reprint, Delhi: Oriental Books Reprint Corporation, 1969), pp. xxxvii–xxxviii. Reprinted by permission of Motilal Banarsidass Publishers Pvt. Ltd., Delhi, India.

The Development of "Classical" Indian Civilization (ca. 300–1000 C.E.)

The Guptas' support of Brahmanic traditions and Vaishnava[3] devotionalism reflected the waning of Buddhist traditions in the mainstream of Indian religious life. In Gupta times and subsequently, down to the advent of Islamic rule, Indian civilization assumed its classical shape, its enduring "Hindu" forms of social, religious, and cultural life.

[3] *Vaishnava* or *Vaishnavite* means "related to Vishnu"; similarly, *Shaiva* or *Shaivite* refers to Shiva worship (compare with *Jaina/Jain* for devotees of the way of the *Jinas* such as Mahavira).

Society

In these centuries, the fundamentally hierarchical character of Hindu/Indian society solidified. The oldest manual of legal and ethical theory, the *Dharmashastra* of Manu, dates from about 200 C.E. Based on Vedic tradition, it treats the **dharma** appropriate to one's class and stage of life, rules for rites and study of the Veda, pollution and purification measures, dietary restrictions, royal duties and prerogatives, and other legal and moral questions.

In it we find the classic statement of the four-class theory of social hierarchy. This ideal construct rests on the basic principle that every person is born into a particular station in life (as a result of *karma* from earlier lives), and every station has its particular *dharma*, or appropriate duties and responsibilities, from the lowest servant to the highest prince or Brahman. The Brahmans' ancient division of Aryans into the four *varnas*, or classes, of *Brahman* (priest), *Kshatriya* (noble/warrior), *Vaishya* (tradesperson), and *Shudra* (servant) provides a schematic structure. These divisions reflect an attempt to fix the status and power of the upper three groups, especially the Brahmans, at the expense of the Shudras and the "fifth estate" of non-Aryan "outcasts," who performed the most polluting jobs in society. Although class distinctions had already hardened before 500 B.C.E., the classes were, in practice, somewhat fluid. If the traditional occupation of a varna was closed to a member, he could often take up another, all theory to the contrary. When Brahmans, Vaishyas, or even Shudras gained political power as rulers (as was evidently the case with the Mauryas, for example), their family gradually became recognized as *Kshatriyas*, the appropriate class for princes.

Although the four classes, or **varnas**, are the theoretical basis for caste relations, much smaller and far more numerous subgroups, or **jatis**, are the units to which our English term *caste* best refers. (*Caste* comes from *casta*, the word the Portuguese used for *jati*.) These divisions (most representing occupational groups) were already the primary units of social distinction in Gupta times. *Jati* groupings are hereditary and distinguished essentially on principles of purity and pollution, which are expressed in three kinds of regulation: (1) commensality (one may take food only from or with persons of the same or a higher group); (2) endogamy (one may marry only within the group); and (3)

Dancing Shiva. A magnificent South Indian bronze of Shiva. The fluid, balanced image depicts the so-called "dancing Shiva" engaged in his dance of simultaneous destruction and creation of the universe, an artistic-mythical rendering of the eternal flux of all worldly existence (13th century; bronze; 33.5 × 24.8 cm). © The Nelson-Atkins Museum of Art, Kansas City, MO. (Purchase: Nelson Trust) 50-20.

trade or craft limitation (one must practice only the trade of one's group).[4]

The caste system has been the basis of Indian social organization for at least two millennia. It enabled Hindus to accommodate foreign cultural, racial, and religious communities within Indian society by treating them as new caste groups. It enabled everyone to tell by dress and other marks how to relate to another person or group, thus giving stability and security to the individual and to society. It represented also the logical extension of the doctrine of *karma* into society—whether as justification, result, or partial cause of the system itself (see Chapter 2).

SOURCE Xuanzang on the caste system in India

Religion

Hindu Religious Life Gupta and later times saw the growth of devotional cults of deities, preeminently Vishnu and Shiva, who were unknown or unimportant in Vedic religion. The temple worship of a particular deity has ever since been a basic form of Hindu piety. After Vishnu (especially in his form as the hero-savior Krishna) and Shiva (originally a fertility god), the chief focus of devotion came to be the Goddess in one of her many forms, such as Parvati, Shakti, Durga, or Kali. Vishnu and Shiva, like Parvati, have many forms and names and have always been easily identified with other deities, who are then worshiped as one form of the Supreme Lord or Goddess. Animal or nature deities were presumably part of popular piety from Indus Valley days forward. Indian reverence for all forms of life and stress on *ahimsa*, or "noninjury" to living beings (see Chapter 2), are most vivid in the sacredness of the cow, which has always been a mainstay of life in India.

In the development of Hindu piety and practice, a major strand was the tradition of ardent theism known as *bhakti*, or "loving devotion." *Bhakti* was already evident, at the latest by 200 C.E., in the Bhagavad Gita's treatment of

---

[4] A. L. Basham, *The Wonder That Was India* (New York: 1963), pp. 148–149.

Devoting Oneself to Krishna

Document

The Bhagavad Gita is the most widely revered and often quoted of all Hindu religious texts. In these verses (Bhagavad Gita 9:22–34), Krishna (Vishnu) tells his friend and disciple, the young warrior Arjuna, of the highest path to salvation, which involves both renouncing one's attachment to the objects ("fruits") of one's actions and devoting oneself in pure faith to the Supreme Lord Krishna.

◆ How is the understanding of older Indian religious practices and ideals (about sacrifice, for example) transformed here? How does the Lord Krishna present himself in relation to other deities? Does the passage present a sharp dichotomy between faith and works? What are the social implications of the message here?

GOD AND THE DEVOTEE

Those persons who, meditating on Me without any thought of another god, worship Me—to them, who constantly apply themselves [to that worship], I bring attainment [of what they do not have] and preservation [of what they have attained].

Even the devotees of other divinities, who worship them, being endowed with faith—they, too, O son of Kunti [actually] worship Me alone, though not according to the prescribed rites.

For I am the enjoyer, as also the lord of all sacrifices. But those people do not comprehend Me in My true nature and hence they fall.

Worshipers of the gods go to the gods; worshipers of the manes go to the manes; those who sacrifice to the spirits go to the spirits; and those who worship Me, come to Me.

A leaf, a flower, a fruit, or water, whoever offers to Me with devotion—that same, proffered in devotion by one whose soul is pure, I accept.

Whatever you do, whatever you eat, whatever you offer in sacrifice, whatever you give away, whatever penance you practice—that, O son of Kunti, do you dedicate to Me.

Thus will you be freed from the good or evil fruits which constitute the bondage of actions. With your mind firmly set on the way of renunciation [of fruits], you will, becoming free, come to Me.

Even-minded am I to all beings; none is hateful nor dear to Me. Those, however, who worship Me with devotion, they abide in Me, and I also in them.

Even if a person of extremely vile conduct worships Me being devoted to none else, he is to be reckoned as righteous, for he has engaged himself in action in the right spirit.

Quickly does he become of righteous soul and obtain eternal peace. O son of Kunti, know for certain that My devotee perishes not.

For those, O son of Prith, who take refuge in Me, even though they be lowly born, women, vaishyas, as also shûdras—even they attain to the highest goal.

How much more, then, pious brôhmans, as also devout royal sages? Having come to this impermanent, blissless world, worship Me.

On Me fix your mind; become My devotee, My worshiper; render homage unto Me. Thus having attached yourself to Me, with Me as your goal, you shall come to Me. . . .

From *Sources of Indian Tradition,* by William Theodore De Bary. Copyright © 1988 by Columbia University Press. Reprinted with permission of the publisher.

Krishna. (See Document, "Devoting Oneself to Krishna.") Gupta and later times saw the rise, especially in the Tamil-speaking south, of schools of bhakti poetry and worship. The central *bhakti* strand in Hindu life derives in good part from Tamil and other vernacular poets who first sang the praises of Shiva or Vishnu as Supreme Lord. Here, pre-Aryan religious sensibilities apparently reasserted themselves through the non-Aryan Dravidian peoples of the south. The great theologian of devotional Hinduism, Ramanuja (d. ca. 1137),

would later come from this same Dravidian tradition. Of major importance also to devotional piety was the development in this era of the Puranas—epic, mythological, and devotional texts. They are still today the functional sacred scriptures of grass-roots Hindu religious life (the Vedic texts remaining the special preserve of the Brahmans).

Whatever god or goddess a Hindu worships, it is usual to also pay homage on proper occasions also to other appropriate deities. Most Hindus view one deity as Supreme Lord

The Four Main Hindu Castes Overview

Traditional Hindu/Indian society is fundamentally hierarchic in character. There are four main classes (*varnas*) into which a person is born according to how he or she lived in a previous life. Every class has its appropriate duties and responsibilities. In addition, there are numerous subgroups (*jatis*) based probably originally on distinctions of occupation. The English word "*caste*" is used rather crudely to refer to all of these groups, which are in practice distinguished by norms involving purity and pollution, especially as regards commensality (regulation of whom one may share food with).

In addition, there is a fifth group of "outcastes" who performed the necessary but most polluting tasks in society, such as removing human waste. Persons in this category were considered "untouchable," and contact with them was considered morally and spiritually unclean.

Brahman	Priest. This is the highest caste in terms of prestige and purity.
Kshatriya	Warrior or aristocrat. This is considered the appropriate caste for rulers.
Vaishya	Tradespeople and merchants.
Shudra	Servant. It includes peasants and manual laborers as well as domestic servants.

but see others as manifestations of the Ultimate at lower levels. Hindu polytheism is not "idolatry," but rather a vivid affirmation of the infinite forms that transcendence takes in this world. The sense of the presence of the Divine everywhere is evident in the importance attached to sacred places. India is the land of religious pilgrimage *par excellence*. Sacred mountains, rivers, trees, and groves are all *tirthas*, or "river fords" to the Divine.

The intellectual articulation of Hindu polytheism and relativism found its finest expression in post-Gupta formulations of Vedanta ("the end of the Veda"). The major Vedantin thinker, Shankara (d. 820), stressed a strict "nonduality" of the Ultimate, teaching that Brahman was the only Reality behind the "illusion" (*maya*) of the world of sense experience. Yet he accepted the worship of a lesser deity as appropriate for those who could not follow his extraordinary norm—the intellectual realization of the formless Absolute beyond all "name and form."

Buddhist Religious Life   The major developments of these centuries were (1) the solidification of the two main strands of Buddhist tradition, the **Mahayana** and the **Theravada**, and (2) the spread of Buddhism abroad from its Indian homeland. The Mahayana ("Great Vehicle [of salvation]") arose in the first century B.C.E. Its proponents differentiated it sharply from the older, more conservative traditions of monk-oriented piety and thought, which they labeled the Hinayana ("Little Vehicle"). In Mahayana speculation Buddhas were seen as manifestations of a single principle of "Ultimate" Reality, and Siddhartha Gautama was held to be only one Buddha among many. The Mahayana stressed the model of the

Buddha's infinite compassion for all beings. The highest goal was not a *nirvana* of "selfish" extinction but the status of a **bodhisattva**, or "Buddha-to-be," who postpones his own nirvana until he has helped all other beings become enlightened. (See Document, "The Bodhisattva Ideal.")

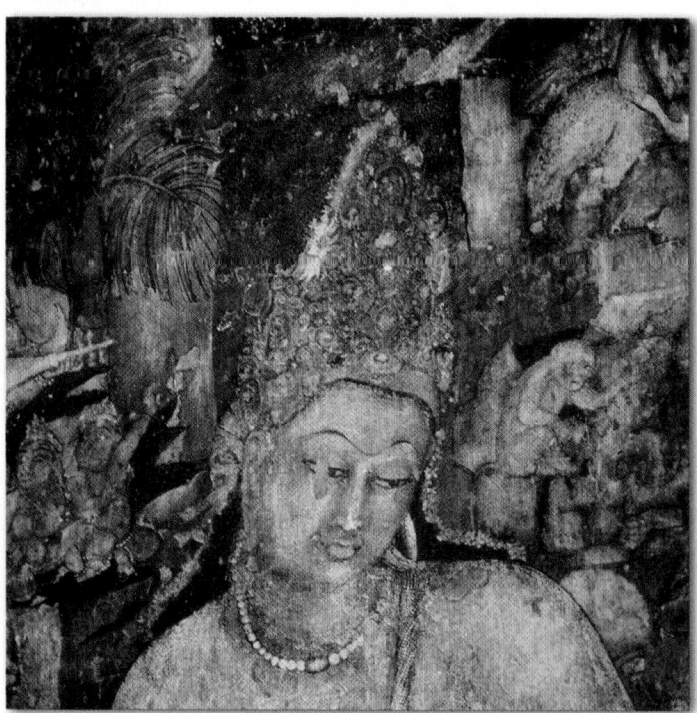

The Bodhisattva Avalokiteshvara. Detail of a Buddhist wall painting from the cave shrines at Ajanta (Maharashtra, India), Gupta period, ca. 475 C.E. Avalokiteshvara (known in China as Kwan-yin and in Japan as Kannon) is the supreme figure of infinite mercy. *Art Resource, N.Y.*

The Bodhisattva Ideal

Document

The following passages from two "perfection of wisdom" texts highlight the Mahayana doctrine of the bodhisattva, who becomes a divine savior as well as an example for others. The Mahayana tradition sees all who enter the Buddhist path as bodhisattvas in the making, beings bound to become Buddhas. It sees its bodhisattva ideal as a higher one than that of the older ideal of the Enlightened Being (Arahant), or the pratyeka, or "private," Buddha of the Theravada tradition whose goal is to achieve nirvana for himself.

◆ The ideal of compassion for all beings is held up as the central one in the Mahayana. How is this developed in the first passage? How is it used in the second to polemicize against the ideals of the Theravada? What might be the appeal of the bodhisattva ideal as opposed to the older Buddhist ideal of the self-perfected Enlightened One, the Arahant?

1. The bodhisattva is endowed with wisdom of a kind whereby he looks on all beings as though victims going to the slaughter. And immense compassion grips him. His divine eye sees . . . innumerable beings, and he is filled with great distress at what he sees, for many bear the burden of past deeds which will be punished in purgatory, others will have unfortunate rebirths which will divide them from the Buddha and his teachings, others must soon be slain, others are caught in the net of false doctrine, others cannot find the path [of salvation], while others have gained a favorable rebirth only to lose it again.

   So he pours out his love and compassion upon all those beings, and attends to them, thinking, "I shall become the savior of all beings, and set them free from their sufferings."

2. "What do you think, Shāriputra? Do any of the disciples and Private Buddhas ever think, 'After we have gained full enlightenment we will bring innumerable beings . . . to complete Nirvāna'?"

   "Certainly not, Lord!"

   "But," said the Lord, "the bodhisattva (has this resolve). . . . A firefly . . . doesn't imagine that its glow will light up all India or shine all over it, and so the disciples and Private Buddhas don't think that they should lead all beings to Nirvāna . . . after they have gained full enlightenment. But the disc of the sun, when it has risen, lights up all India and shines all over it. Similarly the bodhisattva, . . . when he has gained full enlightenment, brings countless beings to Nirvāna."

From *Sources of Indian Tradition*, by William Theodore de Bary. Copyright © 1988 by Columbia University Press. Reprinted with permission of the publisher.

The *bodhisattva* can offer this aid because his long career of self-sacrifice has gained him infinite merit. Salvation becomes possible not only through individual effort, but also through devotion to the Buddhas and *bodhisattvas*. At the popular level, this idea translated into devotional cults of transcendent Buddhas and *bodhisattvas* conceived of as cosmic beings. One of the most important events was that of the Buddha Amitabha, who personifies infinite compassion. Amitabha presides over a Western Paradise, or Pure Land, to which (through his infinite compassion) all who have faith in him have access. (See Chapter 9 for a discussion of Pure Land Buddhism in Japan.)

The older, more conservative "Way of the Elders" (Theravada) always focused on the monastic community but taught that service and gifts to the monks were a major source of merit for the laity. It emphasized gaining merit for a better rebirth through high standards of conduct, lay devotion to the Buddha, and pilgrimage to his relics at various shrines, or **stupas**. The Mahayana also held up monastic life as the ideal, but some of its greatest attractions were its strong devotionalism and virtually polytheistic delight in divine Buddhas and *bodhisattvas* to whom one could pray for mercy, help, and rebirth in paradise. The basis of Theravada piety and practice was the scriptural collection of the traditional teachings ascribed to the Buddha, as reported by his disciples. Theravadins rejected the Mahayana claim that later texts (e.g., the Lotus Sutra) contained the highest teachings of the Buddha.

Map 10–3. Spread of Buddhism Throughout Southeast Asia. By the 12th century C.E., Buddhism had taken root in many parts of Southeast Asia, often blending with local customs, as well as Hindu traditions that had been introduced earlier.

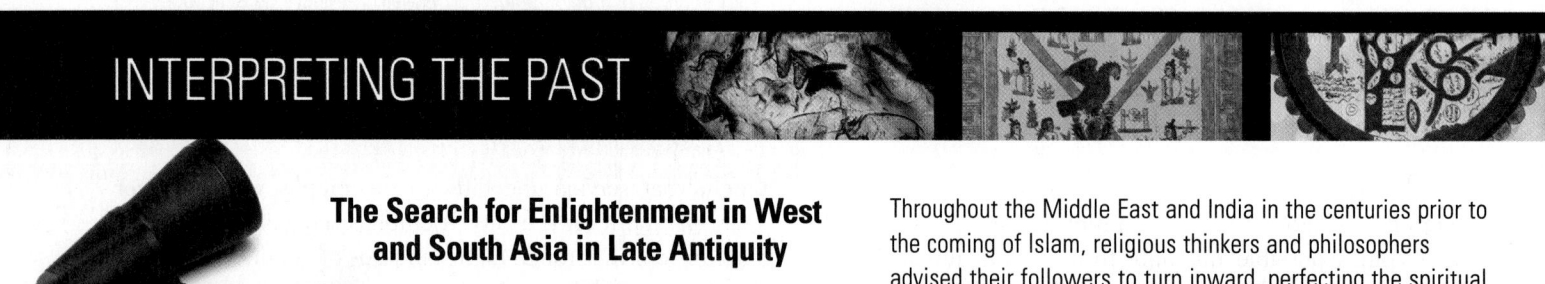

INTERPRETING THE PAST

The Search for Enlightenment in West and South Asia in Late Antiquity

As a young man, the Christian theologian and autobiographer St. Augustine (354-430 C.E.) was attracted to a sect of Manichees in his native North Africa. A man who struggled throughout his life to meet the demands of spiritual improvement while resisting the temptations of the physical body (such as his famous quote, "God give me chastity, but not yet"), Augustine sympathized with the sharp division the followers of Mani drew between the physical and spiritual worlds.

Throughout the Middle East and India in the centuries prior to the coming of Islam, religious thinkers and philosophers advised their followers to turn inward, perfecting the spiritual side of their natures and to de-emphasize the physical world around them. Using the documents and visual images in this chapter, explain how the quest for a satisfying inner life is reflected in the materials created by these civilizations. Relate the images to the documents, where possible.

Text Sources from Chapter 10

A Report of Mani's Words About His Mission (p. 316)
A Chinese Traveler on the Gupta Realm (p. 321)
Devoting Oneself to Krishna (p. 323)
The Bodhisattva Ideal (p. 325).

PRENTICE HALL
myhistorylab
Where it's a good time to connect to the past!

India gave Theravada Buddhism to Ceylon, Burma, and parts of Southeast Asia (see Map 10–3). Mahayana Buddhism predominated in Central Asia and China, from which it spread in the fifth through eighth centuries to Korea and Japan. Tantric Buddhism, an esoteric Mahayana tradition heavily influenced by Hinduism, entered Tibet from North India in the seventh century and became the dominant tradition there.

Summary

Iran. Under the Parthians (247 B.C.E.–223 C.E.) and the Sasanids (224–651 C.E.), Iran was a rival to Roman and Byzantine power in the Near East. The Sasanids, in particular, sought to restore the glory of the ancient Achaemenid Persian Empire and promoted native Persian culture. They also based their rule on orthodox Zoroastrianism and suppressed the Manichaeans as heretics. Although foreign trade flourished, the Parthian and Sasanid rulers favored the landed aristocracy at the expense of the peasantry, who were heavily taxed. The long wars with Rome and Byzantium ultimately sapped Sasanid strength and left the empire vulnerable to Islamic Arab invasion in the seventh century.

India. The Gupta period (320–467 C.E.) is considered one of the highlights of Indian civilization. Art, especially architecture and sculpture, flourished, and Indian civilization took on its enduring "Hindu" social, religious, and cultural shape. Indian contacts with Southeast Asia and China increased during this period. In society the fundamentally hierarchic nature of the caste system solidified. Hindu piety emphasized devotional cults to deities, especially Vishnu and Shiva. Indian Buddhism developed two main schools,

the Mahayana and the Theravada, which spread to other parts of Asia.

Review Questions

1. What are the key elements of Manichaean religion? How was it related to Christian and Zoroastrian traditions?

2. How did the Sasanid Empire develop after the fall of the Parthians? What were the principal economic bases of the Sasanid state?

3. What were the major religious issues in the Sasanid Empire? What role did Zoroastrian "orthodoxy" play in Sasanid affairs? What changes did Zoroastrianism undergo? Who were the main opponents of Zoroastrian tradition? In what ways did Nestorian Christianity influence the Sasanids?

4. How did the Silk Road bring new religious ideas to Central Asia in these centuries?

5. In what sense can the high Gupta period (ca. 320–450) be considered a "golden age"? What was the extent of the empire? Why did it collapse? Where did the locus of Indian culture move after the fifth century and why?

6. What factors in Persia and India in the seventh century might have made the Arab invasions possible? What was the role of Nestorianism in weakening the Sasanid rule?

7. What major affinities do you see between the classical Buddhist and Hindu traditions that crystallized in the first half of the first millennium C.E.? What major differences?

Visual Sources from Chapter 10

1) Manichaean Priests (p. 317)
2) Gupta Sculpture (p. 318)

Questions

How do these items reflect an "inward turn" in the cultures that created them?

Were there any consequences of this search for inner nirvana in the real world?

What instances of cross-cultural connection do you see in these materials?

Key Terms

bodhisattva (p. 324)
jatis (p. 322)
Mahayana (p. 324)
Manichaeism (p. 316)

stupa (p. 325)
Theravada (p. 324)
dharma (p. 322)
varnas (p. 322)

Note: To learn more about the topics in this chapter, please turn to the Suggested Readings at the end of the book. For additional sources related to this chapter please see the Primary Source DVD at the back of this text or MyHistoryLab.

The Formation of Islamic Civilization, 622–1000

- ◆ Origins and Early Development
- ◆ Women in Early Islamic Society
- ◆ Early Islamic Conquests
- ◆ The New Islamic World Order
- ◆ The High Caliphate
- ◆ Islamic Culture in the Classical Era

SLAMIC TRADITION AND CULTURE HAVE FORMED THE LAST GREAT WORLD CIVILIZATION to appear to date. On the one hand, its rise is the story of the creative and intellectual dynamism of distinctive Islamic religious, social, and political institutions within an initially Arab-dominated empire in the eastern Mediterranean and western Asian lands. On the other, it is the story of how Islamic ideas and institutions evolved from their Arabian beginnings into a cosmopolitan array of other cultures and societies. Each was a new creation of a particular place and particular circumstances, yet each was part of a larger, international Islamic culture and civilization.

The basic ideas and ideals of the Islamic worldview derived from a single, prophetic-revelatory event. Muhammad the Prophet's proclamation of the Qur'an.[1] This event galvanized the polytheist Arabs into a new kind of unity—that of the monotheist community of Muslims, or "submitters" to God, all of whom were to be held in equal regard. This community spread far beyond Arabia, and Persians, Indians, and others raised it to new heights. Arab military prowess and cultural pride joined with a new religious orientation to effect one of the most permanent revolutions in historical memory, but the peoples of the older cultural heartlands sustained this revolution and built a new culture and civilization upon it. Their acceptance of a new vision of society (and also of reality) as more compelling than any older vision—Jewish, Roman, Greek, Persian, Christian, Buddhist—gave rise to the multifaceted Islamic civilization. ■

---

[1] The common English transliteration of this Arabic word, *Koran,* is today being replaced by the more accurate *Qur'an;* similarly, *Muhammad* is preferable to *Mohammed, Muslim* to *Moslem, emir* to *amir,* and *ulama* to *ulema.*

والعشرين الذي على طرف و اليد اليمنى من العابة و هى علم و مع نخ فانشان
شاليان منها في قسط المجرة والاثنان الجنوبيان في الطرف الشرقي عنا
العاثر الوارد لا نهاية أشبهت المجرة نهر والنعام قد ورد النهر ويسمى البدوى
الذي على المنكب الايسر والسابع الذي على فوق السهم والحادى والعشرين
الذي على الكف والثاني على واحد والعشرين الذي تحت الابط وهى على مربع محجن
الهناء عيبه من المجرة الناحية المشرق والنعام الصادر يشبه النعام قتى
الماء وصدر عن النهر ويسمى الرابع الذي على الطرف الشمال ويلقى الذي
فن صارى بن النعامين في الشاه وقد صير بما صار القدر والخامس الذي
على السببه الثما ليمو القوس الطليمين ويسمى الموضع الذي بين النعلين
الوصل وهو المنزل العشرون ومن منازل القمر ويسمى التاسع والعاشر
والحادى عشر والثاني عشر والثالث عشر والرابع عشر وهو الستة التى
على خط مقتن من جنب السحان الذي على عين الرامي القلادة والفقارص
ايضا وهذه الستة المقت ستى التى قدر ابو حنيفان ان هذا البرج ستى أقوى
بها نهايتيند القوس ويسمى ايضا الى الموجى ويسمى الموضع المخالفت
القلادة الذي ليسرف وكوكب البلدة وهو المنزل الحادى والعشرين
منازل القمر ويقال ان القمر يا تصور فنر با بالقلادة ويجوز أ يكون كذلك
لان كوكبها فريبه من المنطقة ويسمى السادس والعشرين والسابع والعشرين
اللذين على الفخذ اليسرى والثاث الموخرة اليمنى الصردين
وهذه صورة الرامى

صورة الرامي على ما يرى فى الكرة

صورة

Islamic Astronomy. Initially Muslim astronomers believed that the earth rested motionless at the center of a series of eight spheres, the last of which was studded with fixed stars revolving daily from east to west, and at times from west to east. Muslim astronomers were influenced by Sanskrit, Sasanian, Syriac, and Greek texts on astronomy, which they amended. *Rami*, the Sagittarius in this illustration from an eighteenth-century copy of a book by 'Abd al-Rahman ibn 'Ubmar al-Sufi (d. 986), has a set of twenty-nine gold spots that represents a stellar constellation.

The Early Islamic Worlds of Arab and Persian Cultures

Mecca

The rise of Arabic, Persian, and Turkish Islamic cultures as core elements of the religious and cultural worlds of Islamic civilization is one of the great pivotal moments in world history. In its first three centuries, the Islamic polity was one of the most dynamic and expansive multi-ethnic and multi-lingual imperial states of its day. During the same centuries Chinese emperors of the Tang rebuilt and renovated the previous Han imperium; Charlemagne and the Carolingians struggled to hammer out a much smaller, more homogeneous empire in relatively underdeveloped Western Europe; Byzantium fought to survive against Arab and Turkish arms and turned inward to conserve its traditions; and post-Gupta India was divided into diverse regional kingdoms and remained still vulnerable to new forces (including those of Islam) moving into north-western India.

Only China compared favorably with the Islamic Arab world during this period in political and military power, cultural unity, creativity, and self-consciousness. The Tang and the Abbasids wielded commensurate power in their heydays, although the Chinese held together as a centralized state much longer than the original Islamic Arab empire. Certainly they were the two greatest political and cultural units in the world at the time. They each had one cultural language, and while variations of Chinese were spoken by a greater percentage of Chinese, Arabic quickly became the administrative and religious *lingua franca* of their empire, from Morocco to India and the South China Sea; it was learned across this vast expanse by Islamic subjects who became literate in Arabic by virtue of their Qur'an-based religious studies. The two civilizations also shared the military primacy of pastoral cavalry as well as the adaptive ability to incorporate new peoples into their larger culture—although Islamic cultures proved more flexible on this count. Indeed, the great elasticity and adaptability of Islamic

Origins and Early Development

The Setting

By 600 C.E., the dominant Eurasian political powers, Christian Byzantium and Zoroastrian Sasanid Persia, had confronted one another for over four centuries. This rivalry did not continue much longer. In the wake of one final, mutually exhausting conflict (608–627), a new Arab power broke in from the southern peninsular lands to weaken the one and destroy the other.

Pre-Islamic Arabia was not just a land of deserts, camels, and pastoralists. Byzantium and Persia had kept the nomads of the Syrian and northern Arabian steppe at bay by enlisting small Arab client kingdoms on the edge of the desert as buffer states. One of the biggest of these was Christian in faith. Arab kingdoms had long existed in the agriculturally rich highlands of southern Arabia, which had direct access to the international trade that moved along its

coasts (see Chapter 4). Some of these kingdoms, including a Jewish one in the sixth century, had been independent; others had been under Persian or Abyssinian control. In the western Arabian highland of the Hijaz, astride its major trade route, the town of Mecca was a center of the caravan trade and a pilgrimage site because of its famous sanctuary, the **Ka'ba** (or Kaaba), where pagan Arab tribes enshrined gods. The settled Arabs of Mecca ran a merchant republic in which older tribal values were breaking down under the strains of urban and commercial life. But none of the settled Arabs were cut off from the nomads, who lived on herding and by raiding settlements and caravans.

The Arabic language, a Semitic tongue of the Afro-Asiatic family (see Chapter 4), defined and linked the Arab peoples, however divided they were by religion, blood feuds, rivalry, and conflict. From the Yemen north to Syria-Palestine and Mesopotamia, the Arabs shared a highly developed poetic idiom. Every tribe had a poet to exhort its warriors and insult its enemies before battle. Poetry contests religious traditions and the attendant social order belie its current reputation in present-day Europe and elsewhere as an inherently inflexible system of values and practices.

Nevertheless, the bases of Islamic rule were clearly different, because its component states were spread over vastly more culturally heterogeneous and widely dispersed geographical areas than that of China. Conquest initially fueled the economy of the new Islamic imperial state, but in the long run, trade, artisan crafts, seafaring technology, and urban commercial centers became the backbone of the Islamic lands' prosperity, as well as the prime means of disseminating Islamic concepts and traditions to new lands, even as regional Islamic states replaced the original centralized imperial state of the early Caliphate.

The Islamic Arab, Persian, and Turkish achievement was unique in this period in that it resulted from an effort to build something new rather than to recapture old traditions, whether religious, social, or political. In later centuries the early Arab impact on Islamic culture and religion was tempered and changed by the vast numbers of Persian- and Turkish-speaking Muslims and also the many regional groups, from Swahili speakers in East Africa to the Malays and Indonesians of Southeast Asia. Nevertheless, Arabic went abroad with the holy Qur'an as the sacred medium of God's final revelation. Since Islam's emergence from the Arabian Peninsula, individual Muslims worldwide have always learned something of Arabic and the sacred book.

This achievement was a new historical phenomenon, at least in its global scale. Although the Muslim faith can be seen as an evolution and even reformation of Jewish and Christian monotheism, it was fundamentally an effort to do something new—not merely to reform, but to subsume older traditions of Jews or Christians in a more comprehensive vision of God's plan on earth. And just as Islam can be seen as an extension or (in Muslim eyes) reform of Jewish and Christian monotheism, Muslims also built on previous Arab, Persian, and Turkish traditions; they adopted and adapted those of the neighboring African-European-Asian cultures. Yet as both a civilization and a religious tradition, Islamic peoples developed their own distinctive stamp that persisted wherever Muslims extended the *Umma*.

Focus Questions

◆ Why did only China compare favorably with the Islamic world during the first centuries after the birth of Islam? How were the two civilizations similar, and how were they different?

◆ What is unique about the Islamic achievement? In what ways was it built on the traditions of earlier religions?

---

were also held, often in conjunction with the annual trade fairs that brought tribes together under a general truce.

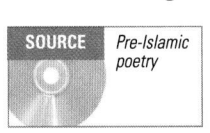
SOURCE *Pre-Islamic poetry*

Islam is not a "religion of the desert." It began in a commercial urban center and first flourished in an agricultural oasis and small merchant towns of the Hijaz region of the western Arabian peninsula. Its first converts were Meccan townsfolk and date farmers of Yathrib (Medina). Before becoming Muslims, most of these Arabs were animists, but some were Jews or Christians, or influenced by Jews or Christians. Caravans passed north and south from Damascus through Mecca to Aden and the Indian Ocean, and no merchant involved in this traffic, as Muhammad himself was, could have been unfamiliar with the many diverse cultures along the trade routes. Early Muslim leaders used the Arab tribes as warriors and looked to Arab culture for their own traditional roots long after the locus of Islamic power had left Arabia. But the empire and civilization they gradually created were centered in the heartlands of Mediterranean and West Asian urban and rural cultures and based more on settled communal existence than on rural and desert tribal societies and economies.

Muhammad and the Qur'an

Muhammad (ca. 570–632) was raised an orphan in one of the commercial families of the old Meccan tribe of Quraysh. Later, in the midst of a successful business career made possible by his marriage to Khadija (d. ca. 619), an older wealthy Meccan widow and entrepreneur, he grew troubled by the idolatry, worldliness, and lack of social conscience around him. These traits would have equally offended sensitive Jewish or Christian morality, with which he was familiar. Yet these traditions remained foreign to most Arabs, even though some Arab tribes were Jewish or Christian.

When he was about forty years old, Muhammad felt himself called by the one true God to "rise and warn" his

The Ka'ba in Mecca. The Ka'ba is viewed in Muslim tradition as the site of the first "house of God," held to have been founded by Adam, then rebuilt by Abraham and his son Ishmael at God's command. It is held to have fallen later into idolatrous use until Muhammad's victory over the Meccans and his cleansing of the holy cubical structure (*Ka'ba* means "cube"). The Ka'ba is the geographical point toward which all Muslims face when performing ritual prayer. It and the plain of Arafat outside Mecca are the two foci of the pilgrimage of Hajj that each Muslim aspires to make at least once in a lifetime. *Mehmet Biber/Photo Researchers, Inc.*

fellow Arabs about their frivolous disregard for morality and the worship due their Creator. On repeated occasions revelation came to him through a figure who was gradually identified as God's messenger angel, Gabriel. It took the form of a "reciting" (**qur'an**) of God's Word—now rendered in "clear Arabic" for the Arabs, just as it had been given to previous prophets in Hebrew or other languages for their peoples.

The message of the Qur'an was clear: The Prophet is to warn his people against worship of false gods and all immorality, especially injustice to the poor, orphans, widows, and women in general. At the end of time, on Judgment Day, every person will be bodily resurrected to face eternal punishment in hellfire or eternal joy in paradise, according to how he or she has lived. The way to paradise lies in gratitude to God for the bounties of creation, his prophetic and revelatory guidance, and his readiness to forgive the penitent. Social justice and obedient worship of the

one Lord are required of every person. Each is to recognize his or her creatureliness and God's transcendence. The proper response is "submission" (**islam**) to God's will, becoming *muslim* ("submissive" or "surrendering") in one's worship and morality. All of creation praises and serves God by nature except humans, who can choose to obey or to reject him. (See Document, "The Qur'an, or 'Recitation,' of God's Word.")

In this Qur'anic message, the ethical monotheism of Judaic and Christian tradition (probably reinforced by Zoroastrian and Manichaean ideas) reached its logical conclusion in a radically theocentric vision; it demanded absolute obedience to the one Lord of the Universe. The Qur'anic revelations explicitly state that Muhammad is only the last in a long line of prophets chosen to bring God's word: Noah, Abraham, Moses, Jesus, and nonbiblical Arabian figures like Salih had been sent before on similar mis-

The Qur'an, or "Recitation," of God's Word $\quad$ Document

The Qur'an has many themes, from moral admonition, social justice, eternal punishment for the ungodly and exemplary stories of past peoples and their prophets to God's majesty and uniqueness, his bountiful natural world and compassion for humankind, and the joys of paradise.

◆ Can you identify at least four major Qur'anic themes in the selections below? To what end are the bounties of creation cited? What is the image of God conveyed in these selections? What can you infer about the Qur'anic conception of prophethood? of the Judgment Day?

The revelation of the Book is from God who is mighty and wise. There are signs for men of faith, in the heavens and in the earth, in your being created and in God's scattered throng of creatures—signs for people with a grasp of truth.

There are signs, too—for those with a mind to understand—in the alternation of night and day, and in the gracious rain God sends from heaven to renew the face of the parched earth, and in the veering of the winds.

These are the signs of God which truly We recite to you. Having God and His signs, in what else after that will you believe as a message?

—*Sura 45:1–6*

Were you set to count up the mercies of God you would not be able to number them. God is truly forgiving and merciful.

—*Sura 16:18*

Such is God your Lord. There is no god but He, creator of all things. Then worship Him who is guardian over all there is. No human perception comprehends Him, while He comprehends all perception. He is beyond all conceiving, the One who is infinitely aware.

—*Sura 6:102–103*

To God belong the east and the west, and wheresoever you turn there is the face of God. Truly God is all-pervading, all-knowing.

—*Sura 2:115*

You people of the Book, why are you so argumentative about Abraham, seeing that the Torah and the Gospel were only sent down after his time? Will you not use your reason? You are people much given to disputing about things within your comprehension: why insist on disputing about things of which you have no knowledge? Knowledge belongs to God and you lack it!

Abraham was not a Jew, nor was he a Christian. He was a man of pure worship (a *hanif*,) and a Muslim: he was not one of those pagan idolaters. . .

—*Sura 3:65–67*

Yet you [people] deny the reality of the judgment. There are guardians keeping watch over you, noble beings keeping record, who know your every deed. The righteous will dwell in bliss. The evil-doers will be in *Jahim*, in the burning on Judgment Day, and there will be no absconding for them.

What can make you realize the Day of judgment as it is? . . . the Day when there is no soul that can avail another soul. For the authority on that Day is God's alone.

Sura 82.1–5, 9, 19

Excerpt from *Readings in the Qur'an*, by Kenneth Cragg. Copyright © 1988 by Kenneth Cragg. Reprinted by permission of HarperCollins, Inc.

sions. The Qur'an is in fact filled with references and stories of earlier Biblical figures, most prominently Abraham and Moses. The person from the Christian New Testament who is mentioned most frequently in the Qur'an is Mary, mother of Jesus. Because the communities of these earlier prophets had strayed from their scriptures' teachings or altered them, Muhammad was given one final iteration of God's message. Jews and Christians, like pagans, were summoned to respond to the moral imperatives of the Qur'an.

The Prophet's preaching fell largely on deaf ears in the first years after his calling. However, a few did follow the lead of his wife, Khadija, in recognizing him as a divinely chosen reformer of individual and communal life. Some prominent Meccans joined him, but the merchant aristocracy as a whole resisted. His preaching against their traditional gods and goddesses threatened both their ancestral ways and also the Meccan pilgrimage shrine and the lucrative trade it attracted. The Meccans began to persecute

Muhammad's followers. After the deaths of Khadija and Muhammad's uncle and protector, Abu Talib, the situation worsened, and the Prophet even had to send a small band of Muslims to seek temporary refuge in Abyssinia. Then, as a result of his growing reputation as a moral and holy man, Muhammad was called to Yathrib (an important agricultural oasis about 240 miles north of Mecca) to arbitrate among its five quarrelsome tribes, three of which were Jewish. Having sent his Meccan followers ahead, Muhammad fled Mecca in July 622 for Yathrib, afterward to be known as Medina (al-Madina, "the City [of the Prophet]"). Some dozen years later, this "emigration," or **hegira**, became the starting point for the Islamic calendar, the event marking the creation of a distinctive Islamic community, or **umma**.[2]

Muhammad quickly cemented ties between the Meccan emigrants and the Medinans, many of whom became converts. Raids on his Meccan enemies' caravans established his leadership. They reflect the economic dimension of the Medinan-Meccan struggle. The Arab Jews of Medina largely rejected his religious message and authority. They even made contact with his Meccan enemies, moving Muhammad to turn on them, kill or enslave some, banish others, and take their lands. Many of the continuing revelations of the Qur'an from this period pertain to communal order or to the Jews and Christians who rejected Islam.

The basic Muslim norms took shape in Medina: allegiance to the *Umma;* honesty in public and personal affairs; modesty in personal habits; abstention from alcohol and pork; fair division of inheritances; improved treatment of women, especially as to property and other rights in marriage; careful regulation of marriage and divorce; ritual ablution before any act of worship, be it Qur'an reciting or prayer; three (later five) daily rites of worship, facing the Meccan shrine of the Ka'ba; payment of a kind of tithe to support less fortunate Muslims; daytime fasting for one month each year (Ramadan) and, eventually, pilgrimage to Mecca (**hajj**) at least once in a lifetime, if one is able. Thus at the core of Islam are the so-called Five Pillars: (1) *Shahada*, or the Muslim Creed ("There is no God but God and Muhammad is God's prophet"; (2) *Salat*, or prayer; (3) *Sawm*, fasting during Ramadan; (4) *Zakat*, or alms; and (5) *Hajj*, the pilgrimage.

Acceptance of Islamic political authority brought tolerance. A Jewish oasis yielded to Muhammad's authority and was allowed, unlike the resistant Medinan Jews, to keep its lands, practice its faith, and receive protection in return for

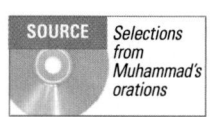

SOURCE Selections from Muhammad's orations

paying a head tax. This practice was followed ever after for Jews, Christians, and other "people of Scripture" who accepted Islamic rule. After long conflict, the Meccans surrendered to Muhammad, and his generosity in accepting them into the *Umma* set the pattern for the later Islamic conquests. Following an age-old practice, Muhammad cemented many of his alliances with marriage (although while Khadija was alive, he did not take a second wife). In the last years of the Prophet's life, the once tiny band of Muslims became the heart of a pan-Arabian tribal confederation, bound together by personal allegiance to Muhammad, submission (*islam*) to God, and membership in the community, or *umma*.

Women In Early Islamic Society

The *umma* is a central concern in Islam, and at the basis of the *umma* is the family. As a result, family law played a central role in the development of Islamic Law. It is in the context of Islamic family law that the rights of women and men are stipulated.

The Qur'an introduced into Arabian society radical new ideas that drastically improved the status of women. For example, it prohibited the common practice of female infanticide stating that all children regardless of sex should have the opportunity to live. The Qur'an recognizes a woman's right to contract her own marriage and that she, and not her male relatives, should receive the dowry from her husband. Legally speaking a woman entering marriage was not an object that was bought and sold but rather a party to a negotiated contract. A woman was also guaranteed the right to inherit, own, and manage property.

Women are therefore afforded many rights in the Qur'an. Yet the Qur'an does not assume the full gender equality such as that advocated in some modern societies in the twenty-first century. Islamic Law stipulates that the father or the senior male controls and guides the family unit. A male receives a larger share in inheritance and has fewer restrctions to initiate a divorce; also, a man's eyewitness testimony is more valid in court than a woman's. Even though the Qur'an introduced many positive changes for women, it also legitimized and presupposed a patriarchial society. The Qur'an did not outlaw particular customs that practically and symbolically prevented women from reaching full equality.

Polygamy is a practice that is often closely identified with Islam. The Qur'an tolerates the practice but seeks to control it. It regulates the number of spouses that a man can have. It states that a man can have up to four wives provided he can treat them all equally and fairly (Q. 4:3). Some Muslims interpret that verse as essentially prohibiting the

---

[2] The twelve-month Muslim lunar year is shorter than the Christian solar year by about eleven days, giving a difference of about three years per century. Muslim dates are reckoned from the month in 622 in which Muhammad began his Hegira (Arabic: *Hijra*). Thus Muslims celebrated the start of their lunar year 1401 in November 1980 (1979–1980 C.E. = A.H. [Anno Hegirae] 1400), whereas it was only 1,358 solar years from 622 to 1980.

Veiled Women. Women mourning the death of martyrs in combat. Safavid fresco, 17th century, Isfahan, Iran. *Art Resource, N.Y.*

SOURCE *Rabia al-Adawiyya, "Brothers, my peace is in my aloneness."*

that are both Islamic and in concert with modern ideas of equality. And of course different Islamic cultures, from Indonesia to North Africa to Europe and America, differ greatly in how literally or liberally they apply traditional practices and customs.

In early Islamic history, many women—such as the wives of Muhammad (Khadija and A'isha)—played influential roles in the development of Islam. They were instrumental in defining certain aspects of Islamic law and even commanded troops in warfare. In medieval times, however, women were not, with a few notable exceptions, prominent in the public sphere. As in many other places around the world, women were largely cut off from public political, social, and educational activities. These negative effects are still visible today in many parts of the Mediterranean and West Asian regions even as women generally are increasingly negotiating their way into the public sphere.

practice because it is impossible to guarantee that you treat and love two or more women "equally." Thus one finds monogamy as the predominant marital practice overall in Muslim communities globally.

Another practice that is commonly associated with Muslim women is veiling, which is understood as the practice of modesty or hijab. The veil is a generic term that applies to a variety ways of dress such as *chador*, and *burqa*. The veiling of women was a customary practice in a number of pre-Islamic societies, especially among upper-class women in the Byzantine and Sasanian Empires. It was, and still is, common in many parts of the Mediterranean.

Islam did not invent the veil. The Qur'an does not specifically stipulate veiling. On the contrary, it emphasizes that both men and women are responsible for their actions and should strive for the common good. However, the Qur'an stipulates that women should guard their modesty and that they "should draw their veils over their bosom and display their beauty only to their husbands and their fathers." (Q. 24:31). The call for modesty is also applicable to men.

As with the spirit of many religious dictums, the implementation of the letter of this imperative has proven problematic. Though the original intention of the veil was to protect women and their honor, the veil and the corollary idea of seclusion in effect largely barred women from public life until the twentieth century. These verses, along with other verses of the Qur'an, have been used to justify patriarchy and militated against women utilizing the full rights that the Qur'an affords them. With more education in modern times, many Muslim women have turned to the Qur'an to interpret these verses anew to stipulate more actions and practices

Early Islamic Conquests

In 632 Muhammad died, leaving neither a son nor a designated successor. The new *umma* faced its first major crisis. A political struggle between Meccan and Medinan factions ended in a pledge of allegiance to Abu Bakr, the most senior of the early Meccan converts. Following old Arabian patterns, many tribes renounced their allegiance to the Prophet at his death. Nevertheless, Abu Bakr's rule (632–634) as Muhammad's successor, or "caliph" (Arabic: *khalifa*), reestablished Medinan hegemony and at least nominal religious conformity for all Arabia. The Arabs were forced to recognize in the *umma* a new kind of supratribal community that demanded more than allegiance to a particular leader.

Course of Conquest

Under the next two caliphs, Umar (634–644) and Uthman (644–656), Arab armies burst out of the peninsula, intent on more than traditional Bedouin booty raids. In one of history's most astonishing military operations, by 643 they had conquered the Byzantine and Sasanid territories of the Fertile Crescent, Egypt, and most of Iran. For the first time in centuries the lands from Egypt to Iran came under one rule. Finally, Arab armies swept west over the Byzantine-controlled Libyan coast and, in the east, pushed to the Oxus, defeating the last Sasanid ruler by 651.

An interlude of civil war followed during the contested caliphate of Muhammad's cousin and son-in-law Ali (656–661). Then the fifth caliph, Mu'awiya (661–680), directed further expansion and consolidated the new

Map Exploration

To explore this map further, go to http://www.prenhall.com/craig_maps

Map 11–1. Muslim Conquests and Domination of the Mediterranean to about 750 C.E. The rapid spread of Islam (both religion and political-military power) is shown here. Within 125 years of Muhammad's rise, Muslims came to dominate Spain and all areas south and east of the Mediterranean.

empire. In the Mediterranean, an Islamic fleet conquered Cyprus, plundered Sicily and Rhodes, and crippled Byzantine sea power. By 680 control of greater Persia was solidified by permanent Arab garrisoning of Khorasan, much of Anatolia was raided, Constantinople was besieged (but not taken), and Armenia was under Islamic rule.

Succeeding decades saw the eastern Berbers of Libyan North Africa defeated and converted to Islam in substantial numbers. With their help, "the West" (*al-Maghrib*, modern Morocco and Algeria) fell quickly. In 711 raids into Spain began (the name of the Berber Muslim leader of the first invaders, Tariq, lives on in the present-day name of *Gibraltar*, a corruption of *Jabal Tariq*, "Mount Tariq"). By 716 the disunited Spanish Visigoth kingdoms had fallen, and much of Iberia was under Islamic control. Pushing north into France, the Arabs were finally checked by a defeat at the hands of Charles Martel at Poitiers (732). At the opposite end of the empire, buoyed by large-scale Arab immigration, Islamic forces consolidated their holdings as far as the Oxus River (Amu Darya) basin. In 710 Arab armies reached the Indus region. Islamic power was supreme from the Atlantic to central Asia (see Map 11–1).

Factors of Success

The basic factor behind this rapid expansion was the weakened military and economic condition of the Byzantines and Sasanids—the result of their chronic warfare with one another. The new Islamic vision of society and life also united the Arabs and attracted others. Its corollary was the commitment among the Islamic leadership to extend "the abode of submission" (*Dar al-Islam*) abroad. However, too

The Five Pillars of Islam

Overview

The five pillars of Islam constitute the basic ritual practices that are required of all Muslims. Muslims recognize that these rituals form the foundations of their practice. Yet not all Muslims observe them or do so only partially. As is common among adherents of other religions, the reality of practice is often far from the ideal.

The five pillars of Islam are

1. *Shahahda* ("witnessing" or testifying to the Muslim creed)
2. *Salat* (formal prayer or worship, alone or communally)
3. *Sawm* (fasting in the month of Ramadan)
4. *Zakat* (alms giving in proportion to one's wealth)
5. *Hajj* (pilgrimage to Mecca at least once in a lifetime, if possible)

Some Muslims regard *jihad* (to struggle justly or strive justly for God; sometimes translated as "holy war" but more commonly understood as personal religious striving having nothing to do with warfare) as a sixth pillar.

much has been made of Muslim zeal for martyrdom. Assurance of paradise for those engaged in **jihad**, or "just struggle (in the path of God)," is less likely to have motivated the average Arab tribesman—who, at least at the beginning, was usually only nominally a Muslim—as much as promise of booty. Life in the Arabian Peninsula was so hard that the hope of greater prosperity must have been compelling.

Still, religious zeal was important, especially as time went on. The early policy of sending Qur'an reciters among the Arab armies to teach essentials of Muslim faith and practice had its effects. Another major factor was the leadership of the first caliphs and field generals, which, combined with Byzantine and Iranian exhaustion, gave Arab armies a distinct advantage. Many subject populations also accepted, even welcomed, Islamic rule as a relief from Byzantine or Persian oppression. Crucial here was the Muslim willingness to allow Christian, Jewish, and even Zoroastrian groups to continue as minorities (with their own legal systems and no military obligations) under protection of Islamic rule. In return, they had to recognize Islamic political authority, pay a non-Muslim head tax (*jizya*), and not proselytize or interfere with Muslim religious practice. (Ironically, as time went on, the head tax and other strictures on non-Muslims encouraged many Christians and Jews to convert.)

Finally, the astute policies of the early leaders helped give the conquests overall permanence: relatively little bloodshed, destruction, or disruption in conquest; adoption of existing administrative systems (and personnel) with minimal changes; adjustment of unequal taxation; appointment of capable governors; and strategic siting of new garrison towns like Basra, Kufa, and Fustat (later Cairo).

The New Islamic World Order

Although they were quick to adopt and adapt existing traditions in the lands they conquered, the Muslims brought with them a new worldview that demanded a new political, social, and cultural reality, however long it might take to effect it. Beyond military and administrative problems loomed the more important question of the nature of Islamic society. Under the Prophet the new community of the *Umma* had replaced, at least in theory and basic organization, the tribal, blood-based sociopolitical order in Arabia. Yet once the Arabs (most of whom became Muslims) had to rule non-Arabs and non-Muslims, new problems tested the ideal of an Islamic polity. Chief among these were leadership and membership qualifications, social order, and religious and cultural identity.

The Caliphate

Allegiance to Muhammad had rested on his authority as a divine spokesperson and gifted leader. His first successors were chosen much as were Arab *shaykhs* ("sheiks"), or tribal chieftains: by agreement of the leaders, or elders, of the new religious "tribe" of Muslims on the basis of superior personal qualities and the precedence in faith conferred by piety and association with the Prophet. The true line of succession to Muhammad was known as the **caliphate**, and the successors' titles were "successor" (*khalifa*, or caliph), "leader" (**imam**—literally, the one who stands in front to lead the ritual prayer), and "commander (**emir**) of the faithful." These names underscored religious and political authority, both of which most Muslims were willing to recognize in the caliphs Abu Bakr and Umar, and potentially in Uthman and Ali. Unfortunately, by the time of Uthman and Ali, dissension led to civil war. Yet the first four caliphs had all been close to Muhammad, and this closeness gave their reigns a nostalgic aura of pristine purity, especially as the later caliphal institution was based largely on sheer power legitimized by hereditary succession. (See Document, "Al-Mawardi and al-Hilli.")

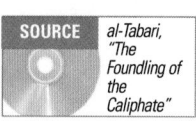 **SOURCE** *al-Tabari, "The Foundling of the Caliphate"*

The nature of Islamic leadership became an issue with the first civil war (656–661) and the recognition of Mu'awiya, a kinsman of Uthman, as caliph. He founded the first dynastic caliphate, that of his Meccan clan of Umayya (661–750). Umayyad descendants held power until they were ousted in 750 by the Abbasid clan, which based its legitimacy on descent from Abbas, an uncle of the Prophet. The Umayyads had the prestige of the office held by the first four, "rightly guided" caliphs. But many also deemed them to be worldly kings compared to the first four, who were seen as true Muslim successors to Muhammad.

The Abbasids won the caliphate by open rebellion in 750, aided by exploitation of pious dissatisfaction with Umayyad worldliness, non-Arab Muslim resentment of Arab preference (primarily in Iran), and dissension among Arab tribal factions in the garrison towns. For all their stress on the Muslim character of their caliphate, the Abbasids were scarcely less worldly and continued the hereditary rule begun by the Umayyads. This they did well enough to retain control of most of the far-flung Islamic territories until 945. Thereafter, although their line continued until 1258, the caliphate was primarily a titular office representing an Islamic unity that existed politically in name only.

The Dome of the Rock in Jerusalem. An early example of Islamic architecture, it dates from the seventh century and the first wave of Arab expansion. It is built on the rock from which Muslims believe Muhammad had an experience of ascent into heaven and on which Jews believe Abraham prepared to sacrifice Isaac. The Dome of the Rock has special symbolic significance for Muslims because the site is associated with the life and story of the Prophet. For a few years of Muhammad's time in Medina, Muslims even faced Jerusalem when they prayed, before a new Qur'anic revelation changed the direction to Mecca. *Scala/Art Resource, N.Y.*

The *Ulama*

Although the caliph could exert his power to influence religious matters, he was never "emperor and pope combined," as European writers have claimed. Religious leadership in the *umma* devolved instead on another group. The functional successors of the Prophet in society at large were those Muslims recognized for piety and learning and sought as informal or even formal (as with state-appointed judges) authorities. Initially, they were the "Companions" (male and female) of Muhammad with greatest stature in the old Medinan *umma*—including the first four caliphs. This generation was replaced by those younger followers most concerned with preserving, interpreting, and applying the Qur'an and with maintaining the norms of the Prophet's original *umma*. Because the Qur'an contained few actual legal prescriptions, they had to draw on precedents from Meccan and Medinan practice, as well as on oral traditions from and about the Prophet and Companions. They also had to develop and standardize grammatical rules for a common Arabic language based on the Qur'an and pre-Islamic poetry. Furthermore, they had to improve the phonetic, cursive Arabic script, a task done so well that the script was gradually applied as the standard written medium for languages wherever Islamic religion and culture became dominant: among Iranians, Turks, Indians, Indonesians, Malays, East Africans, and others. Along with these and other religious, intellectual, and cultural achievements, they developed an enduring pattern of education based on study under those persons highest in the unbroken temporal chain of trustworthy Muslims linking the current age with that of the earliest *umma*.

These scholars came to be known as **ulama** ("persons of right knowledge," the Anglicized Arabic plural of *alim*). Their personal legal opinions and collective discussions of issues, from theological doctrine to criminal punishments, established a basis for religious and social order. By the ninth century they had largely defined the understanding of the divine Law, or *Shari'a*, that Muslims ever after have held to be definitive for legal, social, commercial, political, ritual, and moral concerns. This understanding and the methods by which it was derived form the Muslim science of jurisprudence, the core discipline of Islamic learning.

The centers of *ulama* activity were Medina, Mecca, and especially Iraq (primarily Basra and Kufa, later Baghdad), then Khorasan, Syria, North Africa, Spain, and Egypt. In Umayyad times, the *ulama* had already become the guardians of the Muslim conscience, often criticizing caliphal rule when it strayed too far from Muslim norms. In time the *ulama* became a new elite, one eventually identified with the upper class of each regional society under Islamic rule. Caliphs and their governors regularly sought their advice, but often only for moral or legal (the two are, in Muslim view, the same) sanction of a contemplated (or accomplished) action. Some *ulama* gave dubious sanctions and compromised themselves. Yet incorruptible *ulama* were seldom persecuted for their opinions (except when they supported sectarian rebellions), mostly because of their status and influence among rank-and-file Muslims.

Thus, without building a formal clergy, Muslims developed a workable moral-legal system based on a formally trained, if informally organized, scholarly elite and a tradition of concern with religious ideals in matters of public affairs and social order. If the caliphs and their deputies were seldom paragons of piety and were often ruthless, they had at least to act with circumspection and support pious standards in public. Thus the *ulama* shared leadership in Muslim societies with the rulers, even if unequally—an enduring pattern in Islamic states.

Ritual Worship. These illustrations show the sequence of movement prescribed for the ritual prayers of Salat that each Muslim should perform five times a day. Various words of praise, prayer, and recitation from the Qur'an accompany each position and movement. The ritual symbolizes the Muslim's complete obedience to God and recognition of God as the one, eternal, omnipotent Lord of the universe. *Library of Congress.*

The *Umma*

A strength of the Qur'anic message was its universality. By the time of the first conquests, the new state was already so rooted in Islamic ideals that non-Arab converts had to be accepted, even if it meant loss of tax revenue. The social and political status of new converts was, however, clearly second to that of Arabs. Umar had organized the army register, or *diwan*, according to tribal precedence in conversion to, or (in the unique case of Christian Arab tribes) fighting for, Islam. The *diwan* served as the basis for distributing and taxing the new wealth, which perpetuated Arab precedence. The new garrisons, which rapidly became urban centers of Islamic culture, kept the Arabs enough apart that they were not simply absorbed into the cultural patterns or traditions of the new lands. The dominance of the Arabic language was ensured by the centrality of the Qur'an in Muslim life and the notion of its perfect Arabic form, together with the increasing administrative use of Arabic to replace Aramaic, Greek, Middle Persian, or Coptic.

Non-Arab converts routinely attached themselves to Arab tribes as "clients," which assured protection and a place in the **diwan**. Still, this meant accepting a permanent second-class citizenship alongside the Arabs. Although many non-Arabs, especially Persians, mastered Arabic and prospered, dissatisfaction among client Muslims led to uprisings against caliphal authority. Persian-Arab tensions were especially strong in Umayyad and early Abbasid times. Nevertheless, a Persian cultural renaissance eventually raised the Islamicized, or modern Persian language to high status in Islamic culture. Consequently, it profoundly affected Islamic religion, art, and literature.

Caliphal administration joined with the evolution of legal theory and practice and the consolidation of religious norms to give stability to the emerging Islamic society. So powerful was the Muslim vision of society that, upon the demise of a caliph, or even a dynasty such as the Umayyads, the *umma* and the caliphal office continued. There were, however, conflicting notions of that vision. In the first three Islamic centuries, two major interpretations crystallized that reflected idealistic interpretations of the *Umma*, its leadership, and membership. When neither proved practical, they became minority visions that continued to fire the imaginations of some but failed to win broad-based support. A third, "centrist," vision found favor with the majority because it spoke to a wide spectrum and accommodated inevitable compromises in the cause of Islamic unity.

The Kharijites   The most radical idealists traced their political origin to the first civil war (656–661). They were the Kharijites, or "seceders" from Ali's camp because, in their view, he compromised with his enemies. The Kharijites' position was that the Muslim polity must be based on strict Qur'anic principles. They espoused total equality of the faithful and held that the leader of the *Umma* should be the best Muslim, whoever that might be. They took a rigorist view of membership in the *Umma*: anyone who committed a major sin was no longer a Muslim. Extreme Kharijites called on true Muslims to rebel against the morally compromised reigning caliph. The extremist groups were constant rallying points for opposition to the Umayyads and the Abbasids.

More moderate Kharijites tolerated less-than-ideal Muslims and caliphs, yet they retained a strong sense of the moral imperatives of Muslim duty. Their ideals influenced wider Muslim pietism and even today moderate Kharijite groups survive in Oman and North Africa.

The Shi'a   A second position was defined largely in terms of leadership of the *Umma*. Muhammad had no surviving sons, and his son-in-law and cousin Ali claimed the caliphate in 656, partly on the basis of his blood tie to the Prophet. His claim was contested by Mu'awiya in the first Islamic civil war. When Mu'awiya took over after a Kharijite murdered Ali in 661, many of Ali's followers felt that Islamic affairs had gone awry. The roots of the "partisans of Ali" (*Shi'at Ali*, or simply the **Shi'a**, or *Shi'ites*), go back to Ali's murder and especially to that of his son Husayn at Karbala, in Iraq, at the hands of Umayyad troops (680).

While all Muslims esteemed Ali for his closeness to Muhammad, Shi'ites believed him to be the Prophet's appointed successor. Ali's blood tie with Muhammad was

Iraqi Shi'ites flagellate themselves during a procession in Karbala in March 2006 to mark the fortieth and final day of mourning for Husayn, Muhammad's grandson, who was killed by Umayyad forces in 680 C.E.

Al-Mawardi and al-Hilli

Document

After the death of the Prophet Muhammad, the Islamic community faced a serious political crisis. Muhammad did not provide his followers with specific instructions on who should rule the Muslim community and how it should be ruled. The question of political authority became a hotly contested issue and resulted in the split between Sunni and Shi'a Muslim that has prevailed to this day. Below are two early and important interpretations on political legitimacy by an influential Sunni official, al-Mawardi (974–1058), and al-Hilli (1250–1326), a leading Shi'a theologian.

◆ What are the essential characteristics of a ruler according to both thinkers? What do these thinkers have in common and what are their differences?

AL-MAWARDI

The *Imamate*: God, whose power be glorified, has instituted a chief of the Community as a successor to Prophethood and to protect the Community and assume the guidance of its affairs. Thus the *Imamate* is a principle on which stands the bases of the religious Community and by which its general welfare is regulated, so that the common good is assured by it. Hence rules pertaining to the *Imamate* take precedence over any other rules of government. . . .

Thus the obligatory nature of the *Imamate* is established, and it is an obligation performed for all by a few, like fighting in a holy war, or the study of the religious sciences, and if no one is exercising it, then there emerge two groups. . . .

As for those persons fitted for the *Imamate*, the conditions related to them are seven: . . . Justice in all its characteristics. . . . Knowledge requisite for independent judgment (*ijtihad*) about revealed and legal matters. . . . Soundness of the senses in hearing, sight, and speech, in a degree to accord with their normal functioning. . . . Soundness of the members from any defect that would prevent freedom of movement and agility. . . . Judgment conducive to the governing of subjects and administering matters of general welfare. . . . Courage and bravery to protect Muslim territory and wage the *jihad* against the enemy. . . . Pedigree: he must be of the tribe of Quraysh, since there has come down an explicit statement on this, and the consensus has agreed. . . .

He must maintain the Religion according to the principles established and agreed upon by the earliest Muslims (*salaf al-umma*), and if an innovator appears, or someone with dubious opinions who deviates from those principles, then he must clarify matters by logical proofs, and show him the correct way, and finally apply the rules and punishments to which he is bound, that religion may be preserved from disorder, and the Community from stumbling. . . .

AL-HILLI

He who is worthy of the *Imamate* is a person appointed and specified by God and His Prophet, not any chance person; it is not possible that there be more than one person at any one period who is worthy of it. . . . Hence the *Imamate* is *lutf* [what God does, directly or indirectly, to make it easier for people to obey the divine will]. . . .

It is necessary that the *Imām* be immune to sin [really, free from error, otherwise he would also need an *Imām*, or spiritual guide] and that is impossible. And also if he committed sin, he would lose his place in men's hearts, and the value of his appointment would be nullified. And because he is the guardian of the law, in which case he must be immune to sin . . . which no one perceives but God the most high. Hence . . . the *Imām* must be appointed by God, not by the people. Agreement has been reached that in appointing the *Imām* the specification can be male by God and His Prophet, or by a previous *Imām* in an independent way (without the voice of the people). [There is disagreement over] whether or not his appointment can be in a way that is other than specification (by God and the Prophet). He who knows the unseen make[s] it known. And that comes about in two ways: (1) by making it known to someone immune to sin, such as the Prophet, and then he tells us of the *Imām's* immunity to sin and of this appointment; (2) by the appearance of miracles wrought by his hand to prove his veracity in claiming the *Imamate*. Sunnis say that whenever the people [*umma*] acknowledge any person as chief, and [give the *baya* or allegiance, they] are convinced of his ability and his power increases, he becomes the *Imām*.

The *Imām* [must] be absolutely the best of the people of his age, because he takes precedence over all [or he is above everyone else]. And if there were among them one better than he then the worse would have to take precedence over the better, and that would be evil.

From *The Middle East and Islamic World Reader* by Marvin Gettlemen and Stuart Schar © 2003 by Marvin Gettlemen and Stuart Schar. Reprinted by permission of Grove Press.

Chronology

Origins and Early Development of Islam

ca. 570	Birth of Muhammad
622	The Hegira (*Hijra*, "emigration") of Muslims to Yathrib (henceforward *al-Madina*, "The City [of the Prophet]"); beginning of Muslim calendar
632	Death of Muhammad; Abu Bakr becomes first "successor" (*Khalifa*, caliph) to leadership, reigns 632–634
634–644	Caliphate of Umar; rapid conquests in Egypt and Iran
644–656	Caliphate of Uthman (member of Umayyad clan); more conquests; Qur'an text established; growth of sea power
656–661	Contested Caliphate of Ali; first civil war
661–680	Caliphate of Mu'awiya; founding of Umayyad dynasty (661–750); capital moved to Damascus; more expansion
680	Second civil war (680–692) begins with death of al-Husayn at Karbala

augmented in Shi'ite thinking by belief in the Prophet's designation of him as the true *imam*, or Muslim leader, after him. Numerous rebellions in Umayyad times rallied around persons claiming to be such a true successor, whether as an Alid or merely a member of Muhammad's clan of Hashim. Even the Abbasids based their right to the caliphate on their Hashimite ancestry. The major Shi'ite pretenders who emerged in the ninth and tenth centuries based their claims on both the Prophet's designation and their descent from Ali and Fatima, Muhammad's daughter. They also stressed the idea of a divinely inspired knowledge passed on by Muhammad to his designated heirs. Thus the true Muslim was the faithful follower of the *imams*, who carried Muhammad's blood and spiritual authority.

Shi'ites saw Ali's assassination and the massacre of Husayn and his family as proofs of the evil nature of this world's rulers, and as rallying points for true Muslims. The martyrdom of Ali and Husayn was extended to a line of Alid *imams* that varied among different groups of Shi'ites. True Muslims, like their *imams*, must suffer. But they would be vindicated by a *mahdi*, or "guided one," who would usher in a messianic age and a judgment day that would see the faithful rewarded. (In the Sunni tradition, which we discuss next, similar "mahdist" movements arose throughout Islamic history.)

In later history Shi'ite rulers did head Islamic states, but only after 1500, in Iran, did Shi'ism prevail as the majority faith in a major Muslim state. The Shi'ite vision of the true *Umma* has not been able to dominate the larger Islamic world.

The Centrists   Most Muslims ultimately accepted a third, less sharply defined position on the nature of leadership and membership in the *umma*. In some ways a compromise, it proved acceptable not only to lukewarm Muslims or pragmatists, but also to persons of intense piety. We may term the proponents of this position *centrists*. To emphasize the correctness of their views, they eventually called themselves *Sunnis*—followers of the tradition (**sunna**) established by the Prophet and the Qur'an. Sunnis encompass a wide range of reconcilable ideas and groups. They have made up the broad middle spectrum of Muslims who tend to put communal solidarity and maintenance of the Islamic polity above purist adherence to particular theological tenets. They have been inclusivist rather than exclusivist, a trait that has typified the Islamic (unlike the Jewish or Christian) community through most of its history.

The centrist position was the most workable framework for the new Islamic state. Its basic ideas were threefold. (1) The *umma* is a theocratic entity, a state under divine authority; this translates into a nomocracy, or *umma*, under the authority of God's Law, the Shari'a. The sources of guidance are, first, the Qur'an; second, Muhammad's precedent; and, third and fourth, the interpretive efforts and consensus of the Muslims (in practice, the *ulama*). (2) The caliph is the absolute temporal ruler, charged with administering and defending the Abode of Islam and protecting Muslim norms and practice; he possesses no greater authority than other Muslims in matters of faith. (3) A person who professes to be Muslim by witnessing that "There is no god but God, and Muhammad is his Messenger" should be considered a Muslim (because "only God knows what is in the heart"), and not even a mortal sin excludes such a person automatically from the *Umma*.

Under increasingly influential *ulama* leadership, these and other basic premises of Muslim community became the theological underpinnings of both the caliphal state and the international Islamic social order.

The High Caliphate

The consolidation of the caliphal institution began with the victory of the Umayyad caliph Abd al-Malik in 692 in the second civil war. The ensuing century and a half mark the era of the "high caliphate," the politically strong, culturally vibrant, wealthy, and centralized institution that flourished first under the Umayyads in Damascus and then in the

The Great Mosque of Samarra. Built in the middle of the ninth century by the Abbasid caliph al-Mutawakkil, this Friday, or congregational, mosque has a prayer space larger than nine football fields, making it the largest such enclosed space in the Islamic world. The style of the minaret recalls the ziggurats of ancient Babylon. *Aerofilms.*

Abbasid capital of Baghdad.[3] The height, or "golden age," of caliphal power and splendor came in the first century of Abbasid rule, during the caliphates of the fabled Harun al-Rashid (786–809) and his son, al-Ma'mun (813–833).

The Abbasid State

The Abbasids' revolution effectively ended Arab dominance as well as Umayyad ascendancy (except in Spain). The shift of the Islamic imperial capital from Damascus to the new "city of peace" built at Baghdad on the Tigris (762–766) symbolized the West Asian shift in cultural and political orientation under the new regime. In line with this shift, more Persians entered the bureaucracy. The Abbasids' disavowal of Shi'ite hopes for a divinely inspired imamate reflected their determination to gain the support of a broad spectrum of Muslims, even if they still stressed their descent from al-Abbas (ca. 565–653), uncle of both Muhammad and Ali.

Whereas the Umayyads had relied on Syrian Arab forces, the Abbasids used Khorasanian Arabs and Iranians and, in the provinces, regional mercenaries for their main troops. Beginning in the ninth century, however, they enlisted slave

[3] This periodization of early Islamic government follows that of M. G. S. Hodgson, *The Venture of Islam*, Vol. 1 (Chicago: University of Chicago Press, 1984), pp. 217–236.

soldiers (**mamluks**), mostly Turks from the northern steppes, as their personal troops. The officers of these forces, themselves *mamluks*, soon seized the positions of power in the central and provincial bureaucracies and the army. Eventually the caliphs were dominated by their *mamluk* officers. This domination led to increasing alienation of the Muslim populace from their own rulers. This was evident in Iraq itself, where unrest with his overbearing Turkish guard led the Abbasid caliph to remove the government from Baghdad to the new city of Samarra sixty miles up the Tigris, where it remained from 836 to 892 (see Map 11–2).

Society

The deep division between rulers and populace—the functionally secular state and its subjects—was ever after typical of most Islamic societies. However, even while the independence of provincial rulers reduced Abbasid central power after the mid–ninth century, such rulers generally recognized caliphal authority at least nominally. This gave them legitimacy as guardians of the Islamic socioreligious order, which meanwhile found its real cohesiveness in the Muslim ideals being standardized and propagated by the *ulama*.

However, full conversion of the populace of the Islamic empire lagged behind centralization of political power and development of Islamic socioreligious institutions. Iraq and Iran saw the fullest Islamization of local elites before the mid–twelfth century, followed by Spain, North Africa, and

Chronology

Early Period of the High Caliphate

680–694	Second civil war
685–705	Caliphate of Abd al-Malik; consolidation, Arabization of administration
705–715	Caliphate of al-Walid; Morocco conquered, Spain invaded; Arab armies reach the Indus
ca. 750	Introduction of paper manufacture from China through Samarqand to Islamic world
750	Abbasids seize caliphate from Umayyads, begin new dynasty (750–1258)
756	Some Umayyads escape to Spain, found new dynasty (756–1030) there
762–766	New Abbasid capital built at Baghdad

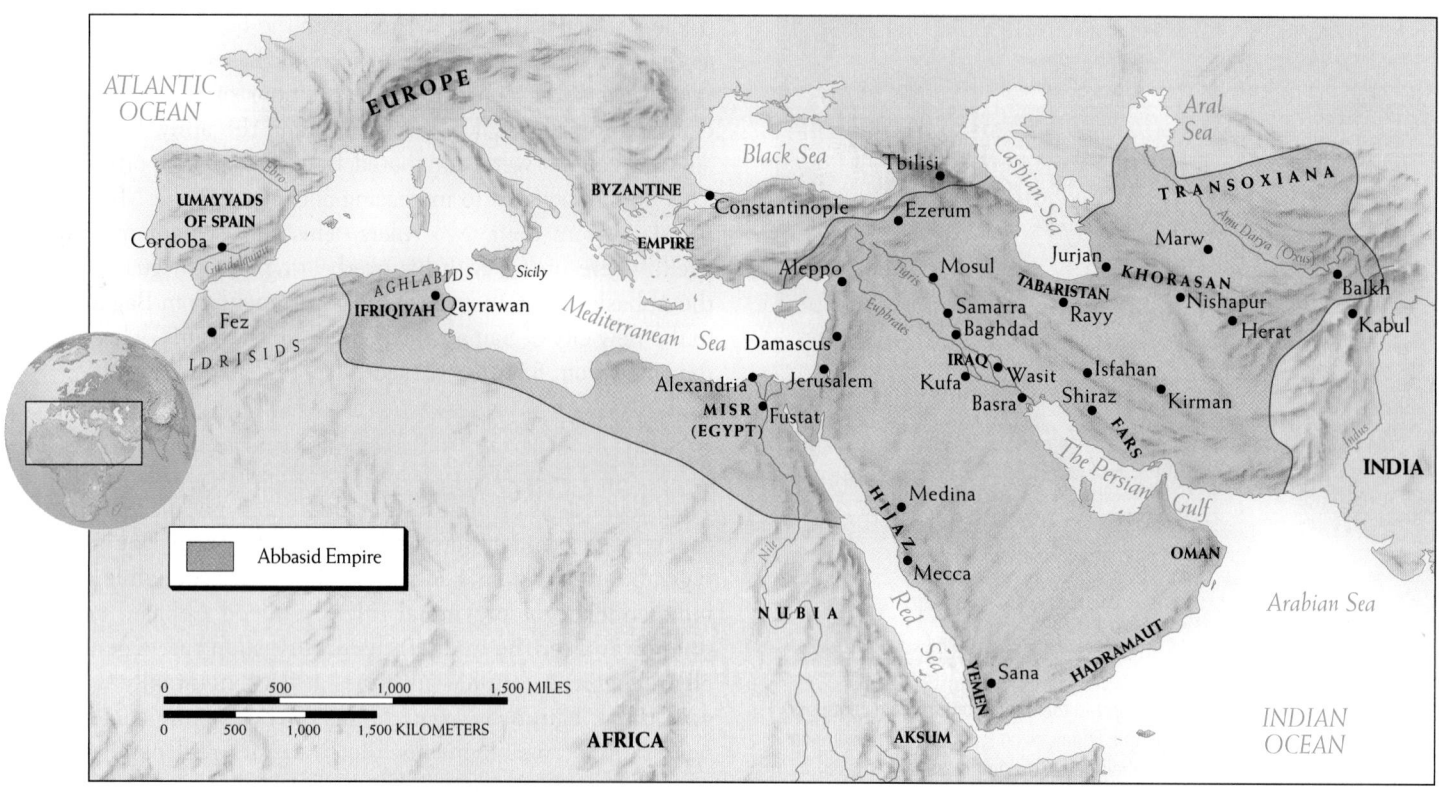

Map 11–2.   The Abbasid Empire, ca. 900 C.E. A great diversity of peoples and nations were united by the Abbasids. Their capital at Baghdad became the center of a trading network that linked India, Africa, and China.

Syria. Conversion and fuller Islamization increased Muslim self-confidence and diminished the need for centralized caliphal power.[4]

Decline

The eclipse of the caliphal empire was foreshadowed at the outset of Abbasid rule, when one of the last Umayyads fled west to Spain, where he founded a Spanish Islamic state (756–1030) that produced the spectacular Moorish or Andalusian culture of Spain. The Spanish Umayyads even claimed the title of caliph in 929, so strong were they and so weak the Abbasids by this time. In all the Abbasid provinces, regional governments were always potential independent states. In North Africa in 801 Harun al-Rashid's governor set up an independent state in modern Tunisia. In Egypt, the Fatimids set up Shi'ite rule in 969 and claimed to be the only true caliphate.

In the East, the Iranian lands grew ever harder for Baghdad to control. Beginning in 821 in Khorasan, Abbasid governors or rebels started independent dynasties repeatedly for the next two centuries, and the caliph usually had to recognize their sway. Among the longest lived of these Iranian

dynasties were the Samanids, who ruled at Bukhara as nominal Abbasid vassals from 875 until 999. They gave northeastern Iran a long period of economic and political security from Turkish steppe invaders. Under their aegis, Persian poetry and Arabic scientific studies began a Persian Islamic cultural renaissance and an influential scientific tradition.

Of greatest consequence for the Abbasid caliphate, however, was the rise in the mountains south of the Caspian of a Shi'ite clan, the Buyids, who took over Abbasid rule in 945. Henceforth the caliph and his descendants were largely puppets in the hands of a Buyid "commander" (*amirs* or *emirs*; later, **sultans**). In 1055 the Buyids were replaced by the more famous Turkish-speaking Seljuk *sultans*. By this time the caliphal office had long been under the control of the ruler in Baghdad, and this was to remain the case until the Mongols final death-blow to even the nominal Abbasid caliphal authority in 1258 (see below, Chapter 13).

Islamic Culture in the Classical Era

The pomp and splendor of the Abbasid court were grand enough to become the stuff of Islamic legends, such as those preserved much later in *A Thousand and One Nights*. Their rich cultural legacy was made possible by a strong

---

[4] Richard W. Bulliet, *Conversion to Islam in the Medieval Period* (Cambridge, MA: Harvard University Press, 1979), especially pp. 7–15, 128–138.

Arabic Astronomy in the Middle Ages attempted to correct Ptolemaic astronomy by means of direct observation and new calculations. As the following diagram from a fourteenth-century Syrian astronomer indicates, they sought to demonstrate how the earth and the moon orbit the sun. *Bodleian Library, University of Oxford.*

army and central government and vigorous internal and external trade, which may have been stimulated by the prosperous Tang Empire of China, with which the Islamic world had much overland and sea contact. Material factors, such as the introduction of paper manufacture (introduced from China through Samarkand about 750) or the flight of Byzantine scholars east to new Abbasid centers of learning, contributed also to making the early Abbasid era special.

Intellectual Traditions

The Abbasid heyday was marked by sophisticated tastes and an insatiable thirst for knowledge—not simply religious knowledge, but *any* knowledge. An Arab historian called Baghdad "the market to which the wares of the sciences and arts were brought, where wisdom was sought as a man seeks after his stray camels, and whose judgment of values was accepted by the whole world."[5] Contacts (primarily among

intellectuals) between Muslims and Christian, Jewish, Zoroastrian, and other "protected" religious communities contributed to the cosmopolitanism of the age. Some older intellectual traditions experienced a revival in early Abbasid times, as in the case of Hellenistic learning. Philosophy, astronomy, mathematics, medicine, and other natural sciences enjoyed strong interest and patronage. In Islamic usage, philosophy and the sciences were subsumed under *falsafa* (from Greek *philosophia*). Islamic culture took over the tradition of rational inquiry from the Hellenic world and developed and preserved it when Europe was a cultural backwater. (See Document, "Ibn Sina on Medicine, ca. 1200 C.E.")

Arabic translations of Greek and Sanskrit works stimulated progress in astronomy and medicine. Translation reached its peak in al-Ma'mun's new academy headed by a Nestorian Christian, Hunayn ibn Ishaq (d. 873), noted for his medical and Greek learning. There were Arabic translations of everything from the Greek authors Galen, Ptolemy, Euclid, Aristotle, Plato, and the Neo-Platonists to the Indian Sanskrit fables that had been translated into Middle Persian under the Sasanids. Such translations stimulated

An Illustration from *The Maqamat* of al Hariri (d. 1122), one of the great masterpieces of Arabic literature of the later Middle Ages. It is a narrative written in rhymed prose for the purposes of entertainment. *Maquamat of Al Harira, Library in a mosque, Arab manuscript, thirteenth century (1237). Paris, France, Bibliothèque Nationale (National Library), Photos 12.com-ARS.*

---

[5] See Oleg Grabar, *The Formation of Islamic Art* (New Haven, CT: Yale University Press, 1973), especially pp. 1–103, 206–213.

Ibn Sina on Medicine, ca. 1020 C.E.

Document

Abu Ali al-Husayn ibn Abdallah Ibn Sina al-Balkhi, or Ibn Sina, known also as Avicenna (980–1037), born in the Tajiki city of Balkh and died in Hamadan, Iran, was a leading Persian physician, philosopher, and scientist. He wrote nearly 450 books on a wide range of subjects focusing on philosophy and medicine. Among his famous were *The Canon of Medicine* and *The Book of Healing*, which were standard medical books for almost 500 years in many European universities. He based his medical system on that of Galen, combining it with Aristotelian metaphysics and traditional Persian and Arab lore.

◆ What are some of the more obvious philosophical concepts in this medical treatise? Can you identify a scientific methodology in Ibn Sina's presentation? Are there any modern concepts in the document?

Material causes, on which health and sickness depend, are: the affected member, which is the immediate subject, and the humors; and in these are the elements. And these two are subjects that, according to their mixing together, alter. In the composition and alteration of the substance which is thus composed, a certain unity is attained.

Efficient causes are the causes changing and preserving the conditions of the human body; as airs, and what are united with them; and evacuation and tetention; and districts and cities and habitable places, and what are united with them; and changes in age and diversities in it, and in races and arts and manners, and bodily and animate movings and restings, and sleepings and wakings on account of them; and in things which befall the human body when they touch it, and are either in accordance or at variance with nature.

Formal causes are physical constitutions, and combinations and virtues which result from them. Final causes are operations. And in the science of operations lies the science of virtues, as we have set forth. These are the subjects of the doctrine of medicine; whence one inquires concerning the disease and curing of the human body. One ought to attain perfection in this research; namely, how health may be preserved and sickness cured. And the causes of this kind are rules in eating and drinking, and the choice of air, and the measure of exercise and rest; and doctoring with medicines and doctoring with the hands. All this with Physicians is according to three species: the well, the sick, and the medium of whom we have spoken.

Charles F. Horne, ed., *The Sacred Books and Early Literature of the East* (New York: Parke, Austin & Lipscomb, 1917), Volume VI: *Medieval Arabia*, pp. 90–91.

---

not only Arabic learning, but later also that of the less advanced European world, especially in the twelfth and thirteenth centuries.

Language and Literature

Arabic language and literature developed greatly in the expanded cultural sphere of the new empire. There developed a significant genre of Arabic writing known as *adab*, or "manners" literature. It included essays and didactic literature influenced by earlier Persian letters. Poetry also flourished by building on the tradition of the Arabic ode, or **qasida**. Grammar was central to the interpretation of the Qur'an that occupied the *ulama* and undergirded an emerging curriculum of religious learning. Historical, geographical,

and biographical writings became major genres of Arabic writing. They owed much to the ancient Bedouin accounts of "the battle days of the Arabs" but arose primarily to record, first, the lives and times of the Prophet and earliest companions, then those of subsequent generations of Muslims. This information was crucial to judging the reliability of the "chains" of transmitters included with each traditional report, or **hadith**. A *hadith* reports words or actions ascribed to Muhammad and the Companions; it became the chief source of Muslim legal and religious norms alongside the Qur'an, as well as the basic unit of most prose genres, from history to Qur'an exegesis. Collections of the *hadith* were mined by preachers and the schools of legal interpretation, whose crowning glory was the work of al-Shafi'i (d. 820) on legal reasoning.

Chronology

"Classical" Period of the High Caliphate

786–809	Caliphate of Harun al-Rashid; apogee of caliphal power
813–833	Caliphate of al-Ma'mun; strong patronage of translations of Greek, Sanskrit, and other works into Arabic; first heavy reliance on slave soldiers (*mamluks*)
875	Rise of Samanid power at Bukhara; patronage of Persian poetry paves way for Persian literary renaissance
909	Rise of Shi'ite Fatimid dynasty in North Africa
945–1055	Buyid emirs rule the eastern empire at Baghdad; the Abbasid caliphs continue largely as figureheads
1055	Buyid emirs replaced by Seljuk sultans as effective rulers at Baghdad and custodians of the caliphate

Art and Architecture

In art and architecture the Abbasid era saw the crystallization of a "classical" Islamic style by about 1000 C.E. Except for ceramics and Arabic calligraphy, most elements of Islamic art and architecture had clear antecedents in Graeco-Roman, Byzantine, or Persian art. What was innovative was the use of older forms and motifs for new purposes and in new combinations, and the spread of such elements to new locales; generally from east (especially the Fertile Crescent) to west (Syria, Egypt, North Africa, and Spain). Sasanid stucco decoration techniques and designs turned up, for example, in Egypt and North Africa. Chronologically, urban Iraq developed an Islamic art first, then made its influence felt east and west, whether in Bukhara or in Syria and North Africa. Also new were the combination and elaboration of discrete forms, as in the case of the colonnade (or hypostyle) mosque or complex arabesque designs.

The Muslims had good reason to be self-confident about their faith and culture and to want to distinguish them from others. Most monuments of the age express the distinctiveness they felt. Particular formal items, such as calligraphic motifs and inscriptions on buildings, came to characterize Islamic architecture and define its functions. Most striking was the avoidance of pictures or icons in pub-

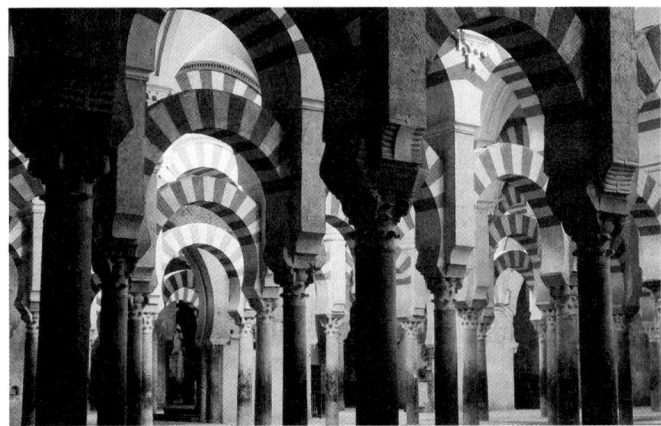

The Congregational Mosque. Two examples of the finest great mosques of the classical Islamic world. Such buildings were designed not only for worship; their large courtyards and pillared halls were also intended to hold the population of a given city and could be used for governmental purposes or for mustering troops in time of war. Their splendor also announced the power and wealth of Islamic rule. The top photo shows the Great Mosque at Qayrawan in modern Tunisia, built during the eighth and nineth centuries. The bottom photo shows the Spanish Umayyad mosque in Cordoba, built and added to from the eighth to the tenth centuries, in a series of roofed extensions—unlike that in Qayrawan, which has only covered colonnades and one great hall. *(A) Werner Forman Archive, Art Resource, N.Y.; (B) Adam Lubroth, Art Resource, N.Y. Muhammad Leading Muslims in Prayer.*

lic art. This was, of course, in line with the Muslim aversion both to any hint of idolatry and to the strongly iconic Byzantine Christian art. Although this iconoclasm later diminished, it was a telling expression of the general thrust of Muslim faith and the culture it animated. Overall, the Muslims' artistic achievements before the year 1000 impress us with an identifiable quality that is both distinctively and "classically" Islamic, whatever the details of a particular example.[6]

---

[6] Grabar, *Formation of Islamic Art*, pp. 1–103, 206–213.

The Qur'an. The page from an eighth- or ninth-century Qur'an in Kufic script (23.8 × 35.5 cm). The earliest Qur'ans were horizontal and written in the formal Kufic script (named for the city of Kufa in Iraq). Note the use of gold.

Summary

Muhammad. The Prophet Muhammad (ca. 570–632) was the founder of Islam. Born in the Arabian commercial city of Mecca, he was influenced by contact with Arab Christians and with Jews. At about age 40, he had a religious experience during which, Muslims believe, God's messenger angel Gabriel repeatedly performed recitation (*qur'an*) of God's word to him. The message of the Qur'an was (1) social justice and worship of the one true God are required of every person; (2) at the end of time, people will be resurrected and judged by God to be rewarded or punished according to how they have lived; and (3) the proper response to God is submission (*islam*) to his will by becoming a muslim ("one who submits").

Islamic Conquest. By the time of Muhammad's death, his followers had conquered all of Arabia. Under his successors, the caliphs, Muslim Arab armies conquered most of the Near East, North Africa, Spain, Sasanid Iran, and northwest India. Many of the peoples of these territories welcomed Islamic rule as liberation from Persian or Byzantine domination and eventually converted to Islam and became part of the *umma*, the community of Islamic believers. The status of women improved under Islam.

INTERPRETING THE PAST

Creating a Community in Early Islam

One of the challenges facing the first Muslims was that of creating a "community" for adherents to the new religion of Islam. The Qur'an was addressed to this new community, and many of the specific injunctions in the book required communal activity, fostering a sense of ethics and shared values among a large and rapidly growing group of people.

Analyzing the documents and images contained in this chapter and in the Primary Source, DVD/MyHistoryLab, comment on the role of this "community" in early Islamic thought and practice. Begin with the excerpts from the Qur'an itself, and then consider visual examples of collective behavior in the context of Islam, such as the photo of the Ka'ba, the fresco painting showing female mourners, and scenes of group prayer.

Of course, like other religions, Islam also faced the challenge of diversity in its ranks. On this problem, comment on the Shi'a and Sunna split reflected in the al-Mawardi document and the excerpt from Muhammad's orations.

Text Sources from MyHistoryLab / PrimarySource DVD

Excerpts from the Qur'an
Muhammad's Orations

Text Source from Chapter 11

Al-Mawardi and al-Hilli (pp. 341)

Visual Source from MyHistoryLab / PrimarySource DVD

Mecca
Medina

PRENTICE HALL
myhistorylab
Where it's a good time to connect to the past!

The Classical Period of the Caliphate Under the Abbasid caliphs who ruled from the city of Baghdad, Islamic culture enjoyed its "classical" phase. Arabic translations of Greek and Sanskrit works stimulated progress in astronomy and medicine. Arabic literature and poetry flourished. As the sacred medium of God's final revelation, the Arabic language spread throughout the Islamic world. Arabic artists and architects built on Greco-Roman, Byzantine, and Persian traditions to develop a distinctive Islamic style in decoration, painting, and architecture. The *ulama*, Islamic religious and legal scholars, played a prominent part in Islamic society as interpreters of Islamic tradition and law.

Decline of the Caliphate The Islamic empire began to splinter early. Disputes over the succession to the Prophet divided Muslims. Large parts of the empire—Spain, North Africa, Iran—seceded. Military commanders (*amirs*) in Baghdad reduced the caliphs to mere figureheads by the tenth century.

Review Questions

1. Describe Arabian society before Islam. What were the prime targets of the Qur'anic message in that society?

Visual Sources from Chapter 11

The Ka'ba in Mecca (p. 332)
Veiled Women (p. 335)
Ritual Worship (p. 339)

Questions

How was Islam designed to be a communal experience?

How was the Muslim community organized after the death of Muhammad?

Were Muslims successful in preserving the community envisioned in the Qur'an?

2. What are the main features of the Islamic worldview? How do Islamic ideas about history, salvation, law, social justice, and other key issues compare to those of Christianity and Judaism?

3. What were the primary kinds of leadership in the early Islamic polities? To what extent were political and religious leadership separated in different offices and functions?

4. Discuss the conversion of subject populations in the early centuries of Islamic empire. What were incentives and obstacles to conversion?

5. Why were the initial Arab armies so successful? Why was the imperial caliphal state eclipsed? What were some of the lasting accomplishments of the Umayyad and Abbasid Empires?

6. Discuss the "classical" culture of the golden age of the caliphate. What role did foreign traditions play in it? What were some of its prominent achievements?

Key Terms

caliphate (p. 337)	**Ka'ba** (p. 330)
diwan (p. 340)	**qur'an** (p. 332)
emir (p. 337)	**Shi'a** (p. 340)
hadith (p. 346)	**sunna** (p. 342)
hajj (p. 334)	**ulama** (p. 339)
hegira (p. 334)	**umma** (p. 334)
imam (p. 337)	**mamluk** (p. 343)
islam (p. 332)	**sultans** (p. 344)
jihad (p. 337)	**qasida** (p. 346)

Note: To learn more about the topics in this chapter, please turn to the Suggested Readings at the end of the book. For additional sources related to this chapter please see the Primary Source DVD at the back of this text or MyHistoryLab.

The Byzantine Empire and Western Europe to 1000

12

◆ The End of the Western Roman Empire

◆ The Impact of Islam on East and West

◆ The Developing Roman Church

◆ The Kingdom of the Franks

◆ Feudal Society

HE EARLY MIDDLE AGES (OR EARLY MEDIEVAL period) marks the birth of Europe as a geographical entity. This period of recovery from the collapse of Roman civilization was also a time of forced experimentation with new ideas and institutions. Within what had been the northern and western provinces of the Roman Empire, Graeco-Roman culture combined with Germanic culture and an evolving Christianity to create distinctive political and cultural forms. In government, religion, and language, as well as geography, these regions grew separate from the eastern Byzantine world and an Islamic Arab world that extended across North Africa from Spain to the eastern Mediterranean. Yet as they did so they also drew vital knowledge and resources from both.

German tribes had been settling peacefully around the Roman Empire since the first century B.C.E., but in the fourth century C.E. they began to migrate directly into it from the north and east. During the fifth century they turned fiercely against their hosts, largely because the Romans,

Hagia Sophia. One of the greatest achievements of Byzantine civilization, Hagia Sophia (the Church of Holy Wisdom) was completed in 537 C.E. by Anthemius of Tralles and Isidore of Miletus. Circled with numerous windows, the great dome floods the hall with light and, together with the church's many other windows, mosaics, and open spaces, gives the interior a remarkable airiness and luminosity. After the Turkish conquest of Constantinople in 1453 Hagia Sophia was transformed into a mosque. *Hagia Sophia, Istanbul. Erich Lessing/Art Resource. N.Y.*

The Early Middle Ages

Western Europe

Byzantium

In Western Europe, the centuries between 400 and 1000 witnessed both the decline of classical civilization and the birth of a new European civilization. Beginning with the fifth century, a series of barbarian invasions separated Western Europe culturally from its Classical age. This prolonged separation was unique to Western Europe. Along with the invasions themselves and the new cultural traits they brought into Europe, it was pivotal to the development of European civilization. Although some important works and concepts survived from antiquity due largely to the Christian church, Western civilization labored for centuries to recover its rich classical past in "renaissances" stretching into the sixteenth century. Out of this mixture of barbarian and surviving (or recovered) classical culture, Western civilization was born. With the aid of a Christian church eager to restore order and centralized rule, the Carolingians created a new, albeit fragile, imperial

tradition. But Western society remained highly fragmented politically and economically during the early Middle Ages. Meanwhile, many of the world's other great civilizations of the first millennium C.E. were peaking.

In China, particularly in the seventh and eighth centuries, Tang dynasty rulers also sought ways to secure their borders against foreign expansion, mainly pastoral nomads. China at this time was far more cosmopolitan and politically unified than Western Europe, and also centuries ahead in technology. By the tenth century, the Chinese were printing with movable type, an invention the West did not achieve until the fifteenth century, and then very likely borrowed in prototype from China. The effective authority of Chinese rulers extended far beyond their immediate centers of government. The Tang dynasty held sway over their empire in a way Carolingian rulers could only imagine.

In Japan, the Yamato court (300–680), much like the court of the Merovingians and Carolingians, struggled to unify and control the countryside. Shintō, a religion friendly to royalty, aided the Yamato. As in the West, a Japanese identity evolved

who regarded them as uncultured barbarians, treated them so cruelly. To the south, Arab dominance transformed the Mediterranean into an often inhospitable "Islamic lake," challenging Western trade with the East. Surrounded and assailed from north, east, and south, Western Europe became insular and even stagnant, its people losing touch with classical, especially Greek, learning and science. But forced to manage by themselves, they also learned to develop their native resources. The reign of Charlemagne saw a modest renaissance of antiquity aided by Byzantium and Arabia. And the peculiar social and political forms that emerged during this period—manorialism and feudalism—not only were successful at coping with unprecedented chaos on local levels but also proved to be

fertile seedbeds for the growth of distinctively Western institutions. ■

The End of the Western Roman Empire

In the early fifth century, Italy and the "eternal city" of Rome suffered a series of devastating blows. In 410 the Visigoths, under Alaric (ca. 370–410), revolted and sacked Rome. In 452 the Huns, led by Attila—known to contemporaries as the "scourge of God"—invaded Italy. And in 455 Rome was overrun yet again, this time by the Vandals.

By the mid–fifth century, power in Western Europe had passed decisively from the hands of the Roman emperors to those of barbarian chieftains. In 476, the traditional date given for the fall of the Roman Empire, the barbarian Odovacer (ca. 434–493) deposed and replaced the Western emperor Romuthrough struggle and accommodation with outside cultures, especially with the Chinese, the dominant influence on Japan between the seventh and twelfth centuries. But foreign cultural influence, again as in the West, never managed to eradicate the indigenous culture. By the ninth century a distinctive Sino-Japanese culture existed. But Japan, again like Western Europe, remained a fragmented land during these centuries, despite a certain allegiance and willingness to pay taxes to an imperial court. Throughout Japan, as in Western Europe, the basic unit of political control consisted of highly self-conscious and specially devoted armed retainers. A system of lordship and vassalage evolved around bands of local mounted warriors known as samurai. Through this system, local order was maintained in Japan until the fifteenth century. Like the Merovingian and Carolingian courts, the Japanese court had to tolerate strong and independent regional rulers.

While Western Europe struggled for political and social order in the fourth and fifth centuries, Indian civilization basked in a golden age under the reign of the Guptas (320–467). In this era of peace and stability, when a vocationally and socially limiting caste system neatly imposed order on Indian society from Brahmans to outcasts, culture, religion, and politics flourished.

In the seventh century, Islamic armies emerged from the Arabian Peninsula, conquered territory from India to Spain by 710, and gave birth to a powerful new international civilization. Cosmopolitan and culturally vibrant, this civilization flourished despite the breakdown of Islamic political unity beginning in the ninth and tenth centuries. Islamic cultural strides in this era overshadowed the modest cultural renaissance in the West under Charlemagne.

Focus Questions

◆ What caused the prolonged separation of Western European civilization from its Classical past? What were the consequences of this separation for Western Europe?

◆ Which other society most resembled that of Western Europe during this period? Why?

◆ While Western Europe struggled to regain order, unity, and contact with its Classical past, what was happening in the other great civilizations of the world?

lus Augustulus. The Eastern emperor Zeno (r. 474–491) recognized Odovacer's authority in the West, and Odovacer acknowledged Zeno as sole emperor, contenting himself to serve as Zeno's Western viceroy. By the end of the fifth century the barbarians had thoroughly overrun the Western Empire. The Ostrogoths settled in Italy, the Franks in northern Gaul, the Burgundians in Provence, the Visigoths in southern Gaul and Spain, the Vandals in Africa and the western Mediterranean, and the Angles and Saxons in England (see Map 12–1).

The barbarian military victories, however, did not result in a great defeat of Roman culture; Western Europe's new masters were willing to learn from the people they had conquered. They admired Roman culture and had no desire to destroy it. Except in Britain and northern Gaul, Roman law, Roman government, and Latin, the Roman language, coexisted with the new Germanic

SOURCE Excerpts from the Hildebra-ndslied

institutions. In Italy under Theodoric, tribal custom gradually gave way to Roman law. Only the Vandals and the Anglo-Saxons—and, after 466, the Visigoths—refused to profess at least titular obedience to the emperor in Constantinople.

The Visigoths, the Ostrogoths, and the Vandals entered the West as Christians, which helped them accommodate to Roman culture. They were, however, followers of the Arian creed, which had been condemned at the Council of Nicaea in 325 and was considered heretical in the West. Later, around 500, the Franks, who had settled in Gaul, would convert to the Orthodox, or "Catholic," form of Christianity supported by the bishops of Rome. As we will see, the Franks ultimately dominated most of Western Europe, helping convert the Goths and other barbarians to Roman Christianity.

All things considered, rapprochement and a gradual interpenetration of two strong cultures—a creative tension—marked the period of the Germanic migrations. The stronger

Map Exploration

To explore this map further, go to http://www.prenhall.com/craig_maps

Map 12–1. Barbarian Migrations into the West in the Fourth and Fifth Centuries. The forceful intrusion of Germanic and non-Germanic tribes into the empire from the last quarter of the fourth century through the fifth century made for a constantly changing pattern of movement and relations. The map shows the major routes taken by the usually unwelcome newcomers and the areas most deeply affected by the main groups.

culture was the Roman, and it became dominant in a later fusion. Despite Western military defeat, the Goths and the Franks became far more romanized than the Romans were germanized. Latin language, Nicene Christianity, and eventually Roman law and government were to triumph in the West during the Middle Ages.

The Byzantine Empire

As the Roman Empire in the West succumbed to Germanic and other barbarian invasions, imperial power shifted to the eastern part of the Roman Empire, whose center was the city of Byzantium (modern day Istanbul). Between 324 and 330, the emperor Constantine the Great rebuilt and renamed the city after himself: Constantinople. It remained the capital of both the old Roman and the new Byzantine Empire until the eighth century, when Charlemagne revived the Western Empire and reclaimed its imperial title. In its historical usage, the term *Byzantine* indicates the Greek, Hellenistic Roman, and Judaic monotheistic elements that distinguish the culture of the East from the Latin West.

Between 324 and 1453, the Byzantine Empire passed from an early period of expansion and splendor to a time of sustained contraction and splintering and finally catastrophic defeat. Historians divide its history into three distinct periods:

1. From the rebuilding of Byzantium as Constantinople in 324 to the beginning of the Arab expansion and the spread of Islam in 632

Barbarian Invasions of the Western Roman Empire

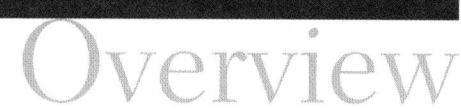
Overview

The Germanic tribes—the barbarians—who overran the Western Roman Empire had coexisted with the Romans for centuries in a relationship marked more by the commingling of cultures and trade than by warfare. The arrival of the Huns from the east in the late fourth century, however, caused many of the tribes, beginning with the Visigoths in 376, to flee westward and seek refuge within the empire. They found the western half of the empire weakened by famine, disease, overtaxation, and an enfeebled military. The Romans lost control of their frontiers, and in the fifth century, the tribes overran the West and set up their own domains. The following is a list of the most important tribes and the areas they controlled by the year 500.

TRIBES	AREA OF CONTROL
Anglo-Saxons	Most of England
Franks	Northeast France
Burgundians	Eastern-central France
Alemanni	Switzerland
Visigoths	Most of Spain and southern France
Suevi	Northwest Spain
Vandals	North Africa
Ostrogoths	Italy, Austria, Croatia, Slovenia

2. From 632 to the conquest of Asia Minor by the Seljuk Turks in 1071, or, as some prefer, to the fall of Constantinople to the Western Crusaders in 1204

3. From 1071, or 1204, to the fall of Constantinople to the Ottoman Turks in 1453, the end of the empire in the East

The Reign of Justinian

In terms of territory, political power, and cultural achievement, the first period of Byzantine history (324–632) was far the greater. Its pinnacle was the reign of Emperor Justinian (r. 527–565) and his like-minded wife, Empress Theodora (d. 548). (See Document, "The Character and 'Innovations' of Justinian and Theodora.") A strongman ruler who expected all his subjects, clergy, and laity, high and low, to submit absolutely to his hierarchical control, Justinian spent, built, and destroyed on a grand scale. Theodora, the daughter of a circus bear trainer, had been an entertainer in her youth and, if Justinian's tell-all court historian, Procopius, is believed, a prostitute as well. Whatever the source, she possessed an intelligence and toughness that matched, and might even have exceeded, those of her husband. An influential counselor, Theodora was a true co-ruler. In 532, after massive tax riots—the so-called Nika Revolt—rocked the city, threatening its destruction and the end of Justinian's brief rule, a panicked emperor contemplated abdication and flight. Theodora stiffened his resolve, insisting that he reestablish his authority unambiguously, which he thereafter did by ordering a bloodbath that left tens of thousands of protesters dead in the Hippodrome.

Cities During Justinian's thirty-eight-year reign, the empire's strength lay in its more than 1,500 cities. Constantinople, with perhaps 350,000 inhabitants, was the largest and the cultural crossroads of Asian and European civilizations. The large, dominant provincial cities had populations of 50,000. A fifth-century record suggests the size and splendor of Constantinople at its peak: 5 imperial and 9 princely palaces; 8 public and 153 private baths; 4 public forums; 5 granaries; 2 theaters; 1 hippodrome; 322 streets; 4,388 substantial houses; 52 porticoes; 20 public and 120 private bakeries; and 14 churches. The most popular entertainments were the races at the Hippodrome and the theater, where, according to clerical critics, nudity and immorality were on display. Many public taverns dotted the cities as well (See Map 12–2).

Justinian as Conqueror. A classical ivory carving of Justinian celebrating his conquests in Italy, North Africa, and West Asia, c. 500 c.e.

Between the fourth and fifth centuries, councils of roughly two hundred members, known as *Decurions,* all local, wealthy landowners, governed the cities. Being the intellectual and economic elite of the empire, they were heavily taxed, which did not make them the emperor's most docile or loyal servants. By the sixth century, fidelity had become the coin of the realm, and special governors, lay and clerical, chosen from the landholding classes, replaced the *decurion* councils as more reliable instruments of the emperor's sovereign will. As the sixth and seventh centuries saw the beginning of new barbarian invasions of the empire from the north and the east, such political tightening became imperative.

Law The imperial goal reflected in Justinian's policy of "one God, one empire, one religion" was to centralize government by imposing legal and doctrinal conformity throughout. To this end, the emperor ordered a collation and revision of Roman law. Such a codification became a pressing matter because of the enormous number of legal decrees, often contradictory, that had been piling up since the mid–second century, as the empire grew ever more Christian and imperial rule increasingly autocratic. The goal: loyal and docile subjects guided by clear and enforceable laws.

The projected *Corpus Juris Civilis,* or "body of civil law," was a fourfold compilation undertaken by a committee of the most learned lawyers. The first compilation, known as the *Code,* appeared in 533, and revised imperial edicts issued since the reign of Hadrian (r. 117–138). A second compilation, the *Novellae,* or "new things," presented the decrees issued by Justinian and his immediate successors since 534. The third compilation, the *Digest,* gathered the major opinions of the old legal experts. And the goal of the fourth compilation, the *Institutes,* was to put in the hands of young scholars a practical textbook that drew its lessons from the *Code* and the *Digest.* Although these various works had little immediate effect on medieval common law, they became the foundation for most subsequent European law between the Renaissance and the nineteenth century. Because bringing subjects under the authority of a single sovereign was the fundamental feature of Roman Law, rulers aspiring to centralize their states especially benefited from Justinian's legal legacy.

Empress Theodora and her Attendants
c. 547 c.e. A mosaic from the Basilica of S. Vitale in Ravenna, Italy.

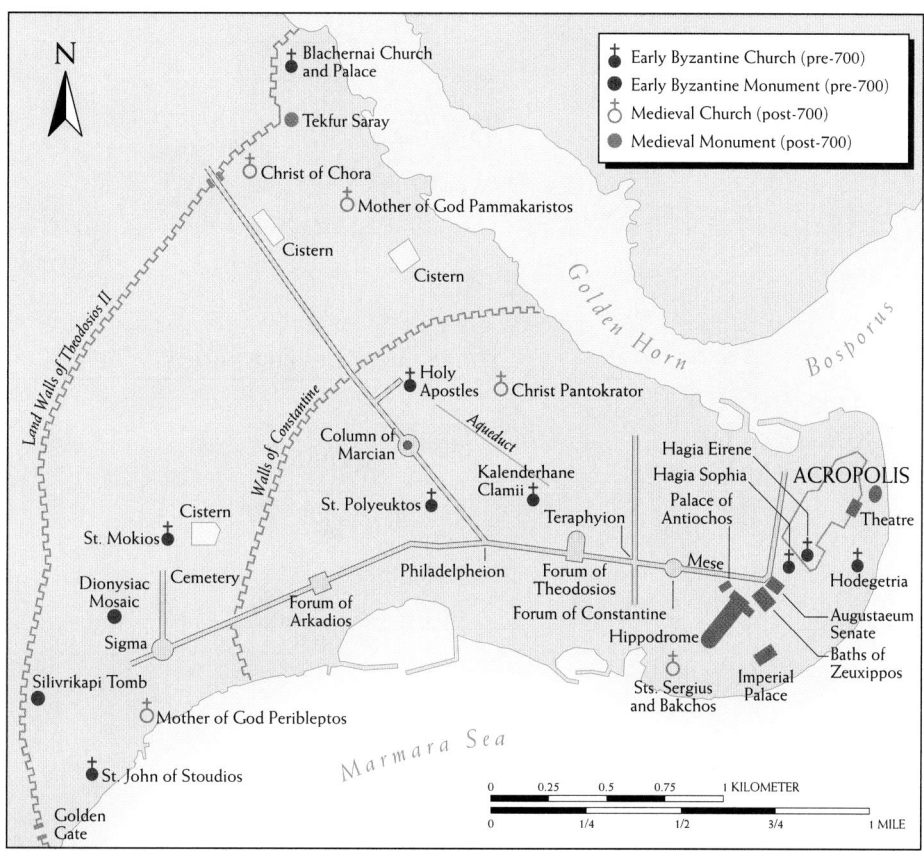

Map 12–2. Constantinople. The city's strategic location was the source of its wealth and made it virtually impregnable to invasion.

Prologue from the Corpus Juris Civilis

This strengthening of empire did not, however, enable Justinian to retrieve the Western imperial lands conquered and occupied by barbarians in Italy, North Africa, and Spain. The harder he tried to do so, the greater the price he paid (See Map 12–3).

Avars, Slavs, and Bulgars

In the sixth and seventh centuries, nomadic barbarian tribes of Avars, Slavs, and Bulgars invaded and occupied the Eastern Empire, threatening a "dark age" there. Although initially fierce raiders, the Slavs later converted to Eastern Orthodoxy or Byzantine Christianity. Hoping to build a cultural-linguistic firewall against menacing Franks who were then attempting to convert his people to Roman Catholicism in a language they did not understand (Latin), King Rastislav of Moravia turned to Constantinople for help. In response, the Byzantine emperor sent two learned missionaries to evangelize the Moravians. They were the priests Constantine, later known as Cyril, and Methodius, both of whom later became saints. In Moravia, the two created a Greek-based alphabet for the Slavs, which allowed them to develop a written language of their own. Through that language the Christian gospels and

Byzantine theology found a lasting Slavic home. Later, after the Bulgars conquered and absorbed the Slavs, that same alphabet was elevated to a broader script known as Cyrillic, after the priest Cyril. Today known as Old Church Slavonic, it has ever since been the international Slavic language through which Byzantine Christianity penetrated eastern Europe: Bohemia, Bulgaria, Macedonia, Rumania, Serbia, Ukraine, and Kievan Russia. In prior centuries, the Byzantines had given Goths, Georgians, Armenians, and Syrians similar native tools for accessing Byzantine culture and religion.

Jvari monastery, Georgia

Persians and Muslims

During the reign of Emperor Heraclius (r. 610–641), the empire took a decidedly Eastern, as opposed to a Roman, direction. Heraclius spoke only Greek, not Latin. He spent his entire reign resisting Persian and Islamic invasions, the former successfully, the latter in vain. In 628 he defeated the Persian king Chosroes and took back one of Western Christendom's great lost relics: a piece of Christ's Cross that had been taken by Chosroes when he captured Jerusalem in 614. After 632, Islamic armies progressively overran the empire, directly attacking Con-

Map 12–3.   The Byzantine Empire at the Death of Justinian. The inset shows the empire in 1025, before its losses to the Seljuk Turks.

stantinople for the first time in the mid-670s. Not until the reign of Leo III of the Isaurian dynasty (r. 717–740) did the Byzantines repel Arab armies and regain at least most of Asia Minor, having lost forever its larger Mediterranean empire. The setback was traumatic and forced a major restructuring of the downsized empire. That was done by creating locally governed and garrisoned provincial strongholds under the direct authority of imperially appointed generals. A major break with the old hierarchical governance of the empire, the new system made possible a more disciplined and flexible use of military power in time of crisis.

In the eleventh century, Byzantine fortunes rapidly reversed as the Muslim Seljuk Turks overran vital Anatolia. A devastating defeat of the Byzantine army at Manzikert in 1071 signaled the end of the empire. That end—at the hands of the Seljuks' cousins, the Ottoman Turks—was still several centuries away. However, after two decades of steady

Turkish advance, the Eastern emperor Alexius I Comnenus (r. 1081–1118) invoked Western aid in 1092. Three years later, the West launched the first Crusade. A century later (1204), the Fourth Crusade stopped in Constantinople en route to Jerusalem, not however to rescue the Eastern capital, but to inflict more damage on the holy city and Eastern Christendom than all previous non-Christian invaders had done. (See Chapter 16.)

The Religious Diversity of Christendom   In both East and West, religious belief and controversy alternately served and undermined imperial political unity. Since the fifth century, the patriarch of Constantinople crowned Byzantine emperors in that city (the "second Rome"), attesting the close ties between rulers and the Eastern Church. In 391, Christianity became the official faith of the Eastern Empire, while all other religions and sects were deemed "demented and

The Character and "Innovations" of Justinian and Theodora

According to their court historian and biographer, Procopius, the emperor and his wife were tyrants, pure and simple. His *Secret History* (sixth century), which some historians distrust as a source, had only criticism and condemnation for the two rulers. Procopius especially resented Theodora, and he did not believe that the rule of law was respected at the royal court.

◆ Is Procopius being fair to Justinian and Theodora? Is the *Secret History* an ancient tabloid? How does one know when a source is biased and self-serving and when it is telling the truth? What does Procopius most dislike about the queen? Was Theodora the last woman ruler to receive such criticism?

Formerly, when the senate approached the Emperor, it paid homage in the following manner. Every patrician kissed him on the right breast; the Emperor [then] kissed the patrician on the head, and he was dismissed. Then the rest bent their right knee to the Emperor and withdrew. It was not customary to pay homage to the Queen.

But those who were admitted [in] to the presence of Justinian and Theodora, whether they were patricians or otherwise, fell on their faces on the floor, stretching their hands and feet out wide, kissed first one foot and then the other of the Augustus [i.e., the emperor], and then retired. Nor did Theodora refuse this honor; and she even received the ambassadors of the Persians and other barbarians and gave them presents, as if she were in command of the Roman Empire: a thing that had never happened in all previous time.

And formerly intimates of the Emperor called him Emperor and the Empress, Empress. . . . But if anybody addressed either of these two as Emperor or Empress

without adding "Your Majesty" or "Your Highness," or forgot to call himself their slave, he was considered either ignorant or insolent, and was dismissed in disgrace as if he had done some awful crime or committed some unpardonable sin.

And [whereas] before, only a few were sometimes admitted to the palace . . . when these two came to power, the magistrates and everybody else had no trouble in fairly living in the palace. This was because the magistrates of old had administered justice and the laws according to their conscience . . . but these two, taking control of everything to the misfortune of their subjects, forced everyone to come to them and beg like slaves. And almost any day one could see the law courts nearly deserted, while in the hall of the Emperor there was a jostling and pushing crowd that resembled nothing so much as a mob of slaves.

From Procopius, *Secret History*, in *The Early Middle Ages, 500–1000*, ed. by Robert Brentano (New York: Free Press, 1964), pp. 70–71.

insane." Between the fourth and sixth centuries, the patriarchs of Constantinople, Alexandria, Antioch, and Jerusalem received generous endowments of land and gold from rich pious donors, empowering the church to act as the state's welfare agency. That great wealth and prestige swelled clerical ranks and bound the clergy tightly to state service.

While Orthodox Christianity was the religion that mattered most, it was not the only religion in the empire with a significant following. Nor did Byzantine rulers view religion as merely a political tool. From time to time, Christian heresies were also given imperial support. And beyond outright persecution, absorption into tolerated, popular forms of

Christianity became a peaceful way for rulers to curtail pagan religious practices.

The empire was also home, albeit less hospitably, to large numbers of Jews. Non-Christian Romans viewed Jews as narrow, dogmatic, and intolerant by comparison with Christians. Under Roman law, Jews had legal protection as long as they did not proselytize among Christians, build new synagogues, or enter sensitive public offices and professions. Whereas the emperor most intent on religious conformity within the empire, Justinian, encouraged Jews to convert voluntarily, later emperors commanded them to be baptized and gave tax breaks to those who freely complied.

Virgin and Child with Saints and Angels. A sixth-century icon of the Virgin and Child surrounded by warrior saints (Theodore on the left; George on the right) and wary angels. A rare survivor of eighth-century iconoclasm.

However, neither persuasion nor coercion succeeded in converting the empire's Jews.

The differences between Eastern and Western Christianity became no less irreconcilable. One issue divided Justinian and Theodora lifelong. Whereas Justinian remained strictly orthodox in his Christian beliefs, Theodora supported a divisive Eastern teaching condemned as a heresy in the West in 451, namely, the teaching that Christ had a single, immortal nature and was not eternal God and mortal man in one and the same person. Still embraced by Coptic and Syrian Christians, the so-called Monophysite heresy exaggerated Orthodox Christianity's determination to protect the sovereignty of God, a concern apparent in Byzantine art, which portrays Christ, a self-same person with God, as impassive and transcendent, not as a suffering

mortal man. In the sixth century, the Monophysites became a separate church in the East, particularly in Armenia.

A similar dispute appeared in Eastern debates over the relationship among the members of the Trinity, specifically whether the Holy Spirit proceeded "from the Son" (*filioque*) as well as from the Father in its generation. Again at issue was God's majesty, the theologians fearing a loss of divine unity and dignity if the Holy Spirit proceeded from both. Some perceive here a hidden political concern, important in the East. By protecting the unity and majesty of the Father, Eastern theology was safeguarding the unity and majesty of the emperor himself, from whom all power on earth was believed properly to flow. The idea of a divisible Godhead, no matter how abstract and subtle, suggested the divisibility of imperial power, particularly in an emperor who associated himself so closely with God.

Another major disagreement between the Christian East and West concerned the veneration of images in worship. In 726, Eastern emperor Leo III (717–714) forbade the use of images and icons throughout Christendom. As their veneration had been commonplace, the decree came as a shock, especially to the West. The change in policy may have been a pretext to close cloisters and secularize monastic lands. Or the emperor may have wished to accommodate Muslim sensitivities at a time when he was at war with the Arabs (Islam strictly forbade image worship). Regardless of the reason, the emperor's decree drove Western popes into the camp of the Franks, where they found in Charlemagne an effective protector against the Byzantine world. Although images were restored in the Eastern churches in the mid–ninth century, many masterpieces went missing during a century of theology- inspired iconoclasm.

A third difference between East and West was the Eastern emperor's pretension to absolute sovereignty, both secular and religious. Expressing his sense of sacred mission, he presented himself in the trappings of holiness and directly interfered in matters of church and religion, what is called Caesaropapism, or the emperor acting as if he held authority over the church as well as over his kingdom. To a degree

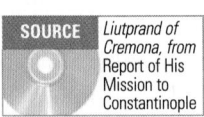 **SOURCE** *Liutprand of Cremona, from Report of His Mission to Constantinople*

unknown in the West, Eastern emperors appointed and managed the clergy, convening church councils and enforcing church decrees. By comparison, the West nurtured a separation of church and state that began to flower in the eleventh century.

The Eastern church rejected several disputed requirements of Roman Christianity. It denied the existence of Purgatory, permitted lay divorce and remarriage, allowed priests, but not bishops, to marry, and embraced vernacular liturgies in place of Greek and Latin. In these matters Eastern Christians gained opportunities and rights Christians in the West would not enjoy, and then only in part, until the Protestant Reformation in the sixteenth century.

Having accumulated over the centuries, these various differences resulted in a schism between the two churches in 1054. In that year a Western envoy of the pope, cardinal Humbertus, visited the patriarch of Constantinople, Michael Cerularius, in the hope of overcoming the differences that divided Christendom. The patriarch was not welcoming, however. As he departed the scene, Humbertus left a bull of excommunication on the altar of Hagia Sophia. In response, the patriarch proclaimed Western popes to have been heretics since the sixth century! Nine hundred and eleven years would pass before that breach was repaired. In a belated ecumenical gesture in 1965, a Roman pope met with the patriarch of Constantinople to revoke the mutual condemnations of 1054.

The Impact of Islam on East and West

A new drama began to unfold in the sixth century with the rise of a rival far more dangerous to the West than the Germanic tribes: the new faith of Islam (see Chapter 11). During the lifetime of the Prophet Muhammad (ca. 570–632) and thereafter, invading Arab armies claimed the attention and resources of the emperors in Constantinople, who found themselves in a life-and-death struggle. Unlike the Germanic invaders, who absorbed and adopted the culture and religion of Rome, the Arabs, although generally tolerant of Christian and Jewish minorities, ultimately imposed their own culture and religion on the lands they conquered.

After an Arab-Berber army under Tariq ibn Ziyad (Gibraltar, "mountain of Tariq," is named after him) conquered Visigothic Spain in 711, Muslims began a seven-hundred-year reign in what is today Andalusia. By the middle of the eighth century Arabs were masters of the southern and eastern Mediterranean coastline, territories today held, for the most part, by Islamic states. Muslim armies also pushed north and east through Mesopotamia and Persia and beyond. The inhabitants of much of these territories, while Christian, were, like the Arabs, Semitic. Any religious unity they may have felt with the Byzantine Greeks appears to have been offset by their hatred of the Byzantine Greek occupation of their lands. The Christian community was in any case badly divided. Byzantine emperor Heraclius had tried to impose Greek "orthodox" beliefs on the churches of Egypt and Syria, creating enmity between Greek and Semitic Christians. As a result, many Egyptian and Syrian Christians, hoping for deliverance from Byzantine oppression, may have welcomed the Islamic conquerors.

The Muslim conquerors generally tolerated Christians and Jews, provided they paid taxes, kept their distance, and made no efforts to proselytize Muslim communities. Always anxious to maintain the purity of their religion and culture, the Arabs forbade mixed marriages and any conscious cultural interchange. Special taxes on conquered peoples encouraged them to convert to Islam.

Assaulted from East and West and everywhere challenged in the Mediterranean, Christian Europe developed a lasting fear and suspicion of the Muslims. In both the East and the West, the Muslim invasion was confronted and halted. Byzantine Emperor Leo III (r. 717–740) stopped Arab armies at Constantinople after a year's siege (717–718). In subsequent centuries the Byzantines further secured their borders and for a time expanded militarily and commercially into Muslim lands. In the West, the Franks under Charles Martel defeated a raiding party of Arabs on the western frontier of the Frankish kingdom near Tours (today in central France) in 732, ending the possibility of Arab expansion into the heart of Europe by way of Spain. To the extent that the Mediterranean remained something of a "Muslim lake" during the high Middle Ages, the center of the evolving West European civilization was shifted north, away from the Mediterranean. Yet, that did not mean the end of positive contact and influence between Muslims and Christians. Although carried on in keen awareness of a powerful Muslim presence in the Mediterranean, Western trade with the East continued to be of great importance to the Carolingians and was pursued in these centuries.

The Western Debt to Islam

Arab invasions and presence in the Mediterranean area during a crucial part of the early Middle Ages contributed both directly and indirectly to the formation of Western Europe. They did so indirectly by driving West Europeans back onto their native tribal and inherited Judeo-Christian, Graeco-Roman, and Byzantine resources, from which they created a Western culture of their own. Also, by diverting the attention and energies of the Byzantine Empire during the formative centuries, the Arabs prevented it from expanding into and reconquering Western Europe. That allowed two Germanic peoples to gain ascendancy: first the Franks and then the Lombards, who invaded Italy in the sixth century and settled in the Po valley.

Despite hostilities between the Christian West and the Muslim world, there was creative interchange between them, with the West having the most to gain. At this time, Arab civilizations were the more advanced, enjoying their golden age, and they had much to teach a

Religious Diversity. A Muslim and a Christian play the *ud* or lute together, from a thirteenth-century *Book of Chants* in the Escorial Monastery of Madrid. Medieval Europe was deeply influenced by Arab-Islamic culture, transmitted particularly through Spain. Some of the many works in Arabic on musical theory were translated into Latin and Hebrew, but the main influence on music came from the arts of singing and playing spread by minstrels. *A Moor and a Christian playing the lute, miniature in a book of music from the "Cantigas" of Alfonso X "the Wise" (1221–1284). Thirteenth century (manuscript). Monastero de El Escorial, El Escorial, Spain/index/bridgeman Art Library.*

Greek works on astronomy, mathematics, and medicine became available in Latin translation to Western scholars. Down to the sixteenth century, the basic gynecological and child-care manuals guiding the work of Western midwives and physicians were compilations made by the Baghdad physician Al-Razi (Rhazes), the philosopher and physician Ibn-Sina (Avicenna) (980–1037), and Ibn Rushd (Averröes) (1126–1198), who was also Islam's greatest authority on Aristotle. Jewish scholars also throve amid the intellectual culture Islamic scholars created. The greatest of them all, Moses Maimonides (1135–1204), wrote in both Arabic and Hebrew. Also the great poets and philologists of the Middle Ages, the Arabs gave the West its most popular book, *The Arabian Nights*, poetic folk tales that are still read and imitated in the West.

The Developing Roman Church

Throughout the period of imperial decline, Germanic invasions, and Islamic expansion, one Western institution remained firmly entrenched and gained in strength: the Christian church. The church sought to organize itself according to the centralized, hierarchical administrative structure of the empire, with strategically placed "viceroys" (bishops) in European cities who looked for spiritual direction to their leader, the bishop of Rome (later pope). As the Western Empire crumbled, local bishops and cathedral chapters (ruling bodies of clergy) filled the resulting vacuum of authority. The local cathedral became the center of urban life and the local bishop the highest authority for those who remained in the cities. In Rome, on a larger and more fateful scale, the pope took control of the city as the Western emperors gradually departed and died out. Left to its own devices, Western Europe soon discovered that the Christian church was its best repository of Roman administrative skills and classical culture.

The Christian church had been graced with special privileges, great lands, and wealth by Emperor Constantine and his successors. In 313 Constantine issued the Edict of Milan, giving Christians legal standing and a favored status within the empire. In 380 Emperors Theodosius I (r. ca. 379–395) and Gratian I (r. 367–383), in a joint declaration, raised Christianity to the official religion of the empire. Both Theodosius and his predecessors acted as much for political effect as out of religious conviction; in 313 Christians composed about one fifth of the population of the empire, making Christianity the strongest

toddling West. Between the eighth and tenth centuries, Moorish Cordoba was a model multicultural city embracing Arabs, Berbers, Spanish Christian converts to Islam, and native Jews. The Iberian Peninsula's largest city in the tenth century, it was a conduit for the finest Arabian tableware, leather, silks, dyes, aromatic ointments, and perfumes into the West. The Arabs taught Western farmers how to irrigate fields and Western artisans how to tan leather and refine silk. The West also gained from its contacts with Arabic scholars. Thanks to the skills of Islamic philosophers and translators, ancient

The Benedictine Order Sets Its Requirements for Entrance

Document

The religious life had great appeal in a time of political and social uncertainty. Entrance into a monastery was not, however, escapism. Much was demanded of the new monk, both during and after his probationary period, which is described here. Benedict's contribution was to prescribe a balanced blend of religious, physical, and intellectual activities within a well-structured community.

◆ Why did the religious life have such great appeal at this time in history? Were there materialistic as well as spiritual reasons for entering a cloister? What are Benedict's reasons for not allowing a monk to change his mind and leave the cloister, once vows have been taken?

When anyone is newly come for the reformation of his life, let him not be granted an easy entrance, but, as the Apostle says, "Test the spirits to see whether they are from God." If the newcomer, therefore, perseveres in his knocking, and if it is seen after four or five days that he bears patiently the harsh treatment offered him and the difficulty of admission, and that he persists in his petition, then let entrance be granted him, and let him stay in the guest house for a few days.

After that let him live in the novitiate, where the novices study, eat, and sleep. A senior shall be assigned to them who is skilled in winning souls, to watch over them with the utmost care. Let him examine whether the novice is truly seeking God, and whether he is zealous for the Work of God, for obedience and for humiliations. Let the novice be told all the hard and rugged ways by which the journey to God is made.

If he promises stability and perseverance, then at the end of two months let this Rule be read through to him,

and let him be addressed thus: "Here is the law under which you wish to fight. If you can observe it, enter; if you cannot, you are free to depart." If he still stands firm, let him be taken to the above-mentioned novitiate and again tested in all patience. And after the lapse of six months let the Rule be read to him, that he may know on what he is entering. And if he still remains firm, after four months let the same Rule be read to him again.

Then, having deliberated with himself, if he promises to keep it in its entirety and to observe everything that is commanded him, let him be received into the community. But let him understand that, according to the law of the Rule, from that day forward he may not leave the monastery nor withdraw his neck from under the yoke of the Rule which he was free to refuse or to accept during that prolonged deliberation.

Leonard J. Doyle, *St. Benedict's Rule for Monasteries* (Collegeville, Minn.: Liturgical Press, 1948), pp. 79–80.

---

among the empire's competing religions. Mithraism, a religion popular among army officers and restricted to males, was its main rival.

Challenged by Rome's decline to become a major political force, the church survived the period of Germanic and Arab invasions as a somewhat spiritually weakened and compromised institution. Yet it remained a potent civilizing and unifying force. It had a religious message of providential purpose and individual worth that could give solace and meaning to life at its worst. It had a ritual of baptism and a creedal confession that united people beyond the traditional barriers of social class, education, and gender. And alone in the West, the church retained an effective hierarchical administration, scattered throughout the old empire, staffed by the best-educated minds in Europe and centered in emperorless Rome.

Monastic Culture

The church also enjoyed the services of growing numbers of monks, who were not only loyal to its mission, but also objects of great popular respect. Monastic culture proved again and again to be the peculiar strength of the church during the Middle Ages.

The first monks were hermits who withdrew from society to pursue a more perfect way of life. They were inspired by the Christian ideal of a life of complete self-denial in imitation of Christ. The popularity of monasticism began to grow as Roman persecution of Christians waned and Christianity became the favored religion of the empire during the fourth century. Embracing the biblical "counsels of perfection" (chastity, poverty, and obedience), the monastic life became the purest form of religious practice.

Anthony of Egypt (ca. 251–356), the father of hermit monasticism, was inspired by Jesus' command to the rich young man: "If you will be perfect, sell all that you have, give it to the poor, and follow me" (Matthew 19:21). Anthony went into the desert to pray and work, setting an example followed by hundreds in Egypt, Syria, and Palestine in the fourth and fifth centuries. This hermit monasticism was soon joined by the development of communal monasticism. In the first quarter of the fourth century, Pachomius (ca. 286–346) organized monks in southern Egypt into a highly regimented community. Such monastic communities grew to contain 1,000 or more inhabitants. They were little "cities of God," trying to separate themselves from the collapsing Roman and the nominal Christian world. Basil the Great (329–379) popularized communal monasticism throughout the East, providing a rule that lessened the asceticism of Pachomius and directed monks beyond their segregated enclaves of perfection into such social services as caring for orphans, widows, and the infirm in surrounding communities.

Athanasius (ca. 293–373) and Martin of Tours (ca. 315–ca. 397) introduced monasticism into the West, where the teaching of John Cassian (ca. 360–435) and Jerome (ca. 340–420) helped shape its basic values and practices. The great organizer of Western monasticism was Benedict of Nursia (ca. 480–547). In 529 he established a monastery at Monte Cassino, in Italy, founding the form of monasticism—Benedictine—that bears his name and that quickly came to dominate in the West. Benedict also wrote a sophisticated *Rule for Monasteries*, a comprehensive plan that both regimented and enriched monastic life. Following the *Rule*, Benedictine monasteries were hierarchically organized and directed by an abbot, whose command was beyond question. Periods of study

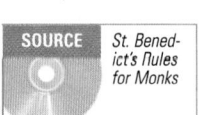
SOURCE: *St. Benedict's Rules for Monks*

and religious devotion (about four hours each day of prayers and liturgical activities) alternated with manual labor (up to eight hours, including copying manuscripts)—a program that permitted not a moment's idleness and carefully promoted the religious, intellectual, and physical well-being of the monks. During the early Middle Ages Benedictine missionaries Christianized both England and Germany. Their disciplined organization and devotion to hard work made the Benedictines an economic and political power as well as a spiritual force wherever they settled (see Document, "The Benedictine Order Sets Its Requirements for Entrance.")

The Doctrine of Papal Primacy

Constantine and his successors, especially the Eastern emperors, ruled religious life with an iron hand and consistently looked on the church as little more than a department of the state. The bishops of Rome, however, never accepted such royal intervention and opposed it in every way they could. Taking advantage of imperial weakness and distraction, they developed for their own defense the doctrine of "papal primacy." This doctrine raised the bishop of Rome to an unassailable supremacy within the church when it came to defining church doctrine and maintaining clerical allegiance. As the "pope," he was both head of the Roman Catholic Church and Christ's vicar on earth continuing the line of Christ's apostles from St. Peter. The new title also put him in a position to claim power within the secular world, giving rise to repeated conflicts between church and state, pope and emperor, throughout the Middle Ages.

Pope Damasus I (r. 366–384) took the first step towards establishing the doctrine when he declared Rome's **apostolic primacy**. Pointing to Jesus' words to Peter in the Gospel of Matthew (16:18) ("Thou art Peter, and upon this rock I will build my church"), he claimed himself and all other popes to be Peter's direct successors as the unique "rock" on which the Christian church was built. Pope Leo I (r. 440–461) took still another step by assuming the title *pontifex maximus*—"supreme priest." He further proclaimed himself to be endowed with a "plenitude of power," thereby establishing the supremacy of the bishop of Rome over all other bishops in the church. During Leo's reign an imperial decree recognized his exclusive jurisdiction over the Western church. At the end of

Chronology

Major Political and Religious Developments of the Early Middle Ages

313	Emperor Constantine issues the Edict of Milan
325	Council of Nicaea defines Christian doctrine
410	Rome invaded by Visigoths under Alaric
413–426	Saint Augustine writes *The City of God*
451–453	Europe invaded by the Huns under Attila
476	Barbarian Odovacer deposes Western emperor and rules as king of the Romans
488	Theodoric establishes kingdom of Ostrogoths in Italy
529	Saint Benedict founds monastery at Monte Cassino
533	Justinian codifies Roman law
732	Charles Martel defeats Arabs at Tours
754	Pope Stephen II and Pepin III ally

the fifth century Pope Gelasius I (r. 492–496) pushed the envelope by proclaiming the authority of the clergy to be "more weighty" than the power of kings because priests had charge 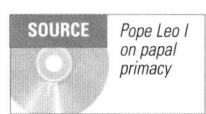 of divine affairs and the means of salvation. That statement laid a foundation for future church-state confrontations, as each side now, while recognizing the other's sphere of power, declared itself to be the superior, like the sun to the moon.

SOURCE *Pope Leo I on papal primacy*

Division of Christendom

As these events suggest, the division of Christendom into Eastern (Byzantine) and Western (Roman Catholic) churches has its roots in the early Middle Ages. The division was due in part to linguistic and cultural differences between the Greek East and the Roman West. As in the West, Eastern church organization closely followed that of the secular state. A "patriarch" ruled over "metropolitans" and "archbishops" in the cities and provinces, who, in turn, ruled over bishops, who stood as authorities over the local clergy. A novel combination of Greek, Roman, and Asian elements shaped Byzantine culture, giving Eastern Christianity a stronger mystical dimension than Western Christianity, a difference in outlook that may have predisposed Eastern patriarchs to submit more passively than Western popes ever could to royal intervention in their affairs.

Contrary to the evolving Western tradition of universal clerical celibacy, which Western monastic culture encouraged, the Eastern church permitted the marriage of parish priests (but not monks), while strictly forbidding bishops to marry. The Eastern church also used leavened bread in the Eucharist, contrary to the Western custom of using unleavened bread. The Roman church also objected to the tendency of the Eastern church to compromise with the politically powerful Arian Christians and the followers of another nonorthodox group, the Monophysite Christians (See "The Byzantine Empire," p. 356). Finally, the Eastern and Western churches both laid claim to jurisdiction over newly converted areas in the northern Balkans.

Beyond these issues, three major factors lay behind the religious break between East and West. The first revolved around questions of doctrinal authority. The Eastern church put more stress on the authority of the Bible and the ecumenical councils of the church in the definition of Christian doctrine than on the counsel and decrees of the bishop of Rome. The claims of Roman popes to a special primacy of authority on the basis of the Apostle Peter's commission from Jesus in the Gospel of Matthew were unacceptable to the East, where the independence and autonomy of regional churches held sway. This basic issue of authority in matters of faith lay behind the mutual excommunication of Pope Nicholas I and Patriarch Photius in the ninth century and that of Pope Leo IX

(through his ambassador to Constantinople, Cardinal Humbert) and Patriarch Michael Cerularius in 1054.

A second major issue in the separation of the two churches, as explained above, was the Western addition of the *filioque* clause to the Nicene-Constantinopolitan Creed. According to this anti-Arian clause, the Holy Spirit proceeds "also from the Son" (*filioque*) as well as from the Father, making clear the Western belief that Christ was fully of one essence with God the Father and not a lesser being.

The third factor dividing the Eastern and Western churches was the iconoclastic controversy of the first half of the eighth century. As noted earlier, after 725 the Byzantine Emperor Leo III (r. 717–741) attempted to force Western popes to abolish the use of images in their churches. This stand met fierce official and popular resistance in the West, where images were greatly cherished, and in the East as well. To punish the West, Leo confiscated valuable papal lands. This direct challenge to the papacy coincided with a threat to Rome and the Western church from the Lombards of northern Italy. Assailed on two fronts, the Roman papacy seemed doomed. But there has not been a more resilient and enterprising institution in Western history than the papacy. Since the pontificate of Gregory the Great (590–604), who 150 years earlier had negotiated a treaty with the Lombards, popes had recognized the Franks of northern Gaul as Europe's ascendant power and seen in them their surest protectors. In 754 Pope Stephen II (r. 752–757), initiating the most fruitful political alliance of the Middle Ages, enlisted the Franks and their ruler, Pepin III, to defend the church against the Lombards and as a Western counterweight to the Eastern emperor. This marriage of religion and politics created a new Western church and empire and determined much of the course of Western history thereafter.

The Kingdom of the Franks

Merovingians and Carolingians: From Clovis to Charlemagne

Around 496, Clovis (ca. 466–511), a warrior chieftain and Arian Christian, won a great victory over a rival tribe after invoking the name of Jesus. His success moved him to convert to Orthodox Christianity, to which his Christian wife had already disposed him. He then founded the first Frankish dynasty, the Merovingians, named after Merovich, an early leader of one branch of the Franks. Clovis and his successors subdued the pagan Burgundians and the Arian Visigoths and established the kingdom of the Franks within ancient Gaul, making the Franks and the Merovingian kings a significant force in Western Europe.

The Franks themselves occupied a broad belt of territory that extended through modern France, Belgium, the Netherlands, and western Germany, while their loyalties remained strictly tribal and local. In attempting to govern their sprawling kingdom, the Merovingians encountered what proved to be the most persistent problem of medieval political history—the competing claims of the "one" and the "many," with the king (the "one") struggling to impose centralized government and transregional loyalty on powerful local magnates (the "many"), determined to preserve their regional autonomy and traditions.

The Merovingian kings addressed this problem by making pacts with the landed nobility and by creating the royal office of count. The counts were men without possessions to whom the king gave great lands in the expectation that they would be, as the landed aristocrats often were not, loyal officers of the kingdom. But like local aristocrats, the Merovingian counts also let their immediate self-interests gain the upper hand. Once established in office for a period of time, they too became territorial rulers in their own right,

St. Mark, from the Gospel Book of Archbishop Ebbo of Reims, 816–835 C.E. A colorful, animated Carolingian portrayal of St. Mark as he writes his gospel. His symbol, a winged lion, appears in the upper right corner.

with the result that the Frankish kingdom progressively fragmented into independent regions and tiny principalities. This centrifugal tendency was aggravated by the Frankish custom of dividing the kingdom equally among the king's legitimate male heirs.

Rather than purchase allegiance and unity within the kingdom, the Merovingian largess occasioned the rise of competing magnates and petty tyrants, who became laws unto themselves within their regions. By the seventh century, the Frankish king was king in title only, lacking effective executive power. Real power was concentrated in the office of the Mayor of the Palace, who was the spokesman at the king's court for the great landowners of the three regions into which the Frankish kingdom was divided: Neustria (roughly western France), Austrasia (roughly central Germany), and Burgundy. Through this office, the Carolingian dynasty rose to power.

The Carolingians, who took their name from the dynasty's greatest ruler, Carolus, later to be known as Charlemagne, controlled the office of the Mayor of the Palace from the ascent to that post of Pepin I of Austrasia (d. 639) until 751, when, with the enterprising connivance of the pope, they simply expropriated the Frankish crown. Pepin II (d. 714) ruled in fact, if not in title, over the Frankish kingdom. His illegitimate son, Charles Martel ("the Hammer," d. 741), created a great cavalry by bestowing lands known as *benefices* or **fiefs** on powerful nobles, who, in return, agreed to be ready to serve as the king's army. It was such an army that checked the Arab probings at Tours in 732.

The fiefs so generously bestowed by Charles Martel to create his army came in large part from landed property that he usurped from the church. His alliance with the landed aristocracy in this grand manner permitted the Carolingians to have some measure of political success where the Merovingians had failed. The Carolingians created counts almost entirely out of the landed nobility from which the Carolingians themselves had risen. The Merovingians, in contrast, had tried to compete directly with these great aristocrats by raising the landless to power. By playing to strength rather than challenging it, the Carolingians strengthened themselves, at least for the short term. The church, by this time dependent on the protection of the Franks against the Eastern emperor and the Lombards, had no choice but to tolerate the seizure of its lands. Later, although they never returned the lands, the Franks partially compensated the church for them.

Frankish Church   The church played a large and enterprising role in the Frankish government. By Carolingian times, monasteries were a dominant force. Their intellectual achievements made them respected repositories of culture.

Their religious teaching and example imposed order on surrounding populations. Their relics and rituals made them magical shrines to which pilgrims came in great numbers. Thanks to their donated lands and serf labor, many had become very profitable farms and landed estates, their abbots rich and powerful magnates. By Merovingian times, the higher clergy were already employed in tandem with counts as royal agents. It was the policy of the Carolingians, perfected by Charles Martel and his successor, Pepin III ("the Short," d. 768), to use the church to pacify conquered neighboring tribes—Frisians, Thuringians, Bavarians, and especially the Franks' archenemies, the Saxons.

Conversion to Nicene Christianity became an integral part of the successful annexation of conquered lands and people; the cavalry broke bodies, while the clergy won hearts and minds. The Anglo-Saxon missionary Saint Boniface (b. Wynfrith, ca. 680–754) was the most important of the German clergy who served Carolingian kings in this way. Christian bishops in missionary districts and elsewhere became lords, appointed by and subject to the king—an ominous integration of secular and religious policy in which lay the seeds of the later Investiture Controversy of the eleventh and twelfth centuries (see Chapter 15).

The church helped the Carolingians with more than territorial expansion. Pope Zacharias (r. 741–752) sanctioned Pepin the Short's termination of the vestigial Merovingian dynasty and the Carolingian accession to kingship of the Franks. With the pope's blessing, Pepin was proclaimed king by the nobility in council in 751. The last of the Merovingians, the puppet king Childeric III, was removed to a monastery and dynastic oblivion. According to legend, Saint Boniface annointed Pepin, thereby investing Frankish rule with a sacral character from the start.

Zacharias' successor, Pope Stephen II (r. 752–757), did not let Pepin forget the favor of his predecessor. Driven from Rome in 753 by the Lombards, Pope Stephen appealed directly to Pepin to cast out the invaders and to guarantee papal claims to central Italy, which was dominated at this time by the Eastern emperor. In 754 the Franks and the church formed an alliance against the Lombards and the Eastern emperor. Carolingian kings became the protectors of the Catholic Church and thereby "kings by the grace of God." Pepin gained the title *patricius Romanorum*, "father-protector of the Romans," a title heretofore borne only by the rep-

resentative of the Eastern emperor. In 755 the Franks defeated the Lombards and gave the pope the lands surrounding Rome, creating what came to be known as the **Papal States**. In this period a fraudulent document appeared—the *Donation of Constantine*, written between 750 and 800—enterprisingly designed to remind the Franks of the church's importance as the heir of Rome. Many believed it to be genuine until fifteenth-century scholars exposed it as a forgery.

The papacy had looked to the Franks for an ally strong enough to protect it from the Eastern emperors. It is an irony of history that the church found in the Carolingian dynasty a Western imperial government that drew almost as slight a boundary between state and church, secular and religious policy, as did Eastern emperors. Although eminently preferable to Eastern domination, Carolingian patronage of the church proved to be no less constraining.

Reign of Charlemagne (768–814)

Charlemagne, the son of Pepin the Short, continued the role of his father as papal protector in Italy and his policy of territorial conquest in the north. After King Desiderius and the Lombards of northern Italy were decisively defeated in 774, Charlemagne took the title "King of the Lombards" in Pavia. He widened the frontiers of his kingdom further by subjugating surrounding pagan tribes, foremost among them the Saxons, whom the Franks brutally Christianized and dispersed in small groups throughout Frankish lands. The Danubian plains were brought into the Frankish orbit by the virtual annihilation of the Avars, a tribe related to the Huns. The Arabs were chased beyond the Pyrenees. By the time of his death on January 28, 814, Charlemagne's kingdom embraced modern France, Belgium, Holland, Switzerland, almost the whole of Germany, much of Italy, a portion of Spain, and the island of Corsica (see Map 12–4).

Charlemagne. An equestrian figure of Charlemagne (or possibly one of his sons) from the early ninth century. *Bronze equestrian statuette of Charlemagne, 3/4 view, from Metz Cathedral, ninth–tenth century. Louvre, Paris, France. Copyright Bridgeman-Giraudon/Art Resource, NY.*

Map 12–4. **The Empire of Charlemagne to 814.** Building on the successes of his predecessors, Charlemagne greatly increased the Frankish domains. Such traditional enemies as the Saxons and the Lombards fell under his sway.

The New Empire Encouraged by his ambitious advisers, Charlemagne came to harbor imperial designs. He desired to be not only king of all the Franks but a universal emperor as well. He had his sacred palace city, Aachen (in French, Aix-la-Chapelle), constructed in conscious imitation of the courts of the ancient Roman and the contemporary Eastern emperors. Although he permitted the church its independence, he looked after it with a paternalism almost as great as that of any Eastern emperor. He used the church above all to promote social stability and hierarchical order throughout the kingdom—as an aid in the creation of a great Frankish

Christian empire. Frankish Christians were ceremoniously baptized, professed the Nicene Creed (with the *filioque* clause), and learned in church to revere Charlemagne.

Charlemagne realized his imperial pretensions on Christmas Day 800, when Pope Leo III (795–816) crowned him emperor. This event created what would later be called the Holy Roman Empire, a revival, based after 870 in Germany, of the old Roman Empire in the West. If the coronation benefited the church, as it certainly did, it also served Charlemagne's designs. Before his coronation, he had been a minor Western potentate in the eyes of Eastern emperors.

After the coronation, Eastern emperors recognized his new imperial dignity, and Charlemagne even found it necessary to disclaim ambitions to rule as emperor over the East.

The New Emperor Charlemagne stood six feet, three and one half inches tall—a fact confirmed when his tomb was opened and exact measurements of his remains were taken in 1861. He was restless, ever ready for a hunt. Informal and gregarious, he insisted on the presence of friends even when he bathed and was widely known for his practical jokes, lusty good humor, and warm hospitality. Aachen was a festive palace city to which people and gifts came from all over the world. In 802 Charlemagne even received from the caliph of Baghdad, Harun-al-Rashid, a white elephant, the transport of which across the Alps was as great a wonder as the creature itself.

Charlemagne had five official wives in succession, and many mistresses and concubines, and he sired numerous children. This connubial variety created problems. His oldest son by his first marriage, Pepin, jealous of the attention shown by his father to the sons of his second wife and fearing the loss of paternal favor, joined with noble enemies in a conspiracy against his father. He spent the rest of his life in confinement in a monastery after the plot was exposed.

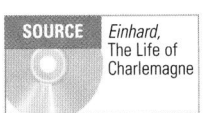
SOURCE Einhard, The Life of Charlemagne

Problems of Government Charlemagne governed his kingdom through counts, of whom there were perhaps as many as 250, strategically located within the administrative districts into which the kingdom was divided. In Carolingian practice, the count tended to be a local magnate, one who already had an armed following and the self-interest to enforce the will of a generous king. He had three main duties: to maintain a local army loyal to the king, to collect tribute and dues, and to administer justice throughout his district.

This last responsibility he undertook through a district law court known as the *mallus*, which heard testimony from the parties involved in a dispute or crime, passed judgment, and assessed a monetary compensation to be paid to the injured party. In very difficult cases, where guilt or innocence was unclear, recourse was often taken to judicial duels or "divine" tests and ordeals. Among these was the length of time a defendant's hand took to heal after immersion in boiling water. In another, the ordeal by water, a defendant was thrown with his hands and feet bound into a river or pond that a priest had blessed. If he floated, he was pronounced guilty, because the pure water had obviously rejected him; if, however, the water received him and he sank, he was deemed innocent.

As in Merovingian times, many counts used their official position and new judicial powers to their own advantage, becoming little despots within their districts. As they grew stronger and more independent, they came to regard the land grants with which they were paid as hereditary positions rather than generous royal donations. This development signaled the impending fragmentation of Charlemagne's kingdom. Charlemagne tried to supervise his overseers and improve local justice by creating special royal envoys known as *missi dominici*, lay and clerical agents (counts, archbishops, and bishops) who made annual visits to districts other than their own. But their impact was marginal. In still another attempt to manage the counts and organize the outlying regions of his realm, the king appointed permanent provincial governors with titles like prefect, duke, or margrave. But as these governors became established in their areas, they proved as corruptible as the others.

Charlemagne never solved the problem of creating a loyal bureaucracy. Ecclesiastical agents proved no better than secular ones in this regard. Landowning bishops had not only the same responsibilities but also the same secular lifestyles and aspirations as the royal counts. Except for their attendance to the liturgy and to church prayers, they were largely indistinguishable from the lay nobility. Capitularies, or royal decrees, discouraged the more outrageous behavior of the clergy. But Charlemagne also sensed—rightly, as the Gregorian reform of the eleventh century would prove—that the emergence of a distinctive and reform-minded class of ecclesiastical landowners would be a danger to royal government. Charlemagne purposefully treated his bishops as he treated his counts, that is, as vassals who served at the king's pleasure.

Alcuin and the Carolingian Renaissance Charlemagne used much of the great wealth his conquests brought him to attract Europe's best scholars to Aachen, where they developed court culture and education. By making scholarship materially as well as intellectually rewarding, Charlemagne attracted such scholars as Theodulf of Orleans (d. 821), Angilbert (d. 814), his own biographer Einhard (ca. 770–840), and the renowned Anglo-Saxon master Alcuin of York (735–804), who at almost fifty became director of the king's palace school in 782. Alcuin brought classical and Christian learning to Aachen and was handsomely rewarded for his efforts with several monastic estates, including that of Saint Martin of Tours, the wealthiest in the kingdom.

Although Charlemagne also appreciated learning for its own sake, his grand palace school was not created simply for love of antiquity. Charlemagne intended it to upgrade the administrative skills of the clerics and officials who staffed the royal bureaucracy. By preparing the sons of nobles to run the religious and secular offices of the realm, court scholarship served kingdom building. With its special concentration on grammar, logic, rhetoric, and basic mathematics, the school provided training in the basic tools of bureaucracy:

Numquid adheret tibi sedes iniqui
tatis: qui fingis laborem in precepto.
Captabunt in animam iusti: ＋san
guinem innocentem condempnabut.

Plowing the Fields. The invention of the moldboard plow greatly improved farming. The heavy plow cut deeply into the ground and furrowed it. This illustration from the Luttrell Psalter (ca. 1340) also shows that the traction harness, which lessened the strangulation effect of the yoke on the animals, had not yet been adopted. Indeed, one of the oxen seems to be on the verge of choking. *Picture Desk, Inc./Kobal Collection.*

reading, writing, speaking, sound reasoning, and counting. Charlemagne's scholars also created a new, clear style of handwriting—Carolingian minuscule—and fostered the use of accurate Latin in official documents, developments that helped increase lay literacy. Charlemagne's sister Gisela oversaw the copying of classical manuscripts, thereby preserving the treasures of antiquity. Through personal correspondence and visitations, Alcuin created a genuine, if limited, community of scholars and clerics at court and did much to infuse the highest administrative levels with a sense of comradeship and common purpose.

A modest renaissance, or rebirth, of antiquity occurred in the palace school as scholars collected and preserved ancient manuscripts for a more curious posterity. Alcuin worked on a correct text of the Bible and made editions of the works of Gregory the Great and the monastic *Rule* of Saint Benedict. These scholarly activities aimed at concrete reforms and served official efforts to bring uniformity to church law and liturgy, educate the clergy, and improve moral life within the monasteries.

The Manor and Serfdom The agrarian economy of the Middle Ages was organized and controlled through village farms known as **manors**. Here peasants labored as farmers in subordination to a lord, that is, a more powerful landowner who gave them land and a dwelling in exchange for their services and a portion of their crops. That part of the land farmed by the peasants for the lord was the **demesne**, on average about one quarter to one third of the arable land. All crops grown there were harvested for the lord.

Peasants were treated according to their social status and the size of their landholdings. A freeman—that is, a peasant with his own modest allodial, or hereditary, property (property free from the claims of an overlord)—became a **serf** by surrendering his property to a greater landowner—a lord—in exchange for protection and assistance. The freeman received his land back from the lord with a clear definition of his economic and legal rights. Although the land was no longer his property, he had full possession and use of it and the number of services and amount of goods he was to supply to the lord were carefully spelled out. Peasants who entered the service of a lord with little real property to bargain with (perhaps only a few farm implements and animals) ended up as unfree serfs and were much more vulnerable to the lord's demands, often spending up to three days a week working the lord's fields. Truly impoverished peasants who lived and worked on the manor as serfs had the lowest status and were the least protected.

Serfs were subject to so-called dues in kind: firewood for cutting the lord's wood, sheep for grazing their sheep on the lord's land, and the like. Thus the lord, who for his part furnished shacks and small plots of land from his vast domain, had at his disposal an army of servants who provided him with everything from eggs to boots. That many serfs were discontented is reflected in the high number of recorded escapes. An astrological calendar from the period marks the days most favorable for escaping. Fugitive serfs roamed the land as beggars and vagabonds, searching for new and better masters.

By the time of Charlemagne, the moldboard plow, which was especially needed in northern Europe where the soil was heavy, and the three-field system of land cultivation were coming into use. These developments greatly improved agricultural productivity. Unlike the older "scratch" plow, which crisscrossed the field with only slight penetration, the moldboard cut deep into the soil and turned it to form a ridge, providing a natural drainage system for the field as well as permitting the deep planting of seeds. Unlike the earlier two-field system of crop rotation, which simply alternated fallow with planted fields each year, the **three-field system** increased the amount of cultivated land by leaving only one third fallow in a given year.

Religion and the Clergy As owners of the churches on their lands, the lords had the right to raise chosen serfs to the post of parish priest, placing them in charge of the churches on the lords' estates. Church law directed the lord to set a serf free before he entered the clergy, but lords were reluctant to do this and risk thereby a possible later challenge to their jurisdiction over the ecclesiastical property with which the serf, as priest, was invested. Lords preferred a "serf priest," one who not only said the Mass on Sundays and holidays but also continued to serve his lord during the week, waiting on the lord's table and tending his steeds. Like Charlemagne with his bishops, Frankish lords cultivated a docile parish clergy.

The ordinary people baptized themselves and their children, confessed the Creed Mass, tried to learn the Lord's Prayer, and received last rites from the priest when death approached. Local priests on the manors were no better educated than their congregations, and instruction in the meaning of Christian doctrine and practice remained at a bare minimum. People understandably became particularly attached in this period to the more tangible veneration of relics and saints.

Charlemagne shared many of the religious beliefs of his ordinary subjects. He collected and venerated relics, made pilgrimages to Rome, frequented the church of Saint Mary in Aachen several times a day, and directed in his last will and testament that all but a fraction of his great treasure be spent to endow Masses and prayers for his departed soul.

Breakup of the Carolingian Kingdom

In the last years of his life, an ailing Charlemagne knew that his empire was ungovernable. The seeds of dissolution lay in regionalism, that is, the determination of each locality, no matter how small, to look first—and often only—to its own

self-interest. In medieval society, a direct relationship existed between physical proximity to authority and loyalty to authority. Local people obeyed local lords more readily than they obeyed a glorious but distant king. Charlemagne had been forced to recognize and even to enhance the power of regional magnates in order to win needed financial and military support.

Louis the Pious The Carolingian kings did not give up easily, however. Charlemagne's only surviving son and successor, Louis the Pious (r. 814–840), had three sons by his first wife. According to Salic or Germanic law, a ruler partitioned his kingdom equally among his surviving sons. Louis recognized that a tripartite kingdom would hardly be an empire and acted early in his reign to break this legal tradition. This he did by making his eldest son, Lothar (d. 855), co-regent and sole imperial heir in 817. To Lothar's brothers he gave important but much lesser appanages, or assigned hereditary lands: Pepin (d. 838) became king of Aquitaine and Louis "the German" (d. 876) became king of Bavaria, over the eastern Franks.

In 823 Louis's second wife, Judith of Bavaria, bore him still a fourth son, Charles (d. 877). Determined that her son should receive more than just a nominal inheritance, the queen incited the brothers Pepin and Louis to war against Lothar and persuaded their father to divide the kingdom equally among his four living sons. As the bestower of crowns upon emperors, the pope had an important stake in the preservation of the revived Western Empire and the imperial title, both of which were threatened by Louis's belated agreement to an equal partition of his kingdom. The pope condemned Louis and restored Lothar to his original magnificent inheritance. But Lothar's regained imperial dignity only stirred anew the resentments of his brothers, including his half-brother, Charles, who joined in renewed war against him.

The Treaty of Verdun and Its Aftermath In 843, with the Treaty of Verdun, peace finally came to Louis's surviving heirs (Pepin had died in 838). The great Carolingian Empire was partitioned into three equal parts. Lothar received a middle section, which came to be known as Lotharingia and embraced roughly modern Holland, Belgium, Switzerland, Alsace-Lorraine, and Italy. Charles the Bald received the western part of the kingdom, or roughly modern France, and Louis the German came into the eastern part, or roughly modern Germany (see Map 12–5). Although Lothar retained the imperial title, the universal empire of Charlemagne and Louis the Pious now ceased to exist. Not until the sixteenth century, with the election in 1519 of Charles I of Spain as the Holy Roman Emperor Charles V, would the Western world again see a kingdom as vast as Charlemagne's.

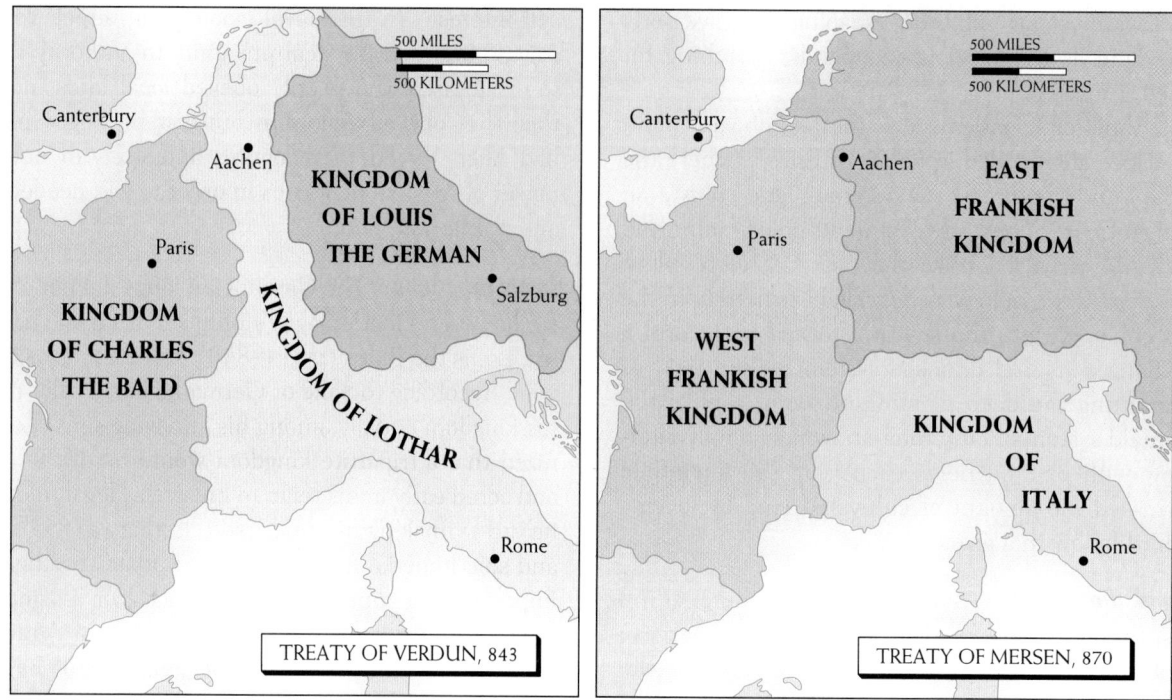

Map 12–5. The Treaty of Verdun (843) and the Treaty of Mersen (870). The Treaty of Verdun divided the kingdom of Louis the Pious among his three feuding children: Charles the Bald, Lothar, and Louis the German. After Lothar's death in 855, the middle kingdom was so weakened by division among his three sons that Charles the Bald and Louis the German divided it between themselves in the Treaty of Mersen.

The Treaty of Verdun proved to be only the beginning of Carolingian fragmentation. When Lothar died in 855 his kingdom was divided equally among his three surviving sons, leaving it much smaller and weaker than the kingdoms of Louis the German and Charles the Bald. Henceforth, Western Europe would be divided into an Eastern and a Western Frankish Kingdom—roughly Germany and France—at war over the fractionalized middle kingdom, a contest that has continued into modern times.

Vikings, Magyars, and Muslims The political breakdown of the Carolingian Empire coincided with new external threats. In the late ninth and tenth centuries, successive waves of Normans (North men), better known as Vikings, swept into Europe from Scandinavia. Vikings was a catchall term for Scandinavian peoples who visited Europe alternately as gregarious traders and savage raiders, and their exploits have been preserved in sagas that reveal a cultural world filled with mythical gods and spirits. Taking to sea in ocean-going longboats of rugged, doubled-hulled construction, they terrified their neighbors to the south, invading and occupying English and European coastal and river towns. In the ninth century, the Danes briefly besieged Paris, while other Vikings turned York into a major trading post for their woolens, jewelry, and ornamental wares. Erik the Red made it to Greenland, and

his son Leif Erikson wintered in Newfoundland and may even have walked on the shores of New England five hundred years before Columbus. In the eleventh century Christian conversions and English defeat of the Norwegians effectively restricted Vikings to their Scandinavian homelands.

Magyars, or Hungarians, who were great horsemen, also swept into Western Europe from the eastern plains, while Muslims made incursions across the Mediterranean from North Africa (see Map 12–6). The Franks built fortified towns and castles in strategic locations as refuges. When they could, they bought off the invaders with grants of land and payments of silver. In the resulting turmoil, local populations became more dependent than ever on local strongmen for life, limb, and livelihood, creating the essential precondition for the maturation of feudal society.

Feudal Society

The Middle Ages were characterized by a chronic absence of effective central government and the constant threat of famine, disease, and foreign invasion. In this state of affairs the weaker sought the protection of the stronger, and the true lords and masters became those who could guarantee

Map 12–6. Viking, Muslim, and Magyar Invasions to the Eleventh Century. Western Europe was sorely beset by new waves of outsiders from the ninth to the eleventh century. From north, east, and south, a stream of invading Vikings, Magyars, and Muslims brought the West at times to near collapse and of course gravely affected institutions within Europe.

immediate protection from rapine and starvation. The term *feudal society* refers to the social, political, military, and economic system that emerged from these conditions.

In a feudal society, what people require most is the firm assurance that others can be depended on in time of dire need. It is above all a system of mutual rights and responsibilities.

During the early Middle Ages, the landed nobility became great lords who ruled over their domains as miniature kingdoms. They maintained their own armies and courts, regulated local tolls, and even minted their own coins. Large groups of warrior **vassals** were created by extensive bestowals of land, and these developed into a prominent professional military class with its own code of knightly conduct. In feudal society, most serfs docilely worked the land, the clergy prayed and gave counsel, and lords and knights maintained law and order.

Origins

The origins of feudal government can be found in the divisions and conflicts of Merovingian society. In the sixth and seventh centuries, individual freemen began placing them-

selves under the protection of more powerful freemen. In this way, the latter built up armies and became local magnates, and the former solved the problem of simple survival. Freemen who so entrusted themselves to others were known as *ingenui in obsequio* (freemen in a contractual relation of dependence). Those who so gave themselves to the king were called *antrustiones*. All men of this type came to be described collectively as *vassi* ("those who serve"), from which evolved the term *vassalage*, meaning the placement of oneself in the personal service of another who promises protection in return.

Landed nobles, like kings, tried to acquire as many vassals as they could, because military strength in the early Middle Ages lay in numbers. Because it proved impossible to maintain these growing armies within the lord's own household, which was the original custom, or to support them by special monetary payments, the practice evolved of simply granting them land as a "tenement." Such land came to be known as a *benefice*, or a **fief**, and vassals were expected to dwell on it and maintain their horses and other accouterments of war in good order. Originally vassals, therefore, were little more than gangs-in-waiting.

Chronology

Carolingian Dynasty (751–987)

750–800	Fraudulent Donation of Constantine created in an effort to counter Frankish domination of church
751	Pepin III "the Short" becomes king of the Franks
755	Franks drive Lombards out of central Italy; creation of Papal States
768–814	Charlemagne rules as king of the Franks
774	Charlemagne defeats Lombards in northern Italy
800	Pope Leo III crowns Charlemagne
814–840	Louis the Pious succeeds Charlemagne as "Emperor"
843	Treaty of Verdun partitions the Carolingian Empire
870	Treaty of Mersen further divides Carolingian Empire
875–950	Invasions by Vikings, Muslims, and Magyars
962	Ottonian dynasty succeeds Carolingian in Germany
987	Capetian dynasty succeeds Carolingian in France

Vassalage and the Fief

Vassalage involved **fealty** to the lord. To swear fealty was to promise to refrain from any action that might in any way threaten the lord's well-being and to perform personal services for him on his request. Chief among the expected services was military duty as a mounted knight. This could involve a variety of activities: a short or long military expedition, escort duty, standing castle guard, or the placement of one's own fortress at the lord's disposal, if the vassal was of such stature as to have one. Continuous bargaining and bickering occurred over the terms of service.

Limitations were placed on the number of days a lord could require services from a vassal. In France in the eleventh century, about forty days of service per year were considered sufficient. It also became possible for vassals to buy their way out of military service by a monetary payment known as *scutage*. The lord, in turn, applied this payment to the hiring of mercenaries, who often proved more efficient than contract-conscious vassals. Beyond his military duty, the vassal was also expected to give the lord advice when he requested it and to sit as a member of his court when it was in session.

The lord's obligations to his vassals were very specific. He was, first of all, obligated to protect the vassal from physical harm and to stand as his advocate in public court. After fealty was sworn and homage paid, the lord provided for the vassal's physical maintenance by the bestowal of a benefice, or fief. The fief was simply the physical or material wherewithal to meet the vassal's military and other obligations. It could take the form of liquid wealth as well as the more common grant of real property. There were so-called money fiefs, which empowered a vassal to receive regular payments from the lord's treasury. Such fiefs created potential conflicts because they made it possible for one country to acquire vassals among the nobility of another. Normally, the fief consisted of a landed estate of anywhere from a few to several thousand acres, but it could also take the form of a castle.

In Carolingian times, a benefice, or fief, varied in size from one or more small villas to several *mansi*, which were agricultural holdings of twenty-five to forty-eight acres.

Lord and Vassal. A seventh-century portrayal of a vassal, who kneels before his lord and inserts his hands between those of his lord in a gesture of mutual loyalty: the vassal promising to obey and serve his lord, the lord promising to support and protect his vassal. *Spanish school (seventh century). Lord and vassal, decorated page (vellum). Archivo de la Corona de Aragon, Barcelona, Spain/Index/Bridgeman Art Library.*

The king's vassals are known to have received benefices of at least 30 and as many as 200 such mansi, truly a vast estate. Royal vassalage with a benefice understandably came to be widely sought by the highest classes of Carolingian society. As a royal policy, however, it proved deadly to the king in the long run. Although Carolingian kings jealously guarded their rights over property granted in benefice to vassals, resident vassals were still free to dispose of their benefices as they pleased. Vassals of the king, strengthened by his donations, in turn created their own vassals. These vassals, in turn, created still further vassals of their own—vassals of vassals of vassals—in a reverse pyramiding effect that fragmented land and authority from the highest to the lowest levels by the late ninth century.

Beginning with the reign of Louis the Pious (r. 814–840), bishops and abbots swore fealty and received their offices from the king as a benefice. The king formally invested these clerics in their offices during a special ceremony in which he presented them with a ring and a staff, the symbols of high spiritual office. This presumptuous practice of lay investiture, like the Carolingian confiscation of church land mentioned earlier, was a sore point for the church. In the eleventh and twelfth centuries it would provoke a great confrontation between church and state as reform-minded clergy rebelled against what they believed to be involuntary clerical vassalage.

Fragmentation and Divided Loyalty

In addition to the fragmentation brought about by the multiplication of vassalage, effective occupation of the land led gradually to claims of hereditary possession. Hereditary possession became a legally recognized principle in the ninth century and laid the basis for claims to real ownership. Fiefs given as royal donations became hereditary possessions and, with the passage of time, in some instances even the real property of the possessor. Further, vassal engagements came to be multiplied in still another way as enterprising freemen sought to accumulate as much land as possible. One man could become a vassal to several different lords. This development led in the ninth century to the concept of a "liege lord"—one master whom the vassal must obey even to the harm of the others, should a direct conflict among them arise.

The problem of loyalty was reflected not only in the literature of the period, with its praise of the virtues of honor and fidelity, but also in the ceremonial development of the very act of "commendation" by which a freeman became a vassal. In the mid–eighth century, an "oath of fealty" highlighted the ceremony. A vassal reinforced his promise of fidelity to the lord by swearing a special oath with his hand on a sacred relic or the Bible. In the tenth and eleventh centuries, paying homage to the lord involved not only the

swearing of such an oath, but also the placement of the vassal's hands between the lord's and the sealing of the ceremony with a kiss.

Despite their problems, feudal arrangements nonetheless provided stability throughout the early Middle Ages and aided the difficult process of political centralization during the high Middle Ages. The genius of feudal government lay in its adaptability. Contracts of different kinds could be made with almost anybody, as circumstances required. The process embraced a wide spectrum of people, from the king at the top to the lowliest vassal in the remotest part of the kingdom. The foundations of the modern nation-state would emerge in France and England from the fine-tuning of essentially feudal arrangements as kings sought to adapt their goal of centralized government to the reality of local power and control.

Summary

The Byzantine Empire. In the fifth century, Roman authority in the West collapsed under the impact of Germanic invasions. However, imperial power shifted to the Eastern part of the Roman Empire—known as the Byzantine Empire—with its capital at Constantinople. The Byzantine Empire would endure until the Ottoman Turks captured Constantinople in 1453. The peak of Byzantine power occurred during the reign of Justinian (527–565), one of whose major achievements was the *Corpus Juris Civilis*, a codification of Roman law on which most European law was based until the nineteenth century. The Byzantine Empire provided a model of civilized society to medieval Europe, helped protect it from Muslim invaders, and preserved much of classical learning.

The Islamic world also acted as a conduit for classical learning to the West, particularly in medicine, astronomy, and mathematics.

The Roman Church. The church was the strongest and most prestigious institution in early medieval Europe, where it filled the vacuum created by the collapse of Roman authority. Monastic culture was especially strong. The greatest organizer of Western monasticism was Saint Benedict of Nursia (480–547). Benedictine monasteries were an economic, political, and spiritual force throughout the West.

With the collapse of imperial authority in the West, the bishops of Rome, the popes, developed the doctrine of papal primacy by which they claimed supreme authority over church doctrine and the clergy. These claims were unacceptable in the East, where a separate Greek Orthodox Church developed under the control of the Byzantine emperors.

Charlemagne's Empire. The Frankish ruler Charlemagne (r. 768–814) sought to re-create a universal Western empire and was crowned emperor by the pope in 800. Charlemagne's realm embraced modern France, Belgium, Holland, and Switzerland, most of Germany, and parts of Italy and Spain. He formed a close alliance with the church and relied on churchmen as royal agents and administrators. His palace school at Aachen was the center of a modest renaissance of classical learning under scholars such as Alcuin of York (735–804).

Yet, despite his efforts at administrative control, Charlemagne's empire proved to be ungovernable. Charlemagne had increased the power of local lords whose support he needed to rule, but their power and wealth became so great that they were able to put their self-interest above royal authority. After Charlemagne's death, his empire dissolved amid quarrels among his heirs, the revolts of powerful nobles, and invasions by Vikings, Magyars, and Muslims.

Feudal Society. The Middle Ages were characterized by a chronic absence of central government and the constant threat of famine, disease, and invasion. Lords were those who could guarantee protection under these conditions.

Feudal society was one in which a local lord was dominant and offered security in return for allegiance from his dependents or vassals. It was a system of mutual rights and responsibilities. Medieval vassals pledged fealty to their lord in return for a fief, or grant of land. They promised to support their "liege lord" with troops or money when he called upon them for aid.

The feudal economy was organized and controlled through agrarian villages known as manors, worked by free peasants, who had their own modest property and economic and legal rights, or by serfs, impoverished peasants who were bound to the land and obliged to provide their lords with an array of services, dues in kind, and products.

Review Questions

1. Trace the history of Christianity to the reign of the emperor Charlemagne. How did the church become a political power in the Western Roman Empire?

2. How did the Franks become the dominant force in Western Europe? What were the characteristics of Charlemagne's rule? Why did his empire break apart?

INTERPRETING THE PAST

Europe in the Dark Ages: The Struggle for Stability

Historians continue to debate the degree to which the removal of the last Roman Emperor in the West (476 C.E.) was a turning point in the history of Europe. Although 476 may or may not be a crucial date to this study, it is clear that many rulers in subsequent centuries attempted to reconstruct the Roman Empire in an effort to reclaim the legitimacy and power of ancient Rome.

Draw on the documents and images contained in this chapter and on the Primary Source DVD/MyHistoryLab, especially those concerning Justinian and Charlemagne, to demonstrate how the idea of

Rome at least partially motivated these kings in their conquests. Examine particularly the documents, images, and maps related to these two emperors. Comment on how successful their quests to re-create the Roman Empire actually were.

Text Sources from MyHistoryLab / PrimarySource DVD

1) Einhard, *Life of Charlemagne*
2) Liutprand of Cremona, *Mission to Constantinople*
3) Prologue from the *Corpus Juris Civilis*
4) Pope Leo I on papal primacy

Visual Source from MyHistoryLab / PrimarySource DVD

1) Hagia Sophia

PRENTICE HALL
myhistorylab
Where it's a good time to connect to the past!

3. How and why was the history of the Eastern or Byzantine half of the Roman Empire so different from the Western half? What were the major political and religious differences? How would you compare Justinian to Charlemagne?

4. Compare and contrast the teaching of Islam, Roman Catholicism, and Byzantine or Orthodox Christianity. Are they irreconcilable?

5. What were the defining features of feudalism? Is a feudal society a "backward" society?

Note: To learn more about the topics in this chapter, please turn to the Suggested Readings at the end of the book. For additional sources related to this chapter please see the Primary Source DVD at the back of this text or MyHistoryLab.

Key Terms

apostolic primacy (p. 364)

demesne (dih-MEEN) (p. 370)

fealty (p. 374)

feudal society (p. 373)

fiefs (p. 366)

Magyars (p. 372)

manors (p. 370)

Papal States (p. 367)

serf (p. 370)

three-field system (p. 371)

vassals (p. 373)

Visual Sources from Chapter 12

1) Map: "Byzantine Empire at the Death of Justinian" (p. 358)
2) "The Empire of Charlemagne, to 814" (p. 368)
3) Charlemagne (p. 367)

Questions

How did Justinian and Charlemagne attempt to revive the Roman Empire, and to what extent were they successful in doing so?

What did Liutprand of Cremona discover in Constantinople when he traveled there? Did it surprise him?

What does the emergence of feudal relations suggest about the long-term success of Charlemagne's revived empire?

13

The Islamic World, 1000–1500

CENTRALIZED CALIPHAL POWER IN THE ISLAMIC world had broken down by the mid–tenth century. Regional Islamic states with distinctive political and cultural identities now dominated—a pattern that would endure to modern times (see Map 13–1). Yet the diverse Islamic lands remained part of a larger civilization. Muslims from Córdoba in Spain could (and did) travel to Bukhara in Transoxiana or Zanzibar on the East African coast and feel at home. Regionalism and cosmopolitanism, diversity and unity, have characterized Islamic civilization ever since.

The next 500 years saw the growth of a truly international Islamic community, united by shared norms of communal order represented and maintained by the Muslim religious scholars (*ulama*). Sufism, the strand of Islam that stressed piety and allegiance to a spiritual master, gained popularity, especially after 1200. The growth of Sufi affiliations or brotherhoods influenced Muslim life everywhere, often countering the more limiting and legalistic aspects of *ulama* conformity. Shi'ite ideas offered another alternative vision of society. Movements loyal to Ali and his heirs challenged but failed to reverse centrist Sunni predominance in most of the Islamic world, even though

Islamic World Map. The geographical treatise and collection of wondrous tales known as *The Wonders of Creation* was popular in medieval and early modern Islamic society. The map shown here portrays several creatures supporting the world in the firmament. North is oriented at the bottom. Africa is the large triangle-shaped landmass jutting upward.

The Expansion of Islamic Civilization, 1000–1500

Africa

Central Asia   India

In Islamic and other Asian territories, the period from about 1000 to the beginning of the sixteenth century is difficult to characterize simply. The spread of Islam to new peoples or to their ruling elites is a theme of this chapter. However, the history of Islam in India is hardly the history of India as a whole. The vast conquests and movements of the Mongols and Central Asian Turks across inner Asia were among the most striking developments in world history in this period. Their effects on the societies they conquered were often cataclysmic, whether in China, south Asia, west Asia, or Eastern Europe. These conquests and migrations wiped out much of the existing orders and forced countless refugees to flee to new areas. After the initial conquests, however, the empires created by the pastoral warriors or *ghazis* of Central Asia helped facilitate the movement across the Eurasian continent of people, merchandise, ideas, and, in the fourteenth century, the Bubonic pandemic. They also contributed, even if unintentionally, new and often significant human resources to existing civilizations, such as those of China, the Islamic heartlands, and South Asia.

In this era, Islam became a truly cosmopolitan tradition of religious, cultural, political, and social values and institutions. This achievement was largely because Islamic culture was highly adaptable and open to "indigenization," or a syncretistic blending of cultural traits, even in the seemingly hostile contexts of polytheistic Hindu, south Asian, and African societies. The ability to adapt while maintaining the core tenets of Islamic religious faith explains the capacity of Islamic religion and culture to take root in so many different regions of the globe. Also in this period, distinct traditions of art, language, and literature, for all their local or regional diversity, became part of a larger Muslim whole. Islamic civilization had none of the territorial contiguity or linguistic and cultural homogeneity of either Chinese or Japanese civilization. Nevertheless, the Islamic world did become a recognizable international reality, a true *Dar al-Islam*, or "House of Islam," in which a Muslim could travel among, encounter, and exchange ideas and goods with other Muslims of radically diverse backgrounds from Morocco to China and have much in common with them. Ibn Battuta (1304–c. 1370), a Moroccan jurist, traveled for thirty years from his country

Shi'ite dynasties ruled much of the Islamic heartlands in the tenth and eleventh centuries.

A cultural renaissance fueled the spread of modern Persian as the major language of Islam alongside Arabic. The Persian-dominated Iranian and Indian Islamic world became more distinct from the western Islamic lands where Arabic prevailed.

Two Asian steppe peoples, the Mongols and the Turks, came to rule much of the Islamic world in these centuries, but with different results. The spread of the Turks added a substantial Turkish element, especially where they became rulers, as happened with the Saljuq sultans in Iran and Anatolia, and with the "slave-sultans" of both the Mamluk sultanate in Egypt, and the Delhi sultanate in north India. The Mongols conquered much of the Islamic heartlands in the thirteenth century, but their culture and religion did not become dominant. Instead, in this age Islam became the major new influence in the Indian subcontinent, Southeast Asia, and sub-Saharan Africa. ∎

through Egypt to India and then to parts of Southeast Asia before returning to dictate his *Travels in Asia and Africa, 1325–1354*. His career as an Islamic judge and an Arabic speaker allowed him to journey the length and breadth of the global Islamic world and feel himself still within the bounds of Islamic civilization.

Indian traditional culture was not bound up with an expanding missionary religious tradition like that of Islam, and the developing caste system closely associated with Hinduism was less adaptable, and thus less portable. Yet in this age Hindu kingdoms flourished in Indonesia, although these kingdoms mostly rejected the caste system and thus accommodated Hinduism and Indian culture to local conditions. Buddhism, another highly adaptable religion, was expanding across much of Central and eastern Asia, thereby solidifying its place as an international missionary tradition.

Christianity, by contrast, was not rapidly expanding in Africa, Asia, or Europe. The somewhat disastrous experience of the Crusades (see Chapter 15) brought Europeans into closer contact with the Islamic world than ever before but did little to attract converts to Christianity, or to increase European power in the Middle East. By 1500, however, the European branch of Christianity was poised on the brink of internal revolution and international expansion. In the year 1000 Europe was almost a backwater of culture and power, compared to major Islamic or Hindu states, let alone China. By 1500, however, European civilization was riding the crest of a commercial and cultural renaissance, enjoying economic and political growth, and starting its global exploration in search of gold and silver to trade with the far-more prosperous and cultured Asian lands. The impact on the Indian Ocean and Chinese-Japanese trade and shipping entrepots was not immediate; it was only after the mid–eighteenth century that European exploration and trade initiatives became full-scale imperial expansion and rule such that the rest of the globe was profoundly changed.

Focus Questions

◆ What impact did the Mongol and Central Asian Turks have on the Islamic world?

◆ Why were Islam and Buddhism more successful than Hinduism and Christianity in expanding during this era? What does this suggest about the characteristics of a successful world religion?

THE ISLAMIC HEARTLANDS

Religion and Society

In this period Islamic society was shaped by the consolidation and institutionalization of Sunni legal and religious norms, Sufi traditions and personal piety, and Shi'ite legal and religious norms.

Consolidation of a Sunni Orthopraxy

The *ulama* (both Sunni and Shi'ite) gradually became entrenched religious, social, and political elites throughout the Islamic world, especially after the breakdown of centralized power in the tenth century. Their integration into local merchant, landowning, and bureaucratic classes led to stronger identification of these groups with Islam.

Beginning in the eleventh century, the *ulama*'s power and fixity as a class were expressed in the institution of the **madrasa**, or college of higher learning. On the one hand, the

Map 13–1.   The Islamic World, 1000–ca. 1500. Compare this map with Map 11–1 on page 336. Though the Muslim world had expanded deep into Africa, India, and Central Asia, it had also lost Spain to Christian reconquest.

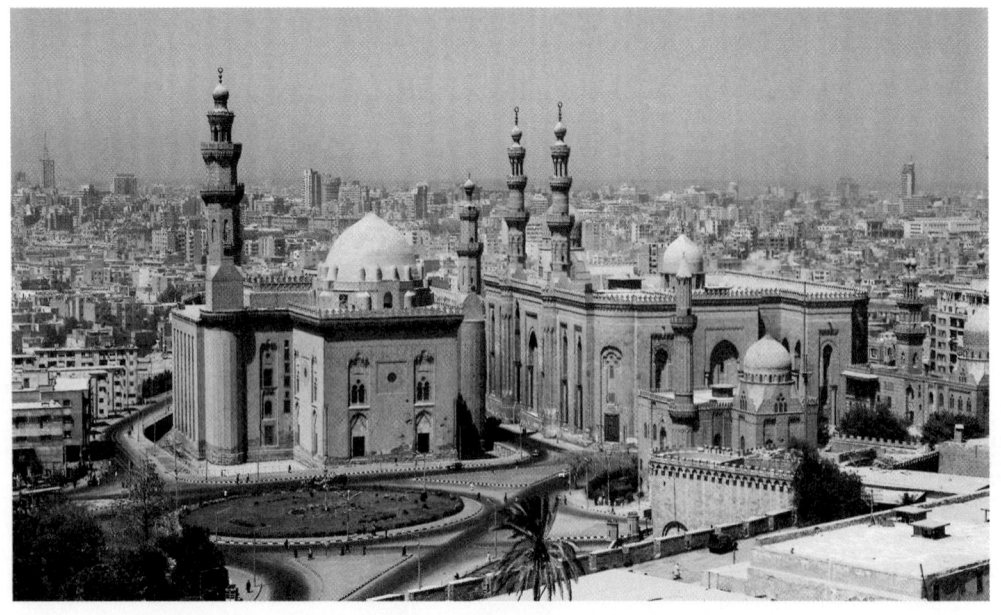

The Sultan Hasan Madrasa and Tomb-Mosque in Cairo, Egypt. This imposing Mamluk building (1356–1363) was built to house teachers and students studying all four of the major traditions or "schools" of Islamic law. Living and teaching spaces are combined here in a building with a mosque and the Sultan's tomb enclosure. *SuperStock, Inc.*

madrasa had grown up naturally as individual experts frequented a given mosque or private house and attracted students seeking to learn the Qur'an, the *Hadith* ("Tradition"), jurisprudence, Arabic grammar, and the like. On the other hand, rulers endowed the *madrasas* with buildings, scholarships, and salaried chairs, so that they could control the *ulama* by appointing teachers and influencing the curriculum. In theory, such control might combat unwelcome sectarianism. Unlike the university, with its corporate organization and institutional degrees, the *madrasa* was a support institution for individual teachers, who personally certified students' mastery of particular subjects. It gave an institutional base to Islam's long-developed system of students seeking out the best teachers and studying texts with them until they received the teachers' formal certification, or "permission" to transmit and teach those same texts themselves.

Largely outside *ulama* control, popular "unofficial" piety flourished in local pilgrimages to saints' tombs, in folk celebrations of Muhammad's birthday, in veneration of him in poetry, and in ecstatic chant and dance among Sufi groups. But the shared traditions that directed family and civil law, the daily worship rituals, fasting in the month of **Ramadan**, and the yearly Meccan pilgrimage united almost all Muslims, even most Kharijites or Shi'ites. In the Christian world, theological dogmas determined sectarian identity. In contrast, Muslims tended to define Islam in terms of what Muslims do—by practice rather than by beliefs. The chief arbiters of "normative" Sunni and Shi'ite Islam among the *ulama* were the *faqihs*, or legal scholars, not the theologians.

Basic Sunni orthopraxy, or "correctness of religious practice," discouraged religious or social innovations. It was well established by the year 1000 as the dominant tradition, even though Shi'ite aspirations often made themselves felt either politically or theologically. The emergence of a conservative theological orientation tied to one of the four main Sunni legal schools, the Hanbalites (after Ibn Hanbal, d. 969) narrowed the scope for creative doctrinal change. The Hanbalites relied on a literalist reading of the Qur'an and the *Hadith*. The *ulama* also became more socially conservative as they became integrated into social aristocracies. The *ulama* were often as committed to the status quo as the rulers.

Sufi Piety and Organization

Sufi piety stresses the spiritual and mystical dimensions of Islam. The term *Sufi* apparently came from the Arabic *suf* ("wool"), based on the old ascetic practice of wearing only a coarse woolen garment. Sufi simplicity and humility had roots with the Prophet and the Companions but developed as a distinctive tendency when, after about 700 C.E., male and female pietists emphasized a godly life over and above

Dancing Dervishes. This image from a 1552 Persian manuscript depicts a Sufi master dancing with his disciples. Sufis often use music and bodily movement to induce a feeling of ecstasy, which they feel brings them closer to God. *Bodleian Library, University of Oxford.*

mere observance of Muslim duties. Some stressed ascetic avoidance of temptations, others loving devotion to God. Sufi piety bridged the abyss between the human and the Divine that the exalted Muslim concept of the omnipotent God of creation implies. Socially, Sufi piety merged with folk piety in such popular practices as saint veneration, shrine pilgrimage, ecstatic worship, and seasonal festivals. Sufi writers collected stories of saints, wrote treatises on the Sufi path, and composed some of the world's finest mystical poetry. (See Document, "Jalaluddin Rumi: Who Is the Sufi?")

Some Sufis were revered as spiritual masters and saints. Their disciples formed brotherhoods with their own distinctive mystical teaching, Qur'anic interpretation, and devotional practice. These fraternal orders became the chief instruments of the spread of Muslim faith, as well as a locus of popular piety in almost all Islamic societies. Organized Sufism has always attracted members from the populace at large (in this, it differs from monasticism), as well as those dedicated to poverty or other radical disciplines. Indeed, Sufi orders became in this age one of the typical social institutions of everyday Muslim life. Whether Sunni or Shi'ite, many Muslims have ever since identified in some degree with a Sufi order.

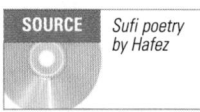

SOURCE *Sufi poetry by Hafez*

Consolidation of Shi'ite Traditions

Shi'ite traditions crystallized between the tenth and twelfth centuries. Many states now came under Shi'ite rulers, but only the Fatimids in Egypt established an important empire.

A substantial Shi'ite populace developed only in Iran, Iraq, and the lower Indus (Sind).

Two Shi'ite groups emerged as the most influential. The first were the "Seveners," or "Isma'ilis," who recognized Isma'il (d. ca. 760), first son of the sixth Alid *imām*, as the seventh *imām*. Their thought drew on Gnostic and Neo-Platonic philosophy, knowledge of which they reserved for a spiritual elite. Isma'ili groups were often revolutionary.

By the eleventh century, however, most Shi'ites accepted a line of twelve *imāms*, the last of whom is said to have disappeared in Samarra (Iraq) in 873 into a cosmic concealment from which he will eventually emerge as the Mahdi, or "Guided One," to usher in the messianic age and final judgment. The "Twelvers," the Shi'ite majority, still focus on the martyrdom of the twelve *imāms* and look for their intercession on the Day of Judgment. They have flourished best in Iran, the home of most Shi'ite thought. The Buyids who took

---

Jalaluddin Rumi: Who Is the Sufi?   Document

Rumi (d. 1273) was one of the greatest and most influential mystics of Islamic history. Born in Mazar-e-Sharif (in a region that was once part of Khorasan), his family moved westward just before the Mongol invasion of Iran to settle finally in Saljuq Konya, in central Anatolia. Rumi succeeded his father as a *madrasa* professor and studied in Syria. The Mevlevi Sufi brotherhood considers him its founder. The following two selections come from Rumi's two longest works of mystical poetry.

◆ What qualities or attributes does the Sufi seem to have, or to seek to develop? What seems to be the Sufi's goal? What might be the aim of the remarks about the "patched mantle" (a common mark of Sufi initiation) and "lust perverse"? What does "Beauty" seem to refer to in the first poem?

What makes the sufi? Purity of heart;
Not the patched mantle and the lust perverse
Of those vile earth-bound men who steal his name.
He in all dregs discerns the essence pure:
In hardship ease, in tribulation joy.
The phantom sentries, who with batons drawn
Guard Beauty's palace gate and curtained bower,
Give way before him, unafraid he passes,
And showing the King's arrow, enters in.

— Mathnawi, p. 54

What to do, Muslims? For I do not recognize myself; not
a Christian I nor Jew, Zoroastrian nor Muslim. . . .
Not of India am I nor China, not Bulgar-land nor Turkistan;
not the Kingdom of Both Iraqs nor the Land of
Khurasan.

Not of this World am I nor the next, not of heaven or hell;
not of Adam nor of Eve, not of Paradise nor Ridwan.
My place is no place, my trace has no trace; not body
nor soul, for I belong to the soul of Love.
Duality have I put aside, I have seen both worlds as one.
One I seek, One I know, One I see, One I call.
He is the first, He the last; he the Outward, He the
inward.

— Diwan-i Shams-i Tabriz

The first poem is from *Rumi: Poet and Mystic*, by R. A. Nicholson. Copyright © 1950 by George Allen and Unwin Ltd., an imprint of HarperCollins Publishers Limited. The second poem trans. from the Arabic by John Alden Williams, reprinted from *The World of Islam*, ed. by John Alden Williams, Copyright © 1994. By permission of the author and the University of Texas Press.

control of the Abbasid caliphate in 945 were Twelvers. The Safavids of Iran made Twelver doctrine the "state religion" in the sixteenth century (see Chapter 21).

Regional Developments

After the tenth century the western half of the Islamic world centered on the Mediterranean developed two regional foci: (1) Spain (*Al-Andalus*), Moroccan North Africa, and, to a lesser extent, West Africa; and (2) Egypt, Syria-Palestine, Anatolia, along with Arabia and Libyan North Africa. The history of the eastern half of the Islamic world in the period between 1000 and 1500 was marked by the violent Mongol incursions of the thirteenth century.

Spain, North Africa, and the Western Mediterranean Islamic World

The grandeur of Spanish Islamic or Andalusian culture is visible still in Córdoba's Great Mosque and the remnants of the Alhambra castle. In European tradition, the *Chanson de Roland* preserves the echo of Charlemagne's retreat through the Pyrenees Mountains after failing to check the first Spanish Umayyad's growing power. That ruler, Abd al-Rahman I (r. 756–788), was the founder of the cosmopolitan tradition of Umayyad Spanish culture at Córdoba, which was the cultural center of the Western world for the next two centuries. Renowned for its medicine, science, literature, intellectual life, commercial activity, public baths and gardens, and courtly elegance, Córdoba reached its zenith under Abd al-Rahman III (r. 912–961), who took the title of caliph in 929. His absolutist, but benevolent, rule saw a largely unified, peaceful Islamic Spain. The mosque-university of Córdoba that he founded attracted students from Europe as well as the Islamic world.

A sad irony of this cosmopolitan world was recurring religious exclusivism, as well as conflict among Muslims and Christians alike. Abroad, Abd al-Rahman III checked both the new Fatimid power in North Africa and the Christian kingdoms in northern Spain, making possible a golden era of Moorish power and culture. But after his

The Alhambra. Built in the fourteenth century, the Alhambra's serene, almost severe aspect belies its wealth of interior ornamentation. Considered one of the greatest examples of Islamic architecture and one of the most beautiful of all surviving medieval buildings, the Alhambra rises within its curtain walls above Grenada, the last of the great Moorish cities of Andalusia.

Getty Images Inc.-Stone Allstock.

death, fragmentation into warring Muslim principalities allowed a resurgence of Spain's Christian states between about 1000 and 1085, when the city of Toledo fell permanently into Christian hands.

Brief Islamic revivals in Spain and North Africa came under the African reform movements of the Almoravids and Almohads. The Almoravids originated as a religious-warrior brotherhood among Berber nomads in West Africa. Having subdued northwestern Africa, in 1086 they carried their zealotry from their new capital of Marrakesh into Spain and reunited its Islamic kingdoms. Under their rule, arabized Christians (Mozarabs) were persecuted, as were some Moorish Jews. The subsequent wars began the last major phase of the Spanish "Reconquest" (*Reconquista*). These conflicts, in which Christian rulers sought to regain and Christianize the peninsula, are best known in the West for the exploits of El Cid (d. 1099), the mercenary adventurer who became the Spanish national hero.

The Almohads ended Almoravid rule in Morocco in 1147 and then conquered much of southern Spain. Before their demise (1225 in Spain; 1275 in Africa), they stimulated a brilliant revival of Moorish culture. During this era, paper manufacture reached Spain and then the rest of Western Europe. The long westward odyssey of Indian fable literature through Iran and the Arab world ended with Spanish and Latin translations in thirteenth-century Spain. The greatest lights of this Spanish Islamic intellectual world were the major philosopher and physician Ibn Rushd (Averroës, d. 1189); the great Muslim mystical thinker Ibn al-Arabi (d. 1240); and the famous Arab-Jewish philosopher Ibn Maymun, or Maimonides (d. 1204). (See Document, "A Muslim Biographer's Account of Maimonides.")

Egypt and the Eastern Mediterranean Islamic World

The Fatimids The major Islamic presence in the Mediterranean from the tenth to the twelfth century was that of the Shi'ite Fatimids, who claimed descent from Muhammad's daughter, Fatima. They began as a Tunisian dynasty, then conquered Morocco, Sicily, and Egypt (969), where they built their new capital, Cairo (*al-Qahira*, "the Victorious"). Their rule as Shi'ite caliphs meant that, for a time, there were three "caliphates"—in Baghdad, Córdoba, and Cairo. The Fatimids were Isma'ilis (see Chapter 11). Content to rule a Sunni majority in Egypt, they sought recognition as true imams by other Isma'ili groups and were able, for a time, to take western Arabia and most of Syria from the Buyid "guardians" of the Abbasid caliphate (see Chapter 11).

Fatimid rule spawned two splinter groups that have played visible, if minor, roles in history. The Druze of modern

Lebanon and Syria originated around 1020 with a few members of the Fatimid court who professed belief in the divinity of one of the Fatimid caliphs. The tradition they founded is too far from Islam to be considered a Muslim sect. The Isma'ili Assassins, on the other hand, were a radical Muslim movement founded by a Fatimid defector in the Elburz mountains of Iran around 1100. The name "Assassins" comes not from the political assassinations that made them infamous, but from a European corruption of the Arabic *Hashishiyyin* ("users of hashish"). It was possibly connected with the story that their assassins were manipulated with drugs to undertake their usually suicidal missions. The Assassins were destroyed by the Mongols in the thirteenth century.

The Fatimids built the al-Azhar mosque in Cairo as a center of learning, a role it maintains today, although for Sunni, not

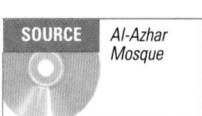

SOURCE *Al-Azhar Mosque*

(as then) Shi'ite, scholarship. Fatimid rulers treated Egypt's Coptic Christians generally as well as they did their Sunni majority, and many Copts held high offices. Jews also usually fared well under the Fatimids.

After 1100 the Fatimids weakened, falling in 1171 to Salah al-Din (Saladin, 1137–1193), a field general and administrator under the Turkish ruler of Syria, Nur al-Din (1118–1174). Saladin, a Sunni Kurd, is well known in the West for his battles (including the retaking of Jerusalem in 1187) with the Crusaders. After Nur al-Din's death, Saladin added Syria-Palestine and Mesopotamia to his Egyptian dominions and founded the Ayyubid dynasty that, under his successors, controlled all three

Decorated Ceramic Bowl. A glazed ceramic bowl decorated with a gazelle or antelope, a symbolic figure of beauty and grace. From North Africa, Tunisian area, Fatimid (tenth–twelfth centuries).

areas until Egypt fell to the Mamluks in 1250 and most of Syria and Mesopotamia to the Mongols by 1260.

Like Nur al-Din, and on the model of the Seljuks (see Chapter 11), Saladin founded *madrasas* to teach and promote Sunni law. His and his Ayyubid successors' reigns in Egypt saw the entrenchment of a self-conscious Sunnism under a program of mutual recognition and teaching of all four Sunni schools of law. Henceforward Shi'ite Islam disappeared from Egypt.

Chronology

Western Islamic Lands

756–1021	Spanish Umayyad dynasty
912–961	Rule of Abd al-Rahman III; height of Umayyad power and civilization
969–1171	Fatimid Shi'ite dynasty in Egypt
ca. 1020	Origin of Druze community (Egypt/Syria)
1056–1275	Almoravid and Almohad dynasties in North Africa, West Africa, and Spain
1096–1291	Major European Christian crusades into Islamic lands; some European presence in Syria-Palestine
1171	Fatimids fall to Salah al-Din (Saladin), Ayyubid lieutenant of the ruler of Aleppo
1189	Death of Ibn Rushd (Averroës), philosopher
1204	Death of Musa ibn Maymun (Maimonides), philosopher and Jewish savant
1240	Death of Ibn al-Arabi, theosophical mystic
1250–1517	Mamluk sultanate in Egypt and (from late 1200s) Syria; claim laid to Abbasid caliphate
1258	Mongols and Hulagu Khan sack Baghdad, ending the Abbasid era
1260	Mamluk victory at Ain Jalut halts Mongol advance into Syria
ca. 1300	Rise of Ottoman state in western Anatolia
1406	Death of Ibn Khaldun, historian and social philosopher
1453	Conquest of Constantinople and the collapse of Byzantium and the Byzantine Empire by the Ottoman forces under Sultan Mehmet I (1451–1481)

The Mamluks The heirs of the Fatimids and Saladin in the eastern Mediterranean were the redoubtable **sultans** ("[those with] authority") of the Mamluk dynasty who were chiefly Circassians from the Caucasus, captured in childhood and trained as slave-bodyguards. The Mamluks were the only Islamic dynasty to withstand the Mongol invasions. Their victory at Ain Jalut in Palestine in 1260 marked the end of the Mongols' westward movement. The first Mamluk sultan, Aybak (r. 1250–1257), and his successors were elite Turkish and Mongol slave-officers drawn originally from the bodyguard of Saladin's dynasty. Whereas the early Mamluks were often succeeded by sons or brothers, succession after the 1390s was more often a survival of the fittest; no sultan reigned more than a few years. The Mamluk state was based on a military fief system and total control by the slave-officer elite.

The Mamluk sultan Baybars (r. 1260–1277), who took the last Crusader fortresses, is a larger-than-life figure in Arab legend. To legitimize his rule, he revived the Abbasid caliphate at least in name after its demise in the fall of Baghdad (1258; discussed later) by installing an uncle of Baghdad's last Abbasid as Caliph at Cairo. He made treaties with Constantinople and with European sovereigns, as well as with the newly converted Muslim ruler, or *khan*, of the Golden Horde—the Mongol Tatars of southern Russia. His public works in Cairo were numerous. He also extended Mamluk rule south to Nubia and west among the Berbers.

As trade relations with the Mongol domains improved after 1300, the Mamluks enjoyed substantial prosperity and commanded a large empire. However, the Black Death epidemic of 1347–1348 in the Arab Middle East hurt the Mamluk and other regional states badly. Still the Mamluks survived even the Ottoman conquest of Egypt in 1517, since Mamluks continued to rule there as Ottoman governors into the nineteenth century.

Architecture, much of which still graces Cairo, remains the most magnificent Mamluk bequest to posterity. In addition, mosaics, calligraphy, and metalwork were among the arts and crafts of special note. The Mamluks were great patrons of scholars who excelled in history, biography, astronomy, mathematics, and medicine. The most important of these was Ibn Khaldun (d. 1406). Born of a Spanish Muslim family in Tunis, he settled in Cairo as an adult. He is still recognized as the greatest Muslim social historian and philosopher of history.

The Islamic East: Asia before the Mongol Conquests

The Persian dynasties of the Samanids at Bukhara (875–999) and the Buyids at Baghdad (945–1055) were the major usurpers of eastern Abbasid dominions. Their

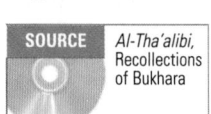

Mamluk Trade. Trade in spices and other precious commodities between the Mamluks and western Europe was of great importance. In this painting from about 1500, we see Venetian ambassadors being received by the governor of Damascus, who sits on a low platform and wears a distinctive, horn-shaped turban. *Erich Lessing/Art Resource, N.Y.*

successes epitomized the rise of regional states that had begun to undermine the caliphate by the ninth century. Similarly, their demises reflected a second emerging pattern: the ascendancy of Turkish slave-rulers (like the Mamluks in the west) and of Oghuz Turkish peoples, known as Turkomans. With the Saljuqs, the process begun with the use of Turkish slave troops in ninth-century Baghdad ended in the permanent presence in the Islamic world of Turkish ruling dynasties. As late converts, they became typically the most zealous of Sunni Muslims.

SOURCE Al-Tha'alibi, Recollections of Bukhara

The Ghaznavids The rule of the Samanids in Transoxiana was finally ended by a Turkoman group in 999, but they had already lost all of eastern Iran south of the Oxus in 994 to one of their own slave governors, Subuktigin (r. 976–997). He set up his own state in modern Afghanistan, at Ghazna, whence he and his son and successor, Mahmud of Ghazna (r. 998–1030), launched successful campaigns against his

former masters. The Ghaznavids are notable for their patronage of Persian literature and culture and for their conquests in northwestern India, which began a lasting Muslim presence in India. Mahmud was their greatest ruler. He is still remembered for his booty raids and destruction of temples in western India. At its peak, his empire stretched from western Iran to the Oxus and to the Indus.

Mahmud attracted to Ghazna numerous Khurasani Persian scholars and artists, notably the great scientist and mathematician al-Biruni (d. 1048), and the epic poet Firdawsi (d. ca. 1020). Firdawsi's *Shahnama* ("The Book of Kings") is the masterpiece of Persian literature, an epic of sixty thousand verses that helped fix the "New Persian" language already developed especially by the prolific writings of another Khurasani poet of an earlier generation, Rudaki (d. ca. 941), the famous Isma'ili Shi'ite. It also helped revive the pre-Islamic cultural traditions of the greater Iranian world, which remained a hallmark of

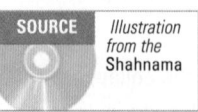

SOURCE Illustration from the Shahnama

A Muslim Biographer's Account of Maimonides

Document

The following are excerpts from the entry on Maimonides (Arabic: Musa ibn Maymun) in the biographical dictionary of learned men by Ibn al-Qifti (d. 1248). In one section (omitted here), Ibn al-Qifti describes how this most famous Spanish Jewish savant at first feigned conversion to Islam when a new Berber ruler demanded the expulsion of Christians and Jews from Spain in about 1133. He tells how Maimonides moved his family to the more tolerant Islamic world of Cairo, where he became the court physician. (Jews and Christians held high office under Muslim rulers.)

◆ Which Islamic dynasty forced Maimonides to leave Spain for Cairo? Why were the Fatimids in Cairo tolerant of Christians and Jews when their Berber co-religionists were not? From the Muslim biographer's treatment of his subject, what can you infer about Islamic societies and the intellectual atmosphere of the time?

. . . This man was one of the people of Andalus, a Jew by religion. He studied philosophy in Andalus, was expert in mathematics, and devoted attention to some of the logical sciences. He studied medicine there and excelled in it. . . .

. . . After assembling his possessions in the time that was needed for this, he left Andalus and went to Egypt, accompanied by his family. He settled in the town of Fustāt [part of greater Cairo], among its Jews, and practiced his religion openly. He lived in a district called al-Masīsa and made a living by trading in jewels and suchlike. Some people studied philosophy under him. . . .

He married in Cairo the sister of a Jewish scribe called Abu'l-Ma'āli, the secretary of the mother of Nŭr al-Dîn 'Alî, known as al-Afdal, the son of Salāh al-Din Yūsuf ibn Ayyūb, and he had a son by her who today is a physician in Cairo after his father. . . .

Mūsā, ibn Maymūn died in Cairo in the year 605 [1208–9].[1] He ordered his heirs to carry his body, when the smell had ceased, to Lake Tiberias and bury him there, seeking to be among the graves of the ancient Israelites and their great jurists, which are there. This was done.

He was learned in the law and secrets of the Jews and compiled a commentary on the Talmud, which is a commentary and explanation of the Torah; some of the Jews approve of it. Philosophic doctrines overcame him, and he compiled a treatise denying the canonical resurrection. The leaders of the Jews held this against him, so he concealed it except from those who shared his opinion in this. . .

In the latter part of his life he was troubled by a man from Andalus, a jurist called Abu'l-'Arab ibn Ma'īsha, who came to Fustāt and met him. He charged him with having been a Muslim in Andalus, accused him [of apostasy] and wanted to have him punished.[2] 'Abd al-Rahīm ibn 'Alī al-Fādil prevented this, and said to him, "If a man is converted by force, his Islam is not legally valid."

Reading the Torah in a Spanish Synagogue. A picture from a Hebrew Haggada, Spain, fourteenth century. Until their expulsion by Christian rulers at the end of the fifteenth century, Jews formed a significant minority in Spain. Their expulsion took many of them to Islamic lands such as North Africa, Egypt, and Anatolia, where they put down lasting roots. *By permission of The British Library.*

From *Islam: From the Prophet Muhammad to the Capture of Constantinople*, Vol. 2: *Religion and Society*, by Bernard Lewis, ed. and trans. Copyright © 1987 by Bernard Lewis. Used by permission of Oxford University Press, Inc.

[1]In fact, he died in 1204.

[2]The penalty for apostasy was death.

later Persian literature. After Mahmud the empire began to break up, although Ghaznavids ruled at Lahore until 1186.

The Saljuqs The Saljuqs were the first major Turkish dynasty of Islam. They were a steppe clan who settled in Transoxiana, became avid Sunnis, and extended their sway over Khorasan in the 1030s. In 1055 they took Baghdad. As the new guardian of the caliphate and master of an Islamic empire, the Saljuq leader Tughril Beg (r. 1037–1063) took the title of *sultan* to signify his temporal power and control. He and his early successors made various Iranian cities their capitals instead of Baghdad.

As new Turkish tribes joined their ranks, the Saljuqs extended Islamic rule for the first time into the central Anatolian plateau at Byzantine expense, even capturing the Byzantine emperor in a victory in Armenia in 1071 (see Map 13–2). They also conquered much of Syria and wrested Mecca and Medina from the Shi'ite Fatimids. The first Turkish rule in Anatolia dates from 1077, when the Saljuq governor there formed a separate sultanate. Known as the Saljuqs of Rum ("Rome," i.e., Byzantium), these latter Saljuqs were only displaced after 1300 by the Ottomans, another Turkish dynasty, who would eventually conquer all of Anatolia and southeastern Europe (see Chapter 21).

The most notable figure of Saljuq rule was the vizier Nizam al-Mulk, the real power behind two sultans from 1063 to 1092. In his time new roads and inns (caravanserais) for trade and pilgrimage were built, canals were dug, mosques and other public buildings were founded (including the first great Sunni *madrasas*), and science and culture were patronized. He also founded in 1067 what some contend was the first Muslim "University," the legal-theological school, or *madrasah*, of the Nizamiyyah in Baghdad; he went on to establish a number of similar *madrasahs* in Mesopotamia and Persia. He supported an accurate calendar reform and authored a major work on the art of governing, the *Siyasatnamah*. Before his murder by an Isma'ili assassin in 1092, he appointed as professor in his Baghdad *madrasa*

SOURCE *al-Ghazzali, excerpt from Confessions*

Muhammad al-Ghazzali (d. 1111), probably the greatest Muslim religious thinker ever. He also patronized the mathematician and astronomer Umar Khayyam (d. 1123), whose Western fame rests on the poetry of his "Quatrains," or *Ruba'iyat*.

After declining fortunes in the early twelfth century, Iranian Saljuq rule crumbled and by 1194 was wholly wiped away by another Turkish slave dynasty from Khwarizm in the lower Oxus basin. By 1200 these Khwarizm-Shahs had built a large, if shaky, empire and sphere of influence covering Iran and Transoxiana. In the same era the Abbasid caliph at Baghdad, al-Nasir (r. 1180–1225), established an independent caliphal state in Iraq, but neither his heirs nor the Khwarizm Shahs were long to survive.

Islamic Asia in the Mongol Age

Mongols and Ilkhanids The building of a vast Mongol empire spanning Asia from China to Poland in the thirteenth century proved momentous not only for eastern Europe and China (see Chapter 8), but also for Islamic Eurasia and India. A Khwarizm Shah massacre of Mongol ambassadors brought down the full wrath of the Great Khan, Genghis (ca. 1162–1227), on the Islamic east. He razed entire cities (1219–1222) from Transoxiana and Khorasan to the Indus. After his death, a division of his empire into four khanates under his four sons gave the Islamic world respite. Then in 1255 Hulagu Khan (r. 1256–1265), a grandson of Genghis, led a massive army again across the Oxus. Adding Turkish troops to his forces (Mongol armies typically included many Turks), he went from victory to victory, destroying every Iranian state. In 1258, when the Abbasid caliph refused to surrender, Hulagu's troops plundered Baghdad, killing at least 80,000 inhabitants, including the caliph and his sons. (See Document, "The Mongol Catastrophe.")

Under the influence of his wife and many Nestorian Christians and Buddhists in his inner circle, Hulagu spared the Christians of Baghdad. He followed this policy in his other conquests, including the sack of Aleppo—which, like Baghdad, resisted. When Damascus surrendered, Western Christians had hopes of the impending fall of Mamluk Cairo and Islamic

Mamluk Bottle. This elegant glass bottle was made in Mamluk workshops in Syria in the mid–fourteenth century for the rulers of the Yemen in southern Arabia. *John Tsantes/Courtesy of the Freer Gallery of Art, Smithsonian Institution, Washington, D.C.*

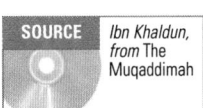

Map 13–2.   The Saljuq Empire, ca. 1095. By the end of the eleventh century the Saljuqs had conquered Persia, Mesopotamia, and Syria and had inflicted a devasting blow against the Byzantine Empire at the battle of Manzikert in 1071, altering the balance of power in the eastern Mediterranean and the Near East.

power, but Hulagu's drive west was slowed by rivalry with his kinsman Berke. A Muslim convert, Berke ruled the khanate of the Golden Horde, the Mongol state centered in southern Russia north of the Caucasus. He was in contact with the Mamluks, and some of his Mongol troops even helped them defeat Hulagu in Palestine (1260), which prevented a Mongol advance into Egypt. A treaty in 1261 between the Mamluk sultan and Berke established a formal alliance that confirmed the breakup of Mongol unity and the autonomy of the four khanates: in China (the Yuan dynasty), in Iran (the Ilkhans), in Russia (the Golden Horde), and in Transoxiana (the Chagatays).

Hulagu and his heirs ruled the old Persian Empire from Azerbaijan for some seventy-five years as the Great Khan of China's viceroys (*Il-Khans*). Here, as elsewhere,

the Mongols did not eradicate the society they inherited. Their native paganism and Buddhist and Christian leanings yielded to Muslim faith and practice, although they practiced religious tolerance. After 1335 Ilkhanid rule fell prey to the familiar pattern of a gradual breaking away of provinces, and for fifty years, Iran was again fragmented.

SOURCE *Ibn Khaldun, from The Muqaddimah*

Timurids and Turkomans   This situation prepared the way for a new Turko-Mongol conquest from Transoxiana, under Timur-i Lang ("Timur the Lame," or "Tamerlane," 1336–1405). Even Genghis Khan's invasions could not match Timur's savage campaigns between 1379 and his death in 1405. These raids were not aimed at building a new

The Mongol Catastrophe

For the Muslim East, the sudden eruption of the Mongol hordes was an indescribable calamity. The shock and despair can be seen in the history of Ibn al-Athir (d. 1233). He writes here about the year 1220–1221, when the Mongols ("Tartars") burst in on the eastern lands.

◆ Is this a positive, negative, or neutral description of the Mongols? Why might the Mongols be compared to Alexander rather than, say, the Huns (see Chapter 6)?

I say, therefore, that this thing involves the description of the greatest catastrophe and the most dire calamity (of the like of which days and nights are innocent) which befell all men generally, and the Muslims in particular; so that, should one say that the world, since God Almighty created Adam until now, hath not been afflicted with the like thereof, he would but speak the truth. For indeed history doth not contain aught which approaches or comes nigh unto it. . . .

Now this is a thing the like of which ear hath not heard; for Alexander, concerning whom historians agree that he conquered the world, did not do so with such swiftness, but only in the space of about ten years; neither did he slay, but was satisfied that men should be subject to him. But these Tartars conquered most of the habitable globe and the best, the most flourishing and most populous part thereof, and that whereof the inhabitants were the most advanced in character and conduct, in about [a] year; nor did any country escape their devastations which did not fearfully expect them and dread their arrival.

Moreover they need no commissariat, nor the conveyance of supplies, for they have with them sheep, cows, horses, and the like quadrupeds, the flesh of which they eat, [needing] naught else. As for their beasts which they ride, these dig into the earth with their hoofs and eat the roots of plants, knowing naught of barley. And so, when they alight anywhere, they have need of nothing from without. As for their religion, they worship the sun when it arises, and regard nothing as unlawful, for they eat all beasts, even dogs, pigs, and the like; nor do they recognise the marriage-tie, for several men are in marital relations with one woman, and if a child is born, it knows not who is its father.

Therefore Islam and the Muslims have been afflicted during this period with calamities wherewith no people hath been visited. These Tartars (may God confound them!) came from the East, and wrought deeds which horrify all who hear of them, and which thou shalt, please God, see set forth in full detail in their proper connection. . . .

From Edward C. Sachau, *Alberuni's India*, Vol. I (London: Kegan Paul, Trench, Truebner, 1910), pp. 17, 19, 20.

empire, but at sheer conquest. In successive campaigns he swept everything before him in a wave of devastation: eastern Iran (1379–1385); western Iran, Armenia, the Caucasus, and upper Mesopotamia (1385–1387); southwestern Iran, Mesopotamia, and Syria (1391–1393); Central Asia from Transoxiana to the Volga and as far as Moscow (1391–1395); North India (1398); and northern Syria and Anatolia (1400–1402). Timur's sole positive contributions seem to have been the buildings he sponsored at Samarkand, his capital. He left behind him ruins, death, disease, and political chaos across the entire eastern Islamic world, which did not soon recover. His was, however, the last great steppe invasion, for firearms soon destroyed the steppe horsemen's advantage.

Timur's sons ruled after him with varying results in Transoxiana and Iran (1405–1494). The most successful Timurid was Shahrukh (r. 1405–1447), who ruled a united Iran for a time. His capital, Herat, became an important center of Persian Islamic culture and Sunni piety. He patronized the famous Herat school of miniature painting as well as Persian literature and philosophy. The Timurids had to share Iran itself with Turkoman dynasties in western Iran, once even losing Herat to one of them. They and the Turkomans were the last Sunnis to rule Iran. Both were eclipsed at the end of the fifteenth century by the militant Shi'ite dynasty of the Safavids, who ushered in a new, Shi'ite era in the Iranian world (see Chapter 21).

 SOURCE A contemporary describes Timur

The Gur-i-mir, the Tomb of Timur in Samarkand. Built from 1490 to 1501 by Timur's grandson, this tile-covered structure houses the tombs of Shahrukh, Ulug Beg, and other Timurids. *Giraudon/Art Resource, N.Y.*

The Spread of Islam Beyond the Heartlands

The period from roughly 1000 to 1500 saw the spread of Islamic civilization as a lasting religious, cultural, social, and political force into new areas (see Map 13–1). Not only from Mesopotamia, Persia, and the Black Sea north to Moscow (under the Golden Horde), but also west to the Balkans and the Danube River basin (through the Ottoman Turks), the greater part of Eurasia came under the control of Islamic rulers in this era (see Chapter 21). Meanwhile, India, Malaysia, Indonesia, inland West Africa, and coastal East Africa all became major spheres of Islamic political,

social, cultural, and commercial presence. In all these regions Sufi orders were most often responsible for converting people and spreading Islamic cultural influences. Merchants, too, were major agents of cultural Islamization in these regions.

Conquest was a third (but demographically less important) means of Islamization (and either Arabization or Persianization) in these regions. Sometimes only ruling elites, sometimes wider circles, became Muslims, but in India, Southeast Asia, and sub-Saharan Africa much, often most, of the populace retained their languages, heritage, and religious traditions even while their elites learned Arabic and/or Persian as second or third languages. Nonetheless, in the most important of these regions, India, the coming of Islam signaled epochal changes.

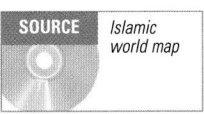

ISLAMIC INDIA AND SOUTHEAST ASIA

Islamic civilization in India (like earlier Indian civilization) was formed by creative interaction between invading foreigners and indigenous peoples. The early Arab and Turkish invaders were a foreign Muslim minority; their heirs were truly "Indian" as well as Islamic, adding a new dimension both to Indian and Islamic civilization. From then on, Indian civilization would both include and enrich Islamic traditions.

The Spread of Islam to South Asia

Well before the Ghaznavids came to the Punjab, Muslims were to be found even outside the original Arab conquest areas in Sind (see Map 13–3). Muslim merchants had settled in the port cities of Gujarat and southern India as diaspora communities to profit from internal Indian trade as well as from trade with the Indies and China. Wherever Muslim traders went, converts to Islam were attracted by business advantages as well as by the straightforward ideology and practice of Islam and its officially egalitarian, "classless" ethic. Sufi orders had also gained a foothold in the central **Deccan** region and in the south, giving today's south Indian Muslims old roots. Sufi piety also drew converts in the north, especially when the Mongol devastation of Iran in the thirteenth century sent refugees into North India. These Muslim refugees strengthened Muslim life in the subcontinent.

Map Exploration

To explore this map further, go to http://www.prenhall.com/craig_maps

Map 13–3. The Indian Subcontinent, 1000–1500. Shown are major kingdoms and regions.

Muslim-Hindu Encounter

From the outset Muslim leaders had to rule a country dominated by utterly different cultural and religious traditions. Much as early Muslim rulers in Iranian territories had given Zoroastrians legal status as "people of Scripture" (like Christians and Jews; see Chapter 11), the first Arab conquerors in Sind (711) had treated Hindus similarly as "protected peoples" under Muslim sovereignty. These precedents gave Indian Muslim rulers a legal basis for coexistence with their Hindu subjects but did not remove Hindu resistance to Islamic rule.

The chief obstacle to Islamic expansion in India was the military prowess of the Hindu warrior class that emerged after the Hun and other Asian invasions of the fifth and sixth centuries. Apparently descended from such invaders

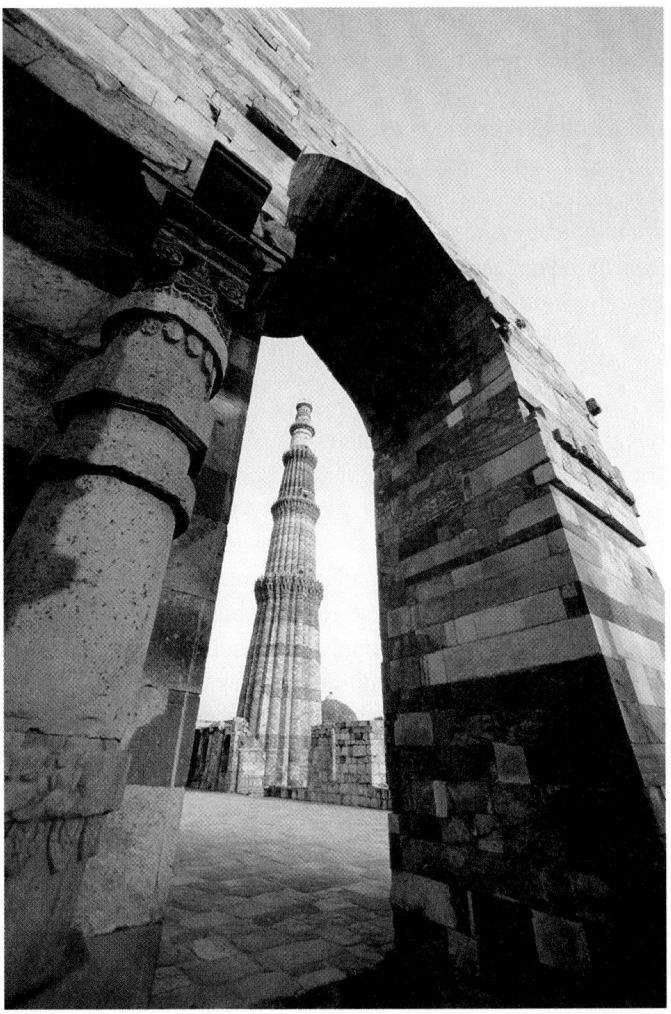

The Qutb Minar (Victory Tower) in Delhi in India is an example of classic Indo-Muslim art and architecture. Constructed in the twelfth century, this soaring tower made from red sandstone commemorated Muslim military victory. *Getty Images, Inc.-Taxi.*

Chronology

Eastern Islamic Lands

875–999	Persian Samanid dynasty, centered at Bukhara
ca. 941	Death of Rudaki, the first Persian epic poet and father of "New Persian"
945–1055	Persian Buyid Shi'ite dynasty in Baghdad controls caliphs
994–1186	Ghaznavid dynasty in Ghazna (modern Afghanistan) and Lahore (modern Pakistan), founded by Subuktigin (r. 976–997) and his son, Mahmud of Ghazna (r. 998–1030)
ca. 1020	Death of Firdawsi, compiler of the Persian epic poem, the *Shahnama*
ca. 1050	Death of al-Biruni, scientist, mathematician, and polyglot
1055–1194	Saljuq rule in Baghdad
1063–1092	Viziership of Nizam al-Mulk
1067	Founding of the Madvasah Nizamiyyah in Bagdad by Nizam al-Mulk
1111	Death of al-Ghazzali, theologian and scholar
1219–1222	Genghis Khan plunders eastern Iran to Indus region
1258	Hulagu Khan conquers Baghdad
1260–1335	Hulagu and his Il-Khanid successors rule Iran
1261	Mamluk-Mongol treaty halts westward Mongol movement
1379–1405	Campaigns of Timur-i Lang (Tamerlane) devastate entire Islamic East
1405–1447	Shahrukh, Timurid ruler at Herat; great patronage of the arts and philosophy
1405–1494	Timurids, successors of Tamerlane, rule in Transoxiana and Iran

and the native warrior (Kshatriya) class of Hindus, this class was known from about the mid–seventh century as *Rajputs*. The Rajputs were a large group of northern Indian clans bound together by a fierce warrior ethic and strong Hindu cultural and religious traditionalism. They fought the Muslims with great tenacity, but their inability to unite brought them eventually under Muslim domination in the sixteenth century (see Chapter 21).

Islamic States and Dynasties

A series of Turkish-Afghan rulers known as the "Slave Sultans of Delhi" extended and maintained Islamic power over North India for nearly a century (1206–1290). Such slaves, or **mamluks**, figured prominently in the leadership and elites of the new regime, much as they did in the Mamluk dynasty in Egypt. Five descendants of Iltutmish ruled after him until 1266. The most vigorous of these was his daughter Raziyya, who ruled as sultana from 1237 to 1241.

Four later Muslim dynasties—the Khaljis, Tughluqs, Sayyids, and Lodis—continued the Delhi sultanate through the fifteenth century. This run of Muslim dynasties was interrupted by the Mongol-Turkish invasion and sack of Delhi by Timur in 1398, from which the city took decades to recover. Even before this devastation, however—roughly from the mid-1300s—the sultanate's central authority began to dwindle. In the two centuries before the advent of the Mughals in the mid–sixteenth century, many regions became partially or wholly independent, smaller sultanates, Rajput kingdoms, or tiny Hindu or Muslim principalities. The sultanate was often only the most prominent among various kingdoms. Regional rule predominated across the subcontinent.

Southeast Asia

The most important independent Islamic state was that of the Bahmanids in the Deccan (1347–1527). These rulers were famous for their architecture and the intellectual life of their court, as well as for their role in containing the powerful South Indian Hindu state of Vijayanagar (1336–1565). (The first documented use of firearms in the subcontinent was in a Bahmani battle with the raja of Vijayanagar in 1366.) Most regional capitals fostered a rich cultural life. Jaunpur, to the north of Benares (Varanasi), for example, became an asylum for artists and intellectuals after Timur's sack of Delhi and boasted an impressive tradition of Islamic architecture. Kashmir, an independent sultanate from 1346 to 1589, was a center of literary activity where many Indian texts were translated into Persian.

Islam spread into Southeast Asia as a result of a natural extension of long-distance Islamic (Arab and Persian) and Indian trade across the Indian Ocean, land and sea migrations of scholars and merchants, and socialization of Indian peoples of South Asia. This extension of much older trade contacts eastward beyond the Indian subcontinent had unique charateristics of its own. Because of their geographic location, the islands in Southeast Asia readily connected India and China and thus became an important trade route by the fifteenth century. The spread of Islam in this region was not a steady, progressive development and was not dominated by one particular tradition. Rather the proliferation of Islam was idiosyncratic, and a number of distinct Islamic traditions emerged centered largely around the five areas: Java, Sumatra, Melaka, Acheh, and Moluccas (see Map 13–4).

In some of the areas, such as in the Moluccas, the traditional beliefs of Islam coexisted with worship and adulation of ancestors, sorcery, or magic. Various central Islamic rites such as the pilgrimage (*hajj*) were perceived to be an Arab custom and thus not required for "true" Muslims. Eventually, however, many political leaders adopted a more stringent Islamic practice largely for political reasons because Islam would allow for greater centralization and consolidation of power.

One of the greatest sources of tension and conflict in this area was not solely due to distinct religious views. Rather it was the struggle between the center and the periphery. Before the arrival of the Dutch in the early seventeenth century, the various urban rulers, typically located in port cities, benefited from the new global economy. They sought to subsume under their control the hereditary chiefs, who had also converted to Islam, by invoking Islam and their vision of a perfect society. The local traditions proved to be durable, especially in the rural areas. Muslims in Southeast Asia therefore adapted Islam to their needs and customs rather than simply replacing the indigenous practices with the new universal and foreign religion.

Map 13–4. The Spread of Islam in Southeast Asia.

Major Islamic Dynasties, 1000s–1500s

Overview

DYNASTY	LOCATION	DYNASTY	LOCATION
(Spanish) Umayyads	Spain (756-1031)	"Great" Saljuqs Saljuqs (of Rum)	Iraq and Persia (1038-1194) Anatolia (1077-1307)
Almoravids	North Africa, Spain (1056-1147)	Abbasids	Iraq and Baghdad (749-1258)
Almohads	North Africa, Spain (1130-1269)	Ghaznavids	Transoxiana and NW India (977-1186)
Fatimids	North Africa, then Egypt, Syria (909-1171)	Khwarzim-Shahs	Central Asia, Persia (c.1077-1231)
Ayyubids	Egypt, Syria, the Yemen (1169-late 1400s)	Ilkhanids	Persia (1256-1353)
Mamluks	Egypt, Syria (1250-1517)	Timurids	Transoxiana, Persia (1370-1506)
Samanids	Khurasan, Transoxiana (819-1005)	Delhi Sultans	Northern India (1206-1555)
Buyids	Persia, Iraq (932-1062)	Bahmanids and successors	Northern Deccan/Central India (1347-1527)

Religious and Cultural Accommodation

Despite the enduring division of the subcontinent into multiple political and administrative units, the five centuries after Mahmud of Ghazna saw Islam become an enduring and influential element of Indian culture—especially in the north and the Deccan. The Delhi sultans were able, except for Timur's invasion, to fend off the Mongol danger, much as the Mamluks had in Egypt. They thereby provided a basic political and social framework within which Islam could take root. Although the ruling class remained a Muslim minority of Persianized Turks and Afghans ruling a Hindu majority, conversion went on at various levels of society. **Ghazis,** ("warriors") also carried Islam by force of arms to pagan groups in eastern Bengal and Assam. Some Hindu converts came from the ruling classes who served the Muslim overlords. Sufi orders converted many Hindus among the lower classes across the north. The Muslim aristocracy, at first mostly foreigners, was usually treated in Indian society as a separate caste group or groups. Lower class or other Hindu converts were assimilated into lower "Muslim castes," often identified by occupation. (See Document, "How the Hindus Differ from the Muslims.")

Sanskrit had long been the Indian scholarly and common language, but in this period regional languages, such as Tamil in the south, gained status as literary and administrative languages, and Persian became the language of intellectual and cultural life for the ruling elites of North India. However, the coming of substantial numbers of Muslims to the subcontinent led to the emergence of a new language, **Urdu-Hindi,** with both Perso-Arabic and indigenous Indian elements. It began to take shape not long after the initial Muslim influx in the eleventh century and developed in response to the increasing need of Hindus and Muslims for a shared language. It became the spoken idiom of the Delhi region and developed into a literary language of North Indian and Deccan Muslims in the seventeenth and eighteenth centuries. Indo-European in grammar, it used Perso-Arabic vocabulary and script and was at first called *Hindi* ("Indian") or *Dakani* ("southern"), then in British times *Hindustani*. Eventually *Urdu* came to serve as the name for the Islamic version of the language that was based on its Persian-Arabic-Turkish heritage, whereas *Hindi* was used for the version associated with Hindu culture and oriented in its further development toward its Hindu and Sanskrit heritage. Each became an official national language: Urdu for modern Pakistan and Hindi for modern India.

Indian Muslims, both immigrants and converts, were always susceptible to Hindu influence (in language, marriage customs, and caste consciousness), much like Muslims in Africa and Asia. However, unlike earlier immigrant elites, they were never utterly absorbed into the predominant Hindu culture but remained in some measure a group apart, conscious of their uniqueness in the Hindu world and proud to be distinct. The Muslim ruling classes saw themselves as the protectors and propagators of Islam in India, and most of the sultans of Delhi sought formal recognition for their rule from the nominal Abbasid caliphs in Baghdad or, in Mamluk times, in Cairo.

Nevertheless, reciprocal influence of Muslims and Hindus was inevitable, especially in popular piety and among the masses as opposed to the ruling elites. Sufi devotion had an appeal similar to that of Hindu devotional, or **bhakti** movements (see Chapter 10), and each influenced the other. Some of India's most revered Sufi and *bhakti* saints date from the fourteenth and fifteenth centuries. During this period, various theistic mystics strove to transcend the mutual antagonism and exclusivism of Muslims and Hindus. They typically preached devotion to a God who saves his worshipers without regard either to Hindu caste obligations or to

Krishna Dancing on the Head of the Serpent Kaliya. This fifteenth-century bronze figure from Vijayanagar is based on a legend, according to which Kaliya was infesting the waters of the Jumna River until Krishna leaped in and emerged dancing on the vanquished snake. *Asian Art Museum of San Francisco. The Avery Brundage Collection B65B72. Sixteenth Century Persian Painting.*

Chronology

India: Major Non-Muslim Dynasties

ca. 900–1300	Chola dynasty in southern India
1336–1565	Hindu dynasty of Vijayanagar

legalistic Muslim observance. The poet-saints Ramananda (d. after 1400) and Kabir (d. ca. 1518) were the two most famous such reformers.

Hindu and Other Indian Traditions

The history of India from 1000 to 1500 was also important for the other religious and cultural communities of India that as a whole vastly outnumbered the Muslims. The Jain tradition flourished, notably in Gujarat, Rajputana, and Karnataka. In the north the Muslim conquests effectively ended Indian Buddhism by the eleventh century. However, Buddhism had already been waning in Indian culture long before Islam arrived.

Hindu religion and culture flourished even under Muslim control, as the continuing social and religious importance of the Brahmans and the popularity of *bhakti* movements throughout India attest. This was an age of Brahmanic scholasticism that produced many commentaries and manuals but few seminal works. *Bhakti* creativity was much greater. The great Hindu Vaishnava Brahman Ramanuja (d. 1137) reconciled *bhakti* ideas with the classical Upanishadic Hindu worldview in the Vedantin tradition. *Bhakti* piety underlies the masterpiece of Hindu mystical love poetry, Jayadeva's *Gita Govinda* (twelfth century), which is devoted to Krishna, the most important of Vishnu's incarnations.

The south continued to be the center of Hindu cultural, political, and religious activity. The most important dynastic state in the south during this age was that of the Cholas, which flourished from about 900 to 1300 and patronized a famous school of bronze sculpture at their capital of Tanjore. Their mightiest successor, the kingdom of Vijayanagar (1336–1565), subjugated the entire south in the fourteenth century and resisted its Muslim foes longer than any other kingdom. Vijayanagar itself was one of India's most lavishly developed cities and a center of the cult of Shiva before its destruction by the Bahmanid sultan of the Deccan.

How the Hindus Differ from the Muslims

Document

Al-Biruni (d. ca. 1050), the greatest scholar-scientist of medieval Islam, was born in northeastern Iran. He spent much of his life at the court of Mahmud of Ghazna, whom he accompanied on expeditions into northwestern India. Alongside his scientific work, he learned Sanskrit, studied India and the Hindus, and wrote the *History of India*. The following selections from this work illustrate the reach and sophistication of his mind.

◆ How does the emphasis on purity and the impurity of foreigners that Biruni imputes to the Hindus compare with the attitudes of Islam and other religions? Does this passage suggest why the Hindu tradition has remained largely an Indian one, while Islam became an international religion? What might be the reference of Biruni's comments about the relative absence of religous controversy among Hindus?

. . . The barriers which separate Muslims and Hindus rest on different causes.

First, they differ from us in everything which other nations have in common. And here we first mention the language, although the difference of language also exists between other nations. If you want to conquer this difficulty (i.e., to learn Sanskrit), you will not find it easy, because the language is of an enormous range, both in words and inflections, something like the Arabic, calling one and the same thing by various names, both original and derived, and using one and the same word for a variety of subjects, which, in order to be properly understood, must be distinguished from each other by various qualifying epithets. . . .

Secondly, they totally differ from us in religion, as we believe in nothing in which they believe, and vice versa.

On the whole, there is very little disputing about theological topics among themselves; at the utmost, they fight with words, but they will never stake their soul or body or their property on religious controversy. On the contrary, all their fanaticism is directed against those who do not belong to them—against all foreigners. They call them *mleecha*, i.e., impure, and forbid having any connection with them, be it by intermarriage or any other kind of

relationship, or by sitting, eating, and drinking with them, because thereby, they think, they would be polluted. They consider as impure anything which touches the fire and the water of a foreigner; and no household can exist without these two elements. Besides, they never desire that a thing which once has been polluted should be purified and thus recovered, as, under ordinary circumstances, if anybody or anything has become unclean, he or it would strive to regain the state of purity. They are not allowed to receive anybody who does not belong to them, even if he wished it, or was inclined to their religion. This, too, renders any connection with them quite impossible, and constitutes the widest gulf between us and them.

In the third place, in all manners and usages they differ from us to such a degree as to frighten their children with us, with our dress, and our ways and customs, and as to declare us to be devil's breed, and our doings as the very opposite of all that is good and proper. By the by, we must confess, in order to be just, that a similar depreciation of foreigners not only prevails among us and the Hindus, but is common to all nations towards each other.

From Edward C. Sachau, *Alberuni's India*, Vol. 1 (London: Kegan Paul, Trench, Truebner, 1910), pp. 17, 19, 20.

Summary

Religion. Between 1000 and 1500, the most important developments for the shape of Islamic society were of Sunni and Shi'ite legal and religious norms and of Sufi traditions and personal piety. Sunnism was the dominant tradition across the Islamic world, but in both main branches of Islam, the *ulama* became the religious, social, and political elites and discouraged religious innovation. Shi'ism flourished in Iran under the Savafid rulers. Sufi piety stresses the spiritual and mystical dimensions of Islam. Sufi fraternal orders, whether Sunni or Shi'ite, became the chief instruments of the spread of Muslim faith in most Islamic societies.

Regional Developments. Despite general religious tolerance and high cultural achievements, the Muslims were gradually pushed out of Spain by the Spanish Christian states between 1000 and 1492. In Egypt, the Shi'ite Fatamids established a separate caliphate from 969 to 1171. The Mamluks, whose rule in Egypt lasted from 1260 to 1517, were the only Muslim dynasty to withstand the Mongol invasions. The Seljuks, based in Anatolia and Iraq, were the first major Turkish dynasty of Islam. Other notable Islamic dynasties were the Ghaznavids in Transoxiana and the Khwarizam-shahs in Persia.

Mongol Invasions. In 1255 the Mongols invaded the Muslim world and swept all before them, conquering Transoxiana, Persia, and Iraq, where they captured Baghdad and killed the last Abbasid caliph in 1258, before being defeated by the Mamluks in Syria in 1260. Thereafter, the Mongols established the Ilkhanid dynasty in Persia and converted to Islam. Another wave of Turko-Mongol conquest under Timur-i Lang further devastated much of the Near East between 1379 and 1405.

India and Southeast Asia. Muslim invaders and rulers, as well as Sufi brotherhoods, spread Islam in India, where it became an enduring and influential part of Indian civilization. A new language, Urdu-Hindi, combined Persian-Arabic and indigenous Indian elements. There was reciprocal influence between Muslims and Hindus.

Buddhism all but disappeared from India during these years, but Hindu religion and culture flourished, even under Muslim control. Hindu devotional, or *bhakti*, movements were especially creative.

In Southeast Asia, Islam was spread by Muslim merchants and traders, as well as by Sufi brotherhoods, and wherever it took root, it blended with local customs.

INTERPRETING THE PAST

Islam and the Challenge of Outside Influences

While Western Europe foundered in its Dark Ages, the Islamic world experienced a renaissance of learning and philosophy, scientific advance, artistic expression, and multicultural cooperation in many parts of the *umma*. To a great extent, this efflorescence rested on the ability of Islamic rulers to accommodate religious and cultural differences in the interests of greater societal stability.

Analyze the documents and images contained in this chapter and in MyHistoryLab / Primary Source to comment on the degree to which Muslims tolerated non-Islamic ideas and individuals. It appears that many Muslims were able to put aside religious differences in the interest of learning.

For a few examples, one might address the Muslim account of Maimonides, the various images of Islamic science, and al-Ghazzali's commentaries on the search for truth.

Text Sources from MyHistoryLab / PrimarySource DVD

Ibn Khaldun, the *Muqaddimah*
Al-Ghazzali's *Confessions*

Text Sources from Chapter 13

"A Muslim Biographer's account of Maimonides" (p. 389)
"The Mongol Catastrophe" (p. 392)
"How the Hindus Differ from the Muslims" (p. 399).

Review Questions

1. In 1000–1500, why did no Muslim leader build a unified large-scale Islamic empire of the extent of the early Abbasids?

2. How were the *ulama* educated? What was their relationship to political leadership? What social roles did they play? What was the role of the *madrasahs* in Islamic culture and civilization?

3. What was the role and impact of religious sectarianism in this period? of the institutionalization of Sufi piety and thought? of the social and political role of Sufism?

4. Discuss the cultural developments in Spain before 1500. Why was Córdoba such a model of civilized culture? What were some of the distinguishing features of *al-Andalus*?

5. Why did Islam survive the successive invasions by steppe peoples (Turks and Mongols) from 945 on? What were the lasting results of these "invasions" for the Islamic world?

6. What were the primary obstacles to stable rule for India's Muslim invaders and immigrants? How did they deal with them?

Key Terms

Al-Andalus (p. 385)

bhakti (p. 398)

Deccan (p. 393)

ghazis (p. 397)

madrasa (p. 381)

mamluk (p. 396)

Ramadan (p. 383)

Reconquista (p. 386)

Sufi (soo-FEE) (p. 383)

sultans (p. 387)

Urdu-Hindi (p. 397)

Note: To learn more about the topics in this chapter, please turn to the Suggested Readings at the end of the book. For additional sources related to this chapter please see the Primary Source DVD at the back of this text or MyHistoryLab.

Visual Sources from MyHistoryLab / PrimarySource DVD

Islamic Science and Alchemy
Islamic Astronomy and Astrology
Islamic World Map

Questions

How does the account of a Muslim traveler in India (p. 399) reveal Islam's cosmopolitan character during this period?

What do the visual sources of Islamic science say about Islam's incorporation of non-Islamic science?

How did political science develop in this period? Read the excerpt from Ibn Khaldun (the *Muquddimah*).

14 Ancient Civilizations of the Americas

UMANS FIRST SETTLED THE AMERICAN CONTINENTS between 12,000 and 40,000 years ago. At that time glaciers locked up much of the world's water, lowering the sea level and opening a bridge of dry land between Siberia and Alaska. The earliest undisputed evidence of humans in Tierra del Fuego, at the southern tip of South America, dates to 11,000 years ago, indicating that at least by then the immigrants and their descendants had spread over all of both North and South America. When the glaciers receded the oceans rose, flooding the Bering Straits and severing Asia from America. Despite some continued contact in the Arctic and perhaps sporadic contacts elsewhere, the inhabitants of the Americas were now isolated from the inhabitants of Africa and Eurasia and would remain so until overwhelmed by European invaders after 1492.

Although isolated from one another, the peoples of the Americas and the peoples of Africa and Eurasia experienced similar cultural changes at the end of the Paleolithic. In the Americas, as in the Eastern Hemisphere, people in some regions gradually

A Mixtec View of Creation. In this manuscript, which predates the Spanish conquest, the Mixtec Indians of Oaxaca, Mexico, illustrate how their gods created the world. The complex narrative depicted here relates the creation of the Mother and Father of the gods by Lord and Lady One-Deer.

Ancient Civilizations of the Americas

The Americas

Civilization in the Americas before 1492 developed independently of civilization in the Old World. As the pharaohs of Egypt were erecting their pyramid tombs, the people of the desert coast of Peru were erecting temple platforms. While King Solomon ruled in Jerusalem, the Olmec were creating their monumental stone heads. As Rome reached its apogee and then declined, so did the great city of Teotihuacán in the Valley of Mexico. As Islam spread from its heartland, the rulers of Tikal brought their city to its greatest splendor before its abrupt collapse. Maya mathematics and astronomy rivaled those of any other peoples of the ancient world. And as the aggressive nation-states of Europe were emerging from their feudal past, the Aztecs and Incas were consolidating their great empires. The

agriculture, engineering, and public works of these states—as exemplified by the famous Aztec drainage systems, the floating gardens or *chiampas* of Lake Texcoco, and the Inca system of roads—exquisitely demonstrate an ability to master the most challenging environments.

The encounter between Old World and New, however, proved devastating for American civilization. The technology that allowed Europeans to embark on the voyages of discovery and fight destructive wars among themselves caught the great native empires unprepared. More important, however, was what historian Alfred Crosby has called the "Columbian Exchange." The peoples of the New World exchanged trade goods, ideas, technology, and microbes among themselves, along north–south trade routes that linked the American Southeast and Southwest to Mesoamerica, and the peoples of the northern Andes to those of the central and southern

shifted from hunting and gathering to a settled, agricultural way of life. And in some places civilization emerged as society grew increasingly stratified, villages coalesced into urban centers, monumental architecture appeared, and craft specialists developed sophisticated artistic traditions.

The two most prominent centers of civilization—and the focus of this chapter—were Mesoamerica, in what is today Mexico and Central America, and the Andean region of South America. Both regions have a long, rich history of civilization that reaches back thousands of years. At the time of the European conquest of the Americas in the sixteenth century, both regions were dominated by powerful expansionist empires—the Aztecs, or Mexica, in Mesoamerica, and the Inca in the Andes. In both regions Spanish conquerors obliterated the native empires and nearly succeeded in obliterating native

culture. But in both, Native American traditions have endured, overlaid and combined in complex ways with Hispanic culture, to provide clues to the pre-Hispanic past. ■

Problems in Reconstructing the History of Native American Civilization

Several difficulties confront scholars trying to understand the ancient civilizations of the Americas. One is simply the nature of the evidence. Andean civilizations never developed writing, and in Mesoamerica much of the written record was destroyed by time and conquest, and what remained was until recently undeciphered. The primary source of information has thus been archaeology, the study of the physical remains left by past cultures. Archaeologists have been successful at teasing out many details of the American past. Turning from the study of monumental regions, as well as east–west routes linking eastern North America with the Great Lakes region and beyond. The coming of the Spanish profoundly disturbed both the patterns of trade and the ecological balance. Most significant, the Spanish introduced new epidemic diseases against which the peoples of the New World did not possess immunity. During the first century after the encounter these diseases, killing vast numbers of people and affording the Europeans a psychological edge, played key role in the conquest of the peoples of the New World.

Equally important in understanding the ability of small numbers of Europeans to conquer these advanced civilizations, however, was the nature of the civilizations themselves. Neither they nor their cultures were static or immobile; they were definitely not, in one historian's words, "a people without history," even if much of that history is lost to us because of the absence of written records. The European invaders succeeded most rapidly in toppling the most organized of the societies in the New World, the Aztecs and the Inca, precisely because these societies were organized, centralized, and hierarchical. It is important to remember that the history of New World civilizations, like that of any other civilization, was tightly linked to internal developments before the arrival of Europeans.

It is also important to recall that the Aztecs and Incas, in particular, ruled over different peoples, many of whom resented their subjugation and saw in the arrival of the Europeans an opportunity to assert their autonomy. Thus the Spanish in Mexico and, to a lesser extent, in Peru, found allies among the native peoples willing to do much of the fighting for them. When Cortés faced the Aztecs in the decisive battle for their capital city, Tenochtitlán, he did so with at least 30,000 native warriors by his side.

Focus Questions

◆ Why is it important to bear in mind that the civilizations of the New World had long and rich histories before the arrival of Europeans? Why is it so difficult to discover the details of the history of the peoples of the Americas? What are our major sources of information?

◆ What role did the environment play in the formation of American civilizations?

remains in great urban centers to the study of the remains left by ordinary people in their everyday lives, they have been able to create an increasingly rich picture of the economic and social organization of ancient American civilizations. But archaeology alone cannot produce the kind of narrative history that thousands of years of written records have made possible for Eurasian civilization. For at least one ancient Mesoamerican people, however—the Maya—this situation is changing. Scholars have recently been able to decipher their writing and attach specific names, dates, and events to heretofore silent ruins.

We also have accounts of the history and culture of the Aztecs and Inca, the last great Native American civilizations, that were related to Spanish missionaries and officials in the wake of the conquest. Although these accounts are invaluable sources of information, it is almost impossible to know how much they are colored by the conquest and the needs and expectations of the conquerors. This dilemma raises another: The long physical separation of the peoples of the Americas from the peoples of Asia and Europe created a great cultural separation as well. Since the conquest, however, European culture has predominated. Both the Spanish conquerors seeking to make sense of the wonders they encountered and later scholars seeking to understand preconquest Native American civilization and reconstruct its history have had to rely on the language and categories of European thought to describe and analyze peoples and cultural experiences that had nothing to do with Europe. Cultural blinders and arrogance have exacerbated this gap—for example, the Spaniards, who sought to eradicate Native American religion and replace it with Christianity.

Again and again, European words, categories, and values have been used to describe the experience of America before it was America. Columbus and other early explorers (see Chapter 18), believing they had reached the East Indies, called the people they met in the Caribbean "Indians." This misnomer stuck, extending to all Native American peoples who, of course, have other names for

Aztec Calendar Stone. When the Aztec "calendar" was unearthed in Mexico in 1790 it confirmed the greatness and complexity of the Americas' pre-Columbian civilizations.

themselves. The name *America* itself is European, taken from Amerigo Vespucci (1451–1512), a Florentine who explored the coast of Brazil in 1501 and 1502.

Mesoamerica

Mesoamerica (the name means "middle America") extends from central Mexico into Central America (see Map 14–1). This is a region of great physical diversity, ranging from lowland tropical rain forests to temperate highlands with fertile basins and valleys. Lowland regions include the Yucatán Peninsula and the Gulf and Pacific coasts. Highland regions include Mexico's central plateau, with the Valley of Mexico and the Oaxaca region, and the mountainous areas of Guatemala. Most of Mesoamerica's mineral resources are found in the highlands. The lowlands were the source of many important trading goods, including hardwoods, plant dyes, and the prized feathers of exotic birds.

Mesoamerica also designates a distinctive and enduring cultural tradition that emerged in this region between 1000 and 2000 b.c.e., manifested itself in a succession of impressive and powerful states until the coming of European conquerors in the sixteenth century, and continues to express itself in the lives of the region's Native American peoples. This is not to say that Mesoamerica was or is culturally homogeneous. The peoples of Mesoamerica were and are ethnically and linguistically diverse. There was no single Mesoamerican civilization, nor was there a single linear development of civilization in the region. Nonetheless, Mesoamerican civilizations shared many traits, including writing, a sophisticated calendrical system, many gods and religious ideas, a ritual ball game, and urban centers with religious and administrative buildings symmetrically arranged around large plazas.

Throughout its history the peoples of the region were linked by long-distance trade. Unlike the Andean region, where sophisticated metallurgy developed early, metallurgy came late to Mesoamerica. When it did come, it was used primarily for ceremonial objects rather than for weapons and tools. Instead, Mesoamericans made weapons and other

tools from **obsidian,** a volcanic glass capable of holding a razor-sharp edge, and for that reason a valued trade commodity.

Mesoamerican history before the Spanish conquest is conventionally divided into four major periods: The term *Classic*, with its associations to ancient Greece and its connotations of "best" or "highest," derives from European historical frameworks. It reflects the view of many early Mesoamericanists that the Classic period, which corresponds more or less to the time during which the Maya civilizations of the southern Yucatán erected dated stone monuments, was the high point of Mesoamerican civilization. That view is no longer so prevalent, but the terminology has endured. The chronology continues to provide a useful framework for understanding Mesoamerican history.

The transition from hunting and gathering to settled village life occurred gradually in Mesoamerica during the Archaic period. The cornerstone of the process was the domestication of maize (corn) and other staple crops, including beans and squash. Other plants native to the Americas that were domesticated in this period include tomatoes, chili peppers, and avocado. Maize and beans were particularly important because together they provide a rich source of protein compared to the grains that were the basis of the Neolithic revolution in the ancient Near East and China. In those regions domesticated animals supplied the protein settled agriculturalists needed in their diet. Mesoamerica, however, was poor in sources of animal protein. It had only a few small domesticated animals—among them dogs and turkeys—and no large herd animals like the cattle, sheep, and goats of the Old World (see Figure 14–1).

The domestication of maize, beans, and other plants secured the people of Mesoamerica an adequate and dependable diet. Over time they devised myriad ways to prepare and store these staples. Maize has also been one of Mesoamerica's major contributions to the world. Since the conquest, maize cultivation has spread to many other parts of the world. Corn is now one of North America's most important crops, and it is used to feed livestock in both North and South America.

Probably because they had no large draft animals—no horses or oxen—the people of the Americas, including

Figure 14.1. Number of Domesticated Species Compared*

	Continent			
	Eurasia	Sub-Saharan Africa	The Americas	Australia
Domesticated Species	13	0	1	0

*A species is defined as a wild mammal weighing on the average over 100 pounds. Thirteen species were domesticated in Eurasia in antiquity: sheep, goats, cows, pigs, horses, Arabian camels, Bactrian camels, donkeys, reindeer, water buffalo, yak, Bali cattle, and mithan. Only one species was domesticated in the Americas: llamas (alpacas), which are found in the Andes. *Adapted from Jared Diamond,* Guns, Germs, and Steel. *W. W. Norton.*

The Formative Period and the Emergence of Mesoamerican Civilization

By about 1500 B.C.E. Mesoamerica's agricultural villages were beginning to coalesce into more complicated societies, with towns and monumental architecture, the division of society into elite and commoner classes, long-distance trade among regions, and the emergence of sophisticated artistic traditions (see Map 14–1).

The Olmec

The most prominent of the Early Formative period cultures is that of the Olmec, centered on the lowlands of Mexico's Gulf coast. This is a densely vegetated region with slow, meandering streams bordered by areas of rich, alluvial soil. The Olmec were once thought of as Mesoamerica's "mother culture," but evidence is accumulating that similarly complex societies were emerging about the same time throughout Mesoamerica.

Most of what is known about the Olmecs comes from the archaeological sites of San Lorenzo and La Venta. Other Olmec centers have not been as intensively studied. San Lorenzo was first occupied about 1500 B.C.E. and had developed into a prominent center by about 1200 B.C.E. It included public buildings, a drainage system linked to artificial ponds, and what was probably the earliest court for the Mesoamerican ball game. The center flourished until about

Mesoamerica, never developed the wheel, although they made wheeled toys. In Mesoamerica humans did all the carrying. And because there were no horses and chariots, warfare in Mesoamerica (and in Andean South America) was always between armies of foot soldiers.

Between 5000 and 2500 B.C.E. villages began to appear in both highland and lowland regions of Mesoamerica. By about 2000 B.C.E. settled agricultural life had taken hold in much of the region. As in the Old World when this happened, people began to make fired clay vessels, and ceramic technology appeared. Nomadic hunter-gatherers have little need of storage, but farmers do, and clay vessels filled that need. Pottery is also a medium for artistic expression, and it played a role in religion and ritual observance throughout Mesoamerican history.

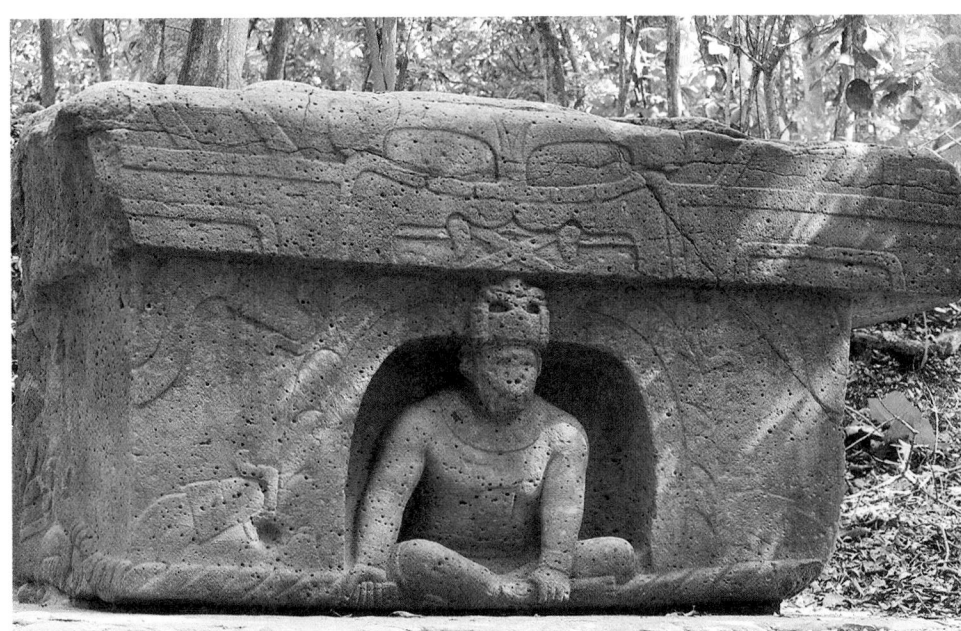

Olmec Monument. A large carved monument from the Olmec site of La Venta with a naturalistically rendered human figure. *Robert and Linda Mitchell Photography.*

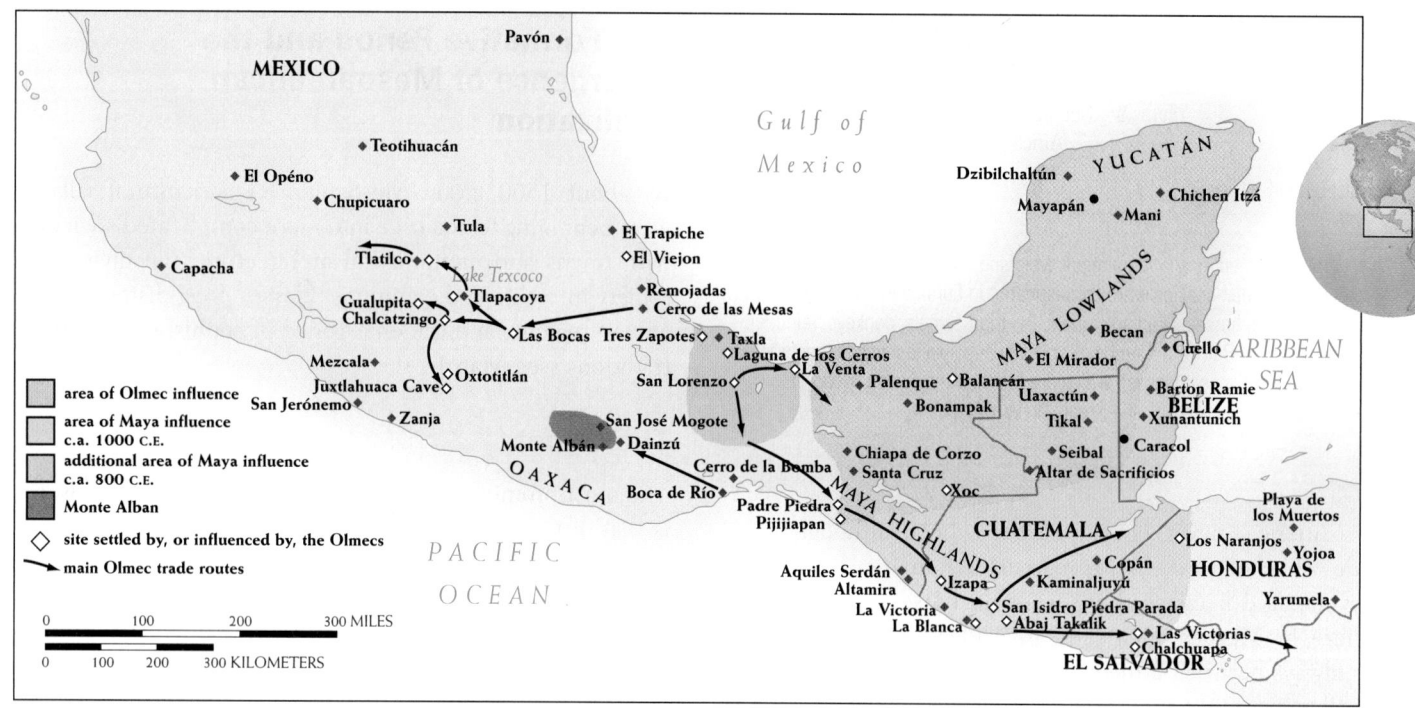

Map 14–1. Mesoamerica: The Formative and Classic Periods.

900 B.C.E. but then went into decline and had been abandoned by about 400 B.C.E. As San Lorenzo declined, La Venta rose to prominence, flourishing from about 900 to 400 B.C.E. La Venta's most conspicuous feature is a 110-foot, scalloped pyramid, known as the Great Pyramid, which stands at one end of a group of platforms and plazas aligned along a north–south axis. Archaeologists have recovered many caches of carved jade, serpentine, and granite artifacts that had been buried along the center line of this axis. Like San Lorenzo, La Venta also had an elaborate drainage system.

Probably the best known Olmec works of art are the massive stone heads, some weighing more than twenty tons, that have been found at both San Lorenzo and La Venta.

Thought to be portraits of Olmec rulers, these were carved from basalt from quarries as much as sixty-five miles distant and transported, probably by raft, to the centers. The Olmec also carved other large basalt monuments, including altars and seated figures.

The population of San Lorenzo and La Venta was never great, probably less than 1,000 people. The monumental architecture and sculpture at these sites nonetheless suggests that Olmec society was dominated by an elite class of ruler-priests able to command the labor of the rest of the population. The elite probably lived in the centers, supported by farmers who lived in villages of pole-and-thatch houses.

Among the most pervasive images in Olmec art is that of the were-jaguar, a half-human, half-feline creature. The were-jaguar may have been a divine ancestor figure, perhaps providing the elite with the justification for their authority. Similarities between the were-jaguar iconography and that of later Mesoamerican deities suggests some of the underlying continuities linking Mesoamerican societies over time.

The raw material for many Olmec artifacts, such as jade and obsidian, comes from other regions of Mesoamerica. Likewise, Olmec goods and Olmec iconography like the were-jaguar are found in other regions, all suggesting that from an early time the parts of Mesoamerica were linked in a web of trade. These contacts would

Chronology

Major Periods in Ancient Mesoamerican Civilization

8000–2000 B.C.E.	Archaic
2000 B.C.E.–150 C.E.	Formative (or Pre-Classic)
150–900 C.E.	Classic
900–1521 C.E.	Post-Classic

have fostered the spread of ideas, contributing to the formation of common Mesoamerican traditions. Control of trade in high-status materials like jade and obsidian by the Olmec elite would also have contributed to their prestige and authority.

The Valley of Oaxaca and the Rise of Monte Alban

Olmec civilization faded after about 400 B.C.E. and had disappeared by about 200 B.C.E. Other regions, however, were rising to prominence. Some of the most significant developments in the Late Formative period occurred in the Valley of Oaxaca. The site of San José Mogote, located in one branch of the valley, had arisen at about the same time as San Lorenzo. By about 600 B.C.E. San José Mogote was a thriving center of perhaps 1,000 people. Around 500 B.C.E. a new center, Monte Alban, was built on a hill where three branches of the valley meet. Monte Alban's population soon grew to about 5,000, and it emerged as the capital of a state that dominated the Oaxaca region. Carved images of bound prisoners at Monte Alban suggest that warfare played a role in establishing its authority. They also suggest an early origin for the practice of ritual human sacrifice that characterized most Mesoamerican cultures. Monte Alban retained its authority in Oaxaca into the Classic period, maintaining its independence against the growing power of the greatest Classic city, Teotihuacán.

The Emergence of Writing and the Mesoamerican Calendar

The earliest evidence of writing and the Mesoamerican calendar have been found in the Valley of Oaxaca at San José Mogote and Monte Alban. The Mesoamerican calendar is based on two interlocking cycles, each with its own day and month names. One cycle, tied to the solar year, was of 365 days; the other was of 260 days. Combining the two cycles produced a "century" of fifty-two years, the amount of time required before a particular combination of days in each cycle would repeat itself. The hieroglyphs found in Oaxaca relate to the 260-day cycle.

At the time of the Spanish conquest, all the peoples of Mesoamerica used this fifty-two-year calendrical system. As we will see, only the Maya developed a calendar based on a longer time period, anchored—like the Jewish, Christian, or Muslim calendars—to a fixed starting point in the past.

The Classic Period in Mesoamerica

The Classic period was a time of cultural florescence in Mesoamerica. In Central Mexico, it saw the rise of Teotihuacán, a great city that rivaled the largest cities of the world at the time. The Maya, who built densely populated cities in the seemingly inhospitable rain forests of the southern Yucatán, developed a sophisticated system of mathematics and Mesoamerica's most advanced hieroglyphic writing.

Pyramid of the Sun. This monumental structure stands near the southern end of Teotihuacán's great central thoroughfare, the Avenue of the Dead.
Kal Muller/Woodfin Camp & Associates.

Indeed, Classic urban life in Mesoamerica was richer and on a larger scale than in Europe north of the Alps at the same time.

Archaeologists and art historians have recently made enormous strides in understanding Classic civilization. Progress in deciphering Maya hieroglyphics has opened a window on the politics and statecraft of the Maya elite. Archaeological studies have broadened our understanding of Teotihuacán and Maya cities, revealing their extent and structure and providing clues to the lives of the people who lived in them.

Classic cities, with their many temples, plazas, and administrative buildings, were religious and administrative centers whose rulers combined secular and religious authority. It was once thought that Classic society was composed of peaceful theocracies, without the chronic warfare charac-

terizing Mesoamerica at the time of the Spanish conquest. It is now clear, however, that warfare was common during the Classic period and that Classic rulers did not hesitate to use force to expand their influence and maintain their authority. The ritual sacrifice of captive enemies was also a feature of Classic societies.

Teotihuacán

In the Late Formative period two centers competed for dominance over the rapidly growing population of the Valley of Mexico. One of these, Cuicuilco, was located at the southern end of the valley. The other, Teotihuacán, was located about thirty miles northeast of Mexico City. When a volcano destroyed Cuicuilco in the first century C.E., Teotihuacán was left unopposed and grew explosively into a great city, perhaps Mesoamerica's first true city-state, dominating central Mexico for many centuries and strongly influencing the rest of Mesoamerica.

Several natural advantages contributed to Teotihuacán's rise. The original source of its prestige may have been a network of caves recently discovered under its most prominent monument, the Pyramid of the Sun (the name by which the Aztecs knew it). These caves may have been considered an entrance to the underworld. Recent studies indicate that stone quarried from them was used to construct the city, creating a direct symbolic link between the city's buildings and its sacred origins. Teotihuacán is also located near an important source of obsidian, straddling a trade route to the Gulf coast and southern Mesoamerica. The quarrying of obsidian and the manufacture and trade of obsidian goods were apparently major sources of the city's wealth and influence. Finally, Teotihuacán is surrounded by fertile farmland susceptible to intensive cultivation with terracing and irrigation.

At its height about 500 C.E. this remarkable city extended over almost nine square miles and had a population of more than 150,000, making it one of the largest cities in the world at the time. Its size and organization suggest that it was ruled by a powerful, centralized authority. It was laid out on a rigid grid plan dominated by a

Teotihuacán. Temple façade showing Quetzalcoatl, the feathered serpent, as well as the god Tlalc, with round eyes.

broad, three-mile-long thoroughfare known as the Avenue of the Dead. Religious and administrative structures and a market occupy the center of the city. At one end of the Avenue of the Dead is the so-called Pyramid of the Moon, and near it, to one side, is the 210-foot-high Pyramid of the Sun. More than 2,000 residential structures surround the city center. The most lavish of these, the homes of the city's elite, lie nearest the center. Most of the city's residents lived in walled apartment compounds farther from the center. These compounds were also centers of craft manufacture, with neighborhoods devoted to pottery, obsidian work, and other specialties. Some parts of the city were reserved for foreign traders. One neighborhood, for example, was home to people from Monte Alban and the Oaxaca region. Paintings and murals adorned the interiors of many buildings, including those of the common people as well as the elite. The humble dwellings of poor farmers occupied the city's periphery. As the city grew, local farmers had apparently been forced to abandon their villages and move to Teotihuacán, another indication of the power of the city's rulers.

Teotihuacán's influence extended throughout Mesoamerica. In the central highlands, dispersed settlements were consolidated into larger centers laid out similarly to Teotihuacán, suggesting conquest and direct control— a Teotihuacán empire. The city's influence in other, more distant regions may have reflected close trading ties rather than conquest. Buildings in Teotihuacán's distinctive architectural style at the site of Kaminaljuyu in the highlands of modern Guatemala, for example, may have been residences for Teotihuacano merchants. The city's obsidian and pottery were exchanged widely for items like the green feathers of the quetzal bird and jaguar skins, valued for ritual garments.

Many of the buildings in Teotihuacán were decorated with striking, skillfully made sculptures and murals of the city's gods and ritual practices. Among the deities of Teotihuacán are a storm god and his goddess counterpart, whose representation suggests a link to the Aztec's rain god, Tlaloc, and his consort, Chalchiuhtlicue. The people of Teotihuacán also worshiped a feathered serpent who is recognizably antecedent to the god the Aztecs worshiped as Quetzalcoatl and the Maya as Kukulcan. Murals also suggest that the Teotihuacán elite, like the Maya and later Mesoamerican peoples, drew their own blood as a form of sacrifice to the gods. A mass burial under one of the city's principal temples indicates that they also practiced human sacrifice.

After 500 C.E. Teotihuacán's influence began to wane, and some time in the eighth century, for reasons that are still poorly understood, its authority collapsed.

Tikal. The staircased temple on the left was built as a tomb for King Jasaw Chan Kawill in the eighth century.

A fire swept through the city, destroying the ritual center and the residences of the elite and hinting at an internal revolt. Although a substantial population lived on in the city, it never regained its former status. It retained its hold on the imagination of succeeding generations of Mesoamericans, however, much like the ruins of ancient Greece and Rome on the imaginations of later Europeans. The name by which we know it, Teotihuacán, is an Aztec word meaning "City of the Gods," and it was still a revered pilgrimage site at the time of the Spanish conquest.

The Maya

Maya civilization arose in southern Mesoamerica, which includes modern Guatemala, the Yucatán Peninsula, Belize, and parts of Honduras and El Salvador. Village life established itself in this region during the first millennium B.C.E., and thereafter the population began to rise steadily. The earliest distinctively Maya urban sites date to around 300 B.C.E., in the Late Formative period. During the Classic period, Maya civilization experienced a remarkable florescence in the lowland jungles of the southern Yucatán.

All the pre-Spanish societies of Mesoamerica were literate, recording historical and religious information on scrolled or screenfold books made with deerhide or bark paper. Only a handful of these books, four of them Mayan, have survived the ravages of time and the Spanish conquest. (Spanish priests, who viewed native religious texts as

A Maya Myth of Creation

Document

This segment of the Maya creation myth is from the *Popol Vuh*, a compendium of Maya mythology and history transcribed into European script by a Quiche Maya noble in the sixteenth century.

◆ How does this myth describe the world before creation? Who are the beings that exist before creation and decide how it is to be carried out? What did they do to create the earth?

There was not yet one person, one animal, bird, fish, crab, tree, rock, hollow, canyon, meadow, forest. Only the sky alone is there; the face of the earth is not clear. Only the sea alone is pooled under all the sky; there is nothing whatever gathered together. It is at rest; not a single thing stirs. It is held back; kept at rest under the sky.

Whatever might be is simply not there; only murmurs, ripples, in the dark, in the night. Only the Maker, Modeler alone, Sovereign Plumed Serpent, the Bearers, Begetters are in the water, a glittering light. . . .

So there were three of them, as Heart of Sky, who came to the Sovereign Plumed Serpent, when the dawn of life was conceived:

"How should it be sown, how should it dawn? Who is to be the provider, nurturer?"

"Let it be this way, think about it: this water should be removed, emptied out for the formation of the earth's own plate and platform, then comes the sowing, the dawning of the sky-earth. But there will be no high days and no bright praise for our work, our design, until the rise of the human work, the human design," they said.

And then the earth rose because of them; it was simply their word that brought it forth. For the forming of the earth, they said, "Earth." It arose suddenly, just like a cloud, like a mist, now forming, unfolding. Then the mountains were separated from the water, all at once the great mountains came forth. By their genius alone, by their cutting edge alone they carried out the conception of the mountain-plain, whose face grew instant groves of cypress and pine.

Reprinted with the permission of Simon & Schuster Adult Publishing Group, from *Popol Vuh*, by Dennis Tedlock. Copyright © 1996 by Dennis Tedlock.

idolatrous, burned almost all of them.) The Maya of the Classic period, who developed Mesoamerica's most advanced writing system, were unique in the extent to which they inscribed writing and calendrical symbols in stone, pottery, and other imperishable materials.

Thanks to rapid advances in the decipherment of Maya writing and to intensive archaeological work at Maya cities, our understanding of the nature of Classic Maya civilization has changed radically in recent decades. According to earlier views, Maya cities were not really cities but empty ceremonial centers inhabited by scholar-priests. The inscriptions were thought to be concerned entirely with astronomical and calendrical observations tied to Maya ritual. Scattered farming communities were thought to have surrounded the centers, supporting the priestly elite. Relations between centers were thought to be peaceful. Contributing to this view was the belief that intensive agriculture capable of supporting dense populations was impossible in the tropical forests of the southern Yucatán where Classic Maya civilization developed.

Archaeologists have shown that Maya centers were indeed cities, and that the largest of them, Tikal, probably had a population of between 50,000 and 70,000 at its height. They have also found evidence of terracing, irrigation systems, and other agricultural technologies that would have increased yields enough to support dense populations. Powerful ruling families and their elite retainers dominated these cities, supported by a far larger class of farmer-commoners. The inscriptions are almost entirely devoted to recounting important events in the lives of these rulers. Cities competed for dominance, and warfare between them was chronic. As murals and sculptures show, captured prisoners were sacrificed to appease the gods and glorify the victorious ruler.

Religion deeply informed the social and political realm of the Maya. They believed that the world had gone through several cycles of creation before the present one. (See Document, "A Maya Myth of Creation.") They recognized no clear distinction between a natural and a supernatural

Maya Calendar. This copy of a page from the Dresden codex shows detailed calendrical observations and astronomical predictions. The original calendar was inscribed on stone tablets.

world. As was probably true also of Teotihuacán, rulers and the elite combined religious and political authority, mediating between humans and gods through elaborate rituals in the temples and plazas of their cities. Rulers claimed association with the gods to justify their authority. They wore special regalia that symbolized their power, and they performed rituals to sustain the gods and the cosmic order. These rituals included bloodletting ceremonies, the sacrifice of captives, and ball games.

The significance of sacrifice and the ball game in Maya ideology is reflected in a Maya creation myth recorded in the *Popol Vuh*, a Maya book transcribed into European script by a Maya noble in the sixteenth century. Imagery in Classic Maya art has been linked to this myth, which tells how the Hero Twins defeated the gods of the underworld in the ball game and returned to life after being sacrificed. One became the sun and the other Venus, and in their regular rising and setting reenact their descent into the underworld and their subsequent rebirth. All Maya cities had ball courts. The games played there were a symbolic reenactment of the confrontation between the Hero Twins and the lords of the underworld, and the losing team was sometimes sacrificed.[1]

The Classic Maya developed a sophisticated mathematics and were among the first peoples in the world to invent the concept of zero. In addition to the 52–year calendar round based on interlocking 260- and 365-day cycles they shared with other Mesoamerican societies, the Maya developed an absolute calendar, known as the **Long Count,** tied to a fixed point in the past. The calendar had great religious as well as practical significance for the Maya. They viewed the movements of the celestial bodies to which the calendar was tied—including the sun, moon, and Venus—as deities. The complexity and accuracy of their calendar reflect Maya skills in astronomical observation. They adjusted their lunar calendar for the actual length of the lunar cycle (29.53 days) and may have had provisions like our leap years for the actual length of the solar year. They also made accurate observations of Venus and recognized before other peoples that it is both the morning and the evening star. The importance of the calendar, its association with divine forces, and the esoteric knowledge required to master it must have been important sources of prestige and power for its elite guardians.

Scholars have been able to correlate the Long Count calendar with the European calendar, and so can date Maya monuments with a precision unknown for other ancient Mesoamerican societies. The commemorative monuments

---

[1] Robert J. Sharer, *The Ancient Maya*, 5th ed. (Stanford, CA: Stanford University Press, 1994), p. 522.

Mayan Mural. This reproduction of one of the remarkable murals found at the Maya site of Bonampak shows the presentation of captives to the city's ruler, Chan Muan. *Copyright © President and Fellows of Harvard College 1998. All rights reserved. Peabody Museum, Harvard University. Photograph by Hillel Burger.*

erected by Classic Maya rulers to record their accomplishments almost always have Long Count dates. As a result, it is now possible to reconstruct the dynastic histories of many Maya cities in detail, keeping in mind, of course, that Maya rulers—like rulers everywhere throughout history—may have exaggerated their accomplishments to put themselves in a favorable light.

During the Classic period no single center dominated the Maya region. Rather, many independent units, each composed of a capital city and smaller subject towns and villages, alternately vied and cooperated with each other, rising and falling in relative prominence. Tikal, at its height the largest Classic Maya city, is also one of the most thoroughly studied. The residential center covers more than fourteen square miles and has more than 3,000 structures. The city follows the uneven terrain of the rain forest and is not, unlike Teotihuacán, laid out on a grid. Monumental causeways link the major structures of the site.

Tikal emerged as an important center in the Late Formative, benefiting from its strategic position. The city is located near a source of flint, valued as a raw material for stone tools. It is also located near swamps that, with modification, might have been agriculturally productive. And it has access to river systems that lead both to the Gulf and the Caribbean coasts, giving it control of the trade between those regions.

A single dynasty of thirty-nine rulers reigned in Tikal from the Early Classic until the eighth century. The early rulers in this Jaguar Paw line were buried in a structure known as the North Acropolis, and the inscriptions associated with their tombs provide us with details about them, including in many cases their names, the dates of their rule, and the dates of major military victories. Monuments associated with the ruler Great Jaguar Paw, for example, suggests that in 378 C.E. he conquered the city of Uaxactún and installed a relative on its throne.

Late in the fourth century links developed between Tikal and Teotihuacán. One ruler, Curl Nose, who ascended to the throne in 379, may have married into the ruling family from the Teotihuacán-dominated city of Kaminaljuyu in the southern highlands.

For about 100 years beginning in the mid–sixth century, Tikal and most other lowland Maya sites experienced a hiatus during which there was little new construction. The city lost much of its influence and may have suffered a serious defeat at the hands of the city of Caracol. Then in 682 the ruler Ah Cacau (r. 682–723?) ascended the throne and initiated a new period of vigor and prosperity for Tikal, again expanding its influence through conquest and strategic marriage alliances. He and his two immediate successors, Yax Kin (r. 734–?) and Chitam (r. 769–?), began an ambitious building program, creating most of Tikal's surviving monumental structures, including the dramatic, soaring temples that dominate the site. Chitam was the last ruler in the Jaguar Paw dynasty. After he died Tikal again declined and, like other sites in the southern lowlands, it never recovered.

Similar dynastic histories have been emerging from research at other Classic Maya sites. Inscriptions in the shrine above the tomb of Lord Pacal (r. 615–683), the greatest ruler of the city of Palenque, located in the west of the Maya region in hills overlooking the Gulf coast plain, record the city's entire dynastic history back to mythic ancestors. Two of the rulers in this genealogy were women, one of them Pacal's mother, Lady Zac Kuk (r. 612–640), and another predecessor, Lady Kanal Ikal (r. 583–604). Palenque is also remarkable for its architectural innovations, which permitted its architects to build structures with thinner walls and larger rooms than at other Classic sites.

Between 800 and 900 C.E. Classic civilization collapsed in the southern lowlands. The ruling dynasties all came to an end, the construction of monumental architecture and sculpture with Long Count dates ceased, and the great cities were virtually abandoned. The cause of the collapse has long been a subject of intense speculation, and is still not known for sure. The factors that may have contributed to it, however, are becoming clearer. Among them are intensifying warfare, population growth, increased population concentration, and attempts to increase agricultural production that ultimately backfired. As the urban areas around the ceremonial centers grew, so did the demand for food. Ambitious building projects continued in the centers right up to the collapse, and some scholars believe that as a growing proportion of the population was employed in these projects, fewer were left to produce food. Overfarming may then have led to soil exhaustion. Some archaeologists also believe a major drought may have occurred. Clearly the Maya exceeded the capacities of their resources, but exactly why and how remain unknown.

After the abandonment of the Classic sites in the southern lowlands, the focus of Maya civilization shifted to the northern Yucatán. There the site of Chichén Itzá, located next to a sacred well, flourished from the ninth to the thirteenth century. Stylistic resemblances between Chichén Itzá and Tula, the capital of the Post-Classic Toltec Empire in central Mexico (see "The Toltecs," p. 415) suggest ties between the two cities, but archaeologists are uncertain of their nature. Chichén Itzá had the largest ball court in the Maya area. After Chichén Itzá's fall, Mayapan became the main Maya center. By the time of the Spanish conquest it too had lost sway, and the Maya had divided into small, competing centers.

The Post-Classic Period

No new strong, centralized power arose immediately to replace Teotihuacán in the wake of its collapse in the eighth century. Warfare increased, and several smaller, militaristic states emerged, many centered around fortified hilltop

Tula Statuary. Tula, now Hidalgo, Mexico, was the capital of the Toltec civilization. These enormous statues, known as the Atlantes, stand atop the remains of the ancient Toltec pyramid raised in ancient Tula. *Sexto Sol/Getty Images, Inc.-Photodise.*

The Founding of Tenochtitlán. According to legend, the tribal god Huitzilopochtli led the Aztecs/Mexica to a spot where an eagle sat atop a prickly pear cactus (*tenochtli*) growing out of a rock and told them to build their capital there. This symbol now graces the Mexican flag. This image first appeared in the *Codex Mendoza*, a pictorial history of the Aztecs, presumably prepared for the first viceroy of New Spain, Antonio Mendoza, around 1541.

an important source of obsidian. The Toltecs themselves were apparently descendants of one of many "barbarian" northern peoples (like the later Aztecs) who began migrating into Mesoamerica during the Late Classic.

Aztec mythology glorified the Toltecs, seeing them as the fount of civilization and attributing to them a vast and powerful empire to which the Aztecs were the legitimate heirs. Other Mesoamerican peoples at the time of the conquest also attributed legendary status to the Toltecs. The archaeological evidence for a Toltec empire, however, is ambiguous. Although a substantial city with a population of between 35,000 and 60,000 people, Tula was never as large or as organized as Teotihuacán. Toltec influence reached many regions of Mesoamerica—as already noted, there were many stylistic affinities between Tula and the Maya city of Chichén Itzá—but archaeologists are uncertain whether that influence translated into political control.

Toltec iconography, which stresses human sacrifice, death, blood, and military symbolism, supports their warlike reputation. Their deities are clearly antecedent to those worshiped by the Aztecs, including the feathered serpent Quetzalcoatl and the warlike trickster Tezcatlipoca.

Whatever the reality of Toltec power, it was short-lived. By about 1100 Tula was in decline and its influence gone.

The Aztecs

The people commonly known as the Aztecs referred to themselves as the **Mexica,** a name that lives on as *Mexico.* At the time of the arrival of the Spanish in 1519 the Aztecs controlled a powerful empire that dominated much of Mesoamerica. Their capital city, Tenochtitlán, was the most populous yet seen in Mesoamerica. Built on islands and landfill in the southern part of Lake Texcoco in the Valley of Mexico, it was home to some 200,000 to 300,000 people. Its great temples and palaces gleamed in the sun. Bearing tribute to its rulers and goods to its great markets, canoes crowded the city's canals and people on foot thronged its streets and the great causeways linking it to the mainland. The city's traders brought precious goods from distant regions; vast wealth flowed in constantly from subject territories. Yet the people responsible for these accomplishments were relative newcomers, the foundation of their power being less than two hundred years old.

Because of the dramatic clash with Spanish adventurers that brought their empire to an end, we have more direct

cities. At the same time interregional trade and market systems became increasingly important, and secular and religious authority, closely linked during the Classic period, began to diverge.

The Toltecs

About 900 c.e. a people known as the Toltecs rose to prominence. Their capital, Tula, is located near the northern periphery of Mesoamerica. Like Teotihuacán, it lay close to information about the Aztecs than any other preconquest Mesoamerican people. Many of the conquistadors recorded their experiences, and postconquest administrators and missionaries collected valuable information about their new subjects while at the same time seeking to extirpate their religion and culture. Although filtered through the bitterness of defeat for the Aztecs and the biases of the conquerors, these records nevertheless provide detailed information about Aztec society and Aztec history.

According to their own legends, the Aztecs were originally a nomadic people inhabiting the shores of a mythical Lake Aztlán somewhere to the northwest of the Valley of Mexico. At the urging of their patron god Huitzilopochtli, they began to migrate, arriving in the Valley of Mexico early in the thirteenth century. Scorned by the people of the cities and states already there, but prized and feared as mercenaries, they ended up in the marshy land on the shores of Lake Texcoco. They finally settled on the island that became Tenochtitlán in 1325 after seeing an eagle perched there on a prickly pear cactus, an omen Huitzilopochtli had said would identify the end of their wandering.

The Aztecs accepted a position as tributaries and mercenaries for Azcazpotzalco, then the most powerful state in the valley, but soon became trusted allies with their own tribute-paying territories. They further consolidated their position with marriage alliances to the ruling families of other cities. These alliances gave their own rulers claim to descent from the Toltecs. In 1428, under their fourth ruler, Itzcoatl (r. 1427–1440), the Aztecs formed a triple alliance with Texcoco and Tlacopan, turned against Azcazpotzalco, and became the dominant power in the Valley of Mexico. It was at this time, less than 100 years before the arrival of Hernán Cortés, that the Aztecs, as head of the Triple Alliance, began the aggressive expansion that brought them their vast tribute-paying empire (see Map 14–2).

Itzcoatl also laid the foundation of Aztec imperial ideology. He ordered the burning of all the ancient books in the valley, expunging any history that conflicted with Aztec pretensions, and restructured Aztec religion and ritual to support and justify Aztec preeminence. The Aztecs now presented themselves as the divinely ordained successors to the ancient Toltecs, and with each new conquest and the growing splendor of Tenochtitlán, they seemed to ratify that claim. (See Document, "Nezahualcoyotl of Texcoco Sings of the Giver of Life.")

Aztec conquests ultimately included almost all of central Mexico. To the west, however, they were unable to conquer the rival Tarascan Empire with its capital of Tzintzuntzan. And within the Aztec realm several pockets, most prominently Tlaxcala, remained unsubdued but nonetheless locked into a pattern of ritual warfare with the Aztecs.

The Aztec Extractive Empire The Aztec Empire was extractive. After a conquest, the Aztecs usually left the local elite intact and in power, imposing their rule indirectly. But they demanded heavy tribute in goods and labor. Tribute included goods of all kinds, including agricultural products, fine craft goods, gold and jade, textiles, and precious feathers. (See Document, "The Aztecs Economically Isolate an Enemy.") Tribute lists in Tenochtitlán, which the Spanish preserved because they, too, wished to exploit the empire they had conquered, indicate the immense quantity of goods that flowed into Tenochtitlán's coffers as a result. In a given year, for example, tribute included as much as 7,000 tons of maize and 2 million cotton cloaks. One nearby province alone was responsible for "12,800 cloaks, . . . 1600 loin cloths, 1600 women's tunics, 8 warriors' costumes, . . . 32,000 bundles of paper, 8000 bowls, and 4 bins of maize and beans."[2] It was this wealth that underwrote the grandeur of Tenochtitlán, making it, as one commentator has described it, "a beautiful parasite, feeding on the lives and labour of other peoples and casting its shadow over all their arrangements."[3]

Aztec Religion and Human Sacrifice Aztec imperial exploitation did not end with food, cotton, and valued craft goods. Human sacrifice on a prodigious scale was central to Aztec ideology. The Aztecs believed that Huitzilopochtli, as sun god, required human blood to sustain him as he battled the moon and stars each night to rise again each day, and that it was their responsibility to provide the victims. The prime candidates for sacrifice were war captives, and the Aztecs often engaged in "flowery wars" with traditional enemies like Tlaxcala just to obtain captives. On major festivals, thousands of victims might perish. Led up the steps of the temple of Huitzilopochtli, a victim was thrown backward over a stone, his arms and legs pinned, while a priest cut out his heart. He would then be rolled down the steps of the temple, his head placed on a skull rack, and his limbs butchered and distributed to be eaten. Small children were sacrificed to the rain god Tlaloc, who, it was believed, was pleased by their tears.

Victims were also selected as god impersonators, stand-ins for particular gods who were sacrificed after a series of rituals. The rituals involved in the festivals honoring the powerful god Tezcatlipoca were particularly elaborate. A beautiful male youth was chosen to represent the god for an entire year, during which he was treated with reverence. He

---

[2] Frances F. Berdan, *The Aztecs of Central Mexico: An Imperial Society* (New York: Holt, Rinehart and Winston, 1982), p. 36.

[3] Inga Clendinnen, *Aztecs: An Interpretation* (Cambridge: Cambridge University Press, 1991), p. 8.

Map Exploration

To explore this map further, go tohttp://www.prenhall.com/craig_maps

Map 14–2.   The Aztec and Inca Empires on the Eve of the Spanish Conquest.

Nezahualcoyotl of Texcoco Sings of the Giver of Life

Document

Nezahualcoyotl, ruler of Texcoco, lived from 1402 to 1472 and was admired as a philosopher-king. In this poem he sings of the presence of the Giver of Life who invents himself and of the ability of human beings to invoke this divinity, but at the same time he emphasizes the impossibility of achieving any close relationship with the divinity.

◆ In what ways does this song remind you of the thought and religious traditions of the early civilizations of China, India, Egypt, and Greece? What are the characteristics of "He Who invents Himself"? What kind of relationship can human beings achieve with this being? Why does the singer compare seeking the Giver of Life with seeking someone among flowers?

In no place can be the house of He Who invents Himself.
But in all places He is invoked,
in all places He is venerated,
His glory, His fame are sought on the earth.
It is He Who invents everything
He is Who invents Himself: God.
In all places He is invoked,
in all places He is venerated,
His glory, His fame are sought on the earth.
No one here is able,
no one is able to be intimate
with the Giver of Life;
only He is invoked, at His side,
near to Him,
one can live on the earth.
He who finds Him,
knows only one thing; He is invoked,
at His side, near to Him,
one can live on the earth.
In truth no one is intimate with You,
O Giver of Life!

Only as among the flowers,
we might seek someone,
thus we seek You,
we who live on the earth,
while we are at Your side.
Our hearts will be troubled,
only for a short time,
we will be near You and at Your side.
The Giver of Life enrages us,
He intoxicates us here.
No one can be perhaps at His side,
be famous, rule on the earth.
Only You change things
as our hearts know it:
No one can be perhaps at His side,
be famous, rule on the earth.

Excerpt (pp. 86–88) from *Fifteen Poets of the Aztec World,* by Miguel León-Portilla. Copyright © 1992 by Miguel León-Portilla. Reprinted by permission of University of Oklahoma Press.

wandered through the city dressed as the god and playing the flute. A month before the end of his reign he was given four young women as wives. Twenty days before his death he was dressed as a warrior and for a few days he was virtually ruler of the city. Then he and his guardians left the city for an island in the lake. As he ascended the steps of the temple, there to be sacrificed, the new Tezcatlipoca began playing his flutes in Tenochtitlán.

As we have seen, human sacrifice had long been characteristic of Mesoamerican societies, but no other Mesoamerican people practiced it on the scale of the Aztecs. Whatever other reasons for it there might have been, one effect must certainly have been to intimidate subject peoples. It may also have had the effect of reducing the population of fighting-age men from conquered provinces, and with it the possibility of rebellion. Together with the heavy burden of tribute, human sacrifice may also have fed resentment and fear, explaining why so many subject peoples were willing to throw in their lot with Cortés when he challenged the Aztecs.

Tenochititlán Three great causeways linked Tenochtitlán to the mainland. These met at the ceremonial core of the city, dominated by a double temple dedicated to Huitzilopochtli and the rain god Tlaloc. It was here that most of the Aztec's sacrificial victims met their fate. The palaces of the ruler and

The Aztecs Economically Isolate an Enemy Document

Diego Muñoz Camargo (1528?–1599) was a mestizo who wrote a history of the Tlascala people, who had been neighbors of the Aztecs, and who through remarkable perseverance and stubbornness remained independent of Aztec control, but at a very high price. The Aztecs had built a remarkable empire. Often they did so through warfare and have been known over the centuries for their ferocity. They did, however, pursue other modes of political dominance. The Tlascalans were a warlike people living east of the Valley of Mexico. The Aztecs attempted to conquer them militarily but failed. Then the Aztecs turned to a different tactic. They isolated the Tlascalans and permitted them to have no trade with other peoples. As a result the Tlascalans retained their independence, but at the cost of a much diminished standard of living and culture.

◆ What claims of political sovereignty did the Aztecs make? How did the Tlascalans respond? What kinds of goods did the Aztecs keep the Tlascalans from receiving? Why was the difficulty in the Tlascalans importing plumes important? How did the standard of living of the Tlascalans suffer?

The Tlascalans, seeing the great enmity of the Mexicans [that is the Aztecs] towards them, defended their interests as best they could. . . . Engaged in this strife, they sent ambassadors to the Mexican princes, asking why they made war upon them, since they had given no cause for hostilities or for the maltreatment of their people. . . . To which the Mexican replied that the great lord of Mexico was the lord of the whole world, to whom all men were vassals . . . and whoever would not yield obedience to them he would destroy and raze their towns to their foundations, settling them with new people. . . . To which the ambassadors of Tlascala replied: "Most powerful lords, Tlascala is no vassal of yours; furthermore, not since they came out of the seven caves have the Tlascalans paid tribute or tax to any king or prince in the world, for they have always retained their freedom, and . . . they will not obey you, for they would rather die than consent to such a thing. . . ."

[T]he people of Tlascala thenceforth lived on their guard against whatever misfortune might before them; and since the Mexicans had conquered the greater part of this New World, . . . they thought that they could

easily seize the province of Tlascala and subjugate it as they had done with the others. And so they fell upon the Tlascalans and engaged them in so many class and skirmishes that within a few years they had forced them back into their own lands and provinces. They kept the Tlascalans encircled for more than sixty years, depriving them of all their human wants, for they had no cotton with which to clothe themselves, nor gold and silver for their adornment, nor green plumes (which they favor most for their emblems and plumages), nor plumes of any other color for their festivals, nor cocoa to drink, nor salt for their food. All these and other things they lacked during the more than sixty years that they were encircled. They became so accustomed to eating no salt that to this day they have no taste for it and attach no worth to it, and even their children who have been reared among us use very little salt. . . .

Diego Muñoz Camargo, *Historia de Tlaxcala* (Mexico, 1947), pp 119–123, Benjamin Keen, trans., as reprinted in Benjamin Keen, ed., *Readings in Latin American Civilization 1492 to the Present* (Boston: Houghton Mifflin Company, 1955), pp. 13–14.

high nobles lay just outside the central precinct. The ruler's palace was the empire's administrative center, with government officials, artisans and laborers, gardens, and a zoo of exotic animals. The rest of the city was divided into four quarters, and these further divided into numerous wards (**calpulli**). Some *calpulli* were specialized, reserved for merchants (*pochteca*) or artisans. The city was laid out on a grid

formed of streets and canals. Agricultural plots of great fertility known as *chinampas* bordered the canal and the lake shores. Aqueducts carried fresh water from springs on the lake shore into the city. A massive dike kept the briny water of the northern part of Lake Texcoco from contaminating the waters around Tenochtitlán. The neighboring city of Tlatelolco was noted for its great marketplace.

Human Sacrifice. Illustration from a colonial-era manuscript volume, known as the *Codex Magliabecchiano*, presenting Aztec ritual sacrifice on a temple altar. *Scala/Art Resource*

Society   Aztec society was hierarchical, authoritarian, and militaristic. It was divided into two broad classes, noble and commoner, with merchants and certain artisans forming an intermediate category. The nobility enjoyed great wealth and luxury. Laws and regulations relating to dress reinforced social divisions. Elaborate and brilliantly colored regalia distinguished nobles from commoners and rank within the nobility. Commoners were required to wear rough, simple garments.

The Aztecs were morally austere. They valued obedience, respectfulness, discipline, and moderation. Laws were strict and punishment severe. Standards for the nobility were higher than for commoners, and punishments for sexual and social offenses were more strictly enforced the higher one stood in the hierarchy. Drunkenness was frowned upon and harshly punished among the elite. Parents would even execute their own children for breaking moral laws and customs.

The highest rank in the nobility was that of *tlatoani* (plural *tlatoque*), or ruler of a major political unit. Of these, the highest were the rulers of the three cities of the Triple Alliance; of them, the highest was the *tlatoani* of Tenochtitlán. Below them were the *tetcutin*, lords of subordinate units. And below them were the *pipiltin,* who filled the bureaucracy and the priesthood.

The bulk of the population was commoners. It was they who farmed the *chinampas*, harvested fish from the lake, and provided labor for public projects. All commoners belonged to a *calpulli*, each of which had its own temple. Children received training in ritual and ideology in the song houses attached to these temples. Young men received military training in the *telpochcalli*, or young men's house. *Calpulli* officials were responsible for assuring that the *calpulli* fulfilled its tribute obligations. Commoners unable to pay debts or their required tribute might become slaves. They might also become slaves for some criminal offenses. A class of serfs worked the estates of noblemen.

Professional traders and merchants—*pochteca*—were important figures in Aztec society. Their activities, backed by the threat of force from Aztec armies, were a key factor in spreading Aztec influence. Their far-reaching expeditions brought back precious luxury goods for the lords of Tenochtitlán. They organized their own guilds and established their own laws and customs for doing business. Their wealth put them in an ambiguous position in Aztec society. As a result, they tended to be self-effacing and avoided ostentatious display. Artisans of luxury goods—including lapidaries, feather workers, and goldsmiths—also had their own *calpulli* and enjoyed a special status.

Markets were central to Aztec economic life. The great market at Tlatelolco impressed the Spaniards for its great size, orderliness, and the variety of goods traded there. More than 60,000 people went there daily. Market administrators, women as well as men, regulated transactions. Cacao beans and cotton cloaks served as mediums of exchange.

Above all else, Aztec society was organized for war. Although there was no standing army as such, the entire society stood on a war footing. All young men received military training, nobles in special schools reserved for

Chronology

Periods of Andean Civilization

ca. 3000–ca. 2000 B.C.E.	Preceramic
ca. 2000–ca. 800 B.C.E.	Initial
ca. 800–ca. 200 B.C.E.	Early Horizon
ca. 200 B.C.E.–ca. 600 C.E.	Early Intermediate
ca. 600 C.E.–ca. 800/1000 C.E.	Middle Horizon
ca. 800/1000–ca. 1475	Late Intermediate
ca. 1475–1532	Late Horizon (Inca Empire)

them, commoners in their *calpulli* schools. Battles were fought to capture new territory, punish rebellious or recalcitrant tributaries, protect trading expeditions, and secure access to important natural resources. Some battles—the flowery wars—were fought just to secure sacrificial victims. Combat was a matter of individual contests, not the confrontation of massed infantry. A warrior's goal was to subdue and capture prisoners for sacrifice. Prowess in battle, as measured by the number of prisoners a warrior captured, was key to social advancement and rewards for both commoners and nobles. Failure in battle brought social disgrace.

Women in Aztec society could inherit and own property. They traded in the marketplace and served as market officials. With their craftwork they could provide their families with extra income. Girls and boys alike were educated in the song houses, and women had access to priestly roles, although they were barred from high religious positions. In general, however, the Aztec emphasis on warfare left women in a subordinate position, tending hearth and home and excluded from positions of high authority. As a man's primary role was to be a warrior, a woman's was to bear children, and childbirth was compared to battle. Death in childbirth, like death in battle, guaranteed rewards in the afterlife.

Andean South America

The Andean region of South America—primarily modern Peru and Bolivia—had, like Mesoamerica, a long history of indigenous civilization when Spanish conquerors arrived in the sixteenth century. This is a region of dramatic contrasts.

From near the equator south, a narrow strip of desert, one of the driest in the world, lines the Pacific coast. Beyond this strip the Andes Mountains rise abruptly. Small river valleys descend the western face of the mountains, cutting the desert plain to create a series of oases from north to south. The cold waters of the Humboldt current sweep north along the coast from the Antarctic, carrying rich nutrients that support abundant sea life. Within the Andes are regions of high peaks and steep terrain, regions of grassland (*puna*), and deep, warm, fertile intermontane valleys. The eastern slopes of the mountains, covered with dense vegetation, descend into the great tropical rain forest of the Amazon basin (see Figure 14–2).

From ancient times, the people of the coast lived by exploiting the marine resources of the Pacific and by cultivating maize, beans, squash, and cotton. They also engaged in long-distance trade by sea along the Pacific coast.

The people of the highlands domesticated several plants native to the Andean region, including the potato, other tubers, and a grain called quinoa. They cultivated (and still cultivate) these crops on the high slopes of the Andes. In the intermontane valleys they cultivated maize. And in the *puna* grasslands they kept herds of llamas and alpacas—the Andean camelids—using them for their fur, their meat, and as beasts of burden. Highland communities since ancient times have maintained access to the different resources available in different altitude zones, with holdings in each zone that can be far distant from each other. They share this adaptation, which anthropologists sometimes call *verticality*,

Grassy plain 13,000 ft. above sea level
Uplands: 10,500–12,500 ft. above sea level
Frost-free valleys 7,500–10,000 ft. above sea level
Lower slopes of mountains: 2,400–7,000 ft. above sea level
Dry coastal region: 2,400 ft. above sea level

Figure 14–2. The Andean environment packs tremendous ecological diversity into a small space.

with people in other mountainous regions, such as the Alps and the Himalayas.[4]

Andean civilization is conventionally divided into seven periods: The Early, Middle, and Late Horizons are periods in which a homogeneous art style spread over a wide area. The Intermediate periods are characterized by regional stylistic diversity.

The Preceramic and the Initial Periods

The earliest monumental architecture in Peru dates to the early third millennium B.C.E., roughly contemporary with the Great Pyramids of Egypt. Located on the coast mostly near the shore, these earliest centers consist of ceremonial mounds and plazas and predate the introduction of pottery to Peru.

Coastal people at this time subsisted primarily on the bounties of the sea, supplementing their diets with squash, beans, and chili peppers cultivated in the floodplains of the coastal rivers. They also cultivated gourds—for use as containers and utensils—and cotton. The cotton fishing nets and other textiles of this period represent the beginning of the sophisticated Andean textile tradition.

The earliest public buildings in the highlands date to before 2500 B.C.E. These are typically stone-walled structures enclosing a sunken fire pit used to burn ritual offerings. The distribution of these structures, first identified at the site of Kotosh, suggests that highland people shared a set of religious beliefs that archaeologists have called the *Kotosh religious tradition*. Highland people were more dependent on agriculture than coastal people during the late preceramic, cultivating maize as well as potatoes and other highland tubers. Llamas and alpacas were fully domesticated by about 2500 B.C.E.

There is little evidence of social stratification for the late preceramic. The public structures of both the coast and the highlands appear to have been centers of community ritual for relatively egalitarian societies.

The introduction of pottery to Peru around 2000 B.C.E. marks the beginning of the Initial period and corresponds to a major shift in settlement and subsistence patterns on the coast. People became increasingly dependent on agriculture as well as on maritime resources. They moved their settlements inland, built irrigation systems, began cultivating maize, and built large and impressive ceremo-

nial centers. The form of these centers varied by region. On the central coast, for example, they consisted primarily of large U-shaped structures that faced inland, toward the mountains and the source of the water that nourished the coastal crops. On the north coast they consisted of large circular sunken courts and large platform structures. Centers were adorned with stone and adobe sculpture, and their façades were brightly painted. Population grew and society became gradually but increasingly stratified. Incised carvings of bodies with severed heads at Cerro Sechín and Sechín Alto in the Casma suggest growing conflict. Centers apparently remained independent of one another, however, with little evidence to suggest larger political groupings.

Chavín de Huantar and the Early Horizon

The large coastal centers of the Initial period declined early in the first millennium B.C.E. At about the same time, beginning around 800 B.C.E., a site in the highlands, Chavín de Huantar, was growing in influence (see Map 14–3). Located on a trade route between the coast and the lowland tropical rain forest, Chavín was the center of a powerful religious cult with a population of perhaps 3,000 at its height. The

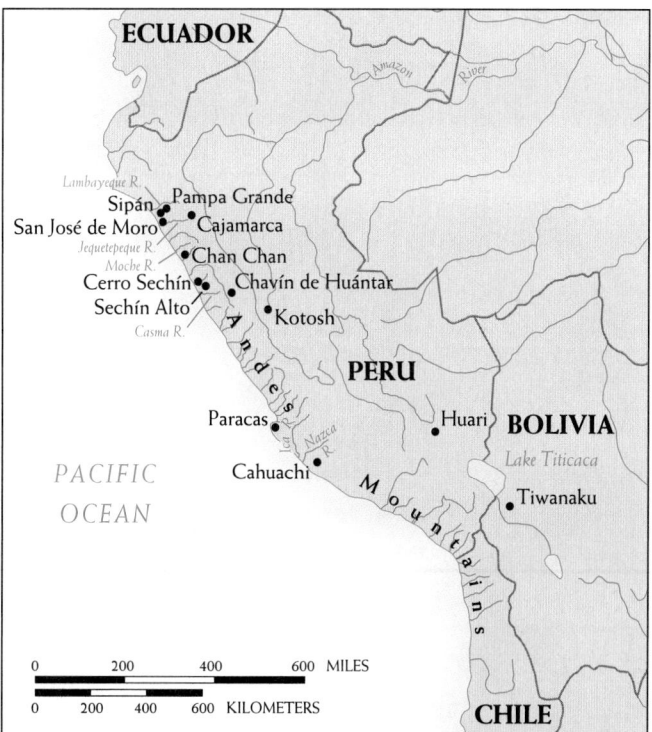

Map 14–3. **Pre-Inca sites** discussed in this chapter.

[4] Michael Mosley, *The Incas and Their Ancestors* (New York and London: Thames and Hudson, 1992), p. 42.

architecture of its central temple complex, which includes U-shaped structures and a sunken circular courtyard, reflects coastal influence. Its artistic iconography draws on many tropical forest animals, including monkeys, serpents, and jaguars. The structure known as the Old Temple is honeycombed with passageways and drains. Archaeologists think that water could deliberately be channeled through these drains to produce a roaring sound. At the end of the central passageway is an imposing stela in the shape of a knife with the blade in the floor and the handle in the ceiling. Known as the Lanzon, this stela is carved in the image of a fanged deity that combines human and feline features. A small hole in the ceiling above the Lanzon suggests that it may have been an oracle whose "voice" was that of a priest in the gallery above.

Between about 400 and 200 B.C.E. Chavín influence spread widely throughout Peru, from the Nazca valley in the south to beyond Cajamarca in the north. This spread is seen in both the distribution of goods made at Chavín and in the incorporation of Chavín iconography into local traditions. Archaeologists believe Chavín influence reflects the prestige of its cult, not political or military expansion. The florescence of Chavín was also marked by important technological innovations in ceramics, weaving, and metallurgy.

Excavations at Chavín and other Early Horizon sites point to increasing social stratification. Examination of skeletal remains at Chavín, for example, suggests that people who lived closer to the ceremonial center ate better than people living on the margins of the site.

The Early Intermediate Period

Signs of increasing warfare accompany the collapse of the Chavín culture and the ideological unity it had brought to the Andes. The subsequent Early Intermediate period saw increasing regional diversity combined with increasing political centralization and the emergence of what were probably the first territorial states in the Andes. We will discuss briefly here only the two best-known cultures of this period, that of Nazca on the south coast of Peru, and of Moche on the north coast.

Nazca

The Nazca culture, which flourished from about 100 B.C.E. to about 700 C.E., was centered in the Ica and Nazca valleys. The people of the Nazca valley built underground aqueducts to tap ground water in the middle of the valley and divert it into irrigation canals. Cahuachi, the largest Nazca site, was once thought to be a large, permanently occupied

The Nazca Geoglyph located in the Peruvian desert depicts a vast hummingbird. The lines were constructed by the Nazca people probably sometime between 250 C.E. and 600 C.E. They appear to have been sacred paths walked by Nazca people perhaps somewhat as medieval Europeans walked a labyrinth. At the summer solstice the final parallel line points to the sun. The features of this and other geoglyphs can only be discerned from the air, and their exact purpose remains a matter of speculation.
Marilyn Bridges/Corbis Bettman.

urban center. Recent research, however, indicates that it was empty most of the year, filling periodically with pilgrims during religious festivals. It may have been the capital of a Nazca confederation, with each of its many temple platforms representing a member unit.

The earlier Paracas culture on the south coast produced some of the world's finest and most intricate textiles. The Nazca too are renowned for their textiles as well as their fine polychrome pottery, elaborately decorated with images of Andean plants and animals. They may be most famous, however, for their colossal earthworks, or geoglyphs, the so-called Nazca lines. These were created by brushing away the dark gravel of the desert to reveal a lighter-colored surface. Some geoglyphs depict figures like hummingbirds, spiders, and killer whales that appear on Nazca pottery. These are usually located on hillsides visible to passers-by. Others, usually consisting of radiating lines and geometric forms, are drawn on the Nazca pampa flats and are only visible from the air.

Moche

The Moche culture flourished from about 200 to 700 C.E. on the north coast of Peru. At its height it dominated all the coastal river valleys from Piura in the north to Huarmey in the south, a distance of some 370 miles. The culture takes its name from the Moche valley, the location of its largest center next to Cerro Blanco. Two huge structures, the Pyramid of the Sun and the Pyramid of the Moon, overlook this site. The cross-shaped Pyramid of the Sun, the largest adobe structure in the Americas, was some 1,200 feet long by 500 feet wide and rose in steps to a height of 60 feet. It was made with more than 143 million adobe bricks, each of which had a mark that probably identified the group that made it. Archaeologists think the marks enabled Moche lords to be sure that subject groups fulfilled their tribute obligations.

It was once thought that Cerro Blanco was the capital of a unified Moche empire. It appears now, however, that the Moche may not have been so centralized. Instead the Moche area may have been divided into northern and southern realms, and each valley ruled by Moche lords from its own center. Pampa Grande, a Moche site in the Lambayeque valley, was almost as large as Cerro Blanco.

The Moche were skilled potters, producing molded and painted vessels that reveal much about Moche life, religion, and warfare. Realistic portrait vessels may depict actual people. Other vessels provide evidence about the appearance of Moche architecture and the kind of regalia worn by the elite. The discovery in the late 1980s of the undisturbed tombs of Moche rulers at the site of Sipan in the Lambayeque valley and San José de Moro in the Jequete-peque valley suggests that a central theme in Moche iconography—the sacrifice ceremony—was an actual Moche ritual. Depictions of the sacrifice ceremony show elaborately dressed figures drinking the blood of sacrificed prisoners. Archaeologists have labeled one of the central figures the Warrior Priest and another the Priestess. The Moche lord in one of the tombs at Sipan was buried in the regalia of the Warrior Priest, and the occupant of one of the tombs at San José de Moro was buried in the regalia of the Priestess.

The Moche were also the most sophisticated smiths in the Andes. They developed innovative alloys, cast weapons and agricultural tools, and used the lost-wax process to create small, intricate works.

The Middle Horizon Through the Late Intermediate Period

Tiwanaku and Huari

In the fifth century C.E., when the Germanic invasions were leading to the disintegration of the Roman Empire and as Teotihuacán was reaching its height in Mesoamerica, the first expansionist empires were emerging in the Andean highlands. One of these was centered at Tiwanaku in the Bolivian altiplano near the south shore of Lake Titicaca, and the other at Huari, in the south-central highlands of Peru. Although they differ in many ways, both are associated with productive new agricultural technologies, and both show evidence of a form of statecraft that reflects Andean verticality—the practice of sending out settlements to exploit the region's varied ecological zones—and that foreshadows the administrative practices of the later Inca Empire. The artistic symbolism of both also shares many features, suggesting a shared religious ideology. Archaeologists still do not have a firm grip on the chronology of Tiwanaku and Huari or the relationship between them.

Tiwanaku lies at more than 12,600 feet above sea level, making it the highest capital in the ancient world. Construction apparently began at the site about 200 C.E. It began its expansionist phase about 500–600 C.E. and collapsed some 500 years later in the eleventh century. The city occupied one to two square miles, and may have had a population of some 20,000–40,000 people at its height. Laid out on a grid, it is dominated by several large and impressive public structures and ceremonial gateways. The effort expended in transporting the stone for these monuments was enormous and indicates the power of the Tiwanaku rulers over the labor of their subjects.

Moche Earspool. This magnificent ear-spool of gold, turquoise, quartz, and shell was found in the tomb of the Warrior Priest in the Moche site of Sipan, Peru, 300 C.E. *Courtesty of UCLA Fowler Museum of Cultural History/Susan Einstein/Christopher B. Donnan.*

A system of raised-field agriculture on the shores of Lake Titicaca provided Tiwanaku with its economic base. This system involved farming on artificial platforms capped with rich topsoil and separated by basins of water. Experimental reconstructions have shown it to be extremely productive.

Tiwanaku dominated the Titicaca basin and neighboring regions. It probably exerted its influence through its religious prestige and by establishing colonies and religious-administrative structures in distant territories.

The Huari Empire flourished from about 600 to 800 C.E., dominating the highlands from near Cuzco in the south to Cajamarca in the north. For a brief period it also extended a fortified colony into Tiwanaku territory. The capital, Huari, covers about one and a half square miles. It consists of a sprawl of large, high-walled stone enclosures, and had a population of 20,000–30,000 people.

Huari is located in an intermontane valley and its rise is associated with the development of techniques for terracing and irrigating the slopes of the valley to increase their productivity. The spread of this beneficial technology may have facilitated the expansion of the Huari Empire, explaining its acceptance in most places without signs of overt military domination. Huari administrative centers were undefended and built in accessible places. Many archaeologists think they may have functioned like later Inca administrative centers, housing a small Huari elite that organized local labor for state projects. Again like the Inca, Huari administrators used *quipu* record-keeping devices made of string. Inca *quipu*, however, used knots, whereas Huari *quipu* used different colored string.

The Chimu Empire

Although there is evidence of Huari influence on the Peruvian north coast, it is unlikely to have taken the form of direct political control. After the demise of Moche authority, two new states emerged on the north coast. One, named for the site of Sican, was centered in the Lambayeque valley. The central figure in Sican iconography, the Sican Lord, may have been a representation of a mythical founder figure named Nyamlap, mentioned in postconquest Spanish chronicles. Like their Moche predecessors in the Lambayeque valley, the Sican people were skilled smiths who produced sumptuous gold objects.

The other new north coast state, known as Chimu, was centered in the Moche valley. In two waves of expansion the Chimu built an empire that incorporated the Lambayeque Valley and stretched for 800 miles along the coast, from the border of Ecuador in the north to the Chillon valley in the south. The administrative capital of this empire, Chan Chan, in the Moche valley, was a vast city. Its walls enclosed eight square miles and its central core covered over two square miles. The focus of the city are some ten immense adobe-walled enclosures known as *ciudadelas*. With their large open plazas, their administrative and storage facilities, and their large burial mounds, these probably housed the empire's ruling elite. Surrounding them were smaller compounds that probably housed the lesser nobility. And surrounding these were the homes and workshops of the artisans and workers who served the elite. Two areas were apparently transport centers, where llama caravans brought raw materials to the capital from the empire's territories. The total population of the city was between 30,000 and 40,000.

About 1470, only sixty years before the arrival of the Spaniards, the Chimu Empire was swept away by a powerful new state from the southern highlands of Peru, the Inca Empire.

The Inca Empire

In 1532, when Francisco Pizarro and his companions happened on it, the Inca Empire was one of the largest states in the world, rivaling China and the Ottoman Empire in size. Its domains encompassed the area between the Pacific coast and the Amazon basin for some 2,600 miles, from Ecuador to northern Chile (see Map 14–2). Its ethnically and linguistically diverse population numbered in the millions.

The Inca themselves called their domain *Tawantinsuyu,* the Land of the Four Quarters. Their capital, Cuzco, lay at the intersection of these divisions. Home to the ruler (Inca) and the ruling elite, it was a city of great splendor and magnificence. Its principal temples, dedicated to the sun and moon, gleamed with gold and silver.

The origins of the Inca are obscure. According to their own traditions, Inca expansion began only in the fifteenth century in the wake of a revolt of the Chanca people that nearly destroyed Cuzco. Inca Yupanqui, son of the city's aging ruler, led a heroic resistance and crushed the revolt. Assuming the name Pachacuti, he laid the foundations of Inca statecraft; he and his successors expanded their domains to bring the blessings of civilization to the rest of the Andean world. There is clearly an element of imperial propaganda in this legend. The Inca did expand dramatically in the fifteenth century, but archaeological evidence suggests that they had been expanding their influence for decades and perhaps centuries before the Chanca revolt.

The Inca enlarged their empire through a combination of alliance and intimidation as well as conquest. They organized their realm into a hierarchical administrative structure and imposed a version of their language, **Quechua,** as the administrative language of the empire. As a result, Quechua is still widely spoken in the Peruvian Andes. (See Document, "The Incas Organize Their Empire.")

Unlike the Aztecs, who extracted tribute from their subject peoples, the Inca relied on various forms of labor taxation. They divided agricultural lands into several categories, allowing local populations to retain some for their own support and reserving others for the state and the gods. In a system known as the ***mita,*** local people worked for the state on a regular basis, receiving in return gifts and lavish state-sponsored ritual entertainments. Men also served in the army and on public works projects, building cities and roads, for example, and terracing hillsides. In a policy that reflects the Andean practice of colonizing ecologically varied regions, the Inca also designated entire communities as ***Mitimaqs,*** moving them about, sometimes great distances, to best exploit the resources of their empire. They sometimes

Machu Picchu. The Inca city of Machu Picchu perches on a saddle between two peaks on the eastern slopes of the Andes.
Robert Frerk/Odyssey Productions.

The Incas Organize Their Empire
Document

The Incas were remarkable for their ability to organize a vast and diverse empire. One of their chief devices of government was the movement of large groups of people to new, unfamiliar provinces. The Incas were also very sensitive to the power of religion and religious rituals. Once they had moved a population, they required that the chief object of worship belonging to that people be moved to the Inca capital of Cuzco, where it was attended by representatives of its original worshipers. This latter group was changed from time to time, allowing portions of the transferred population to become familiar with the language and customs of the court city of Cuzco. These processes of government are described in the following passage by Bernabé Cobo (1582–1657), a Jesuit, whose account is regarded as among the most complete and accurate discussions of Inca culture.

◆ To what extent did the Incas appear to be following a classic mode of rule by dividing and conquering? How did the Incas use one group to balance the threat to their rule from another group? How did they use religion and language to strengthen their authority?

The first thing that these kings did after conquering a province was to remove six or seven thousand families . . . and to transfer these families to the quiet, peaceful provinces, assigning them to different towns. In their stead they introduced the same number of people, taken from the places to which the former families had been sent or from such other places as seemed convenient. . . . In these transfers of population they saw to it that the migrants, both the newly conquered persons and the others, were moved to lands whose climate and conditions were the same as, or similar to, those which they had left behind them. . . .

The Incas introduced these changes of domicile in order to maintain their rule with greater ease, quiet, and security. . . . [T]hey ordered the majority of the *mitimaes* [the groups transferred] whom they sent to the recently conquered towns to make their homes in the provincial capitals, where they served as garrisons. . . . As soldiers they received certain privileges to make them appear of nobler rank, and they were ordered always to obey the slightest commands of their captains and governors. Under this plan, if the natives revolted, the *mitimaes*, being devoted to the governors, soon reduced them to obedience to the Inca; and if the *mitimaes* rioted they were repressed and punished by

the natives; thus, through this scheme of domiciling the majority of the people of some province in other parts, the king was made secure against revolts in his dominions. . . . The Incas required everyone to absorb their language, laws, and religion with all the beliefs about these matters that were established at Cuzco. . . . In order to introduce and establish these things more effectively, . . . they would remove the principal idol from a conquered province and set it up in Cuzco with the same attendance and worship that it had formerly had; all this was seen to by persons who had come from that province. . . . For this reason Indians from every province of the kingdom were at all times in residence in the capital and court, occupied in guarding and ministering to their own idols. Thus they learned the usages and customs of the court; and when they were replaced by others . . . they taught their people what they had seen and learned in the court.

From *Historia del Nuevo Mundo*, by Bernabé Cobe (Seville, 1890–1893), 3: 222–225; Benjamin Keen, trans., as reprinted in Benjamin Keen, ed., *Readings in Latin American Civilization 1492 to the Present* (Boston: Houghton Mifflin Company, 1955), pp. 29–30.

settled loyal people in hostile regions and moved hostile people to loyal regions.

The Inca employed several groups of people in what amounted to full-time state service. One of these, the **mamakuna,** consisted of women who lived privileged but

celibate and carefully regulated lives in cities and towns throughout the empire. *Mamakuna* might also be given in marriage by Inca rulers to cement alliances. These so-called Virgins of the Sun played an important economic as well as religious role, weaving and brewing the maize beer known as

DEPOCITODELINGA COLLCA

topaynga yupanqui

The Inca *Quipumayoc*. The grand treasurer shown holding a *quipu*, a device made of knotted strings, used to record administrative matters and sacred histories. Information was encoded in the colors of the strings and the style of the knots. *The Granger Collection.*

chicha for the Inca elite. Textiles were highly prized in Andean society, and cloth was a form of wealth among the Incas. *Chicha* had great ritual importance and was consumed at state religious festivals. Another group of full-time state workers, the *yanakuna*, were men whose duties included tending the royal llama herds.

Cloth and clothing were not only a principal source of wealth and prestige in Inca society, they were also a means of communication. Complex textile patterns served as insignia of social status, indicating a person's rank and ethnic affiliation. Textile production was among the forms of labor service required by the state, and Inca warehouses were filled with textiles as well as with food and other craft goods.

The Incas made their presence felt in their empire through regional administrative centers and warehouses linked by a remarkable system of roads. The centers served to organize, house, and feed people engaged in *mita* labor service and to impress upon them the power and beneficence of the state with feasting and ritual. The wealth of the empire, collected in storehouses, sustained the *mita* laborers, fed and clothed the army, and enriched the Inca elite. Although the Inca lacked writing, they kept detailed administrative records on string accounting devices called **quipu**.

To move their armies, administer their domains, and distribute the wealth of their empire efficiently, the Inca built more than 14,000 miles of road. These ranged from narrow paths to wide thoroughfares. Rope suspension bridges crossed gorges and rivers, and stairways eased the ascent of steep slopes. A system of relay runners sped messages to Cuzco from the far reaches of the empire.

Over their long history the people of the Andes developed an adaptation to their challenging environment that allowed them to prosper and grow, bringing more land under cultivation than today. Building on ancient Andean traditions, the Inca appear to have engineered a productive economy that brought its people a measure of well-being that would not survive the destruction of the empire by Spanish invaders.

Summary

Mesoamerica. Mesoamerica means "middle America." It extends from central Mexico to Central America. Although there was no single Mesoamerican civilization, the civilizations of the Olmecs, the peoples of Monte Alban and Teotihuacan, the Maya, the Toltecs, and the Aztecs shared many features: urban centers with monumental buildings arranged on large plazas, writing, a sophisticated calendrical system, religious ideas, including human sacrifice, and the cultivation of certain crops, especially maize and beans. Throughout its history, the cities of Mesoamerica were also linked by trade.

The Aztecs established the largest Mesoamerican state before the coming of the Spanish in the sixteenth century.

The Aztec Empire depended on tribute from conquered peoples. Aztec society was organized for war and was divided into nobles and commoners, with merchants and certain artisans forming intermediate categories. The Aztecs practiced wide-scale human sacrifice; most of the victims were captured warriors. Women could own property and participate in trade but were subordinate to men and excluded from high authority.

Andean South America. Monumental architecture and public buildings in Peru date from the third millennium B.C.E. Over the next 3,000 years, the Andean peoples developed pottery, urban centers, intricate cotton weaving, and sophisticated agriculture. The first expansionist empires emerged in the Andean highlands in the fifth century C.E.

The Incas built the most extensive Andean empire. It extended for 2,600 miles from Ecuador to Chile between the Pacific and the Amazon basin. Inca rule relied on con-

quest, intimidation, and alliances with other peoples. The Inca exacted taxation in terms of forced labor and constructed over 14,000 miles of roads and numerous rope bridges. Although the Inca lacked writing, they kept detailed accounts using knotted strings.

Review Questions

1. Describe the rise of civilization in Mesoamerica and Andean South America. What does it have in common with the rise of civilization in Africa and Eurasia? In what ways was it different?

2. The appearance of monumental architecture in the ancient world was often associated with hierarchical agricultural societies. Was this the case for the Peruvian coast?

INTERPRETING THE PAST

Empires in the New World

In the following primary source documents, very different perspectives of Mesoamerican and South American cultures are readily apparent. These primary sources describe indigenous American cultures in Mesoamerica and South America during the early period of contact by the Spanish in the sixteenth century.

Having built complex societies that were politically expansive, economically prosperous, and religiously devout as well as brutally warlike, indigenous Americans posed something of a contradictory puzzle to the arriving Spanish. Use the following sources to examine how the Aztecs and Incas organized and ruled their empires.

Sources from Chapter 14

"The Aztecs Economically Isolate an Enemy" (p. 420).
"The Incas Organize their Empire" (p. 428)

PRENTICE HALL
myhistorylab
Where it's a good time to connect to the past!

3. What were some of the accomplishments of the Classic civilizations of Mesoamerica? How do they compare with contemporary civilizations elsewhere in the world?

4. How was the Aztec Empire organized? the Inca Empire? How do they compare to the early empires of the ancient world in the Near East, Europe, and Asia?

5. Both the Aztec and Inca Empires fell in the early sixteenth century when confronted with Spanish forces of a few hundred men. What factors might have contributed to their defeat?

Key Terms

calpulli (p. 420)

chicha (p. 429)

Long Count (p. 413)

Mexica (p. 416)

mita (p. 427)

Mitimaqs (p. 427)

mamakuna (p. 428)

obsidian (p. 406)

Quechua (p. 427)

quipu (p. 429)

Note: To learn more about the topics in this chapter, please turn to the Suggested Readings at the end of the book. For additional sources related to this chapter please see the Primary Source DVD at the back of this text or MyHistoryLab.

Questions

After reading the primary sources make note of the specific characteristics of the Tlscalans, Aztecs capital Tenochtitlan, and the Inca empire as described by European chroniclers. What types of development and organization are described. How are the economies of the societies organized? What are the implications of the evident high degree of regulation and hierarchy? How do the writers react to these scenes of a foreign culture?

Selectively choose several details in each account that provide an idea of the writer's attitudes towards these subjects. What factors might explain these reactions by Europeans?

Based on the relations between the Aztecs and the Tlascalans, and the Incas with their neighbors that are portrayed in these sources, how would Europeans use these tensions to their advantage?

Africa ca. 1000–1700

- ◆ North Africa and Egypt
- ◆ The Spread of Islam South of the Sahara
- ◆ Sahelian Empires of the Western and Central Sudan
- ◆ The Eastern Sudan
- ◆ The Forestlands—Coastal West and Central Africa
- ◆ East Africa
- ◆ Southern Africa

THE HISTORY OF AFRICA IN THE FIRST HALF OF THE second millennium C.E. varied considerably for different parts of the continent. Many African regions had substantial interactions with the Islamic and European worlds, while others engaged in trade and cultural exchanges within the continent.

The Atlantic slave trade was the major phenomenon that affected almost all of Africa between the fifteenth and nineteenth centuries and is treated in Chapter 18. However, in this chapter we cannot overlook its importance in disrupting and reconfiguring African economies, social organization, and political life.

We begin with Africa above the equator, where the influence of Islam increased and where substantial empires and kingdoms developed. Then we discuss West, East, central, and southern Africa and the effects of first Arab-Islamic and then European influence in these regions. ◼

Benin Plaque. Some of the world's finest works of art were made by the artists of Benin and Ife, though much is still unknown about them. Rarely found elsewhere in Africa, bronze panels like the plaque shown here adorned the royal palace and are considered examples of "court art." The figures are typical of the Benin style in their proportions of head to body— about one to four—perhaps emphasizing the head's importance as a symbol of life and behavior. *Benin Plaque. Brass. Lost wax. W. Africa 16th–17th century c.e. Hillel Burger/Peabody Museum, Harvard University © President and Fellows of Harvard College. All rights reserved.*

Africa, 1000–1700

Africa

Long-distance trade—the movement of goods, people, and, inevitably, cultural practices and ideas, in patterns driven by supply and demand—is typically an engine of historical change. This was as true in Africa in the early centuries of the second millennium as it was in the Americas, Europe, Asia, or anywhere in the world. Different regions in Africa were oriented differently in relation to trade routes and trading partners, and these regions developed in markedly different ways between 1000 and 1700.

The North African coast and the Sahel were situated amidst trading networks that linked the Mediterranean world, the growing **dar-al-Islam** (the "House of Submission," or Islamic world), and the rich kingdoms of West Africa. The East African coast was integrated into the trading and cultural networks of the Indian Ocean basin and was firmly engaged with the Muslim world. The rest of Sub-Saharan Africa was culturally diverse; people here engaged primarily in intra-African trade with cultures that occupied other ecological niches. It is important to remember that Africa is a continent that is home to many societies with different histories, languages, religions, and cultures. In this way it is similar to Europe, but Africa is also much larger than Europe, and more ethnically and culturally diverse.

Along the Mediterranean, the key new factor in African history at this time was the Ottomans' imperial expansion into Egypt and the **Maghreb**. The long Ottoman hegemony altered the political configuration of the Mediterranean world. Merchants and missionaries carried Islam and Arabian cultural influences across the Sahara from North Africa and the Middle East to the western, central, and Nilotic Sudan (see Map 15-2), where Muslim conversion played a growing social and political role, especially among the ruling elites who profited most from brokering trade between their lands and the Islamic north. Islam provided a shared arena of expression for at least some classes and groups in societies over a vast area from Egypt to Senegambia. In Africa as elsewhere, new converts modified Islam through a process of

North Africa and Egypt

As we saw in Chapter 13, Egypt and other North African societies played a central role in Islamic and Mediterranean history after 1000 C.E. From Tunisia to Egypt, Sunni religious and political leaders and their Shi'ite, especially Isma'ili, counterparts struggled for the minds of the masses. By the thirteenth century, however, the Shi'ites had become a small minority of the Muslim population of Mediterranean Africa. In Egypt a Sunni revival confirmed the Sunni character of Egyptian religiosity and legal interpretation. In general, a feisty regionalism characterized states, city-states, and tribal groups north of the Sahara and along the lower Nile. No single power controlled them for long. Regionalism persisted even after 1500, when most of North Africa came under the influence—and often direct control—of the Ottoman Empire centered in Istanbul and felt the pressure of Ottoman-European naval rivalry in the Mediterranean.

By 1800 the nominally Ottoman domains from Egypt to Algeria were effectively independent. In Egypt the Ottomans had established direct rule after their defeat of the Mamluks in 1517, but by the seventeenth and eighteenth centuries, power had passed to Egyptian governors descended from the earlier Mamluks. These Mamluk governors survived until the rise of Muhammad Ali in the wake of the French invasion of 1800 (see Chapter 27). The Mediterranean coastlands between Egypt and Morocco were officially Ottoman provinces, or regencies. By the eighteenth century, however, Algiers was a separate, locally run principality with an economy based on piracy. Tripoli (in modern Libya) was ruled by a family of hereditary, effectively independent rulers, and Tunisia was virtually independent of its nominal Ottoman overlords.

Morocco, ruled by a succession of *Sharifs* (leaders claiming descent from the family of the Prophet Muhammad), was the only North African sultanate to remain fully independent after 1700. The most important *Sharifian* syncretism. Distinctively African forms of Islam emerged, faithful to the central tenets of the religion, but differing in observances and customs from those of the Arabian cultural sphere, especially in attitudes towards women and relationships between the sexes.

South of the Sahara, dynamic processes of state-building and trade were the main forces for cultural change. In central and southern Africa, except along the east coast, and in the West African forests, older African traditions held sway, and there was little or no evidence of Islam beyond individual Muslims involved in trade. On the east coast, however, Islam influenced the development of the Swahili culture and language, a unique blend of African, Indian, and Arabian traditions, and Islamic traders linked the region to India, China, and the Indies. In sub-Saharan Africa, the spread of Islam took place almost entirely through peaceful means.

Along the Atlantic and Indian Ocean coasts of Africa, the key development of the fifteenth century was the arrival of ships carrying traders and missionaries from Christian Europe. The strength of African societies and the biological dangers to Europeans venturing into the interior meant that most of the trade between the African interior and

Europeans on both coasts remained under the control of Africans for generations. Even before Europeans themselves reached the interior, however, the trade in slaves, weapons, and gold that they fostered greatly altered African political and social structures not only along the coasts but in regions untouched by the outsiders. The European voyages of discovery of the fifteenth and sixteenth centuries presaged the African continent's involvement in a new, expanding and, by the eighteenth century, European-dominated global trading system. This system generally exploited rather than bolstered African development, as the infamous Atlantic slave trade (see Chapter 18) and the South African experience illustrate.

◆ Where in Africa was Islamic influence concentrated? How did Islam spread? What does this reveal about the relationship between commerce and cultural diffusion?

◆ Why did different regions in Africa develop in different ways between 1000 and 1700?

dynasty was that of the Sa'dis (1554–1659). One major reason for Morocco's independence was that its Arab and Berber populations united after 1500 to oppose the Portuguese and the Spaniards.

The Spread of Islam South of the Sahara

Islamic influence in sub-Saharan Africa began as early as the eighth century and by 1800 affected most of the Sudanic belt and the coast of East Africa as far south as modern Zimbabwe. The process was mostly peaceful, gradual, and partial. Conversion to Islam was rare beyond the ruling or commercial classes, and Islamic faith tended to coexist or blend with indigenous ideas and practices. Nevertheless, agents of Islam brought commercial and political changes as well as the Qur'an, new religious practices, and literate culture, which proved as important for subsequent history as any other development. Many

innovations, from architecture and technology to intellectual life and administrative practice, depended on writing and literacy, two major bases for developing large-scale societies and cultures.

Comparison of the spread of Islam in West and central Africa with that in East Africa is instructive. In East Africa, Muslim traders moving down the coastline with the ancient monsoon trade routes had begun to "Islamize" ports and coastal regions even before 800 C.E. From the thirteenth century on, Islamic trading communities and city-states developed along the coast from Mogadishu to Kilwa.

By contrast, in the western and central parts of the continent, Islam was introduced south of the Sahara into the Sudan by overland routes, primarily by traders from North Africa and the Nile valley. Berbers who plied the desert routes (see Chapter 5) to trading towns such as Awdaghast on the edge of the Sahel as early as the eighth century were Islam's chief agents. From there Islam spread south to centers such as Kumbi Saleh and beyond,

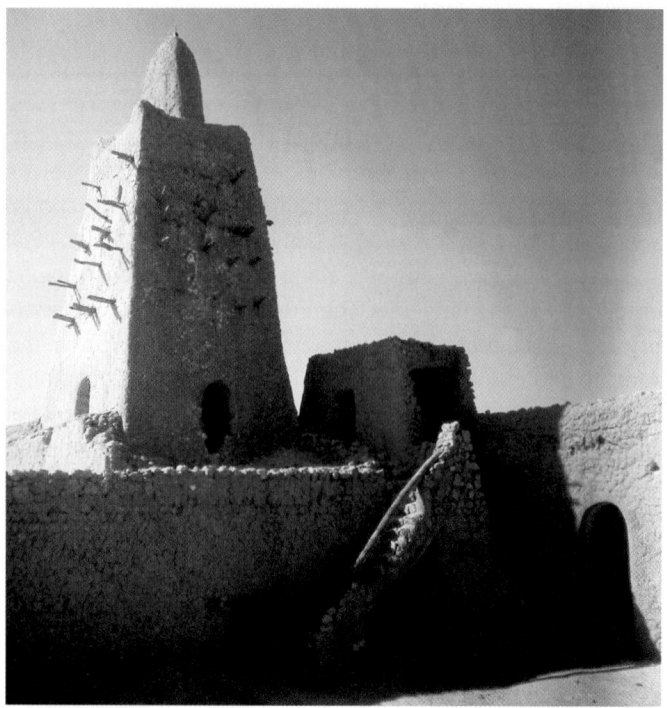

The Great Mosque in Timbuktu. This mud and wood building is typical of western Sudanese mosques. The distinctive tower of the mosque was a symbol of the presence of Islam, which came to places like Timbuktu in central and West Africa by way of overland trade routes. *Werner Forman/ Art Resource, N.Y.*

southeast across the Niger, and west into Senegambia. Another source for the gradual spread of Islam into the central and western Sudan were emigrants from Egypt and the Nilotic Sudan. In particular, migrating Arab tribal groups in search of new land came west to settle in the central sub-Saharan Sahel.

Some Muslim conversion in the western and central Sudan came early, again virtually always through the agency of Muslim traders. The year 985 marks the first time a West African royal court—that of the kingdom of Gao, east of the Niger bend—officially became Muslim (see Chapter 5). The Gao rulers did not, however, try to convert their subjects. By contrast, as we shall see later in the chapter, the rulers of the later kingdom of Ghana long maintained their indigenous traditions even though they traded with Muslims and had Muslim advisers.

From the 1030s zealous militants known as Almoravids (see Chapter 13) began an overt conversion campaign that extended to the western Sahel and Sahara. This movement eventually swept into Ghana's territory, taking first Awdaghast and later, in 1076, Kumbi Saleh. Thereafter, the forcibly converted Soninke ruling group of Ghana spread Islam among their own populace and farther south in the savannah. Here they converted Mande-speaking traders, who brought Islam south into the

forests. Farther west, the Fulbe rulers of Takrur along Senegal became Muslim in the 1030s and propagated their new faith among their subjects. The Fulbe, or Fulani, remained important carriers of Islam over the next eight centuries as they migrated gradually into new regions as far east as Lake Chad, where some rulers were Muslim as early as 1100.

Major groups in West Africa strongly resisted Islamization, especially the Mossi kingdoms founded in the Volta region at Wagadugu around 1050 and Yatenga about 1170.

Sahelian Empires of the Western and Central Sudan

As we noted in Chapter 5, substantial states had risen in the first millennium C.E. in the Sahel regions just south of the Sahara proper.[1] From about 1000 to 1600, four of these developed into relatively long-lived empires: Ghana, Mali, and Songhai in the western Sudan, and Kanem-Bornu in the central Sudan.

Ghana

Ghana established the model for later empires of the Sahel region of the western Sudan. It was located well north of modern Ghana (and unrelated to it except by name) in the region between the inland Niger Delta and the upper Senegal to the north. A Ghanaian kingdom originated as early as 400–600 C.E., but Ghana emerged as a regional power only near the end of the first millennium and flourished for about two centuries. Its capital, Kumbi (or Kumbi Saleh), on the desert's edge, was well sited for the Saharan and Sahelian trade networks. Ghana's major population group was the Soninke. (*Ghana* is the Soninke term for "ruler.")

The Ghanaian rulers were descended matrilineally (through the previous king's sister). They ruled through a council of ministers. The reports we have, especially from the eleventh-century Muslim writer al-Bakri (see Document, "Ghana and Its People in the Mid–Eleventh Century"), indicate that the king was supreme judge and held court regularly to hear grievances. The royal ceremonies reported to have been held in Kumbi Saleh were embellished with the full trappings of regal wealth and power appropriate to a king held to be divinely blessed if not semidivine himself.

In Ghana's hierarchical society, slaves were at the bottom; farmers and draftsmen above them; merchants above

---

[1] S. K. and R. J. McIntosh, *Prehistoric Investigations at Jenne, Mali* (1980), pp. 41–59, 434–461; R. Oliver, *The African Experience* (New York: Harper-Collins, 1991), pp. 90–101.

them; and the king, his court, and the nobility on top. Ghana's power rested on a solid economic base. Tribute from the empire's many chieftaincies and taxes on royal lands and crops supplemented duties levied on all incoming and outgoing trade. This trade, both north–south between the Sahara and the savannah and especially east–west through the Sahel between Senegambia and more easterly trading towns like Gao on the Niger Bend, involved a variety of goods. Most notably, imported salt, cloth, and metal goods such as copper from the north were probably exchanged for gold and perhaps kola nuts from the south. The regime apparently also controlled the gold (and, presumably, the slave) trade that originated in the savannah to the south and west, in the tributary regions of the Bambuk and Galam regions of the middle Senegal and its southern tributary, the Faleme, and in the Boure region of the upper Niger and its tributaries.

Although the king and court of Ghana did not convert to Islam, they made elaborate arrangements to accommodate Muslim traders and government servants in their own settlement a few miles from the royal preserve in Kumbi Saleh. Muslim traders were prominent in the court, literate Muslims administered the government, and Muslim legists advised the ruler.

A huge, well-trained army secured royal control and enabled the kings to extend their sway in the late tenth century to the Atlantic shore and to the south (see Map 15–1).

Ghana and Its People in the Mid–Eleventh Century

Document

The Spanish Muslim geographer al-Bakri (d. 1094) seems never to have visited West Africa himself. Nonetheless, his writings were considered authoritative. Here he describes customs of the ruler and people of the capital of Ghana based on information he carefully gleaned from other Arabic sources and travelers.

◆ How did the ruler of Ghana deal with the differing religious groups in his capital?

Ghana is a title given to their kings; the name of the region is Awkar, and their king today, namely in the year 460 [1067–8 C.E.], is Tanka Manin. . . . This Tanka Manin is powerful, rules an enormous kingdom, and possesses great authority.

The city of Ghana consists of two towns situated on a plain. One of these towns, which is inhabited by Muslims, is large and possesses twelve mosques, in one of which they assemble for the Friday prayer. There are salaried imams and muezzins, as well as jurists and scholars. In the environs are wells with sweet water, from which they drink and with which they grow vegetables. The king's town is six miles distant from this one and bears the name of Al-Ghaba. Between these two towns there are continuous habitations. The houses of the inhabitants are of stone and acacia wood. The king has a palace and a number of domed dwellings all surrounded with an enclosure like a city wall. In the king's town, and not far from his court of justice, is a mosque where the Muslims who arrive at his court . . . pray. Around the king's town are domed buildings and groves and thickets where the sorcerers of these people, men in charge of the religious cult, live. In them too are their idols and the tombs of their kings. . . .

All of them shave their beards, and women shave their heads. The king adorns himself like a woman [wearing necklaces] round his neck and [bracelets] on his forearms, and he puts on a high cap (tartur) decorated with gold and wrapped in a turban of fine cotton. He sits in audience or to hear grievances against officials (mazalim) in a domed pavilion around which stand ten horses covered with gold-embroidered materials. Behind the king stand ten pages holding shields and swords decorated with gold, and on his right are the sons of the [vassal] kings of his country wearing splendid garments and their hair plaited with gold. The governor of the city sits on the ground before the king and around him are ministers seated likewise. . . . When the people who profess the same religion as the king approach him they fall on their knees and sprinkle dust on their heads, for this is their way of greeting him. As for the Muslims, they greet him only by clapping their hands.

Their religion is paganism and the worship of idols (dakakir). When their king dies they construct over the place where his tomb will be an enormous dome of saj wood. Then they bring him on a bed covered with a few carpets and cushions and place him beside the dome. At his side they place his ornaments, his weapons, and the vessels from which he used to eat and drink, filled with various kinds of food and beverages.

From J. F. P. Hopkins, trans.; N. Levtzion and J. F. P. Hopkins, eds., *Corpus of Early Arabic Sources for West African History*. Reprinted with permission of Cambridge University Press, pp. 79–80.

Map Exploration

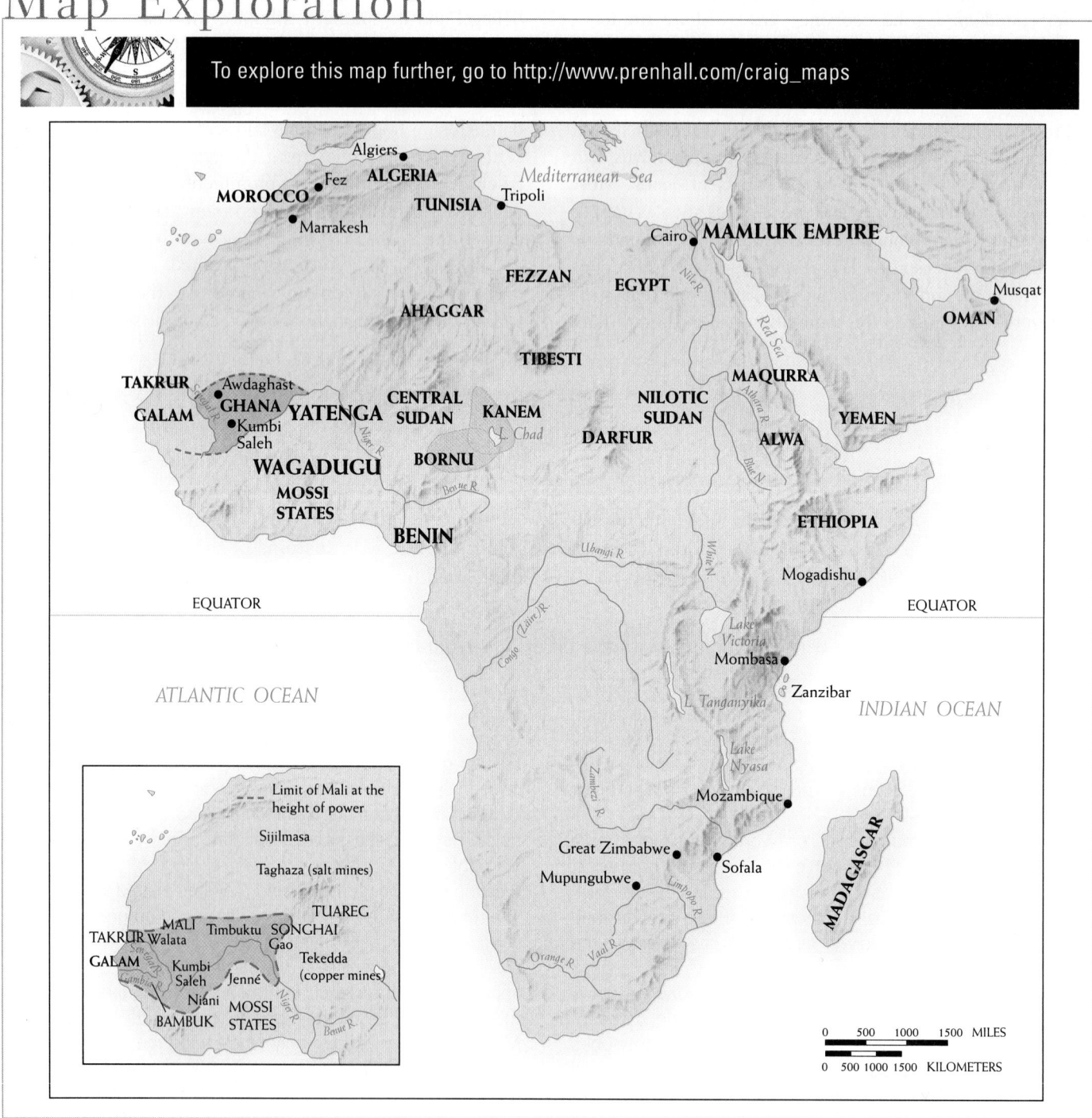

To explore this map further, go to http://www.prenhall.com/craig_maps

Map 15–1. Africa ca. 900–1500. Shown are major cities and states referred to in the text. The main map shows the region of West Africa occupied by the empire of Ghana from ca. 990 to ca. 1180. The inset shows the region occupied by Mali between 1230 and 1450.

Ghanaian troops captured Awdaghast, the important southern terminus of the trans-Saharan trade route to Morocco, from the Berbers in 992. The empire was, however, vulnerable to attack from the desert fringe, as Almoravid Berber forces proved in 1054 when they took Awdaghast in a single raid.

Ghana's empire was probably destroyed in the late twelfth century by the anti-Muslim Soso people from the mountains southeast of Kumbi Saleh; they were a Malinke clan who had long been part of the Ghanaian Empire. Their brief ascendancy between 1180 and 1230 apparently spelled the end of the once great transregional power centered at Kumbi.[2]

Mali

With Ghana's collapse and the Almoravids' failure to build a new empire below the Sahara (largely because of their focus on North Africa), the western Sudan broke up into smaller kingdoms. The former Ghanaian provinces of Mande and Takrur were already independent before 1076, and in the early twelfth century Takrur's control of the Senegal valley and the gold-producing region of Galam made it briefly the strongest state in the western Sudan. Like Ghana, however, it was soon eclipsed, first by the brief Soso ascendancy and then by the rise of Mali.

In the mid–thirteenth century the Keita ruling clan of a Ghanaian successor kingdom, Mali, forged a new and lasting empire. This empire seems to have been built on the same economic base as that of Ghana and Takrur earlier: monopolization of the lucrative north–south gold trade. The Keita kings dominated enough of the Sahel to control the flow of West African gold from the Senegal regions and the forest lands south of the Niger to the trans-Saharan trade routes, and the influx of copper and salt in exchange. Because they were farther south than their Ghanaian predecessors had been, in the fertile land along the Niger, they were better placed to control all trade on the upper Niger and to add to it the Gambia and Senegal trade to the west. They also used captives for plantation labor in the Niger inland delta to produce surplus food for trade.

Agriculture and cattle farming were the primary occupations of Mali's population and, together with the gold trade, the mainstays of the economy. Rice was grown in the river valleys and millet in the drier parts of the Sahel. Together with beans, yams, and other agricultural products, this made for a plentiful food supply. Fishing flourished along the Niger and elsewhere. Cattle, sheep, and goats were plentiful. The chief craft specialties were metalworking (iron and gold) and weaving of cotton grown within the empire.

The Malinke, a southern Mande-speaking people of the upper Niger region, formed the core population of the new state. They apparently lived in walled urban settlements typical of the western savannah region. Each walled town was surrounded by its own agricultural land, held perhaps 1,000 to 15,000 people, and presumably had enough arable land within its walls to deal with siege. Each was linked to neighboring cities by trade and possibly intermarriage.

The Keita dynasty had converted early to Islam, around 1100 C.E. Keita's rulers even claimed descent from Muham-

The Great Mosque at Jenne. Jenne was one of the important commercial centers controlled by the empire of Mali in the thirteenth and fourteenth centuries. The thriving market in front of the mosque reflects the enduring vitality of trade and commerce in the region.

mad's famous ***muezzin*** Bilal ibn Ribah, a former black slave from Abyssinia whose son was said to have settled in the Mande-speaking region. During Mali's heyday in the thirteenth and fourteenth centuries, its kings often made the pilgrimage to Mecca. From their travel in the central Islamic lands, they brought back with them not only military aids, such as large Barbary war horses, but also new ideas about political and military organization. Through Muslim traders' networks, Islam also connected Mali to other areas of Africa, especially those to the east.

Mali's imperial power was built largely by the Keita King Sundiata (or Sunjaata, r. 1230–1255). Sundiata and his successors exploited their agricultural resources, significant population growth, and Malinke commercial skills to build an empire even more powerful than that of Ghana. Sundiata extended his control west to the Atlantic coast and east

---

[2] D. Conrad and H. Fisher, "The Conquest That Never Was: Ghana and the Almoravids, 1076," *History in Africa* 9 (1982): 1–59; 10 (1983): 53–78.

Mansa Musa, King of Mali. The fourteenth century Catalan Atlas shows King Mansa Musa of Mali, seated on a throne holding a nugget of gold. A rider on a camel approaches him. *The Granger Collection.*

beyond Timbuktu. By controlling the commercial entrepôts of Gao, Walata, and Jenne, he dominated the Saharan as well as the Niger trade. He built his capital, Niani, into a major city. Niani was located on a tributary of the Niger in the savannah at the edge of the forest in a gold- and iron-rich region. It had access to the forest trade products of gold, kola nuts, and palm oil; it was easily defended by virtue of its surrounding hills; and it was readily reached by river.

The empire that Sundiata and his successors built ultimately encompassed three major regions and language groups of Sudanic West Africa: (1) the Senegal region (including Takrur), occupied by speakers of the West Atlantic Niger-Kongo language group (including Fulbe, Tukulor, Wolof, Serer); (2) the central Mande states between Senegal and Niger, occupied by the Niger-Kongo-speaking Soninke and Mandinke peoples; and (3) the peoples of the Niger in the Gao region who spoke Songhai, the only Nilo-Saharan language west of the Lake Chad basin. Mali was less a centralized bureaucratic state than the center of a vast sphere of influence that included provinces and tribute-paying kingdoms. Many individual chieftaincies were independent but recognized the sovereignty of the supreme, sacred **mansa**, or "emperor," of the Malian realms.

The greatest Keita king proved to be Mansa Musa (r. 1312–1337), whose pilgrimage through Mamluk Cairo to Mecca in 1324 became famous. He paid out or gave away so much gold in Cairo alone that he started massive inflation lasting over a decade. He returned with many Muslim scholars, artists, and architects. At home, he consolidated Mali's power, securing peace for most of his reign throughout his vast dominions. Musa's devoutness as a Muslim fostered the spread of Islam in the empire and beyond. Under his rule, Timbuktu

SOURCE *Al-Umari Describes Mansa Musa*

became famous for its *madrasas* and libraries, and for its poets, scientists, and architects, making it the leading intellectual center of sub-Saharan Islam and a major trading city of the Sahel—roles it retained long after Mali's imperial sway ended.[3]

Mali's dominance waned after Musa, evidently as the result of rivalries for the throne. Eventually the empire withered, and after 1450 a new Songhai power in Gao to the east ended Mali's imperial authority.

Songhai

Evidence suggests that as early as the eleventh or twelfth century there was a Songhai kingdom around Gao, on the eastern arc of the great bend of the Niger. In 1325 Mansa Musa brought this kingdom and the Gao region under the control of Mali and the Malinke. Mali's domination ended with the rise of a dynasty in Gao known as the Sunni or Sonni around 1375. The kingdom became an imperial power, under the greatest Sunni ruler, Sonni Ali (r. 1464–1492). For more than a century thereafter the Songhai Empire was arguably the most powerful state in Africa (see Map 15–2). With a strong military built around a riverboat flotilla and cavalry, Sonni Ali took Jenne and Timbuktu. He pushed the Tuareg Berbers back into the northern Sahel and Sahara and stifled threats from the southern forestland.

His successor Askia Muhammad al-Turi (r. 1493–1528) continued Sonni Ali's expansionist policies. Between them, Sonni Ali and Askia Muhammad built an empire that stretched west nearly to the Atlantic, northwest into the

---

[3] For more on Mali, especially its wealth and Timbuktu's role as a center of scholarship, see E. Gilbert and J. T. Reynolds, *Africa in World History: From Prehistory to the Present* (Upper Saddle River: Prentice Hall, 2004), pp. 91–93.

Sahara, and east into the central Sudan. Taking advantage of their control of access to the gold and other desirable commodities of West Africa, they emulated their Ghanaian predecessors in cultivating and expanding the ancient caravan trade across the Sahara to the North African coasts of Libya and Tunisia. This provided their major source of wealth.

Unlike Sonni Ali, who held to the traditional African religious faith of his people, Muhammad al-Turi was an enthusiastic Muslim. He built up the Songhai state after the model of the Islamic empire of Mali. (See Document, "Muslim Reform in Songhai.") In his reign, many Muslim scholars came to Gao, Timbuktu, and Jenne. He

Map Exploration

To explore this map further, go to http://www.prenhall.com/craig_maps

Map 15–2. Africa ca. 1500–1700. Important towns, regions, peoples, and states. The inset shows the empire of Songhai at its greatest extent in the early sixteenth century.

Muslim Reform in Songhai

Document

Around 1500 Askia Muhammad al-Turi, the first Muslim among the rulers of Songhai, wrote to the North African Muslim theologian Muhammad al-Maghili (d. 1504) about proper Muslim practices. In these excerpts from al-Turi's seventh question, we see the zeal of the new convert to conform to traditional religious norms, as well as the king's desire for bettering social order and his concern for justice. The answers from al-Maliki reflect the puritanical "official line" of the conservative *ulama* who did not want to allow syncretism to emerge among newly converted groups.

◆ What are the problems and corresponding solutions described in the letters? Which problem did al-Maghili find most serious? Why? Which do you think would have been most serious? Why?

FROM ASKIA MUHAMMAD AL-TURI'S SEVENTH QUESTION

Among the people [of the Songhay Empire], there are some who claim knowledge of the supernatural through sand divining and the like, or through the disposition of the stars . . . [while] some assert that they can write (talismans) to bring good fortune . . . or to ward off bad fortune. . . . Some defraud in weights and measures. . . .

One of their evil practices is the free mixing of men and women in the markets and streets and the failure of women to veil themselves . . . [while] among the people of Djenné [Jenne] it is an established custom for a girl not to cover any part of her body as long as she remains a virgin . . . and all the most beautiful girls walk about naked among people. . . .

So give us legal ruling concerning these people and their ilk, and may God Most High reward you!

FROM MUHAMMAD AL-MAGHILI'S ANSWER

The answer—and God it is who directs to the right course—is that everything you have mentioned concerning people's behavior in some parts of this country is gross error. It is the bounden duty of the commander of the Muslims and all other believers who have the power to change every one of these evil practices.

As for any who claims knowledge of the supernatural in the ways you have mentioned . . . he is a liar and an unbeliever. . . . Such people must be forced to renounce it by the sword. Then whoever renounces such deeds should be left in peace, but whoever persists should be killed with the sword as an unbeliever; his body should not be washed or shrouded, and he should not be buried in a Muslim graveyard. . . .

As for defrauding in weights and measures it is forbidden (*haram*) according to the Qur'an, the Sunna and the consensus of opinion of the learned men of the Muslim community. It is the bounden duty of the commander of the Muslims to appoint a trustworthy man in charge of the markets, and to safeguard people's means of subsistence. He should standardize all the scales in each province. . . . Similarly, all measures both large and small must be rectified so that they conform to a uniform standard. . . .

Now, what you mentioned about the free mixing of men and women and leaving the pudenda uncovered is one of the greatest abominations. The commander of the Muslims must exert himself to prevent all these things. . . . He should appoint trustworthy men to watch over this by day and night, in secret and in the open. This is not to be considered as spying on the Muslims; it is only a way of caring for them and curbing evildoers, especially when corruption becomes widespread in the land as it has done in Timbuktu and Djenné [Jenne] and so on.

From *The African Past*, trans. by J. O. Hunwick, reprinted in Basil Davidson (Grosset and Dunlap, The Universal Library), pp. 86–88. Reprinted by permission of Curtis Brown Ltd. Copyright © 1964 by Basil Davidson.

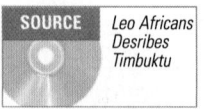

SOURCE Leo Africans Desribes Timbuktu

appointed Muslim judges (*qadis*) in towns throughout the empire and made Timbuktu a major intellectual and legal training center for the whole Sudan. He also replaced native Songhais with Arab Muslim immigrants as government officials to strengthen his centralized power. Like Mansa Musa before him, Muhammad made a triumphal pilgrimage to Mecca, where he was hailed as "Caliph of the western Sahara." From his vast royal treasury he supported the poor and the

Chronology

Sahelian Empires of the Western Sudan

ca. 990–ca. 1180?	Empire of Ghana
1076	Ghana loses Awdaghast to Almoravids
1180–1230	Soso clan briefly controls the old Ghanaian territories
ca. 1230–1450	Empire of Mali, founded by Sundiata
1230–1255	Reign of Sundiata
1312–1337	Reign of Mansa Musa
1374	Independent Songhai state emerges in Gao after throwing off Malian rule
ca. 1450–1600	Songhai Empire at Gao
1464–1492	Reign of Sonni Ali
1464–1591	Askia dynasty
1493–1528	Reign of Askia Muhammad al-Turi
1549–1583	Reign of Askia Dawud
1590s	Collapse of the Songhai Empire

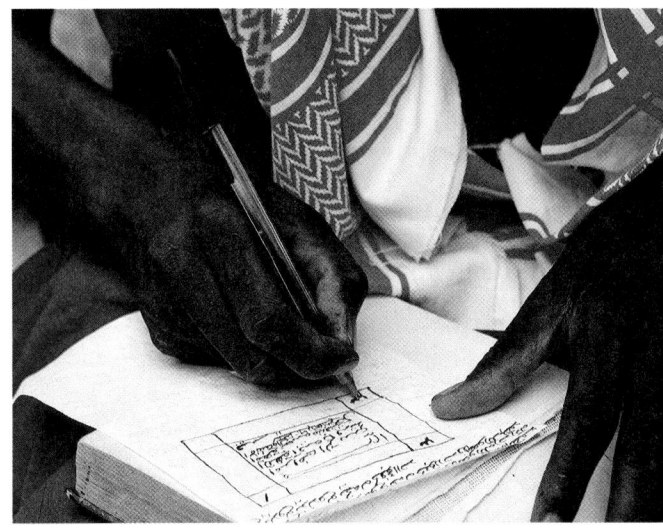

A Marabout Creates a *Grigri*. A verse from the Koran is copied onto a piece of paper, which will be folded and put in a leather pouch. The pouch is worn as an amulet, to protect the wearer from sickness, harm, or evil.

Sufi leaders, or ***marabouts***, and built mosques throughout the realm. Nevertheless, he failed to Islamize the empire or to ensure a strong central state for his successors.

The last powerful Askia leader was Askia Dawud (r. 1549–1583), under whom Songhai economic prosperity and intellectual life achieved its apogee. The trans-Saharan trade reached new heights, and royal patronage of the arts rose to new levels. Still, difficulties mounted. The Askia battled the Mossi to the south and Berber forces from the north. Civil war broke out over succession to the throne in 1586, and the empire was divided. In 1591 an assay sent by the Sa'dis of Morocco used superior gunpowder weapons, coupled with the aid of disaffected Songhai princes, to defeat the last Askia of Gao at Tondibi, and the Gao Empire collapsed.

Kanem and Kanem-Bornu

A fourth sizable Sahelian empire—in the central Sudan—arose after 1100. Called Kanem, it began as a southern Saharan confederation of the nomadic tribes known as Zaghawah that were spread over much of the south-central and southeastern Sahara. By the twelfth century a Zaghawah group known as the Kanuri had apparently settled in Kanem, and from there they began a campaign of military expansion during the thirteenth century. Their key leader in this, Mai Dunama Dibbalemi (r. ca. 1221–1259), was a contemporary of Sundiata in Mali. Like Sundiata, Dibbalemi was a Muslim, and Islam appears to have entrenched itself among the Kanuri ruling class during his reign. Dibbalemi used it to sanction his rule, which otherwise had the familiar African trappings of sacred kingship. It also provided a rationale for expansion through *jihad*, or holy "struggle" against polytheists.

Dibbalemi and his successors expanded Kanuri power north into the desert to include the Fezzan in modern Libya and northeast along the Sahel-Sahara fringe toward Nilotic Africa. In both directions they controlled important trade routes—north to Libya and east to the Nile and Egypt. The next two centuries saw the mixing of Kanuri and local Kanembu peoples, primarily those known as the So. There was a corresponding transformation of the Kanuri leader from a nomadic ***shaykh*** to a Sudanic king and a shift of Kanem from a nomadic to a largely sedentary kingdom with quasi-feudal institutions. Like Mali to the west, Kanem's dominion was of two kinds: direct rule over and taxation of core territories and groups, and indirect control over and collection of tribute from a wider region of vassal chieftaincies. Islamic acculturation progressed most rapidly in the core territories under direct rule.

Civil strife, largely over the royal succession, weakened the Kanuri state in the later fourteenth and fifteenth centuries. After 1400 the locus of power shifted from Kanem proper westward, to the land of Bornu, southwest of Lake Chad. Here, at the end of the fifteenth century, a new Kanuri empire arose almost simultaneously with the collapse of the Askia dynasty of the Songhai Empire at Gao. Near the end of

Chronology

Central Sudanic Empires

ca. 1100–1500	Kanuri empire of Kanem
ca. 1220s–1400	Height of empire of Kanem
ca. 1221–1259	Reign of Mai Dunama Dibbalemi
ca. 1575–1610	Reign of Idris Alawma, major architect of the state
ca. 1575–1846	Kanuri empire of Kanem-Bornu

the sixteenth century firearms and Turkish military instructors enabled the Kanuri leader Idris Alawma (r. ca. 1575–1610) to unify Kanem and Bornu. He set up an avowedly Islamic state and extended his rule as far as Hausaland, between Bornu and the Niger River. The center of trading activity as well as political power and security now shifted from the Niger Bend east to the territory under Kanuri control.

Deriving its prosperity from the trans-Saharan trade, Idris Alawma's regional empire survived for nearly a century. It was finally broken up by a long famine, repeated Tuareg attacks, lack of strong leadership, and loss of control over trade to smaller, better-organized Hausa states. The ruling dynasty held out until 1846, but by 1700 its power had been sharply reduced by the growing Hausa states to the west in what is now northern Nigeria. Their real power came only in the nineteenth century with their unification under the Fulani sultanate of Sokoto (see Chapter 27).

The Eastern Sudan

The Christian states of Maqurra and Alwa in the Nilotic Sudan, or Nubia, lasted for more than 600 years from their early-seventh-century beginnings and maintained political, religious, and commercial contact with Egypt, the Red Sea world, and much of the Sudan.

After 1000 C.E. Maqurra and Alwa continued treaty relations with their more powerful northern Egyptian neighbors. However, the Mamluks intervened repeatedly in Nubian affairs, and Arab nomads constantly threatened the Nubian states. From late Fatimid times onward, both Maqurra and Alwa were increasingly subject to immigrating Muslim Arab tribesmen, and to traders and growing Muslim minorities. The result was a long-term intermingling of Arabic and Nubian cultures and the creation of a new Nilotic Sudanese people and culture.

A significant factor in the gradual disappearance of Christianity in Nubia was its elite character there and its association with the foreign Egyptian world of Coptic Christianity. Maqurra became officially Muslim at the beginning of the fourteenth century, although Christianity survived until late in the same century. The Islamization of Alwa came somewhat later, most effectively under the long-lived Funj sultanate that replaced the Alwa state.

The Funj state flourished between the Blue and White Niles and to the north along the main Nile from just after 1500 until 1762. The Funj were originally cattle nomads who apparently adopted Islam soon after setting up their kingdom. During the late sixteenth and the seventeenth centuries, the Funj developed an Islamic society whose Arabized character was unique in sub-Saharan Africa. A much reduced Funj state held out until an Ottoman Egyptian invasion in 1821.

The Forestlands—Coastal West and Central Africa

West African Forest Kingdoms: The Example of Benin

Many states, some with distinct political, religious, and cultural traditions, had developed in the southern and coastal regions of West Africa before the fifteenth century. Even those states like Asante or the Yoruba kingdoms of Oyo and Ife, which reached their height only after 1500, had much earlier origins. Benin, the best known of these forest kingdoms, reflects the sophistication of West African culture before 1500; its art, in particular, is renowned for its enduring beauty.

Benin State and Society The Edo speakers of Benin have occupied the southern Nigerian region between Yorubaland and the Ibo peoples east of the lower Niger for millennia. Traditional Edo society is organized according to a patrilineal system emphasizing primogeniture. The village is the fundamental political unit, and authority is built around the organization of males into age-grade units.[4]

According to archaeological evidence, the local traditions of the Edo culture of Benin were closely linked to those of Ife, one of the most prominent Yoruba states northwest of Benin. Some kind of distinct kingdom of Benin likely existed as early as the twelfth century, and traditional accounts of both Ife and Edo agree that an Ife prince was sent to rule in Benin around 1300. There are indications that the power of the *oba*, or king, at this time was sharply limited by the Edo leaders who invited the foreign ruler. These leaders were known as the ***uzama***, an order of hereditary indigenous chiefs. Accord-

---

[4] A. F. C. Ryder, *Benin and the Europeans, 1485–1897* (New York: Longman, 1969), p. 1. Ryder's work is a basic reference for the following brief summary about Benin.

ing to tradition, the fourth **oba** managed to wrest more control from these chiefs and instituted something of the ceremonial authority of absolute monarchy. However, only in the fifteenth century, with King Ewuare, did Benin become a royal autocracy and a large state of major regional importance.

Ewuare rebuilt the capital—known today as Benin City—and named it and his kingdom Edo. He apparently established a government in which he had sweeping authority, although he exercised it in light of the deliberations of a royal council. Ewuare formed this council not only from the palace *uzama*, but also from the townspeople. He gave each chief specific administrative responsibilities and rank in the government hierarchy. Ewuare and his successors developed a tradition of military kingship and engaged in major wars of expansion, both into Yorubaland to the west and Ibo country to the east, across the Niger River. They also claimed for the office of *oba* an increasing ritual authority that presaged more radical developments in the king's role.

In the seventeenth century the *oba* was transformed from a military leader into a religious figure with supernatural powers. Human sacrifice, specifically of slaves, seems to have accompanied the cult of deceased kings and became even more frequent later, in the nineteenth century. The succession by primogeniture was discontinued, and the *uzama* chose *obas* from any branch of the royal family.

Benin Art   The global significance of Benin, however, lies in its court art, especially its famous brass sculptures. The splendid terra-cotta, ivory, and brass statuary sculpture of Ife-Benin are among the glories of human creativity. Some scholars trace the artistic and technical lineage of these magnificent sculptures to the sculptures of the Nok culture of ancient West Africa (see Chapter 5).

The best sculptures are cast bronze plaques depicting legendary and historical scenes. These were mounted in the royal palace in Benin City before the sixteenth century. There are also brass heads, apparently of royalty, that resemble the many life-size terra-cotta and brass heads found at Ife. The heads at Ife are held to represent the Oni, or religious chief of ancient Ife, or particular ancestors, who are thereby reverently remembered by their descendants.

Head of a King, from Ife, ca. thirteenth century C.E. The serene classicism of Ife art is equaled only by that of ancient Greece. *Head of a King, from Ife. c. thirteenth century C.E. Brass, height 11⁷/₁₆" (29 cm). © Frank Willett.*

Similar sculptures have been found both to the north and in the Niger Delta. Recent excavations east of the Niger at Igbo-Ukwu have unearthed stunning terra cottas and bronzes that belong to the same general artistic culture, which is dated as early as the ninth century. These artifacts testify to the high cultural level attained in traditional African societies.

European Arrivals on the Coastlands

Along the coasts of West and central Africa, many important changes occurred between 1500 and 1800. Those wrought by the burgeoning Atlantic slave trade are the most notorious (see Chapter 18). Of comparable importance are changes connected with trade in West African gold and other commodities and the effects associated with the importation and spread in West and central Africa of food crops, such as maize, peanuts, squash, sweet potatoes, cocoa, and cassava (manioc) from the Americas. The gradual involvement of Africa in the emerging global economic system paved the way

Chronology

Benin

ca. 1100–1897	Benin state
ca. 1300	First Ife king of Benin state
1440–1475	Reign of Ewuare

Benin Bronze Plaque.   From the palace of the *obas* of Benin, it dates to the Edo period of Benin culture, 1575–1625. It depicts two Portuguese males, perhaps a father and son, holding hands. The figures probably represent the traders or government officials who came to the African coasts in increasing numbers from the end of the fifteenth century on. *Werner Forman, Art Resource, N.Y.*

for eventual colonial domination of the continent, especially its coastal regions, by the Europeans. The European names for segments of the coastline—the Grain (or Pepper) Coast, the Ivory Coast, the Gold Coast, and the Slave Coast—identify the main exports that could be extracted by ship.

Senegambia In West Africa, Senegambia—which takes its name from the Senegal and Gambia Rivers—was one of the earliest regions affected by European trade. Its interior had long been involved in both trans-Saharan trade and east–west trade in the Sahel and the savannah, especially in the heydays of the empires of Ghana, Mali, and Songhai. Senegambia's maritime trade with European powers, like the older overland trade, was primarily in gold and products such as salt, cotton goods, hides, and copper. For roughly a century Senegambian states also provided slaves for European purchase; indeed, perhaps a third of all African slaves exported during the sixteenth century came from Senegambia. Thereafter, however, the focus of the slave trade shifted

south and east along the coast (see Chapter 18). Over time, Portuguese-African mulattos and the British came to control the Gambia River trade, while the French won the Senegal River markets.

The Gold Coast The Gold Coast, like Senegambia, was one of the West African coastal districts most affected by the arrival of international maritime trade. The name derives from the region's importance after 1500 as the outlet for the more southern of West Africa's gold fields in the forestland of Akan. Here, beginning with the Portuguese at Elmina in 1481, but primarily after 1600, European states and companies built coastal forts to protect their trade and to serve as depots for inland goods. The trade in gold, kola nuts, and other commodities seems to have encouraged the growth of larger states in the region, perhaps because they could better handle and control the overland commerce.

The intensive contact of the Gold Coast with Europeans also led to the importation and spread of American crops, notably maize and cassava. The success of these crops in West and central Africa likely contributed to substantial population growth in the sixteenth and seventeenth centuries.

The Gold Coast escaped the ravages of the slave trade for some decades; it was even an importer of slaves until long after 1500. Slaves, however, became big business here in the late seventeenth century, especially in the Accra region. The economy was so disrupted by the slave trade that gold mining declined sharply. Eventually more gold came into the Gold Coast from the sale of slaves than went out from its mines (see Chapter 18).

Central Africa

The vast center of the continent is bounded by swamps in the north, coastal rain forests to the west, highlands to the east, and deserts in the south. Before 1500 these natural barriers impeded international contact and trade with the interior. They also shaped the two-pronged route by which Bantu peoples and languages moved, over many centuries, from western and west-central Africa south into the Zaire basin and east around the equatorial forest into the lakes of highland East Africa. In the tropical central area, regional interaction in movements of peoples and in trade and culture had always been the norm. Here as elsewhere in Africa, however, large as well as small political, economic, and social units could be found. Peoples such as the Lunda and the Luba, for example, on the southern savannah below the rain forest, carved out sizable kingdoms by the fifteenth century and expanded their control over neighboring areas into the eighteenth century.

The Portuguese came to the western coastal regions looking for gold and silver but found none. Ultimately, their main export was slaves. These slaves were taken first for gang labor to the Portuguese sugar plantations on Sao Thomé island in the Gulf of Guinea and then, in vast numbers, to perform similar plantation labor in Brazil. In the 1640s the Dutch briefly succeeded the Portuguese as the major suppliers of African slaves to English and French plantations in the Caribbean.

The Kongo Kingdom Kongo was the major state with which the Portuguese dealt after coming to central Africa in 1483. Dating from probably the fourteenth century, the Kongo kingdom was located on a fertile, well-watered plateau south of the lower Zaïre River valley, between the coast and the Kwango River in the east. Here, astride the border between forest and grassland, the Kongo kings had built a central government based on a pyramid structure of tax or tribute collection. The king's authority was tied to acceptance of him as a kind of spiritual spokesman of the gods or ancestors. By 1600 Kongo was half the size of England and boasted a high state of specialization in weaving and pottery, salt production, fishing, and metalworking.

The Portuguese brought Mediterranean goods, preeminently luxury textiles from North Africa, to trade for central African goods. Such imported luxuries augmented the prestige and wealth of the ruler and his elites. Slaves became the primary export that could be used to obtain foreign luxuries. Meanwhile, imports such as fine clothing, tobacco, and alcohol did nothing to replace the labor pool lost to slavery.

At first the Portuguese put time and effort into education and Christian proselytizing, but the need for more slaves eventually outweighed these concerns. Regional rulers sought to procure slaves from neighboring kingdoms, as did Portuguese traders who went inland themselves. As the demand grew, local rulers increasingly attacked neighbors to garner slaves for Portuguese traders (see Chapter 18).

The Kongo ruler Affonso I (r. ca. 1506–1543), a Christian convert, at first welcomed Jesuit missionaries and supported conversion. But in time he broke with the Jesuits

Queen Nzinga of Ndongo, who ruled from 1615 to 1660. This contemporary engraving shows her negotiating a treaty with the Portuguese. She is seated on the back of a slave.

and encouraged traditional practices, even though he himself remained a Christian. Affonso had constant difficulty curbing the more exploitative slaving practices and independent-minded provincial governors, who often dealt directly with the Portuguese, undermining royal authority. (See Document, "Affonso I of Kongo Writes to the King of Portugal.") Affonso's successor finally restricted Portuguese activity to Mpinda harbor and the Kongo capital of Mbanza Kongo (São Salvador). A few years later, Portuguese attempts to name the Kongo royal successor caused a bloody uprising against them that led in turn to a Portuguese boycott on trade with the kingdom.

Thereafter, disastrous internal wars shattered the Kongo state. Slavery apparently contributed significantly to provincial unrest. Independent Portuguese traders and adventurers soon did their business outside government channels and tried to manipulate the Kongo kings.

Kongo, however, enjoyed renewed vigor in the seventeenth century. The Kongo kings, all descended from Affonso, ruled as divine-right monarchs at the apex of a complex sociopolitical pyramid that rose from district headmen through provincial governors to the court nobility and king. Royal power came to depend on a guard of musket-armed hired soldiers. The financial base of the kingdom rested on tribute from officials and taxes and tolls on commerce. Christianity, the state religion, was accommodated to the traditional ancestor cult, magic, and sorcery. Sculpture, iron and copper technology, dance, and music flourished.

Angola To the south, in Portuguese Angola, the experience was even worse than in Kongo. The Ndongo kingdom

Chronology

Central Africa

1300s	Kongo kingdom founded
1483	Portuguese come to central African coast
ca. 1506–1543	Reign of Affonso I as king of Kongo
1571	Angola becomes Portuguese proprietary colony

Affonso I of Kongo Writes to the King of Portugal

In 1526 Affonso, the Christian African king of Kongo, wrote to the Portuguese monarch ostensibly to complain about the effects of slaving on the Kongo people and economy. But the real issue was that the Portuguese were circumventing his own royal monopoly on the inland slave trade. One of the insidious effects of the massive demand of the Atlantic trade for slaves was the ever-increasing engagement in it of African monarchs, chieftains, and merchants.

◆ How had the introduction of Portuguese merchants and European goods upset the social and political situation in Kongo? How had these goods tempted Affonso's subjects into the slave trade? How did Affonso wish to change the relationship of his people to Portugal? Was the king more worried about human rights or his economic losses?

Sir, Your Highness [of Portugal] should know how our Kingdom is being lost in so many ways that it is convenient to provide for the necessary remedy, since this is caused by the excessive freedom given by your factors and officials to the men and merchants who are allowed to come to this Kingdom to set up shops with goods and many things which have been prohibited by us, and which they spread throughout our Kingdoms and Domains in such an abundance that many of our vassals, whom we had in obedience, do not comply because they have the things in greater abundance than we ourselves; and it was with these things that we had them content and subjected under our vassalage and jurisdiction, so it is doing a great harm not only to the service of God, but the security and peace of our Kingdoms and State as well.

And we cannot reckon how great the damage is, since the mentioned merchants are taking every day our natives, sons of the land and the sons of our noblemen and vassals and our relatives, because the thieves and men of bad conscience grab them wishing to have the things and wares of this Kingdom which they are ambitious of; they grab them and get them to be sold; and so great, Sir, is the corruption and licentiousness that our country is being completely depopulated, and Your Highness should not agree with this nor accept it as in your service. And to avoid it we need from those [your] Kingdoms no more than some priests and a few people to teach in schools, and no other goods except wine and flour for the holy sacrament. That is why we beg of Your Highness to help and assist us in this matter, commanding your factors that they should not send here either merchants or wares, because it is *our will that in these Kingdoms there should not be any trade of slaves nor outlet for them.**

Concerning what is referred above, again we beg of Your Highness to agree with it, since otherwise we cannot . . . remedy such an obvious damage. Pray Our Lord in His mercy to have Your Highness under His guard and let you do for ever the things of His service. I kiss your hands many times. . . .

From *The African Past*, trans. by J. O. Hunwick, reprinted in Basil Davidson (Grosset and Dunlap, The Universal Library), pp. 191–193. Reprinted by permission of Curtis Brown Ltd. Copyright © 1964 by Basil Davidson.

*Emphasis in the original

---

flourished among the Mbundu people during the sixteenth century, though the Portuguese controlled parts of Angola as a proprietary colony (the first white colonial enterprise in black Africa). By the end of the 1500s Angola was exporting thousands of slaves yearly through the port of Luanda. In less than a century the hinterland had been depopulated. New internal trade in salt and the spread of American food crops such as maize and cassava (which became part of the staple diet of the populace) produced some positive changes in the interior, but in the coastal region the Portuguese brought catastrophe.

East Africa

Swahili Culture and Commerce

The participation of East African port towns in the lucrative South Seas trade was ancient. Arabs, Indonesians, and even some Indians had trafficked there for centuries. Many had been absorbed into what had become, during the first millennium C.E., from Somalia south, a predominantly Bantu-speaking population. From the eighth century onward Islam traveled with Arab and Persian sailors and merchants to

Visiting Mogadishu (1331)

Document

Ibn Battuta (d. 1369 or 1377), a native of Tangier, became one of history's most famous travelers through his voluminous and entertaining writings about his years of journeying from West and East Africa to India and China. In the following excerpt from his description of his trip down the East African coast in 1331, he describes first the daily proceedings at the grievance and petitions court presided over by the Sultan of Mogadishu. The East Africans referred to their Sultan as "Shaikh." A *qadi* is a judge; a *faqih*, a jurisconsult or legal scholar; a *wazir*, a government minister; an *amir*, a military commander; and a *sharif*, a descendant of the Prophet Muhammad (which carries special social status).

◆ **What Muslim values and practices does the report seem to describe? As an Arab Muslim, and an outsider, does Ibn Battuta seem to approve or disapprove of what he reports?**

MOGADISHU

When it is Saturday, the people come to the door of the shaikh (the local term for the Sultan), and they sit in covered halls outside the house. The *qadi*, the *faqihs*, the *sharifs*, the men of piety, the shaikhs and the men who have performed the pilgrimage enter the second council room. They sit on wooden platforms prepared for the purpose. The *qadi* is on a platform by himself and each group on a platform reserved for them which nobody shares with them. Then the shaikh sits in his council and sends for the *qadi* who sits on his left. Then enter the *faqihs* and their leaders sit in front of him while the rest of them salute and go away. Then the *sharifs* enter, their leaders sit before him, the rest of them salute and go away. If they are guests, they sit on his right. Then enter the shaikhs and those who have performed the pilgrimage, and their great ones sit and the rest salute and go away. Then enter the *wazirs* and *amirs*; the heads of the soldiers, rank upon rank, they salute and go. Food is brought and the *qadi*, the *sharifs* and whoever is sitting in that

session eat with the shaikh and the shaikh eats with them. If he wishes to honour one of the leaders of his *amirs*, he sends for him that he should eat with them. The rest of the people eat in the dining hall and their eating is according to precedence in the manner of their entrance before the shaikh. Then the shaikh goes into his house and the *qadi*, the *wazirs*, the private secretary, and four of the leading *amirs* sit for hearing litigation between the members of the public and hearing the cases of people with complaints. In a matter connected with the rules of the *shari'a* [religious law] the *qadi* passes judgement; in a matter other than that, the members of the council pass judgement, that is, the ministers and the *amirs*. In a matter where there is need of consultation with the sultan, they write about it to him and he sends out the reply to them immediately on the back of the note in accordance with his view. And such is always their custom.

From Said Hamdun and Noèl King, ed. and trans., *Ibn Battuta in Black Africa*, (Princeton, NJ: Markus Wiener, rev. ed., 1994), pp. 20–21. Reprinted by permission of Markus Wiener Publishers, Inc.

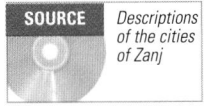
SOURCE *Descriptions of the cities of Zanj*

these southerly trading centers of what the Arabs called the land of the *Zanj*, or "Blacks" (hence "Zanzibar"). Conversion to Islam, however, occurred only along the coast. In the thirteenth century Muslim traders from Arabia and Iran began to dominate the coastal cities from Mogadishu to Kilwa. By 1331 the traveler Ibn Battuta writes of Mogadishu as a thoroughly Islamic port and of the ruler and inhabitants of Kilwa as Muslims. He also notes that towns there had mosques for the faithful.[5] (See Document, "Visiting Mogadishu [1331].")

By this time a common language called **Swahili**, or *Kiswahili*, from the Arabic plural *sawahil*, "coastlands," had developed from the interaction of Bantu and Arabic speakers along the coast. Its structure is Bantu; its vocabulary is largely Bantu but incorporates many words with Arabic roots, and it is written in Arabic script.

Current theory suggests that, like the language, Swahili culture is basically African with a large contribution by Arab, Persian, and other extra-African elements. This admixture created a new consciousness and identity. Today, the many coastal peoples who share Swahili language join African to Persian, Indian, Arab, and other ancestry.

Swahili language and culture probably developed first in the northern towns of Manda, Lamu, and Mombasa, then

[5] *Travels in Asia and Africa, 1325–1354*, trans. and selected by H. A. R. Gibb (New York: Robert M. McBride, 1929), pp. 110–113.

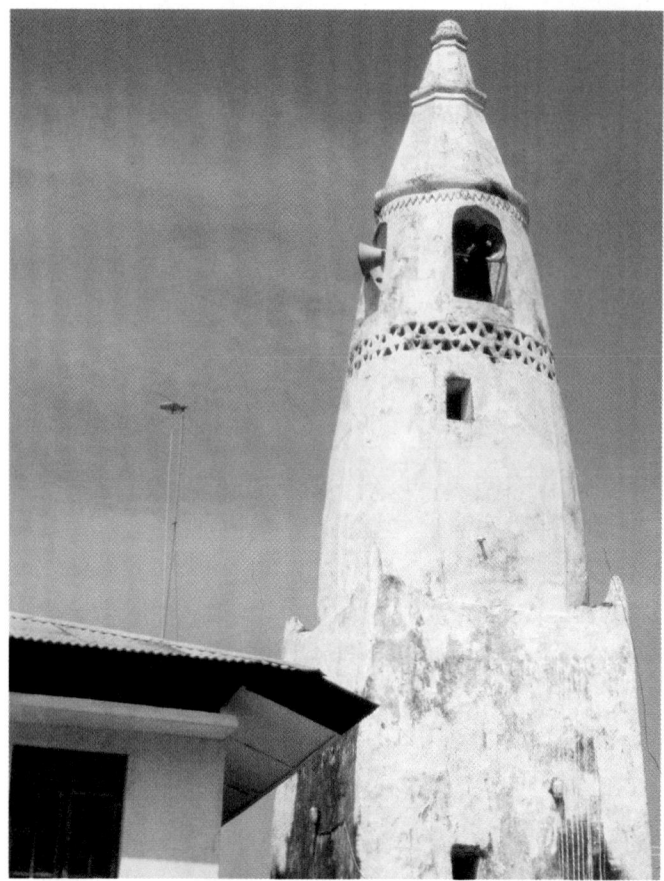

The Malindi Mosque on Zanzibar Island is an example of the influence of Islam on Swahili culture.

Chronology

East and Southeast Africa

900–1500	"Great Zimbabwe" civilization
ca. 1200–1400	Development of Bantu Kiswahili language
ca. 1300–1600	Height of Swahili culture
1698	Omani forces take Mombasa, oust Portuguese from East Africa north of the port of Mozambique
1741–1856	United sultanate of Oman and Zanzibar

and earned their living by farming or fishing. Society seems to have consisted of three principal groups: the local nobility, the commoners, and resident foreigners engaged in commerce. Slaves constituted a fourth class, although their local extent (as opposed to their sale) is disputed.

The flourishing trade of the coastal centers was fed mainly by export of inland ivory. Other exports included gold, slaves, turtle shells, ambergris, leopard skins, pearls, fish, sandalwood, ebony, and cotton cloth. The chief imports were cloth, porcelain, glassware, glass beads, and glazed pottery.

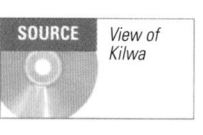

Certain exports tended to dominate particular ports: cloth, sandalwood, ebony, and ivory at Mogadishu, ivory at Manda, and gold at Kilwa (brought up the coast from Sofala, still farther south). Cowrie shells were a common currency in the inland trade, but coins minted at Mogadishu and Kilwa from the fourteenth century on were increasingly used in the major trading centers.

farther south along the coast to Kilwa. They remained localized largely along the coast until recently. Likewise, the spread of Islam was largely limited to the coastal civilization, with the possible exception of the Zambezi valley, where Muslim traders penetrated upriver. This contrasts with the Horn of Africa, where Islamic kingdoms developed both in the Somali hinterland and on the coast.

Swahili civilization reached its apogee in the fourteenth and fifteenth centuries. The harbor trading towns were the administrative centers of the local Swahili states, and most of them were sited on coastal islands or easily defended peninsulas. To these ports came merchants from abroad and from the African hinterlands. These towns were impressive. Stone mosques, fortress-palaces, harbor fortifications, fancy residences, and commercial buildings have their own distinctive cast, which combines African and Arabo-Persian elements.

The Swahili states' ruling dynasties were probably African in origin, though elite families often included Arab or Persian members. Swahili coastal centers boasted an advanced, cosmopolitan culture; by comparison, most of the populace in the small villages lived in mud and sometimes stone houses

The Portuguese and the Omanis of Zanzibar

The original Swahili civilization declined in the sixteenth century. The trade that had originally made everything possible waned with the arrival of the Portuguese and their destruction of both the old oceanic trade (in particular, the Islamic commercial monopoly) and the main Islamic city-states along the eastern coast. Decreases in rainfall or invasions of Zimba peoples from inland regions may also have contributed to the decline.

Nevertheless, the Portuguese undoubtedly intended to gain control of the South Seas trade (see Chapter 18). In Africa, as everywhere, they saw the **Moors** (the Spanish and Portuguese term for Muslims) as their implacable enemies and viewed the struggle to wrest the commerce and the parts of Africa and Asia from Islamic control as a Christian crusade.

The initial Portuguese victories along the African coast led to the submission of many small Islamic ports and states. Still, there was no concerted effort to spread Christianity beyond the fortified settlements established in places like Sofala, Zanzibar, Mozambique, and Mombasa. Thus the long-term cultural and religious consequences of the Portuguese presence were slight.

The Portuguese did, however, cause widespread economic decline on the east coast. When the inland Africans refused to cooperate with them, the formerly heavy gold trade up the Zambezi from Sofala dried up. The militant Portuguese presence also sharply reduced Muslim coastal shipping from India and Arabia. Ottoman efforts in the late sixteenth century failed to defeat the Portuguese, but after 1660 the strong eastern Arabian state of Oman raided the African coast with impunity. In 1698 the Omanis took Mombasa and ejected the Portuguese everywhere north of Mozambique.

Under the Omanis, Zanzibar became a new and major power center in East Africa. Their control of the coastal ivory and slave trade seems to have fueled a substantial recovery of prosperity by the later eighteenth century. Zanzibar itself benefited from the introduction of clove cultivation in the 1830s; cloves became its staple export thereafter. (The clove plantations became also the chief market for a new, devastating internal slave trade, which flourished in East Africa into the late nineteenth century even as the external trade in slaves was crushed.) Omani African sultans dominated the east coast until 1856. Thereafter, Zanzibar and its coastal holdings became independent under a branch of the same family that ruled in Oman. Zanzibar passed eventually to the British when they, the Germans, and the Italians divided East Africa in the late 1880s. Still, the Islamic imprint on the whole coast survives today.

Southern Africa

Southeastern Africa: "Great Zimbabwe"

About the same time that the east-coast trading centers were beginning to flourish, a different kind of civilization was enjoying its heyday farther south, in the rocky, savannah-woodland watershed between the Limpopo and Zambezi Rivers, in modern southern Zimbabwe. This civilization was sited far enough inland never to have felt the impact of Islam. It was founded in the tenth or eleventh century by a Bantu-speaking Shona people, who still inhabit the same general area today. It seems to have become a large and prosperous state between the late thirteenth and the late fifteenth centuries. We know it only through the archaeological remains of an estimated 150 settlements in the Zambezi-Limpopo region.

Great Zimbabwe. Ruins of a stone wall called "The Great Enclosure" and other structures are part of the Great Zimbabwe site.

The most impressive of these ruins, and the apparent capital of this ancient Shona state, is known today as "Great Zimbabwe"—a huge, sixty-odd-acre site encompassing two major building complexes. One—the so-called acropolis—is a series of stone enclosures on a high hill. It overlooks another, much larger enclosure that contains many ruins and a circular tower, all surrounded by a massive wall some thirty-two feet high and up to seventeen feet thick. The acropolis complex may have contained a shrine, whereas the larger enclosure was apparently the royal palace and fort. The stonework reflects a wealthy and sophisticated society. Artifacts from the site include gold and copper ornaments, soapstone carvings, and imported beads, as well as glass and porcelain of Chinese, Syrian, and Persian origins.

The state itself seems to have had partial control of the increasing gold trade between inland areas and the east-coast port of Sofala. Its territory lay east and south of substantial gold-mining enterprises. We can speculate that this large settlement was the capital city of a prosperous empire and the residence of a ruling elite. Its wider domain was made up mostly of smaller settlements whose inhabitants lived by subsistence agriculture and cattle raising and whose culture was different from that of the capital.

We are not sure why the Great Zimbabwe civilization flourished. The evidence suggests first general population growth and increasing economic prosperity in the Zambezi-Limpopo region before 1500 C.E. Even earlier Iron Age sites farther south suggest that other large state entities may have preceded the heyday of Great Zimbabwe proper. The specific impetus for Great Zimbabwe may have been a significant immigration around 1000 C.E. of Late Iron Age Shona speakers who brought with them mining techniques

Carving from Great Zimbabwe. This carving (steatite, 40.5 cm high) is thought to represent a mythical eagle that carries messages from man to the gods. It dates to ca. 1200–1400 C.E. *Werner Forman Archive/Art Resource, N.Y.*

and farming innovations, along with their ancestor cults. Improved farming and animal husbandry could have led to substantial population growth. The gold trade between the inland gold mining areas and Sofala may also have expanded. Great Zimbabwe may have been the chief beneficiary of this trade. This hypothesis links the flourishing of Zimbabwe to that of the East African coast from about the thirteenth century.

However, without new sources, we may never know why this impressive civilization developed and dominated its region for nearly 200 years. The reasons for its demise are also obscure. It appears that the northern and southern sectors of the state split up, and people moved away from Great Zimbabwe, probably because the farming and grazing land there was exhausted. The southern successor kingdom was known as Changamire, which became powerful from the late 1600s until about 1830. The northern successor state, stretched along the middle and lower course of the Zambezi, was known to the first Portuguese sources as the kingdom ruled by the Mwene Mutapa, or "Master Pillager," the title of its sixteenth-century ruler, Mutota, and his successors.

The Portuguese in Southeastern Africa

The Portuguese destroyed Swahili control of both the inland gold trade and the multifaceted overseas trade. Their chief object was to obtain gold from the Zambezi region of the interior. However, because the gold production of the entire region was small and because they encountered repeated difficulties trying to control it, the Portuguese derived little lasting profit from the enterprise. When they had problems sustaining the Zambezi gold trade by trying simply to supplant the Swahili merchants on the coast, they established fortified posts up the Zambezi and meddled in the regional politics of the Shona who controlled the region. This tactic led to ongoing strife between the invaders and the Shona kingdoms. In the 1690s the Changamire Shona dynasty conquered the northern Shona territory and pushed the Portuguese out of gold country.

All along the Zambezi, however, a lasting and destabilizing consequence of Portuguese intrusion was the creation of quasi-tribal chiefdoms. These were led by mixed-blood Portuguese landholders, or ***prazeros***, descended from the first Portuguese estate holders along the Zambezi, who had built up huge estates. Their descendants eventually formed a few clanlike groups of mixed-blood members (from unions with Africans, Indian immigrants, or other estate families). By the end of the eighteenth century, they controlled vast land holdings, commanded armies (often made up largely of slaves), and were a disruptive force in the region because they were too strong for either the Portuguese or the regional African rulers to control. They remind us of how diverse the peoples of modern Africa are.

South Africa: The Cape Colony

In South Africa the Dutch planted the first European colonials almost inadvertently, yet the consequences of their action were to be ultimately as grave and far-reaching as any European incursion onto African soil. The first Cape settlement was built in 1652 by the Dutch East India Company as a resupply point and way station for Dutch vessels on their way back and forth between the Netherlands and the East Indies. The support station grew gradually into what became by century's end a 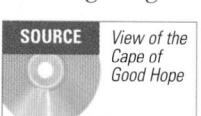 large settler community (the population of the colony in 1662, including slaves, was 392; by 1714 it had reached 3,878).[6] These settlers were the forebears of the Afrikaners of modern South Africa.

SOURCE — *View of the Cape of Good Hope*

Many of the less powerful Khoikhoi people of the region were gradually incorporated into the new colonial economy. The local Khoikhoi (see Chapter 5) were almost exclusively pastoralists; they had neither traditions of strong political organization nor an economic base beyond their herds. At first they bartered livestock freely to Dutch ships and then to the Company settlement for iron, copper, and tobacco. However, when settlers began to displace the Khoikhoi in the southwestern Cape, conflicts ensued. The results were

---

[6] R. Elphick and H. Giliomee, *The Shaping of South African Society, 1652–1820* (Cape Town: Longman, 1979), p. 4.

Cape of good Hope.

A man and woman att the Cape of good Hope

The Table

Souldanja bay

Early European View of Khoikhoi. This seventeenth-century illustration of Khoikhoi near the Cape of Good Hope reflects European prejudices. The facial features of the woman and baby are exaggerated, and because the viewer has no way to know what the woman is doing, she is made to look ridiculous.

the consolidation of European landholdings and a breakdown of Khoikhoi society. Dutch military success led to even greater Dutch control of the Khoikhoi by the 1670s. Treated as free persons, they became the chief source of colonial wage labor—labor in ever-greater demand as the colony grew.

The colony also imported slaves from all along the southern-seas trade routes, including India, East Africa, and Madagascar. Slavery set the tone for relations between the emergent, and ostensibly "white," Afrikaner population and the "coloreds" of other races. Free or not, the latter were eventually all too easily identified with slave peoples.

After the first settlers spread out around the Company station, nomadic white livestock farmers, or **Trekboers**, moved more widely afield, leaving the richer, but limited, farming lands of the coast for the drier interior tableland. There they contested still wider groups of Khoikhoi cattle herders for the best grazing lands. To this end, they developed military techniques—notably the "commando," a collective civilian punitive raid—to secure

Chronology

Southern Africa

1652	First Cape Colony settlement of Dutch East India Company
1795	British replace Dutch as masters of Cape Colony

their way of life by force where necessary. Again the Khoikhoi were the losers. By 1700 they were stripped almost completely of their own pasturages, and their way of life was destroyed. More and more Khoikhoi took up employment in the colonial economy, among the Trekboers as well as the settled colonists. Others moved north to join with other refugees from Cape society (slaves, mixed bloods, and some freedmen) to form raiding bands operating along the frontiers of Trekboer territory close to the Orange River. The disintegration of Khoikhoi society continued in the eighteenth century, accelerated sharply by smallpox—a European import against which this previously isolated group had no immunity.

The Cape society in this period was thus a diverse one. The Dutch Company officials (including Dutch Reformed ministers), the emerging Afrikaners (both settled colonists and Trekboers), the Khoikhoi, and the slaves played differing roles in the emerging new society radiating from Capetown. Intermarriage and cohabitation of masters and slaves added to the social complexity, despite laws designed to check such mixing. Accommodation of nonwhite minority groups within Cape society went on apace; the slow emergence of **Afrikaans**, a new vernacular language of the colonials, shows that the Dutch immigrants themselves were also subject to acculturation processes. By the time of English domination after 1795, the sociopolitical foundations—and the bases of **apartheid**—of modern South Africa were firmly laid.

Summary

North Africa. Developments in African history from 1000 to 1700 varied from region to region. In North Africa, the key new factor was the imperial expansion of the Ottoman Empire as far west as Morocco. But the development of independent regional rulers soon rendered Ottoman authority in North Africa purely nominal.

Empires of the Sudan. Several substantial states arose south of the Sahara: Ghana, Mali, Songhai, and Kanem. The ruling elites of these states converted to or were heavily influenced by Islam, although most of their populations practiced local religions or engaged in syncretism. Much of the wealth of these states was tied to their control of the trans-Saharan trade routes. Farther south, in the coastal forestlands of Central Africa, another substantial kingdom arose in Benin, famous for its brass sculptures.

East Africa. On the east coast, Islam influenced the development of the distinctive Swahili culture and language, and Islamic traders linked the region to India and East Asia.

The Coming of the Europeans. The key development of the fifteenth century was the arrival of European traders, missionaries, and warships. The Portuguese and later Europeans came in search of commerce, converts to Christianity, and spheres of influence. Their arrival disrupted indigenous African culture and political relations and presaged Africa's involvement in and exploitation by a new, expanding global trading system dominated by Europeans.

Review Questions

1. Why did Islam succeed in sub-Saharan and East Africa? What role did warfare play in its success? What role did trade have in it?

2. What was the importance of the empires of Ghana, Mali, and Songhai to world history? Why was the control of the trans-Saharan trade so important to these kingdoms? What was the importance of Islamic culture to them? Why did each of these empires break up?

3. What was the impact of the Portuguese on East Africa? on Central Africa? How did European coastal activities affect the African interior?

4. Why did Ottoman influence decline in northern Africa in the eighteenth century?

INTERPRETING THE PAST

Africa and Islam

Sources from My History Lab / Primary Source DVD

1. Ibn Battuta in Mali
2. Al-Umari describes Mansa Musa of Mali

Sources from Chapter 15

1. Ibn Battuta: Visiting Mogadishu (p. 449).
2. Al-Bakri: Ghana and its People in the Mid-eleventh century (p. 437).
3. Great Mosque at Jenne (p. 439)

The primary source documents and images listed above chronicle the interaction of African and Islamic cultures in sub-Saharan Africa from the tenth to the fourteenth centuries.

As the text sources indicate, Islam coexisted with indigenous ideas and practices, which are usually characterized as "pagan" by these Muslim writers and in later centuries, by Christians. Paganism in Africa can be more accurately defined as *animism*, the belief that souls or spirits inhabit inanimate aspects of the natural world (the stars, sea, rivers, mountains) as well as plants and non-human animals.

The two Ibn Battuta texts document his visits to East Africa (Mogadishu) and, two decades later, to West Africa (Mali), noting how indigenous African customs coexisted with Islamic practices. The al-Bakri text focuses on Ghana more than two centuries earlier, also observing the ways in which the local monarch dealt with differing religious groups. Al-Umari's description of Mansa Musa, the great fourteenth century king of Mali, and his *hajj* (pilgrimage) to Mecca, also includes valuable information about indigenous customs, which predate the introduction of Islam.

Use the source documents along with the photo of Jenne Mosque to address the following thematic questions focusing on the spread of Islam, and the reasons for the continuation of indigenous customs and animistic beliefs. Use specific examples from the documents to support your assertions.

5. How did the Portuguese and Dutch differ from or resemble the Arabs and other Muslims who came as outsiders to sub-Saharan Africa?

6. Discuss the diversity of Cape society in South Africa before 1700. Who were the Trekboers and what was their conflict with the Khoikhoi? How was the basis for apartheid formed in this period?

Key Terms

Afrikaans (p. 453)

apartheid (p. 453)

dar-al-Islam (p. 434)

Maghreb (p. 434)

mansa (p. 440)

marabouts (p. 443)

Moors (p. 450)

muezzin (p. 439)

oba (p. 445)

prazeros (p. 452)

sharifs (p. 434)

shaykh (p. 443)

Swahili (p. 449)

Trekboers (p. 453)

uzama (p. 444)

Note: To learn more about the topics in this chapter, please turn to the Suggested Readings at the end of the book. For additional sources related to this chapter please see the Primary Source DVD at the back of this text or MyHistoryLab.

Questions

What indigenous African customs and spiritual beliefs are recorded by al-Bakri, Battuta, and al-Umari in their accounts? Carefully note and assess the Ibn writer's attitudes (each of the writers are Muslims). Do they seem impartial, positive, or negative in these descriptions? How would you characterize the nature of these customs and beliefs (religious/social/economic)?

How are Islamic beliefs and customs revealed in Mali, Ghana, and East Africa? While the leaders of Mali and East Africa (Mogadishu and Kilwa) are evidently Muslim, the leader of Ghana is not. What are the writer's attitudes toward each ruler and their adherence to the Islamic faith?

Are there differences between East African (Mogadishu) and West African (Mali, Ghana) manifestations of Islam? Specifically, are their any indications of Islam being modified through the process of syncretism (combining elements of several spiritual traditions)? Are they more apparent in West or East Africa? If so, why?

Europe to the Early 1500s: Revival, Decline, and Renaissance

THE HIGH MIDDLE AGES (FROM THE ELEVENTH through the thirteenth century) were a period of political expansion and consolidation and of intellectual flowering and synthesis. The Latin, or Western, church established itself as a spiritual authority independent of secular monarchies, which became more powerful and self-aggrandizing. The parliaments and popular assemblies that accompanied the rise of these monarchies laid the foundations of modern representative institutions. ■

The High Middle Ages saw a revolution in agriculture that increased food supplies and populations. Trade and commerce revived, towns expanded, protomodern forms of banking and credit developed, and a "new rich" merchant class became ascendant in Europe's cities. Universities sprouted. Contact with the Arab world made possible the discovery of antiquity in the writings of the ancient Greek philosophers. Those sources in turn stimulated the great expansion of Western education and culture during the late Middle Ages and the Renaissance.

The late Middle Ages and the Renaissance, roughly 1300–1500, were a time of both unprecedented calamity and bold new beginnings in Europe. France and England

The Medieval Universe. In medieval Europe, the traditional geocentric or earth-centered universe was usually depicted by concentric circles. In this popular German work on natural history, medicine, and science, Konrad von Megenberg (1309–1374) depicted the universe in a most unusual but effective manner. The seven known planets are contained within straight horizontal bands that separate the earth below from heaven, populated by the saints, above.

Konrad von Megenberg. Buch der Natur (Book of Nature). Augsburg: Johannes Bämler, 1481. Rosenwald Collection, Rare Book and Special Collections Division.

The High Middle Ages in Western Europe

Europe

With its borders finally secured, Western Europe during the High Middle Ages was able to concentrate on its political institutions and cultural development, which had been ignored during the early Middle Ages. For Western Europe, the High Middle Ages were a period of clearer self-definition during which individual lands gained much of the geographic shape we recognize today. Europe also began to escape its relative isolation from the rest of the world, which had prevailed since the early Middle Ages. Two factors contributed to this increased engagement: the Crusades and renewed trade along the Silk Road linking China and Europe, made possible by the Mongol conquests in Asia.

Under the Song dynasty (960–1279), before Mongol rule, China continued its technological advance. In addition to the printing press, the Chinese invented the abacus and gunpowder. They also enjoyed a money economy unknown in the West. But culturally, these centuries between 1000 and 1300 were closed and narrow by comparison with those of the Tang dynasty. Politically, the Song were far more autocratic. This was also an era of expansion for Chinese trade, and one of the few in Chinese history in which merchants as a group were able to advance in wealth and status. Although the imperial reach of the Song was limited, Chinese culture in this period was more open to outside influences than in any previous era.

In the late twelfth century Japan shifted from civilian to military rule; the Kamakura *bakufu* governed by mounted warriors who were paid with rights to income from land in exchange for their military services. This rise of a military aristocracy marked the beginning of Japan's "medieval," as distinct from its "classical," period. Three Mongol invasions in

grappled with each other in a bitter conflict known as the Hundred Years' War (1337–1453). Bubonic plague, which contemporaries called Black Death, killed as much as one third of the population in many regions between 1348 and 1350. Thereafter a schism occurred in the church (1378–1417). If that were not calamity enough, in 1453 the Turks captured Constantinople and seemed to be taking dead aim at Western Europe.

The late Middle Ages also witnessed a rebirth that would continue into the seventeenth century. Scholars began to criticize medieval assumptions about the nature of God, humankind, and society. Italian and northern humanists made a full recovery of classical knowledge and languages and ignited new cultural fires that would burn bright throughout Europe. The "divine art" of printing was invented. The **vernacular**, the local language, took its place alongside Latin. In the independent nation-states of Europe, patriotism and incipient nationalism became major forces.

Revival of Empire, Church, and Towns

Otto I and the Revival of the Empire

The fortunes of both the old empire and the papacy began to revive when the Saxon Henry I ("the Fowler"; d. 936) became the first non-Frankish king of Germany in 918. Henry rebuilt royal power and left his son and successor Otto I (r. 936–973) in a strong position. Otto maneuvered his own kin into power in Bavaria, Swabia, and Franconia and then invaded Italy and proclaimed himself its king in 951. In 955 he defeated the Hungarians at Lechfeld, securing German borders against new barbarian attacks and earning the title "the Great."

As part of a royal rebuilding program, Otto enlisted the strong hands of the church. Bishops and abbots, men who possessed a sense of universal empire, yet did not marry and found competitive dynasties, were made royal princes and agents of the king. On February 2, 962, Otto, who had long the thirteenth century also fostered a strong military to resist them. With a civilian court also in existence, Japan actually had a dual government (that is, two emperors and two courts) until the fourteenth century. However, this situation differed greatly from the deep and permanent national divisions developing at this time among the emerging states and autonomous principalities of Western Europe.

Within the many developing autonomous Islamic lands at this time, the teachings of Muhammad created an international culture. Religious identity enabled Muslims to transcend their new and often very deep regional divisions. Similarly, Christianity allowed Englishmen, Frenchmen, Germans, and Italians to think of themselves as one people and to unite in crusades to the Holy Land. As these Crusades got under way in the late eleventh century, Islam too was on the march, penetrating Anatolia and Afghanistan and impinging upon India, where it met a new challenge in Hinduism.

The legacy of the Crusades was mixed. They accomplished few of the goals that originally motivated the European Crusaders; the Holy Land remained under Islamic control, the Crusader kingdoms there collapsed within a few generations of their founding, and the animosity toward Christians fostered by the Crusades resonates even today in the Middle East. Still, the Crusades brought Europeans into more direct and frequent contact with the non-European world than they had known since the heyday of the Roman Empire. Crusaders sampled and sent home products from the Middle East, Asia, and North Africa, creating new tastes in food, art, and even fashion. The resulting growth in demand for these products impelled rising numbers of European merchants to seek these products beyond Europe. Eventually Europeans sought to bypass the Islamic world entirely and secure supplies of Eastern products, especially spices, by going directly to the sources in India and East Asia. By such development European isolation was ended.

Focus Questions

◆ How did the High Middle Ages in Europe differ from the early Middle Ages?

◆ What was the legacy of the Crusades for Europe? In what ways did they signal the start of new relationships between Europe and the wider world?

aspired to the imperial crown, gained it from Pope John XII (955–964) after having rescued the pope from his Italian enemies in the previous year. Thereafter, the church came more than ever under royal control and increasingly determined to be free of it.

The Reviving Catholic Church

With the royal focus shifted from Germany to Italy, Otto's successors, transfixed by their Italian possessions, allowed their German base to deteriorate. As the German empire began to crumble in the eleventh century, the church, long unhappy with imperial domination, declared its independence by embracing a reform movement that had erupted in a monastic order.

Cluny Reform Movement In a great monastery at Cluny, founded in 910 in east-central France, a reform movement, aimed at freeing the church from secular political influence and control, was born. The reformers of Cluny were aided in their efforts by popular respect for the church that found expression in both religious fervor among laypersons and generous baronial patronage of religious houses. People admired clerics and monks because the church was medieval society's most open institution as far as lay participation was concerned. In the Middle Ages any man could theoretically become pope, since the pope was supposed to be elected by the people and the clergy of Rome. All people were candidates for the church's grace and salvation. The church promised a better life to come to the great mass of ordinary people, who found their present existence brutish and without hope.

The Cluny reformers condemned uncompromisingly the contemporary mixing of religious and secular institutions on the part of the state and the subservience of the clergy to royal authority. They taught that the pope in Rome alone commanded the clergy and demanded a clear demarcation between ecclesiastical and secular authority. They further denounced the transgression of ascetic piety by "secular" parish clergy, who lived openly with concubines in a relationship akin to marriage. Although in narrow religious guise, both the celibacy of the clergy and the separation of church and state found precedents in this powerful monastic reform movement. From Cluny, reformers were dispatched throughout France and Italy in the late eleventh century to save the clergy from wives and the church from the state. In both cases, the pope embraced their reforms.

Investiture Struggle: Gregory VII and Henry IV

In 1075 Pope Gregory VII (r. 1073–1085), a fierce advocate of church reform, condemned under penalty of excommunication lay investiture of the clergy in their religious offices at any level. He had in mind primarily the emperor's well-established custom of installing favored bishops to administer his royal estates. This was done by presenting them with the ring and staff of episcopal office at the very same time they received their new secular titles and endowments. Henry IV considered Gregory's action a direct challenge to his ability to administer his realm, while Gregory believed the emperor was usurping the keys to his kingdom. Perceiving that such a measure would weaken royal power vis-à-vis their own, the German princes eagerly supported Gregory's edict. (See Document, "Pope Gregory VII Asserts the Power of the Pope.")

The lines of battle were quickly drawn. Henry assembled his loyal German bishops at Worms in January 1076 and had them proclaim their independence from Gregory. Gregory promptly excommunicated Henry and absolved all Henry's subjects from loyalty to him. The German princes were delighted, and Henry now faced a general revolt. He had no choice but to come to terms with Gregory. In a famous scene, he prostrated himself outside the pope's castle retreat at Canossa in northern Italy on January 25, 1077. There he reportedly stood barefoot in the snow off and on for three days before the pope gave him absolution. Papal power had reached a pinnacle.

The Investiture Controversy was finally settled in 1122 with the Concordat of Worms. There, the new Emperor Henry V (r. 1106–1125) formally renounced his power to invest bishops with ring and staff. In exchange, the new Pope Calixtus II (r. 1119–1124) recognized the emperor's right to be present and to invest bishops with fiefs before or after their investment with ring and staff by the church. The emperor also effectively retained the right to nominate, or veto, candidates. Despite the continuing cooperation between church and state, which was desirable for both sides, distinctive spheres of ecclesiastical and secular

A Black Crusader Saint. St. Maurice was a third-century Egyptian Christian who commanded an Egyptian legion of the Roman army in Gaul. The Romans executed him in 286 C.E. for refusing to worship their gods. Thereafter his Christian cult grew. He was a favorite saint of Charlemagne and other warring medieval German kings. In the era of the Crusades, Western rulers believed that the dark-skinned, Eastern-appearing patron saint of Magdeburg, Germany, would help them win trust in the Eastern lands they occupied and traded in—for which reason artists painted him ever darker.

authority had been stipulated to by both sides. In settling the Investiture Controversy in this way, pope and emperor had also set the stage for greater conflicts and division between church and state.

The Crusades

If an index of popular piety and support for the pope in the High Middle Ages is needed, the **Crusades** amply provide it. What the Cluny reform was to the clergy, the Crusades to the Holy Land were to the laity: an outlet for the heightened religiosity of the late eleventh and twelfth centuries.

Late in the eleventh century, the Byzantine Empire was under severe pressure from the Seljuk Turks, and the Eastern emperor, Alexius I Comnenus, appealed for Western aid. At the Council of Clermont in 1095, Pope Urban II responded positively to that appeal, setting the First Crusade in motion. (See Document, "Pope Urban II (r. 1088–1099) Preaches the First Crusade.") This event has puzzled some historians, because the First Crusade was a very risky venture. But the pope, the nobility, and Western society at large had much to gain by removing large numbers of nobility temporarily from Europe. Too many idle, restless noble youths spent too great a part of their lives feuding with each other and raiding other people's lands. The pope saw that peace and tranquility might more easily be gained at home by sending these factious aristocrats abroad, 100,000 of whom marched off with the First Crusade (see Map 16–1). The nobility, in turn, saw that fortunes could be made in foreign wars. That was especially true for the younger sons of noblemen, who, in an age of growing population and shrinking landed wealth, found in crusading the opportunity to become landowners. Pope Urban may well have also believed that the Crusade would reconcile and reunite Western and Eastern Christianity.

Map 16–1. The Early Crusades. Routes and several leaders of the Crusades during the first century of the movement are shown. The names on this map do not exhaust the list of great nobles who went on the First Crusade. The even showier array of monarchs of the Second and Third Crusades still left the Crusades, on balance, ineffective in achieving their goals.

Religion was not the only motive inspiring the Crusaders; hot blood and greed were no less strong. But unlike the later Crusades, which were undertaken for mercenary reasons, the early Crusades were inspired by genuine religious piety and carefully orchestrated by a revived papacy. Popes promised the first Crusaders a plenary indulgence should they die in battle. That was a complete remission of the temporal punishment due them for unrepented mortal sins, and hence a release from suffering for them in purgatory. In addition to this spiritual reward, the prospect of Holy War against the Muslim infidel also propelled the Crusaders. The Crusade to the Holy Land was also a romantic pilgrimage. All these motives combined to make the First Crusade a Christian success.

En route the Crusaders began a general cleansing of Christendom that would intensify during the thirteenth-century papacy of Pope Innocent III. Accompanied by the new mendicant orders of Dominicans and Franciscans, Christian knights attempted to rid Europe of Jews as well as

Muslims. Along the Crusaders' routes, especially in the Rhineland, Jewish communities were subjected to pogroms.

The First Victory The Eastern emperor welcomed Western aid against advancing Islamic armies. However, the Crusaders had not assembled merely to defend Europe's outermost borders against Muslim aggression. Their goal was to rescue the holy city of Jerusalem, which had been in the hands of the Seljuk Turks since the seventh century. To this end, three great armies—tens of thousands of Crusaders—gathered in France, Germany, and Italy and taking different routes reassembled in Constantinople in 1097.

The convergence of these spirited soldiers on the Eastern capital was a cultural shock that deepened antipathy toward the West. The Eastern emperor suspected their motives, and the common people, whose villages they plundered and suppressed, did not consider them to be Christian brothers in a common cause. Nonetheless the Crusaders accomplished what no Byzantine army had been able to do.

Pope Gregory VII Asserts the Power of the Pope

Document

In the Investiture Controversy between Emperor Henry IV and Pope Gregory VII, the pope's assertion of the powers of his office drew a line in the sand between church and state. Although Gregory's statement bore the modest title, DICTATUS PAPAE ("Dictates of the Pope"), it was dynamite in the history of church-state relations.

◆ In defining his powers as pope, on what authority does Pope Gregory base his power? How many of his assertions are historically verifiable by actual events in church history?

That the Roman Church was founded by God alone.

That the Roman Pontiff alone is rightly to be called universal.

That the Pope may depose the absent.

That for him alone it is lawful to enact new laws according to the needs of the time, to assemble together new congregations, to make an abbey of a canonry; and . . . to divide a rich bishopric and unite the poor ones.

That he alone may use the imperial insignia.

That the Pope is the only one whose feet are to be kissed by all princes.

That his name alone is to be recited in churches.

That his title is unique in the world.

That he may depose emperors.

That he may transfer bishops, if necessary, from one See to another.

That no synod may be called a general one without his order.

That no chapter or book may be regarded as canonical without his authority.

That no sentence of his may be retracted by any one; and that he, alone of all, can retract it.

That he himself may be judged by no one.

That the Roman Church has never erred, nor ever, by the witness of Scripture, shall err to all eternity.

That the Pope may absolve subjects of unjust men from their featly.

Church and State Through the Centuries: A Collection of Historic Documents, trans. and ed. by S. Z. Ehler and John B. Morrall (New York: Biblo and Tannen, 1967), pp. 43–44. Reprinted by permission of Biblio-Moser Book Publishers.

They soundly defeated one Seljuk army after another in a steady advance toward Jerusalem, which they captured on July 15, 1099. The Crusaders owed their victory to superior military discipline and weaponry and were also helped by the deep political divisions within the Islamic world that prevented a unified Muslim resistance.

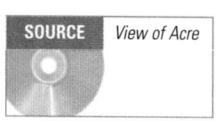

SOURCE *View of Acre*

The victorious Crusaders divided conquered territories into the feudal states of Jerusalem, Edessa, and Antioch, which were apportioned to them as fiefs from the pope. Godfrey of Bouillon, leader of the French-German army, and after him his brother Baldwin, ruled over the kingdom of Jerusalem. The Crusaders, however, remained small islands within a great sea of Muslims, who looked on the Western invaders as savages to be slain or driven out. Once settled in the Holy Land, the Crusaders found themselves increasingly on the defensive. Now an occupying rather than a conquering army, they became obsessed with fortification, building castles and forts throughout the Holy Land, the ruins of which can still be seen today.

Once secure within their new enclaves, the Crusaders ceased to live off the land as they had done since departing Europe and increasingly relied on imports from home. As they developed the economic resources of their new possessions, the once fierce warriors were transformed into international traders and businessmen. The Knights Templar, originally a military-religious order, remade themselves into castle stewards and escorts for Western pilgrims going to and from the Holy Land. Through such endeavors, they became very rich, ending up as wealthy bankers and moneylenders.

The Second and Third Crusades   Native resistance broke the Crusaders' resolve around midcentury, and the forty-year-plus Latin presence in the East began to crumble. Edessa fell to Islamic armies in 1144. A Second Crusade, preached by Christendom's most eminent religious leader, the Cistercian monk Bernard of Clairvaux (1091–1153), attempted a rescue but met with dismal failure. In October 1187, Saladin (r. 1138–1193), king of Egypt and Syria, reconquered Jerusalem, a victory so completely brilliant and unexpected that Pope Urban III was said to have dropped dead upon hearing it. Save for a brief interlude in the thirteenth century, the holiest of cities remained thereafter in Islamic hands until the twentieth century.

A Third Crusade in the twelfth century (1189–1192) attempted yet another rescue, led by the most powerful

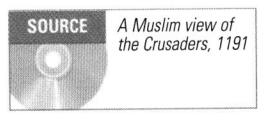
SOURCE *A Muslim view of the Crusaders, 1191*

Western rulers: Hohenstaufen emperor Frederick Barbarossa, Richard the Lion-Hearted, king of England, and Philip Augustus, king of France. It became instead a tragicomic commentary on the passing of the original crusading spirit. Frederick Barbarossa accidentally drowned while fording the Saleph River, a small stream, near the end of his journey across Asia Minor. Richard the Lion-Hearted and Philip Augustus reached the outskirts of

Pope Urban II (r. 1088–1099) Preaches the First Crusade

Document

When Pope Urban II summoned the First Crusade in a sermon at the Council of Clermont on November 26, 1095, he painted a most savage picture of the Muslims who controlled Jerusalem. Urban also promised the Crusaders, who responded by the tens of thousands, remission of their unrepented sins and assurance of heaven. Robert the Monk is one of four witnesses who has left us this summary of the sermon, which exists in five different accounts, a sign of its wide reporting and dissemination.

◆ Is the pope engaging in a propaganda and smear campaign? What images of the enemy does he create and how accurate and fair are they? Did the Christian church have a greater claim to Jerusalem than the people then living there? Does a religious connection with the past entitle one group to confiscate the land of another?

From the confines of Jerusalem and the city of Constantinople a horrible tale has gone forth and very frequently has been brought to our ears, namely, that a race from the kingdom of the Persians [that is, the Seljuk Turks], an accursed race, a race utterly alienated from God, a generation forsooth which has not directed its heart and has not entrusted its spirit to God, has invaded the lands of those Christians and has depopulated them by the sword, pillage and fire; it has led away a part of the captives into its own country, and a part it has destroyed by cruel tortures; it has either entirely destroyed the churches of God or appropriated them for the rites of its own religion. They destroy the altars, after having defiled them with their uncleanness. They circumcise the Christians, and the blood of the circumcision they either spread upon the altars or pour into the vases of the baptismal font. When they wish to torture people by a base death, they perforate their navels, and dragging forth the extremity of the intestines, bind it to a stake; then with flogging they lead the victim around until the viscera having gushed forth and the victim falls prostrate upon the ground. Others they bind to a post and pierce with arrows. Others they compel to extend their necks and then, attacking them with naked swords, attempt to cut through the neck with a single blow. What shall I say of the abominable rape of the women? The king-

dom of the Greeks is now dismembered by them and deprived of territory so vast in extent that it can not be traversed in a march of two months. On whom therefore is the labor of avenging these wrongs and of recovering this territory incumbent, if not upon you? . . .

Jerusalem is the navel of the world; the land is fruitful above others, like another paradise of delights. This the Redeemer of the human race has made illustrious by His advent, has beautified by residence, has consecrated by suffering, has redeemed by death, has glorified by burial. This royal city, therefore, situated at the centre of the world, is now held captive by His enemies, and is in subjection to those who do not know God, to the worship of the heathens. She seeks therefore and desires to be liberated, and does not cease to implore you to come to her aid. From you especially she asks succor, because, as we have already said, God has conferred upon you above all nations great glory in arms.

Accordingly undertake this journey for the remission of your sins, with the assurance of the imperishable glory of the kingdom of heaven.

Translations and reprints from *Original Sources of European History*, Vol. 1 (Philadelphia: Department of History, University of Pennsylvania, 1910), pp. 5–7.

Chronology

The Crusades

1095	Pope Urban II launches the First Crusade
1099	The Crusaders take Jerusalem
1147–1149	The Second Crusade
1187	Jerusalem retaken by the Muslims under Saladin
1189–1192	Third Crusade
1202–1204	Fourth Crusade

Jerusalem, only to shatter the Crusaders' unity and chances of victory by their intense personal rivalry. Philip Augustus returned to France and made war on Richard's continental territories. Richard, in turn, fell captive to the Emperor Henry VI while returning to England.

The English paid a handsome ransom for their adventurous king's release. Popular resentment of taxes levied for that ransom became part of the background of the revolt against the English monarchy that led to royal recognition of English freedoms in the Magna Carta of 1215.

The long-term results of the first three Crusades had little to do with their original purpose. Politically and religiously they were a failure. The Holy Land reverted as firmly as ever to Muslim hands. But the Crusades had been a safety valve for violence-prone Europeans. More importantly, they stimulated Western trade with the East, as Venetian, Pisan, and Genoan merchants followed the Crusaders across Byzantium to lucrative new markets. The need to resupply the Christian settlements in the Near East also created new trade routes and reopened old ones long closed by Islamic warships in the Mediterranean.

The Fourth Crusade

It is a commentary on both the degeneration of the original crusading ideal and the Crusaders' true historical importance that a Fourth Crusade transformed itself into a piratical commercial venture controlled by the Venetians. Launched in 1202, 30,000 crusaders arrived in Venice to set sail for Egypt. When they could not pay the price of transport, the Venetians negotiated an alternative venture: the conquest of Zara, a rival Christian port city on the Adriatic. As a shocked world watched, the Crusaders obliged the Venetians. Zara, however, proved to be only their first digression; in 1204, they besieged Constantinople itself.

This stunning event brought Venice new lands and maritime rights that assured its domination of the eastern

Mediterranean. Constantinople was now the center for Western trade throughout the Near East. Although its capture embarrassed reigning Pope Innocent III, the papacy was soon sharing the spoils, gleeful at the prospect of extending Roman Christianity East. A confidant of the pope became patriarch of Constantinople and launched a mission to win the Greeks and the Slavs to the Roman Church. Western control of Constantinople continued until 1261, when Eastern emperor Michael Paleologus, helped by the Genoese, who envied their great rival's windfall in the East, finally recaptured the city. This fifty-year-plus occupation of Contstantinople did nothing to heal the political and religious divisions between East and West.

Towns and Townspeople

In the eleventh and twelfth centuries, most towns were small and held only about 5 percent of Western Europe's population, but they contained the most creative segments of medieval society.

The Chartering of Towns

Towns were originally dominated by feudal lords, both lay and clerical, who granted charters to those who would agree to live and work within them. The charters guaranteed the towns' safety and gave their inhabitants an independence unknown to peasants who worked the land. The purpose was originally to concentrate skilled laborers who could manufacture the finished goods desired by lords and bishops.

As towns grew and beckoned, many serfs took their skills to the new urban centers. There they found the freedom and profits that could lift an industrious craftsperson

Foundry in Florence. Skilled workers were an integral component of the commerce of medieval towns. This scene shows the manufacture of cannons in a foundry in Florence. *Scala/Art Resource, N.Y.*

into higher social ranks. As this migration of serfs to the towns accelerated, the lords in the countryside offered serfs more favorable terms of tenure to keep them on the land. The growth of towns thus improved the lot of serfs generally.

The Rise of Merchants Rural society not only gave the towns their craftspeople and day laborers, but the first merchants themselves may also have been enterprising serfs. Certainly, some of the long-distance traders were people

who had nothing to lose and everything to gain from the enormous risks of foreign trade. They traveled together in armed caravans and convoys, buying goods and products as cheaply as possible at the source and selling them for all they could get in Western ports (see Map 16–2).

At first the merchants were disliked because they were outside the traditional social groups of nobility, clergy, and peasantry. Over time, however, the powerful grew to respect the merchants, and the weak always tried to imitate them,

Map Exploration

To explore this map further, go to http://www.prenhall.com/craig_maps

Map 16–2. Medieval Trade Routes and Regional Products. Trade in Europe varied in intensity and geographical extent in different periods during the Middle Ages. The map shows some of the channels that came to be used in interregional commerce. Labels tell part of what was carried in that commerce.

because the merchants left a trail of wealth behind them wherever they went.

As the traders established themselves in towns, they grew in wealth and numbers, formed their own protective associations, and soon found themselves able to challenge traditional seigneurial authority. Merchants especially wanted to end the arbitrary tolls and tariffs regional magnates imposed over the surrounding countryside. Such regulations hampered the flow of commerce on which both merchant and craftsman in the growing urban export industries depended.

Townspeople needed simple and uniform laws and a government sympathetic to their new forms of business activity, not the fortress mentality of the lords of the countryside. The result was often a struggle with the old nobility within and outside the towns. This conflict led towns in the High and late Middle Ages to form their own independent communes and to ally themselves with kings against the nobility in the countryside, a development that would eventually rearrange the centers of power in medieval Europe and dissolve classic feudal government.

Because the merchants were the engine of the urban economy, small shopkeepers and artisans identified far more with them than with aloof lords and bishops, who had been medieval society's traditional masters. The lesser nobility (small knights) outside the towns also recognized the new mercantile economy as the wave of the future. During the eleventh and twelfth centuries, the burgher upper classes increased their economic strength and successfully challenged the old noble urban lords for control of the towns.

New Models of Government

With urban autonomy came new models of self-government. Around 1100 the old urban nobility and the new burgher upper class merged into an urban patriciate. It was a marriage between those wealthy by birth (inherited property) and those whose fortunes came from long-distance trade. From this new ruling class was born the aristocratic town council, which henceforth governed towns.

Enriching and complicating the situation, small artisans and craftspeople also slowly developed their own protective associations or **guilds** and began to gain a voice in government. The towns' opportunities for the "little person" had created the slogan "Town air brings freedom." Within town walls people thought of themselves as citizens with basic rights, not subjects at the mercy of their masters' whim.

Towns and Kings

By providing kings with the resources they needed to curb factious noblemen, towns became a major force in the transition from feudal societies to national governments. Towns were a ready source of educated bureaucrats and lawyers who knew Roman law, the tool for running the state. Money was also to be found in the towns in great quantity, enabling kings to hire their own armies and free themselves from dependence on the nobility. In turn towns won royal political recognition and had their constitutions guaranteed. In France, towns became integrated early into royal government. In Germany, they fell under ever-tighter control by the princes. In Italy, uniquely, towns became genuine city-states during the Renaissance.

Jews in Christian Society

Towns also attracted Jews who plied trades in small businesses. Many became wealthy as moneylenders to kings, popes, and businesspeople. Jewish intellectual and religious culture both dazzled and threatened Christians. These various factors encouraged suspicion and distrust among Christians and led to an unprecedented surge in anti-Jewish sentiment in the late twelfth and early thirteenth centuries.

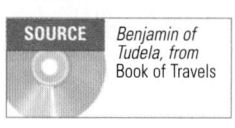

SOURCE *Benjamin of Tudela, from Book of Travels*

Schools and Universities

In the twelfth century, Byzantine and Spanish Islamic scholars made it possible for the philosophical works of Aristotle, the writings of Euclid and Ptolemy, the texts of Greek physicians and Arab mathematicians, and the corpus of Roman law to circulate among Western scholars. Islamic scholars wrote thought-provoking commentaries on Greek texts that were subsequently translated into Latin and made available to Western scholars and

The University of Bologna in central Italy was distinguished as the center for the revival of Roman law. This carving on the tomb of a Bolognese professor of law shows students attending one of his lectures. *Scala/Art Resource, N.Y.*

Student Life at the University of Paris

Document

As the following account by Jacques de Vitry makes clear, not all students at the University of Paris in the thirteenth century were there to gain knowledge. Students fought constantly and subjected each other to ethnic insults and slurs.

◆ Why were students from different lands so prejudiced against one another? Was the rivalry among faculty members as intense as that among students? What are the student criticisms of the faculty? Do they sound credible?

Almost all the students at Paris, foreigners and natives, did absolutely nothing except learn or hear something new. Some studied merely to acquire knowledge, which is curiosity; others to acquire fame, which is vanity; others still for the sake of gain, which is cupidity and the vice of simony. Very few studied for their own edification, or that of others. They wrangled and disputed not merely about the various sects or about some discussions; but the differences between the countries also caused dissensions, hatreds and virulent animosities among them, and they impudently uttered all kinds of affronts and insults against one another.

They affirmed that the English were drunkards and had tails; the sons of France proud, effeminate and carefully adorned like women. They said that the Germans were furious and obscene at their feasts; the Normans, vain and boastful; the Poitevins, traitors and always adventurers. The Burgundians they considered vulgar and stupid. The Bretons were reputed to be fickle and changeable, and were often reproached for the death of Arthur. The Lombards were called avaricious, vicious and cowardly; the Romans, seditious, turbulent and slanderous; the Sicilians,

tyrannical and cruel; the inhabitants of Brabant, men of blood, incendiaries, brigands, and ravishers; the Flemish, fickle, prodigal, gluttonous, yielding as butter, and slothful. After such insults from words they often came to blows.

I will not speak of those logicians [professors of logic and dialectic] before whose eyes flitted constantly "the lice of Egypt," that is to say, all the sophistical subtleties, so that no one could comprehend their eloquent discourses in which, as say Isaiah, "there is no wisdom." As to the doctors of theology, "seated in Moses' set," they were swollen with learning, but their charity was not edifying. Teaching and not practicing, they have "become as sounding brass or a tinkling cymbal," or like a canal of stone, always dry, which ought to carry water to "the bed of spices." They not only hated one another, but by their flatteries they enticed away the students of others; each one seeking his own glory, but caring not a whit about the welfare of souls.

Translations and reprints from the *Original Sources of European History*, Vol.2 (Philadelphia: Department of History, University of Pennsylvania, 1902), pp. 19–20.

students. The resulting intellectual ferment gave rise to Western universities as we know them today. The first important one was established in 1158 in Bologna, which became the model for the universities of Spain, Italy, and southern France, and gained renown for the revival of Roman law. The University of Paris became the model for northern European universities and the study of theology. (See Document, "Student Life at the University of Paris.")

In the High Middle Ages the learning process was basic. People assumed that truth was already known and only needed to be properly organized, elucidated, and defended. Students wrote commentaries on authoritative texts, especially those of Aristotle and the church fathers. Teachers did not encourage students to strive independently for undis-

covered truth beyond the received knowledge of the experts. Rather, students learned to organize and harmonize the accepted truths of tradition, which were drilled into them.

This method of study was known as **Scholasticism**. Students summarized and compared the traditional authorities in their field, elaborated their arguments pro and con, and drew the logical conclusions. With the arrival of Aristotle's works in the West, logic and dialectic became the new tools for disciplining thought and knowledge. Dialectic was the art of discovering a truth by pondering the arguments against it. Together with aspiring philosophers, theologians, and lawyers, even medical students learned their vocation by debating the authoritative texts in their field, not by clinical medical practice.

Abelard No one promoted the new Aristotelian learning more boldly and controversially than Peter Abelard (1079–1142), the leading philosopher and theologian of his time and the first European scholar to gain a large student audience. He ended up, however, not as an academic superstar, but as an obscure abbot of a monastery in Brittany. That was because his bold subjection of church teaching to Aristotelian logic and critical reasoning made him many powerful enemies at a time when there was no tenure to protect genius and free speech in schools and universities. Accused of multiple transgressions of church doctrine, he wrote an autobiography recounting the "calamities" that befell him over a lifetime. His critics especially condemned his subjective interpretations. He likened the trinitarian bonds among God the Father, the Son, and the Holy Spirit to those created among people by sworn documents and covenants. Rather than a God-begotten cosmic ransom of humankind from the Devil, Christ's crucifixion was said to redeem Christians by virtue of its impact on their hearts and minds when they heard and pondered the story. Abelard's ethical teaching stressed intent: The consent of the doer made an act good or evil, not the deed itself. Inner feelings were also said to be more important for receiving divine forgiveness than the sacrament of penance performed by the priest.

Between his native genius and youthful disrespect for seniority and tradition, Abelard gained powerful enemies in high places. He gave those enemies the opportunity to strike him down when in Paris, where he was Master of Students at Notre Dame, he seduced the bright, seventeen-year-old niece of a powerful canon (her name was Heloise), who hired Abelard to be her tutor in his home. The passionate affair ended in public scandal, with Heloise pregnant. Unable to marry her officially (university teachers had to be single and celibate), they wed secretly. Intent on punishing Abelard and ending his career, the enraged uncle not only exposed their affair and secret marriage but also hired men to castrate Abelard.

Thereafter both entered cloisters in nearby Paris: Heloise at Argenteuil, Abelard at St. Denis. She continued to love Abelard and relive their passion in her mind, while Abelard became a self-condemning monk's monk, who assured Heloise in his letters that his "love" for her had only been wretched desire. The famous philosopher ended his life as a platitudinous monk. In 1121, a church synod ordered his writings burned. Another synod in 1140 condemned nineteen propositions from his works as heresy. Retracting his teaching, Abelard lived out the remaining two years of his life in the monastery of St. Denis. Heloise lived another twenty years and gained renown for her positive efforts to reform the rules for the cloistered life of women, under which she had suffered so much. Their story is a revelation of contemporary academic and religious life, the relationship of men and women, and the power of a reform-minded and controlling church.

Ekkehard and Uta. ca. 1240–50. This famous noble pair founded Naumburg Cathedral in Germany in the middle of the thirteenth century and are exemplary studies of medieval nobility.

Society

The Order of Life

In the art and literature of the Middle Ages, three basic social groups were represented: those who fought as mounted knights (the landed nobility), those who prayed (the clergy), and those who labored in fields and shops (the peasantry and village artisans). After the revival of towns in the eleventh century, a fourth social group emerged: the long-distance traders and merchants.

Nobles By the late Middle Ages, a distinguishable higher and lower nobility had evolved, living in both town and country. The higher were the great landowners and territorial magnates, long the dominant powers in their regions; the lower were petty landlords, the descendants of minor knights, newly rich merchants, or wealthy farmers.

Dominicans (left) and Franciscans (right). Unlike the other religious orders, the Dominicans and Franciscans did not live in cloisters but wandered about preaching and combating heresy. They depended for support on their own labor and the kindness of the laity. *Cliche Bibliothèque Nationale de France, Paris.*

Arms were the nobleman's profession, waging war his sole occupation. The nobility accordingly celebrated physical strength, courage, and the constant activity of warfare. Warring brought new riches and a chance to gain honor and glory, whereas peace meant boredom and economic stagnation. In the eighth century the adoption of stirrups by mounted knights gave armies the edge.

No medieval social group was absolutely uniform. Noblemen formed a broad spectrum—from minor vassals without subordinate vassals to mighty barons, the principal vassals of a king or prince, who had many vassals of their own. Dignity and status within the nobility were directly related to the exercise of authority over others; a chief with many vassals far excelled the small country nobleman who was lord over none but himself.

By the late Middle Ages, several factors forced the landed nobility into a steep economic and political decline from which it never recovered. Climatic changes and agricultural failures created large famines, while the great plague (see below) brought about unprecedented population losses. Changing military tactics occasioned by the use of infantry and heavy artillery during the Hundred Years' War made the noble cavalry nearly obsolete. And the alliance of wealthy towns with the king weakened the nobility within their own domains. After the fourteenth century, land and wealth counted for far more than lineage as qualification for entrance into the highest social class.

Clergy   Unlike the nobility and the peasantry, the clergy was an open estate: One was a cleric by religious training and ordination, not because of birth or military prowess.

There were two basic types of clerical vocation: regular and secular. The **regular clergy** comprised the orders of monks who lived according to a special ascetic rule (*regula*) in cloisters separated from the world. In the thirteenth century, two new orders—the Franciscans and the Dominicans—gained the sanction of the church. Their members went out into the world to preach the church's mission and to combat heresy.

The **secular clergy**, those who lived and worked directly among the laity in the world (*saeculum*), formed a vast hierarchy. At the top were the wealthy cardinals, archbishops, and bishops who were drawn almost exclusively from the nobility. Below them were the urban priests, the cathedral canons, and the court clerks. Finally, there was the great mass of poor parish priests, who were neither financially nor intellectually much above the common people they served.

During most of the Middle Ages, the clergy were the first estate, and theology was the queen of the sciences. How did the clergy attain such prominence? A lot of it was self-proclaimed. However, there were also popular respect and reverence for the clergy's role as mediator between God and humanity. The priest brought the Son of God down to earth when he celebrated the sacrament of the Eucharist; his absolution released penitents from punishment for sin. It was declared improper for mere laypeople to sit in judgment on such a priest.

Peasants   The largest and lowest social group in medieval society was one on whose labor the welfare of all others depended: the agrarian peasantry. Many peasants lived and worked on the manors of the nobility, the vital cells of rural social life. The lord of the manor required a certain amount of produce (grain, eggs, and the like) and services from the peasant families and held both judicial and police powers. He owned and operated the machines that processed crops into food and drink. The lord also had the right to subject his tenants to exactions known as *banalities*. He could, for example, force them to breed their cows with his bull, and to pay for the privilege; to grind their bread grains in his mill; to bake their bread in his oven; to make their wine in his wine press; to buy their beer from his brewery; and even to surrender to him the choice parts of all animals slaughtered on his lands. The lord also collected as an inheritance tax a serf's best animal. Without the lord's permission, a serf could neither travel nor marry outside the manor in which he served.

However, the serfs' status was not chattel slavery. It was to a lord's advantage to keep his serfs healthy and happy; his welfare, like theirs, depended on a successful harvest. Serfs had their own dwellings and modest strips of land, and they lived off the produce of their own labor and organization. They could also market for their own profit any surpluses that remained after the harvest. And serfs could pass their property (their dwellings and field strips) on to their children, along with their worldly goods.

Two basic changes occurred in the evolution of the manor from the early to the later Middle Ages. The first was the increasing importance of the single-family holding. As family farms replaced manorial units, land and property remained in the possession of a single family from generation to generation. Second was the conversion of the serf's dues into money payments, a change made possible by the revival of trade and the rise of the towns. This development, completed by the thirteenth century, permitted serfs to hold their land as rent-paying tenants and to overcome their servile status.

By the mid–fourteenth century, a declining nobility in England and France, faced with the ravages of the great plague and the Hundred Years' War, tried to turn back the historical clock by increasing taxes on the peasantry and restricting their migration to the cities. The response was

armed revolt. The revolts of the agrarian peasantry, like those of the urban proletariat, were brutally crushed. They stand out at the end of the Middle Ages as violent testimony to the breakup of medieval society. As growing national sentiment would break its political unity, and heretical movements end its nominal religious unity, the peasantry's revolts revealed the absence of medieval social unity.

Medieval Women

The image and the reality of medieval women are two very different things. The image was strongly influenced by the views of male Christian clergy, whose ideal was the celibate life of chastity, poverty, and obedience. Drawing on both the Bible and classical medical, philosophical, and legal writings predating Christianity, Christian theologians depicted women as physically, mentally, and morally weaker than men. On the basis of such assumptions, Christian clergy considered marriage a debased state by comparison with the religious life, and in their writings praised virgins and celibate widows over wives. In marriage, a woman's role was to be obedient to her husband, who, as the stronger partner, had a duty to protect and discipline her.

This image suggests that medieval women had two basic options in life: to become either a subjugated housewife or a confined nun. In reality, the vast majority of medieval women were neither.

Medieval Marketplace. A fifteenth-century rendering of an 11th- or 12th-century marketplace. Medieval women were active in all trades, but especially in the food and clothing industries. *Scala/Art Resource, N.Y.*

Image and Status   Both within and outside the Church, this image of women is contradicted. Together with the cult of the Virgin Mary, the chivalric romances and courtly love literature of the twelfth and thirteenth centuries put women on pedestals and treated them as superior to men in purity. If the church harbored misogynist sentiments, it also condemned them, as in the case of the thirteenth-century *Romance of the Rose* and other popular bawdy literature.

The learned churchman Peter Lombard (1100–1169) asked why God created Eve from Adam's rib rather than taking her from his head or one of his feet. His answer: God took Eve from Adam's side because woman was created neither to rule over man nor to be enslaved by him but rather to stand squarely at his side, as a companion and partner in mutual aid and trust. By such insistence on the spiritual equality of men and women and their shared responsibility to one another, the church also helped raise the dignity of women.

Germanic law treated women better than Roman law had done, recognizing basic rights that forbade their treatment as chattel. Unlike Roman women, who as teens married much older men, German women married husbands of similar age. Another practice unknown to the Romans was the groom's conveyance of a portion, or dowry (*dos*), to his bride, which became her own in the event of his death. All major Germanic law codes recognized the economic freedom of women: their right to inherit, administer, dispose of, and confer property and wealth on their children. They could also press charges in court against men for bodily injury and rape, the latter receiving punishments ranging from fines, flogging, and banishment to blinding, castration, and death.

Life Choices The nunnery was an option for single women from the higher social classes. Entrance required a dowry and could be almost as expensive as a wedding, although usually cheaper. Within the nunnery, a woman could rise to leadership as an abbess or a mother superior, exercising a degree of authority denied her in much of secular life. However, the nunneries of the established religious orders remained under male supervision, so that even abbesses had to answer to higher male authority.

In the ninth century, under the influence of Christianity, the Carolingians made monogamy official policy. Heretofore they had practiced polygamy and concubinage and permitted divorce. The result was both a boon and a burden to women. On one hand, wives gained a greater dignity and legal security. On the other hand, a wife's labor as household manager and bearer of children greatly increased. And the Carolingian wife was now also the sole object of her husband's wrath and pleasure. Such demands clearly took their toll. The mortality rates of Frankish women increased and their longevity decreased after the ninth century.

Under such conditions, the cloister became an appealing refuge for women. However, the number of women in cloisters was never very large. In late medieval England no more than 3,500 women entered the cloister.

Working women The vast majority of medieval women were neither housewives nor nuns, but working women. The evidence suggests they were respected and loved by their husbands, perhaps be,cause they worked shoulder by shoulder with them in running the household and often also home-based businesses. Between the ages of ten and fifteen, girls were apprenticed in a trade and learned to be skilled workers much like boys. If they married, they often continued their trade, operating their bake or dress shops next to their husbands' business, or becoming assistants and partners in

the shops of their husbands. Women appeared in virtually every "blue-collar" trade, from butcher to goldsmith, but mostly worked in the food and clothing industries. Women belonged to guilds, just like men, and they became craftmasters. By the fifteenth century, townswomen increasingly had the opportunity to go to school and gain vernacular literacy.

Although women did not have as wide a range of vocations as men, their vocational destinies were just as fixed. Unlike men, however, women were excluded from the learned professions of scholarship, medicine, and law by reason of gender alone. Their freedom of movement within a profession was often more regulated than a man's and their wages for the same work were not as great. Still, women remained as prominent and as creative a part of workaday medieval society as men.

Growth of National Monarchies

England and France: Hastings (1066) to Bouvines (1214)

William the Conqueror The most important change in English political life was occasioned in 1066 by the death of the childless Anglo-Saxon ruler Edward the Confessor (r. 1042–1066), so named because of his reputation of piety. Edward's mother was a Norman princess, which gave Duke William of Normandy (d. 1087) a hereditary claim to the English throne. The Anglo-Saxon assembly, however, chose instead Harold Godwinsson (ca. 1022–1066), who had earlier solemnly promised the throne to William. That reneging brought the swift conquest of England by the powerful Normans. William's forces defeated Harold's army at Hastings on October 14, 1066, and William was crowned king of England in Westminster Abbey within weeks of the invasion.

Thereafter William established a strong monarchy but kept the Anglo-Saxon tax system, the practice of court writs (legal warnings) as a flexible form of central control over localities, and the Anglo-Saxon quasi-democratic tradition of frequent *parleying*—that is, the holding of conferences between the king and lesser powers who had vested interests in royal decisions. The result was a balancing of monarchical and parliamentary elements that remains true of English government today.

Popular Rebellion and the Magna Carta William's grandson, Henry II (r. 1154–1189), brought to the throne greatly expanded French holdings through inheritance from his father (Maine, Touraine, and Anjou) and his marriage to Eleanor of Aquitaine (1122–1204), a union that created the so-called Angevin or English-French empire. As Henry II acquired new lands abroad, he became more autocratic at home. The result was strong political resistance from both the nobility and the clergy.

Battle of Hastings. William the Conqueror on horseback urging his troops into combat with the English at the Battle of Hastings (October 14, 1066). From the Bayeux Tapestry, about 1073–1083. *Giraudon/Art Resource, N.Y.*

Under Henry's successors, the brothers Richard the Lion-Hearted (r. 1189–1199) and John (r. 1199–1216), burdensome taxation in support of foreign Crusades and a failing war with France turned resistance into outright rebellion. The danger of despotism became acute under the rule of King John, prompting the English barons to take matters into their own hands. With the full support of the clergy and the townspeople, they forced the king's grudging recognition of the **Magna Carta** ("Great Charter") in 1215, a document that reaffirmed traditional rights and personal liberties still enshrined in English law.

This famous cornerstone of modern English law put limits on royal power and secured the rights of the privileged to be represented at the highest levels of government in important matters like taxation. The Great Charter enabled the English to avoid both a dissolution of the monarchy by the nobility and the abridgment of the rights of the nobility by the monarchy.

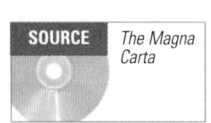

SOURCE *The Magna Carta*

Philip II Augustus Powerful feudal princes dominated France from the beginning of the Capetian dynasty (987) until the reign of Philip II Augustus (1180–1223). During this period the Capetian kings wisely concentrated their limited resources on securing the territory surrounding Paris known as the Île-de-France. By the time of Philip II, Paris had become the center of French government and culture, and the Capetian dynasty a secure hereditary monarchy. Thereafter, the kings of France were able to impose their will on the French nobles.

The Norman Conquest of England enabled the Capetian kings to establish a truly national monarchy. The Duke of Normandy, who after 1066 was master of England, was also a vassal of the French king in Paris. Capetian kings understandably watched with alarm as the power of their Norman vassal grew.

Philip Augustus faced both an internal and an international struggle, and he succeeded at both. His armies occupied all the English territories on the French coast except for Aquitaine. At Bouvines on July 27, 1214, the French won handily over the English and their German allies. The victory unified France around the monarchy and thereby laid the foundation for French ascendancy in the late Middle Ages.

France in the Thirteenth Century: Reign of Louis IX

Louis IX (r. 1226–1270), the grandson of Philip Augustus, embodied the medieval view of the perfect ruler. He inherited a unified and secure kingdom.

Louis' greatest achievements lay at home. The efficient French bureaucracy became under him an instrument of order and fair play in local government. He sent forth royal commissioners to monitor the royal officials responsible for local governmental administration and ensure justice. These royal ambassadors were received as genuine tribunes of the people. Louis further abolished private wars and serfdom within his own royal domain, gave his subjects the right of appeal from local to higher courts, and made the tax system more equitable. The French people came to associate their king with justice, and national feeling, the glue of nationhood, grew strong during his reign.

During Louis's reign, French society and culture became an example to all of Europe, a pattern that would continue into the modern period. Northern France became the showcase of monastic reform, chivalry, and Gothic art and architecture. Louis' reign also coincided with the golden age of Scholasticism, which saw the convergence of Europe's greatest thinkers on Paris, among them Saint Thomas Aquinas.

The Hohenstaufen Empire (1152–1272)

While stable governments developed in both England and France during the Middle Ages, the Holy Roman Empire fragmented in disunity and blood feuding (see Map 16–3).

Frederick I Barbarossa Frederick I Barbarossa (1152–1190), the first of the Hohenstaufens, reestablished imperial authority but also initiated a new phase in the contest between popes and emperors. Never have rulers and popes despised and persecuted one another more than they did during the Hohenstaufen dynasty. Frederick attempted to hold the empire together by stressing feudal bonds, but his reign ended with stalemate in Germany and defeat in Italy. In 1186 his son—the future Henry VI (r. 1190–1197)—married Constance, heiress to the kingdom of Sicily. That alliance became a fatal distraction for the Hohenstaufens. This union of the empire with Sicily left Rome encircled, thereby ensuring the undying hostility of a papacy already thoroughly distrustful of the emperor.

When Henry VI died in September 1197, chaos followed. Germany was thrown into anarchy and civil war. Meanwhile, Henry VI's four-year-old son, Frederick, who had a direct hereditary claim to the imperial crown, had for his own safety been made—fatefully, it would prove—a ward of Pope Innocent III (r. 1198–1215), who proclaimed and practiced as none before him the doctrine of the plenitude of papal power. Innocent had both the will and the means to challenge the Hohenstaufens.

Frederick II Hohenstaufen support had meanwhile remained alive in Germany, where in December 1212 young Frederick, with papal support, became Emperor Frederick II. But Frederick soon disappointed papal hopes. He was Sicilian and only nine of his thirty-eight years as emperor were spent in Germany. To secure the imperial title for himself and his sons, he gave the German princes what they wanted. The German princes became undisputed lords over their territories, in effect, petty kings.

Frederick had an equally disastrous relationship with the papacy, which excommunicated him four times and led the German

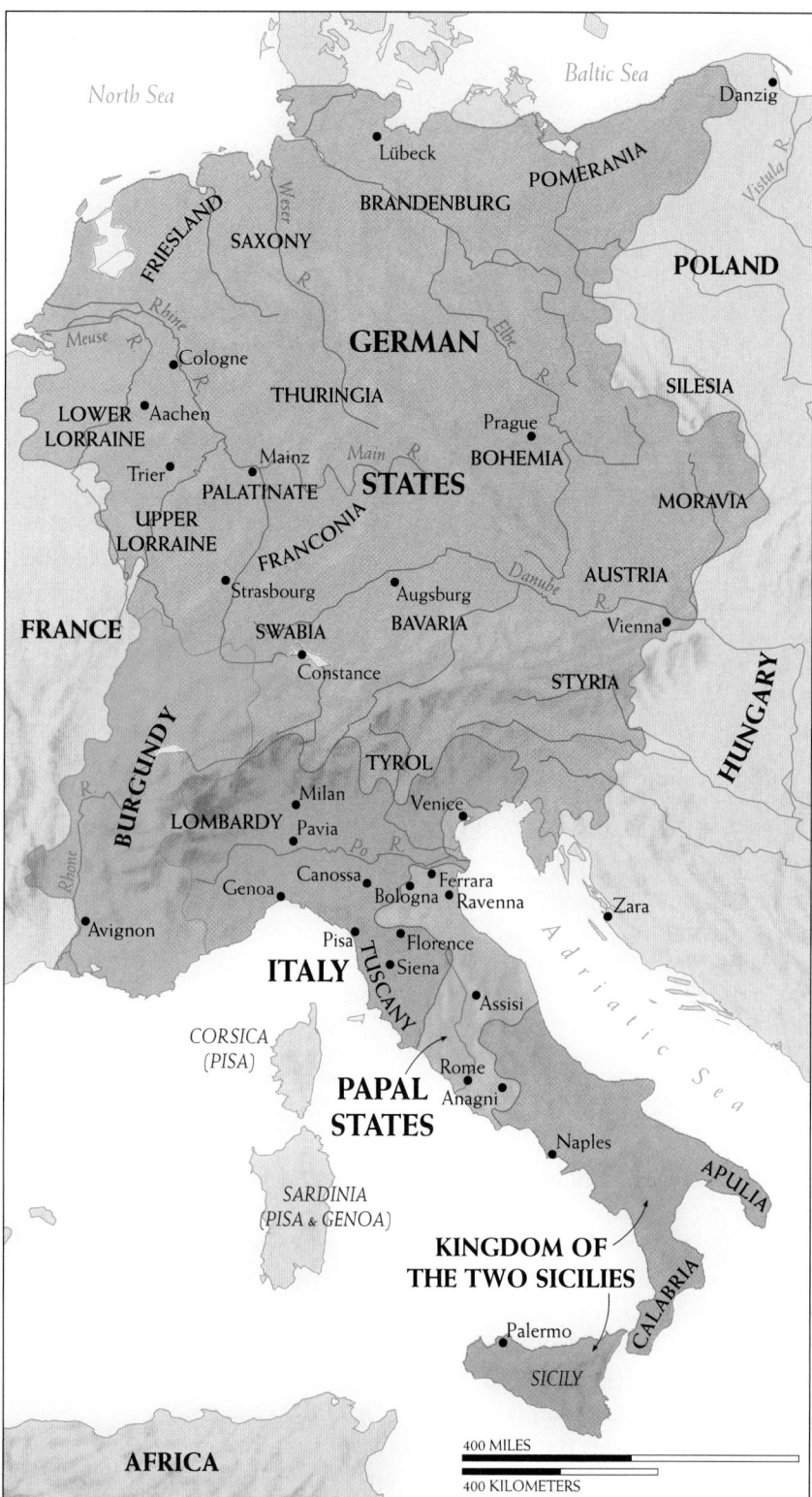

Map 16–3.   Germany and Italy in the Middle Ages. Medieval Germany and Italy were divided lands. The Holy Roman Empire (Germany) embraced hundreds of independent territories that the emperor ruled only in name. The papacy controlled Rome and tried to enforce its will in central Italy. Under the Hohenstaufens (mid–twelfth to mid–thirteenth century), internal German divisions and papal conflict reached new heights; German rulers sought to extend their power to southern Italy and Sicily.

Gothic Cathedral. The portal of Reims Cathedral, where the kings of France were crowned. The cathedral was built in the Gothic style—emblematic of the High Middle Ages—that originated in France in the mid–twelfth century. The earlier Romanesque (Roman-like) style from which it evolved is characterized by fortresslike buildings with thick stone walls, rounded arches and vaults, and few windows. The Gothic style, in contrast, is characterized by soaring structures, their interiors flooded with colored light from vast expanses of stained-glass.

princes against him, launching the church into European politics on a massive scale. This transformation of the papacy into a formidable political and military power soon made the church highly vulnerable to criticism from religious reformers and royal apologists.

When Frederick died in 1250, the German monarchy died with him. The princes established an electoral college in 1257 to pick the emperor, and the "king of the Romans" became their puppet. Between 1250 and 1272 the Hohenstaufen dynasty slowly faded into oblivion.

Political and Social Breakdown

Hundred Years' War

The Causes of the War The Hundred Years' War, which began in May 1337 and lasted until October 1453, started when the English king Edward III (r. 1327–1377), the

grandson of Philip the Fair of France (r. 1285–1314), claimed the French throne. But the war was more than a dynastic quarrel. England and France were territorial and economic rivals with a long history of prejudice and animosity between them. These factors made the Hundred Years' War a struggle for national identity.

Although France had three times the population of England, was far wealthier, and fought on its own soil, most of the major battles were stunning English victories. The primary reason for these French failures was internal disunity caused by endemic social conflicts. Unlike England, France was still struggling to make the transition from a fragmented feudal society to a centralized modern state.

France's defeats also resulted from incompetent leadership and English military superiority. The English infantry was more disciplined than the French, and English archers could fire six arrows a minute with enough force to pierce an inch of wood or the armor of a knight at 200 yards. Eventually, thanks in part to the inspiring leadership of Joan of Arc (1412–1431), and a sense of national identity and self-confidence, the French were able to expel the English from France. By 1453, all that remained to the English was their coastal enclave of Calais.

Charles forgot his liberator as quickly as he had embraced her. When the Burgundians captured Joan in May 1430, he could have secured her release but did not. The Burgundians and the English wanted her publicly discredited, believing this would demoralize French resistance. She was turned over to the Inquisition in English-held Rouen, where, after ten weeks of interrogation, she was executed on May 30, 1431.

The Hundred Years' War had lasting political and social consequences. It devastated France, but it also awakened French nationalism and hastened the country's transition from a feudal monarchy to a centralized state. In both France and England the burden of the war fell most heavily on the peasantry, who were forced to support it with taxes and services.

The Black Death

Preconditions and Causes In the fourteenth century, nine-tenths of the population worked the land. The three-field system of crop production increased the amount of arable land and with it the food supply. But as that supply grew, so did the population. It is estimated that Europe's population doubled between the years 1000 and 1300 and began thereafter to outstrip food production. There were now more people than there was food to feed them or jobs to employ them, and the average European faced the probability of extreme hunger at least once during his or her expected thirty-five-year life span.

Popular wisdom held that a corruption in the atmosphere caused the disease. Some blamed poisonous fumes released by earthquakes. Many wore aromatic amulets as a remedy. According to the contemporary observations of Boccaccio, who recorded the reactions in the *Decameron* (1353), some sought a remedy in moderation and a temperate life, others gave themselves over entirely to their passions (sexual promiscuity ran high within the stricken areas), and still others, "the most sound, perhaps, in judgment" chose flight and seclusion as the best medicine.

One extreme reaction was processions of flagellants, religious fanatics who beat themselves in ritual penance, believing such action would bring divine intervention. The terror created by the flagellants, whose dirty bodies may have transported the disease, became so socially disruptive and threatening that the church finally outlawed such processions.

In some places, Jews were cast as scapegoats. Centuries of Christian propaganda had bred hatred towards Jews, as had their role as society's moneylenders. Pogroms occurred in several cities, sometimes incited by the flagellants.

Social and Economic Consequences Whole villages vanished in the wake of the plague. Among the social and economic consequences of such high depopulation were a shrunken labor supply and a decline in the value of the estates of the nobility. As the number of farm laborers decreased, wages increased and those of skilled artisans soared. Many serfs chose to commute their labor services by money payments and pursue more interesting and rewarding jobs in skilled craft industries in the cities. Agricultural prices fell because of lowered demand, and the price of luxury and manufactured goods—the work of skilled artisans—rose. The noble landholders suffered the greatest decline in power. They were forced to pay more for finished products and for farm labor, while receiving a smaller return on their agricultural produce. Everywhere rents declined after the plague.

Peasants Revolt To recoup their losses, some landowners converted arablland to sheep pasture, substituting more profitable wool production for labor-intensive grain crops. Others abandoned the farms, leasing them to the highest bidder. Landowners also sought to reverse their misfortune by new repressive legislation that forced peasants to stay on their farms while freezing their wages at low levels. In 1351, the

Between 1315 and 1317, cold weather and crop failures produced the greatest famine of the Middle Ages. Densely populated urban areas such as the industrial towns of the Netherlands experienced great suffering. Decades of overpopulation, economic depression, famine, and bad health progressively weakened Europe's population and made it highly vulnerable to a virulent bubonic plague that struck with full force in 1348.

The **Black Death**, so called by contemporaries because of the way it discolored the body, was most likely introduced by rats from Black Sea areas, the epidemic following the trade routes from Asia into Europe. 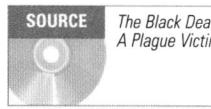 *The Black Death: A Plague Victim* Appearing in Sicily in late 1347, it entered Europe through the port cities of Venice, Genoa, and Pisa in 1348, and from there it swept rapidly through Spain and southern France and into northern Europe. Areas that lay outside the major trade routes, like Bohemia, appear to have remained virtually unaffected. Bubonic plague made numerous reappearances in succeeding decades. It is estimated that Western Europe had lost as much as two fifths of its population by the early fifteenth century. (See Map 16–4.)

Popular Remedies Transmitted by rat- or human-borne fleas, the plague often reached a victim's lungs during the course of the disease. From the lungs, it was spread from person to person by the victim's 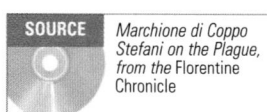 *Marchione di Coppo Stefani on the Plague, from the* Florentine Chronicle sneezing and wheezing. Contemporary physicians had little understanding of these processes, so the most rudimentary prophylaxis was lacking. Throughout much of Western Europe, the plague brought with it an obsession with death and dying, engendering a deep pessimism that endured for decades.

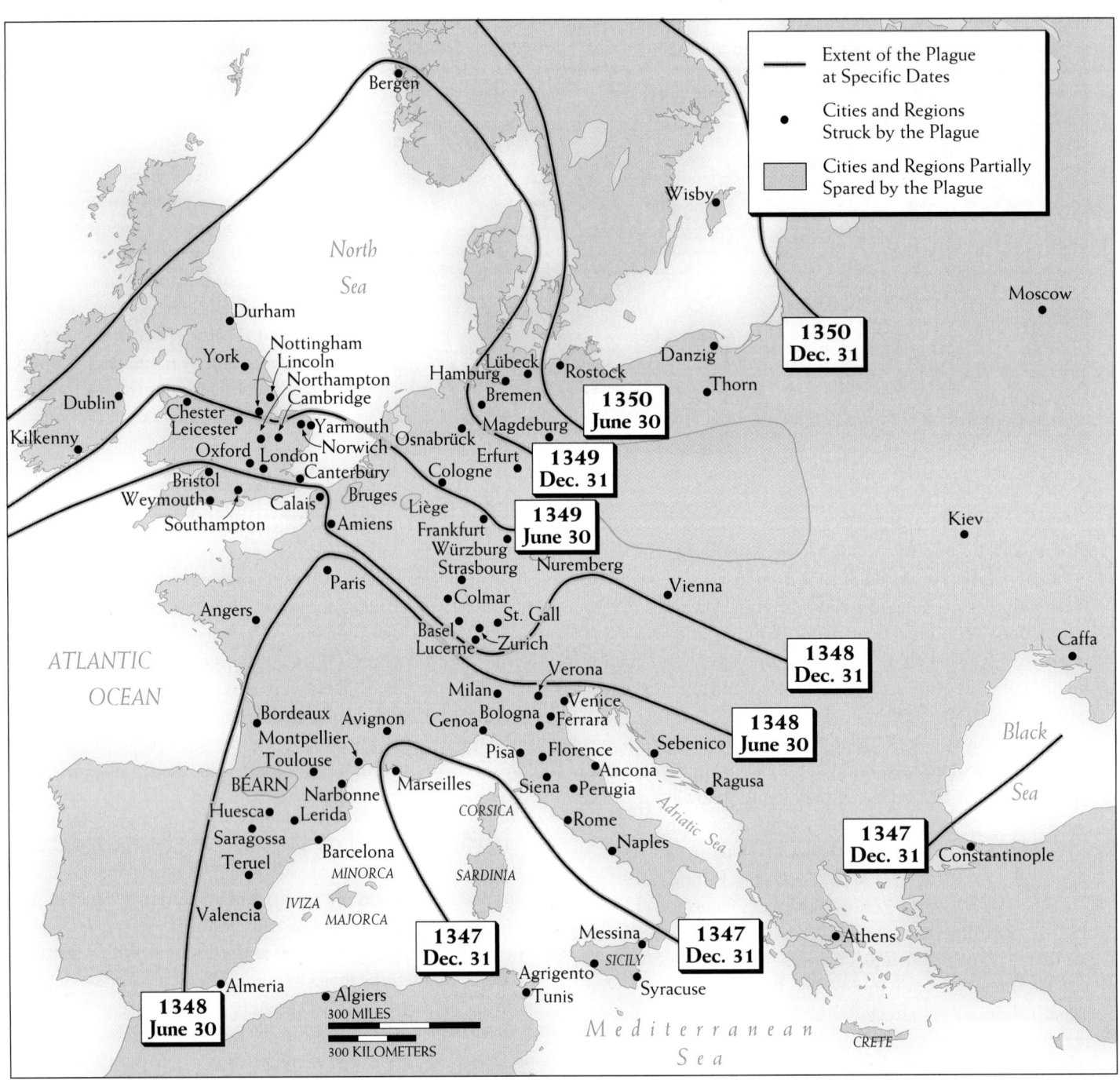

Map 16–4. Spread of the Black Death. Apparently introduced by sea-borne rats from areas around the Black Sea where plague-infested rodents have long been known, the Black Death had great human, social, and economic consequences. According to one of the lower estimates, it killed 25 million in Europe. The map charts the spread of the plague in the mid–fourteenth century. Generally following trade routes, it reached Scandinavia by 1350, and some believe it then went on to Iceland and even Greenland. Areas off the main trade routes were largely spared.

English Parliament passed a Statute of Laborers, which limited wages to preplague levels and restricted the ability of peasants to leave the land of their masters. Opposition to such legislation was also a prominent factor in the English peasants' revolt in 1381. In France the direct tax on the peasantry, the **taille**, was increased, and opposition to it helped ignite the French peasant uprising known as the Jacquerie.

The consequences of both revolts were modest compared to the German Peasant's Revolt in 1525 (see Chapter 17).

Cities Rebound Although the plague hit urban populations hard, the cities and their skilled industries came in time to prosper from its effects. Cities had always protected their interests, passing legislation as they grew to regulate competition from rural areas and to control immigration. After the plague, the reach of such laws extended beyond the cities to include the surrounding lands of nobles and landlords, many of whom now peacefully integrated into urban life.

The omnipresence of death also whetted the appetite for goods that only skilled industries could produce. Expensive cloths and jewelry, furs from the north, and silks from the south were in great demand in the decades after the plague. Initially this new demand could not be met. The basic unit of urban industry, the master and his apprentices (usually one or two), purposely kept its numbers low, jealously guarding its privileges. The first wave of plague turned this already restricted supply of skilled artisans into a shortage almost overnight. As a result, the prices of manufactured and luxury items rose to new heights, which in turn encouraged workers to migrate from the countryside to the city and learn the skills of artisans. Townspeople profited coming and going. As wealth poured into the cities and per capita income rose, agricultural products from the countryside, now less in demand, declined.

There was also gain and loss for the church. It suffered as a landholder and was politically weakened, yet at the same time it received new revenues from the vastly increased demand for religious services for the dead and the dying, along with new gifts and bequests.

New Conflicts and Opportunities

By increasing the importance of skilled artisans, the plague contributed to new social conflicts within the cities. The economic and political power of local artisans and trade guilds grew steadily in the late Middle Ages, along with the demand for their goods and services. The merchant and patrician classes found it increasingly difficult to maintain their traditional dominance and grudgingly gave guild masters a voice in city government. As the guilds won political power, they encouraged restrictive legislation to protect local industries. The restrictions, in turn, caused conflict between master artisans, who wanted to keep their numbers low and expand their industries at a snail's pace, and the many journeymen, who were eager to rise to the rank of master. To the long-existing conflict between the guilds and the ruling urban patriciate was now added a conflict within the guilds themselves.

Also after 1350, the two traditional "containers" of monarchy—the landed nobility and the church—were put on the defensive as a consequence of the plague. Kings now exploited growing national sentiment in an effort to centralize their governments and economies. At the same time, the battles of the Hundred Years' War demonstrated the military superiority of paid professional armies over the traditional noble cavalry, thus bringing into question the latter's future role. The plague also killed many members of the clergy—perhaps one third of the German clergy fell victim as they dutifully ministered to the sick and dying. This reduction in clerical ranks occurred in the same century that saw the pope move from Rome to Avignon (1309–1377) and the Great Schism (1378–1417) divide the church into warring factions.

Ecclesiastical Breakdown and Revival: The Late Medieval Church

Boniface VIII and Philip the Fair

By the fourteenth century popes faced rulers far more powerful than the papacy. When Pope Boniface VIII (r. 1294–1303) issued a bull, *Clericis Laicos*, which forbade lay taxation of the clergy without prior papal approval, King Philip the Fair of France (r. 1285–1314) unleashed a ruthless antipapal campaign. Boniface made a last-ditch stand against state control of national churches on November 18, 1302, when he issued the bull *Unam Sanctam*, which declared that temporal authority was "subject" to the spiritual power of the church.

The French responded with force. Philip sent troops who beat the pope badly and might even have executed him had not an aroused populace liberated the pope and returned him safely to Rome.

There was no papal retaliation. No pope ever again so seriously threatened kings and emperors. Future relations between church and state would henceforth tilt towards state control of religion within particular monarchies.

Papal Authority. Pope Boniface VIII (r. 1294–1303), who opposed the taxation of the clergy by the kings of France and England, issued one of the strongest declarations of papal authority, the bull *Unam Sanctam*. This statue is in the Museo Civico, Bologna, Italy. *Scala/Art Resource, N.Y.*

The Great Schism (1378–1417) and the Conciliar Movement to 1449

After Boniface VIII's death, his successor, Clement V (r. 1305–1314), moved the papal court to Avignon on the southeastern border with France, where it remained until Pope Gregory XI (r. 1370–1378) reestablished the papacy in Rome in January 1377. His successor, Pope Urban VI (r. 1378– 1389), proclaimed his intention to reform the papal government in the **Curia**. This announcement alarmed the cardinals, most of whom were French. Not wanting to surrender the benefits of a papacy under French influence, the French king, Charles V (r. 1364–1380), supported a schism in the church, known thereafter as the **Great Schism**. On September 20, 1378, thirteen cardinals, all but one of whom were French, elected a cousin of the French king as Pope Clement VII (r. 1378–1397). Clement returned to Avignon. Thereafter allegiance to the two papal courts divided along political lines: Acknowledging Urban VI were England and its allies—the **Holy Roman Empire** (based on the old Roman Empire, mostly Germany and Northern Italy), Hungary, Bohemia, and Poland. Supporting Clement VII were France and its orbit—Naples, Scotland, Castile, and Aragon. Only the Roman line of popes, however, is recognized as official by the church.

In 1409 a council at Pisa deposed both the Roman and the Avignon popes and elected its own new pope. But neither Rome nor Avignon accepted its action, so after 1409 there were three contending popes. This intolerable situation ended when the emperor Sigismund (r. 1410–1437) prevailed on the Pisan pope to summon a legal council of the church in Constance in 1414, a council also recognized by the reigning Roman pope Gregory XII (r. 1406–1415). After the three contending popes had either resigned or been deposed, the council elected a new pope, Martin V (r. 1417–1431), in November 1417, reuniting the church.

Under Pope Eugenius IV (r. 1431–1447), the papacy regained much of its prestige and authority, and in 1460 the papal bull *Execrabilis* condemned all appeals to councils as "completely null and void." But the conciliar movement had planted deep within the conscience of all Western peoples the conviction that the leader of an institution must be responsive to its members and not act against their best interests.

The Renaissance in Italy (1375–1527)

The **Renaissance** is the term used to describe fourteenth- and fifteenth-century efforts to revive ancient learning. Most scholars agree that it was a transition from the medieval to the modern world. Medieval Europe, especially before the twelfth century, had been a fragmented feudal society with an agricultural economy, its thought and culture dominated by the church. Renaissance Europe, especially after the fourteenth century, was characterized by growing national consciousness and political centralization, an urban economy based on organized commerce and capitalism, and ever-greater lay and secular control of thought and culture.

The distinctive features and achievements of the Renaissance are most strikingly revealed in Italy from roughly 1375 to 1527, the year of the infamous sack of Rome by imperial soldiers. What was achieved in Italy during these centuries also deeply influenced northern Europe.

The Italian City-State: Social Conflict and Despotism

Renaissance society took distinctive shape within the cities of late medieval Italy. Italy was the natural gateway between East and West. Venice, Genoa, and Pisa traded uninterruptedly with the Near East throughout the Middle Ages and maintained vibrant urban societies. During the thirteenth and fourteenth centuries, the trade-rich Italian cities became powerful city-states, dominating the political and economic life of the surrounding countryside. By the fifteenth century, the great Italian cities had become the bankers for much of Europe. There were five such major, competitive states in Italy: the duchy of Milan, the republics of Florence and Venice, the Papal States, and the kingdom of Naples (see Map 16–5).

Social strife and competition for political power were so intense within the cities that for survival's sake, most had evolved into despotisms by the fifteenth century. Venice, ruled by a successful merchant oligarchy, was the notable exception. Elsewhere, the new social classes and divisions within society produced by rapid urban growth fueled chronic, near-anarchic conflict.

In Florence, these social divisions produced conflict at every level of society. True stability was not established until the ascent to power in 1434 of Cosimo de' Medici (1389–1464). The wealthiest Florentine and a most astute statesman, Cosimo controlled the city internally from behind the scenes, skillfully manipulating the constitution and influencing elections. His grandson Lorenzo the Magnificent (1449–1492, r. 1478–1492) ruled Florence in an almost totalitarian fashion.

Despotism was less subtle elsewhere in Italy. To prevent internal social conflict and foreign intrigue from paralyzing their cities, the dominant groups in many cities cooperated in the hiring of a strongman, known as a *podesta*, to maintain law and order. Because these despots could not depend on the divided populace, they operated through mercenary armies.

Political turbulence and warfare also gave birth to diplomacy, through which the various city-states stayed abreast of foreign military developments and, if shrewd enough, gained

Duchy of Milan	Republic of Venice
Republic of Genoa	Papal States
Republic of Florence	Kingdom of Naples

Map 16–5. Renaissance Italy. The city-states of Renaissance Italy were self-contained principalities whose internal strife was monitored by their despots and whose external conflicts were successfully controlled by treaties.

power and advantage without actually going to war. Most city-states established resident embassies during the fifteenth century, their ambassadors watchful eyes and ears at rival courts. Renaissance culture was promoted as vigorously by despots as by republicans and by popes as enthusiastically as by humanists.

Humanism

Humanism was the scholarly study of the Latin and Greek classics and the ancient Church Fathers, both for their own sake and to promote a rebirth of ancient norms and values.

Humanists advocated the *studia humanitatis*, a liberal arts program that embraced grammar, rhetoric, poetry, history, politics, and moral philosophy.

The first humanists were orators and poets. They wrote original literature in both the classical and vernacular languages, inspired by the newly discovered works of the ancients, and they taught rhetoric within the universities. They were sought as secretaries, speech writers, and diplomats in princely and papal courts.

Classical and Christian antiquity had been studied before the Italian Renaissance—during the Carolingian renaissance of the ninth century, for example. However, the Italian Renaissance of the late Middle Ages was more secular and lay dominated, had broader interests, recovered more manuscripts, and possessed far superior technical skills than earlier rebirths of antiquity.

Unlike their Scholastic rivals, humanists were not content only to summarize and compare the views of recognized authorities on a question but instead went directly to the original source and drew their own conclusions. Avidly searching out manuscript collections, Italian humanists made the full sources of Greek and Latin antiquity available to scholars during the fourteenth and fifteenth centuries. Mastery of Latin and Greek was their surgeon's tool. There is a kernel of truth—but only a kernel—in the arrogant boast of the humanists that the period between themselves and classical civilization was a "dark middle age."

Petrarch, Dante, and Boccaccio Francesco Petrarch (1304–1374) was the father of humanism. He left the legal profession to pursue his love of letters and poetry. Petrarch celebrated ancient Rome in his writings and tirelessly collected ancient manuscripts; among his finds were letters by Cicero. His critical textual studies, elitism, and contempt for the allegedly useless learning of the Scholastics were shared by many later humanists.

Petrarch was far more secular in orientation than Dante Alighieri (1265–1321), whose *Vita Nuova* and *Divine Comedy*—together with Petrarch's sonnets—form the cornerstones of Italian vernacular literature. Also pioneering humanist studies was Petrarch's student and friend Giovanni Boccaccio (1313–1375), author of the *Decameron*, 100 bawdy tales told by three men and seven women in a country retreat from the plague that ravaged Florence in 1348. An avid collector of manuscripts, Boccaccio assembled an encyclopedia of Greek and Roman mythology.

Educational Reforms and Goals The classical ideal of a useful education that produces well-rounded, effective people inspired far-reaching reforms in traditional education. The most influential Italian Renaissance tract on education, Pietro Paolo Vergerio's (1349–1420) *On the Morals That Befit*

Jan van Eyck, "Adam and Eve" (1432). In the wings of the Dutch painter Jan van Eyck's earliest work, the Ghent Altarpiece, Adam and Eve appear after their fall. Unlike the Italian Renaissance masters, the Netherlandish master portrays them as true-to-life humans, not heroic, idealized figures. Above their heads their son Cain kills his brother Abel, a commentary humankind after the Fall."

a Free Man, was written directly from classical models. Vittorino da Feltre (d. 1446) directed his students to a highly disciplined reading of ancient authors, together with vigorous physical exercise and games with intellectual pursuits.

Educated and cultured noblewomen also had a prominent place at Renaissance courts, among them Christine de Pisan (1363?–1434). She was an expert in classical, French, and Italian languages and literature and became a well-known woman of letters in the courts of Europe. Her most famous work, *The City of Ladies*, describes the accomplishments of the great women of history.

Renaissance Art in and Beyond Italy

Throughout Renaissance Europe, the values and interests of the laity were less subordinated to those of the clergy than in previous centuries. In education, culture, and religion, a more this-worldly spirit was evident. The secular world and secular learning along with many purely human pursuits were again appreciated as ends in themselves.

This perspective on life is especially prominent in the painting and sculpture of the High Renaissance, the late fifteenth and early sixteenth centuries, when Renaissance art reached its maturity. In imitation of Greek and Roman art, painters and sculptors created well-proportioned and even heroic figures, as they strove to present the perfect human form. Whereas Byzantine and Gothic art had been religious and edgy in their representation of the human body, Renaissance art, especially in the fifteenth century, reproduced nature and human nature realistically, in both its physical beauty and grotesqueness.

Italian Renaissance artists led the way. They took advantage of new technical skills and materials developed during the fifteenth century: oil paints, the technique of shading to enhance realism (**chiaroscuro**), and sizing figures to convey to the viewer a feeling of continuity with a painting (linear perspective).Compared with their flat, two-dimensional Byzantine and Gothic counterparts, the new artists could fill a canvas or wood panel with energy and life in three dimensions.

The Italian artists Leonardo da Vinci (1452–1519) and Michelangelo Buonarroti (1475–1564) personified the Renaissance ideal of the universal person, one who is a master

of many skills and trades. A military engineer and advocate of scientific experimentation, Leonardo dissected corpses to learn anatomy and was a self-taught botanist. He foresaw such modern machines as airplanes and submarines. The variety of his interests tended to shorten his attention span, so that he constantly moved from one activity to another. As a painter, his great skill lay in conveying inner moods through complex facial features, such as that seen in the most famous of his paintings, the Mona Lisa.

The melancholy genius Michelangelo also excelled in a variety of arts and crafts. His eighteen-foot godlike sculpture *David* is a perfect example of the Renaissance artist's devotion to harmony, symmetry, and proportion, which can also be seen in his extreme glorification of the human form. Four different popes commissioned his works, the best known of which are the frescoes for the Sistine Chapel, painted for Pope Julius II (r. 1503–1513). His later works mark, artistically and philosophically, the passing of High Renaissance painting and the advent of a modernizing, experimental style

Michelangelo's "Scene from the Last Judgment" The High Italian Renaissance obsession with the beefy, pumped-up, heroic body finds expression in this detail of a fresco in Michelangelo's rendering of the "Last Judgment" in the Sistine Chapel.

known as **Mannerism**, which reached its peak in the late sixteenth and early seventeenth centuries. It derived its name from the fact that it permitted the artist to express his own individual perceptions and feelings to paint, compose, or write in a "mannered" or "affected" way. Tintoretto (d. 1594) and the Spaniard El Greco (d. 1614) would become its supreme representatives.

Italy's Political Decline: The French Invasions (1494–1527)

Autonomous city-states of Italy had always preserved their peace and safety from foreign invasion by cooperation with each other. However, in 1494 Naples, supported by Florence and the Borgia pope Alexander VI (1492–1503), prepared to attack Milan. At this point, the Milanese despot Ludovico il Moro (r. 1476–1499) invited the French to revive their dynastic claim to Naples. But France also had dynastic claims to Milan, and the French appetite for new territory became insatiable once French armies had crossed the Alps and reestablished themselves in Italy.

The French king Charles VIII (r. 1483–1498) responded rapidly to Ludovico's call. Within five months he had crossed the Alps (August 1495) and raced as conqueror through Florence and the Papal States into Naples.

Charles's lightning march through Italy alarmed Ferdinand of Aragon (r. 1479–1516), who was also king of Sicily, and helped to create a counteralliance: the League of Venice, which was able to force Charles to retreat.

The French returned to Italy under Charles's successor, Louis XII (r. 1498–1515), this time assisted by the Borgia pope Alexander VI (1492–1503). Alexander, probably the most corrupt pope in history, sought to secure a political base in Romagna, officially part of the Papal States, for his son Cesare.

Seeing that a French alliance could allow him to reestablish control over the region, Alexander agreed to abandon the League of Venice, which made the league too weak to resist a French reconquest of Milan. Louis successfully invaded Milan in August 1499. In 1500 he and Ferdinand of Aragon divided Naples between themselves, while the pope and Cesare Borgia conquered the Romagna without opposition.

In 1503 Cardinal Giuliano della Rovere became Pope Julius II (1503–1513). He suppressed the Borgias and placed their newly conquered lands in Romagna under papal jurisdiction. After fully securing the Papal States with French aid, Julius changed sides and sought to rid Italy of his former ally, the French invaders. Julius, Ferdinand of Aragon, and Venice formed a Holy League in October 1511, and soon Emperor Maximilian I (r. 1493–1519) and the Swiss joined them. By 1512 the French were in full retreat.

The French invaded Italy again under Louis' successor, Francis I (r. 1515–1547). French armies massacred Swiss soldiers of the Holy League at Marignano in September 1515. That victory won from the Medici pope Leo X (r. 1513–1521) an agreement known as the Concordat of Bologna (August 1516), which gave the French king control over the French clergy and the right to collect taxes from them, in exchange for French recognition of the pope's superiority over church councils. This helped keep France Catholic after the outbreak of the Protestant Reformation. But the new French entry into Italy also led to the first of four major wars with Spain in the first half of the sixteenth century: the Habsburg-Valois wars, none of which France won.

Niccolò Machiavelli

The foreign invasions made a shambles of Italy. One who watched as French, Spanish, and German armies wreaked havoc on his country was Niccolò Machiavelli (1469–1527). The more he saw, the more convinced he became that Italian political unity and independence were ends that justified any means. Machiavelli admired the heroic acts of ancient Roman rulers, what Renaissance people called their

Niccolò Machiavelli. Santi di Tito's portrait of Machiavelli, perhaps the most famous Italian political theorist, who advised Renaissance princes to practice artful deception and inspire fear in their subjects if they wished to succeed. *Scala/Art Resource, N.Y.*

Virtù. Romanticizing the old Roman citizenry, he lamented the absence of heroism among his compatriots. Such a perspective caused his interpretation of both ancient and contemporary history to be exaggerated.

The juxtaposition of what Machiavelli believed the ancient Romans had been with the failure of contemporary Romans to realize such high ideals made him the famous cynic we know in the popular epithet *Machiavellian*. Only an unscrupulous strongman, he concluded, using duplicity and terror, could impose order on so divided and selfish a people. Machiavelli seems to have been in earnest when he advised rulers to discover the advantages of fraud and brutality. He apparently hoped to see a strong ruler emerge from the Medici family. The Medicis, however, were not destined to be Italy's deliverers. The second Medici pope, Clement VII (r. 1523–1534), watched helplessly as Rome was sacked by the army of Emperor Charles V (r. 1519–1556) in 1527, the year of Machiavelli's death.

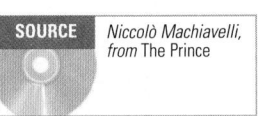

SOURCE · *Niccolò Machiavelli, from* The Prince

Pico della Mirandola States the Renaissance Image of Man

Document

One of the most eloquent Renaissance descriptions of the abilities of humankind comes from the Italian humanist Pico della Mirandola (1463–1494). In his famed *Oration on the Dignity of Man* (ca. 1486), Pico described humans as free to become whatever they choose.

◆ In what does the dignity of humankind consist? Does Pico reject the biblical description of Adam and Eve's fall? Does he exaggerate a person's ability to choose freely to be whatever he or she wishes? What inspired such seeming hubris during the Renaissance?

The best of artisans [God] ordained that that creature (man) to whom He [God] had been able to give nothing proper to himself should have joint possession of whatever had been peculiar to each of the different kinds of being. He therefore took man as a creature of indeterminate nature and, assigning him a place in the middle of the world, addressed him thus: "Neither a fixed abode nor a form that is thine alone or any function peculiar to thyself have we given thee, Adam, to the end that according to thy longing and according to thy judgment thou mayest have and possess what abode, what form, and what functions thou thyself shalt desire. The nature of all other beings is limited and constrained within the bounds of laws prescribed by Us. Thou, constrained by no limits, in accordance with thine own free will, in whose hand We have placed thee, shall ordain for thyself the limits of thy nature. We have set thee at the world's center that thou mayest from thence more easily observe whatever is in the world. We have made thee neither of heaven nor of earth, neither mortal nor immortal, so that with freedom of choice and with honor, as though the maker and molder of thyself, thou mayest fashion thyself in whatever shape thou shalt prefer. Thou shalt have the power to degenerate into the lower forms of life, which are brutish. Thou shalt have the power, out of thy soul's judgment, to be reborn into the higher forms, which are divine." O supreme generosity of God the Father, O highest and most marvelous felicity of man! To him it is granted to have whatever he chooses, to be whatever he wills.

From Giovanni Pico della Mirandola, *Oration on the Dignity of Man*, in *The Renaissance Philosophy of Man*, ed. by E. Cassirer et al. Phoenix Books, 1961, pp. 224–225. Reprinted by permission of The University of Chicago Press.

Chronology

Major Political Events of the Italian Renaissance (1375–1527)

1378–1382	Ciompi revolt in Florence
1434	Medici rule in Florence established by Cosimo de' Medici
1454–1455	Treaty of Lodi allies Milan, Naples, and Florence (in effect until 1494)
1494	Charles VIII of France invades Italy
1495	League of Venice unites Venice, Milan, the Papal States, the Holy Roman Empire, and Spain against France
1499	Louis XII invades Milan (the second French invasion of Italy)
1500	The Borgias conquer Romagna
1512–1513	The Holy League (Pope Julius II, Ferdinand of Aragon, Emperor Maximilian I, and Venice) defeat the French
1513	Machiavelli writes *The Prince*
1515	Francis I leads the third French invasion of Italy
1516	Concordat of Bologna between France and the papacy
1527	Sack of Rome by imperial soldiers

Revival of Monarchy: Nation Building in the Fifteenth Century

With the emergence of sovereign rulers after 1450, unified national monarchies progressively replaced fragmented and divisive feudal governance, but the dynastic and chivalric ideals of feudalism did not disappear. Minor territorial princes survived, and representative assemblies even grew in influence in some regions. But by the late fifteenth and early sixteenth centuries, the old problem of the one and the many was being decided clearly in favor of monarchy.

In the feudal monarchy of the High Middle Ages, the basic powers of government were divided between the king and his semi-autonomous vassals. The nobility and the towns acted with varying degrees of unity and success through such evolving representative bodies as the English Parliament, the French Estates General, and the Spanish Cortes to thwart the centralization of royal power. However, as a result of the Hundred Years' War and the schism in the church, the landed nobility and the clergy were in decline in the late Middle Ages. The increasingly important towns now began to ally with the king. Loyal, businesswise townspeople, not the nobility and the clergy, staffed the royal offices, becoming the king's lawyers, bookkeepers, military tacticians, and diplomats. This new alliance between king and town would slowly break the bonds of feudal society and make possible the rise of the modern sovereign state.

In a sovereign state, the powers of taxation, war making, and law enforcement are no longer the local right of semi-autonomous vassals but are concentrated in the monarch and exercised by his chosen agents. Taxes, wars, and laws become national rather than merely regional matters. Only because monarchs were able to act independently of the nobility and the representative assemblies could they overcome the decentralization that had been the basic obstacle to nation building.

Monarchies also began to create standing national armies in the fifteenth century. As the noble cavalry receded and the infantry and the artillery became the backbone of armies, mercenary soldiers were recruited from Switzerland and Germany to form the mainstay of the "king's army."

The growing cost of warfare increased the need to develop new national sources of royal income. The expansion of royal revenues was especially hampered by the stubborn belief among the highest classes that they were immune from government taxation. The nobility guarded their properties and traditional rights and despised taxation as an insult and a humiliation. Royal revenues accordingly grew at the expense of those least able to resist and least able to pay. Monarchs had several options. As feudal lords they could collect rents from their royal domain. They might also levy national taxes on basic food and clothing, such as the *gabelle* or salt tax in France and the *alcabala* or 10 percent sales tax on commercial transactions in Spain. Kings could also levy direct taxes on the peasantry and on commercial transactions in towns under royal protection. This they did through agreeable representative assemblies of the privileged classes in which the peasantry did not sit. The French *taille* was such a tax. Sale of public offices and the issuance of high-interest government bonds appeared in the fifteenth century as innovative fund-raising devices. But kings did not levy taxes on the powerful nobility. They turned for loans to rich nobles, as they did to the great bankers of Italy and Germany, bargaining with the privileged classes, who often remained as much the kings' creditors and competitors as their subjects.

Medieval Russia

In the late tenth century Prince Vladimir of Kiev (r. 972–1015), then Russia's dominant city, received delegations of Muslims, Roman Catholics, Jews, and Greek Orthodox Christians, each group hoping to win the Russians to its religion. Prince Vladimir chose Greek Orthodoxy, which became the religion of Russia, adding a new cultural bond to the long-standing commercial ties the Russians had with the Byzantine Empire.

Vladimir's successor, Yaroslav the Wise (r. 1016–1054), developed Kiev into a magnificent political and cultural center, but after his death, rivalry among princes challenged Kiev's dominance, and it became just one of several national centers.

Mongol Rule (1243–1480) and Russian Liberation Mongol (or Tatar) armies (see Chapters 8 and 13) invaded Russia in 1223, and Kiev fell in 1240. Russian cities became tribute-paying principalities of the segment of the Mongol Empire called the **Golden Horde**, which had its capital at Sarai, on the lower Volga. Mongol rule further divided Russia from the West but left Russian political institutions and religion largely intact. Thanks to their far-flung trade, the Mongolians brought most Russians greater peace and prosperity than they had enjoyed before.

The princes of Moscow cooperated with the Mongols and grew wealthy. They then gradually expanded the principality through land purchases, colonization, and conquest. In 1380 Grand Duke Dimitri of Moscow (1350–1389) defeated Tatar forces at Kulikov Meadow in a victory that marked the beginning of the decline of Mongolian hegemony. Another century would pass before Ivan III, called Ivan the Great (d. 1505), would bring all of northern Russia under Moscow's control and end Mongol rule in 1480 (See Map 16–6). By the last quarter of the fifteenth century, Moscow had replaced Kiev as the political and religious center of Russia. In Russian eyes it was destined to become the "third Rome" after the fall of Constantinople to the Turks in 1453.

France

There were two cornerstones of French nation building in the fifteenth century. The first was the collapse of the English holdings in France following the Hundred Years' War. The second was the defeat of Charles the Bold (r. 1467–1477) and the duchy of Burgundy. Perhaps Europe's strongest political power in the mid–fifteenth century, Burgundy aspired to lead a dominant middle kingdom between France and the Holy Roman Empire. It might have succeeded had not the Continental powers joined together in opposition. When Charles the Bold was killed at Nancy in 1477, the dream of Burgundian empire died with him.

The dissolution of Burgundy ended its constant intrigue against the French king and left Louis XI (r. 1461–1483) free to secure the monarchy. The newly acquired Burgundian lands and his own Angevin inheritance permitted the king to double

Map 16–6. Russia, ca. 1500.

the size of his kingdom. Louis harnessed the nobility and expanded trade and industry.

A strong nation is a two-edged sword. It was because Louis' successors inherited such a secure and efficient government that France was able to pursue Italian conquests in the 1490s and to fight a long series of losing wars with the Habsburgs in the first half of the sixteenth century. By the mid–sixteenth century France was again a defeated nation and almost as divided internally as it had been during the Hundred Years' War.

Spain

Spain, too, became a strong country in the late fifteenth century. Both Castile and Aragon had been poorly ruled, divided kingdoms in the mid–fifteenth century. The marriage of Isabella of Castile (r. 1474–1504) and Ferdinand of Aragon (r. 1479–1516) changed that situation. The two future sovereigns married in 1469, despite strong protests from neighboring Portugal and France, both of which foresaw the formidable European power such a union would create. Castile was by far the richer and more populous of the two, having an estimated 5 million inhabitants to Aragon's population of under 1 million. Castile was also distinguished by its lucrative sheep-farming industry, which was run by a government-backed organization called the *Mesta*, another example of developing centralized economic planning. Although the two kingdoms were dynastically united by the marriage of Ferdinand and Isabella in 1469, each retained its own government agencies—separate laws, armies, coinage, and taxation—and cultural traditions.

Ferdinand and Isabella could do together what neither was able to accomplish alone, namely, subdue their realms, secure their borders, and venture abroad militarily. Townspeople allied themselves with the crown and progressively replaced the nobility within the royal administration. The crown also extended its authority over the wealthy chivalric orders, a further circumscription of the power of the nobility.

Spain had long been remarkable as a place where three religions—Islam, Judaism, and Christianity—coexisted with a certain degree of toleration. This toleration ended dramatically under Ferdinand and Isabella, who made Spain the prime example of state-controlled religion. Ferdinand and Isabella exercised almost total control over the Spanish church as they placed religion in the service of national unity. They appointed the higher clergy and the officers of the Inquisition. The Inquisition, run by Tomás de Torquemada (d. 1498), Isabella's confessor, was a key national agency established in 1479 to monitor the activity of converted Jews (*conversos*) and Muslims (*Moriscos*) in Spain. In 1492 the Jews were exiled and their properties were confiscated. In 1502 nonconverting Moors in Granada were driven into exile.

Spanish spiritual life remained largely uniform and regimented, a major reason for Spain's remaining a loyal Catholic country throughout the sixteenth century and providing a base of operation for the European Counter-Reformation.

Ferdinand and Isabella had wide horizons. They contracted anti-French marriage alliances that came to determine much of European history in the sixteenth century. In 1496 their eldest daughter, Joanna, later known as "the Mad" (1479–1555), married Archduke Philip (1478–1506), the son of Emperor Maximilian I (r. 1493–1519). Their son, Charles I, the first ruler over a united Spain, came by his inheritance and election as Emperor Charles V in 1519 to rule over a European kingdom almost equal in size to that of Charlemagne. A second daughter, Catherine of Aragon (1485–1536), married King Henry VIII of England. The failure of this latter marriage became the key factor in the emergence of the Anglican Church and the English Reformation.

The new Spanish power was also evident in Ferdinand and Isabella's promotion of overseas exploration. Their patronage of the Genoese adventurer Christopher Columbus (1451–1506), who discovered the islands of the Caribbean while sailing west in search of a shorter route to the spice markets of the Far East, led to the creation of the Spanish Empire in Mexico and Peru, whose gold and silver mines helped to make Spain Europe's dominant power in the sixteenth century.

England

The last half of the fifteenth century was a period of especially difficult political trial for the English. Following the Hundred Years' War, a defeated England was subjected to internal warfare between two rival branches of the royal family, the House of York and the House of Lancaster. This conflict, known to us today as the Wars of the Roses (as York's symbol, according to legend, was a white rose, and Lancaster's a red rose), kept England in turmoil from 1455 to 1485.

The Lancastrian monarchy of Henry VI (r. 1422–1461) was consistently challenged by the Duke of York and his supporters in the prosperous southern towns. In 1461 Edward IV (r. 1461–1483), son of the Duke of York, seized power and, assisted by loyal and able ministers, effectively bent Parliament to his will. His brother and successor was Richard III (r. 1483–1485), whose reign saw the growth of support for the exiled Lancastrian Henry Tudor. Henry returned to England to defeat Richard on Bosworth Field in August 1485.

Henry Tudor ruled as Henry VII (r. 1485–1509), the first of the new Tudor dynasty that would endure until 1603. To bring the rival royal families together and to make the hereditary claim of his offspring to the throne uncontestable, Henry married Edward IV's daughter, Elizabeth of York. He succeeded in disciplining the English nobility through a special and much-feared instrument of the royal will known as the Court of Star Chamber. Henry shrewdly construed legal precedents to the advantage of the crown, using English law to further his own ends. He confiscated so much noble land and so many fortunes that he governed without dependence on Parliament for royal funds, always a cornerstone of strong monarchy. Henry thus began to shape a monarchy that became one of early modern Europe's most exemplary governments during the reign of his granddaughter, Elizabeth I (r. 1558–1603).

Summary

Medieval Society. In theory, medieval society was divided into three main groups: clergy (those who prayed), nobility (those who fought as mounted warriors), and laborers (peasants and artisans). The rise of merchants, self-governing towns, and universities helped break down this division. By supporting rulers against the nobility, towns gave kings the resources—money and university-trained bureaucrats and lawyers—to build national governments. Much of medieval history involved the struggle by rulers to assert their authority over powerful local lords and the church.

Church and State. The medieval papacy sought to extend its power over both church and state. In the tenth century, the Cluny reform movement increased popular respect for the church and strengthened the papacy. In the Investiture Struggle, the papacy secured the independence of the clergy by enlisting the support of the German princes against the Holy Roman Emperors, thus weakening imperial power in Germany. The First Crusade further strengthened papal prestige. But, by the end of the thirteenth century, kings had become more powerful than popes, and the French king, Philip the Fair, was able to defy the papacy. In the fourteenth century, the Great Schism further weakened papal prestige. Although it was able to fend off a movement to make church councils superior to popes, the papacy never recovered its authority over national rulers.

The Renaissance. The Renaissance, which began in the Italian city-states in the late fourteenth century, marks the transition from the medieval to the modern world. Humanism, the scholarly study of the Greek and Latin classics and the ancient Church fathers, promoted a rebirth of ancient norms and values and the classical ideal of an educated, well-rounded person. The growth of secular values led to a great burst of artistic activity by artists such as da Vinci, Raphael, and Michelangelo. The political weakness of the Italian states invited foreign intervention by France, Spain, and the Habsburgs. The sack of Rome by imperial forces in 1527 marks the end of the Renaissance.

Nation Building. By the fifteenth century, England, France, and Spain had developed into strong national monarchies with

INTERPRETING THE PAST

Struggles for Authority in Medieval and Early Modern Europe

Text Sources from My History Lab / Primary Source DVD

1. Magna Carta, 1215
2. Behâ ed-Din: Richard I Massacres Prisoners
3. Peter Abelard Defends Himself

Text Sources from Chapter 16

1. Pope Urban II Preaches the First Crusade (p. 463)

Visual Sources from My History Lab / Primary Source DVD

1. Albrecht Dürer, woodcut showing use of perspective
2. Leonardo da Vinci, sketches and drawings

As he recalled the episode in his *History of my Calamities*, the professor Peter Abelard (1079–1142) claimed to have been a victim of ignorance and intolerance during a debate over one of his books. Refuting a charge that he had made heretical arguments about the Christian Trinity, Abelard attempted to reason with his opponents, but they merely exclaimed, "We don't care about rational argument or any interpretation you might have. The only thing that matters is the word of authority."

In the period 1000–1500, however, the nature and claims of "authority" were in flux, in many specific respects. The period was characterized by a series of ongoing debates about where and how the line between various powers and institutions centralized bureaucracies and professional armies. Although medieval institutions, such as the English Parliament, in theory limited royal power, in practice monarchs in these countries held unchallenged authority. The Great Schism, the Hundred Years' War, and the Black Death had weakened the church and the nobility, while townspeople supported the kings. A similar process was beginning in Russia where the rulers of Moscow were extending their authority after throwing off Mongol rule. In the Empire, however, regional lords had defeated the emperors' attempts to build a strong central state.

Review Questions

1. How do you account for the success of the Cluny reform movement? Can major features of the modern Catholic Church be found in the Cluny reforms?

2. Was the Investiture Controversy a political or a religious conflict? Summarize the respective arguments of Gregory VII and Henry IV. Is the conflict a precedent for the modern doctrine of the separation of church and state?

3. Why did Germany remain divided while France and England began to coalesce into reasonably strong states during the High Middle Ages?

4. How did the responsibilities of the nobility differ from those of the clergy and the peasantry during the High Middle Ages? How did each social class contribute to the stability of society?

5. Describe the circumstances that gave rise to towns. How did towns change traditional medieval society?

6. How did the Hundred Years' War, the Black Death, and the Great Schism in the church affect the course of history? Which had the most lasting effects on the institutions it touched?

7. Was the church an aggressor or a victim in the late Middle Ages and the Renaissance? How successful was it in its confrontations with Europe's emerging dynastic states?

8. What was "reborn" in the Renaissance? Were the humanists the forerunners of modern secular education and culture, or eloquent defenders of a still-medieval Christian view of the world against the church's secular and pagan critics?

9. Historians find features of modern states developing in Europe during the late Middle Ages and Renaissance. What modern features can you identify in the governments of the Italian city-states and the northern monarchies? in Russia?

Key Terms

Black Death (p. 475)	**Magna Carta** (p. 472)
chiaroscuro (p. 480)	**mannerism** (p. 481)
Crusades (p. 460)	**regular clergy** (p. 469)
Curia (p. 478)	**Renaissance** (p. 478)
Golden Horde (p. 484)	**Scholasticism** (p. 467)
Great Schism (p. 478)	**secular clergy** (p. 469)
guilds (p. 466)	*studia humanitatis* (p. 479)
Holy Roman Empire (p. 478)	*taille* (p. 476)
humanism (p. 479)	**vernacular** (p. 458)

could be drawn. Using the documents and images here, demonstrate how Europeans debated the following issues:

◆ Kings v. Nobles—the Magna Carta excerpts.
◆ Christians v. Muslims—Urban II's call for a crusade and Behâ ed-Din on the Massacre at Acre in 1191.
◆ Reason v. Authority—document by Peter Abelard on reason and religion.
◆ Tradition v. Innovation—specifically in the arts, as reflected in the images created by Dürer and da Vinci.

Questions

Did the proponents of each position need their opponents?

How did people in this period construct their identities in terms of "the Other"?

Note: To learn more about the topics in this chapter, please turn to the Suggested Readings at the end of the book. For additional sources related to this chapter please see the Primary Source DVD at the back of this text or MyHistoryLab.

The sixteenth through the eighteenth centuries were a period of great transition in world history, both in terms of social change and in the expansion of trade and migration. The European voyages of discovery and subsequent colonization of the New World created a new global economy linking the world together for the first time.

NORTH
AMERICA

SOUTH
AMERICA

Emanual de Witte, "Portuguese Synagogue, Amsterdam," 1680. One of the significant changes in Old Regime Europe was the creation of an independent Dutch state in which Sephardic Jewish refugees from the Spanish and Portuguese Inquisitions could live and worship openly as Jews. *(See pages 637–639.)*

Schematic plan for a slave ship showing the amount of slaves it could carry. The creation of transatlantic economy linked Africa, Europe, and the Americas for the first time in vast circuits moving people and goods. Slavery became a lynchpin of this trade and forced the migration of millions of people from Africa to the New World, usually in wretched conditions. *(See pages 547–557.)*

THE WORLD IN TRANSITION, 1500 TO 1850

Katharina von Bora, a former nun who became Martin Luther's wife in 1525. One of the great changes the Reformation wrought was the closure of convents in Protestant lands. *(See pages 498–562.)*

Porcelain jar, Qing Dynasty, mid–seventeenth century. Porcelain such as this was in high demand in both China and Europe and became a staple of Chinese exports during the Ming and Qing dynasties. *(See pages 563–577.)*

ASIA

EUROPE

AFRICA

AUSTRALIA

Ottoman coin depicting Mehmed II, c. 1500. For the most of the early-modern period the Ottoman Empire was the strongest Islamic state in the world and a serious threat to European power in the Mediterranean and central Europe. *(See pages 647–651.)*

Making Connections

1

What were the benefits and costs of the creation of a global economy in the seventeenth and eighteenth centuries?

2

How did shifts in the balance of power alter societies around the world between 1500 and 1800?

17

Europe 1500–1650: Expansion, Reformation, and Religious Wars

◆ The Discovery of a New World

◆ The Reformation

◆ The Reformation's Achievements

◆ The Wars of Religion

◆ Superstition and Enlightenment: The Battle Within

I N THE SECOND DECADE OF THE SIX-TEENTH CENTURY, a powerful religious movement began in Saxony in Germany and rapidly spread throughout northern Europe, deeply affecting society and politics as well as the spiritual lives of men and women. Attacking what they believed to be burdensome superstitions and corrupt practices that robbed people of both their money and their peace of mind, Protestant reformers led a revolt against the medieval church. In a short period of time, hundreds of thousands of people from all social classes set aside the beliefs of centuries and adopted a more simplified religious practice.

The Protestant Reformation challenged aspects of the Renaissance, especially its tendency to follow classical sources in glorifying human nature and its loyalty to traditional religion. Protestants were more impressed by the human potential for evil than by the inclination to do good, and encouraged parents, teachers, and magistrates to be firm disciplinarians. On the other hand, Protestants also embraced many Renaissance values, especially humanist educational reforms

Allegory of the Jesuits and their missions in the four continents from the church of San Pedro, Lima, Peru. Anonymous painter (eighteenth century). St. Ignatius is flanked on his left by Francis Xavier, sporting a chasuble with Asian motifs. In the background, Jesuits living all over the world and occupying a variety of hierarchies within the church, including those wearing Chinese costumes and prelate robes, preside over the conversion of the faithful in India, China, Africa, and the Americas. Like Atlas, the Jesuits carry the globe on their shoulders.

European Expansion

Europe

The European turn to the Atlantic was a consequence of its weakness in the East due to Muslim domination there. However, a recovering Europe was now able to compete for access to valuable goods in eastern markets by navigating the high seas. In the late fifteenth and the sixteenth centuries, Europeans sailed far from their own shores to Africa, southern and eastern Asia, and the New World of the Americas. From Japan to Peru, they directly confronted civilizations other than their own and that of Islam, with which they already had contact in the form of trade and, more often, by force of arms. A major motivation for the voyages, which began with a reconnaissance of the West African coast, was to circumvent the Muslim monopoly on the movement of spices from the Indian Ocean into Europe, a grip that had only strengthened with the rise of the Ottomans. A wealthier, more self-confident Europe, now recovered from the great plague-induced population decline of the fourteenth century—its taste for Asian spices long-since whetted during the Crusades—was ready to take those spices at their sources.

For much the same reasons (trade and self-aggrandizement) voyages of exploration also set forth from Ming China—especially between 1405 and 1433—reaching India, the Arabian Gulf, and East Africa. Had those voyages been followed up, they might have prevented Europeans from establishing a presence in the Indian Ocean. But the Chinese now faced both serious pressures on their northern and western borders and the problem of administrating a vast, multicultural empire stretching into Central Asia, where non-Chinese rivals had to be kept under control. Moreover, the dominant Neo-Confucian philosophy espoused by the scholar-bureaucrats in the imperial court disdained merchants and commerce, extolling instead a peasant agrarian economy.

These factors led the Chinese to turn inward and abandon overseas trade and exploration precisely at the moment and the study of ancient languages. Here they found tools to master Scripture and challenge the papacy.

Protestantism was not the only reform movement to grow out of the religious grievances and reforms of the late Middle Ages. Within the church itself a reform was emerging that would give birth to new religious orders, rebut Protestantism, and win back a great many of its converts.

As different groups identified their political and social goals with either Protestantism or Catholicism, a hundred years of bloody opposition between Protestants and Catholics darkened the second half of the sixteenth century and the first half of the seventeenth. The political conflict that had previously been confined to central Europe and a struggle for Lutheran rights and freedoms then shifted to Western Europe—to France, the Netherlands, England, and Scotland—and became a struggle for Calvinist recognition. In France Calvinists fought Catholic rulers for the right to form their own communities, practice their chosen religion openly, and exclude from their lands those they deemed heretical. During the Thirty Years' War (1618–1648), international armies of varying religious persuasions clashed in central and northern Europe. By 1649 English Puritans had overthrown the Stuart monarchy and the Anglican Church.

For Europe the late fifteenth and the sixteenth centuries were a period of unprecedented territorial expansion. Permanent colonies were established in the Americas and the exploitation of the New World's human and mineral resources had begun. Imported American gold and silver spurred scientific invention and a new weapons industry. The new bullion helped create an international traffic in African slaves as rival tribes eagerly sold their captives to the Portuguese. Slaves came in ever-increasing numbers to work the mines and the plantations of the New World as replacements for faltering American natives. ■

when Europeans were exploring the coast of Africa on their way to the Indian Ocean. It was a fateful choice, because it meant that the Asian power best able to resist the establishment of European commercial and colonial empires in the Indian Ocean had abdicated that role, leaving a vacuum of power for Europeans to fill. Still, Chinese merchants continued to ply ocean trade routes and settle as far from home as the Philippines and, in later centuries, the west coasts of North and South America. Wherever there was commerce in Chinese goods, there were Chinese merchants, albeit now operating without support from their government.

Although parallels may be drawn between the court culture of the Forbidden Palace in Beijing and that of King Louis XIV in seventeenth-century France, the Chinese government, with its philosophy of Confucianism, remained more unified and patriarchal than its counterparts in the West. The Chinese, at first, tolerated other religions, warmly embracing Jesuit missionaries, doing so in part because political power in China was not bound to a particular religion. The Japanese were also admirers of the Jesuits, who arrived in Japan with the Portuguese in 1543. The admiration was mutual, leading to three hundred thousand Christian converts by 1600. Tolerance of Christianity did not last as long in Japan as in China. Hideyoshi, in his drive for internal unity, banned Christianity in the late sixteenth century. Nonetheless China and Japan, as well as many Islamic societies, including the Ottomans and the Mughals, demonstrated more tolerance for foreign religions, such as Christianity, than did the West for Islam, or Asian religious traditions.

Focus Questions

◆ Why did Europeans launch voyages of exploration in the fifteenth and sixteenth centuries? What role did the Crusades and the rise of the Ottoman Empire play in this enterprise?

◆ Why did the Chinese voyages of exploration under the Ming come to a halt? What were the consequences for world history?

◆ What was the biological impact of the European discovery of America?

The Discovery of a New World

The discovery of the Americas dramatically expanded the horizons of Europeans, both geographical and intellectual. Knowledge of the New World's inhabitants and exploitation of its mineral and human wealth set new cultural and economic forces in motion throughout Western Europe. Beginning with the successful voyages of the Portuguese and Spanish in the fifteenth century, commercial supremacy progressively shifted from the Mediterranean and Baltic Seas to the Atlantic seaboard, setting the stage for global expansion (see Map 17–1).

The Portuguese Chart the Course

Seventy-seven years before Columbus, who sailed under the flag of Spain, set foot in the Americas, Prince Henry "the Navigator" (1394–1406), ruler of a strong and united Portugal, captured the West African Muslim city of Ceuta at the mouth of the Mediterranean Sea. There began the Portuguese exploration of the African coast, first in search of Guinea gold and slaves, and by century's end a sea route to Asia's spice markets (see Chapter 15). Topping the list of spices were pepper and cloves as they both preserved and enhanced the dull diet of most Europeans. Initially the catch of raiders, African slaves were soon taken effortlessly by Portuguese traders in direct exchanges with tribal chiefs, who readily swapped their captured enemies for horses, corn, and finished goods (cloth and brassware). Over the second half of the fifteenth century, Portuguese ships delivered 150,000 slaves to Europe.

Before there was a sea route to the Orient, spices could only be obtained through the Venetians, who bought or bartered them from Eastern Muslim merchants. This was a powerful Venetian-Mameluk (Turkish) monopoly the Portuguese resolved to beat by going directly to the source by sea. Overland routes to India and China had long existed, but their transit had become too difficult and unprofitable by the fifteenth century. The route by sea posed a different obstacle and risk: fear of the unknown, making the first voyages of exploration slow and tentative.

SOURCE A sixteenth-century portolan

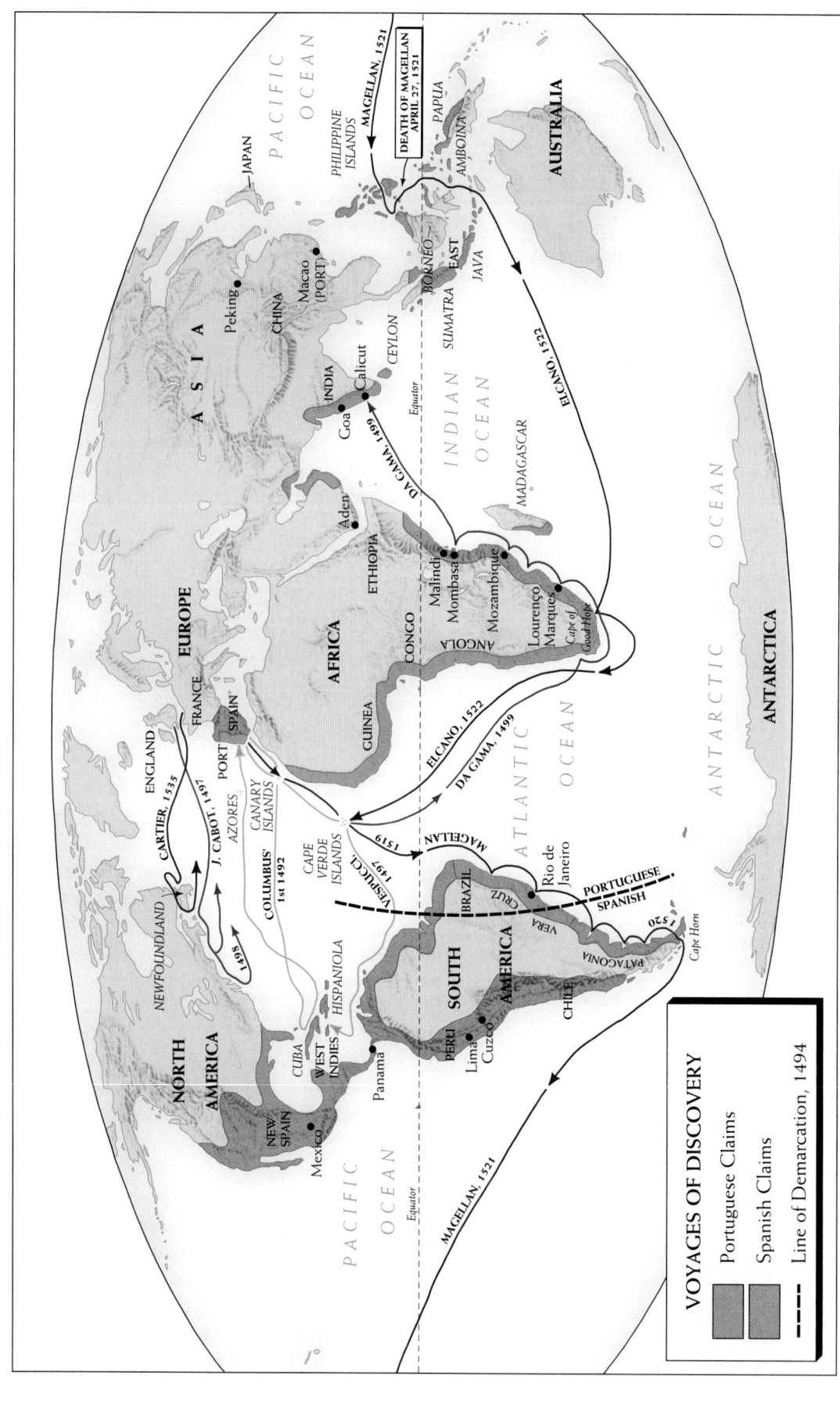

Map 17–1. European Voyages of Discovery and the Colonial Claims of Spain and Portugal in the Fifteenth and Sixteenth Centuries. The map dramatizes Europe's global expansion in the fifteenth and sixteenth centuries.

Christopher Columbus in old age (d. 1506) by Sebastiano del Piombo

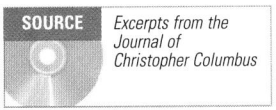

SOURCE *Excerpts from the Journal of Christopher Columbus*

Venturing down the African coast Portuguese square riggers were turned out into the deep ocean by cape after cape, and the farther out they sailed to round them, the greater the sailors' fear that they would not have the sail power to return home. Each cape successfully rounded became a victory and a lesson, allowing the crews to discover the rigging and the skills they would need to cross the oceans to the Americas and the Orient.

In addition to spice markets, the voyages of discovery also sought allies against Western Europe's archenemies, the Muslims. In 1455, a very self-interested pope gave the Portuguese explorers virtual carte blanche from the coast of Guinea to the Indies, granting them all the spoils of war: land, goods, and slaves. The church expected mass conversions in the wake of conquest, a Christian coup as well as mercantile advantage. The explorers also kept an eye out for a reportedly friendly Eastern potentate known as Prester John. Rumored to be a potential Christian ally against the Muslim infidel, he was real enough for Vasco da Gama to carry a letter of introduction to him from the Portuguese king, when he sailed East in 1497.

Bartholomew Dias pioneered the eastern Portuguese Empire after safely rounding the Cape of Good Hope at the tip of Africa in 1487. A decade later, in 1498, Vasco da Gama stood on the shores of India. When he returned to Portugal, he carried a cargo worth sixty times the cost of the voyage. Later, the Portuguese established successful colonies in Goa

and Calcutta, whence they successfully challenged the Arabs and the Venetians for control of the European spice trade.

The Portuguese had concentrated their explorations on the Indian Ocean. Initially following in their wake, the Spanish turned out into the Atlantic Ocean, believing they could find a shorter route to the East Indies by sailing due West. Rather than beating the Portuguese to Asia, Columbus instead discovered the Americas—although he did not know that on his first voyage.

The Spanish Voyages of Christopher Columbus

Thirty-three days after departing the Canary Islands, on October 12, 1492, Columbus landed in San Salvador (Watlings Island) in the eastern Bahamas. Thinking he was in the East Indies, he mistook his first landfall as an outer island of Japan. The error was understandable given the information he relied on: Marco Polo's thirteenth-century account of his years in China and Nuremberg mapmaker Martin Behaim's spherical map of the presumed world. That map showed nothing but ocean between the west coast of Europe and the east coast of Asia, with Cipangu, or Japan, in between (see Map 17–2).

Naked and extremely friendly natives met Columbus and his crew on the beaches of the New World. They were Taino Indians, who spoke a variant of a language known as Arawak. Believing the island on which he landed to be the East Indies, Columbus called the native people who met him Indians, a name that stuck even after it was known that he had actually discovered a new continent. The natives' generosity amazed Columbus, as they freely gave his men all the corn and yams they desired, along with many sexual favors. "They never say no," Columbus marveled, as he observed how easily they could be enslaved by the Spanish.

On the heels of Columbus, Amerigo Vespucci (1451–1512), after whom America is named, and Ferdinand Magellan (1480–1521) carefully explored the coastline of South America. Their travels proved that the new lands discovered by Columbus were not the outermost territory of the Far East, but an entirely unknown continent that opened on the still greater Pacific Ocean. Magellan, who was continuing the search for a westward route to the Indies, made it all the way to the Philippines, where he died.

Impact on Europe and America

Unknowingly to those who undertook and financed it, Columbus' first voyage marked the beginning of more than three centuries of Spanish conquest, exploitation, and administration of a vast American empire. What began as voyages of discovery became expeditions of conquest similar to the warfare Christian Aragon and Castile waged against

Map 17–2. Martin Behaim's "Globe Apple." What Columbus knew of the world in 1492 was contained in this map by Nuremberg geographer Martin Behaim (1440–1507), creator of the first spherical globe of the earth. The ocean section of Behaim's globe is reproduced here. Departing the Canary Islands (in the second section from the right), Columbus expected his first major landfall to be Japan, or what he calls Cipangu (in the second section from the left). When he landed at San Salvador, he thought he was on an outer island of Japan; after reaching Cuba, he believed it to be Japan. Only slowly did it dawn on him that these new lands had never before been seen by Europeans. *From Admiral of the Ocean Sea by Samuel Eliot Morison. Copyright 1942 © renewed 1970 by Samuel Eliot Morison. By permission of Little, Brown and Company, Boston, MA.*

Islamic Moors. Those wars had just ended in 1492, and their conclusion imbued the early Spanish explorers with a zeal for conquering and converting other non-Christian peoples.

The voyages to the New World had important consequences for the cultures of both Europe and America. Much to the benefit of Spain, they created Europe's largest and longest-surviving trading bloc and spurred other European countries to undertake their own colonial ventures. The wealth extracted from its American possessions financed Spain's commanding role in the religious and political wars of the sixteenth century, while fueling a Europe-wide economic expansion.

European expansion also had a profound biological impact. Europeans introduced numerous species of fruits, vegetables, and animals from Europe into the Americas, and vice versa. European expansion also led to a spread of European diseases. Vast numbers of indigenous American peoples died from measles and smallpox, which broke out in massive epidemics among populations with no natural or acquired immunity. Likewise, syphillis killed a million Europeans (see the discussion of the "Columbian Exchange" in Chapter 18).

For the native peoples of America, the voyages began a long period of conquest during which native populations were devastated by warfare, new diseases, and slave labor. In both South and North America, Spanish rule left a lasting footprint of Roman Catholicism, economic dependency, and hierarchical social structure, all of which is still visible today (see Chapter 18).

The Reformation

The **Reformation** was the sixteenth-century religious movement that sought to reform the Church and led to the establishment of Protestantism. It began in Germany.

Religion and Society

The Reformation broke out first in the free imperial cities of Germany and Switzerland. There were about sixty-five such cities, and each was in a sense a little kingdom unto itself. Most had Protestant movements, but with mixed success and duration. Some quickly turned Protestant and remained so. Some were Protestant only for a short time. Others developed mixed confessions, frowning on sectarianism and aggressive proselytizing, letting Catholics and Protestants coexist.

What seemed a life-and-death struggle with higher princely or royal authority was not the only conflict cities were experiencing. They also suffered deep internal social and political divisions. Certain groups favored the Reformation more than others. In many places, guilds like that of the printers, whose members were prospering both socially and economically and who had a history of conflict with local authority, were in the forefront of the Reformation. Evidence suggests that people who felt pushed around and bullied by either local or distant authority—a guild by an autocratic local government, a city or region by a prince or king—perceived in the Protestant movement an ally, at least initially.

Social and political experience thus coalesced with the larger religious issues in both town and countryside. When Martin Luther and his comrades wrote, preached, and sang about a priesthood of all believers, scorned the authority of ecclesiastical landlords, and ridiculed papal laws as arbitrary human inventions, they touched political as well as religious nerves in German and Swiss cities. This was also true in the villages, for the peasants on the land also heard in the Protestant sermon and pamphlet a promise of political liberation and even a degree of social betterment.

Popular Movements and Criticism of the Church

The Protestant Reformation could also not have occurred without the monumental crises of the late medieval church and the Renaissance papacy. For many people, the church had ceased to provide a viable foundation for religious piety. Laity and clerics alike began to seek a more heartfelt, idealistic, and often—in the eyes of the pope—increasingly heretical religious piety. The late Middle Ages were marked by independent lay and clerical efforts to reform local religious practice and by widespread experimentation with new religious forms that shared a common goal of religious simplicity in imitation of Christ.

A variety of factors contributed to the growth of lay criticism of the church. The laity in the cities were becoming increasingly knowledgeable about the world and those who controlled their lives. They traveled widely—as soldiers, pilgrims, explorers, and traders. New postal systems and the printing press increased the information at their disposal. The new age of books and libraries raised literacy and heightened curiosity. Laypersons were increasingly able to take the initiative in shaping the cultural life of their communities.

Secular Control over Religious Life

On the eve of the Reformation, Rome's international network of church offices began to fall apart in many areas, hurried along by a growing sense of regional identity—incipient nationalism—and local secular administrative competence. The late medieval church had permitted important ecclesiastical posts ("benefices") to be sold to the highest bidders and had not enforced residency requirements in parishes. Rare was the late medieval German town that did not have complaints about the maladministration, concubinage, or fiscalism of its clergy, especially the higher clergy (bishops, abbots, and prelates).

City governments also sought to restrict the growth of ecclesiastical properties and clerical privileges and to improve local religious life by bringing the clergy under the local tax code and by endowing new clerical positions for well-trained and conscientious preachers.

The Gutenberg Bible. Print and Protestantism would drive the history of the sixteenth century. Well established by the mid–fifteenth century, the printing press made possible the diffusion of both secular and religious learning. In addition to Humanistic scholarship, print also served the educational and propaganda campaigns of princes and religious reformers, increasing literacy in both Latin and vernacular languages. Among the printed works preparing the way none was more stimulating than Gutenberg's Latin Bible. In the mid-1520s Martin Luther made separate German translations of the New and the Old Testaments, henceforth to become the battering rams of the Protestant Reformation.

The Northern Renaissance

The scholarly works of northern humanists created a climate favorable to religious and educational reforms. Northern humanism was initially stimulated by the importation of Italian learning through such varied intermediaries as students who had studied in Italy, merchants, and the Brothers of the Common Life. The northern humanists tended to come from more diverse social backgrounds and to be more devoted to religious reforms than were their Italian counterparts. They were also more willing to write for lay audiences.

The growth of schools and lay education combined with the invention of cheap paper to create a mass audience for printed books. In response, Johann Gutenberg (d. 1468) invented printing with movable type in the German city of Mainz around 1450. Thereafter, books were rapidly and handsomely produced on topics both profound and practical. By 1500, printing presses operated in at least 60 German cities and in more than 200 throughout Europe. A new medium now existed for politicians, humanists, and reformers alike.

The most famous of the northern humanists was Desiderius Erasmus (1466–1536), the "prince of the humanists." Idealistic and pacifistic, Erasmus gained fame as both an educational and a religious reformer. He aspired to unite the classical ideals of humanity and civic virtue with the Christian ideals of love and piety. He believed that disciplined study of the classics and the Bible, if begun early enough, was the best way to reform

SOURCE *Erasmus, "Pope Julius Excluded from Heaven," 1513*

both individuals and society. He summarized his own beliefs with the phrase *philosophia Christi*, a simple, ethical piety in imitation of Christ. He set this ideal against what he believed to be the dogmatic, ceremonial, and factious religious practice of the late Middle Ages. To promote his own religious beliefs, Erasmus edited the works of the Church Fathers and made a Greek edition of the New Testament (1516), which became the basis for a new, more accurate Latin translation (1519). Martin Luther later used both these works as the basis for his famous German translation.

The best known of early English humanists was Sir Thomas More (1478–1535), a close friend of Erasmus. It was while visiting More that Erasmus wrote his most famous work, *The Praise of Folly* (1511), an amusing and profound exposé of human self-deception that was quickly translated from the original Latin into many vernacular languages. More's *Utopia* (1516), a criticism of contemporary society, depicts an imaginary society based on reason and tolerance that requires everyone to work and has rid itself of all social and political injustice. Although More would remain staunchly Catholic, humanism in England, as in Germany, paved the way for the English Reformation. A circle of English humanists, under the direction of Henry VIII's minister Thomas Cromwell, translated and disseminated late medieval criticisms of the papacy and many of Erasmus's satirical writings as well.

Whereas in Germany, England, and France, humanism helped the Protestants, in Spain it entered the service of the Catholic Church. Here the key figure was Francisco Jiménez de Cisneros (1437–1517), a confessor to Queen Isabella, and after 1508 Grand Inquisitor—a position from which he was able to enforce the strictest religious orthodoxy. Jiménez was a conduit for humanist scholarship and learning. He founded the University of Alcalá near Madrid in 1509, printed a Greek edition of the New Testament, and translated many religious tracts that aided clerical reform and control of lay religious life. His greatest achievement, taking fifteen years to complete, was the Complutensian Polyglot Bible, a six-volume work that placed the Hebrew, Greek, and Latin versions of the Bible in parallel columns. Such scholarly projects and internal church reforms joined with the repressive measures of Ferdinand and Isabella to keep Spain strictly Catholic.

Martin Luther and German Reformation to 1525

Unlike France and England, late medieval Germany lacked the political unity to enforce "national" religious reforms during the late Middle Ages. There were neither lasting Statutes of Provisors and Praemunire, as in England, nor a Pragmatic Sanction of Bourges, as in France, both limiting papal jurisdiction and taxation on a national scale. What happened on a unified national level in England and France occurred only locally and piecemeal within German territories and towns. As popular resentment of clerical immunities and ecclesiastical abuses, especially over the selling of indulgences, spread among German cities and towns, an unorganized "national" opposition to Rome formed. German humanists had long given voice to such criticism, and by 1517 it was pervasive enough to provide a solid foundation for Martin Luther's reform.

Luther (1483–1546) was the son of a successful Thüringian miner. He was educated in Mansfeld, Magdeburg (where the Brothers of the Common Life were his teachers),

The Electoral Princes of Saxony, by Lucas Cranach the Elder (ca. 1532). The three princes Luther served: Frederick the Wise, John the Constant, and John Frederick the Magnanimous. *Hamburg, Kunsthalle (also available via Germanisches National museum); Lucas Cranach: Ein Maler-Unternehmer aus Franken, ed. Claus Grimm, et al., Verlag Friedrich Pustet, Regensburg, 1994), no. A 4, p. 32*

and Eisenach. Between 1501 and 1505 he attended the University of Erfurt, where the nominalist teachings of William of Ockham and Gabriel Biel (d. 1495) prevailed. After receiving his master of arts degree in 1505, Luther registered with the law faculty, following his parents' wishes, but he never began the study of law. To the disappointment of his family, he instead entered the Order of the Hermits of Saint Augustine in Erfurt on July 17, 1505. This decision had apparently been building for some time and was resolved during a lightning storm in which Luther, terrified and crying out to Saint Anne for assistance (Saint Anne was the patron saint of travelers in distress), promised to enter a monastery if he escaped death.

Ordained in 1507, Luther pursued a traditional course of study. In 1510, he journeyed to Rome on the business of his order, finding there justification for the many criticisms of the church he had heard in Germany. In 1511, he moved to the Augustinian monastery in Wittenberg, where he earned his doctorate in theology in 1512. Thereafter, he became a leader within the monastery, the new university, and the spiritual life of the city.

Justification by Faith Alone Reformation theology grew out of a problem then common to many of the clergy and the laity: the failure of traditional medieval religion to provide either full personal or intellectual satisfaction. Luther was especially plagued by the disproportion between his own sense of sinfulness and the perfect righteousness that God required for salvation, according to medieval theology. Traditional church teaching and the sacrament of penance proved no consolation. Luther wrote that he came to despise the phrase "righteousness of God," for it seemed to demand of him a perfection he knew neither he nor any other human being could ever achieve. His insight into the meaning of "justification by faith alone" was a gradual process that extended between 1513 and 1518. The righteousness that God demands, he concluded, did not result from many religious works and ceremonies but was given in full measure to those who believe and trust in Jesus Christ, who alone is the perfect righteousness satisfying to God. To believe in Christ meant to stand before God clothed in Christ's sure righteousness.

The Attack on Indulgences An **indulgence** was a remission of the temporal penalty imposed by priests on penitents as a "work of satisfaction" for their mortal sins. According to medieval theology, after the priest absolved a penitent of guilt for the sins, the penitent remained under an eternal penalty, a punishment God justly imposed for sin. After absolution, however, this eternal penalty was said to be transformed into a temporal penalty, a manageable "work of satisfaction" that the penitent might perform here and now (for example, through prayers, fasting, almsgiving, retreats, and pilgrimages). Penitents who defaulted on such prescribed works of satisfaction could expect to suffer for them in purgatory.

At this point, indulgences, which had earlier been given to Crusaders who did not complete their penances because they had fallen in battle, became an aid to laity, made genuinely anxious by their belief in a future suffering in purgatory for neglected penances or unrepented sins. In 1343, Pope Clement VI (r. 1342–1352) had proclaimed the existence of a "treasury of merit," an infinite reservoir of good works in the church's possession that could be dispensed at the pope's discretion. On the basis of this declared treasury, the church sold "letters of indulgence," which covered the works of satisfaction owed by penitents. In 1476, Pope Sixtus IV (r. 1471–1484) extended indulgences also to cover purgatory.

Originally, indulgences had been given only for the true self-sacrifice of going on a Crusade to the Holy Land. By Luther's time, they were regularly dispensed for small cash payments (very modest sums that were regarded as a good work of almsgiving). They were presented to the laity as remitting not only their own future punishments, but also those of their dead relatives presumed to be suffering in purgatory.

In 1517, Pope Leo X (r. 1513–1521) revived a plenary Jubilee Indulgence that had first been issued by Pope Julius II (r. 1503–1513), whose proceeds were to be used to rebuild St. Peter's Basilica in Rome. Such an indulgence promised forgiveness of all outstanding unrepented sins upon the completion of certain acts. That kind of indulgence was subsequently preached on the borders of Saxony in the territories of the future Archbishop Albrecht of Mainz, who was much in need of revenues because of the large debts he had incurred in order to hold, contrary to church law, three ecclesiastical appointments. The selling of the indulgence was a joint venture by Albrecht, the Augsburg banking house of Fugger, and Pope Leo X, with half the proceeds going to the pope and half to Albrecht and his creditors. The famous indulgence preacher John Tetzel (d. 1519) was enlisted to preach the indulgence in Albrecht's territories because he was a seasoned professional who knew how to stir ordinary people to action. As he exhorted on one occasion:

> *Don't you hear the voices of your dead parents and other relatives crying out, "Have mercy on us, for we suffer great punishment and pain. From this you could release us with a few alms. . . . We have created you, fed you, cared for you, and left you our temporal goods. Why do you treat us so cruelly and leave us to suffer in the flames, when it takes only a little to save us?"*[1]

When Luther, according to tradition, posted his ninety-five theses against indulgences on the door of Castle Church in Wittenberg, on October 31, 1517, he protested especially against the impression created by Tetzel that indulgences actually remitted sins and released the dead

---

[1] *Die Reformation in Augenzeugen Berichten,* ed. by Helmar Junghans (Dusseldorf: Karl Rauch Verlag, 1967), p. 44.

Map 17–3. The Empire of Charles V. Dynastic marriages and good fortune concentrated into Charles's hands rule over the lands shown here, plus Spain's overseas possessions. Crowns and titles rained down on him; election in 1519 as emperor gave him new burdens and responsibilities.

from punishment in purgatory. Luther believed these claims went far beyond the traditional practice and seemed to make salvation something that could be bought and sold.

Election of Charles V   Luther's **ninety-five theses** made him famous overnight. They were embraced by humanists and

other proponents of reform, but they prompted official proceedings against him. In October, he was called before the general of the Dominican order in Augsburg. As sanctions were being prepared against Luther, however, Emperor Maximilian I died (January 12, 1519), and this event, fortunate for the Reformation, turned attention away from heresy in Saxony to the contest for a new emperor.

The pope backed the French king, Francis I. However, Charles I of Spain, a youth of nineteen, succeeded his grandfather and became Emperor Charles V. (See Map 17–3) Charles was assisted by both a long tradition of Habsburg imperial rule and a massive Fugger campaign chest, which secured the votes of the seven electors. The electors, who traditionally enhanced their power at every opportunity, wrung new concessions from Charles for their votes. The

emperor agreed to a revival of the Imperial Supreme Court and the Council of Regency and promised to consult with a diet of the empire on all major domestic and foreign affairs that affected the empire. These measures also helped the development of the Reformation by preventing unilateral imperial action against the Germans, something Luther could be thankful for in the early years of the Reformation.

Luther's Excommunication and the Diet of Worms   In the same month in which Charles was elected emperor, Luther entered a debate in Leipzig (June 27, 1519) with the Ingolstadt professor John Eck. During this contest, Luther challenged the infallibility of the pope and the inerrancy of church councils, appealing for the first time to the sovereign authority of Scripture alone. He burned all his bridges to the old church when he further defended certain teachings of John Huss that had been condemned by the Council of Constance.

In 1520, Luther described the pillars of his reform in three pamphlets. The *Address to the Christian Nobility of the German Nation* urged the German princes to force reforms on the Roman church, especially to curtail its political and economic power in Germany. Here, Luther also famously

A Catholic Portrayal of Martin Luther Tempting Jesus (1547).
Reformation propaganda often portrayed the pope as the Antichrist or the devil. Here Catholic propaganda turns the tables on the Protestant reformers by portraying a figure of Martin Luther as the devil (note the monstrous feet and tail under his academic robes). *Versuchung Christi, 1547, Gemälde, Bonn, Landschaftsverband Rheinland/Rheinisches Landesmuseum, Bonn. Inv. Nr. 58.3.*

declared "all Christians to be of the same estate," by which he meant one Christian people under God's law and grace"—a strictly spiritual equality that the leaders of later peasant revolts willfully interpreted as social and political equality. The *Babylonian Captivity of the Church* examined the traditional seven sacraments of the church, arguing that only two, baptism and the Eucharist, were biblical, and exalted the authority of Scripture, church councils, and secular princes over that of the pope. The *Freedom of a Christian* summarized the new theology for the laity, describing a "happy union" between the soul and Christ by faith alone, in which everything the soul had (sin, death, and damnation) became Christ's and everything Christ had (purity, life, and heaven) became the believer's.

In April 1521, Luther defended his religious teaching before the imperial **Diet of Worms**, over which newly elected Emperor Charles V presided. Ordered to recant, Luther declared that he could not act against Scripture, reason, and his own conscience. On May 26, 1521, he was placed under the imperial ban and thereafter became an "outlaw" to secular as well as religious authority. For his own protection, friends hid him in a secluded castle, where he spent almost a year, from April 1521 to March 1522. During his stay, he translated the New Testament into German, using Erasmus's new Greek text and Latin translation, and he attempted, by correspondence, to oversee the first stages of the Reformation in Wittenberg.

Imperial Distractions: France and the Turks The Reformation was greatly helped in these early years by the emperor's war with France and the advance of the Ottoman Turks into eastern Europe. Against both adversaries Charles V, who also remained a Spanish king with dynastic responsibilities outside the empire, needed German troops, and to that end he promoted friendly relations with the German princes. Between 1521 and 1559, Spain (the Habsburg dynasty) and France (the Valois dynasty) fought four major wars over disputed territories in Italy and along their borders. In 1526, the Turks overran Hungary at the Battle of Mohacs; in Western Europe the French-led League of Cognac formed against Charles for the second Habsburg-Valois war.

Thus preoccupied, the emperor agreed through his representatives at the German Diet of Speyer in 1526 that each German territory was free to enforce the Edict of Worms (1521) against Luther "so as to be able to answer in good conscience to God and the emperor." That concession, in effect, gave the German princes territorial sovereignty in religious matters and gave the Reformation time to put down deep roots. Later, in 1555, the Peace of Augsburg would enshrine such local princely control over religion in imperial law.

How the Reformation Spread In the late 1520s and on into the 1530s, the Reformation passed from the hands of the theologians and pamphleteers into those of the magistrates and princes. In many cities, the magistrates quickly followed the lead of the Protestant preachers and their sizable congregations in mandating the religious reforms they preached. In numerous instances, magistrates had themselves worked for decades to bring about basic church reforms and thus welcomed the preachers as new allies. Reform now ceased to be merely slogans and became laws that all townspeople had to obey.

The religious reform became a territorial political movement as well led by the elector of Saxony and the prince of Hesse, the two most powerful German Protestant rulers. Like the urban magistrates, the German princes quickly recognized the political and economic opportunities offered

Execution of a Peasant Leader. The punishment of a peasant leader in a village near Heilbronn. After the defeat of rebellious peasants in and around the city of Heilbronn, Jacob Rorbach, a well-to-do peasant leader from a nearby village, was tied to a stake and slowly roasted to death. © *Badische Landesbibliothek*

them by the demise of the Roman Catholic Church in their regions. Soon they, too, were pushing Protestant faith and politics onto their neighbors. By the 1530s, Protestant cities and lands formed powerful defensive alliances and prepared for war with the Catholic emperor.

The Peasants' Revolt In its first decade, the Protestant movement suffered more from internal division than from imperial interference. By 1525, Luther had become as much an object of protest within Germany as was the pope. Original allies, sympathizers, and fellow travelers declared their independence from him. Like the German humanists, the German peasantry also had at first believed Luther to be an ally. Since the late fifteenth century, the peasantry had been organized against efforts by territorial princes to override their traditional laws and customs and to subject them to new regulations and taxes. Peasant leaders, several of whom were convinced Lutherans, saw in Luther's teaching about Christian freedom and his criticism of monastic landowners a point of view close to their own. They openly solicited Luther's support of their political and economic rights, including their revolutionary request for release from serfdom.

Lutheran pamphleteers made Karsthans, the burly, honest peasant who earned his bread by the sweat of his brow and sacrificed his comfort for the well-being of others, a symbol of the simple life God desired all people to live. Lutherans were not, however, social revolutionaries. Luther

believed the freedom of the Christian to be an inner release from guilt and anxiety, not any right to create an egalitarian society by violent revolution, as the German peasants (mis)interpreted him. When the peasants revolted against their landlords in 1524–1525, Luther predictably condemned them as "un-Christian" and urged the princes to crush their revolt. An estimated 70,000 to 100,000 peasants may have died by the time the revolt was put down. Had Luther supported the peasants' revolt, not only would he have contradicted his own teaching, he would surely also have ended any chance of the survival of his reform beyond the 1520s.

Luther and the Jews Also controversial is Luther's stand toward the Jews. In 1523, as part of a heady program of civic reform, he published a pamphlet entitled "Jesus Christ Was Born a Jew." Therein, he urged Christians to be kinder and gentler to German Jews in the hope that "some" or "many" might assimilate to Christian society and eventually convert to the new reformed Christianity. By the late 1530s, Luther's Protestant reform was only one among many and even faltering, and some Christians in Bohemia and Moravia, he was told, were even converting to Judaism. He tells the story of three rabbis even coming to him in Wittenberg in the hope of "finding a new Jew in me." Was his kindness to Jews to be repaid by Jewish proselytization of the great reformer himself? From that suspicion on, he regretted his 1523 pamphlet and viewed the Jews as just another in a long history of foreign predators threatening German Christians. He took his anger at Jews out in several new pamphlets published in the late 1530s and early 1540, in which he urged German princes forcibly to remove noncoverting Jews to a land of their own, as France, Spain, and Bohemia had already done. Although far short of making Judaism a capital crime, as imperial law had done with Anabaptism in 1529, Luther's proposals ran along a similar line: assimilation or exile. Fortunately, the shocked and disappointed Jews had a protector in Emperor Charles V, and Luther's colleagues had no heart to replace traditional Christian watchful waiting on the Jews with forced conversions and exile. In Hesse and Saxony around this time, rulers tightened traditional restrictions on Jews. Had Luther been willing, he might have softened these restrictions or prevented them altogether as expectant Jewish leaders had asked him to do.

Zwingli and the Swiss Reformation

Although Luther's was the first, Switzerland and France had their own independent reform movements almost simultaneously with Germany's. Switzerland was a loose confederacy of thirteen autonomous cantons or states and allied areas. Some became Protestant, some remained Catholic, and a few managed to effect a compromise. The two preconditions of the Swiss Reformation were the growth of national sentiment and a desire for church reform.

The Reformation in Zurich Ulrich Zwingli (1484–1531), the leader of the Swiss Reformation, was widely known for opposition to the sale of indulgences and religious superstition. The people's priest in Zurich, he made the city his base for reform. Zwingli's reform guideline was simple and effective: whatever lacked literal support in Scripture was to be neither believed nor practiced. After a public disputation in January 1523, based on his Scripture test, Zurich became, to all intents and purposes, a Protestant city and the center of the Swiss Reformation. Its harsh discipline in pursuit of its religious ideals made it one of the first examples of a "puritanical" Protestant city.

The Marburg Colloquy Landgrave Philip of Hesse (1504–1567) sought to unite Swiss and German Protestants in a mutual defense pact, a potentially significant political alliance. His efforts were spoiled, however, by theological disagreements between Luther and Zwingli over the nature of Christ's presence in the Eucharist. Zwingli maintained a symbolic interpretation of Christ's words, "This is my body." Christ, he argued, was only spiritually, not bodily, present in the bread and wine of the Eucharist. Luther, to the contrary, insisted that Christ's human nature shared the properties of his divine nature; hence, where Christ was spiritually present, he could also be bodily present, this because of his special nature as man and God. For Luther, the Eucharistic miracle was not **transubstantiation**, as Rome taught it, but "consubstantiation": Christ's body and blood being one with, but not of, the bread and wine of the Eucharist, fulfilling Christ's biblical promise that he would be present to faith in the Eucharistic meal whenever it was served.

Philip of Hesse brought the two Protestant leaders together in his castle in Marburg in early October 1529, but they were unable to work out their differences on this issue. Luther left thinking Zwingli a dangerous fanatic. The disagreement splintered the Protestant movement theologically and politically.

Anabaptists and Radical Protestants

The moderate pace and seemingly small ethical results of the Lutheran and Zwinglian reformations discontented many people, among them some of the original co-workers of Luther and Zwingli. Many desired a more rapid and thorough implementation of primitive Christianity and accused the major reformers of going only halfway. The most important of these radical groups were the Anabaptists, the sixteenth-century ancestors of the modern Mennonites and Amish. The Anabaptists were especially distinguished by

Christ Blessing the Children, by Lucas Cranach the Elder (1538). This novel painting was a Lutheran protest against the Anabaptists, who refused to recognize the efficacy of infant baptism. Appealing to the example of Jesus, who had been baptized as an adult, Anabaptists (the name means "rebaptism") disavowed their infant baptism and sought another when they were old enough to grasp what it meant. Here, Jesus joins a throng of new mothers to caress, kiss, and commend their babies to God. After 1529, Anabaptism became a capital offense in the Holy Roman Empire. *Lucas Cranach the Elder,* Christus segnet die Kinder, *Hamburg, Kunsthalle (ca. 1540), copy also in Dresden and Harvard's Fogg Museum*

their rejection of infant baptism and their insistence on only adult baptism (*Anabaptism* derives from the Greek word meaning "to rebaptize"), believing that baptism as a consenting adult conformed to Scripture and was more respectful of human freedom.

Anabaptists physically separated from society to form a more perfect community in imitation of what they believed to be the example of the first Christians. Due to the close connection between religious and civic life in this period, the political authorities viewed such separatism as a threat to basic social bonds.

At first Anabaptism drew its adherents from all social classes. But as Lutherans and Zwinglians joined with Catholics in opposition to it, a more rural, agrarian class came to make up the great majority of Anabaptists. In 1529 rebaptism became a capital offense throughout the Holy Roman Empire. It has been estimated that from 1525 to 1618, between one and five thousand men and women were executed for rebaptizing themselves as adults.

John Calvin and the Genevan Reformation

Calvinism was the religious ideology that inspired or accompanied massive political resistance in France, the Netherlands, and Scotland. Believing in both divine predestination and the individual's responsibility to create a godly society, Calvinists became zealous reformers. In a

German Peasants Protest Rising Feudal Exactions

Document

In the late fifteenth and early sixteenth centuries, German feudal lords, both secular and ecclesiastical, tried to increase the earnings from their lands by raising demands on their peasant tenants. As the lords restricted the traditional freedoms and property rights of peasants, massive revolts occurred in southern Germany in 1525. The following, representative statement of peasant grievances, summarized in twelve articles, came from the town of Memmingen.

◆ Are the peasants more interested in material than in spiritual freedom? Which of their demands are the most revolutionary, and which are the least problematic for their lords to grant? Why do some centuries exhibit greater social and political equality than others?

1. It is our humble petition and desire that in the future each community should choose and appoint a pastor, and that we should have the right to depose him should he conduct himself improperly. . .

2. We are ready and willing to pay the fair tithe of grain. . . The small tithes [of cattle], whether [to] ecclesiastical or lay lords, we will not pay at all, for the Lord God created cattle for the free use of man. . .

3. We . . . take it for granted that you will release us from serfdom as true Christians, unless it should be shown us from the Gospel that we are serfs.

4. It has been the custom heretofore that no poor man should be allowed to catch venison or wildfowl or fish in flowing water, which seems to us quite unseemly and unbrotherly as well as selfish and not agreeable to the Word of God. . .

5. We are aggrieved in the matter of woodcutting, for the noblemen have appropriated all the woods to themselves. . .

6. In regard to the excessive services demanded of us which are increased from day to day, we ask that this matter be properly looked into so that we shall not continue to be oppressed in this way. . .

7. We will not hereafter allow ourselves to be further oppressed by our lords, but will let them demand only what is just and proper according to the word of the agreement between the lord and the peasant. The lord should no longer try to force more services or other dues from the peasant without payment. . .

8. We are greatly burdened because our holdings cannot support the rent exacted from them. . . We ask that the lords may appoint persons of honor to inspect these holdings and fix a rent in accordance with justice. . .

9. We are burdened with a great evil in the constant making of new laws. . . In our opinion we should be judged according to the old written law. . .

10. We are aggrieved by the appropriation . . . of meadows and fields which at one time belonged to a community as a whole. These we will take again into our own hands. . .

11. We will entirely abolish the due called Todfall [that is, *heriot* or *death tax*, by which the lord received the best horse, cow, or garment of a family upon the death of a serf] and will no longer endure it, nor allow widows and orphans to be thus shamefully robbed against God's will, and in violation of justice and right. . .

12. It is our conclusion and final resolution, that if any one or more of the articles here set forth should not be in agreement with the Word of God, as we think they are, such article we will willingly retract.

Translations and Reprints from the Original Sources of European History, Vol. 2 (Philadelphia: Department of History, University of Pennsylvania, 1897).

famous and controversial study, *The Protestant Ethic and the Spirit of Capitalism* (1904), the German sociologist Max Weber argued that this combination of religious confidence and self-disciplined activism produced an ethic congenial to emergent capitalism, bringing Calvinism and later Puritanism into close association with the development of modern capitalist societies.

Political Revolt and Religious Reform in Geneva Whereas in Saxony religious reform paved the way for a political revolution against the emperor, in Geneva a political revolution against the local prince-bishop laid the foundation for religious change. In late 1533 the Protestant city of Bern sent Protestant reformers to Geneva and by the summer of 1535, after much internal turmoil, the Protestants triumphed.

A Portrait of the Young John Calvin. *Bibliothéque Publique et Universitaire, Geneva.*

On May 21, 1536, the city voted officially to adopt the Reformation: "to live according to the Gospel and the Word of God . . . without . . . any more masses, statues, idols, or other papal abuses."

John Calvin (1509–1564), a reform-minded humanist and lawyer, arrived in Geneva after these events, in July 1536. The local Protestant reformer persuaded him to stay and assist the Reformation. Before a year had passed, Calvin had drawn up articles for the governance of the new church, as well as a catechism to guide and discipline the people. As a result of the strong measures proposed to govern Geneva's moral life, many suspected the reformers of trying to create a "new papacy." In February 1538 they were exiled from the city.

Calvin went to Strasbourg, a model Protestant city, where he became pastor to the French exiles. During his two years in Strasbourg he wrote biblical commentaries and a second edition of his masterful *Institutes of the Christian Religion,* which many consider the definitive theological statement of the Protestant faith. He also married and participated in the ecumenical discussions urged on Protestants and Catholics by Charles V. Most important, he learned from the Strasbourg reformer Martin Bucer (1491–1551) how to implement the Protestant Reformation successfully.

SOURCE *Calvin, Ecclesiastical Ordinances*

Calvin's Geneva In 1540 Geneva elected officials favorable to Calvin, and he was invited to return. Within months of his arrival, new ecclesiastical ordinances were implemented that allowed the magistrates and the clergy to cooperate in matters of internal discipline.

Calvin and his followers were motivated above all by a desire to make society godly. The "elect," Calvin taught, should live a manifestly God-pleasing life, if they are truly God's elect. The majesty of God demanded nothing less. The consistory, a judicial body composed of clergy and laity, became his instrument of power. It enforced the strictest moral discipline, meting out punishments for a broad range of moral and religious transgressions and became unpopular with many Genevans.

After 1555 the city's magistrates were all devout Calvinists, and Geneva became home to thousands of exiled Protestants who had been driven out of France, England, and Scotland. Refugees—more than five thousand strong—most of them utterly loyal to Calvin, now made up over one third of the population of Geneva. Thanks to this influx of supporters, Calvin's position in the city was greatly strengthened and the magistrates were very cooperative.

"Liberal thinkers" challenged Calvin's theology of predestination and the bondage of the will both in his life-time and after his death. Michael Servetus (1511–1553), a physician, and Jacobus Arminius (1560–1609), a leading Dutch theologian, stand out among them. Both studied in Geneva and Basel after Calvin's death. Servetus, who had long ridiculed Calvin, made the mistake of coming to Geneva, where he was apprehended and executed with Calvin's blessing for alleged blasphemies against the Holy Trinity. Arminius had studied in Geneva and Basel after Calvin's death and long outlived Calvin.

Political Consolidation of the Lutheran Reformation

By 1530 the Reformation was in Europe to stay. It would, however, take several decades and major attempts to eradicate it before all would recognize this fact. With the political triumph of Lutheranism in the empire by the 1550s, Protestant movements elsewhere gained a new lease on life.

Expansion of the Reformation In the 1530s German Lutherans formed regional consistories, which oversaw and administered the new Protestant churches. These consistories replaced the old Catholic episcopates. Under the leadership of Philip Melanchthon (1497–1560), Luther's most admired colleague, educational reforms were enacted that provided for compulsory primary education, schools for girls, a humanist revision of the traditional curriculum, and catechetical instruction of the laity in the new religion.

Chronology

Progress of Protestant Reformation on the Continent

1517	Luther posts ninety-five theses against indulgences
1519	Charles I of Spain elected Holy Roman emperor (as Charles V)
1519	Luther challenges infallibility of pope and inerrancy of church councils at Leipzig Debate
1521	Papal bull excommunicates Luther for heresy
1521	Diet of Worms condemns Luther
1521–1522	Luther translates the New Testament into German
1524–1525	Peasants' Revolt in Germany
1529	Marburg Colloquy between Luther and Zwingli
1530	Diet of Augsburg fails to settle religious differences
1531	Formation of Protestant Schmalkaldic League
1536	Calvin arrives in Geneva
1540	Jesuits, founded by Ignatius of Loyola, recognized as order by pope
1545–1563	Council of Trent institutes reforms and responds to the Reformation
1546	Luther dies
1547	Armies of Charles V crush Schmalkaldic League
1555	Peace of Augsburg recognizes rights of Lutherans to worship as they please

The Reformation also dug in elsewhere. Introduced into Denmark by Christian II (r. 1513–1523), Lutheranism became the state religion under Christian III (r. 1536–1559). In Sweden, Gustavus Vasa (r. 1523–1560), supported by a nobility greedy for church lands, confiscated church property and subjected the clergy to royal authority at the Diet of Vesteras (1527). In politically splintered Poland, Lutherans, Calvinists, and others found room to practice their beliefs. The absence of a central political authority made Poland a model of religious pluralism and toleration in the second half of the sixteenth century.

Reaction Against Protestants: The "Interim" Charles V made abortive efforts in 1540–1541 to enforce a compromise agreement between Protestants and Catholics. As these and other conciliar efforts failed, he turned to a military solution. In 1547 imperial armies crushed the Protestant Schmalkaldic League.

The emperor established puppet rulers in Saxony and Hesse and issued as imperial law the Augsburg Interim, a new order that Protestants everywhere must readopt Catholic beliefs and practices. But the Reformation was too entrenched by 1547 to be ended even by brute force. Confronted by fierce Protestant resistance and weary from three decades of war, the emperor was forced to relent.

The Peace of Augsburg in September 1555 made the division of Christendom permanent. This agreement recognized in law what had already been well established in practice: *cuius regio, eius religio*, meaning that the ruler of a land would determine the religion of the land. Lutherans were permitted to retain all church lands forcibly seized before 1552. Those discontented with the religion of their region were permitted to migrate to another.

Calvinism was not recognized as a legal form of Christian belief and practice by the Peace of Augsburg. Calvinists remained determined not only to secure the right to worship publicly as they pleased, but also to shape society according to their own religious convictions. They organized to lead national revolutions throughout northern Europe.

The English Reformation to 1553

Late medieval England had a well-earned reputation for defending the rights of the crown against the pope. It was, however, the unhappy marriage of King Henry VIII (r. 1509–1547) that ensured the success of the English protest against the church.

The King's Affair Henry married Catherine of Aragon (d. 1536), a daughter of Ferdinand and Isabella of Spain and the aunt of Emperor Charles V, in 1509. By 1527 the union had produced only a single surviving child, a daughter, Mary. People at this time believed it unnatural for women to rule over men, and Henry was justifiably concerned about the political consequences of leaving behind only a female heir. At best, a woman ruler meant a contested reign; at worst, turmoil and revolution. Henry came to believe that his union with Catherine, who had numerous miscarriages and stillbirths, had been cursed by God, because Catherine had briefly been the wife of his late brother, Arthur.

By 1527 Henry was thoroughly enamored of Anne Boleyn (ca. 1504–1536), one of Catherine's ladies in waiting, and determined to put Catherine aside and marry Anne. This he could not do, however, in Catholic England without a papal annulment of his marriage to Catherine. Therein lay a grave problem for the English king. Not only had eighteen years of marriage passed with offspring, but also in 1527 the reigning pope, Clement VII (r. 1523–1534), was a prisoner of Emperor Charles V, Catherine's nephew. The pope could hardly annul a marriage that had been created by a papal dispensation in the first place, nor did he want to see his aunt dismissed by the English king.

These difficulties did not, however, discourage the king from pursuing a divorce against all odds. After Cardinal Wolsey (1475–1530), Lord Chancellor of England since 1515, failed to secure the papal annulment, Henry turned to his heavy-handed ministers, Thomas Cranmer (1489–1556) and Thomas Cromwell (1485–1540) to find a way out. Both harbored Lutheran sympathies and neither was squeamish. Finding the way to a papal annulment closed, Henry's new advisers proposed a simple, fail-safe solution: Why not have the king simply declare his supremacy over English spiritual affairs, as he did over English temporal affairs? Then the king could settle his own affair.

Reformation Parliament In 1529 Parliament convened for what would be a seven-year session that earned it the title of "Reformation Parliament." It passed a flood of legislation that harassed and finally placed royal reins on the clergy. In January 1531 the clergy publicly recognized Henry as head of the church in England "as far as the law of Christ allows." In 1533 Parliament passed the Submission of the Clergy, effectively placing canon law under royal control and thereby the clergy under royal jurisdiction.

In January 1533 Henry wed the pregnant Anne Boleyn, with Thomas Cranmer officiating. In 1534 Parliament ended all payments by the English clergy and laity to Rome and gave Henry sole jurisdiction over high ecclesiastical appointments. The Act of Succession in the same year made Anne Boleyn's children legitimate heirs to the throne, and the Act of Supremacy declared Henry "the only supreme head on earth of the church of England."

The Protestant Reformation Under Edward VI Despite his political break with Rome, Henry remained decidedly conservative in his religious beliefs, and Catholic doctrine remained prominent in a country seething with Protestant sentiment. Henry forbade the English clergy to marry and threatened to execute clergy caught twice in concubinage. The Six Articles of 1539 reaffirmed transubstantiation, denied the Eucharistic cup to the laity, declared celibate vows inviolable, provided for private Masses, and ordered the continuation of auricular confession.

Edward VI (r. 1547–1553), Henry's son by his third wife, Jane Seymour, became king at age ten. Under his regents, England enacted much of the Protestant Reformation. Henry's Six Articles and laws against heresy were repealed, and clerical marriage and Communion with the cup were sanctioned. An Act of Uniformity imposed

Thomas Cranmer's Book of Common Prayer on all English churches, which were stripped of their images and altars. His forty-two-article confession of faith set forth a moderate Protestant doctrine.

These changes were short-lived because in 1553 Catherine of Aragon's daughter, Mary Tudor (d. 1558), succeeded to the throne and restored Catholic doctrine and practice with a single-mindedness that rivaled that of her father. It was not until the reign of Anne Boleyn's daughter, Elizabeth I (r. 1558–1603), that a lasting religious settlement was worked out in England.

Catholic Reform and Counter-Reformation

The Protestant Reformation did not take the medieval church completely by surprise. There were many internal criticisms and efforts at reform before there was a **Counter-Reformation** in reaction to Protestant successes.

Sources of Catholic Reform Before the Reformation began, ambitious proposals had been made for church reform. But sixteenth-century popes, mindful of how the Councils of Constance and Basel had stripped the pope of his traditional powers, quickly squelched such efforts to bring about basic changes in the laws and institutions of the church. Despite such papal foot-dragging, the church was not without its reformers. Many new religious orders sprang up in the sixteenth century to lead a broad revival of piety within the church.

Ignatius of Loyola and the Society of Jesus Of the various reform groups, none was more instrumental in the success of the Counter-Reformation than the Society of Jesus, the new order of Jesuits. Organized by Ignatius of Loyola in the 1530s, it was officially recognized by the church in 1540. Within a century the society had more than fifteen thousand members scattered throughout the world, with thriving missions in India, Japan, and the Americas.

Ignatius of Loyola (1491–1556) was a heroic figure. A dashing courtier and caballero in his youth, he began his spiritual pilgrimage in 1521 after having been seriously wounded in the legs during a battle with the French. During a lengthy and painful convalescence, he read Christian classics. So impressed was he with the heroic self-sacrifice of the church's saints and their methods of overcoming mental anguish and pain that he underwent a profound religious conversion. Henceforth, he too would serve the church as a soldier of Christ.

After recuperating, Ignatius applied the lessons he had learned during his convalescence to a program of religious and moral self-discipline that came to be embodied in the *Spiritual Exercises*. This psychologically perceptive

The Miracle of St. Ignatius of Loyola, by Peter Paul Rubens. Here, the founder of the Society of Jesus, surrounded by angels and members of the new Jesuit Order, preaches to an aroused assembly. *Erich Lessing/Art Resource, N.Y.*

devotional guide contained mental and emotional exercises designed to teach one absolute spiritual self-mastery. A person could shape his or her own behavior, even create a new religious self, through disciplined study and regular practice.

Whereas in Jesuit eyes Protestants had distinguished themselves by disobedience to church authority and by religious innovation, the exercises of Ignatius were intended to teach good Catholics to submit without question to higher church authority and spiritual direction. Perfect discipline and self-control were the essential conditions of such obedience. To these were added the enthusiasm of traditional spirituality and mysticism and uncompromising loyalty to the church's cause above all else. (See Document, "Ignatius of Loyola's 'Rules for Thinking with the Church.'") This potent combination helped counter the Reformation and win many Protestants back to the Catholic fold, especially in Austria and Germany.

The Council of Trent (1545–1563) The broad success of the Reformation and the insistence of emperor Charles V forced Pope Paul III (r. 1534–1549) to call a general council of the church to reassert church doctrine. The pope also appointed a reform commission, whose report, presented in February 1537, bluntly criticized the fiscality and simony[2] of the papal Curia (court) as the primary source of the church's loss of esteem. The report was so critical that Pope Paul attempted

---

[2] The sin of selling sacred or spiritual things, in this instance church offices.

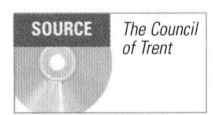

unsuccessfully to suppress its publication; Protestants reprinted and circulated it widely.

The long-delayed council met in 1545 in the imperial city of Trent in northern Italy. There were three sessions, spread over eighteen years, with long interruptions due to war, plague, and politics. Unlike the general councils of the fifteenth century, Trent was strictly under the pope's control, with high Italian prelates prominent in the proceedings.

The council's most important reforms concerned internal church discipline. The selling of church offices and other religious goods was forbidden. Trent strengthened the authority of local bishops so they could effectively discipline popular religious practice. Bishops who resided in Rome were forced to move to their appointed seats of authority. They had to preach regularly and conduct annual visitations. Parish priests were required to be neatly dressed, better educated, strictly celibate, and active among their parishioners. To train better priests, Trent also called for the establishment of a seminary in every diocese.

The Council did not make a single doctrinal concession to the Protestants, however. In the face of Protestant criticism, the Council of Trent reaffirmed the traditional scholastic education of the clergy; the role of good works in salvation; the authority of tradition; the seven sacraments; transubstantiation (see page 501), the withholding of the Eucharistic cup from the laity; clerical celibacy; the reality of purgatory; the veneration of saints, relics, and sacred images; and the granting of letters of indulgence.

Rulers initially resisted Trent's reform decrees, fearing a revival of papal political power within their lands. But in time the new legislation took hold, and parish life revived under the guidance of a devout and better-trained clergy.

The Reformation's Achievements

Although politically conservative, the Reformation brought about far-reaching changes in traditional religious practices and institutions in many lands. By the end of the sixteenth century, what had disappeared or was radically altered was often dramatic.

Religion in Fifteenth-Century Life

In the fifteenth century, on the streets of the great cities of central Europe that later turned Protestant (for example, Zurich, Strasbourg, Nuremberg, and Geneva), the clergy and the religious were everywhere. They made up 6 to 8 percent of the total urban population, and they exercised consider-

Ignatius of Loyola's "Rules for Thinking with the Church"

Document

As leaders of the Counter-Reformation, the Jesuits attempted to live by and instill in others the strictest obedience to church authority. The following are some of the eighteen rules included by Ignatius in his *Spiritual Exercises* to give Catholics positive direction. These rules also indicate the Catholic reformers' refusal to compromise with Protestants.

◆ Would Protestants find any of Ignatius's "rules" acceptable? Might any of them be controversial among Catholic laity as well as among Protestant laity?

In order to have the proper attitude of mind in the Church Militant we should observe the following rules:

1. Putting aside all private judgment, we should keep our minds prepared and ready to obey promptly and in all things the true spouse of Christ our Lord, our Holy Mother, the hierarchical Church.
2. To praise sacramental confession and the reception of the Most Holy Sacrament once a year, and much better once a month, and better still every week. . . .
3. To praise the frequent hearing of Mass. . . .
4. To praise highly the religious life, virginity, and continence; and also matrimony, but not as highly. . . .
5. To praise the vows of religion, obedience, poverty, chastity, and other works of perfection and supererogation. . . .
6. To praise the relics of the saints . . . [and] the stations, pilgrimages, indulgences, jubilees, Crusade indulgences, and the lighting of candles in the churches.
7. To praise the precepts concerning fasts and abstinences . . . and acts of penance. . . .
8. To praise the adornments and buildings of churches as well as sacred images. . . .

9. To praise all the precepts of the church. . . .
10. To approve and praise the directions and recommendations of our superiors as well as their personal behaviour. . . .
11. To praise both the positive and scholastic theology. . . .
12. We must be on our guard against making comparisons between the living and those who have already gone to their reward, for it is no small error to say, for example: "This man knows more than St. Augustine"; "He is another Saint Francis, or even greater." . . .
13. If we wish to be sure that we are right in all things, we should always be ready to accept this principle: I will believe that the white that I see is black, if the hierarchical Church so defines it. For I believe that between . . . Christ our Lord and . . . His Church, there is but one spirit, which governs and directs us for the salvation of our souls.

From *The Spiritual Exercises of St. Ignatius*, trans. by Anthony Mottola, pp. 139–141. Copyright © 1964 by Doubleday, a division of Bantam, Doubleday, Dell Publishing Group, Inc. Used by permission of Doubleday, a division of Random House, Inc.

able political as well as spiritual power. They legislated and taxed; they tried cases in special church courts; and they enforced their laws with threats of excommunication.

The church calendar regulated daily life. About one third of the year was given over to some kind of religious observance or celebration. There were frequent periods of fasting. On almost a hundred days out of the year a pious Christian could not, without special dispensation, eat eggs, butter, fat, or meat.

Monasteries and especially nunneries were prominent and influential institutions. The children of society's most powerful citizens resided there. Local aristocrats were closely identified with particular churches and chapels, whose walls recorded their lineage and proclaimed their generosity. On the

streets, friars from near and far begged alms from passersby. In the churches the Mass and liturgy were read entirely in Latin. Images of saints were regularly displayed, and on certain holidays their relics were paraded about and venerated.

There was a booming business at local religious shrines. Pilgrims gathered there by the hundreds, even thousands—many sick and dying, there in search of a cure or a miracle, but many were there for diversion and entertainment. Several times during the year special preachers arrived in the city to sell letters of indulgence.

Many clergy walked the streets with concubines and children, although they were sworn to celibacy and forbidden marriage. The church tolerated such relationships upon payment of penitential fines.

People everywhere could be heard complaining about the clergy's exemption from taxation and, in many instances, also from the civil criminal code. People also grumbled about having to support church offices whose occupants actually lived and worked elsewhere. Townspeople also expressed concern that the church had too much influence over education and culture.

Religion in Sixteenth-Century Life

In these same cities after the Reformation had firmly established itself, few changes in politics and society were evident. The same aristocratic families governed as before, and the rich generally got richer and the poor poorer. But overall numbers of clergy fell by two thirds and religious holidays shrank by one third. Monasteries and nunneries were nearly absent. Many were transformed into hospices for the sick and poor or into educational institutions, their endowments also turned over to these new purposes. A few cloisters remained for very devout old monks and nuns, who could not be pensioned off or who lacked families and friends to care for them. But these remaining cloisters died out with their inhabitants.

In the churches, which had also been reduced in number by at least a third, worship was conducted almost completely in the vernacular. In some, particularly those in Zwinglian cities, the walls were stripped bare and whitewashed to make sure the congregation meditated only on God's Word. The laity observed no obligatory fasts. Indulgence preachers no longer appeared. Local shrines were closed down, and anyone found openly venerating saints, relics, and images was subject to fine and punishment.

Copies of Luther's translation of the New Testament, or more often excerpts from it, could be found in private homes, and meditation on them was encouraged by the new clergy. The clergy could marry, and most did. They paid taxes and were punished for their crimes in civil courts. Domestic moral life was regulated by committees composed of roughly equal numbers of laity and clergy, over whose decisions secular magistrates had the last word.

Not all Protestant clergy remained enthusiastic about this new lay authority in religion. And the laity themselves were also ambivalent about certain aspects of the Reformation. Over half of the original converts returned to the Catholic fold before the end of the sixteenth century. Whereas half of Europe could be counted in the Protestant camp in the mid–sixteenth century, only a fifth would be there by the mid–seventeenth century.[3]

---

[3] Geoffrey Parker, *Europe in Crisis, 1598–1648* (Ithaca, NY: Cornell University Press, 1979), p. 50.

Family Life in Early Modern Europe

Changes in the timing and duration of marriage, family size, and infant and child care suggest that family life was under a variety of social and economic pressures in the sixteenth and seventeenth centuries. The Reformation was only one factor in these changes and not the major one.

Later Marriages   Between 1500 and 1800, men and women in Western Europe and England married at later ages than they had in previous centuries: men in their mid- to late twenties, and women in their early to mid-twenties. The canonical, or church-sanctioned, age for marriage remained fourteen for men and twelve for women. The church also recognized as valid free, private exchanges of vows between a man and a woman otherwise qualified. After the Reformation, which condemned such clandestine unions, both Protestants and Catholics required parental consent and public vows in church before a marriage could be deemed fully licit.

Late marriage in the West reflected the difficulty couples had supporting themselves independently. It simply took the average couple a longer time than before to prepare themselves materially for marriage. In the sixteenth century, one in five women never married, and these, combined with the estimated 15 percent who were widows, constituted a large unmarried female population. A later marriage was a marriage of shorter duration, since couples who married in their thirties did not spend as much time together as couples who married in their twenties. And because women who bore children for the first time at advanced ages had higher mortality rates, late marriage meant more frequent remarriage for men. As evidenced by the rapid growth of orphanages and foundling homes between 1600 and 1800, delayed marriage also increased premarital sex and the number of illegitimate children.

Arranged Marriages   Marriage tended to be "arranged" in the sense that the parents met and discussed the terms of the marriage before the prospective bride and bridegroom became directly party to the preparations. But the wealth and social standing of the bride and the bridegroom were not the only things considered when youth married. By the fifteenth century, it was usual for the future bride and bridegroom to have known each other and to have had some prior relationship. Also, their emotional feeling for one another was respected by parents. Parents did not force total strangers to live together, and children had a legal right to protest and resist a coerced marriage, which was by definition invalid. The best marriage was one desired by the bride and groom and their families.

Family Size   The West European family was conjugal, or nuclear, consisting of a father and a mother and two to four children who survived into adulthood. This nuclear family

G.1431; Rδ. MGVK fl Taming of the Lion [334 x 477] 1524 *Berlin*

Taming the Lion

A No man is ever so high or good
That he cannot be managed by a woman
Who does his will
In friendly love and service.

B Although he is tyrannical wild,
He is soon calmed by a woman.
She boldly strokes his open mouth,
His anger fades, he does not bite.

C The lion, most lordly of beasts,
Famous for his strength and nobility,
Favors us women with heartfelt gifts
And good humor accompanies his
kindness.

D How wonderfully you reflect
Your taming at woman's hand,
Bearing patiently what another
Does to you against your will.

E O powerful king and greatest lord
Your equal is neither near nor far.
Excelling all, both large and small,
Upon your head should lie a crown.

F Lord lion, although you are feared
by all,
A woman knows how to saddle you,
Bending you to her will by love.
True love finds a home with a
good man.

G How well you have been groomed!
Now how lively and cheerful!
One so spirited
May have the company of women.

H Lord lion, you may have your
every wish.
Cover your trail with your tail
And you will not be tracked down.
Those who love in secret know this well.

Lion I let the women amuse themselves by
serving me.
What harm can they possibly do me?
If I want, I can suddenly turn fierce
again.
He is a fool who lets himself be taught
by women.

Taming the Lion. The words of the attendants (wives) serving the lion (husband) raise the question: who really controls the relationship between the sexes?

lived within a larger household, including in-laws, servants, laborers, and boarders. The average husband and wife had six to seven children, a new birth about every two years. Of these, an estimated one third died by age five, and one half by their teens. Rare was the family, at any social level, that did not experience infant mortality and child death.

Birth Control Artificial birth control (sponges, acidic ointments) has existed since antiquity. The church's condemnation of coitus interruptus (male withdrawal before ejaculation) during the thirteenth and fourteenth centuries suggests the existence of a contraceptive mentality, that is, a conscious, regular effort at birth control. Early birth control measures, when applied, were not very effective, and for both historical and moral reasons the church opposed them. According to Saint Thomas Aquinas, a moral act must aid and abet, never frustrate, nature's goal and the natural end of sex was the birth of children and their godly rearing within the bounds of holy matrimony and the community of the church.

Wet Nursing The church allied with the physicians of early modern Europe on another intimate family matter. Both condemned women who hired wet nurses to suckle their newborn children. The practice was popular among upper-class women and a reflection of their social standing. The practice appears to have increased the risk of infant mortality by exposing infants to a strange and shared milk supply from women who were often not as healthy as the infants' own mothers and lived under less sanitary conditions. But nursing was distasteful to some upper-class women, whose husbands also preferred that they not do it. Among women, vanity and convenience appear to have been motives for hiring a wet nurse, while for husbands, even more was at stake. Because the church forbade sexual intercourse to lactating women, a nursing wife often became a reluctant lover. In addition, nursing had a contraceptive effect (about 75 percent effective). Some women prolonged nursing their children to delay a new pregnancy, and some husbands cooperated in this form of family planning. For other husbands, however, especially noblemen and royalty who desired an abundance of male heirs, nursing seemed to rob them of offspring and jeopardize their patrimony—hence their support of hired wet nurses.

Loving Families? The traditional Western European family had features that seem cold and distant. Children between the ages of eight and thirteen were routinely sent from their homes into apprenticeships, school, or employment in the

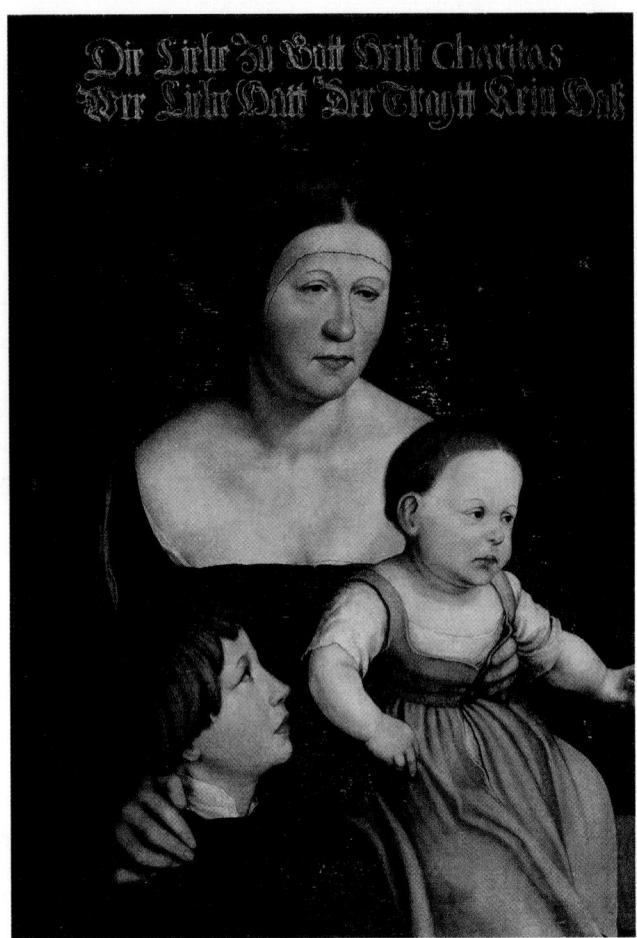

Portrait of His Wife and Two Elder Children, by Hans Holbein the Younger (1528). German-English painter Hans Holbein's painting of his wife and two of his children. *Basel, Kunstmuseum. Gert von der Osten & Horst Vey, Painting and Sculpture in Germany and the Netherlands: 1500–1600 (London: Penguin, 1969), no. 208.*

homes and businesses of relatives, friends, and occasionally strangers. The emotional ties between spouses also seem to have been as tenuous as those between parents and children. Widowers and widows often married again within a few months of their spouses' deaths, and marriages with extreme disparity in age between partners suggest limited affection.

In response to modern-day criticism, an early modern parent might well have asked, "What greater love can parents have for their children than to equip them well for a worldly vocation?" A well-apprenticed child was a self-supporting child, and hence a child with a future. In light of the comparatively primitive living conditions, contemporaries also appreciated the purely utilitarian and humane side of marriage and understood when widowers and widows quickly remarried. Marriages with extreme disparity in age, however, were no more the norm in early modern Europe than the practice of wet nursing, and they received just as much criticism and ridicule.

The Wars of Religion

After the Council of Trent adjourned in 1563, Catholics began a Jesuit-led counteroffensive against Protestants. At the time of John Calvin's death in 1564, Geneva had become both a refuge for Europe's persecuted Protestants and an international school for Protestant resistance, producing leaders fully equal to the new Catholic challenge.

Genevan Calvinism and the reformed Catholicism of the Council of Trent were two equally dogmatic, aggressive, and irreconcilable church systems. Calvinists may have looked like "new papists" to critics when they dominated cities like Geneva, but when as minorities they found their civil and religious rights denied in the empire and elsewhere, they became true firebrands and revolutionaries.

Calvinism adopted a presbyterian organization that magnified regional and local religious authority. Boards of presbyters, or elders, representing the many individual Calvinist congregations, directly shaped the policy of the church at large. By contrast, the Counter-Reformation sponsored a centralized episcopal church system, hierarchically arranged from pope to parish priest and stressing absolute obedience to the person at the top. The high clergy—the pope and his bishops—not the synods of local churches, ruled supreme. Calvinism attracted proponents of political decentralization who opposed totalitarian rulers, whereas Catholicism remained congenial to proponents of absolute monarchy determined to maintain "one king, one church, one law."

The wars of religion were both internal national conflicts and truly international wars. Catholic and Protestant subjects struggled to control France, the Netherlands, and England. The Catholic governments of France and Spain conspired and finally sent armies against Protestant regimes in England and the Netherlands. The outbreak of the Thirty Years' War in 1618 made the international dimensions of the religious conflict especially clear; before it ended in 1648, the war drew every major European nation directly or indirectly into its deadly net.

French Wars of Religion (1562–1598)

When Henry II (r. 1547–1559) died accidentally during a tournament in 1559, his sickly fifteen-year-old son, Francis II (d. 1560), came to the throne under the regency of the queen mother, Catherine de Médicis (1519–1589). With the monarchy so weakened, three powerful families began to compete to control France. They were the Bourbons, whose power lay in the south and west; the Montmorency-Châtillons, who controlled the center of France; and the Guises, who were dominant in eastern France. The Guises were by far the strongest, and the name of *Guise* was interchangeable with militant, ultra-Catholicism. The Bourbon and Montmorency-Châtillon families, in contrast, developed strong Huguenot sympathies, largely for political reasons. (French Protestants were called **Huguenots** after Besançon Hughes, the leader of Geneva's political revolt against the Savoyards in the late 1520s.) The Bourbon Louis I, prince of Condé (d. 1569), and the Montmorency-Châtillon admiral Gaspard de Coligny (1519–1572) became the political leaders of the French Protestant resistance.

Often for quite different reasons, ambitious aristocrats and discontented townspeople joined Calvinist churches in opposition to the Guise-dominated French monarchy. In 1561 over two thousand Huguenot congregations existed throughout France. Although they made up only about a fifteenth of the population, Huguenots held important geographic areas and represented the more powerful segments of French society. Over two fifths of the French aristocracy became Huguenots. Many apparently hoped to establish within France a principle of territorial sovereignty akin to that secured within the Holy Roman Empire by the Peace of Augsburg (1555). Calvinism thus indirectly served the forces of political decentralization.

Catherine de Médicis and the Guises

Following Francis II's death in 1560, Catherine de Médicis continued as regent for her second son, Charles IX (r. 1560–1574). Fearing the Guises, Catherine, whose first concern was always to preserve the monarchy, sought allies among the Protestants. Early in 1562 she granted Protestants freedom to worship publicly outside towns—although only privately within them—and to hold synods, or church assemblies. In March of the same year this royal toleration ended when the Duke of Guise surprised a Protestant congregation worshiping illegally at Vassy in Champagne and proceeded to massacre several score—an event that marked the beginning of the French wars of religion. Perpetually caught between fanatical Huguenot and Guise extremes, Queen Catherine always sought to play the one side against the other. She wanted a Catholic France but not a Guise-dominated monarchy.

On August 22, 1572, four days after the Huguenot Henry of Navarre had married Charles IX's sister—another sign of growing Protestant power in the queen mother's eye—the Huguenot leader Coligny, who increasingly had the king's ear, was wounded by an assassin's bullet. Catherine had apparently been a part of this Guise plot to eliminate Coligny. After its failure, she feared both the king's reaction to her complicity and the Huguenot response under a recovered Coligny. Catherine convinced Charles that a Huguenot coup was afoot, inspired by Coligny, and that only the swift execution of Protestant leaders could save the crown from a Protestant attack on

The St. Bartholemew's Day Massacre. In this notorious event, here depicted by the contemporary Protestant painter François Dubois, three thousand Protestants were slaughtered in Paris and an estimated twenty thousand others died throughout France. The massacre transformed the religious struggle in France from a contest for political power into an all-out war between Protestants and Catholics. *Le Massacre de la St-Barthélémy, entre 1572 et 1584. Oil on wood, 94 × 154 cm. Musée Cantonal des Beaux-Arts, Lausanne. Photo: J.-C. Ducret Musée Cantonal des Beaux-Arts, Lausanne.*

Paris. On the eve of Saint Bartholomew's Day, August 24, 1572, Coligny and three thousand fellow Huguenots were butchered in Paris. Within three days an estimated twenty thousand Huguenots were executed in coordinated attacks throughout France.

This event changed the nature of the struggle between Protestants and Catholics both within and beyond the borders of France. It was thereafter no longer an internal contest between Guise and Bourbon factions for French political influence, nor was it simply a Huguenot campaign to win basic religious freedoms. Henceforth, in Protestant eyes, it became an international struggle to the death for sheer survival against an adversary whose cruelty justified any means of resistance.

The Rise to Power of Henry of Navarre

Henry III (r. 1574–1589), who was Henry II's third son and the last Valois king, found the monarchy wedged between a radical Catholic League, formed in 1576 by Henry of Guise, and vengeful Huguenots. Like the queen mother, Henry III sought to steer a middle course, and in this effort he received support from a growing body of neutral Catholics and Huguenots who put the political survival of France above its religious unity. Such *politiques*, as they were called, were prepared to compromise religious creeds to save the nation.

Theodore Beza Defends the Right to Resist Tyranny

Document

"Although having long urged their flocks not to take up arms in defense of religion, after the St. Bartholomew's Day Massacre of French Protestants, Protestant pamphleteers defended the right of the persecuted to resist tyrants with armed force. In 1574 Calvin's successor in Geneva, Theodore Beza reminded kings of their obligation to protect their subjects and lower magistrates to remove higher ones, if the latter fail to keep their oaths of office. Finally "the People, who are prior to all magistrates" may also deprive tyrants of their power."

◆ What makes Beza's political theories radical?
◆ Are there similarities between Beza's argument and the American Declaration of Independence? If so, how?

It is apparent that there is mutual obligation between the king and the officers of a kingdom; that the government of the kingdom is not in the hands of the king in its entirety, but only the sovereign degree; that each of the officers has a share in accord with his degree; and that there are definite conditions on either side. If these conditions are not observed by the inferior officers, it is the part of the sovereign to dismiss and punish them. . . . If the king, hereditary or elective, clearly goes back on the conditions without which he would not have been recognized and acknowledged, can there be any doubt that the lesser magistrates of the kingdom, of the cities, and of the provinces, the administration of which they have received from the sovereignty itself, are free of their oath, at least to the extent that they are entitled to resist flagrant oppression of the realm which they swore to defend and protect according to their office and their particular jurisdiction? . . .

We must now speak of the third class of subjects, which though admittedly subject to the sovereign in a certain respect, is, in another respect, and in cases of necessity the protector of the rights of the sovereignty itself, and is established to hold the sovereignty to his duty, and even, if need be, constrain and punish him. . . . The people is prior to all the magistrates, and does not exist for them, but they for it. . . . Whenever law and equity prevailed, nations neither created nor accepted kings except upon definite conditions. From this it follows that when kings flagrantly violate these terms, those who have the power to give them their authority have no less power to deprive them of it.

Constitutionalism and Resistance in the Sixteenth Century: Three Treatises by Hotman, Beza, and Mornay, trans. and ed. by Julian H. Franklin (New York: Pegasus, 1969). pp. 111–114.

In the mid-1580s the Catholic League, supported by the Spanish, became completely dominant in Paris. Henry III failed to rout the league with a surprise attack in 1588 and had to flee Paris. Forced by his weakened position into guerrilla tactics, the king had both the Duke and the Cardinal of Guise assassinated. The Catholic League reacted with a fury that matched the earlier Huguenot response to the Massacre of Saint Bartholomew's Day. The king was now forced to strike an alliance with his Protestant cousin and heir, Henry of Navarre, in April 1589.

As the two Henrys prepared to attack Paris, however, a fanatical Dominican friar murdered Henry III. Thereupon the Bourbon Huguenot Henry of Navarre became Henry IV of France (r. 1589–1610).

Henry IV came to the throne as a *politique*, weary of religious strife and prepared to place political peace above absolute religious unity. He believed that a royal policy of tolerant Catholicism would be the best way to achieve such peace. On July 25, 1593, he publicly abjured the Protestant

faith and embraced the traditional and majority religion of his country. "Paris is worth a Mass," he is reported to have said.

The Edict of Nantes   Five years later, on April 13, 1598, Henry IV's famous Edict of Nantes proclaimed a formal religious settlement. In 1591 he had already assured the Huguenots of at least qualified religious freedoms. The Edict 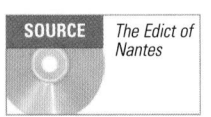 of Nantes made good that promise. It recognized and sanctioned minority religious rights within what was to remain an officially Catholic country. This religious truce—and it was never more than that—granted the Huguenots, who by this time numbered well over a million, freedom of public worship, the right of assembly, admission to public offices and universities, and permission to maintain fortified towns. Most of the new freedoms, however, were to be exercised within their own localities. Concession of the right to fortify towns reveals the continuing distrust between French Protestants and Catholics. The edict only transformed a long hot war between irreconcilable enemies into a long cold war. To its critics, it created a state within a state.

A Catholic fanatic assassinated Henry IV in May 1610. Although Henry is best remembered for the Edict of Nantes, the political and economic policies he put in place were equally important. They laid the foundations for the transformation of France into the absolutist state it would become in the seventeenth century. Ironically, in pursuit of the political and religious unity that had escaped Henry IV, his grandson Louis XIV (r. 1643–1715), calling for "one king, one church, one law," would later revoke the Edict of Nantes in 1685 (see Chapter 20). This action would force France and Europe to learn again by bitter experience the hard lessons of the wars of religion. Rare is the politician who learns from the lessons of history rather than repeat its mistakes.

Imperial Spain and the Reign of Philip II (1556–1598)

Until the English defeated his mighty Armada in 1588, no one person stood larger in the second half of the sixteenth century than Philip II of Spain. During the first half of his reign, attention focused on the Mediterranean and Turkish expansion. On October 7, 1571, a Holy League of Spain, Venice, and the pope defeated the Turks at Lepanto in the largest naval battle of the sixteenth century. Before the engagement ended, thirty thousand Turks had died and over one third of the Turkish fleet was sunk or captured.

Revolt in the Netherlands The spectacular Spanish military success in southern Europe was not repeated in northern Europe when Philip attempted to impose his will within the Netherlands and on England and France. The resistance of the Netherlands especially proved the undoing of Spanish dreams of world empire.

The Netherlands were the richest area in Europe. The merchant towns of the Netherlands were Europe's most independent, however; many, like magnificent Antwerp, were also Calvinist strongholds. A stubborn opposition to the Spanish overlords formed under William of Nassau, the Prince of Orange (r. 1533–1584). Like other successful rulers in this period, William of Orange was a *politique* who placed the Netherlands' political autonomy and well-being above religious creeds. He personally passed through successive Catholic, Lutheran, and Calvinist stages.

The year 1564 saw the first fusion of political and religious opposition to Spanish rule, the result of Philip II's unwise insistence that the decrees of the Council of Trent be enforced throughout the Netherlands. A national covenant was drawn up called the Compromise, a solemn pledge to resist the decrees of Trent and the Inquisition.

Philip dispatched the Duke of Alba (1508–1582) to suppress the revolt. His army of ten thousand men

The Milch Cow. This sixteenth-century satirical painting depicts the Netherlands as a land all the great powers of Europe wish to exploit. Elizabeth of England is feeding her (England had long-standing commerical ties with Flanders); Philip II of Spain is attempting to ride her (Spain was trying to reassert its control over the entire region); William of Orange is trying to milk her (he was the leader of the anti-Spanish rebellion); and the king of France holds her by the tail (France hoped to profit from the rebellion at Spain's expense). *The "Milch Cow." Rijksmuseum, Amsterdam.*

marched northward from Milan in 1567 in a show of combined Spanish and papal might. A special tribunal, known to the Spanish as the Council of Troubles and among the Netherlanders as the Council of Blood, reigned over the land. Several thousand suspected heretics were publicly executed before Alba's reign of terror ended.

William of Orange had been an exile in Germany during these turbulent years. He now emerged as the leader of a broad movement for the Netherlands' independence from Spain.

After a decade of persecution and warfare, the ten largely Catholic southern provinces (what is roughly modern Belgium) came together in 1576 with the seven largely Protestant northern provinces (what is roughly the modern Netherlands) in unified opposition to Spain. This union, known as the Pacification of Ghent, declared internal regional sovereignty in matters of religion. It was a Netherlands version of the Peace of Augsburg.

After more fighting, in January 1579 the southern provinces formed the Union of Arras and made peace with Spain. The northern provinces responded with the formation of the Union of Utrecht and continued the struggle. Spanish preoccupation with France and England in the 1580s permitted the northern provinces to drive out all Spanish soldiers by 1593. In 1596 France and England formally recognized the independence of these provinces. However, the northern provinces did not formally conclude peace with Spain until 1609, when the Twelve Years' Truce concluded their virtual independence. But Spain did not fully recognize that independence until the Peace of Westphalia in 1648.

Elizabeth I (1558–1603) Standing on a Map of England in 1592. An astute, if sometimes erratic, politician in foreign and domestic policy, Elizabeth was one of the most successful rulers of the sixteenth century. *National Portrait Gallery, London/SuperStock.*

England and Spain (1558–1603)

Elizabeth I Elizabeth I (r. 1558–1603), the daughter of Henry VIII and Anne Boleyn, was perhaps the most astute politician of the sixteenth century in both domestic and foreign policy. She repealed the anti-Protestant legislation of her predecessor Mary Tudor and guided a religious settlement through Parliament that prevented England from being torn asunder by religious differences in the sixteenth century, as the Continent was.

Catholic extremists hoped to replace Elizabeth with the Catholic Mary Stuart, Queen of Scots. But Elizabeth acted swiftly against Catholic assassination plots and rarely let emotion override her political instincts.

Elizabeth dealt cautiously with the Puritans, Protestants who sought to "purify" the national church of every vestige of "popery" and to make its Protestant doctrine more precise. The Puritans had two special grievances: (1) the retention of Catholic ceremony and vestments within the Church of England, and (2) the continuation of the episcopal system of church governance.

Sixteenth-century Puritans were not separatists, however. They worked through Parliament to create an alternative national church of semi-autonomous congregations governed by representative presbyteries (hence, Presbyterians), following the model of Calvin and Geneva. The more extreme Puritans wanted every congregation to be autonomous, a law unto itself, with no higher control. They came to be known as Congregationalists. Elizabeth refused to tolerate this group, whose views she considered subversive.

Deterioration of Relations with Spain A series of events led inexorably to war between England and Spain, despite the sin-

cere desires of both Philip II and Elizabeth to avoid it. Following Spain's victory at Lepanto in 1571, England signed a mutual defense pact with France. Also in the 1570s, Elizabeth's famous seamen, John Hawkins (1532–1595) and Sir Francis Drake (?1545–1596), began to prey regularly on Spanish shipping in the Americas. Drake's circumnavigation of the globe between 1577 and 1580 was one in a series of dramatic demonstrations of English ascendancy on the high seas. In 1585 Elizabeth signed a treaty that committed English soldiers to the Netherlands. These events made a tinderbox of English-Spanish relations. The spark that finally touched it off was Elizabeth's reluctant execution of Mary, Queen of Scots (1542–1587) on February 18, 1587, for complicity in a plot to assassinate Elizabeth. Philip II ordered his Armada to make ready.

On May 30, 1588, a mighty fleet of 130 ships bearing 25,000 sailors and soldiers under the command of the Duke of Medina-Sidonia set sail for England. But the day belonged completely to the English. The barges that were to transport Spanish soldiers from the galleons onto English shores were prevented from leaving Calais and Dunkirk. The swifter English and Netherlands ships, assisted by an "English wind," dispersed the waiting Spanish fleet, over a third of which never returned to Spain. The Armada's defeat gave heart to Protestant resistance everywhere. Spain never fully recovered from it. By the time of Philip's death on September 13, 1598, his forces had been rebuffed by the French and the Dutch. His seventeenth-century successors were all inferior leaders who never knew responsibilities equal to Philip's; nor did Spain ever again know such imperial grandeur. The French soon dominated the Continent, while the Dutch and the English whittled away Spain's overseas empire.

Elizabeth died on March 23, 1603, leaving behind her a strong nation poised to expand into a global empire.

The Thirty Years' War (1618–1648)

The Thirty Years' War in the Holy Roman Empire was the last and most destructive of the wars of religion. Religious and political differences had long set Catholics against Protestants and Calvinists against Lutherans. What made the Thirty Years' War so devastating was the now entrenched hatred of the various sides and their seeming determination to sacrifice all for their territorial sovereignty and religious beliefs. As the conflicts multiplied, virtually every major European land became involved either directly or indirectly. When the hostilities ended in 1648, the peace terms shaped much of the map of northern Europe as we know it today.

Fragmented Germany During the second half of the sixteenth century, Germany was an almost ungovernable land of 360 autonomous political entities. The Peace of Augsburg (1555) had given each a significant degree of sovereignty within its own borders. Each levied its own tolls and tariffs and coined its own money, practices that made land travel and trade between the various regions difficult, if not impossible. Many of these little "states" also had great power pretensions. Political decentralization and fragmentation characterized Germany as the seventeenth century opened; it was not a unified nation like Spain, England, or even strife-torn France (see Map 17–4).

Religious Division   Religious conflict accentuated the international and internal political divisions. The Holy Roman Empire was about equally divided between Catholics and Protestants, the latter having perhaps a slight numerical edge by 1600 (see Map 17–5). The terms of the Peace of Augsburg (1555) had attempted to freeze the territorial holdings of the Lutherans and the Catholics. In the intervening years, how-

ever, the Lutherans had gained political control in many Catholic areas, as had the Catholics in a few previously Lutheran areas. There was also religious strife between liberal and conservative Lutherans and between Lutherans and the growing numbers of Calvinists.

As elsewhere in Europe, Calvinism was the political and religious leaven within the Holy Roman Empire. Unrecognized as a legal religion by the Peace of Augsburg, Calvinism established a strong foothold within the empire when Elector Frederick III (r. 1559–1576), a devout convert to Calvinism, made it the official religion within the Palatinate in 1559. By 1609 Palatine Calvinists headed a Protestant defensive alliance supported by Spain's sixteenth-century enemies: England, France, and the Netherlands.

Map 17–4.   The Holy Roman Empire ca. 1618. On the eve of the Thirty Years' War the empire was politically and religiously fragmented, as this somewhat simplified map reveals. Lutherans dominated the north and Catholics the south, while Calvinists controlled the United Provinces and the Palatinate and also had an important presence in Switzerland and Brandenburg.

Map Exploration

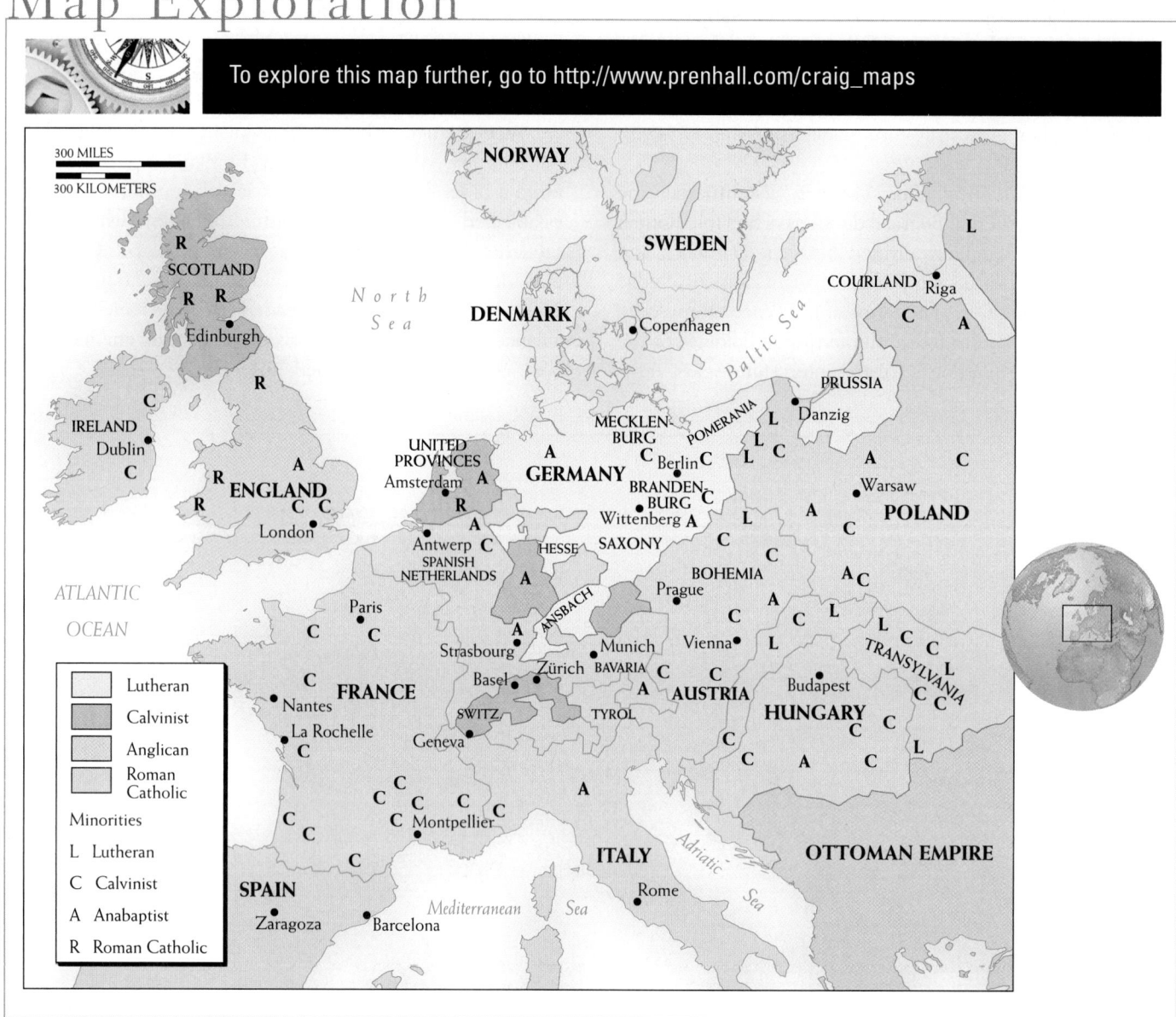

To explore this map further, go to http://www.prenhall.com/craig_maps

Map 17–5. Religious Division ca. 1600. By 1600 few could expect Christians to return to a uniform religious allegiance. In Spain and southern Italy Catholicism remained relatively unchallenged, but note the existence elsewhere of large religious minorities, both Catholic and Protestant.

If the Calvinists were active within the Holy Roman Empire, so also were their Catholic counterparts, the Jesuits. Staunchly Catholic Bavaria, supported by Spain, became militarily and ideologically for the Counter-Reformation what the Palatinate was for Protestantism. From Bavaria, the Jesuits launched successful missions throughout the empire. In 1609 Maximilian, Duke of Bavaria (1573–1651), organized a Catholic League to counter a new Protestant alliance that had been formed by the Calvinist Elector Palatine, Frederick IV (r. 1583–1610). When the league fielded a great army under the command of Jean't Senclaes, Count of Tilly (1559–1632), the stage was set, internally and internationally, for the Thirty Years' War, the worst European catastrophe since the Black Death of the fourteenth century.

The Treaty of Westphalia In 1648 all hostilities within the Holy Roman Empire were brought to an end by the Treaty of Westphalia. It firmly reasserted the major feature of the religious settlement of the Peace of Augsburg (1555), as rulers were again permitted to determine the religion of their lands. The treaty also gave the Calvinists their long-sought legal recognition while still denying it to sectarians. The independence of the Swiss Confederacy and the United Provinces of Holland, long recognized in fact, now became law.

By confirming the territorial sovereignty of Germany's many political entities, the Treaty of Westphalia perpetuated German division and political weakness into the modern period. However, two German states attained international significance during the seventeenth century: Austria and Brandenburg-Prussia. The petty regionalism within the empire also reflected on a small scale the drift of larger European politics. During the seventeenth century distinctive nationstates, each with its own political, cultural, and religious identity, reached maturity and firmly established the competitive nationalism of the modern world.

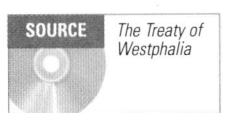
SOURCE The Treaty of Westphalia

Superstition and Enlightenment: The Battle Within

Religious reform and warfare permanently changed religious institutions in major European lands. They also moved intellectuals to rethink human nature and society. One side of that reconsideration was dark and cynical, perhaps because the peak years of religious warfare had also been those of the great European witch hunts. Another side, however, was brilliantly skeptical and constructive, reflecting the growing scientific movement of the years between 1500 and 1700.

Witch Hunts and Panic

Nowhere is the dark side of early modern thought and culture better seen than in the witch hunts and panics that erupted in almost every Western land. Between 1400 and 1700, courts sentenced an estimated 70,000 to 100,000 people to death for harmful magic (*maleficium*) and diabolical witchcraft. In addition to inflicting harm on their neighbors, witches were said to attend mass meetings known as *sabbats*, to which they were believed to fly. They were also accused of indulging in sexual orgies with the devil, who appeared in animal form, most often as a he-goat. Still other charges against them were cannibalism (especially the devouring of small Christian children) and a variety of ritual acts and practices, often sexual, that denied or perverted Christian beliefs.

Why did great witch panics occur in the second half of the sixteenth and early seventeenth centuries? The misfortune created by religious division

Two Witches by Hans Baldung Grien (1523) German artist Hans Baldung Grien presents the powers and temptations of two enchanted, monumental witches as they sow the wind. *Frankfurt, Staedelsches Kunstinstitut, no. 201. Osten & Vey, Painting and Sculpture in Germany and the Netherlands: 1500–1600, no. 201.*

and warfare was a major factor. Some argue that the Reformation spurred the panics by ridiculing the traditional church defenses against the devil and demons, compelling people to protect themselves by searching out and executing witches. Political consolidation by secular governments and the papacy probably played a greater role, with both aggressively conforming their realms and eliminating competition for the loyalty of their subjects.

Village Origins The roots of witch beliefs are found in both popular and elite culture. In village societies, feared and respected "cunning folk" helped people cope with natural disasters and disabilities by magical means. For local people, these were important services that kept village life moving forward in times of calamity.

The possession of magical powers, for good or ill, made one an important person within village society. Claims to such powers were often made by those who were most in need of security and influence, particularly women, and especially old, impoverished single or widowed women. In village society witch beliefs may also have been a way to defy urban Christian society's attempts to impose its orthodox beliefs, laws, and institutions on the countryside. Under church persecution local fertility cults, whose customary semipagan practices were intended to ensure good harvests, acquired the features of diabolical witchcraft.

Influence of the Clergy Popular belief in magic was the essential foundation of the witch hunts. Had ordinary people not believed that "gifted persons" could help or harm by magical means, and had they not been willing to make accusations against them, the hunts would never have occurred. The contribution of learned, Christian society was equally great. The Christian clergy also practiced magic, that of the holy sacraments, transforming bread and wine into the body and blood of Christ, and eternal punishments for sins into temporal ones. And they also exorcised demons.

In the late thirteenth century the church declared its magic the only legitimate magic. Since such power was not human, the theologians reasoned, it came either from God or from the devil. That from God was properly exercised within and by the church. Any who practiced magic outside and against the church did so on behalf of the devil. From such reasoning grew allegations of "pacts" between non-Christian magicians and Satan. Attacking accused witches became a way for the church to extend its spiritual hegemony, especially in new areas being conformed by church and state to higher Christian society. As spiritual authorities revered and feared by villagers or townspeople, local cunning folk posed an obstacle to that mission. To accuse, try, and execute witches was a declaration of moral and political authority over a village or territory.

Why Women?   Roughly 80 percent of the victims of witch hunts were women, most single and between forty-five and sixty years of age. This suggests that misogyny fueled the witch hunts. Inspired by male hatred and sexual fear of women, and occurring at a time when women were also breaking out from under male control, witch hunts were simply a conspiracy of males against females.

Older single women claiming supernatural powers may, however, have been vulnerable for more basic social reasons. As a dependent social group ever in need of public assistance, they were natural targets for the peculiar "social engineering" of the witch hunts. Because of their economic straits, more women than men laid claim to the supernatural powers that made them influential in village society. Such women thus found themselves on the front lines in disproportionate numbers when the church declared war against those who practiced magic without its special blessing. Also, many of these women were midwives—an activity that associated them with the deaths of beloved mothers and infants during childbirth; this misfortune made them targets of local resentment and accusations. Both the church and their neighbors were prepared to think and say the worst about them, a deadly combination.

End of the Witch Hunts   Many factors helped end the witch hunts. The emergence of a more scientific worldview made it difficult to believe in the powers of witches. In the seventeenth century mind and matter came to be viewed as two independent realities, making it harder to believe that words and thoughts could impact physical things. A witch's curse was merely words. With advances in medicine, the rise of insurance companies, and the availability of lawyers, people could protect themselves when physical affliction and natural calamity struck. Witch hunts also tended to get out of hand. Tortured witches sometimes alleged having seen leading townspeople at sabbats; even the judges themselves! At this point the trials ceased to serve the interests of those conducting them. They not only became dysfunctional but threatened anarchy as well.

Writers and Philosophers

By the end of the sixteenth century, many could no longer embrace either old Catholic or new Protestant absolutes. Intellectually as well as politically, the seventeenth century would be a period of transition, one already well prepared by the humanists and scientists of the Renaissance and post-Renaissance (see Chapter 22), who reacted strongly against medieval intellectual traditions.

The writers and philosophers of the late sixteenth and seventeenth centuries were aware that they lived in a period of transition. Some embraced the emerging new science wholeheartedly (Hobbes and Locke), some tried to straddle the two ages (Cervantes and Shakespeare), and still others ignored or opposed the new developments that seemed mortally to threaten traditional values (Pascal).

Miguel de Cervantes Saavedra   Spanish literature of the sixteenth and seventeenth centuries was influenced by the peculiar religious and political history of Spain in this period. Spain was dominated by the Catholic Church, whose piety was strongly promoted by the state. The intertwining of Catholic piety and Spanish political power underlay literary preoccupation with medieval chivalric virtues—in particular, honor and loyalty.

Generally acknowledged to be the greatest Spanish writer of all time, Cervantes (1547–1616) was preoccupied in his work with the strengths and weaknesses of religious idealism. He was the son of a nomadic physician. Having received only a smattering of formal education, he educated himself by insatiable reading in vernacular literature and immersion in the school of life. As a young man, he worked in Rome for a Spanish cardinal. In 1570 he became a soldier and was decorated for gallantry at Lepanto (1571). He conceived and began to write his most famous work, *Don Quixote*, in 1603, while languishing in prison after conviction for theft.

The first part of *Don Quixote* appeared in 1605 and a second part in 1615. If, as many argue, the intent of this work was to satirize the chivalric romances so popular in Spain, Cervantes failed to conceal his deep affection for the character he had created as an object of ridicule, Don Quixote. Don Quixote, a none-too-stable middle-aged man, is driven mad by reading too many chivalric romances. He comes to believe that he is an aspirant to knighthood and must prove his worthiness. To this end, he acquires a rusty suit of armor, mounts an aged horse, and chooses for his inspiration a quite unworthy peasant girl whom he fancies to be a noble lady to whom he can, with honor, dedicate his life.

Don Quixote's foil in the story—Sancho Panza, a clever, worldly, wise peasant who serves as his squire—watches with bemused skepticism, but also with genuine sympathy, as his lord does battle with a windmill (which he mistakes for a dragon) and repeatedly makes a fool of himself as he gallops across the countryside. The story ends tragically with Don Quixote's humiliating defeat by a well-meaning friend, who, disguised as a knight, bests Don Quixote in combat and forces him to renounce his quest for knighthood. The humiliated Don Quixote does not, however, come to his senses as a result. He returns sadly to his village to die a shamed and broken-hearted old man.

Throughout *Don Quixote*, Cervantes juxtaposed the down-to-earth realism of Sancho Panza with the old-fashioned religious idealism of Don Quixote. Cervantes admired the one as much as the other. He wanted his readers to remember that to be truly happy, men and women need dreams, even impossible ones, just as much as a sense of reality.

William Shakespeare There is much less factual knowledge about William Shakespeare (1564–1616), the greatest playwright in the English language, than one would expect of such an important figure. He apparently worked as a schoolteacher for a time and in this capacity acquired his broad knowledge of Renaissance learning and literature. His work shows none of the Puritan distress over worldliness. He took the new commercialism and the bawdy pleasures of the Elizabethan Age in stride and with amusement. In politics and religion, he was a man of his time and not inclined to offend his queen.

That Shakespeare was interested in politics is apparent from his history plays and the references to contemporary political events that fill all his plays. He seems to have viewed government simply, however, through the character of the individual ruler, whether Richard III or Elizabeth Tudor, not in terms of ideal systems or social goals. By modern standards he was a political conservative, accepting the social rankings and the power structure of his day and demonstrating unquestioned patriotism.

Shakespeare knew the theater as one who participated in every phase of its life. A member and principal dramatist of a famous company of actors known as the King's Men, he was a playwright, actor, and part owner of a theater. His work brought together in an original synthesis the best past and current achievements in the dramatic arts. He particularly mastered the psychology of human motivation and passion and had a unique talent for psychological penetration.

Shakespeare wrote histories, comedies, and tragedies. The tragedies are considered his unique achievement. Four of these were written within a three-year period: *Hamlet* (1603), *Othello* (1604), *King Lear* (1605), and *Macbeth* (1606). The most original of the tragedies, *Romeo and Juliet* (1597), transformed an old popular story into a moving drama of "star-cross'd lovers."

In his lifetime and ever since, Shakespeare has been immensely popular with both audiences and readers. As Ben Jonson (1572–1637), a contemporary classical dramatist who created his own school of poets, put it in a tribute affixed to the *First Folio* edition of Shakespeare's plays (1623): "He was not of an age, but for all time."

Blaise Pascal Blaise Pascal (1623–1662) was a French mathematician and a physical scientist widely acclaimed by his contemporaries. Torn between the continuing dogmatism and the new skepticism of the seventeenth century, he aspired to write a work that would refute two groups: the Jesuits,

whose casuistry (i.e., confessional tactics designed to minimize and even excuse sinful acts) he considered a distortion of Christian teaching, and the skeptics, who either denied religion altogether (atheists) or accepted it only as it conformed to reason (deists). Pascal never realized such a definitive work, and his views on these matters exist only in piecemeal form. He wrote against the Jesuits in his *Provincial Letters* (1656–1657), and he left behind a provocative collection of reflections on humankind and religion that was published posthumously under the title *Pensées*.

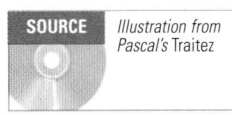
SOURCE Illustration from *Pascal's Traitez*

Early on Pascal was influenced by the Jansenists, seventeenth-century Catholic opponents of the Jesuits. Although good Catholics, the Jansenists shared with the Calvinists Saint Augustine's belief in the total sinfulness of human beings, their eternal predestination by God, and their complete dependence on faith and grace for knowledge of God and salvation.

Pascal believed that reason and science, although attesting to human dignity, remained of no avail in religion. Here only the reasons of the heart and a "leap of faith" could prevail. Pascal saw two essential truths in the Christian religion: A loving God, worthy of human attainment, exists, and human beings, because they are corrupted in nature, are utterly unworthy of God. Pascal believed that the atheists and deists of the age had spurned the lesson of reason. For him, rational analysis of the human condition attested to humankind's utter mortality and corruption, and it exposed the weakness of reason itself in resolving the problems of human nature and destiny. Reason should rather drive those who truly heed it to faith and dependence on divine grace.

Pascal made a famous wager with the skeptics. It is a better bet, he argued, to believe that God exists and to stake everything on his promised mercy than not to do so; if God does exist, everything will be gained by the believer, whereas the loss incurred by having believed in God should he prove not to exist is, by comparison, very slight.

Pascal was convinced that belief in God measurably improved earthly life psychologically and disciplined it morally, regardless of whether God proved in the end to exist. He thought that great danger lay in the surrender of traditional religious values. Pascal urged his contemporaries to seek self-understanding by "learned ignorance" and to discover humankind's greatness by recognizing its misery. Thereby he hoped to counter what he believed to be the false optimism of the new rationalism and science.

Baruch Spinoza The most controversial thinker of the seventeenth century was Baruch Spinoza (1632–1677), the son of a Jewish merchant of Amsterdam. Spinoza's philosophy caused his excommunication by his own synagogue in 1656. In 1670 he published his *Treatise on Religious and Political Philosophy*, a work that criticized the dogmatism of Dutch Calvinists and championed freedom of thought. During his lifetime, both Jews and Protestants attacked him as an atheist.

Spinoza's most influential writing, *Ethics*, appeared after his death in 1677. Religious leaders universally condemned it for its apparent espousal of pantheism. God and nature were so closely identified by Spinoza that little room seemed left either for divine revelation in Scripture or for the personal immortality of the soul, denials equally repugnant to Jews and to Christians.

The most controversial part of *Ethics* deals with the nature of substance and of God. According to Spinoza there is only one substance, which is self-caused, free, and infinite, and God is that substance. From this definition, it follows that everything that exists is in God and cannot even be conceived of apart from him. Such a doctrine is not literally pantheistic, because God is still seen to be more than the created world that he, as primal substance, embraces. Nonetheless, in Spinoza's view, statements about the natural world are also statements about divine nature. Mind and matter are seen to be extensions of the infinite substance of God; what transpires in the world of humankind and nature is a necessary outpouring of the Divine.

Such teaching clearly ran the danger of portraying the world as eternal and human actions as unfree and inevitable, the expression of a divine fatalism. Such points of view had been considered heresies by Jews and Christians because these views deny the creation of the world by God and destroy any voluntary basis for personal reward and punishment.

Thomas Hobbes Thomas Hobbes (1588–1679) was the most original political philosopher of the seventeenth century. Although he never broke with the Church of England, he came to share basic Calvinist beliefs, especially the low view of human nature and the ideal of a commonwealth based on a covenant, both of which find eloquent expression in his political philosophy.

Hobbes was an urbane and much-traveled man and one of the most enthusiastic supporters of the new scientific movement. During the 1630s he visited Paris, where he came to know Descartes; after the outbreak of the Puritan Revolution (see Chapter 20) in 1640, he lived as an exile in Paris until 1651. Hobbes also spent time with Galileo (see Chapter 22) in Italy and took a special interest in the works of William Harvey. Harvey was a physiologist famed for the discovery of how blood circulated through the body; his scientific writings

Leviathan. Thomas Hobbes's political treatise, *Leviathan*, portrayed rulers as absolute lords over their lands, incorporating in their persons the individual wills of all their people.

influenced Hobbes's own tracts on bodily motions.

Hobbes was driven to the vocation of political philosophy by the English Civil War (see Chapter 20). In 1651 his *Leviathan* appeared. Its subject was the political consequences of human passions, and its originality lay in (1) its making natural law, rather than common law (i.e., custom or precedent), the basis of all positive law, and (2) its defense of a representative theory of absolute authority against the theory of the divine right of kings. Hobbes maintained that statute law found its justification only as an expression of the law of nature and that rulers derived their authority from the consent of the people.

Hobbes viewed humankind and society in a thoroughly materialistic and mechanical way. Human beings are defined as a collection of material particles in motion. All their psychological processes begin with and are derived from bare sensation, and all their motivations are egotistical, intended to increase pleasure and minimize pain.

Despite this seemingly low estimate of human beings, Hobbes believed much could be accomplished by the reasoned use of science. All was contingent, however, on the correct use of that greatest of all human powers, one compounded of the powers of most people: the commonwealth, in which people are united by their consent in one all-powerful person.

The key to Hobbes's political philosophy is a brilliant myth of the original state of humankind. According to this myth, human beings in the natural state are generally inclined to a "perpetual and restless desire of power after power that ceases only in death."[4] As all people desire—and in the state of nature have a natural right to—everything, their equality breeds enmity, competition, and diffidence, and the desire for glory begets perpetual quarreling—"a war of every man against every man."[5]

Whereas earlier and later philosophers saw the original human state as a paradise from which humankind had fallen, Hobbes saw it as a corruption from which only society had delivered people. Contrary to the views of Aristotle and of Christian thinkers like Thomas Aquinas, Hobbes saw human beings not as sociable, political animals, but as self-centered beasts, laws unto themselves, utterly without a master unless one is imposed by force.

---

[4] *Leviathan,* Parts I and II, ed. by H. W. Schneider (Indianapolis, IN: Bobbs-Merrill, 1958), p. 86.

[5] Ibid., p. 106.

John Locke Explains the Sources of Human Knowledge

Document

An Essay Concerning Human Understanding (1690) may be the most influential philosophical work ever written in English. Locke's most fundamental idea, which is explicated in the passage below, is that human knowledge is grounded in the experiences of the senses and in the reflection of the mind on those experiences. He rejected any belief in innate ideas. His emphasis on experience led to the wider belief that human beings are creatures of their environment. After Locke, numerous writers argued that human beings could be improved if the environment in which they lived were reformed.

◆ How did Locke's views on sensation and experience influence the way people viewed the world?

◆ Why is Locke's explanation for the sources of human knowledge so important?

Let us then suppose the mind to be, as we say, white paper void of all characters, without any *ideas*. How comes it to be furnished? Whence comes it by that vast store which the busy and boundless fancy of man has painted on it with an almost endless variety? Whence has it all the materials of reason and knowledge? To this I answer, in one word, from *experience*; in that all our knowledge is funded, and from that it ultimately derives itself. Our observation, employed either about *external sensible objects, or about the internal operations of our minds perceived and reflected on by ourselves, is that which supplies our understanding with all the materials of thinking.* These two are the fountains of knowledge, from whence all the ideas we have, or can naturally have, do spring.

First, *our senses,* conversant about particular sensible objects, do *convey into the mind* several distinct *perceptions* of things, according to those various ways wherein those objects do affect them. And thus we come by those *ideas* we have of *yellow, white, heat, cold, soft, hard, bitter, sweet,* and all those which we call sensible qualities. . . . This great source of most of the *ideas* we have, depending wholly upon

our senses, and derived by them to the understanding. I call SENSATION.

Secondly, the other fountain from which experience furnisheth the understanding with *ideas* is the *perception of the operations of our own minds* within us, as it is employed about the ideas it has got. . . . And such are *perception, thinking, doubting, believing, reasoning, knowing, willing,* and all the different actings of our own minds. . . . I call this REFLECTION, the *ideas* it affords being such only as the mind gets by reflecting on its own operations within itself. . . . These two, I say, viz. external material things as the objects of SENSATION, and the operations of our own minds within as the objects of REFLECTION, are to me the only originals from whence all our *ideas* take their beginnings. . . .

The understanding seems to me not to have the least glimmering of any *ideas* which it doth not receive from one of these two.

John Locke, *An Essay Concerning Human Understanding,* Vol. 1 (London: Everyman's Library, 1961), pp. 77–78.

According to Hobbes, people escape the impossible state of nature only by entering a social contract that creates a commonwealth tightly ruled by law and order. The social contract obliges every person, for the sake of peace and self-defense, to agree to set aside personal rights to all things. We should impose restrictions on the liberty of others only to the degree that we would allow others to restrict our own.

Because words and promises are insufficient to guarantee this state, the social contract also establishes the coercive force necessary to compel compliance with the covenant. Hobbes believed that the dangers of anarchy were far greater than those of tyranny, and he conceived of the ruler's power as absolute and unlimited. There is no room in Hobbes's political philosophy for political protest in the name of individual conscience, nor for resistance to legitimate authority by private individuals—features of *Leviathan* criticized by his contemporary Catholics and Puritans alike.

John Locke John Locke (1632–1704) has proved to be the most influential political thinker of the seventeenth century.[6] His political philosophy came to be embodied in the so-called Glorious Revolution of 1688–1689 (Chapter 20). Although he was not as original as Hobbes, his political writings were a major source of the later Enlightenment criticism of absolutism, and they gave inspiration to both the American and French Revolutions.

Locke's two most famous works are the *Essay Concerning Human Understanding* (1690) (discussed in Chapter 22) and *Two Treatises of Government* (1690). Locke wrote *Two Treatises of Government* against the argument that rulers were absolute in their power. Rulers, Locke argued, remain bound to the law of nature, which is the voice of reason, teaching that "all

---

[6] Locke's scientific writings are discussed in Chapter 24.

mankind [are] equal and independent, [and] no one ought to harm another in his life, health, liberty, or possessions,"[7] inasmuch as all human beings are the images and property of God. According to Locke, people enter social contracts, empowering legislatures and monarchs to "umpire" their disputes, precisely to preserve their natural rights, and not to give rulers an absolute power over them. (See Document, "John Locke Explains the Sources of Human Knowledge.")

"Whenever that end [namely, the preservation of life, liberty, and property for which power is given to rulers by a commonwealth] is manifestly neglected or opposed, the trust must necessarily be forfeited and the power devolved into the hands of those that gave it, who may place it anew where they think best for their safety and security."[8] From Locke's point of view,

---

[7] *The Second Treatise of Government*, ed. by T. P. Peardon (Indianapolis, IN: Bobbs-Merrill, 1952), chap. 2, sects. 4–6, pp. 4–6.

[8] Ibid., chap. 13, sect. 149, p. 84.

[9] Ibid.

absolute monarchy was "inconsistent" with civil society and could be "no form of civil government at all."[9]

Summary

Voyages of Discovery. In the late fifteenth century, Europe began to expand around the globe. Driven by both mercenary and religious motives, the Portuguese pioneered a sea route around Africa to India and the Far East, and the Spanish discovered the Americas. Social, political, and biological consequences were immense for Europeans, Native Americans, Africans, and Asians. In time, a truly global world would emerge.

The Reformation. The Reformation began in Germany with Martin Luther's attack on indulgences in 1517. Despite the opposition to the Reformation by Emperor Charles V, Luther had the support of many German princes. The Reformation shattered the religious unity of Europe. In Switzerland, Zwingli and Calvin launched their own versions of Protestantism. In England, Henry VIII repudiated papal authority

INTERPRETING THE PAST

European Expansion and Conquest

The primary source documents and visual sources below chronicle the beginnings of Europe's exploration, conquest, and exploitation of the non-Western world that began in the fifteenth century. As the text sources indicate, explorers like Columbus and Da Gama were the eyes and ears of their sovereigns, intently observing the landscape, resources, and cultures of the Americas, Africa, and India. Without available indigenous written accounts describing their first meetings with Europeans, we must carefully analyze European texts to discern the nature of these momentous encounters. In the following exercise, use the source documents along with the images to address the following thematic questions. Use specific examples from the documents to back up your assertions.

Text Sources

1. *Columbus,* Journal Excerpt and Letter (Primary Source DVD)
2. Excerpt from *The* travel journal of *Vasco da Gama,* (Primary Source DVD)
3. *Duarte Barbosa, Account of His Journeys in Africa and India* (Primary Source DVD)

Visual Sources

1. *Indians planting corn* (Primary Source DVD)
2. American *cannibals* (Primary Source DVD)

The text sources vary widely in the geographic areas they describe, but they were written within several decades of each other, and the authors are all European explorers or colonizers encountering a distant culture for the first time. Christopher Columbus's Journal and Letter offers great detail, although much of it is of questionable accuracy. In reading this revealing journal excerpt and letter, keep in mind these questions: Who was Columbus writing to? What were the possible motives shaping his narrative? In the excerpts from the travel journal of Vasco da Gama, the author discusses encountering the people and culture of the coastal Indian city of Calicut. It too includes a number of inaccuracies along with much valuable information. The third text source, by Duarte Barbosa, written in 1518, recounts Portuguese efforts to trade as well as to dominate East Africa very early in the colonial era. The images listed above also show indigenous cultures, in this case North American (Indians planting corn) and South American (American cannibals) from the perspective of Europeans.

PRENTICE HALL
myhistorylab
Where it's a good time to connect to the past!

when the pope refused to grant him a divorce. The different protestant sects were often as hostile to each other as they were to Catholicism. The Reformation also led to far-reaching changes in religious practices and social attitudes, including steps towards the advancement of women.

The Roman Catholic Church also acted to reform itself. The Council of Trent tightened church discipline and reaffirmed traditional doctrine. The Jesuits converted many Protestants back to Catholicism.

The Wars of Religion. The religious divisions of Europe led to more than a century of warfare from the 1520s to 1648. The chief battlegrounds were in France, the Netherlands, and Germany. When the Thirty Years' War ended in 1648, Europe was permanently divided into Catholic and Protestant areas.

Superstition and Enlightenment. The Reformation led to both dark and constructive views of human nature. Perhaps the darkest view was the witch crazes that erupted across Europe. Thousands of innocent people, mostly women, were persecuted and executed as witches between 1400 and 1700 by both Catholic and Protestant authorities.

Questions

Discuss the observations of Europeans, their accuracy or inaccuracy if it can be determined, and their motives. Also assess how their activities and behavior would have been perceived to indigenous peoples living in the Americas, Africa, or India.

Specifically, in reading each of these texts, analyze the goals, explicit or implied, espoused by Columbus, da Gama, and Barbosa. Are they religious, economic, a combination of both, or something else? What actions do they take to achieve their goals? How do the Europeans perceive the indigenous inhabitants—civilized or uncivilized? peaceful or violent? intelligent or ignorant? Are these descriptions consistent? How accurate do you think these descriptions are? (One example of a rather important inaccuracy—da Gama's journal states that the inhabitants of Calicut are Christians, and includes a description of a Christian church. The residents of Calicut, however, were Hindus, and the journal describes a Hindu temple.)

What are the consequences of the European's encounters? Analyze the short-term results of these encounters first. Did the Europeans indicate a desire to fundamentally change the environment or culture of the lands they visited?

In literature and philosophy, however, these years witnessed an outpouring of creative thinking. Among the greatest writers of the age were Cervantes, Shakespeare, Pascal, Spinoza, Hobbes, and Locke.

Review Questions

1. What impact did European expansion have on the societies of both the Old and New Worlds?

2. What were the main problems of the church that contributed to the Protestant Reformation? Why was the church unable to suppress dissent as it had earlier?

3. How did the theologies of Luther, Zwingli, and Calvin differ? Were their differences only religious, or did they have political consequences for the Reformation as well?

4. Why did the Reformation begin in Germany and not in France, Italy, England, or Spain?

5. What was the Catholic Reformation? Did the Council of Trent alter the character of traditional Catholicism?

6. Why did Henry VIII break with the Catholic Church? Was the "new" religion he established really Protestant?

7. Were the wars of religion really over religion? Explain.

8. Henry of Navarre (later Henry IV of France), Elizabeth I, and William of Orange have been called *politiques*. What does that term mean, and how might it apply to each?

9. Why was England more successful than other lands in resolving its internal political and religious divisions peacefully during the sixteenth and seventeenth centuries?

10. "The Thirty Years' War is the outstanding example in European history of meaningless conflict." Evaluate this statement and provide specific reasons.

Key Terms

Counter-Reformation (p. 507)   **ninety-five theses** (p. 500)

Diet of Worms (p. 501)   **Reformation** (p. 496)

Huguenots (p. 513)   **transubstantiation** (p. 503)

indulgence (p. 499)

Note: To learn more about the topics in this chapter, please turn to the Suggested Readings at the end of the book. For additional sources related to this chapter please see the Primary Source DVD at the back of this text or MyHistoryLab.

Christianity is based on the teaching of Jesus of Nazareth, a Jew who lived in Palestine during the Roman occupation. His simple message of faith in God and self-sacrificial love of one's neighbor attracted many people. The Roman authorities, perceiving his large following as a threat, crucifed him. After Jesus' crucifixion, his followers proclaimed that he had been resurrected from the dead and that he would return in glory to defeat sin, death, and the devil, and take all true believers with him to heaven—a radical vision of judgment and immortality that has driven Christianity's appeal since its inception. In the teachings of the early church, Jesus became the Christ, the son of God, the long-awaited Messiah of Jewish prophecy. His followers called themselves Christians.

Christianity proclaimed the very incarnation of God in a man, the visible presence of eternity in time. According to early Christian teaching, the power of God's incarnation in Jesus lived on in the preaching and sacraments of the church under the guidance of the Holy Spirit. According to the Christian message, in Jesus, eternity has made itself accessible to every person here and now and forevermore.

The new religion attracted both the poor and powerless and the socially rising and well-to-do. For some, the gospel of Jesus promised a better material life. For others, it imparted a sense of spiritual self-worth regardless of one's place or prospects in society.

In the late second century the Romans began persecuting Christians as "heretics" (because of their rejection of the traditional Roman gods) and as social revolutionaries (for their loyalty to a lord higher than the emperor of Rome). At the same time dissenting Christians, particularly sects claiming direct spiritual knowledge of God apart from Scripture, internally divided the young church. To meet these challenges the church established effective weapons against state terrorism and Christian heresy: an ordained clergy, a hierarchical church organization, orthodox creeds, and a biblical canon (the New Testament). Christianity not only gained legal status within the Roman Empire, but also, by the fourth century, most favored religious status thanks to Emperor Constantine's embrace of it.

After the fall of the Western Roman Empire in the fifth century C.E., Christianity became one of history's great success stories. Aided by the enterprise of its popes and the example of its monks, the church cultivated an appealing lay piety centered on the Lord's Prayer, the Apostles' Creed, veneration of the Virgin, and the sacrament of the Eucharist. Clergy became both royal teachers and bureaucrats within the kingdom of the Franks. Despite a growing schism between the Eastern (Byzantine) and Western churches, and a final split in 1054, by 1000 the church held real economic and political power. In the eleventh century reform-minded prelates put an end to presumptuous secular interference in its most intimate spiritual affairs by ending the lay investiture of clergy in their spiritual offices. For several centuries thereafter the church remained a formidable international force, able to challenge kings and emperors and inspire crusades to the Holy Land.

Pentecost. This exquisite enamel plaque, from the Mosan school that flourished in France in the eleventh and twelfth centuries, shows the descent of the Holy Spirit upon the apostles, fifty days after the resurrection of Jesus, on the ancient Jewish festival called the "feast of weeks," or Pentecost. *Courtesy Metropolitan Museum of Art.*

By the fifteenth century the new states of Europe had stripped the church of much of its political power. It was thereafter progressively confined to spiritual and moral authority. Christianity's greatest struggles ever since have been not with kings and emperors over political power, but with materialistic philosophies and worldly ideologies, matters of spiritual and moral hegemony within an increasingly pluralistic and secular world. Since the sixteenth century a succession of humanists, skeptics, Deists, Rationalists, Marxists, Freudians, Darwinians, and atheists have attempted to explain away some of traditional Christianity's most basic teachings. In addition, the church has endured major internal upheavals. After the Protestant Reformation (1517–1555) made the Bible widely available to the laity, the possibilities for internal criticism of Christianity multiplied geometrically. Beginning with the split between Lutherans and Zwinglians in the 1520s, Protestant Christianity has fragmented into hundreds of sects, each claiming to have the true interpretation of Scripture. The Roman Catholic church, by contrast, has maintained its unity and ministry throughout perilous times, although present-day discontent with papal authority threatens the modern Catholic church almost as seriously as the Protestant Reformation once did.

Christianity has remained remarkably resilient. It possesses a simple, almost magically appealing gospel of faith and love in and through Jesus. In a present-day world whose religious needs and passions still run deep, evangelical Christianity has experienced a remarkable revival. The Roman Catholic church, still troubled by challenges to papal authority, has become more pluralistic than in earlier periods. The pope has become a world figure, traveling to all continents to represent the church and advance its position on issues of public and private morality. A major ecumenical movement emerging in the 1960s has promoted unprecedented cooperation among evangelical Christian denominations. Everywhere Christians of all stripes are politically active, spreading their divine, moral, and social messages. Meanwhile, old hot-button issues, such as the ordination of women, are being overtaken by new ones, particularly the marriage of gay men and women and the removal of clergy who do not maintain the moral discipline of their holy orders.

◆ **Over the centuries what have been some of the chief factors attracting people to Christianity?**

◆ **What forces have led to disunity among Christians in the past; what factors cause tensions among modern Christians?**

Gay bishop. V. Gene Robinson is applauded after his investiture as the Episcopal Church's bishop of New Hampshire in March 2004. Robinson is the Episcopal Church's first openly gay bishop. The issue of homosexuality has divided Christian churches across the world.

Conquest and Exploitation: The Development of the Transatlantic Economy

- Periods of European Overseas Expansion
- Mercantilist Theory of Economic Exploitation
- Establishment of the Spanish Empire in America
- Economies of Exploitation in the Spanish Empire
- Colonial Brazil
- French and British Colonies in North America
- The Columbian Exchange: Disease, Animals, and Agriculture
- Slavery in the Americas
- Africa and the Transatlantic Slave Trade

THE LATE-FIFTEENTH-CENTURY EUROPEAN encounter with the American continents changed the entire world. The more than two and a half centuries of European domination and government that followed the encounter made the Americas a region where European languages, legal and political institutions, trade patterns, and religion prevail. African populations, economies, and political structures were altered by the slave trade. These developments gave Europe more influence over other world cultures and civilizations than it would otherwise have achieved.

Within decades of the European voyages of discovery, Native Americans, Europeans, and Africans began to interact in a manner unprecedented in human history. The Native Americans of North and South America encountered bands of European conquerors and European Roman Catholic missionaries. Technological and military superiority as well as political divisions among the Native Americans allowed the Europeans to realize their material and religious ambitions. By the middle of the sixteenth century

Slave Auction Notice. Africans who survived the voyage across the Atlantic were immediately sold into slavery in the Americas. This eighteenth-century advertisement relates to a group of slaves whose ship had stopped at Charleston, South Carolina, and then landed elsewhere in the region to auction its human cargo. Notice the concern to assure potential buyers that the slaves were healthy, as a smallpox epidemic was then raging on the mainland.

The Atlantic World

The Atlantic World

The exchanges of people, goods, ideas, and plants, animals, and microcosms between the American, European, and African continents in the fifteenth and sixteenth centuries transformed world history. In the Americas, the native peoples—whose ancestors had migrated from Asia millennia before—had established a wide variety of civilizations. Some of their most remarkable architectural monuments and cities were constructed during the very centuries when European civilizations were reeling from the collapse of Roman power. While trade and culture had long linked parts of Africa and regions in Eurasia (see Chapter 15) the civilizations of the Americas and the civilizations of Eurasia and Africa had had no significant contact with each other prior to the era of European exploration.

Within half a century of the landing of Columbus, millions of America's native peoples in Florida, the Caribbean islands, Mesoamerica, and South America had encountered Europeans intent on conquest, exploitation, and religious conversion. The Europeans' rapid conquest was the result of several factors—their advanced weapons and navies; the new diseases they brought with them; and internal divisions among the Native Americans. Thereafter, Spain and Portugal dominated Central and South America (what we now, as a result of this history, term Latin America), and England, France, and Holland set out to settle North America. The Europeans imported their own food crops, such as wheat and apples, while also taking advantage of American plants, such as potatoes, corn, and tobacco.

Throughout the Americas and the Caribbean basin, Europeans established economies of exploitation. In Latin America, they developed various institutions to extract native labor. Plantation owners from the Mid-Atlantic English colonies through the Caribbean and into Brazil preferred slaves forcibly imported from Africa. African slaves were hardier than indigenous laborers, who lacked immunity to European diseases, and they could be better controlled than indentured servants from Europe. With the exception of tobacco, plantation crops derived largely from the Old

Europeans had begun to import Africans into the American continents as chattel slaves, converting them to Christianity in the process. Consequently, by the close of the sixteenth century Europe, the Americas, and Africa had become linked in a vast transatlantic economy that extracted material and agricultural wealth from the American continents largely on the basis of the nonfree labor of impressed Native Americans and imported African slaves.

The next century would see English and French colonists settling in North America and the Caribbean, introducing different political values and, through the English, Protestantism. These North American colonists were also part of the transatlantic economy, and many would become economically involved directly or indirectly with African slavery. As they exploited the American wilderness, the colonists interacted with the Native Americans of North America, sometimes destroying indigenous cultures, sometimes converting Native Americans to Christianity; Native Americans, too, were drawn into the transatlantic economy.

Beginning in the sixteenth century the importation of African slaves and the use of slave labor were fundamental to the plantation economy that eventually extended from Maryland to Brazil. The slave trade intimately connected the economy of certain sections of Africa to the transatlantic economy. The slave trade had a devastating effect on the African people and cultures involved in it, but it also enriched the Americas with African culture and religion. ■

Periods of European Overseas Expansion

It may be useful to see the establishment of this vast new transatlantic economy in the larger context of European overseas expansion. That expansion loosed the forces that created the transatlantic economy.

World; some Africans were already familiar with the cultivation of, for example, rice. The emergent Atlantic World drew the economies and peoples of Europe, Africa, and the Americas into a vast worldwide web of production based on slave labor.

Slavery had its most striking impact on the lives of the millions of humans who were torn from their birthplaces, their families, and their cultures. African slaves suffered from high mortality and sharply reduced birthrates; they were subjected to harsh working conditions and brutally dehumanizing treatment.

Beyond the egregious harms done to individual slaves and their descendents, slavery influenced political, economic, and social history throughout the Atlantic world. The slave trade corroded the political and social structures of African societies. Some historians have suggested that the plantation economy's efficient organization and use of labor created models of efficient productive organization and use of labor that became adapted in the Industrial Revolution in Europe and North America (see Chapter 20). Recent historical scholarship has highlighted ways in which the inherent contradictions between the institution of slavery, Enlightenment ideals of human will and behavior, and new political philosophies of the state in Europe and the Americas contributed some of the underpinnings for the wave of revolutions in the eighteenth and nineteenth centuries (see Chapters 22 and 23).

Focus Questions

◆ How did the encounter of Europe and Africa, with the Americas change the global ecological balance?

◆ Why was the Spanish Empire based on economies of exploitation? How was the labor of non-European peoples drawn into the economy of this empire?

◆ How and why did the plantation economy develop? Why did it rely on African slaves for its labor? What were the consequences of the slave trade for individuals and institutions in each of the three continents constituting the Atlantic world?

◆ Why do we think of the plantation economy as a global, rather than regional, system of production? Why was it the "engine" of Atlantic basin trade?

Since the late fifteenth century, European contacts with the rest of the world have gone through four distinct stages. The first was that of the European discovery, exploration, initial conquest, and settlement of the Americas and commercial expansion elsewhere in the world. By the close of the seventeenth century Spain governed South America, except for Portuguese-ruled Brazil. French and British colonies had been established in North America. France, Britain, the Netherlands, and Spain controlled various islands in the Caribbean. The French, British, and Dutch held outposts in Asia.

The second era was one of colonial trade rivalry among Spain, France, and Great Britain. The Anglo-French side of the contest has often been compared to a second Hundred Years' War. During this second period both the British colonies of the North American seaboard and the Spanish colonies of Mexico and Central and South America emancipated themselves from European control. This era may be said to have closed during the 1820s (see Chapter 23).

El Morro, Puerto Rico. This fortress was built by the Spanish in the sixteenth century to protect Spain's valuable trading rights against British, Dutch, and pirate ships.

The third stage of European contact with the non-European world occurred in the nineteenth century when European governments carved formal empires in Africa and Asia. Those nineteenth-century empires also included new areas of European settlement such as Australia, New Zealand, and South Africa. The bases of these empires were trade, national honor, racial theories, religious expansion, and military superiority (see Chapter 25).

The last phase of European dominion occurred during the mid–twentieth century with the decolonization of peoples who had previously been under European colonial rule (see Chapters 32 and 33).

During the four and a half centuries before decolonization, Europeans exerted political dominance over much of the rest of the world that was out of all proportion to Europe's size or population. Europeans frequently treated other peoples as social, intellectual, and economic inferiors. They ravaged existing cultures because of greed, religious zeal, or political ambition. These actions significantly affect the contemporary relationship between Europe and its former colonies. What allowed the Europeans to exert such influence and domination for so long over so much of the world was not any innate cultural superiority, but rather a technological supremacy related to naval power and gunpowder. Ships and guns allowed the Europeans to exercise their will almost wherever they chose.

Mercantilist Theory of Economic Exploitation

The early modern European empires of the sixteenth through the eighteenth centuries—empires based on commerce—existed primarily to enrich trade. Extensive trade rivalries sprang up around the world. The protection of these empires required naval power. Spain dominated the largest of these empires and constructed elaborate naval, commercial, and political structures to exploit and govern it. Finally, these empires depended largely on slave labor. Indeed, the Atlantic slave trade was a major way in which European merchants enriched themselves. That trade in turn forcibly brought together the lives and cultures of peoples in Africa and the New World.

To the extent that any formal economic theory lay behind the conduct of these empires, it was mercantilism, that practical creed of hard-headed business people. The terms **mercantilism** and *mercantile system* (coined by later opponents) designate a system in which governments heavily regulate trade and commerce in hope of increasing individual national wealth. Economic writers of the time believed that a nation had to gain a favorable trade balance

of gold and silver bullion. A nation was truly wealthy only if it amassed more bullion than its rivals.

From beginning to end, the economic well-being of the home country was the primary concern of mercantilist writers. Colonies existed to provide markets and natural resources for the industries of the home country. In turn, the home country furnished military security and political administration for the colonies. For decades both sides assumed that the colonies were the inferior partner in the relationship. The mercantilist statesmen and traders regarded the world as an arena of scarce resources and economic limitation. They assumed that one national economy could grow only at the expense of others. The home country and its colonies were to trade exclusively with each other. To that end, they tried to forge trade-tight systems of national commerce through navigation laws, tariffs, bounties to encourage production, and prohibitions against trading with the subjects of other monarchs. National monopoly

Mercantilism. As this painting of the Custom House Quay in London suggests, trade from European empires and the tariffs imposed on it were expected to generate revenue for the home country. But behind many of the goods carried in the great sailing ships in the harbor and landed on these docks lay the labor of African slaves working on the plantations of North and South America. *Samuel Scott, "Old Custom House Quay" Collection. V&A Images, the Victoria and Albert Museum, London.*

Jacques Savary Praises Trade

Document

During the seventeenth century certain writers believed it necessary to justify trade and commerce. Many people at the time associated wealth and social prestige with the aristocracy and with landed estates. Wealth in land appeared more certain and less likely to disappear through speculation than commercial wealth. Jacques Savary was a Frenchman who in the 1670s wrote a treatise on merchants. He sought to explain why trade and commerce was part of the divine plan for humankind. He also explained how such trade could expand the wealth and power of monarchs. In writing for a French audience, Savary would appear to have in mind the commercial achievements of the Dutch with whom France was then at war as well as of the English. (See Chapter 20)

◆ How does Savary justify trade as part of God's plan for human society? How does he relate trade to the prosperity of kingdoms and to parts of the economy not directly engaging in overseas trade? How does he see commerce enriching monarchs?

By the manner in which Divine Providence has dispersed things throughout the world, it is clear that God wished to create unity and love among all men, because He imposed upon them the state of always having need one of another. He did not choose to permit necessities of existence to be found in one place, but rather spread out his gifts, in order that men might have to trade together . . . it is this endless exchange of the commodities of life which gives birth to Trade, and it is also Trade which adds sweetness to life. . . .

It was not enough that Trade be necessary; it was also essential that it be profitable, in order to compel some men to devote their energies to it; for there are a number of provinces, in which the plentiful supply of most of the goods needed for everyday life would have given rise to laziness, had not the desire for profit and social advancement been a goad which forced them to enter Trade.

One cannot question its usefulness; firstly, with reference to the individuals who practise commerce, because

the largest part of the population makes an honest living by this occupation. . . .

The usefulness of Trade extends also to kingdoms and to the princes who rule them; the more Trade there is within a country, the greater its wealth. There have been states which have gained immense wealth in a short time, but when war has disrupted Trade, their provinces have suffered, have sometimes been unable to pay their taxes, and in the end their fields have lain uncultivated.

The kings can also derive great benefit from Trade; because, apart from the dues which are paid to them on goods entering or leaving the kingdom, it is indeed true that all the ready money which is in the hands of the merchants and business men draw the immense sums of which the kings sometimes have need for financing great enterprises.

Jacques Savary, *The Compleat Merchant* (first published 1675) as quoted in Roger Mettam, ed., *Government and Society in Louis XIV's France* (London: The Macmillan Press Ltd., 1977), pp. 172–173.

was the ruling principle (See Document "Jacques Savary Praises Trade.")

Mercantilist ideas were always neater on paper than in practice. By the early eighteenth century, mercantilist assumptions were far removed from the economic realities of the colonies. The colonial and home markets simply did not mesh. Spain could not produce enough goods for South America. Economic production in the British North American colonies challenged English manufacturing and led to British attempts to limit certain colonial industries, such as iron and hat making.

Colonists of different countries wished to trade with each other. English colonists could buy sugar more cheaply from the French West Indies than from English suppliers. The traders and merchants of one nation always hoped to break the monopoly of another. For all these reasons, the eighteenth century became the "golden age of smugglers."[1] The governments could not control the activities of all their subjects. Clashes among colonists could

[1] Walter Dorn, *Competition for Empire, 1740–1763* (New York: Harper, 1940), p. 266.

and did lead to war between governments. Consequently, the problems associated with the European mercantile empires led to conflicts around the world.

This brief overview of the periods of the European empire and of mercantile theory should provide a clearer context for understanding the character of the conquest of America and the establishment of the transatlantic economy.

Establishment of the Spanish Empire in America

Conquest of the Aztecs and the Incas

Within twenty years of the arrival of Columbus (1451–1506), Spanish explorers in search of gold had claimed the major islands of the Caribbean and brutally suppressed the native peoples. These actions presaged what was to occur on the continent. The Caribbean islands became the staging areas for the further exploration and conquest of other parts of the Americas (see Map 18–1).

In 1519 Hernán Cortés (1485–1547) landed in Mexico with about 500 men and a few horses. He opened

Map 18–1. European Explorations and Conquests, ca. 1550. By the middle of the sixteenth century, Spain controlled vast territories in the Americas.

communication with nearby communities and then with Moctezuma II (1466–1520), the Aztec emperor. Moctezuma may initially have believed Cortés to be the god

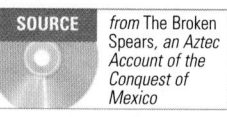

SOURCE *from The Broken Spears, an Aztec Account of the Conquest of Mexico*

Quetzalcoatl, who, according to legend, had been driven away centuries earlier but had promised to return. Whatever the reason, Moctezuma hesitated to confront Cortés, attempting at first to appease him with gifts of gold that only whetted Spanish appetites. Cortés succeeded in forging alliances with some subject peoples and, most importantly, with Tlaxcala, an independent state and traditional enemy of the Aztecs. His forces then marched on the Aztec capital of Tenochtitlán (modern Mexico City), where Moctezuma welcomed him. Cortés soon seized Moctezuma, making him a prisoner in his own capital. Moctezuma died in unexplained circumstances, and the Aztecs' wary acceptance of the Spaniards turned to open hostility. The Spaniards were driven from Tenochtitlán and nearly wiped out, but they ultimately returned and laid siege to the city. The Aztecs, under their last ruler, Cuauhtemoc (ca. 1495–1525), resisted fiercely but were finally defeated in late 1521. Cortés razed Tenochtitlán, building his own capital over its ruins, and proclaimed the Aztec Empire to be New Spain. (See Document, "A Spaniard Describes the Glory of the Aztec Capital.")

In 1532, largely inspired by Cortés's example in Mexico, Francisco Pizarro (ca. 1478–1541) landed on the western coast of South America to take on the Inca Empire, about which he knew almost nothing. His force included about 200 men armed with guns, swords, and horses, the military power of which the Incas did not understand. Pizarro lured the Inca ruler Atahualpa (ca. 1500–1533) into a conference and then seized him. The imprisoned Atahualpa tried to ransom himself with a hoard of gold, but instead of releasing him Pizarro treacherously had him garroted in 1533. The Spaniards fought their way to Cuzco, the Inca capital, and captured it, effectively ending the Inca Empire. The Spanish faced insurrections, however, and fought among themselves for decades. Effective royal control was not established until the late 1560s.

The conquests of Mexico and Peru are among the most dramatic and brutal events in modern world history. Small military forces armed with advanced weapons and in alliance with indigenous enemies of the ruling Aztecs and Incas subdued, in a remarkably brief time, these two advanced, powerful peoples. The spread of European dis-

Spanish Conquest of Mexico. A sixteenth-century drawing depicts a battle during the Spanish conquest of Mexico. The Aztecs are on the right. Note how the Spaniards bring up the rear, behind their native allies, the Tlaxcalteca.

eases, especially smallpox, among the Native Americans also aided the conquest. The native populations had long lived in isolation, and many of them succumbed to the new diseases. But beyond the drama and bloodshed, these conquests, as well as those of other Native American peoples, marked a fundamental turning point. Whole civilizations with long histories and a record of enormous social, architectural, and technological achievement were effectively destroyed. Native American cultures endured, accommodating to European dominance, but there was never any doubt about which culture had the upper hand.

The Roman Catholic Church in Spanish America

The Spanish conquest of the West Indies, Mexico, and the South American continent opened that vast region to the Roman Catholic faith. Roman Catholic priests followed in the steps of the explorers and conquerors. As it had in the Castilian reconquest of the Iberian Peninsula from the Moors, religion played a central role in the conquest of the New World. In this respect the crusade against Islamic civilization in Spain and the crusade against the indigenous religions of the Americas were closely related. In both cases the Castilian monarchy received approval from church authorities for a policy of military conquest on the grounds of converting non-Christians to the Christian faith and eradicating their indigenous religious practices. The mission of conversion justified military conquest and the extension of political control and dominance. As a consequence of this

policy, the Roman Catholic Church in the New World was always a conservative force working to protect the political power and prestige of the conquerors and the interests of the Spanish authorities.

The relationship between political authority and the propagation of religious doctrine was even closer in the New World than on the Iberian Peninsula. The papacy recognized that it could not from its own resources support so extensive a missionary effort, the full requirements for which became clear only after the conquests of Mexico and Peru. The papacy therefore turned over much of the control of the church in the New World directly to the Spanish monarchy. There was thus always a close relationship between the political and economic goals of the monarchy and the role of the church. The zeal of both increased early in the sixteenth century as the papacy and the Habsburg monarchy fought the new enemy of Protestantism, which they were determined should have no foothold in America. As a consequence, the Roman Catholicism that spread throughout the Spanish domains of America took the form of the increasingly zealous faith associated with the Counter-Reformation.

During the sixteenth century the Roman Catholic Church, represented more often than not by the mendicant orders such as the Franciscans and Dominicans, and later by

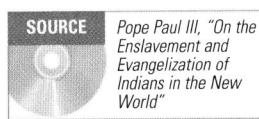

SOURCE *Pope Paul III, "On the Enslavement and Evangelization of Indians in the New World"*

the newly formed Jesuits, sought to convert the Native Americans. In the early decades these conversions often occurred shortly before the Spanish exterminated Native Americans or after they had conquered them. The conversion effort also involved attempts to eradicate surviving indigenous religious practices. The Roman Catholic authorities tended to tolerate some residual traditional ceremonies in the sixteenth century but worked to prohibit them during the seventeenth century. Thus religious conversion represented, among other things, an attempt to destroy still another part of the Native American culture. Furthermore, conversion did not bring acceptance; even until late in the eighteenth century, there were few Native American Christian priests.

Real tension, however, existed between the early Spanish conquerors and the mendicant friars who sought to minister to the Native Americans. Without conquest

A Spaniard Describes the Glory of the Aztec Capital

Document

On November 8, 1519, a group of approximately four hundred Spaniards under the command of Hernán Cortés entered the Aztec capital of Tenochtitlán. One of them was Bernal Díaz del Castillo (b. 1492) who later wrote *The Conquest of New Spain*, a chronicle of his experience. This excerpt gives some sense of the magnificence of the Aztec capital.

◆ **Which elements of Aztec life especially astonished Díaz? What can one conclude about the social and political life of the Aztec elite from the manner in which Moctezuma was attended? Which forms of wealth were most apparent?**

Early next day we left Iztapalapa [where Cortés forces had been camped] with a large escort of these great Caciques [Aztec nobles], and followed the causeway, which is eight yards wide and goes so straight to the city of Mexico [Tenochtitlán] that I do not think it curves at all. Wide though it was, it was so crowded with people that there was hardly room for them all. Some were going to Mexico and others coming away, besides those who had come out to see us, and we could hardly get through the crowds that were there. For the towers and the cues [temples] were full, and they came in canoes from all parts of the lake. No wonder, since they had never seen horses or men like us before.

With such wonderful sights to gaze on we did not know what to say, or if this was real that we saw before our eyes. On the land side there were great cities, and on the lake many more. The lake was crowded with canoes. At intervals along the causeway there were many bridges, and before us was the great city of Mexico. . . .

We marched along our causeway to a point where another small causeway branches off to another city . . . and there, beside some towerlike buildings, which were their shrines, we were met by many more Caciques and dignitaries in very rich cloaks. The different chieftains wore different brilliant liveries, and the causeways were full of them. . . .

. . . When we came near to Mexico, at the place where there were some other small towers, the great Moctezuma descended from his litter, and these other great Caciques supported him beneath a marvelously rich

canopy of green feathers, decorated with gold work, silver, pearls . . . which hung from a sort of border. It was a marvelous sight. The great Moctezuma was magnificently clad, in their fashion and wore sandals . . . the soles of which are of gold and the upper parts ornamented with precious stones. And the four lords who supported him were richly clad also in garments that seem to have been kept ready for them on the road so they could accompany their master . . . and many more lords . . . walked before the great Moctezuma, sweeping the ground on which he was to tread, and laying down cloaks so that his feet should not touch the earth. Not one of these chieftains dared to look him in the face. All kept their eyes lowered most reverently except those four lords, his nephews, who were supporting him.

. . . Who could now count the multitude of men, women, and boys in the streets, on the rooftops and in canoes on the waterways, who had come out to see us? . . .

They led us to our quarters, which were in some large houses capable of accommodating us all and had formerly belonged to the great Moctezuma's father. . . . Here Moctezuma now kept the great shrines of his gods, and a secret chamber containing gold bars and jewels. This was the treasure he had inherited from his father, which he never touched.

From *The Conquest of New Spain*, by Bernal Díaz, trans. by J. M. Cohen (New York: Penguin Books, 1963), copyright © J. M. Cohen, 1963, pp. 216–218.

the church could not convert the Native Americans, but the priests often deplored the harsh conditions imposed on the native peoples. By far the most effective and outspoken clerical critic of the Spanish conquerors was Bartolomé de Las Casas (1474–1566), a Dominican. He contended that conquest was not necessary for conversion. One result of his campaign was new royal regulations after 1550.

Another result of Las Casas's criticism was the emergence of the **Black Legend**, according to which all Spanish treatment of the Native Americans was unprincipled and inhumane. Those who created this view of Spanish behavior drew heavily on Las Casas's writings. Although substantially true,

SOURCE *From A Brief Account of the Devastation of the Indies*

the "Black Legend" nonetheless exaggerated the case against Spain. Certainly the rulers of the native empires—as the Aztec demands for sacrificial victims attest—had often themselves been exceedingly cruel to their subject peoples.

By the end of the sixteenth century the church in Spanish America had become largely an institution upholding the colonial status quo. Although individual priests did defend the communal rights of Native American tribes, the colonial church prospered as the Spanish elite prospered through its exploitation of the resources and peoples of the New World. The church became a great landowner through crown grants and through bequests from Catholics who died in the New World. The monasteries took on an economic as well as a spiritual life of their own. Whatever its concern for the spiritual welfare of the Native Americans, the church remained one of the indications that Spanish America was a conquered world. Those who spoke for the church did not challenge Spanish domination or any but the most extreme modes of Spanish economic exploitation. The church at best only modestly moderated the forces exploiting human labor and material wealth. By the end of the colonial era in the late eighteenth century, the Roman Catholic Church had become one of the single most conservative forces in Latin America and would continue to be so for at least the next century and a half.

Economies of Exploitation in the Spanish Empire

The colonial economy of Spanish America was an economy of exploitation in two senses. First, the organization of labor within the Spanish Empire in one situation after another involved structures of highly dependent servitude or slavery. Second, the resources of the continent were exploited in mercantilist fashion for the economic advantage of Spain.

Varieties of Economic Activity

The early **conquistadores** ("conquerors") had primarily been interested in gold, but by the middle of the sixteenth century silver mining provided the chief source of metallic wealth. The great silver mining centers were Potosí in present-day Bolivia and smaller sites in northern Mexico. The Spanish crown was particularly interested in mining because it received one fifth (the *quinto*) of all mining revenues. The crown thus maintained a monopoly over the production and sale of mercury, which was required for separating silver from the other impurities in the ore. Silver mining was a flourishing source of wealth for the Spanish until the early seventeenth century, when the industry underwent a recession

because of lack of new investment and the increasing costs involved in deeper mines. Nonetheless, silver predominated during the colonial era and experienced a major boom, especially in Mexico, during the eighteenth century. Its production for the benefit of Spaniards and the Spanish crown epitomized the wholly extractive economy on which Latin American colonial life was based.

The activities associated with this extractive economy—mining the ore, smelting it, harvesting wood to feed the smelters' fires—required labor. From the initial contact with America, there were too few Spanish colonists to provide the needed labor. Furthermore, the social status and expectations of those colonists who did come to the Americas made them unlikely to provide wage labor. Consequently, the Spaniards looked first to the Native American population and then to imported African slaves. Indigenous labor dominated on the continent and African labor in the Caribbean. (See Document, "A Contemporary Describes Forced Indian Labor at Potosí.")

Encomienda The Spanish devised a series of institutions to exploit Native American labor. The first was the **encomienda**, a formal grant by the crown of the right to the labor of a specific number of Native Americans for a particular time. An *encomienda* usually involved a few hundred Native Americans but might grant the right to the labor of several thousand. The *encomienda* was first used on Hispaniola but spread to the continent as the conquest took place. *Encomienda* as an institution persisted in some parts of Latin America well into the eighteenth century but had generally declined by the middle of the sixteenth. Some Native Americans substituted payments in kind or cash for labor.

The Spanish crown disliked the *encomienda* system. The monarchy was distressed by reports from concerned clergy that the Native Americans were being mistreated under the system and feared that *encomienda* holders were attempting to transform themselves into a powerful independent nobility in the New World.

Repartimiento The passing of the *encomienda* led to another arrangement of labor servitude, the **repartimiento**, which was largely copied from the draft labor practices of the Incas. *Repartimiento*, in an adaptation of the Incan *mita*, required adult male Native Americans to devote a set number of days of labor annually to Spanish economic enterprises. In the mines of Potosí, the *repartimiento* was known as the *mita*. The time limitation on *repartimiento* led some Spanish managers to use their workers in an extremely harsh manner, under the assumption that more fresh workers would soon be appearing on the scene. Native Americans sometimes did not survive their days of labor rotation.

A Contemporary Describes Forced Indian Labor at Potosí

Document

The Potosí range in Bolivia was the site of the great silver-mining industry in the Spanish Empire. The vast wealth of the region became legendary almost as soon as mining commenced there in the 1540s. Native Americans, most of whom were forced laborers working under the *mita* system of conscription, did virtually all of the work underground. This description, written by a Spanish friar in the early seventeenth century, portrays both the large size of the enterprise and the harsh conditions that the Native Americans endured. At any one time only one-third of the 13,300 conscripted Native Americans were employed. The labor force was changed every four months.

◆ How efficient does the description suggest the mines were? What would have been the likely effects of working so long underground surrounded by burning candles?

According to His Majesty's warrant, the mine owners on this massive range have a right to the *mita* [conscripted labor] of 13,300 Indians in the working and exploitation of the mines, both those which have been discovered, those now discovered, and those which shall be discovered. It is the duty of the Corregidor [municipal governor] of Potosí to have them rounded up and to see that they come in from all the provinces between Cuzco over the whole of El Collao and as far as the frontiers of Tarija and Tomina. . . .

The *mita* Indians go up every Monday morning to the locality of Guayna Potosí which is at the foot of the range; the Corregidor arrives with all the provincial captains or chiefs who have charge of the Indians assigned them, and he there checks off and reports to each mine and smelter owner the number of Indians assigned him for his mine or smelter; that keeps him busy till 1 P.M., by which time the Indians are already turned over to these mine and smelter owners.

After each has eaten his ration, they climb up the hill, each to his mine, and go in, staying there from that hour until Saturday evening without coming out of the mine; their wives bring them food, but they stay constantly underground, excavating and carrying out the ore from which they get the silver. They all have tallow candles, lighted day and night; that is the light they work with, for as they are underground, they have need of it all the time. . . .

These Indians have different functions in the handling of the silver ore; some break it up with bar or pick, and dig down in, following the vein in the mine; others bring it up; others up above keep separating the good and the poor in piles; others are occupied in taking it down from the range to the mills on herds of llamas; every day they bring up more than 8,000 of these native beasts of burden for this task. These teamsters who carry the metal do not belong to the *mita*, but are mingados—hired.

From Antonio Vázquez de Espinosa, *Compendium and Description of the Indies* (ca. 1620), trans. by Charles Upson Clark (Washington, DC: Smithsonian Institution Press, 1968), p. 62, quoted in Helen Delpar, ed., *The Borzoi Reader in Latin American History* (New York: Alfred A. Knopf, 1972), pp. 92–93.

The Hacienda Outside the mines, the major institution using dependent labor in the Spanish colonies was the **hacienda**. This institution, which dominated rural and agricultural life in Spanish colonies on the continent, developed when the crown, partly to counter the extension of the *encomienda*, made available grants of land. These grants led to the establishment of large landed estates owned by **peninsulares**, whites born in Spain, or Creoles, whites born in America. The crown thus continued to use the resources of the New World for patronage without directly impinging on the Native Americans because the grazing that occurred on the *haciendas* required far less labor than did the mines. The establishment of *haciendas* represented the transfer of the principle of the large unit of privately owned land, which was characteristic of Europe and especially of Spain, to the New World. Such estates would become one of the most important features of Latin American life. Laborers on the *hacienda* usually stood in some relation of formal servitude to the owner. Furthermore, they were usually required to buy goods for everyday living on credit from the owner. They were rarely able to repay the resulting debts and thus could not move to work for new landowners. This system was known as **debt peonage**. There were two major products of the *hacienda* economy: foodstuffs for mining areas and urban centers, and leather goods used in vast quantities on min-

The Silver Mines of Potosí. Worked by conscripted Indian laborers under extremely harsh conditions, these mines provided Spain with a vast treasure in silver.

ing machinery. Both farming and ranching were thus subordinate to the mine economy.

Commercial Regulation and the Flota System

Because Queen Isabella of Castile (r. 1474–1504) had commissioned Columbus, the technical legal link between the New World and Spain was the crown of Castile. Its powers both at home and in America were subject to few limitations. Government of America was assigned to the Council of the Indies, which, in conjunction with the monarch, nominated the viceroys of New Spain and Peru. These viceroys were the chief executives in the New World and carried out the laws promulgated by the Council of the Indies. Each of the viceroyalties included subordinate judicial councils known as *audiencias*. There were also a variety of local officers, the most important of which were the *corregidores*, who presided over municipal councils. These offices provided the monarchy with a vast array of opportunities for patronage, usually bestowed on persons born in Spain. Virtually all political power flowed from the top of this political structure downward; in effect, there was little or no local initiative or self-government (see Map 18–2).

The colonial political structures existed largely to support the commercial goals of Spain. Spanish control of its American empire involved a system of monopolistic trade regulation that was more rigid in appearance than in practice. The trade monopoly was often breached. The Casa de Contratación (House of Trade) in Seville regulated all trade with the New World. Cádiz was the only Spanish port to be used for the American trade. In America there were similarly specific ports for trade both to Spain and with non-Spanish merchants. The latter trade was highly restricted. The Casa de Contratación was the single most influential institution of the Spanish Empire, and its members worked closely with the Consulado (Merchant Guild) of Seville and other groups involved with the American commerce in Cádiz. The entire organization was geared to benefit the Spanish monarchy and these privileged merchant groups.

A complicated system of trade and bullion fleets administered from Seville provided the key for maintaining the trade monopoly. Each year a fleet of commercial vessels (the *flota*) controlled by Seville merchants, escorted by warships, carried merchandise from Spain to a few specified ports in America. These included Portobello, Veracruz, and Cartagena. There were no authorized ports on the Pacific coast. Areas far to the south, such as Buenos Aires, received goods only after the shipments had been unloaded at one of the authorized ports. After selling their wares, the ships were loaded with silver and gold bullion, usually wintered in heavily fortified Caribbean ports, and then sailed back to Spain. Each year a Spanish ship also crossed the Pacific from Manila, in the Spanish colony of the Philippines, to the Mexican port of Acapulco, bringing Chinese silk and porcelain. It returned to Manila laden with Mexican silver. So the Spanish Empire became part of a global exchange of trade. The flota system always worked imperfectly, but trade outside it was illegal. Regulations prohibited the Spanish colonists within the American empire from trading directly with each other and from building their own shipping and commercial industry. Foreign merchants were also forbidden to breach the Spanish monopoly.

Colonial Brazil

Spain and Portugal originally had rival claims to the Americas. In 1494, by the Treaty of Tordesillas, the pope divided the seaborne empires of Spain and Portugal by drawing a line west of the Cape Verde Islands. In 1500 a Portuguese explorer landed on the coast of what is present-day Brazil, which extended east of the papal line of division, and thus Portugal gained a major hold on the South American continent.

Portugal had fewer human and material resources to devote to its New World empire than did Spain. The crown granted captaincies to private persons that permitted them to attempt to exploit the region. The native people in the lands that Portugal governed lived for the most part in small, nomadic groups. In this they differed from the native peoples of Spanish America, with their centralized empires, cities, and organized political structures. As a result, labor practices in the two regions were also different. The Portuguese

Map Exploration

To explore this map further, go to http://www.prenhall.com/craig_maps

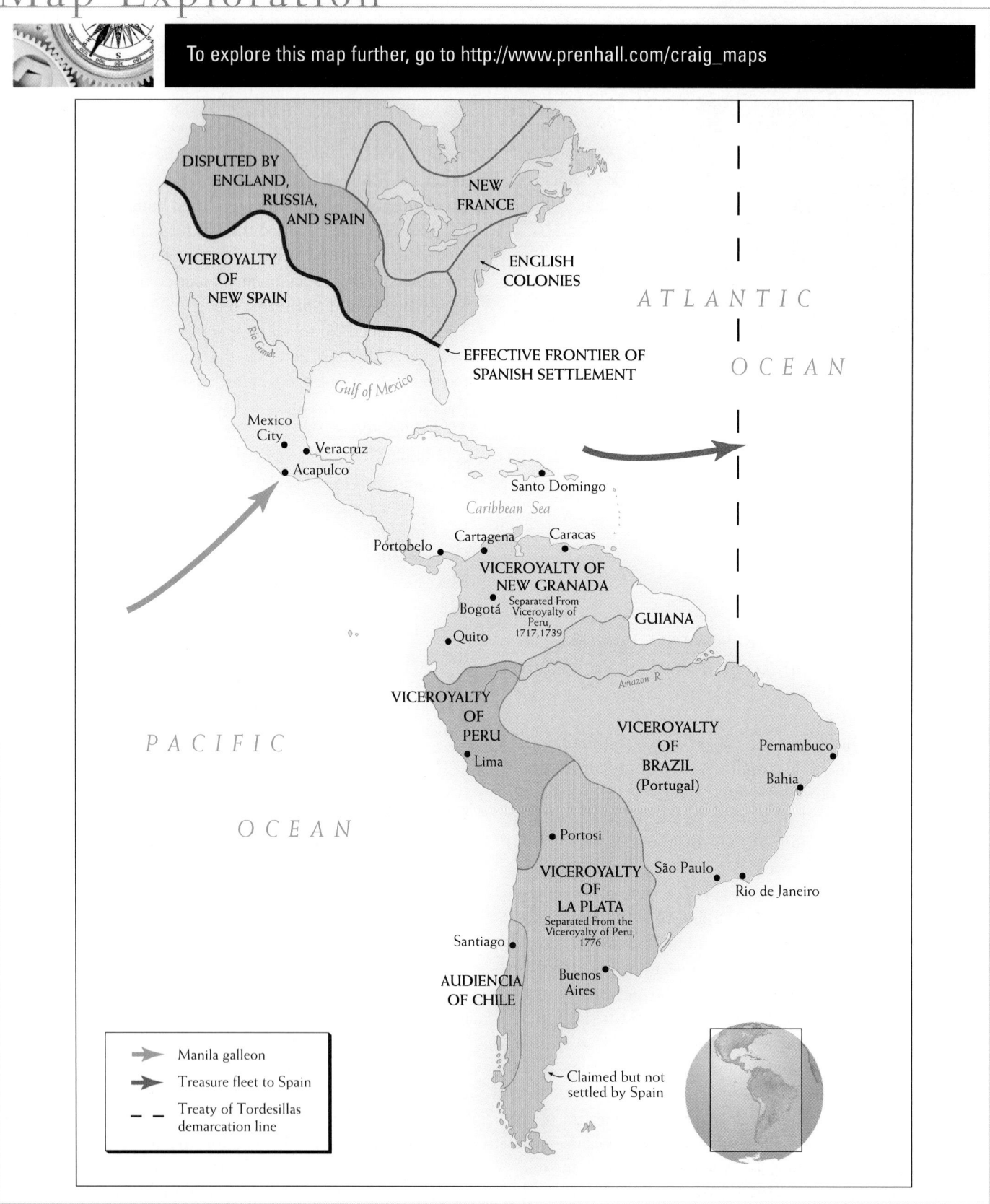

Map 18–2.   The Americas, ca. 1750. Spain organized its vast holdings in the New World into viceroyalties, each of which had its own governor and other administrative officials. The English colonies clung to the North American seaboard. French possessions centered on the St. Lawrence River and the Great Lakes. Portuguese holdings in Brazil were mostly confined to the coast.

Sugar plantations of Brazil and the West Indies were a major source of the demand for slave labor. Slaves are here shown grinding sugar cane and refining sugar, which was then exported to the consumer markets in Europe. © *Hulton-Deutsch Collection/Corbis.*

imported Africans as slaves rather than using the Native American population, as did the Spanish in most areas.

By the mid–sixteenth century, sugar production had gained preeminence in the Brazilian economy, although some minerals were discovered and some cattle raised. Because sugar cane was grown on large estates (*fazendas*) with African slave labor, the dominance of sugar meant also the dominance of slavery.

Towards the close of the seventeenth century, sugar prices declined and the economy suffered. In the early eighteenth century, however, significant deposits of gold were discovered in southern Brazil. Immigrants from Portugal joined the ensuing gold rush, and economic activity moved suddenly towards the south. This shift, however, did not reduce Brazil's reliance on slave labor. In fact, the expansion of gold mining also led to the increased importation of African slaves. Nowhere, except perhaps in the West Indies, was slavery as important as it was in Brazil, where it persisted until 1888.

The taxation and administration associated with gold mining brought new, unexpected wealth to the eighteenth-century Portuguese monarchy, allowing it to rule without recourse to the Cortés or traditional parliament for taxation. Through transatlantic trade the new wealth generated from Brazilian gold also filtered into all the major trading nations, which could sell their goods to Portugal as well as profit from the slave trade.

As in the Spanish Empire, the Portuguese crown attempted to establish a strong network of regulation around Brazilian trade. Brazil, however, required less direct control by the Portuguese than the Spanish Empire required from Spain, and as a result, Brazil's colonial settlers may have felt less resentment towards the Portuguese government than the settlers of the Spanish Empire felt towards the Spanish administrators. In Brazil, where the basic unit of production was the plantation, there were fewer large cities than in Spanish America. The crown's

determination in Spanish America to have precious metals sent to Spain required a vast colonial administration. The sugar plantations of Brazil, in contrast, did not require such direct administration. Consequently, the Portuguese were willing to allow more local autonomy than was Spain. More local officials were allowed to serve in the government in Brazil than in Spanish America, where the administration was dominated by officials born in Spain. In Spanish America the use of Native American labor, which was important to the colonial economy, required government supervision. Brazil, less dependent on Native American labor, felt no such constraints. Indeed, the Portuguese government condoned policies whereby indigenous tribes were driven into the back country or exterminated. Throughout the eighteenth century the Portuguese government also favored the continued importation of slaves.

French and British Colonies in North America

French explorers had pressed down the St. Lawrence River valley in Canada during the seventeenth century. French fur traders and Roman Catholic Jesuit missionaries had followed in their wake, with the French government supporting the missionary effort. By the end of the seventeenth century a significant but sparsely populated French presence existed in Canada (see Map 18–2). Trade rather than extensive settlements characterized the French effort. The largest settlement was Quebec, founded in 1608. Some French settlers married Native American women; the absence of a drive to permanently claim land reduced conflict between the French and the Native Americans. It was primarily through the fur trade that French Canada functioned as part of the early transatlantic economy.

For most readers of this volume, the story of the founding of the English-speaking colonies along the Atlantic seaboard is relatively familiar, but it needs to be set in the larger world context. Beginning

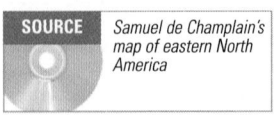

SOURCE   *Samuel de Champlain's map of eastern North America*

with the first successful settlement in Jamestown, Virginia, in 1607 and ending with the establishment of Georgia in 1733, the eastern seaboard of the United States became populated by a series of English colonies. Other nations, including the Dutch and Swedes, had founded settlements, but all of them were eventually taken over during the seventeenth century by the English.

A wide variety of reasons led to the founding of the English colonies. Settlement for enrichment from farming and trade accounted for some settlements, such as Virginia and New Amsterdam (after 1664, New York). Others, such as the Carolinas, were developed by royal favorites who were given vast land tracts. James Oglethorpe founded Georgia as a refuge for English debtors. But the pursuit of religious liberty constituted the major driving force of the Pilgrim and Puritan founders of Massachusetts, the Baptist Roger Williams in Rhode Island, the Quaker William Penn in Pennsylvania, and the Roman Catholic Lord Baltimore in Maryland.

With the exception of Maryland, these colonies were Protestant. The Church of England dominated the southern colonies. In New England, varieties of Protestantism associated with or derived from Calvinism were in the ascendancy. In their religious affiliations, the English-speaking colonies manifested two important traits derived from the English experience. First, much of their religious life was organized around self-governing congregations. Second, their religious outlook derived from those forms of Protestantism that were suspicious of central political authority and especially of potentially despotic monarchs. In this regard, their cultural and political outlook differed sharply from the cultural and political outlook associated with the Roman Catholicism of the Spanish Empire. In a sense the values of the extreme Reformation and Counter-Reformation confronted each other on the two American continents.

The English colonists had complex interactions with the Native American populations. Unlike the Spanish to the south or the French to the north, they had only modest interest in missionary enterprise. As in South America, new diseases imported from Europe took a high death toll among the native population. Unlike Mexico and Peru, however, North America had no large Native American cities. The Native American populations were far more dispersed, and intertribal animosity was intense. The English often encountered well-organized resistance, as from the Powhatan conspiracy in Virginia and the Pequots in New England. The most powerful of the Native American groups was the Iroquois Nation, organized in the early eighteenth century in New York. The Iroquois battled successfully against other tribes and long negotiated successfully with both the Dutch and the English. The English also often used one tribe against another, and the Native Americans also tried to use the English or the French in their own conflicts. The outcome of these struggles between the English settlers and the Native Americans was rarely full victory for either side, but rather mutual exhaustion, with the Native Americans temporarily retreating beyond the reach of English settlements and the English temporarily restraining their initial claims. From the late seventeenth century through the American Revolution, however, the Native Americans of North America were drawn into the Anglo-French Wars that were fought in North America as well as Europe. Indeed, Native American alliances became important for the Anglo-French conflict on the Continent, which was intimately related to their rivalry over transatlantic trade (see Chapter 20).

The largest economic activity throughout the English-speaking colonies was agriculture. From New England through the Middle Atlantic states there were mostly small farms tilled by free white labor; from Virginia southward it was the plantation economy, dependent on slavery. During the early eighteenth century the chief products raised on these plantations were tobacco, indigo, rice, and sugar. Although slavery was a dominant institution in the South, all of the colonies included slaves. The principal port cities along the seaboard—Boston, Newport, New York, Philadelphia,

Fur Trade. A Native American hands a pelt to a European buyer while two spectators—one European, one Indian—nonchalantly observe the transaction. By 1700 the fur trade had decimated the beaver population in southern Canada and New England.

Baltimore, and Charleston—resembled small provincial English cities. They were primarily trading centers through which goods moved back and forth between the colonies and England and the West Indies. The commercial economies of these cities were all related to the transatlantic slave trade.

Until the 1760s the political values of the Americans resembled those of their English counterparts. The colonials were thoroughly familiar with events in England. They 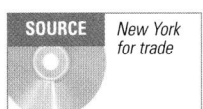 sent many of their children there to be educated. They were monarchists but, like their English counterparts, suspicious of monarchical power. Their politics involved vast amounts of patronage and individual favors. Their society was clearly hierarchical, with an elite that functioned like a colonial aristocracy and many ordinary people who were dependent on that aristocracy. Throughout the colonies during the eighteenth century, the Anglican Church grew in influence and membership. The prosperity of the colonies might eventually have led them to separate from England, but in 1750 few people thought that would occur.

Both England and France had important sugar islands in the Caribbean. England held Jamaica and Barbados, and France held Saint Domingue (Haiti), Guadeloupe, and Martinique. The plantations on these islands were worked by African slaves, and the trade and commerce of the northern British colonies were closely related to meeting the needs of these islands.

The Columbian Exchange: Disease, Animals, and Agriculture

The European encounter with the Americas produced remarkable ecological transformations that have shaped the world to the present moment (see Map 18–3). Alfred Crosby, the leading historian of the process, has named this cross-continental flow the **Columbian Exchange**.

Diseases Enter the Americas

With the exception of a few ships that had gone astray or, in the case of the Vikings, that had gone in search of new lands, the American continents had been biologically separated from Europe, Africa, and Asia for tens of thousands of years. In the Americas no native animals could serve as major beasts of burden except for the llama, which could not transport more than about a hundred pounds. Nor did animals constitute a major source of protein for Native Americans, whose diets consisted largely of maize, beans,

Roanoke. The first successful English colonies in North America in the seventeenth century were preceded by two failed efforts on Roanoke Island in what is now North Carolina in the late sixteenth century. John White accompanied both attempts, the second as governor. White was a perceptive and sensitive observer whose watercolor paintings provide invaluable information about Native American life in the coastal Carolina region at the time of contact. This painting shows the Algonquin village of Secoton. The houses were bark covered. In the lower left is a mortuary temple. The dancers in the lower right are performing a fertility ceremony. The man sitting in the platform in the upper right is keeping birds away from the corn crop. *The Bridgeman Art Library International Ltd.*

peppers, yams, and potatoes. At the same time, the American continents included areas of vast grassland without grazing animals that would have transformed those plants into animal protein. Moreover, it also appears that native peoples had lived on the long-isolated American continents without experiencing such major epidemics as would decimate their populations in the decades after the encounter.

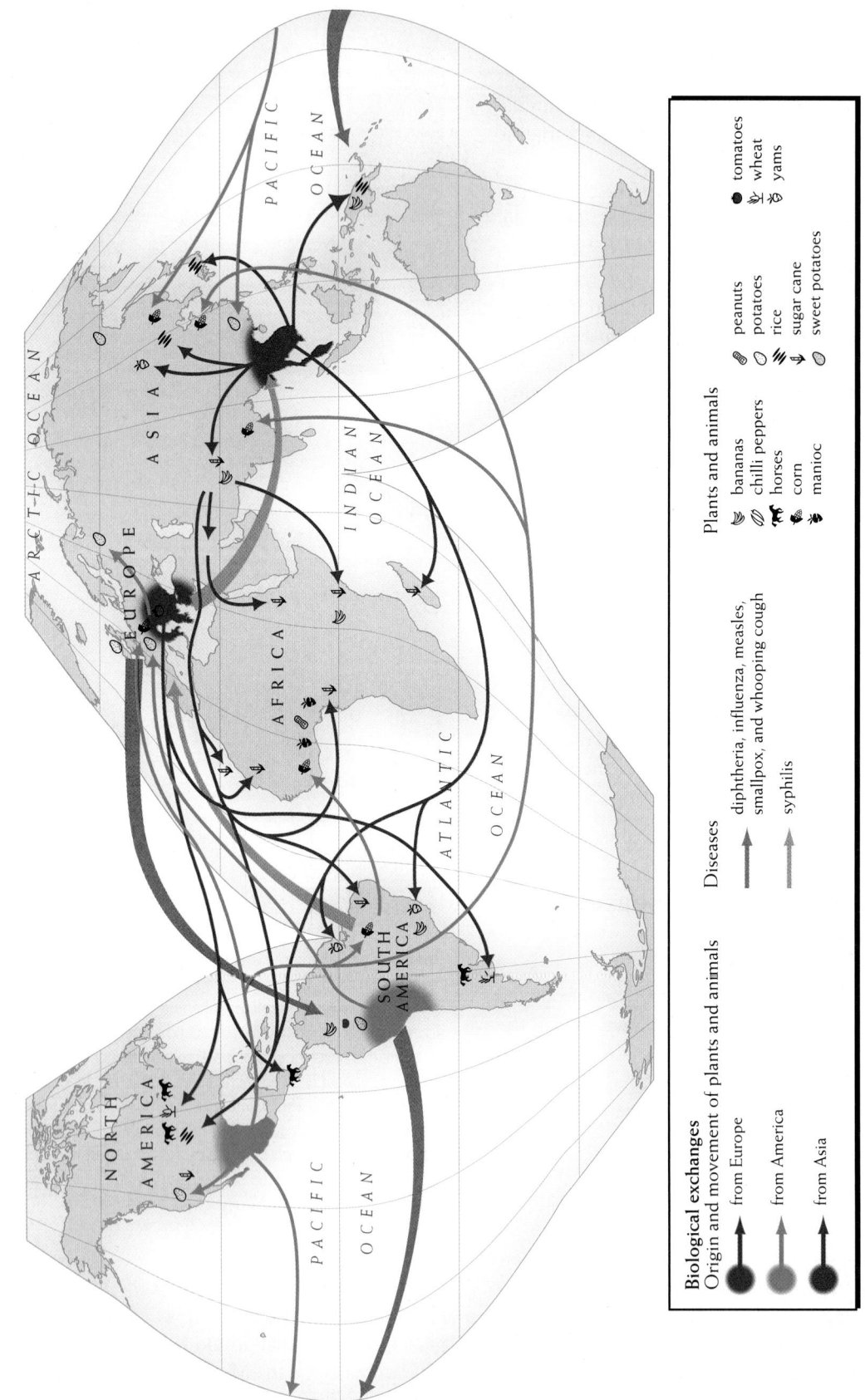

Biological exchanges
Origin and movement of plants and animals

from Europe

from America

from Asia

Diseases

diphtheria, influenza, measles,
smallpox, and whooping cough

syphilis

Plants and animals

bananas	peanuts	tomatoes
chilli peppers	potatoes	wheat
horses	rice	yams
corn	sugar cane	
manioc	sweet potatoes	

Map 18–3.   **Biological Exchanges.**   The world-wide movement of plants, animals, and diseases.

By the second voyage of Columbus (1493), that picture began to change in remarkable ways. On his return voyage to Hispaniola and other islands of the Caribbean, Columbus brought a number of animals and plants that were previously unknown to the New World. The men on all his voyages and those on subsequent European voyages also carried diseases novel to the Americas.

The diseases thus transported by Europeans ultimately accounted for the conquest of the people of the Americas as much as the advanced European weaponry. Much controversy surrounds the question of the actual size of the populations of Native Americans in the Caribbean islands, Mexico, Peru, and the North Atlantic coast. All accounts present those populations as quite significant, with those of Mexico in particular numbering many millions. Yet in the first two centuries after the encounter, wherever Europeans went either as settlers or as conquerors, extremely large numbers of Native Americans died from diseases they had never before encountered. The most deadly such disease was smallpox, which destroyed millions of people. Beyond the devastation wrought

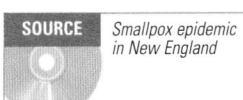

SOURCE *Smallpox epidemic in New England*

by that disease, bubonic plague, typhoid, typhus, influenza, measles, chicken pox, whooping cough, malaria, and diphtheria produced deadly results in more localized epidemics. For example, an unknown disease, but quite possibly typhus, caused major losses among the Native Americans of New England between approximately 1616 and 1619.

On the reverse side of the equation it appears almost certain that syphillis, which became a rampant venereal disease in Europe at the close of the fifteenth century and eventually spread around the globe, originated in the New World. Until the discovery of penicillin in the 1940s, syphillis remained a major concern of public health throughout the world.

Animals and Agriculture

The introduction of European livestock to the Americas quite simply revolutionized the agriculture of two continents. The most important new animals were pigs, cattle, horses, goats, and sheep. Once transported to the New World, these animals multiplied at unprecedented rates. The place where this first occurred was in the islands of the Caribbean, during the first forty years of Spanish settlement and exploitation. This situation established the foundation for the later Spanish conquest of both Mexico and Peru by providing the Spanish with strong breeds of animals, especially horses, acclimated to the Americas when they set out to conquer the mainland of South America.

The horse became first the animal of the conquest and then the animal of colonial Latin American culture. Native Americans had no experience with such large animals who would obey the will of a human rider. The mounted Spanish horseman struck fear into Native Americans, and for good reason. After the conquest, however, the Americas from Mexico southward became the largest horse-breeding region of the world, with ranches raising thousands of animals. Horses became relatively cheap, and even Native Americans could acquire them. By the nineteenth century, the possession of horses would allow the Plains Indians of North America to resist the advance of their white conquerors.

Smallpox. Introduced by Europeans to the Americas, smallpox had a devastating effect on Native American populations. It swept through the Aztec capital of Tenochtitlán soon after the Spaniards arrived, contributing to the fall of the city. This illustration of the effect of the plague in the Aztec capital is from a postconquest history known as the Florentine Codex compiled for Spanish church authorities by Aztec survivors.

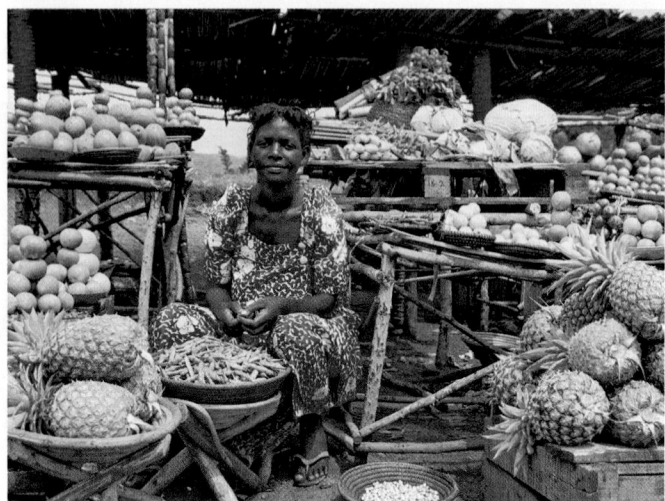

Global Foods. A woman in the African country of Uganda offers beans and pineapples for sale, both of which originated in the Americas.

The flourishing of pigs, cattle, and sheep allowed a vast economic exploitation of the Americas. These animals produced enormous quantities of hides and wool. Their presence in such large numbers also meant the Americas from the sixteenth century through the present would support a diet more plentiful in animal protein than anywhere else in the world.

Europeans also brought their own plants to the New World, including peaches, oranges, grapes, melons, bananas, rice, onions, radishes, and various green vegetables. Socially, for three centuries the most significant of these was sugarcane, whose cultivation created the major demand for slavery throughout the transatlantic plantation economy. Nutritionally, European wheat would, over the course of time, allow the Americas not only to feed themselves, but also to export large amounts of grain throughout the world.

No significant animals from the Americas, except the turkey, actually came to be raised in Europe. The Americas did send to Europe, however, a series of plants that eventually changed the European diet: maize, potatoes, sweet potatoes, peppers, beans, manioc (tapioca), peanuts, squash, pumpkins, pineapples, cocoa, and tomatoes. Africa as well was the recipient of many of these same foodstuffs. All of these, to a greater or lesser degree, eventually entered the diet of Europeans and Africans and of European settlers and their descendants in the Americas. Maize and the potato had the most transforming impact. Each of these two crops became a major staple in European farming, as well as in the European diet. Both crops grow rapidly, supplying food quickly and steadily if not attacked by disease. Tobacco, we should note, originated in the Americas, too.

Maize was established as a crop in Spain within thirty years of the country's encounter with the New World. A cen-

tury and a half later it was commonplace in the Spanish diet, and its cultivation had spread to Italy and France. Maize produced more grain for the seed and farming effort than wheat did. Throughout Europe, maize was associated primarily with fodder for animals. As early as the eighteenth century, travelers noted the presence of polenta in the peasant diet, and other forms of maize dishes, such as fried mush, spread.

The potato established its European presence more slowly than maize. The Spanish encountered the potato only when Pizarro conquered Peru, where it was a major part of the Native American food supply. It was adopted slowly by Europeans because it needed to be raised in climates more temperate than that of Spain and the Mediterranean. The potato appears to have become a major peasant food in Scotland, Ireland, and parts of Germany during the eighteenth century where it provided nutrient insurance against failure of the grain harvest. There is good reason to believe the cultivation of the potato was one of the major causes of the population increase in eighteenth- and nineteenth-century Europe. It was the quintessential food of the poor. In the middle of the 1840s, an American parasite infected the Irish potato crop. The result of the failure of the crop was the death of hundreds of thousands of Irish peasants and the migration of still more hundreds of thousands to the Americas and elsewhere in the world.

Slavery in the Americas

Slavery was the final mode of forced or subservient labor in the New World. Unlike the labor exploitation of Native Americans discussed earlier in this chapter, enslavement of Africans and their descendents extended throughout not only the Spanish Empire but also Portuguese Brazil and the English-speaking colonies of North America. The heartland of transatlantic slavery lay in the Caribbean islands.

The Background of Slavery

Slavery seems to have been one of the tragic facts of human societies as far back as we can trace its history. Although linked to warfare and the age-old practice of taking captives, it cannot be fully explained by military or economic necessity.

Virtually every premodern state around the globe depended on slavery to some extent (see Map 18–4). The Mediterranean and African worlds were no exception, in both the pre-Islamic and the Islamic periods. Slave institutions in sub-Saharan Africa were ancient and included traffic with the Mediterranean world. The Islamic states of southwestern Asia and North Africa continued and even increased this traffic, importing slaves from both the Sudan

Map Exploration

To explore this map further, go to http://www.prenhall.com/craig_maps

Map 18–4.   The Slave Trade, 1400–1860.   Slavery is an ancient institution, and complex slave-trading routes were in existence in Africa, the Middle East, and Asia for centuries, but it was the need to supply labor for the plantations of the Americas that led to the greatest movement of peoples across the face of the earth.

and Horn of Africa as well as the East African coast, although they took fewer slaves from Africa than from eastern Europe and Central Asia. Central Asia, for example, was the source of most of the (largely Turkish) slave-soldier dynasties that came to rule many Islamic states from India to North Africa. (Hence it is not surprising that the word *slave* is derived ultimately from *Slav*.) Both Mediterranean Christian and Islamic peoples were using slaves—mostly Greeks, Bulgarians, Turkish prisoners of war, and Black Sea Tartars, but also Africans—well before the voyages of discovery opened sub-Saharan sources of slaves for the new European colonies overseas.

The Columbian Exchange

Overview

TO THE AMERICAS

Diseases

smallpox, influenza, bubonic plague, typhoid, typhus, measles, chicken pox, malaria, and diphtheria

Animals

pigs, cattle, horses, goats, sheep, chickens

Plants

apples, peaches, pears, apricots, plums, oranges, mangos, lemons, olives, melons, almonds, grapes, bananas, cherries, sugar cane, rice, wheat, oats, barley, onions, radishes, okra, dandelions, cabbages, and other green vegetables

FROM THE AMERICAS

Diseases

syphillis (?)

Animals

turkeys

Plants

maize, tomatoes, sweet peppers, chilis, potatoes, sweet potatoes, squash, pumpkins, manioc (tapioca), beans, cocoa, peanuts, pecans, pineapples, guavas, avocados, blueberries, and tobacco

---

Not all forms of slavery were as dehumanizing as the **chattel slavery** that came to predominate (with the sanction of Christian authorities) during the colonization of the Americas. Islamic law, for example, although permitting slavery, also ameliorated it. All slavery, however, involved the forceful exploitation and degradation of some human beings for the profit of others, the denial of basic freedoms, and sometimes the sundering, often violently, of even the closest family ties. Although there were some variations in the legal and social structures of slavery in the Atlantic world, slaves brought from Africa and their descendents were invariably chattel slaves: they were outright possessions of their masters, indistinguishable from any material possession; they were not recognized as persons under the law, so they had no legal rights; they could not claim any control over their bodies, their time, their labor, or even their own children.

African societies suffered immense political, economic, and social devastation when they were the chief supplier of slaves to the world. The New World societies that were built to a great extent on the exploitation of African slavery also suffered enduring consequences, not the least of which, many believe, is racism.

Establishment of Slavery

As the numbers of Native Americans in South America declined due to disease and exploitation, the Spanish and the Portuguese turned to the labor of imported African slaves.

By the late sixteenth century, in the islands of the West Indies and the major cities of South America, the population of black slaves equaled or surpassed the white European population.

On much of the South American continent dominated by Spain, the number of slaves declined during the late seventeenth century, and the institution became less fundamental there than elsewhere. Slavery continued to prosper, however, in Brazil and especially in the Caribbean. Starting

Sugar plantation. African slaves on the Caribbean island of Antigua bring sugar cane to a windmill where it will be crushed into juice. A white overseer closely watches the proceedings.

African American Culture. This eighteenth-century painting depicts a celebration in the slave quarters on a South Carolina plantation. One planter's description of a slave dance seems to fit this scene: the men leading the women in "a slow shuffling gait, edging along by some unseen exertion of the feet, from one side to the other—sometimes curtseying down and remaining in that posture while the edging motion from one side to the other continued." The women, he wrote, "always carried a handkerchief held at arm's length, which was waved in a graceful motion to and fro as she moved." *Abby Aldrich Rockefeller Folk Art Museum, Colonial Williamsburg Foundation, VA.*

with the importation of slaves to Jamestown in 1619, slavery spread into the British North American colonies and later became a fundamental institution there.

One of the forces that led to the spread of slavery in Brazil and the West Indies was the cultivation of sugar. Sugar cane required a large investment in land and equipment, and only slave labor could provide enough workers for the extremely profitable sugar plantations. As the production of sugar expanded, so did the demand for slaves, and more slaves were imported.

By the close of the seventeenth century the Caribbean islands were the world center for sugar production. As the European appetite for sugar continued to grow, the slave population continued to expand. By 1725, slaves may have constituted almost 90 percent of the population of Jamaica. The situation was similar throughout the West Indies. There and elsewhere, in Brazil and the southern British colonies, prosperity and slavery went hand in hand. The wealthiest and most prized of the colonies were those that raised consumer staples, such as sugar, rice, tobacco, or cotton, by slave labor.

The Plantation Economy and Transatlantic Trade

The **plantation economy** was composed of plantations that stretched from Maryland through the West Indies and into Brazil. They formed a vast corridor of slave societies in which social and economic subordination was based on both involuntary servitude and race. This kind of society, in its total dependence on slave labor and racial differences, was something novel in world history; it had not existed before the European discovery and exploitation of the Americas. The social and economic influence of plantation slavery touched not only the plantation societies themselves, but also West

Africa, western Europe, and New England. It persisted from the sixteenth century through the second half of the nineteenth century, ending with the British effort to outlaw the slave trade during the first half of the nineteenth century, the Latin American Wars of Independence, the Emancipation Proclamation of 1862 in the United States, and the Brazilian emancipation of 1888. Every society in which it existed still contends with its long-term effects.

The slave trade was part of the larger system of transatlantic trade that linked Europe, Africa, and the European colonies in South America, the Caribbean, and North America. In this system the Americas supplied labor-intensive raw materials like tobacco, sugar, coffee, precious metals, cotton, and indigo. Europe supplied manufactured goods like textiles, liquor, guns, metal wares, and beads, not to mention various forms of cash, including even gold. And Africa supplied gold, ivory, wood, palm oil, gum, and other products, as well as the slaves who provided the labor to create the American products. By the eighteenth century slaves were the predominant African export.

Slavery on the Plantations

The plantations in the Americas at which the African slaves eventually arrived were always in a fairly isolated rural setting. Their products, however, were agricultural goods produced for an external overseas market that was part of a larger integrated transatlantic economy. The plantation might raise food for its owners and their slaves, but the main production—whether sugar, tobacco, or, later, cotton and coffee—was intended for export. In turn, plantation owners imported from other parts of the world virtually all the finished or manufactured goods they used or consumed.

King Affonso I of the Kongo holds an audience with European ambassadors who kneel before him. *Courtesy of the Library of Congress.*

The life conditions of plantation slaves differed from colony to colony. Most owners possessed relatively few slaves, and vast slaveholdings were the exception. Black slaves living in Portuguese areas had the fewest legal protections. In the Spanish colonies the church attempted to provide some small protection for black slaves but devoted much more effort towards protecting the Native Americans. Slave codes were developed in the British and the French colonies during the seventeenth century, but they provided only the most limited protection. Virtually all slave owners feared a slave revolt; slave-related legislation and other regulations were intended to prevent such an event. Slave laws favored the master rather than the slave. Masters were permitted to punish slaves by whipping and other harsh corporal punishment. Furthermore, slaves were often forbidden to gather in large groups lest they plan a revolt. In most slave-owning societies, the marriages of slaves were not recognized by law. The child of an enslaved woman was born a slave, the property of the mother's owner. Slave families could be separated at whim by the owner or the owner's heirs.

The daily life of most slaves during these centuries was one of hard agricultural labor, poor diet and clothing, and inadequate housing. The death rate among slaves was high. Their welfare and their lives were sacrificed to the ongoing expansion of the plantations that made their owners wealthy and that produced goods demanded by consumers in Europe. Scholars have argued that slaves in one area or another had a better existence than others, but it is gener-

ally accepted that slaves in all plantation societies suffered under difficult conditions. The specifics of those conditions may have varied, but they were not significantly better in one place than another.

The African slaves who were transported to the Americas were, like the Native Americans, converted to Christianity: in the Spanish domains to Roman Catholicism, and in the English colonies to various forms of Protestantism. In both cases, they were forbidden to practice their traditional faiths. Slave owners often did not know whether particular activities were religious, but they erred on the side of caution: activities that were not directly related to economic production, or that suggested links to African culture, were suppressed. Although some African practices survived in muted forms, and slaves did manage to mix Christianity with African religion, the conversion of Africans to Christianity nonetheless represented another example of the crushing of a set of non-European cultural values in the context of the New World economies and social structures.

The European settlers in the Americas and the slave traders were also prejudiced against black Africans. Many Europeans thought Africans were savage or less than civilized. Others looked down on them simply because they were slaves. These attitudes had been shared by both Christians and Muslims in the Mediterranean world, where slavery had long existed. Furthermore, many European languages and European cultures attached negative connotations to the idea and image of blackness. In virtually all plantation societies, race was an important element in keeping black slaves subservient. Although racial thinking in regard to slavery became more important in the nineteenth century, the fact that slaves were differentiated from the rest of the population by race as well as by their status as chattel property was fundamental to the system.

SOURCE African American Spirituals

Africa and the Transatlantic Slave Trade

It was the establishment of plantations demanding the use of slave labor that drew Africa and its peoples into the heart of the transatlantic economy. As Native American peoples were decimated by conquest and European diseases or proved unsatisfactory as plantation laborers, colonial entrepreneurs

Chronology

Conquest of the Americas and the Transatlantic Slave Trade

1494	Treaty of Tordesillas divides the seaborne empires of Spain and Portugal
1500	The Portuguese arrive in Brazil
1519–1521	Hernan Cortés conquers the Aztec Empire
1531–1533	Francisco Pizarro conquers the Inca Empire
1607	Jamestown, Virginia, first permanent English settlement in North America
1608	The French found Quebec
1619	First African slaves brought to British North America
1700s	Over 6 million slaves imported from Africa to the Americas
1794	Slavery abolished throughout the French empire
1807	The importation of slaves abolished in British domains
1808	The importation of slaves abolished in the United States
1817–1820	Spain abolishes the slave trade
1833	Slavery abolished throughout the British empire
1850	Importation of slaves abolished in Brazil
1874–1928	Indigenous African slavery abolished
1888	Slavery abolished in Brazil

briefly became the chief carriers. The French and the English came into the trade only in the late seventeenth century, yet during the eighteenth century, which saw the greatest number of slaves shipped, they carried almost half the total traffic. Americans, too, were latecomers but avid slavers who managed to make considerable profits before and even after Britain and the United States outlawed the transatlantic slave trade in 1807 and 1808 respectively.

If gold and the search for a sea route to Asia brought the first European ships to Africa, slaves were the main commodity for which they returned for a long time. Slaving was 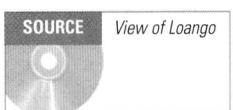 an important part of the massive new overseas trade that financed much European and American economic development that so dramatically changed the West during the nineteenth century. The success and considerable profits of this trade, bought at the price of immense human suffering, helped propel Europe and some of its colonial offshoots in the Americas into world dominance.

Slavery and Slaving in Africa

The trade that long before the fifteenth century supplied African slaves to the Islamic lands of the Mediterranean and to southwestern and southern Asia has conventionally been termed the "Oriental" slave trade. The savannas of the Sudan and the Horn of Africa were the two prime sources of slaves for this trade. The Afro-European trade, conventionally called the **"Occidental" slave trade**, can be traced at least to the thirteenth century, when Europeans established sugar cane plantations on Cyprus soon after Muslim forces had driven them out of the Holy Land. In Cypress, as later in Brazil and the Caribbean islands, slaves proved an especially profitable workforce for the labor-intensive process of sugar production. This industry subsequently spread westward to Crete and Sicily and, in the fifteenth century, to the Portuguese Atlantic islands of Madeira and São Tomé.

The Portuguese in particular developed the plantation system of slave labor as they began their expansion into the Atlantic and beyond. Although the savanna and Horn regions were the earliest sources for this trade, voyages beginning in the fifteenth century by first the Portuguese and then other Europeans opened the western coasts of Africa as far south as Angola, making them the prime slaving areas. A third but less important source region for both Occidental and Oriental trades was the eastern coast of Africa below the Horn.

Prior to the full development of the transatlantic slave trade by about 1650, slavery and slave trading had been no

began to look elsewhere for people to work their plantations. First the Portuguese, and then the Spanish, Dutch, French, and English (others would follow, including Americans) turned to west, central, and, to a lesser degree, southeastern Africa for an ample supply of slaves. Thus the transatlantic slave trade was not overtly the result of racist principles, but of the economic needs of the colonial powers and their willingness to exploit weaker peoples to satisfy them. However, this willingness was based on the tacit racist assumption that non-European, nonwhite tribal peoples were subhuman and could be enslaved for European purposes.

The Portuguese, who were the principal carriers throughout most of the early history of the trade, had a virtual monopoly until the Dutch broke it in the 1640s and

Slaves in the streets of Zanzibar, nineteenth century. Slaving was a part of East African trade for centuries. *Corbis-Bettmann.*

more significant in Africa than anywhere else in the world.[2] Indigenous African slavery resembled that of other premodern societies. It was apparently most common, if still limited, in the areas of the savannah and Horn, presumably because these areas were involved in external slave trading. In the western and central Sudan, slavery came largely to be regulated by Islamic norms, but in the Horn, specifically in Ethiopia, slavery was practiced in both Christian and Muslim communities. Estimates suggest that about 10,000 slaves per year, most of them female, were taken from sub-Saharan Africa through the Oriental slave trade.

By about 1650 the newer Occidental slave trade of the Europeans had become as large as the Oriental trade and for the ensuing two centuries far surpassed it. It affected adversely all of Africa, disrupting especially western and central African societies. As a result of the demand for young male slaves on the plantations of the Americas, West Africa experienced a sharp drain on its productive male population. Between 1640 and 1690, although the price of a slave at the coast remained constant, the number of slaves sold to European carriers doubled, indicating the increasing participation of Africans in the expanding trade. With the growing demand for slaves came an increase in internal warfare in western and central Africa. Moreover, as the external trade destroyed the regional male-female population balance, an internal market for female slaves in particular arose.

These developments accelerated during the eighteenth century—at the height of the Occidental trade. It was also during this period that African states and slave traders were most heavily involved as regulators and suppliers of the

trade. Slave prices at times increased accordingly. Owing to population depletion and regional migrations, however, the actual number of slaves sold declined in some areas. The population declined sharply in the coastal and inland areas hardest hit by the ravages of the trade in the later eighteenth century and continued to decline in places even until 1850.

As European nations, followed by nations in the Americas, slowly began to outlaw first the slave trade and then slavery itself in the nineteenth century, occidental demand slowed and prices for slaves sank. The result was that the Oriental and internal trades increased. Slave exports from East Africa and the Sudan and Horn increased significantly after about 1780, and indigenous African slavery, predominantly of women, also expanded. Indeed, by about 1850 the internal African trade surpassed the combined Oriental and (now outlawed and decreasing) Occidental trade. This traffic was dominated by the same figures—merchants, warlords, and rulers—who had previously profited from external trade.

Indigenous African slavery began a real decline only at the end of the nineteenth century, in part because of the dominance of European colonial regimes and in part because of internal changes. The formal end of African indigenous slavery occurred over a long period, beginning in 1874 in the Gold Coast and ending only in 1928 in Sierra Leone. Late in the twentieth century, however, in various locations around the world—mostly places with endemic, severe poverty and weak civil authority, including the Sudan—patterns emerged of involuntary servitude and human-trafficking that constitute modern-day slavery.

The African Side of the Transatlantic Trade

Africans were actively involved in the transatlantic slave trade. Except for the Portuguese in central Africa, European slave traders generally obtained their human cargoes from private or government-sponsored African middlemen at coastal forts or simply at anchorages along the coast. A system of forts built by Europeans mostly between 1640 and 1750, for example, dominated the Gold Coast. This situation was the result of both the desire and ability of Africans to control inland trade and the vulnerability of Europeans to tropical disease (a new European arrival stood a less than 50 percent chance of surviving a year on the tropical African coast). Thus it was largely African middlemen who undertook the actual capture or procurement of slaves and the difficult, dangerous task of marching them to the coast. These middlemen were generally either wealthy merchants who could mount slaving expeditions inland or the agents of African chieftaincies or kingdoms who sought to profit from the trade.

The media of exchange were varied. At first they usually involved mixed barter for goods that ranged from gold dust or firearms to beads and alcohol. As time went on they came

---

[2] The summary follows closely that of P. Manning, *Slavery and African Life: Occidental, Oriental, and African Slave Trades* (Cambridge: Cambridge University Press, 1990), pp. 127–140.

Map 18–5.   Origins of African Slaves Sent to the Americas. Captive Africans came from eight regions. West Central Africa sent more captives to the Americas than any other region.

Pie chart percentages:
- Senegambia 7%
- Sierra Leone 4%
- Windward Coast 2%
- Gold Coast 10%
- Brigth of Benin 20%
- Bight of Biafra 13%
- West-Central Africa 39%
- Southeast Aftica 5%

SOURCE   Willem Bosman on the slave trade

increasingly to involve some form of monetary payment. This exchange drained productive resources (human beings) in return for nonproductive wealth.

The chief western and central African slaving regions provided different numbers of slaves at different times, and the total number of exported slaves varied sharply between periods (see Map 18–5). When one area was unable to produce sufficient numbers to meet demand (whether as a result of depopulation of choice areas, local warfare, or changing state policies), the European traders shifted their buying to other points. Thus, between 1526 and 1550 the major sources of the slaves for the transatlantic trade were the Kongo-Angola region (34 percent), the Guinea coast of Cape Verde (25.6 percent), and Senegambia (23.5 percent).[3] By

contrast, between 1761 and 1810 the French drew some 52 percent of their slaves from Angola and 24 percent from the Bight of Benin, but only 4.8 percent from Senegambia, whereas the British relied most heavily on the Bight of Biafra and central Africa.[4] Traders naturally went where population density and the presence of active African merchant or state suppliers promised the best numbers and prices, although prices do not seem to have varied radically in a given period.

The Extent of the Slave Trade

Historians now estimate that from the sixteenth through the nineteenth centuries there were over 35,000 transatlantic slave ship voyages forcibly transporting more than 11 million Africans to America; many other Africans were lost in passage

---

[3] Scholars have spent decades attempting to assemble trustworthy statistics on the slave trade; the recent database by Eltis, et al., (*The Trans-Atlantic Slave Trade: A Database on CD-ROM* [Cambridge and New York: Cambridge University Press, 2000], has marshaled a great deal of information in one spot, but new data continue to emerge. Philip Curtin, *The Atlantic Slave Trade: A Census* (Madison: University of Wisconsin Press, 1969), p. 101.

[4] Curtin, *The Atlantic Slave Trade*, pp. 101, 129; James A. Rawley, *The Trans-Atlantic Slave Trade: A History* (New York: W. W. Norton, 1981), p. 129. Note that precise statistics are subject to revision in light of more recent scholarship; see, for example, Eltis, et al., *The Trans-Atlantic Slave Trade: A Database on CD-ROM*.

Slave Ship. Loading plan for the main decks of the 320-ton slave ship *Brookes*. The *Brookes* was only 25 feet wide and 100 feet long, but as many as 609 slaves were crammed on board for the nightmarish passage to the Americas. The average space allowed each person was only about 78 inches by 16 inches. Note how humans were grouped by size, and how every adult depicted on the C and D decks has one leg shackled. *Photographs and Prints Division, Schomburg Center for Research in Black Culture, The New York Public Library, Astor, Lenox, and Tilden Foundations.*

or through other brutality associated with the trade. The slave trade varied sharply in extent from period to period (see Figure 18–1). Only about 3 percent of the total Occidental trade occurred before 1600, and only about 14 percent between 1600 and 1700. The period of greatest activity, 1701–1810, accounted for over 60 percent of the total, and even the final half-century of slaving until 1870 accounted for over 20 percent of the total. Despite Great Britain's abolishing the slave trade in its colonies in 1807 and the United States in 1808, the Portuguese still transported more than a million slaves to Brazil between 1811 and 1870. Other nations also continued to trade in slaves in the nineteenth century. In fact, more slaves landed in the Americas in these final years of the trade than during the entire seventeenth century.[5] We would do well to remember how long it actually took the "modern" western nations to abolish the trade in African slaves.

The overall number of African slaves exported during the Occidental trade—effectively, between 1451 and 1870—is still debated and must be seen in the larger context of all types of slaving in Africa in the same period. A major unknown—for both the Occidental and the Oriental trades—is the number of slaves who died under the brutal conditions to which they were subjected when captured and transported overland and by sea. The **Middle Passage**, the portion of the slave's journey that saw Africans packed onto dangerous and unhealthy boats for the voyage across the Atlantic Ocean, claimed untold numbers. The most reliable estimates pertain only to those slaves who actually landed abroad, and these estimates are more reliable for the Occidental trade than for the older, smaller, and more dispersed Oriental trade. As already noted, those who actually reached an American or Old World destination in the Occidental trade totaled more than 10 million.

Another 5 million or more were lost to the Oriental trade. Finally, the Occidental trade spurred an apparently huge increase in internal slavery, and according to the estimate of one expert, an additional 15 million people were enslaved within African societies themselves.[6]

Consequences of the Slave Trade for Africa

The statistics in the previous section hint at the massive impact slave trading had on African life and history. Still, the question of specific effects remains difficult and disputed.

Figure 18–1. The Atlantic Slave Trade, 1400–1800. *From Cañizares-Esguerra, Jorge; Seeman, Eric, The Atlantic in Global History; 1500–2000, © 2007. Electronically reproduced by permission of Pearson Education, Inc., Upper Saddle River, New Jersey.*

[5] Rawley, *The Transatlantic Slave Trade*, p. 429; Curtin, *Atlantic Slave Trade*, p. 268.

[6] Manning, *Slavery and African Life*, pp. 37, 170–171.

Modern scholarship has tended to emphasize the importance for African history of the coming of the maritime European powers in general and the transatlantic slave trade in particular. Regarding the slave trade, it is safe to say that the impact was considerable, however much that general conclusion must be qualified in the light of particular cases. (See Document, "Olaudah Equiano Recalls His Experience at the Slave Market in Barbados.") Consider some examples.

We do not know for certain if the transatlantic trade brought net population loss or gain to specific areas of West Africa. The wide and rapid spread of maize and cassava cultivation in forest regions after these plants had been imported from the Americas may have

SOURCE Portrait of Olaudah Equiano

fueled African population increases that offset regional human loss through slaving. We know, however, that slaving took away many of the strongest young men in many areas and, in the Oriental trade zones, most of the young women.

Similarly, we do not know if more slaves were captured as byproducts of local wars or from targeted slave raiding, but we do know they were captured and removed from their societies.

Nor do we know if slaving always inhibited development of trade or perhaps sometimes stimulated it because commerce in a range of African products—from ivory to wood and hides—often accompanied that in slaves. Still, we do know that in general, the exchange of productive human beings for money or goods that were generally not used to build a productive economy was a great loss for African society as a whole.

Finally, because we do not yet have accurate estimates of the total population of Africa at different times over the four centuries of the transatlantic slave trade, we cannot determine with certainty its demographic impact. We can, however, make some educated guesses. If, for example, tropical Africa had possibly 50 million inhabitants in 1600, it would then have had 30 percent of the combined popu-

Job ben Solomon. Captured by Mandingo enemies and sold to a Maryland tobacco planter, Job ben Solomon accomplished the nearly impossible feat of returning to Africa as a freeman. By demonstrating his talents as a Muslim scholar, including his ability to write the entire Qur'an from memory, he astonished his owners and eventually convinced them to let him go home. *"The Fortunate Slave," An Illustration of African Slavery in the early eighteenth century by Douglas Grant (1968). From "Some Memoirs of the Life of Job," by Thomas Bluett 1734. Photo by Robert D. Rubic/Precision Chromes, Inc., Rare Books Division, the New York Public Library, Lenox and Tilden Foundations/Art Resource, NY, .*

lation of the Americas, the Middle East, Europe, and North Africa. If in 1900, after the depredations of the slave trade, it had 70 million inhabitants, its population would have dropped to only slightly more than 10 percent of the combined population of the same world regions. Accordingly, current best estimates indicate that overall African population growth suffered significantly as a result of the devastating numbers of people lost to enslavement or to the increased warfare and decreased birthrate tied to the slave trade. Figures like these also give some idea of slavery's probable impact on Africa's ability to engage with developments that, elsewhere in the world, led to the emergence of the modern industrializing world.[7]

It is important to remember that even in West and central Africa, which bore the brunt of the transatlantic trade, its impact and the response to it were so varied in different places and times that even accurate overall statistics could be misleading for particular cases. In a few cases, kingdoms such as Dahomey (the present Republic of Benin) seem to have sought and derived immense economic profit for a time by making slaving a state monopoly. Other kingdoms, such as Benin, sought to stay almost completely out of slaving and derived no gain from it. In

---

[7] On all of the preceding points regarding probable impact of the trade, see Manning, *Slavery and African Life*, pp. 126–148, 168–176. Also consult Eltis, et al., *The Trans-Atlantic Slave Trade: A Database on CD-ROM (an expanded and enhanced version is published in 2008.*

Olaudah Equiano Recalls His Experience at the Slave Market in Barbados

Document

Olaudah Equiano composed one of the most popular and influential slave narratives of the late eighteenth and early nineteenth centuries. He had led a remarkable life. Born in West Africa in what is today Nigeria, he spent his early life among the Ibo. He was captured and sold into slavery, making the dreaded Atlantic crossing described in the previous document. In the passage that follows, he recounts his arrival in Barbados and the experience of cultural disorientation, sale into slavery, and seeing Africans separated from their families. Equiano's life did not end in slavery, the most destructive aspects of which he also described in vivid detail. He achieved his freedom and then led an adventuresome life on various commercial and military ships plying the Caribbean, the Atlantic, and the Mediterranean. He also made a trip to the Arctic Ocean. Equiano's account consequently describes not only the life of a person taken from Africa and sold into American slavery, but also the life of a person who, once free, explored the entire transatlantic world. His autobiographical narrative, which first appeared in 1789 and displayed Equiano's wide reading, served two purposes for the antislavery campaign that commenced in the second half of the eighteenth century. First, it provided a firsthand report of the slave experience in crossing from Africa to America. Second, his powerful rhetoric and clear arguments demonstrated that, if free, Africans could achieve real personal independence. Many defenders of slavery had denied that Africans possessed the character and intelligence to be free persons.

◆ What were the fears of the Africans on the slave ship as they approached the port? How were older slaves in Barbados used to calm their fears? How did the sale of slaves proceed? What happened to African families in the process of the sale?

At last, we came in sight . . . of Barbados, . . . and we soon anchored . . . off Bridgetown. Many merchants and planters now came on board. . . . They put us in separate parcels, and examined us attentively. They also made us jump, and pointed to the land, signifying we were to go there. We thought by this we should be eaten by these ugly men, as they appeared to us; and when, soon after we were all put down under the deck again, there was much dread and trembling among us, and nothing but bitter cries to be heard all the night from these apprehensions, insomuch that at last the white people got some old slaves from the land to pacify us. They told us we were not to be eaten, but to work, and were soon to go on land, where we should see many of our country people. This report eased us much. . . . We were conducted immediately to the merchant's yard, where we were all pent up together like so many sheep in a fold, without regard to sex or age. As every object was new to me, everything filled me with surprise . . . and indeed I thought these people were full of nothing but magical arts. . . . We were not many days in the merchant's custody before we were sold after their usual manner which was this: On a signal given (as the beat of a drum), the buyers rush at once into the

yard where the slaves are confined, and make choice of that parcel they like best. The noise and clamour with which this is attended, and the eagerness visible in the countenances of the buyers, serve not a little to increase the apprehension of the terrified Africans, who may well be supposed to consider them as the ministers of that destruction to which they think themselves devoted. In this manner, without scruple, relations and friends separate, most of them never to see each other again. I remember in the vessel in which I was brought over, in the men's apartment, there were several brothers who, in the sale, were sold in different lots; and it was very moving on this occasion to see and hear their cries at parting. . . . Surely this is a new refinement in cruelty, which, while it has no advantage to atone for it, thus aggravates distress, and adds fresh horrors even to the wretchedness of slavery.

From *The Interesting Narrative of the Life of Olaudah Equiano or Gustavus Vassa, The African, Written by Himself* (first published 1789), as quoted in Henry Louis Gates Jr, and William L. Andrews, eds., *Pioneers of the Black Atlantic: Five Slave Narratives from the Enlightenment, 1772–1815* (Washington, DC: Counterpoint, 1998), pp. 221–223.

many instances, including the rise of Asante power or the fall of the Yoruba Oyo Empire, it now appears that increased slaving was in part a result as well as a cause of regional instability and change. Increased warfare meant increased prisoners to be enslaved and a surplus to be sold off; however, whether slaving gave good cause for war is still a major question in each regional context.

Similarly, if one can establish, as seems evident, a major increase in indigenous slavery as a result of the external trade to occident and orient during the centuries in question, we have to assume major social consequences for African society as a whole, but the specific consequences would differ according to the specifics of regional situations. For example, in West Africa relatively more men were taken as slaves than women, whereas in the Sahelian Sudanic regions relatively more women than men were taken. In the west the loss of so many men increased the pressures for polygamy and possibly the regional use of women slaves as well, whereas in the Sahelian Sudanic regions the loss of women may have stimulated polyandry and reduced the birthrate significantly.

Even though slavery existed previously in Africa, the scale of the transatlantic trade was unprecedented and hence had an unprecedented impact on indigenous social, political, and economic realities. In general, the slave trade measurably changed patterns of life and balances of power in the main affected areas, whether by stimulating trade or warfare (or at least raiding for new supplies), by disrupting previous market and political structures, by substantially increasing slavery inside Africa, or by disturbing the male-female ratio (and hence the workforce balance and birthrate patterns) and consequently the basic social institution of monogamous marriage.

If the overseas slave trade did not substantially and irrevocably change every region it touched, at the least it siphoned indigenous energy into ultimately counterproductive or destructive directions. This, in turn, meant the inhibition of true economic development, especially in central and coastal West Africa. The transatlantic slave trade must by any standard be described as one of the most tragic aspects of European involvement in Africa.

Summary

European Conquest of the New World. The contact between the native peoples of the American continents and the European explorers of the fifteenth and sixteenth centuries transformed world history. In the Americas, the native peoples had established a wide variety of civilizations. Some of their most remarkable architectural monu-

ments and cities were constructed during the centuries when European civilizations were feeble in comparison. Until the European explorations, the civilizations of the Americas, Eurasia, and Africa had had no significant contact with each other.

Within half a century of the landing of Columbus, millions of America's native peoples had encountered Europeans intent on conquest, exploitation, and religious conversion. Because of their advanced weapons, navies, and the new diseases they brought with them, as well as internal divisions among the Native Americans, the Europeans achieved a rapid conquest.

The Transatlantic Economy. In both North and South America, economies of exploitation were established. In Latin America, various institutions were developed to extract native labor. From the Mid-Atlantic English colonies through the Caribbean and into Brazil, slave-labor plantation systems were established. The slaves were forcibly imported from Africa and sold in the Americas to plantation owners. The economies and peoples of Europe, Africa, and the Americas were thus drawn into a vast worldwide web of production based on slave labor.

Slavery. The impact of slavery in the Americas was not limited to the life of the black slaves. Whites in the New World numbered about 12 million in 1820, compared to some 6 million blacks. However, only about 2 million whites had migrated there, compared to some 10 million or more Africans forcibly imported as slaves. Such numbers reveal the effects of brutal slave conditions and the high mortality and low birthrates of slave populations.

None of these statistics, however, enables us to assess the role that slavery has played in the Americas or, in particular, the United States. The United States actually received only a bit more than a quarter as many slaves as did Brazil alone or the British and French Caribbean regions together, yet the forced migration of Africans as slaves into the United States had profound consequences. Consider just the American Civil War and the endurance of racism and inequality or, more positively, the African contribution to American industrial development, language, music, literature, and artistic culture.

On the African continent, the impact of the slave trade was immense, though difficult to document specifically for many areas. The social, economic, and personal effects were enormous in any case, given the extent and duration of the trade. Certainly the loss of population and productive resources helped set the stage for European colonization. The Atlantic slave trade's impact continues to be felt at both ends of the original "trade."

Review Questions

1. How were small groups of Spaniards able to conquer the Aztec and Inca Empires?

2. What was the basis of the mercantilist theory of economics? What was the relationship between the colonial economies and those of the homelands?

3. Describe the economies of Spanish America and Brazil. What were the similarities and differences between them and the British and French colonies in the Caribbean and North America? What role did the various colonies play in the transatlantic economy?

4. Explain the chief factors involved in the Columbian Exchange. Which animals from Europe flourished in the Americas? Why? Which American plants produced broad impact in Europe and elsewhere in the world?

5. Why did forced labor and slavery develop in tropical colonies? How was slavery in the Americas different from slavery in earlier societies?

6. What historical patterns emerged in the slave trade(s) within and out of Africa? Consider the gender and age distribution of slaves, their places of origin, and their destinations.

7. Compare and contrast the Oriental and Occidental slave trades. What was the effect of the transatlantic slave trade on West African societies? On East Africa? What role did Africans themselves play in the slave trade?

INTERPRETING THE PAST

Seeing Both Sides of Slavery: African Americans in the New World

Text Sources from MyHistoryLab / PrimarySource DVD

1. Bryan Edwards, excerpts from *Observations on the Maroon Negroes on Jamaica*
2. Olaudah Equiano, excerpt from *The Interesting Narrative*
3. Phillis Wheatley, *To the Right Honorable William Early of Dartmouth*
4. Five African Spirituals
5. Willem Bosman describes the slave trade

Visual Sources from MyHistoryLab / PrimarySource DVD

1. Advertisement for a slave auction
2. The slave ship *Brookes*

These primary source documents and images focus on the lives of African Americans in the New World from the end of the seventeenth century to the end of the eighteenth century—the height of the Transatlantic slave trade. Three of the documents—written by Olaudah Equiano, Phillis Wheatley, and *African American Spirituals*—are authored by African Americans, and two are written from the perspective of Europeans who supported and participated in the slave trade. Taken together, these accounts tell a complex tale of resistance, accommodation, and exploitation.

Common to the life stories of Equiano and Wheatley is the theme of self-improvement, a virtue championed by Benjamin Franklin, their contemporary and that came to define America's self-images. The five spirituals, like the chronicle of Bryan Edwards's experience in Jamaica, detail both overt and covert resistance to the slave-owning establishment. Finally, Captain Willem Bosman's description of the slave trade offers a perspective that contrasts with Equiano's account of his enslavement and passage to America.

Use the source documents and the images to address the following thematic questions focusing on how Africans resisted a seemingly inexorable system of enslavement. Also evaluate the reactions of European participants in the transatlantic slave trade. Use specific examples from the documents to back up your assertions.

Key Terms

Black Legend (p. 536)

chattel slavery (p. 548)

Columbian Exchange (p. 543)

conquistadores (p. 537)

debt peonage (p. 538)

encomienda (p. 537)

hacienda (p. 538)

mercantilism (p. 532)

Middle Passage (p. 554)

"Occidental" slave trade (p. 551)

peninsulares (p. 538)

plantation economy (p. 549)

repartimiento (p. 537)

Note: To learn more about the topics in this chapter, please turn to the Suggested Readings at the end of the book. For additional sources related to this chapter please see the Primary Source DVD at the back of this text or MyHistoryLab.

Questions

What evidence is there in these documents for the survival of African culture in the Americas? Would African customs and traditions help Africans survive in the New World?

Equiano and Wheatley took different paths as pioneering and popular black writers. A committed abolitionist, Equiano devoted much effort and time to combatting slavery, whereas Wheatley expressed herself mostly in elegant poetry. However, Wheatley also questioned how a slave-owning society could hope to find "Divine acceptance with th' Almighty mind – / While yet (O deed ungenerous!) they disgrace / And hold in bondage afric's blameless race . . ." In the poem, addressed to the Earl of Dartmouth, Wheatley pleads with the newly appointed Secretary to the North American colonies to support increased liberty for the American colonies. How does she invoke her African heritage and the experience of slavery?

What are the attitudes of the two white writers toward Africans they encounter? Are there signs of accommodation with Africans who have gained a measure of power in the Americas (the Maroons)?

East Asia in the Late Traditional Era

LATE IMPERIAL CHINA

◆ Ming (1368–1644) and Qing (1644–1911) Dynasties

JAPAN

◆ Warring States Era (1467–1600)

◆ Tokugawa Era (1600–1868)

KOREA AND VIETNAM

◆ Korea

◆ Vietnam

O NE DIFFICULTY IN COMPARING EAST ASIAN countries is that although they shared many cultural elements, their institutions and history were very different. Their cultural affinity is immediately apparent if we look at Chinese, Japanese, Korean, and Vietnamese paintings side by side. Less visible, but no less basic, was a range of social values shared, at least by their elites. To the extent that it was based on Confucianism, the similarity may have been greatest in the mid–nineteenth century, when Japan, Korea, and Vietnam had become more Confucian than ever before.

But when we compare their histories and institutions, the similarities diminish. China and Japan were furthest apart. Each had gone its own way. Korea and Vietnam, even while forging an identity in reaction to China, were more directly influenced by China in their history and closer to China in their culture and institutions.

For China, the Ming (1368–1644) and Qing dynasties (1644–1911) were just two more centralized bureaucratic regimes of a kind that had been

Seventeenth-century screen painting of a Shintō river festival in Tsushima (a town near Nagoya city) held annually in July to ward off epidemics in the heat of the summer. Among the throng of spectators at the river's edge are shopkeepers, other townspeople, Buddhist priests, and palanquin bearers (at the left). Of the five boats on the river (which are not shown), each with 550 lanterns, only one mast with five red lanterns can be seen at the center of the panel.

East Asia in the Late Traditional Era

East Asia

Why did the West, and not East Asia or anywhere else, open the door to modernity? Why did an industrial revolution not develop within the sophisticated commercial economies of Japan and China? The answer, obviously, must be found within Western history. Still, a few comparisons with the West may illuminate aspects of premodern East Asia.

1. The sociologist Max Weber saw Western capitalism as inspired by the Protestant ethic—which he found lacking in India, China, and Catholic Europe. But is the East Asian family-centered ethic of frugality, savings, and hard work not a "Protestant ethic" of sorts? And if a deeper Calvinist anxiety about salvation is required, as Weber stated, then why has East Asia achieved such explosive growth since World War II?

2. Was the scientific revolution of the seventeenth century critical to the industrial revolution? Some historians say that revolution was well under way before science made a substantial contribution.

3. The self-educated technicians of England who invented the water loom and steam engine reaped enormous honors and rewards. In China and Japan no patents protected inventors and no economists wrote of inventors as the benefactors of society. Wealth and honors were reserved for officials and gentry, who were literary and political in orientation and despised those who worked with their hands. (Of course, in earlier dynasties, Chinese had been brilliantly inventive without patent protection.)

4. Bureaucracy is sometimes viewed as a key component of modernity. Bureaucracy does for administration what the assembly line does for production: it breaks complex tasks into simple ones, to achieve huge gains in efficiency. In the West bureaucracies appeared only in recent centuries. They strengthened monarchies and nation-states against landed aristocrats; they represented the triumph of ability over hereditary privilege.

---

in place for centuries. In the Tang (618–907) the Chinese had forged a pattern of government so efficient and closely geared to the deeper familial and educational constitution of the society that, thereafter, they rebuilt it after each dynastic breakdown. This pattern continued during the Ming and the Qing, giving their histories a recognizable cyclical cast, even though they are also replete with historical trends that cut across dynastic lines.

Japanese political history, in contrast, is not cyclical. Each period of Japanese history reflects a new and different configuration. The centralized governments of the Nara and early Heian gave way to a manorial social order in which a powerful, local warrior class emerged. From this "feudal" class arose first the Kamakura *bakufu*, and then the Ashikaga. These in turn were followed by an era of Warring States and then a lengthy period of centralized "feudalism." Superficially at least, Japan's history was more like that of Europe than of China. Neither Europe nor Japan ever found a pattern of rule that worked so well, was so satisfactory to the rulers, and was so deeply embedded in the institutions of the society that it was re-created over and over again. In fact, from a Japanese or European point of view, that is not how history works.

This chapter underlines the dynamism of both China and Japan during these late centuries. "Late traditional society" does not mean "late static society." In both countries the society became more integrated and

Chinese bureaucrats shared many of the same virtues. They were an elite of talent educated in the Confucian classics as British officials were educated in those of Greece and Rome. But they were somehow different. They had wielded power for at least a millennium, and were a segment of the landed gentry class in a country from which hereditary aristocrats had long since disappeared. Despite their talent, in the nineteenth century they would constitute a major obstacle to modernity.

Putting aside comparisons with Europe, we also note the difference between Chinese and Japanese attitudes towards outside civilizations. When the Jesuits tried to introduce science, the Chinese response was occasional curiosity and general indifference. A few Jesuits were appointed as interpreters or court astronomers, or were used to cast cannons for China's armies. The Chinese lack of interest in foreign cultures can be explained by the coherence of China's core institutions: the emperor, bureaucracy, examination system, Confucian schools, and gentry. These were so deeply rooted and highly appreciated as to constitute a closed system. In contrast, despite a national policy of seclusion, the Japanese reached out for Dutch medicine and science—as they had earlier reached out for Chinese Neo-Confucianism. In the middle of the nineteenth century, this greater openness helps explain their rapid advance.

That Vietnam and Korea did not achieve industrial revolutions requires less explanation. They were smaller and less commercially developed than China or Japan. Vietnam was preoccupied with wars and its expansion to the south. In Korea—sometimes called the "hermit Kingdom," the elites were open only to Chinese culture and engaged in endless factional struggles.

◆ What features of Japan or China, other than those mentioned above, bear on their lack of progress from commerce to industry? Are there still other factors treated in the chapters on Europe that are also relevant?

◆ Why was Tokugawa Japan more open to Western learning that Qing China? Was population a plus, a minus, or a factor that did not matter?

the apparatus of government more sophisticated than ever before. These advances shaped Chinese and Japanese responses to the West during the nineteenth century. Even Korea and Vietnam did not lack dynamism, but we must also note that it was during these centuries that the West was transformed. In fact, Greece and Rome apart, most of what seems important in Western history—the Renaissance, the Reformation, the Scientific Revolution, the formation of nation-states, the Industrial Revolution, the Enlightenment, and the democratic revolution—happened while the Ming and the Qing dynasties were reigning in China. As we view East Asia from the perspective of Europe, it appears to have been caught in a tar pit of slow motion. But in fact the West had simply accelerated. ■

LATE IMPERIAL CHINA

Ming (1368–1644) and Qing (1644–1911) Dynasties

The Ming and the Qing were China's last dynasties. The first was Chinese; the second was a dynasty of conquest in which the ruling house and an important segment of the military were foreign (Manchus). They were nevertheless remarkably similar in their institutions and pattern of rule, so much so that historians sometimes speak of "Ming-Qing despotism" as if it were a single system. The two dynasties are also coupled as a result of certain demographic and economic trends that began during the Ming and continued through the Qing.

Land and People

China's population doubled from about 60 or 90 million in 1368 at the start of the Ming dynasty to about 125 million in 1644 at its end. The population then tripled during the early and middle Qing dynasty, reaching about 410 million people several decades into the mid–nineteenth century. This population density stimulated the growth of commerce and gave new prominence to the scholar-gentry class.

An increase in the food supply paralleled population growth. During the Ming, the spread of Song agricultural technology and new strains of rice accounted for 40 percent of the higher yields, and newly cultivated lands accounted for the rest. During the Qing, half the increased food supply was due to new lands and the other half to better seeds, fertilizers, and irrigation. New crops introduced from America during the late Ming, such as maize, sweet potatoes, and peanuts (which could be planted on dry sandy uplands and did not compete with rice), also bolstered the food supply. By the nineteenth century maize was grown in all parts of China.

In north China the population had declined from 32 million to 11 million during the Mongol conquests. The Ming government repopulated its open lands, resettling villages, building water control systems, and reopening the Grand Canal in 1415. The movement of people to the north continued until the nineteenth century. In the north, most farmers owned the land they worked and at times used hired labor. The land consisted mainly of irrigated dry fields, and the chief crops were millet, sorghum, and wheat.

South and southwest China also saw an influx of migrants from the densely populated lower Yangzi region, many settling in hilly or mountainous border areas that were agriculturally marginal. The White Lotus Rebellion of 1796–1804 occurred in such a recently settled area far from centers of governmental authority. The Miao Wars of the late eighteenth century also were precipitated by the movement of Chinese settlers into southwestern uplands previously left to the slash-and-burn agriculture of the Miao tribes. Other Chinese crossed over to Taiwan or emigrated overseas. During the Qing dynasty, large Chinese mercantile communities became established in Southeast Asia.

The Yangzi basin, meanwhile, became even more densely populated. The lower Yangzi region and the delta, well supplied with waterways, had long been the rice basket of China, but from the late Ming agricultural cash crops, such as silk and cotton, predominated. Cotton was so widely grown in the delta that food had to be brought in from other areas by the early nineteenth century. In the lower Yangzi absentee landlords owned almost half of the land. A typical landlord's holdings were subdivided among tenants, who paid fixed rents in kind. South China also had extensive absentee landlordism, but far more land was owned collectively by clans, which managed the land and distributed rents among their members.

There are many unanswered questions regarding the population growth during these six centuries (1368–1911). Was there a decline in the death rate and, if so, why? Or was it simply that new lands and technology enabled more mouths to be fed? Did the population oblige by promptly increasing? Certainly the Ming-Qing era was the longest continuous period of good government in Chinese history. The good years of Ming rule were longer than such periods in earlier dynasties, and the transition to Qing rule was quicker and less destructive. How much did these long periods of good government contribute to the population growth? Epidemic disease was not absent. In the great

Fishermen on Autumn River, a Ming dynasty scroll painting by Dai Qin (1390–1460). *Tai Chin, "Fisherman on an Autumn River," (1390–1460). Painting Ink and color on paper. Courtesy of Freer Gallery of Art, Smithsonian Institution, Washington, D.C.*

plagues from 1586 to 1589 and from 1639 to 1644, as many as 20 to 30 percent of the people died in the most populous regions of China, and in specific counties and villages the figure was often higher. Another epidemic occurred in 1756 and a cholera epidemic from 1820 to 1822. The growth of China's population more than overcame such losses. Because of the growth in agriculture and population, most accounts view the eighteenth century as the most prosperous in Chinese history. But by the early nineteenth century the Chinese standard of living may have begun to decline. An ever-increasing population was no blessing.

China's Third Commercial Revolution

Commerce in China flourished between 300 B.C.E. and 220 C.E. (the late Zhou through the Han dynasties), only to decline in the centuries of disunity that followed. In Chapter 7 we read Sima Qian's description of wealthy Han merchants. Between 850 and 1250 (late Tang through Song) commerce again surged, only to contract during the Mongol conquest. At the end of the Mongol dynasty, warlords confiscated merchant wealth. Early Ming emperors, isolationist and agrarian in orientation, restricted the use of foreign goods, required licenses for junks (coastal sailing ships), and attempted to encase foreign trade within the constraints of the tribute system. The early Ming also operated government monopolies that stifled enterprise and depressed the southeastern coastal region by their restrictions on maritime trade and shipping. In the mid–sixteenth century commerce started to grow again, buoyed by the surge of population and agriculture and aided by a relaxation of government controls. If the growth during the Han and Song dynas-

ties may be called, respectively, China's first and second commercial revolutions, then the expansion between 1500 and 1800 was the third. This revolution was partly the extension to other parts of China of changes begun earlier in the Yangzi area, but it had new features as well. By the early nineteenth century China was the most highly commercialized nonindustrial society in the world.

One stimulus to commerce was imported silver, which played the role in the Ming-Qing economy that copper cash had played in the Song dynasty. The Chinese balance of trade was favorable. Beginning in the mid–sixteenth century silver from mines in western Japan entered China, and from the 1570s, Spanish galleons sailing from Acapulco to China via Manila brought in Mexican and Peruvian silver. In exchange, Chinese silks and porcelains were sold in the shops of Mexico City. The late Ming court also opened silver mines in Guizhou and Yunnan provinces. In the eighteenth century copper mines were opened in south China. Also, private Shaanxi banks opened branches throughout China to facilitate the transfer of funds from one area to another and extend credit for trade. Eventually they opened offices in Singapore, Japan, and Russia, as well.

As in Europe, so in China, the influx of silver and the overall increase in liquidity led to inflation and commercial growth. The price of land rose steadily. During the sixteenth century

A porcelain enameled plate, from the Ming dynasty, late sixteenth century.

the thirty or fourty early Ming taxes on land that were payable in grain, labor service, and cash were consolidated into one tax payable in silver, the so-called Single Whip Reform. To obtain the silver, farmers sold their grain in the market, and some switched from grain to cash crops. Moreover, by the early nineteenth century there were six times as many farm families as in the mid–fourteenth century.

Urban growth between 1500 and 1800, responding to flourishing local markets, was mainly at the level of intermediate market towns. These towns grew more rapidly than the population as a whole and provided the link between the local markets and the larger provincial capitals and cities such as Beijing, Hangzhou, or Guangzhou. The commercial integration of local, intermediate, and large cities was not entirely new, having occurred during the Song dynasty in the lower Yangzi region, but now it spread over all of China. Interregional trade also gained. Where Song trade between regions was mainly in luxury goods such as silk, lacquerware, porcelains, medicines, and paintings, early Qing traders also dealt in staples, such as grain, timber, salt, iron, and cotton. This is not to suggest that China developed a national economy. Seven or eight regional economies, each the size of a large European nation, were still the focus for most economic activity. However, a new level of trade developed among them, especially where water transport made such trade economical. A final feature of eighteenth-century Chinese economic life was the so-called "putting out" system in textiles, under which merchant capitalists organized and financed each stage of production from fiber to dyed cloth.

Women and the Commercial Revolution The Confucian family ideal changed little during the Ming and Qing dynasties. A woman was expected first to obey her parents, then her husband, and finally her son—when he became the new family head. Physically, women became more restricted. Footbinding, which had begun among the elite during the Song dynasty, spread through the upper classes during the Ming and to some commoners during the mid to late Qing (see Figure 19–1). Most girls were subjected to this cruel and deformative procedure. Even in villages, women with big—that is to say, normal—feet were sometimes considered unmarriageable. One exception to the rule was the Hakka people of south China. Hakka women with unbound feet worked in the fields alongside their male kinsmen. Another exception was the Manchus. One Manchu (Qing) emperor even issued an edict banning footbinding, but the Chinese ignored it.

As population grew and the size of the average landholding shrank, more women worked at home, spinning, weaving, and making other products for the burgeoning commercial markets. As their contribution to the household income grew, their voice in household decisions often became larger than Confucian doctrines would suggest. But at the same time, women's property rights—to inheritance and control of dowries—became more limited than in previous dynasties. Furthermore, the same commercial revolution increased the number of rich townsmen who could afford concubines and patronize tea houses, restaurants, and brothels. (See Document, "The Thin Horse Market.")

Political System

One might expect these massive demographic and economic changes to have produced, if not a bourgeois revolution, at least some profound change in the political superstructure of China. They did not. Government during the Ming and Qing was much like that of the Song or Yuan, only improved and made stronger. Historians sometimes describe it as the "perfected" late imperial system. This system, they argue, was able to contain and use the new economic energies that destroyed the weaker late feudal polities of Europe. The sources of strength of the perfected Ming-Qing system were the spread of education, Confucianism ideology, stronger emper-

Figure 19–1. A Bound Foot. This diagram shows the twisted and cramped bone structure of a bound ("lily") foot, as compared with that of a normal foot. Bound tightly with cloth from the age of five, a little girl's foot grew painfully into this deformed but erotically admired shape. *From East Asia, The Great Tradition, E.O. Reischauer, JK Fairbank, Houghton Mifflin 1960.*

The Thin Horse Market

Document

In China, ancestors without descendants to perform the rites ran the danger of becoming hungry ghosts or wandering spirits. Consequently, having a son who would continue the family line was an act of filial piety. If a wife failed to produce an heir, an official, merchant, or wealthy landowner might take a concubine and try again. Or he might do so simply because he was able to, because it gave him pleasure, and because it was socially acceptable. For a poor peasant household, after a bad harvest and faced with high taxes, the sale of a comely daughter often seemed preferable to the sale of ancestral land.

◆ Concubines usually had no choice in the matter, but neither did many brides in premodern China. Was a woman better off as the wife of a poor peasant, experiencing hardship, hunger, and want, or as the concubine in a wealthy household with servants, good food, and the likelihood that her children would receive an education? What does the following passage tell us about attitudes towards women in premodern China?

Upwards of a hundred people in Yangzhou earn a living in the "thin horse" business.[*] If someone shows an interest in taking a concubine, a team of a broker, a drudge, and a scout stick to him like flies. Early in the morning, the teams gather to wait outside the doors of potential customers, who usually give their business to the first team to arrive. Any teams coming late have to wait for the next opportunity. The winning team then leads their customer to the broker's house. The customer is then served tea and seated to wait for the women. The broker leads out each of them, who do what the matchmaker tells them to do. After each of her short commands, the woman bows to the customer, walks forward, turns toward the light so the customer can see her face clearly, draws back her sleeves to show him her hands, glances shyly at him to show him her eyes, says her age so he can hear her voice, and finally lifts her skirt to reveal whether her feet are bound. An experienced customer could figure out the size of her feet by listening to the noise she made as she entered the room. If her skirt made noise when she walked in, she had to have a pair of big feet under her skirt. As one woman finishes, another comes out, each house having at least five or six. If the customer finds a woman to his liking, he puts a gold hairpin in her hair at the temple, a procedure called "inserting the ornament." If no one satisfies him, he gives a few hundred cash to the broker or the servants.

If the first broker gets tired, others will willingly take his place. Even if a customer has the stamina to keep looking for four or five days, he cannot finish visiting all the houses. Nevertheless, after seeing fifty to sixty white-faced, red-dressed women, they all begin to look alike and he cannot decide which are pretty or ugly. It is like the difficulty of recognizing a character after writing it hundreds or thousands of times. Therefore, the customer usually chooses someone once his mind and eyes can no longer discriminate. The owner of the woman brings out a piece of red paper on which are listed the "betrothal presents," including gold jewelry and cloth. Once he agrees to the deal, he is sent home. Before he even arrives back at his lodgings, a band and a load of food and wine are already waiting there. Before long, presents he was to send are prepared and sent back with the band. Then a sedan chair and all the trimmings—colorful lanterns, happy candles, attendants, sacrificial foods—wait outside for the customer's arrangement. The cooks and the entertainer for the wedding celebration also arrive together with foods, wine, candy, tables, chairs, and tableware. Without the customer's order, the colorful sedan chair for the girl and the small sedan chair for her companion are dispatched to get the girl. The new concubine performs the bowing ceremony with music and singing and considerable clamor. The next morning before noon the laborers ask for rewards from the man, then leave to prepare another wedding for another customer in the same manner.

---

[*]A horse market is for the sale of horses. A "thin horse" market is the market for concubines. The name implies a measure of criticism.

ors, better government finances, more competent officials, and a larger gentry class with an expanded role in local society.

Role of Confucianism Confucian teachings were more widespread in late imperial China than ever before. There were more schools in villages and towns. Academies preparing candidates for the civil service examinations multiplied. Publishing flourished, bookstores abounded, and literacy outpaced population growth. The Confucian view of society was patriarchal. The family, headed by the father, was the basic unit. The emperor, the son of heaven and the ruler-father of the empire, stood at its apex. In between were the district magistrates, the "father-mother officials." The idea of the state as the family writ large was not just a matter of metaphor but carried with it duties and obligations that were binding at every level.

The sociopolitical worldview of Confucianism was also buttressed by Neo-Confucian metaphysics, which gave a unitary character to Ming and Qing culture. This is not, of course, to deny the existence of different schools of Confucian thought. The vitality of late Ming thinkers was especially notable. Still, in comparison to Europe, where religious philosophies were less involved with the state and where a revolution in science was reshaping both religious and political doctrines, the greater unity and integration of the Chinese worldview cannot be denied.

Emperor In Ming-Qing times the emperor was stronger than ever. The Secretariat of high officials that had coordinated government affairs during the Song and the Yuan was abolished by the first Ming emperor, who himself made all important and many unimportant decisions. His successors, often aided by Grand Secretaries, continued this pattern of direct, personal rule. During the late fourteenth and fifteenth centuries the emperor was the bottleneck official, without whose active participation the business of government would bog down.

Then, during the sixteenth and early seventeenth centuries, a series of emperors appeared who were not interested in government. One spent his days on wine, women, and sports; another on Daoist rites; and still another emperor, who never learned to write, passed his days making furniture. During this era Grand Secretaries or eunuchs exercised the emperor's authority. But the Qing reestablished the pattern of personal government by emperors.

Emperors wielded despotic powers at their courts. They had personal secret police and prisons where those who gave even minor offense might be tortured. Even high officials might suffer the humiliating, and sometimes fatal, punishment of having their bared buttocks beaten with bamboo rods at court—a practice inherited from the Mongols. The dedication and loyalty even of officials who were mistreated

attest to the depth of their Confucian ethical formation. One censor who had served three emperors ran afoul of a powerful eunuch. The eunuch obtained an imperial order and had the official tortured to death in 1625. In his deathbed notes to his sons, the official blamed the villain for his agonies but wrote that he welcomed death because his body belonged to his "ruler-father." An earlier mid–sixteenth century incident involved Hai Rui, the most famous censor of the Ming period:

> *Hai presented himself at the palace gate to submit a memorial denouncing some of the emperor's notorious idiosyncrasies. The emperor flew into a rage and ordered that Hai not be permitted to escape. "Never fear, sire," the eunuch go-between told the emperor. "He has said goodbye to his family, has brought his coffin with him, and waits at the gate!" Shih-tsung [the emperor] was so taken aback by this news that he forgave Hai for his impertinence.[1]*

During the Qing the life-and-death authority of emperors did not diminish, but officials were generally better treated. As foreign rulers, the Manchu emperors took care not to alienate Chinese officials.

The Forbidden Palace in Beijing, rebuilt when the third Ming emperor moved the capital from Nanjing to Beijing, was an icon of the emperor's majesty. Unlike the Kremlin, which consists of an assortment of buildings inside a wall, the entire palace complex in Beijing focused on the single figure of the ruler. Designed geometrically, its massive outer and inner walls, vast courtyards, and halls progress stage by stage to the raised area of the audience hall. During the Tang, emperors sat together with their grand councilors while discussing matters of government. In the Song, officials stood in the emperor's presence. By the Ming, the emperor sat on an elevated dais above the officials, who knelt before him. Behind the audience hall were the emperor's private chambers and his harem. In 1425 the palace had 6300 cooks serving 10,000 persons daily. These numbers later increased. By the seventeenth century there were 9,000 palace ladies and perhaps 70,000 eunuchs. The glory of the emperor extended to his family, whose members were awarded vast estates in North China.

Bureaucracy A second component of the Ming-Qing system was the government itself. The formal organization of offices was little different from that in the Tang or the Song. At the top were the military, the censorate, and the administrative branch, and beneath the administration were the six

---

[1] C. O. Hucker, *China's Imperial Past* (Stanford, CA: Stanford University Press, 1975), p. 206.

ministries and the web of provincial, prefectural, and district offices. But government was better financed at this time than during earlier dynasties. The productivity of China became steadily greater, whereas the apparatus of government grew only slowly. Government finances had ups and downs, but as late as the 1580s huge surpluses were still being accumulated at both the central and the provincial levels. These surpluses probably braked the process of dynastic decline. Only during the last fifty years of the Ming did soaring military expenses bankrupt government finances.

In the second half of the seventeenth century the Manchus reestablished a strong central government and restored the flow of taxes to levels close to those of the Ming. In fact, revenues were so ample that early in the eighteenth century the emperors were able to freeze taxes on agriculture at the 1711 level and fix quotas for each province.

This contributed to the general prosperity of the eighteenth century but led to problems during the nineteenth century. Because agricultural productivity continued to rise, even though local officials collected some of the surplus, fixed quotas meant a declining share of the product. Both cultivators and gentry probably benefited from the new wealth, with the latter obtaining the larger share.

If the Ming-Qing system can be spoken of as perfected, the good government it brought to China was largely a product of the ethical commitment and the exceptional ability of its officials. No officials in the world today approach in power or prestige those of the Ming and the Qing. When the Portuguese arrived early in the sixteenth century, they called these officials "mandarins." (This term began as a Sanskrit word for "counselor" that became Hindi, entered Malay, and was then picked up by the Portuguese and adopted by other Europeans.) As in the Song, the rewards of an official career were so great that the competition to enter it was intense.

As population and the number of schools grew, entrance became increasingly competitive. (See Document, "The Seven Transformations of an Examination Candidate.")

After being screened at the district office, a candidate took the county examination. If he passed he became a member of the gentry. He gained the cap and sash of the scholar and exemption from state labor service. Even this examination required years of arduous study. About half a million passed each year. The second hurdle was the provincial examination held every third year. Only one in a hundred or more was successful. The final hurdle was the metropolitan examination, also held triennially. During the Ming fewer than ninety passed each year. As in earlier dynasties, regional quotas were set to prevent the Yangzi region from dominating the officialdom.

Gentry A final component in the Ming-Qing system—if not new, at least vastly more significant than in earlier dynasties—was the **gentry** class. It was an intermediate layer between the elite bureaucracy above and the village below. The lowest level of bureaucratic government was the office of the district magistrate. Although the population increased sixfold during the Ming and the Qing, the number of district magistrates increased only from 1,171 to 1,470. Thus the average district, which had had a population of 50,000 in the early Ming and 100,000 in the late Ming, had two or three times that number by the early nineteenth century. The district magistrate came to his district as an outsider. The "law of avoidance," designed to prevent conflicts of interest, prevented him from serving in his home province. His office compound had a large staff of secretaries, advisers, specialists, clerks, and runners; but even then, he could not govern such a large population directly. To govern effectively, the magistrate had to obtain the cooperation of the local literati or gentry.

Examination Stalls. The dilapidated remains of the examination stalls at Nanjing. Doors to individual cubicles can be seen to the right and left of the three-story gate. Thousands of such cubicles made up the old examination stalls. Those who passed the exams governed China. *Corbis-Bettmann.*

By *gentry* we do not mean a rural elite, like English squires. The Chinese gentry was largely urban, living in market towns or district seats. Socially and educationally, its members were of the same class as the magistrate—a world apart from clerks, runners, or village headmen. They usually owned land, which enabled them to avoid manual labor and to send their children to private academies. As absentee landlords whose lands were worked by sharecroppers, they were often exploitative; rebels at the end of the Ming attacked landlords as they did government offices. But the gentry were also local leaders. They represented community interests, which they interpreted conservatively, vis-à-vis the bureaucracy. They also performed quasi-official functions on behalf of their communities: maintaining schools and Confucian temples; repairing roads, bridges, canals, and dikes; and writing local histories.

The gentry class was the matrix from which officials arose; it was the local upholder of Confucian values. During the mid–nineteenth century, at a time of crisis, it would become the sustainer of the dynasty.

Pattern of Manchu Rule   The collapse of the Ming dynasty in 1644 and the establishment of Manchu rule was less of a break than might be imagined. First, the transition was short. Second, the Manchus, unlike the Mongols, were already partially Sinicized at the time of the conquest. They had been vassals of the Chinese state during the Ming, organized by tribal units into commanderies. Even before entering China, they had had the experience of ruling over Chinese who had settled in Manchuria to the north of the Great Wall.

In the late sixteenth century an able leader unified the Manchurian tribes and proclaimed a new dynasty. While still based in Mukden (more recently, Shenyang), the dynasty established a Confucian government with six ministries, a censorate, and other Chinese institutions. When the Ming collapsed and rebel forces took over China, the Manchus presented themselves as the conservative upholders of the Confucian order. The Chinese gentry preferred the Manchus to Chinese rebel leaders, whom they regarded as bandits. After the Manchu conquest, a few scholars and officials became famous as Ming loyalists. Most, however, served the new dynasty. The Qing as a Chinese dynasty dates from 1644, when the capital was moved from Shenyang (Mukden) to Beijing. All of south China was taken by 1659, with the aid of Ming generals who switched their allegiance to the new regime.

The Seven Transformations of an Examination Candidate

Document

The Chinese civil service examination was a grueling ordeal. Like a chess tournament, it required physical strength. Chinese critics said, "To pass the provincial examination a man needed the spiritual strength of a dragon-horse, the physique of a donkey, the insensitivity of a wood louse, and the endurance of a camel." The following selection is by a seventeenth-century writer who never succeeded in passing.

◆ Is the style of this passage overdone or effective? What is distinctively Chinese about it?

When he first enters the examination compound and walks along, panting under his heavy load of luggage, he is just like a beggar. Next, while undergoing the personal body search and being scolded by the clerks and shouted at by the soldiers, he is just like a prisoner. When he finally enters his cell and, along with the other candidates, stretches his neck to peer out, he is just like the larva of a bee. When the examination is finished at last and he leaves, his mind in a haze and his legs tottering, he is just like a sick bird that has been released from a cage. While he is wondering when the results will be announced and waiting to learn whether he passed or failed, so nervous that he is startled even by the rustling of the trees and the grass and is unable to sit or stand still, his restlessness is like that of a monkey on a leash. When at last the results are announced and he has definitely failed, he loses his vitality like one dead, rolls over on his side, and lies there without moving, like a poisoned fly. Then, when he pulls himself together and stands up, he is provoked by every sight and sound, gradually flings away everything within his reach, and complains of the illiteracy of the examiners. When he calms down at last, he finds everything in the room broken. At this time he is like a pigeon smashing its own precious eggs. These are the seven transformations of a candidate.

From I. Miyazaki, *China's Examination Hell*, trans. by C. Schirokauer. Copyright © 1976 Weatherhill, pp. 57–58.

As a tiny fraction of China's population, the Manchus adopted institutions to maintain themselves as an ethnically separate elite group. One was their military organization. The basic unit was the banner—the unit took the name of its flag. There were eight Manchu banners, eight Mongol, and eight Chinese. There were more companies (of 300 men each) in the Manchu banners than in either of the other two; together with their steppe allies, the Mongols, the Manchu troops outnumbered Chinese troops by more than two to one. Furthermore, the Chinese banners were mainly Manchurian Chinese, who had been a part of the regime from its inception. Manchu garrison forces were segregated and were not under the jurisdiction of Chinese officials. They were given stipends and lands to cultivate. They were forbidden to marry Chinese, their children had to study Manchu, and they were not permitted to practice footbinding. In 1668 northern and central Manchuria were cordoned off by a willow palisade as a Manchu strategic tribal territory and closed to Chinese immigrants.

In addition to the Manchu banners, there were also Chinese constabulary forces known as "armies of the green standard." At first the distinction between the banners and the Chinese military was critical. Later, as the dynasty became Sinicized and accepted, the ethnic basis of its military strength became less important.

The second institutional feature of Manchu government was what has been termed "dyarchy": the appointment of two persons, one Chinese and one Manchu, to each key post in the central government. Early in the dynasty the Chinese appointments were often bannermen or bondservants who were personally loyal to the Manchus. At the provincial level Manchu governor-generals oversaw Chinese governors. Most officials and virtually all district magistrates beneath the governors were Chinese.

A particular strength of the Manchu dynasty was the long reigns of two extremely able emperors, Kangxi (1661–1722) and Qianlong (1736–1795). Kangxi was born in 1654, ten years after the start of the dynasty. He ascended the throne at the age of seven, began to rule at thirteen, and held sway until his death in 1722. He was a man of great vigor. He rose at dawn to read memorials (official documents) before beginning his daily routine of audiences with officials. He sired thirty-six sons and twenty daughters by thirty consorts. He presided over palace examinations. Well versed in the Confucian classics, he won the support of scholars by his patronage of the *Ming History*, a new dictionary, and a 5,000-volume encyclopedia.

Kangxi also displayed an interest in European science: He studied with Jesuit court astronomers whom the Qing had inherited from the Ming. He opened four ports to foreign trade and carried out public works, improving the

Emperor Qianlong. The great Manchu emperor Qianlong (r. 1736–1795). *Unidentified Artist. © Metropolitan Museum of Art, Rogers Fund, 1942.*

SOURCE *The Beijing observatory*

dikes on the Huai and Yellow Rivers and dredging the Grand Canal. During his reign he made six tours of China's southern provinces. Kangxi, in short, was a model emperor. But he was also responsible for the various policies that sought to

Chronology

Late Imperial China

Ming Dynasty 1368–1644

1368–1398	Reign of first Ming emperor; Chinese armies invade Manchuria, Mongolia, and eastern Central Asia
1402–1424	Reign of third Ming emperor; Chinese armies invade Vietnam and Mongolia
1405–1433	Voyages of Zheng He to India and Africa
1415	Grand Canal reopened
1472–1529	Wang Yangming, philosopher
1592–1598	Chinese army battles Japanese army in Korea

Qing (Manchu) Dynasty 1644–1911

1668	Manchuria closed to Chinese immigrants (by Willow Palisade)
1661–1722	Reign of Kangxi
1681	Suppression of revolts by Chinese generals
1683	Taiwan captured
1689	China and Russia sign Treaty of Nerchinsk
1736–1795	Reign of Qianlong
1793	Macartney mission

preserve a separate Manchu identity. Like Kublai Khan (r. 1271–1294) before him, he built a summer palace on the plains of Manchuria, where he hunted, hawked, and rode horseback with the freedom of a steppe lord.

Qianlong began his reign in 1736, fourteen years after the death of his grandfather Kangxi, and ruled until 1795. During his reign the Qing dynasty attained its highest level of prosperity and power. Like Kangxi, he was vigorous, wise, conscientious, careful, and hard-working. He visited south China on inspection tours. He patronized scholars on a grand scale: His *Four Treasures* of the classics, treating history, letters, and philosophy, put 15,000 copyists to work for almost fifteen years. (But he also carried out a literary inquisition against works critical of Manchu rule.)

Only in his last years did Qianlong lose his grip and permit a court favorite to practice corruption on an almost unprecedented scale. In 1796 the White Lotus Rebellion broke out. Qianlong's successor put down the rebellion and permitted the corrupt court favorite to take his own life. The

ample financial reserves that had existed throughout the eighteenth century were never reestablished. China nevertheless entered the nineteenth century with its government intact and with a peaceful and stable society. There were few visible signs of what was soon to come.

Ming-Qing Foreign Relations

Ming Some scholars have contended that post-Song China was not an aggressive or imperialist state. They cite its inability to resist foreign conquest; the civility, self-restraint, and gentlemanliness of its officials; and the Song adage that good men should not be used to make soldiers, just as good iron is not used to make nails. The early Ming convincingly disproves this contention. The first Ming emperor (r. 1368–1398) oversaw the vigorous expansion of China's borders. At his death, China controlled the northern steppe from Hami at the gateway of Central Asia to the Sungari River in Manchuria and had regained control of the southern tier of Chinese provinces as well. The Mongols were expelled from Yunnan in 1382 (see Map 19–1).

During the reign of the third Ming emperor (1402–1424), China became even more aggressive. The emperor sent troops into northern Vietnam, which became a Chinese province for two decades. He also personally led five expeditions into the Gobi Desert in pursuit of Mongol troops.

Whenever possible, the third emperor and his successors "managed" China's frontiers with the tribute system. In this system the ambassadors of vassal kings acted out their political subordination to the universal ruler of the celestial kingdom. An ambassador approached the emperor respectfully, performed the kowtow (kneeling three times and each time bowing his head to the floor three times), and presented his gifts. In return, the vassal kings were sent seals confirming their status, given permission to use the Chinese calendar and year-period names, and appointed to the Ming nobility.

The system conferred notable benefits on those willing to participate. While in Beijing the ambassadors were housed and fed in a style appropriate to their status. The gifts they received were often more valuable than those they brought. In addition, they were permitted to trade private goods in the markets of the city. So attractive were these perquisites that some Central Asian merchants invented imaginary kingdoms of which they appointed themselves the emissaries. Eventually China had to set limits on the size, frequency, and cargos of these missions.

The most far-ranging ventures of the third Ming emperor were the maritime expeditions that sailed to Southeast Asia, India, the Arabian Gulf, and East Africa between 1405 and 1433. They were commanded by the eunuch Zheng He, a Muslim from Yunnan (see Map 19–1). The first

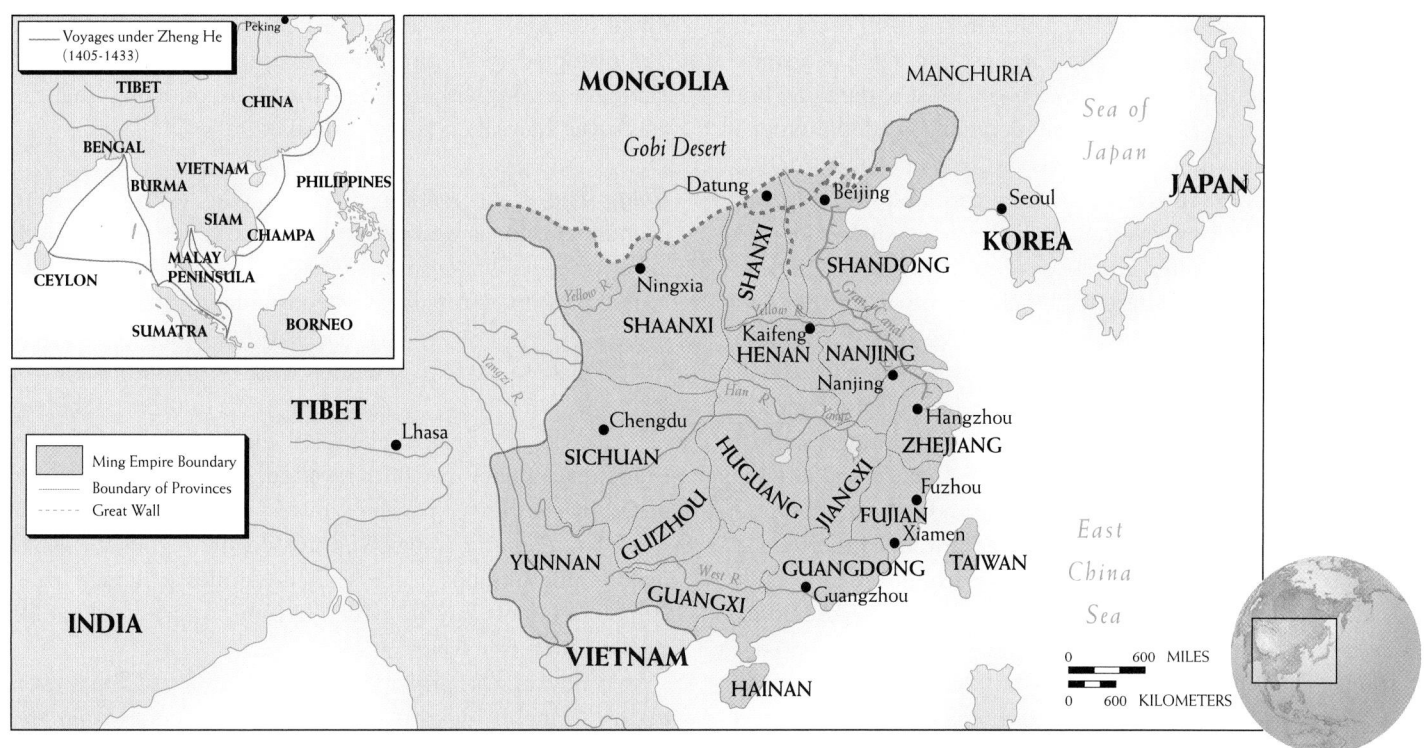

Map 19–1.   The Ming Empire and the Voyages of Zheng He. The inset map shows the voyages of Zheng He to Southeast Asia and India. Some ships of his fleet even reached East Africa. (Zheng himself did not.)

of these armadas had sixty-two major ships and hundreds of smaller vessels and carried 28,000 sailors, soldiers, and merchants. Navigating by compass, the expeditions followed the sea routes of the Arab traders. Trade was not the primary purpose of the expeditions, although some eunuchs used the opportunity to make fortunes, and records show that giraffes, zebras, and other exotic items were presented at the Chinese court. Probably the expeditions were intended to make China's glory known to distant kingdoms and to enroll them in the tribute system. Zheng He's soldiers installed a new king in Java. They captured and brought back to China hostile kings from Borneo and Ceylon, and they signed up nineteen other states as Chinese tributaries.

The expeditions ended as abruptly as they had begun. They were costly and offered little return at a time when the dynasty was fighting in Mongolia and building the new capital at Beijing. What was remarkable about these expeditions was not that they came half a century earlier than the Portuguese voyages of discovery, but that China had the necessary maritime technology and yet decided not to use it. China lacked the combination of restlessness, greed, religious faith, and curiosity that would motivate the Portuguese.

The chief threat to the Ming dynasty was the Mongols. In disarray after the collapse of their rule in China, the Mongols had broken up into eastern, western, and southern tribes. The Chinese, "using the barbarian to control the

Giraffe with Attendant. Some emperors had private zoos and gladly received exotic animals as gifts from tribute states. A painting by Shen Du (1357–1438). *Philadelphia Museum of Art: Given by John T. Dorrance.*

barbarian," made allies of the southern tribes (those settled just north of the Great Wall) against the more fearsome grassland Mongols. This policy worked most of the time, but twice the Mongols formed confederations—pale imitations of the war machine of Genghis—strong enough to defeat Chinese armies: In the 1430s they captured the emperor, and in 1550 they overran Beijing. The Mongol forces involved in the latter attack were defeated by a Chinese army in the 1560s and signed a peace treaty in 1571.

A second foreign threat to the Ming dynasty was the Japanese and the Chinese pirates associated with them. Warrior-lords of decentralized Japan had begun raids on Korea and the northeastern Chinese coast during the thirteenth and early fourteenth centuries; they extended their activities down the coast to southeastern China and beyond during the fifteenth and sixteenth centuries. Hitherto, the coast had been China's most secure frontier. China built defenses and used a scorched-earth policy to make raiding less profitable but mostly had to put up with the depredations. The most serious threat from Japan was its invasions of Korea in 1592 and 1597–1598. Korea resisted with some

initial success. China sent troops only after Japanese armies had occupied the entire Korean peninsula. Eventually the Japanese armies withdrew, but the strain on Ming finances had severely weakened the dynasty.

Qing The final foreign threat to the Ming was the Manchus, who, as we have seen, were the mouse that swallowed the elephant. After coming to power in 1644, the Manchu court spent decades consolidating its rule within

SOURCE *Letters of Zheng Zhilong*

China. The last Ming prince was pursued into Burma and killed in 1662. But then the three Chinese generals who had helped the Manchus conquer the south revolted. The Qing was also opposed by the Sino-Japanese pirate state of Koxinga on Taiwan. The emperor Kangxi suppressed the revolts by 1681; most Chinese troops in the Manchu armies remained loyal. In 1683 he took Taiwan, which became a part of China for the first time (see Map 19–2).

As always, the principal foreign threats to China, even to the Manchu dynasty, which had itself come from the

Map 19–2. The Qing Empire at its Peak. The Willow Palisade was the line of demarcation between the Manchurian homeland of the Qing rulers and China. Chinese were excluded from Manchuria.

north, came from the north and northwest. Russia had begun expanding east across Siberia and south against the remnants of the Golden Horde during the reign of Ivan the Terrible (1533–1584). By the 1660s Russian traders, trappers, and adventurers had reached northern Manchuria, where they built forts and traded with the eastern Mongols. One is reminded of the French penetration of Canada during the same decades. To prevent a rapprochement between the Russians and Mongols, Kangxi set up military colonies in Manchuria during the 1680s and drove the Russians from the lower Amur River. This victory during the early years of the reign of Peter the Great (1682–1725) led to the 1689 Treaty of Nerchinsk. Negotiated with the assistance of Jesuit translators, this treaty excluded Russia from northern Manchuria while permitting its caravans to visit Beijing.

In the west the situation was more complex, with a three-corner relationship among Russia, the western Mongols, and Tibet. Kangxi, and then Qianlong, campaigned against the Mongols, invaded Tibet, and in 1727 signed a new treaty with Russia. During the campaigns the Chinese temporarily came to control millions of square miles of new territories. These areas became protectorates under a "barbarian management office," separate from the administration for China itself. It is a telling comment on the persistence of the Chinese concept of empire that ever since that time, even after China's borders contracted during the nineteenth century, the Chinese have insisted that the Manchu conquests of non-Chinese peoples define their legitimate borders.

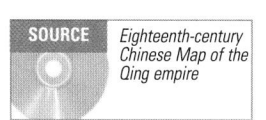 SOURCE *Eighteenth-century Chinese Map of the Qing empire*

The roots of the present-day contention over borders between China and the countries of the former Soviet Union go back to these events during the eighteenth century, as does the Chinese claim to Tibet.

Contacts with the West Europeans had made their way to China during the Tang and the Yuan dynasties. But only with Europe's oceanic expansion in the sixteenth century did they arrive in large numbers. Some came as missionaries, of whom the most calculating, disciplined, enterprising, and successful were the Jesuits. On first arriving in Ming China, they put on the robes of the Buddhist monk; on learning something of the country, they switched to the gowns of the Confucian scholar. They studied Chinese and the Confucian classics and engaged in conversations with scholars. They used their knowledge of astronomy, geography, engraving, and firearms to win entry to the court at Beijing and appointments in the bureau of astronomy.

When the Manchus came to power in 1644, the Jesuits kept their position. They appealed to the curiosity of the court with instruments such as telescopes, clocks, and clavichords. They tried to propagate Christianity. They attacked

Jesuit Missionary. A late seventeenth-century color engraving of the Jesuit missionary Johann Adam Schall depicts him in traditional Confucian dress holding a sextant and a compass. A globe is behind him on the left.

Daoism and Buddhism as superstitions but argued that Confucianism as a rational philosophy complemented Christianity, just as Aristotle's teaching complemented Christian theology in Europe. They handled the problem of the Confucian rites of ancestor worship by interpreting them as secular and nonantagonistic to Christianity. A few high court officials were converted. Kangxi was sympathetic to the scholarly personalities of the Jesuits and appreciated the cannon they cast

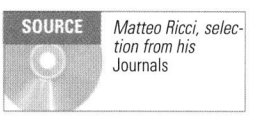 SOURCE *Matteo Ricci, selection from his Journals*

but was unsympathetic to their religion: "I had asked [the Jesuit] Verbiest why God had not forgiven his son without making him die, but though he had tried to answer I had not understood him.[2]

Meanwhile, their Franciscan and Dominican rivals had reported to Rome that the Jesuits condoned the Confucian rites. The ensuing debate was long and complex, but in the end, papal bulls issued in 1715 and 1742 decided against the Jesuits and forbade Chinese Christians to participate in the family rites of ancestor worship. Thereupon the emperor banned Christianity in China, churches were seized, missionaries were forced to flee, and congregations declined.

Other Europeans came to China to trade. The Portuguese came first in the early sixteenth century but behaved badly and were expelled. They returned in midcen-

[2] J. Spence, *Emperor of China: Self-Portrait of K'ang-Hsi* (New York: Alfred A. Knopf, 1974), p. 84.

Qianlong's Edict to King George III of England

Document

The Chinese emperor rejected the requests of the 1793 Macartney mission for change in the restrictive Canton system. His edict reflects the Chinese sense of their superiority to other peoples and their belief that China was the "central kingdom" of the world.

◆ What philosophical principles underlie the emperor's sense of superiority?

You, O King, are so inclined toward our civilization that you have sent a special envoy across the seas to bring to our Court your memorial of congratulations on the occasion of my birthday and to present your native products as an expression of your thoughtfulness. On perusing your memorial, so simply worded and sincerely conceived, I am impressed by your genuine respectfulness and friendliness and greatly pleased. . . .

The Celestial Court has pacified and possessed the territory within the four seas. Its sole aim is to do its utmost to achieve good government and to manage political affairs, attaching no value to strange jewels and precious objects. The various articles presented by you, O King, this time are accepted by my special order to the office in charge of such functions in consideration of the offerings having come from a long distance with sincere good wishes. As a matter of fact, the virtue and prestige of the Celestial Dynasty having spread far and wide, the kings of the myriad nations come by land and sea with all sorts of precious things. Consequently there is nothing we lack, as your principal envoy and others have themselves observed. We have never set much store on strange or ingenious objects, nor do we need any more of your country's manufactures. . . .

Reprinted by permission of the publisher from *China's Response to the West: A Documentary Survey, 1839–1923,* by Ssu-yu Teng and John K. Fairbank, pp. 24–27, 155–156, 240–241. Cambridge, MA: Harvard University Press. Copyright © 1954, 1979 by the President and Fellows of Harvard College.

tury and were permitted to trade on a tiny peninsula at Macao that was walled off from China. They were followed by Dutch from the East Indies (Indonesia), by the British East India Company in 1699, and by Americans in 1784.

At first the Westerners mingled with ships from Southeast Asia in a fairly open multiport pattern of trade. Then, during the early eighteenth century, the more restrictive "Canton system" evolved. Westerners could trade only at Guangzhou—or

SOURCE *View of Guangzhou*

"Canton" as it was known to Westerners. They were barred from entering the city proper but were assigned land outside its walls along the river. They could not bring their wives to China. They were subject to the harsh dispositions of Chinese law. They were under the control of official merchant guilds. Nevertheless, the trade was profitable to both sides.

The British East India Company developed a triangular commerce among China, India, and Britain that enabled the English to drink tea and wear silk. Private fortunes were built. For China this trade produced a huge influx of specie, and the Chinese officials in charge grew immensely wealthy. Chafing under the various restrictions, the British government in 1793 sent the Macartney mission to China to nego-

tiate the opening of other ports, fixed tariffs, representation at Beijing, and so on. The emperor Qianlong graciously permitted Lord Macartney (1736–1806) to present his gifts—which the Chinese described as tribute, even though Macartney refused to perform the kowtow—but he turned down Macartney's requests. (See Document, "Qianlong's Edict to King George III of England.") Western trade remained encapsulated at Guangzhou, distant from Beijing and little noted elsewhere in China.

Ming-Qing Culture

One thing that can be said of Ming-Qing culture, like population or agricultural productivity, is that there was more of it. Whether considering gentry, scholar officials, or a professionalized class of literati, their numbers and works were far greater than in previous dynasties. Even local literary figures or philosophers were likely to publish their collected works or have them published by admiring disciples. Bookstores came of age in the Ming, selling the Confucian classics; commentaries on them; collections of Tang and Song poetry; and also colored prints, novels, erotica, and model answers for the civil service examinations.

Chinese culture had begun to turn inward during the Song in reaction to Buddhism. This tendency was accelerated by the Chinese antipathy to Mongol rule and continued into the Ming and Qing, when Chinese culture became virtually impervious to outside influences. Even works on mathematics and science translated into Chinese by the Jesuits left few traces in Chinese scholarly writings. Chinese cultural self-sufficiency, of course, reflected a tradition and a social order that had stood the test of time, but it also indicated a closed system of ideas with weaknesses that would become apparent in the nineteenth century. Orthodox thought during these five centuries was Zhu Xi Neo-Confucianism. From the mid- to the late Ming, some perturbations were caused by the Zen-like teachings of the philosopher Wang Yangming (1472–1529), whose activism caused him to be jailed, beaten, and exiled at one point in an otherwise illustrious official career.

Several other original thinkers' refusal to accept bureaucratic posts under the Qing won them plaudits during the anti-Manchu nationalism of the early twentieth century, but they had only a limited influence on their own times. The most interesting was Gu Yanwu, who wrote on both philology and statecraft. He used philology and historical phonetics to get at the original meanings of the classics and contrasted their practical ethics with the "empty words" of Wang Yangming. Gu's successors extended his philological studies, developing empirical methods for textual studies, but lost sight of their implications for politics. The Manchus clamped down on unorthodox thought, and the seventeenth-century burst of creativity guttered out into a narrow, bookish, conservative scholasticism. Not until the end of the nineteenth century did thinkers draw from these studies the kind of radical inferences that philological studies of the Bible had produced in Europe.

Ming and Qing Chinese esteemed most highly, and not without reason, the traditional categories of high culture: painting, calligraphy, poetry, and philosophy. Porcelains of great beauty were also produced. In the early Ming the blue-on-white glazes predominated. During the later Ming and Qing more decorative wares with enamel painted over the glaze became widespread. The pottery industry of Europe was begun during the sixteenth century to imitate these wares, and Chinese and Japanese influences have dominated Western ceramics down to the present. Chinese today, however, look back and see the novel as the characteristic cultural achievement of the Ming and Qing.

The novel in China grew out of plot-books used by earlier storytellers. Like the stories, Chinese novels consisted of episodes strung together, and chapters in early novels often ended with an admonition to the reader not to miss the next exciting development. Ming and Qing novels were

Ming Dynasty Ink Painting by Wu Wei (1479–1508). The seated human figure is a part of the tranquility of nature. Nature, densely concentrated at the left and lower portions of the painting, stretches off into space in the middle and upper-right portion. *Wu Wei, "Scholar Seated Under a Tree," China. Ink and traces of color on silk. Courtesy of Museum of Fine Arts, Boston.*

usually written by scholars who had failed the examinations, which may account for their caustic comments on officials. As most novels were written in colloquial Chinese, which was not quite respectable in the society of scholars, their authors wrote under pseudonyms.

Two collections of lively short stories are available in English: *Stories from a Ming Collection* and *The Courtesan's Jewel Box*. Many other stories were pornographic. In fact, the Ming may have invented the humorous pornographic novel. One example available in English is *The Carnal Prayer Mat*. This genre was suppressed in China during the Qing and rediscovered in Japanese collections in the twentieth century.

Short descriptions of several major novels may convey something of their flavor:

1. *The Romance of the Three Kingdoms*, published in 1522, tells of the political and military struggles in China in the aftermath of the Han dynasty. Like Shakespeare, the author, whose identity is uncertain, used a historical setting to create a dramatic world in which human character determines the outcome of events. More than twenty editions had appeared by the end of the Ming, and the novel was also extremely popular in Japan and Korea.

2. *All Men Are Brothers* (also translated as *The Water Margin*) tells of 108 bandit heroes who flee government repression during the late northern Song, establish a hideout on a mountain amid marshes, and like Robin Hood, avenge the wrongs perpetrated by corrupt officials. Separate episodes tell why each had to leave society and of their many daring and funny adventures. Of all Chinese novels, this was the most popular. It was officially banned as subversive during the Qing but was widely read nonetheless.

3. *The Golden Lotus* is a pornographic novel about the sexual adventures of an urban merchant. It gives vivid descriptions of individual women and satirical descriptions of venal officials and greedy monks. In the end the hero dies of his excesses and his family—all six wives and their children—disintegrates. The early English translation of this novel had long passages in Latin to protect those whose minds were not disciplined by the study of that language. Despite its literary merits, the book, like all of its genre, was proscribed during the era of Mao Zedong. In the recent decade it has become available again.

4. *The Dream of the Red Chamber* (also translated as *The Story of the Stone*) is generally considered China's greatest novel. It tells the story of a youth growing up in a wealthy but declining family during the early Qing. Critics praise its subtlety and psychological insight. Anthropologists mine the novel for information on the Chinese extended family and for its depiction of social relations. Like other Ming and Qing novels, it was recognized as a respectable work of art only during the twentieth century, after Western novels entered China.

5. *The Scholars* is a social satire of the early Qing that pokes fun at scholars and officials. (See Document, "A Star in Heaven.")

JAPAN

The two segments of "late traditional" Japan could not be more different. The Warring States era (1467–1600), really the last phase of Japan's medieval history, saw the unleashing of internal wars and anarchy that scourged the old society from the bottom up. Within a century all vestiges of the old manorial or estate system had been scrapped and virtually all of the Ashikaga lords had been overthrown. The Tokugawa era (1600–1868) that followed saw Japan reunited and stable, with a more competent government than ever. The culture was also brilliantly transformed, preparing it for the challenge it would face during the mid–nineteenth century.

Warring States Era (1467–1600)

War is the universal solvent of old institutions. Nowhere in history was this clearer than in Japan between 1467 and 1600. In 1467 a dispute arose over who would be the next Ashikaga shōgun. The dispute led to war between two territorial lords who supported the respective contenders. Other lords used the opportunity to gain territory at the expense of weaker neighbors, and wars raged throughout Japan for eleven years. Most of Kyoto was destroyed in the fighting, and the authority of the Ashikaga *bakufu* came to an end. This first war ended in 1477, but the fighting resumed and continued for more than a century.

War of All Against All

Even before 1467 the Ashikaga equilibrium had been precarious. Regional **daimyo** lords had relied on their relationship to the *bakufu* to hold their stronger vassals in check, while relying on these vassals to preserve their independence against strong neighbors. The collapse of *bakufu* authority after 1467 pulled the linchpin from the system. It left the regional lords standing alone, removing the last barrier to internecine wars.

The regional lords, however, were too weak to stand alone. A region was a hodgepodge of competing jurisdictions. Lands might be "public," or in estates, and some were starting to look like private fiefs. Revenues might be paid to nobles in Kyoto, to regional lords, or to local samurai strongmen. Most regions contained military bands that were not the vassals of the daimyo. Several daimyo had lands in the territories of other lords. Occasionally vassals were militarily more powerful than their daimyo lords. Some local vassals commanded bands of village warriors. Once the regional daimyo were forced to stand alone, they became prey to the stronger among their vassals as well as to neighboring states.

By the end of the sixteenth century all Ashikaga daimyo had fallen, with one exception in remote southern Kyushu. In their place emerged hundreds of little "Warring States daimyo," each with his own warrior band. In one prefecture along the Inland Sea, the remains of 200 hillside castles of such daimyo have been identified. The constant wars among these men were not unlike those of the early feudal era in Europe.

A Star in Heaven

Among the officials whose stories are told in *The Scholars* is Fan Chin, thin and sallow with a grizzled beard and threadbare linen gown, who finally passes the county examination at the age of fifty-four. On his return home, he is given a feast and advice by his domineering father-in-law, Butcher Hu. But when Fan Chin asks Hu for money to travel to the provincial examination, he gets the following reaction.

◆ Why did a satire such as *The Scholars* not undermine the premises on which Qing society rested?

Butcher Hu spat in his face and let loose a stream of abuse. "Don't forget who you are!" he bellowed. "Just passing one examination and you become like a toad thinking to dine on the flesh of a swan. I hear you passed the examination not because of your essay, but because the examiner took pity on your old age. Now, like a fool, you aspire to be an official. Don't you know that those who have passed the higher examination are all stars in heaven! Haven't you seen the Changs in the city? Those officials all have tons of money and generously proportioned faces and ears. Now look at you with your protruding mouth and monkey chin. Piss on the ground and take a good look at yourself in the puddle! A miserable creature like you can't even hope to swallow a swan's fart! Forget it!

[Fan Chin takes the examination anyway. When he returns home, he discovers that his family has been hungry for two days. Fan goes to the market to sell a chicken. In the meantime, heralds on horseback arrive to proclaim he has passed the provincial examination. Returning home, Fan sees the posted announcement and falls into a dead faint. When revived, he begins ranting incoherently. A herald suggests that Butcher Hu, whom Fan fears, bring him to his senses with a slap. Butcher Hu demurs.]

"He may be my son-in-law," he said, "but now he has become a member of the gentry, a star in heaven. How can I hit a star in heaven? I've heard from Buddhist priests that whoever strikes a star in heaven will be carried away by the King of Hell, struck one hundred times with an iron rod, consigned to the eighteenth hell, and never return to human form again. I wouldn't dare do it."

[Eventually Butcher Hu slaps him, and Fan recovers in time to receive a visit from a member of the local gentry, who is wearing "an official's gauze cap, sunflower-coloured gown, gilt belt and black shoes." "Sir," he says to Fan, "although we live in the same district, I regret that we have never become acquainted." After paying his respects, the visitor presents Fan with fifty taels of silver and a more appropriate house. Soon others give him land, goods, money, rice, and servants. The chapter ends with the maids cleaning up under the supervision of Fan Chin's wife after several days of feasting. Fan Chin's mother enters the courtyard.]

"You must be very careful," the old lady warned her daughter-in-law and the maids. "These things all belong to someone else, so don't break them."

The maids replied:" How can you say they belong to others, madam? They all belong to you."

"Oh no! How could our house have such things?" she said with a smile. "How can you talk of their belonging to others?" the maids replied in unison. "And not only these things, but all of us and the house, too, belong to you."

When the old lady heard this, she picked up the bowls and dishes of fine porcelain and the cups and chopsticks inlaid with silver and examined them one by one. She burbled: "These things are all mine." Laughing wildly, she fell over backward, choked on phlegm, and lost consciousness.

If you want to know what became of the old lady, please read the next chapter.

Translation by Shang Wei.

A Japanese term for "survival of the fittest"—"the strong eat and the weak become the meat"—is often applied to this century of warfare. Of the daimyo bands, the most efficient in revamping their domain for military ends survived. The less ruthless, who clung to old ways, were defeated and absorbed. It was an age, as one Warring States general put it, "when only muscle counts." Another said, "The warrior doesn't care if he's called a dog or beast, the main thing is winning.[3]

Early in this period, when there were hundreds of small states, castles were built on a bluff above a river or on a

---

[3] G. Elison and B. L. Smith, eds., *Warlords, Artists, and Commoners* (Honolulu: Hawaii University Press, 1981), p. 57.

Daimyo Castle. Construction of the "White Heron" castle in Himeji was begun during the Warring States era and was completed shortly after 1600. During the Tokugawa peace, it remained as a monument to the glory of the daimyo. Today it can be seen from the "bullet train." *Morris Simoncelli, Japan Airlines Photo.*

mountainside with natural defenses against surprise attacks. Inuyama Castle, today a thirty-minute bus ride from Nagoya, is the most impressive surviving example.

As fighting continued, hundreds of local states gave way to tens of regional states. The castles of such regional states were often located on plains, and as castle towns grew up around them, merchants flocked to supply the needs of their growing soldiery. Eventually, alliances of these regional states fought it out, until in the late sixteenth century all of Japan was brought under the hegemony of a single lord. Oda Nobunaga (1534–1582) completed the initial unification of central Honshu and would have finished the job had a treacherous vassal not assassinated him in 1582. Toyotomi Hideyoshi (1536–1598), who had begun life as a lowly foot soldier, completed the unification in 1590. After his death his vassal generals once again went to war, and it was only with the victory of Tokugawa Ieyasu (1542–1616) at the Battle of Sekigahara in 1600 that true unification was finally achieved. Ieyasu's unification of 1600 superficially resembled that of the Minamoto in 1185 but was in fact based on a sweeping transformation of Japan's society.

Foot Soldier Revolution

During the Warring States period, the foot soldier replaced the aristocratic mounted warrior as the backbone of the military in Japan. Soldiers were still called *samurai*. They were still the vassals of daimyo or, sometimes, the vassals of vassals

of daimyo, but their numbers, social status, and techniques of warfare changed dramatically. As a result, Japanese society changed from what it had been only a century earlier.

The changes began on the land. Ashikaga daimyo had diverted more and more land revenues for their own use, but Warring States daimyo took them all. Public lands and estates, including those of the imperial house, were seized and converted into fiefs. Soldiers were paid stipends from the revenues of the daimyo's lands, and important vassals, usually the officers or commanders of the daimyo's army, were awarded fiefs of their own. The governance of fiefs was essentially private, in the hands of the fief holder.

Inheritance patterns changed to fit the new circumstances. Multigeniture—the division of a warrior's rights to revenues from land among his children—was not appropriate to a society with a hereditary military class. It had impoverished the Kamakura vassals. To protect the integrity of the warrior's household economy, multigeniture had begun to give way to single inheritance during the Ashikaga period. After 1467 single inheritance became universal. As the fief was often passed to the most able son, not necessarily the eldest, the pattern is usually called *unigeniture* rather than *primogeniture*.

With larger revenues, Warring States daimyo built bigger armies. They recruited mainly from the peasantry. Some of the new soldiers moved to the castle town of the daimyo. Others lived on the land or remained in their villages, farming in peace and fighting in war. The growth of the military class had begun earlier. Accounts of twelfth-century battles tell of fighting by tens of hundreds of warriors, sometimes more. Scroll paintings of the Heiji wars corroborate these figures. By the fourteenth century battles involved thousands or tens of thousands of troops. By the late sixteenth century hundreds of thousands were deployed in major campaigns. Screen paintings show massed troops in fixed emplacements with officers riding about on horseback. Of course, special cavalry strike forces were still used.

In the mid–fourteenth century a new weapon was developed: a thrusting spear with a thick shaft and a heavy chisel-like blade. Held in both hands, it could penetrate medieval armor as a sword could not. It could also be swung about like a quarterstaff. It was used by soldiers positioned at intervals of three feet, in a pincushion tactic to impale charging cavalry. The weapon spelled the end of the aristocratic warrior in Japan, just as the pikes used by Swiss soldiers ended knighthood in northern Europe during the fifteenth century. After 1467 this spear became the principal weapon of Warring States Japan. Not surprisingly, its spread coincided with the recruitment of peasant soldiers, for it required only short training. By the early sixteenth century it was every warrior's dream to be the "number one spearman" of his lord. Even generals trained in its use. One famous general wrote that "one hundred spearmen are more effective than ten thousand swords."

A second change in military technology was the introduction of the musket by the Portuguese in the mid–sixteenth century. Warring States generals quickly adopted it. Its superiority was proved in the Battle of Nagashino in 1575, in which Oda Nobunaga and Tokugawa Ieyasu used spear and musket platoons against the cavalry of a famous military tactician. Massing 3,000 muskets behind a bamboo barrier-fence and firing in volleys, Nobunaga decimated the forces of his enemy. As individual combat gave way to mass armies, warfare became pitiless, cruel, and bloody.

How, then, should one characterize the society that emerged from the Warring States? Does the word *feudal* apply, with its suggestion of lords and vassals and manorial life on the fiefs of aristocratic warriors? In some respects, it does: By the late sixteenth century all warriors in Japan were part of a pyramid of vassals and lords headed by a single overlord; warriors of rank held fiefs and vassals of their own.

In other respects Japan resembled postfeudal Europe. First, most of the military class was soldiers, not aristocrats. Even though they were called samurai and were vassals, they were something new. They were not given fiefs but were paid

SOURCE *Tokugawa Shogunate, The Lans for the Military House, 1615*

with stipends of so many bales of rice. Second, unlike, say, feudal England, where the military class was about one quarter of 1 percent of the population, in mid–sixteenth-century Japan it may have reached 7 or 8 percent. It was more of a size with the

Chronology

Warring States Japan and the Era of Unification (1467–1600)

1467–1568	Battles throughout Japan
1543	Portuguese arrive in Japan
1568	Oda Nobunaga takes Kyoto and partially unifies Japan
1575	Battle of Nagashino
1582	Nobunaga assassinated
1588	Hideyoshi starts sword hunt
1590	Hideyoshi completes unification
1592, 1597–1598	Hideyoshi sends armies to Korea
1597	Hideyoshi bans Christianity
1598	Hideyoshi dies, his generals battle for succession
1600	Battle of Sekigahara; Tokugawa Ieyasu reunifies Japan

mercenary armies of Europe during the fifteenth or sixteenth centuries. Third, the recruitment of village warriors added significantly to the power of Warring States daimyo but gave rise to problems as well. Taxes became harder to collect. Local samurai were often involved in uprisings. When organized by Pure Land Buddhist congregations, these uprisings sometimes involved whole provinces. Again, the parallels with postfeudal Europe seem closer. Fourth, even in a feudal society, not everything is feudal. The commercial growth of the Kamakura and Ashikaga periods continued through the dark decades of the Warring States era.

Foreign Relations and Trade

Japanese pirate-traders plied the seas of East Asia during the fifteenth and sixteenth centuries. To halt their depredations, the Ming emperor invited the third Ashikaga shōgun to trade with China. An agreement was reached in 1404 and the shōgun was appointed the "King of Japan." During the next century and a half, periodic "tribute missions" were sent to China. The opening of official trade channels did not, however, end piracy. It stopped only after Japan was reunified at the close of the sixteenth century.

The content of the trade reflected the progress of Japanese crafts. Early Japanese exports to China were raw materials such as raw copper, sulfur, or silver, but by the sixteenth century manufactured goods were rising in importance and included swords, spears, wine bottles, folding fans, picture scrolls, screen paintings, ink slabs, and the like. In exchange, Japan received copper cash, porcelains, paintings, books, and medicines.

After establishing his hegemony over Japan, Hideyoshi permitted only ships with his vermilion seal to trade with China, a policy the Tokugawa continued. Between 1604 and 1635 over 350 ships went to China in this "vermilion-seal trade." Then, in 1635, the imposition of seclusion ended Japan's foreign trade: No Japanese could leave Japan; the construction of large ships was prohibited; trade with the continent was limited to a small community of Chinese merchants in Nagasaki, and to quiet trading with China and Korea through the Ryukyu and Tsushima Islands.

Overlapping Japan's maritime expansion in the seas of East Asia was the arrival of European ships. Portuguese pirate-traders made their way to Goa in India, to Malacca, to Macao in China, and arrived in Japan in 1543. Spanish galleons came in 1587 via Mexico and the Philippines. These eastern and western waves of Iberian expansion were followed by the Dutch and the English after the turn of the century.

The Portuguese, from a tiny country with a population of 1.5 million, were motivated by a desire for booty and profits and by religious zeal. Their ships were superior. Taking advantage of the Chinese ban on maritime commerce, they became important as shippers. They carried Southeast Asian goods and Japanese silver to China and Chinese silk to Japan and then used their profits to buy Southeast Asian spices for the European market. The Portuguese, initially at least, found it easier to trade with the daimyo of a disunited Japan than to deal with the authorities of a united China. A few Kyushu daimyo, thinking to attract Portuguese traders, even converted to Christianity.

Traders brought with them Jesuit missionaries. The Society of Jesus had been founded in 1540 to act as soldiers in the pope's campaign against the Reformation. Only nine years later Saint Francis Xavier (1506–1552) arrived in Japan. He soon wrote back that the Japanese were "the best [people] who have yet been discovered." Another Jesuit wrote that the Japanese "are all white, courteous, and highly civilized, so much so that they surpass all other known races of the world." The Japanese, for their part, also appeared to admire the Jesuits for their asceticism, devoutness, and learning.

As they had attempted to convert scholar-officials in China, so the Jesuits in Japan directed their efforts towards

SOURCE *Japan encounters the West*

Arrival of the Portuguese in Japan. Portuguese merchants arrived in Japan in 1543 from India and the East Indies. Their crews were multiethnic, and they brought Jesuit priests as well. *"Arrival of the Portuguese in Japan" Detail—central section of the boat, 1594–1618. Screen. Paint, gold, paper. Museo Soares Dos Reis, Porto, Portugal. Bridgeman-Giraudon/Art Resource, N.Y.*

the samurai. Moving to Kyoto, they won the favor of Nobunaga, who was engaged in campaigns against warrior monks on Mount Hiei and against Pure Land strongholds in Osaka. Portuguese and Christian objects became fashionable. Painters produced "Southern Barbarian screens" that depicted the "black ships" of the Portuguese. Christian symbols were used on lacquer boxes and saddles. Nobunaga himself occasionally wore Portuguese clothes and a cross and said he might become a Christian if only the Jesuits would drop their insistence on monogamy. Christian converts increased from a few in the early years to 130,000 in 1579, and to about 300,000 in 1600. That is to say, in the late sixteenth century a higher percentage of Japanese were Christian than today.

It is difficult to explain why Christianity met with greater success in Japan than in other Asian lands. When introduced, it was seen as a new Buddhist sect. There seemed little difference to the Japanese between the cosmic Buddha of Shingon and the Christian God, between the paradise of Amida and the Christian heaven, or between prayers to Kannon—the female *bodhisattva* of mercy—and to the Virgin Mary. The Japanese also noted the theological similarity between the pietism of the Pure Land sect and that of Christianity. To Japanese ears, the passage in Romans 10:13, "whosoever shall call upon the name of the Lord shall be saved," was reminiscent of the Pure Land practice of invoking the name of Amida. The Jesuits, too, noted these parallels and felt that the devil had established these sects in Japan to test their faith. Xavier, who, despite his admirable personal characteristics, was narrow-minded, referred to the historical Buddha and Amida as "two demons." Although this intolerance gave rise to certain tensions and animosities, Christianity spread, and to no small measure as a result of the personal example of the Jesuits.

The fortunes of Christianity began to decline in 1597, when Hideyoshi banned Christianity and had six Spanish Franciscans and twenty Japanese converts crucified in Nagasaki. Hideyoshi was aware of Spanish colonialism in the Philippines, and it was rumored that a Spanish pilot had boasted that merchants and priests represented the first step towards the conquest of Japan. Sporadic persecutions continued until 1614, when Tokugawa Ieyasu began a serious movement to extirpate the foreign religion. Faced with torture, some Christians recanted. More than 3,000 others were martyred.

The last resistance was an uprising near Nagasaki in 1637 and 1638 in which 37,000 Christians died. After that, Christianity survived in Japan only as a hidden religion with secret rites and devotions to "Maria-Kannon," the mother of Jesus represented or disguised as the Buddhist goddess of mercy holding a child in her arms. A few of these "hidden Christians" reemerged in the later nineteenth century. Otherwise, apart from muskets and techniques of castle building, all that remained of the Portuguese influence were certain loan words that became a permanent part of the Japanese language: *pan* for bread, *birōdo* for velvet, *kasutera* for sponge cake, *karuta* for playing cards, and *tempura* for that familiar Japanese dish.

SOURCE *Jesuit Martyrs in Japan*

Tokugawa Era (1600–1868)

Political Engineering and Economic Growth During the Seventeenth Century

From 1467 to 1590 Japan's energies were absorbed in ever bigger wars. But after the unifications of 1590 and 1600 Japan's leaders sought to create a peaceful, stable, orderly society. Like a great tanker that requires many times its

"Picture-treading" Plaque. *Fumi-e,* or "picture-treading" plaques are bronze images representing Christ or the Virgin, used by the Tokugawa with increasing intensity from 1614 onward to extirpate the foreign religion. In the *fumi-e* ceremony suspected converts were obliged to tread on the plaques to show that they rejected Christianity.

own length to come about, Japan made this transition slowly. Many of the values and habits of mind of the Warring States era continued into the seventeenth century. By the middle or late seventeenth century, however, its society and political system had been radically reengineered. Vigorous economic and demographic growth had also occurred. This combination of political and economic change made the seventeenth century a period of great dynamism.

Hideyoshi's Rule One pressing problem faced by Japan's unifiers was how to cope with an armed peasantry. In war, village warriors fought for their lord: The benefit they offered the lord was greater than their cost. In peace, only the cost remained: their resistance to taxation and the threat of local uprisings. Accordingly, in the summer of 1588 Hideyoshi ordered a "sword hunt" to disarm the peasants. Records of the collected weaponry exist for only one county of 3,400 households in Kaga, a domain on the Sea of Japan: 1,073 swords, 1,540 short swords, 700 daggers, 160 spears, 500 suits of armor, and other miscellaneous items. Once the hunt was completed, the 5 percent of the population who remained samurai used their monopoly on weapons to control the other 95 percent.

Hideyoshi next moved to freeze the social classes. Samurai were prohibited from quitting the service of their lord. Peasants were barred from abandoning their fields to become townspeople. This policy was continued by the Tokugawa after 1600, and by and large succeeded. Samurai, farmers, and townspeople tended to marry within their respective classes, and each class developed a unique cultural character. The authorities even attempted to dictate lifestyles, prescribing who could ride in palanquins, who could wear silk, and who was permitted to build fancy gates in front of their houses.

But to grasp the class structure of Tokugawa society, we must note the vast range of social gradations within each class. A farmer who was a landlord and a district official was a more important figure than most lower samurai and lived in a different social world from a landless "water-drinking" peasant too poor to buy tea. A townsman could be the head of a great wholesale house, or a humble street peddler or clog mender. A samurai could be an elder, a key decision maker of his domain, with an income of thousands of bushels of rice and several hundred vassals of his own, or an impecunious foot soldier who stood guard at the castle gate.

Having disarmed the peasantry, Hideyoshi ordered cadastral surveys on his own lands and on those of his vassals. The surveys defined each parcel of land by location, size, soil quality, product, and cultivator's name. For the first time, an attempt was made to standardize the rods used to measure land and the boxes used to measure quantities of rice. These standards marked the beginning of the detailed record keeping that characterized the Tokugawa era. Hideyoshi's survey laid the foundations for a systematic land tax. Based on these surveys, domains and fiefs were henceforth ranked in terms of their assessed yield.

Establishment of Tokugawa Rule Bedazzled by his own power and military successes, and against all the evidence of Warring States political behavior, Hideyoshi assumed that his vassals would honor their sworn oaths of loyalty to his heir. He was especially trustful of his great ally Tokugawa Ieyasu, whose domains were larger than his own. His trust was misplaced. After his death in 1598, Hideyoshi's former vassals, paying little attention to his heir, broke apart into two opposing camps and fought a great battle in 1600 from which the alliance headed by Tokugawa Ieyasu emerged victorious. Ieyasu was wise, effective in maintaining alliances, and a master strategist, but above all patient. In comparing the three unifiers, the Japanese tell the story that when a cuckoo failed to sing, Nobunaga said, "I'll kill it if it doesn't sing"; Hideyoshi said, "I'll make it sing"; but Ieyasu sat down and said, "I'll wait until it sings."

Like the Minamoto of twelfth-century Kamakura, Ieyasu spurned the Kyoto court and established his headquarters in Edo (today's Tokyo), in the center of his military holdings in eastern Japan (see Map 19–3). He took the title of shōgun in 1603 and called his government the *bakufu*. In Edo he built a great castle, surrounded by massive fortifications of stone and concentric moats. The inner portion of these moats and stone walls remains today as the Imperial Palace. Ieyasu then used his military power to reorganize Japan.

Ieyasu's first move was to confiscate the lands of his defeated enemies and to reward his vassals and allies. During the first quarter of the seventeenth century the *bakufu* confiscated the domains of 150 daimyo, some of former enemies and some for infractions of the Tokugawa legal code, and transferred 229 daimyo from one domain to another. The transfers completed the work of Hideyoshi's sword hunt by severing long-standing ties between daimyo and their disarmed former village retainers. When a daimyo was transferred to a new fief, he took his samurai retainers with him. During the second quarter of the seventeenth century transfers and confiscations ended and the system settled down.

The reshuffling of domains had not been random. The configuration that emerged was, first, of a huge central Tokugawa domain. It contained the following: most of the domains of "house daimyo"—those who had been Tokugawa vassals before 1600; the fiefs of the 5,000 Tokugawa bannermen (upper samurai); and the lands that furnished the stipends of the other 17,000 Tokugawa direct retainers (middle and lower samurai). Then, strategically placed around the Tokugawa heartland were the domains of the "related daimyo." These domains had been founded by the second and third sons of early shōgun and furnished a successor to the main Tokugawa line when a shōgun had no heir. Beyond the related daimyo was a second tier of "outside daimyo" who had fought as allies of Tokugawa Ieyasu in 1600 but became his vassals only after the battle was over.

Finally, at the antipodes of the system were those outside daimyo who had been permitted to survive despite having fought against the Tokugawa in 1600. Their domains were drastically reduced. They remained the "enemies" within the system, although they had submitted and become Tokugawa vassals after 1600. Thus, the entire layout of domains constituted a defensive system, with the staunchest Tokugawa supporters nearest to the center.

The Tokugawa also established other systemic controls. Legal codes regulated the imperial court, temples and shrines, and daimyo. Military houses were enjoined to use men of ability and to practice frugality. They were prohibited from engaging in drinking par-

SOURCE Sumptuary Laws, Tokugawa Shogunate, 1640

Map Exploration

To explore this map further, go to http://www.prenhall.com/craig_maps

Major outside daimyo domains that played key roles in the 1853-68 restoration period

Main areas of Shogunal Rule

Tōkaidō (Trunk Road)

Map 19–3. Tokugawa Japan and the Korean Peninsula. The area between Edo and Osaka in central Honshu was both the political base of the Tokugawa *bakufu* and its rice basket. The domains that would overthrow the Tokugawa *bakufu* in the late nineteenth century were mostly in outlying areas of southwestern Japan.

ties, wanton revelry, sexual indulgence, habitual gambling, or the ostentatious display of wealth. Only with *bakufu* consent could daimyo marry or repair their castles.

A second control was a hostage system, firmly established by 1642, that required the wives and children of daimyo to reside permanently in Edo and the daimyo themselves to spend every second year in Edo. Like the policy of Louis XIV (r. 1643–1715) at Versailles, this requirement transformed feudal lords into courtiers. The palatial Edo compounds of the daimyo contained hundreds or thousands of retainers and servants and occupied much of the city.

A third key control, established during the 1630s, was the national policy of seclusion. Seclusion was no barrier to cultural imports from China and Korea. But except for small Chinese and Dutch trading contingents at Nagasaki, no foreigners were permitted to enter Japan, and on pain of death, no Japanese were allowed to go abroad. Nor could ocean-going ships be built. This policy was strictly enforced until

Edo Castle. Edo first became a castle town in the mid–fifteenth century. Tokugawa Ieyasu made the castle his residence and headquarters in 1590, and, after his great victory in 1600, rebuilt and extended it. This early Edo period screen painting shows (upper right) the keep or inner citadel, which was not rebuilt after a fire in 1657. Korean envoys (bottom center) enter the castle grounds. They have brought tiger skins and other gifts. Onlookers gawk at their unfamiliar garb. Warriors (top, far right) practice archery. The inner castle compounds shown in the painting were only the central part of an elaborate system of moats, stone-block ramparts, and gates. In 1868, after the Meiji Restoration, Edo was renamed Tokyo (Eastern Capital) and became the residence of the emperor. *Courtesy Albert Craig.*

1854. Like the case of a watch, seclusion enclosed the workings of the entire system. Cut off from substantial outside political contacts, for Japanese, Japan became the world.

An interesting parallel can be drawn between Europe and Tokugawa Japan. Between the fifteenth and eighteenth centuries France moved from a late feudal pattern towards ever greater centralization, whereas Germany moved toward a decentralized order of many independent states. In Japan these two tendencies were delicately balanced. On the one hand, representing the forces of centralization was the *bakufu*, which governed its own domain and also administered the controls over the whole system. Its offices were staffed by its vassals—

its highest councils by house daimyo and high-ranking bannermen, and lesser posts by lower-ranking vassals of ability. The pool of rank was always larger than that of the available posts.

On the other hand, representing decentralization were the domains of the 260 or so daimyo. Except for the house daimyo, they were excluded from service in the *bakufu*. Their domain governments, like miniature *bakufu*, were staffed by their samurai vassals. Each domain had its own autonomous military, finances, judiciary, schools, paper money, and so on. This balance between centralization and decentralization has led Japanese scholars to label the Tokugawa polity the "*bakufu*-domain system."

The Seventeenth-Century Economy

The political dynamism of the period from Hideyoshi through the first century of Tokugawa rule was matched by economic growth. By the late sixteenth century there existed a backlog of agricultural techniques, the spread of which had been impeded by regionalism and wars: methods of water control and irrigation that made double-cropping easier, better tools, new seed strains, the use of bony fish or of night

Daimyo. A daimyo seated in a palanquin carried by commoner porters. The screen at the side is rolled up so that he can observe the sights of Edo. Surrounding the palanquin are several dozen of his samurai retainers. In the right foreground are Edo townsmen. *Courtesy Albert Craig.*

soil from cities as fertilizers, and so on. During the seventeenth century these techniques were widely applied. Resources no longer needed for war were allocated to land reclamation. The result was a doubling of agricultural production, as well as a doubling of population from 12 million in 1600 to 24 million in 1700. The production of agricultural byproducts—cotton, silk, indigo, lumber, dyes, *sake*, and so on—also grew, especially in central Japan and along the shores of the Inland Sea.

Peace also sustained growth in commerce. The merchants in Warring States Japan, like geese who lay golden eggs, had always been at risk. They had to pay for security; they operated within cramped regional economies. On coming to power, Nobunaga and Hideyoshi knew that political unification alone was not enough. They recognized that prosperity would make their rule easier and, acknowledging the enterprise of merchants, they abolished the medieval guilds and freed Japan's central markets from monopolistic restrictions. The result was a burgeoning of trade and the formation of a national market network atop the domain economies. As this network expanded during the seventeenth century, economic functions became more differentiated and efficient. The economic chain that began with a local buyer might extend to a merchant house in a regional port, to coastal shippers, to warehousers in Osaka or Edo, and then to great wholesale houses.

Seclusion ended much foreign trade. One might expect the sharp decline in trade to have dampened Japan's domestic economy. Instead, commerce continued to grow for the remainder of the seventeenth century.

To explain this growth, we must look at the tax system and the pattern of consumption in the castle towns and Edo. Tokugawa tax policy was based on land, not commerce. Taxes took about one third of the peasant's production. It was a heavier tax rate than that in neighboring China and bespeaks the effective grasp that the military class had on Japanese society. Most taxes were paid in grain. Even as late as the mid–nineteenth century, only a third was collected in money payments. Thus, the 87 percent of the population who lived in the countryside paid almost one third of the country's agricultural wealth to the 5 percent in the military class. The remaining 8 percent of townspeople also lived off the tax flow by providing goods and services for samurai. This distribution of benefits was mirrored in the three-area city planning common to all castle towns: a large parklike area with castle, trees, stone walls, and moats for the daimyo and his government; an extensive samurai quarter; and a meaner townspeople's quarter. Moreover, just as the castle towns were the consumption centers of the regional tax economies, so was Edo the national consumption center and a super-castle town. It had the same three-area layout, although on a far grander scale. When the daimyo of Kaga, from a great domain on the Japan Sea, was in attendance at Edo, he was served by 8,000 samurai. When he returned to his domain, 4,000 stayed on in Edo to manage the Kaga estates: 267 acres of houses and gardens, barracks, schools, warehouses, and so on. One of these estates, with its magnificent red gate still intact, is today the main campus of Tokyo University. Other daimyo had establishments proportional to their domains. By 1700 Edo had a population of about 1 million.

To support their Edo establishments, the daimyo sold tax rice in Osaka. The "kitchen of Japan," Osaka became the redistribution center from which competing fleets of coastal shippers brought to Edo food, clothing, lumber, oil, and other supplies. By 1700 Osaka's population was about 400,000. Kyoto, rebuilt after its destruction in the early Warring States period, was almost as big. It continued as a center of handicraft production. It also was the location of the "captive" imperial court, which, after suffering penury during the Warring States era, was given support lands equivalent in revenues to those of a small daimyo.

The Commercial District of Osaka, the "kitchen" of Tokugawa Japan. Warehouses bear the crests of their merchant houses. Ships (upper right) loaded with rice, cotton goods, *sake,* and other goods are about to depart for Edo (Tokyo). Their captains vied with one another to arrive first and get the best price. *Courtesy Albert Craig.*

The system of alternate-year attendance at Edo contributed to the development of overland transportation. The most traveled grand trunk road was the Tōkaidō Road between Edo and Kyoto (see Map 19–3). The artist Hiroshige (1797–1858) made a series of woodblock prints that depicted the scenery at its fifty-three post stations. The post stations had official inns for traveling daimyo and requisitioned supplies and horses as a tax obligation from adjacent villages. These stations often grew into thriving local towns.

SOURCE *View of the Tōkaidō Road*

The growth of a national economy led to a richness and diversity in urban life. Townsmen governed their districts. Samurai city managers watched over the city as a whole. Public schools, police, and companies of firefighters provided public services—a proverb of the time was "Fires are the flowers of Edo." But there were also servants, cooks, messengers, restaurant owners, priests, doctors, teachers, sword sharpeners, book lenders, instructors in the martial arts, prostitutes, and bathhouse attendants. In the world of popular arts there were woodblock printers and artists, book publishers, puppeteers, acrobatic troupes, storytellers, and **Kabuki** and **Nō** actors. Merchant establishments included money changers, pawnbrokers, peddlers, small shops, single-price retail establishments like the House of Mitsui, and great wholesale merchants. Merchant households furnished the raw materials for the personae of Edo fiction: the skin-flint merchant who pinches every penny, the profligate son who runs through an inheritance to an inevitable bankruptcy, an erring wife, or the clerk involved in a hopeless affair with a prostitute. (See Document, "The Virtuous Wife.")

Eighteenth and Early Nineteenth Centuries

By the late seventeenth century the political engineering of the Tokugawa state was complete. After that, few major new laws were enacted, and few important changes were made in governing institutions. In the economy, too, from the early eighteenth century, dynamic growth gave way to slower growth within a high-level equilibrium. In the words of some historians, the society had become "frozen," "unchanging," or "strangely preserved." Yet changes of a different kind were under way.

The Forty-Seven Rōnin The eighteenth century began with high drama. In the spring of 1701 a daimyo on duty at Edo Castle drew his sword and slightly wounded a *bakufu* official who had insulted him. Even to unsheath a sword within the castle was punishable by death. On the same day the daimyo was ordered to commit *harakiri* (literally, to cut his stomach), and his domain was confiscated. Fearing an attempt at revenge, the *bakufu* police kept an eye on the daimyo's

retainers—now *rōnin*, or "masterless samurai." The retainers dissembled, working at lowly jobs, staying at home with their families, or leading lives of drunkenness and debauchery.

Twenty-one months later, on a snowy night in January, forty-seven of the retainers gathered in Edo, attacked the residence of the *bakufu* official, took his head, and then surrendered to the authorities. Their act struck the imagination of the citizenry of Edo and was widely acclaimed. But the *bakufu* council, after deliberating for two months, ordered all forty-seven to commit *harakiri*. The incident embodied the perennial theme of duty versus human feelings. Writers of Kabuki drama and puppet theater quickly took up the incident, and to this day it has been reworked into novels, movies, and television scripts. Just as in Western theater there have been different Hamlets, so have there been many characterizations of Ōishi Kuranosuke, the leader of the band of forty-seven.

Viewed historically, three points may be noted about the incident. First, in a similar situation the more practical samurai of the Warring States period would have forgotten their former lord and rushed to find a new one. Loyalty was highly valued because disloyalty was a live option. But this was no longer true in the Tokugawa era. With the authority of the daimyo backed by that of the shōgun, there was no room for disloyalty. So loyalty became deeply internalized and was viewed almost as a religious obligation. It was also easier for Tokugawa samurai to be loyal unto death because, for the most part, there was so little likelihood in an era of peace that such a loyalty would be called for. In any case, in 1701 it was this Tokugawa species of absolute loyalty that moved the forty-seven rōnin.

Second, the incident tells something of the state in Tokugawa Japan. The 1615 "Laws for the Military Houses" contains the passage: "Law is the basis of the social order. Reason may be violated in the name of law, but law may not be violated in the name of reason. Those who break laws deserve heavy punishments."[4] One Tokugawa law forbade private vendettas. So, despite the moral purity of their act—which all recognized, even those who condemned them to death—the forty-seven "virtuous warriors" had to die. The state was above ethics. Their death sentence was a bureaucratic necessity.

Third, loyalty and idealism were not a monopoly of the males. In the drama, at least, samurai wives and daughters displayed the same heroic spirit of self-sacrifice.

Cycles of Reform Most political history of late Tokugawa Japan is written in terms of alternating cycles of laxity and reform. Even during the mid–seventeenth century the ex-

---

[4] R. Tsunoda, W. T. de Bary, and D. Keene, eds., *Sources of the Japanese Tradition* (New York: Columbia University Press, 1958), p. 336.

penses of the *bakufu* and daimyo states were often greater than their income. In part, the reason was structural: Taxes were based on agriculture in an economy that was becoming commercial. In part, it was simple mathematics: After the samurai were paid their stipends, not enough was left for the expenses of domain governments and the costs of the Edo establishments. In part, it was the toll of extraordinary costs, such as a *bakufu* levy, the wedding of a daimyo's daughter, or the rebuilding of a castle after a fire. And finally, in part, it was a growing taste for luxury among daimyo and retainers of rank.

Over the years a familiar pattern emerged. To make ends meet, domains would borrow from merchants. Then, as finances became even more straitened, a reformist clique of officials would appear, take power, retrench the domain's finances, eliminate extravagance, and return the domain to a more frugal and austere way of life. Debts would be repaid or repudiated. A side effect of reform was the depression of the local merchant economy. But no one likes to practice frugality forever. So, after some of the goals of the reform had been achieved, a new clique would take over the government and a new round of spending would begin. The *bakufu* carried out three great reforms on Tokugawa lands:

1716–1733	Tokugawa Yoshimune	17 years
1787–1793	Matsudaira Sadanobu	6 years
1841–1843	Mizuno Tadakuni	2 years

The first two were long and successful; the third was not. Its failure set the stage for the ineffective response of the *bakufu* to the West in the mid–nineteenth century. Daimyo domains also carried out reforms. Some were successful, enabling them to respond more effectively to the political crisis of the mid–nineteenth century.

Bureaucratization The balance between centralization and decentralization lasted until the end of the Tokugawa era. Not a single domain ever tried to overthrow the *bakufu* hegemony. Nor did the *bakufu* ever try to extend its control over the domains. But bureaucracy grew steadily both within the *bakufu* and within each domain. One development was the extension of public authority into areas that had been private. In 1600 most samurai fiefs were run by their samurai fief holders. They collected the taxes, often at a heavier rate than the domain set, and appointed fief stewards to oversee the fiefs. By 1850, however, district officials administered all but the largest of samurai fiefs. They collected the standard domain taxes and forwarded their income to the samurai. In periods of retrenchment, samurai were often paid only half the amount due.

Along with the growth of bureaucracy was the proliferation of administrative codes and government by paperwork. Surviving domain archives house room after room of records of every imaginable kind, mostly from the late eighteenth and early nineteenth centuries: records of births,

Bridal Procession. The bridal procession of Yohime, the twenty-first daughter of the eleventh Tokugawa shōgun, approaches the Edo mansion of the Kaga daimyo. The red gate (upper right), built in 1827 for this occasion, is today an entrance to the main campus of Tokyo University. The eleventh shōgun had twenty-eight sons and twenty-seven daughters by his more than forty concubines. Of his children, thirteen sons and twelve daughters survived to maturity. This woodblock print by Kunisada is a "national treasure." *Courtesy Albert Craig.*

adoptions, name changes, samurai ranks, fief registers, stipend registers, land and tax registers, court proceedings, domain history, and so on. Administrative codes for the *bakufu* exchequer, for example, grew from a single page during the seventeenth century to forty pages in the late Tokugawa. They define among other things an elaborate structure of offices and suboffices, their jurisdictional boundaries, and detailed instructions about how many copies of each document should be made and to which offices they should be forwarded.

Of course, bureaucratization had limits. Only samurai could aspire to official posts. They came to the office wearing their two swords. Decision-making posts were limited to upper ranking samurai. In periods of financial crises—endemic in the late Tokugawa—a demand arose for men of ability, and middle- or lower-middle-ranking samurai joined domain decision making by becoming staff assistants to bureaucrats of rank.

The Later Tokugawa Economy   By 1700 the economy approached the limit of expansion within the available technology. The population, an important index, reached 26 million early in the eighteenth century and was at the same figure in the mid–nineteenth century, a period during which the population of China more than doubled. Within this constant figure were various smaller movements. Population declined during epidemics in the 1750s and the 1760s, and during famines in the 1780s. The northeast never fully recovered. Southwestern Japan along the Inland Sea gained in population. Central Japan stayed even; it was more urban, and like most premodern cities, Tokugawa cities had higher death rates.

After 1700 taxes became stabilized and land surveys were few. Evidence suggests little increase in grain production and only slow growth in agricultural byproducts. Some families, to raise their standard of living, made conscious efforts to limit their size. Contraception and abortion were commonplace, and infanticide (euphemistically called *mabiki*, the term for thinning out rice shoots in a paddy) was practiced in hard times. But periodic disease, shortages of food, and late marriages among the poor were more important factors. A study of one rural village showed the daughters of poor farmers marrying at twenty-two and having an average of 4.6 children, whereas for the daughters of rich farmers the figures were nineteen and 6.2. A study of another domain showed that the size of the average farm household declined from 7 to 4.25 members.

During the Tokugawa some farmers remained independent small cultivators, but others became landlords or tenants. By the mid–nineteenth century tenants worked about a quarter of all cultivated lands. Most landlords were small, lived in their villages, and often were village leaders.

They were not at all like the Chinese gentry. The misery of the lower stratum of rural society contributed to an increase in peasant uprisings during the late eighteenth and early nineteenth centuries. Authorities had no difficulty in quelling them, although some involved thousands of protestors and were locally destructive. No uprising in Japan even remotely approached those of late Manchu China.

Commerce grew slowly during the late Tokugawa. In the early eighteenth century it was reencased within guilds. Merchants paid set fees, usually not especially high, in return for monopoly privileges in central marketplaces. Guilds were also reestablished in the domains, and some domains established domain-run monopolies on products such as wax, paper, indigo, or sugar. The problem facing domain leaders was how to tax profits without injuring the competitive standing of domain exports. Most late Tokugawa commercial growth was in countryside industries—*sake*, soy sauce, dyes, silks, or cotton—and was especially prominent in central and western Japan. Some were organized and financed by city merchants under the putting-out system. Others competed with city merchants, shipping directly to end markets to circumvent monopoly controls. The expansion of labor in such rural industries contributed to the population shrinkage in late Tokugawa cities.

The largest question about the Tokugawa economy concerns its relation to Japan's amazing industrialization, which began later in the nineteenth century. Some scholars have suggested that Japan had a "running start." Others have stressed Japanese backwardness in comparison with European late developers. The question is still unresolved.

Tokugawa Culture

If *The Tale of Genji* represents the classical culture of the aristocratic Heian court, and if Nō drama or an ink painting by Sesshū represents the austere samurai culture of medieval Japan, then a satire by Saikaku (1642–1693), a drama by Chikamatsu (1653–1724), or a woodblock print of a beauty by Utamaro (1753–1806) may be taken to represent the new urban culture of the Tokugawa era. In such works, one discerns a new secular consciousness, an exquisite taste put to plebeian ends, occasional vulgarities, and a sense of humor only occasionally encountered in the earlier Japanese tradition.

But there was more to Tokugawa culture than the arts and literature of the townspeople. Two hundred and fifty years of peace and prosperity provided a base for an ever more complex culture and a broader popular participation in cultural life. In the villages Buddhism became more deeply rooted; new folk religions proliferated; by the early nineteenth century most well-to-do farmers could read and write. The aristocratic culture of the ranking samurai houses and a sculptor. His autobiographical writings have been translated as *The Embossed Tea Kettle*.

Some scholars have argued that Tokugawa urban culture had a double structure. On the one hand were the samurai, serious and high-minded, who produced a vast body of Chinese-style paintings, poetry, and philosophical treatises. On the other hand was the culture of the townspeople: low-brow, irreverent, secular, satirical, and often scatological. The samurai esteemed Song-style paintings of mountains or waterfalls, often adorned with quotations from the Confucian classics or Tang poetry. The townspeople collected prints of local beauties, actors, courtesans, and scenes from everyday life. Samurai moralists saw money as the root of evil. Merchants saw it as their goal in life; in Osaka, they even held an "abacus festival," at which their adding machines were consecrated to the gods of wealth and commerce.

In poetry, too, a double structure appeared. Bashō (1644–1694) was born a samurai but gave up his status to live as a wandering poet. He is famous for his travel journal, *The Narrow Road of Oku*, and especially for his haiku, little word-picture poems:

Such stillness—
The cries of the cicadas
Sink into the rocks.

A crow perches
On a leafless branch
An autumn evening.

Or, on visiting a battlefield of the past, he wrote:

The summer grass
All that is left
Of a warrior's dream.[5]

Contrast Bashō's sense of the transience of life with the worldly humor of the townsman:

From a mountain temple
The snores of a monk and
the voice of the cuckoo.

Showing a love-letter
to her mother
From a man she doesn't love.

Even the most virtuous woman
will undo her sash
For a flea.[6]

Mother Bathing Her Son. Woodblock print by Kitagawa Utamaro (1753–1806). Utamaro was so popular a master of his genre that publishers hired unknown artists to produce fakes in his name. This led him to sign some works "the genuine Utamaro." He boasted of his high fees, comparing himself to a great courtesan and his imitators to streetwalkers. Note the tub's skillful design, the mother's wooden clog and her simple yet elegant kimono. A second kimono hangs to dry at the upper-right corner. *The Nelson-Atkins Museum of Art, Kansas City, Missouri (Purchase: Nelson Trust).* © *The Nelson Gallery Foundation. All Reproduction Rights Reserved.*

also remained vigorous. Nō plays continued to be staged. The medieval tradition of black ink paintings was continued by the Kanō school and other artists.

The Ashikaga tradition of restraint, simplicity, and naturalness in architecture was extended. The imperial villa in Katsura outside of Kyoto has its roots in medieval architecture and to this day inspires Japanese architects. The gilded and colored screen paintings that had surged in popularity during Hideyoshi's rule developed further, culminating in the powerful works of Ogata Kōrin (1658–1716).

Zen Buddhism, having declined during the Warring States period, was revitalized by the monk Hakuin (1686–1769). One of the great cultural figures of the Tokugawa era, Hakuin was also a writer, a painter, a calligrapher,

[5] D. Keene, ed., *Anthology of Japanese Literature* (New York: Grove Press, 1955), p. 371. Used by permission of Grove/Atlantic, Inc.

[6] R. H. Blyth, *Japanese Humor* (Tokyo: Japanese Travel Bureau, 1957), p. 141.

This is not to say, of course, that townspeople did not write proper haiku as well.

Literature and Drama   Is cultural creativity more likely during periods of economic growth and political change or during periods of stability? The greatest works of literature

and philosophy of Tokugawa Japan were produced between 1650 and 1725, just as the initial political transformation was being completed but the economy was still growing and the society was not yet set in its ways.

One of the major literary figures and certainly the most entertaining was Ihara Saikaku (1642–1693), who is gener-

---

The Virtuous Wife

Document

The three-generation stem family, composed of the older parents, their eldest son and his "bride," and their children, was the ideal during the Edo period. The principal family bond was between the parents and their elder son. The son's "bride," at least until she produced children of her own, was less than a full family member, as the adage "the womb is borrowed" suggests. Kaibara Ekken (1630–1714), an early Confucian moralist, propounded an ethic appropriate to such a family in his *Greater Learning for Women*. It reflects the "wisdom" of his age.

◆ Can people accept and practice any ethic that serves their society? Or are some ethics more "natural" than others? How did a girl raised in Tokugawa society feel? Could she embrace Ekken's teachings? Or does the following passage suggest, at least obliquely, that some human feelings are universal and difficult to deny?

GIRL'S INSTRUCTION

Seeing that it is a girl's destiny, on reaching womanhood, to go to a new home, and live in submission to her father-in-law, it is even more incumbent upon her than it is on a boy to receive with all reverence her parents' instructions. Should her parents, through their tenderness, allow her to grow up self-willed, she will infallibly show herself capricious in her husband's house, and thus alienate his affection; while, if her father-in-law be a man of correct principles, the girl will find the yoke of these principles intolerable. She will hate and decry her father-in-law, and the end of these domestic dissensions will be her dismissal from her husband's house and the covering of herself with ignominy. Her parents, forgetting the faulty education they gave her, may, indeed, lay all the blame on the father-in-law. But they will be in error; for the whole disaster should rightly be attributed to the faulty education the girl received from her parents.

THE INFIRMITIES OF WOMAN

The five worst infirmities that afflict the female are indocility, discontent, slander, jealousy, and silliness. Without any doubt, these five infirmities are found in seven or eight out of every ten women, and it is from these that arises the inferiority of women to men. A woman should cure them by self-inspection and self-reproach.

THE WIFE'S MISCELLANEOUS DUTIES

A woman has no particular lord. She must look to her husband as her lord, and must serve him with all worship and reverence, not despising or thinking lightly of him. The great lifelong duty of a woman is obedience. In her dealings with her husband, both the expression of her countenance and style of her address should be courteous, humble, and conciliatory, never peevish and intractable, never rude and arrogant—that should be a woman's first and chiefest care. When the husband issues his instructions, the wife must never disobey them. In doubtful cases she should inquire of her husband, and obediently follow his commands. If ever her husband should inquire of her, she should answer to the point—to answer in a careless fashion would be a mark of rudeness. Should her husband be roused at any time to anger, she must obey him with fear and trembling, and not set herself up against him in anger and forwardness. A woman should look on her husband as if he were Heaven itself, and never weary of thinking how she may yield to her husband and thus escape celestial castigation.

Kaibara Ekken, *Greater Learning for Women*, in K. Hoshino, *The Way of Contentment* (London: John Murray, 1913, reprinted 1979), pp. 33–34, 44–45.

ally credited with having re-created Japanese fiction. Saikaku was heir to an Osaka merchant house. He was raised to be its master, but after his wife died he let the head clerk manage the business and devoted himself to poetry, theater, and the pleasure quarters. At the age of forty he wrote and illustrated *The Life of an Amorous Man*, the story of a modern and bawdy Prince Genji who cuts a swath through bathhouse girls, shrine maidens, courtesans, and boy actors. The overnight success of the work led to a sequel, *The Life of an Amorous Woman*, the tale of a woman undone by passion and of her downward spiral through the minutely graded circles of the Osaka demimonde. Saikaku also wrote more than twenty other works, including *The Japanese Family Storehouse*, which humorously chronicles the contradictions between the pursuit of wealth and the pursuit of pleasure.

A second major figure of Osaka culture at the turn of the century was the dramatist Chikamatsu Monzaemon (1653–1724). Born a samurai in Echizen province, Chikamatsu entered the service of a court aristocrat in Kyoto and then, in 1705, moved to Osaka to write for both the Kabuki and the puppet theater. Kabuki had begun early in the seventeenth century as suggestive skits and erotic dances performed by troupes of actresses. In 1629 the *bakufu* forbade women to perform on the stage. By the 1660s Kabuki had evolved into a more serious drama with male actors playing both male and female roles. Actors entered the stage on a raised runway or "flower path" through the audience. Famous actors took great liberties in interpreting plays, to roars of approval from the audience. There was a ready market for woodblock prints of actors in their most famous roles—like posters of rock musicians today, but done with incomparably greater artistry.

The three main types of Kabuki plays were dance pieces, which were influenced by the tradition of the Nō; domestic dramas; and historical pieces. Chikamatsu wrote all three. In contrast to Saikaku's protagonists, the men and women in Chikamatsu's dramas struggle to fulfill the duties and obligations of their stations in life. Only when their passions become uncontrollable, which is generally the case, do the plays end in tragedy. The emotional intensity of the ending is heightened by the restraint shown by the actors before they reach their breaking point. In some plays the hero and heroine leave duty behind and, hoping for felicity in the next world, set out on a flight to death. Indeed, this ending was banned by *bakufu* authorities when the excessive popularity of the drama led to its imitation in real life.

It is interesting to compare Kabuki and the Nō drama. Nō is like early Greek drama in that the chorus provides the narrative line. In Nō, the stylization of action is

extreme. In Kabuki, as in Elizabethan drama, the actors declaim their lines in the dramatic realism demanded by the commoner theatergoers of seventeenth-century Japan. But to convey the illusion of realism required some deviation from it. As Chikamatsu himself noted about Kabuki: "Many things are said by the female characters which real women could not utter. . . . It is because they say what could not come from a real woman's lips that their true emotions are disclosed." For him, "Art is something that lies in the slender margin between the real and the unreal.[7] Yet, for all that Chikamatsu was concerned with the refinements of his craft and the balance between emotional expressiveness and unspoken restraints, he never talked of the mysterious "no mind" as the key to an actor's power. His dramas are a world removed from the religiosity of the medieval Nō.

In the early eighteenth century Kabuki was displaced in popularity by the puppet theater (Bunraku). Many of Chikamatsu's plays were written for this genre. The word *puppet* does not do justice to the half-life-sized human figures, which rival Nō masks in their artistry. Manipulated by a team of three, a puppet does not only kneel and bow or engage in swordplay but can also mimic brushing a tear from the eye with its kimono sleeve or threading a needle. In the late eighteenth century the puppet theater, in turn, declined, and as the center of culture shifted from Osaka to Edo, Kabuki again blossomed as Japan's premier form of drama.

Confucian Thought The most important change in Tokugawa intellectual life was that the ruling elite abandoned the religious teachings of Buddhism in favor of the more secular worldview of Confucius, opening many avenues for further changes. (See Document, "A Tokugawa Skeptic.") The reworking occurred slowly. During the seventeenth century samurai were enjoined never to forget the arts of war and to be ever ready to die for their lord. One samurai in his deathbed poem lamented dying on *tatami*—with his boots off, as it were. In this period, most samurai were illiterate and saw book learning as unmanly. Nakae Tōju (1608–1648), a samurai and a Confucian scholar, recounted that as a youth he swaggered around with his friends during the day and studied secretly at night so as not to be thought a sissy. Schools, too, were slow to develop. One Japanese scholar has noted that in 1687 only four domains had proper domain schools; in 1715, only ten.

The great figures of Tokugawa Confucianism lived during the same years as Saikaku and Chikamatsu, in the late

---

[7] Tsunoda, de Bary, Keene, *Japanese Tradition*, p. 448.

seventeenth and early eighteenth centuries. They are great because they succeeded in the difficult task of adapting Chinese Confucianism to fit Japanese society. One problem, for example, was that in Chinese Confucianism there was no place for a shōgun, whereas in the Japanese tradition of sunline emperors there was no room for the Mandate of Heaven. Most Tokugawa thinkers handled this discrepancy by saying that Heaven gave the emperor his mandate and that the emperor then entrusted political authority to the shōgun. One philosopher suggested that the divine emperor acted for Heaven and gave the mandate to the shōgun. Neither solution was very comfortable, for, in fact, the emperor was as much a puppet as those in the Osaka theater.

Another problem was the difference between China's centralized bureaucratic government and Japan's "feudal" system of lord-vassal relationships. Samurai loyalty was clearly not that of a scholar-official to the Chinese emperor. Some Japanese thinkers solved this problem rather ingeniously by saying that it was China that had deviated from the feudal society of the Chou sages, whereas in Japan, Tokugawa Ieyasu had re-created just such a society.

A third problem concerned the "central flowery kingdom" and the barbarians around it. No philosopher could quite bring himself to say that Japan was the real middle kingdom and China the barbarian, but some argued that centrality was relative, and still others suggested that China under barbarian Manchu rule had lost its claim to universality. These are just a few of a large range of problems related to Japanese political organization, Shinto, and to Japanese family practices. By the early eighteenth century these problems had been addressed, and a revised Confucianism acceptable for use in Japan had come into being.

Another point to note is the continuing vitality of Japanese thought—Confucian and otherwise—into the mid–nineteenth century. This vitality is partly explained by the disputes among different schools of Confucianism and partly, perhaps, by Japan's lack of an examination system. The best energies of its samurai youth were not channeled into writing the conventional and sterile "eight-legged essay" that was required in the Chinese examination system. Official preferment—within the constraints of Japan's hereditary system—was often obtained by writing a proposal for domain reforms, although this could sometimes lead to punishments as well.

The vitality was also a result of the rapid expansion of schools from the early eighteenth century. By the early nineteenth century every domain had its own official school and a school on its Edo estate. Commoner schools (*terakoya*), in which reading, writing, and the rudiments of Confucianism were taught, grew apace. In the first half of the nineteenth century private academies also appeared throughout the country. By the late Tokugawa era about 40 to 50 percent of the male population and 15 to 20 percent of the female population was literate—a far higher rate than in most of the world, and on a par with European late developers.

Other Developments in Thought   For Tokugawa scholars, the emotional problem of how to deal with China was vexing. Their response was usually ambivalent. They praised China as the teacher country and respected its creative tradition. They studied its history, philosophy, and literature, and began a tradition of scholarship on China that has remained powerful to this day. But they also sought to retain a separate Japanese identity. Most scholars dealt with this problem by adapting Confucianism to fit Japan. But two schools—never in the mainstream of Tokugawa thought, but growing in importance during the eighteenth and early nineteenth centuries—arrived at more radical positions. The schools of National Studies and Dutch Studies were diametrically opposed in most respects but alike in criticizing the Chinese influence on Japanese life and culture.

National Studies began as philological studies of ancient Japanese texts. One source of its inspiration was Shinto; another was the Neo-Confucian School of Ancient Learning. Just as the School of Ancient Learning had sought to discover the original, true meanings of the Chinese classics before they were contaminated by Song metaphysics, so the scholars in the National Studies tradition tried to find in the Japanese classics the original true character of Japan before it had been contaminated by Chinese ideas. On studying the *Record of Ancient Matters, The Collection of Myriad Leaves*, or *The Tale of Genji*, they found that the early Japanese spirit was free, spontaneous, clean, lofty, and honest, in contrast to the Chinese spirit, which they characterized as rigid, cramped, and artificial. Some writings of this school appear to borrow the anti-Confucian logic of Daoism.

A second characteristic of **National Studies** was its reaffirmation of Japan's unique creation, and by extension, the uniqueness of its emperor. Motoori Norinaga (1730–1801) wrote of Shinto creationism as the "Right Way":

> *Heaven and Earth, all the gods and all phenomena, were brought into existence by the creative spirits of two deities. . . . This . . . is a miraculously divine act the reason for which is beyond the comprehension of the human intellect.*
>
> *But in foreign countries where the Right Way has not been transmitted, this act of divine creativity is not known. Men there have tried to explain the principle of Heaven and earth and all phenomena by such theories as the yin and yang, the hexagrams of the Book of Changes, and the Five Elements. But all of these are fallacious theories stemming from the assumptions of the human intellect and they in no wise represent the true principle.*

Chronology

Tokugawa Era (1600–1868)

1600	Tokugawa Ieyasu reunifies Japan
1615	"Laws of Military Houses" issued
1639	Seclusion policy adopted
1642	Edo hostage system in place
1644–1694	Bashō, poet
1653–1724	Chikamatsu Monzaemon, dramatist
1701	The forty-seven rōnin avenge their lord
1853, 1854	Commodore Matthew Perry visits Japan

The "special dispensation of our Imperial Land" means that ours is the native land of the Heaven-Shining Goddess who casts her light over all countries in the four seas. Thus our country is the source and fountainhead of all other countries, and in all matters it excels all the others.[8]

National Studies became influential during the late Tokugawa era. It had a small but not unimportant influence on the Meiji Restoration. Its doctrines continued thereafter as one strain of modern Japanese ultranationalism. Its most enduring achievement was in Japanese linguistics. Even today, scholars admire Motoori's philology. Moreover, in an age when the prestige of things Chinese was overwhelming, Motoori helped redress the balance by appreciating and giving a name to the aesthetic sensibility found in the Japanese classics. The phrase he used was *mono no aware*, which means, literally, "the poignancy of things."

But National Studies had several weaknesses that prevented it from becoming the mainstream of Japanese thought. First, even the most refined sensibility is no substitute for philosophy. In its celebration of the primitive, National Studies ran headlong into the greater rationality of Confucian thought. Second, National Studies was chiefly literary, and apart from its enthusiasm for the divine emperor, it had little to offer politically in an age when political philosophy was central in both the domain and the *bakufu* schools.

Dutch Studies A second development was Dutch Studies. After Christianity had been proscribed and the policy of seclusion adopted, all Western books were banned in Japan.

Some knowledge of Dutch was maintained among the official interpreters who dealt with the Dutch at Nagasaki. The ban on Western books (except for those propagating Christianity) was ended in 1720 by the shōgun Tokugawa Yoshimune (r. 1716–1745), following the advice of a scholar whom he had appointed to reform the Japanese calendar.

During the remainder of the eighteenth century, a school of "Dutch medicine" became established in Japan. Japanese pioneers early recognized that Western anatomy texts were superior to Chinese. The first Japanese dissection of a corpse occurred in 1754. In 1774 a Dutch translation of a German anatomy text was translated into Japanese. By the mid–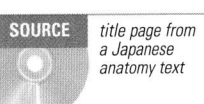nineteenth century there were schools of Dutch Studies in the main cities of Japan, and instruction was available in some domains as well. Fukuzawa Yukichi (1835–1901), who studied Dutch and Dutch science during the mid-1850s at a school begun in 1838 in Osaka, wrote in his *Autobiography* of the hostility of his fellow students towards Chinese learning:

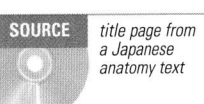
SOURCE — title page from a Japanese anatomy text

> *Though we often had discussions on many subjects, we seldom touched upon political subjects as most of us were students of medicine. Of course, we were all for free intercourse with Western countries, but there were few among us who took a serious interest in that problem. The only subject that bore our constant attack was Chinese medicine. And by hating Chinese medicine so thoroughly, we came to dislike everything that had any connection with Chinese culture. Our general opinion was that we should rid our country of the influences of the Chinese altogether. Whenever we met a young student of Chinese literature, we simply felt sorry for him. Particularly were the students of Chinese medicine the butt of our ridicule.*[9]

While medicine was the primary occupation of those who studied Dutch, some knowledge of Western astronomy, geography, botany, physics, chemistry, and arts also entered Japan. Works on science occasionally influenced other thinkers as well. Yamagata Bantō (1748–1821) was a rich and scholarly Osaka merchant who devised a rationalistic philosophy based on a synthesis of Neo-Confucianism and Western science. After studying a work on astronomy, he wrote in 1820 that conditions on other planets "varied only according to their size and their proximity to the sun." Bantō also speculated that "grass and trees will appear, insects will develop; if there are insects, fish, shellfish, animals and birds will not be absent, and finally there will be people too." Bantō qualified his argument with the naturalistic supposition that

---

[8] Tsunoda, de Bary, Keene, *Japanese Tradition*, pp. 521, 523.

[9] E. Kiyooka, trans., *The Autobiography of Fukuzawa Yukichi* (New York: Columbia University Press, 1966), p. 91.

A Tokugawa Skeptic

Document

Confucian teachings, while hardly scientific, placed a premium on rational argument. Some scholars used this rationalism to attack Buddhism. Others directed their attack against superstitions and explanations of natural phenomena that they found wanting. The following passages by Miura Baien (1723–1789), the son of a Kyushu doctor, exemplify such a rationalism.

◆ **Does modern science answer the kind of question that Baien is raising? Are some superstitions in modern societies still vulnerable to his critique?**

Why do a pair of dark things on the forehead see; why do a pair of holes in the head hear? Why don't eyes hear, why don't ears see? When most people come to these points they just leave them alone, but I simply can't leave them alone. . . . They refer the question to past authority, and when they find a book that deals with it, they accept whatever answer it gives. I can't convince myself entirely in that way. When they discuss the natural world, they do so in a wild, hit-or-miss manner; when they talk of life and death, they do so in an absurd or obscure manner. Though their evidence may be flimsy and their arguments preposterous, this does not disturb people at all.

[It is] a human peculiarity . . . to view everything as human. Take, for example, children's picture books, *The Betrothal of Rats* or *Monsters and Goblins*. Rats are never kept as rats in their true shape; instead all of them are turned into human forms. The bridegroom appears in the book in ceremonial robes with a pair of swords, while the bride is shown with a flowing gown on and snowy cap of cotton,

and is carried in a palanquin with an escort of footmen and young guards. In the book of *Monsters and Goblins*, no cases are found of an umbrella turning into a tea-mortar, or of a broom changing into a bucket. But all monsters and goblins are given eyes and noses and hands and feet, so as to look like members of the human family. . . .

It is such an imagination as this that populates heaven with a supreme God, and earth with gods of wind and thunder. Monstrous in form, they all move by foot, and do their work by hand. Wind is put in bags, thunder is beaten out on drums. If they are real bags, how are they made? And there must be skin to make a drum. If such imaginings are carried further, the sun will be unable to go on revolving unless it gets feet, and nature will be helpless in her work unless she has hands.

R. Tsunoda, W. T. de Bary, and D. Keene, eds., *Sources of the Japanese Tradition* (New York: Columbia University Press, 1960), pp. 490, 493–494. Reprinted with permission.

Mercury and Venus would probably lack human life, "since these two planets are near to the sun and too hot." He contrasted his rational arguments regarding evolution with the "slap-dash" arguments of Buddhists and Shintoists.[10]

From the late eighteenth century the Japanese began to be aware of the West, and especially of Russia, as a threat to Japan. In 1791 a concerned scholar wrote *A Discussion of the Military Problems of a Maritime Nation*, advocating a strong navy and coastal defenses. During the early nineteenth century such concerns mounted. A sudden expansion in Dutch Studies occurred after Commodore Matthew Perry's visits to Japan in 1853 and 1854.

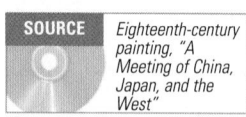 **SOURCE** *Eighteenth-century painting, "A Meeting of China, Japan, and the West"*

During the 1860s Dutch Studies became Western Studies, as English, French, German, and Russian were added to the languages studied at the *bakufu* Institute for the Investigation of Barbarian Books. In sum, Dutch Studies was not a major influence on Tokugawa thought. It cannot begin to compare with Neo-Confucianism. But it laid a foundation on which the Japanese built quickly when the need arose.

KOREA AND VIETNAM

A feature of world history, noted earlier, is the spread of heartland civilizations into their surrounding areas. In East Asia the heartland civilization was that of China; the surrounding areas that were able to take in Chinese learning were Japan, Korea, and Vietnam. Like the Japanese, Koreans and

---

[10] M. Jansen, ed., *Changing Japanese Attitudes Toward Modernization* (Princeton, NJ: Princeton University Press, 1965), p. 144.

Vietnamese learned to write using Chinese ideographs. They partially modeled their governments on those of China. They accepted Chinese Buddhism and Confucianism, and with them Chinese conceptions of the universe, state, and human relationships. The Confucian definitions of the relations between ruler and minister, father and son, and husband and wife were emphasized in Korea and Vietnam as they were in China. But at the same time, Koreans and Vietnamese, who spoke non-Chinese tongues, saw themselves as separate peoples, and gradually came to take pride in their independence. In Europe, Germany might be a parallel case: It became civilized by borrowing the heartland Graeco-Christian culture of the Mediterranean area, but it kept its original tongue and elements from its earlier culture.

Korea

A range of mountains along its northern rim divides the Korean peninsula from Manchuria, making it a distinct geographical unit. Mountains continue south through the eastern third of Korea, while in the west and south are coastal plains and broad river valleys. The combination of mountains, rice paddies, and sea makes Korea a beautiful land. The traditional name for Korea may be translated as the "land of the morning calm." Two further geographical factors affected Korean history. One was that the northwestern corner of Korea was only 300 miles from the northeastern corner of historical China: close enough for Korea to be vulnerable to invasions by its powerful neighbor but far enough away so that most of the time China found it easier to treat Korea as a tributary than to control it directly. The other factor was that the southern rim of Korea was just one hundred miles distant from the Japanese southern island of Kyushu across the Tsushima Straits.

Early History

During its old and new stone ages, Korea was peopled by Tungusic tribes moving south from northeast Asia. They spoke an Altaic tongue—distantly related to Japanese and to Manchurian, Mongolian, and Turkic. They lived by hunting, gathering, and fishing, and, like other early peoples of northeast Asia, made comb-patterned pottery and practiced an animistic religion. During the first millennium B.C.E. agriculture, bronze, and iron were introduced, transforming their primitive society. But Koreans were still ruled by tribal chiefdoms in 108 B.C.E. when the Han emperor Wudi sent an army into north Korea to menace the flank of the Hunnish (Xiongnu) empire that spread across the steppe to the north of China. Wudi built a Chinese city—near the present-day capital of North Korea—which survived into the

fourth century C.E., and established commanderies and prefectures to administer the land.

Between the fourth and seventh centuries three archaic states emerged from earlier tribal confederations. Silla, one of the three, aided by armies from Tang China, conquered the other two in the seventh century. The Tang armies wanted to stay and rule Korea, but after battles with Silla troops they withdrew, and Silla was recognized by China in 675 as an autonomous tribute state. The period of Silla rule may be likened to Nara Japan: Korea borrowed Chinese writing, established some government offices on the Chinese model, sent annual embassies to the Tang court, and took in Chinese Buddhism and Chinese arts and philosophies. Yet within the Silla government, birth mattered more than scholarship and rule by aristocrats continued, while in village Korea, the worship of nature deities was only lightly touched by the Buddhism that spread among the ruling elites.

Silla underwent a normal end-of-dynasty decline, and in 918 a warlord general founded a new dynasty, the Koryo. The English word "Korea" is derived from this dynastic name. This was a creative period. Korean scholars advanced in their mastery of Chinese principles of government. New genres of poetry and literature appeared. Korean potters made celadon vases rivaling those of China. The craft of history advanced: The earliest surviving history of Korea was compiled in 1145. Printing using moveable metallic type was invented during the thirteenth century. But most important of all was the growth of Buddhism. Temples, monasteries, and nunneries were built throughout the land, and Buddhist arts flourished. During the thirteenth century, Buddhist scholars produced in classical Chinese a printed edition of the Tripitaka, a huge compendium of sutras and other sacred writings.

Despite cultural advances, the Koryo state was weak. For one thing, the Koryo economy was undeveloped: Trade was by barter, money did not circulate, and Chinese missions commented on the extravagance of officials in the capital and the squalor of commoners and slaves in Korea's villages. For another, the dynasty was aristocratic from the start, and as centuries passed, private estates and armies arose, and civil officials were replaced by military men. For still another, frequent incursions from across Korea's northern border weakened the state. The cost of wars with the Mongols was particularly high. The Koryo court survived as long as it did by becoming in succession the tributary of the Song, Liao, Chin, and Mongol dynasties.

Korea: The Choson Era

In 1392, a Koryo general, Yi Songgye, deposed the Koryo king and founded a new dynasty. He had been sent to fight against invading Ming armies and decided that assuming power in Korea was the better part of valor. The amazing longevity of the Yi or Choson dynasty, which lasted for 518 years, from 1392 until 1910, was directly related to its status as a tributary of Ming-Qing China (see Map 19–4).

One perspective on this half millennium of Korean history is cultural. If the Koryo was Korea's Buddhist age of faith, the Choson was its Neo-Confucian age. Confucian teachings as interpreted by Zhu Xi became firmly established as the state orthodoxy. By the late fifteenth century, Korean philosophers were making original contributions to Zhu Xi philosophy, that later influenced thinkers in Japan. Schools increased in number. The civil service examinations became the primary route to official promotion. This pattern of changes may be seen as "East Asian" in that it paralleled changes that had occurred in China during the Song dynasty and would occur in Japan during the Tokugawa era.

Another approach to Korean history is to examine the ups and downs of kings and their courts. Not unlike events at European courts during the era of feudal monarchy, Korean history is colorful, filled with usurpations, assassinations, purges, reforms, evil ministers, and struggles between factions. King Sejong (r. 1418–1450) illustrates the potential of a wise monarch. He reformed land taxes, made loans of grain to farmers during spring planting, and encouraged the spread of better agricultural technology. After reforming the army and navy, he attacked pirate strongholds on Tsushima Island and expanded Korea's borders north of the Yalu River. In 1420, he established a Hall of Worthies to encourage scholarship, much like the Hanlin Academy of China. Scholars at his court produced sundials, water clocks, and astronomical instruments. But there were limits that even Sejong could not overcome. The greatest achievement of the Hall of Worthies was to create an alphabetic script (hangul), but it was never used: the prestige of Chinese writing was too great and the entrenched interests of the aristocracy too deep. Sejong promoted the use of coins and paper money to stimulate commerce, but they never caught on. Barter and artisans attached to aristocratic households remained the rule. Sejong was also unable to provide for an orderly succession: he had twenty sons and fourteen daughters, but after his death, his uncle usurped the Korean throne.

Still another interpretation of the Choson centuries is to emphasize the disruption caused by invasions during the middle of the dynasty. Hideyoshi, having brought all of Japan under his control, decided to conquer China, and the path to China was through Korea. His samurai armies devastated Korea twice, once in 1592 and again in 1597. The invasions ended with his death in 1598. On both occasions the Ming court sent troops to aid its tributary, but the rescuing Chinese armies, in turn, devastated the land almost as much as had the Japanese. A third disaster occurred in 1627 and 1637 when Manchu troops invaded pro-Ming Korea,

laying waste to the northwest and to Seoul. The result of these multiple incursions was a drop in taxable land to about a quarter of its late-sixteenth-century level. Behind this statistic lay a grim reality of famine, death, and misery.

The Choson era, however, is, perhaps, best viewed in terms of a seesaw equilibrium between kings, who in theory had absolute powers, and the deeply entrenched **yangban** aristocracy. The yangban of the Koryo era had maintained their position in the transition to the Choson; only those opposed to the new dynasty were dispossessed. The yangban were the heart of the Neo-Confucian revolution. They dominated the civil service examinations, since commoners could not afford the years of study required, and slaves, merchants, and the sons of concubines were barred from the exam. The yangban domination of the bureaucracy enabled them to resist any reform by the throne that would have injured their propertied interests.

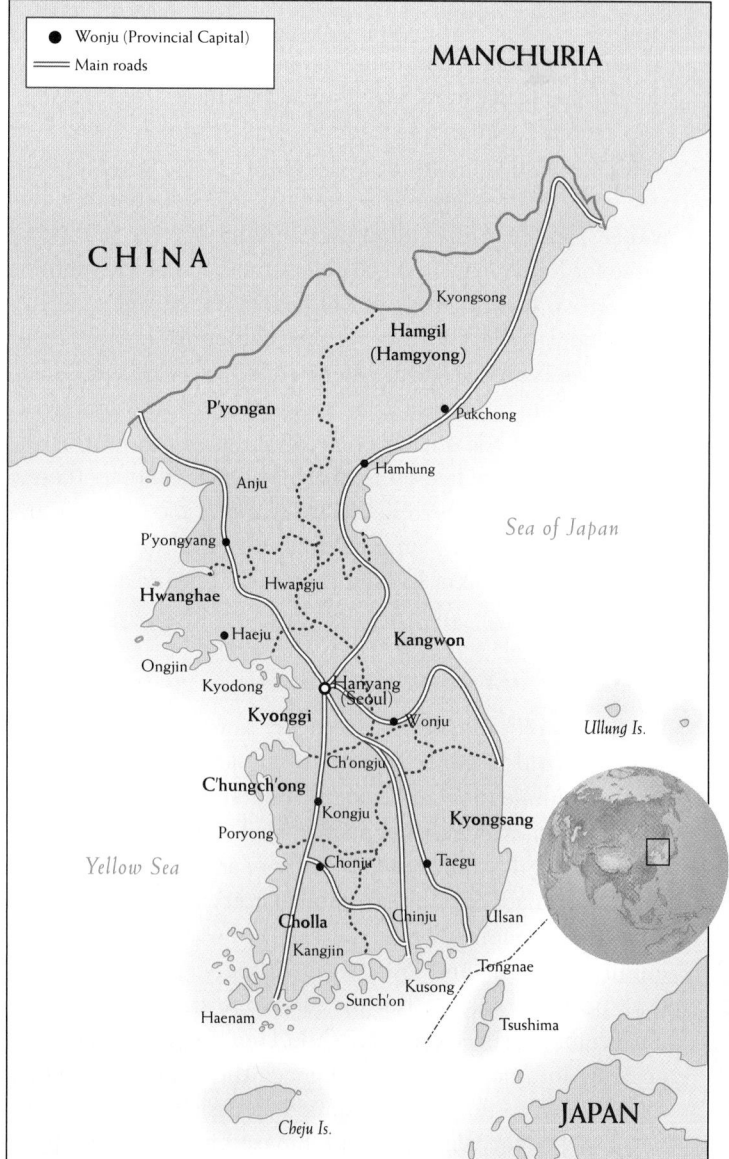

Map 19–4. Korea During the Choson Era.

But they were united only in defense of their prerogatives. For the rest, they divided into factions that waged bitter struggles for control of the government. Losers were often executed or imprisoned. As the struggles became more fierce, the effectiveness of government declined, except for a brief recovery during the early eighteenth century. Successful high officials in Seoul used their power to garner private agricultural estates and establish schools to prepare their kinsmen for examinations.

The aristocracy was also the slave-owning class. Korean slaves, scholars argue, were not like slaves in other lands, since there were no slave auctions, and, following Confucian teachings, husbands were not separated from their wives. But slaves were nonetheless property. They were often attached to land, they could be given as gifts, and their children were slaves to be used as their owners willed. It is estimated that about 30 percent of the Choson population consisted of slaves, and in the mid–seventeenth century, 75 percent of the population of Seoul.

From the mid–seventeenth century on, Korea offers a mixed picture. Literacy rose and a new popular fiction of fables, romances, and novels appeared. Women writers became important for the first time. Among some *yangban* there was a philosophic reaction against what was perceived as the emptiness of Neo-Confucianism. Calling for "practical learning" to effect a renewal of Korean society, scholars criticized the Confucian classics and outlined plans for administrative reforms and the encouragement of com-

A Badge of Rank. In Choson Korea—as in China—the rank of an official was indicated by the embroidered square affixed to his gown. Some squares showed ducks, pheasants, egrets, leopards, or tigers. Here we see a crane flying among the clouds and rainbows below.

merce. Unfortunately, their recommendations were not adopted, and the society continued its decline. More Koreans died in the famine of 1671 than during Hideyoshi's invasions. Overtaxation, drought, floods, pestilence, and famine became commonplace. Robberies occurred in daytime Seoul, and bandits plagued the countryside. Disgruntled officials led peasants in month-long revolts in 1811 and 1862. Because of the concentration of officials, wealth, and military power at Seoul, and because of Manchu support for the ruling house, neither revolt succeeded in toppling the dynasty, but the revolts left Korea with neither the will nor the means to meet the challenges it would soon face.

Vietnam

Early History

Ten major revolts occurred during the thousand years when Vietnam was under Chinese rule—not an unusual number for a Chinese border region with a non-Chinese population. The last revolt, which took place in 939, when China was weak, led to the establishment of an independent Vietnamese government. Vietnam never again became a part of China.

The history of Vietnam's second millennium is conventionally broken into dynastic blocks named after the ruling family:

Ly	1009–1225
Tran	1225–1400
Le	1428–1787
Nguyen	1802–1880s

Vietnamese dynasties, however, were not the strong, centralized, bureaucratic states found in Chinese history. From the beginnings of dynasties, there were tensions between center and periphery. At the center were the social elites who ruled the population of the Red River delta. At the periphery were magnates—powerful local figures who controlled upland peoples. Of these peripheral areas, the province of Thanh Hoa, one hundred miles south of the Hanoi capital, was of particular importance with magnates who were usually autonomous and often opposed the dynasty. Both center and periphery maintained military forces and sometimes engaged in wars. Often, several independent states coexisted during the timespan of a single "dynasty."

Chinese invasions also affected Vietnamese history. Most Chinese dynasties, as they expanded, attempted to reconquer the "south" that had once been ruled by China. Such invasions were repelled—though Ming armies occupied Vietnam for twenty years from 1407. But rather than defying China altogether, Vietnamese rulers found it easier to accommodate: Every Vietnamese dynasty became a "tributary" of China and

Chronology

Korea and Vietnam

Korea

1392	Yi Songgye founds Choson dynasty
1592, 1587	Japanese invasions
1627, 1637	Invasions by Manchu troops
1671	Famine
1811, 1862	Peasant revolts

Vietnam

1471	Vietnam conquers Champa
1483	Confucian legal code promulgated by Le Thanh Tong
1644	Fall of Ming dynasty leads to wave of Chinese immigration
1698	Nguyen court extends rule south to Saigon
1757	Nguyen rule extended over entire Mekong delta
1802	Nguyen unifies Vietnam and establishes a new dynasty

sent missions that professed the Vietnamese ruler's submission to the Chinese emperor. In official communications with the Chinese "emperor," the Vietnamese rulers styled themselves as "kings," indicating their subordinate status.

Such submission, however, was purely formal. Within Vietnam, Vietnamese rulers styled themselves as "emperors" and claimed that their mandate to rule came directly from Heaven, separate but equal to the mandate received by the Chinese emperor. They also denied the universality of the Chinese imperium by referring to China not as the Middle Kingdom but as the Northern Court—their own government being the Southern Court. In 1076, a Vietnamese general fighting Chinese troops wrote the following poem:

> *The Southern emperor rules the Southern land*
> *Our destiny is writ in Heaven's Book*
> *How dare you bandits trespass on our soil*
> *You shall meet your undoing at our hands*[11]

One should note that the poem was in Chinese, Vietnam's only written language, and couched in the terminology of Chinese political thought.

---

[11] S. T. Huynh, *The Heritage of Vietnamese Poetry* (1979), p. 3. Reprinted by permission. Yale University Press.

Late Traditional Vietnam

The first four centuries of an independent Vietnam, the Ly and Tran dynasties (1009–1400), were not remarkable. Vietnam was often divided into regional states that frequently fought wars with each other or with Champa to the south. The Tran dynasty weakened at the end; Vietnam was conquered by Chinese armies in 1407 and was ruled by a Chinese governor for twenty years. Chinese rule, however, proved so exploitative that a rebellion rose against it. The rebellion was led by Le Loi, a landowner from Thanh Hoa, who, in southeast Asian style, used war-elephants against the Chinese troops. After his victory, he went on to establish the Le dynasty (1428–1787).

Two momentous developments began in Vietnam during the fifteenth century under Le, and continued during the centuries that followed. One was centralization and a more extensive use of Chinese institutions. For Vietnam, Chinese institutions and culture were an advanced technology that could be used to strengthen government. The reforms of Le Thanh Tong (1442–1497), an immensely talented early ruler, were especially notable. He divided his realm into thirteen provinces and then into prefectures, counties, and departments. He weakened the nobility by holding civil service examinations for the selection of officials, and set up nine ranks of civil and military officials. He established schools, introduced Neo-Confucian learning, and promoted public works. He registered the population and reinstituted a Chinese-type land tax. In the decades after his death, many reforms broke down, but in time other reformers appeared and carried the process a step further. Overall, the influence of Chinese culture was greater than that of occupation by Chinese armies.

The second development, which also was begun by Le Thanh Tong, was what Vietnamese historians call "the march to the south." Vietnamese armies conquered the state of Champa in 1471. This opened the way for a centuries-long movement of Vietnamese into the central and southern portions of what is today Vietnam (See Map 19–5). To secure the lands he had conquered, Le established self-supporting colonies of Vietnamese soldier-peasants along the coast of the former kingdom. These became a part of the local population. To rule the Muslim Chams, in 1483 he promulgated a Confucian-tinged legal code that remained in effect through most of the dynasty. It appealed to "universal" values that could be accepted by both Vietnamese and Chams—not unlike the *jus gentium* used by the Romans to rule the diverse peoples of their empire. Le's successors were unable to maintain control over the central coast, and autonomous Vietnamese states arose in the area. These impeded the passage of settlers to the south during the sixteenth and early seventeenth centuries.

Politics and demography became entwined. During the complex history of the middle and late Le dynasty, northern Vietnam was governed, in fact, by the Trinh family, and

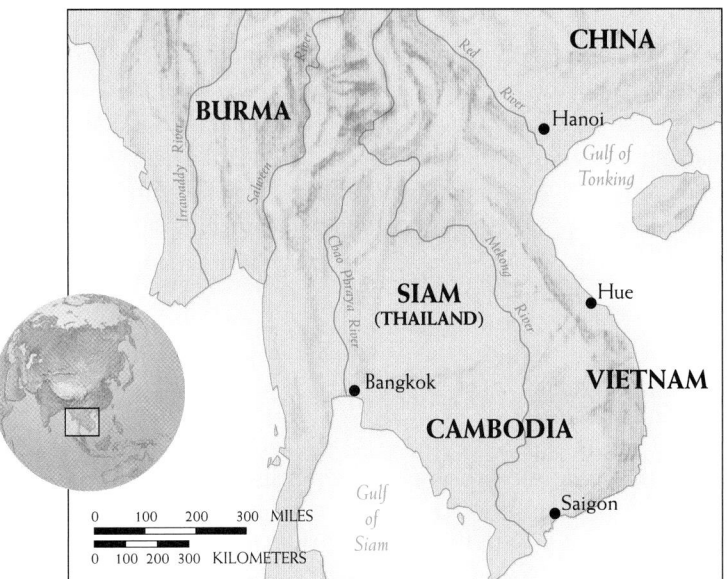

Map 19–5.   Vietnam and Neighboring Southeast Asia

central Vietnam was ruled by the Nguyen from their capital city of Hue. In the seventeenth century, the Mekong delta (today's south Vietnam) was sparsely settled, mostly by Chams and Cambodians. The Nguyen court in Hue extended its rule south to Saigon in 1698 by sending an official to settle a commercial dispute between a Chinese and a Cambodian. By 1757, the Nguyen had further extended their control over the entire Mekong delta westward to the Gulf of Siam. Political control facilitated the continued movement of Vietnamese from the densely settled north to the south, though they remained a minority in southern Vietnam throughout the eighteenth century.

Another phenomenon affecting Vietnam was the Chinese diaspora to southeast Asia. The fall of the Ming dynasty in 1644 led to the first wave of Chinese emigrants. By the century's end substantial numbers of Chinese had settled and formed communities in the Mekong delta. Some became Saigon merchants, selling rice to Chinese merchants in Singapore. Today, about a million partially assimilated Chinese live in southern Vietnam and play a major role in its economy.

In the late eighteenth century, wars broke out between the north and the Nguyen in Hue. By 1802 the Nguyen had defeated the northern armies, unified the country, and established a new dynasty. It kept its capital at Hue. In coming to power the new emperor had been aided by French advisers and adventurers, several of whom were rewarded with high official posts. But from the time of the second emperor, the Nguyen dynasty turned against the French and became anti-Christian in its policies.

The Nguyen dynasty thus became more Chinese than any previous dynasty. (See Document, "On Husband-Sharing.") It adopted the law codes of Manchu China and established institutions such as the Six Boards, Hanlin Academy, Censorate, and a hierarchy of civil and military officials recruited by examinations. The reasons for these initiatives were to placate Confucian scholars in the north, to strengthen the court, and to weaken the military figures who had helped the dynasty's rise.

During the first half of the nineteenth century, Vietnam was probably governed better than in any previous era and better than any other Southeast Asian state. By any traditional standard, it was governed competently, but it had weaknesses. There were tensions between the north, which was overpopulated, well schooled, and furnished most of the official class,

---

On Husband-Sharing   Document

The position of women in Vietnam may have been higher than in China, but Vietnamese officials still had concubines when they could afford them. The eighteenth-century poet Ho Xuang Huong gives her view on the subject.

◆ Should this poem be read as a criticism of the prevailing Confucian ethos?

> One rolls in warm blankets,
> The other freezes:
> Down with this husband-sharing!
> You're lucky ever to have him,
> He comes perhaps twice a month,
> Or less.
> Ah—to fight for—this!

> Turned to a half-servant, an unpaid maid!
> Had I known
> I would have stayed single.

From *A Thousand Years of Vietnamese Poetry*, by Nguyen Ngoc Bich. Copyright © 1975 by The Asia Society. Reprinted by permission.

Hue. A gate from the imperial citadel.

and the south, which was ethnically diverse, educationally backward, and poorly represented in government. Trade and artisanal industries were less developed than in China and Japan, only small amounts of specie circulated, and periodic markets were more common than market towns. The government rested on a society composed largely of self-sufficient villages. In sum, Vietnam entered the second half of the nineteenth century even less prepared than China or Japan for the challenges it would soon face.

Summary

China. China's last two imperial dynasties were the Ming (1368–1644) and the Qing or Manchus (1644–1911). Although China could not match the dynamism of the West during these years, its society became more integrated and its government more sophisticated. The population reached 410 million, cities grew, and commerce expanded.

INTERPRETING THE PAST

Japan, the Shōgunate, and the West

Text Sources from MyHistoryLab / Primary Source DVD

1. Tokugawa Shōgunate, The Laws for the Military House
2. Japan Encounters the West, 1587–1640

Visual Sources from MyHistoryLab / Primary Source DVD

1. The Tokaido Road
2. Jesuit Martyrs in Japan
3. Title Page from a Japanese Anatomy Text, 1775

The primary sources for this chapter illustrate Japan's unique social system and government that existed from the late traditional era to the middle of nineteenth century. Japanese military leaders (*shoguns*) created what has been termed "a premodern police state" as well as heavily restricting contact with Westerners by the early seventeenth century. The first document lists some of the rules that *shoguns* imposed on daimyos (regional nobility and warlords) within their own provinces as well as at the *shōgun's* court at Edo (Tokyo) where they were required to be in attendance at certain times of the year. The second document details the gradual "closing of Japan" from the 1580s to the 1630s. The visual sources add context to the shōgun's policy of insulating Japan from foreign influence for over two centuries.

Use the sources to address the following thematic questions that deal with Japanese leadership's harsh domestic policies, as well as their efforts to strictly control contacts with Westerners and their culture. Use specific examples from the documents to back up your assertions.

Chinese government rested a bureaucracy educated in Confucian teachings and the gentry class. Under the Manchus, China expanded to the west and east, establishing claims to Tibet, Central Asia, and Taiwan. Trade with the West grew, especially with Britain, but it was controlled by Chinese officials.

Japan. After more than a century of civil war among warrior states (the Warring States era, 1467–1600), the Tokugawa shōgun (1600–1868) restored order. Their Edo government controlled the military houses and encouraged economic growth. Japan became closed to the outside world except for a small Dutch presence at Nagasaki. Japanese drama, literature, and art flourished, as did commercial life.

Korea and Vietnam. The fact that "late traditional" history is not the same as "early modern" history is made clear by the development of Korea and Vietnam prior to the nineteenth century. Both countries were tributaries of China, a status that Korea took seriously. Both developed according to their own internal dynamics. Vietnam was notable for its conquest

and peopling of the Mekong delta. Korea, for its Confucian culture, yangban aristocracy, and the institution of slavery.

Review Questions

1. What factors led to economic and population growth in late traditional China? Was the pattern the same in Japan during those centuries?

2. How was Manchu rule like Mongol rule during the Yuan dynasty? How was it like the rule by Chinese emperors during the Ming?

3. What were the social and administrative foundations of the absolute power of Ming-Qing emperors?

4. How did advances in military technology change warfare in sixteenth-century Japan? How was the strategic balance of power reflected in the government created by Tokugawa Ieyasu?

5. Did literacy ruin the samurai or improve them? How did literate samurai "fit" the changed society of the late eighteenth century?

6. "Without some notion of 'human rights,' there can be no imperialism. Hideyoshi's invasion of Korea, the Chinese conquest of Tibet, and the Vietnamese 'march to the south' were all healthy and normal actions by strong states". Discuss.

Key Terms

daimyo (dye-myoh) (p. 578)

gentry (p. 569)

Kabuki (p. 588)

Nō (p. 588)

National Studies (p. 594)

yangban (yahng-bahn) (p. 598)

Questions

What methods did the Tokugawa Shogunate employ in its efforts to maintain strict control over regional *daimyo*? Would these methods help or hinder the shōguns attempts to limit the spread of Christianity?

In viewing the Tokaido Road color print, how did the Japanese environment assist the shogun's policy of insulating Japan from outside influence?

What policy changes are evident in the *Japan Encounters the West* documents dating from 1587 to 1640? How are Europeans depicted? How are Japanese depicted?

Considering the title page from a Japanese anatomy text from 1775 and the excerpt, how and why would Western knowledge (medicine and science) be able to penetrate Japan's formidable policy of isolation?

Note: To learn more about the topics in this chapter, please turn to the Suggested Readings at the end of the book. For additional sources related to this chapter please see the Primary Source DVD at the back of this text or MyHistoryLab.

20

State Building and Society in Early Modern Europe

ETWEEN THE EARLY SEVENTEENTH AND MID–TWENTIETH centuries no region so dominated other parts of the world politically, militarily, and economically as Europe. Such had not been the situation before that time and would not be the situation after World War II. However, for approximately three and a half centuries northwestern Europe became the chief driving force in one world historical development after another. Two broad factors accounted for this situation.

First, by the mid–eighteenth century five major states had come to dominate European politics and would continue to do so until at least World War I. They were Great Britain, France, Austria, Prussia, and Russia. These states established their dominance at the expense of Spain, Portugal, the United Provinces of the Netherlands, Poland, Sweden, and the Ottoman Empire. Equally essential to their rise was the weakness of the Holy Roman Empire after the Peace of Westphalia (1648).

Commencing in the late seventeenth century these five successful states entered upon over a

Schonbrunn Palace, Vienna. To symbolize his vast royal authority Louis XIV of France constructed a vast new palace at Versailles outside Paris as the center of his government. Subsequently, other European monarchs built similar palaces. Between 1743 and 1763 the Austrian Empress Maria Theresa carried out the construction of the Schonbrunn Palace on the outskirts of Vienna to symbolize Habsburg authority.

Early Modern Europe

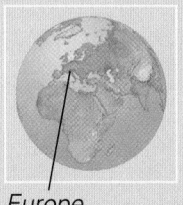

Europe

During the seventeenth and eighteenth centuries political and economic developments occurred in Europe that set the continent on a path that by the nineteenth century resulted in a period of European world domination that ultimately proved temporary. The major states of northwestern Europe consolidated themselves politically and militarily in strong, often aggressive political units. The economy of this region of Europe would take the first steps towards industrialization and the capacity to produce vast quantities of both consumer and capital goods. These same states developed sophisticated financial structures that fueled their overseas commercial empires, which in the cases of the Netherlands, France, and Great Britain could be protected by strong navies.

It is important to recognize that all of those world-transforming developments occurred slowly. At the beginning of this era of political and economic consolidation much of Europe resembled other major world civilizations. By the second quarter of the eighteenth century, the major European powers were not yet nation-states in which the citizens felt themselves united by a shared sense of community, culture, language, and history. They were still monarchies in which the personality of the ruler and the personal relationships of the great noble families considerably influenced public affairs. As yet they differed little in political and social structures from many other societies in the world, and they still lagged behind India, China, and some parts of the Islamic world in population density and urbanization. However, industry and military technology were beginning to reverse the global balance of power between Europe and Asia.

These European states displayed certain problems that also characterized the governments of China and Japan during the same epochs. In particular, as in Japan, the problem of a balance between centralization and decentralization arose in virtually all the European states. In France, Russia, and Prussia, the forces of centralization proved quite strong. In Austria the forces of decentralization were powerful. England achieved a rather delicate balance. Furthermore, as in Tokugawa, Japan, European states of the eighteenth century generally saw an increase in legal codification and in the growth of bureaucracy. Only in Prussia did the military influence on society resemble that in Japan.

The role of the personality of the monarch in Europe bore some resemblance to that of certain Manchu emperors in China, such as Kangxi (1662–1722) and Qianlong (r. 1736–1795). Louis XIV and Peter the Great had no less influence on their nations than did these great Manchu emperors. All of them built up military strength and fostered innovation. However, although European rulers developed state bureaucra-

hundred years of warfare among themselves. These wars were fought first in Europe and then in both Europe and the European colonial empires, making them the first extensive world wars. These conflicts produced the most extensive European impact on the non-European world since the early sixteenth century when the Spanish had conquered the civilizations of Mexico and Peru.

The second factor in the dominance of Europe on the world scene was that during these decades the peoples living primarily in northwestern Europe undertook a series of economic advances that laid the foundation for the social and economic transformation of the world. Europeans began for the first time in their history to achieve a more or less stable food supply. For reasons still much debated, the population of Europe commenced a major period of growth. New inventions in the manufacture of textiles transformed Europe's productive capacity, and the invention of the steam engine, powered by coal as a fuel, opened the way for moving manufacturing from the countryside to cities. Furthermore, the production of iron greatly expanded. These developments, known collectively as the Industrial Revolution, gave Europe a productive capacity previously unknown in human history.

cies, none of them put together so brilliant a group of trained civil servants as those who administered China. The roots of the Chinese civil service went back centuries, and Chinese civil servants, unlike those in Europe, tended to resist modernization of the Chinese government and economy for both practical and ideological reasons. Civil servants in Europe, perhaps because they rose to power simultaneously with Europe's industrialization, tended to foster rather than obstruct modernization, which posed no threat to their power or worldview.

The global commercial empires of the Netherlands, France, Spain, and England gave rise to fierce commercial rivalries. The drive for empire and commercial supremacy propelled these states into contact with Africa, Latin America, India, China, and Japan. Spain and Portugal had long exploited Latin America as their own monopoly, an arrangement that England challenged in the eighteenth century. China's lack of interest in dominating the Indian Ocean opened the way for European adventurers and traders in India. France and England fought for commercial supremacy in India, and by the 1760s England had, in effect, conquered the subcontinent. The slave trade between Africa and the New World flourished throughout the seventeenth and the eighteenth century. European merchants and navies also sought to penetrate East Asia, although their success was limited until the advent of nineteenth-century "gunboat diplomacy." As this term implies, European success in Africa, Asia, and the Indian Ocean was always closely linked to its sophisticated military technology, and especially the construction of sturdy ships able to carry heavy cannons. As a result of these developments, European commerce dominated the world for the next two centuries. Europe and its colonists extracted labor and other natural resources from virtually all the other continents of the world. These assets in turn only widened the growing gap in wealth and power that separated Europe from the rest of the world in the nineteenth and twentieth centuries.

Consequently, by the mid–eighteenth century, the European states that just two centuries earlier lagged behind China in wealth and technology, had made their power and influence felt throughout the world. Beginning in the early eighteenth century with the slow but later steady growth of industrialism, the political power of the European states became linked to a qualitatively different economic base than any seen elsewhere in the world. That political and economic combination allowed Europe to dominate the world from the 1750s to the Second World War.

Focus Questions

◆ How did European states resemble those in other parts of the world in the mid–eighteenth century? How did they differ?

◆ What was the relationship between military technology, especially naval power, and the growth of European colonial empires?

◆ What factors led to the political and economic transformation of western Europe and its emergence as a region that would eventually (for a time) dominate much of the world?

That state of economic advance provided Europeans with the tools to dominate much of the world both economically and militarily. ■

European Political Consolidation

Two Models of European Political Development

In the second half of the sixteenth century, changes in European military organization, weapons, and tactics sharply increased the cost of warfare. Because traditional sources of state income could not finance these growing military costs, monarchs sought new revenues. Monarchies that succeeded in building a secure financial base independent of the support of noble estates, diets, or assemblies achieved what later became known as absolute rule. The French monarchy was the most successful example of such centralized government. The English monarchy, by contrast, failed to make itself absolute, but rather by the end of the seventeenth century could govern only with and through Parliament. These differing paths of political development led to the two distinct models of government—**absolutism** in France and **parliamentary monarchy** in England—that shaped subsequent political development in Europe.

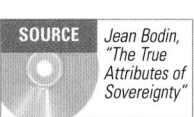

SOURCE Jean Bodin, "The True Attributes of Sovereignty"

Towards Parliamentary Government in England

When Elizabeth I died in 1603 without children, the English crown passed to James VI of Scotland, the son of Mary, Queen of Scots, who became James I of England, the first of the Stuart dynasty. In their pursuit of adequate income, Stuart monarchs of seventeenth-century England threatened the local political interests and economic well-being of the nobility and the landed and commercial elites represented in Parliament. These groups in turn over the course of the decades invoked traditional English liberties to effectively resist the monarchs. Furthermore, **Puritans** in the Church of England, whose Protestant religious views derived from John Calvin, wished to see a more radical reformation carried out in England. While attempting to rule as much as possible without Parliament, both James I (r. 1603–1625) and his son Charles I (r. 1625–1649) also resisted the Puritan demands and at the same time favored peaceful relations with the Roman Catholic powers Spain and France. Consequently the first two Stuarts confronted a combined political and religious opposition to their efforts to make the English monarchy the supreme power in the land. Many of the same political leaders who saw themselves defending traditional English liberties against the monarchy also saw themselves as having to protect the Protestant Reformation in England. Throughout both reigns Parliament sought to assert its rights and to place limitations on royal power particularly in regard to taxation and other royal efforts to exercise arbitrary power. (See Document, "Parliament Presents Charles I with the Petition of Right.")

By 1642 the conflict between Charles I and Parliament over religion and arbitrary taxation erupted into civil war. In 1645 the parliamentary and Puritan forces triumphed. Disputes continued, and in 1649 a rump Parliament from whom any opposing members had been removed voted for the execution of Charles I. Thereafter, Parliament abolished the monarchy, the House of Lords, and the established Church of England. What replaced them was a Puritan republic led by Oliver Cromwell (1599–1658), the victorious general in the civil war. Cromwell himself soon encountered difficulties with Parliament and from 1653 onward governed as a military dictator.

After Cromwell died in 1658, disillusionment with Puritan strictness and political uncertainty led to the restoration of the Stuart monarchy under Charles II (r. 1660–1685). The restored monarch would have extended very considerable religious toleration, but the restored Parliament dominated by conservative members of the Church of England imposed a restrictive religious code on the land. Thereafter the Church of England found itself opposed by both Protestant Non-Conformists and Roman Catholics. Charles II in 1670 entered a secret treaty with Louis XIV of France to oppose the

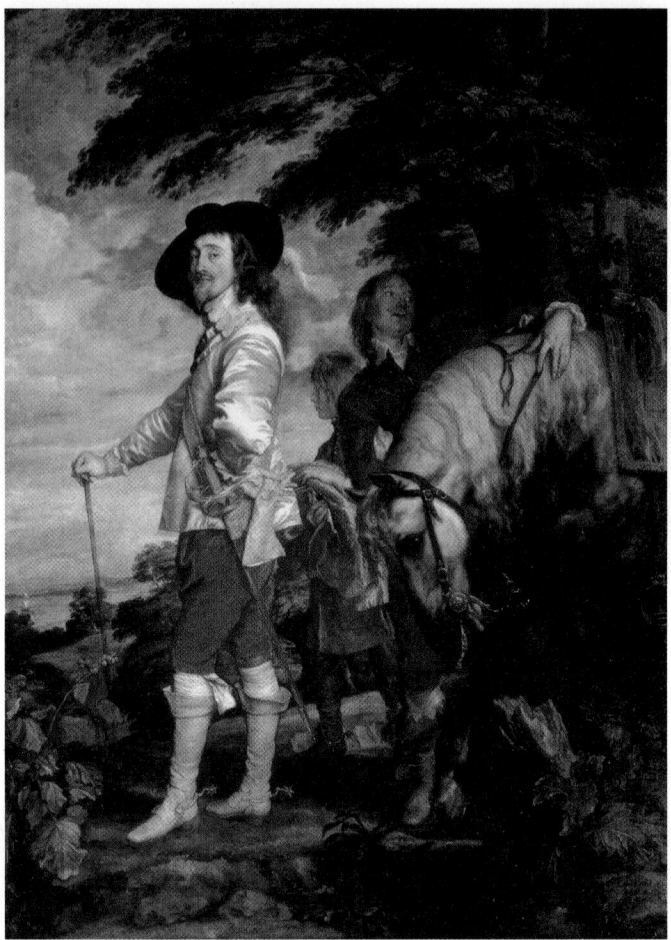

Charles I ruled for several years without calling Parliament, but once he began a war with Scotland, he needed revenues that only Parliament could supply. *Musée du Louvre, Pans/Superstock*

Dutch. As a result of that treaty, Charles again attempted to extend religious toleration. Parliament resisted by passing a Test Act that required all officials to take an oath, which no Roman Catholic could in good conscience take.

James, Duke of York, Charles's brother, was a Roman Catholic and became monarch in 1685. Immediately he extended toleration to both Roman Catholics and the Protestant Non-Conformists. In June 1688 James II (r. 1685–1688) imprisoned seven Anglican bishops who had refused to publicize his suspension of laws against Catholics. Under the guise of a policy of enlightened toleration, James was actually seeking to subject all English institutions to the power of the monarchy.

The English political classes had hoped that James would be succeeded by Mary (r. 1689–1694), his Protestant eldest daughter. She was the wife of William of Orange (1650–1702), stadtholder of the Netherlands, great-grandson of William the Silent (1533–1584), and the leader of European opposition to Louis XIV. But on June 20, 1688, James II's Catholic second wife gave birth to a son. There was now a Catholic male heir to the throne. The Parliamen-

Parliament Presents Charles I with the Petition of Right

Document

After becoming monarch in 1625 Charles I (r. 1625–1649) had imposed unparliamentary taxes, coerced freemen, and quartered troops in transit in private homes. These actions deeply offended Parliament, which in 1628 refused to grant him any funds until he rescinded those practices by recognizing the Petition of Right (June 1628). The Petition constituted a general catalog of the offenses associated with the exercise of arbitrary royal authority. Note, however, that both the Parliament and the King refer to the role of law and recognized limitations on political power and that neither appeals to any kind of divine authority. Compare this document with the document "Bishop Bossuet Defends the Divine Right of Kings" on p. 612.

◆ What limits does the Petition attempt to place on royal taxation? How did the Petition criticize arbitrary arrest? Why was the quartering of soldiers in private homes so offensive?

[The Lords Spirit and Temporal, and commons in Parliament assembled] do humbly pray your Most Excellent Majesty, that no man hereafter be compelled to make or yield any gift, loan, benevolence, tax, or such like charge, without common consent by Act of parliament; and that none be called to make answer, to take such oath, or to give attendance, or be confined, or otherwise molested or disquieted concerning the same, or for refusal thereof; and that no freeman, in any such manner as in before-mentioned, be imprisoned or detained; and that your Majesty will be pleased to remove the said soldiers and mariners [who have been quartered in private homes], and that your people may not be so burdened in time to come; and that the foresaid commissions for proceeding by martial law, may be revoked and annulled; and that hereafter no commissions of like nature may issue forth to any person or persons whatso-

ever, to be executed as aforesaid, lest by colour of them any of your Majesty's subjects be destroyed or put to death, contrary to the laws and franchise of the land.

All which they most humble pray of your Most Excellent Majesty, as their rights and liberties according to the laws and statues of this realm.

The King's Reply: The King willeth that right be done according to the laws and customs of the realm; and that the statutes be put in due execution, that his subjects may have no cause to complain of any wrong or oppressions, contrary to their just rights and liberties, to the preservation whereof he holds himself as well obliged as of his prerogative.

Samuel R. Gardiner, ed., *The Constitutional Documents of the Puritan Revolution* (Oxford: Clarendon Press, 1889), pp. 4–5.

tary opposition invited William to invade England to preserve its "traditional liberties," that is, the Anglican Church and parliamentary government.

The "Glorious Revolution"

William of Orange arrived with his army in November 1688 and was received without opposition by the English people. James fled to France, and Parliament in 1689 proclaimed William III and Mary II the new monarchs, thus completing the bloodless **Glorious Revolution**. William and Mary, in turn, recognized a Bill of Rights that limited the powers of the monarchy and guaranteed the civil liberties of the English privileged classes. Henceforth, England's monarchs would be subject to law and would rule by the consent of Parliament, which was to be called into session every three years. The Bill of Rights also prohibited Roman Catholics from occupying the English throne. The Toleration Act of 1689 permitted

worship by all Protestants but outlawed Roman Catholics and those who denied the Christian doctrine of the Trinity.

The measure closing this century of strife was the Act of Settlement in 1701. This bill provided for the English crown to go to the Protestant House of Hanover in Germany if Anne (r. 1702–1714), the second daughter of James II and the heir to the childless William III, died without issue. Thus, at Anne's death in 1714, the Elector of Hanover became King George I of England (r. 1714–1727), the third foreigner to occupy the English throne in just over a century.

Under the Hanoverians, Britain achieved political stability and economic prosperity during the first quarter of the eighteenth century. Robert Walpole (1676–1745) eventually became George I's chief minister. Walpole's ascendancy from 1721 to 1742 was based on royal support, his ability to handle the House of Commons, and his iron-fisted control of government patronage. He maintained peace abroad and promoted the status quo at home. Britain's foreign trade spread

Chronology

England

1603	James VI of Scotland becomes James I of England
1625	Charles I becomes king of England
1629	Charles I dissolves Parliament and embarks on eleven years of personal rule
1640	April–May, Short Parliament; November, Long Parliament convenes
1642	Outbreak of the Civil War
1649	Charles I executed
1649–1660	Various attempts at a Puritan Commonwealth
1660	Charles II restored to the English throne
1670	Secret Treaty of Dover between France and England
1672	Parliament passes the Test Act
1685	James II becomes king of England
1688	Glorious Revolution
1689	William III and Mary II come to the throne of England
1701	Act of Settlement provides for Hanoverian Succession
1702–1714	Queen Anne, the last of the Stuarts
1714	George I of Hanover becomes king of England
1721–1742	Ascendancy of Sir Robert Walpole

from New England to India. Agriculture became more productive. Because the dominant economic groups were represented in Parliament, they were willing to pay the taxes to support a powerful military force, particularly a strong navy. As a result, Great Britain became not only a European power of the first order, but also eventually a world power.

The power of the British monarchs and their ministers had real limits. Parliament could not wholly ignore popular pressure. Even with the extensive use of patronage, many members of Parliament maintained independent views. Newspapers and public debate flourished. Free speech could be exercised, as could freedom of association. There was no large standing army. Walpole's enemies could and did openly oppose his policies in a fashion impossible on the Continent.

Consequently, the English state embodied both very considerable military power and political liberty. British political life became the model for all progressive Europeans who questioned the absolutist political developments of the Continent. Furthermore, many of the political values that had emerged in the British Isles during the seventeenth century also took deep root among their North American colonies.

Rise of Absolute Monarchy in France: The World of Louis XIV

The French monarchy trod a very different political path. Louis XIV (r. 1643–1715) came to the throne at the age of five. During his childhood Cardinal Mazarin (1602–1661), his chief minister, tried to impose direct royal administration on France. These efforts aroused a series of widespread rebellions among French nobles between 1649 and 1652 known as the Fronde (after the slingshot used by street boys).

Louis XIV of France (r. 1643–1715) was the dominant European monarch in the second half of the seventeenth century. The powerful centralized monarchy he created established the prototype for the mode of government later termed absolutism. *Bridgeman-Giraudon/Art Resource, N.Y.*

Years of Personal Rule

On the death of Mazarin in 1661 Louis XIV assumed personal control of the government at the age of twenty-three. Convinced by the Fronde that heavy-handed policies could endanger the monarchy, Louis concentrated unprecedented authority in the monarchy, but he took care not to intrude excessively on local social and political institutions. He appointed no chief minister. Rebellious nobles would now be challenging the king directly; they could not claim to be resisting only a bad minister.

Louis ruled through powerful councils that controlled foreign affairs, the army, domestic administration, and economic regulations. Each day he spent hours with the chief ministers of these councils, whom he chose from families long in royal service or from among people just beginning to rise in the social structure. Unlike the more ancient noble families, they had no real or potential power bases in the provinces and depended solely on the king for their standing in both government and society.

More than any other monarch of the day, Louis XIV used the physical setting of his court to exert political control. The palace at Versailles, built between 1676 and 1708 on the outskirts of Paris, became Louis' permanent residence after 1682. It was a temple to royalty, architecturally designed and artistically decorated to proclaim the glory of the Sun King, as Louis was known. A spectacular estate with magnificent fountains and gardens, it housed thousands of the more important nobles, royal officials, and servants. Moments near the king were important to most court nobles because they were effectively excluded from the real business of government. The king's rising and dressing were times of rare intimacy, when nobles could whisper their special requests in his ear. Fortunate nobles held his night candle as they accompanied him to his bed.

Versailles. Louis XIV constructed his great palace at Versailles, as painted here in 1668 by Pierre Patel the Elder (1605–1676), to demonstrate the new centralized power he sought to embody in the French monarchy. The central building is the hunting lodge his father Louis XIII had built earlier in the century. Its interior and that of the wings added to it were decorated with themes from mythology presenting Louis XIV as the "Sun King" around whom all his kingdom revolved. The gardens and ponds behind the main structure were the sites of elaborate entertainment, concerts, and fireworks. *Pierre Patel, "Perspective View of Versailles." Châteaux de Versailles et de Trianon, Versailles, France. Photo copyright Bridgeman-Giraudon/Art Resource, N.Y.*

An important source for Louis' concept of royal authority was his devout tutor, the political theorist Bishop Jacques-Bénigne Bossuet (1627–1704). In direct contrast to the English Puritan challenges to royal authority, Bossuet defended what he called the **"divine right of kings."** He cited examples of Old Testament rulers divinely appointed by and answerable only to God. Medieval popes had insisted that only God could judge a pope; so Bossuet argued that only God could judge the king. Although kings might be duty bound to reflect God's will in their rule, as God's regents on earth they could not be bound to the dictates of mere nobles and parliaments. Such assumptions lay behind Louis XIV's alleged declaration: *"L'état, c'est moi"* ("I am the state"). (See Document, "Bishop Bossuet Defends the Divine Right of Kings.")

Louis was determined to unify France religiously. In October 1685 he revoked the Edict of Nantes (1598), which had extended protections to the Huguenots. Protestant churches and schools were closed, Protestant ministers exiled, nonconverting laity forced to be galley slaves, and Protestant children ceremonially baptized by Catholic priests. The revocation prompted the emigration of more than a quarter of a million people, who formed new communities and joined the resistance to France in England, Germany, Holland, and the New World.

Bishop Bossuet Defends the Divine Right of Kings

Document

The revolutions of the seventeenth century caused many to fear anarchy far more than tyranny, among them the influential French bishop Jacques-Bénigne Bossuet (1627–1704), the leader of French Catholicism in the second half of the seventeenth century. Louis XIV made him court preacher and tutor to his son, for whom Bossuet wrote a celebrated *Discourse on Universal History*. In the following excerpt, Bossuet defends the divine right and absolute power of kings. He depicts kings as embracing in their person the whole body of the state and the will of the people they govern and, as such, as being immune from judgment by any mere mortal. Compare this document with the assertions of Parliamentary authority and the rule of law in the document, "Parliament Presents Charles I with the Petition of Right" on page 609.

◆ Why might Bossuet have wished to make such extravagant claims for absolute royal power? How might these claims be transferred to any form of government? What are the religious bases for Bossuet's argument? How does this argument for absolute royal authority lead also to the need for a single uniform religion in France?

The royal power is absolute. . . . The prince need render account of his acts to no one. "I counsel thee to keep the king's commandment, and that in regard of the oath of God. Be not hasty to go out of his sight; stand not on an evil thing for he doeth whatsoever pleaseth him. Where the word of a king is, there is power; and who may say unto him, What doest thou? Whoso keepeth the commandment shall feel no evil thing" [Eccles. 8:2–5]. Without this absolute authority the king could neither do good nor repress evil. It is necessary that his power be such that no one can hope to escape him, and finally, the only protection of individuals against the public authority should be their innocence. This confirms the teaching of St. Paul: "Wilt thou then not be afraid of the power? Do that which is good" [Rom. 13:3].

God is infinite, God is all. The prince, as prince, is not regarded as a private person: he is a public personage, all the state is in him; the will of all the people is included in his. As all perfection and all strength are united in God, so all the power of individuals is united in the person of the prince. What grandeur that a single man should embody so much! . . .

Behold an immense people united in a single person; behold this holy power, paternal and absolute; behold the secret cause which governs the whole body of the state, contained in a single head: you see the image of God in the king, and you have the idea of royal majesty. God is holiness itself, goodness itself, and power itself. In these things lies the majesty of God. In the image of these things lies the majesty of the prince.

From *Politics Drawn from the Very Words of Holy Scripture*, as quoted in James Harvey Robinson, ed., *Readings in European History*, vol. 2 (Boston: Athenaeum, 1906), pp. 275–276.

As will be seen later in the chapter, Louis used most of the wealth and authority he had amassed to lead France into a long series of wars that ultimately weakened the nation by the time of his death in 1715. Yet despite those failures he had established a model of strong centralized monarchy that other monarchs in central and eastern Europe would copy. They believed Louis had been more successful than the Stuart monarchs of Great Britain, who by the early eighteenth century could rule only with and through Parliament.

Russia Enters the European Political Arena

The emergence of Russia as an active European power was a wholly new factor in European politics. Previously, Russia had been considered part of Europe only by courtesy, and before 1673 it did not send permanent ambassadors to Western Europe. Geographically and politically, it lay on the periphery. Hemmed in by Sweden on the Baltic and by the Ottoman Empire on the Black Sea, Russia had no warm-water ports. Its chief outlet for trade to the west was Archangel on the White Sea, which was ice-free for only part of the year.

Chronology

France

1649–1652	The *Fronde,* a revolt of nobility and townspeople against the crown
1661	Louis assumes personal rule
1667	Louis XIV invades Flanders
1672	France invades the United Provinces
1678–1679	Peace of Nijmwegen
1682	Louis establishes his court at Versailles
1685	Edict of Nantes revoked
1689–1697	Nine Years' War between France and the League of Augsburg
1697	Peace of Ryswick
1702–1714	War of the Spanish Succession
1713	Treaty of Utrecht between England and France
1714	Treaty of Rastadt between the emperor and France

Birth of the Romanov Dynasty

The second half of the sixteenth century had witnessed enormous political turmoil during the last half of the reign of Ivan IV (r. 1533–1584), later known as Ivan the Terrible. A period known as the Time of Troubles followed his death. In 1613, hoping to end the uncertainty, an assembly of nobles elected as tsar a seventeen-year-old boy named Michael Romanov (r. 1613–1645). Thus began the dynasty that ruled Russia until 1917. Though a new dynasty had been established, Russia remained weak and impoverished. The **boyars,** the old nobility, controlled the bureaucracy, while the **streltsy,** or guards of the Moscow garrison, persistently posed the danger of mutiny.

Peter the Great

In 1682, another boy—ten years old at the time—ascended the fragile Russian throne as co-ruler with his half brother. His name was Peter (r. 1682–1725), and Russia would never be the same after him. He and his sickly brother, who died in 1696, had come to power on the shoulders of the *streltsy,* who expected to be rewarded for their support. Like Louis XIV, the dangers and turmoil of his youth convinced Peter of two things: First, the power of the tsar must be made secure from the jealousy of the *boyars* and the greed of the *streltsy;* second, the military power of Russia must be increased.

Northwestern Europe, particularly the military resources of the maritime powers, fascinated Peter I, who eventually became known as Peter the Great. In 1697, he made a famous visit in transparent disguise to Western Europe. There he spent his happiest moments inspecting shipyards, docks, and the manufacture of military hardware in England and the Netherlands. Peter returned to Moscow determined to copy the technology he had seen abroad, for he knew warfare would be necessary to make Russia a great power. But he also understood his goal would require him to confront the long-standing power and traditions of the Russian nobles.

Taming the Streltsy and Boyars In 1698, before Peter's return from abroad, the *streltsy* had rebelled. On his return, Peter brutally suppressed the revolt with private tortures and public executions, in which his own ministers took part. Approximately a thousand of the rebels were put to death, and their corpses remained on public display to discourage future disloyalty.

Peter then built a new military establishment that would serve the tsar and not itself. He introduced effective and ruthless policies of conscription, drafting an unprecedented 130,000 soldiers during the first decade of the eighteenth century and almost 300,000 troops by the end of his

Peter the Great (r. 1682–1725), seeking to make Russia a military power, reorganized the country's political and economic structures. His reign saw Russia enter fully into European power politics. Here he is depicted as a latter-day St. George, slaying a dragon. *Art Archive/Picture Desk Inc./ Kobal Collection.*

reign. He adopted policies for the officer corps and general military discipline patterned on those of West European armies.

Peter also determined to make a sustained attack on the *boyars* and their attachment to traditional Russian culture. After his European journey, he personally shaved the long beards of the court *boyars* and sheared off the customary long hand-covering sleeves of their shirts and coats, which had made them the butt of jokes among other European courts. Peter became highly skilled at balancing one group against another, while never completely excluding any, as he set about to organize Russian government and military forces along the lines of the more powerful European states.

Developing a Navy   In the mid-1690s, Peter oversaw the construction of ships to protect his interests in the Black Sea against the Ottoman Empire. In 1695, he began a war with the Ottomans. Part of the reason for Peter's trip to

Western Europe in 1697 was to learn how to build still better warships, this time for combat on the Baltic. The construction of a Baltic fleet, largely constructed on the Finnish coast, was essential in the Great Northern War with Sweden (1700–1721), a struggle that over the years accounted for many of Peter's major steps towards Westernizing his realm. When the Great Northern War came to a close in 1721, the Peace of Nystad confirmed the Russian conquest of Estonia, Livonia, and part of Finland. Henceforth, Russia possessed ice-free ports and a permanent influence on European affairs.

Founding St. Petersburg   At one point, the domestic and foreign policies of Peter the Great intersected. This was at the site on the Gulf of Finland where he founded his new capital city of St. Petersburg in 1703. There he built government structures and compelled the *boyars* to construct town houses. He thus imitated those European monarchs who had copied Louis XIV by constructing smaller versions of Versailles. The founding of St. Petersburg went beyond establishing a central imperial court, however; it symbolized a new Western orientation of Russia and Peter's determination to hold his position on the Baltic coast.

The Case of Peter's Son Aleksei and Reforms of Peter the Great's Final Years   Other reforms arose from Peter's family difficulties. Peter's son Aleksei had been born to his first wife whom he had divorced in 1698. Peter was jealous of the young man, who had never demonstrated strong intelligence or ambition. Increasingly distrustful of his son, Peter became convinced by late 1717 that his court opponents looked to Aleksei as a focus for possible sedition while Russia remained at war with Sweden. Peter undertook an investigation during which he personally interrogated Aleksei, who was eventually condemned to death and died under mysterious circumstances on June 26, 1718.

The interrogations surrounding Aleksei had revealed greater degrees of court opposition than Peter had suspected. Recognizing he could not eliminate his numerous opponents the way he had attacked the *streltsy* in 1698, Peter undertook radical administrative reforms designed to bring the nobility and the Russian Orthodox Church more closely under the authority of persons loyal to the tsar.

Administrative Colleges   In December 1717 Peter reorganized his domestic administration to sustain his own personal authority and to fight rampant corruption. To achieve this goal, Peter looked to Swedish institutions called *colleges*—bureaus of several persons operating according to written instructions rather than departments headed by a single minister. These colleges, eight of which he imposed on Russian administration, were to look after matters such as the collection of taxes, foreign relations, war, and eco-

Vûe des bords de la Neva en descendant la rivière entre le Palais d'hyver de Sa Majesté Impériale & les batimens de l'Academie des Sciences

St. Petersburg. Peter the Great built St. Petersburg on the Gulf of Finland to provide Russia with better contact with Western Europe. He moved Russia's capital there from Moscow in 1703. This is an eighteenth-century view of the city. *The Granger Collection.*

nomic affairs. Each college was to receive advice from a foreigner. Peter used his appointive power to balance the influence in these colleges between nobles and persons he was certain would be personally loyal to himself.

Achieving Secular Control of the Church Peter also moved to suppress the independence of the Russian Orthodox Church, where some bishops and clergy had displayed sympathy for the tsar's son. In 1721, Peter simply abolished the position of *patriarch*, the bishop who had been head of the church. In its place he established a government department called the *Holy Synod*, which consisted of several bishops headed by a layman called the *procurator general*. This body would govern the church in accordance with the tsar's secular requirements.

Table of Ranks In 1722 Peter published a **Table of Ranks** intended to draw the nobility into state service. That table equated a person's social position and privileges with his rank in the bureaucracy or the military, rather than with his lineage among the traditional landed nobility, many of whom continued to resent the changes Peter had introduced into Russia. Peter thus made the social standing of individual *boyars* a function of their willingness to serve the central state.

For all the numerous decisive actions Peter had taken since 1717, he still had not settled on a successor. Consequently, when he died in 1725, there was no clear line of succession to the throne. For more than thirty years, soldiers

Chronology

Rise of Russian Power

1533–1584	Reign of Ivan the Terrible
1584–1613	Time of Troubles
1613	Michael Romanov becomes tsar
1682	Peter the Great becomes tsar as a boy
1689	Peter assumes personal rule
1697	European tour of Peter the Great
1698	Peter suppresses the *streltsy*
1700	The Great Northern War opens between Russia and Sweden; Russia defeated at Narva by Charles XII
1703	Saint Petersburg founded
1709	Russia defeats Sweden at Poltava
1718	Death of Aleksei, son of Peter the Great
1721	Peace of Nystad ends the Great Northern War
1721	Peter establishes control over the Russian church
1722	The Table of Ranks
1725	Peter dies, leaving an uncertain succession

and nobles again determined who ruled Russia. Peter had laid the foundations of a modern Russia, but not the foundations of a stable state.

The Habsburg Empire and the Pragmatic Sanction

After 1648 the Habsburg family retained a firm hold on the title of Holy Roman Emperor, but the power of the emperor depended less on force of arms than on the cooperation he could elicit from the various political bodies in the empire. These included large German units (such as Saxony, Hanover, Bavaria, and Brandenburg) and scores of small German cities, bishoprics, principalities, and territories of independent knights. While establishing their new dominance among the German states, the Habsburgs also began to consolidate their power and influence within their hereditary possessions outside the Holy Roman Empire, which included the Crown of Saint Wenceslas, encompassing the kingdom of Bohemia (in modern Czechoslovakia) and the duchies of Moravia and Silesia; and the Crown of Saint Stephen, which ruled Hungary, Croatia, and Transylvania. In each of their many territories, the Habsburgs ruled by virtue of a different title and needed the cooperation of the local nobility, which was not always forthcoming. They

repeatedly had to bargain with nobles in one part of Europe to maintain their position in another.

Despite these internal difficulties, Leopold I (r. 1658–1705) managed to resist the advances of the Turks into central Europe, which included a siege of Vienna in 1683, and to thwart the aggression of Louis XIV. He achieved Ottoman recognition of his sovereignty over Hungary in 1699 and extended his territorial holdings over much of the Balkan Peninsula and present-day western Romania (see Map 20–1).

In the early eighteenth century the Habsburg emperor Charles VI (r. 1711–1740) had no male heir, and there was only a weak precedent for a female ruler of the Habsburg domains. Charles feared that on his death the Austrian Habsburg lands might fall prey to the surrounding powers. Determined to prevent that disaster and to provide his domains with the semblance of legal unity, he devoted most of his reign to seeking the approval of his family, the estates of his realms, and the major foreign powers for a document called the **Pragmatic Sanction**.

This instrument provided the legal basis for a single line of inheritance within the Habsburg dynasty through Charles VI's daughter Maria Theresa (1740–1780). After extracting various concessions from Charles, the nobles of the various Habsburg domains and the other European rulers did likewise. Consequently, when Charles VI died in October 1740,

Map 20–1.　The Austrian Habsburg Empire, 1521–1772. The empire had three main units—Austria, Bohemia, and Hungary. Expansion was mainly eastward: eastern Hungary from the Ottomans (seventeenth century) and Galicia from Poland (1772). Meantime, Silesia was lost after 1740, but the Habsburgs remained Holy Roman Emperors.

he believed that he had secured legal unity for the Habsburg Empire and a safe succession for his daughter. Despite the Pragmatic Sanction, however, his failure to provide his daughter with a strong army or a full treasury left her inheritance open to foreign aggression. Less than two months after his death, the fragility of the foreign agreements became apparent. In December 1740 Frederick II of Prussia invaded the Habsburg province of Silesia. Maria Theresa had to fight for her inheritance.

The Rise of Prussia

The rise of Prussia occurred within the German power vacuum created by the Peace of Westphalia. It is the story of the extraordinary Hohenzollern family, which had ruled Brandenburg since 1417. Through inheritance the family had acquired a series of territories, most of which were not contiguous with Brandenburg. By the late seventeenth cen-

tury, however, the scattered Hohenzollern holdings represented a block of territory within the Holy Roman Empire second in size only to that of the Habsburgs.

Beginning in the mid–seventeenth century, Hohenzollern rulers forged their geographically separated holdings into a powerful state by collecting taxes simply on their own authority and then building an army that allowed them to continue to enforce their will without the approval of the nobility.

There was, however, a political and social tradeoff between the Hohenzollerns and their various nobles. These *Junkers*, or German noble landlords, were allowed almost complete control over the serfs on their estates. In exchange for their obedience to the Hohenzollerns, the *Junkers* received the right to demand obedience from their serfs. Furthermore taxes fell most heavily on the backs of the peasants and the urban classes. As the years passed, *Junkers* increasingly dominated the army officer corps, and this became even more pronounced during the eighteenth

A Prussian Military Camp. This print shows a Prussian encampment in the Pomerania, on the south coast of the Baltic Sea. By 1800 this entire region had come under Prussian control.

century. All officials and army officers took an oath of loyalty directly to the Hohenzollern rulers. The army and the Elector thus came to embody the otherwise absent unity of the state. The army made Prussia a valuable potential ally. As a result of providing aid to the Habsburg emperor in 1701, the Hohenzollerns were permitted the title of "King" in Prussia, one of their parcels of territory that lay inside Poland and outside the authority of the Holy Roman Emperor.

Frederick William I (r. 1713–1740) of Prussia organized the bureaucracy along military lines. The Prussian military grew from about 39,000 in 1713 to over 80,000 in 1740, making it the third- or fourth-largest army in Europe. Prussia's population, in contrast, ranked thirteenth in size. Separate laws applied to the army and to civilians. Laws, customs, and royal attention made the officer corps the highest social class of the state. Military service thus attracted the sons of *Junkers*. In this fashion the army, the *Junker* nobility, and the monarchy became forged into a single political entity. Military priorities and values dominated Prussian government, society, and daily life as in no other state in Europe. It has often been said that whereas other nations possessed armies, the Prussian army possessed its nation.

Although Frederick William I built the best army in Europe, he avoided conflict. His army was a symbol of Prussian power and unity, not an instrument for foreign adventures or aggression. At his death in 1740 he passed to his son Frederick II (Frederick the Great, r. 1740–1786) this superb military machine, but not the wisdom to refrain from using it. Almost immediately on coming to the throne, Frederick II upset the Pragmatic Sanction and invaded Silesia (see Map 20–2). He thus crystallized the Austrian-Prussian rivalry for the control of Germany that would dominate central European affairs for over a century.

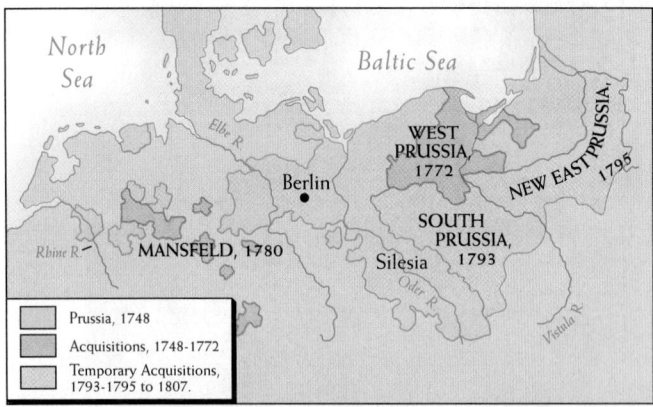

Map 20–2. Prussian Expansions 1748–1795. In the seventeenth century Brandenburg-Prussia expanded mainly by acquiring dynastic titles in geographically separated lands. In the eighteenth century it expanded through aggression to the east, seizing Silesia in 1740 and various parts of Poland in 1772, 1793, and 1795.

European Warfare: From Continental to World Conflict

Without exception the emergence of Great Britain, France, Russia, the Habsburg Empire, and Prussia as the major European powers involved warfare. Whereas religious zeal had largely fueled the European wars of the Reformation era, dynastic and commercial rivalry drove wars from the reign of Louis XIV through the conclusion of the Seven Years' War in 1763. Each round of warfare was geographically more widespread than the last, and eventually these wars became genuinely worldwide. Through these conflicts the European powers extended their military and political presence to match their expanding commercial presence in the Americas and in Asia. At the same time, through their conflicts with each other the European powers developed the military weapons and naval prowess that they also turned against non-European peoples. Thus these European wars are important for both their political and technological character.

The Wars of Louis XIV

By the late 1660s France had become superior to any other European nation in administrative bureaucracy, armed forces, and national unity. Louis XIV could afford to raise and maintain a large and powerful army and was in a position to dominate Europe.

Commencing in 1667, Louis XIV led France into four major wars of expansion, each with a widening scope. In 1667 and then again in 1672 Louis invaded Flanders. His second war, during which he was allied with England, led the Dutch to rally around the leadership of William Prince of Orange, the future William III of England. He forged an alliance with the Holy Roman Emperor, Spain, Lorraine, and Brandenburg against Louis, by then regarded as a menace to the whole of Western Europe, Catholic and Protestant alike. Louis' second war ended inconclusively with the Peace of Nijmwegen, signed with different parties in successive years (1678, 1679).

In 1681 Louis' forces occupied the free city of Strasbourg, prompting new defensive coalitions to form against him. One of these, the League of Augsburg, grew to include England, Spain, Sweden, the United Provinces, and the major German states including the Habsburg emperor. One of the chief reasons that in 1688 William of Orange consented to become monarch of England was to draw that nation and its wealth into the coalition against France. Between 1689 and 1697 the League of Augsburg and France battled each other on European fronts in the Nine Years' War, while England and France struggled to control

Map Exploration

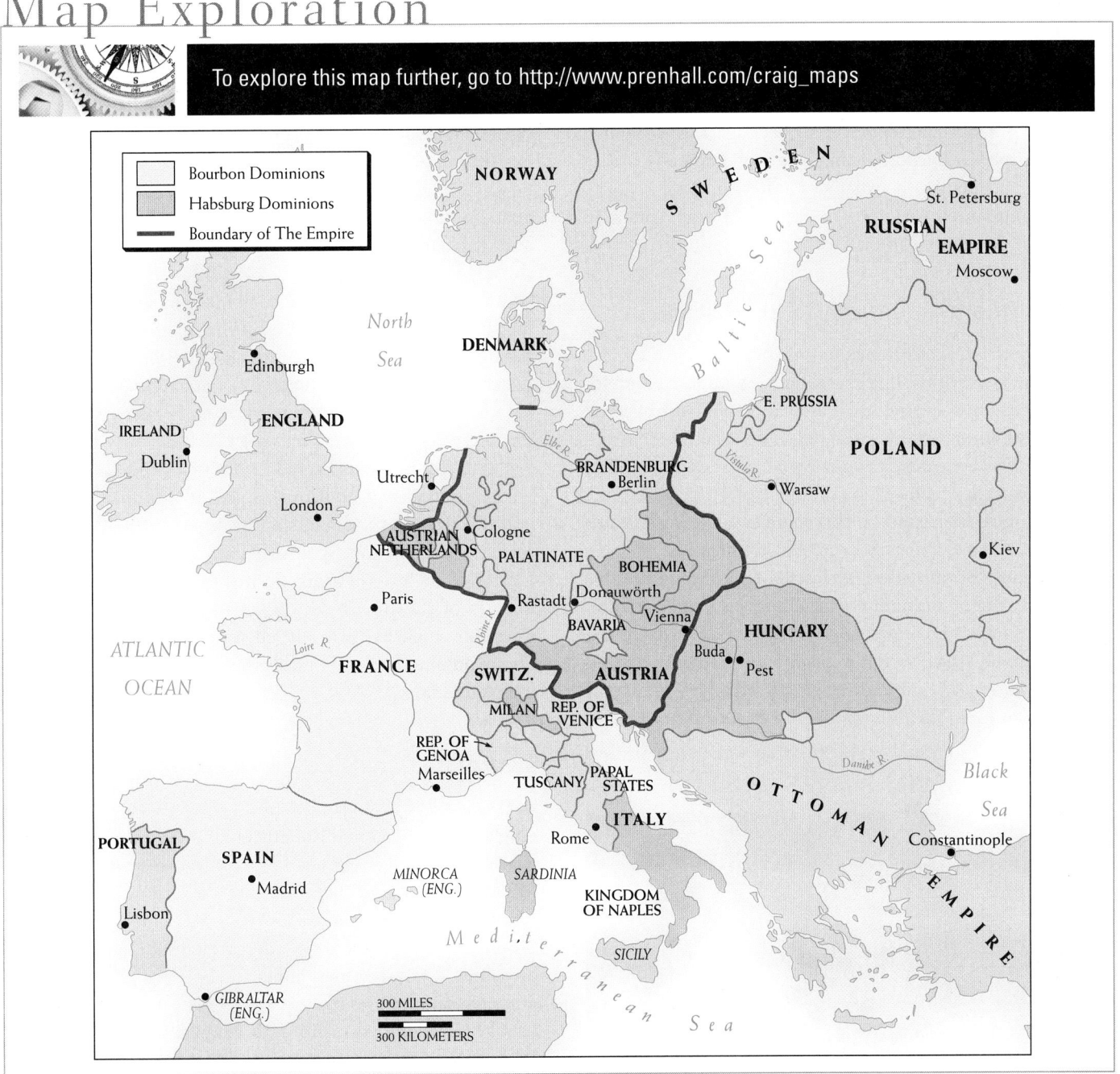

To explore this map further, go to http://www.prenhall.com/craig_maps

Map 20–3. Europe in 1714. The War of the Spanish Succession ended a year before the death of Louis XIV. The Bourbons had secured the Spanish throne, but Spain had forfeited its possessions in Flanders and Italy.

North America. The Peace of Ryswick, signed in September 1697, secured Holland's borders and thwarted Louis' expansion into Germany.

Then on November 1, 1700, Charles II of Spain (r. 1665–1700) died without direct heirs. He left his entire inheritance to Louis' grandson Philip of Anjou, who became Philip V of Spain (r. 1700–1746). Spain and the trade with its American empire appeared to have fallen to France. In

September 1701 England, Holland, and the Holy Roman Empire formed the Grand Alliance to preserve the balance of power by once and for all securing Flanders as a neutral barrier between Holland and France and by gaining for the emperor his fair share of the Spanish inheritance.

The War of the Spanish Succession (1701–1714) soon enveloped Western Europe (see Map 20–3). France finally made peace with England at Utrecht in July 1713 and with

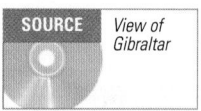
SOURCE *View of Gibraltar*

Holland and the emperor at Rastadt in March 1714. Philip V remained king of Spain, but England got Gibraltar, at the southern tip of Spain, making it a Mediterranean power. Louis also formally recognized the right of the House of Hanover to accede to the English throne. At the conclusion of this long war, France was economically and politically exhausted. The European wars of the next generation occurred not only in Europe but also throughout the European overseas empires.

The Eighteenth-Century Colonial Arena

The Treaty of Utrecht established the boundaries of empire during the first half of the eighteenth century. Except for Brazil, which was governed by Portugal, Spain controlled all of mainland South America, as well as Florida, Mexico, and the entire western half of what is the present-day United States. Spain also ruled Cuba and half of Hispaniola. The British Empire consisted of the colonies along the North Atlantic seaboard, Nova Scotia, Newfoundland, Jamaica, and Barbados. Britain also possessed a few trading stations on the Indian subcontinent. The Dutch controlled Surinam, or Dutch Guiana, in South America; Cape Town at the southern tip of Africa; various trading stations in Ceylon and Bengal; and, most important, the trade with Java in what is today Indonesia.

The French had also established an empire in America and southern Asia. It covered the Saint Lawrence River valley; the Ohio and Mississippi river valleys; Saint Domingue (Haiti), Guadeloupe, and Martinique in the West Indies; and trading stations in India and West Africa. The economy of their West Indian islands resembled those of the Spanish and the British. Their holdings in Canada were sparsely populated, Quebec being the largest settlement, and the economy was based on agriculture and the fur trade. French and English settlers in North America clashed throughout the eighteenth century.

Each of the powers sought to make its imperial holdings into impenetrable trading areas. The Spanish Empire, however, especially stood on the defensive throughout the eighteenth century. The Spanish government lacked the capacity to maintain a commercial monopoly over its sprawling territory.

The Treaty of Utrecht gave the British a thirty-year *asiento*, or contract, to furnish slaves to the Spanish Empire and the right to send one ship each year to the trading fair at Portobello on the Spanish Main (present-day Panama). Nothing but friction arose from these rights. Much to the chagrin of the British, the Spanish government under the Bourbons took its own alleged trading monopoly seriously and maintained coastal patrols that searched English vessels for contraband.

War of Jenkins's Ear

In 1731, during one such search, there was a fight, and an English captain named Robert Jenkins had his ear cut off by the Spaniards. Thereafter, he preserved his ear in a jar of brandy. This incident was of little importance until 1738, when Jenkins appeared before the British Parliament, reportedly brandishing his ear as an example of Spanish atrocities to British merchants in the West Indies. British commercial interests put great pressure on Parliament to do something about Spanish interference in their trade. Robert Walpole could not resist these pressures, and in late 1739 Great Britain went to war with Spain. This might have been a relatively minor clash, but as a result of the Prussian invasion of Silesia, it became the opening encounter in a series of worldwide European wars.

The War of the Austrian Succession (1740–1748)

In December 1740, as noted earlier in the chapter, the new king of Prussia, Frederick II, ignored the Pragmatic Sanction and seized the Austrian province of Silesia. In response to the Prussian aggression, the young Maria Theresa of

A Dutch Merchant and His Wife in Batavia (Java). Attributed to Jacob Cuyp (1594–1651), this painting from 1650 shows the Dutch merchant Jacob Mathieusen and his wife in front of Batavia's harbor, on the island of Java in the East Indies. The merchant points to his ships while a slave shelters the couple from the tropical sun with a parasol.

Chronology

European Conflicts of the Mid–Eighteenth Century

1739	Outbreak of War of Jenkins's Ear between England and Spain
1740	War of the Austrian Succession commences
1748	Treaty of Aix-la-Chapelle
1756	Convention of Westminster between England and Prussia
1756	Seven Years' War opens
1759	British forces capture Quebec
1763	Treaty of Hubertusburg
1763	Treaty of Paris

Austria recognized Hungary as the most important of her crowns and promised the Magyars considerable local autonomy. She thus preserved the Habsburg state, but at great cost to the power of the central monarchy.

The war over the Austrian succession and the British-Spanish commercial conflict could have remained separate disputes. What united them was the role of France, whose aggressive court aristocrats drove the government to support the Prussian aggression against Austria, the traditional enemy of France.

This proved to be one of the most fateful decisions in world history. French aid to Prussia helped consolidate a new and powerful German state that could, and indeed later did, endanger France itself. The French move against Austria also brought Great Britain into the Continental war against France and Prussia in an attempt to assure that Belgium remained in the friendly hands of Austria. In 1744 the British-French conflict expanded beyond the Continent when France decided to support Spain against Britain in the New World. The war ended in military stalemate in 1748 with the Treaty of Aix-la-Chapelle. Prussia retained Silesia, but the treaty was a truce rather than a permanent peace.

The Seven Years' War (1756–1763)

Before the rivalries again erupted into war, a dramatic shift of alliances took place. In 1756 Prussia and Great Britain signed the Convention of Westminster, a defensive alliance aimed at preventing the entry of foreign troops into the Germanies. Frederick feared invasions by both Russia and France. The convention meant that Great Britain, the ally of

Austria since the wars of Louis XIV, had now joined forces with Austria's major eighteenth-century enemy. Later in 1756 Austria achieved a defensive alliance with France. Thus the traditional European alliances of the previous century were reversed.

In August 1756, what would become the Seven Years' War opened when Frederick II invaded Saxony. Frederick considered this a preemptive strike against a conspiracy by Saxony, Austria, and France to destroy Prussian power. In the spring of 1757 France and Austria made a new alliance dedicated to the destruction of Prussia. They were eventually joined by Sweden, Russia, and the smaller German states. Two factors, in addition to Frederick's strong leadership (it was after this war that he came to be called Frederick the Great), saved Prussia—British financial aid and the death in 1762 of Empress Elizabeth of Russia (r. 1741–1762). Her successor Tsar Peter III (d. 1762), a fervent admirer of Frederick, immediately made peace with Prussia, thus allowing Frederick to hold off Austria and France. The Treaty of Hubertusburg of 1763 closed the Continental conflict with no significant changes in prewar borders.

More impressive to the rest of Europe than the survival of Prussia were the victories of Great Britain in every theater of conflict. The architect of victory was William Pitt the Elder (1708–1778). Although Pitt had previously criticized British involvement with the Continent, once he was named secretary of state in charge of the war in 1757 he reversed himself and pumped huge financial subsidies to Frederick the Great. But North America was Pitt's real concern. Put simply, he wanted all of North America east of the Mississippi for Great Britain, and that was exactly what he won as he directed unprecedented resources into the overseas colonial conflict. In what Americans know as the French and Indian War, the French government was unwilling and unable to direct similar resources against the English in America. In September 1759 the British took Quebec City. Montreal fell the next year. The French empire in Canada was coming to an end.

Pitt's colonial vision, however, was global. The French West Indies fell to the British fleets. On the Indian subcontinent the British forces under Robert Clive (1725–1774) defeated the French in 1757 at the Battle of Plassey. This victory opened the way for the eventual conquest of all India by the British East India Company. Never had any other European power experienced such a complete worldwide military victory. Never had a European military victory affected so many non-Europeans.

The Treaty of Paris of 1763 was somewhat less triumphant. Pitt was no longer in office. George III (r. 1760–1820) had succeeded to the British throne and by 1762 had replaced Pitt with a new minister who was responsible

The Taking of Quebec. The capture of Quebec in September 1759 by British forces, followed by the seizure of Montreal a year later, signaled the demise of French power in Canada. *General James Wolfe's expedition against Quebec in 1759: English engraving, 1760. The Granger Collection, New York.*

for the peace settlement, in which Britain received all of Canada, the Ohio river valley, and the eastern half of the Mississippi river valley. France retained footholds in India at Pondicherry and Chandernagore and regained the West Indies sugar islands of Guadeloupe and Martinique.

The midcentury wars among European powers resulted in a new balance of power on the European continent and the high seas (see Map 20–4). Great Britain gained a world empire, and Prussia was recognized as a great continental power. With the surrender of Canada, France retreated from North America and thus opened the way for a continent largely dominated by the English language and Protestantism. By contrast, Latin America remained dominated by the Spanish and Portuguese languages and Roman Catholicism. For many years, West Africa would continue to furnish slaves to the economies of both Americas. On the subcontinent of India the foundations were laid for almost two centuries of British dominance.

By the mid–eighteenth century, the European states that just two centuries earlier had only started to settle the Americas and to engage in limited long-range trade had made their power and influence felt throughout the world. As those wars of the midcentury came to an end, the political power of the European states became linked to a qualitatively different economic base than any seen elsewhere in

the world. That political and economic combination allowed Europe to dominate the world from the 1750s to the Second World War.

The Old Regime

During the turmoil of the French Revolution and its aftermath, it became customary to refer to the patterns of social, political, and economic relationships that had existed in France before 1789 as the *ancien régime*, or the **Old Regime**. The term has come to be applied generally to the life and institutions of all prerevolutionary Continental Europe. Politically, it meant the rule of theoretically absolute monarchies with growing bureaucracies and aristocratically led armies. Economically, the Old Regime was characterized by food shortages, the predominance of agriculture, slow transport, a low level of iron production, comparatively unsophisticated financial institutions, and, in some cases, competitive commercial overseas empires. Socially, men and women saw themselves less as individuals than as members of distinct corporate bodies that possessed certain privileges or rights as a group.

Maintenance of Tradition

Few persons outside the political, commercial, and intellectual elite actually wanted change or innovation. This was especially true of social relationships. Both nobles and peasants repeatedly called for the restoration of traditional or customary rights. The nobles asserted what they considered their ancient rights against the intrusion of the expanding monarchical bureaucracies. The peasants, through petitions and revolts, called for the revival or the maintenance of the customary manorial rights that allowed them access to particular lands, courts, or grievance procedures.

Except for the early industrial development in Britain, the economy was also predominantly traditional. The quality and quantity of the grain harvest remained crucial for most of the population and the gravest concern for governments.

Hierarchy and Privilege

The medieval sense of hierarchy became more rigid during the century. Several cities retained sumptuary laws forbidding persons in one class or occupation from dressing like their social superiors. These laws were largely ineffective.

Map 20–4. The Colonial Arena. The acquisition of overseas colonies by European powers led to intense rivalries on a global scale. Territories frequently changed hands during the eighteenth century.

What really enforced the hierarchy was the corporate nature of social relationships.

Each state or society was considered a community composed of numerous smaller communities. Eighteenth-century Europeans did not enjoy what Americans regard as individual rights. Instead, persons enjoyed such rights and privileges as were guaranteed to whatever communities or groups of which they were a part. The "community" might include the village, the municipality, the nobility, the church, the guild, a university, or the parish. In turn, each of these bodies enjoyed certain privileges—some great, some small. The privileges might involve exemption from taxation or degrading punishment, the right to practice a trade or craft, the right of one's children to pursue a particular occupation, or for the church, the right to collect the tithe.

Aristocracy

The eighteenth century was the great age of the aristocracy. The nobility constituted approximately 1 to 5 percent of the population of any given country. In every European state, it was the single wealthiest sector of the population; possessed the widest degree of social, political, and economic power; and dominated polite society. Land provided the aristocracy with its largest source of income, but the influence of aristocrats was felt in every area of life. Across the Continent, to be an aristocrat was a matter of birth and legal privilege, but in almost every other respect, aristocrats differed markedly from country to country. The smallest, wealthiest, best defined, and most socially responsible aristocracy resided in Great Britain. As one moved eastward across Europe the aristocracy became more numerous, not always wealthy, but possessing increasing degrees of arbitrary, repressive power over those below them in the social structure.

Throughout the century, in a Europe-wide **aristocratic resurgence**, the various nobilities sought to protect their social position and privileges against the expanding power of the monarchies and the growing wealth of commercial groups. First, all nobilities attempted to restrict entry into their ranks and institutions.

Second, they also attempted to monopolize appointments to the officer corps of the armies, the bureaucracies, the government ministries, and the church. The nobles thus hoped to control the power of the monarchies.

Third, the nobles attempted to use institutions they already controlled against the monarchies. These institutions included the British Parliament, the French *parlements*, local aristocratic estates, and provincial diets.

Fourth, the aristocracies pressed the peasantry for higher rents or long-forgotten feudal dues. This was part of an effort by the nobility to shore up its position by appealing to tradition and reasserting old privileges that had lapsed. To contemporaries, this aristocratic resurgence was one of the most fundamental political facts of the day.

The Land and Its Tillers

Land was the economic basis of eighteenth-century life in Europe as it was throughout the rest of the world. Well over three fourths of all Europeans lived on the land, and most never traveled more than a few miles from their birthplaces. With the exception of the nobility and the wealthier landowners, the dwellers on the land were poor, and by any modern standard, their lives were hard.

Peasants and Serfs

Those people who worked the land were subject to immense influence and in some cases direct control by the landowners. This situation prevailed in different degrees for free peasants, such as English tenants and most French cultivators, and for the serfs of Germany, Austria, and Russia, who were legally bound to a particular plot of land and a partic-

An Aristocratic Couple. Portraits such as this one of the English landowner Robert Andrews and his wife, by Thomas Gainsborough (1728–1788), contain many clues to the aristocratic dominance of landed society: Andrews's gun and dog indicate his exclusive right to hunt game on his land. His wife's sitting against the expanse of his landed estate suggests the character of their legal relationship, whereby he could have controlled her property, which would have thus become an extension of his. The market price of the wheat raised on his estate (known in England as corn) would have been protected by various import laws enacted by the English Parliament whose membership was dominated by landowners such as Andrews himself. © *National Gallery, London*

ular lord. In all cases, the class that owned the land also controlled the local government and the courts.

Landlord power increased as one moved from west to east. Most French peasants owned some land, but a few were serfs. However, nearly all peasants were subject to certain feudal dues and to forced labor on the lord's estate for a certain number of days each year. Because French peasants rarely owned enough land to support their families, they were also subject to feudal dues attached to the plots of land they rented.

In Prussia and Austria, despite attempts by the monarchies late in the century to improve the lot of the serfs, the landlords continued to exercise almost complete control over them. Moreover, throughout Continental Europe the burden of state taxation fell on the tillers of the soil. Many peasants, serfs, and other agricultural laborers were forced to undertake supplemental work to pay the tax collector. Through various legal privileges and the ability to demand further concessions from the monarchs, the landlords escaped the payment of numerous taxes. They also presided over the manorial courts.

The condition of the serfs was the worst in Russia. The Russian custom of reckoning one's wealth by the number of owned "souls" (that is, male serfs) rather than by the size of an estate reveals the contrast between Russia and Western Europe. Russian serfs were, in effect, regarded merely as eco-

nomic commodities. Their services were attached to an individual lord rather than to a particular plot of land. Russian landlords could demand as many as six days a week of labor, and like Prussian and Austrian landlords, they could punish their serfs or even exile them to Siberia. Although serfs had little recourse against their lords, custom, tradition, and law did provide a few protections. For example, the marriages of serfs, unlike those of most slaves throughout the world, were legally recognized. The landlord could not disband the family of a serf. (See Document, "Russian Serfs Lament Their Condition.")

The Russian monarchy itself contributed to the degradation of the serfs. Peter the Great gave whole villages to favored nobles. Catherine the Great (r. 1762–1796) confirmed the authority of the nobles over their serfs in exchange for the nobility's political cooperation. This situation led to considerable unrest. There were more than fifty peasant revolts between 1762 and 1769. They culminated between 1773 and 1774 in Pugachev's Rebellion, during which all of southern Russia was in ferment. Emelyan Pugachev (1726–1775) promised the serfs land and freedom. The rebellion was brutally suppressed, and any thought of liberalizing the condition of the serfs was set aside for a generation.

Pugachev's was the largest peasant uprising of the eighteenth century. Smaller peasant revolts or disturbances occurred in Bohemia in 1775, in Transylvania in 1784, in

Road Work. Eighteenth-century France had some of the best roads in the world, but they were often built with forced labor. French peasants were required to work part of each year on such projects. This system, called the *corvée*, was not abolished until the French Revolution in 1789. *Joseph Vernet, "Construction of a Road." Louvre, Paris, France/Bridgeman-Giraudon/Art Resource, N.Y.*

Russian Serfs Lament Their Condition

Document

As with other illiterate groups in European history, it is difficult to recapture the voices of Russian serfs. The following verses from "The Slaves' Lament," a popular ballad from the era of the Pugachev Rebellion (1773–1775), indicate that the serfs were aware of how the legislation of that era, which favored the landowning classes, affected their lives. The verses embody the resentment that Pugachev's Rebellion ignited. Note how the verses suggest that the tsar may be more favorable to serfs than their landowners are. Pugachev claimed to be Tsar Peter III, and many Russian serfs believed him and thus considered him a liberator from landlord tyranny. Throughout this ballad, serfs present themselves as slaves.

◆ What specific complaints about landlords are expressed in these verses? What charges indicate that serfs may believe their situation has worsened? What hope do they seem to place in the tsar? What idealized picture of the world do the serfs believe they would themselves create?

O woe to us slaves living for the masters!
We do not know how to serve their ferocity!
Service is like a sharp scythe;
And kindness is like the morning dew.
Brothers, how annoying it is to us
And how shameful and insulting
That another who is not worthy to be equal with us
Has so many of us in his power.
And if we steal from the lord one half kopeck,
The law commands us to be killed like a louse.
And if the master steals ten thousand,
Nobody will judge who should be hanged.
The injustice of the Russian sheriffs has increased:
Whoever brings a present is right beyond argument.
They have stopped putting their trust in the Creator
*   for authority,*
And have become accustomed to own us like cattle.
All nations rebuke us and wonder at our stupidity,
That such stupid people are born in Russia.
And indeed, stupidity was rooted in us long ago,
as each honour here has been given to vagrants.
The master can kill the servant like a gelding;
The denunciation by a slave cannot be believed.
Unjust judges have composed a decree
That we should be tyrannically whipped with a
*   knout for that.*
Better that we should agree to serve the tsar.
Better to live in dark woods

Than to be before the eyes of these tyrants;
They look on us cruelly with their eyes
And eat us as iron eats rye. No one wants to
*   serve the tsar*
But only to grind us down to the end.
And they try to collect unjust bribes,
And they are not frightened that people die cruelly.
Ah brothers, if we got our freedom,
We would not take the lands or the fields for ourselves.
We would go into service as soldiers, brothers,
And would be friendly among ourselves,
Would destroy all injustice
And remove the root of evil lords.
They [the landlords] sell all the good rye
*   to the merchants,*
And give us like pigs the bad.
The greedy lords eat meat at fast time,
And even when meat is allowed, the slaves
must cook meatless cabbage soup.
O brothers, it is our misfortune
always to have rye kasha.
The lords drink and make merry,
And do not allow the slaves even to burst out laughing.

From Paul Dukes, trans. and ed., *Russia under Catherine the Great: Select Documents on Government and Society* (Oriental Research Partners, 1978), pp. 115–117. Reprinted by permission of Oriental Research Partners.

Moravia in 1786, and in Austria in 1789. Western Europe was more tranquil, but England experienced numerous enclosure riots. Rural rebellions were violent, but the peasants and serfs normally directed their wrath against property rather than persons. The rebels usually sought to reassert traditional or customary rights against practices they perceived as innovations. In this respect, the peasant revolts were conservative in nature.

Family Structures and the Family Economy

In preindustrial Europe, the household was the basic unit of production and consumption. That is to say, very few productive establishments employed more than a handful of people not belonging to the owner's family. These rare establishments were located in cities. Most Europeans lived in rural areas; there, as well as in small towns and cities, the household mode of organization predominated on farms, in artisans' workshops, and in small merchants' shops. With that mode of economic organization, there developed what is known as the **family economy**.

The Family Economy

Throughout Europe people thought and worked in terms of sustaining the economic life of the family, and family members saw themselves as working together in an interdependent rather than an independent or individualistic manner. The goal of the family household was to produce or secure through wages enough food to support its members. In the countryside, that effort virtually always involved farming. In cities and towns, artisan production or working for another person was the usual pattern. Almost everyone lived within a household because ordinary people could rarely support themselves independently. Indeed, except for members of religious orders, people living outside a household were viewed with great suspicion as potentially criminal or disruptive or, at least, potentially dependent on the charity of others.

Marriage and the family within this economy meant that everyone in the household had to work. On a farm, much of the effort went directly into raising food or producing other agricultural goods that could be exchanged for food. In Western Europe, however, few people had enough land to support their households from farming alone. For this reason, one or more family members might work elsewhere and send wages home. For example, the father or older children might be migrant workers, perhaps many miles from home. The burden of the farm work would then fall on the wife and the younger children. This was not uncommon. Within this family economy, all of the goods and income produced went to the benefit of the household rather than to the individual

family member. Depending on their ages and skills, everyone worked. The need to survive poor harvests or economic slumps meant that no one could be idle.

The family economy also dominated the life of skilled urban artisans. The father was usually the chief craftsman. He generally had one or more servants in his employ, but he would also expect his children to work in the enterprise. His eldest child was usually trained in the trade. His wife often sold the wares or had a small shop. The wife of a merchant also often ran the husband's business, especially when he traveled to purchase new goods. In any case, everyone in the family was involved. If business was poor, family members would look for employment elsewhere, not to support themselves but to help the family unit survive.

Farm Family. Painted by the English artist Francis Wheatley (1747–1801) near the close of the eighteenth century, this scene is part of a series illustrating a day in the life of an idealized farm family. Note the artist's assumptions about the division of labor by gender. Men work in the fields, women work in the home or look after the needs of men and children. As other illustrations in this chapter show, many eighteenth-century women in fact worked outside the home, but considerable social pressure was developing at this time to restrict them to domestic roles. This painting and the others in the series are thus more prescriptive than descriptive, intended in part to persuade their viewers that women belonged in their separate family sphere. Many, perhaps most, families living in the countryside could not maintain the closeness that these paintings extol. To survive, many had to send members to work on other farms or even to other regions. *Francis Wheatley (RA) (1747–1801), "Evening," signed and dated 1799, oil on canvas, 17 1/2 × 21 1/2 in. (44.5 × 54.5 cm), Yale Center for British Art, Paul Mellon Collection, Bridgman Art Library (B1977.14.118).*

Women and the Family Economy

The family economy established many of the chief constraints on the lives and the personal experiences of women in preindustrial society. Most of the historical research that has been undertaken on this subject relates to Western Europe. There, a woman's life experience was largely the function of her capacity to establish and maintain a household. For women, marriage was an institution of economic necessity as well as one that fulfilled sexual and psychological needs. A woman outside a household was highly vulnerable. Unless she was an aristocrat or a member of a religious order, she could probably not support herself by her own efforts alone. Consequently, much of a woman's life was devoted first to aiding the maintenance of her parents' household and then to getting her own household to live in as an adult. In most cases, bearing and rearing children were subordinate to these goals.

As a child, certainly by the age of seven, a girl was expected to begin to contribute to the household work. On a farm, she might look after chickens or water animals or carry food to adult men and women working the land. In an urban artisan's household, she would do some form of light work, perhaps involving cleaning or carrying and later sewing or weaving. The girl would remain in her parents' home as long as she made a real contribution to the family enterprise or until her labor elsewhere was more valuable to the family. An artisan's daughter might not leave home until marriage because she could learn increasingly valuable skills from her parents.

The labor of the much larger number of girls growing up on farms quickly became of little value to the family. These girls would then leave home, usually by the age of twelve or fourteen. They might go to another farm but were more likely to migrate to a nearby town or city. They would rarely travel more than thirty miles from their parents' household and would then normally become servants in the household of an employer. (See Document, "Priscilla Wakefield Demands More Occupations Be Opened to Women.")

Having migrated from home, the young woman's chief goal was to accumulate a dowry. Her savings would allow her to make the necessary contribution to form a household with her husband. Marriage within the family economy was a joint economic undertaking, and the wife was expected to make an immediate contribution of capital for the establishment of the household. A young woman might well work for ten years or more to accumulate a dowry. This practice meant that marriage was usually postponed until a woman's mid- to late twenties.

Within the marriage, earning enough money or producing enough farm goods to ensure an adequate food supply was always the dominant concern. Domestic duties, childbearing, and child rearing were subordinate to economic survival.

Consequently, couples would often practice birth control, usually through *coitus interruptus*, or withdrawal of the male before ejaculation. Young children were often placed with wet nurses so the mother could continue to contribute to the household economy. The wet nurse, in turn, was contributing to her own household. The child would be fully reintegrated into its family when it was weaned and would be expected to aid the family at an early age. (See Document, "An Edinburgh Physician Describes the Dangers of Childbirth.")

A married woman's work was in many ways a function of her husband's occupation. If the peasant household possessed enough land to support itself, the wife spent much of her time literally carrying things for her husband—water, food, seed, harvested grain, and the like. But few peasants had such adequate landholdings. If the husband had to do work other than farming, such as fishing or migrant labor, the wife might do the plowing, planting, and harvesting. In the city, the wife of an artisan or merchant often acted as a business manager. She might manage the household finances and participate in the trade or business. When her husband died, she might take over the business, perhaps hiring an artisan.

Finally, if economic disaster struck the family, more often than not it was the wife who took the lead in sending off family members to find work elsewhere or even to beg in the streets.

In all phases of life within the family economy, women led active, often decisive roles. Industriousness rather than idleness was their lot in life. Finding a functional place in the household was essential to their well-being, but once that place had been found, their function was essential to the ongoing well-being of the household.

The Revolution in Agriculture

The main goal of traditional European peasant society was to ensure the stability of the local food supply. That supply was never certain and became more uncertain the farther east one traveled. A failed harvest meant not only hardship, but also death from either outright starvation or protracted debility. Food was often harder to find in the country than in cities because city governments usually stored reserve supplies of grain.

Poor harvests also played havoc with prices. Smaller supplies or larger demand raised grain prices. Even small increases in the cost of food could squeeze peasant or artisan families. If prices increased sharply, many of those families fell back on poor relief from their local government or the church. What made the situation of food supply and prices so difficult was the peasants' sense of helplessness before the whims of nature and the marketplace. Despite differences in rural customs throughout Europe, peasants

Priscilla Wakefield Demands More Occupations Be Opened to Women

At the end of the eighteenth century, several English women writers began to demand a wider life for women. Priscilla Wakefield was among such authors. She was concerned that women found themselves able to pursue only occupations that paid poorly. Often they were excluded from work on the grounds of their alleged physical weakness. She also believed that women should receive equal wages for equal work. Many of the issues she raised have yet to be adequately addressed on behalf of women.

◆ From reading this passage, what do you understand to have been the arguments at the end of the eighteenth century to limit the kinds of employment that women might enter? Why did women receive lower wages for work similar to or the same as that done by men? What occupations traditionally filled by men does Wakefield believe women might also pursue?

Another heavy discouragement to the industry of women, is the inequality of the reward of their labor, compared with that of men; an injustice which pervades every species of employment performed by both sexes.

In employments which depend on bodily strength, the distinction is just; for it cannot be pretended that the generality of women can earn as much as men, when the produce of their labor is the result of corporeal exertion; but it is a subject of great regret, that this inequality should prevail even where an equal share of skill and application is exerted. Male stay-makers, mantua-makers, and hairdressers, are better paid than female artists of the same professions; but surely it will never be urged as an apology for this disproportion, that women are not as capable of making stays, gowns, dressing hair, and similar arts, as men; if they are not superior to them, it can only be accounted for upon this principle, that the prices they receive for their labor are not sufficient to repay them for the expense of qualifying themselves for their business; and that they sink under the mortification of being regarded as artisans of inferior estimation. . . .

Besides these employments which are commonly performed by women, and those already shown to be suitable for such persons as are above the condition of hard labor, there are some professions and trades customarily in the hands of men, which might be conveniently exercised by either sex.—Watchmaking requiring more inge-

nuity than strength, seems peculiarly adapted to women; as do many parts of the business of stationer, particularly, ruling account books or making pens. The compounding of medicines in an apothecary's shop, requires no other talents than care and exactness; and if opening a vein occasionally be a indispensable requisite, a woman may acquire the capacity of doing it, for those of her own sex at least, without any reasonable objection. . . . Pastry and confectionery appear particularly consonant to the habits of women, though generally performed by men; perhaps the heat of the ovens, and the strength requisite to fill and empty them, may render male assistants necessary; but certain women are most eligible to mix up the ingredients, and prepare the various kinds of cakes for baking.— Light turnery and toy-making depend more upon dexterity and invention than force, and are therefore suitable work for women and children. . . .

Farming, as far as respects the theory, is commensurate with the powers of the female mind: nor is the practice of inspecting agricultural processes incompatible with the delicacy of their frames if their constitution be good.

From Priscilla Wakefield, *Reflections on the Present Condition of the Female Sex* (1798), (London, 1817), pp. 125–127, as quoted in Bridget Hill, ed., *Eighteenth-Century Women: An Anthology.* Copyright © 1984 George Allen & Unwin, pp. 227–228.

resisted changes that they felt might endanger the sure supply of food, which they generally believed traditional cultivation practices ensured.

During the century, historians now believe, bread prices slowly but steadily rose, spurred largely by population

growth. This put pressure on all of the poor. The prices rose faster than urban wages and brought no appreciable advantage to the small peasant producer. On the other hand, the rise in grain prices benefited landowners and those wealthier peasants who had surplus grain to sell.

English Children. Few children in the eighteenth century were as privileged as the ones in this landed English family. Most began working to help support their families as soon as they were physically able. It was during the eighteenth century, however, that Europeans apparently began to view childhood as a distinct period in human development. Even though Arthur Devis has painted these children to look something like little adults, he has included various toys associated with chidhood. *Arthur Devis (c. 1711–1787), "Children in an Interior," © 1742–1743, oil on canvas, 39 × 49 3/4 in. (99.0 × 125.5 cm), Yale Center for British Art, Paul Mellon Collection, B1978.43.5.*

An Edinburgh Physician Describes the Dangers of Childbirth

Death in childbirth was a common occurrence throughout Europe until the twentieth century. This brief letter from an Edinburgh physician illustrates how devastating infectious diseases could be to women at the time of childbirth.

◆ How does this passage illustrate a health danger that only women confronted? How might the likelihood of the death of oneself or a spouse in childbirth have affected one's attitudes towards children? How does this passage illustrate limitations on knowledge about disease in the eighteenth century?

We had puerperal fever in the infirmary last winter. It began about the end of February, when almost every woman, as soon as she was delivered, or perhaps about twenty-four hours after, was seized with it; and all of them died, though every method was tried to cure the disorder. What was singular, the women were in good health before they were brought to bed, though some of them had been long in the hospital before delivery. One woman had been dismissed from the ward before she was brought to bed; came into it some days after with her labor upon her; was easily delivered, and remained perfectly well for twenty-four hours, when she was seized with a shivering and the other symptoms of the fever. I caused her to be removed to another ward; yet notwithstanding all the care that was taken of her she died in the same manner as the others.

From a letter to Mr. White from a Dr. Young of Edinburgh, 21 November 1774, cited in C. White, *Treatise on the Management of Pregnant and Lying-In Women* (London, 1777), pp. 45–46, as quoted in Bridget Hill, ed., *Eighteenth-Century Women: An Anthology.* Copyright © 1984 George Allen & Unwin, p. 102.

The increasing price of grain allowed landlords to improve their income and lifestyle. They began a series of innovations in farm production that is known as the **agricultural revolution**.

New Crops and New Methods

This movement began during the sixteenth and seventeenth centuries in the Low Countries, where Dutch landlords and farmers devised better ways to build dykes and to drain land so that they could farm more extensive areas. They also experimented with new crops, such as clover and turnips, that would increase the supply of animal fodder and replenish the soil.

These methods were extensively adopted in England during the early eighteenth century. There, new methods of farming, new crops, and new modes of landholding eventually led to greater productivity. This advance in food production was necessary for an industrial society to develop. It ensured adequate food for the cities and freed surplus agricultural labor for industrial production. The changing modes of agriculture sponsored by the landlords undermined the assumptions of traditional peasant production. Farming now took place not only to provide the local food supply but also to earn the landlord a handsome profit.

Enclosure Replaces Open-Field Method   Many of the agricultural innovations, which were adopted only slowly, were incompatible with the existing organization of land in Britain. Small cultivators who lived in village communities still farmed most of the soil. Each farmer tilled an assortment of unconnected strips. The two- or three-field systems of rotation left much land fallow and unproductive each year. Animals grazed on the common land in the summer and on the stubble of the harvest in the winter. Until at least the middle of the eighteenth century the decisions about which crops would be planted were made communally. The entire system discouraged improvement and favored the

The Lincolnshire Ox. (1790) by George Stubbs. The "Lincolnshire Ox" was a prize Hereford that grew to an enormous size by being fed solely on grass. The fascination with the Lincolnshire Ox, which was displayed for over a year in London, was characteristic of the general interest in agricultural improvements.

poorer farmers, who needed the common land and stubble fields for their animals. The village method made it almost impossible to increase pasture land and with it the size of herds and the production of manure for fertilizer. Traditional methods aimed to produce a steady, but not a growing, supply of food.

In 1700 approximately half the arable land in Britain was farmed by this open-field method. By the second half of the century the rising price of wheat encouraged landlords to consolidate or enclose their lands to increase production. The **enclosures** were intended to use land more rationally and to raise profits. The process involved the fencing of common lands, the reclamation of previously untilled waste, and the transformation of strips into block fields. These procedures disrupted the economic and social life of the countryside. Riots often ensued. Because many British farmers either owned their strips or rented them in a manner that amounted to ownership, the larger landlords usually had to resort to parliamentary acts to legalize the enclosure of the land, which they owned but rented to the farmers. Because the large landowners controlled Parliament, such measures passed easily. Between 1761 and 1792, almost 500,000 acres were enclosed through parliamentary act, as compared with 75,000 acres between 1727 and 1760. In 1801 a general enclosure act streamlined the process.

The enclosures have remained controversial. By permitting the extension of both farming and innovation, they increased food production on larger agricultural units. However, they also disrupted the small traditional communities. They forced off the land some independent farmers, who had needed the common pasturage, and very poor cottagers, who had lived on the reclaimed waste land. However, the enclosures did not depopulate the countryside. In some counties where the enclosures took place, the population increased. New soil had come into production, and services subsidiary to farming also expanded.

Population Expansion

Agricultural improvement was both a cause and a result of an immense expansion in the population of Europe. The current population explosion seems to have had its origins in the eighteenth century. Exact figures are lacking, but the best estimates suggest that in 1700 Europe's population, excluding the European provinces of the Ottoman Empire, was between 100 million and 120 million people. By 1800 the figure had risen to over 180 million, and by 1850 to 260 million (see Figure 20–1). The population of England and Wales rose from 6 million in 1750 to over 10 million in 1800. France grew from 18 million in 1715 to approximately 26 million in 1789. Russia's population increased from 19 million in 1722 to 29 million in 1766. Such extraordinary

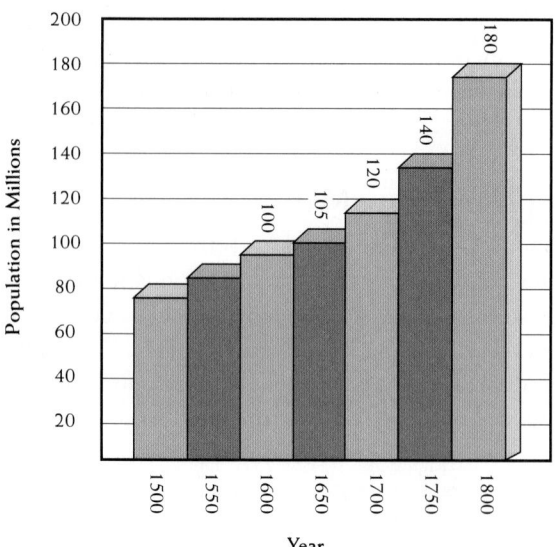

Figure 20-1. Population of Europe, 1500–1800.

sustained growth put new demands on all resources and considerable pressure on existing social organization.

The population expansion occurred across the Continent in both the country and the cities. Only a limited consensus exists about the causes of this growth. There was a clear decline in the death rate. There were fewer wars and somewhat fewer epidemics in the eighteenth century. Hygiene and sanitation also improved. But changes in the food supply itself may have been the chief reason for sustained population growth. One contributing factor was improved and expanding grain production. Another, even more important, was the introduction in the eighteenth century of widespread cultivation of a New World tuber, the potato. Enough potatoes could be raised on a single acre to feed one peasant's family for an entire year. With this more certain food supply, more children could be reared, and more could survive.

SOURCE *Thomas Malthus, from* Essay on the Principle of Population

The Eighteenth-Century Industrial Revolution: An Event in World History

In the second half of the eighteenth century the European economy began very slowly to industrialize. This development, more than any other single factor, distinguished Europe and eventually North America from the rest of the world for the next two centuries. While this economic development was occurring, people did not call it a *revolution*. That term came to be applied to the experience of British technological advances in productivity only after the French

Revolution, when Continental writers contended that what had taken place in Britain was the economic equivalent of the political events in France. From this comparison arose the concept of an *industrial* revolution. The process, however, was revolutionary less in its pace, which was on the whole rather slow, than in its implications for the future of European society.

The European **Industrial Revolution** of the eighteenth century constituted the achievement of sustained economic growth. Previously, production had been limited. The economy of a province or a country might grow but soon reached a plateau. However, since the late eighteenth century the economy of Europe has expanded relatively uninterruptedly. Depressions and recessions, however disruptive, have been temporary, and even during such economic downturns the Western economy has continued to grow.

At considerable social cost and dislocation, industrialism produced more goods and services than ever before in human history. Industrialism in Europe eventually overcame the economy of scarcity. The new means of production 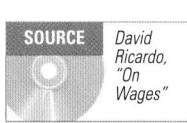 demanded new kinds of skills, new discipline in work, and a large labor force. The produced goods met immediate consumer demand and created new demands. In the long run, industrialism clearly raised the standard of living; the poverty in which most Europeans had always lived was overcome. Industrialization provided human beings greater control over the forces of nature than they had ever known.

SOURCE David Ricardo, "On Wages"

Over time the wealth produced by industrialism upset the political and social structures of the Old Regime and led to political and social reforms. The economic elite of the emerging industrial society would eventually challenge the political dominance of the aristocracy. Industrialization also undermined traditional communities and, along with the growth of cities, displaced many people. These processes repeated themselves virtually everywhere that industrialization occurred during the next two centuries.

The consumer products of the industrializing businesses gave Europeans vast amounts of new goods to sell throughout the world and thus encouraged more international trade in which Western nations supplied the finished goods in exchange for raw materials. As a consequence, the prosperity of other areas of the globe became economically dependent on European and American demand. The wealth achieved through this uneven commerce allowed Europeans to dominate world markets for almost two centuries.

Furthermore, by the early nineteenth century iron and steel production and the new technologies of manufacture allowed European states and later the United States to build more powerful military forces, especially navies, than those

of Africa, Latin America, or Asia. Both the economic and the military dominance of the West arose directly from the industrial achievement.

Much of the history of the non-Western world from the middle of the eighteenth century to the present can be understood in terms of how the nonindustrialized nations initially reacted to the penetration of their world by Europeans and Americans made wealthy and powerful through industrialized economies. Africa and Latin America became generally dependent economies. Japan, by the middle of the nineteenth century, decided it must imitate the European pattern and did so successfully. China did not make that decision and became indirectly ruled by Europeans. The Chinese revolutions of the twentieth century have largely represented efforts to achieve real self-direction. Southeast Asia and the Middle East became drawn into the network of resource supply to the West; they could achieve movement towards economic independence only through imitation or, like Arab nations in the early 1970s, by refusing to supply oil to the West. The process of industrialization that commenced in small factories in eighteenth-century Europe has changed the world more than any other single development in the last two centuries.

Industrial Leadership of Great Britain

Great Britain was the home of the Industrial Revolution and, until the late nineteenth century, remained the industrial leader of Europe and the world (see Map 20–5). Several factors contributed to the early start of industrialization in Britain. Britain was the single largest free-trade area in Europe, with good roads and waterways without tolls or other internal trade barriers. There were rich deposits of coal and iron ore. The political structure was stable, and property was absolutely secure. A sound system of banking and public credit created a good investment climate. Taxation in Britain was heavy, but it received legal approval from Parliament. Taxes were efficiently and fairly collected, largely from indirect taxes, with all regions and persons from all classes paying the same taxes. Besides satisfying domestic consumer demand, the British economy also benefited from the demand for goods from the North American colonies. 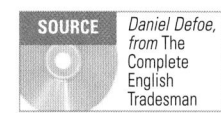 Finally, British society was relatively mobile. Persons who had money or could earn it could rise socially.

SOURCE Daniel Defoe, from The Complete English Tradesman

New Methods of Textile Production Although eighteenth-century European society was devoted primarily to agriculture, small-scale household manufacturing permeated the countryside. The same peasants who tilled the land in spring and summer often spun thread or wove textiles in

---

Why the Industrial Revolution Began in Britain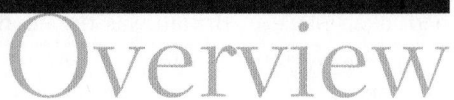

Great Britain was the home of the Industrial Revolution, and until the middle of the nineteenth century, it maintained the industrial leadership of Europe. Several factors contributed to the early industrialization of Britain.

Natural Resources	Britain had extensive deposits of coal and iron ore.
Infrastructure	Britain had an extensive network of roads and canals that facilitated the shipment of raw materials and goods.
Society	**1.** The predominance of London: London was the largest city in Europe and the social, commercial, financial, and political center of Britain. It was thus both an enormous market for consumer goods itself and created a demand for these goods in the rest of Britain, which sought to emulate London fashions.
	2. The prevalence of newspapers: Newspapers thrived in Britain, and advertisements in them increased consumer demand for goods.
	3. Wealth in Britain brought status: British society was relatively mobile. Wealthy merchants and entrepreneurs could rise socially, enter the aristocracy, and enjoy political influence.
Government, Financial Institutions, and Empire	**1.** The rule of law: Britain had a stable government that guaranteed property rights.
	2. Britain was a free trade area. No internal tolls inhibited the shipment of goods and raw materials within Britain.
	3. Britain had a sound system of banking and public credit that created a stable climate for investing in commerce and industry.
	4. Taxes were collected efficiently and fairly. No class was exempt from paying taxes.
	5. The colonial empire: British colonies were both a market for British goods and sources of raw materials for British manufacturers.

---

winter. Under the **domestic or putting-out system**, agents of urban textile merchants took wool or other unfinished fiber to the homes of peasants, who spun it into thread. The agent then transported the thread to other peasants, who wove it into the finished product. The merchant sold the wares. In literally thousands of peasant cottages from Ireland to Austria stood either a spinning wheel or a hand loom. Sometimes the spinners or weavers owned their own equipment, but more often than not, by the middle of the century, the merchant capitalist owned the machinery as well as the raw material.

What must be kept constantly in mind is that eighteenth-century industrial development took place within this rural setting. The peasant family living in a one- or two-room cottage, not the factory, was the basic unit of production. The family economy, rather than the industrial factory economy, characterized the century.

By midcentury production bottlenecks had developed within the domestic system. The demand for cotton textiles was growing more rapidly than production. This demand arose particularly in Great Britain, whose growing population wanted cotton textiles, as did its colonies in North America. The most famous inventions of the Industrial Revolution were devised in response to this consumer demand for cotton textiles.

Cotton textile weavers had the technical capacity to produce enough fabric to satisfy demand. However, the spinners could not produce as much thread as the weavers needed and could use. This imbalance had been created during the 1730s by John Kay's invention of the flying shuttle, which increased the productivity of the weavers. Thereafter, manufacturers and merchants offered prizes for the invention of a machine to eliminate this bottleneck. In about 1765 James Hargreaves (d. 1778) invented the

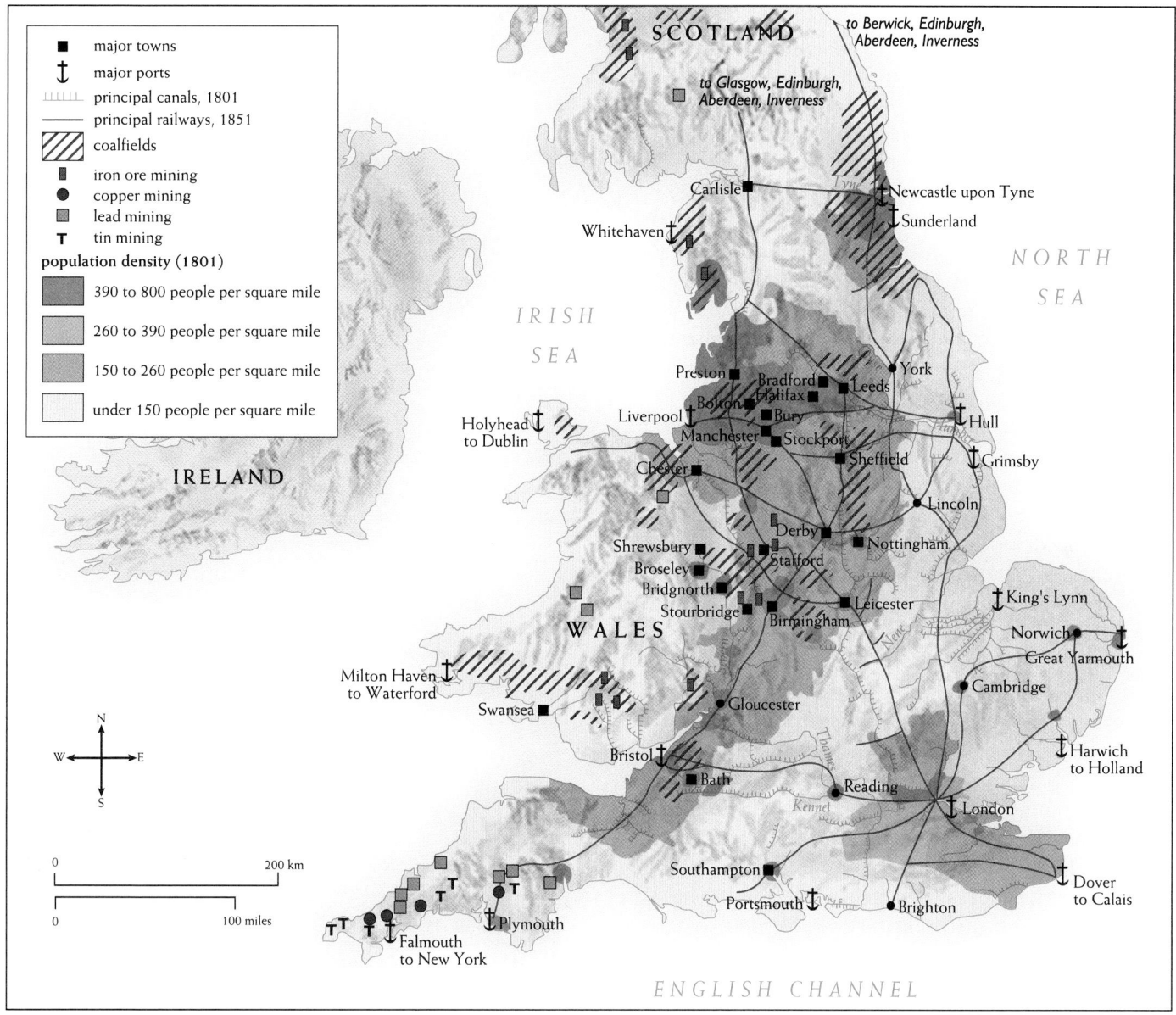

Map 20–5. The Industrial Revolution in Britain. Richly endowed with coal and iron ore and possessing many natural ports and a network of navigable waterways, Britain exploited these advantages to become the world's first industrial nation.

spinning jenny. Initially this machine allowed 16 spindles of thread to be spun, but by the close of the century it included as many as 120 spindles.

The spinning jenny broke the bottleneck between the productive capacity of the spinners and the weavers, but it was still a piece of machinery that was used in the cottage. The invention that took cotton textile manufacture from the home to the factory was Richard Arkwright's (1732–1792) **water frame**, patented in 1769. It was a water-powered device designed to permit the production of a purely cotton

fabric rather than a cotton fabric containing linen fiber for durability. Eventually Arkwright lost his patent rights, and other manufacturers were able to use his invention freely. As a result, numerous factories sprang up in the countryside near streams that provided the necessary water power. From the 1780s onward the cotton industry could meet an ever-expanding demand. Between 1780 and 1800 cotton output increased by 800 percent. By 1815 cotton composed 40 percent of the value of British domestic exports, and by 1830 just over 50 percent.

The Steam Engine The new technology in textile manufacture vastly increased cotton production and revolutionized a major consumer industry. But the invention that more than any other enabled industrialization to grow on itself and expand into one area of production after another was the steam engine. This machine provided for the first time in human history a steady and essentially unlimited source of inanimate power. Unlike engines powered by water or wind, the steam engine, driven by the burning of coal, was a portable source of industrial power that did not fail or falter as the seasons of the year changed. Unlike human or animal power, the steam engine depended on mineral energy that never tired. Finally, the steam engine could be applied to many industrial and, eventually, transportation uses.

The first practical engine using steam power was invented by Thomas Newcomen (1663–1729) in the early eighteenth century. It was large, inefficient in its use of energy, and practically untransportable. Nonetheless, English mine operators used it to pump water out of coal and tin mines. By the late eighteenth century almost a hundred Newcomen machines were operating in the mining districts of England.

During the 1760s James Watt (1736–1819) began to experiment with a model of a Newcomen machine at the University of Glasgow. He gradually understood that if the condenser were separated from the piston and the cylinder, much greater efficiency would result. In 1769 he patented his new invention, but his design required exceedingly precise metalwork. Watt soon found a partner in Matthew Boulton (1728–1809), a toy manufacturer in Birmingham, the city with the most skilled metalworkers in Britain. Watt and Boulton in turn consulted with John Wilkinson (1728–1808), a cannon manufacturer, to find ways to drill the precise metal cylinders required by Watt's design. In 1776 the Watt steam engine found its first commercial application pumping water from mines.

The use of the steam engine spread slowly because until 1800 Watt retained the exclusive patent rights and was reluctant to modify the engine. Boulton eventually persuaded him to adapt the engines for use in running cotton mills. By the early nineteenth century the steam engine had become the prime mover for all industry. With its application to ships and then to wagons on iron rails, it also revolutionized transportation.

Iron Production The manufacture of high-quality iron has been basic to modern industrial development. It constitutes the chief element of all heavy industry and land or sea transport and is the material out of which most productive machinery itself has been manufactured. During the early eighteenth century British ironmakers produced less than 25,000 tons annually. Three factors held back the production of the metal. First, charcoal rather than coke was used to smelt the ore. Charcoal, which is derived from wood, was becoming scarce, and it did not burn at as high a temperature as coke, which is derived from coal. Second, until the perfection of the steam engine, insufficient blasts could be achieved in the furnaces. Finally, the demand for iron was limited. The elimination of the first two problems eliminated the third.

In the course of the century, British ironmakers began to use coke, and the steam engine provided new power for the blast furnaces. Coke was abundant because of Britain's large coal deposits. The steam engine both improved iron production and increased the demand for iron.

In 1784 Henry Cort (1740–1800) introduced a new method for melting and stirring the molten ore. Cort's process produced a purer iron. He also developed a rolling mill that continually shaped the still-molten metal into bars, rails, or other forms. Previously, the metal had been pounded into these forms.

Blacksmith Shop. During the eighteenth century, most goods were produced in small workshops, such as this English blacksmith shop shown in a painting by Joseph Wright of Derby (1734–1797), or in the homes of artisans. Not until very late in the century, with the early stages of industrialization, did a few factories appear. *The Bridgman Art Library International.*

Chronology

Major Inventions in the Textile-Manufacturing Revolution

1733	John Kay's flying shuttle
1765	James Hargreaves's spinning jenny (patent 1770)
1769	James Watt's steam engine patent
1769	Richard Arkwright's water frame patent
1787	Edmund Cartwright's power loom

All of these innovations achieved a better, more versatile, and cheaper product. The demand for iron grew as its price went down. By the early nineteenth century annual British iron production amounted to over a million tons. The lower cost of iron in turn lowered the cost of steam engines and allowed them to be used more widely.

European Cities

Patterns of Preindustrial Urbanization

Remarkable changes occurred in the pattern of city growth between 1500 and 1800. In 1500 there were approximately 156 cities within Europe (excluding Hungary and Russia) with a population greater than 10,000. Only four of those cities—Paris, Milan, Venice, and Naples—had more than 100,000 inhabitants. By 1800 approximately 363 cities had 10,000 or more inhabitants, and 17 of those had populations larger than 100,000. The percentage of the European population living in urban areas had risen from just over 5 percent to just over 9 percent. The urban concentration had also shifted from southern Mediterranean Europe to the north.

Urban Classes

Social divisions were as marked in the cities of the eighteenth century as they were in the industrial centers of the nineteenth.

The Upper Classes   At the top of the urban social structure stood a generally small group of nobles, large merchants, bankers, financiers, clergy, and government officials. These men (and they were always men) controlled the political and economic affairs of the town. Normally they constituted a self-appointed and self-electing oligarchy who governed the city through its corporation or city council. These rights of self-government had generally been granted by a royal charter that gave the city corporation its authority and the power to select its own members. In a few cities on the Continent artisan guilds controlled the corporations, but most councils were under the influence of the local nobility and the commercial elite.

The Middle Class   The prosperous but not immensely wealthy merchants, tradesmen, bankers, and professional people were the most dynamic element of the urban population and constituted the group traditionally regarded as the middle class, or *bourgeoisie*. The middle class had less wealth than most nobles, but more than urban artisans. Middle-class people lived in the cities and towns, and their sources of income had little or nothing to do with the land. The middle class normally supported reform, change, and economic growth. Middle-class businessmen and professionals often found their pursuit of profit and prestige blocked by aristocratic privilege and social exclusiveness. The bourgeoisie (and some progressive aristocrats) also wanted more rational regulations for trade and commerce.

During the eighteenth century the middle class and the aristocracy frequently collided. The former often imitated the lifestyle of the latter, and nobles increasingly embraced the commercial spirit of the middle class. The bourgeoisie was not rising to challenge the nobility; both were seeking to enhance their existing power and prestige. However, tradition and political connection gave the advantage to the nobility. Consequently, as the century passed, the middle class increasingly resented the aristocracy. That resentment became more bitter as the bourgeoisie grew wealthier and more numerous, and the aristocratic control of political and ecclesiastical power tightened. The growing influence of the nobility seemed to mean that the middle class would continue to be excluded from the political decisions of the day.

On the other hand, the middle class tended to fear the lower urban classes as much as they resented the nobility. The lower orders constituted a potentially violent element in society; a potential threat to property; and, in their poverty, a drain on national resources. The lower orders, however, were much more varied than either the city aristocracy or the middle class cared to admit.

Artisans   The segment of the urban population that suffered from both the grasping of the middle class and the local nobility was made up of shopkeepers, artisans, and wage earners. These people constituted the single largest

Dress Shop. Consumption of all forms of consumer goods increased greatly in the eighteenth century. This engraving illustrates a shop, probably in Paris. Here women, working apparently for a woman manager, are making dresses and hats to meet the demands of the fashion trade. *Bildarchiv Preussischer Kulturbesitz.*

group in any city. They included grocers, butchers, fishmongers, carpenters, cabinetmakers, smiths, printers, handloom weavers, and tailors, to give but a few examples. They had their own culture, values, and institutions. Like the peasants of the countryside, they were in many respects conservative. Their economic position was highly vulnerable. If a poor harvest raised the price of food, their own businesses suffered.

The entire life of these artisans and shopkeepers centered on their work. They usually lived near or at their place of employment. Most of them worked in shops with fewer than a half-dozen other craftsmen. Their primary institution had historically been the guild, but by the eighteenth century most guilds had lost influence.

Nevertheless, the guilds were not to be ignored. They played a conservative role. They did not seek economic growth or innovation. They attempted to preserve the jobs and the skills of their members. They still were able in many countries to determine who might and might not pursue a particular craft. They attempted to prevent too many people from learn-

ing a particular skill. The guilds also provided a framework for social and economic advancement. A young boy might become an apprentice to learn a craft or trade. After several years he would be made a journeyman. Still later, if successful, he might become a master. The artisan could also receive certain social benefits from the guilds, including aid for his family during sickness or the promise of admission into the guild for his son. The guilds constituted the chief protection for artisans against the operation of the commercial market. They were particularly strong in central Europe.

The Jewish Population: Age of the Ghetto

Although the small Jewish communities of Amsterdam and other Western European cities became famous for their intellectual life and financial institutions, most European Jews lived in eastern Europe. In the eighteenth century and thereafter, no fewer than 3 million Jews dwelled in Poland, Lithuania, and Ukraine. There were perhaps 150,000 in the Habsburg lands, primarily in Bohemia, around 1760. Fewer than 100,000 lived in Germany and approximately 40,000 in France. England and Holland had Jewish populations of fewer than 10,000. There were even smaller groups of Jews in Italy.

In 1762 Catherine the Great of Russia specifically excluded Jews from a manifesto that welcomed foreigners to settle in Russia. (See Document, "Belorussian Jews Petition Catherine the Great.") She relaxed the exclusion a few years later. After the first partition of Poland in 1772, to be

---

Belorussian Jews Petition Catherine the Great

Document

In the 1780s, through military expansion, Empress Catherine the Great of Russia annexed Belorussia, bringing a new Jewish minority under her imperial government. In response to her decree governing many aspects of the region's law and economy, Belorussian Jews petitioned the empress to protect certain of their traditional rights regarding distillation and sale of spirits. They also petitioned for protection in court and for the right to retain their own traditional practices and courts for matters relating to their own community. The petition indicates how in Russia, as elsewhere in Europe, Jews were treated as a people apart. It also illustrates how Jews, like other minorities in Old Regime Europe, sought both to receive the protection of monarchies against arbitrary local officials and to maintain the integrity of long-standing social practices. The document also illustrates the Jews' dependence on the goodwill of the surrounding non-Jewish community.

◆ In the first part of the petition, how do the petitioners attempt to appeal to long-standing custom to defend their interests? How do both parts of the petition suggest that Jewish law and practice, distinct from the rest of the society, governed Jewish social life? In the context of this petition, which non-Jewish authorities may actually or potentially influence Jewish life?

. . . 2. According to an ancient custom, when the squires built a new village, they summoned the Jews to reside there and gave them certain privileges for several years and then permanent liberty to distill spirits, brew beer and mead, and sell these drinks. On this basis, the Jews built houses and distillation plants at considerable expense. . . . A new decree of Her Imperial Majesty . . . reserved [this right] to the squires. . . . But a decree of the governor-general of Belorussia has now forbidden the squires to farm out distillation in their villages to Jews, even if the squires want to do this. As a result, the poor Jews who built houses in small villages and promoted both this trade and distillation have been deprived of these and left completely impoverished. But until all the Jewish people are totally ruined, the Jewish merchants suffer restraints equally with the poor rural Jews, since their law obliges them to assist all who share their religious faith. They therefore request an imperial decree authorizing the squire, if he wishes, to farm out distillation to Jews in rural areas.

3. Although, with Her Imperial Majesty's permission, Jews may be elected as officials . . . Jews are allotted fewer votes than other people and hence no Jew can ever attain office. Consequently, Jews have no one to defend them in courts and find themselves in a desperate situation—given their fear and ignorance of Russian—in case of misfortune, even if innocent. To consummate all the good already bestowed, Jews dare to petition that an equal number of electors be required from Jews as from others (or, at least, that in matters involving Jews and non-Jews, a representative from the Jewish community hold equal rights with non-Jews, be present to accompany Jews in court, and attend the interrogation of Jews). But cases involving only Jews (except for promissory notes and debts) should be handled solely in Jewish courts, because Jews assume obligations among themselves, make agreements and conclude all kinds of deals in the Jewish language and in accordance with Jewish rites and laws (which are not known to others). Moreover, those who transgress their laws and order should be judged in Jewish courts. Similarly, preserve intact all their customs and holidays in the spirit of their faith, as is mercifully assured in the imperial manifesto.

From *From Supplication to Revolution: A Documentary Social History of Imperial Russia* edited by Gregory L. Freeze. Copyright © 1988 by Oxford University Press, Inc. Used by permission of Oxford University Press, Inc.

discussed in Chapter 23, Russia had a large Jewish population. The partition also resulted in larger Jewish communities in Prussia and Austria.

Jews dwelled in most nations without enjoying the rights and privileges of other subjects of the monarchs, unless such rights were specifically granted to them. They were regarded as aliens whose status might well be changed at the whim of local rulers or the monarchical government.

No matter where they dwelled, the Jews of Europe under the Old Regime lived apart from non-Jews. In cities they usually lived in distinct districts known as **ghettos**; in the countryside, in primarily Jewish villages. Thus this period in Jewish history, which may be said to have begun with the expulsion of the Jews from Spain in 1492, is known as the age of the ghetto, or separate community. Jews were also treated as a distinct people religiously and legally. In Poland for much of the century they were virtually self-governing. Elsewhere they lived under the burden of discriminatory legislation. Except in England, Jews could not mix in the mainstream of the societies in which they dwelled.

During the seventeenth century a few Jews helped finance the wars of major rulers. These financiers often grew close to the rulers and came to be known as "court Jews." They tended to marry among themselves. Perhaps the most famous was Samuel Oppenheimer (1630–1703), who helped the Habsburgs finance their struggle against the Turks, including the defense of Vienna. Their position at court and their financial abilities may have brought them privilege and fame, but court Jews, including Oppenheimer, often failed to have their loans repaid.

Ghetto in Cracow. During the Old Regime, European Jews were separated from non-Jews, typically in districts known as ghettos. Relegated to the least desirable section of a city or to rural villages, most lived in poverty. This watercolor painting depicts a street in Kazimlesz, the Jewish quarter of Cracow, Poland. *Judaica Collection. Max Berger, Vienna Austria/©Erich Lessing/Art Resource, N.Y.*

Unlike the court Jews, however, most European Jews lived in poverty. They occupied the most undesirable sections of cities or poor rural villages. A few were moneylenders, but most worked at the lowest occupations. Their religious beliefs, rituals, and community set them apart. A wall of laws and social institutions—as well as the physical walls of the ghetto—kept them in positions of social inferiority.

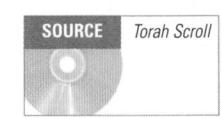

Under the Old Regime, it is important to emphasize, this discrimination was based on religious separateness. Jews who converted to Christianity were welcomed, even if not always warmly, into the major political and social institutions of European society. But until the late eighteenth century those Jews who remained loyal to their faith were subject to various religious, civil, and social disabilities. They were not free to pursue the professions or often change residence, and they stood outside the political structures of the nations in which they lived. Jews could be expelled from the cities where they dwelled, and their property could be confiscated. They were regarded as socially and religiously inferior. They could be required to listen to sermons that insulted them and their religion. Their children could be taken away from them and given Christian instruction. And they knew their non-Jewish neighbors might suddenly turn violently against them. As will be seen in subsequent chapters, however, the end of the Old Regime brought major changes in the lives of Jews and in their relationship to the larger culture.

Summary

Models of European Political Development. In the seventeenth and eighteenth centuries, five great powers emerged in Europe: France, Britain, Austria, Prussia, and Russia. Through their military strength, economic development, and in some cases colonial empires, they would affect virtually every other world civilization.

Britain. In the seventeenth century, conflict between the Stuart kings and Parliament arising out of political, religious, and economic issues led to civil war, the execution of Charles I, a short-lived English republic under Oliver Cromwell, and in 1688–1689 the Glorious Revolution that finally limited royal authority and established the supremacy of Parliament. Although eighteenth-century England was not a democracy, its people had more rights and liberties than the subjects of the absolutist monarchs who ruled the other great European powers.

In a series of worldwide colonial struggles with France, Britain used its commercial resources and navy to profit from France's entanglements in Europe and emerge supreme in North America and India.

France. Under Louis XIV (r. 1643–1715), France became the model of an absolute monarchy. Louis used his splendid court at Versailles to overawe the French aristocracy and promote a glittering image of French culture that impressed all of Europe. However, he was not able completely to overcome opposition from the French elites who sought to reassert their influence under his successors. His revocation of the Edict of Nantes weakened France by driving thousands of French Protestants into exile.

Louis pursued an aggressive foreign policy that expanded France's borders but cost France dearly in wealth and resources and provoked strong opposition from the other European powers. In the War of the Spanish Succession, he succeeded in placing his grandson on the throne of Spain, but the war left France exhausted.

Russia. Russia became a great power under Peter the Great (r. 1682–1725). Peter curbed the power of the Russian church and aristocracy and opened Russia to Western technology and military and commercial influences. He built his new capital at Saint Petersburg. He also built an efficient army and navy and established a centralized bureaucracy to collect revenue.

Central Europe. The Habsburgs remained Holy Roman Emperors, but their power rested on their hereditary domains—Austria, Hungary, Bohemia, and northern Italy. Although the Habsburgs reconquered Hungary from the Ottomans, the rise of Prussia under the Hohenzollerns challenged Habsburg dominance in Central Europe. The Hohenzollern rulers built Prussia from a collection of scattered German states into a great power by developing an efficient bureaucracy and a powerful army. Under Frederick II (r. 1740–1786), Prussia emerged from a series of wars with Austria, France, and Russia as one of the strongest European states and the rival to Habsburg power in central Europe.

The Old Regime. Eighteenth-century European society was traditional, hierarchical, corporate, and privileged—features that had characterized Europe and the world for centuries. All societies also confronted the scarce food supplies. For the eighteenth century, however, an improved food supply helped support a larger population. New agricultural techniques and the expanding population created pressures on social structures.

Commerce also grew during the eighteenth century. Agriculture became more commercialized, with more money payments; cities expanded.

Changes in European Society. European society stood on the brink of a new era in which the social, economic, and political relationships of centuries would be destroyed. The commercial spirit and the values of the marketplace clashed with the traditions of peasants and guilds. That commercial spirit brought social change; by the early nineteenth century it led to a conception of human beings as individuals rather than as members of communities.

The expansion of the European population further stimulated change and challenge to tradition, hierarchy, and corporateness. The traditional economic and social organization (the family economy) had presupposed a stable or declining population. A larger population created the need for new ways to solve old problems. The social hierarchy had to accommodate more people. Corporate groups, such as the guilds, had to confront an expanded labor force. New wealth meant that birth would cease to determine social relationships.

Furthermore, the eighteenth century witnessed the beginning of industrial production in response to the demands for consumer goods by the expanding population. New inventions greatly increasing productive capacity first appeared in the English textile industry. Thereafter industrial modes of production spread to the manufacture of iron. The steam engine provided a portable source of energy allowing factories to be moved from the countryside into cities.

Industrialization also affected Europe's relations with much of the non-European world. For the first time in history, major changes in one region of Europe left virtually no corner of the globe untouched. By the close of the eighteenth century, a movement towards world interconnectedness and interdependence had begun.

Review Questions

1. By the end of the seventeenth century, England and France had different systems of government with different religious policies. What were the main differences? Similarities? Why did each nation develop as it did?

2. How and why did Russia emerge as a great power? Discuss the character of Peter the Great. How were his domestic reforms related to his military ambitions? What were his methods of reform? To what extent did he succeed?

3. What were the main points of conflict between Britain and France in North America, the West Indies, and India? What were the results of these conflicts by 1763? Which countries emerged stronger from the Seven Years' War and why?

4. Why were so many people living in the European countryside dependent upon the aristocracy?

5. How would you define the term *family economy*? In what ways were the lives of women constrained by the family economy in preindustrial Europe? What active roles were possible for women?

6. What caused the agricultural revolution? How did technological innovations help change European agriculture? To what extent did the English aristocracy contribute to the agricultural revolution? What were some of the reasons for peasant revolts in Europe in the eighteenth century?

7. What factors led to the Industrial Revolution of the eighteenth century? What were some of the technological innovations and why were they important? Why did Great Britain take the lead in the Industrial Revolution? How did the consumer contribute to the Industrial Revolution?

8. Describe city life during the eighteenth century. Were all European cities of the same character? What changes had taken place in the distribution of population in cities and towns? Compare the lifestyle of the upper class with those of the middle and lower classes.

INTERPRETING THE PAST

State Building, Modern Society, and Aristocracy in Europe

Text Sources from MyHistoryLab / Primary Source DVD

1. Jean Domat: *On Social Order and Absolutist Monarchy*
2. The Marquis de Mirabeau, *The Friend of Men; or, Treatise on Population (1756)*
3. Louis Sebastian Mercier, *Portrait of Paris: The Saint-Marcel Neighborhood*
Voltaire on Social Conditions in Eighteenth-Century France

Visual Sources from Chapter 20

1. Louis XIV of France (p. 610)
3. Road Work (p. 625)

Europe experienced a resurgence of aristocratic power in the eighteenth century, and absolute monarchs such as France's Louis XIV, Frederick II of Prussia, and Peter the Great of Russia dominated society and politics. Yet within a century almost every major European country had removed monarchs from power and were well on the way to eliminating nearly all traditional aristocratic privileges. Why? This exercise endeavors to answer this question by considering some of

the evidence for and against preserving royal and aristocratic control.

The changes between the mid–eighteenth and mid–nineteenth century occurred in a relatively brief time. Historically speaking, European monarchies had developed over a period of almost two thousand years.

These primary source documents and images illustrate Europe's sharp class divisions and the various perspectives that justified, condemned, and depicted them. First, Jean Domat, a well-respected French legal philosopher during the reign of Louis XIV (1661–1715), offers an explanation of why absolutism is such an important and valuable tradition, and how it conforms with natural law, ethics and religious principles. The second document, authored by the Marquis de Mirabeau, who despite being a highly educated aristocrat, offers prescient warnings about the French countryside and those who purchased lands, replacing traditional nobility, and lacking a sense of *noblesse oblige* (sense of social responsibility) towards the peasants who worked and lived on the land.

The third document, by Louis Sebastien Mercier, describes life among the commoners in Paris and the problems encountered by those who moved from the country to the city. The final document, authored by Francois-Marie Arouet (Voltaire) discusses the realities of day-to-day living in a country and a world where "endless numbers of useful men . . . possess nothing at all."

PRENTICE HALL
myhistorylab
Where it's a good time to connect to the past!

9. What was the status of European Jews in the Old Regime? How were they made to live as a people apart from the rest of the European population? What were the sources of prejudice against Jews in Europe?

Key Terms

absolutism (p. 607)

agricultural revolution (p. 631)

aristocratic resurgence (p. 624)

Use the source documents and the images to address the following thematic questions that focus on the benefits and drawbacks of traditional (aristocratic and royal) rule.

Questions

How does Jean Domat justify absolute monarchy and the legal and social inequality that accompanied it in France under Louis XIV?

Why is the Marquis de Mirabeau, himself an aristocrat, so concerned about the tensions between landowners and peasants? Economic inequality had been an integral part of European life for centuries, and Mirabeau offers a number of justifications for aristocratic control of peasant life. What kinds of problems does he foresee? Were these concerns justified?

How does Mercier's depiction of urban Paris life among common workers and newly arrived peasants conform with the writings of Domat, Mirabeau, and Voltaire? Why might these city-dwellers have inordinate influence on the future political course?

Voltaire's passage is from his notorious and controversial *Philosophical Dictionary* (1764), which was widely condemned because of its critique of the French political system, the Roman Catholic Church, and many other symbols of the establishment. How does his social analysis of French and European society conform with the passages by the three other authors? What position does he ultimately take on the social, economic, and legal inequalities that existed?

boyars (p. 613)

divine right of kings (p. 612)

domestic or putting-out system (p. 634)

enclosures (p. 632)

family economy (p. 627)

ghettos (p. 640)

Glorious Revolution (p. 609)

Industrial Revolution (p. 633)

Junkers (p. 617)

Old Regime (p. 622)

parliamentary monarchy (p. 607)

Pragmatic Sanction (p. 616)

Puritans (p. 608)

spinning jenny (p. 635)

streltsy (p. 613)

Table of Ranks (p. 615)

water frame (p. 635)

Note: To learn more about the topics in this chapter, please turn to the Suggested Readings at the end of the book. For additional sources related to this chapter please see the Primary Source DVD at the back of this text or MyHistoryLab.

21

The Last Great Islamic Empires, 1500–1800

ETWEEN 1450 AND 1650 ISLAMIC CUL-
TURE, SOCIETY, AND statecraft blossomed. The creation of three powerful
empires and several strong regional
states was the culmination of long
processes in Islamic East Mediterranean and West Asian history. During
this time the ideal of a universal Islamic
caliphate yielded to the reality of multi-
ple secular, albeit distinctively "Islamic," sultanates.

The simultaneous growth of the Ottoman,
Safavid, and Mughal Empires, sometimes called the
"gunpowder empires," marked the global apogee of
Islamic society, culture, and economic power. By
about 1600 the Ottoman Turks controlled Asia
Minor, the Fertile Crescent, the Balkans, Crimean
Europe, the Eastern Mediterranean, and Arabia; the
Safavids ruled all of greater Iran; and descendants of
Timur—the Timurid line known as the Mughals—
governed Afghanistan and most of the Indian subcontinent. Around these empires were arrayed Muslim khanates of Central Asia and Russia, sultanates
of Southeast Asia, Islamic savannah-land empires
of West Africa, the city-ports of East Africa, the

Akbar Inspecting the Construction of Fatehpur-Sikri, ca. 1590. Sometime around 1570, work began on the construction of a new Mughal capital, Fatehpur-Sikri ("City of Victory"), a few miles southwest of Agra. Akbar (r. 1556–1605), the great emperor who ordered the building of Fatehpur-Sikri, had a keen interest in architecture, and here he stands at the construction site, gesturing to one of the masons as the imperial entourage looks on. In every sense, he lived up to his epithet as the "architect of the spiritual and material world."

The Last Great Islamic Empires

Ottomans

Safavids

Mughals

The Islamic region's vitality between 1450 and 1800 was exemplified by the three prosperous and great empires and societies of the Ottomans, the Safavids, Qajars, and the Mughals. All built extensive civilian and military bureaucracies using inspired military and civilian leaders, revived Islamic social and cultural ties, and improved tactics and strategies learned from their predecessors.

While Islamic ideology, society, and culture accounted for some of the Ottoman, Safavid, and Mughal successes, each of their own imperial military, social, and commercial innovations marked their respective rise to global importance. They also built arguably the greatest cities in the world of their time, such as Istanbul, Isfahan, and Dehli, and patronized the arts, stimulating important new traditions of Islamic literature, calligraphy, painting, and architecture. Yet they were essentially conservative societies. Economically they remained closely tied to agricultural production, long-distance trade, and taxation based on land. Perhaps because

they were such powerful, wealthy, and successful societies, they did not undergo the kind of social or religio-political revolutions that rocked Europe after 1500. Thus, much like the societies of China and Japan in the same period, they did not experience the sort of generative changes in material and intellectual life that the still comparatively underdeveloped Western Europe experienced in the sixteenth, seventeenth, and eighteenth centuries (although European intellectual culture was vibrant and diverse in regions such as Italy, Germany, and France). There was no compelling challenge to traditional Islamic ideals of societal organizations and human responsibility, even though many Islamic movements of the eighteenth century did call for communal and personal reform.

As one historian has put it, the striking growth of Islamic societies and cultures in this age was "not one of *origination*, but rather one of *culmination* in a culture long already mature." Even in their heydays, these empires produced much scientific work, but no scientific revolution; much art, architecture, and literature of high quality, but none that departed radically in concept or inspiration from previous traditions; political consolidation and also expansion, but no

Sharifian state of Morocco, and regional empires of the Sudan in which Islam played a significant role (see Map 21–1).

In 1600 Islamic civilization seemed as strong and vital as that of Western Europe, China, or Japan, yet military preeminence and economic and political strength were partially deceiving. By the late seventeenth and early eighteenth centuries Ottoman, Safavid, and Mughal military power was struggling before the emergence of Western European military and economic trading expansion and empire building, even though Islamic social and cultural life continued to flourish, and the Ottomans, Safavids, and Mughals continued to enjoy widespread acceptance globally between 1500 and the early nineteenth century.

Hindus were the chief religious group the Muslims displaced in some regions of Southeast Asia. Islam never ousted the Indian Buddhist cultures of Burma, Thailand, and Indochina. Islam did, however, succeed in most of Malaysia, Sumatra, Java, and the "Spice Islands" of the Moluccas. By the end of the fifteenth century, Islam, long a part of Saharan and savannah West and Central Africa, had also spread along the East African coast.

In this chapter we focus first on the three major Islamic empires of the period and then turn briefly to the smaller Islamic political and cultural centers of Central Asia and the coastlands of southern Asia and the Indies where European power was having an impact on what had been a virtual Muslim monopoly on maritime trade. ∎

conquest of significant new markets or territories; commercial prosperity in long-distance trade, but no beginnings of a real commercial or industrial revolution. By the mid–nineteenth century, all were at various stages of economic, political, social, and military disarray in comparison to Europe. By contrast, Western Europe, having lagged behind the Islamic world in economic, social, and cultural development as well as political and military might during the Middle Ages and much of the early modern period, was by the nineteenth century in the midst of industrial, financial, social, and military revolutions and finally poised to challenge successfully the Islamic empires from the Mediterranean to the Indian Ocean.

Thus it is not entirely surprising that European global expansionism gradually dominated Africa, India, Indonesia, and the heartland culture of the Islamic world, rather than the reverse. Neither the great imperial Islamic states, the smaller Islamic sultanates and emirates, the diverse Hindu kingdoms, nor the varied African states (let alone the smaller societies of Africa, the Americas, and the South Pacific) fared well in their eventual clashes with Europeans during this age. The growing European domination of the seas, of the flow of gold and silver, and of global consumable products allowed Europeans to contain as well as to bypass the major Islamic lands in their quest for commercial empires.

Industrial development and military technology joined economic wealth, social prosperity, and political stability by the early 1800s to give Western Europe global military supremacy for the first time. Before 1800 the Europeans were able to bring only minor Islamic states under colonial administrations. However, the footholds they gained in Africa, India, and Southeast Asia laid the groundwork for rapid colonial expansion by the 1850s. The age of the last great Islamic empires was the beginning of the rise of the first great modern European empires. The colonialism of the nineteenth century accompanied the aggressive advance of West European industrial, commercial, and military power that held sway into the mid–twentieth century.

Focus Questions

◆ How did the trajectory of development between the Islamic empires and Europe differ in the period from 1500–1850?

◆ Why, after centuries as the "underdog," was Europe by the early nineteenth century finally able to challenge the power of the Islamic empires?

◆ Why was the Islamic world, more than China and Japan, increasingly subject to European intrusion during the early modern period?

The Ottoman Empire and the East Mediterranean World

Origins and Development of the Ottoman State Before 1600

The Ottomans were a Turkish dynasty that rose to prominence—originally one of various groups of western Oghuz Turks from the steppes of Central Asia who came to Anatolia as settlers and Muslim frontier warriors.[1] The Ottomans reached Anatolia (Asia Minor) in the time of the Seljuks of Rum (1098–1308), who were the first western Turks to have founded a lasting state there (see Chapter 13). By about 1300, the newcomers had built one of several small military states along the Byzantine-Seljuk frontier in western Anatolia. In the fourteenth century several vigorous leaders expanded their territories east into central Anatolia and west across the Dardanelles (in 1356) onto European soil in the Byzantine lands of Macedonia and modern Bulgaria. Exchanging grants of revenue-producing conquered land (*timars*) for military service, the Ottomans built both a formidable fighting force and a loyal military aristocracy.

By 1402 the center of Ottoman rule had shifted northwest to Edirne on the Balkan Peninsula itself. Ottoman control then extended northwest as far as the Danube and east across central Anatolia. Only encircled Constantinople formed an alien pocket within these dominions, and it finally fell in 1453 to Sultan Mehmed II, "the Conqueror" (r. 1451–1481). Constantinople, now renamed "Istanbul," became the Ottoman capital. After hundreds of years proud Byzantium, the center of Eastern Christendom, was no

---

[1] The Ottomans, sometimes called *Osmanlis*, are named after Osman (1259–1326), also rendered *Othman* or *Uthman*, a *ghazi* said to have founded the dynasty when he set up a border state about 1288 on the Byzantine frontier in northwestern Anatolia.

Map Exploration

To explore this map further, go to http://www.prenhall.com/craig_maps

The Muslim Heartland, c.1700

- Muslim-Ruled Lands by 1700
- Muslim-Ruled Lands lost by 1700
- Ottoman Empire
- Safavid Empire
- Mughal Empire

Map 21–1. The Islamic Heartlands, ca. 1700. The three rival "gunpowder" empires—the Safavid, Mughal, and Ottoman empires—dominated the Islamic heartlands. Despite variations, the three empires demonstrated similar organizational structures.

more, although the Ottomans allowed the Christian patriarch to preside in Istanbul over the Eastern church. The fall of Constantinople, or the "liberation of Istanbul," was both the culmination of previous war efforts and also a springboard for Ottoman European ambitions. As their expansionist and extraordinary conquests continued, often justified in the name of Islam, they became in Christian European eyes the scourge of God.

By 1512 Ottoman rule was secure in virtually all of southeastern Europe and north of the Black Sea in most of the Ukraine. Under Selim I (r. 1512–1520) and Süleyman, "the Lawgiver" (known in the West as "Süleyman the Magnificent," r. 1520–1566), this sovereignty was greatly expanded. Selim subjugated the Egyptian Mamluks (1517) and annexed Syria-Palestine, most of North Africa, the Yemen, and western Arabia, including Mecca and Medina. Selim also nullified the Shi'ite threat from Iran in the east (see below). Süleyman extended Ottoman control over Kurdistan and Georgia (in the Caucasus), as well as Mesopotamia and Iraq. He also advanced Ottoman borders in eastern Europe. Having won much of Hungary and nearly taken Vienna by siege in 1526–1529, he was able by battle and treaty to bring virtually all of Hungary under direct Ottoman rule in the 1540s.

Istanbul, from a 1537 Turkish map. Its strategic location on the Bosphorus straits gave it a commanding position to dominate trade in the eastern Mediterranean.

The Ottoman ruler could now claim to be the Abbasid heir and caliph for all Muslims. This claim was symbolized

SOURCE *Ogier Ghiselin de Busbecq, "Suleyman the Lawgiver"*

by the addition (begun by Selim I, after the Mamluk conquest in 1517) of the title "Protector of the Sacred Places [Mecca and Medina]" to that of emperor, **padishah**. At this point, Ottoman military might was unmatched by any state in the world, except possibly China. It controlled a large geographical area—home to numerous linguistic and ethnic groups—making the Ottoman an empire in every sense of the word (see Map 21–2).

The "Classical" Ottoman Order

Mehmed II was the true founder of the Ottoman order. He replaced the tribal chieftains with loyal servants of the ruler; he initiated a tradition of formal governmental legislation with his **Qanun-name** (*"Lawbook"*); and he organized the *ulama* into a hierarchy under a single "Sheikh of Islam." In the next century Süleyman earned his title "Lawgiver" by his legislation touching all aspects of life and all social ranks, his reconciliation of customary law and **Shari'a**, religious law, and his efforts to regularize both law and bureaucracy.

The entire Ottoman state was organized as one vast military institution. All members, whatever their function, held

military ranks as the standing "army" of the state under the hereditary leadership of the Sultan. This centralized state was supported by the productivity of its Muslim and non-Muslim subjects, such as Jewish and Armenian merchants. The ruling class was Muslims, shared the common Ottoman culture, and had to give utter allegiance to the sultan. The state organization included the palace and three other functional divisions: the administrative or ruling institution, the military institution, and the religious or learned institution. The palace included the sultan, his **harem**, his ministers, and the servants. The privy council, headed by the grand vizier, together with the chancery, the imperial treasury, and the remaining civil bureaucracy, formed the backbone of the ruling or administrative institution. Although men held the keys to power, women also had certain important roles, most often concealed to the public eye. Traditional Turkish customs assumed that power was vested collectively in the family. Women had some ceremonial functions; they also played vital roles in court politics, especially in selection of officers and in negotiating economic policy.

Several measures helped ensure the ongoing strength of the sultan at the apex of the ruling institution. Young Ottoman princes were given administrative and leadership training in the provinces, which kept them from being sheltered in the palace and gave them experience of life outside the capital. Stability of succession was traditionally guaranteed by the practice of fratricide in the ruling family, which, legalized formally in Mehmed II's *Qanun-name*, continued until the late sixteenth century. Thus the succession was theoretically left to God, the strongest aspirant to the sultanate having to assert himself and seize power, after which he was expected to execute his brothers to eliminate future competing claims to the throne.

The Ottomans co-opted the legal-religious and educational-intellectual roles of the religious scholars, or *ulama*, for the service of the state, making them an arm of the government under a single religious authority, the **Grand Mufti** or "Sheikh of Islam." This highly organized branch of the state was open only to Muslim men and included the entire system of courts and judges. It was based on a comprehensive network ranging from local mosque schools to the four elite madrasas built around the Süleymaniye Mosque in Istanbul during Süleyman's reign. Scholars' ranks within the graded hierarchy of the *ulama* reflected the level of schooling and teaching they had attained.

While the *ulama* were thus under state control, the state itself was formally committed to maintaining the divinely ordained *Shari'a*, and the *ulama* enjoyed great esteem. This structure may account for the fact that whereas the *ulama* in both Safavid Iran and Mughal India often differed with their rulers, the Ottoman *ulama* usually functioned tamely as part of the state apparatus.

Map 21–2. The Ottoman Empire at Its Zenith. This large and multiethnic empire spanned three continents and lasted for more than 400 years.

Although the religious establishment upheld the supremacy of the *Shari'a* and the sultan recognized its authority, the functional law of the land was the highly organized state administrative law—the practical code, or **Qanun**, established by the ruler. The *Shari'a* as interpreted by the *ulama* theoretically governed the *Qanun*, and often the sultan formally applied traditional religious norms in his regulations. The conformity of these regulations to the *Shari'a* sometimes came from the genuine piety of a particular administrator or ruler and was sometimes only a pious fiction, something also true for Safavid Iran and Mughal India.

The key ingredient to Ottoman power, however, was the military. The Ottoman rulers kept the military's loyalty by two means: checks on the power of the old landed aristocracy by careful registry and control of *timar* lands, and the use of slave soldiers with allegiance only to the sultan. The army was based originally on the provincial cavalry whose officers were supported with *timar* land revenues in lieu of cash wages. The state held all conquered agricultural land as its direct property, granting peasants hereditary land use but not ownership. Careful records were kept of the revenue due on all lands, and as long as the state was strong, so too was its control over productive land and the cavalry-gentry

Süleyman the Lawgiver. Süleyman giving advice to the Crown Prince, Mehmed Khan. From a contemporaneous Ottoman miniature. *Suleyman I (Kanuni); Shehzade by Talikizade Suphi. Folio 79a of the Talikizade Shehnamesi, Library at the Topkapi Palace Museum, A3592, Photograph courtesy of Talat Halman.*

whom *timar* revenues supported. But even as early as 1400 the Ottoman rulers tried to reduce the cavalry-gentry's pre-eminence by employing specialized infantry troops of well-trained and well-paid slave soldiers (equipped, unlike the cavalry, with firearms) whose loyalty was to the sultan alone.

To sustain the quality of these slave troops, the Ottomans developed a unique institution: the provincial slave levy, or **devshirme**. This institution selected young Christian boys from the provincial peasantry to be raised as Muslims; most came from the Balkan peasantry. They were trained to serve in both army and bureaucracy at all levels, from provincial officer to grand vizier. The most famous slave corps was the *yeni cheri* (young troops), or **Janissaries**, the elite infantry troops of the empire. Muslim boys were not allowed into the slave corps, although some parents

tried to buy them a place in what offered the most promising careers in the empire. Until 1572 marriage was forbidden to the slave soldiers, which further ensured loyalty and prevented hereditary claims on office.

After Süleyman: Challenges and Change

The reign of Süleyman marked the peak of Ottoman prestige and power. Further territorial gains were made in the seventeenth century, and the Ottoman state long remained a major force in European and Asian politics, but beginning with the reign of Süleyman's weak son, Selim II (1566–1574), the empire was plagued by military corruption, governmental decentralization, and maritime setbacks. Economically there were agricultural failures, commercial imbalances, and inflation. Yet culturally and intellectually, the seventeenth and eighteenth centuries were periods of impressive accomplishments and lively activity. Overall, these ensuing two centuries witnessed a see-saw pattern between decline and vitality.

Political and Military Developments   The post-Süleyman era began on a sour note with the loss of territory in the Caucasus and Mesopotamia to the Safavids of Iran (1603). By this time the Ottoman military apparatus was already weakened, partly from fighting two-front wars with the Safavids and the Habsburgs and partly because of European advances in military and naval technology. The Janissaries became increasingly disruptive. By 1600 they had largely replaced the provincial cavalry as new warfare styles made cavalry obsolete. By 1600 Muslims were allowed into the Janissary corps, marriage was possible, and the *devshirme* was declining in use (it ended just over a century later). During the seventeenth century, the Janissaries became increasingly corrupt as they tampered with politics, trying to influence decision making and even dynastic succession. Finally, the increasing employment of mercenaries resulted—during peacetime—in the release of masses of unemployed armed men into the countryside, leading to the sacking of provincial towns, banditry, and revolts, all of which disrupted society.

Murad IV (r. 1623–1640) introduced reforms and ruled with an iron hand, but his death left again a weak central authority. The Koprülüs, father and son, two capable viziers (r. 1656–1676), briefly renewed strong administrative control and military success, but thereafter the central institutions decayed.

Economic Developments   Financing the Ottoman state grew ever more difficult. The increase in the Janissary corps from 12,000 to 36,000 men between the early 1500s and 1600 drained state coffers. Inflation grew as the coinage was

Topkapi Palace, Istanbul. Inside the imperial harem, this elegant room was used to entertain the Sultan who watched the proceedings from his large throne. *Tony Souter © Dorling Kindersley.*

important writers were the great historian of the Ottomans, Na'ima (d. 1716), the tireless traveler and travel writer Evliya Chelebi (d. ca. 1685), and probably the greatest Ottoman poet, Nedim (d. 1730). Ottoman art had been highly eclectic in the first century after Mehmed II, but in the later sixteenth century a more conservative turn produced distinctively Ottoman artistic and architectural forms. The greatest name here is that of the imperial master architect Sinan (d. 1578). The first half of the eighteenth century was the golden age of Ottoman poetry and art; it also saw the first Ottoman printing press and the beginning of strong European influence in the arts, architecture, and manners. In the popular sphere, the now classical form of Turkish theater (in which two men play male and female parts) began as early as the sixteenth century, perhaps under Jewish immigrant influence.

Socially, the period saw the consolidation of Ottoman society as a multi-ethnic and multireligious state. The

debased. In contrast to the mercantilist and protectionist policies of European powers, the Ottomans discouraged exports and encouraged imports since too many exports would have raised domestic prices. This damaged the economy in the long run. The population doubled in the sixteenth century, and unemployment grew after 1600. Increased decentralization paved the way for the rise of provincial notables (**ayan**), who became virtually independent in the eighteenth century. Tax farming also went hand-in-glove with the rise of large private estates. New taxes were imposed and old emergency levies regularized, and taxes were required in cash rather than in kind and increasingly on a communal rather than an individual basis.

Culture and Society   The seventeenth and eighteenth centuries were an era of genuine vitality in poetry, prose, music, painting, cartography, historiography, astronomy, and other fields. The Ottoman patronage of the arts and sciences was one way to assert the Ottoman claim to Islamic and universal authority. The seventeenth century saw especially lively intellectual exchange, both religious and secular. But it was also a time when the *ulama* became an aristocratic and increasingly corrupt elite. Major religious posts became hereditary sinecures for sons and other relatives of a handful of families who had produced prominent *ulama*, and the posts were often sold or leased. (See Document, "The Distinctiveness of Ottoman Identity and Culture.")

In literature and the arts, the seventeenth and eighteenth centuries were highly productive. Of the many individuals who were learned in many fields, Katib Chelebi (d. 1657) was the most illustrious; he wrote histories, social commentary, geographies, and encyclopedic works. Other

Devshirme. An Ottoman portrayal of the *devshirme*. This miniature painting from about 1558 depicts the recruiting of young Christian children for the Sultan's elite Janissary corps. The children, dressed in red, are at the bottom, while their parents, who look pleased, congregate on the right. *Arifi, "Suleymanname," Topkapi Palace Museum, II 1517, fol. 31b, photograph courtesy of Talat Halman.*

The Distinctiveness of Ottoman Identity and Culture

Document

Presiding over a pluralistic culture, the Ottoman Turks, themselves a people from the periphery of the central Islamic lands, developed a distinctive "Ottoman" identity and culture that was most evident in their ruling elite. The following selections from members of that elite describe some of the values and qualities they saw as important to Ottoman identity. In the first, Mustafa Ali (d. 1600), a major historian, intellectual, and official of the Ottoman state, lists the special divine favors granted the Ottoman rulers. In the second, another historian, Kinalizade Ali, adopts an ancient political saying attributed to Aristotle and others to describe the prerequisites for an ordered polity under the Shari'a.

◆ Compare the two passages. What common themes emerge?

1 THE GIFTS OF DIVINE FAVOR GIVEN THE OTTOMAN DYNASTY

The first gift: They reside all by themselves in a palace like unique jewels in the depth of the oyster-shell, and totally sever all relations with relatives and dependents. The slave girls and slave pages that have access to their honored private quarters (harem), who are evidently at least three to four thousand individuals, are all strangers and the person of the monarch is like a single gem in their midst. . . .

The second gift: Their religious convictions being immaculate and their character like a shining mirror, it has never happened that a single member of that noble family ever swerved from the road of orthodoxy or that one valiant sultan befriended himself with an unseemly doctrine.

The third gift: The Lord, the Creator and Protector, has always hidden that great race under His protection and it has never been heard that the plague would have entered their flourishing palace or that an individual belonging to that blemishless progeny would have been struck by the horror of the pestilence and would have died of it.

The fourth gift: Whenever they conquered a province and, destroying and eradicating its castles and estates, were confronted with the necessity of appointing a magistrate and assigning a substantial force on their own authority they considered it a sign of weakness, like Alexander the Great, to appoint again one of the great of that province and to assign him certain revenues; may [that province] be as far away as can be, they would opt to send one of the attendants of their Gate of Happiness [there] as san-jaq begi, and to Yemen and Ethiopia and to very remote places like Algeria a begler-begi. No such absolute power was given to the earlier sovereigns.

The fifth gift: The various special troops in their victory-oriented army and the various tools of war and battle use that are given to them were not available to the brawny fists of anyone of the countless armies [of previous times]. To their attacks going downward and going upward are the same, to their victory-imprinted military music low and high notes are of the same level and equal. In their eyes, as it were, the conquest of a castle is like destroying a spider's web, and in their God-assisted hands to beat the enemies is clearly like pulling out a hair from the beard of a decrepit old man.

The sixth gift: The coherence of the figures in the registers of their revenues and the order of the recordings in the ledgers of their expenses are so strict that they and their salaried classes are free of worries. Consequently, their income exceeds their necessary expenses, their gain is larger than [the expenses for] the important affairs of state.

2 THE NEED OF AUTHORITY TO UPHOLD THE SHARI'A

There can be no royal authority without the military
There can be no military without wealth
The subjects produce the wealth
Justice preserves the subjects' loyalty to the sovereign
Justice requires harmony in the world
The world is a garden, its walls are the state
The Holy Law [Shari'a] orders the state
There is no support for the Holy Law except through royal authority.

Selection 1 from Andreas Tietze, *Mustafa Ali's Counsel for Sultans of 1581*, Verlag Der Osterreichischen Akademie Der Wissenshaften, Vienna, 1979, pp. 38–39. Selection 2 from Cornell H. Fleischer, *Bureaucrat and Intellectual in the Ottoman Empire: The Historian Mustafa Ali (1541–1600)*, Princeton University Press, 1986, p. 262.

empire encompassed a dizzying array of languages, religions, and ethnic identities. All subjects, both Muslim and non-Muslim, were organized into small communities called **millets** that were responsible for their community members from the cradle to the grave. The millets thus administered their educational, charitable, and judicial affairs and assisted the central government to collect taxes. Typically the millets were headed by a religious leader and enjoyed some degree of internal autonomy. Thus early on the Ottoman Empire proved to be a haven for a number of minority groups, especially Jews. Considerable immigration of Jews into Ottoman societies following their expulsion from Spain during the Spanish Inquisition (1492) had brought new craftsmen, physicians, bankers, scholars, and even entertainers. The large Christian population of the empire was generally well treated, but in the eighteenth and nineteenth centuries they began to suffer from increasing taxes and other discrimination. As a result the Christians looked as never before to Christian Europe and Russia for liberation.

Still, state policy encouraged just treatment of all subjects; for example, "rescripts of justice" (mostly against the malpractices of tax collectors) were often issued. Although royal decrees reserved special privileges for Muslims, they seldom affected mass behavior. In the eighteenth century, however, relations between Muslims and non-Muslims deteriorated, in part because of the remarkable rise in the economic and social status of non-Muslims—in particular the rich mercantile middle class. Non-Muslims virtually monopolized foreign trade, and in the eighteenth century European countries gave many of them citizenship, which allowed them the trade privileges granted to foreign governments by the sultan.

 SOURCE De Busbecq, "Women in Ottoman Society"

One of the major social institutions of later Ottoman society, the coffeehouse, flourished from the mid–sixteenth century on. Probably originally a Sufi institution that came with coffee to the Mediterranean from the Yemen, the Ottoman coffeehouse rapidly became a major common space for socializing. Here people gathered to drink coffee, play games, watch puppet shows, read books, discuss public affairs, and even engage in political agitation. Despite bans by the sheikh of Islam because of the stimulant qualities of coffee, both the coffee habit and coffeehouses, like the similarly new imported habit of cigarette smoking, could not be suppressed. Different types of coffeehouses developed, each identified by its focus: music, theater, recitation, poetry, or Janissary or other professional affiliation (e.g., firefighting). The coffeehouse stimulated the development of a common Ottoman urban culture among lower and middle classes.

Chronology

The Ottoman Empire

1301	Foundation of early Ottoman principality in Bursa by Osman
1356	Ottomans cross Dardanelles into Europe
1451–1481	Rule of Sultan Mehmed II, "the Conqueror"
1453	Fall of Constantinople to Mehmed the Conqueror
1512–1520	Rule of Selim I
1517	Ottoman conquest of Egypt, assumption of claim to Abbasid caliphal succession from Mamluks
1520–1566	Rule of Süleyman, "the Lawgiver"
1526–1529	First Ottoman siege of Vienna
1578	Death of Ottoman master architect, Sinan
1656–1676	Governance of Koprülüs as viziers
1683	Second Ottoman siege of Vienna
1699	Treaty of Karlowitz, loss of Hungarian and other European territory
1774	Loss of Crimea to Russia; Tsar becomes formal protector of Ottoman Orthodox Christians
1918	End of empire

The Decline of Ottoman Military and Political Power

After their failure in 1683 to take Vienna, the Ottomans were driven out of Hungary and Belgrade and never again seriously threatened Europe. In 1774 Russia took the Crimea and became the formal protector of the Orthodox Christians in the Islamic empire (1774). Whereas in the seventeenth century the Ottoman Empire was a relatively self-contained and self-sufficient empire, by the late eighteenth century the empire was increasingly more dependent on the international market systems, particularly those of Western Europe. Previously its economic growth had been based on conquest and the control of land as a source of wealth. But as soon as its expansion was stopped, the Ottoman Sultans were not fully prepared to adjust to changes in an increasingly West European world economy that was increasingly geared towards capitalist accumulation and industrialization. Henceforth, the Ottomans were prey to the West, never regaining their earlier power and influence before their collapse in 1918.

Outflanked by Russia to the north and by European sea power to the south and west, the Ottomans were blocked in the east by their implacable Safavid foes in Iran. They could not sustain the level of external trade needed to support their expensive wars, especially when, in the eighteenth century, Italian, French, British, and Dutch traders obtained special concessions for their trade in the Fertile Crescent, Persian Gulf, and Red Sea regions that Ottoman merchants did not have. Ultimately, their dependence on a decentralized agrarian-age, local market economy proved insufficient to face the rising global commercial and industrial powers of Europe.

The Safavid Empire and the West Asian World

Origins

As noted in Chapter 13, Iranian history changed under the Safavid dynasty after 1500. The Safavids had begun in the

fourteenth century as hereditary Turkish spiritual leaders of a Sunni **sufi** order, in the northwestern Iranian province of Azerbaijan. In the fifteenth century the Safavid order evolved a new and militant Shi'ite sufi ideology. By claiming descent from the imams of Twelver Shi'ism (see Chapter 13), the Safavid spiritual masters (*sheikhs* and **pirs**) became the focus of Shi'ite religious allegiance. Many adherents were won to the *tariqa*, or sufi brotherhood, and eventually to Shi'ism from among the Turkoman tribesmen of eastern Anatolia, northern Syria, and northwestern Iran. These mounted warriors were called *Qizilbash* ("Red Heads") because of their distinctive red uniform hats, which signaled their allegiance to the twelve Shi'ite imams and their Safavid sufi master.

The growing strength of the Safavid brotherhood brought about conflicts with the dominant Sunni Turkoman groups in the region around Tabriz. The Safavids emerged victorious in 1501 under the leadership of the young Safavid sufi master-designate Isma'il. Recognized as a divinely appointed representative of the "hidden" imam (see Chapter 11), Isma'il extended his sovereignty over the southern Caucasus, Azerbaijan, the Tigris-Euphrates valley, and all of western Iran by 1506 (see Map 21–3). Unified under a

A Turkish Coffeehouse. This early nineteenth-century view of a coffeehouse in Istanbul captures the exoticism that made the Ottoman Empire so intriguing to Western visitors.

Map 21–3.   The Safavid Empire. The Safavid Empire had a difficult time maintaining cohesive borders in the face of numerous invasions from both east and west.

common religious identity and in league with Babur, the Timurid ruler of Kabul, the Safavids by 1512 had taken from the Uzbek Turks all of eastern Iran from the Oxus River in the north to the Arabian Sea in the south. Thereafter, the Uzbeks became implacable foes of the Safavids because of the loss of lands to the Safavids and the Uzbek (and later nineteenth-century Turcoman) pastoral migratory life and border raids. Throughout the ensuing century the Safavids were often forced to fight a debilitating two-front war, against Uzbeks in the east and Ottomans in the west.

A strong central rule now united traditional Iranian lands for the first time since the heyday of the Abbasid caliphate. It was a regime based on the existing Persian bureaucratic institutions, which in turn were based on Seljuk institutions. Shah Isma'il ruthlessly enforced Shi'ite conformity, which slowly took root across the realm—perhaps bolstered by a rising Iranian sufi self-consciousness and identity in the face of the Sunni Ottomans, Arabs,

Uzbeks, and Mughals who surrounded Iran. In the latter part of his reign, Shah Isma'il began to develop a more centralized bureaucracy at the expense of his **Sufi** enthusiasts. The shah was determined to rule no longer as a leader of a Sufi brotherhood but rather to govern, both culturally and politically, through a reconstruction of the historic Iranian monarchy. Although the shah had loyal tribal and religious support within his domain, Isma'il had tenuous ties with his neighbors, especially the leaders of the Ottoman Empire, who vigorously ensured that this Sufi–inspired monarchy would not spread farther into Ottoman eastern Anatolian lands widely populated by other sufi orders.

In 1514 the better-armed Ottoman army of Selim I soundly defeated the Safavid forces at Chaldiran in Iranian

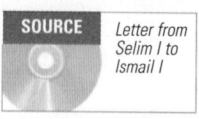 **SOURCE** *Letter from Selim I to Ismail I*

Azerbaijan, marking the beginning of an extended series of Ottoman-Safavid border wars over the next two centuries. Chaldiran also marked the

Dancing Sufis, their arms raised in ecstasy, congregate at the tomb of the great Persian medieval poet, Sa'adi.

beginning of Qizilbash disaffection with Shah Isma'il and consequent efforts to take over power from the Safavids. Furthermore, this defeat gave the Ottomans control of the Fertile Crescent and forced the Safavids to move their capital and their focus eastward, first to Qazwin, and then to Isfahan.

Shah Abbas I

Isma'il's successor, Tahmasp I (r. 1524–1576), survived repeated attacks by both Ottomans and Uzbeks, in part through the strength of Shi'ite religious feeling and the allegiance of the Iranian bureaucracy. A few years later, however, the most able of the Safavid rulers, Shah Abbas I (r. 1588–1629) brought able leadership to the Safavid domains. He regained provincial land for the state and used the revenue to pay for new troops from his Caucasian territories, thereby providing a counterweight to the sometimes

unruly Qizilbash, who (like the Ottoman *chifliks*, or cavalry) were supported by land revenue assignments. Shah Abbas not only pushed the Ottomans out of Azerbaijan and Iraq but also turned back new Uzbek invasions in Khorasan. He also sought alliances with the Ottomans' European enemies. This latter tactic, used by a number of the Safavid rulers, reflected one of the several military and economic divisions in the assumed unity within the Islamic world. Empires, whether Islamic or not, were essentially divided from each other over their own self interests: that is, absolute control of the empire's land and all its resources. Abbas also broke the century-long Portuguese monopoly on trade along Persian shores and opened trade relations with the English and Dutch East India commercial companies. His reign brought considerable prosperity to Iran, symbolized by the magnificent capital he built at Isfahan, which epitomized Safavid grandeur and vision—shown most vividly in its regal central piazza-like square, the Maydan-i Shah.

The most enduring aspect of Safavid consolidation of power in Iran was the replacement of Sunni Islam with Shi'ite Islam as the official religion. Because Twelver Shi'ism was not widely grounded in Iranian religious tradition, although various sufi traditions were, the Safavid Shahs imported religious scholars (*ulama*) primarily from today's Lebanon and Syria, placing them squarely in the service of the state to give legitimacy to the government. The Safavids discouraged pilgrimage to Mecca but instead emphasized visits to Karbala, or to the shrine of Husayn, the grandson of the Prophet Muhammad. Eventually, however,

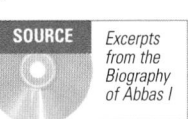

the relations between the government and the *ulama* became strained. By the seventeenth century, the *ulama* withdrew from political participation and refused to bestow direct legitimacy on the Shah.

Safavid Decline

After Shah Abbas, the empire rarely again enjoyed able leadership. This contributed finally to its decline and collapse, the chief causes of which were (1) continued two-front pressure from Ottoman and Uzbek armies, (2) economic decline, (3) social unrest among the provincial elites, and (4) the increasing landholding power of the Shi'ite *ulama*. The conservative *ulama* not only introduced a form of Islamic legalism but also emphasized their own authority as

Maydan-i-Shah. The enormous rectangular-shaped plaza at the top of this aerial photo connects with the equally impressive Masjd-i-Shah Mosque, constructed between 1611 and 1638.

interpreters of the law over that of the monarch. They also persecuted religious minorities and encouraged hatred of Sunni Muslims. Some of the Iranian *ulama* and *tujjar* or merchants sought closer ties with the European commercial communities. Local administrators were content to maintain the traditional decentralized Safavid system in their own respective interests, which only accelerated the country's dependency on the introspective and corrupt Safavid family.

In the end, an Afghan leader captured Isfahan and forced the abdication of Husayn I (1694–1722). A few of

the Safavid princes managed to retake control of western Iran, but the empire's greatness was gone. A revived, but officially Safavid, monarchy under the talented Qizilbash tribal leader Nadir Shah (r. 1736–1747) and several successors restored much of Iran's lost territories. However, Nadir Shah's military ventures, which included an invasion of Northwest India and the conquest of Delhi, sapped the empire's finances. After Nadir's autocratic and brutal reign ended in 1747, Iran's provincial elites, *ulama*, and merchants struggled to regain some of the previous political and economic stability over the next sixty years. By early in the

Chronology

The Safavid Empire

1334	Death of Safi al-Din, founder of Safavid Sufi order
1501	Rise of the Sufi Safavid shahs under Shah Isma'il I ·
1501–1510	Safavid conquest of greater Iran; Shi'i state founded
1588–1629	Rule of Shah Abbas I
1722	The Afghan invasion and forced abdication of Sultan Husayn
1722–1737	The rise of pretenders to the Safavid throne under the Safavid banner of Tahmasp II and his son, Abbas III
1736–1747	Rule of the Sunni Afshar leader, Nadir Shah; revival of Sunni monarchy in Iran
1739	Nadir Shah invades northern India, sacks Delhi

nineteenth century, some success was achieved under the Qajar kings (see Chapter 27).

Culture and Learning

In the long run, the most impressive aspect of Safavid times, in addition to the conversion of Iran to Shi'ite Islam, was the cultural and intellectual renaissance of the sixteenth and seventeenth centuries. The traditions of painting, with their origins in the powerful miniatures of the preceding century—notably those from Herat after 1450, exemplified by the work of the painter Bihzad (1440–1514) in late Timurid times—were cultivated and modified in Safavid times. Portraiture and scenes from everyday life became popular. Among the most developed crafts were ceramic tile, porcelain, shawls, and carpets. The magnificent architecture of Isfahan, especially evident in the exquisite gardens and grand arches and domes constructed in Shah Abbas's time, gives breathtaking evidence of the developed sense of proportion, color, and design in addition to the superb architectural technology and urban planning of Safavid taste. So

SOURCE *Eighteenth-century view of Isfahan*

impressive and ambitious was the scope of Isfahan that it became known as being "half the world," a lofty epithet that offers the notion that it was the quintessence of the religious and imperial Iranian world. It

marks a high point in the sophisticated use of space and lavish use of ceramic tiles to decorate the facades and especially the great domes of major buildings.

The lasting visible legacies of Safavid rule were the Iranian cultural artifacts, buildings, roads, town squares, homes, gardens, and bridges. These were handsomely decorated and financed by the Safavid fortunes from trade in silk, silver and other long-distance commercial products, as well as the Safavid patronage in literature, theology, philosophy, painting, crafts, and architecture. The Safavid age also saw a distinctively Shi'i and sufi piety develop and give a firmly Shi'i Islamic character to Iranian culture and traditions. It focused on commemorating the suffering of the imams, life as a struggle for social justice, and loyalty to the Shi'i *ulama*, who alone provided guidance in the absence of the hidden imam (see Chapter 11).

In intellectual life, the *Ishraqi* or "illuminationist" school of theological-philosophical thought brought together the mystical and sufi bent of Iranian Islamic thought and the long Islamic traditions of Aristotelianism and Platonism in the form of Shi'i religious speculation into the nature of divine truth and its accessibility to human reason and imagination. The illuminationists' two key ideas were the concept of transcendence and the notion of a "realm of images." They conceived of transcendence in terms of a divine light identified with the Light of Truth, which was expressed most fully in Muhammad and the Shi'i imams. The realm of images was a sphere of being in which the attuned spirit could experience true visions. These ideas reconceived human experience of the Divine in a way that transcended logic and had to be experienced individually. At stake were

Safavid Art. *Woman with a Veil*, by Riza Abbasi, ca. 1595. During Safavid times, Persian artists began to depict everyday life and people, such as this graceful and sinuous young woman. *Opaque watercolor, ink, and gold on paper, 34.2 × 21.5 cm. Arthur M. Sackler Gallery, Smithsonian Institution, Washington, D.C. Lent by the Art and History Trust, LTS 1995. 2.80.*

basic notions of the human psyche and the larger cosmos. The most prominent exponent of the *Ishraqi* school was Mulla Sadra (d. 1640).

The Mughals

Origins

In the early sixteenth century, invaders from beyond the Oxus River to the northwest, in the age-old pattern of Indian history, began a new era in the subcontinent: They ended the political fragmentation that by 1500 had reduced the Delhi sultanate to only one among many Indian states. These invaders were Chaghatay Turks descended from Timur (Tamerlane) and known to history as the **Mughals** (a Persianate form of *Mongol*). In 1525 to 1527 the founder of the Mughal dynasty, Babur, marched on India, replaced the last sultan of Delhi, and then defeated a Rajput confederacy. Before his death in 1530 he ruled an empire stretching from the Oxus to Bihar, and the Himalayas to the Deccan (see Map 21–4). But the real founder of the Mughal Empire and the greatest Indian ruler since Ashoka (ca. 264–223 B.C.E.) was Akbar "the Great" (r. 1556–1605). Indeed, he was as great a ruler as, if not greater than, his famous contemporaries, Elizabeth I of England (r. 1558–1603), the Holy Roman Emperor Charles V (r. 1519–1556), and Shah Abbas I (r. 1587–1629).

Akbar's Reign

Akbar began his reign, like so many other illustrious rulers, with an impressive record of military success. He added North India and the northern Deccan to the Mughal dominions. Even more significant, however, were his governmental reforms, cultural patronage, and religious toleration. He completely reorganized the central and provincial governments and rationalized the tax system. His marriages with Rajput princesses and his appointment of Hindus to positions of power eased Muslim-Hindu tensions. So did his cancellation of the poll tax on non-Muslims (1564) and his efforts to reduce the power of the more literalist, "hard-line" *ulama*. Under his leadership the Mughal Empire became a truly Indian empire.

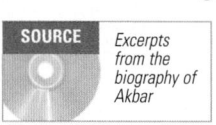

SOURCE *Excerpts from the biography of Akbar*

Akbar was a religious eclectic who showed not only tolerance of all faiths but also unusual interest in different religious traditions. He frequently brought together representatives of all faiths—Jain and Buddhist monks, Brahmans, *ulama*, Parsis (Zoroastrians), and Jesuits—to discuss religion. These debates took place in a special hall in Akbar's magnificent palace complex at Fatehpur-Sikri outside the Mughal capital, Agra.

Map 21–4. India Under the Mughals.

The Last Great Mughals

Akbar's three immediate successors were Jahangir (r. 1605–1627), Shah Jahan (r. 1628–1658), and Awrangzeb (r. 1658–1707). They left behind significant achievements, but the problems of sustaining an Indian empire took their toll on Mughal power. The reigns of Jahangir and Shah Jahan were arguably the golden age of Mughal culture, notably in architecture and painting, which developed its own Mughal style based on traditional Hindi and Persian styles. But the burdens imposed by new building, by military campaigns, and by the erosion of Akbar's administrative and tax reforms led to economic decline. Jahangir set a fateful precedent in permitting English merchants to establish a trading post, or "factory," at Surat on the western coast in Gujarat. Shah Jahan brought the Deccan wholly under Mughal control but lost Kandahar to Safavid forces in 1648.

His wars further strained the Mughal economy. No less a burden on the treasury were his elaborate building projects, the most magnificent of which was the white-stoned Taj Mahal (built 1632–1653), the unparalleled tomb with its Persian-styled dome that he built for his beloved consort, Mumtaz.

With Shah Jahan, religious toleration retreated; under his son, Awrangzeb, a narrow religious fanaticism all but reversed Akbar's earlier policies. The resulting internal disorder and instability hastened the decline of Mughal power. Awrangzeb persecuted non-Muslims, destroying Hindu temples, reimposing the poll tax (1679), and alienating the Rajput leaders, whose forebears Akbar had so carefully cultivated. His intransigent policies coincided with and perhaps contributed to the spread of the militant reformism of the Sikh movement throughout the Punjab and the rise of Hindu Maratha nationalism in Western India.

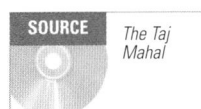

SOURCE · *The Taj Mahal*

Sikhs and Marathas

In the late sixteenth and early seventeenth centuries the Sikhs, who trace their origins to the irenic teachings of Guru Nanak (d. 1538), developed into a distinctive religious movement. Neither Muslim nor Hindu, they had their own scripture, ritual, and moralistic and reformist ideals. Awrangzeb earned their lasting enmity by persecution that culminated in the martyrdom of their ninth leader, or guru, Teg Bahadur, in 1675. Thereafter, the tenth and last Sikh guru, Gobind Singh (d. 1708), developed the Sikhs into a formidable military force. Awrangzeb and his successors had to contend with repeated Sikh uprisings.

The Hindu Marathas, led by the charismatic Shivaji (d. 1680), rose in religious and nationalistic fervor to found their own regional empire in about 1646. On Shivaji's death, the Maratha state controlled the mountainous Western coast, and its army was the most disciplined force in India. Despite Awrangzeb's subsequent defeat of the Marathas and

Fatehpur-Sikri. The Diwan-i-Khas, one of the many pavilions found in the enormous imperial palace complex.

Jahangir and Shaykh Husain. Jahangir showing preference to the Chishti Sufi *shaykh* and saint Husain over three temporal rulers: the Ottoman emperor, the King of England, and a Hindu prince. The Timurid emperor presents a book to Shaykh Husain, the descendant of the great Chishti saint Mu'inuddin, while ignoring the temporal rulers in the lower-left corner. The artist copied the likeness of King James I from an English portrait given to Jahangir by Sir Thomas Roe, the British ambassador from 1615 to 1619. The magnificent floral borders to the miniature (ca. 1615–1618) were added in 1727 by Muhammad Sadiq. *Bichitr, Jahangir Preferring a Sufi Shakikh to Kings, ca. 1660–70, Album Page; Opaque watercolor, gold and ink on paper, 25.3 × 18.1 cm. Courtesy of the Freer Gallery of Art, Smithsonian Institution, Washington, D.C.*

his conquest of the entire south of India, the Marathas continued to fight him. After his death they brought about a confederation of almost all the Deccan states under their leadership. While formally acknowledging Mughal sovereignty, the Marathas actually controlled far more of India after about 1740 than did the Mughals.

Political Decline

In addition to the Rajput, Sikh, and Maratha wars, other factors sealed the fate of the once-great Mughal empire

after Awrangzeb's death in 1707: the rise in the Deccan of the powerful Islamic state of Hyderabad in 1724; the Persian invasion of North India by Nadir Shah in 1739; the invasions (1748–1761) by the Afghan tribal leader Ahmad Shah Durrani (r. 1747–1773), "founder of modern Afghanistan"; and the British victories over Bengali forces at Plassey in Bengal (1757) and over the French on the southeastern coast (1740–1763). By 1819 the dominance of the British East India Company had eclipsed Mughal as it did Maratha and almost all regional Indian power, even though the Mughal line did not officially end until 1858.

Religious Developments

The period from about 1500 to 1650 was of major importance for Indian religious life. Akbar's eclecticism mirrored the atmosphere of the sixteenth century in India. A number of religious figures preached a spiritually or mystically oriented piety that transcended the legalism of both the *ulama* and the Brahmans and rejected caste distinctions. In these ideas, we can see both Muslim Sufi and Hindu *bhakti* influ-

Chronology

India: The Mughals and Contemporary Indian Powers

1525–1527	Rule of Babur, founder of Indian Timurid state
1538	Death of Guru Nanak, founder of Siteh religious tradition
1556–1605	Rule of Akbar "the Great"
1605–1627	Rule of Jahangir
1628–1658	Rule of Shah Jahan, builder of the Taj Mahal
1646	Founding of Maratha Empire
1658–1707	Rule of Awrangzeb
1680	Death of Maratha leader, Shivaji
1708	Death of tenth and last Sikh guru, Gobind Singh
1724	Rise of Hyderabad state
1739	Iranian invasion of North India under Nadir Shah
1757	British East India Company victory over Bengali forces at Plassey
1857–1858	Indian Uprising and the death of the last Mughal ruler, Bahadur Shah II

Guru Arjun's Faith

These lines are from the pen of the fifth guru of the Sikh community, Arjun (d. 1606). In them he repeated the teaching of Kabir, a fifteenth-century Indian saint whose teachings are included with those of Guru Nanak and other religious poets in the Sikh holy scripture, the Adi Granth. This teaching focuses on the error of clinging to a doctrinaire communalist faith, be it that of the Hindus or of the Muslims.

◆ **Why might syncretic teachings, such as those of the Sikhs, have been appealing in seventeenth-century India?**

I practice not fasting, nor observe the [month of] Ramadan:
I serve Him who will preserve me at the last hour.
The one Lord of the earth is my God,
Who judgeth both Hindus and Muslims.
I go not on a pilgrimage to Mecca, nor worship at Hindu places of Pilgrimage.
I serve the one God and no other.
I neither worship as the Hindus, nor pray as the Muslims.
I take the Formless God into my heart, and there make obeisance unto Him.

I am neither a Hindu nor a Muslim.
The soul and the body belong to God whether He be called Allah or Ram.
Kabir hath delivered this lecture.
When I meet a true guru or pir, I recognize my own Master.

From Max Arthur Macauliffe, *The Sikh Religion*, 6 vols. (Oxford: Clarendon Press, 1909), p. 422.

---

ences at work. We mentioned in Chapter 13 two forerunners of such reformers, Ramananda and Kabir. Guru Nanak, the spiritual father of the Sikh movement, took up Kabir's ideas and preached faith and devotion to one loving and merciful God. (See Document, "Guru Arjun's Faith.") He opposed narrow allegiance to particular creeds or rites and excessive pride in external religious observance. Nanak's hymns of praise contain both Hindu and Muslim ideas and imagery. Dadu (d. 1603) preached a similar message. He was born a Muslim but, like Kabir and Nanak, strove to get people to go beyond either Muslim or Hindu allegiance to a more spiritual love and service of God.

There was also an upsurge of *bhakti* devotionalism that amounted to a Hindu revival. It was epitomized by the Bengali Krishna devotee Chaitanya (d. ca. 1533), who stressed total devotion to Lord Krishna. The forebears of present-day Hare Krishna devotees, his followers spread widely his ecstatic public praise of God and his message that all are equal in God's sight. The other major figure in Hindu devotionalism in this era was Tulasidas (d. 1623), whose Hindi retelling of the story of the Sanskrit *Ramayana* remains among the most popular works of Indian literature. Tulasidas used the story of Rama's adventures to present *bhakti* ideas that remain as alive in current everyday Hindu life as do his verses.

Muslim eclectic tendencies came primarily from the Sufis. By 1500 many Sufi retreat centers had been established in India. Sufis' enthusiastic forms of worship and their inclination to play down the externals of religion proved particularly congenial to Indian sensibilities. Such Sufis were, however, often opposed by the more puritanical *ulama*, many of whom held powerful positions as royal advisers and judges. To check puritan bigotry among the *ulama*, Akbar named himself the supreme spiritual authority in the empire and then ordered that toleration be the law of the land.

After Akbar's death the inevitable reaction set in. It was summed up in the work of the Indian leader of the central Asian Sufi order of the Naqshbandiya, Ahmad Sirhindi (d. 1624). He sought to purge Sufism of its extreme tendencies and of all popular practices not sanctioned by the schools of law. He crusaded against any practices that smacked of Hindu influence and also against tolerant treatment of the Hindus themselves. Among Akbar's royal successors, Awrangzeb, as noted above, was known for his strictures against non-Muslims. His intolerance has often been unfairly exaggerated, but in the end its spirit won the day. The possibilities for Hindu-Muslim rapprochement that had emerged in Akbar's time waned, presaging the communal strife that has so marred southern Asian history in recent times.

Central Asia: Islamization in the Post-Timur Era

We can trace the solid footing of Islam in Central Asia to the post-Timur era of the fifteenth century. Even in the preceding century, as the peoples of Western Central Asia had begun to shift from nomadic to settled existence, the familiar pattern of Islamic diffusion from trading and urban centers to the countryside had set in. Islamization by Sunni and Shi'i Sufis, traders, and tribal rulers went on apace thereafter, even as far as Western China and Mongolia. It was slowed only in the late sixteenth century by the conversion of the tribes of Mongolia proper to the Buddhism of the Tibetan lamas. Thus, after 1500 the Safavid Shi'i empire was bounded by Islamic Sunni states in India, Afghanistan, Anatolia, Mesopotamia, Transoxiana, and Western Turkestan (Khwarizm, the region between the Aral and Caspian Seas). In these last two areas, the most important states were those founded by Uzbek and Chaghatay Turks, both of whom were ruled by Muslim descendants of Genghis Khan.

Uzbeks and Chaghatays

During the fifteenth century Timur's heirs had ruled Transoxiana and most of Iran (see Chapter 13). To the north, above the Jaxartes River (Syr Darya) and the Aral Sea, a new steppe khanate had been formed by the unification in 1428 of assorted clans of Turks and Mongols known as the Uzbeks. In time, an Uzbek leader who was descended from Genghis Khan, Muhammad Shaybani (d. 1510), invaded Transoxiana (1495–1500). There he founded a new Uzbek Islamic empire that replaced Timurid rule, which shifted south to Kabul and eventually India, as described earlier. Muhammad's line continued Uzbek rule in Transoxiana at Bukhara into the eighteenth century, while another Uzbek line ruled the independent khanate of Khiva in Western Turkestan from 1512 to 1872.

Of the other Central Asian Islamic states after 1500, the most significant was that of the Chaghatay Turks. The Chaghatays had been the successors of Genghis Khan in the whole region from the Aral Sea and the Oxus River to China (see Map 21–1). After 1350 Timur's invasion broke up their khanate. From about 1514 a revived Chaghatay state flourished in eastern Turkestan—the Tarim basin and the territory

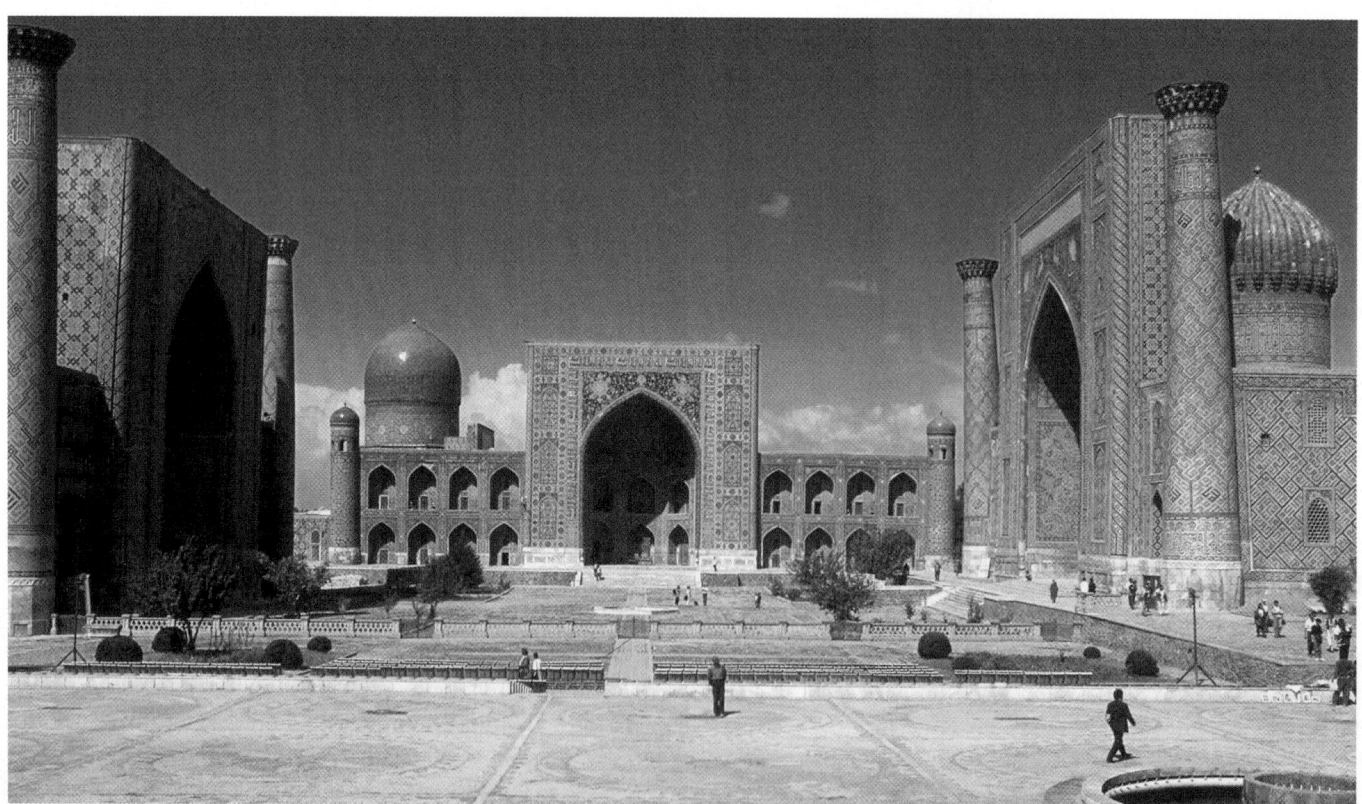

The Great Central Square of the Registan, in Samarkand, with the seventeenth-century Shir Dar Madrasa on the right and the fifteenth-century Ulugh Beg Madrasa on the left. Samarkand and other major Central Asian cities were centers of Islamic culture and learning as well as political power. *Michel Gotin/Ouzebekistan.*

north of it, between Tashkent in the west and the Turfan oasis in the east. Although the Chaghatay rulers lasted until 1678 in one part of the Tarim basin, their real power was lost after about 1555 to various Khoja princes, Sunni zealots who claimed to be *Sharifs* (descendants of the Prophet).

Consequences of the Shi'ite Rift

On the face of it, the Ottoman, Mughal, Safavid, and Central Asian Islamic states had much in common: Muslim faith and culture, similar systems of taxation and law, the Persian language, and Turkish rulers. Yet the deep religious division between the Shi'ite Safavids and all their Sunni neighbors proved stronger than their common bonds. The result was a serious geographic division that isolated Central Asian Muslims in particular.

Shi'ite-Sunni political competition was sharpened by Safavid militancy, to which the Sunni states responded in kind. Attempts to form alliances with non-Muslim states, previously unheard of in the Islamic world, became a commonplace of Shi'ite political strategy. The Sunnis also resorted to such tactics: The Ottomans, for example, made common cause with Protestants against their Catholic Habsburg enemies. Although trade continued, the presence of a militant Shi'ite state astride the major overland trade routes of the larger Islamic world hurt the international flow of Islamic commerce.

The Safavid Shi'ite schism also changed the shared cultural traditions of the "Abode of Islam." This change was especially reflected in the fate of Persian literary culture. As a result of its ever stronger association with Shi'ite religious ideas after the rise of the Safavids, Persian made little further progress as a potential common language alongside Arabic—let alone above it—in Sunni lands. Outside Iran it was destined to remain a language of high culture, the court, and bureaucracy, where it (much like French in eighteenth and nineteenth century Europe) was the mark of the educated and cultural person: Persian language and mastery of the Persian classics defined to a great extent what it meant to be an Ottoman or Mughal "gentlemen." In India, Urdu became the common Muslim idiom (see Chapter 13), and in Ottoman and Central Asian lands, one or another Turkic tongue was spoken in everyday life. The Persian classics inspired Persian learning among educated Sunnis, but Safavid Persian literature was largely ignored.

Central Asia was ultimately the Islamic region most decisively affected by the Shi'ite presence in Iran. Combined with the growing pressure of Christian Russian power from the West, the militant Shi'ism of Iran isolated Central Asia from the rest of the Muslim world. Political and economic relations with other Islamic lands became increasingly difficult after 1500, as did religious and cultural inter-

Afro-Indian merchant. This superb painting of an Indian of African origin shows the many connections that bound the Indian Ocean world. The man in this image is a merchant, probably a member of the Janjeera people, originally from Ethiopia. Janjeera merchants immigrated to India in the Middle Ages. Some remained there and during the fifteenth century they and their descendants obtained positions of power and authority in local governments. The sumptuous dress and dignified bearing of this man suggest wealth and influence. *K.L. Kamat.*

change. However healthy Islam remained in this region, its contact with the original Islamic heartlands (and even with India) shrank. Contact came primarily through a few pilgrims, members of Sufi orders, *ulama*, and students. Central Asian Islam mostly developed in isolation, a large but peripheral area to the Islamic mainstream communities.

Power Shifts in the Southern Oceans

Southern-Oceans Trade

Along the southern rim of Asia, from the Red Sea and East Africa to Indonesia and the South China Sea, the period from 1000 to 1500 witnessed the gradual spread of Islamic religion and culture into new regions and among new peoples. In ports in Java, Sumatra, the Malay Peninsula, South India, Gujarat, East Africa, Madagascar, and Zanzibar, Islamic traders established thriving communities. Their enclaves in these cities often became the dominant presence. Initially the Muslims' economic stature attracted especially the socially and religiously mobile peoples of these cosmopolitan centers; many of them also found the ideas and practices of Islam compelling. Typically this first stage of conversion was followed by Islam's transmission to surrounding areas and finally to inland centers. In this transmission, Sufi orders and their preachers and holy men played the main role. However, conquest by Muslim coastal states quickened the process in Indonesia and East Africa.

The international trade network that the Muslims inherited in the Indian Ocean to South-China sea areas was ancient. Before 1200 much of the trade in these waters had been dominated by Hindu or Buddhist kingdoms on the Malay Peninsula or Sumatra (see Chapter 13). Arab traders had also been active at least in the Indian Ocean. Hindu culture had been carried, along with an Indonesian language, as far as Madagascar in the first millennium C.E. Hindus were the chief religious group the Muslims displaced. In the East, Islam never ousted the Indian Buddhist cultures of Burma, Thailand, and Indochina, although Muslim traders lived in their ports. Islam did, however, gradually win most of Malaysia, Sumatra, Java, and the "Spice Islands" of the Moluccas—always the coastal areas first, then the inland regions (see Map 21–5).

Control of the Southern Seas

The Portuguese reached the East African coast in 1498. In the following three centuries, the history of the lands along the trade routes of the southern Asian seas, from the shores of East Africa to Indonesia and Malaysia, was bound closely not only with Islamic religious, cultural, and commercial networks, but also with the rising power of Christian West-

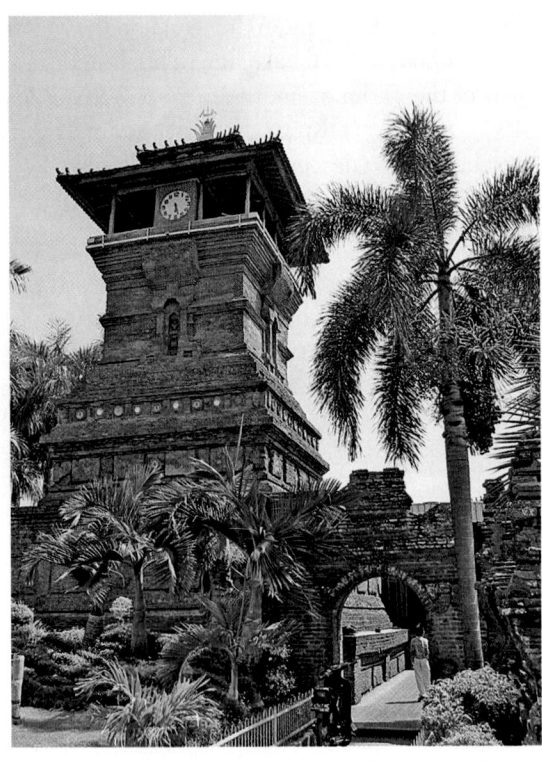

Kudus Mosque. On the island of Java (present-day Indonesia) dates to the first half of the sixteenth century. The Mosque combines Hindu, Buddhist, and Islamic architectural elements.

ern Europe. The key attractions of these diverse lands were their commercial and strategic possibilities (see Map 21–6).

Map 21–5. The Spread of Islam in Southeast Asia, 1300–1900.

The Religions of Southeast Asia

Overview

Predominately Buddhist	Burma
	Thailand, but with a significant Muslim minority
	Cambodia
	Laos
	Vietnam, but with a large Roman Catholic minority
	Singapore, includes Muslim, Christian, and Hindu minorities
Predominately Muslim	Indonesia; but the island of Bali is Hindu, and there is a large Christian minority
	Malaysia, but with Hindu, Buddhist, Chineese, and Christian minorities
	Brunei
Predominately Christian	Philippines, but with a sizable Muslim minority
	East Timor

In the sixteenth century the Europeans began to displace by armed force the Muslims who, by 1500, had come to dominate the maritime southern rim of Asia. European success was based on two key factors. One was that their naval and commercial ventures were backed by national support systems. The other, for a time at least, was their superior warships. This combination enabled the Portuguese to carve out a major power base in the early sixteenth century along the west coast of India at the expense of the Muslims who dominated Indian maritime trade. They did so through superior naval power, and by exploiting indigenous rivalries and terrorizing all who opposed them.

 SOURCE *Doming Navarrete, "Of My Stay in the Kingdom of Macassar"*

However, in the southern-seas trade centers, Islamization continued, even in the face of Christian proselytizing and growing European political and commercial presence. The Muslims, unlike most of the European Christians, never kept aloof from the native populations and were largely assimilated everywhere. They rarely abandoned their faith, which proved generally attractive to new peoples they encountered. The result was usually an Islamized and racially mixed population.

As a result, while European gunboat imperialism had considerable military and economic success, often at the expense of Islamic states, European culture and Christianity made little headway against Islam. From East Africa to the Pacific, only in the northern Philippines did a substantial population become largely Christian.

The East Indies: Acheh

The history of the Indonesian archipelago has always revolved around the international demand for its spices, peppers, and other produce. By the fifteenth century the

Chronology

The Southern Seas: Arrival of the Europeans

1498	The Portuguese come to the East African coast and to the west coast of India
1500–1512	The Portuguese establish bases on west Indian coast, replace Muslims as Indian Ocean power
early 1500s	Muslim sultanates replace Hindu states in Java, Sumatra
1524–1910	State of Acheh in northwestern Sumatra
1600s	Major increase in Islamization and connected spread of Malay language in the archipelago
1641	Dutch conquest of Malacca
ca. 1800	Dutch replace Muslim states as main archipelago power
1873–1910	War between Holland and Acheh

Map 21–6. European Commercial Penetration of Southeast Asia. Beginning with the Portuguese and Spanish in the sixteenth century, and then the Dutch and British in the seventeenth, West European powers established commercial bases throughout Southeast Asia, often cooperating with local Islamic, Hindi, or Buddhist rulers.

coastal Islamic states were centered on the trading ports of the Malay Peninsula, the north shores of Sumatra and Java, and the Moluccas, or "Spice Islands." The last great Hindu kingdom of inland Java was defeated by an Islamic coalition of states in the early 1500s. Several substantial Islamic sultanates arose in the sixteenth and seventeenth centuries, even as Europeans were carving out their own

economic empires in the region. The most powerful of these Islamic states was Acheh, in northwestern Sumatra (ca. 1524–1910).

In its early years Acheh provided the only counterweight to the Portuguese presence across the straits in Malacca (Malaysia). Although the Acheh sultans were unable to drive out the better-armed invaders, neither could the Portuguese subdue them. Despite Portuguese control of Indies commerce, Acheh managed to dominate the pepper trade of Sumatra and to thrive until the end of the sixteenth century. In the first half of the seventeenth century the sultanate controlled both coasts of Sumatra and parts of the Malay Peninsula. Meanwhile, the Dutch had replaced the Portuguese in the business of milking the Indies of their wealth, and by the eighteenth century they were doing it just as ruthlessly and more efficiently. In the early twentieth century the Dutch finally won full control in the region, but only after nearly forty years of intermittent war with Acheh (1873–1910).

SOURCE *Jan van Linschoten on Dutch business in the Indian Ocean*

Summary

The Last Islamic Empires from the Mediterranean Sea to the Indian Ocean. The period from 1500 to 1800 marks the cultural and political blossoming of the last Islamic empires and their gradual demise. The Islamic social, economic, political, and military vitality in the first half of this period was exemplified in the Ottoman, Safavid, and Mughal Empires. All three built vast bureaucracies and arguably the greatest cities in the world of their time. They patronized the arts. Yet they were conservative societies. Economically they remained tied to agricultural production, local trade, and taxation based on land. They did not undergo the social or religio-political revolutions that rocked Western Europe after 1500 or changes in material and intellectual life similar to that experienced in the West European world during the same period. There was no compelling challenge to traditional Islamic ideals, even though numerous Islamic movements of the eighteenth century did call for reform.

Decline. By the latter half of this period, all these empires were in economic, political, and military decline, even if intellectual and artistic vigor held on.

Thus, it is not surprising that European expansionism's invasions and conquests in these three centuries upon Africa, India, Indonesia, and the Islamic heartland caused in great part the decline of these global regions rather than the reverse. None of the Islamic states fared well in their clashes with Europeans during this age. Europeans' growing domination of the world's seas and continents allowed them to contain or to bypass the major Islamic lands in their quest for gold, silver, spices and plantation cash crops for their economic empires.

By the early 1800s industrial development joined economic wealth, social privileges, and political stability to give Europe global military supremacy for the first time. Before 1850, the Europeans were able to bring only minor Islamic states under colonial administration. However, the footholds they gained in Africa, India, and Southeast Asia laid the groundwork for rapid colonial expansion after 1850. The age of the last great Islamic empires was the beginning of the first great modern European empires.

Review Questions

1. Why did the Ottoman Empire expand so rapidly into Europe? Why did the empire fail to hold certain areas in Europe?

2. Why did the Safavid Empire succeed in Iran? What role did Islamic religion, a favorable geographic position, and access to the Indian Ocean have in this development? Who were the major foes of this empire?

3. What were the most important elements that united all Islamic states? Why was there a lack of unity between these states from 1500 to 1850? How and why were the European powers able to promote division among these various states?

4. What were Akbar's main policies towards the Hindu population? Why did he succeed and his followers fail in this area? What were his main governmental reforms?

5. How and why did the Sikhs develop into a formidable military power? Why did they become separatist in their orientation to the larger Indian world?

6. What were the main tenets of the *Ishraqi* or "illumination" school of theological-philosophical thought? Define the concepts of "transcendence" and a "realm of images."

7. Compare the Sunni-Shi'ite differences and similarities within the Islamic world (1500–1800) with that of the Protestant-Catholic split within the Christian world during that same period. For example, can we compare relations between England and Spain in the sixteenth century to those between the Ottomans and the Safavids? Explain.

8. Why were outside powers attracted to the southern-seas lands? Why did the European powers triumph in the struggle to control this area?

Key Terms

ayan (p. 652)

devshirme (p. 651)

Grand Mufti (p. 649)

harem (p. 649)

Janissaries (p. 651)

millets (p. 654)

Mughals (p. 660)

padishah (p. 649)

pirs (p. 655)

Qanun (p. 650)

Qanun-name (p. 649)

Shari'a (p. 649)

sufi (SOO-fee) (pp. 665, 656)

INTERPRETING THE PAST

Islamic Empires: The Importance of Leadership

Text Sources from MyHistoryLab /Primary Source DVD

1. Abdu'l Faz Allami: *Biography of Emperor Akbar of India*
2. Sunni vs. Shi'ite: *Letter from Selim I to Ismail I*
3. Ogier Ghiselin de Busbecq: *Süleyman the Lawgiver*
4. Fathers Simon and Vincent: *Report on Shah Abbas I, the Safavid Ruler of Persia*

Visual Sources from MyHistoryLab/Primary Source DVD.

1. Safavid Battle Tunic
2. Ottoman Law Book, 1517

Islamic societies prospered throughout Southwest Asia in the years between 1450 and 1800, while three imperial states vied for dominance: the Ottomans (Turkey/Mesopotamia), the Safavids (Iran/Mesopotamia/Afghanistan), and the Mughals (India/Pakistan). Each state favored a different sect of Islam, depending on the religious orientation of its rulers and population. Yet each also faced the challenge of ruling

a heterogeneous population with peoples of different religions, ethnicities, and economic interests. A second and equally difficult task was the necessity of maintaining secure borders.

This exercise will involve reading four primary sources, from 1550 to about 1605 that document Ottoman, Safavid, and Mughal rulers and their methods. Because several of the writers lavishly praise the imperial rulers they were describing, you must read carefully "between the lines" in order to better analyze the historical events and circumstances being discussed.

The first document, part of a biography written by Abdu'l Fazl 'Allami, Emperor Akbar's key aide (also a historian and theorist), records the life of the imperial household and the ruler's methods in a highly flattering, but also revealing manner. The second text is a letter from the Ottoman leader Selim I to the Safavid ruler Ismail I, offering a succinct and rather pointed summary of the reasons why Ismail should cease attacking Ottoman borders. The third text, *Süleyman the Lawgiver*, offers an outsider's assessment of the Ottoman emperor, his court, and society. It is highly complimentary, contrasting the Ottomans with European society and its aristocratic leadership. Finally, two Catholic friars (members of the Carmelite religious order) who visited Safavid Persia in 1605 present their views of their host, Shah Abbas, who freely allowed them to seek converts, as well as to gather information.

Use the text sources and the images to gain understanding about how these rulers governed their societies and attempted to secure the borders of their realms from encroachments from aggressive neighbors, including fellow Muslims. Use specific examples from the documents to back up your assertions.

Questions

What were the challenges of running a sizable empire, and what kind of skills were necessary to achieve a stable, prosperous state? Compare each of the documents.

What roles do women perform in Mughal society, according to the biography of Akbar?

How did rulers deal with disputes with other leaders and states (see the Letter from Selim I to Ismail I, especially)? How was religion used in the effort to dissuade further attacks?

Compare the traits of each of the leaders discussed in these texts—were there any common features? Akbar, Abbas, and Süleyman are considered some of the most successful world leaders in history—are any of their potential weaknesses in evidence?

Note: To learn more about the topics in this chapter, please turn to the Suggested Readings at the end of the book. For additional sources related to this chapter please see the Primary Source DVD at the back of this text or MyHistoryLab.

Between approximately 1700 and 1850 extraordinary changes occurred in Western civilization. Although of immediate significance primarily for the nations of Europe and the Americas, in the long run these developments had an immense impact throughout the world. Europe became a great exporter of ideas and technologies that in time would transform human experience.

NORTH
AMERICA

The death of General Warren at the Battle of Bunker Hill, June 17, 1775. The art of the eighteenth century in Europe mirrored the contrasts of the age, at once reflecting the confidence and rationality of the Enlightenment, and the romantic passions of revolutions that shattered the institutions of the Old Regime. *(See pages 708–712).*

Portrait of the Marquis de Pompal. He insisted that Lisbon be reconstructed according to rational principles after the earthquake that destroyed the city. *(See pages 680–682).*

SOUTH
AMERICA

ENLIGHTENMENT AND REVOLUTION IN THE ATLANTIC WORLD, 1700–1850

Cameo of Marie Antoinette, Queen of France.
Marie Antoinette embodies the contrasts of what has often been called the "Age Revolution" in the eighteenth century, culminating in the French Revolution. She met her end at the guillotine in 1793. *(See pages 712–717).*

Chinese Clock.
During the eighteenth century the exchange of ideas and knowledge increased between the West and the East and vice versa. This Chinese clock, from about 1790, is built according to Western techniques. *(See page 575).*

ASIA

Francisco Goya, *The Third of May, 1808*, 1814-1815.
In this painting of Napoleon's soldiers executing resistors to French rule in Spain, the focus is on the common people who fell victim to the destructive force of modern war. *(See pages 725–728).*

EUROPE

AFRICA

AUSTRALIA

French Soldiers in Egypt.
Many of the wars of the eighteenth century were global in character, such as Napoleon's campaign against the Ottoman Empire in 1799. *(See pages 722–728).*

Focus Questions

1
What was the relationship between the Enlightenment and the American, French, and Haitian revolutions of the eighteenth century?

2
Is it ironic that ideas and technologies that contributed to an awakening of European power also fostered critiques that non-European peoples would employ against Western dominance?

The Age of European Enlightenment

22

- ◆ The Scientific Revolution
- ◆ The Enlightenment
- ◆ The Enlightenment and Religion
- ◆ The Enlightenment and Society
- ◆ Enlightened Absolutism

 O SINGLE INTELLECTUAL FORCE DURING the past three centuries has so transformed every region of the world as has Western science and the technology that has flowed from its understanding of nature. Although throughout the world today there has arisen much interest in nontraditional methods of healing, the impact of Western science on every area of human life remains a dominant force. Furthermore, the attainment of scientific knowledge, often for the purposes of military advantage as well as medical and economic advance, has become a goal of most modern states.

The impact of science could make itself felt first in Europe and then elsewhere only as the conviction came to spread that change and reform were both possible and desirable. This attitude is now commonplace, but it came into its own in Europe only after 1700. The capacity and even eagerness to embrace change, especially change as justified on the grounds of science, represents one of the primary intellectual inheritances from that age. The movement of people and ideas that fostered such

Denis Diderot was the heroic editor of the *Encyclopedia*, which was published in seventeen volumes of text and eleven volumes of prints between 1751 and 1772. Through its pages many of the chief ideas of the Enlightenment reached a broad audience of readers.

The European Enlightenment

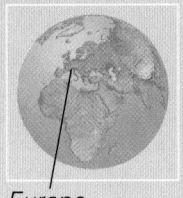

Europe

Of all the movements of modern European thought, the most influential are the Scientific Revolution and the Enlightenment. A direct line of intellectual descent exists from those movements to the science and social criticism of the present day. Wherever modern science and technology are pursued and their effects felt, the spirit of the Enlightenment persists. From the eighteenth century to the present, the writers of the Enlightenment provided a pattern for intellectuals who wished to make their societies more rational, scientific, and secular, and thus "modern." Moreover, the Enlightenment model of society has become so influential in the West (and via the West in the rest of the world) that it has become synonymous with "modern." As a result, societies worldwide are judged to be modernized to the extent that their economies are industrialized and market-oriented and their societies scientific and secular.

The Enlightenment writers valued emotions and passions as well as reason, but they used reason as a weapon for reform and the basis for a more productive economic life. In the two centuries since the Enlightenment, such a use of critical reason has become a mark of reforming and progressive social and intellectual movements. The Enlightenment writers first used reason against Christianity and the strong influence of churches in European society and politics. However, reason came to be used against other world religions as well, leading to the tendency in the modern world to view science and religion in potential conflict and to consider less scientifically advanced societies as inherently culturally backward. This particular view of modernization tended to make the European and later North American experience regarded as the necessary pattern for all advanced society. This outlook originated with the majority of Enlightenment writers themselves. A minority of those writers of the eighteenth century, as with many present-day commentators, questioned whether even a rational, critical, and economically productive Europe should be the pattern for all human societies. Virtually all Enlightenment writers believed in some form of religious toleration or recognition of religious pluralism in their societies.

thinking is called the *Enlightenment*. Its leading voices combined confidence in the human mind inspired by the Scientific Revolution and faith in the power of rational criticism to challenge the intellectual authority of tradition and revealed religion. Its writers believed that human beings could comprehend the operation of physical nature and mold it to the ends of material and moral improvement. The rationality of the physical universe became a standard against which the customs and traditions of society could be measured and criticized. Such criticism penetrated every corner of contemporary society. As a result, the spirit of innovation and improvement came to characterize modern Western society. This outlook would become perhaps the most important European cultural export to the rest of the world. ■

The Scientific Revolution

The sixteenth and seventeenth centuries witnessed a sweeping change in the scientific view of the universe. From being considered the center of the universe, the Earth was now seen as only another planet orbiting about the sun. The sun itself became one of millions of stars. This transformation led to a vast rethinking of moral and religious matters as well as of scientific theory. Science and the scientific method became so impressive and so influential that they set a new standard for evaluating knowledge in the Western world.

In terms of political thought the heritage of the Enlightenment was complex with different strands of political thought often in tension or outright conflict with each other. One strand of Enlightenment political thought that often drew upon the English political experience contributed to constitutionalism and modes of government in which the power and authority of the central government stand sharply circumscribed. Montesquieu, for example, influenced the Constitution of the United States and the numerous constitutions that document later influenced. Another strand of Enlightenment political thought, found in Voltaire, contributed to the growth of strong monarchial governments, which was the case with enlightened absolutism. Advocates of this mode of government believed that a monarch and a strong central bureaucracy could formulate and impose rational solutions to political and social problems and hence overcome competing interests. Still another strand of political thought, arising from Rousseau, led to the socialist concern with inequality of wealth and a desire for radical democratic government. Because of the complexity of Enlightenment political thought, modern governments displaying liberalism, socialism, and bureaucratic centralism may find roots in eighteenth-century thinkers. Modern political movements finding themselves essentially at odds with the Enlightenment heritage are those attached to radical Islamic groups who define themselves in opposition to most Western values. Those Western values tend to be values derived from the Enlightenment.

Much of what has been best about the Western cultural legacy to global culture derives from the Enlightenment. It is also important to remember that, as we observed in Chapter 18, the seventeenth and eighteenth centuries, whose ideas fostered the Enlightenment also saw the rise of European colonial empires and the establishment of plantation economies based on slavery. Europeans' treatment of non-Europeans, as well as their warfare against each other in this era, often belied the principles of the Enlightenment. By the same token, some of the most admirable principles of Western culture, including advocacy of democracy and human rights, can be traced to Enlightenment roots.

Focus Questions

◆ How did Enlightenment values as well as Enlightenment admiration of science become one of the chief defining qualities of societies regarded as advanced, progressive, and modern?

◆ How has the political thought of the Enlightenment influenced the development of modern political philosophies and modern governments?

◆ How could modes of thought developed to criticize various aspects of eighteenth-century European society be transferred to other traditions of world civilizations?

The process that established the new view of the universe is normally termed the *Scientific Revolution*. The revolution-in-science metaphor must be used carefully, however. Not everything associated with the "new" science was necessarily new. Sixteenth- and seventeenth-century natural philosophers were often reexamining and rethinking theories and data from the ancient world and the late middle ages. Moreover, the word *revolution* normally denotes rapid, collective political change involving large numbers of people. The Scientific Revolution was *not* rapid. It was a complex movement with many false starts and brilliant people suggesting wrong as well as useful ideas. Nor did it involve more than a few hundred people who labored in widely separated studies and crude laboratories located in Poland, Italy, Bohemia, France, and Great Britain. Furthermore, the achievements of the new science were not simply the function of isolated brilliant scientific minds. The leading figures of the Scientific Revolution often drew upon the aid of artisans and craftspeople to help them construct new instruments for experimentation and to carry out their experiments. Thus, the Scientific Revolution involved a reappropriation of older knowledge as well as new discoveries. Additionally, because the practice of science involves social activity as well as knowledge, the revolution also saw the establishment of new social institutions to support the emerging scientific enterprise.

From the early seventeenth century through the end of the twentieth century science achieved greater cultural authority in the Western world than did any other form of intellectual activity, and the authority and application of scientific knowledge became one of the defining characteristics of modern Western civilization. Although new knowledge emerged in many areas during the sixteenth and seventeenth centuries, including medicine, chemistry, and natural history, the scientific achievements that most captured the learned imagination and persuaded people of the cultural power of natural knowledge were those that occurred in astronomy.

Nicolaus Copernicus Rejects an Earth-Centered Universe

Nicolaus Copernicus (1473–1543) was a Polish astronomer who enjoyed a high reputation during his life. He had been educated first in Cracow and later in Italy, and he had not been known for strikingly original or unorthodox thought. In 1543, the year of his death, Copernicus published *On the Revolutions of the Heavenly Spheres*. Copernicus' book was "a revolution-making rather than a revolutionary text."[1] What Copernicus did was to provide an intellectual springboard for a complete criticism of the then-dominant view of the position of the Earth in the universe.

The Ptolemaic System At the time of Copernicus, the standard explanation of the place of the Earth in the heavens was the **Ptolemaic system**. It combined the mathematical astronomy of Ptolemy, contained in his work entitled the *Almagest* (150 C.E.), with the physical cosmology of Aristotle. Over the centuries, commentators on Ptolemy's work had developed several alternative Ptolemaic systems, on the basis of which they made mathematical calculations relating to astronomy. Most of these writers assumed that the Earth was the center of the universe, an outlook known as *geocentricism*. Drawing upon Aristotle, these commentators assumed that above the Earth lay a series of concentric spheres, probably fluid in character, one of which contained the moon, another the sun, and still others the planets and the stars. At the outer regions of these spheres lay the realm of God and the angels. The Earth had to be the center because of its heaviness. The stars and the other heavenly bodies had to be enclosed in the spheres so that they could move, since nothing could move unless something was actually moving it. The state of rest was presumed natural; motion required

explanation. This was the astronomy found in such works as Dante's *Divine Comedy*.

Numerous problems were associated with the Ptolemaic model, and these had long been recognized. The most important was the observed motions of the planets. At certain times the planets actually appeared to be going backwards. The Ptolemaic model accounted for these motions primarily through *epicycles*. The planet moved uniformly about a small circle (an epicycle), while the center of the epicycle moved uniformly about a larger circle (called a deferent), with the Earth at or near its center. The combination of these two motions, as viewed from the Earth, was meant to replicate the changing planetary positions among the fixed stars—and did so to a high degree of accuracy. The circles employed in Ptolemaic systems were not meant to represent the actual paths of anything; that is, they were not orbits. Rather, they were the components of purely mathematical models meant to predict planetary positions. Other intellectual, but nonobservational, difficulties related to the immense speed at which the spheres had to move around the Earth. To say the least, the Ptolemaic systems were cluttered. They were effective, however, as long as one assumed Aristotelian physics.

Copernicus' Universe Copernicus' *On the Revolutions of the Heavenly Spheres* challenged the Ptolemaic picture in the most conservative manner possible.

The Ptolemaic System.
The "Emperor's Astronomy" (dedicated to the Holy Roman emperor Charles V) elegantly depicts the cosmos and heavens according to the 1,400-year-old Ptolemaic system, which maintained that the sun revolved around the Earth. By means of hand-colored maps, Petrus Apianus (1495–1552) laid out the mechanics of a universe that was earth- and human-centered. Within three years of Apianus' book, this view was challenged by Copernicus's assertion that the Earth revolved around the sun. Petrus Apianus. *Astronomicum Caesareum* (The Emperor's Astronomy). Ingolstadt, Germany: 1540. Rosenwald Collection, Rare Book and Special Collections Division.

[1] Thomas S. Kuhn, *The Copernican Revolution: Planetary Astronomy in the Development of Western Thought* (New York: Vintage, 1959), p. 135.

Copernicus adopted many elements of the Ptolemaic model but transferred them to a *heliocentric* (sun-centered) model, which assumed that the Earth moved about the sun in a cir-

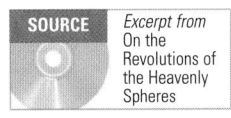

SOURCE *Excerpt from On the Revolutions of the Heavenly Spheres*

cle. Copernicus' model, which retained epicycles, was actually no more accurate than Ptolemy's. However, Copernicus could claim certain advantages over the ancient model. In particular, the epicycles were smaller. The retrograde motion of the planets now stood explained as a result of an optical illusion arising from an observer viewing the planets from a moving Earth. The order of the planets from the sun became more clearly intelligible when it was understood as a result of their increasing periods of revolution based on the planets' increasing distance from the sun.

The repositioning of the Earth had not been Copernicus' goal. Rather, Copernicus appears to have set out to achieve new intelligibility and mathematical elegance for astronomy. The means of doing so was to reject Aristotle's cosmology and to remove the Earth from the center of the universe. His system was no more accurate than the existing ones for predicting the location of the planets, as he had used no new evidence. The major impact of his work was to provide another way of confronting some of the difficulties inherent in Ptolemaic astronomy. The Copernican system did not immediately replace the old astronomy, but it allowed other people who were also discontented with the Ptolemaic view to think in new directions. Indeed, for at least a century, the Copernican system was embraced by a distinct minority of natural philosophers and astronomers.

Tycho Brahe and Johannes Kepler

The next major step towards the conception of a sun-centered system was taken by the Danish astronomer Tycho Brahe (1546–1601). He spent most of his life opposing Copernicus and advocating a different kind of Earth-centered system. He suggested that the moon and the sun revolved around the Earth and that the other planets revolved around the sun. However, in attacking Copernicus, he gave the latter's ideas more publicity. More important, his major weapon against Copernican astronomy was a series of new astronomical observations made with the naked eye. Brahe constructed the most accurate tables of observations that had been drawn up for centuries.

When Brahe died, these tables came into the possession of Johannes Kepler (1571–1630), a German astronomer. Kepler was a convinced Copernican, but for philosophical, not scientific, reasons. Kepler was deeply influenced by Renaissance Neo-Platonists who, following upon Plato's (ca. 428–ca. 328 B.C.E.) association of knowl-

Tycho Brahe in the Uranienburg observatory on the Danish island of Hven (1587). Brahe made the most important observations of the stars since antiquity. Kepler used his data to solve the problem of planetary motion in a way that supported Copernicus's sun-centered view of the universe. Ironically, Brahe himself had opposed Copernicus' view. *Bildarchiv Preussischer Kulturbesitz.*

edge with light, honored the sun. These Neo-Platonists were also determined to discover mathematical harmonies that would support a sun-centered universe. After much work, Kepler discovered that to keep the sun at the center of things, he must abandon the Copernican concept of circular orbits. The mathematical relationships that emerged from a consideration of Brahe's observations suggested that the orbits of the planets were elliptical. Kepler published his findings in 1609 in a book entitled *On the Motion of Mars.* He had solved the problems of planetary orbits by using Copernicus' sun-centered universe and Brahe's empirical data.

Kepler had, however, also defined a new problem. None of the available theories could explain why the planetary orbits were elliptical. That solution awaited the work of Sir Isaac Newton.

Galileo Galilei

From Copernicus to Brahe to Kepler, there had been little new information about the heavens that might not have been known to Ptolemy. However, in 1609 an Italian scientist named Galileo Galilei (1564–1642) first turned a telescope on the heavens. He saw stars where none had been known to exist, mountains on the moon, spots moving across the sun, and moons orbiting Jupiter. The heavens were far more complex than anyone had formerly suspected. None of these dis-

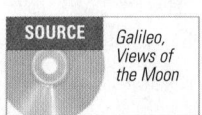
SOURCE   *Galileo, Views of the Moon*

coveries proved that the earth orbited the sun, but they did suggest the complete inadequacy of the Ptolemaic system. It simply could not accommodate these new phenomena. Some of Galileo's colleagues at the University of Padua were so unnerved that they refused to look through the telescope, because it revealed the heavens to be different from the teachings of the church and from Ptolemaic theories. (See Document, "Galileo Discusses the Relationship of Science to the Bible.")

Galileo publicized his findings and arguments for the Copernican system in numerous works, the most famous of which was his *Dialogues on the Two Chief Systems of the World* (1632). This book brought down on him the condemnation of the Roman Catholic Church. He was compelled to recant his opinions. However, he is reputed to have muttered after the recantation, "*E pur si muove*" ("It [the earth] still moves").

Galileo's most important achievement was to articulate the concept of a universe totally subject to mathematical laws. More than any other writer of the century, he argued that nature in its most minute details displayed mathematical regularity. Copernicus had thought that the heavens conformed to mathematical regularity; Galileo saw this regularity throughout all physical nature. He believed that the smallest atom behaved with the same mathematical precision as the largest heavenly sphere.

Galileo stood as one of the foremost champions of the application of mathematics to scientific investigation and of the goal of reducing phenomena to mathematical formulas. However, earlier in the century the English philosopher Francis Bacon had advocated a method based solely on empiricism. As the century passed, both empirical induction and mathematical analysis proved fundamental to scientific investigation.

Francis Bacon: The Empirical Method

Bacon (1561–1626) was an Englishman of almost universal accomplishment. He was a lawyer, a high royal official, and the author of histories, moral essays, and philosophical

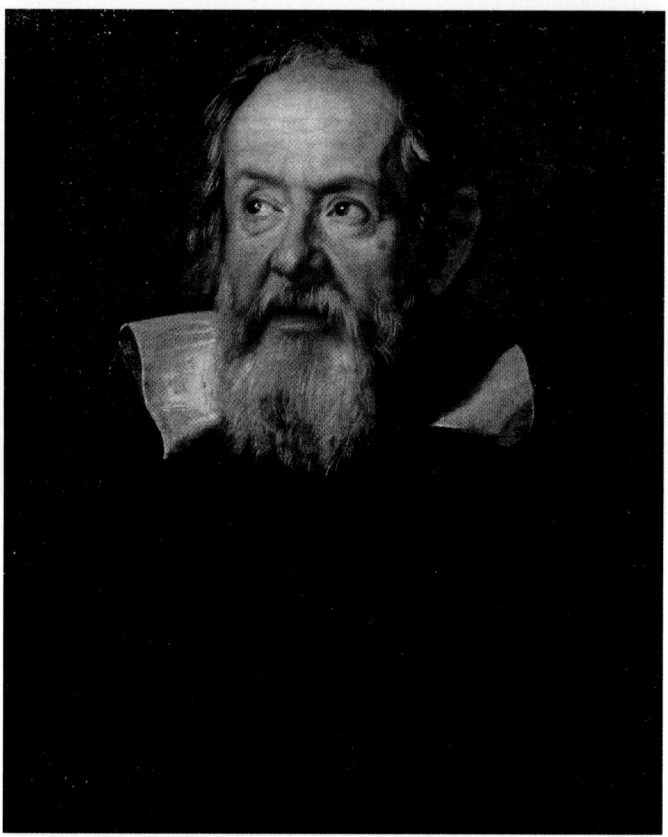

Portrait of Galileo Galilei (1636) by the Flemish Baroque painter Justus Sustermans.

discourses. Traditionally, he has been regarded as the father of **empiricism** and of experimentation in science. Much of this reputation was actually unearned. Bacon was not a natural philosopher, except in the most amateur fashion. His real accomplishment was setting an intellectual tone and helping to create a climate conducive to scientific work.

In books such as *The Advancement of Learning* (1605), the *Novum Organum* (1620), and the *New Atlantis* (1627), Bacon attacked the scholastic belief that most truth had already been discovered and only required explanation, as well as the scholastic reverence for authority in intellectual life. He believed that scholastic thinkers paid too much attention to tradition and to the knowledge of the ancients. He urged contemporaries to strike out on their own in search of a new understanding of nature. He wanted seventeenth-century Europeans to have confidence in themselves and their own abilities rather than in the people and methods

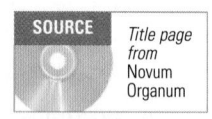
SOURCE   *Title page from Novum Organum*

of the past. Bacon was one of the first major European writers to champion the desirability of innovation and change.

Bacon believed that human knowledge should produce useful results—deeds rather than words. In particular,

Galileo Discusses the Relationship of Science to the Bible

Document

Both Protestant and Roman Catholic religious authorities were often critical of the discoveries and theories of sixteenth- and seventeenth-century science because of tensions with the literal reading of the Bible. For years before his condemnation by the Roman Catholic Church in 1633, Galileo had contended that scientific theory and religious piety were compatible. In his *Letter to the Grand Duchess Christiana* (of Tuscany), written in 1615, he argued that God had revealed truth in both the Bible and physical nature and that the truth of physical nature did not contradict the Bible if the latter were properly understood. Galileo encountered difficulties regarding this letter because it represented a layman telling Roman Catholic Church authorities how to read the Bible.

◆ Why does Galileo see a difference between the text of scripture and the knowledge of nature achieved through the senses? To which does he seem to give priority? Why might church authorities have difficulty with his arguments? Why might some Roman Catholic authorities think he was behaving as a Protestant might?

The reason produced for condemning the opinion that the Earth moves and the sun stands still is that in many places in the Bible one may read that the sun moves and the Earth stands still. . . .

With regard to this argument, I think in the first place that it is very pious to say and prudent to affirm that the holy Bible can never speak untruth—whenever its true meaning is understood. But I believe nobody will deny that it is often very abstruse, and may say things which are quite different from what its bare words signify. . . .

This being granted, I think that in discussions of physical problems we ought to begin not from the authority of scriptural passages, but from sense-experiences and necessary demonstrations; for the holy Bible and the phenomena of nature proceed alike from the divine Word, the former as the dictate of the Holy Ghost and the latter as the observant executrix of God's commands. It is necessary for the Bible, in order to be accommodated to the understanding of every man, to speak many things which appear to differ from the absolute truth so far as the bare meaning of the words is concerned. But Nature, on the other hand, is inexorable and immutable; she never transgresses the laws imposed upon her, or cares a whit whether her abstruse reasons and methods of operation are understandable to men. For that reason it appears that nothing physical which sense-experience sets before our eyes, or which necessary demonstrations prove to us, ought to be called in question (much less condemned) upon the tes-

timony of biblical passages which may have some different meaning beneath their words. For the Bible is not chained in every expression to conditions as strict as those which govern all physical effects; nor is God any less excellently revealed in Nature's actions than in the sacred statements of the Bible. . . .

From this I do not mean to infer that we need not have an extraordinary esteem for the passages of holy Scripture. On the contrary, having arrived at any certainties in physics, we ought to utilize these as the most appropriate aids in the true exposition of the Bible and in the investigation of those meanings which are necessarily contained therein for these must be concordant with demonstrated truths. I should judge the authority of the Bible was designed to persuade men of those articles and propositions which, surpassing all human reasoning, could not be made credible by science, or by any other means than through the very mouth of the Holy Spirit. . . .

But I do not feel obliged to believe that the same God who has endowed us with senses, reason, and intellect has intended to forgo their use and by some other means to give us knowledge which we can attain by them.

knowledge of nature should be brought to the aid of the human condition. These goals required the modification or abandonment of scholastic modes of learning and thinking. Bacon contended, "The [scholastic] logic now in use serves more to fix and give stability to the errors which have their foundation in commonly received notions than to help the search after truth."[2] Scholastic philosophers could not escape from their syllogisms to examine the foundations of their thought and intellectual presuppositions. Bacon urged that philosophers and investigators of nature examine the evidence of their senses before constructing logical speculations. In a famous passage, he divided all philosophers into "men of experiment and men of dogmas" and then observed:

> *The men of experiment are like the ant, they only collect and use; the reasoners resemble spiders, who make cobwebs out of their own substance. But the bee takes a middle course: it gathers its material from the flowers of the garden and of the field, but transforms and digests it by a power of its own. Not unlike this is the true business of philosophy.*[3]

By directing natural philosophy towards an examination of empirical evidence, Bacon hoped that it would achieve new knowledge and thus new capabilities for humankind.

Most of the people in Bacon's day, including the intellectuals, thought that the best era of human history lay in antiquity. Bacon dissented vigorously from that view. He looked to a future of material improvement achieved through the empirical examination of nature. His own theory of induction from empirical evidence was unsystematic, but his insistence on appealing to experience influenced others whose methods were more productive. He and others of his outlook received almost daily support from the reports not only of European explorers, but also of ordinary seamen who now sailed all over the world and could describe wondrous cultures, as well as plants and animals, unknown to the European ancients.

Bacon believed that science had a practical purpose and its goal was human improvement. Some scientific investigation does have this character. Much pure research does not. Bacon, however, linked science and material progress in the public mind. This was a powerful idea and has continued to influence Western civilization to the present day. It has made science and those who can appeal to the authority of science major forces for change and innovation. Thus, though not making any major scientific contribution himself, Bacon directed investigators of nature to a new method

and a new purpose. As a person actively associated with politics, Bacon also believed that the pursuit of new knowledge would increase the power of governments and monarchies. Again, his thought in this area opened the way for the eventual strong linkage between governments and the scientific enterprise.

Isaac Newton Discovers the Laws of Gravitation

The question that continued to perplex seventeenth-century scientists who accepted the theories of Copernicus, Kepler, and Galileo was how the planets and other heavenly bodies moved in an orderly fashion. The Ptolemaic and Aristotelian answer had been the spheres and a universe arranged in the order of the heaviness of its parts. Many unsatisfactory theories had been set forth to deal with the question. It was this issue of planetary motion that the Englishman Isaac Newton (1642–1727) addressed and, in so doing, established a basis for physics that endured for more than two centuries.

In 1687 Newton published *The Mathematical Principles of Natural Philosophy*, better known by its Latin title of *Principia Mathematica*. Much of the research and thinking

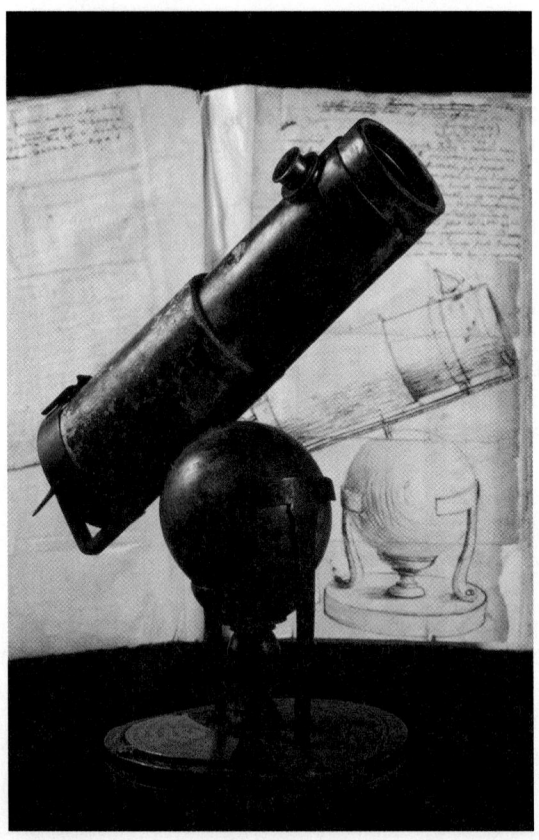

Newton's Telescope. Behind it is a copy of *Principia Mathematica*, his most famous work. © *James A. Sugar/Corbis.*

[2] Quoted in Franklin Baumer, *Main Currents of Western Thought*, 4th ed. (New Haven, CT: Yale University Press, 1978), p. 281.
[3] Quoted in Baumer, p. 288.

for this great work had taken place more than fifteen years earlier. Galileo's mathematical bias permeated Newton's thought, as did his view that inertia applied to bodies both at rest and in motion. Newton reasoned that the planets and all other physical objects in the universe moved through mutual attraction, or gravity. Every object in the universe affected every other object through gravity. The attraction of gravity explained why the planets moved in an orderly, rather than a chaotic, manner. Newton had found that "the force of gravity towards the whole planet did arise from and was compounded of the forces of gravity towards all its parts, and towards every one part was in the inverse proportion of the squares of the distances from the part."[4] Newton proved this relationship mathematically; he made no attempt to explain the nature of gravity itself.

Newton was a great mathematical genius, but he also upheld the importance of empirical data and observation. Like Francis Bacon, he believed that one must observe phenomena before attempting to explain them. The final test of any theory or hypothesis for him was whether it described what was actually observed. Newton was a great opponent of the rationalism of the French philosopher René Descartes (1596–1650), which he believed included insufficient guards against error. Consequently, as Newton's own theory of universal gravitation became increasingly accepted, so, too, was Baconian empiricism.

Women in the World of the Scientific Revolution

The absence of women in the emergence of the new science of the seventeenth century has been a matter of much historical speculation. What characteristics of early modern European intellectual and cultural life worked against extensive contributions by women? Why have we heard so little of the activity by women that did actually occur in regard to the new science?

The same factors that had long excluded women from participating in most intellectual life continued to exclude them from working in the emerging natural philosophy. Traditionally, the institutions of European intellectual life had all but excluded women. Both monasteries and universities had been institutions associated with celibate male clerical culture. Except for a few exceptions in Italy, women had not been admitted to either medieval or early modern European universities; they would continue to be excluded from them until the end of the nineteenth century. Women could and

Women and Learning. René Descartes, the French philosopher, is on the right, tutoring Queen Christina (1626–1689) of Sweden, seated on the left.

did exercise much influence over princely courts where natural philosophers, such as Galileo, sought patronage, but they usually did not determine those patronage decisions or benefit from them. Queen Christina of Sweden was an exception by engaging René Descartes to provide the regulations for a new science academy. When various scientific societies were founded, women were not admitted to membership. In that regard, there were virtually no social spaces that might have permitted women easily to pursue science.

Yet a few isolated women from two different social settings did manage to engage in the new scientific activity—noblewomen and women from the artisan class. In both cases, they could do so only through their husbands or other men in their families.

The social standing of certain noblewomen allowed them to command the attention of ambitious natural philosophers who were part of their husband's social circle. Margaret Cavendish (1623–1673) actually made significant contributions to the scientific literature of the day. After she had been privately tutored and become widely read, her

---

[4] Quoted in A. Rupert Hall, *From Galileo to Newton, 1630–1720* (London: Fontana, 1970), p. 300.

marriage to the duke of Newcastle introduced her into a circle of natural philosophers. She understood the new science, quarreled with the ideas of Descartes and Hobbes, and criticized the Royal Society for being more interested in novel scientific instruments than in solving practical problems. Her most important works were *Observations upon Experimental Philosophy* (1666) and *Grounds of Natural Philosophy* (1668). She was the only woman in the seventeenth century to be allowed to visit a meeting of the Royal Society of London.

Women associated with artisan crafts actually achieved greater freedom in pursuing the new sciences than did noblewomen. Traditionally, women had worked in artisan workshops, often with their husbands; and might take over the business when their spouse died. In Germany, much astronomy occurred in these settings, with women assisting their fathers or husbands. One such German female astronomer, Maria Cunitz, published a book on astronomy that many people thought her husband had written until he added a preface supporting her sole authorship. Elisabetha and Johannes Hevelius constituted a wife-and-husband astronomical team, as did Maria Winkelmann and her husband Gottfried Kirch. In each case, the wife served as the assistant to an artisan astronomer. Although Winkelmann discovered a comet in 1702, not until 1930 was the discovery ascribed to her rather than to her husband. Nonetheless, contemporary philosophers did recognize her abilities and understanding of astronomy. Winkelmann had worked jointly with her husband who was the official astronomer of the Berlin Academy of Sciences and was responsible for establishing an official calendar published by the Academy. When her husband died in 1710, Winkelmann applied for permission to continue the work, basing her application for the post on the guild's tradition of allowing women to continue their husband's work, in this case the completion of observations required for creating an accurate calendar. After much debate, the Academy formally rejected her application on the grounds of her gender, although its members knew of her ability and previous accomplishments. Years later, she returned to the Berlin Academy as an assistant to her son, who had been appointed astronomer. Again, the Academy insisted that she leave, forcing her to abandon astronomy. She died in 1720.

Such policies of exclusion, however, did not altogether prevent women from acquiring knowledge about the scientific endeavors of the age. Margaret Cavendish had composed a *Description of a New World, Called the Blazing World* (1666) to introduce women to the new science. Other examples of scientific writings for a female audience were Bernard de Fontenelle's *Conversations on the Plurality of Worlds* and Francesco Algarotti's *Newtonianism for Ladies* (1737). During the 1730s, Emilie du Châtelet aided Voltaire in his composition of an important French popularization of Newton's science. Her knowledge of mathematics was more extensive than his and crucial to his completing his book.

Still, with only a few exceptions, women were barred from science and medicine until the late nineteenth century, and not until the twentieth century did they enter these fields in any significant numbers. Not only did the institutions of science exclude them, but also the ideas associated with medical practice, philosophy, and biology suggested that women and their minds were essentially different from, and inferior to, men and theirs. By the early eighteenth century, despite isolated precedents of women pursuing natural knowledge, reading scientific literature, and engaging socially with natural philosophers, it had become a fundamental assumption of European intellectual life that the pursuit of natural knowledge was a male vocation.

John Locke

John Locke (1632–1704) attempted to achieve for philosophy a lawful picture of the human mind similar to that which Newton had presented of nature. Locke's three most famous works were the *Essay Concerning Human Understanding* (1690), *Two Treatises of Government*, and his *Letter Concerning Toleration* (1689). Each of them sounded philosophical themes that later writ-

John Locke (1632–1704), defender of the rights of the people against rulers who think their power is absolute. *By courtesy of the National Portrait Gallery, London.*

Major Figures in the Scientific Revolution

Overview

Nicolaus Copernicus (1473–1543)	On the basis of mathematical analysis argued that the Earth moved around the sun.
Tycho Brahe (1546–1601)	Compiled accurate tables of astronomical observations.
Johannes Kepler (1571–1601)	Used Brahe's data to argue that the orbits of the planets were elliptical.
Galileo Galilei (1564–1642)	First astronomer to use a telescope. Argued that mathematical laws governed the universe.
Francis Bacon (1561–1626)	Argued that scientific thought must conform to empirical evidence. Championed innovation and change.
René Descartes (1596–1650)	Invented analytical geometry. Argued that the world was governed by mathematical laws that could be deduced by reason.
Isaac Newton (1642–1727)	Described the effect of gravity mathematically and established a theoretical basis for physics that endured until the late nineteenth century.
John Locke (1632–1704)	Argued that the human mind is a blank slate that may be molded by modifying the environment. Human beings could thus take charge of their own destiny without divine aid.

ers of the Enlightenment found welcome. No other philosopher had so profound an impact on European and American thought during the eighteenth century.

In the *Essay Concerning Human Understanding*, Locke envisioned the human mind as being blank at the time of an individual's birth. In Locke's view, contrary to that of much medieval philosophy, there are no innate ideas (i.e., ideas people are born with); all knowledge is derived from actual sense experience. Each individual mind grows through experience as it confronts the world of sensation. Human ideas are either simple (that is, passive receptions from daily experience) or complex (that is, products of sustained mental exercise). What people know is not the external world in itself, but the results of the interaction of their minds with the outside world. Locke's thinking thus represented an early form of behaviorism. Human nature is changeable and can be molded by modifying the surrounding physical and social environment. Locke also, in effect, rejected the Christian view that human beings were creatures permanently flawed by original sin. Human beings do not need to wait for the grace of God or other divine aid to better their lives. They can take charge of their own destiny.

Locke wrote *Two Treatises of Government* during the reign of Charles II (r. 1660–1685). Locke argued that rulers are not absolute in their power. They remain bound to the law of nature. That law is the voice of reason, teaching that human beings are equal and independent and that they should not harm one another or disturb one another's property because all persons are the images and property of God. According to Locke, people enter political contracts, empowering legislatures and monarchs to judge their disputes in order to preserve their natural rights (which include the possession of property) but not to give rulers an absolute power over them. Locke also contended that a monarch who violated the trust that had been placed in him could be overthrown. This argument reappeared in the American Declaration of Independence in 1776. But in eighteenth-century Europe it was Locke's argument against absolutism and in favor of limited government that was most influential. Like his philosophy, it opened a wider arena for individual action.

Locke's *Letter Concerning Toleration* contended that each person was responsible for his own religious salvation. Governments existed to protect property and the civil order. Matters only became confused when governments undertook to legislate on religion and require conformity to a single church. Yet Locke himself drew the line in England against toleration of Roman Catholics and Unitarians. During the eighteenth century, however, the logic of his argument was extended to advocate toleration for those faiths as well.

The Enlightenment

The movement that came to be known as the **Enlightenment** included a number of writers living at different times in various countries. Its early exponents, known as the *philosophes*, popularized the rationalism and scientific ideas of the seventeenth century. They worked to expose contemporary social and political abuses and argued that reform was necessary and possible. The advancement of their cause and ideas was anything but steady. They confronted vested interests, political oppression, and religious condemnation. Yet by midcentury they had brought enlightened ideas to the European public in a variety of formats.

Voltaire

One of the earliest and by far the most influential of the *philosophes* was François Marie Arouet, known to posterity as Voltaire (1694–1778). During the 1720s Voltaire had offended the French authorities by certain of his writings. He was arrested and briefly imprisoned. Later he went to England, visiting its best literary circles, observing its tolerant intellectual and religious climate, relishing the freedom he felt in its moderate political atmosphere, and admiring its science and economic prosperity. In 1733 he published *Letters on the English*, which appeared in French the next year. The book praised the virtues of the English and indirectly criticized the abuses of French society. In 1738 he published *Elements of the Philosophy of Newton*, which popularized the thought of the great scientist. Both works enhanced his reputation.

Thereafter, Voltaire lived part of the time in France and part near Geneva, just across the French border, where the royal authorities could not bother him. His essays, history, plays, stories, and letters made him the literary dictator of Europe. He turned the bitter venom of his satire and sarcasm against one evil after another in French and European life. His most famous satire is *Candide* (1759), in which he attacked war, religious persecution, and what he regarded as unwarranted optimism about the human condition. Like most *philosophes*, Voltaire believed that human society could and should be improved. But he was never certain that reform, if achieved, would be permanent. The optimism of the Enlightenment constituted a tempered hopefulness rather than a glib certainty. Pessimism was an undercurrent in most of the works of the period.

The *Encyclopedia*

The midcentury witnessed the publication of the *Encyclopedia*, one of the greatest monuments of the

Voltaire. Philosopher, dramatist, poet, historian, and popularizer of scientific ideas, Voltaire (1694–1778) was the most famous and influential of the eighteenth-century philosophers. His sharp satire and criticism of religious institutions opened the way for a more general critique of the European political and social status quo. *Nicholas de Largilliere/Art Resource/Bildarchiv Preussischer Kulturbesitz.*

Enlightenment. Under the heroic leadership of Denis Diderot (1713–1784) and Jean le Rond d'Alembert (1717–1783), the first volume appeared in 1751. When completed in 1772, it numbered seventeen volumes of text and eleven of plates. The *Encyclopedia* was the product of the collective effort of more than one hundred authors, and its editors had solicited articles from all the major French *philosophes*. The project reached fruition only after numerous attempts to censor it and to halt its publication. The *Encyclopedia* set forth the most advanced critical ideas in religion, government, and philosophy. This criticism often had to be hidden in obscure articles or under the cover of irony. The articles represented a collective plea for freedom of expression. However, the large volumes also provided important information on manufacturing, canal building, ship construction, and improved agriculture.

Between 14,000 and 16,000 copies of various editions of the *Encyclopedia* were sold before 1789. The project had been designed to secularize learning and to undermine the intellectual assumptions remaining from the Middle Ages and the Reformation. The articles on politics, ethics, and

The Enlightenment and Religion

Throughout the century, in the eyes of the *philosophes*, the chief enemy of the improvement of humankind and the enjoyment of happiness was the church. The hatred of the *philosophes* for the church and Christianity was summed up in Voltaire's cry of "Crush the Infamous Thing." Almost all varieties of Christianity, but especially Roman Catholicism, invited the criticism of the *philosophes*. Intellectually, the churches perpetuated a religious rather than a scientific view of humankind and physical nature. (See Document, "Voltaire Attacks Religious Fanaticism.") The clergy taught that human beings were basically sinful and that they required divine grace to become worthy creatures. The doctrine of original sin in either its Catholic or its Protestant formulation suggested that meaningful improvement in human nature was impossible. Religious concerns turned human interest away from this world to the world to come. For the *philosophes*, the concept of predestination suggested that the fate of the human soul after death bore little or no relationship to virtuous living. Through their disagreements over obscure doctrines, the various churches favored the politics of intolerance and bigotry that in the past had caused human suffering, torture, and war.

Deism

The *philosophes* believed that religion should be reasonable and lead to moral behavior. The Newtonian worldview had convinced many writers that nature was rational. Therefore, the God who had created nature must also be rational, and the religion through which that God was worshiped should be rational. Moreover, Lockean philosophy, which limited human knowledge to empirical experience, cast doubt on whether divine revelation was possible. These considerations gave rise to a movement for enlightened religion known as ***deism***.

The title of one of its earliest expositions, *Christianity Not Mysterious* (1696) by John Toland, indicates the general tenor of this religious outlook. Toland and later writers wished to consider religion a natural and rational, rather than a supernatural and mystical, phenomenon. In this respect the deists differed from Newton and Locke, who had regarded themselves as distinctly Christian. Newton had believed that God might interfere with the natural order, whereas the deists regarded God as resembling a divine watchmaker who had set the mechanism of nature to work and then let them operate without intervention.

There were two major points in the deists' creed. The first was a belief in the existence of God, which they thought could be empirically deduced from the contemplation of nature.

Illustration from the *Encyclopedia*. Denis Diderot in the *Encyclopedia* included illustrations of machinery and working people from across the globe. Diderot was also deeply hostile to slavery. This engraving illustrated a sugar mill and sugar boiling house run with slave labor in the New World. The sugar produced in such mills was used in the European coffee houses where the ideas of the *philosophes* were often discussed. *University of Virginia Library.*

society ignored concerns about divine law and concentrated on humanity and its immediate well-being. The encyclopedists looked to antiquity rather than to the Christian centuries for their intellectual and ethical models. The future welfare of humankind lay not in pleasing God or following divine commandments, but rather in harnessing the power of the earth and its resources and in living at peace with one's fellow human beings. The good life was to be achieved through the application of reason to human relationships.

With the publication of the *Encyclopedia*, enlightened thought became more fully diffused over the Continent. Enlightened ideas penetrated German and Russian intellectual and political circles (see Map 22–1).

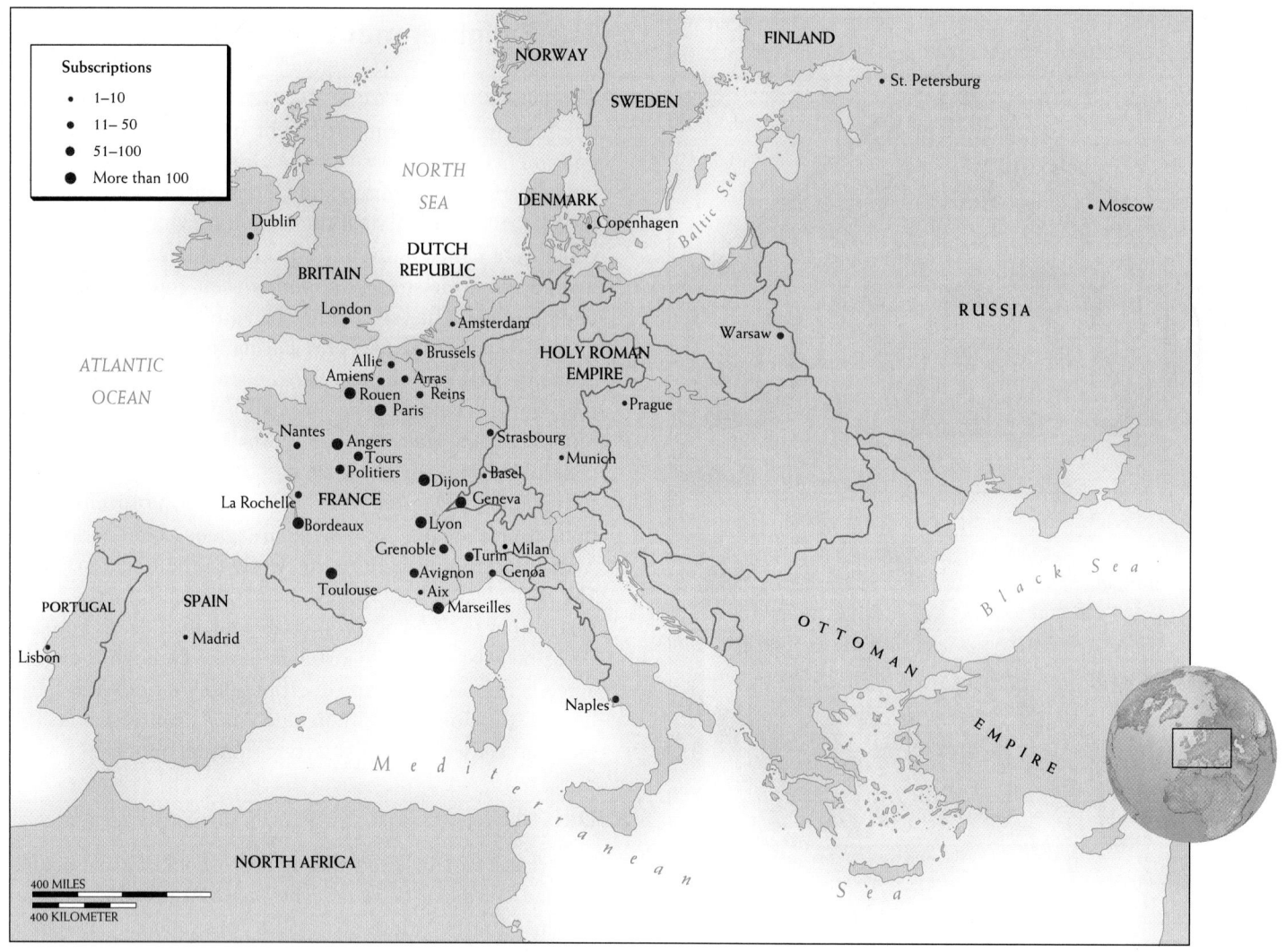

Map 22–1. Subscriptions to Diderot's *Encyclopedia* throughout Europe.

Because nature provided evidence of a rational God, that Deity must also favor rational morality. Consequently, the second point in the deists' creed was a belief in life after death, when rewards and punishments would be meted out according to the virtue of the life a person led on this earth.

Deism was empirical, tolerant, reasonable, and capable of encouraging virtuous living. It was the major positive religious component of the Enlightenment. Voltaire declared:

The great name of Deist, which is not sufficiently revered, is the only name one ought to take. The only gospel one ought to read is the great book of Nature, written by the hand of God and sealed with his seal. The only religion that ought to be professed is the religion of worshiping God and being a good man.[5]

[5] Quoted in J. H. Randall, *The Making of the Modern Mind*, rev. ed. (New York: Houghton Mifflin, 1940), p. 292.

If such a faith became widely accepted, it would overcome the fanaticism and rivalry of the various Christian sects. Religious conflict and persecutions would end. There would also be little or no necessity for a priestly class to foment fanaticism, denominational hatred, and bigotry.

Toleration

A primary social condition for such a life was the establishment of religious toleration. Voltaire took the lead in championing this cause. In 1762 the political authorities in Toulouse ordered the execution of a Huguenot named Jean Calas (1698–1762). He stood accused of having murdered his son to prevent him from converting to Roman Catholicism. Calas had been viciously tortured and publicly strangled without ever having confessed his guilt. The confession would not have saved his life, but it would have given the Catholics good propaganda to use against Protestants.

Voltaire Attacks Religious Fanaticism

The chief complaint of the philosophes against Christianity was that it bred a fanaticism that led people to commit crimes in the name of religion. In this passage from Voltaire's *Philosophical Dictionary* (1764), he directly reminds his readers of the intolerance of the Reformation era and indirectly referred to examples of contemporary religious excesses. He argues that the philosophical spirit can overcome fanaticism and foster toleration and more humane religious behavior. Shocking many of his contemporaries, he praises the virtues of Confucianism over those of Christianity. Voltaire was reacting to specific occurrences of religious intolerance that had occurred in France during his lifetime.

◆ What concrete examples of religious fanaticism might Voltaire have had in mind? Why does Voltaire contend that neither religion nor laws can contain religious fanaticism? Why does Voltaire admire the Chinese?

Fanaticism is to superstition what delirium is to fever and rage to anger. The man visited by ecstasies and visions, who takes dreams for realities and his fancies for prophecies, is an enthusiast; the man who supports his madness with murder is a fanatic. . . .

The most detestable example of fanaticism was that of the burghers of Paris who on St. Bartholomew's Night [1572] went about assassinating and butchering all their fellow citizens who did not go to mass, throwing them out of windows, cutting them in pieces.

Once fanaticism has corrupted a mind, the malady is almost incurable. . . .

The only remedy for this epidemic malady is the philosophical spirit which, spread gradually, at last tames men's habits and prevents the disease from starting; for once the disease has made any progress, one must flee and wait for the air to clear itself. Laws and religion are not strong enough against the spiritual pest; religion, far from being healthy food for infected brains, turns to poison in them. . . .

Even the law is impotent against these attacks of rage; it is like reading a court decree to a raving maniac. These fellows are certain that the holy spirit with which they are filled is above the law, that their enthusiasm is the only law they must obey.

What can we say to a man who tells you that he would rather obey God than men, and that therefore he is sure to go to heaven for butchering you?

Ordinarily fanatics are guided by rascals, who put the dagger into their hands; these latter resemble that Old Man of the Mountain who is supposed to have made imbeciles taste the joys of paradise and who promised them an eternity of the pleasures of which he had given them a foretaste, on condition that they assassinated all those he would name to them. There is only one religion in the world that has never been sullied by fanaticism, that of the Chinese men of letters. The schools of philosophy were not only free from this pest, they were its remedy; for the effect of philosophy is to make the soul tranquil, and fanaticism is incompatible with tranquility. If our holy religion has so often been corrupted by this infernal delirium, it is the madness of men which is at fault.

Voltaire, *Philosophical Dictionary*, trans. by P. Gay (New York: Basic Books, 1962), pp. 267–269.

Voltaire learned of the case only after Calas's death. He made the dead man's cause his own. In 1763 he published

a *Treatise on Tolerance* and hounded the authorities for a new investigation. Finally, in 1765 the judicial decision against the unfortunate man was reversed. For Voltaire, the case illustrated the fruits of religious fanaticism and the need for rational reform of judi-

cial processes. Somewhat later in the century the German playwright and critic Gotthold Lessing (1729–1781) wrote *Nathan the Wise* (1779) as a plea for toleration not only of different Christian sects, but also of religious faiths other than Christianity. All of these calls for toleration stated, in effect, that human life should not be subordinated to religion. Secular values and considerations were more important than religious ones.

Chronology

Major Publication Dates of the Enlightenment

1687	Newton's *Principia Mathematica*
1690	Locke's *Essay Concerning Human Understanding*
1696	Toland's *Christianity Not Mysterious*
1733	Voltaire's *Letters on the English*
1738	Voltaire's *Elements of the Philosophy of Newton*
1748	Montesquieu's *Spirit of the Laws*
1750	Rousseau's *Discourse on the Moral Effects of the Arts and Sciences*
1751	First volume of the *Encyclopedia* edited by Diderot and d'Alembert
1755	Rousseau's *Discourse on the Origin of Inequality*
1762	Rousseau's *Social Contract*
1763	Voltaire's *Treatise on Tolerance*
1776	Smith's *Wealth of Nations*
1779	Lessing's *Nathan the Wise*
1792	Wollstonecraft's *A Vindication of the Rights of Woman*

Islam in Enlightenment Thought

Islam, except in the Balkan Peninsula, had few adherents in eighteenth-century Europe. Although European merchants traded with the Ottoman Empire or with those parts of South Asia where Islam prevailed, most Europeans came to know what little they did know about the Islamic world and Islam as a religion through books—the religious commentaries of Christian missionaries, histories, and the reports of travelers—that with rare exceptions were hostile to Islam and deeply misleading.

Islam continued to be seen as a rival to Christianity. European writers repeated what other Christian critics had said for centuries. They portrayed Islam as a false religion and Muhammed as an impostor and a false prophet because he had not performed miracles. Furthermore, they also attacked Islam as an exceptionally carnal or sexually promiscuous religion because of its teaching that heaven was a place of sensuous delights, its permission for a man to have more than one wife, Muhammed's own polygamy, and the presence of harems in the Islamic world.

Christian authors also ignored the Islamic understanding of the life and mission of Muhammed. They referred to Islam as Muhammedanism, thus implying that Muhammed was divine rather than a human being with whom God had chosen to communicate. For Muslims, the suggestion that Muhammed was divine is blasphemous.

Several European universities did endow professorships for the study of Arabic during the seventeenth century. But these university scholars generally agreed with theological critics that Islam too often embodied religious fanaticism. Even relatively well-informed works based on considerable knowledge of Arabic and Islamic sources, such as Barthélemy d'Herbelot's *Bibliothèque Orientale (Oriental Library)*, a reference book published in 1697, Simon Ockley's *History of the Saracens* (1718), and George Sale's introduction to the first full English translation of the Qur'an (1734) were largely hostile to their subject. All these books continued to be reprinted and remained influential well into the nineteenth century, demonstrating how little disinterested information was available to Europeans about Islam.

Enlightenment philosophes spoke with two voices regarding Islam. Voltaire indicated his opinion along with that of many of his contemporaries in the title of his 1742 tragedy, *Fanaticism, or Mohammed the Prophet*. Although he sometimes spoke well of the Qur'an, Voltaire declared in a later historical work, "We must suppose that Muhammed, like all enthusiasts, violently impressed by his own ideas, retailed them in good faith, fortified them with fancies, deceived himself in deceiving others, and finally sustained with deceit a doctrine he believed to be good."[6] Thus for Voltaire, Muhammed and Islam in general represented simply one more example of the religious fanaticism he had so often criticized among Christians.

Some Enlightenment writers, however, spoke well of the Islamic faith. The deist John Toland, who opposed prejudice against both Jews and Muslims, contended that Islam derived from early Christian writings and was thus a form of Christianity. These views so offended most of his contemporaries that Toland became known as a "Mohametan" Christian. Edward Gibbon (1737–1794), who blamed Christianity for contributing to the fall of the Roman Empire, wrote with respect of Muhammed's leadership and Islam's success in conquering so vast a territory in the first century of its existence. Other commentators approved of Islam's tolerance and the charitable work of Muslims.

---

[6] Quoted in Theodore Besterman, *Voltaire* (New York: Harcourt, Brace, & World, 1969), p. 409.

Map of Turkey and View of Constantinople (Istanbul).
Few Europeans visited the Ottoman Empire. What little they knew about it came from reports of travelers and from illustrations such as this view of Istanbul, the empire's capital. © *Historical Picture Archive/Corbis.*

Some *philosophes* criticized Islam on cultural and political grounds. In *The Persian Letters* (1721), supposedly written by two Muslim Persians visiting Europe, Charles Louis de Secondat, baron de Montesquieu (1689–1755), who became a major political philosopher, used Islamic culture as a foil to criticize his own European society. But by the time he wrote his more influential *Spirit of the Laws* (1748), discussed more fully later in this chapter, Montesquieu associated Islamic society with the passivity that he ascribed to people subject to political despotism. Like other Europeans, Montesquieu believed the excessive influence of Islamic religious leaders prevented the Ottoman Empire from adapting itself to new advances in technology.

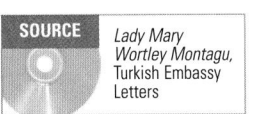

One of the most positive commentators on eighteenth-century Islam was a woman. Between 1716 and 1718, Lady Mary Wortley Montagu (1689–1762) lived in Constantinople with her husband, the British ambassador to Turkey. She wrote a series of letters about her experiences there that were published the year after her death. In these *Turkish Embassy Letters*, she praised much about Ottoman society and urged the English to copy the Turkish practice of vaccination against smallpox. Unlike European males, Montagu had access to the private quarters of women in Istanbul. In contrast to the constraints under which English women found themselves, she thought upper-class Turkish women were remarkably free and well treated by their husbands despite having to wear clothing that completely covered them in public. In fact, Montagu thought the anonymity these coverings bestowed allowed Turkish women to move freely about Istanbul. She also considered the magnificent Ottoman architecture better than anything in Western Europe. Montagu repeatedly criticized the misinformation that prevailed in Europe about the Ottoman Empire and declared that many of the hostile comments about Islam and Islamic morality were simply wrong.

Yet the European voices demanding fairness and expressing empathy for Islam were rare throughout the eighteenth century. As one historian has commented, "The basic Christian attitude was still what it had been for a millennium: a rejection of the claim of Muslims that Muhammed was a prophet and the Qur'an the word of God, mingled with a memory of periods of fear and conflict, and also, a few thinkers and scholars apart, with legends, usually hostile and often contemptuous."[7]

Nor were Muslims very curious about the Christian West. Only a handful of people from the Ottoman or Safavid empires visited Western Europe in the eighteenth century, and no Islamic writers showed much interest in contemporary European authors. The Ulama, the Islamic religious establishment, reinforced these attitudes. They taught that God's revelations to Muhammed meant Islam had superceded Christianity as a religion and therefore there was little to be learned from the Christian culture of Europe.

The Enlightenment and Society

Although the *philosophes* wrote much about religion, humanity was the center of their interest. As one writer in the *Encyclopedia* observed, "Man is the unique point to which we must refer everything, if we wish to interest and please amongst considerations the most arid and details the most dry."[8] The *philosophes* believed that the application of human reason to society would reveal laws in human relationships similar to those found in physical nature. Although the term did not appear until later, the idea of social science originated with the Enlightenment. The purpose of discovering social laws was to remove the inhumanity that existed through ignorance of them.

Montesquieu and *The Spirit of the Laws*

Charles Louis de Secondat, Baron de Montesquieu, was a French noble of the robe and a magistrate. His work *The Spirit of the Laws* (1748), perhaps the single most influential book of the century, exhibits the internal tensions of the Enlightenment. Montesquieu pursued an empirical method, taking illustrative examples from the political experience of both ancient and modern nations. From them he concluded that no single set of political laws could apply to

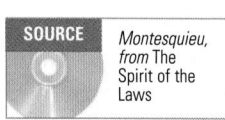
SOURCE Montesquieu, from The Spirit of the Laws

all peoples at all times and in all places. Rather, the good political life depended on the relationship of many political variables. Whether a monarchy or a republic was the best form of government depended on the size of the political unit and its population, its social and religious customs, economic structure, traditions, and climate. Only a careful examination and evalua-

tion of these elements could reveal what mode of government would prove most beneficial to a particular people. A century later such speculations would have been classified as sociology.

As far as France was concerned, Montesquieu believed in a monarchy whose power was tempered and limited by various intermediary institutions, including the aristocracy, the towns, and the other corporate bodies that enjoyed particular liberties that the monarch must respect. These corporate bodies might be said to represent various segments of the general population and thus of public opinion. In France he regarded the *parlements*, judicial courts dominated by aristocrats like himself, as the major example of an intermediary association. Their role was to limit the power of the monarchy and thus to preserve the liberty of the subjects. In championing these aristocratic bodies and the general role of the aristocracy, Montesquieu was a political conservative. He adopted that stance, however, in the hope of achieving reform, for he considered the oppressive and inefficient absolutism of the monarchy responsible for the degradation of French life.

One of Montesquieu's most influential ideas was that of division of power. He took Great Britain for his model of a government with power wisely separated among different branches. There he believed he had found a system in which executive power resided in the king, legislative power in the Parliament, and judicial power in the courts. He thought any two branches could check and balance the power of the other. His perception of the eighteenth-century British constitution was incorrect, because he failed to see how patronage and electoral corruption allowed a handful of aristocrats to dominate the government. Moreover, he was also unaware of the emerging cabinet system, which meant that the executive power was slowly becoming a creature of the Parliament. Nevertheless, the analysis illustrated Montesquieu's strong sense of the need to limit the exercise of power through a constitution and for legislatures, not monarchs, to make laws. Although Montesquieu set out to defend the political privileges of the French aristocracy, his ideas had a profound and enduring effect on the liberal democracies of the next two centuries.

Adam Smith on Economic Growth and Social Progress

The most important economic work of the Enlightenment was Adam Smith's (1723–1790) *Inquiry into the Nature and Causes of the Wealth of Nations* (1776). Smith, who was for a time a professor at Glasgow, believed that economic liberty was the foundation of a natural economic system. As a result, he urged that the mercantile system of England—

---

[7] A. Hourani, *Islam in European Thought* (Cambridge: Cambridge University Press, 1991), p. 136.
[8] Quoted in F. L. Baumer, *Main Currents of Western Thought*, 4th ed. (New Haven, CT: Yale University Press, 1978), p. 374.

Printing Shops. Shops such as this were the productive centers for the book trade and newspaper publishing, which spread the ideas of the Enlightenment. *The Granger Collection.*

including the navigation acts, the bounties, most tariffs, special trading monopolies, and the domestic regulation of labor and manufacture—be abolished. These regulations were intended to preserve the wealth of the nation, to capture wealth from other nations, and to maximize the work available for the nation's laborers. Smith argued, however, that they hindered the expansion of wealth and production. The best way to encourage economic growth, he maintained, was to unleash individuals to pursue their own selfish economic interests. As self-interested individuals sought to enrich themselves by meeting the needs of others in the marketplace, the economy would expand. Consumers would find their wants met as manufacturers and merchants competed for their business.

It was a basic assumption of mercantilism that the earth's resources are limited and scarce, so that one nation can acquire wealth only at the expense of others. Smith's

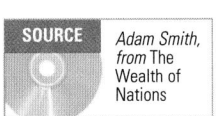

SOURCE *Adam Smith, from The Wealth of Nations*

book challenged this assumption. He saw the resources of nature—water, air, soil, and minerals—as boundless. To him, they demanded exploitation for the enrichment and comfort of humankind. In effect, Smith was saying that the nations and peoples of Europe need not be poor.

Smith is usually regarded as the founder of ***laissez-faire*** economic thought and policy, which favors a limited role for the government in economic life. *The Wealth of Nations* was, however, a complex book. Smith was no simple dogmatist. For example, he did not oppose all government activity touching the economy. The state, he argued, should provide schools, armies, navies, and roads. It should also undertake certain commercial ventures, such as the opening of danger-

ous new trade routes that were economically desirable, but too expensive or risky for private enterprise.

Within *The Wealth of Nations*, Smith, like other Scottish thinkers of the day, embraced an important theory of human social and economic development, known as the *four-stage theory*. According to this theory, human societies can be classified as hunting and gathering, pastoral or herding, agricultural, and commercial. The hunters and gatherers have little or no settled life. Pastoral societies are groups of nomads who tend their herds and develop some private property. Agricultural or farming societies are settled and have clear-cut property arrangements. Finally, in the commercial state there exist advanced cities, the manufacture of numerous items for wide consumption, extensive trade between cities and the countryside, and elaborate forms of property and financial arrangements. Smith and other Scottish writers described the passage of human society through these stages as a movement from barbarism to civilization.

The four-stage theory implicitly evaluated the later stages of economic development and the people dwelling in them as higher, more progressive, and more civilized than the earlier ones. A social theorist using this theory could thus very quickly look at a society and, on the basis of the state of its economic development and organizations, rank it in terms of the stage it had achieved. In point of fact, the commercial stage, the highest rank in the theory, described society as it appeared in northwestern Europe. Thus, Smith's theory allowed Europeans to look about the world and always find themselves dwelling at the highest level of human achievement. This outlook served as one of the major justifications in the minds of Europeans for their economic and imperial domination of the world during the next century. They repeatedly portrayed themselves as bringing a higher level of civilization to people elsewhere who, according to the four-stage theory, lived in lower stages of human social and economic development. Europeans thus imbued with the spirit of the Enlightenment presented themselves as carrying out a civilizing mission to the rest of the world.

Rousseau

Jean-Jacques Rousseau (1712–1778) held a different view of political power. Rousseau was a strange, isolated genius who never felt comfortable with the other *philosophes*. Yet perhaps more than any other writer of the mid–eighteenth century, he transcended the thought and values of his own time. Rousseau had a deep antipathy towards the world and the society in which he lived. It seemed impossible for human beings living according to contemporary commercial values to achieve moral, virtuous, or sincere lives. In 1750, in his *Discourse on the Moral Effects of the Arts and Sciences*, he contended that civilization and enlightenment had corrupted human nature. Human beings in the state of nature had been more dignified. In 1755, in a *Discourse on the Origin of Inequality*, Rousseau blamed much of the evil in the world on maldistribution of property.

In both works, Rousseau directly challenged the social fabric of the day. He questioned the concepts of material and intellectual progress and the morality of a society in which commerce and industry were regarded as the most important human activities. He felt that the real purpose of society was to nurture better people. Rousseau's vision of reform was much more radical than that of other contemporary writers.

Rousseau carried these same concerns into his political thought. His most extensive discussion of politics appeared in *The Social Contract* (1762). Compared to Montesquieu's *The Spirit of the Laws, The Social Contract* is an abstract book. It does not propose specific reforms but outlines the kind of political structure that Rousseau believed would overcome the evils of contemporary politics and society.

In the tradition of John Locke, most eighteenth-century political thinkers regarded society as a collection of independent individuals pursuing personal, selfish goals. These writers wished to liberate these individuals from the undue bonds of government. Rousseau picked up the stick from the other end. His book opens with the declaration, "All men are born free, but everywhere they are in chains."[9] The rest of the volume constitutes a defense of the chains of a properly organized society over its members. Rousseau sug-

Rousseau. The writings of Jean-Jacques Rousseau (1712–1778) raised some of the most profound social and ethical questions of the Enlightenment. This portrait by Maurice Quentin was made ca. 1740. *Bildarchiv Preussischer Kulturbesitz Maurice Quentin de la Tour/Bildarchiv Preussicher Kulturbesitz.*

gested that society is more important than its individual members, because they are what they are only as a result of their relationship to the larger community. Independent human beings living alone can achieve little. Through their relationship to the larger community, they become moral creatures capable of significant action. The question then becomes what kind of community allows people to behave morally. Rousseau sought to project the vision of a society in which each person could maintain personal freedom while also behaving as a loyal member of the larger community. He drew on the traditions of Plato and Calvin to define freedom as obedience to law. In his case, the law to be obeyed was that created by the general will. This concept normally indicated the will of the majority of voting citizens who acted with adequate information and under the influence of virtuous customs and morals. Such democratic participation in decision making would bind the individual citizen to the community. Rousseau believed that the general will must always be right and that to obey the general will was to be free. This argument led him to the notorious conclusion that some people must be forced to be free. His politics thus

---

[9] Jean-Jacques Rousseau, *The Social Contract and Discourses*, trans. by G. D. H. Cole (New York: Dutton, 1950), p. 3.

constituted a justification for radical direct democracy and for collective action against individual citizens.

Rousseau had, in effect, assaulted the eighteenth-century cult of the individual and the fruits of selfishness. He stood at odds with the commercial spirit that was transforming society. Adam Smith wanted people to be prosperous; Rousseau wanted them to be good even if it meant they might remain poor. He saw human beings not as independent individuals, but as creatures enmeshed in necessary social relationships. He believed that loyalty to the community should be encouraged. As one device to that end, he suggested a civic religion based on deism. Such a shared tolerant religious faith would unify society. Rousseau's chief intellectual inspiration arose from his study of Plato and the ancient Greek *polis*. Especially in Sparta, he thought he had discovered human beings dwelling in a moral society inspired by a common purpose. He hoped that modern human beings might also create such a moral commonwealth in which virtuous living would not become subordinate to commercial profit.

Enlightened Critics of European Empire

Most European thinkers associated with the Enlightenment favored the extension of European empires across the world. Like the Scottish writers who embraced the four-stage theory, they believed that the extension of the political structures and economies of northwestern Europe amounted to the spread of progress and civilization. The Scottish commentators and their followers were not without their criticisms of European civilization, but on the whole they believed it superior.

There were, however, a few minority Enlightenment voices who criticized the European empires. The topic that most frequently allowed such criticism were discussions of the European conquest of the Americas, the treatment of Native Americans, and the enslavement of Africans on the two American continents. The most important of these crit-

 SOURCE *Immanuel Kant defines the Enlightenment*

ics were Denis Diderot and two German philosophers, Immanuel Kant (1724–1804) and Johann Gottfried Herder (1744–1803). (See Document, "Denis Diderot Condemns European Empires.")

What sets of ideas allowed these figures from the Enlightenment to criticize empire? As Sankar Muthu has recently written, "The first and most basic idea is that human beings deserve some modicum of moral and political respect simply because of the fact that they are human."[10] In other words, the Enlightenment critics of empire argued

for the existence of a form of shared humanity that the sixteenth-century European conquerors and their successors in the Americas and in other areas of imperial conquest had ignored. Immanuel Kant, the German philosopher, wrote, "When America, the Negro countries, the Spice Islands, the Cape, and so forth were discovered, they were to them [the Europeans], countries belonging to no one, since they counted the inhabitants as *nothing*."[11] Kant, Denis Diderot, and the German philosopher of history Herder rejected this dismissive outlook and the harsh policies that had flowed from it. They believed no single definition of human nature could be made the standard throughout the world and then used to dehumanize people whose appearance or culture differed from that standard.

A second of these critical ideas was the conviction that the people whom Europeans had encountered in the Americas had actually possessed cultures that should have been respected and understood rather than being destroyed. Some Europeans in the early years of the encounter with America had actually argued that the native peoples were human, but that their way of life was so low, they could not be treated a being equally human with Europeans. In the late eighteenth century Herder directly rejected such a view, "'European culture' is a mere abstraction, an empty concept. Where does or did it actually exist in its entirety? In which nation? In which period? . . . Only a misanthrope could regard European culture as the universal condition of our species. The culture of man is not the culture of the European; it manifests itself according to time and place in every people."[12] For Herder, human beings living in different societies possessed the capacity as human beings to develop in culturally different fashions. He thus strongly embraced an outlook later known as cultural relativism.

A third idea, closely related to the second, was that human beings may develop distinct cultures possessing intrinsic values that cannot be directly compared. The reason they may not be compared one to the detriment of another is that each culture possesses deep inner social and linguistic complexities that make any simple comparison impossible. Indeed, Diderot, Kant, and Herder argued that one fundamental aspect of humanity is the ability to develop a variety of distinctly different cultures.

These arguments critical of empire often involved criticism of New World slavery and were part of the antislavery movement to be discussed in a later chapter. Whereas the antislavery arguments took strong hold in both Europe and America from the late eighteenth century onward, the arguments critical of empire did not. They stand generally isolated

---

[10] Sankar Muthu, *Enlightenment Against Empire* (Princeton: Princeton University Press, 2003), p. 268. This section draws primarily from this excellent recent book.

[11] Quoted in Muthu, *Enlightenment Against Empire*, p. 267.
[12] F. M. Barnard, *Self-direction and Political Legitimacy: Rousseau and Herder* (Oxford: Clarendon Press, 1988), p. 227.

Denis Diderot Condemns European Empires

Document

Denis Diderot was one of the most prolific writers of the Enlightenment. He is most famous as editor of the *Encyclopedia*. Some of his writings were published without being directly attributed to him. Among these were his contributions to Abbé G. T. Raynal's *History of the Two Indies*, published in various changing editions after 1772. Diderot's contributions appear to have been made in 1780. The entire *History* was critical of the European colonial empires that had arisen since the Spanish encounter with the New World. Diderot was particularly concerned to condemn the inhumane treatment of the native populations of the Americas, the greed displayed by all Europeans, and the establishment of various forms of forced labor.

◆ What is the basis for Diderot's view that Europeans have behaved tyrannically? How does he portray the behavior of Europeans once they have left their own native countries and find themselves in foreign areas? What are the specific social results he associates with European greed?

Let the European nations make their own judgment and give themselves the name they deserve. . . . Their explorers arrive in a region of the New World unoccupied by anyone from the Old World, and immediately bury a small strip of metal on which they have engraved these words: *This country belongs to us*. And why does it belong to you? . . . You have no right to the natural products of the country where you land, and you claim a right over your fellow-men. Instead of recognizing this man as a brother you only see him as a slave, a beast of burden. Oh my fellow citizens! You think like that and you behave like that; and you have ideas of justice, a morality, a holy religion . . . in common with those whom you treat so tyrannically. This reproach should especially be addressed to the Spaniards.

Beyond the Equator a man is neither English, Dutch, French, Spanish, nor Portuguese. He retains only those principles and prejudices of his native country which justify or excuse his conduct. He crawls when he is weak; he is violent when strong; he is in a hurry to acquire, in a hurry to enjoy, and capable of every crime which will lead him most quickly to his goals. He is a domestic tiger returning to the forest; the thirst for blood takes hold of him once more. This is how all the Europeans, every one of them, indistinctly, have appeared in the countries of the New World. There they have assumed a common frenzy—the thirst for gold.

The Spaniard, the first to be thrown up by the waves onto the shores of the New World, thought he had no duty to people who did not share his color, customs, or religion. He saw in them only tools for his greed, and he clapped them in irons. These weak men, not used to work, soon died in the foul air of the mines, or in other occupations which were virtually as lethal. Then people called for slaves from Africa. Their number has gone up as more land has been cultivated. The Portuguese, Dutch, English, French, Danes, all the nations, free or subjected, have without remorse sought to increase their fortune in the sweat, blood and despair of these unfortunates. What a horrible system!

Denis Diderot, *Political Writings*, John Hope Mason and Robert Wokler, eds., (Cambridge: Cambridge University Press, 1998), pp. 177, 178, 186.

---

from the rest of Enlightenment political thought and would not be strongly revived until new anticolonial voices were raised in Europe and the non-European world at the close of the nineteenth century.

Women in the Thought and Practice of the Enlightenment

Women, especially in France, helped significantly to promote the careers of the *philosophes*. In Paris the salons of women such as Marie-Thérèse Geoffrin (1699–1777), Julie de Lespinasse (1733–1776), and Claudine de Tencin (1689–1749) gave the *philosophes* access to useful social and political contacts and a receptive environment for their ideas. These women were well connected to major political figures who could help protect the *philosophes* and secure them pensions. The marquise de Pompadour (1721–1764), the mistress of Louis XV, for example, played a key role in overcoming efforts to censor the *Encyclopedia*. She also helped block the circulation of works attacking the *philosophes*.

Enlightenment Salon. The salon of Madame Marie-Thérèse Geoffrin (1699–1777) was one of the most important gathering spots for Enlightenment writers during the middle of the eighteenth century. Well-connected women such as Madame Geoffrin were instrumental in helping the *philosophes* they patronized to bring their ideas to the attention of influential people in French society and politics. *Châteaux de Malmaison et Bois-Preau, Rueil-Malmaison. Bridgeman-Giraudon/Art Resource, N.Y.*

Nonetheless, the *philosophes* were on the whole not strong feminists. Although many criticized the education women received as overly religious and tended to reject ascetic views of sexual relations, the *philosophes* advocated no radical changes in the social condition of women.

Montesquieu, for example, maintained in general that the status of women in a society was the result of climate, the political regime, culture, and women's physiological nature. He believed women were not naturally inferior to men and should have a wider role in society. He was well aware of the personal, emotional, and sexual repression women endured in his day. Yet there were limits to his willingness to consider change in women's social role. He retained a traditional view of marriage and family and expected men to dominate those institutions. Furthermore, although he supported the right of women to divorce and opposed laws that directly oppressed them, he upheld the ideal of female chastity.

The views about women expressed in the *Encyclopedia* were less generous. The editors, Diderot and d'Alembert, recruited men almost exclusively as contributors and saw no need to include many articles by women. Most of the articles that dealt with women specifically or that discussed women in connection with other subjects often emphasized their physical weakness and inferiority, usually attributed to menstruation or childbearing. Contributors disagreed on the social equality of women. Some favored it, others opposed it, and still others were indifferent. The articles conveyed a general sense that women were reared to be frivolous and unconcerned with important issues. The encyclopedists discussed women primarily in a family context—as daughters, wives, and mothers—and considered motherhood their most important occupation. On sexual behavior, the encyclopedists upheld an unquestioned double standard.

In contrast to the articles, however, illustrations in the *Encyclopedia* showed women deeply involved in the economic activities of the day. The illustrations also showed the activities of lower- and working-class women, about whom the articles have little to say.

Rousseau urged a traditional role for women. In his novel *Émile* (1762) he declared that women should be educated for a position subordinate to men, emphasizing especially women's function in bearing and rearing children. He portrayed them as weaker and inferior to men in virtually all respects except perhaps for their capacity for feeling and giving love. He excluded them from political life. Women were assigned the domestic sphere alone. Many of these attitudes were not new—some have roots as ancient as Roman law—but Rousseau's powerful presentation and the influence of his other writings gave them new life, including in the legislation of the French Revolution. (See Document, "Rousseau Argues for Separate Spheres for Men and Women.")

Paradoxically, despite these views and his own ill treatment of the many women who bore his many children, Rousseau achieved a vast following among women in the eighteenth century. He is credited with persuading thousands of upper-class women to breast-feed their own children rather than putting them out to wet nurses. One explanation for this influence is that his writings, although they did not advocate liberating women or expanding their social or economic roles, did stress the importance of their emotions and subjective feelings. He portrayed the domestic life and the role of wife and mother as a noble and fulfilling vocation, giving middle- and upper-class women a sense that their daily occupations had purpose. He assigned them a degree of influence in the domestic sphere that they could not have competing with men outside it.

In 1792 in *A Vindication of the Rights of Woman*, Mary Wollstonecraft, (1759–1797) brought Rousseau before the judgment of the rational Enlightenment ideal of progressive knowledge. Wollstonecraft (who, like so many women of her day, died shortly after childbirth of puerperal fever) accused Rousseau and others after him who upheld traditional roles for women of attempting to narrow women's vision and limit their experience. She argued that to confine women to the separate domestic sphere because of their supposed physiological limitations was to make them the sensual slaves of men. Confined in this separate sphere, as the victims of male

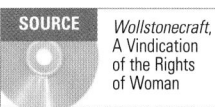

SOURCE *Wollstonecraft, A Vindication of the Rights of Woman*

Rousseau Argues for Separate Spheres for Men and Women

Document

Rousseau published *Émile*, a novel about education, in 1762. In it he made one of the strongest and most influential arguments of the eighteenth century for distinct social roles for men and women. Furthermore, he portrayed women as fundamentally subordinate to men. See page 699 for a contemporary rebuttal.

◆ How does Rousseau move from the physical differences between men and women to an argument for distinct social roles and social spheres? What would be the proper kinds of social activities for women in Rousseau's vision? What kind of education would he think appropriate for women?

There is no parity between the two sexes in regard to the consequences of sex. The male is male only at certain moments. The female is female her whole life or at least during her whole youth. Everything constantly recalls her sex to her; and, to fulfill its functions well, she needs a constitution which corresponds to it. She needs care during her pregnancy; she needs rest at the time of childbirth; she needs a soft and sedentary life to suckle her children; she needs patience and gentleness, a zeal and an affection that nothing can rebuff in order to raise her children. She serves as the link between them and their father; she alone makes him love them and gives him the confidence to call them his own. How much tenderness and care is required to maintain the union of the whole family! And, finally, all this must come not from virtues but from tastes, or else the human species would soon be extinguished.

The strictness of the relative duties of the two sexes is not and cannot be the same. When woman complains on this score about unjust man-made inequality, she is wrong. This inequality is not a human institution—or, at least, it is the work not of prejudice but of reason. It is up to the sex that nature has charged with the bearing of children to be responsible for them to the other sex. Doubtless it is not permitted to any one to violate his faith, and every unfaithful husband who deprives his wife of the only reward of the austere duties of her sex is an unjust and barbarous man. But the unfaithful woman does more; she dissolves the family and breaks all the bonds of nature. . . .

Once it is demonstrated that man and woman are not and ought not be constituted in the same way in either character or temperament, it follows that they ought not to have the same education. In following nature's directions, man and woman ought to act in concert, but they ought not to do the same things. The goal of their labors is common, but their labors themselves are different, and consequently so are the tastes directing them. . . .

The good constitution of children initially depends on that of their mothers. The first education of men depends on the care of women. Men's morals, their passions, their tastes, their pleasures, their very happiness also depend on women. Thus the whole education of women ought to relate to men. To please men, to be useful to them, to make herself loved and honored by them, to raise them when young, to care for them when grown, to counsel them, to console them, to make their lives agreeable and sweet—these are the duties of women at all times, and they ought to be taught from childhood. So long as one does not return to this principle, one will deviate from the goal, and all the precepts taught to women will be of no use for their happiness or for ours.

From Émile; or, On Education, by Jean-Jacques Rousseau, by Allan Bloom, trans. Copyright © 1979 by Basic Books, a member of Perseus Books L.L.C.

tyranny, they could never achieve their own moral or intellectual identity. Denying good education to women would impede the progress of all humanity. Wollstonecraft was demanding for women the kind of intellectual liberty that male writers of the Enlightenment had been championing for men for more than a century. (see Document, "Mary Wollstonecraft Criticizes Rousseau's View of Women.")

Enlightened Absolutism

During the last third of the century it seemed that several European rulers had embraced many of the reforms set forth by the *philosophes*. *Enlightened absolutism* is the term used to describe this phenomenon. The phrase indicates monarchical government dedicated to the rational strengthening of

Mary Wollstonecraft Criticizes Rousseau's View of Women

Document

Mary Wollstonecraft published *A Vindication of the Rights of Woman* in 1792, thirty years after Rousseau's *Émile* had appeared. She criticized and rejected Rousseau's argument for distinct and separate spheres for men and women as defending the continued bondage of women to men and as hindering the wider education of the entire human race.

◆ What specific criticisms does Wollstonecraft direct against Rousseau's views? Why does Wollstonecraft put so much emphasis on a new kind of education for women?

The most perfect education . . . is such an exercise of the understanding as is best calculated to strengthen the body and form the heart. Or, in other words, to enable the individual to attain such habits of virtue as will render it independent. In fact, it is a farce to call any being virtuous whose virtues do not result from the exercise of its own reason. This was Rousseau's opinion respecting men: I extend it to women. . . .

I may be accused of arrogance; still I must declare what I firmly believe, that all the writers who have written on the subject of female education and manners from Rousseau to Dr. Gregory [a Scottish physician], have contributed to render women more artificial, weak characters, than they would other wise have been; and, consequently, more useless members of society. . . .

. . . Strengthen the female mind by enlarging it, and there will be an end to blind obedience; but, as blind obedience is ever sought for by power, tyrants and sensualists are in the right when they endeavour to keep women in the dark, because the former only wants slaves, and the latter a play-thing. The sensualist, indeed, has been the most dangerous of tyrants, and women have been duped by their lovers, as princes by their ministers, whilst dreaming that they reigned over them.

. . . Rousseau declares that a woman should never, for a moment, feel herself independent, that she should be governed by fear to exercise her natural cunning, and made a coquettish slave in order to render her a more alluring object of desire, a sweeter companion to man, whenever he chooses to relax himself. He carries the arguments, which he pretends to draw from the indications of nature, still further, and insinuates that truth and fortitude, the corner stones of all human virtue, should be cultivated with certain restrictions, because, with respect to the female character, obedience is the grand lesson which ought to be impressed with unrelenting rigour.

What nonsense! When will a great man arise with sufficient strength of mind to put away the fumes which pride and sensuality have thus spread over the subject! If women are by nature inferior to men, their virtues must be the same in quality, if not in degree, or virtue is a relative idea; consequently, their conduct should be founded on the same principles, and have the same aim.

Connected with man as daughters, wives, and mothers, their moral character may be estimated by their manner of fulfilling those simple duties; but the end, the grand end of their exertions should be to unfold their own faculties and acquire the dignity of conscious virtue. . . .

But avoiding . . . any direct comparison of the two sexes collectively, or frankly acknowledging the inferiority of women, according to the present appearance of things, I shall only insist that men have increased that inferiority till women are almost sunk below the standard of rational creatures. Let their faculties have room to unfold, and their virtues to gain strength, and then determine where the whole sex must stand in the intellectual scale. . . .

. . . I . . . will venture to assert, that till women are more rationally educated, the progress of human virtue and improvement in knowledge must receive continual checks. . . .

The mother, who wishes to give true dignity of character to her daughter, must regardless of the sneers of ignorance, proceed on a plan diametrically opposite to that which Rousseau has recommended with all the deluding charms of eloquence and philosophical sophistry: for his eloquence renders absurdities plausible, and his dogmatic conclusions puzzle, without convincing, those who have not ability to refute them.

From Mary Wollstonecraft, *A Vindication of the Rights of Woman*, ed. by Carol H. Poston. Copyright © 1975 W. W. Norton & Co., Inc., pp. 21, 22, 24–26, 35, 40, 41.

the central absolutist administration at the cost of lesser centers of political power. The monarchs most closely associated with it—Frederick II of Prussia, Joseph II of Austria, and Catherine II of Russia—often found that the political and social realities of their realms caused them to moderate both their enlightenment and their absolutism. Frederick II corresponded with the *philosophes*, invited Voltaire to his court, and even wrote history and political tracts. Catherine II, who was a master of what would later be called public relations, consciously sought to create the image of being enlightened. She read the works of the *philosophes*, became a friend of Diderot and Voltaire, and made frequent references to their ideas, all in the hope that her nation might seem more modern and Western. Joseph II continued numerous initiatives begun by his mother, Maria Theresa, and imposed a series of religious, legal, and social reforms that contemporaries believed he had derived from suggestions of the *philosophes*.

Despite such appearances, the relationship between these rulers and the writers of the Enlightenment was more complicated. The rulers did wish to see their subjects enjoy better health, more accessible education, a more rational political administration, and economic prosperity. In many of these policies, they were more advanced than the rulers of western Europe. However, the humanitarian and liberating zeal of the Enlightenment directed only part of their policies. Frederick II, Joseph II, and Catherine II were also determined to play major diplomatic and military roles in Europe. In no small measure they sought the rational economic and social integration of their realms, so they could achieve military strength. After the Seven Years' War all the states of Europe understood that they would require stronger armed forces, which meant they needed new revenues. The search for new revenues and for more political support for their rule led these monarchs to make "enlightened" reforms. Consequently, they and their advisers used rationality to pursue many goals admired by the *philosophes* but also to further what the *philosophes* considered irrational militarism.

Joseph II of Austria

No eighteenth-century ruler so embodied rational, impersonal force as the emperor Joseph II of Austria. He was the son of Maria Theresa (r. 1740–1780) and co-ruler with her from 1765 to 1780. During the next ten years he ruled alone. He lived very simply, sleeping on straw and eating little but beef. He lived in a town house in Vienna rather than the elaborate royal palace on the outskirts of the city. He prided himself on a narrow, passionless rationality, which he sought to impose by his own will on the various Habsburg

domains. Despite his eccentricities and cold personality, Joseph II genuinely and sincerely wished to improve the lot of his peoples. His well-intentioned efforts led to a series of aristocratic and peasant rebellions from Hungary to the Austrian Netherlands.

Of all the rising states of the eighteenth century, Austria was the most diverse in its people and problems. The Habsburgs never succeeded in creating either a unified administrative structure or a strong aristocratic loyalty. The price of preserving the monarchy during the War of the Austrian Succession (1740–1748) had been guarantees of considerable aristocratic independence, especially in Hungary.

During and after the conflict, however, Maria Theresa had strengthened her powers in Austria and Bohemia. Through major administrative reorganization she imposed a much more efficient system of tax collection that extracted funds even from the clergy and the nobles, and she established several central councils to deal with governmental problems. She was particularly concerned about bringing all educational institutions into the service of the crown so that she could have enough educated officials, and she expanded primary education on the local level.

Maria Theresa was also concerned about the welfare of the peasants and serfs. The extension of the authority of the royal bureaucracy over that of the local nobilities helped the peasants, as did the empress's decrees limiting the services that landowners could demand from them. This concern arose from her desire to assure a good military recruitment pool. In all these policies and in her general desire to stimulate prosperity and military strength by royal initiative, Maria Theresa anticipated the policies of her son.

Joseph II, however, was more determined, and his projected reforms were more wide ranging than his mother's. He was ambitious to expand at the expense of Poland, Bavaria, and the Ottoman Empire. But his greatest ambition was to change the authority of the Habsburg emperor over his various realms. He sought to overcome the pluralism of the Habsburg holdings by increasing the power of the central monarchy in areas of political and social life that Maria Theresa had wisely not disturbed. In particular, Joseph sought to lessen Hungarian autonomy. He refused to have himself crowned king of Hungary and even had the Crown of Saint Stephen sent to Vienna. He thus avoided having to guarantee existing or new Hungarian privileges in a coronation oath. He reorganized local government in Hungary to increase the authority of his own officials, and he required the use of the German language in all governmental matters. But the Magyar nobility resisted, and in 1790 Joseph had to rescind most of his centralizing measures.

Another target of Joseph's assertion of royal absolutism was religion. In October 1781 Joseph extended freedom of worship to Lutherans, Calvinists, and the Greek Orthodox. They were permitted to have their own churches, sponsor schools, enter skilled trades, and to hold academic appointments and positions in the public service. From 1781 through 1789 Joseph relieved the Jews of certain taxes and signs of personal degradation and gave them the right of private worship. Despite these benefits the Jews still did not enjoy general legal rights equal to those of other Habsburg subjects.

Above all, Joseph sought to bring the various institutions of the Roman Catholic Church directly under his control. He forbade direct communication between the bishops of his realms and the pope. He regarded most orders of monks and nuns as unproductive. Consequently, he dissolved over 600 monasteries and confiscated their lands, although he excepted certain orders that ran schools or hospitals. He also dissolved the traditional Roman Catholic seminaries, which he believed taught priests too great a loyalty to the papacy and too little concern for their future parishioners. In their place he sponsored eight general seminaries that emphasized parish duties. In effect, Joseph's policies made Roman Catholic priests the employees of the state and ended the influence of the church as an independent institution in Habsburg lands. In many respects, the ecclesiastical policies of Joseph II, known as *Josephinism*, prefigured those of the French Revolution.

Towards serfdom and the land, Joseph II again pursued policies initiated by Maria Theresa to more far-reaching ends. During his reign he introduced reforms that touched the heart of rural society. He abolished the legal status of serfdom defined in terms of servitude to another person. He gave peasants much more personal freedom. They could marry, engage in skilled work, or have their children trained in such skills without permission of the landlord. The procedures of the manorial courts were reformed, and avenues of appeal to royal officials were opened. Joseph also encouraged landlords to change land leases, so that it would be easier for peasants to inherit them or to transfer them to another peasant without bringing into doubt the landlord's title of ownership. Joseph believed that reducing traditional burdens would make the peasant tillers of the land more productive and industrious.

In 1789 Joseph proposed a new and daring system of land taxation. All proprietors were to be taxed, regardless of social status. No longer were the peasants alone to bear the burden of taxation. He commuted compulsory service into a monetary tax, split between the landlord and the state. The decree was drawn up, but resistance from the nobles delayed its implementation. Then in 1790 Joseph died, and the decree never went into effect. However, his measures had stirred up turmoil throughout the Habsburg realms.

Peasants revolted over disagreements about the interpretation of their newly granted rights. The nobles of the various realms protested the taxation scheme.

On Joseph's death, the crown went to his brother Leopold II (r. 1790–1792). Although sympathetic to Joseph's goals, Leopold had to repeal many of the most controversial decrees, such as that changing taxation.

Catherine the Great of Russia

Joseph II never grasped the practical necessity of cultivating political support for his policies. Catherine II (r. 1762–1796), who had been born a German princess, understood only too well the fragility of the Romanov dynasty's power base.

After the death of Peter the Great in 1725, the court nobles and the army had determined the Russian succession. As a result, the crown fell into the hands of people with little talent until 1741, when Peter's daughter Elizabeth came to the throne. At her death in 1762 Elizabeth was succeeded by Peter III, one of her nephews. He was a weak and possibly insane ruler who had been married in 1745 to a

Catherine the Great ascended to the Russian throne after the murder of her husband. She tried initially to enact major reforms, but she never intended to abandon absolutism. She assured the nobility of their rights and by the end of her reign had imposed press censorship. *The Granger Collection.*

Chronology

Russia from Peter the Great Through Catherine the Great

1725	Death of Peter the Great
1741–1762	Elizabeth
1762	Peter III
1762	Catherine II (the Great) becomes empress
1767	Legislative Commission summoned
1768	War with Turkey
1771–1774	Pugachev's Rebellion
1772	First Partition of Poland
1774	Treaty of Kuchuk-Kainardji ends war with Turkey
1775	Reorganization of local government
1783	Russia annexes the Crimea
1785	Catherine issues the Charter of the Nobility
1793	Second Partition of Poland
1795	Third Partition of Poland
1796	Death of Catherine the Great

young German princess, the future Catherine the Great. Catherine had neither love nor loyalty for her demented husband. After a few months of rule Peter III was deposed and murdered with Catherine's approval, if not aid. On his deposition she was immediately proclaimed empress.

Catherine's familiarity with the Enlightenment and the general culture of Western Europe convinced her that Russia must make major reforms if it were to remain a great power. Since she had come to the throne through a palace coup, she understood that any major reform must enjoy wide political and social support.

Consequently, in 1767 Catherine summoned a Legislative Commission to advise her on revising the law and government of Russia. There were over 500 delegates drawn from all sectors of Russian life. Before the commission convened, Catherine wrote a set of *Instructions*, containing ideas drawn from the political writings of the *philosophes*. The revision of Russian law, however, did not occur for more than half a century. In 1768 Catherine dismissed the commission before several of its key committees had reported.

Yet the commission had gathered a vast amount of information about the conditions of local administration and economic life throughout Russia. The inconclusive debates and the absence of programs from the delegates themselves suggested that most Russians saw no alternative to an autocratic monarchy. Catherine herself had no intention of departing from absolutism.

Catherine proceeded to carry out limited reforms on her own authority. She supported the rights and local power of the nobility. In 1775 she reorganized local government to solve problems brought to light by the Legislative Commission. She put most local offices into the hands of nobles rather than creating a royal bureaucracy. In 1785 Catherine issued the Charter of the Nobility, which guaranteed many noble rights and privileges. She issued a similar charter to

Charter of Nobility. Granted by Empress Catherine II in 1785, this charter concluded the legal consolidation of Russian nobility as a class and provided for its political and corporate rights, privileges, and principles of self-organization. In this printing, the imperial title is hand written in gold and is surrounded by engraved coats of arms of the provinces of the Russian Empire. *Zhalovannaia Gramota Dvorianstvu* (Charter Granted to the Nobility), *1785. Rare Book Collection. Law Library*, Library of Congress.

Map 22–2. Expansion of Russia, 1689–1796. The overriding territorial aim of the two most powerful Russian monarchs of the eighteenth century, Peter the Great (in the first quarter of the century) and Catherine the Great (in the last half of the century) was to secure navigable outlets to the sea in both the north and the south for Russia's vast empire; hence Peter's push to the Baltic Sea and Catherine's to the Black Sea. Russia also expanded into Central Asia and Siberia during this time period.

the towns of her realms. In part, the empress had to favor the nobles. There were too few educated subjects in her realm to establish an independent bureaucracy, and the treasury could not afford an army strictly loyal to the crown. So Catherine wisely made a virtue of necessity. She strengthened the stability of her crown by a convenient alliance with her nobles and urban leaders.

Catherine continued the Russian drive for warm-water ports (see Map 22–2). This led to warfare with the Turks between 1768 and 1774, when the Treaty of Kuchuk-Kainardji gave Russia a direct outlet on the Black Sea, free navigation rights in its waters, and free access through the Bosphorus. Moreover, the Crimea became an independent state, which Catherine painlessly annexed in 1783.

The Partition of Poland

These Russian military successes made the other states of Eastern Europe uneasy. Their anxieties were allayed by the First Partition of Poland. The Russian victories along the Danube River in what is today Romania were most unwelcome to Austria, which had its own ambitions there. At the same time, the Ottoman Empire was pressing Prussia for aid against Russia. Frederick the Great made a proposal to Russia and Austria that would give each something it wanted, prevent conflict among them, and save appearances. After long, complicated, secret negotiations, the three powers agreed that Russia would abandon the Danubian provinces in return for a large chunk of Polish territory with almost 2 million inhabitants. As a reward for remaining neutral, Prussia annexed most of the Polish territory between East Prussia and Prussia proper, which allowed Frederick to unite two previously separate sections of his realm. Finally, Austria took Galicia, with its important salt mines, and other Polish territory with over 2.5 million inhabitants. The Polish state had lost approximately one third of its territory.

There were two additional partitions of Poland by Russia and Prussia, and one more by Austria. They occurred in 1793 and 1795 and removed Poland from the map of Europe until 1919. The great powers contended that they were saving themselves, and by implication the rest of Europe, from Polish anarchy. The argument was plausible to some contemporaries because of the fears spurred by the French Revolution. However, the truth was that the political weakness of Poland made the country and its resources a rich field for plunderous aggression.

Summary

The Scientific Revolution. The scientific ideas of the sixteenth and seventeenth centuries changed the way Western intellectuals thought about the world and humankind. Instead of a view of nature and humanity based on Scripture and Divine Revelation, Western thinkers came to rely on mathematical laws, empirical data, and experimentation. Copernicus, Kepler, and Galileo overturned the ancient idea, sanctioned by the Bible, that the Earth was the center of the universe and that the sun and the planets revolved around it. Galileo and Descartes maintained that the world was governed by mathematical laws. Francis Bacon urged the necessity for observation and experimentation. Newton showed the effects of gravity and established an enduring basis for physics. Locke argued that human beings are shaped by their sense experiences and are hence creatures of their environment subject to reform and possible progress.

The Enlightenment. The Enlightenment *philosophes* used reason as a basis for reform and to advocate progressive social, economic, and political movements. Voltaire attacked religious intolerance and advocated strong central government to impose rational solutions to social and political problems. Montesquieu and other *philosophes* argued for limited, constitutional government. Rousseau wished to reform society in the name of virtue rather than material happiness. He maintained that in the pursuit of virtue the needs of society were more important than those of the individual. The competing strands of the Enlightenment continue to pervade Western society.

Enlightened Absolutism. Enlightened absolutism was a form of monarchical government dedicated to the rational

strengthening of the central government. Many of the reforms enlightened monarchs imposed were influenced by the ideas of the *philosophes*, but the chief goal of these rulers was to increase their own authority and military strength, as witnessed by the partitions of Poland among Russia, Prussia, and Austria at the end of the eighteenth century. The most important enlightened monarchs were Frederick II of Prussia, Joseph II of Austria, and Catherine the Great of Russia.

Review Questions

1. What was the Scientific Revolution? What were the major contributions of Copernicus, Brahe, Kepler, Galileo, Bacon, and Newton? Do you think they regarded themselves as revolutionaries?

2. Define the Enlightenment. Is it best seen as a single movement or a series of related movements? What was the relationship of the Enlightenment to the New Sci-

INTERPRETING THE PAST

The Enlightenment and the Quest for Practical Knowledge

Text Sources from MyHistory Lab/ Primary Source DVD

1. Lady Mary Wortley Montagu: *Letters*
2. James Lind, *A Treatise on Scurvy*
3. Immanuel Kant, *Defining the Enlightenment*

Visual Sources from MyHistoryLab/ Primary Source DVD

1. *Drawing of Queen Anne of England Visiting Anton Van Leeuwenhoek* (1698)
2. *Jewish Medical Book: Illustration of the Human Body Compared to a House*
3. Illustration of a *camera obscura* from the *Encyclopedia*

The European Enlightenment was a multifaceted phenomenon, with competing strands of political thought, new social and philosophical theories, and innovative scientific developments that contributed to a public debate about the nature of society. Using reason and empiricism, the *philosophes* attempted to publicize injustice and abuse, particularly by traditional

authority—hereditary monarchs, the aristocracy, and the Church. In so doing, they hoped to reform society by using reason and humor in order to advance the cause of science and rationalism. Their primary tool was the printed word, disseminated in books, journals, and newspapers read by growing numbers of literate people throughout Europe.

This exercise will involve reading three eighteenth century primary sources that document the attempt to develop practical solutions to improve society through the use of rational thought and scientific methods. Although today we take the application of science and technology to solve problems as routine, during this era these were pioneering and often controversial methods, since they intruded on the customary authority of the Church and monarchy.

The first document is written by Lady Mary Wortley Montagu, the wife of the ambassador to Constantinople (capital of the Ottoman Empire) who discusses her observations of Muslim society and particularly the practice of smallpox vaccination. The second document, from James Lind, a Scottish naval surgeon, describes his search for a cure for scurvy, a disease that he discovered was caused by insufficient intake of vitamin C and was fatal if untreated. The third document is from the German *philosophe* Immanuel Kant, who seeks to define the Enlightenment as an empowerment of individuals to think rationally by actively challenging traditional authorence? How did the Enlightenment further the idea of progress and the superiority of European civilization?

3. Why did the *philosophes* believe they must comment so extensively on religion? Why did they criticize Christianity? Why did some of them champion deism? What were the differing views of the philosophes towards Islam?

4. Was there a single Enlightenment view of politics? Why could writers so dedicated to reform have so many different political paths to achieve reform? Why did some Enlightenment writers argue for the superiority of European culture? Why did others criticize European empires?

5. Define enlightened absolutism. What were the similarities in the policies of Frederick the Great, Joseph II, and Catherine the Great? To what extent do their policies actually seem to stem from the ideas of the Enlightenment *philosophes*?

ity. The accompanying images illustrate how information about technological and medical advances were circulated in printed images.

Use the source documents and the images to enter the world of the *philosophes* and those allied with them in the effort to use reason to improve society. Use specific examples from the documents to back up your assertions.

Questions

How did the experience of living in Constantinople (Istanbul) change Lady Mary's outlook? How would she have come to be aware of Ottoman medical practices such as vaccination? How does she compare the life of the elites in Ottoman society with the life of peasants?

How did James Lind discover a cure for scurvy? Was the "scientific method" involved? If so, how?

How do the visual sources for this exercise illustrate the use of reason, science, and technology to improve human society?

How do the authors of the first two documents adhere to (or not adhere to) Immanuel Kant's plea for individuals to empower themselves in the quest for knowledge?

Key Terms

deism (p. 687)

empiricism (p. 680)

Enlightenment (p. 686)

laissez-faire (p. 693)

philosophes (p. 686)

Ptolemaic system (p. 678)

Scientific Revolution (p. 677)

Note: To learn more about the topics in this chapter, please turn to the Suggested Readings at the end of the book. For additional sources related to this chapter please see the Primary Source DVD at the back of this text or MyHistoryLab.

23

Revolutions in the Transatlantic World

- ◆ Revolution in the British Colonies in North America
- ◆ Revolution in France
- ◆ Wars of Independence in Latin America
- ◆ Towards the Abolition of Slavery in the Transatlantic Economy

ETWEEN 1776 AND 1824 A WORLD-TRANSFORMING series of revolutions occurred in France and the Americas. In half a century the peoples of the two American continents established their independence of European political control. In Europe the French monarchy collapsed from the forces of aristocratic resistance and popular revolution. All the revolutionary leaders sought to establish new governments based largely, though never entirely, on Enlightenment principles.

From start to finish these revolutions were connected. The financial pressures from the Seven Years' War (1756–1763) had led Britain, Spain, and France to undertake a search for revenue that politically destabilized the Americas and France itself. Once the American Revolution began, France aided the colonists, thus exacerbating its own financial problem. In turn the French Revolution and the ensuing

Guerilla Warfare. Haitian slaves ambush French forces during their successful revolt led by Toussaint L'Ouverture and Jean-Jacques Dessalines in 1794. The Haitian revolution was the largest emancipation of slaves to occur in the eighteenth century.

The Transatlantic Revolutions

The Atlantic World

The revolutions and the crusade against slavery that occurred throughout the transatlantic world between 1776 and the 1830s transformed the political, social, and economic life of three continents. First in North America, then in France and other parts of Europe, and finally in South America bold political experiments challenged colonial government, monarchies, and aristocratic governments and laid the foundations for modern liberal democracy. These revolutions and the effort to abolish slavery owed much to the philosophical inspiration of the Enlightenment and bear witness to the immense influence of the Enlightenment in world history.

As a result of the events of this age of transatlantic revolution the largest republic since ancient times was established in North America. In Europe the absolutist governments were overthrown across the continent by the impact of the French Revolution and the armies of Napoleon. Slaves on Haiti overthrew the French colonial regime and established the first black republic. By the close of the first quarter of the nineteenth century wars of independence across Latin America had closed the era of European empire with the establishment of republics everywhere except Brazil.

No less important this era witnessed the beginning of an international effort to bring about the abolition of the slave economies that had long dominated the transatlantic economy.

The expanding forms of political liberty found their counterparts in an economic life freed from the constraints of the old colonial empires and eventually from the economies based on plantation slave labor. The new American republic constituted a vast free trade zone with its commerce and ports open to the entire world.

For the first time since the encounter with Europe, all of Latin America could trade freely with its own peoples and those of the rest of the world.

In Europe the reforms of the French Revolution and the new Napoleonic Code of law removed many regional economic barriers and led to more standard weights and measures.

National law formed the framework for economic activity. The movement to abolish slavery fostered a wage economy

Napoleonic Wars created situations in Spain and Portugal to which the colonial elites in Latin America responded by seeking independence. Thus the transatlantic revolutions, despite their individual characters and developments, were interconnected events in world history. Furthermore, the era witnessed the commencement of a vast international crusade, first to abolish the slave trade and then to abolish slavery in the transatlantic world. The same Enlightenment ideas that inspired many of the revolutionaries also inspired the opponents of slavery as did religious convictions. The political and economic dislocations of the revolutionary era helped the anti-slavery forces achieve their goals. The political, social, and economic life of the transatlantic world would never be the same again. ∎

Revolution in the British Colonies in North America

Resistance to the Imperial Search for Revenue

After the Treaty of Paris in 1763 ended the Seven Years' War (see Chapter 20), the British government faced two imperial problems. The first was the sheer cost of empire, which the of free laborers. That kind of economy generated its own set of problems and social dislocation, including a sort of share-cropping serfdom for many former slaves, but it was nonetheless an economy of free human beings who were the chattel of no other human being.

Finally, the age of transatlantic revolutions saw the emergence of nationalism as a political force. All of the revolutions, because of their popular political base, had given power to the idea of nations defined by their own character and historical past rather than by dynastic rulers. Americans saw themselves as forming a new kind of nation. The French had demonstrated the power of a nation fully mobilized for military purposes. In turn the aggression of France had aroused national sentiment, especially in Great Britain, Spain, and Germany. The new nations of Latin America also sought to define themselves by their heritage and historical experience rather than by their past in the Spanish and Portuguese empires.

These various revolutions, their political doctrines, and their social and economic departures provided examples to peoples elsewhere in the world. But even more important, the transformations of the transatlantic revolutions and eventual abolition of slavery meant that new political classes and newly organized independent nations would become actors on the world scene. Europeans would have to deal with a score of new nations in the Americas. The rest of the world confronted new nations freed from the direction and authority of European powers. In turn, the political changes in Europe meant that those nations and their relationships with the rest of the world would be directed by a broader range of political groups and forces than in the past. Ironically, however, by the close of the nineteenth century several of the European nations as well as the United States that had become liberal democratic states would commence a new wave of colonialism throughout Africa and Asia and would impose new economic dominance on the republics of Latin America.

Focus Questions

◆ What is the relationship between the Enlightenment and the transatlantic revolutions? Between the Enlightenment and the crusade against slavery?

◆ How did the transatlantic revolutions fundamentally alter the relationship between Europe and the Americas?

◆ What is the relationship between the transatlantic revolutions and nationalism? Why did such a relationship exist?

British felt they could no longer carry alone. The second was that the defeat of the French required the British to organize a vast expanse of new territory: all of North America east of the Mississippi, with its French settlers and, more important, its native Indian population (see Map 23–1).

The British drive for revenue began in 1764 with the Sugar Act, which attempted to produce more revenue from imports into the colonies by the rigorous collection of what was actually a reduced tax on sugar. Smugglers were to be tried in admiralty courts without juries. The next year, Parliament passed the Stamp Act, which put a tax on legal documents and certain other items such as newspapers. The British considered these taxes legal and just because they had been approved by Parliament and because the revenue was to be spent in the colonies. The Americans responded that they alone through their assemblies had the right to tax themselves and that they were not represented in Parliament. Furthermore, the Americans feared that if colonial government were financed from Britain, they would cease to control it.

In October 1765 the Stamp Act Congress met in America and drew up a protest to the Crown. (See Document, "The Stamp Act Congress Addresses George III.") There was much disorder in the colonies, particularly in Massachusetts, led by groups known as the Sons of Liberty. The colonists agreed to boycott British goods. In 1766 Parliament repealed the Stamp Act but, through the Declaratory Act, claimed the power to legislate for the colonies.

Map 23–1.   North America in 1763. In the year of the victory over France, the English colonies lay along the Atlantic seaboard. The difficulties of organizing authority over the previous French territory in Canada and west of the Appalachian Mountains would contribute to the tensions that would precipitate the American Revolution.

American Political Ideas

The political ideas of the American colonists had largely arisen from the struggle of seventeenth-century English aristocrats and gentry against the absolutism of the Stuart monarchs. The American colonists believed that the English Revolution of 1688 had established many of their own fundamental political liberties. The colonists claimed that, through the measures imposed from 1763 to 1776, George III (r. 1760–1820) and the British Parliament were attacking those liberties and dissolving the bonds of moral and political allegiance that had formerly united the two peoples. Consequently, the colonists employed a theory that had originally been developed to justify an aristocratic rebellion in England to support their own popular revolution.

These Whig political ideas, largely derived from John Locke (1632–1704), were only a part of the English ideological heritage that affected the Americans. Throughout the eighteenth century they had become familiar with a series of British political writers called the *Commonwealthmen*. These writers held republican political ideas that had their intellectual roots in the most radical thought of the Puritan revolution. They had relentlessly criticized the government patronage and parliamentary management of Robert Walpole (1676–1745) and his successors. They argued that such government was corrupt and that it undermined liberty. They regarded much parliamentary taxation as simply a means of financing political corruption. They also attacked standing armies as instruments of tyranny. In Great Britain this republican political tradition had only a marginal impact. Most Britons regarded themselves as the freest people in the world. In the colonies, however, these radical books and pamphlets were read widely and were often accepted at face value. The policy of Great Britain towards America after the Treaty of Paris made many colonists believe that the worst fears of the Commonwealthmen were coming true.

Crisis and Independence

In 1767 Charles Townshend (1725–1767) led Parliament to regulate and tax colonial imports. The colonists again resisted. The ministry sent over its own customs agents to administer the laws. To protect these new officers, the

Boston Massacre. This view of the Boston Massacre of March 5, 1770, by Paul Revere owes more to propaganda than to fact. There was no order to fire, and the innocent citizens portrayed here were really an angry, violent mob. *The Granger Collection, New York.*

The Stamp Act Congress Addresses George III

Document

In 1765 the Stamp Act Congress met to protest the British imposition of taxes on the colonies. American leaders believed Great Britain had no right to impose such taxation. Their argument was that they were not and could not be represented in Parliament and that they were subject to the taxation only of their own assemblies. Later clauses implied that the taxation would prevent the colonists from purchasing manufactured goods from Britain and demanded the repeal of the act.

◆ Why does the Congress insist on the same rights for subjects born in the colonies as those born in England? On what grounds does the Congress declare that Parliament may not levy taxes in the colonies? Why is the Congress so concerned about what courts may try cases arising from the Stamp Act?

The Members of this Congress, sincerely devoted, with the warmest sentiments of affection and duty to His Majesty's person and government . . . and with minds deeply impressed by a sense of the present and impending misfortunes of the British colonies on this continent; having considered as maturely as time will permit, the circumstances of the said colonies, esteem it our indispensable duty to make the following declarations of our humble opinion, respecting the most essential rights and liberties of the colonists, and of the grievances under which they labor, by reason of several late acts of Parliament.

1. That His Majesty's subjects in these colonies, owe the same allegiance to the crown of Great Britain, that is owing from his subjects born within the realm, and all due subordination to that august body the Parliament of Great Britain.
2. That His Majesty's liege subjects in these colonies are entitled to all the inherent rights and liberties of his natural born subjects, within the kingdom of Great Britain.
3. That it is inseparably essential to the freedom of a people, and the undoubted right of Englishmen, that no taxes be imposed on them but with their own consent, given personally, or by their representatives.

4. That the people of these colonies are not, and cannot, be represented in the House of Commons in Great Britain.
5. That the only representatives of the people of these colonies are persons chosen therein by themselves, and that no taxes ever have been, or can be constitutionally imposed on them, but by their respective legislatures.
6. That all supplies to the crown being free gifts of the people, it is unreasonable and inconsistent with the principles and spirit of the British constitution, for the people of Great Britain to grant to His Majesty the property of the colonists.
7. That trial by jury, is the inherent and invaluable right of every British subject in these colonies.
8. That the late act of Parliament entitled, *An act for granting and supplying certain stamp duties, and other duties, in the British colonies and plantations, in America, etc.* by imposing taxes on the inhabitants of these colonies, and the said act, and several other acts, by extending the jurisdiction of the courts of admiralty beyond its ancient limits, have a manifest tendency to subvert the rights and liberties of the colonists.

From *Journal of the First Congress of the American Colonies . . .* 1765 (New York, 1845), pp. 27–29, as quoted in Oscar Handlin, ed., *Readings in American History.* Copyright © 1957 Alfred A. Knopf, pp. 116–117.

British sent troops to Boston in 1768. The obvious tensions resulted, and in March 1770 British troops killed five citizens in the Boston Massacre. In that same year Parliament repealed the Townshend duties except for the one on tea.

In May 1773 Parliament allowed the East India Company to import tea directly into the American colonies. Although the law lowered the price of tea, it retained the tax without the colonists' consent. In some cities the colonists refused to

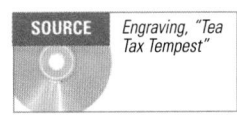
SOURCE Engraving, "Tea Tax Tempest"

permit the tea to be unloaded; in Boston, a shipload of tea was thrown into the harbor, an event known since as the Boston Tea Party.

The British ministry of Lord North (1732–1792) was determined to assert the authority of Parliament over the resistant colonies. In 1774 Parliament passed a series of laws known in American history as the Intolerable Acts. These measures closed the port of Boston, reorganized the government of Massachusetts, allowed troops to be quartered in private homes, and removed the trials of royal customs officials to England. In the same year Parliament approved the Quebec Act, which extended the boundaries of Quebec to include the Ohio River valley. The Americans regarded the Quebec Act as an attempt to prevent the extension of their mode of self-government westward beyond the Appalachian Mountains.

During these years committees of correspondence, composed of citizens critical of Britain, had been established throughout the colonies. In September 1774 these committees organized the First Continental Congress in Philadelphia. This body hoped to persuade Parliament to restore self-government in the colonies and to abandon its attempt at direct supervision of colonial affairs. Conciliation, however, was not forthcoming. By April 1775 the battles of Lexington and Concord had been fought. In June the colonists were defeated at the Battle of Bunker Hill.

The Second Continental Congress gathered in May 1775. It still sought conciliation with Britain but soon undertook the government of the colonies. By August 1775 George III had declared the colonies in rebellion. During the winter Thomas Paine's (1737–1809) pamphlet *Common Sense* galvanized public opinion in favor of separation from Great Britain. A colonial army and navy were organized. In April 1776 the Continental Congress opened American ports to the trade of all nations. Finally, on July 4, 1776, the Continental Congress adopted the Declaration of Independence. Thereafter, the War of the American Revolution continued until 1781, when the forces of George Washington (1732–1799) defeated those of Lord Cornwallis (1738–1805) at Yorktown. Early in 1778, however, the war had widened into a European conflict when Benjamin Franklin (1706–1790) persuaded the French government to support the rebellion. In 1779 the Spanish also came to the aid of the colonies. The 1783 Treaty of Paris concluded the conflict, and the thirteen American colonies had established their independence.

As the crisis with Britain unfolded during the 1760s and 1770s, the American colonists came to see themselves as first preserving traditional English liberties against a tyrannical Crown and corrupt Parliament and then as developing a new sense of liberty. By the mid-1770s the colonists had embraced republican political ideals. They would govern themselves through elected assemblies without any monarchical authority. The Constitutional Convention met in 1787. After the constitution was adopted in 1788, Americans would insist on a bill of rights specifically protecting civil liberties. The Americans would reject the aristocratic social hierarchy that had existed in the colonies. They would embrace democratic ideals, even if the franchise remained limited. They would assert the equality of white male citizens not only before the law but also in ordinary social relations. They would reject social status

based on birth and inheritance and assert the necessity of liberty for all citizens to improve their social standing and economic lot by engaging in free commercial activity. They did not free their slaves, nor did they address the rights of women or Native Americans, but the American Revolution produced a society freer than any the world had seen, one that would expand the circle of political and social liberty. The American Revolution was a genuinely radical movement, the influence of which would increase as Americans moved across the continent and as other peoples began to question traditional European government. The political and social values of the American Revolution would inspire the wars of independence in Latin America and, to a lesser extent, both liberal and radical political movements in Europe.

Revolution in France

The French monarchy emerged from the Seven Years' War both defeated and deeply in debt. The later French support for the American Revolution exacerbated the financial difficulties. Given the economic vitality of France, the government debt

Chronology

The American Revolution

1760	George III becomes king
1763	Treaty of Paris concludes the Seven Years' War
1764	Sugar Act
1765	Stamp Act
1766	Sugar Act repealed and Declaratory Act passed
1767	Townshend Acts
1770	Lord North becomes George III's chief minister
1770	Boston Massacre
1773	Boston Tea Party
1774	Intolerable Acts
1774	First Continental Congress
1775	Second Continental Congress
1776	Declaration of Independence
1778	France enters the war on the side of America
1781	British forces surrender at Yorktown
1783	Treaty of Paris concludes War of the American Revolution

was neither overly large nor disproportionate to the debts of other European powers. The problem was the government's inability to collect sufficient taxes to service and repay the debt.

Between 1786 and 1788 Louis XVI (r. 1774–1792) appointed several different ministers to deal with the financial crisis. All failed to persuade the aristocracy and the church to pay more taxes. As these negotiations dragged on, the *parlement* of Paris declared that only the Estates General could institute new taxes. The Estates General had not met since 1614. Consequently, in July 1788, Louis XVI agreed to convene the Estates General the next year.

Revolutions of 1789

The Estates General Becomes the National Assembly The Estates General had three divisions: the First Estate of the clergy, the Second Estate of the nobility, and the **Third Estate**, representing everyone else in the kingdom. Before the Estates General met at Versailles in May 1789, there had been much public debate over its organization. The monarchy had agreed that the Third Estate should have twice as many members as either the nobility or the clergy. Then there arose the question of how voting should be organized. The nobility wanted all votes to be taken by Estate, which would have allowed the nobles and clergy to outvote the Third Estate. The Third Estate wanted each member to vote individually so that, with its larger membership, it would dominate.

From the beginning the Third Estate, composed largely of local officials, professional men, and lawyers, refused to sit as a separate order as the king desired. For several weeks there was a stand-off. Then, on June 1 the Third Estate invited the clergy and the nobles to join it in organizing a new legislative body. A few of the lower clergy did so. On June 17 that body declared itself the National Assembly.

Three days later, finding themselves accidentally locked out of their usual meeting place, the National Assembly moved to a nearby tennis court, where its members took the famous Tennis Court Oath to continue to sit until they had given France a constitution. Louis XVI ordered the National Assembly to desist, but shortly afterward most of the clergy and many nobles joined the assembly. On June 27 the king capitulated and formally requested the First and Second Estates to meet with the National Assembly, where voting would occur by head rather than by order. Government by the privileged orders thus ended, and the National Assembly became the National Constituent Assembly.

Fall of the Bastille Two new factors soon intruded. First, Louis XVI attempted to regain the initiative by mustering troops near Versailles and Paris. This was the beginning of a steady, and consistently poorly executed, royal attempt to halt the revolution. Most of the National Constituent Assembly

Storming of the Bastille. On July 14, 1789, crowds stormed the Bastille, a prison in Paris. This event, whose only practical effect was to free a few prisoners, marked the first time the populace of Paris redirected the course of the revolution. *Anonymous, France, eighteenth century, "Seige of the Bastille, 14 July, 1789." Musée de la Ville de Paris, Musée Carnavalet, Paris, France. Bridgeman-Giraudon/Art Resource, N.Y.*

wished to create some form of constitutional monarchy, but from the start Louis's refusal to cooperate thwarted that effort.

The second new factor was the populace of Paris. The mustering of royal troops created anxiety in the city, where there had been several bread riots. By June the Parisians were organizing a citizen militia and collecting arms.

On July 14 around 800 people, mostly small shopkeepers, tradespeople, artisans, and wage earners, marched to the Bastille in search of weapons for the militia. This great fortress had once held political prisoners. Through miscalculations and ineptitude by the governor of the fortress, the troops in the Bastille fired into the crowd, killing ninety-eight people and wounding many others. The crowd then stormed the fortress, released its seven prisoners, none of whom was there for political reasons, and killed several soldiers and the governor. They found no weapons.

This was the first of many crucial *journées*, or days, when the populace of Paris would redirect the course of the revolution. The fall of the Bastille signaled that the political future of the nation would not be decided solely by the National Constituent Assembly. As the news spread, similar disturbances took place in the provincial cities. A few days later Louis XVI, again bowing to events, came to Paris and recognized both the new elected government of the city and its National Guard. The citizens of Paris were, for the time, being satisfied.

The Great Fear and Surrender of Feudal Privileges As popular urban disturbances erupted in various cities, a movement known as the *Great Fear* swept across much of the French countryside. Peasants were reclaiming rights and property that they had lost through the aristocratic resurgence of the last quarter century, as well as venting their anger against the injustices of rural life. The Great Fear, which was an intensification of peasant disturbances that had begun during the spring, witnessed the burning of châteaux, the destruction of records and documents, and the refusal by peasants to pay feudal dues.

On the night of August 4, 1789, aristocrats in the National Constituent Assembly attempted to halt the disorder in the countryside. By prearrangement, liberal nobles and churchmen rose in the assembly and surrendered hunting and fishing rights, judicial authority, tithes, and special exemptions. In a sense, these nobles gave up what they had already lost and what they could not have regained without civil war. Later, many would also be compensated for their losses. Nonetheless, after August 4 all French citizens were subject to the same and equal laws.

Declaration of the Rights of Man and Citizen

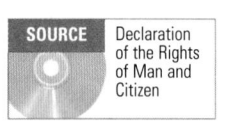

On August 27, 1789, the assembly issued the *Declaration of the Rights of Man and Citizen*. This declaration drew together much of the political language of the Enlightenment and was also influenced by the Declaration of Rights adopted by Virginia in America in June 1776. The French declaration proclaimed that all men were "born and remain free and equal in rights." Their natural rights were "liberty, property, security, and resistance to oppression." Governments existed to protect those rights. All political sovereignty resided in the nation and its representatives. All citizens were to be equal before the law and were to be "equally admissible to all public dignities, offices and employments, according to their capacity, and with no other distinction than that of their virtues and talents." There were to be due process of law and presumption of innocence until proof of guilt. Freedom of religion was affirmed. Taxation was to be apportioned equally according to capacity to pay. Property constituted "an inviolable and sacred right."[1]

Louis XVI stalled before ratifying both the declaration and the aristocratic renunciation of feudalism. His hesitations fanned suspicions that he might try to resort to force. Moreover, bread shortages continued. On October 5 several thousand Parisian women marched to Versailles, demanding more bread. This was one of several occasions when women played a major role in the actions of the Parisian crowd. (See Document, "French Women Petition to Bear Arms.") On this day they milled about the palace, and many stayed the night. Under this pressure the king agreed to sanction the

---

[1] Quoted in Georges Lefebvre, *The Coming of the French Revolution,* trans. by R. R. Palmer (Princeton, NJ: Princeton University Press, 1967), pp. 221–223.

Women's March. The women of Paris marched to Versailles on October 7, 1789. The following day the royal family was forced to return to Paris with them. Henceforth, the French government would function under the constant threat of mob violence. *Anonymous, eighteenth century, "To Versailles, to Versailles." The Women of Paris going to Versailles, October 7, 1789. French, Musée de la Ville de Paris, Musée Carnavalet, Paris, France. Photograph copyright Bridgeman-Giraudon/Art Resource, N.Y.*

decrees of the assembly. The Parisians believed that the king had to be kept under the watchful eye of the people. Consequently they demanded that Louis and his family return to Paris. The monarch had no real choice. On October 6, 1789, his carriage followed the crowd into the city, where he and his family settled in the palace of the Tuileries. The National Constituent Assembly soon followed. Thereafter, both Paris and France remained relatively stable and peaceful until the summer of 1792.

Reconstruction of France

Once established in Paris, the National Constituent Assembly set about reorganizing France. Throughout its proceedings the Assembly was determined to protect property and to limit the impact on national life of small-property owners as well as of the unpropertied elements of the nation. While championing civic equality before the law, the Assembly spurned social equality and extensive democracy. The Assembly thus charted a general course that, to a greater or lesser degree, nineteenth-century liberals across Europe and in other areas of the world would follow.

Political Reorganization

The Constitution of 1791, the product of the National Constituent Assembly's deliberations, established a constitutional monarchy. There was a unicameral Legislative Assembly vested with powers of war and peace. The monarch could delay but not halt legislation. The system of voting was complex and restricted. Only about 50,000 citizens of the French nation of 26 million could actually elect or serve in the Legislative Assembly.

French Women Petition to Bear Arms

The issue of women serving in the revolutionary French military appeared early in the revolution. In March 1792 Pauline Léon presented a petition to the National Assembly on behalf of more than 300 Parisian women asking the right to bear arms and train for military service for the revolution. Similar requests were made during the next two years. Some women did serve in the military, but in 1793 legislation specifically forbade it on the grounds that women belonged in the domestic sphere and that military service would lead them to abandon family duties.

◆ "Citoyenne" is the feminine form of the French word for citizen. How does this petition seek to challenge the concept of citizenship in the French *Declaration of the Rights of Man and Citizen*? How do these petitioners relate their demand to bear arms to their role as women in French society? How do the petitioners relate their demands to the use of all national resources against the enemies of the revolution?

Patriotic women come before you to claim the right which any individual has to defend his life and liberty.

. . . We are citoyennes [female citizens], and we cannot be indifferent to the fate of the fatherland.

. . . Yes, Gentlemen, we need arms, and we come to ask your permission to procure them. May our weakness be no obstacle; courage and intrepidity will supplant it, and the love of the fatherland and hatred of tyrants will allow us to brave all dangers with ease. . . .

No, Gentlemen, We will [use arms] only to defend ourselves the same as you; you cannot refuse us, and society cannot deny the right nature gives us, unless you pretend the *Declaration of Rights* does not apply to women and that they should let their throats be cut like lambs, without the right to defend themselves. For can you believe the tyrants would spare us? . . . Why then not terrorize aristocracy and tyranny with all the resources of civic effort and the pure zeal, zeal which cold men can well call fanaticism and exaggeration, but which is only the natural result of a heart burning with love for the public weal? . . .

. . . If, for reasons we cannot guess, you refuse our just demands, these women you have raised to the ranks of citoyennes by granting that title to their husbands, these women who have sampled the promises of liberty, who have conceived the hope of placing free men in the world, and who have sworn to live free or die—such women, I say, will never consent to concede the day to slaves; they will die first. They will uphold their oath, and a dagger aimed at their breasts will deliver them from the misfortunes of slavery! They will die, regretting not life,

but the uselessness of their death; regretting moreover, not having been able to drench their hands in the impure blood of the enemies of the fatherland and to avenge some of their own!

But, Gentlemen, let us cast our eyes away from these cruel extremes. Whatever the rages and plots of aristocrats, they will not succeed in vanquishing a whole people of united brothers armed to defend their rights. We also demand only the honor of sharing their exhaustion and glorious labors and of making tyrants see that women also have blood to shed for the service of the fatherland in danger.

Gentlemen, here is what we hope to obtain from your justice and equity:

1. Permission to procure pikes, pistols, and sabres (even muskets for those who are strong enough to use them), within police regulations.
2. Permission to assemble on festival days and Sundays on the Champ de la Fédération, or in other suitable places, to practice maneuvers with these arms.
3. Permission to name the former French Guards to command us, always in conformity with the rules which the mayor's wisdom prescribes for good order and public calm.

From "French Women Petition to Bear Arms" in *Women in Revolutionary Paris, 1789–1795*, trans. by Darline Gay Levy, Harriet Branson Applewhite, and Mary Durham Johnson. © 1979 by the Board of Trustees of the University of Illinois. Used with permission of the authors and the University of Illinois Press.

The exclusion of women from both voting and holding office did not pass unnoticed. In 1791 Olympe de Gouges (d. 1793), a butcher's daughter who became a major radical in Paris, composed a *Declaration of the Rights of Woman*, which she ironically addressed to Queen Marie Antoinette (1755–1793). Much of the document reprinted the *Declaration of the Rights of Man and Citizen*, adding the word *woman* to the various original clauses. That strategy demanded that women be regarded as citizens and not merely as daughters, sisters, wives, and mothers of citizens. Olympe de Gouges further outlined rights that would permit women to own property and require men to recognize the paternity of their children. She called for equality of the sexes in marriage and improved education for women. She declared, "Women, wake up; the tocsin of reason is being heard throughout the whole universe; discover your rights."[2] Her demands illustrated how the public listing of rights in the *Declaration of the Rights of Man and Citizen* created universal civic expectations even among those it did not cover.

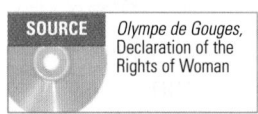

The National Constituent Assembly abolished the ancient French provinces, such as Burgundy, and replaced them with eighty-three departments (*départements*) of generally equal size named after rivers, mountains, and other geographical features. The ancient judicial courts, including the seigneurial courts and the *parlements*, were suppressed and replaced by established uniform courts with elected judges and prosecutors. Legal procedures were simplified, and the most degrading punishments abolished.

Economic Policy

In economic matters the National Constituent Assembly suppressed the guilds and liberated the grain trade. The assembly established the metric system to provide the nation with uniform weights and measures. These policies of economic freedom and uniformity disappointed both peasants and urban workers caught in the cycle of inflation. By the decrees of 1790 the Assembly placed the burden of proof on the peasants to rid themselves of the residual feudal dues for which compensation was to be paid. On June 14, 1791, the Assembly enacted the Chapelier Law forbidding worker associations, thereby crushing the attempts of urban workers to protect their wages. Peasants and workers were to be left to the mercy of the free marketplace.

The National Constituent Assembly decided to pay the troublesome royal debt by confiscating and then selling the lands of the Roman Catholic Church in France.

The Assembly then authorized the issuance of **assignats**, or government bonds, the value of which was guaranteed by the revenue to be generated from the sale of church property. When the *assignats* began to circulate as currency, the Assembly issued even larger quantities of them to liquidate the national debt. However, within a few months the value of *assignats* began to fall. Inflation increased and put new stress on the lives of the urban poor.

Civil Constitution of the Clergy

In July 1790 the National Constituent Assembly issued the Civil Constitution of the Clergy, which transformed the Roman Catholic Church in France into a branch of the secular state. This measure reduced the number of bishoprics, made borders of dioceses conform to those of the new departments, and provided for the election of priests and bishops, who henceforth became salaried employees of the state. The Assembly consulted neither the pope nor the French clergy about these broad changes. The king approved the measure only with the greatest reluctance.

The Civil Constitution of the Clergy was the major blunder of the National Constituent Assembly. The measure roused immense opposition within the French church, even from bishops who had long championed Gallican liberties over papal domination. Faced with this resistance, the Assembly unwisely ruled that all clergy must take an oath to support the Civil Constitution. Only seven bishops and about half the clergy did so. In reprisal, the assembly designated the clergy who had not taken the oath as "refractory" and removed them from their clerical functions. Refractory priests immediately attempted to celebrate Mass.

In February 1791 the pope condemned not only the Civil Constitution of the Clergy but also the *Declaration of the Rights of Man and Citizen*. That condemnation marked the opening of a Roman Catholic offensive against liberalism in Europe and revolution throughout the world that continued for over a century. Within France itself, the pope's action meant that religious devotion and revolutionary loyalty became incompatible for many people. French citizens quickly divided between those who supported the constitutional priests and those who resorted to the refractory clergy. Louis XVI and his family favored the latter.

Counterrevolutionary Activity

In the summer of 1791 the queen and some nobles who had already left the country persuaded Louis XVI also to flee. The escape failed when Louis, along with his family, was recognized and stopped in the town of Varennes. On June 24 soldiers escorted the royal family back to Paris. Thereafter, the leaders of the National Constituent Assembly knew that the chief counterrevolutionary sat on the French throne.

---

[2] Quoted in Sara E. Melzer and Leslie W. Rabine, eds., *Rebel Daughters: Women and the French Revolution* (New York: Oxford University Press, 1992), p. 88.

Two months later, on August 27, 1791, Emperor Leopold II of Austria (r. 1790–1792), who was the brother of Marie Antoinette, and Frederick William II (r. 1786–1797), the king of Prussia, issued the Declaration of Pillnitz. The two monarchs promised to intervene in France to protect the royal family and to preserve the monarchy if the other major European powers agreed. The latter provision rendered the statement meaningless because Great Britain would not have given its consent. In France, however, the revolutionaries felt surrounded by aristocratic and monarchical foes.

Near its close in September 1791 the National Constituent Assembly forbade any of its own members to sit in the Legislative Assembly then being elected. This new body met on October 1 to confront immense problems.

A Second Revolution

Since the earliest days of the revolution, various clubs of politically like-minded persons had organized themselves in Paris. The best organized were the **Jacobins**, whose name derived from the fact that the group met in a former Dominican (Jacobin) monastery located in the Rue St. Jacques. The Paris club was linked to other local clubs in the provinces. In the Legislative Assembly a group of Jacobins known as the *Girondists* (because many of them came from the department of the Gironde) assumed leadership.[3] They led the Legislative Assembly on April 20, 1792, to declare war on Austria, by this time governed by Francis II (r. 1792–1835) and allied to Prussia.

End of the Monarchy The war radicalized the revolution and led to what is usually called the *second revolution*, which overthrew the constitutional monarchy and established a republic. The war initially went poorly, and the revolution seemed in danger. Late in July, under radical working-class pressure, the government of Paris passed from the elected council to a committee, or commune, of representatives from the sections (municipal wards) of Paris. On August 10, 1792, a large crowd invaded the Tuileries and forced Louis XVI and Marie Antoinette to take refuge in the Legislative Assembly itself. During the disturbance several hundred of the royal Swiss guards and many Parisians died. Thereafter, the royal family was imprisoned in comfortable quarters, but the king was suspended from his political functions.

The Convention and the Role of Sans-Culottes During the first week of September, in what are known as the September Massacres, the Paris Commune summarily killed about

1,200 people in the city jails. Many were aristocrats or priests, but most were simply common criminals. The crowd had assumed that the prisoners were all counterrevolutionaries. The Paris Commune then compelled the Legislative Assembly to call for the election, by universal manhood suffrage, of a new assembly to write a democratic constitution. That body, called the **Convention** after its American counterpart of 1787, met on September 21, 1792.

As its first act the Convention declared France a republic, that is, a nation governed by an elected assembly without a king. The second revolution had been the work of Jacobins more radical than the Girondists and of the people of Paris known as the ***sans-culottes***. The name of the latter means "without breeches," and was derived from the long trousers that, as working people, they wore instead of aristocratic knee breeches. The *sans-culottes* were shopkeepers, artisans, wage earners, and a few factory workers. The politics of the Old Regime had ignored them, and the policies of the National Constituent Assembly had left them victims of unregulated economic liberty. (See Document, "A Pamphleteer Describes a *Sans-Culotte*.")

The *sans-culottes*, whose labor and military service were needed for the war effort, generally knew what they wanted. They sought immediate price controls for relief from food shortages and rising prices. They believed that all people had a right to subsistence and profoundly resented most forms of social inequality. They felt intense hostility towards the aristocracy and the original leaders of the revolution, whom they believed simply wanted to take over the social privileges of the aristocracy. They did not demand the abolition of property, but advocated a community of relatively small-property owners. They were antimonarchical, strongly republican, and suspicious even of representative government.

In contrast, the Jacobins were republicans who sought representative government. Their hatred of the aristocracy did not extend to a general suspicion of wealth. Basically, the Jacobins favored an unregulated economy. However, from Louis XVI's flight to Varennes onward, the more extreme Jacobins began to cooperate with leaders of the Parisian *sans-culottes* and the Paris Commune to overthrow the monarchy. Once the Convention began its deliberations, these advanced Jacobins, known as the Mountain because of their seats high in the assembly hall, worked with *sans-culottes* to carry the revolution forward and win the war.

In December 1792 Louis XVI was put on trial as mere "Citizen Capet" (Capet was the family name of medieval forebears of the royal family). The Girondists sought to spare his life, but the Mountain defeated the effort. By a narrow majority, Louis was convicted of conspiring against the liberty of the people and the security of the state. Condemned to death, he was beheaded on January 21, 1793.

---

[3] The Girondists are also frequently called the *Brissotins* after Jacques-Pierre Brissot (1754–1793), who was their chief representative in early 1792.

A Pamphleteer Describes a *Sans-Culotte*

Document

This document from 1793 describes a *sans-culotte* as a hardworking, useful, patriotic citizen who sacrifices himself to the war effort. It contrasts those virtues with the lazy and unproductive luxury of the noble and the self-interested plottings of the politician.

◆ What social resentments appear in this description? How could these resentments create solidarity among the *sans-culottes* to defend the revolution? How does this document relate civic virtue to work? Where does this document suggest that the *sans-culotte* may need to confront enemies of the republic?

A *sans-culotte* you rogues? He is someone who always goes on foot, who has no millions as you would all like to have, no chateaux, no valets to serve him, and who lives simply with his wife and children, if he has any, on a fourth or fifth story.

He is useful, because he knows how to work in the field, to forge iron, to use a saw, to use a file, to roof a house, to make shoes, and to shed his last drop of blood for the safety of the Republic.

And because he works, you are sure not to meet his person in the Café de Chartres, or in the gaming houses where others conspire and game; nor at the National theatre . . . nor in the literary clubs. . . .

In the evening he goes to his section, not powdered or perfumed, or smartly booted in the hope of catching the eye of the citizenesses in the galleries, but ready to support good proposals with all his might, and to crush those which come from the abominable faction of politicians.

Finally, a *sans-culotte* always has his sabre sharp, to cut off the ears of all enemies of the Revolution; sometimes he even goes out with his pike; but at the first sound of the drum he is ready to leave for the Vendée, for the army of the Alps or for the army of the North. . . .

From "Reply to an Impertinent Question: What Is a Sans-culotte?" April 1793. Reprinted in Walter Markov and Albert Soboul, eds., *Die Sansculotten von Paris*, and republished trans. by Clive Emsley in Merryn Williams, ed., *Revolutions: 1775–1830* (Baltimore, MD: Penguin Books, in association with the Open University, 1971), pp. 100–101.

Execution of Louis XVI. On January 21, 1793, the Convention executed Louis XVI. *Execution of Louis XVI. Aquatint. French, eighteenth century. Musée de la Ville de Paris, Musée Carnavalet, Paris, France. Giraudon/Art Resource, N.Y.*

The next month, the Convention declared war on Great Britain, Holland, and Spain. France was now at war with virtually all of Europe. Civil war soon followed. In March 1793 aristocratic officers and priests commenced a royalist revolt in the Vendée in western France and roused much local popular support. The Girondists had led the country into the war but had proved themselves incapable either of winning it or of suppressing the enemies of the revolution at home. The Mountain stood ready to take up the task.

The Reign of Terror and Its Aftermath

The **Reign of Terror** is the name given to the months of quasijudicial executions and murders stretching from the autumn of 1793 to the midsummer of 1794. The Terror can be understood only in the context of the internal and external wars, on the one hand, and the revolutionary expectations of the Convention and the *sans-culottes*, on the other.

Committee of Public Safety In April 1793 the Convention established a Committee of General Security and a Committee of Public Safety to perform the executive duties of the government. The latter committee eventually enjoyed almost dictatorial power. The committee conceived of their task as saving the revolution from mortal enemies at home and abroad. They generally enjoyed a working political relationship with the *sans-culottes* of Paris, but it was an alliance of expediency for the committee.

The major problem was to secure domestic support for the war. In early June 1793 the Parisian *sans-culottes* invaded the Convention and secured the expulsion of the Girondist members. That gave the Mountain complete control. On June 22 the Convention approved a fully democratic constitution but suspended its operation until after the war emergency. August 23 saw a ***levée en masse***, or general military requisition of population, which conscripted males into the army and directed economic production for military purposes. On September 29 a maximum on prices was established in accord with *sans-culottes'* demands. During these same months the armies of the revolution also crushed many of the counterrevolutionary disturbances in the provinces.

The Society of Revolutionary Republican Women Revolutionary women established their own distinct institutions to fight the internal enemies of the revolution. In May 1793 Pauline Léon and Claire Lacombe founded the Society of Revolutionary Republican Women. Its members and other women filled the galleries of the Convention to hear the debates and cheer their favorite speakers. The Society became increasingly radical, however. Its members sought stricter controls on the price of food and other commodities, worked to ferret out food hoarders, and brawled with working market women thought to be insufficiently revolutionary. The women of the Society also demanded the right to wear the revolutionary cap or cockade usually worn only by male citizens. By October 1793 the Jacobins in the Convention had begun to fear the turmoil the Society was causing and banned all women's clubs and societies.

There were other examples of repression of women in 1793. Olympe de Gouges, author of the *Declaration of the Rights of Woman*, opposed the Terror and accused certain Jacobins of corruption. She was tried and guillotined in November 1793. In the same year women were formally excluded from the French army and from attending the galleries of the Convention.

Revolutionary Calendar. To symbolize the beginning of a new era in human history, French revolutionary legislators established a new calendar. This calendar for Year Two (1794) proclaims the indivisible unity of the revolution and the goals of Liberty, Equality, and Fraternity. *Art Resource/ Bildarchiv Preussischer Kulturbesitz.*

Chronology

The French Revolution

1789	May 5	Estates General opens at Versailles
	June 17	Third Estate declares itself the National Assembly
	June 20	National Assembly takes the Tennis Court Oath
	July 14	Fall of the Bastille
	August 4	Nobles surrender their feudal rights in a meeting of the National Constituent Assembly
	August 27	*Declaration of the Rights of Man and Citizen*
	October 5–6	Parisian women march to Versailles and force Louis XVI and his family to return to Paris
1790	July 12–14	Civil Constitution of the Clergy adopted and accepted by the king
1791	June 20–24	Louis XVI and his family attempt to flee France and are stopped at Varennes
1792	April 20	France declares war on Austria
	August 10	Tuileries palace stormed, and Louis XVI takes refuge in the Legislative Assembly
	September	September Massacres; monarchy abolished
1793	January 21	Louis XVI executed
	February 1	France declares war on Great Britain
	March	Counterrevolution breaks out in the Vendée
	April 6	Committee of Public Safety formed
	July	Robespierre enters Committee of Public Safety
	August 23	*Levée en masse* proclaimed
	October 16	Queen Marie Antoinette executed
	November 10	Cult of Reason proclaimed; revolutionary calendar beginning in September
1794	May 7	Cult of the Supreme Being proclaimed
	June 8	Robespierre leads the celebration of Festival of the Supreme Being
	July 28	Robespierre executed
1795	August 22	Constitution of the Year III adopted, establishing the Directory

The Republic of Virtue   The pressures of war made it relatively easy to dispense with legal due process. However, the people in the Convention and the Committee of Public Safety also believed they had made a new departure in world history. They had established a republic in which civic virtue rather than aristocratic and monarchical corruption might flourish.

Dechristianization   The most dramatic departure of the republic of virtue was an attempt to dechristianize France. In October 1793 the Convention proclaimed a new calendar dating from the first day of the French Republic. There were twelve months of thirty days with names associated with the seasons and climate. Every tenth day, rather than every seventh, was a holiday. Many of the most important events of the next few years became known by their dates on the revolutionary calendar.[4]

In November 1793 the convention decreed the Cathedral of Notre Dame to be a Temple of Reason. The legislature then sent trusted members, known as deputies on mission,

---

[4] From summer to spring, the months on the revolutionary calendar were *Messidor, Thermidor, Fructidor, Vendémiaire, Brumaire, Frimaire, Nivose, Pluviose, Ventose, Germinal, Floréal,* and *Prairial.*

The Paris Jacobin Club Alerts the Nations to Internal Enemies of the Revolution

Document

By early 1793, the revolutionary groups in Paris stood sharply divided amongst themselves. The Girondists, who had led the nation into war, faced military reversals. General Dumouriez, a former revolutionary commander, had changed sides and was leading an army against France. At this point, on April 5, the radical Jacobin Club of Paris sent a circular to its provincial clubs, painting a dire picture of the fate of the revolution. While Dumouriez was marching against Paris, they accused members of the government and its administrators of conspiring to betray the revolution. The circular suggested that some people were cooperating with England in the war against France. The Jacobins also portrayed as counterrevolutionaries all those political figures who had opposed the execution of Louis XVI. The distortion of the motives of political enemies, the appeal to a possible reversal of the revolution, and the accusations of internal conspiracy served to justify the demand for justice against enemies of the revolution.

◆ How did the Jacobins use the war to call for actions against their own domestic political enemies? What real and imagined forces did they see threatening the revolution?

Friends, we are betrayed! To arms! To arms! The terrible hour is at hand when the defenders of the *Patrie* must vanquish or bury themselves under the bloody ruins of the Republic. Frenchmen, never was your liberty in such great peril! At last our enemies have put the finishing touch to their foul perfidy, and to complete it their accomplice Dumouriez is marching on Paris. . . .

But Brothers, not all your dangers are to be found there! . . . You must be convinced of a grievous truth! Your greatest enemies are in your midst, they direct your operations. O Vengeance!!! . . .

Yes, brothers and friends, yes, it is in the Senate that patricidal hands tear at your vitals! Yes, the counterrevolution is in the Government. . . , in the National Convention. It is there, at the center of your security and your hope, that criminal delegates hold the threads of the web that they have woven with the horde of despots who come to butcher us! . . . It is there that a sacriligious cabal is directed by the English court . . . and others. . . .

Let us rise! Yes, let us rise! Let us arrest all the enemies of our revolution, and all suspected persons. Let us

exterminate, without pity, all conspirators, unless we wish to be exterminated ourselves. . . .

Let the departments, the districts, the municipalities, and all the popular societies unite and concur in protesting to the Convention, by dispatching thereto a veritable rain of petitions manifesting the formal wish for the immediate recall of all unfaithful members who have betrayed their duty by not wishing the death of the tyrant, and above all, against those who have led astray so many of their colleagues. Such delegates are traitors, royalists, or fatuous men. The Republic condemns the friends of kings! . . .

Let us all unite equally to demand that the thunder or indictments be loosed against generals who are traitors to the Republic, against prevaricating ministers, against postal administrators, and against all unfaithful agents of the government. Therein lies our most salutary means of defence; but let us repel the traitors and tyrants.

From John Hall Stewart, *Documentary Survey of the French Revolution*, 1st Edition, © 1951. Reprinted by permission of Pearson Education, Inc., Upper Saddle River, NJ.

into the provinces to enforce dechristianization by closing churches, persecuting clergy and believers, and occasionally forcing priests to marry. This religious policy roused much opposition and deeply separated the French provinces from the revolutionary government in Paris.

Progress of the Terror During late 1793 and early 1794 Maximilien Robespierre (1758–1794) emerged as the

chief figure on the Committee of Public Safety. The Jacobin Club provided his primary forum and base of power. A shrewd and sensitive politician, he had opposed the war in 1792, believing it to be a measure that might aid the monarchy. He largely depended on the support of the *sans-culottes* of Paris but continued to dress as he had before the revolution and opposed dechristianization as a political blunder. For him, the republic of virtue meant wholehearted support of republican government and the renunciation of selfish gains from political life. He once told the Convention:

> If the mainspring of popular government in peacetime is virtue, amid revolution it is at the same time virtue and terror: virtue, without which terror is fatal; terror, without which virtue is impotent. Terror is nothing but prompt, severe, inflexible justice; it is therefore an emanation of virtue.[5]

The Reign of Terror manifested itself through a series of revolutionary tribunals established by the Convention during the summer of 1793. The tribunals were to try the enemies of the Republic, but the definition of enemy remained uncertain and shifted as the months passed. The first victims were Marie Antoinette, other members of the royal family, and aristocrats, who were executed in October 1793. They were followed by Girondist politicians who had been prominent in the Legislative Assembly. (See Document, "The Paris Jacobin Club Alerts the Nations to Internal Enemies of the Revolution.")

By early 1794 the Terror had moved to the provinces, where the deputies on mission presided over the summary execution of thousands of people who had allegedly supported internal opposition to the revolution. In Paris during the late winter of 1794 Robespierre turned the Terror against republican political figures of the left and right. On March 24 he secured the execution of certain extreme sans-culottes leaders. Shortly thereafter he moved against more conservative republicans. Robespierre thus exterminated the leadership from both groups that might have threatened his own position. Finally, on June 10 he secured passage of a law that permitted the revolutionary tribunal to convict suspects without hearing substantial evidence.

In May 1794, at the height of his power, Robespierre, considering the worship of reason too abstract for most citizens, abolished it and established the Cult of the Supreme Being. He did not long preside over this new religion. On June 26 he made an ill-tempered speech in the Convention, declaring the existence of a conspiracy among other leaders of the government against him and the revolution. Such accusations against unnamed persons had usually preceded his earlier attacks. On July 27 (the Ninth of Thermidor) members of the Convention, by prearrangement, shouted him down when he rose to speak. Robespierre was arrested that night and executed the next day.

The Reign of Terror soon ended, having claimed as many as 40,000 victims. Most were peasants and sans-culottes who had rebelled against the revolutionary government. By the late summer of 1794 those provincial uprisings had been crushed, and the war against foreign enemies was also going well. Those factors, combined with the feeling in Paris that the revolution had consumed enough of its own children, brought the Terror to an end. (See Document, "Burke Denounces the Extreme Measures of the French Revolution.")

The Thermidorian Reaction: End of the Terror and Establishment of the Directory

The tempering of the revolution, called the **Thermidorian Reaction**, began in July 1794. It destroyed the machinery of terror and set up a new constitutional regime. The influence of generally wealthy middle-class and professional people replaced that of the sans-culottes. Many of the people responsible for the Terror were removed from public life. The Paris Jacobin Club was closed, and provincial Jacobin clubs were forbidden to correspond with each other.

The Thermidorian Reaction also involved still further political reconstruction. In place of the fully democratic constitution of 1793, which had never gone into effect, the Convention issued the Constitution of the Year III. It was a conservative document that provided for a bicameral legislative government heavily favoring property owners. The executive body, consisting of a five-person Directory, was elected by the upper legislative house, known as the Council of Elders.

By the Treaty of Basel of March 1795, the Convention concluded peace with Prussia and Spain. With the war effort succeeding, the Convention severed its ties with the sans-culottes. True to their belief in an unregulated economy, the Thermidorians repealed the ceiling on prices. When food riots resulted during the winter of 1794–1795, the Convention put them down to prove that the era of the sans-culottes journées had ended. On October 5, 1795 (13 Vendémiaire) the sections (municipal units, each with its own assembly) of Paris rebelled against the Convention. For the first time in the history of the revolution, artillery was turned against the people of Paris. A general named Napoleon Bonaparte (1769–1821) commanded the cannon and with what he termed a "whiff of grapeshot" dispersed the crowd. Other enemies of the Directory would be more difficult to disperse.

The Napoleonic Era

Napoleon Bonaparte was born in 1769 to a poor family of lesser nobles in Corsica. Because France had annexed Cor-

---

[5] Quoted in Richard T. Bienvenu, *The Ninth of Thermidor: The Fall of Robespierre* (New York: Oxford University Press, 1968), p. 38.

sica in 1768, he went to French schools, pursued a military career, and in 1785 obtained a commission as a French artillery officer. He strongly favored the revolution and was a fiery Jacobin. In 1793 he played a leading role in recovering the port of Toulon from the British. As a reward the government appointed him a brigadier general. His defense of the new regime on 13 Vendémiaire won him another promotion and a command in Italy. By October 1797 he had crushed the Austrian army in Italy and concluded on his own initiative the Treaty of Campo Formio, which took

Burke Denounces the Extreme Measures of the French Revolution

Edmund Burke was undoubtedly the most important and articulate foreign critic of the French Revolution. His first critique, *Reflections on the Revolution in France*, appeared in 1790. He continued to attack the revolution in later years. In 1796 he published *Letters on a Regicide Peace*, which opposed a peace treaty between Great Britain and revolutionary France. In that work he enumerated what he regarded as the most fundamental evils of the revolutionary government: the execution of the king, the confiscation of property of the church and nobles, and the policy of dechristianization.

◆ To which of the major events in the French Revolution does Burke make reference? Why by 1796 would Burke and others have attached so much importance to the religious policies of the revolution? Did Burke exaggerate the evils of the revolution? Who might have been persuaded by Burke's condemnation?

A government of the nature of that set up at our very door has never been hitherto seen, or even imagined in Europe. . . . France, since her revolution, is under the sway of a sect, whose leaders have deliberately, at one stroke, demolished the whole body of that jurisprudence which France had pretty nearly in common with other civilized countries. . . .

Its foundation is laid in regicide, in Jacobinism, and in atheism, and it has joined to those principles a body of systematic manners, which secures their operation. . . .

I call a commonwealth regicide, which lays it down as a fixed law of nature, and a fundamental right of man, that all government, not being a democracy, is an usurpation. That all kings, as such, are usurpers; and for being kings may and ought to be put to death, with their wives, families, and adherents. That commonwealth which acts uniformly upon those principles . . .—this I call regicide by establishment.

Jacobinism is the revolt of the enterprising talents of a country against its property. When private men form themselves into associations for the purpose of destroying the pre-existing laws and institutions of their country; when they secure to themselves an army, by dividing amongst the people of no property the estates of the ancient and lawful proprietors, when a state recognizes those acts; when it does not make confiscations for crimes, but makes crimes for confiscations; when it has its principal strength, and all its resources, in such a violation of property . . .—I call this Jacobinism by establishment.

I call it atheism by establishment, when any state, as such, shall not acknowledge the existence of God as a moral governor of the world; . . .—when it shall abolish the Christian religion by a regular decree;—when it shall persecute with a cold, unrelenting, steady cruelty, by every mode of confiscation, imprisonment, exile, and death, all its ministers;—when it shall generally shut up or pull down churches; when the few buildings which remain of this kind shall be opened only for the purpose of making a profane apotheosis of monsters, whose vices and crimes have no parallel amongst men . . . When, in the place of that religion of social benevolence, and of individual self-denial, in mockery of all religion, they institute impious, blasphemous, indecent theatric rites, in honour of their vitiated, perverted reason, and erect altars to the personification of their own corrupted and bloody republic; . . . when wearied out with incessant martyrdom, and the cries of a people hungering and thirsting for religion, they permit it, only as a tolerated evil—I call this atheism by establishment.

When to these establishments of regicide, of Jacobinism, and of atheism, you add the correspondent system of manners, no doubt can be left on the mind of a thinking man concerning their determined hostility to the human race.

The Works of the Right Honourable Edmund Burke (London: Henry G. Bohn, 1856), 5: 206–208.

Austria out of the war. Soon all of Italy and Switzerland lay under French domination.

In November 1797 the triumphant Bonaparte returned to Paris to be hailed as a hero and to confront France's only remaining enemy, Britain. Judging it impossible to cross the Channel and invade England at that time, he chose to capture Egypt from the Ottoman Empire. He thus hoped to drive the British fleet from the Mediterranean, cut off British communication with India, damage British trade, and threaten the British Empire. But the invasion of Egypt was a failure. Admiral Horatio Nelson (1758–1805) destroyed the French fleet at Aboukir on August 1, 1798. The French army could then neither accomplish anything of importance in the Near East nor get home. The French invasion of Egypt had alarmed Russia, which had its own ambitions in the Near East. The Russians, the Austrians, and the Ottomans joined Britain to form the Second Coalition. In 1799 the Russian and Austrian armies defeated the French in Italy and Switzerland and threatened to invade France.

Having heard of these misfortunes, Napoleon abandoned his army in Egypt and returned to France in October 1799. On November 10, 1799 (19 Brumaire) his troops overthrew the Directory. Bonaparte issued the Constitution of the Year VII in December 1799, establishing himself as the First Consul. The constitution received overwhelming approval from the electorate in a largely rigged plebiscite. The establishment of the **Consulate**, in effect, closed the revolution in France.

The Consulate in France (1799–1804) Bonaparte quickly justified the public's confidence by achieving peace with France's enemies. Russia had already left the Second Coalition. A campaign in Italy brought another victory over Austria at Marengo in 1800. The Treaty of Lunéville early in 1801 took Austria out of the war and confirmed the earlier settlement of Campo Formio. Britain was now alone and, in 1802, concluded the Treaty of Amiens, which temporarily brought peace to Europe.

Bonaparte also restored peace and order at home. Although he used generosity, flattery, and bribery to win over some of his enemies, issued a general amnesty, and employed persons from all political factions, Bonaparte was ruthless and efficient in suppressing political opposition. He established a highly centralized administration in which all departments were managed by prefects directly responsible to the central government in Paris. He employed secret police. He stamped out, once and for all, the royalist rebellion in the west and moved against other royalist plots.

Napoleon also alleviated the hostility of French Catholics. In 1801 he concluded a concordat with Pope Pius VII (r. 1800–1823), to the shock and dismay of his anticlerical supporters. The concordat declared that "Roman Catholicism is the religion of the great majority of French citizens." This was merely a statement of fact and fell far short of what the pope had wanted—religious dominance for the Roman Catholic Church. Both refractory and constitutional clergy were forced to resign. Their replacements received their spiritual investiture from the pope, but the state named the bishops and paid their salaries and the salary of one priest in each parish. In return, the church gave up its claims to its confiscated property. The clergy had to swear an oath of loyalty to the state, and the Organic Articles of 1802, which were actually distinct from the concordat, established the supremacy of state over church. Similar laws were applied to the Protestant and Jewish religious communities, reducing still further the privileged position of the Catholic Church.

Napoleon. In December 1799 Napoleon seized power and established himself as First Consul. The title of "Consul" came from the ancient Roman Republic; by 1894 Napoleon would assume the title of "Emperor" as the French Republic gave way to the Napoleonic Empire. The simplicity of this modest military dress as First Consul also gave way to flowing imperial robes. *© Historical Picture Archive/CORBIS.*

In 1802 another plebiscite appointed Napoleon consul for life, and he soon produced still another new constitution, which granted him what amounted to full power. He transformed the basic laws and institutions of France on the basis of both liberal principles derived from the Enlightenment and the early years of the revolution and conservative principles going back to the Old Regime, on the one hand, and the spirit that had triumphed at Thermidor, on the other. This was especially true of the Civil Code of 1804, usually called the Napoleonic Code. However, these laws stopped far short of the full equality advocated by liberal rationalists. Fathers were granted extensive control over their children and men over their wives. Labor unions were still forbidden, and the rights of workers were inferior to those of their employers.

In 1804 Bonaparte seized on a bomb attack on his life to make himself emperor. He argued that the establishment of a dynasty would make the new regime secure and make further attempts on his life useless. Still another new constitution, ratified by a plebiscite, was promulgated, designating Napoleon Emperor of the French instead of First Consul of the Republic. Napoleon summoned the pope to Notre Dame to take part in the coronation. But at the last minute the pope agreed that Napoleon should actually crown himself. The emperor had no intention of allowing anyone to think that his power and authority depended on the approval of the church. Henceforth he was called Napoleon I.

Napoleon's Empire (1804–1814)
Between his coronation as emperor and his final defeat at Waterloo (1815), Napoleon conquered most of Europe in military campaigns that astonished the world. France's victories changed the map of Europe, ended the Old Regime and its feudal trappings in Western Europe, and forced the eastern European states to reorganize themselves to resist Napoleon's armies. Everywhere, Napoleon's advance unleashed the powerful force of nationalism. (See Document, "Napoleon Advises His Brother to Rule Constitutionally.")

The Treaty of Amiens with Britain (1802) could not last. Napoleon intervened militarily to extend French influence in Europe. The British issued an ultimatum. When Napoleon ignored it, Britain declared war, in May 1803. William Pitt the Younger (1759–1806) returned to office as prime minister in 1804 and began to construct the Third Coalition. By August 1805 he had persuaded Russia and Austria to move once again against French aggression. On October 21, 1805, Lord Nelson destroyed the combined French and Spanish fleets at the Battle of Trafalgar just off the Spanish coast. Nelson was killed, but the British lost no ships. Trafalgar put an end to the French hope of invading Britain and guaranteed British control of the sea.

On land, however, the story was different. Between mid-October 1805 and July 1807 Napoleon had defeated the armies of Austria, Prussia, and Russia in stunning victories. The most famous of the victories was that of Austerlitz on December 2, 1805. Through these campaigns he forced Austria to withdraw from northern Italy, where Napoleon himself was recognized as king. He replaced the ancient Holy Roman Empire with the Confederation of the Rhine. On July 7, 1807, Napoleon and Emperor Alexander I (r. 1800–1825) of Russia concluded the Treaty of Tilsit, which confirmed France's gains in central and eastern Europe. Prussia and Russia became allies of Napoleon.

Napoleon knew that he could not be genuinely secure until he had defeated Britain. Unable to compete with the British navy, he adopted economic warfare to cut off all British trade with the European continent. He thus hoped to cripple British commercial and financial power, cause domestic unrest and revolution, and drive the British from the war. On November 21, 1806, he had issued the Berlin Decrees forbidding his allies to import British goods. The Milan Decree of 1807 attempted to halt neutral nations, such as the United States, from trading with Britain. Nonetheless, the British economy survived because of its access to the growing markets of North and South America and the eastern Mediterranean. Known as the Continental System, Napoleon's policies harmed the European economies and roused resentment against France.

The Wars of Liberation
In 1807, as part of the strategy of crippling the British economy, a French army invaded the Iberian Peninsula to force Portugal to abandon its traditional alliance with Britain. The army stayed in Spain to protect lines of supply and communication. When a revolt broke out in Madrid in 1808, Napoleon deposed the Bourbons and placed his brother Joseph (1768–1844) on the Spanish throne. Attacks on the privileges of the church increased public outrage.

In Spain Napoleon faced a kind of warfare not vulnerable to his usual tactics. Guerrilla bands cut communications, killed stragglers, destroyed isolated units, and then disappeared. The British landed an army under Sir Arthur Wellesley (1769–1852), later the Duke of Wellington, to support the Spanish insurgents. Thus began the long peninsular campaign that would drain French strength and play a critical role in Napoleon's eventual defeat.

Encouraged by the French troubles in Spain, the Austrians renewed the war in 1809. The French army nonetheless marched swiftly into Austria and won the battle of Wagram. The resulting peace deprived Austria of much territory and 3.5 million subjects. Another spoil of victory was the Archduchess Marie Louise (1791–1847), Francis I's eighteen-year-old daughter, whom Napoleon

Napoleon Advises His Brother to Rule Constitutionally

Document

As Napoleon swept through Europe, he set his relatives on the thrones of various conquered kingdoms and then imposed written constitutions on them. In this letter of November 1807, Napoleon sent his brother Jerome (1784–1860) a constitution for the Kingdom of Westphalia in Germany. The letter shows how Napoleon spread the political ideas and institutions of the French Revolution across Europe. Napoleon ignored, however, the nationalistic resentment that French conquest aroused, even when that conquest brought more liberal political institutions. Such nationalism would contribute to his downfall.

◆ **What benefits does Napoleon believe his conquest and subsequent rule by his brother will bring to their new subjects? Why does he believe that these, rather than military victory, will achieve new loyalty? How does Napoleon suggest playing off the resentment of the upper classes to consolidate power? What is the relationship between having a written constitution such as the one Napoleon is sending his brother and the power of public opinion that he mentions towards the close of the letter?**

I enclose the constitution for your Kingdom. You must faithfully observe it. I am concerned for the happiness of your subjects, not only as it affects your reputation, but my own, but also for its influence on the whole European situation.

Don't listen to those who say that your subjects are so accustomed to slavery that they will feel no gratitude for the benefits you give them. There is more intelligence in the Kingdom of Westphalia than they would have you believe; and your throne will never be firmly established except upon the trust and affection of the common people. What German opinion impatiently demands is that men of no rank, but of marked ability, shall have an equal claim upon your favour and your employment, and that every trace of serfdom, or of a feudal hierarchy between the sovereign and the lowest class of his subjects shall be done away with. The benefits of the Code Napoleon, public trial, and the introduction of juries, will be the leading features of your Government. And to tell you the truth, I count more upon their effects, for the extension and consolidation of your rule, than upon the most resounding victories. I want your subjects to enjoy a degree of liberty, equality, and prosperity hitherto unknown to the German people. . . . Such a method of government will be a stronger barrier between you and Prussia than the Elbe, the fortresses, and the protection of France. What people will want to return under the arbitrary Prussian rule, once it has tasted the benefits of a wise and liberal administration? In Germany, as in France, Italy, and Spain, people long for equality and liberalism. I have been managing the affairs of Europe long enough now to know that the burden of the privileged classes was resented everywhere. Rule constitutionally. Even if reason, and the enlightenment of the age, were not sufficient cause, it would be good policy for one in your position; and you will find that the backing of public opinion gives you a great natural advantage over the absolute kings who are your neighbors.

From J. M. Thompson, ed., *Napoleon's Letters* (London: Dent, 1954), pp. 190–191, as quoted in Maurice Hutt, ed., *Napoleon* (Englewood Cliffs, NJ: Prentice-Hall, 1972), p. 34.

---

married for dynastic purposes after divorcing his wife Josephine de Beauharnais (1763–1814), who had borne him no children.

The Franco-Russian alliance concluded at Tilsit was faltering. The Continental System had harmed the Russian economy. Napoleon's organization of a Polish state, the Grand Duchy of Warsaw, on the Russian doorstep and its enlargement in 1809 after the battle of Wagram angered Alexander I. Napoleon's annexation of Holland in violation of the Treaty of Tilsit, his recognition of the French Marshal Bernadotte as the future king of Sweden (r. 1818–1844), and his marriage to an Austrian princess further disturbed the tsar. At the end of 1810 Russia withdrew from the Continental System and began to prepare for war (see Map 23–2).

Determined to stifle the Russian military threat, Napoleon amassed an army of over 600,000 men, including

William Pitt and Napoleon. In this early nineteenth-century cartoon, England, personified by a caricature of William Pitt, and France, personified by a caricature of Napoleon, are carving out their areas of interest around the globe. *Cartoon by Gillray/Corbis-Bettmann.*

over 400,000 non-French soldiers drawn from his empire and allies. He intended the usual short campaign crowned by a decisive battle, but the Russians retreated before his advance. His vast superiority in numbers—the Russians had only about 160,000 troops—made it foolish for them to risk a battle. Instead, they destroyed all food and supplies as they retreated. The so-called Grand Army of Napoleon could not live off the country, and Russia was too vast for supply lines. Terrible rains, fierce heat, shortages of food and water, and the courage of the Russian rear guard eroded the morale of Napoleon's army.

In September 1812 Russian public opinion forced the army to stand and fight. At Borodino, not far west of Moscow, the bloodiest battle of the Napoleonic era cost the French 30,000 casualties and the Russians almost twice as many. Yet the Russian army was not destroyed. Napoleon had won nothing substantial. By October, after occupying Moscow, the Grand Army was forced to retreat. By December Napoleon realized that the Russian fiasco would encourage plots against him at home. He returned to Paris, leaving the remnants of his army to struggle westward. Perhaps only as many as 100,000 lived to tell the tale of their terrible ordeal. Even as the news of the disaster reached the West, the total defeat of Napoleon was far from certain. He was able to suppress his opponents in Paris and raise another 350,000 men.

Francisco de Goya, *The Third of May, 1808,* 1814–1815. Napoleon sent troops into Spain in 1807 after the king of Spain had agreed to aid France against Portugal, which was assisting Britain. By early 1808 Spain had essentially become an occupied nation. On May 2 riots took place in Madrid between French troops and Spanish civilians. In response to the riots, the French marshall Joachim Murat ordered numerous executions, especially of artisans and clergy, during the night of May 2 and 3. *Francisco de Goya, "Los fusilamientos del 3 de Mayo, 1808," 1814. Oil on canvas, 8′ 6″ × 11′ 4″. © Museo Nacional Del Prado, Madrid.*

Map 23–2. Napoleonic Europe in late 1812. By mid-1812 the areas shown in peach were incorporated into France, and most of the rest of Europe was directly controlled by or allied with Napoleon. But Russia had withdrawn from the failing Continental System, and the decline of Napoleon was about to begin.

In 1813 patriotic pressure and national ambition brought together the last and most powerful coalition against Napoleon. Financed by the British, the Russians drove westward to be joined by Prussia and then Austria. From the west Wellington marched his peninsular army into France. Napoleon waged a skillful campaign in central Europe and defeated the allies at Dresden. In October, however, he met decisive defeat at Leipzig from the combined armies of his enemies, in what the Germans called the Battle of the Nations. At the end of March 1814 the allied army marched into Paris. Napoleon abdicated and went into exile on the island of Elba off the coast of northern Italy.

The Congress of Vienna and the European Settlement

Once Napoleon was removed, the allies began to pursue their own separate ambitions. The key person in achieving eventual agreement among the allies was Robert Stewart, Viscount Castlereagh (1769–1822), the British foreign secretary. Even before the victorious armies had entered Paris, he achieved the Treaty of Chaumont on March 9, 1814, providing for the restoration of the Bourbons to the French throne and the contraction of France to its 1792 frontiers. Even more important, Britain, Austria, Russia, and Prussia formed a Quadruple Alliance for twenty years to

Chronology

Napoleonic Europe

1797	Napoleon concludes Treaty of Campo Formio
1798	Nelson defeats French navy at Aboukir
1799	Consulate established
1801	Concordat between France and papacy
1802	Treaty of Amiens
1803	War renewed between France and Britain
1804	Execution of Duke of Enghien; Napoleonic Civil Code issued; Napoleon crowned emperor
1805	Nelson defeats French fleet at Trafalgar (October 21); Austerlitz (December 2)
1806	Continental System established by Berlin Decrees
1807	Treaty of Tilsit
1808	Beginning of Spanish resistance to Napoleonic domination
1809	Wagram; Napoleon marries Archduchess Marie Louise of Austria
1812	Invasion of Russia
1813	Leipzig (Battle of the Nations)
1814	Treaty of Chaumont (March) establishes Quadruple Alliance; Congress of Vienna convenes (September)
1815	Napoleon returns from Elba (March 1); Waterloo (June 18); Holy Alliance formed (September 26); Quadruple Alliance renewed (November 20)
1821	Napoleon dies on Saint Helena

preserve whatever settlement they later agreed on. Remaining problems—and there were many—and final details were left for a conference to be held at Vienna.

The Congress of Vienna assembled in September 1814 but did not conclude its work until November 1815. The four great powers conducted the important work of the conference. The victors agreed that no single state should be allowed to dominate Europe. They constructed a series of states to serve as barriers to any new French expansion (see Map 23–3). Thus, they established the kingdom of the Netherlands, including Belgium in the north, and added Genoa to Piedmont in the south. Prussia, whose power was increased by acqui-

sitions in eastern Europe, was given important new territories in the west to deter French aggression along the Rhine River. Austria was given full control of northern Italy to prevent a repetition of Napoleon's conquests there. Most of Napoleon's arrangements in the rest of Germany were left untouched. The Holy Roman Empire was not revived. The Congress established the rule of legitimate monarchs and rejected any hint of the republican and democratic politics that had flowed from the French Revolution.

However, the settlement of Eastern Europe sharply divided the victors. Alexander I wanted Russia to govern all of Poland. Prussia was willing if it received all of Saxony. Austria, however, refused to surrender its share of Poland or to see Prussian power grow and Russia penetrate deeper into central Europe. The Polish-Saxon question enabled France to rejoin the great powers. The French Foreign Minister Talleyrand (1754–1838) suggested that the weight of France, added to that of Britain and Austria, might bring Alexander to his senses. When news of a secret treaty among the three leaked out, the tsar agreed to become ruler of a smaller Poland, and Frederick William III of Prussia (r. 1797–1840) agreed to settle for part of Saxony. Thereafter, France was included as a fifth great power in all deliberations.

Napoleon's escape from Elba on March 1, 1815, further restored unity among the victors. He promised a liberal constitution and a peaceful foreign policy, but the allies declared him an outlaw (a new device under international law) and sent their armies to crush him. Wellington, with the crucial help of the Prussians, defeated Napoleon at Waterloo in Belgium on June 18, 1815. Napoleon again abdicated and was exiled to Saint Helena, a tiny Atlantic island off the coast of Africa, where he died in 1821.

The Hundred Days, as the period of Napoleon's return is called, made the peace settlement somewhat harsher for France, but the other main outlines of the Vienna Settlement remained in place. The Quadruple Alliance between England, Austria, Prussia, and Russia was renewed on November 20, 1815. Henceforth, it was as much a coalition for the maintenance of peace as for the pursuit of victory over France. A coalition with such a purpose had not previously existed in European international relations. Its existence and later operation represented an important new departure in European affairs. Unlike the situation in the eighteenth century, certain European powers were determined to prevent the outbreak of future war. The statesmen at Vienna, unlike their eighteenth-century counterparts, had seen the armies of the French Revolution change major frontiers of the European states and overturn the political and social order of much of the Continent. They had seen unprecedented military destruction. They were determined to prevent a recurrence of those upheavals. The shared

Map Exploration

To explore this map further, go to http://www.prenhall.com/craig_maps

Map 23–3. Europe 1815, after the Congress of Vienna. The Congress of Vienna achieved the post-Napoleonic territorial adjustments shown on the map. The most notable arrangements dealt with areas along France's borders (the Netherlands, Prussia, Switzerland, and Piedmont) and in Poland and northern Italy.

purpose of the diplomats was to establish a framework for future stability, not to punish a defeated France. The great powers through the Vienna Settlement framed international relations in such a manner that the major powers would respect that settlement and not as in the eighteenth century use military force to change it.

The Congress of Vienna succeeded in preventing future French aggression and in arranging an acceptable settlement for Europe that produced a long-lasting peace. Its work has been criticized for failing to recognize and provide for the great forces that would stir the nineteenth century—nationalism and democracy—but such criticism is inappro-

Political Cartoon of the Congress of Vienna. In this cartoon depiction, Talleyrand simply watches which way the wind is blowing; Castlereagh hesitates, while the monarchs of Russia, Prussia, and Austria form the dance of the Holy Alliance. The King of Saxony holds onto his crown and the republic of Geneva pays homage to the Kingdom of Sardinia. *Bildarchiv Preussischer Kulturbesitz.*

priate. The settlement, like all such agreements, was aimed at solving past ills, and in that it succeeded. The Vienna Settlement remained essentially intact for almost half a century and spared Europe a general war until 1914.

Wars of Independence in Latin America

The wars of the French Revolution, particularly those of Napoleon, sparked movements for independence throughout Latin America. Between 1804 and 1824 France was driven from Haiti, Portugal lost control of Brazil, and Spain was forced to withdraw from all of its American empire except for Cuba and Puerto Rico. Three centuries of Iberian colonial government over the South American continent ended.

Eighteenth-Century Developments

Spain was one of the defeated powers in 1763. Charles III (r. 1759–1788) and the government circles in Spain were convinced that the American colonial system had to be changed. After 1765 the monarch abolished the monopolies of Seville and Cádiz and permitted other Spanish commercial centers to trade with America. He also opened more South American and Caribbean ports to trade and author-

ized commerce between American ports. In 1776 he organized a fourth viceroyalty in the region of the Río de la Plata, which included much of present-day Argentina, Uruguay, Paraguay, and Bolivia. Charles III also attempted to make tax collection more efficient and to eliminate bureaucratic corruption. To achieve those ends, he introduced into the empire *intendents*, who were royal bureaucrats loyal only to the Crown.

These reforms, which took place during the same years as the unsuccessful British effort to reorganize its authority in its North American colonies, largely succeeded in returning the empire to direct Spanish control. Many **peninsulares**, whites born in Spain, went to the New World to fill new posts at the expense of **creoles**, whites born in America. Expanding trade likewise brought more Spanish merchants to Latin America. The economy retained its export orientation, and economic life continued to be organized for the benefit of Spain. There matters stood until the early nineteenth century.

First Movements Towards Independence

Haiti achieved independence from France in 1804, following a slave revolt that commenced in 1794 led by Toussaint L'Ouverture (1744–1803) and Jean-Jacques Dessalines (ca. 1756–1806). Haiti's revolution involved the popular uprising of a repressed social group, which proved to be the great exception in the Latin American drive for liberty from European masters. Generally speaking, on the South American continent it was the Creole elite—merchants, landowners, and professional people—who led the movements against Spain and Portugal. Few Indians, blacks, mestizos, mulattos, or slaves became involved in or benefited from the end of Iberian rule. Indeed, the Haitian slave revolt haunted the Creoles, as did an Indian revolt in the Andes in 1780 and 1781. The Creoles were determined that political independence from Spain and Portugal should not cause social disruption or the loss of their social and economic privileges. In this respect the Creole revolutionaries were not unlike American revolutionaries in the Southern colonies who wanted to reject British rule but keep their slaves, or French revolutionaries who wanted to depose the king but not extend liberty to the French working class.

Creole complaints resembled those of the American colonists against Great Britain. Latin American merchants wanted to trade more freely within the region and with North American and European markets. They wanted commercial regulations that would benefit them rather than Spain.

Creoles also feared that Spanish imperial regulations might affect landholdings, access to commissions in the army, local government policy, and the treatment of slaves and Indians in ways that would harm their interests. They also deeply resented Spanish policies favoring *peninsulares* for political patronage, including appointments in the colonial government, church, and army. They believed the *peninsulares* improperly secured all the best positions. Seen in this light, the royal patronage system represented another device with which Spain extracted wealth and income from America for its own people rather than its colonial subjects.

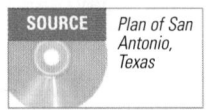
SOURCE Plan of San Antonio, Texas

From the 1790s onward Spain suffered military reverses in the wars associated with the French Revolution and Napoleon, and the commercial situation turned sharply against the inhabitants of the Spanish Empire. The military pressures led the Spanish monarchy into a desperate search for new revenues, including increased taxation and the confiscation of property in the American Empire. The policies harmed the economic life of the Creole elite.

Creole leaders had read the Enlightenment *philosophes* and regarded their reforms as potentially beneficial to the region. They were also well aware of the events and the political philosophy of the American Revolution. But something more than reform programs and revolutionary example was required to transform Creole discontent into revolt against the Spanish government. That transforming event occurred in Europe when Napoleon toppled the Portuguese monarchy in 1807 and the Spanish government in 1808 and then placed his own brother on the thrones of both countries. The Portuguese royal family fled to Brazil and established its government there. But the Bourbon monarchy of Spain seemed wholly vanquished.

The Creole elite feared that a liberal Napoleonic monarchy in Spain would impose reforms in Latin America harmful to their economic and social interests and would drain the region of the wealth and resources needed for Napoleon's wars. To protect their interests, various Creole juntas, or political committees, between 1808 and 1810 claimed the right to govern different regions of Latin America. After the establishment of these local juntas, the Spanish would not again directly govern the continent and after ten years of politically and economically exhausting warfare were to recognize the permanence of Latin American independence.

San Martín in Río de la Plata

The first region to assert its independence was the Río de la Plata, or modern Argentina. As early as 1806 the citizens of Buenos Aires had fought off a British invasion and thus had learned that they could look to themselves rather than Spain for effective political and military action. In 1810 the junta in Buenos Aires not only thrust off Spanish authority but also sent liberation forces against Paraguay and Uruguay. The armies were defeated, but Spain nonetheless soon lost control in the two areas. Paraguay asserted its own independence. Uruguay was eventually absorbed by Brazil.

Undiscouraged by these early defeats, the Buenos Aires government remained determined to liberate Peru, the greatest stronghold of royalist power and loyalty on the continent. By 1814 José de San Martín (1778–1850), the leading general of the Río de la Plata forces, had organized and led a disciplined army in a daring march over the Andes Mountains. By early 1817 he had occupied Santiago in Chile, and established the Chilean independence leader Bernardo O'Higgins (1778–1842) as supreme dictator. San Martín then constructed a naval force that in 1820 transported his army to Peru. The next year, he drove royalist forces from Lima and assumed the title of Protector of Peru (see Map 23–4).

Simón Bolívar's Liberation of Venezuela

While San Martín had been liberating the southern portion of the Continent, Simón Bolívar (1783–1830) had been pursuing a similar task in the north. In 1810, as a firm advocate

Toussaint L'Ouverture. L'Ouverture (1744–1803) began the revolt that led to Haitian independence in 1804.

capital of New Granada (including modern Colombia, Bolivia, and Ecuador), as a base for attacking Venezuela. By the summer of 1821 his forces had captured Caracas, and he had been named president.

A year later, in July 1822, the armies of Bolívar and San Martín joined to liberate Quito. At a famous meeting in Guayaquil the two leaders sharply disagreed about the future political structure of Latin America. San Martín believed that monarchies were required; Bolívar maintained his republicanism. Not long thereafter San Martín quietly retired from public life and went into exile in Europe. Meanwhile, Bolívar purposefully allowed the political situation in Peru to fall into confusion, and in 1823 he sent troops to establish his control. On December 9, 1824, at the Battle of Ayacucho, the Spanish royalist forces suffered a major defeat at the hands of the liberating army. The battle marked the conclusion of Spain's effort to retain its American empire.

Independence in New Spain

The drive for independence in New Spain, which included present-day Mexico as well as Texas, California, and the rest of the southwestern United States, clearly illustrates the socially conservative outcome of the Latin American colonial revolutions. As elsewhere, a local governing junta was organized. But before it had undertaken any significant measures, a Creole priest, Miguel Hidalgo y Costilla (1753–1811), issued a call for rebellion to the Indians in his parish. They and other repressed groups of black and mestizo urban and rural workers responded. Father Hidalgo set forth a program of social change, including hints of land reform. Soon he stood at the head of a rather unorganized group of 80,000 followers and marched on Mexico City. Both Hidalgo's forces and the royalist army that opposed them committed numerous atrocities. In July 1811 he was captured and executed. Leadership of his movement then fell to José María Morelos y Pavón (1765–1815), a mestizo priest. Far more radical than Hidalgo, he called for an end to forced labor and for substantial land reforms. He was executed in 1815, ending five years of popular uprising.

In 1820, however, the conservative political groups in Mexico, both Creole and Spanish, found their recently achieved security challenged from an unexpected source. A revolution in Spain had forced Ferdinand VII (r. 1813–1833) to accept a liberal constitution. Conservative Mexicans feared that the new liberal monarchy would attempt to impose liberal reforms on Mexico. Therefore, for the most conservative of reasons, they rallied to a former royalist general, Agustín de Iturbide (1783–1824),

Map 23–4. The Independence Campaigns of San Martín and Bolívar. This print of 1774 illustrates rowdy Bostonians tormenting a tarred and feathered exciseman or tax collector who had attempted to collect taxes imposed by the British Parliament. They are forcing tea down his throat while other Bostonians pour the contents of tea boxes into the harbor. On the tree in the back is a copy of the Stamp Act posted upside down. That act had been passed by Parliament in 1765 but repealed a year later after widespread American protest. *The Granger Collection.*

of both independence and republicanism, Bolívar had helped organize a liberating junta in Caracas, Venezuela. Between 1811 and 1814 civil war broke out throughout Venezuela as both royalists, on the one hand, and slaves and *llaneros* (Venezuelan cowboys), on the other, challenged the authority of the republican government. (See Document, "Bolívar Denounces Spanish Rule in Latin America.") Bolívar had to go into exile. In 1816, with help from Haiti, he launched a new invasion against Venezuela. He first captured Bogotá,

Bolívar Denounces Spanish Rule in Latin America

In September 1815 Simón Bolívar published a long statement, often called *The Jamaica Letter,* in which he explained the political and economic difficulties under which the Creole elite of the Spanish Empire had lived. He defined Americans as referring to those persons in Latin America who were neither Indian nor European by birth. He also implicitly excluded black slaves. Consequently his attack on Spain was voiced on behalf of the white population of the South American continent who had been born there and who demanded rights of political participation and economic freedom.

◆ Why does Bolívar describe the Creole elite as having lived in a permanent political infancy? What are the economic disadvantages that he describes, and why had those become more burdensome in the half century before he wrote this letter? How had Spanish economic regulation prevented the Creole elite from achieving positions of responsibility in Latin America? How does this document compare with others concerned with movements of independence and nationalism?

The role of the inhabitants of the American hemisphere has for centuries been purely passive. Politically they were non-existent. We are still in a position lower than slavery, and therefore it is more difficult for us to rise to the enjoyment of freedom.... We have been harassed by a conduct which has not only deprived us of our rights but has kept us in a sort of permanent infancy with regard to public affairs. If we could at least have managed our domestic affairs and our internal administration, we could have acquainted ourselves with the processes and mechanics of public affairs....

Americans today, and perhaps to a greater extent than ever before, who live within the Spanish system occupy a position in society no better than that of serfs destined for labor, or at best they have no more status than that of mere consumers. Yet even this status is surrounded with galling restrictions, such as being forbidden to grow European crops, or to store products which are royal monopolies, or to establish factories of a type the [Spanish] Peninsula itself does not possess. To this add the exclusive trading privileges, even in articles of prime necessity, and the barriers between American provinces, designed to prevent all exchange of trade, traffic, and

understanding. In short, do you wish to know what our future held?—simply the cultivation of the fields of indigo, grain, coffee, sugar cane, cacao, and cotton; cattle raising on the broad plains; hunting wild game in the jungles; digging in the earth to mine its gold—but even these limitations could never satisfy the greed of Spain.

So negative was our existence that I can find nothing comparable in any other civilized society, examine as I may the entire history of time and the politics of all nations. Is it not an outrage and a violation of human rights to expect a land so splendidly endowed, so vast, rich, and populous, to remain merely passive?

As I have just explained, we were cut off and, as it were, removed from the world in relation to the science of government and administration of the state. We were never viceroys or governors, save in the rarest of instances; seldom archbishops and bishops; diplomats never; as military men, only subordinates; as nobles, without royal privileges. In brief, we were neither magistrates nor financiers and seldom merchants....

From Harold A. Bierck Jr., ed., *Selected Writings of Bolívar,* Vol. 1. Copyright © 1951 The Colonial Press, pp. 110–112.

who in 1821 declared Mexico independent of Spain. Shortly thereafter, Iturbide was declared emperor. His own regime did not last long, but an independent Mexico, governed by persons determined to resist any significant social reform, had been created.

Great Britain was highly sympathetic to the independence movements in the different regions of Latin America. By breaking the hold of the Spanish empire the movement towards independence opened the markets of the continent to British trade and investment. Consequently in

Simón Bolívar. Bolívar was the liberator of much of Latin America. He inclined towards a policy of political liberalism.

Chronology

The Wars of Latin American Independence

1759–1788		Charles III of Spain carries out imperial reforms
1776		Organization of Viceroyalty of Río de la Plata
1780–1781		Revolt of Indians in the Andes
1794		Toussaint L'Ouverture leads slave revolt in Haiti
1804		Independence of Haiti
1807		Portuguese royal family flees to Brazil
1808		Spanish monarchy falls to Napoleon
1808–1810		Creole Committees organized to govern much of Latin America
1810		Buenos Aires junta sends forces to liberate Paraguay and Uruguay
1811		Miguel Hidalgo y Costilla leads rebellion in New Spain and is executed
1811–1815		José María Morelos y Pavón leads rebellion in New Spain and is executed
1814		San Martín organizes army
1815		Brazil declared a kingdom
1816		Bolívar invades Venezuela
1817		San Martín occupies Santiago, Chile
1820		Revolution in Spain
1821	February 24	New Spain declares independence
	June 29	Bolívar captures Caracas, Venezuela
	July 28	San Martín liberates Peru
1822	July 26–27	San Martín and Bolívar quarrel at Guayaquil; San Martín goes into exile in Europe
	September 7	Dom Pedro declares Brazilian independence
1824		Battle of Ayacucho—final Spanish defeat

1823 Great Britain supported the American Monroe Doctrine that prohibited further colonization and intervention by European powers in America. Britain soon recognized the Spanish colonies as independent states. Through the rest of the century, British commercial interests dominated Latin America.

Brazilian Independence

Brazilian independence, in contrast to that of Spanish Latin America, came relatively simply and peacefully. As already noted, the Portuguese royal family, along with several thousand government officials and members of the court, took refuge in Brazil in 1807. Their arrival immediately transformed Rio de Janeiro into a court city. The prince regent Joao (r. 1816–1826) addressed many of the local complaints, equivalent to those of the Spanish Creoles. In 1815 he made Brazil a kingdom, which meant that it was no longer to be regarded merely as a colony of Portugal. This transformation was in many respects long overdue because Brazil was far larger and more prosperous than Portugal itself. Then in 1820 a revolution occurred in

Portugal, and its leaders demanded Joao's return to Lisbon. They also demanded the return of Brazil to colonial status. Joao, who had become Joao VI in 1816, returned to Portugal but left his son Pedro (r. 1822–1831) as regent in Brazil, encouraging him to be sympathetic to the political aspirations of the Brazilians. In September 1822 Pedro embraced Brazilian independence against the recolonializing efforts of Portugal. By the end of the year he had become emperor of an independent Brazil, which remained a monarchy until 1889. Thus in contrast to virtually all other nations of Latin America, Brazil achieved independence in a way that left no real dispute as to where the center of political authority lay.

Another factor aided the peaceful transition to independence in Brazil. The political and social elite there were determined to preserve slavery against the forces (see pages xx-xx) that were challenging that institution. The wars of independence elsewhere had led to the abolition of slavery or moved the independent states closer to abolition. Any attempt to gain independence from Portugal through warfare might have caused social as well as political turmoil that would open the slavery question.

Towards the Abolition of Slavery in the Transatlantic Economy

In 1750 almost no one seriously questioned the institution of slavery; by 1888 slavery no longer existed in the transatlantic economy. This vast transformation of economic and social life occurred as the result of an international effort, first to abolish the slave trade and then to abolish the institution of slavery itself. At no previous time in world history had a society actually attempted to abolish slavery. Its eventual abolition in the transatlantic world stands as one of the most permanent achievements of the forces unleashed by the eighteenth-century Enlightenment and revolutions.

The eighteenth-century crusade against slavery in the plantation economy that stretched from Maryland south to Brazil (see Chapter 18) originated among writers of the Enlightenment and religious critics of slavery. Although some authors associated with the Enlightenment, including John Locke, were reluctant to question slavery or even defended it, the general Enlightenment rhetoric of equality stood in sharp contrast to the radical inequality of slavery. Montesquieu satirized slavery in *The Spirit of the Laws*. Adam Smith's emphasis in *The Wealth of Nations* on free labor and the efficiency of free markets undermined economic defenses of slavery. Much eighteenth-century

literature idealized primitive peoples living in cultures very different from those of Europe and portrayed them as embodying a lost human virtue. This literature allowed some Europeans to look upon African slaves in the Americas as having been betrayed and robbed of an original innocence. In such a climate, slavery, once considered the natural and deserved result of some deficiency in slaves themselves, grew to be regarded as undeserved and unacceptable. Other Enlightenment ethical thinking led reformers to believe that by working against slavery, for virtually the first time defined as an unmitigated evil, they would realize their own highest moral character.

The initial religious protest against slavery originated among English Quakers, a radical Protestant religious group founded by George Fox in the seventeenth century. By the early eighteenth century it had solidified itself into a small, but relatively wealthy, sect in England. Members of Quaker congregations at that time actually owned slaves in the West Indies and participated in the transatlantic slave trade. During the Seven Years' War (1756–1763), however, many Quakers experienced economic hardship. Furthermore, the war created other difficulties for the English population as a whole. Certain Quakers decided that the presence of the evil of slavery in the world explained these troubles. They then sought to remove this evil from their own lives and from the lives of their congregations by taking action against the whole system of slavery that characterized the transatlantic economy.

Just as the slave system was a transatlantic affair, so was the crusade against it. There were Quaker communities in America, and soon Quakers in both Philadelphia and England wrote and organized against the institution. By the earliest stages of the American Revolution small groups of reformers, usually spearheaded by Quakers, had established an antislavery network. The turmoil of the American Revolution and the founding of the American republic gave these groups the occasion for some of their earliest successes. Emancipation gradually, but nonetheless steadily, spread among the northern states. In 1787 the Continental Congress forbade slavery in the newly organized Northwest Territory north of the Ohio River.

Despite these American developments, Great Britain became and remained the center for the antislavery movement. In 1772 a decision by the chief justice affirmed that slaves brought into Great Britain could not forcibly be removed. During the early 1780s the antislavery reformers in Great Britain decided to work towards ending the slave trade rather than the institution of slavery itself. The horrors of the slave trade caught the public's attention in 1783 when the captain of the slave ship *Zong* threw more than 130 slaves overboard in order to collect insurance. Soon after, groups from the Church of England and the English Quakers formed the Society for the Abolition of the Slave Trade. The most famous of the new leaders was William Wilberforce, who, each year for the rest of his life, introduced a bill to end the slave trade.

For the reformers, attacking the trade rather than the institution appeared a less radical and more achievable reform. To many, the slave trade appeared a more obvious crime than the holding of slaves, which seemed a more passive act. Furthermore, attacking slavery itself involved serious issues of property rights, which might alienate potential supporters of the abolition of the slave trade. The antislavery groups also believed that if the trade were ended, planters would have to treat their remaining slaves more humanely.

While the British reformers worked for the abolition of the slave trade, slaves themselves in certain areas took matters into their own hands. Indeed, the largest emancipation of slaves to occur in the eighteenth century came on the island of Saint Domingue (Haiti), France's wealthiest colony, as a result of the slave revolt of 1794 led by Toussaint L'Ouverture and Jean-Jacques Dessalines (see Map 23–5). The revolt in Haiti and Haiti's eventual independence in 1804 stood as a warning to slave owners throughout the West Indies. Other slave revolts occurred, such as those in Virginia led by Gabriel Prosser in 1800 and by Nat Turner in 1831, in South Carolina led by Denmark Vesey in 1822, in British-controlled Demarra in 1823 and 1824, and in Jamaica in 1831. Each of these was brutally suppressed.

For complicated economic reasons some British West Indies planters began to consider abolition of the slave trade useful to their interests. Within the West Indies themselves the planters were experiencing soil exhaustion and competition from newly tilled islands opened for sugar cultivation. Some older plantations were being abandoned while others operated with low profitability. With the new islands there was a glut of sugar on the market, and as a consequence the price was falling. Under these conditions some British West Indies planters, for reasons that had nothing to do with religion or enlightened humanitarianism, began to favor curtailing the slave trade. Without new slaves, competing French planters would lack the labor they needed to exploit their islands.

Then, during the Napoleonic Wars, the British captured a number of the valuable French islands. In 1805 to protect the planters of the older British West Indies islands, the British Cabinet forbade the importation of slaves into the newly acquired French islands. By 1807 the abolition sentiment was strong enough for Parliament to pass Wilberforce's often proposed measure prohibiting slave trading from any British port.

Thereafter the suppression of this trade became one of the fundamental pillars of nineteenth-century British foreign policy. The British navy maintained a squadron of ships around the coast of West Africa to halt slave traders. Although the French and Americans also patrolled the West African coast, neither was deeply committed to ending the slave trade. Nonetheless, in 1824 the American Congress had made slave trading a capital offense.

Leaders of the Latin American wars of independence, disposed by Enlightenment ideas to disapprove of slavery, had sought the support of slaves by promises of emancipation. Once free of Spanish domination, the newly independent nations slowly freed their slave populations in order to maintain good relations with Great Britain from whom they needed economic support. Despite the gradual nature of this abolition, slavery would disappear from all nations of Latin America by the middle of the century with the important exception of Brazil.

Map 23–5. The Haitian Revolution.

Spanish Slave Ship. After 1807 the British Royal Navy patrolled the West African coast attempting to intercept slave-trading ships. In 1846 the British ship HMS *Albatross* captured a Spanish slave ship, the *Albanoz*, and freed the slaves. A British officer depicted the appalling conditions in the slavehold in this watercolor. *The Granger Collection, N.Y.*

the Danes, in 1848, but the Dutch not until 1863. France had witnessed a significant antislavery movement throughout the first half of the century but did not abolish slavery in its West Indian possessions until the revolutions of 1848.

Despite all of these considerable achievements of the antislavery movement, during the first thirty years of the nineteenth century the institution of slavery actually revived and achieved new footholds in the transatlantic world. These areas included the lower south of the United States for the cultivation of cotton, Brazil for the cultivation of coffee, and Cuba for the cultivation of sugar. World demand for those products made the slave system economically viable in those regions. Slavery would end in the United States only after American abolitionists brought it to the center of American politics in the 1850s and the Civil War was fought during the next decade. In Cuba it would persist until 1886, and full emancipation would occur in Brazil only in 1888 (see Chapters 25, 26, and 27).

The emancipation crusade, like slave trading itself, drew Europeans into African affairs. In 1787 the British established a colony for poor free blacks from Britain in Sierra Leone, which actually succeeded only after the British navy began to settle Africans rescued from captured slave-trading ships. The French established a smaller experiment at Libreville in Gabon. The most famous and lasting attempt to settle former black slaves in Africa was the establishment of Liberia through the efforts of the American Colonization Society after 1817. Liberia became an independent republic in 1847. All of these efforts to move former slaves back to Africa had only modest success, but they did affect the future of West Africa itself.

Other antislavery reformers were less interested in establishing outposts for settlement of former slaves than in transforming the African economy itself. These reformers attempted to spread both Christianity and free trade to Africa, hoping to exchange British manufactured goods, particularly textiles, for tropical goods produced by Africans. These commercial efforts of the antislavery movement marked the first serious intrusions of European powers well beyond the coast of West Africa into the heart of the continent.

After the American Civil War finally halted any large-scale demand for slaves from Africa, the antislavery

Having slowly recognized that the abolition of the slave trade had not actually improved the lot of slaves, British reformers in 1823 adopted as a new goal the gradual emancipation of slaves and founded the Abolition Society. The savagery with which West Indian planters put down slave revolts in 1823 and 1824 and again in 1831 strengthened the resolve of the antislavery reformers. By 1830 the reformers abandoned the goal of gradual abolition and demanded immediate complete abolition of slavery. In 1833, following the passage of the Reform Bill in Great Britain, they achieved that goal when Parliament abolished the right of British subjects to hold slaves. In the British West Indies, 750,000 slaves were freed within a few years.

The other old colonial powers in the New World tended to be much slower in their abolition of slavery. Portugal did little or nothing about slavery in Brazil, and when that nation became independent, its new government continued slavery. Portugal ended slavery elsewhere in its American possessions in 1836; the Swedes, in 1847;

reformers began to focus on ending the slave trade in East Africa and the Indian Ocean. This new drive against slavery and the slave trade in Africa itself became one of the rationales for European interference in Africa during the second half of the century and served as one of the foundations for the establishment of the late-century colonial empires.

Summary

The Transatlantic Revolutions. The revolutions and the crusade against slavery that occurred throughout the transatlantic world between 1776 and the 1830s transformed three continents. In North America, in France and other parts of Europe, and in South America, political experiments challenged government and the rule of monarchies and aristocracies. The foundations of modern liberal democracy were laid. The largest republic since ancient times had been established in North America. In Latin America, republicanism triumphed everywhere except Brazil. Never again could government be undertaken in these regions without some form of participation by the governed.

Economic and Social Liberalization. The expanding forms of political liberty found their counterparts in an economic life freed from the constraints of the old colonial empires and the slavery that marked their plantations. The new American republic constituted a vast free trade zone. Its commerce was open to the world. And for the first time since the encounter with Europe, Latin America could trade freely among its own peoples and those of the rest of the world. In France and Europe, where the Napoleonic armies had carried the doctrines of the rights of man, economic life had been rationalized and freed from the domination of local authorities and local weights and measures. National law formed the framework for economic activity. The movement to abolish slavery fostered a wage economy of free laborers. That kind of economy would generate its own set of problems and social dislocation, but it was nonetheless an economy of free human beings.

Nationalism. Finally, the age of transatlantic revolutions saw the emergence of nationalism as a political force, a development that will be more fully discussed in chapter 24. All of the revolutions, because of their popular political base, had given power to the idea of nations defined by their own character and historical past rather than by dynastic rulers. The Americans saw themselves as forming a new kind of nation. The French had demonstrated the power of a nation mobilized for military purposes. In turn, the aggression of France had aroused national sentiment, especially in Great Britain, Spain, and Germany. The new nations of Latin America also sought to define themselves by their heritage and historical experience rather than by their past in the Spanish and Portuguese Empires.

These various revolutions, their political doctrines, and their social and economic departures provided examples to peoples elsewhere in the world. But even more important, the transatlantic revolutions and eventual abolition of slavery meant that new political classes and independent nations would become actors on the world scene. Europeans would have to deal with a score of new nations in the Americas. The rest of the world confronted new nations freed from the direction and authority of European powers. The political changes in Europe meant that those nations and their relationships with the rest of the world would be directed by a broader range of groups than in the past.

Review Questions

1. Discuss the American Revolution in the context of transatlantic history. To what extent were the colonists influenced by their position in the transatlantic economy? To what extent were they influenced by European ideas and political developments? How did their demands for liberty compare and contrast with the ideas of liberty championed during the French Revolution?

2. How was the Estates General transformed into the National Assembly? How does the *Declaration of the Rights of Man and Citizen* reflect the social and political values of the eighteenth-century Enlightenment? What were the chief ways in which France and its government were reorganized in the early years of the revolution? Why has the Civil Constitution of the Clergy been called the greatest blunder of the National Assembly?

3. Why were some political factions dissatisfied with the constitutional settlement of 1791 in France? What was the revolution of 1792, and why did it occur? What were the causes of the Reign of Terror, and what political coalitions made it possible?

4. How did Napoleon rise to power? What were his major domestic achievements? Did his rule more nearly fulfill or betray the ideals of the French Revolution? Why did

Napoleon decide to invade Russia? Why did he fail? What were the major outlines of the peace settlement achieved by the Congress of Vienna?

5. What political changes took place in Latin America in the twenty years between 1804 and 1824? What were the main reasons for Creole discontent with Spanish rule? Who were some of the primary leaders of Latin American independence, and why were they successful? How were the movements to Latin American independence influenced by the American and French Revolutions? What were the factors that made the Latin American wars of independence different from those two revolutions?

6. A motto of the French Revolution was "liberty, equality, and fraternity." How might one compare the American Revolution, the French Revolution, and the Latin American wars of independence in regard to the achievement of these goals? Which groups in each country or region benefited from the revolution, and which gained little or nothing from the changes?

7. What intellectual and religious factors contributed to the rise of the antislavery movement? To what extent did nonhumanitarian forces contribute to it? What opposition did it meet? Why did slavery receive a new lease on life during the same years that the antislavery movement emerged?

INTERPRETING THE PAST

Women Activists and the French Revolution

Text Sources from MyHistoryLab /Primary Source DVD

   1. *Declaration of the Rights of Man and Citizen*
   2. Olympe de Gouges: *Declaration of the Rights of Woman and Female Citizen*

Text Sources from Chapter 23

   1. *French Women Petition to Bear Arms* (page 715)
   2. *A Pamphleteer Describes a Sans-Culotte* (page 718)

The French revolutionary era aroused widespread expectations among the country's citizens that the feudal system would be eliminated and that democracy would replace the hereditary aristocracy that ruled France. Women were at the forefront of the marches, strikes, and riots that prodded the representatives of the Third Estate (commoners) to push for radical changes in 1789. The resulting reorganization of the French government by the National Assembly and the Constitution of 1791 offered a number of reforms but did not provide for universal suffrage (right to vote) for men or women, or other truly democratic measures. The stage was

thus set for the second and more radical, stage of the Revolution to commence.

In this exercise you will read primary sources that focus on the role of women during the French Revolution, as active participants on the street, in public meetings, and in organizations such as the Society of Revolutionary Republican Women. The exclusion of women from participation in the political system, even after the events of 1789, led to an increase in demands for equal rights, unhindered by their traditionally subservient roles.

The first document here is the *Declaration of Rights of Man and Citizen*, issued by the National Assembly in late 1789 to declare men born free and forever equal in rights before the law. It was a formal acknowledgement that the individual freedoms that were the hallmark of the American Revolution should apply to France. The second document, from Olympe de Gouges, a writer and playwright, reacted to the *Declaration of Rights of Man* by issuing her own proclamation that called for equal rights for women. The third document is a petition from more than 300 Parisian women asking for the right to bear arms, and train for military service during the war with Austria, which had been provoked by the Emperor of Austria's threat to intervene in France to preserve the monarchy. The fourth document is a brief description of a *sans-culotte*, the working-class artisans who were at the heart of revolutionary activity and symbolized "civic virtue."

PRENTICE HALL **myhistorylab** *Where it's a good time to connect to the past!*

Key Terms

assignats (p. 716)

Consulate (p. 724)

Convention (p. 717)

creoles (p. 731)

Jacobins (p. 717)

levée en masse (p. 719)

peninsulares (p. 731)

Reign of Terror (p. 719)

sans-culottes (p. 717)

Thermidorean Reaction (p. 722)

Third Estate (p. 713)

Note: To learn more about the topics in this chapter, please turn to the Suggested Readings at the end of the book. For additional sources related to this chapter please see the Primary Source DVD at the back of this text or MyHistoryLab.

Use the source documents to explore the reasoning and evidence offered by the men and women of the revolutionary era in their demands for expanded rights. Use specific examples from the documents to back up your assertions.

Questions

How do the *French Women Petition to Bear Arms* and *Declaration of the Rights of Woman* challenge the idea of citizenship embodied in the *Declaration of the Rights of Man?*

How do the authors of the *French Women Petition to Bear Arms* relate their appeal to bear arms to their gender in French society?

What are the characteristics of the *sans-culottes* depicted in *A Pamphleteer Describes a Sans-Culotte?* How does the author suggest they will achieve solidarity against the enemies of the French Revolution? What are the similarities (and differences) of purpose and identity between the *sans-culottes*, who seem uniformly identified as male, and the authors of the *French Women Petition to Bear Arms?*

What elements are common to the *French Women Petition to Bear Arms*, the *Declaration of the Rights of Woman*, and *The Declaration of the Rights of Man?* What are the differences?

24

Political Consolidation in Nineteenth-Century Europe and North America

- ◆ The Emergence of Nationalism in Europe
- ◆ Early-Nineteenth-Century Political Liberalism
- ◆ Efforts to Liberalize Early-Nineteenth-Century European Political Structures
- ◆ Testing the New American Republic
- ◆ The Canadian Experience
- ◆ Midcentury Political Consolidation in Europe
- ◆ Unrest of Nationalities in Eastern Europe
- ◆ Racial Theory and Anti-Semitism

D URING THE NINETEENTH CENTURY TWO fundamental long-term developments occurred in the northern transatlantic world that would have a profound impact over the decades in every culture on the face of the earth. First, in both Europe and North America there took place a process of political consolidation that made the nation-states of that region the strongest of the period. Second, and directly contributing to that political strength, there emerged in Europe and North America powerful, new industrial economies with a new kind of society no longer based primarily on the land. As a direct result of this political consolidation and industrialization, the nations of the northern transatlantic became the world's major military powers. By the close of the nineteenth century and well into the twentieth this political and military power allowed the nations of Europe and the United States to exert unprecedented political, military, and economic influence around the globe. It was on the basis of that power that many people in Europe and North America came to claim superiority over people

One of the Extraordinary Figures of the Nineteenth Century, Giuseppe Garibaldi (1807–1882), here seen towards the end of his life serenely dressed in his trademark poncho (a mode of dress he adopted in the 1830s and 1840s as a freedom fighter in South America), was the forceful and spiritual leader of the movement for Italian unification, which was achieved, after many conflicts, in 1861.

European and North American Political Consolidation

Europe, North America

During the first three quarters of the nineteenth century the nations of Europe and North America underwent major political consolidation. Great Britain emerged from the Napoleonic Wars as the strongest power on the globe and maintained that position for more than a century. France experienced decades of changing political regimes but remained a major political and military force. However, the third quarter of the century saw Germany and Italy transformed from relatively soft regions of small principalities into major unified nation states. Similarly the Austrian Empire reorganized itself. As will be seen in Chapter 25, Russia also undertook major political and social reforms to consolidate the strength of the tsarist government. On the other side of the Atlantic the United States became a major nation aspiring to stretch across the North American continent as did Canada. These developments laid the foundation for the major transatlantic state-system of the late nineteenth and early twentieth centuries.

The movement towards strong, centralized national states in Europe and North America during the nineteenth century had counterparts elsewhere in the world. In Asia during this same period, Japan sought to imitate the military and economic power of the European states. Late nineteenth-century Latin America enjoyed one of its most successful and stable periods. The governments of that region established centralized regimes on the basis of relatively prosperous economies. In the United States the Civil War established the power of the central federal government over that of the individual states. The role of the war in the forging of a single American nation was similar to the role that military force played in the unifications of Italy and Germany and the suppression of the Paris Commune.

In Italy and Germany many people regarded the triumph of nationalism as a positive achievement. However, the last half of the century also saw various national and ethnic groups use the power of the national state to repress or dominate other groups. Examples include the Hungarian treatment of smaller subject nationalities and the British treatment of the Irish. To some extent, this phenomenon can be explained by the geographical borders of the new nations that were carved out of former European monarchies and empires, such as the Austro-Hungarian Empire. In many cases, the boundaries ignored the reality that many, perhaps most, regions were home to more than one ethnic group, with religions, languages, and ethnicities different from those of their rulers and the governing class. In the premodern dwelling in other cultures and other regions. Moreover, the manner in which Europeans and to a lesser extent Americans developed sets of ideas to explain what was happening politically and economically in their region would later be used by peoples elsewhere in the world as they responded to the worldwide power that the northern transatlantic powers exerted.

The present chapter will examine the process of political consolidation in the northern transatlantic world while Chapter 25 will explore the social changes that occurred there in the nineteenth century. Although we will consider the two processes separately, each contributed to the other. ■

The Emergence of Nationalism in Europe

Nationalism proved to be the single most powerful European political ideology of the nineteenth and early twentieth centuries. As a political idea, **nationalism** is based on world, loyalty to a ruling dynasty, rather than shared history, language, or ethnicity, was the primary determinant of group identity or membership in a polity above the local level. People saw themselves first as members of a tribe, clan, village, or town, and second as the subjects of a ruler who might not even speak their language and whose authority often impinged very little on their daily lives. Thus ethnic or linguistic minorities posed less of an obstacle to monarchical rulers than to governments of nation-states, where national identity is often based on shared language and ethnicity. This problem has continued to bedevil national states in Europe and elsewhere in the world into the modern era and is an important cause for many recent conflicts in regions as diverse as Eastern Europe, Asia, and Africa.

Elsewhere around the globe during the nineteenth century strong central governments often simply repressed minority populations, especially indigenous peoples, or allowed them fewer rights of civic participation and protection. In almost all cases the repression of minority groups generated social and political problems that haunted the twentieth century. Native Americans failed to gain rights in Latin America. In the United States the westward movement brought warfare against Native Americans, and legislation facilitated the segregation of American black citizens. In Canada, English speakers fared better than French speakers. In Australia, Aborigines were killed or forcibly relocated in many regions before and after that country's government gained sovereignty from England.

Finally, the emergence of strong European nation-states set the stage for the transfer of their rivalries from Europe to other areas of the globe. The militarily and economically strong states of Europe soon turned to foreign adventures that subjugated vast areas of Africa and Asia. This imperialism led many colonized peoples to become aware that only strong nationalistic movements of their own could eventually end subjugation by the militarily stronger Europeans. Consequently, during the first quarter of the twentieth century, the nationalistic principle that less than fifty years earlier had dominated European politics began to influence the politics of the peoples on whom Europeans had imposed their government and administration. As these former colonies achieved independence and established their own nation-states, however, their governments experienced problems similar to those of the European nations in balancing the demands for unity of the majority with the rights of the diverse ethnic and religious minorities inhabiting their territory.

Focus Questions

◆ What role has military and economic power played in strengthening nation-states?

◆ Why do most nation-states have ethnic minorities? Why have these minorities tended to be oppressed?

◆ How did the rivalry among the European nation-states affect other regions of the world? What relationship did it have on the development of nationalism outside of Europe?

the relatively modern concept that a nation is composed of people who are joined together by the bonds of common language, customs, culture, and history, and who, because of those bonds, should share the same government. That is to say, political and ethnic boundaries should coincide. This idea came into its own in Europe during the late eighteenth and early nineteenth centuries. Early-nineteenth-century nationalists directly opposed the principle upheld at the Congress of Vienna in 1814–1815 that legitimate monarchies or family dynasties, rather than ethnicity, should provide the basis for political unity. Nationalists naturally protested multinational states such as the Austrian or Russian Empires, which embraced a wide variety of diverse ethnic groups who were often hostile to each other. Nationalists also objected to peoples of the same ethnic group, such as Germans and Italians, dwelling in political units smaller than that of the ethnic nation. Consequently, nationalists challenged both the domestic and the international order of the Vienna settlement.

SOURCE *Joseph Mazzini on nationalism*

Creating Nations

Nationalists actually created nations in the nineteenth century. During the first half of the century a group of nationalistically minded writers using the printed word spread a nationalistic concept of the nation. They were frequently historians who chronicled a people's past or writers and literary scholars who established a national literature by collecting and publishing earlier writings in the people's language. In effect, they gave a people a sense of their past and a literature of their own. In time schoolteachers, by imparting a nation's official language and history, spread nationalistic ideas. The language to be used in the schools and in government offices was always a point of contention for nationalists. In France and Italy official versions of the national language were imposed in the schools and replaced local dialects. In parts of Scandinavia and eastern Europe nationalists attempted to resurrect from earlier times what they regarded as purer versions of the national language. Often these resurrected languages were

virtually invented by modern scholars or linguists. This process of establishing national languages led to far more linguistic uniformity within European nations than had existed before the nineteenth century. In most countries spoken and written proficiency in the official printed language became a path to social and political advancement and employment within government bureaucracies. The growth of a uniform language helped to persuade people who had not thought of themselves as constituting a nation that they were a nation. Yet even in 1850, perhaps less than half of the inhabitants of France, for example, spoke official French (see Map 24–1).

Meaning of Nationhood

Nationalists used a variety of arguments and metaphors to express what they meant by nationhood. Some argued, for example, that gathering Italians into a unified Italy or Germans into a unified Germany, thus eliminating the petty

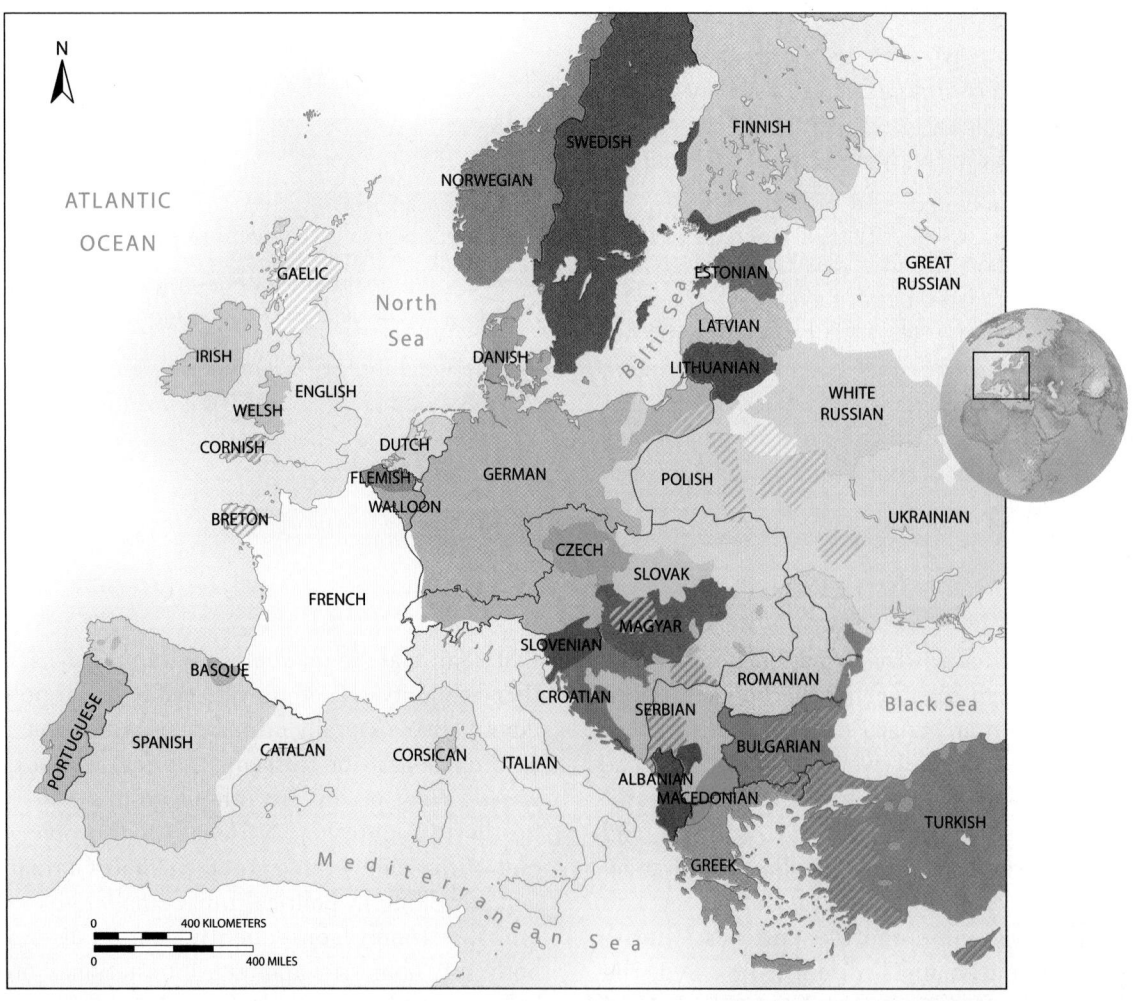

Map 24–1.   Languages of Europe. Although this map provides a good overview of the main languages of nineteenth-century Europe, it does not show the vast number of dialects that were the primary tongue of most speakers. A speaker of the Piedmont dialect from northwestern Italy, for example, would not understand a speaker from Sicily.

dynastic states that governed those regions, would promote economic and administrative efficiency. Some nationalists claimed that nations, like biological species in the natural world, were distinct creations of God. Other nationalists claimed a place for their nations in the divine order of things. Throughout the nineteenth century, for example, Polish nationalists portrayed Poland as the suffering Christ among nations, thus implicitly suggesting that Poland, like Christ, would experience resurrection and a new life. (See Document, "Mazzini Defines Nationality.")

A significant difficulty for nationalism was, and is, determining which ethnic groups could be considered nations, with claims to territory and political autonomy. In theory, any of them could, but in reality nationhood came to be associated with groups that were large enough to support a viable economy, that had a history of significant cultural association, that possessed a cultural elite that could nourish and spread the national language, and that could conquer other peoples to establish and protect their own independence. Throughout the century many smaller ethnic groups claimed to fulfill

Mazzini Defines Nationality

Document

No political force in the nineteenth century was stronger than nationalism. It replaced dynastic political loyalty with loyalty based on ethnicity. In 1835 the Italian nationalist and patriot Giuseppe Mazzini (1805–1872) explained his understanding of the concept. Note how he combined a generally democratic view of politics with a religious concept of the divine destiny of nations.

◆ What specific qualities of a people does Mazzini associate with nationalism? How and why does Mazzini relate nationalism to divine purposes? How does this view of nationality relate to the goals of liberal freedom? How does it compare to other perspectives on nationalism and independence movements (for example, "William Gladstone Pleads for Irish Home Rule" and "Herzl Calls for the Establishment of a Jewish State") in this chapter?

The essential characteristics of a nationality are common ideas, common principles and a common purpose. A nation is an association of those who are brought together by language, by given geographical conditions or by the role assigned them by history, who acknowledge the same principles and who march together to the conquest of a single definite goal under the rule of a uniform body of law.

The life of a nation consists in harmonious activity (that is, the employment of all individual abilities and energies comprised within the association) towards this single goal. . . .

But nationality means even more than this. Nationality also consists in the share of mankind's labors which God assigns to a people. This mission is the task which a people must perform to the end that the Divine Idea shall be realized in this world; it is the work which gives a people its rights as a member of Mankind; it is the baptismal rite which endows a people with its own character and its rank in the brotherhood of nations. . . .

Nationality depends for its very existence upon its sacredness within and beyond its borders.

If nationality is to be inviolable for all, friends and foes alike, it must be regarded inside a country as holy, like a

religion, and outside a country as a grave mission. It is necessary too that the ideas arising within a country grow steadily, as part of the general law of Humanity which is the source of all nationality. It is necessary that these ideas be shown to other lands in their beauty and purity, free from any alien mixture, from any slavish fears, from any skeptical hesitancy, strong and active; embracing in their evolution every aspect and manifestation of the life of the nation. These ideas, a necessary component in the order of universal destiny, must retain their originality even as they enter harmoniously into mankind's general progress.

The people must be the basis of nationality; its logically derived and vigorously applied principles its means; the strength of all its strength; the improvement of the life of all and the happiness of the greatest possible number its results; and the accomplishment of the task assigned to it by God its goal. This is what we mean by nationality.

From *Absolutism to Revolution, 1648–1848*, 2nd ed., Herbert H. Rowen, ed. Copyright © 1969. Reprinted by permission of Prentice Hall, Upper Saddle River, NJ.

these criteria but could not effectively achieve either independence or recognition. They could and did, however, create domestic unrest within the political units they inhabited. Such was the situation in Europe. A similar situation, though in many ways quite different, prevailed for a time in the United States, where by the middle of the century leaders of many Southern states began to make statements that resembled those of nationalist leaders in Europe. One can view the defeat of the Confederate States of America, discussed later in this chapter, as an example of the military failure of a region to establish itself as a kind of nationality.

Regions of Nationalistic Pressure in Europe

During the nineteenth century nationalists challenged the political status quo in six major areas of Europe. England had brought Ireland under direct rule in 1800, allowing the Irish to elect members to the British Parliament in Westminster. Irish nationalists, however, wanted independence or at least self-government. The "Irish problem" would haunt British politics for the next two centuries. German nationalists sought political unity for all German-speaking peoples, challenging the multinational Austrian Empire and pitting Prussia and Austria against each other. Italian nationalists sought to unify the peninsula and drive out the Austrians. Polish nationalists struggled, primarily against Russia, to restore Poland as an independent nation. In eastern Europe a host of national groups, including Hungarians, Czechs, Slovenes, and others, sought either autonomy or formal recognition within the Austrian Empire. Finally, in the Balkans national groups, including Serbs, Greeks, Albanians, Romanians, and Bulgarians, sought independence from Ottoman and Russian control. Although there were never simultaneous disturbances in all six areas, any one of them could erupt into turmoil. In each area, nationalist activity ebbed and flowed. The dominant governments often thought they needed only to repress the activity or ride it out until stability returned. During the century, however, nationalists changed the political map and political culture of Europe in a way that the Confederate States of America failed to do in the mid–nineteenth-century United States.

Early-Nineteenth-Century Political Liberalism

In the present-day United States, the word *liberal* carries meanings and connotations that have little or nothing to do with its significance for nineteenth-century Europeans. European conservatives of the last century saw liberals as more radical than they actually were; present-day

Americans often think of nineteenth-century liberals as more conservative than they were. In any case, the term *liberal* as used in present-day American political rhetoric has virtually no relationship to its nineteenth-century counterpart.

Politics

European **liberalism** derived from the Enlightenment, the example of English liberties, and the so-called principles of 1789 as embodied in the French *Declaration of Rights of Man and Citizen*. Liberal political figures sought to establish a framework of legal equality, religious toleration, and freedom of the press. They sought to limit the arbitrary power of the government against the persons and property of individual citizens. They generally believed that the legitimacy of government emanated from the freely given consent of the governed expressed through elected representative or parliamentary bodies. Most important, free government required that state or crown ministers be responsible to the representatives of the nation rather than to the monarch.

These goals were limited. Such responsible government, however, existed in none of the major European countries in 1815. Even in Great Britain the ministers were at least as responsible to the monarch as to the House of Commons. The people who espoused these changes in government tended to be those who were excluded from the existing political processes, but whose wealth and education made them believe such exclusion was unjustified. Liberals were often academics, members of the learned professions, and people involved in the rapidly expanding commercial and manufacturing sectors. They believed in and were products of the career open to talent. The existing monarchical and aristocratic regimes often failed to recognize sufficiently their new status and to provide for their economic and professional interests.

Although European liberals wanted broader political participation, they were not Democrats. Second only to their hostility to the privileged aristocracies was their general contempt for the lower, unpropertied classes. Liberals transformed the eighteenth-century concept of aristocratic liberty into a new concept of privilege based on wealth and property instead of birth. By midcentury this widely shared attitude meant that throughout Europe, liberals had separated themselves from both the rural and the urban working class. In the first half of the nineteenth century political liberals did not generally support the extension of political rights to women, but liberal political principles provided women with strong arguments to do so, as seen for example in the *Declaration of Female Independence* issued by the Seneca Falls convention in the United States in 1848.

Economics

The economic goals of the liberals also furthered their separation from the working class. Here, the Enlightenment and the economic thought deriving from Adam Smith set the pattern. The manufacturers of Great Britain, the landed and manufacturing middle class of France, and the commercial interests of Germany and Italy wanted to be able to manufacture and sell goods freely. They thus favored the removal of international tariffs as well as internal barriers to trade. To that end, liberals across the Continent and those who imitated them outside of Europe favored the rapid construction of railways from the 1830s onward.

European economic liberals opposed the old paternalistic legislation that established wages and labor practices by government regulation or by guild privileges. Labor was simply one more commodity to be bought and sold freely. Liberals sought an economic structure in which people were free to use their talents and property to enrich themselves. The liberals contended that this would lead to more goods and services for everyone at lower prices. Economic liberty was to provide the basis for material progress.

The economic goals of European liberals found many followers outside Europe among groups that favored the expansion of free trade, new transport systems, and a free market in labor. In the United States people of this outlook often attacked slavery as an inefficient, paternalistic institution. In Latin America political liberals sought to remove paternalistic legislation that had protected Native Americans during the centuries of the Spanish Empire.

Relationship of Nationalism and Liberalism

Nationalism was not necessarily or logically linked to liberalism, and some conservative nationalists, for example, ignored the rights of national minorities. Liberalism and nationalism, however, were often complementary. Behind the concept of a people joined naturally together by the bonds of common language, customs, culture, and history lurked the idea of popular sovereignty. The idea of the career open to talent could be applied to suppressed national groups who were not permitted to realize their cultural or political potential. The efficient government and administration required by commerce and industry would mean

A CONVENTION OF HEMMERS AND STITCHERS HELD AT LYNN, FEB. 28, FOR ADOPTING A LIST OF PRICES; MRS. E. HALL, PRESIDING.—(See page 284.)

Female Liberal Political Activism. The ideas of political liberalism spoke deeply to the situation of women throughout the transatlantic world. Women demanded entrance into the political forum as demonstrated by the first women's rights convention in Seneca Falls, New York in 1848, and this meeting of women strikers in Lynn, Massachusetts in 1860.

replacing the small German and Italian states with larger political units. Moreover, nationalist groups in one country could gain the sympathy of liberals in other nations by espousing representative government and political liberty.

Liberalism and Nationalism in Modern World History

The wars of the French Revolution in Europe had demonstrated by the early nineteenth century that the ideals of political liberalism could easily spread across dynastic borders. In time those liberal ideals as well as those of nationalism would spread around the globe. It is for this reason that what began as a European development is so important not just for Europe but also for global history. The concept of the rights of man and citizen could be used during the wars of independence in Latin America to challenge Spanish government. By the close of the nineteenth century those same ideals could be turned against the colonial government that Europeans imposed on Africa and Asia (see Chapter 27). Furthermore, the belief that people should have the right to govern themselves would inspire the settlers who spread across both the United States and Canada as well as those who came to live in Australia and New Zealand. Similarly, the belief that individual ethnic groups should constitute independent nations became a major political idea whereby peoples living under European colonial government during the late nineteenth and even more importantly the twentieth century would challenge the right of Europeans and later Americans to govern them or to dominate their lives informally through economic power. Thus the political developments in Europe during the early nineteenth century would produce a profound impact around the globe during the next century.

Efforts to Liberalize Early-Nineteenth-Century European Political Structures

European nations certainly did not move towards liberal political structures rapidly or without considerable conflict. Indeed after the Congress of Vienna most conservatives hoped that they had established walls against liberal advances. Three examples will indicate the different experiences that different European liberals confronted early in the nineteenth century.

Russia: The Decembrist Revolt of 1825 and the Autocracy of Nicholas I

In the process of driving Napoleon's army across Europe and then occupying defeated France, many officers in the Russian army were introduced to the ideas of the French Revolution and the Enlightenment. They realized how economically backward and politically stifled Russia was. Under these conditions, groups within the officer corps formed secret societies. These societies were small and divided in their goals; they agreed only that the government of Russia must change. Sometime during 1825 they seem to have decided to carry out a coup d'état in 1826.

Other events intervened. In late November 1825 Tsar Alexander I suddenly and unexpectedly died. His death created two crises. The first was a dynastic one: Alexander had no direct heir. His brother Constantine stood next in line to the throne. However, Constantine, who was the commander of Russian forces in Poland, had renounced any claim to be tsar. Through a series of secret instructions made public only after his death, Alexander had named his younger brother, Nicholas (r. 1825–1855), as the new tsar. Once Alexander was dead, the legality of these instructions became uncertain. Constantine acknowledged Nicholas as tsar, and Nicholas acknowledged Constantine. This family muddle continued for about three weeks, during which Russia actually had no ruler, to the astonishment of Europe. Then, in early December, the army command reported to Nicholas the existence of a conspiracy among certain officers. Able to wait no longer, Nicholas had himself declared tsar.

The second crisis now unfolded—a plot by junior officers to rally the troops under their command to the cause of reform. On December 26, 1825, the army was to take the oath of allegiance to Nicholas, who was less popular than Constantine and was regarded as more conservative. Nearly all of the regiments did so. But the Moscow regiment, whose chief officers, surprisingly, were not secret society members, marched into the Senate Square in Saint Petersburg and refused to swear allegiance. Rather, they called for Constantine and a constitution. Attempts to settle the situation peacefully failed. Late in the afternoon Nicholas ordered cavalry and artillery to attack the insurgents. Five of the plotters were executed, and over one hundred other officers were exiled to Siberia.

The immediate result of the revolt was the crushing of liberalism as even a moderate political influence in Russia. Nicholas I also manifested extreme conservatism in foreign affairs. Russia under Nicholas became the policeman of Europe, ever ready to provide troops to suppress liberal and nationalist movements. Except for a modest experiment early in the twentieth century tsarist Russia would never know genuinely liberal political structures.

Revolution in France (1830)

In 1824 Louis XVIII (r. 1814–1824), the Bourbon restored to the throne of France by the Congress of Vienna, died. He was succeeded by his brother, Charles X (r. 1824–1830). The new king considered himself a monarch by divine right and he also moved to restore lands that the French aristocrats had lost during the revolution. He also pressed other conservative measures through the Chamber of Deputies. Opposition soon developed. After elections in 1827 Charles began to govern somewhat less conservatively, but French liberals wanted a genuinely constitutional regime. Matters came to a head in 1829 when Charles abandoned efforts to accommodate liberals and appointed an ultraroyalist ministry, but his efforts backfired.

In 1830 Charles X called for new elections, in which the liberals scored a stunning victory. Instead of attempting to accommodate the new Chamber of Deputies, the king and his ministers decided to undertake a royalist seizure of power. In June and July 1830 the ministry had sent a naval expedition against Algeria. On July 9 reports of its victory, and the consequent foundation of a French empire in North Africa, reached Paris. On July 25, 1830, under the euphoria of this foreign diversion, Charles X issued the Four Ordinances, which restricted freedom of the press, dissolved the recently elected Chamber of Deputies, and called for new elections under a franchise restricted to the wealthiest people in the country.

Decembrist Revolt. When the Moscow regiment refused to swear allegiance to Nicholas, he ordered the cavalry and artillery to attack them. Although a total failure, the Decembrist Revolt came to symbolize the yearnings of all Russian liberals in the nineteenth century for a constitutional government. *The Insurrection of the Decembrists at Senate Square, St. Petersburg on 14th December, 1825 (w/c on paper) by Russian School (nineteenth century). Private Collection/ Bridgeman Art Library.*

Liberal newspapers immediately called on the nation to reject the monarch's actions. The laboring populace of Paris, burdened since 1827 by an economic downturn, took to the streets and erected barricades. The king called out troops, and more than 1,800 people died during the ensuing battles in the city. On August 2 Charles X abdicated and left France for exile in England. The liberals in the Chamber of Deputies named a new ministry composed of constitutional monarchists. They proclaimed Louis Philippe (r. 1830–1848), the Duke of Orléans, the head of the liberal branch of the royal family, the new monarch. Under what became known as the **July Monarchy**, Louis Philippe was called the king of the French rather than of France. The king had to cooperate with the Chamber of Deputies; he could not dispense with laws on his own authority. The revolutionary tricolor replaced the white flag of the Bourbons. The Charter, or constitution, was regarded as embodying the rights of the people rather than a concession granted by the monarch. Catholicism was recognized only as the religion of the majority of the people, not the official religion. Censorship was abolished. The franchise, though still restricted, was extended. Socially, however, the Revolution of 1830 proved quite conservative. The landed oligarchy retained its economic, political, and social influence. Money became the path to power and influence in the government. There was much corruption. Most important, the liberal monarchy displayed scant sympathy for the lower and working classes.

The Great Reform Bill in Britain (1832)

The passage of the **Great Reform Bill**, which became law in 1832, was the result of events different from those that occurred on the Continent. In Britain the forces of conservatism and reform compromised with each other. As a result, during the century Great Britain became for most

Liberty Leading the People by Eugene Delacroix is a famous evocation of the Revolution of 1830. *Giraudon/Art Resource, N.Y.*

parliamentary reform were returned to Parliament. Even some Tories believed that parliamentary reform was necessary because they had concluded that Catholic emancipation could have been passed only by a corrupt House of Commons. The Wellington ministry soon fell. The Tories were badly divided, and King William IV (r. 1830–1837) turned to the Whigs under the leadership of Earl Grey (1764–1845) to form a government.

The Whig ministry soon presented the House of Commons with a major reform bill that had two broad goals. The first was to replace "rotten" boroughs, which had few voters, with representatives for the previously unrepresented manufacturing districts and cities. The second was to increase the number of voters in England and Wales. In 1831 the House of Commons narrowly defeated the bill. Grey called for a new election, in which a majority in favor of the bill was returned to the Commons. The House of Commons passed the reform bill, but the House of Lords rejected it. Mass meetings were held throughout the country, and riots broke out in

people the exemplary liberal state not only of Europe but also of the world.

English determination to maintain the union with Ireland caused the first step in the reform process. England's relationship to Ireland was not unlike that of Russia's to Poland or Austria's to Hungary. The Act of Union in 1800 between England and Ireland suppressed the separate Irish Parliament. The Irish now sent representatives to the British Parliament at Westminster, but only Protestant Irishmen could be elected to represent overwhelmingly Catholic Ireland.

During the 1820s, under the leadership of Daniel O'Connell (1775–1847), Irish nationalists organized the Catholic Association to agitate for **Catholic emancipation**, as the movement for legal rights for Roman Catholics was known. In 1828 O'Connell was elected to Parliament but could not legally take his seat. The British ministry of the Duke of Wellington (1769–1852) realized that henceforth Ireland might elect a predominantly Catholic delegation to Parliament. If they were not seated, civil war might erupt. Consequently, in 1829 Wellington and Robert Peel (1788–1850) steered the Catholic Emancipation Act through Parliament. Roman Catholics could now become members of Parliament. This measure, together with the repeal in 1828 of restrictions against Protestant nonconformists, ended the monopoly held by members of the Church of England on British political life.

Catholic emancipation alienated many of Wellington's Tory supporters. In the election of 1830 many supporters of

Daniel O'Connell, known as the "Liberator," was the preeminent leader of Catholic emancipation in the first half of the nineteenth century.

several cities. Finally, William IV agreed to create enough new peers to give a third reform bill a majority in the House of Lords. Under this pressure, the measure became law in 1832.

The Great Reform Act expanded the size of the English electorate, but it was not a democratic measure. The electorate was increased by over 200,000 persons, or by almost 50 percent. The basis of voting, however, remained a property qualification. Some working-class voters actually lost the vote when their old franchise rights were abolished. New urban boroughs gave the growing cities a voice in the House of Commons. Yet the passage of the Reform Act did not, as it was once thought, constitute the triumph of the middle-class interest in England. For every new urban electoral district, a new rural district was also drawn. It was expected that the aristocracy would dominate the rural elections.

Although passed with much turmoil and conflict, the Great Reform Act established the foundations for long-term political stability in Britain. During the 1840s a major working-class political movement known as **Chartism** would bring the demands of industrial workers into the political process. Despite the tensions created by Chartism, British political structures maintained themselves. Throughout the second half of the nineteenth century Great Britain continued to symbolize the confident liberal state. A large body of ideas emphasizing competition and individualism was accepted by the members of all classes. Even the leaders of trade unions during these years asked only to receive some of the fruits of prosperity and to prove their own social respectability. Parliament itself continued to provide an institution that permitted the absorption of new groups and interests into the existing political processes.

The most important example of the opening of parliamentary processes was the Second Reform Act passed by a Conservative government in 1867. It increased the number of voters from approximately 1,430,000 to 2,470,000. Britain had taken a major step towards democracy. Benjamin Disraeli (1804–1881), who led the Conservatives in the House of Commons, thought significant portions of the working class would eventually support Conservative candidates who were responsive to social issues. He also thought the growing suburban middle class would become more conservative.

Gladstone and Disraeli The election of 1868, however, which followed the Second Reform Act, dashed Disraeli's hopes. William Gladstone (1809–1898) became the new prime minister. His ministry of 1868–1874 witnessed the culmination of classical British liberalism. Gladstone introduced competitive examinations into the civil service, abolished the purchase of army officers' commissions, and introduced the secret ballot. He opened Oxford and Cambridge universities to students of all religious denominations and, by the Education Act of 1870, made the British government responsible for establishing and running elementary schools, which had been supported by the various churches.

The liberal policy of creating popular support for the nation by extending political liberty and reforming abuses had its conservative counterpart in concern about social reform. Disraeli succeeded Gladstone as prime minister in

A House of Commons Debate. William Ewart Gladstone, standing on the right, is attacking Benjamin Disraeli, who sits with legs crossed and arms folded. Gladstone served in the British Parliament from the 1830s through the 1890s. Four times the Liberal Party prime minister, he was responsible for guiding major reforms through Parliament. Disraeli, regarded as the founder of modern British conservatism, served as prime minister from 1874 to 1880. *Mary Evans Picture Library.*

1874. Whereas Gladstone looked to individualism, free trade, and competition to solve social problems, Disraeli believed the state should protect weaker citizens. In his view, paternalistic legislation would alleviate class antagonism. His most important measures were the Public Health Act of 1875, which consolidated and extended previous sanitary legislation, and the Artisans Dwelling Act of 1875, through which the government became actively involved in providing housing for the working class.

The Irish Question Ireland remained a major issue for the British government. From the late 1860s onward, Irish nationalists had sought to achieve **home rule** for Ireland, by which they meant more Irish control of local government. Their demands of the British government very much resembled the demands that first the Hungarians and then the Czechs made towards the Habsburg government, which will be considered later in this chapter. The Irish, like the Hungarians and Czechs in the Habsburg Empire, proved a profoundly disruptive force in British politics.

The leader of the Irish movement for home rule was Charles Stewart Parnell (1846–1891). By 1885 Parnell had organized eighty-five Irish members of the House of

William Gladstone Pleads for Irish Home Rule

Document

Since 1800 Ireland had been governed as part of Great Britain, sending representatives to the British Parliament in Westminster. Throughout the century, there had been tension and violent conflict between the Irish and their English governors. Agitation for home rule, whereby the Irish would directly control many of their own affairs, reached a peak in the 1880s. In 1886 William Gladstone introduced a Home Rule Bill into Parliament. The evening when Parliament voted on the measure Gladstone made a long speech, part of which is quoted here, asking Parliament to reject the traditions of the past and to grant Ireland this measure of independence. That night the Home Rule Bill of 1886 went down to defeat. The problem of Irish home rule continues to vex British politics today.

◆ **Why did Gladstone support Irish home rule in 1886? How does he pose the issue as a matter of redeeming the reputation of England?**

What is the case of Ireland at this moment? . . . Can anything stop a nation's demand, except its being proved to be immoderate and unsafe? But here are multitudes, and, I believe, millions upon millions, out-of-doors, who feel this demand to be neither immoderate nor unsafe. In our opinion, there is but one question before us about this demand. It is as to the time and circumstance of granting it. There is no question in our minds that it will be granted. . . .

Ireland stands at your bar expectant, hopeful, almost suppliant. Her words are the words of truth and soberness. She asks a blessed oblivion of the past, and in that oblivion our interest is deeper than even hers. My right honourable friend the Member [of Parliament] for East Edinburgh ask us tonight to abide by the traditions of which we are the heirs. What traditions? By the Irish traditions? Go into the length and breadth of the world, ransack the literature of all countries, find, if you can, a single voice, a single book, find, I would almost say, as much as a single newspaper article, unless the product of the [present] day, in which the conduct of England towards

Ireland is anywhere treated except with profound and bitter condemnation. Are these the traditions by which we are exhorted to stand? No, they are a sad exception to the glory of our country. They are a broad and black blot upon the pages of its history; and what we want to do is to stand by the traditions of which we are the heirs in all matters except our relations with Ireland, and to make our relations with Ireland conform to the other traditions of our country. So we treat our traditions—so we hail the demand of Ireland for what I call a blessed oblivion of the past. She also asks a boon [a favor] for the future; and that boon for the future, unless we are much mistaken, will be a boon to us in respect of honour, no less than a boon to her in respect of happiness, prosperity, and peace. Such . . . is her prayer. Think, I beseech you, think well, think wisely, think, not for the moment, but for the years that are to come, before you reject this Bill.

Quoted in Hans Kohn, ed., *The Modern World: 1848 to the Present*, 2nd ed. (New York: Macmillan; London: Collier-Macmillan Ltd., 1968), pp. 116, 118.

Commons into a tightly disciplined party that often voted as a bloc. In the election of 1885 the Irish Party emerged holding the balance of power between the English Liberals and Conservatives. The Irish could decide which party would take office. In December 1885 Gladstone announced support for home rule for Ireland, and Parnell gave his votes to the formation of a Liberal ministry. (See Document, "William Gladstone Pleads for Irish Home Rule.") However, the issue split the Liberal Party. In 1886 a group known as the Liberal Unionists joined with the Conservatives to defeat Gladstone's Home Rule Bill. Gladstone called for a new election, which the Liberals lost. They remained permanently divided. The new Conservative ministry of Lord Salisbury (1830–1903) attempted to reconcile the Irish to the English government through public works and administrative reform. The policy had only marginal success.

In 1892 Gladstone returned to power and sponsored a second Home Rule Bill that passed the House of Commons but was defeated in the House of Lords. With the failure of this bill, further action on the Irish question was suspended until a Liberal ministry passed the third Home Rule Bill in the summer of 1914. However, the implementation of home rule was suspended for the duration of World War I.

As already noted, the Irish question affected British politics much the way that the nationalities problem affected Austria. Normal British domestic issues could not be adequately addressed because of the political divisions created by Ireland. The split of the Liberal Party hurt the cause of further social and political reform. The people who could agree about reforms could not agree on Ireland, and Ireland seemed more important. Because the two traditional parties failed to deal with the social questions, by the turn of the century a newly organized Labour Party began to fill the vacuum.

1848: Year of Revolutions in Europe

In 1848 a series of liberal and nationalistic revolutions and revolts spread across Europe (see Map 24–2). No single factor caused this general revolutionary groundswell; rather, similar conditions existed in several countries. Severe food shortages had prevailed since 1846 due to poor harvests. The commercial and industrial economy was in recession, with widespread unemployment. However, the dynamic for

Map 24–2. Centers of Revolution in 1848–1849. The revolution that toppled the July Monarchy in Paris in 1848 soon spread to Austria and many of the German and Italian states. Yet by the end of 1849, most of these uprisings had been suppressed.

change in 1848 originated not with the working classes but with the political liberals, who were generally drawn from the middle classes. Throughout the Continent liberals were pushing for more representative governments, civil liberty, and unregulated economic life.

To put additional pressure on their governments, the liberals began to appeal for the support of the urban working classes, even though the goals of the two groups were different. The working classes sought improved employment and better working conditions rather than political reform for its own sake. The liberals refused to follow political revolution with social reform and thus isolated themselves from their temporary working-class allies. Once separated from potential mass support, the liberal revolutions became an easy prey to the armies of reactionary governments. As a result, the revolutions of 1848 failed to establish genuinely liberal or national states.

What are known in European history as the Revolutions of 1848 were confined to the Continent, where the results were important for the individual nation-states. In France the monarchy of Louis Philippe was overthrown and briefly replaced by a republic. In 1851 the republic was in turn overthrown in a military coup led by Louis Napoleon, a nephew of the first Napoleon. Thereafter Louis Napoleon created the Second Empire and took the title of Napoleon III. In Prussia and the Austrian Empire short-lived revolutions brought political liberals and nationalists to the fore, but in each case those revolutions were suppressed by the military. The same was true of efforts by Italian nationalists to thrust off Austrian rule of Italy.

From the standpoint of world history, however, the chief importance of the failed liberal and national Revolutions of 1848 was the emergence on the European continent of strongly conservative governments that would dominate the scene for the next quarter century. The turmoil of 1848 through 1850 ended the era of liberal revolution that had begun in 1789. Liberals and nationalists had discovered that rational argument and local insurrections would not help them to achieve their goals. The working class also adopted new tactics and organization. The era of the riot and urban insurrection was ending. In the future, workers would turn to trade unions and political parties to achieve their political and social goals. Finally, after the Revolutions of 1848, the political initiative in Europe passed for a time to the conservative political groups.

The defeat of liberal political forces in 1848 and the triumph of conservative powers also influenced the modernization of Japan. Within a few years Japan would emerge from its long self-imposed isolation. After the Meiji Restoration the new leaders of Japan looked to European examples of successful modern nations. The nation they would most clearly copy was the conservative, militaristic Germany that emerged after the defeat of the liberals of 1848.

Testing the New American Republic

Towards Sectional Conflict

While the nations of Western Europe very slowly embraced political liberalism, the United States of America was continuing its bold republican political experiment. By the first quarter of the century, however, serious sectional tensions had arisen, the most important of which related to the presence of black slavery in the Southern states.

The Constitutional Convention of 1788 had debated the sectional difference in a dispute over what proportion of the slave population, if any, would be counted in determining how many seats the Southern states were allotted in the House of Representatives. A compromise allowed the slaveholding states to count three fifths of their slaves when calculating their population for representation in Congress. The Constitution also forbade any federal attempt to prevent the importation of slaves before 1808. Between 1788 and 1808 thousands of slaves were imported into the United States.

The westward movement, however, meant that slavery could not permanently be ignored. The Ordinance of 1787, passed by Congress under the Articles of Confederation, had prohibited slavery in the Northwest Territory, which embraced the future states of Ohio, Indiana, Illinois, Michigan, and Wisconsin. Territory south of the Ohio River and beyond the Mississippi River was, however, open to slavery, and there it spread. By 1820 the number of slave and free states was evenly divided; this meant an equal number of senators from slave and free states. That year, Missouri was admitted as a slave state and Maine as a free one. It was also decided that in the future no slave states would be carved out of land north of the southern border of Missouri. For the time being, this Missouri Compromise ended congressional debate over slavery. Nonetheless, the economies of the North and the South were rapidly diverging.

Northern Economic Development Family farms, free labor, commerce, and early industrialization in textiles characterized the economy of the Northern states. Northern farmers tended primarily to produce foodstuffs for their local communities. The farms were relatively small and worked by families. Farm laborers were free. Similarly, free laborers worked in the towns, on the ships, and in the factories of the North. The political spokesmen for the North tended to favor tariffs to protect their young industries from cheaper foreign competition. In this favoring of tariffs, many Americans whose political views otherwise often resembled European liberals differed from their European counterparts.

The North was the site of the earliest textile factories in the United States. Samuel Slater had established the first textile mill in Rhode Island in 1790. He had learned how to manufacture textiles in the new mills of industrializing Great Britain. His transfer of that technology to America illustrates how important British and European advances were transported to the United States. Much of the early industrialization of the United States depended on such technological transfers. By the second decade of the nineteenth century the North had hundreds of cotton factories. These mills used cotton that was produced in the South, but most Southern cotton was sold overseas, mainly to the growing British textile industry.

During the second quarter of the century innovations in transportation led to the fuller integration of different parts of the Northern economy. Canals were built to link the major rivers with manufacturing and agricultural markets. The most famous was the Erie Canal, which connected the Hudson River to the Great Lakes. Other canals linked the Great Lakes to the Ohio River. Major efforts were undertaken to make the Ohio, Mississippi, and Missouri Rivers navigable, which allowed steamboats to transport goods. But by the late 1840s, in America as in Europe, the major transportation innovation was the railroad. Most of the railways linked the Northeast and the West and fostered the commercial agriculture of the Midwest. Its products were sold in the Northeast and exported from Northern ports. Hence, the development of east–west railways undermined the older river-based trade routes along the Ohio and down the Mississippi. Few major lines ran north and south, so former ties between the sections based on the rivers weakened. The building of the early railways also aided the development of the Northern coal and iron industries. The further expansion of railways at midcentury caused new sectional tensions, as it became clear the railways could open vast territories for settlement and could thus also open a national debate over the future of slavery. That prospect sharpened the sectional debate and led to civil war (see Map 24–3).

Rivers, canals, and railways allowed the upper Midwest to develop into a rich area for agriculture. In this sense much of the Northern economy was as rural and agricultural as the Southern. What most distinguished the two regions

The Excelsior Iron Works, located in New York City. This print from the 1840s shows the works as a beehive of activity. Iron mills produced the material for railroads, ships, and machinery.

was free versus slave labor. The Southern economy depended on slavery and could expand only if slavery were allowed to expand as well.

The Southern Economy The overwhelmingly rural economy of the American South was dependent on cotton and slavery. In those respects, the Southern economy resembled the economies of many Latin American countries, which were based on exporting a single crop or natural resource and on slave labor. The South had to export goods, primarily raw cotton, either to the North or to Europe, primarily to Great Britain, to maintain its standard of living.

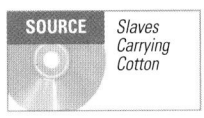

SOURCE Slaves Carrying Cotton

Cotton was king. The invention of the cotton gin by Eli Whitney (1765–1825) in 1793 made cotton cultivation much more profitable because the seed no longer had to be laboriously picked by hand out of the new cotton. The industrial revolution in textiles kept cotton prices high, and the expansion in world population kept the demand for cotton cloth steady. The South profited from growing the cotton, New England from shipping it, and other parts of the North from supplying the manufactured goods the South needed. The South had virtually no incentive to diversify its agriculture.

Slavery in the American South Slavery was abolished in the North by the early nineteenth century largely in response to the egalitarian values of the American Revolution. In any case, slavery had never been fundamental to the Northern

Map Exploration

To explore this map further, go to http://www.prenhall.com/craig_maps

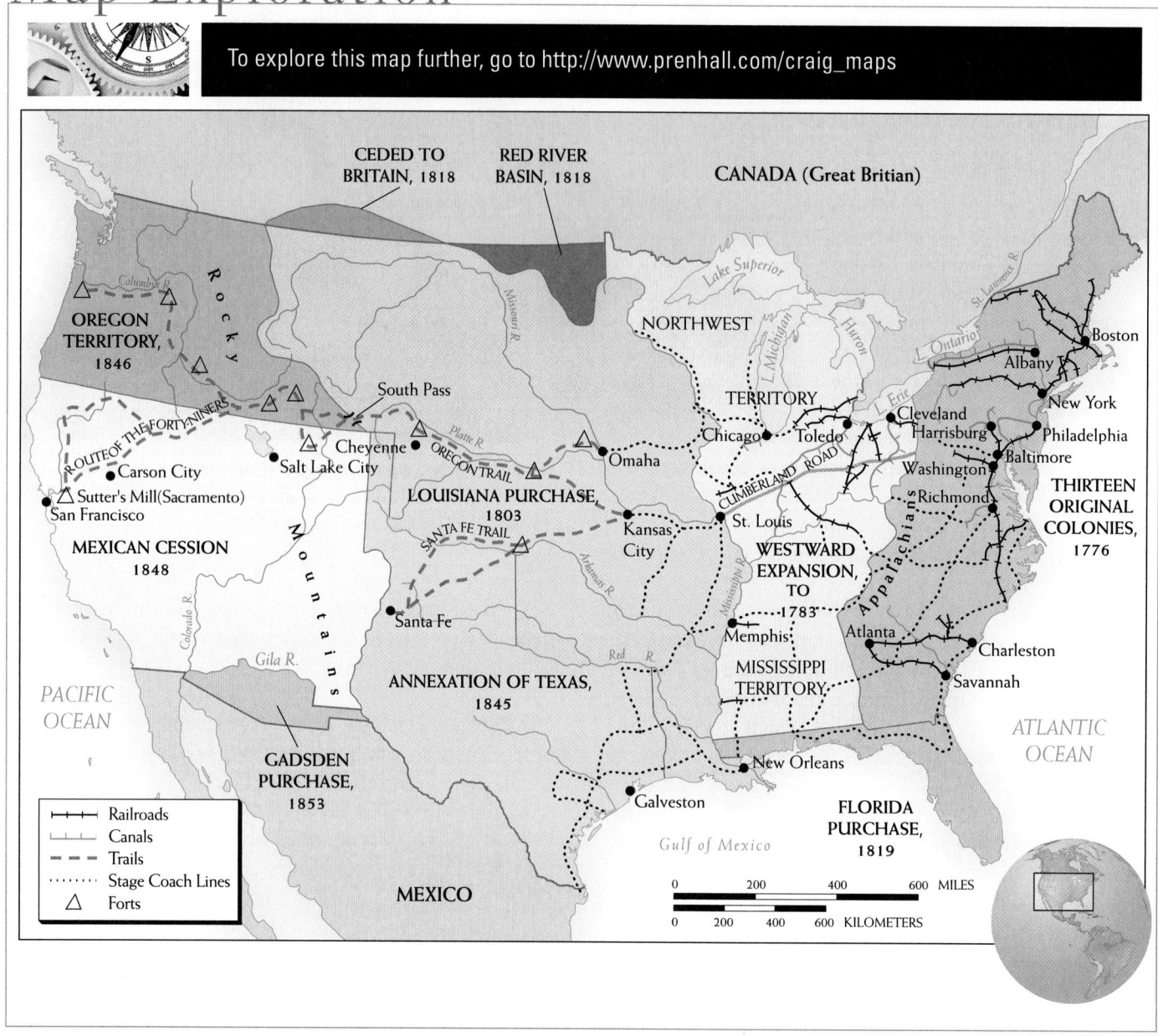

Map 24–3. The United States, 1776–1850. During the nineteenth century the United States expanded across the entire North American continent. The revolutionary settlement had provided most of the land east of the Mississippi. The single largest addition thereafter was the Louisiana Purchase of 1803. The annexation of Texas, and later the Mexican Cession following the Mexican War, added the major Southwestern territories. The borders of the Oregon Territory were settled through long, difficult negotiations with Great Britain.

economy. But in the South, the expansion of the cotton empire in the Mississippi Delta in the early nineteenth century gave slavery a new lease on life. Although most Southern families never owned slaves and relatively few slave owners had possessed more than a few slaves, the institution of slavery survived for many reasons. For one, it was economically viable, and no one could devise a way politically or socially acceptable to white Southerners to abolish it. No less impor-

tant was the strong commitment to the protection of private property, which included slaves, throughout American society in both the North and the South. Perhaps the most basic reason for the endurance of slavery after the early nineteenth century, however, was racist thinking that saw blacks as fundamentally inferior to whites. Such thinking was not peculiar to the South, but it functioned there as one more argument against abolishing slavery.

What was the life of an American slave like? All American slaves were nonwhite, the descendants of Africans who had been forcibly captured and shipped in the most wretched of conditions to the United States (see Chapter 17). Despite much miscegenation among Africans and their white slave owners and Native Americans, the various slave codes defined as black virtually anyone who had African antecedents. Slaves were regarded as chattel property; that is, they could be sold, given away, or even gambled away like any other piece of property. They had no recourse to law or constitutional protections and could be, and often were, treated badly by their masters. Whipping and beating were permitted. State laws protected slaves from extreme violence but were laxly enforced; slaves lived with no serious protection from the law or legal authorities. Their standard of living was generally poor. Although owners wanted to see their slave investments reproduce themselves, slaves suffered from overwork and from diseases associated with poor nutrition, substandard sanitation, and inferior housing.

Slaves worked primarily in the fields, where they plowed, hoed, and harvested cotton, rice, sugar, tobacco, or corn. They were usually organized into work gangs supervised by white overseers. This work was, like all farming, seasonal, but during planting or harvest seasons, labor would persist from sunrise to sunset. Children would work in the fields as helpers. Older or more privileged slaves might work in the house, cleaning, cooking, or taking care of children.

Recent scholarship has emphasized how the slave communities helped preserve the family life and inner personalities of the slaves. Some elements of African culture persisted in the slave communities. African legends were passed on orally. Religion proved extraordinarily important. Slaves also adopted for their own cultural needs the Old Testament stories of the Jews' liberation from Egypt. They also often combined elements of African religion with evangelical Protestantism. Yet despite these efforts to preserve a sense of community and even of family, the marriages and family lives of slaves had no legal recognition. The integrity of the slave family could be violated at the master's whim or changing economic circumstances. White masters and their sons often sexually exploited black slave women. Because slaves were property, they could be sold for profit or transported when the owner moved to a different region. Consequently, families could be, and were, separated by sale or perhaps after an owner's death. Many young children were reared and cared for by other slaves to whom they were not related. In a world of white dominance, the institutions, customs, and religions of the slave community were the only means black slaves had to protect the autonomy of their own personalities.

Scars of Slavery. This Louisiana slave named Gordon was photographed in 1863 after he had escaped to Union lines during the Civil War. He bears the permanent scars of the violence that lay at the heart of the slave system. Few slaves were so brutally marked, but all lived with the threat of beatings if they failed to obey. *National Archives and Records Administrations.*

The Abolitionist Movement

During the 1830s a militant antislavery movement emerged in the North. Its leaders and followers refused to accept what they regarded as the moral compromise of living in a nation that tolerated slavery. Abolitionists such as William Lloyd Garrison, editor of the *Liberator*, condemned the Union and the Constitution as structures that perpetuated slavery. Former slaves who had escaped slavery, such as Frederick Douglass and Sojourner Truth, and freeborn black Americans, such as Daniel A. Payne, also joined the cause. (See Document, "Daniel A. Payne Denounces American Slavery.") The antislavery movement, which was initially only one of many American reform movements, gained new adherents during the 1840s as the question of extending slavery into the new territories came to the fore in 1847 towards the end of the Mexican War (1846–1848). That military victory added significant new territory in the Southwest and California, in addition to Texas, which had been annexed in 1845. Through negotiations with Britain the United States also acquired the vast Oregon Territory in the Northwest in 1846 (see Map 24–3).

Daniel A. Payne Denounces American Slavery

Document

Daniel A. Payne was an African American who became an ordained Lutheran minister. He delivered this speech in June 1839, at his ordination. Though born in Charleston, South Carolina, he was the son of free African Americans. As a young man he had opened a school in that state to educate African-American children. He had to abandon this effort after the legislature prohibited teaching free or enslaved African Americans to read and write. Later he became president of Wilberforce University in Xenia, Ohio, which was dedicated to the education of African Americans.

◆ On what grounds does Payne condemn slavery? What examples of moral brutalization does Payne associate with slavery? How does he bring religious arguments against the evils of slavery?

. . . I am opposed to slavery, not because it enslaves the black man, but because it enslaves *man*. And were all the slaveholders in this land men of color, and the slaves white men, I would be as thorough and uncompromising an abolitionist as I now am; for whatever and whenever I may see a being in the form of a man, enslaved by his fellow man, without respect to his complexion, I shall lift up my voice to plead his cause, against all the claims of his proud oppressor; and I shall do it not merely from the sympathy which man feels towards suffering man, but because God, *the living God*, whom I dare not disobey, has commanded me to open my mouth for the dumb, and to plead the cause of the oppressed.

Slavery brutalizes man. . . . This being God created but a little lower than the angels, and crowned him with glory and honor; but slavery hurls him down from his elevated position, to the level of brutes, strikes this crown of glory from his head and fastens upon his neck the galling yoke, and compels him to labor like an ox, through summer's sun and winter's snow, without remuneration. Does a man take the calf from the cow and sell it to the butcher? So slavery tears the child from the arms of the reluctant mother, and barters it to the soul trader for a young colt, or some other commodity! Does the bird catcher tear away the dove from his mate? So slavery separates the groaning husband from the embraces of his distracted and weeping wife! . . . The very moment that a man conceives the diabolic design of enslaving his brother's body, that very moment does he also conceive the still more heinous design of fettering his will, for well does he know that in order to make his dominion supreme over the body, he must fetter the living spring of all its motions. Hence, the first lesson the slave is taught

is to yield his will unreservedly and exclusively to the dictates of his master. And if a slave desires to educate himself or his children, in obedience to the dictates of reason or the laws of God, he does not, he cannot do it without the consent of his master. . . .

In view of the moral agency of man, God hath most wisely and graciously given him a code of laws, and certain positive percepts, to control and regulate moral actions. This code of laws, and these positive percepts, with the divine influence which they are naturally calculated to exert on the mind of man, constitutes his moral government. . . .

Now, slavery nullifies these laws and percepts—weakens and destroys their influence over the human mind, and hinders men from yielding universal and entire obedience to them; therefore slavery subverts the moral government of God. This is the climax of the sin of slavery. . . .

. . . Slavery never legislates for the religious instruction of slaves, but, on the contrary, legislates to perpetuate their ignorance; and there are laws this very moment in the statute books of South Carolina and other states, prohibiting the religious instruction of slaves. . . .

In a word, slavery tramples the laws of the living God under its unhallowed feet—weakens and destroys the influence which those laws are calculated to exert over the mind of man, and constrains the oppressed to blaspheme the name of the Almighty.

Speech originally printed in the *Lutheran Herald and Journal of the Fort Plain, N. Y., Franckean Synod*, Vol. 1, No. 15 (August 1, 1839) as reprinted in Philip S. Foner, ed., *The Voice of Black America: Major Speeches by Negroes in the United States, 1797–1971*. Copyright © 1972, New York: Simon & Schuster, pp. 67–71.

Victory in the Mexican War opened debate on the extension of slavery into the huge new territory it created. Southerners feared that the changing climate of national debate and the opening of territories where slavery might be prohibited would give the South a minority status and thus eventually overturn its political and social culture. Northerners came to believe that a slave-power conspiracy controlled the federal government. The Compromise of 1850 temporarily restored political calm and stability and reassured the South; but many Northerners came to believe that the compromise only demonstrated the strength of the slave-power conspiracy in Washington.

In 1854 the introduction of the Kansas-Nebraska Bill renewed the formal national political debate over slavery and galvanized the antislavery forces. The principle of the bill, introduced by Stephen A. Douglas (1813–1861), was that of popular sovereignty. The people of each new territory would 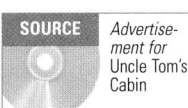 decide whether slavery was to be permitted within its borders. Douglas was thus willing to repeal the Missouri Compromise, which had prohibited slavery in most of the Louisiana Territory. Popular sovereignty meant that every newly organized territory had to debate slavery. In 1854 the new Republican Party was organized largely in opposition to the Kansas-Nebraska Bill. Not everyone, however, was willing just to argue. For example, John Brown went to Kansas, where armed conflict had already broken out, and carried out virtual guerrilla warfare against slaveholding settlers. During 1854 "Bleeding Kansas" was in a state of civil war.

In 1857, in the Dred Scott decision, the Supreme Court effectively repealed the Missouri Compromise by declaring that Congress could not prohibit slavery in the territories. The decision further declared that slaves did not become free by living in free states and that slaves did not have rights that others were bound to respect. For radical antislavery Northerners, the decision raised the most serious questions about the morality of the Union itself, and it demonstrated again a Southern conspiracy to protect slavery. Thereafter, slavery dominated national political debate.

In 1859 John Brown seized the federal arsenal at Harpers Ferry, Virginia, as part of an effort to foment a possible slave rebellion. He was captured, tried, and hanged, further increasing sectional polarization. Radical Southerners feared more than ever a Northern conspiracy to attack the institution of slavery, while Northern radicals feared that the South would use the federal government to protect slavery. Thus the politics of both sections became radicalized.

The Republican Party had become the party that opposed slavery, although most Republicans did not favor outright abolition. In 1858 Abraham Lincoln (1809–1865) ran against Stephen Douglas for the U.S. Senate in Illinois. Lincoln lost but made a national reputation for himself in the debates leading up to the election. In 1860 Lincoln, the Republican candidate, was elected president. Neither he nor the Republican Party had campaigned for the abolition of slavery. Nonetheless, Southerners perceived his election as the victory of a party and a president dedicated to the eradication of slavery. In December 1860 Southern states began to secede and formed the Confederate States of America. Attempts at political compromise to maintain the Union failed, and when Confederate forces fired on Fort Sumter in Charleston harbor in April 1861, the most destructive war in U.S. history began.

The Civil War lasted almost exactly four years, and a different nation emerged from the violence. In 1863 Lincoln emancipated the slaves in the rebelling states. The Emancipation Proclamation transformed the Northern cause from that of suppressing a Southern rebellion into that of extending liberty. By the time the Confederacy was defeated in 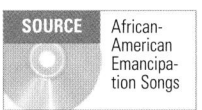 1865, the South was occupied by Northern armies, its farms were often fallow, its transportation network disrupted, and many of its cities in ruins. Southern political leaders had virtually no impact on the immediate postwar decisions. The Thirteenth, Fourteenth, and Fifteenth Amendments to the Constitution largely recast the character of the Union. The Thirteenth abolished slavery, the Fourteenth granted citizenship to the former slaves, and the Fifteenth allowed them to vote. The Fourteenth Amendment also prohibited much political activity by people who had taken up arms against the Union. These amendments resolved the issues of slavery and the relative roles of the state and federal governments.

The Civil War and the Reconstruction era that followed it overturned the antebellum social and political structures of the South. The slaves were freed and for a time participated broadly and actively in the politics of the Southern states. For more than ten years federal troops occupied parts of the South. Many of the antebellum Southern leaders left political life. Economically, the South remained generally rural and still dependent on cotton. For the first time since the earliest colonial days, it became an area of free labor. Many of the freed slaves and poor whites who tilled the land remained hopelessly in debt to wealthier landowners. Attempts to bring manufacturing into the South met with limited success. Rampant racism also blocked free economic development. For the rest of the century the South remained in a semicolonial relationship to the North. More than ever, in order to pay for the goods and services it needed, the South had to export raw materials or partially finished goods to the North, according to the economic rules set by Northern manufacturers and financiers. Throughout the rural South, poverty was the norm.

SOURCE   Advertisement for Uncle Tom's Cabin

SOURCE   African-American Emancipation Songs

Within the context of world history, the American Civil War is important for several reasons. With the exception of the Taiping Rebellion in China from 1851 to 1864, it was the greatest war that occurred anywhere in the world between the defeat of Napoleon in 1815 and the onset of World War I in 1914. It resulted in the establishment of a continent-wide free labor market, even though freed blacks lived in great poverty, and an economic dependence not unlike that of the rural classes of Latin America. The free labor market, purged of slavery, helped open the entire North American continent to economic development. The war also allowed American political and economic interests to develop without the distraction of the debates over states' rights and the morality of slavery. Thereafter, free labor would become the American norm, and the debates over the role of industrial labor in the United States resembled those in Europe to be discussed in Chapter 25.

The Canadian Experience

Under the Treaty of Paris of 1763, all of Canada came under the control of Great Britain. Canada then, as now, included both an English-speaking and a French-speaking population. The latter was concentrated primarily in Quebec. The Quebec Act of 1774, which had so disturbed the English colonists along the Atlantic seaboard, made the Roman Catholic Church the established church in Quebec. During the American Revolution approximately 30,000 English loyalists fled the colonies and settled in Canada. They thus established a larger English presence and were strongly loyal to the British Crown.

Harvest of death. Corpses of dead soldiers are strewn across the battlefield in Gettysburg, Pennsylvania. The battle, which lasted from July 1-3, 1863, resulted in 51,000 casualties.

The tension between the French and English populations led, in part, to the Constitutional Act of 1791, which divided the colony into Upper Canada (primarily English in ethnic composition) and Lower Canada (primarily French). Each section had its own legislature, and a governor-general presided over the two provinces on behalf of the British Crown. Newfoundland, Nova Scotia, New Brunswick, Cape Breton Island, and Prince Edward Island remained separate colonies.

In the early nineteenth century relations with the United States were often tense. There were local disputes over the fur trade and fear that the United States would dominate Canada. That apprehension, along with the Anglo-French ethnic divisions, came to constitute two of the major themes of Canadian history.

By the late 1830s the political situation in Canada was beginning to generate considerable internal pressure. Tension arose between long-established families with powerful economic interests in both Upper and Lower Canada and new settlers who hoped to achieve prosperity for themselves. There were quarrels over the influence of the British Crown in local affairs. In 1837 rebellions occurred in both Upper and Lower Canada. Although there were relatively few casualties, the British realized that some action had to be taken.

Road to Self-Government

The British government, operating in the more liberal political climate following the first Reform Act (1832), was determined to avoid another North American revolution. Consequently, it sent the Earl of Durham (1792–1840) to Canada with extensive powers to make reforms. In 1839 his *Report on the Affairs of British North America* advocated responsible government for Canada. Durham contended that both Canadian provinces should be united into one political unit. He thought that such political unification would eventually lead to a thoroughly English culture throughout Canada which would overwhelm the French influence in Quebec. He also believed that most Canadian affairs should be in the hands of a Canadian legislature and that only foreign policy and defense should remain under British control. In effect, Durham wanted Canadians generally to govern themselves, so that English culture would dominate. His policy was carried out in the Canada Act of 1840, which gave the nation a single legislature composed of two houses.

The Durham *Report* established the political pattern that the British government would, to a greater or lesser extent, follow with its other English-speaking colonies during the nineteenth century. Britain sought to foster responsible self-government in Australia, New Zealand, and South Africa. The Canadian experience thus had a considerable impact throughout the world. But, until well into the twentieth century, the

Canadian rail passengers board a train of the Great Western Railway at Clifton Depot in southern Ontario, sometime in the late 1850s. As in the United States, the growth of railroads transformed Canada in the nineteenth century.

British government, like other Western imperial powers, also generally believed that nonwhite peoples, such as those of India, required direct British colonial administration.

Keeping a Distinctive Culture

Canadians did learn to exercise self-government, but distinct English and French cultures continued to exist. Within the legislature there were almost always tradeoffs between the eastern and western sections of the nation. Furthermore, during the American Civil War, fears arose that the American republic might seek to invade or dominate Canada. One response to this fear was an attempt to unite the Maritime Provinces in 1862. Those discussions led to broader considerations of the desirability of a stronger federation among all the parts of Canada.

The result of those debates and discussions was the British North America Act of 1867, which created a Canadian federation. Canadians hoped to avoid what they regarded as flaws in the constitution of the United States. The Canadian system of government was to be federal, but with much less emphasis on states' rights than in the United States. Canadians established a parliamentary mode of government but also chose to retain the presence of the British monarchy in the person of the governor-general as head of state. The person who was most responsible for establishing this new government and who led it for most of the period between 1867 and 1891 was John A. MacDonald (1815–1891).

Midcentury Political Consolidation in Europe

During the same period that the United States and Canada established themselves as strong unified political entities in North America, major political consolidation occurred in Europe that would have an enormous impact on the rest of the world. As has so often been true in modern European history, war made change possible. In this case a conflict disrupted the international balance that had prevailed since 1815 and quickly unleashed forces that upset the political situation in several of the involved states. The war itself was in some respects less important than the political consequences that flowed from it during the next decade.

The Crimean War

The Crimean War (1854–1856), named after the Black Sea peninsula on which it was largely fought, originated from a long-standing rivalry between Russia and the Ottoman Empire. Russia wanted to extend its influence over the Ottoman provinces of Moldavia and Walachia (now in Romania). In 1853 Russia went to war against the Ottomans on the pretext that the Ottomans had given Roman Catholic France, instead of Orthodox Russia, the right to protect Christians and Christian shrines in the Holy Land. The next year France and Great Britain supported the Ottoman Empire to protect their interests in the eastern Mediterranean, while Austria and Prussia remained neutral. The war quickly bogged down after the French and the British invaded the Crimea. In March 1856 a peace conference in Paris concluded a treaty highly unfavorable to Russia.

The Crimean War shattered the image of an invincible Russia that had prevailed since the close of the Napoleonic Wars. It also shattered the power of the Concert of Europe to settle international disputes on the Continent. The major European powers were no longer willing to cooperate to maintain the existing borders between themselves and their neighbors. For the next twenty-five years instability prevailed in European affairs, allowing a largely unchecked adventurism in foreign policy.

Italian Unification

Italian nationalists had long wanted to unite the small absolutist principalities of the peninsula into a single state but could not agree on how to do it. Romantic republicans such as Giuseppe Mazzini (1805–1872) and Giuseppe Garibaldi (1807–1882) sought to drive out the Austrians by popular military force and then to establish a republic. They not only failed but also frightened more moderate Italians. The person who eventually achieved unification was Count Camillo Cavour (1810–1861), the prime minister of Piedmont.

Piedmont (officially styled the "Kingdom of Sardinia"), in northwestern Italy, was the most independent state on the peninsula (see Map 24–4). It had unsuccessfully fought against Austria in 1848 and 1849. Following the second defeat, King Charles Albert (r. 1831–1849) abdicated in favor of his son, Victor Emmanuel II (r. 1849–1878). In 1852 the new monarch chose Cavour—a moderate liberal in economics and a strong monarchist who rejected republicanism—as his prime minister.

Cavour believed that if Italians proved themselves to be efficient and economically progressive, the great powers might decide that Italy could govern itself. He worked for free trade, railway construction, credit expansion, and agricultural improvement. He also fostered the Nationalist Society, which established chapters in other Italian states to press for unification under the leadership of Piedmont. Cavour furthermore believed that Italy could be unified only with the aid of France.

Cavour joined the French and British side in the Crimean War to be able to raise the question of Italian unification at the peace conference. There he gained no specific rewards but did achieve the sympathy of Napoleon III (r. 1852–1870) of France. In 1858 Cavour and the French emperor met and plotted to start a war with Austria.

During the winter and spring of 1859 tension grew between Austria and Piedmont as the latter mobilized its army. In late April war erupted, and France came to Piedmont's aid. On June 4 the Austrians were defeated at Magenta, and on June 24, at Solferino in Lombardy. Fearing too extensive a Piedmontese victory, Napoleon III concluded a separate peace with Austria on July 11 at Villafranca. Piedmont received Lombardy, but the Veneto remained under Austrian control. Cavour felt betrayed by France, but nonetheless the war had driven Austria from most of northern Italy. Later that summer Parma, Modena, Tuscany, and the Romagna voted to unite with Piedmont.

At this point the forces of romantic republican nationalism compelled Cavour to pursue the complete unification of northern and southern Italy. In May 1860 Garibaldi landed in Sicily with more than 1,000 troops. He captured Palermo and prepared to attack the mainland. By September the city and kingdom of Naples, probably the most corrupt example of Italian absolutism, lay under his control. To forestall a republican victory Cavour rushed troops south to confront Garibaldi. On the way Cavour's troops conquered the Papal States except for the area around Rome, which remained under the direct control of the pope.

Garibaldi's nationalism won out over his republicanism, and he unhappily accepted the Piedmontese domination. In late 1860 Naples and Sicily voted to join the northern union forged by Piedmont. In March 1861 Victor Emmanuel II was

Chronology

German and Italian Unification

1854		Crimean War opens
1855		Cavour leads Piedmont into war on side of France and England
1856	July 20	Treaty of Paris concludes Crimean War
1858		Secret conference between Louis Napoleon and Cavour
1859		War of Piedmont and France against Austria
1860		Garibaldi lands his forces in Sicily and conquers southern Italy
1861	March 17	Proclamation of the Kingdom of Italy
	June 6	Death of Cavour
1862		Bismarck becomes prime minister of Prussia
1864		Danish War
1866		Austro-Prussian War; Veneto ceded to Italy
1867		North German Confederation formed
1870	June 6	Crisis over Hohenzollern candidacy for the Spanish throne
	July 12	
	July 13	Bismarck publishes edited press dispatch
	July 19	France declares war on Prussia
	September 1	France defeated at Sedan and Napoleon III captured
	September 4	French Republic proclaimed
	October 2	Italian state annexes Rome
1871	January 18	Proclamation of the German Empire at Versailles
	March 18	Paris Commune
	May 28	
	May 10	Treaty of Frankfurt between France and Germany

proclaimed king of Italy. Three months later Cavour died. The new state was governed by the conservative constitution promulgated in 1848 by Charles Albert. Italy gained the Veneto in

Map 24–4. The Unification of Italy. Beginning with the association of Sardinia and Piedmont by the Congress of Vienna in 1815, unification was achieved through the expansion of Piedmont between 1859 and 1870. Both Cavour's statesmanship and the campaigns of ardent nationalists played large roles.

Map 24–5. The Unification of Germany. Under Bismarck's leadership, and with the strong support of its royal house, Prussia used diplomatic and military means, on both the German and international stages, to forcibly unify the German states into a strong national entity.

1866 as a result of the war between Austria and Prussia, and Rome in 1870 as a result of the Franco-Prussian War.

German Unification

A united German nation was the single most important political development in Europe between 1848 and 1914. Germany was united by the conservative army and monarchy of Prussia and by Prussia's conservative prime minister, who sought to outflank the Prussian liberals.

William I (r. 1861–1888) regarded the Prussian army as his first concern. In 1860 his war minister and chief of staff proposed to enlarge the army and to increase the period of conscription from two to three years. The Prussian parliament, created by the constitution of 1850, refused to approve the necessary taxes. A deadlock continued for two years between the monarch and the Parliament dominated by liberals.

Bismarck In September 1862 William I turned for help to the person who, more than any other single individual, shaped the next thirty years of European history: Otto von Bismarck (1815–1898). Bismarck came from Junker stock,

and his outlook was deeply informed by the most traditional Prussian values, including admiration for the monarchy, the nobility, and the army. After being appointed prime minister and foreign minister in 1862, Bismarck immediately moved against the liberal parliament. He contended that the Prussian constitution permitted the government to function on the basis of previously granted taxes. Therefore, taxes could be collected and spent, despite the parliamentary refusal to vote them. The army and most of the bureaucracy supported this interpretation of the constitution. However, in 1863 new elections sustained the liberal majority in the parliament. Bismarck had to find some way to attract popular support away from the liberals and towards the monarchy and the army. To that end, he set about uniting Germany through the conservative institutions of Prussia. The tactic amounted to diverting public attention from domestic matters to foreign affairs. It also meant that Prussia now assumed a position of leadership in the effort to unify Germany.

Bismarck pursued what was known as the **_kleindeutsch_**, or small German, solution to unification. Austria was to be excluded from German affairs when an opportunity

Heinrich von Treitschke Demands the Annexation of Alsace and Lorraine

The Franco-Prussian War witnessed outbursts of extreme nationalistic rhetoric on both sides. One such voice was that of the German historian Heinrich von Treitschke (1834–1896). In a newspaper article, he demanded the annexation of Alsace and Lorraine from France. He did so even though the population of Alsace wished to remain part of France and German was not the dominant language in the region. He appealed to an earlier time when the region had been German in language and culture, and he asserted a policy that "might makes right" to assure German domination. Read this passage in conjunction with Lord Acton's condemnation of nationalism. (See "Lord Acton Condemns Nationalism," p. 769.)

◆ On what grounds does Treitschke base the German claim to Alsace and Lorraine? Why does he contend it is proper to ignore the wishes of the people involved? What, if any, political morality informs his views?

The sense of justice to Germany demands the lessening of France. . . .

What is demanded by justice is, at the same time, absolutely necessary for our security. . . .

Every State must seek the guarantees of its own security in itself alone. . . .

In view of our obligation to secure the peace of the world, who will venture to object that the people of Alsace and Lorraine do not want to belong to us? The doctrine of the right of all the branches of the German race to decide on their own destinies, the plausible solution of demagogues without a fatherland, shiver to pieces in presence of the sacred necessity of these great days. These territories are ours by the right of the sword, and we shall dispose of them in virtue of a higher right—the right of the German nation, which will not permit its lost children to remain strangers to the German Empire. We Germans, who know Germany and France, know better than these unfortunates themselves what is good for the people of Alsace. . . . Against their will we shall restore them to their true selves. We have seen with joyful wonder the undying power of the moral forces of history, manifested far too frequently in the immense changes of these days, to place much confidence in the value of a mere popular disinclination. The spirit of a nation lays hold, not only of the generation which live beside it, but of those who are before and behind it. We appeal from the mistaken wishes of the men who are there to-day to the wishes of those who were there before them. We appeal to all those strong German men who once stamped the seal of our German nature on the language and manners, the art and the social life of the Upper Rhine. Before the nineteenth century closes the world will recognize that . . . we were only obeying the dictates of

national honor when we made little account of the preferences of the people who live in Alsace to-day. . . .

At all times the subjection of a German race to France has been an unhealthy thing; today it is an offence against the reason of History—a vassalship of free men to half-educated barbarians . . .

There is no perfect identity between the political and national frontier of any European country. Not one of the great Powers, and Germany no more than the rest of them, can ever subscribe to the principle that "language alone decides the formation of States." It would be impossible to carry that principle into effect. . . .

The German territory which we demand is ours by nature and by history. . . . In the tempests of the great Revolution the people of Alsace, like all the citizens of France, learned to forget their past. . . .

Most assuredly, the task of reuniting there the broken links between the ages is one of the heaviest that has ever been imposed upon the political forces of our nation. . . .

The people of Alsace are already beginning to doubt the invincibility of their nation, and at all events to divine the mighty growth of the German Empire. Perverse obstinancy, and a thousand French intrigues creeping in the dark, will make every step on the newly conquered soil difficult for us: but our ultimate success is certain, for on our side fights what is stronger than the lying artifices of the stranger—nature herself and the voice of common blood.

From Heinrich von Treitschke, "What We Demand from France" (1870), in Heinrich von Treitschke, *Germany, France, Russia and Islam* (New York: G. P. Putnam's Sons, 1915), pp. 100, 102, 106, 109, 120, 122, 134–135, 153, 158.

Creating Nations. The proclamation of the German Empire in the Hall of Mirrors at Versailles, January 18, 1871, after the defeat of France in the Franco-Prussian War. Kaiser Wilhelm I is standing at the top of the steps under the flags; Otto von Bismarck is in the center in a white uniform. The new nation possessed enormous economic resources and nationalistic ambitions. *Bildarchiv Preussicher Kulturbesitz/Original: Friedrichsruher Fassung, Bismarck-Museum.*

presented itself. To achieve that end, Bismarck undertook two brief wars.

In 1864 he went to war with Denmark over the question of the duchies of Schleswig and Holstein, German-speaking areas that had long been administered by the Danish monarchy (see Map 24–5). The Austrians helped defeat Denmark and then with Prussia undertook the joint administration of the two duchies. Thereafter, Bismarck concluded various alliances with France and Italy to gain their support against Austria. War between Prussia and Austria broke out in the summer of 1866. This Seven Weeks' War led to the decisive defeat of Austria at Koniggratz. The Prussian victory and the consequent Treaty of Prague excluded the Habsburgs from German affairs. Prussia became the only major power among the German states.

In 1867 Hanover, Hesse, Nassau, and the city of Frankfurt, all of which had supported Austria during the war, were annexed by Prussia, and their rulers deposed. Prussia and these newly incorporated territories, plus Schleswig and Holstein and the rest of the German states north of the Main River, constituted the North German Confederation. Prussia was its undisputed leader.

The Franco-Prussian War and the German Empire

Bismarck now awaited an opportunity to complete unification by bringing the states of southern Germany into the confederation. The occasion arose as a result of complex diplomacy surrounding the possibility of a cousin of William I of Prussia becoming king of Spain. France was, of course, opposed to the idea of a second state on its borders ruled by a Hohenzollern. Bismarck personally edited a press dispatch surrounding these negotiations to make it appear that William I had insulted the French ambassador, even though the king had not done so. Bismarck intended to goad France into war, and he succeeded. (See Document, "Heinrich von Treitschke Demands the Annexation of Alsace and Lorraine.") On July 19 France declared war. Napoleon III hoped that victory would give his regime a new and stronger popular base. Once the war began, the states of southern Germany supported Prussia. On September 1, at Sedan, the Germans not only defeated the French army but also captured Napoleon III. By late September, Paris was besieged. It finally capitulated on January 28, 1871. Ten days earlier, in the Hall of Mirrors at the Palace of Versailles, the German Empire had been proclaimed. The rulers of the states of south Germany had requested William I to accept the imperial title. They, in turn, retained their thrones.

The unification of Germany established a strong, coherent state in the middle of Europe. It had been forged by the Prussian army and would be dominated by Prussian institutions. Its center of power rested on the monarchy and the military. It possessed enormous economic resources and nationalistic ambitions. For the next eighty years Europe would have to come to grips with this new political reality both on the Continent and abroad. The unification of Italy and Germany proved to many people that nationalistic goals could only be achieved by armed force. After its defeat at the hands of Prussia, France would within five years become a republic—the Third Republic—governed by a chamber of deputies, a senate, and a president.

Unrest of Nationalities in Eastern Europe

In the age of national states, liberal institutions, and industrialism, the Habsburg domains remained primarily dynastic, absolutist, and agrarian. Following the Revolutions of 1848 Emperor Francis Joseph (r. 1848–1916) and his ministers attempted to impose a centralized administration on the multinational empire. The system amounted to a military and bureaucratic government dominated by German-speaking Austrians. This situation was especially annoying to the Hungarians. The defeats in 1859 and 1866 and the

Lord Acton Condemns Nationalism

Lord Acton (1834–1902) was a major nineteenth-century English historian and commentator on contemporary religious and political events. In all his writings, he was deeply concerned with the character and preservation of liberty. His was one of the earliest voices to warn against the political dangers of nationalism.

◆ Why does Acton see the principle of nationality as dangerous to liberty? Why does he see nationalism as a threat to minority groups? Why does he see nationalism as a threat to democracy?

The greatest adversary of the rights of nationality is the modern theory of nationality. By making the State and the nation commensurate with each other in theory, it reduces practically to a subject condition all other nationalities that may be within the boundary. It cannot admit them to an equality with the ruling nation which constitutes the State, because the State would then cease to be national, which would be a contradiction of the principle of its existence. According, therefore, to the degree of humanity and civilization in that dominant body which claims all the rights of the community, the inferior races are exterminated, or reduced to servitude, or outlawed, or put in a condition of dependence.

If we take the establishment of liberty for the realization of moral duties to be the end of civil society, we must conclude that those states are substantially the most perfect which, like the British and Austrian Empires, include various distinct nationalities without oppressing them. Those in which no mixture of races has occurred are imperfect; and those in which its effects have disappeared are decrepit. A State which is incompetent to satisfy different races condemns itself; a State which labors to neutralize, to absorb, or to expel them, destroys its own vitality; a State which does not include them is destitute of the chief basis of self-government. The theory of nationality, therefore, is a retrograde step in history. . . .

[N]ationality does not aim either at liberty or prosperity, both of which it sacrifices to the imperative necessity of making the nation the mold and measure of the State. Its course will be marked with material as well as moral ruin, in order that a new invention may prevail over the works of God and the interests of mankind. There is no principle of change, no phrase of political speculation conceivable, more comprehensive, more subversive, or more arbitrary than this. It is a confutation of democracy, because it sets limits to the exercise of the popular will, and substitutes for it a higher principle.

From John Emerich Edward Dalbert-Acton, *First Baron Acton, Essays in the History of Liberty*, ed. by J. Rufus Fears (Indianapolis IN: Liberty Classics, 1985), pp. 431–433.

---

exclusion of Austria from Italy and from German affairs compelled Francis Joseph to come to terms with the Hungarian nobility. The subsequent **Ausgleich**, or Compromise, of 1867 transformed the Habsburg Empire into a dual monarchy. Francis Joseph was crowned king of Hungary in Budapest. Except for the common monarch, foreign policy, and army, Austria and Hungary became almost separate states (see Map 24–6).

Many of the other national groups within the empire—including the Czechs, the Ruthenians, the Romanians, and the Serbo-Croatians—opposed the Compromise because it permitted the German-speaking Austrians and the Hungarian Magyars to dominate all other nationalities in their respective states. The Czechs of Bohemia were the most vocal group. For over twenty years they were conciliated by generous Austrian patronage and posts in the bureaucracy. By the turn of the century the Czechs had become more vocal. They and German-speaking groups in the Austrian Reichsrat disrupted Parliament rather than permit a compromise on language issues. The emperor ruled thereafter by imperial decree with the support of the bureaucracy. Constitutionalism was dead in Austria. It flourished in Hungary only because the Magyars used it to dominate competing national groups.

Nationalist unrest within the Habsburg Empire not only caused internal political difficulties, but also constituted one of the major sources of political instability for all of central and eastern Europe. Virtually all the nationality problems had a foreign policy as well as a domestic political dimension. Both the Serbo-Croatians and the Poles believed they deserved a wholly independent state in union with their fellow

SOURCE   Serbian Society of National Defense, "Program for Nationalism"

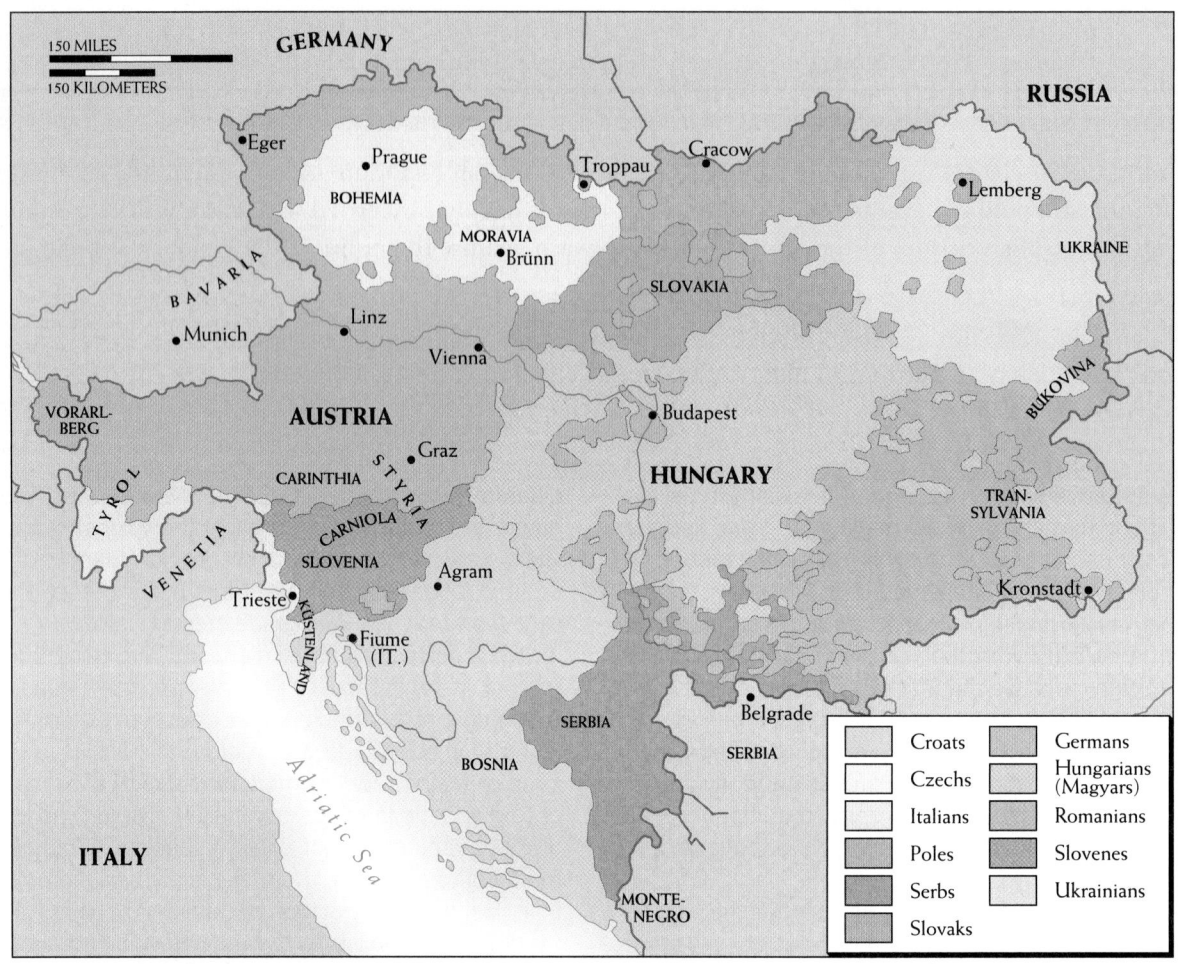

Map 24–6. Nationalities within the Habsburg Empire. The patchwork appearance reflects the unusual problem of the numerous ethnic groups that the Habsburgs could not, of course, meld into a modern national state. Only the Magyars were recognized in 1867, leaving nationalist Czechs, Slovaks, and the others chronically dissatisfied.

nationals who lived outside the empire. Other national groups, such as Ukrainians, Romanians, and Bosnians, saw themselves as potentially linked to Russia, to Romania, to Serbia, or to a larger yet-to-be-established Slavic state. Many of these nationalities looked to Russia for protection. Out of these nationalistic tensions emerged much of the turmoil that would spark the First World War. (See Document, "Lord Acton Condemns Nationalism.") The dominant German population of

Revolutionary. In 1848, Ana Ipatescu helped to lead Transylvanian revolutionaries against Russian rule. (Transylvania is part of present-day Romania.) The revolutions of 1848 in Eastern Europe were primarily the rising of nationalist groups. Although generally repressed in the revolutions of that year, subject nationalities would prove a source of political upheaval and unrest in the region throughout the rest of the century, ultimately providing the spark for the outbreak of World War I. *The Art Archive/Picture Desk, Inc./Kobal Collection.*

Austria proper was generally loyal to the emperor. However, a significant segment of the Austrian German population was strongly nationalistic and yearned to be part of the united German state being established by Bismarck. These nationalistic Germans in the Austrian Empire often hated the non-German national groups, particularly the Jews. Such attitudes would influence the youth and young adulthood of Adolf Hitler (1889–1945) and shape many of his political opinions.

Nationality problems touched each of the three great central and eastern European empires—the German, the Russian, and the Austrian. All had Polish populations. Each shared at least two other major national groups. Each nationality regarded its own aspirations and discontents as more important than the larger good or even survival of the empire they inhabited. The stirrings of nationalism affected the fate of all three empires from the 1860s through the outbreak of World War I. The government of each would be overturned during the war, and the Austrian Empire would disappear. These same unresolved problems of central and eastern European nationalism would then lead directly to World War II. During more recent years they have led to civil war in what was formerly Yugoslavia and to the breakup of what used to be called Czechoslovakia.

Racial Theory and Anti-Semitism

Articulated racial theory constituted a new component of late-century nationalistic unrest. Racial thinking, or **racism**, had long existed in Europe. Renaissance explorers had displayed considerable prejudice against nonwhites. Since at least the eighteenth century, biologists and anthropologists had classified human beings according to the color of their skin, their language, and their stage of civilization. Late-eighteenth-century linguistic scholars had observed similarities between many of the European languages and Sanskrit. They then postulated the existence of an ancient race called the Aryans, who had spoken the original language from which the rest derived. During the Romantic period, writers had called the different cultures of Europe *races*. The debates over slavery in the European colonies and the United States had given further opportunity for the development of racial theory. However, in the late nineteenth century the concept of race emerged as a single dominant explanation of the history and the character of large groups of people.

Arthur de Gobineau (1816–1882), a reactionary French diplomat, enunciated the first important theory of race as the major determinant of human history. In his four-volume *Essay on the Inequality of the Human Races* (1853–1854) Gobineau portrayed the troubles of Western civilization as being the result of the long degeneration of the original

white Aryan race. It had unwisely intermarried with the inferior yellow and black races, thus diluting the greatness and ability that originally existed in its blood. Gobineau saw no way to reverse this degeneration.

Gobineau's essay remained relatively obscure for years. Houston Stewart Chamberlain (1855–1927), an Englishman who settled in Germany, put racial theory on an alleged scientific basis in his widely read two-volume work entitled *Foundations of the Nineteenth Century* (1899). He championed the concept of biological determinism through race. Through the use of contemporary genetic theory, Chamberlain argued in opposition to Gobineau that the human race could be improved and even that a superior race could be developed. Chamberlain then added another element. He pointed to the Jews as the major enemy of European racial regeneration. Chamberlain's book and the lesser works on which it drew thus aided the spread of **anti-Semitism**. Other writings in Germany emphasized the supposed racial and cultural dangers posed by the Jews to traditional German national life.

Anti-Semitism and the Birth of Zionism

Political and racial anti-Semitism, which cast such dark shadows across the twentieth century, emerged in part from this atmosphere of racial thought. Religious anti-Semitism

Theodor Herzl. Herzl's visions of a Jewish state would eventually lead to the creation of Israel in 1948. *BBC Hulton/Corbis-Bettmann.*

dated from at least the Middle Ages. Since the French Revolution Western European Jews had gradually gained entry into the civil life of Britain, France, Austria, and Germany (see Chapter 25). Popular anti-Semitism, which identified the Jewish community with money and banking interests, persisted. During the last third of the century, as finance capitalism changed the economic structure of Europe, people pressured by the changes became hostile towards the Jewish community. In Austria, Germany, and France various political leaders and parties used such anti-Semitism for their own considerable political advantage.

To this already ugly atmosphere, racial thought contributed the belief that no matter to what extent Jews assimilated themselves and their families into the culture and even the religion of their country, their Jewishness—and thus their alleged danger to the society—would remain. The problem of race was not in the character, but in the blood of the Jew. An important Jewish response to this new, rabid outbreak of anti-Semitism was the launching in 1896 of the Zionist movement to found a separate Jewish state. Its founder was the Austro-Hungarian Theodor Herzl (1860–1904). The advance of political anti-Semitism, especially in Austria and France,

---

Herzl Calls for the Establishment of a Jewish State

Document

In 1896 Theodor Herzl published his pamphlet *The Jewish State*. Herzl had become convinced that only the establishment of a separate state for Jews would halt the outbreaks of anti-Semitism that characterized late-nineteenth-century European political and cultural life. Following the publication of this pamphlet, Herzl began to organize the Zionist movement among Jews in both Eastern and Western Europe.

◆ Why does Herzl define what he calls the Jewish Question as a national question? What objections does he anticipate to the founding of a Jewish state? Why does he believe that a Jewish state will prevent anti-Semitism?

The idea which I develop in this pamphlet is an age-old one: the establishment of a Jewish State.

The world resounds with outcries against the Jews, and this is what awakens the dormant idea. . . .

I believe I understand anti-Semitism, a highly complex movement. I view it from the standpoint of a Jew, but without hatred or fear. I think I can discern in it the elements of vulgar sport, of common economic rivalry, of inherited prejudice, of religious intolerance—but also of a supposed need for self-defense. To my mind, the Jewish Question is neither a social nor a religious one, even though it may assume these and other guises. It is a national question, and to solve it we must first of all establish it as an international political problem which will have to be settled by the civilized nations of the world in council.

We are a people, one people.

Everywhere we have sincerely endeavored to merge with the national communities surrounding us and to preserve only the faith of our fathers. We are not permitted to do so. . . . :

And will some people say that the venture is hopeless, because even if we obtain the land and the sovereignty only the poor people will go along? They are the very ones we need first! Only desperate men make good conquerors.

Will anybody say, Oh yes, if it were possible it would have been done by now?

It was not possible before. It is possible now. As recently as a hundred, even fifty years ago it would have been a dream. Today it is all real. The rich, who have an epicurean acquaintance with all technical advance, know very well what can be done with money. And this is how it will be: Precisely the poor and plain people, who have no idea of the power that man already exercises over the forces of Nature, will have the greatest faith in the new message. For they have never lost their hope of the Promised Land. . . .

Now, all this may seem to be a long-drawn-out affair. Even in the most favorable circumstances it might be many years before the founding of the State is under way. In the meantime, Jews will be ridiculed, offended, abused, whipped, plundered, and slain in a thousand different localities. But no; just as soon as we begin to implement the plan, anti-Semitism will immediately grind to a halt everywhere. . . .

From Theodor Herzl, *The Jewish State*. © 1970 The Herzl Press, pp. 27, 33, 109, as quoted in William W. Hallo, David B. Ruderman, and Michael Stanislawski, eds., *Heritage: Civilization and the Jews Source Reader*. © 1984 Praeger, pp. 234–235.

as well as Herzl's personal experiences of discrimination, convinced him that liberal politics and the institutions of the liberal state could not protect the Jews in Europe or ensure that they would be treated justly. In 1896 Herzl published *The Jewish State*, in which he called for a separate state in which the Jews of the world might be assured of those rights and liberties that they should be enjoying in the liberal states of Europe. (See Document, "Herzl Calls for the Establishment of a Jewish State.") Furthermore, Herzl followed the tactics of late-century mass democratic politics by directing his appeal in particular to the economically poor Jews who lived in the ghettos of Eastern Europe and the slums of Western Europe. The original call to **Zionism** thus combined a rejection of the anti-Semitism of Europe with a desire to establish some of the ideals of both liberalism and socialism in a state outside Europe.

Racial thinking and revived anti-Semitism were part of a wider late-century aggressive nationalism. Previously, nationalism had been a literary and liberal movement. From the 1870s onward, however, nationalism became a movement with mass support, well-financed organizations, and political parties. Nationalists tended to redefine nationality in terms of race and blood. The new nationalism opposed the internationalism of both liberalism and socialism. The ideal of nationality was used to overcome the pluralism of class, religion, and geography. The nation and its duties replaced religion for many secularized people. It sometimes became a secular religion in the hands of state schoolteachers, who were replacing the clergy as the instructors of youth. This aggressive, racist nationalism would prove to be the most powerful ideology of the early twentieth century.

Summary

Nationalism. Nationalism is the modern concept that people who share the same customs, culture, language, and history should also share the same government. It became the most powerful European political ideology of the nineteenth and early twentieth centuries. Nationalists challenged both the domestic and the international order of the Vienna settlement in the decades after 1815.

Liberalism. Politically, nineteenth-century liberals sought to establish constitutional governments that recognized civil liberties and made the executive responsible to a legislature elected by men of wealth and property. Economically, liberals wanted a laissez-faire economy with minimal government involvement. People should be free to use their talents and property to enrich themselves without the state intervening to protect the working classes or the poor. Liberals often

supported nationalists' efforts to create a single national state that could function as a more efficient economic unit. Although efforts to liberalize tsarist Russia failed, liberalism largely triumphed in France after the Revolution of 1830 and in Britain after the passage of the Great Reform Bill. The British were, however, unable to resolve the problem of Irish nationalism in the nineteenth century.

Italian and German Unification. With French assistance, Piedmont and its premier Count Camillo Cavour managed to unite most of the Italian peninsula by 1860. The new Kingdom of Italy was formed from the northern Italian duchies, Austrian Lombardy, the Papal States, and the Kingdom of the Two Sicilies. Austrian Venetia was added in 1866, and Italy occupied Papal Rome in 1870.

German unification was achieved by Prussia under the leadership of Otto von Bismarck between 1864 and 1871. In three victorious wars against Denmark, Austria, and France, Bismarck forged the German states into a German Empire dominated by Prussia. Germany was henceforth the dominant power on the European continent.

North America. In the United States, westward expansion and war against Mexico brought vast new territories under the republic from the Mississippi River to the Pacific, but sectional conflict between North and South over economic issues and slavery led to the outbreak of the Civil War in 1861. Northern victory led to the abolition of slavery, the creation of a continent-wide free labor market, and enormous economic development that would make the United States the world's leading industrial power in the twentieth century.

Canada in these years achieved self-government from Britain and created a united Canadian federation in 1867. However, Canada remained part of the British Empire and retained its connection with the British monarchy.

Eastern Europe. Nationalism created problems for the three Eastern European empires: Germany, Russia, and Austria, but Habsburg Austria faced the greatest challenge from nationalism because it was a dynastic, not a national, state. Eleven different nationalities made up the Habsburg monarchy, each with its own national aspirations. In 1867 the Habsburgs worked out the *Ausgleich*, or Compromise, with the Magyars, by which Hungary became an autonomous kingdom under the Habsburg emperor. Thereafter the Habsburg monarchy became known as Austria-Hungary. However, Czechs, Croats, and other Slavs in the monarchy became increasingly dissatisfied.

Racism and Anti-Semitism. In the late nineteenth century, biological determinism, the concept that some peoples or races were inherently superior to others, took root in Western thought. In Germany, Austria, and France, some nationalists used the concept of race to blame the Jews for their countries' economic and political problems. Part of the Jewish response was the launching of the Zionist movement to found a separate Jewish state.

Review Questions

1. Define nationalism. What were the goals of nationalists? What were the difficulties they confronted in realizing those goals? Why was nationalism a special threat to the Austrian Empire? What areas saw significant nationalist movements between 1815 and 1830? Which were successful and which unsuccessful?

2. What were the tenets of liberalism? Who were the liberals and how did liberalism affect the political developments of the early nineteenth century? What relationship does liberalism have to nationalism?

3. Compare and contrast the movement towards political liberalism between 1815 and 1830 in Russia, France, and Great Britain.

4. What economic differences between the American North and South gave rise to sectional conflict? Why was slavery the core issue in that conflict? How did the westward movement contribute to making slavery so important an issue?

5. Why was it so difficult to unify Italy? What were the contributions of Mazzini, Cavour, and Garibaldi to Italian unification?

6. Who was Otto von Bismarck, and why did he try to unify Germany? What was Bismarck's method of unification, and why did he succeed? What effect did the unification of Germany have on the rest of Europe?

INTERPRETING THE PAST

The Promises and Perils of Nationalism

Sources from Chapter 24

1. *Mazzini Defines Nationality* (p. 747)
2. *William Gladstone Pleads for Irish Home Rule* (p. 754)
3. *Heinrich von Treitschke Demands Annexation of Alsace and Lorraine* (p. 767)
4. *Lord Acton Condemns Nationalism* (p. 769)

As the most potent and influential political ideology in Europe during the nineteenth and much of the twentieth centuries, nationalism helped unify previously disparate peoples and offered new possibilities for the development of democratic governments. The concept that people with shared language, customs, and culture should share the same government lay at the core of nationalism. It directly contradicted the traditional role of monarchies and family dynasties.

In this exercise, you will read documents that spotlight a number of the positive and negative attributes of nation-

alism during the nineteenth century. The perspectives will vary, from the "liberal nationalists" like Giusepe Mazzini, who argued for a democratic national state based on "common ideas, common principles, and a common purpose," to more extreme nationalistic rhetoric espoused by Heinrich von Treitschke, who argued for the expansion of Germanic power, no matter what the wishes of the people involved. In exploring the attributes of nationalism, and its purposes and justifications, you will compare the perspectives from the authors of four primary sources.

The first document here is a definition of nationalism by Mazzini, a philosopher and politician who was one of the founders of the modern Italian state. The second source is an excerpt from a speech by William Gladstone, a British prime minister of the late nineteenth century who sought "home rule" for Ireland. The third source is a newspaper article written by the German historian Treitschke, who believed that the Alsace-Lorraine region of eastern France should be annexed to Germany because its culture was German. The final excerpt was written by Lord Acton, an English historian who warned of the dangers of nationalism.

7. How did British politicians handle the Irish Question? What were the parallels between England's relationship with Ireland and the nationality problem of the Austrian Empire?

8. What were the origins of the modern idea of racial theory? Who were its major proponents? How did the rise of such a theory change European anti-Semitism?

Key Terms

anti-Semitism (p. 771)

Ausgleich (p. 769)

Catholic emancipation (p. 752)

Chartism (p. 753)

Great Reform Bill (p. 751)

home rule (p. 754)

July Monarchy (p. 751)

kleindeutsch (p. 766)

liberalism (p. 748)

nationalism (p. 744)

racism (p. 771)

Zionism (p. 773)

Note: To learn more about the topics in this chapter, please turn to the Suggested Readings at the end of the book. For additional sources related to this chapter please see the Primary Source DVD at the back of this text or MyHistoryLab.

Use the source documents to analyze and compare perspectives regarding nationalism and to answer the following questions. Use specific examples from the documents to back up your assertions.

Questions

What qualities does Giuseppe Mazzini attribute to nationalism? What kind of justification does he offer for his positive endorsement of this ideology?

What reasons does William Gladstone give for the Irish desire for home rule? How does he use world opinion to support his argument?

What specific justifications does von Treitschke offer for the German claim to the French provinces of Alsace and Lorraine? How does he deal with the opposition to the German claim from the residents of the disputed territory, many of whom are of German ancestry?

What elements of nationalism does Lord Acton view as potentially dangerous?

Between approximately 1850 and 1945 Western Europe achieved an unprecedented measure of political, economic, and military power across the globe. The century may thus quite properly be regarded as the European era of world history. But no less impressive than the vast reach of European influence was its brevity. By 1945 much of Europe, from Britain to the Soviet Union, literally lay in ruins.

George Caleb Bingham, "Fur Traders Descending the Missouri," ca. 1845. Romantic painters of the nineteenth century created paintings idealizing the beauty of nature in Europe and North America just as industrialization and urbanization began to alter the landscape. *(See pages 800–807).*

NORTH AMERICA

SOUTH AMERICA

Male and female laborers of African descent have large bags of coffee beans on a plantation in Brazil. Other workers scoop the beans or pick them from trees. American economies relied on export economy in the nineteenth to twentieth centuries. *(See pages 824–827.)*

INTO THE
MODERN WORLD,
1815–1949

Tbilisi, Georgia, in the late nineteenth century.
Even cities far removed from major industrial zones experienced rapid growth in the nineteenth century. Tbilisi (Tiflis), in the Caucasus, which came under Russian rule in 1801, saw its population increase from 68,000 in 1865 to 160,000 by 1900.
(See pages 797–800.)

Twentieth-century Japanese woodblock print.
Japan more than any other East Asian society eagerly industrialized, yet traditional culture, including the art of woodblock printing, endured as well.
(See pages 898–915.)

ASIA

French Indochina.
The city hall of Saigon, Vietnam reflects the colonial legacy of the French Empire.
(See page 888).

EUROPE

AFRICA

Three carved wooden African figures of colonial officials.
These figures are carved using traditional African woodmaking techniques, but their subject matter represents the reality of European colonization in nineteenth-century Africa.
(See pages 867–874).

AUSTRALIA

Making Connections

1
How special were the circumstances that allowed Western Europe and America to achieve global power?

2
How did technology and new ideas about equality and democracy transform societies in Asia, Africa, and the Americas?

Northern Transatlantic Economy and Society, 1815–1914

◆ European Factory Workers and Urban Artisans

◆ Nineteenth-Century European Women

◆ Jewish Emancipation

◆ European Labor, Socialism, and Politics to World War I

◆ North America and the New Industrial Economy

◆ The Emergence of Modern European Thought

◆ Islam and Late-Nineteenth-Century European Thought

URING THE NINETEENTH CENTURY NORTHWESTERN Europe and the United States developed major industrial economies. These economies produced more goods and services than ever before in world history. This economic achievement undergirded the enormous international political power exerted by the industrial nations of the West from that time to the present.

The first half of the nineteenth century witnessed in Europe and to a lesser extent in the United States the emergence of a new kind of industrial labor force. These laborers worked in factories rather than in their homes or in small artisan workshops. More often than not the new industrial working class dwelled in cities. The presence and growth of this new labor force were the most important social developments of the century and would produce a vast influence on European and American political life. It was out of the social and political experience of this work force that the political movement known as socialism arose.

Russian society. A detail from the "Parade on Tsarina's Meadow" by G.G. Chernetson, 1831. Tsarina's Meadow was a vast space outside St. Petersburg that often held military parades and reviews in nineteenth-century Russia. The different classes and ethnic groups of the Russian empire can be seen mingling about.

The Building of Northern Transatlantic Supremacy

North Atlantic

Between 1850 and 1914 Europe had more influence throughout the world than it had before or has had since. Although Europe and North America together were the most industrially advanced regions of the world, the preponderance of economic power lay with Europe. Its industrial base was more advanced than that of any other region, including the still-developing United States. European banks exercised vast influence across the globe. Europeans financed the building of railways in Africa, Asia, and the Americas. Financial power brought political influence. The armaments industry gave European armies and navies predominant power over the peoples of Africa and Asia, whereas the United States began to exercise such power only as a result of the Spanish-American War. These economic developments established a pattern that still persists. First European, and later American, banks, companies, and corporations penetrated the economies and societies of Asia, Africa, and Latin America. These nonpolitical groups often expected their own governments to protect their interests. Thus, what started as commercial contact often evolved into the exercise of direct political influence even over nations that had never been European colonies.

During these years European culture was probably also enjoying its greatest influence. Capital cities in Latin America, especially Buenos Aires and Montevideo, adopted European-style architecture. Paris became synonymous with high fashion. Paris, London, and Vienna were world intellectual centers. The rest of the world regarded advanced industrial and urban civilization of Europe as a model, in part because more non-Europeans were visiting and studying in Europe than ever before. During this period many American artists and writers flocked to Europe to absorb its culture. Another cultural feature of Western Europe and the United States that affected the rest of the world during the era was the emerging role of women. In particular, the demand for the entrance of women into the political process and the professions became a hallmark of the twentieth century. On both sides of the Atlantic, women assumed leadership roles in social reform movements.

In the second half of the nineteenth century European and American political, economic, and social life assumed many characteristics of our present-day world. In Europe nation-states with large electorates, political parties, centralized bureaucracies, and universal military service emerged. In the United States the politics associated with the Progressive movement brought the presidency to the center of American political life. On both sides of the North Atlantic, business adopted large-scale corporate structures, and the labor force organized itself into trade unions. The number of white-collar laborers grew as urban life became predominant throughout Western Europe. But even as new vast cities arose in the United States, farming continued to spread across the central Midwest and upper Southwest. During this period, too, women began to assert new political awareness and to become politically active in both Europe and America.

During these same years Europe quietly became dependent on the resources and markets of the rest of the world. Farms in the United States, Canada, Latin America, Australia, and New Zealand supplied food to much of the world. Consequently climate changes in Kansas, Argentina, or New Zealand might now affect the European economy. However, before World War I the dependence was concealed by Europe's industrial, military, and financial supremacy. At the time Europeans assumed their supremacy to be natural, but the twentieth century

The nation that most clearly understood the nature of European power and sought to imitate it was Japan. After the Meiji restoration (1868), Japanese administrators came to Europe to study the new technology, political structures, and military organizations. The Japanese political and military reorganization that resulted proved sufficiently successful to allow them to defeat Russia in 1905, providing the first example of a non-European nation using Western weapons, organizations, and economic power to defeat a European nation. In the twentieth century other non-European nations found ways to import or manufacture technology that permitted them to challenge European and later American hegemony. Indeed, today the proliferation of weaponry usually developed in the United States or Europe has allowed regional powers to challenge Western dominance. This destabilizing arms trade began in the second half of the nineteenth century.

In contrast to Japan, China, India, the countries of the Middle East, and Africa were overwhelmed by the economic and military power of Europe. In time, however, the peoples of those lands under European domination embraced the ideologies of revolutionary protest, most particularly those of nationalism and socialism. As people from the colonial world came to work or study in Europe, they encountered ideas and criticisms that were most effective against European and Western culture. They adapted those ideas to their own cultural contexts and then turned them against their colonial governors.

Europeans eventually turned their military power against each other in 1914. World War I destroyed the late-nineteenth-century European self-confidence. At home, the Bolsheviks brought revolution to Russia. Abroad after the war, anticolonial movements began to grow, especially in India, in a manner that most Europeans in 1900 could not have imagined. In turn, those movements found many sympathetic supporters in Europe as a result of the spread of ideas regarding social justice and public policy. Furthermore, because the political and economic systems of the world had become so interconnected during the second half of the nineteenth century, the influence and impact of the European conflict could not be limited to Europe. The United States again was drawn into World War I and was never again able to avoid worldwide responsibilities.

Focus Questions

- What was the relationship between nineteenth-century Europe's economic power and its political hegemony around the globe?

- How did European colonies use ideologies fostered in Europe against their colonial rulers?

would reveal it to have been temporary. Nevertheless, while it prevailed, Europeans dominated most of the other peoples of the earth and displayed extreme self-confidence. Towards the close of the nineteenth century the United States, having achieved the status of a major industrial power as well as an agricultural supplier, now entered the world stage as a military power, defeating Spain in the Spanish-American War in 1898. With that victory, the United States also acquired its first colonial territories.

During these same decades a number of major new sets of ideas arose. Theories of evoution in biology, relativity in physics, the irrational philosophy, and psychoanalysis in psychology came to the fore, shaping much of the intellectual outlook for the next century. ▦

European Factory Workers and Urban Artisans

Although the seeds of industrial production had been sown in the eighteenth century, it was only in the nineteenth century that much of Europe headed towards a more fully industrial society. By 1830 only Great Britain had already attained that status, but new factories and railways were beginning to be constructed elsewhere in Europe. However, what characterized the second quarter of the century was less the triumph of industrialism than the final gasps of those economic groups that opposed it and were displaced by it. Intellectually, the period saw the formulation of the major creeds supporting and criticizing the new society.

The specter of poor harvests still haunted Europe. The worst such experience of the century was the Irish famine of 1845 to 1847. Perhaps as many as half a million Irish peasants with no land or small plots simply starved when disease blighted the potato crop. Hundreds of thousands emigrated. By midcentury, the revolution in landholding had led to greater agricultural production. It also resulted in a vast uprooting of people from the countryside into cities and from Europe into the rest of the word. The countryside thus provided many of the workers for the new factories, as well as people with few economic skills who slowly immigrated to cities in hope of finding work.

In much of northern Europe both artisans and factory workers underwent a process of **proletarianization**. This term

SOURCE Benjamin Disraeli, excerpt from Sybil

indicates the entry of workers into a wage economy and their gradual loss of significant ownership of the means of production, such as tools and equipment, and control over the conduct of their own trades. The process occurred rapidly wherever the factory system arose. The factory owner provided the financial capital to construct the factory, purchase the machinery, and secure the raw materials. The factory workers contributed their labor for a wage. Those workers also submitted to factory discipline, which meant that work conditions became largely determined by the demands for smooth operation of the machines. Closing of factory gates to late workers, fines for lateness, dismissal for drunkenness, and public scolding of faulty laborers constituted attempts to enforce regularity on humans that would match the regularity of cables, wheels, and pistons. The factory workers had no direct say over the quality of the product or its price. It should be noted that for all their difficulties, factory conditions were often better than those of textile workers who resisted the factory mode of production. In particular, English hand-loom weavers, who continued to work in their homes, experienced decades of declining trade and growing poverty in their unsuccessful competition with power looms.

Urban artisans in the nineteenth century experienced proletarianization more slowly than factory workers, and machinery had little to do with the process. The emergence of factories in itself did not harm urban artisans. Many even prospered from the development. For example, the construction and maintenance of the new machines generated demand for metal workers, who consequently did well. The actual erection of factories and the expansion of cities benefited all craftsmen in the building trades, such as carpenters, roofers, joiners, and masons. The lower prices for machine-made textiles aided artisans involved in the making of clothing, such as tailors and hatters, by reducing the costs of their raw materials. Where the urban artisans encountered difficulty, and found their skills and livelihood threatened, was in the organization of production.

In the eighteenth century a European town or city workplace had usually consisted of a few artisans laboring for a master, first as apprentices and then as journeymen, according to established guild regulations and practices. The master owned the workshop and the larger equipment, and the apprentices and journeymen owned their tools. The journeyman could expect to become a master. This guild system had allowed considerable worker control over labor recruitment and training, production pace, product quality, and price.

In the nineteenth century the situation of the urban artisan changed. It became increasingly difficult for artisans to continue to exercise corporate or guild direction and

Il Quarto Stato (The Fourth Estate), 1901. Giuseppe Pellizza da Volpedo (1868–1907) was a powerfully committed Italian socialist artist. The title of his painting is taken from the French socialist Jean Jaurès, who believed that workers would soon displace the traditional three estates of the clergy, aristocracy, and commoners. Pellizza and other artists embracing social realism moved painting away from nostalgic, sentimental depictions of peasants to images of industrial or farm laborers experiencing hunger, poverty, and awakening political consciousness. *Oil on canvas, 283 cm × 550 cm. Civica Galleria d'Arte Moderna-Milano. Photo by Marcello Saporetti.*

Overview

Major European Cities, 1850–1914

	1850	1880	1914
Berlin	419,000	1,122,000	2,071,000
Birmingham	233,000	437,000	840,000
Frankfurt	65,000	137,000	415,000
London	2,685,000	4,470,000	7,256,000
Madrid	281,000	398,000	600,000
Paris	1,053,000	2,269,000	2,888,000
Vienna	444,000	1,104,000	2,031,000

control over their trades. The French Revolution had outlawed such organizations in France. Across Europe, political and economic liberals disapproved of labor and guild organizations and attempted to make them illegal.

Other destructive forces were also at work. The masters often found themselves under increased competitive pressure from larger, more heavily capitalized establishments or from the possibility of the introduction of machine production into a previously craft-dominated industry. In many workshops masters began to follow a practice, known in France as *confection*, whereby goods such as shoes, clothing, and furniture were produced in standard sizes and styles rather than by special orders for individual customers. This practice increased the division of labor in the workshop. Each artisan produced a smaller part of the uniform final product. Consequently, less skill was required of each artisan, and the particular skills possessed by a worker became less valuable. Masters also attempted to increase production and reduce their costs for piecework. Those attempts often led to work stoppages or strikes. Migrants from the countryside or small towns created, in some cases, a surplus of relatively unskilled workers who were willing to work for lower wages or under less favorable and protected conditions than traditional artisans. The dilution of skills and lower wages, caused not by machinery but by changes in the organization of artisan production, made it much more difficult for urban journeymen ever to hope to become masters with their own workshops where they would be in charge. Increasingly, these artisans became lifetime wage laborers whose skills were simply bought and sold in the marketplace. (See Document, "A French Physician Describes a Working-Class Slum in Lille").

In the United States defenders of slavery frequently compared what they claimed to be the protected situation of slaves living on plantations with the plight of factory workers in both Europe and the northern United States. They argued that a free market in wage labor left workers worse off than slaves. But the situation in the European labor market as in the American North was much more complicated than the defenders of slavery contended.

Nineteenth-Century European Women

Women in the Early Industrial Revolution

The industrial economy ultimately produced an immense impact on the home and the family life of women. First, it took virtually all productive work out of the home and allowed many families to live on the wages of the male spouse alone. That transformation prepared the way for a new concept of gender-determined roles in the home and in general domestic life. Women came to be associated with domestic duties such as housekeeping, food preparation, child rearing and nurturing, and household management. The man came to be associated almost exclusively with breadwinning. Children were reared to match these gender patterns. Previously, this domestic division of labor had prevailed only among the relatively small middle and gentry class. During the nineteenth century it came to characterize the working class as well. Second, industrialization created new modes of employment that allowed many young women to earn enough money to marry or, if necessary, to support themselves independently. Third, industrialism, although fostering more employment for women, lowered the skills required of them.

Because the early Industrial Revolution had begun in textile production, women and their labor were deeply involved from the start. While both

SOURCE *Parliamentary report on female miners, 1842*

spinning and weaving were still domestic industries, women usually worked in all stages of production. Hand spinning was virtually always a woman's task. When spinning was moved into factories and involved large machines, however, men displaced women. The higher wages commanded by male cotton-factory workers allowed many women to stop working or to work only to supplement their husbands' wages.

With the next generation of machines in the 1820s, unmarried women rapidly became employed in the factories. However, their jobs tended to require less skill than most work done by men and than women had previously exercised in the home production of textiles. There was thus a certain paradox in the impact of the factory on women. Many new jobs opened

A French Physician Describes a Working-Class Slum in Lille

Document

The work of medical doctors frequently carried them into working-class areas of industrial cities rarely visited by the middle class. Louis Villermé was such a French physician. He described the slums and living conditions of industrial workers. The passage here, published in 1840, describes a particularly notorious section of Lille, a major cotton-manufacturing town in northern France.

◆ What does this physician find most disturbing about the scene he describes? How is his description designed to evoke concern from a middle-class reader? How might the conditions described have led the poor of France towards socialism or radical politics? How would addressing the problems described have increased the role of government?

The poorest live in the cellars and attics. These cellars . . . open onto the streets or courtyards, and one enters them by a stairway which is very often at once the door and the window. . . . Commonly the height of the ceiling is six or six and a half feet at the highest point, and they are only ten to fourteen or fifteen feet wide.

It is in these somber and sad dwellings that a large number of workers eat, sleep, and even work. The light of day comes an hour later for them than for others, and the night an hour earlier.

Their furnishings normally consist, along with the tools of their profession, of a sort of cupboard or a plank on which to deposit food, a stove . . . a few pots, a little table, two or three poor chairs, and a dirty pallet of which the only pieces are a straw mattress and scraps of a blanket. . . .

In their obscure cellars, in their rooms, which one would take for cellars, the air is never renewed, it is infected; the walls are plastered with garbage. . . . If a bed exists, it is a few dirty, greasy planks; it is damp and putrescent straw; it is a coarse cloth whose color and fabric are hidden by a layer of grime; it is a blanket that resembles a sieve. . . .

The furniture is dislocated, worm-eaten, covered with filth. Utensils are thrown in disorder all over the dwelling. The windows, always closed, are covered by paper and glass, but so black, so smoke-encrusted, that the light is unable to penetrate . . . everywhere are piles of garbage, of ashes, of debris from vegetables picked up from the streets, of rotten straw; of animal nests of all sorts; thus, the air is unbreathable. One is exhausted, in these hovels, by a stale, nauseating, somewhat piquante odor, odor of filth, odor of garbage. . . .

And the poor themselves, what are they like in the middle of such a slum? Their clothing is in shreds, without substance, consumed, covered, no less than their hair, which knows no comb, with dust from the workshops. And their skin? . . . It is painted, it is hidden, if you wish, by indistinguishable deposits of diverse exudations.

From Louis René Villermé, *Tableau de l'état et de soie* (Paris, 1840), as quoted and trans. in William H. Sewell Jr., *Work and Revolution in France: The Language of Labor from the Old Regime to 1848.* Copyright © 1980 Cambridge University Press, p. 224.

to them, but those jobs were less skilled than those that had been available to them before. Moreover, the women in the factories were almost always young and single or widows. At marriage or perhaps at the birth of the first child, a woman usually found that her husband earned enough money for her to leave the factory. Factory owners also disliked employing married women because of the likelihood of pregnancy, the influence of husbands, and the duties of child rearing.

In Britain and elsewhere by midcentury, industrial factory work accounted for less than half of all employment for women. The largest group of employed women in France continued to work on the land. In England they were

domestic servants. Domestic industries, such as lace glove and garment making and other kinds of needlework, employed many women. Their conditions of labor were almost always harsh, whether they worked in their homes or sweated in workshops. Generally all work done by women commanded low wages and involved low skills. They had virtually no way to protect themselves from exploitation. The charwoman was a common sight across the Continent and symbolized the plight of working women.

One of the most serious problems facing working women was the uncertainty of employment. Because they virtually always found themselves in the least skilled jobs and trades, their employment was never secure. Much of their work was seasonal. This was one reason so many working-class women feared they might be compelled to turn to prostitution. On the other hand, cities and the more complex economy did allow a greater variety of jobs. Movement to cities and entrance into the wage economy also gave women wider opportunities for marriage. Cohabitation before marriage seems to have been common. Parents did not arrange marriages as frequently as in the past. Marriage also generally meant that a woman would leave the work force to live on her husband's earnings. If all went well, that arrangement might improve her situation, but if the husband became ill or died, or deserted her, she would have to reenter the market for unskilled labor at a much advanced age.

Women in Textile Factories. As textile production became increasingly automated in the nineteenth century, textile factories required fewer skilled workers and more unskilled attendants. To fill these unskilled positions, factory owners turned increasingly to unmarried women and widows, who worked for lower wages than men and were less likely to form labor organizations. The two women shown here, holding "shuttles" used in textile factories, worked in the Lowell Mills, in Massachusetts, around 1860. *American Textile History Museum.*

Nonetheless, many of the traditional practices associated with the family economy survived into the industrial era. As a young woman came of age, both family needs and her desire to marry still directed what she would do with her life. The most likely early occupation for a young woman was domestic service. A girl born in the country normally migrated to a nearby town or city for such employment, often living initially with a relative. As in the past, she would attempt to earn enough in wages to give herself a dowry so she might marry and establish her own household. If she became a factory worker, she would probably live in a supervised dormitory. Such dormitories were one of the ways factory owners attracted young women workers, by convincing parents that their daughters would be safe. The life of young women in the cities seems to have been more precarious than it had been earlier. There seem to have been fewer family and community ties. There were also perhaps more available young men. These men, who worked for wages rather than in the older apprenticeship structures, were more mobile, so relationships between men and women were often more fleeting. In any case, illegitimate births increased. That is to say, fewer women who became pregnant before marriage found the father of the child willing to marry them.

Marriage in the wage industrial economy was also different. It still involved the starting of a separate household, but the structure of gender relationships within the household was different. Marriage was less an economic partnership: The husband might be able to support the entire family. The wage economy and the industrialization that separated workplace and home made it difficult for women to combine domestic duties with work. When married women worked, it was usually in the nonindustrial sector of the economy. More often than not children rather than the wife were sent to work, which may help explain the increase of fertility within marriages, since children in the wage economy tended to be an economic asset. Married women worked outside the home only when family needs or illness or the death of a spouse really required them to do so.

Within the home, the domestic duties of working-class women were an essential factor in the family wage economy. Homemaking came to the fore when a life at home had to be organized that was separate from the place of work. Wives were primarily concerned with food and cooking, but they often also were in charge of the family's finances. The role of the mother expanded when the children still living at home became wage earners. She was then providing home support for her entire wage-earning family. She created the environment to which the family members returned after work. The longer period of home life of working children may also have strengthened the affection between those children and their hardworking, homebound mothers.

Social Disabilities Confronted by All Women

During the early nineteenth century virtually all European women faced social and legal disabilities in property rights, family law, and education. By the close of the century each area had shown improvement. In this period European women, like European men, led lives that reflected their social rank. Yet within each rank, the experience of women was distinct from that of men. Women remained, generally speaking, economically dependent and legally inferior, whatever their social class. Their position thus resembled that of women around the world in that all women found their lives circumscribed by traditional social customs and expectations. (See Document, "English Women Industrial Workers Explain Their Economic Situation.")

Women and Property Until the last quarter of the nineteenth century in most European countries no married women, whatever their social class, could own property in their own names. In effect, upon marriage women lost to their husbands' control any property they owned or that they might inherit or earn by their own labor. Their legal identities were subsumed into their husbands', and they had no independent standing before the law. The courts saw the theft of a woman's purse as a theft of her husband's property. Because European society was based on private property and wage earning, these disabilities put married women at a great disadvantage, limiting their freedom to work, save, and relocate.

Reform of women's property rights came slowly. By 1882 Great Britain allowed married women to own property in their own right. In France, however, a married woman could not even open a savings account in her own name until 1895, and not until 1907 were married women granted possession of their own wages. In 1900 Germany allowed women to take jobs without their husbands' permission, but a German husband retained control of most of his wife's property except for her wages. Similar laws prevailed elsewhere in Europe.

Family Law European family law also worked to the disadvantage of women. Legal codes required wives to obey their husbands. The Napoleonic Code and the remnants of Roman law made women legal minors throughout Europe. Divorce was difficult for most of the century. In England until 1857 divorce required an act of Parliament. Most nations did not permit divorce by mutual consent. French law forbade divorce between 1816 and

1884. Thereafter the chief recognized legal cause for divorce was cruelty and injury, which had to be proven in court. In Great Britain adultery was the usual cause for divorce, but a woman had to prove her husband's adultery plus other offenses, whereas a man only had to prove his wife's adultery. In Germany only adultery or serious maltreatment was recognized as grounds for divorce. Across Europe extramarital sexual relations of husbands were more tolerated than those of wives. Everywhere, divorce required legal hearings and proof, making the process expensive and all the more difficult for women who did not control their own property.

The authority of husbands also extended to children. A husband could take children away from their mother and give them to someone else to rear. Only the husband, in most countries, could permit his daughter to marry. In some countries he could virtually force his daughter to marry the man of his choice. In cases of divorce and separation, the husband normally assumed authority over children no matter how he had treated them previously.

The sexual and reproductive rights of women, which have been so widely debated recently, could hardly be discussed in the nineteenth century. Both contraception and

Middle-Class Family. Family was central to the middle-class conception of a stable and respectable social life. This portrait of the Bellelli family is by Edgar Degas. Notice that the husband and father sits at his desk, suggesting his association with business and the world outside the home, whereas the wife and mother stands with their children, suggesting her domestic role. *Edgar Degas (1834–1917), The Bellelli Family, c. 1858–60. Musée d'Orsay, Paris, France. Photograph Copyright Bridgeman-Giraudon/Art Resource, N.Y.*

English Women Industrial Workers Explain Their Economic Situation

Document

In 1832, there was much discussion in the British press about factory legislation. Most of that discussion was concerned with the employment of children, but the *Examiner* newspaper made the suggestion that any factory laws should not only address the problem of child labor, but also, in time, eliminate women from employment in factories. That article provoked the following letter to the editor, composed by or on behalf of women factory workers, which stated the necessity of such employment for women and the unattractive alternatives.

◆ **What reasons do these women give to prove the necessity of their holding manufacturing jobs? What changes in production methods have led women from the home to the factory? How does the situation of these women relate to the possibility of their marrying?**

Sir, Living as we do, in the densely populated manufacturing districts of Lancashire, and most of us belonging to that class of females who earn their bread either directly or indirectly by manufactories, we have looked with no little anxiety for your opinion on the Factory Bill. . . . You are for doing away with our services in manufactories altogether. So much the better, if you had pointed out any other more eligible and practical employment for the surplus female labour, that will want other channels for a subsistence. If our competition were withdrawn, and short hours substituted, we have no doubt but the effects would be as you have stated, "not to lower wages, as the male branch of the family would be enabled to earn as much as the whole had done," but for the thousands of females who are employed in manufactories, who have no legitimate claim on any male relative for employment or support, and who have, through a variety of circumstance, been early thrown on their own resources for a livelihood, what is to become of them?

In this neighbourhood, hand-loom has been almost totally superseded by power-loom weaving, and no inconsiderable number of females, who must depend on their own exertions, or their parishes for support, have been forced, of necessity into the manufactories, from their total inability to earn a livelihood at home.

It is a lamentable fact, that, in these parts of the country, there is scarcely any other mode of employment for female industry, if we except servitude and dressmaking. Of the former of these, there is no chance of employment for one-twentieth of the candidates that would rush into the field, to say nothing of lowering the wages of our sisters of the same craft; and of the latter, galling as some of the hardships of manufactories are (of which the indelicacy of mixing with the men is not the least), yet there are few women who have been so employed, that would change conditions with the ill-used genteel little slaves, who have to lose sleep and health, in catering to the whims and frivolities of the butter-flies of fashion.

We see no way of escape from starvation, but to accept the very tempting offers of the newspapers, held out as baits to us, fairly to ship ourselves off to Van Dieman's Land [Tasmania] on the very delicate errand of husband hunting, and having safely arrived at the "Land of Goshen," jump ashore, with a "Who wants me?" . . .

—*The Female Operatives of Todmorden*

From *The Examiner*, February 26, 1832, as quoted in Ivy Pinchbeck, *Women Workers and the Industrial Revolution, 1750–1850* (New York: Augustus M. Kelley, 1969), pp. 199–200.

abortion were illegal. The law on rape normally worked against women. Wherever they turned—whether to physicians or lawyers—women confronted an official or legal world populated and controlled by men.

Educational Barriers Throughout the nineteenth century women had less access to education than men, and what was available to them was inferior. Not surprisingly, the percentage of illiterate women exceeded that of men. Most

women were educated only enough for the domestic careers they were expected to follow.

University and professional education remained reserved for men until at least the third quarter of the century. The University of Zurich opened its doors to women in the 1860s. The University of London admitted women for degrees in 1878. Women were not awarded degrees at Oxford until 1920 or at Cambridge until 1921. They could not attend Sorbonne lectures until 1880. Just before the turn of the century universities and medical schools in the Austrian Empire allowed women to matriculate, but Prussian universities did not until after 1900. Russian women did not attend universities before 1914, but other institutions that awarded degrees were open to them. Italian universities were more open to both women students and women instructors than similar institutions elsewhere in Europe.

The absence of a system of private or public secondary education for women prevented most of them from gaining the qualifications they needed to enter a university whether or not the university prohibited them. Considerable evidence suggests that educated, professional men feared the competition of women. Women who attended universities and medical schools were sometimes labeled political radicals.

Chronology

Major Dates in Late-Nineteenth-Century and Early-Twentieth-Century European Women's History

1857	Revised English divorce law
1865	University of Zurich admits women for degrees
1869	John Stuart Mill's *The Subjection of Women*
1878	University of London admits women as candidates for degrees
1882	English Married Woman's Property Act
1894	Union of German Women's Organizations founded
1901	National Council of French Women founded
1903	British Women's Social and Political Union founded
1907	Norway permits women to vote on national issues
1910	British suffragettes adopt radical tactics
1918	Vote extended to some British women
1918	Weimar constitution allows German women to vote
1920–1921	Oxford and Cambridge Universities award degrees to women
1922	French Senate defeats bill extending vote to women
1928	Britain extends vote to women on same basis as men

By 1900 men in the educated elites also feared the challenge educated women posed to traditional gender roles in the home and workplace. Restricting their access to secondary and university education helped bar women from social and economic advancement. Women would benefit only marginally from the expansion of professional employment that occurred during the late nineteenth and early twentieth centuries. Although a few women did enter the professions, especially medicine, most nations prevented women from becoming lawyers until after World War I.

Schoolteaching at the elementary level, which was seen as a female job because of its association with the nurturing of children, became a professional haven for women. Trained at institutions that were equivalent to normal schools, women schoolteachers were regarded as educated, but not as university educated. Secondary education remained largely the province of men.

The few women who pioneered in the professions and on government commissions and school boards or who dispersed birth control information faced grave social obstacles, personal humiliation, and often outright bigotry. These women and their male supporters were challenging that clear separation of life into male and female spheres that had emerged in middle-class European society during the nineteenth century. Women themselves often hesitated to support feminist causes or expanded opportunities for themselves because they had been so thoroughly acculturated into the recently stereotyped roles. Many women saw a real conflict between family responsibilities and feminism.

New Employment Patterns for Women

During the late nineteenth century two major developments affected the economic lives of women. The first was an expansion in the variety of jobs available outside the better paying learned professions. The second was a withdrawal of married women from the work force. These two seemingly contradictory developments require explanation.

Availability of New Jobs The expansion of governmental bureaucracies, the emergence of corporations and other large-scale businesses, and the expansion of retail stores opened many new employment opportunities for women. The need for elementary schoolteachers, usually women, grew with compulsory education laws. Technological inventions and innovations, such as the typewriter and eventually the telephone exchange, also fostered female employment. Women by the thousands became secretaries and clerks for governments and private businesses. More thousands became shop assistants.

Although these jobs did open new and often better employment opportunities for women, they nonetheless

Women Working at a Telephone Exchange. The invention of the telephone opened new employment opportunities for women. *Mary Evans Picture Library.*

required low-level skills and involved minimal training. They were occupied primarily by unmarried women or widows. Few women had prominent positions.

Employers continued to pay women low wages because they assumed, often knowing better, that a woman did not need to support herself independently but could expect additional financial support from her father or husband. Consequently, a woman who did need to support herself independently could rarely find a job paying an adequate income or a position that paid as well as one held by a man who was supporting himself independently.

Withdrawal from the Labor Force Most of the women filling these new service positions were young and unmarried. After marriage, or certainly after the birth of her first child, a woman normally withdrew from the labor force. She either did not work or she worked at home. This pattern was not new, but it had become more common by the end of the nineteenth century. The industrial occupations that women had filled in the mid–nineteenth century, especially textile and garment making, were shrinking. Those industries thus offered fewer jobs for either married or unmarried women. Employers in offices and retail stores preferred young, unmarried women whose family responsibilities would not interfere with their work. The decline in the number of births also meant that fewer married women were needed to look after other women's children.

The real wages paid to male workers increased during this period, thus reducing families' need for a second income. Also, thanks to improving health conditions, men lived longer than before, and so wives were less likely to be thrust into the work force by an emergency. Smaller families also lowered the need for supplementary wages. Working children stayed longer at home and continued to contribute to the family's wage pool.

Finally, the cultural dominance of the middle class, with its generally idle wives, established a pattern of social expectations. The more prosperous a working-class family became, the less involved in employment its women were supposed to be. Indeed, the less income-producing work a wife did, the more prosperous and stable the family was considered.

Yet behind these generalities stands the enormous variety of social and economic experience late-nineteenth-century women actually encountered. As might be expected, social class largely determined these individual experiences.

Late-Nineteenth-Century Working-Class Women

Although less dominant than earlier in the century, the textile industry and garment making continued to employ many women. The German clothing-making trades illustrate the kind of vulnerable economic situation that women could encounter as a result of their limited skills and the organization of the trade. The manufacture of mass-made clothes in

Women Laundry Workers. Although new opportunities opened to them in the late nineteenth century, many working-class women, like these women ironing in a laundry, remained in traditional occupations. As the wine bottle suggests, alcoholism was a problem for women as well as men engaged in tedious work. The painting is by Edgar Degas (1834–1917). *Réunion des Musées Nationaux/Art Resource, N.Y.*

The Rise of Political Feminism

As can be seen from the previous discussion, liberal society and its values neither automatically nor inevitably improved the lot of women. In particular, it did not give them the vote or access to political activity. Male liberals feared that granting the vote to women would benefit political conservatives, because women were thought to be unduly controlled by the clergy. Consequently, anticlerical liberals often had difficulty working with feminists.

Obstacles to Achieving Equality Women were also often reluctant to support feminist causes. Political issues relating to gender were only one of several priorities for many women. Some were sensitive to their class and economic interests. Others subordinated feminist political issues to national unity and nationalistic patriotism. Still others would not support particular feminist organizations because of differences over tactics. The various social and tactical differences among women often led to sharp divisions within the feminists' own ranks. Except in England, it was often difficult for working-class and middle-class women to cooperate. Roman Catholic feminists were uncomfortable with radical secularist feminists.

Although liberal society and law presented women with many obstacles, they also provided feminists with many of their intellectual and political tools. As early as 1792 in Britain, Mary Wollstonecraft (1759–1797), in *The Vindication of the Rights of Women*, had applied the revolutionary doctrines of the rights of man to the predicament of the members of her own sex (see Chapter 22). John Stuart Mill (1806–1873), with his wife Harriet Taylor (1804–1858), had applied the logic of liberal freedom to the position of women in *The Subjection of Women* (1869). The arguments for utility and efficiency so dear to middle-class liberals could be used to expose the human and social waste implicit in the inferior role assigned to women.

Furthermore, the socialist criticism of capitalist society often, though by no means always, included a harsh indictment of the social and economic position to which women

Germany was designed to require minimal capital investment by manufacturers and to protect them from significant risk. A major manufacturer would arrange to produce clothing through a putting-out system. He would purchase the material and then put it out for tailoring. The clothing was made not in a factory but usually in independently owned, small sweatshops or by workers in their homes.

In Berlin in 1896 there were more than 80,000 garment workers, mostly women. When business was good, employment for these women was high. If business became poor, however, less and less work was put out, idling many of them. In effect, the workers who actually sewed the clothing carried much of the risk of the enterprise. Some women did work in factories, but they too were subject to layoffs. Furthermore, women in the clothing trade were nearly always in positions less skilled than those of the male tailors or the male middlemen who owned the workshops.

The expectation of separate social and economic spheres for men and women and the definition of women's chief work as pertaining to the home contributed mightily to the exploitation of women workers outside the home. Because their wages were regarded merely as supplementing their husbands', they became particularly vulnerable to the economic exploitation that characterized the German putting-out system for clothing production. Women were nearly always treated as casual workers in Europe.

had been relegated. The earliest statements of feminism arose from critics of the existing order and were often associated with people who had unorthodox opinions about sexuality, family life, and property. This hardened resistance to the feminist message, especially on the Continent.

These difficulties prevented Continental feminists from raising the kind of massive public support or mounting the large demonstrations that feminists in Great Britain and the United States could. Everywhere in Europe, however, including Britain, the feminist cause was badly divided over both goals and tactics.

Votes for Women in Britain Europe's most advanced women's movement was in Great Britain. There Millicent Fawcett (1847–1929) led the moderate National Union of Women's Suffrage Societies. She believed Parliament would grant women the vote only when convinced that women would be respectable and responsible in their political activity. In 1908 this organization could rally almost half a million women in London. Fawcett was the wife of a former Liberal Party cabinet minister and economist. Her tactics were those of English liberals.

Emmeline Pankhurst (1858–1928) led a different and much more radical branch of British feminists. Pankhurst's husband had been active in both labor and Irish nationalist politics. Irish nationalists had developed numerous disruptive political tactics. Early labor politicians had also sometimes had confrontations with police over the right to hold meetings. In 1903 Pankhurst and her daughters

founded the Women's Social and Political Union. For several years they and their followers, known derisively as **suffragettes**, lobbied publicly and privately for women's suffrage. By 1910, having failed to move the government, they turned to the violent tactics of arson, window breaking, and sabotage of postal boxes. They marched en masse on Parliament. The Liberal government of Herbert Asquith (1852–1928), prime minister from 1908 to 1916, imprisoned many of the demonstrators and force-fed those who went on hunger strikes in jail. The government refused to extend the franchise. Only in 1918, and then as a result of their contribution to the war effort, did some British women receive the vote.

Political Feminism on the Continent The contrast of France and Germany shows how advanced the British women's movement was. In France, when Hubertine Auclert (1848–1914) began campaigning for the vote in the 1880s, she stood virtually alone. During the 1890s several women's organizations emerged. In 1901 the National Council of French Women (CNFF) was organized among upper-middle-class women, but it did not support the vote for women for several years. French Roman Catholic feminists, such as Marie Mauguet (1844–1928), supported the franchise. Almost all French feminists, however, rejected violence: They were also never able to organize mass rallies. The leaders of French feminism believed that the vote could be achieved through careful legalism. In 1919 the French Chamber of Deputies granted the vote to women, but in 1922 the French Senate defeated the bill. French women did not receive the right to vote until 1944 at the end of World War II.

In Germany feminist awareness and action were even more underdeveloped. German law actually forbade German women from political activity. Because no group in the German Empire enjoyed extensive political rights, women were not certain that they would benefit from demanding them. Any such demand would be regarded as subversive of both the state and society.

In 1894 the Union of German Women's Organizations (BDFK) was founded. By 1902 it was calling for the right to vote, but it was largely concerned with improving women's social conditions, their access to education, and their right to other protections. The group also worked to see women admitted to political or civic

Women's Suffrage. The creator of this poster cleverly reveals the hypocrisy and foolishness of denying the vote to women. *Private collection/Bridgeman Art Library.*

activity on the municipal level. Their work usually included education, child welfare, charity, and public health. The German Social Democratic Party supported women's suffrage, but that Socialist party was so disdained by the German authorities and German Roman Catholics that this support only made suffrage more suspect in their eyes. Women received the vote in Germany only in 1918 under the constitution of the Weimar Republic. Before World War I, only in Norway (1907) could women vote on national issues.

Jewish Emancipation

One of the most important social changes to occur throughout Europe during the nineteenth century was the emancipation of European Jews from the narrow life of the ghetto into a world of equal or nearly equal citizenship and social status. This transformation represented one of the major social impacts of political liberalism on European life.

Early Steps to Equal Citizenship

Emancipation, slow and never fully completed, began in the late eighteenth century and continued throughout the nineteenth. It moved at different paces in different countries. In 1782 Joseph II (r. 1765–1790), the Habsburg emperor, issued a decree that placed the Jews of his empire under more or less the same laws as Christians. In France the National Assembly recognized Jews as French citizens in

1789. During the Napoleonic Wars Jewish communities in Italy and Germany were allowed to mix on a generally equal footing with the Christian population.

These various steps towards political emancipation were frequently limited or partially repealed with changes in rulers or governments. Even in countries that granted them political rights, Jews could not own land and could be subject to discriminatory taxes. Nonetheless, by the first half of the nineteenth century Jews in Western Europe and to a much lesser extent in central and Eastern Europe had begun to acquire equal or nearly equal citizenship.

In Russia, however, the traditional modes of prejudice and discrimination continued unabated until World War I. Jews were treated as aliens under Russian rule. The government undermined Jewish community life, limited publication of Jewish books, restricted areas where Jews might live, required internal passports from Jews, banned them from many forms of state service and from many institutions of higher education. The police and others were allowed to conduct **pogroms**—organized riots—against Jewish neighborhoods and villages.

Broadened Opportunities

After the revolutions of 1848, and especially in Western Europe, the situation of European Jews improved for several decades. Throughout Germany, Italy, the Low Countries, and Scandinavia, Jews were allowed full rights of citizenship. After 1858 Jews in Great Britain could sit in Parliament. In Austria-Hungary full legal rights were extended to Jews in 1867. From approximately 1850 to 1880

Dedication of a New Synagogue. The social life of Europe became transformed in numerous ways during the nineteenth century. Beyond the expansion of cities and the rise of industrial society, there also occurred numerous changes in religious life. One of the most important of these was the gradual emancipation of European Jews from sharply restricted lives in urban ghettos to fuller political participation and social assimilation. This painting by G. E. Opitz portrays the dedication of a new synagogue in Alsace in 1820.
The Jewish Museum, N.Y./Art Resource, N.Y.

there was relatively little organized or overt prejudice towards Jews. They entered the professions and other occupations once closed to them. They participated fully in the literary and cultural life of their nations. They were active in the arts and music. They became leaders in science and education. Jews intermarried freely with non-Jews as legal prohibitions against such marriages were repealed during the last quarter of the century.

Outside of Russia, Jewish political figures served in the highest offices of the state. Politically they tended to be aligned with liberal parties because such groups had championed equal rights. Later in the century, especially in Eastern Europe, many Jews became associated with the Socialist parties.

The prejudice that had been associated with religious attitudes towards Jews seemed to have dissipated, although it still appeared in rural Russia and Eastern Europe. From these regions hundreds of thousands of European Jews immigrated to the United States. Almost anywhere in Europe Jews might encounter prejudice on a personal level. But in Western Europe, including England, France, Italy, Germany, and the Low Countries, the Jewish populations seem to have felt relatively secure from the old dangers of legalized persecution and discrimination.

That began to change during the last two decades of the nineteenth century. In the 1870s anti-Semitic sentiments attributing the economic stagnation of that decade to Jewish bankers and financial interests began to be voiced. In the 1880s organized anti-Semitism erupted in Germany as it did in France in the 1890s. As we saw in the previous chapter, those developments gave birth to Zionism, the movement to establish a Jewish state in Palestine. However, Zionism was initially a minority movement within the Jewish community. Most Jewish leaders believed the attacks on Jewish life to be temporary recurrences of older prejudice; they felt that their communities would remain safe under the legal protections that had been extended during the century. That analysis would be proved disastrously wrong during the 1930s and 1940s.

European Labor, Socialism, and Politics to World War I

The Working Classes in the Late Nineteenth Century

After 1848 European workers ceased taking to the streets to voice their grievances in the form of riots. They also stopped trying to revive the old paternalistic guilds. After midcentury the labor force accepted the fact of modern industrial production and its general downgrading of skills and attempted

to receive more benefits from that system. Workers turned to new institutions and ideologies. Chief among them were trade unions, democratic political parties, and socialism.

Trade Unions Trade unionism came of age as legal protections were extended to unions throughout the second half of the century. Unions became fully legal in Great Britain in 1871 and were allowed to picket in 1875. In France the Third Republic fully legalized unions in 1884. After 1890 they could function in Germany with little disturbance. Initially, most trade unions were slow to enter the political process directly. As long as the traditional governing classes looked after labor interests, members of the working class rarely sought office themselves.

The midcentury organizational efforts of the unions aimed to improve the wages and working conditions of skilled workers. By the close of the century large industrial unions for unskilled workers were also being organized. They confronted extensive opposition from employers, and

Trade Union Membership Certificate. Trade unions continued to grow in late nineteenth-century Great Britain. The effort to curb the unions eventually led to the formation of the Labour Party. The British unions often had quite elaborate membership certificates, such as this one for the National Union of Gas Workers and General Labourers of Great Britain and Ireland. *The Granger Collection.*

were often recognized only after long strikes. In the decade before 1914 strikes were common throughout Europe as the unions attempted to raise wages to keep up with inflation. However, despite the advances of unions and the growth of their membership in 1910 to approximately 3 million in Britain, 2 million in Germany, and 977,000 in France, they never included a majority of the industrial labor force. The unions did represent a new collective fashion in which workers could associate to confront the economic difficulties of their lives and attain better security.

Democracy and Political Parties The democratic franchise gave workers direct political influence, which meant they could no longer be ignored. Except for Russia, all the major European states adopted broad-based, if not perfectly democratic, electoral systems. Democracy brought new modes of popular pressure to bear on all governments. It meant that discontented groups could now voice their grievances and advocate their programs within government rather than from outside it.

The advent of democracy witnessed the formation for the first time in Europe of organized mass political parties, such as had existed throughout the nineteenth century in the United States. In the liberal European states with narrow electoral bases, most voters had been men of property who understood what they had at stake in politics. Organization had been minimal. The expansion of the electorate brought into the political processes many people whose level of political consciousness and interest was low. This electorate had to be organized and taught the nature of power and influence in the liberal democratic state. The organized political party—with its workers, newspapers, offices, social life, and discipline—was the vehicle that mobilized the new voters. The largest single group in these mass electorates was the working class. The democratization of politics presented the Socialists with opportunities and required the traditional ruling class to vie with them for the support of the new voters.

Marxist Critique of the Industrial Order

During the 1840s Karl Marx (1818–1883) produced the most influential of all critiques of the newly emerged industrial order. His analysis became very important because later in the century it was adopted by the leading Socialist political party in Germany, which in turn influenced most other European Socialist parties including a small group of exiled Russian Socialists led by V. I. Lenin. Marx was born in the Rhineland. His Jewish middle-class parents sent him to the University of Berlin, where he became deeply involved in radical politics. During 1842 and 1843 he edited the radical *Rhineland Gazette*. Soon the German

Karl Marx. Marx's Socialist philosophy eventually triumphed over most alternative versions of socialism in Europe, but his monumental work has been subject to varying interpretations, criticisms, and revisions that continue to this day. *Bildarchiv Preussischer Kulturbesitz.*

authorities drove him into exile—first in Paris; then in Brussels; and finally, after 1849, in London.

In 1844 Marx met Friedrich Engels (1820–1895), another young middle-class German, whose father owned a textile factory in Manchester, England. The next year, Engels published *The Condition of the Working Class in England*, which presented a devastating picture of industrial life. The two men became fast friends. Late in 1847 they were asked to write a pamphlet for a newly organized and ultimately short-lived secret Communist league. *The Communist Manifesto*, published in German, appeared early in 1848. Marx, Engels, and the league had adopted the name *Communist* because the term was more self-consciously radical than *Socialist*. *Communism* implied the outright abolition of private property rather than some less extensive rearrangement of society. The *Manifesto* itself was a work of fewer than fifty pages. It would become the most influential political document of modern European history, but that development lay in the future. At the time it was simply one more political tract. Moreover, neither Marx nor his thought had any effect on the revolutionary events of 1848.

In *The Communist Manifesto* Marx and Engels contended that human history must be understood rationally and as a whole. According to their analysis, history is the record of humankind's coming to grips with physical nature to produce the goods necessary for survival. That basic productive process determines the structures, values, and ideas of a society. Historically, the organization of the means of production has always involved conflict between the classes who owned and controlled the means of production and those classes who worked for them. That necessary conflict has provided the engine for historical development; it is not an accidental byproduct of mismanagement or bad intentions. Consequently, only a radical social transformation, not piecemeal reforms, can eliminate the social and economic evils inherent in the very structures of production. Such a revolution will occur as the inevitable outcome of the development of capitalism.

In Marx's and Engels's eyes, during the nineteenth century the class conflict that had characterized previous Western history had become a struggle between the bourgeoisie and the proletariat, or between the middle class and the workers. The character of capitalism ensured the sharpening of the struggle. Capitalist production and competition would steadily increase the size of the unpropertied proletariat. Large-scale mechanical production crushed both traditional and smaller industrial producers into the ranks of the proletariat. As the business structures grew larger and larger, smaller middle-class units would be squeezed out by the competitive pressures. Competition among the few remaining gigantic concerns would lead to more intense suffering by the proletariat. As the workers suffered increasingly from the competition among the ever-enlarging firms, they would foment revolution and finally overthrow the few remaining owners of the means of production. For a time the workers would organize the means of production through a dictatorship of the proletariat, which would eventually give way to a propertyless and classless communist society.

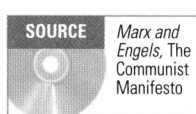

SOURCE Marx and Engels, The Communist Manifesto

This proletarian revolution was inevitable, according to Marx and Engels. The structure of capitalism required competition and consolidation of enterprise. Although the class conflict involved in the contemporary process resembled that of the past, it differed in one major respect. The struggle between the capitalistic bourgeoisie and the industrial proletariat would culminate in a wholly new society that would be free of class conflict. The victorious proletariat, by its very nature, they contended, could not be a new oppressor class: "The proletarian movement is the self-conscious, independent movement of the immense majority, in the interest of the immense majority."[1] The result of the proletarian victory would be "an association, in which the free development of each is the condition for the free development of all."[2] The victory of the proletariat over the bourgeoisie represented the culmination of human history. For the first time, one group of people would not be oppressing another. Marx's analysis was conditioned by his own economic environment. The 1840s had seen much unemployment and deprivation. Capitalism, however, did not collapse as he predicted, nor did the middle class during the rest of the century or later become proletarianized.

Rather, more and more people came to benefit from the industrial system. Nonetheless, within a generation Marxism had captured the imagination of many Socialists and large segments of the working class. Its doctrines were allegedly based on the empirical evidence of hard economic fact. This much proclaimed scientific aspect of **Marxism** helped the ideology, as science became more influential during the second half of the century. Marx had made the ultimate victory of socialism seem certain. His works also suggested that the path to socialism lay with revolution rather than reform. As Marxist thought permeated the international Socialist movement during the next seventy-five years, it would provide the ideological basis for some of the most momentous and ultimately repressive political movements in the history of virtually the entire modern world.

Germany: Social Democrats and Revisionism

That the thought of Karl Marx ultimately came to exercise such vast influence was the result of his ideas becoming adopted by the German Social Democratic Party (SPD). Founded in 1875, the SPD suffered twelve years of persecution by Otto von Bismarck (1815–1898), who believed socialism would undermine German politics and society. In 1878 there was an attempt to assassinate Emperor William I (r. 1861–1888). Bismarck unfairly blamed the Socialists and steered antisocialist laws through the Reichstag, the German Parliament. These measures suppressed the organization, meetings, newspapers, and other public activities of the SPD. Nonetheless, the SPD steadily polled more votes in elections to the Reichstag.

When repression failed, Bismarck enacted social welfare legislation to wean German workers from socialist loyalties. These measures provided health insurance, accident insurance, and old age and disability pensions. The German state itself thus organized a system of social security that did not change the system of property holding or politics.

---

[1] Robert C. Tucker, ed., *The Marx-Engels Reader* (New York: W. W. Norton, 1972), p. 353.
[2] Ibid.

In 1891, after forcing Bismarck's resignation, Emperor William II (r. 1888–1918) allowed the antisocialist legislation to expire. The SPD then had to decide how to operate as a legalized party. Their new direction was announced in the Erfurt Program of 1891. In good Marxist fashion, the program declared the imminent doom of capitalism and the necessity of socialist ownership of the means of production. However, these goals were to be achieved by legal political participation rather than by revolutionary activity. Since the revolution was inevitable, it was argued, the immediate task of Socialists was to improve workers' lives. In theory, the SPD was vehemently hostile to the German Empire, but in practice the party functioned within its institutions.

This situation of the SPD, however, generated the most important internal socialist challenge to the orthodox Marxist analysis of capitalism and the socialist revolution. Eduard Bernstein (1850–1932) wrote what was regarded as his socialist heresy. Bernstein, who was familiar with the British **Fabians**, questioned whether Marx and his later orthodox followers had been correct in their pessimistic appraisal of capitalism and the necessity of revolution. In *Evolutionary Socialism* (1899), Bernstein pointed to the rising standard of living in Europe, the ongoing power of the middle class, and the opening of the franchise to the working class. He argued that a humane socialist society required not revolution, but more democracy and social reform. Bernstein's doctrines, known as **revisionism**, were widely debated among German Socialists and were finally condemned as theory, although the party actually pursued a peaceful, reformist program. His critics argued that evolution towards social democracy might be possible in liberal, parliamentary Britain but not in authoritarian, militaristic Germany with its basically powerless Reichstag. Therefore, the German SPD continued to advocate revolution.

The German debate over revisionism became important for the later history of Marxist socialism. The German SPD was, as noted, the most successful prewar Socialist party. Its rejection of an ideology of reform socialism in favor of revolutionary socialism influenced all Socialists who looked to the German example. Most significant, Lenin adopted this position, as did the other leaders of the Russian Revolution. Thereafter, wherever Soviet Marxism was influential, the goal of its efforts would be revolution rather than reform.

Great Britain: The Labour Party and Fabianism

No form of socialism made significant progress in Great Britain, the most advanced industrial society of the day. The members of the growing trade unions normally supported Liberal Party candidates. The "new unionism" of the late 1880s and the 1890s organized the dock workers, the gas

workers, and similar unskilled groups. Employer resistance to unions heightened class antagonism. In 1892 Keir Hardie (1856–1915) became the first independent worker elected to Parliament. In 1893 the Socialist Independent Labour Party was founded, but it remained ineffective.

In 1901, however, a decision by the House of Lords (Britain's supreme court) removed the legal protection previously accorded union funds. The Trades Union Congress responded by launching the Labour Party, which sent twenty-nine members to Parliament in the election of 1906. Their goals did not yet encompass socialism. The British labor movement also became more militant. In scores of strikes, workers fought for wages to meet the rising cost of living. The government intervened to mediate these strikes, which in 1911 and 1912 involved the railways, the docks, and the mines.

British socialism itself remained primarily the preserve of intellectuals. The Socialists who exerted the most influence were from the Fabian Society, founded in 1884. The society took its name from Q. Fabius Maximus (d. 203 B.C.E.), the Roman general who defeated Hannibal by waiting before

Beatrice and Sidney Webb. These most influential British Fabian Socialists, shown in a photograph from the late 1920s, wrote many books on governmental and economic matters, served on special parliamentary commissions, and agitated for the enactment of socialist policies.
UPI/Corbis/Bettmann.

attacking. Its name thus indicated a gradualist approach to social reform. Its leading members were Sydney Webb (1859–1947) and Beatrice Webb (1858–1943), H. G. Wells (1866–1946), and George Bernard Shaw (1856–1950). Many of the Fabians were civil servants who believed that the problems of industry, the expansion of ownership, and the state direction of production could be solved and achieved gradually, peacefully, and democratically. They sought to educate the country to the rational wisdom of socialism. They were particularly interested in collective ownership on the municipal level, or so-called gas-and-water socialism.

Russia: Industrial Development and the Birth of Bolshevism

Following its defeat in the Crimean War, the tsarist government in Russia had undertaken a series of major internal reforms. The most important of these was the emancipation of the serfs in 1861. That measure was extremely complicated and in effect required serfs to pay for their land. The poverty of the emancipated serfs became a political cause for groups of urban revolutionaries in Russia, the most important of which was named The People's Will, who succeeded in assassinating Tsar Alexander II (r. 1855–1881) in 1881. Thereafter, the government pursued a policy of general political repression. (See Document "The People's Will Issues a Revolutionary Manifesto.")

At the same time in the late nineteenth century the tsarist government was determined to make Russia an industrial power. It favored the growth of heavy industries, such as railways, iron, and steel. A small, but significant, industrial proletariat arose. By 1900 Russia had approximately 3 million factory workers. Their working and living conditions were bad by any standard.

New political departures accompanied this economic development. In 1901 the Social Revolutionary Party was founded. It opposed industrialism and looked to the communal life of rural Russia as a model for the economic future. In 1903 the Constitutional Democratic Party, or Cadets, was formed. Liberal in outlook, the Cadets were drawn from people who participated in the *zemstvos* (local governments). They wanted a parliamentary regime with responsible ministries, civil liberties, and economic progress. The Cadets hoped to model themselves on the Liberal parties of Western Europe.

Lenin's Early Thought and Career The situation for Russian Socialists differed radically from that in other major European countries. Russia had no representative political institutions and only a small working class. The compromises and accommodations achieved elsewhere were meaningless in Russia, where socialism in both theory and practice had

to be revolutionary. The Russian Social Democratic Party had been established in 1898. It was Marxist, and its members greatly admired the German SPD, but tsarist repression meant that it had to function in exile.

The leading late-nineteenth-century Russian Marxist was Georgii Plekhanov (1857–1918), based in Switzerland. His chief disciple was Vladimir Illich Ulyanov (1870–1924), who took the name of Lenin. The future leader of the communist revolution was the son of a high bureaucrat. His older brother had been executed in 1887 for participating in a plot against Alexander III (r. 1881–1894). In 1893 Lenin moved to Saint Petersburg, where he briefly practiced law. Soon he, too, was drawn to the revolutionary groups among the factory workers. In 1895 he was exiled to Siberia. After his release in 1900, Lenin spent most of the next seventeen years in Switzerland.

In Switzerland Lenin became deeply involved in the organizational and policy disputes of the exiled Russian Social Democrats. They all considered themselves Marxists but quarreled about the proper nature of a Marxist revolution in primarily rural Russia and the structure of their own party. The Social Democrats were modernizers who favored further industrial development. Most believed that Russia

Chronology

Major Dates in the Development of Socialism

1864	International Working Men's Association (the First International) founded
1875	German Social Democratic Party founded
1876	First International dissolved
1878	German antisocialist laws passed
1884	British Fabian Society founded
1889	Second International founded
1891	German antisocialist laws permitted to expire
1891	German Social Democratic Party's Erfurt Program
1895	French *Confédération Générale du Travail* founded
1899	Eduard Bernstein's *Evolutionary Socialism*
1902	Formation of the British Labour party
1902	Lenin's *What Is to Be Done?*
1903	Bolshevik-Menshevik split

The People's Will Issues a Revolutionary Manifesto

Document

In the late 1870s, an extreme revolutionary movement appeared in Russia calling itself The People's Will. It advocated the overthrow of the tsarist government and the election of an Organizing Assembly to form a government based on popular representation. It directly embraced terrorism as a path towards its goal of the Russian people governing themselves. Members of this group assassinated Alexander II in 1881.

◆ Which of the group's seven demands might be associated with liberalism, and which go beyond liberalism in their radical intent? Why does the group believe it must engage in terrorism as well as propaganda? Would there have been any reforms or steps towards reform that the Russian government might have taken that might have satisfied this group or dissuaded them from terrorist action?

Although we are ready to submit wholly to the popular will, we regard it as none the less our duty, as a party, to appear before the people with our program. . . . It is as follows:

1. Perpetual popular representation, . . . having full power to act in all national questions.
2. General local self-government, secured by the election of all officers, and the economic independence of the people.
3. The self-controlled village commune as the economic and administrative unit.
4. Ownership of the land by the people.
5. A system of measures having for their object the turning over to the laborers of all mining works and factories.
6. Complete freedom of conscience, speech, association, public meeting, and electioneering activity.
7. The substitution of a territorial militia for the army. . . .

In view of the stated aim of the party its operations may be classified as follows:

1. Propaganda and agitation. Our propaganda has for its object the popularization, in all social classes, of the idea of a political and popular revolution as a means of social reform, as well as popularization of the party's own program. Its essential features are criticism of the existing order of things, and a statement and explanation of revolutionary methods. The aim of agitation should be to incite the people to protest as generally as possible against the present state of affairs, to demand such reforms as are in harmony with the party's purposes, and, especially, to demand the summoning of an Organizing Assembly. . . .

2. Destructive and terroristic activity. Terroristic activity consists in the destruction of the most harmful persons in the Government, the protection of the party from spies, and the punishment of official lawlessness and violence in all the more prominent and important cases in which such lawlessness and violence are manifested. The aim of such activity is to break down the prestige of Governmental power, to furnish continuous proof of the possibility of carrying on a contest with the Government, to raise in that way the revolutionary spirit of the people and inspire belief in the practicability of revolution, and, finally, to form a body suited and accustomed to warfare.

Quoted in George Kennan, *Siberia and the Exile System*, vol. 2 (New York: The Century Co., 1891), pp. 495–499.

---

must develop a large proletariat before the revolution could come. This same majority hoped to mold a mass political party like the German SPD.

Lenin dissented from both positions. In *What Is to Be Done?* (1902), he condemned any accommodations. He also criticized a trade unionism that settled for short-term gains rather than true revolutionary change for the working class. Lenin further rejected the concept of a mass party composed of workers. Revolutionary consciousness would not arise spontaneously from the working class. It must be carried to them by a small, elite party, "people who make revolutionary activity their profession."[3] The guiding principle of that party should be "the strictest secrecy, the strictest selection of members, and the training of professional revolutionaries."[4]

---

[3] Quoted in Albert Fried and Ronald Sanders, eds., *Socialist Thought: A Documentary History* (Garden City, NY: Anchor Doubleday, 1964), p. 459.
[4] Ibid., p. 468.

Establishment of the Bolsheviks In 1903, at the London Congress of the Russian Social Democratic Party, Lenin split the party ranks. Although it lost most of the votes during the congress, Lenin's group mustered a slim majority near the close. Thereafter, his faction assumed the name **Bolsheviks**, meaning "majority," and the other, more moderate, democratic revolutionary faction became known as the **Mensheviks**, or "minority." There was, of course, a considerable public relations advantage to the name *Bolshevik*. (In 1912 the Bolsheviks organized separately from other Social Democrats.) In 1905 Lenin complemented his organizational theory with a program for revolution in Russia. His *Two Tactics of Social Democracy in the Bourgeois-Democratic Revolution* urged that the socialist revolution unite the proletariat and the peasants. He grasped better than any other revolutionary the profound discontent in the Russian countryside. He knew that an alliance of workers and peasants in rebellion probably could not be suppressed. Lenin's two principles of an elite party and a dual social revolution allowed the Bolsheviks, in late 1917, to capture the leadership of the Russian Revolution and to transform the political face of the modern world.

The Revolution of 1905 and Its Aftermath The quarrels among the Russian Socialists had no immediate influence within Russia itself. In 1904 Russia went to war with Japan, but the result was defeat and political crisis. The Japanese captured Port Arthur, Russia's base on the eastern coast of China, early in 1905. A few days later, on January 22, a priest named Father Gapon (1870–1906) led thousands of workers to petition the tsar for improvements in industrial conditions. As the petitioners approached the Winter Palace in Saint Petersburg, troops opened fire. About 100 people were killed, and many more were wounded.

Revolutionary disturbances spread throughout Russia: Sailors mutinied, peasants revolted, and property was attacked. An uncle of the tsar was assassinated. Liberal Constitutional Democratic leaders from the *zemstvos* demanded political reform. University students went on strike. In early October 1905 strikes broke out in Saint Petersburg, and worker groups, called **soviets**, virtually controlled the city. Tsar Nicholas II (r. 1894–1917) promised Russia constitutional government.

Early in 1906 the tsar announced the election of a parliament, the **Duma**, with two chambers. However, he reserved for himself ministerial appointments, financial policy, and military and foreign affairs. Nicholas named as his chief minister P. A. Stolypin (1862–1911). Neither the tsar nor his minister was sympathetic to the Duma. It would meet, disagreements would occur, and it would be dismissed. In 1906, however, the government canceled any

Chronology

Major Dates in Turn-of-the-Century Russian History

1895	Lenin arrested and sent to Siberia
1897	Eleven-and-a-half-hour workday established
1898	Russian Social Democratic Party founded
1900	Lenin leaves Russia for Western Europe
1901	Social Revolutionary Party founded
1903	Constitutional Democratic Party (Cadets) founded
1903	Bolshevik-Menshevik split
1904	Russo-Japanese War begins
1905 January	Japan defeats Russia
January 22	Revolution breaks out in Saint Petersburg after Bloody Sunday massacre
October 20	General strike
October 26	*October Manifesto* establishes constitutional government
1906 May 10	Meeting of first *Duma*
June	Stolypin appointed prime minister
July 21	Dissolution of first *Duma*
November	Land redemption payments canceled for peasants
1907 March 5–June 16	Second *Duma* seated and dismissed
1907	Franchise changed and a third *Duma* elected, which sits until 1912
1911	Stolypin assassinated by a social revolutionary
1912	Fourth *Duma* elected
1914	World War I breaks out

redemptive payments the peasants still owed from the emancipation of the serfs in 1861. Thereafter Stolypin repressed rural discontent.

After Stolypin's assassination in 1911 by a social revolutionary, the tsarist government simply muddled along. But

Bloody Sunday. On Bloody Sunday, January 22, 1905, troops of Tsar Nicholas II fired on a peaceful procession of workers who sought to present a petition at the Winter Palace in Saint Petersburg. After this event, there was little chance of reconciliation between the tsarist government and the Russian working class. *Bildarchiv Preussischer Kulturbesitz.*

the imperial family became surrounded by scandal over the influence of Grigori Rasputin (1871?–1916), who seemed able to heal the tsar's hemophilic son, the heir to the throne. The undue influence of this strange and uncouth man, the continued social discontent, and the conservative resistance to liberal reforms rendered the position and policy of the tsar uncertain after 1911.

European Socialism in World History

The debates among late-nineteenth- and early-twentieth-century European Socialists were complicated and in some respects obscure. They proved significant, however, not only for European politics but also for political developments around the world and that is the reason we have discussed them in some detail. The impact arose for two reasons. First, Europeans who immigrated to North and South America carried many of these socialist ideas and quarrels with them. They continued to debate the issues they had debated in Europe in their new homelands. Second, by the end of the nineteenth century numerous students from different parts of the European empires in Africa and Asia traveled to Europe for education. There they confronted these debates among European Socialists. Many of those students later returned home to become leaders of anticolonial political movements and carried

with them again the ideas and quarrels about methods, theory, and tactics they had encountered among European Socialists.

North America and the New Industrial Economy

The full industrialization of the United States followed a pattern not unlike that of nineteenth-century Europe. The first industry to become thoroughly mechanized was textile manufacture, followed by growth in the iron and steel industries. There were certain significant differences, however. The United States industrialized considerably later than Great Britain. Its major expansion in iron and steel took place after the Civil War and was thus approximately contemporary to the economic rise of the newly united Germany. In the United States there had always been enormous social respect for entrepreneurial enterprise. American manufacturers and commercial developers thus encountered little of the prejudice against trade and commerce that existed among the European aristocracy. Wealthy American businessmen had considerable political influence. The United States possessed an immense internal market that functioned without trade restraints for the shipment of unprocessed goods to factories or of finished products to their markets. Much of the capital for American industrial expansion came from British bankers who saw the United States as an area of secure investment. Finally, the United States had a relative shortage of labor and consequently relatively high wages, the factors that attracted so many immigrants to the industrial sector during the second half of the century.

In America as in Europe, however, the railways spurred the most intense industrial growth. The number of railway miles increased from approximately 50,000 in the mid-1860s to almost 200,000 by 1900. Much of the construction was made possible by vast European investments in the United States. The railways created enormous demand for iron, steel, coal, and lumber. They also stimulated settlement, vastly expanded markets, and helped to knit the country together.

Immigrant Labor. Chinese laborers, known as "coolies," performed most of the backbreaking work on the construction of the railroads in the American West. The workers depicted here are laying down track near Promontory, Utah.

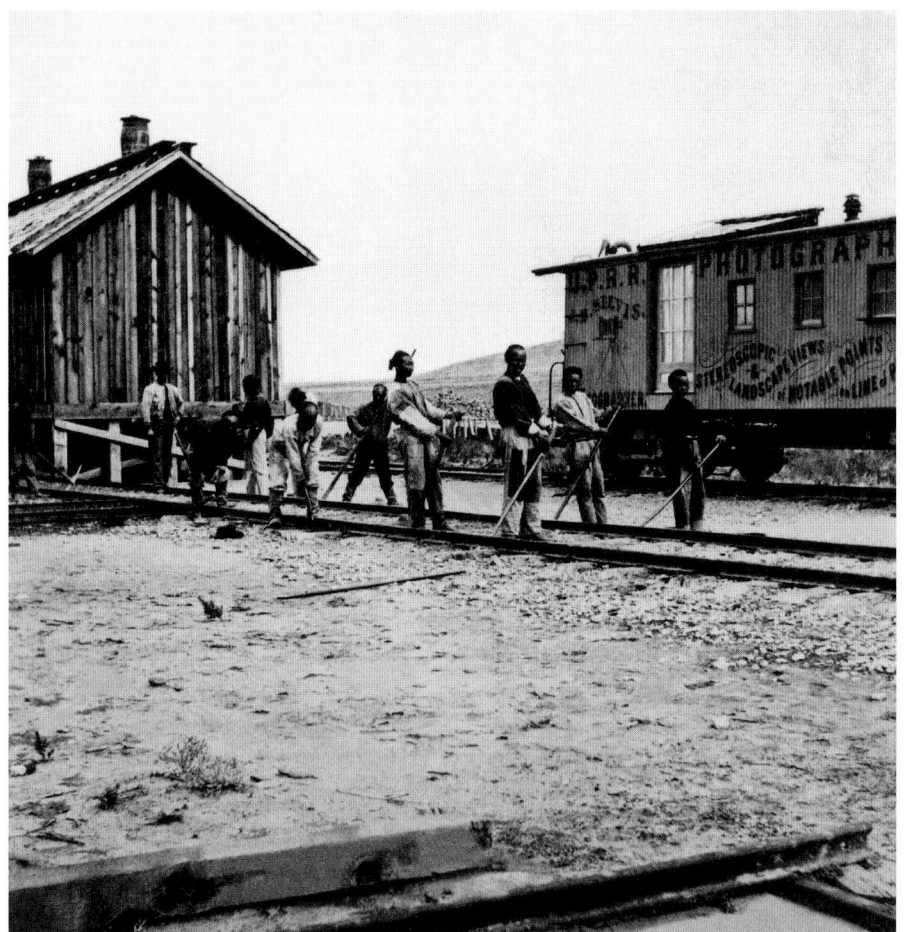

European Immigration to the United States

The same conditions that made American life so difficult for black people and Native Americans (see Chapter 23) turned the United States into a land of vast opportunity for white European immigrants. These immigrants faced religious and ethnic discrimination as well as frequent poverty in the United States; however, for many of them and their children, the social and economic structures of the United States allowed for assimilation and remarkable upward social mobility. This was especially true of those immigrants, mostly from northern and Western Europe, who arrived between approximately 1840 and 1890—the great period of German, English, Welsh, Scottish, and Irish immigration (see Map 25–1). Among this group, the Irish undoubtedly encountered the most difficulties and resistance.

Towards the end of the century and well into the next—in what is sometimes known as the New Immigration—millions of people arrived from the Mediterranean, Eastern Europe, and the Balkans. Most of these peoples left economically depressed areas and financed their immigration themselves. However, some American companies did send ships to Italy for immigrants to work in American factories and mines. These new immigrants, who generally came to work in the growing industrial cities, were perceived as fundamentally different from those who had come before them. They were seen and treated as of a lower class and inherently more difficult to assimilate than the earlier immigrants. Predominately Roman Catholic, Orthodox, and Jewish, they encountered much intolerance. The same kind of racial theory that spread through Europe during these years was present in the United States. These new immigrants were often regarded as being from less desirable racial stocks. As a result, turn-of-the-century immigrants often encountered serious prejudice and endured lives of enormous poverty. They also often settled into communities of people from their own ethnic background. What ultimately held them together

Map Exploration

To explore this map further, go to http://www.prenhall.com/craig_maps

Map 25–1. **Patterns of Global Migration, 1840–1900.** Emigration was a global process by the late nineteenth century. But more immigrants went to the United States than to every other nation combined.

Italian immigrants

were various private organizations, such as churches and synagogues, clubs, newspapers in their own languages, and social agencies they organized for themselves.

Although none of these immigrants faced the same legal discrimination as did American black people, the Jews encountered restricted covenants on real estate, obstacles to joining private clubs, and quotas for admission to many schools and universities. Asian immigrants to the West Coast of the United States faced harsher prejudice.

Unions: Organization of Labor

The expansion of industrialism led to various attempts to organize labor unions. In America as in Europe, workers faced great resistance from employers and those who feared that labor unions might lead to socialism. Another difficulty arose from the social situation of the labor force itself. White laborers would not organize alongside black workers.

Different ethnic minorities would not cooperate. The ongoing flood of immigration ensured a supply of workers willing to work for low wages. The owners of businesses more often than not could divide and conquer the sprawling, ethnically mixed labor force.

The first effort at labor organization occurred in the 1870s with the National Labor Union and railroad unions. In 1881 the American Federation of Labor (AFL) was founded. In contrast to earlier organizations and the advanced European socialist movement, such as that in Germany, it did not seek to transform the life of workers in a radical fashion but rather focused on higher wages and better working conditions. The AFL concentrated on organizing skilled workers; it did not seek to organize whole industries. Among its most effective leaders was Samuel Gompers (1850–1924). Other unions, such as the United Mine Workers and the Railway Brotherhoods, organized workers by industry.

The industrialization of the United States—again, like that of Europe—saw major periods of business crisis or

Ellis Island. In 1892 the federal government opened the immigration station on Ellis Island, located in New York City's harbor, where about 80 percent of the immigrants to the United States landed. As many as 5,000 passengers per day reported to federal immigration officers for questions about their background and for physical examinations, such as this eye exam. Only about 1 percent were quarantined or turned away for health problems. *Brown Brothers.*

downturn. Serious depressions occurred in both the 1870s and the 1890s. There was no government relief. What little relief there was came from local authorities and private charities. This pattern would continue until the Great Depression of the 1930s. The economic turmoil of the 1880s and 1890s spawned violent strikes. Perhaps the most famous of these incidents was the breaking of the Pullman strike in Chicago in 1894 by federal troops. The major goal of labor thereafter was to achieve the full legal right to organize. Although the Clayton Act of 1914 moved in that direction, the clear right to organize with the protection of the federal government was achieved only through the legislation of Franklin Roosevelt's (1882–1945) New Deal in the 1930s.

Socialism was a path not taken by American labor and one not allowed to be taken. The leaders of the conservative unions worked against the Socialists, and spokesmen for business did everything possible to block their influence. The federal and state governments actively sought to repress socialist activities wherever they appeared. After the Bolshevik Revolution of 1917 virtually all American Socialists were persecuted as Bolshevists during the 1920s and beyond. The United States thus became the land where many social issues tended to be addressed by trade unions rather than by Socialist parties. Furthermore, although many conservative American political and business leaders disliked them, unions were not legally attacked here as they were in Britain, which led to the founding of the British Labour Party after the turn of the century.

In many European countries, Socialist parties, or ministers like Bismarck who attempted to outflank the Socialists, had pressed their governments to pass legislation providing social security and other social services. As with so many other policies favorable to labor, no significant legislation of this kind was passed in the United States, at either the federal or state level, until the New Deal.

The Progressives

Much of the power in American politics in the decades after the Civil War, especially in cities, often lay in the hands of political bosses. This system depended on patronage at every level of government. In return for jobs, contracts, licenses, favors, and sometimes actual services, the boss expected and received political support. Government was a vehicle for distributing spoils. The point of boss politics was not merely venality; it was also a way, however crude and unattractive, of organizing the disorderly social and economic forces of the great cities. It was a way of managing cities that were growing as never before with highly diverse populations.

Towards the close of the century, reform-minded political figures began to emerge on the city and state levels. These reformers feared that people such as themselves from the white upper-middle classes might soon lose political and social influence. Deeply disturbed by the corruption of much of political life, these reformers found the urban environment with its slums an unacceptable picture of disorder. They wanted to see more efficient and less corrupt government. They also wanted the government to become a direct agent of change and reform. Pursuing these goals, they ushered in what has been called the *Progressive era*, which lasted from approximately 1890 through 1914. Although the Progressives were reformers, they were not always liberal by later standards. For example, Progressives in the South often disenfranchised blacks and poor whites by imposing literacy tests and similar devices.

The Progressives began their reform work on the local level, especially in the cities, before they launched into national politics. The disorder and extreme disparity of wealth and poverty in the cities disturbed them. Urban reformers believed that the politics of bosses and patronage robbed cities of the money needed to make them livable places. In place of patronage, they demanded social and municipal services to clean up the cities. They repeatedly attacked special interests who blocked reform. Progressive mayors called for lower utility rates and streetcar fares and also attacked police corruption.

Social Reform

Not only politicians joined the progressive crusade. Churches began to address the question of social reform. It

 SOURCE *New York street scene, 1900*

was in this era that the "Social Gospel" was first preached, with its message that Christianity involved civic action. Young men and women began to work in settlement houses in the slums. The most famous was Chicago's Hull House, led by Jane Addams (1860–1935). Other young persons from the middle class became active in housing and health reform, education, and charities. They conducted extensive surveys of the poorest parts of the great cities. These people believed that the urban environment could be cleaned up and social order made to prevail. Their vision of such social order was that of the white middle class.

Beginning in the mid-1890s, progressivism began to affect state governments. There the impulse towards reform involved various attempts to protect whole classes of persons who were perceived as unable to protect themselves against exploitation, especially children and women working

Tenement House, New York City, ca. 1890. Social reformers, such as the journalist Jacob Riis, drew the attention of millions to urban poverty and the plight of industrial workers. In his pathbreaking book, *How the Other Half Lives* (1890), Riis shocked Americans with a portrait of New York City's poor. Here seven members of an immigrant family living in a one-room tenement apartment in New York's Lower East Side sullenly confront the viewer.

under unwholesome conditions for low wages. Other aspects of progressivism at the state level involved the civil-service requirements and the regulation of railways. Virtually all of these reformers partook of the cult of science that was so influential in the late nineteenth century. They believed that the problems of society were susceptible to scientific, rational management. The general public interest should replace special interests.

The Progressive Presidency

Roosevelt Theodore Roosevelt became president in 1901 after the assassination of William McKinley (1843–1901). He had been police commissioner of New York City and later a reforming governor of New York State. Roosevelt, in effect, created the modern American presidency. By force of personality and intelligence, he began to make the presidency the most important and powerful branch of government. As president, he began to set the agenda for national affairs and to

define the problems that the federal government was to address. He surrounded himself with strong advisers and Cabinet members. He used his own knowledge of party patronage to beat the bosses at their own game. (See Document, "Theodore Roosevelt States His Progressive Creed.")

In domestic policy, Roosevelt was determined to control the powerful business trusts. No centers of economic power should, through their organization, be stronger than the federal government. He successfully moved against some of the most powerful financiers in the country, such as J. P. Morgan and John D. Rockefeller. Through legislation associated with the term "Square Deal," Roosevelt attempted to assert the public interest over that of the various powerful special interests. He was not opposed to big business in itself, but he wanted it to operate according to rules established by the government for the public good.

In 1902 Roosevelt brought the moral power of the presidency to the aid of mine workers who were on strike. He appointed a commission to arbitrate the dispute. This

Theodore Roosevelt States His Progressive Creed

Document

In 1912 Theodore Roosevelt ran unsuccessfully for the presidency on the Progressive ticket challenging both traditional Republicans and Democrats. At the party convention he set forth his most important progressive convictions. The issues Roosevelt raised in this speech still echo in American politics.

◆ Why does Roosevelt attack the old established parties? What political reforms does he advocate? What social reforms? Why have some people seen Roosevelt as one of the first presidents to be concerned with the environment?

The Old parties are husks, with no real soul within either, divided on artificial lines, boss-ridden and privilege-controlled, each a jumble of incongruous elements, and neither daring to speak out wisely and fearlessly what should be said on the vital issues of the day. This new movement is a movement of truth, sincerity, and wisdom, a movement which proposes to put at the service of all our people the collective power of the people, through their governmental agencies. . . .

The first essential in the Progressive program is the right of the people to rule. . . . We should provide by a national law for presidential primaries. We should provide for the election of United States Senators by popular vote . . . there must be stringent and efficient corrupt-practices acts, applying to the primaries as well as the elections; and there should be publicity of campaign contributions during the campaign. . . .

We stand for a living wage. Wages are subnormal if they fail to provide a living for those who devote their time and energy to industrial occupations. The monetary equivalent of a living wage varies according to local conditions, but must include enough to secure the elements of a normal standard of living—a standard high enough to make morality possible, to provide for education and recreation, to care for immature members of the family, to maintain the family during periods of sickness, and to permit of reasonable saving for old age.

Hours are excessive if they fail to afford the worker sufficient time to recuperate and return to his work thoroughly refreshed. We hold that the night labor of women and children is abnormal and should be prohibited. We hold that the seven-day working week is abnormal, and we hold that one day of rest in seven should be provided by law. . . . Working women have the same need to combine for protection that working men have; the ballot is as necessary for one class as for the other . . . and therefore we favor woman suffrage.

I believe in a protective tariff, but I believe in it as a principle, approached from the standpoint of the interest of the whole people, and not as a bundle of preferences to be given to favored individuals. . . .

There can be no greater issue than that of conservation in this country. Just as we must conserve our men, women and children, so we must conserve the resources of the land on which they live. . . .

Our cause is based on the eternal principle of righteousness; and even though we who now lead may for the time fail, in the end the cause itself shall triumph. . . . I say in closing: We stand at Armageddon, and we battle for the Lord.

From Theodore Roosevelt's "Confession of Faith Before the Progressive National Convention," August 6, 1912, as quoted in Oscar Handlin, ed., *Readings in American History.* Copyright © 1957 Alfred A. Knopf, pp. 477–480.

---

was a major intrusion of the federal government into the economic system. It reversed the policies that had prevailed a decade earlier, when the government had used federal troops to break strikes. Roosevelt sought to make the presidency and the federal government the guarantor of fairness in economic relations. Thus he fostered the passage of the Pure Food and Drug Act and the Meat Packing Act in 1906, which protected the public against adulterated foodstuffs. Here again, the regulatory principle

came to the fore. His conservation policies ensured that millions of acres of national forests came under the care of the federal government.

Roosevelt was associated with a vigorous, imperialistic foreign policy that had roots in the 1890s. In 1898 McKinley had led the nation into the Spanish-American War, and the United States had emerged as an imperial power with control of Cuba, Puerto Rico, Guam, and the Philippines. Roosevelt believed that the United States should be a major world power, and he sent a war fleet around the world. In Latin America naval intervention assured the success of the Panamanian revolt of 1903 against Colombia. A treaty with the new Panamanian government allowed the United States to construct and control a canal across the Isthmus of Panama. The United States was thus following the model of the European great powers, which had been intervening in Africa and Asia. Like the other great powers, the imperialist policies of the United States were built on a conviction of racial superiority.

Roosevelt was succeeded in 1909 by William Howard Taft (1857–1930), his hand-picked successor. Taft disappointed Roosevelt, and in 1912 the election was a three-way contest among Taft, Roosevelt (running as a third-party candidate), and Woodrow Wilson. The Democrat Wilson won and brought a different concept of progressivism to the White House.

Wilson Woodrow Wilson (1856–1924) was a former president of Princeton University and a reforming governor of New Jersey, where he had battled the bosses. While still an academic, he had criticized the weak presidency of the late nineteenth century. Wilson, like Roosevelt, accepted a modern industrialized nation. However, unlike Roosevelt, Wilson disliked big business almost in and of itself. He believed in economic competition in which the weak would receive protection from the government. Wilson termed his attitude and policy the New Freedom. Although he had pressed this idea during the campaign, in office he followed a policy of moderate regulation of business.

Wilson also had a different view of the presidency. He saw the office as responsible for leading Congress to legislative decisions. Wilson was the first American president since 1800 to deliver the State of the Union address to Congress in person. He presented Congress with a vast agenda of legislation and then worked carefully with the Democratic leadership to see that it was passed. Although Wilson appeared to be an advanced reformer, he retained many beliefs that have disappointed his later admirers. For example, he reinstated racial segregation in the federal civil service and opposed female suffrage.

Wilson had long seen his real goals in terms of domestic reform. But war broke out in Europe in August 1914. Although Wilson was reelected in 1916 on the slogan "He Kept Us Out of War!" in April 1917 he led the nation into the European conflict. The expertise that he and other Progressives had brought to the task of efficient domestic government was then turned to making the nation an effective military force. These two impulses—the first towards domestic reform, the second towards a strong international role—had long marked the progressive movement and would shape American history in the years after the war.

The American Progressives resembled political leaders of their generation in Great Britain. The Conservative Benjamin Disraeli (1804–1881) and Liberals William Gladstone (1809–1898) and David Lloyd-George (1863–1945) had supported various measures of social reforms. Elsewhere in Europe political leaders in France and Germany had undertaken reforms in housing and urban life to forestall the advance of socialism and to address the problems of industrialization and urbanization. These leaders had favored unprecedented use of central government authority and the establishment of stronger governments.

The Emergence of Modern European Thought

Parallel with the striking changes in European economic and social life there emerged major new departures in thought. The roots of these developments lay largely in the Enlightenment with its championing of science and self-criticism. More than ever European thinkers looked to the relationship of human beings to their immediate earthly environment and increasingly less to religious ideas.

In about 1850, Voltaire would have felt at home in a general discussion of scientific concepts. The basic Newtonian picture of physical nature that he had popularized still prevailed. Scientists continued to believe that nature operates as a vast machine according to mechanical principles. At mid-century, learned persons regarded the physical world as rational, mechanical, and dependable. Its laws could be ascertained objectively through experiment and observation. Scientific theory purportedly described physical nature as it really existed. Moreover, by 1850, science had a strong institutional life in French and German universities and in new professional societies. The word *scientist* had been invented in the early 1830s by William Whewell of Cambridge University and was in common use by the end of the century.

The last quarter of the nineteenth century and the first decade of the twentieth century were the crucible of modern Western thought. Philosophers, scientists, psychologists, and artists began to portray physical reality, human nature, and society in ways different from those of the past. The vast change in thinking commenced in the realm of biology.

Darwin's Theory of Natural Selection

In 1859, Charles Darwin (1809–1882) published *On the Origin of Species*, which carried the mechanical interpretation of physical nature into the world of living things. (See Document, "Darwin Defends a Mechanistic View of Nature.")

Darwin Defends a Mechanistic View of Nature

Document

In the closing paragraphs of *On the Origin of Species* (1859), Charles Darwin contrasted the view of nature he championed with that of his opponents. He argued that an interpretation of organic nature based on mechanistic laws was actually nobler than an interpretation based on divine creation. In the second edition, however, Darwin added the term *Creator* to these paragraphs.

◆ Why does Darwin believe a mechanistic creation suggests no less dignity than creation by God? How does the insertion of the term *Creator* change this passage? What is the grandeur that Darwin finds in his view of life?

Authors of the highest eminence seem to be fully satisfied with the view that each species has been independently created. To my mind it accords better with what we know of the laws impressed on matter by the Creator, that the production and extinction of the past and present inhabitants of the world should have been due to secondary causes, like those determining the birth and death of the individual. When I view all beings not as special creations, but as the lineal descendants of some few beings which lived long before the first bed of the Cambrian [geological] system was deposited, they seem to me to become ennobled. . . .

It is interesting to contemplate a tangled bank, clothed with many plants of many kinds, with birds singing on the bushes, with various insects flitting about, and with worms crawling through the damp earth, and to reflect that these elaborately constructed forms, so different from each other, and dependent upon each other in so complex a manner, have all been produced by laws acting around us. These laws, taken in the largest sense, being

Growth with Reproduction; Inheritance which is almost implied by reproduction; Variability from the indirect and direct action of the conditions of life, and from use and disuse: a Ratio of Increase so high as to lead to a Struggle for Life, and as a consequence to Natural Selection, entailing Divergence of Character and the Extinction of less-improved forms. Thus, from the war of nature, from famine and death, the most exalted object which we are capable of conceiving, namely the production of the higher animals, directly follows. There is grandeur in this view of life, with its several powers, having been originally breathed by the Creator into a few forms or into one; and that, whilst this planet has gone cycling on according to the fixed law of gravity, from so simple a beginning endless forms most beautiful and most wonderful have been, and are being evolved.

Charles Darwin, *On the Origin of Species and the Descent of Man* (New York: Modern Library, n.d.), pp. 373–374.

Both Darwin and his book have been much misunderstood. He did not originate the concept of evolution, which had been discussed widely before he wrote. What he and Alfred Russel Wallace (1823–1913) did, working independently, was to formulate the principle of natural selection, which explained how species had changed or evolved over time. Earlier writers had believed evolution might occur; Darwin and Wallace explained how it could occur.

The two scientists contended that more living organisms come into existence than can survive in their environment. Those organisms with a marginal advantage in the struggle for existence live long enough to propagate. This principle of survival of the fittest Darwin called **natural selection**. It was naturalistic and mechanistic, requiring no guiding mind behind the development in organic nature.

What neither Darwin nor anyone else in his day could explain was the origin of those chance variations that provided some living things with the marginal chance for survival. Only after 1900, when the work on heredity of the Austrian monk Gregor Mendel (1822–1884) received public attention, did the mystery of those variations begin to be unraveled.

Darwin and Wallace's theory represented the triumph of naturalistic explanation, which removed the idea of preconceived divine purpose from organic nature. Eyes were not made for seeing according to the rational wisdom and purpose of God but had developed mechanistically over time. Thus the theory of evolution through natural selection not only contradicted the biblical narrative of the Creation, but it also undermined both the deistic argument for the existence of God from the design of the universe and the whole concept of fixity in nature or the universe at large. The world was a realm of flux. The idea that physical and organic nature might be constantly changing allowed people to believe that society, values, customs, and beliefs should also change.

In 1871, in *The Descent of Man*, Darwin applied the principle of evolution by natural selection to human beings. Darwin was hardly the first person to treat human beings as animals, but he contended that humankind's moral nature and religious sentiments, as well as its physical frame, had developed naturalistically largely in response to the requirements of survival. Neither the origin nor the character of humankind, in Darwin's view, required the existence of a god for their explanation. Not since Copernicus had removed the earth from the center of the universe had the pride of Western human beings received so sharp a blow.

Darwin's theory of evolution by natural selection was controversial from the moment *On the Origin of Species* appeared. It encountered criticism from both the religious and the scientific communities. By the end of the century, scientists widely accepted the concept of evolution, but not yet Darwin's mechanism of natural selection. The acceptance

Darwin's theories about the evolution of humankind from the higher primates aroused enormous controversy. This caricature shows him with a monkey's body holding a mirror to an apelike creature. *National History Museum, London, UK/Bridgeman Art Library.*

of the latter really dates from the 1920s and 1930s, when Darwin's theory was combined with modern genetics.

The Revolution in Physics

By the late 1870s, discontent arose over the belief of many physical scientists that their mechanistic models, solid atoms, and absolute time and space actually described the real universe.

In 1883, Ernst Mach (1838–1916) published *The Science of Mechanics*, in which he urged that scientists consider their concepts descriptive not of the physical world, but of the sensations experienced by the scientific observer. Scientists could describe only the sensations, not the physical world that underlay those sensations. In line with Mach, the French scientist Henri Poincaré (1854–1912) urged that the theories of scientists be regarded as hypothetical constructs of the human mind rather than as true descriptions of nature. In 1911, Hans Vaihinger (1852–1933) suggested the concepts of science be considered "as if" descriptions of the physical world. By World War I, few scientists believed they could portray the "truth" about physical reality. Rather, they saw themselves as recording the observations of instruments and as offering useful hypothetical or symbolic models of nature.

X Rays and Radiation Discoveries in the laboratory paralleled the philosophical challenge to earlier physical science. In December 1895, Wilhelm Roentgen (1845–1923) published a paper on his discovery of X rays, a form of energy that penetrated various opaque materials. Major steps in the exploration of radioactivity followed within months of the publication of his paper.

In 1896, Henri Becquerel (1852–1908) discovered that uranium emitted a similar form of energy. The next year, J. J. Thomson (1856–1940), at Cambridge University, formulated the theory of the electron. The interior world of the atom had become a new area for human exploration. In 1902, Ernest Rutherford (1871–1937) explained the cause of radiation through the disintegration of the atoms of radioactive materials. Shortly thereafter, he speculated on the immense store of energy present in the atom.

Theories of Quantum Energy, Relativity, and Uncertainty The discovery of radioactivity and discontent with the existing mechanical models led to revolutionary theories in physics. In 1900, Max Planck (1858–1947) pioneered the articulation of the quantum theory of energy, according to which energy is a series of discrete quantities, or packets, rather than a continuous stream. In 1905, Albert Einstein (1879–1955) published his first epochmaking papers on **relativity**, in which he contended that time and space exist not separately, but rather as a combined continuum.

Marie Curie (1869–1934) and Pierre Curie (1859–1906) were two of the most important figures in the advance of physics and chemistry. Marie was born in Poland but worked in France for most of her life. She is credited with the discovery of radium, for which she was awarded the Nobel Prize in Chemistry in 1911. *Ullstein Bilderdienst.*

Moreover, the measurement of time and space depends on the observer as well as on the entities being measured.

In 1927, Werner Heisenberg (1901–1976) set forth his uncertainty principle, according to which the behavior of subatomic particles is a matter of statistical probability rather than of exactly determinable cause and effect. Much that had seemed unquestionable about the physical universe had now become ambiguous.

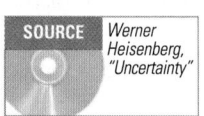

The mathematical complexity of twentieth-century physics meant science would rarely again be successfully popularized. At the same time, through applied technology and further research in chemistry, physics, and medicine, science affected daily living more than ever before. Scientists from the late nineteenth century onward became the most successful group of Western intellectuals in gaining the financial support of governments and private institutions for the pursuit of their research. They did so by relating the success of science to the economic progress, military security, and the health of their nations. Science, through research, medicine, and technological change, has thus affected modern life more significantly than any other intellectual activity.

Friedrich Nietzsche and the Revolt Against Reason

During the second half of the century, philosophers began to question the adequacy of rational thinking to address the human situation. No writer better exemplified this new attitude than the German philosopher Friedrich Nietzsche (1844–1900). His books remained unpopular until late in his life, when his brilliance had deteriorated into insanity. He was wholly at odds with the values of the age and attacked Christianity, democracy, nationalism, rationality, science, and progress. He sought less to change values than to probe their sources in the human character. He wanted not only to tear away the masks of respectable life, but also to explore how human beings made such masks.

His first important work was *The Birth of Tragedy* (1872), in which he urged that the nonrational aspects of human nature are as important and noble as the rational characteristics. He insisted on the positive function of instinct and ecstasy in human life. To limit human activity to strictly rational behavior was to impoverish human life. In this work, Nietzsche regarded Socrates as one of the major contributors to Western decadence because of the Greek philosopher's appeal for rationality. In Nietzsche's view, the strength for the heroic life and the highest artistic achievement arise from sources beyond rationality.

In later works, such as the prose poem *Thus Spake Zarathustra* (1883), Nietzsche criticized democracy and Christianity. Both would lead only to the mediocrity of sheepish masses. He announced the death of God and proclaimed the coming of the *Overman* (Übermensch), who would embody heroism and greatness. The term was frequently interpreted as some mode of superman or super-race, but such was not Nietzsche's intention. He was critical of contemporary racism and anti-Semitism. He sought a return to the heroism that he associated with Greek life in the Homeric age. He thought the values of Christianity and of bourgeois morality prevented humankind from achieving life on a heroic level.

Two of Nietzsche's most profound works are *Beyond Good and Evil* (1886) and *The Genealogy of Morals* (1887).

Both are difficult books. Nietzsche sought to discover not what is good and what is evil, but the social and psychological sources of the judgment of good and evil. He declared, "There are no moral phenomena at all, but only a moral interpretation of phenomena."[5] He dared to raise the question of whether morality itself was valuable: "We need a critique of moral values; the value of these values themselves must first be called in question."[6] In Nietzsche's view, morality was a human convention that had no independent existence. For Nietzsche, this discovery liberated human beings to create life-affirming values instead. Christianity, utilitarianism, and middle-class respectability could, in good conscience, be abandoned. Human beings could create a new moral order that would glorify pride, assertiveness, and strength rather than meekness, humility, and weakness.

The Birth of Psychoanalysis

A determination to probe beneath surface or public appearance united the major figures of late-nineteenth-century science, art, and philosophy. They sought to discern the undercurrents, tensions, and complexities that lay beneath the calm surfaces of hard atoms, respectable families, rationality, and social relationships. No intellectual development more exemplified this trend than psychoanalysis through the work of Sigmund Freud (1856–1939).

Development of Freud's Early Theories Freud was born into an Austrian Jewish family that settled in Vienna. He planned to become a lawyer but soon moved to the study of physiology and medicine. In 1886, he opened his medical practice in Vienna, where he lived until driven out by the Nazis in 1938. Freud conducted all his research and writing from the base of his medical practice. His earliest medical interests had been psychic disorders, to which he sought to apply the critical method of science. In late 1885, he had studied in Paris with Jean-Martin Charcot (1825–1893), who used hypnosis to treat cases of hysteria. In Vienna, he collaborated with another physician, Josef Breuer (1842–1925), and in 1895 they published *Studies in Hysteria*.

In the mid-1890s, Freud abandoned hypnosis and allowed his patients to talk freely and spontaneously about themselves. He found that they associated their particular neurotic symptoms with experiences related to earlier experiences, going back to childhood. He also noted that sexual matters were significant in his patients' problems. For a time, he thought that perhaps sexual incidents during childhood accounted for their illnesses.

By 1897, however, Freud had rejected this view. In its place he formulated a theory of infantile sexuality, according to which sexual drives and energy already exist in infants and do not simply emerge at puberty. For Freud, human beings are sexual creatures from birth through adulthood. He thus questioned in the most radical manner the concept of childhood innocence. He also portrayed the little acknowledged matter of sexuality as one of the bases of mental order and disorder.

Freud's Concern with Dreams During the same decade, Freud also examined the psychic phenomena of dreams. Romantic writers had taken dreams seriously, but few psychologists had examined them scientifically. Freud believed the seemingly irrational content of dreams must have a reasonable, scientific explanation. His research led him to reconsider the general nature of the human mind. He concluded that dreams allow unconscious wishes, desires, and drives that had been excluded from everyday conscious life to enjoy freer play in the mind. "The dream," he wrote, "is the [disguised] fulfillment of a [suppressed, repressed] wish."[7] During the waking hours, the mind represses or censors certain wishes, which are as important to the individual's psychological makeup as conscious thought is. In fact, Freud argued, unconscious drives and desires contribute to conscious behavior. Freud developed these concepts and related them to his idea of infantile sexuality in his most important book, *The Interpretation of Dreams*, published in 1900.

Freud's Later Thought In later books and essays, Freud developed a new model of the internal organization of the mind as an arena of struggle and conflict among three entities: the id, the superego, and the ego. The **id** consists of amoral, irrational, driving instincts for sexual gratification, aggression, and general physical and sensual pleasure. The **superego** embodies the external moral imperatives and expectations imposed on the personality by society and culture. The **ego** mediates between the impulses of the id and the asceticism of the superego and allows the personality to cope with the inner and outer demands of its existence. Consequently, everyday behavior displays the activity of the personality as its inner drives are partially repressed through the ego's coping with external moral expectations, as interpreted by the superego.

Despite his interest in the nonrational forces in human life and thought, Freud was a son of the Enlightenment. Like the *philosophes*, he was a realist who wanted human beings to live free of fear and illusions by rationally understanding themselves and their world. He saw the personalities of human beings as being determined by finite physical

---

[5] *The Basic Writings of Nietzsche*, ed. and trans. by Walter Kaufman (New York: The Modern Library, 1968), p. 275.
[6] Ibid., p. 456.

[7] *The Basic Writings of Sigmund Freud*, trans. by A. A. Brill (New York: The Modern Library, 1938), p. 235.

Freud in the United States. In 1909 Freud and his then-devoted disciple Carl Jung visited Clark University in Worcester, Massachusetts, during Freud's only trip to the United States. Here Freud sits on the right holding a cane. Jung is sitting on the far left. *Archives of the History of American Psychology—The University of Akron. Courtesy Clark University Special Collections.*

and mental forces in a finite world. He was hostile to religion and spoke of it as an illusion. Freud, like the writers of the eighteenth century, wished to see civilization and humane behavior prevail. More fully than those predecessors, however, he understood the immense sacrifice of instinctual drives required for rational civilized behavior. It has been a grave misreading of Freud to see him as urging humankind to thrust off all repression. He did indeed believe that excessive repression could lead to mental disorder, but he also believed civilization and the survival of humankind required some repression of sexuality and aggression. Freud thought the sacrifice and struggle were worthwhile, but he was pessimistic about the future of civilization in the West.

Islam and Late-Nineteenth-Century European Thought

The few late-nineteenth-century European thinkers who wrote about Islam interpreted it in terms of the growing contemporary scientific outlook as a historical religious phenomenon without any

Al-Afghani. One of the most influential thinkers in the Muslim world in the nineteenth century, al-Afghani tried to reconcile modern science with Islam.

reference to the supernatural. Islam, like the other great world religions, was seen as a product of a particular culture and the same kind of analysis was applied to the Qur'an. In the works of scholars such as the influential French writer Ernest Renan (1823–1892), Islam was, like Judaism, a manifestation of the ancient Semitic mentality, which had given rise to a powerful monotheistic vision. Renan, and sociologists such as the German Max Weber, also dismissed Islam as a religion and culture incapable of developing science and closed to new ideas.

However, Renan's views were opposed in a French journal by Jamal al-din al-Afghani (1839–1897), an Egyptian intellectual, who argued that over time Islam, which had arisen six hundred years after Christianity, would eventually produce cultures as modern as those in Europe. Al-Afghani was one of the rare Islamic writers who directly contested a European thinker (see Chapter 27).

The European racial and cultural outlooks that denigrated nonwhite peoples and their civilizations were also directed towards the Arab world. European authors who championed white racial superiority looked to India and the Aryan civilization that was supposed to have risen there and later influenced northern European life as the source of Europe's cultural superiority.

Christian missionaries reinforced these anti-Islamic attitudes. They blamed Islam for Arab economic backwardness, for mistreating women, and for condoning slavery. They also often came into conflict with Islamic religious authorities. Because the penalty for abjuring Islam is death, the missionaries made few converts among Muslims. So they turned their efforts to founding schools and hospitals, hoping these Christian foundations would eventually lead some Muslims to Christianity. Few Muslims converted, but these institutions did educate young Arabs in Western science and medicine, and many of their students became leaders in the Middle East. Eventually, as missionary families came to live for long periods of time among Arabs, they became more sympathetic to Arab political aspirations.

Within the Islamic world, and especially in the decaying Ottoman Empire, as political leaders continued to champion Western scientific education and technology, they confronted a variety of responses from religious thinkers. Some of these thinkers sought to combine modern thought with Islam. For example, the Salafi, or the salafiyya movement, believed there was no inherent contradiction between science and Islam. They believed Muhammad had wisely and properly addressed the issues of his day, and a reformed Islamic faith could do so again. The Arab world should cease direct imitation of the West and modernize itself on the basis of a pure, restored Islamic faith. The Salafi emphasized a rational reading of the Qur'an and saw Ottoman decline as the result of Muslim religious error. This outlook, which had originally sought to reconcile Islam with the modern world, eventually led many Muslims in the twentieth century to oppose Western influence.

Other Islamic religious leaders simply rejected the West and modern thought. They included the Mahdist movement in Sudan, the Sanussiya in Libya, and the Wahhabi movement in the Arabian peninsula (see Chapter 27). Such religious-based opposition was strongest in those portions of the Middle East where the European presence was least direct, which is to say outside of Morocco, Algeria, Egypt, and Tunisia, which for all intents and purposes were under the control of Western powers by 1900, and Turkey, where Ottoman leaders had long been deeply involved with the West.

Summary

Workers. During the course of the nineteenth century, European workers underwent a process of proletarianization as the process of industrialization spread across the Continent. To protect their interests, European workers joined trade unions and socialist parties, such as the Labour Party in Britain. The Marxist critique of modern capitalism strongly influenced European socialism when the German Social Democratic Party adopted the thought of Karl Marx. In Russia, Lenin founded the Bolsheviks as an elite Marxist party that advocated the overthrow of the tsarist regime through a revolution of workers and peasants.

Women. Nineteenth-century women were divided along class lines. Unlike working-class women, most women of the upper and middle classes adopted a cult of domesticity and did not work outside the home. Most jobs available to women were low paying and insecure. Women of all classes faced social, political, and legal disabilities that were only gradually improved in the late nineteenth and early twentieth centuries. Before World War I, only Norway allowed women to vote, and few women could earn university degrees or enter the professions.

Jewish Emancipation. With the exception of Russia, European countries had abolished their legal restrictions on Jews by the mid–nineteenth century. Jews became more fully integrated into European political and economic life. After 1880, however, anti-Semitism increased as Jews were blamed for economic and social problems.

The United States. By 1914, the United States had become the world's leading industrial power. However, despite the creation of a mass industrial work force, socialism did not take root in the United States. Under presidents Theodore Roosevelt and Woodrow Wilson, the Progressive movement enacted a number of social and political reforms. The United States also embarked on a more aggressive foreign policy with the Spanish-American War, the acquisition of a colonial empire, interventions in Latin America, and, under Wilson, participation in World War I.

Modern European Thought. In 1850, learned Europeans regarded the physical world as rational, mechanical, and dependable. By the first decades of the twentieth century philosophers, scientists, psychologists, and artists began to portray physical reality, human nature, and society in ways that seem familiar to us today. Physicists probed the mysteries of the atom. The theories of evolutionary biology contended that human nature is part of the order of nature and does not stand apart from nature. Traditional morality and the primacy of reason were challenged by Nietzsche and Freud. Within the Islamic world, modern European thought produced a variety of often-conflicting responses.

Review Questions

1. What were the chief factors accounting for the proletarianization of the European labor force? How much of the change in the situation of workers was a result of technology and how much of the change in their organization?

2. How would you describe living conditions in European cities during the late nineteenth century? What factors contributed to those conditions? How did urban reform emerge?

3. How did the class position of a European woman determine much of her experience? How did industrialization change the social experience of working-class women? What were the social factors that limited the opportunities of women regardless of their class? Why

did women grow discontented with their lot? What factors led to change? To what extent had they improved their position by 1914? Was the emancipation of women inevitable? How did women approach their situation differently from country to country?

4. What were the major characteristics of Jewish emancipation in the nineteenth century? How did late-century economic developments contribute to increasing prejudice against Jews?

5. How did the ideas of Karl Marx come to dominate so much late-nineteenth-century European socialism?

6. What was the status of the working-class groups in the United States and Europe in 1860? What improvements if any had been achieved by 1914?

7. What caused the emergence of trade unions and organized mass political parties in Europe?

8. How did the American Progressives, as reformers, differ from the various European Socialists? Why were the debates of "opportunism" and "revisionism" important to the socialist parties? Why were there so many disputes among Socialists?

9. Assess the value of industrialism for Russia. Were the tsars wise in attempting to modernize their country or would they have been better off leaving it as it was? How did Lenin's view of socialism differ from that of Socialists in Western Europe? Why did socialism not emerge as a major political force in the United States?

10. What were the major changes in science in the late nineteenth century? How did both Darwin and Einstein challenge assumptions of earlier science? How may both Nietzsche and Freud be seen to challenge confidence in human rationality?

INTERPRETING THE PAST

Workers and Factory Owners

Source from Chapter 25

1. *A French Physician Describes a Working-Class Slum* (page 784)

Sources from MyHistoryLab/Primary Source DVD

1. *The Sadler Report—Child Labor in the United Kingdom, 1832*
2. Edwin Chadwick, *Summary from Poor Law Commissioners*
3. Andrew Ure, *Philosophy of Manufactures*

The development of industrial economies in Western Europe and the United State during the nineteenth century also produced a labor force that differed from any in world history. Working in factories instead of their homes, small workshops, or marketplaces, these workers posed unique challenges to industry owners as well as European and American political leaders. The social and political responses to worker concerns shaped later-nineteenth-century and twentieth-century life.

In this exercise you will read documents that spotlight some of the most intractable problems posed by the industrial labor force and the rapidly growing urban centers where they lived and worked. The primary issues that arose during the period covered by this chapter—1815–1914—were the working conditions and polices of factory employment and equally, if not more important, living conditions in the working-class housing districts of the increasing number of industrial cities throughout Britain, Europe, and America.

The document from Chapter 25, from page 784, is written by a French physician describing living conditions in Lille, a major cotton-manufacturing city in northern France. From MyHistoryLab, Primary Source, the first source is an excerpt of the result of a British Parliamentary investigation of working conditions in textile factories in England—the Sadler Report. The second document is a report by Edwin Chadwick, a British lawyer responsible for writing a report on sanitary conditions and public health for a royal commission. The final document is an excerpt from an essay that forcefully argues the case for factory owners against potential reformers.

Use the source documents and images to analyze and compare viewpoints relating to the living and working conditions of nineteenth-century industrial labor. Answer the following questions in an essay. Use specific examples from the documents to back up your assertions.

11. What were the chief characteristics of Western attitudes towards Islam in the nineteenth century? How did Islamic thinkers respond to modern Western thought.

Key Terms

Bolsheviks (p. 799)

Duma (p. 799)

ego (p. 811)

Fabians (p. 796)

id (p. 811)

Marxism (p. 795)

Mensheviks (p. 799)

natural selection (p. 808)

pogroms (p. 792)

proletarianization (p. 782)

relativity (p. 809)

revisionism (p. 796)

soviets (p. 799)

suffragettes (p. 791)

superego (p. 811)

Note: To learn more about the topics in this chapter, please turn to the Suggested Readings at the end of the book. For additional sources related to this chapter please see the Primary Source DVD at the back of this text or MyHistoryLab.

Questions

What is most problematic about the scenes described by the French physician in Lille? The Sadler Report? What would be the effect on their readers?

What would be the benefits of improving public health, according to Chadwick? What key innovation is central to improving sanitary conditions for the working classes?

What is Andrew Ure's argument in defense of the factory system and its owners? How does he view unions and workers organizing to improve conditions? How does he view factory and mill owners?

26

Latin America from Independence to the 1940s

◆ Independence Without Revolution

◆ Economy of Dependence

◆ Search for Political Stability

◆ Three National Histories

Y THE MID-1820S, LATIN AMERICANS HAD DRIVEN out their colonial rulers and broken the colonial trade monopolies. Although rich in natural resources, the region did not achieve widespread prosperity and long-lasting political stability for more than a century after independence. The wars of independence had not been popular grass-roots movements. They had originated with the creole elite, who were seeking to resist the imposition of European liberalism by Napoleon or, later, the Spanish liberals.

In effect, the wars had been fought to break the colonial trade monopolies and to preserve the existing social structure. The military leaders of the wars held much of the political power in the new nations the wars had created.

The wars also destroyed much of the economic infrastructure of the region. Mines had been flooded, livestock depleted, and the work force disrupted. Whereas previously colonial Latin America had been dependent on Spain for its exports and financial credits, it now became dependent on Great Britain and later on the United States.

Mexico City. Juan O'Gorman (1905–1982) was best known as an architect whose most famous work is the library at the Universidad Nacional Autónima de Mexico. In 1932, he took the helm of Mexico City's department of building and construction. His interests in architecture, art (he became a renowned muralist), and the development of Mexico City are all on display in his 1949 painting, "El Ciudad de Mexico." The painting, complete with angels heralding "Viva Mexico," shows the city and the country as a work in progress. *Temple sobre masonite, 66 × 122 cm, Col. Museo de Arte Moderno. Reproduction authorized by the Instituto Nacional de Bellas Artes y Literatura-CONACULTA.*

Latin American History

Latin America

Since the early nineteenth century, Spanish- and Portuguese-speaking America stretching from the Rio Grande to Cape Horn has posed a paradox. Languages, religion, economic ties, and many political institutions render the area part of the Western world. Yet the economics, politics, and social life of Latin America have developed differently from other parts of the West. Exceedingly rich in natural resources, possessing gold, silver, nitrates, and oil, the region has been plagued with extreme poverty. As other Western nations have moved towards liberal democracy and social equality, the states of Latin America have had millions of citizens living in situations of marked inequality and social dependence. For over a century and a half, the political life of Latin America has been characterized by uncertain democracy, authoritarian regimes, and a general tendency towards instability. Three major explanations have been set forth to account for these difficulties that have led to so much tragedy and human suffering.

The first and most widely accepted view contends that after the wars of independence the new states of Latin America remained economically and culturally dependent on Europe and, later, the United States. In effect, proponents of this view—called **dependency theory**—argue that the colonial framework was never abolished. Under Spanish and Portuguese rule, Latin America's wealth was extracted and exported for the benefit of those powers. After independence, the creole elite turned towards foreign investors, first British and then American, to finance economic development and to provide the technology for mining, transport, and industry. As a result, Latin America became dependent on wealthy foreign powers for investment and for markets. These foreign powers, more interested in strong governments that would protect their interests than in developing the economies and political structures of the Latin American states, threw their support behind dictators whose policies impoverished their people and suppressed democratic dissent.

A second explanation emphasizes the Iberian heritage. Its advocates contend that Latin America should be viewed as a region on the periphery of the Western world in the same manner that Spain, Portugal, and Italy lie on the Mediterranean periphery of Europe. All of these Latin nations, dominated by Roman Catholicism, have had similar

Latin America shares many cultural features with Europe and North America. Its languages are primarily European, although much of its population speaks Native American languages. Its primary religion is Roman Catholicism. Its nations have often adopted the constitutional traditions of Europe and the United States. Many of its elite have studied abroad. Despite these important similarities, however, the economic and political development of Latin America has been different from that of much of Europe or the United States.

The reasons for these differences have long puzzled historians. Why has Latin America been less stable and less prosperous than Europe and North America? The answers appear to lie in the role Latin America played in the integrated global economic system that began to develop in the nineteenth century, just when it achieved political independence. This system prevented Latin Americans from achieving economic independence. The region's leaders thought they could best satisfy the economic interests of their nations by providing raw materials to the world economy. Most Latin American nations consequently developed export economies devoted to raw materials or semifinished goods. Unfortunately, this decision made their export products vulnerable to worldwide fluctuations in demand. They were also susceptible to undue influence from foreign business and banking interests and to political interference by the governments of the United States and Europe.

unstable and often authoritarian governments. They have frequently tended towards some version of dictatorship, uneven development, anticlericalism, and social cleavage between urban and rural areas and between wealthy middle-class or landed elites and poor peasant populations. Viewed in this Iberian-Mediterranean context, Latin America seems less puzzling than when it is viewed in the context of northern Europe.

A third explanation emphasizes conscious political, economic, and cultural decisions the Latin American **creole** elite took after independence. This explanation contends that the elite, including the army officers who won the wars, sought to enrich themselves and to maintain their positions at the cost of all other segments of the population, who in many of these countries differed ethnically and racially from the elite. These officers, landowners, and urban middle-class leaders aligned their national economies with the industrializing regions of Europe and North America, with which they aligned themselves culturally as well, thus differentiating themselves from the lower classes and indigenous peoples and culture. They also adopted European liberal political and economic ideologies to justify unlimited exploitation of economic resources on the basis of individualist enterprise. They then used the wealth generated by this exploitation to maintain their power. They embraced European concepts of progress to dismiss the legitimacy of the culture and communal values of the Indians or the peasants.

To understand the region and its past, all three viewpoints are relevant. In addition, it helps to view Latin America within a global perspective. Beginning in the nineteenth century much of the region, like much of Asia and Africa, was drawn into an integrated worldwide economic system dominated by Europe and North America. Many nations in Latin America and elsewhere developed narrow economies based on the export of one or a few raw materials or semifinished products. They were vulnerable to fluctuations in worldwide demand for these products and to political and economic interference from Europe and North America. The results were often economic turbulence and political instability.

Focus Questions

◆ What is dependency theory? How can it help to understand the history of Latin America since independence?

◆ Is Latin America's Iberian heritage a likely explanation of why Latin America has developed along such different lines from those of North America?

◆ What role did the creole elite play in the economic and political instability that has characterized Latin America in the modern era?

Latin America had much in common with other regions of the world—Africa and Asia, for example—during the nineteenth and early twentieth centuries. In all three regions, particular nations or areas would specialize in a particular niche in the increasingly integrated world economy. In Asia and Africa vast plantations produced products such as rubber; in Latin America plantations might produce sugar or coffee. In all three regions huge mining industries extracted resources such as copper, phosphates, gold, and diamonds. Virtually all such enterprises were dominated by Europeans or North Americans. Filling a particular niche by supplying a particular raw product might bring initial prosperity but provided too narrow an economic base for sustained economic well-being. In contrast, the economic advance of the United States and Europe was largely due to their ability to exploit niche economies around the globe. ■

Independence Without Revolution

Immediate Consequences of Latin American Independence

The wars of independence left Latin America by the late 1820s liberated from direct European control, but economically exhausted and politically unstable (see Map 26–1). Only Brazil tended to prosper immediately after independence. In contrast, the new republics of the former Spanish empire felt themselves weak and vulnerable. Because the wars of independence had been largely civil wars, the new governments

Map Exploration

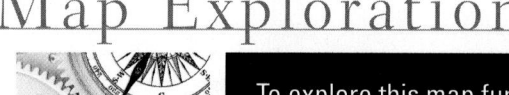

To explore this map further, go to http://www.prenhall.com/craig_maps

CANADA (Great Britian)

CALIFORNIA

UNITED STATES

ATLANTIC

OCEAN

Rio Grande

TEXAS

• San Antonio

MEXICO
1821

Gulf of Mexico

Mexico City
• Veracruz

CUBA (Spain)

HAITI 1804

PUERTO (Spain)
RICO

BR. HONDURAS

Caribbean Sea

Guatemala
UNITED PROVINCES OF
CENTRAL AMERICA
1823–1839

Panama

TRINIDAD

Caracas

BRITISH GUIANA

DUTCH GUIANA

FRENCH GUIANA

Bogotá
GRAN
COLOMBIA
1819–1830

GALAPAGOS IS.

Quito

Amazon R.

INDEFINITE BOUNDARY

PERU
1821

Lima

PACIFIC

*A
n
d
e
s*

EMPIRE OF BRAZIL
1822

Bahia

BOLIVIA
1825

Sucre

*M
o
u
n
t
a
i
n
s*

PARAGUAY
1811

• Asunción

Rio de Janeiro

OCEAN

CHILE
1818

*P
a
m
p
a
s*

Santiago •

URUGUAY 1828

Buenos
Aires •

• Montevideo

UNITED PROVINCES
OF LA PLATA
1816

*P
a
t
a
g
o
n
i
a*

500 MILES

500 KILOMETERS

Map 26–1. **Latin America in 1830.** By 1830 most of Latin America had been liberated from Europe. This map shows the initial borders of the states of the region with the dates of their independence. The United Provinces of La Plata formed the nucleus of what later become Argentina.

knew that many of their populations might welcome their collapse. Economic life on the continent contracted, and in 1830 overall production was lower than it had been in 1800. Difficult terrain over vast distances made interregional trade complicated, and few institutions fostered it. The old patterns of overseas trade had been disrupted. There was an absence of funds for investment. Many wealthy *peninsulares* returned to Spain or departed for Cuba. Consequently, Latin American governments and businesses looked to Britain for protection, markets, and capital investment.

Independence itself also created several new sources of discontent. There was much disagreement about the character of the future government, even among those who had most wanted to oust the Spanish. Certain institutions, such as the Roman Catholic Church, that had enjoyed a privileged status in the colonial period sought to maintain those privileges under new and often unfriendly governments. Native American communities, which had also been somewhat protected by paternalistic colonial policies, found themselves subject to new exploitation once they were made equal citizens under the law. Major disagreements arose between the creole elites of different regions of the new nations. The agricultural hinterlands resented the predominance of the port cities, whose merchants set the terms of trade. Investors or merchants from one Latin American nation found themselves in conflict with those of others over transport tariffs on rivers or over mining regulations. Civilians often became rivals of the military for political authority.

Absence of Social Change

Yet no matter what the actual or potential conflict among various groups in the literate political and economic elites might be, they all opposed substantial social reform. The creole victors in the wars of independence granted equal rights to all persons, and except for Brazil, the independent states had 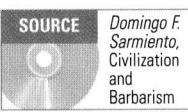 abolished slavery by 1855. However, the right to vote depended on a property qualification, and peasants remained dependent on and often subservient to their landlords. The racial codes of the colonial empires disappeared, but not the racial prejudice. Although **mestizos**, **mulattos**, and even Indians who achieved economic success were assimilated into the higher ranks of the social structure, persons of white or nearly white complexion tended to constitute the elite of Latin America. The creole elite generally discriminated against the peoples of color in their midst. Most important, no major changes in landholding accompanied the wars of independence; the ruling classes of all the newly independent nations protected the interests of landholders.

SOURCE Domingo F. Sarmiento, Civilization and Barbarism

Except for Mexico in 1910, no Latin American nation, from the wars of independence until the 1950s, experienced a fundamental revolution that overthrew the social and economic structures dating from the colonial period. The absence of such social revolution, which would necessarily have involved changes in landholding, is perhaps the single most important factor in Latin American history during the first century of independence. The rise and fall of political regimes represented quarrels among the elite and did not substantially change the structures or expectations of everyday life for most of the population. Throughout the social structure there was no mutually shared trust or allegiance to the political system.

Control of the Land

Most Latin Americans during the nineteenth century lived in the countryside. Agriculture continued to be dominated by large *haciendas*, or plantations. The landowners virtually ruled these estates as small domains. They were nearly a law unto themselves. The *latifundia* (the large rural estates) actually grew larger during the nineteenth century. Confiscated church lands and conquered Indian territories augmented existing estates or led to the establishment of new ones. These estates might include tens of thousands of acres yet be attended by a relatively sparse work force. Work was labor intensive because little machinery was available; virtually none was manufactured in Latin America. Herding and stock raising produced salted meat, leather, tallow, and wool for the export market. For some products—salted meats, for example—there was a limited manufacturing stage in Latin America. Other agricultural exports included cereal crops, tobacco, sugar, coffee, and cacao.

SOURCE Argentine Gaucho

Landowners constituted a society of their own. Their families intermarried. They sometimes formed friendships or family alliances with members of the wealthy urban classes who were involved in export commerce or the law. Younger sons might enter the army or the church. The landowners served in the various postindependence national parliaments or congresses. Their wealth, literacy, and social connections made them the rulers of the countryside, and the army would protect them from any social uprising.

The landowners lived well and comfortably, although often on isolated estates. Most of the rural work force were socially and economically dependent on them. In Brazil 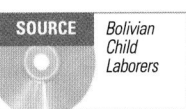 slavery persisted until 1888. Although it was once argued that slavery in Roman Catholic Latin America was more paternalistic and less harsh than elsewhere, that view has long been abandoned among scholars who now believe Latin American slavery was as harsh as

SOURCE Bolivian Child Laborers

A Chilean Cattle Estate. The great landowners of Latin America ruled their huge estates as small domains. *Sergio Larrain/Magnum Photos Inc.*

	1870	1914
Rio de Janiero	275,000	1,000,000
Sao Paulo	31,000	450,000
Buenos Aires	178,000	1,200,000
Lima	90,000	200,000
Guayaquil, Ecuador	12,000	75,000
Mexico City	200,000	700,000

Figure 26–1. Population of Latin American Cities, 1870–1914
Source: United Nations.

which increased the size of the white population; Asian immigration was a source of inexpensive labor. Throughout this period there arose a political and social trade-off between the urban and rural elites. Each more or less permitted the other to pursue its economic self-interest, to profit from the commodity export economy through commerce or production, and to repress any discontent. Nonetheless, the growth of the urban centers shifted political influence from the countryside to the cities and gave rise to an urban working class and all the social discontents associated with vast numbers of relatively poor people working in difficult situations. Urban growth in Latin America created social and political difficulties not unlike those that arose in Europe and the United States at about the same time. (See Document, "An Observer Describes Vagabonds of Nineteenth-Century Mexico City.")

Submissive Political Philosophies

The political philosophies embraced by the educated and propertied creole elites also discouraged any real challenge to the social order. The political ideas associated with European liberalism, which flourished in Latin America immediately after independence, supported republican government but also limited the franchise to property holders. Thus in Latin America, as in Europe, liberalism protected property and tended to ignore the social problems of the poor and propertyless. In addition, the creole elite frequently exhibited racial prejudice towards the mulatto, mestizo, and Indian populations.

Economic liberalism and the need for British investment led to the championing of free trade. During the decades immediately after independence, Latin America actually exported less than it had under colonial rule. The region achieved a trade balance by exporting precious metals. Because these metals often came from stocks mined years earlier, this in effect amounted to a flight of capital. The general economic view was that Latin America would produce

that in North America and perhaps more so. In other rural areas many people lived as virtual slaves. **Debt peonage** was widespread and often tied a peasant to the land like a European serf. A peon would become indebted to his landlord and could never repay the debt. Later in the nineteenth century the new lands that were opened were generally organized as large holdings with tenants rather than as small landholdings with independent farmers. This was markedly different from both the United States and Canada. Poor roads and limited railways made internal travel difficult and kept many people on the land. Little effort was made to provide even a primary education, leaving millions of Latin American peasants ignorant, lacking any significant technological skills, and incapable of improving their condition or of protesting or escaping their bondage to the land and its owners.

The second half of the nineteenth century witnessed a remarkable growth in Latin American urban life (see Figure 26–1). There was some movement from the countryside to the city and an influx of European immigrants as well as some from Asia. The creole elite favored European immigration,

An Observer Describes Vagabonds of Nineteenth-Century Mexico City

Poverty characterized large areas of nineteenth-century Latin American cities as it did those elsewhere in the world. Guillermo Prieto (1818–1897) was active in the political and civic life of Mexico in the decades immediately after independence, serving as both finance minister and postmaster. He commenced writing his memoirs in 1886. In those he described vagabonds known as *léperos* who dwelled in the slums of Mexico City. Prieto wrote about these people from the standpoint of a political and economic liberal. His attitudes towards poverty and crime resembled those of contemporary European liberals. Note how he concentrates on observing and implicitly criticizing the character of these vagabonds and pays little or no attention to the economic situation that gave rise to much of their behavior. Also note how Prieto who was also a poet, somewhat romanticizes them by pointing to behaviors of loyalty that he obviously admires.

◆ **What are the characteristics of character and background that Prieto associates with the *lépero*? Does he believe these vagabonds chose their life? Does he think they can change their lives? What qualities about them does he perhaps admire?**

The lower classes, who inhabited the suburbs and some central points of the city, lived in a misery that today, fortunately, must appear completely incredible. . . .

The men like domino pieces of six, and blank, bar skin above and cotton trousers below; the women with a short woolen shawl floating over the breast and shoulder, and wrapped about in a long cloth. Pull it back, and you make the wearer spin like a top.

The true *lépero*, generally speaking, is a mestizo, illegitimate, born out of adultery, sacrilegious, and full of mischief. To his rascality he joins a sprightly wit, capacity for generous actions, courage, and really remarkable traits of gratitude, all on a base of idleness, fanaticism, and a powerful inclination toward robbery, drunkenness and love. . . .

The *lépero* is shrewd, and knows how to adopt an abject manner; he appears most submissive when he is most vindictive and harbors the worst intentions; he tends to be an unbeliever and a mocker of religion; he delights in tormenting lay priests, sacristans, and church people in general; he hates cops and soldiers, . . . he is a skilful but unsteady worker, a swindler, a vagrant, and a gambler. . . .

Jail doesn't scare him, although he distrusts and keeps out of the way of informers, scribes, and clerks of the courts of justice. . . .

To add to the contradictions of his character . . . the *lépero* is courageous; he hates ingratitude and perfidy toward a comrade; he prides himself on his disinterest; very rarely will he betray an accomplice or abandon a friend in misfortune.

His mind is a chaos. Bestial superstitions, perverted moral maxims, confused notions of liberty and rights, collusion with the saints to commit robbery . . . a very sea!

Guillermo Prieto, *Memorias de mis tiempos* (1948) excerpted by Benjamin Keen, trans., as reprinted in Benjamin Keen, ed., *Readings in Latin-American Civilization 1492 to the Present* (Boston: Houghton Mifflin Company, 1955), pp. 299–298.

---

raw materials for export in exchange for manufactured goods imported from Europe, and especially from Britain.

For most of the nineteenth century the landed sector of the economy dominated because cheap imports from abroad and a shortage of local capital discouraged indigenous attempts at industrialism. Latin American liberals championed the extension of great landed estates and all the forms of social dependence associated with them. The produce of the new land could contribute raw materials or lightly processed goods for export to pay for the import of finished goods. Liberals thus favored confiscating land owned by the church and the Indian communities, because these groups did not exploit their lands in a progressive manner, according to the liberals.

During the second half of the century, **positivism**—the political ideas stemming from the French positivist philosopher Auguste Comte (1798–1857)—swept across Latin America.

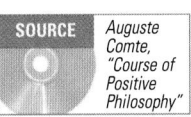
SOURCE Auguste Comte, "Course of Positive Philosophy"

Comte and his followers had advocated the cult of science and technological progress. This highly undemocratic outlook suggested that either technocrats or dictatorial governments could best achieve modernization. It was especially popular among military officers and influenced the ongoing Latin American struggle between civilian and military elites. The great slogan of Latin American positivism, emblazoned on the flag of the Brazilian republic, was "Order and Progress." Social or political groups that created disorder or challenged the existing social order were by definition unprogressive.

Towards the close of the century the military forces in various countries—following the model of European armies, especially Germany's—became more professionalized. Their new training often made the officer corps the most important educated elite in a country. Their education and attachment to the armies they served gave them considerable influence, generally of a conservative character.

Finally, the late-nineteenth-century European theories of "scientific" racism were used to preserve the Latin American social status quo and the dominance of those of white or more nearly white complexions. Racial theory could attribute the economic backwardness of the region to its vast nonwhite or mixed-blood population. This explanation, of course, shifted responsibility for the economic difficulties of Latin America away from the mostly white governing elites towards Indians, blacks, mestizos, and mulattos, who had long been exploited or repressed.

This conservative intellectual heritage continued to affect twentieth-century political thought. First, it can be seen in the ongoing tendency of military groups in Latin America to view themselves as the guarantors of order. These groups were ready to intervene in political affairs and seize control from civilians to protect the status quo or to thwart social change. Second, it can be seen in the way the political elites of Latin America naturally and actively opposed communism after the Russian Revolution. Although many Latin American nations had small organized communist parties, governments used the fear of communism to resist virtually all political movements—communist or not—that advocated social reform or questioned property arrangements. From the 1920s onward, in Latin America as in Europe, the fear of communism brought support to conservative governments, whether civilian or military. Communism would become an even more powerful issue throughout the region after the successful Cuban Revolution of 1957 installed an actual Soviet-dominated communist state in Latin America.

Economy of Dependence

The wars of independence destroyed the Spanish and Portuguese colonial trade monopolies. Where previously only a few dozen ships called annually at any port, hundreds laden with goods from all over the world could now drop anchor. Consequently, Latin America had many new trading partners, but it remained heavily dependent on non-Latin American economies. Trade was free and the nations were politically independent, but other nations continued to shape Latin American economic life in the most fundamental manner.

One of the chief reasons for this dependence on foreign trading partners was the absence of large internal markets. Had such markets existed during the colonial period itself, the newly independent nations might have been able to trade with each other rather than primarily with nations outside the region. Trade after independence flowed in the same direction that trade had flowed before independence because Europe remained the source of imports of finished goods. Furthermore, then as now, geographical barriers hindered internal trade. The jungles of the Amazon and the Andes Mountains prevented any easy east–west trade. No road systems allowed goods to travel between countries or even easily within them, and there was little domestic investment in transport. European and American investments in railways generally facilitated exports rather than internal trade.

New Exploitation of Resources

As previously noted, the wars of independence sharply disrupted the Latin American economy. In both Mexico and Peru, mines were flooded; machinery was in disrepair; labor was dispersed. Agricultural production was also disrupted. Between 1825 and 1850 the new nations attempted to set their economic houses in order, but with mixed results. Capital financing to restore the mining industry and establish new industries was totally inadequate. Virtually no domestic industries existed to manufacture heavy equipment or build ships. Both to restore old industries, such as mining, and to have access to modern transport, such as steamships and railroads, Latin Americans had to turn to Europe and North America. For many decades Britain exer-

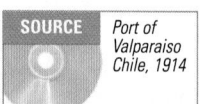

SOURCE *Port of Valparaiso Chile, 1914*

cised the predominant economic influence over Latin America. Britain had sought to break the old colonial monopoly. Once it was gone, the British rapidly established their own economic dominance. This desire to pour manufactured goods into Latin America also led Britain and other nations to discourage the development of manufacturing industries there. Europeans and Americans had no desire to see competitors emerge. Foreign investment did help revive the mining industry in Mexico, Peru, and Chile, but mining produces raw materials, not manufactured goods.

To pay for imports and foreign services, Latin American nations turned to the production of agricultural commodities for which there was great European demand. This shift meant that the rural areas of Latin America and the commercial centers serving agriculture became politically and economically more important than many of the old colonial urban centers. The production of wheat, beef, hides, hemp, coffee, cocoa, and other foodstuffs for the export market also raised the value of land and led governments to expand into previously unsettled territory and to confiscate the lands of the church. Because so much land was available, agricultural production was increased by putting more land under cultivation rather than by finding more efficient ways to farm areas already under cultivation. So much wealth could be accumulated through land speculation and land development that little incentive existed for alternative investments in manufacturing. It would also have been difficult, if not impossible, for new Latin American industries to compete with the cheap goods imported from more established industrial economies abroad.

After 1850 the Latin American republics became, relatively speaking, more prosperous. Chile exported copper and nitrates as well as wheat. Peru exported guano to be used as fertilizer. Coffee was becoming king in Venezuela, Brazil, Colombia, and Central America. Sugar continued to be produced in the West Indies as well as in Cuba, which remained under Spanish control. Argentina supplied hides and tallow. However, this limited prosperity and recovery were based on the export of agricultural commodities, extracted minerals, or nonreplenishable resources, such as guano, and the importation of finished goods from abroad.

Nevertheless, the period from approximately 1870 through 1930 came to be seen as a kind of golden age for the Latin American economy. There was more prosperity than ever before, especially in Chile, Argentina, Brazil, and Mexico. The export economy seemed to foster genuine economic growth. The economies of the Latin American nations grew because industrial production in Europe and the United States created a demand for more exports. The Latin American export economy also allowed large quantities of new products to be imported from Europe and the United States. Both the exports and the imports drew Latin America more deeply than ever into the world economy.

There were three broad varieties of late-nineteenth-century Latin American exports. First were foodstuffs raised in Latin America that were more or less like those that could be raised in Europe, chiefly wheat and beef products, for which Argentina became the great exporter. Second were distinctly tropical products, such as bananas, sugar, and coffee. Third were natural resources, including metals, of which

Brazilian Coffee being loaded onto a British ship. Most Latin American countries developed an export economy based on the exchange of agricultural products, raw materials, and semifinished goods for finished goods and services from abroad. Until recently, the coffee industry dominated both the political and economic life of Brazil. *Corbis-Bettmann.*

copper was the most important; minerals, such as nitrates; and later, oil.

Both the trading patterns for these goods and the internal improvements in Latin American production deeply and inextricably linked the economy of the region to Europe and, after 1900, to the United States. Europeans and North Americans provided capital and the technological and managerial skills to build bridges, roads, railroads, steam lines, and new mines. Most of the transport system was constructed to service the existing export economy rather than to foster the development of alternative forms of domestic economic development. Furthermore, whenever the economy of Europe or the United States floundered, Latin America was hurt. The region could not control its own economic destiny. A decline in the prices of commodities and raw materials could, of course, force Latin America to reduce the amount of goods it imported, harming its European and North American trading partners. But the major economic difficulties almost always struck Latin America first and lasted there longest.

Increased Foreign Ownership and Influence

During the late nineteenth century the relative prosperity of the export sector increased the degree of dependence. The growing European demand generated by spreading industrialism gave Latin Americans a false sense of the long-term security of their export markets. The vast profits to be made through mining and agricultural exports discouraged investment in local industry, except as it served the export economy. Land still remained the most favored form of domestic investment. Foreigners saw no reason to capitalize local industry that might replace goods being imported. By late in the century the wealthy classes in Latin America had, in

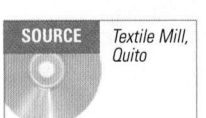 SOURCE Textile Mill, Quito

effect, lost control and even ownership of some of the most valuable sectors of their economy. For example, in 1901 British and other foreign investors owned approximately 80 percent of the Chilean nitrate industry. Foreigners also owned and operated most of the steamship lines and railroads.

The European and American economic penetration of Latin America was more subtle than that experienced by India or China, but it was no less real. Foreign ownership was not the only indication of economic dependence. Foreign powers used their political and military influence to protect their economic interests. Britain was the dominant power until the turn of the century. Its diplomats and military and naval officers were frequently involved directly or indirectly in the domestic political affairs of the Latin American nations. From the Spanish American War of 1898 onward the United States began to exercise more direct influence in the region. In 1903, to facilitate its plans to build a canal across the Isthmus of Panama, the United States participated in the rebellion that allowed Panama to separate from Colombia. There were numerous other instances of U.S. military intervention in the Caribbean and in Central America. By the 1920s U.S. investments had become dominant as a result of two decades of "Dollar Diplomacy." During that decade, largely as a result of economic dislocations arising from World War I, the United States generally replaced Great Britain as the dominant trading partner of Latin American nations. The role of the United States remains controversial, but from a structural standpoint it was just one more example of a dominant foreign power treating Latin America as a junior and dependent economic partner.

The United States interventions were one cost to Latin America of being a dependent economy. More significant costs, however, arose from fundamental shifts in world trade that were brought on by World War I and continued through the 1920s. First, the overall amount of trade carried on by European countries decreased, particularly during the war, when traditional trading partners divided into two warring

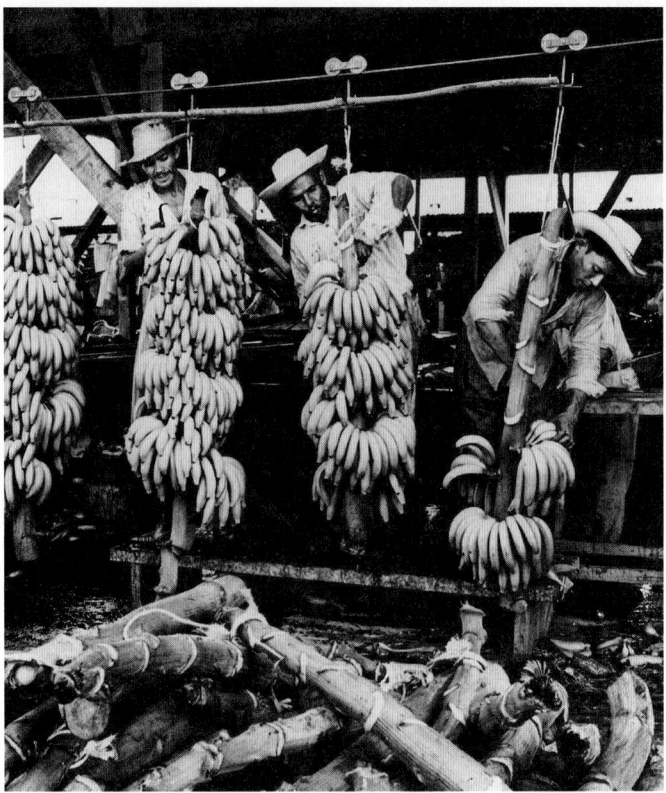

Banana Republic. For most of the twentieth century the United Fruit Company, an American conglomerate, exerted tremendous economic influence throughout Central America, with extensive coffee and banana plantations throughout the region. The company also wielded significant political power, especially in Guatemala, where workers in this photograph hang banana bunches from a pole.

camps. Second, during the 1920s world prices of agricultural commodities dropped steadily. Latin American nations had to produce more goods to pay for their imports, and no easy or rapid adjustment was possible. Third, various synthetic products manufactured in Europe or North America replaced the natural products long supplied by Latin American producers. Most important among these products were synthetic nitrates. Finally, petroleum began to replace other natural products as an absolute percentage of world trade. This shift meant that petroleum-exporting countries, such as Mexico, gained a greater share of export income.

Economic Crises and New Directions

The Great Depression turned the difficult economic conditions of the 1920s into a genuine crisis. Commodity prices virtually collapsed. The economic decline in Europe and the United States also lessened the demand for Latin American products. The republics of Latin America could not repay their debts to foreign banks, and a number of them suspended interest payments. Those decisions in turn worsened the economic crisis in the more developed creditor nations. The depression led eventually to the beginning of a new economic era in Latin America. The new era, which really began after the conclusion of World War II, was marked by strong economic nationalism and a determination to create sectors of the various national economies that were not wholly dependent on events and wealth outside Latin America. These various drives towards economic independence have had mixed success, but they date only from the turmoil of the depression.

Where did industrialism fit into this general picture of a dependent economy, or what is sometimes termed a **neo-colonial economy**. The brief answer is, almost always, on the periphery of the export sector. Until the 1940s major industrialization did not occur in Latin America. There were, however, significant earlier developments. Before World War I light manufacturing was done in connection with preparing exports, such as beef processing in Argentina. Light-manufactured goods such as textiles were also produced. With the depression, however, it became necessary to substitute domestically manufactured goods for those traditionally imported from abroad. Various nations pursued different policies of what was called **import substitution**, but all of these policies were undertaken because of the collapse of the export economy rather than because of any independent decision to industrialize. In that regard, the effort to industrialize was itself a result of being dependent.

By the mid-1940s there were three major varieties of manufacturing in Latin America. First, there were industries that, as in the past, transformed raw materials for export. They included sugar and other food processing, tin and copper mining, and petroleum refining. Second, there were industries addressing local demands, such as power plants, textiles, foundries, machine shops, and food companies. Third, there were industries depending generally on the transformation of imported materials. These industries were basically assembly plants whose owners could take advantage of inexpensive labor. None of this manufacturing was particularly sophisticated, and none of it involved heavy industry. Not until the 1950s would significant steel production, for example, occur in the region.

Search for Political Stability

The new states of independent Latin America, unlike the British colonies of North America, had little or no experience in self-government. The Spanish empire had been ruled directly by the monarchy and by Spanish-born royal bureaucrats. Spain had persistently discriminated against the creole elite as well as against mulattos, mestizos, and Indians. This monarchical or paternalistic heritage survived in two forms. First, many traditionalists and conservatives favored the establishment of monarchies in Latin America, including José de San Martín (1778–1850). Monarchy was briefly established in Mexico. In Brazil, an emperor from the Portuguese royal family governed until 1889.

The second heritage of the colonial monarchy was the proclivity of the Latin American political elites to tolerate or actively to support strong executives. Few of the early republic constitutions endured or established a stable political life. They were frequently suspended or rewritten, so that a strong leader could consolidate his own power. Such figures, who appeared throughout Latin America during the nineteenth century, were called **caudillos**. They usually came from the army officer corps or enjoyed strong ties to the army. Whatever constitutional justification they provided for themselves, the real basis of their rule was force and repression. *Caudillos* might support conservative causes, such as protection of the church or strong central government, or they might pursue liberal policies, such as the confiscation of church land, the extension of landed estates, and the development of education.

Initially, such dictatorial government was accepted simply to ensure political stability when republican regimes floundered. In many countries the early years of independence saw internal conflicts among regions. In this situation, a national *caudillo* might reach a compromise with various regional *caudillos* that allowed them to retain substantial local control.

These strongmen also encountered little opposition because of their repressive policies. Later in the century the new relative prosperity of expanding economies quieted potential discontent. The dictators became more skilled at both repression and patronage. The political and social elites also rallied to their support when, around the turn of the century, the young labor movement called strikes.

Even when *caudillos* were forced from office and parliamentary government was more or less restored, the regimes that replaced them were neither genuinely liberal nor democratic. Parliamentary governments usually ruled by courtesy of the military and in the economic interest of the existing elites. No matter who ruled, the life of the overwhelming mass of the population changed little. Except for the Mexican Revolution of 1910, Latin American politics was run by and for the elite.

Three National Histories

Three Latin American nations possess over 50 percent of the land, people, and wealth of the region. They are Argentina, Mexico, and Brazil. Their national histories illustrate the more general themes of Latin American history.

Argentina

Argentine history from independence to World War II can be divided into three general eras. From the rebellion against Spain in 1810 until midcentury, the question of which region of the nation would dominate political and economic life was foremost. From 1853 until 1916 Argentina experienced extraordinary economic expansion and large-scale immigration from Europe, which transformed its society and its position in the world. From 1916 to 1943 Argentines failed to establish a democratic state and struggled with the ramifications of an economy they did not really control.

Buenos Aires Versus the Provinces In 1810 the junta in Buenos Aires had overturned Spanish government in the viceroyalty of Río de la Plata. However, the other regions of the viceroyalty refused to accept the leadership of the province and city of Buenos Aires. Paraguay, Uruguay, and Upper Peru (Bolivia) went their separate ways. Conflicts between Buenos Aires and the remaining provinces dominated the first seventy years of Argentine history. It was the story of *porteños*, as the inhabitants of Buenos Aires were called, versus provincials. Eventually Buenos Aires established its primacy because of its capacity to dominate trade on the Río de la Plata and its control of the international customhouse, which assured revenue.

Between 1821 and 1827 Bernardino Rivadavia (1780–1845) worked to create a liberal political state but could not overcome the centrifugal forces of regionalism. His major accomplishment was a commercial treaty in 1823 that established Great Britain as a dominant trading partner. Thus began a deep intermeshing of trade and finance between the two nations that would continue for over a century. After Rivadavia's resignation in 1827 came the classical period of *caudillo* rule in Argentina. The strongman of the province of Buenos Aires was Juan Manuel de Rosas (1793–1877). In 1831 he negotiated the Pact of the Littoral, whereby Buenos Aires was put in charge of foreign relations, trade, and the customhouse, while the other provinces were left to run their own internal affairs. Within Buenos Aires, Rosas set up what amounted to dictatorial rule. He tolerated no dissent, no civil liberties, and no political power distinct from his own. One of his devices was the secret *Mazorca* (ear of corn) association, which terrorized his opponents. His major policies were expansion of trade and agriculture, suppression of the Indians, and nationalism. In Argentine history Rosas symbolized government by a single strong figure.

Expansion and Growth of the Republic Rosas' success in strengthening Buenos Aires bred resentment in other provinces. In 1852 Justo José de Urquiza (1800–1870), the *caudillo* of the state of Entre Rios, overthrew Rosas. The next

Juan Manuel de Rosas (1793–1877), a *caudillo* of Buenos Aires from 1827 to 1852. De Rosas was the archetypal *caudillo*, waging relentless war on the natives of Patagonia. *Corbis-Bettmann.*

year a federal constitution was promulgated for the Argentine Republic. Buenos Aires remained aloof until the republic conquered the province in 1859. Disputes continued. In 1880 the city of Buenos Aires was made a distinct federal province, separate from its rich hinterland. Provincials had hoped that this arrangement would lessen the influence of the city; however, the economic prosperity of the end of the century simply gave the capital new prominence.

The Argentine economy was overwhelmingly agricultural, the chief exports at midcentury being animal products. Internal transportation was poor and the country was sparsely populated. Technological advances changed this situation during the last quarter of the century. In 1876 the first refrigerator ship, *La Frigiorique*, steamed into Buenos Aires. Henceforth, it would be possible to transport large quantities of Argentine beef to Europe. Furthermore, at about the same time it became clear that wheat farming could be extended throughout the pampas. In 1879 and 1880 a government army under General (and later President) Julio Roca (president 1880–1886, 1898–1904) carried out a major campaign against the Indian population known as the

SOURCE *Portrait of an Auracanian Indian Chief*

Conquest of the Desert. The British soon began to construct and manage railways to carry wheat from the interior to the coast, where it would be loaded on British and other foreign steamships. Government policy made the purchase of land by wealthy Argentines simple and cheap. The owners, in turn, rented the land to tenants. The predominance of both large landowners and foreign business interests thus continued throughout the most significant economic transformation in Argentine history.

The development of the **pampas** and the vastly increased production of beef and wheat made Argentina one of the wealthiest nations of Latin America and a major agricultural rival of the United States. The opening of land, even if only for tenant farming and not ownership, encouraged hundreds of thousands of Europeans, particularly from Spain and Italy, to immigrate to Argentina. The immigrants also provided workers for the food-processing, service, and transportation industries in Buenos Aires. By 1900 the new economic life and the thousands of new citizens had drastically changed Argentina. It became much more urbanized and industrialized. More people had reason to be politically discontent. Moreover, the children of the nineteenth-century immigrants often became the strongest Argentine nationalists during the twentieth century.

The prosperity of economic expansion quieted most political opposition for some time. The conservative landed oligarchy continued to govern under presidents who sought

Chronology

Argentina

1810	Junta in Buenos Aires overthrows Spanish government
1827–1852	Era of Rosas' dictatorial government
1876	Ship refrigeration makes possible export of beef around the world
1879–1880	General Roca carries out *Conquest of the Desert* against the Indian population
1914–1918	Argentina remains neutral in World War I
1930s	Period of strong influence of nationalist military
1943–1956	Era of Juan and Eva Perón

to perpetuate a strong export economy. Like similar groups elsewhere, they ignored the social questions raised by urbanization and industrialization. However, they also ignored the political aspirations of the urban middle and professional classes, whose members wanted a greater share in political life and an end to political corruption. In 1890 these groups founded the Radical Party, which for many years achieved few successes. However, in 1912 the conservative government expanded the franchise and provided for the secret ballot.

Four years later, Hipólito Irigoyen (1850–1933), leader of the Radical Party, was elected president (first term 1916–1922). Without significant support in the legislature, his presidency brought fewer changes than might have been expected. He remained neutral in World War I, so Argentina could trade with both sides. Nonetheless, the war put great pressure on the economy, and much labor agitation resulted. Although previously sympathetic towards labor, Irigoyen as president used troops against strikers. The most violent labor clash occurred in January 1919, when troops quelled a general strike in Buenos Aires during what became known as the *Semana Trágica*, or Tragic Week. Thereafter, the Radical Party

Immigrant Hotel, Buenos Aires, ca. 1900. More than 8 million people from Europe and Asia immigrated to South America and the Caribbean between 1860 and 1920. In this photograph, European immigrants dine in a communal hall at a hotel set aside specifically for them.

attempted to consolidate support among conservatives and pursued policies that benefited landowners and urban business interests. This was possible because of the close relationship between agricultural producers and processors and because both the landed and the middle classes wanted to resist concessions to the working classes.

The Military in Ascendence By the end of the 1920s the onetime reformist Radical Party had become corrupt and directionless. The worldwide commodity depression hurt exports. In 1930 the military staged a coup against the aged Irigoyen, who had returned to the presidency in 1928. The officers eventually returned power to conservative civilians, and Argentina remained heavily dependent on the British export market. U.S. interests also began to establish plants in Argentina, removing still more economic activity from Argentine control.

Throughout the 1930s a right-wing nationalistic movement, **nacionalismo**, arose among writers, political journalists, and a few active politicians. This movement resembled the Fascist political movements then active in Europe. Its supporters were angered by British and American domination of the economy, equating their influence with imperialism. In politics the movement's supporters rejected liberalism and spread the fear of international communism. They also exhibited a strong anti-Semitic spirit and warmly supported the Roman Catholic Church. *Nacionalismo* was associated with a relatively progressive social policy rooted in the social values of the late-nineteenth-century papacy of Leo XIII. It advocated social reforms that recognized the needs of workers and the poor but that also sought to promote social harmony rather than communist revolution or socialist reconstruction of the economy. The various writers who set forth these ideas also looked back to Rosas as a role model for Argentine politics. In effect these groups were anti-imperialistic, socially concerned, authoritarian, and sympathetic to the rule of a modern *caudillo*. The pressures that came to the fore as a result of World War II gave these attitudes and their supporters influence that they had not previously enjoyed.

The war closed almost all of Europe to Argentine exports, creating a sudden economic crisis. The country's leadership seemed incapable of responding to the crisis, and in 1943 the military again seized control. Its leaders had lost patience with politicians more interested in patronage than in patriotism. Many of the officers were children of immigrants and were fiercely nationalistic. They regarded liberal politics as a system that permitted politicians to look after themselves. Some officers had become deeply impressed by the Fascist and Nazi movements and their rejection of European liberal politics. The officers also shared the Fascist and Nazi hostility to Britain. They contended that the government must address social questions, industrialize the country, and liberate it from foreign economic control. In all these respects, they echoed the *nacionalistas*.

Between 1943 and 1946 Juan Perón (1895–1974), one of the colonels involved in the 1943 coup, forged this social discontent and these authoritarian political attitudes into a remarkable political movement known as **Perónism**. It was authoritarian, initially militaristic, anti-communist, and socially progressive. Perón understood better than his fellow officers that political power could be exerted by appeals to the Argentine working class, particularly in Buenos Aires. He gained the support of the trade unions that were opposed to communism. In 1945 he had been arrested by other military leaders, but he was freed when it became clear that he alone could silence working-class discontent. In 1946 he made himself the voice of working-class democracy, even though after his election to the presidency he created an authoritarian regime that only marginally addressed industrial problems. He was greatly aided by his wife, the former actress Eva Duarte (1919–1952). She enjoyed charismatic support among trade-union members and the working class. (See Document, "Eva Perón Explains the Sources of Her Popularity.")

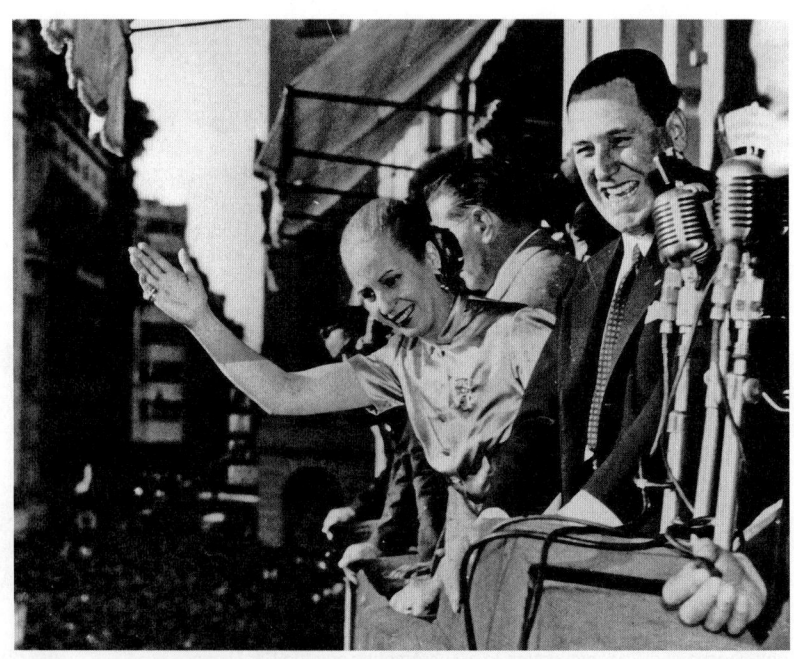

Argentine president Juan Domingo Perón and his wife Eva address a throng of supporters from a balcony in Buenos Aires.

Eva Perón Explains the Sources of Her Popularity

Document

The Perónist movement in Argentina drew broad support from workers and the poor. The movement involved a cult of personality around both Perón and his wife, Eva. In 1951 Eva Perón published a book entitled *My Mission in Life (La Razón de mi Vida)*. Here she explains how she sought to relate to her husband's political supporters.

◆ Why was Eva Perón's acceptance of the name "Evita" a political act? How did her use of this name separate her from the ruling elites of Argentina? What is the role she projects for herself in her relationship to various social groups in Argentina? Do you believe her discussion of herself to be sincere or politically opportunistic?

When I chose to be "Evita," I chose the path of my peole. . . .

Only the people call me "Evita." Only the *descamisados* [the "unshirted," as Perón's working-class followers were termed] learned to call me so. . . .

I appeared to them thus the day I went to meet the humble of my land, telling them that I preferred being "Evita" to being the wife of the president, if that "Evita" could help to mitigate some grief, or dry a tear.

If a man of the government, a leader, a politician, an ambassador, who normally calls me "Señora," should call me "Evita," it would sound as strange and out of place to me as if a street-urchin, a workingman, or a humble person of the people should call me "Señora." . . .

Now, if you ask me which I prefer, my reply would be immediately that I prefer the name by which I am known to the people.

When a street-urchin calls me "Evita," I feel as though I were the mother of all urchins, and of all the weak and the humble of my land.

When a working man calls me "Evita," I feel glad to be the companion of all the workingmen of my country and even of the whole world.

When a woman of my country calls me "Evita," I imagine myself her sister, and that of all the women of humanity.

And so, almost without noticing it, I have classified in these three examples the principal activities of "Evita" relating to the humble, the workers, and women.

The truth is that, without any artificial effort, at no personal cost, as though I had been born for all this, I feel myself responsible for the humble as though I were the mother of all of them; I fight shoulder to shoulder with the workers as though I were another of their companions from the workshop or factory; in front of the women who trust in me, I consider myself something like an elder sister, responsible to a certain degree for the destiny of all of them who have placed their hopes in me.

And certainly I do not deem this an honor but a responsibility. . . .

Yes. I confess that I have an ambition, one single, great personal ambition: I would like the name of "Evita" to figure somewhere in the history of my country.

From Sara Castro-Klarén, Sylvia Malloy, and Beatriz Sarlo, *Women's Writing in Latin America: An Anthology.* Selection trans. by Ethel Cherry. Copyright © 1991 by Westview Press. Reprinted by permission of Westview Press.

Perón became the most famous of the postwar Latin American dictators, but his power and appeal were rooted in the antiliberal attitudes that had been fostered by the corruption and aimlessness of Argentine politics during the depression. He was the supreme twentieth-century embodiment of the *caudillo*. He was ousted in 1956, but long-term stability would elude Argentine politics after his departure.

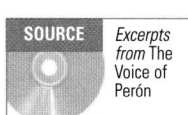
SOURCE Excerpts from The Voice of Perón

Mexico

The heritage of Mexican independence was a combination of the thwarted social revolution led by Father Hidalgo and José María Morelos between 1811 and 1815 and the conservative political coup carried out in 1820 by the creole elite against a potentially liberal Spanish crown. For the first century of independence conservative forces held sway, but in 1910 the Mexican people launched the most far-reaching revolution in Latin American history.

Turmoil Follows Independence The years from 1820 to 1876 were a time of political turmoil, economic floundering, and national humiliation. Newly independent Mexico attempted no liberal political experiments. Its first ruler was Agustín de Iturbide (1783–1824), who ruled until 1823 as an emperor. After this unsuccessful effort to adopt monarchical rule, Mexico was governed by a succession of presidents, most of whom were *caudillos* from the army or depended on the army for support. The strongest of these figures was Antonio López de Santa Anna (1795–1863), a general and a political opportunist always willing to modify his principles and policies to attain or retain power. Usually he supported conservative political and social interests. He ruled in a thoroughly dictatorial manner. More than once he was driven from office, but he inevitably returned until finally exiled in 1855.

The midcentury movement against Santa Anna's autocracy was called **La Reforma**. In theory, its supporters were liberal, but Mexican liberalism was associated primarily with anticlericalism, confiscation of church lands, and opposition to military influence on national life and politics. *La Reforma* aimed to produce political stability, civilian rule, and an economic policy that would attract foreign capital and immigrants. Having deposed Santa Anna, the leaders of the reform movement passed legislation to break up large landed estates, particularly those owned by the church, and to promote the establishment of small farms. However, the actual content of the laws permitted existing large landowners to purchase additional land cheaply and thus made great estates even larger. The legislative attack on privileges of the church led to further civil war between 1857 and 1860. In January 1861 Benito Juárez (1806–1872) entered Mexico City as the temporary victor.

Political instability was matched by economic stagnation. After 1820 many Spanish officials and merchants fled Mexico, taking with them large quantities of gold and silver. The mines that had produced Mexico's colonial wealth were in poor condition, and the country lacked the investment capital or technological knowledge to repair them. The inefficiencies of the *hacienda* system left farming in a backward condition. Cheap imports of manufactured goods spelled the end of domestic industries. Transportation was primitive. The government's remedy for these weaknesses was massive foreign borrowing; as a result, interest payments became one of the largest portions of the national budget.

Foreign Intervention Political weakness and economic disarray invited foreign intervention. The territorial ambitions of the United States impinged on Mexico in two ways. In 1823 the Mexican government allowed Stephen F. Austin (1793–1836) to begin the colonization of Texas. During the

Benito Juarez led *La Reforma*, a mid–nineteenth-century movement opposed to the autocracy of Santa Anna. Juarez is portrayed with the tools of an engineer in front of a background of railway building to suggest his dedication to economic progress and modernization in Mexico.

next decade, the policies of Santa Anna stirred resentment among the Texas settlers, and in 1835 they rebelled. The next year Santa Anna destroyed the defenders of the Alamo but was decisively defeated at the battle of San Jacinto. Texas became an independent republic that was annexed by the United States in 1845. Border clashes between Mexican and U.S. forces enabled President James Polk to launch a war against Mexico in 1846 that saw the United States army occupy Mexico City. Through the treaty of Guadalupe Hidalgo (1848), the United States gained a vast portion of Mexican territory, including what is now New Mexico, Arizona, and California.

Further foreign intervention occurred as a direct result of Juárez's liberal victory in 1861. Mexican conservatives and clerics invited the Austrian Habsburg Archduke Maximilian

The Execution of Maximilian of Mexico, June 19, 1867, by the French Impressionist painter Edouard Manet. Between 1867 and 1869 Manet completed a series of compositions depicting the execution of the Mexican emperor. This is the final and largest work.

(1832–1867) to become the emperor of Mexico. Napoleon III (r. 1852–1870) of France, who portrayed himself as a defender of the Roman Catholic Church, provided support for this imperial venture. In May 1862 French troops invaded Mexico, and two years later Maximilian became emperor. He disappointed his conservative supporters by accepting much of the former government's liberal policy towards the church but was unable to gain support from other segments of the population. By 1867 Juárez had organized strong resistance forces. He captured the unhappy emperor and executed him. The Mexicans had been victorious, but their vulnerability to foreign powers had again been exposed.

Díaz and Dictatorship Once restored to office, the liberal leaders continued their measures against the church but failed to rally significant popular support. Consequently, in 1876 Porfirio Díaz (1830–1915), a liberal general, led a revolt on the grounds that he was restoring a true republic. Except for four years in the 1880s, when a surrogate held office, Díaz retained the presidency until 1911. He maintained what became one of the most successful dictatorships in Latin American history by giving almost every political sector something it wanted. He allowed landowners to purchase public land cheaply; he favored the army, whose support he required; and he made peace with the church by not enforcing anticlerical measures. Later, he freely used repression against opponents to diffuse their political activity and bribery to cement the loyalty of his supporters. Wealthy Mexicans grew even richer under Díaz, and Mexico became a respectable member of the international financial community. Unprecedented quantities of foreign capital flooded the nation. Foreign companies, especially from the United States, invested heavily in what, by 1900, appeared to be a thoroughly stable country.

Yet problems remained. The peasants wanted land and resented the ever-growing power of the landlords. Because food production actually declined during the Díaz regime, many Mexicans were malnourished. Labor unrest and strikes afflicted the textile and mining industries. Like other Latin American rulers and governments in Europe and the United States, Díaz used military force against workers. Due to inflation, real wages for the working class declined in the first decade of this century. The Panic of 1907 in the United States disrupted the Mexican economy. By 1910 the so-called *Pax Porfiriana* was unraveling.

Revolution In 1908 the elderly Díaz announced that he would not seek reelection. Although he later changed his mind and was reelected in 1910, his first announcement spurred public discussion of Mexico's political and social future. In 1910 Díaz was opposed by Francisco Madero (d. 1913), a wealthy landowner and moderate liberal. Madero's campaign slogan was "Effective Suffrage—No Reelection," which ironically Díaz himself had coined two generations earlier. Díaz won, but Madero then led an insurrection that drove the dictator into European exile by May 1911.

Shortly thereafter, Madero was elected president. He recognized the rights of trade unions to organize and to strike, but he was unwilling to undertake significant agrarian reform that might have changed the pattern of landholding. He ended by being distrusted both by conservatives, who wanted little or no change from the days of Díaz, and by reformist leaders, who thought the time had come for extensive social and political restructuring. Far more radical leaders emerged, calling for social change. Pancho Villa (1874–1923) in the north and Emiliano Zapata (1879–1919) in the south rallied mass followings of peasants who demanded fundamental structural changes in rural landholding. In late 1911 Zapata proclaimed his Plan of Ayala, which in effect set forth a program of large-scale peasant confiscation of land. Much of the struggle during the next ten years would be between supporters and opponents of such agrarian reform. (See Document, "Emiliano Zapata Issues the Plan of Ayala.")

Emiliano Zapata Issues the Plan of Ayala   Document

By November 1911 the Díaz regime had fallen in Mexico, and Francisco Madero was attempting to establish a moderately liberal government. He was confronted by a major popular peasant revolution led in the valley of Morelos by Emiliano Zapata. On November 28 the rebel leader set forth his opposition to Madero and announced sweeping goals of land reform. Zapata never took dominant control of the Mexican Revolution, but the radical economic demands of his *Plan of Ayala* would influence the course of Mexican social development for the next thirty years.

◆ Why did Zapata place so much emphasis on collective ownership of natural resources? What is Zapata's vision of future economic life? Who would be the winners and losers from his proposed policies?

. . . be it known: that the lands, woods, and water usurped by the *hacendados* [great landowners] . . . henceforth belong to the towns or citizens in possession of the deeds concerning these properties of which they were despoiled through the devious action of our oppressors. The possession of said properties shall be kept at all costs, arms in hand. The usurpers who think they have right to said goods may state their claims before special tribunals to be established upon the triumph of the Revolution.

. . . the immense majority of Mexico's villages and citizens own only the ground on which they stand. They suffer the horrors of poverty without being able to better their social status in any respect, or without being able to dedicate themselves to industry or agriculture due to the fact that the lands, woods, and water are monopolized by a few. For this reason, through prior compensation, one-third of such monopolies will be expropriated from their powerful owners in order that the villages and citizens of Mexico may obtain *ejidos* [agricultural communities], colonies, town sites, and rural properties for sowing or tilling, and in order that the welfare and prosperity of the Mexican people will be promoted in every way.

The property of those *hacendados* . . . who directly or indirectly oppose the present plan shall be nationalized, and two-thirds of their remaining property shall be designated for war indemnities—pensions for the widows and orphans of the victims that succumb in the struggle for this plan.

From James W. Wilkie and Albert L. Michaels, eds., *Revolution in Mexico: Years of Upheaval, 1910–1940*. Copyright © 1969 by Alfred A. Knopf, p. 46.

Madero found himself squeezed between the conservative supporters of the deposed Díaz and the radical peasant revolutionaries. No one trusted him, and in early 1913 he was overthrown by General Victoriano Huerta (1854–1916), who had the help of the United States and was assassinated not long thereafter. Huerta, who was basically a dictator, failed to quash the peasant rebellion. His attacks against the forces of Zapata involved considerable loss of life. In the meantime, Venustiano Carranza (1859–1920), a wealthy landowner, joined Villa's cause. He soon put himself at the head of a large Constitutionalist Army—so called because it advocated the restoration of constitutional government in opposition to the political dictatorship of Huerta—that initially received the support of both Zapata and Villa. Huerta's government collapsed on August 15, 1914, when Constitutionalist forces entered Mexico City. Thereafter disputes erupted between Carranza and Villa and then between Carranza and Zapata. These conflicts arose both from simple political rivalry and from Carranza's refusal to embrace the kind of radical agrarian reform the two peasant leaders sought. Carranza eventually won out, thanks to his political skills and the effectiveness of his army.

Carranza's political skills also helped him build a broad base and edge out both Villa and Zapata as the chief leader of the revolution. One particularly skillful move followed an attempt by President Woodrow Wilson (1856–1924) of the United States to support Carranza by sending U.S. Marines to Veracruz in April 1914. Carranza shrewdly denounced the United States for this action, thus casting himself in the role of patriot and nationalist, and the Marines departed. In another skillful move, he addressed himself to the concerns of urban industrial workers as well as the land hunger of rural peasants, successfully separating the two groups. This division ultimately doomed the effort to implement an agrarian revolution. Carranza made many promises, especially about agrarian reform, that he had little or no intention of carrying out.

The Mexican Revolution. The forces of Emiliano Zapata march on Xochimilco in 1914. Women fought alongside men and played other prominent roles during the Mexican Revolution. *UPI/Corbis-Bettman.*

Beginning in early 1915 Carranza's military forces began an ultimately successful campaign against Villa and Zapata. The peasant leaders still commanded regional support but could not win control of the nation. During 1916 Carranza confronted U.S. military intervention along the border that continued until early 1917, when the United States became involved in World War I in Europe. Throughout the turmoil in Mexico, the government of the United States attempted to protect American interests. These activities involved ongoing diplomatic initiatives with the various groups in Mexico as well as the threat of military action.

By 1917, after years of deadly and destructive civil war, Carranza's forces were sufficiently confident to write a constitution. The Constitution of 1917 set forth a program for ongoing social revolution—never pursued with any vigor—and political reform. Perhaps its two most famous provisions were Articles 27 and 123. Article 27 provided for the government, on behalf of the nation, to become the owner of water and mineral rights and other subsoil property rights. This article abrogated all prerevolutionary contracts with foreign companies in regard to oil and minerals. Together with other provisions, it meant that peasant villages could reclaim land they had lost over the past half century. Article 123 guaranteed certain rights for the organization of labor. Many years would pass before all the provisions of the constitution could be enforced, but from 1917 onward it provided the ongoing goals of the revolution and the ideals towards which Mexican governments were expected to strive.

Carranza and his immediate subordinates were much more conservative than either Villa or Zapata. They recognized the agrarian problem but were cautious about changing existing property arrangements.

Carranza and his chief supporters were associated with northwestern Mexico and admired the economic development they had seen in California. They were determined to modernize Mexican political life and attract capital investment; Mexican leaders would share these goals from that time onward. Thus despite all the radical rhetoric associated with the revolution and the vast upheaval among peasants that it involved, the Mexican Revolution saw the victory of a more or less middle-class political and economic elite who would attempt to govern the country through enlightened paternalism. Although turmoil would persist for many years, with Carranza's victory the general direction of Mexican political life had been established.

The decade after 1917 witnessed both confusion and consolidation. In 1919 Zapata was lured into an ambush and killed. Carranza was assassinated in 1920. Three years later Villa was also assassinated. In this turmoil, Carranza's generals provided stability. During the 1920s military leaders drawn from Carranza's revolutionary Constitutionalist Army served as presidents. They moved cautiously and hesitated to press land redistribution too quickly. They were opposed by the Roman Catholic Church, which at one point suspended all services for more than two years. In 1929 Plutarco Elías Calles (1877–1945) organized the **PRI**, the Institutional Revolutionary Party, which quickly became the most important political force in the nation. The Mexican political system became one dominated by a single party within which most political debate occurred, rather than a system dominated by a single strong leader. Despite external criticism and internal tensions, the PRI has overseen the longest period of political stability experienced by any Latin American nation in the twentieth century.

In 1934 Lázaro Cárdenas (1895–1970) was elected president. More than any of the other leaders to emerge after the revolution, he moved directly to fulfill the promises and programs of 1917. He turned tens of millions of acres of land over to peasant villages. In 1938, when Mexico was the third largest producer of petroleum, he expropriated the oil industry. His nationalization policy established PeMex, which remains the Mexican national oil company. Cárdenas left other mineral industries in private and generally foreign hands. His extensive reforms went through smoothly because he worked through bureaucratic and administrative means.

With the election of Manuel Ávila Camacho (1897–1955) in 1940, the era of revolutionary politics ended. Thereafter, the major issues in Mexico were those generally associated with postwar economic development. But unlike other Latin American nations, Mexico, because of its revolution, could confront those issues with a democratic perspective and a sense of collective social responsibility, no matter how imperfectly those goals might be realized.

Brazil

Postcolonial Brazil, the largest Latin American country, differed in several important respects from other newly independent nations in the region. Its language and colonial heritage were Portuguese rather than Spanish. For the first sixty-seven years of its independence it had a relatively stable monarchical government. And most distinctively, it retained the institution of slavery until 1888.

Brazil had moved directly from being part of the Portuguese monarchy to becoming an independent empire in 1822. The first emperor, Pedro I (r. 1822–1831), while serving as regent for his father, the king of Portugal, had put himself at the head of the independence movement. Although he granted Brazil a constitution in 1823, Pedro's high-handed rule and his patronage of Portuguese courtiers rather than Brazilians led to his forced abdication in 1831. Brazilians then took hold of their own destinies.

After a decade of political uncertainty under a regency, Pedro II (r. 1831–1889), the fifteen-year-old son of Pedro I, assumed direct power in 1840 and governed Brazil until 1889. Pedro II made wise and shrewd use of patronage. He established a reputation as a constitutional monarch by asking leaders of both the conservative and the liberal political parties to form ministries. Consequently, Brazil enjoyed remarkable political stability. However, the government took few initiatives to develop the economy.

The Slavery Issue The great divisive issue in Brazil's social and political life was slavery. Sugar production remained the mainstay of the economy until the middle of the nineteenth century. Most sugar plantations were located

Chronology

Mexico

1820–1823	Agustín de Iturbide rules unsuccessfully as emperor
1833–1855	Santa Anna dominates Mexican political scene
1846–1848	Mexico defeated by United States and loses considerable territory
1861	Victory of liberal forces under Juárez
1862–1867	French troops led by Archduke Maximilian of Austria unsuccessfully invade Mexico
1876–1911	Era of Porfirio Díaz
1911	Beginning of Mexican Revolution
1911	Zapata proclaims Plan of Ayala
1917	Forces of Carranza proclaim constitution
1929	Institutional Revolutionary Party organized

in the coastal provinces of the northeast. Their owners were conservative and resistant to changes in production. Soil exhaustion and inefficient farming methods made profits impossible without the cheap labor of slaves. From about 1850 coffee cultivation began to spread in the southern provinces, marking a key shift in Brazilian agriculture. Coffee would soon become the nation's most important product. Coffee producers also used slave labor and wanted to retain slavery, but their profits were much larger than those of the sugar producers, so a transition to free labor would have been easier for them. Coffee planters also tended to see themselves as being on the side of economic progress. Hence, people investing in coffee were more open to emancipation than those who had invested in sugar.

As early as 1826 the Brazilian government had made a treaty with Great Britain, agreeing to suppress the slave trade. For many years Brazil refused to honor these treaty provisions but by 1850 had virtually ceased importing slaves, putting the sugar planters on the defensive and freeing the capital once spent on slaves for investments in coffee. The end of slave imports effectively doomed the institution of slavery because the birthrate among slaves was too low for the slave population to reproduce itself. It was nonetheless one thing to face this technical inevitability and another to abolish slavery.

The Paraguayan War of 1865–1870 postponed consideration of the slave question. This conflict, which pitted Brazil, Argentina, and Uruguay against Paraguay, originated in border disputes and in larger commercial conflicts about ongoing Paraguayan access to the ports on the lower Plate River, in particular Montevideo. The conflict

Antislavery Print. Slavery lasted longer in Brazil than in any other nation in North or South America. Antislavery groups circulated prints such as this one published in France to illustrate the brutality of slave life in Brazil.
The Granger Collection N.Y.

became a long, exceedingly destructive struggle because the dictator of Paraguay, Francisco Solano López (1827–1870), mobilized his entire country into a war of attrition and refused to surrender. His death in battle in 1870 finally ended the war, but only after more than half (and perhaps a larger portion) of the adult male population of Paraguay had been killed. The victorious powers installed a friendly government in Paraguay, which sold off state lands to foreign speculators.

The end of the war returned slavery to the forefront of Brazilian politics. Brazil and the Spanish colonies of Puerto Rico and Cuba were now the only slaveholding countries in the hemisphere. The emperor favored gradual emancipation. A law of 1871 set the stage for such emancipation by freeing slaves owned by the crown and by decreeing legal freedom for future children of slaves. The law actually had little effect because it required the children of slaves to work on plantations until the age of twenty-one. However, throughout the 1870s and 1880s the abolition movement grew in Brazil. Public figures from across the entire political spectrum called for an end to slavery. (See Document, "A Brazilian Liberal Denounces Slavery.") Abolitionists helped slaves to escape. The army, many of whose officers held political views associated with positivism, resented having to enforce laws protecting slavery. In 1888 Pedro II was in Europe for medical treatment, and his daughter was regent. She favored abolition rather than gradual emancipation. When Parliament in that year passed a law abolishing slavery without any compensation to the slave owners, she signed it, thus ending slavery in Brazil.

A Republic Replaces Monarchy The abolition of slavery brought to a head other issues that in 1889 caused the collapse of the monarchy. Planters who received no financial compensation for their slaves were resentful. Roman Catholic clerics were disaffected by disputes with the emperor over education. Pedro II was unwell; his daughter, the heir to the throne, was unpopular and distrusted. The officer corps of the army had been dissatisfied with what it regarded as insufficient political influence since its victory in the Paraguayan War. In November 1889 the army sent Pedro II into exile in France.

The Brazilian republic lasted from 1891 to 1930. Like the monarchy, it was dominated by a small group of wealthy persons, the most dominant of whom were the coffee planters. The political arrangement that allowed the republic to function smoothly was an agreement among the state governors. The president was to be chosen alternately from the states of São Paulo and Minas Gerais. In turn, the other eighteen governors had considerable local political latitude. Fixed elections and patronage kept the system in operation.

A Brazilian Liberal Denounces Slavery

Document

Critics sharply attacked slavery in Brazil from the mid–nineteenth century onward. The first major attempt to emancipate slaves occurred in 1871. That law proposed gradual emancipation by liberating the children of slaves. The abolitionist movement continued to grow resulting in the final emancipation of slaves in Brazil in 1888. In 1883 Joaquim Nabuco, a major leader of the abolitionist movement, published *O Abolicionismo*, which stands as one of the chief examples of Brazilian antislavery literature. Although not quoted in the passage below, Nabuco drew extensive parallels between the slavery of Brazil and that which had existed in the United States before the Civil War. Here Nabuco seeks to demonstrate the manner in which the continuation of slavery prevents commercial economic development in Brazil and inhibits the country from embracing the progressive forces of the day. Note the manner in which Nabuco has absorbed the ideas of the eighteenth-century Enlightenment and nineteenth-century European liberalism.

◆ What are the values and outlooks that Nabuco associates with the expansion of commerce? Why does he see slavery as undermining those values? How and why does he see slavery inhibiting progressive social and intellectual forces? In this passage, what are possible arguments against slavery that Nabuco does not raise?

Slavery does not permit the existence of a true working class, nor is it compatible with the wage system and the personal dignity of the artisan. . . . [T]here can be no strong, respected, and intelligent working class where the employers of labor are accustomed to order slaves about. . . .

Slavery and industry are mutually exclusive terms, like slavery and colonization. The spirit of the former, spreading through a country, kills every one of the human faculties from which industry springs—initiative, inventiveness, individual energy, and every one of the elements that industry requires—the formation of capital, an abundance of labor, technical education of the workers, confidence in the future. . . .

. . .[C]ommerce, in the absence of industry and free labor, can function only as an agent of slavery, buying whatever it offers and selling whatever it needs. This is why in Brazil commerce does not develop or open new perspectives for the country. . . . Slavery distrusts commerce, as it distrusts any agency of progress, whether it is a business man's office, a railroad station, or a primary school; yet slavery needs commerce. . . . But so long as slavery endures, commerce must always be the servant of a class, and not an independent national agent. . . .

Of the classes whose growth slavery artificially stimulates, none is more numerous than that of government employees. . . . Officeholding is . . . the asylum of the descendants of formerly rich and noble families that have squandered the fortunes made from slavery. . . . But officeholding is also our political olive tree, that shelters all those young men of brains and ambition but no money who form the great majority of our talented people. . . .

Among the forces of progress and change around which slavery has created a vacuum as hostile to its interests, the press is notable—and not only the newspaper but the book, and everything that concerns education. . . . The slave hut and the school are poles that repel each other. . . .

Among the forces whose emergence slavery has impeded is public opinion, the consciousness of a common destiny. Under slavery there cannot exist that powerful force called public opinion, that simultaneously balances and offers a point of support to the individuals who represented the most advanced thought of the country. Just as slavery is incompatible with spontaneous immigration, so will it prevent the influx of new ideas. Itself incapable of invention, it will have nothing to do with progress.

Joaquim Nabuco, *O Abolicionismo* (São Paulo, 1938), excerpted from Benjamin Keen, trans., as reprinted in Benjamin Keen, ed., *Readings in Latin-American Civilization-1492 to the Present* (Boston: Houghton Mifflin Company, 1955), pp. 339–343.

Literacy replaced property as the qualification for voting, leaving few people qualified to vote. There was consequently little organized opposition and, for that matter, little political life at all within the republic.

From the 1890s onward the coffee industry dominated both the political and the economic life of the nation. Around 1900 Brazil was producing over three-fourths of the world's coffee. The crop's success led almost inevitably to overproduction. To meet this problem, the government devised policies for maintaining high prices that required large loans from foreign banks. High world coffee prices encouraged competition from other Latin American producers, which in turn required more price supports in Brazil. In addition to the international loans, maintaining the price of coffee required considerable payments to the government from all of the non-coffee-related sectors of the economy. These sectors in turn felt exploited by the coffee interests. As a result of these arrangements, throughout the life of the republic Brazil remained essentially a country producing a single product for export and few goods for internal consumption.

Economic Problems and Military Coups The end of slavery, the expansion of coffee production, and the beginning of a slow growth of urban industry attracted foreign immigrants to Brazil. They tended to settle in the cities and constituted the core of the early industrial labor force. In Brazil, as elsewhere, World War I caused major economic disruption. Urban labor discontent appeared. There was a general strike in São Paulo in 1917, with the inevitable military action against the strikers. The failure to address urban and industrial social problems and the political corruption of the republic led to attempted military coups in 1922 and 1924. Both revolts failed to bring down the republic, but they indicated profound discontent with a political structure designed primarily to protect the producers of a single agricultural commodity. The revolts also demonstrated that certain segments of the military were determined to change the political system. They wanted a modern nation that was not dependent on a single exportable product and a political system that depended on more than corruption and recognized interests besides those of the coffee planters.

Coffee had ruled as the economic "king" of the Brazilian republic, and its collapse brought the republic down with it. In 1929 coffee prices hit record lows; currency exchange rates fell; and foreign loans were unavailable. Millions of bags of coffee lay in warehouses. Government reserves were depleted in an unsuccessful attempt to hold up the price of coffee and to pay for imports no longer being funded by coffee exports. The economic structure of the republic lay in shambles. In October 1930 a military coup installed Getulio Vargas (1883–1954) in the presidency. Vargas governed Brazil until 1945.

The Vargas years represent a major turning point in Brazilian history. Vargas was initially supported by the reform elements in the military, by professional middle-class groups, and by urban workers. In office, he moved first to the right and

Latin American Products for Export 1820–1930

Overview

Argentina	animal products (meat, leather, wool), grain
Bolivia	tin, silver, wool
Brazil	coffee, sugar, rubber
Chile	copper
Colombia	coffee, cattle
Ecuador	bananas
Mexico	silver, cattle, oil
Peru	nitrates, silver
Uruguay	animal products (meat, leather)
Venezuela	coffee, cattle

SOURCE *Coffee Plantation, Brazil*

Vargas and the Military. Getulio Vargas became ruler of Brazil in 1930 through a military coup. Here he stands with his military supporters. One of the purposes of such pictures was to remind the public that any serious opposition might be put down by the military. *UPI/Corbis-Bettmann.*

then to the left and then back again. He was an experimentalist and pragmatist who primarily wanted to hold on to power and to make Brazil a modern nation. Vargas was able to recognize the new social and economic groups shaping Brazilian political life. First with constitutionalism and then with dictatorship, he attempted to allow the government to act on behalf of those groups without allowing them to influence or direct the government in a genuinely democratic manner. However, despite the personal power that accrued to him, he did not form his own political party or movement as Perón would later do in Argentina or as the Mexican revolutionaries had done. Rather, Vargas attempted to function like a ringmaster directing the various forces in Brazilian life. His failure to establish a genuinely stable institutional political framework for a Brazil that included many interest groups besides the coffee planters has influenced Brazil to the present day.

Vargas and his supporters sought to lessen dependence on coffee by fostering industries that would produce domestically goods that had previously been imported from abroad. They thus attempted to create internal suppliers for goods needed in the internal Brazilian economy. The policy succeeded, and by the mid-1930s domestic manufacturing was increasing. These years mark the real beginning of Brazilian manufacturing. In the constitution of 1934 Vargas established a legal framework for labor relations. The structures were paternalistic but included an eight-hour day and a minimum wage. The constitution also asserted government responsibility to protect mineral and water rights.

In the Brazilian context these measures appeared reformist, if not necessarily liberal, and marked a departure from government policy dominated by the coffee oligarchy and politics by patronage. However, in the late 1930s Vargas confronted major political opposition from both the Brazilian Communist Party (founded in 1922) and a new right-wing movement called *Integralism*. In 1937, facing these political opponents, Vargas assumed personal dictatorial power. His regime thereafter was repressive. He claimed to have established an ***Estado Novo*** ("new state"). He wrapped himself in the flag of nationalism and order and presented himself as the protector of national stability against factions that would foster instability and of the national interest against international opponents.

Like the European dictators of the same era, Vargas used censorship, secret police, and torture against his political opponents. He also used his newly assumed power to diversify and modernize the economy. In 1940 a five-year plan provided more state direction for the

SOURCE *Rio de Janiero Street Scene, 1940s*

economy. His government favored the production of goods from heavy industry that would be used in Brazil itself. To maintain the support of workers and trade unions, the state also issued a progressive labor code. Siding with the Allies in World War II, Brazil built up large reserves of foreign currency through the export of foodstuffs. This economic activity and imposed political stability allowed the government to secure foreign loans for still further economic development. By the end of the war Brazil was becoming the major Latin American industrial power.

Participation in World War II on the side of the Allies had led many in Brazil to believe that they should not remain subject to a dictatorship. This attitude was widespread in the military, which had fought in Europe and established close contact with the United States. In 1945 Vargas promised that he would lead the nation towards democracy and hold presidential as well as congressional elections. His actions, however, suggested that he planned to manipulate the elections. In response, the military carried out a coup, and Vargas retired temporarily from political life.

The new regime, which was democratic, continued the general policy of economic development through foreign-financed industrialization. The state, however, assumed a much smaller role. When in 1950 Vargas was elected president, his return to office was anticlimactic. He was by then an elderly man, well past his prime. Yet in 1953 he established Petrobas, a state-owned petroleum exploration company. His presidency remained controversial. There was much criticism of him and of the corruption of his appointments. A member of his staff became involved in the assassination of a prominent civilian journalist. The military demanded that Vargas resign. Instead he took his own life in 1954, leaving a public testament in which he presented himself as the protector of the poor and of the broad national interest.

In the decade after Vargas' death, Brazil remained a democracy, although a highly unstable one. The government itself began to undertake vast projects such as the enormously costly construction of the new capital of Brasília, begun in 1957. Located far inland, Brasília required the creation of a vast road system. With Brasília under way, the government of Juscelino Kubitschek (1902–1976), who had supported the building of the new capital, fostered the establishment of a large automobile industry. The rapid growth of cities and the expansion of a working class radicalized political life. The political system could not readily accommodate itself to the concerns of workers and the urban poor. Widespread poverty and illiteracy continued to plague both the cities and the countryside. In a structural problem created by the constitution of 1946, the presidency was controlled by urban voters, whereas the congress was controlled by rural voters.

Chronology

Brazil

1822	Brazil becomes an independent empire
1840	Pedro II assumes personal rule
1840s and 1850s	Spread of coffee cultivation
1865–1870	Paraguayan War
1871	First law curbing slavery
1888	Slavery abolished
1889	Fall of the monarchy
1917	General strike in São Paulo
1929	Collapse of coffee prices
1930–1945	Vargas era
1957	Construction of Brasília begins
1964	Military takes control of the government

By the early 1960s, when President João Goulert (1918–1977) took office, Brazilian political life was in turmoil. Goulert's predecessors, including Vargas, had always attempted to balance interests or to move among various political forces without firmly favoring a single sector. After months of wavering, however, Goulert committed himself to a policy favored by the left. In 1964 he announced his support for land reform. Peasants had already tried to seize land, and landowners had fought them. Political conservatives and moderates expected some favors to urban radicals, which they might have tolerated, but vigorously resisted any hint of significant political or land reform in the countryside. Goulert also questioned the authority of the military hierarchy. Moreover, Brazil faced economic problems: Both industrial and farm production had fallen from the levels achieved in 1960, fostering discontent. In March 1964 the military, claiming to protect Brazil from communism, seized control of the government, ending its post–World War II experiment with democracy.

Summary

Economic Dependence. In the 1820s, Latin America threw off Spanish and Portuguese rule, but the traditional elites—landowners, military officers, the church—remained in control. A series of strongmen called *caudillos* dominated most Latin American republics. Nor did independence bring economic prosperity. Because Latin American economies remained dependent on producing agricultural commodities for export, foreign nations, particularly Britain, dominated Latin American economic life. When commodity prices collapsed during the Great Depression, Latin American economies were devastated. The crisis did, however, lead to the beginnings of manufacturing in many Latin American countries in an effort to avoid dependence on imports.

Argentina. After independence, Buenos Aires came to dominate Argentina economically and politically. Agricultural exports, the growth of industry, and large-scale European immigration contributed to a strong export economy. However, urban social discontent and the growth of nationalism in the 1930s led to military intervention in politics and the corporatist dictatorship of Juan Perón from 1946 to 1956.

Mexico. In the first decades after independence Mexico was politically and economically unstable. Mexico lost half its territory to the United States and was invaded by France in the 1860s. The long-lasting dictatorship of Porfirio Díaz brought political stability but led to increasing discontent. The Mexican Revolution that began in 1911 produced cautious social and economic reform under the one-party rule of the PRI, the Institutional Revolutionary Party, which remained in power until the end of the century.

Brazil. Brazil was a stable constitutional monarchy after independence until 1889. It also retained slavery until 1888. The establishment of a republic did not change Brazil's economic dependence on coffee exports, however, and the collapse of coffee prices in 1929 led to the dictatorship of Getulio Vargas. Although politically repressive, Vargas instituted social reforms and promoted industrial development, which continued to expand in the decade after his death in 1954.

Review Questions

1. What was the condition of the Latin American economies after independence? What was their relation to Britain? Why were most Latin American states slow to develop an industrial base? What role did their economies play in the worldwide economy that developed in the nineteenth century?

2. Did the structure of Latin American societies change after independence? What role did the traditional elites

INTERPRETING THE PAST

Latin America: Dependence, Dictators, and Democracy

Sources from MyHistoryLab / Primary Source DVD

1. Francisco Bilbao, *America in Danger* (1862)
2. Friederich Hassaurek, *How to Conduct a Latin American Revolution* (1865)

Source from Chapter 26

1. *A Brazilian Liberal Denounces Slavery* (1883)
   (page 838)

PRENTICE HALL
myhistorylab
Where it's a good time to connect to the past!

Since gaining independence from European states in the early nineteenth century, Latin American states have been unstable politically, inclined to authoritarian regimes and frequent coups. Economic dependency accompanied this political instability. Natural resources and agricultural products were extracted and exported for the benefit of European and North American investors, primarily large corporations.

In this exercise you will examine three documents that spotlight some of the most intractable problems relating to the economic, social, and political life in Latin America in the period after independence. The first document, written by Francisco Bilbao, a liberal political reformer, recapitulates the justifications for the military dictatorships that were prevalent throughout Latin America. The second document is a step-by-step "guide" to the process of revolution, which occurred play in the economic and political life of their nations? What was the condition of the mass of the population?

3. How did European and United States investment in Latin America affect the region economically? Politically?

4. Why did so many Latin American nations find it difficult to develop stable political regimes? What role did the military play?

5. What was the effect of increased European immigration on Argentina? How did the Argentine elite cope with growing urbanization and industrialization? Why was Juan Perón able to seize and hold power?

6. Did Mexico experience a real revolution in the early twentieth century? How does this experience distinguish Mexico from other Latin American countries? What caused the turmoil?

7. Why was the Brazilian experience of independence and early nationhood different from that of Spanish-speaking Latin America? What was the role of coffee in Brazil's economy? How did the Vargas regime change the Brazilian economy? Why did Brazilian democracy end in a military coup in 1964?

Key Terms

caudillos (p. 827)

creole (p. 819)

debt peonage (p. 822)

dependency theory (p. 818)

Estado Novo (p. 840)

import substitution (p. 827)

La Reforma (p. 832)

mestizos (p. 821)

mulattos (p. 821)

nacionalismo (p. 830)

neo-colonial economy (p. 827)

pampas (p. 829)

Perónism (p. 830)

positivism (p. 823)

PRI (p. 836)

frequently, as observed by the American Minister to Ecuador in the 1860s. The third primary source, from Chapter 28, is written by a Brazilian abolitionist, who discusses the social and political dimensions of slavery, which existed in that country until 1888.

Assignment

After reading the documents relate the authors' point of view to the three major explanations for these problems, which are outlined in the "Global Perspective" section an pages 818–819.

Then write an essay that outlines the parallels between the sources and the ways in which they support or undermine the above explanations.

Note: To learn more about the topics in this chapter, please turn to the Suggested Readings at the end of the book. For additional sources related to this chapter please see the Primary Source DVD at the back of this text or MyHistoryLab.

27

India, the Islamic Heartlands, and Africa, 1800–1945

T HE ENCROACHMENT OF THE EUROPEAN NATIONS ON the rest of the world from the late fifteenth century onward brought radical, often devastating changes. In the West itself, spiritual and material disruption accompanied the Renaissance, the Reformation, the Enlightenment, and the Industrial and Scientific Revolutions. When Western expansion brought the ideas and innovations of these watershed European developments to Asia and Africa, the challenges and changes that ensued came much more rapidly than they had in the West. Furthermore, this development occurred simultaneously with the spread of European military and economic power, which provided a context for both virulent resistance and cautious adaptation.

To speak of these complex processes under the rubric of "modernization" still does not reflect the acute differences between the relatively lengthy and gradual processes of change in Western Europe and the more rapid and disruptive changes that European imperialism and colonialism brought to other parts of the world. Nor does it do justice to the

The Emir of Bukhara and His Ministers, ca. 1870. In 1868, Russia defeated the Emir of Bukhara, who ruled one of several petty states in Central Asia that came under Russian domination in the latter half of the nineteenth century. The emir was permitted to rule a greatly diminished territory under Russian protection.

The Challenge of Modernity: India, Islam, and Africa

Africa — Middle East — India

The century and a half that began in 1800 was bleak for the fortunes of the Indian subcontinent, Africa, and the Islamic societies of the Middle East and elsewhere. For centuries there had been a rough but long-term balance in advances and setbacks in material and intellectual culture, commercial development, and political stability among the major cultural regions of the world. Suddenly, over a period of 150 years, Europe, long a relative backwater in world history, came to dominate the rest of the world.

The Middle East, Africa, Iran, Central Asia, India, and Southeast Asia, along with Central and South America—later the so-called "Third World" of "developing nations"— were most drastically affected by European imperialism and colonialism. Notwithstanding indigenous developments in these regions, the overarching and decisive development of this era was new and unprecedented domination of the world's economy, intellectual life, and political and military history by a single segment of the global community. Certainly the histories of the less "developed" nations of the world ("developed" in the sense of evolving towards European-style economic, political, and cultural systems) in this age have their own internal dynamics; in fact, many smaller African or South American societies were not even directly affected by Western dominance until recently. Still, the impact of Western military, economic, and cultural power and influence was considerable. While not synonymous with "progress" as Westerners and modernization theorists have often liked to believe, it has been, nevertheless, a hallmark of the "modern" age in most of Asia, Africa, and South America. Whether by rejection, adaptation

degree to which the West appropriated the very concept of "modernity." Although every advanced society in any age has presumably viewed its culture as "modern," the dominance of the West in recent centuries has identified modernity with a novel set of ideas and institutions that evolved in Europe between the Renaissance and the early twentieth century and was then gradually exported to, or imposed upon, other societies around the globe. The expression "the impact of modernity" refers to how "modern" Western civilization affected traditional cultures.

The consequences of the spread of Western culture have been so massive that today non-Western peoples are often seen as merely its passive recipients. The American or European view of the world often reflects a simplistic dualism that enhances Western self-esteem by portraying the "modern" West

on one side and the "backward" "Orient" on the other, as though all of the world outside Europe, North America, and their most Westernized offshoots were some monolithic, archaic entity. Popular Western stereotypes of the Arab, the African, the Indian, the Chinese, and so on reinforce the Westerner's sense of being the true "modern" of recent history.

As parochial as such chauvinistic generalizations are, these generalizations may nonetheless have a certain grim historical core, as suggested by the crises that many non-Western cultures experienced under the material and spiritual impact of Western modernity and its agents. The impingement of the West has been a major element in the recent history of African, Asian, and Indian civilizations. Not all non-Western societies have had equal success in either retaining or reasserting their precolonial independence and identity, nor in and syncretism, or outright imitation, peoples worldwide had to contend with the immense power of the West.

The vitality of so many of the cultures and traditions that bore the brunt of the Western onslaught has been striking. Arab, Iranian, Indian, African, and other encounters with Western material and intellectual domination produced different and often very creative responses and initiatives. These have borne full fruit in political, economic, and intellectual independence only since 1945, although most began much earlier. For example, modern Islamic reform and resurgence began in the eighteenth century, although it has only recently become a major global factor. Indian national, as opposed to regional, consciousness developed from the late eighteenth century onward in response to British imperial and colonial domination, even though it led to national union and independence only after World War II. Ironically, exposure of the indigenous elite to European political and social philosophies gave future leaders of colonial independence drives vital intellectual ammunition with which to develop ideologies of self-rule. Creative thinkers like Mohandas K. Gandhi (1869–1948) merged these European philosophies with ideas drawn from their own cultures to create distinctive new ideologies that could inspire sympathizers from the West as well as their own indigenous followers to oppose European imperialism and oppression of all kinds. African nationalist leaders such as Julius Nyerere (1922–1999) and Jomo Kenyatta (1889–1978) similarly found creative ways to merge European nationalist models with indigenous cultural ones.

Certainly one result of the imperial-colonial experience almost everywhere has been to sharpen the cultural self-consciousness and self-confidence of those peoples most negatively affected by Western dominance. The imperial-colonial experiences of the Third World nations may well prove to have been not only ones of misery and reversal, but also of transition to positive development and resurgence, despite the problems that plague many of these nations.

Focus Questions

◆ How did Western domination affect the Indian subcontinent, the Islamic heartlands, and Africa in the nineteenth century?

◆ How did these societies eventually develop ideologies of resistance that helped them achieve independence?

responding creatively to the ongoing challenges of Western-style modernity. The spectrum of postimperial or postcolonial experience ranges from the largely positive response of Japan or the mixed experience of China to the painful and often destructive experiences of most African societies, with India, Iran, South America, and the Middle East somewhere in between.

Nevertheless, in all of these Third World areas, Western modernity entered cultures that had flourishing social, religious, and political traditions of their own. These traditions did not simply melt away on the arrival of the Westerners. Rather, a profound transformation took place that sought to delicately balance the unforeseen challenges of modernity with the familiarity of tradition. That transformation reverberates to this day. It took place throughout Asia and Africa as these continents also became the sites of a fierce European competion for their raw materials and influence. The "great game" and the "scramble for colonies" would permanently alter the cultural, economical, and political landscape in both Asia and Africa, and in Europe as well. ■

THE INDIAN EXPERIENCE

British Dominance and Colonial Rule

In the eighteenth century Britain became the dominant power in the southern seas, overshadowing Portugal and Holland. In India the British defeated the French and regional Indian powers for domination of the subcontinent (see Chapter 21). By the early nineteenth century they had built the largest European colonial empire in the Afro-Asian

Map 27–1.   British India, 1820 and 1856.

world. India, the greatest traditional civilization of Africa or Asia to come under direct European colonial rule, was the "jewel in the crown" of that empire.

Building the Empire: The First Half of the Nineteenth Century

Penetrating the multi-ethnic, multilingual, and multiconfessional area known as India was not a simple task for Britain but required a multipronged approach. In order for British imperial plans to succeed, the British gradually had to secure the economic and cultural basis for their control. This involved identifying how to be able to extract as many natural resources as possible with minimal costs and also how to convince various strata of Indian society and the various ethnic groups that cooperation with the British imperial enterprise was in their best interests.

As early as half a century before the British Crown asserted direct rule over India in 1858, the British wielded effective imperial control through the East India Company. As the Company's pressure on smaller states to pay "subsidies" for military "protection" brought ever more of them to either collapse or rebellion, the British annexed more territory. Those areas not annexed were recognized as independent princely states. Ranging in size from less than a square mile to more than 80,000 square miles (Hyderabad), these independent states retained their status only as long as they remained faithfully allied to Britain and contributed money to their

common "defense." Members of Indian elites often colluded with the British against local rulers. The state of Mysore, the Maratha confederation, and the Sikhs of the Panjab were overpowered between 1797 and 1853. The India that resulted was a mixture of small and large tributary states and provinces that the British administered directly (see Map 27–1).

The economic impact of Company rule was extensive. To pay the debts incurred by their military actions, the Company's administrators organized and exploited Indian land revenues. Squeezed by these demands, many peasants deserted their land; by the 1830s land revenues were in sharp decline. In addition, demand for Indian indigo, cotton, and opium in the China and British trade also slacked off in the 1830s, and famines brought widespread suffering. The economic and social reforms (1828–1836) of Governor General Lord William Bentinck (1774–1839) were not sufficient to turn things around substantially.

Company rule, especially in the early nineteenth century, also affected the physical face of India. Company policies encouraged settled agriculture and small commodity production at the expense of the nomadic and pastoralist cultures that had been a major presence across North and central India. British "pacification" involved the clearing of land to deny natural cover to military enemies and the often forced settlement of peasants as pioneer farmers in new regions. Early in the nineteenth century European entrepreneurs also undertook massive commercial logging opera-

SOURCE *Lord William Bentinck on the Suppression of Sati*

The Indian Mutiny of 1857. The mutinous Sepoy cavalry attacking a British infantry division at the battle of Cawnpore. Although the uprising was suppressed, it was not easily forgotten. In its aftermath the British reorganized the government of India. *The Granger Collection, New York.*

tions. These activities caused extensive deforestation throughout the subcontinent. This ecological destruction was a major by-product of the transformation of India into a more homogeneous peasant farming society that provided a better base for colonial administration.[1]

The Indians were by no means passive in the face of this misuse of their lands and peoples. The first half of the nineteenth century saw almost constant revolt in one place or another. The revolts included peasant movements of noncooperation, Muslim farm workers' attacks on British and Hindu estate owners, grain riots, and tribal warfare. They culminated in a watershed event, the Indian Uprising of 1857 (the so-called Sepoy Mutiny or Rebellion). Thus the commonly accepted image of this era as one of general tranquillity prior to a "mutiny" against British custodianship turns out to have been a product of British propaganda.

The immediate trigger of the Uprising of 1857 was the concern among Bengal troops that animal grease on newly issued rifles exposed them to ritual pollution. Behind this issue, however, lay a variety of grievances, including the recent addition of Sikhs, Gurkhas, and lower caste soldiers to the army; the deteriorating economic conditions of many of the Hindu troops' higher-caste relatives back home; outrage at excessive tax rates, especially among troops from Meerut; and anger at the 1856 British annexation of the rich princely state of Awadh (home to many of the troops). One can also see in the revolt the desire to recover and rebuild a pre-British political order in North India. The revolt was not

an all-India affair. It centered on Delhi, where the last Mughal emperor joined in the rebel cause, and involved uprisings in other cities and towns from Chittagong in Bengal to Lahore and even Peshawar in the Panjab. Uprisings in the countryside around Delhi and Lucknow involved the peasantry.

Because their real power bases in Bengal and the Panjab were not destroyed, and their ability to communicate and move new troops was not impaired, the British eventually won the day. With their forces augmented by Sikhs from the Panjab and Gurkhas from Nepal, they overcame the internally divided Indian opposition. By autumn 1857, the revolt was broken, often with great brutality, and it was finished before the end of the year. In the next year the East India Company was dissolved, and India came under direct rule of the British crown.

The "Mutiny" of 1857 was not a nationalist revolution, but rather a series of antiforeigner, anti-British spontaneous uprisings. Still, it presaged the rise of an effective unified response and highlighted underlying resentment of the burdens of foreign domination that were to grow increasingly oppressive for Indians of all regions and religions over the ensuing ninety years of Crown rule, known as the **raj**.

British-Indian Relations

The overall impact of British presence on the Indian masses, under both Company and Crown rule, was brutal but impersonal, in that it was largely economic. India was effectively integrated into Britain's economy, becoming a market for British goods and providing Britain with raw materials and other products. Britain's involvement in

---

[1] C. A. Bayly, *Indian Society and the Making of the British Empire* (Cambridge: Cambridge University Press, 1988), pp. 138–146.

India's internal affairs included politics, education, the civil-service infrastructure, communications, and transportation, but the consequences of its domination and exploitation of India's labor and resources were especially far-reaching.

British cultural imperialism was never a major nor even an official policy of the East India Company. In fact, like Warren Hastings (1732–1818), governor general of the Company from 1774 to 1785, many Britons expressed interest in and some openness to Indians and their culture. A few mixed and even intermarried with Indians. The Company itself required many of its India officers to learn Persian and Sanskrit. Nor did it try to propagate Christianity or impose Western culture; indeed, it opposed Christian missionary activity in India until the 1830s and 1840s, partly because the caste system enabled the implementation of imperial policy. Nonetheless the British-Indian relationship had a paternalistic and patronizing dimension, both before and after the events of 1857. Even with the improved access of Indians to English education and to civil-service positions of greater responsibility in the late nineteenth and early twentieth centuries, the fundamental imbalance between overlords and subjects remained and was frequently expressed in racial terms. The ethos of the British rulers included the understanding that they had the task of governing an inferior "race" that could not handle the job by itself. Even Indians whose university degrees or army training gave them impeccable British qualifications were never accepted as true equals. From army to civil-service ranks, the upper echelon of command was British; the middle and lower echelons of administration were Indian.

Despite this unequal relationship, British ideas and ways of doing things influenced a small but powerful Indian elite in both their business and political life and their manners and customs. Conversion to Christianity was rare, but Christian and secular values associated with the European Enlightenment—the ideals of British liberalism, for example—influenced Hindu and Muslim educated classes.

In the nineteenth century, probably the most influential and controversial member of the Indian elite to engage the British on their own ground was Ram Mohan Roy (1772–1833). Roy, a Bengali Hindu, rose to the top of the native ranks of East India Company service and became a strong voice for reform, both of Hindu life and practice and of British colonial policy where it deviated from European and Christian ideals. The spiritual father of the Brahmo Samaj (1828), a Hindu reform movement opposed to "barbarous" practices that ranged from *sati* (immolation of widows on their husbands' funeral pyres) to "idol worship" and Brahmanic "ritualism," Roy was an avowed modernist who wanted to meld the best of European-Christian morality and thought with the best of Hindu piety and thought. He

Portrait of Ram Mohan Roy, the most influential Indian thinker in the early nineteenth century.

was quick to oppose autocratic and unfair British legal and commercial practices and campaigned in India and in England to reform the Company's policies. He was influenced by the Christian Scriptures and the great thinkers of European civilization and drew upon them in his Hindu reform efforts. His wide-ranging writings and public campaigns for education, political involvement, and social progress and against the "backward" practices and ideas of many of his Hindu compatriots alienated most of the leading Hindu thinkers and activists of his age, but twentieth-century Indians have often seen him as a visionary.

The cultural relationship between Britain and India was not, of course, a one-way affair. During the Company era, and increasingly after 1858, Britons at home became aware of India and Indians. The image that came to them, however, was filtered through the experience of other Britons who had spent time in the subcontinent and were not always either sympathetic or objective interpreters. Even many of those officers of the Company who made India a career developed little interest in Indians beyond what they needed to know to extract economic gain from them. Others, however, studied Indian cultures and languages and got to know at least some of the Indian elite as friends. However, after the implementation of direct Crown rule in 1858, a stricter social segregation of white rulers from Indian subjects set in.

Despite the keen interest in Indian culture that many of them had, the British, much more than their Central Asian Mughal predecessors, treated Indians all too often as backward heathens in need of the "civilizing" influences of their own "enlightened" culture, law, political system, education,

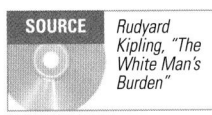 **SOURCE** *Rudyard Kipling, "The White Man's Burden"*

and religion. A vivid example of this dismissive attitude to Indian culture is evident in the argument of the nineteenth-century British historian and statesman Lord Macaulay (1800–1859) in favor of an English-language curriculum in Indian schools. (See Document, "Macaulay Writes on Indian Education.")

Macaulay Writes on Indian Education

Document

The decision in 1835 to encourage English-language study and the British school curriculum in Indian schools was hotly disputed by both the English and the Indians. In the end it bred a new generation of elite Indians prepared to act as advocates for their nation, as well as a class of bureaucrats for the British raj. It also worked to the advantage of Hindus because Muslims tended to reject English schooling and lost ground in the long run. This famous position paper by Thomas Babington Macaulay expresses the thinking of the "Anglicists," who prevailed over the "Orientalists," and reveals British prejudices about the superiority of Western culture over Indian culture.

◆ When Macaulay writes "that English is better worth knowing than Sanscrit or Arabic," is he making an objective judgment or is he engaging in "cultural imperialism"? From your perspective, which are the laudable, and which the problematic, intentions and goals of the writer?

We now come to the gist of the matter. We have a fund to be employed as government shall direct for the intellectual improvement of the people of this country. The simple question is, what is the most useful way of employing it?

All parties seem to be agreed on one point, that the dialects commonly spoken among the natives of this part of India contain neither literary nor scientific information, and are, moreover, so poor and rude that, until they are enriched from some other quarter, it will not be easy to translate any valuable work into them. It seems to be admitted on all sides that the intellectual improvement of those classes of the people who have the means of pursuing higher studies can at present be affected only by means of some language not vernacular amongst them.

What then shall that language be? One-half of the committee maintain that it should be the English. The other half strongly recommend the Arabic and Sanscrit. The whole question seems to me to be, which language is the best worth knowing?

To sum up what I have said, I think it clear that we are free to employ our funds as we choose; that we ought to employ them in teaching what is best worth knowing; that English is better worth knowing than Sanscrit or Arabic; that

the natives are desirous to be taught English, and are not desirous to be taught Sanscrit or Arabic; that neither as the languages of law, nor as the languages of religion, have the Sanscrit and Arabic any peculiar claim to our engagement; that it is possible to make natives of this country thoroughly good English scholars; and that to this end our efforts ought to be directed. In one point I fully agree with the gentlemen to whose general views I am opposed. I feel with them, that it is impossible for us, with our limited means, to attempt to educate the body of the people. We must at present do our best to form a class who may be interpreters between us and the millions whom we govern; a class of persons, Indian in blood and color, but English in taste, in opinions, in morals, and in intellect. To that class we may leave it to refine the vernacular dialects of the country, to enrich those dialects with terms of science borrowed from the Western nomenclature, and to render them by degrees fit vehicles for conveying knowledge to the great mass of the population.

British Officer Reclining. This photograph of a British officer reclining while being fanned and served by two Indian attendants provides a glimpse into the colonial lifestyle in British India. It also gives insight into race, class, and labor divisions.

Most Indians resented their subordinate status. The nationalist movement at the end of the nineteenth century extended to the grass-roots level—among tribal groups, peasant farmers, and home or small-industry workers. Whatever their status, the distrust and animosity most Indians felt towards their foreign rulers continued to grow.[2]

From British Crown Raj to Independence

The Burden of Crown Rule

The Revolt of 1857 had numerous consequences beyond the transfer of the administration of India from the East India Company to the British Crown. The bloody conflict

exacerbated mutual fear and hatred. Before the revolt, the British had maintained a largely native army under British officers. After the revolt, they tried to maintain a ratio of at least one British to three Indian soldiers. Because the army was financed by Indian, not British, revenues, it imposed a huge economic burden on India, diverting one-third of its total annual revenues to pay for its own military occupation.

British economic policies and accelerating population growth put great strains on India's poor. Cheap

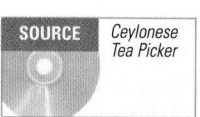

British machine-produced goods were exchanged for Indian raw materials and the products of its home industries, harming or destroying Indian craft industries and forcing multitudes into poverty or onto the land. Industrialization, which might have provided work for India's unemployed masses, was avoided. During the Civil War in the United States (1861–1865), which interrupted Britain's source of cotton from the American South, there was a shift from food to cotton farming in India. This shift intensified the effects of a drought in the 1870s, leading to widespread famine. Many peasants were forced to immigrate to Britain's dominions in South Africa, where they worked as indentured servants.

The Revolt of 1857 also created a poisonous distrust of Indians within the British colonial administration. **Cantonments** segregating white masters from "untrustworthy" natives became the rule in Indian towns and cities. Despite the just intentions expressed in royal statements and the opening of the civil service, at least nominally, to Indian candidates, the *raj* discouraged equality between Indian and Britisher. One bright exception to this trend was the tenure (1880–1884) of the Marquess of Ripon (1827–1909) as viceroy of India. Ripon fought to erase legal racial discrimination by allowing Indian judges to try British as well as Indian citizens. His efforts earned him the hatred of most of his British compatriots in India, but he was an example to emerging Indian leaders of the best that British egalitarianism could produce. Although his British foes managed by agitation to dilute his measures, in doing so they unwittingly gave Indians a model for political agitation of their own.[3]

Indian Resistance

Indians soon took up political activism. Late in the nineteenth century they founded the institutions that would help overcome traditional regionalism, build national feeling, and ultimately end colonial rule. In 1885

---

[2] See, for example, Bayly, *Indian Society and the British Empire*, pp. 169–199; David Arnold, "Rebellious Hillmen: The Gudem-Rampa Risings, 1839–1924," in Ranajit Guha, ed., *Subaltern Studies* (Delhi: Oxford University Press, 1982), pp. 88–142; Ranajit Guha, *Elementary Aspects of Peasant Insurgency in Colonial India* (New Delhi, 1984); cf. Eric Stokes, *The Peasant and the Raj: Studies in Agrarian Society and Peasant Rebellion in Colonial India* (Cambridge: Cambridge University Press, 1978).

[3] Stanley Wolpert, *A New History of India*, 2nd ed. (New York: Oxford University Press, 1982), pp. 256–257.

Amrita Cal Roy, "English Rule in India, 1886" Indian modernists formed the Indian National Congress to reform traditional Hindu and Muslim practices that were out of line with their liberal ideals and to change British Indian policies that were equally out of line with British democratic ideals. Other Indians agitated for the rejection of British rule altogether. The Muslim League developed as a counterbalance to the Hindu-dominated Congress. The League eventually made common cause with the Congress in the quest for home rule but ultimately worked for, and gained, a separate independent Muslim state, Pakistan. Heavy-handed and erratic British policies in legal administration, political representation, and taxation strengthened the growing desire for nationhood and independence.

Indian internal divisions were a major obstacle to independence. These divisions included the many language groups and subject princely states of the subcontinent. These, however, were not the only divisions or even the most critical. For much of British rule, every Indian politician was first a representative of his own region or state and second an Indian nationalist. Furthermore, the educated Indian elite had little in common with the masses of farmers and laborers beyond antagonism to foreign rule, making unified resistance or political action difficult. Mistrust and conflict among Hindus, Muslims, Sikhs, and Jains also impeded concerted political action.

Nonetheless, a nationalist movement with many subbranches took root. There were three principal elements within the independence movement that led to the creation of India and Pakistan in 1947.

The first consisted of those in the National Congress organization who sought gradual reform and progress towards

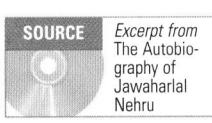

Excerpt from The Autobiography of Jawaharlal Nehru Indian self-governance, or *svarāj*. This position did not preclude outright opposition to the British, but it did mean trying to deal with the colonial rulers to change the system from within wherever possible. Among the proponents of this approach were G. K. Gokhale (1866–1915), the champion of moderate, deliberate, peaceful work towards self-determination; the spiritual and political genius Mohandas K. Gandhi (1869–1948); and his follower Jawaharlal Nehru (1889–1964), who became the first prime minister of India. Gandhi was the principal Indian leader after World War I and directed the all-India drive that finally forced the British out. An English-trained lawyer, Gandhi drew on not only his own native Hindu (and Jain and Buddhist) heritage, but also on the ideas of Western liberal and Christian thinkers like Henry David Thoreau (1817–1862) and Leo Tolstoy (1828–1910). In the end, Gandhi became a world figure as well as an Indian leader. (See Document, "Gandhi on Passive Resistance and Svarāj.")

The "Great Soul," "Mahatma" Mohandas K. Gandhi, father of the modern state of India.

The second element consisted of the militant Hindu nationalists, whose leader, the extremist B. G. Tilak (1856–1920), stressed the use of Indian languages and a revival of Hindu culture and learning. Tilak also subscribed to an anti-Muslim, Hindu communalist vision of Indian "self-governance." Where earlier in the nineteenth century foreign ideas had stimulated a Hindu renaissance and various reform movements, the Hindu extremists now looked to a return to traditional Indian values and self-sufficiency. Although their movement dissipated in the common resistance effort after 1914, their religious and political ideas still influence Indian political life, as witnessed by the resurgence of Hindu extremist groups in recent years and the communal strife, especially of Hindus with Muslims.

Muslims made up the third element but there were many divergent regional and even sectarian Muslim constituencies. Generally their leaders could be brought to make common cause only by the fear that as a minority they stood to lose what power they had in a Hindu-majority, all-India state. Muslims had been slower than the Hindus to take up British

Gandhi on Passive Resistance and Svarāj

Document

Gandhi's powerful thinking and prose were already evident in his Hind Svarāj, or Indian Home Rule, of 1909. This work was to remain his basic manifesto. The following excerpts reflect important points in his philosophy. *Svadeshī* refers to reliance only on what one produces at home (rather than on foreign goods).

◆ How does Gandhi relate the ideas of passive resistance and svarāj to his theory of Indian self-rule? What are the advantages and disadvantages of his strategy for effecting political and social change? How does this document compare with others concerned with movements of independence and nationalism? See "The Stamp Act Congress Addresses George III" (Chapter 23) and "Mazzini Defines Nationality" (Chapter 24).

Passive resistance is a method of securing rights by personal suffering; it is the reverse of resistance by arms. When I refuse to do a thing that is repugnant to my conscience, I use soul-force. For instance, the government of the day has passed a law which is applicable to me. I do not like it. If by using violence I force the government to repeal the law, I am employing what may be termed body-force. If I do not obey the law and accept the penalty for its breach, I use soul-force. It involves sacrifice of self.

Everybody admits that sacrifice of self is infinitely superior to sacrifice of others. Moreover, if this kind of force is used in a cause that is unjust, only the person using it suffers. He does not make others suffer for his mistakes. . . .

. . . The real meaning of the statement that we are a law-abiding nation is that we are passive resisters. When we do not like certain laws, we do not break the heads of law-givers but we suffer and do not submit to the laws. . . .

If man will only realize that it is unmanly to obey laws that are unjust, no man's tyranny will enslave him. This is the key to self-rule or home-rule. . . .

Let each do his duty. If I do my duty, that is, serve myself, I shall be able to serve others. Before I leave you, I will take the liberty of repeating:

1. Real home-rule is self-rule or self-control.
2. The way to it is passive resistance: that is soul-force or love-force.
3. In order to exert this force, *Svadeshī* in every sense is necessary.
4. What we want to do should be done, not because we object to the English or because we want to retaliate, but because it is our duty to do so. Thus, supposing that the English remove the salt-tax, restore our money, give the highest posts to Indians, withdraw the English troops, we shall certainly not use their machine-made goods, nor use the English language, nor many of their industries. It is worth noting that these things are, in their nature, harmful; hence we do not want them. I bear no enmity towards the English but do towards their civilization. In my opinion, we have used the term *Svadeshī* without understanding its real significance. I have endeavored to explain it as I understand it, and my conscience testifies that my life henceforth is dedicated to its attainment.

From *Sources of Indian Tradition*, ed. by William Theodore de Bary. Copyright © 1958 by Columbia University Press. Reprinted with permission of the publisher.

ideas and education and thus lagged behind the Hindu intelligentsia in numbers and influence with the British or other Indians. Because of the prominence of Muslims in the 1857 Revolt, the British were at first much less inclined to foster their advancement than that of Hindus. Nonetheless, the Muslims, distrusting the largely Hindu National Congress after its founding in 1885, sought rapprochement with the British at first, rather than risk being submerged in Hindu-led movements of opposition.

The man who did the most to win back respect and a voice for the Muslims in India under the Crown was Sayyid Ahmad Khan (1817–1898). A long-time supporter of modernist ideas and of cooperation with the British, he could also be sharply critical of their mistakes in India. His opposition to Muslim participation in the National Congress foreshadowed the tensions and conflict in Hindu-Muslim relations. He was also the founder of the Muslim educational initiative that led to the creation of

Chronology

India

1772–1833	Ram Mohan Roy, Hindu reformer
1774–1785	Administration of Warren Hastings
1817–1898	Sayyid Ahmad Khan, Muslim reformer
1835	Introduction of English education
1857–1858	Sepoy Revolt, or "Mutiny," followed by direct Crown rule as a British colony
1869–1948	Mohandas K. Gandhi
1873–1938	Muhammad Iqbal
1876–1949	Muhammad Ali Jinnah
1885	Indian National Congress formed
1889–1964	Jawaharlal Nehru
1947	Independence and partition

The Founding Father of Pakistan. Muhammad Ali Jinnah was the president of India's Muslim League who in the 1930s advanced the "two nations" theory and made the first formal demand for a separate Muslim homeland. His ideas led to the establishment of Pakistan. *AP Wide World Photos.*

the Muhammadan Anglo-Oriental College at Aligarh, which became the center for modernist Muslim attempts to integrate Muslim faith with modern Western thought and learning. It is still a major Muslim intellectual center in India today.

Hindu-Muslim Friction on the Road to Independence

In the twentieth century the rift between Muslims and Hindus in the subcontinent grew wider, despite periods of cooperation against the British. Arguments for coexistence with Hindus floundered, and Muslim fears of loss of communal identity and rights grew. In the end the great Indo-Muslim poet, thinker, and "spiritual father of Pakistan," Muhammad Iqbal (1873–1938), and the "founder of Pakistan," Muhammad Ali Jinnah (1876–1949), helped move Muslims to separatism.

The independence of India and Pakistan from Western domination was achieved only with suffering and violence. Blood was spilled in the long battle with the British, in communal violence among Indians themselves, in the violence between Hindus and Muslims that accompanied partition in 1947, and in the subsequent (and still festering) dispute over Kashmir between India and Pakistan. Still, the victory of 1947 gave the peoples of the subcontinent, Indians and Pakistanis, at last a sense of participation in the world of nations on their own terms instead of on those dictated by a

foreign power. The British influence was in some ways a good one. The British left a legacy of administrative and political unity and egalitarian and democratic ideals that Indian nationalists turned to their own uses.

THE ISLAMIC EXPERIENCE

Islamic Responses to Declining Power and Independence

The eighteenth century saw the weakening of the great Muslim empires and the increasing ascendancy of the West in international trade, military-political power, imperialist expansion, industrial specialization and productivity, and technological progress. The diverse Islamic peoples and states were thrust from positions of global power into a struggle for survival. As with India, the decline of Islamic preeminence was due both to the rise of the modern West and to internal problems.

Map 27–2. West Asia, Central Asia, and the Mediterranean, ca. 1850. Compare this map with Map 21–2 on p. 650. Though the Ottoman Empire still technically ruled a large area, in actuality it had lost much control over regions on the periphery.

By the nineteenth century all of the largest Muslim empires—Mughal, Ottoman, Safavid/Qajar, Moroccan, and Central Asian—had declined politically, militarily, and economically in relation to Western European empires (see Map 27–2).

They had grown increasingly decentralized, were less stable economically and politically, and were increasingly dominated by entrenched hereditary elites. Furthermore, the circumnavigation of the globe meant that it was no longer necessary to cross through the Middle East to get from Europe to Asia and back. For millennia, the Middle East benefited commercially from its geographic middle-man status. The shift in trade routes, however, resulted in changes in Middle Eastern and Mediterranean economies that caused them to become more peripheral to the world economy now centered on Western Europe. Yet once the various European nations had established a foothold in South and Southeast Asia, they turned their attention in the early nineteenth century to the Islamic heartlands in the Middle East. The Middle East became enmeshed in European imperial competition for its industrial resources such as oil, and most of the area came under Western political and economic domination. The interaction between the people of the Middle East and these new imperial powers was varied. There were some examples of cooperation and accommodation, but for the most part, the prevailing tone in the nineteenth century was one of conflict.

Ultimately, the fundamental question that engrossed Muslim reformers, politicians, and intellectuals was the basis of European ascendancy. Was the secular learning and technological superiority of Europe something transferable to the Middle East or other non-European regions? Could the once dominant Islamic word regain its vitality by importing European values and education as well as technology? Could the Islamic tradition of values itself be adapted or reformed to support and foster the kind of societal progress that Europe seemed to have managed without succombing to secularization entirely?

During the eighteenth and nineteenth centuries a variety of reform movements sought to revive Islam as a comprehensive guide for living and to purify it of the effects of many of the more stultifying developments in Islamic societies during the preceding centuries. In the major urban areas such as Cairo, Istanbul, and Damascus, influential reformers such as Muhammad Ali (see p. 859) and the sultan Mahmud II proposed adaptionist reform that sought to reengineer the armies, institutions, and societies of the Middle East to conform to the political reality of European domination. In these same urban settings, a variety of intellectuals sought to redefine what it meant to be Muslim in a modern age by emphasizing the malleability of the religion in relation to contemporary society. The most famous of such reform efforts was *Tanzimat* (see p. 860) in the Ottoman Empire. In the more rural areas, where neither urban Muslim ideas nor European power had penetrated to the same extent, other reformers stressed rejection of more flexible forms of Islam and of any Western or other values that might be held up as models.

Frontispiece from the Arab Literary-Scientific Journal *al-Muqtataf,* founded by Yaqub Sarruf in the 1860s. A group of such periodicals provided a public arena for political debate despite Ottoman, Egyptian, and British censors. They were a way for the burgeoning educated middle class of the Arab world (especially in Egypt) to construct national identities and debate social, economic, and political issues and policies. The crossed pen and hammer suggest a call to action while the floral border is reminiscent of traditional Islamic manuscripts.

The most famous of these movements that emphasized a strict construction of what "true" Islam entails was that of the **Wahhabis**, the followers of Ibn Abd al-Wahhab (1703–1792) in Arabia. It sought to combat excesses of popular and Sufi piety, such as saint worship, visitations to saints' tombs, and faith in the intercession of Sufi masters and saints. It also sought to break the stranglehold of the *ulama*'s conformist interpretations of legal and religious issues, favoring instead the exercise of independent judgment. The only authorities were to be the Qur'an and the traditions of the Prophet, not the scholastic edifices of the traditional schools of legal and theological interpretation. Allied with a local Arab prince, Sa'ud, the Wahhabi movement swept much of the Arabian Peninsula. It was crushed in the early nineteenth century by Egyptian military forces acting for the Ottoman regime. Still, the movement finally saw victory under a descendant of Sa'ud at the onset of this century and is the guiding ideology of present-day Saudi Arabia.

Other Muslim reform movements reflected similar revivalist and even militantly pietist responses to Islamic decadence and decline. Examples include that of Usman Dan Fodio in Africa in the late eighteenth century (discussed later in this chapter) and the Muslim Brotherhood in modern Egypt (see Chapter 34). Such groups called for a pristine Islam divested of the authoritarianism of the medieval legal schools, *ulama* theological conformity, and degenerate Sufi orders. Furthermore, these movements inspired a noncritical nostalgia for a time when Islamic societies were in ascendance and even dominating. This memory still rallies movements from Africa to Indonesia. In Islamic societies everywhere it has provided a response to the challenge of Western-style "modernity" and a model for cultural and religious life.

Western Political and Economic Encroachment

From the late 1700s until World War II the political fortunes of Arab, Turkish, Persian, Indian, Southeast Asian, and African Islamic states were increasingly dictated from outside by Western powers—including Britain, Russia, Germany, and France—and were at the mercy of the rivalries among them.

Western governments extracted capitulations favorable to their own economic and political interests from indigenous governments in exchange for promises of military protection or other considerations. These capitulations granted commercial concessions, protection, and "extraterritorial" legal status to European merchant enclaves. Such concessions (the earliest had been granted in the sixteenth century) had originally been reciprocal and had also served the commercial purposes of Muslim rulers and merchants. However, they eventually provided Western powers with pretexts for direct intervention in Ottoman, Iranian, Indian, and African affairs. The Ottoman Empire, like the Mughal Empire, suffered from internal disunity; its provincial rulers, or *pashas*, were virtually independent. This, combined with the increasing economic problems facing all the agrarian societies of Asia and Africa, made it easy for the Western powers—with their rapidly industrializing economies and increasingly effective militaries—to take control almost at will. Repeated Ottoman diplomatic and military defeats made that once great imperial power "the sick man of Europe" after 1800; similar weakness allowed Westerners to control the destinies of Indian and Iranian states and principalities.

The event that marked symbolically the onset of European domination of the Islamic heartlands was Napoleon Bonaparte's (1769–1821) invasion of Egypt in 1798 (see Chapter 23). The ease with which the French army was able to invade Egypt and topple the local government was suggestive of the weakened military status of the Middle East and the wider Muslim world. It also demonstrated the technical advances of European field artillery and infantry rifles. Eventually the French were forced by Britain, Russia, and the Ottomans to evacuate Egypt in 1801, but the invasion heralded a new era of European imperialism in the region. The British had already wrested control over India and the Persian Gulf from the French; they now became the preeminent European power in the eastern Mediterranean as well. The French continued to contest British ascendancy in the larger Middle Eastern area, but Russia presented the most serious nineteenth-century challenge to Britain's colonial empire.

Russia, which had already won control of the Black Sea from the Ottomans, sought to gain as much territory and influence in Iran, the Caucasus, and Central Asian regions as possible. Afghanistan, an independent kingdom established by Ahmad Shah Durrani (r. 1737–1773), acted as a buffer that prevented Russia from penetrating into British India. In the Iranian and Ottoman regions, however, Russia and Britain struggled for supremacy. The Crimean War of 1854–1856 (see Chapter 24) was one result of this conflict.

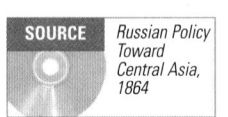

SOURCE *Russian Policy Toward Central Asia, 1864*

The Western Impact

Beyond the overt political and commercial impact of the West, Western political ideology, culture, and technology proved to be critical factors for change in Islamic societies. Outside of India, this effect was most strongly felt in Egypt, Lebanon, North Africa, and Anatolia (modern Turkey), as we shall see. Of all the Islamic states, including those in Africa and India, the ones least and last affected by Western "modernity" were Iran, Afghanistan, and the Central Asian khanates. The Iranian case deserves at least brief attention.

Iran The rulers of Iran from 1794 to 1925 were the Qajar shahs, a Turkoman dynasty whose absolutist reign was not unlike that of the Safavids. However, unlike the Safavids, the Qajars did not make religious claims to descent from the Shi'ite *imams*. Under Qajar rule, in marked contrast to Safavid rule, the *ulama* of the Shi'ite community became less and less strongly connected with the state apparatus. This period also saw the emergence of a Shi'i traditionalist doctrine that encouraged all Shi'ites, in the absence of a living *imam*, to choose a **mujtahid**—a qualified scholarly guide—from among the *ulama* and follow him in all matters requiring religious-legal interpretation. As a result, the *ulama* gained strength as an independent power in the state. As the guardians of law and faith, they were often the chief critics of the government (not least for its attempts to admit Western influences) and exponents of the people's grievances.

A prime demonstration of *ulama* power occurred when the Qajar Shah granted a fifty-year monopoly on tobacco sales to a British corporation in 1890. In 1891 the leading authority in the *ulama* spearheaded a tobacco boycott to protest the concession. This popular action, the first successful mass protest in modern Iranian history, was also supported by modernist-nationalist opponents of the Qajar regime who had strong connections to Iran's commercial, or **bazaari**, middle classes. In the face of such widespread opposition, the shah had to rescind the concession. On the one hand, this was a stunning victory for the power of public opinion and a symbolic triumph over the penetration of Western commercial interests in Iran. Yet ironically this action only made Iran more dependent on Western capital. The Iranian government was forced to pay an exorbitant compensation of around £500,000 sterling to the British corporation, which necessitated a foreign loan from a British bank. This was Iran's first foreign debt and caused it to be more reliant on Western institutions thereafter.

Linking Asia and Europe. The opening of the Suez Canal in 1869 was a major engineering achievement. It also became a major international waterway, reducing the distance from London to Bombay by half.

Subject as it was to the machinations of outsiders, such as Russia, Britain, and France, Iran inevitably felt the impact of Western ideas about education, science, law, and government. This occurred especially in the latter half of the century, when younger Iranian intellectuals began to warm to Western liberalism on economic, social, and political issues. As in other Islamic countries, the seeds of a new, secular nationalism were being sown where, previously, sectarian or communalist religious sentiments had held sway. It coincided and worked with a growing desire for a voice in government. An uneasy alliance of Iranian radical nationalists, liberal *bazaaris*, and conservative *ulama* proved, on occasion, an effective counterforce to Qajar absolutism, beginning with the successful 1891–1892 Tobacco Boycott and ending with the revolutionary *mashruteh* or Iranian Constitutional Movement of 1906–1911, when the Qajar shahs were forced to yield up their powers of treaty making and control of the country's finances to the *majlis* or National Consultative Assembly. Yet such alliances were not to last the twentieth century.

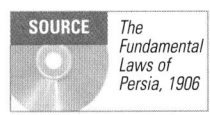
SOURCE *The Fundamental Laws of Persia, 1906*

Muhammad Ali (1769–1849), the famous viceroy of Egypt.

Islamic Responses to Foreign Encroachment

As the Iranian case shows, Western impingement on the Islamic world in the nineteenth and twentieth centuries elicited varied responses. Every people or state had a different experience, according to its particular circumstances and history. Yet there were at least three typical styles of reaction: (1) a tendency to emulate Western ideas and institutions; (2) the attempt to join Western innovations with traditional Islamic institutions; and (3) a traditionalist rejection of things Western in favor of either the status quo or a return to a purified Islamic community, or *Umma*. Of course, none of these styles was confined to one class or group in Islamic societies, and none was uniform within a country or across political, ethnic, and cultural boundaries.

Emulation of the West

The career of the virtually independent Ottoman viceroy Muhammad Ali (ca. 1769–1849), pasha of Egypt from 1805 to 1849, exemplifies a strategy of emulation. Ali, who arrived in Alexandria as part of an Albanian regiment of Ottoman forces sent to fight the French in 1801, set out to rejuvenate Egypt's failing agriculture, introduce modern mechanized industry, modernize the army with European help, and introduce European education and culture in government schools. Although he ultimately failed to make

Egypt as powerful as the European states of his day, Muhammad Ali did set his country on the path to becoming a nation state. His successors' financial and political successes such as the building of the Suez Canal also led to catastrophes such as indebtedness and the eventual occupation of Egypt by Britain in spite of the heroic 1881–1882 uprising led by Urabi Pasha (1839–1911). From 1882 to 1956, Britain occupied the Suez Canal and parts of Egypt, and while some consider Muhammad Ali to be "the father of modern Egypt," others consider Urabi Pasha, an Egyptian-born military officer, to be the "father of Egyptian nationalist movements." But Muhammad Ali and Urabi Pasha were not alone in the evolution of Egyptian political and militant identities. Sa'd Zaghlul Pasha (1857–1927), an Egyptian statesman and patriot, led a *Wafd* or delegation to Paris in 1919 to protest the 1914 British protectorate imposed on Egypt and to demand immediate independence. Zaghlul Pasha and his companions did not defeat the British occupation, but the *Wafd* party continued into contemporary times well beyond the last occupying British troop.

Efforts to appropriate Western experience and success were made by several Ottoman sultans and viziers after

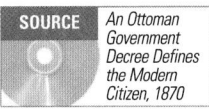
SOURCE *An Ottoman Government Decree Defines the Modern Citizen, 1870*

the devastating defeat of the Turks by Russia in 1774. Most notable were the reforms of Selim III (r. 1762–1808), Mahmud II (r. 1808–1839), and the

Tanzimat. A sitting of the new (1909) Turkish parliament following the abolition of the 1876 Constitution in 1878 by the Sultan Abdul Hamid II. The sessions were held in a lavish chamber with the delegates from the Balkans, Anatolia, and Fertile Crescent (Syria, Lebanon, Iraq, Jordan, and Palestine) seated facing a high podium at the front of the chamber.

so-called **Tanzimat**, or beneficial "legislation" (literally, "[re]ordering") era, from about 1839 to 1880. Selim made serious efforts at economic, administrative, and military reform. He brought European officers in to train new military corps that were to supplant the conservative Janissaries. Mahmud's reforms were much like those of Muhammad Ali. Most important were his destruction of the Janissary corps, tax and bureaucratic reforms, and encouragement of Western military and educational methods among the Ottoman elites. Like Selim and Muhammad Ali, he was less interested in promoting European enlightenment ideas about citizen rights and equity than in building a stronger, more modern centralized government, which often resulted in the consolidation of political power among a select few.

The Tanzimat reforms, introduced by several liberal Ottoman ministers of state, continued the efforts of Selim and Mahmud to bring the Ottoman state into line with ideals espoused by the European states. They were also intended to give European powers less cause to intervene in Ottoman affairs and to regenerate domestic confidence in the state.

The nineteenth-century Ottoman reforms failed to save the empire or truly to revive it as an economically

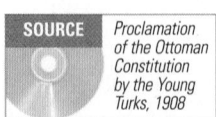

SOURCE *Proclamation of the Ottoman Constitution by the Young Turks, 1908*

sound, culturally vibrant, or militarily and politically powerful state. Nevertheless, they paved the way for the rise of Turkish nationalism, the "Young Turk" revolution of 1908, and ultimately the nationalist revolution of the 1920s that produced modern Turkey. (Ironically and tragically, this development simultaneously frustrated similar nationalist aspirations among old Ottoman minorities like the Greeks, the Armenians, and the Kurds.)

The creation of the Turkish republic out of the ashes of the Ottoman state after World War I is probably the most extreme example of an effort to modernize and nationalize an Islamic state on a Western model, although others would argue that it is the most successful case of integration. This state was largely the child of Mustafa Kemal (1881–1938), known as "Atatürk" ("father of the Turks"), its founder and first president (1922–1938). Atatürk led Turkey through an intensive period of reform that sought to eliminate vestiges of the Ottoman past and orient Turkey even more towards the West. His wide-ranging reforms were based on six principles that Atatürk defined as the foundation of the doctrine known as "Kemalism." These were: reformism, secularism, republicanism, nationalism, statism, and populism. Though these major reforms ranged from the introduction of a European-style code of civil law to the abolition of the caliphate, Sufi orders, Arabic script, and the Arabic call to prayer, Atatürk attempted to inculcate pride in the idea of a modern secular Turkish nation that appealed to all segments of society. On the surface, Atatürk's reforms constituted a truly radical attempt to secularize an Islamic state and to separate religious from political and social institutions. Yet at the same time, his reforms were largely a continuation of the transformation that had begun in the Ottoman era and had essentially the same goal as the Tanzimat movement, i.e., to make Turkey more responsive to the challenges of modernity. In the intervening years, Turkey has maintained its independence, reaffirmed its commitment to democratic government, and emerged with a unique, but still distinctly Islamic, identity.

Kemal Atatürk at the Wedding of His Adopted Daughter, Nebile, in 1929. Everything about this photo—the bride's dress, her father's white tie—suggests a European setting.

Integration of Western and Islamic Ideas

The attempt to join modernization with traditional Islamic institutions and ideas is exemplified in the thought of famous Muslim intellectuals, such as Jamal al-Din al-Afghani

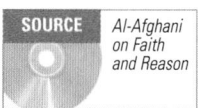
SOURCE Al-Afghani on Faith and Reason

(1839–1897), Muhammad Abduh (1845–1905), and Muhammad Iqbal (1873–1938). These thinkers argued for a progressive Islam rather than a materialist Western secularism as the best answer to life in the modern world.

Afghani is best known for his emphasis on the unity of the Islamic world, or **pan-Islamism**, and on a populist, constitutionalist approach to political order. His ideas and his charismatic personality influenced political activist movements in Egypt, Iran, Ottoman Turkey, and elsewhere.

His Egyptian disciple, Muhammad Abduh, sought to modernize Muslim education. He argued that a firm, revealed Qur'anic base could be combined harmoniously with modern science and its open questioning of reality. Through his efforts as Grand Mufti and head of state education, he introduced modernist reforms that affected even the curriculum

of the most venerable traditionalist institution of higher learning in the Islamic world, the great al-Azhar in Cairo.

Muhammad Iqbal, the most celebrated Indian Muslim thinker of the twentieth century, argued for a modernist revival of Muslim faith focused on purifying and uplifting the individual self above enslavement either to reason or to traditionalist conformity. Often credited with the original idea of a separate Muslim state in the Indian subcontinent (today's Pakistan), Iqbal still felt that Islam was essentially nonexclusivist and supranationalist:

> The truth is that Islam is not a church. It is a state conceived as a contractual organism . . . and animated by an ethical ideal which regards man not as an earth-rooted creature, defined by this or that portion of the earth, but as a spiritual being understood in terms of a social mechanism, and possessing rights and duties as a living factor in that mechanism. . . .[4]

Although Iqbal's poetry and essays excited Muslim fervor and dynamism, it is difficult to say how great his actual impact on Islamic political and social life really was.

Women and Reform in the Middle East

Though the discussion of reform, religion, and modernity in the Middle East was dominated by men, there were also a number of Middle Eastern women who started to address the status of women in modern society. Most important were those women who demanded political involvement for women in their country's affairs: the Iranian women who confronted their fathers and brothers in the Iranian Parliament in December 1911 concerning the possibility that the men might capitulate to the Russian-British demands to remove the American reforming administrator, Morgan Schuster; the Egyptian women who upon their return with their politician husbands in 1919 from Paris, where the latter had been humiliated as the Egyptian delegation (or *Wafd*), by the Versailles powers, threw off their veils and declared themselves the new Egyptian women; or the Palestinian women who convened in 1929 a Women's Congress of Palestine to address the political issues that ensued after the Wailing Wall riots of the same year. It is also noteworthy that there emerged in the late nineteenth and early twentieth centuries a number of journals and magazines that were devoted to women's concerns. These mainly focused on traditional issues such as cooking, parenting, and fashion, but there were other journals that sought to enlarge the domain of women and their role in the public sphere. Some articles

---

[4] Quoted in K. Cragg and R. M. Speight, eds., *Islam from Within* (Belmont, CA: Wadsworth, 1980), p. 213.

stressed that women were an essential part of society and should not be excluded from participation in commerce and politics. Some movements or demonstrations likewise carried forward such concerns. For example, the Egyptian Feminist Union was founded in 1923 by Huda Sha'rawi (1879–1947) to fight for women's suffrage, reform of marriage laws, and equal access to education. In a well-publicized event, Sha'rawi and her colleague Saize Nabrawi made a dramatic gesture to highlight the objective of the feminist movement. Standing in the midst of Cairo's bustling train station they publicly removed their veils to emphasize that women should no longer be concealed from the rest of society. Sha'rawi's act, like that of the women returned from Versailles in 1919, indicated that the veil was symbolic of the inadequate public status of women in Egypt and other Middle Eastern countries. For those outside the Middle East today, veiling is often seen as the most important gender issue. Many Middle Eastern feminists stress, however, that women's inequality is rooted in wide-ranging cultural, political, and economical structures that need to be addressed long before the issue of the veil.

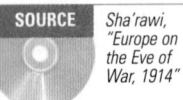
SOURCE Sha'rawi, "Europe on the Eve of War, 1914"

Purification and Revival of Islam

A third kind of Muslim reaction to Western domination has emphasized Islamic values and ideals to the exclusion of "outside" forces. This approach has involved either the kind of purist or reformist revivalism already seen in Wahhabism or the kind of conservatism often associated with Sunni or Shi'ite "establishment" *ulama*, as in the case of Iran since 1979. Both conservative and revivalist Muslim thinkers share the conviction that it is within, not outside, the Islamic tradition that answers to the questions facing Muslims in the modern world are to be found.

Traditionalist conservatism is much harder to pin down as the ethos of particular movements and organized groups than is reformist revivalism. Whereas Muslim revivalism (today commonly called "Islamism") usually focuses on Qur'an and Prophetic example as the sole authorities for Islamic life, Muslim conservatism commonly champions those forms of Islamic life and thought embodied in traditional law, theology, and even Sufism. It is seen in the legalistic tendencies that have often resurfaced when Islamic norms have been threatened by the breakdown of traditional society and the rise of secularism. Although such conservatism has often been associated with the most reactionary forces in Islamic society, it has often also served to preserve basic Muslim values while allowing for gradual change in a way that reformist revivalism could not accept. Where conservatives have formed alliances with governments or simply been co-opted by them, the

Chronology

Islamic Lands, 1700–1938

1703–1792	Ibn Abd al-Wahhab
1737–1773	Rule of Ahmad Shah Durrani, founder of modern Afghanistan
1794–1925	Qajar shahs of Iran
1798	Invasion of Egypt by Napoleon Bonaparte
1805–1849	Rule of Muhammad Ali in Egypt
ca. 1839–1880	Era of the Tanzimat reforms of the Ottoman Empire
1839–1897	Jamal al-Din al-Afghani
1845–1905	Muhammad Abduh
1882–1922	British occupation of Egypt
1908	"Young Turk" revolution
1922–1938	Mustafa Kemal, "Atatürk," in power

credibility of the establishment *ulama* has often been destroyed. This is because the masses of Muslims have been increasingly attracted to Islamist agendas for change.

Nationalism

Nationalism is a product of modern European history (see Chapter 24). Although not merely a response to Western encroachment, nationalist movements in the Islamic world have been either largely stimulated by Western models or produced in direct reaction to Western imperialist exploitation and colonial occupation. During the late nineteenth century, many intellectuals in Asia or Africa grappled with the question of identity and whether or not their ethnic or linguistic group constituted a distinct nation or whether they were part of a larger whole. (See Document, "Tâhâ Hussein, 'The Future of Culture in Egypt.'") The answer was not always self-evident and was in fact quite complicated given the mosaic of ethnicities, religions, and language groups across Africa and Asia. Yet the often arbitrary or artificial division of the colonial world by European administrators eventually demanded an answer to these questions in Asia and Africa. In the European capitals new "nations" were created and drawn on the map in the African and Asian continents especially after World War I. These new nations, such as Nigeria, Lebanon, Congo, or Iraq, reflected realities and interests of imperialism rather than

Tâhâ Hussein, "The Future of Culture in Egypt"

Document

Tâhâ Hussein (1889–1973) was the Egyptian Minister of Education from 1950 to 1952 and a leading Arab intellectual. He was born in a poor village in upper Egypt and became blind by the age of three. He studied at the important Al-Azhar University and eventually finished his doctorate at the Sorbonne in Paris. Hussein, like so many intellectuals around the world at this time, was very concerned with nationalism and how to reconcile the challenges of modernity with traditional thought and practice. In his writings, he argued that Egypt was part of Mediterranean civilization and that Egypt should follow European ideas in its quest to build up a modern nation. In the following piece, "The Future of Culture in Egypt," written in 1938, Hussein argues that Egypt had historical connections to Europe. Westernization thus constituted a return to Egypt's real roots.

◆ What is Hussein trying to achieve by emphasizing Egypt's historic ties to Europe?

The subject to be treated in this discourse is the future of culture in Egypt, now that our country has regained her freedom through the revival of the constitution and her honor through the realization of independence. We are living in an age characterized by the fact that freedom and independence do not constitute ends in themselves, but are merely means of attaining exalted, enduring, and generally practical goals. . . .

I know of nothing that causes me more worry than this newly won independence and freedom of ours. I fear that they may beguile us into thinking that we have come to the end of the road when in fact we have just reached the beginning. . . .

I do not want us to feel inferior to the Europeans because of our cultural shortcomings. This would cause us to despise ourselves and admit that they are not treating us unjustly when they are being arrogant. It is obnoxious for a man who is sensitive to dignity and honor to be compelled to acknowledge that he is not yet deserving of them. Let us keep this disgrace from ourselves and the nation. The way to do it is to take hold of our affairs with determination and vigor from today on, discard useless words for meaningful action, and establish our new life on a sound, constructive basis. . . .

At the outset we must answer this fundamental question: Is Egypt of the East or of the West? Naturally, I mean East or West in the cultural, not the geographical sense. It seems to me that there are two distinctly different and bitterly antagonistic cultures on the earth. Both have

existed since time immemorial, the one in Europe, the other in the Far East. . . .

The Egyptian mind had no serious contact with the Far Eastern mind; nor did it live harmoniously with the Persian mind. The Egyptian mind has had regular, peaceful, and mutually beneficial relations only with the Near East and Greece. In short, it has been influenced from earliest times by the Mediterranean Sea and the various peoples living around it. . . .

In order to become equal partners in civilization with the Europeans, we must literally and forthrightly do everything that they do; we must share with them the present civilization, with its pleasant and unpleasant sides, and not content ourselves with words or mere gestures. Whoever advises any other course of action is either a deceiver or is himself deceived. Strangely enough we imitate the West in our everyday life, yet hypocritically deny the fact in our words. If we really detest European life, what is to hinder us from rejecting it completely? And if we genuinely respect the Europeans, as we certainly seem to do by our wholesale adoption of their practices, why do we not reconcile our words with our actions? Hypocrisy ill becomes those who are proud and anxious to overcome their defects.

From *The Future of Culture in Egypt*, by Tâhâ Hussein, trans. by Sidney Glazer, Washington, D.C.: American Council of Learned Societies, 1954, pp. 1–5, 7–9, 15–17, 20, 25. No. 9 in ACLS Near Eastern Translation Project, copyright 1954. Reprinted in *The Islamic World*, eds. William H. McNeill and Marilyn Robinson Waldon, The University of Chicago Press 1973.

actual facts on the ground. In due time, these borders have taken on an aura of legitimacy. However, forging nations from artificial parameters has proven to be a difficult and sometimes violent process. As in India, nationalism has been an important aspect of the response to Western

domination in the Islamic heartlands. In Turkey in the 1920s it took a secularist form; in Libya, Iran, and elsewhere since the 1970s and 1980s it has taken an Islamic-revivalist form. As an Afro-Asian phenomenon, it will reappear in the next section ("The African Experience") and in Chapter 34.

THE AFRICAN EXPERIENCE

The century and a half between 1800 and 1945 saw striking change throughout Africa, but especially in sub-Saharan Africa. North Africa and Egypt were more closely bound up in the politics of the Ottoman Empire and Europe through-out this period. Except for South Africa below the Transvaal, tropical and southern Africa did not come under colonial control until after 1880. Before then, internal develop-ments—first, demographic and power shifts and then the rise of Islamic reform movements—overshadowed the increasing European presence in the continent.

New States and Power Centers

Southern Africa

In the south, below the Limpopo River, the first quarter of the nineteenth century saw devastating internal warfare, depopulation, and forced migrations of many Bantu peoples in what is known as the *mfecane*, or "crushing" era. Likely brought on by a population explosion and perhaps fueled by increasing economic competition, the *mfecane* was marked by the rapid rise of sizable military states among the northern Nguni-speaking Bantu. Its result was a period of warfare and chaos; widespread depopulation by death and

Moshoeshwe, king and founder of Lesotho. Not all of the Bantu peoples followed the militaristic example of Shaka. Moshoeshwe, prince of a subtribe of the Sotho Bantus, fought off Zulu attacks and led his people to a mountain stronghold in southern Africa, where, through diplomacy and determination, he founded a small nation that has endured to the present. The kingdom became the British protectorate of Basutoland in 1868. In 1966 it achieved independence as the kingdom of Lesotho under Moshoeshwe's great-grandson, King Moshoeshwe II. *Courtesy of the Library of Congress.*

emigration; and the creation of new, multitribal, multilingual Bantu states in the regions of modern Zimbabwe, Mozambique, Malawi, Zambia, and Tanzania.

The Nguni warrior-king Dingiswayo formed the first of the new military states between about 1800 and 1818. The

most important state was formed by his successor, Shaka, leader of the Nguni-speaking Zulu nation and kingdom (ca. 1818–1828). Shaka's brutal military tactics led to the Zulu conquest of a vast dominion in south-eastern Africa and the virtual depopulation of some 15,000 square miles. Refugees from Shaka's "total war" zone fled north into Sotho-speaking Bantu territory or south to put increasing pressure on the southern Nguni peoples. Virtual chaos ensued, both north and south of Zululand.

The net result, beyond widespread suffering and death, was the creation of many diverse new states. Some people tried to imitate the unique military state of Shaka; others fled to mountainous areas and built up new, largely defensive states; others even went west into the Kalahari. The most famous new state was Lesotho, the Sotho kingdom of King Moshoeshwe, which survived as long as he lived (from the 1820s until 1870). Moshoeshwe defended his people from

Chronology

Southern Africa

ca. 1800–1818	Dingiswayo, Nguni Zulu king, forms new military state
ca. 1800–1825	The *mfecane* among the Bantu of southeastern Africa
1806	British take Cape Colony from the Dutch
ca. 1818–1828	Shaka's reign as head of the Nguni state; major warfare, destruction, and expansion
ca. 1825–1870	Sotho kingdom of King Moshoeshwe in Lesotho region
1835–1841	Great Trek of Boers into Natal and north onto the high veld beyond the Orange
1843	British annexation of Natal province
1852–1860	Creation of the Orange Free State and South African Republic

the Zulu and held off the Afrikaners, missionaries, and British until his death.

The new state-building spawned by the *mfecane* was nullified by Boer expansion and British annexation of the Natal province (1843). These developments stemmed from the **Great Trek** of Boer *voortrekers*, which took place between 1835 and 1841. This migration brought about 6,000 Afrikaners from the eastern Cape Colony northeastward into the more fertile regions of southern Africa, Natal, and especially the high veld above the Orange River. It resulted in the creation after 1850 of the Afrikaner republics of the Orange Free State between the Orange and Vaal Rivers, and the South African Republic north of the Vaal.

East and Central Africa

Farther north in East and East Central Africa, increasing external trade was the basis for the formation of several strong regional states. In the Lakes region, peoples such as the Nyamwezi to the east of Lake Tanganyika and the Baganda west of Lake Victoria gained regional power from as early as the late eighteenth century through trade with the Arab-Swahili eastern coast and the states of the eastern Congo to the west. The chief traffic in this east–west commerce across central Africa involved slaves, ivory, copper, and from the outside Indian cloth, firearms, and other manufactured goods.

West Africa

In West Africa the slave trade was only slowly curtailed. European demand for other products, however—notably palm oil and gum arabic—became more important by the 1820s. In the first half of the century *jihad* (holy struggle) movements of the Fulbe (or Fulani) and others shattered the stability of the western savannah and forest regions from modern Senegal and Ghana through southern Nigeria. Protracted wars and dislocation resulted in the rise of regional kingdoms, such as those of Asante and Dahomey (modern Benin), which flourished before succumbing to internal dissension and the colonial activities of Britain and France.

Islamic Reform Movements

The expansive vitality of Islam was one of the significant agents of change in sub-Saharan Africa before the European rush for colonies in the 1880s. It has remained a factor on the wider African scene ever since. In 1800 Islam was already a long-established tradition from West Africa across the Sudan to the Red Sea and along the East African coast, as well as over all of Arabic-speaking North Africa. It had long been widespread in the southern Sahara and northern Sahel and was common among merchant classes in various parts of West Africa. Islam was the law of the land in states such as the sultanate of Zanzibar on the eastern coast and the waning Funj sultanate on the Blue Nile in the eastern Sudan. Even so, the rural populace were still often semipagan, or wholly pagan, and even the ruling and urban elites of the towns were frequently only nominally Muslim.

The nineteenth century is notable for the number and strength of a series of militant Islamic revivalist and reform movements of *jihad*. Aimed at a more truly Muslim society and

Elephant Tusks, Congo. Ivory was a prized possession used for decorative purposes and jewelry. *National Museum of African Art/Smithsonian Institution.*

wider allegiance to Muslim values, these movements both fixed and spread Islam as a lasting part of the African scene. The West African *jihad* movements originated in the seventeenth century with the activities of militant, reformist Sufi brotherhoods that had penetrated West Africa from the north, especially through Mauritania. These movements eventually spread to other regions and flourished, especially in the eighteenth century among widely dispersed groups of people.

The most important *jihad* movement came at the beginning of the nineteenth century and was led by a Fulbe Muslim scholar from Hausa territory in the central Sahel. Usman Dan Fodio (1754–1817) was influenced by the reformist ideas that spread throughout the Muslim world in the eighteenth century, from India to Saudi Arabia and Africa. Shortly after 1804 he gathered an immense army of fervent supporters and conquered most of the Hausa lands of modern Nigeria, bringing an explicitly Islamic order to the area. Dan Fodio left behind an impressive sultanate centered on the new capital of Sokoto and governed by one of his sons, Muhammad Bello, until 1837. In his wake the Fulbe became the ruling class in the Hausa regions, and Islam spread into the countryside, where it still predominates. (See Document, "Usman Dan Fodio on Evil and Good Government.")

Usman Dan Fodio on Evil and Good Government

Document

Following in the tradition of the Wahhabis in Arabia and virtually all previous Islamic reform movements, Dan Fodio (1754–1817) stressed adherence to Muslim norms as expressed in the Shari'a, the Divine Law. In the two excerpts that follow, he enumerated some of the evils of the previous Hausa rulers and their "law," and then listed five principles of proper Islamic government.

◆ What does the first principle of good government, that "authority shall not be given to one who seeks it," mean? What abuses by government listed by Dan Fodio might be most appalling to the average Muslim? Why?

One of the ways of their government [that is, of the Hausa or Habe kings] is succession to the emirate by hereditary right and by force to the exclusion of consultation. And one of the ways of their government is the building of their sovereignty upon three things: the people's persons, their honour, and their possessions; and whomsoever they wish to kill or exile or violate his honour or devour his wealth they do so in pursuit of their lusts, without any right in the Shari'a. One of the ways of their government is their imposing on the people monies not laid down by the Shari'a, being those which they call janghali and kurdin ghari and kurdin salla. One of the ways of their governments is their intentionally eating whatever food they wish, whether it is religiously permitted or forbidden, and wearing whatever clothes they wish, whether religiously permitted or forbidden, and drinking what beverages [ta'am] they wish, whether religiously permitted or forbidden, and riding whatever riding beasts they wish, whether religiously permitted or forbidden, and taking what women they wish without marriage contract, and living in decorated palaces, whether religiously permitted or forbidden, and spreading soft (decorated) carpets as they wish, whether religiously permitted or forbidden. . . .

And I say—and help is with God—the foundations of government are five things: the first is that authority shall not be given to one who seeks it. The second is the necessity for consultation. The third is the abandoning of harshness. The fourth is justice. The fifth is good works. And as for its ministers, they are four. (The First) is a trustworthy wazir to wake the ruler if he sleeps, to make him see if he is blind, and to remind him if he forgets, and the greatest misfortune for the government and the subjects is that they should be denied honest wazirs. And among the conditions pertaining to the wazir is that he should be steadfast in compassion to the people, and merciful towards them. The second of the ministers of government is a judge whom the blame of a blamer cannot overtake concerning the affairs of God. The third is a chief of police who shall obtain justice for the weak from the strong. The fourth is a tax collector who shall discharge his duties and not oppress the subjects. . . .

From translation of Usman Dan Fodio's *Kitab al-Farq* by M. Hiskett, *Bulletin of the School of Oriental and African Studies*, London, 1960, Part 3, p. 558. Reprinted by permission of Oxford University Press, Oxford, Great Britain.

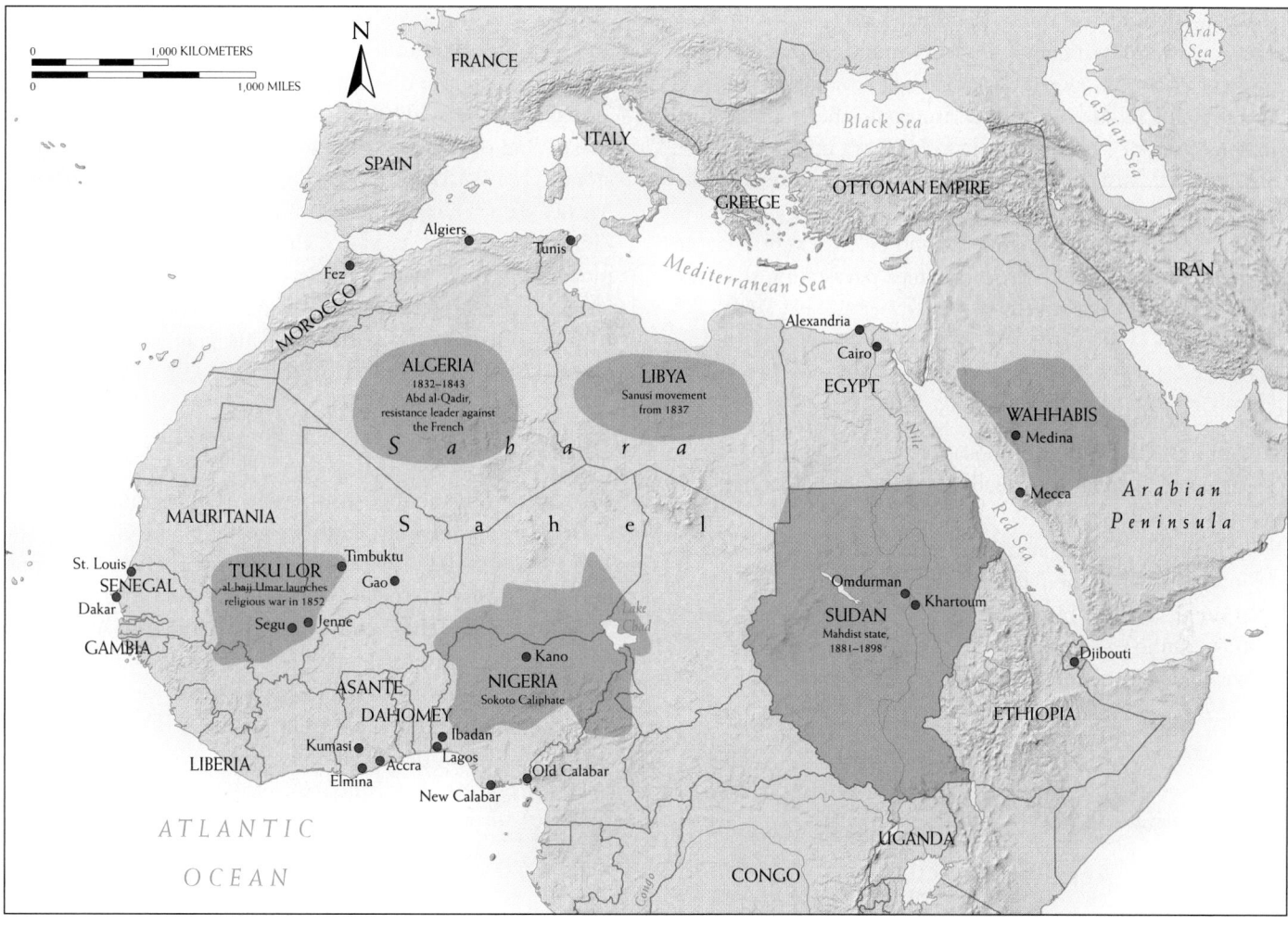

Map 27–3. **Islamic Reform Movements in Africa and Arabia in the Nineteenth Century.**

Other nineteenth-century reform movements had similar success both in gaining at least ephemeral political power and in spreading a revivalist, reformist Islamic message among the masses. Most notable alongside several West African *jihad* movements were the Sanusi movement of Libya and the eastern Sahara (after about 1840) and the famous Mahdist uprising of the eastern

Sudan (1880s and 1890s). The Libyan movement provided the focus for resistance to the Italian invasion of 1911. The Sudanese Muhammad Ahmad (1848–1885) condemned the widespread corruption of basic Islamic ideals and declared himself the awaited deliverer, or **Mahdi**, in 1881. He led the northern Sudan in rebellion against Ottoman-Egyptian control, defeating even the British forces from Egypt under Charles George Gordon (1833–1885) at Khartoum. His successor governed the Sudan until the British finally destroyed the young Islamic state in 1899 (see Map 27–3).

Chronology

Islamic Reform Movements

1810	Dan Fodio founds Islamic sultanate in lands of former Hausa states of northern and central Nigeria
after 1840	Sanusi movement in Libya and eastern Sahara
1881	Muhammad Ahmad declares himself the Mahdi (Sudan)

Increasing European Involvement: Exploration and Colonization

During the nineteenth century, the growing involvement of Europe in African affairs led to European domination of the continent's politics and economy. Before the mid-1800s, Europeans had rarely ventured beyond coastal areas, although the transatlantic slave trade had affected areas farther inland. This changed drastically as, first, trading companies and explorers, then missionaries and, finally, colonial troops and governments moved into Africa. Ironically, the gradual elimination of the slave trade (largely through the efforts of British abolitionists) was accompanied by increased European exploration and increased Western Christian missionary activity in Africa, which ushered in imperial and colonial ventures that had consequences perhaps even more devastating than the slave trade for Africa's future.

Explorers

The nineteenth-century European explorers—mostly English, French, and German—gradually uncovered for Westerners the great "secrets" of Africa: the sources and courses of the Niger, Nile, Zambezi, and Congo Rivers; natural wonders, such as Mount Kilimanjaro and Lake Tanganyika; and fabled places like Timbuktu. The history of European exploration is one of fortune hunting, self-promotion, violence, and mistakes as well as patience, perseverance, bravery, and dedication.

Henry Morton Stanley and His Servant Kalula. Stanley was a journalist-turned-explorer who "found" abolitionist-turned-explorer David Livingstone near Lake Tanganyika in 1871. Stanley claimed to have greeted him with, "Dr. Livingstone, I presume."

Many of the explorers were also accomplished authors and lecturers; tales of their adventures stimulated European interest in Africa and opened the way for traders, missionaries, and finally soldiers and governors from the Christian West. One of the greatest explorers was Dr. David Livingstone (1813–1873); among other things, he re-named Mosioa-Tunya ("smoke that thunders"), on what is now the Zimbabwe-Zambia border, "Victoria Falls," after Britain's monarch at the time. Livingstone was a Scottish Presbyterian missionary, physician, and abolitionist who was in love with and dedicated to Africa and its peoples as were few other Westerners before or after him.

Christian Missions

The latter nineteenth century saw a mounting influx of Christian missionaries, both Protestant and Catholic (by 1900, some 10,000). They vied—sometimes with one another, sometimes with Muslims—for the souls of Africans. Part of their motivation for coming to Africa was to eradicate the remaining slave trade, especially the trade in East Africa run by Arabs from Zanzibar.

The missionaries came to know the African peoples far better than did the explorers. Their accounts of Africa contained, to be sure, chauvinistic and misleading descriptions of the "degraded" state of African culture and religion, but they did bring real knowledge of and interest in Africa to Europe. Their translation work and mission schools also brought alphabetic culture and literacy to Africans. Although their settlements, often in remote areas, provided European governments with convenient pretexts for intervention in the affairs of African tribes and states, the missionaries themselves were more often idealists than opportunists and often worked in opposition to the colonial officers. Half of those who went into the tropical regions succumbed to indigenous diseases, such as malaria, yellow fever, and sleeping sickness. If they were often paternalistic and virtual instruments of the imperialism of their home countries, they also sought to provide Africans with medicine and education. Through the ideals of their faith, they provided Africans—sometimes intentionally, sometimes inadvertently—with a weapon of principle to use against their European exploiters. African Christian churches, for example, later played a leading role in the resistance to apartheid in South Africa, despite white Christian oppression and collusion with racism in that country and elsewhere in Africa (see Chapter 34). As this discussion suggests, the role of Christian missionaries in the European domination of Africa was not simple or by any means wholly positive.

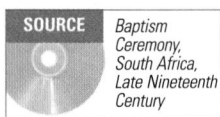

SOURCE   *Baptism Ceremony, South Africa, Late Nineteenth Century*

A Missionary Visit to a Zulu Kraal. The nineteenth-century European and American enthusiasm for working towards "the evangelization of the world in our time" found one of its major outlets in missionary efforts in Africa. *Courtesy of the Library of Congress.*

The Colonial "Scramble for Africa"

Before 1850 the only significant conflict between Europeans and Africans over European attempts to take African territory was in South Africa and Algeria. In South Africa, as we have noted, the Boers came into conflict with Bantu tribes after leaving the British-ruled Cape Colony on their Great Trek to find new lands. The French invaded Algeria in 1830, settled Europeans on choice farmlands, and fought native resistance fighters. Over most of the continent, however, the European presence was felt with real force only from the 1880s. Yet by World War I virtually all of Africa (Ethiopia and Liberia were the only exceptions) was divided into a patchwork of large territories ruled by European colonial administrations (see Map 27–4).

This foreign takeover of Africa was supported by mounting European popular and commercial interest fueled by the publicity given African exploration and missionary work. The European desire for the industrial markets and natural resources of Africa, together with intra-European competition for power and prestige, pushed one European state after another to claim whatever segments of Africa they could (see Chapter 29).

The superior economic, technological, and military power the West commanded made this wholesale takeover possible. In particular, technical expertise gave Europeans access to the interior of the continent in the late nineteenth century. Except for the Nile and the Niger, all the great African rivers have impassable waterfalls only a short way inland from the sea, where the coastal plains rise sharply to the largely highland interior. European-built steamboats above the falls and railroads around them (or where no navigable rivers ran) permitted new levels of commercial and colonial exploitation.

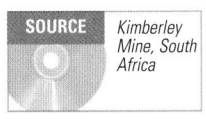

SOURCE *Kimberley Mine, South Africa*

Men Sorting Diamonds, Kimberley, South Africa. Diamond mining in South Africa took off in the late 1860s. By 1880 Kimberley, the biggest mine in the region, had 30,000 people, second only to Cape Town. Whites such as these diamond sorters, monopolized the well-paid skilled jobs.

Map Exploration

To explore this map further, go to http://www.prenhall.com/craig_maps

SPANISH MOROCCO

ALGERIA   TUNISIA   *Mediterranean Sea*   Suez Canal   OTTOMAN EMPIRE   PERSIA

MOROCCO

LIBYA   EGYPT

RIO DE ORO

FRENCH WEST AFRICA   *Red Sea*   ARABIA

Nile R.

SENEGAL
GAMBIA
PORT. GUINEA   DAHOMEY   *Niger R.*   ERITREA   FRENCH SOMALILAND

SIERRA LEONE   NIGERIA   ANGLO-EGYPTIAN SUDAN   ETHIOPIA
BRITISH SOMALILAND

LIBERIA

IVORY COAST   GOLD COAST   TOGO   RIO MUNI   CAMEROON   SOMALIA

GABON   FRENCH EQUATORIAL AFRICA   *Congo R.*   BRITISH EAST AFRICA

CABINDA   BELGIAN CONGO   *L. Victoria*   INDIAN OCEAN

ATLANTIC   GERMAN EAST AFRICA   PEMBA

OCEAN   *L. Tanganyika*   ZANZIBAR

L. Nyasa

ANGOLA

RHODESIA   MOZAMBIQUE   MADAGASCAR

Zambezi R.

GERMAN SOUTHWEST AFRICA   BECHUANALAND   TRANSVAAL

UNION OF SOUTH AFRICA   NATAL

ORANGE FREE STATE

Legend:
- British
- French
- German
- Portuguese
- Italian
- Belgian
- Spanish
- Independent State

1,200 MILES

1,200 KILOMETERS

Map 27–4. Partition of Africa, 1880–1914. By 1914 the only countries in Africa that remained independent were Liberia and Ethiopia. The occupying powers included most large European states.

Great Britain and France were the vanguard of the European nations that sought to include African lands in their imperial domains. The British had the largest involvement. On one axis, it ranged from South Africa (begun when they took the Cape Colony from the Dutch in 1795) to their effective **protectorate** in Egypt (from 1882). On another axis, it extended from trading interests in West Africa to colonies such as Sierra Leone and Gambia, set up in 1807, to protectorate rule, as in the Niger districts after 1885, and to a Zanzibar-based sphere of influence in East Africa in the 1870s (and finally a protectorate for Zanzibar in 1890).

The British long resisted African colonial involvement and then chose "indirect" as preferable to "direct" colonial administration. Their rule was only slightly more enlightened than that of the French, who had earlier carved out a colonial empire under their direct control. The French had long had government-supported trading outposts in Senegal and other parts of West Africa. After a bitter struggle (1830–1847) they conquered Algeria, creating the first major European colony in Africa. Tunisia and the Ivory Coast became French protectorates in the 1880s, Dahomey was bloodily annexed in 1894, and French Equatorial Africa was proclaimed in 1910.

Beginning in the mid-1880s the major European powers sought mutual agreement to their claims on particular segments of Africa. Leopold II of Belgium (r. 1865–1909) and Otto von Bismarck (1815–1898) in Germany established their own claims to parts of Africa. France and England set about consolidating their African interests. Italy, too, eventually took African colonial territory in Eritrea, Somaliland, and Libya, but Ethiopia used its newly modernized army to defeat an Italian invasion in 1896. Italy finally conquered Ethiopia in 1935. The **scramble for Africa** was largely over by the outbreak of World War I. After the war Germany lost its African possessions to other colonial powers. Europe's colonies in Africa did not gain independence until the changes in the worldwide balance of power and in attitudes towards colonial rule that followed World War II (see Chapter 34).

Patterns in European Colonial Rule and African Resistance

European colonial rule in Africa is one of the uglier chapters of modern history. If German, French, Belgian, Portuguese, and Boer rule were notoriously brutal and produced worse atrocities, Britain also had its share of misrule

and exploitation. The paternalistic attitudes of late-nineteenth-century Europe and America amounted in the end to sheer racism when applied in Africa. The regions with large-scale white settlement produced the worst exploitation at the expense of vastly greater native populations. Everywhere, white minorities exercised disproportionate power over the lives of black or brown majorities. Among the worst legacies of the European presence was the white racist state of modern South Africa, which did not end until 1994. No Western nation can have a clear conscience about its involvement in Africa.

African states were not, of course, simply passive objects of European manipulation and conquest. Many astute native rulers sought, by diplomacy, trade, and warfare, to use the European presence to their own advantage. The Bagandan king Mutesa in the 1870s (in what is today Uganda), is an example of an African ruler who benefited, at least for a while, from European interest in his territory. Direct armed resistance was always (even for Ethiopia) doomed because of European technological superiority. Nevertheless, such resistance was widespread and continued into the twentieth century in many places. In the end, colonial rule was the product of ongoing conflict and negotiation between European desires, backed up by technological superiority, and the enduring power "on the ground" of African individuals and institutions.

British taxpayers were reluctant to fund colonial ventures. British colonial officials attempted to make a virtue of necessity; since they could afford to pay the salaries of only

Mutesa of Buganda and His Court. Noted for his cunning and diplomatic skill and for his autocratic and often cruel conduct, Mutesa was one of the few African rulers who was able to maintain a powerful and successful army and court, which enabled him to deal effectively with Egyptian and British efforts to encroach on his sphere of influence. *Brown Brothers.*

Oginga Odinga on European Influences   Document

Oginga Odinga (ca. 1911–1994) was an early Kenyan nationalist leader. After Kenya's independence in 1963, he opposed many of President Jomo Kenyatta's policies. When he published his biography in 1967, he titled the book *Not Yet Uhuru*; "Uhuru" is a Swahili word meaning "freedom" or "independence." In his book, Odinga argues that leaders of Kenya's post-colonial government emphasized the creating of a new African elite (themselves) rather than serving the masses of Africans who worked for independence.

Odinga was born into a leading family of the Luo tribe. He grew up in western Kenya, near Lake Victoria. These are his recollections of his first experiences with Europeans.

◆ What seems to have made the strongest impression on Odinga? What overall attitude does Odinga seem to have towards Europeans? What can you infer from this passage about Luo culture?

We connected Whites and Government with five main things. There were the inoculations against the plague from which the children ran in fear. There were the tax collections. There was the order to the villagers to work on the roads. There were clothes, *kanzu*, the long robes copied from Arab garb at the coast, given free to the chiefs and elders to wear to encourage others in the tribe to clothe themselves in modern dress. There were the schools, which came later, and to which, in the beginning, only orphans, foster children, poor nieces and nephews and never the favourite sons were sent, for the villagers distrusted the pressure on them to send their children out of the home and away from herding the animals; and the more alert objected to the way the Christian missions taught 'This custom (yours) is bad, and this (ours) is good', for they could see that the children at the missions would grow up to despise Luo ways. . . .

a very small contingent of British administrators, they put British men at the top of existing African political structures, and ruled through indigenous leaders. Often, in the early days of colonial rule, the British would make a show of removing a few high-profile, independent-minded indigenous leaders. In Uganda, for example, the British deposed Mutesa's successor and sent him into exile. The remaining leaders—"native chiefs," in colonial parlance—and their British supervisors would then engage in a delicate balancing act: the chiefs and the colonists came to depend on each other for power and legitimacy, but neither the chiefs nor the colonists could command perfect loyalty from their subjects.

Frederick Lugard, whose British parents were missionaries in India, had been an explorer, entrepreneur, and military leader in various parts of Africa before being appointed high commissioner of Northern Nigeria in 1900. During his tenure there, he formalized this British style of colonial administration and named it, appropriately enough, **indirect rule**.

Other European powers generally ruled their colonies directly: they were willing to bankroll the placement of greater numbers of Europeans in the colonies themselves, and they hired local Africans to work under them within European-style political structures. The French were the most explicit about their intentions, claiming that their goal

was for Africans to "evolve"—through education, imitation, assimilation (and, perhaps, over many generations)—into French citizens. In practice, however, French colonial officials were loathe to share the prestige of citizenship.

Another important variation in the African colonial experience is between settler and non-settler colonies. Colonies with relatively high settler populations tended to be places where the environment could support plantation-style, export-oriented agriculture, and where the diseases to which Europeans were most susceptible were less prevalent. Settler colonies included Kenya, Mozambique, Rhodesia (now Zimbabwe), South Africa, and Algeria.[5]

Africans resisted European domination in all its guises, throughout the continent. Often the most efficient way for Africans to resist was to simply disengage, attempting to avoid payment of colonial taxes or participation in forced labor schemes. (See Document, "Oginga Odinga on European Influences.") Riots, marches, and rebellions, however, were more frequent and forceful than colonial administrators wanted to admit, and accounts of such events were some-

---

[5] See E. Gilbert & J. T. Reynolds, *Africa in World History* (Upper Saddle River, NJ: Pearson Prentice Hall, 2004) chapter 15 for more detailed coverage.

Mau Mau freedom fighters in a Kenyan hideout, around 1950.

mon European tongue and through the assimilation of European thought and culture by a growing educated native elite. These elites were typically educated in mission schools and sometimes foreign universities. Their ranks gradually increased in the early twentieth century. From them came the leaders of Africa's nationalist movements between the two world wars and of Africa's new independent nations after World War II.

Mass political parties emerged in the postwar period, including the Convention People's Party in the Gold Coast (Ghana) under Kwame Nkrumah (1909–1972), and the African Democratic Assembly that drew members from a number of French West African colonies under the leadership of Félix Houphouët-Boigny (1905–1993), who became the first president of the Ivory Coast.

It is important to note, however, a countervailing trend, which was the emergence of movements seeking to transcend both colonial boundaries and ethnic or "tribal" divisions and foster an inclusive African identity. One example is **Negritude**, a literary and intellectual movement to celebrate all aspects of African civilization that was exemplified by the writings of

times suppressed during the colonial era. Resistance tended to be more overt and sustained in settler colonies, where Africans and Europeans were most likely to come into direct contact. In places where large swaths of fertile land had been seized by Europeans—the highlands of Kenya, for example—resistance could become violent and chronic, as in the **Mau Mau** uprising that began as a protest against land alienation among Kenya's Kikuyu people. Through the course of the 1950s, tens of thousands of Kenyans were killed, and the British imprisoned many more suspected insurgents and sympathizers in detention camps, while the Mau Mau revolt became a nationalist insurgency.[6]

The Rise of African Nationalism

The most important factor in the end of the European colonial period was the rise of nationalism across Africa, especially after World War I. However little the colonial partition of Africa reflected native linguistic, racial, or cultural divisions, it still influenced both nationalist movements and the eventual shape of African states. The "national" consciousness of the diverse peoples of a given colonial unit was fueled by common opposition to foreign rule. It was also fed by the use of a com-

Champion of Negritude, Leopold Senghor during a visit to France in 1949. He later became president of Senegal.

[6] The history of Mau Mau is still contested. British administrators deliberately destroyed much of the documentary evidence. For recent attempts to reconstruct events and their meanings, see D. Anderson, *Histories of the Hanged: The Dirty War in Kenya and the End of Empire* (New York: W.W. Norton &Co., 2005), and C. Elkins, *Imperial Reckoning: The Untold Story of Britain's Gulag in Kenya* (New York: Henry Holt & Co., 2004).

Leopold Senghor (1906–2001), who later became the first president of Senegal.

The most severe indigenous critiques of the Western treatment of Africa often drew on Western religious and political ideals. The African leaders of the twentieth century learned well from the West and used their learning to help end Western domination. The process culminated in the creation of more than forty self-governing African nations after 1945 (see Chapter 34). African independence movements were based on modern nationalist models from Europe and America rather than ancient ones derived from native tradition. The nationalist and independence movements typically sought to eject the colonial intruders and not to return to an earlier status quo. Their aim was to take over and to run for themselves the Western institutions that colonialism had introduced. This legacy from the West is still visible today.

Summary

Western Encroachment. The century and a half that began in 1800 was a bleak one for the Indian subcontinent, Africa, and the Islamic societies. For centuries there had been a rough balance in material and intellectual culture, commerce, and political stability among the major cultural

regions of the world. Suddenly, over 150 years, the European sector of the global community came to dominate the rest of the world.

The Middle East, Africa, Iran, Central Asia, India, and Indonesia-Malaysia, along with Central and South America—what is today referred to as "the Third World" of "developing nations"—were most drastically affected by European imperialism and colonialism. Regardless of indigenous developments in these regions, the decisive development of this era was unprecedented domination by a single segment of the global community. Western dominance, sometimes positive, often sordid and ugly, was by no means synonymous with "progress," as Westerners have often liked to think. Nevertheless, it has been a hallmark of the "modern" age in most of Asia, Africa, and South America.

Indigenous Reactions. The vitality of so many of the cultures and traditions that bore the brunt of the Western onslaught has been striking. Arab, Iranian, Indian, African, and other encounters with Western material and intellectual domination produced different responses and initiatives. These have borne full fruit in political, economic, and intellectual independence only since 1945; however, most began much earlier, some even well before 1800. For example, modern Islamic reform and resurgence began in the eighteenth century, although it has become a major global factor

INTERPRETING THE PAST

The Indian Encounter with Great Britain in the Nineteenth Century

Source from Chapter 27

1. Macaulay Writes on Indian Education (1835), page 851

Sources from MyHistoryLab/ PrimarySource DVD-ROM

1. Dadabhai Naoroji, *The Benefits of British Rule in India* (1871)
2. Amrita Lal Roy, *English Rule in India* (1886)

By the mid–nineteenth century Britain dominated India's economy and politics and was actively intervening in its cultural and social life. British policies focused on expanding settled

agriculture and commodity production, clearing land, and forced resettlement of peasants. Another British initiative encouraged commercial logging on a large scale, which resulted in deforestation and ecological destruction across large areas of the subcontinent. While reaping economic rewards from India as a result of high taxes levied for "protection," the British also introduced modern technological innovations such as railroads and telegraphs, along with their educational system. These progressive innovations have spurred an active debate about the relative value of Western technology and education compared to the poverty, famine, and other problems caused by British encroachment in almost every facet of India's economy, life, and culture.

The first document is authored by Thomas Babington Macaulay. He argues for English-language study in Indian schools as a way to improve and modernize society. Macaulay was an English politician and historian who served on the Supreme Council of India in the 1830s. The second primary source is written by Dadabhai Naoroji, an Indian scholar, only in recent years. Indian national consciousness also developed from the eighteenth century onward in response to British domination, even though it led to national union and independence only after World War II.

One result of the imperial-colonial experience almost everywhere has been the sharpening of cultural self-consciousness and self-confidence among those peoples most negatively affected by Western dominance. The imperial-colonial experiences of the Third World nations included both misery and reversal, and transition to positive development and resurgence. Nonetheless, it is important to recognize that many of the economic, educational, and demographic problems that plague former colonies trace their origins to colonial policies.

Review Questions

1. What does the "impact of modernity" mean to traditional Afro-Asian-Indian cultures? What patterns of reaction can you discern? Why was the West able to impose itself on these cultures?

2. Why was India called the "jewel in the crown" of the British Empire? How did the British gain control of India? What policies did they follow in government and economics?

3. What kinds of political activism against British rule can you cite from Indian history after 1800? What kinds of success or failure did they have?

4. How was the Islamic world internally divided after 1800? How did those divisions influence the coming of European powers?

5. How did nationalism affect European control in south Asia, Africa, and the Middle East? How and when did its various manifestations arise? Were there any successful "national states" from these regions before 1945?

6. Discuss the new African states and power centers of sub-Saharan Africa before 1870. Why did no modern nation-state develop in the area? How did Islam affect the development of new entities? What role did trade play?

7. What were Europeans' three main interests in Africa? Why were Africans unable to stop the "scramble for Africa"?

8. What factors influenced Africans' experience of colonial rule in different regions?

9. What was the role of African nationalism in resisting foreign control?

Key Terms

bazaari (p. 858)	**Negritude** (p. 873)
cantonments (p. 852)	**pan-Islamism** (p. 861)
Great Trek (p. 865)	**protectorate** (p. 871)
indirect rule (p. 872)	**raj** (p. 849)
Mau Mau (p. 873)	**scramble for Africa** (p. 871)
Mahdi (p. 867)	**Tanzimat** (p. 860)
mfecane (p. 864)	**Wahhabis** (p. 857)
mujtahid (p. 858)	

businessman, and political leader who actively sought a measure of political and economic reform of the colonial system in the decades after 1860. Naoroji's essay argues for a continuation of British rule, couched in positive and even-handed terms. The third source is by Amrita Lal Roy, whose "English Rule in India" was published in the *North American Review*, the oldest literary journal in the United States and an influential voice for reform.

Questions

How does Macaulay support his judgment that English should be the language taught in Indian schools? Is his argument objective or subjective?

What main points do Naoroji and Roy employ in their arguments for and against British rule? What are the areas of agreement between the two articles? Disagreement?

Do some online research to find out more about the authors of these three source documents. How might their positions and backgrounds influence their views?

Note: To learn more about the topics in this chapter, please turn to the Suggested Readings at the end of the book. For additional sources related to this chapter please see the Primary Source DVD at the back of this text or MyHistoryLab.

The Islamic tradition is one of the youngest major world religions. Since its inception during the lifetime of the Prophet Muhammad (632 B.C.E.) it has grown, like the Christian and Buddhist traditions, into a worldwide community not limited by national boundaries or defined in racial or ethnic terms. It began among the Arabs but spread widely. Islam's historical heartlands are those Arabic-, Turkic-, and Persian-speaking lands of the Near East between Egypt and Afghanistan. However, today more than half of its faithful live in Asia east of Karachi, Pakistan; and more Muslims live in sub-Saharan Africa than in all of the Arab lands. There are also growing Muslim minorities in the United States and Europe.

The central vision of Islam is a just and peaceful society where people can freely worship God. It focuses on a human community of worshipers who recognize the absolute sovereignty and oneness of God and strive to do God's will. Muslims believe that divine will is found first in god's revealed word, the Qur'an; then as elaborated and specified in the actions and words of his final prophet, Muhammad; and finally as interpreted and extended in the scriptural exegesis and legal traditions of the Muslim community over the past thirteen and a half centuries.

The Muslim vision thus centers on one God who has guided humankind throughout history by means of prophets or apostles and repeated revelations. God is the Creator of all, and in the end all will return to God. God's majesty would seem to make him a distant, threatening deity of absolute justice; there is such an element in the Muslim understanding of the wide chasm between the human and the Divine. Still, there is an immanent as well as a transcendent side to the Divine in the Muslim view. Indeed, Muslims have given us some of the greatest images of God's closeness to his faithful worshiper, images that have a special place in the thought of the Muslim mystics, who are known as *Sufis* (taken originally from *suf*, "wool," because of the early Muslim ascetics' use of simple wool dress).

Muslims understand God's word in the Qur'an and the elaboration of that word by tradition to be a complete prescription for human life. Thus Islamic law is not law in the Western sense of civil, criminal, or international systems. Rather, it is a comprehensive set of standards for the moral, ritual, social, political, economic, aesthetic, and even hygienic and dietary dimensions of life. By being faithful to God's law the Muslim hopes to gain salvation on the Last Day, when human history shall end and all of God's creatures who have ever lived will be resurrected and called to account for their thoughts and actions during their lives on earth. Some will be saved, but others will be eternally damned.

Thus *Islam*, which means "submission [to God]," has been given as a name to the religiously defined system of life that Muslims have sought to institute wherever they have lived. Muslims have striven to organize their societies and political realities around the ideals represented in the traditional picture of the Prophet's community in Medina and Mecca. This approach necessitated compromise in which power was given to temporal rulers and accepted by Muslim religious leaders as long as those rulers protected God's Law, the *Shari'ah*. The ideal of a single international Muslim community, or *Umma*, has never fully been realized politically, but it remains an ideal.

Many movements of reform over the centuries have called for greater adherence to rigorist interpretations of Islamic law and greater dominance of piety and religious values in sociopolitical as well as individual life. The most famous of these movements, that of the Wahhabis in eighteenth-century Arabia, remains influential in much of the Muslim world, including Saudi Arabia. The Wahhabis' puritanical zeal in fighting what they consider "innovations" in many regional Islamic contexts, such as Shi'ism, Sufi traditions, and all more liberal forms of Islamic practice, continues to the present day. Wahhabism has had considerable success in the past half century and was apparently

Muhammad and Ali. This sixteenth-century Persian miniature shows the prophet Muhammad and his kinsman Ali purifying the Ka'ba in Mecca of pagan idols. The Ka'ba is the geographical point towards which all Muslims face when performing ritual prayer. *Art Resource/Bildarchiv Preussischer Kulturbesitz.*

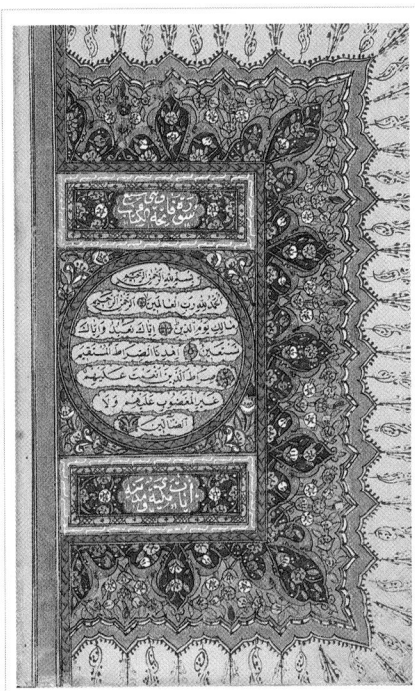

The Qur'an's First Chapter. This nineteenth-century hand-copied Koran in Arabic is open to the *Fatiha*, the opening chapter of Islam's holy book. In seven very short verses, the Fatiha sums up man's relation to God in prayer. The first verse, "In the name of God, Most Gracious, Most Merciful," is said out loud by Muslims at the beginning of every major action they undertake each day. *Koran. Hand-copied in Arabic by Kohazadeh Ahmad Rashid Safi. Decorated by Adham Gharbaldesh at Balawi, Probably Persian, nineteenth century. African and Middle Eastern Division, Library of Congress*

Muslim School Children in Malaysia, 1997. Though most non-Muslims associate Islam with the Middle East, Islam has deep roots in Southeast Asia. About 212 million Muslims live in Indonesia, making it the most populous Muslim country in the world.

the spawning ground of the extremist views of Osama bin Laden's al-Qa'ida terrorist movement, which is largely Arab in its ethnic makeup and which has turned from fighting Muslim states it regards as un-Islamic to opposing what it considers the U.S. intrusion into the Arab Islamic world and its unpopular foreign policy in the region. While meainstream Muslims everywhere reject bin Laden's extremism, Wahhabi zealotry has adherents on the fringes of Islamic communities around the world. In this respect, Islam is not unlike Christianity, Judaism, Hinduism, or other major religions, each of which has over its history spawned literalists, zealots, and extremists, who have urged violence in the name of their version of their parent faith.

The major sectarian, or minority, groups among Muslims are those of the Shi'ites, who have held out for an ideal of a temporal ruler who is also the spiritual heir of Muhammad and God's designated deputy on earth. Most Shi'ites, notably those of Iran, hold that after eleven designated blood descendants of the prophets had each failed to be recognized by the majority of Muslims as the rightful leader, or *Imam*, the twelfth disappeared and remains to this day physically absent from the world, although not dead. He will come again at the end of time to vindicate his faithful followers.

Muslim piety takes many forms. The common duties of Muslims are central for Muslims everywhere: faith in God and trust in his Prophet; regular performance of ritual worship (*Salat*); fasting during daylight hours every day in Ramadan (the ninth month of the lunar year); giving one's wealth to the needy (*zakat*); and at least once in a lifetime, if able, making the pilgrimage to Mecca and its environs (*Hajj*). Other more regional or popular, but ubiquitous, practices are also important. Celebration of the Prophet's birthday indicates the exalted popular status of Muhammad, even though any divine status for him is strongly rejected theologically. Recitation of the Qur'an permeates all Muslim practice, from daily worship to celebrations of all kinds. Visitation of saints' tombs is a prominent form of popular devotion. Sufi chanting or even ecstatic dancing are also practiced by Muslims around the world.

Muslims vary enormously in their physical environment, language, ethnic background, and cultural allegiances. What binds them now as in the past are not political allegiances but religious affinities and a shared heritage of religious faith and culture. How these allegiances and sensibilities will fare in the face of global challenges will be an important factor in shaping the world of the twenty-first century.

◆ **How has the ideal of a single, international Muslim community influenced Islamic history? World history?**

◆ **What impact have reform movements had on Islam since its inception? What impact do they have today?**

28

Modern East Asia

ROM THE MID–NINETEENTH CENTURY, THE West was the expanding, aggressive, imperialistic force in world history. Its industrial goods and gunboats reached every part of the globe. It believed in free trade and had the military might to impose it on others. It was the trigger for change throughout the world. But the response to the Western impact depended on the internal array of forces in each country. In fact, the "response to the West" was only one small, though vital, part of the history of each country. Japan and China were both relatively successful in their responses, for although each was subject to "unequal treaties," neither became a colony.

The two countries were also similar in that their governing elites were educated in Confucianism. Unlike the otherworldly religions of Buddhism, Islam, or Christianity, Confucianism was just secular enough to crumble in the face of the more powerful secularism of nineteenth-century science and the doctrines associated with it. In both Japan and China, although much more rapidly in Japan, the leading intellectuals abandoned Confucianism in

Woodblock, Munakata Shikō, 1945. In modern Japan, woodblock prints are divided between modernists who, initially at least, took their inspiration from the West, and those who went through a "Western phase" and then built on the native folk art tradition. Among the latter, the greatest was Munakata Shikō (1903–1975). Munakata was born in Aomori Prefecture, a sparsely populated area in north-ernmost Honshu known for its long bitter winters, rocky soil, and strong folk religion tradition. At age 24 Munakata went to Tokyo, where for two years he experimented with oils, but then he switched to print-making. In 1937, at age 34, he took up the Buddhist subjects for which he is best known. His most famous prints are sensuous Buddhist deities and Bodhisattvas such as the one depicted here.

Modern East Asia

East Asia

From the late nineteenth century most countries wanted to become modern. They coveted the wealth and power of the West. But what does it mean to be modern?

Three stages may be noted in Japan's development as the world's first and most advanced non-Western modernizer: preconditions, Westernization, and assimilation.

Even before contact with the modern West, Japan had some of the preconditions needed for industrialization: a fairly literate people, an ethic of duty and hard work, a market economy, secular thought, some bureaucracy, and a protonationalism. In sum, an adequate base for an "external modernization."

Building on these preconditions, Japan Westernized after 1868, adopting a range of new institutions: post offices, banks, custom houses, hospitals, police forces, joint stock companies, universities with faculties of science and engineering, and so on. Japanese thinkers brought in modern ideas and values:

Spencer and Guizot, Turgenev and Tolstoy, Adam Smith and Marx. Japanese writers began experimenting with new forms.

Little by little Japan *assimilated* what it had borrowed. The *zaibatsu* combines were modern, with the most recent technologies, yet their business organizations were unlike those of the West. The spare beauty of traditional architecture was transferred to the glass, steel, concrete, and stone of the modern. A new literature, completely Japanese yet also completely modern, appeared.

Japan may serve as a useful model in that its modernization—as analyzed in terms of the above three stages—has gone further than that in any other non-Western country. We note the absence in India or the Islamic world of comparable preconditions. After the end of colonialism, countries in these areas had to create the necessary preconditions even as they borrowed the new technologies. The difficulty explains their limited success. In Africa the dearth of preconditions was even more pronounced.

China, like Japan but unlike countries of South Asia, the Middle East, or Africa, had many of the necessary favor of Western secular doctrines. To be sure, many Confucian values, deeply embedded in the societies, survived the philosophies of which they had once been a part. In fact, one of the "breakdown products" of the Confucian sociopolitical identity was a strong new nationalism in both China and Japan.

But there the similarities end. In most other respects, modern Japan and China could hardly be more different. Perhaps the difference was only to be expected, given the pattern of recurrent dynasties in China's premodern history and of feudal evolution in Japan's.

The coming of Commodore Matthew Perry (1794–1858) in 1853–1854 precipitated a rapid political change in Japan. Within fifteen years the old Tokugawa regime had collapsed, and the Japan-

ese were building a modern state. Economic growth followed. By 1900 Japan had defeated China and within five years would defeat tsarist Russia in war. Sustained economic growth continued during the early twentieth century. After the Great Depression, Japan, like Italy and Germany, became an aggressive and militarized state and was eventually defeated in World War II. But after the war Japan reemerged more stable, more productive, and with a stronger parliamentary government than before.

The Chinese polity, in contrast, easily weathered the Opium War (1839–1842), an event of considerably greater magnitude than Perry's visit to Japan. The hold of tradition in China was remarkable, as was the effectiveness of traditional remedies in dealing with political ills. Only in its preconditions—they might be called East Asian preconditions—in place. But when it came to Westernization, the government by Confucian literati that had long been China's outstanding asset became its greatest liability. It took decades to topple the dynasty and to advance beyond Confucian ideas.

Then, in the maelstrom of the May Fourth Movement, intellectual change occurred at a furious pace, but new doctrines alone could not provide a stable polity. Nationalism emerged as the common denominator of Chinese thought. The nationalists (or Guomindang) drew on it at the Huangpu Academy, during the march north, and in the Nanjing government. But other groups could also appeal to it. The Chinese Communists won out by 1949.

It is beguiling to view the CCP cadres as a new class of literati operating the machinery of a monolithic, centralized state, with the teachings of Marx and Lenin replacing those of Confucius, and local party organization replacing the Confucian gentry. But this interpretation is too simple. Communism stressed science, materialism, and class conflict. It broke with the Chinese past.

Communism itself was also modified in China. Marx had predicted that socialist revolutions would break out in advanced economies where the contradictions of capitalism were sharpest. Lenin had shifted the emphasis from spontaneous revolutions by workers to the small but disciplined revolutionary party, the vanguard of the proletariat. He thereby changed communism into what it has been ever since: a movement capable of seizing power only in backward nations. At the level of doctrine, Mao Zedong modified Lenin's ideas only slightly—by theorizing that "progressive" peasants were a part of the proletariat. But he went beyond this theory in practice, virtually ignoring city workers while relying on China's villages for recruits for his armies, who were then indoctrinated using Leninist techniques.

Yet, the organizational techniques that were so effective in creating a party and army would prove less so for economic development. It soon became clear that mass mobilization was no substitute for individual incentives.

Focus Questions

◆ Why are the preconditions necessary for modernization along Western lines? Why are they so important?

◆ Compare and contrast the process of modernization in Japan and China in the twentieth century. Which country was more successful? Why?

relations with the Western powers did traditional patterns not work. In one sense the strength of tradition was China's weakness, for it took seventy years after the Opium War to overthrow the dynasty. Only then were Chinese able to begin the modernization that Japanese had started in 1868, and even then they were unsuccessful. Along with warlordism and the other problems that had accompanied the dissolution of past dynasties, new ills arose from the rending of the very fabric of the dynastic pattern. To these was added the unprecedented experience of being confronted by nations more powerful than itself. That China in some sense "failed" during this modern century is not a Western view imposed on China; it is the view the Chinese themselves hold. ▪

MODERN CHINA (1839–1949)

China's modern century was not the century in which it became modern as much as it was the century in which it encountered the modern West. Its first phase, from the Opium War to the fall of the Qing or Manchu dynasty (1912), was remarkably little affected by Western impact. Indeed, it was only during the decade before 1912 that the Confucian tradition began to be discarded in favor of new ideas from the West. The second phase of China's modern history, from 1912 to the establishment of a communist state in 1949, was a time of turmoil and suffering. The fighting incidental to the collapse of the dynasty gave way to decades of warlord rule; to partial military unification and continual military campaigns; to war with Japan; and then, while most countries were returning to peace, to four bitter years of civil war.

Close of Manchu Rule

The Opium War

The eighteenth-century three-country trade—British goods to India, Indian cotton to China, and Chinese tea to Britain—was in China's favor. The silver flowing into China spurred the monetization of Chinese markets. Then the British replaced cotton with Indian opium. By the 1820s the balance of trade was reversed, and silver began to flow out of China.

A crisis arose in the 1830s when the British East India Company lost its monopoly on British trade with China. The opium trade became wide open. To check the evil of opium and outflow of specie, the Chinese government banned opium in 1836, closing the dens where it was smoked and executing Chinese dealers. In 1839 the government sent Imperial Commissioner Lin Zexu (1785–1850) to Guangzhou (Canton) to superintend the ban. He continued the crackdown on Chinese dealers and destroyed over 20,000 chests—a six-month supply—of opium belonging to foreign merchants. This action led to a confrontation between the Chinese and the British. (See Document, "Commissioner Lin Urges Morality on Queen Victoria.")

War broke out in November 1839 when Chinese war junks clashed with a British merchantman. The following June sixteen British warships arrived at Guangzhou, and for the next two years the British bombarded forts, fought battles, seized cities, and attempted negotiations. The Chinese troops, with their antiquated weapons and old-style cannon, were ineffective. The war was finally ended in August 1842 by the Treaty of Nanjing, the first of the "unequal treaties."

The treaty not only ended the "Canton system," which restricted Western trade, but also provided Britain with a superb deep-water port at Hong Kong, a huge indemnity, and

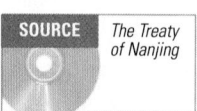 **SOURCE** *The Treaty of Nanjing*

the opening of five ports: Guangzhou, Shanghai, Xiamen (Amoy), Ningbo, and Fuzhou. British merchants and their families could reside in the ports and engage in trade; Britain could appoint a consul for each city; and British residents gained extraterritoriality, under which they were subject to British and not Chinese law. The treaty also contained a "most-favored-nation" clause, a provision that any further rights gained by any other nation would automatically accrue to Britain as well. The treaty with Britain was followed in 1844 by similar treaties with the United States and France. The American treaty permitted churches in treaty ports, and the French treaty permitted the propagation of Catholicism.

After the signing of the treaties, Chinese imports of opium rose from 30,000 chests to 87,000 in 1879. Thereafter, imports declined to 50,000 chests in 1906, and ended during World War I. But other kinds of trade did not grow as much as had been hoped, and Western merchants blamed the lack of growth on artificial restraints imposed by Chinese officials. They also complained that, despite the treaties, Guangzhou remained closed to trade. The Chinese authorities, for their part, were incensed by the export of coolies to

The Opium War, 1840. Armed Chinese junks were no match for British warships. The war ended in 1842 with the Treaty of Nanjing.

Commissioner Lin Urges Morality on Queen Victoria

Document

In 1839 the British in China argued for free trade and protection for the legal rights of their citizens. The Chinese position was that behind such lofty arguments, the British were pushing opium.

◆ What does this document suggest about the Qing dynasty's view of China's place in the world in 1839? Does the dynasty still view China as a universal empire? Do Lin's arguments leave the British queen any ground to stand on?

A communication: magnificently our great Emperor soothes and pacifies China and the foreign countries, regarding all with the same kindness. If there is profit, then he shares it with the peoples of the world; if there is harm, then he removes it on behalf of the world. This is because he takes the mind of heaven and earth as his mind.

The kings of your honorable country by a tradition handed down from generation to generation have always been noted for their politeness and submissiveness. We have read your successive tributary memorials saying, "In general our countrymen who go to trade in China have always received His Majesty the Emperor's gracious treatment and equal justice," and so on. Privately we are delighted with the way in which the honorable rulers of your country deeply understand the grand principles and are grateful for the Celestial grace. For this reason the Celestial Court in soothing those from afar has redoubled its polite and kind treatment. The profit from trade has been enjoyed by them continuously for two hundred years. This is the source from which your country has become known for its wealth. But after a long period of commercial intercourse, there appear among the crowd of barbarians both good persons and bad, unevenly. Consequently there are those who smuggle opium to seduce the Chinese people and so cause the spread of the poison to all provinces. Such persons who only care to profit themselves, and disregard their harm to others, are not tolerated by the laws of heaven and are unanimously hated by human beings. His Majesty the Emperor, upon hearing of this, is in a towering rage. . . .

We find that your country is sixty or seventy thousand li [three li make one mile, ordinarily] from China. Yet there are barbarian ships that strive to come here for trade for the purpose of making a great profit. The wealth of China is used to profit the barbarians. That is to say, the great profit made by barbarians is all taken from the rightful share of China. By what right do they then in return use the poisonous drug to injure the Chinese people? Even

though the barbarians may not necessarily intend to do us harm, yet in coveting profit to an extreme, they have no regard for injuring others. Let us ask, where is your conscience? I have heard that the smoking of opium is very strictly forbidden by your country; that is because the harm caused by opium is clearly understood. Since it is not permitted to do harm to your own country, then even less should you let it be passed on to the harm of other countries—how much less to China!

Suppose there were people from another country who carried opium for sale to England and seduced your people into buying and smoking it; certainly your honorable ruler would deeply hate it and be bitterly aroused. We have heard heretofore that your honorable ruler is kind and benevolent. Naturally you would not wish to give unto others what you yourself do not want.

Now we have set up regulations governing the Chinese people. He who sells opium shall receive the death penalty and he who smokes it also the death penalty. Now consider this: if the barbarians do not bring opium, then how can the Chinese people resell it, and how can they smoke it? The fact is that the wicked barbarians beguile the Chinese people into a death trap. How then can we grant life only to those barbarians? He who takes the life of even one person still has to atone for it with his own life; yet is the harm done by opium limited to the taking of one life only? Therefore in the new regulations, in regard to those barbarians who bring opium to China, the penalty is fixed at decapitation or strangulation. This is what is called getting rid of a harmful thing on behalf of mankind.

[However] all those who within the period of the coming one year (from England) or six months (from India) bring opium to China by mistake, but who voluntarily confess and completely surrender their opium, shall be exempt from their punishment. This may be called the height of kindness and the perfection of justice.

Reprinted by permission of the publisher from Ssu-Yu Teng and John K. Fairbank, *China's Response to the West* (Cambridge, MA: Harvard University Press). Copyright 1954, 1979 by the President and Fellows of Harvard College.

work under harsh conditions in Cuba and Peru. A second war broke out in 1856, which continued sporadically until Lord Elgin (1811–1863), the British commander, together with a French contingent, captured Beijing in 1860. A new set of conventions and treaties provided for indemnities, the opening of eleven new ports, the stationing of foreign diplomats in Beijing, the propagation of Christianity anywhere in China, and the legalization of the opium trade.

While the British fought China for trading rights, the Russians were encroaching on China's northern frontier. During the 1850s Russia established settlements along the Amur River. In 1858 China signed a treaty ceding the north bank of the Amur to Russia, and in 1860 China gave Russia the Maritime Province between the Ussuri River and the Pacific.

Rebellions Against the Manchu

Far more immediate a threat to Manchu rule than foreign gunboats and unequal treaties were the Taiping, Nian, and Muslim Rebellions that convulsed China between 1850 and 1873 (see Map 28–1). The torment and suffering they caused were unparalleled in world history. Estimates of those killed during the twenty years of the **Taiping Rebellion** range from 20 to 30 million. If one adds in losses due to other rebellions, droughts, and floods, China's population dropped by 60 million and did not recover to prerebellion levels until almost the end of the dynasty in 1912.

The Taipings were begun by Hong Xiuquan (1814–1864), a schoolteacher from a poor family in a minority Hakka group in the southern province of Guangdong. Hong had four times failed to pass the civil service examinations. He became ill and saw visions. Influenced by Protestant tracts he had picked up in Guangzhou, Hong announced that he was the younger brother of Jesus and that God had told him to rid China of evil demons—including Manchus, Confucians, Daoists, and Buddhists. He formed an Association of God Worshipers. His followers cut off their queues as a sign of resistance to the Manchus, who called them "long-haired rebels." The Taipings began by attacking local Confucian temples, arousing the opposition of the gentry. They were soon joined by peasants, miners, and workers. Hong proclaimed the Heavenly Kingdom of Great Peace in 1851 and two years later took Nanjing and made it his capital. The fighting spread until the Taipings controlled most of the Yangzi basin; their expeditions eventually entered sixteen of the eighteen Chinese provinces. By that time their army numbered almost a million.

The Taiping ideology joined Old Testament Christianity with an ancient text often used by reformers, the *Zhou Rites*. The puritanical ethics of the Taipings came from the former, and the notion of sharing property equally came from the latter. The Taipings prohibited opium, tobacco, alcohol, gambling, adultery, prostitution, and footbinding. They upheld filial piety. They maintained that women were men's equals and appointed them to administrative and military posts. In short, like earlier rebels, the Taipings combined moral reform, religious fervor, and a vision of a transformed egalitarian society.

The movement had several weaknesses. Most Taiping leaders were too poorly educated to govern effectively, and the Taipings could not draw on the gentry. When the Taiping area was divided into kingdoms, dissension broke out. The Taipings failed to cultivate the secret societies, which were also anti-Manchu. They also failed to cultivate Westerners, who had been neutral before the 1860 treaty settlements and aided the Manchus thereafter. In addition, many Taiping ideals remained unfulfilled; for example, land was not redistributed, and, although Taiping teachings emphasized frugality and the sanctity of monogamous marriage, Hong lived with many concubines in the midst of luxury.

The other rebellions were of lesser note but of longer duration. The Nian were located north of the Taipings along the Huai River. They began as bandits who lived in walled villages, were organized in secret societies, and lived by raiding the surrounding countryside. Eventually they built an army, collected taxes, and ruled 100,000 square miles. The Qing court feared that the Nian would join forces with the Taipings. An even longer revolt was of Muslims against Chinese in the southwest and the northwest. One rebel set up an Islamic kingdom with himself as sultan. Like the Taiping Rebellion, these various rebellions took advantage of the weakened state of the dynasty and occurred in areas that had few officials and no Qing military units.

Against these rebellions, the Manchu Banners and the Chinese Army of the Green Standard proved helpless: The one was useful only for defense, the other only against civilians. The first effective step was taken against the rebellions when, in 1852, the court sent Zeng Guofan (1811–1872) to Hunan Province in south-central China to organize a local army. Zeng was a product of the Confucian examination system and had served in Beijing. He saw the Manchu government, of which he was an elite member, as the upholder of morality and the social order, and Chinese rebels as would-be destroyers of that order. Arriving in Hunan, he recruited members of the gentry as officers. They were of the class that, since the late Ming, had been growing in importance and performing many local government functions, in some cases organizing local militia. Not only were they Confucian, but as landlords they had the most to lose from rebel rule. They recruited soldiers from their local areas. Zeng's "Hunan Braves" stopped the Taipings' advance.

Until 1860 the Qing court was dominated by Manchu conservatives who limited Zeng's role and dragged their feet in

Map showing rebellions in China.

Legend:
- Area Dominated by Taipings
- Areas of Muslim Rebellions
- Taiping Northern Expedition
- Taiping Army (1850–1853)
- Further Taiping Expeditions
- Nien Stronghold
- Treaty Ports

Labels on map: Manchuria, INNER MONGOLIA, Sea of Japan, JAPAN, KOREA, Dalian, Beijing, Taku, Tianjin, GREAT WALL, Turkestan, Jinji, Lanzhou, Xian, Kaifeng, Zhihe, Nanjing, Shanghai, Ningbo, East China Sea, Fuzhou, Xiamen, TAIWAN, Guangzhou, Jintian, Macao, Hong Kong, VIETNAM, HAINAN, South China Sea, Yunnan, Tibet, Yellow River, Yangzi River, Grand Canal.

Map 28–1.   The Taiping, Nian, and Muslim Rebellions. Between 1850 and 1873 China was wracked by rebellions that almost ended the Manchu dynasty. The dynasty was saved by Chinese "gentry armies."

upholding the treaties. In 1860 the conservatives lost their footing when the British and the French occupied Beijing. A reform government replaced the conservatives, began internal changes, adopted a policy of cooperation with the Western powers, and put Zeng in charge of suppressing the rebellions. Zeng appointed other able officials to raise regional armies. Li Hongzhang (1823–1901), with his Anhui Army, was especially effective. Foreigners and Shanghai merchants gave their support. Revenues from the customs service and foreign ships and weapons were essential to Zeng's armies. The Taipings collapsed when Nanjing was captured in 1864 after protracted fighting. Zeng and Li suppressed the Nian by 1868, and the Muslim rebellion was put down five years later. Scholar-officials, relying on local gentry, had saved the dynasty.

Self-Strengthening and Decline (1874–1895)

The two decades after the suppression of the midcentury rebellions illustrate the dictum that there is no single "correct" view of history. In comparison, for example, with the

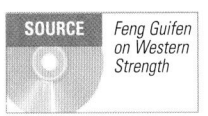
SOURCE *Feng Guifen on Western Strength*

late Song or the late Ming, the last decades of the nineteenth century look good. In view of the dynasty's advanced stage of administrative decentralization, the Chinese resiliency and capacity to rebuild after unprecedented destruction were impressive. Even on its borders the Manchu state was able to maintain or regain some territories while losing others. But if we ask instead how effective China's response was to the West, or if we compare China's progress with that of Japan, then China during the same decades looks almost moribund. Historians often call these years the period of "**self-strengthening**," after a catch phrase in vogue at the time. This term is not inappropriate, as the list of new initiatives taken during the period is long. Yet, since the firepower of Western naval forces doubled each decade, the forces that China faced at the end of the century were vastly more formidable than those of the Opium War. Despite self-strengthening, China was relatively weaker at the end of the period than at the start.

Between 1850 and 1864, China was wracked by a great civil war between the Taiping rebels and the gentry-led militia of the Qing government. The victory of the latter delayed the collapse of the Qing dynasty until 1912. The scene above shows troops arrayed in battle formation.

In 1895 Li Hongzhang met with Itō Hirobumi (1838–1909) of Japan to negotiate a peace treaty after China's defeat in the Sino-Japanese War. Itō asked with uncharacteristic bluntness: "Ten years ago when I was at Tianjin, I talked about reform with the Grand Secretary [Li]. Why is it that up to now not a single thing has been changed or reformed?" Li replied: "Affairs in my country have been so confined by tradition that I could not accomplish what I desired. . . . Now in the twinkling of an eye ten years have gone by, and everything is still the same. I am even more regretful. I am ashamed of having excessive wishes and lacking the power to fulfill them." Itō responded blandly: "The providence of heaven has no affection, except for the virtuous."[1] Considering that Li was the single most powerful figure in China during these decades, Itō's puzzlement was not surprising.

The Court at Beijing   The situation at the court partly explains China's inability to act effectively. Prince Gong (1833–1898) and the empress dowager (1835–1908) were co-regents for the young emperor. For a Manchu noble, Prince Gong was a man of ideas. After signing the treaties of 1860 he established in 1861 a new office directly under the Grand Council to handle the court's relations with foreign diplomats in Beijing. The following year he established a school to train the Chinese in foreign languages. Over time, however, his position at the court grew weaker. Outmaneuvered by the empress dowager, he was ousted in 1884.

The empress dowager was the daughter of a Manchu official. She had become an imperial concubine and had produced the only male child of the former emperor. She was educated, clever, petty, strong-willed, and narrow-

[1] S. Y. Teng and J. K. Fairbank, *China's Response to the West* (Cambridge, MA: Harvard University Press, 1954), p. 126.

minded. She did not oppose change, except by circumstance, nor did she favor it. She had no conception of how to reform China. Her single goal was to gather political power into her own hands. She acquired this by forging a political machine of conservative bureaucrats, military commanders, and eunuchs, and by maintaining a balance between the court and the regional strength of the powerful governors general. The result was a court barely able to survive, too weak to govern effectively, and not inclined to do more than approve of initiatives taken at the provincial level.

Regional Governments   The most vital figures during these decades were a handful of governors general whose names are legendary: Zeng Guofan, Li Hongzhang, Zuo Zongtang (1812–1885), and Zhang Zhidong (1837–1909). Each had a staff of 200 or 300 and an army and was in charge of two or three provinces. They were loyal to the dynasty that they had restored in the face of almost certain collapse, and in return for their allegiance they were allowed great autonomy.

Their first task was reconstruction. The rebellions in central China had destroyed the mulberry trees on which the silkworms fed and those in the northwest, the irrigation systems. Millions were hungry or homeless. The leaders' response to these ills was massive and effective. Just as they had mobilized the gentry to suppress the rebellions, now they obtained their cooperation in rebuilding. They set up refugee centers and soup kitchens, reduced taxes in the devastated Yangzi valley, reclaimed lands gone to waste, began water-control projects, and built granaries. By the early 1890s considerable well-being had been restored to China's late dynastic society.

Their second task was self-strengthening—the adoption of Western arms and technology. The governors general were keenly aware of China's weakness. To strengthen China, they built arsenals and shipyards during the 1860s and 1870s, and during the 1870s and 1880s they began commercial ventures as well. The China Merchants Steam Navigation Company was established in 1872, the Kaiping Coal Mine in 1876, and then a telegraph company, short stretches of railways, and cotton mills. The formula applied in running these enterprises was "official supervision and merchant operation." The major decisions were made by scholar-officials like Zeng, but day-to-day operations were left to the merchants. This division of labor led to contradictions. The Steam Navigation Company, for example, was funded partly by the government because private capital was inadequate.

Li Hongzhang awarded the company a monopoly on shipments of the rice paid in taxes and official cargos to Tianjin and won tariff concessions for the company as well. For a time these advantages enabled it to compete successfully with foreign lines. But Li also used company ships to transport his troops; he took company funds to reward his

The effects of the treaty ports and of Western imperialism on China were largely negative. Under the low tariffs mandated by the treaties, Chinese industries had little protection from imports. Native cotton spinning was almost destroyed by imports of yarn—although the cloth woven from the yarn remained competitive with foreign cloth. Chinese tea lost ground to Indian tea and Chinese silk to Japanese silk, as these countries developed products of standard quality and China did not. China found few products to export: pig bristles, soybeans, and vegetable oils. The level of foreign trade stayed low, and China's interior markets were affected only slightly.

By the 1870s the foreign powers had reached an accommodation with China. They counted on the court to uphold

The Empress Dowager Cixi (1835–1908), with Female Attendants. The empress dowager manipulated the levers of power at the Manchu court in Beijing.

political followers; and he interfered in the company by hiring and firing managers. Under these conditions, both investors and managers took their profits quickly and did not reinvest in the line. Soon British lines once again dominated shipping in China's domestic waters.

Treaty Ports Conditions in the **treaty ports**, of which there were fourteen by the 1860s, were different from the rest of China. The ports were little islands of privilege where foreigners lived in mansions staffed with servants, raced horses at the track, participated in amateur theatricals, drank (in Shanghai, at the longest bar in the world), and went to church on Sunday. But the ports were also islands of security, under the rule of foreign consuls, where capital was safe from confiscation, trade was free, and "squeeze" (extortion by officials) was the exception and not the rule. Foreign companies naturally located in the ports. The Hong Kong and Shanghai Bank, for example, was funded in 1865 by British interests to finance international trade and to make loans to Chinese firms and banks. Chinese merchants were also attracted by these conditions and located their businesses on rented lands in the foreign concessions. Joint ventures, such as steamboats on the Yangzi, were also begun by Chinese and foreign merchants. Well into the twentieth century the foreign concessions (treaty-port lands leased in perpetuity by foreigners) remained the vital sector of China's modern economy.

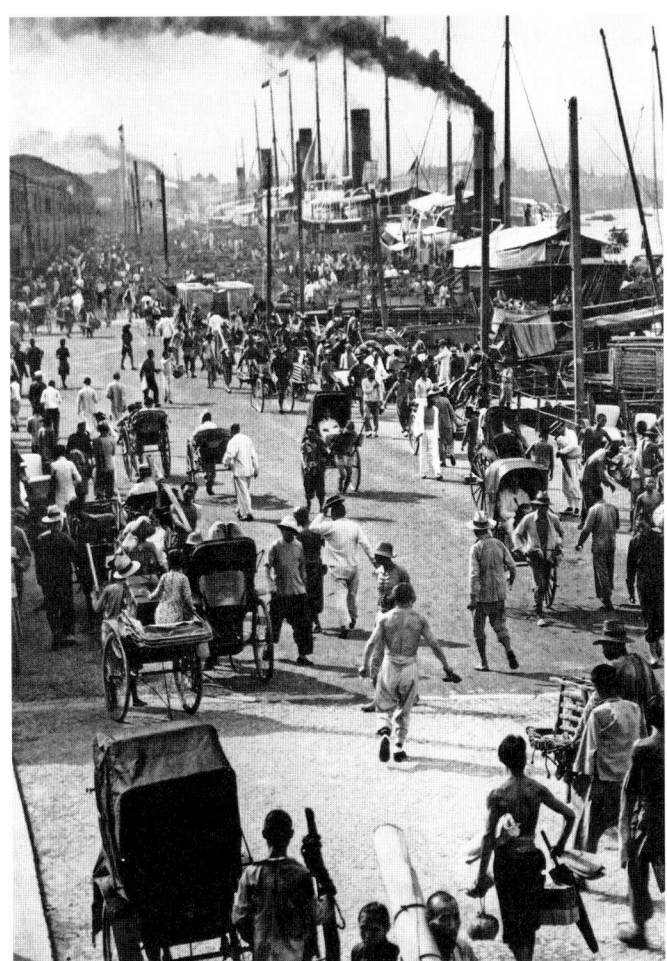

The Bund. After the Opium War, Shanghai became a treaty port in 1842 and foreign settlements arose along the Huangpu River, north of the old walled city. British and other companies built offices along the river's muddy waterfront, which they called the "Bund"—an Anglo-Indian term derived from "band," the Urdu word for embankment. Before World War II, ocean-going ships docked along the Bund in the heart of commercial Shanghai. Today, this stretch of the river is fronted by the Zhongshan (Sun Yat-sen) Road. On one side are banks, insurance companies, and hotels; on the other, a park. Ships no longer dock.

the treaties; in return, they became a prop for the dynasty during its final decades. By 1900, for example, the court's revenues from customs fees were larger than those from any other source, including the land tax. The fees were collected by the Maritime Customs Service, a notably efficient and honest treaty-port institution headed by an Irishman, Sir Robert Hart (1835–1911), who saw himself as serving the Chinese government. In 1895 the Maritime Customs Service had 700 Western and 3,500 Chinese employees.

The Borderlands: The Northwest, Vietnam, and Korea

China's other foreign relations were with fringe lands inhabited by non-Chinese but that China claimed by right of past conquest or as tributaries. Often distant from the pressing concerns of Chinese government, the tributaries were nonetheless the mirrors in which China saw reflected its own self-image as a universal empire. During the late nineteenth century this image was strengthened in the northwest but dealt a fatal blow in Vietnam and Korea.

The Northwest In the northwest, China confronted tsarist Russia. Both countries had been expanding onto the steppe since the seventeenth century (see Chapter 20). Both had firearms. Caught in a pincers between them, the once proud, powerful, and independent nomadic tribes were gradually rendered impotent. Conservatives at the Manchu court ordered Zuo Zongtang, who had suppressed Muslim rebels within China, to suppress a Muslim leader who had founded an independent state in Chinese Turkestan (the Tarim basin, a part of the old Silk Road). Zuo led his army across 3,000 miles of deserts, and by 1878 had reconquered the area, which was subsequently renamed Xinjiang, or the "New Territories." A treaty signed with Russia in 1881 also restored most of the Ili region in western Mongolia to Chinese control. These victories strengthened court conservatives who wished to take a stronger stance towards the West.

Vietnam To the south was Vietnam, which had retained its independence from China since 935. It saw itself as an independent and separate state, but it used the Chinese writing system, modeled its laws and government on those of China, and traded with China within the framework of the tribute system. China, more simply, saw Vietnam as a tributary that could be aided or punished as necessary.

During the 1840s the second emperor of the Nguyen dynasty, which had begun in 1802, moved to reduce French influences and suppress Christianity. Thousands were killed, including French and Vietnamese priests. The French responded by seizing Saigon and the three provinces of Cochin China in 1859, establishing a protectorate over Cam-

The French in Vietnam. Arrival in Saigon of Paul Beau (1857–1927), governor general of Indochina 1902–1907, from "Le Petit Journal," November 1902.

bodia in 1864, and taking three more provinces in 1867 and Hanoi in 1882. China, flush with confidence after its victories in Central Asia, in 1883 sent in troops to aid its tributary. The result was a two-year war in which French warships ranged the coast of China, attacking shore batteries and sinking ships. In 1885 China was forced to sign a treaty abandoning its claims to Vietnam. By 1893 France had brought together Vietnam, Cambodia, and Laos to form the Federation of Indochina, which remained a French colony until 1940.

Korea A third area of contention was Korea. Unlike Vietnam, Korea saw itself as a tributary of China. Even at his own court the Korean ruler styled himself as a king and not an emperor. It was the only rim area of China that accepted the tribute system on Chinese terms.

During the last decades of the long (1392–1910) Choson dynasty, the Korean state was weak. It hung on to power, in part, by enforcing a policy of seclusion almost as total as that of Tokugawa Japan, which won it the name of the Hermit Kingdom. Its only foreign ties were its tribute relations with China and its trade and occasional diplomatic missions to Japan. In 1876 Japan "opened" Korea to international rela-

Students at Nanjing University. University students at Nanjing University study in the Severence Hall Reading Room in the early 1900s.

tions, using much the same tactics that Perry had used twenty-two years earlier against Japan. Japan then contended with China for influence in Korea's internal politics. Conservatives and moderate reformers in Korea looked to China for support. Radical reformers, weaker and fewer in number, looked to Japan, arguing that only sweeping changes such as those that had been made in Japan would enable Korea to survive. The radicals, however, were soon suppressed.

In 1893 a popular religious sect unleashed a rebellion against the weak and corrupt Seoul government. When the government requested Chinese help to suppress the rebellion, China sent troops, but Japan sent more, and in 1894 war broke out between China and Japan. China and the Western powers expected an easy Chinese victory, but they had not understood the changes occurring within Japan. Japan won handily. Neither the Chinese fleet nor the Chinese armies were a match for the discipline and the superior tactics of the Japanese units. It was after this war that Taiwan became Japan's first colony. The defeat by Japan convinced many throughout China that basic changes were inevitable.

From Dynasty to Warlordism (1895–1926)

China was ruled by officials who had mastered the Confucian classics and the historical and literary tradition that had developed alongside them. This intellectual formation was highly resistant to change. For most officials living in China's interior, the foreign crises of the nineteenth century were "coastal phenomena" that, like bee stings, were painful for a time but then forgotten. Few officials realized the magnitude of the foreign threat.

China's defeat in 1895 by Japan, another Asian nation and one for which China had had little regard, came as a shock. The response within China was a new wave of reform proposals. (See Document, "Liang Qichao Urges the Chinese to Reform (1896).") The most influential thinker was Kang Youwei (1858–1927), who described China as "enfeebled" and "soundly asleep atop a pile of kindling." For this state of affairs, Kang blamed the "conservatives." They did not understand, Kang argued, that Confucius himself had been a reformer and not simply a transmitter of past wisdom. Confucius had invented the idea of a golden age in the past in order to persuade the rulers of his own age to adopt his ideas. All of history, Kang continued, was evolutionary—a march forward from absolute monarchy to constitutional monarchy to democracy. Actually, Kang was not well-versed in Western ideas; he equated the somewhat mystical Confucian virtue of humanity (*ren*) with electricity and ether. Nonetheless, his reinterpretation of the essentials of Confucianism removed a major barrier to the entry of Western ideas into China.

In 1898 the emperor himself became sympathetic to Kang's ideas and, on June 11, launched "one hundred days of reform." He took as his models not past Chinese monarchs, but Peter the Great (r. 1682–1725) and the Japanese Meiji emperor (r. 1867–1912). Edicts were issued for sweeping reforms of China's schools, railroads, police, laws, military services, bureaucracy, post offices, and examination system. But the orders were implemented in only one province; conservative resistance was nationwide. Even at the court, the empress dowager regained control and ended the reforms. Kang and most of his associates fled to Japan. One reformer who remained behind was executed.

Liang Qichao Urges the Chinese to Reform (1896)

Document

Next to Kang Youwei, Liang Qichao (1873–1929) was the most influential thinker of late Qing China.

◆ What kind of reform program is Liang advocating? Compare his response to the challenge of the West with that by a Japanese commentator in "A Japanese View of the Inventiveness of the West," on page 901.

On the *Harm of not Reforming*. Now here is a big mansion which has lasted a thousand years. The tiles and bricks are decayed and the beams and rafters are broken. It is still a magnificently big thing, but when wind and rain suddenly come up, its fall is foredoomed. Yet the people in the house are still happily playing or soundly sleeping and as indifferent as if they have seen or heard nothing. Even some who have noted the danger know only how to weep bitterly, folding their arms and waiting for death without thinking of any remedy. Sometimes there are people a little better off who try to repair the cracks, seal up the leaks, and patch up the ant holes in order to be able to go on living there in peace, even temporarily, in the hope that something better may turn up. These three types of people use their minds differently, but when a hurricane comes they will die together. . . . A nation is also like this. . . .

India is one of the oldest countries on the great earth. She followed tradition without change; she has been rendered a colony of England. Turkey's territory occupied three continents and had an established state for a thousand years; yet, because of observing the old ways without change, she has been dominated by six large countries, which have divided her territory. . . . The Moslems in central Asia have usually been well known for their bravery and skill in warfare, and yet they observe the old ways without changing. The Russians are swallowing

them like a whale and nibbling them as silkworms eat mulberry leaves, almost in their entirety.

The age of China as a country is equal to that of India and the fertility of her land is superior to that of Turkey, but her conformity to the defective ways which have accumulated and her incapacity to stand up and reform make her also like a brother of these two countries. . . . Whenever there is a flood or drought, communications are severed, there is no way to transport famine relief, the dead are abandoned to fill the ditches or are disregarded, and nine out of ten houses are emptied. . . . The members of secret societies are scattered over the whole country, waiting for the chance to move. Industry is not developed, commerce is not discussed, the native goods daily become less salable. . . . "Leakage" [i.e., squeeze] becomes more serious day by day and our financial sources are almost dried up. Schools are not well-run and students, apart from the "eight-legged" essays, do not know how to do a thing. The good ones are working on small researches, flowery writing, and miscellaneous trifles. Tell them about the vast oceans, they open their eyes wide and disbelieve it.

The response of the Western powers to China's 1895 defeat has been described as "carving up the melon." Each nation tried to define a sphere of interest, which usually consisted of a leasehold along with railway rights and special commercial privileges. Russia gained a leasehold at Port Arthur; Germany acquired one in Shandong. Britain got the New Territories adjoining Jiulong (Kowloon) at Hong Kong. New ports and cities were opened to foreign trade. The United States, busy acquiring the Philippines and Guam, was in a weaker position in China. So it enunciated an "open-door" policy: equal commercial opportunities for all powers and the preservation of the territorial integrity of China.

There was in China at this time a religious society known as the **Boxers**. The Chinese name translates more literally as the "Righteous and Harmonious Fists." The Boxers had rituals, spells, and amulets that they believed made them impervious to bullets. They rebelled first in Shandung in 1898, and, gaining court support, entered Beijing in 1900. The court declared war on the treaty powers, and there followed a two-month siege of the foreign legation quarter. Pent-up resentments against decades of foreign encroachments fueled support for the rebellion. Eventually an international force captured Beijing, won a huge indemnity, and obtained the right to maintain permanent military forces in the capital. In the aftermath of the Boxer Rebellion, the Russians occupied Manchuria.

The defeat of the Boxers convinced even conservative Chinese leaders of the futility of clinging to old ways. A more powerful reform movement began, with the empress dowager herself in its vanguard. But as the movement gained momentum, the dynasty could not stay far enough in front and eventually was overrun.

Educational reforms began in 1901. Women, for the first time, were admitted as students to newly formed schools. In place of Confucianism, the instructors taught science, mathematics, geography, and an anti-imperialist version of Chinese history that fanned the flames of nationalism. Western doctrines, such as classical economics, liberalism, socialism, anarchism, and social Darwinism, were also introduced into China. Most entered via translations from Japanese, and in the process the modern vocabulary coined by Japanese scholars was implanted in China. By 1906 there were 8,000 Chinese students in Japan, which had become a hotbed of Chinese reformist and revolutionary societies.

Military reforms were begun by Yuan Shikai (1859–1916), whose New Army drew on Japanese and Western models. Young men from gentry families, spurred by patriotism, broke with the traditional Chinese animus against military careers and joined the New Army as officers. Their loyalty was to their commanders and to their country, not to the dynasty.

Political reforms began with a modification of the examination system to accommodate the learning at the new schools. Then in 1905 the examination system was abolished altogether. Henceforth, officials were to be directly recruited from the graduates of the schools and those who had studied abroad. Provincial assemblies were formed in 1909, and a consultative assembly with some elected members was established in Beijing in 1910. These representative bodies were intended to rally the new gentry nationalism in support of the court, but they became forums for the expression of interests at odds with those of the dynasty.

In sum, during the first decade of the twentieth century the three vital components of the imperial system—Confucian education, the bureaucracy, and the gentry—had been discarded or modified in ways that even a few decades earlier would have been unimaginable.

These changes sparked the 1911 revolution. It began with an uprising in Sichuan province against a government plan to nationalize the main railways. The players were:

1. Gentry who stood to lose their investments in the railways.
2. Qing military commanders, who broke with Beijing, declaring their provinces independent.

3. Sun Zhongshan (or Sun Yat-sen) (1866–1925), a republican revolutionary. Born a peasant, he had learned English and become a Christian in Hawaii, then studied medicine in Guangzhou and Hong Kong. He organized the Revolutionary Alliance in Tokyo in 1905 and was associated with the Nationalist Party (Guomindang) formed in 1912.
4. Yuan Shikai, who was called on by the court to preserve the dynasty. Instead, he arranged for the last child emperor to abdicate and for Sun to step aside. He declared himself president of the new Republic of China.

The Nationalists won the election called in 1913. Yuan thereupon had their leader assassinated, crushed the military governors who supported them, and forced Sun Zhongshan and other revolutionaries to flee again to Japan. Yuan emerged as the uncontested ruler of China. Mistaking the temper of the times, he proclaimed a new dynasty with himself as emperor. The idea of yet another dynasty met implacable opposition from all quarters, forcing Yuan to abandon the attempt. He died three months later in June 1916. After Yuan, China fell into the hands of warlord armies. The years until the late twenties were a time of agony, frustration, and travail for the Chinese people. But they were also a time of intense intellectual ferment.

Cultural and Ideological Ferment: The May Fourth Movement

In the century after the Opium War, China's leading thinkers responded to the challenge of the West in terms of four successive modes of thought:

1. During the 1840s and the 1850s, and into the 1860s, the key event in China was the Taiping Rebellion. The success of gentry Confucianism in putting down the rebellion and in reestablishing the social order underlined for most Chinese the effectiveness, vitality, and validity of traditional doctrines.
2. From the 1860s to the 1890s, the dominant intellectual modality was "*ti-yong* reformism." The essence (*ti*) was to remain Chinese, but useful contrivances (*yong*) could be borrowed from the West. This formula enabled a restabilized China to borrow and reform in small ways such as building arsenals and railroads while remaining Chinese at the core. It was the ideology of the "self-strengthening" movement.
3. Then, during the last decade of the Manchu dynasty, the *ti-yong* distinction came to be seen as inadequate. The *ti* itself was reinterpreted. The dominant view was that of Kang Youwei, who argued that Confucius had been a reformer and that Confucianism, properly understood, was a philosophy of change. This kind of thought was behind the rash of reforms of 1900 through 1911.

4. The fourth stage was a period of freedom and vigorous experimentation with new doctrines that began in 1914 and extended into the 1920s. It is called the May Fourth Movement after an incident in Beijing in 1919 in which thousands of students protested the settlement at Versailles that awarded former German possessions in Shandung to Japan. The powerful nationalism that led the students to demonstrate in the streets changed the complexion of Chinese thought. Instead of appealing to tradition, leading thinkers began to judge ideas in terms of their value in solving China's problems. It was also not accidental that this era of intellectual excitement corresponded almost exactly with the period of warlord rule—which afforded a breathing space between the ideological constraints of the old dynasty and those of the Nationalist and Communist eras that would follow.

Scholars who returned from abroad during the last years of Manchu rule often located in the safety of the treaty ports. During the May Fourth era, however, the center of advanced thought was Beijing. Cai Yuanpei (1868–1940), who had been minister of education under the republic, became the chancellor of Beijing University, and Chen Duxiu (1879–1942) became his dean of letters. Both men had had a classical education and had passed the traditional examinations. Cai joined the party of Sun Zhongshan and went to study in Germany. After the fall of Yuan Shikai, he made Beijing University into a haven for scholars who had returned from study in Japan or the West.

Chen Duxiu, a Francophile, had studied in Japan. In 1915 he launched *New Youth*, a magazine that played a role in the intellectual revolution of early-twentieth-century China comparable to the *cahiers* in the French Revolution or the pamphlets of Thomas Paine in the American Revolution. In his magazine Chen placed the blame for Chinese ills on the teachings of Confucius. He called for a generation of progressive, cosmopolitan, and scientific youth who would uphold the values of liberty, equality, and fraternity. (See Document, "Chen Duxiu's 'Call to Youth' in 1915.")

Chen Duxiu's "Call to Youth" in 1915   Document

Struggle, natural selection, and organic process are the images used by Chen Duxiu. How different from those of Confucianism!

◆ **How does Chen's "Call to Youth" relate to the political conditions in China in 1915?**

The Chinese compliment others by saying, "He acts like an old man although still young." Englishmen and Americans encourage one another by saying, "Keep young while growing old." Such is one respect in which the different ways of thought of the East and West are manifested. Youth is like early spring, like the rising sun, like trees and grass in bud, like a newly sharpened blade. It is the most valuable period of life. The function of youth in society is the same as that of a fresh and vital cell in a human body. In the processes of metabolism, the old and the rotten are incessantly eliminated to be replaced by the fresh and living. . . . According to this standard, then, is the society of our nation flourishing, or is it about to perish? I cannot bear to answer. As for those old and rotten elements, I shall leave them to the process of natural selection. . . . I only, with tears, place my plea before the young and vital youth, in the hope that they will achieve self-awareness, and begin to struggle.

What is the struggle? It is to exert one's intellect, discard resolutely the old and the rotten, regard them as enemies and as the flood or savage beasts, keep away from their neighborhood and refuse to be contaminated by their poisonous germs. Alas! Do these words really fit the youth of our country? I have seen that, out of every ten youths who are young in age, five are old in physique; and out of every ten who are young in both age and physique, nine are old in mentality. Those with shining hair, smooth countenance, a straight back and a wide chest are indeed magnificent youths! Yet if you ask what thoughts and aims are entertained in their heads, then they all turn out to be the same as the old and rotten, like moles from the same hill. . . . It is the old and rotten air that fills society everywhere. One cannot even find a bit of fresh and vital air to comfort those of us who are suffocating in despair.

Reprinted by permission of the publisher from Ssu-Yu Teng and John K. Fairbank, *China's Response to the West* (Cambridge, MA: Harvard University Press). Copyright 1954, 1979 by the President and Fellows of Harvard College.

The greatest modern Chinese writer was Lu Xun (1881–1936). Like most other leading intellectuals of the period, he had been born in a scholar-official family. He went to Japan for eight years to study medicine but switched in mid-course to literature. His first work, *A Madman's Diary*, appeared in *New Youth* in 1918. Its protagonist is a pathetic figure whose madness takes the form of a belief that people eat people. Lu Xun's message was that only the vision of a madman could truly comprehend an abnormal and inhumane society.

As the May Fourth Movement developed, ideas propounded in Beijing quickly spread to the rest of China, especially to its urban centers. Protest demonstrations against imperialist privilege broke out in Shanghai, Wuhan, and Guangzhou, as they had in the capital. Nationalism and anti-imperialist sentiment were stronger than liberalism, although few thinkers did not speak out for democracy. Only members of an older generation of reformers, such as Kang Youwei, came full circle and, appalled by the slaughter of World War I and what they saw as Western materialism, advocated a return to traditional Chinese philosophies.

At the onset of China's intellectual revolution, Marxism had small appeal; Marx's critique of capitalist society did not fit Chinese conditions. More persuasive was the anarchism of Peter Kropotkin (1842–1921), who taught that mutual aid was as much a part of evolution as the struggle for survival. But after the Russian Revolution of 1917, Marxism-Leninism entered China. The Leninist definition of imperialism as the last crisis stage of capitalism had an immediate appeal, for it put the blame for China's ills on the West and offered "feudal" China the possibility of leapfrogging over capitalism to socialism. As early as 1919 an entire issue of *New Youth* was devoted to Marxism. Marxist study groups formed in Beijing and other cities. In 1919 a student from Hunan, Mao Zedong, who had worked in the Beijing University library, returned to Changsha to form a study group. Chen Duxiu was converted to Marxism in 1920. Instructed in organizational techniques by a Comintern agent, Chen and others formed the Chinese Communist Party in Shanghai in 1921; Zhou Enlai (1898–1976) formed a similar group in Paris during the same year. The numbers involved were small but grew steadily.

Nationalist China

Guomindang Unification of China and the Nanjing Decade (1927–1937)

Sun Zhongshan had fled to Japan during the 1913–1916 rule by Yuan Shikai. He returned to Guangzhou in 1916, but despite his immense personal attractiveness as a leader he was a poor organizer, and his **Guomindang (GMD)**—or Nationalist Party—made little headway. For a time in 1922 he was driven out of Guangzhou by a local warlord. From 1923 Sun began to receive Soviet advice and support. With the help of Comintern agents like Michael Borodin, he reorganized his party on the Leninist model, with an executive committee on top of a national party congress and, below this, provincial and county organizations and local party cells.

Since 1905 Sun had enunciated his "three principles of the people": nationality, livelihood, and rights. Sun's earlier nationalism had been directed against Manchu rule; it was now redirected against Western imperialism. The principle of people's livelihood was defined in terms of equalizing landholdings and nationalizing major industries. By "people's rights" Sun meant democracy, although he argued that full democracy must be preceded by a preparatory period of tutelage under a single-party dictatorship. Sun sent his loyal lieutenant Jiang Jieshi (Chiang Kai-shek) (1887–1975) to the Soviet Union for study. Jiang returned after four months with a cadre of Russian advisers and established a military academy at Huangpu to the south of Guangzhou in 1924. The cadets of Huangpu were to form a "party army." Sun died in 1925. By 1926 the Academy had graduated several

Jiang Jieshi (or Chiang Kai-shek, 1887–1975), as a young revolutionary officer, stands behind Sun Zhongshan (or Sun Yat-sen, 1866–1925), father of China's 1911–1912 Republican Revolution, taken around 1925.

thousand officers, and the GMD army numbered almost 100,000. The GMD had become the major political force in China, with 200,000 members; its leadership was divided between a left and a right wing.

Changes occurring within Chinese society spurred the growth of the party. Industries arose in the cities. Labor unions were organized in tobacco and textile factories. New ventures were begun outside the treaty ports, and chambers of commerce were established even in medium-sized towns. Entrepreneurs, merchants, officials, journalists, and the employees of foreign firms formed a new and politically conscious middle class.

The quicksilver element in cities was the several million students at government, Catholic, and Protestant schools. In May 1925 students demonstrated against the treatment of workers in foreign-owned factories at Shanghai. Police in the international settlement fired on the demonstrators, killing thirteen and wounding fifty. The incident further inflamed national and anti-imperialist feelings. Strikes and boycotts of foreign goods were called throughout China. Those in Hong Kong lasted for fifteen months.

Under these conditions the Chinese Communist Party (CCP) also grew, and in 1926 it had about 20,000 members. The party was influential in student organizations, labor unions, and even within the GMD. By an earlier agreement Sun had permitted CCP members to join the GMD as individuals but had enjoined them from organizing CCP cells within the GMD. Moscow approved of this policy; it felt that the CCP was too small to accomplish anything on its own, and that by working within the GMD, its members could join in the "bourgeois, national, democratic struggle" against "imperialism and feudal warlordism." Zhou Enlai, for example, became deputy head of the political education department of the Huangpu Academy.

By 1926 the GMD had established a base in the area around Guangzhou, and Jiang Jieshi felt ready to march north against the warlord domains. He worried about the growing communist strength, however, and before setting off he ousted the Soviet advisers and CCP members from the GMD offices in Guangzhou. The march north began in July. By the spring of 1927 Jiang's army had reached the Yangzi, defeating, and often absorbing, warlord armies as it advanced (see Map 28–2).

After entering Shanghai in April 1927 Jiang carried out a sweeping purge of the CCP—against its members in the GMD, against its party organization, and against the labor unions that it had come to dominate. Hundreds were killed. The CCP responded by trying to gain control of the GMD left wing, which had established a government at Wuhan, and by armed uprisings. Both attempts failed. The surviving CCP members fled to the mountainous border region of Hunan

and Jiangxi to the southwest and established the "Jiangxi Soviet." The left wing of the GMD, disenchanted with the Communists, rejoined the right wing at Nanjing, China's new capital. Jiang's army continued north, took Beijing, and gained the nominal submission of most northern Chinese warlords in 1928. By this time most foreign powers had recognized the Nanjing regime as the government of China.

Jiang Jieshi was the key figure in the Nanjing government. By training and temperament he believed in military force. He was unimaginative, strict, feared more than loved, and, amid considerable corruption, incorruptible. Jiang venerated Sun Zhongshan and his three "people's principles." The grandeur of Sun's tomb in Nanjing surpassed that of the Ming emperors. But where Sun, as a revolutionary, had looked back to the zeal of the Taiping rebels, Jiang, trying to consolidate his rule over provincial warlords, looked back to Zeng Guofan, who had put down the rebels and restabilized China. Like Zeng, Jiang was conservative and, though a Methodist, often appealed to Confucian values. The New Life Movement begun by Jiang in 1934 was an attempt to revitalize these values.

Jiang's power rested on the army, the party, and the government bureaucracy. The army was dominated by the Huangpu clique, which was personally loyal to Jiang, and by officers trained in Japan. After 1927 Soviet military advisers were replaced by German advisers, who reorganized Jiang's army along German lines with a general staff system. The larger part of GMD revenues went to the military, which was expanded into a modernized force of 300,000. Huangpu graduates also controlled the secret military police and used it against Communists and any others who opposed the government. The GMD was a dictatorship under a central committee. Jiang became president of the party in 1938.

The densely populated central and lower Yangzi provinces were the area of GMD strength. The party, however, was unable to control the outlying areas occupied by warlords, Communists, and Japanese. Some gains were made during the Nanjing decade: Jiang's armies defeated the northern warlords in 1930, put down a rebellion in the coastal province of Fujian in 1934, and extended their control over southern and southwest China two years later, but warlords ruled some areas until 1949. In 1931 Jiang attacked the Jiangxi Soviet. In 1934 the Communists were forced to abandon their mountain base and flee to the southwest and then to Shaanxi province in northwestern China. Of the 90,000 troops that set out on this epic **Long March** of 6,000 miles, only 20,000 survived (see Map 28–3). It was during this march that Mao Zedong wrested control of the CCP from the Moscow-trained, urban-oriented leaders and established his unortho-

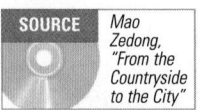

SOURCE Mao Zedong, "From the Countryside to the City"

Map 28–2. The Northern Expeditions of the Guomindang. These expeditions, from 1926 to 1928, unified most of China under the Nationalist (Guomindang) government of Jiang Jieshi, inaugurating the Nanjing decade. Warlord armies continued to hold power on the periphery.

dox view that a revolutionary Leninist party could base itself on the peasantry.

The Japanese had held special rights in Manchuria since the Russo-Japanese War of 1905. When Jiang's march north and the rise of Chinese nationalism threatened the Japanese position, field-grade officers of Japan's forces in Manchuria engineered a military coup in 1931, and in 1932 established a puppet state and proclaimed the independence of Manchuria. In the years that followed, Japanese army units moved south as far as the Great Wall. Chinese national sentiment demanded that Jiang resist, but Jiang, well aware of the disparity between his armies and those of Japan, felt that the internal unification of China should take precedence over war against a foreign power. On a visit to Xian in 1936 Jiang was captured by a northern warlord and held until he agreed to join with the CCP in a united front against Japan.

In the following year, however, a full-scale war with Japan broke out, and China's situation again changed.

War and Revolution (1937–1949)

In 1937 the GMD controlled most of China and was recognized as its government, whereas the CCP survivors of the Long March had just begun to rebuild their strength in arid Shaanxi, an area too remote for Jiang's army to penetrate. But by 1949 CCP forces had conquered China, including border areas never under GMD rule, and Jiang and the GMD were forced to flee to Taiwan. What had happened?

The war with Japan was the key event. It began in July 1937 with an unplanned clash at Beijing and then quickly spread. Battlefield victories soon convinced the

Map 28–3. The Long March, 1934–1935. Arrows trace the Chinese Communist's "Long March," from Jiangxi Soviet to Yun'an in northwestern China.

Japanese military leaders to abandon negotiations in favor of a knockout blow. Beijing and Tianjin fell within a month, Shanghai was attacked in August, and Nanjing fell in December. During the following year the Japanese took Guangzhou and Wuhan and set up puppet regimes in Beijing and Nanjing. In 1940, frustrated by trying to work with Jiang, the leader of the left wing of the GMD and many of his associates joined the Japanese puppet government. Japan proclaimed its "New Order in East Asia," which was to replace the system of unequal treaties. It expected Jiang to recognize his situation as hopeless and to submit. Instead, in 1938 he relocated his capital to Chongqing, far to the west behind the gorges of the Yangzi. He was joined by thousands of Chinese—students and professors, factory

managers and workers—who moved from occupied to free China.

Jiang's stubborn resistance to the Japanese won admiration from all sides. But the area occupied by the Japanese included just those eastern cities, railways, and densely populated Yangzi valley territories that had constituted the GMD base. The withdrawal to Chongqing cut the GMD off from most of the Chinese population; programs for modernization ended; and the GMD's former tax revenues were lost. Inflation increased geometrically, reducing the real income of officials, teachers, and soldiers alike. By the end of World War II and during the early postwar years salaries were paid in large packages of almost worthless money, which was immediately spent for food or goods possessing real value. Inflation led to demoralization and exacerbated the already widespread corruption.

The United States sent advisers and military equipment to strengthen Jiang's forces after the start of the Pacific War. The advisers, however, were frustrated by Jiang, who wanted not to fight the Japanese but to husband his forces for the anticipated postwar confrontation with the Communists. Within his own army a gap divided officers and men. Conditions in the camps were primitive, food poor, and medical supplies inadequate. The young saw conscription almost as a death sentence. Jiang's unwillingness to commit his troops against the Japanese also meant that the surge of anti-Japanese patriotism was not converted to popular support for the GMD.

For the Communists, the Japanese occupation was an opportunity. Headquartered at Yan'an, they consolidated their base in Shaanxi province. They began campaigns to promote literacy and production drives to promote self-sufficiency. Soldiers grew food so as not to burden the peasants. The CCP abandoned its earlier policy of expropriating lands in favor of reductions in rents and interest. (This change led to the widespread American view that the CCP were not Communists but agrarian reformers, despite their protests to the contrary.) The party took only those provincial and county offices needed to ensure their control and shared the rest with the GMD and other parties. It expanded village councils to include tenants and other previously excluded strata. But while compromising with other political and social groups, it strengthened the party internally.

> **SOURCE** Li Shaoqi, "How to Be a Good Communist," 1939

Party membership expanded from 40,000 in 1937 to 1.2 million in 1945. Schools were established in Yan'an to train party cadres. Even as the party expanded, it maintained orthodoxy by a rectification campaign begun in 1942. Those tainted by liberalism, individualism, or other impure tendencies were criticized and made to confess their failings and repent at public meetings. Mao's thought was supreme. To the Chinese at large Mao represented himself as the successor to Sun Zhongshan, but within the Communist Party he presented himself as a theoretician in the line of Marx (1818–1883), Engels (1820–1895), Lenin (1870–1924), and Stalin (1879–1953).

Whereas the GMD ruled through officials and often in cooperation with local landlords, the Communists learned to operate at the grass-roots level. They infiltrated Japanese-controlled areas and also penetrated some GMD organizations and military units. CCP armies were built up from 90,000 in 1937 to 900,000 in 1945. These armies were supplemented by a rural people's militia and by guerrilla forces in nineteen mountainous "base areas." By most accounts the Yan'an leadership and its party, army, and mass organizations possessed a cohesion, determination, and high morale that were conspicuously lacking in Chongqing.

But the strength of the Chinese Communists as of 1945 should not be overstated. Most Chinese villagers were influenced by neither the CCP nor the GMD, and although intellectuals in free China had become disaffected with the GMD, most did not positively support the CCP. When the war in the Pacific ended in 1945, China's future was unclear. The Soviet Union allowed CCP cadres to enter Manchuria, which it had seized during the last few days of the war, and blocked the entry of GMD troops until the following year. But even the Soviet Union recognized the GMD as the government of China and expected it to win the postwar struggle. The Allies directed Japanese armies to surrender to the GMD forces in 1945. The United States flew Jiang's troops from Chongqing to key eastern cities. His armies were by then three times the size of the Communists' and far better equipped.

A civil war broke out early in 1946. Both sides knew that the earlier united front had been a sham. Efforts by U.S. General George Marshall (1880–1959) to mediate were futile. Until the summer of 1947 GMD armies were victorious—even capturing Yan'an. But the tide turned in July as CCP armies went on the offensive in north China. They captured American military equipment left by the GMD forces, and by October 1948 the GMD forces had been driven from Manchuria. In January 1949 Beijing and Tianjin fell. By late spring CCP armies had crossed the

Mao Zedong (1893–1976) at his cave headquarters in Shaanxi province during World War II. He wears a padded winter jacket and writes with a Chinese brush. On his desk are the *Collected Works* of Lu Hsun. *Getty Images, Inc.–Taxi.*

Yangzi, taking Nanjing and Shanghai. A few months later all of China was in communist hands. Many Chinese fled with Jiang to Taiwan or escaped to Hong Kong; they included not only GMD officials and generals, but entrepreneurs and academics as well. Not a few subsequently made their way to the United States.

In China apprehension was mixed with anticipation. The disciplined, well-behaved soldiers of the "Peoples' Liberation Army" were certainly a contrast to those of the GMD. As villages were liberated, lands were taken from landlords and given to the landless. In the cities crowds welcomed the CCP troops as liberators. The feeling was widespread that the future of China was once again in the hands of the Chinese.

Chronology

Modern China

Close of Manchu Rule

1839–1842	Opium War
1850–1873	Taiping and other rebellions
1870s–1880s	Self-strengthening movement
1894–1895	Sino-Japanese War
1898	One hundred days of reform
1898–1900	Boxer Rebellion
1912	Republican revolution overthrows Qing dynasty

Warlordism

1912–1916	Yuan Shikai president of Republic of China
1916–1928	Warlord era
1919	May Fourth incident

Nationalist China

1924	Founding of Huangpu Military Academy
1926–1928	Jiang's march north and Guomindang reunification of China
1928–1937	Nanjing decade
1934–1935	Chinese Communists' Long March to Yan'an
1937–1945	War with Japan
1945–1949	Civil war and the establishment of the People's Republic of China

MODERN JAPAN (1853–1945)

Overthrow of the Tokugawa Bakufu (1853–1868)

From the seventeenth century into the nineteenth, the natural isolation of the islands of Japan was augmented by its policy of seclusion, making Japan into a little world of its own. The 260-odd domains were the states of this world, the *bakufu* in Edo was its hegemon, and the imperial court in Kyoto provided a sacerdotal or religious sanction for the *bakufu*-domain system. Then, in 1853 and 1854, the American ships of Commodore Perry came and forced Japan to sign a Treaty of Friendship, opening it to foreign intercourse. Fourteen years later the entire *bakufu*-domain system collapsed, and a new group of unusually talented leaders seized power. Seclusion, like the case of a watch, had been necessary to preserve the Tokugawa political mechanism. With the case removed, the jolt of the foreign intrusion caused the inner workings to fly apart.

It was surprising how little changed during the first four years after Perry. The *bakufu* attended to its affairs and the domains to theirs. The daimyo continued to spend every

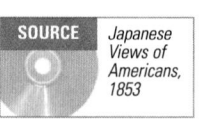 **SOURCE** *Japanese Views of Americans, 1853*

other year living in Edo. Political action consisted mainly of daimyo cliques trying to influence *bakufu* policy. The break came in 1858 when the *bakufu*, ignoring the imperial court's disapproval, was persuaded to sign a commercial treaty with the United States. In reaction, some daimyo, who wanted a voice in national policy making, criticized the treaty as contravening the hallowed policy of seclusion. Younger samurai, frustrated by their exclusion from office, started a movement to "honor the emperor." The *bakufu*, in turn, responded with a purge: Dissident daimyo were forced into retirement, while samurai critics were executed or imprisoned. The purge was effective until 1860, when the head of the *bakufu* council was himself assassinated by extremist samurai. His successors lacked the nerve to continue his tough policies, thus opening the way for a new kind of politics between 1861 and 1868.

In 1861 two domains, Chōshū and Satsuma, emerged to mediate, to heal the breach that had opened between the *bakufu* and the court. Chōshū was the first to come forth: Its officials traveled between Kyoto and Edo, proposing a policy that favored the *bakufu* but made concessions to the court. Next Satsuma sallied forth with a policy that made further concessions and ousted Chōshū as "the friend of the court." In response, the moderate reformist government of Chōshū adopted the pro-emperor policy of its extremist faction and,

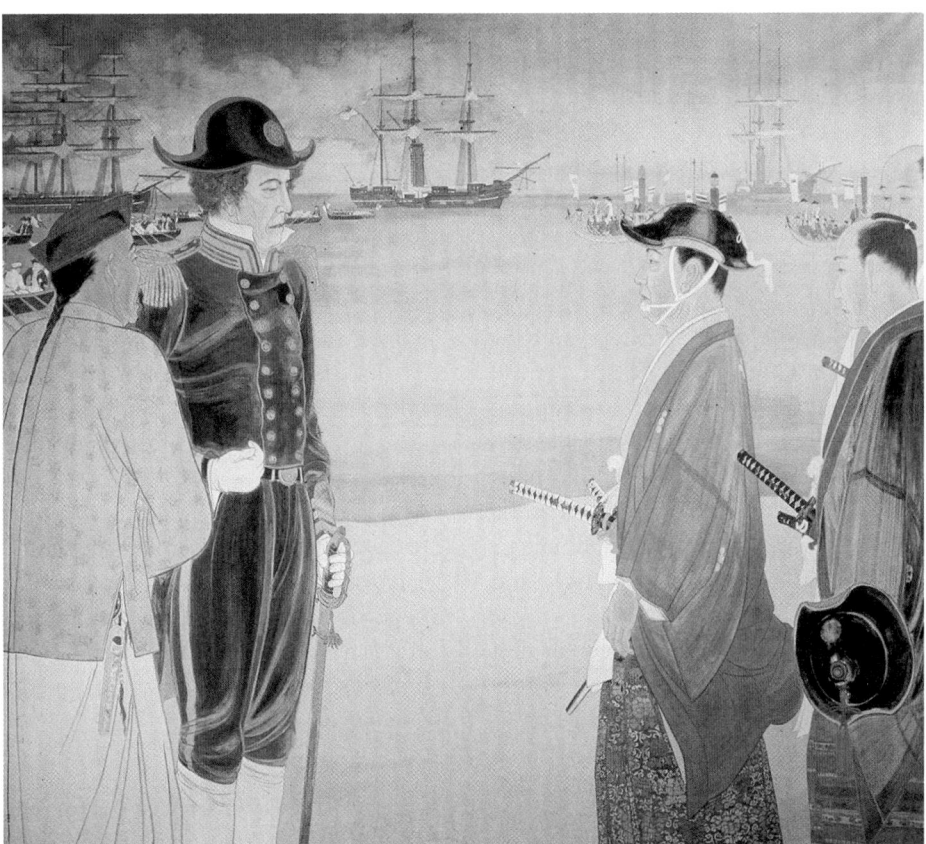

West Meets East. Commodore Matthew Perry Meeting Japanese Officials at Kurigahama in 1853. At the right are two emissaries of the bakufu; at the left is Perry's Chinese translator, who speaks English and communicates with the Japanese in written Chinese. Perry's ships are visible in the background, along with smaller Japanese craft.

in turn, ousted Satsuma. Beaten in the diplomatic game, Satsuma seized the court in 1863 in a military coup, and the Chōshū radicals returned disgruntled to their domain.

Four points may be noted about the 1861–1863 diplomatic phase of domain action: (1) Even after 250 years of *bakufu* rule, several domains were still viable, autonomous units that could act when the opportunity arose; (2) the two domains that acted first and most of those that followed were large domains with many samurai—Chōshū had 10,000 samurai families and substantial financial resources; (3) both Satsuma and Chōshū had fought against the Tokugawa in 1600 and remembered an earlier independence; (4) by the 1861–1863 period, domain politics was no longer in the hands of daimyo and their high-ranking advisers. In both Satsuma and Chōshū the new politics had opened decision making to middle-ranking samurai officials in a way that would have been impossible before 1853.

The 1863 Satsuma coup at the Kyoto court initiated a military phase of politics in which battles would determine every turning point. Events were complicated, for besides the court and the *bakufu*, there were more than 260 domains—somewhat like a circus with too many rings and sideshows. But most domains were too small to carry weight in national politics. Hereditary daimyo, for example, were influential mainly as *bakufu* officials. Of the larger domains, some were insolvent and others too closely associated with the *bakufu* to act independently. As long as Satsuma and Chōshū remained enemies, politics stalemated and the *bakufu* continued as hegemon. But when the two domains became allies in 1866, the *bakufu* was overthrown in less than two years.

The movement for a "union of court and camp" contributed to the *bakufu*'s downfall; daimyo, who earlier had criticized the *bakufu*, campaigned for a new conciliar rule in which they would participate together with the emperor. The movement came to nothing, but it led daimyo to withdraw support that might otherwise have gone to the *bakufu*. A second feature of this period was a strong antiforeignism. Samurai extremists assassinated foreigners as well as *bakufu* officials; one of their slogans was "expel the barbarians." Early on, Chōshū and Satsuma fired on foreign ships. But when Western gunboats bombarded those domains in retaliation, they immediately dropped their xenophobic slogan and set about buying rifles and gunboats.

Another aspect of the military phase of politics from 1863 to 1868 was the formation of new rifle units, commanded mostly by lower samurai. These units transformed political power in Japan. For example, Chōshū troops armed with Spencers and Minies—mostly surplus left over from the U.S. Civil War—defeated a traditionally armed but numerically superior *bakufu* army in mid-1866 with a numbing force.

A final development was a cultural shift in the way Japanese saw themselves. During the Tokugawa era they saw themselves as civilized Confucians. They viewed most of the rest of the world, China and Korea excepted, as barbarians. But in the face of superior Western technology, this view became untenable. In 1868 Fukuzawa Yukichi (1835–1901), a student of Western studies and a *bakufu* translator, introduced a Western theory of stages of history: The West, with its technology, science, and humane laws, was seen as "civilized and enlightened"; China, Japan, and countries like Turkey were seen as half civilized; other areas were seen as barbarian. This theory stood the traditional view almost on its head. Fukuzawa argued, furthermore, that technology was not detachable but grew out of the Western legal, political, economic, and educational systems. James Watt (1736–1819), he suggested, had been moved to invent the steam engine because inventions were protected by patents and inventors were rewarded with profits and honors. Fukuzawa argued further that Western systems required political freedoms and a citizenry with a spirit of independence. Fukuzawa's writings became immensely influential after the Restoration, eventually sparking the "Civilization and Enlightenment Movement" of the 1870s. (See Document, "A Japanese View of the Inventiveness of the West.")

Building the Meiji State (1868–1890)

Most attempts by non-Western nations to build modern states occurred during the twentieth century; the idea of a "developing nation" did not exist in the mid–nineteenth century. Yet Japan after the 1868 **Meiji Restoration** was just such a nation. (The years from 1868 to 1912 are referred to as the "Meiji period," after the era name that accompanied the accession of the new emperor.) It was committed to progress, by which it meant achieving wealth and power of the kind Western industrial nations possessed. In retrospect, we are aware that Japan had important assets that contributed to the attainment of these goals. But it also had liabilities, and they loomed large in the eyes of the Meiji leaders. There was no blue-print for progress. The government faced tough decisions as it advanced by trial and error. It also demanded that the Japanese people make sacrifices for the sake of the future.

The announcement of the restoration of rule by an emperor was made on January 3, 1868. In the battles that followed, Chōshū and Satsuma troops defeated those of the *bakufu*. In May, Edo surrendered to the imperial forces. Within months Edo Castle became the imperial palace and Edo was renamed Tokyo, the "eastern capital." A year later the last *bakufu* holdouts surrendered in Hokkaido. At the start the Meiji government was only a small group of samurai leaders from Chōshū, Satsuma, and a few other domains. These men controlled the youthful emperor through a handful of Kyoto nobles. They controlled their own domains through domain officials and the samurai commanders of the domain armies. They have been described, only half humorously, as twelve bureaucrats in search of a bureaucracy. But such a description belittles the vision with which they defined the goals of the new government.

Centralization of Power

Their immediate goal was to centralize political power. What this entailed, concretely, was using the leverage of the Chōshū and Satsuma domain armies to abolish the domains. This was a ticklish operation in that many in these armies were loyal to their domain rather than to the young samurai leaders, who had left the domains to form the new central government. Nevertheless, by 1871 the young leaders had replaced the domains with prefectures controlled by the Tokyo government. To ensure a complete break with the past, each new prefectural governor was chosen from samurai of other regions. The first governor of the Chōshū area, for example, was a samurai of a former Tokugawa domain.

Having centralized political authority, in 1871 about half of the most important Meiji leaders went abroad for a year and a half—ostensibly to revise the unequal treaties but in fact to study the West. (See Document, "On Wives and Concubines.") They traveled in the United States and Europe visiting parliaments, schools, and factories. On returning to Japan in 1872 they discovered that the stay-at-home officials were planning war with Korea. They quickly quashed the plan, insisting that the highest priority be given to domestic development.

The second task of the Meiji leaders was to stabilize government revenues, which fluctuated with the price of rice since the land tax was collected mostly in grain. The government converted the grain tax to a money tax, shift-

A Japanese View of the Inventiveness of the West

Document

Serious Japanese thinkers reacted to their country's weakness with proposals to adopt Western science and industry. But the "Civilization and Enlightenment Movement" of the 1870s had its lighter side as well. In 1871 the novelist Kanagaki Robun wrote a satire about a man with an umbrella, a watch, and eau de cologne on his hair, eating with a friend in a new beef restaurant. Before the Restoration, Buddhism had banned beef eating as a defilement. The comic hero, however, wonders, "Why we in Japan haven't eaten such a clean thing before." He then goes on to rhapsodize about Western inventions. See also "Liang Qichao Urges the Chinese to Reform" on page 890.

◆ **What do pickled onions have to do with the marvels of Western technology?**

In the West they're free of superstitions. There it's the custom to do everything scientifically, and that's why they've invented amazing things like the steamship and the steam engine. Did you know that they engrave the plates for printing newspapers with telegraphic needles? And that they bring down wind from the sky with balloons? Aren't they wonderful inventions! Of course, there are good reasons behind these inventions. If you look at a map of the world you'll see some countries marked "tropical," which means that's where the sun shines closest. The people in those countries are all burnt black by the sun. The king of that part of the world tried all kinds of schemes before he hit on what is called a balloon. That's a big round bag they fill with air high up in the sky. They bring the bag down and open it, causing the cooling air inside the bag to spread out all over the country. That's a great invention. On the other hand, in Russia, which is a cold country where the snow falls even in summer and the ice is so thick that people can't move, they invented the steam engine. You've got to admire them for it. I understand that they modeled the steam engine after the flaming chariot of hell, but anyway, what they do is to load a crowd of people on a wagon and light a fire in a pipe underneath. They keep feeding the fire inside the pipe with coal, so that the people riding on top can travel a great distance completely oblivious to the cold. Those people in the West can think up inventions like that, one after the other. . . . You say you must be going? Well, good-bye. Waitress! Another small bottle of *sake*. And some pickled onions to go with it!

From *Modern Japanese Literature*, D. Keene, ed. and trans, pp. 32–33. Copyright © 1956 Grove Press. Reprinted by permission of Grove/Atlantic, Inc.

ing the burden of fluctuations onto the shoulders of the nation's farmers. But a third of the revenues still went to pay for samurai stipends, so in 1873 the government raised a conscript army and subsequently abolished the samurai class. The samurai were paid off in government bonds; but as the bonds fell during the inflation of the 1870s, most former samurai became impoverished. What had begun as a reform of government finance ended as a social revolution.

Some samurai rebelled. Those in the domains that had carried out the Restoration were particularly indignant at their treatment. The last and greatest uprising, in 1877, was by Satsuma samurai led by Saigō Takamori (1827–1877), who had broken with the government over the issue of Korea. When the uprising was suppressed in 1877, the Meiji government became militarily secure.

Political Parties

Other samurai opposed the government by forming political parties and campaigning for popular rights, elections, and a constitution. They drew heavily on liberal Western models that had become widely known through the "Civilization-and-Enlightenment" movement. National assemblies, they argued, were the means by which advanced societies tapped the energies of their peoples; parties in a national assembly would unite the emperor and the people, thereby curbing the arbitrary actions of the Satsuma-Chōshū clique. Samurai were the mainstay of the early party movement, despite its doctrines proclaiming all classes to be equal. During the mid-1870s there was some movement between the parties and the rebellions, but as the rebellions ended, the people's rights movement became more stable.

On Wives and Concubines

Document

During the 1870s and 1880s leading Japanese thinkers introduced a wide range of Western ideas into their country. Among them were freedom and equality as rights inherent in human nature. Debating the questions of equality in marriage and the rights of wives, intellectuals voiced a radical criticism of concubinage and prostitution. As a consequence of these debates, laws were passed during the eighties and nineties that strengthened the legal status of wives. Mori Arinori (1847–1889), who had studied in the United States and England, wrote the following passage in 1874. He later became a diplomat and, between 1885 and 1889, the minister of education.

◆ Think of comparable instances in American or European history where new ideas led to dramatic social change. How long did the changes last, and how deeply rooted did they become?

The relation between man and wife is the fundamental of human morals. The moral path will be achieved by establishing this fundamental, and the country will only be firmly based if the moral path is realized. When people marry, rights and obligations emerge between them so that neither can take advantage of the other.

There have hitherto been a variety of marriage practices [in our country]. . . . Sometimes there may be one or even several concubines in addition to the wife, and sometimes a concubine may become the wife. Sometimes the wife and the concubines live in the same establishment. Sometimes they are separated, and the concubine is the favored one while the wife is neglected. . . .

Taking a concubine is by arbitrary decision of the man and with acquiescence of the concubine's family. The arrangement, known as ukedashi, is made by paying money to the family of the concubine. This means, in other words, that concubines are bought with money. Since concubines are generally geisha and prostitutes

patronized by rich men and nobles, many descendants in the rich and noble houses are the children of bought women. Even though the wife is superior to the concubine in households where they live together, there is commonly jealousy and hatred between them because the husband generally favors the concubine. Therefore, there are numerous instances when, the wife and the concubines being scattered in separate establishments, the husband repairs to the abode of the one with whom he is infatuated and willfully resorts to scandalous conduct. . . .

Thus, I have here explained that our country has not yet established the fundamental of human morality, and I hope later to discuss how this situation injures our customs and obstructs enlightenment.

From Meiroku Zasshi, *Journal of the Japanese Enlightenment*, trans. and with introduction by William Reynolds Braisted, assisted by Adachi Yasushi and Kikuchi Yūji (Cambridge, MA: Harvard University Press, 1976), pp. 104–105. © 1976 by the President and Fellows of Harvard College. Reprinted by permission of Harvard University Press.

Then, with the government's formation of prefectural assemblies in 1878, what had been in fact unofficial pressure groups became true political parties. Many farmers joined, wanting their taxes cut; the poor joined too, hoping to improve their condition. The parties were given another boost after a political crisis in 1881, when the government promised a constitution and a national assembly within ten years. During the 1880s the parties had ups and downs. When poorer peasants rebelled, the parties temporarily dissolved to dissociate themselves from the uprisings. But as the date for national elections approached, the parties regrouped and regained strength, and the ties between party notables and local men of influence grew closer.

The Constitution

The government viewed the party movement with distaste but was unsure how to counter it. The promise of a constitution had been one tactic. Itō Hirobumi (1841–1909),

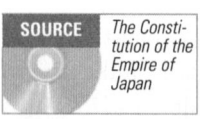 **SOURCE** *The Constitution of the Empire of Japan*

originally from Chōshū, went abroad to shop for a constitution that would serve the needs of the Meiji government. He found principles to his liking in Germany and brought home a German jurist to help adapt the conservative Prussian constitution of 1850 to Japanese uses. As promulgated in 1889, the Meiji Constitution was notable for the extensive powers granted to the

Japan's first foreign mission, headed by Prince Iwakura, Ambassador Extraordinary and Plenipotentiary, leaving Yokohama for the United States and Europe on December 23, 1871. *Scala/Art Resource, N.Y.*

emperor and for the severely limited powers it granted to the lower house in the **Diet** (the English term for Japan's bicameral national assembly).

The emperor was sovereign. According to the constitution, he was "sacred and inviolable." In Itō's commentaries the sacredness was defined in Shinto terms. As in Prussia, the emperor was given direct command of the armed forces. Yamagata Aritomo (1838–1922) had set up a German-type general staff system in 1878. The emperor had the right to name the prime minister and to appoint the cabinet. He could dissolve the lower house of the Diet and issue imperial ordinances when the Diet was not in session. The Imperial Household Ministry, which was outside the cabinet, administered the great wealth given to the imperial family during the 1880s—so that the emperor would never have to ask the Diet for funds. In every case, it was intended and understood that the Meiji leaders would act for the emperor in all of these matters. Finally, the constitution itself was presented as a gift from the emperor to his subjects.

The lower house of the Diet, in contrast, was given the authority only to approve budgets and pass laws. Both of these powers were hedged. The constitution stipulated that the previous year's budget would remain in effect if a new budget was not approved. The appointive House of Peers, the upper house of the Diet, had to approve any bill to become law. Furthermore, to ensure that the parties themselves would represent the stable and responsible elements of Japanese society, the vote was given only to adult males paying fifteen yen or more in taxes. In 1890 this was about 5 percent of the adult male population. In short, Itō had never intended to create a parliamentary system with full deliberative powers. What he devised was a constitutional system that included a parliament as one of its parts.

The government also created institutions designed to limit the future influence of the political parties. In 1884 it created a new nobility, honorable and conservative, with which to stock the future House of Peers. The nobility was composed of ex-nobles and the Meiji leaders themselves. Itō, born a lowly foot soldier in Chōshū, began in the new nobility as a count and ended as a prince. In 1885 he established a cabinet system and became the first prime minister, followed by Kuroda Kiyotaka (1840–1900) of Satsuma, and then by Yamagata Aritomo of Chōshū. In 1887 Itō established a privy council, with himself as its head, to approve the constitution he had written. In 1888 new laws and civil service examinations were instituted to insulate the imperial bureaucracy from the tawdry concerns of political parties. By this time the bureaucracy, which had begun as a loose collection of men of ability and of their protégés, had become highly systematized. Detailed administrative laws defined their functions and governed their behavior. They were well paid. In 1890 there were 24,000 officials; by 1908 there were 72,000.

Growth of a Modern Economy

The late Tokugawa economy was backward and not markedly different from the economies of other East Asian countries. Almost 80 percent of the population lived in the countryside at close to a subsistence level. Sophisticated but labor-intensive paddy-field techniques were used in farming. Taxes were high, as much as 35 percent of the product, and two-thirds of the land tax was paid in kind. That is to say, money had only partially penetrated the rural economy. Japan had not developed factory production with machinery, steam power, or large accumulations of capital.

Early Meiji reforms unshackled the late Tokugawa economy. Occupations were freed, which meant that farmers could trade and samurai could farm. Barriers on roads were abolished, as were the monopolistic guilds that had restricted access to central markets. The abolition of

The Promulgation of the Meiji Constitution in 1889. The emperor, standing under the canopy, was declared "sacred and inviolable." Seated on the throne, at the left, is the empress. *Shosai Ginko (Japanese, act. 1874–1897). View of the Issuance of the State Constitution in the State Chamber of the New Imperial Palace, March 2, 1889. Photograph © The Metropolitan Museum of Art.*

domains threw open regional economies that had been partially self-enclosed. Most large merchant houses were too closely tied to daimyo finances and went bankrupt, but there rose a groundswell of new commercial ventures and of traditional agriculturally based industries.

Silk was the wonder crop. The government introduced mechanical reeling, enabling Japan to win markets previously held by the hand-reeled silk of China. About two-thirds of Japanese silk production was exported, and not until the 1930s did cotton textiles become more important. Silk production rose from 2.3 million pounds in the post-Restoration era to 93 million in 1929.

A parallel unshackling occurred on the land. The land tax reform of the 1870s, although initially lowering taxes only slightly, created a powerful incentive for growth by giving farmers a clear title to their land and by fixing the tax in money. The freedom to buy and sell land led to a rise in tenancy from an estimated 25 percent in 1868 to about 44 percent at the turn of the century. Progressive landlords bought fertilizer and farm equipment. Rice production rose from 149 million bushels a year during 1880–1884 to 316 million during 1935–1937. More food, combined with a drop in the death rate—the result of better hygiene—led to population growth: from about 30 million in 1868 to

45 million in 1900 to 73 million in 1940. Because the farm population remained constant, the extra hands were available for factory and other urban jobs.

First Phase: Model Industries

The development of modern industries was the government's greatest concern. They developed in four phases. The first, which lasted until 1881, was the era of model industries. With military strength a goal, the Meiji government expanded the arsenals and the shipyards that it had inherited from the Tokugawa. It also built telegraph lines, made a start on railroads, developed coal and copper mines, and established factories for textiles, cement, glass, tools, and other products. Every new industry begun during the 1870s was the work of the government; many were initiated by the Ministry of Industry, set up in 1870 under Itō. The quantitative output of these early industries was insignificant, however. Essentially they were pilot-plant operations that doubled as "schools" for technologists and labor.

Just as important to economic development was a variety of other new institutions such as banks, post offices, ports, roads, commercial laws, a system of primary and secondary schools, and a government university. They were pat-

Silk-Weaving Mill in Japan, late nineteenth century. Note the division of labor: the women do the manual labor, while the man, dressed in formal attire, supervises.

terned after European and American examples, although the pattern was often altered to fit Japan's needs. For example, Tokyo Imperial University had a faculty of agriculture earlier than any university in Europe.

Second Phase: 1880s–1890s

More substantial growth in the modern sector took place during the 1880s and 1890s. It was marked by the appearance of what would later become the great industrial combines known as *zaibatsu*. Accumulating capital was the greatest problem for would-be entrepreneurs. Iwasaki Yatarō (1834–1885) used political connections. After the Restoration he gained control of the ships that he had managed as a samurai official for the Tosa domain. He next acquired government ships that had been used to transport troops during the 1874 Taiwan Expedition and the 1877 Satsuma Rebellion. From these beginnings he built a shipping line to compete with foreign companies, started a bank, and invested in the enterprises that later became the Mitsubishi combine.

Shibusawa Eiichi (1840–1931) was another maverick entrepreneur. Born into a peasant family that made indigo dye, he became a merchant, joined the pro-emperor movement, then switched sides and became a retainer of the last shogun. He spent two years in France and after 1868 entered the Finance Ministry. In 1873 he made the so-called heavenly descent from government to private business. Founding the First Bank, he showed a talent for beginning new industries with other people's money. His initial success was the Osaka Cotton Spinning Mill, established as Japan's first joint stock company in 1882. The investors profited hugely, and money poured in to found

new mills; by 1896 the production of yarn had reached 17 million pounds, and by 1913 it was more than ten times that amount. After the turn of the century cotton cloth replaced yarn as the focus of growth: Production rose more than 100-fold, from 22 million square yards in 1900 to 2,710 million in 1936.

Another area of growth was railroads. Before railroads, the bulk of Japan's commerce was carried by coastal shipping. It cost as much during the early Meiji period to transport goods fifty miles overland as it did to ship them to Europe. Railroads gave Japan an internal circulatory system, opening up hitherto isolated regions. In 1872 Japan had 18 miles of track; in 1894, 2,100 miles; and in 1934, 14,500 miles.

Cotton textiles and railroads were followed during the 1890s by cement, bricks, matches, glass, beer, chemicals, and other private industries. One can only admire the foresight and vigor of the bold entrepreneurs who pioneered in these industries. At the same time, the role of government in creating a favorable climate for growth should not be forgotten: The society and the polity were stable, the yen was sound, capital was safe, and taxes on industry were low. In every respect, the conditions enjoyed by Japan's budding entrepreneurs differed from those of China.

Third Phase: 1905–1929

The economy continued to grow after the Russo-Japanese War in 1905 and spurted ahead during World War I. Light industries and textiles were central, but iron and steel, shipping, coal mining, electrical power, and chemicals also grew. An economic slump followed the war, and the economy grew slowly during the twenties. One factor was renewed competition from a Europe at peace; another was the great earthquake that destroyed Tokyo in 1923. Tokyo was rebuilt with loans, but they led to inflation. Agricultural productivity also leveled off during the twenties: It became cheaper to import foodstuffs from the newly acquired colonies of Taiwan and Korea than to invest in new agricultural technology at home.

By the twenties Japanese society, especially in the cities, was becoming modern. The Japanese ate better, were healthier, and lived longer. Personal savings rose with the standard of living. Urban workers opened postal saving accounts, drank beer, went to movies, and read newspapers. In 1890 31 percent of girls and 64 percent of boys went to primary schools; by 1905 the figures were 90 and 96 percent; and by 1925 primary school education was universal. Japan had done what no other non-Western nation had even attempted: It had achieved universal literacy. During the twenties, the thirties, and the war years increasing numbers

Planning began in 1869, one year after the Meiji Restoration, and the first line from the Shiodome station in Tokyo to the port of Yokohama was opened in 1872. In this woodblock print, onlookers (in the foreground) gape outside the fence while passengers in Western dress await the arrival of the train. *Courtesy of the Library of Congress.*

of primary school graduates went on to middle and higher schools, or entered the new technical colleges. Nevertheless, an enormous cultural and social gap remained between the majority who had only a primary school education and the 3 percent who attended university. The gap would prove to be a basic weakness in the political democracy of the twenties.

It should also be noted that despite overall improvements in the condition of the Japanese, the human costs of growth were sometimes high. (See Document, "Natsume Sōseki on the Costs of Rapid Modernization.") Because textiles played a large role in the early phase of growth, well into the twentieth century more than half of the industrial labor force was women. They went to the mills after leaving primary school and returned to their villages before marrying. "Neither silk-reeling maids nor slops are kept for long," went the words of one song. Their working hours were long, their dormitories crowded, and their movements restricted. "Like the money in my employment contract, I remain sealed away," was another verse. Some contracted tuberculosis, the plague of late-nineteenth- and early-twentieth-century Japan, and were sent back to their villages to die. The following verse bluntly captures the public attitude towards women factory workers:

If a woman working in an office is a willow,
A poetess is a violet,
And a female teacher is an orchid,
Then a factory woman is a vegetable gourd.[2]

---

[2] E. Patricia Tsurumi, "Whose History Is It Anyway? And Other Questions Historians Should Be Asking," in *Japan Review* (1995) 6:17–38, p. 21. By permission of the International Research Center for Japanese Studies.

Fourth Phase: Depression and Recovery

A Japanese bank crisis in 1927, followed by the worldwide Great Depression in 1929, plunged Japan into unemployment and suffering. The distress was particularly acute in the rice-producing regions of the northeast. The political consequences of the Depression years were far-reaching. Yet most of Japan had recovered by 1933 and even the northeast by 1935, more rapidly than any other industrial nation.

An export boom and military procurements at home fueled the recovery. During the 1930s the production of pig iron, raw steel, and chemicals doubled. Japan could construct complete electric-power stations and became self-sufficient in machine tools and scientific instruments. Shipbuilding forged ahead; by 1937 Japan had a merchant fleet of 4.5 million tons, the third largest and certainly the newest in the world. Despite continued growth in cotton cloth during the 1930s, textiles slipped relative to the products of heavy industry. The quality of Japan's manufacturers also rose. The outcry in the West against Japanese exports at this time was not so much because of volume—a modest 3.6 percent of world exports in 1936—but because for the first time Japanese products had become competitive in terms of quality.

The Politics of Imperial Japan (1890–1945)

Parliaments began in the West and have functioned better there than in the rest of the world. For Japan to establish a constitution during the nineteenth century was a bold experiment. Even so cautious a constitution as that of Meiji in that age had no precedent outside the West; most Western

Natsume Sōseki on the Costs of Rapid Modernization

Natsume Sōseki (1867–1916) was one of the earliest of a series of great novelists to create a new literature in Japan after the turn of the century. Sōseki could often be humorous. One of his early works, *I Am a Cat*, looks at a Tokyo household from a feline perspective. He advocated ethical individualism as superior to state morality. He also wrote of human isolation in a changing society and of the dark side of human nature.

◆ What were the costs of Japan's rapid modernization? Was the uneasiness experienced by only a few advanced thinkers, or did it cut across the society? Was it different from alienation in the modern West?

THE CIVILIZATION OF MODERN JAPAN

Let us set aside the question of the bragging about the new teachings acquired from the West, which are only superficially mastered. Let us suppose that in forty or fifty years after the Restoration, by the power of education, by really applying ourselves to study, we can move from teaching A to teaching B and even advance to C—without the slightest vulgar fame-seeking, without the slightest sense of vainglory. Let us further suppose that we pass, in a natural orderly fashion, from stage to stage and that we ultimately attain the extreme of differentiation in our internally developed enlightenment that the West attained after more than a hundred years. If, then, by our physical and mental exertions, and by ignoring the difficulties and suffering involved in our precipitous advance, we end by passing through, in merely one-half the time it took the more prosperous Westerners to reach their stage of specialization, to our stage of internally developed enlightenment, the consequences will be serious indeed. At the same time we will be able to boast of this fantastic acquisition of knowledge, the inevitable result will be a nervous collapse from which we will not be able to recover.

PASSERS-BY

This is what your brother said. He suffers because nothing he does appears to him as either an end or a means. He is perpetually uneasy and cannot relax. He cannot sleep and so gets out of bed. But when he is awake, he cannot stay still, so he begins to walk. As he walks, he finds that he has to begin running. Once he has begun running, he cannot stop. To have to keep on running is bad enough, but he feels compelled to increase his speed with every step he takes. When he imagines what the end of all this will be, he is so frightened that he breaks out in a cold sweat. And the fear becomes unbearable.

I was surprised when I heard your brother's explanation. I myself have never experienced uneasiness of this kind. And so, though I could comprehend what he was saying, I could feel no sympathy for him. I was like a man who tries to imagine what it is like to have a splitting headache though he has never had one. I tried to think for a while. And my wandering mind hit upon this thing called "man's fate"; it was a rather vague concept in my mind, but I was happy to have found something consoling to say to your brother.

"This uneasiness of yours is no more than the uneasiness that all men experience. All you have to do is to realize that there is no need for you alone to worry so much about it. What I mean to say is that it is our fate to wander blindly through life."

Not only were my words vague in meaning but they lacked sincerity. Your brother gave me one shrewd, contemptuous glance; that was all my remarks deserved. He then said: "You know, our uneasiness comes from this thing called scientific progress. Science does not know where to stop and does not permit us to stop either. From walking to rickshaws, from rickshaws to horsedrawn cabs, from cabs to trains, from trains to automobiles, from automobiles to airships, from airships to airplanes—when will we ever be allowed to stop and rest? Where will it finally take us? It is really frightening."

"Yes, it is frightening," I said.

Your brother smiled. "You say so, but you don't really mean it. You aren't really frightened. This fear that you say you feel, it is only of the theoretical kind. My fear is different from yours. I feel in my heart. It is an alive, pulsating kind of fear."

First selection from M. Kosaka, *Japanese Thought in the Meiji Era.* Copyright © 1958 Pan-Pacific Press, pp. 447–448; second selection from E. McClellan, *Two Japanese Novelists: Sōseki and Tōson* (Chicago: University of Chicago Press, 1974), pp. 49–50.

observers were skeptical of its chances for success. How are we now, in retrospect, to view the Japanese political experience after 1890?

One view is that because the Japanese were not ready for constitutional government, the militarism of the thirties was inevitable. In terms of an ideal democracy, Japanese society certainly had many weaknesses: a small middle class, weak trade unions, an independent military under the emperor, a strong emperor-centered nationalism, and so on. Still, these weaknesses, as others note, did not prevent the Diet from growing in importance, nor did they block the transfer of power from the bureaucratic Meiji leaders to political party leaders. The transfer fell short of full parliamentary government. But, had it not been derailed by the Great Depression and other events, the advance towards parliamentary government might well have continued.

From Confrontation to the Founding of the Seiyūkai (1890–1900)

Two kinds of political history can be written about Japan under the Meiji Constitution. One would describe what the government did. It would include the drawing up of budgets, the building of modern military forces, the prosecution of wars, the formation of a banking system, the establishment of new universities, the reform of the tax system, and so on—all of those activities that characterize a modernizing state. The other kind of history would deal with politics, the struggles between different groups and bodies for power.

In 1890 the Meiji leaders—sometimes called *oligarchs*, the few who rule—were concerned with nation building, not politics. They saw the cabinet as "transcendental," as serving the emperor and nation above the ruck of partisan interests. They viewed the political parties as noisy, ineffective, and irresponsible. They saw the lower house of the Diet as a safety valve, a place to let off steam without interfering in the government's serious work of building a new Japan. But the oligarchs had miscalculated: The authority of the lower house to approve or turn down the budget made that body more powerful than they had intended. This drew the oligarchs, willy-nilly, into the political struggles they had hoped to avoid.

The first act of the parties in the new 1890 Diet was to slash the government's budget. Prime Minister Yamagata was furious but had to make concessions to get part of the cut restored. This pattern of applying pressure to the annual budget continued for almost a decade. Rising costs meant that the previous year's budget was never enough, and although the government tried to intimidate and bribe the parties, it failed. It even formed a government party and tried to win elections by enlisting the police and local officials for campaign support. The opposing political parties nevertheless maintained their control of the lower house. They were well-organized in the prefectures, where assemblies had begun in 1878, and enjoyed the support of the voters, mostly well-to-do landowners, who opposed the heavy land tax.

Unable either to coerce or defeat the opposing parties, and determined that his Meiji Constitution not fail, in 1900 Itō Hirobumi formed a new party. The party was called the Rikken Seiyūkai, or "Friends of Constitutional Government." The Seiyūkai was composed of ex-bureaucrats associated with Itō and politicians from the Liberal Party that a Tosa samurai, Itagaki Taisuke (1837–1919), had formed in 1881. For most of the next twenty years it was the most important

Russo-Japanese War. Japanese soldiers with flag and bayonets charge across a smoky field to engage Russian troops in the 1904–1905 Russo-Japanese War. Victory over Russia gave Japan Korea and a new international standing. The popularity of postcards, such as this one, reflected the new nationalism of Japan. *Corbis-Bettmann.*

party in Japan, providing parliamentary support for successive governments through its control of the lower house. This arrangement was satisfactory to both sides: Itō and subsequent prime ministers got the Diet support necessary for the government to function smoothly. The party politicians got cabinet posts and pork barrel legislation with which to reward their supporters. Itō had made the constitution work, but at the cost of relinquishing transcendental cabinets.

The Golden Years of Meiji

The years before and after the turn of the century represented the culmination of what the government had striven for since 1868. Economic development was under way. The

unequal treaties were revised in two steps: Japan got rid of extraterritoriality in 1899 (by a treaty signed in 1894) and regained control of its own tariffs in 1911. However, it was events abroad that won Japan recognition as a world power.

The first event was a war with China in 1894–1895 over conflicting interests in Korea. From its victory Japan secured Taiwan, the Pescadores Islands, the Kwantung Peninsula in southern Manchuria, an indemnity, and a treaty giving it the same privileges in China as those enjoyed by the Western powers (see Map 28–4). Russia, however, had its own expansionist plans and, obtaining French and German support, forced Japan to give up the Kwantung Peninsula, which included Port Arthur. Three years later, Russia took Kwantung for itself.

Map 28–4. Formation of the Japanese Empire. The Japanese empire grew in three stages: the Sino-Japanese War of 1894–1895, the Russo-Japanese War of 1904–1905, and Japanese conquests in Manchuria and northern China after 1931.

The second event was Japan's participation in 1900 in the international force that relieved the Boxers' siege of the foreign legations in Beijing. The Japanese troops were notable for their numbers and discipline.

The third event was the Anglo-Japanese Alliance of 1902. For Britain this alliance ensured Japanese support for its East Asian interests and warded off the likelihood of a Russo-Japanese agreement over spheres of influence in northeast Asia. For Japan the alliance meant it could fight Russia without fear that a third party would intervene.

The fourth event was the war with Russia that began in 1904, when Japanese torpedo boats launched a surprise attack on the Russian fleet at Port Arthur. On land, Japanese armies drove the Russians from their railway zones in Manchuria and seized Mukden in March 1905. The Russians sent their Baltic fleet to join the battle, but it was annihilated by Admiral Tōgō (1847–1934) at Tsushima Straits. After months of war, both countries were worn out; and on the home front, Russia was plagued by revolution. President Theodore Roosevelt (1858–1919) proposed a peace conference at Portsmouth, New Hampshire. The resulting treaty gave Japan the Russian lease on the southern portion of the Liaotung Peninsula (which it called the Kwantung Peninsula), the Russian railway in south Manchuria, the southern half of Sakhalin, and a recognition of Japan's "paramount interest" in Korea, which was annexed in 1910.

It is ironic that Japan, a country still not free of the system of unequal treaties, should itself have joined the imperialist scramble for colonies. Neither Japanese tradition, which had rarely looked to foreign expansion, nor Japan's economy, which was just beginning to build its modern industries and could not export capital, explains the desire for colonies. The explanation is simpler: Japan wanted equality with the great Western powers, and military power and colonies were the best credentials. Enthusiasm for empire was shared alike by political party leaders, most liberal thinkers, and conservative leaders.

Rise of the Parties to Power

The founding of the Seiyūkai by Itō in 1900 ended a decade of confrontation between the Diet and the government. The aging oligarch Itō soon found intolerable the day-to-day experience of dealing with party politicians, who, unlike the bureaucrats, neither obeyed him nor paid him the respect that he thought his due. He relinquished the presidency of the party to the noble Saionji Kinmochi (1849–1940) in 1903. Saionji also found it too much to bear and passed the post to Hara Takashi (1856–1921) in 1914. With Hara, the office found the man.

Hara was an outsider. Born a generation after the founding fathers of the Meiji state and in a politically unimportant northeastern domain, he began his political career as a newspaper reporter. He then entered the Foreign Office, eventually becoming ambassador to Korea, and then, in turn, an editor, a bank official, a company president, and a Diet member. He helped Itō to found the Seiyūkai. The most able politician in Japan, he was painstaking, patient, paternalistic, and perspicacious. His goals for Japan centered on the expansion of national wealth and power and were no different from those of Itō or Yamagata. But he felt that they should be achieved by party government, not oligarchic rule, and worked unceasingly to expand the power of his party. The years between 1905 and 1921 were marked by the struggle between these two alternative conceptions of government.

The struggle can be represented as a rising curve of party strength and a descending curve of oligarchic influence. The rising curve had two vectors: a buildup of the Seiyūkai party machine that enabled it to win elections and maintain itself as the majority (or plurality) party in the Diet, and the strengthening of the Diet vis-à-vis other elites within the government in Tokyo. For the former, Hara obtained campaign funds from industrialists and other moneyed interests. He also promoted pork barrel legislation in the Diet: Local constituencies that supported Seiyūkai candidates got new schools, bridges, dams, roads, or even railroad lines. Seiyūkai politicians established ties with local notables, who brokered the votes of their communities. When serving as home minister, Hara was even willing to call on the police and local officials to aid Seiyūkai election campaigns.

In co-opting other governmental elites, the Seiyūkai had mixed success. The party steadily increased its representation in the cabinet. It gained some patronage appointments in the central bureaucracy and in the newly formed colonial bureaucracy, although most bureaucrats remained professionals and resisted the intrusion of outside political appointees. Some career bureaucrats, however, developed working relations with the party and became partly politicized. In the House of Peers, and in the privy council, which ratified treaties, the Seiyūkai fared less well. By and large, these remained independent bodies. The Seiyūkai had no success in penetrating the military services. At most, it exercised some restraints on military budgets in time of peace.

The descending curve of weakening oligarchic control reflected the aging of the "men of Meiji." In 1900 Itō was the last oligarch to become prime minister. From 1901 to 1912 Katsura Tarō (1847–1913), a Chōshū general and Yamagata's protégé, and Saionji, Itō's protégé, took turns in the post. Both had Seiyūkai support. Towards the end of the period Katsura began to resent the fact that he, a grown man, had to go to Yamagata for every important decision.

Changes within the elites also weakened the oligarchs. A younger generation of officers in the military services chafed at the continuing domination by the old Satsuma and Chōshū cliques. In the civil bureaucracy younger officials who had graduated from the law faculty of Tokyo Imperial University were achieving positions of responsibility. Proud of their ability, they saw the bureaucracy as an independent service and resisted oligarchic control almost as much as they resisted that of the parties.

The oligarchs did, however, maintain their power to act for the emperor in appointing prime ministers. With the deaths of Itō in 1909 and Yamagata in 1922 this vital function was taken over by Saionji and, later, by ex-prime ministers.

As the rising and descending curves approached each other, the political parties advanced. Several turning points were critical. One came in 1912: When the army's demands for a larger budget were refused, it withdrew its minister, causing Saionji's cabinet to collapse. Katsura formed a new cabinet and tried to govern using imperial decrees in place of Diet support. This infuriated the parties, and even the usually compliant Seiyūkai withdrew its support. Massive popular demonstrations broke out, a movement was organized for the "Protection of the Constitution," and party orators shouted "Destroy the Satsuma-Chōshū cliques" and "Off with Katsura's head." Katsura tried to counter the popular forces aligned against him by forming a second political party, to rival the Seiyūkai. The party became politically important during the 1920s, but Katsura was forced to resign in 1913. The lower house had brought down an oligarchic prime minister.

The curves finally crossed in 1918 when Hara became prime minister. It was the first time a politician who was not a Meiji founding father or a protégé of one had obtained the post. He enacted reforms but did nothing to remedy the parliamentary shortcomings of the Meiji Constitution.

Another development was the wave of liberalism that began during World War I and culminated in the period of party governments from 1924 to 1932. Japan had joined the Allies in World War I and came under the influence of democratic currents of thought from England and America. Scholars discussed revising the Meiji Constitution. Labor unions were organized, at first liberal and often Christian, and later Marxist. A social movement was launched to improve conditions in Japan's industrial slums and to pass social and labor legislation. The Kenseikai, which had been out of power since 1916, grew steadily more liberal and adopted several of the new social causes as its own, such as universal manhood suffrage. When Hara cut the tax qualification for voting from ten to three yen—a considerable extension of the franchise—the Kenseikai criticized the change as insufficient and the Seiyūkai as the perpetrator of class despotism.

During a brief interlude of nonparty cabinets between 1922 and 1924, the Kenseikai launched the Second Movement for the Protection of the Constitution. Liberal factions of the other big party, the Seiyūkai, joined in the movement, and the two parties formed a coalition government in 1924. For the next eight years the presidents of one or the other of the two major parties were appointed as prime ministers.

The cabinets (1924–1926) of Katō Kōmei are considered the peak of parliamentary power in prewar Japan. Born in 1860, Katō graduated from Tokyo Imperial University at the age of twenty-one and entered the Mitsubishi firm. He married the boss's daughter, spent time in England, and joined the Foreign Ministry, becoming foreign minister at forty. For a country that esteemed age, his rise was meteoric. He subsequently became a Diet member, a newspaper president, an ambassador to England, and, from 1914, president of the Kenseikai. Outspoken, cold, and haughty, Katō was widely respected, if not liked. He was an Anglophile who understood and advocated a British model of government. His ministry passed universal manhood suffrage, increased academic appointments to the House of Peers, and cut the military budget from 42 percent in 1922 to 29 percent in 1925. He also enacted social and labor legislation. In effect, he legalized the moderate socialist movement and outlawed revolutionary socialism. Katō's cabinet brought Japan close to a true parliamentary government, which, although not mandated by the Meiji Constitution, had not been banned by it either.

Militarism and War (1927–1945)

The future of Japan's parliamentary government seemed assured during the mid-1920s. The economy was growing; society was stable; party leaders were experienced. Japan's international position was secure. By a decade later, however, party leaders had lost the gains of thirty-five years. By 1945 Japan had been defeated in a devastating war and was occupied by foreign troops for the first time in its history. How did this come about?

Put simply, a small shift in the balance of power among the governmental elites established by the Meiji Constitution had produced a major change in Japan's foreign policy. The parties had been the obstreperous elite between 1890 and 1926 and had advanced their influence by forcing the other elites to compromise. From the late 1920s the military became the obstreperous elite and did the same. Beginning in 1932 military men replaced party presidents as prime ministers. In 1937 Japan went to war with China; and by the end of 1941 Japan was allied with Germany and Italy, had clashed with the Soviet Union, and had gone to war with the United States.

From their inception, the military services in Japan had been constructed on different principles from Japan's civilian society. Soldiers were not samurai. The rifle companies of Satsuma and Chōshū had broken decisively with that tradition, and universal conscription had put the new military on a changed footing. But the armed services had their own schools, which inculcated the values of discipline, bravery, loyalty, and obedience. Soldiers saw themselves as the true heirs of those who had founded the modern Japanese state and the true guardians of Japanese tradition. They contrasted their loyalty to the emperor and their concern for all Japanese with the pandering to special interests by the political parties.

The military resented its diminished national stature during the 1920s, when military budgets were cut and the prestige of a military career had declined to the point where officers wore civilian clothes when off base. In particular, the fleet wing of the navy resented the decision by moderate admirals to accept a formula at the London Naval Conference of the Great Powers in 1930 that would weaken Japan's naval strength. But even during the liberal 1920s there had been no change in the constitutional position of the services; the general staffs remained directly responsible to the emperor. With the passing of the Meiji oligarchs, this meant they were responsible to no one but themselves.

A Crisis in Manchuria

The new multilateral treaties (the 1921–1922 Washington Conference and the 1930 London Conference) that replaced the earlier system of bilateral treaties (such as the Anglo-Japanese Alliance) recognized the existing colonies of the victors in World War I but opposed new colonial ventures. The Western treaty powers were especially strong in support of the "open door" in China, which in their minds included Manchuria. Japan's position in Manchuria was ambiguous. Because Japan maintained its interests through a tame Chinese warlord, Manchuria was not, strictly speaking, a colony. But because Japan had gained its special position in Manchuria at the cost of 100,000 lives in the 1905 Russo-Japanese War, it saw its claim to Manchuria as similar to that of Western nations and their colonies.

From the late 1920s the Guomindang unification of China and the blossoming of Chinese nationalism threatened Japan's special position. Japanese army units tried to block the march north and murdered the Manchurian warlord when he showed signs of independence. In this crisis the party government in Tokyo equivocated, hoping to preserve a status quo that was crumbling before its eyes. The

Yearning for Military Heroes. Japanese patriotic society members dressed as samurai around 1925.

army saw Manchuria as a buffer between the Soviet Union and the Japanese colony of Korea and was unwilling to make concessions. So in 1931 the army provoked a crisis, took over Manchuria, and proclaimed it an independent state in 1932. When the League of Nations condemned Japan for violating the open door, Japan withdrew from the League in 1933.

The Great Depression

Just as the crisis in Manchuria had called into question Japan's place in the international political order, so did the Great Depression cast doubts on the international economic order and on the *zaibatsu*. The *zaibatsu* were seen as rich capitalist profiteers in a country full of suffering and want, as the backers of the "established parties," and as internationalists at a time of rising nationalism.

Rural Japan was especially hard hit by the Depression. The real income of farmers fell by about a third between 1926 and 1931 and recovered only slowly. Our images of the depression in Japan, which may not be representative, come primarily from the northeast, where a crop failure in 1931 led to famine; children turned to begging for food from passing trains, and tenant farmers were forced to eat the inner bark of pine trees or to dig up the roots of wild plants. Urban workers suffered, too. The value of Japanese exports dropped 50 percent between 1929 and 1931. Workers' real income dropped from an index of 100 in 1929 to 69 in 1931. Unemployment rose to 3 million, and many factory workers returned to their villages, adding to the burden on the farm economy. Only the salaried middle class was better off as prices dropped.

As noted earlier, the government acted effectively to counter the depression. Going off the gold standard led to an export boom, and Japan came out of the depression more quickly than any other nation. By 1936 Japan's heavy industries were growing apace, and real wages were up. The recovery came too late to help the political parties, however; by 1936 political trends that had begun during the worst years of the depression had become irreversible.

The depression galvanized the political left and right. The political left was composed mainly of socialist moderates who won eight Diet seats in 1928, eighteen in 1936, and thirty-seven in 1937. Supported by unionists and white-collar workers, they would reemerge as an even stronger force after World War II. There was also a radical left, consisting of many little Marxist parties and of the Japanese Communist Party, which had been founded in 1922. Although small and subject to growing governmental repression, the radical parties became influential in intellectual and literary circles during the twenties and thirties.

The Radical Right and the Military The political right in pre–World War II Japan is difficult to define. Most Japanese, except for a few Marxist or Christian intellectuals, were imbued with an emperor-centered nationalism. The centrist parties were strongly nationalist and only weakly or sporadically liberal. During the 1930s, however, a new array of right-wing organizations went beyond the usual nationalism to challenge the status quo. Civilian ultranationalists used a combination of Shinto myths and Confucian values to attack the Western liberalism that had begun to enter Japan's urban society. Some bureaucrats looked to the example of Nazi Germany and argued for the exclusion of party politicians from government. Bureaucrats could run it better, serving the interests of all of the people. Military officers envisioned a "defense state" guided by themselves. They argued for military expansion and an autarchic colonial empire insulated from the uncertainties of the world economy. Young officers of the revolutionary right advocated "direct action" against the elites of the parliamentary coalition and called for a second restoration of imperial power.

The last group precipitated political change. On May 15, 1932, junior army and navy officers attacked the Seiyūkai offices, the Bank of Japan, and the Tokyo police headquarters, and murdered Prime Minister Inukai. This attack occurred at the peak of right-wing agitation and the pit of the Depression. In these circumstances Saionji decided that it would be unwise to appoint another party president as the new prime minister; he chose instead a moderate admiral. For the next four years cabinets were led by moderate military men, but with continuing party participation. These cabinets were no more than a holding pattern; they satisfied neither the parties nor the radical young officers.

During 1936 and 1937 Japanese politics were buffeted by crosscurrents but continued to drift to the right. In the election of February 1936 the Minseitō, the successor to the Kenseikai, overturned the Seiyūkai-dominated Diet. It used as its slogan, "What shall it be, parliamentary government or Fascism?" A week later young officers responded with an attempted coup in Tokyo. Leading 1400 soldiers, they attacked government offices, killed cabinet ministers, although missing the prime minister, and occupied the Diet, the Army ministry, and other government buildings. They called for a cabinet made up of military men, but Saionji and other men near the emperor stood firm. The navy also opposed the rebellion, and within three days it was suppressed. It was the last "direct action" by the radical right in prewar Japan. The ringleaders were swiftly tried and executed, and generals sympathetic to them were retired. The officers in charge of the purge within the army were tough-minded technocrats, who throughout the budget cuts of the 1920s had advocated the further modernization of Japan's weaponry. They included General Tōjō Hideki (1884–1948), who would lead Japan into World War II.

Suppression of the radical young officers did not mean a withdrawal of the military from politics. On the contrary, the services interfered more than ever in the formation of cabinets, blocking whenever possible the appointment of party politicians or liberal bureaucrats. As a result, from 1936 on moderate prime ministers gave way to more outspokenly militaristic figures.

Opposition to militarism remained substantial nonetheless. In the 1937 election the prime minister, a former general whose political slogan was "Respect the gods and honor the emperor," tried to win control of the Diet by throwing government support to the Shōwakai, a Nazi-like party. It performed miserably at the polls, gaining only 40 Diet seats, while the two major centrist parties, which had joined in opposition to the government, won 354. The Japanese people were more level-headed than their leaders. But the centrists' victory proved hollow, for although a peacetime government could not rule without the Diet, the Diet could not oppose a government in wartime; by summer, Japan was at war in China.

The Road to Pearl Harbor There were three critical junctures between the outbreak of war with China and the World War II campaign in the Pacific. The first was the decision in January 1938 to strike a knockout blow at the Nationalist Party (GMD) government in Nanjing. The war had begun the previous year when a skirmish broke out between Chinese and Japanese troops near Beijing and quickly spread. The Japanese army's leaders themselves disagreed on whether to continue. Many held that the only threat to Japanese interests in Korea and Manchuria was the Soviet Union, and that a long war in China was unnecessary and foolish. But as Japanese armies advanced, others on the general staff argued that the only way to end the war

Four years before Pearl Harbor, the Japanese invaded and occupied most of eastern China. Early in 1937, Japanese troops captured Nanjing, entering the city through its triple-arched gate. Chinese resistance led to a breakdown of military discipline and the "rape of Nanjing," an event still alive in Chinese memory decades later.

was to convince the Chinese Nationalists that fighting was hopeless. The general staff got its way, and the army quickly occupied most of the cities and railroads of eastern China. When Nationalist leader Jiang Jieshi (1887–1975) refused to give in, a stalemate ensued that lasted until 1945. China was never an active theater in the Pacific War.

The second critical decision was the signing of the **Tripartite Pact** with Germany and Italy in September 1940. Japan had long admired Germany. In 1936 it had joined Germany in the Anti-Comintern Pact directed against international communism. It also wanted an alliance with Germany against the Soviet Union. Germany insisted, however, that any alliance would also have to be directed against the United States and Britain. The Japanese would not agree; the Japanese navy, especially, saw the American Pacific fleet as its only potential enemy and was unwilling to risk being dragged into a German war. After Japanese troops were defeated by Russian troops in an undeclared miniwar from May to September 1939 on the Mongolian border, sentiment rose in favor of an alliance with Germany, but then Germany "betrayed" Japan by signing a nonaggression pact with the Soviet Union. Japan decided to improve its relations with the United States, but America insisted that Japan get out of China. By the late spring of 1940 German victories in Europe—the fall of Britain appeared imminent—again led military leaders in Japan to favor an alliance with Germany.

Japan signed the Tripartite Pact with three objectives in mind: to isolate the United States, to take over the Southeast Asian colonies of the countries defeated by Germany in Europe, and to improve its relations with the Soviet Union through the good offices of Germany. Japan achieved the last objective on its own when it signed a neutrality pact with the Soviet Union in April 1941. Two months later, Germany attacked the Soviet Union without consulting its ally Japan. It compounded this second "betrayal" by asking Japan to attack the Soviet Union in the east. Japan waited and watched. When the German advance was stopped short of Moscow, Japan decided to honor the neutrality pact and turn south. This decision marked, in effect, the end of Japan's participation in the Axis. Thereafter, it fought its own war in Asia. Yet instead of deflecting American criticism as intended, the Tripartite Pact, by linking Japan to Germany, led to a hardening of America's position on China.

The third and fatal decision was to go to war with the United States. In June 1940, following Germany's defeat of France, Japanese troops had moved into northern French Indochina. The United States retaliated by limiting strategic exports to Japan. When Japanese troops took southern Indochina in July 1941, the United States embargoed all exports to Japan; they cut Japanese oil imports by 90 percent, producing the "crisis of the dwindling stockpile." The navy's general staff warned that oil reserves would last only two years; after that the navy would lose its capability to fight. Its general staff pressed for the capture of the oil-rich Dutch East Indies. But it was too dangerous to move against Dutch and British colonies in Southeast Asia with the United States on its flank in the Philippines. The navy, therefore, planned a preemptive strike against the United States, and on December 7, 1941, it bombed Pearl Harbor. The Japanese decision for war wagered Japan's land-based air power, shorter supply lines, and what it saw as greater will power against American productivity. At the Imperial Conference where the all-or-nothing decision was taken, the navy's chief of staff compared the war with the United States to a dangerous operation that might save the life of a critically ill patient. In the end, of course, despite stunning initial victories, the war left Japan defeated and in ruins.

Japanese Militarism and German Nazism

Some of the salient features of Japanese militarism afford an interesting comparison with Nazi Germany. Both countries were late developers with elitist, academic bureaucracies and strong military traditions. Both had patriarchal family systems. The parliamentary systems of both were less well rooted than those of England, France, or the United States. Stricken by the Great Depression, both sought a solution in territorial expansion, justifying it in terms of being have-not nations. Both persecuted Socialists and then liberals. Both were modern enough in their military services, schools, governments, and communications to implement authoritarian regimes, but their values were not sufficiently modern or democratic to resist antiparliamentary forces.

The differences between the two countries are also striking. Despite the gap between its small educated elite and the rest of the population with only a middle-school education, and despite the cultural split between the more traditional rural areas and the Westernized cities, Japan was more homogeneous than Germany. It had no Catholic-Protestant split. It had no *Junker* class, nor was its socialist movement a serious contender for political power. The political process during the 1930s was also different. In Germany parliament ruled, so that to come to power the Nazis

had to win an election. In this they were helped by the combination of the Great Depression and a runaway inflation that destroyed the German middle class and the centrist parties along with it. In Japan's constitutional system, the Diet was weaker. Control of the government was taken away from the Seiyūkai and Minseitō even while they continued

Tōjō Hideki (1884–1948), prime minister at the time of the attack on Pearl Harbor in 1941 and one of the chief figures in the rise of Japanese militarism. *Corbis-Bettmann.*

Chronology

Modern Japan

Overthrow of Tokugawa Bakufu

1853–1854	Perry obtains Treaty of Friendship
1858	*Bakufu* signs commercial treaty
1861–1863	Chōshū and Satsuma emerge
1866	Chōshū defeats *bakufu* army
1868	Meiji Restoration

Nation Building

1868–1871	Shaping a new state
1871–1873	Iwakura mission
1873–1878	Social revolution from above
1877	Satsuma Rebellion
1881	Promise of constitution
1889	Meiji Constitution promulgated
1890	First Diet session

Imperial Japan

1894–1895	Sino-Japanese War
1900	Seiyūkai formed
1904–1905	Russo-Japanese War
1910	Korea annexed

Era of Party Government

1918	Hara becomes prime minister
1924	Katō becomes prime minister
1925	Universal manhood suffrage passed

Militarism

1931	Japan takes Manchuria
1937	War with China
1941	Japan attacks Pearl Harbor
1945	Japan surrenders

to win elections. They remained strong at the polls partly because Japan did not suffer from inflation and the depression did not decimate its middle class.

The process by which the two countries went to war was also different. In Germany the Nazis rose as a mass party, created a totalitarian state, and then made war. The authority of the Nazi Party lasted until Hitler died in a Berlin bunker. In Japan there was neither a mass party nor a single group of leaders in continuous control of the government. The spiritual mobilization of the Japanese population, the implementation of controls over industry, and the formation of a nationalism so intense that university students could be mobilized as suicide (*kamikaze*) pilots all followed the outbreak of hostilities. In Japan it was not the totalitarian state that made war as much as it was war that made the state totalitarian.

The Allies depicted General Tōjō, the prime minister at the outbreak of war, as the Japanese Hitler. Yet when American planes began to bomb Japan in 1944, he was removed from office by the elder statesmen close to the emperor and succeeded by increasingly moderate prime ministers. The military, to be sure, continued to prosecute the war. Even after the devastation of the atomic bombs, the Imperial Conference on August 14, 1945, was divided three to three over the Allied ultimatum demanding unconditional surrender.

The emperor broke the deadlock, saying that the unendurable must be endured. It was the only important decision that he had ever been allowed to make.

Summary

China: The Nineteenth Century. China's bureaucracy centered on the imperial court in Beijing. The court was concerned about governing China and, then, to protecting its land frontiers. For 2,000 years, the only threats to China had come from beyond those frontiers. The expansion of imperial Russia reinforced this orientation. In the east, China was protected by the ocean. Even the Sino-Japanese pirates of the sixteenth century had been more a nuisance than a serious threat, and Europeans were initially viewed in the same light. The Opium War was fought in 1839–1842, and other wars with European powers thereafter, but these were seen as "coastal incursions," which posed little threat to the Qing heartland. Far more serious were the Taiping and other rebellions, which seized villages, threatened gentry control of local society, and attacked officials at both district and provincial levels. For China, the important story of the nineteenth century was the success of gentry armies in suppressing these

INTERPRETING THE PAST

East Asia in the Modern Era: Westernization, Assimilation, and Resistance

Sources from MyHistoryLab/ PrimarySource DVD

1. President Fillmore, *Letter to the Emperor of Japan* (1852)
2. Feng Guifen *on Western Strength* (circa 1860)

Sources from Chapter 28

1. Liang Qichao *Urges the Chinese to Reform* (1896), page 890;
2. Chen Duxiu's "Call to Youth" in 1915, page 892

The process of modernization in East Asia during the nineteenth and early twentieth centuries was inevitably linked to contact with

the West—either through cooperation, trade, diplomatic and technological exchanges, or more

coercive methods characterized by outright military intimidation and colonial subjugation. China and Japan, as the most populous and prosperous nations in East Asia, possessed many of the preconditions required for modernization but had quite different experiences in adapting Western technology, ideas, and values to their own society.

In this exercise you will read four brief primary sources that focus on the encounters between East Asian nations and the West and the process of modernization.

The first document is authored by Liang Qichao, the most influential thinker in late Qing dynasty (1644–1911) China. He advocates reform and transformative change, comparing Chinese society to other regions overtaken and controlled by Western nations. The second source, authored by Chen Duxiu, is an imaginative "Call to Youth" written six years before he helped create the Chinese Communist Party. The third source is the letter that American President Millard Fillmore sent to the Japanese emperor with the naval squadron led by Commodore Matthew Perry in 1854. In this diplomatic but firm dispatch, Fillmore outlines what the Americans would like to obtain from Japan in the short term, rebellions, a success using Western weapons but based on traditional values. Not until the very end of the century after Japan's defeat of China in 1895 and its defeat of Russia in 1905 did the Chinese begin substantial Westernizing reforms—and by then it was too late for the dynasty.

China: The Twentieth Century. After the Qing fell in 1912, China was ruled for a decade and a half by regional warlords, a pattern not unlike the aftermaths of previous dynasties. But the ferment of the newly entering flood of Western ideas fed a growing nationalism. This nationalism permeated the Huangpu Military Academy that trained the officers of the Guomindang (or Nationalist) army; it lent legitimacy to the army's march north and to the establishment of the Nanjing government. By 1934, the Guomindang was winning; Communists were forced to abandon bases in south China and flee to the arid northwest. But then Japan invaded and occupied just those areas on which the Guomindang had depended. The Communists built up their army, extended their influence into "occupied China," and won the civil war that wracked China between 1945 and 1949.

The Transformation of Japan. In contrast to China, the Tokugawa regime collapsed quickly—only 15 years after the arrival of Perry in 1853. With its collapse, an elaborate

as well as his longer-term goal of opening trade relations with the almost totally isolated island nation. The fourth document is written by Feng Guifen, a Chinese teacher and official whose ideas were central to the "Self-Strengthening Movement" that attempted to rapidly adopt Western technology and armaments beginning in the 1860s.

Questions

How do Liang Qichao and Chen Duxiu each approach the task of convincing their fellow citizens that reform and modernization are necessary? What are the differences? Similarities?

How do Liang's and Chen's arguments differ from Feng Guifen's effort to begin a "Self-Strengthening" movement in China ?

What types of suggestions and guidance does the American president offer the Japanese emperor? Why was it necessary for him to forcefully advocate such major changes to isolationist Japan?

structure of vested interests was destroyed. Leon Trotsky once spoke of dislocations in history produced by modern weapons in countries with less advanced technologies. Traditional vested interests in Japan—represented by samurai rebellions using old-fashioned weapons—attempted to fight against the new reformist government in the decade after 1868, but they lost every battle. The new Meiji government began sweeping Westernizing reforms in every field. Economic growth went hand in hand with universal education. The emperor became the unifying symbol for traditional and conservative thinkers. The Diet (Japan's parliament) became the focus for progressives and liberals. A shifting balance between conservatives and liberals ensued, with parliamentary democracy making gains into the 1920s. But then the Great Depression and a crisis in Manchuria opened the way for the rise of militarism in the 1930s. One thing led to another, and Japan went to war with the United States in 1941.

Review Questions

1. Which had the greater impact on China, the Opium War or the Taiping Rebellion?

2. How did the Qing (Manchu) dynasty recover from the Taiping Rebellion? Why was the recovery inadequate to prevent the overthrow of the dynasty in 1912?

3. Did the May Fourth Movement prepare the way for the Nationalist revolution? The Communist revolution? Or was it incidental to both?

4. After the Meiji Restoration, what steps did Japan's leaders take to achieve their goal of "wealth and power"?

5. What were the strengths and weaknesses of Japan's prewar parliamentary institutions? What led to the sudden rise of militarism during the thirties?

Key Terms

Boxers (p. 890)   **Self-strengthening** (p. 885)

Diet (p. 903)   **Taiping Rebellion** (p. 884)

Guomindang (GMD) (p. 893)   **treaty ports** (p. 887)

Long March (p. 894)   **Tripartite Pact** (p. 914)

Meiji Restoration (p. 900)   ***zaibatsu*** (p. 905)

Note: To learn more about the topics in this chapter, please turn to the Suggested Readings at the end of the book. For additional sources related to this chapter please see the Primary Source DVD at the back of this text or MyHistoryLab.

The twentieth century and first years of the new millennium witnessed global conflict and global interaction—made possible by advances in technology and communication unprecedented in history.

Austrian socialist poster from the 1920s.
Economic depression nurtured both socialism and fascism in the 1920s and 1930s throughout Europe, especially in Germany and Austria, whose economies never recovered from World War I. The poster says, the "Red Man Speaks."
(See pages 966–976).

NORTH AMERICA

John F. Kennedy.
John F. Kennedy's presidency, called "Camelot" by its admirers, symbolized American optimism for the future under the youthful president in the 1960s, an optimism that would be sorely tested in the ensuing decades.
(See pages 1021–1024).

SOUTH AMERICA

Yellow star saying "Jude" (Jew) that all Jews in German-occupied Europe had to wear sewn onto their clothing.
The Nazis made Jews a scapegoat for the devastation of Germany's economy and society in the 1920s and 1930s. The result was the Holocaust.
(See pages 973–974, 995–997).

GLOBAL CONFLICT AND CHANGE, 1900–PRESENT

British and Belgian soldiers, World War I.
This image shows the truly global nature of World War I, as it depicts not only soldiers from Great Britain, but also from throughout the British empire.
(See pages 934–941).

Young supporters of Hamas march during a rally in Gaza City, March 2005.
(See pages 1120–1123).

ASIA

Anonymous painting, Industrialization Along the Yangzi River.
This painting masterfully illustrates the synchronizing of tradition and modernity in late twentieth-century China. It meshes the themes of traditional Chinese landscape painting with a vision of a modern urban society.
(See pages 1068–1076).

EUROPE

AFRICA

AUSTRALIA

A hot-air balloon from the activist organization Greenpeace sails past the Taj Mahal, protesting India's, and Pakistan's nuclear tests.
(See pages 1115–1116).

Making Connections

1

How have ethnic, religious, and national tensions contributed to conflict in the twentieth and twenty-first centuries?

2

Has globalization been a force for peace or conflict in the twentieth and early-twenty-first centuries?

Imperialism and World War I

DURING THE SECOND HALF OF THE NINETEENTH century, and especially after 1870, Europe exercised unprecedented influence and control over the rest of the world. North and South America, as well as Australia and New Zealand, almost became part of the European world as great streams of European immigrants populated them. Until the nineteenth century, Asia (with the significant exception of India) and most of Africa had gone their own ways, having little contact with Europe.

But in the latter part of that century, almost all of Africa was divided among a number of European nations (see Chapter 27). Europe also imposed its economic and political power across Asia (see Map 29–1 and Chapter 28). By the next century, European dominance had brought every part of the globe into a single world economy. Events in any corner of the world had significant effects thousands of miles away.

These developments might have been expected to lead to greater prosperity and good fortune. Instead, they helped foster competition and hostility

Queen Victoria's Golden Jubilee. By the late nineteenth century, British manufacturers were commonly printing commemorative wallpapers to celebrate special events. This wallpaper, celebrating Queen Victoria's Golden Jubilee in 1887, uses exotic images of the empire to demonstrate the power of the Queen. It probably would have been displayed in hotels and inns rather than in private homes. The flora and fauna of the empire—a kangaroo (Australia), an ostrich (Africa), a tiger (India)— as well as a couple skating on a frozen pond (Canada) surround the monarch. The distant lands of the Empire have been tamed and absorbed into domestic British culture.

Imperialism and the Great War

Europe

The outburst of European imperialism in the last part of the nineteenth century brought Western countries into contact with almost all the inhabited areas of the world and intensified their activity in places where they had already been interested. The growth of industry, the increased ease of transportation and communication, and the development of a world economic system all tended to bring previously remote and isolated places into the orbit of the West. By the time of the outbreak of World War I, European nations had divided Africa among themselves for exploitation, as the advent of steamships and railroads in the late nineteenth century allowed them to penetrate the African interior for the first time. The vast subcontinent of India had long been a British colony, producing primary products such as raw cotton that fed British industry. Much of China had fallen under European control after American "gunboat diplomacy" and the "Opium War" destabilized Chinese imperial rule in the nineteenth century.

Indochina was under French rule. The islands of the Pacific had been divided among Western powers. Much of the Middle East was under the nominal control of the Ottoman Empire, which was in its death throes and under European influence. The Monroe Doctrine made Latin America a protectorate of the United States. Japan, pushed out of its isolation, had itself become an imperial power at the expense of China and Korea. What all of the Western imperial powers, as well as Japan, had in common was a need to extract raw materials from their colonies to feed their industries. Their colonies in turn were to serve as markets for Western manufactured goods, even at the expense of indigenous manufactures, as in the case of India's ancient cloth weaving industry. This, as well as the prestige that colonies afforded, helps explain why nations were so determined to obtain and retain colonies.

The emergence of a new, powerful German state at the center of Europe upset the old balance of power and threatened the peace established in 1815. Germany's Chancellor Bismarck, however, created a new system of

among the great powers of Europe and to bring on a terrible war that undermined Europe's strength and its influence in the world. The peace settlement, proclaimed as "a peace without victors," disillusioned idealists in the West. It treated Germany almost as harshly as Germany would have treated its foes if it had been victorious. The new system also failed to provide realistic and effective safeguards against a return to power of a vengeful Germany. The withdrawal of the United States into a disdainful isolation from world affairs destroyed the basis for keeping the peace on which the hopes of Britain and France relied. The frenzy for imperial expansion that had seized Europeans in the late nineteenth century had done much to destroy Europe's peace and prosperity and its dominant place in the world. ∎

Expansion of European Power and the "New Imperialism"

The explosive developments in nineteenth-century science, technology, industry, agriculture, transportation, communication, and military weapons provided the chief sources of European power. They made it possible for a few Europeans (or Americans) to impose their will, by force or the threat of force, on other peoples many times their number. Institutional as well as material advantages allowed Westerners to have their way. The growth of national states that commanded the loyalty, service, and resources of their inhabitants to a degree previously unknown was a Western phenomenon. It permitted the European nations to deploy their resources more effectively than ever before.

The Europeans also possessed another, less tangible, weapon: They considered their civilization and way of life to alliances that preserved the peace for as long as he remained in power. The new German emperor, William II, abandoned this policy of restraint and sought greater power and influence for his country. The result was a system of alliances that divided Europe into two armed camps and greatly increased the chances of a general war. What began as yet another Balkan War involving the European powers became a world war that profoundly influenced the rest of the world. As the terrible war of 1914–1918 dragged on, the real motives that had driven the European powers to fight gave way to public affirmations of the principles of nationalism and self-determination. Peoples under colonial rule took seriously the public statements, and sometimes the private promises, made to secure their cooperation in supplying the war effort and sought to win their independence and nationhood. For the most part they were disappointed by the peace settlement. The establishment of the League of Nations and the system of mandates in place of open colonial rule did not change much. The British Empire inherited vast territories from the defeated German and the defunct Ottoman Empires and was larger than ever. The French retained and expanded their holdings in Africa, the Pacific, and the Middle East. The Americans added to the islands they controlled in the Pacific. Japanese imperial ambitions were rewarded at the expense of China.

A glance at the new map of the world could give the impression that the old imperial nations, especially Britain and France, were more powerful than ever. However, that impression would be superficial and misleading. The great Western European powers paid an enormous price in lives, money, and will for their victory in the war. Colonial peoples pressed for the rights that Western nations proclaimed as universal but denied to their colonies; influential minorities in the countries that ruled them sympathized with colonial aspirations for independence. Tension between colonies and their ruling nations was one cause of the instability in the world created by the Paris treaties of 1919.

Focus Questions

◆ Why were Western powers eager to obtain colonies?

◆ Why is World War I a turning point in history?

◆ How did World War I alter the relationship between imperial powers and colonized peoples?

be superior to all others. This gave them a self-confidence that was often unpleasantly arrogant and fostered their expansionist mood.

The expansion of European influence was not new. Spain, Portugal, France, Holland, and Britain had controlled territories overseas for centuries, but by the mid–nineteenth century, only Great Britain still had extensive holdings. The first half of the century was generally hostile to colonial expansion. The loss of the American colonies had sobered even the British. The French acquired Algeria and part of Indochina, and the British added territory to their holdings in Canada, India, Australia, and New Zealand. The dominant doctrine of free trade, however, opposed political interference in other lands as economically unprofitable.

Britain ruled the waves and had great commercial advantages as a result of being the first country to experience the Industrial Revolution. Therefore, the British were usually content to trade and invest overseas without annexations. Yet they were prepared to interfere forcefully if a less industrialized country interfered with their trade. Still, at midcentury, in Britain as elsewhere, most people opposed further political or military involvement overseas.

In the last third of the century, however, the European states swiftly spread their control over perhaps ten million square miles and 150 million people—about one-fifth of the world's land area and one-tenth of its population. During this period, European expansion went forward with great speed, and participation in it came to be regarded as necessary for a great power. The movement has been called the **New Imperialism**.

The New Imperialism

The word *imperialism* is now used so loosely that it has almost lost real meaning. It may be useful to offer a definition that might be widely accepted: "the policy of extending

Map 29–1. Asia, 1880–1914. As in Africa (see Map 27–4), the late nineteenth century saw imperialism spread widely and rapidly in Asia. Two new powers, Japan and the United States, joined the British, French, and Dutch in extending control both to islands and to the mainland and in exploiting an enfeebled China.

a nation's authority by territorial acquisition or by establishing economic and political hegemony over other nations."[1] That definition seems to apply equally well to ancient Egypt

and Mesopotamia and to the European performance in the late nineteenth century, but the latter case had new elements. Previous imperialisms had taken the form either of seizing land and settling it with the conqueror's people or of establishing trading centers to exploit the resources of the dominated area. The New Imperialism did not completely abandon these devices, but it introduced new ones.

---

[1] *American Heritage Dictionary of the English Language* (New York: Houghton Mifflin, 1969), p. 660.

The usual pattern of the New Imperialism was for a European nation to invest capital in a "less industrialized" country, to develop its mines and agriculture, to build railroads, bridges, harbors, and telegraph systems, and to employ many natives in the process. This transformed the local economy and culture. To safeguard its investments, the dominant European state would make favorable arrangements with the local government, either by loaning it money or by intimidating it.

If these arrangements proved inadequate, the dominant power would establish more direct political control. Sometimes this meant full annexation and direct rule as a colony, or it could be a protectorate status, whereby the local ruler became a figurehead controlled by the dominant European state and maintained by its military power. In other instances, the European state established "spheres of influence" in which it received special commercial and legal privileges without direct political involvement.

Motives for the New Imperialism

The predominant interpretation of the motives for the New Imperialism has been economic, in the form given by the English radical economist J. A. Hobson (1858–1928) and later adapted by Lenin. As Lenin put it, "Imperialism is the monopoly stage of capitalism,"[2] the last stage of a dying system. Competition inevitably eliminates inefficient capitalists and therefore leads to monopoly. Powerful industrial and financial capitalists soon run out of profitable areas of investment in their own countries and persuade their governments to gain colonies in "less developed" countries. Here they can find higher profits from their investments, new markets for their products, and safe sources of raw materials.

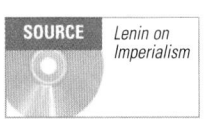
SOURCE — Lenin on Imperialism

Facts do not support this viewpoint, however. The European powers did invest considerable capital abroad, but not in a way that fit the model of Hobson and Lenin. Britain, for example, made heavier investments abroad before 1875 than during the next two decades. Only a small percentage of British and European investments overseas, moreover, went to their new colonies. Most capital went into other European countries or to older, well-established areas like the United States, Canada, Australia, and New Zealand. Even when countries did invest in new areas, they often did not invest in their own colonies.

The facts are equally discouraging for those who emphasize the need for markets and raw materials. Colonies were

[2] V. I. Lenin, *Imperialism, the Highest Stage of Capitalism* (New York: International Publishers, 1939), p. 88.

[3] *The Colonial Empires* (New York: Delacorte, 1966), p. 393.

Knitting the World. The New Imperialism was not restricted to Europe. An advertisement for the Singer Sewing Machine Company, based in New York, shows a seamstress sewing together the two halves of the western hemisphere. By the late nineteenth century, U.S. firms like Singer created a global demand for their goods. Singer sewing machines came with instruction booklets printed in 54 languages. Of the fifteen factories making the machines, only seven were in the United States. *Hartman Center for Sales. Advertising and Marketing History.*

not usually important markets for the great imperial nations, and all these states were forced to rely on areas that they did not control as sources of vital raw materials. It is not even clear that control of the new colonies was particularly profitable, though Britain, to be sure, benefited greatly from its rule of India. It is also true that some European businesspeople and politicians hoped colonial expansion would cure the great depression of 1873 to 1896.

Nevertheless, as one of the leading students of the subject has said, "No one can determine whether the accounts of empire ultimately closed with a favorable cash balance."[3] That is true of the European imperial nations collectively, but it is certain that for some of them, like Italy and Germany, empire was a losing proposition. Some individuals (like King Leopold II of the Belgians, in the Congo) and companies, of course, made great profits from particular colonial ventures, but such people were able to influence national policy only occasionally. Economic motives certainly played a part, but a full understanding of the New Imperialism requires a search for other motives.

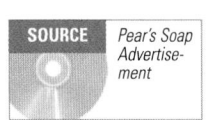
SOURCE — Pear's Soap Advertisement

At the time, advocates of imperialism gave various justifications for it. Some argued that the advanced European nations had a duty to bring the benefits of their higher culture and superior civilization to more so-called backward peoples. Religious groups demanded that Western governments support Christian missionaries politically and even militarily. Some politicians and diplomats supported imperialism as a

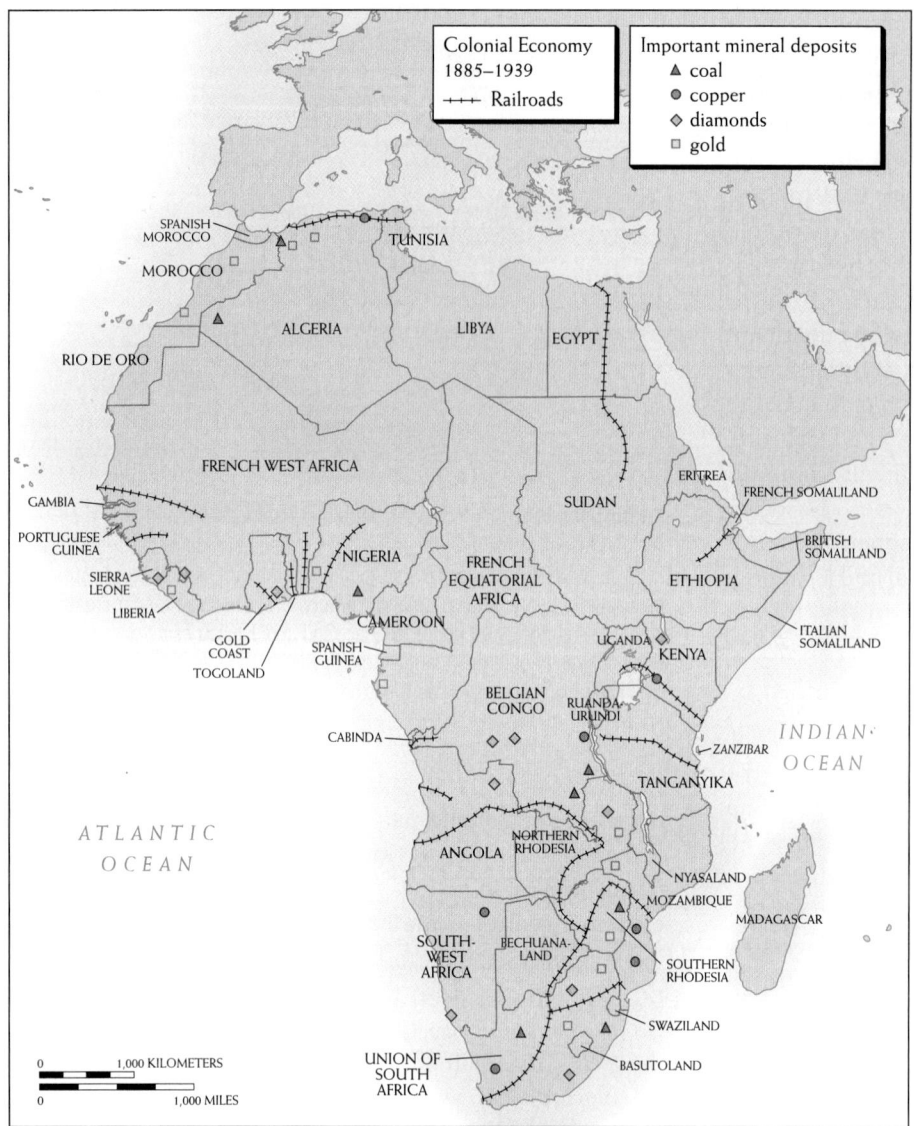

Map 29–2. The Colonial Economy of Africa, 1885–1939. The economies of European colonies in Africa were based largely on the exploitation of natural resources. Note how all of the railroads terminated at a port to link the colonies to the world market.

The "Scramble for Africa"

All of these motives were on display in the late nineteenth century, when European imperial powers expanded their economic and political control of Africa. During this so-called scramble for Africa, which occurred between the late 1870s and about 1900, the European powers sought to maximize their control of African territory and raw materials. Motivated by intense economic and political competition, they rationalized their expansionary policies on both religious and cultural grounds. The imperial powers eventually divided almost all the continent among themselves. The short- and long-term consequences were complex and in most cases devastating for the Africans. Among the long-term effects was that European control forcibly integrated African societies into the modern world economy. In the process, new forms of social organizations emerged and new market economies and political structures developed that would later form the basis for the modern, postcolonial African nations.

For centuries, European slave-trading bases had dotted the African coastline, but few Europeans had penetrated the interior. This changed in the late 1870s. (See Chapter 27). The Congress of Vienna had prohibited the Atlantic slave trade in 1815, a ban that Western, primarily British, naval patrols enforced along the African coast. Those patrols and the abolition of slavery in the Americas during the nineteenth century meant that Africa was no longer a source for slave labor except in Central and East Africa, where Arab slave traders continued to export slaves to the Muslim world until at least the 1890s. Instead, Africa became an important supplier of raw materials, such as ivory, rubber, minerals, and, notably, diamonds and gold to the West. The British, French, Belgians, Germans, Italians, and Portuguese sought to maximize their access to these resources. The competition was so fierce and the scramble for African territories so frantic and volatile that the imperial powers were constantly negotiating with each other about how to parcel Africa among them without the contest leading to war. To set the rules, the German chancellor Otto von Bismarck called a conference in Berlin in 1884–1885 that

tool of social policy. In Germany, for instance, some people suggested that imperial expansion would deflect public interest away from domestic politics and social reform. Yet Germany acquired few colonies, and such considerations played little, if any, role in its colonial policy. In Britain, Joseph Chamberlain (1836–1914), the colonial secretary from 1895 to 1903, argued for the empire as a source of profit and economic security that would finance a great program of domestic reform and welfare, but these arguments were made well after Britain had acquired most of its empire. Another apparently plausible justification for imperialism was that colonies would attract a European country's surplus population. In fact, most European emigrants went to areas their countries did not control, chiefly the Americas and Australia.

British Fort at Alexandria, Egypt. The opening of the Suez Canal in 1869 sharply reduced the time needed for travel from Europe to the Far East, and, for Great Britain, from England to its colony in India. Britain acquired a financial interest in the canal, giving it a strategic interest in Egypt. In 1882 Britain made Egypt a protectorate in order to secure the canal.
Hulton/Corbis/Bettmann.

mapped out a European-controlled Africa. African colonies had become both trophies for European powers and possible bargaining chips in their economic and political competition with each other (See Map 29–2).

The imperial scramble for Africa was not based on a universal policy, and each power acquired and administered its new possessions in different ways. Their goal, however, was the same: to gain control, or at least dominance, through diplomacy or superior force and then either to place Europeans directly in charge of administering the territories or, in some cases, to compel local rulers to accept European "advisers" who would exercise the real authority. The Europeans justified their activities by claiming that this was a civilizing mission—that they were bringing civilization to "savage" and "backward" natives. In fact, the European powers ran Africa primarily for their own benefit.

North Africa In North Africa, the experience of European imperialism was slightly different from that in sub-Saharan Africa. Because much of North Africa was still technically part of the Ottoman Empire, the European powers secured their interests primarily in two ways: through economic penetration (investments and loans) and diplomatic pressure. Force, however, was always an option.

By 1914, European powers controlled all of North Africa. France had begun the conquest of Algeria in 1830 (see Chapter 20). The French also took control of Tunisia in the early 1880s and of Morocco between 1901 and 1912. Italy seized Libya from Turkey in 1911–1912. Egypt, the richest North African country, fell under the control of Britain.

Egypt Egypt was an unusual case. For most of the nineteenth century, it had been a semi-independent province of the Ottoman Empire under the hereditary rule of a Muslim dynasty. The Khedives, as these rulers were titled, had tried to modernize the country by building new harbors, roads, and a European-style army. To pay for these projects, the Egyptian government borrowed money from European creditors. To earn the money to repay these loans, it forced farmers to plant cash crops, particularly cotton that could be sold on the international market. This proved to be a mixed blessing. When cotton prices were high, for example, during the American Civil War (1861–1865), which cut off supplies of cotton from the Southern states, the Egyptian economy boomed, and government revenues soared. When cotton prices fell, as they did after the Civil War, so did Egyptian revenue. Ultimately, the Egyptian government became utterly dependent on European creditors. The construction of the Suez Canal was the final blow to Egypt's finances.

The Suez Canal was opened in 1869. Built by French engineers with European capital, it was one of the most remarkable engineering feats of the day. The canal connected the Mediterranean to the Red Sea, which meant that ships from Europe no longer had to sail around Africa to reach Asia. In particular, the canal reduced the shipping distance from India to Britain from about 12,000 miles to 7,000 miles. The canal therefore increased the speed of international contacts and, by reducing shipping costs, made many goods on the world market more affordable. Yet the tangible benefits to Egypt were not immediately clear. By 1876, the Khedive was bankrupt; most of his shares in the company that ran the canal were sold to Britain. Egypt's European creditors took more than 50 percent of Egyptian revenue each year to repay their loans and forced the Egyptian government to increase taxes to raise more revenue. This provoked a rebellion, and in 1881 the Egyptian army took over the government to defend Egypt from foreign exploitation.

An uncooperative Egyptian government was, however, not in the best interests of the European superpowers. Britain sent a fleet and army to Egypt that easily defeated the Egyptians and established seventy years of British supremacy in the country.

Egypt never became an official part of the British Empire. The Khedives, who became kings after Egypt severed its ties with Turkey during the First World War, continued to reign, but the British exercised control through a relatively small number of British administrators and soldiers. The British used their experience from India to run Egypt.

Their primary goal was stability: Egypt had to repay its debts, and Britain was to retain control of the Suez Canal, which the British regarded as their "lifeline" to their empire

Cruelty in the Belgian Congo. A naked slave, tied to the ground, is whipped by an overseer.

SOURCE Arthur James Balfour, "Problems with which We Have to Deal in Egypt"

in India and the Far East. They built a naval base at Alexandria and installed a large garrison in Cairo. They established municipal governments that were responsible for taxation and public services and further expanded cotton cultivation. They also prevented the Egyptians from establishing a textile industry that would compete with Britain's own textile mills.

Economically, this meant that while the Egyptian economy grew and tax revenues increased, per capita income actually declined among Egyptians, most of whom were peasant farmers who owned little or no land. Politically, it led to the growth of Egyptian nationalism and to increasing demands that the British leave Egypt.

The Belgian Congo Perhaps the most remarkable story in the European scramble for Africa was the acquisition of the Belgian Congo. In the 1880s, the lands drained by the vast Congo River and its tributaries became the personal property of King Leopold II of Belgium (r. 1865–1909). As a young monarch, he had become determined that Belgium, despite its small territory, must acquire colonies. No doubt he was inspired by the great commercial wealth that the neighboring Netherlands had accumulated from its long history of colonial trade.

The Belgian government, however, had no interest at that time in acquiring colonies. So despite being a constitutional monarch, Leopold used his own wealth and political guile to realize his colonial ambitions. He did so under the guise of humanitarian concern for Africans. In 1876, he

gathered explorers, geographers, and antislavery reformers in Brussels and formed the International African Association. He then recruited the English-born journalist and explorer Henry Morton Stanley (1841–1904) to undertake a major expedition into the Congo. Stanley had previously made a great reputation by crossing Africa from east to west. Between 1879 and 1884, Stanley explored the Congo and on Leopold's behalf made "treaties" with local rulers who had no idea what they were signing. Leopold then won diplomatic recognition for those treaties and for his own allegedly humanitarian efforts in the region first from the United States and then in 1885 from a conference of European powers held in Berlin. The larger, stronger European states were willing to let Leopold govern the Congo to keep one another out. Leopold, thus, personally became the ruler of an African domain that was over seventy times the size of Belgium itself. Only after the Belgian government gave him an interest-free loan that he needed to pay for his activities in the Congo did he agree to bequeath the Congo to Belgium upon his death.

Although Leopold continued to cultivate the image of a humanitarian ruler by holding antislavery conferences in Belgium and manipulating public relations, his goal in the

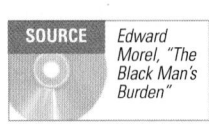

SOURCE Edward Morel, "The Black Man's Burden"

Congo was economic exploitation of the most brutal kind. Leopold's administration used slave labor, intimidation, torture, mutilation, and mass murder to extract rubber and ivory from what

became known as the Congo Free State. Eventually, beginning with the African-American reporter George Washington Williams (1849–1891) and culminating with an international outcry led by the English journalist E. D. Morel (1873–1924) and the diplomat Roger Casement (1864–1916), Leopold's crimes were exposed, and he formally turned the Congo over to Belgium in 1908.

The cruelties in the Congo, which became the basis for Joseph Conrad's classic novel *Heart of Darkness* (1902), were recorded for posterity in photographs, eyewitness

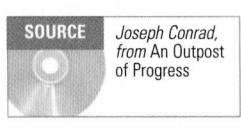

SOURCE Joseph Conrad, from An Outpost of Progress

accounts, newspaper articles, and by an official Belgian commission. The most responsible historical estimates suggest that the exploitation Leopold's administration carried out halved the population of the Congo in about thirty years. Millions of Africans died of murder, exploitation, starvation, and disease.

Southern Africa South Africa's fertile pastures and farm land and its vast deposits of coal, iron ore, gold, diamonds, and copper made it appealing to a host of people. The Afrikaners or Boers, descendants of seventeenth- and eighteenth-century Dutch settlers, had long inhabited the area around the Cape of Good Hope, and the British started to settle there after Britain took over from the Dutch during the Napoleonic Wars.

Though the British met with considerable native resistance, as they expanded in southern Africa, from the Zulu, Shona, and Ndebele peoples, they eventually established colonies in what is now South Africa, Botswana, Zambia, and Zimbabwe. In 1910, after a series of bloody wars with the white Afrikaners, who consistently resented and opposed British rule, the British formed a pact with them that guaranteed the rule of the European minority over the majority black and nonwhite population. Africans and people of mixed race whom the British referred to as "colored" were forbidden to own land, denied the right to vote, and excluded from positions of power. To preserve their political power and economic privileges, the white elite of South Africa eventually enforced a policy of racial apartheid—"separateness"—that turned the country into a totally segregated land. The result was decades of oppression, racial tensions, and economic exploitation.

Asia In Asia, the emergence of Japan as a great power frightened the other powers that were interested in China (see Chapter 28). The Russians were building a railroad across Siberia to Vladivostok and were afraid of any threat to Manchuria. Together with France and Germany, they applied diplomatic pressure that forced Japan out of the Liaotung Peninsula in northern China and its harbor, Port Arthur. All pressed feverishly for concessions in China. Fearing that China, its markets, and its investment opportunities would soon be closed to U.S. citizens, the United States proposed the Open Door Policy in 1899. This policy opposed foreign annexations in China and allowed entrepreneurs of all nations to trade there on equal terms. British support helped win acceptance of the policy by all the powers except Russia.

The United States had only recently emerged as a force in international affairs. After freeing itself of British rule and consolidating its independence during the Napoleonic Wars, the Americans had busied themselves with westward expansion on the North American continent until the end of the nineteenth century. The Monroe Doctrine of 1823 had, in effect, made the entire Western Hemisphere an American protectorate. Cuba's attempt to gain independence from Spain was the spark for the new U.S. involvement in international affairs. Sympathy for the Cuban cause, U.S. investments on the island, the desire for Cuban sugar, and concern over the island's strategic importance in the Caribbean all helped persuade the United States to fight Spain.

Victory in the Spanish-American War of 1898 brought the United States an informal protectorate over Cuba and the annexation of Puerto Rico and drove Spain completely out of the Western Hemisphere. The United States forced Spain to sell the Philippine Islands and Guam, and Germany bought the other Spanish islands in the Pacific. The United States and Germany also divided Samoa between them. France and Britain took the remaining Pacific islands. The United States had dominated Hawaii for some time and annexed it in 1898, five years after an American-backed coup had overthrown the native Hawaiian monarchy. This burst of activity after the Spanish-American War made the United States an imperial and Pacific power (see Map 29–3).

Thus, by the turn of the century, most of the world had come under the control of the industrialized West. The one remaining area of great vulnerability was the Ottoman Empire. Its fate, however, was closely tied up with European developments and must be treated in that context.

Chronology

Expansion of European Power and the New Imperialism

1869	Suez Canal completed
1875	Britain gains control of the Suez Canal
1879–1884	Leopold II establishes his personal rule in the Congo
1880s	Britain establishes protectorate over Egypt
1882	France controls Algeria and Tunisia
1884–1885	Germany establishes protectorate over Southwest Africa (Namibia), Togoland, the Cameroons, and East Africa (Tanzania)
1898	Spanish-American War: United States acquires Puerto Rico, Philippines, and Guam, annexes Hawaiian Islands, and establishes protectorate over Cuba
1899	United States proposes Open Door Policy in Far East
1899–1902	Boer War in South Africa
1908	Belgium takes over the Congo from Leopold II

Map 29–3. The American Domain, ca. 1900. The United States claimed islands in the South Pacific and intervened repeatedly in Latin America to secure its economic interests.

Emergence of the German Empire

Formation of the Triple Alliance (1873–1890)

Prussia's victories over Austria and France and its creation of a large, powerful German Empire in 1871 revolutionized European diplomacy. The sudden appearance of a vast new state that brought together most of the German people to form a nation of great and growing population, wealth, industrial capacity, and military power posed new problems.

The balance of power created at the Congress of Vienna was altered radically. Britain retained its position and so did Russia, even though it was somewhat weakened by the Crimean War. Austria, however, had lost ground, and its position was further threatened by the forces of nationalism within the Austro-Hungarian Empire. French power and prestige were badly damaged by the Franco-Prussian War and the German annexation of Alsace-Lorraine. The

French were both afraid of their powerful new neighbor and resentful of their defeat and their loss of territory and of France's traditional position as the dominant Western European power.

Bismarck's Leadership (1873–1890)

Until 1890 Otto von Bismarck (1815–1898) continued to guide German policy. He insisted after 1871 that Germany was a satisfied power and wanted no further territorial gains, and he meant it. He wanted to avoid a new war that might undo his achievement. He tried to assuage French resentment by cultivating friendly relations and by supporting French colonial aspirations. He also prepared for the worst. If France could not be conciliated, it must be isolated. Bismarck sought to prevent an alliance between France and any other European power—especially Austria or Russia—that would threaten Germany with a war on two fronts.

War in the Balkans Bismarck's first move was to establish the Three Emperors' League in 1873. It brought together the three great conservative empires of Germany, Austria, and Russia. The league collapsed when Russia went to war with Turkey in 1877 as a result of uprisings in the Ottoman Balkan provinces. The tottering Ottoman Empire was preserved chiefly by the competing aims of those powers who awaited its demise. Ottoman weakness encouraged Serbia and Montenegro to come to the aid of their fellow Slavs in Bosnia and Herzegovina. Soon the rebellion spread to Bulgaria.

Then Russia entered the fray and created a major international crisis. The Russians hoped to expand at Ottoman expense and to achieve their most cherished goal: control of Constantinople and the Dardanelles. Russian intervention also reflected the influence of the **Pan-Slavic movement**, which sought to bring all the Slavic peoples, even those under Austrian or Ottoman rule, under the protection of Holy Mother Russia.

Before long the Ottoman Empire was forced to ask for peace. The Treaty of San Stefano of March 1878 was a Russian triumph, but a short-lived one. The Slavic states in the Balkans were freed of Ottoman rule, and Russia itself obtained territory and a heavy monetary indemnity. But the terms of the Russian victory alarmed the other great powers. Austria feared that the new Slav states in the Balkans and the powerful increase in Russian influence there would threaten its own Balkan provinces. The British were alarmed by the damage the Russian settlement would do to the European balance of power and especially by possible Russian control of the Dardanelles. Disraeli (1804–1881) was determined to resist, and British public opinion supported him. A popular song gave the language a new word for superpatriotism—jingoism:

> *We don't want to fight.*
> *But by jingo if we do,*
> *We've got the men,*
> *We've got the ships,*
> *We've got the money too!*
> *The Russians will not have Constantinople!*

Congress of Berlin Even before San Stefano, Disraeli had sent a fleet to Constantinople. After the magnitude of Russia's appetite was known, Britain and Austria forced Russia to agree to an international conference at which the provisions of San Stefano would be reviewed by the other great powers. The resulting Congress of Berlin met in June and July of 1878 under the presidency of Bismarck.

The decisions of the Congress were a blow to Russian ambitions. Bulgaria lost two-thirds of its territory and was deprived of access to the Aegean Sea. Austria-Hungary was given Bosnia and Herzegovina to "occupy and administer," although those provinces remained formally under Ottoman

Bismarck and the Kaiser. Bismarck and the young Kaiser William II meet in 1888. The two disagreed over many issues, and in 1890 William dismissed the aged chancellor. *German Information Center.*

rule. Britain received Cyprus, and France gained permission to occupy Tunisia. These privileges were compensation for the gains that Russia was permitted to keep. Germany asked for nothing, but the Russians were bitterly disappointed. The Three Emperors' League was dead.

The major trouble spot now was in the south Slavic states of Serbia and Montenegro. They deeply resented the Austrian occupation of Bosnia and Herzegovina, as did many of the natives of those provinces. The south Slavic question, no less than the estrangement between Russia and Germany, was a threat to the peace of Europe.

German Alliances with Russia and Austria Bismarck could ignore the Balkans, but not the breach in his eastern alliance system. With Russia alienated, he concluded a secret treaty with Austria in 1879. The resulting Dual Alliance provided that if either Germany or Austria was attacked by Russia, the ally would help the attacked party. If either was attacked by someone else, each promised at least to maintain neutrality. The treaty was renewed every five years until 1918. As the central point in German policy, it was criticized at the time; some have judged it mistaken in retrospect. It appeared to tie the German fortunes to those of the troubled Austro-Hungarian Empire and thus to borrow trouble. It also isolated the Russians and pushed them to alliances in the West.

Bismarck was aware of these dangers but discounted them. He never allowed the alliance to drag Germany into Austria's Balkan quarrels. He made it clear to the Austrians

Bismarck Explains His Foreign Policy

Document

Otto von Bismarck, chancellor of the new German Empire, guided German foreign policy in the years from its establishment of the empire in 1871 until his dismissal from office in 1890. In that period and for another quarter century, Europe was free of war among the great powers. The system of alliances Bismarck took the lead in creating is often given credit for preserving that peace. The following passage from his memoirs, written in his retirement, sets forth in retrospect his intentions in creating this system.

◆ What alliances made up Bismarck's systems? How were they meant to preserve the peace? What is Bismarck's stated purpose for avoiding a war in Europe? Were there other reason too?

The Triple Alliance which I originally sought to conclude after the peace of Frankfurt, and about which I had already sounded Vienna and St. Petersburg, from Meaux, in September 1870, was an alliance of the three emperors with the further idea of bringing into it monarchical Italy. It was designed for the struggle which, as I feared, was before us, between the two European tendencies which Napoleon called Republican and Cossack, and which I, according to our present ideas, should designate on the one side as the system of order on a monarchical basis, and on the other as the social republic to the level of which the antimonarchical development is wont to sink, either slowly or by leaps and bounds, until the conditions thus created become intolerable, and the disappointed populace are ready for a violent return to monarchical institutions in a Cæsarean form, I consider that the task of escaping from this *circulus vitiosus*, or, if possible, of sparing the present generation and their children an entrance

into it, ought to be more closely incumbent on the strong existing monarchies, those monarchies which still have a vigorous life, than any rivalry over the fragments of nations which people the Balkan peninsula. If the monarchical governments have no understanding of the necessity for holding together in the interests of political and social order, but make themselves subservient to the chauvinistic impulses of their subjects, I fear that the international revolutionary and social struggles which will have to be fought out will be all the more dangerous, and take such a form that the victory on the part of monarchical order will be more difficult. Since 1871 I have sought for the most certain assurance against those struggles in the alliance of the three emperors, and also in the effort to impart to the monarchical principle in Italy a firm support in that alliance.

Otto von Bismarck, *Reflections and Reminiscences*, ed. by Theodore S. Hamerow (New York: Harper Torchbooks, 1968), pp. 236–237.

---

that the alliance was purely defensive and that Germany would never attack Russia.

Bismarck expected the news of the Austro-German negotiations to frighten Russia into seeking closer relations with Germany, and he was right. Russian diplomats soon approached him, and by 1881 he had renewed the Three Emperors' League on a firmer basis. Although it did not resolve all conflicts, it helped preserve peace.

The Triple Alliance In 1882 Italy, ambitious for colonial expansion and annoyed by the French preemption of Tunisia, asked to join the Dual Alliance. At this point Bismarck's policy was a complete success. He was allied with three of the great powers and friendly with Great Britain, which held aloof from all alliances. France was isolated and no threat. Although the Three Emperors' League was al-

lowed to lapse, the Triple Alliance (Germany, Austria, and Italy) was renewed for another five years in 1887. To restore German relations with Russia, Bismarck negotiated the Reinsurance Treaty that same year, in which both powers promised to remain neutral if either was attacked. All seemed smooth, but a change in the German monarchy soon overturned Bismarck's system. (See Document, "Bismarck Explains His Foreign Policy.").

In 1888 William II (r. 1888–1918) came to the German throne. Like many Germans of his generation, he was filled with a sense of Germany's destiny as the leading power of Europe. To achieve a "place in the sun," he and his contemporaries wanted a navy and colonies like Britain's. These aims, of course, ran counter to Bismarck's limited continental policy. In 1890 William used a disagreement over domestic policy to dismiss Bismarck.

During Bismarck's time, Germany was a force for European peace and was increasingly understood to be so. This position would not have been possible without its great military power. But it also required the leadership of a statesman who could exercise restraint and make a realistic estimate of what his country needed and what was possible.

Forging the Triple Entente (1890–1907)

Franco-Russian Alliance Almost immediately after Bismarck's retirement, his system of alliances collapsed. His successor, General Leo von Caprivi (1831–1899), refused the Russian request to renew the Reinsurance Treaty, which he considered incompatible with the Austrian alliance. Political isolation and the need for foreign capital unexpectedly drove the Russians towards France. The French, who were even more isolated, were glad to pour capital into Russia if it would help produce an alliance and security against Germany. In 1894 the Franco-Russian alliance was signed.

Britain and Germany Britain now became the key to the international situation. Colonial rivalries pitted the British against the Russians in Central Asia and against the French in Africa. Traditionally, Britain had also opposed Russian control of Constantinople and the Dardanelles and French control of the Low Countries. There was no reason to think that Britain would soon become friendly with its traditional rivals or abandon its usual friendliness towards the Germans. Yet within a decade of William II's accession, Germany had become the enemy in the minds of the British. The problem lay in the foreign and naval policies of the German emperor and his ministers.

At first Germany tried to win the British over to the Triple Alliance, but when Britain clung to "splendid isolation," German policy changed. The idea was to demonstrate Germany's worthiness as an ally by withdrawing support and even making trouble for Britain.

The Germans began to exert pressure against Britain in Africa by barring British attempts to build a railroad from Capetown to Cairo. They also openly sympathized with the Boers of South Africa in their resistance to British expansion. In 1896 William insulted the British by sending a congratulatory telegram to Paul Kruger (1825–1904), president of the Transvaal, for repulsing a British raid "without having to appeal to friendly powers for assistance."

In 1898 William's dream of a German navy began to achieve reality with the passage of a naval law providing for nineteen battleships. In 1900 a second law doubled that figure. The architect of the new navy was Admiral Alfred von Tirpitz (1849–1930), who openly proclaimed that Germany's naval policy was aimed at Britain. His "risk" theory argued that Germany could build a fleet strong enough, not to defeat the British, but to inflict enough damage to make the British navy inferior to those of other powers like France or the United States. The threat posed by the German navy did more to antagonize British opinion than anything else. As the German navy grew and German policies seemed to become more threatening, the British were alarmed enough to abandon their traditional attitudes and policies (see Figure 29–1).

Entente Cordiale The first breach in Britain's isolation came in 1902 when an alliance was concluded with Japan to help defend British interests in the Far East against Russia. Next, Britain in 1904 concluded a series of agreements with the French, collectively called the Entente Cordiale. It was not a formal treaty and had no military provisions, but it settled all outstanding colonial differences between the two nations. The Entente Cordiale was a big step towards aligning the British with Germany's great potential enemy.

First Moroccan Crisis At this point Germany decided to test the new understanding between Britain and France and to press for colonial gains. In March 1905 William II landed at Tangier, challenged the French predominance there in a speech in favor of Moroccan independence, and by implication asserted Germany's right to participate in Morocco's destiny. Germany's chancellor, Prince Bernhard

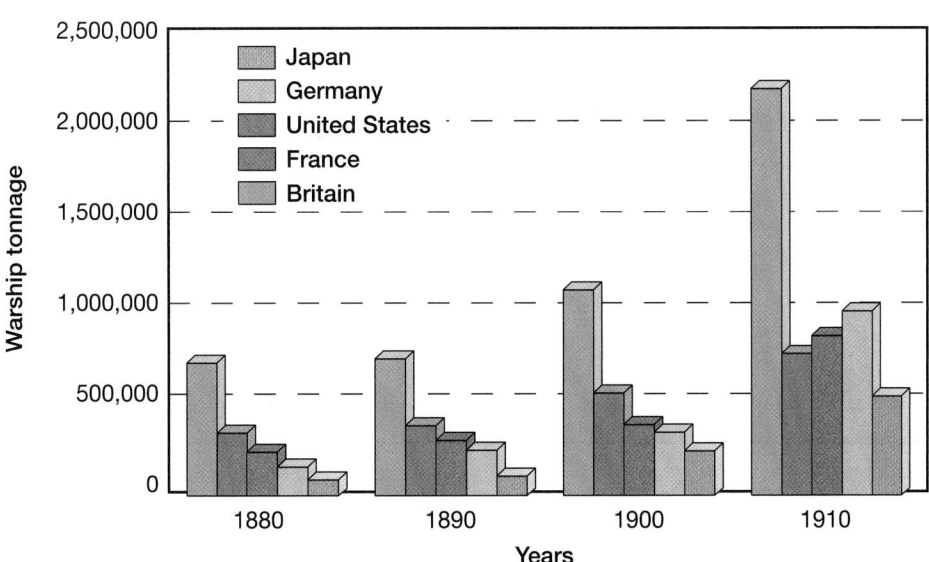

Figure 29–1. Warship Tonnage of the World's Navies, 1880–1910. Naval strength was the primary index of power before World War I. Paul Kennedy, *Rise and Fall of the Great Powers* (New York: Random House, 1987), p. 203.

von Bülow (1849–1929), intended to show France how weak it was and how little it could expect from Britain; he also hoped to gain significant colonial concessions.

The Germans might well have achieved their aims, but they demanded an international conference to exhibit their power more dramatically. The conference met in 1906 at Algeciras in Spain. Austria sided with its German ally, but Spain, Italy, and the United States voted with Britain and France. The Germans had overplayed their hand, and the French were confirmed in their position in Morocco. German bullying had, moreover, driven Britain and France closer together. In the face of a possible German attack on France, Sir Edward Grey (1862–1933), the British foreign secretary, without making a firm commitment, authorized conversations between the British and French general staffs. Their agreements became morally binding as the years passed. By 1914 French and British military and naval plans were so mutually dependent that the two countries were effectively, if not formally, allies.

British Agreement with Russia Britain's new relationship with France was surprising. But hardly anyone believed that the British whale and the Russian bear would ever be allies. The Russo-Japanese War of 1904–1905 made such a development seem even less likely because Britain was allied with Russia's enemy. But Britain had behaved with restraint, and the Russians were chastened by their humiliating defeat. The defeat had also led to the Russian Revolution of 1905, which left Russia weak and reduced British apprehensions. The British were also concerned that Russia might again drift into the German orbit.

With French support, the British made overtures to the Russians and in 1907 concluded an agreement with them that settled Russo-British quarrels in Central Asia and Persia and opened the door for wider cooperation. The Triple Entente, an informal but powerful association of Britain, France, and Russia, was now ranged against the Triple Alliance. Because Italy was unreliable, Germany and Austria-Hungary stood surrounded by two great land powers and Great Britain.

William II and his ministers had turned Bismarck's nightmare of the prospect of a two-front war with France and Russia into a reality and had made it more horrible by adding Britain to the hostile coalition. Bismarck's alliance system had been intended to maintain peace, but the new one increased the risk of war and made the Balkans, where Austrian and Russian ambitions clashed, a likely spot for it. Bismarck's diplomacy had left France isolated and impotent; the new arrangement found France associated with the two greatest powers in Europe, apart from Germany. The Germans could rely only on Austria, where troubles made it more likely to need aid than to provide it.

World War I

The Road to War (1908–1914)

The situation in the Balkans was exceedingly complicated. The weak Ottoman Empire controlled the central strip running west from Constantinople to the Adriatic. North and south of it were the independent states of Romania, Montenegro, Serbia, and Greece; Bulgaria, while technically still part of the empire, was legally autonomous and practically independent. The Austro-Hungarian Empire included Croatia and Slovenia and since 1878 had "occupied and administered" Bosnia and Herzegovina.

Except for the Greeks and the Romanians, most of the inhabitants of the Balkans spoke variants of the same Slavic language and felt a cultural and historical kinship with one another and with Russia. For centuries they had been ruled by Austrians, Hungarians, or Turks, and the growing nationalism that characterized late-nineteenth-century Europe made many of them eager for liberty or at least autonomy. The more radical among them longed for a union of the south Slavic, or Yugoslav, peoples in a single nation. They looked to independent Serbia as the center of the new nation and hoped to detach all the Slavic provinces (especially Bosnia, which bordered on Serbia) from Austria. Serbia was to unite the Slavs at the expense of Austria, as Piedmont had united the Italians, and Prussia the Germans.

In 1908 a group of modernizing reformers called the Young Turks overthrew the Ottoman government. This threatened to revive the empire and to interfere with the plans of the European jackals to pounce on the Ottoman corpse. These events precipitated the first of a series of Balkan crises that would eventually lead to world war.

The Bosnian Crisis In 1908 the Austrian and Russian governments decided to act before Turkey became strong enough to resist. They agreed to call an international conference in which each of them would support the other's demands. Russia would agree to the Austrian annexation of Bosnia and Herzegovina, and Austria would support Russia's request to open the Dardanelles to Russian warships.

Austria, however, declared the annexation unilaterally before any conference was called. The British, ever concerned about their own position in the Mediterranean, rejected the Russian demand. The Russians, feeling betrayed by the British, were humiliated and furious. Their "little brothers," the Serbs, were enraged by the loss of Bosnia, which they had hoped one day to include in an independent south Slavic nation led by themselves. The Russians were too weak to do anything but accept the new situation. The Germans had not been warned in advance of Austria's plans and were unhappy because the action threatened their relations with Russia. But Germany felt so dependent on the Dual Alliance that it assured Austria of its support. Austria had been given a free hand, and to an extent German policy was being made in Vienna. It was a dangerous precedent. At the same time, the failure of Britain and France to support Russia strained the Triple Entente and made it harder for them to oppose Russian interests again if they wanted to retain Russian friendship.

Second Moroccan Crisis The second Moroccan crisis, in 1911, emphasized the French and British need for mutual support. When France sent in an army to put down a rebellion, Germany took the opportunity to "protect German interests" in Morocco as a means of extorting colonial concessions in the French Congo. To add force to their demands, the Germans sent the gunboat *Panther* to the port of Agadir, allegedly to protect German citizens there. Once again, as in 1905, the Germans went too far. The *Panther*'s visit to Agadir alarmed Britain. For some time Anglo-German relations had been deteriorating, chiefly because of the naval race, but negotiations failed to persuade William II and Tirpitz to slow down naval construction.

In this atmosphere, the British heard of the *Panther*'s arrival in Morocco. They mistakenly believed that the Germans meant to turn Agadir into a naval base on the Atlantic. The crisis passed when France yielded some insignificant bits of the Congo and Germany withdrew from Morocco. The main result was to increase British fear of, and hostility to, Germany and to draw Britain closer to France. Specific plans were now formulated for a British expeditionary force to help defend France against German

attack. The British and French navies agreed to cooperate. If France were attacked by Germany, Britain had to help defend the French, for its own security was inextricably tied up with that of France.

The Balkan Wars After the second Moroccan crisis, Italy feared that the recognition of the French protectorate in Morocco would encourage France to move into Libya. Consequently, in 1911 Italy attacked the Ottoman Empire to anticipate the French, defeated the faltering Turks, and obtained Libya and the Dodecanese Islands in the Aegean. The Italian victory encouraged the Balkan states to try their luck. In 1912 Bulgaria, Greece, Montenegro, and Serbia attacked the Ottoman Empire and won easily (see Map 29–4). After this First Balkan War the victors fell out among themselves. The Serbs and the Bulgarians quarreled about the division of Macedonia, and in 1913 a Second Balkan War erupted. This time the Ottoman Empire and Romania joined Greece and Serbia against Bulgaria, which lost much of what it had gained since 1878.

The alarmed Austrians were determined to limit Serbian gains and especially to prevent the Serbs from obtaining a port on the Adriatic. An international conference sponsored by Britain in early 1913 resolved the matter in Austria's favor and called for an independent kingdom of Albania. But Austria felt humiliated by the public airing of Serbian demands. At first the Serbs defied the powers and stayed in Albania. Under Austrian pressure they withdrew, but in September 1913, after the Second Balkan War, the Serbs reoccupied sections of Albania. In mid-October Austria

Map 29–4.   The Balkans, 1912–1913. Two maps show the Balkans before (a) and after (b) the two Balkan Wars; note the Ottoman retreat. In (c) we see the geographical relationship of the Central Powers and their Bulgarian and Turkish allies.

unilaterally issued an ultimatum to Serbia, which again withdrew from Albania. During this crisis many Austrians had wanted an all-out attack on Serbia to remove its threat once and for all. In Russia, Pan-Slavic sentiment pressed Czar Nicholas II (r. 1894–1917) to take a firm stand, but Russia nonetheless once again let Austria have its way.

The lessons learned from this crisis profoundly influenced behavior in the final crisis of 1914. The Russians had, as in 1908, been embarrassed by their passivity, and their allies were now more reluctant to restrain them. The Austrians were embarrassed by the results of accepting an international conference and were determined not to do it again. They had seen that better results might be obtained from a threat of direct force; they and their German allies did not miss the lesson.

Assassination of the Archduke. Above: The Austrian Archduke Franz Ferdinand and his wife in Sarajevo on June 28, 1914. Later in the day the royal couple were assassinated by young revolutionaries trained and supplied in Serbia, igniting the crisis that led to World War I. Below: Moments after the assassination the Austrian police captured one of the assassins. *Brown Brothers.*

Sarajevo and the Outbreak of War (June–August 1914)

The Assassination On June 28, 1914, a young Bosnian nationalist shot and killed the Austrian Archduke Francis Ferdinand (1863–1914), heir to the throne, and his wife as they drove through the Bosnian capital of Sarajevo. The assassin was a member of a conspiracy hatched by a political terrorist society called Union or Death, better known as the Black Hand. The chief of intelligence of the Serbian army's general staff had helped plan the crime. Even though his role was not actually known at the time, it was generally believed that Serbian officials were involved. The glee of the Serbian press supported that belief.

Germany and Austria's Response The assassination was condemned throughout Europe. To those Austrians who had long favored an attack on Serbia as a solution to the empire's Slavic problem, the opportunity seemed irresistible. But it was never easy for the Dual Monarchy to make a decision. Conrad von Hotzendorf (1852–1925), chief of the Austrian general staff, urged an attack as he had often done before. Count Stefan Tisza (1861–1918), speaking for Hungary, resisted. Count Leopold Berchtold (1863–1942), the Austro-Hungarian foreign minister, knew that German support would be required if Russia should decide to protect Serbia. He also knew that nothing could be done without Tisza's approval and that only German support could persuade the Hungarians to accept a war. The question of peace or war, therefore, had to be answered in Berlin.

William II and Chancellor Theobald von Bethmann-Hollweg (1856–1921) readily promised German support for an attack on Serbia. It has often been said that they gave the Austrians a "blank check," but their message was firmer than that. They urged the Austrians to move swiftly, while the other powers were still angry at Serbia. They also indicated that a failure to act would be taken as evidence of Austria-Hungary's weakness and uselessness as an ally. Therefore, the Austrians never wavered in their determination to attack Serbia. They hoped, with the protection of Germany, to fight a limited war that would not bring on a general European conflict. However, they were prepared to risk even the latter. The Germans also knew that they risked a general war, but they hoped to "localize" the fight between Austria and Serbia.

These calculations proved to be incorrect. Bethmann-Hollweg hoped that the Austrians would strike swiftly and present the powers with a *fait accompli* while the outrage of the assassination was still fresh. He also hoped that German support would deter Russian involvement. Failing that, he was prepared for a continental war that would bring rapid victory over France and allow a full-scale attack on the Russians, who were always slow to bring their strength into action. This policy depended on British neutrality, and the German chancellor convinced himself that the British could be persuaded to stand aloof.

However, the Austrians were slow to act. They did not even deliver their deliberately unacceptable ultimatum to Serbia until July 24, when the general hostility towards Serbia had begun to subside. Serbia further embarrassed the Austrians by returning so soft and conciliatory an answer that even the mercurial German emperor thought it removed all reason for war. But the Austrians were determined not to turn back. On July 28 they declared war on Serbia, even though they could not field an army until mid-August.

Chronology

Coming of World War I

1871	End of the Franco-Prussian War; creation of the German Empire; German annexation of Alsace-Lorraine
1873	Three Emperors' League (Germany, Russia, and Austria-Hungary)
1875	Russo-Turkish War
1878	Congress of Berlin
1879	Dual Alliance between Germany and Austria
1881	Three Emperors' League is renewed
1882	Italy joins Germany and Austria in Triple Alliance
1888	William II becomes German emperor
1890	Bismarck dismissed
1894	Franco-Russian alliance
1898	Germany begins to build battleship navy
1902	British alliance with Japan
1904	Entente Cordiale between Britain and France
1904–1905	Russo-Japanese War
1905	First Moroccan crisis
1907	British agreement with Russia
1908–1909	Bosnian crisis
1911	Second Moroccan crisis; Italy attacks Turkey
1912–1913	First and Second Balkan Wars
1914	Outbreak of World War I

The Triple Entente's Response The Russians, previously so often forced to back off, responded angrily to the Austrian demands on Serbia. The most conservative elements of the Russian government feared that war would bring on revolution as it had in 1905. But nationalists, Pan-Slavs, and most of the politically conscious classes in general demanded action. The government ordered partial **mobilization**, against Austria only. This policy was militarily impossible, but its purpose was diplomatic: to pressure Austria to hold back its attack on Serbia.

Mobilization of any kind, however, was dangerous because it was generally understood to be equivalent to an act of war. It was especially alarming to General Helmuth von Moltke (1848–1916), head of the German general staff. The possibility that the Russians might start mobilization before the Germans could move would upset the delicate timing of Germany's only battle plan—the **Schlieffen Plan**, which required an attack on France first—and would endanger Germany. From this point on, Moltke pressed for German mobilization and war. The pressure of military necessity mounted until it became irresistible (see Map 29–5).

The Western European powers were not eager for war. France's president and prime minister were on their way back from a visit to Russia when the crisis flared up again on July 24. The Austrians had, in fact, timed their ultimatum precisely, so that these two men would be at sea at the crucial moment. Had they been in Paris they might have

Map 29–5. The Schlieffen Plan of 1905. Germany's grand strategy for quickly winning the war against France in 1914 is shown by the wheeling arrows on the map. The crushing blows at France were, in the original plan, to be followed by the release of troops for use against Russia on Germany's Eastern Front. But the plan was not adequately implemented, and the war on the Western Front became a long contest instead.

The Western Front. French troops advancing on the Western Front. This scene of trench warfare characterizes the twentieth century's first great international conflict. The trenches were protected by barbed wire and machine guns, which gave defenders the advantage. *Hulton/Corbis-Bettmann.*

attempted to restrain the Russians. But the French ambassador to Russia gave the Russians the same assurances that Germany had given its ally. The British worked hard to avoid trouble by traditional means: a conference of the powers. Austria, still smarting from its humiliation after the London Conference of 1913, would not hear of it. The Germans privately supported the Austrians but were publicly conciliatory in the hope of keeping the British neutral.

Soon, however, Bethmann-Hollweg realized what he should have known from the first: If Germany attacked France, Britain must fight. Until July 30 his public appeals to Austria for restraint were a sham. Thereafter, he sincerely tried to persuade the Austrians to negotiate and to avoid a general war, but it was too late. While Bethmann-Hollweg was urging restraint on the Austrians, Moltke was pressing them to act. The Austrians wondered who was in charge in Berlin, but they could not retreat without losing their own self-respect and that of the Germans.

On July 30 Austria ordered mobilization against Russia. Bethmann-Hollweg resisted the enormous pressure to mobilize, not because he had any further hope of avoiding war but because he wanted Russia to mobilize against Germany first and appear to be the aggressor. Only thus could he win the support of the German nation for war, especially the pacifistic Social Democrats. His luck was good this time. The news of Russian general mobilization came only minutes before Germany would have mobilized in any case. The Schlieffen Plan went into effect. The Germans invaded Luxembourg on August 1 and Belgium on August 3. The lat-

ter invasion violated the treaty of 1839, in which the British had guaranteed Belgian neutrality. This factor undermined the considerable sentiment in Britain for neutrality and united the nation against Germany. Germany then invaded France, and on August 4 Britain declared war on Germany.

The Great War had begun. As Sir Edward Grey put it, the lights were going out all over Europe. They would come on again, but Europe would never be the same.

Strategies and Stalemate (1914–1917)

Throughout Europe jubilation greeted the outbreak of war. No general war had been fought since Napoleon, and the horrors of modern warfare were not yet understood. The dominant memory was of Bismarck's swift and decisive campaigns, in which costs and casualties were light and the rewards great.

Both sides expected to take the offensive, force a battle on favorable ground, and win a quick victory. The Triple Entente powers—or the Allies, as they came to be called—had superior numbers and financial resources as well as command of the sea. Germany and Austria, the Central Powers, had the advantages of internal lines of communication and of having launched their attack first.

After 1905 Germany's only war plan was the one developed by Count Alfred von Schlieffen (1833–1913), chief of the German general staff from 1891 to 1906 (see Map 29–5). It aimed to outflank the French defenses by sweeping through Belgium to the Channel, then wheeling to the south and east to envelop the French and crush them against the German fortresses in Lorraine. In the east the Germans planned to stand on the defensive against Russia until France had been beaten, a task they thought would take only six weeks.

The apparent risk, besides the violation of Belgian neutrality and the consequent alienation of Britain, lay in weakening the German defenses against a direct attack across the frontier. Yet Schlieffen is said to have uttered the dying words, "It must come to a fight. Only make the right wing strong." The execution of his plan, however, was left to Helmuth von Moltke, the nephew of Bismarck's most effective general. Moltke was a gloomy and nervous man who lacked the talent of his illustrious uncle and the theoretical daring of Schlieffen. He added divisions to the left wing and even weakened the Russian front for the same purpose. The consequence of this hesitant strategy was the failure of the Schlieffen Plan by a narrow margin.

Map 29–6. World War I in Europe. Despite the importance of military action in the Far East, in the Middle East, and at sea, the main theaters of activity in World War I were in the European areas shown here.

The War in the West The French had also put faith in the offensive, but with less reason than the Germans. They badly underestimated the numbers and the effectiveness of the German reserves and set too much store on the importance of the courage and spirit of their troops, which proved insufficient against modern weapons, especially the machine gun. The French offensive on Germany's western frontier failed totally. In a sense this defeat was better than a partial success because it released troops for use against the main German army. As a result, the French and the British were able to stop the Germans at the Battle of the Marne in September 1914.

Thereafter, the war in the west became one of position instead of movement. Both sides dug in behind a wall of trenches protected by barbed wire that stretched from the North Sea to Switzerland. Strategically placed machine-gun nests made assaults difficult and dangerous. Both sides, nonetheless, attempted massive attacks initiated by artillery bombardments of unprecedented and horrible force and duration. Still, the defense was always able to prevent a breakthrough.

The War in the East In the east the war began auspiciously for the Allies. The Russians advanced into Austrian territory and inflicted heavy casualties, but Russian incompetence and German energy soon reversed the situation (see Map 29–6). A junior German officer, Erich Ludendorff (1865–1937), under the command of the elderly General Paul von Hindenburg (1847–1934), destroyed or captured an entire Russian army at the Battle of Tannenberg; he also defeated the Russians at the Masurian Lakes. In 1915 the Central Powers pressed their advantage in the east and drove into the Baltic states and western Russia, inflicting over 2 million casualties in a single year. Russian confidence was badly shaken, but the Russian army stayed in the field.

As the battle lines hardened, both sides sought new allies. Turkey (because of its hostility to Russia) and Bulgaria (the enemy of Serbia) joined the Central Powers. Italy seemed an especially valuable prize, and both sides bid for its support with promises of a division of the spoils of victory. Because what the Italians wanted most was held by Austria, the Allies could make the more attractive promises. In a secret treaty of 1915 the Allies agreed to deliver to Italy most of *Italia Irredenta* (i.e., the Trentino, the South Tyrol, Trieste, and some of the Dalmatian Islands) after victory. By the spring of 1915 Italy was engaging Austrian armies. Although the Italian campaign distracted the Central Powers, it never produced significant results. Romania joined the Allies in 1916 but was quickly defeated and driven from the war.

In the Far East, Japan honored its alliance with Britain and entered the war. The Japanese quickly overran the

A German U-Boat, moored in its harbor in 1917. By this date German submarine warfare had been severely curtailed.

German colonies in China and the Pacific and used the opportunity to improve their own position against China.

In 1915 the Allies undertook to break the deadlock in the fighting by going around it. The idea came chiefly from Winston Churchill (1874–1965), First Lord of the British Admiralty. He proposed an attack at Gallipoli on the Dardanelles and the swift capture of Constantinople. This policy would knock Turkey from the war, bring help to the Balkan front, and ease communication with Russia. Success depended on timing, speed, and daring leadership, but all of these qualities were lacking. The execution of the attack was inept and overly cautious. Troops were landed and, as resistance continued, the Allied commitment increased. Before the campaign was abandoned the Allies lost almost 150,000 men and diverted three times that number from more useful fighting.

Return to the West Both sides turned back to the west in 1916 (see Map 29–5). General Erich von Falkenhayn (1861–1922), who had succeeded Moltke in September 1914, sought success by an attack on the French stronghold of Verdun. The commander of Verdun, Henri Pétain (1856–1951), became a hero. "They shall not pass" became a slogan of national defiance. The Allies tried to end the impasse by launching a major offensive along the River Somme in July. Once again, the superiority of the defense was demonstrated. The only result was enormous casualties on both sides. On all fronts the losses were great and the results meager. The war on land dragged on with no end in sight.

The War at Sea As the war continued, control of the sea became more important. The British ignored the distinction between war supplies (which were contraband according to international law) and food or other peaceful cargo, which was not subject to seizure. They imposed a strict blockade meant to starve out the enemy, regardless of international law. The Germans responded with submarine warfare meant to destroy British shipping and to starve the British. They declared the waters around the British Isles a war zone, where even neutral ships would not be safe. Both policies were unwelcome to neutrals, and especially to the United States, which conducted extensive trade in the Atlantic, but the sinking of neutral ships by German submarines was both more dramatic and more offensive than Britain's blockade.

In 1915 the British liner *Lusitania* was torpedoed by a German submarine. Among the 1200 drowned were 118 Americans. President Woodrow Wilson (1856–1924) warned Germany that a repetition would not be accepted, and the Germans desisted rather than further anger the United States. This development gave the Allies a considerable advantage. The German fleet that had cost so much money and had caused so much trouble played no significant part in the war. The only battle it fought was at Jutland in the spring of 1916. The battle resulted in a standoff and confirmed British domination of the surface of the sea.

America Enters the War In December 1916 President Wilson attempted to bring about a negotiated peace, but neither side was willing to give up its hopes for total victory. The war seemed likely to continue until one or both sides reached exhaustion. Two events early in 1917 changed the situation radically. On February 1 the Germans announced the resumption of unrestricted submarine warfare, which led the United States to break off diplomatic relations. On April 6 the United States declared war on Germany.

One of the deterrents to an earlier American intervention had been the presence of autocratic tsarist Russia among the Allies. Wilson could conceive of the war only as an idealistic crusade "to make the world safe for democracy." That problem was resolved in March of 1917 by a revolution in Russia that overthrew the tsarist government.

The Russian Revolution

The March Revolution in Russia was neither planned nor led by any political faction. It was the result of the collapse of the monarchy's ability to govern. Military and domestic failures produced massive casualties, widespread hunger, strikes by workers, and disorganization in the army. The peasant unrest

Petrograd Munitions Workers Demonstrating in 1917. The barely legible slogan at the top of the banner reads, "Victory to the Petrograd Workers!" *Rla-Novosti/Sovfoto/Eastfoto.*

that had plagued the countryside before 1914 did not subside during the conflict. All political factions were discontented.

In early March 1917 strikes and worker demonstrations erupted in Petrograd, as Saint Petersburg had been renamed. The ill-disciplined troops in the city refused to fire on the demonstrators, and the tsar abdicated on March 15. The government of Russia fell into the hands of members of the Duma, who formed a provisional government composed chiefly of Constitutional Democrats with Western sympathies. The various Socialists, including both Social Revolutionaries and Social Democrats of the Menshevik wing, also began to organize the workers into councils called **soviets**. Initially, they allowed the provisional government to function without actually supporting it. But they became estranged as the Constitutional Democratic Party failed to control the army or to purge "reactionaries" from the government.

In this climate the provisional government decided to remain loyal to the existing Russian alliances and to continue the war against Germany. Its fate was sealed when a new offensive in the summer of 1917 collapsed. Disillusionment with the war, shortages of food and other necessities at home, and the growing demand by the peasants for land reform undermined the government, even after its leadership had been taken over by the moderate Socialist Alexander Kerensky (1881–1970).

Ever since April the Bolsheviks had been working against the provisional government. The Germans, in their most successful attempt at subversion, had rushed the brilliant Bolshevik leader V. I. Lenin (1870–1924) in a sealed train from his exile in Switzerland across Germany to Petrograd in the hope that he would cause trouble for the revolutionary government. The Bolsheviks demanded that all political power go to the soviets, which they controlled. The failure of the summer offensive encouraged them to attempt a coup, but it failed. Lenin fled to Finland, and his chief collaborator, Leon Trotsky (1877–1940), was imprisoned.

An abortive right-wing countercoup gave the Bolsheviks another chance. Trotsky, released from prison, led the powerful Petrograd Soviet. Lenin returned in October, insisted to his doubting colleagues that the time was ripe to take power, and by the extraordinary force of his personality persuaded them to act. Trotsky organized the coup that took place on November 6 and that concluded with an armed assault on the provisional government. The Bolsheviks, almost as much to their own astonishment as

Lenin Establishes His Dictatorship

Document

After the Bolshevik coup in October, elections for the Constituent Assembly were held in November. The results gave a majority to the Social Revolutionary Party and embarrassed the Bolsheviks. Using his control of the Red Army, Lenin closed the Constituent Assembly in January 1918, after it had met for only one day, and established the rule of a revolutionary elite and his own dictatorship. Here is the crucial Bolshevik decree.

◆ What reasons does Lenin give for closing the legitimately elected Constituent Assembly? What other reasons might he have had? What were the soviets? Did they have a legitimate claim to the monopoly of political power? Was the dissolution of the assembly a temporary or permanent measure? What defense can be made for the Bolsheviks' action? Is it enough to justify that action?

. . . The Constituent Assembly, elected on the basis of lists drawn up prior to the October Revolution, was an expression of the old relation of political forces which existed when power was held by the compromisers and the Cadets. When the people at that time voted for the candidates for the Socialist-Revolutionary Party, they were not in a position to choose between the Right Socialist-Revolutionaries, the supporters of the bourgeoisie, and the Left Socialist-Revolutionaries, the supporters of Socialism. Thus, the Constituent Assembly, which was to have been the crown of the bourgeois parliamentary republic, could not become an obstacle in the path of the October Revolution and the Soviet power.

The October Revolution, by giving the power to the Soviets, and through the Soviets to the toiling and exploited classes, aroused the desperate resistance of the exploiters, and in the crushing of this resistance it fully revealed itself as the beginning of the socialist revolution . . . the majority in the Constituent Assembly which met on January 5 was

secured by the party of the Right Socialist-Revolutionaries, the party of Kerensky, Avksentyev and Chernov. Naturally, this party refused to discuss the absolutely clear, precise and unambiguous proposal of the supreme organ of Soviet power, the Central Executive Committee of the Soviets, to recognize the program of the Soviet power, to recognize the "Declaration of Rights of the Toiling and Exploited People," to recognize the October Revolution and the Soviet power. . . .

The Right Socialist-Revolutionary and Menshevik parties are in fact waging outside the walls of the Constituent Assembly a most desperate struggle against the Soviet power. . . .

Accordingly, the Central Executive Committee resolves: The Constituent Assembly is hereby dissolved.

From *A Documentary History of Communism*, Vol. 1, R. V. Daniels, ed. Copyright © 1960 Random House, pp. 133–135. Reprinted by permission of the author.

---

to that of the rest of the world, had come to rule Russia. (See Document, "Lenin Establishes His Dictatorship.")

The victors moved to fulfill their promises and to assure their own security. The provisional government had decreed an election for late November to select a Constituent Assembly. The Social Revolutionaries won a large majority over the Bolsheviks. When the assembly gathered in January, it met for only a day before the Red Army, controlled by the Bolsheviks, dispersed it. All other political parties also ceased to function in any meaningful fashion. In November and January the Bolshevik government promulgated decrees that nationalized the land and turned it over to its peasant proprietors. Factory workers were put in charge of their plants. Banks were taken from their owners and seized for the state, and the debt of the

tsarist government was repudiated. Property of the church reverted to the state.

The Bolshevik government also took Russia out of the war, which they believed benefited only capitalism. They signed an armistice with Germany in December 1917. On March 3, 1918, they accepted the Treaty of Brest-Litovsk, by which Russia yielded Finland, Poland, the Baltic states, and the Ukraine. Georgian territory in the Transcaucasus region was ceded to Turkey. The Bolsheviks also agreed to pay a heavy war indemnity. These terms were a terribly high price to pay for peace, but Lenin had no choice. The Bolsheviks needed time to impose their rule on a devastated and chaotic Russia.

SOURCE Bolshevik Revolution Poster

Overview

Casualties of the Major Belligerents in World War I

COUNTRY	KILLED	WOUNDED
Austria-Hungary	1.1 million	3.62 million
Belgium	38,000	44,000
Britain	723,000	1.16 million
Bulgaria	88,000	152,000
France	1.4 million	2 million
Germany	2 million	4.2 million
Italy	578,000	947,000
Ottoman Empire	804,000	400,000
Romania	250,000	120,000
Russia	1.8 million	1.45 million
Serbia	278,000	138,000
United States	114,000	205,000
Total:	**9,173,000**	**14,436,000**

Until 1921 the New Bolshevik government confronted massive domestic resistance. A civil war erupted between the "Red" Russians supporting the revolution and the **"White" Russians**, who opposed the Bolshevik triumph. In the summer of 1918 the tsar and his family were murdered. Loyal army officers continued to fight the revolution and received aid from the Allies. However, led by Trotsky, the Red Army eventually overcame the domestic opposition. By 1921 Lenin and his supporters were in firm control.

End of World War I

Military Resolution

The Treaty of Brest-Litovsk brought Germany to the peak of its success. The Germans controlled Eastern Europe and its resources, especially food. By 1918 they were free to concentrate their forces on the Western Front. This turn of events would probably have been decisive had it not been balanced by American intervention. Still, American troops would not arrive in significant numbers for about a year, and both sides tried to win the war in 1917. An Allied attempt to break through in the west failed disastrously, bringing heavy losses to

the British and the French and causing a mutiny in the French army. The Austrians, supported by the Germans, defeated the Italians at Caporetto and threatened to overrun Italy, before they were checked with the aid of Allied troops. The deadlock continued, but time was running out for the Central Powers.

In 1918 the Germans, persuaded chiefly by Ludendorff—second in command to Hindenburg, but the real leader of the army—decided to gamble everything on one last offensive. The German army pushed forward and even reached the Marne again but got no farther. They had no more reserves, and the entire nation was exhausted. The Allies, on the other hand, were bolstered by the arrival of American troops in ever-increasing numbers. They launched a counteroffensive that was irresistible. As the Austrian fronts in the Balkans and Italy collapsed, the German high command knew that the end was imminent.

Ludendorff was determined that peace should be made before the German army could be thoroughly defeated in the field and that the responsibility should fall on civilians. For some time he had been the effective ruler of Germany under the aegis of the emperor. He now allowed a new government to be established on democratic principles and to seek peace immediately.

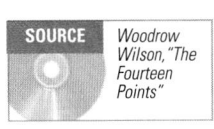 SOURCE Woodrow Wilson, "The Fourteen Points"

The new government, under Prince Max of Baden (1867–1928), asked for peace on the basis of the **Fourteen Points** that President Wilson had declared as the American war aims. These were idealistic principles, including self-determination for nationalities, open diplomacy, freedom of the seas, disarmament, and establishment of a League of Nations to keep the peace. Wilson insisted that he would deal only with a democratic German government because he wanted to be sure he was dealing with the German people and not merely their rulers.

The disintegration of the German army forced William II to abdicate on November 9, 1918. The majority branch of the Social Democratic Party proclaimed a republic to prevent the establishment of a soviet government under the control of their radical Leninist wing, which had earlier broken away as the Independent Socialist Party. Two days later this Republican, Socialist led government signed the armistice that ended the war by accepting German defeat. The German people were, in general, unaware that their army had been defeated in the field and was crumbling. No foreign soldier stood on German soil. Many Germans expected a negotiated and mild settlement. The real peace embittered the German people, many of whom came to believe that Germany had not been defeated but had been tricked by the enemy and betrayed—even stabbed in the back—by Republicans and Socialists at home.

The victors rejoiced, but they also had much to mourn. The casualties on all sides came to over 9 million dead and over 14 million wounded. The economic and financial

John Singer Sargent, *Gassed*, 1918–1919. Many new weapons were used extensively for the first time in the Great War of 1914–1918, including machine guns, barbed wire, tanks, airplanes, and several kinds of poison gas. The Germans were the first to employ gas as a weapon, firing a nonlethal kind of tear gas at the Russians on the Eastern Front in January 1915. By April, they had learned how to use the poison gas chlorine against the Allies on the Western Front. *Gassed*, by the American painter John Singer Sargent, can be compared to ancient Greek friezes depicting mythical battles. There is, however, an important difference in treatment: While Greek sculptures always portray an element of heroism along with death and suffering, Sargent's painting reveals only the horror of battle. *Imperial War Museum, London.*

resources of the European states were badly strained. The victorious Allies, formerly creditors to the world, became debtors to the new American colossus, itself barely touched by the calamities of war.

The old international order, moreover, was dead. Russia was ruled by a Bolshevik dictatorship that preached world revolution and the overthrow of capitalism everywhere. Germany was in chaos. Austria-Hungary had disintegrated into a swarm of small states competing for the remains of the ancient empire. These kinds of change stirred the colonial territories ruled by the European powers; overseas empires would never again be as secure as they had seemed before the war. Europe was no longer the center of the world, free to interfere when it wished or to ignore the outer regions if it chose. Its easy confidence in material and moral progress was shattered by the brutal reality of four years of horrible war. The memory of that war lived on to shake the nerve of the victorious Western powers as they confronted the new conditions of the postwar world.

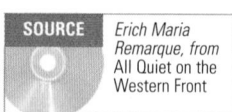

SOURCE Erich Maria Remarque, from All Quiet on the Western Front

Settlement at Paris

The Peacemakers The representatives of the victorious states gathered at Versailles and other Parisian suburbs in the first half of 1919. Wilson speaking for the United States, David Lloyd George (1863–1945) for Britain, Georges Clemenceau (1841–1929) for France, and Vittorio Emanuele Orlando (1860–1952) for Italy made up the Big Four. Japan,

now recognized for the first time as a great power, also had an important part in the discussions.

Wilson's idealism came into conflict with the more practical war aims of the victorious powers and with many of the secret treaties that had been made before and during the war. The British and French people had been told that Germany would be made to pay for the war. Russia had been promised control of Constantinople in return for recognition of the French claim to Alsace-Lorraine and British control of Egypt. Romania had been promised Transylvania at the expense of Hungary. Some of the agreements contradicted others; Italy and Serbia had competing claims to the islands and shore of the Adriatic. During the war the British had encouraged Arab hopes of an independent Arab state carved out of the Ottoman Empire; those plans conflicted with the Balfour Declaration (1917), in which the British seemed to accept Zionism and to promise the Jews a national home in Palestine. Both of these plans conflicted with an Anglo-French agreement to divide the Near East between themselves.

The continuing national goals of the victors presented further obstacles to an idealistic "peace without victors." France was keenly conscious of its numerical inferiority to Germany and of the low birthrate that would keep it inferior. Naturally, France was eager to achieve a settlement that would permanently weaken Germany and preserve French political and military superiority. Italy sought the acquisition of *Italia Irredenta* ("unredeemed Italy"); Britain looked to its imperial interests; Japan pursued its own advantage in Asia; and the United States insisted on freedom of the seas,

Versailles. The German delegation signs the peace treaty ending the First World War in the Hall of Mirrors of the Palace of Versailles on June 28, 1919. This painting by Sir William Orpen, completed in 1921, now hangs in the Imperial War Museum in London. U.S. President Woodrow Wilson is seated in the center, holding a clutch of papers. *Museum, London/Bildarchiv Preussischer Kulturbesitz.*

which favored American commerce, and on its right to maintain the Monroe Doctrine.

Finally, the peacemakers of 1919 faced a world still in turmoil. The greatest immediate threat appeared to be the spread of bolshevism. While Lenin and his colleagues were distracted by civil war, the Allies landed small armies in Russia to help overthrow the Bolshevik regime. Communist governments were established in Bavaria and Hungary. Berlin also experienced a dangerous communist uprising led by the "Spartacus group" (Communist extremists). The Allies were sufficiently worried by these developments to allow and to support suppression of these communist movements by right-wing military forces. They even permitted an army of German volunteers to operate against the Bolsheviks in the Baltic states.

The fear of the spread of communism played a part in the thinking of the diplomats at Versailles, but it was far from dominant. The Germans kept playing on such fears as a way of getting better terms, but the Allies, especially the French, would not hear of it. Fear of Germany remained the chief concern for France; attention to interests that were more traditional and more immediate governed the policies of the other Allies.

The Peace The Paris settlement consisted of five separate treaties between the victors and the defeated powers. Formal sessions began on January 18, 1919, and the last treaty was signed on August 10, 1920. The notion of "a peace without victors" became a mockery when the Soviet Union (as Russia was now called) and Germany were excluded from the peace conference. The Germans were simply presented with a treaty and compelled to accept it, which fully justified their complaint that the treaty had not been negotiated but dictated. The principle of national self-determination was violated many times, as it was unavoidable. Nevertheless, the diplomats of the small nations were angered by their exclusion from decision making. The undeserved adulation accorded Wilson on his arrival gradually turned into equally undeserved scorn. He had not abandoned his ideals lightly but had merely given way to the irresistible force of reality.

The League of Nations Wilson put great faith in a new instrument for peace and justice, the **League of Nations**. Its covenant was an essential part of the peace treaty. The 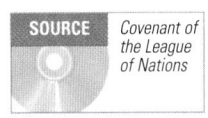 league was not intended as an international government, but as a body of sovereign states that agreed to pursue common policies and to consult in the common interest, especially when war threatened. In that case the members promised to submit the matter to arbitration, to an international court, or to the League Council. Refusal to abide by this agreement would justify league intervention in the form of economic and even military sanctions.

But the league was unlikely to be effective because it had no armed forces at its disposal. Action required the unanimous consent of its council, consisting of Britain, France, Italy, the United States, Japan, and four other states that had temporary seats. The Covenant of the League bound its members to "respect and preserve" the territorial integrity of all its members, which was generally seen as a device to ensure the security of the victorious powers. The exclusion from the League Assembly of Germany and the Soviet Union further undermined the league's claim to even-handedness.

Colonies Another provision of the covenant dealt with colonial areas. They were to be placed under the "tutelage" of one of the great powers under league supervision and encouraged to advance towards independence. Because there were no teeth in this provision, little advance was made. Provisions for disarmament were equally ineffective. Members of the league remained fully sovereign and continued to pursue their own national interests.

Germany In the West, the main territorial issue was the fate of Germany (see Map 29–7). Although a united Germany was less than fifty years old, no one seems to have thought of undoing Bismarck's work and dividing it into its component parts. The French would have liked to set up the Rhineland as a separate buffer state, but Lloyd George and Wilson would not permit that. Still, they could not ignore France's need for protection against a resurgent Germany. France received Alsace-Lorraine and the right to work the coal mines of the Saar for fifteen years. Germany west of the Rhine, and fifty kilometers east of it, was to be a demilitarized zone; Allied troops could stay on the west bank for fifteen years. In addition to this physical barrier to a new German attack, the treaty provided that Britain and the United States would guarantee to aid France if it were attacked by Germany. Such an attack was made more unlikely by the permanent disarmament of Germany. Its army was limited to 100,000 men on long-term service; its fleet was all but eliminated; and it was forbidden to have war planes, submarines, tanks, heavy artillery, or poison gas. As long as these provisions were observed, France would be safe.

The East The settlement in the East ratified the collapse of the great defeated empires that had ruled it for centuries.

Germany's frontier lost much of Silesia and part of Prussia. East Prussia was cut off from the rest of Germany by a corridor carved out to give the revived state of Poland access to the sea. The Austro-Hungarian Empire disappeared. Most of its German-speaking people were gathered in the small Republic of Austria, cut off from the Germans of Bohemia and forbidden to unite with Germany. The Magyars occupied the much-reduced kingdom of Hungary.

The Czechs of Bohemia and Moravia joined with the Slovaks and Ruthenians to the east to form Czechoslovakia, and this new state also included several million unhappy Germans. The southern Slavs were united in the kingdom of Serbs, Croats, and Slovenes, or Yugoslavia. Italy gained the Trentino and Trieste. Romania gained Transylvania from Hungary and Bessarabia from Russia. Bulgaria lost territory to Greece and Yugoslavia. Finland, Estonia, Latvia, and Lithuania became independent states, and much of Poland was carved out of formerly Russian soil. Similarly, in the Caucasus, the new nations of Georgia, Armenia, and Azerbaijan took advantage of the turmoil following the Russian revolution to enjoy a period of independence from 1918 to 1921. Autonomy was also achieved by Ukraine and Russia during this brief period.

The old Ottoman Empire also disappeared. The new Republic of Turkey was limited to little more than Constantinople and Asia Minor. Palestine and Iraq came under British control and Syria and Lebanon under French control as mandates of the League of Nations. Germany's former colonies in Africa were divided among Britain, France, Belgium, and South Africa. The German Pacific possessions went to Australia, New Zealand, and Japan.

In theory, the mandate system was meant to have the "advanced nations" govern the former colonies in the interests of the native peoples until they became ready to govern themselves. They were thus divided into three categories—A, B, and C—in descending order of their readiness for independence. In practice, most mandated

Peacemakers. The Allies promoted Arab efforts to secure independence from Turkey in an effort to remove Turkey from the war. Delegates to the peace conference of 1919 in Paris included British Colonel T. E. Lawrence, who helped lead the rebellion against Turkey, and representatives from the Middle East. Prince Feisal, the third son of King Hussein, stands in the foreground of this picture; Lawrence is in the middle row, second from the right; and Brigadier General Nuri Pasha Said of Baghdad is second from the left. *Corbis-Bettmann.*

Map 29–7. World War I Peace Settlement in Europe and the Middle East. The map of central and Eastern Europe, as well as that of the Middle East, underwent drastic revision after World War I. The enormous territorial losses suffered by Germany, Austria-Hungary, the Ottoman Empire, Bulgaria, and Russia were the other side of the coin represented by gains for France, Italy, Greece, and Romania and by the appearance, or reappearance, of at least eight new independent states from Finland in the north to Yugoslavia in the south. The mandate system for former Ottoman territories outside Turkey proper laid foundations for several new, mostly Arab, states in the Middle East.

Legend (map key):
- Autonomous states, 1917-1921
- Austria-Hungary, 1914
- Germany, 1914
- Areas lost by Germany in 1919
- Areas lost by Bulgaria
- Areas lost by Russia
- Areas lost by The Ottoman Empire

territories were treated as colonies by the powers under whose "tutelage" they came. Not even one Class A mandate had achieved full independence twenty years after the signing of the treaty. Colonialism was to remain a problem even after World War II.

Reparations Perhaps the most debated part of the peace settlement dealt with reparations for the damage done by Germany during the war. Before the armistice the Germans promised to pay compensation "for all damages done to the civilian population of the Allies and their property." The Americans judged that the amount would be between $15 billion and $25 billion and that Germany would be able to pay that amount. However, France and Britain, worried about repaying their war debts to the United States, were eager to have Germany pay the full cost of the war, including pensions to survivors and dependents. There was general agreement that Germany could not afford to pay such a sum, whatever it might be, and no sum was fixed at the conference. In the meantime Germany was to pay $5 billion annually until 1921. At that time a final figure would be set, which Germany would have to pay within thirty years. The French did not regret the outcome. Either Germany would pay and be bled into impotence, or Germany would refuse to pay and justify French intervention.

To justify these huge reparations, the Allies inserted the notorious Clause 231, the **war guilt clause**, into the treaty:

> The Allied and Associated Governments affirm, and Germany accepts, the responsibility of Germany and her allies for causing all the loss and damage to which the Allied and Associated Governments and their nationals have been subjected as a consequence of the war imposed upon them by aggression of Germany and her allies.

The Germans, of course, bitterly resented the charge. They had lost territories containing millions of Germans and great quantities of badly needed natural resources; they were presented with an astronomical and apparently unlimited reparations bill. To add insult to injury, they had to admit to a war guilt that they did not feel. Finally, they had to accept the entire treaty as it was written by the victors, without any opportunity for negotiation. Germany's Chancellor Philipp Scheidemann (1865–1939) spoke of the treaty as the imprisonment of the German people and asked, "What hand would not wither that binds itself and us in these fetters?" But there was no choice. The Social Democrats and the Catholic Center Party formed a new government, and their representatives signed the treaty. These parties formed the backbone of the Weimar government that ruled Germany until 1933; they never overcame the stigma of accepting the Treaty of Versailles.

Evaluation of the Peace

Few peace settlements have been more attacked than the one negotiated in Paris in 1919. It was natural that the defeated powers should have objected to it, but the peace was soon bitterly criticized in the victorious countries as well. Many of the French thought that it failed to provide adequate security for France, because it tied that security to promises of aid from the unreliable Anglo-Saxon countries. In England and the United States, liberals complained that the treaty violated the idealistic and liberal aims and principles that the Western leaders had professed. It was not a peace without victors. It did not end imperialism but attempted to promote the national interests of the winning nations. It violated the principles of national self-determination by leaving significant pockets of minorities outside the borders of their national homelands.

The most influential critic was John Maynard Keynes (1883–1946), a brilliant British economist who took part in the peace conference. When he saw the direction it was taking, he resigned in disgust and wrote a book called *The Economic Consequences of the Peace* (1920). It was a scathing attack, especially on reparations and the other economic clauses of the treaty. It was also a skillful assault on the negotiators, particularly on Wilson, who was depicted as a fool and a hypocrite. Keynes argued that the Treaty of Versailles was both immoral and unworkable. He called it a Carthaginian peace, referring to the utter destruction of Carthage by Rome after the Third Punic War (149–146 B.C.E.). He argued that such a peace would bring economic ruin and war to Europe unless it were repudiated. Keynes had a great effect on the British, who were already suspicious of France and glad of an excuse to withdraw from continental affairs. The decent and respectable position came to be one that aimed at revision of the treaty in favor of Germany.

Even more important was the book's influence in the United States. It fed the traditional tendency towards isolationism and gave powerful weapons to Wilson's enemies. Wilson's own political mistakes helped prevent American ratification of the treaty. Consequently, America was out of the League of Nations and not bound to defend France. Britain, therefore, was also free from its obligation to France. France was left to protect itself without adequate means to do so for long.

Many of the attacks on the Treaty of Versailles are unjustified. It was not a Carthaginian peace. Germany was neither dismembered nor ruined. Reparations could be and were scaled down, and until the great world depression of the 1930s the Germans recovered a high level of prosperity. Complaints against the peace should also be measured against the peace the victorious Germans had imposed on Russia at Brest-Litovsk and their plans for a European settlement in case of victory. Both were far more severe than anything enacted at Versailles. The attempt at achieving self-determination for nationalities was less than perfect, but it was the best solution Europe had ever accomplished in that direction.

The peace, nevertheless, was unsatisfactory in important ways. The elimination of the Austro-Hungarian Empire, however inevitable that might seem, created serious problems. Economically it was disastrous, for it separated raw materials from manufacturing areas and producers from their markets by new boundaries and tariff walls. In hard times, this separation created friction and hostility that aggravated other quarrels also created by the peace treaties. Poland and especially Czechoslovakia contained unhappy German minorities. Czechoslovakia itself was a collection of nationalities that did not find it easy to live together as a nation. Disputes over territories in Eastern Europe promoted further tension. The peace was inadequate on another level as well. It rested on a defeat that Germany did not admit. The Germans believed they had been cheated rather than defeated. The high moral principles proclaimed by the Allies also undercut the validity of the peace, for it plainly fell far short of those principles.

Finally, the great weakness of the peace was its failure to accept reality. Germany and Russia were inevitably to play an important part in European affairs, yet they were excluded from the settlement and from the League of Nations. Given the many discontented parties, the peace was not self-enforcing, yet no satisfactory machinery for enforcing it was established. The league was never a serious force for this purpose. It was left to France, with no guarantee of support from Britain and no hope of help from the United States, to defend the new arrangements. Finland, the Baltic states, Poland, Romania, Czechoslovakia, and Yugoslavia were created or strengthened as a barrier to the westward expansion of Russian communism and as a safeguard to deter German revival. Most of these states, however, would have to rely on France in case of danger. France was simply not strong enough for the task if Germany were to rearm.

The tragedy of the Treaty of Versailles was that it was neither conciliatory enough to remove the desire for change, even at the cost of war, nor harsh enough to make another war impossible. A lasting peace required enforcing German disarmament while the more obnoxious clauses of the peace treaty were revised. Such a policy demanded continued attention to the problem, unity among the victors, and far-sighted leadership; none of these was present in adequate supply during the next two decades.

Summary

The New Imperialism. European imperialism in the last part of the nineteenth century brought the Western countries into contact with most of the world. By 1914, European nations had divided Africa among themselves and controlled large parts of Asia and the islands of the Pacific. Much of the Middle East was under the nominal control of the Ottoman Empire, which was in its death throes and under European influence. The Monroe Doctrine made Latin America a protectorate of the United States. Japan had become an imperial power at the expense of China and Korea.

World War I. The emergence of a new, powerful German state at the center of Europe upset the old balance of power. Bismarck, however, preserved the peace for as long as he remained in power. The new German emperor, William II, abandoned the policy of restraint and sought more power and influence for his country. The result was a system of alliances that divided Europe into two armed camps. What began as yet another Balkan War involving the European powers became a world war that influenced the rest of the world. As the terrible war of 1914–1918 dragged on, the real motives that had driven the European powers to fight gave way to public affirmations of the principles of nationalism and self-determination.

The Peace Settlement. The peoples under colonial rule took these statements seriously and sought to win their own independence and nationhood. For the most part they were disappointed by the peace settlement. The British and French Empires were larger than ever. The Americans added to the islands they controlled in the Pacific. Japanese imperial ambitions were rewarded at the expense of China.

However, the old imperial nations, especially Britain and France, had paid an enormous price in lives, money, and will for their victory in the war. Colonial peoples pressed for the rights that were proclaimed as universal by the West but denied to their colonies; influential minorities in the countries that ruled them sympathized with colonial aspirations for independence. Tension between colonies and their ruling nations was a cause of instability in the world created by the Paris treaties of 1919.

Review Questions

1. What role did Bismarck envisage for the new Germany after 1871? How successful was he in carrying out his vision? Was he wise to tie Germany to Austria-Hungary?

2. Why and in what stages did Britain abandon "splendid isolation" at the turn of the century? Were the policies it pursued instead wise ones, or should Britain have followed a different course?

3. How did developments in the Balkans lead to the outbreak of World War I? What was the role of Serbia? Of Austria? Of Russia? What was the aim of German policy in July 1914? Did Germany want a general war?

4. Why did Germany lose World War I? Could Germany have won, or was victory never a possibility? Assess the settlement of Versailles. What were its benefits to Europe, and what were its drawbacks? Was the settlement too harsh or too conciliatory? Could it have secured lasting peace in Europe? How might it have been improved?

INTERPRETING THE PAST

The New Imperialism: Motives, Justifications, and Costs

Text Sources from MyHistoryLab/ PrimarySource DVD

1. Jules Ferry, *Le Tonkin et la Mere-Patrie* (1896)
2. Charles Seignobos, "*The Great African Hunt*" (1909)
3. Rudyard Kipling, *The White Man's Burden* (1899)
4. Edward Morel, *The Black Man's Burden* (1920)

Visual Sources from MyHistoryLab/ PrimarySource DVD-ROM

1. *Pygmies, 1904 World's Fair*
2. *Pear's Soap Advertisement*

The "New Imperialism" of nineteenth century was characterized by European (the late) acquisition of new territories and the establishment of economic and political hegemony over other nations. More than a century later, it is still a hot topic for debate. While it is clear that imperialism brought some economic benefits to Western nations in the form of inexpensive commodities

extracted by low-cost (or slave) labor and captive markets for their products, the overall profitability is still in doubt. Just as important, Western nations sought strategic and political advantages through their extensive overseas holdings. Yet basic questions remain: What were the primary motives of European imperialists? What are the lasting historical and cultural impacts on the West and non-Western nations?

In this exercise you will read four primary sources from the late nineteenth and early twentieth centuries and examine two images that illustrate the political, military, economic, and cultural impacts of imperialism. You will then answer the following questions in the process of completing the assignment below.

The first document is written by Jules Ferry (1832–1893), a French statesman who advocated aggressive colonial expansion for France. The second source, by Charles Seignobos, describes "the scramble for Africa" in which European nations raced to obtain territories and influence after the Berlin Conference of 1885. The third source is the classic poem, "The White Man's Burden" by Rudyard Kipling that communicates the then widely held view (among Westerners) that colonization benefited African and Asian peoples. The fourth primary source was written by Edward D. Morel, a British journalist and reformer, who forcefully refutes "The White Man's Burden," by illustrating the effects of Western exploitation on the people and culture of Africa.

5. Why was Lenin successful in establishing Bolshevik rule in Russia? What role did Trotsky play? Was it wise policy for Lenin to take Russia out of the war?

Key Terms

Fourteen Points (p. 943)

Italia Irredenta (p. 940)

League of Nations (p. 945)

mobilization (p. 937)

New Imperialism (p. 923)

Pan-Slavic movement (p. 931)

reparations (p. 948)

Schlieffen Planb (p. 937)

soviets (p. 941)

war guilt clause (p. 948)

"White" Russians (p. 943)

Note: To learn more about the topics in this chapter, please turn to the Suggested Readings at the end of the book. For additional sources related to this chapter please see the Primary Source DVD at the back of this text or MyHistoryLab.

The two accompanying images offer evidence of how Africans were viewed by Westerners a century ago—the first shows members of a tribe of African pygmies who were displayed at the St. Louis World's Fair of 1904, and the second is an advertisement for Pear's soap, graphically illustrating the negative associations of "darkness."

Questions

What are Ferry's chief reasons for promoting colonial expansion? What consequences does Ferry predict for European countries should they not expand their markets?

How does "The Great African Hunt" by Charles Seignobos depict African culture and history? What might explain this view from an eminent French scholar?

In the same "Scramble for Africa" reading, "A Natural Inclination to Submit to Higher Authority," author Frederick Lugard, a British colonial administrator, explains why Britain must gain new colonies, and what the benefits would be to Africans. What are his main contentions, and how does he connect nationalism to economic arguments for imperialism?

What is the "White Man's Burden," according to Kipling? What is the "Black Man's Burden," according to Morel? How does Morel view capitalism in the African colonial context?

30 Depression, European Dictators, and the American New Deal

I N THE TWO DECADES THAT FOLLOWED THE CONCLUSION OF the Paris Settlement, the Western world saw a number of experiments in politics and economic life. Two broad factors accounted for these experiments. First, the war, the Russian Revolution, and the peace treaty had transformed the political face of Europe. New political regimes had emerged in the wake of the collapse of the monarchies of Germany, Austria-Hungary, and Russia. These new governments immediately faced the problems of postwar reconstruction, economic dislocation, and nationalistic resentments. Most of these nations also included large groups who questioned the legitimacy of their governments.

Second, beginning in the early twenties, economic dislocations that led to the economic downturn that became known as the Great Depression began to spread across the world. It occurred through the combination of financial turmoil in the more advanced industrial nations and a collapse of commodity prices in the commodity-exporting countries. Faced with political instability and economic crisis, governments

Nazi Party Rally. Young women among an enthusiastic crowd extend the Nazi salute at a party rally in 1938. Note the gender divisions in this photograph. Nazi ideology encouraged women to favor traditional domestic roles over employment in the workplace and to bear many children. The men are portrayed as defenders of the homeland. *Bildarchiv Preussischer Kulturbesitz.*

The Interwar Period in Europe and the United States

The West

The two decades between the great wars marked a period of immense political and economic transition around the globe. Many regions endured political turmoil and economic instability, followed by the establishment of militaristic authoritarian regimes. In Italy, it was the Fascists; in Germany, the Nazis; in the Soviet Union, Stalin's regime. Spain too came under the rule of a military dictator who rose to power with the assistance of the Nazis. Many Europeans, battered by the global economic crisis of the 1930s and, in the case of Germany, the harsh terms of the Treaty of Versailles, believed that only strong leaders could lead their countries to prosperity again in the global competition for resources and territory. In East Asia, Japan came into the grip of a right-wing militaristic government. China saw more than twenty years of civil war and revolution that would culminate with the rise to power of the Communists under Mao. Most of Latin America came under the sway of dictators or governments heavily influenced by the military.

With the exception of Russia (and later China), all of these governments were right-wing. In fact, the Russian Revolution was a pivotal factor in the rise of right-wing and fascist dictators, who often justified their power on the basis of their firm opposition to the "Red Menace" and the growing popularity enjoyed by socialism and communism in many European countries during the economic crisis of the 1930s.

To many observers in the late 1930s, the day of liberal parliamentary democracy appeared to be ending. The disruptions arising from World War I and the social and economic turmoil of the depression seemed to pose problems that liberal governments could not address. Only the radical medicine of socialism, communism, or right-wing dictatorships seemed capable of resolving the crisis. Some countries, such as France in the mid-1930s, were brought to the brink of civil war by the deep divisions between the right and left in their populations. Spain became engulfed in the civil war that brought General Francisco Franco (1892–1975) to power in 1939.

contrived various political and economic responses. In Europe these efforts often produced authoritarian regimes. In the United States the response to the depression led to a much-increased role for the federal government in the life of the nation. ∎

After Versailles: Demands for Revision and Enforcement

The Paris settlement fostered both resentment and discontent. Those resentments counted among the chief political factors in Europe for the next two decades. Germany had been humiliated. The arrangements for reparations led to endless haggling over payments. Various national groups in the successor states of the Austro-Hungarian Empire felt

that injustice had been done in their particular cases of self-determination. There were demands for further border adjustments. On the other side, the victorious powers, and especially France, often believed that the provisions of the treaty were being inadequately enforced. Consequently, throughout the 1920s and into the 1930s demands either to revise or to enforce the Paris treaties contributed to domestic political turmoil across the Continent. All too many political figures were willing to fish in these troubled international waters for a large catch of domestic votes.

Towards the Great Depression in Europe

Three factors combined to bring about the intense severity and the extended length of the **Great Depression** with its accompanying extensive unemployment and loss of social

The interwar period also departed from the nineteenth-century ideal of *laissez-faire* economics, in which central governments assumed little responsibility for guiding the economies of their countries. The German inflation of the early 1920s, the worldwide financial collapse of the late 1920s, the vast unemployment of the early 1930s, and the agricultural crisis of both decades roused demands for government action as millions of people experienced very real, and often sudden, economic hardship and suffering. One reason for these demands was simply that more governments throughout the world were responsible to mass democratic electorates. Governments that failed to adequately address the problems were put out of office. This happened to the Republicans in the United States, the Socialist and Liberal parties in Germany, the left-wing parties in Japan, and various political parties in Latin America that failed to deal with the depression. Paradoxically, many democratic electorates actually turned themselves over to politically authoritarian regimes as they searched for social and economic stability.

Extreme forms of nationalism in both Europe and Japan also spawned authoritarianism. The authoritarian governments of Germany, Italy, and Japan all had agendas of nationalistic aggression. They shared the nineteenth-century conviction that territorial expansion was essential to national prestige and economic security. As a result they were prepared to move wherever they saw fellow nationals living outside their borders (a legacy of the creation of nation-states in the eighteenth and nineteenth centuries) or where they could establish dominance over other peoples and thus become imperial powers. Japan moved against Manchuria and later other parts of Asia. Italy invaded Ethiopia. Germany sought union with German-speaking peoples in Austria and Czechoslovakia and then sought to expand throughout Eastern Europe. In turn, those actions challenged the dominance of Great Britain and the vital security interests of the United States. By the end of the 1930s the authoritarian regimes and the liberal democracies stood on the brink of a major confrontation.

Focus Questions

◆ Why did many people in the 1930s lose faith in liberal democracy and *laissez-faire* economics?

◆ What led many countries to adopt authoritarian regimes during this period? Why did authoritarian governments seem to pose a solution to economic hardship and social instabililty?

◆ What was the relationship between extreme nationalism and the outbreak of World War II?

security for millions of people around the globe. First, a financial crisis stemmed directly from the war and the peace settlement. To this was added a crisis in the production and distribution of goods in the world market. These two problems became intertwined in 1929, and as far as Europe was concerned they reached the breaking point in 1931. Finally, both of these difficulties became worse than they might have been because no major Western European country or the United States provided strong, responsible economic leadership.

Financial Tailspin

As one of the chief victors in the war, France was determined to collect reparations from Germany. The United States was no less determined that its allies repay the wartime loans it had extended to them. The European allies also owed various debts to each other. German reparations were to provide the means of repaying the American and other allied debts. Most of the money that the Allies collected from each other also went to the United States.

The quest for payment of German reparations caused one of the major diplomatic crises of the 1920s; the crisis itself resulted in further economic upheaval. In early 1923 the Allies—France in particular—declared Germany to be in technical default of its reparation payments. On January 11, to ensure receipt of the hard-won reparations, French troops occupied the Ruhr mining and manufacturing district. The **Weimar Republic** ordered passive resistance that amounted to a general strike in the largest industrial region of the nation. Confronted with this tactic, the French government sent French civilians to run the German mines and railroads. France got its way. The Germans paid, but its victory cost France dearly. The English were alienated by the French heavy-handedness and took no part in the occupation. Britain became more suspicious of France and more sympathetic to Germany. The cost of the Ruhr occupation, moreover, vastly increased French as well as German inflation and damaged the French economy.

The political and economic turmoil of the Ruhr invasion led to international attempts to ease the German payment of reparations. The most famous of these were the Dawes Plan of 1924 and the Young Plan of 1929, both devised by Americans. At the same time, large amounts of American investment capital were pouring into Europe. However, by 1928 this lending decreased as American money became diverted into the booming New York stock market. The crash of Wall Street in October 1929—the result of virtually unregulated financial speculation—saw the loss of large amounts of money. Credit sharply contracted in the United States as numerous banks failed. Thereafter, little American capital was available for investment in Europe.

As the credit for Europe began to run out, a major financial crisis struck the Continent. In May 1931 the Kreditanstalt collapsed. The Kreditanstalt was a primary lending institution and major bank for much of central and Eastern Europe. The German banking system consequently came under severe pressure and was saved only through government guarantees. As the German difficulties increased, U.S. president Herbert Hoover (1874–1964) announced in June 1931 a one-year moratorium on all payments of international debts. The Hoover moratorium was a prelude to the end of reparations. The Lausanne Conference of the summer of 1932 brought, in effect, the era of reparations to a close. The next year the debts owed to the United States were settled either through small token payments or simply through default.

Problems in Agricultural Commodities

The 1920s witnessed a contraction in the market demand for European goods relative to the Continent's productive capacity. This problem originated both within and outside Europe. In both instances the difficulty arose from agriculture. Better methods of farming, improved strains of wheat, expanded tillage, and more extensive transport facilities all over the globe vastly increased the quantity of grain. World wheat prices fell to record lows. Although this helped consumers, it decreased the income of European farmers. At the same time, higher industrial wages raised the cost of the industrial goods that farmers or peasants used. Consequently, they also had great difficulty paying off their mortgages and normal annual operation debts. These problems were especially acute in central and Eastern

Europe and abetted farmers' disillusionment with liberal politics. German farmers, for example, would become prime supporters of the National Socialist Workers Party (Nazis).

Outside Europe similar problems affected other producers of agricultural commodities. The prices they received for their products plummeted. Government-held reserves reached record levels. This glut of major world commodities involved the supplies of wheat, sugar, coffee, rubber, wool, and lard. The people who produced these goods in underdeveloped nations could no longer make enough money to buy finished goods from industrial Europe. As world credit collapsed, the economic position of these commodity producers worsened. Commodity production had simply outstripped world demand.

The results of the collapse in the agricultural sector of the world economy and the financial turmoil were stagnation and depression for European industry. Coal, iron, and textiles had depended largely on international markets. Unemployment spread from these industries to those producing finished consumer goods. Persistent unemployment in Great Britain and, to a lesser extent, in Germany during the 1920s had created "soft" domestic markets. The policies of reduced spending with which the governments confronted the depression further weakened domestic demand. By the early 1930s the depression was feeding on itself.

Jarrow Crusade. In what was known as the "Jarrow Crusade" during the autumn of 1936 a group of approximately 200 protesters marched from the town of Jarrow in northeastern England to London to demonstrate their need for employment and the plight of their town where the previous year the shipyard had been closed. *Getty Image, Inc./Hulton Archive Photos.*

Depression and Government Policy

The depression did not mean absolute economic decline or total unemployment. However, the economic downturn spread potential as well as actual insecurity. People in nearly all walks of life feared the loss of their own economic security and lifestyles. The depression also frustrated normal social and economic expectations. Even the employed often seemed to make no progress; and their anxieties created a major source of social discontent.

The governments of the late 1920s and the early 1930s were not particularly well suited in either structure or ideology to confront these problems. The electorates demanded action. The government response depended largely on the severity of the Depression in a particular country and on the self-confidence of the nation's political system.

Great Britain and France undertook moderate political experiments. In 1924 the Labour Party in Great Britain established itself as a viable governing party by forming a short-lived government. It again formed a ministry in 1929.

Under the pressure of the Depression and at the urging of King George V (r. 1910–1936), the Labour prime minister Ramsay MacDonald (1866–1937) organized a National Government, which was a coalition of the Labour, Conservative, and Liberal Parties. It remained in power until 1935, when a Conservative ministry led by Stanley Baldwin (1867–1947) replaced it. (See Document "George Orwell Observes a Woman in the Slums.")

The most important French political experiment was the **Popular Front** Ministry, which came to office in 1936. It was composed of Socialists, Radicals, and Communists—the first time that Socialists and Communists had cooperated in a ministry. The Popular Front addressed major labor problems in the French economy. By 1938 various changes in the cabinet in effect brought the Popular Front to an end.

The political changes in Britain and France were only of domestic significance. But the political experiments of the 1920s and 1930s that reshaped world history and civilization involved the establishment of a Soviet government in Russia, a Fascist regime in Italy, and a Nazi dictatorship in Germany.

George Orwell Observes a Woman in the Slums

Document

Although Great Britain was beginning to emerge from the Great Depression by the late 1930s, much poverty and human degradation remained. This scene, described in 1937 by the social critic and novelist George Orwell (1903–1950), captures a glimpse of the sadness and hopelessness that many British citizens as well as vast numbers of other Europeans experienced every day of their lives during the Depression.

◆ How does Orwell's descriptive language evoke sympathy for the woman he portrays? What economic conditions led to such poverty? What class attitudes does Orwell begin to explore in this passage?

The train bore me away, through the monstrous scenery of slag-heaps, chimneys, piled scrap-iron, foul annals, paths of cindery mud crisscrossed by the prints of clogs. . . . As we moved slowly through the outskirts of the town we passed row after row of little grey slum houses running at right angles to the embankment. At the back of one of the houses a young woman was kneeling on the stones, poking a stick up the leaden waste-pipe which ran from the sink inside, and which I suppose was blocked. I had time to see everything about her—her sacking apron, her clumsy clogs, her arms reddened by the cold. . . . She had a round pale face, the usual exhausted face of the slum girl who is twenty-five and looks forty, thanks to miscarriages and drudgery; and its work, for the second in which I saw it, the most desolate, hopeless expression I have ever seen. It struck me then that we are mistaken when we say that "it isn't the same for them as it would be for us", and that people bred in the slums can imagine nothing but the slums. For what I saw in her face was not the ignorant suffering of an animal. She knew well enough what was happening to her—understood as well as I did how dreadful a destiny it was to be kneeling there in the bitter cold, on the slimy stones of a slum backyard, poking a stick up a found drain-pipe.

George Orwell, *The Road to Wigan Pier* (New York: Berkley Medallion Books, 1967; originally printed in 1937), p. 29. (Copyright © George Orwell, 1937) by permission of Bill Hamilton as Literary Executor of the Estate of the Late Sonia Brownell Orwell and Secker & Warburg Ltd.

The Soviet Experiment

The consolidation of the Bolshevik Revolution in Russia established the most extensive and durable of all twentieth-century authoritarian governments.

SOURCE The Bolshevik seizure of power

The Communist Party of the Soviet Union retained power from 1917 until the end of 1991, and its presence influenced the political history of Europe and much of the rest of the world, as did no other single factor. Unlike the Italian Fascists or the German National Socialists, the Bolsheviks seized power violently through revolution. For several years they confronted armed opposition, and their leaders long felt insecure about their hold on the country. The Communist Party was neither a mass party nor a nationalistic one. Its early membership rarely exceeded

Lenin. Anxiety over the spread of the Bolshevik Revolution was a fundamental factor of European politics during the 1920s and 1930s. Images like this Soviet portrait of Lenin as a heroic revolutionary conjured fears among people in the rest of Europe of a political force determined to overturn their social, political, and economic institutions. *Gemalde von A. M. Gerassimow, "Lenin as Agitator"/Bildarchiv Preussischer Kulturbesitz.*

more than 1 percent of the Russian population. The Bolsheviks confronted a much less industrialized economy than that in Italy or Germany. They believed in and practiced the collectivization of economic life attacked by the right-wing dictatorships. The Marxist-Leninist ideology was broader than the nationalism of the Fascists and the racism of the Nazis. Communism was an exportable commodity. The Communists regarded their government and their revolution not as part of a national history but as epoch-making events in the history of the world and the development of humanity. (See Document, "A Communist Woman Demands a New Family Life.") Fear of communism and determination to stop its spread became one of the leading political forces in Western Europe and the United States for most of the rest of the century. Policies flowing from that opposition would influence their relationships with much of the rest of the world.

War Communism

Within the Soviet Union the Red Army under the organizational genius of Leon Trotsky (1879–1940) had suppressed internal and foreign military opposition to the new government. Within months of the revolution, a new secret police, known as *Cheka*, appeared. Throughout the civil war Lenin (1870–1924) had declared that the Bolshevik Party, as the vanguard of the revolution, was imposing the dictatorship of the proletariat. Political and economic administration became highly centralized. All major decisions flowed from the top in a nondemocratic manner. Under the economic policy of **War Communism,** the revolutionary government confiscated and then operated the banks, the transport facilities, and heavy industry. The state also forcibly requisitioned grain and shipped it from the countryside to feed the army and the workers in the cities. The fact of the civil war permitted suppression of possible resistance to this economic policy.

War Communism helped the Red Army defeat its opponents. The revolution had survived and triumphed. The policy, however, generated domestic opposition to the Bolsheviks, who in 1920 numbered only about 600,000 members. The alliance of workers and peasants forged by the slogan of "Peace, Bread, and Land" had begun to dissolve. Many Russians were no longer willing to make the sacrifices demanded by the central party bureaucrats. In 1920 and 1921 serious strikes occurred. Peasants were discontented and resisted the requisition of grain. In March 1921 the navy mutinied at Kronstadt. The Red Army crushed the rebellion with grave loss of life. Each of these incidents suggested that the proletariat itself was opposing the dictatorship of the proletariat. Also, by late 1920 it had

A Communist Woman Demands a New Family Life

Document

While Lenin sought to consolidate the Bolshevik Revolution against internal and external enemies, there existed within the young Soviet Union a vast utopian impulse to change and reform virtually every social institution that had existed before the revolution or those Communists associated with capitalist society. Alexandra Kollontai (1872–1952) was a spokesperson of the extreme political left within the early Soviet Union. There had been much speculation on how the end of bourgeois society might change the structure of the family and the position of women. In this passage written in 1920 Kollontai states one of the most radically utopian visions of this change. During the years immediately after the revolution, extreme rumors circulated in both Europe and America about sexual and family experimentation in the Soviet Union. Statements such as this fostered such rumors and raised profound moral anxieties about the possible spread of communism beyond the borders of the Soviet Union. Kollontai herself later became a supporter of Stalin and a Soviet diplomat.

◆ Why did Kollontai see the restructuring of the family as essential to the establishment of a new kind of communist society? Would these changes make people loyal to that society? What changes in society does the kind of economic independence she seeks for women presuppose? What might childhood be like in this society?

There is no escaping the fact: the old type of family has seen its day. It is not the fault of the Communist State, it is the result of the changed conditions of life. The family is ceasing to be a necessity of the State, as it was in the past; on the contrary, it is worse than useless, since it needlessly holds back the female workers from more productive and far more serious work. . . . But on the ruins of the former family we shall soon see a new form rising which will involve altogether different relations between men and women, and which will be a union of affection and comradeship, a union of two equal members of the Communist society, both of them free, both of them independent, both of them workers. No more domestic "servitude" of women. No more inequality within the family. No more fear on the part of the woman lest she remain without support or aid with little ones in her arms if her husband should desert her. The woman in the Communist city no longer depends on her husband but on her work. It is not her husband but her robust arms which will support her. There will be no more anxiety as to the fate of her children. The State of the Workers will assume responsibility for these. Marriage will be purified of all its material elements, of all money calculations, which constitute a hideous blemish on family life in our days. . . .

The woman who is called upon to struggle in the great cause of the liberation of the workers—such a woman should know that in the new State there will be no more

room for such petty divisions as were formerly understood: "These are my own children, to them I owe all my maternal solicitude, all my affection; those are your children, my neighbour's children; I am not concerned with them. I have enough to do with my own." Henceforth the worker-mother, who is conscious of her social function, will rise to a point where she no longer differentiates between yours and mine; she must remember that there are henceforth only our children, those of the Communist State, the common possession of all the workers.

The Worker's State has need of a new form of relation between the sexes. The narrow and exclusive affection of the mother for her own children must expand until it embraces all the children of the great proletarian family. In place of the indissoluble marriage based on the servitude of woman, we shall see rise the free union, fortified by the love and mutual respect of the two members of the Workers' State, equal in their rights and in their obligations. In place of the individual and egotistic family there will arise a great universal family of workers, in which all the workers, men and women, will be, above all, workers, comrades.

From Alexandra Kollontai, *Communism and the Family*, as reprinted in Rudolf Schlesinger, ed. and trans., *The Family in the USSR* (London: Routledge and Kegan Paul, 1949), pp. 67–69. Reprinted by permission.

become clear that further revolution would not sweep across the rest of Europe. For the time being the Soviet Union would constitute a vast island of revolutionary socialism in the larger sea of worldwide capitalism.

The New Economic Policy

Under these difficult conditions Lenin made a crucial strategic retreat. In March 1921, following the Kronstadt mutiny, he outlined the **New Economic Policy**, normally referred to as NEP. Apart from what he termed "the commanding heights" of banking, heavy industry, transportation, and international commerce, considerable private economic enterprise was allowed. In particular, peasants could farm for a profit. They would pay taxes like other citizens, but they could sell their surplus grain on the open market. The NEP was consistent with Lenin's earlier conviction that the Russian peasantry held the key to the success of the revolution. After 1921 the countryside did become more stable, and a secure food supply seemed assured for the cities. Similar free enterprise flourished within light industry and domestic retail trade. By 1927 industrial production had reached its 1913 level. The revolution seemed to have transformed Russia into a land of small family farms and privately owned shops and businesses.

Stalin versus Trotsky

The NEP had caused sharp disputes within the Politburo, the highest governing committee of the Communist Party. The partial return to capitalism seemed to some members nothing less than a betrayal of sound Marxist principles. These frictions increased as Lenin's firm hand disappeared. In 1922 he suffered a stroke and never again dominated party affairs; in 1924 Lenin died. In the ensuing power vacuum, an intense struggle for leadership of the party commenced. Two factions emerged. One was led by Trotsky; the other by Joseph Stalin (1879–1953), who had become general secretary of the party in 1922. Shortly before his death Lenin had criticized both men. He was especially harsh towards Stalin. However, the general secretary's base of power lay with the party membership and with the daily management of party affairs. Consequently, he was able to withstand the posthumous strictures of Lenin.

Each faction wanted to control the party, but the struggle was fought over the question of Russia's path towards industrialization and the future of the communist revolutionary movement. Trotsky, speaking for what became known as the left wing, urged rapid industrialization and looked to voluntary collectivization of farming by poor peasants as a means of increasing agricultural production. Trotsky further argued that the revolution in Russia could succeed only if new revolutions took place elsewhere. Russia needed the skills and wealth of other nations to build its own economy. As Trotsky's influence within the party began to wane, he also demanded that party members be permitted to criticize the policies of the government and the party. Trotsky, however, was a latecomer to the advocacy of open discussion. When in control of the Red Army, he had been an unflinching disciplinarian.

A right-wing faction opposed Trotsky. Although its chief ideological voice was that of Nikolai Bukharin (1888–1938), the editor of *Pravda*, the official party paper, Stalin was its true political manipulator. In the mid-1920s this group pressed for the continuation of Lenin's NEP and a policy of relatively slow industrialization.

Stalin was the ultimate victor in these intraparty rivalries. Unlike the other early Bolshevik leaders, he had not spent a long exile in Western Europe. He was much less an intellectual and internationalist. He was also much more brutal. His handling of various recalcitrant national groups within Russia after the revolution had shocked even Lenin. Stalin's power lay in his command of bureaucratic and administrative methods. He was neither a brilliant writer nor an effective public speaker; however, he mastered the crucial, if dull, details of party structure, including admission and promotion. That mastery meant that he could draw on the support of the lower levels of the party apparatus when he clashed with other leaders.

In the mid-1920s Stalin supported Bukharin's position on economic development. In 1924 he also enunciated, in opposition to Trotsky, the doctrine of "socialism in one country." He urged that socialism could be achieved in Russia alone. Russian success did not depend on the fate of the revolution elsewhere. Stalin thus nationalized the previously international scope of the Marxist revolution. He cunningly used the apparatus of the party and his control over the Central Committee of the Communist Party to edge out Trotsky and his supporters. By 1927 Trotsky had been removed from all his offices, ousted from the party, and exiled to Siberia. In 1929 he was expelled from Russia and eventually moved to Mexico, where he was murdered in 1940 by one of Stalin's agents. With the removal of Trotsky, Stalin was firmly in control of the Soviet state. It remained to be seen where he would direct its course and what "socialism in one country" would mean in practice.

Decision for Rapid Industrialization

While the capitalist economies of Western Europe floundered during the depression, the Soviet Union registered tremendous industrial advance. As usual in Russia, the direction and impetus came from the top. Stalin far exceeded his tsarist predecessors in the intensity of state coercion and

Kulaks. During Stalin's drive to collectivize agriculture, wealthy peasants known as *kulaks* become the object of his wrath. Here a group of mostly peasant women demonstrate against the *kulaks*. *AP Wide World Photos.*

terror he brought to the task. Russia achieved its stunning economic growth during the 1930s only at the cost of literally millions of human lives and the degradation of millions more. Stalin's economic policy clearly proved that his earlier rivalry with Trotsky had been a matter of political power rather than one of substantial ideological difference.

Through 1928 Lenin's NEP, as championed by Bukharin with Stalin's support, had steered Soviet economic development. Private ownership and enterprise were permitted to flourish in the countryside to ensure enough food for the workers in the cities. A few farmers, the *kulaks*, had become prosperous. They probably numbered less than 5 percent of the rural population. During 1928 and 1929 they and other farmers withheld grain from the market because prices were too low. Food shortages occurred in the cities and caused potential unrest. The goals of the NEP were no longer being fulfilled. Sometime during these troubled months, Stalin came to a momentous decision: Russia must industrialize rapidly to match the economic and military power of the West. Agriculture must be collectivized to produce sufficient grain for food and export and to free peasant labor for the factories. This program, which basically embraced Trotsky's earlier economic position, unleashed a second Russian revolution. The costs and character of "socialism in one country" now became clear.

Agricultural Policy In 1929 Stalin ordered party agents into the countryside to confiscate any hoarded wheat. The *kulaks* bore the blame for the grain shortages. As part of the general plan to erase the private ownership of land and to collectivize

farming, the government undertook a program to eliminate the *kulaks* as a class. A *kulak*, however, soon came to mean any peasant who opposed Stalin's policy. In the countryside, peasants and farmers at all levels of wealth resisted stubbornly. They were determined to keep their land. They wreaked their own vengeance on the policy of **collectivization** by slaughtering more than 100 million horses and cattle between 1929 and 1933. The situation in the countryside amounted to open warfare. The peasant resistance caused Stalin to call a brief halt to the process in March 1930. He justified the slowdown on the grounds of "dizziness from success."

Soon thereafter, the drive to collectivize the farms was renewed with vehemence, and the costs remained high. As many as 10 million peasants were killed, and millions of others were sent forcibly to collective farms or labor camps. Initially, because of the turmoil on the land, agricultural production fell. There was famine in 1932 and 1933. Milk and meat remained in short supply because of the livestock slaughter. Yet Stalin persevered. The *kulaks* were uprooted from their farms and sent to Siberia or other regions far from their homes. Peasants who remained had their lands incorporated into large collective farms. The state provided the machinery for these units through machine-tractor stations. The state thus retained control over major farm machines, a monopoly that was a powerful weapon.

Collectivization dramatically changed Russian farming. In 1928 approximately 98 percent of Russian farmland consisted of small peasant holdings. Ten years later, despite all the opposition, over 90 percent of the land had been collectivized, and the quantity of farm produce directly handled by the government had risen by 40 percent. The government now had primary direction over the food supply. The farmers and peasants could no longer determine whether there would be stability or unrest in the cities. Stalin and the Communist Party had won the battle of the wheat fields, but they had not solved the problem of producing enough grain. That difficulty has plagued the former Soviet Union to the present day.

Five-Year Plans The revolution in agriculture had been undertaken for the sake of industrialization. The increased grain supply was to feed the labor force and provide exports to finance the imports required for industrial development. The industrial achievement of the Soviet Union between 1928 and World War II was one of the most striking accomplishments of the twentieth century. Russia made a more rapid advance towards economic

Propaganda. Stalin used intimidation and propaganda to support his drive to collectivize Soviet agriculture. The poster shows an idealized Soviet collective farm on which tractors owned by the state have replaced peasant labor. In reality, collectivization provoked fierce resistance and caused famines in which millions of peasants died. *1932 (colour litho) by Klutchis (fl. 1932). Deutsches Plakat Museum, Essen, Germany/Archives Charmet/The Bridgeman Art Library.*

growth than any other nation in the Western world has ever achieved during any similar period of time. By even the conservative estimates of Western observers, Soviet industrial production rose approximately 400 percent between 1928 and 1940. The production of iron, steel, coal, electrical power, tractors, combines, railway cars, and other heavy machinery was emphasized. Few consumer goods were produced. The labor for this development was supplied internally. Capital was raised from the export of grain, even at the cost of internal shortage. The technology was generally borrowed from already industrialized nations.

The organizational vehicle for industrialization was a series of Five-Year Plans first begun in 1928. The State Planning Commission, or Gosplan, oversaw the program. It set goals of production and organized the economy to meet

them. Coordinating all facets of production was immensely difficult and complicated. Deliveries of materials from mines or factories had to be assured before the next unit could carry out its part of the plan. There was many a slip between the cup and the lip. The troubles in the countryside were harmful. A vast program of propaganda was undertaken to sell the Five-Year Plans to the Russian people and to elicit cooperation. The industrial labor force, however, soon became subject to regimentation similar to that being imposed on the peasants. By the close of the 1930s the accomplishment of the three Five-Year Plans was truly impressive and probably allowed the Soviet Union to survive the German invasion. Industries that had never existed in Russia now challenged and in some cases, such as tractor production, surpassed their counterparts in the rest of the world. Large, new industrial cities had been built and populated by hundreds of thousands of people.

Many non-Russian contemporaries looked at the Soviet economic experiment quite uncritically. While the capitalist world lay in the throes of the depression, the Soviet economy had grown at a pace never realized in the West. The American writer Lincoln Steffens (1866–1936) reported after a trip to Russia, "I have seen the future and it works." Beatrice Webb (1858–1943) and Sydney Webb (1859–1947), the British Fabian Socialists, spoke of "a new civilization" in the Soviet Union. These and other similar writers ignored the shortages in consumer goods and the poor housing. More important, they seem to have had little idea of the social cost of the Soviet achievement. Millions of people had been killed and millions more uprooted. The total picture of suffering and human loss during those years will probably never be known; the deprivation and sacrifice of Soviet citizens far exceeded anything described by Marx and Engels in relation to nineteenth-century industrialization in Western Europe.

The Purges

Stalin's decisions to industrialize rapidly and to move against the peasants aroused internal political opposition because they were departures from the policies of Lenin. In 1929 Stalin forced Bukharin, the fervent supporter of the NEP and his own former ally, off the Politburo. Little detailed information is known about further opposition, but it does seem to have existed among lower level party followers of Bukharin and other previous opponents of rapid industrialization. Sometime in 1933 Stalin began to fear that he would lose control over the party apparatus and that effective rivals might emerge. These fears were probably produced as much by his own paranoia as by real plots. Nevertheless, they resulted in the **Great Purges**, among the most

Party Congress, 1936. By the mid-1930s Stalin's purges had eliminated many leaders and other members form the Soviet Communist Party. This photograph of a meeting of a party congress in 1936 shows a number of the surviving leaders with Stalin, who sits fourth from the right in the front row. To his left is Vyacheslav Molotov, long-time foreign minister. The first person on the left in the front row is Nikita Khrushchev, who headed the Soviet Union in the late 1950s and early 1960s. *Itar-Tass/Sovfoto/Eastfoto.*

labor camps, and still others left unmolested. After the civilian party members had been purged, the prosecutors turned against the army. Important officers, including heroes of the civil war, were killed. Within the party itself, hundreds of thousands of members were expelled, and applicants for membership were removed from the rolls. The exact numbers of executions, imprisonments, and expulsions are unknown but certainly ran into the millions.

The trials and purges astonished observers from outside the Soviet Union. Nothing quite like this phenomenon had ever been seen. Political murders and executions were not new, but the absurd confessions were novel. The scale of the political turmoil was also unprecedented. The Russians themselves did not believe or comprehend what was occurring. There existed no national emergency or crisis. There were only accusations of sympathy for Trotsky or of complicity in Kirov's murder or of other nameless crimes. If a rational explanation is to be sought, it probably must be found in Stalin's concern for his own power. In effect, the purges created a new party structure absolutely loyal to him. The "old Bolsheviks" of the October Revolution were among his earliest targets. They and others active in the first years of the revolution knew how far Stalin had moved from Lenin's policies. New, younger party members replaced those executed or expelled. The newcomers knew little of old Russia or of the ideals of the original Bolsheviks. They had not been loyal to Lenin, Trotsky, or any Soviet leader except Stalin himself.

Despite the flagrant violence and widespread repression of the Soviet experiment, it found many sympathizers throughout the world. Some people did not know of its repression; others ignored those events. The Soviet Union almost immediately after the Bolshevik seizure of power had fostered the organization of Communist parties subservient to Moscow influence throughout the world. Others who were not formally members of these parties often sympathized with what they believed or hoped were the goals of the Soviet Union. During at least the first fifty years of its existence the Soviet Union managed to capture the imagination of some intellectuals in the West and in other parts of the

mysterious and horrendous political events of this century. The purges were not understood at the time and are still not fully comprehended today.

On December 1, 1934, Sergei Kirov (1888–1934), the popular party chief of Leningrad (formerly Saint Petersburg and Petrograd) and a member of the Politburo, was assassinated. In the wake of the shooting thousands of people were arrested, and still more were expelled from the party and sent to labor camps. At the time it was believed that Kirov had been murdered by opponents of the regime. Direct or indirect complicity in the crime became the normal accusation against those whom Stalin attacked. It now seems practically certain that Stalin himself authorized Kirov's assassination to forestall any threat from the Leningrad leader.

The purges after Kirov's death were just the beginning of a larger process. Between 1936 and 1938 spectacular show trials were held in Moscow. Previous high Soviet leaders, including former members of the Politburo, publicly confessed political crimes. They were convicted and executed. It is still not certain why they made their palpably false confessions. Still other leaders and lower level party members were tried in private and shot. Thousands of people received no trial at all. The purges touched persons in all areas of party life. It is inexplicable why some were executed, others sent to

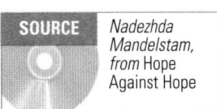
SOURCE *Nadezhda Mandelstam, from Hope Against Hope*

globe who hoped for a utopian egalitarian transformation of society. During much of the 1930s, to these and other people, the Soviet Union also appeared as an enemy to the fascist experiments in Italy and Germany. The Marxist ideology championed by the Soviet Union appeared to many people living in the European colonial empires as a vehicle for freeing themselves from the colonial situation. The Soviet Union welcomed and trained many such anticolonial leaders and offered other support to their causes. In the wake of the collapse of the Soviet Union at the close of the century and what is now known about its repression it is difficult to understand the power its presence exercised over many people's political imaginations around the world, but that attraction was one of the most fundamental factors in world politics from the 1920s through at least the early 1970s.

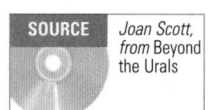
SOURCE Joan Scott, from Beyond the Urals

The Fascist Experiment in Italy

The first authoritarian political experiment in Western Europe that arose in part from fears of the spread of bolshevism occurred in Italy. The general term *fascist*, which has been used to describe the various right-wing dictatorships that arose between the wars, was derived from the Italian Fascist movement of Benito Mussolini (1883–1945).

While scholars still dispute the exact meaning of **fascism** as a political term, the governments regarded as fascist were antidemocratic, anti-Marxist, antiparliamentary, and frequently anti-Semitic. They hoped to hold back the spread of bolshevism, which seemed a real threat at the time. They sought a world that would be safe for the middle class, small businesses, owners of moderate amounts of property, and small farmers. The Fascist regimes rejected the political inheritance of the French Revolution and of nineteenth-century liberalism. Their adherents believed that normal parliamentary politics and parties sacrificed national honor and greatness to petty party disputes. They wanted to overcome the class conflict of Marxism and the party conflict of liberalism by consolidating the various groups and classes within the nation for great national purposes. As Mussolini declared in 1931, "The fascist conception of the state is all-embracing, and outside of the state no human or spiritual values can exist, let alone be desirable."[1] Fascist governments were usually single-party dictatorships characterized by terrorism and police surveillance. These dictatorships were rooted in the base of mass political parties.

---

[1] Quoted in Denis Mack Smith, *Italy: A Modern History* (Ann Arbor: University of Michigan Press, 1959), p. 412.

Rise of Mussolini

The Italian *Fasci di Combattimento* ("Band of Combat") was founded in 1919 in Milan. Most of its members were war veterans who felt that the sacrifices of World War I had been in vain. They resented Italy's failure to gain the city of Fiume, towards the northern end of the Adriatic Sea, at the Paris conference. They feared socialism, inflation, and labor unrest.

Their leader or **Duce**, Benito Mussolini, was the son of a blacksmith. After having been a schoolteacher and a day laborer, he became active in Italian Socialist politics and by 1912 had become editor of the socialist newspaper *Avanti*. In 1914 Mussolini broke with the Socialists and supported Italian entry into the war on the side of the Allies. His interventionist position lost him the editorship of *Avanti*. He then established his own paper, *Il Popolo d'Italia*. Later he served in the army and was wounded. In 1919 Mussolini was just another Italian politician. His *Fasci* organization was one of many small political groups in a country characterized by such entities. As a politician, Mussolini was an opportunist par excellence. He could change his ideas and principles to suit every new occasion. Action for him was always more important than thought or rational justification. His one real rule was political survival.

Postwar Italian politics was a muddle. During the war the Italian Parliament had virtually ceased to function. Ministers had ruled by decree. However, many Italians were dissatisfied with the parliamentary system as it then existed. They felt that Italy had emerged from the war as less than a victorious nation, had not been treated as a great power at the peace conference, and had not received the territories it deserved. The main spokesman for this discontent was the extreme nationalist writer Gabriele D'Annunzio (1863–1938). In 1919 he captured Fiume with a force of patriotic Italians. The Italian army, enforcing the terms of the Versailles Treaty, eventually drove him out. D'Annunzio had provided the example of the political use of a nongovernmental military force. Removing him from Fiume made the parliamentary ministry seem unpatriotic.

Between 1919 and 1921 Italy was also wracked by social turmoil. Numerous industrial strikes occurred, and workers occupied factories. Peasants seized uncultivated land from large estates. Parliamentary and constitutional government seemed incapable of dealing with this unrest. The Socialist Party had captured a plurality of seats in the Chamber of Deputies in 1919. A new Catholic Popular Party had also done well. Both appealed to the working and agrarian classes. However, neither party would cooperate with the other, and parliamentary deadlock resulted. Under these conditions, many Italians honestly—and still others conveniently—believed that a communist revolution might break out.

Initially, Mussolini was uncertain which way the political winds were blowing. He first supported the factory occupa-

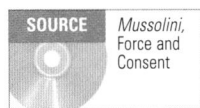

SOURCE *Mussolini, Force and Consent*

tions and land seizures. Never one to be concerned with consistency, however, he soon reversed himself. He had discovered that many upper-class and middle-class Italians who were pressured by inflation and who feared property loss had no sympathy for the workers or the peasants. They wanted order rather than some vague social justice that might harm their own interests. Consequently, Mussolini and his Fascists took direct action in the face of the government inaction. They formed local squads who terrorized Socialist supporters. They attacked strikers and farm workers and protected strikebreakers. Conservative land and factory owners were grateful to the terrorists. The officers and institutions of the law simply ignored these crimes. By early 1922 the Fascists controlled the local government in many parts of northern Italy.

In 1921 Mussolini and thirty-four of his followers had been elected to the Chamber of Deputies. Their importance grew as the local Fascists gained more direct power. The Fascist movement now had hundreds of thousands of supporters. In October 1922 the Fascists, dressed in their characteristic black shirts, began a march on Rome. Intimidated, King Victor Emmanuel III (r. 1900–1946) refused to authorize using the army against the marchers. No other single decision so ensured a Fascist seizure of power. The cabinet resigned in protest. On October 29 the monarch telegraphed Mussolini in Milan and asked him to become prime minister. The next day Mussolini arrived in Rome by sleeping car and, as head of the government, greeted his followers when they entered the city.

Technically, Mussolini had come into office by legal means. The monarch did have the power to appoint the prime minister. Mussolini, however, had no majority in the Chamber of Deputies. Behind the legal façade of his assumption of power lay the months of terrorist disruption and intimidation and the threat of the Fascists' October march itself.

The Fascists in Power

Mussolini had not really expected to be appointed prime minister. He moved cautiously to consolidate his power. He succeeded because of the impotence of his rivals, his own effective use of his office, his power over the masses, and his sheer ruthlessness. On November 23, 1922, the king and Parliament granted Mussolini dictatorial authority for one year to bring order to the lower levels of the government. Wherever possible, Mussolini appointed Fascists to office. Late in 1924, at Mussolini's behest, Parliament changed the election law. Previously parties had been represented in the Chamber of Deputies in proportion to the popular vote cast for them. According to the new election law, the party that gained the largest popular vote (with a minimum of at least 25 percent) received two thirds of the seats in the chamber.

Coalition government, with all its compromises and hesitations, would no longer be necessary. In the election of 1924 the Fascists won a great victory and complete control of the Chamber of Deputies. They used that majority to end legitimate parliamentary life. A series of laws passed in 1925 and 1926 permitted Mussolini, in effect, to rule by decree. In 1926 all other political parties were dissolved, and Italy was transformed into a single-party, dictatorial state.

The Italian dictator made one important domestic departure that brought him significant political dividends. Through the Lateran Accord of February 1929 the Roman Catholic Church and the Italian state made peace with each other. Ever since the armies of Italian unification had seized papal lands in the 1860s the church had been hostile to the state. The popes had remained virtual prisoners in the Vatican after 1870. The agreement of 1929 recognized the pope as the temporal ruler of Vatican City. The Italian government agreed to

Mussolini and the Black Shirts. Mussolini poses with supporters the day after the Black Shirt March on Rome intimidated the King of Italy into making him prime minister. *Bildarchiv Preussischer Kutturbesitz.*

pay an indemnity to the papacy for confiscated land. The state also recognized Catholicism as the religion of the nation, exempted church property from taxes, and allowed church law to govern marriage. The Lateran Accord brought further respectability to Mussolini's authoritarian regime.

German Democracy and Dictatorship

The Weimar Republic

The Weimar Republic was born from the defeat of the imperial army, the revolution of 1918 against the Hohenzollerns, and the hopes of German Liberals and Social Democrats. Its name derived from the city in which its constitution was written and promulgated in August 1919. While the constitution was being debated, the republic, headed by the Social Democrats, accepted the humiliating terms of the Versailles Treaty. Although its officials had signed only under the threat of an Allied invasion, the republic was nevertheless permanently associated with the national disgrace and the economic burdens of the treaty. Throughout the 1920s the government of the republic was required to fulfill the economic and military provisions imposed by the Paris settlement. It became all too easy for nationalists and military figures whose policies had brought on the tragedy and defeat of the war to blame the young republic and the Socialists for the results of the conflict. In Germany, more than in other countries, the desire to revise the treaty was closely related to a desire to change the mode of domestic government.

The Weimar Constitution was a highly enlightened document. It guaranteed civil liberties and provided for direct election, by universal suffrage, of the **Reichstag** and the president. It also, however, contained certain crucial structural flaws that eventually allowed it to be overthrown. Seats in the Reichstag were allotted according to a complicated system of proportional representation. This made it relatively easy for small political parties to gain seats and resulted in shifting party combinations that led to considerable instability. Ministers were technically responsible to the Reichstag, but the president appointed and removed the chancellor, the head of the cabinet. Perhaps most important, Article 48 allowed the president, in an emergency, to rule by decree. The constitution thus permitted the possibility of presidential dictatorship.

The new government suffered major and minor humiliations as well as considerable economic instability. In March 1920 the right-wing Kapp Putsch, or armed insurrection, erupted in Berlin. Led by a conservative civil servant and supported by army officers, the attempted coup failed, but only after government officials had fled the city and workers had carried out a general strike. In the same month, strikes took place in the Ruhr mining district. The government sent in troops. Such extremism from both the left and the right would haunt the republic for all its days. In May 1921 the Allies presented a reparations bill for 132 billion gold marks. The German Republican government accepted this preposterous demand only after new Allied threats of occupation. Throughout the early 1920s there were numerous assassinations or attempted assassinations of important Republican leaders. Violence was the hallmark of the first five years of the republic.

Invasion of the Ruhr and Inflation Inflation brought on the major crisis of this period. The financing of the war and continued postwar deficit spending generated an immense rise in prices. Consequently, the value of German currency fell. By early 1921 the German mark traded against the American dollar at a ratio of 64 to 1, compared with a ratio of 4.2 to 1 in 1914. The German financial community contended that the value of the currency could not be stabilized until the reparations issue had been solved. In the meantime, the printing presses kept pouring forth paper money, which was used to redeem government bonds as they fell due.

The French invasion of the Ruhr in January 1923, to secure the payment of reparations, and the German response of passive economic resistance produced cataclysmic

Inflation in Germany. During the German inflation of 1923 currency literally was not worth the paper upon which it was printed. Here German children play with batches of worthless banknotes. *Bettmann/Hulton Deutsch Collection.*

inflation. The Weimar government paid subsidies to the Ruhr labor force, who had laid down their tools. Unemployment soon spread from the Ruhr to other parts of the country, creating a new drain on the treasury and also reducing tax revenues. The printing presses by this point had difficulty providing enough paper currency to keep up with the daily rise in prices. Money was literally not worth the paper it was printed on. Stores were unwilling to exchange goods for the worthless currency, and farmers withheld produce from the market.

The moral and social values of thrift and prudence were thoroughly undermined. Middle-class savings, pensions, and insurance policies were wiped out, as were investments in government bonds. Simultaneously, debts and mortgages could not be paid off. Speculators in land, real estate, and industry made great fortunes. Union contracts generally allowed workers to keep up with rising prices. Thus inflation was not a disaster for everyone. To the middle class and the lower middle class, however, the inflation was still one more trauma coming hard on the heels of the military defeat and the peace treaty. Only when the social and economic upheaval of these months is grasped can one understand the later German desire for order and security at almost any cost.

Hitler's Early Career Late in 1923 Adolf Hitler (1889–1945) made his first significant appearance on the German political scene. The son of a minor Austrian customs official, he had gone to Vienna, where his hopes of becoming an artist were soon dashed. He lived off money sent by his widowed mother and later off his Austrian orphan's allowance. He also painted postcards for further income and later found work as a day laborer. In Vienna he encountered Mayor Karl Lueger's (1844–1910) Christian Socialist Party, which prospered on an ideology of anti-Semitism and from the social anxieties of the lower middle class. Hitler absorbed the rabid German nationalism and extreme anti-Semitism that flourished in Vienna. He came to hate Marxism, which he associated with Jews. During World War I Hitler fought in the German army, was wounded, rose to the rank of corporal, and won the Iron Cross for bravery. The war gave him his first sense of purpose.

After the conflict, Hitler settled in Munich. There he became associated with a small nationalistic, anti-Semitic political party that in 1920 adopted the name of National Socialist German Workers Party, better known simply as the **Nazis**. In the same year the group began to parade under a red banner with a black swastika. It issued a platform, or program, of Twenty-Five Points. Among other things, this platform called for the repudiation of the Versailles Treaty, the unification of Austria and Germany, the exclusion of Jews from German citizenship, agrarian reform, the prohibition of

Weimar Germany. In this painting, which reflects the mood of social and political disillusionment that prevailed in much of Europe in the 1920s, George Grosz satirized conservative and rightwing groups in Weimar Germany, including the army, the courts, the newspapers, and the Nazi Party. *Grosz George (1893–1959) © VAGA, NY, Stuetzen der Gesellschaft (pillars of Society), 1926. Oil on canvas, 2000,0 × 108,0 cm. Photo: Joerg P. Anders. Nationalgalerie, Staatliche Museen zu Berlin, Berlin, Germany.*

land speculation, the confiscation of war profits, state administration of the giant cartels, and the replacement of department stores with small retail shops. Originally the Nazis had called for a broad program of nationalization of industry in an attempt to compete directly with the Marxist political parties for the vote of the workers. As the tactic failed, the Nazis redefined the meaning of the word *socialist* in the party name, so that it suggested a nationalistic outlook. In 1922, Hitler said

> Whoever is prepared to make the national cause his own to such an extent that he knows no higher ideal than the welfare of his nation; whoever has understood our great national anthem, Deutschland, Deutschland, über Alles ["Germany, Germany, over All"], to mean that nothing in the wide world surpasses in his eyes this Germany, people and land, land and people—that man is a Socialist.[2]

This definition, of course, had nothing to do with traditional German socialism. The "socialism" that Hitler and the Nazis had in mind was not state ownership of the means of production but the subordination of all economic enterprise to the welfare of the nation. It often implied protection for small economic enterprises. Increasingly, the Nazis discovered their party appealed to virtually any economic group that was at risk and under pressure. They often tailored their messages to the particular local problems these groups confronted in different parts of Germany. The Nazis also found considerable support among war veterans, who faced economic and social displacement in Weimar society. The ongoing Nazi demand for revision of the Versailles Treaty appealed to a broad spectrum of economic groups as well as the disaffected war veterans. (See Document "Hitler Denounces the Versailles Treaty.")

Soon after the promulgation of the Twenty-Five Points, the storm troopers, or **SA** (*Sturm Abteilung*), were organized under the leadership of Captain Ernst Roehm (1887–1934). It was a paramilitary organization that initially provided its members with food and uniforms and, later in the decade, with wages. In the mid-1920s the SA adopted its famous brown-shirted uniform. The storm troopers were the chief Nazi instrument for terror and intimidation before the party came into control of the government. They were a law unto themselves. The organization constituted a means of preserving military discipline and values outside the small army permitted by the Paris settlement. The existence of such a private party army was a sign of the potential for violence in the Weimar Republic and the widespread contempt for the law and the institutions of the republic.

The social and economic turmoil following the French occupation of the Ruhr and the German inflation gave the

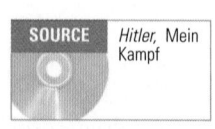

SOURCE
Hitler, Mein Kampf

fledgling party an opportunity for direct action against the Weimar Republic, which seemed incapable of providing military or economic secu-

rity. By this time, because of his immense oratorical skills and organizational abilities, Hitler personally dominated the Nazi Party. On November 9, 1923, Hitler and a band of followers, accompanied by General Erich Ludendorff (1865–1937), attempted an unsuccessful putsch at a beer hall in Munich. When the local authorities crushed the rising, sixteen Nazis were killed. Hitler and Ludendorff were arrested and tried for treason. The general was acquitted. Hitler used the trial to make himself into a national figure. In his defense, he condemned the republic, the Versailles Treaty, the Jews, and the weakened condition of his adopted country. He was convicted and sentenced to five years in prison. He actually spent only a few months in jail before being paroled. During this time, he dictated **Mein Kampf** ("My Struggle"). Another result of the brief imprisonment was his decision to seize political power by legal methods.

The Stresemann Years The officials of the republic were attempting to repair the damage from the inflation. Gustav Stresemann (1878–1929) was responsible primarily for reconstruction of the republic and for its achievement of a sense of self-confidence. Stresemann abandoned the policy of passive resistance in the Ruhr. The country simply could not afford it. Then, with the aid of banker Hjalmar Schacht (1877–1970), he introduced a new German currency. The rate of exchange was 1 trillion of the old German marks for one new Rentenmark. Stresemann also moved against challenges from both the left and the right. He supported the crushing of both Hitler's abortive putsch and smaller communist disturbances. In late November 1923, after four months as chancellor, he resigned to become foreign minister, a post he held until his death in 1929. In that office he continued to influence the affairs of the republic.

In 1924 the Weimar Republic and the Allies renegotiated the reparation payments. The Dawes Plan lowered the annual payments and allowed them to fluctuate according to the fortunes of the German economy. The last French troops left the Ruhr in 1925. The same year, Field Marshal Paul von Hindenburg (1847–1934), a military hero and a conservative monarchist, was elected president of the republic. He governed in strict accordance with the constitution, but his election suggested that German politics had become more conservative. Conservative Germans seemed reconciled to the republic. This conservatism was in line with the prosperity of the latter 1920s. Foreign capital flowed into Germany, and employment, which had been poor throughout most of the postwar years, improved smartly. Giant industrial combines spread. The prosperity helped to establish broader acceptance and appreciation of the republic.

---

[2] Alan Bullock, *Hitler: A Study in Tyranny*, rev. ed. (New York: Harper & Row, 1964), p. 76.

Hitler Denounces the Versailles Treaty

Document

Demands for revision of the Versailles Treaty of 1919 existed in many European nations during the 1920s, but such demands were especially fundamental to German politics and constituted a fundamental platform of the National Socialist Movement. Hitler and his followers made denunciation of the treaty their single most uncompromising declaration. In this speech of April 17, 1923, Hitler explained how the treaty had undermined the German nation.

◆ How might the French invasion of the Ruhr and the resulting inflation have made this speech particularly effective? To what extent was Hitler's condemnation of the control the Versailles Treaty imposed on Germany correct? How does Hitler contrast his young Nazi movement with the young Weimar Republic? Why does the one appear a strong and the other a weak supporter of German national goals?

With the armistice begins the humiliation of Germany. If the Republic on the day of its foundation had appealed to the country: "Germans, stand together! Up and resist the foe! The Fatherland, the Republic expects of you that you fight to your last breath," then millions who are now the enemies of the Republic would be fanatical Republicans. Today they are the foes of the Republic not because it is a Republic but because this Republic was founded at the moment when Germany was humiliated, because it so discredited the new flag that men's eyes must turn regretfully towards the old flag.

It was no Treaty of Peace which was signed, but a betrayal of Peace.

The Treaty was signed which demanded from Germany that she should perform what was for ever impossible of performance. But that was not the worst; after all that was only a question of material values. This was not the end: Commissions of Control were formed! For the first time in the history of the modern world there were planted on a State agents of foreign Powers to act as Hangmen and German soldiers were set to serve the foreigner. And if one of these Commissions was "insulted," a company of the German army had to defile before the French flag. We no longer feel the humiliation of such an act; but the outside world says, "What a people of curs!"

So long as this Treaty stands there can be no resurrection of the German people: no social reform of any kind is possible! The Treaty was made in order to bring 20 million Germans to their deaths and to ruin the German nation. But those who made the Treaty cannot set it aside. At its foundation our Movement formulated three demands;

1. Setting aside of the Peace Treaty.
2. Unification of all Germans.
3. Land and soil to feed our nation.

Our Movement could formulate these demands, since it was not our Movement which casued the War, it has not made the Republic, it did not sign the Peace Treaty.

There is thus one thing which is the first task of this Movement: it desires to make the German once more National, that his Fatherland shall stand for him above everything else. It desires to teach our people to understand afresh the truth of the old saying: He would not be a hammer must be an anvil. An anvil are we today, and that anvil will be beaten until out of the anvil we fashion once more a hammer, a German sword!

From speech delivered in Munich, April 17, 1923, by Adolph Hitler, from *The Speeches of Adolf Hitler, April 1922–August 1939*, trans. by Norman H. Baynes, 1969, pp. 56–57.

In foreign affairs, Stresemann pursued a conciliatory course. He fulfilled the provisions of the Versailles Treaty even as he attempted to revise it by diplomacy. He was willing to accept the settlement in the West but was a determined, if sometimes secret, revisionist in the East. He aimed to recover German-speaking territories lost to Poland and Czechoslovakia and possibly to unite with Austria, chiefly by diplomatic means. The first step, however, was to achieve respectability and economic recovery. That goal required a policy of accommodation and "fulfillment," for the moment at least.

Locarno These developments gave rise to the Locarno Agreements of October 1925. The spirit of conciliation led foreign ministers Austen Chamberlain (1863–1937) for Britain and Aristide Briand (1862–1932) for France to accept Stresemann's proposal for a fresh start. France and Germany both accepted the western frontier established at Versailles as legitimate. Britain and Italy agreed to intervene against the aggressor if either side violated the frontier or if Germany sent troops into the demilitarized Rhineland. Significantly, no such agreement was made about Germany's eastern frontier, but the Germans made treaties of arbitration with Poland and Czechoslovakia, and France strengthened its ties with those countries. France supported German membership in the League of Nations and agreed to withdraw its occupation troops from the Rhineland in 1930, five years earlier than specified at Versailles.

Germany was pleased to have achieved respectability and a guarantee against another Ruhr occupation, as well as the possibility of revision in the east. Britain enjoyed playing a more even-handed role. Italy was glad to be recognized as a great power. The French were happy, too, because the Germans voluntarily accepted the permanence of their western frontier, which was also guaranteed by Britain and Italy, and France maintained its allies in the east.

The Locarno Agreements brought new hope to Europe. Germany's entry into the League of Nations was greeted

Chronology

Major Political Events of the 1920s and 1930s

1919 August	Constitution of the Weimar Republic promulgated
1920	Kapp Putsch in Berlin
1921 March	Kronstadt mutiny leads Lenin to initiate his New Economic Policy
1922 October	Fascist march on Rome leads to Mussolini's assumption of power
1923 January	France invades the Ruhr
November	Hitler's Beer Hall Putsch
1924	Death of Lenin
1925	Locarno Agreements
1928	Kellogg-Briand Pact; first Five-Year Plan launched in USSR
1929 January	Trotsky expelled from USSR
February	Lateran Accord between the Vatican and the Italian state
October	New York stock market crash
November	Bukharin expelled from his offices in the Soviet Union; Stalin's central position thus affirmed
1930 March	Bruning government begins in Germany
	Stalin calls for moderation in his policy of agricultural collectivization because of "dizziness from success"
September	Nazis capture 107 seats in German Reichstag
1931 August	National Government formed in Britain
1932 March 13	Hindenberg defeats Hitler for German presidency
May 31	Franz von Papen forms German Cabinet
July 31	German Reichstag election
November 6	German Reichstag election
December 2	Kurt von Schleicher forms German Cabinet
1933 January 30	Hitler made German chancellor
February 27	Reichstag fire
March 5	Reichstag election
March 23	Enabling Act consolidates Nazi power
1934 June 30	Blood purge of the Nazi Party
August 2	Death of Hindenburg
December 1	Assassination of Kirov leads to the beginning of Stalin's purges
1936 May	Popular Front government in France
July–August	Most famous of public purge trials in Russia

with enthusiasm. Chamberlain, Briand, and Stresemann all received the Nobel Peace Prize in 1925 and 1926. The spirit of Locarno was carried even further when the leading European states, Japan, and the United States signed the Kellogg-Briand Pact in 1928, renouncing "war as an instrument of national policy." The joy and optimism were not justified. France had merely recognized its inability to coerce Germany without help. Britain had shown its unwillingness to uphold the settlement in the east. Austen Chamberlain declared that no British government ever would "risk the bones of a British grenadier" for the Polish corridor. Germany was not reconciled to the eastern settlement. It maintained clandestine military connections with the Soviet Union and planned to continue to press for revision.

In both France and Germany, moreover, the conciliatory politicians represented only a part of the nation. In Germany especially, most people continued to reject Versailles and regarded Locarno as only an extension of it. When the Dawes Plan ran out in 1929 it was replaced by the Young Plan, which lowered the reparation payments, put a term on how long they must be made, and removed Germany entirely from outside supervision and control. The intensity of the outcry in Germany against the continuation of any reparations showed how far the Germans were from accepting their situation. Despite these problems, war was by no means inevitable. Europe, aided by American loans, was returning to prosperity. German leaders like Stresemann would certainly have continued to press for change, but there is little reason to think that they would have resorted to force, much less to a general war. Continued prosperity and diplomatic success might have won the loyalty of the German people for the Weimar Republic and moderate revisionism, but the Great Depression of the 1930s brought new forces to power.

Depression and Political Deadlock

The outflow of foreign, and especially American, capital from Germany that began in 1928 undermined the economic prosperity of the Weimar Republic. The resulting economic crisis brought parliamentary government to a halt. In 1928 a coalition of center parties and the Social Democrats governed. All went reasonably well until the Depression struck. Then the coalition partners differed sharply on economic policy. The Social Democrats refused to reduce social and unemployment insurance. The more conservative parties, remembering the inflation of 1923, insisted on a balanced budget. The coalition dissolved in March 1930. To resolve the parliamentary deadlock in the Reichstag, President von Hindenburg appointed Heinrich Brüning (1885–1970) as chancellor. Lacking a majority in

the Reichstag, the new chancellor governed through emergency presidential decrees, as authorized by Article 48 of the constitution. The party divisions in the Reichstag prevented the overriding of the decrees. The Weimar Republic was transformed into a presidential dictatorship.

German unemployment rose from 2,258,000 in March 1930 to over 6,000,000 in March 1932. There had been persistent unemployment during the 1920s, but nothing of such magnitude or duration. The economic downturn and the parliamentary deadlock worked to the advantage of the more extreme political parties. In the election of 1928 the Nazis had won only 12 seats in the Reichstag, and the Communists had won 54 seats. Two years later, after the election of 1930, the Nazis held 107 seats and the Communists 77.

The power of the Nazis in the streets was also on the rise. The unemployment fed thousands of men into the 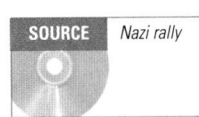 storm troopers, which had 100,000 members in 1930 and almost 1 million in 1933. The SA freely and viciously attacked Communists and Social Democrats. For the Nazis, politics meant the capture of power through terror and intimidation as well as through elections. Decency and civility in political life vanished. Nazi rallies resembled secular religious revivals. The Nazis paraded through the streets and the countryside. They gained powerful supporters and sympathizers in the business, military, and newspaper communities. Some intellectuals were also sympathetic. The Nazis transformed this discipline and enthusiasm born of economic despair and nationalistic frustration into impressive electoral results.

Hitler Comes to Power

For two years Brüning continued to govern through the confidence of Hindenburg. The economy did not improve, and the political situation deteriorated. In 1932 the eighty-three-year-old president stood for reelection. Hitler ran against him and forced a runoff. The Nazi leader garnered 30.1 percent of the vote in the first election and 36.8 percent in the second. Although Hindenburg was returned to office, the vote convinced him that Brüning had lost the confidence of conservative German voters. In May 1932 he dismissed Brüning and appointed Franz von Papen (1878–1969) in his place. The new chancellor was one of a small group of extremely conservative advisers on whom the aged Hindenburg had become increasingly dependent. Others included the president's son and several military figures. With the continued paralysis in the Reichstag, their influence over the president amounted to control of the government. Consequently, the crucial decisions of the next several months were made by only a handful of people.

Papen and the circle around the president wanted to draw the Nazis into cooperation with them without giving Hitler effective power. The government needed the popular support on the right that only the Nazis seemed able to generate. The Hindenburg circle decided to convince Hitler that the Nazis could not come to power on their own. Papen removed the ban on Nazi meetings that Brüning had imposed and then called a Reichstag election for July 1932. The Nazis won 230 seats and polled 37.2 percent of the vote. Hitler would only enter the Cabinet if he were made chancellor. Hindenburg refused. Another election was called in November, partly to wear down the Nazis' financial resources. The Nazis gained only 196 seats, and their percentage of the popular vote dipped to 33.1 percent. The advisers around Hindenburg still refused to appoint Hitler to office.

In early December 1932 Papen resigned, and General Kurt von Schleicher (1882–1934) became chancellor. People were now afraid of civil war between the extreme left and the far right. Schleicher decided to try and fashion a broad-based coalition of conservative groups and trade unionists. The prospect of such a coalition, including groups from the political left, frightened the Hindenburg circle even more than the prospect of Hitler. They did not trust Schleicher's motives, which have never been clear. Consequently, they persuaded Hindenburg to appoint Hitler chancellor. To control him and to see that he did little mischief, Papen was named vice chancellor, and other traditional conservatives were appointed to the Cabinet. On January 30, 1933, Adolf Hitler became the chancellor of Germany.

Hitler had come into office by legal means. All the proper forms and procedures had been observed. This was important, for it permitted the civil service, the courts, and the other agencies of the government to support him in good conscience. He had forged a rigidly disciplined party structure and had mastered the techniques of mass politics and propaganda. He understood how to touch the raw social and political nerves of the electorate. His support appears to have come from across the social spectrum. Pockets of resistance appeared among Roman Catholic voters in the country and small towns. Otherwise, support for Hitler was particularly strong among farmers, war veterans, and the young, who had especially suffered from the insecurity of the 1920s and the Depression of the early 1930s. Hitler promised them security against Communists and Socialists, effective government in place of the petty politics of the other parties, and an uncompromising nationalist vision of a strong, restored Germany.

Much blame was once assigned to German big business for the rise of Hitler. However, there is little evidence that business contributions made any crucial difference to the Nazis' success or failure. Hitler's supporters were frequently suspicious of business and giant capitalism. They wanted a simpler world, one in which small property would be safe from both socialism and large-scale capitalist consolidation. These people looked to Hitler and the Nazis rather than to the Social Democrats because the latter, although concerned with social issues, never appeared sufficiently nationalistic. The Nazis won out over other conservative nationalistic parties because, unlike those conservatives, the Nazis did address the problem of social insecurities.

Hitler's Consolidation of Power

Once in office, Hitler moved with almost lightning speed to consolidate his control. This process had three facets: the capture of full legal authority, the crushing of alternative political groups, and the purging of rivals within the Nazi Party itself. On February 27, 1933, a mentally ill Dutch Communist set fire to the Reichstag building in Berlin. The Nazis quickly turned the incident to their own advantage by claiming that the fire proved the existence of an immediate communist threat against the government. To the public, it seemed plausible that the Communists might attempt some action against the state now that the Nazis were in power. Under Article 48, Hitler made the Emergency Decree suspending civil liberties and proceeded to arrest Communists or alleged Communists. This decree was not revoked as long as Hitler ruled Germany.

In early March another Reichstag election took place. The Nazis still received only 43.9 percent of the vote. However, the arrest of the newly elected communist deputies and the political fear aroused by the fire meant that Hitler could control the Reichstag. On March 23, 1933, the Reichstag passed an Enabling Act that permitted Hitler to rule by decree. Thereafter, there were no legal limits on his exercise of power. The Weimar Constitution was never formally repealed or amended. It had simply been supplanted by the February Emergency Decree and the March Enabling Act.

Perhaps better than anyone else, Hitler understood that he and his party had not inevitably come to power. His potential opponents had stood divided between 1929 and 1933. He intended to prevent them from regrouping. In a series of complex moves, Hitler outlawed or undermined various German institutions that might have served as rallying points for opposition. In early May 1933 the offices, banks, and newspapers of the free trade unions were seized, and their leaders arrested. The Nazi Party itself, rather than any government agency, undertook this action. In late June and early July, the other German political

Hitler. Hitler's mastery of the techniques of mass politics and propaganda—including huge staged rallies like this one in 1938—was an important factor in his rise to power. *Bildarchiv Preussischer Kulturbesitz.*

parties were outlawed. By July 14, 1933, the National Socialists were the only legal party in Germany. During the same months the Nazis had taken control of the governments of the individual federal states in Germany. By the close of 1933 all major institutions of potential opposition had been eliminated.

The final element in Hitler's personal consolidation of power involved the Nazi Party itself. By late 1933 the SA, or storm troopers, consisted of approximately 1 million active members and a larger number of reserves. The commander of this party army was Ernst Roehm, a possible rival to Hitler himself. The German army officer corps, on whom Hitler depended to rebuild the national army, were jealous of the SA leadership. Consequently, to protect his own position and to shore up support with the regular army, on June 30, 1934, Hitler ordered the murder of key SA officers, including Roehm. Others killed between June 30 and July 2 included the former chancellor Kurt von Schleicher and his wife. The exact number of purged victims is unknown, but it has been estimated to have exceeded 100. The German army, which was the only institution in the nation that might have prevented the murders, did nothing. A month later, on August 2, 1934, President Hindenburg died. Thereafter, the offices of chancellor and president were combined. Hitler was now the **Führer**, or sole ruler of Germany and of the Nazi Party.

The Police State

Terror and intimidation had helped propel the Nazis to office. As Hitler consolidated his power, he oversaw the organization of a police state. The chief vehicle of police surveillance was the **SS** (*Schutzstaffel*), or security units, commanded by Heinrich Himmler (1900–1945). This group had originated in the mid-1920s as a bodyguard for Hitler and had become a more elite paramilitary organization than the larger SA. In 1933 the SS had approximately 52,000 members. It was the instrument that carried out the blood purges of the party in 1934. By 1936 Himmler had become head of all police matters in Germany.

The police character of the Nazi regime was all-pervasive, but the people who most consistently experienced its terror were the German Jews. Anti-Semitism had been a key plank of the Nazi program—anti-Semitism based on biological racial theories stemming from late-nineteenth-century thought rather than from religious discrimination. Before World War II the Nazi attack on the Jews went through three stages of increasing intensity. In 1933, shortly after assuming power, the Nazis excluded Jews from the civil service. For a time they also attempted to enforce boycotts of Jewish shops and businesses. The boycotts won relatively little public support. In 1935 the Nuremberg Laws robbed German Jews of their citizenship. All

Anti-Jewish Policies. Soon after seizing power, the Nazi government began harassing German Jewish businesses. Non-Jewish German citizens were urged not to buy merchandise from shops owned by Jews. *Bildarchiv Preussischer Kulturbesitz.*

persons with at least one Jewish grandparent were defined as Jews. The professions and the major occupations were closed to Jews. Marriage and sexual intercourse between Jews and non-Jews were prohibited. Legal exclusion and humiliation of the Jews became the order of the day. (See Document, "The Nazis Pass Their Racial Legislation.")

The persecution of the Jews increased again in 1938. Business careers were forbidden. In November 1938, under orders from the Nazi Party, thousands of Jewish stores and synagogues were burned or otherwise destroyed. The Jewish community itself had to pay for the damage that occurred on this **Kristallnacht** because the government confiscated the insurance money. In all manner of other ways, large and petty, the German Jews were harassed. This persecution allowed the Nazis to inculcate the rest of the population with the concept of a master race of pure German "Aryans" and also to display their own contempt for civil liberties.

After the war broke out, Hitler decided in 1942 to destroy the Jews in Europe. It is thought that over 6 million

Jews, mostly from Eastern European nations, died as a result of that staggering decision, unprecedented in its scope and implementation.

Women in Nazi Germany

The Nazis believed in separate social spheres for men and women. Men belonged in the world of action, women in the home. The two spheres should not mix. Women who sought to liberate themselves and to adopt roles traditionally followed by men in public life were considered symptoms of cultural decline. Respect for women should arise from their function as wives and mothers.

These attitudes stood in direct conflict with many of the social changes that German women, like women elsewhere in Europe, had experienced during the first three decades of the twentieth century. German women had become much more active and assertive. More of them worked in factories or were independently employed, and they had begun to enter the professions. Under the Weimar constitution, they voted. Throughout the Weimar period there was also a lively discussion of women's emancipation. For the Nazis these developments were signs of cultural weakness. They generally urged a much more traditional role for women in their new society. Nazi writers portrayed women as wives and mothers first and foremost.

The Nazis' point of view was supported by women of a generally conservative outlook and women who were following traditional roles as housewives, confirming the choices these women had made about how to lead their lives. In a period of high unemployment, the Nazi attitude also appealed to many men because it discouraged women from competing with them in the work place. Such competition had begun during World War I, and many Nazis considered it symptomatic of the social confusion that had followed the German defeat.

The Nazi discussion of the role of women was also deeply rooted in Nazi racism. Nazi writers argued that the superiority of the pure German race depended on the purity of the blood of each and every individual. It was the special task of German mothers to preserve racial purity. Hitler particularly championed this view of women. They were to breed strong sons and daughters for the German nation. Nazi journalists often compared the role of women in childbirth to that of men in battle. Each served the state in particular social and gender roles. In both cases, the good of the nation was superior to that of the individual.

Most Nazis who discussed the role of women relegated them to the home. They also generally attacked feminist outlooks. Women were encouraged to bear many children, because the Nazis believed the declining German birth rate

The Nazis Pass Their Racial Legislation

Anti-Semitism was a fundamental tenet of the Nazi Party and became a major policy of the Nazi government. This comprehensive legislation of September 15, 1935, carried anti-Semitism into all areas of public life and into some of the most personal areas of private life as well. It was characteristically entitled the Law for the Protection of German Blood and Honor. Hardly any aspect of Nazi thought and action shocked the non-German world as much as this policy towards the Jews.

◆ How would this legislation have affected the normal daily interaction between Jews and non-Jews in Germany? Why are there specific prohibitions against mixed marriages and sexual relations between Jews and non-Jews? How does this legislation separate German Jews from the symbols of German national life?

Imbued with the knowledge that the purity of German blood is the necessary prerequisite for the existence of the German nation, and inspired by an inflexible will to maintain the existence of the German nation for all future times, the Reichstag has unanimously adopted the following law, which is now enacted:

Article I: (1) Any marriages between Jews and citizens of German or kindred blood are herewith forbidden. Marriages entered into despite this law are invalid, even if they are arranged abroad as a means of circumventing this law.

(2) Annulment proceedings for marriages may be initiated only by the Public Prosecutor.

Article II: Extramarital relations between Jews and citizens of German or kindred blood are herewith forbidden.

Article III: Jews are forbidden to employ as servants to their households female subjects of German or kindred blood who are under the age of forty-five years.

Article IV: (1) Jews are prohibited from displaying the Reich and national flag and from showing the national colors.

(2) However, they may display the Jewish colors. The exercise of this right is under state protection.

Article V: (1) Anyone who acts contrary to the prohibition noted in Article I renders himself liable to penal servitude.

(2) The man who acts contrary to the prohibition of Article II will be punished by sentence to either a jail or penitentiary.

(3) Anyone who acts contrary to the provisions of Articles III or IV will be punished with a jail sentence up to a year and with a fine, or with one of these penalties.

Article VI: The Reich Minister of Interior, in conjunction with the Deputy to the Führer and the Reich Minister of Justice, will issue the required legal and administrative decrees for the implementation and amplification of this law.

Article VII: This law shall go into effect on the day following its promulgation, with the exception of Article III, which shall go into effect on January 1, 1936.

From *Documents of German History*, Louis L. Snyder, ed. and trans. Copyright © 1958 Rutgers the State University, pp. 427–428. Reprinted by permission of Rutgers University Press.

was the result of emancipated women who had spurned their natural and proper roles as mothers. The Nazis established special medals for women who bore large families. They also sponsored schools that taught women how to care for and rear children (see photograph on page 953).

The Nazis also saw women as educators of the young and thus the special protectors of German cultural values. Through cooking, dress, music, and stories, mothers were to instill a love for the nation. As consumers for the home, women were to aid German-owned shops, to buy German-produced goods, and to avoid Jewish merchants.

The Nazis realized that in the midst of the Depression many women would need to work, but the party urged them to pursue employment that the Nazis considered natural to their character. These tasks included agriculture, teaching, nursing, social work, and domestic service. Nonetheless, despite some variation in the early and mid-1930s, the percentage of women employed in Germany changed little from the Weimar to the Hitler years: It was 37 percent in 1928 and the same again in 1939. Thereafter, because of the war effort, many more women were recruited into the German work force.

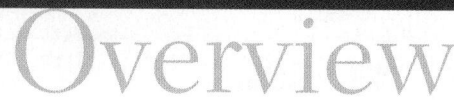

Characteristics Shared by Fascist, Nazi, and Soviet Communist Regimes of the 1920s and 1930s

1. Well-organized, highly disciplined political parties

2. Intense nationalism

3. Programs that promised to cure social, political, and economic malaise

4. A monopoly over mass communications and propaganda

5. Highly effective instruments of terror and police power

6. Real or imagined national, class, or racial enemies who could be demonized to whip up mass support

7. Command over modern technology and its capacity for immense destruction

The Great Depression and the New Deal in the United States

The United States emerged from the First World War as a major world power. However, it retreated from that role when the Senate refused to ratify the Versailles Treaty and subsequently failed to join the League of Nations. In 1920 Warren Harding (1865–1923) became president and urged a return to what he termed "normalcy," which meant minimal involvement abroad and conservative economic policies at home. Business interests clearly remained in the ascendent, with the federal government taking a relatively inactive role in national economic life. Indeed, government inactivity was the virtual creed of Harding's successor, President Calvin Coolidge (1872–1933).

The first seven or eight years of the decade witnessed remarkable American prosperity. New electrical appliances such as the radio, phonograph, washing machine, and vacuum cleaner appeared on the market. Large-scale advertising campaigns attempted to persuade consumers to purchase such items. Real wages rose for many groups of workers. Industry grew at a robust rate. Automobile manufacturers assumed a major role in national economic life. Henry Ford's (1863–1947) Model T exemplified the determination of the automobile industry to produce for a mass market. Increasing numbers of factories became mechanized. Engineers and efficiency experts were the heroes of the business world. For most of the 1920s the New York stock market boomed. All of this remarkable activity stood in marked contrast to the various economic dislocations occurring in Europe.

The material prosperity appeared, however, in a sharply divided society. Segregation remained a basic fact of life for black Americans throughout the South and to a lesser degree in other areas of the country. The Ku Klux Klan, which sought 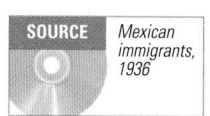 to terrorize blacks, Roman Catholics, and Jews, enjoyed a resurgence. The Prohibition Amendment of 1919 (repealed in 1933) forbade the manufacture and transport of alcoholic beverages. In the wake of this divisive national policy, major criminal operations arose to supply liquor and to disrupt the stability of civic life. Many immigrants came from Mexico and Puerto Rico. They settled in cities where their labor was desired, but where they were often not welcomed or assimilated. Finally, the wealth of the nation was overwhelmingly concentrated in relatively few hands.

SOURCE   *Mexican immigrants, 1936*

Economic Collapse

In March 1929 Herbert Hoover became president, the third Republican in as many elections. On October 29, 1929, the New York stock market crashed. The other financial markets also went into a tailspin. During the next year the stock market continued to fall. The banks that had loaned people money with which to speculate in the market suffered great losses.

The financial collapse of 1929 triggered the Great Depression in America, although there were other underlying domestic causes. During the 1920s manufacturing firms had not made sufficient capital investment. The disproportionate amount of profits going to about 5 percent of the U.S. population had by the end of the decade begun to undermine the purchasing power of other consumers. Furthermore, agriculture had been in trouble for years. Finally, the economic difficulties in Europe and

Women members of the Ku Klux Klan in New Castle, Indiana, August 1, 1923. The revived Klan was a powerful presence in scores of American communities during the early 1920s, especially among native-born white Protestants, who feared cultural and political change. In addition to preaching "100 percent Americanism," local Klan chapters also served a social function for members and their families. *Ball State University Libraries, Archives & Special Collections, W. A. Swift Photo Collection.*

Unemployed Workers. The Great Depression brought unprecedented unemployment to the United States. In 1930 unemployed workers were photographed standing outside the Municipal Lodging House in New York City. *Corbis-Bettmann.*

Latin America, which predated those in the United States, meant foreigners were less able to purchase products produced in the United States.

The most pervasive problem of the Great Depression was the spread of unemployment. Joblessness hit poor unskilled workers most rapidly but then worked its way up the job ladder to touch factory and white-collar workers. As unemployment spread, small retail businesses suffered. In the major American manufacturing cities, hundreds of thousands of workers could not find jobs. The price of corn fell so low in some areas that it was not profitable to harvest the crop. By the early 1930s banks across the country began to fail, and people lost their savings.

The federal government was not really equipped to address the emergency. There was no tradition of federal action to alleviate economic distress. President Hoover organized economic conferences in Washington and encouraged the Federal Reserve to make borrowing easier. He supported the ill-advised Hawley-Smoot Tariff Act of 1930, with which Congress had hoped to protect American industry by a high tariff barrier. But fundamentally Hoover believed relief was a matter for local government and voluntary organizations. In many areas the local relief agencies had actually run out of money by 1931.

New Role for Government

The election of 1932 was one of the most crucial in American history. Franklin Delano Roosevelt (1882–1945), in accepting the Democratic nomination, pledged his party to a "new deal for the American people." He overwhelmingly defeated Hoover, and quickly set about redirecting federal policy towards the Depression.

Roosevelt had been born into a moderately wealthy New York family. A distant cousin of Theodore Roosevelt (1858–1919), he had been educated at Harvard College and Columbia Law School. After serving in World War I as assistant secretary of the navy, in 1920 he ran as the Democratic vice presidential candidate. The next year, however, he was struck with polio and his legs became paralyzed. With extraordinary determination he went on to be elected governor of New York in 1928. As the newly elected president he attempted to convey to the nation the same kind of optimistic spirit that had informed his own personal struggle of the 1920s.

Roosevelt's first goal was to give the nation a sense that the federal government was acting to meet the economic challenge. The first 100 days of his administration became legendary. Coming into office at the height of the crisis in the banking system, he immediately closed all the banks and permitted only sound institutions to reopen. Congress convened in a special session and rapidly passed a new banking act. Shortly thereafter, Congress enacted the Agricultural Adjustment Act and the Farm Credit Act to aid the farm sector of the economy. To provide jobs, Roosevelt's administration sponsored the Civilian Conservation Corps. The Federal Emergency Relief Act provided funding for state and local relief agencies. To restore confidence, Roosevelt began making speeches, known as his "fireside chats," to the American people.

Roosevelt's most ambitious program was the National Industrial Recovery Act (NIRA), which established the National Recovery Administration (NRA). This agency attempted to foster codes written by various industries to regulate wages and prices. It was hoped that competition might be thus regulated to protect jobs and assure production.

The NIRA and other New Deal legislation, such as the Wagner Act of 1935, which established the National Labor Relations Board and the Fair Labor Standards Act of 1938, provided a larger role in the American economy for organized labor. It became easier for unions to organize. Union membership grew rapidly and steadily. American unionism took on a new character during these years. Previously, most unions had organized by craft and had been affiliated with the American Federation of Labor.

The major union gains of the 1930s, however, occurred through the organization of whole industries composed of workers in various crafts in a single union. The most important of these organizations were the United Mine Workers and United Automobile Workers. These new unions organized themselves into the Congress of Industrial Organizations. The CIO and the AFL were rivals until they merged in the 1950s. These new strong industrial labor organizations introduced a powerful new force into the American economic scene.

In 1935 the U.S. Supreme Court declared the NRA unconstitutional. Thereafter, Roosevelt deemphasized centralized economic planning. There were no fewer federal agencies—indeed, their number increased—but they operated in general independence from each other.

Through New Deal legislation, the federal government was far more active in the economy than it had been in the past. The government itself attempted to provide relief for the unemployed in the industrial sector. The major institution of the relief effort was the **Works Progress Administration**. Created in 1935, the WPA began a massive program of large public works.

The programs of the New Deal years also involved the federal government directly in economic development rather than turning such development over to private enterprise. Through the Tennessee Valley Authority (TVA), the government became directly involved in the economy of the four states of the Tennessee river valley. The TVA built dams and then produced and sold hydroelectricity. Never had the government undertaken so

The Works Progress Administration was one of the chief New Deal agencies designed to create public works projects that would generate employment, such as this group of men repairing a street. *Corbis/Bettmann.*

extensive an economic role. Another major new function for the government was providing security for the elderly, through the establishment of the Social Security Administration in 1935.

Hence, in one area of American life after another, it was decided that individual voluntary effort could not provide sufficient personal economic security and that the government must act to do so. These actions established a mixed economy in the United States—that is, one in which the federal government would play an ongoing active role alongside the private sector.

The New Deal changed much of American life. Yet despite its programs and new initiatives, it did not solve the unemployment problem. Indeed, in the late 1930s the economy began to falter again. It was the entry of the nation into World War II that brought the U.S. economy to full employment.

However, the New Deal did preserve American democracy and capitalism. The experience of the United States under the New Deal stood in marked contrast to the economic and political experiments taking place in Europe. Many businesspeople found Roosevelt far too liberal and his policies too activist. Nonetheless, the New Deal fundamentally preserved capitalism in a democratic setting, where, in contrast to Europe, there was a broad spectrum of political debate—much of it highly critical of the administration. The United States had demonstrated that a nation with a vast industrial economy could confront its gravest economic crisis and still preserve democracy.

Summary

Postwar Problems. The Versailles settlement bred political discontent and resentment throughout Europe among both victors and the defeated. In the 1920s there were endless wrangles over reparations between Germany and the Allied powers. After World War I, Europe never recovered its prewar prosperity or stability. The onset of the Great Depression in 1929 caused severe problems in both Europe and the United States and led to the Nazi seizure of power in Germany and FDR's New Deal in the United States.

The Soviet Union. The Bolsheviks had expected communist revolutions to break out across Europe. When that did not happen, they were forced to consolidate their regime within Russia. Lenin's New Economic Policy gave the state control over heavy industry, transportation, and international commerce but allowed for small-scale private enterprise and peasant farms. Stalin abandoned this policy to push for rapid industrialization. He abolished private enterprise, collectivized agriculture, and eliminated his opponents in a series of purges in which millions were imprisoned or killed. Despite the violence and oppression, Marxist parties around the world were subservient to the Soviet Union as the world's only communist state and the enemy of fascism.

Fascist Italy. Benito Mussolini came to power in Italy in 1922. Many Italians were dissatisfied with the terms of the Versailles Treaty and frightened by the social unrest that followed World War I. Mussolini promised order and a strong state. Although he achieved power by legal means, he soon transformed Italy into a single-party dictatorship. In 1929 he came to terms with the Catholic Church by negotiating the Lateran Accord, which recognized the pope as the independent ruler of Vatican City.

Nazi Germany. The postwar Weimar Republic in Germany was buffeted by social, political, and financial instability. Many Germans refused to accept Germany's defeat in World War I or the terms of the Versailles Treaty. Rampant inflation destroyed the savings of the middle class. The Great Depression brought financial collapse and massive unemployment. Many Germans looked to Adolf Hitler and the Nazi Party for solutions. Once Hitler came to power in 1933, he quickly established a one-party dictatorship based on police terror, propaganda, racial anti-Semitism, and the cult of Hitler as supreme leader. The Jews, in particular, were persecuted. Hitler also formed an alliance with the German army and began a program of rapid rearmament.

The United States. The United States emerged from World War I as a world power but retreated into isolation during the 1920s. The prosperity of the 1920s ended in the Great Depression. Franklin Delano Roosevelt's New Deal greatly expanded the power of the federal government in social and economic affairs and preserved capitalism in a democratic setting.

Review Questions

1. Explain the causes of the Great Depression. Why was it more severe, and why did it last longer than previous economic downturns? Could it have been avoided?

2. How did Stalin achieve supreme power in the Soviet Union? Why did he decide that Russia had to industrialize rapidly? Why did this require the collectivization of agriculture? Was the policy a success? How did it affect the Russian people? What were the causes of the great purges?

3. Why was Italy dissatisfied and unstable after World War I? How did Mussolini achieve power? What were the characteristics of the fascist state?

4. Why did the Weimar Republic collapse in Germany? Discuss Hitler's rise to power. Which groups in Germany supported Hitler, and why were they pro-Nazi? How did he consolidate his power?

5. Compare the authoritarian regimes in the Soviet Union, Italy, and Germany. What characteristics did they have in common? What role did terror play in each?

6. Why did the United States economy collapse in 1929? What policies did Roosevelt use to combat the Depression? How did his policies affect the role of the federal government in national life?

INTERPRETING THE PAST

Fascism, Collective Action, and Women's Rights

Sources from MyHistoryLab/ PrimarySource DVD

1. Benito Mussolini, *The Political and Social Doctrine of Fascism*
2. John Maynard Keynes, *The End of Laissez-Faire*

Source from Chapter 30

3. *A Communist Woman Demands a New Family Life* (page 959)

The authoritarian ideologies that developed in the 1920s and 1930s did so as a result of the failure of traditional governing philosophies and institutions to cope with financial collapse, agricultural crisis, and political uncertainties in Europe after World War I.

Fascism and one of its variants, Nazism, were each associated with fervent and aggressive nationalism, combined with a contempt for liberal principles of individual liberty and the democratic political system. Communism, an ideology that first developed in the nineteenth century, was refined by Russian Bolsheviks in the early twentieth century and also disdained individual freedoms and democratic principles.

In this exercise you will read three primary sources from the early twentieth century that focus on fascism, the role of the government in the economy, and women's rights. You will then answer the following questions in the process of completing the assignment below.

The first document is written by Benito Mussolini, the leader of the Italian state from 1922 to 1943, and fascism's most articulate spokesman. In this explanation of the movement, he outlines the roles of an all-powerful state and the individual citizen in the modern era. The second document, from 1926, is by British economist John Maynard Keynes, who advocated government of the economy to protect individuals from capitalisms down cycle. The third document

Key Terms

collectivization (p. 961)

Duce (p. 964)

fascism (p. 964)

Führer (p. 973)

Great Depression (p. 954)

Great Purges (p. 962)

Kristallnacht (p. 974)

Mein Kampf (p. 968)

Nazis (p. 967)

New Economic Policy (NEP) (p. 960)

Popular Front (p. 957)

Reichstag (p. 966)

SA (p. 968)

SS (p. 973)

War Communism (p. 958)

Weimar Republic (p. 955)

Works Progress Administration (p. 978)

Note: To learn more about the topics in this chapter, please turn to the Suggested Readings at the end of the book. For additional sources related to this chapter please see the Primary Source DVD at the back of this text or MyHistoryLab.

details how the Communist party (and the state) could assist in restructuring family life, and the role of women in pursuit of a shared common goal.

Questions

How does Mussolini justify the lack of individual freedom under a fascist state? What are the primary doctrines of fascism? How does he explain the development of the fascist ideology?

What does Keynes mean when he advocates "collective action" to improve the "technique of modern capitalism"? How does Keynes' views on the role of government contrast with Mussolini's?

The Kollontai document focuses on women and their role in society. What changes in their traditional role does she envision as desirable?

World War II

THE MORE IDEALISTIC SURVIVORS OF THE FIRST World War, especially in the United States and Great Britain, thought of it as "the war to end all wars" and "a war to make the world safe for democracy." Only thus could they justify the awful slaughter, expense, and upheaval. How appalled they would have been had they known that only twenty years after the peace treaties a second great war would break out that would be more truly global than the first. In this war the democracies would be fighting for their lives against militaristic, nationalistic, authoritarian, and totalitarian states in Europe and Asia. Great Britain and the United States would be allied with the communist Soviet Union. The defeat of the militarists and dictators would not bring the longed-for peace, but rather a Cold War in which the European states became second-class powers, subordinate to the two new great powers, partially or fully non-European: the Soviet Union and the United States. ■

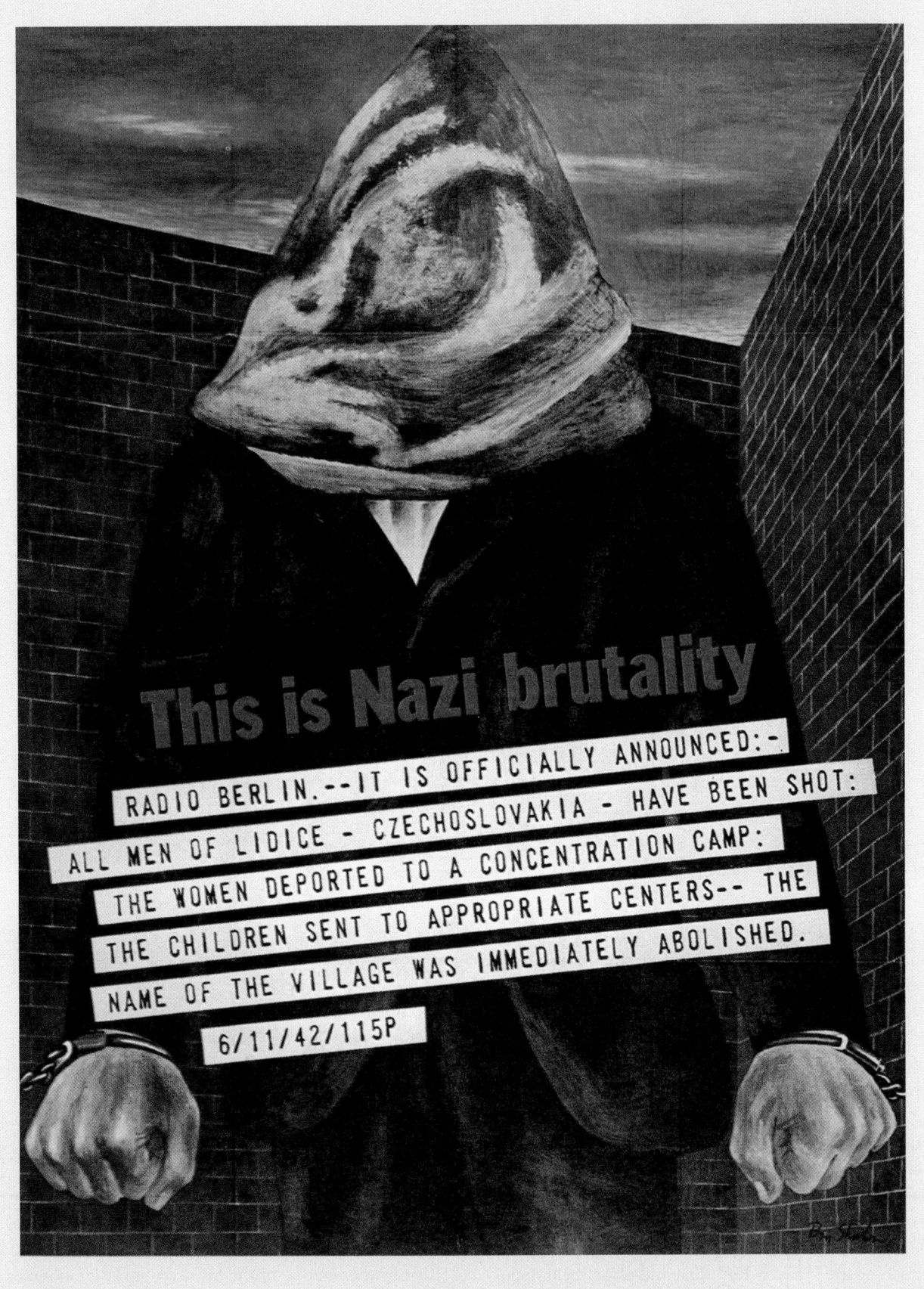

Nazi Terror. In this vivid poster, the artist Ben Shahn (1898–1969) memorialized the destruction of Lidice. The Czechoslovakian town was obliterated by the Nazis on June 11, 1942, in vengeance for the resistance by Czechs against their Nazi rulers. *The Granger Collection, N.Y.*

World War II

World War II

The second great war of the twentieth century (1939–1945) grew out of the unsatisfactory resolution of the first. In retrospect, the two wars appear to some people to be one continuous conflict—a kind of twentieth-century Thirty Years' War—with the two main periods of fighting separated by an uneasy truce. To others, that point of view distorts the situation by implying that the second war was the inevitable result of the first and its inadequate peace treaties.

The latter opinion seems more sound. Whatever the flaws of the treaties of Paris, the world suffered an even more terrible war than the first as a result of failures of judgment and will on the part of the victorious democratic powers. The United States, which had become the wealthiest and potentially the strongest nation in the world, disarmed almost entirely and withdrew into a shortsighted and foolish isolation; it could play no important part in restraining the angry and ambitious dictators who brought on the war.

Britain and France refused to face the reality of the threat the Axis powers posed until the most deadly war in history was required to put it down. If the victorious democracies had remained strong, responsible, and realistic, they could have remedied whatever injustices or mistakes arose from the treaties without endangering the peace.

Equally important, however, was the unwillingness of the victorious powers to adjust the peace treaties from World War I, especially to lessen the burden on the devastated German economy, even in the face of the obvious inability of Germany to pay the enormous war reparations the victors demanded. Here too, the isolationism of the United States played a pivotal role, as the government insisted that its allies in World War I, France and Britain, whose economies were also struggling after the war, repay their debts to the United States. France and Britain, in turn, sought to fund their war debts using reparations extracted primarily from Germany, whose economy was also burdened by the occupation of the Ruhr Valley and the ensuing loss of some of its best industrial infrastructure and resources. A vicious cycle ensued,

Again the Road to War (1933–1939)

World War I and the Versailles Treaty had only a marginal relationship to the world depression of the 1930s. But in Germany, where the reparations settlement had contributed to the vast inflation of 1923, economic and social discontent focused on the Versailles settlement as the cause of all ills. Throughout the late 1920s Adolf Hitler and the Nazi Party had never ceased denouncing Versailles as the source of all Germany's trouble; the economic woes of the early 1930s seemed to bear them out.

Nationalism and attention to the social question, along with party discipline, had been the sources of Nazi success. They continued to influence Hitler's foreign policy after he became chancellor in early 1933. Moreover, the Nazi destruction of the Weimar Republic and of political opposition meant that German foreign policy lay in Hitler's own

hands. Consequently, it is important to know his goals and the plans he had for achieving them. (See Document, "Hitler Describes His Goals.")

Hitler's Goals

From first to last, Hitler's racial theories and goals held the central place in his thought. He meant to go far beyond Germany's 1914 boundaries, which were the limit of the vision of his predecessors. He intended to bring the entire German people (*Volk*), understood as a racial group, together into a single nation. The new Germany would include all the Germanic parts of the old Habsburg Empire, including Austria. This virile and growing nation would need more space to live (**Lebensraum**), which would be taken from the Slavs, a lesser race, fit only for servitude. The new Germany would be purified by the removal of the Jews, the most inferior race in Nazi theory. The plan always required the conquest of Poland and which the advent of the Great Depression only exacerbated. The inability of the democratic German government of the Weimar Republic to negotiate a better deal from the inflexible victors of World War I added to the perception of ordinary Germans that it was weak and inept and thus contributed to its downfall. One of the legacies of World War II was a realization on the part of the Western World of the dangers excessively high foreign debts can pose to the world order, as poor countries, unable to repay or renegotiate their debt structures, can be tempted to secede from international institutions and invade their neighbors in an effort to salvage their economies and shore up their governments.

The second war itself was plainly a global war. The Japanese occupation of Manchuria in 1931, while not technically a part of that war, was a significant precursor. Italy attacked Ethiopia in 1935. Italy, Germany, and the Soviet Union intervened in the Spanish Civil War (1936–1939). Japan attacked China in 1937. European colonies or former colonies, such as Australia and other South Pacific islands, the Philippines, and regions of the Middle East and North Africa became theaters of war or, like India, were drawn into the conflict by helping to supply the combatants. Men and women from all the inhabited continents thus took part. The use of atomic weapons

brought the frightful struggle to a close, but what are called conventional weapons did almost all the damage while state-sponsored genocide, such as the Holocaust, killed millions of civilians. The world reached a level of destructiveness that threatened the very survival of civilization, even without the use of atomic or nuclear devices.

The aftermath of World War II, and the analysis on the part of the victors of the causes of the conflict, led to the creation of the United Nations, an international organization designed to forestall future conflict through improved international diplomacy. Imperfect as the United Nations is, most scholars agree that it has helped preserve world peace.

Focus Questions

◆ What was the relationship between World War I and World War II? Why was the isolationism of the United States after World War I such an important factor in the advent of World War II?

◆ Why was World War II truly a global war?

◆ What lessons did the world learn from the experiences of World War I and World War II?

the Ukraine as the primary areas for the settlement of Germans and for the provision of badly needed food. However, neither *Mein Kampf* nor later statements of policy were blueprints for action. Hitler was a brilliant improviser who exploited opportunities as they arose. But he never lost sight of his goal, which would almost certainly require a major war.

Destruction of Versailles

When Hitler came to power, Germany was too weak to permit the direct approach to his goals. The first problem was to shake off the fetters of Versailles and to make Germany a formidable military power. In October of 1933 Germany withdrew from an international disarmament conference and also from the League of Nations. These acts alarmed the French but were merely symbolic. In January of 1934 Germany made a nonaggression pact with Poland that was of greater concern, for it put into question France's chief means of containing the

Germans. At last, in March 1935 Hitler formally renounced the disarmament provisions of the Versailles Treaty with the formation of a German air force, and soon he reinstated conscription, which aimed at an army of half a million men.

His path was made easier because the League of Nations was ineffective at keeping the peace. In September 1931 Japan occupied Manchuria, provoking an appeal to the League of Nations by China. The league responded by sending out a commission under the Earl of Lytton (1876–1951). The Lytton Report condemned the Japanese for resorting to force, but the powers were unwilling to impose sanctions. Japan withdrew from the league and kept control of Manchuria.

The league formally condemned Hitler's decision to rearm Germany, but it took no steps to prevent it. France and Britain felt unable to object because they had not carried out their own promises to disarm. Instead, they met with Mussolini (1883–1945) in June 1935 to form the so-called Stresa Front and agreed to maintain the status quo in Europe

Hitler Describes His Goals

From his early career, Hitler had certain long-term general views and goals. They were set forth in his *Mein Kampf*, which appeared in 1925, and included consolidation of the German *Volk* ("People"), provision of more land for the Germans, and contempt for such "races" as Slavs and Jews. Here are some of Hitler's views.

◆ What is the basic principle on which Hitler's policy is founded? How does he justify his plans for expansion? What reasons does he give for hostility to France and Russia? What is the basis for Hitler's claim of a right of every man to own farmland? Was that a practical goal for Germany in the 1930s? Was there any way for Hitler to achieve his goals without a major war?

The National Socialist movement must strive to eliminate the disproportion between our population and our area—viewing this latter as a source of food as well as a basis for power politics—between our historical past and the hopelessness of our present impotence. . . .

The demand for restoration of the frontiers of 1914 is a political absurdity of such proportions and consequences as to make it seem a crime. Quite aside from the fact that the Reich's frontiers in 1914 were anything but logical. For in reality they were neither complete in the sense of embracing the people of German nationality, nor sensible with regard to geomilitary expediency. . . .

As opposed to this, we National Socialists must hold unflinchingly to our aim in foreign policy, namely, to secure for the German people the land and soil to which they are entitled on this earth. . . .

. . . The soil on which some day German generations of peasants can beget powerful sons will sanction the investment of the sons of today, and will some day acquit the responsible statesmen of blood-guilt and sacrifice of the people, even if they are persecuted by their contemporaries. . . .

Much as all of us today recognize the necessity of a reckoning with France, it would remain ineffectual in the long run if it represented the whole of our aim in foreign policy. It can and will achieve meaning only if it offers the rear cover for an enlargement of our people's living space in Europe. . . .

If we speak of soil in Europe today, we can primarily have in mind only Russia and her vassal border states. . . .

. . . See to it that the strength of our nation is founded, not on colonies, but on the soil of our European homeland. Never regard the Reich as secure unless for centuries to come it can give every scion of our people his own parcel of soil. Never forget that the most sacred right on this earth is a man's right to have earth to till with his own hands, and the most sacred sacrifice the blood that a man sheds for this earth.

by force if necessary. But Britain was desperate to maintain superiority at sea. Contrary to the Stresa accords and at the expense of French security needs, Britain soon made a separate naval agreement with Hitler, allowing him to rebuild the German fleet to 35 percent of the British navy.

Italy Attacks Ethiopia

The Italian attack on Ethiopia underscored the impotence of the League of Nations and the timidity of the Allies. Using a border incident as an excuse, Mussolini attacked Ethiopia in October 1935. His real intent was to avenge a humiliating defeat that the Italians had suffered in 1896, to begin the restoration of Roman imperial glory, and perhaps

to divest Italians from the corruption of the Fascist regime and Italy's economic troubles.

The League of Nations condemned Italian aggression and voted economic sanctions. It imposed an arms embargo that limited loans and credits to and imports from Italy. But Britain and France were afraid of alienating Mussolini, so they refused to place an embargo on oil, the one economic sanction that could have prevented Italian victory. Even more important, the British did not prevent the movement of Italian troops and munitions through the Suez Canal. This wavering policy was disastrous. The League of Nations and collective security were totally discredited, and Mussolini turned to Germany. By November 1, 1936, he could speak publicly of a Rome-Berlin "Axis."

Remilitarization of the Rhineland

The Ethiopian affair also influenced Hitler's evaluation of the strength and determination of the Western powers. On March 7, 1936, he took his greatest risk yet, sending a small armed force into the demilitarized Rhineland. This was a breach not only of the Versailles Treaty but also of the Locarno Agreements of 1925, agreements that Germany had voluntarily made. It also removed one of the most important elements of French security. France and Britain had every right to resist. The French especially had a claim to retain the only element of security left after the failure of the Allies to guarantee France's defense. Yet Britain and France made only a feeble protest with the League of Nations. British opinion would not support France. The French themselves were paralyzed by internal division and by military planning that was exclusively defensive. Both countries were further weakened by a growing pacifism.

A Germany that was rapidly rearming and had a defensible western frontier presented a completely new problem to the Western powers. Their response was the policy of **appeasement**. It was based on the assumption that Germany had real grievances, that Hitler's goals were limited and ultimately acceptable, and that the correct policy was to negotiate and make concessions before a crisis could lead to war. Behind this approach was the general horror of another war. Memories of the last war were still fresh, and the prospect of aerial bombardment was terrifying. A firmer policy, moreover, would have required rapid rearmament. But British leaders especially were reluctant to pursue this path because of the expense and widespread belief that the arms race had been a major cause of the last war. As Germany armed, the French huddled behind their defensive wall, the Maginot Line, and the British hoped for the best.

The Spanish Civil War

The new European alignment that found the Western democracies on one side and the Fascist states on the other was made clearer by the Spanish Civil War, which broke out in July 1936. In 1931 the Spaniards had established a democratic republic. Elections in February 1936 brought to power a government ranging from Republicans of the left to Communists and anarchists. The defeated groups, especially the Falangists, the Spanish version of Fascists, would not accept defeat at the polls. In July, General Francisco Franco (1892–1975) led an army from Spanish Morocco against the republic (see Map 31–1).

Thus began a civil war that lasted almost three years, killed hundreds of thousands, and provided a training ground for World War II. Germany and Italy aided Franco with troops and supplies. The Soviet Union sent equipment and advisers to the Republicans. Liberals and leftists from Europe and America volunteered to fight in the Republican ranks against fascism.

Pablo Picasso, *Guernica*, 1937. The Spanish Civil War divided Europe, with Fascist Italy and Nazi Germany assisting Franco, and Soviet Russia aiding the republic. Before its end in 1939, the war in Spain took some 500,000 lives. On April 26, 1937, planes from the German Condor Legion bombed the Basque town of Guernica, killing some 1,000 men, women, and children and destroying about 70 percent of the buildings. It was the most effective aerial bombardment of a city up to that time, and its purpose was simply to create terror. *Museo Nacional Centro de Arte Reina Sofia/© 1998 Estate of Pablo Picasso/Artists Rights Society (ARS), New York. Oil on Canvas. 119599 × 2595 3/499.*

Map 31–1.   The Spanish Civil War, 1936–1939. The purple area on the map shows the large portion of Spain quickly overrun by Franco's insurgent armies during the first year of the war. In the following two years progress came more slowly for the Fascists as the war became a kind of international rehearsal for the coming World War II. Madrid's fall to Franco in the spring of 1939 had been preceded by that of Barcelona a few weeks earlier.

The civil war, fought on blatantly ideological lines, profoundly affected world politics. It brought Germany and Italy closer together, leading to the Rome-Berlin **Axis** Pact.

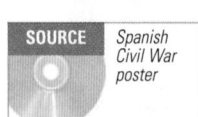

The Axis powers were joined in the same year by Japan in the Anti-Comintern Pact, ostensibly against communism but really a new and powerful diplomatic alliance. In Western Europe, the appeasement mentality reigned. Although international law permitted the sale of weapons and munitions to the legitimate Republican government, France and Britain forbade the export of war materials to either side. The United States passed new neutrality legislation to the same end. By early 1939 the Fascists had won effective control of Spain.

Austria and Czechoslovakia

Hitler made good use of his new friendship with Mussolini. In 1934 Mussolini, not yet allied with Hitler, had frustrated a Nazi coup in Austria by threatening military intervention. In 1938 the new diplomatic situation encouraged Hitler to try again. He seems to have hoped to achieve his goal by propaganda, bullying, and threats, but the Austrian Premier, Kurt von Schuschnigg (1897–1977), refused to collapse.

On March 9 the premier announced a plebiscite for March 13, in which the Austrian people could decide whether to unite with Germany for themselves. Hitler dared not let the plebiscite take place and invaded Austria on March 12. Mussolini made no objection, and Hitler marched into Vienna to the cheers of his Austrian sympathizers.

The **Anschluss**, or union of Germany and Austria, had great strategic significance, especially for Czechoslovakia, one of the bulwarks of French security. The Czechs were now surrounded by Germany on three sides.

The very existence of Czechoslovakia was an affront to Hitler. It was democratic and pro-Western; it had been created as a check on Germany and was allied to both France and the Soviet Union. It also contained about 3.5 million ethnic Germans who lived in the Sudetenland near the German border. These Germans had been the dominant class in the old Austro-Hungarian empire, and they resented their new minority position. Supported by Hitler, they agitated for privileges and autonomy within the Czech state. The Czechs made many concessions; Hitler's motivation, however, was not to improve the lot of the Sudeten Germans but to destroy Czechoslovakia.

The French, as usual, deferred to British leadership. The British prime minister was Neville Chamberlain (1869–1940), a man thoroughly committed to the policy of appeasement. He was determined not to allow Britain to go to war again. He pressured the Czechs to make further concessions to Germany, but no concession was enough.

On September 12, 1938, Hitler made a provocative speech that led to rioting in the Sudetenland and the declaration of martial law by the Czech government. German intervention seemed imminent. Chamberlain sought to appease Hitler at Czech expense and thus to avoid war. At Hitler's mountain retreat, Berchtesgaden, on September 15 Chamberlain accepted the separation of the Sudetenland from Czechoslovakia. Moreover, he and the French premier, Edouard Daladier (1884–1970), threatened to desert the Czechs if they did not agree. A week later Chamberlain flew again to Germany only to find that Hitler had raised his demands: He wanted cession of the Sudetenland in three days and its immediate occupation by the German army.

Munich

France and Britain prepared for war. At the last moment Mussolini proposed a conference of Germany, Italy, France, and Britain. It met on September 29 at Munich. Hitler received almost everything he had demanded. The Sudetenland, the key to Czech security, became part of Germany, thus depriving the Czechs of any chance of self-defense (see

Agreement at Munich. On September 29–30, 1938, Hitler met with the leaders of Britain and France at Munich to decide the fate of Czechoslovakia. The Allied leaders abandoned the small democratic nation in a vain attempt to appease Hitler and avoid war. Hitler sits in the center of the picture. To his right is British Prime Minister Neville Chamberlain. *Ullstein Bilderdienst.*

Map 31–2). In return, the rest of Czechoslovakia was spared. Hitler promised, "I have no more territorial demands to make in Europe." Chamberlain told a cheering crowd that he had brought "peace with honour. I believe it is peace for our time." (See Document, "Winston Churchill Warns of the Effects of the Munich Agreement.")

Even in the short run, the appeasement of Hitler at Munich was a failure. Soon Poland and Hungary also tore bits of territory from Czechoslovakia, and the Slovaks demanded autonomy. Finally, on March 15, 1939, Hitler broke his promise and occupied Prague, putting an end to Czech independence and to illusions that his only goal was to restore Germans to the Reich. Munich remains an example of short-sighted policy that helped bring on a war in disadvantageous circumstances as a result of the very fear of war and the failure to prepare for it.

Hitler's occupation of Prague discredited appeasement in the eyes of the British people. In the summer of 1939 a Gallup Poll showed that three-quarters of the British public believed it worth a war to stop Hitler. Although Chamberlain himself had not lost all faith in his policy, he felt the need to respond to public opinion, and he responded to excess.

It was apparent that Poland was the next target of German expansion. In the spring of 1939 the Germans put pressure on Poland to restore the formerly German city of Danzig and to allow a railroad and a highway through the Polish Corridor to connect East Prussia with the rest of Germany. When the Poles would not yield, the pressure mounted. On March 31 Chamberlain announced a

Winston Churchill Warns of the Effects of the Munich Agreement

Document

Churchill delivered a speech on the Munich Agreement before the House of Commons on October 5, 1938. Following are excerpts from it.

◆ What was decided at Munich? Why were the representatives of Czechoslovakia not at the meeting? Why did Chamberlain think the meeting was successful? Munich was the high point of the policy called "appeasement." How would its advocates defend this policy? Churchill was a leading opponent of appeasement. What are his objections to it?

The Chancellor of the Exchequer [Sir John Simon] said it was the first time Herr Hitler had been made to retract—I think that was the word—in any degree. We really must not waste time after all this long Debate upon the difference between the positions reached at Berchtesgaden, at Godesberg and at Munich. They can be very simply epitomized, if the House will permit me to vary the metaphor. One pound was demanded at the pistol's point. When it was given, £2 were demanded at the pistol's point. Finally, the dictator consented to take £17s. 6d. and the rest in promises of good will for the future. . . .

I do not grudge our loyal, brave people, who were ready to do their duty no matter what the cost, who never flinched under the strain of last week—I do not grudge them the natural, spontaneous outbursts of joy and relief when they learned that the hard ordeal would no longer be required of them at the moment; but they should know the truth. They should know that there has been gross neglect and deficiency in our defenses; they should know that we have sustained a defeat without a war, the consequences of which will travel far with us along our road; they should know that we have passed an awful milestone in our history, when the whole equilibrium of Europe has been deranged, and that the terrible words have for the time being been pronounced against the Western democracies: "Thou art weighed in the balance and found wanting." And do not suppose that this is the end. This is only the beginning of the reckoning. This is only the first sip, the first foretaste of a bitter cup which will be proffered to us year by year unless, by a supreme recovery of moral health and martial vigor, we arise again and take our stand for freedom as in the olden time.

Franco-British guarantee of Polish independence. Hitler did not take the guarantee seriously. He had come to hold the Western leaders in contempt. He knew that both countries were unprepared for war and that many of their populations were opposed to war for Poland.

Belief in the Polish guarantee was further undermined by the inability of France and Britain to get effective help to the Poles. The French, still dominated by the defensive mentality of the Maginot Line, had no intention of attacking Germany's western front. The only way to defend Poland was to bring Russia into the alliance against Hitler, but a Russian alliance posed many problems. Each side was profoundly suspicious of the other. The French and British were hostile to Russia's communist ideology, and since Stalin's purge of the officer corps of the Red Army, they questioned the military value of an alliance with Russia. Besides, the Russians could not help Poland without the right to cross Romania and enter Poland. Both nations, suspicious of Russian intentions—and with good reason—refused to grant these rights. As a result, Western negotiations with Russia were slow and cautious.

The Nazi-Soviet Pact

The Russians also had good reason to hesitate. They resented being left out of the Munich Agreement. They were annoyed by the low priority that the West seemed to give to negotiations with Russia, compared with the urgency with which they dealt with Hitler. They feared, rightly, that the Western powers meant them to bear the burden of the war against Germany. As a result, they opened negotiations with Hitler, and on August 23, 1939, the world was shocked to learn of a Nazi-Soviet non-aggression pact. Its secret provisions, which were easily guessed and soon carried out, divided Poland between the two powers and allowed Russia to annex the Baltic states and to take Bessarabia from Romania. The most bitter ideological enemies had become

Map Exploration

To explore this map further go to http://www.prenhall.com/craig_maps

Map 31–2. Partitions of Czechoslovakia and Poland, 1938–1939. The immediate background of World War II is found in the complex international drama unfolding on Germany's eastern frontier in 1938 and 1939. Germany's expansion inevitably meant the victimization of Austria, Czechoslovakia, and Poland. With the failure of the Western powers' appeasement policy and the signing of a German-Soviet pact, the stage for the war was set.

allies; communist parties in the West changed their line overnight from the ardent advocacy of resistance to Hitler to a policy of peace and quiet.

The Nazi-Soviet pact sealed the fate of Poland, and the Franco-British commitment guaranteed a general war. On September 1, 1939, the Germans invaded Poland. Two days later Britain and France declared war on Germany. World War II had begun.

World War II (1939–1945)

World War II was truly global. Fighting took place in Europe and Asia, the Atlantic and the Pacific Oceans, the Northern and Southern Hemispheres. The demand for the fullest exploitation of material and human resources for increased

production, the use of blockades, and the intensive bombing of civilian targets made the war of 1939 even more "total"— that is, comprehensive and intense—than that of 1914.

German Conquest of Europe

The speed of the German victory over Poland astonished everyone, not least the Russians, who hastened to collect their share of the booty before Hitler could deprive them of it. On September 17 they invaded Poland from the east, dividing the country with the Germans. They then absorbed Estonia, Latvia, and Lithuania into the Soviet Union. In November 1940 the Russians invaded Finland, but the Finns fought back fiercely. Although they were finally compelled to yield territory and bases to Russia, they retained their independence. Russian difficulties in Finland may well

Chronology

Events leading to World War II

1919 June	Versailles Treaty
1923 January	France occupies the Ruhr
1925 October	Locarno Agreements
1931 Spring	Onset of Great Depression in Europe
1933 January	Hitler comes to power
October	Germany withdraws from League of Nations
1935 March	Hitler renounces disarmament, starts an air force, and begins conscription
October	Mussolini attacks Ethiopia
1936 March	Germany reoccupies and remilitarizes the Rhineland
July	Outbreak of Spanish Civil War
October	Formation of the Rome-Berlin Axis
1938 March	Anschluss with Austria
September	Munich Conference and partition of Czechoslovakia
1939 March	Hitler occupies Prague; France and Great Britain guarantee Polish independence
August	Nazi-Soviet pact
September 1	Germany invades Poland
September 3	Britain and France declare war on Germany

have encouraged Hitler to invade the Soviet Union in June 1941, just twenty-two months after the 1939 treaty.

Meanwhile, the Western Front was quiet. The French remained behind the Maginot Line while Hitler and Stalin swallowed Poland and the Baltic states. Britain hastily rearmed and imposed the traditional naval blockade. Cynics in the West called it the phony war, or Sitzkrieg, but Hitler shattered the stillness in the spring of 1940. In April, without warning and with swift success, the Germans invaded Denmark and Norway. Hitler now had both air and naval bases closer to Britain. A month later a combined land and air attack struck Belgium, the Netherlands, and Luxembourg. German air power and armored divisions were irresistible. The Dutch surrendered in a few days, and the Belgians, although aided by the French and the British, surrendered less than two weeks later. The British and French armies in

Belgium were forced to flee to the English Channel to seek escape from the beaches of Dunkirk. By the heroic effort of hundreds of Britons manning small boats, over 200,000 British and 100,000 French soldiers were saved, but casualties were high and much valuable equipment was abandoned.

The Maginot Line ran from Switzerland to the Belgian frontier. Until 1936 the French had expected the Belgians to continue the fortifications along their German border. After Hitler remilitarized the Rhineland without opposition, the Belgians lost faith in their French alliance and returned to neutrality, leaving the Maginot Line exposed on its left flank. Hitler's swift advance through Belgium therefore circumvented France's main line of defense. The French army, poorly and hesitantly led by generals who lacked a proper understanding of how to use tanks and planes, collapsed. Mussolini, eager to claim the spoils of victory when it was clearly safe to do so, attacked France on June 10, though without success. Less than a week later the new French government, under the ancient hero of Verdun, Henri Philippe Pétain (1856–1951), asked for an armistice. In two months Hitler had accomplished what Germany had failed to achieve in four years of bitter fighting in the previous war.

The terms of the armistice, signed June 22, 1940, allowed the Germans to occupy more than half of France, including the Atlantic and English Channel coasts. To prevent the French from fleeing to North Africa to continue the fight, and even more to prevent them from turning their fleet over to Britain, Hitler left southern France unoccupied. Pétain set up a dictatorial regime at the resort city of Vichy and collaborated with the Germans to preserve as much autonomy as possible. Most of the French were too stunned to resist. Many thought that Hitler's victory was certain and saw no alternative to collaboration. A few, most notably General Charles de Gaulle (1890–1969), fled to Britain, where they organized the French National Committee of Liberation, or "Free French." The Vichy government controlled most of French North Africa and the navy. But the Free French began operating in central Africa and from London radioed messages of hope and defiance to France. As expectations of a quick German victory faded, a French Resistance movement arose.

Battle of Britain

Hitler expected the British to come to terms. He was prepared to allow Britain to retain its empire in return for a free hand for Germany in Europe. If there was any chance that the British would consider such terms, that chance disappeared when Winston Churchill (1874–1965) replaced Chamberlain as prime minister in May 1940.

One of Churchill's greatest achievements was establishing a close relationship with the American president Franklin D. Roosevelt (1882–1945), who found ways to help the British

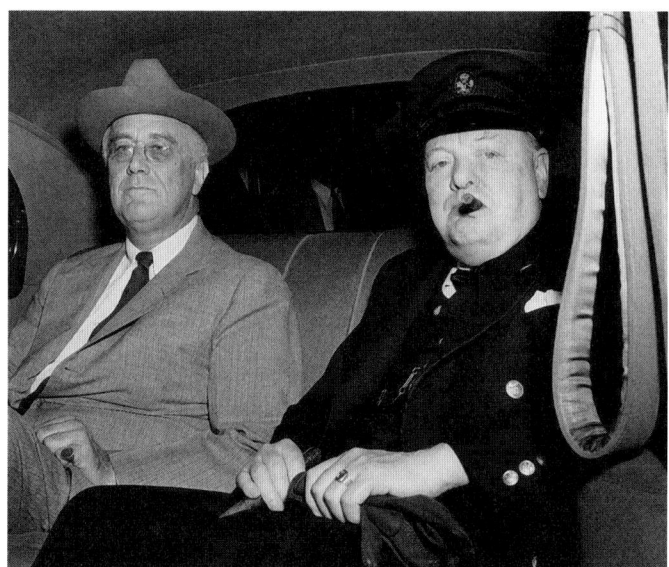

Churchill and Roosevelt. The close cooperation between Prime Minister Winston Churchill of Britain and President Franklin Roosevelt of the United States helped to assure the effective alliance of their two countries in World War II. *UPI/Corbis-Bettmann.*

Battle of Britain. A rubble-strewn street in London after the city had experienced a night of German bombing. Despite many casualties and widespread devastation, the German bombing of London did not break British morale or prevent the city from functioning. *The Granger Collection, N.Y.*

despite strong political opposition. In 1940 and 1941, before the United States was at war, America sent military supplies, traded destroyers for leases on British naval bases, and even convoyed ships across the Atlantic to help the British survive.

As Britain remained defiant, Hitler was forced to contemplate an invasion, which required control of the air. The first strikes by the German air force (**Luftwaffe**), directed against the airfields and fighter planes in southeastern England, began in August 1940. Had these attacks continued, Germany might soon have gained control of the air and, with it, the chance of a successful invasion. In early September, however, seeking revenge for British bombing raids on German cities, the *Luftwaffe* made London its major target. For two months, London was bombed every night. Much of the city was destroyed, and about 15,000 people were killed, but the theories of victory through air power alone proved vain. Casualties were much less than expected, and the bombings made the British people more resolute.

Moreover, the Royal Air Force (RAF), aided by the newly developed radar and an excellent system of communications, inflicted heavy losses on the *Luftwaffe*. Hitler lost the Battle of Britain in the air and was forced to abandon his plans for invasion.

German Attack on Russia

Operation Barbarossa, the code name for the invasion of Russia, was aimed at knocking Russia out of the war before winter could set in. Success depended in part on an early start, but here Hitler's Italian alliance proved costly. Mussolini was jealous of Hitler's success and annoyed at German condescension.

Consequently, Mussolini launched an attack against the British in Egypt and drove them back some sixty miles. Encouraged by this success, he also invaded Greece. But in North Africa the British counterattacked and drove into Libya, and the Greeks also repulsed the Italians. In March 1941 the British sent help to the Greeks, and Hitler was forced to divert his attention to the Balkans and to Africa. General Erwin Rommel (1891–1944), later to earn the title "The Desert Fox," went to Africa and soon drove the British back into Egypt. In the Balkans the German army swiftly occupied Yugoslavia and crushed Greek resistance, but the price was a delay of six weeks for Barbarossa (see Map 31–3). This proved to be costly the following winter in the Russian campaign.

Operation Barbarossa was launched against Russia on June 22, 1941, and it almost succeeded. Stalin panicked. He had not fortified his frontier or ordered his troops to withdraw when attacked. Two thousand planes were destroyed on the ground. By November Hitler had gone farther into Russia than had Napoleon: The German army stood at the gates of Leningrad, on the outskirts of Moscow, and on the Don River. Of the 4.5 million troops with which the Russians had begun the fighting, they had

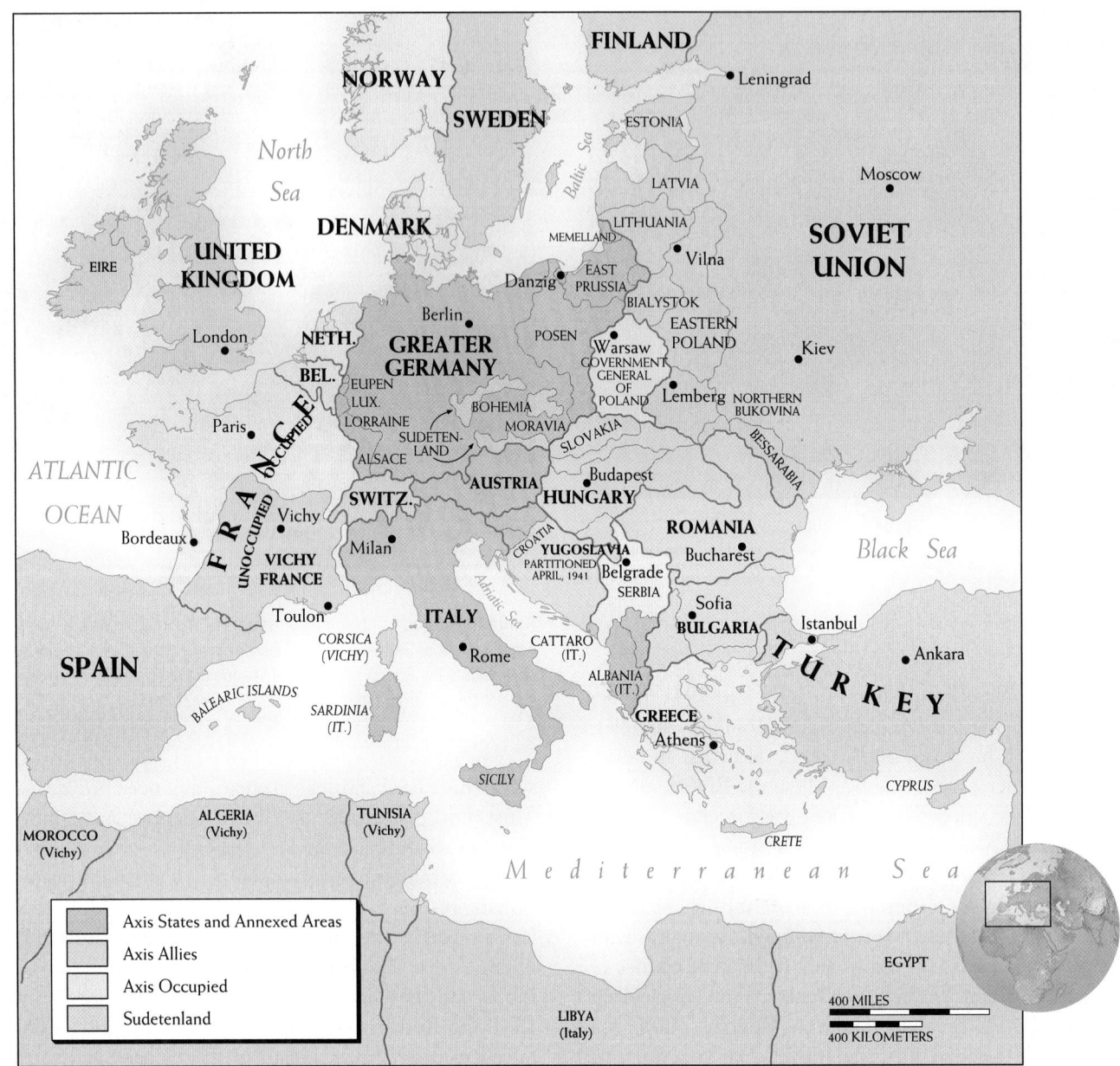

Map 31–3. Axis Europe 1941. On the eve of the German invasion of the Soviet Union, the Germany-Italy Axis bestrode most of Western Europe by annexation, occupation, or alliance—from Norway and Finland in the north to Greece in the south and from Poland to France. Britain, the Soviets, a number of insurgent groups, and, finally, the United States had before them the long struggle of conquering this Axis "fortress Europe."

lost 2.5 million; of their 15,000 tanks, only 700 were left. A German victory seemed imminent.

But the Germans could not deliver the final blow. In August there was a delay in their advance to decide on a course of action. One plan was to take Moscow before winter. Such a plan might have brought victory, for Moscow was Russia's transportation hub. Hitler, however, diverted significant forces to the south. By the time he was ready to return to the offensive near Moscow, it was too late. Winter struck the German army, which was not equipped to face it. Given precious time, Stalin was able to restore order and fortify the

city. Even more important, troops had arrived from Siberia, where they had been placed to check a possible Japanese attack. In November and December the Russians counterattacked. The war had turned into one of attrition, and the Germans began to have visions of Napoleon's retreat.

Hitler's Europe

The demands and distractions of war and Hitler's defeat prevented him from fully carrying out his plans. Therefore, it is hard to be sure what his intentions were, but the measures he took before his death give evidence of a regime probably unmatched in history for carefully planned terror and inhumanity. To give *Lebensraum* to the Germans at the expense of people he deemed inferior, Hitler established colonies of Germans in Poland, driving the local people from their land and using them as cheap labor. He had worse plans for Russia. The Russians would be driven to Central Asia and Siberia, where they would be kept in check by frontier colonies of German war veterans. Germans would settle the more desirable lands of European Russia.

Hitler's long-range plans included Germanization as well as colonization. In lands inhabited by people racially akin to the Germans, like Scandinavia, the Netherlands, and Switzerland, the natives would be absorbed into the German nation. Such peoples would be reeducated and purged of dissenting elements, but there would be little or no colonization. He even had plans, only slightly realized, of adopting selected people from those he considered the lesser races into those he considered the master race.

Hitler regarded the conquered lands merely as a source of plunder. From Eastern Europe he removed everything useful, including entire industries. In Russia and Poland the Germans simply confiscated the land. In the west the conquered countries were forced to support the occupying army at a rate several times the real cost. The Germans used the profits to strip the conquered peoples of most necessities. The Nazis were frank about their policies. One of Hitler's high officials said, "Whether nations live in prosperity or starve to death interests me only insofar as we need them as slaves for our culture."[1]

Racism and the Holocaust

The most horrible aspect of the Nazi rule in Europe arose from the inhumanity and brutality inherent in Hitler's racial doctrines. He considered the Slavs *Untermenschen*, subhuman creatures like beasts who need not be treated as people. In Poland the upper and professional classes were either jailed, deported, or killed. Schools and churches were closed; marriage was controlled to keep down the Polish birthrate; and harsh living conditions were imposed. In Russia things were even worse. Hitler spoke of his Russian campaign as a war of extermination. Heinrich Himmler (1900–1945), head of Hitler's elite SS guard, formed

SOURCE *Emmanuel Ringelblum*, Notes from the Warsaw Ghetto, 1942

---

[1] Quoted by Gordon Wright, *The Ordeal of Total War, 1939–1945* (New York: Harper & Row, 1968), p. 117.

Roundup of Warsaw Jews. World War II resulted in the near-total destruction of the Jews of Europe, victims of the Holocaust spawned by Hitler's racial theories of the superiority and inferiority of particular ethnic groups. Hitler placed special emphasis on the need to exterminate the Jews, to whom he attributed particular wickedness. This picture shows a roundup of Jews in Warsaw, where there was a large Jewish population, ultimately on their way to concentration or death camps. *Corbis-Bettmann.*

Mass Murder at Belsen

Hitler's calculated plan to wipe out Europe's Jews, was not widely known during the war. Kurt Gerstein, a colonel in the SS, was part of the apparatus of extermination. However, unlike most people involved, he tried to tell the world what was taking place. The following is an account of what he saw at the death camp at Belsen, Germany, in 1942.

◆ What were the reasons for Hitler's policy of exterminating millions of people? Why did many Germans take part in the process? Why did Colonel Gerstein not resist?

A train arrived from Lemberg [Lvov]. There were forty-five cars containing 6,700 people, 1,450 of whom were already dead. Through the gratings on the windows, children could be seen peering out, terribly pale and frightened, their eyes filled with mortal dread. . . . The train entered the station, and two hundred Ukrainians wrenched open the doors and drove the people out of the carriages with their leather whips. Instructions came through a large loudspeaker telling them to remove all their clothing, artificial limbs, glasses, etc. They were to hand over all objects of value at the counter. . . . Shoes were to be carefully tied together, for otherwise no one would ever again have been able to find shoes belonging to each other in a pile that was a good eighty feet high. Then the women and girls were sent to the barber who, with two or three strokes of his scissors, cut off all their hair and dropped it into potato sacks. . . .

Then the column moved off. Headed by an extremely pretty young girl, they walked along the avenue, all naked, men, women, and children, with artificial limbs removed. I myself was stationed up on the ramp between the [gas] chambers with Captain Wirth.

Mothers with babies at their breasts came up, hesitated, and entered the chambers of death. At the corner stood a burly SS man with a priestlike voice. "Nothing at all is going to happen to you!" he told the poor wretches. "All you have to do when you get into the chambers is to breathe in deeply. That stretches the lungs. Inhaling is necessary to prevent disease and epidemics." When asked what would be done with them, he replied: "Well, of course, the men will have to work building houses and roads, but the women won't need to work. They can do housework or help in the kitchen, but only if they want to." For some of these poor creatures, this was a small ray of hope that was enough to make them walk the few steps to the chambers without resistance. Most of them knew what was going on. The smell told them what their fate was to be. They went up the small flight of steps and saw everything. Mothers with their babies clasped to their breasts, small children, adults, men, women, all naked; they hesitated, but they entered the chambers of death, thrust forward by the others behind them or by the leather whips of the SS [Storm Troopers]. Most went in without a word. . . . Many were saying prayers. I prayed with them. I pressed myself into a corner and cried aloud to my God and theirs. How gladly I should have gone into the chambers with them; how gladly I should have died with them. Then they would have found an SS officer in uniform in their gas chambers; they would have believed it was an accident and the story would have been buried and forgotten. But I could not do that yet. First, I had to make known what I had seen here. The chambers were filling up. The people were treading on each other's feet. There were 700–800 of them in an area of 270 square feet, in 1,590 cubic feet of space. The SS crushed them together as tightly as they possibly could. The doors closed. Meanwhile, the rest waited out in the open, all naked. "It's done exactly the same way in winter," I was told. "But they may catch their death!" I said "That's what they're here for," an SS man said. . . . The diesel exhaust gases were intended to kill those unfortunates. But the engine was not working. . . . The people in the gas chambers waited, in vain. I heard them weeping, sobbing. . . . After 2 hours and 49 minutes, measured by my stopwatch, the diesel started. Up to that moment, men and women had been shut up alive in those four chambers, four times 750 people in four times 1,590 cubic feet of space. Another twenty-five minutes dragged by. Many of those inside were already dead. They could be seen through the small window when the electric light went on for a moment and lit up the inside of the chamber. After twenty-eight minutes, few were left alive. At the end of thirty-two minutes, all were dead.

extermination squads to eliminate 30 million Slavs to make room for the Germans. Some 6 million Russian prisoners of war and deported civilian workers may have died under Nazi rule.

Hitler had special plans for the Jews. He meant to make all Europe *Judenrein* ("free of Jews"). For a time he thought of sending them to Madagascar but later decided on the "final solution of the Jewish problem": extermination. The

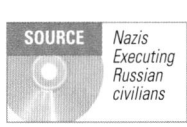 Nazis built extermination camps in Germany and Poland and used the latest technology to kill millions of men, women, and children just because they were Jews. (See Document, "Mass Murder at Belsen.") Before the war was over, 6 million Jews had died in what has come to be called the **Holocaust**. Only about a million remained alive, mostly in pitiable condition (see Map 31–4).

Map 31–4. The Holocaust. The Nazi policy of ethnic cleansing—targeting Jews, Gypsies, political dissidents, and "social deviants"—began with imprisoning them in concentration camps, but by 1943 the *Endlösung*, or Final Solution, called for the systematic extermination of "undesirables."

The Road to Pearl Harbor

The war took on truly global proportions in December 1941. The Japanese were already at war with China, and between the outbreak of that war in 1937 and the opening of the World War II campaign in the Pacific, there were three critical junctures. The first was the decision in January 1938 to destroy the Chinese Nationali st Party government in Nanjing. The army quickly occupied most of the cities and

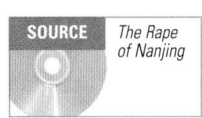 railroads of eastern China, killing over 300,000 people and brutally raping 7,000 women (known today as the Rape of Nanjing), but Jiang Jieshi (Chiang Kai-shek) refused to give in. The result was a stalemate that lasted until 1945. China was never a major theater of the war in the Pacific.

The second critical decision was the Tripartite Pact with Germany and Italy in September 1940. Japan had long admired Germany. In 1936 it had joined Germany in the Anti-Comintern Pact directed against international communism. It also wanted an alliance with Germany against the Soviet Union. Germany insisted, however, that any alliance also be directed against the United States and Britain, to which the Japanese would not agree. The Japanese navy, especially, was not interested in being dragged into a German war. After an undeclared miniwar with Russia from May to December 1939 on the Mongolian border, sentiment rose for an alliance with Germany, but then Germany "betrayed" Japan by signing a nonaggression pact with the Soviet Union. For a time Japan decided to improve its relations with the United States, but America insisted that Japan get out of China. By the late spring of 1940 German victories in Europe—the fall of Britain appeared imminent—again led the Japanese military to favor an alliance with Germany.

When Japan signed the Tripartite Pact it had three objectives: to isolate the United States, to take over the Southeast Asian colonies of Britain, France, and the Netherlands, and to improve its relations with the Soviet Union through the good offices of Germany.

The last objective was reached when Japan signed a neutrality pact with the Soviet Union in April 1941. Two months later Germany attacked the Soviet Union, without consulting Japan. It compounded this second "betrayal" by asking Japan to attack the Soviet Union in the east. Japan waited and watched. When the German advance faltered, Japan decided to honor the neutrality pact and turn south. This, in effect, was the end of Japan's participation in the Axis. Thereafter, it fought its own war in Asia. Yet instead of deflecting American criticism as intended, the pact, by linking Japan to Germany, hardened America's position on China.

The third and fateful decision was to go to war with the United States. In June 1941, following Germany's defeat of France, Japanese troops had occupied northern French Indochina. The United States retaliated by limiting strategic exports to Japan. In July 1941 Japanese troops took southern Indochina, and the United States embargoed all exports to Japan, cutting Japanese oil imports by 90 percent. The navy pressed for the capture of the oil-rich Dutch East Indies, but it would be too dangerous to move against Dutch and British colonies in Southeast Asia with the United States on its flank in the Philippines. The navy, therefore, planned a preemptive strike against the United States. The Japanese

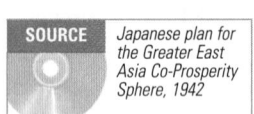 SOURCE — *Japanese plan for the Greater East Asia Co-Prosperity Sphere, 1942*

decision for war wagered Japan's land-based air power, shorter supply lines, and what it saw as greater will power against American productivity. At the Imperial Conference where the all-or-nothing decision was taken, the navy's chief of staff compared the war with the United States to a dangerous operation that might save a critically ill patient.

America's Entry into the War

On Sunday morning, December 7, 1941, even while Japanese representatives were discussing a settlement in Washington, Japan launched an air attack on Pearl Harbor, Hawaii, the chief American naval base in the Pacific. The next day, the United States and Britain declared war on Japan. Three days later, Germany and Italy declared war on the United States.

The Tide Turns

The potential power of the United States was enormous, but America was ill prepared for war. Although conscription had been introduced in 1940, the army was tiny, inex-

Pearl Harbor. The successful Japanese attack on the American base at Pearl Harbor in Hawaii on December 7, 1941, together with simultaneous attacks on other Pacific bases, brought the United States into war against the Axis powers. For Japan, it was the opening phase of a campaign to capture European and American colonies in Southeast Asia.

perienced, and poorly supplied. American industry was not ready for war. The Japanese swiftly captured Guam, Wake Island, and the Philippines (see Map 31–5). They also attacked Hong Kong, Malaya, Burma, and Indonesia. By the summer of 1942, the Japanese Empire stretched from the western Aleutian Islands south almost to Australia, and from Burma east to the Gilbert Islands in the mid-Pacific.

In the same year, the Germans almost reached the Caspian Sea in their drive for Russia's oil fields. In Africa, Rommel drove the British back towards the Suez Canal and was finally stopped at El Alamein, only seventy miles from Alexandria. Relations between the democracies and their

Soviet ally were not close; German submarines were threatening British supplies; the Allies were being thrown back on every front, and the future looked bleak.

The tide turned at the Battle of Midway in June 1942. A month earlier, both sides had suffered massive losses in the Battle of the Coral Sea, but greater U.S. ship production made such trade-offs unprofitable for Japan. At Midway, American planes destroyed four Japanese aircraft carriers. Soon American Marines landed on Guadalcanal in the Solomon Islands and began to reverse the momentum of the war. The war in the Pacific was far from over, but Japan was checked sufficiently to allow the Allies to concentrate their efforts first in the West.

Map 31–5. The War in the Pacific. As in Europe, the Allies initially had trouble recapturing areas that the Japanese had quickly seized early in the war. The map shows the initial expansion of the Japanese and the long struggle of the Allies to push them back to their homeland and defeat them.

Allied Landings in Africa, Sicily, and Italy In November 1942, an Allied force landed in French North Africa. Even before that landing, the British Field Marshal Bernard Montgomery (1887–1976), after stopping Rommel at El Alamein, had begun a drive to the west (see Map 31–6). The American general Dwight D. Eisenhower (1890–1969) had pushed eastward through Morocco and Algeria. The German army was trapped in Tunisia and crushed. The Mediterranean was now under Allied control, and southern Europe was exposed. In July and August 1943 the Allies took Sicily. Mussolini was driven from power, the Allies landed in Italy, and Marshal Pietro Badoglio (1871–1956), the leader of the new Italian government, declared war on Germany. Churchill had spoken of Italy as the "soft underbelly" of the Axis, but German resistance was tough and determined. Still, the need to defend Italy strained the Germans' energy and resources and left them vulnerable on other fronts.

Battle of Stalingrad The Russian campaign became especially demanding. In the summer of 1942 the Germans resumed the offensive on all fronts but did not get far, except in the south. Their goal there was the oil fields near the Caspian Sea, and they got as far as Stalingrad on the Volga, a key point for protecting the flank of their southern army. Hitler was determined to take the city and Stalin to hold it. The Battle of Stalingrad raged for months with unexampled ferocity. The Russians lost more men than the Americans lost in combat during the entire war, but their heroic defenses prevailed. Because Hitler again overruled his generals and would not allow a retreat, an entire German army was lost.

Stalingrad marked the turning point of the Russian campaign. Thereafter, as the German military and material resources dwindled, the Russians advanced westward inexorably.

Strategic Bombing In 1943 the Allies also gained ground in production and logistics. The industrial might of the United States began to come into full force. New technology and tactics made great strides in eliminating the submarine menace. In the same year the American and British air forces began a series of massive bombardments of Germany by night and day. This bombing did not have much effect on the war until 1944. Then the Americans introduced long-range fighters that could protect the bombers and allow accurate missions by day. By 1945 the Allies could bomb at will.

Map 31–6. North African Campaigns, 1942–1945. Control of North Africa was important to the Allies if they were to have access to Europe from the south. The map diagrams this theater of the war from Morocco to Egypt and the Suez Canal.

Stalingrad. Russian soldiers, in their heroic defense of Stalingrad, dug trenches from building to building in the city. The German defeat at Stalingrad in February 1943 marked the turning point of the Russian campaign. Thereafter the Russians advanced inexorably westward.

Defeat of Nazi Germany

On June 6, 1944 (D-Day), in one of greatest amphibious assaults ever attempted, Allied troops landed in force on the coast of Normandy (see Map 31–7). By the beginning of September France had been liberated.

All went smoothly until December, when the Germans launched a counterattack called the Battle of the Bulge through the Forest of Ardennes. However, it was their last gasp. The Allies recovered the momentum and pushed eastward. They crossed the Rhine in March 1945, and German resistance crumbled. This time there could be no doubt that the Germans had lost the war on the battlefield.

In the east, the Russians were within reach of Berlin by March 1945. Because the Allies insisted on unconditional surrender, the Germans fought on until May. Hitler committed suicide in an underground hideaway in Berlin on May 1, 1945. The Russians occupied Berlin by agreement with their Western allies. The Third Reich had lasted a dozen years instead of the millennium predicted by Hitler.

Fall of the Japanese Empire

The war in Europe ended on May 8, 1945, and by then victory over Japan was in sight (see also Chapter 28). The original

D-Day. Allied troops landed in Normandy on D-Day, June 6, 1944. This photograph, taken two days later, shows long lines of men and equipment moving inland from the beach to reinforce the troops leading the invasion.

Map 31–7.   Defeat of the Axis in Europe, 1942–1945. Here we see some major steps in the progress towards Allied victory against Axis Europe. From the south through Italy, the west through France, and the east through Russia, the Allies gradually conquered the continent to bring the war in Europe to a close.

Japanese attack on the United States had been a calculated risk against the odds. The longer the war lasted, the greater the impact of American superiority in industrial production and human resources. Beginning in 1943 American forces began a campaign of "island hopping," selecting major bases and places strategically located along the enemy supply line. Starting from the Solomons, they moved northeast towards the Japanese homeland. American bombers launched a terrible wave of bombings that destroyed Japanese industry and disabled the Japanese navy. But still the Japanese government, dominated by a military clique, refused to surrender.

Confronted with Japan's determination, the Americans made plans for a frontal assault on the Japanese homeland,

which, they calculated, would cost unacceptable American casualties and even greater losses for the Japanese. At this point, science and technology presented the Americans with another choice. Since early in the war a secret program had been in progress. Its staff was working to use atomic energy for military purposes.

On August 6, 1945, an American plane dropped an atomic bomb on the city of Hiroshima. More than 70,000 of its 200,000 residents were killed. Two days later the Soviet Union declared war on Japan and invaded Manchuria. The next day a second atomic bomb fell, this time on Nagasaki. Even then the Japanese were prepared to face an invasion rather than give up. It was only the unprecedented intervention of Emperor Hirohito (r. 1926–1989) that forced the government to surrender on August 14. Even then, the Cabinet made the condition that Japan could keep its emperor. President Harry Truman (1884–1972), who had come to office on April 12, 1945, on the death of Franklin D. Roosevelt, accepted the condition. Peace was formally signed on September 2, 1945.

The Cost of War

World War II was the most terrible war in history. Military deaths are estimated at 15 million, and at least as many civilians were killed. If deaths linked indirectly to the war are included, as many as 40 million may have died. Most of Europe and significant parts of Asia were devastated. Yet the end of so terrible a war brought little opportunity for relaxation. The dawn of the Atomic Age that brought a dramatic end to the war made people conscious that another major war might destroy humanity. Everything depended on the conclusion of a stable peace, but even as the fighting ended, the victors began to quarrel.

The Domestic Fronts

World War II represented an effort of total war by all the belligerents. Never before in world history had so many men and women and so many resources been devoted to military effort. One result was the carnage that occurred on the battlefields and at sea. Another was an unprecedented organization of civilians on the various home fronts. Each

Hiroshima. This photo, taken a few days after an atomic bomb was dropped, poignantly captures the total devastation wreaked on the city. *Corbis-Bettmann.*

domestic effort and experience was different, but almost no one escaped the impact of the conflict. Shortages, propaganda campaigns, and new political developments were ubiquitous. In this section we look at the home fronts of the principal European belligerents.

Germany: From Apparent Victory to Defeat

Hitler had expected to defeat all his enemies by rapid strokes, or **blitzkrieg**. Such campaigns would scarcely have affected Germany's society and economy. During the first two years of the war, in fact, Hitler demanded few important sacrifices from the German people. Spending on domestic projects continued, and food was plentiful; the economy was not on a full wartime footing. The failure to knock out the Soviet Union changed everything. Because enough food could no longer be imported from the east, Germany had to mobilize for total war, and the government demanded major sacrifices.

A great expansion of the army and military production began in 1942. As minister for armaments and munitions, Albert Speer (1905–1981) guided the economy, and Germany met its military needs instead of making consumer goods. Major German business enterprises aided the growth of wartime production. Between 1942 and late 1944 the output of military products tripled, but as the war went on the army absorbed more men from industry, hurting the production of even military goods.

Beginning in 1942 everyday products became scarce. Prices and wages were controlled, but the standard of living of German workers fell, Burdensome food rationing began in April 1942, and shortages were severe until the Nazi government seized food from occupied Europe. To preserve their own home front, the Nazis passed on the suffering to their defeated neighbors.

By 1943 there were also serious labor shortages. The Nazis required German teenagers and retired workers to work in the factories, and increasing numbers of women joined them. To achieve total mobilization the Germans closed retail businesses, raised the maximum age of women eligible for compulsory service, shifted non-German domestic workers to wartime industry, moved artists and entertainers into military service, closed theaters, and reduced such basic public services as mail and railways. Finally, the Nazis forced thousands of people from conquered lands to labor in Germany.

Hitler assigned women a special place in the war effort. The celebration of motherhood continued, with an emphasis on women who were the mothers of important military figures. Films portrayed ordinary women who became especially brave and patriotic during the war and remained faithful to their husbands who were at the front. Women were thereby

Youth Rally. Members of the Nazi German Women's Youth Movement perform calisthenics. *Getty Images Inc.—Hulton Archive Photos.*

depicted as mothers and wives who would send their sons and husbands off to war. The government portrayed other wartime activities of women as the natural fulfillment of their maternal roles. As air raid wardens they protected their families; as factory workers in munitions plants they aided their sons on the front lines. Women working on farms were providing for their soldier sons and husbands; as housewives they were helping to win the war by conserving food and managing their households frugally. Finally, by their faithful chastity, German women were protecting racial purity. They were not to marry or to engage in sexual relations with men who were not Germans. German women were thus supposed to demonstrate the kind of service and courage required by the war.

The war years also saw an intensification of political propaganda on the domestic front beyond what occurred in other countries. Hitler and other Nazis genuinely believed that weak domestic support had led to Germany's defeat in World War I, and they were determined that this would not happen again. Nazi propaganda blamed the outbreak of the war on the British and its prolongation on the policies of Germany's opponents. It also stressed the might of Germany and the inferiority of its foes.

Propaganda Minister Josef Goebbels (1897–1945) used radio and films to boost the Nazi cause. Movies of the collapse of Poland, Belgium, Holland, and France demonstrated German military might. Throughout the conquered territories the Nazis used the same mass media to frighten inhabitants about the possible consequences of an Allied victory. Later in the war the ministry broadcast exaggerated claims of Nazi victories. As the German armies were checked on the battlefield, especially in Russia, propaganda became a substitute for victory. To stiffen German resolve, the propaganda also aimed to frighten the German population about the consequences of defeat.

After May 1943, when the Allies began their major bombing offensive over Germany, the German people had much to fear. One German city after another endured heavy bombing, fires, and destruction. But the bombing did not undermine German morale—on the contrary, it may have confirmed the general fear of defeat at the hands of such savage opponents and increased German resistance.

World War II brought increased power to the Nazi party in Germany. Every area of the economy and society came under the direct influence or control of the party. The Nazis were determined that they, rather than the traditionally honored German officer corps, would profit from the new authority flowing to the central government because of the war effort. Throughout the war years there was virtually no serious opposition to Hitler or his ministers. In 1944 a small group of army officers made an attempt to assassinate Hitler; the effort failed, and there was no significant popular support for this act.

The war brought great changes to Germany, but what transformed the country afterward was the experience of defeat accompanied by vast physical destruction, invasion, and occupation. Hitler and the Nazis had brought the nation to such a complete and disastrous end that only a new kind of state with new political structures could emerge.

France: Defeat, Collaboration, and Resistance

In France the Vichy government cooperated closely with the Germans for a variety of reasons. Some of the collaborators believed that the Germans were sure to win and wanted to be on the victorious side. A few sympathized with the ideas and plans of the Nazis. Many conservatives regarded the French defeat as a judgment on what they saw as the corrupt, secularized, liberal Third Republic. But most of the French were not active collaborators and remained helpless and demoralized by defeat and German power.

Many conservatives and extreme rightists saw the Vichy government as a device to reshape the French national character and halt the decadence they associated with political and religious liberalism. The Roman Catholic clergy, who had lost power and influence under the Third Republic, gained status under Vichy. The church supported Pétain; his government supported religious education. Vichy adopted the church's views of the importance of family and spiritual values. Divorce was forbidden during the first three years of marriage and difficult thereafter; large families were rewarded.

Bombing of Cologne. The Allied campaign of aerial bombardment did terrible damage to German cities. This photograph shows the devastation it delivered to the city of Cologne on the Rhine. *UPI/Corbis-Bettmann.*

The Vichy regime embraced an intense, chauvinistic nationalism. It encouraged the long-standing prejudice against foreigners working in France and persecuted those who were not regarded as genuinely and thoroughly French. The chief victims were French Jews. Anti-Semitism was not new in France, as the Dreyfus affair had demonstrated. Even before Germany undertook Hitler's "final solution" in 1942, the French had begun to remove Jews from government, education, and publishing. In 1941 the Germans began to intern Jews living in occupied France; soon they carried out killings and imposed large fines collectively on the Jews of the occupied zone. In the spring of 1942 the Germans began deporting Jews, ultimately over 60,000, to the extermination camps of Eastern Europe. The Vichy government had no part in these decisions, but it made no protest, and its own anti-Semitic policies facilitated the process.

A few Frenchmen had fled to join de Gaulle's Free French forces soon after the defeat of 1940. Serious internal resistance to the German occupiers and to the Vichy government, however, developed only late in 1942. The Germans attempted to force young people in occupied France to work in German factories; some of them fled and joined the Resis-

tance, but the total number of resisters was small. Many were deterred by fear. Some disliked the violence that resistance inevitably entailed. As long as it appeared that the Germans would win the war, moreover, resistance seemed imprudent and futile. In all, less than 5 percent of the adult French population appear to have been involved.

By early 1944 the tide of battle had shifted. An Allied victory appeared inevitable, and the Vichy government was clearly doomed. Only then did an active Resistance assert itself. General de Gaulle urged the French people to resist their conquerors and their lackeys in the Vichy government. Within France, Resistance groups joined forces to plan for a better day. From Algiers on August 9, 1944, the Committee of National Liberation declared the authority of Vichy illegitimate. Soon French soldiers joined in the liberation of Paris and established a government for Free France. On October 21, 1945, France voted to adopt a new constitution as the basis of the Fourth Republic. The French people had experienced defeat, disgrace, deprivation, and suffering. Hostility and bitter quarrels over who had done what during the occupation and the Vichy period divided them for decades.

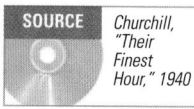

Vichy Poster. "The National Revolution" was the name the Vichy regime gave to its program to remake France. The house on the left, representing the Third Republic, carries the name "France and Company," which implies that the Third Republic was run like a corrupt business firm. It tilts precariously on shaky supports: egoism, radicalism, capitalism, communism, Jewry, antimilitarism, and disorder. The house on the right represents the Vichy government. It sits safe, strong, neat, and orderly, on solid columns: school, craftsmanship, the peasantry, and the military. These rest on equally firm bases: discipline, order, thrift, and courage. Underlying all are the three basic values—work, family, and fatherland— which Vichy made its national slogan. *Philippe Noyer, "Révolution nationale." Bibliothèque de Documentation Internationale Contemporaine. © ARS-Artists Rights Society, New York.*

Great Britain: Organization for Victory

On May 22, 1940, the British Parliament gave the government emergency powers. The government could now institute compulsory military service, food rationing, and various controls over the economy.

Churchill and the British war cabinet moved as quickly as possible to mobilize the nation. By the end of 1941 British production had already surpassed Germany's. To meet the heavy demands on the labor force, factory hours were extended, and women were brought into the work force in great numbers. Unemployment disappeared, and the working classes had more money to spend than they had enjoyed for many years. To avoid inflation caused by increased demand for an inadequate supply of consumer goods, savings were encouraged, and taxes raised to absorb the excess purchasing power.

The bombing "blitz" conducted by the German *Luftwaffe* against British targets in the winter and spring of 1940 to 1941 was the most immediate and dramatic experience of the war for the British people. The German air raids killed thousands and destroyed the homes of many more. Many families removed their children to the countryside. Gas masks were issued to thousands of city dwellers, who were frequently compelled to take shelter from the bombs in the London subways.

After the spring of 1941 Hitler needed most of his air force for the Russian front, but the bombing of Britain continued, killing more than 30,000 people. Terrible as it was, this toll was much smaller than the number of Germans killed by Allied bombing later in the war. In England as in Germany, however, the bombing did not break the people's spirit but seems to have made them more determined.

During the worst months of the "blitz" the remarkable speeches of Winston Churchill cheered and encouraged the British people. He united them with a sense of common suffering and purpose. They were called upon to make many sacrifices: Transportation facilities were strained simply from carrying enough coal for domestic heating and for running factories. Food and clothing for civilians were in short supply, and the government adopted strict rationing to achieve a fair distribution. Every scrap of land was farmed, increasing the productive portion by almost 4 million acres. Gasoline was in short supply, so private vehicles almost disappeared.

The British established their own propaganda machine to influence the Continent. The British Broadcasting Company (BBC) sent programs to every country in Europe in the local language to encourage resistance against the Nazis. At home the government used the radio to unify the nation. Soldiers at the front heard the same programs as their families at home.

For most of the population, strangely enough, the standard of living improved over the course of the war. The general health of the nation also improved for reasons that are still not clear. These gains should not be exaggerated, but many connected them with the active involvement of the government in the economy and the lives of the citizens.

This wartime experience may have contributed to the Labour Party's victory in 1945; many feared that a return to Conservative rule would bring a return to the economic misery of the 1930s.

The United States: American Women and African Americans in the War Effort

In the United States, the withdrawal of millions of men from the work force and their induction into the armed forces created a demand for new workers, especially in the burgeoning defense industries. In part, it was filled by millions of women leaving the home to enter the labor force, some of them taking jobs in defense plants doing work usually done only by men. Economic pressures caused by the Great Depression of the 1930s had already brought many more women into the work force than had been common before. Most came from poor families and worked in white-collar jobs to support themselves or to help their families eke out a living. Even so, the heavy burden of housework and the widespread hostility to the idea of women working outside the home kept the vast majority of women at home.

America's entry into the war changed things quickly. The need for vast amounts of equipment to wage the war

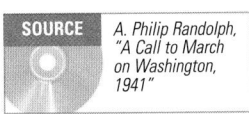

SOURCE A. Philip Randolph, "A Call to March on Washington, 1941"

called for and attracted new groups to seek work in the many enlarged and newly created factories. African Americans from the South came to Northern and Western cities to seek well-paying jobs, and women, too, came forward in greater numbers than ever before. Prejudices of various kinds had kept them from many opportunities, but the needs of war overcame such prejudice. In October 1942, President Roosevelt made the new situation clear: "In some communities employers dislike to hire women. In others they are reluctant to hire Negroes. We can no longer afford to indulge such prejudice."

Many women already working moved over to jobs in the defense industries; others entered the work force for the first time, lured less by wages than by patriotism. Their brothers and boyfriends were risking their lives for their country and its ideals of freedom and democracy. They were eager to do their part to support them, to be, in the words of a current song, the woman "behind the man behind the gun." Another popular song, "Rosie the Riveter," told of a young woman working in an aircraft factory to provide protection for her boyfriend in the Marines. Rosie came to be one of the best known symbols of the war effort when she appeared on the cover of the *Saturday*

Rosie the Riveter, as drawn by Norman Rockwell on the May 29, 1943, edition of the *Saturday Evening Post*. She chomps on a sandwich during a break at a defense plant. A copy of *Mein Kampf* serves as a footstool.

Evening Post. With her rivet gun on her lap she stamped on a copy of Hitler's *Mein Kampf*, the hated symbol of the enemy's evil.

The Soviet Union: "The Great Patriotic War"

No nation suffered greater loss of life or more extensive physical destruction during World War II than the Soviet Union. Perhaps as many as 16 million people were killed, and vast numbers of Soviet troops were taken prisoner. Hundreds of cities and towns and well over half the industrial and transportation facilities of the country were devastated. The Germans sent thousands of Soviet prisoners to work in factories in Germany as forced labor. The Germans also confiscated grain supplies and drew mineral resources and oil from the Soviet Union to serve their own war effort.

Stalin (1879–1953) conducted the war as virtual chief of the armed forces, and the State Committee for Defense provided strong central coordination. In the decade before the war, Stalin had already made the Soviet Union a highly centralized nation; he had attempted to manage the entire economy centrally through the Five-Year Plans, the collectivization of agriculture, and the purges. The country was thus on what amounted to a wartime footing long before the conflict erupted. When the war began, millions of citizens entered the army, but the army did not grow in influence at the expense of the state and the Communist Party— that is, Stalin.

Soviet propaganda differed from that of other nations. Because the Soviet government distrusted the loyalty of its citizens, it confiscated radios to prevent the people from listening to German propaganda. In large cities the government erected large loudspeakers to broadcast to the people in place of radios. Soviet propaganda emphasized Russian patriotism, not Marxist class conflict. The struggle was called "The Great Patriotic War." As in other countries, writers and playwrights helped sustain public support for the war. Sometimes they drew on communist themes, but they also portrayed the common Soviet citizen as contributing to a great patriotic struggle.

Great Russian novels of the past reappeared; more than half a million copies of Tolstoy's *War and Peace* were published during the siege of Leningrad. Other authors wrote straightforward propaganda fostering hatred of the Germans. Serge Eisenstein (1898–1948), the great filmmaker, produced a vast epic entitled *Ivan the Terrible*, which glorified one of the most brutal tsars of Russia's past. Musicians, such as Dimitri Shostakovich (1906–1975), wrote scores that sought to contribute to the struggle and evoke heroic emotions. The most important of these was Shostakovich's Seventh Symphony, also known as the "Leningrad Symphony."

Stalin even made peace with the Russian Orthodox Church. He pursued friendly relations with church leaders and allowed them to enter the Kremlin. Stalin hoped that this new policy would give him more support at home and permit the Soviet Union to be viewed more favorably in those parts of Eastern Europe where the Orthodox Church predominated.

Within occupied portions of the western Soviet Union, an active resistance movement arose against the Germans. The swiftness of the German invasion had stranded thousands of Soviet troops, some of whom escaped and carried on irregular resistance warfare behind enemy lines. Stalin supported partisan forces in lands held by the enemy for two reasons: He wanted to cause as much difficulty as possible for the Germans; and the Soviet-sponsored resistance reminded the peasants in the conquered regions that the Soviet government, with its policies of collectivization, had

Home front. Russian women apply grease to howitzer shells at a munitions plant during World War II. *Getty Images Inc.—Hulton Archive Photos.*

not disappeared. Stalin feared that the peasants' hatred of the communist government might lead them to collaborate with the invaders. When the Soviet army moved westward toward the end of the war, it incorporated the partisans into the regular army.

As the Soviet armies reclaimed the occupied areas and then moved across Eastern and central Europe, the Soviet Union established itself as a world power second only to the United States. Stalin had been a reluctant belligerent, but he emerged a major victor. In that respect, the war and the extraordinary patriotic effort and sacrifice it generated consolidated the power of Stalin and the party more effectively than had the political and social policies of the previous decade.

Preparations for Peace

The split between the Soviet Union and its wartime allies that followed the war and began to emerge as it ended should cause no surprise. As the self-proclaimed center of world communism, the Soviet Union was openly dedicated to the overthrow of the capitalist nations, although this message was muted when the occasion demanded. On the other side, the Western allies were no less open about their hostility to communism and its chief purveyor, the Soviet Union.

Although cooperation against a common enemy and strenuous propaganda efforts in the West helped improve

Western feeling towards the Soviet ally, Stalin remained suspicious and critical of the Western war effort. Likewise, Churchill never ceased planning to contain the Soviet advance into Europe. For some time Roosevelt seems to have hoped that the Allies could continue to work together after the war, but even he was losing faith by 1945. Differences in historical development and ideology, as well as traditional conflicts over political power and influence, soon dashed hopes of a mutually satisfactory peace settlement and continued cooperation to uphold it.

The Atlantic Charter

In August 1941, even before America entered the war, Roosevelt and Churchill had met off Newfoundland and agreed to the Atlantic Charter. A broad set of principles in the spirit of Wilson's Fourteen Points, it provided a theoretical basis for the peace they sought. When Russia and the United States joined Britain in the war, the three powers entered a purely military alliance in January 1942, leaving all political questions aside. The first political conference was the meeting of foreign ministers in Moscow in October 1943. The ministers reaffirmed earlier agreements to fight on until the enemy surrendered unconditionally and to continue cooperating after the war in a united-nations organization.

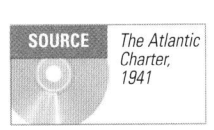
SOURCE *The Atlantic Charter, 1941*

Tehran

The first meeting of the three leaders took place at Tehran, the capital of Iran, in 1943. Western promises to open a second front in France the next summer (1944) and Stalin's agreement to join in the war against Japan (when Germany was defeated) created an atmosphere of goodwill in which to discuss a postwar settlement. Stalin wanted to retain what he had gained in his pact with Hitler and to dismember Germany. Roosevelt and Churchill made no firm commitments.

The most important decision was for the Western Allies to attack Germany from Europe's west coast instead of from southern Europe by way of the Mediterranean. This decision meant, in retrospect, that Soviet forces would occupy Eastern Europe and control its destiny. At Tehran in 1943 the Western Allies did not foresee this clearly, for the Russians were still fighting deep within their own frontiers, and military considerations were paramount everywhere.

By 1944 the situation was different. In August, Soviet armies were in sight of Warsaw, which had risen in expec-

tation of liberation. But the Russians turned south into the Balkans, allowing the Polish rebels to be annihilated. The Russians gained control of Romania and Hungary, gaining advances of which centuries of expansionist tsars had only dreamed. Alarmed by these developments, Churchill went to Moscow and met with Stalin in October. They agreed to share power in the Balkans on the basis of Soviet predominance in Romania and Bulgaria, Western predominance in Greece, and equality of influence in Yugoslavia and Hungary. These agreements were not enforceable without American approval, and the Americans were known to be hostile to such un-Wilsonian devices as "spheres of influence."

The three powers easily agreed on Germany's disarmament and denazification and on its division into four zones of occupation by France and the Big Three (the USSR, Britain, and the United States). Churchill, however, began to balk at Stalin's plan to dismember Germany and objected to his demand for reparations in the amount of $20 billion as well as for forced labor from all the zones, with Russia to get half of everything. These matters were left to fester and cause dissension in the future.

The settlement of Eastern Europe remained a problem. Everyone agreed that the Soviet Union deserved neighboring governments that were friendly, but the West insisted that they also be independent, autonomous, and democratic. The Western leaders, and especially Churchill, were not eager to see Eastern Europe fall under Russian domination. They, especially Roosevelt, were also truly committed to democracy and self-determination.

However, Stalin knew that independent, freely elected governments in Poland and Romania would not be safely friendly to Russia. He had already established a subservient government in Poland at Lublin in competition with the Polish government in exile in London. Under pressure from the Western leaders, however, Stalin agreed to reorganize the government and to include some Poles friendly to the West. He also signed a Declaration on Liberated Europe, promising self-determination and free democratic elections. Stalin was never free of the fear that the Allies might still make an arrangement with Germany and betray him. Yet he appeared eager to avoid conflict before the war with Germany was over, and he probably thought it worth endorsing some meaningless principles as the price of continued harmony. In any case, he wasted little time violating these agreements.

Yalta

The next meeting of the Big Three was at Yalta in the Crimea in February 1945. The Western armies had not yet crossed the Rhine, and the Soviet army was within 100 miles of Berlin. The war with Japan continued, and no atomic explosion had yet taken place. Roosevelt, faced with an invasion of Japan and prospective heavy losses, was eager to bring the Russians into the Pacific war as soon as possible.

As a true Wilsonian, Roosevelt also suspected Churchill's determination to maintain the British Empire and Britain's colonial advantages. The Americans thought that Churchill's plan to set up British spheres of influence in Europe would encourage the Russians to do the same and lead to friction and war. To encourage Russian participation in the war against Japan, Roosevelt and Churchill made extensive concessions to Russia in Asia. Again in the tradition of Wilson, Roosevelt stressed a United Nations organization: "Through the United Nations, he hoped to achieve a self-enforcing peace settlement that would not require American troops, as well as an open world without spheres of influence in which American enterprise could work freely."[2] Soviet agreement on these points seemed well worth concessions elsewhere.

SOURCE *The Charter of the United Nations, 1945*

Potsdam

The Big Three met for the last time in the Berlin suburb of Potsdam in July 1945. Much had changed since the last conference. Germany was defeated, and news of the successful experimental explosion of an atomic weapon reached the American president during the meetings. The cast of characters was also different: President Truman replaced Roosevelt; and Clement Attlee (1883–1967), leader of the Labour Party, replaced Churchill during the conference. Previous agreements were reaffirmed, but progress on undecided questions was slow.

Russia's western frontier was moved far into what had been Poland and included part of German East Prussia (see Map 31–8). In compensation, Poland was allowed "temporary administration" over the rest of East Prussia and Germany east of the Oder-Neisse river line, a condition that became permanent. In effect, Poland was moved about 100 miles west, at the expense of Germany, to accommodate the Soviet Union. The Allies agreed that Germany would be divided into occupation zones until the final peace treaty was signed, and the country remained divided until the end of the Cold War more than forty years later.

[2] Robert O. Paxton, *Europe in the Twentieth Century* (New York: Harcourt Brace Jovanovich, 1975), p. 487.

Map 31–8. Territorial Changes in Europe After World War II. The map shows the shifts in territory that followed the defeat of the Axis. No treaty of peace formally ended the war with Germany.

A Council of Foreign Ministers was established to draft peace treaties for Germany's allies. Growing disagreements made the job difficult, and it was not until February 1947 that Italy, Romania, Hungary, Bulgaria, and Finland signed treaties. The Russians signed their own agreements with the Japanese in 1956. These disagreements were foreshadowed at Potsdam.

Big Three at Potsdam. This photograph shows the "Big Three" at Potsdam. By the summer of 1945 only Stalin remained of the original leaders of the major Allies. Roosevelt and Churchill had been replaced by Harry Truman and Clement Attlee. *Corbis-Bettmann.*

many, and the Soviet Union intervened in the Spanish Civil War (1936–1939). Japan attacked China in 1937. These developments revealed that aggressive forces were on the march around the globe and that the defenders of the world order lacked the will to stop them. The formation of the Axis among Germany, Italy, and Japan guaranteed that the war would be fought around the world. There were fighting and suffering in Asia, Africa, the islands of the Pacific, and Europe. The use of atomic weapons brought the struggle to a close, but what are called conventional weapons did almost all the damage. The survival of civilization was threatened even without the use of nuclear devices.

This was ended not with unsatisfactory peace treaties but with no treaty at all in the European area where it had begun. The world quickly split into two unfriendly camps: the Western led by the United States, and the Eastern led by the Soviet Union. This division hastened the liberation of former colonial territories.

Summary

The Coming of War. The second great war of the twentieth century (1939–1945) grew out of the unsatisfactory resolution of the first. In retrospect, the two wars appear to some people to be one continuous conflict, with the two main periods of fighting separated by an uneasy truce. To others, that point of view distorts the situation by implying that the second war was the inevitable result of the first and its inadequate peace treaties.

The latter opinion seems more sound. Whatever the flaws of the treaties of Paris, the world suffered an even more terrible war than the first as a result of failures of judgment and will on the part of the victorious democratic powers. The United States, which had become the wealthiest and potentially the strongest nation in the world, disarmed almost entirely and withdrew into foolish isolation; it could play no important part in restraining the ambitious dictators who would bring on the war. Britain and France refused to face the threat posed by the Axis powers until the most deadly war in history was required to put it down. If the victorious democracies had remained strong, responsible, and realistic, they could have remedied whatever injustices or mistakes arose from the treaties without endangering the peace.

World War II. The second war itself was plainly a world war. The Japanese occupation of Manchuria in 1931 was a precursor. Italy attacked Ethiopia in 1935. Italy, Ger-

Review Questions

1. What were Hitler's foreign policy aims? Was he bent on conquest in the East and dominance in the West, or did he simply want to return Germany to its 1914 boundaries?

2. Why did Britain and France adopt a policy of appeasement in the 1930s? What were its main features? Did the appeasers buy the West valuable time to prepare for war by their actions at Munich in 1938?

3. How was Hitler able to defeat France so easily in 1940? Why was the air war against Britain a failure? Why did Hitler invade Russia? Why did the invasion ultimately fail? Could it have succeeded?

4. Why did Japan attack the United States at Pearl Harbor? What was the significance of American intervention in the war? Why did the United States drop atomic bombs on Japan? Did President Truman make the right decision when he ordered the bombs used?

5. What impact did World War II have on the civilian population of Europe? How did experiences on the domestic front of Great Britain differ from those of Germany and France? What impact did "The Great Patriotic War" have on the people of the Soviet Union? Did participation in World War II solidify Stalin's hold on power?

6. What was Hitler's "final solution" to the Jewish problem? Why did Hitler want to eliminate Slavs as well? Some historians have looked at the twentieth century and have seen a period of great destruction as well as of great progress. Was the twentieth century truly a "century of Holocaust"? Discuss the ramifications of these questions.

Axis (p. 988)

blitzkrieg (p. 1003)

Holocaust (p. 997)

Lebensraum (p. 984)

Luftwaffe (p. 993)

Key Terms

Anschluss (p. 989)

appeasement (p. 987)

INTERPRETING THE PAST

Totalitarian States and Total War

Text Sources from MyHistoryLab/ PrimarySource DVD

1. Kita Ikki, *Outline for the Reconstruction of Japan*
2. Franklin Delano Roosevelt, *The Four Freedoms*
3. Nadezhda Mandelstam, from *Hope Against Hope: A Memoir*

Text Source from Chapter 31

1. *Hitler Describes his Goals* (page 986)

Visual Sources from MyHistoryLab/Primary Source DVD

1. *The Warsaw Ghetto*
2. *Civilian Refugees in Europe*

Militarism and nationalism, along with the authoritarian ideologies that grew popular in the 1920s and 1930s, were significant contributing factors to the start of World War II. Economic crises and the high debts and repayments required of Western nations allowed leaders who offered simplistic and forceful answers to gain power. Hitler in Germany, Mussolini in Italy, Franco in Spain, as well as the military-dominated government in Japan advocated aggressive military action, extreme social regimentation, and the demonization of specific ethnic and racial groups to restore their countries to a mythical age of virtuous unity.

In this exercise you will read four primary sources from the early twentieth century and examine two images that focus on authoritarian nationalism and the response from a Western democratic leader in the World War II era.

The first document is written by Kita Ikki, who outlines the policies of the militaristic nationalists responsible for Japan's entry in World War II and its invasion of China in the 1930s. The second source is a speech given by United States president Franklin Roosevelt almost a year before Japan attacked American forces at Pearl Harbor. In it, the president defines American policy as diametrically opposed to the authoritarian dictatorships of Germany and Japan. The third document offers graphic evidence of the impact of Russian dictator Josef Stalin's authoritarian methods on the behavior of the country's citizens. The final document is an excerpt from Adolf Hitler's book *Mein Kampf*, which describes the principles upon which the Nazi party would later rule Germany.

PRENTICE HALL
myhistorylab
Where it's a good time to connect to the past!

The two accompanying visual sources illustrate the impact on civilians of the policies of the militaristic ultranationalists in Europe during World War II.

Questions

What are Kita Ikki's primary goals in reorganizing Japan? How would you characterize the rights of individuals versus the rights of the state in Ikki's view?

How do the programs and policies advocated by Ikki differ from those proposed by Adolf Hitler? How are they similar? Are their any similarities between Ikki's and Mussolini's beliefs about war?

What is the basic principle of Hitler's vision of his party's role in German political life?

What are Roosevelt's "four freedoms"? How do the national polices he announces differ from those that Hitler and Ikki promote?

How did the authoritarian policies of the Russian state affect those who were arrested? How did the state create the "terror" and fear throughout society?

Note: To learn more about the topics in this chapter, please turn to the Suggested Readings at the end of the book. For additional sources related to this chapter please see the Primary Source DVD at the back of this text or MyHistoryLab.

32

The West Since World War II

IN THE MORE THAN HALF A CENTURY SINCE THE CONCLUSION of World War II, Europe's influence on the world scene has been transformed. The destruction and financial strains of the war left Europe exhausted and incapable of exercising the kind of power it had formerly exerted. Almost immediately after the war, the Cold War developed between the United States and the Soviet Union. Europe along with other parts of the world became a divided and contested territory, with America dominant in Western Europe and the Soviets dominant in Eastern Europe. The European powers themselves could not determine the outcome of that struggle for world dominance between the superpowers. Furthermore, less than five years after the war Europeans began to lose control of their overseas empires.

Within both the world context and the more narrow Western context, the greatest change that took place after 1945 was the emergence of the United States as a fully active great power. The American retreat from leadership that occurred in

The "beautiful game," by way of Europe. In the twentieth century the sport of soccer became the most popular game in the world. The World Cup, which takes place every four years, is a truly global event. The 2006 Cup attracted over 28 billion television viewers—the most watched event in history. Here Florent Malouda from France is taken down by two Italian players in the final in Berlin on July 10, 2006. Like several other players from the French squad, Malouda was an emigré. Indeed, the captain of the French team, Zinedine Zidane, who was ejected in a controversial call late in the game, has been quoted as saying, "First I am an Algerian from Marseille, and then a Frenchman." Italy went on to the win the match 5–3 in penalty kicks.

The West Since 1945

The West

The history of the West since the end of World War II has been full of paradoxes. Europe, which gave birth to Western civilization and remained its center from the eighteenth century until the war, declined in world influence. During the four decades immediately after the war, the United States and the Soviet Union rose to predominance and replaced Western Europe as the major powers on the world scene. Consequently, while the traditional center of Western influence exerted little power, both new great Western powers came to exert more political and military power than any other previous nation of continental Europe. But they did so in conflict with each other.

Immediately after 1945 the nations of the West entered the Cold War. That ideological, economic, and military rivalry between the United States and the Soviet Union dominated political struggles throughout the world for more than half a century. It divided Europe between NATO and Warsaw Pact military forces and forced nations outside of Europe, in Asia, Africa, and Latin America, to side with one or the other of the superpowers. Hence the Cold War too became a world war that had an important impact on non-Western nations. At times these other nations became theaters of conflict in which indigenous civil wars melded into the struggle between the United States and the Soviet Union, as in the case of Cuba, Angola, Korea, and Vietnam. A neutral stance in this conflict became extremely difficult for any nation to sustain.

In the later 1980s, however, the Cold War unexpectedly ended as the Soviet Union and the nations of Eastern Europe, their economies exhausted from failed experiments in central planning and repression, experienced enormous internal political changes and began the difficult transition to democracy and capitalism. These changes have clearly opened a new epoch of Western history. The United States has emerged from the Cold War as the single remaining superpower. Western Europe has achieved a new level of economic and political unity under the auspices of the European Union, although its peoples and governments are hesitant to press the process too far too rapidly. The economic success of the European Union has inspired other regional global treaties to promote free markets, including NAFTA (North Atlantic Free Trade Association), as well

1919 was not repeated. The decision by the United States to take an activist role in world affairs touched virtually every aspect of the postwar world. As a result of this acceptance of a leadership role, American domestic politics and its foreign policy became intertwined as in no previous period of American history.

Europe did not stagnate in this situation. Rather its society continued to develop in new directions. Population, agricultural production, and general consumption increased, especially in Western Europe. As in virtually every other part of the world, Europe experienced the impact of American culture through military alliances, trade, tourism, and popular entertainment. Europeans also began to build structures for greater economic cooperation.

Yet for forty-five years after the Second World War, Europe remained divided between a Western region generally characterized by democracies and an Eastern region characterized by Communist Party authoritarian states dominated by the Soviet Union. From the late 1970s onward there were political stirrings and economic stagnation in Eastern Europe and the Soviet Union. These culminated in 1989 with revolutions throughout Eastern Europe and in 1991 with the collapse of communist government in the Soviet Union itself. Since those events Europeans have been seeking to forge a new political direction. The movement towards unification, most particularly of the currency, continues in Western Europe. But the several nations that emerged from the former Soviet Union continue to as the global WTO (World Trade Organization). Europe has also been more ambitious than the United States in promoting international organizations such as the World Court designed to discipline countries that oppress their neighbors or threaten world peace. Eastern Europe and the former Soviet Union are experiencing economic turmoil and political uncertainty. Although some Eastern European countries such as Poland, the Czech Republic, and Hungary are better prepared than others to join the European Union, the shared aspiration of all Eastern European nations to become EU members bodes well for the future of this region. Except for Latvia, Estonia, and Lithuania, newly independent former regions of the Soviet Union such as Ukraine, Georgia, and Belarus have an even more difficult path ahead of them in developing their economies and societies. Together with the Islamic countries, such as Uzbekistan, Turkmenistan, and Kazakhstan, these countries face added difficulties from the legacy of repressive authoritarian government and centrally planned economies. The security of Europe's eastern borders will depend on the success of these Eastern European nations and former Soviet republics in making the transition to democracy.

Another important factor in the history of both the United States and Europe since World War II has been the rising immigration from the rest of the world. Germany has seen the influx of significant numbers of *gastarbeiters* (guest workers) from Turkey, while France, Italy, and Spain receive more immigrants from North Africa and the Middle East, many from their former colonies. The United States, with its long history as an immigrant nation, has been more comfortable dealing with the influx of non-European immigrants, but struggles persist over language, cultural identity, and assimilation. Europe, less accustomed to non-European immigration, has found it even more difficult to accommodate immigrants whose religions, languages, and appearance differ from those of Europeans.

experience political confusion and economic stagnation. The attacks of September 11, 2001, on the United States and the international events flowing therefrom have challenged the post–World War II Western alliance. ■

The Cold War Era

Initial Causes

The tense relationship between the United States and the Soviet Union that dominated world history during the second half of the twentieth century originated in the closing months of World War II. In part, the new coldness between the Allies arose from the mutual feeling that each had violated previous agreements. The Russians were plainly asserting permanent control of Poland and Romania under puppet communist governments. The United States, on the other hand, was taking a harder line on the extent of German reparations to the Soviet Union.

In retrospect, however, it appears unlikely that friendlier styles on either side could have avoided a split that rested on basic differences of ideology and interest. The Soviet Union's attempt to extend its control westward into central Europe and the Balkans and southward into the Middle East was a continuation of the policy of tsarist Russia. It had been Britain's traditional role to restrain Russian expansion into these areas; the United States inherited that task as Britain's power waned. The alternative was to permit a major change in the balance of power in the world in favor of a huge, traditionally hostile nation. That nation, dedicated in its official ideology to the overthrow of nations like the United States, was governed by Stalin

(1879–1953), an absolute dictator, who had repeatedly demonstrated his capacity for the most amazing deceptions and the most horrible cruelties. Few nations would be likely to take such risks.

In the aftermath of World War II, however, the Americans made no attempt to roll back Soviet power where it already existed. This was true even though American military forces were the greatest in their history, American industrial power

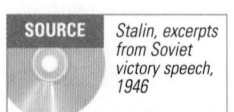

SOURCE Stalin, excerpts from Soviet victory speech, 1946

was unmatched in the world, and America had a monopoly on atomic weapons. In less than a year from the war's end, the Americans reduced their forces in Europe from 3.5 million to half a million. The speedy withdrawal reflected pressure to "get the boys home," but it was also fully in accord with America's peacetime plans and goals. These goals included support for self-determination, autonomy, and democracy in the political sphere; and free trade, freedom of the seas, no barriers to investment, and the Open Door in the economic sphere. As the strongest, richest nation in the world—the one with the greatest industrial plant and the strongest currency—the United States would benefit handsomely if an international order based on such goals were established.

American hostility to colonial empires created tensions with France and Britain, but these stresses were minor. The main conflict was with the Soviet Union. From the Soviet perspective, extending the borders of the USSR and dominating the formerly independent states of Eastern Europe would provide needed security and would compensate the Soviet people for the fearful losses they had endured in the war. The Soviets could thus see American resistance to their expansion as a threat to their security and their legitimate aims. American objections over Poland and other states could be seen as attempts to undermine regimes friendly to Russia and to encircle the Soviet Union with hostile neighbors.

The growth in France and Italy of large communist parties plainly taking orders from Moscow led the Americans to believe that Stalin was engaged in a great worldwide plot to subvert capitalism and democracy. In the absence of reliable evidence about Stalin's intentions, it is impossible to know for certain if these suspicions were justified, but most people in the West considered them plausible.

Areas of Early Cold War Conflict

The new mood of hostility among the former allies appeared quickly. In February 1946 both Stalin and his

SOURCE Winston Churchill, the "Iron Curtain" speech

foreign minister, Vyacheslav Molotov (1890–1986), gave public speeches in which they spoke of the Western democracies as enemies. A month

later Churchill (1874–1965) delivered a speech in Fulton, Missouri, in which he spoke of an Iron Curtain that had descended on Europe, dividing a free and democratic West from an East under totalitarian rule. He warned against communist subversion and urged Western unity and strength to counter the new menace. In this atmosphere, difficulties grew.

The attempt to deal cooperatively with the problem of atomic energy was an early victim of the **Cold War**. The Americans put forward a plan to place the manufacture and control of atomic weapons under international control, but the Russians balked at proposed requirements for on-site inspection and for limits on veto power in the United Nations. The plan fell through. The United States continued to develop its own atomic weapons in secrecy, and the Russians did the same. By 1949, with the help of information obtained by Soviet spies in Britain and the United States, the Soviet Union had exploded its own atomic bomb, and the race for nuclear weapons was on.

The resistance of Westerners to what they increasingly perceived as Soviet intransigence and communist plans for subversion and expansion took clearer form in 1947. Since 1944 civil war had been raging in Greece between the royalist government restored by Britain and insurgents supported by the communist countries, chiefly Yugoslavia. In 1947

H-bomb Shelter. In 1950 Albert Einstein wrote that "Radioactive poisoning of the atmosphere and hence annihilation of any life on earth has been brought within the range of technical possibilities. . . . In the end, there beckons more and more clearly general annihilation." The U.S. government, however, fostered belief in manageable atomic warfare in spite of the evidence from Japan, and backyard bomb shelters were a 1950s fad. This one could house a small family for up to five days. Standard features included canned food and water, sterno stove, battery-powered radio, chemical toilet, flashlight, blankets, and first-aid kit. During peacetime, the shelter could be used as a spare bedroom, for storage space, or even to cultivate mushrooms.

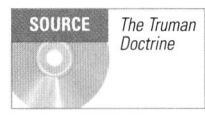

Britain informed the United States that it was financially no longer able to support the Greeks. On March 12 President Truman (1884–1972) asked Congress for legislation that would provide funds to support Greece and also Turkey, which was under Soviet pressure to yield control of the Dardanelles, and Congress complied. In what became known as the Truman Doctrine, the American president advocated a policy of supporting "free people who are resisting attempted subjugation by armed minorities or by outside pressures," by implication anywhere in the world.

American aid to Greece and Turkey took the form of military equipment and advisers. For Western Europe, where the menacing growth of communist parties was fueled by postwar poverty and hunger, the Americans devised the European Recovery Program. Named the **Marshall Plan** after George C. Marshall (1880–1959), the secretary of state who introduced it, this program provided broad economic aid to European states on condition only that they work together for their mutual benefit. The Soviet Union and its satellites were invited to participate. Finland and Czechoslovakia were willing, and Poland and Hungary showed interest. The Soviets, however, forbade them to take part.

The Marshall Plan helped restore prosperity to Western Europe and set the stage for Europe's unprecedented post-

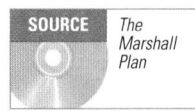

war economic growth. It also led to the waning of communist strength in the West and to the establishment there of solid democratic regimes.

From the Western viewpoint, this policy of "containment" was a new and successful response to the Soviet and communist challenge. Stalin may have considered it a renewal of the old Western attempt to isolate and encircle the USSR. His answer was to replace all multiparty governments behind the Iron Curtain with thoroughly communist regimes completely under his control. He also called a meeting of all communist parties around the world at Warsaw in the autumn of 1947. There they organized the Communist Information Bureau (Cominform), a revival of the old Comintern, dedicated to spreading revolutionary communism throughout the world.

In February 1948 a more dramatic and brutal display of Stalin's new policy took place in Prague. The Communists expelled the democratic members of what had been a coalition government and murdered Jan Masaryk (1886–1948), the foreign minister and son of the founder of Czechoslovakia, Thomas Masaryk (1850–1937). President Eduard Benes (1884–1948) was forced to resign, and Czechoslovakia was brought fully under Soviet rule.

These Soviet actions, especially those in Czechoslovakia, increased American determination to go ahead with its own arrangements in Germany. The Russians swiftly dismantled German industry in the eastern zone, but the Americans chose to try to make Germany self-sufficient, which meant restoring rather than destroying its industrial capacity. To the Soviets the restoration of a powerful industrial Germany, even in the western zones only, was frightening and unacceptable.

Disagreement over Germany produced the most heated postwar debate. When the Western powers agreed to go forward with a separate constitution for the western sectors of Germany in February 1948, the Soviets walked out of the joint Allied Control Commission. In the summer of that year the Western powers issued a new currency in their zone. Berlin, although well within the Soviet zone, was governed by all four powers. The Soviets chose to seal off the city by closing all railroads and highways to West Germany. Their purpose was to drive the Western powers out of Berlin.

The Western allies responded to the Berlin Blockade with an airlift of supplies to the city that lasted almost a year. In May 1949 the Russians were forced to back down and to open access to Berlin. The incident greatly increased tensions and suspicions between the opponents. It hastened the separation of Germany into two states, a situation that prevailed for forty years. West Germany formally became the German Federal Republic in September 1949, and the eastern region became the German Democratic Republic a month later.

Berlin Airlift. The Allied airlift in action during the Berlin Blockade. Every day for almost a year Western planes supplied the city until Stalin lifted the blockade in May 1949. *Bildarchiv Preussischer Kulturbesitz.*

NATO and the Warsaw Pact

Meanwhile, the nations of Western Europe had been coming closer together. The Marshall Plan encouraged international cooperation. In March 1948 Belgium, the Netherlands, Luxembourg, France, and Britain signed the Treaty of Brussels, providing for cooperation in economic and military matters. In April 1949 these nations joined Italy, Denmark, Norway, Portugal, and Iceland to sign a treaty with Canada and the United States that formed the North Atlantic Treaty Organization (NATO). NATO committed its members to mutual assistance in case any of them was attacked. For the first time in history the United States committed itself to defend allies outside the Western Hemisphere. NATO formed the West into a bloc. A few years later West Germany, Greece, and Turkey joined the alliance (see Map 32–1).

Soviet relations with the states of Eastern Europe were governed by a series of bilateral treaties providing for close ties and mutual assistance in case of attack. In 1949 the Council of Mutual Assistance (COMECON) was formed to integrate the economies of these states. Unlike the NATO states, the Eastern alliance system was under direct Soviet domination through local communist parties controlled from Moscow and overawed by the presence of the Red Army. The Warsaw Pact of May 1955, which included Albania, Bulgaria, Czechoslovakia, East Germany, Hungary, Poland, Romania, and the Soviet Union, merely gave formal recognition to a system that already existed. Europe stood divided into two unfriendly blocs.

In 1953 Stalin died; later that year an armistice was concluded in Korea (see Chapter 33). Both events produced hope that international tensions might lessen, but the rivalry of power and polemics soon resumed.

Crises of 1956

The events of 1956 had considerable significance both for the Cold War and for what they implied about the realities of European power in the postwar era.

Suez In July 1956 President Gamal Abdel Nasser (1918–1970) of Egypt nationalized the Suez Canal. Great Britain and France feared that this action would close the canal to their supplies of oil in the Persian Gulf. In October 1956 war broke out between Egypt and Israel. The British

Map 32–1. Major Cold War European Alliance Systems. The North Atlantic Treaty Organization, which includes both Canada and the United States, stretches as far east as Turkey. By contrast, the Warsaw Pact nations were the contiguous communist states of Eastern Europe, with the Soviet Union, of course, as the dominant member.

and French seized the opportunity to intervene; however, the United States refused to support their action. The Soviet Union protested vehemently. The Anglo-French forces had to be withdrawn, and control of the canal remained with Egypt.

The Suez intervention proved that without the support of the United States the nations of Western Europe could no longer undertake meaningful military operations to impose their will on the rest of the world. It also appeared that the United States and the Soviet Union had restrained their allies from undertaking actions that might have resulted in a wider conflict. The fact that neither of the superpowers wanted war constrained both Egypt and the Anglo-French forces.

Poland The autumn of 1956 also saw important developments in Eastern Europe that demonstrated similar limitations on independent action among the Soviet bloc nations. When the prime minister of Poland died, the Polish Communist Party leaders refused to choose as his successor the person selected by Moscow. Considerable tension developed. The Soviet leaders even visited Warsaw to make their opinions known. In the end, Wladyslaw Gomulka (1905–1982) emerged as the new Communist leader of Poland. He was the choice of the Poles, and he proved acceptable to the Soviets because he promised continued economic and military cooperation and most particularly continued Polish membership in the Warsaw Pact. Within those limits he halted the collectivization of Polish agriculture and improved the relationship between the communist government and the Polish Roman Catholic Church.

Uprising in Hungary Hungary provided the second trouble spot for the Soviet Union. (See Document, "The Church and the Communist Party Clash over Education in Hungary.") In late October demonstrations of sympathy for the Poles occurred in Budapest. The Communist government moved to stop the demonstrations, and street fighting erupted. A new ministry headed by former premier Imre Nagy (1896–1958) was installed by the Hungarian Communist Party. Nagy was a Communist who sought a more independent position for Hungary. He went much further in his demands than Gomulka and directly appealed for political support from non-communist groups in Hungary. Nagy called for the removal of Soviet troops and the ultimate neutralization of Hungary. He even called for Hungarian withdrawal from the Warsaw Pact. These demands were wholly unacceptable to the Soviet Union. In early November Soviet troops invaded Hungary; deposed Nagy, who was later executed; and imposed Janos Kadar (1912–1989) as premier.

The Cold War Intensified

The events of 1956 ended the era of fully autonomous action by the European nation-states. In different ways and to differing degrees, the two superpowers had demonstrated the new political realities. After 1956 the Soviet Union began to talk about "peaceful coexistence" with the United States. In 1958 negotiations began between the two countries for limitations on the testing of nuclear weapons. However, in the same year the Soviet Union also announced that the status of West Berlin had to be changed and the Allied occupation forces withdrawn. The demand was refused. In 1959 tensions relaxed sufficiently for several Western leaders to visit Moscow and for Soviet Premier Nikita Khrushchev (1894–1971) to tour the United States. A summit meeting was scheduled for May 1960 in Paris, and American President Dwight D. Eisenhower (1890–1969) was to go to Moscow.

Just before the gathering, the Soviet Union shot down an American U-2 aircraft that was flying reconnaissance over Soviet territory. Khrushchev demanded an apology from

Chronology

Major Dates in the Era of the Cold War

1948	Berlin Blockade
1949	Formation of the North Atlantic Treaty Organization (NATO)
1950	Outbreak of the Korean War
1953	Death of Stalin
1956 July	Egypt seizes the Suez Canal
October	Anglo-French attack on the Suez Canal; Hungarian Revolution
1957	Treaty of Rome establishes the European Economic Community (EEC)
1960	Paris Summit Conference collapses
1961	Berlin Wall erected
1962	Cuban Missile Crisis
1963	Russian-American Test Ban Treaty
1968	Russian invasion of Czechoslovakia
1975	Helsinki Accords
1979	Russian invasion of Afghanistan
1981	Military crackdown on Solidarity Movement in Poland
1985	Reagan-Gorbachev summit
1987	Major American-Soviet Arms Limitation Treaty
1989	Berlin Wall comes down
1991	Soviet Union dissolves

The Church and the Communist Party Clash over Education in Hungary

Document

Throughout Eastern Europe, the Roman Catholic Church became one of the strongest opponents of the postwar Communist Party governments. It raised issues relating to church schools, free worship, participation in church-sponsored organizations, and the erection of new church buildings. One of the harshest clashes took place in Hungary. Following are two statements that illustrate the opposing positions of the church and the party. Cardinal Mindszenty (1892–1975) was later imprisoned and became one of the best-known political prisoners in Eastern Europe.

◆ How does Mindszenty relate the position of church-supported schools to the nature and rights of parenthood? How does he compare the actions of the Communist Party to those of Hitler? How does the Minister of Public Worship set party members against the church? How does he attempt to place loyalty to the party above private beliefs? What does the Communist Party fear from religious education and participation in religious activities on the part of its members and their children?

STATEMENT OF JOSEF CARDINAL MINDSZENTY, MAY 20, 1946

The right of the Church to have schools is entirely in concord with the right of parents to educate their children. What is incumbent upon the parents in all questions of natural life is incumbent upon the Church with regard to the supernatural life. Parents are prior to the state, and their rights were always and still are, acknowledged by the Church. The prerogative of parents to educate their children cannot be disputed by the state, since it is the parents who give life to the child. They feed the child and clothe it. The child's life is, as it were, the continuation of theirs. Hence it is their right to demand that their children are educated according to their faith and their religious outlook.

It is their right to withhold their children from schools where their religious convictions are not only disregarded but even made the object of contempt and ridicule. It was this parental right which German parents felt was violated when the Hitler government deprived them of their denominational schools. The children came home from the new schools like little heathens, who smiled derisively or laughed at the prayers of their parents.

You Hungarian parents will likewise feel a violation of your fundamental rights if your children can no longer attend the Catholic schools solely because the dictatorial State closes down our schools by a brutal edict or renders their work impossible.

STATEMENT OF THE HUNGARIAN COMMUNIST MINISTER OF PUBLIC WORSHIP, JUNE 7, 1950

We must start a vast work of enlightenment, and in the first place explain to our party colleagues and also to all workers that any father who sends his child to religion classes, places it in the hands of the enemy and entrusts his soul and thinking to the enemies of peace and imperialistic warmongers.

A part of our working people believes that participation of children in religious instruction is a private matter which has nothing to do with the political conviction of their parents. They are wrong. To send children to a reactionary pastor for religious instruction, is a political movement against the People's Democracy, whether intentional or not. . . .

In carrying out the basic principles, religion within the party is no private matter, but we must take a difference between plain party members and party officials, and must not in any case make party membership dependent on the fact whether our party members are religious. In the first place, we must expect from our party officials, our leading men, that they do not send their children to religious instruction courses, do not take part in religious ceremonies and train their wives in the spirit of communistic conception.

Also, we must patiently endeavor to enlighten our members, and ensure through training and propaganda that they realize; "In going to Church, taking part in processions, sending our children to religious instruction, we unconsciously further the efforts of clerical reaction."

From Colman J. Barry, O.S.B., *Readings in Church History* © 1965 by The Missionary Society of Saint Paul the Apostle in the State of New York. Used by permission of Paulist Press, Inc.

President Eisenhower, who accepted responsibility but refused to apologize. Khrushchev then refused to take part in the summit conference, and Eisenhower's trip to the Soviet Union was canceled.

The Soviet actions to destroy the possibility of the summit conference on the eve of its opening were not simply the result of the American spy flights. The Soviets had long been aware of the American flights but chose to protest at this time for two reasons. Khrushchev had hoped that the leaders of Britain, France, and the United States would be sufficiently divided over the future of Germany so that a united Allied front would be impossible. (The divisions did not come about as he had hoped.) Consequently, the conference would have been of little use to him. Second, by 1960 the communist world itself had become split between the Soviets and the Chinese. The latter accused the Russians of lacking revolutionary zeal. Khrushchev's action was, in part, a response to those charges and proof of the hard-line attitude of the Soviet Union towards the capitalist world.

The abortive Paris conference opened the most difficult period of the Cold War. In 1961 the new U.S. president, John F. Kennedy (1917–1963), and Premier Khrushchev met in Vienna. The conference was inconclusive, but Kennedy left wondering if the two nations could avoid war. Throughout 1961 thousands of refugees from East Germany had fled to West Berlin. This outflow was a political and economic embarrassment to East Germany. In August 1961 the East Germans erected a concrete wall along the border between East and West Berlin. Henceforth, until November 1989, it was possible to cross only at designated checkpoints and with proper papers.

A year later the Cuban Missile Crisis brought the most dangerous days of the Cold War. The Soviet Union placed missiles in Cuba, a nation friendly to Soviet aims lying less

Cuban Missile Crisis of 1962. The American ambassador to the United Nations displayed photographs to persuade the world of the threat to the United States less than one hundred miles from its own shores. *Corbis/Bettmann.*

than 100 miles from the United States. The United States blockaded Cuba, halted the shipment of new missiles, and demanded the removal of existing installations. After a tense week the Soviets backed down and the crisis ended.

Détente and Afterward

In 1963 the two powers concluded a Nuclear Test Ban Treaty. This agreement marked the start of a lessening in the sharp tensions between the United States and the Soviet Union that had commenced just after the end of World War II. In 1968 the Soviet Union invaded Czechoslovakia to block its

Soviet Invasion of Czechoslovakia. In the summer of 1968 Soviet tanks rolled into Czechoslovakia, ending that country's experiment in liberalized communism, known as the Prague spring. This picture shows defiant, flag-waving Czechs passing a Soviet tank in the immediate aftermath of the invasion. *Hulton Archive Photos/Getty Images, Inc.*

President Ronald Reagan and Premier Mikhail Gorbachev confer at a summit meeting in December 1989. *AP/Wide World Photos.*

sented the most significant agreement since World War II between the two superpowers.

Thereafter, the political upheavals in Eastern Europe and the Soviet Union overwhelmed the issues of the Cold War. The Soviet Union abandoned its support for communist governments in Eastern Europe. By the close of 1991 the Soviet Union itself had collapsed and been replaced by the Commonwealth of Independent States. The era of the Cold War had concluded in a manner that virtually no one had predicted.

European Society in the Second Half of the Twentieth Century and Beyond

The sharp division of Europe into a democratic West and communist East for most of the second half of the twentieth century makes generalizations about social and economic developments difficult. Prosperity in the West contrasted with shortages in the Eastern economies, which were managed to benefit the Soviet Union. Most of the developments discussed in this chapter took place in Western Europe.

Towards Western European Unification

Since 1945, the nations of Western Europe have taken unprecedented steps towards economic cooperation. The process of economic integration has not been steady, nor is it completed. The collapse of the Soviet Union and the emergence of new free governments in Eastern Europe have further complicated an already difficult process.

The Marshall Plan and NATO gave the involved countries new experience in working with each other and demonstrated the productivity, efficiency, and simple possibility of cooperative action. In 1950 France, West Germany, Italy, and the "Benelux" countries (Belgium, the Netherlands, and Luxembourg) organized the European Coal and Steel Community. Its success reduced the suspicions of government and business groups about the concept of coordination and economic integration.

It took more, however, to draw European leaders towards further unity. The unsuccessful Suez intervention and the resulting diplomatic isolation of France and Britain persuaded many Europeans that only through unified action could they significantly influence the two superpowers or control their own destinies. Consequently, in 1957, through the Treaty of Rome, the six members of the Coal and Steel Community agreed to form a new organization: the **European Economic Community**. The members of the Common Market, as the EEC soon came to be called, sought to achieve the eventual elimination of tariffs, a free flow of capital and labor, and similar wage and social benefits in all

growing independence and to overthrow the government of its relatively liberal leader, Alexander Dubcek (1921–1974). Although deplored by the United States, this action led to no renewal of tensions. During the presidency of Richard Nixon (1913–1994) the United States embarked on a policy of détente, or reduction of tension, with the Soviet Union. This policy involved trade agreements and mutual reduction of strategic armaments. The Soviet invasion of Afghanistan in 1979, although not directly affecting Europe, hardened relations between Washington and Moscow, and the U.S. Senate refused to ratify the Strategic Arms Limitation Treaty of 1979.

The administration of President Ronald Reagan (1911–2004) initially slowed arms limitation negotiations and successfully deployed a major new missile system in Europe. The United States also launched a new arms proposal, known as the Strategic Arms Defense Initiative, to create a system that would use highly developed technology in space to defend against nuclear attack. The proposal was controversial at home but played a major role in arms negotiations between the United States and the Soviet Union. One of the purposes of the Reagan arms buildup was simply to outspend the Soviet Union and force it to exhaust its own financial resources and continue to starve consumer industries.

President Reagan and Soviet leader Mikhail S. Gorbachev (b. 1931) held a friendly summit meeting in 1985, the first East-West summit in six years. Other meetings followed. Arms negotiations continued until, in December 1987, the United States and the Soviet Union agreed to dismantle over 2,000 medium- and shorter-range missiles. The treaty provided for mutual inspection. This action reprethe participating countries. The chief institutions of the EEC were a Council of Foreign Ministers and a High Commission composed of technocrats. The former came to be the dominant body.

The Common Market was a stunning success. By 1968 all tariffs among the six members had been abolished well ahead of the planned schedule. Trade and labor migration among the members grew steadily. Moreover, nonmember states began to copy the Community and seek membership. In 1959 Britain, Denmark, Norway, Sweden, Switzerland, Austria, and Portugal formed the European Free Trade Area. However, by 1961 Great Britain had decided to seek Common Market membership. Twice—in 1963 and 1967—France vetoed British membership on the grounds that Britain was too closely tied to the United States and its policies to support the EEC wholeheartedly.

Nevertheless, the Common Market survived and continued to prosper. In 1973 Great Britain, Ireland, and Denmark became members. Discussions continued on further steps towards integration, including proposals for a common currency. Throughout the late 1970s, however, and into the 1980s momentum slowed. Norway and Sweden, with relatively strong economies, declined to join. Although in 1982 Spain, Portugal, and Greece applied for membership and were eventually admitted, there continued to be sharp disagreements and a sense of stagnation within the Community.

Finally, the leaders of the Community reached an important decision in early 1988. They targeted the year 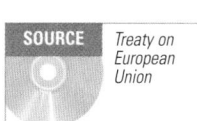 1992 for achieving a virtual free-trade zone throughout the Community, entailing the elimination of remaining trade barriers and other restrictive trade policies. In 1991 the leaders of the Community signed the Treaty of Maastricht, which made a series of specific institutional proposals that would lead to a unified currency and a strong central bank. This treaty was submitted to referendums in a number of European states. It failed to be adopted in Denmark and only narrowly passed in France, making clear that it could not be enforced without wider popular support. When the treaty went into effect in November 1993, the European Community was renamed the **European Union (EU)**.

The troubles of the Maastricht Treaty illustrate a new phase in the process of European unity. Until recently the process of establishing greater unity has been carried out primarily by political leaders and by bureaucrats in the individual governments and the Community High Commission in Brussels. As the prospect of unity becomes imminent, however, the people of Europe have begun to raise issues about the democratic nature of the emerging political entity they are being asked to join. They are clearly in favor of some kind of close cooperation and perhaps union, but they are unwilling to see it set forth only by politicians and bureaucrats. They wish to see a wider European market, but they want that market to be genuinely free and not overregulated. Finally, the European Community, now the European Union, has recently had to deal with how it should relate to the newly independent states in Eastern Europe.

The most striking recent element of the expanding momentum of economic cooperation was the adoption of a common currency, the **euro**. Twelve nations including Austria, Belgium, Finland, France, Germany, Greece, Ireland, Italy, Luxembourg, the Netherlands, Portugal, and Spain constitute the region using this new currency. In January 1, 1999, the currencies of these nations were fixed according to the value of the euro. In January 2002 the national currencies of these nations were replaced by new coins and notes denominated in the euro. Such a widespread common currency is unprecedented in European history.

In 2004 the European Union embraced the largest expansion in its history. Ten new members entered the Union. They were Cyprus, the Czech Republic, Estonia, Hungary, Latvia, Lithuania, Malta, Poland, Slovakia, and Slovenia (see Map 32–2). On one day the Union came to include an additional seventy-five million people with nine languages. This expansion will present enormous challenges because the economies in these nations, most of whom are from the former Eastern Soviet bloc, are much less developed. They come to the Union in hopes that membership will foster prosperity; their needs will place new political strains on the existing structures. They will be permitted to adopt the euro only when their economies have become sufficiently strong.

The Euro. Some thousand people stand around a huge euro symbol in a park in Frankfurt's banking district in Germany, January, 1, 1997. *AP/Wide World Photos.*

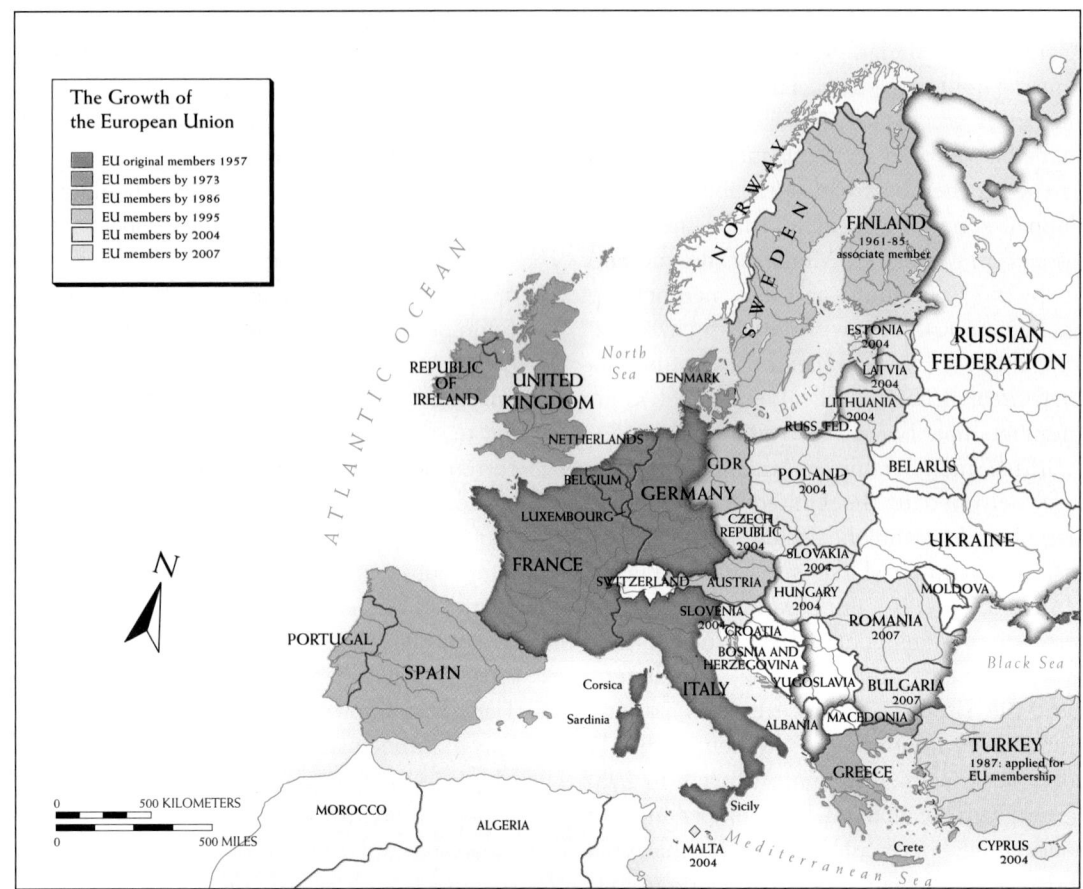

Map 32–2.   The Growth of the European Union. This map traces the growth of membership in the European Union from its founding in 1957 through the introduction of its newest members in 2004. Note that even though Turkey has applied for membership it has not yet been admitted.

The most public challenge that now faces and divides the nations of the European Union is the possible future admission of Turkey. Some European political leaders strongly favor this step when Turkey has achieved the economic and democratic structures requisite for European Union membership. Other leaders oppose future admission of Turkey, seeing Turkey as not having been historically a part of Europe. They are also apprehensive about the influence of Islamist political activity in Turkey. The debate over possible admission of Turkey serves as a proxy for debate over the future cultural and religious character of the Union itself. Religion has not been a major topic of discussion within the Union, but the possible admission of a nation with an overwhelmingly Islamic population has brought the issue to the fore.

Towards a Welfare State Society

The Great Depression, the rise of authoritarian states in the wake of economic dislocation and mass unemployment, and World War II, which involved more people in a war effort than ever before, changed how many Europeans thought

about social welfare. Governments began to spend more on social welfare than they did on the military. This reallocation of funds was a reaction to the state violence of the first half of the century and was possible because the NATO defense umbrella, which the United States primarily staffed and funded, protected Western Europe.

Creation of European Welfare States The modern European welfare state was broadly similar across the Continent. Before World War II, except in Scandinavia, the two basic models for social legislation were the German and the British. Bismarck had introduced social insurance in Germany during the 1880s to undermine the German Social Democratic Party. In effect, the imperial German government provided workers with social insurance and thus some sense of social security while denying them significant political participation. In early-twentieth-century Britain, where all classes had access to the political system, social insurance was targeted toward the poor. In both the German and British systems, workers were insured only against the risks from disease, injury on the job, and old age. Unemployment was assumed to be only a short-term problem and often one that workers brought on themselves. People higher in the social structure could look out for themselves and did not need government help.

After World War II, the concept emerged that social insurance against predictable risks was a social right and should be available to all citizens. In Britain, William B. Beveridge (1879–1963) famously set forth this concept in 1942. Paradoxically, making coverage universal, as Beveridge recommended, appealed to conservatives as well as socialists. If medical care, old-age pensions, and other benefits were available to all, they would not become a device to redistribute income from one part of the population to another.

The first major European nation to begin to create a welfare state was Britain, in 1945–1951 under the Labour Party ministry of Clement Attlee (1883–1967). The most important element of this early legislation was the creation of the National Health Service. France and Germany did not adopt similar health care legislation until the 1970s, because their governments initially refused to make coverage universal.

The spread of welfare legislation (including unemployment insurance) within Western Europe was related to both the Cold War and domestic political and economic policy. The communist states of Eastern Europe were promising their people social security as well as full employment. The capitalist states came to believe they had to provide similar security for their people, but, in fact, the social security of the communist states was often more rhetoric than reality.

Resistance to the Expansion of the Welfare State

Western European attitudes towards the welfare state have reflected three periods that have marked economic life since the end of the war. The first period was one of reconstruction from 1945 through the early 1950s. It was followed by the second period—almost twenty-five years of generally steady and expanding economic growth. The third period brought first an era of inflation in the late 1970s and then one of relatively low growth and high unemployment from the 1990s to the present. During each of the first two periods, a general conviction existed, based on Keynesian economics, that the foundation of economic policy was government involvement in a mixed economy. From the late 1970s, more people came to believe the market should be allowed to regulate itself and that government should be less involved in, though not completely withdraw from, the economy.

The most influential political figure in reasserting the importance of markets and resisting the power of labor unions was Margaret Thatcher (b. 1925) of the British Conservative Party who served as Prime Minister from 1979 to 1990. She cut taxes and sought to curb inflation. She and her party were determined to roll back many of the socialist policies that

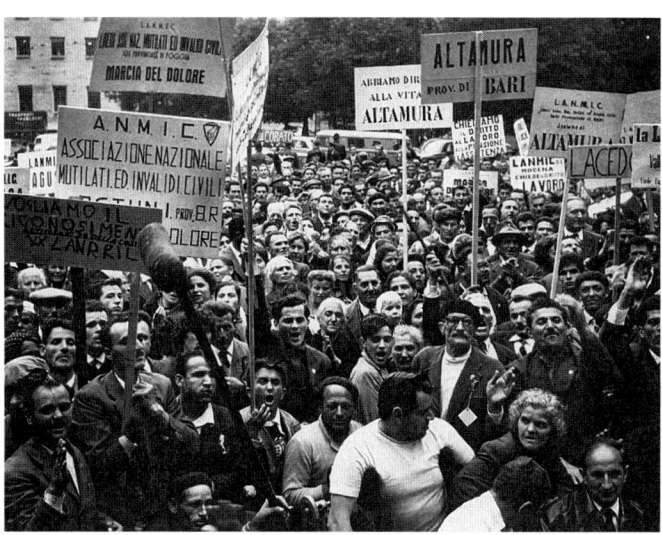

The March of Pain. Under the banner "The March of Pain," a crowd of angry protesters from the southern Italian city of Bari, members of an association for the handicapped, lobby for more government assistance. The demands of special interest groups on the welfare state increased dramatically in the sixties and seventies.

Britain had enacted since the war. Her administration privatized many industries that Labour Party governments had nationalized. She also curbed the power of the trade unions in a series of bitter and often violent confrontations. Her goal was to make the British economy more efficient and competitive. Although her administration roused enormous controversy, she was able to push these policies through Parliament. Furthermore, over time the British Labour Party itself largely came to accept what was at the time known as the Thatcher Revolution. (See Document, "Margaret Thatcher Asserts the Need for Individual Responsibility.")

While Thatcher redirected the British economy, the government-furnished welfare services now found across continental Europe began to encounter resistance. The funding on which they are based assumed a growing population and low unemployment. As the proportion of the population consuming the services of the welfare state—the sick, the injured, the unemployed, and the elderly—increases relative to the number of able-bodied workers who pay for them, the costs of those services have risen.

The leveling off of population growth in Europe discussed in the previous section has thus imperiled the benefits of the welfare state, which Europeans have come to take for granted. Furthermore, during the past two decades, significant levels of unemployment in major Western European nations have increased welfare payments. The low fertility rates across the Continent mean the next working generation will have fewer people to support the retired elderly population. Middle-class taxpayers have also become reluctant to support existing systems.

Margaret Thatcher Asserts the Need for Individual Responsibility

Document

No single European political figure so challenged and criticized the assumptions of the welfare state and of state intervention in general than Margaret Thatcher, British Prime Minister from 1979 to 1990. Known as the "Iron Lady," Thatcher repeatedly demanded that people take individual responsibility rather than rely on state-sponsored support. Yet her administration did not dismantle the key structures of the British welfare state.

◆ How and why does Thatcher contend that there is no such thing as society? Does she criticize all government aid to citizens? How does she emphasize the reciprocal character of social relationships? How does she argue in favor of personal and private charity to aid persons in need?

I think we have gone through a period when too many children and people have been given to understand "I have a problem, it is the Government's job to cope with it!" or "I have a problem, I will go and get a grant to cope with it!" "I am homeless, the Government must house me!. And so they are casting their problems on society, and who is society? There is no such thing! There are individual men and women and, there are families, and no government can do anything except through people. And people look to themselves first. It is our duty to look after ourselves and then also to help look after our neighbour. Life is a reciprocal business and people have got the entitlements too much in mind without the obligations, because there is no such thing as an entitlement unless someone has first met an obligation. And it is, I think, one of the tragedies that ... there are some people who have been manipulating the system and so some of those help and benefits that were meant to say to people: "All right, if you cannot get a job, you shall have a basic standard of living!" . . . [lead] people

[to] come and say: "But what is the point of working? I can get as much on the dole!" You say: "Look" It is not from the dole. It is your neighbour who is supplying it and if you can earn your own living then really you have a duty to do it and you will feel very much better!" There is also something else I should say to them: "If that does not give you a basic standard, you know, there are ways in which we top up the standard. You can get your housing benefit." But it went too far. If children have a problem, it is society that is at fault. There is no such thing as society. There is living tapestry of men and women and people, and the beauty of that tapestry and the quality of our lives will depend upon how much each of us is prepared to take responsibility for ourselves and each of us prepared to turn round and help by our own efforts those who are unfortunate.

This extract derives from a transcript of the original interview rather than the published text. Reprinted with permission from margaretthatcher.org, the official website of the Margaret Thatcher Foundation.

The general growth of confidence in the ability of market forces rather than government intervention to sustain social cohesion has also spread in the past twenty-five years and has raised questions about the existing welfare structures. Governments across the Continent, including those normally associated with left-of-center politics, such as the British Labour Party and the German Social Democratic Party, have limited further growth of the welfare state and have reduced benefits. In that respect, Europeans in the next few decades may look at the second half of the twentieth century as the Golden Age of welfare states and may find their own societies dealing with social welfare differently.

The Movement of Peoples

Many people migrated from, to, and within Europe during the half century following World War II.

External Migration In the decade and a half after 1945 approximately half a million Europeans each year settled elsewhere in the world. This was the largest outward migration since the 1920s, when the rate was approximately 700,000 persons annually. While the earlier migrants had mostly been from rural areas, the later migrants often included educated city dwellers.

Decolonization in the postwar period contributed to an inward flow of European colonials from overseas (see Chapter 34). The most dramatic example of this phenomenon was the more than 1 million French colonials who moved to France after the end of the Algerian War. British citizens returned from various parts of the British Empire; Dutch people came back to the Netherlands from Indonesia, and Portuguese returned from Africa.

Decolonization also provoked a migration of non-European inhabitants of the former colonies to Europe. Great Britain, for example, received thousands of immigrants from

India and Pakistan, as well as from its former African and Caribbean colonies. France received many immigrants from its former colonies in Indochina and the Arab world. This influx caused social tension and conflict. In Great Britain, for example, during the 1980s there were angry clashes between the police and non-European immigrants. France has had similar difficulties, which have contributed to the emergence there of the National Front, an extreme right-wing group led by Jean-Marie Le Pen (b. 1928). This group has drawn strength from the racial and ethnic tensions that have developed as a tight job market provokes resentment among some working-class voters towards North African immigrants.

As a result of this external migration into Europe, large Islamic populations now exist in several European nations and have become political factors in France and Germany.

Internal Migration World War II and its aftermath created a vast refugee problem. Millions of people were displaced from their homes. Many cities in Germany and in central and Eastern Europe had been bombed or overrun by invading armies. Hundreds of thousands of foreign workers had been moved into Germany to contribute to the war effort. There were thousands of prisoners of war. Some of these people were returned to their homeland willingly; others, unwillingly. Changes in borders after the war also caused many people to move or be moved. For example, Poland, Czechoslovakia, and Hungary sent millions of ethnic Germans to Germany. Hundreds of thousands of Poles left from territory taken over by the Soviet Union. An estimated 3 million East Germans migrated to West Germany (see Map 32–3).

Map 32–3.   Displaced Peoples in East and Central Europe, 1945–1950. World War II left millions of Europeans displaced. In an attempt to reestablish ethnic and linguistic uniformity within political boundaries, more than 31 million people were resettled between 1945 and 1952.

Once the Cold War set in, Soviet domination made it impossible for Eastern Europeans to migrate to other parts of Europe, whether for political or economic reasons. As a result, until the collapse of the Soviet empire, most internal migration in Europe after the immediate postwar years occurred outside the Communist bloc.

The major motivation for internal migration from the late 1950s onward was economic opportunity. The prosperous nations of northern and Western Europe had jobs that paid good wages and provided excellent benefits, often financed in part by the governments. Thus, there was a flow of workers from the poorer countries of Turkey, Greece, Yugoslavia, Italy, Spain, and Portugal into the wealthier countries of France, West Germany, Switzerland, and the Benelux nations. The establishment of the European Economic Community in 1957 facilitated this movement.

The migration of workers into northern Europe snowballed after 1960. Several hundred thousand workers entered France and Germany each year. Virtually all these migrants settled in cities. They were usually welcomed during years of prosperity and resented later when European economies began to slow in the mid-1980s. In Germany during the early 1990s, they were attacked.

In the late 1980s politics again became a major factor in European migration. The pressure of thousands of refugees seeking to escape from Eastern Europe to the West contributed to the collapse of the Communist governments of Eastern Europe in 1988 and 1989. Since 1989 people from all over Eastern Europe have migrated to the West. The civil war in the former Yugoslavia has also created many refugees. Europe has been in recession, however, and the new migrants are generating tension, resentment, and strife. Several nations have taken legal and administrative steps to restrict migration.

The New Muslim Population

Well into the twentieth century the European relationship with most of the Muslim world was either at arm's length or colonialist. Muslims from the Ottoman Empire, the greatest Muslim state, rarely traveled in Europe, and few Europeans traveled in the empire. Europeans encountered Muslims mainly as subjects, in colonies, such as Algeria, Egypt, the Indian subcontinent, sub-Saharan Africa, and the East Indies. In all of these regions from at least the mid–nineteenth century onward, Christian missionaries often clashed with Muslim religious teachers.

At the same time most Europeans, with the exception of a few minority communities in the Balkans and the former Soviet Empire, regarded themselves and their national cultures as either Christian or secular. Indeed, until recently most Europeans paid little attention to Islam.

That indifference began to change in the 1960s and had dissolved by the end of the twentieth century as a sizable Muslim population settled in Europe. This highly diverse immigrant community had become an issue in Europe even before the events of September 11, 2001, discussed later in this chapter.

The immigration of Muslims into Europe and particularly Western Europe arose from two chief sources: European economic growth and decolonization. As the economies of Western Europe began to recover in the quarter century after World War II, a labor shortage developed. To fill this demand, Western Europe imported laborers, many of whom came from Muslim nations. For example, Turkish "guest workers" were invited to move to West Germany—on a temporary basis, it was presumed—in the 1960s, and Britain welcomed Pakistanis. The aftermath of decolonization and the quest for a better life led Muslims from East Africa and the Indian subcontinent to settle in Great Britain. The Algerian war brought many Muslims from North Africa into France. Today there are approximately 1.3 million Muslims in Great Britain, 3.2 million in Germany, and 4.2 million in France. Smaller but still significant numbers have settled in Italy, Spain, Sweden, Denmark, and the Netherlands, nations that had previously had generally homogeneous populations.

These Muslim immigrant communities share certain social and religious characteristics. Originally, many Muslims came to Europe expecting they would eventually

Muslim Women Wearing Headscarves, France. The presence of foreign-born Muslims whose labor is necessary for the prosperity of the European economy is a major issue in contemporary Europe. Many of these Muslims, such as these women, live in self-contained communities. *Figaro Magazine/Torregano/Getty Images, Inc.*

return to their homes, an expectation their host countries shared. Neither the immigrants nor the host nations gave much thought to assimilation. Moreover, except for Great Britain, where all immigrants from the Commonwealth may vote immediately upon settling there, European governments made it difficult for Muslim, or any other, immigrants to take part in civic life. Unlike the United States, few European countries had any experience in dealing with large-scale immigration. The various Muslim communities have therefore generally remained unassimilated and self-contained. This apartness has provided internal community support for Muslim immigrants but prevented them from fully engaging with the societies in which they live. Many of their children have not learned European languages well, and Muslim women tend to remain strictly confined to their homes.

But the world around these communities has changed. Many of the largely unskilled jobs that the immigrants originally filled have disappeared. Most of the Muslim immigrants to Europe, unlike many who have settled in the United States and Canada, were nei-

SOURCE *Justin Vaïse, from "Veiled Meaning," 2004*

ther highly skilled nor professionally educated. As a result, they and their adult children who may have grown up in Europe find it difficult to get jobs in the modern service economy. Furthermore, as European economic growth has slowed, European Muslims have become the target of politicians, such as Le Pen in France, who seek to blame the immigrants for a host of problems, from crime to unemployment.

The radicalization of parts of the Islamic world has also touched the Muslim communities in Europe. Although Turkish Muslims living in Germany come from a nation that has been secularized since the 1920s and thus tend to be less religiously observant than Pakistani Muslims dwelling in Great Britain, Muslims from both countries have been involved in radical Islamic groups, and some belonged to organizations involved in the September 11, 2001, attack on the United States. By contrast, the French government has exerted more control over its Muslim community.

Nonetheless, European Muslims are not a homogeneous group. They come from different countries, have different class backgrounds, and espouse different Islamic traditions. Many European Muslims and Muslim clerics disagree strongly with each other. Some emphasize a more traditional message; others preach a more radical one that is highly critical of the West. At the same time, these Muslim communities so often now marked by deep poverty and unemployment have become a major concern for European social workers who disagree among themselves about how their governments should respond to them.

New Patterns in the Work and Expectations of Women

In the decades since World War II the work patterns and social expectations of women have changed markedly. In all social ranks women have begun to assume larger economic and political roles. Women have entered the learned professions and are filling more major managerial positions than ever before in European history. (See Document, "Simone de Beauvoir Urges Economic Freedom for Women.")

Feminism Certain more or less traditional patterns continue to describe the position of women in both family and economic life. Despite enormous gains during the second half of the twentieth century, and despite the collapse of those authoritarian governments whose social policies inhibited the advancement of women into the mainstream of society, gender inequality remained a major characteristic of the social life of Europe at the opening of the twenty-first century.

Since World War II, European feminism, although less highly organized than American feminism, has set forth a new agenda. The most widely read postwar work on women's issues was undoubtedly Simone de Beauvoir's (1908–1986) *The Second Sex*, published in 1949. In that work, de Beauvoir explored the difference being a woman rather than a man had made in her life. She was part of the French intellectual establishment and thus wrote from a privileged position. Over the years, however, she and other European feminists argued that at all levels, European women experienced distinct social and economic disadvantages. In the courts, for

Simone de Beauvoir, here with her companion, the philosopher Jean-Paul Sartre, was the major feminist writer in postwar Europe. *Getty Images Inc./Hulton Archive Photos.*

Simone de Beauvoir Urges Economic Freedom for Women

Document

Simone de Beauvoir was the single most important feminist voice of mid–twentieth-century Europe. In *The Second Sex*, published in France in 1949, she explored the experience of women coming of age in a world of ideas, institutions, and social expectations shaped historically by men. Much of the book discusses the psychological strategies that modern European women had developed to deal with their status as "the second sex." Towards the end of her book, de Beauvoir argues strongly that economic freedom and advancement for women are fundamental to their personal fulfillment.

◆ Why does de Beauvoir argue that the achievement of civic rights must be accompanied by economic freedom for women? Why does the example of the small number of professional women illustrate issues for European women in general? How does she indicate that even professional women must overcome a culture in which the experience of women is fundamentally different from that of men? Do de Beauvoir's comments seem relevant for women at the opening of the twenty-first century? What similarities do you see with the views of Priscilla Wakefield (Chapter 20) and Mary Wollstonecraft (Chapter 22)?

According to French law, obedience is no longer included among the duties of a wife, and each woman citizen has the right to vote; but these civil liberties remain theoretical as long as they are unaccompanied by economic freedom. . . . It is through gainful employment that woman has traversed most of the distance that separated her from the male; and nothing else can guarantee her liberty in practice. Once she ceases to be a parasite, the system based on her dependence crumbles; between her and the universe there is no longer any need for a masculine mediator. . . .

When she is productive, active, she regains her transcendence; in her projects she concretely affirms her status as subject; in connection with the aims she pursues, with the money and the rights she takes possession of, she makes trial of and senses her responsibility. . . .

There are . . . a fairly large number of privileged women who find in their professions a means of economic and social autonomy. These come to mind when one considers woman's possibilities and her future. . . . [E]ven though they constitute as yet only a minority; they continue to be the subject of debate between feminists and antifeminists. The latter assert that the emancipated women of today succeed in doing nothing of importance in the world and that furthermore they have difficulty in achieving their own inner equilibrium. The former exaggerate the results obtained by professional women and are blind to their inner confusion. There is no good reason. . . . to say they are on the wrong road; and still it is certain that they are not tranquilly installed in their new realm: as yet they are only halfway there. The woman who is economically emancipated from man is not for all that in a moral, social, and psychological situation identical with that of man. The way she carried on her profession and her devotion to it depends on the context supplied by the total pattern of her life. For when she begins her adult life she does not have behind her the same past as does a boy; she is not viewed by society in the same way; the universe presents itself to her in a different perspective. The fact of being a woman today poses peculiar problems for an independent human individual.

Simone de Beauvoir, *The Second Sex*, trans. by H. M. Parshley. Copyright 1952 and renewed 1980 by Alfred A. Knopf, Inc. Reprinted by permission of Alfred A. Knopf, a division of Random House Inc.

example, divorce and family laws favored men. European feminists also called attention to the social problems that women faced, including spousal abuse.

More Married Women in the Work Force The number of married women in the work force has risen sharply. Both middle-class and working-class married women have sought jobs outside the home. Because of the rather low birthrate in the 1930s, there were few young single women to be employed just after the war. Married women entered the job market to replace them. Some factories changed their work shifts to accommodate the needs of married women. Consumer conveniences and improvements in health care also made it easier for married women to enter the work force by reducing the demands of child care on their time.

In the twentieth century children were no longer expected to make substantial contributions to family income. They spent much of their time in compulsory schools. When families needed more income than one worker can provide, both parents worked. Even without financial necessity, both parents were now likely to work when both were motivated to pursue careers.

New Work Patterns   In the late twentieth century the work pattern of European women displayed much more continuity than it did in the nineteenth century. Single women entered the work force after their schooling and continued to work after marriage. They might withdraw from the work force to care for young children but return when the children begin school. Several factors created this new pattern, but women's increasing life expectancy is one of the most important.

When married women died relatively young, child rearing filled much of their lives. The lengthening life-span has meant that child rearing occupies much less of women's lives.

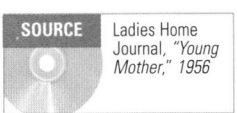

SOURCE   Ladies Home Journal, "Young Mother," 1956

Consequently, women throughout the Western world have new concerns about how they will spend those years when they are not involved with rearing children. The age at which women have decided to bear children has risen. Women have tended to bear children in their early twenties in Eastern Europe and in their late twenties in Western Europe. In urban areas, childbearing occurs later and the birthrate is lower than elsewhere.

Many women have begun to limit sharply the number of children they bear or to forgo childbearing and child rearing altogether. Both men and women continue to expect to marry, but the new careers open to women and the desire of couples to maintain as high a standard of living as possible have contributed to a declining birthrate.

Women in the New Eastern Europe   Many paradoxes surround the situation of women in Eastern Europe now that it is no longer governed by Communists. Under communism women generally enjoyed social equality as well as a broad spectrum of government-financed benefits. A significant proportion (normally well over 50 percent) of women worked in these societies both because they could and because it was expected of them. There were, however, no significant women's movements since they, like all independent associations, were frowned on.

The new governments of the region are free but have so far shown little concern toward women's issues. The economic difficulties the new governments face may endanger the funding of various health and welfare programs that benefit women and children. For example, a free market economy may not allow Eastern European women the extensive maternity benefits they used to enjoy. Moreover, the high proportion of women in the work force could leave them more vulnerable than men to the region's economic troubles. Women may well find themselves being laid off before men and hired for new jobs later than men.

American Domestic Scene Since World War II

Three major themes have characterized the postwar American experience—an opposition to the spread of communism, an expansion of civil rights to blacks and other minorities at home, and a determination to achieve ongoing economic growth. Virtually all of the major postwar political debates and social divisions have arisen from these issues.

Truman and Eisenhower Administrations

The foreign policy of President Harry Truman was directed against communist expansion in Europe and East Asia. He enunciated the Truman Doctrine in regard to Greece and Turkey and initiated the Marshall Plan for European reconstruction. As will be discussed more fully in Chapter 33 he led the United States to support the UN intervention against aggression in Korea. Domestically, the Truman administration pursued what may be regarded as a continuation of the New Deal. However, Truman encountered considerable opposition from conservative Republicans. The major achievement of those Republicans was the passage in 1947 of the Taft-Hartley Act, which limited labor union activity. Truman won the 1948 election against great odds. Through policies he termed the Fair Deal, he sought to extend economic security.

Those efforts, however, were frustrated as fear of a domestic communist menace swept much of the country.

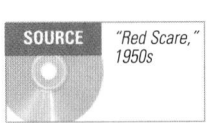

SOURCE   "Red Scare," 1950s

Senator Joseph McCarthy (1909–1957) of Wisconsin led the campaign against the perceived communist danger within the ranks of American citizens and government agencies. The patriotism and loyalty of scores of prominent Americans were challenged. That development, a frustration with the war in Korea, and perhaps the natural weariness of the electorate after twenty years of Democratic Party government led to the election of war hero Dwight Eisenhower in 1952.

In retrospect, the Eisenhower years now seem a period of calm after the war years of the 1940s and before the turmoil of the 1960s. Eisenhower, personally popular, ended the Korean War. The country was generally prosperous. Home building increased dramatically, and the vast interstate highway system was initiated. The president was less activist than either Roosevelt or Truman had been.

Beneath the apparent quiet of the Eisenhower years, however, stirred several forces that would lead to the disruptions of the 1960s. One of them flowed from the injustices of segregation and racial inequality. Another flowed from the long-term implications of some of the major foreign policy commitments the Eisenhower administration made in its effort to oppose the advance of communism. One of those commitments led to American involvement in Vietnam; indeed, that involvement began under Eisenhower.

Civil Rights

In 1954 the United States Supreme Court, in the decision of *Brown v. Board of Education of Topeka*, declared unconstitutional the segregation of the black and white races. Shortly thereafter the Court ordered the desegregation of schools. For the next ten years the struggle over school integration and civil rights for black Americans stirred the nation. Southern states attempted to resist school desegregation. In 1957 Eisenhower sent troops into Little Rock, Arkansas, to integrate the schools, but resistance continued in other Southern states.

While the battle raged over the schools, American blacks began to protest segregation in other areas. In 1955 the Reverend Martin Luther King Jr. (1929–1968) organized a boycott in Montgomery, Alabama, against segregated buses. The Montgomery bus boycott marked the beginning

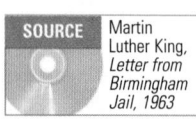 **SOURCE** Martin Luther King, *Letter from Birmingham Jail, 1963*

of the use of civil disobedience to fight racial discrimination in the United States. Drawing on the ideas of Henry David Thoreau (1817–1862) and the experience of Mohandas Gandhi (1869–1948) in India, the leaders of the civil rights movement went to jail rather than obey laws they considered unjust. The civil rights struggle continued well into the 1960s. One of its most dramatic moments was the 1963 march on Washington by tens of thousands of supporters of civil rights legislation. The greatest achievements of the movement were the Civil Rights Act of 1964, which desegregated public accommodations, and the Voting Rights Act of 1965, which cleared the way for black Americans to vote. This legislation as well as ongoing protests against housing and job discrimination brought black citizens nearer to the mainstream of American life than they had ever been.

Martin Luther King Jr., pictured here with his wife Coretta, was the most prominent civil rights leader in the United States. Here he leads a protest march in 1965. *Battmann-Corbis.*

However, much yet remained undone. In 1967 major race riots occurred in several American cities, resulting in significant loss of life. Those riots, followed by the assassination of Martin Luther King Jr., in 1968, weakened the civil rights movement. Despite new efforts to fight discrimination, the movement lacked a major national leader. Not until the late 1980s did a new leader emerge in the person of the Reverend Jesse Jackson (b. 1941), who raised new issues of racial equality and promoted drives that led to the registration of many black voters. There was, however, little follow-up to this campaign.

Race relations continue to plague the social life of the United States. Although black Americans have more access to education and public office, especially in urban areas, they lag behind other Americans economically and in their prospects for good health. Furthermore, as other groups, particularly Latino Americans, began to enter the political process in the 1980s and raise issues on behalf of their own communities, racial relations became more complicated. In 1992 one of the most destructive riots in American history—triggered by a court decision relating to the treatment of black Americans by the police—devastated parts of Los Angeles.

New Social Programs

The advance of the civil rights movement in the late 1950s and early 1960s represented the cutting edge of a new advance of political liberalism. In 1960 John F. Kennedy narrowly won the presidential election. He saw himself as attempting to set the country moving again after the years of Eisenhower torpor. Kennedy defined his aims as seeking to move towards a New Frontier. One goal was to put a man on the moon. He also attempted unsuccessfully to expand medical care under the social security program. In the civil rights movement, however, he basically reacted rather than led.

Nevertheless, the reaction to Kennedy's assassination in 1963 provided the occasion for his successor, Lyndon Johnson (1908–1973), to press for activist legislation. Johnson set forth a bold domestic program known as the War on Poverty, which established major federal programs to create jobs and provide job training. Furthermore, new entitlements were added to the social security program, including Medicare, which provides medical services for the elderly and disabled. Johnson's drive for what he termed the Great Society brought to a close the era of major federal initiatives that had begun under Franklin Roosevelt. The liberal impulse remained alive in American politics, but by the late 1960s the electorate had begun to become much more conservative.

The Vietnam War and Domestic Turmoil

Johnson's activist domestic vision quickly was overshadowed by the U.S. involvement in Vietnam (to be considered more fully in Chapter 33). By 1965 Johnson had decided to send tens of thousands of Americans to Vietnam. This policy led to the longest of American wars. At home, the war and particularly the draft provoked vast public protests. Most young American men who were drafted went into the armed forces, but significant numbers, especially college and university students, resisted. Large-scale protests involving civil disobedience, often patterned after those of the civil rights movement, erupted on campuses throughout the country. In some cases units of the National Guard were sent to restore calm. At Kent State University in Ohio in 1970 the National Guard killed four protestors. In all these respects, the Vietnam War divided the nation as had no conflict since the Civil War.

The national unrest led Lyndon Johnson to decide not to seek reelection in 1968. Richard Nixon led the Republicans

Kent State Protest. The clash between protesting students and the Ohio National Guard at Kent State University was the most violent moment in the protests against the U.S. involvement in Vietnam. *AP/Wide World Photos.*

to victory. His election marked the beginning of an era of American politics dominated by conservative policies. Nixon campaigned on a platform of law and order. He also stressed his former experience in foreign policy as vice president (under Eisenhower). Perhaps the most important act of his administration was his reestablishment of diplomatic relations with the People's Republic of China. Initially, Nixon's policies towards Vietnam were no more successful than those of Johnson. Half of the casualties in the war occurred under his administration. Nonetheless, he concluded the war in 1972. That same year he was reelected, but soon thereafter the Watergate scandal began to erode his administration.

The Watergate Scandal

On the surface, the Watergate scandal involved only the burglary of the Democratic Party national headquarters by White House operatives in 1972. The deeper issues related to questions of the extent of presidential authority and the right of the government to intrude into the personal lives of citizens. In 1973 Congress established a committee to investigate the scandal. Testimony before that committee revealed that President Nixon had recorded conversations in the White House. The Special Prosecutor, who had been appointed to investigate the charges, finally gained access to the tapes in the summer of 1974 through a decision of the Supreme Court. In the meantime the Judiciary Committee of the House of Representatives voted three articles of impeachment against Nixon. Shortly thereafter, some of the newly released tapes revealed that Nixon had ordered federal agencies to try to cover up White House participation in the burglary. After this revelation, Nixon became the only American president to resign.

The Watergate scandal further shook public confidence in the government. It was also a distraction from the major problems facing the country, especially inflation, which had resulted from fighting the war in Vietnam while expanding federal domestic expenditures. The subsequent administrations of Gerald Ford (1974–1977, b. 1913) and Jimmy Carter (1977–1981, b. 1924) battled inflation and high interest rates without significant success. Furthermore, the Carter administration became bogged down in the Iran hostage crisis of 1980 after Iranians took more than forty Americans hostage and held them for over a year.

The Triumph of Political Conservatism

In 1980 Ronald Reagan was elected president by a large majority and reelected four years later. Reagan was the first fully ideological conservative to be elected in the postwar era. Reagan sought to reduce the role of the federal government in American life. The chief vehicle to this end was a major tax cut and reform of the taxation system. The consequence of America's vastly increased defense spending and the tax policy was the largest fiscal deficit in American history. However, inflation was controlled, and the American economy experienced its longest peacetime expansion.

The straightforward conservatism of the Reagan administration proved offensive to many Americans who had traditionally supported a liberal political and social agenda. His policies were regarded as hostile to blacks and women. High officials were involved in scandals, particularly the sale of arms to Iran in exchange for the promised release of American hostages in Lebanon. Despite these difficulties, Reagan left office as probably the most popular and successful of the post–World War II American presidents.

In 1988 Vice President (under Reagan) George Bush (b. 1924) was elected to succeed Reagan. He was immediately confronted by the major changes that Gorbachev was carrying out in the Soviet Union and the extraordinary transformations occurring in Eastern Europe that are discussed later in this chapter. Bush kept the NATO alliance strong and close to the United States at a time when observers had begun to question its utility. In 1989 he sent troops into Panama to oust its dictator, Manuel Noriega (b. 1940). In the summer of 1990, in response to the invasion of Kuwait by Iraq, he initiated the largest mobilization of American troops since the Vietnam War. Using the United Nations, he forged a broad worldwide coalition against Iraq's aggression. In early 1991 the coalition launched Operation Desert Storm and forced Iraq out of Kuwait.

The victory in the Persian Gulf War was the high point of the Bush presidency. Thereafter, he stumbled in the face of the serious economic problems confronting the nation. In 1992 the Democratic nominee, Governor William Clinton (b. 1946) of Arkansas, won the election.

The Clinton presidency encountered difficulties almost from the beginning. During his first two years in office he tried to bring about a dramatic change in health care finance and delivery. This effort ultimately failed and left the Clinton presidency with a reputation for being poorly managed.

In 1994, in one of the most far-reaching changes in recent American politics, the Republican Party won majorities in both houses of Congress. The new Republican-controlled Congress undertook major changes in the funding of welfare, taxation, and government regulation. This Congress continued the conservative redirection of federal policy that had begun with the election of Ronald Reagan.

The presidential election of 1996 saw the reelection of President Clinton and of a Republican-dominated Congress and Senate. Scandals plagued both parties. The House of Representatives censured and fined Newt Gingrich, the Speaker of the House. A personal sexual scandal and allegations of perjury plagued President Clinton during 1998, although the Republicans lost seats in the House of Representatives in that year's election. In the wake of the election loss, Gingrich resigned from the House, and President Clinton was impeached. He was acquitted in early 1999 by the Senate. In terms of policy, Clinton was seen as moving the Democractic Party into a more conservative stance.

The presidential election of 2000 between Texas governor George W. Bush (the son of the former president) and Vice President Al Gore was the closest in modern American history. Gore won a majority of the popular vote but failed to win a majority in the electoral college. The pivotal electoral votes depended on which candidate carried Florida, where the final vote count was disputed for more than a month after the November election. After complicated legal disputes over how, or indeed whether, to recount the Florida vote, the U.S. Supreme Court voted 5 to 4 to halt the recount, which resulted in Bush being declared the winner in Florida and thus in the presidential election as well.

On September 11, 2001, a surprise terrorist attack on New York City and Washington, D.C., transformed the political life of the United States. As the nation rallied to respond, a period of remarkable bipartisan cooperation followed. In October 2001, the United States began a war against terrorism with air attacks against terrorist positions in Afghanistan.

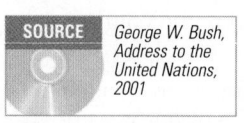
SOURCE   George W. Bush, Address to the United Nations, 2001

U.S. forces also attacked the forces of the extremist Islamic Taliban regime in Afghanistan, which had tolerated the presence of Islamic terrorists within the part of Afghanistan that was under its control. In 2003 as a second step in the response to the terrorist threat the United States invaded Iraq, an event fully discussed in the last section of this chapter and in Chapter 34.

In 2004 President Bush successfully overcame the challenge of Democratic candidate John Kerry to achieve reelection with a majority of both the popular and electoral college vote. In the subsequent congressional elections of 2006 the Democratic Party regained control of both houses of Congress in an election fought out largely over the American intervention in Iraq.

The Soviet Union to 1989

The Soviet Union emerged from World War II as a major world power, but Stalin did little or nothing to modify the repressive regime he had fostered. The police remained ever present. The cult of personality around Stalin expanded, and the central bureaucracy continued to grow. Heavy industry was still favored in place of production for consumers. Agriculture continued to be troubled. Stalin's personal authority over the party and the nation remained unchallenged. In foreign policy he solidified Soviet control over Eastern Europe for the purposes of both Communist expansion and Soviet national security. The Soviet army assured subservience to the goals of the Soviet Union. Such continued to be the situation until Stalin died on March 6, 1953.

The Khrushchev Years

No single leader immediately replaced Stalin, but by 1956 Nikita Khrushchev became premier, remaining in that position until 1964. He never enjoyed the extraordinary powers of Stalin.

In 1956, at the Twentieth Congress of the Communist Party, Khrushchev made a secret speech (later published outside the Soviet Union) in which he denounced Stalin and his crimes against Socialist justice during the purges of the 1930. (See Document, "Khrushchev Denounces the Crimes of Stalin: The Secret Speech.") The speech caused shock and consternation in party circles and opened the way for limited, but genuine, internal criticism of the Soviet government. By 1958 all of Stalin's former supporters were gone, but none had been executed.

Under Khrushchev, intellectuals were somewhat freer to express their opinions. This so-called thaw in the cultural life of the country was closely related to the premier's interest in the opinions of experts on problems of industry and agriculture. He often went outside the usual bureaucratic

The Kitchen Debate. One of the most famous incidents of the Cold War was a spontaneous debate between Nikita Khrushchev and Vice President Richard Nixon at a trade fair in Moscow. Because it took place at a display of kitchen appliances, it was sometimes called the Kitchen Debate. *Elliott Erwitt/Magnum Photos, Inc.*

channels in search of information and new ideas. Novels such as Aleksandr Solzhenitsyn's (b. 1918) *One Day in the Life of Ivan Denisovich* (1963) could be published. However, Boris Pasternak (1890–1960), the author of *Dr. Zhivago*, was not permitted to accept the Nobel Prize for literature in 1958. The intellectual liberalization of Soviet life during this period looked favorable largely in comparison with what had preceded it and continued to seem so later when freedom of expression declined again in the two decades after Khrushchev's fall.

In economic policy Khrushchev made moderate efforts to decentralize economic planning and execution. During the late 1950s he often boasted that Soviet production of consumer goods would overtake that of the West. Steel, oil, and electric power production continued to grow, but the consumer sector including housing improved only marginally. The ever-growing defense budget and the space program that successfully launched the first human-engineered earth satellite, *Sputnik*, in 1957 made major demands on the nation's productive resources.

Khrushchev strongly redirected Stalin's agricultural policy. He recognized that despite the collectivization of the

SOURCE *Soviet Collective, 1950s*

1930s the Soviet Union could not feed its own people. Khrushchev removed many of the most restrictive regulations on private cultivation. The machine-tractor stations were abandoned. Existing collective farms were further amalgamated. The government undertook an extensive "virgin lands" program to extend wheat cultivation by hundreds of thousands of acres. This policy initially

Khrushchev Denounces the Crimes of Stalin: The Secret Speech

Document

In 1956 Khrushchev denounced Stalin in a secret speech to the Party Congress. *The New York Times* published a text of that speech smuggled from Russia.

◆ What are the specific actions on the part of Stalin that Khrushchev denounced? Why does Khrushchev pay so much attention to Stalin's creation of the concept of an "enemy of the people"? Why does Khrushchev draw a distinction between the actions of Stalin and those of Lenin?

Stalin acted not through persuasion, explanation, and patient cooperation with people, but by imposing his concepts and demanding absolute submission to his opinion. Whoever opposed this concept or tried to prove his viewpoint and the correctness of his position was doomed to removal from the leading collective [group] and to subsequent moral and physical annihilation. . . .

Stalin originated the concept of "enemy of the people." This term automatically rendered it unnecessary that the ideological errors of a man or men engaged in a controversy be proved; this term made possible the usage of the most cruel repression violating all norms of revolutionary legality, against anyone who in any way disagreed with Stalin, against those who were only suspected of hostile intent, against those who had bad reputations.

This concept "enemy of the people" actually eliminated the possibility of any kind of ideological fight or the making of one's views known on this or that issue, even those of a practical character. In the main, and in actuality, the only proof of guilt used, against all norms of current legal science, was the "confession" of the accused himself; and, as a subsequent probing proved, "confessions" were acquired through physical pressures against the accused. . . .

Lenin used severe methods only in the most necessary cases, when the exploiting classes were still in existence and were vigorously opposing the revolution, when the struggle for survival was decidedly assuming the sharpest forms, even including civil war.

Stalin, on the other hand, used extreme methods and mass repressions at a time when the revolution was already victorious, when the Soviet State was strengthened, when the exploiting classes were already liquidated and Socialist relations were rooted solidly in all phases of national economy, when our party was politically consolidated and had strengthened itself both numerically and ideologically. It is clear that here Stalin showed in a whole series of cases his intolerance, his brutality and his abuse of power. Instead of proving his political correctness and mobilizing the masses, he often chose the path of repression and physical annihilation, not only against actual enemies, but also against individuals who had not committed any crimes against the party and the Soviet Government. . . .

---

increased grain production to new records. The applied farming techniques, however, proved inappropriate for the soil, and the new lands soon underwent severe erosion. The agricultural problem continued to grow over the decades. By the 1970s the Soviet Union imported vast quantities of grain from the United States and other countries. United States grain imports constituted a major facet of the policy of détente.

By 1964 high Communist Party leaders and many people lower in the party had concluded that Khrushchev had tried to do too much too soon and had done it too poorly. His foreign policy, culminating in the backdown over the Cuban Missile Crisis, appeared a failure. On October 16, 1964, after defeat in the Central Committee of the

Communist Party, Khrushchev resigned. Leonid Brezhnev (1906–1982) eventually emerged as his successor.

Brezhnev

Domestically the Soviet government became markedly more repressive after 1964. Intellectuals enjoyed less and less freedom and had little direct access to the government leadership. In 1974 the government expelled Solzhenitsyn. Jewish citizens of the Soviet Union were harassed. Bureaucratic obstacles impeded emigration to Israel.

The internal repression gave rise to a dissident movement. Certain Soviet citizens dared to criticize the regime in public and to carry out small demonstrations against it. They accused the Soviet government of violating the human rights provisions of the 1975 Helsinki Accords. The dissidents included prominent citizens, such as the Nobel Prize–winning physicist Andrei Sakharov (1921–1989). The Soviet government responded with further repression.

In foreign policy the Brezhnev years witnessed attempts both to reach accommodation with the United States and to continue to expand Soviet influence and maintain Soviet leadership of the communist movement. Nonetheless, growing Soviet spending on defense, and particularly on naval expansion, put ongoing pressures on the consumer side of the economy.

In December 1979 the Soviet Union invaded Afghanistan. A Soviet presence had already existed in that country, but for reasons that still remain unclear, the Soviet government felt required to send in troops to ensure its influence in Central Asia. The Afghanistan invasion, in addition to exacerbating tensions with the United States, tied the hands of the Soviet government in its own sphere of influence in Eastern Europe. There seems little doubt that the Soviet hesitation to react more strongly to events in Poland during the 1980s, which are discussed in "Communism and Solidarity in Poland," stemmed in part from having committed military resources to Afghanistan and from the broad condemnation the invasion provoked from some Western European Communist Parties and from the governments of nations not aligned with the West. The Soviet government also clearly lost internal support as its army became bogged down and suffered steady losses.

Communism and Solidarity in Poland

In early July 1980 the Polish government raised meat prices. The result was hundreds of protest strikes across the country. On August 14 workers occupied the Lenin shipyard at Gdansk. The strike soon spread to other shipyards, transport facilities, and factories connected with the shipbuilding industry. The most important leader to emerge from among the strikers was Lech Walesa (b. 1944). The strike leaders refused to negotiate with the government through any of the government-controlled unions. The Gdansk strike ended on August 31 after the government promised the workers the right to organize an independent union. Less than a week later the Polish communist head of state was replaced; later that year the Polish courts recognized Solidarity as an independent union, and the state-controlled radio—for the first time in thirty years—broadcast a Roman Catholic Mass.

In the summer of 1981, for the first time in any European communist state, secret elections for the Polish

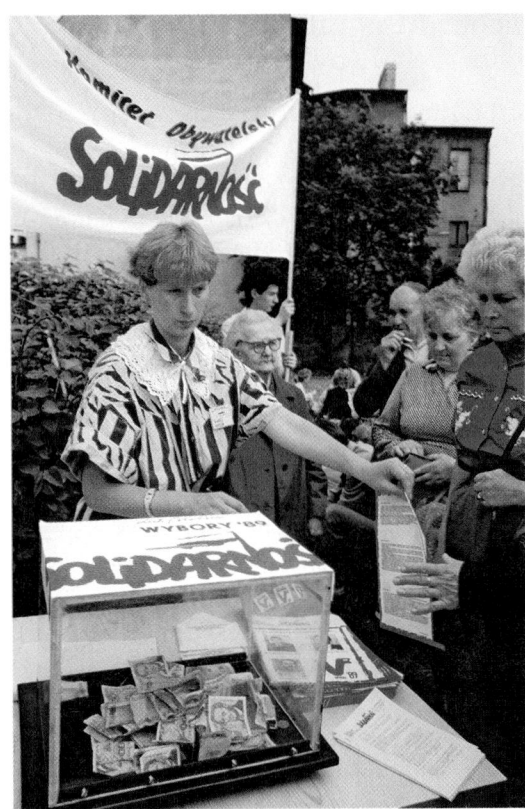

The Polish Trade Union "Solidarity" in 1989 successfully forced the Polish Communist government to hold free elections. In June of that year Solidarity, whose members here are collecting funds for their campaign, won overwhelmingly. *Bernard Bisson/CORBIS/Bettmann.*

party congress permitted real choices among the candidates. Poland remained a nation governed by a single party, but real debate was temporarily permitted within the party congress. This extraordinary Polish experiment came to a rapid close in late 1981. General Wojciech Jaruzelski (b. 1923) became head of the party, and the army moved into the center of Polish events. In December 1981 martial law was declared. The government arrested several Solidarity leaders. Martial law would continue until late in the 1980s.

By the time of Brezhnev's death in 1982, the entire Soviet system had grown rigid and seemed hardly capable of meeting the needs of its people or pursuing a successful foreign policy. Until the middle of the 1980s, however, no observers expected rapid change in the Soviet Union or its satellites. The nations of Eastern Europe were expected to continue with one-party governments, their aspirations for self-determination smothered, and only limited possibilities for independent political action. What had lasted forty years, it was assumed, would endure into the future. No one anticipated the vast changes that were imminent.

Gorbachev Attempts to Redirect the Soviet Union

Both of Brezhnev's immediate successors, Yuri Andropov (1914–1984) and Constantin Chernenko (1911–1985), died after holding office for short periods. In 1985 Mikhail S. Gorbachev (b. 1931) came to power. In what proved to be the last great attempt to reform the Soviet system and eliminate its repressive Stalinist heritage, he immediately set about making the most remarkable changes that the Soviet Union had witnessed since the 1920s. His reforms unloosed forces that within seven years would force him to retire and end both communist rule and the Soviet Union as it had existed since the Bolshevik Revolution of 1917.

Initially, Gorbachev and his supporters challenged the way the party and bureaucracy had traditionally managed the Soviet government and economy. Under the policy of **perestroika**, or restructuring, they proposed major economic and political reforms. The centralized economic ministries were reduced in size. A larger role was allowed for private enterprise on the local level. By early 1990, in a clear abandonment of traditional Marxist ideology, Gorbachev had begun to advocate private ownership of property. He and his advisers considered policies to liberalize the economy and move it rapidly towards a free market. Despite these organizational changes the Soviet economy, instead of growing, stagnated and even declined. Shortages of food, consumer goods, and housing became chronic. In a pattern that has continued to characterize Russian political life, old-fashioned Communists blamed these results on the abandonment of centralized planning. Democratic critics blamed overly slow reform and urged a more rapid move to a free market economy.

Gorbachev also allowed, within the Soviet context, an extraordinarily broad public discussion and criticism of Soviet history and Soviet Communist Party policy. This development was termed **glasnost**, or openness. Certain communist figures from the 1920s, such as Bukharin (1888–1938), who had been executed by Stalin, once again received official public recognition for their positive contributions to Soviet history. Within factories, workers were permitted to criticize party officials and the economic plans of the party and the government. Censorship was relaxed and free expression encouraged. Dissidents were released from prison. In the summer of 1988 Gorbachev presided over a party congress that witnessed full debates. In 1988 a new constitution permitted openly contested elections. After real political campaigning, a novel experience for the Soviet Union, the Congress of People's Deputies was elected in 1989 and then formally elected Gorbachev as president.

The Soviet Union was a vast empire of diverse peoples and nationalities. Some of those groups had been conquered under the tsars; others, such as the Baltic states, had been incorporated into the Soviet Union under Stalin. Glasnost quickly brought to the fore the discontents of all such peoples, no matter how or when they had been incorporated into the Soviet state. Gorbachev proved particularly inept in addressing these ethnic complaints.

1989: Year of Revolutions in Eastern Europe

In 1989 Soviet domination and communist rule in Eastern Europe came to an abrupt end. None of these revolutions could have taken place without the refusal of the Soviet Union to intervene militarily as it had done in 1956 and 1968. For the first time since the end of World War II the peoples of Eastern Europe could shape their own political destiny without the almost certain military intervention of the Soviet Union. Once they realized the Soviets would stand back, thousands of ordinary citizens denounced Communist Party domination and asserted their desire for democracy.

The generally peaceful character of most of these revolutions was not inevitable. It may, in part, have resulted from the shock with which much of the world responded to the violent repression of prodemocracy protesters in Beijing's Tienanmen Square by the People's

Statue of Lenin. The collapse of Communist Party governments in Eastern Europe and the Soviet Union was the most important political event of the closing years of the twentieth century. It was accompanied by the destruction of the public symbols of those governments. Throughout the region gigantic statues of Communist Party leaders were torn down. Here, Hungarians explore a toppled statue of Lenin.

Republic of China in the late spring of 1989. The Communist Party officials of Eastern Europe and the Soviet Union clearly decided at some point in 1989 that they could not offend world opinion with a similar attack on democratic demonstrators.

Solidarity Reemerges in Poland

During the mid-1980s, Poland's government relaxed martial law. By 1984 several leaders of Solidarity had been released from prison and began again to work for free trade unions and democratic government. An active underground press and several new dissenting political organizations emerged. Poland's economy continued to deteriorate, demonstrating the inability of communist governments to deliver economic growth and prosperity.

During 1987 the government released the last of its Solidarity prisoners in a sweeping amnesty. In 1988 new strikes occurred that even the leaders of Solidarity had not anticipated. This time the communist government failed to reimpose control. Solidarity was legalized.

Jaruzelski, with the tacit consent of the Soviet Union, repealed martial law and promised free elections to a parliament with increased powers. When elections were held in 1989, the Communists lost overwhelmingly to Solidarity candidates. Late in the summer Jaruzelski, unable to find a Communist who could forge a majority coalition in parliament, turned to Solidarity. On August 24, 1989, after negotiating with Lech Walesa, Jaruzelski named Tadeusz Mazowiecki (b. 1927) the first non-Communist prime minister of Poland since 1945. The appointment was made with the express approval of Gorbachev.

Hungary Moves Towards Independence

Hungary had for some time shown the greatest national economic independence of the Soviet Union in Eastern Europe. The Hungarian government had emphasized the production of food and consumer goods. It had also permitted a small stock exchange. In early 1989, as events unfolded in Poland, the Hungarian communist government began to take other independent actions. In January its parliament permitted independent political parties. Soon thereafter the government permitted free travel between Hungary and Austria, opening the first breach in the Iron Curtain. Thousands of East Germans then moved into Austria through Hungary. From Austria they went to West Germany.

In May 1989 Premier Janos Kadar (1912–1989), who had been installed after the Soviet intervention in 1956, was voted from office by the parliament. Thousands of people

The Fall of the Berlin Wall. The most dramatic moment in the weeks of the collapse of communist regimes in Eastern Europe occurred in November 1989 when crowds destroyed the Berlin Wall, the most prominent symbol of the Cold War divisions in Europe. *A. Avarkian/Time Life Pictures/Getty Images, Inc.*

gave an honorary burial to the body of Imre Nagy, who had been executed in 1958. The Hungarian Communist Party changed its name to the Socialist Party and permitted the emergence of other opposition political parties. In October, Hungary promised free elections. By 1990 a coalition of democratic parties controlled the Parliament and governed the country.

The Breach of the Berlin Wall and German Reunification

In the autumn of 1989 popular demonstrations erupted in many East German cities. The most important occurred in Leipzig. The streets filled with people demanding democracy and an end to Communist Party rule.

Gorbachev told the leaders of the East German Communist Party that the Soviet Union would no longer support them. With startling swiftness, the communist leaders of the East German government resigned, making way for a younger generation of Communist Party leaders. These new leaders, who remained in office for just weeks, promised political and economic reform. They convinced few East Germans, however, and the emigration to the West continued. In November 1989, in one of the most emotional moments in European history since 1945, the government of East Germany ordered the opening of the Berlin Wall. Tens of thousands of East Berliners crossed into West Berlin to celebrate, to visit families, and to shop with money provided by the West German government. Shortly thereafter, free travel began between East and

West Germany. By early 1990 the communist government of East Germany, after failing to reorganize itself, had been swept away in free elections.

The revolution in East Germany had broad ramifications for international relations. The citizens of the two Germanies were determined to reunify. With the collapse of Communist Party government in East Germany, there was no longer a viable distinction between them. Late in 1989 the ministers of the European Economic Community accepted in principle the unification of Germany. By February 1990 reunification had become a foregone conclusion, accepted by the United States, the Soviet Union, Great Britain, and France.

SOURCE *Helmut Kohl, speech to the American Council of Germany, 1990*

The Velvet Revolution in Czechoslovakia

Late in 1989, in "the velvet revolution," communist rule in Czechoslovakia quickly unraveled. In November, under popular pressure from street demonstrations and well-organized political opposition, the Communist Party began to retreat from office. The patterns were similar to those occurring elsewhere. The old leadership resigned, and younger Communists replaced them. The changes they offered were inadequate.

The popular new Czech leader who led the forces against the party was Václav Havel (b. 1936), a playwright and philosopher of international standing whom the government had frequently imprisoned. Havel and the group he represented, which called itself Civic Forum, negotiated changes with the government. These included an end to the political dominance of the Communist Party (which had been written into the constitution), inclusion of non-Communists in the government, elimination of traditional Marxist education, removal of travel restrictions, and relaxation of censorship.

Early in December the tottering communist government admitted that the invasion of 1968 had been a mistake. The Soviet Union and other Warsaw Pact states did likewise. Shortly thereafter Civic Forum succeeded in forcing the resignation of Gustav Husak (b. 1913), who had been president of Czechoslovakia since 1968, and in guaranteeing a free election for his successor. In late December 1989 Havel was elected president.

Violent Revolution in Romania

The most violent upheaval of 1989 occurred in Romania, where President Nicolae Ceausescu (1918–1989) had governed without opposition for almost a quarter century.

Romania was a one-party state with total centralized economic planning. Ceausescu, who had been at odds with the Soviet government for some time, maintained his Stalinist regime in the face of Gorbachev's reforms. He was supported by an army and a security force loyal to him. He had also placed his closest relatives in major political positions where they personally profited through corrupt practices.

On December 15 troubles erupted in the city of Timisoara in western Romania. The security forces sought to arrest a clergyman who had tried to protect the rights of ethnic Hungarians within Romania's borders. Over the next two days the Romanian security forces fired on demonstrators in Timisoara. Casualties ran into at least the hundreds. A few days later demonstrators in Bucharest publicly shouted against Ceausescu at a major rally, and by December 22 the city was in full revolt. Fighting, with many casualties, broke out between the army, which supported the revolution, and the security forces loyal to Ceausescu. The revolutionaries gained control of the television station and broadcast reports of the spreading revolution. Ceausescu and his wife attempted to flee the country but were captured, tried, and executed by firing squad on December 25. His death ended the shooting between the army and security forces. The provisional government in Bucharest announced that the first free elections since the end of World War II would take place in the spring of 1990.

The Collapse of the Soviet Union

Gorbachev clearly believed, as shown by his behavior towards Eastern Europe in 1989, that the Soviet Union could no longer afford to support communist governments in that region or intervene to uphold their authority. He was beginning to advance a similar view of the nature of the authority of the Communist Party within the Soviet Union.

Renunciation of Communist Political Monopoly

In early 1990 Gorbachev formally proposed to the Central Committee of the Soviet Communist Party that the party abandon its monopoly of power. (See Document "Gorbachev Proposes that the Soviet Communist Party Abandon Its Monopoly of Power.") After intense debate the Committee adopted his proposal, abandoning the Leninist position that only a single elite party could act as the vanguard of the revolution and forge a new Soviet society.

Gorbachev Proposes That the Soviet Communist Party Abandon Its Monopoly of Power

On February 5, 1990, President Mikhail Gorbachev proposed to the Central Committee of the Soviet Communist Party that it abandon its position as the single legal party as provided in Article 6 of the Soviet constitution. His proposal followed similar actions by several of the Communist Parties of Eastern Europe. From the time of Lenin through Brezhnev, the Soviet Communist Party portrayed itself as the sole vanguard of the revolution. Gorbachev argued that it should abandon that special role and compete for political power with other political parties. Within two years, the party was no longer in power, Gorbachev had resigned, and the Soviet Union no longer existed.

◆ Why did Gorbachev argue that the Soviet Communist Party must reform itself? To what extent did his speech call for the abandonment of traditional Communist Party goals? How did he think the Soviet Communist Party could function in a pluralistic political system?

The main thing that now worries Communists and all citizens of the country is the fate of *perestroika*, the fate of the country and the role of the Soviet Communist Party at the current, probably most crucial, stage of revolutionary transformation.

[It is important to understand. . . that the party will only be able to fulfill the mission of political vanguard if it drastically restructures itself, masters the art of political work in the present conditions and succeeds in cooperating with forces committed to *perestroika*.

The crux of the party's renewal is the need to get rid of everything that tied it to the authoritarian–bureaucratic system, a system that left its mark not only on methods of work and inter-relationships within the party, but also on ideology, ways of thinking and notions of socialism.

The [newly proposed] platform says: our ideal is a humane, democratic socialism, expressing the interests of the working class and all working people; and relying on the great legacy of Marx, Engels and Lenin, the Soviet Communist Party is creatively developing socialist ideals to match present-day realities and with due account for the entire experience of the 20th century.

The platform states clearly what we should abandon. We should abandon the ideological dogmatism that became ingrained during past decades, outdated stereotypes in domestic policy and outmoded views on the

world revolutionary process and world development as a whole.

We should abandon everything that led to the isolation of socialist countries from the mainstream of world civilization. We should abandon the understanding of progress as a permanent confrontation with a socially different world. . . .

The party's renewal presupposes a fundamental change in its relations with state and economic bodies and the abandonment of the practice of commanding them and substituting for their functions.

The party in a renewing of society can exist and play its role as vanguard only as a democratically recognized force. This means that its status should not be imposed through constitutional endorsement.

The Soviet Communist Party, it goes without saying, intends to struggle for the status of the ruling party. But it will do so strictly within the framework of the democratic process by giving up any legal and political advantages, offering its program and defending it in discussions, cooperating with other social and political forces, always working amidst the masses, living by their interests and their needs.

Gorbachev confronted challenges from three major political forces by 1990. One consisted of those groups—considered conservative in the Soviet context—whose members wanted to maintain the influence of the Communist Party and the Soviet army. They were deeply

disturbed by the country's economic stagnation and political and social disorder. They still appeared to control significant groups in the economy and society. During late 1990 and early 1991 Gorbachev, who himself seems to have been disturbed by the nation's turmoil, began to appoint members of these factions to key positions in the government. In other words, Gorbachev seemed to be making a strategic retreat. He apparently believed that only these more conservative forces would give him the support he needed.

Gorbachev made this calculation because he was now facing opposition from members of a second group, those who wanted much more extensive and rapid change. Their leading spokesman was Boris Yeltsin (1931–2007). He and those supporting him wanted to move quickly to a market economy and a more democratic government. Like Gorbachev, Yeltsin had risen through the Communist Party and then become disillusioned with its policies. Throughout the late 1980s he had been critical of Gorbachev. In 1990 he was elected president of the Russian Republic, the largest and most important of the Soviet Union's constituent republics. In the new political climate, that position gave him a firm political base from which to challenge Gorbachev's authority and increase his own.

The third force was regional unrest. Some of the republics of the Soviet Union had experienced considerable discontent in the past, but it had been repressed by the military or the Communist Party. Initially, the greatest unrest came from the three Baltic republics of Estonia, Latvia, and Lithuania.

During 1989 and 1990 the parliaments of the Baltic republics tried to increase their independence, and Lithuania actually declared independence. Discontent also arose in the Soviet Islamic republics in Central Asia. Riots broke out in Azerbaijan and Tajikistan. Throughout 1990 and 1991 Gorbachev sought to negotiate new constitutional arrangements between the republics and the central government. His failure to do so may have been the most important reason for the rapid collapse of the Soviet Union.

The August 1991 Coup

The turning point in all of these events came in August 1991 when the conservative forces that Gorbachev had brought into the government attempted a coup. Armed forces occupied Moscow, and Gorbachev himself was placed under house arrest while on vacation in the Crimea. The forces of political and economic reaction—led by people who, at the time, were associated with Gorbachev—had at last attempted to seize control. Boris Yeltsin denounced the coup and asked the world to help maintain the Soviet Union's movement towards democracy.

Within two days the coup collapsed. Gorbachev returned to Moscow, but in humiliation, having been victimized by the groups to whom he had turned for support. One of the largest public demonstrations in Russian history, perhaps the largest, celebrated the failure of the coup in Moscow. From that point

on, Yeltsin steadily became the dominant political figure in the nation. In the months immediately after the coup the Communist Party, compromised by its participation in the coup, totally collapsed. The constitutional arrangements between the central government and the individual republics were revised. On December 25, 1991, the Soviet Union ceased to exist, Gorbachev left office, and the Commonwealth of Independent States came into being (see Map 32–4).

The Yeltsin Years

As president of Russia, Boris Yeltsin was the head of the largest and most powerful of the new states. His popularity was high both in Russia and in the Commonwealth in 1992, but by 1993 he faced serious economic and political problems. Opposition to Yeltsin personally and to his economic and political reforms grew in the Russian parliament. Its members were mostly former Communists who wanted to slow or halt the movement towards reform. The impasse between the president and the parliament crippled the government. In September 1993 Yeltsin suspended parliament, which responded by deposing him. Parliament's leaders tried to provoke popular uprisings against Yeltsin in Moscow. The military, however, backed Yeltsin and eventually surrounded the parliament building with troops and tanks. On October 4, 1993, after pro-parliament rioters rampaged through Moscow, Yeltsin ordered the tanks to attack the parliament building, crushing the revolt.

These actions temporarily consolidated Yeltsin's position and authority. The major Western powers, deeply concerned by the turmoil in Russia, supported him. The crushing of parliament left Yeltsin far more dependent than before on the military, and the country's continuing economic problems bred unrest. In the December elections, for example, radical nationalists openly intolerant of non-Russian ethnic groups and advocating rebuilding Russia's empire made an uncomfortably strong showing, nearly capturing more seats in the new parliament than supporters of Yeltsin. In 1994 the central government found itself at war in the province of Chechnya, a conflict from which the central government eventually emerged as the loser. This conflict demonstrated the very limited capacity of the government to exercise its authority when faced with significant resistance.

The parliamentary elections of late 1995 saw the Communist Party reassert its political presence as it achieved control of over one-third of the seats in the Russian parliament. The communist leadership claimed that it did not intend to return to its former authoritarian ways. The parliamentary elections represented a major rebuff to the Yeltsin government, which had become increasingly

Map 32–4.   The Commonwealth of Independent States. In December 1991 the Soviet Union broke up into its fifteen constituent republics. Eleven of these were loosely joined in the Commonwealth of Independent States. Also shown is the autonomous region of Chechnya, which has waged two bloody wars with Russia in the last decade.

unpopular. Yet by very deft political actions, Yeltsin defeated the Communist Party candidate for the presidency in the summer of 1996.

Thereafter Russian politics remained highly confused. President Yeltsin, who suffered from poor health, faced steady opposition in the Russian parliament. The economic life of the nation remained stagnant at best. In 1998 Russia defaulted on its debt payments. Political assassinations occurred. The economic downturn contributed to further political unrest. In the face of these problems, Yeltsin resigned the presidency just as the new century opened. His resignation made the premier, Vladimir Putin, acting president. Putin was elected president in his own right in March 2001. Putin renewed the war against the rebels in Chechnya, which not only resulted in heavy casualties and enormous destruction there, but also strengthened Putin's political support in Russia itself. After the terrorist

attacks on the United States, Putin extended cooperation with the American assault on Afghanistan largely because the Russian government was afraid that Islamic extremism would spread beyond Chechnya to other regions in Russia and to the largely Muslim nations that bordered Russia in Central Asia and the Caucasus.

The Chechen war spawned one of the major acts of recent terrorism. In September 2004, a group of Chechens captured an elementary school in Beslan, a community in the Russian republic of North Ossetia (in the north Caucasus), on the opening day of the term. Approximately 1,200 students, teachers, and parents were held hostage for several days. When government troops stormed the school, approximately 330 of the hostages were killed.

In the wake of this event and as part of his determination that the central Russian government would dominate the

Chechnya. A Chechen fighter points his rifle at the head of a Russian prisoner of war outside the Chechen capital Grozny in August 1996. *AP/Wide World Photos.*

economy and political life, Putin has pursued policies of strong governmental centralization. Power has been taken away from local political units and placed in the hands of central government. The central government has also moved against citizens who have accumulated great wealth in the past decade. Overall it must be concluded that the future of democratic processes faces great difficulty in Russia. At the same time that the power of the central government in Russia grows, there have been tensions between Russia and the United States. Putin is particularly apprehensive over the growth of NATO on the eastern borders of Russia and the implicit growth of American influence there, most especially in Poland. Further tensions with the United States arise as the new nations that were once part of the old Soviet Union seek greater independence from Russia and friendship with the United States. Resolution of stability in the Middle East, particularly in relationship to Iraq and Iran, also present another arena of tension between the United States and Russia.

The Collapse of Yugoslavia and Civil War

Yugoslavia was created after World War I. Its borders included six major national groups—Serbs, Croats, Slovenes, Montenegrins, Macedonians, and Bosnians (Muslims)—among whom there have been ethnic disputes for centuries (see Map 32–5). The Croats and Slovenes are Roman Catholic and use the Latin alphabet. The Serbs, Montenegrins, and Macedonians are Eastern Orthodox and use the Cyrillic alphabet. The Bosnians are Islamic. Most members

of each group reside in a region with which they are associated historically—Serbia, Croatia, Slovenia, Montenegro, Macedonia, and Bosnia-Herzegovina—and these regions formerly constituted individual republics within Yugoslavia. Many Serbs, however, lived outside Serbia proper.

Yugoslavia's first communist leader, Marshal Tito (1892–1980), had acted independently of Stalin in the late 1940s and pursued his own foreign policy. He succeeded in muting ethnic differences by encouraging a cult of personality around him and by complex political power sharing. After his death serious economic difficulties undermined the authority of the central government, and Yugoslavia gradually dissolved into civil war.

In the late 1980s the old ethnic differences came to the fore again in Yugoslav politics. Nationalist leaders—most notably Slobodan Milošević (b. 1941) in Serbia and Franjo Tudjman (b. 1922) in Croatia—gained increasing authority. The Serbs contended that Serbia did not exercise sufficient influence in Yugoslavia and that Serbs living in Yugoslavia, but outside Serbia, encountered systematic discrimination, especially from Croats. Ethnic tension and violence soon resulted. During the summer of 1990, in the wake of the changes in the former Soviet bloc nations, Slovenia and Croatia declared independence from the central Yugoslav government and were soon recognized by several European nations, including, most importantly, Germany. Recognition from the full European community soon followed.

From this point on, violence escalated steadily. Serbia—concerned about Serbs living in Croatia and about the loss of lands and resources there—was determined to maintain a unitary Yugoslav state that it would dominate. Croatia was equally determined to secure independence. Croatian Serbs demanded safeguards against discrimination and violence, providing the Serbian army with a pretext to move against Croatia. By June 1991 full-fledged war had erupted between the two republics. Serbia accused Croatia of reviving fascism, while Croatia accused Serbia of maintaining a Stalinist regime. At its core, however, the conflict was ethnic; as such, it highlighted the potential for violent ethnic conflict within the former Soviet Union.

The conflict took a new turn in 1992 as Croatian and Serbian forces determined to divide Bosnia-Herzegovina. The Muslims in Bosnia—who had lived alongside Serbs and Croats for generations—soon became crushed between the opposing forces. The Serbs in particular, pursuing a policy called "ethnic cleansing," a euphemism redolent of some of the worst horrors of World War II, killed or forcibly moved many Bosnian Muslims.

More than any other single event, the unremitting bombardment of Sarajevo, the capital of Bosnia-Herzegovina,

Map Exploration

To explore this map further, go to http://www.prenhall.com/craig_maps

AUSTRIA

HUNGARY

ROMANIA

Ljubljana
SLOVENIA
Zagreb

CROATIA

Vojvodina

Vukovar
Novi Sad

Banja Luka

Belgrade

**BOSNIA AND
HERZEGOVINA**

SERBIA

Split
Sarajevo

Montenegro

Podgorica

Pristina
Kosovo

ITALY

BULGARIA

Skopje

Adriatic Sea

ALBANIA
MACEDONIA

GREECE

100 MILES
100 KILOMETERS

Legend:
- Albanian
- Bulgarian
- Croat
- Hungarian
- Macedonian
- No Majority Present
- Montenegrin
- Muslim
- Serb
- Slovak
- Slovene

Map 32–5. Ethnic Composition in the Former Yugoslavia. The rapid changes in Eastern Europe during the close of the 1980s intensified longstanding ethnic tensions in the former Yugoslavia. This map shows where Yugoslavia's ethnic population lived in 1991, before internal conflicts escalated.

brought the violence of the Yugoslav civil war to the attention of the world. The United Nations attempted unsuccessfully to mediate the conflict and imposed sanctions, which had little influence. Early in 1994, however, a shell exploded in the marketplace in Sarajevo, killing dozens of people. Thereafter, NATO forced the Serbs to withdraw their artillery from around Sarajevo.

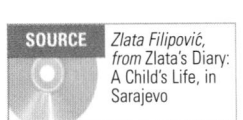

SOURCE *Zlata Filipović, from Zlata's Diary: A Child's Life, in Sarajevo*

The events of the civil war came to a head in 1995 when NATO forces carried out strategic air strikes. Later that year under the leadership of the United States, the leaders of the warring forces completed a peace agreement in Dayton, Ohio. The agreement was of great complexity but recognized an independent Bosnia. The terms of the agreement

have been enforced by the presence of NATO troops, including many from the United States.

In the late 1990s Serbian aggression against ethnic Albanians in the province of Kosovo again provoked a NATO response. For months the world watched as the Serbian military drove Albanians from Kosovo where the Albanians constituted the majority of the population. Casualties, atrocities, and deaths were daily occurrences. These tactics resembled those that had been used earlier in the decade in Bosnia. In early 1999 NATO intervened and launched an air attack against the Serbian forces that was the largest military action in Europe since the close of World War II. Belgrade was repeatedly bombed. As a result, the Serbian army withdrew from Kosovo, and NATO ground forces entered the province to protect the ethnic Albanians.

Destruction of Sarajevo. An elderly parishioner walks through the ruins of St. Mary's Roman Catholic Church in Sarajevo. The church was destroyed by Serb shelling in May 1992. *Reuters/Corbis-Bettmann.*

In 2000 a revolution overthrew the regime of Slobodan Milošević, and the new Yugoslav government handed him over in June 2001 to the International War Crimes Tribunal at the Hague for trial as a war criminal (Milošević died in prison in 2006 of natural causes).

Challenges to the Atlantic Alliance

Challenges on the International Security Front

NATO has continued to exist following the collapse of the Soviet Union and has moved to expand its membership to include Poland, the Czech Republic, and Hungary. Yet the exact present purpose of NATO remains ill defined. Although initially taking a reluctant role in settling the civil war in the former Yugoslavia, NATO eventually attempted to assume the role of internal peacekeeper in the new Europe. The role was not welcomed by all NATO members or the broad European publics.

The sense of drift in the purpose of NATO and the inward-looking tendency of continental Europe manifested itself in new and unexpected ways after the September 11, 2001, attacks by al Qaeda on the United States. Initially Europeans deeply sympathized with the tragedy and loss of life experienced by Americans. After all many Europeans as well as many other non-Americans died in the collapse of the Twin Towers. NATO aircraft patrolled the skies of the United States. Not long thereafter, however, a significant

split developed as the United States government of President George W. Bush responded to the terrorist assault.

The September 11 attacks on the United States transformed and redirected American foreign policy into what the administration of President George W. Bush termed "a war on terrorism." In late 2001, the United States attacked the Taliban government of Afghanistan, rapidly overthrowing it. The defeat of the Taliban destroyed al Qaeda's Afghan bases, but not its leadership, which appears to have survived, although it was dispersed and remains in hiding.

Following the Afghan campaign, the Bush administration set forth a policy of preemptive strikes and intervention against potential enemies of the United States. The administration argued that the danger of weapons of mass destruction—then believed to have been developed by governments such as that of Iraq—falling into the hands of international terrorist organizations posed so severe a danger to the security of the United States that the nation could not wait to respond to an attack but must stand prepared to take preemptive action. This argument, which aroused controversy both at home and abroad, marked a major departure from previous United States foreign policy.

The sharpest and thus far most lasting division arose in the months immediately before and after the American invasion of Iraq in 2003. The American invasion, which will be discussed more fully in Chapter 34, received the support of

Chronology

The Breakup of Yugoslavia

1991 June	Slovenia declares independence
	Croatia declares independence
1992 January	Macedonia declares independence
April	Serbia and Montenegro proclaim a new Federal Republic of Yugoslavia
April	War erupts in Bosnia and Herzegovina after Muslims and Croats vote for independence
1995 November	Peace agreement reached in Dayton, Ohio
1998 March	War breaks out in Kosovo, a province of Serbia
1999 March	NATO bombing of Serbia begins
2000	Milošević Regime overthrown

numerous European governments including most notably the United Kingdom, Italy, Poland, Bulgaria, and Spain. Other traditional European allies of the United States, however, most particularly, France and Germany, sharply criticized American decision making and actions. Popular political opinon across Europe dissented vocally from American policy.

Once the invasion had been carried out and the occupation commenced, terrorists struck in Europe itself. On March 11, 2004, at least 190 people were killed in commuter train bombings in Madrid, Spain. The Madrid bombings were the largest act of terrorism against civilians in Europe since World War II. The al Qaeda–sponsored attack demonstrated that such terrorist attacks can directly influence European political processes. The terrorist attack occurred just before the Spanish election, in which the Spanish government, which had supported the American invasion of Iraq, was voted from office. The new Spanish government announced that it would withdraw Spanish troops from the conflict.

In the years following the American invasion of Iraq profound divisions have arisen between the United States and many of its historic postwar allies. Many Europeans see

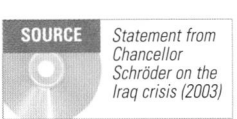
SOURCE Statement from Chancellor Schröder on the Iraq crisis (2003)

themselves, their values, and their emerging political community as different from Americans and their values and political community. The long-term relationship will no doubt be worked through on many issues beyond the immediate one of Iraq. More than likely, external events and the wider conflict between the West and radical political Islam will be the determining factors characterizing the Atlantic alliance, as was the division between a democractic West and a communist Eastern block in the past.

Strains over Environmental Policy

Commencing in the 1960s and growing in intensity over the past two decades significant concern has arisen in all the major industrialized countries over the impact of economic development on the environment. This concern has involved issues of pollution of water from industrial and urban waste and the pollution of the atmosphere from the emissions of hydro-carbons set loose in the air by industrial plants and the ever-growing number of automobiles and other vehicles using internal combustion engines as well as coal-burning utility plants and other industrial sites. One result of this new interest in the environment has been the rise of politically active environmental movements around the world. Some of these have worked within the existing political system; others have taken more radical courses of

Terrorist Bombing Madrid. Police search for clues from the debris of one of the trains destroyed in the terrorist attack of March 11, 2004. *AP/Wide World Photos.*

action including ecological terrorism, sabotage, and confrontation with police at major meetings of world leaders, particularly at the G-8 Summit meetings.

Environmental issues have proved divisive within the industrial democracies. Environmental activist groups and environmental political parties have urged action in various areas of concern. Other political groups have sought either slower action or little action on the grounds that addressing the threats to the environment may halt economic growth.

During the past decade the political tensions arising from environmentalism have begun to impinge upon international relations. The chief issue in debate has been the emission of what are termed "greenhouse gases," which the scientific community has concluded is raising the temperature of the planet in such a way as to have a major negative impact around the globe.

In 1997 various members of the United Nations signed the Kyoto Protocol on Climate Change. This treaty set

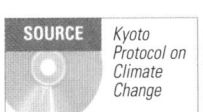
SOURCE Kyoto Protocol on Climate Change

specific mandatory goals for the reduction of the emission of greenhouse gases in the most developed industrial countries against 1990 benchmarks. Those gases include carbon dioxide, methane, hydrofluorocarbons, and sulphur hexafluoride among others. The Kyoto Protocol received the support of numerous major nations including Japan, Russia, and the European Union and became binding on its signatories in 2005. Whether the various targets that have been set by the treaty and by subsequent statements of various governments will be able to do so or not remains to be seen. Some developing nations have actually been permitted to increase their emissions.

A British Newspaper Editorial Criticizes American Environmental Policies

Document

In 2001 the United States government, under the leadership of President George W. Bush, withdrew from the Kyoto environment accords of 1997 that had been reached under United Nations sponsorship. This led to much strain between the U.S. and its partners. In 2007 President Bush—modifying his earlier position on setting targets for the reduction of greenhouse gases—proposed a series of negotiations among all major nations contributing to pollution, including China and India, who were exempted from the Kyoto Accords. Following President Bush's proposal for a new set of negotiations in effect led by the United States, *The Guardian Unlimited*, a major British on-line newspaper, editorialized on the new situation. The editorial is somewhat more accommodating to the United States than might appear on first reading. It sharply criticizes previous U.S. policy. At the same time it suggests that European and other nations might be well advised to permit the United States government to take a lead in these negotiations if the question of greenhouse gas emissions can effectively be addressed. Note that because this editorial appeared in the on-line version of the newspaper, it will be read around the world. Thus, its argument is intended to go well beyond the Atlantic community.

◆ What are the criticisms of the Bush administration policy? How does the editorial, while critical, still suggest some cooperation with the United States? What factors might account for both the modification of the U.S. policy and the accommodations suggested by the editorial?

George W Bush's announcement last week that he wants to convene a global summit on climate change would have been laudable had it come earlier in his presidency. Much earlier. His stated goal of setting fixed targets for reducing carbon-dioxide emissions might have looked like leadership, were it not for the awkward fact that most of the world's developed nations already have targets. That is because, unlike the US, they signed the 1996 Kyoto Protocol.

What is more, the leading developed nations already have a summit. Leaders of the G8 are meeting this week to discuss . . . implementing a more stringent regime of emissions cuts. . . .

. . . If the stage is already set, if all of the key players, including the new generation of polluters from the developing world such as China, India and Brazil, have been invited, . . . why wait? What need is there for Mr Bush's alternative summit?

The answer lies in the Bush administration's scorn for any international agreement that is not brokered by the US. . . . Since the US is the world's biggest polluter, any deal to cut emissions will put disproportionate pressure on Washington. So if Mr Bush is going to be seen to acquiesce to anything, for face-saving rea-

sons he needs it to be something ostensibly American in origin.

Fortunately, there are now domestic US forces pushing for action on climate change. Public opinion was way ahead of President Bush in accepting the scientific evidence that the planet is in peril. Several US states, most notably California, have responded by taking measures of their own to curb emissions. That, in turn, has led US business, anticipating ever more stringent controls, to stop lobbying for climate-change denial and start investing in alternative energy. Demand for green technology is growing. Agile American capitalists do not need to be motivated by ecological principle to get into that market. . . .

That doesn't mean that the rest of the G8 should snub the US President and reject his alternative summit. . . .

This week presents an opportunity to turn Mr Bush's newfound interest in climate change into a commitment to do something about it soon. That is better than confirming his fear that environmental talks are just an excuse to vilify America. . . .

Protesters at the UN Climate Change Conference, Montreal. Thousands of people march through the streets of Montreal on December 3, 2005, as part of a worldwide day of protest against global warming. The demonstration coincided with a United Nations Climate Change Conference.

The United States, along with Australia, has not ratified the protocol. The United States in 2001 withdrew entirely from the protocol. The Bush administration indicated that it feared implementation of the treaty would harm economic growth in the United States. The administration also criticized those parts of the treaty that permit developing nations such as China and India, who contribute major pollution, not to reduce their emissions. The administration has contended this portion of the treaty works to the disadvantage of the United States in world trade.

This stance on the part of the United States put it at odds with traditional European allies as well as Japan. Moreover, as the United States pursued its intervention in Iraq, numerous European governments saw American government as pressing unilateral policies on a number of fronts. Even supporters of the United States in Iraq, such as Great Britain, have been critical of the environmental policies of the Bush administration. (See Document, "A British Newspaper Editorial Criticizes American Environmental Policies.")

In the spring of 2007 the United States sought to modify its position and to gain some measure of agreement on the environment with other nations. The United States has offered to enter into negotiations with all nations who are major contributors to greenhouse emissions including India and China. Moreover, in a reversal of policy the United States offered to enter into negotiations for setting specific targets for elimination of emissions. At the same time the conservative government of Germany wanted the nations of the G-8 to promise to reduce their 1990 levels of greenhouse emissions by fifty percent by 2050. Other nations have proposed similar ambitious goals for the reduction of these gases.

Numerous factors account for these recent shifts in environmental policy statements. The American National Academy of Sciences has determined the rate of worldwide greenhouse emissions is growing faster than anyone has predicted. Many industrial and commercial companies have found it to their advantage to embrace the environmental cause. Several companies and industries have come to believe they can actually prosper by addressing climatic issues. Across the globe advocates for more rapid dealing with the growing environmental challenge appear to have been making great strides in persuading public opinion of the validity and urgency of their case, a development reflected by changes in the stance of various governments—even if they have not embraced the Kyoto Protocol.

Two developments clearly lie ahead in the immediate future. First, environmental pollution will continue to grow. Second, a period of protracted negotiations will ensue. Those negotiations will contribute to the ongoing tension between the United States and its traditional Atlantic partners.

Summary

The Cold War. U.S.-Soviet cooperation did not survive World War II. After 1945 Europe was divided into a Soviet-dominated zone in the East (the Warsaw Pact) and a U.S. led zone in the West (NATO). U.S.-Soviet rivalry played itself out around the world from the 1950s to the 1980s, although gradually a spirit of détente arose between the two powers, especially under President Ronald Reagan and Soviet leader Mikhail Gorbachev. The Cold War ended with the collapse of communist rule in Eastern Europe in 1989 and the disappearance of the Soviet Union in 1991.

Postwar European Society. Since World War II, European society has been marked by a rise in prosperity and consumerism, more rights and opportunities for women, moves towards political and economic unification symbolized by the adoption of a common currency, the euro, in 2002, and the publication of a draft constitution for a united Europe in 2003.

The United States. The major themes in postwar American history were opposition to communism at home and abroad, the expansion of civil rights to African Americans, and economic prosperity. Politically, the relatively liberal years from the late 1950s through the 1970s were succeeded by a growing conservatism especially under the presidencies of Ronald Reagan, George Bush, and George W. Bush. Even the democratic President Bill Clinton was more a centrist than a liberal. After the terrorist attacks of September 11, 2001, the United States embarked on a war on terrorism that led to wars in Afghanistan and Iraq.

Eastern Europe. The failure of the communist regimes in Eastern Europe and the Soviet Union to produce economic prosperity or political liberalization led to their growing unpopularity. Soviet economic difficulties led Mikhail Gorbachev to institute liberal reforms that led to the collapse of the communist rule first in Eastern Europe, then in the Soviet Union itself. The disappearance of the Soviet Union led to independence for much of the former Soviet empire. Russia itself has experienced social, economic, and political turmoil under presidents Boris Yeltsin and Vladimir Putin.

In the former Yugoslavia, the end of communist rule led to dismemberment and civil war. In the 1990s the NATO powers, led by the United States, intervened to halt the fighting and end a pattern of ethnic atrocities.

INTERPRETING THE PAST

Feminism and Civil Rights after World War II

Source from Chapter 32

1. *Simone de Beauvoir Urges Economic Freedom for Women* (page 1032)

Sources from MyHistoryLab / PrimarySource DVD

2. *Ladies Home Journal,* "Young Mother," 1956
3. *Martin Luther King, Letter from Birmingham Jail*

As the global economy and society changed in the years after World War II, women assumed larger roles in the work force and in politics. Married women were no longer relegated to the domestic sphere, and increasing numbers of younger women entered college, slowly gaining a foothold in the higher-paid professions. Yet resistance to women in the workplace continued, and gender inequality was predominant throughout the second half of the twentieth century. As a result, the feminist movement stimulated by authors such as Simone de Beauvoir in France and Betty Friedan *(The Feminine Mystique)* in America, grew steadily more influential.

The Civil Rights movement in the United States grew out of continuing efforts of African-Americans to gain their full rights as citizens after the Civil War in 1865. The 1950s and 1960s proved to be a crucial period in the movement, as black World War II veterans and their families joined with clergymen such as Martin Luther King, Jr., and a new wave of younger supporters to engage in strikes as well as demonstrations to end the restrictive laws and traditions that made blacks second-class citizens.

In this exercise you will read three primary sources relating to feminism and the Civil Rights movement. Then answer the following questions in the process of completing the assignment below.

The first document is an excerpt from *The Second Sex*, by Simone de Beauvoir, one of the pioneering feminists of the post-World War II era. The second source is a 1956 article from *The Ladies Home Journal*, a popular magazine for American women, exploring the world of a suburban housewife, whose experience differs radically from the professional women discussed by de Beauvoir. The third source Martin Luther King, Jr.'s *Letter from Birmingham Jail,* written to a group of white Alabama clergyman who stated their support of King's cause while disagreeing with his tactics.

Review Questions

1. What were the causes of the Cold War? How did the United States and the Soviet Union each react to what it perceived to be the other's hostility? What was the effect of the Cold War on Europe?

2. How did the outcome of World War II affect Europe's position in the world? What were the factors behind the movement towards European unification? How successful has this movement been?

3. What were the chief characteristics of Western European society in the decades since 1945? What was the experience of Eastern Europe during the same period and why was it different?

4. What were the most important developments in the domestic history of the United States between 1945 and 1968? How did the Vietnam War affect American society? When did the shift to political conservatism occur in the United States? What did it mean for the role of the federal government?

5. Describe the Soviet economy between 1945 and 1990. Did it meet the needs of the Soviet people? What were the causes for the collapse of the Soviet Union? What role did Gorbachev play in that process?

6. Describe the collapse of communist rule in Eastern Europe. Why was it a relatively bloodless revolution? What problems have followed the collapse of communist rule?

7. Was the old Yugoslavia a national state? Why did it break apart and slide into civil war? How did the West respond to this crisis?

8. How did the American response to the attacks of September 11, 2001, cause significant rifts in the NATO alliance? Why do some European nations feel able to dissent from the U.S. position in the Middle East when they rarely did so during the Cold War?

9. What are the major factors in regard to environmental policy that have divided the United States and European nations?

Key Terms

Cold War (p. 1018)

euro (p. 1025)

European Economic Community (p. 1024)

European Union (EU) (p. 1025)

glasnost (p. 1040)

Marshall Plan (p. 1019)

perestroika (p. 1040)

Questions

What are de Beauvoir's arguments on behalf of economic rights for women? How does she link them to women's civil rights?

How does the *Ladies Home Journal* article depict suburban life for the young mother being profiled? What is her role? How does it differ from the roles envisioned by de Beauvoir?

In King's *letter* how does he justify the breaking of laws and peaceful demonstrations against injustice? What is his response to the white clergymen who urge him to wait for the courts to act on civil rights?

How does King respond to the charge of being an extremist? How does he invoke an economic dimension to racial injustice?

Note: To learn more about the topics in this chapter, please turn to the Suggested Readings at the end of the book. For additional sources related to this chapter please see the Primary Source DVD at the back of this text or MyHistoryLab.

East Asia: The Recent Decades

- ◆ Japan
- ◆ China
- ◆ Taiwan
- ◆ Korea
- ◆ Vietnam

THE HISTORY OF EAST ASIA SINCE THE END OF World War II may be divided into two phases. During the first from 1945 to 1980, several East Asian nations became communist but achieved only a small improvement in the lives of their peoples. In stark contrast, the nations that used a mixture of state guidance and market-oriented economies made East Asia the most dynamic region in the postwar world. Japan led the way, achieving economic growth that has often been spoken of as miraculous but can

more sensibly be described as single-minded. Japan also developed into a robust parliamentary democracy with freedoms comparable to those of Western Europe or the United States.

Taiwan and South Korea began their economic development a decade or two later and from a much lower level, and though lacking the political freedom of Japan, they attained stunning economic growth, as did the tiny British colony of Hong Kong and the even tinier ex-British colony of Singapore. Viewing the progress of these countries, it would appear that the values of the East Asian heritage—hard work,

The Price of Growth. A coal-powered plant in Hebei province, northern China, February 2006. According to the Worldwatch Institute, sixteen of the world's twenty most polluted cities are in China. On average, China builds one coal-fired plant a week.

Modern East Asia

East Asia

Before World War II, only Europe, the United States, and Japan had successfully combined the ingredients needed for modern economic growth. It was as though these countries had a magic potion that the rest of the world lacked. Industrialization in East Asia during the second half of the twentieth century made clear that there was no magic potion: The West and Japan just got there first. The industrialization of East Asia raises issues that powerfully affect relations among nations.

One question is whether high-wage nations will be able to compete with those low-wage nations that have found the formula for growth. Until recently, advanced nations were satisfied with their share of world trade. They sold the products of their heavy industries and advanced technologies and bought raw materials and the labor-intensive products of light industries. They assumed that their technological advantage was permanent, and that they could always stay sufficiently ahead of the less-developed nations to maintain high wages for their workers. This assumption has now been challenged. Since the 1960s, Taiwan, South Korea, Hong Kong, and Singapore have

not only achieved modern economic growth but have also moved rapidly into high technology—well before their wages reached Western levels. This has made them formidable competitors in precisely those areas in which the West has considered itself preeminent. Since the late 1980s, China has done the same. The United States, by keeping its market open, regained competitiveness during the 1990s, but at the cost of holding down wages, drastic corporate restructuring, relocating jobs abroad, and accumulating huge trade deficits. Will it be willing to continue paying this price? Will competition combined with runaway immigration create a permanent two-tier system of wages? China, the most recent East Asian industrializer, will possess the economic advantages of cheap labor for decades. If it succeeds in its development goals, the impact on high-wage nations will be massive.

A second issue raised by East Asian economic growth concerns natural resources. An oil crisis occurred in the early 1970s when demand outran supply. There were shortages at the pumps, a steep rise in the price of oil, and a transfer of wealth from industrial to oil-rich nations. Experts pointed out that the world's reserves were dwindling. Market forces, however, uncovered new sources of supply and the crisis

frugality, family orientation, thirst for education, and concern for getting ahead—lead almost automatically to economic development if given half a chance.

The communist nations—China, North Korea, and Vietnam—did poorly. China was wracked by continuous political convulsions. Despite gaining undisputed political authority over a vast area comparable to that of the Qing Empire, the government was unable to tap the energies and talents of its people. The contrast between the low productivity of the Chinese in China and the remarkable productivity of the same people in Hong Kong and Taiwan was remarkable.

Vietnam, plagued by wars during these early decades, did not develop at all. North Korea, where

most of the industry of Japan's prewar colony was located, did slightly better during the decade after the Korean War, but then plummeted to a state of misery.

The second phase of postwar East Asian history began during the 1980s. Those nations that had prospered earlier continued to grow. Japan's per capita product zoomed to European levels. Taiwan, South Korea, Hong Kong, and Singapore (sometimes referred to as the "tiger" economies) also achieved amazing advances. Growth went hand in hand with social stability and an increasingly varied cultural life. Especially notable were advances in democracy in Taiwan and South Korea (see Map 33–1).

faded, yet oil reserves are still being used up faster than ever as demand rises. At some point demand, including new demand from China and India, will again outstrip supply. Soaring gas prices suggest the point is near at hand. Will struggles over scarce resources become a central feature in future international relations?

A third issue is population. Japan's population quadrupled in the course of its industrialization and then began to level off without a need for draconian measures. Its pattern resembled that of the advanced nations of the West. China, in contrast, already had a huge population when it began its recent industrialization. Since it could ill afford a further quadrupling, it adopted extremely tough policies to limit births. Its population may peak at 1.6 billion in 2030. Whether other less-developed nations in the world follow the Japanese or Chinese pattern will depend on their particular circumstances, but for many, the Chinese model may be unavoidable. More people are no blessing.

A fourth issue concerns the political consequences of economic growth. The recent history of Taiwan and South Korea suggests that East Asian dictatorships can evolve towards democracy as standards of living rise. Will this happen in China? China is prospering, and its people are caught up in consumerism, but the Chinese Communist Party, so far, shows no signs of relaxing its monopoly on government. Also, postwar Taiwan and South Korea were less thoroughly authoritarian to begin with and were strongly influenced by the United States. It is too early to speak with any confidence.

A final issue, the dark companion of industrial and population growth, is pollution. As long as most of the world remained underdeveloped, the industrial nations assumed that their wastes would harmlessly vanish into the vast reaches of surrounding lands and seas. But as populations encroach on forested lands, and Eastern Europe, India, Russia, South America, and East Asia industrialize, pollution becomes more threatening. Even apart from disasters such as Minamata and Chernobyl, automobile fumes, industrial effluents, chimney gases, pesticides, garbage, and sewage cause lakes to die, forests to wither, and level of toxins to rise.

Focus Questions

◆ What is the impact of East Asian economic growth on the world's natural resources? on international relations?

◆ Does recent history suggest that the Chinese government will become more democratic as its citizens become more prosperous?

The most notable positive changes occurred in China, which in 1978 launched a market economy within a communist dictatorship. Explosive growth and an export boom resulted. Long suppressed entrepreneurial abilities surfaced, and China quickly became a player in global markets. As the economy grew, the society was also transformed. Vietnam adopted a weaker version of the same policy. It permitted private enterprises and opened its markets to some foreign capital. Only North Korea resisted the changes sweeping the rest of the communist world. The rigidities of its singular brand of communism took their toll: in the early years of the twenty-first century, its people suffered hunger and misery, and its government pursued desperate policies. ∎

Japan

For Japan, already bogged down in its occupation of China, the decision in 1941 to go to war with the United States and its allies was a desperate gamble. By all objective measures—steel production, oil, machine tools, heavy chemicals, shipping—Japan was far weaker than the United States. The Japanese military, however, misread statements of isolationist sentiment in the United States during 1940 and 1941 and concluded that Americans had no stomach for a drawn-out war in the western Pacific. In terms of strategy,

Map 33–1. Contemporary East Asia.

they bet Japan's shorter lines of supply against American productivity.

By early 1945, the Japanese were poor, hungry, and ill-clothed. Cities were burned out, factories scarred by bomb-

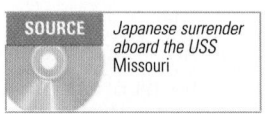

SOURCE *Japanese surrender aboard the USS* Missouri

ings; shipping had been sunk, railways were dilapidated, and trucks and cars were scarce. Yet, despite their wretched condition, the Japanese people steeled themselves for invasion and a final battle in defense of their homeland. Then, in early

August, atomic bombs were dropped on Hiroshima and Nagasaki, and the Soviet Union declared war on Japan and invaded Manchuria. Even after these disasters, opinion at the imperial conference—hastily convened to decide on a national policy—was split, with three favoring surrender and three for continuing the war. The emperor broke the deadlock, and Japan accepted the Allied terms of unconditional surrender. On August 15, the emperor broadcast Japan's surrender to the Japanese people, saying that the "unendurable must be endured."

After years of wartime propaganda, the Japanese reacted with shock to the fact of surrender, deep sadness at having lost the war, relief that the bombing was over, and apprehension about what would come next. They expected a harsh and vindictive occupation, but when they found it constructive, they turned to positive cooperation. Their receptivity to new democratic ideas and their repudiation of militarism led one Japanese writer to label the era "the second opening of Japan."

The Occupation

General Douglas MacArthur was the Supreme Commander for the Allied Powers in Japan. His headquarters in Tokyo was staffed almost entirely by Americans, and the Occupation forces themselves were American, apart from British Commonwealth troops on the island of Shikoku. The chief concern of the first phase of the Occupation was demilitarization and democratization. Civilians and soldiers abroad were returned to Japan and the military was demobilized. Ultranationalist organizations were dissolved and the Home Ministry was abolished. The police were decentralized, and political prisoners were freed. Following the model of the Nuremberg trials in Germany, wartime leaders were brought to trial for "crimes against humanity." In addition, 210,000 officers, businessmen,

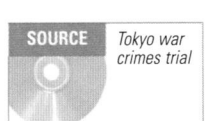 SOURCE *Tokyo war crimes trial*

teachers, and officials—the leaders of wartime Japan—were removed from office. The thoroughness of these reforms reflected the Occupation view that Japanese society had been tainted by feudal and militaristic values and that Japan's leaders had been joined in a huge conspiracy to wage aggressive war.

As a part of democratization, Shinto was disestablished as the state religion, labor unions were encouraged, and the holding companies of zaibatsu combines were dissolved. The old educational system, which had forced students at an early age to choose either an elite or a mass track, was changed to a single-track system that kept open longer the option of continuing in school. The most radical undertaking was a land reform that expropriated landlord holdings and sold them to landless tenants at a fractional cost. The effect, ironically, was to create a countryside of politically conservative small farmers. Needless to say, some of these reforms merely accelerated changes already under way in Japan, and all of the reforms depended on the cooperation—at times enthusiastic and at times reluctant—of Japanese officials.

Of all the Occupation reforms, none was more important than the new constitution, written by the Government Section of MacArthur's headquarters in 1947 and passed

Emperor Hirohito and General MacArthur. The two men met at the U.S. Embassy in Tokyo in 1945. MacArthur felt the emperor contributed to the stability of Japan and made the work of the Occupation easier. The emperor was glad to be of use and relieved he was not hanged as a war criminal. *Corbis/Bettmann.*

into law by the Japanese Diet. It fundamentally changed Japan's polity in five respects:

1. A British-style parliamentary state was established in which the cabinet became a committee of the majority party or coalition in the Diet. This broke with the Meiji Constitution, which had permitted the emperor or those who acted in his name to appoint prime ministers without regard for the Diet. The new constitution also added an American-style independent judiciary and a federal system of prefectures with elected governors and local leaders.
2. Women were given the vote.
3. The rights to life, liberty, the pursuit of happiness, a free press, and free assembly were guaranteed. These were joined by newer rights, such as academic freedom, collective bargaining, sexual equality in marriage, and minimal standards of wholesome and cultural living.
4. **Article 9**, the no-war clause, stipulated: "The Japanese people forever renounce war as a sovereign right of the

nation" and will never maintain "land, sea, and air forces" or "other war potential." This article would make Japan into something unique in the world: a major power without commensurate military strength.

5. The constitution defined a new role for the emperor as "the symbol of the state deriving his position from the will of the people with whom resides sovereign power."

The Japanese people accepted the new constitution and embraced democracy with uncritical enthusiasm. The no-war clause was viewed by most as the guarantee of a peaceful future. Although it did not preclude the formation of a Self-Defense

SOURCE   *Japanese elections, 1946*

Force, it acted as a brake on military expenditures, which half a century later were only about 1 percent of Japan's gross domestic product. The Japanese had been readied for the changed status of the emperor by his speech on January 1, 1946, in which he renounced all claims to divinity. The Occupation saw to it that the emperor traveled about Japan in a manner appropriate to his new status as a symbol of the state. No one who saw this mild, rumpled-looking, and inarticulate man mistook him for a Shinto god. During the 1960s and 1970s, most, though not all, Japanese came to feel a considerable affection for Emperor

---

Two Views of the "Symbol Emperor"

Document

The murkiest aspect of Japan's prewar emperor-centered ideology was the juxtaposition of the emperor as a modern monarch and the emperor as a living deity, ultimately descended from the sun goddess. In the first selection, former Prime Minister Yoshida Shigeru, a product of Meiji Japan, basically accepts the prewar ideology but argues that because in fact the emperor exercised little power before World War II, nothing was changed by the postwar constitution. In the second selection, Nobel Prize winner Ōe Kenzaburō, a humanistic and slightly leftist novelist, recognizes that the emperor has been stripped of his former authority but worries about a revival of his Shinto identity.

◆ What does Yoshida mean by "as naturally," and why does Ōe call the prewar emperor an "absolute ruler"?

1. In regard to the question of the Imperial structure of government, as it existed in Japan, I pointed out that the Meiji Constitution had originated in the promises made to the Japanese people by the Emperor Meiji at the beginning of his reign, and there was little need to dwell on the fact that democracy, if we were to use the word, had always formed part of the traditions of our country, and was not—as some mistakenly imagined—something that was about to be introduced with the revision of the Constitution. As for the Imperial House, the idea and reality of the Throne had come into being among the Japanese people as naturally as the idea of the country itself; no question of antagonism between Throne and people could possibly arise; and nothing contained in the new Constitution could change that fact. The word "symbol" had been employed in the definition of the Emperor because we Japanese had always regarded the Emperor as the symbol of the country itself—a statement which any Japanese considering the issue dispassionately would be ready to recognize as an irrefutable fact.

2. Japan's emperor system, which had apparently lost its social and political influence after the defeat in the

Pacific War, is beginning to flex its muscles again, and in some respects it has already recouped much of its lost power—with two differences: first, the Japanese today will not accept the prewar ideology-cum-theology that held the emperor to be both absolute ruler and living deity. Nevertheless, imperial rites performed quite recently were done in such a manner as to impress upon us that the emperor's lineage can be traced to a deity; I am referring here to the rituals associated with the present emperor's enthronement and the so-called Great Thanksgiving Service that followed it. These ceremonies provoked little objection from either the government or the people, indeed most Japanese seemed to take it all very much for granted.

1. Yoshida Shigeru, *The Yoshida Memoirs*. Copyright © 1961 Heineman Books, p. 139.
2. From "Speaking on Japanese Culture Before a Scandinavian Audience," *Japan, The Ambiguous and Myself: The Nobel Prize Speech and Other Lectures by Kenzaburō Ōe*. Published by Kodansha International, Ltd., 1995. Copyright © 1992 by Kenzaburō Ōe. All rights reserved. Reprinted by permission.

Hirohito, who, they felt, had shared in their wartime and postwar hardships. They were saddened by his death in 1989 (See Document, "Two Views of the 'Symbol Emperor'.")

By the end of 1947, most of the planned reforms had been carried out. To create a climate in which the new democracy could take root and flourish, the Occupation in its second phase turned to Japan's economic recovery. It dropped plans to deconcentrate big business further, encouraged the Japanese government to curb inflation, and cracked down on communist unions that used strikes for political ends. The United States also gave Japan $2 billion in economic aid.

The outbreak of the Korean War in 1950 marked the start of the third and final phase of the Occupation. The American military, fully engaged in the peninsular war, no longer had time for Japan. Consequently, Japanese officials began to look to the cabinet and the Diet for policy decisions, not to the occupying forces. By the time Japan regained its sovereignty in April 1952, the effect of the changeover was hardly noticeable in the daily life of the Japanese people. On the same day as the peace treaty, Japan signed a security treaty with the United States, which provided for American bases and committed the United States to Japan's defense. Although attacked by the political left, the security treaty became the cornerstone of Japan's minimalist defense policy.

Parliamentary Politics

In 1945, Japan had a parliamentary potential that harked back to the rise of party power in the Diet between 1890 and 1932. It also had an authoritarian potential compounded of those factors that had led to the rise of militarism. Had the country been occupied by the Soviet Union, the efficiency of its bureaucracy, its wartime economic planning organs, its educated and disciplined work force, and its receptivity to change after defeat would doubtless have made Japan a model communist state. Occupied by the United States, the parliamentary potential emerged.

Japan's postwar politics can be divided into three periods. The first, from 1945 to 1955, was the continuation of prewar party politics as modified to fit the new political environment. Two conservative parties and a socialist party emerged. The Liberals and the Democrats—the conservative parties—were the successors to the two mainstream prewar parties. They resumed their struggle for power in the early postwar elections. The Japanese Socialist Party, which won 26 percent of the vote in 1947, was the heir of the moderate prewar Socialist Party, which had received 9 percent of the vote in 1937.

For most of this first decade, the Liberals held power under Prime Minister Yoshida Shigeru (1878–1967). Before the war, Yoshida had been an ardent imperialist but had favored close ties with Britain and the United States and opposed the rise of militarism. After the war, as president of the Liberal Party, he cooperated closely with MacArthur and

Chronology

Japan Since 1945

1948–1954	Yoshida ministries
1950–1953	Korean War
1952	Peace and security treaties
1955	Liberal and Democratic Parties merge to form the LDP
1955–1973	Double-digit economic growth
1972	Japan recognizes the People's Republic of China
1973–1989	Economic growth continues at slower pace
1990	Bubble bursts and recession begins
1993	Socialists lose half of their Diet seats
1994–1996	Non-LDP coalitions govern; LDP-led coalitions reestablished
2001–2006	Koizumi Junichirō of the LDP as prime minister
2003	Japan sends troops to Iraq
2006	Abe Shinzō of the LDP becomes prime minister
2007	Fukuda Yasuo of the LDP becomes prime minister

worked to rebuild Japan's economy. Probusiness and anticommunist, he was so autocratic in his dealings with bureaucrats and lesser politicians that he was nicknamed "one-man Yoshida."

The long second period from 1955 to 1993 has been called the one-and-a-half party system. The "one" party was the Liberal Democratic Party (**LDP**), formed by a merger of the two conservative parties in 1955. It held power throughout this period. The "half party," so called because it was permanently out of power, was the Japanese Socialist Party. It had split in two in 1951 and come back together in 1955.

What did one-party rule for thirty-eight years mean? One-party rule is not usually associated with representative government. In the immediate postwar years, the strength of the conservatives was simply the continuation of prewar constituencies, that is to say, the network of ties between local men of influence, prefectural assemblymen, and Diet politicians, and their ties to business and the bureaucracy. From the 1960s onward, the LDP became identified as the party that was rebuilding Japan and maintaining Japan's security through close ties with the United States. It was widely recognized as more able than other parties. Despite the cozy relationships that developed between the LDP and business, periodic scandals, and a general distrust of politicians, the

Opening the Olympics. In the 1964 Tokyo Olympics Japan stepped back onto the international stage after the disasters of the war years. Holding the Olympic torch was Yoshinori Sakai, who was born in Hiroshima on August 6, 1945, when the atomic bomb was dropped on the city.

Japanese people voted to keep it in power. Rule by a single party for such a long period provided for an unusual continuity in government policies. Within the larger pattern of the LDP hegemony, several trends were notable:

1. From 1955 to 1960, Japanese politics was marked by ideological strife. The LDP was led by wartime figures who had been purged after the war but had resumed their political careers. These leaders rather high-handedly modified several Occupation reforms, recentralized the police, strengthened central government controls over education, and even considered a revision of the constitution. The opposition was led by Marxist socialists, many of whom had been persecuted during the war. The socialists branded LDP rule as the "tyranny of the majority," since legislation was often passed by "snap votes," and warned of the revival of authoritarianism. Diet sessions were marked by confrontation, rancor, and occasional violence. After 1960, confrontation politics declined. Adopting a "low posture," the new LDP prime minister dropped controversial political issues and drew up a plan to double the national income in ten years. These moves inaugurated a more peaceful era. As prosperity grew during the seventies and eighties, ideological confrontation declined further. In many areas a consensus emerged as LDP consulted opposition politicians before presenting bills to the Diet.

2. Another trend was a steady decline in the LDP popular vote from 63 percent in 1955, to 55 percent in 1963, to 43 percent in 1976. The decline mirrored Japan's economic growth: Farmers, small shopkeepers, and others, who traditionally voted for the LDP, became a smaller part of the population, while unionized laborers and white-collar workers, who tended to vote for the Socialists, increased. By the late seventies, the conservatives faced the possibility that they would have to form a coalition to stay in power. But in the 1979 election the steady twenty-year decline in the LDP popular vote came to an end. For the next fourteen years the party enjoyed a stable majority in the powerful Lower House of the Diet—though not always in the Upper House—and maintained its rule.

3. Although it received less than half of the popular vote, the LDP maintained its Diet majority because its opposition fragmented: In 1960, non-Marxist members broke from the Socialist Party to form a competing Democratic Socialist Party. In 1964, the Value Creating Society (*Sōka Gakkai*), a Nichiren Buddhist sect that grew to include almost one-tenth of the Japanese population, formed the Clean Government Party (*Kōmeitō*). The Japanese Communist Party, which became less militant after the end of the Korean War, also gained ground, and during the 1970s received almost 10 percent of the popular vote. Competition at the polls between candidates of these smaller opposition parties benefited the larger LDP.

The third and recent era of politics began in 1993. The notable feature of this era was the decline and fall of the left. The Japanese Socialist Party had been the principal opposition party for almost fifty years. But the end of the Cold War, the worldwide rejection of Marxism, the decline of labor union membership and militancy, and the widespread Japanese view that Socialist politicians had little to contribute to their recession-ridden country signaled the demise of socialism in Japan. In the 1993 election the Socialists dropped from 136 to 70 seats in the Lower House of the Diet. In 1994, hungry for a taste of power after decades in the wilderness, they set aside their principles and joined the LDP in a coalition government. In the 1996 general election, voters showed their disapproval by stripping the Socialists of all but 26 seats; in the 2000 election the total dropped further to 19 seats. The Communist Party also slumped. In the 2003 election, Socialists and Communists together garnered less than 5 percent of the seats in the 480-member Lower House.

The collapse of the left inaugurated an era of multiparty conservative politics. The players were the LDP, still the largest party, a shifting number of smaller conservative parties, and the Clean Government Party. Japanese electoral politics during the 1990s was punctuated by scandals and factional strife, but the single overriding issue was the economy. In 1993 the LDP lost 52 of its 275 seats, a consequence of its failure to end the recession. In its place, a non-LDP Conservative coalition held power between 1994 and 1996. Political scientists saw this as the beginning of the two-party conservative government. The possibility was not absent. But as the economic crisis continued, voters again turned to the LDP in the hope that its more seasoned politicians would be better able to cope with the lagging economy. After the turn of the millennium, the economy strengthened and with it the fortunes of the LDP. From 2001 to 2006, the popular Koizumi Junichiro was party president and prime minister. He was followed as prime minister by the belligerent and less popular Abe Shinzō, and in 2007, by the dovish Fukuda Yasuo. For the time being the LDP maintains its popular hegemony.

Economic Growth

The extraordinary story of the economic rise of East Asia after World War II began with Japan. Japanese productivity in 1945 was about the same as it had been in 1918. By 1955 it had recovered to prewar levels, but just as growth was expected to moderate, it forged ahead and continued at a double-digit pace for almost two decades. Shipbuilding, machine tools, steel, heavy chemicals, automobiles, and consumer electronics and optics led the way. Before the war, "made in Japan" had meant cheap, ten-cent-store goods. By the late 1970s Sony, Toyota, Honda, Panasonic, Toshiba, Seiko, and Canon were known throughout the world for the quality of their products.

Several factors explain this growth. An infrastructure of banking, marketing, and manufacturing skills had carried over from prewar Japan. The international situation was also favorable: Oil was cheap, access to raw materials and export markets was easy, and under American sponsorship Japan gained early entry into the World Bank, the International Monetary Fund, and other international organizations. A rate of savings close to 20 percent helped reinvestment. This reflected a traditional frugality but was also a modern necessity in view of inadequate pensions.

A revolution in education contributed as well. In the prewar years education for most Japanese ended with middle school and only 2 or 3 percent of students went to university. By the early 1980s, almost all middle school graduates went on to high school, and a rising percentage of high school graduates went on to higher education. Even more telling is the fact that by the early eighties Japan was graduating more engineers than the United States, and that virtually all of them were employed in productive, nonmilitary industries. (At the time, the total number of lawyers in Japan roughly equaled a single year's graduating class from American law schools.) This upgrading of human capital and channeling of its best minds into productive careers enabled Japan to tap the huge backlog of technology that had developed in the United States during and after the war years. It proved far cheaper to license or buy technology than to invent it. After "improvement engineering," Japan sold its products to the world.

Another factor was an abundance of high-quality, cheap labor. The population in 1950 was 83 million; by 2004 it rose to 127 million. It was expected to stabilize and then decline early in the twenty-first century. Immediately after the war about 47 percent of Japan's labor force was in agriculture; by 2005 only a tiny fraction worked on the land. Until the mid-1960s more labor was available than jobs, which kept wages low. Labor organization proved no bar to economic growth. Industrial workers in Japan during the immediate postwar decades were more highly unionized than those in the United States, but the basic component of labor organization was the company-based union, rather than a trade union. Company-based unions regularly engaged in spring offensives and marched with red flags on May Day, but they also took great pains not to impair their companies' productivity. Since the 1980s the strength of unions has declined. In 2005, about one-fifth of the labor force belonged to unions.

The government aided manufacturers with tariff protection, foreign exchange, and special depreciation allowances. Industries in advanced technologies benefited from cheap loans, subsidies, and products from government research laboratories. Small budgets for defense spending and welfare kept corporate taxes low. The Finance Ministry and the Ministry of Trade and Industry encouraged the Bank of Japan to back private banks in refinancing Japan's industries. Critics who spoke of "Japan Inc.", as though Japan were a single gigantic corporation, overstated the case: Competition between companies within Japan was fierce, but government was more supportive of business than it was regulative.

By 1973 the Japanese economy had become "mature." Double-digit growth gave way to 4 percent growth. Labor became more expensive, research budgets grew as the backlog of cheap technology declined, welfare costs rose, and tough but costly antipollution policies were implemented. Behind the statistic of slower growth was a change in the composition of the economy: Smokestack industries declined while service industries, pharmaceuticals, specialty chemicals, scientific equipment, computers, and robots grew. Japan's trade, hitherto balanced, began to generate huge surpluses. The surpluses were mainly due to the growing appetite of world markets for Japanese products but were also a result of protectionist policies. These policies

Nissan Motors Assembly Line. An almost completely automated assembly line at Nissan Motors' Zama factory. The high cost of labor in Japan makes such robot-intensive production economical. *Reuters/Susumu Takahashi/ Archive Photos.*

led to friction and to demands from the United States and Europe for their abolition.

Sluggish growth, or no growth at all, characterized the nineties. Convinced that their boom would never end, Japanese had bid up the price of corporate shares and land to unrealistic levels—several times those of Europe and America. In 1991 the "bubble" burst: The price of land and stocks plummeted. Japanese who had bought shares of stock or real estate at exaggerated prices were hard hit; banks that had made housing or margin loans incurred huge losses. As banks and individuals retrenched, the economy slowed. Thousands of small companies went bankrupt; large companies restructured and cut their research budgets; some workers were laid off or retired early; and fewer new graduates were hired. Unemployment rose.

In 2002 an export-led recovery began. The reviving American economy and the soaring Chinese economy were critical. Japanese economists began to speak of the "complementarity" of Japanese and Chinese markets. In 2004 consumers—who had increased their savings during the recession—began to spend, and stock valuations also rose.

Problems left over from the nineties persisted. Banks still carried many bad debts. Public debt was high, but the Japanese, still protected by lifetime employment, were unwilling to

shoulder new taxes. As in the developed economies of the United States and Europe, industrial production continued to move abroad in pursuit of cheap, skilled labor. Sony television sets were no longer manufactured in Japan.

But Japanese strengths were also formidable: Industry was restructured during the nineties, with greater rewards for talent. Japanese automobiles were coveted throughout the world, and the Japanese export surplus grew. Even Japan's redoubtable management skills seemed exportable: Nissan's Tennessee plant took 17.37 hours to assemble an automobile, while at General Motors the average was 26.75. Equally notable was Japan's determination to maintain its lead in flat screens, fermentation chemistry, robotics, and materials research and to become a world force in biotechnology, medical instruments, and airplanes. Today, new science and engineering buildings on the Tokyo University campus dwarf the dreary prewar brick buildings of the faculties of law, letters, economics, and education.

At the dawn of the third millennium Japan's economy loomed large. It was second only to the United States, larger than the other East Asian economies combined, or almost as large as the economies of Germany and France combined. See the comparative data in Figure 33–1 and in the Overview table on p. 1065. Income figures always require qualification, but the salient fact remains: Japan achieved a near-European level of affluence through the peaceful development of human resources in a free society.

Society and Culture

The triple engines of change—Occupation reforms, economic growth, and rapid expansion of higher education—transformed Japanese society. In 1945, almost half of the population lived in villages organically rooted in the past; sixty years later most Japanese lived in cities, more than a quarter in the Tokyo-Osaka industrial corridor. As in the United States and Europe, a tiny percentage of the population produced the food for the rest. Families changed, too. In

A Comparison of Japan with Germany and France in the Year 2006 (IMF Estimates)		
	GDP (in billions)	Population (in millions)	Per Capita GDP
Germany	$2,872	82	$35,024
France	$2,149	64	$33,578
Total	$5,021	146	$34,390 (average)
Japan	$4,883	127	$38,449

Figure 33–1.   A Comparison of Japan with Germany and France in the Year 2006 (IMF Estimates).

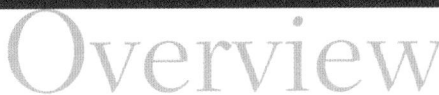

Gross Domestic Products (GDP) of Japan, Other East Asian Nations, and Other Asian Nations in 2006 (in billions of dollars)

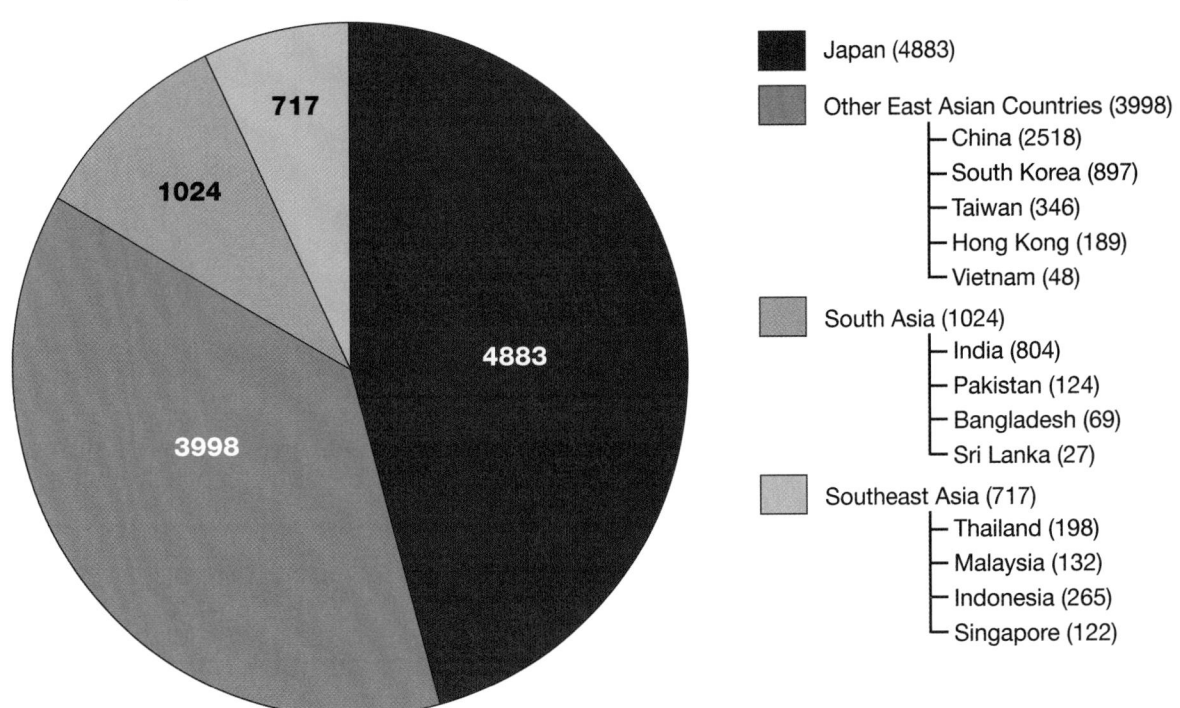

Japan (4883)

Other East Asian Countries (3998)
- China (2518)
- South Korea (897)
- Taiwan (346)
- Hong Kong (189)
- Vietnam (48)

South Asia (1024)
- India (804)
- Pakistan (124)
- Bangladesh (69)
- Sri Lanka (27)

Southeast Asia (717)
- Thailand (198)
- Malaysia (132)
- Indonesia (265)
- Singapore (122)

1945 the three-generation extended family of grandparents, parents, and children was held up as the ideal, and most marriages were arranged. Fifty years later the nuclear family of parents and children was the norm, and most marriages were "love matches." In the 1950s and 1960s, companies and government offices built huge apartment blocks for their employees on the edges of cities. The apartments were small, but wives welcomed life without mothers-in-law. In the 1960s and 1970s, larger apartments, called "mansions" in Japanese, were built in cities and purchased by middle- and higher-income families; only the rich could afford city houses. As incomes rose, people bought rice cookers, washing machines, dryers, televisions, computers, and other electronic equipment. Consumerism was constrained only by the small size of living units.

The status of women rose. Occupation reforms had given women the vote, legal equality, and an equal share of the family inheritance. Women's colleges gained the right to award degrees, and women were admitted to hitherto all-male universities, including the former imperial universities. Rising incomes and smaller families enabled parents to give daughters as well as sons a higher education. Co-ed excursions to ocean beaches or ski slopes became commonplace. Most women worked for a few years after completing their education and married later: The average age of marriage rose from 24 in 1970 to 28 in 2002. Wives usually stayed at home while their children were small, but many returned to work when their children entered middle school. In 1980, almost twice as many wives stayed at home than worked, while in 2002 more wives worked than stayed at home. A working wife had a greater say in household matters. With the shift towards nuclear families, wives became household authority figures, at least during the long hours that their husbands commuted and worked. Greater economic leeway also made divorce an option: The number tripled to European levels between 1970 and 2002.

In the new Japan more than ever, getting ahead depended on education. Middle school was compulsory, and by 2007 over half of high school graduates—about the same percentage as in the United States—went on to some form of higher education. The pressure to enter good schools started in kindergarten. Mothers routinely compared children's test scores and sent their children to after-school tutoring classes. Examinations determined admissions at every level, even for

Middle School Students in A Japanese Literature Class. Girls and boys wear school uniforms and study together. Desks are pushed together to accomodate large classes. The teacher is dressed like a businessman. *Charles Gupton/Getty Images Inc.–Stone Allstock.*

Comic Book. Raised from childhood in the arts of *ninja*, the young heroine Azumi slays evil men. The popularity of this *Bigu Komikku* (Big Comic) led to a movie (*anime*, or animated) version. Was this the Japanese model for "Kill Bill"? Japan has specialized comics for every demographic group—for children, teenage boys, teenage girls, and adults. *Clive Streeter © Dorling Kindersley.*

the cram schools that prepped failed candidates to retake university entrance examinations. Magazine articles regularly lamented the excesses of Japan's "examination society." They claimed that Japan's lockstep education was appropriate to the needs of assembly-line production but not to the needs of "the information age." But little was done to change the system. A few students rebelled against their parents or bullied their schoolmates, but most students realized that the pressure to excel was for their own good and limited their rebellion to reading violent and sadistic *manga* (comics).

On the positive side, the enormous prewar gap between the tiny educated elite and the masses with only a middle school education disappeared. Whatever the reality, more than 90 percent of Japanese saw themselves as middle class. This consciousness was the social base for the new democracy and for the growing number of voters who described themselves as independents. More education also explains Japan's tremendous consumption of newspapers, magazines, and books. Bookstores stock every variety of books imaginable: serious fiction, mysteries, histories, poetry, science fiction, romances, cookbooks, and translations, as well as books on investing, self-improvement, and home repairs.

In prewar Japan, the claims of the individual vis-à-vis the family, community, and state were generally weak. Postwar prosperity brought greater personal autonomy. Public opinion polls of workers showed a desire for more meaningful work and a larger sphere of independence apart from their jobs. Small pleasures did not replace duties but became an expected part of everyday life. The young, who took affluence for granted, met with friends at coffeehouses or McDonald's, watched American movies or Japanese *anime*, and frequently traveled abroad.

Attitudes towards minorities, about 2 percent of the population, improved during the postwar decades. The Ainu of Hokkaido, long despised and neglected, had mostly died off or been absorbed into the majority population during the prewar century. In the postwar years, the 20,000 or 30,000 who maintained or regained an ethnic identity formed political organizations, enlisted the support of leftist parties, and obtained welfare legislation. A larger problem was the *burakumin* or outcast communities, which were especially numerous in western Japan. Though physically indistinguishable from other Japanese, their members were

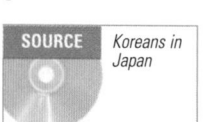

SOURCE   Koreans in Japan

shunned as marriage partners and frequently barred from good jobs. Political and legal action improved their condition, though social prejudices persisted. A less tractable problem was the 900,000 Koreans in Japan. By the 1980s, most had been born and educated in Japan but were not citizens, since citizenship was determined by blood, not birthplace. Early on, many supported North Korea, though few wished to live there. As South Korea industrialized, Japanese Koreans were no longer seen as the people of a backward nation, but they were still viewed as separate from Japanese and suffered social and occupational prejudices.

As the new millennium began, a serious social problem facing Japan was the aging of its population. In 1980, there were five workers for every retired person; by 2010 there will be fewer than two. Corporate pensions were underfunded, private savings were inadequate, and government and public pensions (the Japanese equivalent of Social Security) added to government deficits. A recurring question is how the old will be supported and how they will vote in elections. This problem, of course, is not unique to Japan. All developed nations have experienced a shift from high to lower fertility and mortality, but the imbalance is particularly severe in Japan, Italy, and Germany, where wartime population losses and postwar baby booms skewed age group distribution.

Urban Japan is extremely crowded and would be more livable with fewer people. With an estimated birthrate in 2007 of 8.1 and a deathrate of 8.98 per 1000, a slow decline was already under way. Some Japanese welcome this opportunity to reduce population. Until Japan returns to a more normal population distribution, the problem of too few workers, they argue, can be solved by raising the retirement age, starting pensions later, and tapping the reservoir of nonworking, middle-aged women. Others, however, advocate incentives to encourage marriage and larger families. The average Japanese family today has 1.23 children, one of the lowest figures in the world. During the past two decades, people of Japanese descent from Brazil and Peru and illegal immigrants from other parts of Asia have come to take the lowly jobs that Japanese despise. Some illegals have been deported; the numbers, overall, do not offset the decline in births.

The postwar transformation of Japanese society might be expected to have produced deep cultural strains and social dislocations. At the margin, these did occur. The growth among the urban poor of "new religions" such as the Value Creating Society was interpreted by some as an attempt to re-create a sense of community within an increasingly impersonal urban society. One aberrant apocalyptic cult released nerve gas in a Tokyo subway in 1995, leaving the Japanese shocked that something so "un-Japanese" could happen. White-collar workers, or "salary men," spent hours commuting to work in crowded buses and trains. In Japan's corporate world *karōshi*, or death from overwork, became a recognized phenomenon.

Yet the ability of the society—family, school, office, and workshop—to absorb strains and lend support to the individual was impressive. Lifetime employment—only slightly affected by the bursting of the bubble in 1991—gave both workers and salaried employees a sense of security. Even during the long recession of the nineties, layoffs were exceptional. Japanese wives, according to public opinion polls, felt they were better off than their American counterparts. Of children born in Japan, about 1 percent were to unwed mothers; in the United States the figure was thirty times greater. Infant mortality was

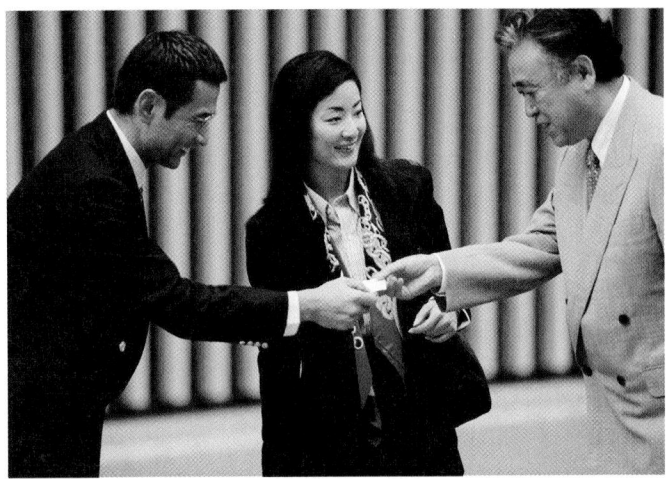

Body Language. Japanese businessmen exchange business cards in Tokyo. A businesswoman stands and observes. An almost diplomatic formality governs such occasions. *Getty Images, Inc.*

the lowest in the world and longevity the highest. Japan also had far less crime. Even big cities were safe at night. Drugs were not a problem. Effective gun control had predictable results: in 2002, 24 persons, mostly gang members, were killed by guns in Japan; the figure for the United States was almost 10,000. In 2000 the prison population in the United States was thirty times greater than that of Japan. Despite crowded housing and omnipresent social pressures, by most objective measures Japanese society was stable and healthy.

Japanese culture also remained vital. The traditional arts were maintained—poetry, painting, pottery, fabrics, tea ceremony, flower arrangement, the Kabuki, and Nō drama. The best artists were designated as Living National Treasures and held in respect. In architecture, literature, painting, and dance, the prewar tradition of vigorous experiments with new or hybrid forms continued. The awareness of nature, so evident in films like Kurosawa Akira's *Rashomon* or *The Seven Samurai*, carried over to television dramas. Films by Itami Jūzō (*Tanpopo*) and Suo Masayuki (*Shall We Dance*) combined humor and social satire. Symphony orchestras in Japan's major cities played Mozart and Stravinsky as well as native compositions with haunting passages played on the Japanese flute and zither. Clothing designers competed in Tokyo, New York, and Paris. College students formed rock bands, listened to jazz, watched *anime*, and read Japanese science fiction along with the writings of serious novelists. Postwar Japan amply supports an argument for parallelism between economic and cultural dynamics.

Japan and the World

At the start of the new millennium, Japan had three sets of critical international relationships: with the world, East Asia, and the United States. With the world, Japan was a trading partner and, as it described itself, a "UN nation." It gave more foreign aid to developing countries than did other nations. It was a member of major international economic organizations. Its economy depended on free trade, and it worked assiduously to ensure the requisite conditions. A second set was with its East Asian neighbors. For reasons of history and proximity, Japan was extraordinarily alert (and at moments insensitive) to developments in Korea, Taiwan, China, and the Russian Far East. Newspapers covered these nations in detail. Japan's relations with China, South Korea, and Taiwan have improved during recent decades, though specific grievances remain. Towards China, Japanese felt a growing ambivalence. They appreciated Chinese imports of Japanese goods, which had resuscitated the Japanese economy, but they worried that China's growing military strength was altering the political balance in East Asia, if not posing a future threat. They envisioned a peaceful balance of powers in East Asia, not a Chinese hegemony. The third critical relationship was with the United States. The two countries were political allies, major trading partners, and linked by mutual security concerns. The 1952 security treaty, several times amended, remained the cornerstone of Japanese defense planning. Until the eighties Japan contributed little. In recent decades Japan has moved towards more positive military cooperation—within the limits of its constantly reinterpreted "peace constitution." When terrorists struck at the United States in September 2001, Prime Minister Koizumi spoke out in support of the United States and against terrorism. The Diet passed new laws permitting the Self-Defense Forces to play for the first time an active, noncombat role in a war zone in support of U.S. forces. In 2003 Japan sent troops to Iraq. In 2006 the Self-Defense Agency became a cabinet ministry. In an East Asia in which China, Russia, and the United States have arsenals of atomic weapons and even North Korea has a few, Japanese feel increasingly vulnerable. If its trust in the U.S. "nuclear umbrella" should ever waver, Japan would become a nuclear power overnight.

China

The story of China after 1949 might begin with the four Ma's: Malthus, Marx, Ma Yinchu, and Mao Zedong. Malthus had claimed that population would expand geometrically whereas food would increase only arithmetically. Marx rejected the Malthusian hypothesis, along with classical economics, as myths of the capitalist stage of history. Professor Ma Yinchu (1882–1982), the chancellor of Beijing University, published in 1957 *New Principles on Chinese Population*, in which he argued that unchecked population growth would impede capital accumulation and depress living standards. Mao Zedong,

faithfully following the teachings of Marx, purged Professor Ma, and closed down population institutes at Chinese universities. What followed was a population increase from 550 million in 1949 to nearly a billion in 1981. Real growth occurred in the Chinese economy during the 1960s and 1970s, but the gains were eaten up by the extra mouths. In the face of this crisis, in 1981 the Chinese government adopted a national policy of one child per family. It recognized that the policy ran contrary to the deep-rooted Chinese sense of family but argued that without it, China's future would be bleak. Thereafter the increase slowed dramatically, but the population still crossed the 1.3 billion mark in 2005. The median age in China in 2007 is 33. Consequently, the birth rate is high—despite the one-child policy. Population will continue to grow until sometime before the middle of the century.

Soviet Period (1950–1960)

Civil war in China ended in 1949 as the last of Jiang Jieshi's troops fled to Taiwan. The People's Republic of China was proclaimed in October. The following year, China entered into an alliance with the Soviet Union. The decade that followed is often called the "Soviet period" because the Soviet model was adopted for the government, the army, the economy, and higher education.

The first step taken by the communist government was military consolidation. Even after the republic was proclaimed, Chinese armies continued to push outward, conquering vast areas with non-Chinese populations. Tibet, for example, was seized in 1950. Once subdued, the areas inhabited by Tibetans, Uighur Turks, Mongols, and other minorities were designated autonomous regions, but they were occupied by the Chinese army and were settled by a growing number of Chinese immigrants. Although members of the indigenous populations staffed their governments, the Chinese Communist Party exercised a tight control.

SOURCE *Chinese artillery class*

Political consolidation followed. The most powerful elite was the Communist Party. Its members held the key levers of power in the government, army, and security forces. Mao was both party chairman and head of state. He ruled through the Standing Committee of the Political Bureau (Politburo) of the party's Central Committee. Below the Politburo were regional, provincial, and district committees with party cells in every village, factory, school, and government office. The party expanded from 2.7 million members in 1947 to 17 million in 1961. Party members were exhorted to energize and enforce the local enactment of government policies.

Economic reconstruction began immediately. An attempt was made to integrate the industries in Manchuria and former treaty ports with the rest of China. Huge numbers of workers were mobilized to build new bridges, dams, roads, and railways. China's first five-year plan for economic development began in 1953. The Soviet Union sent financial aid as well as engineers and planners.

Rural society underwent two fundamental changes: land redistribution and then collectivization. In the early fifties, party cadres visited villages and held meetings at which landlords were denounced and forced to confess their crimes. Some were rehabilitated, others were sent to labor camps, and hundreds of thousands—some scholars estimate several million—were killed. Their holdings were redistributed to the landless, and local responsibilities formerly borne by landlord gentry were shifted to associations dominated by former tenant farmers. Then in 1955 and 1956, before the new landowners had time to put down roots as private landowners, all lands were seized by the state and collectivized. The timing was important: There was the earlier example of the Soviet Union, where collectivization came six years after redistribution; it was resisted by the *kulaks*, who had had time to put down roots.

During the early 1950s, intellectuals and universities also became a target for thought reform; the Chinese slang term was **brainwashing**. This involved study and indoctrination in Marxism, group pressure to produce an atmosphere of insecurity and fear, which would be followed by confession, repentance, and reacceptance by society. The indoctrination was intended to strengthen party control. But beyond this was the optimistic belief that the inculcation of correct moral doctrines could mobilize human energies on behalf of the state—perhaps a belief with distant Confucian roots. In 1956 Mao felt that intellectuals had been adequately indoctrinated and, concerned lest creativity be stifled, he said in a speech, "Let the hundred flowers bloom"—a reference to the lively discourse among the many schools of philosophy in ancient Zhou China. To his surprise, intellectuals responded with a torrent of criticism that did not spare the Communist Party. Mao thereupon reversed his position, sending many leading writers and intellectuals to labor camps.

By the late 1950s Mao was disappointed with the results of collectivization as it had developed during the first Five-Year Plan. In 1958 he scrapped a second plan (and the Soviet model) in favor of a mass mobilization to unleash the productive energies of the people. He called it the **Great Leap Forward**. One slogan was "Hard work for a few years and happiness for a thousand." Campaigns were organized to

Trial of a landlord. The judges, seated at tables with their hats beneath, are former tenants and Communist Party cadres. The accused, bound and guarded by PRC soldiers, is a former landlord or village head. During the land reform of the early 1950s, the sentence was often death.

accomplish vast projects; iron smelters were built in "back-yards" and instant industries were the order of the day. In the countryside, village-based collective farms gave way to communes of 30,000 persons or more. The results were disastrous. Homemade iron was unusable, instant industries failed, and agricultural production plummeted. Scholars estimate that between 1958 and 1962 as many as 20 to 30 million Chinese starved to death. To control the damage, communes were broken into production brigades in 1959, and two years later these were further broken into production teams of forty households. But even these actions could not overcome the ills of low incentives and collective responsibility; agricultural production fell through the 1970s.

It was also during these years that Sino-Soviet relations deteriorated. Disputes arose over borders. China was dissatisfied with the level of Soviet aid. It was also embarrassed by the Soviet debunking of Stalin's cult of personality, since within China Mao was still venerated as the "great helmsman." For its part, the Soviet Union condemned the Great Leap Forward as leftist fanaticism and resented Mao's view of himself, after Stalin's death, as the foremost theoretician and exponent of world communism. In 1960, the Soviet Union halted economic aid and withdrew its engineers from China, and by 1963 the split was visible to the outside world. Each country deployed about a million troops along their mutual border. Had relations between the two communist giants been amicable, these troops, deployed elsewhere, might have changed the course of history in Southeast Asia and Eastern Europe. The Sino-Soviet split was arguably the single most important development in postwar international politics.

The years between 1960 and 1965 saw conflicting trends. The utter failure of the Great Leap Forward led some Chinese leaders to turn away from Mao's reckless radicalism towards more moderate policies. Mao kept his position as the head of the party but was forced to give up his post as head of state to another veteran communist official. Yet even as the government moved towards realistic goals and stable bureaucratic management, General Lin Biao (1908–1971) reestablished within the army the party committees and procedures for ideological indoctrination that had lapsed after the failure of the Great Leap Forward. A new mass movement was also begun to transform education.

The Great Proletarian Cultural Revolution (1965–1976)

In 1965, Mao once again emerged to dominate Chinese politics. Mao the revolutionary had never been able to make the transition to Mao the ruler of an established state. When he looked at the Chinese Communist Party and the government bureaucracy, he saw a new privileged elite; when he

looked at younger Chinese, he saw a generation with no experience of revolution. Mao feared that the Chinese revolution—his revolution—would end up as a Soviet-style bureaucratic communism run for the benefit of officials, so he called for a new revolution to create a truly egalitarian culture.

Obtaining army support, Mao urged students and teenaged youth to form bands of Red Guards. In the early feverish phase of the **Cultural Revolution**, the guards invoked Mao's sayings contained in the "Little Red Book" almost as holy scripture. Mass rallies were held. One rally in Beijing was attended by "millions" of youths, who then made "long marches" back to their home provinces to carry out Mao's program. Universities were shut down as student factions fought among themselves. Teachers were beaten, imprisoned, and subjected to such extremes of humiliation that many committed suicide. Books and artworks were destroyed in a campaign against "the four olds." Stone Buddhas that had endured since the Song dynasty were smashed or defaced. Things foreign also came under attack. Homes were ransacked for foreign books, and Chinese who had studied abroad were persecuted. Even the borrowing of foreign technology was denigrated as "sniffing after the farts of foreigners and calling them sweet." Red Guards attacked local party headquarters and beat to death persons they regarded as reactionaries, including some party cadres. High officials were purged. Revolutionary committees replaced the crippled apparatus of party and government. Chinese today recall these events as a species of mass hysteria that defies understanding.

SOURCE *May Day Celebrations, Beijing*

Eventually Mao tired of the violence and near anarchy. In 1968 and 1969 he called in the army to take over the revolutionary committees. In 1969, a new Central Committee, composed largely of military men, was established, and General Lin Biao was named as Mao's successor. Violence came to an end as millions of students and intellectuals were sent to the countryside to work on farms. In 1970 and 1971 the revolutionary committees were reconstituted as party committees. Worsening relations with the Soviet Union also made China's leaders desire greater stability at home. In 1969, a pitched battle had broken out between Chinese and Russian troops over an island in the Ussuri River. After this encounter, the Chinese built bomb shelters in their main cities. It was just at this time that President Nixon began to withdraw U.S. troops from Vietnam. When he proposed a renewal of ties, China quickly responded. Nixon visited Beijing in 1972, opening a new era of diplomatic relations.

The second phase of the Cultural Revolution between 1969 and 1976 was moderate only in comparison with what had gone before. On farms and in factories, ideology was still

Performance During Cultural Revolution. Members of the Xiangyang Commune in Jiangsu Province take part in the campaign to "Criticize Lin Biao and Confucius," one of the last large "campaigns" dictated by members of Chinese government in charge of the Cultural Revolution. Here, the commune's amateur art troupe performs a ballad criticizing Confucius. The campaign began after the death of Lin Biao, who, though for a time was Mao Zedong's chosen successor, was accused of attempting to seize power.

Chronology

China Since 1949

1949	Communist victory; People's Republic of China established
1950	Sino-Soviet alliance; China invades Tibet
1953	First Five-Year Plan
1958	Great Leap Forward
1960–1963	Sino-Soviet split
1965–1976	Cultural Revolution
1972	Nixon visits Beijing
1976	Mao Zedong dies
1978–1997	Deng Xiaoping in power
1980–2007	China's economy grows at double-digit rate
1989	Tienanmen Square incident
2003	Hu Jintao becomes premier

seen as an adequate substitute for economic incentives. Universities reopened, but students were admitted by class background, not by examination. In 1971, Lin Biao was purged. According to the official account of his death, Lin had tried to kill Mao and seize the government, but when his coup failed, he died in a plane crash while attempting to escape to the Soviet Union. Lin's place was taken by the so-called Gang of Four, which included Mao's wife and was abetted by the aging Mao. Class struggle was revived, and an official campaign was launched attacking the rightist "political swindlers" Lin Biao and Confucius.

China After Mao

Political Developments Mao's death in 1976 brought immediate changes. Within four weeks the Gang of Four and their radical supporters had been arrested. In their place, Deng Xiaoping (1904–1997) emerged as the dominant figure in Chinese politics. Twice purged for rightist tendencies—once during the Cultural Revolution he was paraded around Beijing wearing a dunce cap—Deng was determined that such things not happen again. He ousted his enemies, rehabilitated those purged during the Cultural Revolution, and put his supporters in power. Portraits and statues of Mao were removed from most public places in August 1980. After the lunacy of the Cultural Revolution, the establishment of a normal Communist dictatorship came as a welcome relief. The people began to enjoy a measure of security and the prospect of better lives.

There arose, however, a tension between the determination of the ruling party to maintain its grip on power and its desire to obtain the benefits of some liberalization. The tension was most visible in China's intellectual life. The government's repudiation of the Cultural Revolution had led to an outpouring of stories, plays, and reports. In *Nightmare* by Xu Hui, the mother of a son killed during the Cultural Revolution asks, "Why? Why? Can anyone tell me why?" Liu Binyan wrote of corrupt officials who had "degenerated into parasitical insects that fed off the people's productivity and the socialist system." But criticism of Deng's rule was not allowed. Writers were regularly enjoined to be "led by the Communist Party and guided by Marx-Leninism." When a writer in 1983 overstepped the invisible line separating what was permissible from what was not, a short campaign was launched against "spiritual pollution." In 1985 and 1987 as well, the government organized campaigns against "capitalist thinking" and "bourgeois democracy."

Universities returned to normal in 1977. Entrance examinations were reinstituted, purged teachers were returned to their classrooms, and scientists and scholars were sent to study in Japan and the West. During the late seventies and eighties students still spent one afternoon a week discussing party directives or the writings of Deng Xiaoping. But far more influential was the new openness within China and the growing contacts with the wider world as scholars returned from the West. Students became aware of the prosperity achieved by Japan, Hong Kong, and Taiwan. They began to demand greater freedoms and even political democracy. During the late 1980s, the ferment that marked Eastern Europe and the Soviet Union under Gorbachev also appeared in China: it was as if a new virus had entered the communist world.

The new spirit came to a head in April and May of 1989, when hundreds of thousands of students, workers, and people from all walks of life demonstrated for democracy in Tienanmen Square in Beijing and in dozens of other cities. Hunger strikes were held. Students published prodemocracy newspapers. Banners proclaimed slogans, among them "Give us freedom or give us death." A twenty-seven-foot polystyrene-and-plaster Goddess of Democracy and Freedom was erected in the square. At first, government leaders could not agree on how to respond, but the hardline faction led by Deng won out and in early June sent in tanks and troops. Hundreds of students were killed, and leaders who did not escape abroad were jailed. The event defined the political climate in China in the years that followed: No challenge to Communist Party rule was tolerated, though considerable freedom was allowed in other areas of life.

Economic Growth

In the economic sphere, China's leaders repudiated the policies of Mao. After taking power, Deng

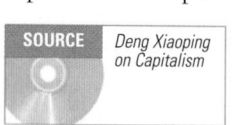

SOURCE *Deng Xiaoping on Capitalism*

said in a speech (or is said to have said) that "to be rich is glorious." His greatest achievement in the years after 1978 was to demonstrate in China the superiority of market incentives to central planning. In 1985, Hu Yaobang, the General Secretary of the CCP, expressed a similarly realistic view, that China "had wasted twenty years" on "radical leftist nonsense."

In China's villages, as the family farm once again became the basic unit of production, grain production rose from about 300 million tons in the 1980s to more than 500 million in the late 1990s. A local leader commented, "When people work for themselves, they work better." Then, as farmers living near

Goddess of Democracy and Freedom. Student activists construct a "Goddess of Democracy and Freedom," taking the Statue of Liberty as their model. The goddess was in place in Tienanmen Square shortly before tanks drove students from the square in June 1989. *Reuters/Ed Nachtrieb/ Archive Photos.*

cities found it much more profitable to abandon grains in favor of specialty crops such as fruit or the feedgrains required by China's rising consumption of meat, grain production declined to 431 million tons in 2003. Family farm incomes continued to gain, though still only a third of those of city dwellers. Worried about rising imports of grains and future self-sufficiency, in 2003 the government announced agricultural subsidies to promote grain production.

State-operated enterprises—the surviving portion of the old, centrally planned, command economy—as late as 1982 generated 74 percent of total industrial production. More than half ran at a loss, and because they employed twice the labor needed to run them efficiently, they were a constant drain on China's state-owned banks. Their workers were paid little and had little incentive to work hard, since they enjoyed the security of the so-called iron ricebowl. In 1999 the government announced a plan to sell off many of these enterprises. The state ownership required by China's constitution would give way to public (that is to say, private) ownership. The temporary costs would be high in terms of defaulted loans, bankruptcies, unemployed workers, and a rise in pensioners, but the drain on the state budget would end. Since 1999, the picture has changed: Some industries were sold off. Some were made more efficient and continued as a "strategically important" government sector, including industries involved in military equipment, electrical power, oil, telecommunications, aviation, and shipping.

The main driver of the economy, however, has been the free market sector. The figures are dazzling. Between 1980 and 2007 the Chinese economy grew at an average of 10 percent. In 2006, the rate was 10.7 percent. Industrial production grew at twice that rate. Exports rose steadily from $7 billion in 1975 to $974 billion in 2006. The surge in new enterprises began in special economic zones established along the border with Hong Kong and quickly spread along the coast. Shanghai, with a population of 14 million, became a city of industrialists and skyscrapers and the site of China's first stock exchange. Shandong Province in the northeast attracted huge investments from Japan, South Korea, and the United States and achieved stunning growth. As entrepreneurs, cities, and local governments joined in, the tide of enterprise swept inland. Wuhan, a major communications hub and automobile manufacturer in central China, averaged growth of 16 or 17 percent during the early 1990s. In the hinterlands large regions lagged behind and clamored for government assistance, but to achieve growth the government was willing to tolerate personal and regional inequities.

The factors that fueled this growth were clear: a huge surplus of good quality, cheap labor, a savings rate of 35–40 percent, a level of protectionism higher than other Asian nations, large investments from abroad, and open world markets. The rate of literacy in China is 91 percent and rising. At Peking University, it is easier to gain admission to the medical school than to the business school or the Department of Economics. China, initially, used tariffs to shield its markets, while making use of cheap labor to flood foreign markets with goods and build up its currency reserves—which in 2007 were more than 1 trillion dollars, the highest in the world. China joined the World Trade Organization in 2001; since then its protectionism has become less blatant.

Social Change During the Mao years, farmers had been tied to their village collective. Cities were closed to those without residence permits. City dwellers, whether they worked in factories, hospitals, schools, newspapers, or government offices, were members of "units." Units, like company towns, provided

Cheap Labor. Wages at this Beijing shirt factory are low by Western standards but high by Chinese standards. This is not a sweatshop but a modern factory. Should Western nations leave the production of textiles to low-wage nations? What of steel or micro electronics?
A. Raney/Photo Edit.

their members with jobs, housing, food, child care, medical services, and pensions. Party cadres controlled the units and, through them, every aspect of their members' lives. Block organizations exercised surveillance over the inhabitants and reported infractions of socialist morality to the authorities.

Under Deng, controls were loosened. The police became less active (except against political dissidents), censorship was reduced, and ties with the outside world were allowed to develop. The "unit" also diminished in importance as food became widely available in free markets, and apartments were sold to their inhabitants on easy terms. Private housing brought with it the freedom to change jobs. As workers with higher salaries began to provide for their own needs, life became freer and more enjoyable. The market economy placed a premium on individual decisions and initiatives.

The new prosperity and changing mores became increasingly visible. The blue Mao uniforms of the 1960s were followed by suits, however ill-fitting and later, for the young, blue jeans, sneakers, and colorful jackets. By the 1990s, innovative Chinese designers were holding fashion shows in Shanghai and Beijing. Young people associated freely, and in urban areas earlier taboos against public displays of affection were relaxed. The household treasures of the 1960s, radios and bicycles, gave way to stoves and refrigerators in the 1970s, and in the next decade, to washing machines and color televisions. Crowds gathered around displays of motorbikes in department stores. By the early nineties, motorbikes and privately owned cars competed in crowded streets with the ceaseless flow of bicycles. Private restaurants opened, and travel for pleasure became commonplace.

Chinese Affluence. Shoppers at Pacific Place in Hong Kong, one of the many new upscale shopping malls that are found throughout China.

In 1988, most passengers on domestic airline flights were foreign; ten years later, most were Chinese.

The estimated Chinese per capita GDP, as measured by the exchange value of its currency, was about $1,902 in 2006. While this is low, in purchasing power the figure is closer to $7,600. Chinese are keenly aware that their living standard has improved sharply over the past two decades and expect similar improvements in the future.

The new wealth, quite naturally, was unevenly distributed. The more successful entrepreneurs bought houses, cars, microwaves, computers, and cell phones. They traveled abroad and sent their children to private schools. As their lifestyle became more Western, they were sometimes called China's new middle class, but in fact they constituted an upper class. Other city dwellers participated in the new prosperity but to a lesser extent, and many barely scraped by. In villages, the pace of change was slower: In prosperous belts surrounding cities, farmers built brick houses and owned tractors, but in the hinterlands an older poverty remained the rule. In the West envy is green. In China the envy and resentment by have-nots towards the newly affluent is called the "red-eye disease."

China and the World   The Cold War largely defined foreign relations in the China of Mao. It was amicable towards its communist neighbors—the Soviet Union, North Korea, and North Vietnam, and hostile towards South Korea, Japan,

U.S.-protected Taiwan, and the United States. It sent troops to rescue North Korea during the latter phase of the Korean War (1950–1953), and it sent material aid to the North Vietnamese during the Vietnam War (1959–1975). However, its rupture with the Soviet Union in 1960 isolated it from relations with the other major communist power in East Asia. China's fear of the Soviet Union and America's despair over its war in Vietnam opened the way for President Nixon's visit to China in 1972. The visit notwithstanding, China's foreign relations until after Mao's death in 1976 were largely a reflection of the revolutionary tumult within.

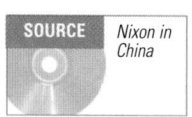
SOURCE   *Nixon in China*

Deng Xiaoping's embrace of market capitalism after 1978 was, necessarily, coupled with an about face in foreign relations, since world trade was critical for export-led economic growth. China reestablished relations with the Soviet Union. It welcomed increased trade and investments from Japan, South Korea, and Taiwan. It developed a growing trade with the European Economic Community.

Relations with the United States were complicated, despite the U.S. recognition of China in 1979. American military alliances with Japan and South Korea, its unofficial support of Taiwan, and its ties to the non-communist nations of Southeast Asia continued to act as the main countervailing force to Chinese hegemony in the region. China resented the U.S. presence in what it considered—in Middle Kingdom fashion—its own proper sphere of influence. The United States was appreciative of the benefits of trade with China but was critical of the extreme imbalance: China's exports to the United States increased from $62 billion in 1997 to $288 billion in 2006 and still rise; its imports from the United States during the same period increased from $13 to $55 billion. The United States also protested the continuing Chinese piracy of hundreds of millions of dollars' worth of U.S. movies, computer software, and CDs each year. It criticized as well human rights abuses, nuclear testing, and arms sales to Iran and Pakistan (See Document, "U.S. Foreign Policy: A Chinese Dissident's View.")

A third phase of Chinese foreign policy—of China as a great power—began to take form at the turn of the century. As Japan had earlier, China moved to establish relations with Africa, South America, and the Middle East to secure stable

sources of the raw materials needed to feed its industries. It also stepped up the transformation of its military forces from a mass army to a smaller but more powerful, hi-tech, modern military. Unlike Japan, it possessed an arsenal of atomic and hydrogen bombs. The rapid growth of its military budget will soon enable China to project its military strength beyond its borders.

U.S. policy towards the new China rested on the assumption that a wider Chinese engagement with the world would lead to better relations. The Chinese premier visited the United States in 1997, and the U.S. president returned the visit the following year. In 2000, the U.S. House of Representatives accorded China a most-favored nation trade status; the following year China was admitted to the World Trade Organization. When terrorists destroyed the World Trade Center in September 2001, China saw this as an opportunity

---

U.S. Foreign Policy: A Chinese Dissident's View

Document

Wei Jingsheng, a Chinese advocate of democratic rights, was deported to the United States in late 1997. A year later, in an op-ed page essay in *The New York Times,* he criticized U.S. policy as pandering to Chinese tyranny.

◆ Should U.S. foreign policy be used to promote human rights even in poor countries with cultural traditions different from those in the West? Or should the United States avoid interference in the domestic politics of other nations and aim primarily at furthering American economic and security goals? What can foreign policy achieve? Where should the balance be struck?

CHINA'S DIVERSIONARY TACTICS

One year ago, after 18 years in a Chinese prison, I was "released" and sent here. A Chinese official said that if I ever set foot in China again, I would immediately be returned to prison. . . .

The State Department, in a report last January, used my forced exile as evidence that China was taking "positive steps in human rights" and that "Chinese society continued to become more open." These "positive steps" led the United States and its allies to oppose condemnation of China at a meeting of the United Nations Commission on Human Rights in April. In the months that followed, President Clinton and other Western leaders traveled to China, trumpeting increased economic ties and muting criticism on human rights.

Thus, without fear of sanction, the Chinese Government intensified its repression in 1998. Once the leaders achieved their diplomatic victories, they turned to

their main objective: the preservation of tyrannical power. This year, about 70 people are known to have been arrested. . . .

Li Peng, the speaker of the National People's Party Congress, declared recently, "If an organization's purpose is to promote a multiparty system in China and to negate the leadership prerogatives of the Chinese Communist Party, then it will not be permitted to exist."

This statement clearly shows that the Communist Party's primary objective is to sustain its tyranny, and to do so it must deny the people basic rights and freedoms. We must measure the leaders' progress on human rights not by the "release" of individuals but by the people's ability to speak, worship and assemble without official interference and persecution.

Wei Jingsheng, *The New York Times,* 24 December 1998. Copyright © 1998 by *The New York Times.* Reprinted by permission.

Reviewing the Troops in Hong Kong. Chinese President Hu Jintao inspects the People's Liberation Army garrison during a three day visit to the Stonecutter's Naval Base in Hong Kong in 2007. Hu was on a three day visit to celebrate the tenth anniversary of Hong Kong's handover to Chinese rule.

to move against pro-independence Muslim groups in its own western provinces and gave verbal backing to the U.S. campaign against terrorism. Since 2003, China has cooperated with the United States, Japan, Russia, and South Korea to end the development of nuclear weapons by North Korea. A generational change in Chinese leadership occurred when Hu Jintao became General Secretary of the CCP in 2002 and premier in 2003. He introduced a more open style of administration but did not relinquish the CCP's monopoly on government. In 2005, Hu visited Washington and Seattle, where he had dinner with Bill Gates.

Taiwan

Taiwan is a mountainous island less than 100 miles off the coast of central China. A little larger than Belgium or Massachusetts, it has a population of 22.9 million. Originally populated by aborigines, and then lightly settled by Chinese immigrants, it became a distant and backward part of the Qing empire. In 1895, it became a Japanese colony as a spoil of the Sino-Japanese War. The Japanese found it easy to rule since the Taiwanese lacked a sense of national identity and were accustomed to rule by officials who came from across the seas and spoke a language they could not understand. (Standard Chinese and the Fujian dialect spoken by Taiwanese are mutually unintelligible.) The Japanese colonial government quickly suppressed opium and bandits and eradicated epidemic diseases. It built roads and railroads, reformed the land system, and introduced improvements in agriculture. Before 1895 education had been the privilege of a tiny elite; sixty years later, 71 percent of school-age children attended the "common schools" established by the Japanese. (In the Dutch East Indies and French Indochina

the figure was about 10 or 15 percent.) Light industries were introduced, and during the thirties, textiles, chemicals, ceramics, and machine tools. Though mostly owned by Japanese and run in their interest, more benefits seem to have accrued to the local population than was the case in Korea, another Japanese colony.

Anticolonial feelings rose slowly. During the twenties Taiwanese petitioned for political reforms and received a few concessions, but after the China war began in 1937, the Japanese reverted to strict controls and assimilationist policies. At the end of the war the Taiwanese were happy to see the Japanese leave and welcomed GMD (Guomindang) officials as liberators. The new officials, however, viewing the Taiwanese as Japanese collaborators, looted the economy and ruled harshly. When Taiwanese protested in February 1947, the GMD police put down the demonstrators and over several months killed almost 10,000 Taiwanese, many of them community leaders. By the time Jiang Jieshi (Chiang Kai-shek) and 2 million more military and civilian mainlanders fled to the island in 1949, its economy and society were in disarray. Mainlanders looked down on the Taiwanese, who in turn hated their new rulers and in private often compared them unfavorably to the Japanese.

From the 1950s onward three interdependent developments occurred: the growth of the economy, the rise of democratic politics, and a changing relation to the mainland of China.

The economic story is interesting in that the GMD, which had failed in China, succeeded in Taiwan. Part of the reason is that its control of the island was complete and the times were peaceful. It had restored order by the mid-fifties, and rapid growth followed. Heavy industries were put under state control; other former Japanese industries were sold to private parties. With the outbreak of the Korean War in

1950, U.S. aid became substantial. Foreign investment was welcomed. Light industries were followed by consumer electronics, steel, and petrochemicals and then by computers and semiconductors. Private industries led the way. During the late eighties, substantial Taiwanese investments in China began; by 2005 they totaled over $47 billion. The two economies moved closer together. By the late nineties, Taiwan was the world's largest producer of monitors, keyboards, motherboards, and computer mice; it was second in notebook PCs and fourth in integrated circuits. Many of these were actually manufactured in Taiwanese-owned plants in mainland China. Estimated Taiwanese per capita product in 2006 was $12,500 (or nearer to $29,000 in actual purchasing power), several times that of mainland China.

The transition in Taiwan from authoritarian to democratic government was not unlike that in South Korea, and coupled with the earlier example of Japan, suggests that democracy is a viable option for "East Asian" societies. For the first twenty years, the GMD government of Taiwan was a dictatorship, and it ruled as it had on the mainland: opposition parties were banned, and martial law was in effect. It maintained that it was the government of all of China, and through its control of the "central government," dominated the "provincial government" in which Taiwanese were permitted to participate. Social changes began during the 1960s. Education advanced, with rising numbers entering universities. Taiwanese and mainlanders began to intermarry. As the economy advanced, a new middle class emerged, a class more concerned with economic wellbeing than past history. Taiwanese entered the GMD and moved from provincial to central government posts. Jiang Jieshi died in 1975, a year earlier than Mao. Under his son Jiang Jingguo, who was president from 1978 to 1988, Taiwan inched towards representative government. In 1987, he permitted opposition parties to form and ended martial law.

The next advance occurred in 1988, when Li Denghui, a Taiwanese who had risen within the GMD, became president. This ended the pattern of mainlander rule. An academic before becoming a politician, Li was a graduate of a Taiwanese high school, Kyoto Imperial University, and Cornell. In 1996, in what he billed as "the first free election in 5,000 years of Chinese history," Li became the first "elected" president of Taiwan. A further advance towards a fully democratic system occurred in 2000, when Chen Shuibian, the candidate of the leading opposition party, was elected as Li's successor. Also a Taiwanese, Chen was born in poverty, rose to become a corporate lawyer, and in 1994, became mayor of Taipei. His election, which ended fifty years of GMD rule, was hailed by one scholar as "the first peaceful transition of power from one political party to another in Taiwanese history, and probably in all of Chinese history." In 2004 Chen was reelected as president. The next presidential election in 2008 will doubtless be free and open.

Since 1949, the communist government in Beijing has claimed that Taiwan is a province of China unlawfully controlled by a "bandit" government. It spoke of taking Taiwan by force. It maintained that its relation with the island was a matter of internal Chinese politics and refused diplomatic ties with any nation maintaining such ties with Taiwan. For almost thirty years, from the outbreak of the Korean War in 1950 until 1979, Taiwan was a

The World's Tallest Building. Evening traffic swirls around the world's tallest building, the Taipei 101, completed in 2004, with 101 floors. At 1,671 feet, it is the only building in the world to be over a half kilometer in height. The design is inspired by traditional Chinese architecture.

protégé of the United States, which ignored the mainland, supported Taiwan's claim to be the legitimate government of all of China, and provided military protection for the island. In 1979, however, the United States formally broke off relations with Taipei and recognized Beijing as the legitimate government of a China that included Taiwan. The United States, nevertheless, continued informal relations with Taiwan, and continued to trade with it and sell it arms. Curiously, it was during the years of diplomatic limbo after the 1979 break that Taiwan's economy grew and its society became democratic.

At the onset of the twenty-first century, both China and the United States were apprehensive about Taiwan. China was concerned that a democratically elected government would give Taiwan a claim to legitimacy in the eyes of the world. It also worried that Taiwan's prosperity would make its peoples less willing to rejoin the mainland—a view lent credence by public opinion polls in Taiwan. It spoke anew of using force to retake the island, but it was aware that an invasion of the island would disrupt China's own world trade. China also knew that the growing economic dependence of Taiwan on China might, eventually, make an invasion unnecessary. The United States, for its part, feared that within a decade or two China would have the military power to attempt the conquest of Taiwan. It cautioned Taiwan's president not to speak of independence. He responded that a declaration of independence was unnecessary since Taiwan already functioned as an independent state. Some in the U.S. Congress felt that the United States could not stand by and see this prosperous and democratic state, which it had helped to create, be forcibly taken over by China.

Korea

Korea and Vietnam, the other two countries in the East Asian zone of civilization, both became colonies: Vietnam became a part of French Indochina in 1883; Korea was annexed by Japan in 1910. In both countries, the imposition of colonialism on a people with a high indigenous culture and a strong sense of national identity engendered a powerful anticolonial nationalism. After World War II, both were divided into a communist north and a non-communist south, Korea immediately and Vietnam years later. Both experienced civil war. In each instance the United States entered the conflicts to stem the spread of communism. Never before had the United States fought in countries about which it knew so little.

Korea as a Japanese Colony

The social ills and political and economic weaknesses that had plagued the Choson dynasty in 1800 continued through the nineteenth century. As the century drew to a close,

a three-cornered, imperialist rivalry arose among China, Japan, and Russia, with Korea as the prize. Japan won. Defeating China in the Sino-Japanese War (1894–1895) and Russia in the Russo-Japanese War (1904–1905), it made Korea a protectorate in 1905 and annexed it in 1910.

Annexation was followed by efforts to make Korea a model colony. A land survey and land tax reform clarified land ownership. Public hygiene was enforced, infectious diseases dropped sharply, and the population grew from 14 million in 1910 to 24 million in 1940. Attendance at common schools increased from 20,000 in 1910 to 1.2 million in 1939, while attendance at higher common schools, girls' higher schools, and trade schools also rose. New money was issued and banks established. As in Taiwan, a huge investment was made in roads, railways, and telegraph lines. The 1920s saw further investments in hydroelectric power, nitrogenous fertilizer plants, and mining. Most large-scale industries were Japanese-owned, but Korean entrepreneurs began textile mills, shipping lines, and small industries. Even excluding mining and transport, employment in industry rose from 385,000 in 1932 to 1,322,000 in 1943.

The colonial transformation was not just a matter of economics. Koreans who studied at Japanese universities came into contact with the full range of political, social, literary, and artistic currents of the modern world and brought their new knowledge back to Korea. By the 1930s a modern culture was forming in Korea's cities. In sum, experiencing a truncated version of Meiji-type reforms, Korea became vastly different from what it had been in 1910.

Being a Japanese colony was nonetheless a hard road to modernity. The colonial government was authoritarian. Its goal was to make Korea into a part of Imperial Japan—albeit a subordinate part—any benefits to Koreans were incidental. Education was Japan-oriented, and instruction was given in Japanese. The land tax reform primarily benefited landowners. Japanese and Korean land companies bought up former crown lands, and tenancy rose from 42 percent in 1913 to 69 percent in 1945. The Japanese in Korea received better salaries, medical care, education, and jobs than their Korean counterparts. Whether in government, banking, or industry, Koreans were mainly relegated to the lower echelons. To be sure, this was also the case in all European colonies, but it particularly rankled in Korea because Korea was an older culture and racially close to Japan. The colonial regime, moreover, suppressed all nationalist movements and political opposition, denying Koreans the experience of self-government. Some political activists fled to China or the Soviet Union. The police, half of whom were Koreans, earned a reputation for brutality and were hated by the populace. After 1937, the Japanese policy of "assimilation" grew even harsher: Koreans were pressured to adopt Japanese names, drafted to fight in Japan's wars, and sent to labor in factories in Japan. "Comfort women" were recruited, occasionally by force, to service Japanese troops. In recent years, this bitter colonial legacy has only begun to subside.

North and South

Immediately upon Japan's defeat in 1945, Soviet troops entered the North; a month later U.S. forces occupied Korea south of the Thirty-Eighth Parallel. There had been a promise of unification, but two separate states developed. In the South, the United States initially aimed at the formation of a democratic, self-governing nation but settled for the anti-communist and somewhat authoritarian government of Syngman Rhee (1875–1965), a longtime nationalist leader whose party won the 1948 election. With Rhee's installation as the first president of the Republic of Korea, the United States formally ended its military government of Korea. Many of Rhee's officials and officers had formerly served in the colonial government or the Japanese military. His government was strongly supported by conservative Koreans and by the million or so Koreans who had fled the North.

Comfort Women. South Korean women who were forced to become sex slaves by the Japanese during World War II protest near the Japanese embassy in Seoul, January 2003.

In the North, the Russians established a communist government under Kim Il Sung (1912–1994). Kim had worked with the Chinese Communists during the 1930s and subsequently with the Soviet Union. When the South held elections in 1948, the North hurriedly followed suit. In September, the Democratic People's Republic of Korea was established. Not a few of its officers and officials had fought on the communist side in the Chinese Civil War. At the end of 1948 the Soviet Union withdrew its troops from North Korea. During 1949 and early 1950 the United States withdrew most of its troops from the South. The withdrawal was part of a larger American disengagement from continental Asia after the communist victory in China. The United States at the same time dissociated itself from the Chinese nationalist regime on Taiwan as a part of its policy of "letting the dust settle."

Civil War and U.S. Involvement

On June 25, 1950, North Korea invaded the South in an attempt to reunite the Korean peninsula. Kim Il Sung, the North Korean leader, had received Stalin's permission for the invasion and a promise from Mao to send Chinese troops in case the United States entered the war. He planned for a quick victory before the United States had time to intervene. But the Cold War had already begun in Europe, and the invasion, coming four months after the signing of the Sino-Soviet Alliance, was seen by the United States as an act of aggression by world communism. The United States rushed

troops from Japan to South Korea and obtained United Nations backing for its action. It also sent naval forces to the Taiwan Straits to protect Taiwan, and over the next several years, entered into military alliances with South Korea, Japan, Taiwan, the Philippines, and the non-communist states of Southeast Asia. The Korean War was a catalyst for a major turn in postwar American foreign policy.

During the first months of the war, the unprepared American and South Korean forces were driven southward into a small area around Pusan on the southeastern rim of the peninsula (see Map 33–2). But then, amphibious units led by the United Nations commander General Douglas MacArthur landed at Inchon in the middle of Korea's western coast and drove the North Korean armies beyond the Thirty-Eighth Parallel deep into North Korea. In midwar, American policy had shifted from the containment of communism to a rollback.

The UN forces in Korea were half American and two-fifths Korean; the rest were contingents from Britain, Australia, Turkey, and twelve other nations. In the final phase of the war, China sent in "volunteers" to rescue the beleaguered North Korean forces. Chinese troops pushed the overextended UN forces back to a line close to the Thirty-Eighth Parallel. After months of fierce fighting, the war became stalemated in 1951 and ended with an armistice on July 27, 1953. Thereafter the two Koreas maintained a hostile peace. On each side of the heavily guarded border were about 600,000 troops. The 142,000 American casualties made the war the fourth largest in U.S. history.

Map 33–2.   The Korean War, 1950–1953.

South Korea: Democracy and Growth

After the armistice, two remarkable and intertwined stories unfolded in South Korea: stunning economic growth and the rise of a democratic polity.

Rhee remained in office until 1960, when at age eighty-five he was forced to retire in the wake of massive student demonstrations. There followed twenty-seven years of rule by two generals and then twenty years of democratic government. The first general, Park Chung-hee, seized power in a military *coup d'état* in 1961. Shedding his uniform, he then won a controlled election and became a civilian president. His rule was semiauthoritarian: Opposition parties were legal and active but their leaders were often jailed. Students were able to mount protest demonstrations but were usually blocked by riot

police and frequently tear-gassed. South Koreans could read non-communist foreign books and magazines and travel abroad. In time, even Koreans who approved of Park's economic policies came to resent his use of police and intelligence agencies to sustain his rule. Park was assassinated by his intelligence chief in 1979. Another general seized power the following year, transformed himself into a civilian president, and ruled until 1987 in the pattern established by his predecessor.

At the inception of Park's rule, unemployment had been rife and poverty widespread. Park and his successor were determined to promote economic growth. Emphasizing science and technology, they supported business and swiftly expanded higher education. Management drew on skills learned during the colonial era; labor was disciplined, hardworking, and cheap. The United States gave large amounts of aid and provided an open market for Korean exports. The result was double-digit growth. Especially notable was the growth of **chaebol** such as Hyundai or Daewoo, which resembled the Mitsui or Mitsubishi *zaibatsu* of prewar Japan. The policies of the two leaders, and of their successors after 1987, were successful beyond their expectations. Korea's gross national product rose dramatically (see Figure 33–2).

With an estimated per capita product in 2006 of $17,720 (and a purchasing power considerably higher), South Korea moved into the ranks of developed nations and became the world's tenth largest economy. The country's voice in world affairs grew with its economy.

Ironically, the industrialization and urbanization wrought by the two generals created an affluent and educated middle class that was no longer willing to tolerate authoritarian rule.

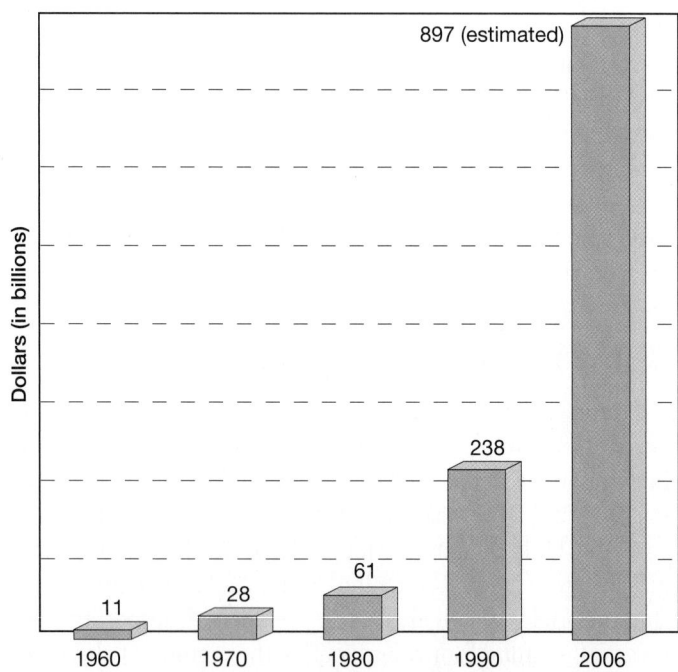

Figure 33–2.   South Korean Gross Domestic Product 1960–2006.

In 1987, an era of increasingly democratic politics began. In the election of that year—an election seen as free and democratic—a former general was elected as president. Five years later in 1992, a moderate, conservative party politician with no ties to the military was voted into office. He purged the generals who had supported the two previous presidents and replaced them with officers willing to work with party governments. He also launched investigations of his predecessors' finances. Though one reporter commented that corruption was as Korean as *kimchee* (a traditional dish of spicy, pickled cabbage), the hundreds of millions of dollars in secret bank accounts uncovered by investigators astonished even the Koreans. In 1995, the previous presidents and several top *chaebol* leaders were arrested, found guilty, and sent to prison, though they were later released.

Further evidence of the durability of representative government in South Korea was demonstrated in the election of 1997, in which the leader of an opposition party, Kim Dae-jung, became president. A longtime pro-democracy campaigner, Kim had earlier been the target of assassination attempts and once condemned to die. He was pro-labor, a populist, a Catholic, and an idealist. He took office with high hopes but encountered difficulties that proved insurmountable. The economy sagged; layoffs and fear of further job losses left public opinion unsettled. Kim also adopted a "sunshine policy" of openness, reconciliation, and material aid towards North Korea. His efforts to reduce tensions on the

The Two Kims. South Korean President Kim Dae-jung traveled to Pyongyang in June 2000 to promote his "sunshine policy." As he departed he hugged Kim Jong-il, the North Korean leader. But when the North Korean leader failed to respond with a visit to Seoul or with an easing of tensions, sunshine turned to rain, and Kim Dae-jung's popularity sagged. *Koren Pool/Yonhap/AP/Wide World Photos.*

peninsula earned him a Nobel Peace Prize in 1998, but it later came out that North Korea had agreed to a summit only after receiving a bribe from the South. When North Korea failed to reciprocate Kim's overtures, Kim's popularity fell.

However, the underlying trend continued: in 2002 another opposition politician, Roh Moo-hyun, was elected president. Roh was younger, more liberal, and represented a generation with no memory of the Korean War. He was backed by a minority party and resented by the conservative majority party in the National Assembly. In March 2004 the conservatives voted to impeach him. The Korean people felt the impeachment improper, and in the April election they gave Roh's URI Party a majority of National Assembly seats. In May, the Constitutional Court overturned the impeachment and Roh returned to office. Critical of the United States and open to closer relations with China and the government in the North, Roh's presidency suggested a change in South Korea's international stance. By the end of his term, however, Roh had lost his popularity, and some predicted that conservative politicians would be returned to power in the December 2007 election.

North Korea

Before 1945, most Japanese industries in Korea were located in the North, giving its industrialization an early edge. But North Korea's planned economy was enclosed within a tightly sealed, authoritarian state, which stressed heavy industry, organized its farmers in collectives, and totally controlled education and the media. By the 1970s, its economy became sluggish, and shortages of food, clothing, and necessities were chronic. During the 1990s there were periods in which famines led to a drop in population.

The misery of the North Korean people was highlighted by the caviar and Mercedes Benz lifestyle of its leaders. The cult of personality surrounding "the great leader" Kim Il Sung went beyond that of even Stalin or Mao. The Korean Communist Party was Marxist-Leninist, but the kinship terminology used to describe the fatherly leader, the mother party, and the familial North Korean state gave the official state philosophy an almost Confucian coloration. Kim designated his son, "the beloved leader" Kim Jong-Il (b. 1942), as his successor, and when the father died in 1994, the son became the leader of North Korea—the only instance of hereditary succession in a communist state.

International Relations

Since the Korean War, South Korea was allied with the United States, which guaranteed its defense. Even in 2007, a small U.S. military force remained in the South. North Korea was backed by the Soviet Union and China, the latter asserting that their solidarity was "as close as lips and teeth." However, after the collapse of the Soviet Union, Russia lost interest in its former ally. China continued to offer aid and trade but was more attracted by the allure of a vibrant South Korea, with which it established diplomatic relations in 1992. Since then, South Koreans have invested billions in China, trade between the two nations has flourished, and in 1995 the Chinese president visited Seoul. North Korea was increasingly an orphan.

The North Korean record was poor. To obtain hard currency, it had engaged in counterfeiting and drug smuggling. It ran prison camps like those of the former Soviet Union. It had kidnapped Japanese citizens, fired missiles into Japanese waters, and threatened Japan, saying that Tokyo would be reduced to "a sea of fire" if Japan continued its security arrangement with the United States. Increasingly isolated, and with a garrison state mentality, it used a Pakistani connection to import nuclear technology. When charged with this in 2003, it first denied and then boasted of the development. The United States, China, Russia, South Korea, and Japan moved to persuade North Korea to abandon its development of such weapons. Even China did not want a nuclear North Korea on its doorstep. But both China and South Korea with its "sunshine policy" were reluctant to apply pressure, fearing a North Korean collapse and a flood of refugees. In October 2006 North Korea exploded its first atomic bomb. This led China, North Korea's principal trading partner, to toughen its stance, and in February 2007 an agreement settling some issues was reached between North Korea and the six powers: food and aid in exchange for an abandonment of nuclear weapons. What kind of final settlement would be reached was still unclear. All that can be said with certainty was that a small, isolated, bankrupt dictatorship had kept the attention of its larger neighbors for more than a decade.

Vietnam

The Colonial Backdrop

The Nguyen dynasty that reunited Vietnam in 1802 was still vigorous in 1858 when France began its conquest of the area, but it proved no match. France completed its conquest of Vietnam and Cambodia in 1883, formed the Indochinese Union in 1887, and added Laos to the Union in 1893.

In many ways Indochina was a classic example of colonial rule: a people of one race and culture, for the sake of economic benefits and national glory, controlling and exploiting a people of another race and culture in a far-off land. To obtain access to the country's natural resources, the French built harbors, roads, and a railway linking Saigon, Hanoi, and southern China. They established rubber plantations in the Mekong Delta and tea plantations in the highlands. They

introduced modern mining technology for the extraction of coal and built breweries, rice and paper mills, and glass and cement factories. Large industries were dominated by the French, smaller enterprises by Vietnamese-Chinese. Workers were paid poorly. Vietnamese were mainly laborers, except for the few that became landlords. In the South, 3 percent of landowners owned 45 percent of the land and received 60 percent of the crop grown by their tenants. Although new irrigation works in the Mekong Delta quadrupled the area of rice fields, the consumption of rice by peasants declined. The skewed distribution of wealth meant that no indigenous middle class developed, apart from the landlords and Chinese merchants whose commercial acumen was resented by the Vietnamese. The French also did little to educate the Vietnamese: in 1939, over 80 percent of the population was illiterate, possibly a higher percentage than in the early nineteenth century under the Nguyen.

During the early decades of French rule, the Vietnamese made futile attempts to restore the dynasty. By the early twentieth century, Vietnamese nationalists in exile in China, Japan, and France had formed political parties. But when they tried to organize within Vietnam, the parties were suppressed and their leaders jailed or executed. Within Vietnam, only clandestine parties survived. The most skilled organizer of such parties was Ho Chi Minh (1892–1969), who had participated in the founding of the French Communist Party in 1920, studied in Moscow in 1923, and worked under the Comintern agent Mikhail Borodin in Canton in 1925. Ho founded the Revolutionary Youth League of Vietnam in 1925 and sent its cadres to China and the Soviet Union for training. He then founded the Indochinese Communist Party in 1930. When the Popular Front gained power in France (1936–1938), opposition parties were tolerated in Vietnam and Ho's party emerged the strongest. After 1938 the French again suppressed all opposition groups. Shortly before the outbreak of the Pacific War, the Japanese occupied Vietnam. For their own convenience, until March 1945, they ruled through Vichy French puppets. Ho, who in 1941 had formed the **Viet Minh** (League for the Independence of Vietnam) as a popular front organization to resist the Japanese, proclaimed the Democratic Republic of Vietnam after Japan's defeat in 1945 and became the preeminent nationalist leader in his country. There followed three cycles of war and almost three decades of peace.

The Anticolonial War

The first war lasted from 1946 to 1954. On one side was the Viet Minh, led by Ho. It was controlled by Communists but also included some representatives of nationalist parties. On the other side were the French, who had reoccupied Vietnam immediately after the war, and their conservative Vietnamese

Ho Chi Minh (1892–1969). Ho became a Communist in France in 1920, studied in Moscow, and founded the Indochinese Communist Party in 1930. He fought, in succession, against the Japanese, French, and Americans. He did not live to see the communist victory in 1975. *Corbis/Bettmann.*

allies. The French tried to legitimize their rule by setting up in 1948 a puppet government under Bao Dai, the last in the line of Nguyen emperors. After years of war, the French lost a major battle at Dien Bien Phu in 1954 and, with it, the will to continue what critics at home called the "dirty war." They departed in defeat.

A conference at Geneva divided the country into a communist North and a non-communist South. In the South, Ngo Dinh Diem, a nationalist leader who had not collaborated with the French, came to power and established the Republic of Vietnam. Much of his political support came from the 900,000 Vietnamese who had fled from the North.

The Vietnam War

The second cycle of war, from 1959 to 1975, involved the United States. During the 1940s, in line with its wartime anticolonial position, the United States had urged the French to reach an accommodation with Ho Chi Minh. But after the rise of communist China and the outbreak of the Korean War, it came to see French actions in Vietnam as an attempt to stem the tide of communism—a view encouraged by the French. It recognized the French-sponsored government of Bao Dai and gave $4 billion in aid between 1950 and 1954. When the French withdrew, it transferred its support to Diem in the South.

Fighting began with guerrilla attacks against Southern troops in the late 1950s. Some said these were a local response to Diem's suppression of his political enemies, while others, including North Vietnamese after the war, said they were directed from the North. Local incidents eventually turned into a full-scale war between the North and the South (see Map 33–3). The North received material aid from the Soviet Union and China, although, unlike the Korean War, China sent no "volunteers." The South was aided by the United States, whose forces increased from 600 military advisers in 1961, to 16,000 troops in 1963, 70,000 in 1965, and over half a million in 1969. Despite such massive support, South Vietnam—and the United States—lost the war. The reasons for the defeat were several.

1. The South was difficult to govern. In comparison to the North, the region had been less deeply influenced by Chinese culture. It was ethnically diverse, with Chinese, Cambodians, and Chams as well as Vietnamese. In religion, it was divided among several varieties of Buddhism, Catholicism, and two powerful "new religions," the Cao Dai in the eastern provinces and the Hoa Hao in the western provinces. The two millenarian sects possessed private armies, and though opposed to the Communists, they stood apart from the South Vietnamese government, at times warring among themselves. Throughout this era, the inability of successive Southern governments to unify their fragmented society was a basic weakness in their struggles with the communist North.

2. All too often corrupt, the South Vietnamese government inspired little loyalty in its citizens.

3. Ho Chi Minh was a national hero to many South Vietnamese as well as to Northerners. Even non-Communists sometimes viewed the United States as the successor to the French—despite its total lack of colonial ambitions in Southeast Asia—and supported communist guerrillas as the heirs of the earlier anticolonial struggle.

4. Both the communist guerrillas in the South and the North Vietnamese troops fought better than the soldiers of the South Vietnamese government.

5. In the jungle terrain of Vietnam, the technological edge of the United States was blunted. A greater tonnage of bombs was dropped on supply trails in Cambodia than on Japan in World War II, yet supplies continued to flow to the South.

At the beginning, the U.S. government saw the war, like the earlier war in Korea, as a part of the broader struggle against world communism. After the gravity of the Sino-Soviet split became apparent, the government saw it more narrowly as a war to halt the spread of Chinese communism.

Map Exploration

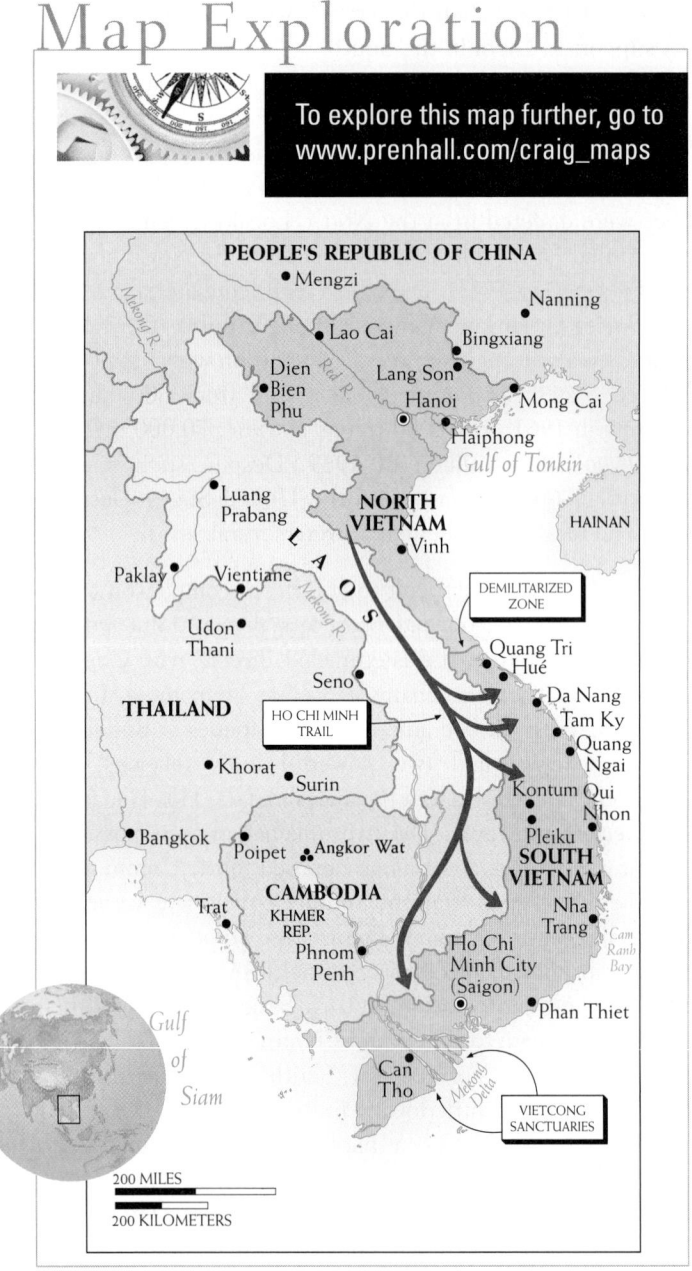

To explore this map further, go to
www.prenhall.com/craig_maps

Map 33–3. Vietnam and Its Southeast Asian Neighbors. The map identifies important locations associated with the war in Vietnam.

Few in the United States understood the depth of the tradi-

SOURCE *Truong Nhu Tang, "Myth of a Liberation"*

tional Vietnamese ambivalence towards China, which would resurface shortly after the war. As the war dragged on and casualties mounted, opposition to the war grew and public opinion split. In 1968, Lyndon Johnson announced he would not run for reelection. When Richard Nixon became president, he called for the "Vietnamization" of the war and began to with-

draw American troops. In January 1973, a ceasefire was arranged in Paris, and two months later the last U.S. troops left. Fighting broke out anew between North and South, the South Vietnamese forces collapsed in 1975, and the country was reunited under the Hanoi government in the North. Saigon was renamed Ho Chi Minh City.

In the mid-1970s, few areas of the world were as devastated as Vietnam and its neighbors. After unifying the country, Hanoi sent many thousands of those associated with the former South Vietnamese government to labor camps, collectivized its agricultural lands, and in 1976 began a five-year plan for the economy. Several hundred thousand Vietnamese and ethnic Chinese fled by boat or across the Chinese border.

War with Cambodia

Vietnam's third and smallest cycle of war was with Cambodia, its neighbor to the west. Pol Pot (1926–1998) and the communist **Khmer Rouge** ("Red Cambodia") had come to power in 1975. During the next three years, his government evacuated cities and towns, abolished money and trade, banned Buddhism, and executed or caused to die of starvation an estimated 1 million persons, roughly 15 percent of the Cambodian population. Schoolteachers and the educated were singled out as special targets.

Clashes occurred between Khmer Rouge troops and Vietnamese troops along their common border. Vietnam was Cambodia's historical enemy, as China was Vietnam's. When Pol Pot purged the Khmer Rouge of pro-Vietnamese elements, Vietnam retaliated in 1978 by invading and occupying most of Cambodia and setting up a puppet government. Most Cambodians accepted Vietnamese rule: They feared Pol Pot more than they hated Vietnam. But Vietnamese troops were unable to completely suppress Pol Pot's guerrilla forces.

In its international relations, the unified Vietnam of 1975 became an ally of the Soviet Union and gave the Soviets a naval base at Cam Ranh Bay in return for economic, military, and diplomatic support. But relations with China soured. Vietnam had long feared Chinese domination and resented China's invitation to Nixon in 1972, when American troops were still fighting on its soil. China, in turn, felt its wartime aid had not been duly appreciated, resented Vietnam's treatment of its ethnic Chinese, and feared Vietnam's close ties to the Soviet Union. In 1979, China decided to "teach Vietnam a lesson" and invaded four Northern provinces. Seasoned Vietnamese troops repelled the invaders, but losses were heavy on both sides. For years thereafter China supported Pol Pot's guerrillas and maintained pressure on Vietnam's northern border with occasional shellings and attacks.

Skulls. A worker cleans a skull excavated from a mass grave in Cambodia. The Khmer Rouge, under Pol Pot, murdered about one-sixth of the Cambodian population. Doctors, teachers, and other educated people were especially targeted. *AP Wide World Photos.*

Recent Developments

During the late 1980s, the situation changed abruptly, as if a kaleidoscope had been shaken. The collapse of the Soviet Union destroyed Vietnam's primary international relationship. In 1989, Vietnam tired of its costly occupation of Cambodia and withdrew in favor of a UN-sponsored government made up of contending Cambodian factions. One of these factions, led by a pro-Vietnamese communist leader, staged a coup in 1997 and took over the government. His rule was strengthened when Pol Pot died in 1998 and the Khmer Rouge collapsed. This, in turn, opened the way to better relations with China: cross-border trade began and China's landlocked Yunnan province began to use the Vietnamese port of Haiphong as an outlet for its products. In 1995, Vietnam joined ASEAN (Association of Southeast Asian Nations)—an important advance in its relations with its closest and richer neighbors—and reestablished diplomatic relations with the United States. It moved towards "normal" relations with the rest of the world. Europeans and Americans began to take package tours to Vietnam, visiting scenic spots that only two decades earlier had been the battle zones of a bitter war.

By the late 1990s, a "Chinese pattern" had emerged in Vietnam. On the one hand, the communist government in Hanoi monopolized political power and controlled the army, police, and media. On the other, the leaders, aware that victories in wars were hollow as long as their people remained

destitute, embraced capitalism as the road to growth. In place of collective agriculture, farmers were allowed to keep the rice they grew; as a result Vietnam went from near starvation to become the world's second largest exporter of rice. Stock markets were established in Hanoi and Ho Chi Minh City. Taxes were kept low and a premium was put on education. Garment manufacturing, food processing, and the production of other consumer goods grew apace. Between 1991 and 2007, the economy averaged over 8 percent growth and received more offers of foreign investment than it could absorb. Taiwan and Singapore were the largest investors, but Intel, Nike, and other American companies were not far behind. Vietnam's exports to the United States in 2006 were nine times greater than its imports, a problem for relations between the two nations. By the turn of the millennium, shops in Vietnam were full of food and goods, when only a decade or so earlier there had been regional famine. During the first decade of the millennium, Vietnam was the second fastest growing economy in the world—only China was faster. In this new climate the South was the engine of the economy. It also served as a model—slightly more open, pluralistic, and cosmopolitan—which even most North Vietnamese saw as attractive.

Population offered a mixed picture. With 86 million persons in 2007, Vietnam was one of the world's most densely populated nations. The government limited families to two children—in contrast to China's one. Hanoi's population increased from 130,000 in the 1930s to about 4 million, Ho Chi Minh City's (Saigon's) from less than a million in the 1970s to 4.5 million. The gap in the standard of living between urban and rural Vietnamese grew wider, an uncomfortable fact for a communist government. More than half of the population was born after the end of the Vietnam War, its youth and low medical costs made labor cheap. In 2007, Vietnam's estimated per capita income was a low $800 but rising (as measured by purchasing power, it was over $3,600). It had begun the trajectory that all East Asian nations but North Korea had in common.

Summary

Japan. The U.S.-led occupation after World War II established a democratic government and set Japan on the way to its remarkable postwar prosperity. By the twenty-first century, Japan had the second largest economy in the world. Politically, the conservative Liberal Democratic Party has remained dominant, despite occasional electoral losses. Socially, Japan has remained stable, with the world's highest longevity rate.

China. Communist rule was established in 1949. Until his death in 1976, Mao Zedong controlled China. Mao broke with the Soviet Union in the 1960s and launched the disastrous Cultural Revolution in 1965. After Mao's death, China opened its economy to free-market reforms. The result has been surging economic growth and rising prosperity. Politically, the Communist Party has blocked democratic reform, even using force in 1989 to crush a prodemocratic movement.

Taiwan. The Nationalist Party set up a separate state in Taiwan under U.S. protection after their defeat in the Chinese civil war in 1949. Since then Taiwan has moved from poverty to prosperity, from dictatorship to democracy. The Chinese government insists that Taiwan is a province of China. The status of Taiwan is an outstanding issue between the United States and China.

Korea. The postwar occupation of Korea by the Soviet Union and the United States led to its division into the communist state of North Korea and pro-Western South Korea. This division survived the Korean War of 1950–1953. The prosperity of democratic South Korea contrasts with the poverty and hunger of North Korea. Although contacts between the two Koreas have increased, the North remains a closed society.

Vietnam. From the end of World War II until the 1970s, Vietnam was almost continuously involved in war, first against the reimposition of French colonial rule, then against the United States and its South Vietnamese allies. North Vietnam's victory over the South in 1975 reunified the country. Vietnam remains relatively poor; only recently has it embraced free market principles.

INTERPRETING THE PAST

The Transformation of Postwar East Asia

Text Sources from MyHistoryLab/ PrimarySource DVD

1. James Schnabel, *The United States Army in the Korean War*
2. Truong Nhu Tang, *Myth of a Liberation*
3. Deng Xiaoping, *On Introducing Capitalism*

Visual Sources from MyHistoryLab/ PrimarySource DVD

1. *Japanese Election, 1946*

2. *Asian Games, Tokyo, 1958*

East Asia faced numerous challenges in the decades following World War II as economic, political, and social changes engulfed the vast and populous region. After more than a century of being economically dominated and often directly controlled by the West, East Asian nations began to effectively compete with Europe and the United States. Rapid industrialization first occurred in Japan, as it recovered from the devastating bombings

of World War II, followed by Taiwan, South Korea, Singapore, Thailand, and China.

Along with economic gains, East Asian nations have had to change their ancient cultures and antiquated bureaucracies and political systems to conform with their citizens' needs and expectations, as well as those of their international business partners. One of the key problems in many countries in East Asia is the need to adapt nationalism to the complicated reality of ethnic, regional, and local differences, in which competing agendas often transcend the ideal of national unity.

In this exercise you will read four primary sources relating to the politics and economies of East Asia, especially focusing on how nationalism has changed since World War II. You will then answer the following questions in the process of completing the assignment below.

The first document is an excerpt from a U.S. Army history detailing the partitioning of the Korean peninsula at the conclusion of World War II. The momentous economic changes that would propel this East Asian nation to the forefront of the global economy were still decades in the future, but the decisions made in 1945 are still being felt in Korea today. The second source is written by Truong Nhu Tang, a South Vietnamese leader of the "National Liberation Front," which fought the French and Americans from the 1950s to the 1970s. The third document is a portion of a speech by Deng Xiaoping, China's leader in the 1980s and early 1990s, in

Review Questions

1. Is postwar Japan better understood as a return to the relative liberalism of the 1920s or as a fresh start based on Occupation reforms? Why did the Occupation of Japan go so smoothly in contrast to the American occupation of Iraq?

2. Compare present-day Chinese and Japanese income levels and standards of living. In Japan, what factors led double-digit growth to turn into single-digit growth? Will the same factors come into play in China?

3. Is China from 1949 until the death of Mao better understood as an outgrowth of its earlier history or as a communist state comparable, say, to the old Soviet Union? And to what country would you compare post-Deng China?

4. How did the precolonial and colonial eras of Korea and Vietnam shape their history after World War II? How did the Cold War shape their history?

5. If you were the U.S. secretary of state, what long-term China policy would you propose to the president?

Key Terms

Article 9 of the No-War Constitution (p. 1059)

brainwashing (p. 1069)

chaebol (p. 1080)

Cultural Revolution (p. 1070)

Great Leap Forward (p. 1069)

Khmer Rouge (p. 1084)

LDP (p. 1061)

Viet Minh (p. 1082)

which he justifies the need for capitalism and a market economy in the country's socialist system. The fourth document combines two brief statements by Japanese scholars who focus on the changing role of the emperor of Japan after World War II.

The two accompanying images illustrate similar processes of social and political change: the first depicting the first elections after World War II in Japan, and the second depicting large-scale multinational athletic games in Tokyo in 1958.

Questions

Schnabel's account details the partition of Korea in 1945. What were the main considerations in the decision to partition the country? What were its consequences?

While Truong Nhu Tang was allied with the North Vietnamese in the fight against the French and the Americans, he was a southerner and a founder of the National Liberation Front. What was his attitude towards the North Vietnamese leadership? Had this been understood, might it have affected the outcome of the war?

What are Deng Xiaoping's reasons for introducing capitalism into China's socialist system? How would capitalism affect China's chances of becoming a democracy? What does it mean to build capitalism within socialism?

Note: To learn more about the topics in this chapter, please turn to the Suggested Readings at the end of the book. For additional sources related to this chapter please see the Primary Source DVD at the back of this text or MyHistoryLab.

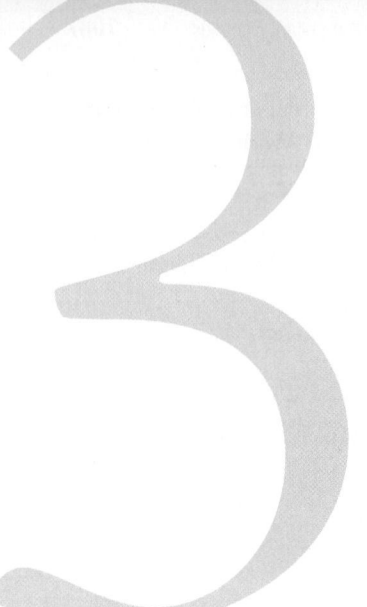

Postcolonialism and Beyond: Latin America, Africa, Asia, and the Middle East

- ◆ Beyond the Postcolonial Era
- ◆ Latin America Since 1945
- ◆ Postcolonial Africa
- ◆ The Islamic Heartlands, from North Africa to Indonesia
- ◆ The Postcolonial Middle East

THE SIX DECADES SINCE WORLD WAR II SAW Europe eclipsed by the rise of the two superpowers—the United States and the Soviet Union—and then witnessed the collapse of the Soviet Union (see Chapter 32). Elsewhere in the world, especially in the industrializing regions, the post–World War II decades witnessed the end of Western colonialism and challenges to European and superpower imperialism. New nations emerged in Africa and Asia.

Two developments in Asia have particularly affected the entire world and will continue to do so for the foreseeable future. First, as explored in the previous chapter, East Asia, Japan, and more recently China have emerged as major political and economic powers. Second, the rise of militant political Islam as a result of developments in the postcolonial Middle East now presents a political and military challenge across much of the globe.

The waning of colonial and imperial dominance of the many by the few and the emergence of new powerful forces from the previous colonial

Darfur, Western Sudan. Distraught Sudanese refugees wait at a food and clothing aid distribution point. The conflict, which began in February 2003, has killed as many as 300,000 people through violence, hunger, and disease. Some 2.5 million people have been displaced by the fighting.

Democratization, Globalization, and Terrorism

The World

Two remarkable political and economic developments have shaped our era: democratization and globalization. The apparent progress of these two processes seemed to be challenged, at least symbolically, most dramatically.

Since 1970, on one continent or another, democratic political rights have expanded. Authoritarian regimes of both the right and the left have been reformed or collapsed. Democracies have replaced dictatorships, military juntas, or one-party communist autocracies. Progress has not been uniform, but more and more people everywhere aspire to have a voice in how they are governed. This process of political change, usually termed democratization, involves expanding the number of people who participate in the political processes, and the orderly change in, or confirmation of, executive and legislative leaders through elections and the establishment of viable civil societies. Although there are still many autocracies and authoritarian states, never before have so many nations around the world seen such an extension of democratic government.

An unprecedented series of economic linkages, generally termed globalization, has paralleled the spread of democracy. This process has included the forging of new trade and manufacturing agreements, such as NAFTA, among the leading industrial nations. Globalization has reduced trade barriers, including tariffs and other regulations that have hindered the circulation of goods, services, and labor among nations. The emergence of such worldwide trading and investment networks has led to the consolidation of economic enterprises as owners of capital seek to locate their centers of production in the most advantageous labor and resource markets. The giant corporations of the United States, Europe, and Asia now operate in a multinational setting.

Globalization's supporters believe that it will produce more goods and services at a lower cost to consumers than a highly regulated economy could. Its critics argue that globalization will concentrate power in the hands of unregulated corporations and that governments have surrendered too

world must be set within a larger historical perspective, however. Since the sixteenth century the various Asian, African, and Latin American regions of the globe had been drawn steadily into the European sphere of economic and political influence. Those areas to be treated here—Latin America, Africa, Central Asia, South and Southeast Asia, and the Middle East—were often conquered, exploited, and colonized by European powers. The period of colonialism that began in earnest in the seventeenth century was a fateful, but relatively

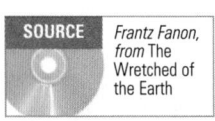

SOURCE *Frantz Fanon, from* The Wretched of the Earth

brief, episode in world history. The last significant colonial holdings gained their independence in the 1970s. ■

Beyond the Postcolonial Era

It may be argued, with the collapse of apartheid in South Africa, the fall of the Berlin Wall, and recent economic growth in India and China, that the postcolonial era has also ended. Others, however, point out that the lingering remnants of colonialism from both the World War I and World War II eras continue to persist in many global regions to this day. At present those who live in industrial much of their authority to regulate the economy, preserve the environment, and protect workers. The critics also believe that the new economic structures mean that poor nations, many of them the emerging nations discussed in this chapter, become poorer so that rich nations can become richer. Globalization rode the wave of prosperity that seems to have crested in the late 1990s. It remains to be seen what will occur in the more difficult times of our present decade.

The debate over globalization has made both its admirers and detractors more aware of the vast areas of deep poverty that persist around the world, especially in South and Central America, the Caribbean, Africa, and much of Asia—regions that still struggle with the legacy of European colonialism. Most of these regions were impoverished by early stages of globalization in the late nineteenth century before globalization achieved its present momentum, but the enormous and widely advertised prosperity of so much of the Northern Hemisphere has made the poorer regions more conscious of their poverty and, especially in Africa and the Middle East, ripe for political extremism. Among Muslims, such extremism has often come to be associated with political Islamism. As the most prosperous nation and the unchallenged superpower, the United States has become the target of those suffering from and opposed to globalization.

The economic, military, and diplomatic involvement of the United States in other regions of the globe has led some people to view it as an imperial power and to attack it using terrorist tactics. Its overwhelming support for the state of Israel, the festering Israeli-Palestinian conflict, and, most recently, the U.S. invasion of Iraq have also convinced many peoples, especially those in the Muslim world, that the United States is the enemy of Islam and that using terrorist tactics to attack it is justified. Within the United States, as well as around the world, debate continues over the future role of the United States and whether the United States can best protect the interests of its citizens and the peace and prosperity of the world through unilateral and preemptive invasions such as that of Iraq or through greater cooperation with international bodies such as the United Nations.

Focus Questions

◆ What are the arguments of the proponents and opponents of globalization?

◆ How has the legacy of European colonialism affected the Middle East, Asia, and Africa?

◆ Why has the United States become a prime target for terrorists? What is the debate over how the United States should best respond to this threat?

nations are witnessing waves of economic growth, much like those of the early 1990s in East Asia; the forging of new political alignments, both regional and transregional; internal struggles to build political systems that allow the development of civil society and limit the domination of corrupt oligarchic or dictatorial regimes; and, most dramatically, the determination of radical Islamists to confront the influence on the rest of the world of the European past in general and the United States present in particular.

Since 1945 two distinct developments occurred in the world. The first—in a process that is generally termed **decolonization**—was the emergence of the various parts of Africa and Asia from the direct government and administration of foreign powers and the organization of those previous colonial

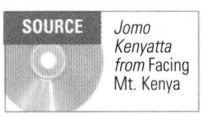

SOURCE *Jomo Kenyatta from Facing Mt. Kenya*

dependencies into independent states. Included in this category are India, Pakistan, most Arab states, the Latin American nations, and the new nations of Africa (see Map 34–1). Each of the newly independent states of Africa and Asia attempted to live within the colonial borders and frontiers created by the earlier colonial European powers.

As the process of decolonization took place and new nations then established themselves with greater or lesser degrees of stability, there have been four stages in their relationship to the industrial European and Europeanized nations. First, until the breakup of the Soviet Union, its rivalry with the United States manifested itself on every continent and added to the tensions and turmoil of the era.

The End of Empire. A statue of Queen Victoria is removed from the front of the Supreme Court building in Georgetown, former capital of the British colony of Guyana, in February 1970, in preparation for the transition to independence.

New emerging nations tended to be under the patronage of one superpower or the other (or, less often, that of China). However artificially conceived, that bipolar division of the colonial world has ended.

Second, in the years since the end of the Cold War and collapse of the Soviet Union, the character of the world economy, including issues of trade, financial investments, and resource allocation, has led to new phases of economic, social, and cultural interdependence, now usually termed **globalization**, that remain ill-defined and troublesome, whether they relate to automobile production, oil reserves, trade restrictions, currency failures, or international debt.

Third, the ideas of civil society and participatory government, often symbolized by the democracies of the United States, Europe, Japan, and a number of Asian, African, and Latin American countries have gained ground even in those regions where autocratic, authoritarian regimes have been the primary forms of government, at least since World War II. In all three kinds of interactions, change has often outpaced peoples' and leaders' awareness of it. The world may look and feel different today from just thirty, let alone fifty, years ago, but the rhetoric of decolonization is still used, though applied to different realities.

These stages of development that seemed relatively steady and peaceful, however, have given way to a fourth, largely unanticipated, set of developments, in which forces of society, culture, and religion have asserted themselves in aggressive and dramatic ways throughout much of the world. A central question for the present era is whether to see the global variety of social, cultural, and religious traditions as a creative or divisive force in the twenty-first century and beyond. One much-discussed contemporary model for understanding the complex international scene today is that of "the West versus the Rest," in which the European and Europeanized world and its ethos are seen as the hope of the future, while all other social, religious, and cultural traditions are depicted as rallying points for opposition to the spread of European-style "modernity." In this model, the future is seen as involving potentially less conflict and competition between nation states. Instead, this perspective forecasts a **clash of civilizations** dominating world

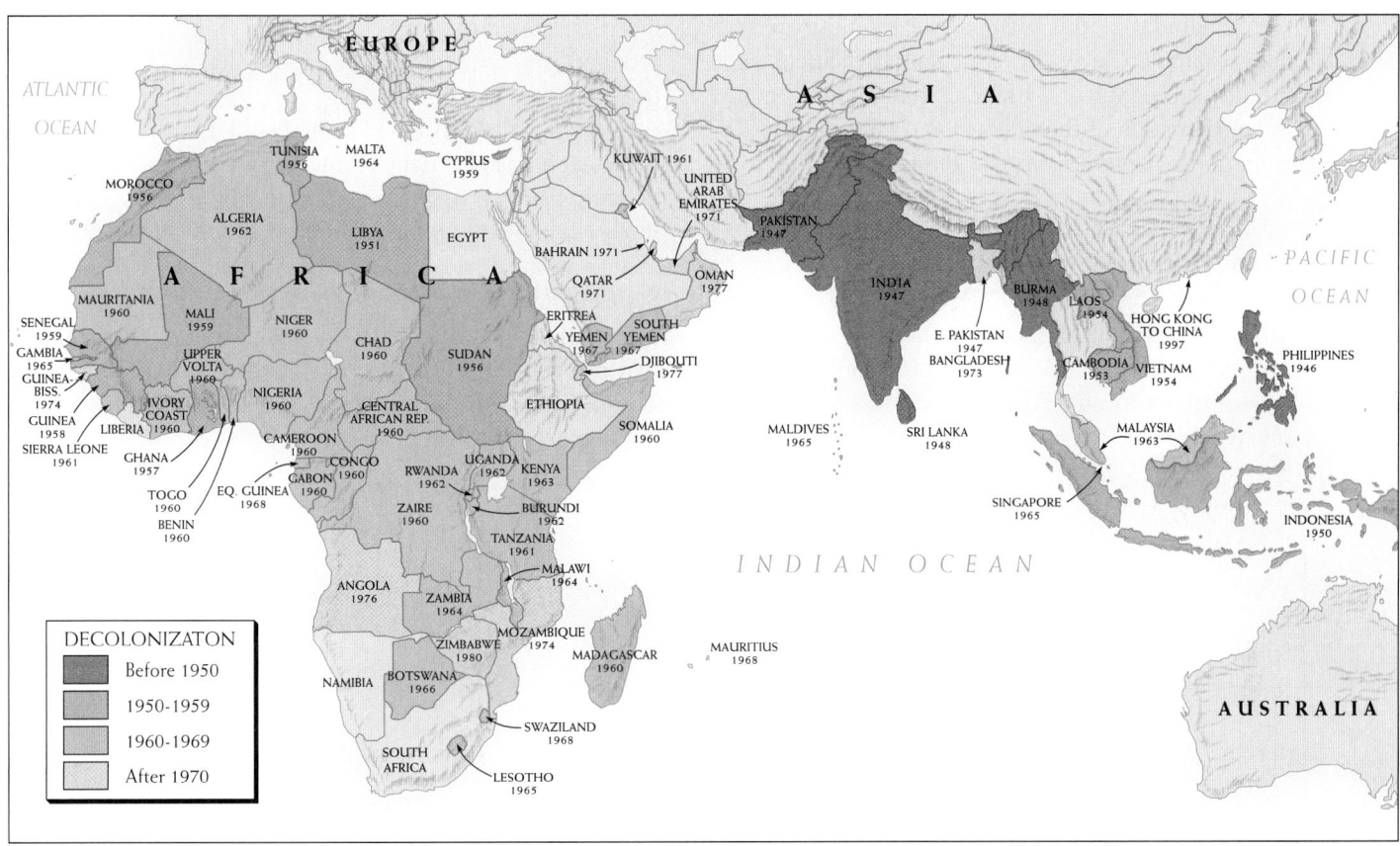

Map 34–1. Decolonizaton since World War II. Europe's rapid retreat from imperialism after World War II is graphically depicted on this map, showing half the globe—from Africa to the Pacific.

affairs.[1] This analysis pits Islamic, European and Eastern Orthodox Christian, Buddhist, Hindu, Confucian, and other religious, social, and cultural traditions of ."civilizations" against one another in a resurgence of religious, social, ethnic, and cultural chauvinism that portends new bloodletting and international conflict. This analysis has found favor among some observers in the wake of international political developments following the attacks of September 11, 2001, on the United States.

Other observers believe this analysis glosses over the vast variety within every religious or cultural tradition and overstates the effects of religious resurgence and the differences in values among the major religious or cultural traditions and world views of humankind. They instead urge that much of the value of studying the varied traditions of world culture and their modern representatives and derivatives is to be able to gain a more nuanced view of the modern world as a domain in which many cultural and religious and political traditions interact and compete, but in which people of all kinds can get along. Population control, the environment, political accommodation, food supply, public health, and the like thus become the focus of shared international concern and partnership; our common need for solutions to such transnational, planetwide problems must take precedence, it is argued, over wide "civilizational" differences. That the task will not be easy is evident from the troubled history of the past century.

However, if we seek to understand the larger global scene, we must at least recognize the persistent influence of the great religious and moral traditions of humankind, however we may interpret that influence. In particular, Buddhist, Christian, and Islamic faith and values continue to claim the allegiance of major sectors of our globe, not only in Africa and Asia, but also in Europe and the Americas. No longer can we assume that secular rationalism will easily monopolize ideology during the process of material modernization. Rather we can expect a pluralistic global community in which diverse traditions best coexist and learn from one another.

---

[1] See Samuel P. Huntington, "The Clash of Civilizations?" *Foreign Affairs* 72, 3 (Summer 1993): pp. 22–49, and a vast array of articles around the world written in response to this provocative and simplistic piece. This article was followed by a whole book devoted to the so-called "Huntington thesis": *The Clash of Civilizations and the Remaking of World Order* (New York: 1996), in which Huntington somewhat refined his ideas.

In the remainder of this chapter, we shall survey the traditionally examined areas of postcolonial political and economic developments and then conclude with more extensive consideration of the political and cultural conflict emerging from the contemporary Middle East.

Latin America Since 1945

During the second half of the twentieth century and beyond, the nations of Latin America experienced divergent paths of political and economic change. Their leaders tried repeatedly to alleviate their people's dependence on the more developed portions of the globe. At best, these efforts produced mixed results; at worst, they led to repression and tragedy (see Map 34–2).

Before World War II the states of Latin America had been economically dependent on the United States and Western Europe. Beginning in the 1950s a shift occurred in those dependent relationships without any significant change in the general situation of dependency. The United States loomed larger than ever; the Soviet Union also for a time came to play a far larger economic and political role. In that respect Latin America, like so many other parts of the world, dwelled in the shadow of the rival superpowers and became an arena for confrontations between them.

Map 34–2.   Contemporary Central and South America.

The economic life of the region reflected those new facts of dependence. Attempts were made to expand the industrial base and the agricultural production of the various national economies. Virtually all the financing came from U.S. and Western European banks or from Soviet subsidies. Enormous debts were contracted to Western banks, and these debts made Latin American economies virtual prisoners to the fluctuations of world interest rates and the international banking community. Subsidies and special market arrangements with the Soviet Union made other Latin American nations no less dependent on outside economic forces. These new relationships, however, did not alter the underlying character of the national economies of most Latin American countries, which overwhelmingly remain exporters of agricultural commodities and mineral resources.

Since the 1970s, Latin America has shipped massive amounts of cocaine to the United States and Europe; this has led to political turmoil and civil war in Colombia. The desire to halt this drug trafficking has led to formal and informal intervention by the United States at one time or another in the affairs of several Latin American countries.

The social structures of the Latin American nations have become more complicated since World War II. A culture of poverty remains the dominant social characteristic of the area. (See Document, "Lourdes Arizpe Discusses the Silence of Peasant Women.") Even periods of economic boom, such as that fostered in Mexico by oil production in the late 1970s, have proved brief and have almost inevitably been followed by decline. Migration into the cities from the countryside has created tremendous urban overcrowding and slums inhabited by the desperately poor (see Figure 34–1). In many countries the standards of health and nutrition have fallen. The growth of service industries in the cities has also fostered the emergence of a professional, educated middle class, often possessed with a strong desire to imitate the affluent lifestyle of their social counterparts in the United States and Western Europe. This new professional middle class has displayed little taste for radical politics, major social

reform, or revolution. They and the more traditional landed and industrial elites were willing, especially during the 1960s and 1970s, to support military governments pledged to maintain order and the status quo.

Political events in Latin America led to the establishment of authoritarian governments of both the left and the right and to a retreat from the ideal and model of parliamentary democracy. Only Mexico, Colombia, Venezuela, and Costa Rica remained parliamentary states throughout this period. Elsewhere, two paths of political development were followed. In Cuba and Nicaragua, and for a short time in Chile, revolutionary socialist governments with close ties to the Soviet Union were established. Elsewhere, often in response to the fear of revolution or communist activity, military governments held power for long periods, sometimes punctuated with brief interludes of civilian rule. Such were the situations in Chile, Brazil, Argentina, Paraguay, Bolivia, Peru, and Uruguay. Governments of both the left and the right engaged in repression, suspending civil liberties and arresting enemies.

These political changes fostered new roles for two traditional Latin American institutions: the military and the Roman Catholic Church. The armies of the various nations have played key political roles since the wars of independence, but towards the close of the twentieth century they frequently assumed the direct government of nations rather than use indirect influence. In the clash between the forces of social revolution and reaction, many Roman Catholic priests and bishops protested social and economic inequalities and attacked the repression of opposition forces. Certain Roman Catholic theologians combined traditional Christian ideas of concern for the poor with Marxist ideology to formulate what came to be known as a **liberation theology**. Generally speaking, the Vatican under both Pope John Paul II and Pope Benedict XVI has attacked this Latin American theological initiative, and as a result its impact has diminished.

During the last decade and a half, Latin America has changed significantly. Several nations, including Argentina, Chile, and Brazil, like the rest of the world, have moved towards democratization. In a departure from earlier policies there has been a strong tendency throughout the continent to allow private markets rather than the state to address economic issues. Yet these changes have remained tenuous, as several nations have had difficulty paying their foreign debts and protecting the value of their currency. In most nations, the military keeps a watchful eye on democratic developments and remains apprehensive about disorder. The end of the Cold War brought to a close one source of external political challenge, but the internal social problems of these nations have continued to raise major

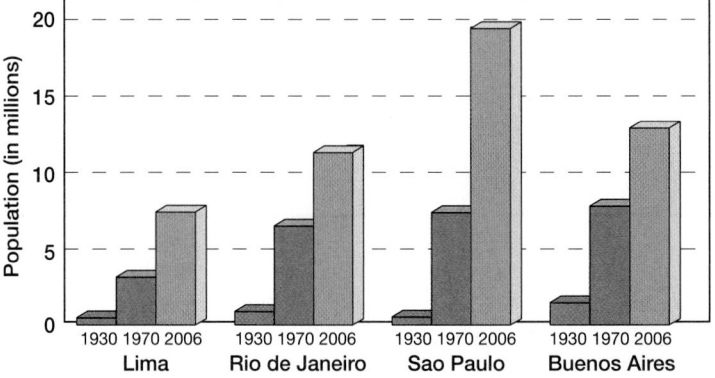

Figure 34–1. Population of Major South American Cities, 1930–2006.

Lourdes Arizpe Discusses the Silence of Peasant Women

Document

Lourdes Arizpe, a Mexican anthropologist, wrote extensively on the plight of peasant women in the 1970s. In this passage she discusses how the lives and history of Mexican peasant women are shrouded in silence. Though her remarks are directed towards the situation in Mexico, they may well apply to peasant women in other cultures as well.

◆ What are the factors that Arizpe cites as leading to the historical silence of peasant women? Why does she believe it is important for such women to learn to speak with their own voices? How do the stereotypes of Mexican peasant women both contribute to and arise from the silence? Why does she believe peasant women to be the most marginalized of all women?

History has imposed a greater silence on peasant women than on any other social group. Perhaps it is the solitude of the plains or the obligatory circumspection of their gender or merely political repression, but circumstances combine to force them to live in a secret world. Doubtless there are those who would assert that their tie to nature leads them to express themselves with actions rather than words. But the male peasant lives in the natural world without being silenced.

Silence, when not deliberate (although, how can we be sure it isn't?) could be anger or wisdom or, simply, a gesture of dignity. When there is no one worth talking to, I stay silent. If someone doesn't want to recognize my existence, I stay silent. In the spectrum of invisibility that history has imposed on women, perhaps the most invisible of the invisibles have been the peasants.

When direct expression is not permitted, the possibility of knowledge is lost and we fill that disturbing vacuum with phantoms. It is therefore not surprising that the Mexican mentality is filled with myths and stereotypes about peasant women. There is the submissive Indian woman who is a product of condescending maternalism; the wild woman both fantasized about and feared by men;

the brazen hussy of melodramatic soap operas; the faint-hearted but treacherous small-town woman invented by the urban mind. Silence is also created by everyone's desire to hear what they want to hear rather than listen to what women are trying to say.

Today it seems that everyone mouths concerns about peasant women without any sincere interest.

. . . What is important today is to create opportunities for peasant women to speak.

It is not that they have never spoken, only that their words have never been recognized. Because their words are discomforting when they denounce exploitation; disturbing when they display a deep understanding of the natural world not shared by their city sisters; strange when they describe an integrating vision of the universe; and because, being women's words, they are not important to androcentric [male-centered] history. Of all the marginalized peoples, peasant women are the most marginalized.

Lourdes Arizpe, "Peasant Women and Silence," trans. by Laura Beard Milroy in *Women's Writing in Latin America: A Anthology*, by Sara Castro-Klarén, Sylvia Malloy, and Beatriz Sarlo. Copyright © 1992 by Westview Press. Reprinted by permission of Westview Press.

difficulties for their governments. Several nations have faced new sources of disorder in the post–Cold War era from powerful drug-producing cartels that have challenged the authority of governments.

Revolutionary Challenges

There were four major attempts among the nations of Latin America to establish genuinely revolutionary governments pursuing major social and economic change. They occurred in Cuba in 1959, in Chile in 1970, in Nicaragua in 1979,

and in Peru in the 1980s. In recent years leftist governments led by Hugo Chavez in Venezuela and Evo Morales in Bolivia have embraced policies reminiscent of those regimes. Each of the four revolutionary initiatives involved some form of Marxist political organization, and with the exception of the Shining Path revolutionary movement in Peru, each revolutionary government pursued a close relationship with the Soviet Union. All three had immense symbolic importance not only in Latin America, but also anywhere the colonial influence of Europeans and the economic dominance of the United States once prevailed.

The Turn to the Left in Latin American politics is represented by Hugo Chavez, who has oil wealth to fund his ambitions, and Evo Morales, the first indigenous president of Bolivia. Chavez assumed power in 1999; Morales in 2006.

The establishment of these governments provoked active resistance and intervention by the United States. It also encouraged opposition to social and political change by traditional elites throughout Latin America.

The Cuban Revolution Cuba had remained a colony of Spain until the Spanish-American War of 1898. Thereafter, it achieved independence within a sphere of U.S. influence, which took the form of economic domination and occasional military intervention. The fluctuating governments of the island had been both ineffective and corrupt. During the 1950s Fulgencio Batista (1901–1973), a dictator supported by the U.S. government, ruled Cuba.

Historically, Cuba had been politically restive. During the 1940s university student groups led antigovernment agitation. Among the students thus politicized in those years was Fidel Castro Ruz (b. 1926), the son of a wealthy landowner. On July 26, 1953, he and others attacked a government army barracks. The revolutionary movement that he thereafter came to lead in exile took its name from that date: the Twenty-Sixth of July Movement. In 1956 Castro and a handful of followers set sail on a yacht from Mexico and landed in Cuba. They took refuge in the Sierra Maestra Mountains, from which they organized guerrilla attacks on Batista's supporters. By late 1958 Castro's forces were positioned to topple Batista, who fled Cuba on New Year's Day in 1959. By the middle of January, Castro had arrived in Havana as the revolutionary victor.

Castro undertook the most extensive political, economic, and social reconstruction in recent Latin American history. He rejected parliamentary democracy and governed Cuba as a dictator. For approximately the first decade of the revolution he ruled in a personal manner; by the early 1970s, although Castro continued to dominate, executive power was vested in a council. The revolutionary government carried out major land redistribution. In some cases, groups of relatively small landowners were established. On other parts of the island, large state farms became the model.

The Cuban Revolution spurned an industrial economic model and concentrated on improving the agricultural sector. Despite an attempt to turn towards more mixed agriculture, the production of sugar kept its leading role, and the Cuban economy remained monocultural.

Efforts to expand sugar production were disappointing, because too much was attempted too quickly by people who had had too little experience in raising and processing sugar cane. The sugar industry came to depend on large Soviet subsidies and on the Soviet bloc nations for its market. In that respect, the Cuban economy did not escape the cycle of external dependence.

Fidel Castro, waving to cheering crowds acknowledging his triumph over the Batista regime on January 1, 1959. *UPI/Corbis-Bettmann.*

In foreign affairs, the Cuban Revolution was characterized by a sharp break with the United States and a close relationship with the Soviet Union. Shortly after achieving power, Castro aligned himself with the Cuban Communist Party and thereafter with the Soviet bloc. The United States, under both Republican and Democratic administrations, was hostile towards Castro and towards the presence of a communist state less than 100 miles from the Florida mainland. In 1961 the United States and Cuban exiles launched the unsuccessful Bay of Pigs invasion. The close Cuban relationship to the Soviet Union prepared the ground for the missile crisis of 1962, which is generally regarded as the most dangerous incident of the entire Cold War. Thereafter followed about a decade of cool relations between Cuba and the United States without overt hostility. During the late 1970s and the 1980s a dialogue of sorts was undertaken between Cuba and the United States, but formal diplomatic relations have not resumed. Mutual distrust continues.

With the collapse of the Soviet Union and the end of the Cold War, the future of Castro's Cuba became uncertain, but the Castro government continued firmly in charge as a remarkably enduring authoritarian regime. Cuba remains the only state closely associated with the former Soviet Bloc that has not experienced substantial political or economic reform. The subsidies that flowed from the Soviet Union to support the Cuban economy are no longer available, however, creating a shortage of everyday consumer goods. The Marxist political and economic ideology stands discredited throughout the world, but the aging Castro's leadership has remained intact. In 2006 Castro experienced serious problems with his health and disappeared from public sight. His brother Raul assumed the daily oversight of the government. However, as of this writing, Castro has begun to make limited public appearances. Some observers believe his death will see a collapse of the government; others believe that the bureaucracy Castro created may actually endure. It would appear that whatever transition occurs when Castro finally passes from the scene will be slower than once anticipated.

Throughout the Cold War, Cuba assumed an importance far greater than its size might suggest. After 1959 it served as a center for the export of communist revolution

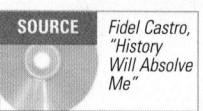

throughout Latin America and, after it sent troops to Angola in the late 1970s, in Africa as well. A key policy of the U.S. government, pursued with differing intensities and strategies under different administrations, was to prevent a second Cuba or Communist-dominated state in Latin America. That goal led to direct and indirect intervention in other revolutionary situations and to support for authoritarian governments in Latin America that were dedicated to resisting Marxist revolution.

Chile Until the 1970s Chile was the single most enduring model of parliamentary democracy in Latin America. It had experienced political turmoil and governments of the left and the right, but its parliamentary structures had remained in place. During the 1960s, however, as economic life became more difficult and class relationships deteriorated, Chilean politics became more polarized. Unemployment and labor unrest rose alarmingly. There was profound resentment of the economic domination of Chile by large U.S. corporations.

The situation came to a head in 1970 when Salvador Allende (1908–1973), the candidate of the left-wing political coalition and a Marxist, was elected president with a plurality of the votes. His coalition did not control the Chilean congress, nor did it have the support of the military. For a few months the center and right-wing political groups took a watch-and-wait attitude. Allende nationalized some businesses. The congress blocked policies related to land redistribution, wage improvement, and resistance to foreign economic influence, so Allende began to expropriate foreign property, much of which belonged to U.S. corporations, by decree. This policy frightened the Chilean owners of small and medium-sized businesses. Workers were dissatisfied with the relatively modest effect that socialization had on their daily lives. Inflation ballooned. Despite the expropriation of large estates and the reorganization of agriculture, harvests were poor.

In the autumn of 1973 Allende found himself governing a nation in turmoil without significant domestic political support and with many foreign enemies. He proved unwilling to make significant political compromises. In

Pariah. A 1977 poster from a New York protest highlights the enormous international opposition to the policies of General Pinochet.

Thereafter, for fifteen years Chile was governed by a military junta, whose most important member, General Augusto Pinochet (1915–2006), served as president. The military government pursued a close relationship with the United States and a policy of strong resistance to Marxism in the hemisphere. It also suggested a state-directed free-market economy and reversed the expropriations of the Allende years. After a brief period of economic improvement, inflation and unemployment resumed. The rule of the Chilean military was marked by harsh political repression.

In a referendum held in late 1988, Chileans rejected Pinochet's bid for another term as president. Democratization has been relatively smooth. Civilian governments have investigated the political repression of the Pinochet years and uncovered thousands of cases of torture and murder. The government nonetheless moved slowly, not wishing to provoke the army or revisit the most controversial era of the nation's history. In 1999, while in Great Britain for a medical consultation, General Pinochet was arrested when the government of Spain sought to extradite him to that country to stand trial for the disappearances of Spanish citizens under his rule. Pinochet was ultimately returned to Chile where he was judged too sick to stand trial. He died in 2006 and received no state funeral. The politics of Chile had moved on with Micelle Bachelet, whose air-force general father had opposed Pinochet and had died shortly after being arrested by the Pinochet government.

During the past two decades Chile has moved towards a more liberal constitutional government. In 2006 the length of the presidential term was reduced from six to four years. Presidential and congressional elections will henceforward coincide. The direct political influence of the military has been reduced.

The Sandinista Revolution in Nicaragua In the summer of 1979 a Marxist guerrilla force, the **Sandinistas**, overthrew the corrupt dictatorship of the Somoza family in Nicaragua. The Somozas had governed Nicaragua more or less as their own personal preserve since the 1930s with moderate, but rarely enthusiastic, support from the United States. The Sandinistas established a collective government that pursued social and economic reform and reconstruction. The movement—with Roman Catholic priests on its leadership council—epitomized the new political and social forces in Latin America. The exact direction of the revolutionary government remained unclear because it confronted significant domestic political opposition and direct military challenge from the contra guerrilla movement.

the wake of strikes and disorder, the army became hostile. The government of the United States was deeply disturbed by the Allende experiment and by the prospect of a Marxist nation on the western coast of South America. The Nixon administration actively supported the discontent within the Chilean army. In mid-September 1973 an army coup overthrew Allende, who was killed in the presidential palace. Chile's short-lived experiment in Marxist socialism ended.

The government of the United States, particularly under the Reagan administration (1981–1989), was hostile to the Sandinistas. It provided both direct and indirect aid to the opposition guerrillas and criticized the Sandinistas. The U.S. government feared the spread of Marxist revolutionary activity in Central America, a fear reinforced by the close ties between the Sandinistas and the Soviet Union. For the United States, the Sandinista government represented a Central American version of Castro's Cuba.

The rule of the Sandinistas came to a relatively quick end. In early 1990, after a negotiated peace settlement with the contras, they lost the presidential election to an opposition coalition that also captured control of the National Assembly. A floundering economy and U.S. aid had contributed to the electoral victory. Nicaraguans were also tired of the civil war that had shaken the country for a decade. The Sandinistas relinquished power peacefully, and a democratic government supported by the United States has remained in control despite persistent economic weaknesses.

Pursuit of Stability Under the Threat of Revolution

Argentina In 1955 the Argentine army revolted against the excesses and corruption of the Perón dictatorship, and Juan Perón (1895–1974) went into exile. Two decades of economic stagnation and social unrest followed. Neither the army nor the civilian political leaders could forge the kind of political coalition involving the working class that Perón had created. Nor could any of the post-Perón governments cope with unemployment and inflation. In 1973 Perón was recalled from exile in a desperate and futile attempt to restore the fragile stability of a generation earlier. He died about a year later.

By 1976 the army had undertaken direct rule. There was widespread repression; thousands of citizens simply disappeared, never to be heard of again. The leading army officers played something like a game of musical chairs as they moved in and out of an ever-changing ruling junta. In April 1982 General Leopoldo Galtieri (b. 1926), in an effort to score a political success, launched a disastrous invasion of the Islas Malvinas (Falkland Islands). Argentina was decisively defeated by Britain, and the military junta was thoroughly discredited.

In 1983 civilian rule was restored, and Argentina set out on the road to democratization. The major political figure responsible for this achievement was President Raul Alfonsín (b. 1927). Under his leadership, many of the former military figures responsible for the years of repression received prison sentences. Civilian courts took over the role formerly assigned

to military tribunals. Alfonsín also sought to turn more real political authority over to the Argentine congress. In all respects Argentina has provided the most extensive example in Latin America of the restoration of democratic practices after military rule. Peaceful elections and transitions of governments have occurred for almost two decades.

The Argentine government easily survived a brief attempted military coup in 1990. Thereafter its major difficulties have been economic. There is rising labor discontent. Many businesses and industries, such as telephone communications, formerly owned by the government have been privatized. Argentina has thus attempted to encourage foreign investment to sustain economic growth. Nonetheless, in 2001 it became clear that Argentina would be unable to repay its foreign debts. Rising unemployment, a currency devaluation, and drastic cuts in basic government services led to political turmoil. In recent years the government has taken a stance of intervening in the economy particularly in efforts to control inflation. Significant economic growth has occurred for the past several years.

Brazil In 1964 the military assumed the direct government of Brazil and did not fully relinquish it until the mid-1980s. The military government stressed order and used repression to maintain it. The army itself, however, was divided about the wisdom of the military's move into the political realm. Many officers were concerned that the corruption of everyday politics would undermine the army reputation and sap its *esprit de corps*. They also feared that respect for the army would come to depend on its success in the political arena. Consequently, within the army itself, certain forces sought to restore a more nearly normal or democratic government. In 1985 civilian government returned under the military's watchful eye.

The military government fostered denationalized industrial development. Non-Brazilian corporations were invited to spearhead the drive towards industrialization. In this respect Brazil opted for an industrial model, but an industrialism guided and dominated from the outside. One result was the accumulation of a massive foreign debt, the servicing and repayment of which have become perhaps Brazil's most important national problem. The relative success of the government's industrialization policy also made Brazil the major industrialized nation in Latin America, which has had a huge impact on the Brazilian rain forest. Subsidies and tax incentives have made the clearing of the Amazon rain forest especially profitable for large landholders involved in cattle ranching. By 1998, 12 percent of Brazil's rain forest had been cleared.

The great question now is how the social changes wrought by industrialism, such as growing urbanization, will be able to receive political accommodation. In Brazil, as in

Deforestation in the Amazon. A cut and burned section of trees on federal land in Brazil's Amazonian state of Para. The problems of deforestation, wood trafficking, habitat destruction, slave labor, land grabbing, and violence are all intertwined as colonization of the region accelerates.

Argentina, the economic and social pressures of the society have spawned conditions ripe for political agitation. It was just that possibility that in the past had led so many citizens—within both the traditional and the new professional elites—to support authoritarian government.

The civilian government of President Fernando Collor de Mello that came to office in 1990, like numerous other governments in the region, advocated privatization. He and his advisers favored allowing market forces to stimulate growth. They also attempted to contain inflation. During 1992, however, President Collor was impeached by the Brazilian Senate on charges of corruption and using his office to enrich himself. In 1995 Fernando Henrique Cardoso won the presidency, and he has pursued economic policies led by technocrats in hopes of achieving economic growth along with democratic stability.

In 1995, Fernando Henrique Cardoso won the presidency and was reelected to a second term. He pursued economic policies led by technocrats in hopes of achieving economic growth along with economic stability. By 2003, however, Brazil's economic growth had sharply slowed and required international assistance. In 2003 in the wake of the economic turmoil, Luiz Inácio Lula da Silva became the first person from a working-class background to achieve election to the Brazilian presidency. He was reelected in 2006. His administration combined socialist concern for social services along with an austere economic policy.

Mexico Institutionally, Mexico has undergone relatively few political changes since World War II. In theory at least, the government continued to pursue the goals of the revolution. Power remained firmly in the control of the Partido Revolucionario Institucional (PRI), which until the late 1980s had maintained the appearance of stability.

Yet shifts had occurred under this apparently stable surface. The government retreated from some of the aims of the revolution and appeared conservative when compared to Marxist Cuba or Allende's Chile. In the early 1950s certain large landowners were exempted from the expropriation and redistribution of land. The Mexican government maintained open relations with Cuba and the other revolutionary regimes of Latin America but also resisted any intrusion of

Zapatistas. Named after the revolutionary hero Emiliano Zapata (depicted on the banner, see Chapter 26) the Zapatistas demanded rights for the impoverished Native American population of Mexico, especially in the southern state of Chiapas, where this photograph was taken in 1997. *AP/Wide World Photos.*

Marxist doctrines into Mexico. When necessary, it arrested political malcontents.

Mexico experienced an oil boom from 1977 to 1983. Oil revenues brought immense new wealth into the nation, but the world oil glut burst that bubble. The aftermath revealed the absence of any policy of stable growth. Like so many other states in the region, Mexico amassed large foreign debts and, in doing so, surrendered real economic independence.

In 1988 the PRI encountered a major challenge at the polls. Opposition candidates received much of the vote in a hotly contested election. Whether the election results were honestly reported may never be known. The PRI remained in power, but with the knowledge that it would not be able to dominate the political scene in the manner it had for over half a century. Thereafter, the internal leadership of the party began to move towards greater decentralization in the way the party was run. The newly elected president, Carlos Salinas, moved rapidly to privatize economic enterprise. He also favored free-trade agreements. The most important of these was the North American Free Trade Agreement (NAFTA), which created a vast free-trade area among Mexico, Canada, and the United States. Under Salinas' policies the economic growth rate of Mexico became the best it had been in ten years. In 1991 Salinas came to a new accommodation with the Roman Catholic Church, thus moving away from the traditional anticlericalism that had characterized Mexican politics. By 1991 the PRI appeared to have regained its former political ascendancy.

The situation was largely a façade, however. Beginning in 1994 Mexico underwent a series of political shocks. Its government had to call out troops to quell armed rebellion in Chiapas. During the election of that year, the leading candidate of the PRI was assassinated, and party members were openly charged with complicity in the deed. Party corruption received increasing publicity. Early in 1995 Mexico suffered a major economic downturn, and the peso was sharply devalued. Only loans from the United States saved the economy. Ernesto Zedillo, elected president in 1994, blamed Salinas and his family for the situation, and Salinas went into exile abroad. Thereafter Mexico entered a period of political uncertainty and economic austerity; further unrest occurred in Chiapas. In the election of 2000 the PRI candidate for president lost to Vicente Fox of the National Action Party (PAN). For the first time in seventy years the PRI were out of power. The Fox presidency achieved less than had been expected. His term ended in late 2006 with a sharply contested election in which Felipe Calderon, also a candidate of PAN, came into office with considerable opposition and controversy as the result of a very narrow electoral win. He was not a PRI candidate so that party remains out of office and deeply divided. Whether Calderon will prove more successful than Fox remains to be seen.

Continuity and Change in Recent Latin American History

The most striking aspect of the history of the past six decades in Latin America is its tragic continuity with the region's previous history. Revolution has brought moderate social change, but at the price of authoritarian government, economic stagnation, and dependence on different foreign powers. Real independence has not been achieved. Throughout the region for much of the period, parliamentary democracy has been fragile at best; it was the first element of national life to be sacrificed to the conflicting goals of socialism, economic growth, or resistance to revolution.

The recent trends towards democratization and market economics may mark a break in that pattern, however. The region might well enjoy healthy economic growth if inflation can be contained and investment fostered. The challenge—difficult both politically and economically—will be to see that the fruits of any new prosperity are shared in a way that prevents new political resentment and turmoil. Furthermore, as in the past, economic turmoil far from Latin America may have an adverse impact on its destiny. Each time such turmoil has occurred, the governments of Latin America have found themselves economically dependent upon either the United States or European governments and bankers.

Postcolonial Africa

Africa represents the clearest example of continuity between arbitrarily constructed colonial territories and emergent independent states. Most of its modern nations are direct inheritors of their colonial predecessors' boundaries, just as the former colonial capitals have typically become the post-independence national capitals. Despite the obvious reasons for such continuity, it is remarkable that the colonial frontiers, which had little to do with the boundaries of traditional tribal territories or indigenous empires and states, should have managed to persist so consistently. If nationalism was a European export to the rest of the world, Africa provides striking examples of how attractive it can be as a motive for supratribal and transregional state formation.[2] The rise of African nationalism can generally be dated to the period between the two world wars, when previously fragmented or regional opposition to European colonial occupation began to be replaced by larger scale anti-imperialist movements. In World War II the important roles that Africa was called on to play with its natural and human resources, as well as the experience of thousands of Africans who were conscripted or volunteered to fight or labor abroad, proved a catalyst for African nationalism. Further, in the aftermath of war, Europe was largely disposed to give up its colonial empires (see Chapter 32).

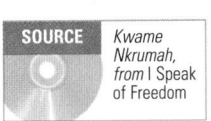

SOURCE *Kwame Nkrumah, from* I Speak of Freedom

The Transition to Independence

The "scramble for Africa" and European colonization in Africa took place in the historical blink of an eye (see Chapters 27 and 29). Independence came almost as quickly. In 1950, only Egypt, Liberia, Ethiopia, and white-controlled South Africa were sovereign states. By 1980 no African territory (except for two tiny Spanish holdings on the Moroccan coast) was ruled by a European state, although South Africa and Namibia continued to be white-dominated. African leaders, such as Kwame Nkrumah (1909–1972) in the Gold Coast (modern Ghana), Jomo Kenyatta (1893–1978) in Kenya, Julius Nyerere (1922–1999) in Tanganyika (later Tanzania), and

President Jomo Kenyatta is congratulated on Kenya's independence as England's Queen Elizabeth II looks on, December 12, 1963.

Patrice Lumumba (1925–1961) in the Congo became symbols of African self-determination and freedom from foreign domination. (SeeDocument, "The Pan-African Congress Demands Independence.")

The actual transition from colonial administrative territories to independent national states was generally peaceful. In the few cases involving extended violent conflict with colonial powers, however, the battles were ferocious. The most protracted and bloody wars of independence from European overlords were the guerrilla struggles fought in French Algeria from 1955 to 1962; in Portuguese Angola and Mozambique from 1961 to 1975; and in the Democratic Republic of Congo (formerly the Belgian Congo, later Zaire), Zambia (formerly Northern Rhodesia), and Zimbabwe (formerly Southern Rhodesia) from 1960 to 1980. Violence was more likely in colonies with large populations of European settlers (such as Algeria) or lucrative exports of minerals or other resources (Congo, for example).

In contrast to the peaceful "handing over" from colonial rule, the internal conflicts that arose in many of the newly independent states were often fierce. Much of the instability in African states has been a legacy of both the colonial powers' generally minimal efforts to prepare their colonial subjects for self-government, and the haphazard nineteenth-century division of the continent into arbitrary colonial units.

Until World War II, the colonial powers tended to assume they would govern their African colonies for many generations. Colonial administrators were in no rush to create the physical, economic, political, and social infrastructures that would allow their territories to function independently.

---

[2] We are especially indebted to Roland Oliver, *The African Experience* (London and New York, 1991), pp. 227–264, for many of the broader interpretations put forward in the current section.

The Pan-African Congress Demands Independence

Document

For more than two centuries before World War II European powers had dominated or directly ruled large parts of Africa. Before World War II nationalist political movements came to the fore in a number of these colonial empires. After the war, nationalist movements burgeoned throughout most of the colonial world.

The costs of fighting World War II meant the European powers had less wealth with which to govern their colonies. In addition, the principles of the victorious Allies in Europe were inconsistent with colonialism, as was the foreign policy of the United States, now the dominant Western power.

In the following passage, representatives to the 1945 Fifth Pan-African Congress meeting in Manchester, England, set forth their demand for freedom.

◆ What are these African leaders' social and political goals? How did World War II help to allow such goals to be voiced? Why did these leaders believe they were entitled to use force?

DECLARATION TO THE COLONIAL POWERS

The delegates believe in peace. How could it be otherwise, when for centuries the African peoples have been the victims of violence and slavery? Yet if the Western world is still determined to rule mankind by force, then Africans, as a last resort, may have to appeal to force in the effort to achieve freedom, even if force destroys them and the world.

We are determined to be free. We want education. We want the right to earn a decent living; the right to express our thoughts and emotions, to adopt and create forms of beauty. We demand for Black Africa autonomy and independence so far and no further than it is possible in this One World for groups and peoples to rule themselves subject to inevitable world unity and federation.

We are not ashamed to have been an age-long patient people. We continue willingly to sacrifice and strive. But we are unwilling to starve any longer while doing the world's drudgery, in order to support by our poverty and ignorance a false aristocracy and a discarded imperialism.

We condemn the monopoly of capital and the rule of private wealth and industry for private profit alone. We welcome economic democracy as the only real democracy.

Therefore, we shall complain, appeal and arraign. We will make the world listen to the fact of our condition. We will fight in every way we can for freedom, democracy, and social betterment.

Molefi Kete Asante and Abus S. Abarry, *African Intellectual Heritage: A Book of Sources* (Philadelphia: Temple University Press, 1996), pp. 520–521. © 1996 by Temple University. All Rights Reserved.

None of the nascent states had enough educated, trained, and experienced African citizens to staff the political, administrative, economic, and social apparatuses of a sovereign country, and this alone made for difficult times after independence. Corruption among new officials proved rife; military coups often provided the only stable governance available; the attempt to implement planned economies on a socialist model often brought economic catastrophe; and ethnic and regional revolts led to civil wars.

Most dangerous and costly to the new states were the separatist struggles, civil wars, and border wars between new states that grew out of the independence struggles. The Nigerian civil war of 1967–1970 was an especially bloody example (see p. 1105). Other new nations caught for periods in open warfare have been Morocco and the western Sahara; Libya and Chad; South African–held Namibia; Ethiopia and Eritrea; Kenya, Uganda, and Tanzania; Rwanda and Burundi; Somalia; and the Sudan. Strikingly, whatever the original goals of the parties involved, these conflicts universally served to ratify rather than repudiate the postcolonial state divisions.

Every African state has had a different experience and history since World War II. The new independent states of Africa have been anything but models. Thus far, with the notable exception of Zanzibar and Tanganyika uniting in the new state of Tanzania, any ideas of a union or unions of nations have failed. Nevertheless, it is important to note that African polities did not revert to tiny tribal or regional political units. Here we briefly examine the histories of four nations: Nigeria, South Africa, Congo, and Rwanda.

Nigeria The modern Republic of Nigeria is the most populous state in Africa, with about 120 million inhabitants in 2005. Nigeria achieved independence from Britain in 1960 and ratified a republican constitution in 1964 that federated the three major provincial regions—the Eastern, Western, and Northern—under a national government based in Lagos, the former British administrative capital. Nigeria's largest ethnic and linguistic groups are the major ones of the same three regions: Igbo in the Eastern, Yoruba in the Western, and Hausa and Fulani in the Northern province. Although these languages have been recognized since 1980 as acceptable for federal business, the official Nigerian language is English.

Nowhere was the aftermath of independence bloodier than in Nigeria, which was, at its inception, arguably the most powerful and potentially successful state in independent Africa. The three-province federation soon proved unworkable, and a 1966 *coup d'état* brought a military government into power. Its leader was himself soon assassinated, and Lieutenant Colonel Yakubu Gawon (b. 1934) took over amid ethnic unrest that ended in massacres in the fall of 1966. Gawon's government subdivided the three provinces into states, three each in the Western and Eastern Provinces, and six in the Northern. In May 1967, the Eastern Province's assembly empowered its leader, Lieutenant Colonel Chukwuemeka Odumegwu Ojukwu (b. 1933), to form a new, independent state of Biafra out of the three states of the Eastern Province. Ojukwu was an Igbo nationalist but aspired to control lands beyond those of the Igbos—in particular, those containing the important off-shore oil reserves of the Eastern Province. The new Biafran state was able to gain recognition from several African states; secure arms and support from France, South Africa, and Portugal; and develop successful worldwide propaganda depicting Biafra as a small, brave, mostly Christian country fighting for its survival against a hostile, oppressive, mostly Muslim central government.

The ensuing two and a half years saw a tragic and bloody civil war pitting elements of independent Africa's best national army against each other. The larger federal forces slowly chipped away at the Biafran state. The estimated death toll soared above a million—the overwhelming majority of whom were Igbo civilians, mostly refugees who died of starvation—before the Biafrans surrendered in January 1970. In the end, at great cost, Nigerians had purchased an increased sense of unity, along with a major role for the military in Nigerian politics. The struggle also contributed to the development of African diplomacy and of international aid efforts in Africa.[3]

Biafran War Refugees, such as this young child, attracted international attention.

Gawon was overthrown by another military commander in 1975. In the ensuing years Nigeria was plagued by political instability at the top, with its leadership passing usually from one military ruler to another, except for the four-year Second Republic under President Shehu Usman Aliyu Shagari (b. 1925), a Fulani Muslim from the north whose rule ended in a military coup in 1983. A decade later, the military regime nullified the 1993 election of Yoruba leader Moshood Abiola to the presidency. This debacle ended in a coup by General Sani Abacha, who instituted four years of repressive military rule. Novelist and environmental activist Kenule "Ken" Saro-Wiwa (b. 1941) was executed in 1995.

Nobel laureate author Wole Soyinka (b. 1934) led protest demonstrations against the military government in 1994 and later went into exile, where in 1996 he helped found a seventeen-member National Liberation Council. Abacha died in June 1998 and was replaced by General Abubakar, who reversed some of Abacha's policies. Soyinka was able to return in October 1998 to a hero's welcome, and some political prisoners were released. Finally, military rule was replaced in 1999 by civilian government under an elected president, Olusegun Obasanjo, and a new constitution was ratified and implemented. Umaru Musa Yar'Adua succeeded Obasanjo as president after an election in April 2007 that was widely believed to be flawed. Problems of religious animosities and ethnic divisions remain. Despite the nation's wealth, corruption and mismanagement have hindered Nigeria's development.

[3] Oliver, *African Experience,* pp. 235–236.

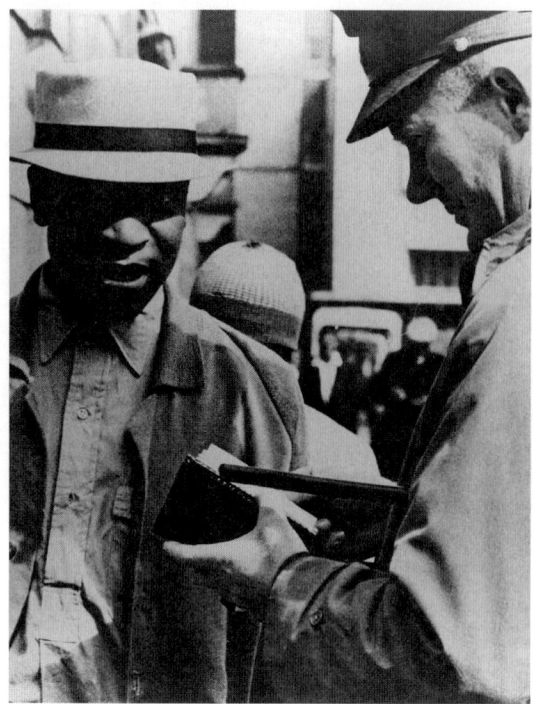

Apartheid. A police officer checks a black African's identification card, under the *apartheid* system's hated pass laws.

South Africa The radical separation of white from nonwhite peoples in all areas of life endured as official government policy in South Africa for nearly fifty years. From the time the Afrikaner-led National Party (NP) came to power in 1948, the Union of South Africa was governed according to the avowedly racist policy of **apartheid** ("apartness"). Until the dismantling of this policy after 1991, the white minority (in 1991, 5.4 million persons) ran the country, maintaining economic and political control and privilege. Its 31 million blacks, 3.7 million "coloreds" (people with dual ancestry), and 1 million Indians were kept strictly segregated—treated, at best, as second-class citizens or, in the case of blacks, as noncitizens or even nonhumans. This system was maintained chiefly by repression, most visibly direct military and police action, to quell dissent and enforce apartheid laws.

The history of apartheid and its passing is a bloody and tortured, but finally triumphant, one. In part as a result of worldwide opposition to apartheid, South Africa saw itself become increasingly isolated from the 1960s onward. Meanwhile, the rest of Africa—including other white-run states like Rhodesia (Zimbabwe)—progressed to majority, African rule. In 1961 South Africa withdrew from the British Commonwealth of Nations. In the sixties and seventies the government created three tiny "independent homelands" for blacks inside the country, allowing the white minority to treat blacks as immigrant "foreigners" in the

parts of South Africa where most had to work. The international community refused to recognize the homelands, or "Bantustans." South Africa's isolation was further dramatized when two anti-apartheid black leaders, the Zulu chief Albert Luthuli (1898?–1967) in 1960 and the Anglican bishop Desmond Tutu (b. 1931) in 1984, were awarded the Nobel Prize for their work against apartheid.

By 1978, as Pieter Botha (1916–2006) came to power, apartheid was failing: The homelands were economic and political catastrophes; the country was in an inflationary recession; skilled whites were emigrating; and with other white colonial regimes progressing to majority, African rule, South Africa was becoming a pariah state. Threats from guerrilla forces prompted the government to send its troops on preemptive raids into neighboring countries. Botha's concessions on issues such as interracial marriage and public-transportation segregation were not enough to calm the situation. Internal opposition and international pressure grew.

Beginning in 1986 many nations responded to Tutu's call and imposed economic sanctions against the government. Anti-apartheid movements in the United States and elsewhere convinced companies and individuals to liquidate investments in South Africa. Strikes by black workers in 1987 led the government to declare a state of emergency, but the resulting violent confrontation created widespread support among Western nations for a complete trade embargo. In June 1988 more than 2 million black workers went on strike to protest new repressive labor laws and a ban on political activity by trade unions and anti-apartheid groups. President Botha resigned in August 1989.

In February 1990 the new president, F. W. de Klerk (b. 1936), began a series of landmark government actions: the lifting of the ban on the African National Congress (ANC), the main anti-apartheid organization; the release of ANC leader Nelson Mandela after twenty-seven years of imprisonment; and the repeal of the Separate Amenities Act, the legal basis for segregation in public places. In early 1991 de Klerk announced plans to end all apartheid laws, and in June the race registration law was repealed. In March 1992, in a whites-only referendum in which over 85 percent of voters turned out, 67.8 percent voted to grant constitutional equality to all races. De Klerk and Mandela, despite terrorist attempts from both black and white extremists, were able to bring their own and eighteen other parties to endorse a new interim constitution. For their leadership, Mandela and de Klerk shared the Nobel Peace Prize for 1993.

Multi-racial elections were held in April 1994. The ANC won 63 percent of the vote, the NP 20 percent, and other parties the remainder. Nelson Mandela was elected president of what Tutu termed the Rainbow Nation, in honor of South Africa's racial and political diversity. The

Nelson Mandela campaigning for the presidency of post-apartheid South Africa.

nonracial constitution of December 1996 provided a new structure for national politics. Meanwhile, the **Truth and Reconciliation Commission** (TRC), established in 1995, offered an unprecedented way to come to terms with the country's past: rather than attempting to bring to justice the many perpetrators of human-rights abuses during the apartheid era, the TRC offered amnesty in exchange for testimony and provided victims a platform for detailing their losses. The TRC's premises were controversial—some victims of apartheid atrocities, for example, protested that their perse-cutors were evading punishment—but it is unlikely that any other mechanism could have generated a more comprehen-sive account of apartheid's abuses.

 *Nelson Mandela, from* Freedom, Justice, and Dignity for all South Africa

The government of Thabo Mbeki, who succeeded Mandela in 1999 and was reelected in 2004, is striving to deal with the challenges that the majority of the population face. Despite substantial mineral resources, and the highest GNP in Africa, South Africa still faces huge problems: one of the world's highest rates of HIV/AIDS infection; high unemployment, poverty, and crime rates; extreme income inequality; insufficient educational and economic infra-structure; woefully inadequate public services in much of the country; potentially severe water-supply and water-quality problems; and difficulties fulfilling the promises of a new era of economic and social progress.

Congo   European rule in Africa was nowhere benign, but it may have reached its nadir in the Congo Free State. In this personal fiefdom of Belgium's King Leopold II between 1885 and 1908, Africans were routinely mutilated or killed for offenses such as failing to meet local officials' quotas for rubber collection. As a Belgian colony, Congo fared slightly better, but from independence onward Congo's history has had more than its share of atrocities.

The Republic of Congo gained independence on June 30, 1960, with Patrice Lumumba (1925 – 1961) as prime minister and Joseph Kasavubu (1910–1969) as president. Lumumba and Kasavubu belonged to different parties; almost immediately, the government began to factionalize. Two provinces, Katanga and South Kasai, separately attempted to secede. Kasavubu dismissed Lumumba from office. Lumumbu resisted, and in the ensuing crisis the Congolese Army's chief of staff, Joseph-Désiré Mobutu (1930–1997), overthrew them both. Lumumbu was assas-sinated in Katanga Province on January 17, 1961. Various presidents served brief terms until 1965, when Mobutu again seized power. This time he had the backing of the United States Central Intelligence Agency—in the Cold

War calculus of influence, he was seen as a defense against African socialism—and this time he kept power for more than 30 years.

Mobutu outlawed all political parties except his own, the Popular Movement of the Revolution, from 1967 to 1990. He launched the Authenticité campaign to celebrate African culture by, among other measures, discouraging Western clothing, Africanizing place-names (Congo was renamed Zaire, Leopoldville became Kinshasa, and many others) and personal names (he became Mobutu Sese Seko Kuku Ngbendu Wa Za Banga, which can be translated as, "The all-powerful warrior who, because of his endurance and inflexible will to win, goes from conquest to conquest, leaving fire in his wake and arising from the blood and ashes of his enemies like the Sun which conquers the night"). As his new name suggests, he also developed a powerful cult of personality. Mobutu's regime became increasingly corrupt, and Mobutu was rumored to be a multi-billionaire. His rule became a kleptocracy.

Mobutu played his Cold War cards well, fostering close relationships with Western powers (particularly the United States) while formally proclaiming nonaligned status. The combination of the end of the Cold War and Mobutu's failing health created an opening for opposition leaders, which they were quick to seize. Refugees from Rwanda's genocide (see "Rwanda") further destabilized the country, and, starting in 1996, insurgents supported by Rwanda, Uganda, Zambia, and Angola captured much of eastern Zaire. Most of these outsiders backed Laurent Kabila (1939–2001) when he was sworn in as president on May 29, 1997. The country was again renamed the Democratic Republic of the Congo (DRC).

Since then, what has been called the Second Congo War (the revolt against Mobutu being the first) or even the African World War has roiled the DRC. International alliances have been made and broken, ceasefires have been negotiated and violated. In 2001, Kabila was assassinated; his son, Joseph Kabila, took office; in 2006, in hotly contested and subsequently disputed elections, he defeated other candidates for the presidency.

The DRC is immense and has a wealth of natural resources, particularly valuable minerals. Nonetheless its future is uncertain; fighting continues, much infrastructure has been destroyed, and most citizens have little reason to trust their government. Estimates vary wildly, but probably close to 4 million people have died as a result of fighting in the DRC since the mid-1990s.

Rwanda Rwanda is roughly one one-hundredth the size of the Democratic Republic of the Congo, but during and after the Rwandan genocide of 1994 the two countries' histories became intertwined. Under Belgian administration, ethnicity in Ruanda-Urundi (now, Rwanda and Burundi) was

Rwandan Refugees carry their belongings as they stream out of the Mugunga refugee camp in Zaire (Congo) back towards Rwanda, in the aftermath of the 1994 genocide. *David Guttenfelder/AP Wide World Photos.*

determined by wealth: since the minority Tutsi tribe already constituted the elite, anyone deemed wealthy by the Belgians became a "Tutsi" and most others were designated as belonging to the largest pre-existing ethnic group, the "Hutu." (There is also a significant minority population of Twa forest people, or "pygmies.") At independence in 1961, Rwanda and Burundi separated, and—despite the tradition of rulership by a Tutsi monarchy—Rwanda became a republic with Hutu leadership.

Over the following decades, there were many cross-border clashes between Rwanda, Burundi, and Uganda. Although this violence was usually labeled as Tutsi-versus-Hutu, there is no way to determine the extent to which ethnic animosity actually drove these conflicts, or how much ethnicity was a convenient cover for other agendas. In any case, on April 6, 1994, when a helicopter carrying the (Hutu) presidents of both Rwanda and Burundi was shot down over Rwanda's capital, killing both presidents, Tutsis were blamed. The groundwork had been laid for inter-ethnic civil war. Over the following months, approximately 800,000 Tutsis and moderate Hutus were killed in a massive genocide. The Uganda-based, Tutsi-led Rwandan Patriotic Front (RPF) under Paul Kagame (b. 1957), meanwhile, gradually took control of the country, and millions of Hutu refugees fled to Zaire. RPF and Ugandan forces pursued them into Zaire, creating one of the triggers for Mobutu's overthrow.

. The Rwandan genocide sparked soul-searching, but little effective action, in the West. United Nations peacekeepers were on the ground in Rwanda when the genocide began, but under the terms of their deployment they were unable to intervene. United States President Bill Clinton was harshly criticized for failing to take action; indeed, U.S. officials studiously avoided referring to events in Rwanda as "genocide" until late May 1994.

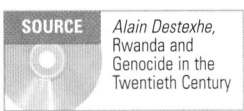 *Alain Destexhe,* Rwanda and Genocide in the Twentieth Century

Following a period under a transitional government, a new constitution was approved and Kagame was elected president in 2003. Although Kagame has been criticized for stifling dissent, most observers believe that Rwanda is undergoing a remarkable recovery.

The African Future

Most African states have not achieved peace and prosperity. And, it must be noted, some struggles—most notably in the Democratic Republic of the Congo and the Darfur region of Sudan—are still ongoing, their human consequences catastrophic, and their ultimate outcomes not clear. However, the last half-century has seen radical change and development. Overall, the prospects for future government stability are stronger than ever. Economic problems still loom extremely large, but even in that sphere progress is being made after decades of failed schemes. The often heavy burdens of the past—be they regional rivalries and hatreds, religious and linguistic divisions, major economic and social policy mistakes in early independence, or the crippling experience of apartheid—still present formidable hurdles. Probably even more serious are the newer problems with which almost all of Africa's nations have to contend as they strive to build civil societies and achieve economic health. Each African state faces unique problems and must draw on its unique resources if it is to be successful in the present century.

Health and Environment There are a variety of health and environmental challenges facing Africa, the most notorious of which is **HIV/AIDS**. In late 2005, nearly 25 million people in sub-Saharan Africa were infected with HIV. There are significant regional variations in HIV infection rates: in general, rates are highest (over 20 percent of the adult population) in southern African nations, followed by East and central Africa, while rates are generally relatively low (often under 5 percent) in West African nations (see Map 34–3). Governments have also varied tremendously in their responses to HIV/AIDS. Uganda, for example, embarked on an aggressive public education campaign in the 1990s, which seems to have helped reduce infection rates

there. In contrast, in early 2000, South African President Thabo Mbeki publicly questioned whether HIV causes AIDS and made other statements that contributed to an atmosphere of denial and shame surrounding HIV/AIDS in South Africa.

Other diseases, while less likely to capture headlines in the West, sicken or kill millions of Africans every year. The World Health Organization declared the prevalence of tuberculosis an emergency in Africa in 2005, and the situation has not improved since then. Malaria and other primarily tropical diseases reduce life expectancy, increase absenteeism from school and work, and reduce economic productivity in almost all parts of Africa. Only very recently have significant global health initiatives, such as the Global Network for Neglected Tropical Diseases (established in 2006), begun to target Africa's interrelated health challenges.

African environmental challenges run the gamut from wildlife poaching to soil erosion to improper disposal of hazardous waste. Africans have been in the forefront of the environmental justice movement, with activists including Ken Saro-Wiwa (see p. 1105) and Nobel laureate Wangari Maathai, leader of Kenya's Green Belt Movement, building grassroots environmental campaigns.

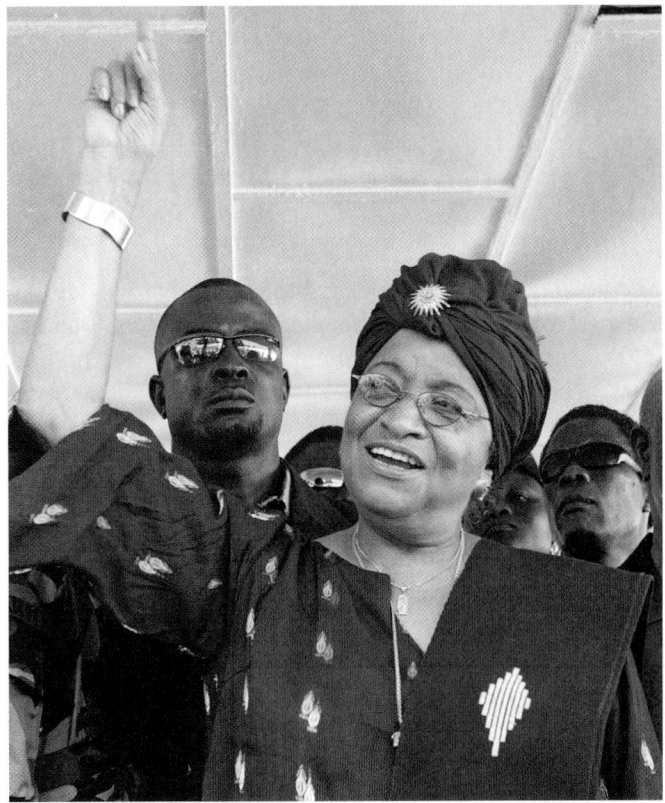

Ellen Sirleaf-Johnson was elected president of Liberia in 2005. She is the first woman elected to lead an African nation.

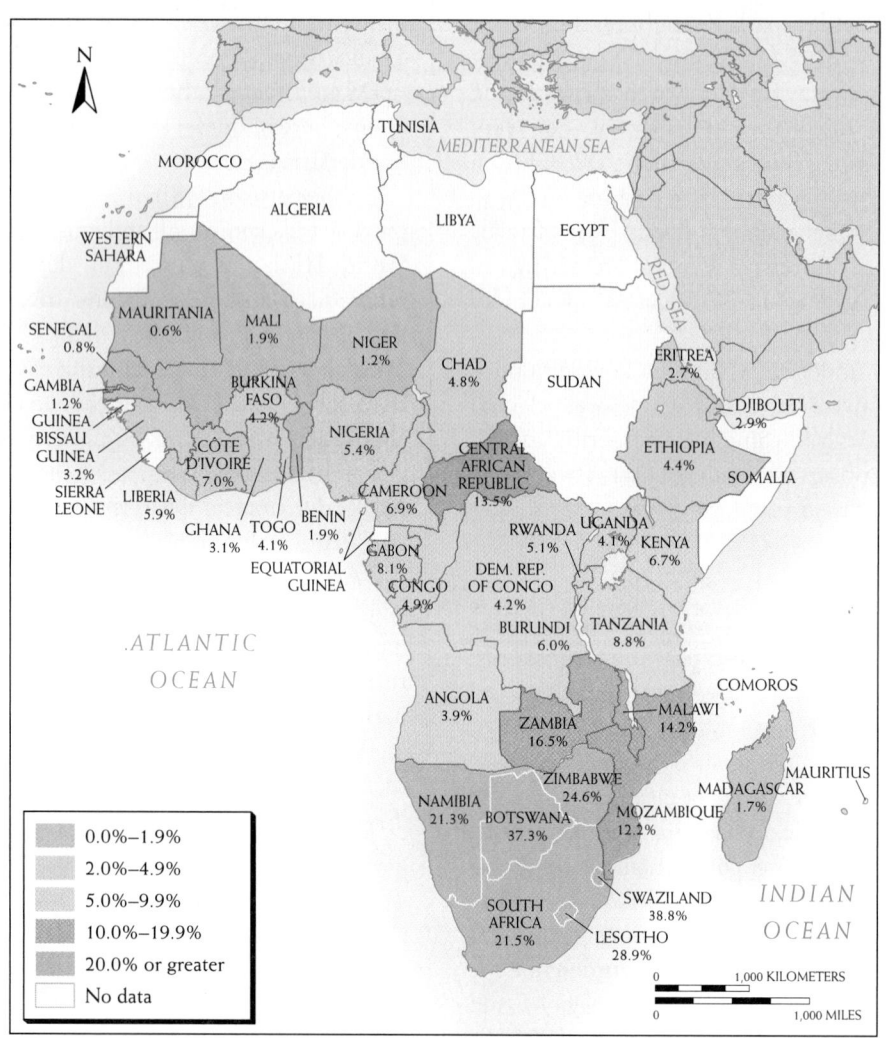

Map 34–3.   Distribution of HIV Infection Rates in Africa.

Social Change African society has changed rapidly during the postcolonial period, though many traditions endure.

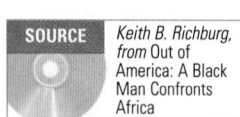

Keith B. Richburg, *from* Out of America: A Black Man Confronts Africa

Rapid urbanization is a trend that began in the colonial period and has continued to the present. The explosive growth of new urban centers at the expense of rural areas has disrupted the continent's traditionally agrarian-based societies, age-old family and tribal allegiances, religious values, and sociopolitical systems. Migrants come to cities in search of wage labor, but African urban economies have never grown as quickly as their populations; many African cities include large slum areas where masses of people live in substandard housing, lacking plumbing and other essential infrastructure. In general, men have been more likely to migrate from rural to urban areas than women, so there are often significant gender imbalances in both rural and urban areas.

In a significant discontinuity with the colonial era, African women have been elected to many national offices. Women were active in anti-colonial and anti-apartheid movements and took leadership roles in some post-independence rebellions (for example, in Uganda), but it is only since the mid-1990s that large numbers of women have been elected to national parliaments and other high offices. Ellen Sirleaf-Johnson, the first woman elected to lead an African nation, won the presidency of Liberia in 2005.

Population growth has been rapid throughout Africa, creating economic, social, and political challenges. Deaths from HIV/AIDS have created new population trends, such as the large numbers of "AIDS orphans," children whose parents have been killed or incapacitated by disease.

Religion is an important force in the lives of most individual Africans and in the structures of African societies. Christianity and Islam both continue to gain converts. Evangelical Christianity, in particular, is growing rapidly.

Trade and Development

During the Cold War, one of the areas in which the West and the Soviet bloc competed was in dispensing development aid in Africa. Starting in the 1990s, trade has been emphasized as the best mechanism for growing African economies and improving standards of living. Under President Bill Clinton, for example, the United States encouraged private-sector trade and investment through the Partnership for Economic Growth and Opportunity in Africa. President Bush supported the African Global Competitiveness Initiative (AGCI) to build sub-Saharan Africa's capacity for trade and competitiveness. A factor of rapidly growing importance is trade with, and direct investment by, China. African economies still need to grow tremendously to meet their populations' needs.

The Islamic Heartlands, from North Africa to Indonesia

The lands today dominated or significantly marked by Islamic culture and containing either Muslim majority populations or major Muslim minority numbers stretch from North and West Africa to the Philippines. More specifically, they are found in the Arab world from Morocco to Iraq and the Gulf, in West and East Africa, in the Balkans and the Turkish-speaking world of Turkey and the former Soviet Central Asian republics, in Persian-speaking Iran and parts of Central Asia, in western China, and in South and Southeast Asia. India, Bangladesh, Pakistan, and Indonesia have the four largest Muslim populations in the world, the first three having about 132, 109, and 125 million Muslims, respectively, and the last more than 240 million. The Muslims of the entire Arab world number no more than 250 million. The various nations of this huge region of Central, South, and Southeast Asia illustrate the many different ways in which Islamic faith and practice may manifest themselves and affect political life.

Turkey

Turkey represents a modernist republican experiment that has attempted to create a civil society and a democratically elected government despite struggles over the roles of the military, ethnicity, culture, and religion in society. However, the Turkish military has repeatedly deposed elected governments and supervised the selection of new leadership. Economically, Turkey has certainly had its difficulties, but along

with Israel it is still the most economically advanced Middle Eastern country. With the creation of new Turkic-language-speaking states in Central Asia after the breakup of the Soviet Union, Turkey is making a bid, and may succeed, to strengthen its ties with this underdeveloped part of the world and to be a major factor in its emergence over the next generation. (See Document, "A Modernist Muslim Poet's Eulogy for His Mother.")

Geographically and culturally Turkey is part of both Europe and Asia. Istanbul, its main commercial and cultural center, is located in continental Europe. In recent years, Turkey, already a member of NATO, has sought admission into the European Union, thus far without success.

Turkey also participates in several significant European cultural events such as the European soccer competition and the widely watched (in Europe at least) Eurovision song contest. In coming years, the issue of Turkish membership in the European Union will be contested because many across Europe are skeptical about admitting an overwhelmingly Muslim nation into the Union and about the less-than-stellar Turkish human-rights record. Up to now, the longtime persecution of the ten-to-twelve-million-strong Kurdish minority in Turkey has been a sticking point for European acceptance of the idea of admitting Turkey to the European Union. Human-rights violations such as imprisonment of journalists, repression of the Kurdish language, and repression of freedom of speech, as well as serious indebtedness to the International Money Fund have worked against Turkey's case for EU admission also. In addition, various Islamist parties have emerged in Turkey and complicated the political landscape. It remains to be seen whether Turkey will align itself more with Europe, the Middle East, or Central Asia in the years ahead, even though it is making a strong effort to join Europe while reaching out to Central Asia.

Iran and Its Islamic Revolution

Iran, the most important state of west Asia, was ruled from 1925 to 1941 as a monarchy by a former army commander, Reza Khan, who had come to power by military takeover and the support of the British governing Reza Shah with the ancient Persian name of Pahlavi. He attempted to introduce modernist economic, educational, and governmental reforms. He saw himself much like his contemporary in Turkey, Ataturk (1881–1938), creating a rich landlord and industrial class with few benefits for the pastoral, peasant, and urban laborers of his time. Reza Shah was not interested in a parliamentary, popularly oriented state, but rather a highly centralized autocratic monarchy. His reforms differed from Ataturk's in that Reza Shah did not

A Modernist Muslim Poet's Eulogy for His Mother

Document

The following is a poem drawn from the autobiography of Aziz Nesin, *That's How It Was but Not How It's Going to Be* (1966). Nesin (b. 1915) is a prolific Turkish writer, political commentator, and social critic whose writing career began in 1946 with his publication of a satirical weekly paper. The following poem is a eulogy for his long-dead mother, a reflection on the deprivations she endured, and a determined promise to ensure women a better life in the future. It reflects the widespread feeling among secular modernists in Turkey and elsewhere that one of the hallmarks of modernity is the emancipation of women. The final two lines repeat the original Turkish title of Nesin's book.

◆ What is the impact of addressing the poem to his own mother rather than to some other female figure? What specific things is Nesin criticizing in the poem?

VOW TO MY MOTHER'S MEMORY

All mothers, the most beautiful of mothers,
You are the most beautiful of the beautiful,
At thirteen you married;
At fifteen you gave me birth.
You were twenty-six,
You died before you lived.
I owe you this heart overflowing with love.
I don't even have your picture;
It was a sin to have a photograph taken.
You saw neither movie, nor play.
Electricity, gas, water, stove,
Nor even a bedstead was found in your home.

You could never bathe in the sea,
You couldn't read nor write.
Your lovely eyes
Looked at the world from behind a black veil.
When you were twenty-six
You died, before you lived.
Henceforward, mothers will not die before they live.
That's how it was,
But not how it's going to be!

Aziz Nesin, *Istanbul Bay: The Autobiography of Aziz Nesin, Part I,* p. 9. Copyright © 1977 Center for Middle Eastern Studies. Reprinted by permission.

---

have to deal with a battle-tested and heavily armed military or an experienced and eager middle class, both of whom Ataturk had to placate in order to realize his social and industrialization projects.

By the time Russian and British forces deposed Reza Shah in 1941 and installed his son, Muhammad Reza, as shah, the activism of radical trade unionists and socialist-minded intelligentsia had been quickly crushed, and the power of the Shi'ite religious leaders, or *ulama*, had been muted along the way to a strong, centralized Pahlavi state. The son, much more than his father, sought to legitimize Pahlavi by linkage with the imperial dynasties of pre-Islamic Persia. He continued his father's secular and industrial state building from the end of World War II until 1978, with one interruption from 1951 to 1953. Those three years saw Muhammad Mosaddeq (1881–1967), after decades of parliamentary experience, reach the pinnacle of political power through his successful drawing together of a broad coalition of workers, *bazari* merchants, religious leaders, the intelli-

gentsia, and government workers into a political force called "The National Front" that rode its way into the minds and hearts of Iranians with the nationalization of the British-owned Anglo-Iranian Oil Company in Abadan. The 1951 Nationalization Act sent Iranians dancing into the streets of Tehran for days. Mossadeq's years as Iran's most popular Prime Minister came to an end, however, on August 19, 1953, through a covert U.S. Central Intelligence Agency and British Military Intelligence *coup d'etat* called Operation Ajax. Though denied for decades, the U.S. quietly admitted to its intervention into Iranian politics in the 1990s, thereby confirming Iranians' past suspicions and earning both the U.S. and Britain several generations of deep hatred and distrust by Iran.

SOURCE *Pro-Mosaddeq rally, Tehran, 1951*

In the 1960s Muhammad Reza Shah faced two groups of opposition; one led by educated secularists and the other by the *ulama*. While land reform and other Pahlavi "white revolutions" were opposed by both groups for different rea-

Khomeini. The bearded ayatollah waves to a cheering throng in Tehran, Iran, in February 1979. *Reuters/Corbs-Bettmann.*

sons, the Shah's heavy-handed and at times very brutal repression of any form of protest, including nonviolent street marches, critical publications, and political meetings, forced the two groups to reassess the close association of the shah with the U.S. and the need for militant confrontations. While the *ulama* preferred the continuation of nonviolent opposition through the 1970s and 1980s, the middle- and upper-class professionals including students, industrial workers, and leftists opted for tactical violent clashes with the Shah's regime and his U.S. ally. For all of the modernizing and the military and economic buildup that the U.S. and the Shah initiated, his reign failed to narrow the gap between the extremely wealthy few and the extremely poor masses. The fact that fully half of Iran's 60-odd million inhabitants are Turkish, Kurdish, Arabic, and other minorities did little to help him consolidate and strengthen his centralized Iranian monarchy.

Finally, in 1978 religious leaders and secularist professional revolutionaries joined forces to end the shah's long regime with a revolution filled with a wide spectrum of emo-

tion, ideology, and secular as well as religious symbolism. What had begun as an "Iranian Revolution", ended up as an "Islamic Revolution", so that in 1979 the constitution of a new post-shah republic was not a secular but an Islamic one adapted under the guidance of the Shi'ite religious leader, Ayatollah Ruhollah Khomeini (1902–1989).

Subsequent years followed with a protracted war with Iraq (1980–1988) and the institution of repressive and violent measures against enemies of the new regime not unlike those methods used under the shah. Still, the new state—with religious leaders exercising a degree of influence over politics not seen since early Safavid times in the sixteenth century—has survived. Khomeini and his successors, Hashemi Rafsanjani (b. 1934) and Ali Khameini (b. 1939), however, were not free of or untainted by politics. They had to struggle to find a new formula for combining Muslim values and norms with twentieth-century *realpolitik*, and this will continue to be a major challenge for their successors.

The immediate successor to Rafsanjani, Mohammad Khatami, was elected to the great surprise of many to the presidency in 1997 by a resounding majority in the first real national leadership election since the 1979 revolution. Khatami, a moderate cleric himself as well as former minister of culture with a reputation as a liberal among the major figures in Iranian politics, tried to steer Iran on a more moderate, liberal course. Many think his election and administration represented a key step in Iran's movement after its watershed revolution towards a more stable government and more internationally engaged and accepted power globally, particularly in the Middle Eastern and Indian Ocean sphere. The wide-ranging reforms that people expected from Khatami, however, failed to materialize. There have been sporadic and unsuccessful student protests against the clerical government. In 2003, Shirin Ebadi, an Iranian lawyer, won the Nobel Peace Prize for her decades of dedicated work to improve the legal protections and general status of women and children in Iran. The Islamic leaders of Iran paid no attention to that singular honoring of the first Muslim woman to ever receive such an international award. In 2005, Mahmud Ahmadinejad (b. 1956), a former officer of the *Basij* or Youth Corps, veteran of the eight-year Iraq-Iran war, and former mayor of Tehran, surprisingly defeated the veteran liberal religious politician and former two-term Islamic Republic president, Ali Akbar Hashemi Rafsanjani (b. 1956), introducing a new style of bombast and straight talk to Iranian national and international politics. As a result the U.S. and its allies (particularly Israel) concluded that a regime change due to Iran's policies on nuclear energy and its alleged military involvement in the U.S. occupation of Iraq was overdue. The future is very uncertain.

Iranian Nobel Prize Winner Shirin Ebadi at the Street Children's Home That She Founded in Tehran. Ebadi was awarded the prestigious prize for her work in defending human rights. She was the first Muslim woman to be awarded a Nobel.

Afghanistan and the Former Soviet Republics

North of Iran, 40 million Central Asian Muslims predominate in the broad region that stretches across the south-central reaches of the former Soviet Union between the Crimea and China, and 30 million or more Muslims live in Chinese Central Asia. These people have had to sustain their religious and intellectual traditions in the face of Russian and Chinese cultural, linguistic, and political imperialism. In the 1980s both Soviet and Chinese Muslims appeared to be asserting themselves. The 1979 Soviet invasion and occupation of Afghanistan, whose people had close ties to the Muslim peoples in the Soviet Union, reflected the potential importance of this movement. The phased withdrawal of Soviet forces from Afghanistan in 1988 looked surprisingly like the U.S. withdrawal from South Vietnam in 1974. It was soon followed by a much more momentous aboutface in the form of the collapse of the Soviet Union in 1990 into many separate states, most of which remain loosely connected through the Commonwealth of Independent States (CIS). The Central Asian republics within the Commonwealth include Kazakhstan, Kyrgyzstan, Tajikistan, Turkmenistan, and Uzbekistan, as well as the Caucasian republics of Armenia, Azerbaijan, Georgia, and Moldova. Suddenly the Central Asian Islamic republics of the former Soviet Union found themselves effectively independent states, with little of the infrastructure to manage such a transition. The great challenge now is whether they and their sister states of the Commonwealth can attain political viability without first being destroyed by economic collapse or ethnic or regional conflict.

The Soviet invasion of Afghanistan produced a major unexpected result. Thousands of Muslims, mostly fundamentalist in outlook, had arrived in Afghanistan to oust the Soviets and their Afghan puppets. Conservative Arab states and the United States supported this effort, which succeeded by the late 1980s. The conservative Arab states saw the Afghan War as an opportunity both to resist the expansion of Soviet influence into their sphere and to divert the energies of their own religious extremists. The United States saw the Afghan War as another round in the Cold War. The militant Muslim fundamentalists saw it as a religious struggle against an impious non-Muslim power.

After the Soviets withdrew, a power vacuum in Afghanistan lasted almost a decade. By 1998, however, rigorist Muslims known as the *Taliban* had seized control of the country. They imposed their own version of Islamic law, which involved strict regimentation of women and public executions and mutilations for criminal offenses. The Taliban also allowed groups of Muslim terrorists known as *al Qaeda*, which means "Base," to establish training camps in their country. The terrorists who attacked the United States on September 11, 2001, came from these camps. As will be seen later in the chapter, one response of the United States to those attacks was a military campaign against the Taliban government of Afghanistan.

India

India, a largely Hindu state, and Pakistan, a largely Muslim state, gained independence in 1947 after the British agreed to a partition of the subcontinent. Much of their subsequent history has been one of mutual antagonism. This was born out of the Hindu-Muslim communal violence and the disputes over Kashmir and other areas that accompanied the partition. The tragedy of the massive displacement of Muslims from the new India and of Hindus and Sikhs from the new Pakistan (about 8 million people in each case) was and is still immense for millions of families and individuals. The two states still have not resolved their major differences, including their conflicting claims to Kashmir. Their rivalry has been exacerbated recently by a new round of saber rattling, this time a nuclear one begun by five Indian underground nuclear tests carried out in mid-May 1998, which were closely followed by similar Pakistani tests two weeks later. Since that time there have been a number of crises between the two nations in which there have been fears of a nuclear exchange.

Bereft of its spiritual and material father, Mohandas Gandhi (1869–1948), after his assassination in 1948 at the hands of a Hindu fanatic, India has been directed for most of its existence by the leaders of Gandhi's Congress Party. First came Gandhi's follower and nationalist colleague, Jawaharlal Nehru (1889–1964), who developed India's famous theory of political neutrality vis-à-vis world alignments, such as that of the superpowers in the Cold War. Nehru's long leadership carried India through the critical organizational period of early independence and not only Pakistani disputes but also a brief Himalayan war with China in 1962. His secularist, reconciliatory policies reduced the communal hatreds, religious zealotry, and regional tensions of the postpartition era, and he also made progress in the huge task of economic development of the overpopulated, underdeveloped new nation. His government oversaw the nuts-and-bolts internal work of damping such potentially divisive movements as Sikh religious separatism and of forging a national federation from states divided by religious, cultural, and political history as well as by languages.

In this era Hindi and English were set as the national languages, and fourteen major regional languages, each associated with a state, were recognized for regional official use. Nehru's resolute opposition to caste privilege also helped improve equality of citizenship beyond universal suffrage.

Nehru was succeeded by another Congress leader, Lal Bahadur Shastri (1904–1966), who saw India through a debilitating nine-month war and standoff with Pakistan in

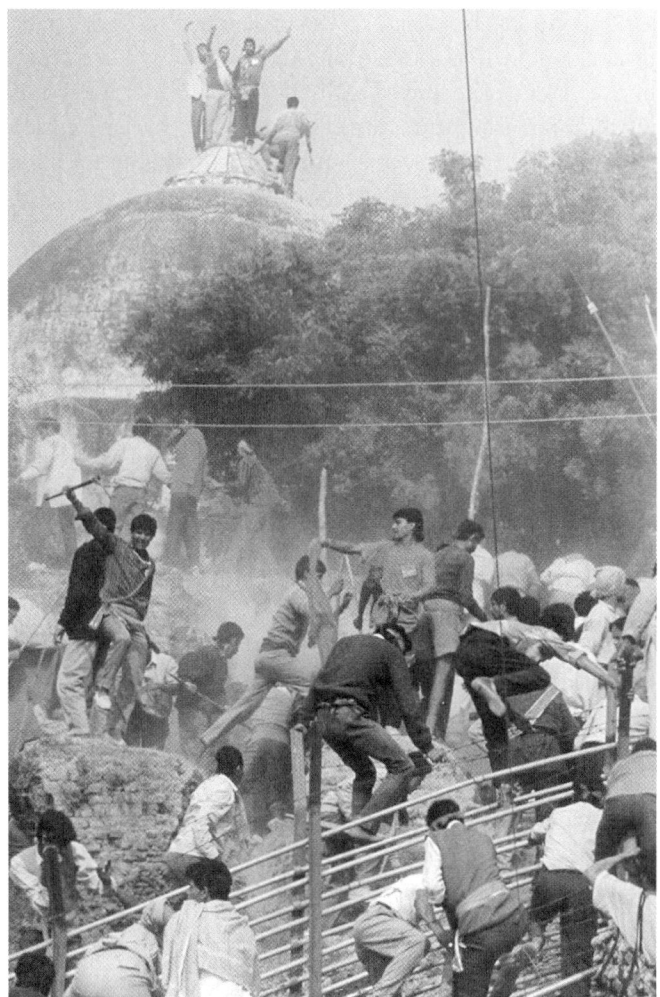

Hindu Militants. Hindu militants attack a Muslim mosque in Ayodhya, India, December 6, 1992. The razing of this mosque at the hands of a mob led by Hindu communalist extremists touched off a wave of Hindu-Muslim violence in India. The Hindus claimed the mosque, built some 500 years ago, occupied the site of what had originally been a Hindu temple and sought to have a new temple built once the mosque was cleared away. *Sunil Malhotra/ Reuters/Corbis-Bettmann.*

1965. His successor was Nehru's daughter, Indira Gandhi (1917–1984; prime minister, 1966–1977, 1980–1984; no familial relation to Mohandas Gandhi). She carried on most of her father's policies and similarly managed to steer a tricky course of neutralism during the Cold War and its East–West tensions. India's 1971 victory over Pakistan and the subsequent creation of Bangladesh to replace East Pakistan cemented for some years her often shaky political control; this war and the subsequent development, with Russian help, of an atomic bomb confirmed India as the major power in South Asia. The failure of her efforts to reduce national poverty and improve India's general economic health soon overcame her postwar popularity. After her efforts to assume virtual dictatorial power in the face of calls for her resignation, in 1977 she and the Congress Party were ousted by the voters for three years. She was reelected prime minister in an amazing turnaround and served until her resolute efforts to quell Sikh separatism brought about her assassination in 1984 by two Sikhs from her own palace guard.

Indira Gandhi's son, Rajiv Gandhi (1944–1991), was elected prime minister after her, and his handling of the thorny Sikh issue was generally applauded. Indications that he and Prime Minister Bhutto might work together to resolve some of the old India-Pakistan hostilities were also promising. Charges of corruption in his government led to his party's temporary fall and the prime ministership of V. P. Singh (b. 1931), who worked in his brief period of leadership to defuse Hindu-Sikh and Hindu-Muslim communal tensions. Singh's resignation gave Gandhi as leader of the Congress Party a chance in the national and state elections of 1991, but during the campaign he was assassinated by a Sri Lankan Tamil suicide bomber. Because no party won the subsequent national vote, the leader of the Congress Party, P. V. Narasimha Rao, was asked to form a government. He and the Congress managed afterwards to make substantial economic progress and, despite failures such as the 1992 radical Hindu riot and attack on the Babri Mosque in Ayodhya, to keep the lid generally on a wide variety of communal and separatist problems, from the Sikhs in the Punjab to Muslims in Kashmir and the south, Hindu extremists, and Uttarakhand separatists in the Himalayas. In 1997, Vice President K. R. Narayanan, a former academic and foreign service officer, assumed the presidency. He and his party were displaced in 2004 by an unexpected Congress Party victory.

India's problems remain large. Poverty and disease, including plague outbursts, remain serious. Separatist movements based on regional linguistic affinity, such as that of the Tamil peoples of the south, or religious affinity, such as that of the Sikhs of the Punjab, have pulled at the unity of the Indian state. Industrialization and agricultural modernization have recently made great strides, yet the neutralizing force of runaway population growth has yet to be countered enough to ensure a brighter future for India's masses. India's population is now at about 1 billion and growing at nearly 2 percent per year. The growing strength of militant Hindu nationalists and fundamentalists and new outbreaks of communal violence between Hindus and India's large Muslim minority pose serious threats to the country's political stability. As the world's largest functioning democracy, India will be an important model of representative government and pluralistic society if it succeeds in staying together and solving or even reducing its harshest problems: overpopulation and mass poverty.

Pakistan and Bangladesh

The architect and first president of Pakistan, Muhammad Ali Jinnah (1876–1948), oversaw the creation of a Muslim state comprising the widely separated East and West Pakistan in the two predominantly Muslim areas of northwest India and East Bengal. New constitutions, war with India, religious versus secularist ideological strife, repeated military rule, and consistent return to the ballot box have marked the often-baffling pendulum swings of the new nation in its first half century. In 1971 East Pakistan seceded and became the new Islamic nation of Bangladesh. Indian and Bangladeshi relations have been troubled since then. However, the main political division in the subcontinent remains that between India and Pakistan.

Pakistan's groping efforts to create a fully Islamic society and to solve its massive economic problems have been hampered by periodic lapses into dictatorship. Such lapses are usually punctuated by bloodshed and military coups, the most recent being that which brought the military leader Zia ul-Haqq (1924–1988) to power in 1977. The elections of November 1988, following his death in a suspicious air crash, opened the door to the possible success of parliamentary government rule. The new prime minister, Benazir Bhutto (b. 1953), was the daughter of the man whom Zia ul-Haqq overthrew and executed. She was also the first female leader of a major Islamic state in the twentieth century. Her time in office was cut short by the president's dismissal of her government in August 1990.

Benazir Bhutto returned to the prime ministership, only to be deposed by the president on charges of corruption in 1996 and convicted in 1999. The successor government did not last long, for in 1999, General Parviz Musharraf, Chief of Army Staff (a post he resigned in 2007), took over as chief executive of Pakistan and has continued to govern, despite increasing protest, since that time. Of all central Asian governments, that of Pakistan has confronted the most direct challenge from radical Islam.

Indonesia and Malaysia

The new East Indies state of Indonesia came into being in 1949 as a nominal republic succeeding the long Dutch and brief Japanese colonial dominions in the East Indies. The much smaller territory of Malaya received its independence from British colonial rule in 1957 as a federation under a rotating monarch; it was later joined by the states of Sarawak and Sabah in northern Borneo, forming the federation of Malaysia. Each of these two new sovereign states faces different challenges.

Indonesia, the largest Muslim country in the world (about 216 million of its estimated 245 million people are Muslim), is trying to achieve a consensus among its disparate and scattered parts. It must determine how Muslim religious faith is to be reconciled with secularist government. The overriding problem for Malaysia (population 20 million) has been the cleft between the largely Chinese (32 percent) and partly Indian (9 percent) non-Muslim minority on the one hand, and the largely Muslim majority of Malay and other indigenous peoples (59 percent) on the other. Both nations have rich cultural traditions and natural resources; it remains to be seen how each will choose to preserve them while meeting the demands of modern global politics and participation in the global economy. An important part of the future of Islam as a global religious and cultural tradition, as well as the future of these two Asian states, is at stake.

The Postcolonial Middle East

Today no other part of the world so dominates international concern and conflict as those in the Middle East region. The issues have arisen as a result of the French and British successor nations established in the region since World War I, the coming of the Jewish state of Israel and resulting Palestine wars, the rise of militant Islamists, and the recent military interventions and occupations by the United States in Iraq and Afghanistan.

Postcolonial Nations in the Middle East

The modern Middle East arose as a result of the collapse of the Ottoman Empire and the subsequent division of the region by France and Britain following World War I and the Versailles Peace Conference. Those powers in effect carved out their own colonial nations and protectorates in the Middle East. Saudi Arabia, Iraq, and Egypt became semi-independent states after World War I, and Lebanon and Syria were officially recognized as independent by France during World War II. In 1948 Britain abandoned its Mandate or colony over Palestine, and the United Nations recognized the state of Israel and established 60 U.N. Relief and Works Agency (UNRWA) Palestinian refugee camps in Gaza, the West Bank, Jordan, Lebanon, Syria, and Egypt. Another 4 million Palestinians live today in the Palestinian diaspora from Turkey to Texas, and six regional wars and two internal uprisings (*intifada*) have erupted so far involving Israel, with apparently no end in sight as regional and international attempts to end the occupation of Palestinian lands continues into the twenty-first century.

During the late 1940s and thereafter, other Arab states gained official political independence: Jordan in 1946; Libya in 1951; Morocco and Tunisia in 1956; Algeria in 1962; and, by 1971, Yemen, Oman, and the Arabian/Persian Gulf shaykhdoms. (See Map 34–4.)

As elsewhere in the industrializing world, these states have sought political self-determination amidst political instability and autocratic rule. All share the classical Arabic written language (*fuśha*), whereas the spoken colloquial language (*amiyya*) varies from country to country and even region to region. Various attempts to create pan-Arab alliances or federations have all failed primarily because regional differences and political self-interests of autocratic and elite families have overcome the common social, cultural, and political denominators. The heritage of these efforts to establish a common and even pan-Arab nationalism remains important to many today.

In the wake of World War II, many of the foremost leaders of Arab nationalism, such as Gamal Abdul Nasser of Egypt (1918–1970), were sympathetic to socialism or to the Soviet Union. While socialism was in part a European ideology, Arab socialism was not overtly anti-European, but rather an adoption of European concepts to the conditions and traditions within the Middle East world. Popular among both secular and religious middle-class supporters, "Islamic socialism" had gained considerable support in the 1980s until discredited by the contradictory actions of their Arab, Turkish, Iranian, and Kurdish leaders. Soviet-style communism, however, was so overtly secular and anti-religious, many Arab, Turkish, and Iranian Muslims tended to be tentative if not hostile to their secular-minded contemporaries who embraced communist parties and trade union politics so readily.

Nationalism in the basic sense of "patriotism to the homeland" and "Egypt for Egyptians" remains the most important ideology from Morocco to India, and thus has the broadest range of supporters from autocratic leaders, traditional monarchies, military juntas, and single-party dictatorships to regional factions, sectarian militias, and student groups. It is safe to say that no ideology currently resonates at its highest level today than the feeling of "solidarity" among Arab, Turkish, Iranian, and Kurdish peoples. The social and political distinctions and sectarian and secular lines are drawn not so much by commonality of political cultures but by access to wealth, income, land, and arms. Thus, the elites of the oil-producing countries such as Syria, Iraq, Saudi Arabia, and the Gulf states who have ready access to wealth, income, land, and arms act "nationalistically" both when such actions serve their own and their largest supporters' interests while regional and local elites who have less access to wealth, income, land, and arms are allied with the oil-producing "giants" as long as it serves their regional and local interests and needs. All too often, the oil-producing "giants" act in their own state and family interests in alliance

Map 34–4. The Modern Middle East and the Distribution of Major Religious Communities. The inset shows Israel and the Occupied Territories.

with the U.S. and the European Union as guarantors of their continued elite status while the regional and local elites and families are often left to their own devices, frequently changing alliances, and responsive to the immediate needs of food, housing, education, and health of their constituents. Any attempt by a foreign power to intervene, manipulate, or tinker with the delicate social, economic, political, and cultural alliances of the state, regional, and local elites is at great risk. Such alliances shift quickly, are based on historic as well as contemporary interests, and respond to a range of other needs unseen and little understood by the foreign power. The rising poverty, refugee displacements, urban crimes, and social violence in the Middle East and North African regions during the past decades dictate the directions and redirections of local and regional alliances more often than not.

The King-Crane Commission Report, August 28, 1919

In the postwar peace settlements following World War I it proved impossible to reconcile the claims of the Arabs, the Zionists, the British, and the fact-finding French. The American President Woodrow Wilson sent a fact-finding mission to the region to determine what the people of the region really wanted. The King-Crane Commission was headed by Henry C. King, the president of Oberlin College, and Charles R. Crane, a businessman and philanthropist. The commission spent several weeks in the Middle East meeting with representatives of the various ethnic, religious, and national communities.

Although the commission's report had no influence on policy in the region, it is remarkable because it captured the uncertain political mood in the Middle East immediately following World War I. As the following section reveals, the United States was held in high regard in the region. The report also anticipated some of the problems relating to Arab-Jewish relations.

◆ What are some of the major political issues highlighted by the commission? Why did the commission find such a positive attitude towards the United States?

We recommend . . . serious modification of the extreme Zionist programme for Palestine of unlimited immigration of Jews, looking finally to making Palestine distinctly a Jewish state.

If, however, the strict terms of the Balfour Statement are adhered to, favouring the establishment in Palestine of a national home for the Jewish people, "it being clearly understood that nothing shall be done which may prejudice the civil and religious rights of existing non-Jewish communities in Palestine"—it can hardly be doubted that the extreme Zionist programme must be greatly modified. For a national home for the Jewish people is not equivalent to making Palestine into a Jewish State; nor can the erection of such a Jewish State be accomplished without the grave trespass upon the civil and religious rights of existing non-Jewish communities in Palestine. . . .

Then it is to be remembered that the non-Jewish population of Palestine—nearly nine-tenths of the whole—are emphatically against the entire Zionist programme. The tables show that there was no one thing upon which the population of Palestine was more agreed than upon this. To subject a people so minded to unlimited Jewish immigration, and to steady financial and social pressure to surrender the land, would be a gross violation of the principle just quoted, and of the people's rights, though it kept within the forms of law. It is to be noted also that the feeling against the Zionist programme is not confined to Palestine, but shared very generally by the people throughout Syria, as our conferences clearly showed. More than seventy-two percent—1.350 in all the petitions in the whole of Syria were directed against the Zionist programme. Only two requests—those for a united Syria and for independence had a larger support. . . .

In view of all these considerations, and with a deep sense of sympathy for the Jewish cause, the Commissioners feel bound to recommend that only a greatly reduced Zionist programme be attempted by the Peace Conference, and even that, only very gradually initiated. This would have to mean that Jewish immigration should be definitely limited, and that the project for making Palestine distinctly a Jewish commonwealth should be given up. . . . Nevertheless, upon the face of the returns, America was the first choice of 1,152 of the petitions presented—more than sixty percent—while no other Power had as much as fifteen per cent for first choice.

And the conferences showed that the people knew the grounds upon which they registered their choice for America. They declared that their choice was due to knowledge of America's record; the unselfish aims with which she had come into the War; the faith in her felt by multitudes of Syrians who had been in America; the spirit revealed in American educational institutions in Syria, especially the College in Beirut, with its well-known and constant encouragement of Syrian national sentiment; their belief that America had no territorial or colonial ambitions, and would willingly withdraw when the Syrian State was well established as her treatment both of Cuba and the Philippines seemed to them to illustrate; her genuinely democratic spirit; and her ample resources. From the point of view of the desires of the "people concerned," the Mandate should clearly go to America.

U.S. government

Arab governments, defining themselves according to the values of nationalism, worked out arrangements with local Muslim authorities. For example, the Saudi royal family turned over its educational system to adherents of a rigorist, puritanical form of Islam called *Wahhabism* (see Chapter 27) while modernizing the country's infrastructure. The Egyptian government attempted to play different Islamic militant and professional groups off against one another. These governments retained the support of prosperous, devout middle-class Muslims while doing little about the plight of the poor. In general, Muslim religious leaders were highly critical of the Soviet Union and its influence in the region. Consequently, for many in the Middle East today the memory of Arab nationalism and socialism remains the memory of deceptions, self-interest, and a failed Arab identity.

The Arab-Israeli Conflict

Nowhere in the affairs of the Middle East has the influence of the superpowers and Europe been more sharply felt than in the 1948 creation of the state of Israel out of the former British mandate territory of Palestine.

SOURCE *Israel's proclamation of independence, 1948*

This event was the achievement principally of the world Zionist movement founded in 1897 by Theodor Herzl (1860–1904) in Europe. The British Balfour Declaration of 1917, issued during the middle of World War I and thus reflecting British wartime goals and concerns, favored the establishment of a national homeland for the Jews in Palestine as long as the "non-Jewish" rights were preserved. In 1920, however, there were only about 60,000 Jews and ten times that number of Christian and Muslim Arabs in Palestine. As some voices at the time, such as the American fact-finding mission, the 1919 King-Crane Commission sent by the American president Woodrow Wilson foresaw, and time would bear out, serious trouble lay ahead. (See Document, "The King-Crane Commission Report, August 28, 1919.") The Commission had concluded that the Zionist program would not accomplish its goal of an independent state except by force.

The interwar years saw increasing Jewish colonies and growing clashes between Jews and Palestinians poorly mediated by the often contradictory policy of the British. Immigration of Jews, largely from Eastern Europe, increased in the 1920s and 1930s until Britain tried in 1936 to restrict it severely in response to the Palestinian six-month General Strike. For the time being, European Jews escaping the Nazi Holocaust had to seek other refuge in other lands. After the war the Zionist movement received a tremendous boost from Jews worldwide and

Holy City. Jews pray at the Wailing Wall in Jerusalem during Passover, immediately below the Dome of the Rock, Islam's third holiest site.

from the Allied nations, who felt the need to atone for the indescribable horror of the Holocaust by helping to secure a refuge for Jews from around the world. Because of the great numbers of immigrants from around the world into the United States, Jewish immigrants faced many obstacles in entering the U.S. as the quota system was still in use by Immigration officials.

The concept of return to the Holy Land had a long history in Judaism. However, translating the concept into the creation of a national state was difficult because, for centuries, the land, administered by the Ottoman Empire, had been the home of Arabic-speaking Palestinians, primarily Muslims, but also Christians and Jews, all of whom were without voice in the matter of the fate of their own land over much of the twentieth century. The Palestinians have understandably not been able to accept why they should be displaced and persecuted, whether because of another people's historic religious attachment to the land or as reparation for Europe's sins against Europe's Jewish communities. On the other hand, especially in the light of nineteenth- and twentieth-century European anti-Semitic persecutions, European Jews themselves felt the desperate need for a homeland exclusively Jewish where they might be safe from European persecution and to which Jews everywhere might flee from the nagging anti-Semitism that still rears its ugly head around the globe. For the past 60 years, displaced Palestinians and militant Israelis continue to clash over the 1947 U.N. Partition plan and the subsequent occupation of lands and territories not approved by the U.N. but seized by Israeli military forces and Jewish colonists.

In 1945 Britain found itself beset in Palestine by Jews seeking to settle there and by Jewish underground and terrorist organizations aiming to oust the British while Palestinian resistance though sporadic had become increasingly violent. In 1947 the British washed their hands of Palestine, and the United Nations called for partition of the former mandate territory into a Jewish state. The plan was 30 percent of arable land for Jews (who represented about 30 percent of the total population) and a Muslim/Christian Arab state of 70 percent of the arable land (about 70 percent of the former Palestinian Mandate). The existing Arab states refused to accept the U.N. resolution, but in May 1948 Jews in Palestine proclaimed the independent state of Israel anyway. This declaration led to the Israeli-Arab states war of 1948–1949. In this war Syria, Iraq, Lebanon, Jordan, and Egypt armies of approximately 40,000 troops attacked Israel but lost to the 92,000 Israeli forces who were better armed, better trained, better connected with European countries, and more resolute. The combined Israeli forces not only occupied all the U.N.–proposed

SOURCE *Palestinian declaration of independence, 1988*

Israeli territory, but also seized a substantial portion of that designated by the U.N. for a Palestinian state. In addition to the plight of Palestinians subjected to Israeli rule or occupation, the creation of Israel also produced a massive Palestinian refugee problem that has yet to be resolved by anyone—the Arab nations, Israel itself, the United Nations, or other interested parties. Over the half-century since 1948, nearly seventy-five percent of the Palestinians in the world have been refugees from their homes and homeland. The wars of 1956, 1967, 1973, 1975–1990, and 2005, as well as the two *intifadas* only added additional refugees to the original ones.

Since 1948 there has been, at best, an armed truce between Israel and its neighbors and, at worst, open warfare. The Arab nations and the Palestinian people displaced by the new state have generally not wanted to accept Israel's right to exist as a state, and Israel (with the

support of the United States) has taken aggressive measures, often in defiance of world opinion and international law regarding **occupied territories**, to ensure its survival. The most serious military confrontations were the Suez Crisis of 1956, when Israel (and briefly France and England) invaded the Sinai; the 1967 June war (often referred to as the "Six Day War"), when Israel occupied the Sinai, the Golan Heights, and the West Bank (of the Jordan River); the October war of 1973, or the Yom Kippur war, when the Egyptians and Syrians staged a surprise attack on Israel in the Sinai and the Golan that ended in a standoff; and the Israeli invasions of Lebanon in 1978 and 1982 in the context of the Lebanese-Syrian conflict and the professed determination of Israel to extirpate anti-Israeli terrorist havens.

Ever since the fall of 2000, the region has spiraled into an abyss of violence in the midst of the second Palestinian *intifada* with repeated Israeli military assaults on towns and refugee camps in the West Bank and Gaza and regular Palestinian extremist suicide attacks on mainly civilian targets.

Most recently, the highly provocative construction by Israel of a massive 200+ mile "separation barrier" through the West Bank is currently asserting Israeli control over still more Palestinian West-Bank territory, ostensibly in the name of increased Israeli security from suicide bombings. The virtual pull-back of the United States from any serious effort at bringing either Israel or the Palestinians back into negotiations has now left the future of the region in still greater danger and uncertainty.

Simultaneously, in a cycle of violence familiar from Northern Ireland to Vietnam, the frustrations of an embattled Israel have made it increasingly ready to meet terrorist atrocities with preemptive military actions and violent reprisals, both at home and abroad. Israel has responded to extremist terrorist attacks and civilian resistance such as the ***Intifada***, or uprising (literally, "shaking off"), in the occupied territories with air and commando raids on Arab states thought to support Palestinian terrorism; with repressive, even punitive, measures against the Palestinian populations in the occupied territories; and generally with a hard-line stance against negotiation over the status of the territories seized in 1967.

Arab and some non-Arab states have been equally intransigent about recognizing Israel's right to exist, have supported guerrilla groups attacking Israel, and have refused until recently to deal directly with Israel to reach a long-term Middle East solution. Egypt was the first notable exception to this policy. In the late 1970s, under Gamal Abdel Nasser's successor, President Anwar Sadat (1918–1981), and through the mediation of U.S. President Jimmy Carter (b. 1924), Egypt entered into direct negotiations with Israel's prime minister Menachem Begin

Confrontation. Israeli soldiers guard blindfolded Palestinian militants at the Herez border crossing in February 2004.

(1913–1994). The two countries reached an agreement—the Camp David Accords—in 1978, and in 1979 signed a formal peace treaty. Sadat was assassinated in 1981 by Egyptian Muslim extremists, but the treaty has held up under his successor, Husni Mubarak (b. 1928).

Nonetheless, despite the Egyptian-Israeli accords, violence and political impasse—tragic, morally debilitating, and materially draining for all the peoples of the area—continued through the 1980s and 1990s and has only accelerated since 2000. Recent Israeli military actions in the occupied territories were provoked by, but in turn have brought on, more Palestinian terrorist bombings in Israel and abroad.

Added to this bleak history and current struggle is the ugly legacy of hate instilled in many on both sides over the past fifty years. Arabs and even many Muslims outside the Arab world have come to label non-Israeli Jews, Israelis, and both religious and political Zionists as oppressors and enemies, making virtually no distinction among them. Many Israelis and some Jews around the world have similarly vilified all Arabs and Muslims. In many ways Arab-Israeli and Muslim-Jewish relations are at an all-time low, and it may require a generation or more to displace the prejudice, stereotyping, and hatred so long accumulated. The human crisis is far from over, even if peace were to arrive tomorrow.

Some events of recent years gave at least brief hope for an eventual resolution to the conflict. In 1991, in the wake of

the Gulf War that followed Iraq's invasion of Kuwait, the parties to the Arab-Israeli conflict began peace negotiations. The negotiations ended with the 1993 Middle East Peace Agreement, also known as the Oslo Agreement, which raised hopes for a negotiated settlement and the creation of an independent Palestinian state alongside the Jewish state of Israel.

In fact, there has been little substantive progress made in the fourteen years since the 1993 agreement. Jordan and Egypt did agree in 1994 to a peace treaty with Israel, but some other Arab states—foremost among them Syria—have still not been willing to negotiate with Israel, and Israel has preferred to keep developing settlements and roads in such a way as to preclude any contiguous territory with which to form a viable state. Extremists on both sides have tried to put up obstacles to the success of the peace initiative. In early 1994 an American-born Israeli Jewish fanatic machine-gunned worshipers in a mosque in Hebron. In November 1995 another Jewish Israeli extremist assassinated Prime Minister Yitzhak Rabin for trying to make peace and to allow the eventual creation of even a circumscribed Palestinian state. Then, in the run-up to the Israeli elections of May 29, 1996, called in the wake of Rabin's death, Palestinian extremists carried out a series of savage bombings on buses and in crowded shopping areas. The subsequent victory in the elections of a Likud conservative hard-liner, Benjamin Netanyahu (b. 1949), over Rabin's Labor successor, Shimon Peres, by a margin of less than 1 percent of the vote, cast new uncertainty on peace prospects.

The leadership on both sides proved unable to implement the ideals of the Oslo Agreement. The Netanyahu regime repeatedly took hard-line stands and even provocative actions such as the determined expansion of Jewish West Bank settlements. To the latter end, new roads and building projects were implemented to divide further the Palestinian population in the occupied territories. Other actions included curtailment of water supplies to Palestinian areas and public declarations of Israel's determination to retain all of Jerusalem and much of the territories even in the face of international censure. Nor did the Palestinian Authority created by the 1993 peace agreement prove any better. Under the leadership of Yasser Arafat (1929–2004), it grew steadily more corrupt, ineffective, and out of touch with its constituencies, and the suffering of the masses in the West Bank and Gaza in particular only grew steadily worse after the agreement. Despite the efforts of the Palestinian and Israeli security forces, Palestinian guerrillas of the extremist wing of the resistance organization Hamas found ways to kill Israelis—overwhelming civilians in daylight bombings, even during religious holidays such as Passover, in a sustained effort to torpedo the already shaky **peace process**. These terrorist attacks led Israel to seal its borders, resulting in the additional loss of 11 percent of West Bank Palestinian farm lands, a source of livelihood for thousands of Arabs in the occupied territories who normally work in Israel proper, and this has exacerbated the already dire plight of Gaza in particular, keeping thousands of Palestinian families in poverty and starvation and in turn feeding the extremist resistance groups.

The Netanyahu era ended after a scandal involving the prime minister himself, and in March 2000, Ariel Sharon became prime minister. Sharon is the former army general charged with responsibility for the camp massacres by Christian militias operating in the 1982–1983 Israeli invasion of south Lebanon. His administration has been marked by an escalation of violence on both sides. Sharon, however, has also proposed that Israel withdraw from Gaza and close Israeli settlements in that region, a proposal that has proved controversial on both sides. His government has also begun to erect a fence separating Israeli and Palestinian territory. Arafat died in late 2004. His passing may present a new opportunity for negotiations in the region—with the Palestinians now led by Mahmoud Abbas (Abu Mazen), elected to Palestinian presidency in January 2005.

Middle Eastern Oil

The oil wealth of the Arab and Iranian world has been another significant factor in the recent history the region. Oil has been both a blessing and a curse for the people and countries of the Middle East. Ever since the discovery of oil in Iran in 1908, but especially after Saudi Arabia's first oil production in 1939, the world demand for oil has surged. In the mid-1970s, oil became a major bargaining chip in international diplomacy; one the Arab and other oil-rich Third World states—such as Venezuela, Nigeria, Iran, and Indonesia—have used to their advantage. In the Arab countries of North Africa and especially of Arabia and the Gulf, oil production and wealth have changed every aspect of life. Oil has propelled formerly peripheral and virtually unknown countries of the Sahara or the Arabian deserts into major roles in the world of international banking and finance. Oil has also boosted the damaged self-confidence of the Arab world after a century and a half of European domination. A testimony to the global importance

of Middle Eastern oil was the willingness of the United States and European nations to form a coalition with some Arab countries and to commit massive forces to the region to expel Iraq from Kuwait after Iraq's invasion of its neighbor in 1990. Though the economic benefits of oil are all too obvious, this resource has not necessarily had the corresponding political remuneration for people in the Middle East. Because of its importance to the world economy, the Middle East has been subject to considerable foreign involvement, whether from Europe, the United States, or the former Soviet Union. This involvement has sometimes been detrimental to political development. The most famous example of this feature is the 1953 CIA and British coup in Iran, which overthrew the popular government of Muhammad Mossadeq who had sought to nationalize the Iranian oil industry. In 2000, Madeline Albright, then the U.S. Secretary of State, apologized to the Iranian nation for the role of the United States in this coup and for the negative effects it may have had on Iranian political development.

The Rise of Militant Islamism

The increase in the global importance of the oil-producing states of the Middle East has coincided with a new round of Muslim efforts in the Middle East and elsewhere to revive pristine Muslim values and standards and to reform the perceived evils and failures in Muslim societies. In the spirit, and often in the footsteps, of earlier Muslim resurgents such as those of the eighteenth century in India, Arabia, and Africa, many Muslims have sought to return to the "fundamentals" of Islamic life, faith, and society. They see this as a means of rejuvenation, of social and economic as well as political justice, and of defense against the encroachment of foreign, usually Western secularist and materialist, values and norms. Indeed, a major new element in twentieth-century Muslim revivalism is its consciousness of being a viable response to the destructive influence of Western-style "modernity" on the mores, values, and religious faith and practice of Muslim peoples.

Much of the appeal of Islamist groups everywhere is their willingness and ability to address the needs of the underclasses in Middle Eastern, North African, and Asian cities and countries. Many Muslims around the world may generally agree with the critique of modern society that these movements present, but they are most often in strong disagreement with their proposed militant solutions to the current economic and cultural predicament. Where government after government of Muslim-majority countries has failed to provide social services such as housing, medical care, education, and jobs, the Islamist groups have succeeded under the banner of a just, moral Muslim societal

Social Service. Lebanese Shi'ite families in a Hezbollah-run shelter in Beirut take refuge from the Israeli airstrikes that pummeled the country in July 2006. Hezbollah has an extensive social-service network in southern Lebanon.

ideal. While the world press, and especially the U.S. press, have heard only of the relatively small fringe groups of Islamist extremists, Muslims at the grassroots level have seen the major Islamist groups in the dictatorships or military regimes under which most of them live providing services for which the state has long abdicated its responsibility.

Such Muslim fundamentalism—or, to give it a more correct name, "Islamist reformism"—motivated many of the revolutionaries who overthrew the government of Muhammed Reza Shah (r. 1941–1978) in Iran in 1978, as discussed earlier in the chapter. It is also seen in the Muslim Brethren movement in Egypt and elsewhere, in the Welfare Party in Turkey, and in many other groups, from Morocco to the Persian Gulf, and also outside the Middle East proper. All such Islamist groups see themselves as traditionalist—whether radical, conservative, or liberal/moderate—in that they feel their approach is one that is true to basic Muslim values and norms. The political actions of the reformist groups range from revolutionary action (Iran) to democratic participation (Turkey) to complete political quietism (the Tablighi international revivalist movement begun in Pakistan). Whether these movements will bring lasting change to Islamic societies is an open question for the Muslim world generally and the Middle East in particular. There is no question, however, of their present-day attraction and influence.

The background to modern Islamist reform lies in the European expansion over much of the globe in just a few centuries. This expansion brought far more social and political change than religious or even cultural change to the Islamic world. It saw the emergence globally of European-style nationalism and the idea of the nation-state; of post-Enlightenment ideals of individual liberties and rights and representative government; and of the concept of one's religious faith and affiliation as a strictly private, "religious" matter and one's citizenship as a public, "secular" matter. Such ideas proved revolutionary, or at the least disruptive, in the Islamic world, especially in this century.

The twentieth century in Islamic parts of the world presents a checkered history of autocratic governments generally at least as far removed from their citizenries as any of the medieval or premodern, often foreign (primarily Turkish) dynasties that had ruled Arab, Persian, Indian, or other regions of the Muslim-majority world. Experiments with European-style parliamentary government have only rarely taken hold in the Islamic world (or the rest of the Third World); nor have either liberal democratic or Marxist-socialist political and social ideals proven viable for the long term. Even so, until recently little of the political discourse in Islamic lands has given serious attention to specifically *Islamic* alternatives.

With the rise and postcolonial independence of many national states and the flourishing of diverse nationalisms, politics became often theoretically as well as actually divorced from Islamic religious tradition and its norms. This breach occurred in overt ways that it had not before, however large the actual gap always was between the religious ideals of government as guardian of the Shari'ah order on the one hand and the political realities of governing as power politics on the other. Where leaders had previously claimed Muslim faith and allegiance, some, such as the Arab nationalists of the post–World War I era, came to espouse secular ideologies and to ignore religion except to use it as a political weapon. And used as a weapon it was; in the late twentieth and early twenty-first centuries as in those earlier, Islamic religious allegiance has commonly been invoked to bolster a ruler's claim to legitimacy and often to cloak in pious garb much more mundane objectives and programs.

In short, the recent past has seen no realization of an "ideal" Islamic state in which religious and political authority is conjoined. If anything, the gap has widened typically between Islamic norms and ideals on the one hand and political and social realities on the other. Even in the post-revolutionary Islamic Republic of Iran there has been a clear division between political necessity and reality and religious values and standards. However sincerely the latter are claimed as the basis of state policy and procedure, no one can miss the frequent stretching of those standards to justify pragmatic political decisions. Nonetheless, the ideals championed in the Iranian Revolution proved a powerful counterweight to the secular ideas of Arab nationalism.

When we look at the Islamist movements of recent decades, we find that the calls for a congruence of religion

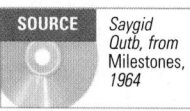

SOURCE   *Saygid Qutb, from Milestones, 1964*

and politics in the Islamic world trace less to some kind of ideal model of a religious state or so-called **theocracy** than to a sorely felt need for simple social and political justice, such as that which Islam (or any of the other great religious traditions) has always demanded for individuals and groups alike. The cries for a "jihad" of Muslims are aimed less often outward than inward, less at foreign "devils" and more at domestic tyrants, corruption, and social and economic injustice. Indeed, perhaps the most international and widely influential of all contemporary Islamic revivalist or reform movements, that of the Tabligh-i Jama'at, is even explicitly apolitical in its tenets; it looks to convert the individual person of faith to true submission (*islam*) rather than lip service: Reform of the world begins with oneself.

As for those reform movements that are avowedly political, be they activist but nonviolent (the majority) or extremist and violent (the minority), they live upon the deep sense of socioeconomic and political injustice that citizens of most Islamic countries (like most other Third-World countries) rightfully feel. Such feelings can, however, go over the edge and end in extremism and even terrorism. Osama Bin Laden, the dispossessed Saudi millionaire who founded and has led his own violent movement, al Qaeda, from the 1990s to the present, stunned the world, and especially the United States, with suicide attacks using civilian airliners to destroy the World Trade Center towers and part of the Pentagon building on September 11, 2001. His motive was primarily to get revenge for the American military presence in Saudi Arabia, the American-led blockade of Iraq, and the American support of Israel against the Palestinians. (See Document, "Jihad Against Jews and Crusaders: World Islamic Front Statement, 1998.")

These carefully executed and massively destructive attacks have led the United States into still heavier military involvement in the Middle East and Central Asia. In October 2001, the United States attacked the Taliban government of Afghanistan, rapidly overthrowing it. The defeat of the Taliban destroyed al Qaeda's Afghan bases, but not its high-profile leadership, which appears to have survived, although it was dispersed and remains in hiding. Whether this military response to the threat of terrorism is successful remains to be seen. What is clearer, however, is that the ongoing war on terrorism is radically changing the security needs of the United States. The U.S. military is transferring many of its troops and bases that were previously located in Western Europe and East Asia closer to the Middle East. It would appear that American troops will not soon leave this part of the world. Further United States intervention followed in 2003 with the invasion of Iraq.

Iraq and United States: Intervention and Occupation

The modern nation of Iraq was established by the British after World War I. For millennia, this area of Mesopotamia was home to powerful empires. More recently, it was part of the Ottoman Empire. Iraq as such had never been a distinct political unit and until 1921 was primarily a geographic term, referring to today's southern Iraq. Postwar imperial concern and the potential of oil under Iraqi soil motivated the British government to oversee the creation of Iraq, which they felt would best protect their interests in the region. Given the disparate ethnic and religious groups in the country, the British could not identify a suitable leader within Iraq. Instead, the British imported a politician from Arabia named Faysal ibn Husayn and crowned him king of the Hashemite Monarchy of Iraq. Until 1958, the monarchy ruled Iraq with the help of British advisers. A consortium of foreign oil companies, largely British, dominated the Iraqi oil industry and the British army maintained their military bases in Iraq.

Many Iraqis came to resent this arrangement and the foreign presence in their country. A bloody *coup d'état* in 1958 under the leadership of Abd al-Karim Qasem brought

 SOURCE *Saddam Hussein's invasion of Kuwait*

a violent end to the monarchy. By this time, Iraqis had developed a distinct sense of national identity that was highly critical of foreign involvement in Iraq affairs. By 1979, the Ba'ath party was the dominant force in Iraq policy. That year Saddam Hussein started his tyrannical reign. Shortly after he took power he invaded Iran and initiated the tragic and bloody Iran-Iraq War (1980–1988). He also invaded and occupied Kuwait in 1990. An international

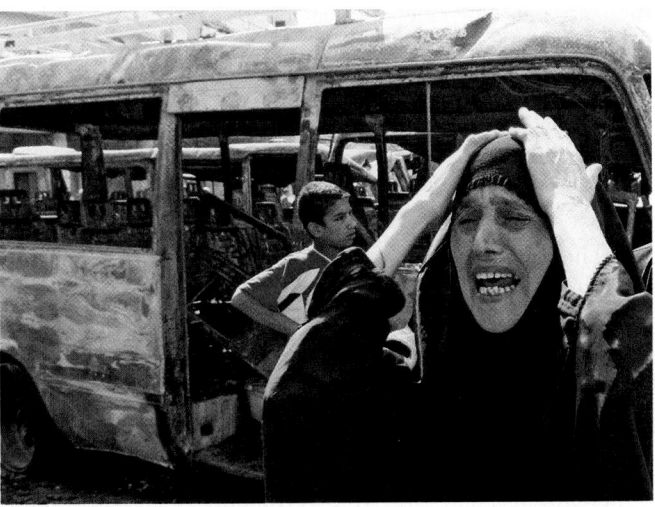

Suicide Car Bomb Explosion, Iraq, 2007. An Iraqi woman reacts at the site of a car bomb explosion in Baghdad that killed more than 85 civilians and wounded dozens of others.

Jihad Against Jews and Crusaders: World Islamic Front Statement, 1998

Document

Osama Bin Laden is one of the leaders of the al Qaeda terrorist organization that was responsible for the attacks on September 11, 2001. He came from a privileged background in Saudi Arabia and eventually volunteered to oust the Soviet Union from Afghanistan in the 1980s. The success that Bin Laden and his associates had in driving out the Soviets convinced them that a similar "holy war" should be implemented in the rest of the Islamic world. Their goal was to re-create an Islamic state that would replace the debased and secular governments of the Middle East. Because a vast majority of Muslims do not agree with their political views and their terrorist tactics, al Qaeda started increasingly to couch its rhetoric in xenophobic terms. Utilizing anti-American and anti-Semitic statements, Bin Laden and his followers hoped to grab the attention of Muslims around the world by commenting on prominent political issues and problems in the region. In 1998, Bin Laden issued a legal proclamation, based on his questionable and invalid interpretation of the Islamic faith, that called for the killing of Americans. When this proclamation was first issued it did not garner considerable attention nor did it inspire many Muslims around the world.

◆ On what religious authority does Bin Laden rest his claims? How does Bin Laden hope to ignite a mass revolution and support for his agenda?

The Arabian Peninsula has never—since God made it flat, created its desert, and encircled it with seas—been stormed by any forces like the crusader armies spreading in it like locusts, eating its riches and wiping out its plantations. All this is happening at a time in which nations are attacking Muslims like people fighting over a plate of food. In the light of the grave situation and the lack of support, we and you are obliged to discuss current events, and we should all agree on how to settle the matter.

No one argues today about three facts that are known to everyone; we will list them, in order to remind everyone:

First, for over seven years the United States has been occupying the lands of Islam in the holiest of places, the Arabian Peninsula, plundering its riches, dictating to its rulers, humiliating its people, terrorizing its neighbors, and turning its bases in the Peninsula into a spearhead through which to fight the neighboring Muslim peoples.

military coalition under the leadership of the United States (Operation Desert Storm) expelled the Iraqi army from Kuwait. During the 1990s, Iraq was an international pariah subject to extensive economic sanctions monitored by the United Nations. The Iraqi government eventually expelled the United Nations inspectors in 1998, and the United Nations was unable to reinsert them for almost five years.

The United States government adopted a policy of regime change in Iraq during the last years of the Clinton administration, though it did little to carry out that policy. In the wake of 9/11, however, the Bush administration, became convinced that the government of Saddam Hussein had to be removed and with it any threat of Iraqi weapons of mass destruction. During late 2002 and early 2003 the United States and British governments sought to obtain passage of the United Nations Security Council resolutions that would require Iraq to disarm on its own or to face disarmament by military force. The efforts to obtain an effective United Nations Security Council resolution failed

primarily because the governments of France and Russia threatened to veto the measure. In the face of the United Nations failure to pass a resolution the United States, Great Britain, and Australia, backed by the support of a coalition of over forty other nations, called the "Coalition of the Willing," invaded Iraq in the middle of March 2003. After three weeks of fighting, the Coalition succeeded in removing the government of Saddam Hussein from power. The announced goals of the invasion, in addition to toppling the Iraqi regime, were to destroy Iraq's capacity to manufacture or deploy weapons of mass destruction and to bring consensual government to the Iraqi people.

The invasion of Iraq was undertaken with considerable international opposition, most notably from France, Germany, and Russia. It also provoked large antiwar demonstrations in the United States and other parts of the world. The war has created strains within the European Union and NATO. It also marks a new era in relations between the United States and Europe and also with the rest of the world.

If some people have in the past argued about the fact of the occupation, all the people of the Peninsula have now acknowledged it. The best proof of this is the Americans' continuing aggression against the Iraqi people using the Peninsula as a staging post, even though all its rulers are against their territories being used to that end, but they are helpless.

Second, despite the great devastation inflicted on the Iraqi people by the crusader-Zionist alliance, and despite the huge number of those killed, which has exceeded 1 million. . . despite all this, the Americans are once again trying to repeat the horrific massacres, as though they are not content with the protracted blockade imposed after the ferocious war or the fragmentation and devastation.

So here they come to annihilate what is left of this people and to humiliate their Muslim neighbors.

Third, if the Americans' aims behind these wars are religious and economic, the aim is also to serve the Jews' petty state and divert attention from its occupation of Jerusalem and murder of Muslims there. The best proof of this is their eagerness to destroy Iraq, the strongest neighboring Arab state, and their endeavor to fragment all the states of the region such as Iraq, Saudi Arabia, Egypt, and Sudan into paper statelets and through their disunion and weakness to guarantee Israel's survival and the continuation of the brutal crusade occupation of the Peninsula.

All these crimes and sins committed by the Americans are a clear declaration of war on Allah, his messenger, and Muslims. And ulema have throughout Islamic history unanimously agreed that the jihad is an individual duty. . . .

On that basis, and in compliance with Allah's order, we issue the following fatwa to all Muslims:

The ruling to kill the Americans and their allies—civilians and military—is an individual duty for every Muslim who can do it in any country in which it is possible to do it, in order to liberate the al-Aqsa Mosque and the holy mosque [Mecca] from their grip, and in order for their armies to move out of all the lands of Islam, defeated and unable to threaten any Muslim. This is in accordance with the words of Almighty Allah, "and fight the pagans all together as they fight you all together," and "fight them until there is no more tumult or oppression, and there prevail justice and faith in Allah."

This is in addition to the words of Almighty Allah: "And why should ye not fight in the cause of Allah and of those who, being weak, are ill-treated (and oppressed)?".women and children, whose cry is: "Our Lord, rescue us from this town, whose people are oppressors; and raise for us from thee one who will help!"

We—with God's help—call on every Muslim who believes in Allah and wishes to be rewarded to comply with God's order to kill the Americans and plunder their money wherever and whenever they find it. We also call on Muslim ulema, leaders, youths, and soldiers to launch the raid on Satan's U.S. troops and the devil's supporters allying with them, and to displace those who are behind them so that they may learn a lesson.

U.S. government translation

Currently, it is immensely difficult to ensure peace and stability in Iraq. Many Iraqis have resisted the occupation of Iraq by foreign forces, and historical factors militate against a unified government. The unpreparedness of the Americans and their allies to deal with the chaos of postwar Iraq has exacerbated matters. At the same time, the American-led Coalition Authority had a difficult time formulating a clear policy amidst a difficult and dangerous situation that has laid the American government open to criticism in the region and around the world. The failure to find weapons of mass destruction in Iraq led to wide questioning of the rationale for the war.

Throughout Iraq an insurgency has been launched against the Coalition forces and against Iraqis, particularly those in the security services, which had cooperated with the Coalition and the recently installed Iraqi government. In the United States itself, President George W. Bush secured reelection in 2004 and commenced his second term indicating that he would continue to pursue his existing policies in the Middle East. In late January 2005, an election was held in Iraq under

conditions of insurgent attacks to elect the Assembly that will write a new constitution. With voter turnout much higher than had been widely anticipated, the election did succeed. However, the challenges of securing ever-wider internal support for the construction of democratic processes now confront the emerging Iraqi government and American policy makers. Internal violence and effective civil war still continue to resist resolution.

Summary

The Postcolonial World. Since 1945 the European colonies have disappeared from Africa and Asia and have been replaced by a multitude of independent and semi-independent states. These states have had to adjust their political and economic relations first to one or other of the superpowers during the Cold War and then, since the disappearance of the Soviet Union, to the United States.

Latin America. Most Latin American countries remain politically and economically dependent on the United States. Except in Cuba, no revolutionary movement has been able to overturn the traditional structure of Latin American society. Despite social and economic problems, Argentina and Brazil have managed to move from military rule to stable democratic, civilian government. In Mexico, the long dominance of the PRI ended in 2000.

Africa. Independent Africa has faced severe problems: arbitrary boundaries, disease, economic dependence, and political instability. While Nigeria has experienced ethnic and religious strife under a succession of military dictatorships, South Africa has emerged as a stable, multi-ethnic democracy with the end of white rule in the 1990s. The challenge for Africa as a whole is to build a truly civil society and achieve economic health and political stability.

The Middle East. Oil and Arab Muslim and Christian objections to the creation of the State of Israel, and then its occupation of Palestinian lands, have dominated the politics of the Middle East since the 1940s. While the possession of vast deposits of oil has made some Middle Eastern governments wealthy, it has not led to the creation of prosperous democratic societies. The existence of Israel has inflamed the Middle East for more than six decades. Although efforts by the United States to sponsor an Israeli-Palestinian peace have made some progress, the cycle of terror and retaliatory violence has persisted, and it is unclear whether a lasting peace between Israel and its neighbors can be achieved or a viable Palestinian state created.

Militant Islamists, although hardly a monolithic movement or majority of Middle East Muslims, have proved increasingly disruptive to a battle-scarred region and to lands beyond. In the wake of the terrorist attacks of September 11, 2001, the United States overthrew the Taliban regime in Afghanistan and Saddam Hussein in Iraq. The United States finds itself increasingly embroiled in a chaotic and unstable region of the world, partly due to U.S. political and economic policies, and partly due to social, economic, and political

INTERPRETING THE PAST

Poverty, Power, and Globalization

Text Document from Chapter 34

1. Lourdes Arizpe Discusses Silence of Peasant Women (page 1096)

Text Documents from MyHistoryLab / Primary Source DVD

1. *United Nations Universal Declaration of Human Rights*
2. *Frantz Fanon, The Wretched of the Earth*
3. *Juan Perón, The Voices of Perón,*

Visual Sources from MyHistoryLab / PrimarySource DVD

1. *Indonesian Guerillas*
2. *Cocoa Harvesting, Ghana*

Democracy and globalization have transformed societies around the world in the six decades since the end of World War II. The decline of authoritarian regimes, and the spread of economic linkages among the United States, Europe, Asia, Africa, and Latin America led

to more efficient and global trade networks. As a result, large-scale demographic changes have occurred in emerging economies as millions have migrated to cities from the countryside. Staggering poverty still exists side by side with great prosperity, exacerbated by the availability of relatively inexpensive communication technologies: cable and satellite television, cell phones, movies, and radio. As a result, developing countries in Latin America, the Caribbean, Africa, and Asia are again vulnerable to those who promise an end to poverty and exploitation by offering extremist policies.

In this exercise you will read four primary sources relating to the problems of poverty and powerlessness in non-Western regions. The first document is a Mexican anthropologist's discussion of the silence of peasant women in that country. Hard-working and marginalized within their communities as well as their families, peasant women are now part of the industrial work force in the great shanty towns surrounding manufacturing plants across the globe. The second primary source is taken from the 1948 United Nations *Universal Declaration of Human Rights.* Linking many principles of the American and French Revolutions, the *Universal Declaration* updates them for the twentieth century. The third document is written by Frantz Fanon, an author, psychiatrist, and revolutionary who describes the effect of colonialism and oppression, economic and otherwise, on colo-inequities, poor national leadership, and continued weaknesses in family-dominated centralized states.

Review Questions

1. Are the nations of Latin America still economically dependent on the United States and Western Europe? If so, why? How did the superpower rivalry of the Cold War affect Latin America? How successful has the worldwide trend towards democratization been in Latin America? Describe the transition from military rule to civilian democracy in Brazil, Argentina, and Chile. Has Mexico made a similar transition?

2. What factors contributed to the spread of decolonization in sub-Saharan Africa? What challenges did many newly independent states share? Has postcolonial Nigeria lived up to its potential? Why is Nigeria's record significant for Africa as a whole? Describe the apartheid regime in South Africa. Why was it dismantled in the 1990s? What problems does the Democratic Republic of the Congo face? What factors contributed to the 1994 genocide in Rwanda?

3. Compare and contrast the roles of social change, religion, and economics in Turkey, Iran, Pakistan, and Malaysia. How does the profound influence of Islam in this and other regions of the world suggest the power of religious tradition in modern politics and society? Compare the nationalization process and results in 1951 Iran and in 1956 Egypt.

4. What have been the major factors in the creation of the modern Middle East? How have interventions by European powers and the United States affected this region? Compare and contrast the roles of religion and nationalism in the Middle East.

5. Explain the origin and course of the Israeli-Palestinian conflict. What have been the major turning points? Have there been moments when the conflict might have reached a peaceful resolution?

6. Describe the origins and character of political and militant Islam. Why has it taken so radical a political course in the post–Iranian Revolution era (1979)? Why was the Soviet invasion of Afghanistan an important event in its development? Why has the United States become the primary target of militant Islamists?

nized peoples. The fourth source comprises several excerpts of speeches delivered by Juan Perón, the president and dictator of Argentina from 1946 to 1956. Perón's philosophy is characterized by extreme nationalism and authoritarianism, as well as astute coalition-building and an emphasis on economic revitalization.

The two accompanying images show peasants engaged in traditional and in political protests.

Questions

What factors are cited by Arizpe as important in the historical silence of peasant women? Why is ending this silence so important, according to the author?

What rights in the Declaration are universal? Are all of the rights listed important? Would the application of these rights help the marginalized peasant women discussed by Arizpe? Why or why not?

What are the similarities and differences in the approaches of Fanon and Perón to helping the marginalized and powerless? Compare Fanon's observations of the effects of colonization with those of Arizpe's discussion of peasant women.

Does Fanon's observations of the effects of colonization compare in any way to the exploitation of peoples in developing nations by multinational corporations in the post-colonial era? Explain.

Key Terms

apartheid (p. 1106)

clash of civilizations (p. 1092)

decolonization (p. 1091)

globalization (p. 1092)

HIV/AIDS (p. 1109)

Intifadah (p. 1121)

liberation theology (p. 1095)

occupied territories (p. 1121)

peace process (p. 1123)

Sandinistas (p. 1099)

theocracy (p. 1125)

Truth and Reconciliation Commission (TRC) (p. 1107)

Note: To learn more about the topics in this chapter, please turn to the Suggested Readings at the end of the book. For additional sources related to this chapter please see the Primary Source DVD at the back of this text or MyHistoryLab.

Glossary

absolutism. Term applied to strong centralized continental monarchies that attempted to make royal power dominant over aristocracies and other regional authorities.

Acropolis. The religious and civic center of Athens. It is the site of the Parthenon.

Afrikaans. The new language, derived from Dutch, that evolved in the seventeenth- and eighteenth-century Cape Colony.

Afro-Asiatic. A language family that includes Semitic languages, Kushitic, and others.

agape. Meaning "love feast." A common meal that was part of the central ritual of early Christian worship.

agora. The Greek marketplace and civic center. It was the heart of the social life of the polis.

agricultural revolution. The innovations in farm production that began in the eighteenth century and led to a scientific and mechanized agriculture.

Ahura Mazda. Supreme god in ancient Iranian religion, especially in the religious system of the Iranian prophet Zoroaster (7th century–6th century B.C.). Ahura Mazda was worshiped by the Persian king Darius I (reigned 522 B.C.–486 B.C.) and his successors as the greatest of all gods and protector of the just king.

Aksum. A powerful Christianized trading state in the Ethiopian highlands.

Al-Andalus. The Arabic name given to those parts of the Iberian Peninsula governed by Muslims, or Moors, at various times between 711 and 1492.

amir/emir. An Islamic military commander.

Amitabha Buddha. The Buddhist Lord of the Western Paradise, or Pure Land.

Annam. The name given by the Chinese to modern-day Vietnam, meaning "peaceful" or "pacified South."

Anschluss. Meaning "union." The annexation of Austria by Germany in March 1938.

anti-Semitism. Prejudice, hostility, or legal discrimination against Jews.

apartheid. "Apartness," the term referring to racist policies enforced by the white-dominated regime that existed in South Africa from 1948 to 1992.

apostolic primacy. The doctrine that the popes are the direct successors to the Apostle Peter and as such heads of the church.

appeasement. The Anglo-French policy of making concessions to Germany in the 1930s to avoid a crisis that would lead to war. It assumed that Germany had real grievances and Hitler's aims were limited and ultimately acceptable.

Areopagus. The governing council of Athens, originally open only to the nobility. It was named after the hill on which it met.

Arianism. The belief formulated by Arius of Alexandria (ca. 280–336 C.E.) that Jesus was a created being, neither fully man nor fully God, but something in between.

aristocratic resurgence. Eighteenth-century aristocratic efforts to resist the expanding power of European monarchies.

Article 9 of the No-War Constitution. Article 9 of the Japanese Constitution not only forbids the use of force as a means to settling international disputes but also forbids Japan from maintaining an army, navy, or air force.

Aryans. The Indo-European speakers who invaded India and Iran in the second and first millenia B.C.E.

assignats. Government bonds based on the value of confiscated church lands issued during the early French Revolution.

Atman-Brahman. The unchanging, infinite principle of reality in Indian religion.

Atomists. School of ancient Greek philosophy founded in the fifth century B.C.E. by Leucippus of Miletus and Democritus of Abdera. It held that the world consists of innumerable, tiny, solid, indivisible, and unchangeable particles called atoms.

Augustus. The title given to Octavian in 27 B.C.E. and borne thereafter by all Roman emperors.

Ausgleich. Meaning "compromise." The agreement between the Habsburg Emperor and the Hungarians to give Hungary considerable administrative autonomy in 1867. It created the Dual Monarchy, or Austria-Hungary.

Austronesian. A widely dispersed language family with origins in the Pacific. Malagasy, spoken in Madagascar, is an Austronesian language.

Axis. The alliance between Nazi Germany and fascist Italy. Also called the Pact of Steel.

ayan. Ottoman notables.

ayatollah. A major Shi'ite religious leader.

Bakufu. "Tent government." The military regime that governed Japan under the shōguns.

Bantu. A large sub-group of the Niger-Congo language family; also, the people who speak Bantu languages.

bazaari. The Iranian commercial middle class.

bhakti. Hindu devotional movements.

bishop. Originally a person elected by early Christian congregations to lead them in worship and supervise their funds. In time, bishops became the religious and even political authorities for Christian communities within large geographical areas.

Black Death. The bubonic plague that killed millions of Europeans in the fourteenth century.

Black Legend. The argument that Spanish treatment of native Americans was uniquely inhumane.

blitzkrieg. Meaning "lightning war." The German tactic early in World War II of employing fast-moving, massed armored columns supported by airpower to overwhelm the enemy.

bodhisattva. A "Buddha to be" who postpones his own nirvana until he has helped all other beings become enlightened.

Bolsheviks. Meaning the "majority." Term Lenin applied to his faction of the Russian Social Democratic Party. It became the Communist Party of the Soviet Union after the Russian Revolution.

Boxers. A nationalistic Chinese religious society that attacked foreigners and their encroachments on China in the late nineteenth century.

boyars. The Russian nobility.

Brahmanas. Texts dealing with the ritual application of the Vedas.

Bronze Age. The name given to the earliest civilized era, ca. 4000 to 1000 B.C.E. The term reflects the importance of the metal bronze, a mixture of tin and copper, for the peoples of this age for use as weapons and tools.

caliphate. The true line of succession to Muhammad.

calpulli. The wards into which the Aztec capital, Tenochtitlan, was divided.

cantonments. The segregation of areas in which Europeans lived in British-ruled India from those areas inhabited by native Indians.

Cataract. A waterfall or steep rapids. Major cataracts on the Nile River are numbered.

Catholic. Meaning "universal." The body of belief held by most Christians enshrined within the church.

Catholic Emancipation. The grant of full political rights to Roman Catholics in Britain in 1829.

caudillo. Latin American strongman, or dictator, usually with strong ties to the military.

censor. Official of the Roman republic charged with conducting the census and compiling the lists of citizens and members of the Senate.

Censorate. The branch of the imperial Chinese government that acted as a watchdog, reporting instances of misgovernment directly to the emperor and remonstrating when it considered the emperor's behavior improper.

Chartism. The first large-scale European working-class political movement. It sought political reforms that would favor the interests of skilled British workers in the 1830s and 1840s.

chattel slavery. A form of slavery in which humans are owned as goods; the slave has no legal standing as a person and few, if any, rights.

chiaroscuro. The use of shading to enhance naturalness in painting and drawing.

chicha. A maize beer brewed by the ***mamakuna*** for the Inca elite.

civilization. A form of human culture marked by urbanism, metallurgy, and writing.

clash of civilizations. Political theory, most often identified with Harvard political scientist Samuel P. Huntington, which con-

tends that conflict between the world's religio-cultural traditions or "civilizations" increasingly dominates world affairs.

Cold War. The ideological and geographical struggle between the United States and its allies and the USSR and its allies that began after World War II and lasted until the dissolution of the USSR in 1989.

collectivization. The bedrock of Stalinist agriculture, which forced Russian peasants to give up their private farms and work as members of collectives, large agricultural units controlled by the state.

Columbian Exchange. Biological exchange of plants, animals, and diseases between the Americas and the rest of the world.

conquistadores. Meaning "conquerors." The Spanish conquerors of the New World.

Consulate. French government dominated by Napoleon from 1799 to 1804.

Convention. French radical legislative body from 1792 to 1794.

corvée. A French labor tax requiring peasants to work on roads, bridges, and canals.

Counter-Reformation. The sixteenth-century reform movement in the Roman Catholic Church in reaction to the Protestant Reformation.

Creoles. Persons of European descent who were born in the Spanish colonies.

Crusades. Religious wars directed by the church against infidels and heretics.

Cultural Revolution. A movement launched by Mao between 1965 and 1976 against the Soviet-style bureaucracy that had taken hold in China. It involved widespread disorder and violence.

culture. The ways of living built up by a group and passed on from one generation to another.

cuneiform. A writing system invented by the Sumerians that used a wedge-shaped stylus, or pointed tool, to write on wet clay tablets that were then baked or dried (*cuneus* means "wedge" in Latin). The writing was also cut into stone.

Curia. The papal government.

daimyo. Meaning "great name," these men were the most powerful feudal leaders in Japan from the tenth to the nineteenth century.

Daoism. A Chinese philosophy that teaches that wisdom lies in becoming one with the Tao, the "way," which is the creative principle of the universe.

dar-al-Islam. In Arabic, the "House of Submission," or Islamic world. There are many shades of meaning, ranging from a place where the government is under Muslim control, to a place where individuals are free to practice Islamic beliefs.

debt peonage. A system that forces agricultural laborers (peons) to work and live on large estates (*haciendas*) until they have repaid their debts to the estate's owner.

Deccan. Large plateau with varying terrain that constitutes most of southern India.

deism. A belief in a rational God who had created the universe, but then allowed it to function without his interference according to the mechanisms of nature and a belief in rewards and punishments after death for human action.

Delian League. An alliance of Greek states under the leadership of Athens that was formed in 478–477 B.C.E. to resist the Persians.

demesne. The part of a manor that was cultivated directly for the lord of the manor.

dependency theory. Theory that contends that after the states of Latin America achieved independence in the early-mid nineteenth century, they remained economically and culturally dependent on Europe and later the United States.

devshirme. The system under the Ottoman Empire that required each province to furnish a levy of Christian boys who were raised as Muslims and became soldiers in the Ottoman army.

dharma. Moral law or duty.

Diet. The bicameral Japanese parliament.

Diet of Worms. The meeting of the representative (diet) of the Holy Roman Empire presided over by the Emperor Charles V at the Germain city of Worms in 1521 at which Martin Luther was ordered to recant his ninety-five theses. Luther refused and was declared outlaw although he was protected by the Elector of Saxony and other German princes.

diffusion. The spread of ideas, objects, or traits from one culture to another.

divine right of kings. The theory that monarchs are appointed by and answerable only to God.

Diwan. High governmental body in many Islamic states.

domestic or putting-out system of textile production. Method of producing textiles in which agents furnished raw materials to households whose members spun them into thread and then wove cloth, which the agents then sold as finished products.

Duce. Meaning "leader." Mussolini's title as head of the Fascist Party.

Duma. The Russian parliament, after the revolution of 1905.

dynastic cycle. The term used to describe the rise, decline, and fall of China's imperial dynasties.

ego. According to Freudian theory, the part of the mind that mediates between the impulses of the id and the asceticism of the superego and allows the personality to cope with the inner and outer demands of its existence.

empiricism. The use of experiment and observation derived from sensory evidence to construct scientific theory or philosophy of knowledge.

enclosures. The consolidation or fencing in of common lands by British landlords to increase production and achieve greater commercial profits. It also involved the reclamation of waste land and the consolidation of strips into block fields.

encomienda. The grant by the Spanish crown to a colonist of the labor of a specific number of Indians for a set period of time.

Enlightenment. The eighteenth-century movement led by the **philosophes** that held that change and reform were both desirable through the application of reason and science.

Epicureans. School of philosophy founded by Epicurus of Athens (342–271 B.C.E.). It sought to liberate people from fear of death and the supernatural by teaching that the gods took no interest in human affairs and that true happiness consisted in pleasure, which was defined as the absence of pain.

equestrians. Literally "cavalrymen" or "knights." In the earliest years of the Roman Republic, those who could afford to serve as mounted warriors.

Estado Novo. The "new state" based on political stability and economic and social progress supposedly established by the dictator Getulio Vargas after 1937.

Etruscans. A people of central Italy who exerted the most powerful external influence on the early Romans.

Eucharist. Meaning "thanksgiving." The celebration of the Lord's Supper. Considered the central ritual of worship by most Christians. Also called Holy Communion.

euro. The common currency created by the EEC in the late 1990s.

European Economic Community (EEC). The economic association formed by France, Germany, Italy, Belgium, the Netherlands, and Luxembourg in 1957. Also known as the Common Market.

European Union. The new name given to the EEC in 1993. It included most of the states of Western Europe.

Fabians. British socialists in the late nineteenth and early twentieth century who sought to achieve socialism through gradual, peaceful, and democratic means.

family economy. The basic structure of production and consumption in preindustrial Europe.

fascism. Political movements that tend to be antidemocratic, anti-Marxist, antiparliamentary, and often anti-Semitic. Fascists were invariably nationalists and exalted the nation over the individual. They supported the interests of the middle class and rejected the ideas of the French Revolution and nineteenth-century liberalism. The first fascist regime was founded by Benito Mussolini (1883–1945) in Italy in the 1920s.

fealty. An oath of loyalty by a vassal to a lord, promising to perform specified services.

feudal society. The social, political, military, and economic system that prevailed in the Middle Ages and beyond in some parts of Europe.

fief. Land granted to a vassal in exchange for services, usually military.

Fourteen Points. President Woodrow Wilson's (1856–1924) idealistic war aims.

Führer. Meaning "leader." The title taken by Hitler when he became dictator of Germany.

gentry. In China, a largely urban, landowning class that represented local interests and functioned as quasi-bureaucrats under the magistrates.

ghazis. Warriors who carried Islam by force of arms to pagan groups.

ghettos. Separate communities in which Jews were required by law to live.

glasnost. Meaning "openness." The policy initiated by Mikhail Gorbachev in the 1980s of permitting open criticism of the policies of the Soviet Communist Party.

globalization. Term used to describe the increasing economic and cultural interdependence of societies around the world.

Glorious Revolution. The largely peaceful replacement of James II by William and Mary as English monarchs in 1688. It marked the beginning of constitutional monarchy in Britain.

Golden Horde. Name given to the Mongol rulers of Russia from 1240 to 1480.

Grand Mufti. The chief religious authority of the Ottoman Empire. Also called "the Shaykh of Islam."

Great Depression. A prolonged worldwide economic downturn that began in 1929 with the collapse of the New York Stock Exchange.

Great Leap Forward. Mao's disastrous attempt to modernize the Chinese economy in 1958.

Great Purges. The imprisonment and execution of millions of Soviet citizens by Stalin between 1934 and 1939.

Great Reform Bill (1832). A limited reform of the British House of Commons and an expansion of the electorate to include a wider variety of the propertied classes. It laid the groundwork for further orderly reforms within the British constitutional system.

Great Schism. The appearance of two and at times three rival popes between 1378 and 1415.

Great Trek. The migration between 1835 and 1847 of Boer pioneers (called *voortrekkers*) north from British-ruled Cape Colony to establish their own independent republics.

guild. An association of merchants or craftsmen that offered protection to its members and set rules for their work and products.

Guomingdang (GMD). China's Nationalist Party, founded by Sun Yat-sen.

hacienda. Large landed estates in Spanish America.

hadith. A saying or action ascribed to Muhammad.

Hajj. The pilgrimage to Mecca that all Muslims are enjoined to perform at least once in their lifetime.

Harappan. Term used to describe the first civilization of the Indus Valley.

harem. The wives, concubines, female relatives, and servants in a Muslim household—usually confined to a section of a house or palace.

Hegira. The flight of Muhammad and his followers from Mecca to Medina in 622 C.E. It marks the beginning of the Islamic calendar.

heliocentric theory. The theory, now universally accepted, that the earth and the other planets revolve around the sun. First proposed by Aristarchos of Samos (310–230 B.C.E.).

Helots. Hereditary Spartan serfs.

heretics. People who publicly dissent from officially accepted dogma.

hieroglyphics. The complicated writing script of ancient Egypt. It combined picture writing with pictographs and sound signs. Hieroglyph means "sacred carvings" in Greek.

Hindu. Term applied to the diverse social, racial, linguistic, and religious groups of India.

HIV/AIDS. Collection of symptoms and infections resulting from the specific damage to the immune system caused by the human immunodeficiency virus (HIV) in humans, and similar viruses in other species (SIV, FIV, etc.). The late stage of the condition leaves individuals susceptible to opportunistic infections and tumors. Although treatments for AIDS and HIV exist to decelerate the virus's progression, there is currently no known cure.

Holocaust. The Nazi extermination of millions of European Jews between 1940 and 1945. Also called the "final solution to the Jewish problem."

Holy Roman Empire. The revival of the old Roman Empire, based mainly in Germany and northern Italy, that endured from 870 to 1806.

home rule. The advocacy of a large measure of administrative autonomy for Ireland within the British Empire between the 1880s and 1914.

hoplite phalanx. The basic unit of Greek warfare in which infantrymen fought in close order, shield to shield, usually eight ranks deep.

Huguenots. French Calvinists.

humanism. The study of the Latin and Greek classics and of the Church Fathers both for their own sake and to promote a rebirth of ancient norms and values.

humanitas. The Roman name for a liberal arts education.

id. According to Freudian psychoanalysis, the part of the mind that consists of amoral, irrational, driving instincts for sexual gratification, aggression, and physical and sensual pleasure.

The *Iliad* and the *Odyssey*. The epic poems by Homer about the "Dark Age" heroes of Greece who fought at Troy. The poems were written down in the eighth century B.C.E. after centuries of being sung by bards.

Il-khans. One of the four khananats within the Mongol Empire, comprising largely what is modern-day Iran.

imams. Islamic prayer leader.

impact of modernity. The effect of western political, economic, and social ideas and institutions on traditional societies.

imperator. Under the Roman Republic, it was the title given to a victorious general. Under Augustus and his successors, it became the title of the ruler of Rome, meaning "emperor."

import substitution. The replacement of imported goods with those manufactured domestically.

Indirect Rule. The British practice of administering African colonies through indigenous political structures and leaders.

Indo-European. A widely distributed language group that includes most of the languages spoken in Europe, Persian, Sanskrit, and their derivatives.

Indo-Greeks. Bactrian rulers who broke away from the Seleucid Empire to found a state that combined elements of Greek and Indian civilizations.

indulgences. Remission of the temporal penalty of punishment in purgatory that remained after sins had been forgiven.

Industrial Revolution. Mechanization of the European economy that began in Britain in the second half of the eighteenth century.

intifadah. Literally, "shaking." Uprisings by the Palestinians against Israeli occupation.

Islam. Meaning "submission." The religion founded by the prophet Muhammad.

Islamic fundamentalism. A movement among many Muslims to return to the "fundamentals" of Islamic faith, life, and society.

Italia Irredenta. Meaning "unredeemed Italy." Italian-speaking areas that had been left under Austrian rule at the time of the unification of Italy.

Jacobins. The radical republican party during the French Revolution that displaced the Girondins.

Jains. An Indian religious community that teaches compassion for all beings.

Janissaries. Elite Ottoman troops who were recruited through the ***devshirme***.

jatis. The many subgroups that make up the Hindu caste system.

jihad. "Struggle in the path of God." Although not necessarily implying violence, it is often interpreted to mean holy war in the name of Islam.

July Monarchy. The French regime set up after the overthrow of the Bourbons in July 1830.

Junkers. The noble landlords of Prussia.

junzi. The Confucian term for a person who behaves ethically, in harmony with the cosmic order.

Ka'ba. A black meteorite in the city of Mecca that became Islam's holiest shrine.

Kabuki. A realistic form of Japanese theater similar to English Elizabethan drama.

Kalahari. A large desert in southwestern Africa that partially isolates southern Africa from the rest of the continent.

kamikaze. "Divine winds" that sank a portion of the invading Mongol fleet in Japan in 1281.

karma. The Indian belief that every action has an inevitable effect. Good deeds bring good results; evil deeds have evil consequences.

Khmer Rouge. Meaning "Red Cambodia." The radical Communist movement that ruled Cambodia from 1975 to 1978.

Khoisan. The language group spoken by the Khoikhoi, the San, and other peoples; also, the Khoikhoi and San peoples.

kleindeutsch. Meaning "small German." The argument that the German-speaking portions of the Habsburg Empire should be excluded from a united Germany.

Kristallnacht. Meaning "crystal night" because of the broken glass that littered German streets after the looting and destruction of Jewish homes, businesses, and synagogues across Germany on the orders of the Nazi Party in November 1938.

Kush. An ancient Nubian kingdom that in some periods dominated, and in others was dominated by, pharaonic Egypt.

La Reforma. The nineteenth-century Mexican liberal reform movement that opposed Santa Ana's dictatorship and sought to foster economic progress, civilian rule, and political stability. It was strongly anti-clerical.

laissez-faire. French phrase meaning "allow to do." In economics, the doctrine of minimal government interference in the working of the economy.

latifundia. Large plantations for growing cash crops owned by wealthy Romans.

LDP. The Liberal Democratic Party. A conservative party that has dominated postwar Japanese politics.

League of Nations. The association of sovereign states set up after World War I to pursue common policies and avert international aggression.

Lebensraum. Meaning "living space," the Nazi plan to colonize and exploit Eastern Europe.

Legalism. The Chinese philosophical school that argued that a strong state was necessary in order to have a good society.

levée en masse. The French revolutionary conscription (1792) of all males into the army and the harnessing of the economy for war production.

liberalism. In the nineteenth century, support for representative government dominated by the propertied classes and minimal government interference in the economy.

liberation theology. The effort by certain Roman Catholic theologians to combine Marxism with traditional Christian concern for the poor.

Logos. Divine reason, or fire, which according to the Stoics, was the guiding principle in nature.

Long Count. A Mayan calendar that dated from a fixed point in the past.

Long March. The flight of the Chinese communists from their Nationalist foes to northwest China in 1934.

Luftwaffe. The German air force in World War II.

madrasa. An Islamic college of higher learning.

Maghreb. Literally, in Arabic, "place of sunset," or the west; refers to the northwest of Africa, and specifically what is now Morocco.

magi. A tribe from ancient Media, who, prior to the conquest of the Medes by the Achaemenid Empire in 550 B.C., were responsible for religious and funerary practices. The best known magi were the "Wise Men from the East" in the Bible.

Magna Carta. The "Great Charter" limiting royal power that the English nobility forced King John to sign in 1215.

Magna Graecia. Meaning "Great Greece" in Latin, it was the name given by the Romans to southern Italy and Sicily because there were so many Greek colonies in the region.

Magyars. The majority ethnic group in Hungary.

Mahabharata and *Ramayana*. The two classical Indian epics.

Mahayana. The "Great Vehicle" for salvation in Buddhism. It emphasized the Buddha's infinite compassion for all beings.

mamluk. Slave soldiers who converted to Islam, the mamluks eventually became a powerful military caste and even governed Egypt from 1250 to 1517.

manakuna. Inca women who lived privileged but celibate lives and had important economic and cultural roles.

Mandate of Heaven. The Chinese belief that Heaven entrusts or withdraws a ruler's or a dynasty's right to govern.

Manichaeism. One of the major dualistic religions in ancient Persia, in which good and evil were constantly at odds with one another.

Mannerism. A style of art in the mid to late sixteenth century that permitted artists to express their own "manner" or feelings in contrast to the symmetry and simplicity of the art of the High Renaissance.

manor. Village farms owned by a lord.

mansa. Malian emperor, from Mandinka word meaning "king of kings."

marabout. In Sunni Islam as practiced in West Africa, a marabout is a spiritual leader, versed in the Koran, who often guides the personal lives of his followers.

Marshall Plan. The U.S. program, named after Secretary of State George C. Marshall, that provided economic aid to Europe after World War II.

Marxism. The theory of Karl Marx (1818–1883) and Friedrich Engels (1820–1895) that history is the result of class conflict, which will end in the inevitable triumph of the industrial proletariat over the bourgeoisie and the abolition of private property and social class.

Mau Mau. An uprising that began among the Kikuyu of the Kenya highlands and lasted through the 1950s. The British referred to it as the "Kenya Emergency."

Meiji Restoration. The overthrow of the Tokugawa *bakufu* in Japan in 1868 and the transfer, or "restoration," of power to the imperial government under the Emperor Meiji.

Mein Kampf. Meaning "My Struggle." Hitler's statement of his political program, published in 1924.

Mensheviks. Meaning the "minority." Term Lenin applied to the majority moderate faction of the Russian Social Democratic Party opposed to him and the Bolsheviks.

mercantilism. Term used to describe close government control of the economy that sought to maximize exports and accumulate as much precious metals as possible to enable the state to defend its economic and political interests.

Meroe. The capital city of the ancient Napatan empire, which at one time rivaled Aksum.

Mesoamerica. The part of North America that extends from the central part of modern Mexico to Central America.

Mesopotamia. Modern Iraq. The land between the Tigris and Euphrates Rivers where the first civilization appeared around 3000 B.C.E.

Messiah. The redeemer whose coming Jews believed would establish the kingdom of God on earth. Christians considered Jesus to be the Messiah (Christ means Messiah in Greek).

mestizos. Persons of mixed Native American and European descent.

Mexica. The Aztecs name for themselves.

mfecane. A period of widespread warfare and chaos among Bantu peoples in east-central Africa during the early nineteenth century.

Middle Passage. The transatlantic crossing of ships carrying slaves from Africa to the Americas and Caribbean.

millets. Within the Ottoman Empire, ethnic communities that administered their own educational, charitable, and judicial affairs.

Minoan. The Bronze Age civilization that arose in Crete in the third and second millennia B.C.E.

mita. The Inca system of forced labor in return for gifts and ritual entertainments.

Mitimaqs. Communities whom the Incas forced to settle in designated regions for strategic purposes.

mobilization. The placing of a country's military forces on a war footing.

Monophysite. Adhering to the dogma of the single, unitary nature of Christ (in opposition to the orthodox doctrine that Christ had two natures: human and divine).

Monotheism. The worship of one universal God.

Moors. The Spanish and Portuguese term for Muslims.

muezzin. The leader of a mosque's call to prayers.

Mughals. Descendants of the Mongols who established an Islamic empire in India in the sixteenth century with its capital at Delhi.

mujtahid. A Shi'ite religious-legal scholar.

mulattos. Persons of mixed African and European descent.

Mycenaean. The Bronze Age civilization of mainland Greece that was centered at Mycenae.

mystery religions. The cults of Isis, Mithras, and Osiris, which promised salvation to those initiated into the secret or "mystery" of their rites.

nacionalismo. A right-wing Argentine nationalist movement that arose in the 1930s and resembled European fascism.

nationalism. The belief that one is part of a nation, defined as a community with its own language, traditions, customs, and history that distinguish it from other nations and make it the primary focus of a person's loyalty and sense of identity.

National Studies. A Japanese intellectual tradition that emphasized native Japanese culture and institutions and rejected the influence of Chinese Confucianism.

natural selection. According to Darwin, the process in nature by which only the organisms best adapted to their environment tend to survive and transmit their genes, while those less adapted tend to be eliminated.

Nazis. The German Nationalist Socialist Party.

neocolonial economy. An economic relationship between a former colonial state and countries with more developed economies in which the former colony exports raw materials to and imports manufactured goods from the more developed nations.

Negritude. A movement begun among African students in 1930s Paris to celebrate African culture and thought.

Neo-Daoism. A revival of Taoist "mysterious learning" that flourished as a reaction against Confucianism during the Han dynasty.

Neolithic Revolution. The shift beginning 10,000 years ago from hunter-gatherer societies to settled communities of farmers and artisans. Also called the Age of Agriculture, it witnessed the invention of farming, the domestication of plants and animals, and the development of technologies such as pottery and weaving. "Neolithic" comes from the Greek words for "new stone."

New Economic Policy (NEP). A limited revival of capitalism, especially in light industry and agriculture, introduced by Lenin in 1921 to repair the damage inflicted on the Russian economy by the Civil War and War Communism.

New Imperialism. The extension in the late nineteenth and early twentieth centuries of Western political and economic dominance to Asia, the Middle East, and Africa.

Nicene Creed. A statement of Christian belief, formulated by the council of Christian bishops at Nicaea in 324 C.E., that rejected Arianism in favor of the doctrine that Christ is both fully human and fully divine.

Niger-Kongo. A language family that originated in the savanna and woodlands of west and south-central Africa.

Nilo-Saharan. A language family concentrated in the band between the Nile and Rift highlands of Morocco.

Nilotic Africa. The lands along the Nile River.

ninety-five theses. Document posted on the door of Castle Church in Wittenberg, Germany, on October 31, 1517, by Martin Luther protesting, among other things, the selling of indulgences.

Nirvana. In Buddhism the attainment of release from the wheel of **karma**.

Nok. A west African Iron Age culture renowned for its artistry.

Nō play. A highly stylized form of Japanese drama in which the chorus provides the narrative line as in classical Greek plays.

oba. Title of the king of Benin.

obsidian. A hard volcanic glass that was widely used in Mesoamerica.

Occidental slave trade. The trade in slaves from Africa to the Islamic Mediterranean and Asia that predated the transatlantic slave trade.

occupied territories. Land occupied by Israel as a result of wars with its Arab neighbors in 1948–1949, 1967, and 1973.

Old Regime. Term applied to the pattern of social, political, and economic relationships and institutions that existed in Europe before the French Revolution.

orthodox. Meaning "holding the right opinions." Applied to the doctrines of the Catholic Church.

Ottoman Empire. The imperial Turkish state centered in Constantinople that ruled large parts of the Balkans, North Africa, and the Middle East until 1918.

padishah. Meaning "emperor." One of the titles of the Ottoman monarchs.

Paleolithic Age. The earliest period when stone tools were used, from about 1,000,000 to 10,000 B.C.E. From the Greek meaning "old stone."

Pampas. The fertile South American lowlands that include the Argentine provinces of Buenos Aires, La Pampa, Santa Fe, and Córdoba, most of Uruguay, and the southernmost end of Brazil, Rio Grande do Sul, covering more than 750,000 km² (289,577 sq mi).

Panhellenic ("all-Greek"). The sense of cultural identity that all Greeks felt in common with each other.

pan-Islamism. The movement that advocates that the entire Muslim world should form a unified political and cultural entity.

Pan-Slavic movement. The movement to create a nation or federation that would embrace all the Slavic peoples of Eastern Europe.

Papal States. Territory in central Italy ruled by the pope until 1870.

parlement. French regional court dominated by hereditary nobility. The most important was the Parlement of Paris, which claimed the right to register royal decrees before they could become law.

parliamentary monarchy. A state headed by a monarch but whose power is shared with a national representative body.

pastoralists. People whose way of life centers on the raising and herding of livestock; nomads.

patricians. The hereditary upper class of early Republican Rome.

peace process. Efforts, chiefly by the United States, to broker a peace between the State of Israel and the PLO.

Peloponnesian Wars. The protracted struggle between Athens and Sparta to dominate Greece between 465 and Athens' final defeat in 404 B.C.E.

peninsulares. Native-born Spaniards who emigrated from Spain to settle in the Spanish colonies.

perestroika. Meaning "restructuring." The attempt in the 1980s to reform the Soviet government and economy.

Perónism. An authoritarian, nationalist movement founded in Argentina in the 1940s by the dictator Juan Perón.

pharaoh. The god-kings of ancient Egypt. The term originally meant "great house" or palace.

Pharisees. The group that was most strict in its adherence to Jewish law.

philosophes. The eighteenth-century writers and critics who forged the new attitudes favorable to change. They sought to apply reason and common sense to the institutions and societies of their day.

Phoenicians. The ancient inhabitants of modern Lebanon. A trading people, they established colonies throughout the Mediterranean.

pipiltin. Aztec bureaucrats and priests.

pirs. Shi'ite holy men.

plantation economy. The economic system stretching between Chesapeake Bay and Brazil that produced crops, especially sugar, cotton, and tobacco, using slave labor on large estates.

plebeians. The hereditary lower class of early Republican Rome.

plenitude of power. The teaching that the popes have power over all other bishops of the church.

pochteca. Aztec merchants.

pogroms. Organized riots against Jews in the Russian Empire.

polis. The basic Greek political unit. Usually, but incompletely, translated as "city-state," the Greeks thought of the *polis* as a community of citizens theoretically descended from a common ancestor.

political Islamism. Political movement that seeks to return to the fundamentals of Islamic life through rejuvenation of Muslim faith and society and the rejection of Western, materialist, and secularist values and norms.

polytheism. The worship of many gods.

Popular Front. A government of all left-wing parties that took power in France in 1936 to enact social and economic reforms.

populares. Roman politicians who sought to pursue a political career based on the support of the people rather than just the aristocracy.

positivism. The philosophy of Auguste Comte that science is the final, or positive, stage of human intellectual development because it involves exact descriptions of phenomena, without recourse to unobservable operative principles, such as gods or spirits.

Pragmatic Sanction. The legal basis negotiated by the Emperor Charles VI (r. 1711–1740) for the Habsburg succession through his daughter Maria Theresa (r. 1740–1780).

prazeros. Portuguese and mixed-race owners of large estates in the Zambezi valley.

PRI. The Institutional Revolutionary Party, which emerged from the Mexican revolution of 1911 and governed Mexico until the end of the twentieth century.

Proletarianization. The process whereby independent artisans and factory workers lose control of the means of production and of the conduct of their own trades to the owners of capital.

Protectorate. A variation on colonial rule in which, at least in theory exerts local authority over domestic issues.

Ptolemaic system. The pre-Copernican explanation of the universe, which placed the Earth at the center of the universe.

Punic Wars. Three wars between Rome and Carthage for dominance of the western Mediterranean that were fought from 264 B.C.E. to 146 B.C.E.

Pure Land Buddhism. A variety of Japanese Buddhism that maintained that only faith was necessary for salvation.

puritans. English Protestants who sought to "purify" the Church of England of any vestiges of Catholicism.

Qanun. Ottoman administrative law.

qasida. Some of the most elaborate poems in the world, they generally run 50–100 lines, have a single, unifying theme, regular rhyme and meter and speak in praise of a ruler or idea.

Quechua. The Inca language.

quipu. Knotted string used by Andean peoples for recordkeeping.

Qur'an. Meaning "a reciting." The Islamic bible, which Muslims believe God revealed to the prophet Muhammad.

racism. The pseudoscientific theory that biological features of race determine human character and worth.

raj. The years from 1858 to 1947 during which India was governed directly by the British Crown.

raja. An Indian king.

Ramadan. The month each year when Muslims must fast during daylight hours.

Reconquista. The Christian reconquest of Spain from the Muslims from 1000 to 1492.

Reformation. The sixteenth-century religious movement that sought to reform the Roman Catholic Church and led to the establishment of Protestantism.

regular clergy. Monks and nuns who belong to religious orders.

Reichstag. The German parliament, which existed in various forms until 1945.

Reign of Terror. The period between the summer of 1793 and the end of July 1794 when the French revolutionary state used extensive executions and violence to defend the Revolution and suppress its alleged internal enemies.

relativity. Theory of physics, first expounded by Albert Einstein in 1905, in which time and space exist not separately, but rather as a combined continuum.

Renaissance. The revival of ancient learning and the supplanting of traditional religious beliefs by new secular and scientific values that began in Italy in the fourteenth and fifteenth centuries.

reparations. The requirement incorporated into the Versailles Treaty that Germany should pay for the cost of World War I.

repartimiento. A labor tax in Spanish America that required adult male native Americans devote a set number of days a year to Spanish economic enterprises.

revisionism. The advocacy among nineteenth-century German socialists of achieving a humane socialist society through the evolution of democratic institutions, not revolution.

SA. The Nazi parliamentary forces, or stormtroopers.

Sahara. The world's largest desert. It extends across Africa from the Atlantic to the eastern Sudan. Historically, the Sahara has hindered contact between the Mediterranean and sub-Saharan Africa.

Sahel. An area of steppe and semidesert that borders the Sahara.

samsara. The endless cycle of existence, of birth and rebirth.

samurai. Professional Japanese warriors.

Sandinistas. The Marxist guerrilla force that overthrew the Somoza dictatorship in Nicaragua in 1979.

sans-culottes. Meaning "without breeches." The lower-middle classes and artisans of Paris during the French Revolution.

satraps. Governors of provinces in the Persian Empire.

savanna. An area of open woodlands and grassy plains.

Schlieffen Plan. Germany's plan for achieving a quick victory in the West at the outbreak of World War I by invading France through Belgium and Luxembourg.

Scholasticism. Method of study based on logic and dialectic that dominated the medieval schools. It assumed that truth already existed; students had only to organize, elucidate, and defend knowledge learned from authoritative texts, especially those of Aristotle and the Church Fathers.

Scientific Revolution. The sweeping change in the scientific view of the universe that occurred in the West in the sixteenth and seventeenth centuries.

scramble for Africa. The late nineteenth-century takeover of most of Africa by European powers.

secular clergy. Parish clergy who did not belong to a religious order.

serfs. Peasants tied to the land they tilled.

Shahanshah. "King of kings," the title of the Persian ruler.

Shari'a. Islamic religious law.

sharifs. A term for leaders who are direct descendents of the prophet Muhammad through his first grandson, Hasan ibn Ali.

shaykh. Arabic word for a tribal elder or Islamic scholar; can also be rendered as sheikh, sheik, or sheikh.

Shi-a. The minority of Muslims who trace their beliefs from the caliph Ali who was assassinated in 661 C.E.

Shintō. "The way of the gods." The animistic worship of the forces of nature that is the indigenous religion of Japan.

Shōgun. A military official who was the actual ruler of Japan in the emperor's name from the late 1100s until the mid–nineteenth century.

Silk Road. Trade route from China to the West that stretched across Central Asia.

Sophists. Professional teachers who emerged in Greece in the mid–fifth century B.C.E. who were paid to teach techniques of rhetoric, dialectic, and argumentation.

soviets. Workers' and soldiers' councils formed in Russia during the Revolution.

spinning jenny. A machine invented in England by James Hargreaves around 1765 to mass-produce thread.

SS. The chief security units of the Nazi state.

Steppe peoples. Nomadic tribespeople who dwelled on the Eurasian plains from eastern Europe to the borders of China and Iran. They frequently traded with or invaded more settled cultures.

Stoics. A philosophical school founded by Zeno of Citium (335–263 B.C.E.) that taught that humans could be happy only with natural law.

streltsy. Professional troops who made up the Moscow garrison. They were suppressed by Peter the Great.

studia humanitatis. During the Renaissance, a liberal arts program of study that embraced grammar, rhetoric, poetry, history, philosophy, and politics.

stupa. A Buddhist shrine.

Sudan. The broad band of Sahel and savanna that crosses the African continent south of the Sahara.

suffragettes. British women who lobbied and agitated for the right to vote in the early twentieth century.

Sufi. Sufism is a mystic tradition within Islam that encompasses a diverse range of beliefs and practices dedicated to Divine love and the cultivation of the elements of the Divine within the individual human being. The chief aim of all Sufis is to let go of all notions of duality, including a conception of an individual self, and to realize the Divine unity.

sultans. Rulers who have almost complete sovereignty over a certain domain without claiming the title of Caliph.

Sunna. Meaning "tradition." The dominant Islamic group whose followers are called Sunnis.

superego. According to Freud, the part of the mind that embodies the external moral imperatives and expectations imposed on the personality by society and culture.

Swahili. A language and culture that developed from the interaction of native Africans and Arabs along the East African coast.

symposion. The carefully organized drinking party that was the center of Greek aristocratic social life. It featured games, songs, poetry, and even philosophical disputation.

syncretism. Blending or fusion of different systems of religious or philosophical beliefs.

Table of Ranks. An official hierarchy established by Peter the Great in imperial Russia that equated a person's social position and privileges with his rank in the state bureaucracy or army.

taille. The direct tax on the French peasantry.

Taiping rebellion. A nineteenth-century revolt against China's Manchu dynasty that was inspired by quasi-Christian ideas and that led to enormous suffering and destruction before its collapse in 1868.

Tanzimat. Reform movement that started in 1839 in an attempt to bring the Ottoman Empire into the modern era and to help integrate non-Muslims and non-Ottomans into the Empire.

Tennō. "Heavenly emperor." The official title of the emperor of Japan.

tetcutin. Subordinate Aztec lords.

tetrarchy. Diocletian's (r. 306–337 C.E.) system for ruling the Roman Empire by four men with power divided territorially.

theocracy. A state ruled by religious leaders who claim to govern by divine authority.

Theravada. The "Way of the Elders." A school of Buddhism that emphasized the monastic ideal.

Thermidorean Reaction. The reaction against the radicalism of the French Revolution that began in July 1794. Associated with the end of terror and establishment of the Directory.

Third Estate. The branch of the French Estates General representing all of the kingdom outside the nobility and the clergy.

three-field system. A medieval innovation that increased the amount of land under cultivation by leaving only one-third fallow in a given year.

tlatoani. An Aztec ruler.

transubstantiation. The doctrine that the entire substances of the bread and wine are changed in the Eucharist into the body and blood of Christ.

treaty ports. Chinese ports ruled by foreign consuls where foreigners enjoyed commercial privileges and immunity from Chinese laws.

Trekboers. White livestock farmers in Cape Colony.

tribunes. Roman officials who had to be plebeians and were elected by the plebeian assembly to protect plebeians from the arbitrary power of the magistrates.

Tripartite Pact. The alliance between Japan and Nazi Germany and Fascist Italy that was signed in 1940.

typanosomiasis. Sleeping sickness, a parasitic disease that is transmitted by tsetse flies. If untreated, it is fatal both to humans and animals.

ulama. "Persons with correct knowledge." The Islamic scholarly elite who served a social function similar to the Christian clergy.

Umma. The Islamic community.

"unequal treaties." Agreements imposed on China in the nineteenth century by European powers, the United States, and Japan that granted their citizens special legal and economic privileges on Chinese soil.

Upanishads. The Upanishads, which date to about the seventh century B.C.E., have been perennial sources of spiritual knowledge for Hindus. The word *upanishad* means "secret and sacred knowledge." This word occurs in the Upanishads themselves in more than a dozen places in this sense. The word also means "texts incorporating such knowledge." There are ten principal Upanishads.

Urdu-Hindi. A language that combines Persian-Arabic and native Indian elements. Urdu is the Muslim version of the language. Hindi is the Hindu version.

uzama. An order of hereditary chiefs in Benin.

varnas. The four main classes that form the basis for Hindu caste relations.

vassal. A person granted an estate or cash payments in return for accepting the obligation to render services to a lord.

Vedas. The sacred texts of the ancient Aryan invaders of India. The Rig Vedas are the oldest materials in the Vedas.

vernacular. The everyday language spoken by the people, as opposed to Latin.

Viet Minh. The Communist-dominated popular front organization formed by Ho Chi Minh to establish an independent Vietnamese republic.

Wahhabis. Followers of Ibn Abd al-Wahhab (1703–1792) who sought to combat the excesses of popular and Sufi piety in Islam and looked to the Qur'an and the traditions of the Prophet as the sole authoritative guidance in religion.

War Communism. The economic policy adopted by the Bolsheviks during the Russian Civil War to seize the banks, heavy industry, railroads, and grain.

war guilt clause. Clause of the Versailles Treaty, which assigned responsibility for World War I solely to Germany.

water frame. A water-powered device invented by Richard Arkwright to produce a more durable cotton fabric. It led to the shift in the production of cotton textiles from households to factories.

Weimar Republic. The German democratic regime that existed between the end of World War I and Hitler's coming to power in 1933.

White Russians. Those Russians who opposed the Bolsheviks (the "Reds") in the Russian Civil War of 1918–1921.

Works Progress Administration (WPA). New Deal program created by the Roosevelt administration in 1935 that provided relief for the unemployed in the industrial sector during the Great Depression in the United States.

yangban. Elite Korean families of the Choson period.

zaibatsu. Large industrial combines that came to dominate Japanese industry in the late nineteenth century.

Zen. A form of Buddhism, which taught that Buddha was only a man and exhorted each person to attain enlightenment by his or her own efforts.

Zionism. The movement to create a Jewish state in Palestine (the Biblical Zion).

Zoroastrianism. A quasi-monotheistic Iranian religion founded by Zoroaster (ca. 628–551 B.C.E.) who preached a message of moral reform and exhorted his followers to worship only Ahura Mazda, the Wise Lord.

Suggested Readings

Chapter 1

General Prehistory

P. BOGUCKI, The Origins of Human Society (1999). An excellent summary of recent scholarship on the earliest origins of human societies.

F. BRAY, The Rice Economies: Technology and Development in Asian Societies (1986). Still the best authority on the origins of rice cultivation and its effect on the develepment of ancient Asia.

M. EHRENBERG, Women in Prehistory (1989). An account of the role of women in early times.

C. FREEMAN, Egypt, Greece and Rome: Civilizations of the Ancient Mediterranean (2004). Good comparative study of Egypt with Greece and Rome.

D.C. JOHNSON and M.R. EDEY, Lucy: The Beginning of Mankind (1981). An account of the African origins of humans.

S.M. NELSON, ed., Ancient Queens: Archaeological Explorations (2003). Reassesses women rulers and female power in the ancient world.

S.M. NELSON and M. ROSEN-AYALON, In Pursuit of Gender: Worldwide Archaeological Approaches (2002). Essays on gender and the archaeology of the ancient world.

D.L. NICHOLS and T.H. CHARLTON, eds., The Archaeology of CityStates: Cross-cultural Approaches (1997). One of a growing body of books and essay collections employing cross-cultural and comparative approaches to world history and archaeology.

M. OLIPHANT, The Atlas of the Ancient World: Charting the Great Civilizations of the Past (1992). An excellent comprehensive atlas of the ancient world.

P.L. SHINNIE, Ancient Nubia (1996). A study of the African state most influenced by Egyptian culture.

Near East

M.E. AUBER, The Phoenicians and the West (1996). A new study of an important sea-going people who served as a conduit between East and West.

BEN-TOR, ed., The Archaeology of Ancient Israel (1992). A useful and up-to-date survey.

J. BOTTÉRO, Everyday Life in Ancient Mesopotamia (2001). Interesting vignettes of ancient Mesopotamian life.

H. CRAWFORD, Sumer and the Sumerians (1991). A discussion of the oldest Mesopotamian civilization.

I. FINKELSTEIN and N.A. SILBERMAN, The Bible Unearthed: Archaeology's New Vision of Ancient Israel and the Origin of Its Sacred Texts (2001). An interesting discussion of the insights of recent archaeological finds on the history of the Bible and ancient Israel.

G. LEICK, Mesopotamia: The Invention of the City (2002). Good discussion of the urban history of ancient Mesopotamia.

J.N. POSTGATE, Early Mesopotamia (1992). An excellent study of Mesopotamian economy and society from the earliest times to about 1500 B.C.E., helpfully illustrated with drawings, photos, and translated documents.

D.B. REDFORD, Akhenaten (1987). A study of the controversial religious reformer.

W.F. SAGGS, The Might That Was Assyria (1984). A history of the northern Mesopotamian Empire and a worthy companion to the author's account of the Babylonian Empire in the south.

M. VAN DE MIEROOP, A History of the Ancient Near East, ca. 3000–323 B.C. (2004). An up-to-date comprehensive survey of ancient Near Eastern history.

India

D.P. AGRAWAL, The Archaeology of India (1982). A fine survey of the problems and data. Detailed, but with excellent summaries and brief discussions of major issues.

C. CHAKRABORTY, Common Life in the Rigveda and Atharvaveda—An Account of the Folklore in the Vedic Period (1977). An interesting attempt to reconstruct everyday life in the Vedic period from the principal Vedic texts.

J.R. McINTOSH, A Peaceful Realm: The Rise and Fall of the Indus Civilization (2002). Discusses what archaeologists have managed to unearth so far regarding Harrapan civilization.

W.D. O'FLAHERTY, The Rig Veda: An Anthology (1981). An excellent selection of Vedic texts in prosaic but very careful translation, with helpful notes on the texts.

J.E. SCHWARTZBERG, ed., A Historical Atlas of South Asia (1978). The definitive reference work for historical geography. Includes chronological tables and substantive essays.

R. THAPAR, Early India: From the Origins to A.D. 1300 (2003). A comprehensive introduction to the early history of India.

China

M. LOEWE and E. Shaughnessy, eds., The Cambridge History of Ancient China: From the Origins of Civilization to 221 B.C. (1999). A comprehensive and authoritative history of ancient China.

K. C. CHANG, The Archeology of Ancient China, 4th ed. (1986). The standard work on the subject.

K.C. CHANG, Art, Myth, and Ritual: The Path to Political Authority in Ancient China (1984). A study of the relation between shamans, gods, agricultural production, and political authority during the Shang and Zhou dynasties.

N. DI COSMO, Ancient China and Its Enemies: The Rise of Nomadic Power in East Asian History (2002). An excellent study of the relationship between China and nomadic peoples that was a powerful force in shaping Chinese and Central Asian history.

C.Y. HSU, Western Chou Civilization (1988).

D.N. KEIGHTLEY, The Origins of Chinese Civilization (1983).

M.E. LEWIS, Sanctioned Violence in Early China (1990).

X.Q. LI, Eastern Zhou and Qin Civilizations (1986). This work includes fresh interpretations based on archaeological finds.

Americas

R.L. BURGER, Chavín and the Origins of Andean Civilization (1992). A lucid and detailed account of the rise of civilization in the Andes.

M.D. COE and R. KOONTZ, Mexico: From the Olmecs to the Aztecs (2002). Good survey of ancient Mexico.

D. DREW, The Lost Chronicles of the Maya Kings (1999). Fine introduction to the history of Maya civilization.

V.W. FITZHUGH and A. CROWELL, Crossroads of Continents: Cultures of Siberia and Alaska (1988). Covers the area where the immigration from Eurasia to the Americas began.

R. FORD, ed., Prehistoric Food Production in North America (1985). Examines the origins of agriculture in the Americas.

P.D. HUNT, Indian Agriculture in America: Prehistory to the Present (1987). Includes a discussion of preconquest agriculture.

A. KNIGHT, Mexico: From the Beginning to the Spanish Conquest (2002). First of a three-volume comprehensive history of Mexico.

C. MORRIS and A. VON HAGEN, The Inka Empire and Its Andean Origins (1993). An overview of Andean civilization with excellent illustrations.

M. MOSELEY, The Incas and Their Ancestors: The Archaeology of Ancient Peru (1992). An overview of Peruvian archaeology.

J.A. SABLOFF, The New Archaeology and the Ancient Maya (1990). A lively account of recent research in Maya archaeology.

I. SILVERBLATT, Moon, Sun, and Witches: Gender Ideologies and Class in Inca and Colonial Peru (1987). A controversial but thought-provoking discussion of Incan ideas about gender.

Chapter 2

China

R. BERSTEIN, Ultimate Journey: Retracing the Path of an Ancient Buddhist Monk Who Crossed Asia in Search of Enlightenment (2001). Discusses the diffusion of Buddhism from India to China.

H.G. CREEL, What Is Taoism? And Other Studies in Chinese Cultural History (1970).

W.T. DE BARY ET AL., Sources of Chinese Tradition (1960). A reader in China's philosophical and historical literature. It should be consulted for the later periods as well as for the Zhou.

H. FINGARETE, Confucius—The Secular as Sacred (1998).

Y.L. FUNG, A Short History of Chinese Philosophy, ed. by D. Bodde (1948). A survey of Chinese philosophy from its origins down to recent times.

A. GRAHAM, Disputers of the Tao (1989).

D. HAWKES, Ch'u Tz'u: The Songs of the South (1985).

D.C. LAU, trans., Lao-tzu, Tao Te Ching (1963).

D.C. LAU, trans., Confucius, The Analects (1979).

C. LI, ed., The Sage and the Second Sex: Confucianism, Ethics, and Gender (2000). A good introduction to gender and ethics in Confucian thought.

B.I. SCHWARTZ, The World of Thought in Ancient China (1985).

A. WALEY, Three Ways of Thought in Ancient China (1956). An easy yet sound introduction to Confucianism, Daoism, and Legalism.

A. WALEY, The Book of Songs (1960).

B. WATSON, trans., Basic Writings of Mo Tzu, Hsun Tzu, and Han Fei Tzu (1963).

B. WATSON, trans., The Complete Works of Chuang Tzu (1968).

H. WELCH, Taoism, The Parting of the Way (1967).

India

A.L. BASHAM, The Wonder That Was India, rev. ed. (1963). Still unsurpassed by more recent works. Chapter VII, "Religion," is a superb introduction to the Vedic Aryan, Brahmanic, Hindu, Jain, and Buddhist traditions of thought.

W.N. BROWN, Man in the Universe: Some Continuities in Indian Thought (1970). A penetrating yet brief reflective summary of major patterns in Indian thinking.

W.T. DE BARY ET AL., Sources of Indian Tradition (1958). 2 vols. Vol. I, From the Beginning to 1800, ed. and rev. by Ainslie T. Embree (1988). Excellent selections from a variety of Indian texts, with good introductions to chapters and individual selections.

P. HARVEY, An Introduction to Buddhism (1990). Chapters 1–3 provide an excellent historical introduction.

T.J. HOPKINS, The Hindu Religious Tradition (1971). A first-rate, thoughtful introduction to Hindu religious ideas and practice.

K. KLOSTERMAIER, Hinduism: A Short History (2000). A relatively compact survey of the history of Hinduism.

J.M. KOLLER, The Indian Way (1982). A useful, wide-ranging handbook of Indian thought and religion.

R.H. ROBINSON and W.L. JOHNSON, The Buddhist Religion, 3rd ed. (1982). An excellent first text on the Buddhist tradition, its thought and development.

R.C. ZAEHNER, Hinduism (1966). One of the best general introductions to central Indian religious and philosophical ideas.

Israel

A. BACH, ed., Women in the Hebrew Bible: A Reader (1999). Excellent introduction to the ways in which biblical scholars are exploring the role of women in the Bible.

BRIGHT, A History of Israel (1968), 2nd ed. (1972). One of the standard scholarly introductions to biblical history and literature.

W.D. DAVIES and L. FINKELSTEIN, eds., The Cambridge History of Judaism. Vol. I, Introduction: The Persian Period (1984). Excellent essays on diverse aspects of the exilic period and later.

J. NEUSNER, The Way of Torah: An Introduction to Judaism (1979). A sensitive introduction to the Judaic tradition and faith.

The Oxford History of the Biblical World, M. D. COOGAN, ed. (1998).

Greece

The Cambridge Companion to Greek and Roman Philosophy, D. SEDLEY ed., (2003).

G.B. KERFERD, The Sophistic Movement (1981). An excellent description and analysis.

J. LEAR, Aristotle: The Desire to Understand (1988). A brilliant yet comprehensible introduction to the work of the philosopher.

T.E. RIHIL, Greek Science (1999). Good survey of Greek science incorporating recent reseach on the topic.

J.M. ROBINSON, An Introduction to Early Greek Philosophy (1968). A valuable collection of the main fragments and ancient testimony to the works of the early philosophers, with excellent commentary.

G. VLASTOS, The Philosophy of Socrates (1971). A splendid collection of essays illuminating the problems presented by this remarkable man.

G. VLASTOS, Platonic Studies, 2nd ed. (1981). A similar collection on the philosophy of Plato.

G. VLASTOS, Socrates, Ironist and Moral Philosopher (1991). The results of a lifetime of study by the leading interpreter of Socrates in our time.

Comparative Studies

(Increasingly world historians are looking at ancient civilizations in relationship to each other rather than as isolated entities to try to understand commonalities and differences in social and cultural development.)

W. DONIGER, Splitting the Difference: Gender and Myth in Ancient Greece and India (1999).

G.E.R. LLOYD, The Ambitions of Curiosity: Understanding the World in Ancient Greece and China (2002).

G.E.R. LLOYD, The Way and the Word: Science and Medicine in Early China and Greece (2002).

T. MCEVILLEY, The Shape of Ancient Thought: Comparative Studies of Greek and Indian Philosophies (2002).

Chapter 3

The Rise of Greek Civilization

P. CARTLEDGE, The Spartans (2003). A readable account of this enigmatic people.

J. CHADWICK, The Mycenaean World (1976). A readable account by a man who helped decipher Mycenaean writing.

R. DREWS, The Coming of the Greeks (1988). A fine discussion of the Greeks' arrival as part of the movements of the Indo-European peoples.

J.V. FINE, The Ancient Greeks (1983). An excellent survey that discusses historical problems and the evidence that gives rise to them.

M.I. FINLEY, World of Odysseus, rev. ed. (1965). A fascinating attempt to reconstruct Homeric society.

P. GREEN, Xerxes at Salamis (1970). A lively and stimulating history of the Persian War.

D. HAMEL, Trying Neaira (2003). A lively account of the events surrounding a famous jury trial that sheds interesting light on Athenian society in the fourth century B.C.E.

V.D. HANSON, The Western Way of War (1989). A brilliant and lively discussion of the rise and character of the hoplite phalanx and its influence on Greek society.

V.D. HANSON, The Other Greeks (1995). A revolutionary account of the Greek invention of the family farm and its centrality for the shaping of the polis.

D. KAGAN, The Great Dialogue: A History of Greek Political Thought from Homer to Polybius (1965). A discussion of the relationship between the Greek historical experience and political theory.

W.K. LACEY, The Family in Ancient Greece (1984).

J.F. LAZENBY, The Defense of Greece, 490–479 B.C. (1993). A new and valuable study of the Persian Wars.

J.F. MCGLEW, Tyranny and Political Culture in Ancient Greece (1993). A recent account of political developments in the Archaic period.

O. MURRAY, Early Greece (1980). A lively and imaginative account of the early history of Greece to the end of the Persian War.

A.M. SNODGRASS, The Dark Age of Greece (1972). A good examination of the archaeological evidence.

B.S. STRAUSS, The Battle of Salamis: The Naval Encounter That Saved Greece and Western Civilization (2004). A lively account of the major naval battle of the Persian Wars and its setting.

A.G. WOODHEAD, Greeks in the West (1962). An account of the Greek settlements in Italy and Sicily.

W.J. WOODHOUSE, Solon the Liberator (1965). A discussion of the great Athenian reformer.

S.G. MILLER, Ancient Greek Athletics (2004). The most complete and most useful account of the subject.

Classical and Hellenistic Greece

W. BURKERT, Greek Religion (1987). An excellent study by an outstanding student of the subject.

J.R. LANE FOX, Alexander the Great (1973). An imaginative account that does more than the usual justice to the Persian side of the problem.

Y. GARLAN, Slavery in Ancient Greece (1988). An up-to-date survey.

P. GREEN, Alexander to Actium: The Historical Evolution of the Hellenistic Age (1990). A remarkable synthesis of political and cultural history.

C.D. HAMILTON, Agesilaus and the Failure of Spartan Hegemony (1991). An excellent biography of the king who was the central figure in Sparta during its domination in the fourth century B.C.E.

N.G.L. HAMMOND, Philip of Macedon (1994). A new biography of the founder of the Macedonian Empire.

N.G.L. HAMMOND and G.T. GRIFFITH, A History of Macedonia, Vol. 2, 550–336 B.C. (1979). A thorough account of Macedonian history that focuses on the careers of Philip and Alexander.

R. JUST, Women in Athenian Law and Life (1988). An account of women's place in Athenian society.

D. KAGAN, The Peloponnesian War (2003). A narrative history of the war.

B.M.W. KNOX, The Heroic Temper: Studies in Sophoclean Tragedy (1964). A brilliant analysis of tragic heroism.

D.M. LEWIS, Sparta and Persia (1977). A valuable discussion of relations between Sparta and Persia in the fifth and fourth centuries B.C.E.

A.A. LONG, Hellenistic Philosophy: Stoics, Epicureans, Sceptics (1974). An account of Greek science in the Hellenistic and Roman periods.

R. MEIGGS, The Athenian Empire (1972). A fine study of the rise and fall of the empire, making excellent use of inscriptions.

J.J. POLLITT, Art and Experience in Classical Greece (1972). A scholarly and entertaining study of the relationship between art and history in classical Greece, with excellent illustrations.

J.J. POLLITT, Art in the Hellenistic Age (1986). An extraordinary analysis that places the art in its historical and intellectual context.

E.W. ROBINSON, Ancient Greek Democracy (2004). A stimulating collection of ancient sources and modern interpretations.

D.M. SCHAPS, Economic Rights of Women in Ancient Greece (1981).

B.S. STRAUSS, Athens After the Peloponnesian War (1987). An excellent discussion of Athens' recovery and of the nature of Athenian society and politics in the fourth century B.C.E.

B.S. STRAUSS, Fathers and Sons in Athens (1993). An unusual synthesis of social, political, and intellectual history.

V. TCHERIKOVER, Hellenistic Civilization and the Jews (1970). A fine study of the impact of Hellenism on the Jews.

G. VLASTOS, Socrates, Ironist and Moral Philosopher (1991). The results of a lifetime of study by the leading interpreter of Socrates in our time.

Chapter 4

Iran

M. BOYCE, Zoroastrians: Their Religious Beliefs and Practices (1979). The most recent survey, organized historically and based on extensive research.

M. BOYCE, ed. and TRANS., Textual Sources for the Study of Zoroastrianism (1984). Well-translated selections from a broad range of ancient Iranian materials.

J.M. COOK, The Persian Empire (1983). Survey of the Achaemenid period.

J. CURTIS, Ancient Persia (1989). Excellent portfolio of photographs of artifacts and sites, with a clear historical survey of the arts and culture of ancient Iran.

W.D. DAVIES and L. FINKLESTEIN, ed., The Cambridge History of Judaism, Vol. 1, Introduction; "The Persian Period." Good articles on Iran and Iranian religion as well as Judaism.

J. DUCHESNE-GUILLEMIN, TRANS., The Hymns of Zarathushtra, trans. by M. Henning (1952, 1963). The best short introduction to the original texts of the Zoroastrian hymns.

R.N. FRYE, The Heritage of Persia (1963, 1966). A first-rate survey of Iranian history to Islamic times: readable but scholarly.

R. GHIRSHMAN, Iran (1954). Good material on culture, society, and economy as well as politics and history.

W.W. MALANDRA, TRANS. and ed., An Introduction to Ancient Iranian Religion: Readings from the Avesta and Achaemenid Inscriptions (1983). Helpful especially for texts of inscriptions relevant to religion.

India

A.L. BASHAM, The Wonder That Was India, rev. ed. (1963). Excellent material on Mauryan religion, society, culture, and history.

A.L. BASHAM, ed., A Cultural History of India (1975). A fine collection of historical-survey essays by a variety of scholars. See Part I, "The Ancient Heritage" (Chapters 2–16).

N.N. BHATTACHARYYA, Ancient Indian History and Civilization: Trends and Perspectives (1988). Covers Mauryan and Gupta times as well as earlier periods, with chapters on political systems, cities and villages, ideology and religion, and art.

W.T. DE BARY ET AL., COMP., Sources of Indian Tradition, 2nd ed. (1958). Vol. I: From the Beginning to 1800, ed. and rev. by Ainslie T. Embree (1988). Excellent selections from a wide variety of Indian texts, with good introductions to chapters and selections.

B. ROWLAND, The Art and Architecture of India: Buddhist/Hindu/Jain, 3rd rev. ed. (1970). The standard work, lucid and easy to read. Note Part Three, "Romano-Indian Art in North-West India and Central Asia."

V.A. SMITH, ed., The Oxford History of India, 4th rev. ed. by Percival Spear et al. (1981), pp. 71–163. A dry, occasionally dated historical survey. Includes useful reference chronologies.

R. THAPAR, Ashoka and the Decline of the Mauryans (1973). The standard treatment of Ashoka's reign.

R. THAPAR, A History of India, Part I (1966), pp. 50–108. Three chapters that provide a basic survey of the period.

S. WOLPERT, A New History of India, 2nd ed. (1982). A basic survey history. Chapters 5 and 6 cover the Mauryans, Guptas, and Kushans.

Greek and Asian Dynasties

A.K. NARAIN, The Indo-Greeks (1957. Reprinted with corrections, 1962). The most comprehensive account of the complex history of the various kings and kingdoms.

F.E. PETERS, The Harvest of Hellenism (1970), pp. 222–308. Helpful chapters on Greek rulers of the Eastern world from Seleucus to the last Indo-Greeks.

J.W. SEDLAR, India and the Greek World: A Study in the Transmission of Culture (1980). A basic work that provides a good overview.

D. SINOR, ed., The Cambridge History of Early Inner Asia (1990). See especially Chapters 6 and 7.

Chapter 5

R. BATES, V.Y. Mudimbe, and Jean O'Barr, eds., Africa and the Disciplines (1993). Explores how knowledge of Africa has shaped various fields of scholarship. The essay on history by Steven Feierman is particularly relevant to this chapter.

P. BOHANNAN and P. CURTIN, Africa and Africans, rev. ed. (1995). An enjoyable and enlightening discussion of African history and prehistory and of major African institutions (e.g., arts, family life, religion).

R. BULLIET, The Camel and the Wheel (1990). Explains why the camel was chosen over the wheel as a means of transport in the Sahara.

P. CURTIN, On the Fringes of History: A Memoir (2005). An engaging autobiography by one of the pioneers in African Studies in the United States; explores what it means to be a historian in the modern world.

P. CURTIN, S. FEIERMANN, L. THOMPSON, and J. VANSINA, African History rev. ed . (1995). The classic survey history, written by four of the leaders in the field.

T.R.H. DAVENPORT and CHRISTOPHER SAUNDERS, South Africa: A Modern History, rev. ed. (2000). A comprehensive survey, beginning with coverage of prehistoric southern Africa, the Khoisan peoples, and the Bantu migrations.

B. DAVIDSON, Africa in History rev. ed. (1995). A sweeping history of the diverse parts of Africa, emphasizing cultural exchange within the continent and beyond.

C.A. DIOP, Precolonial Black Africa (1988). A seminal work by the pioneering Afro-centric scholar; his conclusions are controversial, but his writings are always provocative.

P.A. EBRON, Performing Africa (2002). Analyzes the role of performance in the creation and global circulation of African history and identity.

P. GARLAKE, Early Art and Architecture of Africa (2002). Highlights the diversity and sophistication of early African art and discusses the social context in which it was created.

E. GILBERT and J. REYNOLDS, Africa in World History (2004). The best new survey of African history, placing it in a global context. In conversational prose, the authors attend to environmental factors in African history and emphasize the roles of Western bias in shaping what we now know (and think we know) about Africa.

J. ILIFFE, Africans: The History of a Continent (1995). A thematic survey of African history, from the paleontological record to the end of apartheid, with a focus on environment and demography.

E. ISICHEI, A History of Christianity in Africa: From Antiquity to the Present (1995). An amazing survey of Christianity's role on the African continent, from the time of Christ through European missionaries to the present popularity of Christian faith.

R. OLIVER, The African Experience (1991). A masterly, balanced, and engaging sweep through African history.

I. VAN SERTIMA, Black Women in Antiquity rev. ed. (1988). From Lucy to Hatshepsut and beyond, essays explore the role and status of women in African societies of the past.

L. WHITE, et al., eds., African Words, African Voices: Critical Practices in Oral History (2001). A lively group of essays offer various perspectives on the uses of oral history in African research.

Chapter 6

From Republic to Empire

R. BAUMANN, Women and Politics in Ancient Rome (1995). A study of the role of women in Roman public life.

A.H. BERNSTEIN, Tiberius Sempronius Gracchus: Tradition and Apostasy (1978). A new interpretation of Tiberius's place in Roman politics.

T.J. CORNELL, The Beginnings of Rome: Italy and Rome from the Bronze Age to the Punic Wars, c. 1000–264 B.C. (1995). A consideration of the royal and early republican periods of Roman history.

T. CORNELL and J. MATTHEWS, Atlas of the Roman World (1982). Much more than the title indicates, this book presents a comprehensive view of the Roman world in its physical and cultural setting.

J-M. DAVID, The Roman Conquest of Italy (1997). A good analysis of how Rome united Italy.

A. GOLDSWORTHY, Roman Warfare (2002). A good military history of Rome.

A. GOLDSWORTHY, In the Name of Rome: The Men Who Won the Roman Empire (2004). The story of Rome's greatest generals in the republican and imperial periods.

E.S. GRUEN, Diaspora: Jews Amidst Greeks and Romans (2002). A fine study of Jews in the Hellenistic and Roman world.

E.S. GRUEN, The Hellenistic World and the Coming of Rome (1984). A new interpretation of Rome's conquest of the eastern Mediterranean.

W.V. HARRIS, War and Imperialism in Republican Rome, 327–70 B.C. (1975). An analysis of Roman attitudes and intentions concerning imperial expansion and war.

A. KEAVENEY, Rome and the Unification of Italy (1988). The story of how Rome organized its defeated opponents.

S. LANCEL, Carthage, A History (1995). Includes a good account of Rome's dealings with Carthage.

J.F. LAZENBY, Hannibal's War: A Military History of the Second Punic War (1978). A careful and thorough account.

F.G.B. MILLAR, The Crowd in Rome in the Late Republic (1999). A challenge to the view that only aristocrats counted in the late republic.

M. PALLOTTINO, The Etruscans, 6th ed. (1974). Makes especially good use of archaeological evidence.

H.H. SCULLARD, A History of the Roman World, 753–146 B.C., 4th ed. (1980). An unusually fine narrative history with useful critical notes.

G. WILLIAMS, The Nature of Roman Poetry (1970). An unusually graceful and perceptive literary study.

Imperial Rome

W. BALL, Rome in the East: The Transformation of an Empire (2001). A thorough account of the influence of the East on Roman history.

T. BARNES, The New Empire of Diocletian and Constantine (1982).

K.R. BRADLEY, Slavery and Society at Rome (1994). A study of the role of slaves in Roman life.

P. BROWN, The Rise of Western Christendom: Triumph and Diversity, 200–1000 (1996). A vivid picture of the spread of Christianity by a master of the field.

A. FERRILL, The Fall of the Roman Empire, The Military Explanation (1986). An interpretation that emphasizes the decline in the quality of the Roman army.

K. GALINSKY, Augustan Culture (1996). A work that integrates art, literature, and politics.

A.H.M. JONES, The Later Roman Empire, 3 vols. (1964). A comprehensive study of the period.

D. KAGAN, ed., The End of the Roman Empire: Decline or Transformation? 3rd ed. (1992). A collection of essays discussing the problem of the decline and fall of the Roman Empire.

J.E. Lendon, Empire of Honor, The Art of Government in the Roman World (1997). An original and path-breaking interpretation.

E.N. Luttwak, The Grand Strategy of the Roman Empire (1976). An original and fascinating analysis by a keen student of modern strategy.

R. MacMullen, Roman Social Relations, 50 B.C. to A.D. 284 (1981).

R. MacMullen, Corruption and the Decline of Rome (1988). A study that examines the importance of changes in ethical ideas and behavior.

R.W. Mathison, Roman Aristocrats in Barbarian Gaul: Strategies for Survival (1993). An unusual slant on the late empire.

J.F. Matthews, Laying Down the Law: A Study of the Theodosian Code (2000). A study of the importance of Roman law as a source for the understanding of Roman history and civilization.

W.A. Meeks, The Origins of Christian Morality: The First Two Centuries. An account of the shaping of Christianity in the Roman Empire.

F. Millar, The Emperor in the Roman World, 31 B.C.–A.D. 337 (1977). A study of Roman imperial government.

F. Millar, The Roman Empire and Its Neighbors, 2nd ed. (1981).

H.M.D. Parker, A History of the Roman World from A.D. 138 to 337 (1969). A good survey.

M.I. Rostovtzeff, Social and Economic History of the Roman Empire, 2nd ed. (1957). A masterpiece whose main thesis has been much disputed.

V. Rudich, Political Dissidence Under Nero: The Price of Dissimulation (1993). A brilliant exposition of the lives and thoughts of political dissidents in the early empire.

E.T. Salmon, A History of the Roman World, 30 B.C. to A.D. 138 (1968). A good survey.

R. Syme, The Roman Revolution (1960). A brilliant study of Augustus, his supporters, and their rise to power.

R. Syme, The Augustan Aristocracy (1985). An examination of the new ruling class shaped by Augustus.

L.A. Thompson, Romans and Blacks (1989).

Chapter 7

D. Bodde, China's First Unifier (1938). A study of the Qin unification of China, viewed through the Legalist philosopher and statesman Li Si.

T.T. Ch'u, Law and Society in Traditional China (1961). Treats the sweep of Chinese history from 202 B.C.E. to 1911 C.E.

T.T. Ch'u, Han Social Structure (1972).

A. Cotterell, The First Emperor of China (1981). A study of the first Qin emperor.

R. Coulborn, Feudalism in History (1965). One chapter interestingly compares the quasi feudalism of the Zhou with that of the Six Dynasties period.

J.K. Fairbank, E.O. Reischauer, and A.M. Craig, East Asia: Tradition and Transformation (1989). A fairly detailed single-volume history covering China, Japan, and other countries in East Asia from antiquity to recent times.

J. Gernet, A History of Chinese Civilization (1982). A survey of Chinese history.

D.A. Graff and R. Higham, A Military History of China (2002).

C.Y. Hsu, Ancient China in Transition (1965). On social mobility during the Eastern Zhou era.

C.Y. Hsu, Han Agriculture (1980). A study of the agrarian economy of China during the Han dynasty.

J. Levi, The Chinese Emperor (1987). A novel about the first Qin emperor based on scholarly sources.

M. Loewe, Everyday Life in Early Imperial China (1968). A social history of the Han dynasty.

J. Needham, The Shorter Science and Civilization in China (1978). An abridgment of the multivolume work on the same subject with the same title—minus Shorter—by the same author.

S. Owen, ed. and Trans., An Anthology of Chinese Literature: Beginnings to 1911 (1996).

I. Robinet, Taoism: Growth of a Religion (1987).

M. Sullivan, The Arts of China (1967). An excellent survey history of Chinese art.

D. Twitchett and M. Loewe, eds., The Ch'in and Han Empires, 221 B.C.E.–C.E. 220 (1986). Vol. 1 of The Cambridge History of China.

Z. S. Wang, Han Civilization (1982).

B. Watson, Ssu-ma Ch'ien, Grand Historian of China (1958). A study of China's premier historian.

B. Watson, Records of the Grand Historian of China, Vols. 1 and 2 (1961). Selections from the Shiji by Sima Qian.

B. Watson, The Columbia Book of Chinese Poetry (1986).

F. Wood, The Silk Road: Two Thousand Years in the Heart of Asia (2003). A lively narrative combined with photographs and paintings.

A. Wright, Buddhism in Chinese History (1959).

Y.S. Yu, Trade and Expansion in Han China (1967). A study of economic relations between the Chinese and their neighbors.

Chapter 8

General

P. Bol, This Culture of Ours (1992). An insightful intellectual history of the Tang through the Song dynasties.

J. Cahill, Chinese Painting (1960). An excellent survey.

J.K. Fairbank and M. Goldman, China: A New History (1998). The summation of a lifetime engagement with Chinese history.

F.A. Kierman Jr., and J.K. Fairbank, eds., Chinese Ways in Warfare (1974). Chapters by different authors on the Chinese military experience from the Zhou to the Ming.

Sui and Tang

P.B. Ebrey, The Aristocratic Families of Early Imperial China (1978).

D. McMullen, State and Scholars in T'ang China (1988).

S. Owen, The Great Age of Chinese Poetry: The High T'ang (1980).

S. Owen, trans. and ed., An Anthology of Chinese Literature: Beginnings to 1911 (1996).

E.G. Pulleyblank, The Background of the Rebellion of An Lu-shan (1955). A study of the 755 rebellion that weakened the central authority of the Tang dynasty.

E.O. Reischauer, Ennin's Travels in T'ang China (1955). China as seen through the eyes of a ninth-century Japanese Marco Polo.

E.H. Schafer, The Golden Peaches of Samarkand (1963). A study of Tang imagery.

So. Teiser, The Ghost Festival in Medieval China (1988). On Tang popular religion.

D. Twitchett, ed., The Cambridge History of China, Vol. III: Sui and T'ang China, 589–906 Part 1, (1979).

G. W. Wang, The Structure of Power in North China During the Five Dynasties (1963). A study of the interim period between the Tang and the Song dynasties.

A. F. Wright, The Sui Dynasty (1978).

Song

B. Birge, Women, Property, and Confucian Reaction in Song and Yuan China (960–1366) (2002). The rights of women to property—whether in the form of dowries or inheritances—were considerable during the Song but declined thereafter.

C.S. Chang and J. Smythe, South China in the Twelfth Century (1981). China as seen through the eyes of a twelfth-century Chinese poet, historian, and statesman.

E.L. Davis, Society and the Supernatural in Song China (2001).

J.W. Haeger, ed., Crisis and Prosperity in Song China (1975).

R. Hymes, Statesmen and Gentlemen (1987). On the transformation of officials into a local gentry elite during the twelfth and thirteenth centuries.

R. Hymes, Way and Byway: Taoism, Local Religion, and Models of Divinity in Sung and Modern China (2002).

M. ROSSABI, China Among Equals (1983). A study of the Liao, Qin, and Song Empires and their relations.

W.M. TU, Confucian Thought, Selfhood as Creative Transformation (1985).

K. YOSHIKAWA, An Introduction to Song Poetry, trans. by B. Watson (1967).

Yuan

T.T. ALLSEN, Mongol Imperialism (1987).

J.W. DARDESS, Conquerors and Confucians: Aspects of Political Change in Late Yuan China (1973).

DE RACHEWILTZ, TRANS., The Secret History of the Mongols: A Mongolian Epic Chronicle of the Thirteenth Century (2003). A new translation of a key historical work on the life of Genghis.

H. FRANKE and D. TWITCHETT, eds., The Cambridge History of China, Vol. VI: Alien Regimes and Border States, 710–1368 (1994).

J.D. LANGLOIS, China Under Mongol Rule (1981).

R.LATHAM, TRANS., Travels of Marco Polo (1958).

H.D. MARTIN, The Rise of Chingis Khan and His Conquest of North China (1981).

D. MORGAN, The Mongol Empire and Its Legacy (1999). Genghis, the several khanates, and the aftermath of empire.

P. RATCHNEVSKY, Genghis Khan, His Life and Legacy (1992). The rise to power of the Mongol leader, with a critical consideration of historical sources.

Chapter 9

M. ADOLPHSON, The Gates of Power: Monks, Courtiers, and Warriors in Premodern Japan (2000). A new interpretation stressing the importance of temples in the political life of Heian and Kamakura Japan.

B.L. BATTEN, To the Ends of Japan: Premodern Frontiers, Boundaries, and Interactions. (2003). An interesting treatment of Heian Japan, topic by topic.

C. BLACKER, The Catalpa Bow (1975). An insightful study of folk Shinto.

R. BORGEN, Sugawara no Michizane and the Early Heian Court (1986). A study of a famous courtier and poet.

D.M. BROWN, ed., The Cambridge History of Japan: Ancient Japan (1993). This series of six volumes sums up several decades of research on Japan.

D. BROWN and E. ISHIDA, eds., The Future and the Past (1979). A translation of a history of Japan written in 1219.

The Cambridge History of Japan, D.M. BROWN, ed.; Vol. 1, Ancient Japan, W. McCullough and D. H. Shively eds; Vol. 2, Heian Japan, K. Yamamura, ed. Vol. 3, Medieval Japan. Fine multi-author works.

M. COLLCUTT, Five Mountains (1980). A study of the monastic organization of medieval Zen.

T.D. CONLON, State of War: The Violent Order of Fourteenth Century Japan (2003). Compare Conlon's account with those of Souyri and Friday.

P. DUUS, Feudalism in Japan (1969). An easy survey of the subject.

W.W. FARRIS, Population, Disease, and Land in Early Japan, 645–900 (1985). An innovative reinterpretation of early history.

W.W. FARRIS, Heavenly Warriors: The Evolution of Japan's Military, 500–1300 (1992).

W.W. FARRIS, Sacred Texts and Buried Treasures (1998). Studies of Japan's prehistory and early history, based on recent Japanese research.

K.F. FRIDAY, Samurai, Warfare and the State in Early Medieval Japan (2004). Weapons and warfare in Japan from the tenth to fourteenth centuries.

A.E. GOBLE, GDaigo's Revolution (1996). A provoking account of the 1331 revolt by an emperor who thought emperors should rule.

J.W. HALL, Government and Local Power in Japan, 500–1700: A Study Based on Bizen Province (1966). A splendid and insightful book.

J.W. HALL and T. TOYODA, Japan in the Muromachi Age (1977). Another collection of essays.

D. KEENE, ed., Anthology of Japanese Literature from the Earliest Era to the Mid-Nineteenth Century (1955).

D. KEENE, ed., Twenty Plays of the N Theatre (1970).

T. LAMARRE, Uncovering Heian Japan: An Archeology of Sensation and Inscription (2000). The "archeology" in the title refers to digging into literature.

I.H. LEVY, The Ten Thousand Leaves (1981). A fine translation of Japan's earliest collection of poetry.

J.P. MASS and W. HAUSER, eds., The Bakufu in Japanese History (1985). Topics in bakufu history from the twelfth to the nineteenth centuries.

I. MORRIS, TRANS., The Pillow Book of Sei Shnagon (1967). Observations about the Heian court life by the Jane Austen of ancient Japan.

S. MURASAKI, The Tale of Genji, trans. by A. Waley (1952). A comparison of this translation with that of Seidensticker is instructive.

S. MURASAKI, The Tale of Genji, trans. by E. G. Seidensticker (1976). The world's first novel and the greatest work of Japanese fiction.

R.J. PEARSON ET AL., eds., Windows on the Japanese Past: Studies in Archaeology and Prehistory (1986).

D.L. PHILIPPI, TRANS., Kojiki (1968). Japan's ancient myths.

J. PIGGOT, The Emergence of Japanese Kingship (1997).

E.O. REISCHAUER, Ennin's Diary, the Record of a Pilgrimage to China in Search of the Law and Ennin's Travels in T'ang China (1955).

E.O. REISCHAUER and A.M. CRAIG, Japan: Tradition and Transformation (1989). A more detailed work covering the sweep of Japanese history from the early beginnings through the 1980s.

H. SATO, Legends of the Samurai (1995). Excerpts from various tales and writings.

D.H. SHIVELY and W.H. McCULLOUGH, eds., The Cambridge History of Japan: Heian Japan (1999).

D.T. SUZUKI, Zen and Japanese Culture (1959).

H. TONOMURA, Community and Commerce in Late Medieval Japan (1992).

R. TSUNODA, W.T. DE BARY, and D. KEENE, COMPS., Sources of the Japanese Tradition (1958). A collection of original religious, political, and philosophical writings from each period of Japanese history. The best reader. A new edition should be out soon.

H.P. VARLEY, Imperial Restoration in Medieval Japan (1971). A study of the 1331 attempt by an emperor to restore imperial power.

A. WALEY, TRANS., The N Plays of Japan (1957). Medieval dramas.

K. YAMAMURA, ed., Cambridge History of Japan: Medieval Japan (1990).

Chapter 10

Iran

M. BOYCE, Zoroastrians: Their Religious Beliefs and Practices (1979). A detailed survey by the current authority on Zoroastrian religious history. See Chapters 7–9.

M. BOYCE, ed. and TRANS., Textual Sources for the Study of Zoroastrianism (1984). A valuable anthology with an important introduction that includes Boyce's arguments for a revision of the dates of Zoroaster's life (to between 1400 and 1200 B.C.E.).

R.N. FRYE, The Heritage of Persia (1963). Still one of the best surveys, Chapter 6 deals with the Sasanid era.

R. GHIRSHMAN, Iran (1954 [orig. ed. 1951]). An introductory survey of similar extent to Frye, but with differing material also.

R. GHIRSHMAN, Persian Art: The Parthian and Sasanid Dynasties (1962). Superb photographs, and a very helpful glossary of places and names. The text is minimal.

GEO WIDENGRAN, Mani and Manichaeism (1965). Still the standard introduction to Mani's life and the later spread and development of Manichaeism.

India

A.L. BASHAM, The Wonder That Was India (1963). The best survey of classical Indian religion, society, literature, art, and politics.

W.T. DE BARY ET AL., comp., Sources of Indian Tradition, 2nd ed. (1958), Vol. I, From the Beginning to 1800, ed. and rev. by Ainslie T. Embree (1988). Excellent selections from a wide variety of Indian texts, with good introductions to the text selections.

S. DUTT, Buddhist Monks and Monasteries of India (1962). The standard work. See especially Chapters 3 ("Bhakti") and 4 ("Monasteries Under the Gupta Kings").

D.G. MANDELBAUM, Society in India (1972). 2 vols. The first two chapters in Volume I of this study of caste, family, and village relations are a good introduction to the caste system.

B. ROWLAND, The Art and Architecture of India: Buddhist/Hindu/Jain, 3rd rev. ed. (1970). See the excellent chapters on Sungan, Andhran, and other early Buddhist art (6–8, 14), the Gupta period (15), and the Hindu Renaissance (17–19).

V.A. SMITH, The Oxford History of India, 4th rev. ed. (1981). See especially pages 164–229 (the Gupta period and following era to the Muslim invasions).

R. THAPAR, A History of India, Part I (1966), pp. 109–193. Three chapters covering the rise of mercantilism, the Gupta "classical pattern," and the southern dynasties to ca. 900 C.E..

P. YOUNGER, Introduction to Indian Religious Thought (1972). A sensitive attempt to delineate classical concerns of Indian religious thought and culture.

Chapter 11

O. GRABAR, The Formation of Islamic Art (1973). A critical and creative interpretation of major themes in the development of distinctively Islamic forms of art and architecture.

A. HOURANI, A History of the Arab Peoples (1991). A masterly survey of the Arabs down through the centuries and a clear picture of many aspects of Islamic history and culture that extend beyond the Arab world.

H. KENNEDY, The Prophet and the Age of the Caliphates: The Islamic Near East from the Sixth to the Eleventh Century (1986). The best survey of early Islamic history.

I. LAPIDUS, A History of Islamic Societies (1988). A comprehensive overview of the rise and development of Islam all over the world.

F.E. PETERS, Muhammad and the Origins of Islam (1994). A balanced analysis of the life of Muhammad.

F. RAHMAN, Major Themes of the Qur'an (1980). The best introduction to the basic ideas of the Qur'an and Islam, seen through the eyes of a perceptive Muslim modernist scholar.

F. SCHUON, Understanding Islam (1994). Compares the Islamic worldview with Catholic Christianity. A dense, but intellectually stimulating, discussion.

M. SELLS, Approaching the Qur'an. The Early Revelations (1999). A fine introduction and new translations of some of the more common earlier Qur'anic revelations.

B. STOWASSER, Women in the Qur'an, Traditions and Interpretation (1994). An outstanding systematic study of statements regarding women in the Qur'an.

Chapter 12

K. ARMSTRONG, Muhammad: A Biography of the Prophet (1992). Strong on religion.

R. BARTLETT, The Making of Europe, 950–1350 (1992). A study of the way immigration and colonial conquest shaped the Europe we know.

M. BLOCH, Feudal Society, Vols. 1 and 2, trans. by L. A. Manyon (1971). A classic on the topic and as an example of historical study.

P. BROWN, Augustine of Hippo: A Biography (1967). Late antiquity seen through the biography of its greatest Christian thinker.

J.H. BURNS, The Cambridge History of Medieval Political Thought c. 350–c. 1450 (1991). The best scan.

R.H.C. DAVIS, A History of Medieval Europe: From Constantine to St. Louis (1972). Unsurpassed in clarity.

R. FLETCHER, The Barbarian Conversion: From Paganism to Christianity (1998). Up-to-date survey.

J.B. GLUBB, The Great Arab Conquests (1995). Jihadists.

G. GUGLIELMO, ed., The Byzantines (1997). Updates key issues.

D. GUTAS, Greek Thought, Arabic Culture (1998). A comparative intellectual history.

G. HOLMES, ed., The Oxford History of Medieval Europe (1992). Overviews of Roman and northern Europe during the "Dark Ages."

B. LEWIS, The Middle East: A Brief History of the Last 2,000 Years (1995)

C. MANGO, Byzantium: The Empire of New Rome (1980).

J. MARTIN, Medieval Russia 980–1584 (1995). A concise narrative history.

R. MCKITTERICK, ed., Carolingian Culture: Emulation and Innovation (1994). Fresh essays.

J.J. NORWICH, Byzantium: The Decline and Fall (1995).

J.J. NORWICH, Byzantium: The Apogee (1997). The whole story in two volulmes.

R.I. PAGE, Chronicles of the Vikings: Records, Memorials, and Myths (1995). Sources galore.

F. ROBINSON, ed., The Cambridge Illustrated History of the Islamic World (1996). Spectacular.

S. RUNCIMAN, Byzantine Civilization (1970). Succinct, comprehensive account by a master.

P. SAWYER, The Age of the Vikings (1962). Old but solid account.

C. STEPHENSON, Medieval Feudalism (1969). Excellent short summary and introduction.

L. WHITE JR., Medieval Technology and Social Change (1962). Often fascinating account of how primitive technology changed life.

H. WOLFRAM, The Roman Empire and Its Germanic Peoples (1997). Challenging, but most rewarding.

Chapter 13

The Islamic Heartlands

L. AHMED, Women and Gender in Islam: Historical Roots of a Modern Debate (1992). A good historical survey of the status of women in Middle Eastern societies.

J. BERKEY, The Formation of Islam: Religion and Society in the Near East, 600–1800 (2002). An interesting new synthesis focusing on political and religious trends.

C.E. BOSWORTH, The Islamic Dynasties: A Chronological and Genealogical Handbook (1967). A handy reference work for dynasties and families important to Islamic history in all periods and places.

M.A. COOK, Commanding Right and Forbidding Wrong in Islamic Thought (2001). A masterful anaylsis of the development of Islamic law.

P.K. HITTI, History of the Arabs, 8th ed. (1964). Still a useful English resource, largely for factual detail. See especially Part IV, "The Arabs in Europe: Spain and Sicily."

A. HOURANI, A History of the Arab Peoples (1991). The newest survey history and the best, at least for the Arab Islamic world.

S.K. JAYYUSI, ed., The Legacy of Muslim Spain, 2 vols. (1994). A comprehensive survey of the arts, politics, literature, and society by experts in various fields.

B. LEWIS, ed., Islam and the Arab World (1976). A large-format, heavily illustrated volume with many excellent articles on diverse aspects of Islamic (not simply Arab, as the misleading title indicates) civilization through the premodern period.

D. MORGAN, The Mongols (1986). A recent and readable survey history.

J.J. SAUNDERS, A History of Medieval Islam (1965). A brief and simple, if sketchy, introductory survey of Islamic history to the Mongol invasions.

India

W.T. DE BARY ET AL., COMP., Sources of Indian Tradition, 2nd ed. (1958), Vol. I, From the Beginning to 1800, ed. and rev. by Ainslie T. Embree (1988). Excellent selections from a wide variety of Indian texts, with good introductions to chapters and individual selections.

S.M. IKRAM, Muslim Civilization in India (1964). The best short survey history, covering the period 711 to 1857.

R.C. MAJUMDAR, gen. ed., The History and Culture of the Indian People, Vol. VI, The Delhi Sultanate, 3rd ed. (1980). A comprehensive political and cultural account of the period in India.

F. ROBINSON, ed., The Cambridge History of India, Pakistan, Bangladesh, Sri Lanka, Nepal, Bhutan, and the Maldives (1989). A very helpful quick reference source with brief but well-done survey essays on a wide range of topics relevant to South Asian history down to the present.

A. WINK, Al-Hind: The Making of the Indo-Islamic World, Vol. 1 (1991). The first of five promising volumes to be devoted to the Indo-Islamic world's history. This volume treats the seventh to eleventh centuries.

Southeast Asia

L. ANDAYA, The World of Maluku: Eastern Indonesia in the Early Modern Period (1993). A comprehensive view of the formation of what is now Indonesia.

B.W. ANDAYA and L. ANDAYA, A History of Malaysia (1982). A good overview of Indonesia's smaller but critical northern neighbor.

J. SIEGEL, Shadow and Sound: The Historical Thought of a Sumatran People (1979). An excellent analysis tracing the relation between foreign influences and local practice.

Chapter 14

B.S. BAUER, The Development of the Inca State (1992). An important new work that emphasizes archaeological evidence over the Spanish chronicles in accounting for the emergence of the Inca Empire.

F.F. BERDAN, The Aztecs of Central Mexico: An Imperial Society (1982). An excellent introduction to the Aztecs.

R.E. BLANTON, S.A. KOWALEWSKI, G. FEINMAN, and J. APPEL, Ancient Mesoamerica: A Comparison of Change in Three Regions (1981). Concentrates on ancient Mexico.

K.O. BRUHNS, Ancient South America (1994). A clear discussion of the archaeology and civilization of the region with emphasis on the Andes.

R.L. BURGER, Chavín and the Origins of Andean Civilization (1992). A detailed study of early Andean prehistory by one of the leading authorities on Chavín.

R.M. CARMACK, J. GASCO, and G.H. GOSSEN, The Legacy of Mesoamerica: History and Culture of a Native American Civilization (1996). A survey of Mesoamerica from its origins to the present.

I. CLENDINNEN, Aztecs: An Interpretation (1995). A fascinating attempt to reconstruct the Aztec world.

M.D. COE, Breaking the Maya Code (1992). The story of the remarkable achievement of deciphering the ancient Maya language.

M.D. COE, The Maya (1993). The best introduction.

M.D. COE, Mexico from the Olmecs to the Aztecs (1994). A wide-ranging introductory discussion.

G. CONRAD and A.A. DEMAREST, Religion and Empire: The Dynamics of Aztec and Inca Expansionism (1984). An interesting comparative study.

S.D. GILLESPIE, The Aztec Kings (1989).

R. HASSIG, Aztec Warfare.

J. HYSLOP, Inka Settlement Planning (1990). A detailed study.

M. LEÓN-PORTILLA, Fifteen Poets of the Aztec World (1992). An anthology of translations of Aztec poetry.

M.E. MILLER, The Art of Mesoamerica from Olmec to Aztec (1986). A well-illustrated introduction.

C. MORRIS and A. VON HAGEN, The Inka Empire and Its Andean Origins (1993). A clear overview of Andean prehistory by a leading authority. Beautifully illustrated.

M.E. MOSELY, The Incas and Their Ancestors: The Archaeology of Peru (1992). Readable and thorough.

J.A. SABLOFF, The Cities of Ancient Mexico (1989). Capsule summaries of ancient Mesoamerican cultures.

J.A. SABLOFF, Archaeology and the Maya (1990). A look at changing views of the ancient Maya.

L. SCHELE and M.E. MILLER, The Blood of Kings (1986). A rich and beautifully illustrated study of ancient Maya art and society.

R.S. SHARER, The Ancient Maya, 5th ed. (1994). A classic. Readable, authoritative, and thorough.

M.P. WEAVER, The Aztecs, Maya, and Their Predecessors (1993). A classic textbook.

Chapter 15

J. ABUN-NASR, A History of the Maghrib in the Islamic Period (1987). The most recent North African survey. Pages 59–247 are relevant to this chapter.

E.K. AKYEAMPYONG, ed., Themes in West Africa's History (2006). A wide-ranging collection of essays by leading scholars.

I. BATTUTA, N. KING, S. HAMDUN, Ibn Battuta in Black Africa rev. ed. (2005). Well-selected excerpts from Battuta's extensive journals.

P. BEN-AMOS, Art, Innovation and Politics in Eighteenth-Century Benin (1999). Offers insights into the many levels of meaning and authority in Benin's artworks.

I. BERGER, E.F. White, C. Skidmore-Hess, Women in Sub-Saharan Africa: Restoring Women to History (1999). A valuable resource on the role of women in African history.

D. BIRMINHAM, Central Africa to 1870 (1981). Chapters from the Cambridge History of Africa that give a brief, lucid overview of developments in this region.

P. BOHANNAN and P. CURTIN, Africa and Africans, rev. ed. (1995). Accessible, topical approach to African history, culture, society, politics, and economics.

P.D. CURTIN, S. FEIERMANN, L. THOMPSON, and J. VANSINA, African History rev. ed. (1995). An older, but masterly survey. The relevant portions are Chapters 6–9.

B. DAVIDSON, West Africa Before the Colonial Era (1998). A typically readable survey by one of the great popularizers of African history.

R. ELPHICK, Kraal and Castle: Khoikhoi and the Founding of White South Africa (1977). An incisive, informative interpretation of the history of the Khoikhoi and their fateful interaction with European colonization.

R. ELPHICK and H. GILIOMEE, The Shaping of South African Society, 1652–1820 (1979). A superb, synthetic history of this crucial period.

J.D. FAGE, A History of Africa rev. ed., (2001). Still a readable survey history.

E. GILBERT and J. REYNOLDS, Africa in World History (2004). The best new survey of African history, placing it in a global context. See especially chapters six and seven on Islam, and chapters nine through twelve for the period leading to European colonization.

M. HISKETT, The Development of Islam in West Africa (1984). The standard survey study of the subject. Of the relevant sections (Chapters 1–10, 12, 15), that on Hausaland, which is treated only in passing in this text, is noteworthy.

M. HORTON and J. MIDDLETON, The Swahili (2000).

R.W. JULY, A History of the African People, 3rd ed. (1980). Chapters 3–6 treat Africa before about 1800 area by area; Chapter 7 deals with "The Coming of Europe."

N. LEVTZION, R. Pouwels, eds. History of Islam in Africa (2000). A wide-ranging collection of essays.

N. LEVTZION, D.T. NIANI, ed., Africa from the Twelfth to the Sixteenth Century, UNESCO General History of Africa, Vol. IV (1984). Many survey articles cover the various regions and major states of Africa in the centuries noted in the title.

R. OLIVER, The African Experience (1991). A masterly, balanced, and engaging survey, with outstanding syntheses and summaries of recent research.

C.A. QUINN and F. QUINN, Pride, Faith, and Fear: Islam in Sub-Saharan Africa (2005). A readable account of Islam in Africa, bringing the story up to the present.

A.F.C. RYDER, Benin and the Europeans: 1485–1897 (1969). A basic study.

D. ROBINSON, Muslim Societies in African History (2004). A comprehensive overview.

JOHN K. THORNTON, The Kingdom of Kongo: Civil War and Transition, 1641–1718 (1983). A detailed and perceptive analysis for those who wish to delve into Kongo state and society in the seventeenth century.

M. WILSON and L. THOMPSON, eds., The Oxford History of South Africa, Vol. I., South Africa to 1870 (1969). Relatively detailed, if occasionally dated, treatment.

Chapter 16

M. BRECHT, Martin Luther: His Road to Reformation, 1483–1521 (1985). Best on young Luther.

C. BROWN, ET AL., Rembrandt: The Master and His Workshop (1991). A great master's art and influence.

R. BRIGGS, Witches and Neighbors: A History of European Witchcraft (1996). A readable introduction.

E. DUFFY, The Stripping of the Altars (1992). Strongest argument yet that there was no deep reformation in England.

H.O. EVENNETT, The Spirit of the Counter Reformation (1968). The continuity and independence of Catholic reform.

HANS-JÜRGEN GOERTZ, The Anabaptists (1996). Best treatment of minority Protestants.

O.P. GRELL and A. CUNNINGHAM, Health Care and Poor Relief in Protestant Europe (1997) The civic side of the Reformation.

M. HOLT, The French Wars of Religion, 1562–1629 (1995). Scholarly appreciation of religious side of the story.

J.C. HUTCHISON, Albrecht Durer (1990). The life behind the art.

H. JEDIN, A History of the Council of Trent, Vols. 1, 2 (1957–1961). Comprehensive, detailed, and authoritative.

M. KITCHEN, The Cambridge Illustrated History of Germany (1996). Comprehensive and accessible.

A. KORS and E. PETERS, eds., European Witchcraft, 1100–1700 (1972). Classics of witch belief.

W. MACCAFFREY, Elizabeth I (1993). Magisterial study.

G. MATTINGLY, The Armada (1959). A masterpiece, novel-like in style.

D. MCCOLLOCH, The Reformation (2004). No stone unturned, with English emphasis.

H.A. OBERMAN, Luther: Man Between God and Devil (1989). Authoritative biography

J.W. O'MALLEY, The First Jesuits (1993). Extremely detailed account of the creation of the Society of Jesus and its original purposes.

S. OZMENT, The Age of Reform, 1250–1550: An Intellectual and Religious History of Late Medieval and Reformation Europe (1980). Broad, lucid survey.

S. OZMENT, When Fathers Ruled: Family Life in Reformation Europe (1983). Effort to portray the constructive side of Protestant thinking about family relationships.

S. OZMENT, The Bürgermeister's Daughter: Scandal in a Sixteenth-Century German Town (1996). What a woman could do at law in the sixteenth century.

G. PARKER, The Thirty Years' War (1984). Large, lucid survey.

J.H. PARRY, The Age of Reconnaissance (1964). A comprehensive account of explorations from 1450 to 1650.

W. PRINZ, Durer (1998). Latest biography of Germany's greatest painter.

J.J. SCARISBRICK, Henry VIII (1968). The best account of Henry's reign.

G. STRAUSS, ed. and TRANS., Manifestations of Discontent in Germany on the Eve of the Reformation (1971). A rich collection of sources for both rural and urban scenes.

H. WUNDER, He Is the Sun, She Is the Moon: Women in Early Modern Germany (1998). Best study of early modern women.

Chapter 17

J. ABUN-NASR, A History of the Maghrib in the Islamic Period (1987). The most recent North African survey. Pages 59–247 are relevant to this chapter.

D. BIRMINHAM, Central Africa to 1870 (1981). Chapters from the Cambridge History of Africa that give a brief, lucid overview of developments in this region.

P. BOHANNAN and P. CURTIN, Africa and Africans, rev. ed. (1971). Accessible, topical approach to African history, culture, society, politics, and economics.

P.D. CURTIN, S. FEIERMANN, L. THOMPSON, and J. VANSINA, African History (1978). An older, but masterly survey. The relevant portions are Chapters 6–9.

R. ELPHICK, Kraal and Castle: Khoikhoi and the Founding of White South Africa (1977). An incisive, informative interpretation of the history of the Khoikhoi and their fateful interaction with European colonization.

R. ELPHICK and H. GILIOMEE, The Shaping of South African Society, 1652–1820 (1979). A superb, synthetic history of this crucial period.

J.D. FAGE, A History of Africa (1978). Still a readable survey history.

M. HISKETT, The Development of Islam in West Africa (1984). The standard survey study of the subject. Of the relevant sections (Chapters 1–10, 12, 15), that on Hausaland, which is treated only in passing in this text, is noteworthy.

R.W. JULY, Precolonial Africa: An Economic and Social History (1975). Chapter 10 gives an interesting overall picture of slaving in African history.

R.W. JULY, A History of the African People, 3rd ed. (1980). Chapters 3–6 treat Africa before about 1800 area by area; Chapter 7 deals with "The Coming of Europe."

I.M. LEWIS, ed., Islam in Tropical Africa (1966), pp. 4–96. Lewis's introduction is one of the best brief summaries of the role of Islam in West Africa and the Sudan.

D.T. NIANI, ed., Africa from the Twelfth to the Sixteenth Century, UNESCO General History of Africa, Vol. IV (1984). Many survey articles cover the various regions and major states of Africa in the centuries noted in the title.

R. OLIVER, The African Experience (1991). A masterly, balanced, and engaging survey, with outstanding syntheses and summaries of recent research.

J.A. RAWLEY, The Transatlantic Slave Trade: A History (1981). Impressively documented, detailed, and well-presented survey history of the Atlantic trade; little focus on African dimensions.

A.F.C. RYDER, Benin and the Europeans: 1485–1897 (1969). A basic study.

JOHN K. THORNTON, The Kingdom of Kongo: Civil War and Transition, 1641–1718 (1983). A detailed and perceptive analysis for those who wish to delve into Kongo state and society in the seventeenth century.

M. WILSON and L. THOMPSON, eds., The Oxford History of South Africa, Vol. I., South Africa to 1870 (1969). Relatively detailed, if occasionally dated, treatment.

Chapter 18

B. BAILYN, Atlantic History: Concepts and Contours (2005). An essential overview to this burgeoning area of historical inquiry, written by a leader in the field.

I. BERLIN, Many Thousands Gone: The First Two Centuries of Slavery in North America (1998); Generations of Captivity: A History of African American Slaves (2003). Two volumes representing the most extensive and important recent treatment of slavery in North America; highlights the diversity of slave experiences.

R. BLACKBURN, The Making of New World Slavery from the Baroque to the Modern 1492–1800 (1997). An extraordinary work.

V. CARRETTA, Equiano, the African: The Biography of a Self-Made Man (reprint 2007). Provides context and analysis of the renowned accounts of one-time slave Olaudah Equiano.

B. COBO and R. HAMILTON, History of the Inca Empire rev. ed. (1983). A seventeenth-century account, with a modern translation and interpretation.

N.D. COOK, Born to Die: Disease and New World Conquest, 1492–1650 (1998). A survey of the devastating impact of previously unknown diseases on the native populations of the Americas.

M.S. CREIGHTON and L. NORLING, eds. Iron Men, Wooden Women: Gender and Seafaring in the Atlantic World, 1700–1920 (2006). Eye-opening accounts of life at sea, and how gender-roles were shaped and challenged on the Atlantic.

P. D. CURTIN, The Atlantic Slave Trade: A Census (1969). Remains a basic work.

P.D. CURTIN, The Rise and Fall of the Plantation Complex (1998). Places the plantation economy in the context of world history.

D.B. DAVIS, The Problem of Slavery in Western Culture (1966). A brilliant and far-ranging discussion.

D. ELTIS, The Rise of African Slavery in the Americas (1999). Detailed discussion of the size and scope of the Atlantic market, with attention to the role of Africans on both sides of the Atlantic.

H.L. GATES JR. and W.L. ANDREWS, eds., Pioneers of the Black Atlantic: Five Slave Narratives from the Enlightenment, 1772–1815 (1998). An anthology of autobiographical accounts.

S. GRUZINSKI, The Conquest of Mexico: The Incorporation of Indian Societies into the Western World, 16th–18th Centuries (1993). Interprets the experience of Native Americans, from their own point of view, during the time of the Spanish conquest.

L. HANKE, Bartolomé de Las Casas: An Interpretation of His Life and Writings (1951). A classic work.

R. HARMS, The Diligent: A Voyage through the Worlds of the Slave Trade (2002). A powerful narrative of the voyage of a French slave trader.

J. HEMMING, The Conquest of the Incas, rev. ed., (2003). A lucid account of the conquest of the Inca Empire and its aftermath.

J. HEMMING, Red Gold: The Conquest of the Brazilian Native Americans, 1500–1760 (1978). A careful account with excellent bibliography.

H. KLEIN, The Atlantic Slave Trade (1999). A synthesis of scholarly knowledge.

W. KLOOSTER and A. PADULA, The Atlantic World: Essays on Slavery, Migration, and Imagination (2004). Essays by leading scholars examine important aspects of the creation of a new way of living – and a new way of thinking about the world.

P.E. LOVEJOY, Transformations in Slavery: A History of Slavery in Africa (2000). An important new evaluation of slavery as it was practiced within Africa, and its relation to the Islamic and trans-Atlantic slave trades.

K. MANN, Rethinking the African Diaspora: The Making of a Black Atlantic World in the Bight of Benin and Brazil (2005). This analysis of the dynamics of human and cultural migration and exchange on the busiest route of the slave trade is a significant addition to Atlantic World scholarship.

P. MANNING, Slavery and African Life: Occidental, Oriental, and African Slave Trades (1990). An admirably concise economic-historical synthesis of the evidence, with multiple tables and statistics to supplement the magisterial analysis.

A. PAGDEN, Lords of All the World: Ideologies of Empire in Spain, Britain, and France c. 1500–c. 1800 (1995). An effort to explain the imperial thinking of the major European powers.

S. PEABODY & K. GRINBERG, Slavery, Freedom, and the Law in the Atlantic World: A Brief History with Documents (2007). Examines the legal frameworks through which slavery was institutionalized, and documents the many ways people challenged slavery.

D.K. RICHTER, Facing East from Indian Country: A Native History of Early America (new ed. 2003). Uses the biographies of three Native Americans to offer a fresh perspective on North American history from the time of Columbus to the American Revolution.

S.B. SCHWARTZ, ed., Tropical Babylons: Sugar and the Making of the Atlantic World, 1450–1680 (2003). A comprehensive examination of the role of sugar in the plantation economy.

I.K. STEELE, The English Atlantic, 1675–1740s: An Exploration of Communication and Community (1986). An exploration of culture and commerce in the transatlantic world.

H. THOMAS, Conquest: Montezuma, Cortés, and the Fall of Old Mexico (1993). A splendid modern narrative of the event, with careful attention to the character of the participants.

H. THOMAS, The Slave Trade: The Story of the Atlantic Slave Trade: 1440–1870 (1999). A sweeping narrative overview.

J. THORNTON, Africa and Africans in the Making of the Atlantic World, 1400–1680 (1992). A discussion of the role of Africans in the emergence of the transatlantic economy.

J. THORNTON, The Kongolese Saint Anthony: Dona Beatriz Kimpa Vita and the Antonian Movement, 1684 – 1706 (1998). Describes a fascinating period in Kongolese history, when Beatriz Kimpa Vita led a Christian movement during a time of political and social turmoil.

N. WACHTEL, The Vision of the Vanquished: The Spanish Conquest of Peru Through Indian Eyes, 1530–1570 (1977). A presentation of Incan experience of conquest.

Chapter 19

China

D. BODDE and C. MORRIS, Law in Imperial China (1967). Focuses on the Qing dynasty (1644–1911).

T. BROOK, The Confusions of Pleasure: Commerce and Culture in Ming China (1988).

C.S. CHANG and S.L.H. CHANG, Crisis and Transformation in Seventeenth-century China: Society, Culture, and Modernity (1992).

P. CROSSLEY, Translucent Mirror: History and Identity in Qing Imperial Ideology (1999).

W.T. DE BARY, Learning for One's Self: Essays on the Individual in Neo-Confucian Thought (1991). A useful corrective to the view that Confucianism is simply a social ideology.

M.C. ELLIOTT, The Manchu Way: The Eight Banners and Ethnic Identity in Late Imperial China (2001). The latest word; compare to Crossley above.

M. ELVIN, The Pattern of the Chinese Past: A Social and Economic Interpretation (1973). A controversial but stimulating interpretation of Chinese economic history in terms of technology. It brings in earlier periods as well as the Ming, Qing, and modern China.

J.K. FAIRBANK, ed., The Chinese World Order: Traditional China's Foreign Relations (1968). An examination of the Chinese tribute system and its varying applications.

H.L. KAHN, Monarchy in the Emperor's Eyes: Image and Reality in the Ch'ien-lung Reign (1971). A study of the Chinese court during the mid-Qing period.

P. KUHN, Soulstealers: The Chinese Sorcery Scare of 1768 (1990).

LI YU, The Carnal Prayer Mat, trans. by P. Hanan (1990).

F. MOTE and D. TWITCHETT, eds., The Cambridge History of China: The Ming Dynasty 1368–1644, Vols. VI (1988) and VII (1998).

S. NAQUIN, Peking Temples and City Life, 1400–1900 (2000).

S. NAQUIN and E.S. RAWSKI, Chinese Society in the Eighteenth Century (1987).

J.B. PARSONS, The Peasant Rebellions of the Late Ming Dynasty (1970).

P.C. PERDUE, Exhausting the Earth, State and Peasant in Hunan, 1500–1850 (1987).

D.H. PERKINS, Agricultural Development in China, 1368–1968 (1969).

E. RAWSKI, The Last Emperors: A Social History of Qing Imperial Institutions (1998).

M. RICCI, China in the Sixteenth Century: The Journals of Matthew Ricci, 1583–1610 (1953).

W. ROWE, Hankow (1984). A study of a city in late imperial China.

G.W. SKINNER, The City in Late Imperial China (1977).

J.D. SPENCE, Ts'ao Yin and the K'ang-hsi Emperor: Bondservant and Master (1966). An excellent study of the early Qing court.

J.D. SPENCE, Emperor of China: A Self-Portrait of K'ang-hsi (1974). The title of this readable book does not adequately convey the extent of the author's contribution to the study of the early Qing emperor.

J.D. SPENCE, Treason by the Book (2001). An account of the legal workings of the authoritarian Qing state that reads like a detective story.

L.A. STRUVE, TRANS. and ed., Voices from the Ming-Qing Cataclysm (1993). A reader with translations of Chinese sources.

F. WAKEMAN, The Great Enterprise (1985). On the founding of the Manchu dynasty.

Japan

M.E. BERRY, Hideyoshi (1982). A study of the sixteenth-century unifier of Japan.

M.E. BERRY, The Culture of Civil War in Kyoto (1994). On the Warring States era.

H. BOLITHO, Treasures Among Men: The Fudai Daimyo in Tokugawa Japan (1974). A study in depth.

H. BOLITHO, Bereavement and Consolation: Testimonies from Tokugawa Japan (2003). Instances of how Tokugawa Japanese handled the death of a child.

C.R. BOXER, The Christian Century in Japan, 1549–1650 (1951).

The Cambridge History of Japan; Vol. 4 J.W. Hall (ed.), Early Modern Japan (1991). A multi-author work.

M. CHIKAMATSU, Major Plays of Chikamatsu, trans. by D. Keene (1961).

R.P. DORE, Education in Tokugawa Japan (1965).

G.S. ELISON, Deus Destroyed: The Image of Christianity in Early Modern Japan (1973). A brilliant study of the persecutions of Christianity during the early Tokugawa period.

J.W. HALL and M. JANSEN, eds., Studies in the Institutional History of Early Modern Japan (1968). A collection of articles on Tokugawa institutions.

J.W. HALL, K. NAGAHARA, and K. YAMAMURA, eds., Japan Before Tokugawa (1981).

S. HANLEY, Everyday Things in Premodern Japan: The Hidden Legacy of Material Culture (1997).

H.S. HIBBETT, The Floating World in Japanese Fiction (1959). An eminently readable study of early Tokugawa literature.

M. JANSEN, ed., The Nineteenth Century, Vol. 5 in The Cambridge History of Japan (1989).

K. KATSU, Musui's Story (1988). The life and adventures of a boisterous, no-good samurai of the early nineteenth century. Eminently readable.

D. KEENE, TRANS., Chushingura, the Treasury of Loyal Retainers (1971). The puppet play about the forty-seven men who took revenge on the enemy of their former lord.

O.G. LIDIN, Tanegashima: The Arrival of Europe in Japan (2002). The impact of the musket and Europeans on sixteenth-century Japan.

M. MARUYAMA, Studies in the Intellectual History of Tokugawa Japan, trans. by M. Hane (1974). A seminal work in this field by one of modern Japan's greatest scholars.

J.L. MCCLAIN, ET. AL., Edo and Paris: Urban Life and the State in the Early Modern Era (1994). Comparison of city life and government role in capitals of Tokugawa Japan and France.

K.W. NAKAI, Shogunal Politics (1988). A brilliant study of Arai Hakuseki's conceptualization of Tokugawa government.

P. NOSCO, ed., Confucianism and Tokugawa Culture (1984). A lively collection of essays.

H. OOMS, Tokugawa Village Practice: Class, Status, Power, Law (1996).

A. RAVINA, Land and Lordship in Early Modern Japan (1999). A sociopolitical study of three Tokugawa domains.

I. SAIKAKU, The Japanese Family Storehouse, trans. by G.W. Sargent (1959). A lively novel about merchant life in seventeenth-century Japan.

G.B. SANSOM, The Western World and Japan (1950).

J.A. SAWADA, Confucian Values and Popular Zen (1993). A study of Shingaku, a popular Tokugawa religious sect.

C.D. SHELDON, The Rise of the Merchant Class in Tokugawa Japan (1958).

T.C. SMITH, The Agrarian Origins of Modern Japan (1959). On the evolution of farming and rural social organization in Tokugawa Japan.

P.F. SOUYRI, The World Turned Upside Down: Medieval Japanese Society (2001). After a running start from the late Heian period, an analysis of the overthrow of lords by their vassals.

R.P. TOBY, State and Diplomacy in Early Modern Japan: Asia in the Development of the Tokugawa Bakufu (1984).

C. TOTMAN, Tokugawa Ieyasu: Shgun (1983).

C. TOTMAN, Green Archipelago, Forestry in Preindustrial Japan (1989).

H.P. VARLEY, The 'nin War: History of Its Origins and Background with a Selective Translation of the Chronicle of 'nin (1967).

K. YAMAMURA and S.B. HANLEY, Economic and Demographic Change in Preindustrial Japan, 1600–1868 (1977).

Korea

T. HATADA, A History of Korea (1969).

W.E. HENTHORN, A History of Korea (1971).

KI-BAIK LEE, A New History of Korea (1984).

P. LEE, Sourcebook of Korean Civilization, Vol. I (1993).

Vietnam

J. BUTTINGER, A Dragon Defiant, a Short History of Vietnam (1972).

NGUYEN DU, The Tale of Kieu (1983).

N. TARLING, ed., The Cambridge History of Southeast Asia (1992).

K. TAYLOR, The Birth of Vietnam (1983).

A.B. WOODSIDE, Vietnam and the Chinese Model (1988).

Chapter 20

F. ANDERSON, The Crucible of War: The Seven Years' War and the Fate of Empire in British North America, 1754–1766 (2000). A splendid narrative and analysis.

J. BLUM, Lord and Peasant in Russia from the Ninth to the Nineteenth Century (1961). Remains a thorough and wide-ranging discussion.

P. BURKE, The Fabrication of Louis XIV (1992). Examines the manner in which the public image of Louis XIV was forged in art.

P. BUSHKOVITCH, Peter the Great: The Struggle for Power, 1671–1725 (2001). Replaces previous studies.

L. COLLEY, Britons: Forging the Nation, 1707–1837 (1992) A major study of the making of British nationhood.

P. DEANE, The First Industrial Revolution, (1999). A well-balanced and systematic treatment.

J. DE VRIES, European Urbanization, 1500–1800 (1984). The most important and far-ranging of recent treatments of the subject.

W. DOYLE, The Old European Order, 1660–1800 (1992). The most thoughtful treatment of the subject.

R.J.W. EVANS, The Making of the Habsburg Monarchy, 1550–1700: An Interpretation (1979). Places much emphasis on intellectual factors and the role of religion.

D. FRASER, Frederick the Great: King of Prussia (2001) Excellent on both Frederick and eighteenth-century Prussia.

E. HOBSBAWM, Industry and Empire: The Birth of the Industrial Revolution (1999). A survey by a major historian of the subject.

K. HONEYMAN, Women, Gender and Industrialization in England, 1700–1850 (2000). Emphasizes how certain work or economic roles became associated with either men or women.

O.H. HUFTON, The Poor of Eighteenth-Century France, 1750–1789 (1975). A brilliant study of poverty and the family economy.

L. HUGHES, *Russia in the Age of Peter the Great* (1998). An excellent account.

D.I. KERTZER and M. BARBAGLI, *The History of the European Family: Family Life in Early Modern Times, 1500–1709* (2001). A series of broad-ranging essays covering the entire Continent.

S. KING and G. TIMMONS, *Making Sense of the Industrial Revolution: English Economy and Society, 1700–1850* (2001). Examines the Industrial Revolution through the social institutions that brought it about and were changed by it.

M. KISHLANSKY, *A Monarchy Transformed: Britain 1603–1714* (1996) An excellent synthesis.

P.L ANGFORD, *A Polite and Commercial People: England 1717–1783* (1989). An excellent survey of mid-eighteenth-century Britain covering social history as well as politics, the overseas wars, and the American Revolution.

A. LOSSKY, *Louis XIV and the French Monarchy* (1994). The most recent major analysis.

F.E. MANUEL, *The Broken Staff: Judaism Through Christian Eyes* (1992). An important discussion of Christian interpretations of Judaism.

M.A. MEYER, *The Origins of the Modern Jew: Jewish Identity and European Culture in Germany, 1749–1824* (1967). A general introduction organized around individual case studies.

D. UNDERDOWN, *Fire from Heaven: Life in an English Town in the Seventeenth Century* (1992). A lively account of how a single English town experienced the religious and political turmoil of the century.

D. VALENZE, *The First Industrial Woman* (1995). An elegant work exploring the manner in which industrialization transformed the work of women.

J. WEST, *Gunpower, Government, and War in the Mid–Eighteenth Century* (1991). A study of how warfare touched much government of the day.

Chapter 21

S.S. BLAIR and J. BLOOM, *The Art and Architecture of Islam, 1250–1800* (1994). A fine survey of the period for all parts of the Islamic world.

R. CANFIELD, ed., *Turko-Persia in Historical Perspctive* (1991). A good general collection of essays.

K. CHELEBI, *The Balance of Truth* (1957). A marvelous volume of essays and reflections by probably the major intellectual of Ottoman times.

W.T. DE BARY ET AL., COMP., *Sources of Indian Tradition*, 2nd ed. (1958),Vol. I, From the Beginning to 1800, ed. and rev. by Ainslie T. Embree (1988). Excellent selections from a wide variety of Indian texts, with good introductions to chapters and individual selections.

S. FAROQI, *Towns and Townsmen of Ottoman Anatolia* (1984). Examines the changing balances of economic power between the urban and rural areas.

C.H. FLEISCHER, *Bureaucrat and Intellectual in the Ottoman Empire: The Historian Mustafa Ali (1541–1600)* (1986). A major study of Ottoman intellectual history.

G. HAMBLY, *Central Asia* (1966). Excellent survey chapters (9–13) on the Chaghatay and Uzbek (Shaybanid) Turks.

R.S. HATTOX, *Coffee and Coffee-Houses: The Origins of a Social Beverage in the Medieval Near East* (1985). A fascinating piece of social history.

M.G.S. HODGSON, *The Gunpowder Empires and Modern Times*, Vol. 3 of The Venture of Islam, 3 vols. (1974). Less ample than Vols. 1 and 2 of Hodgson's monumental history, but a thoughtful survey of the great post-1500 empires.

S.M. IKRAM, *Muslim Civilization in India* (1964). Still the best short survey history, covering the period from 711 to 1857.

H. INALCIK, *The Ottoman Empire: The Classical Age, 1300–1600* (1973). An excellent, if dated, survey with solid treatment of Ottoman social, religious, and political institutions.

H. INALCIK, *An Economic and Social History of the Ottoman Empire, 1300–1914* (1994). A masterly survey by the dean of Ottoman studies today.

C. KAFADAR, *Between Two Worlds: The Construction of the Ottoman State* (1995). A readable analysis of theories of Ottoman origins and early development.

N.R. KEDDIE, ed., *Scholars, Saints, and Sufis: Muslim Religious Institutions in the Middle East Since 1500* (1972). A collection of interesting articles well worth reading.

M. MUJEEB, *The Indian Muslims* (1967). The best cultural study of Islamic civilization in India as a whole, from its origins onward.

G. NECIPOGLU, *Architecture, Ceremonial, and Power: The Topkapi Palace in the Fifteenth and Sixteenth Centuries* (1991). A superb analysis of the symbolism of Ottoman power and authority.

L. PIERCE, *The Imperial Harem: Women and Sex in the Ottoman Empire* (1993). Ground-breaking study on the role of women in the Ottoman Empire.

D. QUATARERT, *An Economic and Social History of the Ottoman Empire, 1300–1914* (1994). The authoritative account of Ottoman economy and society.

J. RICHARDS, *The Mughal Empire*, Vol. 5 of The New Cambridge History of India (1993). A impressive synthesis of the varying interpretations of Mughal India.

S.A.A. RIZVI, *The Wonder That Was India*, Vol. II (1987). A sequel to Basham's original The Wonder That Was India; treats Mughal life, culture, and history from 1200 to 1700.

F. ROBINSON, *Atlas of the Islamic World Since 1500* (1982). Brief, excellent historical essays, color illustrations with detailed accompanying text, and chronological tables, as well as precise maps, make this a refreshing general reference work.

R. SAVORY, *Iran Under the Safavids* (1980). A solid and readable survey.

S.J. SHAW, *Empire of the Gazis: The Rise and Decline of the Ottoman Empire, 1280–1808*, Vol. I of History of the Ottoman Empire and Modern Turkey (1976). A solid historical survey with excellent bibliographic essays for each chapter and a good index.

Chapter 22

D. BEALES, *Joseph II: In the Shadow of Maria Theresa, 1741–1780* (1987). The best treatment in English of the early political life of Joseph II.

M. BIAGIOLI, *Galileo Courtier: The Practice of Science in the Culture of Absolutism* (1993). A major revisionist work that emphasizes the role of the political setting on Galileo's career and thought.

D.D. BIEN, *The Calas Affair: Persecution, Toleration, and Heresy in Eighteenth-Century Toulouse* (1960). Classic treatment of the famous case.

T.C.W. BLANNING, *The Culture of Power and the Power of Culture: Old Regime Europe 1660–l789* (2002). The strongest treatment of the relationship of eighteenth-century cultural changes and politics.

R. DARNTON, *The Literary Underground of the Old Regime* (1982). Classic essays on the world of printers, publishers, and booksellers.

P. DEAR, *Revolutionizing the Sciences: European Knowledge and Its Ambitions, 1500–1700* (2001). A broad-ranging study of both the ideas and institutions of the new science.

I. DE MADARIAGA, *Catherine the Great: A Short History* (1990). A good brief biography.

S. GAUKROGER, *Francis Bacon and the Transformation of Early-Modern Philosophy* (2001). An excellent, accessible introduction.

J. GLEIXK, *Isaac Newton* (2003) The best brief biography.

D. GOODMAN, *The Republic of Letters: A Cultural History of the French Enlightenment* (1994). Concentrates on the role of salons.

I. HARRIS, *The Mind of John Locke: A Study of Political Theory in Its Intellectual Setting* (1994). The most comprehensive recent treatment.

J.L. HEILBRON, The Sun in the Church: Cathedrals as Solar Observatories (2000). A remarkable study of the manner in which Roman Catholic cathedrals were used to make astsronomical observations and calculations.

K.J. HOWELL, God's Two Books: Copernican Cosmology and Biblical Interpretqation in Early Modern Science (2003). Best introduction to early modern issues of science and religion.

J. MELTON, The Rise of the Public in Enlightenmen Europe (2001). A superb overview of the emergence of new institutions that made the expression of a broad public opinion possible in Europe.

T. MUNCK, The Enlightenment: A Comparative Social History 1721–1794 (2000). A clear introduction to the social background that made possible the spread of Enlightenment thought.

S. MUTHU, Enlightenment against Empire (2003) A study of philosophes who criticized the European empires of their day.

D. OUTRAM, The Enlightenment (1995). An excellent brief introduction.

R. PORTER, The Creation of the Modern World: The Untold Story of the British Enlightenment (2001). A superb, lively overview.

P. RILEY, The Cambridge Companion to Rousseau (2001). Excellent accessible essays by major scholars.

E. ROTHCHILD, Economic Sentiments: Adam Smith, Condorcet, and the Enlightenment (2001). A sensitive account of Smith's thought and its relationship to the social questions of the day.

S. SHAPIN, The Scientific Revolution (1996). An important revisionist survey emphasizing social factors.

L. STEINBRÜGGE, The Moral Sex: Woman's Nature in the French Enlightenment (1995). Emphasizes the conservative nature of Enlightenment thought on women.

P. ZAGORIN, How the Idea of Religious Toleration Came to the West (2003) An excellent exploration of the rise of toleration.

Chapter 23

R. ANSTEY, The Atlantic Slave Trade and British Abolition, 1760–1810 (1975). A standard overview that emphasizes the role of religious factors.

B. BAILYN, The Ideological Origins of the American Revolution (1967). An important work illustrating the role of English radical thought in the perceptions of the American colonists.

K.M. BAKER, Inventing the French Revolution: Essays on French Political Culture in the Eighteenth Century (1990). Important essays on political thought before and during the revolution.

K.M. BAKER and C. LUCAS, eds., The French Revolution and the Creation of Modern Political Culture, 3 vols. (1987). A splendid collection of important original articles on all aspects of politics during the revolution.

R.J. BARMAN, Brazil: The Forging of a Nation, 1798–1852 (1988). The best coverage of this period.

C. BECKER, The Declaration of Independence: A Study in the History of Political Ideas (1922). Remains an important examination of the political and imperial theory of the Declaration.

J.F. BERNARD, Talleyrand: A Biography (1973). A useful account.

L. BETHELL, The Cambridge History of Latin America, Vol. 3 (1985). Contains an extensive treatment of independence.

R. BLACKBURN, The Overthrow of Colonial Slavery, 1776–1848 (1988). A major discussion quite skeptical of the humanitarian interpretation.

T.C.W. BLANNING, ed., The Rise and Fall of the French Revolution (1996). A wide-ranging collection of essays illustrating the debates over the French Revolution.

J. BROOKE, King George III (1972). The best biography.

R. COBB, The People's Armies (1987). The major treatment in English of the revolutionary army.

O. CONNELLY, Napoleon's Satellite Kingdoms (1965). The rule of Napoleon and his family in Europe.

E.V. DA COSTA, The Brazilian Empire (1985). Excellent coverage of the entire nineteenth-century experience of Brazil.

D.B. DAVIS, The Problem of Slavery in the Age of Revolution, 1770–1823 (1975). A transatlantic perspective on the issue.

F. FEHÉR, The French Revolution and the Birth of Modernity (1990). A wide-ranging collection of essays on political and cultural facets of the revolution.

A. FORREST, The French Revolution and the Poor (1981). A study that expands consideration of the revolution beyond the standard social boundaries.

M. GLOVER, The Peninsular War, 1807–1814: A Concise Military History (1974). An interesting account of the military campaign that so drained Napoleon's resources in western Europe.

J. GODECHOT, The Counter-Revolution: Doctrine and Action, 1789–1804 (1971). An examination of opposition to the revolution.

A. GOODWIN, The Friends of Liberty: The English Democratic Movement in the Age of the French Revolution (1979). A major work that explores the impact of the French Revolution on English radicalism.

L. HUNT, Politics, Culture, and Class in the French Revolution (1986). A series of essays that focus on the modes of expression of the revolutionary values and political ideas.

W.W. KAUFMANN, British Policy and the Independence of Latin America, 1802–1828 (1951). A standard discussion of an important relationship.

E. KENNEDY, A Cultural History of the French Revolution (1989). An important examination of the role of the arts, schools, clubs, and intellectual institutions.

M. KENNEDY, The Jacobin Clubs in the French Revolution: The First Years (1982). A careful scrutiny of the organizations chiefly responsible for the radicalizing of the revolution.

M. KENNEDY, The Jacobin Clubs in the French Revolution: The Middle Years (1988). A continuation of the previously listed study.

H. KISSINGER, A World Restored: Metternich, Castlereagh and the Problems of Peace, 1812–1822 (1957). A provocative study by an author who became an American secretary of state.

G. LEFEBVRE, The Coming of the French Revolution (trans. 1947). A classic examination of the crisis of the French monarchy and the events of 1789.

G. LEFEBVRE, Napoleon, 2 vols., trans. by H. Stockhold (1969). The fullest and finest biography.

J. LYNCH, The Spanish American Revolutions, 1808–1826 (1986). An excellent one-volume treatment.

P. MAIER, American Scripture: Making the Declaration of Independence (1997). Stands as a major revision of our understanding of the Declaration.

G. MASUR, Simón Bolívar (1969). The standard biography in English.

S.E. MELZER and L.W. RABINE, eds., Rebel Daughters: Women and the French Revolution (1992). A collection of essays exploring various aspects of the role and image of women in the French Revolution.

M. MORRIS, The British Monarchy and the French Revolution (1998). Explores the manner in which the British monarchy saved itself from possible revolution.

R. MUIR, Tactics and the Experience of Battle in the Age of Napoleon (1998). Examines the wars from the standpoint of the soldiers in combat.

H. NICOLSON, The Congress of Vienna (1946). A good, readable account.

T.O. OTT, The Haitian Revolution, 1789–1804 (1973). An account that clearly relates the events in Haiti to those in France.

R.R. PALMER, Twelve Who Ruled: The Committee of Public Safety During the Terror (1941). A clear narrative and analysis of the policies and problems of the committee.

R.R. PALMER, The Age of the Democratic Revolution: A Political History of Europe and America, 1760–1800, 2 vols. (1959, 1964). An impressive survey of the political turmoil in the transatlantic world.

C. PROCTOR, Women, Equality, and the French Revolution (1990). An examination of how the ideas of the Enlightenment and the attitudes of revolutionaries affected the legal status of women.

A.J. RUSSELL-WOOD, ed., From Colony to Nation: Essays on the Independence of Brazil (1975). A series of important essays.

P. SCHROEDER, The Transformation of European Politics, 1763–1848 (1994). A fundamental treatment of the diplomacy of the era.

T.E. SKIDMORE and P.H. SMITH, Modern Latin America, 4th ed. (1997). A very useful survey.

A. SOBOUL, The Parisian Sans-Culottes and the French Revolution, 1793–94 (1964). The best work on the subject.

A. SOBOUL, The French Revolution (trans. 1975). An important work by a Marxist scholar.

D.G. SUTHERLAND, France, 1789–1825: Revolution and Counter-revolution (1986). A major synthesis based on recent scholarship in social history.

T. TACKETT, Religion, Revolution, and Regional Culture in Eighteenth-Century France: The Ecclesiastical Oath of 1791 (1986). The most important study of this topic.

T. TACKETT, Becoming a Revolutionary: The Deputies of the French National Assembly and the Emergence of a Revolutionary Culture (1789–1790) (1996). The best study of the early months of the revolution.

J.M. THOMPSON, Robespierre, 2 vols. (1935). The best biography.

D.K. VAN KEY, The Religious Origins of the French Revolution: From Calvin to the Civil Constitution, 1560–1791 (1996). Examines the manner in which debates within French Catholicism influenced the coming of the revolution.

M. WALZER, ed., Regicide and Revolution: Speeches at the Trial of Louis XVI (1974). An important and exceedingly interesting collection of documents with a useful introduction.

I. WOLOCH, The New Regime: Transformations of the French Civic Order, 1789–1820s (1994). An important overview of just what had and had not changed in France after the quarter century of revolution and war.

G. WOOD, The Radicalism of the American Revolution (1991). A major interpretation.

Chapter 24

I. BERLIN, Generations of Captivity: A History of African-American Slaves (2003) A major work.

D. BLACKBOURN, The Long Nineteenth Century: A History of Germany, 1780–1918 (1998). An outstanding survey.

D.G. CREIGHTON, John A. MacDonald (1952, 1955). A major biography of the first Canadian prime minister.

D. DONALD, Lincoln (1995). Now the standard biography.

R.B. EDGERTON, Death or Glory: The Legacy of the Crimean War (2000). Multifaceted study of a badly mismanaged war that transformed many aspects of European domestic politics.

M. HOLT, The Rise and Fall of the American Whig Party: Jacksonian Politics and the Onset of the Civil War (2003) An extensive survey of the Jacksonian era.

R. KEE, The Green Flag: A History of Irish Nationalism (2001). A vast survey.

W. LACQUER, A History of Zionism (1989). The most extensive one-volume treatment.

M.B. LEVINGER, Enlightened Nationalism: The Transformation of Prussian Political Culture, 1806–1848 (2002). A major work based on the most recent scholarship.

J.M. MCPHERSON, The Battle Cry of Freedom: The Civil War Era (1988). An excellent one-volume treatment.

D. MORTON, A Short History of Canada (2001). Useful popular history.

J.P. PARRY, The Rise and Fall of Liberal Government in Victorian Britain (1994). An outstanding study.

A. PLESSIS, The Rise and Fall of the Second Empire, 1852–1871 (1985). A useful survey of France under Napoleon III.

D.M. POTTER, The Impending Crisis, 1848–1861 (1976) A penetrating study of the coming of the American Civil War.

A. SKED, Decline and Fall of the Habsburg Empire, 1815–1918 (2001). A major, accessible survey of a difficult subject.

D.M. SMITH, Cavour (1984). An excellent biography.

C.P. STACEY, Canada and the Age of Conflict (1977, 1981). A study of Canadian foreign relations.

D. WETZEL, A Duel of Giants: Bismarck, Napoleon III, and the Origins of the Franco-Prussian War (2001). Broad study based on most recent scholarship.

Chapter 25

M. ADAS, Machines as the Measure of Men: Science, Technology, and Ideologies of Western Dominance (1989). The best single volume on racial thinking and technological advances as forming ideologies of European colonial dominance.

A. ASCHER and P.A. STOLYPIN, The Search for Stability in Late Imperial Russia (2000). A broad-ranging biography based on extensive research.

I. BERLIN, Karl Marx: His Life and Environment, 4th ed. (1996). A classic volume that remains an excellent introduction.

JANET BROWNE, Charles Darwin, 2 vols. (2002) An eloquent, accessible biography.

J. BURROW, The Crisis of Reason: European Thought, 1848–1914 (2000). The best overview available.

A.D. CHANDLER JR., The Visible Hand: Managerial Revolution in American Business (1977). Remains the best discussion of the innovative role of American business.

A. CLARKE, The Struggle for the Breeches: Gender and the Making of the British Working Class (1995). An examination of the manner in which industrialization made problematical the relationships between men and women.

W. CRONIN, Nature's Metropolis: Chicago and the Great West, 1848–1893 (1991) The best examination of any major American nineteenth-century city.

P. GAY, Freud: A Life for Our Time (1988). The new standard biography.

R.F. HAMILTON, Marxism, Revisionism, and Leninism: Explication, Assessment, and Commentary (2000). A contribution from the perspective of a historically minded sociologist.

S. HAHN, A Nation under Our Feet: Black Political Struggles in the Rural South from Slavey to the Great Migration (2003). A major synthesis.

A. HOURANI, Arab Thought in the Liberal Age 1789–1939 (1967). A classic account, clearly written and accessible to the nonspecialist.

D.I. KERTZER and M. BARBAGLI, eds., Family Life in the Long Nineteenth Century, 1789–1913: The History of the European Family (2002). Wide-ranging collection of essays.

J.T. KLOPPENBERG, Uncertain Victory: Social Democracy and Progressivism in European and American Thought (1986). An extremely important comparative study.

J. KÖHLER, Zarathustra's Secret: The Interior Life of Friedrich Nietzsche (2002). A controversial new biography.

L. KOLAKOWSKI, Main Currents of Marxism: Its Rise, Growth, and Dissolution, 3 vols. (1978). Especially good on the last years of the nineteenth century and the early years of the twentieth.

P. KRAUSE, The Battle for Homestead, 1880–1892 (1992). Examines labor relations in the steel industry.

D. LANDES, The Wealth and Poverty of Nations: Why Some Are So Rich and Some So Poor (1998). A major international discussion of the subject.

M. MCGERR, A Fierce Discontent: The Rise and Fall of the Progressive Moevement in America, 1870–1920 (2003). The best recent synthesis.

E. MORRIS, Theodore Rex (2002). Major survey of Theodore Roosevelt's presidency and personality.

A. PAIS, Subtle Is the Lord: The Science and Life of Albert Einstein (1983). Remains the most accessible scientific biography.

J. RENDALL, The Origins of Modern Feminism: Women in Britain, France and the United States, 1780–1860 (1985). A well-informed introduction.

R. SERVICE, Lenin: A Biography (2002). Based on new sources and will no doubt become the standard biography.

R.M. UTLEY, The Indian Frontier and the American West, 1846–1890 (1984). A broad survey of the pressures of white civilization against Native Americans.

D. VITAL, A People Apart: The Jews in Modern Europe, 1789–1939 (1999). A deeply informed survey.

Chapter 26

S. ARROM, The Women of Mexico City, 1790–1857 (1985). A pioneering study.

E. BERMAN, ed., Women, Culture, and Politics in Latin America (1990). Useful essays.

L. BETHELL, ed., The Cambridge History of Latin America, 8 vols. (1992). The single most authoritative coverage, with extensive bibliographical essays.

V. BULMER-THOMAS, The Economic History of Latin America Since Independence (1994). A major study in every respect.

E.B. BURNS, The Poverty of Progress: Latin America in the Nineteenth Century (1980). Argues that the elites suppressed alternative modes of cultural and economic development.

E.B. BURNS, A History of Brazil (1993). The most useful one-volume treatment.

D. BUSHNELL and N. MACAULAY, The Emergence of Latin America in the Nineteenth Century (1994). A survey that examines the internal development of Latin America during the period.

R. CONRAD, The Destruction of Brazilian Slavery, 1850–1889 (1971). A good survey of the most important problem in Brazil in the second half of the nineteenth century.

R. CONRAD, World of Sorrow: The African Slave Trade to Brazil (1986). An excellent survey of the subject.

E.V. DA COSTA, The Brazilian Empire: Myths and Histories (1985). Essays that provide a thorough introduction to Brazil during the period of empire.

H.S. FERNS, Britain and Argentina in the Nineteenth Century (1968). Explains clearly the intermeshing of the two economies.

M. FONT, Coffee, Contention, and Change in the Making of Modern Brazil (1990). Extensive discussion of the problems of a single-commodity economy.

R. GRAHAM, Britain and the Onset of Modernization in Brazil (1968). Another study of British economic dominance.

S.H. HABER, Industry and Underdevelopment: The Industrialization of Mexico, 1890–1940 (1989). Examines the problem of industrialization before and after the revolution.

G. HAHNER, Emancipating the Female Sex: The Struggle for Women's Rights in Brazil, 1850–1940 (1990). An extensive examination of a relatively understudied issue in Latin America.

C.H. HARING, Empire in Brazil: A New World Experiment with Monarchy (1958). Remains a useful overview.

J. HEMMING, Amazon Frontier: The Defeat of the Brazilian Indians (1987). A brilliant survey of the experience of Native Americans in modern Brazil.

R.A. HUMPHREYS, Latin America and the Second World War, 2 vols. (1981–1982). The standard work on the topic.

F. KATZ, ed., Riot, Rebellion, and Revolution in Mexico: Social Base of Agrarian Violence, 1750–1940 (1988). Essays that put the violence of the revolution in a longer context.

A. KNIGHT, The Mexican Revolution, 2 vols. (1986). The best treatment of the subject.

S. MAINWARING, The Catholic Church and Politics in Brazil, 1916–1985 (1986). An examination of a key institution in Brazilian life.

M.C. MEYER and W.L. SHERMAN, The Course of Mexican History (1995). An excellent survey.

M. MORNER, Adventurers and Proletarians: The Story of Migrants in Latin America (1985). Examines immigration to Latin America and migration within it.

J. PAGE, Perón: A Biography (1983). The standard English treatment.

D. ROCK, Politics in Argentina, 1890–1930: The Rise and Fall of Radicalism (1975). The major discussion of the Argentine Radical Party.

D. ROCK, Argentina, 1516–1987: From Spanish Colonization to Alfonsín (1987). Now the standard survey.

D. ROCK, ed., Latin America in the 1940s: War and Postwar Transitions (1994). Essays examining a very difficult decade for the continent.

R.M. SCHNEIDER, "Order and Progress": A Political History of Brazil (1991). A straightforward narrative with helpful notes for further reading.

T.E. SKIDMORE, Black into White: Race and Nationality in Brazilian Thought (1993). Examines the role of racial theory in Brazil.

P.H. SMITH, Argentina and the Failure of Democracy: Conflict Among Political Elites. 1904–1955 (1974). An examination of one of the major political puzzles of Latin American history.

S.J. STEIN and B.H. STEIN, The Colonial Heritage of Latin America: Essays on Economic Dependence in Perspective (1970). A major statement of the dependence interpretation.

D. TAMARIN, The Argentine Labor Movement, 1930–1945: A Study in the Origins of Perónism (1985). A useful introduction to a complex subject.

H.J. WIARDA, Politics and Social Change in Latin America: The Distinct Tradition (1974). Excellent essays that stress the ongoing role of Iberian traditions.

J.D. WIRTH, ed., Latin American Oil Companies and the Politics of Energy (1985). A series of case studies.

J. WOLFE, Working Women, Working Men: São Paulo and the Rise of Brazil's Industrial Working Class, 1900–1955 (1993). Pays particular attention to the role of women.

J. WOMACK, Zapata and the Mexican Revolution (1968). A classic study.

Chapter 27

General Works

S. COOK, Colonial Encounters in the Age of High Imperialism (1996). A good introduction to the imperial enterprise in Africa and Asia.

D.K. FIELDHOUSE, The West and the Third World. Trade: Colonialism, Depedence and Development (1999). Addresses whether colonialism was detrimental or beneficial to colonized peoples.

D. HEADRICK, The Tentacles of Progress: Technology Transfer in the Age of Imperialism, 1850–1940 (1988). Discusses the roles of new methods of transportation (railroads, steamships), forms of expertise (doctors, botanists), and other types of "technology transfer" in European colonization, and post-independence development.

P. HOPKIRK, The Great Game: The Struggle for Empire in Central Asia (1992). Focuses on the political and economic rivalries of the imperial powers.

India

A. AHMAD, Islamic Modernism in India and Pakistan, 1857–1964 (1967). The standard survey of Muslim thinkers and movements in India during the period.

C.A. BAYLY, Indian Society and the Making of the British Empire, The New Cambridge History of India, II. 1 (1988). One of several major contributions of this author to the ongoing revision of our picture of modern Indian history since the eighteenth century.

A. GHOSH, In an Antique Land: History in the Guise of a Traveler's Tale (1992). An anthropologist traces the footsteps of a premodern slave traveling with his master from North Africa to India. A gripping tale of premodern life in the India Ocean basin and also of contemporary Egypt.

R. GUHA, ed., Subaltern Studies: Writings on South Asian History and Society (1982). Essays on the colonial period that focus on the social, political, and economic history of "subaltern" groups and classes (hill tribes, peasants, etc.) rather than only the elites of India.

S.N. HAY, ed., "Modern India and Pakistan," Part VI of Wm. Theodore de Bary et al., eds., Sources of Indian Tradition, 2nd ed. (1988). A superb selection of primary-source documents, with brief introductions and helpful notes.

F. ROBINSON, ed., The Cambridge Encyclopedia of India, Pakistan, Bangladesh, Sri Lanka, Nepal, Bhutan, and the Maldives (1989). A fine collection of survey articles by various scholars, organized into topical chapters ranging from "Economies" to "Cultures."

Central Islamic Lands

J.J. DONAHUE and J.L. ESPOSITO, eds., Islam in Transition: Muslim Perspectives (1982). An interesting selection of primary-source materials on Islamic thinking in this century.

W. CLEVELAND, A History of the Modern Middle East, 3rd ed. (2004). A balanced and well-organized overview of modern Middle Eastern history.

A. DAWISHA, Arab Nationalism in the Twentieth Century, From Triumph to Despair (2003). A good overview of the development of Arab nationalism.

S. DERINGIL, The Well-Protected Domains: Ideology and the Legitimation of Power in the Ottoman Empire, 1876–1909 (1998). An impressive study on nationalism and reform in the Ottoman Empire.

D.F. EICKELMAN, Knowledge and Power in Morocco: The Education of a Twentieth-Century Notable (1985). A fascinating study of traditional Islamic education and society in the twentieth century through a social biography of a Moroccan religious scholar and judge.

A. HOURANI, Arabic Thought in the Liberal Age, 1798–1939 (1967). The standard work, by which all subsequent scholarship on the topic is to be judged.

N.R. KEDDIE, An Islamic Response to Imperialism (1968). A brief study of al-Afghani, the great Muslim reformer, with translations of a number of his writings.

B. LEWIS, The Emergence of Modern Turkey, 2nd ed. (1968). A concise but thorough history of the creation of the Turkish state, including nineteenth-century background.

J.O. VOLL, Islam: Continuity and Change in the Modern World (1982). Chapters 1–6. An interpretive survey of the Islamic world since the eighteenth century. Its emphasis on eighteenth-century reform movements is especially noteworthy.

Africa

C. ACHEBE, Things Fall Apart (1959). Reading this classic novel may be the best way to get a profound sense of the ways African and European cultures interacted in the early colonial period.

D. ANDERSON, Histories of the Hanged: The Dirty War in Kenya and the End of Empire (2005). This account of the Kikuyu-led Mau Mau movement in Kenya emphasizes the way Mau Mau activities, and the British response, shaped and distorted Kenya's independence movement. (See also C. Elkins' Imperial Reckoning..., below.)

A.A. BOAHEN, Africa Under Colonial Domination, 1880–1935 (1985). Vol. VII of the UNESCO General History of Africa. Excellent chapters on various regions of Africa in the period. Chapters 3–10 detail African resistance to European colonial intrusion in diverse regions.

W. CARTEY and M. KILSON, eds., The Africa Reader: Colonial Africa (1970). Original source materials give a vivid picture of African resistance to colonial powers, adaptation to foreign rule, and the emergence of the African masses as a political force.

P. CURTIN, S. FEIERMANN, L. THOMPSON, and J. VANSINA, African History (1978). The relevant portions are Chapters 10–20.

B. DAVIDSON, Modern Africa: A Social and Political History (1989). A very useful survey of African history.

C. ELKINS, Imperial Reckoning: The Untold Story of Britain's Gulag in Kenya (2004). The Pulitzer Prize–winning account of Britain's appalling response to the Mau Mau movement in colonial Kenya; while Elkins focuses on the British, D. Anderson in Histories of the Hanged (see above) emphasizes the Kenyan side of the story.

J.D. FAGE, A History of Africa (1978). The relevant chapters, which give a particularly clear overview of the colonial period, are 12–16.

B. FREUND, The Making of Contemporary Africa: The Development of African Society Since 1800 (1984). A refreshingly direct synthetic discussion and survey that take an avowedly, but not reductive, materialist approach to interpretation.

E. GILBERT and J.T. REYNOLDS, Africa in World History: From Prehistory to the Present (2004). An engaging overview of the period, with attention to technology, economics, and ideologies, among other factors. See especially chapters 13–15.

D. HEADRICK, Tools of Empire (1982). A provocative evaluation of the roles played by technology in the imperial venture.

A. HOCHSCHILD, King Leopold's Ghost: A Story of Greed, Terror, and Heroism in Colonial Africa (1998). A compelling, well-documented narrative of the atrocities committed in turn-of-the-twentieth-century Congo when it was held as the personal fiefdom of Belgium's monarch.

T. PAKENHAM, The Scramble for Africa (1991). An excellent analysis of the imperialist age in Africa.

A.D. ROBERTS, ed., The Colonial Moment in Africa: Essays on the Movement of Minds and Materials, 1900–1940 (1986). Chapters from The Cambridge History of Africa treating various aspects of the colonial period in Africa, including economics, politics, and religion.

Chapter 28

China

P.M. COBLE, The Shanghai Capitalists and the Nationalist Government, 1927–1937 (1980).

L.E. EASTMAN, The Abortive Revolution: China Under Nationalist Rule, 1927–1937 (1974).

L.E. EASTMAN, Seeds of Destruction: Nationalist China in War and Revolution, 1937–1949 (1984).

M. ELVIN and G.W. SKINNER, The Chinese City Between Two Worlds (1974). A study of the late Qing and Republican eras.

J.W. ESHERICK, The Origins of the Boxer Rebellion (1987).

S. ET, China's Republican Revolution (1994).

J.K. FAIRBANK and M. GOLDMAN, China, a New History (1998). A survey of the entire sweep of Chinese history; especially strong on the modern period.

J.K. FAIRBANK and D. TWITCHETT, eds., The Cambridge History of China. Like the premodern volumes in the same series, the volumes on modern China represent a survey of what is known. Volumes 10–15, which cover the history from the late Qing to the People's Republic, have been published, and the others will be available soon. The series is substantial. Each volume contains a comprehensive bibliography.

J. FITZGERALD, Awakening China: Politics, Culture, and Class in the Nationalist Revolution (1996).

C. HAO, Chinese Intellectuals in Crisis: Search for Order and Meaning, 1890–1911 (1987).

W.C. KIRBY, ed., State and Economy in Republican China (2001).

P.A. KUHN, Rebellion and Its Enemies in Late Imperial China: Militarization and Social Structure, 1796–1864 (1980). A study of how the Confucian gentry saved the Manchu dynasty after the Taiping Rebellion.

P. KUHN, Origins of the Modern Chinese State (2002).

J. LEVENSON, Liang Ch'i-ch'ao and the Mind of Modern China (1953). A classic study of a major Chinese reformer and thinker.

LU XUN, Selected Works (1960). Novels, stories, and other writings by modern China's greatest writer.

S. NAQUIN, Peking: Temples and City Life, 1400–1900 (2000).

E.O. REISCHAUER, J.K. FAIRBANK, and A.M. CRAIG, East Asia: Tradition and Transformation (1989). A detailed text on East Asian history. Contains ample chapters on Japan and China and shorter chapters on Korea and Vietnam.

H.Z. SCHIFFRIN, Sun Yat-sen, Reluctant Revolutionary (1980). A biography.

B.I. SCHWARTZ, Chinese Communism and the Rise of Mao (1951). A classic study of Mao, his thought, and the Chinese Communist Party before 1949.

B.I. SCHWARTZ, In Search of Wealth and Power: Yen Fu and the West (1964). A fine study of a late-nineteenth-century thinker who introduced Western ideas into China.

J.D. SPENCE, The Gate of Heavenly Peace: The Chinese and Their Revolution, 1895–1980 (1981). Historical reflections on twentieth-century China.

J.D. SPENCE, The Search for Modern China (1990). A thick text but well written.

M. SZONYI, Practicing Kinship: Lineage and Descent in Late Imperial China (2002).

S.Y. TENG and J.K. FAIRBANK, China's Response to the West (1954). A superb collection of translations from Chinese thinkers and political figures, with commentaries.

T.H. WHITE and A. JACOBY, Thunder Out of China (1946). A view of China during World War II by two who were there.

Japan

G. AKITA, Foundations of Constitutional Government in Modern Japan (1967). A study of It Hirobumi in the political process leading to the Meiji constitution.

G.C. ALLEN, A Short Economic History of Modern Japan (1958).

A.E. BARSHAY, The Social Sciences in Modern Japan: the Marxian and Modernist Traditions (2004). Different interpretations of history.

J.R. BARTHOLOMEW, The Formation of Science in Japan (1989). The pioneering English-language work on the subject.

W.G. BEASLEY, Japanese Imperialism, 1894–1945 (1987). Excellent short book on the subject.

G.M. BERGER, Parties Out of Power in Japan, 1931–1941 (1977). An analysis of the condition of political parties during the militarist era.

G.L. BERNSTEIN, Recreating Japanese Women, 1600–1945 (1991).

The Cambridge History of Japan, The Nineteenth Century, M.B. Jansen, ed. (1989); The Twentieth Century, P. Duus, ed. (1988). Multi-author works.

A.M. CRAIG, Chsh in the Meiji Restoration (2000). A study of the Chsh domain, a Prussia of Japan, during the period 1840–1868.

A.M. CRAIG and D.H. SHIVELY, eds., Personality in Japanese History (1970). An attempt to gauge the role of individuals and their personalities as factors explaining history.

P. DUUS, Party Rivalry and Political Change in Taisho Japan (1968). A study of political change in Japan during the 1910s and 1920s.

P. DUUS, The Abacus and the Sword: The Japanese Penetration of Korea, 1895–1910 (1995). A thoughtful analysis.

S. ERICSON, The Sound of the Whistle: Railroads and the State in Meiji Japan (1996). An economic and social history of railroads, an engine of growth and popular symbol.

Y. FUKUZAWA, Autobiography (1966). Japan's leading nineteenth-century thinker tells of his life and of the birth of modern Japan.

A. GARON, The State and Labor in Modern Japan (1987). A fine study of the subject.

C.N. GLUCK, Japan's Modern Myths: Ideology in the Late Meiji Period (1988). A brilliant study of the complex weave of late Meiji thought.

A. GORDON, The Evolution of Labor Relations in Japan: Heavy Industry, 1853–1955 (1985). A seminal work.

B.R. HACKETT, Yamagata Aritomo in the Rise of Modern Japan, 1932–1922 (1973). History as seen through the biography of a central figure.

I. HALL, Mori Arinori (1973). A biography of Japan's first minister of education.

T.R.H. HAVENS, The Valley of Darkness: The Japanese People and World War II (1978). Wartime society.

C. IRIYE, After Imperialism: The Search for a New Order in the Far East, 1921–1931 (1965). (Also see other studies by this author.)

D.M.B. JANSEN and G. ROZMAN, eds., Japan in Transition from Tokugawa to Meiji (1986). Contains fine essays.

W. JOHNSTON, The Modern Epidemic: A History of Tuberculosis in Japan (1995). A social history of a disease.

E. KEENE, ed., Modern Japanese Literature, An Anthology (1960). A collection of modern Japanese short stories and excerpts from novels.

F.Y.T. MATSUSAKA, The Making of Japanese Manchuria, 1904–1932 (2001). On railroad strategies in empire building.

J.W. MORLEY, ed., The China Quagmire (1983). A study of Japan's expansion on the continent between 1933 and 1941. (For diplomatic history, see also the many other works by this author.)

R.H. MYERS and M.R. PEATTIE, eds., The Japanese Colonial Empire, 1895–1945 (1984).

T. NAJITA, Hara Kei in the Politics of Compromise, 1905–1915 (1967). A study of one of Japan's greatest party leaders.

K. OHKAWA and H. ROSOVSKY, Japanese Economic Growth: Trend Acceleration in the Twentieth Century (1973).

M. RAVINA, The Last Samurai: The Life and Battles of Saigo Takamori (2004). Unlike the movie, this account of the Satsuma uprising is historical.

G. SHIBA, Remembering Aizu (1999). A stirring autobiographical account of a samurai youth whose domain lost in the Meiji Restoration.

K. SMITH, A Time of Crisis: The Great Depression and Rural Revitalization (2001). An intellectual history of village movements during the 1930s.

J.J. STEPHAN, Hawaii Under the Rising Sun (1984). Japan's plans for rule in Hawaii.

R.H. SPECTOR, Eagle Against the Sun: The American War with Japan (1985). A narrative of World War II in the Pacific.

E.P. TSURUMI, Factory Girls: Women in the Thread Mills of Meiji Japan (1990). A sympathetic analysis of the key component of the Meiji labor force.

W. WRAY, Mitsubishi and the N. Y. K., 1870–1914 (1984). The growth of a shipping zaibatsu, with analysis of business strategies, the role of government and imperialist involvements.

Chapter 29

L. ALBERTINI, The Origins of the War of 1914, 3 vols. (1952, 1957). Discursive but invaluable.

V.R. BERGHAHN, Germany and the Approach of War in 1914 (1973). A work similar in spirit to both of Fischer's (see below) but stressing the importance of Germany's naval program.

S.B. FAY, The Origins of the World War; 2 vols. (1928). The most influential of the revisionist accounts.

F. FISCHER, Germany's Aims in the First World War (1967). An influential interpretation that stirred a great controversy in Germany and around the world by emphasizing Germany's role in bringing on the war.

D. FROMKIN, Europe's Last Summer: Who Started the Great War in 1914? (2004). A lively account that fixes on the final crisis in July 1914.

J.N. HORNE, Labour at War: France and Britain, 1914–1918 (1991). An examination of a major issue on the home fronts.

J. KEEGAN, The First World War (1999). A vivid and readable narrative.

P. KENNEDY, The Rise of the Anglo-German Antagonism 1860–1914 (1980). An unusual and thorough analysis of the political, economic, and cultural roots of important diplomatic developments.

D.C.B. LIEVEN, Russia and the Origins of the First World War (1983). A good account of the forces that shaped Russian policy.

A. MOMBAUER, The Origins of the First World War. Controversies and Consensus (2002). A fascinating survey of the debate over the decades and the current state of the question.

R. PIPES, A Concise History of the Russian Revolution (1996). A one-volume version of a scholarly masterpiece.

Z. STEINER, Britain and the Origins of the First World War (1977). A perceptive and informed account of the way British foreign policy was made in the years before the war.

H. Strachan, The First World War (2004). A fine one-volume account of the war.

A.J.P. Taylor, The Struggle for Mastery in Europe, 1848–1918 (1954). Clever but controversial.

S.R. Williamson, Jr., Austria-Hungary and the Origins of the First World War (1991). A valuable study of a complex subject.

Chapter 30

W.S. Allen, The Nazi Seizure of Power: The Experience of a Single German Town, 1930–1935, rev. ed. (1984). A classic treatment of Nazism in a microcosmic setting.

J. Barnard, Walter Reuther and the Rise of the Auto Workers (1983). A major introduction to the new American unions of the 1930s.

K.D. Bracher, The German Dictatorship (1970). A comprehensive treatment of both the origins and the functioning of the Nazi movement and government.

A. Bullock, Hitler: A Study in Tyranny, rev. ed. (1964). The best biography.

M. Burleigh and W. Wipperman, The Racial State: Germany 1933–1945 (1991). Emphasizes the manner in which racial theory influenced numerous areas of policy.

R. Conquest, The Great Terror: Stalin's Purges of the Thirties (1968). The best treatment of the subject to this date.

G. Craig, Germany, 1866–1945 (1978). A major survey.

I. Deutscher, The Prophet Armed (1954), The Prophet Unarmed (1959), and The Prophet Outcast (1963). Remains the major biography of Trotsky.

I. Deutscher, Stalin: A Political Biography, 2nd ed. (1967). The best biography in English.

B. Eichengreen, Golden Fetters: The Gold Standard and the Great Depression, 1919–1939 (1992). A remarkable study of the role of the gold standard in the economic policies of the interwar years.

E. Eyck, A History of the Weimar Republic, 2 vols. (trans. 1963). The story as narrated by a liberal.

M.S. Fausold, The Presidency of Herbert Hoover (1985). An important treatment.

G. Feldman, The Great Disorder: Politics, Economics, and Society in the German Inflation, 1914–1924 (1993). The best work on the subject.

S. Fitzpatrick, Stalin's Peasants: Resistance and Survival in the Russian Village After Collectivization (1994). A pioneering study.

P. Fussell, The Great War and Modern Memory (1975). A brilliant account of the literature arising from World War I during the 1920s.

J.K. Galbraith, The Great Crash (1979). A well-known account by a leading economist.

R. Gellately, The Gestapo and German Society: Enforcing Racial Policy, 1933–1945 (1990). A discussion of how the police state supported Nazi racial policies.

H.J. Gordon, Hitler and the Beer Hall Putsch (1972). An excellent account of the event and the political situation in the early Weimar Republic.

R. Hamilton, Who Voted for Hitler? (1982). An examination of voting patterns and sources of Nazi support.

J. Held, ed., The Columbia History of Eastern Europe in the Twentieth Century (1992). Individual essays on each country.

P. Kenez, The Birth of the Propaganda State: Soviet Methods of Mass Mobilization, 1917–1929 (1985). An examination of the manner in which the Communist government inculcated popular support.

B. Kent, The Spoils of War: The Politics, Economics, and Diplomacy of Reparations, 1918–1932 (1993). A comprehensive account of the intricacies of the reparations problem of the 1920s.

D. Landes, The Unbound Prometheus: Technological Change and Industrial Development in Western Europe from 1750 to the Present (1969). Includes an excellent analysis of both the Great Depression and the few areas of economic growth.

B. Lincoln, Red Victory: A History of the Russian Civil War (1989). An excellent narrative account.

M. McAuley, Bread and Justice: State and Society in Petrograd, 1917–1922 (1991). A study that examines the impact of the Russian Revolution and Leninist policies on a major Russian city.

D.J.K. Peukert, Inside Nazi Germany: Conformity, Opposition, and Racism in Everyday Life (1987). An excellent discussion of life under Nazi rule.

R. Pipes, The Unknown Lenin: From the Secret Archives (1996). A collection of previously unpublished documents that indicated the repressive character of Lenin's government.

P. Pulzer, Jews and the German State: The Political History of a Minority, 1848–1933 (1992). A detailed history by a major historian of European minorities.

L.J. Rupp, Mobilizing Women for War: German and America Propaganda, 1939–1945 (1978). Although concentrating on a later period, it includes an excellent discussion of general Nazi attitudes toward women.

A.M. Schlesinger Jr., The Age of Roosevelt, 3 vols. (1957–1960). The most important overview.

D.M. Smith, Mussolini's Roman Empire (1976). A general description of the Fascist regime in Italy.

D.M. Smith, Italy and Its Monarchy (1989). A major treatment of an important neglected subject.

A. Solzhenitsyn, The Gulag Archipelago, 3 vols. (1974–1979). A major examination of the labor camps under Stalin by one of the most important contemporary Russian writers.

R.J. Sontag, A Broken World, 1919–1939 (1971). An exceptionally thoughtful and well-organized survey.

A.J.P. Taylor, English History, 1914–1945 (1965). Lively and opinionated.

H.A. Turner Jr., German Big Business and the Rise of Hitler (1985). An important major study of the subject.

H.A. Turner Jr., Hitler's Thirty Days to Power (1996). A narrative of the events leading directly to the Nazi seizure of power.

L. Yahil, The Holocaust: The Fate of European Jewry, 1932–1945 (1990). A major study of this fundamental subject in twentieth-century history.

Chapter 31

A. Adamthwaite, France and the Coming of the Second World War, 1936–1939 (1977). A careful account making good use of the French archives.

O. Bartov, Mirrors of Destruction: War, Genocide, and Modern Identity (2001). Remarkably penetrating essays.

E.R. Beck, Under the Bombs: The German Home Front, 1942–1945 (1986). An interesting examination of a generally unstudied subject.

P.M.H. Bell, The Origins of the Second World War in Europe, 3rd ed. (2007). A comprehensive study of the period and debates surrounding the European origins of the Second World War.

A. Beevor, The Spanish Civil War (2001). Particularly strong on the political issues.

C. Browning, The Origins of the Final Solution: The Evolution of the Nazi Jewish Policy (2004). The story of how Hitler's policy developed from discrimination to annihilation

A. Bullock, Hitler: A Study in Tyranny, rev. ed. (1964). A brilliant biography.

W.S. Churchill, The Second World War, 6 vols. (1948–1954). The memoirs of the great British leader.

A. Crozier, The Causes of the Second World War, 1997. An examination of what brought on the war.

R.B. Frank, Downfall: The End of the Imperial Japanese Empire (1998). A thorough, well-documented account of the last months of the Japanese empire and the reasons for its surrender.

J.L. Gaddis, We Now Know: Rethinking Cold War History (1998). A fine account of the early years of the Cold War, making use of new evidence emerging since the collapse of the Soviet Union.

J.L. Gaddis, P.H. Gordon, E.May, eds., Cold War Statesmen Confront the Bomb: Nuclear Diplomacy Since 1945 (1999). A collection of essays discussing the effect of atomic and nuclear weapons on diplomacy since WWII.

M. Gilbert, The Holocaust: A History of the Jews of Europe During the Second World War (1985). The best and most comprehensive treatment.

A. Iriye, Pearl Harbor and the Coming of the Pacific War (1999). Essays on how the Pacific war came about, including a selection of documents.

J. Keegan, The Second World War (1990). A lively and penetrating account by a master military historian.

I. Kershaw, Hitler: 1889–1936: Hubris (1999) and Hitler: 1936–1945: Nemesis (2001). An outstanding two-volume biography.

W.F. Kimball, Forged in War: Roosevelt, Churchill, and the Second World War, (1998). A study of the collaboration between the two great leaders of the West based on a thorough knowledge of their correspondence.

W. Murray and A.R. Millett, A War to Be Won: Fighting the Second World War, (2000). A splendid account of the military operations in the war.

P. Neville, Hitler and Appeasement: The British Attempt to Prevent the Second World War (2005). A defense of the British appeasers of Hitler.

R. Overy, Why the Allies Won (1997). An anlysis of the reasons for the victory of the Allies, with special emphasis on technology.

N. Rich, Hitler War Aims, 2 vols. (1973–1974). The best study of the subject in English.

P. Wandycz, The Twilight of French Eastern Alliances, 1926–1936 (1988). A well-documented account of the diplomacy of central and eastern Europe in a crucial period.

G.L. Weinberg, A World at Arms: A Global History of World War II (1994). A thorough and excellent narrative account.

Chapter 32

B.S. Anderson and J.P. Pinsser, A History of Their Own: Women in Europe from Prehistory to the Present, Vol. 2 (1988). A broad-ranging survey.

R. Bernstein, Out of the Blue: The Story of September 11, 2001, from Jihad to Ground Zero (2002). An excellent account by a gifted journalist.

A. Brown, The Gorbachev Factor (1996). An important commentary by an English observer.

D. Calleo, Rethinking Europe's Future (2003). A daring book by an experienced commentator.

J.L. Gaddis, What We Know Now (1997). Examines the Cold War in light of newly released documents.

D.J. Garrow, Bearing the Cross: Martin Luther King Jr. and the Southern Leadership Conference, 1955–1968 (1986). The best work on the subject.

W. Hitchcock, Struggle for Europe: The Turbulent History of a Divided Continent, 1945–2002 (2003). The best overall narrative now available.

D. Kearns, Lyndon Johnson and the American Dream (1976). A useful biography.

J. Keep, The Last of the Empires: A History of the Soviet Union, 1956–1991 (1995). A clear narrative.

M. Mandelbaum, The Ideas That Conquered the World: Peace, Democracy, and Free Markets (2002). An important analysis by a major commentator on international affairs.

J. Mann, The Rise of the Vulcans: The History of Bush's War Cabinet (2004). An account of the major foreign policy advisors behind the invasion of Iraq.

R. Mann, A Grand Delusion: America's Descent into Vietnam (2001). The best recent narrative.

J. McCormick, Understanding the European Union: A Concise Introduction (2002). Outlines the major features.

N. Naimark, Fires of Hatred: Ethnic Cleansing in Twentieth-Century Europe (2002). A remarkably sensitive treatment of a tragic subject.

R. Sawka and Anne Stevens, eds., Contemporary Europe (2000). A collection of essays on major topics.

G. Stokes, ed., From Stalinism to Pluralism: A Documentary History of Eastern Europe Since 1945 (1996). An important collection of documents that are not easily accessible elsewhere.

M. Walker, The Cold War and the Making of the Modern World (1994). A major survey.

Chapter 33

China

R. Baum, Burying Mao: Chinese Politics in the Age of Deng Xiaoping (1996).

A. Chan, R. Madsen, J. Unger, Chen Village Under Mao and Deng (1992).

J. Chang, Wild Swans: Three Daughters of China (1991). An intimate look at recent Chinese society through three generations of women. Immensely readable.

J. Feng, Ten Years of Madness: Oral Histories of China's Cultural Revolution (1996).

J. Fewsmith, China Since Tiananmen: The Politics of Transition (2001). Focus is on the rise to power of Jiang Zemin and Chinese politics during the nineties.

B.M. Frolic, Mao's People: Sixteen Portraits of Life in Revolutionary China (1987).

T. Gold, State and Society in the Taiwan Miracle (1986). The story of economic growth in postwar Taiwan.

M. Goldman, Sowing the Seeds of Democracy in China: Political Reform in the Deng Xiaoping Era (1994).

A. Iriye, China and Japan in the Global Setting (1992).

D.M. Lampton, Same Bed, Different Dreams: Managing U.S.–China Relations, 1989–2000 (2001).

H. Liang, Son of the Revolution (1983). An autobiographical account of a young man growing up in Mao's China.

K. Lieberthal, Governing China, from Revolution Through Reform (2004).

B. Liu, People or Monsters? and Other Stories and Reportage from China After Mao (1983). Literary reflections on China.

R. MacFarquhar and J.K. Fairbank, eds., The Cambridge History of China, Vol. 14, Emergence of Revolutionary China (1987), and Vol. 15, Revolutions Within the Chinese Revolution, 1966–1982 (1991).

L. Pan, Sons of the Yellow Emperor: A History of the Chinese Diaspora (1990). A pioneer study that treats not only Southeast Asia but the rest of the world as well.

M.R. Ristaino, Port of Last Resort: The Diaspora Communities of Shanghai (2001).

T. Saich, Governance and Politics of China (2004).

H. Wang, China's New Order (2003). Translation of a work by a Qinghua University professor, a liberal within the boundaries of what is permissable in China.

G. White, ed., In Search of Civil Society: Market Reform and Social Change in Contemporary China (1996).

M. Wolf, Revolution Postponed: Women in Contemporary China (1985).

Zhang X. and Sang Y., Chinese Lives: An Oral History of Contemporary China (1987).

Japan

G.L. Bernstein, Haruko's World: A Japanese Farm Woman and Her Community (1983). A study of the changing life of a village woman in postwar Japan.

T. Bestor, Neighborhood Tokyo (1989). A portrait of contemporary urban life in Japan.

G.L. Curtis, The Logic of Japanese Politics: Leaders, Institutions, and the Limits of Change (1999).

G.L. CURTIS, Policymaking in Japan: Defining the Role of Politicians (2002).

M.H. CUSUMANO, The Japanese Automobile Industry (1985). A neat study of the postwar business strategies of Toyota and Nissan.

R.P. DORE, City Life in Japan (1999). A classic, reissued.

R.P. DORE, Land Reform in Japan (1959). Another classic.

S. GARON, Molding Japanese Minds: The State in Everyday Life (1997).

S.M. GARON, The Evolution of Civil Society from Meiji to Heisei (2002). That is to say, from the mid–nineteenth century to the present day.

A. GORDON, ed., Postwar Japan as History (1993).

H. HIBBETT, ed., Contemporary Japanese Literature: An Anthology of Fiction, Film, and Other Writing Since 1945 (1977). Translations of postwar short stories.

Y. KAWABATA, The Sound of the Mountain (1970). Sensitive, moving novel by Nobel author.

J. NATHAN, Sony, the Private Life (1999). A lively account of the human side of growth in the Sony Corporation.

D. OKIMOTO, Between MITI and the Market (1989). A discussion of the respective roles of government and private enterprise in Japan's postwar growth.

S. PHARR, Losing Face: Status Politics in Japan (1996).

E.F. VOGEL, Japan as Number One: Lessons for America (1979). While dated and somewhat sanguine, this remains an insightful classic.

Korea and Vietnam

B. CUMINGS, Korea: The Unknown War (1988).

B. CUMINGS, The Origins of the Korean War (Vol. 1, 1981; Vol. 2, 1991).

B. CUMINGS, The Two Koreas: On the Road to Reunification? (1990).

C.J. ECKERT, Korea Old and New, A History (1990). The best short history of Korea, with extensive coverage of the postwar era.

C.J. ECKERT, Offspring of Empire: The Koch'ang Kims and the Colonial Origins of Korean Capitalism, 1876–1945 (1991).

G.M.T. KAHIN, Intervention: How America Became Involved in Vietnam (1986).

S. KARNOW, Vietnam: A History. rev. ed. (1996).

L. KENDALL, Shamans, Housewives, and Other Restless Spirits: Women in Korean Ritual and Life (1985).

K.B. LEE, A New History of Korea (1984). A translation by E. Wagner and others of an outstanding Korean work covering the full sweep of Korean history.

T. LI, Nguyen Cochinchina: South Vietnam in the Seventeenth and Eighteenth Centuries (1998).

D. MARR, Vietnam 1945: The Quest for Power (1995).

C.W. SORENSEN, Over the Mountains Are Mountains (1988). How peasant households in Korea adapted to rapid industrialization.

A. WOODSIDE, Vietnam and the Chinese Model (1988). Provides the background for Vietnam's relationship to China.

Chapter 34

General Works

P. FARMER, Pathologies of Power: Health, Human Rights, and the New War on the Poor (2003). Farmer, a physician, uses his experiences at Harvard and in the Caribbean to argue that inadequate healthcare in the third world violates human rights, and imperils us all.

J.H. LATHAM, Africa, Asia, and South America Since 1800: A Bibliographic Guide (1995). A valuable tool for finding materials on the topics in this chapter.

S. POWER, A Problem from Hell: America and the Age of Genocide (2002). A masterful analysis of genocides in the twentieth century (in Armenia, the Holocaust, the Khmer Rouge, Kurds, Rwanda, and Bosnia) and the U.S. response.

J.D. SACHS, The End of Poverty: Economic Possibilities for Our Time (2005). A renowned economist's plan to end extreme poverty around the world by 2025.

Latin America

P. BAKEWELL, A History of Latin America: c. 1450 to the Present (2003). An up-to-date survey.

A. CHOMSKY ET AL., The Cuba Reader: History, Culture, Politics (2004). Very useful, broad-ranging anthology.

J. DOMINGUEZ and M. SHIFTER, Constructing Democratic Governance in Latin America (2003). Contains individual country studies.

G. JOSEPH ET AL., The Mexico Reader: History, Culture, Politics (2003). Excellent introduction to major issues.

P. LOWDEN, Moral Opposition to Authoritarian Rule in Chile (1996). A discussion of Chilean politics from the standpoint of human rights.

J. PRESTON and S. DILLON, Opening Mexico: The Making of a Democracy (2004). Excellent analysis of recent developments in Mexico.

H. WIRARDA, Democracy and Its Discontents: Development, Interdependence, and U.S. Policy in Latin America (1995). A useful overview.

Africa

B. DAVIDSON, Let Freedom Come (1978). Remains a thoughtful commentary of African independence.

P. GOUREVITCH, We Wish to Inform You that Tomorrow We Will Be Killed with Our Families (1999). An account of the Rwandan genocide that is beautifully written, and almost unbearable to read.

J. HERBST, States and Power in Africa (2000). Relates current issues of African state-building to those before the colonial era.

R.W. JULY, A History of the African People, 5th ed. (1995). Provides a careful and clear survey of post–World War I history and consideration of nationalism.

N. MANDELA, Long Walk to Freedom: The Autobiography of Nelson Mandela (1995). Autobiography of the African leader who transformed South Africa.

L. THOMPSON, A History of South Africa (2001). The best survey.

N. VAN DE WALLE, African Economies and the Politics of Permanent Crisis, 1979–1999 (2001). Exploration of difficulties of African economic development.

India and Pakistan

O.B. JONES, Pakistan: Eye of the Storm (2003). Best recent introduction.

R. RASHID, Taliban: Militant Islam, Oil and Fundamentalism in Central Asia (2001). Analysis of radical Isalmist regime in Afghanistan.

R.W. STERN, Changing India: Bourgeois Revolution on the Subcontinent (2003). Overview of forces now changing Indian society.

S. WOLPERT, A New History of India (2003). The closing chapters of this fine survey history are particularly helpful in orienting the reader in postwar Indian history until the mid-1980s.

Islam and the Middle East

A. AHMED, Discovering Islam: Making Sense of Muslim Hisotry and Society, rev. ed. (2003). An excellent and readable overiew of Islamic–Western relations.

J. ESPOSITO, The Islamic Threat: Myth or Reality, 2nd ed. (1992). A useful corrective to some of the polemics against Islam and Muslims today.

J.J. ESPOSITO, ed., The Oxford Encyclopedia of Islam (1999). A thematic survey of Islamic history, particularly strong in the Modern Era.

D. FROMKIN, A Peace to End All Peace: The Fall of the Ottoman Empire and the Creation of the Modern Middle East (2001). Very good on the impact of World War I on the region.

G. FULLER, The Future of Political Islam (2003). A very good overview of Islamist ideology by a former CIA staff member.

J. KEAY, Sowing the Wind: The Seeds of Conflict in the Middle East (2003). A balanced account.

N.R. KEDDIE, Modern Iran: Roots and Results of Revolution (2003). Chapters 6–12 focus on Iran from 1941 through the first years of the 1978 revolution and provide a solid overview of history in this era.

G. KEPEL, Jihad: The Trail of Political Islam (2002). An extensive treatment by a leading French scholar of the subject.

Credits

Index

World History Documents DVD-ROM

- Nine Hindu planets
- Hindu Gods
- Elephanta Water Cave, India
- Daoist scroll
- Confucius
- Jain cosmographical map

Chapter 3   Greek and Hellenistic Civilization

Text Sources

- Hesiod, excerpt from *Works and Days*
- Greece and Persia: The Treaty of Antalcides, 387 B.C.E.
- Aristophanes, excerpt from *The Birds*
- Agatharchides of Cnidos describes Saba
- Homer, Debate Among the Greeks
- Plutarch, from *Life of Lycurgus*: Education and Family in Sparta
- Aristotle, The Creation of the Democracy in Athens
- Sophocles, from *Antigone*
- Thucydides, *Pericles Funeral Oration*

Visual Sources

- Thucydides and Herodotus
- The Parthenon
- Illustration of a paradox of Zeno and Elea
- Greek athletics
- Detail of a statue from Delphi
- Archimedes' mirror

Chapter 4   Iran, India and Inner Asia to 200 C.E.

Text Sources

- Kautilya, from *Arthashastra*, "The Duties of Government Superintendents"
- Excerpts from *The Questions of King Milinda*
- The "Cyrus Cylinder": The First Declaration of Religious Freedom
- Livy, The Rape of Lucretia and the Origins of the Republic
- Slaves in the Roman Countryside
- Augustus' Moral Legislation: Family Values
- Juvenal, A Satirical View of Women
- Gnostic Teachings of Jesus, According to Irenaeus
- Perpetua, The Autobiography of a Christian Martyr
- *The Confession* of Saint Patrick

Visual Sources

Chapter 5   Africa: Early History to 1000 C.E.

Text Sources

- From the Periplus of the Erythraean Sea: Travel and Trade in the Indian Ocean
- Procopius of Caesarea, History of the Wars, ca. 550 C.E.

Visual Sources

Chapter 6   Republican and Imperial Rome

Text Sources

- St. Augustine of Hippo, Theory of the "Just War"
- Sidonius Apollinaris, *Rome's Decay* and *A Glimpse of the New Order*
- Pope Leo I on Bishop Hilary of Aries
- Pliny the Younger, *Epistulae Letters*
- Pliny the Elder, from *The Natural History*
- Paulus Orosius, from *Seven Books of History Against the Pagans*
- Jordanes, *The Origin and Deeds of the Goths,* Book twenty-six
- Horace, "Dulce et Decorum est Pro Patria Mori"
- Excerpts from the *Hildebrandslied*
- Bishop Synesius of Cyrene, Letter to his brother
- *The Acts of the Apostles:* Paul Pronounces the "Good News" in Greece
- Marcus Aurelius, *The Meditations, Book Two* (167 C.E.)
- St. Benedict's Rules for Monks
- From *The Conversion of Kartli* (the life of St. Nino)
- Ammianus Marcellinus on the Huns

Visual Sources

- Statue of Caesar Augustus
- Roman Forum
- Roman aqueduct
- Armenian Monastery
- Tombstone of a Roman soldier

Chapter 7   China's First Empire, 221 B.C.E.–589 C.E.

Text Sources

- Zhang Quian, *Han Shu*, "Descriptions of the Western Regions"
- Sima Qian, *The Life of Meng Tian, Builder of the Great Wall*
- Faxien, *Record of Buddhist Countries,* chapter sixteen
- Chinese description of the Tibetans

Visual Sources

- The Great Wall of China
- Han Chinese house
- Emperor Wudi, Dunhunag, China

Chapter 8   Imperial China, 589–1368

Text Sources

- Treaty between Tibet and China, 821–822
- The Mongols: An Excerpt from the *Novgorod Chronicle*, 1315
- Tang Daizong on the art of government
- Marco Polo, excerpt from *The Travels of Marco Polo*
- Ma Huan, excerpt from *The Overall Survey of the Ocean's Shores*
- Lu You, excerpt from "Diary of a Journey to Sichuan"
- Ibn Wahab, an Arab merchant visits Tang China
- Excerpts from *The History of the Life and Travels of Rabban Bar Sauma*
- Excerpt from William of Rubruck's Account of the Mongols

Visual Sources

- View of Nanjing
- View of Guangzhou (Canton)
- Title page from Japanese anatomy text, ca.1775
- The Tokaido Road in Japan
- The Peking observatory
- Shinto temple
- Profiles of Asian peoples
- Northern Tartary women
- Map of the Yellow River
- Mandarins
- Jesuit martyrs in Japan
- European views of the Chinese
- European views of Tatars and Chinese
- Chinese jade book
- Chinese armillary sphere
- Buddhist world map
- Ongons (Mongolia)
- Eighteenth-century Japanese painting, "A Meeting of China, Japan, and the West"
- The mausoleum of Akbar the Great
- Chinese map of Central Asia

Chapter 20   State Building and Society in Early Modern Europe

Text Sources

- Jean Domat, *On Social Order and Absolutist Monarchy*
- The Marquis de Mirabeau, *The Friend of Men*, or *Treatise on Population*, 1756
- Louis Sébastien Mercier, from *Tableau de Paris*, vol. 1, "The Saint-Marcel Neighborhood"
- Voltaire: On Social Conditions in Eighteenth-century France
- Peter the Great, "Correspondence with Alexis" (Russia), 1715
- Glückel of Hameln, *Memoirs* (The Holy Roman Empire) 1690
- Galileo, "Third Letter on Sunspots" (Italian States), 1612
- Jonathan Swift, "A Description of a City Shower" (Great Britain), 1710
- Jean Bodin, *Six Books of the Commonwealth*, "The True Attributes of Sovereignty"
- Hugo Grotius, selections from *On the Law of War and Peace*
- Thomas Malthus, excerpt from *Essay on the Principle of Population*
- David Ricardo, "The Iron Law of Wages"

Visual Sources

- View of St. Petersburg from the first Russian newspaper, *Vedomosti*
- View of Gibraltar
- Prussian soldiers
- Illustration from *American Magazine*, 1758
- Hobbes, *Leviathan* I
- Hobbes, *Leviathan* II
- Frontspiece from the first national atlas of England
- First Dutch national atlas
- Eighteenth-century powderhorn
- 1755 Battle between British and Indians

- View of Batavia, 1764
- Map of the country of Georgia
- Map of Mauritius, nineteenth century

Chapter 21   The Last Great Islamic Empires, 1500–1800

Text Sources

- Sunni versus Shi'ite: Letter from Selim I to Ismail I
- Paul Rycaut, on the State of the Ottoman Empire, 1668
- Ogier Ghiselin de Busbecq, excerpt from "Women in Ottoman Society"
- Ogier Ghiselin de Busbecq, "Süleyman the Lawgiver"
- Jan Hugghen van Linschoten, on Dutch business in the Indian Ocean
- Fathers Simon and Vincent Report on Shah Abbas I, the Safavid Ruler of Persia
- Excerpts from the Biography of Shah Abbas I
- Excerpts from the Biography of Emperor Akbar of India
- Domingo Navarrete, "Of My Stay in the Kingdom of Macasar"
- Abu'l-Fadl 'Allami's *Ain-i-Akbari*
- Abu Taleb Khan, A Muslim Indian's Reactions to the West
- Portrait of an Ottoman Gentleman
- Excerpt from the Memoirs of Babur
- Shah Isma'il Describes Himself to His Followers
- A Sikh Guru's Testimony of Faith
- Ottoman compass, early nineteenth century
- Daniel Defoe, selection from *The Complete English Tradesman*

Visual Sources

- Eighteenth-century European engraving of Isfahan
- View of Hormuz
- The Taj Mahal
- Safavid battle tunic
- Russian views of "People of the Empire"
- Photograph of an Uzbek woman from the *Turkestanskii Albom*
- Persian miniature painting: Layla and Majnun
- Ottoman naval attack on the island of Gerbi
- Ottoman law book
- Illustration from the *Chronicles of Java*
- Armenian missal
- Armenian creation myth
- Book of Kings: Illustrations from the Shahnamah
- Seventeenth-century Portuguese trading posts in the Indian Ocean
- Seventeenth-century Portuguese map of the Indian Ocean

Chapter 22   The Age of European Enlightenment

Text Sources

- Adam Smith, *The Wealth of Nations* (Great Britain), 1776
- William Harvey, Address to the Royal College of Physicians, 1628
- Voltaire, On Universal Toleration
- René Descartes, *The Discourse on Method* and "I Think, Therefore I Am"

- Nicolaus Copernicus, excerpt from *On the Revolutions of the Heavenly Spheres*
- Mary Wollstonecraft, Introduction to *A Vindication of the Rights of Woman*
- The *Encyclopédie*, "Bakers (Boulanger)" (France) 1763
- John Locke, *Essay Concerning Human Understanding* (Great Britain), 1689
- Denis Diderot, Preliminary Discourse from *The Encyclopedia* (France), 1751
- Voltaire, Letters On England (France), 1733
- French Peasants, *Cahiers de doléances* (Grievances) (France), 1789
- Johann Wolfgang von Goethe, Prometheus, 1773

Visual Sources

- Title page from Vico, *Principii di una Scienza Nuova*
- Title page from Francis Bacon, *Novum Organum*
- The Copernican solar system
- Sixteenth-century anatomical drawings, II
- Sixteenth-century anatomical drawings, I
- Russian charter granted to the nobility
- Ptolemaic world map
- Principles of magnetism: illustration by William Gilbert, 1600
- Pinel's skull types
- Illustration from Newton's *Opticks*
- Jewish medical text by Tobias Cohen
- Illustrations for *The Emperor's Astronomy*
- Illustration showing a vacuum experiment
- Galileo's telescopic drawing of the moon
- Frontispiece from Andreas Vesalius, *On the Fabric of the Human Body*
- First printed medical text with illustrations
- Descartes, illustration from *Optics*
- Descartes's view of the universe
- Blake's image of the creation
- *Birds of America* by John Audubon I
- Visit of Queen Anne of England to Anton von Leeuwenhoek, 1698
- American magnolia tree, 1731
- *Birds of America* by John Audubon II
- Frontispiece from Maimonides's *Guide for the Perplexed*

Chapter 23   Revolutions in the Transatlantic World

Text Sources

- Revolutionary France: *The Declaration of the Rights of Man and of the Citizen*, 1789-1791
- Olympe de Gouges, *Declaration of the Rights of Woman and the Female Citizen*
- Alexis de Tocqueville, excerpt from *Democracy in America*
- Marquis de Condorcet, passage from from *Sketch for a Historical Picture of the Progress of the Human Mind*
- Lady Mary Wortley Montagu, Letters: (a) on Constantinople; (b) on Smallpox; (c) on Vaccination in Turkey
- James Lind, from *A Treatise of the Scurvy*, 1753
- Isaac Newton, from *Opticks*

- Immanuel Kant defines the Enlightenment, 1784
- Francis Bacon, from *Novum Organum*
- David Ricardo, excerpt from *Principles of Political Economy and Taxation*
- Cesare Beccaria, from *An Essay on Crimes and Punishments*
- Baron de Montesquieu, excerpt from *The Spirit of the Laws*
- Robespierre "Speech to National Convention: The Terror Justified" (France), 1794
- Edmund Burke, *Reflections on the Revolution in France* (Great Britain), 1790
- Jose Morelos, *Sentiments of the Nation* (Mexico), 1813
- Simon de Bolívar, "Address to Second National Congress" (Venezuela), 1819

Visual Sources

- Revolutionary ladies, North Carolina
- Origins of the French monarchy
- Illustration from *Poor Richard's Almanack*
- Illustration of the execution of King Louis XVI, 1793
- Illustration of the murder of Jean-Paul Marat, 1793
- Boston Tea Party Revolution
- Battle of Yorktown
- "Tea-Tax Tempest" by Carl Guttenberg
- "Cult of the Supreme Being," French Revolution
- Ironclad warship
- Plan of San Antonio, Texas

Chapter 24   Political Consolidation in Nineteenth-Century Europe and North America, 1815–1880

Text Sources

- Benjamin Disraeli, excerpt from *Sybil, or The Two Nations*
- Anthony Trollope, excerpt from *North America*
- Samuel Smiles, excerpt from *Self-Help, with Illustrations of Character and Conduct*
- Crèvecoeur, from *Letters from an American Farmer*, "What Is an America"
- Crèvecoeur, from *Letters from an American Farmer*

Visual Sources

- A Beethoven sonata manuscript
- Wagon train crossing the Sierra Nevada
- View of Charleston, ca. 1870
- Slaves carrying cotton and picking cotton I
- Slaves carrying cotton and picking cotton II
- Slave shackles
- *Uncle Tom's Cabin* advertisement
- Ironclad warship
- Map of the western United States

Chapter 25   Northern Transatlantic Economy and Society, 1815–1914

Text Sources

- William James, from *Pragmatism*, 1907
- William Hazlitt, selections from *The Spirit of the Age*

- W.E.B. Du Bois, *Souls of Black Folk*, "Of Mr. Booker T. Washington and Others"
- Thorstein Veblen, excerpt from *The Theory of Leisure Class*
- The Sadler Report: Child Labor in the United Kingdom, 1832
- Robert Owen, excerpt from *Address to the Workers of New Lanark*, 1816
- Parliamentary report on English female miners, 1842
- Matthew Arnold, excerpt from *Dover Beach*
- Karl Marx and Fredrich Engels, from the *Communist Manifesto*
- John Stuart Mill, excerpts from *On Liberty*
- James Fenimore Cooper, Author's Introduction to *The Prairie*
- Henrik Ibsen, from *A Doll's House*, Act Three
- Frederick Winslow Taylor, "A Piece Rate System," 1896
- Franz Boas, from *The Mind of Primitive Man*, 1911
- Fanny Kemble, excerpt from *Records of a Girlhood*
- Ellen Key, from *The Century of the Child*
- Eliza Bishee Duffey, from *No Sex in Education; or, an Equal Chance for Both Girls and Boys*, 1874
- Edwin Chadwick, Summary from the Poor Law Commissioners
- Chartist Movement: The People's Petition of 1838
- Charles Darwin, from *The Origins of the Species*
- Booker T. Washington, "Industrial Education for the Negro"
- Andrew Ure, from *The Philosophy of Manufactures*
- African American Emancipation Songs: (a) "Many Thousands Gone;" (b) "Kingdom Coming"
- Abraham Lincoln, The Emancipation Proclamation
- A Luddite pamphlet
- Joseph Mazzini, *Life and Writings of Joseph Mazzini*, 1805–1872
- Mikhail Bakunin, "Principles and Organization of the International Brotherhood," 1866
- Pope Leo XIII, Rerum Novarum (Of New Things), 1891
- George Eliot, "Review: Margaret Fuller and Mary Wollstonecraft" (Great Britain), 1855
- Emile Zola, *Nana* (France), 1880
- Friedrich Nietzsche, *Beyond Good and Evil* (Germany), 1886
- Richard Freiherr von Krafft-Ebing, *Psychopathia Sexualia* (Germany), 1886
- Peters, "A Manifesto for German Colonization" (Germany and Africa), 1884
- Werner Heisenberg, "Uncertainty" (Germany), 1927
- Virginia Woolf, from *A Room of One's Own* (Great Britain), 1929
- Mary Kingsley, *Travels in West Africa* (Great Britain and Africa), 1893 and 1895

Visual Sources

- Women suffrage parade
- Tbilisi in the late nineteenth century
- Tashkent textile mill
- Street scenes, Germany
- Singer sewing machine advertisement
- Portrait of Sequoyah, inventor of the Cherokee alphabet
- San Francisco earthquake
- Reconstruction in the American South
- North-South reconciliation through the Spanish-American war, 1898
- Nineteenth-century whale chart
- Muybridge photos
- Mill on the Brandywine
- Mandan Sioux offering
- Machine exhibit, 1904 Worlds Fair
- Logging in Minnesota, 1893
- Lincoln remembrance
- Italian immigrants in USA
- Immigrants sailing to USA
- Illinois Central Railroad poster
- Homestead steel mill
- Georgian musicians
- Georgian (Caucasus) peasants
- Advertisement for gas-smoothing iron
- Excelsior Iron Works
- Edison's Vitascope
- Slum Life: Dead horse in New York street
- "De Ovi Mamalian," by Karl von Baer
- Cotton plantation, United States of America
- Chinese immigrants in USA
- Child textile worker
- Cherokee Constitution
- Black soldier, United States Civil War
- Architectural iron works catalog
- J. M. Stanley, Araucanian chief
- Apache Indian prinsoners, 1886
- Frontispiece from *Martin Chuzzlewit*

Chapter 26   Latin America from Independence to the 1940s
Text Sources

- Francisco García Calderón, excerpt from *Latin America: Its Rise and Progress*
- Francisco Bilbao, *America in Danger*, 1862
- Friederich Hassaurek, *How to Conduct a Latin American Revolution*, 1865
- Domingo F. Sarmiento, "Civilization and Barbarism"
- José Fernández, *El Gaucho Martín Fierro*
- José Martí, "Our America"
- Platt Amendment
- Auguste Comte, "Course of Positive Philosophy" (France), 1830–1842

Visual Sources

- Unloading coffee in Brazil
- Traffic in Rio de Janiero, 1940
- Quito textile factory, circa 1910
- Port of Valparaiso, Chile
- Pancho Villa
- Buenos Aires coffee bar, 1930s
- Bolivian child laborers
- A Peruvian couple, ca. 1860

Visual Sources

- Tientsin China, 1924
- Signing of the Treaty of Portsmouth, 1905
- Shanghai, 1920s
- Rape of Nanjing, 1937
- Emperor Meiji
- Japanese views of Commodore Perry's mission, 1853, I
- Japanese views of Commodore Perry's mission, 1853, II
- Japanese views of Commodore Perry's mission, 1853, III
- Japanese views of Commodore Perry's mission, 1853, IV
- Japanese views of Commodore Perry's mission, 1853, V
- Japanese views of Commodore Perry's mission, 1853, VI
- Japanese Samurai society, 1920s
- Japanese in Tsingtao, China 1920s
- Illustration from *The Complete Survey of Medical Knowledge*
- Governor's residence of Indonesia
- Engravings showing the military victories of the Emperor Quianlong I
- Chinese pavilion, 1904 Worlds Fair
- Lin Zexu destroying opium
- Chinese acupuncturist
- Canton destruction
- Americans in Yokohama, 1855
- Ainu woman
- Grigorii Chernetsov, "Parade on Tsarina's Meadow," 1831
- Filipino slaves

Chapter 29   Imperialism and World War I

Text Sources

- Watkin Tench, from *A Complete Account of the Settlement at Port Jackson*
- The Scramble for Africa
- The Covenant of the League of Nations
- The Balfour Declaration, 1917
- Woodrow Wilson, "Speech on the Fourteen Points"
- Soldiers' Accounts of Battle
- Sir Henry McMahon, Letter to Ali Ibn Husain, 1915
- Serbian Society of National Defense, Program for Nationalism
- Rudyard Kipling, "The White Man's Burden"
- Roupen of Sassoun, Eyewitness to Armenia's Genocide
- Robert Louis Stevenson, passage from *In the South Seas*
- Nineteenth-century European descriptions of the Pacific island of Lelu
- Carl von Clauswitz, *On War*, "Arming the Nation"
- Jules Ferry, *Le Tonkin et la Mere-Patrie*
- José Rizal, excerpt from *The Reign of Greed*
- Irish National Identity: (a) Irish Declaration of Independence; (b) Ulster's Solemn League and Covenant; (c) Eamon de Valera, radio broadcast
- Fustel de Coulanges, Letter to German Historian Theodor Mommsen, 1870
- François Carlotti, from "World War I: A Frenchman's Recollections"
- Erich Maria Remarque, excerpt from *All Quiet on the Western Front*

- Edward D. Morel, *The Black Man's Burden*
- British Soldiers on the Battle of the Somme
- Bolshevik Seizure of Power, 1917: (a) Lenin, on the Overthrow of the Provisional Government; (b) Isvestia, "Little Good Is to Be Expected"; (c) Lenin, on Censorship of the Press; (d) Lenin, Establishment of the Secret Police

Visual Sources

- Woodrow Wilson on his way to Versailles, 1919
- Women shipyard workers
- Women munitions workers
- Victory parade, Paris
- Trench warfare, I
- Trench warfare, II
- Tin Mining, Indonesia
- The "New Europes": Sydney
- The "New Europes": New York City
- The "New Europes": Johannesburg
- The "New Europes": Detroit
- The "New Europes": Cape Town
- Tattooed Polynesian warrior
- Tattooed native of Nukahiwa
- Spartacist demonstration, Berlin
- Pygmies, 1904 World's Fair
- Portrait of Jose Rizal
- Polynesian mask
- Pears' soap advertisement
- Nineteenth-century globe
- Inuit family, 1918
- Indian School, Pennsylvania
- Illustration from an Uzbek children's book, 1926
- Howkan Indian village, Alaska
- French tanks
- Filipino insurgents, 1900
- US field hospital in the Philippines, Philippine-American War
- Early churches in Hawaii I
- Early churches in Hawaii II
- Black American soldiers, 1918
- Austro-Hungarian soldiers wearing gas masks
- Arab delegates to the Versailles conference, 1919
- Anti-Spartacist demonstration, Germany
- American World War I poster
- American machine gunners
- Afrikaner guerrillas, Second Boer War
- African women protest white rule in South Africa

Chapter 30   Depression, European Dictators, and the American New Deal

Text Sources

- Nadezhda K. Krupskaya on Communism
- John Scott, excerpt from *Behind the Urals: An America Worker in Russia's City of Steel*
- John Maynard Keynes, passage from *The End of Laissez-Faire*
- Filippo Tommaso Marinetti, "Futuristic Manifesto"

- Benito Mussolini, from "The Political and Social Doctrine of Fascism"
- Sofia Pavlova, "Taking Advantage of New Opportunities" (Russia), 1920s
- Irina Ivanovna Kniazeva, "A Life in a Peasant Village" (USSR), 1917–1930s

Visual Sources

- Yugoslavs at well, 1920s
- Women bathers, 1920s
- Viktor Deni, Stalinist poster, 1931
- Spanish Civil War poster
- Soviet poster, 1917
- Segregated movie theatre, Mississippi, 1939
- Russian factory, 1939
- Poverty, southern United States
- Nazi rally
- Nazi party congress, Nuremberg, 1934
- Movie theater, New York, 1926
- Dorothea Lange, Migrant mother, Great Depression
- Dorothea Lange, Mexican migrants in USA, 1936
- Looted food shop, Germany
- London stock exchange, 1920s
- Ku Klux Klan rally, 1924
- Inflation in Germany
- Hoover Dam
- Herbert Hoover speaks to a television audience, 1927
- Execution by guillotine, France, 1929
- Chinatown, San Francisco, 1920s
- Cars on Daytona Beach, 1920s
- British Empire poster, "Growing Markets for Our Goods"
- Bread line, 1930s
- Bolshevik Revolution poster
- Automobile advertisement, 1920s
- Anti-Japanese sentiment, California, 1920s
- 1936 Berlin Olympics
- "There's no way like the American way" billboard

Chapter 31   World War II

Text Sources

- Transcript of the Rape of Nanjing Sentencing, 1947
- Roosevelt and Churchill: The Atlantic Charter, 1941
- Nadezhda Mandelstam, excerpt from *Hope Against Hope: A Memoir*
- Lindsey Parrot, "Tojo Makes Plea of Self-Defense"
- Kita Ikki, Outline for the Reconstruction of Japan
- Japanese Total War Research Institute, Plan for the Greater East Asia Co-Prosperity Sphere, 1942
- Franklin Delano Roosevelt, The Four Freedoms, 1941
- Chicago Commission on Race Relations, *The Negro in Chicago: A Study of Race Relations and a Race Riot*
- American Investigators, from *The Effects of Atomic Bombs on Hiroshima and Nagasaki*
- Adolf Hitler, The *Obersalzberg* Speech, 1939
- Adolf Hitler, excerpt from *Mein Kampf*

- Philip Randolph, A Call to March on Washington, 1941
- Winston Churchill, "Their Finest Hour" (Great Britain), 1940
- Gertrud Scholtz-Klink, "Speech to the Nazi Women's Organization" (Germany), 1935
- Constancia de la Mora, from *In Place of Splendor* (Spain), 1939

Visual Sources

- Warsaw ghetto
- Eisenhower and U.S. troops before D-Day
- U.S. air bombing of Bologna, April 1945
- Tokyo shanty town, September 1945
- Tokyo and Nuremberg war crimes trials I
- Tokyo and Nuremberg war crimes trials II
- The war in the Pacific
- The internment of Japanese Americans I
- The internment of Japanese Americans II
- The internment of Japanese Americans III
- The Holocaust II
- The Holocaust I
- The destruction of Europe, post-WWII
- Summits of the Allied leaders, I
- Summits of the Allied leaders, II
- Rosie the Riveter
- Nazi executing Russian civilians
- Japanese surrender aboard the USS *Missouri*, 2 September 1945
- Japanese bombing of Pearl Harbor
- Hitler and Chamberlain, 1938
- Hiroshima after the dropping of the atomic bomb
- German persecution of the Jews
- Hitler celebrating French surrender
- D-Day
- Gernab civilian refugees in Europe
- Atomic bomb mushroom cloud
- American workers at B-17 bomber plant
- American propaganda poster
- American GIs in Holland
- "United We Win" poster

Chapter 32   The West Since World War II

Text Sources

- Vaclav Havel, "The Need for Transcendence in the Postmodern World"
- The Kyoto Protocol to the United Nations Framework Convention on Climate Change, Article Two
- The Charter of the United Nations, 1945
- Winston Churchill, from the Iron Curtain Speech, 1946
- Pope John Paul II, from *Centesimus Annus*
- Nikita Krushchev, Speech to the Twenty-second Congress of the Communist Party, 1962
- National Organization for Women, Statement of Purpose, 1966
- Martin Luther King, Jr., Letter from Birmingham City Jail, 1963

- *Ladies Home Journal*, "Young Mother," 1956
- Joseph Stalin, excerpts from the "Soviet Victory" Speech, 1946
- John F. Kennedy, Address Before the General Assembly of the United Nations, 1961
- James B. Stockdale, excerpt from *A Vietnam Experience: Ten Years of Reflection*
- Henry A. Myers, "East Berliners Rise Up Against Soviet Oppression"
- Helmut Kohl, Speech to the American Council on Germany, 1990
- Harry S Truman, The Truman Doctrine, 1947
- George F. Kennan, "Long Telegram," 1946
- George C. Marshall, The Marshall Plan, 1947
- François Mitterrand, Speech to the United Nations, 1990
- Dean Acheson, United States Secretary of State, on the failure of the Chinese Nationalist Government, 1949
- Addresses by George W. Bush, 2001: (a) from Address to the Nation, September 11; (b) from Address to the Nation, November 8; (c) from Address to the United Nations, November 10
- Mussolini Heaps Contempt on Political Liberalism, 1923
- Rachel Carson, from *Silent Spring*
- European criticism of American environmental policies, 2007
- Gamal Abdel Nasser, Speech on the Suez Canal (Egypt), 1956
- Zlata Filipovi, from *Zlata's Diary: A Child's Life in Sarajevo* (Bosnia) 1992
- Treaty on European Union, 1992
- Jörg Haider, from *The Freedom I Mean* (Austria), 1995
- Justin Vaïsse, from "Veiled Meaning" (France), 2004
- Statement from Chancellor Schröder on the Iraq Crisis (2003)
- The United Nations, Universal Declaration of Human Rights, 1948

Visual Sources

- Vietnamese refugees
- US and British votes in the UN on the Suez Canal crisis, 1956
- The "kitchen debate" between Nixon and Kruschev
- Stalin monument, Prague
- Soviet collective agriculture, 1950s
- Soviet agriculture
- Smog in Los Angeles, 1954
- Segregation, USA, 1950s II
- Segregation, USA, 1950s I
- Polio vaccination
- Ozone poster
- Outdoor market, Soviet Central Asia
- Nikita Krushchev visiting an Albanian factory
- U.S. newspaper headline showing the "Red Scare", 1950s
- March on Washington, 1963
- Man on the moon, 1969
- Levittown, New York
- Latino rights
- Kennedy in Berlin, 1963
- International space station

- Hurricane Katrina
- Hungarian uprising, 1956
- H-Bomb shelter
- The earth at night
- Disabled Italians demand more government aid
- March on Washington, 1963 II
- Cardinal Francis Spellman conducting mass in New York
- Bulgarian labor brigade
- Anti-Vietnam protesters
- 1955 designer kitchen
- US and Soviet forces meet, 1945

Chapter 33   East Asia: The Recent Decades

Text Sources

- Truong Nhu Trang, "Myth of a Liberation"
- James F. Schnabel, from *United States Army in the Korean War*
- General Douglas MacArthur, "Old Soldiers Never Die," 1951
- Deng Xiaoping, on introducing capitalist principles to China
- Vietnamese National Anthem, 1946
- Resolution Establishing the Viet Minh, 1941
- Chinese peasants attack a local despot, 1948
- China: Marriage Law of 1950
- China: Cultural Revolution Violence at Qinghua University, 1968
- Vietnam: Ho Chi Minh's Last Will and Testament
- China: A Farmer's Prespective, 2002
- Famine in North Korea, 2002
- China: Hu Jintao, A "Harmonious Society," 2006
- Letter of Plan Chu Trinh to the French Governor-General, 1906
- Nguyen Van Vinh's View of the Vietnamese, 1913
- Ho Chi Minh, "Equality!"

Visual Sources

- UN sprays DDT over Seoul
- Nixon in China, 1972
- Meeting between the Chinese, Soviet, Indian foreign ministers, 1962
- May Day celebrations in Tiananmen Square II
- May Day celebrations in Tiananmen Square I
- Koreans in Japan mark homeland
- Korean child receiving food aid during the Korean War
- Japanese election, 1946
- French nurse inoculating Indochinese baby
- Female machinists, Beijing
- Chinese landowner trial, 1950s
- Chinese Communist guerrillas
- Chinese artillery class
- Asian games, Tokyo, 1958
- Albanian-Chinese ties
- American consumer goods, late 1940s

Chapter 34 Postcolonialism and Beyond: Latin America, Africa, Asia, and the Middle East

Text Sources

▪ Sayyid Qutb, from *Milestones*, 1964

▪ Saddam Hussein's Invasion of Kuwait: (a) Saddam Hussein, "Victory Day" Speech; (b) Bishara A. Bahbah, "The Crisis in the Gulf: Why Iran Invaded Kuwait"

▪ Palestinian Declaration of Independence, 1988

▪ Osama bin Laden, World Islamic Front Statement, 1998

▪ Nelson Mandela, excerpt from *Freedom, Justice and Dignity for All South Africa: Statements and Articles by Mr. Nelson Mandela*

▪ Nelson Mandela, Closing Address at the 13th International AIDS Conference, July 2000

▪ Kwame Nkrumah, from *I Speak of Freedom: A Statement of African Ideology*

▪ Keith B. Richburg, excerpt from *Out of America: A Black Man Confronts Africa*

▪ Juan Perón, excerpt from *The Voice of Perón*

▪ Jomo Kenyatta, from *Facing Mt. Kenya: The Tribal Life of the Gikuyu*

▪ Jawaharlal Nehru, from *The Autobiography of Jawaharlal Nehru*

▪ Israel's Proclamation of Independence, 1948

▪ Frantz Fanon, from *The Wretched of the Earth*

▪ Excerpt from the 9/11 Commission Report

▪ Alain Destexhe, excerpt from *Rwanda and Genocide in the Twentieth Century*

▪ Aimé Césaire, from *Return to My Native Land*

▪ Léopold Senghor on Negritude, 1937 and 1964

▪ Fidel Castro, *History Will Absolve Me*, 1953

▪ Abu'l 'Ala Mawdudi on the Scope and Purpose of the Islamic State, 1903–1979

▪ Jawaharlal Nehru, "Why India Is Non-Aligned" (India), 1956

▪ Ho Chi Minh, "Declaration of Independence of the Democratic Republic of Vietnam" (Vietnam) 1945

▪ Nnamdi Azikiwe on imperialism

Visual Sources

▪ The Shah of Iran accepting homage from a peasant, 1953

▪ Tamils protesting adoption of Singhalese as national language

▪ Operation Desert Storm

▪ Mossadegh supporters

▪ Moroccan health care worker

▪ Moroccan child receiving immunization

▪ Midwifery class, Burma

▪ Mayan religious ceremony

▪ La Paz, Bolivia, 1950s

▪ Kwame Nkrumah and Julius Nyere

▪ Iranian students protest

▪ Indonesian political rallies

▪ Indonesian guerillas

▪ Indian women receiving military training

▪ Ghanaian demonstrators

▪ General election, Ceylon (Sri Lanka)

▪ Female Irgun recruits, Israel

▪ Date market, Algeria

▪ Construction of the Aswan Dam, Egypt

▪ Cocoa harvesting in Ghana

▪ Central American market

▪ Cairo traffic

▪ Anti-Western Chinese poster, 1950s

▪ Asante king, early 1950s

▪ Harvesting coca, Ghana, middle of the twentieth century

YOU SHOULD CAREFULLY READ THE TERMS AND CONDITIONS BEFORE USING THE DVD-ROM PACKAGE. USING THIS DVD-ROM PACKAGE INDICATES YOUR ACCEPTANCE OF THESE TERMS AND CONDITIONS.

SINGLE PC OR MAC LICENSE AGREEMENT AND LIMITED WARRANTY

READ THIS LICENSE CAREFULLY BEFORE OPENING THIS PACKAGE. BY OPENING THIS PACKAGE, YOU ARE AGREEING TO THE TERMS AND CONDITIONS OF THIS LICENSE. IF YOU DO NOT AGREE, DO NOT OPEN THE PACKAGE. PROMPTLY RETURN THE UNOPENED PACKAGE AND ALL ACCOMPANYING ITEMS TO THE PLACE YOU OBTAINED THEM.

1. GRANT OF LICENSE and OWNERSHIP: The enclosed computer programs ("Software") are licensed, not sold, to you by Prentice-Hall, Inc. ("We" or the "Company") and in consideration of your purchase or adoption of the accompanying Company textbooks and/or other materials, and your agreement to these terms. We reserve any rights not granted to you. You own only the disk(s) but we and/or our licensors own the Software itself. This license allows you to use and display your copy of the Software at a single location for academic use only, so long as you comply with the terms of this Agreement.

2. RESTRICTIONS: Except for backup, you may not copy the documentation or the Software. You may not reverse engineer, disassemble, decompile, modify, adapt, translate, or create derivative works based on the Software or the Documentation. You may be held legally responsible for any copying or copyright infringement, which is caused by your failure to abide by the terms of these restrictions.

3. TERMINATION: This license is effective until terminated. This license will terminate automatically without notice from the Company if you fail to comply with any provisions or limitations of this license. Upon termination, you shall destroy the Documentation and all copies of the Software. All provisions of this Agreement as to limitation and disclaimer of warranties, limitation of liability, remedies, or damages, and our ownership rights shall survive termination.

4. LIMITED WARRANTY AND DISCLAIMER OF WARRANTY: Company warrants that for a period of 60 days from the date you purchase this SOFTWARE (or purchase or adopt the accompanying textbook), the Software, when properly installed and used in accordance with the Documentation, will operate in substantial conformity with the description of the Software set forth in the Documentation, and that for a period of 30 days the disk(s) on which the Software is delivered shall be free from defects in materials and workmanship under normal use. The Company does not warrant that the Software will meet your requirements or that the operation of the Software will be uninterrupted or error-free. Your only remedy and the Company's only obligation under these limited warranty is, at the Company's option, return of the disk for a refund of any amounts paid for it by you or replacement of the disk. THIS LIMITED WARRANTY IS THE ONLY WARRANTY PROVIDED BY THE COMPANY AND ITS LICENSORS, AND THE COMPANY AND ITS LICENSORS DISCLAIM ALL OTHER WARRANTIES, EXPRESS OR IMPLIED, INCLUDING WITHOUT LIMITATION, THE IMPLIED WARRANTIES OF MERCHANTABILITY AND FITNESS FOR A PARTICULAR PURPOSE. THE COMPANY DOES NOT WARRANT, GUARANTEE, OR MAKE ANY REPRESENTATION REGARDING THE ACCURACY, RELIABILITY, CURRENTNESS, USE, OR RESULTS OF USE, OF THE SOFTWARE.

5. LIMITATION OF REMEDIES AND DAMAGES: IN NO EVENT, SHALL THE COMPANY OR ITS AGENTS, LICENSORS, OR CONTRACTORS BE LIABLE FOR ANY INCIDENTAL, INDIRECT, SPECIAL, OR CONSEQUENTIAL DAMAGES ARISING OUT OF OR IN CONNECTION WITH THIS LICENSE OR THE SOFTWARE, INCLUDING FOR LOSS OF USE, LOSS OF DATA, LOSS OF INCOME OR PROFIT, OR OTHER LOSSES, SUSTAINED AS A RESULT OF INJURY TO ANY PERSON, OR LOSS OF OR DAMAGE TO PROPERTY, OR CLAIMS OF THIRD PARTIES, EVEN IF THE COMPANY OR AN AUTHORIZED REPRESENTATIVE OF THE COMPANY HAS BEEN ADVISED OF THE POSSIBILITY OF SUCH DAMAGES. IN NO EVENT SHALL THE LIABILITY OF THE COMPANY FOR DAMAGES WITH RESPECT TO THE SOFTWARE EXCEED THE AMOUNTS ACTUALLY PAID BY YOU, IF ANY, FOR THE SOFTWARE OR THE ACCOMPANYING TEXTBOOK. BECAUSE SOME JURISDICTIONS DO NOT ALLOW THE LIMITATION OF LIABILITY IN CERTAIN CIRCUMSTANCES, THE ABOVE LIMITATIONS MAY NOT ALWAYS APPLY TO YOU.

6. GENERAL: THIS AGREEMENT SHALL BE CONSTRUED IN ACCORDANCE WITH THE LAWS OF THE UNITED STATES OF AMERICA AND THE STATE OF NEW YORK, APPLICABLE TO CONTRACTS MADE IN NEW YORK, AND SHALL BENEFIT THE COMPANY, ITS AFFILIATES AND ASSIGNEES. THIS AGREEMENT IS THE COMPLETE AND EXCLUSIVE STATEMENT OF THE AGREEMENT BETWEEN YOU AND THE COMPANY AND SUPERSEDES ALL PROPOSALS OR PRIOR AGREEMENTS, ORAL OR WRITTEN, AND ANY OTHER COMMUNICATIONS BETWEEN YOU AND THE COMPANY OR ANY REPRESENTATIVE OF THE COMPANY RELATING TO THE SUBJECT MATTER OF THIS AGREEMENT. If you are a U.S. Government user, this Software is licensed with "restricted rights" as set forth in subparagraphs (a)-(d) of the Commercial Computer-Restricted Rights clause at FAR 52.227-19 or in subparagraphs (c)(1)(ii) of the Rights in Technical Data and Computer Software clause at DFARS 252.227-7013, and similar clauses, as applicable.

Customer Technical Support: To obtain support, please visit us online anytime at http://247 pearsoned.custhelp.com where you can search our knowledgebase for common solutions, view product alerts, read answers to top questions, and review all options for